STRATEGIC MANAGEMENT

COMPETITIVENESS & GLOBALIZATION • 10E

STRATEGIC MANAGEMENT

COMPETITIVENESS & GLOBALIZATION • 10E

MICHAEL A. HITT

Texas A&M University

R. DUANE IRELAND

Texas A&M University

ROBERT E. HOSKISSON

Rice University

SOUTH-WESTERN
CENGAGE Learning·

Australia • Brazil • Japan • Korea • Mexico • Singapore • Spain • United Kingdom • United States

SOUTH-WESTERN
CENGAGE Learning

Strategic Management: Competitiveness & Globalization: Concepts and Cases, 10th edition

Michael A. Hitt, R. Duane Ireland, and Robert E. Hoskisson

Vice President of Editorial, Business:
Jack W. Calhoun

Publisher:
Erin Joyner

Senior Acquisitions Editor:
Michele Rhoades

Senior Developmental Editor:
Julia Chase

Editorial Assistant:
Tamara Grega

Marketing Manager:
Jonathan Monahan

Content Project Manager:
Jana Lewis

Senior Media Editor:
Kristen Meere

Manufacturing Planner:
Ron Montgomery

Senior Marketing Communications Manager:
Jim Overly

Production Service:
Cenveo Publisher Services

Senior Art Director:
Tippy McIntosh

Internal Designer:
Ramsdell Design

Cover Designer:
Ramsdell Design

Cover Image:
©Ryan McVay, Photodisc, Getty Images

Rights Acquisitions Specialist:
Sam Marshall

For product information and technology assistance, contact us at
Cengage Learning Customer & Sales Support, 1-800-354-9706

For permission to use material from this text or product, submit all requests online at **www.cengage.com/permissions**
Further permissions questions can be emailed to
permissionrequest@cengage.com

Exam*View*® is a registered trademark of eInstruction Corp. Windows is a registered trademark of the Microsoft Corporation used herein under license. Macintosh and Power Macintosh are registered trademarks of Apple Computer, Inc. used herein under license.

© 2008 Cengage Learning. All Rights Reserved.

Cengage Learning WebTutor™ is a trademark of Cengage Learning.

Library of Congress Control Number: 2011938797

ISBN-13: 978-1-111-82587-4
ISBN-10: 1-111-82587-4

South-Western
5191 Natorp Boulevard
Mason, OH 45040
USA

Cengage Learning products are represented in Canada by Nelson Education, Ltd.

For your course and learning solutions, visit **www.cengage.com**

Purchase any of our products at your local college store or at our preferred online store **www.cengagebrain.com**

Printed in Canada
1 2 3 4 5 6 7 15 14 13 12 11

To my family, I love each and every one of you. I am blessed that you are a part of my life.
—**MICHAEL A. HITT**

To my entire family, I love each of you dearly and remain so grateful for your incredibly strong support and encouragement over the years. Your words and deeds have indeed showed me how to "keep my good eye to the sun and my blind eye to the dark."
—**R. DUANE IRELAND**

To my father, who lived a simple life, focused on his family, and was an example of honesty and endurance.
—**ROBERT E. HOSKISSON**

BRIEF CONTENTS

Preface xix

Part 1: Strategic Management Inputs   1

1. Strategic Management and Strategic Competitiveness 2
2. The External Environment: Opportunities, Threats, Industry Competition, and Competitor Analysis 34
3. The Internal Organization: Resources, Capabilities, Core Competencies, and Competitive Advantages 70

Part 2: Strategic Actions: Strategy Formulation   99

4. Business-Level Strategy 100
5. Competitive Rivalry and Competitive Dynamics 130
6. Corporate-Level Strategy 162
7. Merger and Acquisition Strategies 192
8. International Strategy 224
9. Cooperative Strategy 260

Part 3: Strategic Actions: Strategy Implementation   291

10. Corporate Governance 292
11. Organizational Structure and Controls 324
12. Strategic Leadership 360
13. Strategic Entrepreneurship 390

Part 4: Cases   1

Name Index I-1
Company Index I-17
Subject Index I-20

CONTENTS

Preface xix

Part 1: Strategic Management Inputs 1

1: Strategic Management and Strategic Competitiveness 2

Once a "Giant," Borders Became a "Weakling" on Its Knees 3

The Competitive Landscape 6

    The Global Economy 7

    Strategic Focus: Huawei Also Needs Guanxi in the United States 8

    Technology and Technological Changes 10

    Strategic Focus: The Core of Apple: Technology and Innovation 12

The I/O Model of Above-Average Returns 14

The Resource-Based Model of Above-Average Returns 16

Vision and Mission 17

    Vision 17

    Mission 18

Stakeholders 19

    Classifications of Stakeholders 19

Strategic Leaders 22

    The Work of Effective Strategic Leaders 23

    Predicting Outcomes of Strategic Decisions: Profit Pools 23

The Strategic Management Process 24

Summary 25 • Review Questions 26 • Experiential Exercises 26

Video Case 27 • Notes 28

2: The External Environment: Opportunities, Threats, Industry Competition, and Competitor Analysis 34

British Petroleum (BP) and Its Environment: How the Deepwater Horizon Offshore Drilling Platform Disaster Is Shaping Its Strategy 35

The General, Industry, and Competitor Environments 38

External Environmental Analysis 39

    Scanning 40

    Monitoring 40

    Forecasting 41

    Assessing 41

Segments of the General Environment 41

    The Demographic Segment 42

    The Political/Legal Segment 44

    The Sociocultural Segment 45

    The Technological Segment 46

    The Global Segment 47

    The Physical Environment Segment 48

    Strategic Focus: Firms' Efforts to Take Care of the Physical Environment in Which They Compete 49

Industry Environment Analysis 50

    Threat of New Entrants 51

    Bargaining Power of Suppliers 54

    Bargaining Power of Buyers 55

    Threat of Substitute Products 55

    Strategic Focus: The Multi-Industry Battle for Mobile and Home Digital Computing and Entertainment 56

    Intensity of Rivalry among Competitors 57

Interpreting Industry Analyses 59

Strategic Groups 60

Competitor Analysis 60

Ethical Considerations 62

Summary 63 • Review Questions 64 • Experiential Exercises 64
Video Case 65 • Notes 65

3: The Internal Organization: Resources, Capabilities, Core Competencies, and Competitive Advantages 70

Subway Restaurants: Core Competencies as the Foundation for Success 71

Analyzing the Internal Organization 73

    The Context of Internal Analysis 73

    Creating Value 75

    The Challenge of Analyzing the Internal Organization 75

    Strategic Focus: Effectively Analyzing the Internal Organization and Deciding How to Best Use the Firm's Assets—It's Hard Work! 78

Resources, Capabilities, and Core Competencies 79

    Resources 79

    Capabilities 81

    Core Competencies 82

    Strategic Focus: Procter & Gamble: Using Capabilities and Core Competencies to Create Value for Customers 83

Building Core Competencies 84

    The Four Criteria of Sustainable Competitive Advantage 84

    Value Chain Analysis 87

Outsourcing 90

Competencies, Strengths, Weaknesses, and Strategic Decisions 90

Summary 91 • Review Questions 92 • Experiential Exercises 92
Video Case 93 • Notes 94

Part 2: Strategic Actions: Strategy Formulation 99

4: Business-Level Strategy 100

Morning Joe in the Afternoon in China, India, and Beyond: The New Starbucks 101

Customers: Their Relationship with Business-Level Strategies 103

    Effectively Managing Relationships with Customers 104

    Reach, Richness, and Affiliation 104

    Who: Determining the Customers to Serve 105

    What: Determining Which Customer Needs to Satisfy 106

    How: Determining Core Competencies Necessary to Satisfy Customer Needs 106

The Purpose of a Business-Level Strategy 107

Types of Business-Level Strategies 108

    Cost Leadership Strategy 110

    Strategic Focus: Walmart, Dollar Stores, and Amazon: Who Is Buying Whose Lunch? 112

    Differentiation Strategy 115

    Focus Strategies 118

    Integrated Cost Leadership/Differentiation Strategy 120

    Strategic Focus: The Li Ning Company: Heading toward Global Market Leadership? 121

Summary 124 • Review Questions 124 • Experiential Exercises 125
Video Case 125 • Notes 126

5: Competitive Rivalry and Competitive Dynamics 130

Disruptive Innovation: Winning Rivalry Battles against Competitors 131

A Model of Competitive Rivalry 134

Competitor Analysis 135

    Market Commonality 135

    Strategic Focus: Market Commonality and Resource Similarity in the Global Automobile Producer Industry 136

    Resource Similarity 138

Drivers of Competitive Actions and Responses 139

Competitive Rivalry 141

    Strategic and Tactical Actions 141

Likelihood of Attack 142

    First-Mover Incentives 142

    Organizational Size 144

    Quality 145

Likelihood of Response 146

    Type of Competitive Action 146

    Actor's Reputation 147

    Dependence on the Market 147

Competitive Dynamics 148

    Slow-Cycle Markets 148

    Fast-Cycle Markets 149

    Strategic Focus: Competition to Sell Cloud Computing Resources 151

    Standard-Cycle Markets 152

Summary 154 • Review Questions 155 • Experiential Exercises 155
Video Case 156 • Notes 157

6: Corporate-Level Strategy 162

General Electric: The Quintessential Diversified Firm 163

Levels of Diversification 165

Low Levels of Diversification 165

Strategic Focus: Relatedness among Business Bears Fruit at the Publicis Groupe 167

Moderate and High Levels of Diversification 168

Reasons for Diversification 168

Value-Creating Diversification: Related Constrained and Related Linked Diversification 170

Operational Relatedness: Sharing Activities 171

Corporate Relatedness: Transferring of Core Competencies 171

Market Power 172

Strategic Focus: The Economic Power of Google and the Competitive Derivatives 174

Simultaneous Operational Relatedness and Corporate Relatedness 175

Unrelated Diversification 175

Efficient Internal Capital Market Allocation 175

Restructuring of Assets 177

Value-Neutral Diversification: Incentives and Resources 178

Incentives to Diversify 178

Resources and Diversification 181

Value-Reducing Diversification: Managerial Motives to Diversify 182

Summary 184 • Review Questions 184 • Experiential Exercises 184 • Video Case 186 Notes 186

7: Merger and Acquisition Strategies 192

Technology Giants' Acquisition Strategies and Their Outcomes 193

The Popularity of Merger and Acquisition Strategies 195

Mergers, Acquisitions, and Takeovers: What Are the Differences? 195

Reasons for Acquisitions 196

Increased Market Power 196

Overcoming Entry Barriers 198

Strategic Focus: Cross-Border Acquisitions by Firms from Emerging Economies: Leverage Resources to Gain a Larger Global Footprint and Market Power 199

Cost of New Product Development and Increased Speed to Market 201

Lower Risk Compared to Developing New Products 201

Increased Diversification 202

Reshaping the Firm's Competitive Scope 203

Learning and Developing New Capabilities 203

Problems in Achieving Acquisition Success 203

Integration Difficulties 205

Inadequate Evaluation of Target 205

Large or Extraordinary Debt 206

Inability to Achieve Synergy 207

Too Much Diversification 207

Managers Overly Focused on Acquisitions 208

Strategic Focus: The Acquisitions and Mergers to Form Citigroup: Divestitures Associated with the Failed Concept of the Financial Supermarket 209

Too Large 210

Effective Acquisitions 211

Restructuring 213

    Downsizing 213

    Downscoping 213

    Leveraged Buyouts 214

    Restructuring Outcomes 214

Summary 216 • Review Questions 216 • Experiential Exercises 217 • Video Case 218
Notes 219

8: International Strategy 224

International Strategy: Critical to Starbucks'
Future Success 225

Identifying International Opportunities 227

    Incentives to Use International Strategy 228

    Three Basic Benefits of International Strategy 229

International Strategies 231

    International Business-Level Strategy 231

    International Corporate-Level Strategy 234

Environmental Trends 237

    Liability of Foreignness 237

    Regionalization 238

Choice of International Entry Mode 239

    Exporting 239

    Licensing 240

    Strategic Alliances 241

    Acquisitions 242

    New Wholly Owned Subsidiary 243

    Dynamics of Mode of Entry 244

    Strategic Focus: Walmart International: Using Multiple Paths to Enter
    International Markets 245

Risks in an International Environment 246

    Political Risks 246

    Economic Risks 247

Strategic Competitiveness Outcomes 248

    International Diversification and Returns 248

    Enhanced Innovation 249

The Challenge of International Strategies 249

    Complexity of Managing International Strategies 249

    Limits to International Expansion 250

    Strategic Focus: Haier Group: A Story of Product and Geographic Diversification 251

Summary 252 • Review Questions 253 • Experiential Exercises 253
Video Case 254 • Notes 255

9: Cooperative Strategy 260

The Renault-Nissan Alliance: Collaborating to Succeed 261

Strategic Alliances as a Primary Type of Cooperative Strategy 263

    Types of Major Strategic Alliances 263

    Strategic Focus: Fujitsu Siemens Computers B.V.—The Beginning and the End 264

    Reasons Firms Develop Strategic Alliances 266

Strategic Focus: Microsoft and Nokia Form a Partnership to Shape the Future 268

Business-Level Cooperative Strategy 270

    Complementary Strategic Alliances 270

    Competition Response Strategy 272

    Uncertainty-Reducing Strategy 273

    Competition-Reducing Strategy 273

    Assessing Business-Level Cooperative Strategies 274

Corporate-Level Cooperative Strategy 275

    Diversifying Strategic Alliance 276

    Synergistic Strategic Alliance 276

    Franchising 276

    Assessing Corporate-Level Cooperative Strategies 277

International Cooperative Strategy 277

Network Cooperative Strategy 279

    Alliance Network Types 279

Competitive Risks with Cooperative Strategies 280

Managing Cooperative Strategies 281

Summary 283 • Review Questions 284 • Experiential Exercises 284 • Video Case 284
Notes 285

Part 3: Strategic Actions: Strategy Implementation 291

10: Corporate Governance 292

Corporate Governance: What Is All the Fuss About? 293

Separation of Ownership and Managerial Control 295

    Agency Relationships 296

    Product Diversification as an Example of an Agency Problem 297

    Agency Costs and Governance Mechanisms 299

Ownership Concentration 301

    The Increasing Influence of Institutional Owners 301

Board of Directors 302

    Enhancing the Effectiveness of the Board of Directors 304

    Executive Compensation 305

    The Effectiveness of Executive Compensation 306

    *Strategic Focus: Executive Compensation: What Are Some of the Issues and
What Might the Future Hold?* 307

Market for Corporate Control 308

    Managerial Defense Tactics 309

International Corporate Governance 310

    Corporate Governance in Germany and Japan 311

    Corporate Governance in China 312

Governance Mechanisms and Ethical Behavior 313

    Strategic Focus: The Many Facets of Corporate Governance: Rio Tinto's Experiences 314

Summary 316 • Review Questions 317 • Experiential Exercises 317
Video Case 318 • Notes 319

11: Organizational Structure and Controls 324

Another One Bites The Dust: Borders Declares Bankruptcy 325

Organizational Structure and Controls 327
>Organizational Structure 327
>Organizational Controls 328

Relationships between Strategy and Structure 330

Evolutionary Patterns of Strategy and Organizational Structure 330
>Simple Structure 331
>Functional Structure 332
>Multidivisional Structure 332
>Matches between Business-Level Strategies and the Functional Structure 333
>Matches between Corporate-Level Strategies and the Multidivisional Structure 336
>*Strategic Focus: Cisco: Cooperation to the Extreme and Back 337*
>Matches between International Strategies and Worldwide Structure 343
>*Strategic Focus: Evaluating Performance in a Large Conglomerate: LG Company 344*
>Matches between Cooperative Strategies and Network Structures 348

Implementing Business-Level Cooperative Strategies 350

Implementing Corporate-Level Cooperative Strategies 351

Implementing International Cooperative Strategies 351

Summary 352 • Review Questions 353 • Experiential Exercises 353
Video Case 354 • Notes 354

12: Strategic Leadership 360

Succession at HP: Can the New CEO Save the Company's Soul? 361

Strategic Leadership and Style 362

The Role of Top-Level Managers 364
>Top Management Teams 365

Managerial Succession 368
>*Strategic Focus: Can Highly Successful Leaders Be Replaced Successfully? The Importance of Succession Planning 371*

Key Strategic Leadership Actions 372
>Determining Strategic Direction 372

Leo Apotheker, former CEO of HP

>Effectively Managing the Firm's Resource Portfolio 373
>Sustaining an Effective Organizational Culture 376
>Emphasizing Ethical Practices 377
>Establishing Balanced Organizational Controls 378
>*Strategic Focus: The Key to E-Commerce Is Trust: Fraud at Alibaba 379*

Summary 382 • Review Questions 383 • Experiential Exercises 383
Video Case 384 • Notes 384

13: Strategic Entrepreneurship 390

Open Innovation: Combining External Technologies and Ideas with Internal R&D Capabilities 391

Entrepreneurship and Entrepreneurial Opportunities 393

Innovation 394

Entrepreneurs 395

International Entrepreneurship 396

Internal Innovation 397

   Incremental and Radical Innovation 397

   Strategic Focus: 3M Has a Culture Focused on Creating Innovation 398

   Autonomous Strategic Behavior 400

   Induced Strategic Behavior 401

Implementing Internal Innovations 402

   Cross-Functional Product Development Teams 402

   Facilitating Integration and Innovation 403

   Creating Value from Internal Innovation 403

Innovation through Cooperative Strategies 404

Innovation through Acquisitions 405

   Strategic Focus: Social Networking Web Sites Facilitate Innovation: Application Software Innovation 406

Creating Value through Strategic Entrepreneurship 407

Summary 409 • Review Questions 409 • Experiential Exercises 410
Video Case 410 • Notes 411

Part 4: Cases

Case 1: Adobe Systems Incorporated 1

Case 2: Apple Inc.: Keeping the "i" in "Innovation" 16

Case 3: AT&T: Another Century of Innovation? 40

Case 4: Finding the Best Buy 57

Case 5: Chipotle: The Challenges of Integrity 71

Case 6: Coinstar: A Sleeping Giant Awakens 88

Case 7: Domino's Pizza: A Case Study in Organizational Evolution 99

Case 8: Dr Pepper Snapple Group 2011: Fighting to Prosper in a Highly Competitive Market 115

Case 9: Ford Motor Company: Staying "Ford Tough" 127

Case 10: Google 155

Case 11: Developing Global Teams to Meet Twenty-First Century Challenges at W. L. Gore & Associates 172

Case 12: Herman Miller: A Case of Reinvention and Renewal 184

Case 13: Luck Companies: Igniting Human Potential 196

Case 14: McDonald's: From Big Mac to P'tit Plaisir 207

Case 15: CIBC Mellon: Managing a Cross-Border Joint Venture 219

Case 16: MGM Resorts International 231

Case 17: Microsoft Corp. 251

Case 18: The Movie Exhibition Industry: 2011 266

Case 19: Navistar: Can It Keep On Truckin'? 277

Case 20: Netflix 300

Case 21: Porsche 317

Case 22: Rite Aid Corporation 327

Case 23: Reynolds American Inc. 339

Case 24: The Entrepreneurs at Twitter: Building a Brand, a Social Tool or a Tech
Powerhouse? 352

Case 25: The Ultimate Fighting Championship and Cultural Viability 359

Case 26: Under Armour: Working to Stay on Top of Its Game 370

Case 27: Union Pacific Corporation 383

Case 28: Valeant Pharmaceuticals International, Inc. 400

Case 29: Victory: The New American Motorcycle Celebrates Its First Decade
on the Road 419

Case 30: Zipcar: The Future of Transportation? 437

Name Index I-1

Company Index I-17

Subject Index I-20

PREFACE

Our goal in writing each edition of this book is to present a new, up-to-date standard for explaining the strategic management process. To reach this goal with the 10th edition of our market-leading text, we again present you with an intellectually rich yet thoroughly practical analysis of strategic management.

With each new edition, we are challenged and invigorated by the goal of maintaining the standard that we established for presenting strategic management knowledge in a readable style. To prepare for each new edition, we carefully study the most recent academic research to ensure that the strategic management content we present to you is highly current and relevant for use in organizations. In addition, we continuously read articles appearing in many different business publications (e.g., *Wall Street Journal, Bloomberg Businessweek, Fortune, Financial Times,* and *Forbes,* to name a few); we do this to identify valuable examples of how companies are actually using (or not using) the strategic management process. Though many of the hundreds of companies we discuss in the book will be quite familiar to you, some companies will likely be new to you. One reason for this is that we use examples of companies from around the world to demonstrate how globalized business has become. To maximize your opportunities to learn as you read and think about how actual companies use strategic management tools, techniques, and concepts (based on the most current research), we emphasize a lively and user-friendly writing style.

Several *characteristics* of this 10th edition of our book will enhance your learning opportunities:

■ This book presents you with the most comprehensive and thorough coverage of strategic management that is available in the market.

■ The research used in this book is drawn from the "classics" as well as the most recent contributions to the strategic management literature. The historically significant "classic" research provides the foundation for much of what is known about strategic management while the most recent contributions reveal insights about how to effectively use strategic management in the complex, global business environment in which firms now compete. Our book also presents you with many up-to-date examples of how firms use the strategic management tools, techniques, and concepts developed by leading researchers. Indeed, although this book is grounded in the relevant theory and current research, it also is strongly application oriented and presents you, our readers, with a vast number of examples and applications of strategic management concepts, techniques, and tools. In this edition, for example, we examine more than 600 companies to describe the use of strategic management. Collectively, no other strategic management book presents you with the *combination* of useful and insightful *research* and *applications* in a wide variety of organizations as does this text. Company examples range from the large U.S.-based firms such as Apple, Starbucks,

Walmart, Walt Disney, Pfizer, Dell, PepsiCo, Coca-Cola, Hewlett-Packard, Ford, and General Motors, to major foreign-based firms such as Alibaba, British Petroleum, Renault-Nissan, Nokia, Volvo, Fujitsu, LG Electronics, Siemens, NTT DOCOMO, Haier, Rosneft, Rio Tinto, CEMEX, Baidu, IKEA, Unilever, Publicis, and Huawei. We also include examples of smaller and medium-sized firms such as LDK Solar, JA Solar, Sementes Guerra (Brazil), Edu-Science (Hong Kong), Green Mountain and Groupon.

■ We carefully *integrate* two of the most popular and well-known theoretical concepts in the strategic management field: industrial-organization economics and the resource-based view of the firm. We do this because research and practical experience indicate that both theories play a major role in understanding the linkage between strategic management and organizational success. Therefore, we integrate these two theoretical perspectives to effectively explain the strategic management process and its application in all types of organizations.

■ We use the ideas of prominent scholars (e.g., Ron Adner, Rajshree Agarwal, Gautam Ahuja, Raffi Amit, Jay Barney, Joel Baum, Paul Beamish, Ming-Jer Chen, Russ Coff, Rich D'Aveni, Kathy Eisenhardt, Javier Gimeno, Luis Gomez-Mejia, Ranjay Gulati, Don Hambrick, Connie Helfat, Amy Hillman, Michael Lennox, Marvin Lieberman, Yadong Luo, Shige Makino, Costas Markides, Danny Miller, Will Mitchell, Margie Peteraf, Michael Porter, C. K. Prahalad, Nandini Rajagopalan, Jeff Reuer, Richard Rumelt, David Sirmon, Ken Smith, David Teece, Mary Tripsas, Wenpin Tsai, Michael Tushman, Oliver Williamson, Anthea Zhang, Maurizio Zollo, and Ed Zajac) to shape the discussion of *what* strategic management is. We describe the practices of prominent executives and practitioners (e.g., Ursula Burns, Jeff Immelt, Jack Ma, Indra Nooyi, and many others) to help us describe *how* strategic management is used in many types of organizations.

The authors of this book are also active scholars. We conduct research on different strategic management topics. Our interest in doing so is to contribute to the strategic management literature and to better understand how to effectively apply strategic management tools, techniques, and concepts to increase organizational performance. Thus, our own research is integrated in the appropriate chapters along with the research of numerous other scholars, some of whom are noted above.

In addition to our book's *characteristics,* there are some specific *features* and *revisions* that we have made in this 10th edition that we are pleased to highlight for you:

■ **New Opening Cases and Strategic Focus Segments.** We continue our tradition of providing all-new Opening Cases and Strategic Focus segments. In addition, new company-specific examples are included in each chapter. Through all of these venues, we present you with a wealth of examples of how actual organizations, most of which compete internationally as well as in their home markets, use the strategic management process for the purpose of outperforming rivals and increase their performance.

■ **New Strategy Right Now Callouts.** Each chapter contains 3 Strategy Right Now icons that direct the student to the CourseMate site. There students can find out how to access the Gale Business & Company Resource Center (BCRC). The BCRC houses recent articles covering most of the concepts and companies highlighted in each of the chapters. In addition, online quizzes are associated with all of the BCRC content in CengageNow.

■ **Thirty All-New Cases** with an effective mix of organizations headquartered or based in the United States and a number of other countries. Many of the cases have full financial data (the analyses of which are in the Case Notes that are available to instructors). These timely cases present active learners with opportunities to apply the strategic management process and understand organizational conditions and contexts and to make appropriate recommendations to deal with critical concerns. These cases can also be found in CengageNow. New to this edition, we have created nine guided cases (Apple, Coinstar, Domino's, Herman Miller, The Movie Exhibition Industry, Porsche, RJ Reynolds, Valeant, and Zipcar). These guided cases can be assigned and auto-graded.

- ■ **More Than 950 New References** (2010, 2011) were included in the endnotes to support new material added or current strategic management concepts used in the book. In addition to demonstrating the classic and recent research from which we draw our material, these data support the fact that this book references the current cutting-edge research and thinking in the field.

- ■ **New Concepts** were added in several chapters. Examples include executive ambidexterity and ambicultural executives (Chapter 1), cloud computing (Chapter 5), private-public partnerships in strategic alliances (Chapter 9), and open innovation (Chapter 13).

- ■ **New Content** was added to several chapters. Examples include the linkage between knowledge spillovers and innovation (Chapter 1), the fact that 85 percent of shareholder value is created by intangible resources (Chapter 1), the notion of mobile ecosystems (Chapter 9), the Dodd-Frank legislation focused on regulating financial services (Chapter 10), the notion that incentive compensation produces positive results with talented executives but negative outcomes with less talented executives (Chapter 12), and more detailed exploration of managerial succession, especially among top executives (Chapter 12).

- ■ **New Information** was provided in several chapters. Examples include the new aggressive actions of firms based in China and other emerging economy countries (Chapter 1), the effects of the tsunami in Japan (Chapter 2), political upheavals in Middle Eastern countries (Chapter 2), and definitions for political risks and economic risks (Chapter 8). New information is also provided in 18 new or highly revised figures and tables across several chapters (e.g., Chapters 3, 4, 8, 9, and 10).

- ■ **All New Video Case Exercises** are included in the end-of-chapter material for each chapter. These engaging videos demonstrate how the concepts students are learning actually connect to the ideas and actions of the interesting individuals and companies highlighted in the videos. Assignable and auto-gradable exercises accompany these videos in CengageNow.

- ■ **New and Revised Experiential Exercises** are at the end of each chapter to support individuals' efforts to understand the use of the strategic management process. These exercises place active learners in a variety of situations requiring application of some part of the strategic management process.

- ■ **An Exceptional Balance** between current research and up-to-date applications of it in actual organizations. The content has not only the best research documentation but also the largest amount of effective real-world examples to help active learners understand the different types of strategies organizations use to achieve their vision and mission.

- ■ **Access to Harvard Business School (HBS) Cases.** We have developed a set of assignment sheets and AACSB International assessment rubrics to accompany 10 of the best-selling HBS cases. Instructors can customize the text to include these cases (www.cengage.com/custom/makeityours/hitt10e) and utilize the accompanying set of teaching notes and assessment rubrics to formalize assurance of learning efforts in the capstone Strategic Management/Business Policy course. Contact your Cengage Learning representative for more information.

Supplements for Instructors

Instructor's Resource CD

Key ancillaries (Instructor's Resource Manual, PowerPoint® slides, ExamView and Word Test Bank files, and Comprehensive Case Notes) are provided, giving instructors the ultimate tool for customizing lectures and presentations.

Case Notes. These notes include directed assignments, financial analyses, and thorough discussion and exposition of issues in the case. Select cases also have assessment rubrics tied to AACSB outcomes standards that can be used for grading each case. The Case Notes provide consistent and thorough support for instructors, following the method espoused by the author team for preparing an effective case analysis. The Case Notes are on the Instructor's Resource CD and Instructor Web site.

Instructor's Resource Manual. The Instructor's Resource Manual, organized around each chapter's knowledge objectives, includes teaching ideas for each chapter and how to reinforce essential principles with extra examples. This support product includes lecture outlines, detailed answers to end-of-chapter review questions, instructions for using each chapter's experiential exercises and video cases, and additional assignments. Available on the Instructor's Resource CD and Instructor Web site.

Test Bank. Thoroughly revised and enhanced, test bank questions are linked to each chapter's knowledge objectives and are ranked by difficulty and question type. We provide an ample number of application questions throughout, and we have also retained scenario-based questions as a means of adding in-depth problem-solving questions. The questions are also tagged to AACSB outcomes, Bloom's Taxonomy, and the Dierdorff/Rubin metrics. The test bank material is also available in computerized Exam View™ format for creating custom tests in both Windows and Macintosh formats. Available on the Instructor's Resource CD and Instructor Web site.

Exam View™. Computerized testing software contains all of the questions in the certified printed test bank. This program is easy-to-use test-creation software that is compatible with Microsoft Windows. Instructors can add or edit questions, instructions, and answers, and select questions by previewing them on the screen, selecting them randomly, or selecting them by number. Instructors can also create and administer quizzes online, whether over the Internet, a local area network (LAN), or a wide area network (WAN). Available on the Instructor's Resource CD and Instructor Web site.

PowerPoint®. An all-new PowerPoint presentation, created for the 10th edition, provides support for lectures, emphasizing key concepts, key terms, and instructive graphics. Slides can also be used by students as an aid to note-taking. eLecture audio content is also available within the PowerPoint slides. Available on the Instructor's Resource CD and Instructor Web site.

DVD Case Program. A collection of 13 new BBC videos have been included in the end-of-chapter material. These new videos are short, compelling, and timely illustrations of today's management world. Topics include Brazil's growing global economy, the aftermath of BP's oil spill, Zappos.com, the Southwest merger with AirTrans, and more. Available on the DVD and Instructor Web site. Detailed case write-ups including questions and suggested answers appear in the Instructor's Resource Manual. Assignable and auto-gradable exercises accompany these videos in CengageNow.

Instructor Web site. Access important teaching resources on this companion Web site. For your convenience, you can download electronic versions of the instructor supplements from the password-protected section of the site, including the Instructor's Resource Manual, Test Bank, PowerPoint® presentations, and Case Notes. To access these additional course materials and companion resources, please visit www.cengagebrain .com. On the CengageBrain.com homepage, use the search box at the top of the page to search for the ISBN of your title (from the back cover of your book). This will take you to the product page where free companion resources can be found.

WebTutor™. Jump-start your course with customizable, rich, text-specific content within this Course Management System! Access a wealth of interactive resources in addition to those on the companion Web site to supplement the classroom experience and further prepare students for professional success. This resource is ideal as an integrated solution for your distance learning or web-enhanced course.

CengageNow. This robust online course management system gives you more control in less time and delivers better student outcomes—NOW. CengageNow™ includes teaching and learning resources organized around lecturing, creating assignments, casework, quizzing, and gradework to track student progress and performance. The 30 comprehensive cases appear in CengageNow in traditional and guided formats. These two models are assignable and gradable, bringing students to a higher level of understanding in preparation for in-class activities. Multiple types of quizzes, including video quizzes that cover the video found at the end of each chapter, are assignable and gradable. We also include assignable and gradable Business & Company Resource Center (BCRC) quizzes that direct students to Gale articles to find expansive, current event coverage for companies, including a wealth of daily updated articles and company financials. Flexible assignments, automatic grading, and a gradebook option provide more control while saving you valuable time. A Personalized Study diagnostic tool empowers students to master concepts, prepare for exams, and become more involved in class.

Cengage Learning Write Experience 2.0. This new technology is the first in higher education to offer students the opportunity to improve their writing and analytical skills without adding to your workload. Offered through an exclusive agreement with Vantage Learning, creator of the software used for GMAT essay grading, Write Experience evaluates students' answers to a select set of assignments for writing for voice, style, format, and originality.

The Business & Company Resource Center (BCRC). Put a complete business library at your students' fingertips! This premier online business research tool allows you and your students to search thousands of periodicals, journals, references, financial data, industry reports, and more. This powerful research tool saves time for students—whether they are preparing for a presentation or writing a reaction paper. You can use the BCRC to quickly and easily assign readings or research projects. Visit http://www.cengage.com/ bcrc to learn more about this indispensable tool. For this text in particular, BCRC will be especially useful in further researching the companies featured in the text's 30 cases as well as the concepts highlighted in the Opening Cases and Strategic Focus segments.

CourseMate. This dynamic interactive learning tool includes online quizzes, flashcards, games, PowerPoint slides, and more, helping to ensure your students come to class prepared!

Micromatic Strategic Management Simulation (for bundles only). The Micromatic Business Simulation Game allows students to decide their company's mission, goals, policies, and strategies. Student teams make their decisions on a quarter-by-quarter basis, determining price, sales and promotion budgets, operations decisions, and financing requirements. Each decision round requires students to make approximately 100 decisions. Students can play in teams or play alone, compete against other players or the computer, or use Micromatic for practice, tournaments, or assessment. You can control any business simulation element you wish, leaving the rest alone if you desire.

Because of the number and type of decisions the student users must make, Micromatic is classified as a medium to complex business simulation game. This helps students understand how the functional areas of a business fit together without being bogged down in needless detail and provides students with an excellent capstone experience in decision making.

Smartsims (for bundles only). MikesBikes Advanced is a premier strategy simulation; providing students with the unique opportunity to evaluate, plan, and implement strategy as they manage their own company while competing online against other students within their course.

Students from the management team of a bicycle manufacturing company make all the key functional decisions involving price, marketing, distribution, finance, operations, HR, and R&D. They formulate a comprehensive strategy, starting with their existing product, and then adapt the strategy as they develop new products for emerging markets.

Through the Smartsims easy-to-use interface, students are taught the cross-functional disciplines of business and how the development and implementation of strategy involves these disciplines. The competitive nature of MikesBikes encourages involvement and learning in a way that no other teaching methodology can, and your students will have fun in the process!

Global Economic Watch. The current global economic crisis leaves more and more questions unanswered every day and presents "one of the most teachable moments of the century." South-Western delivers the solution. The Global Economic Crisis Resource Center is an online one-stop shopping location that provides educators with current news, journal articles, videos, podcasts, PowerPoint slides, test questions, and much more.

Make It Yours – Custom Case Selection

Cengage Learning is dedicated to making the educational experience unique for all learners by creating custom materials that best suit your course needs. With our Make It Yours program, you can easily select a unique set of cases for your course from providers such as Harvard Business School Publishing, Darden, and Ivey. See http://www.custom.cengage.com/makeityours/hitt10e for more details.

Acknowledgments

We express our appreciation for the excellent support received from our editorial and production team at South-Western. We especially wish to thank Michele Rhoades, our Senior Acquisitions Editor; Julia Chase, our Development Editor; Jonathan Monahan, our Marketing Manager; Jana Lewis, our Content Project Manager; and Andrea Clemente, our project lead. We are grateful for their dedication, commitment, and outstanding contributions to the development and publication of this book and its package of support materials.

We are highly indebted to all of the reviewers of past editions. Their comments have provided much insight in the preparation of this current edition:

Lana Belousova
Suffolk University

Erich Brockmann
University of New Orleans

David Cadden
Quinnipiac University

Ken Chadwick
Nicholls State University

Bruce H. Charnov
Hofstra University

Jay Chok
USC Marshall

Peter Clement
State University of New York – Delhi

James Cordeiro
SUNY Brockport

Deborah de Lange
Suffolk University

Irem Demirkan
Northeastern University

Scott Elston
Iowa State University

Robert Goldberg
Northeastern University

Monica Gordillo
Iowa State University

Susan Hansen
University of Wisconsin-Platteville

Glenn Hoetker
Arizona State University

James Hoyt
Troy University

Carol Jacobson
Purdue University

James Katzenstein
California State University, Dominguez Hills

Nancy E. Landrum
University of Arkansas at Little Rock

Mina Lee
Xavier University

Patrice Luoma
Quinnipiac University

Jean McGuire
Louisiana State University

Rick McPherson
University of Washington

Karen Middleton
Texas A&M-Corpus Christi

Raza Mir
William Paterson University

Martina Musteen
San Diego State University

Frank Novakowski
Davenport University

Consuelo M. Ramirez
University of Texas at San Antonio

Barbara Ribbens
Western Illinois University

Manjula S. Salimath
University of North Texas

Deepak Sethi
Old Dominion University

Manisha Singal
Virginia Tech

Warren Stone
University of Arkansas at Little Rock

Len J. Trevino
Washington State University

Edward Ward
Saint Cloud State University

Marta Szabo White
Georgia State University

Michael L. Williams
Michigan State University

Diana J. Wong-MingJi
Eastern Michigan University

William J. Worthington
Baylor University

Wilson Zehr
Concordia University

Finally, we are very appreciative of the following people for the time and care that went into preparing the supplements to accompany this edition:

Charles Byles
Virginia Commonwealth University

Susan Carson

Carol Decker
Tennessee Wesleyan College

Richard H. Lester
Texas A&M University

Paul Mallette
Colorado State University

Kristi L. Marshall

Marta Szabo White
Georgia State University

Michael A. Hitt
R. Duane Ireland
Robert E. Hoskisson

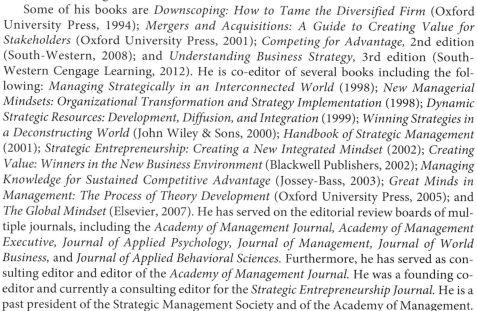

Michael A. Hitt

Michael A. Hitt is a University Distinguished Professor and holds the Joe B. Foster Chair in Business Leadership at Texas A&M University. He received his Ph.D. from the University of Colorado. He has more than 260 publications including 26 co-authored or co-edited books and was cited as one of the 10 most-cited scholars in management over a 25-year period in an article published in the 2008 volume of the *Journal of Management*. In 2010, *Times Higher Education* listed him as one of the top scholars in economics, finance, and management.

Some of his books are *Downscoping: How to Tame the Diversified Firm* (Oxford University Press, 1994); *Mergers and Acquisitions: A Guide to Creating Value for Stakeholders* (Oxford University Press, 2001); *Competing for Advantage,* 2nd edition (South-Western, 2008); and *Understanding Business Strategy,* 3rd edition (South-Western Cengage Learning, 2012). He is co-editor of several books including the following: *Managing Strategically in an Interconnected World* (1998); *New Managerial Mindsets: Organizational Transformation and Strategy Implementation* (1998); *Dynamic Strategic Resources: Development, Diffusion, and Integration* (1999); *Winning Strategies in a Deconstructing World* (John Wiley & Sons, 2000); *Handbook of Strategic Management* (2001); *Strategic Entrepreneurship: Creating a New Integrated Mindset* (2002); *Creating Value: Winners in the New Business Environment* (Blackwell Publishers, 2002); *Managing Knowledge for Sustained Competitive Advantage* (Jossey-Bass, 2003); *Great Minds in Management: The Process of Theory Development* (Oxford University Press, 2005); and *The Global Mindset* (Elsevier, 2007). He has served on the editorial review boards of multiple journals, including the *Academy of Management Journal, Academy of Management Executive, Journal of Applied Psychology, Journal of Management, Journal of World Business,* and *Journal of Applied Behavioral Sciences.* Furthermore, he has served as consulting editor and editor of the *Academy of Management Journal.* He was a founding co-editor and currently a consulting editor for the *Strategic Entrepreneurship Journal.* He is a past president of the Strategic Management Society and of the Academy of Management.

He is a Fellow in the Academy of Management and in the Strategic Management Society. He received an honorary doctorate from the Universidad Carlos III de Madrid and is an Honorary Professor and Honorary Dean at Xi'an Jiao Tong University. He has been acknowledged with several awards for his scholarly research and he received the Irwin Outstanding Educator Award and the Distinguished Service Award from the Academy of Management. He has received best paper awards for articles published in the *Academy of Management Journal, Academy of Management Executive,* and *Journal of Management.*

R. Duane Ireland

R. Duane Ireland is a University Distinguished Professor and holds the Conn Chair in New Ventures Leadership in the Mays Business School, Texas A&M University where he previously served as head of the management department. He teaches strategic management courses at all levels (undergraduate, masters, doctoral, and executive). He has over 200 publications including more than a dozen books. His research, which focuses on diversification, innovation, corporate entrepreneurship, and strategic entrepreneurship, has been published in a number of journals, including *Academy of Management Journal, Academy of Management Review, Academy of Management Executive, Administrative Science Quarterly, Strategic Management Journal, Journal of Management, Strategic Entrepreneurship Journal, Human Relations, Entrepreneurship Theory and Practice, Journal of Business Venturing,* and *Journal of Management Studies,* among others. His recently published books include *Understanding Business Strategy,* 3rd edition (South-Western Cengage Learning, 2012), *Entrepreneurship: Successfully Launching New Ventures,* 4th edition (Prentice-Hall, 2012), and *Competing for Advantage,* 2nd edition (South-Western, 2008). He is serving or has served as a member of the editorial review boards for a number of journals, including *Academy of Management Journal, Academy of Management Review, Academy of Management Executive, Journal of Management, Strategic Entrepreneurship Journal, Journal of Business Venturing, Entrepreneurship Theory and Practice, Journal of Business Strategy, Academy of Management Perspectives,* and *European Management Journal.* He recently completed a term as editor of the *Academy of Management Journal.* He has completed terms as an associate editor for *Academy of Management Journal,* as an associate editor for *Academy of Management Executive,* and as a consulting editor for *Entrepreneurship Theory and Practice.* He has co-edited special issues of *Academy of Management Review, Academy of Management Executive, Journal of Business Venturing, Strategic Management Journal, Journal of High Technology and Engineering Management,* and *Organizational Research Methods.* He received awards for the best article published in *Academy of Management Executive* (1999) and *Academy of Management Journal* (2000). In 2001, his co-authored article published in *Academy of Management Executive* won the Best Journal Article in Corporate Entrepreneurship Award from the U.S. Association for Small Business & Entrepreneurship (USASBE).

He is a Fellow of the Academy of Management, a Fellow of the Strategic Management Society, and a 21st Century Entrepreneurship Research Scholar. He is the current Vice President and Program Chair for the Academy of Management. He received the 1999 Award for Outstanding Intellectual Contributions to Competitiveness Research from the American Society for Competitiveness and the USASBE Scholar in Corporate Entrepreneurship Award (2004).

Robert E. Hoskisson

Robert E. Hoskisson is the George R. Brown Chair of Strategic Management at the Jesse H. Jones Graduate School of Business, Rice University. He received his Ph.D. from the University of California-Irvine. Professor Hoskisson's research topics focus on corporate governance, acquisitions and divestitures, corporate and international diversification, corporate entrepreneurship, privatization, and cooperative strategy. He teaches courses in corporate and international strategic management, cooperative strategy, and strategy consulting, among others. Professor Hoskisson's research has appeared in over 120 publications, including articles in the *Academy of Management Journal, Academy of Management Review, Strategic Management Journal, Organization Science, Journal of Management, Journal of International Business Studies, Journal of Management Studies, Organization Research Methods, Journal of Business Venturing, Entrepreneurship Theory and Practice, Academy of Management Perspectives, Academy of Management Executive, Journal of World Business, California Management Review,* and 26 co-authored books. In 2010, *Times Higher Education* listed him as one of the most highly cited scholars in economics, finance, and management. He is currently an associate editor of the *Strategic Management Journal* and serves on the Editorial Review board of the *Academy of Management Journal*. Professor Hoskisson has served on several editorial boards for such publications as the *Academy of Management Journal* (including consulting editor and guest editor of a special issue), *Journal of Management* (including associate editor), *Organization Science, Journal of International Business Studies* (including consulting editor), *Journal of Management Studies* (guest editor of a special issue), and *Entrepreneurship Theory and Practice*. He has co-authored several books including *Understanding Business Strategy,* 3rd Edition (South-Western Cengage Learning, 2012), *Competing for Advantage,* 2nd edition (South-Western, 2008), and *Downscoping: How to Tame the Diversified Firm* (Oxford University Press, 1994).

He has an appointment as a Special Professor at the University of Nottingham and as an Honorary Professor at Xi'an Jiao Tong University. He is a Fellow of the Academy of Management and a charter member of the Academy of Management Journals Hall of Fame. He is also a Fellow of the Strategic Management Society. In 1998, he received an award for Outstanding Academic Contributions to Competitiveness, American Society for Competitiveness. He also received the William G. Dyer Distinguished Alumni Award given at the Marriott School of Management, Brigham Young University. He completed three years of service as a representative at large on the Board of Governors of the Academy of Management and currently is President-Elect of the Strategic Management Society.

Case Title	Manufacturing	Service	Consumer Goods	Food/Retail	High Technology	Internet	Transportation/Communication	International Perspective	Social/Ethical Issues	Industry Perspective
Adobe		●	●		●	●				●
Apple	●		●		●					●
AT&T		●			●		●			●
Best Buy		●	●	●						●
Chipotle Mexican Grill		●		●					●	
Coinstar (Redbox)							●			●
Domino's Pizza		●	●	●				●		●
Dr Pepper Snapple Group	●			●					●	●
Ford	●		●				●	●		●
Google		●			●	●	●	●		
Gore	●		●					●	●	●
Herman Miller	●		●	●					●	
Luck Company	●						●	●		●
McDonald's		●		●				●	●	●
Mellon		●		●						●
MGM		●		●				●		●
Microsoft	●	●			●	●				●
Movie Exhibition Industry		●								●
Navistar	●						●			●
Netflix		●	●		●		●			●
Porsche	●						●	●		
Rite Aid		●	●	●						
RJ Reynolds	●			●					●	●
Twitter		●			●		●	●		
Ultimate Fighting		●							●	●
Under Armour	●			●	●					●
Union Pacific		●					●		●	●
Valeant	●							●		●
Victory	●						●			●
Zipcar		●				●	●		●	●

Case Title	1	2	3	4	5	6	7	8	9	10	11	12	13
Chapters													
Adobe		●			●	●	●						
Apple			●	●	●				●				●
AT&T				●	●	●			●		●		●
Best Buy				●	●	●	●		●	●			
Chipotle Mexican Grill		●	●	●	●						●	●	
Coinstar (Redbox)	●					●			●		●	●	
Domino's Pizza		●	●	●	●						●	●	●
Dr Pepper Snapple Group	●	●	●	●		●	●				●	●	
Ford	●	●		●	●			●				●	●
Google		●	●	●	●	●		●	●			●	●
Gore		●	●	●		●				●	●		●
Herman Miller		●	●								●		●
Luck Company			●		●				●				●
McDonald's	●	●		●				●		●			
Mellon									●	●	●	●	●
MGM		●		●	●	●	●	●	●			●	
Microsoft			●		●	●	●		●		●	●	
Movie Exhibition Industry		●		●	●								
Navistar		●			●	●	●	●				●	
Netflix		●	●	●	●				●			●	●
Porsche		●	●	●		●	●	●	●	●			
Rite Aid		●		●	●	●	●				●		
RJ Reynolds		●		●		●	●					●	
Twitter				●	●						●	●	●
Ultimate Fighting	●	●	●									●	
Under Armour				●	●			●			●		
Union Pacific	●	●										●	
Valeant		●	●			●	●					●	●
Victory				●		●							●
Zipcar		●	●	●	●							●	●

PART 1
Strategic Management Inputs

1. Strategic Management and
   Strategic Competitiveness, 2

2. The External Environment: Opportunities, Threats,
   Industry Competition, and Competitor Analysis, 34

3. The Internal Organization: Resources, Capabilities,
   Core Competencies, and Competitive Advantages, 70

© Ryan McVay/Getty Images

CHAPTER 1

Strategic Management and Strategic Competitiveness

Studying this chapter should provide you with the strategic management knowledge needed to:

1. Define strategic competitiveness, strategy, competitive advantage, above-average returns, and the strategic management process.

2. Describe the competitive landscape and explain how globalization and technological changes shape it.

3. Use the industrial organization (I/O) model to explain how firms can earn above-average returns.

4. Use the resource-based model to explain how firms can earn above-average returns.

5. Describe vision and mission and discuss their value.

6. Define stakeholders and describe their ability to influence organizations.

7. Describe the work of strategic leaders.

8. Explain the strategic management process.

© Ryan McVay/Getty Images

ONCE A "GIANT," BORDERS BECAME A "WEAKLING" ON ITS KNEES

Borders changed the way books were sold and became the largest book retailer in the world. At one time, it had more than 1,300 large stores and approximately 35,000 employees. But, in February 2011, Borders declared bankruptcy. When it did so, it had shrunk to 674 stores and about 19,500 employees. Borders experienced hard times and paid for the ineffective strategies employed by its executive leadership teams. At its peak in the 1990s, Borders stock sold for more than $35 per share. On the day it declared bankruptcy, Borders stock sold for 23 cents per share.

What went wrong? Many goods are now sold by large chain store retailers. However, the way people buy and what they buy is beginning to change—especially in retail sales of books. Since 1995 and the founding of Amazon.com, books have been sold over the Internet. But with the rise of digital technology, electronic books and devices to read them have become highly popular. Quite obviously, they do not require large "brick-and-mortar" stores to sell them. Borders simply did not adjust quickly or effectively to these changes in the marketplace. Of course, it had to compete against Barnes & Noble, Walmart, Costco, and other large retailers selling books. It did not adjust quickly to Amazon's appearance in the market. It was much slower than Barnes & Noble, and that company required almost two years to launch Barnesandnoble.com. One of Borders' early mistakes was to develop an agreement with Amazon to handle its Internet sales instead of establishing its own Web presence.

Web-based retailing is growing in popularity, especially for electronic books. With eReaders such as Amazon's Kindle, Barnes & Noble's NOOK, and Apple's highly versatile iPad, the old way of selling books is rapidly becoming a dinosaur. While these changes were occurring in the retail book market, Borders invested heavily to enhance the marketing for traditional book selling. Borders tried to lure customers to its stores with promises of an enriching experience. Borders was also harmed by chaos in its executive ranks, having three regular CEOs and an interim CEO within a period of about two years. As a result of poor strategic decisions and ineffective strategic leadership, Borders suffered net losses of $344 million for 2008 and 2009. It also had compiled a massive debt in a campaign to buy back its stock while trying to keep the price high. All of its actions had the opposite effect.

With the bankruptcy, Borders wants to stay in business if it can reach agreement with its debtors. It plans to close about 200 more stores, and obtain reduced rent by renegotiating its current long leases. But it must do much more and quickly if it is to survive in the new book retail market. At the present time, it is difficult to see how Borders can survive without the capabilities to navigate in this new competitive landscape.

Joseph Clemson/Alamy

While Border's primary competitor, Barnes and Noble, beefed up its online presence and created the Nook eReader, Borders chose instead to focus on expanding its physical plants, refurbishing its stores and outsourcing its online sales operation to Amazon. This proved to be the wrong strategy.

Sources: C. Caldwell, 2011, A fate written in the stores, *Financial Times,* http://www.ft.com, March 4; Borders' publishers, landlords band together in bankruptcy, 2011, *The Wall Street Journal,* http://www.wsj.com, February 25; S. Rosenbaum, 2011, Inside the world of local books—a bright future, *Fast Company,* http://www.fastcompany.com, February 21; Borders bankruptcy: What went wrong? 2011, *The Wall Street Journal,* http://www.wsj.com, February 16; M. Frazier, 2011, The three lessons of the Borders bankruptcy, *Forbes,* http://www.forbes.com, February 16; M. Spector & J. A. Trachtenberg, 2011, Chapter 11 for Borders, new chapter for books, *The Wall Street Journal,* http://www.wsj.com, February 12.

As we see from the Opening Case, Borders was highly unsuccessful because of its inability to compete against other major book retailers, especially in the area of Internet book sales. Therefore, we can conclude that Borders was not competitive (unable to achieve *strategic competitiveness*). It clearly was unable to earn *above-average returns*. In fact, it suffered significant net losses and eventually had to declare bankruptcy because of inadequate cash flow and assets that were valued less that its liabilities. Its competitors, Barnes & Noble and Amazon, were more competitive and adjusted more effectively to changes in the book retail market. For example, both firms had eReaders (the NOOK and Kindle, respectively) to sell along with electronic books. They used the strategic management process (see Figure 1.1) as the foundation for the commitments, decisions, and actions they took to pursue strategic competitiveness and above-average terms. Obviously, Borders did not use this process and it cost the firm in major ways, perhaps even its ability to survive. The strategic management process is fully explained in this book. We introduce you to this process in the next few paragraphs.

Strategic competitiveness is achieved when a firm successfully formulates and implements a value-creating strategy. A **strategy** is an integrated and coordinated set of commitments and actions designed to exploit core competencies and gain a competitive advantage. When choosing a strategy, firms make choices among competing alternatives as the pathway for deciding how they will pursue strategic competitiveness.[1] In this sense, the chosen strategy indicates what the firm *will do* as well as what the firm *will not do*.

As explained in the Opening Case, Borders tried to enrich its traditional approach with more marketing and making its stores more attractive. However, because the number of books sold through large chain store retailers has been declining, this strategy had little chance for success. A recent study conducted to identify the factors that contribute to the success of top corporate performers showed why Borders was unsuccessful. This study found that the top performers were entrepreneurial, market oriented (effective knowledge of the customers' needs), used valuable competencies, and offered innovative products and services.[2] Borders displayed none of these attributes. It clearly did not understand its market and customers and it was not innovative. Therefore, its lack of success is not surprising. A firm's strategy also demonstrates how it differs from its competitors. Recently, Ford Motor Company devoted efforts to explain to stakeholders how the company differs from its competitors. The main idea is that Ford claims that it is "greener" and more technically advanced than its competitors, such as General Motors and Chrysler Group LLC (an alliance between Chrysler and Fiat SpA).[3]

A firm has a **competitive advantage** when it implements a strategy that creates superior value for customers and that its competitors are unable to duplicate or find too costly to imitate.[4] An organization can be confident that its strategy has resulted in one or more useful competitive advantages only after competitors' efforts to duplicate its strategy have ceased or failed. In addition, firms must understand that no competitive advantage is permanent.[5] The speed with which competitors are able to acquire the skills needed to duplicate the benefits of a firm's value-creating strategy determines how long the competitive advantage will last.[6]

Above-average returns are returns in excess of what an investor expects to earn from other investments with a similar amount of risk. **Risk** is an investor's uncertainty about the economic gains or losses that will result from a particular investment.[7] The most successful companies learn how to effectively manage risk. Effectively managing risks reduces investors' uncertainty about the results of their investment.[8] Returns are often measured in terms of accounting figures, such as return on assets, return on equity, or return on sales. Alternatively, returns can be measured on the basis of stock market returns, such as monthly returns (the end-of-the-period stock price minus the beginning stock price, divided by the beginning stock price, yielding a percentage return). In smaller, new venture firms, returns are sometimes measured in terms of the amount and

Strategic competitiveness is achieved when a firm successfully formulates and implements a value-creating strategy.

A **strategy** is an integrated and coordinated set of commitments and actions designed to exploit core competencies and gain a competitive advantage.

A firm has a **competitive advantage** when it implements a strategy that creates superior value for customers and competitors are unable to duplicate or find too costly to try to imitate.

Above-average returns are returns in excess of what an investor expects to earn from other investments with a similar amount of risk.

Risk is an investor's uncertainty about the economic gains or losses that will result from a particular investment.

Figure 1.1 The Strategic Management Process

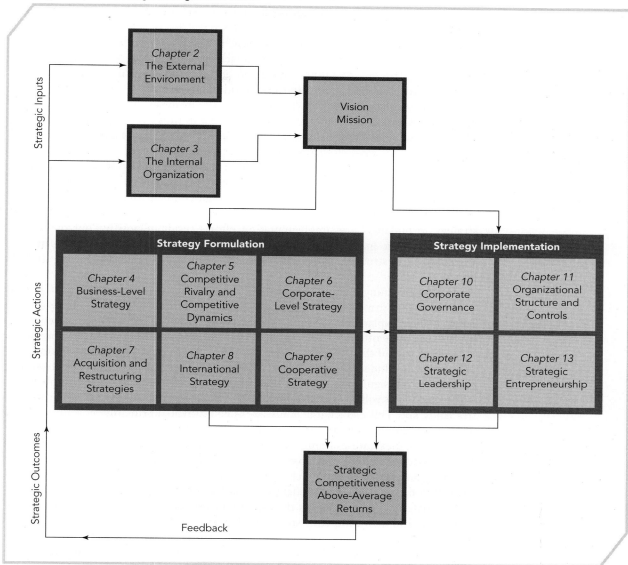

© 2013 Cengage Learning.

speed of growth (e.g., in annual sales) rather than more traditional profitability measures[9] because new ventures require time to earn acceptable returns (in the form of return on assets and so forth) on investors' investments.[10]

Understanding how to exploit a competitive advantage is important for firms seeking to earn above-average returns.[11] Firms without a competitive advantage or that are not competing in an attractive industry earn, at best, average returns. **Average returns** are returns equal to those an investor expects to earn from other investments with a similar amount of risk. In the long run, an inability to earn at least average returns results first in decline and, eventually, failure. Failure occurs because investors withdraw their investments from those firms earning less-than-average returns. This is what happened to Borders when it was unable to earn returns. Indeed, it lost money and because of the investors' lack of confidence in the firm, its stock price fell perilously close to zero.

As we noted above, there are no guarantees of permanent success. This is true for Borders, which enjoyed a considerable amount of success in the 1990s. Even considering

Average returns are returns equal to those an investor expects to earn from other investments with a similar amount of risk.

Apple's excellent current performance, it still must be careful not to become overconfident and continue its quest to be the leader in its markets. (Apple is the topic of a Strategic Focus segment later in this chapter.)

The **strategic management process** (see Figure 1.1) is the full set of commitments, decisions, and actions required for a firm to achieve strategic competitiveness and earn above-average returns. The firm's first step in the process is to analyze its external environment and internal organization to determine its resources, capabilities, and core competencies—the sources of its "strategic inputs." Obviously, Borders' process failed at this point because it did not understand the market in which it competed. It performed poorly against other large chain-store retailers and failed to foresee the major changes in the market with increasing sales of electronic books.

With the information gained from external and internal analyses, the firm develops its vision and mission and formulates one or more strategies. To implement its strategies, the firm takes actions toward achieving strategic competitiveness and above-average returns. Effective strategic actions that take place in the context of carefully integrated strategy formulation and implementation efforts result in positive outcomes. This dynamic strategic management process must be maintained as ever-changing markets and competitive structures are coordinated with a firm's continuously evolving strategic inputs.[12]

In the remaining chapters of this book, we use the strategic management process to explain what firms do to achieve strategic competitiveness and earn above-average returns. These explanations demonstrate why some firms consistently achieve competitive success while others fail to do so.[13] As you will see, the reality of global competition is a critical part of the strategic management process and significantly influences firms' performances.[14] Indeed, learning how to successfully compete in the globalized world is one of the most significant challenges for firms competing in the current century.[15]

Several topics will be discussed in this chapter. First, we describe the current competitive landscape. This challenging landscape is being created primarily by the emergence of a global economy, globalization resulting from that economy, and rapid technological changes. Next, we examine two models that firms use to gather the information and knowledge required to choose and then effectively implement their strategies. The insights gained from these models also serve as the foundation for forming the firm's vision and mission. The first model (the industrial organization or I/O model) suggests that the external environment is the primary determinant of a firm's strategic actions. Identifying and then competing successfully in an attractive (i.e., profitable) industry or segment of an industry are the keys to competitive success when using this model.[16] The second model (resource-based) suggests that a firm's unique resources and capabilities are the critical link to strategic competitiveness.[17] Thus, the first model is concerned primarily with the firm's external environment while the second model is concerned primarily with the firm's internal organization. After discussing vision and mission, direction-setting statements that influence the choice and use of strategies, we describe the stakeholders that organizations serve. The degree to which stakeholders' needs can be met increases when firms achieve strategic competitiveness and earn above-average returns. Closing the chapter are introductions to strategic leaders and the elements of the strategic management process.

The **strategic management process** is the full set of commitment, decisions, and actions required for a firm to achieve strategic competitiveness and earn above-average returns.

The Competitive Landscape

The fundamental nature of competition in many of the world's industries is changing. The reality is that financial capital continues to be scarce and markets are increasingly volatile.[18] Because of this, the pace of change is relentless and ever-increasing. Even determining the boundaries of an industry has become challenging. Consider, for example, how advances in interactive computer networks and telecommunications have blurred the boundaries of the entertainment industry. Today, not only do cable companies and satellite networks compete for entertainment revenue from television, but telecommunication companies are moving into the entertainment business through significant improvements in fiber-optic lines.[19] Partnerships among firms in different segments of the entertainment industry further blur industry boundaries. For example, MSNBC is co-owned by NBC Universal and Microsoft. In turn, General Electric owns 49 percent of NBC Universal while Comcast owns the remaining 51 percent.[20]

Other characteristics of the current competitive landscape are noteworthy. Conventional sources of competitive advantage such as economies of scale and huge advertising budgets are not as effective as they once were in terms of helping firms earn above-average returns. Moreover, the traditional managerial mind-set is unlikely to lead a firm to strategic competitiveness. Managers must adopt a new mind-set that values flexibility, speed, innovation, integration, and the challenges that evolve from constantly changing conditions.[21] The conditions of the competitive landscape result in a perilous business world, one in which the investments that are required to compete on a global scale are enormous and the consequences of failure are severe.[22] Effective use of the strategic management process reduces the likelihood of failure for firms as they encounter the conditions of today's competitive landscape.

Hypercompetition is a term often used to capture the realities of the competitive landscape. Under conditions of hypercompetition, assumptions of market stability are replaced by notions of inherent instability and change.[23] Hypercompetition results from the dynamics of strategic maneuvering among global and innovative combatants.[24] It is a condition of rapidly escalating competition based on price-quality positioning, competition to create new know-how and establish first-mover advantage, and competition to protect or invade established product or geographic markets.[25] In a hypercompetitive market, firms often aggressively challenge their competitors in the hopes of improving their competitive position and ultimately their performance.[26]

Several factors create hypercompetitive environments and influence the nature of the current competitive landscape. The emergence of a global economy and technology, specifically rapid technological change, are the two primary drivers of hypercompetitive environments and the nature of today's competitive landscape.

> A **global economy** is one in which goods, services, people, skills, and ideas move freely across geographic borders.

The Global Economy

A **global economy** is one in which goods, services, people, skills, and ideas move freely across geographic borders. Relatively unfettered by artificial constraints, such as tariffs, the global economy significantly expands and complicates a firm's competitive environment.[27]

Interesting opportunities and challenges are associated with the emergence of the global economy.[28] For example, the European Union (composed of several countries) has become one of the world's largest markets, with 700 million potential customers. "In the past, China was generally seen as a low-competition market and a low-cost producer. Today, China is an extremely competitive market in which local market-seeking MNCs [multinational corporations] must fiercely compete against other MNCs and against those local companies that are more cost effective and faster in product development. While China has been viewed as a country from which to source low-cost goods, lately, many MNCs, such as P&G (Procter

The European Union is composed of more than 25 member states including Austria, Lithuania, and Ireland. While it began as a purely economic union, it has evolved into an organization that spans many areas from economic development to environmental policy.

swissmacky/Shutterstock.com

S T R A T E G I C **F O C U S**

HUAWEI ALSO NEEDS GUANXI IN THE UNITED STATES

Building strong relationships is an important dimension of Chinese culture. In fact, "Guanxi" (strong relationships in which each party feels obligated to help the other) is a major element of doing business in China. Over time, U.S. companies operating in Chinese markets have learned this lesson. Huawei has learned that Guanxi is also important for doing business in the United States.

Huawei is the largest manufacturer of phone network equipment in China and second in global markets to Sweden's Ericsson AB. Huawei first invested in the United States in 2001 and has developed a sizable presence in global markets, yet the portion of its total sales revenue from North and South America is negligible. To help build its competitive-

ness in global markets, it hired John Roese, former Chief Technology Officer at Nortel Networks, to manage its North American R&D activities. It also hired Matt Bross, a former British Telecom executive, to serve as Chief Technology Officer for its U.S. operations. In 2010 it formed Amerilink Telecom Corp, based in Kansas, in an attempt to compete for large U.S. contracts.

Huawei has become a highly innovative company, filing 1,737 patents in 2008 alone. In fact, Fast Company ranked Huawei as the fifth most innovative company in its 2010 listing. The development of major R&D centers (including one in Silicon Valley in the United States) and the development of innovative products are helping Huawei to gain respect from experts in the telecommunications field. It has become a major supplier of telecommunications products such as routers and fiber systems and also has a significant share of the wireless market with its LTE and WiMAX technologies.

Huawei Technologies is entering the booming market for Internet-based computing, expanding its reach to Silicon Valley and beyond.

Despite these significant successes, Huawei has experienced problems in the U.S. market and with the U.S. government. For example, it tried to acquire several U.S. businesses in 2010 and 2011 without success. In 2010, it bid for 2Wire, a consumer electronics and software firm, and also tried to acquire the business telecom unit of Motorola, but both were sold to other companies. The companies said that they did not believe that Huawei would gain the approval from the U.S. government to make the purchase. In 2011, Huawei tried to acquire 3Leaf, a U.S.–based company that developed networking technology. Despite the fact the 3Leaf was insolvent, the Committee on Foreign Investment in the United States recommended against the acquisition. Members of the U.S. Congress and government officials had concerns about Huawei. Thus, Huawei has not built Guanxi with the U.S. government. Some of the concerns stem from the original linkages between Huawei and the Chinese military and because of prior charges against the company suggesting that it stole proprietary technology. Thus, Huawei has barriers to overcome.

Huawei continues to seek better footing in U.S. markets. For example, the company has asked the U.S. government to conduct a formal investigation of its business with the intent to clear its reputation. In addition, Huawei had a major 10-year anniversary celebration for its U.S. operations. The celebration was held in Santa Clara, California, at its new large R&D center. In the invitation, Huawei described the firm as a local global company. The invitation also explained that it has deepened its commitment to the United States in its first 10 years of operations there, and is a consumer-oriented, responsible corporate citizen in the communities where it has operations. These are the right words to say, but Huawei must also convince U.S. government officials of its positive value to the country. It needs to proactively build relationships with federal and state government officials.

AP Photos/Song fan

GLOBALIZATION • GLOBALIZATION • GLOBALIZATION

Some have recommended that it invest in lobbyists to help build and support its relationships as do many large U.S. corporations. Regardless, to achieve the level of success in U.S. markets desired by Huawei, it will need to build Guanxi with U.S. government officials, customers, and suppliers.

Sources: E. Woyke, 2011, Huawei holding 10-year U.S. anniversary event to refine reputation, *Forbes*, www.forbes.com, March 3; A. W. Goldberg & J. P. Galper, 2011, Where Huawei went wrong in America, *The Wall Street Journal*, www .online.wsj.com, March 3; D. Barboza, 2011, China telecom giant, thwarted in U.S. deals, seeks inquiry to clear name, *The New York Times*, www.nytimes.com, February 25; E. Lococo, 2011, Huawei says it's no threat to U.S. security, invites probe, *Bloomberg Businessweek*, www.businessweek.com, February 24; D. Ikenson, 2011, Despite Huawei's experience, America is increasingly open to Chinese investment, *Forbes*, www.forbes.com, February 23; K. Eaton, 2010, U.S. two-faced on China: Happy to spend there, blocks acquisitions here, *Fast Company*, www.fastcompany.com, August 5; S. Saitto & J. McCracken, 2010, Huawei said to have failed in U.S. takeover bid, Bloomberg *Businessweek*, www .businessweek.com, August 31; O. Malik, 2009, Huawei unveils grand ambition in naming Bross CTO, *Businessweek*, www.businessweek.com, September 30.

and Gamble), are actually net exporters of local management talent; they have been dispatching more Chinese abroad than bringing foreign expatriates to China."[29] China has become the second-largest economy in the world, surpassing Japan. India, the world's largest democracy, has an economy that also is growing rapidly and now ranks as the fourth largest in the world.[30] Simultaneously, many firms in these emerging economies are moving into international markets and are now regarded as multinational firms. This fact is explored in the Strategic Focus on Huawei. The discussion shows that barriers to entering foreign markets still exist, however. Essentially, Huawei must build credibility in the U.S. market, and especially build a positive relationship with stakeholders such as the U.S. government.

The statistics detailing the nature of the global economy reflect the realities of a hypercompetitive business environment and challenge individual firms to think seriously about the markets in which they will compete. Consider the case of General Electric (GE). Although headquartered in the United States, GE expects that as much as 60 percent of its revenue growth through 2015 will be generated by competing in rapidly developing economies (e.g., China and India). The decision to count on revenue growth in emerging economies instead of in developed countries such as the United States and European nations seems quite reasonable in the global economy. GE achieved significant growth in 2010 partly because of signing contracts for large infrastructure projects in China and Russia. GE's CEO, Jeffrey Immelt, argues that we have entered a new economic era in which the global economy will be more volatile and that most of the growth will come from emerging economies such as Brazil, China, and India.[31] Therefore, GE is investing significantly in these emerging economies, in order to improve its competitive position in vital geographic sources of revenue and profitability.

The March of Globalization

Globalization is the increasing economic interdependence among countries and their organizations as reflected in the flow of goods and services, financial capital, and knowledge across country borders.[32] Globalization is a product of a large number of firms competing against one another in an increasing number of global economies.

In globalized markets and industries, financial capital might be obtained in one national market and used to buy raw materials in another. Manufacturing equipment bought from a third national market can then be used to produce products that are sold in yet a fourth market. Thus, globalization increases the range of opportunities for companies competing in the current competitive landscape.[33]

Firms engaging in globalization of their operations must make culturally sensitive decisions when using the strategic management process.[34] Additionally, highly globalized firms must anticipate ever-increasing complexity in their operations as goods, services, people, and so forth move freely across geographic borders and throughout different economic markets.

Overall, it is important to note that globalization has led to higher performance standards in many competitive dimensions, including those of quality, cost, productivity, product introduction time, and operational efficiency. In addition to firms competing in the global economy, these standards affect firms competing on a domestic-only basis. The reason is that customers will purchase from a global competitor rather than a domestic firm when the global company's good or service is superior. Because workers now flow rather freely among global economies, and because employees are a key source of competitive advantage, firms must understand that increasingly, "the best people will come from … anywhere."[35] Thus, managers have to learn how to operate effectively in a "multi-polar" world with many important countries having unique interests and environments.[36] Firms must learn how to deal with the reality that in the competitive landscape of the twenty-first century, only companies capable of meeting, if not exceeding, global standards typically have the capability to earn above-average returns.

Although globalization offers potential benefits to firms, it is not without risks. Collectively, the risks of participating outside of a firm's domestic country in the global economy are labeled a "liability of foreignness."[37]

One risk of entering the global market is the amount of time typically required for firms to learn how to compete in markets that are new to them. A firm's performance can suffer until this knowledge is either developed locally or transferred from the home market to the newly established global location.[38] Additionally, a firm's performance may suffer with substantial amounts of globalization. In this instance, firms may over-diversify internationally beyond their ability to manage these extended operations.[39] Overdiversification can have strong negative effects on a firm's overall performance.

Thus, entry into international markets, even for firms with substantial experience in the global economy, requires effective use of the strategic management process. It is also important to note that even though global markets are an attractive strategic option for some companies, they are not the only source of strategic competitiveness. In fact, for most companies, even for those capable of competing successfully in global markets, it is critical to remain committed to and strategically competitive in both domestic and international markets by staying attuned to technological opportunities and potential competitive disruptions that innovations create.[40]

Technology and Technological Changes

Technology-related trends and conditions can be placed into three categories: technology diffusion and disruptive technologies, the information age, and increasing knowledge intensity. Through these categories, technology is significantly altering the nature of competition and contributing to unstable competitive environments as a result of doing so.

Technology Diffusion and Disruptive Technologies

The rate of technology diffusion, which is the speed at which new technologies become available and are used, has increased substantially over the past 15 to 20 years. Consider the following rates of technology diffusion:

It took the telephone 35 years to get into 25 percent of all homes in the United States. It took TV 26 years. It took radio 22 years. It took PCs 16 years. It took the Internet 7 years.[41]

Perpetual innovation is a term used to describe how rapidly and consistently new, information-intensive technologies replace older ones. The shorter product life cycles resulting from these rapid diffusions of new technologies place a competitive premium on being able to quickly introduce new, innovative goods and services into the marketplace.[42]

In fact, when products become somewhat indistinguishable because of the widespread and rapid diffusion of technologies, speed to market with innovative products may be the primary source of competitive advantage (see Chapter 5).[43] Indeed, some argue that the global economy is increasingly driven by or revolves around constant innovations. Not surprisingly, such innovations must be derived from an understanding of global standards and expectations of product functionality.[44] Although some argue that large established firms may have trouble innovating, evidence suggests that today these firms are developing radically new technologies that transform old industries or create new ones.[45] Apple is an excellent example of a large established firm capable of radical innovation. Also, in order to diffuse the technology and enhance the value of an innovation, additional firms need to be innovative in their use of the new technology, building it into their products.[46]

Another indicator of rapid technology diffusion is that it now may take only 12 to 18 months for firms to gather information about their competitors' research and development and product decisions.[47] In the global economy, competitors can sometimes imitate a firm's successful competitive actions within a few days. In this sense, the rate of technological diffusion has reduced the competitive benefits of patents. Today, patents may be an effective way of protecting proprietary technology in a small number of industries such as pharmaceuticals. Indeed, many firms competing in the electronics industry often do not apply for patents to prevent competitors from gaining access to the technological knowledge included in the patent application.

Disruptive technologies—technologies that destroy the value of an existing technology and create new markets[48]—surface frequently in today's competitive markets. Think of the new markets created by the technologies underlying the development of products such as iPods, iPads, WiFi, and the browser. These types of products are thought by some to represent radical or breakthrough innovations.[49] (We discuss more about radical innovations in Chapter 13.) A disruptive or radical technology can create what is essentially a new industry or can harm industry incumbents. However, some incumbents are able to adapt based on their superior resources, experience, and ability to gain access to the new technology through multiple sources (e.g., alliances, acquisitions, and ongoing internal research).[50]

Clearly, Apple has developed and introduced "disruptive technologies" such as the iPod, and in so doing changed several industries. For example, the iPod and its complementary iTunes have revolutionized how music is sold to and used by consumers. In conjunction with other complementary and competitive products (e.g., Amazon's Kindle), Apple's iPad is contributing to and speeding major changes in the publishing industry, moving from hard copies to electronic books. Apple's new technologies and products are also contributing to the new "information age." Thus, Apple provides an example of entrepreneurship through technology emergence across multiple industries.[51]

The Information Age

Dramatic changes in information technology have occurred in recent years. Personal computers, cellular phones, artificial intelligence, virtual reality, massive databases, and multiple social networking sites are only a few examples of how information is used differently as a result of technological developments. An important outcome of these changes is that the ability to effectively and efficiently access and use information has become an important source of competitive advantage in virtually all industries. Information technology advances have given small firms more flexibility in competing with large firms, if that technology can be efficiently used.[52]

Both the pace of change in information technology and its diffusion will continue to increase. For instance, the number of personal computers in use globally is expected to surpass three billion by 2012. More than 335 million were sold in the United States alone in 2011.[53] The declining costs of information technologies and the increased accessibility to them are also evident in the current competitive landscape. The global proliferation of relatively inexpensive computing power and its linkage on a global scale via computer networks combine to increase the speed and diffusion of information technologies. Thus, the competitive potential of information technologies is now available to companies of all sizes throughout the world, including those in emerging economies.[54]

The Internet is another technological innovation contributing to hypercompetition. Available to an increasing number of people throughout the world, the Internet provides an infrastructure that allows the delivery of information to computers in any location. Access to the Internet on smaller devices such as cell phones is having an ever-growing impact on competition in a number of industries. However, possible changes to Internet

STRATEGIC FOCUS

THE CORE OF APPLE: TECHNOLOGY AND INNOVATION

A popular children's game is to take the core of an apple after eating it and say "Apple core, Baltimore, who is your friend?" Another child names a "friend" and the first child throws the apple core at him/her. The child who is a target may not want the apple core thrown at her or him. In the world of business, firms clearly do not want to be targeted by Apple's core with new technology, which is likely in the form of an innovative product. In recent years, Apple has transformed industries with the introduction of new products such as the iPod, iPad (currently causing a transformation), and to some degree, even the iPhone.

Apple has achieved phenomenal success with the introduction of these innovative products. In fact, Steven Jobs was selected by *Fortune* magazine as the CEO of the first decade of the twenty-first century, based on the fact that Apple under his leadership has transformed four industries, three of them in the most recent decade. In addition, in 2011, *Fast Company* named Apple the most innovative company, and *Fortune* ranked Apple as the top company in its annual survey and evaluation of companies based on multiple criteria. In addition, Apple had the second largest market capitalization of all firms in the world. As these data suggest, Apple is one of the top companies in the world based on almost any criterion or set of criteria used. Because of this, Apple is perceived exceptionally well by customers and has what some refer to as "legendary" market power. An executive with one telecommunications company suggested that to negotiate with Apple, one has to start on his knees, implying that you almost have to beg them to partner with your firm. Apple's growth rate has been phenomenal and its financial performance even more impressive. And, the appeal of Apple's products is global. For example, Apple has announced the opening of its fifth store in China to handle growing demand for its products. Currently, Apple's stores in China handle 40,000 people daily, four times the average flow of customers in its U.S. stores.

Tomas Abad/Age Fotostock

This Apple Retail Store on 5th Avenue in New York City enjoys a steady flow of traffic every day, as do many urban Apple retail locations. Even more remarkable is that currently Apple's stores in China handle 40,000 people daily, four times the average flow of customers in its U.S. stores!

Although there are many reasons for its success, the primary reason rests with Apple's new technology development and innovative new products. Apple's most recent successful launch was the iPad. When it was introduced, analysts projected sales somewhere between 1 to 10 million units. In the first nine months after the iPad's introduction, Apple sold 15 million of them. As often happens with highly successful innovations, competitors quickly developed and introduced imitative iPads. In fact, competitors sold almost 1 million units during the first year after the iPad's introduction to the market. One consulting firm announced that 64 different companies introduced a total of 102 different tablets designed to sell to the same market as the iPad. Apple then introduced the iPad 2, which is lighter, faster, and more versatile, yet usually sells for the same price as the original iPad. One executive described the iPad 2 as Secretariat (the famous champion thoroughbred race horse). He suggested that it would lead the imitative competitors' products by 31 lengths (as Secretariat did in the Belmont Stakes). Apple is expected to retain at least 80 percent of the tablet computer market even with the many imitative products on the market.

TECHNOLOGY • TECHNOLOGY • TE

Sources: 2011, World's Most Admired Companies, *Fortune*, www.fortune.com, March 3; B. Worthen, 2011, With new iPad, Apple tries to stay ahead of wave of tablet rivals, *The Wall Street Journal*, www.online.wsj.com, March 3; G. A. Fowler & N. Wingfield, 2011, Apple's showman takes the stage, *The Wall Street Journal*, www.online.wsj.com, March 3; 2011, Apple and the tablets, *Financial Times*, www.ft.com, March 1; N. Louth, 2011, Finding value in Apple's core, *Financial Times*, www.ft.com, February 25; M. Helft, 2011, After iPad's head start, rival tablets are poised to flood offices, *The New York Times*, www.nytimes.com, February 20; L. Chao, 2011, New Shanghai Apple store will be biggest in China, *The Wall Street Journal*, www.online.wsj.com, February 18.

Service Providers' (ISPs) pricing structures could affect the rate of growth of Internet-based applications. Users downloading or streaming high-definition movies, playing video games online, and so forth would be affected the most if ISPs were to base their pricing structure around total usage.

© Nicholas Monu/iStockphoto.com

STRATEGY RIGHT NOW

Find out more about Apple's drive to innovate.
www.cengagebrain.com

Increasing Knowledge Intensity

Knowledge (information, intelligence, and expertise) is the basis of technology and its application. In the competitive landscape of the twenty-first century, knowledge is a critical organizational resource and an increasingly valuable source of competitive advantage.[55] Indeed, starting in the 1980s, the basis of competition shifted from hard assets to intangible resources. For example, "Wal-Mart transformed retailing through its proprietary approach to supply chain management and its information-rich relationships with customers and suppliers."[56] Relationships with customers and suppliers are an example of an intangible resource.

Knowledge is gained through experience, observation, and inference and is an intangible resource (tangible and intangible resources are fully described in Chapter 3). The value of intangible resources, including knowledge, is growing as a proportion of total shareholder value in today's competitive landscape.[57] In fact, the Brookings Institution estimates that intangible resources contribute approximately 85 percent of that value.[58] The probability of achieving strategic competitiveness is enhanced for the firm that develops the ability to capture intelligence, transform it into usable knowledge, and diffuse it rapidly throughout the company.[59] Therefore, firms must develop (e.g., through training programs) and

Julien THOMAZO/PhotoLibrary

The pricing landscape of ISPs may evolve based on the advent of streaming video and the increased use of iPads and other tablets and mobile devices.

acquire (e.g., by hiring educated and experienced employees) knowledge, integrate it into the organization to create capabilities, and then apply it to gain a competitive advantage.[60]

A strong knowledge base is necessary to create innovations. In fact, firms lacking the appropriate internal knowledge resources are less likely to invest money in research and development.[61] Firms must continue to learn (building their knowledge stock) because knowledge spillovers to competitors are common. There are several ways in which knowledge spillovers occur, including the hiring of professional staff and managers by competitors.[62] Because of the potential for spillovers, firms must move quickly to use their knowledge in productive ways. In addition, firms must build routines that facilitate the diffusion of local knowledge throughout the organization for use everywhere that it has value.[63] Firms are better able to do these things when they have strategic flexibility.

Strategic flexibility is a set of capabilities used to respond to various demands and opportunities existing in a dynamic and uncertain competitive environment. Thus, strategic flexibility involves coping with uncertainty and its accompanying risks.[64] Firms should try to develop strategic flexibility in all areas of their operations. However, those working within firms to develop strategic flexibility should understand that the task is not easy, largely because of inertia that can build up over time. A firm's focus and past core competencies may actually slow change and strategic flexibility.[65]

Strategic flexibility is a set of capabilities used to respond to various demands and opportunities existing in a dynamic and uncertain competitive environment.

To be strategically flexible on a continuing basis and to gain the competitive benefits of such flexibility, a firm has to develop the capacity to learn. Continuous learning provides the firm with new and up-to-date skill sets, which allow it to adapt to its environment as it encounters changes.[66] Firms capable of rapidly and broadly applying what they have learned exhibit the strategic flexibility and the capacity to change in ways that will increase the probability of successfully dealing with uncertain, hypercompetitive environments.

The I/O Model of Above-Average Returns

From the 1960s through the 1980s, the external environment was thought to be the primary determinant of strategies that firms selected to be successful.[67] The industrial organization model of above-average returns explains the external environment's dominant influence on a firm's strategic actions. The model specifies that the industry or segment of an industry in which a company chooses to compete has a stronger influence on performance than do the choices managers make inside their organizations.[68] The firm's performance is believed to be determined primarily by a range of industry properties, including economies of scale, barriers to market entry, diversification, product differentiation, and the degree of concentration of firms in the industry.[69] We examine these industry characteristics in Chapter 2.

Grounded in economics, the I/O model has four underlying assumptions. First, the external environment is assumed to impose pressures and constraints that determine the strategies that would result in above-average returns. Second, most firms competing within an industry or within a segment of that industry are assumed to control similar strategically relevant resources and to pursue similar strategies in light of those resources. Third, resources used to implement strategies are assumed to be highly mobile across firms, so any resource differences that might develop between firms will be short-lived. Fourth, organizational decision makers are assumed to be rational and committed to acting in the firm's best interests, as shown by their profit-maximizing behaviors.[70] The I/O model challenges firms to find the most attractive industry in which to compete. Because most firms are assumed to have similar valuable resources that are mobile across companies, their performance generally can be increased only when they operate in the industry with the highest profit potential and learn how to use their resources to implement the strategy required by the industry's structural characteristics.[71]

The five forces model of competition is an analytical tool used to help firms find the industry that is the most attractive for them. The model (explained in Chapter 2) encompasses several variables and tries to capture the complexity of competition. The five forces model suggests that an industry's profitability (i.e., its rate of return on invested capital relative to its cost of capital) is a function of interactions among five forces: suppliers, buyers, competitive rivalry among firms currently in the industry, product substitutes, and potential entrants to the industry.[72]

Firms use the five forces model to identify the attractiveness of an industry (as measured by its profitability potential) as well as the most advantageous position for the firm to take in that industry, given the industry's structural characteristics.[73] Typically, the model suggests that firms can earn above-average returns by producing either standardized goods or services at costs below those of competitors (a cost leadership strategy) or by producing differentiated goods or services for which customers are willing to pay a price premium (a differentiation strategy). (The cost leadership and product differentiation strategies are discussed in Chapter 4.) The fact that "... the fast food industry is becoming a 'zero-sum industry' as companies battle for the same pool of customers"[74] suggests that fast food giant McDonald's is competing in a relatively unattractive industry. However, by focusing on product innovations and enhancing existing facilities while buying properties outside the United States at attractive prices for selectively building new stores, McDonald's is positioned in the fast food (or quick-service) restaurant industry to earn above-average returns.

Figure 1.2 The I/O Model of Above-Average Returns

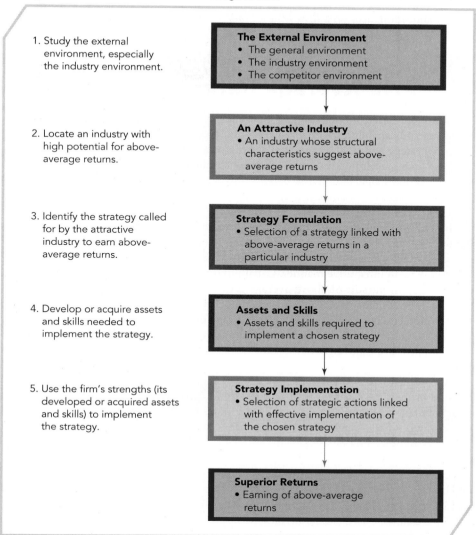

1. Study the external environment, especially the industry environment.

The External Environment
- The general environment
- The industry environment
- The competitor environment

2. Locate an industry with high potential for above-average returns.

An Attractive Industry
- An industry whose structural characteristics suggest above-average returns

3. Identify the strategy called for by the attractive industry to earn above-average returns.

Strategy Formulation
- Selection of a strategy linked with above-average returns in a particular industry

4. Develop or acquire assets and skills needed to implement the strategy.

Assets and Skills
- Assets and skills required to implement a chosen strategy

5. Use the firm's strengths (its developed or acquired assets and skills) to implement the strategy.

Strategy Implementation
- Selection of strategic actions linked with effective implementation of the chosen strategy

Superior Returns
- Earning of above-average returns

© 2013 Cengage Learning.

As shown in Figure 1.2, the I/O model suggests that above-average returns are earned when firms are able to effectively study the external environment as the foundation for identifying an attractive industry and implementing the appropriate strategy. For example, in some industries, firms can reduce competitive rivalry and erect barriers to entry by forming joint ventures. Because of these outcomes, the joint ventures increase profitability in the industry.[75] Companies that develop or acquire the internal skills needed to implement strategies required by the external environment are likely to succeed, while those that do not are likely to fail.[76] Hence, this model suggests that returns are determined primarily by external characteristics rather than by the firm's unique internal resources and capabilities.

Research findings support the I/O model in that approximately 20 percent of a firm's profitability is explained by the industry in which it chooses to compete. However, this research also shows that 36 percent of the variance in firm profitability can be attributed to the firm's characteristics and actions.[77] These findings suggest that the external environment and a firm's resources, capabilities, core competencies, and competitive advantages (see Chapter 3) influence the company's ability to achieve strategic competitiveness and earn above-average returns.

As shown in Figure 1.2, the I/O model assumes that a firm's strategy is a set of commitments and actions flowing from the characteristics of the industry in which the firm has decided to compete. The resource-based model, discussed next, takes a different view of the major influences on a firm's choice of strategy.

The Resource-Based Model of Above-Average Returns

The resource-based model assumes that each organization is a collection of unique resources and capabilities. The *uniqueness* of its resources and capabilities is the basis of a firm's strategy and its ability to earn above-average returns.[78]

Resources are inputs into a firm's production process, such as capital equipment, the skills of individual employees, patents, finances, and talented managers. In general, a firm's resources are classified into three categories: physical, human, and organizational capital. Described fully in Chapter 3, resources are either tangible or intangible in nature.

Individual resources alone may not yield a competitive advantage.[79] In fact, resources have a greater likelihood of being a source of competitive advantage when they are formed into a capability. A **capability** is the capacity for a set of resources to perform a task or an activity in an integrative manner. Capabilities evolve over time and must be managed dynamically in pursuit of above-average returns.[80] **Core competencies** are resources and capabilities that serve as a source of competitive advantage for a firm over its rivals. Core competencies are often visible in the form of organizational functions. For example, Apple's R&D function is likely one of its core competencies. There is little doubt that its ability to produce innovative new products that are perceived as valuable in the marketplace is a core competence for Apple, as suggested in the earlier Strategic Focus.

According to the resource-based model, differences in firms' performances across time are due primarily to their unique resources and capabilities rather than the industry's structural characteristics. This model also assumes that firms acquire different resources and develop unique capabilities based on how they combine and use the resources; that resources and certainly capabilities are not highly mobile across firms; and that the differences in resources and capabilities are the basis of competitive advantage.[81] Through continued use, capabilities become stronger and more difficult for competitors to understand and imitate. As a source of competitive advantage, a capability "should be neither so simple that it is highly imitable, nor so complex that it defies internal steering and control."[82]

The resource-based model of superior returns is shown in Figure 1.3. This model suggests that the strategy the firm chooses should allow it to use its competitive advantages in an attractive industry (the I/O model is used to identify an attractive industry).

Not all of a firm's resources and capabilities have the potential to be the foundation for a competitive advantage. This potential is realized when resources and capabilities are valuable, rare, costly to imitate, and nonsubstitutable.[83] Resources are *valuable* when they allow a firm to take advantage of opportunities or neutralize threats in its external environment. They are *rare* when possessed by few, if any, current and potential competitors. Resources are *costly to imitate* when other firms either cannot obtain them or are at a cost disadvantage in obtaining them compared with the firm that already possesses them. And they are *nonsubstitutable* when they have no structural equivalents. Many resources can either be imitated or substituted over time. Therefore, it is difficult to achieve and sustain a competitive advantage based on resources alone.[84] Individual resources are often integrated to produce integrated configurations in order to build capabilities. These capabilities are more likely to have these four attributes.[85] When these four criteria are met, however, resources and capabilities become core competencies.

As noted previously, research shows that both the industry environment and a firm's internal assets affect that firm's performance over time.[86] Thus, to form a vision and mission, and subsequently to select one or more strategies and determine how to implement them, firms use both the I/O and the resource-based models.[87] In fact, these models complement each other in that one (I/O) focuses outside the firm while the other

Resources are inputs into a firm's production process, such as capital equipment, the skills of individual employees, patents, finances, and talented managers.

A **capability** is the capacity for a set of resources to perform a task or an activity in an integrative manner.

Core competencies are capabilities that serve as a source of competitive advantage for a firm over its rivals.

Figure 1.3 The Resource-Based Model of Above-Average Returns

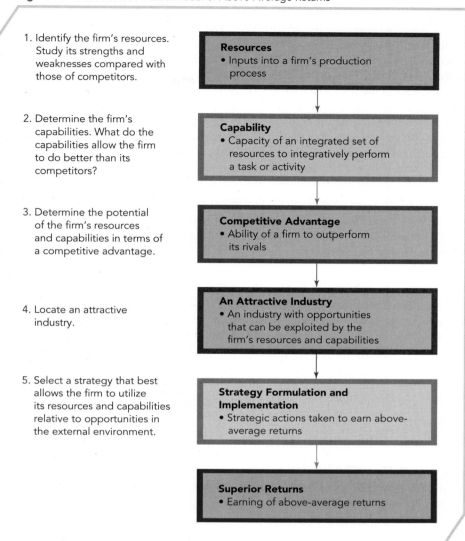

1. Identify the firm's resources. Study its strengths and weaknesses compared with those of competitors.

Resources
• Inputs into a firm's production process

2. Determine the firm's capabilities. What do the capabilities allow the firm to do better than its competitors?

Capability
• Capacity of an integrated set of resources to integratively perform a task or activity

3. Determine the potential of the firm's resources and capabilities in terms of a competitive advantage.

Competitive Advantage
• Ability of a firm to outperform its rivals

4. Locate an attractive industry.

An Attractive Industry
• An industry with opportunities that can be exploited by the firm's resources and capabilities

5. Select a strategy that best allows the firm to utilize its resources and capabilities relative to opportunities in the external environment.

Strategy Formulation and Implementation
• Strategic actions taken to earn above-average returns

Superior Returns
• Earning of above-average returns

© 2013 Cengage Learning.

(resource-based) focuses inside the firm. Next, we discuss the forming of the firm's vision and mission—actions taken after the firm understands the realities of its external environment (Chapter 2) and internal organization (Chapter 3).

Vision and Mission

After studying the external environment and the internal organization, the firm has the information it needs to form its vision and a mission (see Figure 1.1). Stakeholders (those who affect or are affected by a firm's performance, as explained later in the chapter) learn a great deal about a firm by studying its vision and mission. Indeed, a key purpose of vision and mission statements is to inform stakeholders of what the firm is, what it seeks to accomplish, and who it seeks to serve.

Vision

Vision is a picture of what the firm wants to be and, in broad terms, what it wants to ultimately achieve.[88] Thus, a vision statement articulates the ideal description of an organization and gives shape to its intended future. In other words, a vision statement points the firm in

Vision is a picture of what the firm wants to be and, in broad terms, what it wants to ultimately achieve.

the direction of where it would like to be in the years to come.[89] An effective vision stretches and challenges people as well. In her book about Steve Jobs, Apple's phenomenally successful CEO, Carmine Gallo argues that one of the reasons that Apple is so innovative was Jobs' vision for the company. She suggests that he thought bigger and differently than most people—she describes it as "putting a dent in the universe." To be innovative, she explains that one has to think differently about their products and customers—"sell dreams not products"—and differently about the story to "create great expectations."[90] Steve Jobs passed away in October 2011. Apple will be challenged to remain highly innovative without him. Interestingly, many new entrepreneurs are highly optimistic when they develop their ventures.[91]

It is also important to note that vision statements reflect a firm's values and aspirations and are intended to capture the heart and mind of each employee and, hopefully, many of its other stakeholders. A firm's vision tends to be enduring while its mission can change with new environmental conditions. A vision statement tends to be relatively short and concise, making it easily remembered. Examples of vision statements include the following:

Our vision is to be the world's best quick service restaurant. (McDonald's)

To make the automobile accessible to every American. (Ford Motor Company's vision when established by Henry Ford)

As a firm's most important and prominent strategic leader, the CEO is responsible for working with others to form the firm's vision. Experience shows that the most effective vision statement results when the chief executive officer (CEO) involves a host of stakeholders (e.g., other top-level managers, employees working in different parts of the organization, suppliers, and customers) to develop it. In addition, to help the firm reach its desired future state, a vision statement should be clearly tied to the conditions in the firm's external environment and internal organization. Moreover, the decisions and actions of those involved with developing the vision, especially the CEO and the other top-level managers, must be consistent with that vision.

Mission

The vision is the foundation for the firm's mission. A **mission** specifies the business or businesses in which the firm intends to compete and the customers it intends to serve.[92] The firm's mission is more concrete than its vision. However, similar to the vision, a mission should establish a firm's individuality and should be inspiring and relevant to all stakeholders.[93] Together, the vision and mission provide the foundation that the firm needs to choose and implement one or more strategies. The probability of forming an effective mission increases when employees have a strong sense of the ethical standards that guide their behaviors as they work to help the firm reach its vision.[94] Thus, business ethics are a vital part of the firm's discussions to decide what it wants to become (its vision) as well as who it intends to serve and how it desires to serve those individuals and groups (its mission).[95]

Even though the final responsibility for forming the firm's mission rests with the CEO, the CEO and other top-level managers often involve more people in developing the mission. The main reason is that the mission deals more directly with product markets and customers, and middle- and first-level managers and other employees have more direct contact with customers and the markets in which they are served. Examples of mission statements include the following:

Be the best employer for our people in each community around the world and deliver operational excellence to our customers in each of our restaurants. (McDonald's)

Our mission is to be recognized by our customers as the leader in applications engineering. We always focus on the activities customers desire; we are highly motivated and strive to advance our technical knowledge in the areas of material, part design and fabrication technology. (LNP, a GE Plastics Company)

McDonald's mission statement flows from its vision of being the world's best quick-service restaurant. LNP's mission statement describes the business areas (material, part design, and fabrication technology) in which the firm intends to compete.

Learn more about Coca Cola's sustainability vision.

www.cengagebrain.com

A **mission** specifies the businesses in which the film intends to compete and the customers it intends to serve.

Some believe that vision and mission statements provide little value. One expert believes, "Most vision statements are either too vague, too broad in scope, or riddled with superlatives."[96] Clearly, vision and mission statements that are poorly developed do not provide the direction a firm needs to take appropriate strategic actions. Still, as shown in Figure 1.1, a firm's vision and mission are critical aspects of the *strategic inputs* required to engage in *strategic actions* that help to achieve strategic competitiveness and earn above-average returns. Therefore, firms must accept the challenge of forming effective vision and mission statements.

Stakeholders

Every organization involves a system of primary stakeholder groups with whom it establishes and manages relationships.[97] **Stakeholders** are the individuals, groups, and organizations who can affect the firm's vision and mission, are affected by the strategic outcomes achieved, and have enforceable claims on the firm's performance.[98] Claims on a firm's performance are enforced through the stakeholders' ability to withhold participation essential to the organization's survival, competitiveness, and profitability.[99] Stakeholders continue to support an organization when its performance meets or exceeds their expectations.[100] Also, research suggests that firms that effectively manage stakeholder relationships outperform those that do not. Stakeholder relationships can therefore be managed to be a source of competitive advantage.[101]

Although organizations have dependency relationships with their stakeholders, they are not equally dependent on all stakeholders at all times;[102] as a consequence, not every stakeholder has the same level of influence.[103] The more critical and valued a stakeholder's participation, the greater a firm's dependency on it. Greater dependence, in turn, gives the stakeholder more potential influence over a firm's commitments, decisions, and actions. Managers must find ways to either accommodate or insulate the organization from the demands of stakeholders controlling critical resources.[104]

Classifications of Stakeholders

The parties involved with a firm's operations can be separated into at least three groups.[105] As shown in Figure 1.4, these groups are the capital market stakeholders (shareholders and the major suppliers of a firm's capital), the product market stakeholders (the firm's primary customers, suppliers, host communities, and unions representing the workforce), and the organizational stakeholders (all of a firm's employees, including both non-managerial and managerial personnel).

Each stakeholder group expects those making strategic decisions in a firm to provide the leadership through which its valued objectives will be reached.[106] The objectives of the various stakeholder groups often differ from one another, sometimes placing those involved with a firm's strategic management process in situations where trade-offs have to be made. The most obvious stakeholders, at least in U.S. organizations, are *shareholders*—individuals and groups who have invested capital in a firm in the expectation of earning a positive return on their investments. These stakeholders' rights are grounded in laws governing private property and private enterprise.

In contrast to shareholders, another group of stakeholders—the firm's customers—prefers that investors receive a minimum return on their investments. Customers could have their interests maximized when the quality and reliability of a firm's products are improved, but without high prices. High returns to customers, therefore, might come at the expense of lower returns for capital market stakeholders.

Because of potential conflicts, each firm must carefully manage its stakeholders. First, a firm must thoroughly identify and understand all important stakeholders. Second, it must prioritize them in case it cannot satisfy all of them. Power is the most critical criterion in prioritizing stakeholders. Other criteria might include the urgency

Stakeholders are the individuals, groups, and organizations that can affect the firm's vision and mission, are affected by the strategic outcomes achieved, and have enforceable claims on the firm's performance.

Figure 1.4 The Three Stakeholder Groups

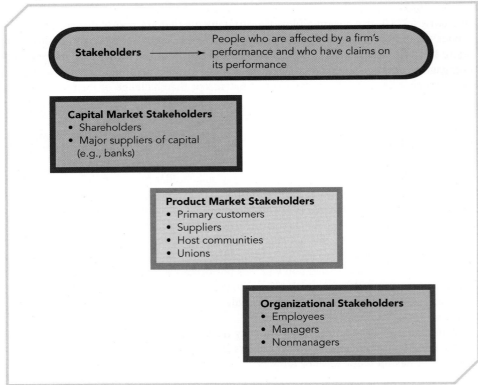

© 2013 Cengage Learning.

of satisfying each particular stakeholder group and the degree of importance of each to the firm.[107]

When the firm earns above-average returns, the challenge of effectively managing stakeholder relationships is lessened substantially. With the capability and flexibility provided by above-average returns, a firm can more easily satisfy multiple stakeholders simultaneously. When the firm earns only average returns, it is unable to maximize the interests of all stakeholders. The objective then becomes one of at least minimally satisfying each stakeholder.

Trade-off decisions are made in light of how important the support of each stakeholder group is to the firm. For example, environmental groups may be very important to firms in the energy industry but less important to professional service firms.[108] A firm earning below-average returns does not have the capacity to minimally satisfy all stakeholders. The managerial challenge in this case is to make trade-offs that minimize the amount of support lost from stakeholders. Societal values also influence the general weightings allocated among the three stakeholder groups shown in Figure 1.4. Although all three groups are served by firms in the major industrialized nations, the priorities in their service vary because of cultural differences. Next, we present additional details about each of the three major stakeholder groups.

Capital Market Stakeholders

Shareholders and lenders both expect a firm to preserve and enhance the wealth they have entrusted to it. The returns they expect are commensurate with the degree of risk accepted with those investments (i.e., lower returns are expected with low-risk investments while higher returns are expected with high-risk investments). Dissatisfied lenders may impose stricter covenants on subsequent borrowing of capital. Dissatisfied shareholders may reflect their concerns through several means, including selling their stock. Institutional investors (e.g., pension funds, mutual funds) often are willing to sell their stock if the returns are not what they desire, or take actions to improve the firm's performance such as pressuring top managers to improve the governance oversight by the board of directors. Some institutions owning major shares of a firm's stock may have conflicting views of the actions needed, which can be challenging for managers. This is because some may want an increase in returns in the short term while the others desire a focus on building long-term competitiveness.[109] Managers may have to balance their desires with other shareholders or prioritize the importance of the institutional owners with different goals. Clearly shareholders who hold a large share of stock (sometimes referred to as blockholders—see Chapter 10 for more explanation) are influential,

RICK WILKING/Reuters/Landov

This Westminster, Colorado Circuit City store shuttered its doors after Circuit City failed to reach a deal to sell the company.

especially in the determination of the firm's capital structure (i.e., the amount of equity versus the amount of debt used). Often large shareholders prefer that the firm minimize its use of debt because of the risk of debt, its cost, and the possibility that debt holders have first call on the firm's assets in case of default over the shareholders.[110]

When a firm is aware of potential or actual dissatisfactions among capital market stakeholders, it may respond to their concerns. The firm's response to stakeholders who are dissatisfied is affected by the nature of its dependency relationship with them (which, as noted earlier, is also influenced by a society's values). The greater and more significant the dependency relationship is, the more likely a direct and significant response by the firm. Before liquidating, Circuit City took several actions to try to satisfy its capital market stakeholders. For example, it closed stores, changed the top management team, and sought potential buyers.[111] However, none of these actions allowed Circuit City to meet the expectations of its capital market stakeholders, and it declared bankruptcy and went out of business.

Product Market Stakeholders

Some might think that product market stakeholders (customers, suppliers, host communities, and unions) share few common interests. However, all four groups can benefit as firms engage in competitive battles. For example, depending on product and industry characteristics, marketplace competition may result in lower product prices being charged to a firm's customers and higher prices being paid to its suppliers (the firm might be willing to pay higher supplier prices to ensure delivery of the types of goods and services that are linked with its competitive success).[112]

Customers, as stakeholders, demand reliable products at the lowest possible prices. Suppliers seek loyal customers who are willing to pay the highest sustainable prices for the goods and services they receive. Although all product market stakeholders are important, without customers, the other product market stakeholders are of little value. Therefore, the firm must try to learn about and understand current and potential customers.[113] Host communities want companies willing to be long-term employers and providers of tax revenue without placing excessive demands on public support services. Union officials are interested in secure jobs, under highly desirable working conditions, for employees they represent. Thus, product market stakeholders are generally satisfied when a firm's profit margin reflects at least a balance between the returns to capital market stakeholders (i.e., the returns lenders and shareholders will accept and still retain their interests in the firm) and the returns in which they share.

Organizational Stakeholders

Employees—the firm's organizational stakeholders—expect the firm to provide a dynamic, stimulating, and rewarding work environment. As employees, we are usually satisfied working for a company that is growing and actively developing our skills, especially those skills required to be effective team members and to meet or exceed global work standards. Workers who learn how to use new knowledge productively are critical to organizational success. In a collective sense, the education and skills of a firm's workforce are competitive weapons affecting strategy implementation and firm performance.[114] Strategic leaders are ultimately responsible for serving the needs of organizational stakeholders on a day-to-day basis. In fact, to be successful, strategic leaders must effectively use the firm's human capital.[115] The importance of human capital to their success is likely why outside directors are more likely to propose layoffs compared to inside strategic leaders, while such insiders are likely to use preventative cost-cutting measures and seek to protect incumbent employees.[116] A highly important means of building employee skills for the global competitive landscape is through international assignments. The process of managing expatriate employees and helping them build knowledge can have significant effects over time on the firm's ability to compete in global markets.[117]

Strategic Leaders

Strategic leaders are people located in different areas and levels of the firm using the strategic management process to select strategic actions that help the firm achieve its vision and fulfill its mission. Regardless of their location in the firm, successful strategic leaders are decisive, committed to nurturing those around them,[118] and committed to helping the firm create value for all stakeholder groups.[119] In this vein, research evidence suggests that employees who perceive that their CEO is a visionary leader also believe that the CEO leads the firm to operate in ways that are consistent with the values of all stakeholder groups rather than emphasizing only maximizing profits for shareholders. In turn, visionary leadership helps to obtain extra effort by employees, thereby achieving enhanced firm performance. These findings are consistent with the argument that "To regain society's trust ... business leaders must embrace a way of looking at their role that goes beyond their responsibility to the shareholder to include a civic and personal commitment to their duty as institutional custodians."[120]

When identifying strategic leaders, most of us tend to think of CEOs and other top-level managers. Clearly, these people are strategic leaders. In the final analysis, CEOs are responsible for making certain their firm effectively uses the strategic management process. Indeed, the pressure on CEOs to manage strategically is stronger than ever.[121] However, many other people help choose a firm's strategy and then determine the actions for successfully implementing it.[122] The main reason is that the realities of twenty-first-century competition that we discussed earlier in this chapter (e.g., the global economy, globalization, rapid technological change, and the increasing importance of knowledge and people as sources of competitive advantage) are creating a need for those "closest to the action" to be making decisions and determining the actions to be taken.[123] In fact, the most effective CEOs and top-level managers understand how to delegate strategic responsibilities to people throughout the firm who influence the use of organizational resources. In fact, delegation also helps to avoid too much managerial hubris at the top and the problems it causes, especially in situations allowing significant managerial discretion.[124]

Organizational culture also affects strategic leaders and their work. In turn, strategic leaders' decisions and actions shape a firm's culture. **Organizational culture** refers to the complex set of ideologies, symbols, and core values that are shared throughout the firm and that influence how the firm conducts business. It is the social energy that drives—or fails to drive—the organization.[125] For example, Southwest Airlines is known for having a unique and valuable culture. Its culture encourages employees to work hard but also to

Strategic leaders are people located in different areas and levels of the firm using the strategic management process to select strategic actions that help the firm achieve its vision and fulfill its mission.

Organizational culture refers to the complex set of ideologies, symbols, and core values that are shared throughout the firm and that influence how the firm conducts business.

have fun while doing so. Moreover, its culture entails respect for others—employees and customers alike. The firm also places a premium on service, as suggested by its commitment to provide POS (Positively Outrageous Service) to each customer.

Some organizational cultures are a source of disadvantage. It is important for strategic leaders to understand, however, that whether the firm's culture is functional or dysfunctional, their effectiveness is influenced by that culture. The relationship between organizational culture and strategic leaders' work is reciprocal in that the culture shapes the outcomes of their leadership while their leadership helps shape an ever-evolving organizational culture.

The Work of Effective Strategic Leaders

Perhaps not surprisingly, hard work, thorough analyses, a willingness to be brutally honest, a penchant for wanting the firm and its people to accomplish more, and tenacity are prerequisites to an individual's success as a strategic leader.[126] In addition, strategic leaders must have a strong strategic orientation while simultaneously embracing change in the dynamic competitive landscape we have discussed.[127] In order to deal with this change effectively, strategic leaders must be innovative thinkers and promote innovation in their organization.[128] Promoting innovation is facilitated by a diverse top management team representing different types of expertise and leveraging relationships with external parties.[129] Strategic leaders can best leverage partnerships with external parties and organizations when their organizations are ambidextrous. That is, the organizations simultaneously promote exploratory learning of new and unique forms of knowledge and exploitative learning that adds incremental knowledge to existing knowledge bases, allowing them to better understand and use their existing products.[130] In addition, strategic leaders need to have a global mindset, or what some refer to as an ambicultural approach to management.[131]

Strategic leaders, regardless of their location in the organization, often work long hours, and their work is filled with ambiguous decision situations.[132] However, the opportunities afforded by this work are appealing and offer exciting chances to dream and to act.[133] The following words, given as advice to the late Time Warner chair and co-CEO Steven J. Ross by his father, describe the opportunities in a strategic leader's work:

There are three categories of people—the person who goes into the office, puts his feet up on his desk, and dreams for 12 hours; the person who arrives at 5 A.M. and works for 16 hours, never once stopping to dream; and the person who puts his feet up, dreams for one hour, then does something about those dreams.[134]

The operational term used for a dream that challenges and energizes a company is vision. The most effective strategic leaders provide a vision as the foundation for the firm's mission and subsequent choice and use of one or more strategies.

Predicting Outcomes of Strategic Decisions: Profit Pools

Strategic leaders attempt to predict the outcomes of their decisions before taking efforts to implement them, which is difficult to do. Many decisions that are a part of the strategic management process are concerned with an uncertain future and the firm's place in that future. As such, managers try to predict the effects on the firm's profits of strategic decisions that they are considering.[135]

Mapping an industry's profit pool is something strategic leaders can do to anticipate the possible outcomes of different decisions and to focus on growth in profits rather than strictly growth in revenues. A **profit pool** entails the total profits earned in an industry at all points along the value chain.[136] (We explain the value chain in Chapter 3 and discuss it further in Chapter 4.) Analyzing the profit pool in the industry may help a firm see something others are unable to see and to understand the primary sources of profits in an industry. There are four steps to identifying profit pools: (1) define the pool's boundaries,

A profit pool entails the total profits earned in an industry at all points along the value chain.

(2) estimate the pool's overall size, (3) estimate the size of the value-chain activity in the pool, and (4) reconcile the calculations.[137]

For example, McDonald's might desire to map the quick-service restaurant industry's profit pools. First, McDonald's would need to define the industry's boundaries and, second, estimate its size (which is large, because McDonald's operates in markets across the globe). The net result of this is that McDonald's tries to take market share away from competitors such as Burger King and Wendy's, and growth is more likely in international markets. Armed with information about its industry, McDonald's could then estimate the amount of profit potential in each part of the value chain (step 3). In the quick-service restaurant industry, marketing campaigns and customer service are likely more important sources of potential profits than are inbound logistics' activities (see Chapter 3). With an understanding of where the greatest amount of profits are likely to be earned, McDonald's would then be ready to select the strategy to use to be successful where the largest profit pools are located in the value chain.[138] As this brief discussion shows, profit pools are a potentially useful tool to help strategic leaders recognize the actions to take to increase the likelihood of increasing profits. Of course, profits made by a firm and in an industry can be partially interdependent on the profits earned in adjacent industries.[139] For example, profits earned in the energy industry can affect profits in other industries (e.g., airlines). When oil prices are high, it can reduce the profits earned in industries that must use a lot of energy to provide their goods or services.

The Strategic Management Process

As suggested by Figure 1.1, the strategic management process is a rational approach firms use to achieve strategic competitiveness and earn above-average returns. Figure 1.1 also features the topics we examine in this book to present the strategic management process to you.

This book is divided into three parts. In Part 1, we describe what firms do to analyze their external environment (Chapter 2) and internal organization (Chapter 3). These analyses are completed to identify marketplace opportunities and threats in the external environment (Chapter 2) and to decide how to use the resources, capabilities, core competencies, and competitive advantages in the firm's internal organization to pursue opportunities and overcome threats (Chapter 3). The analyses explained in Chapters 2 and 3 compose the well-known SWOT analyses (strengths, weaknesses, opportunities, threats).[140] With knowledge about its external environment and internal organization, the firm forms its strategy taking into account the firm's vision and mission.

The firm's strategic inputs (see Figure 1.1) provide the foundation for choosing one or more strategies and deciding how to implement them. As suggested in Figure 1.1 by the horizontal arrow linking the two types of strategic actions, formulation and implementation must be simultaneously integrated to successfully use the strategic management process. Integration happens as decision makers think about implementation issues when choosing strategies and as they think about possible changes to the firm's strategies while implementing a currently chosen strategy.

In Part 2 of this book, we discuss the different strategies firms may choose to use. First, we examine business-level strategies (Chapter 4). A business-level strategy describes the actions a firm takes to exploit its competitive advantage over rivals. A company competing in a single product market (e.g., a locally owned grocery store operating in only one location) has but one business-level strategy while a diversified firm competing in multiple product markets (e.g., General Electric) forms a business-level strategy for each of its businesses. In Chapter 5, we describe the actions and reactions that occur among firms in marketplace competition. Competitors typically respond to and try to anticipate each other's actions. The dynamics of competition affect the strategies firms choose as well as how they try to implement the chosen strategies.[141]

For the diversified firm, corporate-level strategy (Chapter 6) is concerned with determining the businesses in which the company intends to compete as well as how to manage its different businesses. Other topics vital to strategy formulation, particularly in the diversified company, include acquiring other businesses and, as appropriate, restructuring the firm's portfolio of businesses (Chapter 7) and selecting an international strategy (Chapter 8). With cooperative strategies (Chapter 9), firms form a partnership to share their resources and capabilities in order to develop a competitive advantage. Cooperative strategies are becoming increasingly important as firms seek ways to compete in the global economy's array of different markets.[142]

To examine actions taken to implement strategies, we consider several topics in Part 3 of the book. First, we examine the different mechanisms used to govern firms (Chapter 10). With demands for improved corporate governance being voiced by many stakeholders in the current business environment, organizations are challenged to learn how to simultaneously satisfy their stakeholders' different interests.[143] Finally, the organizational structure and actions needed to control a firm's operations (Chapter 11), the patterns of strategic leadership appropriate for today's firms and competitive environments (Chapter 12), and strategic entrepreneurship (Chapter 13) as a path to continuous innovation are addressed.

It is important to emphasize that primarily because they are related to how a firm interacts with its stakeholders, almost all strategic management process decisions have ethical dimensions.[144] Organizational ethics are revealed by an organization's culture; that is to say, a firm's decisions are a product of the core values that are shared by most or all of a company's managers and employees. Especially in the turbulent and often ambiguous competitive landscape of the twenty-first century, those making decisions as a part of the strategic management process are challenged to recognize that their decisions affect capital market, product market, and organizational stakeholders differently and to regularly evaluate the ethical implications of their decisions.[145] Decision makers failing to recognize these realities accept the risk of placing their firm at a competitive disadvantage with regard to ethical business practices.[146]

As you will discover, the strategic management process examined in this book calls for disciplined approaches to serve as the foundation for developing a competitive advantage. These approaches provide the pathway through which firms will be able to achieve strategic competitiveness and earn above-average returns. Mastery of this strategic management process will effectively serve you, our readers, and the organizations for which you will choose to work.

SUMMARY

- Firms use the strategic management process to achieve strategic competitiveness and earn above-average returns. Strategic competitiveness is achieved when a firm develops and implements a value-creating strategy. Above-average returns (in excess of what investors expect to earn from other investments with similar levels of risk) provide the foundation needed to simultaneously satisfy all of a firm's stakeholders.

- The fundamental nature of competition is different in the current competitive landscape. As a result, those making strategic decisions must adopt a different mind-set, one that allows them to learn how to compete in highly turbulent and chaotic environments that produce a great deal of uncertainty. The globalization of industries and their markets and rapid and significant technological changes are the two primary factors contributing to the turbulence of the competitive landscape.

- Firms use two major models to help develop their vision and mission and then choose one or more strategies in pursuit of strategic competitiveness and above-average returns. The core assumption of the I/O model is that the firm's external environment has a large influence on the choice of strategies more than do the firm's internal resources, capabilities, and core competencies. Thus, the I/O model is used to understand the effects an industry's characteristics can have on a firm when deciding what strategy or strategies with which to compete against rivals. The logic supporting the I/O model suggests that above-average returns are earned when the firm locates an attractive industry or part of an industry and successfully implements the strategy dictated by that industry's characteristics. The core assumption of the resource-based model is that the firm's unique resources, capabilities, and core competencies have a major influence on selecting and using strategies more than does the firm's external environment. Above-average returns are earned when the firm uses its valuable, rare, costly-to-imitate, and nonsubstitutable resources and capabilities to compete against its rivals in one or more industries. Evidence indicates that both models yield insights that are linked to successfully selecting and using strategies. Thus, firms want to use their unique resources, capabilities, and core competencies as the foundation to engage in one or more strategies that allow them to effectively compete against rivals.

■ Vision and mission are formed to guide the selection of strategies based on the information from the analyses of the firm's internal and external environments. Vision is a picture of what the firm wants to be and, in broad terms, what it wants to ultimately achieve. Flowing from the vision, the mission specifies the business or businesses in which the firm intends to compete and the customers it intends to serve. Vision and mission provide direction to the firm and signal important descriptive information to stakeholders.

■ Stakeholders are those who can affect, and are affected by, a firm's strategic outcomes. Because a firm is dependent on the continuing support of stakeholders (shareholders, customers, suppliers, employees, host communities, etc.), they have enforceable claims on the company's performance. When earning above-average returns, a firm has the resources it needs to at minimum simultaneously satisfy the interests of all stakeholders. However, when earning only average returns, the firm must carefully manage its stakeholders in order to retain their support. A firm earning below-average returns must minimize the amount of support it loses from unsatisfied stakeholders.

■ Strategic leaders are people located in different areas and levels of the firm using the strategic management process to help the firm achieve its vision and fulfill its mission. In general, CEOs are responsible for making certain that their firms properly use the strategic management process. The effectiveness of the strategic management process is increased when it is grounded in ethical intentions and behaviors. The strategic leader's work demands decision trade-offs, often among attractive alternatives. It is important for all strategic leaders and especially the CEO and other members of the top-management team to conduct thorough analyses of conditions facing the firm, be brutally and consistently honest, and work jointly to select and implement the correct strategies.

■ Strategic leaders predict the potential outcomes of their strategic decisions. To do this, they must first calculate profit pools in their industry (and adjacent industries as appropriate) that are linked to value chain activities. Predicting the potential outcomes of their strategic decisions reduces the likelihood of the firm formulating and implementing ineffective strategies.

REVIEW QUESTIONS

1. What are strategic competitiveness, strategy, competitive advantage, above-average returns, and the strategic management process?

2. What are the characteristics of the current competitive landscape? What two factors are the primary drivers of this landscape?

3. According to the I/O model, what should a firm do to earn above-average returns?

4. What does the resource-based model suggest a firm should do to earn above-average returns?

5. What are vision and mission? What is their value for the strategic management process?

6. What are stakeholders? How do the three primary stakeholder groups influence organizations?

7. How would you describe the work of strategic leaders?

8. What are the elements of the strategic management process? How are they interrelated?

EXPERIENTIAL EXERCISES

EXERCISE 1: STAKEHOLDER ANALYSIS, STRATEGIC PLANNING, AND STRATEGIC LEADERSHIP

Every organization relies on its own unique bundle of organizational stakeholders. Each one of the relationships between the organization and its stakeholders is influential in its ability to serve its mission and achieve above-average profits in the for-profit sector, or to create value in the not-for-profit sector. However, there are many ways that stakeholder management differs between the for-profit and not-for-profit worlds. It is easy to think of a for-profit firm that has product market stakeholders, such as customers, who can add or subtract their support by their decision of whether or not to purchase the firm's products or services. But who is the customer for a not-for-profit, and are the categories of product, market, organization, and capital market stakeholders very different from the for-profit arena? This exercise challenges you to uncover some of the more influential ways in which this is so.

Part One

In this exercise, you will be working in teams of approximately four students per team.

1. Decide which not-for-profit organization you wish to analyze. If you would like assistance in identifying a not-for-profit organization, a good Web source is the IRS; you may search for charities at http://www.irs.gov/app/pub-78/.
2. Determine two or three key strategic initiatives of this not-for-profit organization. Most not-for-profits, particularly well-known ones, are good about posting their strategic plans on their Web sites.
3. Now perform an analysis, such as a macroenvironmental analysis, and list all known or expected stakeholders for the organization. You should place them in the context of product, market, and organizational stakeholders.

Part Two

Now you are ready to start thinking critically about the organization and the challenges it faces among its stakeholders as it attempts to roll out its strategic initiatives.

1. For each strategic initiative that the organization has announced, analyze each stakeholder for the organization, and list areas in which the proposed strategy is likely to be supported, or not, by that particular stakeholder.
2. Organize your listing so as to be able to present to the class a summary of those strategies upon which expected support is likely to be gained and those strategies upon which support is likely to be discouraged.
3. Present to the class your recommendation for how the organization should proceed. For instance, if perceived support is critical to the successful strategic initiative but the strategy is likely to be viewed negatively by the stakeholder, provide some potential actions that the organization might take to mitigate the negative reaction or, alternatively, that might gain the stakeholders' support.

Conflicts are normal among organizational stakeholders, and deciding which must be attended to and at which time for which strategic action is a critical strategic leadership activity for every firm.

EXERCISE 2: CRAFTING A PERSONAL VISION AND MISSION STATEMENT

Drawing on an analysis of internal and external constraints, a firm creates a mission and vision as a cornerstone of its strategy. You can do the same for yourself as an individual. A personal vision will be a broad statement of your intended future, whereas a personal mission statement will emphasize your individuality and inspire you to achieve and be relevant to all of your particular stakeholders. Together they form the foundation for the strategies that you will choose to achieve for your future desired state. The real goal of this assignment is for you to focus on you.

To get started, you may want to view some Web resources, such as the blog offered by Franklin Covey (http://www.franklincovey.com/blog/tag/mission-statement-builder) or "Life on Purpose: 15 Questions to Discover Your Personal Mission" by Tina Su (http://thinksimplenow.com/happiness/life-on-purpose-15-questions-to-discover-your-personal-mission/). You could also do a Web search on personal mission statements, which will reveal a multitude of resources.

Part One

To get started on this assignment, you need to take an inventory of sorts about who you are and who you aspire to be. Therefore, begin rating yourself along the following dimensions (this is not an all-inclusive list; add as you see fit to best describe you):

- Identify your positive personality traits. Describe your character.
- Identify your beliefs and values.
- Identify your passion and talents.

Part Two

Craft your own personal vision and mission statements. You will have one vision statement and one mission statement. Each should be brief: Ideally, the vision statement will be one sentence and the mission statement will be three or four sentences, but these are just guidelines and not hard-and-fast rules.

Part 3

The instructor will ask for volunteers to share their personal statements. The class should be prepared to address the following:

- How difficult was the process, particularly the introspection?
- How did you go about deciding upon your final set of values, beliefs, passions, etc.?
- How different were your final personal statements from what you started with?
- Does this process have value?
- How flexible should these statements be; should they be reviewed and adapted often?
- What are your thoughts, now, about corporate vision and mission statements? Is there real value here for stakeholders?

VIDEO CASE

BRAZIL: AN EMERGING ECONOMY WITH STRATEGIC COMPETITIVENESS

In a world of stagnant growth, Brazil's economy is growing at a rate of 7 percent, which is three times faster than the U.S. growth rate. A country rich in natural resources and sophisticated in hydropower and biofuels, Brazil has emerged with strategic competitiveness. Being one of the greenest economies, Brazil is one of the largest producers of iron ore and one of the leading exporters of many popular commodities. After surviving historic financial collapse, Brazil has risen to have a strong manufacturing base, and the country's poor now have more purchasing power.

Be prepared to discuss the following concepts and questions in class:

Concepts

- Strategic competitiveness
- Strategy
- Hypercompetition
- Global economy
- Resources
- Capabilities
- Core competencies
- Stakeholders
- Strategic leaders

Questions

1. How is Brazil a strategic competitor?
2. What is Brazil's strategy?
3. Is Brazil a hypercompetitor?
4. What impact does Brazil have on the global economy?
5. What resources, capabilities, and core competencies does Brazil have?
6. Identify and explain the stakeholders associated with Brazil's thriving economy.
7. Describe Lula as a strategic leader. What strategies do you think he should employ to handle Brazil's latest issues?

NOTES

1. J. McGregor, 2009, Smart management for tough times, *Businessweek*, http://www.businessweek.com, March 12.
2. K. Matzler, F. Bailom, M. Anschober, & S. Richardson, 2010, Sustaining corporate success: What drives the top performers? *Journal of Business Strategy*, 31(5): 4–13.
3. D. Kiley, 2009, Ford heats out on a road of its own, *Businessweek*, January 19, 47–49.
4. D. G. Sirmon, M. A. Hitt, R. D. Ireland, & B. A. Gilbert, 2011. Resource orchestration to create competitive advantage: Breadth, depth and life cycle effects, *Journal of Management*, 37: in press; D. G. Sirmon, M. A. Hitt, & R. D. Ireland, 2007, Managing firm resources in dynamic environments to create value: Looking inside the black box, *Academy of Management Review*, 32: 273–292.
5. R. D'Aveni, G. B. Dagnino, & K. G. Smith, 2010, The age of temporary advantage, *Strategic Management Journal*, 31: 1371–1385; R. D. Ireland & J. W. Webb, 2009, Crossing the great divide of strategic entrepreneurship: Transitioning between exploration and exploitation, *Business Horizons*, 52(5): 469–479.
6. J. A. Lamberg, H. Tikkanen, T. Nokelainen, & H. Suur-Inkeroinen, 2009, Competitive dynamics, strategic consistency, and organizational survival, *Strategic Management Journal*, 30: 45–60; G. Pacheco-de-Almeida & P. Zemsky, 2007, The timing of resource development and sustainable competitive advantage, *Management Science*, 53: 651–666.
7. K. D. Miller, 2007, Risk and rationality in entrepreneurial processes, *Strategic Entrepreneurship Journal*, 1: 57–74.
8. R. M. Stulz, 2009, 6 ways companies mismanage risk, *Harvard Business Review*, 87(3): 86–94.
9. P. Steffens, P. Davidsson, & J. Fitzsimmons, 2009, Performance configurations over time: Implications for growth- and profit-oriented strategies, *Entrepreneurship Theory and Practice*, 33: 125–148.
10. J. C. Short, A. McKelvie, D. J. Ketchen, Jr., & G. N. Chandler, 2009, Firm and industry effects on firm performance: A generalization and extension for new ventures, *Strategic Entrepreneurship Journal*, 3: 47–65; T. Bates, 2005, Analysis of young, small firms that have closed: Delineating successful from unsuccessful closures, *Journal of Business Venturing*, 20: 343–358.
11. D. G. Sirmon, M. A. Hitt, J.-L. Arregle, & J. T. Campbell, 2010, The dynamic interplay of capability strengths and weaknesses: Investigating the bases of temporary competitive advantage, *Strategic Management Journal*, 31: 1386–1409; A. M. McGahan & M. E. Porter, 2003, The emergence and sustainability of abnormal profits, *Strategic Organization*, 1: 79–108.
12. Y. Zhang & J. Gimeno, 2010, Earnings pressure and competitive behavior: Evidence from the U.S. electronics industry, *Academy of Management Journal*, 53: 743–768; T. R. Crook, D. J. Ketchen, Jr., J. G. Combs, & S. Y. Todd, 2008, Strategic resources and performance: A meta-analysis, *Strategic Management Journal*, 29: 1141–1154.
13. J. Barthelemy, 2008, Opportunism, knowledge, and the performance of franchise chains, *Strategic Management Journal*, 29: 1451–1463.
14. J. Li, 2008, Asymmetric interactions between foreign and domestic banks: Effects on market entry, *Strategic Management Journal*, 29: 873–893.
15. L. Nachum, 2010, When is foreignness an asset or a liability? Explaining the performance differential between foreign and local firms, *Journal of Management*, 36: 714–739.
16. M. A. Delmas & M. W. Toffel, 2008, Organizational responses to environmental demands: Opening the black box, *Strategic Management Journal*, 29: 1027–1055; A. M. McGahan & M. E. Porter, 1997, How much does industry matter, really? *Strategic Management Journal*, 18 (Special Issue): 15–30.
17. J. Barney, D. J. Ketchen, & M. Wright, 2011, The future of resource-based theory: Revitalization or decline? *Journal of Management*, 37: in press; T. R. Holcomb, R. M. Holmes, Jr., & B. L. Connelly, 2009, Making the most of what you have: Managerial ability as a source of resource value creation, *Strategic Management Journal*, 30: 457–485.
18. M. Statman, 2011, Calm investment behavior in turbulent investment times, in *What's Next 2011*, New York: McGraw-Hill Professional, E-Book; E. Thornton, 2009, The new rules, *Businessweek*, January 19, 30–34; T. Friedman, 2005, *The World is Flat: A Brief History of the 21st Century*, New York: Farrar, Strauss and Giroux.
19. D. Searcey, 2006, Beyond cable. Beyond DSL. *Wall Street Journal*, July 24, R9.
20. 2011, NBC Universal, Wikipedia, http://en.wikipedia.org/wiki/NBC Universal, accessed March 20.
21. D. F. Kuratko & D. B. Audretsch, 2009, Strategic entrepreneurship: Exploring different perspectives of an emerging concept, *Entrepreneurship Theory and Practice*, 33: 1–17.
22. J. Hagel, III, J. S. Brown, & L. Davison, 2008, Shaping strategy in a world of constant disruption, *Harvard Business Review*, 86(10): 81–89; G. Probst & S. Raisch, 2005, Organizational crisis: The logic of failure, *Academy of Management Executive*, 19(1): 90–105.
23. D'Aveni, Dagnino, & Smith, The age of temporary advantage; J. W. Selsky, J. Goes, & O. N. Babüroglu, 2007, Contrasting perspectives of strategy making: Applications in "Hyper" environments, *Organization Studies*, 28(1): 71–94.

24. A. V. Izosimov, 2008, Managing hypergrowth, *Harvard Business Review*, 86(4): 121–127.

25. D'Aveni, Dagnino, & Smith, The age of temporary advantage; R. A. D'Aveni, 1995, Coping with hyper-competition: Utilizing the new 7S's framework, *Academy of Management Executive*, 9(3): 46.

26. D'Aveni, Dagnino, & Smith, The age of temporary advantage; D. J. Bryce & J. H. Dyer, 2007, Strategies to crack well-guarded markets, *Harvard Business Review* 85(5): 84–92.

27. S. H. Lee & M. Makhija, 2009, Flexibility in internationalization: Is it valuable during an economic crisis? *Strategic Management Journal*, 30: 537–555; S. J. Chang & S. Park, 2005, Types of firms generating network externalities and MNCs' co-location decisions, *Strategic Management Journal*, 26: 595–615.

28. S. E. Feinberg & A. K. Gupta, 2009, MNC subsidiaries and country risk: Internalization as a safeguard against weak external institutions, *Academy of Management Journal*, 52: 381–399; R. Belderbos & L. Sleuwaegen, 2005, Competitive drivers and international plant configuration strategies: A product-level test, *Strategic Management Journal*, 26: 577–593.

29. Y. Luo, 2007, From foreign investors to strategic insiders: Shifting parameters, prescriptions and paradigms for MNCs in China, *Journal of World Business*, 42(1): 14–34.

30. M. A. Hitt & X. He, 2008, Firm strategies in a changing global competitive landscape, *Business Horizons*, 51: 363–369; A. Ratanpal, 2008, Indian economy and Indian private equity, *Thunderbird International Business Review*, 50: 353–358.

31. S. Malone, 2011, GE's Immelt sees new economic era for globe, *Financial Post*, http://www.financialpost.com, March 13.

32. C. H. Oh, 2009, The international scale and scope of European multinationals, *European Management Journal*, 27(5): 336–343; G. D. Bruton, G. G. Dess, & J. J. Janney, 2007, Knowledge management in technology-focused firms in emerging economies: Caveats on capabilities, networks, and real options, *Asia Pacific Journal of Management*, 24(2): 115–130.

33. A. Ciarione, P. Piselli, & G. Trebeschi, 2009, Emerging markets' spreads and global financial conditions, *Journal of International Financial Markets, Institutions and Money*, 19: 222–239.

34. R. Gulati, 2010, Management lessons from the edge, *Academy of Management Perspectives*, 24(2): 25–27.

35. M. A. Prospero, 2005, The march of war, *Fast Company*, May, 14.

36. J. P. Quinlan, 2011, Speeding towards a messy, multi-polar world, in *What's Next 2011*, New York: McGraw-Hill Professional, E-Book.

37. B. Elango, 2009, Minimizing effects of "liability of foreignness": Response strategies of foreign firms in the United States, *Journal of World Business*, 44: 51–62.

38. D. B. Fuller, 2010, How law, politics and transnational networks affect technology entrepreneurship: Explaining divergent venture capital investing strategies in China, *Asia Pacific Journal of Management*, 27: 445–459; D. J. McCarthy & S. M. Puffer, 2008, Interpreting the ethicality of corporate governance decisions in Russia: Utilizing integrative social contracts theory to evaluate the relevance of agency theory norms, *Academy of Management Review*, 33: 11–31.

39. M. A. Hitt, R. E. Hoskisson, & H. Kim, 1997, International diversification: Effects on innovation and firm performance in product-diversified firms, *Academy of Management Journal*, 40: 767–798.

40. R. D. Ireland & J. W. Webb, 2007, Strategic entrepreneurship: Creating competitive advantage through streams of innovation, *Business Horizons*, 50(1): 49–59; G. Hamel, 2001, Revolution vs. evolution: You need both, *Harvard Business Review*, 79(5): 150–156.

41. K. H. Hammonds, 2001, What is the state of the new economy? *Fast Company*, September, 101–104.

42. D. Dunlap-Hinkler, M. Kotabe, & R. Mudambi, 2010, A story of breakthrough versus incremental innovation: Corporate entrepreneurship in the global pharmaceutical industry, *Strategic Entrepreneurship Journal*, 4: 106–127; B. Peters, 2009, Persistence of innovation: Stylised facts and panel data evidence, *The Journal of Technology Transfer*, 34: 226–243.

43. K. Z. Zhou & F. Wu, 2010, Technological capability, strategic flexibility and product innovation, *Strategic Management Journal*, 31: 547–561; J. L. Boyd & R. K. F. Bresser, 2008, Performance implications of delayed competitive responses: Evidence from the U.S. retail industry, *Strategic Management Journal*, 29: 1077–1096.

44. J. Kao, 2009, Tapping the world's innovation hot spots, *Harvard Business Review*, 87(3): 109–117.

45. L. Jiang, J. Tan, & M. Thursby, 2011, Incumbent firm invention in emerging fields: Evidence from the semiconductor industry, *Strategic Management Journal*, 32: 55–75.

46. R. Adner & R. Kapoor, 2010, Value creation in innovation ecosystems: How the structure of technological interdependence affects firm performance in new technology generations, *Strategic Management Journal*, 31: 306–333.

47. C. W. L. Hill, 1997, Establishing a standard: Competitive strategy and technological standards in winner-take-all industries, *Academy of Management Executive*, 11(2): 7–25.

48. J. L. Funk, 2008, Components, systems and technological discontinuities: Lessons from the IT sector, *Long Range Planning*, 41: 555–573; C. M. Christensen, 1997, *The Innovator's Dilemma*, Boston: Harvard Business School Press.

49. Dunlap-Hinkler, Kotabe, & Mudambi, A story of breakthrough versus incremental innovation; C. M. Christensen, 2006, The ongoing process of building a theory of disruption, *Journal of Product Innovation Management*, 23(1): 39–55.

50. M. Makri, M. A. Hitt, & P. J. Lane, 2010, Complementary technologies, knowledge relatedness and invention outcomes in high technology mergers and acquisitions, *Strategic Management Journal*, 31: 602–628; C. L. Nichols-Nixon & C. Y. Woo, 2003, Technology sourcing and output of established firms in a regime of encompassing technological change, *Strategic Management Journal*, 24: 651–666.

51. J. Woolley, 2010, Technology emergence through entrepreneurship across multiple industries, *Strategic Entrepreneurship Journal*, 4: 1–21.

52. K. Celuch, G. B. Murphy, & S. K. Callaway, 2007, More bang for your buck: Small firms and the importance of aligned information technology capabilities and strategic flexibility, *Journal of High Technology Management Research*, 17: 187–197.

53. 2010, Worldwide PC Market, eTForecasts, http://www.etforecasts.com, accessed on March 23, 2011.

54. M. S. Giarratana & S. Torrisi, 2010, Foreign entry and survival in a knowledge-intensive market: Emerging economy countries' international linkages, technology competences and firm experience, *Strategic Entrepreneurship Journal*, 4: 85–104.

55. R. Agarwal, D. Audretsch, and M. B. Sarkar, 2010, Knowledge spillovers and strategic entrepreneurship, *Strategic Entrepreneurship Journal*, 4: 271–283; C. F. Fey & P. Furu, 2008, Top management incentive compensation and knowledge sharing in multinational corporations, *Strategic Management Journal*, 29: 1301–1323.

56. M. Gottfredson, R. Puryear, & S. Phillips, 2005, Strategic sourcing: From periphery to the core, *Harvard Business Review*, 83(2): 132–139.

57. L. F. Mesquita, J. Anand, & T. H. Brush, 2008, Comparing the resource-based and relational views: Knowledge transfer and spillover in vertical alliances, *Strategic Management Journal*, 29: 913–941; K. G. Smith, C. J. Collins, & K. D. Clark, 2005, Existing knowledge, knowledge creation capability, and the rate of new product introduction in high-technology firms, *Academy of Management Journal*, 48: 346–357.

58. E. Sherman, 2010, Climbing the corporate ladder, *Continental Magazine*, November, 54–56.

59. A. Capaldo, 2007, Network structure and innovation: The leveraging of a dual network as a distinctive relational capability,

Strategic Management Journal, 28: 585–608; S. K. Ethirau, P. Kale, M. S. Krishnan, & J. V. Singh, 2005, Where do capabilities come from and how do they matter? *Strategic Management Journal*, 26: 25–45.

60. Sirmon, Hitt, & Ireland, Managing firm resources.

61. A. Cuervo-Cazurra & C. A. Un, 2010, Why some firms never invest in formal R&D, *Strategic Management Journal*, 31: 759–779.

62. H. Yang, C. Phelps, & H. K. Steensma, 2010, Learning from what others have learned from you: The effects of knowledge spillovers on originating firms, *Academy of Management Journal*, 53: 371–389.

63. A. C. Inkpen, 2008, Knowledge transfer and international joint ventures: The case of NUMMI and General Motors, *Strategic Management Journal*, 29: 447–453; P. L. Robertson & P. R. Patel, 2007, New wine in old bottles: Technological diffusion in developed economies, *Research Policy*, 36(5): 708–721.

64. R. E. Hoskisson, M. A. Hitt, & R. D. Ireland, 2008, *Competing for Advantage*, 2nd ed., Cincinnati: Thomson South-Western; K. R. Harrigan, 2001, Strategic flexibility in old and new economies, in M. A. Hitt, R. E. Freeman, & J. S. Harrison (eds.), *Handbook of Strategic Management*, Oxford, UK: Blackwell Publishers, 97–123.

65. S. Nadkarni & V. K. Narayanan, 2007, Strategic schemas, strategic flexibility, and firm performance: The moderating role of industry clockspeed, *Strategic Management Journal*, 28: 243–270.

66. A. C. Edmondson, 2008, The competitive imperative of learning, *Harvard Business Review*, 86(7/8): 60–67; K. Shimizu & M. A. Hitt, 2004, Strategic flexibility: Organizational preparedness to reverse ineffective strategic decisions, *Academy of Management Executive*, 18(4): 44–59; K. Uhlenbruck, K. E. Meyer, & M. A. Hitt, 2003, Organizational transformation in transition economies: Resource-based and organizational learning perspectives, *Journal of Management Studies*, 40: 257–282.

67. R. E. Hoskisson, M. A. Hitt, W. P. Wan, & D. Yiu, 1999, Swings of a pendulum: Theory and research in strategic management, *Journal of Management*, 25: 417–456.

68. E. H. Bowman & C. E. Helfat, 2001, Does corporate strategy matter? *Strategic Management Journal*, 22: 1–23.

69. M. A. Delmas & M. W. Toffel, 2008, Organizational responses to environmental demands: Opening the black box, *Strategic Management Journal*, 29: 1027–1055; J. Shamsie, 2003, The context of dominance: An industry-driven frame work for exploiting reputation, *Strategic Management Journal*, 24: 199–215.

70. J. Galbreath & P. Galvin, 2008, Firm factors, industry structure and performance variation: New empirical evidence to a classic debate, *Journal of Business Research*, 61: 109–117.

71. M. B. Lieberman & S. Asaba, 2006, Why do firms imitate each other? *Academy of Management Journal*, 31: 366–385; L. F. Feldman, C. G. Brush, & T. Manolova, 2005, Co-alignment in the resource-performance relationship: Strategy as mediator, *Journal of Business Venturing*, 20: 359–383.

72. M. E. Porter, 1985, *Competitive Advantage*, New York: Free Press; M. E. Porter, 1980, *Competitive Strategy*, New York: Free Press.

73. J. C. Short, D. J. Ketchen, Jr., T. B. Palmer, & G. T. M. Hult, 2007, Firm, strategic group, and industry influences on performance, *Strategic Management Journal*, 28: 147–167.

74. P. Ziobro, 2009, McDonald's pounds out good quarter, *Wall Street Journal*, http://www.wsj.com, April 23.

75. T. W. Tong and J. J. Reuer, 2010, Competitive consequences of interfirm collaboration: How joint ventures shape industry profitability, *Journal of International Business Studies*, 41: 1056–1073.

76. C. Moschieri, 2011, The implementation and structuring of divestitures: The unit's perspective, *Strategic Management Journal*, 32: 368–401.

77. A. M. McGahan, 1999, Competition, strategy and business performance, *California Management Review*, 41(3): 74–101; McGahan & Porter, How much does industry matter, really?

78. J. Kraaijenbrink, J.-C. Spender, & A. J. Groen, 2010, The resource-based view: A review and assessment of its critiques, *Journal of Management*, 38: 349–372; S. L. Newbert, 2008, Value, rareness, competitive advantage, and performance: A conceptual-level empirical investigation of the resource-based view of the firm, *Strategic Management Journal*, 29: 745–768.

79. Kraaijenbrink, Spender, & Groen, The resource-based view; E. Verwall, H. Commandeur, & W. Verbeke, 2009, Value creation and value claiming in strategic outsourcing decisions: A resource contingency perspective, *Journal of Management*, 35: 420–444.

80. P. L. Drnevich & A. P. Kriauciunas, 2011, Clarifying the conditions and limits of the contributions of ordinary and dynamic capabilities to relative firm performance, *Strategic Management Journal*, 32:254–279; S. Kaplan, 2008, Cognition, capabilities, and incentives: Assessing firm response to the fiber-optic revolution, *Academy of Management Journal*, 51: 672–694; S. A. Zahra, H. Sapienza, & P. Davidsson, 2006, Entrepreneurship and dynamic capabilities: A review, model and research agenda, *Journal of Management Studies*, 43(4): 927–955.

81. S. L. Newbert, 2007, Empirical research on the resource-based view of the firm: An assessment and suggestions for future research, *Strategic Management Journal*, 28: 121–146.

82. P. J. H. Schoemaker & R. Amit, 1994, Investment in strategic assets: Industry and firm-level perspectives, in P. Shrivastava, A. Huff, & J. Dutton (eds.), *Advances in Strategic Management*, Greenwich, CT: JAI Press, 9.

83. A. A. Lado, N. G. Boyd, P. Wright, & M. Kroll, 2006, Paradox and theorizing within the resource-based view, *Academy of Management Review*, 31: 115–131; D. M. DeCarolis, 2003, Competencies and imitability in the pharmaceutical industry: An analysis of their relationship with firm performance, *Journal of Management*, 29: 27–50.

84. C. Zott, 2003, Dynamic capabilities and the emergence of intraindustry differential firm performance: Insights from a simulation study, *Strategic Management Journal*, 24: 97–125.

85. M. Gruber, F. Heinemann, & M. Brettel, 2010, Configurations of resources and capabilities and their performance implications: An exploratory study on technology ventures, *Strategic Management Journal*, 31: 1337–1356.

86. E. Levitas & H. A. Ndofor, 2006, What to do with the resource-based view: A few suggestions for what ails the RBV that supporters and opponents might accept, *Journal of Management Inquiry*, 15(2): 135–144; G. Hawawini, V. Subramanian, & P. Verdin, 2003, Is performance driven by industry- or firm-specific factors? A new look at the evidence, *Strategic Management Journal*, 24: 1–16.

87. M. Makhija, 2003, Comparing the source-based and market-based views of the firm: Empirical evidence from Czech privatization, *Strategic Management Journal*, 24: 433–451; T. J. Douglas & J. A. Ryman, 2003, Understanding competitive advantage in the general hospital industry: Evaluating strategic competencies, *Strategic Management Journal*, 24: 333–347.

88. R. D. Ireland, R. E. Hoskisson, & M. A. Hitt. 2012, *Understanding Business Strategy*, 3rd ed., Mason, OH: South-Western Cengage Learning.

89. S. Ward, 2009, Vision statement, *About.com*, http://www.sbinfocanada about.com, April 22; R. Zolli, 2006, Recognizing tomorrow's hot ideas today, *Businessweek*, September 25: 12.

90. C. Gallo, 2010, *The Innovation Secrets of Steve Jobs*, NY: McGraw-Hill.

91. G. Cassar, 2010, Are individuals entering self-employment overly optimistic? An empirical test of plans and projections on nascent entrepreneur expectations, *Strategic Management Journal*, 31: 822–840.

92. S. Kemp & L. Dwyer, 2003, Mission statements of international airlines: A content analysis, *Tourism Management*, 24:635–653; R. D. Ireland & M. A. Hitt,

1992, Mission statements: Importance, challenge, and recommendations for development, *Business Horizons*, 35(3): 34–42.

93. J. I. Siciliano, 2008, A comparison of CEO and director perceptions of board involvement in strategy, *Nonprofit and Voluntary Sector Quarterly*, 27: 152–162; W. J. Duncan, 1999, *Management: Ideas and Actions*, New York: Oxford University Press, 122–125.

94. J. H. Davis, J. A. Ruhe, M. Lee, & U. Rajadhyaksha, 2007, Mission possible: Do school mission statements work? *Journal of Business Ethics*, 70: 99–110.

95. L. W. Fry & J. W. Slocum, Jr., 2008, Maximizing the triple bottom line through spiritual leadership, *Organizational Dynamics*, 37: 86–96; A. J. Ward, M. J. Lankau, A. C. Amason, J. A. Sonnenfeld, & B. A. Agle, 2007, Improving the performance of top management teams, *MIT Sloan Management Review*, 48(3): 85–90.

96. M. Rahman, 2009, Why strategic vision statements won't measure up, *Strategic Direction*, 25: 3–4.

97. K. Basu & G. Palazzo, 2008, Corporate social responsibility: A process model of sensemaking, *Academy of Management Review*, 33: 122–136.

98. D. A. Bosse, R. A. Phillips, & J. S. Harrison, 2009, Stakeholders, reciprocity, and firm performance, *Strategic Management Journal*, 30: 447–456; J. P. Walsh & W. R. Nord, 2005, Taking stock of stakeholder management, *Academy of Management Review*, 30: 426–438.

99. N. Darnell, I. Henrique, & P. Sadorsky, 2010, Adopting proactive environmental strategy: The influence of stakeholders and firm size, *Journal of Management Studies*, 47: 1072–1122; G. Donaldson & J. W. Lorsch, 1983, *Decision Making at the Top: The Shaping of Strategic Direction*, New York: Basic Books, 37–40.

100. S. Sharma & I. Henriques, 2005, Stakeholder influences on sustainability practices in the Canadian Forest products industry, *Strategic Management Journal*, 26: 159–180.

101. A. Mackey, T. B. Mackey, & J. B. Barney, 2007, Corporate social responsibility and firm performance: Investor preferences and corporate strategies, *Academy of Management Review*, 32: 817–835; A. J. Hillman & G. D. Keim, 2001, Shareholder value, stakeholder management, and social issues: What's the bottom line? *Strategic Management Journal*, 22: 125–139.

102. G. Van der Laan, H. Van Ees, & A. Van Witteloostuijn, 2008, Corporate social and financial performance: An extended stakeholder theory, and empirical test with accounting measures, *Journal of Business Ethics*, 79: 299–310; J. M. Stevens, H. K. Steensma, D. A. Harrison, & P. L. Cochran, 2005, Symbolic or substantive document? The influence of ethics codes on financial executives' decisions,

103. M. L. Barnett & R. M. Salomon, 2006, Beyond dichotomy: The curvilinear relationship between social responsibility and financial performance, *Strategic Management Journal*, 27: 1101–1122.

104. T. Kuhn, 2008, A communicative theory of the firm: Developing an alternative perspective on intra-organizational power and stakeholder relationships, *Organization Studies*, 29: 1227–1254; L. Vilanova, 2007, Neither shareholder nor stakeholder management: What happens when firms are run for their short-term salient stakeholder? *European Management Journal*, 25(2): 146–162.

105. J. L. Murrillo-Luna, C. Garces-Ayerbe, & P. Rivera-Torres, 2008, Why do patterns of environmental response differ? A stakeholders' pressure approach, *Strategic Management Journal*, 29: 1225–1240; R. E. Freeman & J. McVea, 2001, A stakeholder approach to strategic management, in M. A. Hitt, R. E. Freeman, & J. S. Harrison (eds.), *Handbook of Strategic Management*, Oxford, UK: Blackwell Publishers, 189–207.

106. R. Boutilier, 2009, *Stakeholder Politics: Social Capital, Sustainable Development, and the Corporation*, Sheffield, United Kingdom, Greenleaf Publishing; C. Caldwell & R. Karri, 2005, Organizational governance and ethical systems: A conventional approach to building trust, *Journal of Business Ethics*, 58: 249–267.

107. F. G. A. de Bakker & F. den Hond, 2008, Introducing the politics of stakeholder influence, *Business & Society*, 47: 8–20.

108. Darnell, Henrique, & Sadorsky, Adopting proactive environmental strategy; P. Berrone & L. R. Gomez-Meija, 2009, Environmental performance and executive compensation: An integrated agency-institutional perspective, *Academy of Management Journal*, 52: 103–126.

109. B. L. Connelly, L. Tihanyi, S. T. Certo, & M. A. Hitt, 2010, Marching to the beat of different drummers: The influence of institutional owners on competitive actions, *Academy of Management Journal*, 53: 723–742.

110. X. Zuoping, 2010, Large shareholders, legal institution and capital structure decision, *Nankai Business Review International*, 1: 59–86.

111. 2009, Circuit City to liquidate U.S. stores, *MSNBC*, http://www.msnbc.com, January 16.

112. L. Pierce, 2009, Big losses in ecosystems niches: How core firm decisions drive complementary product shakeouts, *Strategic Management Journal*, 30: 323–347; B. A. Neville & B. Menguc, 2006, Stakeholder multiplicity: Toward an understanding of the interactions between stakeholders, *Journal of Business Ethics*, 66: 377–391.

113. O. D. Fjeldstad & A. Sasson, 2010, Membership matters: On the value of being embedded in customer networks,

114. D. A. Ready, L. A. Hill, & J. A. Conger, 2008, Winning the race for talent in emerging markets, *Harvard Business Review*, 86(11): 62–70; A. M. Grant, J. E. Dutton, & B. D. Rosso, 2008, Giving commitment: Employee support programs and the prosocial sensemaking process, *Academy of Management Journal*, 51: 898–918.

115. M. A. Hitt, K. T. Haynes, & R. Serpa, 2010, Strategic leadership for the 21st century, *Business Horizons*, 53: 437–444.

116. N. Abe & S. Shimizutani, 2007, Employment policy and corporate governance—An empirical comparison of the stakeholder and the profit-maximization model, *Journal of Comparative Economics*, 35: 346–368.

117. R. Takeuchi, 2010, A critical review of expatriate adjustment research through a multiple stakeholder view: Progress, emerging trends and prospects, *Journal of Management*, 36: 1040–1064.

118. J. Welch & S. Welch, 2009, An employee bill of rights, *Businessweek*, March 16, 72.

119. Hitt, Haynes, & Serpa, Strategic leadership for the 21st century; J. P. Jansen, D. Vera, & M. Crossan, 2008, Strategic leadership for exploration and exploitation: The moderating role of environmental dynamism, *The Leadership Quarterly*, 20: 5–18.

120. R. Khurana & N. Nohria, 2008, It's time to make management a true profession, *Harvard Business Review*, 86(10): 70–77.

121. N. Byrnes, 2009, Executives on a tightrope, *Businessweek*, January 19, 43; D. C. Hambrick, 2007, Upper echelons theory: An update, *Academy of Management Review*, 32: 334–339.

122. J. C. Camillus, 2008, Strategy as a wicked problem, *Harvard Business Review* 86(5): 99–106; A. Priestland & T. R. Hanig, 2005, Developing first-level managers, *Harvard Business Review*, 83(6): 113–120.

123. R. J. Harrington & A. K. Tjan, 2008, Transforming strategy one customer at a time, *Harvard Business Review*, 86(3): 62–72; R. T. Pascale & J. Sternin, 2005, Your company's secret change agent, *Harvard Business Review*, 83(5): 72–81.

124. J. Li & Y. Tang, 2010, CEO hubris and firm risk taking in China: The moderating role of managerial discretion, *Academy of Management Journal*, 53: 45–68; Y. L. Doz & M. Kosonen, 2007, The new deal at the top, *Harvard Business Review*, 85(6): 98–104.

125. B. Stevens, 2008, Corporate ethical codes: Effective instruments for influencing behavior, *Journal of Business Ethics*, 78: 601–609; D. Lavie, 2006, The competitive advantage of interconnected firms: An extension of the resource-based view, *Academy of Management Review*, 31: 638–658.

126. H. Ibarra & O. Obodru, 2009, Women and the vision thing, *Harvard Business Review*,

87(1): 62–70; M. Crossan, D. Vera, & L. Nanjad, 2008, Transcendent leadership: Strategic leadership in dynamic environments, The *Leadership Quarterly*, 19: 569–581.

127. R. Shambaugh, 2011, Leading in today's economy: The transformational leadership model, in *What's Next 2011*, NY: McGraw-Hill.

128. Shambaugh, Leading in today's economy; A. Leiponen & C. E. Helfat, 2010, Innovation objectives, knowledge sources and the benefits of breadth, *Strategic Management Journal*, 31: 224–236.

129. T. Buyl, C. Boone, W. Hendriks, & P. Matthyssens, 2011, Top management team functional diversity and firm performance: The moderating role of CEO characteristics, *Journal of Management Studies*, 48: 151–177; S. Nadkarni & P. Hermann, 2010, CEO personality, strategic flexibility and firm performance: The case of Indian business process outsourcing industry, *Academy of Management Journal*, 53: 1050–1073.

130. Q. Cao, Z. Simsek, & H. Zhang, 2010, Modelling the joint impact of the CEO and the TMT on organizational ambidexterity, *Journal of Management Studies*, 47: 1272–1296.

131. M.-J. Chen & D. Miller, 2010, West meets east: Toward an ambicultural approach to management, *Academy of Management Perspectives*, 24(4): 17–37.

132. C. A. Montgomery, 2008, Putting leadership back into strategy, *Harvard Business Review*, 86(1): 54–60; D. C. Hambrick, S. Finkelstein, & A. C. Mooney, 2005, Executive job demands: New insights for explaining strategic decisions and leader behaviors, *Academy*

of *Management Review*, 30: 472–491; J. Brett & L. K. Stroh, 2003, Working 61-plus hours a week: Why do managers do it? *Journal of Applied Psychology*, 88: 67–78.

133. J. A. Byrne, 2005, Great work if you can get it, *Fast Company*, April, 14.

134. M. Loeb, 1993, Steven J. Ross, 1927–1992, *Fortune*, January 25, 4.

135. Y.-C. Tang & F.-M. Liou, 2010, Does firm performance reveal its own causes? The role of Bayesian inference, *Strategic Management Journal*, 31: 39–57.

136. O. Gadiesh & J. L. Gilbert, 1998, Profit pools: A fresh look at strategy, *Harvard Business Review*, 76(3): 139–147.

137. O. Gadiesh & J. L. Gilbert, 1998, How to map your industry's profit pool, *Harvard Business Review*, 76(3): 149–162.

138. C. Zook, 2007, Finding your next CORE business, *Harvard Business Review*, 85(4): 66–75; M. J. Epstein & R. A. Westbrook, 2001, Linking actions to profits in strategic decision making, *Sloan Management Review*, 42(3): 39–49.

139. M. J. Lenox, S. F. Rockart, & A. Y. Lewin, 2010, Does interdependency affect firm and industry profitability? An empirical test, *Strategic Management Journal*, 31: 121–139.

140. M. M. Helms & J. Nixon, 2010, Exploring SWOT analysis—where are we now? A review of the academic research from the last decade, *Journal of Strategy and Management*, 3: 215–251.

141. T. Yu, M. Subramaniam, & A. A. Cannella, Jr., 2009, Rivalry deterrence in international markets: Contingencies governing the mutual forbearance hypothesis, *Academy of Management Journal*, 52: 127–147; D. J. Ketchen ,C.

C. Snow, & V. L. Street, 2004, Improving firm performance by matching strategic decision-making processes to competitive dynamics, *Academy of Management Executive*, 18(4): 29–43.

142. D. Li, L. Eden, M. A. Hitt, & R. D. Ireland, 2011, Governance in multilateral R&D alliances, *Organization Science*, in press; P. Ozcan & K. M. Eisenhardt, 2009, Origin of alliance portfolios: Entrepreneurs, network strategies, and firm performance, *Academy of Management Journal*, 52: 246–279.

143. S. D. Julian, J. C. Ofori-Dankwa, & R. T. Justis, 2008, Understanding strategic responses to interest group pressures, *Strategic Management Journal*, 29: 963–984; C. Eesley & M. J. Lenox, 2006, Firm responses to secondary stakeholder action, *Strategic Management Journal*, 27: 765–781.

144. Y. Luo, 2008, Procedural fairness and interfirm cooperation in strategic alliances, *Strategic Management Journal*, 29: 27–46; S. J. Reynolds, F. C. Schultz, & D. R. Hekman, 2006, Stakeholder theory and managerial decision-making: Constraints and implications of balancing stakeholder interests, *Journal of Business Ethics*, 64: 285–301; L. K. Trevino & G. R. Weaver, 2003, *Managing Ethics in Business Organizations*, Stanford, CA: Stanford University Press.

145. D. Pastoriza, M. A. Arino, & J. E. Ricart, 2008, Ethical managerial behavior as an antecedent of organizational social capital, *Journal of Business Ethics*, 78: 329–341.

146. B. W. Heineman Jr., 2007, Avoiding integrity land mines, *Harvard Business Review*, 85(4): 100–108.

CHAPTER 2

The External Environment: Opportunities, Threats, Industry Competition, and Competitor Analysis

Studying this chapter should provide you with the strategic management knowledge needed to:

1. Explain the importance of analyzing and understanding the firm's external environment.

2. Define and describe the general environment and the industry environment.

3. Discuss the four activities of the external environmental analysis process.

4. Name and describe the general environment's seven segments.

5. Identify the five competitive forces and explain how they determine an industry's profit potential.

6. Define strategic groups and describe their influence on the firm.

7. Describe what firms need to know about their competitors and different methods (including ethical standards) used to collect intelligence about them.

© Ryan McVay/Getty Images

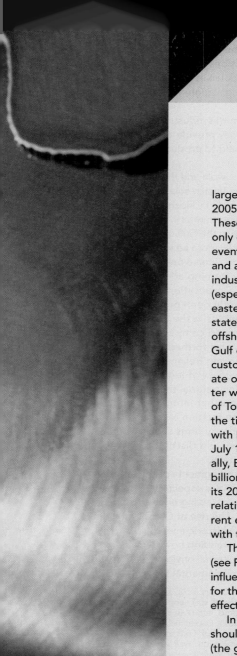

BRITISH PETROLEUM (BP) AND ITS ENVIRONMENT: HOW THE DEEPWATER HORIZON OFFSHORE DRILLING PLATFORM DISASTER IS SHAPING ITS STRATEGY

The explosion that led to the subsequent sinking of the oil and gas drilling platform on April 20, 2010, sent ripples not only across the Gulf of Mexico but also had a huge influence on BP and its two subcontractors, Transocean and Halliburton. The Deepwater Horizon spill was the largest accidental offshore spill in history, at 206 million gallons. In comparison, the 1989 Exxon Valdez tanker wreck spilled 11.3 million gallons of oil. However, this was not BP's only large well-publicized disaster. In 2006 there was an environmental spill in Alaska, and in 2005 there was the largest refinery explosion in Texas City, Texas, which killed 15 people. These events, especially the Deepwater Horizon disaster, have put BP in the crosshairs not only of regulators and government officials but also environmentalists. Furthermore, these events have enabled doubts about its legitimacy with critical stakeholders on Wall Street, and also influenced other industry participants (especially in the southeastern and southwestern states associated with offshore drilling in the Gulf of Mexico) and its customers. One immediate outcome of the disaster was the replacement of Tony Hayward, CEO at the time of the disaster, with Robert Dudley, on July 10, 2010. Additionally, BP announced a $32 billion charge realized on its 2010 balance sheet relative to past and current expenses associated with the disaster.

Workers work feverishly to contain and clean up the largest accidental offshore spill in U.S. history.

Eye Ubiquitous/SuperStock

The strategic actions (see Figure 1.1) that BP will take relative to this disaster and to position for future success will be influenced by continuing pressures from its external environment. One of the main challenges for the firm's strategic leader (Robert Dudley) is to understand what the external environment's effects are on the firm and to predict how its future strategic actions might lead to success.

In the future, BP and all the other oil and gas firms focused on extracting such fuels should expect regulatory change in the political/legal segment of the general environment (the general environment and all of its segments are discussed in this chapter). In August 2010, President Obama appointed a federal commission to investigate the Deepwater Horizon oil spill. Their report, issued in January 2011, concluded that government oversight of the industry needed to be fundamentally reformed and that oil company practices needed to improve dramatically. One co-chairman of that commission, William Reilly, former head of the Environmental Protection Agency, suggested that even with all techniques learned after the Exxon Valdez disaster, and increased technology, the oil capture was rather pathetic; "they collected 5 or 6% of what was spilled." Because of this oversight commission, along with congressional hearings on the report, it is virtually assured that more regulatory and safety inspections of offshore drilling platforms and operations will be undertaken, both from a company standpoint and the government agency responsible for such inspections, the Bureau of Ocean Energy Management, Regulation and Enforcement (BOEMRE). Certainly one of the effects is that regulation of drilling permits has become more intense, and in fact, very few have been approved since the Deepwater Horizon disaster.

The economic segment of the general environment will continue to produce demand for energy, especially with the rise of emerging markets such as China and India; thus exploration for hydrocarbon products will continue. Although demand for energy will persist, the pressure to use alternative sources of energy will be driven by the sociocultural segment of the environment because of the carbon emissions produced by such hydrocarbons. However, the demand for energy and the slowdown in the economy seems to have swamped the possible passage of any CO_2 emission legislation, which is needed for our long-term future and health.

Technology increases have also affected many companies in this industry. Gas drilling and fracturing have dramatically increased gas reserves and may provide a substitute for other CO_2 emission-producing products such as coal. Coal is said to produce about 25 percent of the CO_2 emissions in the United States.

The dramatic earthquake in Sendai, Japan at 9.0 on the Richter scale and the subsequent tsunami have also created questions relative to a critical substitute energy source, nuclear power. Influence from the physical environment produced the problems seen in Japan. This influence created a disaster despite the fact that the Japanese have been very careful in regard to constructing "safe" plants. The physical environment has an influence in the Gulf of Mexico, where drillers have suggested that natural pressure in the Gulf has realized more accidents compared to offshore reserves in the North Sea and Brazil, where deep water reserve pressures are lower.

BP has tried to rectify problems in the Gulf of Mexico by forming additional joint ventures in the global arena. A recent venture with Rosneft Corporation, which is similar to an existing Russian venture with other partners, has recently been proposed. If the deal goes through, BP would help Rosneft explore opportunities in the arctic region. "Rosneft insisted on a share swap, giving the Kremlin-controlled company a 5 percent stake in BP in exchange for 9.4 percent of Rosneft." BP has also formed another international joint venture by investing 7.2 billion with Indian Partner, Reliance Industries, giving it a 30 percent stake in oil and gas fields off the east coast of India. These fields are possibly as large at the fields in the North Sea. These deals signal the importance of the global segment of the external environment that BP and other integrated oil firms have to deal with when contending with scarce reserves. The Russian reserves are 10 years away from producing. Not only do large integrated energy firms such as BP have to source energy globally, they also need to transport, refine, and distribute it through global partnerships, both internal and external, to the company.

As the BP example shows, assessing the influence of various segments of the external environment is critical in assuring future success for any firm. This is especially true for energy firms, which are part of a global integrated process of extracting energy, refining various products, and distributing them around the world. The rise of China and India coupled with the rise of Brazil as an energy power and Russia's historic energy reserves portends to their significant influence in world markets. Understanding how these complex processes work and how to deal with these segments of the external environment are critical in formulating strategies to be successful in such global environmental forces.

Sources: 2011, Business: Dancing with bears, BP in Russia, *The Economist*, February 5, 73; J. Ball, 2011, Environment (special report)—lessons from the gulf—William Reilly on why the oil spill happened, and where the industry goes from here, *Wall Street Journal*, March 7, R5; P. Elkind, D. Whitford, and D. Burke, 2011, An accident waiting to happen, *Fortune*, February 7, 105–132; P. Hunter and P. Russell, 2011, Capitol hill views divided on oil-spill report, *Engineering News-Record*, February 7, 7; A. Peaple, 2011, Reshaped BP finds east is no Eden, *Wall Street Journal*, February 23, C14; R. Gold, 2010, Halliburton faulted over cement job, *Wall Street Journal*, www .wsj.com, September 9; J. Weisman, 2010, BP softens political hit, *Wall Street Journal*, www.wsj.com, June 21.

Find out more about the EXXON Valdez disaster

www.cengagebrain .com

As described in the Opening Case and suggested by research, the external environment affects a firm's strategic actions.[1] For example, British Petroleum (BP) seeks to expand its oil reserves after the Deepwater Horizon oil and gas drilling platform disaster in the Gulf of Mexico by forming joint ventures in Russia with Rosneft Corporation, and in India with Reliance Industries.[2] In addition, it is clear that BP's strategic actions are affected by conditions in other segments of its general environment, such as the political/legal, social/cultural, and physical environment segments. As we explain in this chapter, a firm's external environment creates both opportunities (e.g., the opportunity for BP to enter other global markets) and threats (e.g., the possibility that additional regulations in its markets will reduce opportunities to extract oil and gas). Collectively, opportunities and threats affect a firm's strategic actions.[3]

Regardless of the industry in which they compete, the external environment influences firms as they seek strategic competitiveness and above-average returns. This chapter focuses on how firms analyze their external environment. The understanding of conditions in its external environment that the firm gains by analyzing that environment is matched with knowledge about its internal organization (discussed in the next chapter) as the foundation for forming the firm's vision, developing its mission, and identifying and implementing strategic actions (see Figure 1.1).

As noted in Chapter 1, the environmental conditions in the current global economy differ from historical conditions. For example, technological changes and the continuing growth of information gathering and processing capabilities increase the need for firms to develop effective competitive actions on a timely basis.[4] (In slightly different words, firms have little time to correct errors when implementing their competitive actions.) The rapid sociological changes occurring in many countries affect labor practices and the nature of products demanded by increasingly diverse consumers. Governmental policies and laws also affect where and how firms choose to compete.[5] In addition, changes to nations' financial regulatory systems that were enacted in 2010 and beyond are expected to increase the complexity of organizations' financial transactions.[6]

Viewed in their totality, the conditions that affect firms today indicate that for most organizations, their external environment is filled with uncertainty. To successfully deal with this uncertainty and to achieve strategic competitiveness and thrive, firms must be aware of and fully understand the different segments of the external environment.[7]

Firms understand the external environment by acquiring information about competitors, customers, and other stakeholders to build their own base of knowledge and capabilities.[8] On the basis of the new information, firms take actions, such as building new capabilities and core competencies, in hopes of buffering themselves from any negative environmental effects and to pursue opportunities as the basis for better serving their stakeholders' needs.[9] A firm's strategic actions are influenced by the conditions in the three parts (the general, industry, and competitor) of its external environment (see Figure 2.1).

Figure 2.1 The External Environment

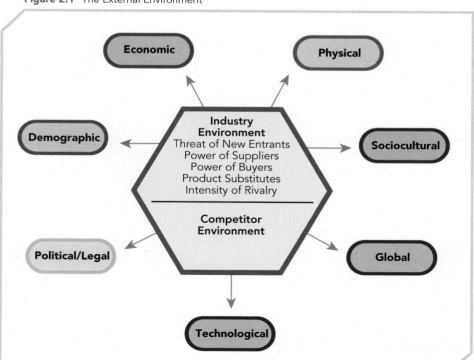

The General, Industry, and Competitor Environments

The **general environment** is composed of dimensions in the broader society that influence an industry and the firms within it.[10] We group these dimensions into seven environmental *segments*: demographic, economic, political/legal, sociocultural, technological, global, and physical. Examples of *elements* analyzed in each of these segments are shown in Table 2.1.

Firms cannot directly control the general environment's segments. The recent bankruptcy filings by General Motors and Chrysler Corporation highlight this fact. These firms could not directly control various parts of their external environment, including the economic and political/legal segments; however, these segments are influencing the actions the firms are taking, including Chrysler's alliance with Fiat.[11] Because firms cannot directly control the segments of their external environment, successful ones learn how to gather the information needed to understand all segments and their implications for selecting and implementing the firm's strategies.

The **industry environment** is the set of factors that directly influences a firm and its competitive actions and responses:[12] the threat of new entrants, the power of suppliers, the power of buyers, the threat of product substitutes, and the intensity of rivalry among competitors. In total, the interactions among these five factors determine an industry's profit potential; in turn, the industry's profit potential influences the choices each firm makes about its strategic actions. The challenge for a firm is to locate a position within an industry where it can favorably influence the five factors or where it can successfully defend against their influence. The greater a firm's capacity to favorably influence its industry environment, the greater the likelihood that the firm will earn above-average returns.

The **general environment** is composed of dimensions in the broader society that influence an industry and the firms within it.

The **industry environment** is the set of factors that directly influences a firm and its competitive actions and competitive responses: the threat of new entrants, the power of suppliers, the power of buyers, the threat of product substitutes, and the intensity of rivalry among competitors.

Table 2.1 The General Environment: Segments and Elements

Demographic segment	• Population size • Age structure • Geographic distribution	• Ethnic mix • Income distribution
Economic segment	• Inflation rates • Interest rates • Trade deficits or surpluses • Budget deficits or surpluses	• Personal savings rate • Business savings rates • Gross domestic product
Political/Legal segment	• Antitrust laws • Taxation laws • Deregulation philosophies	• Labor training laws • Educational philosophies and policies
Sociocultural segment	• Women in the workforce • Workforce diversity • Attitudes about the quality of work life	• Shifts in work and career preferences • Shifts in preferences regarding product and service characteristics
Technological segment	• Product innovations • Applications of knowledge	• Focus of private and government-supported R&D expenditures • New communication technologies
Global segment	• Important political events • Critical global markets	• Newly industrialized countries • Different cultural and institutional attributes
Physical environment segment	• Energy consumption • Practices used to develop energy sources • Renewable energy efforts • Minimizing a firm's environmental footprint	• Availability of water as a resource • Producing environmentally friendly products • Reacting to natural or man-made disasters

How companies gather and interpret information about their competitors is called *competitor analysis.* Understanding the firm's competitor environment complements the insights provided by studying the general and industry environments.[13] This means, for example, that BP wants to learn as much as it can about its major competitors—such as Exxon-Mobil and Royal Dutch Shell plc—while also learning about its general and industry environments.

Analysis of the general environment is focused on environmental trends while an analysis of the industry environment is focused on the factors and conditions influencing an industry's profitability potential and an analysis of competitors is focused on predicting competitors' actions, responses, and intentions. In combination, the results of these three analyses influence the firm's vision, mission, and strategic actions. Although we discuss each analysis separately, performance improves when the firm integrates the insights provided by analyses of the general environment, the industry environment, and the competitor environment.

External Environmental Analysis

Most firms face external environments that are highly turbulent, complex, and global—conditions that make interpreting those environments difficult.[14] To cope with often ambiguous and incomplete environmental data and to increase understanding of the general environment, firms engage in external environmental analysis. This analysis has four parts: scanning, monitoring, forecasting, and assessing (see Table 2.2). Analyzing the external environment is a difficult, yet significant, activity.[15]

Identifying opportunities and threats is an important objective of studying the general environment. An **opportunity** is a condition in the general environment that, if exploited effectively, helps a company achieve strategic competitiveness. For example, recent market research results suggested to Procter & Gamble (P&G) after its acquisition of Gillette, a shaving products company, that an increasing number of men across the globe are interested in fragrances and skin care products. To take advantage of this opportunity, P&G is reorienting toward beauty products to better serve both men and women. The change constitutes an organization change focused on combining product categories rather than its typical organization around a specific branded product.[16]

A **threat** is a condition in the general environment that may hinder a company's efforts to achieve strategic competitiveness.[17] Microsoft is currently experiencing a severe external threat as smartphones are expected to surpass personal computer (PC) sales in the near future. Although Microsoft has a smartphone operating system, Apple, Google, and Research in Motion (BlackBerry phones) have operating platforms that are much more popular than those using Microsoft's platform. Although PC growth will continue to expand, it is not growing at the rate that smartphones are, and possible substitution may happen between PCs, smartphones, and additional devices, such as Apple's iPad and

An **opportunity** is a condition in the general environment that if exploited effectively, helps a company achieve strategic competitiveness.

A **threat** is a condition in the general environment that may hinder a company's efforts to achieve strategic competitiveness.

Table 2.2 Components of the External Environmental Analysis

Scanning	• Identifying early signals of environmental changes and trends
Monitoring	• Detecting meaning through ongoing observations of environmental changes and trends
Forecasting	• Developing projections of anticipated outcomes based on monitored changes and trends
Assessing	• Determining the timing and importance of environmental changes and trends for firms' strategies and their management

similar devices. The main software platform is needed to assure other software producers will develop applications for the platform. Apple has large numbers of applications being developed, and Google's Android system software applications are rapidly increasing as well. As such, Microsoft is in a severe catch-up position relative to its competition. It recently formed a joint venture with Nokia Corporation to establish a firmer platform for its existing software using Nokia's large potential smartphone base. However, this threat remains until this opportunity is realized.[18]

Firms use several sources to analyze the general environment, including a wide variety of printed materials (such as trade publications, newspapers, business publications, and the results of academic research and public polls), trade shows and suppliers, customers, and employees of public-sector organizations. People in *boundary-spanning* positions can obtain a great deal of this type of information. Salespersons, purchasing managers, public relations directors, and customer service representatives, each of whom interacts with external constituents, are examples of boundary-spanning positions.

Scanning

Scanning entails the study of all segments in the general environment. Through scanning, firms identify early signals of potential changes in the general environment and detect changes that are already under way.[19] Scanning often reveals ambiguous, incomplete, or unconnected data and information. Thus, environmental scanning is challenging but critically important for firms, especially those competing in highly volatile environments.[20] In addition, scanning activities must be aligned with the organizational context; a scanning system designed for a volatile environment is inappropriate for a firm in a stable environment.[21]

Many firms use special software to help them identify events that are taking place in the environment and that are announced in public sources. For example, news event detection uses information-based systems to categorize text and reduce the trade-off between an important missed event and false alarm rates.[22] The Internet provides significant opportunities for scanning. Amazon.com, for example, records significant information about individuals visiting its Web site, particularly if a purchase is made. Amazon then welcomes these customers by name when they visit the Web site again. The firm sends messages to customers about specials and new products similar to those they purchased in previous visits. A number of other companies such as Netflix also collect demographic data about their customers in an attempt to identify their unique preferences (demographics is one of the segments in the general environment).

Philip Morris International continuously scans segments of its external environment to detect current conditions and to anticipate changes that might take place in different segments. For example, PMI always studies various nations' tax policies on cigarettes (these policies are part of the political/legal segment). The reason for this is that raising cigarette taxes might reduce sales while lowering these taxes might increase sales.

Monitoring

When *monitoring,* analysts observe environmental changes to see if an important trend is emerging from among those spotted through scanning.[23] Critical to successful monitoring is the firm's ability to detect meaning in environmental events and trends. For example, Tesco, the United Kingdom's largest retailer, plans to add Turkish, Sri Lankan, Latin, Filipino, African, and South African cuisine to its food offerings. One analyst noted, "Britain has become one of the most ethnically diverse nations on earth, and there is a very strong, growing demand by those who have settled here to buy food from their homelands."[24] Tesco already sells Asian, Oriental, Afro-Caribbean, Kosher, Polish, and Halal foods. Continual monitoring of these trends is necessary for a large retailer such as Tesco to maintain the right balance among its products.

Effective monitoring requires the firm to identify important stakeholders and understand its reputation among these stakeholders as the foundation for serving their unique needs.[25] (Stakeholders' unique needs are described in Chapter 1.) Scanning and monitoring are particularly important when a firm competes in an industry with high technological uncertainty.[26] Scanning and monitoring can provide the firm with information; they also serve as a means of importing knowledge about markets and about how to successfully commercialize new technologies the firm has developed.[27]

Forecasting

Scanning and monitoring are concerned with events and trends in the general environment at a point in time. When *forecasting,* analysts develop feasible projections of what might happen, and how quickly, as a result of the changes and trends detected through scanning and monitoring.[28] For example, analysts might forecast the time that will be required for a new technology to reach the marketplace, the length of time before different corporate training procedures are required to deal with anticipated changes in the composition of the workforce, or how much time will elapse before changes in governmental taxation policies affect consumers' purchasing patterns.

Forecasting events and outcomes accurately is challenging. Forecasting demand for new technological products is difficult because technology trends are continually driving product life cycles shorter. This is particularly difficult for a firm like Intel, whose products go into many customers' technological products, which are consistently updated. Increasing the difficulty, each new wafer fabrication or silicone chip technology production plant that Intel invests in becomes significantly more expensive for each generation of chip products. Having tools that allow better forecasting of electronic product demand is increasingly important.[29]

During an economic downturn, forecasting becomes more difficult and more important. For example, Procter & Gamble (P&G), Unilever, and Colgate-Palmolive, which primarily sell branded products, have been pushed by retailers to lower their prices, while at the same time these retailers are selling lower-priced, private-label goods. Thus, these consumer product companies are forecasting the effects of the two trends noted as they seek to project demand. Fortunately, these consumer product companies are seeing demand increase for branded products as the economy improves.[30]

Assessing

The objective of *assessing* is to determine the timing and significance of the effects of environmental changes and trends that have been identified.[31] Through scanning, monitoring, and forecasting, analysts are able to understand the general environment. Going a step further, the intent of assessment is to specify the implications of that understanding. Without assessment, the firm is left with data that may be interesting but of unknown competitive relevance. Even if formal assessment is inadequate, the appropriate interpretation of that information is important.

How accurate senior executives are concerning their competitive environments may be less important for strategy and corresponding organizational changes than correctly interpreting environmental trends. Thus, although gathering and organizing information is important, appropriately interpreting that intelligence to determine if an identified trend in the external environment is an opportunity or threat is paramount.[32]

Segments of the General Environment

The general environment is composed of segments that are external to the firm (see Table 2.1). Although the degree of impact varies, these environmental segments affect all industries and the firms competing in them. The challenge to each firm is to scan, monitor, forecast, and assess the elements in each segment to determine their effects on the

Many Asian countries are home to an aging population with citizens 65 or older. Aging populations are a significant problem for countries because of the need for workers and the burden on the government and taxes necessary for funding retirement programs.

zhang bo/iStockphoto.com

firm. Effective scanning, monitoring, forecasting, and assessing are vital to the firm's efforts to recognize and evaluate opportunities and threats.

The Demographic Segment

The **demographic segment** is concerned with a population's size, age structure, geographic distribution, ethnic mix, and income distribution.[33] Demographic segments are commonly analyzed on a global basis because of their potential effects across countries' borders and because many firms compete in global markets.

Population Size

The world's population doubled (from 3 billion to 6 billion) between 1959 and 1999. Current projections suggest that population growth will continue in the twenty-first century, but at a slower pace. The U.S. Census Bureau projects that the world's population will be 9 billion by 2040.[34] By 2050, India is expected to be the most populous nation in the world (with over 1.8 billion people). China, the United States, Indonesia, and Pakistan are predicted to be the next four most populous nations in 2050. Firms seeking to find growing markets in which to sell their goods and services want to recognize the market potential that may exist for them in these five nations.

While observing the population of different nations and regions of the world, firms also want to study changes occurring within different populations to assess their strategic implications. For example, in 2011, 23 percent of Japan's citizens were 65 or older, while the United States and China will not reach this level until 2036.[35] Aging populations are a significant problem for countries because of the need for workers and the burden of funding retirement programs. In Japan and other countries, employees are urged to work longer to overcome these problems. Interestingly, the United States has a higher birthrate and significant immigration, placing it in a better position than Japan and other European nations.

Age Structure

As noted earlier, in Japan and other countries, the world's population is rapidly aging. In North America and Europe, millions of baby boomers are approaching retirement. However, even in developing countries with large numbers of people under the age of 35, birth rates have been declining sharply. In China, for example, by 2040 there will be more than 400 million people over the age of 60. The more than 90 million baby boomers in North America may postpone retirement given the recent financial crisis. In fact, data now suggest that baby boomers (those born between 1946 and 1965) are struggling to meet their retirement goals and are uncertain if they will actually be able to retire as originally expected. This is partly because of declines in the value of their homes as well as declines in their other retirement investments—a number of baby boomers "are being forced to postpone retirement, find cheaper housing, and cut living expenses" due to a decline in their retirement assets between 2007 and 2009.[36] The possibility of future declines is creating uncertainty for baby boomers about how to invest and when they might be able to retire.[37] On the other hand, delayed retirements by baby boomers with value-creating skills may facilitate firms' efforts to successfully implement their strategies. Moreover, delayed retirements may allow companies to think of creative ways for skilled, long-time employees to impart their accumulated knowledge to younger employees as they work a bit longer than originally anticipated.

The **demographic segment** is concerned with a population's size, age structure, geographic distribution, ethnic mix, and income distribution.

Geographic Distribution

For decades, the U.S. population has been shifting from the north and east to the west and south. Firms should consider the effects of this shift in demographics as well.[38] For example, Florida is the U.S. state with the largest percentage of its population (17.6 percent) 65 years or older. Thus, companies providing goods and services that are targeted to senior citizens might pay close attention to this group's geographic preference for states in the south (such as Florida) and the southwest (such as Texas). Similarly, the trend of relocating from metropolitan to nonmetropolitan areas continues in the United States. These trends are changing local and state governments' tax bases. In turn, business firms' decisions regarding location are influenced by the degree of support that different taxing agencies offer as well as the rates at which these agencies tax businesses.

Geographic distribution patterns are not identical throughout the world. For example, in China, 60 percent of the population lives in rural areas; however, the growth is in urban communities such as Shanghai (with a current population in excess of 18 million) and Beijing (over 15 million). These data suggest that firms seeking to sell their products in China should recognize the growth in metropolitan areas rather than in rural areas. Larger cities are expected to generate more growth in GDP per person than smaller cities and also attract more human capital—people with talent to produce economic growth.[39]

Ethnic Mix

The ethnic mix of countries' populations continues to change. For example, Hispanics are now the largest ethnic minority (16 percent) in the United States, representing more than 50 million of the total U.S. population of 308 million.[40] In fact, the U.S. Hispanic market is the third largest "Latin American" economy behind Brazil and Mexico. Spanish is now the dominant language in parts of U.S. states such as Texas, California, Florida, and New Mexico. Given these facts, some firms might want to assess the degree to which their goods or services could be adapted to serve the unique needs of Hispanic consumers. This is particularly appropriate for companies competing in consumer sectors such as grocery stores, movie studios, financial services, and clothing stores.

Changes in the ethnic mix also affect a workforce's composition. In the United States, for example, the population and labor force will continue to diversify, as immigration accounts for a sizable part of growth. Projections are that the combined Latino and Asian population shares will increase to more than 20 percent of the total U.S. population by 2014. Interestingly, much of this immigrant workforce is bypassing high-cost coastal cities and settling in smaller rural towns. Many of these workers are in low-wage, labor-intensive industries such as construction, food service, lodging, and landscaping. For this reason, if border security is tightened, these industries will likely face labor shortages. In addition, well-trained medical and technical personnel have difficulties migrating to the United States even when their skills are in demand. U.S. migration policies have not maintained the same fluidity as global trade agreements; U.S. trade policies have been liberalized while U.S. immigration policies have been tightened.[41]

Income Distribution

Understanding how income is distributed within and across populations informs firms of different groups' purchasing power and discretionary income. Studies of income distributions suggest that although living standards have improved over time, variations exist within and between nations.[42] Of interest to firms are the average incomes of households and individuals. For instance, the increase in dual-career couples has had a notable effect on average incomes. Although real income has been declining in general in some nations, the household income of dual-career couples has increased, especially in the United States. These figures yield strategically relevant information for firms. For instance, research indicates that whether an employee is part of a dual-career couple can strongly influence the willingness of the employee to accept an international assignment. However, because of the worldwide economic downturn, many companies were still pursuing international assignments but changing them to avoid some of the additional costs of funding expatriates abroad.[43]

The growth of the economy in China has drawn many firms, not only for the low-cost production, but also because of the large potential demand for products, given its large population base. However, the amount of China's gross domestic product that makes up domestic consumption is the lowest of any major economy at less than one-third. In comparison, India's domestic consumption of consumer goods accounts for two-thirds of its economy, or twice China's level. As such, many western multinationals are considering entering India as a consumption market as its middle class grows extensively. Although India as a nation has poor infrastructure, its consumers are in a far better position to spend. Furthermore, the urban-rural income difference has been declining in India more rapidly than in China. Because of situations like this, paying attention to the differences between markets based on income distribution can be very important.[44] Of course, the recent global financial crisis may affect the size of the world's "middle class."

The Economic Segment

The economic environment refers to the nature and direction of the economy in which a firm competes or may compete.[45] In general, firms seek to compete in relatively stable economies with strong growth potential. Because nations are interconnected as a result of the global economy, firms must scan, monitor, forecast, and assess the health of their host nation and the health of the economies outside their host nation.

As firms compete during the second decade of the twenty-first century, the world's economic environment is quite uncertain. Some businesspeople are even beginning to question the ability of economists to provide valid and reliable predictions about trends to anticipate in the world's economic environment.[46] The lack of confidence in predictions from those specializing in providing such predictions complicates firms' efforts to understand the conditions they might face during future competitive battles.

In terms of specific economic environments, companies competing in Japan or desiring to do so might carefully evaluate the economic impact of the earthquake, subsequent tsunami, and radiation leaks at the nuclear power generation plants in Sendai.[47] Although the crisis in Japan is country specific, its ripple effects have been felt around the globe. For example, many industries that source inputs from Japan, such as electronic gear and auto parts, have had to close plants for short periods due to lack of critical inputs.

Because of its acknowledged economic growth, a number of companies are evaluating the possibility of entering Russia to compete or, for those already competing in that nation, to expand the scope of their operations. However, "there is no denying that doing business in Russia is not for the faint at heart."[48] This unique, challenging, and sometimes difficult-to-understand business environment presents significant risks in doing business in Russia. This challenging environment can also be an advantage because it serves as an entry barrier to limit the number of companies willing to enter and learn how to operate effectively to reap the returns. Another country with growth opportunities is Vietnam, as firms across the globe take note of how their government reforms and economic decentralization are creating opportunities for investment for sourcing, as well as their developing consumer market.[49]

The Political/Legal Segment

The political/legal segment is the arena in which organizations and interest groups compete for attention, resources, and a voice in overseeing the body of laws and regulations guiding interactions among nations as well as between firms and various local governmental agencies.[50] Essentially, this segment represents how organizations try to influence governments and how they try to understand the influences (current and projected) of those governments on their strategic actions.

When regulations are formed in response to new laws that are legislated (e.g., the Sarbanes-Oxley Act dealing with corporate governance—see Chapter 10 for more

The **economic environment** refers to the nature and direction of the economy in which a firm competes or may compete.

The **political/legal segment** is the arena in which organizations and interest groups compete for attention, resources, and a voice in overseeing the body of laws and regulations guiding interactions among nations as well as between firms and various local governmental agencies.

information), they often influence a firm's strategic actions. For example, less-restrictive regulations on firms' actions are a product of the recent global trend toward privatization of government-owned or government-regulated firms. Much privatization in recent years has been driven by government budget concerns and the need to raise funds by selling government owned firms to reduce deficits.[51] Some believe that the transformation from state-owned to private firms occurring in multiple nations has substantial implications for the competitive landscapes in a number of countries and across multiple industries.[52]

Firms must carefully analyze a new political administration's business-related policies and philosophies. Antitrust laws, taxation laws, industries chosen for deregulation, labor training laws, and the degree of commitment to educational institutions are areas in which an administration's policies can affect the operations and profitability of industries and individual firms across the globe. For example, President Obama's administration has sought to pursue policies with the intention of reducing the amount of work U.S. companies outsource to firms. This policy could affect information technology outsourcing firms based in countries such as India. When President Obama visited India in 2010, he bypassed visiting Bangalore, which is an outsourcing and technology center and economic hotspot in India.[53] The introduction of legislation in the U.S. Congress during the early tenure of the Obama administration suggested at least some support for these stated intentions. However, the legislation has not been enacted and has less likelihood of passing since the 2010 midterm elections.[54]

To deal with issues such as those we are describing, firms develop a political strategy to influence governmental policies that might affect them. Some argue that developing an effective political strategy is essential to the restructured General Motors' efforts to achieve strategic competitiveness since it received government funding during the economic downturn. In addition, the effects of global governmental policies (e.g., those related to firms in India that are engaging in IT outsourcing work) on a firm's competitive position increase the need for firms to form an effective political strategy.[55]

Firms competing in the global economy encounter an interesting array of political/legal questions and issues. For example, the European sovereign-debt crisis has destabilized the European Union. Starting with Greece and moving on to Ireland, Portugal, and Spain, economies weakened by large public debt burdens have caused fiscal policies to be much more restrictive, and still government debt is at sky-high levels which increases bond rates.[56] The debt crisis has put many banks at risk and discourages investment because consumer consumption is likely to be limited. Another crisis in the Middle East and throughout the Arab world is the political revolutions in country after country demanding political reform. Starting with Tunisia and proceeding to Egypt, Libya, Bahrain, Syria, and other states in the region, there is significant turmoil, which has led to a temporary increase in world oil prices.[57] These are political events which create uncertainty in the world's business affairs and make decision making more difficult.

> The **sociocultural segment** is concerned with a society's attitudes and cultural values.

The Sociocultural Segment

The sociocultural segment is concerned with a society's attitudes and cultural values. Because attitudes and values form the cornerstone of a society, they often drive demographic, economic, political/legal, and technological conditions and changes.

Societies' attitudes and cultural values appear to be undergoing possible changes at the start of the second decade of the twenty-first century. In the United States, attitudes and values about health care are an area in which sociocultural changes might occur. Specifically, while the United States has the highest overall health care expenditure as well as the highest expenditure per capita of any country in the world, millions of the nation's citizens lack health insurance. Although health care

In Cairo's Tahrir Square, demonstrator holds Libya's former national flag, now used by rebels (center), while majority wave Egyptian flags during a protest.

AFP/Getty Images

reform legislation was passed in the early part of the Obama administration, it continues to be a bone of contention—especially since the 2010 midterm elections—with attempts made to repeal it and many states filing lawsuits.[58] Continuing changes to the nature of health care policies can have a significant effect on business firms,[59] so they must carefully examine trends regarding health care in order to anticipate the effects on their operations.

As the U.S. labor force has increased, it has become more diverse, as significantly more women and minorities from a variety of cultures enter the workplace. In 1993, the total U.S. workforce was slightly less than 130 million; in 2005, it was slightly greater than 148 million. It is predicted to grow to more than 192 million by 2050. In the same year, 2050, the U.S. workforce is forecast to be composed of 48 percent female workers, 11 percent Asian American workers, 14 percent African American workers and 24 percent Hispanic workers.[60] The growing gender, ethnic, and cultural diversity in the workforce creates challenges and opportunities, including combining the best of both men's and women's traditional leadership styles. Although diversity in the workforce has the potential to improve performance, research indicates that management of diversity initiatives is required in order to reap these organizational benefits. Human resource practitioners are trained to successfully manage diversity issues to enhance positive outcomes.[61]

Another manifestation of changing attitudes toward work is the continuing growth of contingency workers (part-time, temporary, and contract employees) throughout the global economy. This trend is significant in several parts of the world, including Canada, Japan, Latin America, Western Europe, and the United States. In the United States, the fastest growing group of contingency workers is those with 15 to 20 years of work experience. The layoffs resulting from the recent global crisis and the loss of retirement income of numerous "baby boomers"—many of whom feel they must work longer to recover losses to their retirement portfolios—are a key reason for this. Companies interested in hiring on a temporary basis may benefit by gaining access to the long-term work experiences of these newly available workers. Also, temporary workers are the first to be employed as the economy revives after a downturn.[62]

Although the lifestyle and workforce changes referenced previously reflect the values of the U.S. population, each country and culture has unique values and trends. National cultural values affect behavior in organizations and thus also influence organizational outcomes such as differences in CEO compensation.[63] Likewise, the national culture influences to a large extent the internationalization strategy that firms pursue relative to one's home country.[64] Knowledge sharing is important for dispersing new knowledge in organizations and increasing the speed in implementing innovations. Personal relationships are especially important in China as *guanxi* (personal connections) has become a way of doing business within the country and for individuals to advance their careers in what is becoming a more open market society. Understanding the importance of guanxi is critical for foreign firms doing business in China.[65]

The Technological Segment

Pervasive and diversified in scope, technological changes affect many parts of societies. These effects occur primarily through new products, processes, and materials. The **technological segment** includes the institutions and activities involved in creating new knowledge and translating that knowledge into new outputs, products, processes, and materials. Given the rapid pace of technological change and risk of disruption, it is vital for firms to thoroughly study the technological segment.[66] The importance of these efforts is suggested by the finding that early adopters of new technology often achieve higher market shares and earn higher returns. Thus, both large and small firms should continuously scan the external environment to identify potential substitutes for technologies that are in current use, as well as to identify newly emerging technologies from which their firm could derive competitive advantage.[67]

As a significant technological development, the Internet has become a remarkable capability to provide information easily, quickly, and effectively to an ever-increasing

© Nicholas Monu/iStockphoto.com

Find out more about the sociocultural, political, and legal segments of the general environment at McDonald's.

www.cengagebrain .com

The **technological segment** includes the institutions and activities involved with creating new knowledge and translating that knowledge into new outputs, products, processes, and materials.

percentage of the world's population. Companies continue to study the Internet's capabilities to anticipate how it may allow them to create more value for customers in the future and to anticipate future trends.

In spite of the Internet's far-reaching effects, wireless communication technology is becoming the next significant technological opportunity for companies to apply when pursuing strategic competitiveness. Handheld devices and other wireless communications equipment are used to access a variety of network-based services. The use of handheld computers with wireless network connectivity, Web-enabled mobile phone handsets, and other emerging platforms (e.g., consumer Internet-access devices such as the iPhone and iPad) has increased substantially and should soon become the dominant form of communication and commerce.[68]

For example, eBay's iPhone application has become "by far the largest m[mobile]-commerce application in the world," going from $600 million in volume in 2009 to between $1.5 billion and $2 billion in 2010.[69] Amazon's Kindle is not only a reader but also provides access to the Internet. With each new version of mobile devices such as the iPhone, iPad, and Kindle, amazing additional functionalities and software applications are added.

The Global Segment

The **global segment** includes relevant new global markets, existing markets that are changing, important international political events, and critical cultural and institutional characteristics of global markets.[70] There is little doubt that markets are becoming more global and that consumers as well as companies throughout the world accept this fact. Consider the automobile industry. The global auto industry is one in which an increasing number of people believe that because "we live in a global community," consumers in multiple nations are willing to buy cars and trucks "from whatever area of the world."[71]

When studying the global segment, firms (including automobile manufacturers) should recognize that globalization of business markets may create *opportunities* to enter new markets as well as *threats* that new competitors from other economies may also enter their market. This is both an opportunity and a threat for the world's automobile manufacturers—worldwide production capacity is now a potential threat to all global companies where entering another market to sell a company's products appears to be an opportunity. In China, for example, even though car sales surged 37 percent in 2010, it is expected that by 2015 they will reach production overcapacity and have a glut of extra cars. Because of the global economic slowdown, in order to increase sales many car companies want to enter foreign markets. This has led to overcapacity worldwide. To add to the problem in China, labor unions have organized strikes to demand higher wages. For example at Toyota Motor Corporation and Honda Motor Corporation, as young workers coming from rural areas into urban areas are settling down to permanent work, they expect higher wages. This signals that China is no longer a "bargain-basement market for placid workers." This is especially problematic for foreign automakers because by 2017 J. D. Power projects Chinese brands will account for 45 percent of the country's passenger-vehicle market.[72]

The markets from which firms generate sales and income are one indication of the degree to which they are participating in the global economy. For example, H. J. Heinz Company, a large global food producer, is acquiring a stake in Coniexpress S. A. Industrias Alimenticias, a leading Brazilian manufacturer of tomato-based products, ketchup, condiments, and vegetables. The full fiscal year 2011, which ends April 27, is expected to have a sales growth of 2 to 3 percent, while sales in emerging economies such as its Asia-Pacific area grew 16.8 percent and the rest of the world outside its main North-American group grew 14.5 percent. Thus, much of Heinz's sales growth and its profit margins are coming from emerging markets.[73] Likewise, much of SABMiller's growth in beer is coming from emerging economies. For example, at the 2010 World Cup, its purchase of Castle Lager allowed it to sell an extra 30 million bottles. Similar acquisitions of India's Narang and Columbia's Bavaria brands are part of its $17 billion string of acquisitions since 1999, leading to its increased sales growth in emerging markets.[74] Citigroup's CEO, Vikram S. Pandit, has steered his large financial

The **global segment** includes relevant new global markets, existing markets that are changing, important international political events, and critical cultural and institutional characteristics of global markets.

service company through the financial crisis with the help of a $45 billion taxpayer-funded loan. However, Pandit sees much opportunity in developing markets, and as such, half of Citigroup's profit comes from developing countries. For instance, in Latin America and Asia the bank increased its assets by $470 billion in 2010, an increase of 16 percent, by adding customers in countries such as Brazil, Mexico, and India.[75] Thus, for these companies and so many others, understanding the conditions of today's global segment and being able to predict future conditions are critical to their success.

The global segment presents firms with both opportunities and threats or risks. Because of the threats and risks, some firms choose to take a more cautious approach to competing in international markets. These firms participate in what some refer to as *globalfocusing*. Globalfocusing often is used by firms with moderate levels of international operations who increase their internationalization by focusing on global niche markets.[76] In this way, they build on and use their special competencies and resources while limiting their risks within the niche market. Another way in which firms limit their risks in international markets is to focus their operations and sales in one region of the world.[77] In this way, they can build stronger relationships in and knowledge of their markets. As they build these strengths, rivals find it more difficult to enter their markets and compete successfully.

In all instances, firms competing in global markets should recognize their sociocultural and institutional attributes. Furthermore, Korean ideology emphasizes communitarianism, a characteristic of many Asian countries. Korea's approach differs from those of Japan and China, however, in that it focuses on *inhwa*, or harmony. Inhwa is based on a respect of hierarchical relationships and obedience to authority. Alternatively, the approach in China stresses *guanxi*—personal relationships or good connections—while in Japan, the focus is on *wa*, or group harmony and social cohesion.[78] The institutional context of China suggests a major emphasis on centralized planning by the government. The Chinese government provides incentives to firms to develop alliances with foreign firms having sophisticated technology in hopes of building knowledge and introducing new technologies to the Chinese markets over time.[79] As such, it is important to analyze the strategic intent of foreign firms when pursuing alliances and joint ventures abroad, especially where the local partners are receiving technology which may in the long run reduce the foreign firms' advantages.[80]

The Physical Environment Segment

The **physical environment segment** refers to potential and actual changes in the physical environment and business practices that are intended to positively respond to and deal with those changes.[81] Concerned with trends oriented to sustaining the world's physical environment, firms recognize that ecological, social, and economic systems interactively influence what happens in this particular segment.[82]

There are many parts or attributes of the physical environment that firms should consider as they try to identify trends in this segment.[83] Some argue that global warming is a trend firms and nations should carefully examine in efforts to predict any potential effects on the global society as well as on their business operations. Investors are seeking to take advantage of this trend, calling it "green alpha," by looking to profit by increasing environmental sustainability.[84] Energy consumption is another part of the physical environment that concerns both organizations and nations. In Canada, for example, a representative of the Energy Council of Canada said: "The electricity sector right now is 75 percent clean, and the idea is that over a well-defined period of time we'll be a 90 percent clean electricity sector."[85] Most of this clean power generation comes from hydroelectric produced electricity.

Because of increasing concern about sustaining the quality of the physical environment, a number of companies are developing environmentally friendly policies. Indra K. Nooyi, CEO of PepsiCo, is pursuing a strategy called "capital performance with purpose." This strategy links green efforts in all businesses to the bottom line. Through this approach, PepsiCo hopes to create technologies that can be replicated across its multiple facilities, thereby creating large savings. For example, Frito-Lay, a PepsiCo business unit, operates the world's seventh-largest private delivery fleet. In large urban areas it is

The **physical environment segment** refers to potential and actual changes in the physical environment and business practices that are intended to positively respond to and deal with those changes.

S T R A T E G I C F O C U S

FIRMS' EFFORTS TO TAKE CARE OF THE PHYSICAL ENVIRONMENT IN WHICH THEY COMPETE

The number of companies throughout the world that recognize that they compete within the confines of the physical environment and that they are expected to reduce the negative effect of their operations on the physical environment while competing continues to increase. Also, consumers concerned about the physical environment value this trend.

Producing and selling additional "green" (i.e., environmentally friendly) products is one company response to this trend. Siemens AG, a large diversified engineering firm similar to General Electric in the United States, was traumatized by a global bribery scandal that led to a new outside CEO, Peter Loscher, being appointed. His leadership led to a significant restructuring effort. While Loscher divested telecommunication and information technology businesses, he increased the focus on selling sustainability oriented products to both consumers and industrial customers, including everything from light bulbs to high-speed trains to factory controls.

Siemens generates $38 billion in sales from wind power, solar energy, and energy-conserving electricity grids. It claims to be the lead offshore wind turbine producer, and about one quarter of its 400,000 employees are what Siemens calls "green-collar workers" that are focused on sustainability products. This approach has allowed Siemens' stock to surge 47 percent in 2009, almost twice the gain that GE's stock achieved in the same period. Interestingly, GE has also made a significant emphasis on the green consciousness of its sales orientation.

In addition to products, companies across the globe are committing to or increasing their commitment to environmental sustainability. McDonald's, for example, has pursued green restaurant design, sustainable packaging, and waste management, and seeks to improve energy efficiency to reduce its environmental footprint. More importantly, it has required its supply chain to strive to meet sustainability goals. For example, Cargill, Inc., a large basic food producer, has been recognized by McDonald's as a "Global Best of Green" supplier.

McDonald's is one of Cargill's largest customers, and Cargill partners with them "in every area from menu development, to restaurant operations and risk management solutions." McDonald's supports an annual sustainability conference in which it challenges its suppliers to meet "best practices" to improve environmental sustainability. For instance, Cargill invested millions to install anaerobic reactors at all of its largest beef and pork processing plants. Through this process, Cargill reclaims methane from wastewater lagoons and converts it to fuel the plants' boilers. This process has reduced 30 percent of the natural gas demand at 11 meat plants. Cargill estimates that this process has reduced greenhouse gas emissions by more than 1.3 million metric tons over the last four years: "It reduces pollution, increases our renewable energy and cuts costs."

Procter & Gamble (P&G) recently announced increased targets for its 2012 sustainability goals. Among the goals are those to (1) "develop and market at least $50 billion in cumulative sales of sustainable innovation

PRNewsFoto/The Procter & Gamble Company

Former P&G CEP John Pepper provides the billionth liter of water to Taiwo Faruna in Nigeria in celebration of a new milestone for the Children's Safe Drinking Water Program.

products, (2) deliver a 20 percent reduction (per unit of production) in carbon dioxide emissions, energy consumption, water usage and disposed waste from P&G plants, and (3) enable 300 million children to Live, Learn and Thrive by delivering three billion liters of clean water through P&G's Children's Safe Drinking Water program." Dutch consumer product giant Unilever also has an ongoing commitment to sustainability. The firm's sustainability actions include reducing water usage in its plants, working with its suppliers to encourage sustainability practices on their parts, and improving the eco-efficiency of their manufacturing facilities. Again, an important aspect of these sustainability programs by large companies is that it extends to their supply chain. For example, Walmart's sustainability has an immense impact on both major and minor supply chain partners.

Although many forces are pushing firms to become greener, not all the "green" claims of products on store shelves are valid. According to a recent study reported in the *Wall Street Journal*, 95 percent of consumer products examined committed at least one offense of "green washing," a term used to describe unproven environmental claims. Both TerraChoice and Underwriters Laboratories offer green-certification programs, which could benefit many manufacturers who seek to have third-party verification of their green or environmentally friendly claims.

Although there are many firms whose claims are not verified, the examples noted above signify a growing commitment by firms around the globe in response to emerging trends in the physical environment segment. In addition to positively responding to the observed trends in this segment of the general environment, there is some evidence that firms engaging in these types of behaviors outperform those failing to do so, as the Siemens example illustrates. This emerging evidence suggests that these behaviors benefit companies, their stakeholders, and the physical environment in which they operate.

Sources: 2011, Betting on green, *Economist*, March 12, 22; 2011, Thinking outside (and inside) the box, *Refrigerated and Frozen Foods*, March, 40–41; G. Colvin, 2011, Green forum, *Fortune*, April 11, 90–102; R. Pendrous, 2011, The green giant of sustainable thinking, *Profitable Production*, March, 37; D. Stanford, 2011, Sustainability meets the profit motive, *Bloomberg Businessweek*, April 4, 25–26; R. Weiss & B. Kammel, 2011, How Siemens got its Mojo back, *Bloomberg Businessweek*, http://www.businessweek.com, January 27; G. Bounds, 2010, Health and Wellness: Misleading claims on "green" labeling, *Wall Street Journal*, October 26, D4.

Learn more about Cargill as a green supplier.

www.cengagebrain.com

putting in an all-electric fleet of delivery trucks that it estimates will save 500,000 gallons of diesel fuel a year, curbing greenhouse emissions by 75 percent over combustion engines. This conversion also expects to save $700,000 in maintenance costs.[86]

We discuss other firms' efforts to "reduce their environmental footprint" and to be good stewards of the physical environment as a result of doing so in the preceding Strategic Focus. As we note, the number of "green" products companies are producing continues to increase.

As our discussion of the general environment shows, identifying anticipated changes and trends among external elements is a key objective of analyzing the firm's general environment. With a focus on the future, the analysis of the general environment allows firms to identify opportunities and threats. It is necessary to have a top management team with the experience, knowledge, and sensitivity required to effectively analyze this segment of the environment.[87] Also critical to a firm's choices of strategic actions to take is an understanding of its industry environment and its competitors; we consider these issues next.

Industry Environment Analysis

An **industry** is a group of firms producing products that are close substitutes. In the course of competition, these firms influence one another. Typically, industries include a rich mixture of competitive strategies that companies use in pursuing above-average returns. In part, these strategies are chosen because of the influence of an industry's characteristics.[88]

An **industry** is a group of firms producing products that are close substitutes.

Compared with the general environment, the industry environment has a more direct effect on the firm's strategic competitiveness and ability to earn above-average returns.[89] An industry's profit potential is a function of five forces of competition: the threats posed by new entrants, the power of suppliers, the power of buyers, product substitutes, and the intensity of rivalry among competitors (see Figure 2.2).

The five forces model of competition expands the arena for competitive analysis. Historically, when studying the competitive environment, firms concentrated on companies with which they competed directly. However, firms must search more broadly to recognize current and potential competitors by identifying potential customers as well as the firms serving them. For example, the communications industry is now broadly defined as encompassing media companies, telecoms, entertainment companies, and companies producing devices such as smartphones.[90] In such an environment, firms must study many other industries to identify firms with capabilities (especially technology-based capabilities) that might be the foundation for producing a good or a service that can compete against what they are producing. Using this perspective finds firms focusing on customers and their needs rather than on specific industry boundaries to define markets.

When studying the industry environment, firms must also recognize that suppliers can become a firm's competitors (by integrating forward) as can buyers (by integrating backward). For example, several firms have integrated forward in the pharmaceutical industry by acquiring distributors or wholesalers. In addition, firms choosing to enter a new market and those producing products that are adequate substitutes for existing products can become a company's competitors. Next, we examine the five forces the firm analyzes to understand the profitability potential within the industry (or a segment of an industry) in which it competes or may choose to compete.

Threat of New Entrants

Identifying new entrants is important because they can threaten the market share of existing competitors.[91] One reason new entrants pose such a threat is that they bring additional production capacity. Unless the demand for a good or service is increasing, additional capacity holds consumers' costs down, resulting in less revenue and lower returns for

Figure 2.2 The Five Forces of Competition Model

competing firms. Often, new entrants have a keen interest in gaining a large market share. As a result, new competitors may force existing firms to be more efficient and to learn how to compete on new dimensions (e.g., using an Internet-based distribution channel).

The likelihood that firms will enter an industry is a function of two factors: barriers to entry and the retaliation expected from current industry participants. Entry barriers make it difficult for new firms to enter an industry and often place them at a competitive disadvantage even when they are able to enter. As such, high entry barriers tend to increase the returns for existing firms in the industry and may allow some firms to dominate the industry.[92] Thus, firms competing successfully in an industry want to maintain high entry barriers in order to discourage potential competitors from deciding to enter the industry.

Barriers to Entry

Firms competing in an industry (and especially those earning above-average returns) try to develop entry barriers to thwart potential competitors. For example, the server market is hypercompetitive and dominated by IBM, Hewlett-Packard, and Dell. Historically, the scale economies these firms have developed by operating efficiently and effectively have created significant entry barriers, causing potential competitors to think very carefully about entering the server market to compete against them. Oracle, primarily a software-oriented company, acquired Sun Microsystems, which is primarily a server hardware company, to overcome the barriers to entry that exist in this industry. Oracle intends to preload Oracle software into its new server line. "Hardware makers such as Dell and HP are getting into software, and software companies like Oracle are getting into hardware"; these "companies want to create the integrated hardware and software systems that can satisfy a corporate customer's every IT need."[93] The degree of success Oracle will achieve as a result of its decision to enter the server market via an acquisition remains uncertain.

Several kinds of potentially significant entry barriers may discourage competitors from entering a market.

Economies of Scale *Economies of scale* are derived from incremental efficiency improvements through experience as a firm grows larger. Therefore, the cost of producing each unit declines as the quantity of a product produced during a given period increases. This is the case for IBM, Hewlett-Packard, and Dell in the server market, as previously described.

Economies of scale can be developed in most business functions, such as marketing, manufacturing, research and development, and purchasing.[94] Increasing economies of scale enhances a firm's flexibility. For example, a firm may choose to reduce its price and capture a greater share of the market. Alternatively, it may keep its price constant to increase profits. In so doing, it likely will increase its free cash flow, which is very helpful during financially challenging times.

New entrants face a dilemma when confronting current competitors' scale economies. Small-scale entry places them at a cost disadvantage. Given the size of Sun Microsystems relative to the three major competitors in the server market, Oracle has found it difficult to compete against its scale advantaged competitors.[95] Additionally, large-scale entry through such an acquisition, in which the new entrant manufactures large volumes of a product to gain economies of scale, risks strong competitive retaliation.

Some competitive conditions reduce the ability of economies of scale to create an entry barrier. Many companies now customize their products for large numbers of small customer groups. Customized products are not manufactured in the volumes necessary to achieve economies of scale. Customization is made possible by flexible manufacturing systems (this point is discussed further in Chapter 4). In fact, the new manufacturing technology facilitated by advanced information systems has allowed the development of mass customization in an increasing number of industries. Although it is not appropriate for all products and implementing it can be challenging, mass customization has become increasingly common in manufacturing products.[96] Online ordering has enhanced the ability of customers to obtain customized products. Companies manufacturing customized products learn how to respond quickly to customers' needs in lieu of developing scale economies.

Product Differentiation Over time, customers may come to believe that a firm's product is unique. This belief can result from the firm's service to the customer, effective advertising campaigns, or being the first to market a good or service. The Coca-Cola Company and PepsiCo have established strong brands in the soft drink market. These brands compete with each other not only in the United States but around the world. Because each has used a great deal of resources building their brands, customer loyalty is strong. These companies battle each other for market leadership, which has changed back and forth over the years.[97] Although Diet Coke is currently the lead brand in the soft drink market, PepsiCo is leading the way in regard to innovation in social media, such as advertising on Facebook and Twitter as well as other approaches through the Internet.[98] When considering entry into the soft drink market, a company needs to pause to examine how one can overcome the brand image and consumer loyalty to these two giants in this global industry. One needs significant resources to capture market share, although many firms are doing so that have the resources to produce private label products such as Walmart.

Companies such as Procter & Gamble (P&G) and Colgate-Palmolive spend a great deal of money on advertising and product development to convince potential customers of their products' distinctiveness and of the value buying their brands provides. Customers valuing a product's uniqueness tend to become loyal to both the product and the company producing it. In turn, customer loyalty is an entry barrier for firms thinking of entering an industry and competing against the likes of P&G and Colgate. To compete against firms offering differentiated products to individuals who have become loyal customers, new entrants often allocate many resources. To combat the perception of uniqueness, new entrants frequently offer products at lower prices. This decision, however, may result in lower profits or even losses.

Capital Requirements Competing in a new industry requires a firm to have resources to invest. In addition to physical facilities, capital is needed for inventories, marketing activities, and other critical business functions. Even when a new industry is attractive, the capital required for successful market entry may not be available to pursue the market opportunity.[99] For example, defense industries are difficult to enter because of the substantial resource investments required to be competitive. In addition, because of the high knowledge requirements of the defense industry, a firm might acquire an existing company as a means of entering this industry, but it must have access to the capital necessary to do this. Obviously, Oracle had the capital required to acquire Sun Microsystems as a foundation for entering the server market.

Switching Costs Switching costs are the one-time costs customers incur when they buy from a different supplier. The costs of buying new ancillary equipment and of retraining employees, and even the psychic costs of ending a relationship, may be incurred in switching to a new supplier. In some cases, switching costs are low, such as when the consumer switches to a different brand of soft drink. Switching costs can vary as a function of time. For example, in terms of credit hours toward graduation, the cost to a student to transfer from one university to another as a freshman is much lower than it is when the student is entering the senior year.

Occasionally, a decision made by manufacturers to produce a new, innovative product creates high switching costs for the final consumer. Customer loyalty programs, such as airlines' frequent flyer miles, are intended to increase the customer's switching costs. If switching costs are high, a new entrant must offer either a substantially lower price or a much better product to attract buyers. Usually, the more established the relationships between parties, the greater the switching costs.

Access to Distribution Channels Over time, industry participants typically develop effective means of distributing products. Once a relationship with its distributors has been built a firm will nurture it, thus creating switching costs for the distributors. Access to distribution channels can be a strong entry barrier for new entrants, particularly in consumer nondurable goods industries (e.g., in grocery stores where shelf space is limited) and in international markets. New entrants have to persuade distributors to carry their products, either in addition to or in place of those currently distributed. Price breaks and cooperative advertising allowances may be used for this purpose; however, those practices reduce the new entrant's profit potential. Interestingly, access to distribution is less of a barrier for products that can be sold on the Internet.

Cost Disadvantages Independent of Scale Sometimes, established competitors have cost advantages that new entrants cannot duplicate. Proprietary product technology, favorable access to raw materials, desirable locations, and government subsidies are examples. Successful competition requires new entrants to reduce the strategic relevance of these factors. Delivering purchases directly to the buyer can counter the advantage of a desirable location; new food establishments in an undesirable location often follow this practice.

Government Policy Through licensing and permit requirements, governments can also control entry into an industry. Liquor retailing, radio and TV broadcasting, banking, and trucking are examples of industries in which government decisions and actions affect entry possibilities. Also, governments often restrict entry into some industries because of the need to provide quality service or the need to protect jobs. Alternatively, deregulation of industries, exemplified by the airline and utilities industries in the United States, allows more firms to enter.[100] However, some of the most publicized government actions are those involving antitrust. Often the Antitrust Division of the Justice Department or the Federal Trade Commission will disallow a merger because it creates a firm that is too dominant in an industry and would thus create unfair competition.[101] Such a negative ruling would obviously be an entry barrier for the acquiring firm.

Expected Retaliation

Companies seeking to enter an industry also anticipate the reactions of firms in the industry. An expectation of swift and vigorous competitive responses reduces the likelihood of entry. Vigorous retaliation can be expected when the existing firm has a major stake in the industry (e.g., it has fixed assets with few, if any, alternative uses), when it has substantial resources, and when industry growth is slow or constrained. For example, any firm attempting to enter the airline industry at the current time can expect significant retaliation from existing competitors due to overcapacity.

Locating market niches not being served by incumbents allows the new entrant to avoid entry barriers. Small entrepreneurial firms are generally best suited for identifying and serving neglected market segments. When Honda first entered the U.S. motorcycle market, it concentrated on small-engine motorcycles, a market that firms such as Harley-Davidson ignored. By targeting this neglected niche, Honda avoided competition. After consolidating its position, Honda used its strength to attack rivals by introducing larger motorcycles and competing in the broader market. Competitive actions and competitive responses between firms such as Honda and Harley-Davidson are discussed more fully in Chapter 5.

Bargaining Power of Suppliers

Increasing prices and reducing the quality of their products are potential means suppliers use to exert power over firms competing within an industry. If a firm is unable to recover cost increases by its suppliers through its own pricing structure, its profitability is reduced by its suppliers' actions. A supplier group is powerful when

- It is dominated by a few large companies and is more concentrated than the industry to which it sells.
- Satisfactory substitute products are not available to industry firms.
- Industry firms are not a significant customer for the supplier group.
- Suppliers' goods are critical to buyers' marketplace success.
- The effectiveness of suppliers' products has created high switching costs for industry firms.
- It poses a credible threat to integrate forward into the buyers' industry. Credibility is enhanced when suppliers have substantial resources and provide a highly differentiated product.

The airline industry is one in which suppliers' bargaining power is changing. Though the number of suppliers is low, the demand for major aircraft is also relatively low. Boeing and Airbus aggressively compete for orders of major aircraft, creating more power for buyers in the process. When a large airline signals that it might place a "significant" order for wide-body airliners which either Airbus or Boeing might produce, both companies are likely to battle for the business and include a financing arrangement, highlighting the buyer's power in the potential transaction.

Bargaining Power of Buyers

Firms seek to maximize the return on their invested capital. Alternatively, buyers (customers of an industry or a firm) want to buy products at the lowest possible price—the point at which the industry earns the lowest acceptable rate of return on its invested capital. To reduce their costs, buyers bargain for higher quality, greater levels of service, and lower prices.[102] These outcomes are achieved by encouraging competitive battles among the industry's firms. Customers (buyer groups) are powerful when

- They purchase a large portion of an industry's total output.
- The sales of the product being purchased account for a significant portion of the seller's annual revenues.
- They could switch to another product at little, if any, cost.
- The industry's products are undifferentiated or standardized, and the buyers pose a credible threat if they were to integrate backward into the sellers' industry.

Consumers armed with greater amounts of information about the manufacturer's costs and the power of the Internet as a shopping and distribution alternative have increased bargaining power in many industries. One reason for this shift is that individual buyers incur virtually zero switching costs when they decide to purchase from one manufacturer rather than another or from one dealer as opposed to any other.

Threat of Substitute Products

Substitute products are goods or services from outside a given industry that perform similar or the same functions as a product that the industry produces. For example, as a sugar substitute, NutraSweet (and other sugar substitutes) places an upper limit on sugar manufacturers' prices—NutraSweet and sugar perform the same function, though with different characteristics. Other product substitutes include e-mail and fax machines instead of overnight deliveries, plastic containers rather than glass jars, and tea instead of coffee. Newspaper firms have experienced significant circulation declines over the past decade or more. The declines are due to substitute outlets for news including Internet sources, cable television news channels, and e-mail and cell phone alerts. Likewise, satellite TV and cable and telecommunication companies provide substitute services for basic media services such as television, Internet, and phone. However, as illustrated in the Strategic Focus, the possible switching is becoming more complicated as consumer

STRATEGIC FOCUS

THE MULTI-INDUSTRY BATTLE FOR MOBILE AND HOME DIGITAL COMPUTING AND ENTERTAINMENT

In the Internet era, as media content has moved from a paper, tape, and film (or analog) world to a digital world based on Internet technology, new industry structures are emerging as firms begin to utilize that technology and create commercial opportunities. This process of new technology creation, utilization, and commercialization ultimately leads to changes in organizational patterns, and in particular, strategic alliances and mergers and acquisitions as firms restructure themselves around the utilization and commercial opportunities being created.

At the base of this new digital world are firms that offer digital services. In particular focusing on television subscribers, there are about 64 million cable TV households and 32.5 million satellite consumers. However, although starting at a lower base, telecom TV homes are growing at an increased rate relative to satellite and cable providers. In 2011 telecom television providers are at 8.5 million but are projected to be at 16 million by 2014. Each of these providers is seeking to bundle their services to provide not only television but also broadband and telecommunication services. Many telecom providers are also reaching/pursuing mobile phone services, especially as the penetration rate of landlines is decreasing and mobile phones are increasing.

PSL Images/Alamy

More and more people are choosing to watch movies and television shows via an online streaming service. Google TV, along with Apple TV, Netflix, and Hulu are competing for this base, as are cable companies through video on demand (VOD) services. Many more companies are sure to enter the market vying for a piece of this growing trend.

Industry convergence is also being felt by device producers such as Apple and other PC makers such as Dell and HP. Apple has produced a smartphone, the iPhone, which has sparked all other device makers to try to produce similar products. Such products now are offered by all of the mobile phone producers, including Nokia, Samsung, and Motorola, among others. Not only do the smartphones provide telephone and texting capabilities but also increasingly numerous multimedia applications, including music and video as well as GPS services and general Internet searches. There are new applications almost every day. The opportunities here globally are even more significant than the purchases of personal computers because the price is lower.

The battle for a software platform among these smartphones is also important. The iPhone platform produced by Apple is currently in the lead, but Google has been catching up through its Android platform. Although Microsoft is behind, Nokia has recently moved to adopt the Microsoft platform. Research in Motion's (RIM) platform is also competing but is behind the Apple and Google platforms. RIM has been in the lead among business customers, but this lead is being eroded as well by Apple and Google platforms. The larger the base of users in these platforms the more draw there is for independent software producers to create new application uses for an increasing variety of smartphones, which draws more consumers to the platform and the company's devices.

The platform is also important in the home, where there is a battle for control of the set-top box, which manages the media content available through televisions and other home devices such as the personal computer. Again, Apple TV, Google TV, and firms such as Netflix and Hulu are competing for this base, as are cable companies through video on demand (VOD) services.

Finally, firms that actually produce the media—musicians, news organizations and newspapers, television and movie producers, and publishers—want to make sure that their content is available through all sources. Now, that means mobile as well as home devices, where they can gain access to advertising dollars, which have been the traditional ways of profiting from media. For example, people are going to movies in theaters less than they used to, even with increased use of technology such as three dimensions (3D). More and more people are watching media at home through big screen televisions and via VOD services, which are available not only in the home but on mobile devices, netbooks, laptops, and desktop PCs.

This convergence among players has led to acquisitions between buyers and suppliers and competitors as well as multiple relationships and strategic partnerships through strategic alliances, which have become the norm as firms compete to take advantage of the resources available. A recent trend has been to partner with social network firms such as Twitter and Facebook in order to better utilize social media and gain new advertising dollars. This convergence makes competitor analysis much more difficult than it used to be because it is difficult to say who is a competitor, who is a supplier, who is a buyer, and who is a new entrant into the industry, and what products, services, and processes will be substituted next as the industry structure evolves. One day a firm provides a complementary product such as software to hardware producers, and the next day the complementor (formally defined later in the chapter) makes an acquisition, as Oracle did of Sun Microcomputers, and becomes a competitor to other server producers such as Dell, HP, and IBM. Competitor analysis must take into consideration the technological changes which lead to the utilization and commercialization of technologies. It also must ultimately examine how such technological changes will lead to convergence of competitors or other firms and associated organizational changes through alliances and acquisitions and the possible re-creation of a new set of industry competitors, buyers, and suppliers.

Sources: P. Burrows, 2011, Mobile wars! Apple vs. Google vs. those other guys, *Bloomberg Businessweek*, http://www .businessweek.com, February 16; J. Christensen, 2011, Industrial evolution through complementary convergence: The case of IT security, *Industrial & Corporate Change*, 20(1): 57–89; J. Davis, 2011, Lenovo's tablet, smartphone focus: New business unit created, http://www.channelinsider.com, January 25; G. Rivlin, 2011, The problem with Microsoft, *Fortune*, April 11, 45–52; G. Winslow, 2011, Map to TV everywhere, *Broadcast & Cable*, February 14, 23; 2010, The competitive landscape, *Multichannel News*, http://www.multichannel.com, December 27; A. Pierce, 2010, The convergence of communication technologies, *Tech Directions*, 70(5): 12–13; D. Sullivan & J. Yuening, 2010, Media convergence and the impact of the internet on the M&A activity of large media companies, *Journal of Media Business Studies*, 7(4): 21–40.

demand for content changes through increasing use of mobile devices such as tablets and smartphones.[103] Tablets such as the iPad are reducing the number of PCs sold and this is curtailing the growth of PC producers such as Taiwan's Acer Computers, at least until they can come out with their own successful tablet product.[104] These products are increasingly popular, especially among younger and technologically savvy people, and as product substitutes they have significant potential to continue to reduce traditional media sources such as newspaper circulation sales.

In general, product substitutes present a strong threat to a firm when customers face few, if any, switching costs and when the substitute product's price is lower or its quality and performance capabilities are equal to or greater than those of the competing product. Differentiating a product along dimensions that customers value (such as quality, service after the sale, and location) reduces a substitute's attractiveness.

Intensity of Rivalry among Competitors

Because an industry's firms are mutually dependent, actions taken by one company usually invite competitive responses. In many industries, firms actively compete against one another. Competitive rivalry intensifies when a firm is challenged by a competitor's actions or when a company recognizes an opportunity to improve its market position.

Firms within industries are rarely homogeneous; they differ in resources and capabilities and seek to differentiate themselves from competitors.[105] Typically, firms seek to differentiate their products from competitors' offerings in ways that customers value and in which the firms have a competitive advantage. Common dimensions on which rivalry is based include price, service after the sale, and innovation.

Next, we discuss the most prominent factors that experience shows to affect the intensity of firms' rivalries.

Numerous or Equally Balanced Competitors

Intense rivalries are common in industries with many companies. With multiple competitors, it is common for a few firms to believe they can act without eliciting a response. However, evidence suggests that other firms generally are aware of competitors' actions, often choosing to respond to them. At the other extreme, industries with only a few firms of equivalent size and power also tend to have strong rivalries. The large and often similar-sized resource bases of these firms permit vigorous actions and responses. The competitive battles between Airbus and Boeing exemplify intense rivalry between relatively equal competitors, especially as airlines place bids for the new wide-body planes they are producing. Coca-Cola and PepsiCo have a strong rivalry in drink products as consumers demand not only great taste but real health benefits.[106]

Slow Industry Growth

When a market is growing, firms try to effectively use resources to serve an expanding customer base. Growing markets reduce the pressure to take customers from competitors. However, rivalry in no-growth or slow-growth markets (slow change) becomes more intense as firms battle to increase their market shares by attracting competitors' customers. For example, there is a growing trend for health care of baby boomers, who are now reaching age 65. Growth can be realized by managed-care firms like WellPoint Inc. and Aetna Inc. without strong rivalry.[107] The same is true for home health care, but as regulation becomes more prominent in this industry, growth is likely to slow and rivalry increase.[108]

Typically, battles to protect market share are fierce. Certainly, this has been the case in the airline industry and in the fast-food industry as McDonald's, Wendy's, and Burger King try to win each other's customers. The instability in the market that results from these competitive engagements may reduce the profitability for all firms engaging in such battles.

Burger King, in an attempt to protect market share, often switches up its menu offerings. Some items have met with more success (the Whopper) than others (BK Veggie Burger.)

David H. Wells/CORBIS

High Fixed Costs or High Storage Costs

When fixed costs account for a large part of total costs, companies try to maximize the use of their productive capacity. Doing so allows the firm to spread costs across a larger volume of output. However, when many firms attempt to maximize their productive capacity, excess capacity is created on an industry-wide basis. To then reduce inventories, individual companies typically cut the price of their product and offer rebates and other special discounts to customers. However, these practices, common in the automobile manufacturing industry in the recent past, often intensify competition. The pattern of excess capacity at the industry level followed by intense rivalry at the firm level is observed frequently in industries with high storage costs. Perishable products, for example, lose their value rapidly with the passage of time. As their inventories grow, producers of perishable goods often use pricing strategies to sell products quickly.

Lack of Differentiation or Low Switching Costs

When buyers find a differentiated product that satisfies their needs, they frequently purchase the product loyally over time. Industries with many companies that have successfully differentiated their products have less rivalry, resulting in lower competition for individual firms. Firms that develop and sustain a differentiated product that cannot be easily imitated by competitors often earn higher returns. However, when buyers view products as commodities (i.e., as products with few differentiated features or capabilities), rivalry intensifies. In these instances, buyers' purchasing decisions are based primarily on price and, to a lesser degree, service. Personal computers are a commodity product. Thus, the rivalry between Dell, Hewlett-Packard, Lenovo, and other computer manufacturers is strong and these companies are always trying to find ways to differentiate their offerings (Hewlett-Packard now pursues product design as a means of differentiation). Apple has been able to maintain a differentiation strategy through ease of use of its software applications and its integration capabilities with other software platforms.

High Strategic Stakes

Competitive rivalry is likely to be high when it is important for several of the competitors to perform well in the market. For example, although it is diversified and is a market leader in other businesses, Samsung has targeted market leadership in the consumer electronics market and is doing quite well. This market is quite important to Sony and other major competitors, such as Hitachi, Matsushita, NEC, and Mitsubishi, suggesting that rivalry among these competitors will remain strong.

High strategic stakes can also exist in terms of geographic locations. For example, Japanese automobile manufacturers are committed to a significant presence in the U.S. marketplace because it is the world's largest single market for automobiles and trucks. Due to the high stakes involved in the United States for both Japanese and U.S. manufacturers, rivalry among the global firms from these two countries is intense. With the excess capacity in this industry we mentioned earlier in this chapter, there is every reason to believe that the rivalry among global automobile manufacturers will remain intense in the foreseeable future.

High Exit Barriers

Sometimes companies continue competing in an industry even though the returns on their invested capital are low or negative. Firms making this choice likely face high exit barriers, which include economic, strategic, and emotional factors causing them to remain in an industry when the profitability of doing so is questionable. Exit barriers are especially high in the airline industry. Although earning even average returns is difficult for these firms, they face substantial exit barriers, such as their ownership of specialized assets (e.g., large aircraft).[109] Common exit barriers include the following:

- Specialized assets (assets with values linked to a particular business or location)
- Fixed costs of exit (such as labor agreements)
- Strategic interrelationships (relationships of mutual dependence, such as those between one business and other parts of a company's operations, including shared facilities and access to financial markets)
- Emotional barriers (aversion to economically justified business decisions because of fear for one's own career, loyalty to employees, and so forth)
- Government and social restrictions (often based on government concerns for job losses and regional economic effects; more common outside the United States).

Interpreting Industry Analyses

Effective industry analyses are products of careful study and interpretation of data and information from multiple sources. A wealth of industry-specific data is available to be analyzed by individual countries. Because of globalization, international markets and rivalries must be included in the firm's analyses. In fact, research shows that in some industries, international variables are more important than domestic ones as determinants of strategic competitiveness. Furthermore, because of the development of global markets, a country's borders no longer restrict industry structures. In fact, movement into international markets enhances the chances of success for new ventures as well as more established firms.[110]

Analysis of the five forces in the industry allows the firm to determine the industry's attractiveness in terms of the potential to earn adequate or superior returns. In general, the stronger competitive forces are, the lower the profit potential for an industry's firms. An unattractive industry has low entry barriers, suppliers and buyers with strong bargaining positions, strong competitive threats from product substitutes, and intense rivalry among competitors. These industry characteristics make it difficult for firms to achieve strategic competitiveness and earn above-average returns. Alternatively, an attractive industry has high entry barriers, suppliers and buyers with little bargaining power, few competitive threats from product substitutes, and relatively moderate rivalry.[111] Next, we explain strategic groups as an aspect of industry competition.

Strategic Groups

A set of firms that emphasize similar strategic dimensions and use a similar strategy is called a **strategic group**.[112] The competition between firms within a strategic group is greater than the competition between a member of a strategic group and companies outside that strategic group. Therefore, intrastrategic group competition is more intense than is interstrategic group competition. In fact, more heterogeneity is evident in the performance of firms within strategic groups than across the groups. The performance leaders within groups are able to follow strategies similar to those of other firms in the group and yet maintain strategic distinctiveness to gain and sustain a competitive advantage.[113]

The extent of technological leadership, product quality, pricing policies, distribution channels, and customer service are examples of strategic dimensions that firms in a strategic group may treat similarly. Thus, membership in a particular strategic group defines the essential characteristics of the firm's strategy.[114]

The notion of strategic groups can be useful for analyzing an industry's competitive structure. Such analyses can be helpful in diagnosing competition, positioning, and the profitability of firms within an industry.[115] High mobility barriers, high rivalry, and low resources among the firms within an industry limit the formation of strategic groups.[116] However, research suggests that after strategic groups are formed, their membership remains relatively stable over time, although recent research does examine how change occurs.[117] Using strategic groups to understand an industry's competitive structure requires the firm to plot companies' competitive actions and competitive responses along strategic dimensions such as pricing decisions, product quality, distribution channels, and so forth. This type of analysis shows the firm how certain companies are competing similarly in terms of how they use similar strategic dimensions.

Strategic groups have several implications. First, because firms within a group offer similar products to the same customers, the competitive rivalry among them can be intense. The more intense the rivalry, the greater the threat to each firm's profitability. Second, the strengths of the five industry forces differ across strategic groups. Third, the closer the strategic groups are in terms of their strategies, the greater is the likelihood of rivalry between the groups.

> A set of firms that emphasize similar strategic dimensions and use a similar strategy is called a **strategic group**.

Competitor Analysis

The competitor environment is the final part of the external environment requiring study. Competitor analysis focuses on each company against which a firm directly competes.

Figure 2.3 Competitor Analysis Components

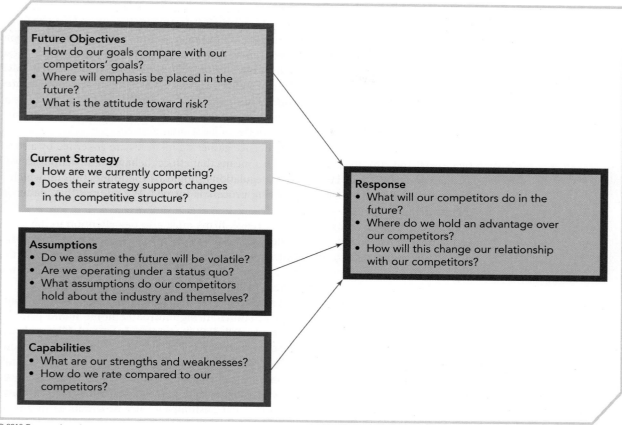

© 2013 Cengage Learning.

For example, Coca-Cola and PepsiCo, Home Depot and Lowe's, and Boeing and Airbus are keenly interested in understanding each other's objectives, strategies, assumptions, and capabilities. Indeed, intense rivalry creates a strong need to understand competitors.[118] In a competitor analysis, the firm seeks to understand the following:

- What drives the competitor, as shown by its *future objectives*
- What the competitor is doing and can do, as revealed by its *current strategy*
- What the competitor believes about the industry, as shown by its *assumptions*
- What the competitor's capabilities are, as shown by its *strengths* and *weaknesses*[119]

Information about these four dimensions helps the firm prepare an anticipated response profile for each competitor (see Figure 2.3). The results of an effective competitor analysis help a firm understand, interpret, and predict its competitors' actions and responses. Understanding the actions of competitors clearly contributes to the firm's ability to compete successfully within the industry.[120] Interestingly, research suggests that executives often fail to analyze competitors' possible reactions to competitive actions their firm takes,[121] placing their firm at a potential competitive disadvantage as a result.

Critical to an effective competitor analysis is gathering data and information that can help the firm understand its competitors' intentions and the strategic implications resulting from them.[122] Useful data and information combine to form **competitor intelligence**, the set of data and information the firm gathers to better understand and anticipate competitors' objectives, strategies, assumptions, and capabilities. In competitor analysis, the firm gathers intelligence not only about its competitors, but also regarding public policies in countries around the world. Such intelligence facilitates an understanding of the

Competitor intelligence is the set of data and information the firm gathers to better understand and better anticipate competitors' objectives, strategies, assumptions, and capabilities.

strategic posture of foreign competitors. Through effective competitive and public policy intelligence, the firm gains the insights needed to make effective strategic decisions on how to compete against its rivals.

When asked to describe competitive intelligence, it seems that a number of people respond with phrases such as "competitive spying" and "corporate espionage." These phrases denote the fact that competitive intelligence is an activity that appears to involve trade-offs.[123] According to some, the reason for this is that "what is ethical in one country is different from what is ethical in other countries." This position implies that the rules of engagement to follow when gathering competitive intelligence change in different contexts.[124] However, firms avoid the possibility of legal entanglements and ethical quandaries only when their competitive intelligence gathering methods are governed by a strict set of legal and ethical guidelines.[125] This means that ethical behavior and actions as well as the mandates of relevant laws and regulations should be the foundation on which a firm's competitive intelligence-gathering process is formed. We address this matter in greater detail in the next section.

When gathering competitive intelligence, firms must also pay attention to the complementors of its products and strategy.[126] **Complementors** are companies or networks of companies that sell complementary goods or services that are compatible with the focal firm's good or service. When a complementor's good or service adds value to the sale of the focal firm's good or service, it is likely to create value for the focal firm.

There are many examples of firms whose good or service complements other companies' offerings. For example, firms manufacturing affordable home photo printers complement other companies' efforts to sell digital cameras. Intel and Microsoft are perhaps the most widely recognized complementors. The Microsoft slogan "Intel Inside" demonstrates the relationship between two firms who do not directly buy from or sell to each other but whose products have a strong complementary relationship. Alliances among airline operations (e.g., the Star Alliance and the SkyTeam Alliance) find these companies sharing their route structures and customer loyalty programs as means of complementing each others' operations. (Each alliance is a network of complementors.) Recently, Continental Airlines announced that it was leaving the SkyTeam Alliance to join the Star Alliance. The primary reason for this change was to provide greater global coverage to Continental's customers by combining its routes with those of the other members of the Star Alliance. In essence, Continental's conclusion was that the complementors of the Star Alliance created more value for its customers than did its complementors in the SkyTeam Alliance. Ultimately, Continental merged with United Airlines, a key Star Alliance member.

As our discussion shows, complementors expand the set of competitors firms must evaluate when completing a competitor analysis. For example, as illustrated in the Strategic Focus, sometimes complementors change, as in the purchase of Sun Microsystems by Oracle. After the acquisition Oracle was no longer a complementor of Dell and HP, but a competitor. Similarly, Intel and Microsoft analyze each other's actions in that those actions might either help each firm gain a competitive advantage or damage each firm's ability to exploit a competitive advantage.

Complementors are companies or networks of companies that sell complementary goods or services that are compatible with the focal firm's good or service.

Ethical Considerations

Firms must follow relevant laws and regulations as well as carefully articulated ethical guidelines when gathering competitor intelligence. Industry associations often develop lists of these practices that firms can adopt. Practices considered both legal and ethical include (1) obtaining publicly available information (e.g., court records, competitors' help-wanted advertisements, annual reports, financial reports of publicly held corporations, and Uniform Commercial Code filings), and (2) attending trade fairs and shows to obtain competitors' brochures, view their exhibits, and listen to discussions about their products. In contrast, certain practices (including blackmail, trespassing, eavesdropping, and stealing drawings, samples, or documents) are widely viewed as unethical and often are illegal.

Some competitor intelligence practices may be legal, but a firm must decide whether they are also ethical, given the image it desires as a corporate citizen. Especially with electronic transmissions, the line between legal and ethical practices can be difficult to determine. For example, a firm may develop Web site addresses that are similar to those of its competitors and thus occasionally receive e-mail transmissions that were intended for those competitors. The practice is an example of the challenges companies face in deciding how to gather intelligence about competitors while simultaneously determining how to prevent competitors from learning too much about them. To deal with these challenges, firms should establish principles and take actions that are consistent with them. Many firms follow the Strategy and Competitive Intelligence Professionals, a professional association, code of professional practice and ethics dealing with this issue.[127]

Open discussions of intelligence-gathering techniques can help a firm ensure that employees, customers, suppliers, and even potential competitors understand its convictions to follow ethical practices for gathering competitor intelligence. An appropriate guideline for competitor intelligence practices is to respect the principles of common morality and the right of competitors not to reveal certain information about their products, operations, and strategic intentions.[128]

SUMMARY

- The firm's external environment is challenging and complex. Because of the external environment's effect on performance, the firm must develop the skills required to identify opportunities and threats existing in that environment.

- The external environment has three major parts: (1) the general environment (elements in the broader society that affect industries and their firms), (2) the industry environment (factors that influence a firm, its competitive actions and responses, and the industry's profit potential), and (3) the competitor environment (in which the firm analyzes each major competitor's future objectives, current strategies, assumptions, and capabilities).

- The external environmental analysis process has four steps: scanning, monitoring, forecasting, and assessing. Through environmental analyses, the firm identifies opportunities and threats.

- The general environment has seven segments: demographic, economic, political/legal, sociocultural, technological, global, and physical. For each segment, the firm has to determine the strategic relevance of environmental changes and trends.

- Compared with the general environment, the industry environment has a more direct effect on the firm's strategic actions. The five forces model of competition includes the threat of entry, the power of suppliers, the power of buyers, product

substitutes, and the intensity of rivalry among competitors. By studying these forces, the firm finds a position in an industry where it can influence the forces in its favor or where it can buffer itself from the power of the forces in order to achieve strategic competitiveness and earn above-average returns.

- Industries are populated with different strategic groups. A strategic group is a collection of firms following similar strategies along similar dimensions. Competitive rivalry is greater within a strategic group than between strategic groups.

- Competitor analysis informs the firm about the future objectives, current strategies, assumptions, and capabilities of the companies with which it competes directly. A thorough analysis examines complementors that sustain a competitor's strategy and major networks or alliances in which competitors participate. When analyzing competitors, the firm should also identify and carefully monitor major actions taken by firms with performance below the industry norm.

- Different techniques are used to create competitor intelligence: the set of data, information, and knowledge that allows the firm to better understand its competitors and thereby predict their likely strategic and tactical actions. Firms should use only legal and ethical practices to gather intelligence. The Internet enhances firms' capabilities to gather insights about competitors and their strategic intentions.

REVIEW QUESTIONS

1. Why is it important for a firm to study and understand the external environment?

2. What are the differences between the general environment and the industry environment? Why are these differences important?

3. What is the external environmental analysis process (four steps)? What does the firm want to learn when using this process?

4. What are the seven segments of the general environment? Explain the differences among them.

5. How do the five forces of competition in an industry affect its profit potential? Explain.

6. What is a strategic group? Of what value is knowledge of the firm's strategic group in formulating that firm's strategy?

7. What is the importance of collecting and interpreting data and information about competitors? What practices should a firm use to gather competitor intelligence and why?

EXPERIENTIAL EXERCISES

EXERCISE 1: STRATEGIC GROUP MAPPING

If a given set of firms emphasize similar strategic dimensions and use a similar strategy, these firms can be said to reside in the same strategic group. Other common definitions of strategic groups typically argue that the firms in a given industry follow similar strategies such as pricing, degree of specialization, research and development commitment, or the like. It is also likely that firms operating in a given industry may have very different profitability profiles, which begs the question of why if one firm is most profitable don't all the others in that industry attempt to move into the same strategic group as the industry leader?

Part One

1. Form teams and pick an industry the team finds interesting. A list of industries and industry leaders may be found at Yahoo! Finance (http://biz.yahoo.com/ic/ind_index.html).

2. Investigate this industry in order to create a strategic group map. You must pick the two dimensions for your map that best represent the key success factors in this industry (e.g., R&D investments, pricing, geographic reach, etc.).

3. For each firm listed on your map, investigate its overall financial performance, not only historically but also its five-year growth forecast. (This information is also available at Yahoo! Finance and other locations).

Part Two

Prepare a presentation to the class that discusses your findings and that answers the following key issues or questions:

1. Who are the most direct competitors and on what basis do they mostly compete (i.e., why did you choose the competitive dimensions that you did)?

2. How does profitability stack up between strategic groups? Which groups are most profitable and why?

3. What would it take for a firm to move from an underperforming (profitability-wise) strategic group to a more profitable strategic group? How likely is it that this could happen?

4. Think about one of the firms in a particular strategic group. Are there any opportunities for this firm that you see because of your strategic group mapping?

5. What conclusions can you reach about why some firms end up where they do among various strategic groups?

EXERCISE 2: WHAT DOES THE FUTURE LOOK LIKE?

A critical ingredient to studying the general environment is identifying opportunities and threats. An opportunity is a condition in the environment that, if exploited, helps a company achieve strategic competitiveness. In order to identify opportunities, you must be aware of trends that affect the world around us now or that are projected to do so in the future.

Thomas Fry, senior futurist at the DaVinci Institute, believes that the chaotic nature of interconnecting trends and the vast array of possibilities that arise from them are somewhat akin to watching a spinning compass needle. From the way we use phones, e-mail, or recruit new workers to organizations, the climate for business is changing and shifting dramatically, and at rapidly increasing rates. Sorting these trends out and making sense of them provides the basis for opportunity decision making. Which ones will dominate and which ones will fade? Understanding this is crucial for business success.

Your challenge (either individually or as a group) is to identify a trend, technology, entertainment, or design that is likely to alter the way in which business is conducted in the future. Once you have identified this, be prepared to discuss:

Which of the six dimensions of the general environment will this affect (may be more than one)?

- Describe the impact.
- List some business opportunities that will come from this.
- Identify some existing organizations that stand to benefit.
- What, if any, are the ethical implications?

You should consult a wide variety of sources. For example, the Gartner Group and McKinsey & Company both produce market research and forecasts for business. There are also a host of Web forecasting tools and addresses such as TED (technology, entertainment, design, where you can find videos of their discussions; see www.ted.com), which hosts an annual conference for path-breaking new ideas. Similarly, the DaVinci Institute, Institute for Global Futures, and a wide host of others have their own unique vision for tomorrow's environment.

VIDEO CASE

THE NEED TO EXAMINE THE EXTERNAL ENVIRONMENT: DISASTER IN THE GULF ONE YEAR LATER

The Gulf Coast oil spill disaster not only resulted in oil and tar balls washing up on local beaches but contributed to the evaporation of the wedding business on the beach. In one family business, 85 percent of the business and $90,000 cash were lost while they only received $20,000 in emergency payments. A year later, resentful wedding business owners are still living day to day. They contend that British Petroleum (BP), which owned the Deepwater Horizon oil rig where the explosion and subsequent leak occurred, has not fulfilled its obligations to them and their true losses won't ever be recovered. With government intervention, the $20 billion fund established by BP has only paid out $3.8 billion. Government attorney, Kenneth Feinberg, emphasizes that 200,000 claimants have been compensated in nine months.

Be prepared to discuss the following concepts and questions in class:

Concepts

- The external environment
- External environmental analysis

- Five forces of competition
- Strategic groups
- Competitor analysis

Questions

1. What external environment (general, industry, and competitive) segments do you think BP considered or didn't consider prior to their drilling off the Gulf Coast? What should the wedding business owners now consider in their external environment?

2. How should BP have handled an external environmental analysis and what environmental changes and trends (opportunities and threats) might they have discovered?

3. Analyze BP using the five forces of competition model to determine the industry's current attractiveness in terms of profit potential.

4. Who might be in BP's strategic group and why?

5. What would a competitor of BP now discover about them in a competitor analysis?

NOTES

1. H. Benbya & M. Van Alstyne, 2011, How to find answers within your company, *MIT Sloan Management Review*, 52(2): 65–75; D. A. Bosse, R. A. Phillips, & J. S. Harrison, 2009, Stakeholders, reciprocity, and firm performance, *Strategic Management Journal*, 30: 447–456.
2. A. Peaple, 2011, Reshaped BP finds east is no Eden, *Wall Street Journal*, February 23, C14.
3. D. Grégoire, P. Barr, & D. Shepherd, 2010, Cognitive processes of opportunity recognition: The role of structural alignment, *Organization Science*, 21(2): 413–431; P. Chattopadhyay, W. H. Glick, & G. P. Huber, 2001, Organizational actions in response to threats and opportunities, *Academy of Management Journal*, 44: 937–955.
4. M. Xu, V. Ong, Y. Duan, & B. Mathews, 2011, Intelligent agent systems for executive information scanning, filtering and interpretation: Perceptions and challenges, *Information Processing & Management*, 47(2): 186–201; C. Weigelt & M. B. Sarkar, 2009, Learning from supply-side agents: The impact of technology solution providers' experiential diversity on clients' innovation adoption,

Academy of Management Journal, 52: 37–60.
5. A. Chacar, W. Newburry, & B. Vissa, 2010, Bringing institutions into performance persistence research: Exploring the impact of product, financial, and labor market institutions, *Journal of International Business Studies*, 41(7): 1119–1140; J. P. Bonardi, G. I. F. Holburn, & R. G. Vanden Bergh, 2006, Nonmarket strategy performance: Evidence from U.S. electric utilities, *Academy of Management Journal*, 49: 1209–1228.
6. S. Hanson, A. Kashyap, & J. Stein, 2011, A macroprudential approach to financial regulation. *Journal of Economic Perspectives*, 25(1): 3–28.
7. M. Lopez-Gamero, J. Molina-Azorin, & E. Claver-Cortes, 2011, Environmental uncertainty and environmental management perception: A multiple case study, *Journal of Business Research*, 64(4): 427–435.
8. J. Harrison, D. Bosse, & R. Phillips, 2010, Managing for stakeholders, stakeholder utility functions, and competitive advantage, *Strategic Management Journal*, 31(1): 58–74; J. Uotila, M. Maula, T. Keil, & S. A. Zahra, 2009, Exploration,

exploitation, and financial performance: Analysis of S&P 500 corporations, *Strategic Management Journal*, 30: 221–231; J. L. Murillo-Luna, C. Garces-Ayerbe, & P. Rivera-Torres, 2008, Why do patterns of environmental response differ? A stakeholder's pressure approach, *Strategic Management Journal*, 29: 1225–1240.
9. M. T. Lucas & O. M. Kirillova, 2011, Reconciling the resource-based and competitive positioning perspectives on manufacturing flexibility, *Journal of Manufacturing Technology Management*, 22(2): 189–203; A. Kacperczyk, 2009, With greater power comes greater responsibility? Takeover protection and corporate attention to stakeholders, *Strategic Management Journal*, 30: 261–285; C. Eesley & M. J. Lenox, 2006, Firm responses to secondary stakeholder action, *Strategic Management Journal*, 27: 765–781.
10. L. Fahey, 1999, *Competitors,* New York: John Wiley & Sons; B. A. Walters & R. L. Priem, 1999, Business strategy and CEO intelligence acquisition, *Competitive Intelligence Review*, 10(2): 15–22.
11. A. P. Kellogg & J. Bennett, 2009, Chrysler's bankruptcy deals blow to

affiliates, *Wall Street Journal Online,* http://www.wsj.com, May 2.

12. E. L. Chen, R. Katila, R. McDonald, & K. M. Eisenhardt, 2010, Life in the fast lane: Origins of competitive interaction in new vs. established markets, *Strategic Management Journal,* 31(13): 1527–1547; J. C. Short, D. J. Ketchen, Jr., T. B. Palmer, & G. T. Hult, 2007, Firm, strategic group, and industry influences on performance, *Strategic Management Journal,* 28: 147–167.

13. G. J. Kilduff, H. A. Elfenbein, & B. M. Staw, 2010, The psychology of rivalry: A relationally dependent analysis of competition, *Academy of Management Journal,* 53(5): 943–969; K. P. Coyne & J. Horn, 2009, Predicting your competitor's reaction, *Harvard Business Review,* 87(4): 90–97.

14. W. K. Smith & M. W. Lewis, 2011, Toward a theory of paradox: A dynamic equilibrium model of organizing, *Academy of Management Review,* 36(2): 381–403; D. Sull, 2009, How to thrive in turbulent markets, *Harvard Business Review,* 87(2): 78–88; J. Hagel, III, J. S. Brown, & L. Davison, 2008, Shaping strategy in a world of constant disruption, *Harvard Business Review,* 86(10): 80–89.

15. J. A. Lamberg, H. Tikkanen, T. Nokelainen, & H. Suur-Inkeroinen, 2009, Competitive dynamics, strategic consistency, and organizational survival, *Strategic Management Journal,* 30: 45–60.

16. E. Bryon, 2011, At P&G beauty makeover needs to prove it has legs, *Wall Street Journal,* January 26, B1.

17. B. Gilad, 2011, The power of blindspots. What companies don't know, surprises them. What they don't want to know, kills them, *Strategic Direction,* 27(4): 3–4; W. B. Gartner, K. G. Shaver, & J. Liao, 2008, Opportunities as attributions: Categorizing strategic issues from an attributional perspective, *Strategic Entrepreneurship Journal,* 2: 301–315.

18. P. Burrows, 2011, Mobile wars! Apple vs. Google vs. those other guys, *Bloomberg Businessweek,* http://www.businessweek.com, February 16; N. Wingfield, 2011, Corporate news: Alliance no sure bet for Windows phone, *Wall Street Journal,* February 12, B3.

19. D. Chrusciel, 2011, Environmental scan: Influence on strategic direction, *Journal of Facilities Management,* 9(1): 7–15; W. H. Stewart, R. C. May, & A. Kalla, 2008, Environmental perceptions and scanning in the United States and India: Convergence in entrepreneurial information seeking? *Entrepreneurship Theory and Practice,* 32: 83–106; K. M. Patton & T. M. McKenna, 2005, Scanning for competitive intelligence, *Competitive Intelligence Magazine,* 8(2): 24–26.

20. A. Graefe, S. Luckner, & C. Weinhardt, 2010, Prediction markets for foresight, *Futures,* 42(4): 394–404; J. O. Schwarz, 2008, Assessing the future of futures studies in management, *Futures,* 40: 237–246; K. M. Eisenhardt, 2002, Has strategy changed? *MIT Sloan Management Review,* 43(2): 88–91.

21. Y. Hsu & C. Liu, 2010, Environmental performance evaluation and strategic management using balanced scorecard, *Environmental Monitoring and Assessment,* 170(1–4): 599–607; J. R. Hough & M. A. White, 2004, Scanning actions and environmental dynamism: Gathering information for strategic decision making, *Management Decision,* 42: 781–793; V. K. Garg, B. A. Walters, & R. L. Priem, 2003, Chief executive scanning emphases, environmental dynamism, and manufacturing firm performance, *Strategic Management Journal,* 24: 725–744.

22. P. G. F. De Abreu, 2010, How good does your early warning system have to be?, *Competitive Intelligence Magazine,* www .scip.org, October–December; C.-P. Wei & Y.-H. Lee, 2004, Event detection from online news documents for supporting environmental scanning, *Decision Support Systems,* 36: 385–401.

23. Fahey, *Competitors,* 71–73.

24. 2010, UK: Tesco extends ethnic food range, *Just-food global news, www .just-food.com,* November 30.

25. C. Dellarocas, 2010, Online reputation systems: How to design one that does what you need, *MIT Sloan Management Review,* 51(3): 33–37; T. M. Jones, W. Felps, & G. A. Bigley, 2007, Ethical theory and stakeholder-related decisions: The role of stakeholder culture, *Academy of Management Review,* 32: 137–155.

26. X. Zhang, S. Majid, & S. Foo, 2010, Environmental scanning: An application of information literacy skills at the workplace, *Journal of Information Science,* 36(6): 719–732; M. J. Leiblein & T. L. Madsen, 2009, Unbundling competitive heterogeneity: Incentive structures and capability influences on technological innovation, *Strategic Management Journal,* 30: 711–735.

27. J. Calof & J. Smith, 2010, The integrative domain of foresight and competitive intelligence and its impact on R&D management, *R & D Management,* 40(1): 31–39; F. Sanna-Randaccio & R. Veugelers, 2007, Multinational knowledge spillovers with decentralized R&D: A game theoretic approach, *Journal of International Business Studies,* 38: 47–63.

28. Fahey, *Competitors.*

29. S. D. Wu, K. G. Kempf, M. O. Atan, B. Aytac, S. A. Shirodkar, & A. Mishra, 2010, Improving new-product forecasting at Intel Corporation, *Interfaces,* 40(5): 385–396.

30. The Associated Press, 2010, Procter, Colgate and Unilever profit as brands sell again, *The New York Times,* www .nytimes.com, April 29; E. Byron, 2009, P&G investors need a little pampering, *Wall Street Journal Online,* http://www .wsj.com, April 30.

31. T. Sueyoshi & M. Goto, 2011, Methodological comparison between two unified (operational and environmental) efficiency measurements for environmental assessment, *European Journal of Operational Research,* 210(3): 684–693; P. E. Bierly, III, F. Damanpour, & M. D. Santoro, 2009, The application of external knowledge: Organizational conditions for exploration and exploitation, *Journal of Management Studies,* 46: 481–509; Fahey, *Competitors,* 75–77.

32. M. Exu, V. Ong, Y. Duan, & B. Mathews, 2011, Intelligent agent systems for executive information scanning, filtering and interpretation: Perceptions and challenges, *Information Processing & Management,* 47(2): 186–201; M. S. Hopkins, S. LaValle, F. Balboni, N. Kruschwitz, & R. Shokley, 2010, 10 insights: A first look at the new intelligent enterprise survey on winning with data, *MIT Sloan Management Review,* 52(1): 22–31.

33. R. King, 2010, Consumer demographics: Use demographic resources to target specific audiences, *Journal of Financial Planning,* 23(12): S4–S6; E. K. Foedermayr & A. Diamantopoulos, 2008, Market segmentation in practice: Review of empirical studies, methodological assessment, and agenda for future research, *Journal of Strategic Marketing,* 16: 223–265.

34. U.S. Census Bureau, 2011, International database, http://www.census.gov/ipc/ www/idb/worldpopinfo.php, March 29.

35. T. Kambayashi, 2011, Brief: Aging Japan sees slowest population growth yet, *McClatchy-Tribune Business News,* http:// www.mcclatchy.com, February 25; S. Moffett, 2005, Fast-aging Japan keeps its elders on the job longer, *Wall Street Journal,* June 15, A1, A8.

36. E. S. Browning, 2011, Retiring boomers find 401k (plans) fall short, *Wall Street Journal,* February 19, A1, A11; S. Armour, 2009, Mortgage crisis robbing seniors of golden years, *USA Today,* June 5–7, A1 & A2.

37. P. Hudomiet, G. Kezdi, & R. J. Willis, 2011, Stock market crash and expectations of American households, *Journal of Applied Econometrics,* 26(3): 393–415; J. M. Nittoli, 2009, Now is no time to skimp on retirement plans, *Wall Street Journal,* http://www.wsj.com, June 5.

38. P. O'Connor & C. Dougherty, 2010, South gains in census—Count dents political clout of snow belt, *Wall Street Journal,* December 22, A1.

39. R. Dobbs, S. Smit, J. Remes, J. Manyika, C. Roxburgh, & A. Restrepo, 2011, Urban world: Mapping the economic power of cities, Chicago: McKinsey Global Institute, March.

40. S. Reddy, 2011, U.S. News: Latinos fuel growth in decade, *Wall Street Journal,* March 25, A2.

41. K. Zaidi, 2010, Harmonizing trade liberalization and migration policy through

shared responsibility: A comparison of the impact of bilateral trade agreements and the GATS in Germany and Canada, *Syracuse Journal of International Law and Commerce*, 37(2): 267–297.

42. A. Mountford & H. Rapoport, 2011, The brain drain and the world distribution of income, *Journal of Development Economics*, 95(1): 4–17; A. K. Fosu, 2008, Inequality and the growth-poverty nexus: Specification empirics using African data, *Applied Economics Letters*, 15: 563–566; A. McKeown, 2007, Periodizing globalization, *History Workshop Journal*, 63(1): 218–230.

43. A. Hain-Cole, 2010, Companies juggle cost cutting with competitive benefits for international assignments, *Benefits & Compensation International: A Magazine for Global Companies*, 40(5): 26.

44. J. Lee, 2010, Don't underestimate India's consumers, *Bloomberg Businessweek*, http://www.businessweek.com, January 21.

45. C. Chua & S. Tsiaplias, 2011, Predicting economic contractions and expansions with the aid of professional forecasts, *International Journal of Forecasting*, 27(2): 438–451; L. Fahey & V. K. Narayanan, 1986, *Macroenvironmental Analysis for Strategic Management (The West Series in Strategic Management)*, St. Paul, Minnesota: West Publishing Company, 105.

46. F. Ackerman, E. A. Stanton, & R. Bueno, 2010, Fat tails, exponents, extreme uncertainty: Simulating catastrophe in DICE, *Ecological Economics*, 69(8): 1657–1665; P. Coy, 2009, What good are economists anyway? *Businessweek*, April 27, 26–31.

47. J. Brinsley, 2011, Global economics: Crisis in Japan, *Bloomberg Businessweek*, March 21, 16–24; J. Simms, 2009, Losses at Japan's electronics companies are no shock, *Wall Street Journal Online*, http://www.wsj.com, February 4.

48. C. F. Fey & S. Shekshnia, 2011, The key commandments for doing business in Russia, *Organizational Dynamics*, 40(1): 57–66; J. Bush, 2009, The worries facing Russia's banks, *Wall Street Journal Online*, http://www.wsj.com, April 13.

49. S. Leung, 2010, Vietnam: An economic survey, *Asian-Pacific Economic Literature*, 24(2): 83–103; A. Peaple & N. P. Muoi, 2009, Vietnam's market—the fizz is deliberate, *Wall Street Journal Online*, http://www.wsj.com, June 11.

50. G. F. Holburne & B. A. Zelner, 2010, Political capabilities, policy risk, and international investment strategy: Evidence from the global electric power generation industry, *Strategic Management Journal*, 31(12): 1290–1315; C. Oliver & I. Holzinger, 2008, The effectiveness of strategic political management: A dynamic capabilities framework, *Academy of Management Review*, 33: 496–520.

51. M. William, 2010, World news: Moscow moves on selling assets, *Wall Street Journal*, October 22, A15.

52. N. Boubakri & L. Bouslimi, 2010, Analysts following of privatized firms around the world: The role of institutions and ownership structure, *International Journal of Accounting*, 45(4): 413–442.

53. I. Williams, 2010, Obama bypasses India's outsourcing capital, *World Blog from NBC News*, http://www.worldblog.msnbc.msn.com, November 8; M. Srivastava, 2009, The sudden chill at an Indian hot spot, *Businessweek*, May 4, 59.

54. J. Hook, 2010, Senate outsourcing bill stalls, *Wall Street Journal*, October 29, A2; 2009, Taking aim at outsourcers on U.S. soil, *Businessweek*, June 15, 10.

55. R. Sachitand, 2010, Politics over business, *Business Today*, November 14, 64; G. L. F. Holburn & R. G. Vanden Bergh, 2008, The effectiveness of strategic political management: A dynamic capabilities framework, *Academy of Management Review*, 33: 521–540.

56. M. Ezrati, 2011, Europe's debt crisis continues, despite Ireland's resolved debt, *On Wall Street*, February, 35–36.

57. D. Strumpf, 2011, Oil-price forecast rises on Libya unrest, *Wall Street Journal*, March 9, C10.

58. R. Daly & J. Zigmond, 2011, Pushing for cost savings: GOP legislation challenges Obama's requests, *Modern Healthcare*, March 7, 8–9.

59. D. W. Brin, 2011, EHealth feels the pain now, *Wall Street Journal*, March 9, B5; T. Fetter, 2010, Tenet chief envisions changing health landscape, *Wall Street Journal*, December 18, B5.

60. 2009, Characteristics of the civilian labor force, U.S. Department of Labor, Bureau of Labor Statistics data, http://www.bls.gov, June.

61. M. DelCarmen Triana, M. F. Garcia, & A. Colella, 2010, Managing diversity: How organizational efforts to support diversity moderate the effects of perceived racial discrimination on affective commitment, *Personnel Psychology*, 63(4): 817–843.

62. 2011, Job creation increasing: Temporary workers benefit, *Journal of Property Management*, 76(2): 8; A. McConnon, 2009, For a temp giant, a boom in boomers, *Businessweek*, June 1, 54.

63. T. Grenness, 2011, The impact of national culture on CEO compensation and salary gaps between CEOs and manufacturing workers, *Compensation & Benefits Review*, 43(2): 100–108.

64. P. Dimitratos, A. Petrou, F. Plakoyiannaki, & J. E. Johnson, 2011, Strategic decision-making processes in internationalization: Does national culture of the focal firm matter?, *Journal of World Business*, 46(2): 194–204; S. Michailova & K. Hutchings, 2006, National cultural influences on knowledge sharing: A comparison of China and Russia, *Journal of Management Studies*, 43: 384–405.

65. C. M. Chan, S. Makino, & T. Isobe, 2010, Does subnational region matter? Foreign affiliate performance in the United States and China, *Strategic Management Journal*, 31(11): 1226–1243; J. B. Knight & L. Yueh, 2008, The role of social capital in the labour market in China, *Economics of Transition*, 16: 389–414; P. J. Buckley, J. Clegg, & H. Tan, 2006, Cultural awareness in knowledge transfer to China—The role of guanxi and mianzi, *Journal of World Business*, 41: 275–288.

66. J. Euchner, 2011, Managing disruption: An interview with Clayton Christensen, *Research Technology Management*, 54(1): 11–17; R. K. Sinha & C. H. Noble, 2008, The adoption of radical manufacturing technologies and firm survival, *Strategic Management Journal*, 29: 943–962.

67. B. I. Park & P. N. Ghauri, 2011, Key factors affecting acquisition of technological capabilities from foreign acquiring firms by small and medium sized local firms, *Journal of World Business*, 46(1): 116–125; K. H. Tsai & J.-C. Wang, 2008, External technology acquisition and firm performance: A longitudinal study, *Journal of Business Venturing*, 23: 91–112.

68. Burrows, Mobile wars!; S. A. Brown, 2008, Household technology adoption, use, and impacts: Past, present, and future, *Information Systems Frontiers*, 10: 397–402.

69. A. Ignatius, 2011, How e-Bay developed a culture of experimentation, *Harvard Business Review*, 89(3): 92–97.

70. J. Spence & C. Gomez, 2011, MNEs and corruption: The impact of national institutions and subsidiary strategy, *Strategic Management Journal*, 32(3): 280–300; L. F. Mesquita & S. G. Lazzarini, 2008, Horizontal and vertical relationships in developing economies: Implications for SMEs' access to global markets, *Academy of Management Journal*, 51: 359–380.

71. K. Kyung-Tae, R. Seung-Kyu, & O. Joongsan, 2011, The strategic role evolution of foreign automotive parts subsidiaries in China, *International Journal of Operations & Production Management*, 31(1): 31–55; J. R. Healey, 2009, Penske-Saturn deal could change how cars are sold, *USA Today*, June 8, B2.

72. B. McClellan, 2010, China success clouded by labor strikes, overcapacity, *Ward's Autoworld*, November, 25.

73. 2011, Heinz agrees to acquire 80% stake in a leading Brazilian food company; Heinz also reports strong third-quarter results with EPS of $0.84 on higher sales, led by emerging markets, top 15 brands and North American consumer products, *Business Wire*, March 3.

74. S. Cendrowski, 2010, SABMiller, *Fortune*, July 26, 18.

75. D. Griffin, 2011, Pandit stakes Citi's future on emerging markets, *Bloomberg Businessweek*, http://www.businessweek.com, March 21.

76. K. E. Meyer, 2009, Uncommon commonsense, *Business Strategy Review*, 20: 38–43; K. E. Meyer, 2006, Globalfocusing: From domestic conglomerates to global specialists, *Journal of Management Studies*, 43: 1110–1144.

77. G. Qian, T. A. Khoury, M. W. Peng, & Z. Qian, 2010, The performance implications of intra- and inter-regional geographic diversification, *Strategic Management Journal*, 31: 1018–1030; C. H. Oh & A. M. Rugman, 2007, Regional multinationals and the Korean cosmetics industry, *Asia Pacific Journal of Management*, 24: 27–42.

78. C. Ho & K. A. Redfern, 2010, Consideration of the role of Guanxi in the ethical judgments of Chinese managers, *Journal of Business Ethics*, 96: 207–221; X.-P. Chen & S. Peng, 2008, Guanxi dynamics: Shifts in the closeness of ties between Chinese coworkers, *Management and Organizational Review*, 4: 63–80; M. A. Hitt, M. T. Dacin, B. B. Tyler, & D. Park, 1997, Understanding the differences in Korean and U.S. executives' strategic orientations, *Strategic Management Journal*, 18: 159–167.

79. T. M. Hout & P. Ghemawat, 2010, China vs the world, *Harvard Business Review*, 88(12): 94–103; M. A. Hitt, D. Ahlstrom, M. T. Dacin, E. Levitas, & L. Svobodina, 2004, The institutional effects on strategic alliance partner selection: China versus Russia, *Organization Science*, 15: 173–185.

80. T. K. Das & R. Kumar, 2011, Regulatory focus and opportunism in the alliance development process, *Journal of Management*, 37(3): 682–708.

81. J. Harris, 2011, Going green to stay in the black: Transnational capitalism and renewable energy, *Perspectives on Global Development & Technology*, 10(1): 41–59; L. Berchicci & A. King, 2008, Postcards from the edge: A review of the business and environment literature, in J. P. Walsh & A. P. Brief (eds.), *Academy of Management Annals*, New York: Lawrence Erlbaum Associates, 513–547.

82. M. Delmas, V. H. Hoffmann, & M. Kuss, 2011, Under the tip of the iceberg: Absorptive capacity, environmental strategy, and competitive advantage, *Business & Society*, 50(1): 116–154; M. J. Hutchins & J. W. Sutherland, 2008, An exploration of measures of social sustainability and their application to supply chain decisions, *Journal of Cleaner Production*, 16: 1688–1698.

83. J. K. Hall, G. A. Daneke, & M. J. Lenox, 2010, Sustainable development and entrepreneurship: Past contributions and future directions, *Journal of Business Venturing*, 25(5): 439–448.

84. K. Gilbert, 2010, Money from trees, *Institutional Investor*, 44(9): 41–89; P. K. Dutta & R. Radner, 2009, A strategic analysis of global warming: Theory and some numbers, *Journal of Economic Behavior & Organization*, 71(2): 187–209.

85. T. Willatt & S. Saylor, 2011, Canada's "clean" image extends to clean power, *Power*, 155(3): 32–34.

86. D. Stanford, 2011, Why sustainability is winning over CEOs, *Bloomberg Businessweek*, http://www.businessweek.com, April 4.

87. V. Souitaris & B. Maestro, 2010, Polychronicity in top management teams: The impact on strategic decision processes and performance of new technology ventures, *Strategic Management Journal*, 31(6): 652–678.

88. C. Yi-Min & L. Feng-Jyh, 2010, The persistence of superior performance at industry and firm levels: Evidence from the IT industry in Taiwan, *Industry & Innovation*, 17(5): 469–486; J. Galbreath & P. Galvin, 2008, Firm factors, industry structure and performance variation: New empirical evidence to a classic debate, *Journal of Business Research*, 61: 109–117.

89. J. J. Tarzijan & C. C. Ramirez, 2011, Firm, industry and corporation effects revisited: A mixed multilevel analysis for Chilean companies, *Applied Economics Letters*, 18(1): 95–100; V. F. Misangyl, H. Elms, T. Greckhamer, & J. A. Lepine, 2006, A new perspective on a fundamental debate: A multilevel approach to industry, corporate, and business unit effects, *Strategic Management Journal*, 27: 571–590.

90. D. Sullivan & J. Yuening, 2010, Media convergence and the impact of the internet on the M&A activity of large media companies, *Journal of Media Business Studies*, 7(4): 21–40.

91. C. Lutz, R. Kemp, & S. Gerhard Dijkstra, 2010, Perceptions regarding strategic and structural entry barriers, *Small Business Economics*, 35(1): 19–33.

92. F. Schivardi & E. Viviano, 2011, Entry barriers in retail trade, *Economic Journal*, 121(551): 145–170; M. R. Peneder, 2008, Firm entry and turnover: The nexus with profitability and growth, *Small Business Economics*, 30: 327–344; A. V. Mainkar, M. Lubatkin, & W. S. Schulze, 2006, Toward a product-proliferation theory of entry barriers, *Academy of Management Review*, 31: 1062–1075.

93. B. Stone & A. Ricadela, 2010. Oracle's Larry Ellison beats up on his rivals—again, *Bloomberg Businessweek*, http://www.businessweek, October 6.

94. S. Siew Kien, C. Soh, & P. Weil, 2010, Global IT management: Structuring for scale, responsiveness, and innovation, *Communications of the ACM*, 53(3): 59–64; S. K. Ethiraj & D. H. Zhu, 2008, Performance effects of imitative entry, *Strategic Management Journal*, 29: 797–817; R. Makadok, 1999, Interfirm differences in scale economies and the evolution of market shares, *Strategic Management Journal*, 20: 935–952.

95. T. Cari, 2011, Corporate News: Oracle's software sales zoom—licensed revenue helps power 78 percent rise in net; Sun hardware sales disappoint, *Wall Street Journal*, March 25, B3.

96. X. Huang, M. Kristal, & R. G. Schroeder, 2010, The impact of organizational structure on mass customization capability: A contingency view, *Production & Operations Management*, 19(5): 515–530; M. J. Rungtusanatham &

F. Salvador, 2008, From mass production to mass customization: Hindrance factors, structural inertia, and transition hazard, *Production and Operations Management*, 17: 385–396.

97. N. Zmuda, 2011, How Pepsi blinked, fell behind Diet Coke, *Advertising Age*, March 21, 1–6.

98. N. Zmuda & K. Patel, 2010, Pass or fail, Pepsi's Refresh will be case for marketing textbooks, *Advertising Age*, February 8, 1–18.

99. T. Rice & P. E. Strahan, 2010, Does credit competition affect small-firm finance?, *Journal of Finance*, 65(3): 861–889.

100. 2011, Airline deregulation, revisited, *Bloomberg Businessweek*, http://www.businessweek.com, January 21.

101. J. Jaeger, 2010, Anti-trust reviews: Suddenly, they're a worry, *Compliance Week*, 7(80): 48–59.

102. S. Bhattacharyya & A. Nain, 2011, Horizontal acquisitions and buying power: A product market analysis, *Journal of Financial Economics*, 99(1): 97–115.

103. G. Winslow, 2011, Map to TV everywhere, *Broadcasting & Cable*, February 14, 23.

104. B. Einhorn & R. Salamat, 2011, iPad causes collateral damage in Taiwan, *Bloomberg Businessweek*, April 11, 31.

105. D. G. Sirmon, M. A. Hitt, J. Arregle, & J. Campbell, 2010, The dynamic interplay of capability strengths and weaknesses: Investigating the bases of temporary competitive advantage, *Strategic Management Journal*, 31(13): 1386–1409; D. G. Sirmon, S. Gove, & M. H. Hitt, 2008, Resource management in dyadic competitive rivalry: The effects of resource bundling and deployment, *Academy of Management Journal*, 51: 919–935.

106. C. Dieroff, 2011, Beverage trends: Consumers want it all, *Prepared Foods*, February: 49–55.

107. 2011, 2010 Managed care industry report, *Medical Benefits*, 28(6), 5–6; S. Nadkarni & V. K. Narayanan, 2007, Strategic schemas, strategic flexibility, and firm performance: The moderating role of industry clockspeed, *Strategic Management Journal*, 28: 243–270.

108. J. Tozzi, 2011, Home-care companies brace for regulation, *Bloomberg Businessweek*, March 21, 60–61.

109. R. García-Castro & M. A. Ariño, 2011, The multidimensional nature of sustained competitive advantage: Test at a United States airline, *International Journal of Management*, 28(1): 230–248; P. Prada & M. Esterl, 2009, Airlines predict more trouble, broaden cuts, *Wall Street Journal Online*, http://www.wsj.com, June 12.

110. S. Nadkarni, P. Herrmann, & P. Perez, 2011, Domestic mindsets and early international performance: The moderating effect of global industry conditions, *Strategic Management Journal*, 32(5): 510–531; S. E. Feinberg & A. K. Gupta, 2009, MNC subsidiaries and country risk: Internalization as a safeguard against weak external institutions,

Academy of Management Journal, 52: 381–399.

111. M. E. Porter, 1980, *Competitive Strategy,* New York: Free Press.

112. S. Kaplan, 2011, Research in cognition and strategy: Reflections on two decades of progress and a look to the future, *Journal of Management Studies,* 48(3): 665–695; M. S. Hunt, 1972, Competition in the major home appliance industry, 1960–1970 (doctoral dissertation, Harvard University); Porter, *Competitive Strategy,* 129.

113. S. Cheng & H. Chang, 2009, Performance implications of cognitive complexity: An empirical study of cognitive strategic groups in semiconductor industry, *Journal of Business Research,* 62(12): 1311–1320; G. McNamara, D. L. Deephouse, & R. A. Luce, 2003, Competitive positioning within and across a strategic group structure: The performance of core, secondary, and solitary firms, *Strategic Management Journal,* 24: 161–181.

114. D. Williams, C. Young, R. Shewchuk, & H. Qu, 2010, Strategic groupings of U.S. biotechnology initial public offerings and a measure of their market influence, *Technology Analysis & Strategic Management,* 22(4): 399–415; F. Zen & C. Baldan, 2008, The strategic paths and performance of Italian mutual banks: A nonparametric analysis, *International Journal of Banking, Accounting and Finance,* 1: 189–214; M. W. Peng, J. Tan, & T. W. Tong, 2004, Ownership types and strategic groups in an emerging economy, *Journal of Management Studies,* 41: 1105–1129.

115. W. S. DeSarbo & R. Grewal, 2008. Hybrid strategic groups, *Strategic Management*

Journal, 29: 293–317; M. Peteraf & M. Shanley, 1997, Getting to know you: A theory of strategic group identity, *Strategic Management Journal,* 18 (Special Issue): 165–186.

116. J. Lee, K. Lee, & S. Rho, 2002, An evolutionary perspective on strategic group emergence: A genetic algorithm-based model, *Strategic Management Journal,* 23: 727–746.

117. P. Ebbes , R. Grewal, & W. S. DeSarbo, 2010, Modeling strategic group dynamics: A hidden Markov approach, *Quantitative Marketing and Economics,* 8: 241–274; J. A. Zuniga-Vicente, J. M. de la Fuente Sabate, & I. S. Gonzalez, 2004, Dynamics of the strategic group membership-performance linkage in rapidly changing environments, *Journal of Business Research,* 57: 1378–1390.

118. T. Yu, M. Subramaniam, & A. A. Cannella, Jr., 2009, Rivalry deterrence in international markets: Contingencies governing the mutual forbearance hypothesis, *Academy of Management Journal,* 52: 127–147.

119. Porter, *Competitive Strategy,* 49.

120. J. E. Prescott & R. Herko, 2010, TOWS: The role of competitive intelligence, *Competitive Intelligence Magazine,* 13(3): 8–17; L. Capron & O. Chatain, 2008, Competitors' resource-oriented strategies: Acting on competitors' resources through interventions in factor markets and political markets, *Academy of Management Review,* 33: 97–121.

121. D. B. Montgomery, M. C. Moore, & J. E. Urbany, 2005, Reasoning about competitive reactions: Evidence from executives, *Marketing Science,* 24: 138–149.

122. K. Xu, S. Liao, J. Li, & Y. Song, 2011, Mining comparative opinions from customer reviews for competitive intelligence, *Decision Support Systems,* 50(4): 743–754; S. Jain, 2008, Digital piracy: A competitive analysis, *Marketing Science,* 27: 610–626.

123. J. G. York, 2009, Pragmatic sustainability: Translating environmental ethics into competitive advantage, *Journal of Business Ethics,* 85: 97–109.

124. R. Huggins, 2010, Regional competitive intelligence: Benchmarking and policy-making. *Regional Studies,* 44(5): 639–658.

125. 2011, SCIP Code of ethics for CI professionals, http://www.scip.org, April 15; K. A. Sawka, 2008, The ethics of competitive intelligence, *Kiplinger Business Resource Center Online,* http://www.kiplinger.com, March.

126. T. Mazzarol & S. Reboud, 2008, The role of complementary actors in the development of innovation in small firms, *International Journal of Innovation Management,* 12: 223–253; A. Brandenburger & B. Nalebuff, 1996, *Co-opetition,* New York: Currency Doubleday.

127. SCIP Code of ethics for CI professionals, http://www.scip.org, April 15.

128. C. S. Fleisher & S. Wright, 2009, Examining differences in competitive intelligence practice: China, Japan, and the West, *Thunderbird International Business Review,* 51: 249–261; A. Crane, 2005, In the company of spies: When competitive intelligence gathering becomes industrial espionage, *Business Horizons,* 48(3): 233–240.

CHAPTER 3

The Internal Organization: Resources, Capabilities, Core Competencies, and Competitive Advantages

Studying this chapter should provide you with the strategic management knowledge needed to:

1. Explain why firms need to study and understand their internal organization.

2. Define value and discuss its importance.

3. Describe the differences between tangible and intangible resources.

4. Define capabilities and discuss their development.

5. Describe four criteria used to determine whether resources and capabilities are core competencies.

6. Explain how firms analyze their value chain for the purpose of determining where they are able to create value when using their resources, capabilities, and core competencies.

7. Define outsourcing and discuss reasons for its use.

8. Discuss the importance of identifying internal strengths and weaknesses.

9. Discuss the importance of avoiding core rigidities.

SUBWAY RESTAURANTS: CORE COMPETENCIES AS THE FOUNDATION FOR SUCCESS

Fred DeLuca and his business partner, Dr. Peter Buck, opened their first submarine sandwich shop in Bridgeport, CT, in 1965 (DeLuca was 17 years old at the time). With a total of close to 35,000 units located in 98 different countries, Subway restaurants are now available to consumers in convenient locations throughout the world. The fact that Subway has a larger number of locations than McDonald's suggests the success this firm is having as well as the breadth and depth of its market presence. Subway believes that its stores are the "leading choice for people seeking quick, nutritious meals that the whole family can enjoy."

A number of factors support privately owned Subway's continuing growth and success, including the fact that in the United States, the recent challenging economic climate found even affluent customers choosing to dine at quick-service restaurants such as Subway and McDonald's rather than spending some of their disposable income to eat in more expensive restaurants. However, much more than the influence of the economic environment (an influence from the external environment that we examined in Chapter 2) affects Subway's success. The way Subway uses its resources and capabilities as the foundation for core competencies (defined in Chapter 1, core competencies are capabilities that serve as a potential source of competitive advantage for a firm over its rivals) demonstrates the value of understanding a firm's internal organization (this chapter's subject). A high-quality product, excel-

Shoosmith Collection/Alamy

Subway's ability to find superior locations is one of its core competencies. This franchise is located in the Aintree Racecourse Retail and Business Park.

lent customer service, and continuously finding superior locations for its stores are core competencies for Subway

Subway's slogan, "Eat Fresh," describes what it believes customers can do when eating there. To produce the products that allow customers to "Eat Fresh," Subway bakes its own bread and offers a consistent set of fresh ingredients (meats, cheeses, and condiments) as choices so customers can customize their order. The products available to Subway customers are both healthy as measured by caloric intake and nutritious as measured by several indicators, such as protein count. The fact that 24.2 percent of those recently surveyed "completely trust" Subway's nutritional claims suggests that its products are creating value for customers. This percentage is double the percentage of the second-most trusted set of nutritional claims (claims offered by Chick-fil-A restaurants). In 2011, Subway received the MenuMasters' Award given by *Nation's Restaurant News* in the "Healthy Innovations" category for its "Build Your Better Breakfast" that was introduced in 2010. These recognitions suggest that Subway's core competence of high-quality foods may indeed be a competitive advantage for the firm.

In terms of customer service, Subway uses its resources to provide continuous training to its franchisees and those working within those units. These efforts are geared to providing standardized yet customized and supportive experiences to customers. Evidence that its customer service is a core competence and potentially a competitive advantage is suggested by the fact that in 2010, Subway was selected for the second consecutive year as "number one" by consumers in the "most popular," "top service," and the "healthy options" categories that are part of Zagat's Fast-Food Survey.

Learn more about McDonald's core competencies.

www.cengagebrain .com

© Nicholas Monu/iStockphoto.com

The location of its units is Subway's third core competence and possible competitive advantage. The firm uses its resources to find the best locations in the world for its units. In the words of a Subway official: "We're continually looking at just about any opportunity for someone to buy a sandwich, wherever that might be . . . [In this sense], the non-traditional [location] is becoming the traditional." An appliance store in Brazil, an automobile show-room in California, a zoo in Taiwan, and a Goodwill store in South Carolina are some of the unusual locations for Subway units. Interestingly, at the end of 2010, Subway had units in countries (such as Tanzania, Bolivia, and Afghanistan) where McDonald's did not, suggesting the firm's commitment to "non-traditional" locations.

Sources: J. Dickler, 2011, Rich Americans flock to fast food, *CNNMoney.com*, http://www.cnnmoney.com, February 28; J. Jargon, 2011, Unusual store locations fuel Subway's growth, *Wall Street Journal Online*, http://www.wsj.com, March 10; J. Jargon, 2011, Subway's hot-selling sandwiches around the world, *Wall Street Journal Online*, http://www.wsj.com, March 8; J. Jargon, 2011, Subway runs past McDonald's chain, *Wall Street Journal Online*, http://www.wsj.com, March 8; J. Jargon, 2011, A Subway, but no McDonald's in Tanzania, *Wall Street Journal Online*, http://www.wsj.com, March 8; J. Rooney, 2010, Subway keeps it real to win the fast-food race, *Advertising Age*, 39: November 1; 2010, Among fast-food restaurants, Subway's nutritional claims are the "most-trusted" by consumers, *Decision Analyst*, http://www.decisionanalyst.com, February 10.

As discussed in the first two chapters, several factors in the global economy, including the rapid development of the Internet's capabilities[1] and globalization in general have made it increasingly difficult for firms to find ways to develop sustainable competitive advantages.[2] Increasingly, innovation appears to be a vital path to efforts to develop such advantages.[3] Subway's introductions of a full breakfast menu and a line of pizza offerings are examples of product innovations this firm introduced recently as part of its efforts to develop a competitive advantage. Of course, Subway's competitors remain committed to innovation as well. McDonald's frozen strawberry-lemonade is an example of a recent product innovation from this firm.[4]

As is the case for Subway and McDonald's, among many firms, Campbell Soup Co. is emphasizing innovation to increase its competitiveness relative to rivals such as General Mills Inc. and those producing lower-priced store brands. The contents of Campbell's well-known condensed soups have been changed to enhance their flavor and the soups are now being offered in microwavable containers as well as in cans. Overall, Campbell's CEO is committed to the firm pursuing innovations in terms of its core categories—simple meals, healthy beverages, and baked snacks—as the source of its success.[5] At General Motors, efforts are underway to reduce the "drag" the firm's bureaucracy creates on innovation. According to a company official, "GM still wastes millions of dollars developing engines and vehicle variants that interest few customers." To remedy this problem, GM is making changes with the intention of having the "right people and the right engineers on the right priorities and products, not just do the most vehicles possible."[6]

People are an especially critical resource for helping organizations learn how to continuously innovate as a means of achieving successful growth.[7] This is the case at 3M, where the director of global compensation says that harnessing the innovative powers of the firm's employees is the means for rekindling growth.[8] At 3M and other companies, people who are able to facilitate their firm's efforts to innovate are themselves a valuable resource with the potential to be a competitive advantage.[9] A sign of the times is the fact that a global labor market now exists as firms seek talented individuals to add to their fold. As Richard Florida argues, "[W]herever talent goes, innovation, creativity, and economic growth are sure to follow."[10]

To identify and successfully use resources over time, those leading firms need to think constantly about how to manage resources for the purpose of increasing the value their goods or services create for customers as compared to the value rivals' products create. As this chapter shows, firms achieve strategic competitiveness and earn above-average returns by acquiring, bundling, and leveraging their resources for the purpose of taking advantage of opportunities in the external environment in ways that create value for customers.[11]

Even if the firm develops and manages resources in ways that create core competencies and competitive advantages, competitors will eventually learn how to duplicate the benefits of any firm's value-creating strategy; thus all competitive advantages have a limited life.[12] Because of this, the question of duplication of a competitive advantage is not if it will happen, but when. In general, a competitive advantage's sustainability is a function of three factors: (1) the rate of core competence obsolescence because of environmental changes, (2) the availability of substitutes for the core competence, and (3) the imitability of the core competence.[13] For all firms, the challenge is to effectively manage current core competencies while simultaneously developing new ones.[14] Only when firms are able to do this can they expect to achieve strategic competitiveness, earn above-average returns, and remain ahead of competitors (see Chapter 5).

We studied the general, industry, and competitor environments in Chapter 2. Armed with knowledge about the realities and conditions of their external environment, firms have a better understanding of marketplace opportunities and the characteristics of the competitive environment in which those opportunities exist. In this chapter, we focus on the firm itself. By analyzing its internal organization, a firm determines what it can do. Matching what a firm *can do* (a function of its resources, capabilities, and core competencies in the internal organization) with what it *might do* (a function of opportunities and threats in the external environment) is a process that yields insights the firm requires to select its strategies.

We begin this chapter by briefly describing conditions associated with analyzing the firm's internal organization. We then discuss the roles of resources and capabilities in developing core competencies, which are the sources of the firm's competitive advantages. Included in this discussion are the techniques firms use to identify and evaluate resources and capabilities and the criteria for identifying core competencies from among them. Resources by themselves typically are not competitive advantages; in fact, resources create value when the firm uses them to form capabilities, some of which become core competencies, and hopefully competitive advantages. Because of the relationship among resources, capabilities, and core competencies, we also discuss the value chain and examine four criteria firms use to determine if their capabilities are core competencies and as such, sources of competitive advantage.[15] The chapter closes with cautionary comments about outsourcing and the need for firms to prevent their core competencies from becoming core rigidities. The existence of core rigidities indicates that the firm is too anchored to its past, which prevents it from continuously developing new capabilities and core competencies.

Analyzing the Internal Organization

The Context of Internal Analysis

One of the conditions associated with analyzing a firm's internal organization is the reality that in today's global economy, some of the resources that were traditionally critical to firms' efforts to produce, sell, and distribute their goods or services such as labor costs, access to financial resources and raw materials, and protected or regulated markets are still important; but, it is now less likely that these resources will become core competencies and possibly competitive advantages.[16] An important reason for this is that an increasing number of firms are using their resources to form core competencies through which they successfully implement an international strategy (discussed in Chapter 8) as a means of overcoming the advantages created by these more traditional resources.

The Volkswagen Group has established "Strategy 2018" as its international strategy. The firm, which sells its products in over 150 countries, employs 400,000 people to operate

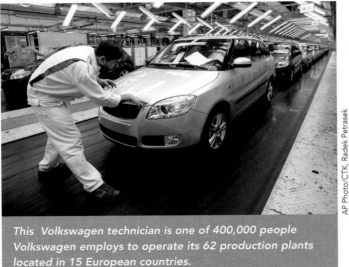

This Volkswagen technician is one of 400,000 people Volkswagen employs to operate its 62 production plants located in 15 European countries.

AP Photo/CTK, Radek Petrasek

its 62 production plants located in 15 European countries. By using its resources to form technological and innovation capabilities, Volkswagen intends to create superior customer service and product quality as core competencies on which it will rely to implement its international strategy.[17]

Increasingly, those analyzing their firm's internal organization should use a global mind-set to do so. A **global mind-set** is the ability to analyze, understand, and manage an internal organization in ways that are not dependent on the assumptions of a single country, culture, or context.[18] Because they are able to span artificial boundaries, those with a global mind-set recognize that their firms must possess resources and capabilities that allow understanding of and appropriate responses to competitive situations that are influenced by country-specific factors and unique cultures. Using a global mind-set to analyze the internal organization has the potential to significantly help the firm in its efforts to outperform rivals.[19] A global mind-set was used to develop Volkswagen Group's "Strategy 2018."

Finally, analyzing the firm's internal organization requires that evaluators examine the firm's entire portfolio of resources and capabilities. This perspective suggests that individual firms possess at least some resources and capabilities that other companies do not—at least not in the same combination. Resources are the source of capabilities, some of which lead to the development of core competencies; in turn, some core competencies may lead to a competitive advantage for the firm.[20] Understanding how to leverage the firm's unique bundle of resources and capabilities is a key outcome decision makers seek when analyzing the internal organization.[21] Figure 3.1 illustrates the relationships among

A global mind-set is the ability to analyze, understand, and manage an internal organization in ways that are not dependent on the assumptions of a single country, culture, or context.

Figure 3.1 Components of an Internal Analysis

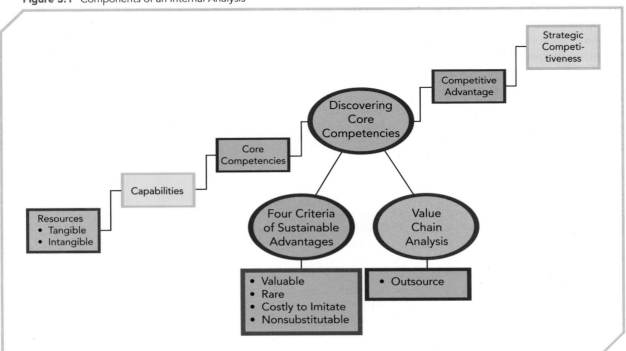

resources, capabilities, core competencies, and competitive advantages and shows how their integrated use can lead to strategic competitiveness. As we discuss next, firms use the assets in their internal organization to create value for customers.

Creating Value

Firms use their resources as the foundation for producing goods or services that will create value for customers.[22] **Value** is measured by a product's performance characteristics and by its attributes for which customers are willing to pay. Firms create value by innovatively bundling and leveraging their resources to form capabilities and core competencies.[23] Firms with a competitive advantage create more value for customers than do competitors.[24] Walmart uses its "every day low price" approach to doing business (an approach that is grounded in the firm's core competencies, such as information technology and distribution channels) to create value for those seeking to buy products at a low price compared to competitors' prices for those products.[25] Mattress manufacturer E. S. Kluft & Company creates value for customers interested in buying what the firm says is the "best mattress in the world." Each of the firm's products is made by hand by skilled craftsmen. Thus, human capital is a core competence and likely the source of a competitive advantage for E. S. Kluft. (The firm's upper-end mattress sells for $50,000 per unit.)[26] The stronger these firms' core competencies, the greater the amount of value they're able to create for their customers.[27]

Ultimately, creating value for customers is the source of above-average returns for a firm. What the firm intends regarding value creation affects its choice of business-level strategy (see Chapter 4) and its organizational structure (see Chapter 11).[28] In Chapter 4's discussion of business-level strategies, we note that value is created by a product's low cost, by its highly differentiated features, or by a combination of low cost and high differentiation, compared with competitors' offerings. A business-level strategy is effective only when it is grounded in exploiting the firm's capabilities and core competencies. Thus, the successful firm continuously examines the effectiveness of current capabilities and core competencies while thinking about the capabilities and competencies it will require for future success.[29]

At one time, the firm's efforts to create value were largely oriented to understanding the characteristics of the industry in which it competed and, in light of those characteristics, determining how it should be positioned relative to competitors. This emphasis on industry characteristics and competitive strategy underestimated the role of the firm's resources and capabilities in developing core competencies as the source of competitive advantages. In fact, core competencies, in combination with product-market positions, are the firm's most important sources of competitive advantage.[30] A firm's core competencies, integrated with an understanding of the results of studying the conditions in the external environment, should drive the selection of strategies.[31] As Clayton Christensen noted, "Successful strategists need to cultivate a deep understanding of the processes of competition and progress and of the factors that undergird each advantage. Only thus will they be able to see when old advantages are poised to disappear and how new advantages can be built in their stead."[32] By emphasizing core competencies when selecting and implementing strategies, companies learn to compete primarily on the basis of firm-specific differences. However, while doing so they must be simultaneously aware of how things are changing in the external environment.[33]

The Challenge of Analyzing the Internal Organization

The strategic decisions managers make about their firm's internal organization are non-routine,[34] have ethical implications,[35] and significantly influence the firm's ability to earn above-average returns.[36] These decisions involve choices about the resources the firm needs to collect and how to best manage them.

Value is measured by a product's performance characteristics and by its attributes for which customers are willing to pay.

Making decisions involving the firm's assets—identifying, developing, deploying, and protecting resources, capabilities, and core competencies—may appear to be relatively easy. However, this task is as challenging and difficult as any other with which managers are involved; moreover, the task is increasingly internationalized.[37] Some believe that the pressure on managers to pursue only decisions that help the firm meet the quarterly earnings expected by market analysts makes it difficult to accurately examine the firm's internal organization.[38]

The challenge and difficulty of making effective decisions are implied by preliminary evidence suggesting that one-half of organizational decisions fail.[39] Sometimes, mistakes are made as the firm analyzes conditions in its internal organization.[40] Managers might, for example, think a capability is a core competence when it is not. This may have been the case at Polaroid Corporation as decision makers continued to believe that the capabilities it used to build its instant film cameras were highly relevant at the time its competitors were developing and using the capabilities required to introduce digital cameras. In this instance, Polaroid's decision makers may have concluded that superior manufacturing was a core competence as was the firm's ability to innovate in terms of creating value-adding features for its instant cameras. If a mistake is made when analyzing and manage a firm's resources, such as appears to have been the case some years ago at Polaroid, decision makers must have the confidence to admit it and take corrective actions.[41]

A firm can improve by studying its mistakes; in fact, the learning generated by making and correcting mistakes can be important to efforts to create new capabilities and core competencies.[42] Today, a substantially slimmed-down Polaroid is introducing a number of new products, including GL20 Camera Glasses. These glasses include a built-in camera and dual LCDs that appear to cover individuals' eyes when wearing the oversized glasses.[43] These products are based on ideas advanced by Lady Gaga, who is now Polaroid's creative director. Thus, Polaroid may be developing marketing and product design as capabilities and hopefully core competencies as the source of hoped-for competitive success.

As we discuss next, three conditions—uncertainty, complexity, and intraorganizational conflict—affect managers as they analyze the internal organization and make decisions about resources (see Figure 3.2).[44]

Figure 3.2 Conditions Affecting Managerial Decisions about Resources, Capabilities, and Core Competencies

Conditions		
	Uncertainty	Uncertainty exists about the characteristics of the firm's general and industry environments and customers' needs.
	Complexity	Complexity results from the interrelationships among conditions shaping a firm.
	Intraorganizational Conflicts	Intraorganizational conflicts may exist among managers making decisions as well as among those affected by the decisions.

Managers face uncertainty because of a number of issues, including those of new proprietary technologies, rapidly changing economic and political trends, transformations in societal values, and shifts in customers' demands.[45] Environmental uncertainty increases the complexity and range of issues to examine when studying the internal environment.[46] Consider how uncertainty affects how to use resources at Peabody Energy Corp.

Peabody is the world's largest private-sector coal company. The firm's coal products fuel approximately 11 percent of all U.S. electricity generation and 2 percent of worldwide electricity. But the firm faces a great deal of uncertainty with respect to how it might best use its resources today to prepare for its future. One reason for this is that at least for some, coal is thought of as a "dirty fuel." Partly to reduce the uncertainty the firm faces because of this, Peabody is using some of its resources to build a "clean" coal-fired plant and has signed two agreements to develop clean coal in China. As a proponent of strong emissions standards, Peabody's leaders argue for more use of "clean coal." One of these agreements calls for Peabody and its partners to develop a green coal energy campus, including a 1200-MW power plant that will capture CO_2 and convert it into green building materials.[47] Obviously, the complexity of the decisions Peabody is making to reduce uncertainty (such as working with partners in China) is quite significant. Biases about how to cope with uncertainty affect decisions made about how to manage the firm's resources and capabilities to form core competencies.[48] For example, Peabody's CEO strongly believes in coal's future, suggesting that automobiles capable of burning coal could be built. Finally, intraorganizational conflict may surface when decisions are made about the core competencies a firm should develop and nurture. Conflict might surface in Peabody about the degree to which resources and capabilities should be used to form core competencies to support current coal technologies relative to the building of core competencies to support newer "clean technologies."

In making decisions affected by these three conditions, judgment is required. *Judgment* is the capability of making successful decisions when no obviously correct model or rule is available or when relevant data are unreliable or incomplete. In such situations, decision makers must be aware of possible cognitive biases, such as overconfidence. Individuals who are too confident in the decisions they make about how to use the firm's resources may fail to fully evaluate contingencies that could affect those decisions.[49]

When exercising judgment, decision makers often take intelligent risks. In the current competitive landscape, executive judgment can become a valuable capability. One reason is that, over time, effective judgment that decision makers demonstrate allows a firm to build a strong reputation and retain the loyalty of stakeholders whose support is linked to above-average returns.[50]

As we discuss in the Strategic Focus, finding individuals who can make the most successful decisions about using the organization's resources is challenging. Being able to do this is important because the quality of leaders' decisions regarding resources and their management affect a firm's ability to achieve strategic competitiveness. Individuals holding these key decision-making positions are called *strategic leaders*. Discussed fully in Chapter 12, for our purposes in this chapter we can think of strategic leaders as individuals with an ability to make effective decisions when examining the firm's resources, capabilities, and core competencies for the purpose of making choices about their use.

Next, we consider the relationships among a firm's resources, capabilities, and core competencies. While reading these sections of materials, keep in mind that organizations have more resources than capabilities and more capabilities than core competencies.

S T R A T E G I C **F O C U S**

EFFECTIVELY ANALYZING THE INTERNAL ORGANIZATION AND DECIDING HOW TO BEST USE THE FIRM'S ASSETS— IT'S HARD WORK!

As we note in Chapter 12, a firm's upper-level managers such as the CEO and members of the top management team may be well compensated. This is particularly the case when a firm's board of directors believes that those individuals are or that they have the potential to be excellent decision makers capable of effectively using the company's resources, capabilities, and core competencies for the purpose of earning above-average returns. As evidence for this, consider that between 2009 and 2010, the median value of salaries, bonuses, and long-term incentive packages for CEOs of 350 major U.S. companies increased 11 percent to $9.3 million.

Sometimes CEOs experience a reasonable amount of success using a firm's resources, as is the case for Judy McGrath, now the former CEO of Viacom Inc.'s MTV Networks. McGrath's leadership was instrumental in developing the MTV brand and its iconoclastic roots through which teenagers, the firm's target customer, were urged to tell their parents, "I want my MTV!" In other instances, an individual's tenure can be short lived, as is the case for Christina Norman, former CEO of the Oprah Winfrey Network (OWN). Just four months after launching the new network's programs, Norman was removed by OWN's board of directors, which concluded that the firm's resources were not being used effectively to develop attractive television programs.

Gap Inc. offers clothing through several brands, including Gap, Old Navy, and Banana Republic. Today, the firm's CEO says that he has a "high sense of urgency" to essentially stop years of bleeding with the firm's namesake brand. Other decisions the CEO is making are related to using the firm's resources to cut bureaucracy so that Gap clothes can reach stores much faster. Additionally, he decided to remove Gap's top designer after "four years of lackluster results." In commenting about the designer's departure, analysts noted that the designer had brought a "needed coolness factor" to Gap clothes but that at the same time, he failed to find a way to use the firm's design-related resources and capabilities to "deliver consistent takes on trends."

JIM WATSON/AFP/Getty Images

Gap Inc.'s Chairman & CEO Glenn Murphy has made many changes as head of the firm's namesake brand.

Other strategic leaders in different companies are currently making decisions about how to use their firm's resources. For example, leaders at Advance Publications Inc., parent company of Condé Nast, a publisher of multiple magazines such as *Vogue, GQ, Golf Digest, Bon Appetit, Conde Nast Traveler,* and *Wired* among others, has decided to invest $500 million of its financial resources (a tangible resource) in digital properties as a way of stimulating growth. Cisco CEO John Chambers recently announced that the firm's internal decision-making processes were being reorganized as a foundation for making tough decisions as to "where to shut off spending to preserve profitability." Thus, some of the upcoming decisions by Cisco's strategic leaders will result in different allocations of the firm's resources. Finally, after assuming the position of CEO for Hewlett-Packard (H-P), Meg Whitman (former eBay CEO) prepared to deal with challenges the firm faced, some of which were at least partly a result of Leo Apotheker's short 11-month tenure as H-P's CEO. In this regard, some analysts concluded that H-P faced a "strategic direction" crisis at the time of Whitman's appointment. The view that "numerous questions remain over H-P's strategy, including its plan to possibly spin off its mainstay personal-computer business" demonstrate the potential strategic direction crisis. Whitman pledged to carefully study the possible divestment of H-P's PC business as she sought to make decisions that would improve the firm's competitiveness.

All of these decisions concerning the use of firms' resources are being made under conditions of uncertainty about a number of factors, including customers' preferences, global economic conditions, and potential changes in various nations' business-related regulations. Time will tell if the resource-related decisions made by the strategic leaders we mention here will have the hoped-for effect of contributing positively to each firm's efforts to earn above-average returns.

Sources: R. Adams, 2011, New business model in vogue at Conde Nast, *Wall Street Journal Online*, http://www.wsj .com, May 31; D. Clark & S. Tibken, 2011, Cisco to reduce its bureaucracy, *Wall Street Journal Online*, http://www .wsj.com, May 6; E. Holmes, 2011, Gap CEO tailors urgent revamp, *Wall Street Journal Online*, http://www.wsj.com, Mary 19; E. Holmes, 2011, Revolving door spins at Gap, *Wall Street Journal Online*, http://www.wsj.com, May 6; J. S. Lublin, 2011, CEO pay in 2010 jumped 11%, *Wall Street Journal Online*, http://www.wsj.com, May 9; S. Schechner & A. E. Schuker, 2011, MTV Networks chief resigns, *Wall Street Journal Online*, http://www.wsj.com, May 6; E .A. E. Schuker, 2011, Oprah Network ousts its CEO, *Wall Street Journal Online*, http://www.wsj.com, May 7; May 1; B. Worthen, J. Scheck, & J. S. Lublin, 2011, H-P defends hasty Whitman hire, *Wall Street Journal*, http://wsj .com, September 23.

© Nicholas Monu/iStockphoto.com

Explore Gap Inc.'s branding strategy.
www.cengagebrain .com

Resources, Capabilities, and Core Competencies

Resources, capabilities, and core competencies are the foundation of competitive advantage. Resources are bundled to create organizational capabilities. In turn, capabilities are the source of a firm's core competencies, which are the basis of establishing competitive advantages.[51] We show these relationships in Figure 3.1. Here, we define and provide examples of these building blocks of competitive advantage.

Resources

Broad in scope, resources cover a spectrum of individual, social, and organizational phenomena.[52] By themselves, resources do not allow firms to create value for customers as the foundation for earning above-average returns. Indeed, resources are combined to form capabilities.[53] Subway links its fresh ingredients with several other resources including the continuous training it provides to those running the firm's units as the foundation for customer service as a capability; as explained in the Opening Case, customer service is also a core competence for Subway. As its sole distribution channel, the Internet is a resource for Amazon.com. The firm uses the Internet to sell goods at prices that typically are lower than those offered by competitors selling the same goods through what are more costly brick-and-mortar storefronts. By combining other resources (such as access to a wide product inventory), Amazon has developed a reputation for excellent customer service. Amazon's capability in terms of customer service is a core competence as well in that the firm creates unique value for customers through the services it provides to them. Amazon also uses its technological core competence to offer AWS (Amazon Web Services), services through which businesses can rent computing power from Amazon at a cost of pennies per hour. In the words of the leader of this effort, "AWS makes it possible for anyone with an Internet connection and a credit card to access the same kind of world-class computing systems that Amazon uses to run its $34 billion-a-year retail operation."[54]

Some of a firm's resources (defined in Chapter 1 as inputs to the firm's production process) are tangible while others are intangible. **Tangible resources** are assets that can

Tangible resources are assets that can be observed and quantified.

be observed and quantified. Production equipment, manufacturing facilities, distribution centers, and formal reporting structures are examples of tangible resources. Subway's food ingredients are a tangible resource. Intangible resources are assets that are rooted deeply in the firm's history and have accumulated over time. Because they are embedded in unique patterns of routines, intangible resources are difficult for competitors to analyze and imitate. Knowledge, trust between managers and employees, managerial capabilities, organizational routines (the unique ways people work together), scientific capabilities, the capacity for innovation, brand name, the firm's reputation for its goods or services and how it interacts with people (such as employees, customers, and suppliers), and organizational culture are intangible resources.[55] The routines Subway uses to develop and use its training procedures are an example of an intangible resource.

The four primary categories of tangible resources are financial, organizational, physical, and technological (see Table 3.1). The three primary categories of intangible resources are human, innovation, and reputational (see Table 3.2).

Tangible Resources

As tangible resources, a firm's borrowing capacity and the status of its physical facilities are visible. The value of many tangible resources can be established through financial statements, but these statements do not account for the value of all the firm's assets, because they disregard some intangible resources.[56] The value of tangible resources is also constrained because they are hard to leverage—it is difficult to derive additional business or value from a tangible resource. For example, an airplane is a tangible resource,

> **Intangible resources** include assets that are rooted deeply in the firm's history, accumulate over time, and are relatively difficult for competitors to analyze and imitate.

Table 3.1 Tangible Resources

Financial Resources	• The firm's capacity to borrow • The firm's ability to generate funds through internal operations
Organizational Resources	• Formal reporting structures
Physical Resources	• The sophistication of a firm's plant and equipment and the attractiveness of its location • Distribution facilities • Product inventory
Technological Resources	• Availability of technology-related resources such as copyrights, patents, trademarks, and trade secrets

Sources: Adapted from J. B. Barney, 1991, Firm resources and sustained competitive advantage, *Journal of Management*, 17: 101; R. M. Grant, 1991, *Contemporary Strategy Analysis*, Cambridge, U.K.: Blackwell Business, 100–102.

Table 3.2 Intangible Resources

Human Resources	• Knowledge • Trust • Skills • Abilities to collaborate with others
Innovation Resources	• Ideas • Scientific capabilities • Capacity to innovate
Reputational Resources	• Brand name • Perceptions of product quality, durability, and reliability • Positive reputation with stakeholders such as suppliers and customers

Sources: Adapted from R. Hall, 1992, The strategic analysis of intangible resources, *Strategic Management Journal*, 13: 136–139; R. M. Grant, 1991, *Contemporary Strategy Analysis*, Cambridge, U.K.: Blackwell Business, 101–104.

but "You can't use the same airplane on five different routes at the same time. You can't put the same crew on five different routes at the same time. And the same goes for the financial investment you've made in the airplane."[57]

Although production assets are tangible, many of the processes necessary to use these assets are intangible. Thus, the learning and potential proprietary processes associated with a tangible resource, such as manufacturing facilities, can have unique intangible attributes, such as quality control processes, unique manufacturing processes, and technologies that develop over time.[58]

Intangible Resources

Compared to tangible resources, intangible resources are a superior source of capabilities and subsequently, core competencies.[59] In fact, in the global economy, "the success of a corporation lies more in its intellectual and systems capabilities than in its physical assets. [Moreover], the capacity to manage human intellect—and to convert it into useful products and services—is fast becoming the critical executive skill of the age."[60]

Because intangible resources are less visible and more difficult for competitors to understand, purchase, imitate, or substitute for, firms prefer to rely on them rather than on tangible resources as the foundation for their capabilities. In fact, the more unobservable (i.e., intangible) a resource is, the more valuable that resource is to create capabilities.[61] Another benefit of intangible resources is that, unlike most tangible resources, their use can be leveraged. For instance, sharing knowledge among employees does not diminish its value for any one person. To the contrary, two people sharing their individualized knowledge sets often can be leveraged to create additional knowledge that, although new to each individual, contributes to performance improvements for the firm.

This brainstorming session allows group members to share ideas and collaborate. Individualized knowledge sets can be leveraged to create additional knowledge.

Rubberball/Jupiter images

Reputational resources (see Table 3.2) are important sources of a firm's capabilities and core competencies. Indeed, some argue that a positive reputation can even be a source of competitive advantage.[62] Earned through the firm's actions as well as its words, a value-creating reputation is a product of years of superior marketplace competence as perceived by stakeholders.[63] A reputation indicates the level of awareness a firm has been able to develop among stakeholders and the degree to which they hold the firm in high esteem.[64]

A well-known and highly valued brand name is a specific reputational resource.[65] A continuing commitment to innovation and aggressive advertising facilitates firms' efforts to take advantage of the reputation associated with their brands.[66] Harley-Davidson has a reputation for producing and servicing high-quality motorcycles with unique designs. Because of the desirability of its reputation, the company also produces a wide range of accessory items that it sells on the basis of its reputation for offering unique products with high quality. Sunglasses, jewelry, belts, wallets, shirts, slacks, belts, and hats are just a few of the large variety of accessories customers can purchase from a Harley-Davidson dealer or from its online store.[67]

Capabilities

The firm combines individual tangible and intangible resources to create capabilities. In turn, capabilities are used to complete the organizational tasks required to produce, distribute, and service the goods or services the firm provides to customers for the purpose of creating value for them.[68] As a foundation for building core competencies and hopefully competitive advantages, capabilities are often based on developing, carrying, and exchanging information and knowledge through the firm's human capital.[69] Hence, the value of human capital in developing and using capabilities and, ultimately, core competencies cannot be overstated.[70] At IBM, for example, human capital is critical to forming and using the firm's capabilities for long-term customer relationships and deep scientific and research skills, and the breadth of the firm's technical skills in hardware, software, and services.[71]

As illustrated in Table 3.3, capabilities are often developed in specific functional areas (such as manufacturing, R&D, and marketing) or in a part of a functional area (e.g., advertising). Table 3.3 shows a grouping of organizational functions and the capabilities that some companies are thought to possess in terms of all or parts of those functions.

Core Competencies

Defined in Chapter 1, core competencies are capabilities that serve as a source of competitive advantage for a firm over its rivals. Core competencies distinguish a company competitively and reflect its personality. Core competencies emerge over time through an organizational process of accumulating and learning how to deploy different resources and capabilities.[72] As the capacity to take action, core competencies are "crown jewels of a company," the activities the company performs especially well compared to competitors and through which the firm adds unique value to the goods or services it sells to customers.[73]

Table 3.3 Examples of Firms' Capabilities

Functional Areas	Capabilities	Examples of Firms
Distribution	• Effective use of logistics management techniques	• Walmart
Human Resources	• Motivating, empowering, and retaining employees	• Microsoft
Management Information Systems	• Effective and efficient control of inventories through point-of-purchase data collection methods	• Walmart
Marketing	• Effective promotion of brand-name products • Effective customer service • Innovative merchandising	• Procter & Gamble • Ralph Lauren Corp. • McKinsey & Co. • Nordstrom Inc. • Crate & Barrel
Management	• Ability to envision the future of clothing	• Hugo Boss • Zara
Manufacturing	• Design and production skills yielding reliable products • Product and design quality • Miniaturization of components and products	• Komatsu • Witt Gas Technology • Sony
Research & Development	• Innovative technology • Development of sophisticated elevator control solutions • Rapid transformation of technology into new products and processes • Digital technology	• Caterpillar • Otis Elevator Co. • Chaparral Steel • Thomson Consumer Electronics

Innovation is thought to be a core competence at Apple. As a capability, R&D activities are the source of this core competence. More specifically, the way Apple has combined some of its tangible (e.g., financial resources and research laboratories) and intangible (e.g., scientists and engineers and organizational routines) resources to complete research and development tasks creates a capability in R&D. By emphasizing its R&D capability, Apple is able to innovate in ways that create unique value for customers in the form of the products it sells, suggesting that innovation is a core competence for Apple.

Excellent customer service in its retail stores is another of Apple's core competencies. In this instance, unique and contemporary store designs (a tangible resource) are combined with knowledgeable and skilled employees (an intangible resource) to provide superior service to customers. A number of carefully developed training and development procedures are capabilities on which Apple's core competence of excellent customer service is based. The procedures that are capabilities include ". . . intensive control of how employees interact with customers, scripted training for on-site tech support and consideration of every store detail down to the pre-loaded photos and music on demo devices."[74]

Consumer products giant Procter & Gamble (P&G) sells branded products that it believes are of superior quality and value to customers located in more than 180 countries. Generating approximately $80 billion in annual sales revenue, P&G has numerous tangible and intangible resources that are used to form capabilities, some of which are core competencies. We examine the relationship between some of the firm's capabilities and competencies in the Strategic Focus. Interestingly, even in light of its size and scale (in terms of the number of products sold and the firm's encompassing geographic reach), P&G apparently has five core competencies (labeled core strengths by the firm).

© Nicholas Monu/iStockphoto.com

STRATEGY RIGHT NOW

Read more about Watervap's core competencies.

www.cengagebrain.com

S T R A T E G I C   F O C U S

PROCTER & GAMBLE: USING CAPABILITIES AND CORE COMPETENCIES TO CREATE VALUE FOR CUSTOMERS

Guided by its slogan of "Touching lives, improving life," Procter & Gamble (P&G) is known throughout the world for its stable of consumer brands. Organized within two global business units (Beauty & Grooming and Household Care), Crest, CoverGirl, Herbal Essences, Ivory, Bold, and Bounce are just a few of the more than 250 branded products the firm's 127,000 employees produce in facilities located in approximately 80 countries. Twenty-four of this firm's branded product lines generate at least $1 billion in annual sales. Estimates are that on average, every person in the world spends $12 annually to buy P&G products. The firm's new CEO wants to increase this annual average expenditure to $14 per person by 2015. Additionally, he wants the firm's annual sales revenue to grow to $100 billion from today's roughly $80 billion mark, and for the number of P&G customers to increase to 5 billion from the current 4.2 billion. How are these objectives to be reached? According to company officials and analysts, in part these objectives are to be reached through plans that are now in place to move quickly and broadly into developing countries such as China and India and to produce products that will appeal to new but lower-income customers. Of course, efforts will simultaneously continue to satisfy the needs of P&G's huge stable of current customers. These intended actions appear to support the view that P&G is a very effective competitor that continuously seeks growth through its competitive actions.

Daniel Acker/Bloomberg/Getty Images

Procter & Gamble (P&G) is organized into two global business units, Beauty & Grooming and Household Care. The Downy product line is managed by the Household Care team.

P&G relies on its capabilities and core competencies to satisfy current customers and to develop products to serve the needs of new customers. Typically, P&G likes to use its capabilities and competencies to grow organically rather than through mergers and acquisitions or through cooperative relationships. In the words of a previous P&G CEO: "Organic growth is more valuable because it comes from your core competencies. Organic growth exercises your innovation muscle. If you use it, it gets stronger." Cutting-edge technology, supply chain management skills, marketing and advertising expertise, a broad product portfolio, and research and development skills with respect to fats, oils, skin chemistry, surfactants, and emulsifiers are a few of P&G's highly-regarded capabilities. All of these capabilities, which result from combinations of the firms' tangible and intangible resources, allow P&G to perform tasks that must be completed to produce, sell, distribute, and service its branded products.

Taking this a step farther, we discover that these capabilities contribute to the firm's five core competencies (called core strengths by P&G). For example, R&D capabilities are foundational to P&G's *innovation* core competence. Similarly, the firm's marketing and advertising skills contribute to its *consumer understanding* and *brand-building* core competencies. The supply chain management capability is critical to the *go-to-market* core competence (a competence through which P&G "reaches retailers and consumers at the right place and time") and to the *scale* competence (a competence allowing P&G to be efficient and to create value for customers as a result). Thus, we see how some of P&G's capabilities are linked to one or more of the firm's five core competencies. From an operational perspective, these core competencies are activities P&G performs especially well relative to competitors and through which the firm is able to create unique value for customers.

Sources: E. Byron, 2011, P&G turns Febreze into a $1 billion brand, *Wall Street Journal*, http://www.wsj.com, March 8; A. K. Reese, 2011, Planning to succeed at Procter & Gamble, *Supply & Demand Chain Executive*, http://www.sdcexe .com, January 12; 2011, Energizer to shut two international battery plants, *Reuters*, http://www.fidelity.com, March 9; 2011, P&G core strengths, *Procter & Gamble Home Page*, http://www.p&g.com, June 6; 2011, Procter & Gamble Co., *Standard & Poor's Stock Report*, http://www.standardandpoors.com, June 11; 2011, P&G's strategy to win market share to pay off, *Treflis*, http://www.treflis.com, January 12; B. Horovitz, 2010, Procter & Gamble looks beyond U.S. borders, *USA Today*, http://www.usatoday.com, March 19.

Building Core Competencies

Two tools help firms identify their core competencies. The first consists of four specific criteria of sustainable competitive advantage that can be used to determine which capabilities are core competencies. Because the capabilities shown in Table 3.3 have satisfied these four criteria, they are core competencies. The second tool is the value chain analysis. Firms use this tool to select the value-creating competencies that should be maintained, upgraded, or developed and those that should be outsourced.

The Four Criteria of Sustainable Competitive Advantage

Capabilities that are valuable, rare, costly to imitate, and nonsubstitutable are core competencies (see Table 3.4). In turn, core competencies can lead to competitive advantages for the firm over its rivals. Capabilities failing to satisfy the four criteria are not core competencies, meaning that although every core competence is a capability, not every capability is a core competence. In slightly different words, for a capability to be a core competence, it must be valuable and unique from a customer's point of view. For a core competence to be a potential source of competitive advantage, it must be inimitable and nonsubstitutable by competitors.[75]

A sustainable competitive advantage exists only when competitors cannot duplicate the benefits of a firm's strategy or when they lack the resources to attempt imitation. For some period of time, the firm may have a core competence by using capabilities that are valuable and rare, but imitable. For example, some firms are trying to develop a core competence and potentially a competitive advantage by out-greening their competitors.

Table 3.4 The Four Criteria of Sustainable Competitive Advantage

Valuable Capabilities	• Help a firm neutralize threats or exploit opportunities
Rare Capabilities	• Are not possessed by many others
Costly-to-Imitate Capabilities	• Historical: A unique and a valuable organizational culture or brand name • Ambiguous cause: The causes and uses of a competence are unclear • Social complexity: Interpersonal relationships, trust, and friendship among managers, suppliers, and customers
Nonsubstitutable Capabilities	• No strategic equivalent

(Interestingly, developing a "green" core competence can contribute to the firm's efforts to earn above-average returns while benefitting the broader society.) Since 2005, Walmart has used its resources in ways that have allowed it to reduce its stores' carbon footprint by more than 10 percent and the carbon footprint of its trucking fleet by several times this percentage. Additionally, progress is being made toward the firm's goal of zero waste going to landfills from its operations. A reduction of its waste by 81 percent in California suggests that this goal may be attainable.[76] Competitor Target is also using its resources and capabilities for the purpose of forming a "green" core competence. "Environmental sustainability is integrated throughout our businesses—from the way we build our stores to the products on our shelves," the store says. Packaging its Archer Farms Balanced Potato Crisps in bags that are manufactured with 25 percent renewable plant-based plastic is one example of actions Target is taking to be environmentally sustainable.

The length of time a firm can expect to create value by using its core competencies is a function of how quickly competitors can successfully imitate a good, service, or process. Value-creating core competencies may last for a relatively long period of time only when all four of the criteria we discuss next are satisfied. Thus, either Walmart or Target would know that it has a core competence and possibly a competitive advantage in terms of green practices if the way the firm uses its resources to complete these practices satisfies the four criteria.

Valuable

Valuable capabilities allow the firm to exploit opportunities or neutralize threats in its external environment. By effectively using capabilities to exploit opportunities or neutralize threats, a firm creates value for customers. For publishers, e-books are both an opportunity (to sell books through a different distribution channels) and a threat (a reduction in publishers' ability to sell books through traditional channels such as physical storefronts). To neutralize the possibility/threat of lower sales revenue from traditional channels, publishers such as Penguin Group are trying to determine how to take advantage of the opportunities digital technologies create to transform their businesses. In partnership with other companies, Penguin sees using the Internet to sell directly to customers as an opportunity to create value for customers. "Penguin is one of three major publishers backing a new Web venture . . . that will highlight new titles and authors, and sell books directly to consumers. The site, Bookish.com is expected to launch" in the summer of 2011.[77]

Rare

Rare capabilities are capabilities that few, if any, competitors possess. A key question to be answered when evaluating this criterion is, "How many rival firms possess these valuable capabilities?" Capabilities possessed by many rivals are unlikely to become core competencies for any of the involved firms. Instead, valuable but common (i.e., not rare) capabilities are sources of competitive parity.[78] Competitive advantage results only when firms develop and exploit valuable capabilities that become core competencies and that differ from those shared with competitors. It is possible that Walmart and Target might reach competitive parity with their sustainability/green initiatives given that the capabilities used to complete green-oriented tasks are valuable but may not be rare.

Valuable capabilities allow the firm to exploit opportunities or neutralize threats in its external environment.

Rare capabilities are capabilities that few, if any, competitors possess.

Costly to Imitate

Costly-to-imitate capabilities are capabilities that other firms cannot easily develop. Capabilities that are costly to imitate are created because of one reason or a combination of three reasons (see Table 3.4). First, a firm sometimes is able to develop capabilities because of *unique historical conditions*. As firms evolve, they often acquire or develop capabilities that are unique to them.[79]

A firm with a unique and valuable *organizational culture* that emerged in the early stages of the company's history "may have an imperfectly imitable advantage over firms founded in another historical period;"[80] one in which less valuable or less competitively useful values and beliefs strongly influenced the development of the firm's culture. Briefly discussed in Chapter 1, organizational culture is a set of values that are shared by members in the organization. We explain this in greater detail in Chapter 12. An organizational culture is a source of advantage when employees are held together tightly by their belief in it.[81] With its emphasis on cleanliness, consistency, and service and the training that reinforces the value of these characteristics, McDonald's culture is thought by some to be a core competence and a competitive advantage. The same appears to be the case for Mustang Engineering (an engineering and project management firm based in Houston, Texas). Established as a place where people are expected to take care of people, Mustang offers "a company culture that we believe is unique in the industry. Mustang is a work place with a family feel. A client once described Mustang as a world-class company with a mom-and-pop culture."[82]

A second condition of being costly to imitate occurs when the link between the firm's core competencies and its competitive advantage is *causally ambiguous*.[83] In these instances, competitors can't clearly understand how a firm uses its capabilities that are core competencies as the foundation for competitive advantage. As a result, firms are uncertain about the capabilities they should develop to duplicate the benefits of a competitor's value-creating strategy. For years, firms tried to imitate Southwest Airlines' low-cost strategy but most have been unable to do so, primarily because they can't duplicate this firm's unique culture.

Social complexity is the third reason that capabilities can be costly to imitate. Social complexity means that at least some, and frequently many, of the firm's capabilities are the product of complex social phenomena. Interpersonal relationships, trust, friendships among managers and between managers and employees, and a firm's reputation with suppliers and customers are examples of socially complex capabilities. Southwest Airlines is careful to hire people who fit with its culture. This complex interrelationship between the culture and human capital adds value in ways that other airlines cannot, such as jokes on flights by the flight attendants or the cooperation between gate personnel and pilots.

Nonsubstitutable

Nonsubstitutable capabilities are capabilities that do not have strategic equivalents. This final criterion "is that there must be no strategically equivalent valuable resources that are themselves either not rare or imitable. Two valuable firm resources (or two bundles of firm resources) are strategically equivalent when they each can be separately exploited to implement the same strategies."[84] In general, the strategic value of capabilities increases as they become more difficult to substitute. The more intangible and hence invisible capabilities are, the more difficult it is for firms to find substitutes and the greater the challenge is to competitors trying to imitate a firm's value-creating strategy. Firm-specific knowledge and trust-based working relationships between managers and nonmanagerial personnel, such as existed for years at Southwest Airlines, are examples of capabilities that are difficult to identify and for which finding a substitute is challenging. However, causal ambiguity may make it difficult for the firm to learn as well and may stifle progress, because the firm may not know how to improve processes that are not easily codified and thus are ambiguous.[85]

In summary, only using valuable, rare, costly-to-imitate, and nonsubstitutable capabilities has the potential for the firm to create sustainable competitive advantages. Table 3.5 shows the competitive consequences and performance implications resulting from

Costly-to-imitate capabilities are capabilities that other firms cannot easily develop.

Nonsubstitutable capabilities are capabilities that do not have strategic equivalents.

Table 3.5 Outcomes from Combinations of the Criteria for Sustainable Competitive Advantage

Is the Capability Valuable?	Is the Capability Rare?	Is the Capability Costly to Imitate?	Is the Capability Nonsubstitutable?	Competitive Consequences	Performance Implications
No	No	No	No	• Competitive disadvantage	• Below-average returns
Yes	No	No	Yes/no	• Competitive parity	• Average returns
Yes	Yes	No	Yes/no	• Temporary competitive advantage	• Average returns to above-average returns
Yes	Yes	Yes	Yes/no	• Sustainable competitive advantage	• Above-average returns

combinations of the four criteria of sustainability. The analysis suggested by the table helps managers determine the strategic value of a firm's capabilities. The firm should not emphasize capabilities that fit the criteria described in the first row in the table (i.e., resources and capabilities that are neither valuable nor rare and that are imitable and for which strategic substitutes exist). Capabilities yielding competitive parity and either temporary or sustainable competitive advantage, however, will be supported. Some competitors such as Coca-Cola and PepsiCo and Boeing and Airbus may have capabilities that result in competitive parity. In such cases, the firms will nurture these capabilities while simultaneously trying to develop capabilities that can yield either a temporary or sustainable competitive advantage.

Value Chain Analysis

Value chain analysis allows the firm to understand the parts of its operations that create value and those that do not.[86] Understanding these issues is important because the firm earns above-average returns only when the value it creates is greater than the costs incurred to create that value.[87]

The value chain is a template that firms use to analyze their cost position and to identify the multiple means that can be used to facilitate implementation of a chosen strategy.[88] Today's competitive landscape demands that firms examine their value chains in a global rather than a domestic-only context.[89] In particular, activities associated with supply chains should be studied within a global context.[90]

We show a model of the value chain in Figure 3.3. As depicted in the model, a firm's value chain is segmented into value chain activities and support functions. **Value chain activities** are activities or tasks the firm completes in order to produce products and then sell, distribute, and service those products in ways that create value for customers. **Support functions** include the activities or tasks the firm completes in order to support the work being done to produce, sell, distribute, and service the products the firm is producing. A firm can develop a capability and/or a core competence in any of the value chain activities and in any of the support functions. When it does so, it has established an ability to create value for customers. In fact, as shown in Figure 3.3, customers are the ones firms seek to serve when using value chain analysis to identify their capabilities and core competencies. When using their unique core competencies to create unique value for customers that competitors cannot duplicate, firms have established one or more competitive advantages. This appears to be the case for P&G as it relies on the five core competencies described earlier in a Strategic Focus to produce unique, high-quality branded products that are sold to customers throughout the world.

The activities associated with each part of the value chain are shown in Figure 3.4 while the activities that are part of the tasks firms complete when dealing with support functions appear in Figure 3.5. All items in both figures should be evaluated relative to competitors'

Value chain activities are activities or tasks the firm completes in order to produce products and then sell, distribute, and service those products in ways that create value for customers.

Support functions include the activities or tasks the firm completes in order to support the work being done to produce, sell, distribute, and service the products the firm is producing.

Figure 3.3 A Model of the Value Chain

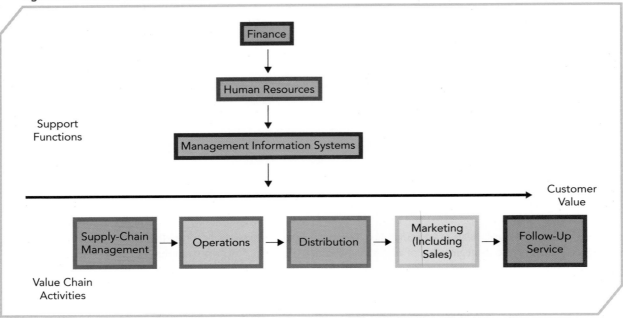

Source: © Copyrighted 2011 by Michael A. Hitt, R. Duane Ireland, and Robert E. Hoskisson.

Figure 3.4 Creating Value through Value Chain Activities

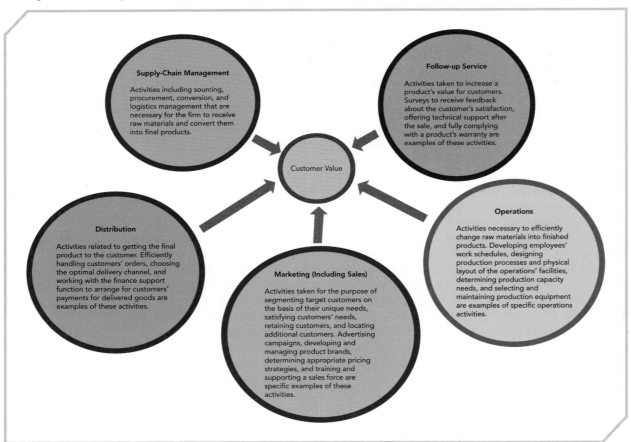

Source: © Copyrighted 2011 by Michael A. Hitt, R. Duane Ireland, and Robert E. Hoskisson.

Figure 3.5 Creating Value through Support Functions

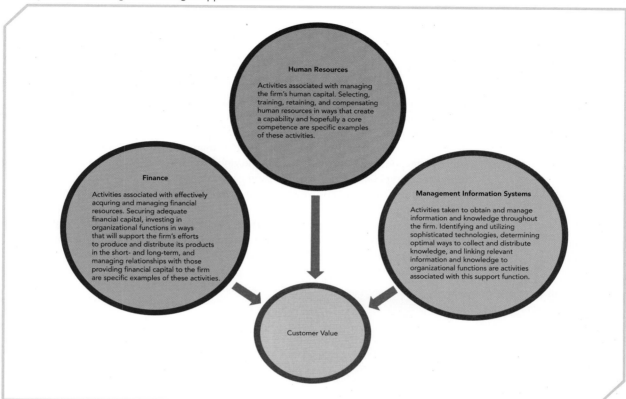

Human Resources

Activities associated with managing the firm's human capital. Selecting, training, retaining, and compensating human resources in ways that create a capability and hopefully a core competence are specific examples of these activities.

Finance

Activities associated with effectively acquiring and managing financial resources. Securing adequate financial capital, investing in organizational functions in ways that will support the firm's efforts to produce and distribute its products in the short- and long-term, and managing relationships with those providing financial capital to the firm are specific examples of these activities.

Management Information Systems

Activities taken to obtain and manage information and knowledge throughout the firm. Identifying and utilizing sophisticated technologies, determining optimal ways to collect and distribute knowledge, and linking relevant information and knowledge to organizational functions are activities associated with this support function.

Customer Value

Source: © Copyrighted 2011 by Michael A. Hitt, R. Duane Ireland, and Robert E. Hoskisson.

capabilities and core competencies. To become a core competence and a source of competitive advantage, a capability must allow the firm (1) to perform an activity in a manner that provides value superior to that provided by competitors, or (2) to perform a value-creating activity that competitors cannot perform. Only under these conditions does a firm create value for customers and have opportunities to capture that value.

Creating value for customers by completing activities that are part of the value chain often requires building effective alliances with suppliers (and sometimes others to which the firm outsources activities, as discussed in the next section) and developing strong positive relationships with customers. When firms have such strong positive relationships with suppliers and customers, they are said to have "social capital."[91] The relationships themselves have value because they produce knowledge transfer and access to resources that a firm may not hold internally.[92] To build social capital whereby resources such as knowledge are transferred across organizations requires trust between the parties. The partners must trust each other in order to allow their resources to be used in such a way that both parties will benefit over time and neither party will take advantage of the other.[93] Trust and social capital usually evolve over time with repeated interactions but firms can also establish special means to jointly manage alliances that promote greater trust with the outcome of enhanced benefits for both partners.[94]

Evaluating a firm's capability to execute its value chain activities and support functions is challenging. Earlier in the chapter, we noted that identifying and assessing the value of a firm's resources and capabilities requires judgment. Judgment is equally necessary when using value chain analysis, because no obviously correct model or rule is universally available to help in the process.

What should a firm do about value chain activities and support functions in which its resources and capabilities are not a source of core competence? Outsourcing is one solution to consider.

Outsourcing

Concerned with how components, finished goods, or services will be obtained, **outsourcing** is the purchase of a value-creating activity or a support function activity from an external supplier.[95] Not-for-profit agencies as well as for-profit organizations actively engage in outsourcing.[96] Firms engaging in effective outsourcing increase their flexibility, mitigate risks, and reduce their capital investments.[97] In multiple global industries, the trend toward outsourcing continues at a rapid pace.[98] Moreover, in some industries virtually all firms seek the value that can be captured through effective outsourcing. As with other strategic management process decisions, careful analysis is required before the firm decides to outsource.[99] And if outsourcing is to be used, firms must recognize that only activities where they cannot create value or where they are at a substantial disadvantage compared to competitors should be outsourced.[100]

Outsourcing can be effective because few, if any, organizations possess the resources and capabilities required to achieve competitive superiority in all value chain activities and support functions. For example, research suggests that few companies can afford to develop internally all the technologies that might lead to competitive advantage.[101] By nurturing a smaller number of capabilities, a firm increases the probability of developing core competencies and achieving a competitive advantage because it does not become overextended. In addition, by outsourcing activities in which it lacks competence, the firm can fully concentrate on those areas in which it can create value.

The consequences of outsourcing cause additional concerns.[102] For the most part, these concerns revolve around the potential loss in firms' innovative ability and the loss of jobs within companies that decide to outsource some of their work activities to others. Thus, innovation and technological uncertainty are two important issues to consider when making outsourcing decisions. However, firms can also learn from outsource suppliers how to increase their own innovation capabilities.[103] Companies must be aware of these issues and be prepared to fully consider the concerns about opportunities from outsourcing suggested by different stakeholders (e.g., employees). The opportunities and concerns may be especially significant when firms outsource activities or functions to a foreign supply source (often referred to as offshoring).[104] Bangalore and Belfast are the newest hotspots for technology outsourcing, competing with major operations in other nations such as China.[105] Yet, IBM recently made the decision to keep outsourced activities in the United States instead of moving them to a foreign location.[106]

This Belfast outsourcing center provides support for a U.S.–based telecom firm. Cities like Bangalore and Belfast are the newest entrants into the growing world of technology outsourcing.

David Silverman/Getty Images

Outsourcing is the purchase of a value-creating activity or a support function activity from an external supplier.

Competencies, Strengths, Weaknesses, and Strategic Decisions

By analyzing the internal organization, firms are able to identify their strengths and weaknesses in resources, capabilities, and core competencies. For example, if a firm has weak capabilities or does not have core competencies in areas required to achieve a competitive advantage, it must acquire those resources and build the capabilities and competencies needed. Alternatively, the firm could decide to outsource a function or activity where it is weak in order to improve its ability to use its remaining resources to create value.[107]

In considering the results of examining the firm's internal organization, managers should understand that having a significant quantity of resources is not the same as having the "right" resources. The "right" resources are those with the potential to be formed into core competencies as the foundation for creating value for customers and developing competitive advantages as a result of doing so. Interestingly, decision makers sometimes become more focused and productive when seeking to find the right resources when the firm's total set of resources is constrained.[108]

Tools such as outsourcing help the firm focus on its core competencies as the source of its competitive advantages. However, evidence shows that the value-creating ability of core competencies should never be taken for granted. Moreover, the ability of a core competence to be a permanent competitive advantage can't be assumed. The reason for these cautions is that all core competencies have the potential to become *core rigidities*.[109] Typically, events occurring in the firm's external environment create conditions through which core competencies can become core rigidities, generate inertia, and stifle innovation. "Often the flip side, the dark side, of core capabilities is revealed due to external events when new competitors figure out a better way to serve the firm's customers, when new technologies emerge, or when political or social events shift the ground underneath."[110]

Historically, Borders Group Inc. relied on its large storefronts that were conveniently located for customers to visit and browse through books and magazines in a pleasant atmosphere as sources of its competitive success. Over the past decade or so, though, digital technologies (part of the firm's external environment) rapidly changed customers' shopping patterns for reading materials. Discussed earlier in the chapter, Amazon.com's use of the Internet significantly changed the competitive landscape for Borders and similar competitors such as Barnes & Noble. It is possible that Borders' core competencies of store locations and a desirable physical environment for customers became core rigidities for this firm, eventually leading to the filing of bankruptcy in early 2011 and subsequent liquidation.[111] Managers studying the firm's internal organization are responsible for making certain that core competencies do not become core rigidities.

After studying its external environment to determine what it might choose to do (as explained in Chapter 2) and its internal organization to understand what it can do (as explained in this chapter), the firm has the information required to select a business-level strategy that it will use to compete against rivals. We describe different business-level strategies in the next chapter.

SUMMARY

- In the current competitive landscape, the most effective organizations recognize that strategic competitiveness and above-average returns result only when core competencies (identified by studying the firm's internal organization) are matched with opportunities (determined by studying the firm's external environment).

- No competitive advantage lasts forever. Over time, rivals use their own unique resources, capabilities, and core competencies to form different value-creating propositions that duplicate the focal firm's ability to create value for customers. Because competitive advantages are not permanently

sustainable, firms must exploit their current advantages while simultaneously using their resources and capabilities to form new advantages that can lead to future competitive success.

- Effectively managing core competencies requires careful analysis of the firm's resources (inputs to the production process) and capabilities (resources that have been purposely integrated to achieve a specific task or set of tasks). The knowledge the firm's human capital possesses is among the most significant of an organization's capabilities and ultimately provides the base for most competitive advantages. The firm must create an organizational culture that allows people to integrate their individual knowledge with that held by others so that, collectively, the firm has a significant amount of value-creating organizational knowledge.

- Capabilities are a more likely source of core competence and subsequently of competitive advantages than are individual resources. How a firm nurtures and supports its capabilities so they can become core competencies is less visible to rivals, making efforts to understand and imitate the focal firm's capabilities difficult.

- Only when a capability is valuable, rare, costly to imitate, and nonsubstitutable is it a core competence and a source of competitive advantage. Over time, core competencies must be supported, but they cannot be allowed to become core rigidities. Core competencies are a source of competitive advantage only when they allow the firm to create value by exploiting opportunities in its external environment. When this is no longer possible, the company shifts its

attention to forming other capabilities that satisfy the four criteria of a sustainable competitive advantage.

- Value chain analysis is used to identify and evaluate the competitive potential of resources and capabilities. By studying their skills relative to those associated with value chain activities and support functions, firms can understand their cost structure and identify the activities through which they can create value.

- When the firm cannot create value in either a value chain activity or a support function, outsourcing is considered. Used commonly in the global economy, outsourcing is the purchase of a value-creating activity from an external supplier. The firm should outsource only to companies possessing a competitive advantage in terms of the particular primary or support activity under consideration. In addition, the firm must continuously verify that it is not outsourcing activities from which it could create value.

REVIEW QUESTIONS

1. Why is it important for a firm to study and understand its internal organization?

2. What is value? Why is it critical for the firm to create value? How does it do so?

3. What are the differences between tangible and intangible resources? Why is it important for decision makers to understand these differences? Are tangible resources more valuable for creating capabilities than are intangible resources, or is the reverse true? Why?

4. What are capabilities? How do firms create capabilities?

5. What four criteria must capabilities satisfy for them to become core competencies? Why is it important for firms to

use these criteria to evaluate their capabilities' value-creating potential?

6. What is value chain analysis? What does the firm gain by successfully using this tool?

7. What is outsourcing? Why do firms outsource? Will outsourcing's importance grow in the future? If so, why?

8. How do firms identify internal strengths and weaknesses? Why is it vital that managers have a clear understanding of their firm's strengths and weaknesses?

9. What are core rigidities? What does it mean to say that each core competence could become a core rigidity?

EXPERIENTIAL EXERCISES

EXERCISE 1: WHAT MAKES A GREAT OUTSOURCING FIRM?

The focus of this chapter is on understanding how firm resources and capabilities serve as the cornerstone for competencies and, ultimately, a competitive advantage. However, when firms cannot create value in either a primary or support activity, outsourcing becomes a potential strategy. Yet with the recession that began in 2007, there seems to be a shift occurring. According to the International Association of Outsourcing Professionals (IAOP) at their 2010 annual conference, their members reported a 24 percent increase from their 2009 business volumes. Their report goes on to suggest that significant trends are emerging. The

IAOP research finds a focus on risk arbitrage to keep flexibility and adaptability forefront (just think Japanese earthquake, social media revolution); that cloud computing is reinventing outsourcing, which allows companies to "rent" computing resources rather than invest themselves; and that allshoring is occurring all over the world, with rural U.S. areas competing with China and India for outsourcing contracts. All of their trends may be found at the following address: http://www.iaop.org/Firmbuilder/ Articles/34/175/3185 from the report titled "The 2011 Global Outsourcing 100: Transforming the Corporation".

During that same 2010 conference, the IAOP announced its Global Outsourcing 100, which represents the world's best outsourcing service providers. The evaluation process mirrors that employed by many top customers and considers four key criteria: (1) size and growth in revenue, employees, centers, and countries served; (2) customer experience as demonstrated through the value being created at the company's top customers; (3) depth and breadth of competencies as demonstrated through industry recognition, relevant certifications, and investment in the development of people, processes, and technologies; and (4) management capabilities as reflected in the experience and accomplishments of the organization's top leaders and investment in management systems that ensure outsourcing success. Here are the first 10 companies on the 2010 list, in alphabetical order.

1. Accenture
2. Aditya Birla Minacs
3. Advanced Technology Services
4. Aegis
5. Amdocs
6. Aon Hewitt
7. API Outsourcing
8. ARAMARK
9. Artezio
10. Auriga

With a team, pick one of the Top 100 Global best outsourcing firms to analyze from the list on the IAOP Web site at http://www.iaop.org/Content/23/196/3117 (a new list is published annually in *Fortune* magazine and updated on the IAOP site). Prepare a brief presentation formed around the contents of the chapter that addresses at a minimum the following questions:

■ Why was this company chosen to be in the top 100? What has been the company's history as regards outsourcing as a source of revenue?
■ How does the firm describe, or imply, its value proposition?
■ What unique competitive advantage does the firm exhibit?

■ Do you consider this to be a sustainable competitive advantage? Utilize the four criteria of sustainable competitive advantage as your guide.

EXERCISE 2: VRIO ANALYSIS—IS THE FIRM'S ADVANTAGE SUSTAINABLE?

In this chapter, the concepts of sustainable competitive advantage and how firms can use their unique bundle of resources to achieve such an advantage were introduced. Remember that a sustainable competitive advantage can only be present if competitors are unsuccessful in duplicating the firm's benefit or the competitor is unable to acquire the resources necessary to imitate.

However, discovering if a competitive advantage is sustainable or merely temporary can be difficult for managers. According to the *Business Insider* War Room online magazine (http://www.businessinsider.com/warroom), there are 6 critical ingredients to achieve a sustainable competitive advantage: (1) real intellectual property; (2) a dynamic rather than a single product line; (3) dramatic cost improvement capabilities; (4) a proven team with inside relationships; (5) a lock on the customer or market; and (6) strong focus and differentiation.

In your teams, prepare for class discussion an analysis of a *Fortune 500* company that your team finds interesting (the 2011 list may be viewed at CNNMoney, http://money.cnn.com/magazines/fortune/fortune500/2011/full_list/). Your team should be prepared, at a minimum, to address the following issues:

1. How does the firm describe its value proposition?
2. List each of the firm's capabilities as represented by your text in Table 3.4.
3. Prepare a list for your firm that replicates the columns represented in Table 3.5.
4. What do you consider to be the firm's core competencies?
5. Do you consider this firm to possess a sustainable competitive advantage, and if so, do you believe this to be sustainable in the future?
6. Categorize the firm's performance over the past few years.

VIDEO CASE

ORGANIZATIONAL CULTURE CREATES STRATEGIC COMPETITIVENESS
Tony Shay/CEO/Zappos.com

Zappos.com, an online shoe retailer, has been listed in *Fortune* magazine's 100 best companies to work for over the past two years because employees feel empowered and respected. Recognized as a thriving company due to its unique organizational culture, from its untimed and unscripted call centers to "bald and blue" days, Zappos gives its employees the opportunity to shine in the workplace. Tony Shay, CEO, believes that Zappos is making the world a better place by allowing employees to be happy and to look at their job as a place to be for life. By receiving job security and benefits on par with competitors, Zappos employees remain dedicated to promoting branding opportunities with every customer. As a result, Amazon.com willingly purchased Zappos for $1.2 billion.

Be prepared to discuss the following concepts and questions in class:

Concepts
■ Value
■ Resources, capabilities, and core competencies
■ Sustainable competitive advantage
■ Value chain
■ Outsourcing

Questions
1. How is Zappos' organizational culture creating value?
2. What resources and resulting capabilities and core competencies do you see within the Zappos organization that gives it strategic competitiveness?
3. Will Zappos' competitive advantage be sustainable?
4. What value chain activities performed by Zappos help to create value for its customers?
5. Why do you think Zappos is not outsourcing its call centers?

NOTES

1. E. Rudea-Sabater & D. Derosby, 2011, The evolving Internet in 2025: Four scenarios, *Strategy & Leadership*, 39: 32–38.

2. H. A. Ndofor, D. G. Sirmon, & X. He, 2011, Firm resources, competitive actions and performance: Investigating a mediated model with evidence from the in-vitro diagnostics industry, *Strategic Management Journal*, 32: 640–657; R. R. Wiggins & T. W. Ruefli, 2002, Sustained competitive advantage: Temporal dynamics and the incidence of persistence of superior economic performance, *Organization Science*, 13: 82–105.

3. D. Dunlap-Hinkler, M. Kotabe, & R. Mudambi, 2010, A story of breakthrough versus incremental innovation: Corporate entrepreneurship in the global pharmaceutical industry, *Strategic Entrepreneurship Journal*, 4: 106–127.

4. 2011, McDonald's: Slow growth in a tough economy, *Bloomberg BusinessWeek*, June 13, 28.

5. J. S. Lublin, 2011, Campbell's chief stirs plans to heat lukewarm soup sales, *Wall Street Journal*, http://www.wsj.com, May 16.

6. S. Terlep, 2011, GM's latest change agent tackles designs, red tape, *Wall Street Journal*, http://www.wsj.com, June 15.

7. R. E. Ployhart & T. P Moliterno, 2011, Emergence of the human capital resource: A multilevel model, *Academy of Management Review*, 36: 127–150; A. Leiponen, 2008, Control of intellectual assets in client relationships: Implications for innovation, *Strategic Management Journal*, 29: 1371–1394.

8. D. DePass, 2006, Cuts in incentives upset 3M supervisors, *Star Tribune*, December 16.

9. M. A. Hitt, R. D. Irel, D. G. Sirmon, & C. A. Trahms, 2011, Strategic entrepreneurship: Creating value for individuals, organizations, and society, *Academy of Management Perspective*, 25: 57–75; C. D. Zatzick & R. D. Iverson, 2007, High-involvement management and work force reduction: Competitive advantage or disadvantage? *Academy of Management Journal*, 49: 999–1015.

10. R. Florida, 2005, *The Flight of the Creative Class*, New York: HarperBusiness.

11. M. Gruber, F. Heinemann, M. Brettel, & S. Hunbeling, 2010, Configurations of resources and capabilities and their performance implications: An exploratory study on technology ventures, *Strategic Management Journal*, 31: 1337–1356; D. G. Sirmon, M. A. Hitt, & R. D. Ireland, 2007, Managing firm resources in dynamic markets to create value: Looking inside the black box, *Academy of Management Review*, 32: 273–292.

12. F. Polidoro Jr. & P. K. Toh, 2011, Letting rivals come close or warding them off? The Effects of substitution threat on imitation deterrence, *Academy of Management Journal*, 54: 369–392; A. W. King, 2007, Disentangling interfirm and intrafirm causal ambiguity: A conceptual model of causal ambiguity and sustainable competitive advantage, *Academy of Management Review*, 32: 156–178.

13. M. Semadeni & B. S. Anderson 2010, The follower's dilemma: Innovation and imitation in the professional services industry, *Academy of Management Journal*, 53: 1175–1193; U. Ljungquist, 2007, Core competency beyond identification: Presentation of a model, *Management Decision*, 45: 393–402.

14. A. Parmigiani & S. S. Holloway, 2011, Actions speak louder than modes: Antecedents and implications of parent implementation capabilities on business unit performance, *Strategic Management Journal*, 32: 457–485.

15. J. A. Adegbesan & M. J. Higgins, 2010, The intra-alliance division of value created through collaboration, *Strategic Management Journal*, 32: 187–211; M. A. Peteraf & J. B. Barney, 2003, Unraveling the resource-based tangle, *Managerial and Decision Economics*, 24: 309–323; J. B. Barney, 2001, Is the resource-based "view" a useful perspective for strategic management research? Yes, *Academy of Management Review*, 26: 41–56.

16. G. Zied & J. McGuire, 2011, Multimarket competition, mobility barriers, and firm performance, *Journal of Management Studies*, 48: 857–890; D. P. Lepak, K. G. Smith, & M. Susan Taylor, 2007, Value creation and value capture: A multilevel perspective, *Academy of Management Review*, 32: 180–194.

17. Strategy, 2011, Volkswagen Home Page, http://www.volkswagen.com, June 1.

18. A. Arino, 2011, Building the global enterprise: Strategic assembly, *Global Strategy Journal*, 1: 47–49; M. Javidan, R. M. Steers, & M. A. Hitt (eds.), 2007, *The Global Mindset*: Amsterdam: Elsevier Ltd; T. M. Begley & D. P. Boyd, 2003, The need for a corporate global mindset, MIT *Sloan Management Review*, 44(2): 25–32.

19. O. Levy, S. Taylor, & N. A. Boyacigiller, 2010, On the rocky road to strong global culture, *MIT Sloan Management Review*, 51: 20–22; O. Levy, S. Beechler, S. Taylor, & N. A. Boyacigiller, 2007, What we talk about when we talk about "global mindset": Managerial cognition in multinational corporations, *Journal of International Business Studies*, 38: 231–258.

20. R. A. D'Aveni, G. B. Dagnino, & K. G. Smith, 2010, The age of temporary advantage, *Strategic Management Journal*, 31: 1371–1385; E. Danneels, 2008, Organizational antecedents of second-order competences, *Strategic Management Journal*, 29: 519–543.

21. H. Hoang & F. T. Rothaermel, 2010, Leveraging internal and external experience: Exploration, exploitation, and R&D project performance, *Strategic Management Journal*, 31: 734–758; K. J. Mayer & R. M. Salomon, 2006, Capabilities, contractual hazards, and governance: Integrating resource-based and transaction cost perspectives, *Academy of Management Journal*, 49: 942–959.

22. P. L. Drnevich & A. P. Kriauciunas, 2011, Clarifying the conditions and limits of the contributions of ordinary and dynamic capabilities to relative firm performance, *Strategic Management Journal*, 32: 254–279; R. Adner & R. Kapoor, 2010, Value creation in innovation ecosystems: How the structure of technological interdependence affects firm performance in new technology generations, *Strategic Management Journal*, 31: 306–333.

23. D. G. Sirmon, S. Gove, & M. A. Hitt, 2008, Resource management in dyadic competitive rivalry: The effects of resource bundling and deployment, *Academy of Management Journal*, 51: 919–935; E. Danneels, 2007, The process of technological competence leveraging, *Strategic Management Journal*, 28: 511–533.

24. J. S. Harrison, D. A. Bosse, & R. A. Phillips, 2010, Managing for stakeholders, stakeholder utility functions, and competitive advantage, *Strategic Management Journal*, 31: 58–74; J. L. Morrow, Jr., D. G. Sirmon, M. A. Hitt, & T. R. Holcomb 2007, Creating value in the face of declining performance: Firm strategies and organizational recovery, *Strategic Management Journal*, 28: 271–283.

25. K. Talley, 2011, Wal-Mart results to grab investor interest, *Wall Street Journal*, http://www.wsj.com, May 13.

26. M. Shank, 2011, Making $50,000 mattresses, selling in Buffett's furniture stores, *Bloomberg.com News*, http://www.bloomberg.com, March 11.

27. V. Rindova, W. J. Ferrier, & R. Wiltbank, 2010, Value from gestalt: How sequences of competitive actions create advantage for firms in nascent markets, *Strategic Management Journal*, 31: 1474–1497.

28. D. G. Sirmon, M. A. Hitt, J.-L. Arregle, & J. T. Campbell, 2010, The dynamic interplay of capability strengths and weaknesses: Investigating the bases of temporary competitive advantage, *Strategic Management Journal*, 31: 1386–1409.

29. F. Aime, S. Johnson, J. W. Ridge, & A. D. Hill, 2010, The routine may be stable but the advantage is not: Competitive implications of key employee mobility, *Strategic Management Journal*, 31: 75–87.

30. K. Z. Zhou & F. Wu, 2010, Technological capability, strategic flexibility, and product innovation, *Strategic Management Journal*, 31: 547–561.

31. M. H. Kunc & J. D. W. Morecroft, 2010, Managerial decision making and firm performance under a resource-based paradigm, *Strategic Management Journal*, 31: 1164–1182; J. Woiceshyn & L. Falkenberg, 2008, Value creation in knowledge-based firms: Aligning problems and resources, *Academy of Management Perspectives*, 22 (2): 85–99; M. R. Haas & M. T. Hansen, 2005, When using knowledge can hurt performance: The value of organizational capabilities in a management consulting company, *Strategic Management Journal*, 26: 1–24.

32. C. M. Christensen, 2001, The past and future of competitive advantage, *Sloan Management Review*, 42(2): 105–109.

33. S. K. Parker & C. G. Collins, 2010, Taking stock: Integrating and differentiating multiple proactive behaviors, *Journal of Management*, 36: 633–662; O. Gottschalg & M. Zollo, 2007, Interest alignment and competitive advantage, *Academy of Management Review*, 32: 418–437.

34. S. M. Mudambi & S. Tallman, 2010, Make, buy or ally? Theoretical perspectives on knowledge process outsourcing through alliances, *Journal of Management Studies*, 47: 1434–1456; D. P. Forbes, 2007, Reconsidering the strategic implications of decision comprehensiveness, *Academy of Management Review*, 32: 361–376.

35. J. Surroca, J. A. Tribo, & S. Waddock, 2010, Corporate responsibility and financial performance: The role of intangible resources, *Strategic Management Journal*, 31: 463–490; T. M. Jones, W. Felps, & G. A. Bigley, 2007, Ethical theory and stakeholder-related decisions: The role of stakeholder culture, *Academy of Management Review*, 32: 137–155.

36. M. S. Gary & R. E. Wood, 2011, Mental models decision rules, and performance heterogeneity, *Strategic Management Journal*, 32: 569–594; Y. Deutsch, T. Keil, & T. Laamanen, 2007, Decision making in acquisitions: The effect of outside directors' compensation on acquisition patterns, *Journal of Management*, 33: 30–56.

37. S. W. Bradley, H. Aldrich, D. A. Shepherd, & J. Wiklund, 2011, Resources, environmental change and survival: Asymmetric paths of young independent and subsidiary organizations, *Strategic Management Journal*, 32: 486–509; A. Phene & P. Almieda, 2008, Innovation in multinational subsidiaries: The role of knowledge assimilation and subsidiary capabilities, *Journal of International Business Studies,* 39: 901–919.

38. Y. Zhang & J. Gimeno, 2010, Earnings pressure and competitive behavior: Evidence from the US Electricity industry, *Academy of Management Journal*, 53: 743–768; L. M. Lodish & C. F. Mela, 2007, If brands are built over years, why are they managed over quarters? *Harvard Business Review*, 85(7/8): 104–112.

39. P. M. Madsen & V. Desai, 2010, Failing to learn? The effects of failure and success on organizational learning in the global orbital launch vehicle industry, *Academy of Management Journal*, 53: 451–476; P. C. Nutt, 2002, *Why Decisions Fail*, San Francisco: Berrett-Koehler Publishers.

40. J. P. Eggers, 2011, All experience is not created equal: Learning, adapting and focusing in product portfolio management, *Strategic Management Journal*, in press.

41. J. D. Ford & L. W. Ford, 2010, Stop blaming resistance to change and start using it, *Organizational Dynamics*, 39: 24–36.

42. Y. Zhang, H. Li, Y Li, & L.-A. Zhou, 2010, FDI spillovers in an emerging market: The role of foreign firms' country origin diversity and domestic firms' absorptive capacity, *Strategic Management Journal*, 31: 969–989; I. Mitroff, 2008, Knowing: How we know is as important as what we know, *Journal of Business Strategy*, 29(3): 13–22.

43. 2011, Polaroid: Trying to make goods out of Gaga, *Boston Globe*, http://www .boston.com, January 17.

44. O.-P. Kauppila, 2010, Creating ambidexterity by integrating and balancing structurally separate interorganizational partnerships, *Strategic Organization*, 8: 283–312; N. P. Tuan & T. Yishi, 2010, Organisational capabilities, competitive advantage and performance in supporting industries in Vietnam, *Asian Academy of Management Journal*, 15: 1–21; R. Amit & P. J. H. Schoemaker, 1993, Strategic assets and organizational rent, *Strategic Management Journal*, 14: 33–46.

45. J. Li & Y. Tang, 2010, CEO hubris and firm risk taking in China: The moderating role of managerial discretion, *Academy of Management Journal*, 53: 45–68; S. J. Carson, A. Madhok, & T. Wu, 2006, Uncertainty, opportunism, and governance: The effects of volatility and ambiguity on formal and relational contracting, *Academy of Management Journal*, 49: 1058–1077; R. E. Hoskisson & L. W. Busenitz, 2001, Market uncertainty and learning distance in corporate entrepreneurship entry mode choice, in M. A. Hitt, R. D. Ireland, S. M. Camp, & D. L. Sexton (eds.), *Strategic Entrepreneurship: Creating a New Integrated Mindset*, Oxford, UK: Blackwell Publishers, 151–172.

46. S. S. K. Lam & J. C. K. Young, 2010, Staff localization and environmental uncertainty on firm performance in China, *Asia Pacific Journal of Management*, 27: 677–695; C. M. Fiol & E. J. O'Connor, 2003, Waking up! Mindfulness in the face of bandwagons, *Academy of Management Review*, 28: 54–70.

47. C. Helman, 2011, Peabody energy chief: Coal is the fastest growing fuel in the world, *Forbes Online*, http://www.forbes .com, March 11.

48. A. Leiponen & C. E. Helfat, 2010, Innovation objectives, knowledge sources, and the benefits of breadth, *Strategic Management Journal*, 31: 224–236; G. P. West, III, 2007, Collective cognition: When entrepreneurial teams, not individuals, make decisions, *Entrepreneurship Theory and Practice*, 31: 77–102.

49. J. W. Fredrickson, A. Davis-Blake, & W. G. Sanders, 2010, Sharing the wealth: Social comparisons and pay dispersion in the CEO's top team, *Strategic Management Journal*, 31: 1031-1053; N. J. Hiller & D. C. Hambrick, 2005, Conceptualizing executive hubris: The role of (hyper-) core self-evaluations in strategic decision making, *Strategic Management Journal*, 26: 297–319.

50. G. Davies, R. Chum, & M. A. Kamins, 2010, Reputation gaps and the performance of service organizations, *Strategic Management Journal*, 31: 530–546.

51. Ndofor, Sirmon, & He, Firm resources, competitive actions and performance; P. A. Geroski, J. Mata, & P. Portugal, 2010, Founding conditions and the survival of new firms, *Strategic Management Journal*, 31: 510–529.

52. J. Bae, F. C. Wezel, & J. Koo, 2011, Cross-cutting ties, organizational density, and new firm formation in the U.S. biotech industry, *Academy of Management Journal*, 54: 295–311; R. H. Lester, A. Hillman, A. Zardkoohi, & A. A. Cannella, 2008, Former government officials as outside directors: The role of human and social capital, *Academy of Management Journal*, 51: 999–1013.

53. J. M. Shaver, 2011, The benefits of geographic sales diversification: How exporting facilitates capital investment, *Strategic Management Journal*, in press; K. Meyer, S. Estrin, S. K. Bhaumik, & M. W. Peng, 2009, Institutions, resources, and entry strategies in emerging economies, *Strategic Management Journal*, 30: 61–80.

54. A. Vance, 2011, The cloud: Battle of the tech titans, *Bloomberg Businessweek*, http://www.businessweek.com, March 3.

55. D. Somaya, Y. Kim, & N. S. Vonortas, 2011, Exclusivity in licensing alliances: Using hostages to support technology commercialization, *Strategic Management Journal*, 32: 159–186; K. G. Smith, C. J. Collins, & K. D. Clark, 2005, Existing knowledge, knowledge creation capability, and the rate of new product introduction in high-technology firms, *Academy of Management Journal*, 48: 346–357; S. G. Winter, 2005, Developing evolutionary theory for economics and management, in K. G. Smith and M. A. Hitt (eds.), *Great Minds in Management: The Process of Theory Development*, Oxford, UK: Oxford University Press, 509–546.

56. A. M. Arikan & L. Capon, 2010, Do newly public acquirers benefit or suffer from their pre-IPO affiliations with underwriters and VCs? *Strategic Management Journal*, 31: 1257–1298; J. A. Parnell, J. E. Spillan, & D. L. Lester, 2010, Crisis aversion and sustainable strategic management (SSM)

in emerging economies, *International Journal of Sustainable Strategic Management*, 2: 41–59; J. A. Dubin, 2007, Valuing intangible assets with a nested logit market share model, *Journal of Econometrics*, 139: 285–302.

57. A. M. Webber, 2000, New math for a new economy, *Fast Company*, January/February, 214–224.

58. E. Danneels, 2011, Trying to become a different type of company: Dynamic capability at Smith Corona, *Strategic Management Journal*, 32: 1–31; M. Song, C. Droge, S. Hanvanich, & R. Calantone, 2005, Marketing and technology resource complementarity: An analysis of their interaction effect in two environmental contexts, *Strategic Management Journal*, 26: 259–276.

59. K. E. Meyer, R. Mudambi, & R. Narula, 2011, Multinational enterprises ad local contexts: The opportunities and challenges of multiple embeddedness, *Journal of Management Studies*, 48: 235–252.

60. J. B. Quinn, P. Anderson, & S. Finkelstein, 1996, Making the most of the best, *Harvard Business Review*, 74(2): 71–80.

61. R. E. Ployhart, C. H. Van Iddekinge, & W. I. Mackenzie, 2011, Acquiring and developing human capital in service contexts: The interconnectedness of human capital resources, *Academy of Management Journal*, 54: 353–368; N. Stieglitz & K. Heine, 2007, Innovations and the role of complementarities in a strategic theory of the firm, *Strategic Management Journal*, 28: 1–15.

62. L. Diestre & N. Rajagopalan, 2011, An environmental perspective on diversification: The effects of chemical relatedness and regulatory sanctions, *Academy of Management Journal*, 54: 97–115.

63. M D. Pfarrer, T. G. Pollock, & V. P. Rindova, 2010, A tale of two assets: The effects of firm reputation and celebrity on earnings surprises and investors' reactions, *Academy of Management Journal*, 53: 1131–1152; T. G. Pollock, G. Chen, & E. M. Jackson, 2010, How much prestige is enough? Assessing the value of multiple types of high-status affiliates for young firms, *Journal of Business Venturing*, 25: 6–23.

64. P. M. Lee, T. G. Pollock, & K. Jin, 2011, The contingent value of venture capitalist reputation, *Strategic Organization*, 9: 33–69; J. J. Ebbers & N. M. Wijnberg, 2011, Nascent ventures competing for start-up capital: Matching reputations and investors, *Journal of Business Venturing*, in press.

65. K. T. Smith, M. Smith, & K. Wang, 2010, Does brand management of corporate reputation translate into higher market value? *Journal of Strategic Marketing*, 18: 201–221.

66. N. Rosenbusch & J. Brinckmann, 2011, Is innovation always beneficial? A meta-analysis of the relationship between innovation and performance in SMEs, *Journal of Business Venturing*, 26: 441–457; J. Blasberg & V. Vishwanath, 2003, Making cool brands hot, *Harvard Business Review*, 81(6): 20–22.

67. 2011, Harley-Davidson Motor Clothes Merchandise, June 3, http://www.harley-davidson.com.

68. T. Isobe, S. Makino, & D. B. Montgomery, 2008, Technological capabilities and firm performance: The case of small manufacturing firms in Japan, *Asia Pacific Journal of Management*, 25: 413–425; S. Dutta, O. Narasimhan, & S. Rajiv, 2005, Conceptualizing and measuring capabilities: Methodology and empirical application, *Strategic Management Journal*, 26: 277–285.

69. R. W. Coff, 2010, The coevolution of rent appropriation and capability development, *Strategic Management Journal*, 31: 711–733; M. Kroll, B. A. Walters, & P. Wright, 2008, Board vigilance, director experience and corporate outcomes, *Strategic Management Journal*, 29: 363–282; J. Bitar & T. Hafsi, 2007, Strategizing through the capability lens: Sources and outcomes of integration, *Management Decision*, 45: 403–419.

70. T. Dalziel, R. J. Gentry, & M. Bowerman, 2011, An integrated agency-resource dependence view of the influence of directors' human and relational capital on firms' R&D spending, *Journal of Management Studies*, in press; T. A. Stewart & A. P. Raman, 2007, Lessons from Toyota's long drive, *Harvard Business Review*, 85(7/8): 74–83.

71. S. Lohr, 2011, Lessons in longevity, from IBM, *The New York Times*, http://www.nytimes.com, June 18.

72. N. P. Tuan & T. Yoshi, 2010, Organisational capabilities, competitive advantage and performance in supporting industries in Vietnam, *Asian Academy of Management Journal*, 15: 1–21; C. Zott, 2003, Dynamic capabilities and the emergence of intraindustry differential firm performance: Insights from a simulation study, *Strategic Management Journal*, 24: 97–125.

73. H. R. Greve, 2009, Bigger and safer: The diffusion of competitive advantage, *Strategic Management Journal*, 30: 1–23; C. K. Prahalad & G. Hamel, 1990, The core competence of the corporation, *Harvard Business Review*, 68(3): 79–93.

74. Y. I. Kane & I. Sherr, 2011, Secrets from Apple's genius bar: Full loyalty, no negativity, *Wall Street Journal*, http://www.wsj.com, June 15.

75. M. Makri, M. A. Hitt, & P. J. Lane, 2010, Complementary technologies, knowledge relatedness, and invention outcomes in high technology mergers and acquisitions, *Strategic Management Journal*, 31: 602–628; S. Newbert, 2008, Value, rareness, competitive advantage, and performance: A conceptual-level empirical investigation of the resource-based view of the firm, *Strategic Management Journal*, 29: 745–768.

76. 2011, Wal-Mart's green initiatives shouldn't be ignored, *Los Angeles Times*, http://www.latimes.com, May 30.

77. J. A. Trachtenberg, 2011, Penguin CEO adjusts to e-books but sees room for the old, *Wall Street Journal*, http://www.wsj.com, May 9.

78. Q. Gu & J. W. Lu, 2011, Effects of inward investment on outward investment: The venture capital industry worldwide—1985–2007, *Journal of International Business Studies*, 42: 263–284; S. A. Zahra, 2008, The virtuous cycle of discovery and creation of entrepreneurial opportunities, *Strategic Entrepreneurship Journal*, 2: 243–257.

79. C. A. Coen & C. A. Maritan, 2011, Investing in capabilities: The dynamics of resource allocation, *Organization Science*, 22: 199–217.

80. J. B. Barney, 1991, Firm resources and sustained competitive advantage, *Journal of Management*, 17: 99–120.

81. C. C. Maurer, P. Bansal, & M. M. Crossan, 2011, Creating economic value through social values: Introducing a culturally informed resource-based view, *Organization Science*, 22: 432–448.

82. K. Stinebaker, 2007, Global company puts focus on people, *Houston Chronicle Online*, http://www.chron.com, February 18.

83. M. H. Kinc & J. D. W. Morecroft, 2010, Managerial decision making and firm performance under a resource-based paradigm, *Strategic Management Journal*, 31: 1164–1182; A. W. King & C. P. Zeithaml, 2001, Competencies and firm performance: Examining the causal ambiguity paradox, *Strategic Management Journal*, 22: 75–99.

84. Barney, Firm resources, 111.

85. K. Srikanth & P. Puranam, 2011, Integrating distributed work: Comparing task design, communication, and tacit coordination mechanisms, *Strategic Management Journal*, 32: 849–875; A. K. Chatterjee, 2009, Spawned with a silver spoon? Entrepreneurial performance and innovation in the medical device industry, *Strategic Management Journal*, 30: 185–206.

86. R. Belderbos, W. van Olffen, & J. Zou, 2011, General and specific social learning mechanisms in foreign investment location choice, *Strategic Management Journal*, 32: in press; A. Leiponen & C. E. Helfat, 2010, Innovation objectives, knowledge sources, and the benefits of breadth, *Strategic Management Journal*, 31: 224–236.

87. M. E. Porter, 1985, *Competitive Advantage*, New York: Free Press, 33–61.

88. Z. G. Zacharia, N. W. Nix, & R. F. Lusch, 2011, Capabilities that enhance outcomes of an episodic supply chain collaboration, *Journal of Operations Management*, 29: 591–603; J. Alcacer, 2006, Location choices across the value chain: How activity and capability influence co-location, *Management Science*, 52: 1457–1471.

89. A. Rugman, A. Verbeke, & W. Yuan, 2011, Re-conceptualizing Bartlett and Ghoshal's classification of national subsidiary roles in the multinational enterprise, *Journal of Management Studies*, 48: 253–277; H. U. Lee & J.-H. Park, 2008, The influence of top management team international exposure on international alliance formation, *Journal of Management Studies*, 45: 961–981; 2007, Riding the global value chain, *Chief Executive Online*, January/February, http://www .chiefexecutive.net.

90. S. M. Mudambi & S. Tallman, 2010, Make, buy or ally? Theoretical perspectives on knowledge process outsourcing through alliances, *Journal of Management Studies*, 47: 1434–1456; R. Locke & M. Romis, 2007, Global supply chain, MIT *Sloan Management Review*, 48(2): 54–62.

91. U. Zander & L. Zander, 2010, Opening the grey box: Social communities, knowledge and culture in acquisitions, *Journal of International Business Studies*, 41: 27–37; C. L. Luk, O. H. M. Yau, L. Y. M. Sin, A. C. B. Tse, R. P. M. Chow, & J. S. Y. Lee, 2008, The effects of social capital and organizational innovativeness in different institutional contexts, *Journal of International Business Studies*, 39: 589–612.

92. R. M. Wiseman, G. Cuevas-Rodriguez, & L. R. Gomez-Mejia, 2011, Towards a social theory of agency, *Journal of Management Studies*, in press; L .F. Mesquita, J. An, & T. H. Brush, 2008, Comparing the resource-based and relational views: Knowledge transfer and spillover in vertical alliances, *Strategic Management Journal*, 29: 913–941.

93. R. E. Hoskisson, J. Covin, H. W. Volberda, & R. A. Johnson, 2011, Revitalizing entrepreneurship: The search for new research opportunities, *Journal of Management Studies*, in press; A. A. Lado, R. R. Dant, & A. G. Tekleab, 2008, Trust-opportunism paradox, relationalism, and performance in interfirm relationships: Evidence from the retail industry, *Strategic Management Journal*, 29: 401–423; S. N. Wasti & S. A. Wasti, 2008, Trust in buyer-supplier relations: The case of the Turkish automotive industry, *Journal of International Business Studies*, 39: 118–131.

94. D. Faems, M. Janssens, A. Madhok, & Van Looy, 2008, Toward an integrative perspective on alliance governance: Connecting contract design, trust dynamics and contract application, *Academy of Management Journal*, 51:1053–1078.

95. A. Hecker & T. Kretschmer, 2011, Outsourcing decisions: The effect of scale economies and market structure, *Strategic Organization*, 8: 155–175.

96. 2011, Not-for-profit organizations, *Outsourcing-law.com*, http://www .outsourcing-law.com, June 8; P. W. Tam, 2007, Business technology: Outsourcing finds new niche, *Wall Street Journal*, April 17, B5.

97. S. Nadkami & P. Hermann, 2010, CEO personality, strategic flexibility, and firm performance: The case of the Indian business process outsourcing industry, *Academy of Management Journal*, 53: 1050–1073.

98. R. Liu, D. J. Feils, & B. Scholnick, 2011, Why are different services outsourced to different countries? *Journal of International Business Studies*, 42: 558–571.

99. F. Castellucci & G. Ertug, 2010, What's in it for them? Advantages of higher-status partners in exchange relationships, *Academy of Management Journal*, 53: 149–166; C. C. De Fontenay & J. S. Gans, 2008, A bargaining perspective on strategic outsourcing and supply competition, *Strategic Management Journal*, 29: 819–839; A. Tiwana & M. Keil, 2007, Does peripheral knowledge complement control? An empirical test in technology outsourcing alliances, *Strategic Management Journal*, 28: 623–634.

100. M. H. Zack & S. Singh, 2010, A knowledge-based view of outsourcing, *International Journal of Strategic Change Management*, 2: 32–53.

101. M. Reitzig & S. Wagner, 2010, The hidden costs of outsourcing: Evidence from patent data, *Strategic Management Journal*, 31: 1183–1201; A. Tiwana, 2008, Does interfirm modularity complement ignorance? A field study of software outsourcing alliances, *Strategic Management Journal*, 29: 1241–1252.

102. C. S. Katsikeas, D. Skarmeas, & D. C. Bello, 2009, Developing successful trust-based international exchange relationships, *Journal of International Business Studies*, 40: 132–155; E. Perez & J. Karp, 2007, U.S. to probe outsourcing after ITT case, *Wall Street Journal* (Eastern Edition), March 28, A3, A6.

103. C. Grimpe & U. Kaiser, 2010, Balancing internal and external knowledge acquisition: The gains and pains from R&D outsourcing, *Journal of Management Studies*, 47: 1483–1509; C. Weigelt & M. B. Sarkar, 2009, Learning from supply-side agents: The impact of technology solution providers' experiential diversity on clients' innovation adoption, 52: 37–60.

104. P. D. O. Jensen & T. Pederson, 2011, The economic geography of offshoring: The fit between activities and local context, *Journal of Management Studies*, 48: 352–372; F. J. Contractor, V. Kumar, S. K. Kundu, & T. Pedersen, 2010, Reconceptualizing the firm in a world of outsourcing and offshoring: The organizational and geographical relocation of high-value company functions, *Journal of Management Studies*, 47: 1417–1433.

105. N. Heath, 2009, Outsourcing: The new hot spots, *BusinessWeek*, http://www .businessweek.com, February 20.

106. S. Hamm, 2009, IBM: Outsourcing at home, *BusinessWeek*, http://www .businessweek.com, January 16.

107. Y. Li, Z. Wei, & Y. Liu, 2010, strategic orientations, knowledge acquisition, and firm performance: The perspective of the vendor in cross-border outsourcing, *Journal of Management Studies*, 47: 1457–1482; M. A. Hitt, D. Ahlstrom, M. T. Dacin, E. Levitas, & L. Svobodina, 2004, The institutional effects on strategic alliance partner selection in transition economies: China versus Russia, *Organization Science*, 15: 173–185.

108. D. M. Sullivan & M. R. Marvel, 2011, Knowledge acquisition, network reliance, and early-stage technology venture outcomes, *Journal of Management Studies*, 48: in press; M. Gibbert, M. Hoegl, & L. Valikangas, 2007, In praise of resource constraints, *MIT Sloan Management Review*, 48(3): 15–17, 126.

109. E. Rawley, 2010, Diversification, coordination costs, and organizational rigidity: Evidence from microdata, *Strategic Management Journal*, 31: 873–891.

110. D. L. Barton, 1995, *Wellsprings of knowledge: Building and sustaining the sources of innovation*, Boston: Harvard Business School Press, 30–31.

111. M. Spector & J. A. Trachtenberg, 2011, Borders mulls piecemeal sale, *Wall Street Journal*, http://www.wsj.com, May 13.

PART 2
Strategic Actions: Strategy Formulation

4. Business-Level Strategy, 100

5. Competitive Rivalry and Competitive Dynamics, 130

6. Corporate-Level Strategy, 162

7. Merger and Acquisition Strategies, 192

8. International Strategy, 224

9. Cooperative Strategy, 260

CHAPTER 4
Business-Level Strategy

Studying this chapter should provide you with the strategic management knowledge needed to:

1. Define business-level strategy.

2. Discuss the relationship between customers and business-level strategies in terms of *who*, *what*, and *how*.

3. Explain the differences among business-level strategies.

4. Use the five forces of competition model to explain how above-average returns can be earned through each business-level strategy.

5. Describe the risks of using each of the business-level strategies.

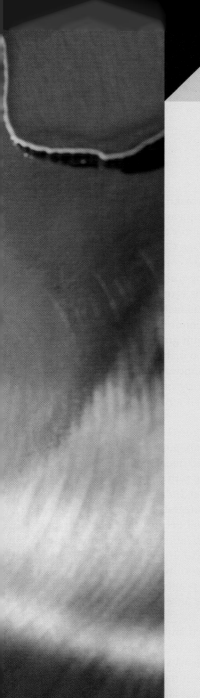

MORNING JOE IN THE AFTERNOON IN CHINA, INDIA, AND BEYOND: THE NEW STARBUCKS

Starbucks changed how people in the United States ordered coffee, how much they paid for it, and how and where they drank it. In other words, this company changed the way that Americans experienced their cup of "joe". They now drink coffee in many places, such as in coffee shops while using Wi-Fi, or on trains and subways, ordering grandes, lattes, and other once strange-sounding names. Most of all, they are willing to pay more than $4 for a cup of "joe". With thousands of stores on street corners, in retail outlets in shopping malls, and in bookstores, among other locations, Starbucks seemed almost on its way toward becoming a generic name for a cup of coffee. It had become one of the "darlings" of Wall Street because almost every action it took appeared to be successful.

But, on the way to the bank, something happened in 2008. A major recession occurred and consumers were less willing to pay the high prices for a premium cup of coffee, leading to a reduction in same-store sales for the first time in Starbucks' history. In addition, competitors (e.g., McDonald's) started to eat away at Starbucks' market share. Finally, Starbucks appeared to be unable to control the quality of the "experience" across the thousands of stores. In short, Starbucks started to lose its "differentiation" and its luster. Howard Schultz stepped up to take over the CEO position again, and shortly thereafter he announced major changes. For one, he announced that Starbucks was closing 900 poorly performing stores in the United

Starbucks Corp., the world's biggest coffee-shop chain, began selling its Via instant coffee in the greater China region, which it forecast will be its biggest growth market in two years.

Bloomberg/Getty Images

States. In addition, Schultz announced that the firm would regain its focus on innovation.

With more than 17,000 stores globally, Starbucks was on the move again in 2011. For example, it has regained its emphasis on innovation by introducing several new products, such as its instant coffee, Via. Although originally Starbucks' customers questioned the sale of instant coffee, Via has been highly successful with sales growing to more than $200 million annually in only two years after its introduction. Starbucks celebrated its 40th anniversary with a new brand/logo, in which the name of the company was deleted. Although some questioned this move, others think it will have a neutral to positive impact. Essentially, the Starbucks name was removed to allow the company to introduce new products well beyond coffee, which has become synonymous with the product. Starbucks also announced an agreement with Green Mountain to distribute Starbucks coffee pods for use with that company's Keurig single cup coffee brewing system.

A significant part of Starbucks' growth goals target China and India. In 2001, Starbucks had 430 stores in China with plans to have 1,500 stores operating in the country by 2015. Additionally, Starbucks signed an agreement with Tata Coffee in India to buy coffee beans and to open stores in hotels and other Tata-affiliated retail stores in India. Along with these developments, Starbucks now allows customers to pay for their purchases with their iPhones. Starbucks continues to display environmental consciousness with the goal of recycling all of its used paper cups. Finally, it continues to offer all of its employees, full-time and part-time, health insurance that costs the company about $250 million annually.

Therefore, Starbucks has stepped up to differentiate the firm from all competitors and many other companies operating in other industries as well.

Sources: C. C. Miller, 2011, A changed Starbucks, a changed CEO, *The New York Times*, www.nytimes.com, March 12; J. Jargon, 2011, Starbucks in pod pack, *Wall Street Journal*, www.online.wsj.com, March 11; F. Hardaway, 2011, Happy birthday Starbucks, *Fast Company*, www.fastcompany.com, March 8; C. C. Miller, 2011, Now at Starbucks: Buy a latte by waving your phone, *The New York Times*, www.nytimes.com, January 16; V. Bajaj, 2011, A Starbucks venture in tea-drinking India, *The New York Times*, www.nytimes.com, January 13; R. Matuson, 2011, The naked truth about Starbucks, *Fast Company*, www.fastcompany.com, January 11; L. Kaufman, 2010, Where does that Starbucks cup go? *The New York Times*, www.nytimes.com, November 30.

Learn more about Starbuck's innovation.

www.cengagebrain .com

Explore Starbucks' global expansion strategy.

www.cengagebrain .com

A **business-level strategy** is an integrated and coordinated set of commitments and actions the firm uses to gain a competitive advantage by exploiting core competencies in specific product markets.

Increasingly important to firm success,[1] strategy is concerned with making choices among two or more alternatives.[2] As we noted in Chapter 1, when choosing a strategy, the firm decides to pursue one course of action instead of others. The choices are influenced by opportunities and threats in the firm's external environment[3] (see Chapter 2) as well as the nature and quality of the resources, capabilities, and core competencies in its internal organization[4] (see Chapter 3). As we see in the Opening Case, Starbucks was once a huge leader in its industry but began to suffer from poor economic times and from competition. It had lost most of its differentiation. Even firms such as McDonald's, not known for offering premium products, began providing premium coffee drinks at a much lower price than Starbucks. As a result, Starbucks sales quit growing and began shrinking at many of its stores. Since that time, Starbucks has taken major steps to regain its differentiation. It closed almost 900 stores and became more innovative, introducing several new products (e.g., Via) and new processes (e.g., allowing payments with an iPhone). Starbucks appears to have recaptured its luster and lead among competitors using its differentiated strategy.

The fundamental objective of using any type of strategy (see Figure 1.1) is to gain strategic competitiveness and earn above-average returns.[5] Strategies are purposeful, precede the taking of actions to which they apply, and demonstrate a shared understanding of the firm's vision and mission.[6] Starbucks' decisions to form an alliance with Green Mountain to offer coffee pods for the Keurig Brewing systems and to enter India's market were quite purposeful. An effectively formulated strategy marshals, integrates, and allocates the firm's resources, capabilities, and competencies so that it will be properly aligned with its external environment.[7] A properly developed strategy also rationalizes the firm's vision and mission along with the actions taken to achieve them.[8] Information about a host of variables including markets, customers, technology, worldwide finance, and the changing world economy must be collected and analyzed to properly form and use strategies. In the final analysis, sound strategic choices that reduce uncertainty regarding outcomes are the foundation for building successful strategies.[9]

Business-level strategy, this chapter's focus, is an integrated and coordinated set of commitments and actions the firm uses to gain a competitive advantage by exploiting core competencies in specific product markets.[10] Business-level strategy indicates the choices the firm has made about how it intends to compete in individual product markets. The choices are important because long-term performance is linked to a firm's strategies.[11] Given the complexity of successfully competing in the global economy, the choices about how the firm will compete can be difficult.[12] For example, MySpace, a social networking site, was the largest networking site in 2006 with approximately 50 million users. But, within two years, it lost the lead to a fast-developing social networking site, Facebook. Facebook quickly enlarged its market share with more than 600 million users in 2011, while MySpace had only about 34 million users.[13] Facebook has made several major competitive moves in recent years challenging MySpace to further adjust or fine-tune its strategy as it engages its major competitor in various competitive battles.

Every firm must form and use a business-level strategy. However, every firm may not use all the strategies—corporate-level, merger and acquisition, international, and cooperative—that we examine in Chapters 6 through 9. A firm competing in a single-product market area in a single geographic location does not need a corporate-level strategy to deal with product diversity or an international strategy to deal with geographic diversity. In contrast, a diversified firm will use one of the corporate-level strategies as well as a separate business-level strategy for each product market area in which it competes. Every firm—from the local dry cleaner to the multinational corporation—must develop and use at least one business-level strategy. Thus business-level strategy is the *core* strategy—the strategy that the firm forms to describe how it intends to compete in a product market.[14]

We discuss several topics to examine business-level strategies. Because customers are the foundation of successful business-level strategies and should never be taken for granted,[15] we present information about customers that is relevant to business-level strategies. In terms of customers, when selecting a business-level strategy the firm determines (1) *who* will be served, (2) *what* needs those target customers have that it will satisfy, and (3) *how* those needs will be satisfied. Selecting customers and deciding which of their needs the firm will try to satisfy, as well as how it will do so, are challenging tasks. Global competition has created many attractive options for customers, thus making it difficult to determine the strategy to best serve them.[16] Effective global competitors have become adept at identifying the needs of customers in different cultures and geographic regions as well as learning how to quickly and successfully adapt the functionality of a firm's good or service to meet those needs.

Descriptions of the purpose of business-level strategies—and of the five business-level strategies—follow the discussion of customers. The five strategies we examine are called *generic* because they can be used in any organization competing in any industry.[17] Our analysis describes how effective use of each strategy allows the firm to favorably position itself relative to the five competitive forces in the industry (see Chapter 2). In addition, we use the value chain (see Chapter 3) to show examples of the primary and support activities necessary to implement specific business-level strategies. Because no strategy is risk-free,[18] we also describe the different risks the firm may encounter when using these strategies. In Chapter 11, we explain the organizational structures and controls linked with the successful use of each business-level strategy.

Customers: Their Relationship with Business-Level Strategies

Strategic competitiveness results only when the firm satisfies a group of customers by using its competitive advantages as the basis for competing in individual product markets.[19] A key reason firms must satisfy customers with their business-level strategy is that returns earned from relationships with customers are the lifeblood of all organizations.[20]

The most successful companies try to find new ways to satisfy current customers and/or to meet the needs of new customers. Being able to do this can be even more difficult when firms and consumers face challenging economic conditions. During such times, firms may decide to reduce their workforce to control costs. This can lead to problems, however, when having fewer employees makes it more difficult for companies to meet individual customers' needs and expectations. In these instances, some suggest that firms should follow several courses of action, including paying extra attention to their best customers and developing a flexible workforce by cross-training employees so they can undertake a variety of responsibilities on their jobs. Amazon.com, insurer USAA, and Lexus have been identified as "customer service champions" because they devote extra care and attention to customer service especially during challenging economic times.[21]

Effectively Managing Relationships with Customers

The firm's relationships with its customers are strengthened when it delivers superior value to them. Strong interactive relationships with customers often provide the foundation for the firm's efforts to profitably serve customers' unique needs.

As the following statement shows, Caesar's Entertainment (the world's largest provider of branded casino entertainment) is committed to providing superior value to customers: "Caesar's Entertainment is focused on building loyalty and value with its customers through a unique combination of great service, excellent products, unsurpassed distribution, operational excellence and technology leadership."[22] Importantly, as Caesar's appears to anticipate, delivering superior value often results in increased customer loyalty. In turn, customer loyalty has a positive relationship with profitability. However, more choices and easily accessible information about the functionality of firms' products are creating increasingly sophisticated and knowledgeable customers, making it difficult to earn their loyalty.[23]

A number of companies have become skilled at the art of *managing* all aspects of their relationship with their customers.[24] For example, Amazon.com is widely recognized for the quality of information it maintains about its customers, the services it renders, and its ability to anticipate customers' needs. Using the information it has, Amazon tries to serve what it believes are the unique needs of each customer; and it has a strong reputation for being able to successfully do this.[25]

As we discuss next, firms' relationships with customers are characterized by three dimensions. Companies such as Acer and Amazon.com understand these dimensions and manage their relationships with customers in light of them.

Reach, Richness, and Affiliation

The *reach* dimension of relationships with customers is concerned with the firm's access and connection to customers. In general, firms seek to extend their reach, adding customers in the process of doing so.

Reach is an especially critical dimension for social networking sites such as Facebook and MySpace in that the value these firms create for users is to connect them with others. As noted earlier, traffic to MySpace has been declining in recent years; at the same time, the number of Facebook users has been dramatically increasing in the United States and abroad. As a result, Facebook had more than 600 million users in 2011, almost 1800 percent more than MySpace[26] Reach is also important to Netflix. Fortunately for this firm, recent results indicate that its reach continues to expand: "Netflix ended 2010 with approximately 20.01 million total subscribers, representing a 17.2 percent increase over the end of 2009."[27]

Packages of DVDs await shipment at the Netflix.com headquarters in San Jose, CA.

Justin Sullivan/Stringer/Getty Images News/Getty Images

Richness, the second dimension of firms' relationships with customers, is concerned with the depth and detail of the two-way flow of information between the firm and the customer. The potential of the richness dimension to help the firm establish a competitive advantage in its relationship with customers leads many firms to offer online services in order to better manage information exchanges with their customers. Broader and deeper information-based exchanges allow firms to better understand their customers and their needs. Such exchanges also enable customers to become more knowledgeable about how the firm can satisfy them. Internet technology and e-commerce transactions have substantially reduced the costs of meaningful information exchanges with current and potential customers.

As we have noted, Amazon is a leader in using the Internet to build relationships with customers. In fact, it bills itself as the most "customer-centric company" on earth. Amazon and other firms use rich information from customers to help them develop innovative new products that better satisfy customers' needs.[28]

Affiliation, the third dimension, is concerned with facilitating useful interactions with customers. Viewing the world through the customer's eyes and constantly seeking ways to create more value for the customer have positive effects in terms of affiliation. This approach enhances customer satisfaction and produces fewer customer complaints. In fact, for services, customers often do not complain when dissatisfied; instead they simply go to competitors for their service needs.[29] Internet navigators such as Microsoft's MSN Autos help online clients find and sort information. MSN Autos provides data and software to prospective car buyers that enable them to compare car models along multiple objective specifications. A prospective buyer who has selected a specific car based on comparisons of different models can then be linked to dealers that meet the customer's needs and purchasing requirements. Information about other relevant issues such as financing and insurance and even local traffic patterns is also available at the site. Because its revenues come not from the final customer or end user but from other sources (such as advertisements on its Web site, hyperlinks, and associated products and services), MSN Autos represents the customer's interests, a service that fosters affiliation.[30]

As we discuss next, effectively managing customer relationships (along the dimensions of reach, richness, and affiliation) helps the firm answer questions related to the issues of *who, what,* and *how.*

Who: Determining the Customers to Serve

Deciding *who* the target customer is that the firm intends to serve with its business-level strategy is an important decision.[31] Companies divide customers into groups based on differences in the customers' needs (needs are discussed further in the next section) to make this decision. Dividing customers into groups based on their needs is called **market segmentation**, which is a process that clusters people with similar needs into individual and identifiable groups.[32] In the animal food products business, for example, the food-product needs of owners of companion pets (e.g., dogs and cats) differ from the needs for food and health-related products of those owning production animals (e.g., livestock). A subsidiary of Colgate-Palmolive, Hill's Pet Nutrition sells food products for pets. In fact, the company's mission is "to help enrich and lengthen the special relationship between people and their pets."[33] Thus, Hill's Pet Nutrition targets the needs of different segments of customers with the food products it sells for animals.

Almost any identifiable human or organizational characteristic can be used to subdivide a market into segments that differ from one another on a given characteristic. Common characteristics on which customers' needs vary are illustrated in Table 4.1.

Market segmentation is a process used to cluster people with similar needs into individual and identifiable groups.

Table 4.1 Basis for Customer Segmentation

Consumer Markets
1. Demographic factors (age, income, sex, etc.)
2. Socioeconomic factors (social class, stage in the family life cycle)
3. Geographic factors (cultural, regional, and national differences)
4. Psychological factors (lifestyle, personality traits)
5. Consumption patterns (heavy, moderate, and light users)
6. Perceptual factors (benefit segmentation, perceptual mapping)

Industrial Markets
1. End-use segments (identified by SIC code)
2. Product segments (based on technological differences or production economics)
3. Geographic segments (defined by boundaries between countries or by regional differences within them)
4. Common buying factor segments (cut across product market and geographic segments)
5. Customer size segments

Source: Based on information in S. C. Jain, 2009, *Marketing Planning and Strategy*, Mason, OH: South-Western-Cengage Custom Publishing.

What: Determining Which Customer Needs to Satisfy

After the firm decides *who* it will serve, it must identify the targeted customer group's needs that its goods or services can satisfy. In a general sense, *needs (what)* are related to a product's benefits and features.[34] Successful firms learn how to deliver to customers what they want, when they want it.[35] Having close and frequent interactions with both current and potential customers helps the firm identify those individuals' and groups' current and future needs.[36]

From a strategic perspective, a basic need of all customers is to buy products that create value for them. The generalized forms of value that goods or services provide are either low cost with acceptable features or highly differentiated features with acceptable cost. In the recent global financial crisis, companies across industries recognized their customers' needs to feel as secure as possible when making purchases. Allowing customers to return their cars if they lose their job within 12 months of the purchase is how Hyundai Motors decided to address this consumer need, creating value in the form of security.[37]

The most effective firms continuously strive to anticipate changes in customers' needs. The firm that fails to anticipate and certainly to recognize changes in its customers' needs may lose its customers to competitors whose products can provide more value to the focal firm's customers. It is also recognized that consumer needs and desires have been changing in recent years. For example, more consumers desire to have an experience rather than to simply purchase a good or service. As a result, one of Starbucks' goals has been to provide an experience, not just a cup of coffee. Customers also prefer to receive customized goods and services. Again, Starbucks has been doing this for some time, allowing customers to design their own drinks, within their menus (which have become rather extensive over time). They also demand fast service. Consumers in the United States have been known for their impatience, but rapid service is now expected by most consumers.[38] Unhappy consumers lead to lost sales, theirs and others who learn of their dissatisfaction. Therefore, it is important to maintain customer satisfaction by meeting and satisfying their needs.[39]

How: Determining Core Competencies Necessary to Satisfy Customer Needs

After deciding *who* the firm will serve and the specific *needs* of those customers, the firm is prepared to determine how to use its capabilities and competencies to develop products that can satisfy the needs of its target customers. As explained in Chapters 1 and 3, *core competencies* are resources and capabilities that serve as a source of competitive advantage for the firm over its rivals. Firms use core competencies (*how*) to implement value-creating strategies and thereby satisfy customers' needs. Only those firms with the capacity to continuously improve, innovate, and upgrade their competencies can expect to meet and hopefully exceed customers' expectations across time.[40] Firms must continuously upgrade their capabilities to ensure that they maintain the advantage over their rivals by providing customers with a superior product.[41] Often these capabilities are difficult for competitors to imitate partly because they are constantly being upgraded but also because they are integrated and used as configurations of capabilities to perform an important activity (e.g., R&D).[42]

Companies draw from a wide range of core competencies to produce goods or services that can satisfy customers' needs. For example, Merck is a large pharmaceutical firm well-known for its R&D capabilities. In recent times, Merck has been building on these capabilities by investing heavily in R&D. In 2011, for example, Merck invested $8.5 billion to conduct research and identify major new drugs. These new drugs are intended to meet the needs of consumers and to sustain Merck's competitive advantage in the industry.[43]

SAS Institute is the world's largest privately owned software company and is the leader in business intelligence and analytics. Customers use SAS programs for data warehousing, data mining, and decision support purposes. SAS serves 50,000 sites in 100 countries and serves 93 percent of the top Fortune 100 firms. Allocating approximately 24 percent of revenues to research and development (R&D), a percentage that exceeds percentages allocated by its competitors, SAS relies on its core competence in R&D to satisfy the data-related needs of such customers as the U.S. Census Bureau and a host of consumer goods firms (e.g., hotels, banks, and catalog companies).[44]

Sometimes, firms may find it necessary to use their core competencies as the foundation for producing new goods or services for new customers. This may be the case for some small automobile parts suppliers in the United States. Given that U.S. auto production in recent years declined about a third from more typical levels, a number of these firms are seeking to diversify their operations, perhaps exiting the auto parts supplier industry as a result of doing so. Some analysts believe that the first rule for these small manufacturers is to determine how their current capabilities and competencies might be used to produce value-creating products for different customers. One analyst gave the following example of how this might work: "There may be no reason that a company making auto door handles couldn't make ball-and-socket joints for artificial shoulders."[45]

Our discussion about customers shows that all organizations must use their capabilities and core competencies (the *how*) to satisfy the needs (the *what*) of the target group of customers (the *who*) the firm has chosen to serve. Next, we describe the different business-level strategies that are available to firms to use to satisfy customers as the foundation for earning above-average returns.

The Purpose of a Business-Level Strategy

The purpose of a business-level strategy is to create differences between the firm's position and those of its competitors.[46] To position itself differently from competitors, a firm must decide whether it intends to *perform activities differently* or to *perform different activities*. Strategy defines the path which provides the direction of actions to be taken by leaders of the organization.[47] In fact, "choosing to perform activities differently or to perform different activities than rivals" is the essence of business-level strategy.[48] Thus, the firm's business-level strategy is a deliberate choice about how it will perform the value chain's primary and support activities to create unique value. Indeed, in the current complex competitive landscape, successful use of a business-level strategy results from the firm learning how to integrate the activities it performs in ways that create superior value for customers.

Firms develop an activity map to show how they integrate the activities they perform. We show the Southwest Airlines activity map in Figure 4.1. The manner in which Southwest has integrated its activities is the foundation for the successful use of its primary cost leadership strategy (this strategy is discussed later in the chapter) but also includes differentiation through the unique services provided to customers. The tight integration among Southwest's activities is a key source of the firm's ability to at least historically operate more profitably than its competitors.

As shown in Figure 4.1, Southwest Airlines has configured the activities it performs into six strategic themes—limited passenger service; frequent, reliable departures; lean, highly productive ground and gate crews; high aircraft utilization; very low ticket prices; and short-haul, point-to-point routes between mid-sized cities and secondary airports. Individual clusters of tightly linked activities make it possible for the outcome of a strategic theme to be achieved. For example, no meals, no seat assignments, and no baggage transfers form a cluster of individual activities that support the strategic theme of limited passenger service (see Figure 4.1).

Southwest's tightly integrated activities make it difficult for competitors to imitate the firm's cost leadership strategy. The firm's unique culture and customer service, both of which are sources of competitive advantages, are features that rivals have been unable to imitate, although some have tried and largely failed (e.g., U.S. Airways' MetroJet

Figure 4.1 Southwest Airlines Activity System

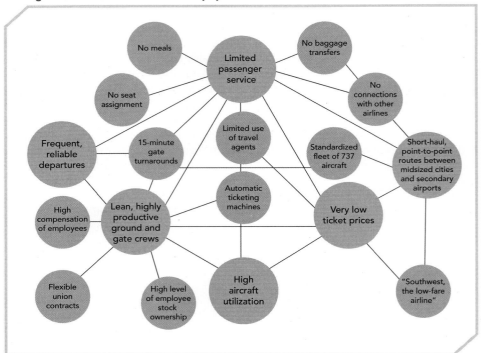

© 2013 Cengage Learning.

subsidiary, United Airlines' United Shuttle, Delta's Song, and Continental Airlines' Continental Lite). Hindsight shows that these competitors offered low prices to customers, but weren't able to operate at costs close to those of Southwest or to provide customers with any notable sources of differentiation, such as a unique experience while in the air. The key to Southwest's success has been its ability to continuously reduce its costs while providing customers with *acceptable* levels of differentiation such as an engaging culture. Firms using the cost leadership strategy must understand that in terms of sources of differentiation that accompany the cost leader's product, the customer defines *acceptable*. Fit among activities is a key to the sustainability of competitive advantage for all firms, including Southwest Airlines. Strategic fit among the many activities is critical for competitive advantage. It is more difficult for a competitor to match a configuration of integrated activities than to imitate a particular activity such as sales promotion, or a process technology.[49]

Types of Business-Level Strategies

Firms choose from among five business-level strategies to establish and defend their desired strategic position against competitors: *cost leadership, differentiation, focused cost leadership, focused differentiation,* and *integrated cost leadership/differentiation* (see Figure 4.2). Each business-level strategy helps the firm to establish and exploit a particular *competitive advantage* within a particular *competitive scope.* How firms integrate the activities they perform within each different business-level strategy demonstrates how they differ from one another.[50] For example, firms have different activity maps, and thus, a Southwest Airlines activity map differs from those of competitors JetBlue, Continental, American Airlines, and so forth. Superior integration of activities increases the likelihood of being able to gain an advantage over competitors and to earn above-average returns.

Figure 4.2 Five Business-Level Strategies

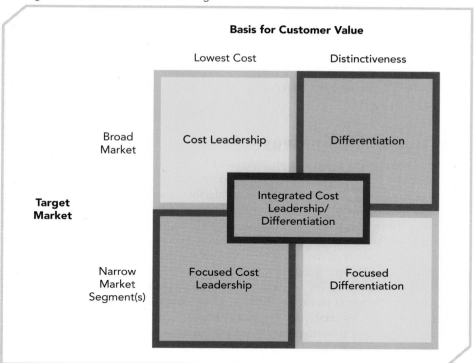

Source: Based on M. E. Porter, 1998, *Competitive Advantage: Creating and Sustaining Superior Performance*, New York: The Free Press; D. G. Sirmon, M. A. Hitt, & R. D. Ireland, 2007, Managing firm resources in dynamic environments to create value: Looking inside the black box, *Academy of Management Review*, 32: 273–292; D. G. Sirmon, M. A. Hitt, R. D. Ireland & B. A. Gilbert, 2011, Resource orchestration to create competitive advantage: Breadth, depth and life cycles effects, *Journal of Management*, in press. © Copyrighted 2011 by Michael A. Hitt, R. Duane Ireland, and Robert E. Hoskisson.

When selecting a business-level strategy, firms evaluate two types of potential competitive advantages: "lower cost than rivals, or the ability to differentiate and command a premium price that exceeds the extra cost of doing so."[51] Having lower cost derives from the firm's ability to perform activities differently than rivals; being able to differentiate indicates the firm's capacity to perform different (and valuable) activities. Thus, based on the nature and quality of its internal resources, capabilities, and core competencies, a firm seeks to form either a cost competitive advantage or a distinctiveness competitive advantage as the basis for implementing its business-level strategy.[52]

Two types of target markets are broad market and narrow market segment(s) (see Figure 4.2). Firms serving a broad market seek to use their capabilities to create value for customers on an industry-wide basis. A narrow market segment means that the firm intends to serve the needs of a narrow customer group. With focus strategies, the firm "selects a segment or group of segments in the industry and tailors its strategy to serving them to the exclusion of others."[53] Buyers with special needs and buyers located in specific geographic regions are examples of narrow customer groups.[54] As shown in Figure 4.2, a firm could also strive to develop a combined low cost/distinctiveness value creation approach as the foundation for serving a target customer group that is larger than a narrow market segment but not as comprehensive as a broad (or industry-wide) customer group. In this instance, the firm uses the integrated cost leadership/differentiation strategy.

None of the five business-level strategies shown in Figure 4.2 is inherently or universally superior to the others.[55] The effectiveness of each strategy is contingent both on the opportunities and threats in a firm's external environment and on the strengths and weaknesses derived from the firm's resource portfolio. It is critical, therefore, for the firm to select a business-level strategy that is based on a match between the opportunities and threats in its external environment and the strengths of its internal organization as shown by its core competencies.[56] After the firm chooses its strategy, it should consistently emphasize actions that are required to successfully use it. Walmart's continuous emphasis on driving its costs lower is thought to be a key to the firm's effective cost leadership strategy.[57]

Cost Leadership Strategy

The **cost leadership strategy** is an integrated set of actions taken to produce goods or services with features that are acceptable to customers at the lowest cost, relative to those of competitors.[58] Firms using the cost leadership strategy commonly sell standardized goods or services (but with competitive levels of differentiation) to the industry's most typical customers. Process innovations, which are newly designed production and distribution methods and techniques that allow the firm to operate more efficiently, are critical to successful use of the cost leadership strategy.[59]

As noted, cost leaders' goods and services must have competitive levels of differentiation that create value for customers. For example, in recent years Kia Motors has emphasized the design of its cars in the U.S. market as a source of differentiation while implementing a cost leadership strategy. Called "cheap chic," some analysts had a positive view of this decision, saying that "When they're done, Kia's cars will still be low-end (in price), but they won't necessarily look like it."[60] It is important for firms using the cost leadership strategy to not only concentrate on reducing costs because it could result in the firm efficiently producing products that no customer wants to purchase. In fact, such extremes could limit the potential for important process innovations and lead to employment of lower-skilled workers, poor conditions on the production line, accidents, and a poor quality of work life for employees.[61]

As shown in Figure 4.2, the firm using the cost leadership strategy targets a broad customer segment or group. Cost leaders concentrate on finding ways to lower their costs relative to competitors by constantly rethinking how to complete their primary and support activities to reduce costs still further while maintaining competitive levels of differentiation.[62]

For example, cost leader Greyhound Lines Inc. continuously seeks ways to reduce the costs it incurs to provide bus service while offering customers an acceptable level of differentiation. Greyhound offers additional services to customers trying to enhance the value of the experience customers have while they pay low prices for their service package. Interestingly, a number of customers now "insist on certain amenities that they receive on planes and trains—such as Internet access and comfortable seats, not to mention cleanliness." To maintain competitive levels of differentiation while using the cost leadership strategy, Greyhound recently starting using over 100 "motor coaches" that have leather seats, additional legroom, Wi-Fi access, and power outlets in every row.[63]

Greyhound enjoys economies of scale by serving more than 25 million passengers annually with about 2,300 destinations in the United States and almost 13,000 daily departures. These scale economies allow the firm to keep its costs low while offering some of the differentiated services today's customers seek from the company. Demonstrating the firm's commitment to the physical environment segment of the general environment is the fact that "one Greyhound bus takes an average of 34 cars off the road."[64]

As primary activities, inbound logistics (e.g., materials handling, warehousing, and inventory control) and outbound logistics (e.g., collecting, storing, and distributing products to customers) often account for significant portions of the total cost to produce

The **cost leadership strategy** is an integrated set of actions taken to produce goods or services with features that are acceptable to customers at the lowest cost, relative to that of competitors.

some goods and services. Research suggests that having a competitive advantage in logistics creates more value with a cost leadership strategy than with a differentiation strategy.[65] Thus, cost leaders seeking competitively valuable ways to reduce costs may want to concentrate on the primary activities of inbound logistics and outbound logistics. In so doing many firms choose to outsource their manufacturing operations to low-cost firms with low-wage employees (e.g., China).[66] However, care must be taken because outsourcing also makes the firm more dependent on firms over which they have little control At best, it creates interdependencies between the outsourcing firm and the suppliers. If dependencies become too great, it gives the supplier more power with which the supplier may increase prices of the goods and services provided. Such actions could harm the firm's ability to maintain a low-cost competitive advantage.[67]

Cost leaders also carefully examine all support activities to find additional potential cost reductions. Developing new systems for finding the optimal combination of low cost and acceptable levels of differentiation in the raw materials required to produce the firm's goods or services is an example of how the procurement support activity can facilitate successful use of the cost leadership strategy.

Big Lots Inc. uses the cost leadership strategy. With its vision of being "The World's Best Bargain Place," Big Lots is the largest closeout retailer in the United States with annual sales of over $5 billion from more than 1,400 stores with approximately 13,000 employees. For Big Lots, closeout goods are brand-name products sold by other retailers provided for sale at substantially lower prices.[68]

As described in Chapter 3, firms use value-chain analysis to identify the parts of the company's operations that create value and those that do not. Figure 4.3 demonstrates the primary and support activities that allow a firm to create value through the cost leadership strategy. Companies unable to link the activities shown in this figure through the activity map they form typically lack the core competencies needed to successfully use the cost leadership strategy.

Effective use of the cost leadership strategy allows a firm to earn above-average returns in spite of the presence of strong competitive forces (see Chapter 2). The next sections (one for each of the five forces) explain how firms implement a cost leadership strategy.

Rivalry with Existing Competitors

Having the low-cost position is valuable to deal with rivals. Because of the cost leader's advantageous position, rivals hesitate to compete on the basis of price, especially before evaluating the potential outcomes of such competition.[69] As described in the Strategic Focus, Walmart has been known for its ability to maintain very low costs, thereby creating value for customers. However, the changes it made to attract upscale customers made its low-cost position vulnerable to rivals. Dollar Store, Amazon.com, and others took advantage of the opportunity. Amazon appears to have become a low-cost leader, and the Dollar Stores provide low costs and easy access for customers. Both of these rivals have begun to siphon off Walmart customers. Because of Walmart's unprecedented loss of sales and market position, it has started to fight back by returning to its former strategy and is implementing new competitive actions as well (e.g., building new express stores).

The degree of rivalry present is based on a number of different factors such as size and resources of rivals, their dependence on the particular market, and location and prior competitive interactions, among others.[70] Firms may also take actions to reduce the amount of rivalry that they face. For example, firms sometimes form joint ventures to reduce rivalry and increase the amount of profitability enjoyed by firms in the industry.[71]

In the past, rivals such as Costco and Target hesitated to compete directly with Walmart strictly on the basis of costs and, subsequently, prices to consumers. Yet, given Walmart's changes, its prices on some products are only slightly below the prices of similar goods at Target. Walmart's changes then also provided an opportunity for Target and Costco. Walmart saw the error in its new direction and has vowed to return to its cost leadership strategy of providing the lowest prices on all goods sold.

STRATEGIC FOCUS

WALMART, DOLLAR STORES, AND AMAZON: WHO IS BUYING WHOSE LUNCH?

Walmart is the largest retailer in the world and has used its economies of scale and distribution system to drive costs exceptionally low. As such, it has been the market leader in low prices for retail goods for many years. However, recently Walmart's same store sales have been declining and those of rivals Family Dollar and Amazon (among others) have been increasing. What happened?

Well, Walmart decided to change its strategy at the margin with the intent of trying to attract more upscale customers. For example, it introduced organic foods, remodeled some stores making the aisles wider and less cluttered, and reduced the variety of products offered. In so doing, its prices also increased on some goods. In fact, on some goods, its prices were not much below those of its rival Target. Additionally, the new strategy appeared designed to take market share away from Target. However, in making this aggressive move to attract Target's customers and other new ones as well, Walmart deviated from its cost leadership strategy and was not protecting its flank.

Walmart's actions provided an opening to several of its rivals. For example, online competitors were allowed to gain a cost/price advantage. One author tells of an experience where he was searching for a new Waste-King garbage disposal (his quit working). He found that Amazon.com offered it for a price that was 20 percent lower than the price it was sold at Walmart. Interestingly, Amazon's sales increased by 40 percent in 2010. At the same time, Family Dollar and some similar rivals have been cleaning up their stores, stocking more name-brand products, and keeping their prices low. By doing so, they attracted former Walmart customers because of their low prices and convenience. Family Dollar, Dollar Tree, and Dollar General all experienced increased sales revenues and are adding hundreds of new stores.

Frances Roberts/Alamy

The rise of Dollar Stores, like this Mr. Dollar Store in Bushwick Brooklyn, NY, are proving to be a challenge for retail giant Walmart.

Walmart realized that it made a mistake. As a result, it has begun to add products back into stores that were eliminated earlier. Additionally, it is focused heavily on keeping its costs and prices low. Finally, Walmart is opening 40 new express stores of only slightly more than 14,000 square feet. Yet analysts question if these actions will be adequate to win back customers that were lost. First, 40 express stores will not offer much competition to the thousands of dollar stores. Also, it must attract customers back with lower prices and/or more product variety than offered by competitors. Only meeting their low prices may be inadequate to get customers to change if they are satisfied with their current stores. Time will tell if Walmart will be able to recapture its cost leadership position in the market after giving it up to rivals.

Sources: M. Alexander, 2011, Make Cents? Walmart to mirror Dollar Store model, Walletpop, www.walletpop.com, March 17; S. Denning, 2011, Wal-Mart and the futility of traditional management, *Forbes*, www.forbes.com, February 23; M. Bustillo, 2011, Wal-Mart tries to recapture Mr. Sam's winning formula, *Wall Street Journal*, www.online.wsj.com, February 22; 2011, Wal-Mart, humbled king of retail, plots rebound, *Wall Street Journal*, www.online.wsj.com, February 6; M. Cardona, 2010, Dollar Stores are taking Walmart's lunch money, *Daily Finance*, www.dailyfinance.com, December 4; M. Alexander, 2010, Dollar stores rival Walmart—here's why, *Walletpop*, www.walletpop.com, August 25; B. Speaker, 2010, FDO, DLTR, NDN beat Walmart at its own game, Investor Place, www.investorplace.com, August 26.

© Nicholas Monu/iStockphoto.com

STRATEGY RIGHT NOW

Explore Dollar Tree's strategic environment.

www.cengagebrain.com

Figure 4.3 Examples of Value-Creating Activities Associated with the Cost Leadership Strategy

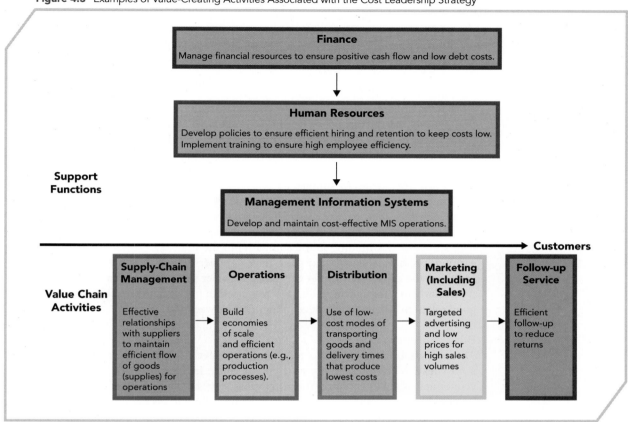

Source: Based on M. E. Porter, 1998, *Competitive Advantage: Creating and Sustaining Superior Performance,* New York: The Free Press; D. G. Sirmon, M. A. Hitt & R. D. Ireland, 2007, Managing firm resources in dynamic environments to create value: Looking inside the black box, *Academy of Management Review,* 32: 273–292; D. G. Sirmon, M. A. Hitt, R. D. Ireland & B. A. Gilbert, 2011, Resource orchestration to create competitive advantage: Breadth, depth and life cycles effects, *Journal of Management,* in press. © Copyrighted 2011 by Michael A. Hitt, R. Duane Ireland, and Robert E. Hoskisson.

Bargaining Power of Buyers (Customers)

Powerful customers can force a cost leader to reduce its prices, but not below the level at which the cost leader's next-most-efficient industry competitor can earn average returns. Although powerful customers might be able to force the cost leader to reduce prices even below this level, they probably would choose not to do so. Prices that are low enough to prevent the next-most-efficient competitor from earning average returns would force that firm to exit the market, leaving the cost leader with less competition and in an even stronger position. Customers would thus lose their power and pay higher prices if they were forced to purchase from a single firm operating in an industry without rivals.

Buyers can also develop a counterbalancing power to the customers' power by carefully analyzing and understanding each of their customers. To help in obtaining information and understanding the customers, buyers can participate in customers' networks. In so doing, they share information, build trust, and participate in joint problem solving with their customers.[72] In turn, they use the information obtained to provide a product that provides superior value to customers by most effectively satisfying their needs.

Bargaining Power of Suppliers

The cost leader operates with margins greater than those of competitors. Cost leaders want to constantly increase their margins by driving their costs lower. Among other benefits, higher gross margins relative to those of competitors make it possible for the cost leader to absorb its suppliers' price increases. When an industry faces substantial increases in the cost of its supplies, only the cost leader may be able to pay the higher prices and continue to earn either average or above-average returns. Alternatively, a powerful cost leader may be able to force its suppliers to hold down their prices, which would reduce the suppliers' margins in the process. Walmart lost its way in this regard. By reducing the number and type of products sold in Walmart stores, it reduced its bargaining power with several suppliers. In so doing, it was unable to gain the best (lowest) prices on goods relative to its competitors. Thus, Amazon and the Dollar Stores began winning market share from Walmart by offering lower prices.

The fact remains that Walmart is the largest retailer in North America, thus giving the firm a great deal of power with its suppliers. Walmart is the largest supermarket operator in the United States and its Sam's Club division is the second largest warehouse club in the United States. Collectively, this sales volume and the market penetration it suggests (over 100 million people visit a Walmart store each week) still allow Walmart to obtain low prices from its suppliers.

Some firms create dependencies on suppliers by outsourcing whole functions. They do so to reduce their overall costs.[73] They may outsource these activities to reduce their costs because of earnings pressures from stakeholders (e.g., institutional investors who own a major stock holding in the company) in the industry.[74] Often when there is such earnings pressure, the firm may see foreign suppliers whose costs are also lower, providing them the capability to offer the goods at lower prices.[75] Yet, when firms outsource, particularly to a foreign supplier, they also need to invest time and effort into building a good relationship, hopefully developing trust between the firms.[76]

Potential Entrants

Through continuous efforts to reduce costs to levels that are lower than competitors', a cost leader becomes highly efficient. Because increasing levels of efficiency (e.g., economies of scale) enhance profit margins, they serve as a significant entry barrier to potential competitors.[77] New entrants must be willing to accept no-better-than-average returns until they gain the experience required to approach the cost leader's efficiency. To earn even average returns, new entrants must have the competencies required to match the cost levels of competitors other than the cost leader. The low profit margins (relative to margins earned by firms implementing the differentiation strategy) make it necessary for the cost leader to sell large volumes of its product to earn above-average returns. However, firms striving to be the cost leader must avoid pricing their products so low that their ability to operate profitably is reduced, even though volume increases.

Product Substitutes

Compared with its industry rivals, the cost leader also holds an attractive position in terms of product substitutes. A product substitute becomes an issue for the cost leader when its features and characteristics, in terms of cost and differentiated features, are potentially attractive to the firm's customers. When faced with possible substitutes, the cost leader has more flexibility than its competitors. To retain customers, it can reduce the price of its good or service. With still lower prices and competitive levels of differentiation, the cost leader increases the probability that customers prefer its product rather than a substitute.

Competitive Risks of the Cost Leadership Strategy

The cost leadership strategy is not risk free. One risk is that the processes used by the cost leader to produce and distribute its good or service could become obsolete because of competitors' innovations.[78] These innovations may allow rivals to produce at costs lower than those of the original cost leader, or to provide additional differentiated features without increasing the product's price to customers.

A second risk is that too much focus by the cost leader on cost reductions may occur at the expense of trying to understand customers' perceptions of "competitive levels of differentiation." Walmart, for example, has been criticized for having too few salespeople available to help customers and too few individuals at checkout registers. These complaints suggest that there might be a discrepancy between how Walmart's customers define "minimal levels of service" and the firm's attempts to drive its costs increasingly lower.

Imitation is a final risk of the cost leadership strategy. Using their own core competencies, competitors sometimes learn how to successfully imitate the cost leader's strategy. When this happens, the cost leader must increase the value its good or service provides to customers. Commonly, value is increased by selling the current product at an even lower price or by adding differentiated features that create value for customers while maintaining price.

Differentiation Strategy

The **differentiation strategy** is an integrated set of actions taken to produce goods or services (at an acceptable cost) that customers perceive as being different in ways that are important to them.[79] While cost leaders serve a typical customer in an industry, differentiators target customers for whom value is created by the manner in which the firm's products differ from those produced and marketed by competitors. Product innovation, which is "the result of bringing to life a new way to solve the customer's problem—through a new product or service development—that benefits both the customer and the sponsoring company"[80] is critical to successful use of the differentiation strategy.[81]

Firms must be able to produce differentiated products at competitive costs to reduce upward pressure on the price that customers pay. When a product's differentiated features are produced at noncompetitive costs, the price for the product may exceed what the firm's target customers are willing to pay. If the firm has a thorough understanding of what its target customers value, the relative importance they attach to the satisfaction of different needs, and

This crowded store could benefit from more attention to service. Too few salespeople to check people out can have a negative impact on the customers' experience.

SuperStock/Alamy

for what they are willing to pay a premium, the differentiation strategy can be effective in helping it earn above-average returns. Of course, to achieve these returns, the firm must apply its knowledge capital (knowledge held by its employees and managers) to provide customers with a differentiated product that provides them with superior value.[82]

Through the differentiation strategy, the firm produces nonstandardized (that is, distinctive) products for customers who value differentiated features more than they value low cost. For example, superior product reliability and durability and high-performance sound systems are among the differentiated features of Toyota Motor Corporation's Lexus products. However, Lexus offers its vehicles to customers at a competitive purchase price relative to other luxury automobiles. As with Lexus products, a product's unique attributes, rather than its purchase price, provide the value for which customers are willing to pay.

To maintain success with the differentiation strategy results, the firm must consistently upgrade differentiated features that customers value and/or create new valuable features (innovate) without significant cost increases.[83] This approach requires firms to constantly change their product lines.[84] These firms may also offer a portfolio of products that complement each other, thereby enriching the differentiation for the customer and perhaps satisfying a portfolio of consumer needs.[85] Because a differentiated product satisfies customers' unique needs, firms following the differentiation strategy are able to charge premium prices. The ability to sell a good or service at a price that substantially exceeds the cost of creating its differentiated features allows the firm to outperform rivals and earn above-average returns. Rather than costs, a firm using the differentiation strategy primarily concentrates on investing in and developing features that differentiate a product in ways that create value for customers.[86] Overall, a firm using the differentiation strategy seeks to be different from its competitors on as many dimensions as possible.

The **differentiation strategy** is an integrated set of actions taken to produce goods or services (at an acceptable cost) that customers perceive as being different in ways that are important to them.

The less similarity between a firm's goods or services and those of competitors, the more buffered it is from rivals' actions. Commonly recognized differentiated goods include Toyota's Lexus, Ralph Lauren's wide array of product lines, Caterpillar's heavy-duty earth-moving equipment, and McKinsey & Co.'s differentiated consulting services.

A good or service can be differentiated in many ways. Unusual features, responsive customer service, rapid product innovations and technological leadership, perceived prestige and status, different tastes, and engineering design and performance are examples of approaches to differentiation.[87] While the number of ways to reduce costs may be finite, virtually anything a firm can do to create real or perceived value is a basis for differentiation. Consider product design as a case in point. Because it can create a positive experience for customers, design is an important source of differentiation (even for cost leaders seeking to find ways to add functionalities to their low-cost products as a way of differentiating their products from competitors) and hopefully, for firms emphasizing it, of competitive advantage.[88] Apple is often cited as the firm that sets the standard in design, with the iPod and the iPhone demonstrating Apple's product design capabilities.[89]

The value chain can be analyzed to determine if a firm is able to link the activities required to create value by using the differentiation strategy. Examples of primary value chain activities and support functions that are commonly used to differentiate a good or service are shown in Figure 4.4. Companies without the skills needed to link

Figure 4.4 Examples of Value-Creating Activities Associated with the Differentiation Strategy

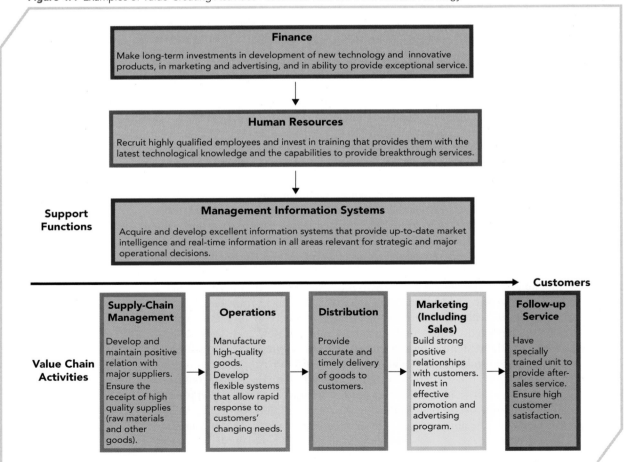

Source: Based on information from, M. E. Porter, 1998, *Competitive Advantage: Creating and Sustaining Superior Performance*, New York: The Free Press; D. G. Sirmon, M. A. Hitt, & R. D. Ireland, 2007, Managing firm resources in dynamic environments to create value: Looking inside the black box, *Academy of Management Review*, 32: 273–292; D. G. Sirmon, M. A. Hitt, R. D. Ireland, & B. A. Gilbert, 2011, Resource orchestration to create competitive advantage: Breadth, depth and life cycles effects, *Journal of Management*, in press. © Copyrighted 2011 by Michael A. Hitt, R. Duane Ireland, and Robert E. Hoskisson.

these activities cannot expect to successfully use the differentiation strategy. Next, we explain how firms using the differentiation strategy can successfully position themselves in terms of the five forces of competition (see Chapter 2) to earn above-average returns.

Rivalry with Existing Competitors

Customers tend to be loyal purchasers of products differentiated in ways that are meaningful to them. As their loyalty to a brand increases, customers' sensitivity to price increases is reduced. The relationship between brand loyalty and price sensitivity insulates a firm from competitive rivalry. Thus, Bose is insulated from intense rivalry as long as customers continue to perceive that its stereo equipment offers superior sound quality at a competitive purchase price. Bose has a strong positive reputation for high-quality and unique products. Thus, reputations can sustain the competitive advantage of firms following a differentiation strategy.[90]

Bargaining Power of Buyers (Customers)

The distinctiveness of differentiated goods or services reduces customers' sensitivity to price increases. Customers are willing to accept a price increase when a product still satisfies their perceived unique needs better than does a competitor's offering. Thus, the golfer whose needs are specifically satisfied by Callaway golf clubs will likely continue buying those products even if their cost increases. Similarly, the customer who has been highly satisfied with a Louis Vuitton wallet will probably replace that wallet with another one made by the same company even though the purchase price is higher than the original one. Purchasers of brand-name food items (e.g., Heinz ketchup and Kleenex tissues) accept price increases in those products as long as they continue to perceive that the product satisfies their distinctive needs at an acceptable cost. In all of these instances, the customers are relatively insensitive to price increases because they do not think that an acceptable product alternative exists.

Bargaining Power of Suppliers

Because the firm using the differentiation strategy charges a premium price for its products, suppliers must provide high-quality components, driving up the firm's costs. However, the high margins the firm earns in these cases partially insulate it from the influence of suppliers in that higher supplier costs can be paid through these margins.[91] Alternatively, because of buyers' relative insensitivity to price increases, the differentiated firm might choose to pass the additional cost of supplies on to the customer by increasing the price of its unique product.

Potential Entrants

Customer loyalty and the need to overcome the uniqueness of a differentiated product present substantial barriers to potential entrants. Entering an industry under these conditions typically demands significant investments of resources and patience while seeking customers' loyalty.

Product Substitutes

Firms selling brand-name goods and services to loyal customers are positioned effectively against product substitutes. In contrast, companies without brand loyalty face a higher probability of their customers switching either to products which offer differentiated features that serve the same function (particularly if the substitute has a lower price) or to products that offer more features and perform more attractive functions.

Competitive Risks of the Differentiation Strategy

One risk of the differentiation strategy is that customers might decide that the price differential between the differentiator's product and the cost leader's product is too large. In this instance, a firm may be offering differentiated features that exceed target customers' needs. The firm then becomes vulnerable to competitors that are able to offer customers a combination of features and price that is more consistent with their needs.

This risk is generalized across a number of companies producing different types of products during an economic recession—a time when sales of luxury goods (e.g., jewelry and leather goods) often suffer. The decline was expected to be more severe in the United States compared to Europe and Japan. A decision made during the last economic recession by Coach Inc., a maker of high-quality, luxurious accessories and gifts for women and men, demonstrates one firm's reaction to the predicted decline in the sales of luxury goods. With an interest in providing products to increasingly cost-conscious customers without "cheapening" the firm's image, Coach introduced a new line of its products called "Poppy"; the average price of items in this line is approximately 20 percent lower than the average price of Coach's typical products.[92]

Another risk of the differentiation strategy is that a firm's means of differentiation may cease to provide value for which customers are willing to pay. A differentiated product becomes less valuable if imitation by rivals causes customers to perceive that competitors offer essentially the same good or service, but at a lower price.[93] A third risk of the differentiation strategy is that experience can narrow customers' perceptions of the value of a product's differentiated features. For example, customers having positive experiences with generic tissues may decide that the differentiated features of the Kleenex product are not worth the extra cost. To counter this risk, firms must continue to meaningfully differentiate their product (e.g., through innovation) for customers at a price they are willing to pay.[94]

Counterfeiting is the differentiation strategy's fourth risk. "Counterfeits are those products bearing a trademark that is identical to or indistinguishable from a trademark registered to another party, thus infringing the rights of the holder of the trademark."[95] Companies such as Hewlett-Packard must take actions to deal with the problems counterfeit goods create for firms whose rights are infringed upon next.

Focus Strategies

The focus strategy is an integrated set of actions taken to produce goods or services that serve the needs of a particular competitive segment. Thus, firms use a focus strategy when they utilize their core competencies to serve the needs of a particular industry segment or niche to the exclusion of others. Examples of specific market segments that can be targeted by a focus strategy include (1) a particular buyer group (e.g., youths or senior citizens), (2) a different segment of a product line (e.g., products for professional painters or the do-it-yourself group), or (3) a different geographic market (e.g., northern or southern Italy by using a foreign subsidiary).[96]

There are many specific customer needs firms can serve by using a focus strategy. For example, Los Angeles–based investment banking firm Greif & Company positions itself as "The Entrepreneur's Investment Bank." Greif & Company is a leader in providing merger and acquisition advice to medium-sized businesses located in the western United States.[97] Goya Foods is the largest U.S.-based Hispanic-owned food company in the United States. Segmenting the Hispanic market into unique groups, Goya offers more than 1,600 products to consumers. The firm seeks "to be the be-all for the Latin community."[98] By successfully using a focus strategy, firms such as these gain a competitive advantage in specific market niches or segments, even though they do not possess an industry-wide competitive advantage.

Although the breadth of a target is clearly a matter of degree, the essence of the focus strategy "is the exploitation of a narrow target's differences from the balance of the industry."[99] Firms using the focus strategy intend to serve a particular segment of an industry more effectively than can industry-wide competitors. They succeed when they effectively serve a segment whose unique needs are so specialized that broad-based competitors choose not to serve that segment or when they satisfy the needs of a segment being served poorly by industry-wide competitors.[100]

Firms can create value for customers in specific and unique market segments by using the focused cost leadership strategy or the focused differentiation strategy.

The **focus strategy** is an integrated set of actions taken to produce goods or services that serve the needs of a particular competitive segment.

Focused Cost Leadership Strategy

Based in Sweden, IKEA, a global furniture retailer with locations in 24 countries and territories and sales revenue of 21.1 billion euros in 2008, uses the focused cost leadership strategy. Young buyers desiring style at a low cost are IKEA's target customers.[101] For these customers, the firm offers home furnishings that combine good design, function, and acceptable quality with low prices. According to the firm, "Low cost is always in focus. This applies to every phase of our activities."[102]

IKEA emphasizes several activities to keep its costs low. For example, instead of relying primarily on third-party manufacturers, the firm's engineers design low-cost, modular furniture ready for assembly by customers. To eliminate the need for sales associates or decorators, IKEA positions the products in its stores so that customers can view

Goya canned food products pack a shelf in this Top Valu market in Long Beach, CA.

different living combinations (complete with sofas, chairs, tables, etc.) in a single room-like setting, which helps the customer imagine how furniture will look in the home. A third practice that helps keep IKEA's costs low is requiring customers to transport their own purchases rather than providing delivery service.

Although it is a cost leader, IKEA also offers some differentiated features that appeal to its target customers, including its unique furniture designs, in-store playrooms for children, wheelchairs for customer use, and extended hours. IKEA believes that these services and products "are uniquely aligned with the needs of [its] customers, who are young, are not wealthy, are likely to have children (but no nanny), and, because they work, have a need to shop at odd hours."[103] Thus, IKEA's focused cost leadership strategy also includes some differentiated features with its low-cost products.

Focused Differentiation Strategy

Other firms implement the focused differentiation strategy. As noted earlier, there are many dimensions on which firms can differentiate their good or service. For example, the new generation of lunch trucks populating cities such as New York, San Francisco, Los Angeles, and even College Station, Texas, use the focused differentiation strategy. Serving "high-end fare such as grass-fed hamburgers, escargot and crème brulee," highly trained chefs and well-known restaurateurs own and operate many of these trucks. In fact, "the new breed of lunch truck is aggressively gourmet, tech-savvy and politically correct." Selling sustainably harvested fish tacos in a vehicle that is fueled by vegetable oil, the Green Truck, located in Los Angeles, demonstrates these characteristics. Moreover, the owners of these trucks often use Twitter and Facebook to inform customers of their locations as they move from point to point in their focal city.[104]

Denver-based Kazoo Toys uses the focused differentiation strategy to create value for parents and children interested in purchasing unique toys while simultaneously having access to unique services. Kazoo offers more than 60,000 distinctive toys.[105] With a focus strategy, firms such as Kazoo Toys must be able to complete various primary value chain activities and support functions in a competitively superior manner to develop and sustain a competitive advantage and earn above-average returns. The activities required to use the focused cost leadership strategy are virtually identical to those of the industry-wide cost leadership strategy (see Figure 4.3), and activities required to use the focused differentiation strategy are largely identical to those of the industry-wide differentiation strategy (see Figure 4.4). Similarly, the manner in which each of the two focus strategies allows a firm to deal successfully with the five competitive forces parallels those of the two broad strategies. The only difference is in the firm's competitive scope; the firm focuses on a narrow industry segment. Thus, Figures 4.3 and 4.4 and the text describing the five competitive forces also explain the relationship between each of the two focus strategies and competitive advantage.

Competitive Risks of Focus Strategies

With either focus strategy, the firm faces the same general risks as does the company using the cost leadership or the differentiation strategy, respectively, on an industry-wide basis. However, focus strategies have three additional risks.

First, a competitor may be able to focus on a more narrowly defined competitive segment and thereby "out-focus" the focuser. This would happen to IKEA if another firm found a way to offer IKEA's customers (young buyers interested in stylish furniture at a low cost) additional sources of differentiation while charging the same price or to provide the same service with the same sources of differentiation at a lower price. Second, a company competing on an industry-wide basis may decide that the market segment served by the firm using a focus strategy is attractive and worthy of competitive pursuit. For example, women's clothiers such as Chico's, Ann Taylor, and Liz Claiborne might conclude that the profit potential in the narrow segment being served by Anne Fontaine is attractive and decide to design and sell competitively similar clothing items. Initially, Anne Fontaine designed and sold only white shirts for women. However, the shirts were distinctive. They were quite differentiated on the basis of their design, craftsmanship, and high quality of raw materials.[106] The third risk involved with a focus strategy is that the needs of customers within a narrow competitive segment may become more similar to those of industry-wide customers as a whole over time. As a result, the advantages of a focus strategy are either reduced or eliminated. At some point, for example, the needs of Anne Fontaine's customers for high-quality, uniquely designed white shirts could dissipate. If this were to happen, Anne Fontaine's customers might choose to buy white shirts from chains such as Liz Claiborne that sell clothing items with some differentiation, but at a lower cost.

Integrated Cost Leadership/Differentiation Strategy

Most consumers have high expectations when purchasing a good or service. In general, it seems that most consumers want to pay a low price for products with somewhat highly differentiated features. Because of these customer expectations, a number of firms engage in primary value chain activities and support functions that allow them to simultaneously pursue low cost and differentiation. Firms seeking to do this use the integrated cost leadership/differentiation strategy. The objective of using this strategy is to efficiently produce products with some differentiated features. Efficient production is the source of maintaining low costs while differentiation is the source of creating unique value. Firms that successfully use the integrated cost leadership/differentiation strategy usually adapt quickly to new technologies and rapid changes in their external environments. Simultaneously concentrating on developing two sources of competitive advantage (cost and differentiation) increases the number of primary and support activities in which the firm must become competent. Such firms often have strong networks with external parties that perform some of the primary and support activities.[107] In turn, having skills in a larger number of activities makes a firm more flexible.

The **integrated cost leadership/ differentiation strategy** involves engaging in primary value chain activities and support functions that allow a firm to simultaneously pursue low cost and differentiation.

Concentrating on the needs of its core customer group (higher-income, fashion-conscious discount shoppers), Target Stores uses an integrated cost leadership/differentiation strategy as shown by its "Expect More. Pay Less" brand promise. Target's annual report describes this strategy: "Our enduring 'Expect More. Pay Less' brand promise helped us to deliver greater convenience, increased savings and a more personalized shopping experience." In 2010, Target remodeled 341 stores and provided a greater assortment of merchandise to include more grocery items and innovative products. It added more privately branded products to offer lower prices, created new mobile applications, and introduced distinctive Web strategies to continue to differentiate the services provided to customers.[108]

European-based Zara, which pioneered "cheap chic" in clothing apparel, is another firm using the integrated cost leadership/differentiation strategy. Zara offers current and desirable fashion goods at relatively low prices. To implement this strategy effectively requires sophisticated designers and means of managing costs, which fits Zara's capabilities. Zara can design and begin manufacturing a new fashion in three weeks, which suggests a highly flexible organization that can adapt easily to changes in the market or with competitors.[109]

THE LI NING COMPANY: HEADING TOWARD GLOBAL MARKET LEADERSHIP?

Li Ning was an Olympic Gold medalist for China in the 1980s. In 1991, he started the Li Ning Company, which manufactures and markets sportswear. Early in the twenty-first century, the company experienced significant growth and became the number two company in China's sportswear market behind market leader Nike. It took over the number two position from Adidas. The company has achieved its growth and success by selling cheaper sportswear products in the smaller cities in China. Nike and Adidas are the leaders in the larger city markets, but Li Ning has done well, with more than 7,900 stores in China at the end of 2010, a 9.2 percent increase over 2009. Its total revenues have grown to $1.2 billion, an increase of more than 400 percent since 2005.

However, Li Ning is not satisfied with this position. It has taken several actions to capture greater market share and to compete in different market segments. It has enhanced its investment in R&D and is developing upscale products to compete with Nike and Adidas. However, these products will still be priced 15 to 20 percent below their Nike and Adidas products. The company is always working on building its brand name to allow it to compete in these markets as well. In addition, Li Ning has recently moved into the U.S. market, where it will face significant competition from other brand name sportswear companies. Its goal is to have 20 percent of its total revenue from sales in international markets by 2018. It is targeting its products for professional athletes and ordinary consumers. In the United States, Li Ning's products are sold through the Champs Sports and Eastbay units of Foot Locker. Li Ning has signed endorsement deals with NBA star Shaquille O'Neal and the second pick in the 2010 NBA Draft, Evan Turner.

Although Li Ning is seemingly taking the right actions to capture new market share, it faces substantial competition in the United States and even in China. For example, both Nike and Adidas plan to expand the sales of their products in the smaller Chinese cities, the bedrock of Li Ning's business in China. In addition, it will be exceptionally challenging to capture U.S. market share from companies such as Nike, as they are embedded in those markets. Perhaps it can do so by providing quality products at cheaper prices.

China Photos/Stringer/Getty Images

Consumers walk past the flagship shop of China's large sports clothing company, the Beijing Li Ning Company, at the Dongdajie Street in Xian of Shaanxi Province, China.

Sources: 2011, Li Ning Reports 2010 Annual Results, Li Ning Company Limited, www.lining.com, March 16; L. Burkitt, 2011, A Chinese run at the United States, Wall Street Journal, www.online.wsj.com, January 19; 2010, Li Ning signs up the no. 2 NBA overall draft pick Evan Turner to further strengthen its world-class sports sponsorship resources, Li Ning Company Limited, www.lining.com, September 16; J. Backaler, 2010, China's homegrown success stories, Forbes, www.forbes.com, Sept. 12; P. Waldmeir, 2010, Asian rival makes big strides on Adidas turf, Financial Times, www.ft.com, August 26; 2010, Li Ning to sell basketball shoes at select Champs Sports stores, SportsBusiness Daily, www.sportsbusinessdaily.com, July 21.

Flexibility is required for firms to complete primary value chain activities and support functions in ways that allow them to use the integrated cost leadership/differentiation strategy in order to produce somewhat differentiated products at relatively low costs. Chinese auto manufacturers have developed a means of product design that provides a flexible architecture that allows low-cost manufacturing but also car designs that are differentiated from competitors.[110] Flexible manufacturing systems, information networks, and total quality management systems are three sources of flexibility that are particularly useful for firms trying to balance the objectives of continuous cost reductions and continuous enhancements to sources of differentiation as called for by the integrated strategy.

The Li Ning Company is implementing an integrated cost leadership/differentiated strategy. The company entered the market and grew large using a cost leadership strategy. It is now seeking to enter the upscale markets in China, in which it will compete with Nike and Adidas. It is also entering the U.S. market, in which it will compete against both of these firms and other brand-name sportswear producers. Thus, it will encounter significant challenges. In fact, it may end up "stuck in the middle" and not compete effectively in any markets. Perhaps its opportunity is to provide high-quality brand-name goods for a lower price than its "upscale" competitors.

Flexible Manufacturing Systems

A flexible manufacturing system (FMS) increases the "flexibilities of human, physical, and information resources"[111] that the firm integrates to create relatively differentiated products at relatively low costs. A significant technological advance, FMS is a computer-controlled process used to produce a variety of products in moderate, flexible quantities with a minimum of manual intervention.[112] Often the flexibility is derived from modularization of the manufacturing process (and sometimes other value chain activities as well).[113]

The goal of an FMS is to eliminate the "low cost versus product variety" trade-off that is inherent in traditional manufacturing technologies. Firms use an FMS to change quickly and easily from making one product to making another. Used properly, an FMS allows the firm to respond more effectively to changes in its customers' needs, while retaining low-cost advantages and consistent product quality.[114] Because an FMS also enables the firm to reduce the lot size needed to manufacture a product efficiently, the firm's capacity to serve the unique needs of a narrow competitive scope is higher. In industries of all types, effective mixes of the firm's tangible assets (e.g., machines) and intangible assets (e.g., people's skills) facilitate implementation of complex competitive strategies, especially the integrated cost leadership/differentiation strategy.[115]

Information Networks

By linking companies with their suppliers, distributors, and customers, information networks provide another source of flexibility. These networks, when used effectively, help the firm satisfy customer expectations in terms of product quality and delivery speed.[116]

Earlier, we discussed the importance of managing the firm's relationships with its customers in order to understand their needs. Customer relationship management (CRM) is one form of an information-based network process that firms use for this purpose.[117] An effective CRM system provides a 360-degree view of the company's relationship with customers, encompassing all contact points, business processes, and communication media and sales channels.[118] The firm can then use this information to determine the trade-offs its customers are willing to make between differentiated features and low cost—an assessment that is vital for companies using the integrated cost leadership/differentiation strategy. Such systems help firms to monitor their markets and stakeholders and allow them to better predict future scenarios. This capability helps firms to adjust their strategies to be better prepared for the future.[119] Thus, to make comprehensive strategic decisions with effective knowledge of the organization's context, good information flow is essential. Better quality managerial decisions require accurate information on the firm's environment.[120]

Total Quality Management Systems

Total quality management (TQM) is a managerial process that emphasizes an organization's commitment to the customer and to continuous improvement of all processes through problem-solving approaches based on empowerment of employees.[121] Firms develop and use TQM systems to (1) increase customer satisfaction, (2) cut costs, and (3) reduce the amount of time required to introduce innovative products to the marketplace.[122]

Firms able to simultaneously reduce costs while enhancing their ability to develop innovative products increase their flexibility, an outcome that is particularly helpful to firms implementing the integrated cost leadership/differentiation strategy. Exceeding customers' expectations regarding quality is a differentiating feature, and eliminating process inefficiencies to cut costs allows the firm to offer that quality to customers at a relatively low price. Thus, an effective TQM system helps the firm develop the flexibility needed to identify opportunities to simultaneously increase differentiation and reduce costs. Yet, TQM systems are available to all competitors. So they may help firms maintain competitive parity, but rarely alone will they lead to a competitive advantage.[123]

Competitive Risks of the Integrated Cost Leadership/Differentiation Strategy

The potential to earn above-average returns by successfully using the integrated cost leadership/differentiation strategy is appealing. However, it is a risky strategy, because firms find it difficult to perform primary value chain activities and support functions in ways that allow them to produce relatively inexpensive products with levels of differentiation that create value for the target customer. Moreover, to properly use this strategy across time, firms must be able to simultaneously reduce costs incurred to produce products (as required by the cost leadership strategy) while increasing products' differentiation (as required by the differentiation strategy).

Firms that fail to perform the primary and support activities in an optimum manner become "stuck in the middle."[124] Being stuck in the middle means that the firm's cost structure is not low enough to allow it to attractively price its products and that its products are not sufficiently differentiated to create value for the target customer. These firms will not earn above-average returns and will earn average returns only when the structure of the industry in which it competes is highly favorable.[125] Thus, companies implementing the integrated cost leadership/differentiation strategy must be able to produce products that offer the target customer some differentiated features at a relatively low cost/price.

Firms can also become stuck in the middle when they fail to successfully implement *either* the cost leadership *or* the differentiation strategy. In other words, industry-wide competitors too can become stuck in the middle. Trying to use the integrated strategy is costly in that firms must pursue both low costs and differentiation. This is the challenge for the Li Ning Company. If it can offer high-quality goods desired by consumers at lower prices, however, it may be able to capture market share from the leaders, such as Nike.

Firms may need to form alliances with other firms to achieve differentiation, yet alliance partners may extract prices for the use of their resources that make it difficult to meaningfully reduce costs.[126] Firms may be motivated to make acquisitions to maintain their differentiation through innovation or to add products to their portfolio not offered by competitors.[127] Research suggests that firms using "pure strategies," either cost leadership or differentiation, often outperform firms attempting to use a "hybrid strategy" (i.e., integrated cost leadership/differentiation strategy). This research suggests the risky nature of using an integrated strategy.[128] However, the integrated strategy is becoming more common and perhaps necessary in many industries because of technological advances and global competition. This strategy often requires a long-term perspective to make it work effectively, and therefore requires dedicated owners that allow the implementation of a long-term strategy that can require several years to produce positive returns.[129]

Total quality management (TQM) is a managerial process that emphasizes an organization's commitment to the customer and to continuous improvement of all processes through problem-solving approaches based on empowerment of employees.

SUMMARY

- A business-level strategy is an integrated and coordinated set of commitments and actions the firm uses to gain a competitive advantage by exploiting core competencies in specific product markets. Five business-level strategies (cost leadership, differentiation, focused cost leadership, focused differentiation, and integrated cost leadership/differentiation) are examined in the chapter.

- Customers are the foundation of successful business-level strategies. When considering customers, a firm simultaneously examines three issues: *who*, *what*, and *how*. These issues, respectively, refer to the customer groups to be served, the needs those customers have that the firm seeks to satisfy, and the core competencies the firm will use to satisfy customers' needs. Increasing segmentation of markets throughout the global economy creates opportunities for firms to identify more distinctive customer needs they can serve with one of the business-level strategies.

- Firms seeking competitive advantage through the cost leadership strategy produce no-frills, standardized products for an industry's typical customer. However, these low-cost products must be offered with competitive levels of differentiation. Above-average returns are earned when firms continuously emphasize efficiency such that their costs are lower than those of their competitors, while providing customers with products that have acceptable levels of differentiated features.

- Competitive risks associated with the cost leadership strategy include (1) a loss of competitive advantage to newer technologies, (2) a failure to detect changes in customers' needs, and (3) the ability of competitors to imitate the cost leader's competitive advantage through their own distinct strategic actions.

- Through the differentiation strategy, firms provide customers with products that have different (and valued) features. Differentiated products must be sold at a cost that customers believe is competitive relative to the product's features as compared to the cost/feature combinations available from competitors' goods. Because of their distinctiveness, differentiated goods or services are sold at a premium price. Products can be differentiated on any dimension that some customer group values. Firms using this strategy seek to differentiate their products from competitors' goods or services on as many dimensions as possible. The less similarity to competitors' products, the more buffered a firm is from competition with its rivals.

- Risks associated with the differentiation strategy include (1) a customer group's decision that the differences between the differentiated product and the cost leader's goods or services are no longer worth a premium price, (2) the inability of a differentiated product to create the type of value for which customers are willing to pay a premium price, (3) the ability of competitors to provide customers with products that have features similar to those of the differentiated product, but at a lower cost, and (4) the threat of counterfeiting, whereby firms produce a cheap imitation of a differentiated good or service.

- Through the cost leadership and the differentiated focus strategies, firms serve the needs of a narrow competitive segment (e.g., a buyer group, product segment, or geographic area). This strategy is successful when firms have the core competencies required to provide value to a specialized market segment that exceeds the value available from firms serving customers on an industry-wide basis.

- The competitive risks of focus strategies include (1) a competitor's ability to use its core competencies to "outfocus" the focuser by serving an even more narrowly defined market segment, (2) decisions by industry-wide competitors to focus on a customer group's specialized needs, and (3) a reduction in differences of the needs between customers in a narrow market segment and the industry-wide market.

- Firms using the integrated cost leadership/differentiation strategy strive to provide customers with relatively low-cost products that also have valued differentiated features. Flexibility is required for firms to learn how to use primary value chain activities and support functions in ways that allow them to produce differentiated products at relatively low costs. The primary risk of this strategy is that a firm might produce products that do not offer sufficient value in terms of either low cost or differentiation. In such cases, the company becomes "stuck in the middle." Firms stuck in the middle compete at a disadvantage and are unable to earn more than average returns.

REVIEW QUESTIONS

1. What is a business-level strategy?

2. What is the relationship between a firm's customers and its business-level strategy in terms of *who*, *what*, and *how*? Why is this relationship important?

3. What are the differences among the cost leadership, differentiation, focused cost leadership, focused differentiation, and integrated cost leadership/differentiation business-level strategies?

4. How can each one of the business-level strategies be used to position the firm relative to the five forces of competition in a way that helps the firm earn above-average returns?

5. What are the specific risks associated with using each business-level strategy?

EXPERIENTIAL EXERCISES

EXERCISE 1: MARKET SEGMENTATION THROUGH BRANDING

The "who" in a firm's target market is an extremely important decision. As discussed in the chapter, firms divide customers into groups based upon differences in customer needs, which is the heart of market segmentation. For example, if you owned a restaurant and your target market was college-aged students, your strategy would be very different than if your target market was business professionals.

In this exercise, your team will be identifying market segmentation strategies used by various companies. Remember that market segmentation "is a process used to cluster people with similar needs into individual and identifiable groups."

Part One

Your team should select an advertised and prominent brand. You may choose a business or consumer product. However, you should choose a brand widely known and widely advertised. Once you have chosen the brand, find and collect at least four instances of this brand being advertised in print or digital media. Find your four or more instances from different publications, if possible.

Part Two

Assemble a poster with the images you collected from your research. Be prepared to present your findings to the class as regards:

1. Why did you choose this brand?

2. Review each of the criteria discussed in Table 4.1 for either your consumer market or industrial market.

EXERCISE 2: CREATE A BUSINESS-LEVEL STRATEGY

This assignment brings together elements from the previous chapters. Accordingly, you and your team will create a business-level strategy for a firm of your own creation. The instructor will assign you an industry from which you will create a strategy for entering that industry using one of the five potential business-level strategies.

Each team is assigned one of the business-level strategies described in the chapter:

- Cost leadership
- Differentiation
- Focused cost leadership
- Focused differentiation
- Integrated cost leadership/differentiation

Part One

Research your industry and describe the general environment and the industry. Using the dimensions of the general environment, identify some factors for each dimension that are influential for your industry. Next, describe the industry environment using the Five Forces model. Database services like Mint Global, Datamonitor, or IBIS World can be helpful in this regard. If those are not available to you, consult your local librarian for assistance. You should be able to clearly articulate the opportunities and the threats that exist.

Part Two

Create on a poster the business-level strategy assigned to your team. Be prepared to describe the following:

- Mission statement
- Description of your target customer
- Picture of your business. Where is it located (downtown, suburb, rural, etc.)?
- Describe trends that provide opportunities and threats for your intended strategy.
- List the resources, both tangible and intangible, required to compete successfully in this market.
- How will you go about creating a sustainable competitive advantage?

VIDEO CASE

DIFFERENTIATION STRATEGY IN TOUGH ECONOMIC TIMES

Howard Schultz/CEO/Starbucks

Starbucks, 17,000 stores strong worldwide, offers 70,000 different ways to order coffee. Unfortunately, Starbucks has announced the closing of 900 underperforming stores in the United States and will cut more than 1,000 jobs. Howard Schultz, Starbucks CEO, admits that Starbucks may have grown too big too fast given today's economy, and a business plan was not in place for the severity of the economic downturn. During this time, competitors like Dunkin Donuts are offering an upgraded coffee experience at a lower cost. However, Schultz maintains that Starbucks will not cut corners but will reduce waste to save the company more than $400 million and continue to sell more than a cup of coffee.

Be prepared to discuss the following concepts and questions in class:

Concepts

- Business-level strategy
- Managing relationship with customers
- Market segmentation
- Differentiation strategy
- Five forces of competition

Questions

1. Describe Starbucks' business-level strategy.
2. How is Starbucks managing its relationship with customers?
3. How would you describe the market segment(s) that Starbucks serves?
4. Is the differentiation strategy appropriate for Starbucks, now or in the future? Why or why not?
5. Using the five forces model of competition, how should Starbucks plan to position itself in these economic times?

NOTES

1. R. D. Ireland, R. E. Hoskisson, & M. A. Hitt, 2012. *Understanding Business Strategy*. Mason, OH: Southwestern-Cengage learning.

2. H. Greve, 2009, Bigger and safer: The diffusion of competitive advantage, *Strategic Management Journal*, 30: 1–23.

3. M. A. Delmas & M. W. Toffel, 2008, Organizational responses to environmental demands: Opening the black box, *Strategic Management Journal*, 29: 1027–1055; S. Elbanna & J. Child, 2007, The influence of decision, environmental and firm characteristics on the rationality of strategic decision-making, *Journal of Management Studies*, 44: 561–591.

4. J. Barney, D. J. Ketchen, & M. Wright, 2011, The future of the resource-based view: Revitalization of decline? *Journal of Management*, in press; D. G. Sirmon, M. A. Hitt, R. D. Ireland, & B. A. Gilbert, 2011, Resource orchestration to create competitive advantage: Breadth, depth and life cycle effects, *Journal of Management*, in press.

5. N. A. Morgan & L. L. Rego, 2009, Brand portfolio strategy and firm performance, *Journal of Marketing*, 73: 59–74; C. Zott & R. Amit, 2008, The fit between product market strategy and business model: Implications for firm performance, *Strategic Management Journal*, 29: 1–26.

6. S. Kaplan, 2008, Framing contests: Strategy making under uncertainty, *Organization Science*, 19: 729–752.

7. S. Maxfield, 2008, Reconciling corporate citizenship and competitive strategy: Insights from economic theory, *Journal of Business Ethics*, 80: 367–377; K. Shimizu & M. A. Hitt, 2004, Strategic flexibility: Organizational preparedness to reverse ineffective strategic decisions, *Academy of Management Executive*, 18(4): 44–59.

8. B. Chakravarthy & P. Lorange, 2008, Driving renewal: The entrepreneur-manager, *Journal of Business Strategy*, 29: 14–21.

9. J. A. Lamberg, H. Tikkanen, T. Nokelainen, & H. Suur-Inkeroinen, 2009, Competitive dynamics, strategic consistency, and organizational survival, *Strategic Management Journal*, 30: 45–60; R. D. Ireland & C. C. Miller, 2005, Decision-making and firm success, *Academy of Management Executive*, 18(4): 8–12.

10. I. Goll, N. B. Johnson, & A. A. Rasheed, 2008, Top management team demographic characteristics, business strategy, and firm performance in the U.S. airline industry: The role of managerial discretion, *Management Decision*, 46: 201–222; J. R. Hough, 2006, Business segment performance redux: A multilevel approach, *Strategic Management Journal*, 27: 45–61.

11. P. Ozcan & K. M. Eisenhardt, 2009, Origin of alliance portfolios: Entrepreneurs, network strategies, and firm performance, *Academy of Management Journal*, 52: 246–279; B. Choi, S. K. Poon, & J. G. Davis, 2008, Effects of knowledge management strategy on organizational performance: A complementarity theory-based approach, *Omega*, 36: 235–251.

12. J. W. Spencer, 2008, The impact of multinational enterprise strategy on indigenous enterprises: Horizontal spillovers and crowding out in developing countries, *Academy of Management Review*, 33: 341–361.

13. MySpace, 2011, *Wikipedia*, http://en.wikipedia.org, March 23; Facebook, 2011, *Wikipedia*, http://en.wikipedia.org, March 23.

14. D. Lei & J. W. Slocum, 2009, The tipping points of business strategy: The rise and decline of competitiveness, *Organizational Dynamics*, 38: 131–147.

15. R. J. Harrington & A. K. Tjan, 2008, Transforming strategy one customer at a time, *Harvard Business Review*, 86(3): 62–72; R. Priem, 2007, A consumer perspective on value creation, *Academy of Management Review*, 32: 219–235.

16. M. Pynnonen, P. Ritala, & J. Hallikas, 2011, The new meaning of customer value: A systemic perspective, *Journal of Business Strategy*, 32(1): 51–57.

17. M. E. Porter, 1980, *Competitive Strategy*, New York: Free Press.

18. M. Baghai, S. Smit, & P. Viguerie, 2009, Is your growth strategy flying blind? *Harvard Business Review*, 87(5): 86–96.

19. D. G. Sirmon, S. Gove, & M. A. Hitt, 2008, Resource management in dyadic competitive rivalry: The effects of resource bundling and deployment, *Academy of Management Journal*, 51: 919–935; D. G. Sirmon, M. A. Hitt, & R. D. Ireland, 2007, Managing firm resources in dynamic environments to create value: Inside the black box, *Academy of Management Review*, 32: 273–292.

20. J. Singh, P. Lentz, & E. J. Nijssen, 2011, First- and second-order effects of institutional logics on firm-consumer relationships: A cross-market comparative analysis, *Journal of International Business Studies*, 42: 307–333.

21. J. McGregor, 2009, When service means survival, *BusinessWeek*, March 2: 26–33.

22. 2011, Company information, http://www.caesars.com, April 26.

23. Y. Liu & R. Yang, 2009, Competing loyalty programs: Impact of market saturation, market share, and category expandability, *Journal of Marketing*, 73: 93–108.

24. P. E. Frown & A. F. Payne, 2009, Customer relationship management: A strategic perspective, *Journal of Business Market Management*, 3: 7–27.

25. H. Green, 2009, How Amazon aims to keep you clicking, *BusinessWeek*, March 2: 34–35.

26. MySpace, 2011, *Wikipedia*, http://en.wikipedia.org, March 23; Facebook, 2011, *Wikipedia*, http://en.wikipedia.org, March 23.

27. 2011, Netflix 2010 4th Quarter Report, http://www.netflix.com, January 26.

28. M. Bogers, A. Afuah, & B. Bastian, 2010, Users as innovators: A review, critique and future research directions, *Journal of Management*, 36: 857–875.

29. L-Y Jin, 2010, Determinants of customers' complaint intention, *Nankai Business Review International*, 1: 87–99.

30. 2011, http://www.autos.msn.com, April 26.

31. S. F. Slater, E. M. Olson, & G. T. Hult, 2010, Worried about strategy implementation? Don't overlook marketing's role, *Business Horizons*, 53: 469–479; I. C. MacMillan & L. Selden, 2008, The incumbent's advantage, *Harvard Business Review*, 86(10): 111–121.

32. C. W. Lamb Jr., J. F. Hair Jr., & C. McDaniel, 2011, *Marketing*, 11th ed., Mason, OH: South-Western Cengage Learning.

33. 2011, About Hill's pet nutrition, http://www.hillspet.com, April 26.

34. S. French, 2009, Re-framing strategic thinking: The research—aims and outcomes, *Journal of Management Development*, 28: 205–224.

35. R. J. Brodie, J. R. M. Whittome, & G. J. Brush, 2009, Investigating the service brand: A customer value perspective, *Journal of Business Research*, 62: 345–355; P. D. Ellis, 2006, Market orientation and performance: A meta-analysis and cross-national comparisons, *Journal of Management Studies*, 43: 1089–1107.

36. L. A. Bettencourt & A. W. Ulwick, 2008, The customer-centered innovation map, *Harvard Business Review*, 86(5): 109–114.

37. A. Feldman, 2009, Wooing the worried, *BusinessWeek*, April 27, 24.

38. R. Lewis & M. Dart, 2010, *The New Rules of Retail*, New York: Palgrave Macmillan.

39. C. A. Funk, J. D. Arthurs, L. J. Trevino, & J. Joireman, 2010, Consumer animosity in the global value chain: The effect of international shifts on willingness to purchase hybrid products. *Journal of International Business Studies*, 41: 639–651.

40. T. Y. Eng & J. G. Spickett-Jones, 2009, An investigation of marketing capabilities and upgrading performance of manufacturers in Mainland China and Hong Kong, *Journal of World Business*, in press; M. B. Heeley & R. Jacobson, 2008, The recency of technological inputs and financial performance, *Strategic Management Journal*, 29: 723–744.

41. P. L. Drnevich & A. P. Kriauciunas, 2011, Clarifying the conditions and limits of the contributions of ordinary and dynamic capabilities to relative firm performance, *Strategic Management Journal*, 32: 254–279.

42. M. Gruber, F. Heinimann, M. Brietel, & S. Hungeling, 2010, Configurations of resources and capabilities and their performance implications: An exploratory study on technology ventures, *Strategic Management Journal*, 31: 1337–1356.

43. T. Randall, 2011, Merck's risky bet on research, *Bloomberg Businessweek*, April 25: 25–26.

44. 2011, About SAS, http://www.sas.com, April 27.

45. K. E. Klein, 2009, Survival advice for auto parts suppliers, *Wall Street Journal Online*, http://www.wsj.com, June 16.

46. M. E. Porter, 1985, *Competitive Advantage*, New York: Free Press, 26.

47. R. Rumelt, 2011, *Good Strategy/Bad Strategy*, New York: Crown Business.

48. M. E. Porter, 1996, What is strategy? *Harvard Business Review*, 74(6): 61–78.

49. Porter, What is strategy?

50. M. Reitzig & P. Puranam, 2009, Value appropriation as an organizational capability: The case of IP protection through patents, *Strategic Management Journal*, 30: 765–789; C. Zott, 2003, Dynamic capabilities and the emergence of intraindustry differential firm performance: Insights from a simulation study, *Strategic Management Journal*, 24: 97–125.

51. M. E. Porter, 1994, Toward a dynamic theory of strategy, in R. P. Rumelt, D. E. Schendel, & D. J. Teece (eds.), *Fundamental Issues in Strategy,* Boston: Harvard Business School Press: 423–461.

52. Porter, What is strategy?, 62.

53. Porter, *Competitive Advantage*, 15.

54. S. Sun, 2009, An analysis on the conditions and methods of market segmentation, *International Journal of Business and Management*, 4: 63–70.

55. J. Gonzales-Benito & I. Suarez-Gonzalez, 2010, A study of the role played by manufacturing strategic objectives and capabilities in understanding the relationship between Porter's generic strategies and business performance, *British Journal of Management*, 21(4): 1027–1043.

56. Ireland, Hoskisson, & Hitt, *Understanding Business Strategy*; G. B. Voss, D. Sirdeshmukh, & Z. G. Voss, 2008, The effects of slack resources and environmental threat on product exploration and exploitation, *Academy of Management Journal*, 51: 147–158.

57. S. McKee, 2009, Customers your company doesn't want, *Wall Street Journal Online*, http://www.wsj.com, June 12.

58. Porter, *Competitive Strategy*, 35–40.

59. M. J. Gehlhar, A. Regmi, S. E. Stefanou, & B. L. Zoumas, 2009, Brand leadership and product innovation as firm strategies in global food markets, *Journal of Product & Brand Management*, 18: 115–126.

60. M. Ihlwan, 2009, Kia Motors: Still cheap, now chic, *BusinessWeek*, June 1, 58.

61. D. Mehri, 2006, The dark side of lean: An insider's perspective on the realities of the Toyota production system, *Academy of Management Perspectives*, 20(2): 21–42.

62. N. T. Sheehan & G. Vaidyanathan, 2009, Using a value creation compass to discover "Blue Oceans," *Strategy & Leadership*, 37: 13–20.

63. A. M. Chaker, 2009, Planes, trains … and buses? *Wall Street Journal Online*, http://www.wsj.com, June 18.

64. 2011, About Greyhound, http://www.greyhound.com, April 27.

65. M. Kotabe & R. Mudambi, 2009, Global sourcing and value creation: Opportunities and challenges, *Journal of International Management*, 15: 121–125; D. F. Lynch, S. B. Keller, & J. Ozment, 2000, The effects of logistics capabilities and strategy on firm performance, *Journal of Business Logistics*, 21(2): 47–68.

66. R. Liu, D. J. Feils, & B. Scholnick, 2011, Why are different services outsources to different countries? *Journal of International Business Studies*, 42: 558–571; J. Hatonen & T. Erikson, 2009, 30+ years of research and practice of outsourcing—Exploring the past and anticipating the future, *Journal of International Management*, 15: 142–155.

67. M. J. Lennox, S. F. Rockart, & A. Y. Lewin, 2010, Does interdependency affect firm and industry profitability? An empirical test, *Strategic Management Journal*, 31: 121–139.

68. 2011, Corporate overview, http://www.biglots.com, May 2.

69. J. Morehouse, B. O'Mera, C. Hagen, & T. Huseby, 2008, Hitting back: Strategic responses to low-cost rivals, *Strategy & Leadership*, 36: 4–13; L. K. Johnson, 2003, Dueling pricing strategies, *The McKinsey Quarterly*, 44(3): 10–11.

70. G. J. Kilduff, H. A. Elfenbein, & B. W. Staw, 2010, The psychology of rivalry: A relationally dependent analysis of competition, *Academy of Management Journal*, 53: 943–969.

71. T. W. Tong & J. J. Reuer, 2010, Competitive consequences of interfirm collaboration: How joint ventures shape industry profitability, *Journal of International Business Studies*, 41: 1056–1073.

72. O. D. Fjeldstad & A. Sasson, 2010, Membership matters: On the value of being embedded in customer networks, *Journal of Management Studies*, 47: 944–966.

73. F. J. Contractor, V. Kumar, S. K. Kundu, & T. Pedersen, 2010, Reconceptualizing the firm in a world of outsourcing and offshoring: The organizational and geographical relocation of high-value company functions. *Journal of Management Studies*, 47: 1417–1433.

74. Y. Zhang & J. Gimeno, 2010, Earnings pressure and competitive behavior: Evidence from the U.S. electricity industry, *Academy of Management Journal*, 53: 743–768.

75. B. Flynn, 2010, Introduction to the special topic forum on global supply chain management, *Journal of Supply Chain Management*, 46(2): 3–4.

76. J. Dyer & W. Chu, 2011, The determinants of trust in supplier–automaker relations in the U.S., Japan and Korea: A retrospective, *Journal of International Business Studies*, 42: 28–34; M-S. Cheung, M. B. Myers, & J. T. Mentzer, 2011, The value of relational learning in global buyer-supplier exchanges: A dyadic perspective and test of the pie-sharing hypothesis, *Strategic Management Journal*, 32: in press.

77. O. Ormanidhi & O. Stringa, 2008, Porter's model of generic competitive strategies, *Business Economics*, 43: 55–64; J. Bercovitz & W. Mitchell, 2007, When is more better? The impact of business scale and scope on long-term business survival, while controlling for profitability, *Strategic Management Journal*, 28: 61–79.

78. K. Z. Zhou & F. Wu, 2010, Technological capability, strategic flexibility and product innovation, *Strategic Management Journal*, 31: 547–561.

79. Porter, *Competitive Strategy*, 35–40.

80. 2009, Product innovation, http://www.1000ventures.com, June 19.

81. D. Dunlap-Hinkler, M. Kotabe, & R. Mudambi, 2010, A story of breakthrough versus incremental innovation: Corporate entrepreneurship in the global pharmaceutical industry, *Strategic Entrepreneurship Journal*, 4: 106–127; R. Cowan & N. Jonard, 2009, Knowledge portfolios and the organization of innovation networks, *Academy of Management Review*, 34: 320–342.

82. Z. Simsek & C. Heavy, 2011, The mediating role of knowledge-based capital for corporate entrepreneurship effects on performance: A study of

small-to medium sized firms, *Strategic Entrepreneurship Journal*, 5: 81–100.

83. R. Kotha, Y. Zheng, & G. George, 2011, Entry into new niches: The effects of firm age and the expansion of technological capabilities on innovative output and impact, *Strategic Management Journal*, 32: in press; D. Ashmos Plowman, L. T. Baker, T. E. Beck, M. Kulkarni, S. Thomas-Solansky, & D. V. Travis, 2007, Radical change accidentally: The emergence and amplification of small change, *Academy of Management Journal*, 50: 515–543.

84. R. Agarwal, D. Audretsch, & M. B. Sarkar, 2010, Knowledge spillovers and strategic entrepreneurship, *Strategic Entrepreneurship Journal*, 4: 271–283; M. J. Benner, 2007, The incumbent discount: Stock market categories and response to radical technological change, *Academy of Management Review*, 32: 703–720.

85. F. T. Rothaermel, M. A. Hitt, & L. A. Jobe, 2006, Balancing vertical integration and strategic outsourcing: Effects on product portfolio, product success and firm performance, *Strategic Management Journal*, 27: 1033–1056; A. V. Mainkar, M. Lubatkin, & W. S. Schulze, 2006, Toward a product-proliferation theory of entry barriers, *Academy of Management Review*, 31: 1062–1075.

86. A. Cuervo-Cazurra & C. A. Un, 2010, Why some firms never invest in R&D, *Strategic Management Journal*, 31: 759–779.

87. E. Levitas & T. Chi, 2010, A look at the value creation effects of patenting and capital investment through a real-option lens: The moderation role of uncertainty, *Strategic Entrepreneurship Journal*, 4: 212–233; L. A. Bettencourt & A. W. Ulwick, 2008, The customer-centered innovation map, *Harvard Business Review*, 86(5): 109–114.

88. M. Abbott, R. Holland, J. Giacomin, & J. Shackleton, 2009, Changing affective content in brand and product attributes, *Journal of Product & Brand Management*, 18: 17–26.

89. B. Charny & J. A. Dicolo, 2009, Apple debuts new iPhones to long lines, *Wall Street Journal Online*, http://www.wsj.com, June 19.

90. B. K. Boyd, D. D. Bergh, & D. J. Ketchen, 2010, Reconsidering the reputation-performance relationship: A resource-based view, *Journal of Management*, 36: 588-609; V. P. Rindova, I. O. Williamson & A. P. Petkova, 2010, Reputation as an intangible asset: reflections on theory and methods in two empirical studies of business school reputations, *Journal of Management*, 36: 610-619.

91. O. Chatain, 2011, Value creation, competition and performance in buyer-supplier relationships, *Strategic Management Journal*, 32: 76–102.

92. S. Berfield, 2009, Coach's new bag, *BusinessWeek*, June 29: 41–43; S. Berfield, 2009, Coach's Poppy line is luxury for recessionary times, *BusinessWeek Online*, http://www.wsj.com, June 18.

93. D. G. Sirmon, J.-L. Arregle, M. A. Hitt, & J. W. Webb, 2008, The role of family influence in firms' strategic responses to threat of imitation, *Entrepreneurship Theory and Practice*, 32: 979–998; F. K. Pil & S. K. Cohen, 2006, Modularity: Implications for imitation, innovation, and sustained advantage, *Academy of Management Review*, 31: 995–1011.

94. M. M. Crossan & M. Apaydin, 2010, A multi-dimensional framework of organizational innovation: A systematic review of the literature, *Journal of Management Studies*, 47: 1154–1180.

95. X. Bian & L. Moutinho, 2009, An investigation of determinants of counterfeit purchase consideration, *Journal of Business Research*, 62: 368–378.

96. Porter, *Competitive Strategy*; K. Blomkvist, P. Kappen, & I. Zander, 2010, Quo vadis? The entry into new technologies in advanced foreign subsidiaries of the multinational enterprise, *Journal of International Business Studies*, 41: 525–549.

97. 2011, Greif & Co., http://www.greifco.com, May 6.

98. 2011, About Goya foods, http://www.goyafoods.com, May 6.

99. Porter, *Competitive Advantage*, 15.

100. Ibid., 15–16.

101. K. Kling & I. Goteman, 2003, IKEA CEO Andres Dahlvig on international growth and IKEA's unique corporate culture and brand identity, *Academy of Management Executive*, 17(1): 31–37.

102. 2009, About IKEA, http://www.ikea.com, June 21.

103. G. Evans, 2003, Why some stores strike me as special, *Furniture Today*, 27(24): 91; Porter, What is strategy? 65.

104. K. McLaughlin, 2009, Food truck nation, *Wall Street Journal Online*, http://www.wsj.com, June 5.

105. B. R. Barringer & R. D. Ireland, 2008, *Entrepreneurship: Successfully Launching New Ventures*, 2nd ed., Upper Saddle River, NJ: Prentice-Hall.

106. 2011, Anne Fontaine, http://www.factio-magazine.com, May 6.

107. H. A. Ndofor, D. G. Sirmon, & X. He, 2011, Firm resources, competitive actions and performance: Investigating a mediated model with evidence from the in-vitro diagnostics industry, *Strategic Management Journal*, 32: 640–657; R. A. D'Aveni, G. B. Dagnino, & K. G. Smith, 2010, The age of temporary advantage, *Strategic Management Journal*, 31: 1371–1385.

108. 2010, Letter to our shareholders, Target Annual Report, http://www.target.com, March 11.

109. 2011, Company, Zara, http://www.zara.com, May 6; K. Capell, 2008, Zara thrives by breaking all the rules, *BusinessWeek*, October 20, 66.

110. H. Wang & C. Kimble, 2010, Low-cost strategy through product architecture: Lessons from China, *Journal of Business Strategy*, 31(3): 12–20.

111. R. Sanchez, 1995, Strategic flexibility in product competition, *Strategic Management Journal*, 16 (Special Issue): 140.

112. M. I. M. Wahab, D. Wu, and C.-G. Lee, 2008, A generic approach to measuring the machine flexibility of manufacturing systems, *European Journal of Operational Research*, 186: 137–149.

113. M. Kotabe, R. Parente, & J. Y. Murray, 2007, Antecedents and outcomes of modular production in the Brazilian automobile industry: A grounded theory approach, *Journal of International Business Studies*, 38: 84–106.

114. T. Raj, R. Shankar, & M. Sunhaib, 2009, An ISM approach to analyse interaction between barriers of transition to flexible manufacturing systems, *International Journal of Manufacturing Technology and Management*, 16: 417–438. E. K. Bish, A. Muriel, & S. Biller, 2005, Managing flexible capacity in a make-to-order environment, *Management Science*, 51: 167–180.

115. S. M. Iravani, M. P. van Oyen, & K. T. Sims, 2005, Structural flexibility: A new perspective on the design of manufacturing and service operations, *Management Science*, 51: 151–166.

116. P. Theodorou & G. Florou, 2008, Manufacturing strategies and financial performance—the effect of advanced information technology: CAD/CAM systems, *Omega*, 36: 107–121.

117. N. A. Morgan & L. L. Rego, 2009, Brand portfolio strategy and firm performance, *Journal of Marketing*, 73: 59–74.

118. D. Elmuti, H. Jia, & D. Gray, 2009, Customer relationship management strategic application and organizational effectiveness: An empirical investigation, *Journal of Strategic Marketing*, 17: 75–96.

119. C. O. Scharmer & K. Kaeufer, 2010, In front of blank canvas: Sensing emerging futures, *Journal of Business Strategy*, 31(4): 21–29

120. D. P. Forbes, 2007, Reconsidering the strategic implications of decision comprehensiveness, *Academy of Management Review*, 32: 361–376.

121. J. D. Westphal, R. Gulati, & S. M. Shortell, 1997, Customization or conformity: An institutional and network perspective on the content and consequences of TQM adoption, *Administrative Science Quarterly*, 42: 366–394.

122. S. Modell, 2009, Bundling management control innovations: A field study of organisational experimenting with total quality management and the balanced scorecard, *Accounting, Auditing & Accountability Journal*, 22: 59–90.

123. A. Keramati & A. Albadvi, 2009, Exploring the relationship between use of information technology in total quality management

and SMEs performance using canonical correlation analysis: A survey on Swedish car part supplier sector, *International Journal of Information Technology and Management*, 8: 442–462; R. J. David & S. Strang, 2006, When fashion is fleeting: Transitory collective beliefs and the dynamics of TQM consulting, *Academy of Management Journal*, 49: 215–233.

124. Porter, *Competitive Advantage*, 16.

125. Ibid., 17.

126. M. A. Hitt, L. Bierman, K. Uhlenbruck, & K. Shimizu, 2006, The importance of resources in the internationalization of professional service firms: The good, the bad, and the ugly, *Academy of Management Journal*, 49: 1137–1157.

127. P. Puranam, H. Singh, & M. Zollo, 2006, Organizing for innovation: Managing the coordination-autonomy dilemma in technology acquisitions, *Academy of Management Journal*, 49: 263–280.

128. S. Thornhill & R. E. White, 2007, Strategic purity: A multi-industry evaluation of pure vs. hybrid business strategies, *Strategic Management Journal*, 28: 553–561.

129. B. Connelly, L. Tihanyi, S. T. Certo, & M. A. Hitt, 2010, Marching to the beat of different drummers: The influence of institutional owners on competitive actions, *Academy of Management Journal*, 53: 723–742.

CHAPTER 5

Competitive Rivalry and Competitive Dynamics

Studying this chapter should provide you with the strategic management knowledge needed to:

1. Define competitors, competitive rivalry, competitive behavior, and competitive dynamics.

2. Describe market commonality and resource similarity as the building blocks of a competitor analysis.

3. Explain awareness, motivation, and ability as drivers of competitive behaviors.

4. Discuss factors affecting the likelihood a competitor will take competitive actions.

5. Describe factors affecting the likelihood a competitor will respond to actions taken against it.

6. Explain the competitive dynamics in each of slow-cycle, fast-cycle, and standard-cycle markets.

DISRUPTIVE INNOVATION: WINNING RIVALRY BATTLES AGAINST COMPETITORS

Clayton Christensen, a Harvard professor and author of *The Innovator's Dilemma*, has focused his career on studying "disruptive innovation." He defines disruptive innovation as "an innovation that makes it so much simpler and so much more affordable to own and use a product that a whole new population of people can now have one." He suggests that some disruptive innovations are "the personal computer, the router, Toyota's automobiles, Kodak's original camera, Xerox's original photocopier and Canon's desktop photocopier."

For example, Xerox was disrupted by Canon. Xerox's main business was selling larger photocopiers to business customers that operated centralized, high-speed photocopier centers. Canon came in with desktop copiers that could make three or four copies a minute but couldn't collate, enlarge, or do grayscale replication. Xerox got no signal from its customers that this little table-top copier was important. However, little by little, Canon made its smaller photocopiers better, faster, more capable, and more convenient to use, and created an entirely new broad-based and more consumer-oriented market. Canon's market increased when its copier became a multi-function printer, scanner, and fax machine, usable by consumers as well as small and medium-sized businesses.

Apple's iPhone has disrupted the cell phone and personal computer markets, creating the smartphone segment. Its application software increases its available

With the rise of online streaming video, Walmart has entered the game and is gaining share with its Vudu service.

functions as compared to a cell phone, which is used primarily for phone, texting, and e-mail services. This has created a disruption across many industries, including laptops (especially once the iPad came out), GPS firms like TomTom who make portable GPS navigation systems, and game platform producers such as Nintendo.

For example, in 2010, when Apple introduced its new operating system (iOS) software that runs the iPhone and iPad, it was announced that the new operating system would include "an Apple-hosted social-gaming service called Game Center." OpenFeint, a video game startup, built a service that let video game players play one another on Apple devices. The overall application software market grew 160 percent in 2010 to $2.2 billion, with Apple's App Store accounting for 83 percent of the total. Interestingly, 17 percent of the 409,000 apps offered in the App Store are games. This is a significant increase in revenue, especially for a company like Apple, which derives most of its money from selling hardware.

At first, Apple prevented interaction between phones, such as for gaming purposes, because it was perceived as a security problem. However, hackers broke the code and started using the platform as a game machine. This serendipitous finding was picked up quickly by Apple, which introduced the update to its iOS software and began racking up sales of more than $1 million a day by August of 2008. Additionally, it cut the price on its iPod touch and started advertising it as a game device besides its other features.

As the iPad continues to improve its graphics power, game platform hardware and software producers are threatened. Steve Jobs was quoted as saying, "That's a big bag of hurt for old school video game companies." This is because Apple's hardware and operating systems are multi-functional (with many uses besides games) and there are a large set of game application software producers creating products for the Apple platform. The products are mobile and the games can be played anywhere. Sony, which makes the PlayStation console, has responded with the Xperia PLAY phone; it has a slide-out controller and is

Read more about Canon's consumer market.

www.cengagebrain .com

"PlayStation-certified," meaning that players can use already-owned games on the PLAY phone. The phone is made by Sony Ericsson (partner in the joint venture) and runs Google's popular Android operating system. Google is an additional player in this market. It has an increasing number of games being produced using its Linux-based operating system, which is an open source software. Compare this to Apple's approach, which requires companies to develop software that fits its closed operating system.

However, in the video-on-demand market, Apple's iTunes service might be disrupted by none other than Walmart. Walmart owns Vudu, a non-subscription video streaming service, which has allowed Walmart to rapidly gain market share. While iTunes flourishes within the Apple family of products (Macs, iPads, iPods, and iPhones), "Vudu is available on 300 different TVs, Blu-ray players and video game consoles from the likes of Sony, Philips, and Samsung." Walmart's objective is to be everywhere because Walmart has spent $3.5 billion in sourcing DVDs from Hollywood studios. It therefore has power to leverage and promote its Vudu service. Although Apple's revenues in 2010 were $385 million from movies and TV shows sold on the Web with a 64 percent market share, Vudu is rapidly increasing. In second place, Microsoft has a distant eight percent share, but Walmart is tied for third with Amazon for the most on-demand movies rented in the last quarter of 2010. Although Vudu is avoiding direct conflict with Netflix, the largest online subscription service, Walmart through its non-subscription Vudu service, represents a David with "a shiny new slingshot" with Apple as the Goliath.

Sources: 2011, Hand to hand combat, *Economist*, February 26, 70–72; B. Caulfield, 2011, Apple says game on, *Forbes*, April 25, 34–36; C. Christensen & J. Euchner, 2011, Managing disruption: An interview with Clayton Christensen, *Research Technology Management*, 54(1): 11–17; D. Pomerantz, 2011, What's on Walmart?, *Forbes*, April 25, 38; C. Sorensen, 2011, Games on the go, *MacLean's*, February 21, 43; A. M. Subramanian, K. Chai, & S. Mu, 2011, Capability reconfiguration of incumbent firms: Nintendo in the video game industry, *Technovation*, 31(5/6): 228–239; D. Tang, 2011, Off to the races, *Wall Street Journal*, February 19, D12; D. Tang, 2011, The new retro, *Wall Street Journal*, March 19, D11; M. Holmes, 2010, The world of disruption, *VIA Satellite*, December, 7; V. Rindova, W. Ferrier & R. Wiltbank, 2010, Value from gestalt: How sequences of competitive actions create advantage for firms in nascent markets, *Strategic Management Journal*, 31(13): 1474–1497; N. Wingfield, 2010, Why we can't stop playing, *Wall Street Journal*, November 30, D1–D2.

Firms operating in the same market, offering similar products, and targeting similar customers are **competitors**.[1] Southwest Airlines, Delta, United, Continental, and JetBlue are competitors, as are PepsiCo and Coca-Cola Company. As described in the Opening Case, Apple's family of products (Macs, iPads, iPods, and iPhones) are currently engaging in a competitive battle in the video game market with stand-alone and mobile game platforms produced by Sony, Microsoft, and Nintendo. As noted in the Opening Case, in response, Sony has produced a PLAY phone that has its own game console and allows one to use "play station certified games" on the mobile device.[2]

Firms interact with their competitors as part of the broad context within which they operate while attempting to earn above-average returns.[3] The decisions firms make about their interactions with their competitors significantly affect their ability to earn above-average returns.[4] Because 80 to 90 percent of new firms fail, learning how to select the markets in which to compete and how to best compete within them is highly important.[5]

Competitive rivalry is the ongoing set of competitive actions and competitive responses that occur among firms as they maneuver for an advantageous market position.[6] Especially in highly competitive industries, firms constantly jockey for advantage as they launch strategic actions and respond or react to rivals' moves.[7] It is important for those leading organizations to understand competitive rivalry, in that "the central, brute empirical fact in strategy is that some firms outperform others,"[8] meaning that competitive rivalry influences an individual firm's ability to gain and sustain competitive advantages.[9]

A sequence of firm-level moves, rivalry results from firms initiating their own competitive actions and then responding to actions taken by competitors.[10] **Competitive behavior** is the set of competitive actions and responses the firm takes to build or defend its competitive advantages and to improve its market position.[11] Through competitive behavior, the firm tries to successfully position itself relative to the five forces of competition (see Chapter 2) and to defend current competitive advantages while building advantages for the future (see Chapter 3). Increasingly, competitors engage in competitive

Competitors are firms operating in the same market, offering similar products, and targeting similar customers.

Competitive rivalry is the ongoing set of competitive actions and competitive responses that occur among firms as they maneuver for an advantageous market position.

Competitive behavior is the set of competitive actions and competitive responses the firm takes to build or defend its competitive advantages and to improve its market position.

Figure 5.1 From Competitors to Competitive Dynamics

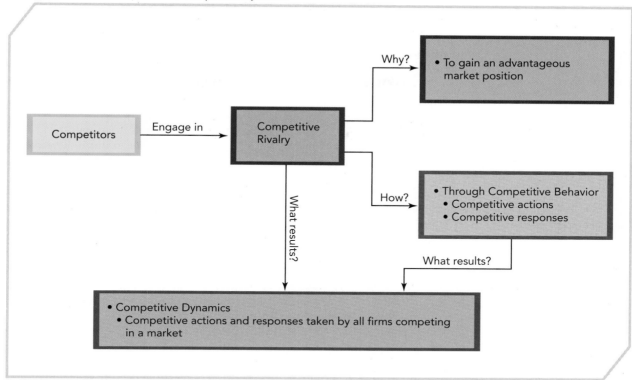

Source: Adapted from M. J. Chen, 1996, Competitor analysis and interfirm rivalry: Toward a theoretical integration, *Academy of Management Review*, 21: 100–134.

actions and responses in more than one market.[12] Firms competing against each other in several product or geographic markets are engaged in **multimarket competition**.[13]

All competitive behavior—that is, the total set of actions and responses taken by all firms competing within a market—is called **competitive dynamics**. The relationships among these key concepts are shown in Figure 5.1.

This chapter focuses on competitive rivalry and competitive dynamics. A firm's strategies are dynamic in nature because actions taken by one firm elicit responses from competitors that, in turn, typically result in responses from the firm that took the initial action.[14] As explained in the Opening Case, Apple, Sony, and other video game producers are changing how they compete as they respond to competitive moves. Likewise, Walmart is seeking to enter the video-on-demand market through Vudu as it responds to iTunes dominance in this market.

Competitive rivalries affect a firm's strategies, as shown by the fact that a strategy's success is determined not only by the firm's initial competitive actions but also by how well it anticipates competitors' responses to them *and* by how well the firm anticipates and responds to its competitors' initial actions (also called attacks).[15] Although competitive rivalry affects all types of strategies (e.g., corporate-level, acquisition, and international), its dominant influence is on the firm's business-level strategy or strategies. Indeed, firms' actions and responses to those of their rivals are the basic building blocks of business-level strategies.[16] Recall from Chapter 4 that business-level strategy is concerned with what the firm does to successfully use its competitive advantages in specific product markets. In the global economy, competitive rivalry is intensifying,[17] meaning that the significance of its effect on firms' business-level strategies is increasing. However, firms that develop and use effective business-level strategies tend to outperform competitors in individual product markets, even when experiencing intense competitive rivalry that price cuts bring about.[18]

Find out more about Apple's cutting-edge technology strategy.
www.cengagebrain.com

Multimarket competition occurs when firms compete against each other in several product or geographic markets.

Competitive dynamics refer to all competitive behaviors—that is, the total set of actions and responses taken by all firms competing within a market.

A Model of Competitive Rivalry

Competitive rivalry evolves from the pattern of actions and responses as one firm's competitive actions have noticeable effects on competitors, eliciting competitive responses from them.[19] This pattern suggests that firms are mutually interdependent, that they are affected by each other's actions and responses, and that marketplace success is a function of both individual strategies and the consequences of their use.[20] Increasingly, too, executives recognize that competitive rivalry can have a major effect on the firm's financial performance.[21] Research shows that intensified rivalry within an industry results in decreased average profitability for the competing firms.[22] For example, Research in Motion (RIM) dominated the smartphone market with its Blackberry operating system platform until Apple's iPhone platform emerged. Likewise, the introduction of the Android platform by Google has cut into RIM's market share and has thereby lowered the company's performance expectations.[23]

Figure 5.2 presents a straightforward model of competitive rivalry at the firm level; this type of rivalry is usually dynamic and complex.[24] The competitive actions and responses the firm takes are the foundation for successfully building and using its capabilities and core competencies to gain an advantageous market position.[25] The model in Figure 5.2 presents the sequence of activities commonly involved in competition between a particular firm and each of its competitors. Companies can use the model to understand how to be able to predict competitors' behavior (actions and responses) and reduce the uncertainty associated with competitors' actions.[26] Being able to predict competitors' actions and responses has a positive effect on the firm's market position and its subsequent financial performance.[27] The sum of all the individual rivalries modeled in Figure 5.2 that occur in a particular market reflect the competitive dynamics in that market.

The remainder of the chapter explains components of the model shown in Figure 5.2. We first describe market commonality and resource similarity as the building blocks of a competitor analysis. Next, we discuss the effects of three organizational characteristics—awareness, motivation, and ability—on the firm's competitive behavior. We then examine competitive rivalry between firms, or interfirm rivalry, in detail, by describing the factors that affect the likelihood a firm will take a competitive action and the factors that affect the likelihood a firm will respond to a competitor's action. In the chapter's final

Figure 5.2 A Model of Competitive Rivalry

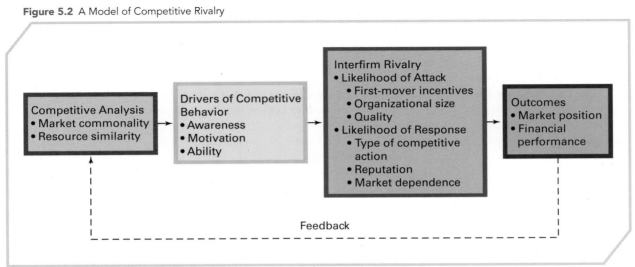

Source: Adapted from M. J. Chen, 1996, Competitor analysis and interfirm rivalry: Toward a theoretical integration, *Academy of Management Review*, 21: 100–134.

section, we turn our attention to competitive dynamics to describe how market characteristics affect competitive rivalry in slow-cycle, fast-cycle, and standard-cycle markets.

Competitor Analysis

As previously noted, a competitor analysis is the first step the firm takes to be able to predict the extent and nature of its rivalry with each competitor. The number of markets in which firms compete against each other (called market commonality, defined on the following pages) and the similarity in their resources (called resource similarity, also defined in the following section) determine the extent to which the firms are competitors. Firms with high market commonality and highly similar resources are "clearly direct and mutually acknowledged competitors."[28] The drivers of competitive behavior—as well as factors influencing the likelihood that a competitor will initiate competitive actions and will respond to its competitors' actions—influence the intensity of rivalry, even for direct competitors.[29]

In Chapter 2, we discussed competitor analysis as a technique firms use to understand their competitive environment. Together, the general, industry, and competitive environments comprise the firm's external environment. We also described how competitor analysis is used to help the firm *understand* its competitors. This understanding results from studying competitors' future objectives, current strategies, assumptions, and capabilities (see Figure 2.3 in Chapter 2). In this chapter, the discussion of competitor analysis is extended to describe what firms study to be able to *predict* competitors' behavior in the form of their competitive actions and responses. The discussions of competitor analysis in Chapter 2 and in this chapter are complementary in that firms must first *understand* competitors (Chapter 2) before their competitive actions and competitive responses can be *predicted* (this chapter).

Such competitive awareness is illustrated in the Strategic Focus on the competitors in the rivalry among the global automobile producers such as Toyota, Ford, General Motors, Honda, Chrysler, Nissan, and others. These analyses are highly important because they help managers to avoid "competitive blind spots," in which managers are unaware of specific competitors or their capabilities. If managers have competitive blind spots, they may be surprised by a competitor's actions, thereby allowing the competitor to increase its market share at the expense of the manager's firm.[30] Competitor analyses are especially important when a firm enters a foreign market. Managers need to understand the local competition and foreign competitors currently operating in the market.[31] Without such analyses, they are less likely to be successful.

Market Commonality

Each industry is composed of various markets. The financial services industry has markets for insurance, brokerage services, banks, and so forth. To concentrate on the needs of different, unique customer groups, markets can be further subdivided. The insurance market, for example, could be broken into market segments (such as commercial and consumer), product segments (such as health insurance and life insurance), and geographic markets (such as Western Europe and Southeast Asia). In general, the capabilities the Internet's technologies generate help to shape the nature of industries' markets along with the competition among firms operating in them. For example, Alex Tosolini, VP of e-commerce for Procter and Gamble (P&G), notes: "Facebook is both a marketing and a distribution channel, as P&G has worked to develop 'f-commerce' capabilities on its fan pages, fulfilled by Amazon, which has become a top 10 retail account for Pampers," a disposable diaper product.[32]

Competitors tend to agree about the different characteristics of individual markets that form an industry. For example, in the transportation industry, the commercial air travel market differs from the ground transportation market, which is served by such

S T R A T E G I C **F O C U S**

MARKET COMMONALITY AND RESOURCE SIMILARITY IN THE GLOBAL AUTOMOBILE PRODUCER INDUSTRY

Although very few automobile producing firms exist in each country around the globe, there is intense rivalry among these large firms because the vehicle market is global. Almost all of the large firms have market commonality; that is, they compete in most of the same segments of the market, from the luxury car to the small fuel-efficient car, as well as hybrids, SUVs, and trucks. Also, because they have similar resources and capabilities, they are continually exploring knowledge in the same general areas to advance their products and make them more desirable for consumers. Due to market commonality and resource similarity, they are aware, motivated, and have the ability to compete for market share in each segment and country they have entered. As such, rivalry among these global giants is very intense.

In 2008 U.S.-centric automakers were caught with lots of gas-guzzling sports utility vehicles and pickup trucks when gas soared to $4.00 a gallon. Because of the recession and high gas prices, consumers turned to smaller, fuel-efficient compact cars and hybrids. Due to the intense rivalry, this sent General Motors and Chrysler into U.S.-funded bankruptcy reorganizations and delayed Ford's return to profitability. However, in 2011, these Detroit-oriented companies have bolstered their fuel-efficiency offerings and are under pressure to increase the overall fuel efficiency of their products. GM has launched the Chevrolet Cruze compact, while the Chevrolet Volt (an electric car which can use gas if needed) appeared in December 2010, and Chevrolet has plans for introducing the Sonic, a new subcompact, later in 2011. Chrysler is introducing the Fiat 500 subcompact into the United States (Fiat has taken a controlling interest in Chrysler) and has remodeled its Sebring compact, called the Chrysler 200. In 2010, Ford launched its fuel-efficient Fiesta subcompact and debuted a restyled version of its Focus compact. Ford also introduced the Fusion hybrid mid-size sedan in 2010.

With its Genesis car, Hyundai aims to attract affluent buyers and raise its image among less wealthy customers.

Transtock/SuperStock

This rebirth is due in part to knowing what had to be done to compete and having the resources necessary to accomplish it. This knowledge and motivation comes from the overlapping market commonality and resource similarity between most global competitors. Once GM felt that it had adequate products, it encouraged Chevrolet dealers to illustrate their competitive parity (especially with the Japanese producers) by buying rival cars and thereby providing opportunities for customers to test drive them to compare to Chevrolet vehicles. One dealer noted that this was done because "it's so tough to change people's perception when Chevrolet spent so many years delivering average cars."

The rivalry drives continuous incremental advances, for example, in battery, power storage, and electrical car technology, to attain better fuel efficiency. Toyota's hybrid power train (for example, the Prius) has been dominant for years, but rivals are challenging it with a number of new innovative systems. Porsche has created a gasoline-electric hybrid that stores energy without batteries. "Porsche's kinetic hybrid system uses a flywheel that holds energy generated by Hub Motor/Generators mounted on the front wheels. Those motor/generators create electricity during braking." Chrysler has developed a hydraulic hybrid that stores energy in pressurized hydraulic fluid. Fluid for the system is stored in a 14.4-gallon high pressure accumulator tank, which is pressurized by an engine-driven pump. When the driver presses the accelerator, the pressure is released from the accumulator tank, powering a hydraulic motor connected to the axle drive. Braking also repressurizes or recharges the hydraulic fluid, much like regenerative brakes in a conventional hybrid. The gasoline engine does not power the wheels directly; the hydraulic motor is directly connected to the drive axle. Hyundai has a hybrid focused more on highway driving at higher speeds through its transmission; conventional hybrids, which are electric-focused, are more efficient at lower speeds. Hyundai's hybrid uses a transmission-mounted electric device which enables 40 mile-per-gallon highway mileage torque from the transmission and allows the gas motor to run more efficiently. GM gets a 25 percent mile-per-gallon increase through an eAssist system on Buick models using "a belt-alternator-starter mild-hybrid system"; the large alternator not only improves efficiency but doubles as a starter. All these systems are new incremental innovations that have helped maintain company competitiveness in the rivalrous hybrid segment.

In 2010, Toyota had a number of recalls and received negative media attention because of braking problems and uncontrolled acceleration in several of its models. This allowed many rivals to attack Toyota, a market leader across many segments. For instance, Lexus, the luxury brand of Toyota and the longtime leader in the luxury segment in the United States, ceded some ground to Mercedes, BMW, and Cadillac as all luxury brands introduced better financing and pricing for their customers to attract Lexus owners. Interestingly, Lexus is not the leader in all markets. It has the least market share among the top luxury models in China. So, the lead can change by country showing the intensity of the rivalry worldwide.

Other companies, such as Hyundai, are seeking to be more competitive at a lower price. Hyundai Motor Corporation has been known for its dependable, low-cost though unexciting cars, but is moving up to luxury models to compete with Cadillac, Mercedes, and BMW. Hyundai launched the Genesis in 2008, and it now plans an even more costly sequel because of the accolades given to the Genesis by car reviewers. Using the strategy of offering luxury cars at a lower price, mirroring what Toyota did when it launched the Lexus line in the 1990s, Hyundai aims not only to attract affluent buyers, but also to raise the company's image among less wealthy customers who remain wary of the brand's cheaper models. AutoNation, Inc., the largest owner of auto retailers in the United States, recently added two Hyundai stores. "Their quality went from some of the lowest in the country to among the best." Not only is Hyundai launching more advanced products, but it's unmistakably more aggressive in a number of areas. The redesigned Sonata won honors in a stringent U.S. crash test. They have also delivered an "onslaught of new drive train technologies." They are not only increasing their R&D internally, but also leveraging their "deep bench" of affiliated suppliers to help develop new technologies.

As a relatively new entrant, Hyundai represents a raft of other companies coming from emerging countries such as China and now India. In the past, these car companies have primarily been parts suppliers and assemblers for more well-known companies. However, because of their growing domestic market, they seek to not only sell their own cars, but enter global markets. They have done so, for instance, through acquisitions of other companies. In 2008, Tata Motors, an Indian company, completed the acquisition of historic U.K. brands Jaguar and Land Rover from Ford. Because these companies from India and China are expected to enter the world marketplace with new capacity, overcapacity is projected. This will increase rivalry even more for the existing companies.

© Nicholas Monu/iStockphoto.com

STRATEGY RIGHT NOW

Learn more about Toyota's market leadership.

www.cengagebrain .com

Sources: M. Kitamura, A. Ohnsman, & Y. Hagiwara, 2011, Why Lexus doesn't lead the pack in China, *Bloomberg Businessweek*, March 28, 32–33; K. Kyung-Tae, R. Seung-Kyu, & O. Joogsan, 2011, The strategic role evolution of foreign automotive parts subsidiaries in China: A case study from the perspective of capabilities evolution, *International Journal of Operations & Production Management*, 31(1): 31–55; K. Linebaugh, M. Dolan, M. Ramsey, & S. Terlep, 2011, Detroit keeps its cool as gas prices heat up, *Wall Street Journal*, January 5, B1–B2; R. Roy, 2011, Batteries and beyond, *Automotive News*, February 14, 6; H. Greimel, 2010, New day at Hyundai, *Automotive News*, December 13, 4; T. Higgins, 2010, Luxury cars are neck and neck in the U.S., *Bloomberg Businessweek*, October 18, 26–27; B. McClellan, 2010, China success clouded by labor strikes, overcapacity, *Ward's Autoworld*, November 25; M. Ramsey, 2010, Can Hyundai sell pragmatic prestige?, *Wall Street Journal*, September 20, B1; A. Sawyers, 2010, Chevy dealer buys rival cars for test drives, *Automotive News*, July 19, 9; A. Taylor III, 2010, Volkswagen's grand plan, *Fortune*, October 18, 24.

firms as YRC Worldwide (one of the largest transportation service providers in the world) and major YRC competitors Arkansas Best, Con-way Inc., and FedEx Freight.[33] Although differences exist, many industries' markets are partially related in terms of technologies used or core competencies needed to develop a competitive advantage. For example, although railroads and truck ground transport compete in a different segment and can be substitutes, different types of transportation companies need to provide reliable and timely service. Commercial air carriers such as Southwest, United, and Jet Blue must therefore develop service competencies to satisfy their passengers, while YRC, railroads, and their major competitors must develop such competencies to serve the needs of those using their services to ship goods.

Firms sometimes compete against each other in several markets that are in different industries. As such these competitors interact with each other several times, a condition called market commonality. More formally, market commonality is concerned with the number of markets with which the firm and a competitor are jointly involved and the degree of importance of the individual markets to each.[34] When firms produce similar products and compete for the same customers, as in the global automobile industry (see Strategic Focus), the competitive rivalry is likely to be high.[35] Firms competing against one another in several or many markets engage in multimarket competition.[36] Coca-Cola and PepsiCo compete across a number of product (e.g., soft drinks, bottled water) and geographic markets (throughout the United States and in many foreign markets). Airlines, chemicals, pharmaceuticals, and consumer foods are examples of other industries in which firms often simultaneously compete against each other in multiple markets.

Firms competing in several markets have the potential to respond to a competitor's actions not only within the market in which the actions are taken, but also in other markets where they compete with the rival. This potential creates a complicated competitive mosaic in which "the moves an organization makes in one market are designed to achieve goals in another market in ways that aren't immediately apparent to its rivals."[37] This potential complicates the rivalry between competitors. In fact, research suggests that a firm with greater multimarket contact is less likely to initiate an attack, but more likely to move (respond) aggressively when attacked. For instance, research in the computer industry found that "firms respond to competitive attacks by introducing new products but do not use price as a retaliatory weapon."[38] Thus, in general, multimarket competition reduces competitive rivalry, but some firms will still compete when the potential rewards (e.g., potential market share gain) are high.[39]

Resource Similarity

Resource similarity is the extent to which the firm's tangible and intangible resources are comparable to a competitor's in terms of both type and amount.[40] Firms with similar types and amounts of resources are likely to have similar strengths and weaknesses and use similar strategies.[41] The competition between FedEx and United Parcel Service (UPS) in using information technology to improve the efficiency of their operations and to reduce costs demonstrates these expectations. Pursuing similar strategies that are supported by similar resource profiles, personnel in these firms work at a feverish pace to receive, sort, and ship packages. Rival DHL is trying to compete with the two global giants supported by the privatized German postal service, Deutsche Post World Net, which acquired it in 2002. DHL has made impressive gains in recent years (though it closed its operations in the United States after acquiring Airborne Express); it competes strongly in Europe and Asia with resources and capabilities similar to those of FedEx and UPS.[42] To survive in the United States, it has negotiated a partnership agreement with UPS and others to make its U.S. deliveries. Such arrangements are often referred to as "coopetition" (cooperation between competitors).[43]

Market commonality is concerned with the number of markets with which the firm and a competitor are jointly involved and the degree of importance of the individual markets to each.

Resource similarity is the extent to which the firm's tangible and intangible resources are comparable to a competitor's in terms of both type and amount.

Figure 5.3 A Framework of Competitor Analysis

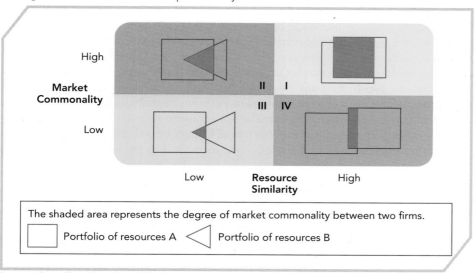

Source: Adapted from M. J. Chen, 1996, Competitor analysis and interfirm rivalry: Toward a theoretical integration, *Academy of Management Review*, 21: 100–134.

When performing a competitor analysis, a firm analyzes each of its competitors in terms of market commonality and resource similarity. The results of these analyses can be mapped for visual comparisons. In Figure 5.3, we show different hypothetical intersections between the firm and individual competitors in terms of market commonality and resource similarity. These intersections indicate the extent to which the firm and those with which it is compared are competitors. For example, the firm and its competitor displayed in quadrant I have similar types and amounts of resources (i.e., the two firms have a similar portfolio of resources). The firm and its competitor in quadrant I would use their similar resource portfolios to compete against each other in many markets that are important to each. These conditions lead to the conclusion that the firms modeled in quadrant I are direct and mutually acknowledged competitors (e.g., as in the global auto industry). In contrast, the firm and its competitor shown in quadrant III share few markets and have little similarity in their resources, indicating that they aren't direct and mutually acknowledged competitors. Thus, a small local, family-owned Italian restaurant does not compete directly against Olive Garden nor does it have resources that are similar to those of Darden Restaurants, Inc. (Olive Garden's owner). The firm's mapping of its competitive relationship with rivals is fluid as firms enter and exit markets and as companies' resources change in type and amount. Thus, the companies with which the firm is a direct competitor change across time.

Drivers of Competitive Actions and Responses

As shown in Figure 5.2 (on page 136), market commonality and resource similarity influence the drivers (awareness, motivation, and ability) of competitive behavior. In turn, the drivers influence the firm's competitive behavior, as shown by the actions and responses it takes while engaged in competitive rivalry.[44]

Awareness, which is a prerequisite to any competitive action or response taken by a firm, refers to the extent to which competitors recognize the degree of their mutual interdependence that results from market commonality and resource similarity.[45] Awareness tends to be greatest when firms have highly similar resources (in terms of types and amounts) to use while competing against each other in multiple markets. Komatsu Ltd., Japan's top construction machinery maker, and U.S.-based Caterpillar Inc. have similar resources and are certainly aware of each other's actions.[46] The same is true for Walmart and France's Carrefour, the two largest supermarket groups in the world. The last two firms' joint awareness has increased as they use similar resources to compete against each other for dominant positions in multiple European and South American markets. Likewise, a new area of this competition is in China: "Carrefour and Walmart, while they make up a small fraction of China's total retail outlets, are two of the biggest retailers in the country. Carrefour operates more than 180 hypermarkets in China and Walmart owns more than 200 stores in the country."[47] Awareness affects the extent to which the firm understands the consequences of its competitive actions and responses. A lack of awareness can lead to excessive competition, resulting in a negative effect on all competitors' performance.[48]

Motivation, which concerns the firm's incentive to take action or to respond to a competitor's attack, relates to perceived gains and losses. Thus, a firm may be aware of competitors but may not be motivated to engage in rivalry with them if it perceives that its position will not improve or that its market position won't be damaged if it doesn't respond.[49] In some cases, firms may locate near competitors in order to more easily access suppliers and customers. For example, Latin American banks have located operations in Miami, Florida, to reach customers from a similar culture and to access employees who understand this culture as well. In Miami, there are several Latin American banks that direct most of their competitive actions at U.S. financial institutions.[50]

Market commonality affects the firm's perceptions and resulting motivation. For example, the firm is generally more likely to attack the rival with whom it has low market commonality than the one with whom it competes in multiple markets. The primary reason is the high stakes involved in trying to gain a more advantageous position over a rival with whom the firm shares many markets. As mentioned earlier, multimarket competition can find a competitor responding to the firm's action in a market different from the one in which the initial action was taken. Actions and responses of this type can cause both firms to lose focus on core markets and to battle each other with resources that had been allocated for other purposes. Because of the high stakes of competition under the condition of market commonality, the probability is high that the attacked firm will respond to its competitor's action in an effort to protect its position in one or more markets.[51]

In some instances, the firm may be aware of the markets it shares with a competitor and be motivated to respond to an attack by that competitor, but lack the ability to do so. *Ability* relates to each firm's resources and the flexibility they provide. Without available resources (such as financial capital and people), the firm lacks the ability to attack a competitor or respond to its actions. For example, smaller and newer firms tend to be more innovative but generally have fewer resources to attack larger and established competitors. Likewise, foreign firms often are at a disadvantage against local firms because of the local firms' social capital (relationships) with consumers, suppliers, and government officials.[52] However, similar resources suggest similar abilities to attack and respond. When a firm faces a competitor with similar resources, careful study of a possible attack before initiating it is essential because the similarly resourced competitor is likely to respond to that action.[53]

Resource *dissimilarity* also influences competitive actions and responses between firms, in that "the greater is the resource imbalance between the acting firm and competitors or potential responders, the greater will be the delay in response"[54] by the firm with a resource disadvantage. For example, Walmart initially used a focused cost leadership strategy to compete only in small communities (those with a population of 25,000 or less). Using sophisticated logistics systems and extremely efficient purchasing practices, among others, to gain competitive advantages, Walmart created a new type of value (primarily in the form of wide selections of products at the lowest competitive prices) for customers in small retail markets. Local competitors lacked the ability to marshal needed resources at the pace required to respond quickly and effectively. However, even when facing competitors with greater resources (greater ability) or more attractive market positions, firms should eventually respond, no matter how daunting the task seems. Choosing not to respond can ultimately result in failure, as happened with at least some local retailers who didn't respond to Walmart's competitive actions. Of course, the actions taken by Walmart were only the beginning. Walmart has become the largest retailer in the world and feared by all competitors, large and small.

Barone Firenze/shutterstock.com

Sony, maker of the PlayStation console, partnered with Sony Ericsson to make the Xperia PLAY phone, which uses "PlayStation-certified games" and runs on Google's Android operating system.

Competitive Rivalry

The ongoing competitive action/response sequence between a firm and a competitor affects the performance of both firms;[55] thus it is important for companies to carefully analyze and understand the competitive rivalry present in the markets they serve to select and implement successful strategies.[56] Understanding a competitor's awareness, motivation, and ability helps the firm to predict the likelihood of an attack by that competitor and the probability that a competitor will respond to actions taken against it.

As we described earlier, the predictions drawn from studying competitors in terms of awareness, motivation, and ability are grounded in market commonality and resource similarity. These predictions are fairly general. The value of the final set of predictions the firm develops about each of its competitors' competitive actions and responses is enhanced by studying the "Likelihood of Attack" factors (such as first-mover incentives and organizational size) and the "Likelihood of Response" factors (such as the actor's reputation) that are shown in Figure 5.2. Evaluating and understanding these factors allow the firm to refine the predictions it makes about its competitors' actions and responses.

Strategic and Tactical Actions

Firms use both strategic and tactical actions when forming their competitive actions and competitive responses in the course of engaging in competitive rivalry.[57] A **competitive action** is a strategic or tactical action the firm takes to build or defend its competitive advantages or improve its market position. A **competitive response** is a strategic or tactical action the firm takes to counter the effects of a competitor's competitive action. A **strategic action** or a **strategic response** is a market-based move that involves a significant commitment of organizational resources and is difficult to implement and reverse. A **tactical action** or a **tactical response** is a market-based move that is taken to fine-tune a strategy; it involves fewer resources and is relatively easy to implement and reverse.

As noted in the Opening Case, Apple opened a service called "Game Center" once it found that users were using its iPhone, iPad, and iPod platforms for video games. With its update to its iOS (operating system) software, game producers began producing game applications to use the Apple system as its graphics became more advanced. This represents a strategic move by Apple. Game platform hardware and software producers such

A **competitive action** is a strategic or tactical action the firm takes to build or defend its competitive advantages or improve its market position.

A **competitive response** is a strategic or tactical action the firm takes to counter the effects of a competitor's competitive action.

A **strategic action** or a **strategic response** is a market-based move that involves a significant commitment of organizational resources and is difficult to implement and reverse.

A **tactical action** or a **tactical response** is a market-based move that is taken to fine-tune a strategy; it involves fewer resources and is relatively easy to implement and reverse.

as Nintendo and Sony then created strategic responses to the Apple threat. For example, Sony, which produces the PlayStation console, partnered with Sony Ericsson to make the Xperia PLAY phone, which uses "PlayStation-certified games" and runs on Google's Android operating system.[58]

Walmart prices aggressively as a means of increasing revenues and gaining market share at the expense of competitors. However, pricing is a tactical strategy and Walmart's performance has lagged recently. In recent tactical moves, it has asserted that it will do a better job on competitive pricing.[59] Although pricing aggressively is at the core of what Walmart is and how it competes, can the tactical action of aggressive pricing continue to lead to the competitive success the firm has historically enjoyed? Is Walmart achieving the type of balance between strategic and tactical competitive actions and competitive responses that is a foundation for all firms' success in marketplace competitions?

When engaging rivals in competition, firms must recognize the differences between strategic and tactical actions and responses and should develop an effective balance between the two types of competitive actions and responses. Airbus, Boeing's major competitor in commercial airliners, is aware that Boeing is strongly committed to taking actions it believes are necessary to successfully launch the 787 jetliner, because deciding to design, build, and launch the 787 is a major strategic action. In fact, many analysts believe that Boeing's development of the 787 airliner was a strategic response to Airbus's new A380 aircraft.[60]

Likelihood of Attack

In addition to market commonality, resource similarity, and the drivers of awareness, motivation, and ability, other factors affect the likelihood a competitor will use strategic actions and tactical actions to attack its competitors. Three of these factors—first-mover incentives, organizational size, and quality—are discussed next.

First-Mover Incentives

A **first mover** is a firm that takes an initial competitive action in order to build or defend its competitive advantages or to improve its market position. The first-mover concept has been influenced by the work of the famous economist Joseph Schumpeter, who argued that firms achieve competitive advantage by taking innovative actions[61] (innovation is defined and described in detail in Chapter 13). In general, first movers "allocate funds for product innovation and development, aggressive advertising, and advanced research and development."[62]

The benefits of being a successful first mover can be substantial.[63] Especially in fast-cycle markets (discussed later in the chapter), where changes occur rapidly and where it is virtually impossible to sustain a competitive advantage for any length of time, a first mover can experience many times the valuation and revenue of a second mover.[64] This evidence suggests that although first-mover benefits are never absolute, they are often critical to a firm's success in industries experiencing rapid technological developments and relatively short product life cycles.[65] In addition to earning above-average returns until its competitors respond to its successful competitive action, the first mover can gain (1) the loyalty of customers who may become committed to the goods or services of the firm that first made them available, and (2) market share that can be difficult for competitors to take during future competitive rivalry.[66] The general evidence that first movers have greater survival rates than later market entrants is perhaps the culmination of first-mover benefits. [67]

The firm trying to predict its competitors' competitive actions might conclude that they will take aggressive strategic actions to gain first movers' benefits. However, even though a firm's competitors might be motivated to be first movers, they may lack the ability to do so. First movers tend to be aggressive and willing to experiment with innovation

A **first mover** is a firm that takes an initial competitive action in order to build or defend its competitive advantages or to improve its market position.

and take higher, yet reasonable, levels of risk.[68] To be a first mover, the firm must have readily available the resources to significantly invest in R&D as well as to rapidly and successfully produce and market a stream of innovative products.[69] If the firm does not have the necessary resources or cannot establish the necessary legitimacy, being a first mover can lead to survival risks.[70]

Organizational slack makes it possible for firms to have the ability (as measured by available resources) to be first movers. *Slack* is the buffer or cushion provided by actual or obtainable resources that aren't currently in use and are in excess of the minimum resources needed to produce a given level of organizational output.[71] As a liquid resource, slack can quickly be allocated to support competitive actions, such as R&D investments and aggressive marketing campaigns that lead to first-mover advantages. This relationship between slack and the ability to be a first mover allows the firm to predict that a first-mover competitor likely has available slack and will probably take aggressive competitive actions to continuously introduce innovative products. Furthermore, the firm can predict that as a first mover, a competitor will try to rapidly gain market share and customer loyalty in order to earn above-average returns until its competitors are able to effectively respond to its first move.

Firms evaluating their competitors should realize that being a first mover carries risk. For example, it is difficult to accurately estimate the returns that will be earned from introducing product innovations to the marketplace.[72] Additionally, the first mover's cost to develop a product innovation can be substantial, reducing the slack available to support further innovation. Thus, the firm should carefully study the results a competitor achieves as a first mover. Continuous success by the competitor suggests additional product innovations, while lack of product acceptance over the course of the competitor's innovations may indicate less willingness in the future to accept the risks of being a first mover.[73]

A **second mover** is a firm that responds to the first mover's competitive action, typically through imitation. More cautious than the first mover, the second mover studies customers' reactions to product innovations. In the course of doing so, the second mover also tries to find any mistakes the first mover made so that it can avoid them and the problems they created. Often, successful imitation of the first mover's innovations allows the second mover to avoid the mistakes and the major investments required of the pioneers (first movers).[74]

Second movers also have the time to develop processes and technologies that are more efficient than those used by the first mover or that create additional value for consumers.[75] The most successful second movers rarely act too fast (so they can fully analyze the first mover's actions) nor too slow (so they do not give the first mover time to correct its mistakes and "lock in" customer loyalty).[76] Overall, the outcomes of the first mover's competitive actions may provide an effective blueprint for second and even late movers (discussed below) as they determine the nature and timing of their competitive responses.[77] Determining whether a competitor is an effective second mover (based on its past actions) allows a first-mover firm to predict that the competitor will respond quickly to successful, innovation-based market entries. The first mover can expect a successful second-mover competitor to study its market entries and to respond with a new entry into the market within a short time period. As a second mover, the competitor will try to respond with a product that provides greater customer value than does the first mover's product. The most successful second movers are able to rapidly and meaningfully interpret market feedback to respond quickly, yet successfully, to the first mover's successful innovations.

For example, Hyundai has traditionally been a second mover in the automobile industry. However, it has decided that "playing follow the leader on R&D isn't good enough anymore."[78] As illustrated in the Strategic Focus on the automobile industry, it is leading the way in a number of new features in its automobiles, such as an "onslaught of new drive train technologies" and a new hybrid drive that makes the transmission—and therefore the car—efficient at higher speeds than traditional hybrids, such as the Toyota Prius.

A **second mover** is a firm that responds to the first mover's competitive action, typically through imitation.

A **late mover** is a firm that responds to a competitive action a significant amount of time after the first mover's action and the second mover's response. Typically, a late response is better than no response at all, although any success achieved from the late competitive response tends to be considerably less than that achieved by first and second movers. However, on occasion, late movers can be successful if they develop a unique way to enter the market and compete. For firms from emerging economies this often means a niche strategy with lower-cost production and manufacturing.[79]

The firm competing against a late mover can predict that the competitor will likely enter a particular market only after both the first and second movers have achieved success in that market. Moreover, on a relative basis, the firm can predict that the late mover's competitive action will allow it to earn average returns only after the considerable time required for it to understand how to create at least as much customer value as that offered by the first and second movers' products.

Organizational Size

An organization's size affects the likelihood it will take competitive actions as well as the types and timing of those actions.[80] In general, small firms are more likely than large companies to launch competitive actions and tend to do it more quickly. Smaller firms are thus perceived as nimble and flexible competitors who rely on speed and surprise to defend their competitive advantages or develop new ones while engaged in competitive rivalry, especially with large companies, to gain an advantageous market position.[81] Small firms' flexibility and nimbleness allow them to develop variety in their competitive actions; large firms tend to limit the types of competitive actions used.[82]

For example, large security firms like ADT serve only single-family homes with home security systems; they don't service apartment dwellers. SimpliSafe, a small firm headquartered in Cambridge, Massachusetts, has a product focused on apartment customers and has entered the security market through this niche. Their product is battery-powered and is fixed to walls near doors and windows. It does not require a complicated installation. Furthermore, it works with cell phones while ADT's products use landlines. Additionally, the system is portable if the customer moves to another apartment, and it is cheaper, costing $300 plus a $15 monthly service fee. It also does not require a contract and there are no added fees like those that larger companies tack on. Moreover, because it is a small firm, it does not have large marketing overhead. SimpliSafe expects sales in 2011 to be around $15 million, up from single-digit millions in 2010.[83]

A **late mover** is a firm that responds to a competitive action a significant amount of time after the first mover's action and the second mover's response.

Large firms, however, are likely to initiate more competitive actions along with more strategic actions during a given period.[84] Thus, when studying its competitors in terms of organizational size, the firm should use a measurement such as total sales revenue or total number of employees. The competitive actions the firm likely will encounter from competitors larger than it is will be different from the competitive actions it will encounter from smaller competitors.

The organizational size factor adds another layer of complexity. When engaging in competitive rivalry, the firm often prefers a large number of unique competitive actions. Ideally, the organization has the amount of slack resources held by a large firm to launch a greater *number* of competitive actions and a small firm's flexibility to launch a greater *variety* of competitive actions. Herb Kelleher, cofounder and former CEO of

SimpliSafe is a battery-powered alarm system that is portable and works with cell phones. In addition it does not require a contract and there are no added fees.

Keypad   Keychain Remote   Entry Sensor   Motion Sensor   Panic Button   Base Station

SimpliSafe.com

Southwest Airlines, addressed this matter: "Think and act big and we'll get smaller. Think and act small and we'll get bigger."[85]

In the context of competitive rivalry, Kelleher's statement can be interpreted to mean that relying on a limited number or types of competitive actions (which is the large firm's tendency) can lead to reduced competitive success across time, partly because competitors learn how to effectively respond to the predictable. In contrast, remaining flexible and nimble (which is the small firm's tendency) in order to develop and use a wide variety of competitive actions contributes to success against rivals.

Walmart is a huge firm and generates annual sales revenue that makes it the world's largest company. Because of its size, scale, and resources, Walmart has the flexibility required to take many types of competitive actions that few—if any—of its competitors can undertake, and at reduced cost. Demonstrating this type of flexibility in terms of competitive actions has proven critical to Walmart's entry into the grocery business and its competition with Albertson's, Safeway, and Kroger as well as competitors such as Costco and Target, among others.[86]

Quality

Quality has many definitions, including well-established ones relating it to the production of goods or services with zero defects[87] and as a cycle of continuous improvement.[88] From a strategic perspective, we consider quality to be the outcome of how a firm competes through its primary and support activities (see Chapter 3). Thus, **quality** exists when the firm's goods or services meet or exceed customers' expectations. Some evidence suggests that quality may be the most critical component in satisfying the firm's customers.[89]

In the eyes of customers, quality is about doing the right things relative to performance measures that are important to them.[90] Customers may be interested in measuring the quality of a firm's goods and services against a broad range of dimensions. Sample quality dimensions in which customers commonly express an interest are shown in Table 5.1. Quality is possible only when top-level managers support it and when its importance is

Table 5.1 Quality Dimensions of Goods and Services

Product Quality Dimensions
1. *Performance*—Operating characteristics
2. *Features*—Important special characteristics
3. *Flexibility*—Meeting operating specifications over some period of time
4. *Durability*—Amount of use before performance deteriorates
5. *Conformance*—Match with preestablished standards
6. *Serviceability*—Ease and speed of repair
7. *Aesthetics*—How a product looks and feels
8. *Perceived quality*—Subjective assessment of characteristics (Product image)

Service Quality Dimensions
1. *Timeliness*—Performed in the promised period of time
2. *Courtesy*—Performed cheerfully
3. *Consistency*—Giving all customers similar experiences each time
4. *Convenience*—Accessibility to customers
5. *Completeness*—Fully serviced, as required
6. *Accuracy*—Performed correctly each time

Source: Adapted from J. Evans, 2008, *Managing for Quality and Performance*, 7th ed., Mason, OH: Thomson Publishing.

Quality exists when the firm's goods or services meet or exceed customers' expectations.

institutionalized throughout the entire organization and its value chain.[91] When quality is institutionalized and valued by all, employees and managers alike become vigilant about continuously finding ways to improve quality.[92]

Quality is a universal theme in the global economy and is a necessary but insufficient condition for competitive success.[93] Without quality, a firm's products lack credibility, meaning that customers don't think of them as viable options. Indeed, customers won't consider buying a product until they believe that it can satisfy at least their base-level expectations in terms of quality dimensions that are important to them.[94] Boeing's new 787 aircraft has been delayed due to quality concerns. Many of its problems have come from its numerous suppliers and supply chain subassemblies, but such media events make large airline customers nervous, and there have been some associated postponements in orders.[95]

Quality affects competitive rivalry. The firm evaluating a competitor whose products suffer from poor quality can predict declines in the competitor's sales revenue until the quality issues are resolved. In addition, the firm can predict that the competitor likely won't be aggressive in its competitive actions until the quality problems are corrected in order to gain credibility with customers.[96] However, after the problems are corrected, that competitor is likely to take more aggressive competitive actions.

Likelihood of Response

The success of a firm's competitive action is affected by the likelihood that a competitor will respond to it as well as by the type (strategic or tactical) and effectiveness of that response. As noted earlier, a competitive response is a strategic or tactical action the firm takes to counter the effects of a competitor's competitive action. In general, a firm is likely to respond to a competitor's action when (1) the action leads to better use of the competitor's capabilities to gain or produce stronger competitive advantages or an improvement in its market position, (2) the action damages the firm's ability to use its capabilities to create or maintain an advantage, or (3) the firm's market position becomes less defensible.[97]

In addition to market commonality and resource similarity and awareness, motivation, and ability, firms evaluate three other factors—type of competitive action, reputation, and market dependence—to predict how a competitor is likely to respond to competitive actions (see Figure 5.2 on 136).

Type of Competitive Action

Competitive responses to strategic actions differ from responses to tactical actions. These differences allow the firm to predict a competitor's likely response to a competitive action that has been launched against it. Strategic actions commonly receive strategic responses and tactical actions receive tactical responses. In general, strategic actions elicit fewer total competitive responses because strategic responses, such as market-based moves, involve a significant commitment of resources and are difficult to implement and reverse.[98]

Another reason that strategic actions elicit fewer responses than do tactical actions is that the time needed to implement a strategic action and to assess its effectiveness can delay the competitor's response to that action.[99] In contrast, a competitor likely will respond quickly to a tactical action, such as when an airline company almost immediately matches a competitor's tactical action of reducing prices in certain markets. Either strategic actions or tactical actions that target a large number of a rival's customers are likely to elicit strong responses.[100] In fact, if the effects of a competitor's strategic action on the focal firm are significant (e.g., loss of market share, loss of major resources such as critical employees), a response is likely to be swift and strong.[101]

Actor's Reputation

In the context of competitive rivalry, an *actor* is the firm taking an action or a response while *reputation* is "the positive or negative attribute ascribed by one rival to another based on past competitive behavior."[102] A positive reputation may be a source of above-average returns, especially for consumer goods producers.[103] Thus, a positive corporate reputation is of strategic value[104] and affects competitive rivalry. To predict the likelihood of a competitor's response to a current or planned action, firms evaluate the responses that the competitor has taken previously when attacked—past behavior is assumed to be a predictor of future behavior.

Competitors are more likely to respond to strategic or tactical actions when they are taken by a market leader.[105] In particular, evidence suggests that commonly successful actions, especially strategic actions, will be quickly imitated. For example, although a second mover, IBM committed significant resources to enter the information service market. When IBM was immediately successful in this endeavor, competitors such as HP, Dell, and others responded with strategic actions to enter the market.[106] IBM's reputation as well as its successful strategic action strongly influenced entry by these competitors.

In contrast to a firm with a strong reputation such as IBM, competitors are less likely to take responses against a company with a reputation for competitive behavior that is risky, complex, and unpredictable. The firm with a reputation as a price predator (an actor that frequently reduces prices to gain or maintain market share) generates few responses to its pricing tactical actions because price predators, which typically increase prices once their market share objective is reached, lack credibility with their competitors.[107] Occasionally, a firm with a minor reputation can sneak up on larger, more resourceful competitors and take market share from them. In recent years, for example, firms from emerging markets have taken market share from major competitors based in developed markets.[108]

Dependence on the Market

Market dependence denotes the extent to which a firm's revenues or profits are derived from a particular market.[109] In general, competitors with high market dependence are likely to respond strongly to attacks threatening their market position.[110] Interestingly, the threatened firm in these instances may not always respond quickly, even though an effective response to an attack on the firm's position in a critical market is important.

Akamai Technologies is the dominant player in a $2.5 billion market for content delivery network (CDN) services. If a person clicks on a Web site to download software or music, or to examine headlines or video clips, Akamai often provides these bigger files to the consumer through its servers rather than through the company computer system from which the download appears to be taking place. As such, Akamai has well-equipped servers to facilitate improved and more reliable download performance, as it handles billions of daily Web interactions for organizations like NBC, the NASDAQ market, and the U.S. Department of Defense. However, because Akamai is dependent on this market (it is not very diversified), rival CDN providers such as Limelight Networks and Level 3 Communications have forced Akamai to lower their basic CDN service prices. Because of this market dependence, the company responds quickly to both tactical and strategic entry moves and hopes to make up the difference through "volume." However,

Microsoft, makers of Kinect for its Xbox, is a company with a positive reputation in the gaming segment.

PHIL MCCARTEN/Reuters /Landov

Akamai may have more competition in the future as telecom companies such as AT&T are adding content distribution capabilities to their phone networks. As such, Akamai's competitive responses are likely to be more dramatic in the future.[111]

Competitive Dynamics

Whereas competitive rivalry concerns the ongoing actions and responses between a firm and its direct competitors for an advantageous market position, *competitive dynamics* concern the ongoing actions and responses among *all* firms competing within a market for advantageous positions. Building and sustaining competitive advantages are at the core of competitive rivalry, in that advantages are the key to creating value for shareholders.[112]

To explain competitive dynamics, we explore the effects of varying rates of competitive speed in different markets (called slow-cycle, fast-cycle, and standard-cycle markets) on the behavior (actions and responses) of all competitors within a given market. Competitive behaviors as well as the reasons for taking them are similar within each market type, but differ across types of markets. Thus, competitive dynamics differ in slow-cycle, fast-cycle, and standard-cycle markets. The sustainability of the firm's competitive advantages differs across the three market types. Research has also shown how firms go through life-cycle stages as markets evolve over time within which a firm is competing.[113] However, understanding what happens within each type of market is more pertinent in knowing how to respond to the competition.

As noted in Chapter 1, firms want to sustain their competitive advantages for as long as possible, although no advantage is permanently sustainable. The degree of sustainability is affected by how quickly competitive advantages can be imitated and how costly it is to do so.

Slow-Cycle Markets

Slow-cycle markets are those in which the firm's competitive advantages are shielded from imitation, commonly for long periods of time, and where imitation is costly.[114] Thus, competitive advantages are sustainable over longer periods of time in slow-cycle markets.

Building a unique and proprietary capability produces a competitive advantage and success in a slow-cycle market. This type of advantage is difficult for competitors to understand. As discussed in Chapter 3, a difficult-to-understand and costly-to-imitate resource or capability usually results from unique historical conditions, causal ambiguity, and/or social complexity. Copyrights, geography, patents, and ownership of an information resource are examples of resources.[115] After a proprietary advantage is developed, the firm's competitive behavior in a slow-cycle market is oriented to protecting, maintaining, and extending that advantage. Thus, the competitive dynamics in slow-cycle markets usually concentrate on competitive actions and responses that enable firms to protect, maintain, and extend their competitive advantage. Major strategic actions in these markets, such as acquisitions, usually carry less risk than in faster-cycle markets.[116]

Walt Disney Co. continues to extend its proprietary characters, such as Mickey Mouse, Minnie Mouse, and Goofy. These characters have a unique historical development as a result of Walt and Roy Disney's creativity and vision for entertaining people. Products based on the characters seen in Disney's animated films are sold through Disney's theme park shops as well as freestanding retail outlets called Disney Stores. Because copyrights shield it, the proprietary nature of Disney's advantage in terms of animated character trademarks protects the firm from imitation by competitors.

Slow-cycle markets are those in which the firm's competitive advantages are shielded from imitation commonly for long periods of time and where imitation is costly.

Consistent with another attribute of competition in a slow-cycle market, Disney protects its exclusive rights to its characters and their use. As with all firms competing in slow-cycle markets, Disney's competitive actions (such as building theme parks in France, Japan, and China) and responses (such as lawsuits to protect its right to fully control use of its animated characters) maintain and extend its proprietary competitive advantage while protecting it.

Patent laws and regulatory requirements such as those in the United States requiring FDA (Food and Drug Administration) approval to launch new products shield pharmaceutical companies' positions. Competitors in this market try to extend patents on their drugs to maintain advantageous positions that the patents provide. However, after a patent expires, the firm is no longer shielded from competition, allowing generic imitations and usually leading to a loss of sales.

The competitive dynamics generated by firms competing in slow-cycle markets are shown in Figure 5.4. In slow-cycle markets, firms launch a product (e.g., a new drug) that has been developed through a proprietary advantage (e.g., R&D) and then exploit it for as long as possible while the product is shielded from competition. Eventually, competitors respond to the action with a counterattack. In markets for drugs, this counterattack commonly occurs as patents expire or are broken through legal means, creating the need for another product launch by the firm seeking a protected market position. It is becoming more difficult for firms like Merck to get drugs approved; patent protected drug approvals are trending down, while risky research spending is rising.[117]

Fast-Cycle Markets

Fast-cycle markets are markets in which the firm's capabilities that contribute to competitive advantages aren't shielded from imitation and where imitation is often rapid and inexpensive.[118] Thus, competitive advantages aren't sustainable in fast-cycle markets. Firms competing in fast-cycle markets recognize the importance of speed; these companies appreciate that "time is as precious a business resource as money or head count—and that the costs of hesitation and delay are just as steep as going over budget or missing a financial forecast."[119] Such high-velocity environments place considerable pressures on top managers to quickly make strategic decisions that are also effective.[120] The often substantial competition and technology-based strategic focus make

> **Fast-cycle markets** are markets in which the firm's capabilities that contribute to competitive advantages aren't shielded from imitation and where imitation is often rapid and inexpensive.

Figure 5.4 Gradual Erosion of a Sustained Competitive Advantage

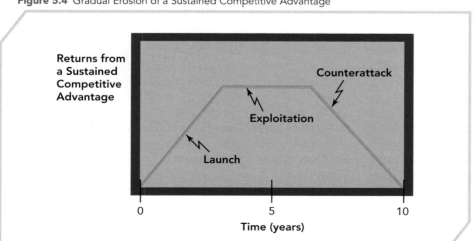

Source: Adapted from I. C. MacMillan, 1988, Controlling competitive dynamics by taking strategic initiative, *Academy of Management Executive*, II(2): 111–118.

the strategic decision complex, increasing the need for a comprehensive approach integrated with decision speed, two often-conflicting characteristics of the strategic decision process.[121]

Reverse engineering and the rate of technology diffusion in fast-cycle markets facilitate rapid imitation. A competitor uses reverse engineering to quickly gain the knowledge required to imitate or improve the firm's products. Technology is diffused rapidly in fast-cycle markets, making it available to competitors in a short period. The technology often used by fast-cycle competitors isn't proprietary, nor is it protected by patents as is the technology used by firms competing in slow-cycle markets. For example, only a few hundred parts, which are readily available on the open market, are required to build a PC. Patents protect only a few of these parts, such as microprocessor chips. Interestingly, research also demonstrates that showing what an incumbent firm knows and its research capability can be a deterrent to other firms to enter the market.[122]

The reality of fast-cycle markets has led to the development of generational products; such products usually start with a substantial technical advance in the performance of a product category and are followed with additional regular, though incremental, technological advances as new generations of products are introduced, as in Intel semiconductor logic chips or HP printer families.[123] Fast-cycle markets are more volatile than slow-cycle and standard-cycle markets. Indeed, the pace of competition in fast-cycle markets is almost frenzied, as companies rely on innovations as the engines of their growth. Because prices often decline quickly in these markets, companies need to profit quickly from their product innovations. Cloud computing as discussed in the Strategic Focus is an example where change is happening rapidly as firms seek to establish space in the market as it evolves rapidly.[124]

Fast-cycle market characteristics, such as cloud computing described in the Strategic Focus, make it virtually impossible for companies in this type of market to develop sustainable competitive advantages. Recognizing this reality, firms avoid "loyalty" to any of their products, preferring to cannibalize their own before competitors learn how to do so through successful imitation. This emphasis creates competitive dynamics that differ substantially from those found in slow-cycle markets. Instead of concentrating on protecting, maintaining, and extending competitive advantages, as in slow-cycle markets, companies competing in fast-cycle markets focus on learning how to rapidly and continuously develop new competitive advantages that are superior to those they replace. They commonly search for fast and effective means of developing new products. For example, it is common in some industries for firms to use strategic alliances to gain access to new technologies and thereby develop and introduce more new products into the market.[125] In recent years, many of these alliances have been offshore (with partners in foreign countries) in order to access appropriate skills while maintaining lower costs to compete. However, getting the appropriate balance is important so that key capabilities are not lost in the offshoring and outsourcing process.[126]

The competitive behavior of firms competing in fast-cycle markets is shown in Figure 5.5. As suggested by the figure, competitive dynamics in this market type entail actions and responses that are oriented to rapid and continuous product introductions and the development of a stream of ever-changing competitive advantages. The firm launches a product to achieve a competitive advantage and then exploits the advantage for as long as possible. However, the firm also tries to develop another temporary competitive advantage before competitors can respond to the first one (see Figure 5.5). Thus, competitive dynamics in fast-cycle markets often result in rapid product upgrades as well as quick product innovations.[127]

As our discussion suggests, innovation plays a critical role in the competitive dynamics in fast-cycle markets. For individual firms, then, innovation is a key source of competitive advantage. Through innovation, the firm can cannibalize its own products before

STRATEGIC FOCUS

COMPETITION TO SELL CLOUD COMPUTING RESOURCES

Cloud computing refers to firms that sell computer processing, storage, and software application access on demand via a computer network, in particular over the Internet. Such computational resources include application software such as word processing, spreadsheets, database management, and e-mail. The traditional model of computing where software and data are fully contained on a user's computer is differentiated from cloud computing, where the user's computer may contain very little software or data and a minimal operating system or Web browser. Through this minimal software, the client uses the focal computer as a display terminal for accessing applications, data, and storage in a distant location. Certainly this is the way mobile smartphones access e-mail and other data sources located on a server elsewhere. Web-based e-mail such as Gmail, Hotmail, and Yahoo! allow services to be provided on local devices through the Internet, making them prime examples of cloud computing. As such, cloud computing involves pooling of many remote computers "in the cloud" to manage tasks, warehouse large storage of data, manage and synchronize multiple documents online, and computationally process intense amounts of data and provide application services.

Large firms and startups are seeking to use the power of cloud computing. Amazon played a key role in the emergence of cloud computing. When it modernized its data centers, they were using as little as 10 percent of their capacity at one time. As their internal efficiency improved, Amazon initiated a service development effort by providing computing power to external customers by launching Amazon Web Services (AWS) in 2006. Now Amazon has thousands of corporate customers who use their cloud computing services, including Pfizer, Netflix, and many small startups. Such services allow large firms to improve their efficiency and change computing to an expense rather than a large capital investment. Furthermore, these services allow small firms access to powerful computational resources that they can purchase rather inexpensively compared to the capital investment that might otherwise be required. For small firms in emerging economies, these services facilitate easier entry into markets in developed countries relative to their previous capabilities if they had to spend significant investment dollars to gain up-to-date information technology resources.

Peter DaSilva/The New York Times/Redux Pictures

Drew Houston, chief executive of Dropbox, and Arash Ferdowsi, co-founder, at their office in San Francisco. A number of companies focused on online storage, like Dropbox, are gaining users and attention, with new investment driving a boom in this niche business.

Another aspect of the business is focused on intra-company cloud computing, or private clouds. Large hardware and software producers such as Oracle, HP, IBM, and Dell are all seeking to sell private cloud computer systems to corporations so that their clients can consolidate their computing power centrally and reduce costs throughout their intra-corporate networks. For example, in 2010, Oracle bought Sun Microsystems, a hardware server manufacturer, even though Oracle's focus has traditionally been focused on producing software which facilitates database management and also affiliated software services to larger corporations. Their intent with the Sun acquisition is to pursue combination hardware and software systems to establish a platform on which to run the various products that are needed in the cloud and establish a standard that client firms can depend on for running their large networks.

Likewise, HP, under its new CEO, Léo Apotheker, has announced plans to have a leading role in cloud computer information technology. HP plans a hybrid approach, offering intra-company systems plus public clouds to sell computational resources to small and medium-sized enterprises, thereby offering a portfolio of cloud services, from private infra-structure to public platform services. To accomplish this, it will need to acquire more soft-ware, especially applications. For instance, it acquired Palm's webOS Mobile Operating System. It hopes to sell 100 million devices installed with webOS, allowing mobile devices to access its client's intra-company or HP's public cloud offerings. An example of how these devices might work is the iPad tablet computer by Apple. One can examine files on the iPad generated by Microsoft Office applications and Adobe's portable document format (PDF) files despite the lack of a USB computer bus on the iPad. To read these documents, the iPad uses a file transferred from the iTunes computer program, which is accessed through remote cloud computing services, sending the file to the iPad as an electronic mail message attachment.

The competition for private intra-company services to shift large data-intensive firms to cloud computing will be intense and include HP, IBM, Oracle, IBM, SAP, and others. This competition will be fast-changing and uncertain, given the disruptive cost reduction incentive for firms to move their data crunching to lower-cost opportunities in the cloud, as well as the lack of standards. Likewise, the competition will be just as intense and uncertain to sell public cloud services to small and medium-sized firms that will seek to have access to increased computing power at a cheaper cost.

Salesforce.com is an example of a specific business function moving to the cloud and sell-ing its services to individual companies as a way to increase the efficiency of sales operations. Salesforce.com sells its Web-based software to large and small firms' sales departments. It has created a $1.4 billion-a-year business by tracking leads, giving detailed histories of who bought what and when, and how to reach particular consumers. Although Salesforce.com is focused on one particular function of cloud computing, their software has developed 170,000 applications written by other firms running on its technology. However, Salesforce.com may have difficulty breaking into other functions on the cloud, given its single focus on sales.

Dropbox is another example of cloud computing focused on individual consumers. It is "cloud computing for the rest of us." Dropbox lets its customers "store digital files includ-ing photos, personal documents, and digital music files in an electronic locker that the owner can access or share on nearly any net-connected device." In other words, Dropbox is a file backup service as well as source to provide access from any net-connect device at an increasingly affordable price. As you can see, this disruptive concept, cloud computing, is likely to change the way that we use and access our computer services, especially as we move farther and farther into mobile computing devices such as smartphones and tablets. This will not only change the nature of competition but likewise increase it in different ways for existing companies.

Sources: V. Barret, 2011, Larry's long reach, *Forbes*, March 14, 18–19; T. Claburn, 2011, Google turns office into Google apps client, *InformationWeek*, March 14, 16; J. P. Mangalindan, 2011, Cloud computing for the rest of us, *Fortune*, March 21, 50; S. Marston, Z. Li, S. Bandyopadhyay, J. Zhang, & A. Ghalsasi, 2011, Cloud computing—The business perspective, *Decision Support Systems*, 51(1): 176–189; A. Ricadela, 2011, Apotheker seeks to save HP's "lost soul" with software growth, *Bloomberg Businessweek*, http://www.businessweek.com, March 10; C. Saran & W. Ashford, 2011, HP aims to be leader of the pack but will new strategy reach the cloud?, *Computer Weekly*, March 22, 8; C. Tuna, 2011, Tech giants look forward to cloudy days, *Wall Street Journal*, March 30, B1; B. Worthen, 2011, Boss Talk: Michael Dell looks beyond PC business, *Wall Street Journal*, April 25, B1; B. Worthen & I. Sherr, 2011, Corporate News: H-P CEO takes the stage, *Wall Street Journal*, March 15, B3; V. Barret, 2010, The web's big upstart, *Forbes*, December 6, 72–80.

competitors successfully imitate them and still maintain an advantage through next generation products.

Standard-Cycle Markets

Standard-cycle markets are markets in which the firm's competitive advantages are partially shielded from imitation and imitation is moderately costly. Competitive advan-tages are partially sustainable in standard-cycle markets, but only when the firm is able to continuously upgrade the quality of its capabilities to stay ahead of competitors. The

Standard-cycle markets are markets in which the firm's competitive advantages are moderately shielded from imitation and where imitation is moderately costly.

Figure 5.5 Developing Temporary Advantages to Create Sustained Advantage

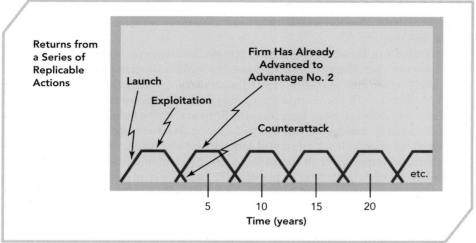

Source: Adapted from I. C. MacMillan, 1988, Controlling competitive dynamics by taking strategic initiative, *Academy of Management Executive*, II(2): 111–118.

competitive actions and responses in standard-cycle markets are designed to seek large market shares, to gain customer loyalty through brand names, and to carefully control a firm's operations in order to consistently provide the same positive experience for customers.[128]

Standard-cycle companies serve many customers in competitive markets. Because the capabilities and core competencies on which their competitive advantages are based are less specialized, imitation is faster and less costly for standard-cycle firms than for those competing in slow-cycle markets. However, imitation is slower and more expensive in these markets than in fast-cycle markets. Thus, competitive dynamics in standard-cycle markets rest midway between the characteristics of dynamics in slow-cycle and fast-cycle markets. Imitation comes less quickly and is more expensive for standard-cycle competitors when a firm is able to develop economies of scale by combining coordinated and integrated design and manufacturing processes with a large sales volume for its products.

Because of large volumes, the size of mass markets, and the need to develop scale economies, the competition for market share is intense in standard-cycle markets. In some markets associated with consumer electronics, fast cycles occur, such as in smartphones and tablet sales. However, in other consumer segments such as the television market, the cycles are more placid and closer to standard-cycle markets. Nonetheless, rivalry is intense as new technologies emerge. For example, prices are coming down in the flat-panel TV market as competition in this market has become relatively more stable. However, some firms are seeking to establish an uptick in the competition by moving towards 3D flat panel televisions. Samsung and LG Electronics were seeking to establish competing platform standards in a 3D format in 2010. These producers were disappointed "when they tried to bring Avatar-like theater experiences with 3D into the living room."[129] However, the demand did not materialize as they had hoped. LG uses a special film on their screens which works like typical 3D glasses. Alternatively, Samsung is trying to commit Sony and others to use battery-powered glasses to facilitate the 3D experience. The competition in this technology is relatively slower to take hold, even in advanced technology segments such as flat panel televisions.

This form of competition is readily evident in the battles among consumer foods' producers, such as candy makers. Hershey competes in different market segments with Mars, Cadbury, Nestle, and Godiva. In addition, similar to other consumer food manufacturers, some candy makers have kept prices constant, selling downsized packages (others, like Hershey, have increased their prices). However, this can change when there is a supply disruption causing a significantly increased price in a commodity such as cocoa, a base ingredient for chocolate.[130] Package design and ease of availability are the competitive dimensions on which these firms sometimes compete to outperform their rivals in this market.

Innovation can also drive competitive actions and responses in standard-cycle markets, especially when rivalry is intense. Some innovations in standard-cycle markets are incremental rather than radical in nature (incremental and radical innovations are discussed in Chapter 13). For example, consumer foods producers are innovating within their lines of healthy products. Overall, many firms are relying on innovation as a means of competing in standard-cycle markets and earning above-average returns.

Overall, innovation has a substantial influence on competitive dynamics as it affects the actions and responses of all companies competing within a slow-cycle, fast-cycle, or standard-cycle market. We have emphasized the importance of innovation to the firm's strategic competitiveness in earlier chapters and do so again in Chapter 13. These discussions highlight the importance of innovation in most types of markets.

SUMMARY

- Competitors are firms competing in the same market, offering similar products, and targeting similar customers. Competitive rivalry is the ongoing set of competitive actions and competitive responses occurring between competitors as they compete against each other for an advantageous market position. The outcomes of competitive rivalry influence the firm's ability to sustain its competitive advantages as well as the level (average, below average, or above average) of its financial returns.

- The set of competitive actions and responses that an individual firm takes while engaged in competitive rivalry is called competitive behavior. Competitive dynamics is the set of actions and responses taken by all firms that are competitors within a particular market.

- Firms study competitive rivalry in order to predict the competitive actions and responses that each of their competitors likely will take. Competitive actions are either strategic or tactical in nature. The firm takes competitive actions to defend or build its competitive advantages or to improve its market position. Competitive responses are taken to counter the effects of a competitor's competitive action. A strategic action or a strategic response requires a significant commitment of organizational resources, is difficult to successfully implement, and is difficult to reverse. In contrast, a tactical action or a tactical response requires fewer organizational resources and is easier to implement and reverse. For example, for an airline company, entering major new markets is an example of a strategic action or a strategic response; changing its prices in a particular market is an example of a tactical action or a tactical response.

- A competitor analysis is the first step the firm takes to be able to predict its competitors' actions and responses. In Chapter 2, we discussed what firms do to *understand* competitors. This discussion was extended in this chapter to describe what the firm does to *predict* competitors' market-based actions. Thus, understanding precedes prediction. Market commonality (the number of markets with which competitors are jointly involved and their importance to each) and resource similarity (how comparable competitors' resources are in terms of type and amount) are studied to complete a competitor analysis. In general, the greater the market commonality and resource similarity, the more firms acknowledge that they are direct competitors.

- Market commonality and resource similarity shape the firm's awareness (the degree to which it and its competitors understand their mutual interdependence), motivation (the firm's incentive to attack or respond), and ability (the quality of the resources available to the firm to attack and respond). Having knowledge of these characteristics of a competitor increases the quality of the firm's predictions about that competitor's actions and responses.

- In addition to market commonality and resource similarity and awareness, motivation, and ability, three more specific factors affect the likelihood a competitor will take competitive actions. The first of these concerns first-mover incentives. First movers, those taking an initial competitive action, often gain loyal customers and earn above-average returns until competitors can successfully respond to their action. Not all firms can be first movers in that they may lack the awareness, motivation, or ability required to engage in this type of competitive behavior. Moreover, some firms prefer to be a second mover (the firm responding to the first mover's action). One reason for this is that second movers, especially those acting quickly, can successfully compete against the first mover. By evaluating the first mover's product, customers' reactions to it, and the responses of other competitors to the first mover, the second mover can avoid the early entrant's mistakes and find ways to improve upon the value created for customers by the first mover's good or service. Late movers (those that respond a long time after the original action was taken) commonly are lower performers and are much less competitive.

■ Organizational size, the second factor, tends to reduce the variety of competitive actions that large firms launch while it increases the variety of actions undertaken by smaller competitors. Ideally, the firm would prefer to initiate a large number of diverse actions when engaged in competitive rivalry. The third factor, quality, is a base denominator to competing successfully in the global economy. It is a necessary prerequisite to achieving competitive parity. It is a necessary but insufficient condition for gaining an advantage.

■ The type of action (strategic or tactical) the firm took, the competitor's reputation for the nature of its competitor behavior, and that competitor's dependence on the market in which the action was taken are studied to predict a competitor's response to the firm's action. In general, the number of tactical responses taken exceeds the number of strategic responses. Competitors respond more frequently to the actions taken by the firm with a reputation for predictable and understandable competitive behavior, especially if that firm is a market leader. In general, the firm can predict that when its competitor is highly dependent for its revenue

and profitability in the market in which the firm took a competitive action, that competitor is likely to launch a strong response. However, firms that are more diversified across markets are less likely to respond to a particular action that affects only one of the markets in which they compete.

■ In slow-cycle markets, where competitive advantages can be maintained for at least a period of time, the competitive dynamics often include firms taking actions and responses intended to protect, maintain, and extend their proprietary advantages. In fast-cycle markets, competition is substantial as firms concentrate on developing a series of temporary competitive advantages. This emphasis is necessary because firms' advantages in fast-cycle markets aren't proprietary and, as such, are subject to rapid and relatively inexpensive imitation. Standard-cycle markets have a level of competition between that in slow-cycle and fast-cycle markets; firms are moderately shielded from competition in these markets as they use capabilities that produce competitive advantages that are moderately sustainable. Competitors in standard-cycle markets serve mass markets and try to develop economies of scale to enhance their profitability. Innovation is vital to competitive success in each of the three types of markets. Companies should recognize that the set of competitive actions and responses taken by all firms differs by type of market.

REVIEW QUESTIONS

1. Who are competitors? How are competitive rivalry, competitive behavior, and competitive dynamics defined in the chapter?

2. What is market commonality? What is resource similarity? What does it mean to say that these concepts are the building blocks for a competitor analysis?

3. How do awareness, motivation, and ability affect the firm's competitive behavior?

4. What factors affect the likelihood a firm will take a competitive action?

5. What factors affect the likelihood a firm will initiate a competitive response to the action taken by a competitor?

6. What competitive dynamics can be expected among firms competing in slow-cycle markets? In fast-cycle markets? In standard-cycle markets?

EXPERIENTIAL EXERCISES

EXERCISE 1: TRAGEDY OF THE COMMONS

The tragedy of the commons is a dilemma that encompasses elements from social psychology and competitive behavior, to name just a couple. The concept first appeared in an article by Garrett Hardin in the Journal *Science* published in 1968. The dilemma arises from a situation in which individuals act in ways that may not necessarily be in everyone's long term interests. In general, the tragedy of the commons occurs when individuals all have equal access to a shared resource and each individual seeks to maximize his or her own self-interest. For a contemporary example, think about global warming in general or localized pollution in particular as instances of the dilemma: there is a distinct advantage for one country/state/business to pollute, which in turn imperils society as a whole.

As explained by R. De Young (1999, Tragedy of the Commons, in D. E. Alexander and R. W. Fairbridge [Eds] *Encyclopedia of Environmental Science*. Hingham, MA: Kluwer Academic Publishers), ecologist Garrett Hardin's parable involves a pasture "open to all." He asks us to imagine the grazing of animals on a common ground. Individuals are motivated to add to their flocks to increase personal wealth. Yet, every animal added to the total degrades the commons a small amount. Although the degradation for each additional animal is small relative to the gain in wealth for the owner, if all owners follow this pattern, the commons will ultimately be destroyed. And, being rational actors, each owner is motivated to add to their flock:

Therein is the tragedy. Each man is locked into a system that compels him to increase his herd without limit—in a world that is limited. Ruin is the destination toward which all men rush, each pursuing his own interest in a society that believes in the freedom of the commons. (Hardin, 1968).

In this exercise, the instructor needs 4 volunteers to participate. You will be asked to come to the front of the class and demonstrate the concept through a short exercise.

You should be familiar with the Tragedy of the Commons (there are many good resources in the library and you are encouraged to read Hardin's original 1968 article in *Science*, volume 162, pages 1243–1248, titled "The Tragedy of the Commons" before attending class.

EXERCISE 2: IS BEING THE FIRST MOVER USUALLY ADVANTAGEOUS?

Henry Ford is often credited with saying that he would rather be the first person to be second. This is strange coming from the innovator of the mass-produced automobile in the United States. So is the first mover advantage really a myth, or is it something that every firm should strive for?

First movers are typically considered to be the ones that initially introduce an innovative product or service into a market segment (in other words, first to market in a new product or service segment). The notion subscribed to first movers is that doing so creates an almost impenetrable competitive advantage that later entrants find difficult to overcome. However, history is replete with situations where second or later movers find success. If the best way to succeed in the future is to understand the past, then an understanding of why certain first movers succeeded

and others failed should be instructive. Accordingly, this exercise requires you to investigate a first mover and identify specifically why, or why not, it was able to hold onto its first-mover advantage.

Part One

Pick an industry that you find of interest. This assignment can be done individually or in a team. Research that industry and identify one or two instances of a first mover; research the introduction of a new offering into new market segments. For example, you might pick consumer electronics and look for firms that initiated new products in new market segments. Your choice of industry must be approved in advance by your instructor as duplication of industries is to be avoided.

Part Two

Each individual or team is to present their findings with the discussion centering on the following at a minimum:

- Brief history and description of the industry chosen (e.g., was this a fast-, standard-, or slow-cycle market at the time the first mover initiated its strategic action)?
- How has innovation of new products traditionally been accomplished in this industry: through new firms entering the market or existing firms launching new offerings?
- Identify one or two first movers and provide a review of what happened. If the product or offering is still considered successful, describe why. If not, why not?
- What did you learn as a result of this exercise? Do you consider the first mover a wise strategy; is your answer dependent upon industry, timing, or luck?

VIDEO CASE

A FOCUS ON COMPETITIVE DYNAMICS: HYUNDAI SOUTH KOREA

With a strategy "to sell more car for less than the competition," consumers are flocking to Hyundai dealerships, and the company is experiencing an 8 percent increase in their U.S. sales. Auto executives both inside and outside the company recognize Hyundai's ability and pursuit to dominate the market through top-level quality. Durability, as evidenced by longer warranties, and greater consumer awareness through major advertising have brought Hyundai from a retrenched state to a strong rebound. With lessons from Toyota, Hyundai remains reactive to industry issues and new automobile manufacturing upstarts.

BE PREPARED TO DISCUSS THE FOLLOWING CONCEPTS AND QUESTIONS IN CLASS:

Concepts
- Competitive behavior
- Competitive dynamics
- Multimarket competition
- Competitive response
- Strategic actions
- Late movers

Questions
1. Describe Hyundai's competitive behavior.
2. What kind of competitive dynamics might you expect from Hyundai and other automakers?
3. Is Hyundai involved in multimarket competition? Why or why not?
4. What impact will market commonality have on competitive responses in the auto industry?
5. What strategic actions may occur as a result of your answer to question 4?
6. Can Hyundai be identified as a late mover? If so, why? What consequences should they be aware of?

NOTES

1. E. L. Chen, R. Katila, R. McDonald, & K. M. Eisenhardt, 2010, Life in the fast lane: Origins of competitive interaction in new vs. established markets, *Strategic Management Journal*, 31(13): 1527–1547; M.-J. Chen, 1996, Competitor analysis and interfirm rivalry: Toward a theoretical integration, *Academy of Management Review*, 21: 100–134.

2. C. Sorensen, 2011, Games on the go, *MacLean's*, February 21, 43.

3. R. Casadesus-Masanell & J. E. Ricart, 2011, How to design a winning business model, *Harvard Business Review*, 89(1/2): 100–107; M. Schrage, 2007, The myth of commoditization, *MIT Sloan Management Review*, 48(2): 10–14.

4. M. Chen, H. Lin, & J. Michel, 2010, Navigating in a hypercompetitive environment: The roles of action aggressiveness and TMT integration, *Strategic Management Journal*, 31(13): 1410–1430; R. D. Ireland & J. W. Webb, 2007, Strategic entrepreneurship: Creating competitive advantage through streams of innovation, *Business Horizons*, 50: 49–59.

5. M. E. Porter & K. R. Kramer, 2011, Creating shared value, *Harvard Business Review*, 89(1/2): 62–77; B. R. Barringer & R. D. Ireland, 2008, *Entrepreneurship: Successfully Launching New Ventures*, 2nd ed., Upper Saddle River, NJ: Prentice Hall.

6. P. J. Derfus, P. G. Maggitti, C. M. Grimm, & K. G. Smith, 2008, The red queen effect: Competitive actions and firm performance, *Academy of Management Journal*, 51: 61–80; C. M. Grimm, H. Lee, & K. G. Smith, 2006, *Strategy as Action: Competitive Dynamics and Competitive Advantage*, New York: Oxford University Press.

7. D. Di Gregorio, D. Thomas, & F. de Castilla, 2008, Competition between emerging market and multinational firms: Wal-Mart and Mexican retailers, *International Journal of Management*, 25(3): 532–545, 593; J. W. Selsky, J. Goes, & O. N. Baburoglu, 2007, Contrasting perspectives of strategy making: Applications in "hyper" environments, *Organization Studies*, 28(1): 71–94.

8. T. C. Powell, 2003, Varieties of competitive parity, *Strategic Management Journal*, 24: 61–86.

9. G. J. Kilduff, H. A. Elfenbein, & B. M. Staw, 2010, The psychology of rivalry: A relationally dependent analysis of competition, *Academy of Management Journal*, 53(5): 943–969; D. G. Sirmon, S. Gove, & M. A. Hitt, 2008, Resource management in dyadic competitive rivalry: The effects of resource bundling and deployment, *Academy of Management Journal*, 51: 919–935.

10. D. B. Montgomery, M. C. Moore, & J. E. Urbany, 2005, Reasoning about competitive reactions: Evidence from executives, *Marketing Science*, 24: 138–149; S. K. Ethitaj & D. H. Zhu, 2008, Performance effects of imitative entry, *Strategic Management Journal*, 29: 797–817.

11. Grimm, Lee, & Smith, *Strategy as Action*; G. Young, K. G. Smith, C. M. Grimm, & D. Simon, 2000, Multimarket contact and resource dissimilarity: A competitive dynamics perspective, *Journal of Management*, 26: 1217–1236.

12. R. Chellappa, V. Sambamurthy, & N. Saraf, 2010, Competing in crowded markets: Multimarket contact and the nature of competition in the enterprise systems software industry, *Information Systems Research*: Special Issue on Digital Systems and Competition, 21(3), 614–630; E. I. Rose & K. Ito, 2008, Competitive interactions: The international investment patterns of Japanese automobile manufacturers, *Journal of International Business Studies*, 39: 864–879.

13. T. Yu, M. Subramaniam, & A. A. Cannella, 2009, Rivalry deterrence in international markets: Contingencies governing the mutual forbearance hypothesis, *Academy of Management Journal*, 52: 127–147; K. G. Smith, W. J. Ferrier, & H. Ndofor, 2001, Competitive dynamics research: Critique and future directions, in M. A. Hitt, R. E. Freeman, & J. S. Harrison (eds.), *Handbook of Strategic Management*, Oxford, UK: Blackwell Publishers, 326.

14. G. Young, K. G. Smith, & C. M. Grimm, 1996, "Austrian" and industrial organization perspectives on firm-level competitive activity and performance, *Organization Science*, 73: 243–254.

15. J. Marcel, P. Barr, & I. Duhaime, 2011, The influence of executive cognition on competitive dynamics, *Strategic Management Journal*, 32(2): 115-138.

16. J. J. Li, K. Z. Zhou, & A. T. Shao, 2009, Competitive position, managerial ties & profitability of foreign firms in China: An interactive perspective, *Journal of International Business Studies*, 40: 339–352; M.-J. Chen & D. C. Hambrick, 1995, Speed, stealth, and selective attack: How small firms differ from large firms in competitive behavior, *Academy of Management Journal*, 38: 453–482.

17. J. M. Mol & N. M. Wijnberg, 2011, From resources to value and back: Competition between and within organizations, *British Journal of Management*, 22(1): 77–95.

18. Porter & Kramer, Creating shared value; A. Sahay, 2007, How to reap higher profits with dynamic pricing, *MIT Sloan Management Review*, 48(4): 53–60.

19. V. Rindova, W. Ferrier, & R. Wiltbank, 2010, Value from gestalt: How sequences of competitive actions create advantage for firms in nascent markets, *Strategic Management Journal*, 31(13): 1474–1497; T. Yu & A. A. Cannella, Jr., 2007, Rivalry between multinational enterprises: An event history approach, *Academy of Management Journal*, 50: 665–686; W. J. Ferrier, 2001, Navigating the competitive landscape: The drivers and consequences of competitive aggressiveness, *Academy of Management Journal*, 44: 858–877.

20. Smith, Ferrier, & Ndofor, Competitive dynamics research, 319.

21. H. Ndofor, D. G. Sirmon, & X. He, 2011, Firm resources, competitive actions and performance: Investigating a mediated model with evidence from the in-vitro diagnostics industry, *Strategic Management Journal*, 32(6): 640–657; E. G. Olson & D. Sharma, 2008, Beating the commoditization trend: A framework from the electronics industry, *Journal of Business Strategy*, 29(4): 22–28.

22. D. G. Sirmon, M. A. Hitt, J. Arregle, & J. Campbell, 2010, The dynamic interplay of capability strengths and weaknesses: Investigating the bases of temporary competitive advantage, *Strategic Management Journal*, 31(13): 1386–1409; J. Li, 2008, Asymmetric interactions between foreign and domestic banks: Effects on market entry, *Strategic Management Journal*, 29: 873–893.

23. J. Beer, 2011, The future of RIM not so dim, *Canadian Business*, April 11, 13–14.

24. S. Cheng & H. Chang, 2009, Performance implications of cognitive complexity: An empirical study of cognitive strategic groups in semiconductor industry, *Journal of Business Research*, 62(12): 1311–1320; G. Leask & D. Parker, 2007, Strategic groups, competitive groups and performance within the U.K. pharmaceutical industry: Improving our understanding of the competitive process, *Strategic Management Journal*, 28: 723–745.

25. Rindova, Ferrier, & Wiltbank, Value from gestalt; Y. Y. Kor & J. T. Mahoney, 2005, How dynamics, management, and governance of resource deployments influence firm-level performance, *Strategic Management Journal*, 26: 489–496.

26. K. G. Fouskas & D. A. Drossos, 2010, The role of industry perceptions in competitive responses, *Industrial Management & Data Systems*, 110(4): 477–494; R. L. Priem, L. G. Love, & M. A. Shaffer, 2002, Executives' perceptions of uncertainty scores: A numerical taxonomy and underlying dimensions, *Journal of Management*, 28: 725–746.

27. J. Chod & E. Lyandres, 2011, Strategic IPOs and product market competition, *Journal of Financial Economics*, 100(1): 45–67; J. C. Bou & A. Satorra, 2007, The persistence of abnormal returns at industry and firm levels: Evidence from Spain, *Strategic Management Journal*, 28: 707–722.

28. Chen, Competitor analysis, 108.

29. Chen, Competitor analysis, 109.

30. 2011, The power of blindspots. What companies don't know, surprises them. What they don't want to know, kills them, *Strategic Direction*, 27(4): 3–4; D. Ng, R. Westgren, & S. Sonka, 2009, Competitive blind spots in an institutional field, *Strategic Management Journal*, 30: 349–369.

31. B. I. Park & P. N. Ghauri, 2011, Key factors affecting acquisition of technological capabilities from foreign acquiring firms by small and medium sized local firms, *Journal of World Business*, 46(1): 116–125; S. J. Chang & D. Xu, 2008, Spillovers and competition among foreign and local firms in China, *Strategic Management Journal*, 29: 495–518.

32. J. Neff, 2011, P&G e-commerce chief sees blurring of sales, marketing, *Advertising Age*, April 11, 8.

33. 2011, http://www.hoovers.com/company/YRC_Worldwide_Inc, April 19.

34. Chen, Competitor analysis, 106.

35. C. Lee, N. N. Venkatraman, H. Tanriverdi, & B. Iyer, 2010, Complementarity-based hypercompetition in the software industry: Theory and empirical test, 1990-2002. *Strategic Management Journal*, 31(13): 1431-1456; A. Kachra & R. E. White, 2008, Know-how transfer: The role of social, economic/competitive, and firm boundary factors, *Strategic Management Journal*, 29: 425–445.

36. J. Anand, L. F. Mesquita, & R. S. Vassolo, 2009, The dynamics of multimarket competition in exploration and exploitation activities, *Academy of Management Journal*, 52(4): 802–821; M. J. Chen, K.-H. Su, & W. Tsai, 2007, Competitive tension: The awareness-motivation-capability perspective, *Academy of Management Journal*, 50: 101–118; J. Gimeno & C. Y. Woo, 1999, Multimarket contact, economies of scope, and firm performance, *Academy of Management Journal*, 42: 239–259.

37. I. C. MacMillan, A. B. van Putten, & R. S. McGrath, 2003, Global gamesmanship, *Harvard Business Review*, 81(5): 62–71.

38. W. Kang, B. Bayus, & S. Balasubramanian, 2010, The strategic effects of multimarket contact: Mutual forbearance and competitive response in the personal computer industry, *Journal of Marketing Research*, 47(3): 415–427; Young, Smith, Grimm, & Simon, Multimarket contact, 1230.

39. V. Bilotkach, 2011, Multimarket contact and intensity of competition: Evidence from an airline merger, *Review of Industrial Organization*, 38(1): 95–115; H. R. Greve, 2008, Multimarket contact and sales growth: Evidence from insurance, *Strategic Management Journal*, 29: 229–249; J. Gimeno, 1999, Reciprocal threats in multimarket rivalry: Staking out "spheres of influence" in the U.S. airline industry, *Strategic Management Journal*, 20: 101–128.

40. Fouskas & Drossos, The role of industry perceptions in competitive responses; S. Jayachandran, J. Gimeno, & P. R. Varadarajan, 1999, Theory of multimarket competition: A synthesis and implications for marketing strategy, *Journal of Marketing*, 63: 49–66; Chen, Competitor analysis, 107.

41. Ndofor, Sirmon, & He, Firm resources, competitive actions and performance; J. Gimeno & C. Y. Woo, 1996, Hypercompetition in a multimarket environment: The role of strategic similarity and multimarket contact on competitive de-escalation, *Organization Science*, 7: 322–341.

42. 2011, Research and markets: International express parcels survey 2011, *Business Wire*, http://www.businesswire.com, April 19.

43. G. B. Dagnino & E. Rocco, 2009, *Coopetition Strategy: Theory, Experiments and Cases*, New York: Rutledge; S. MacMillan, 2008, The issue: DHL turns to rival UPS, *BusinessWeek*, http//:www.businessweek.com, June 11.

44. T. Hutzschenreuter & F. Gröne, 2009, Product and geographic scope changes of multinational enterprises in response to international competition, *Journal of International Business Studies*, 40(7): 1149-1170; Chen, Su, & Tsai, Competitive tension; Chen, Competitor analysis, 110.

45. Ibid.; W. Ocasio, 1997, Towards an attention-based view of the firm, *Strategic Management Journal*, 18 (Special Issue): 187–206; Smith, Ferrier, & Ndofor, Competitive dynamics research, 320.

46. R. A. Carter, 2010, Tracking new developments in dozer design, *Engineering & Mining Journal*, 211(2): 30–32; 2007, Komatsu lifts outlook, outdoes rival Caterpillar, *New York Times Online*, http://www.nytimes.com, July 30.

47. L. Burkitt, 2011, China fines Wal-Mart, Carrefour over pricing, *Wall Street Journal*, http://www.wsj.com, February 22.

48. R. S. Livengood & R. K. Reger, 2010, That's our turf! Identity domains and competitive dynamics, *Academy of Management Review*, 35(1): 48–66; J. F. Porac & H. Thomas, 1994, Cognitive categorization and subjective rivalry among retailers in a small city, *Journal of Applied Psychology*, 79: 54–66.

49. Livengood & Reger, That's our turf; S. H. Park & D. Zhou, 2005, Firm heterogeneity and competitive dynamics in alliance formation, *Academy of Management Review*, 30: 531–554.

50. S. R. Miller, D. E. Thomas, L. Eden, & M. A. Hitt, 2008, Knee deep in the big muddy: The survival of emerging market firms in developed markets, *Management International Review*, 48: 645–666.

51. Chen, Competitor analysis, 113.

52. C. Williams & S. Lee, 2011, Entrepreneurial contexts and knowledge coordination within the multinational corporation, *Journal of World Business*, 46(2): 253–264; M. Leiblein & T. Madsen, 2009, Unbundling competitive heterogeneity: Incentive structures and capability influences on technological innovation, *Strategic Management Journal*, 30: 711–735.

53. R. Makadok, 2010, The interaction effect of rivalry restraint and competitive advantage on profit: Why the whole is less than the sum of the parts, *Management Science*, 56(2): 356–372; R. Belderbos & L. Sleuwaegen, 2005, Competitive drivers and international plant configuration strategies: A product-level test, *Strategic Management Journal*, 26: 577–593.

54. C. M. Grimm & K. G. Smith, 1997, *Strategy as Action: Industry Rivalry and Coordination*, Cincinnati: South-Western Publishing Co., 125.

55. Kang, Bayus, & Balasubramanian, The strategic effects of multimarket contact; B. Webber, 2007, Volatile markets, *Business Strategy Review*, 18(2): 60–67; K. G. Smith, W. J. Ferrier, & C. M. Grimm, 2001, King of the hill: Dethroning the industry leader, *Academy of Management Executive*, 15(2): 59–70.

56. B. Markens, 2011, Be aware of your competition to increase market share, *Paperboard Packaging*, 96(1): 11; S. E. Jackson, 2008, Grow your business without leaving your competitive stronghold, *Journal of Business Strategy*, 29(4): 60–62.

57. B. L. Connelly, L. Tihanyi, S. T. Certo, & M. A. Hitt, 2010, Marching to the beat of different drummers: The influence of institutional owners on competitive actions, *Academy of Management Journal*, 53(4): 723–742; W. J. Ferrier & H. Lee, 2003, Strategic aggressiveness, variation, and surprise: How the sequential pattern of competitive rivalry influences stock market returns, *Journal of Managerial Issues*, 14: 162–180.

58. G. Nimeh, 2011, What mobile has in store, *Marketing*, February 23, 17.

59. M. Bustillo, 2011, Wal-Mart merchandise goes back to basics, *Wall Street Journal*, http://www.wsj.com, April 11.

60. P. Sanders, 2010, Boeing resumes 787 flight testing, *Wall Street Journal*, http://www.wsj.com, December 23.

61. J. Schumpeter, 1934, *The Theory of Economic Development*, Cambridge, MA: Harvard University Press.

62. J. L. C. Cheng & I. F. Kesner, 1997, Organizational slack and response to environmental shifts: The impact of resource allocation patterns, *Journal of Management*, 23: 1–18.

63. F. F. Suarez & G. Lanzolla, 2007, The role of environmental dynamics in building a first mover advantage theory, *Academy of Management Review*, 32: 377–392.

64. G. M. McNamara, J. Haleblian, & B. J. Dykes, 2008, The performance implications of participating in an acquisition wave: Early mover advantages, bandwagon effects, and the moderating influence of industry characteristics and acquirer tactics, *Academy of Management Journal*, 51,

113–130; F. Wang, 2000, Too appealing to overlook, *America's Network*, December, 10–12.

65. R. K. Sinha & C. H. Noble, 2008, The adoption of radical manufacturing technologies and firm survival, *Strategic Management Journal*, 29: 943–962; D. P. Forbes, 2005, Managerial determinants of decision speed in new ventures, *Strategic Management Journal*, 26: 355–366.

66. H. R. Greve, 2009, Bigger and safer: The diffusion of competitive advantage, *Strategic Management Journal*, 30: 1–23; W. T. Robinson & S. Min, 2002, Is the first to market the first to fail? Empirical evidence for industrial goods businesses, *Journal of Marketing Research*, 39: 120–128.

67. J. C. Short & G. T. Payne, 2008, First-movers and performance: Timing is everything, *Academy of Management Review*, 33 (1), 267–270.

68. A. Srivastava & H. Lee, 2005, Predicting order and timing of new product moves: The role of top management in corporate entrepreneurship, *Journal of Business Venturing*, 20: 459–481.

69. Ndofor, Sirmon, & He, Firm resources, competitive actions and performance; M. S. Giarratana & A. Fosfuri, 2007, Product strategies and survival in Schumpeterian environments: Evidence from the U.S. security software industry, *Organization Studies*, 28(6): 909–929.

70. S. D. Dobrev & A. Gotsopoulos, 2010, Legitimacy vacuum, structural imprinting, and the first mover disadvantage, *Academy of Management Journal*, 53(5): 1153–1174.

71. K. Mellahi & A. Wilkinson, 2010, A study of the association between level of slack reduction following downsizing and innovation output, *Journal of Management Studies*, 47(3): 483–508; Z. Simsek, J. F. Veiga, & M. H. Lubatkin, 2007, The impact of managerial environmental perceptions on corporate entrepreneurship: Toward understanding discretionary slack's pivotal role, *Journal of Management Studies*, 44: 1398–1424.

72. A. Tuppura, P. Hurmelinna-Laukkanen, K. Puumalainen, & A. Jantunen, 2010, The influence of appropriability conditions on the firm's entry timing orientation, *Journal of High Technology Management Research*, 21(2): 97–107; M. B. Lieberman & D. B. Montgomery, 1988, First-mover advantages, *Strategic Management Journal*, 9: 41–58.

73. G. Pacheco-de-Almeida, 2010, Erosion, time compression, and self-displacement of leaders in hypercompetitive environments, *Strategic Management Journal*, 31(13): 1498–1526; D. Lange, S. Boivie, & A. D. Henderson, 2009, The parenting paradox: How multibusiness diversifiers endorse disruptive technologies while their corporate children struggle, *Academy of Management Journal*, 52: 179–198.

74. S. Jonsson & P. Regnér, 2009, Normative barriers to imitation: Social complexity of core competences in a mutual fund industry, *Strategic Management Journal*, 30: 517–536; 2001, Older, wiser, webbier, *The Economist*, June 30, 10.

75. M. Poletti, B. Engelland, & H. Ling, 2011, An empirical study of declining lead times: Potential ramifications on the performance of early market entrants, *Journal of Marketing Theory and Practice*, 19(1): 27–38; W. Boulding & M. Christen, 2001, First-mover disadvantage, *Harvard Business Review*, 79(9): 20–21.

76. J. L. Boyd & R. K. F. Bresser, 2008, Performance implications of delayed competitive responses: Evidence from the U.S. retail industry, *Strategic Management Journal*, 29: 1077–1096.

77. S. Bin, 2011, First-mover advantages: Flexible or not?, *Journal of Management & Marketing Research*, 7: 1–13; J. Gimeno, R. E. Hoskisson, B. B. Beal, & W. P. Wan, 2005, Explaining the clustering of international expansion moves: A critical test in the U.S. telecommunications industry, *Academy of Management Journal*, 48: 297–319; K. G. Smith, C. M. Grimm, & M. J. Gannon, 1992, *Dynamics of Competitive Strategy*, Newberry Park, CA: Sage Publications.

78. H. Greimel, 2010, New day at Hyundai, *Automotive News*, December 13, 4.

79. A. Fleury & M. Fleury, 2009, Understanding the strategies of late-movers in international manufacturing, *International Journal of Production Economics*, 122(1): 340–350; J. Li & R. K. Koxhikode, 2008, Knowledge management and innovation strategy: The challenge for latecomers in emerging economies, *Asia Pacific Journal of Management*, 25: 429–450.

80. F. Karakaya & P. Yannopoulos, 2011, Impact of market entrant characteristics on incumbent reactions to market entry, *Journal of Strategic Marketing*, 19(2): 171–185; S. D. Dobrev & G. R. Carroll, 2003, Size (and competition) among organizations: Modeling scale-based selection among automobile producers in four major countries, 1885–1981, *Strategic Management Journal*, 24: 541–558.

81. L. F. Mesquita & S. G. Lazzarini, 2008, Horizontal and vertical relationships in developing economies: Implications for SMEs access to global markets, *Academy of Management Journal*, 51: 359–380; F. K. Pil & M. Hoiweg, 2003, Exploring scale: The advantage of thinking small, *The McKinsey Quarterly*, 44(2): 33–39.

82. C. Zhou & A. Van Witteloostuijn, 2010, Institutional constraints and ecological processes: Evolution of foreign-invested enterprises in the Chinese construction industry, 1993–2006, *Journal of International Business Studies*, 41(3): 539–556; M. A. Hitt, L. Bierman, & J. D. Collins, 2007, The strategic evolution of U.S. law firms, *Business Horizons*, 50: 17–28; D. Miller & M. J. Chen, 1996, The

simplicity of competitive repertoires: An empirical analysis, *Strategic Management Journal*, 17: 419–440.

83. J. Shambora, 2011, David vs. Goliath, *Fortune*, February 28, 26.

84. Young, Smith, & Grimm, "Austrian" and industrial organization perspectives.

85. B. A. Melcher, 1993, How Goliaths can act like Davids, *BusinessWeek*, Special Issue, 193.

86. E. Basker & M. Noel, 2009, The evolving food chain: competitive effects of Wal-Mart's entry into the supermarket industry, *Journal of Economics & Management Strategy*, 18(4): 977–1009.

87. P. B. Crosby, 1980, *Quality Is Free*, New York: Penguin.

88. W. E. Deming, 1986, *Out of the Crisis*, Cambridge, MA: MIT Press.

89. G. C. Avery & H. Bergsteiner, 2011, Sustainable leadership practices for enhancing business resilience and performance, *Strategy & Leadership*, 39(3): 5–15; D. A. Mollenkopf, E. Rabinovich, T. M. Laseter, & K. K. Boyer, 2007, Managing Internet product returns: A focus on effective service operations, *Decision Sciences*, 38: 215–250.

90. X. Luo, 2010, Product competitiveness and beating analyst earnings target, *Journal of the Academy of Marketing Science*, 38(3): 253–264; K. Watanabe, 2007, Lessons from Toyota's long drive, *Harvard Business Review*, 85(7/8): 74–83.

91. F. Pakdil, 2010, The effects of TQM on corporate performance. *The Business Review*, 15(1): 242–248; A. Azadegan, K. J. Dooley, P. L. Carter, & J. R. Carter, 2008, Supplier innovativeness and the role of interorganizational learning in enhancing manufacturing capabilities, *Journal of Supply Chain Management*, 44(4): 14–35.

92. M. Terziovski & P. Hermel, 2011, The role of quality management practice in the performance of integrated supply chains: A multiple cross-case analysis, *The Quality Management Journal*, 18(2): 10–25; K. E. Weick & K. M. Sutcliffe, 2001, *Managing the Unexpected*, San Francisco: Jossey-Bass, 81–82.

93. D. P. McIntyre, 2011, In a network industry, does product quality matter?, *Journal of Product Innovation Management*, 28(1): 99–108; G. Macintosh, 2007, Customer orientation, relationship quality, and relational benefits to the firm, *Journal of Services Marketing*, 21(3): 150–159.

94. S. Thirumalai & K. K. Sinha, 2011, Product recalls in the medical device industry: An empirical exploration of the sources and financial consequences, *Management Science*, 57(2): 376–392.

95. G. Norris, 2010, Tail woes, *Aviation Week & Space Technology*, July 5, 33; J. Wallace, 2009, Boeing at risk of losing more 787 orders, *Seattle-Post-Intelligencer*, http://www.seattlepi.nwsource.com, March 13.

96. M. Su & V. R. Rao, 2011, Timing decisions of new product preannouncement and launch with competition, *International Journal of Production Economics*, 129(1): 51–64.

97. Ndofor, Sirmon, & He, Firm resources, competitive actions and performance; T. R. Crook, D. J. Ketchen, J. G. Combs, & S. Y. Todd, 2008, Strategic resources and performance: A meta-analysis, *Strategic Management Journal*, 29: 1141–1154; Smith, Ferrier, & Ndofor, Competitive dynamics research, 323.

98. C. Lutz, R. Kemp, & S. Gerhard Dijkstra, 2010, Perceptions regarding strategic and structural entry barriers, *Small Business Economics*, 35(1): 19–33; M. J. Chen & I. C. MacMillan, 1992, Nonresponse and delayed response to competitive moves, *Academy of Management Journal*, 35: 539–570; Smith, Ferrier, & Ndofor, Competitive dynamics research, 335.

99. Connelly, Tihanyi, Certo, & Hitt, Marching to the beat of different drummers; M. J. Chen, K. G. Smith, & C. M. Grimm, 1992, Action characteristics as predictors of competitive responses, *Management Science*, 38: 439–455.

100. Chen, Katila, McDonald, & Eisenhardt, 2010, Life in the fast lane; M. J. Chen & D. Miller, 1994, Competitive attack, retaliation and performance: An expectancy-valence framework, *Strategic Management Journal*, 15: 85–102.

101. M. Ritson, 2009, Should you launch a fighter brand?, *Harvard Business Review*, 87(10): 86–94; T. Gardner, 2005, Interfirm competition for human resources: Evidence from the software industry, *Academy of Management Journal*, 48: 237–258; N. Huyghebaert & L. M. van de Gucht, 2004, Incumbent strategic behavior in financial markets and the exit of entrepreneurial start-ups, *Strategic Management Journal*, 25: 669–688.

102. Smith, Ferrier, & Ndofor, Competitive dynamics research, 333.

103. T. Obloj & L. Capron, 2011, Role of resource gap and value appropriation: Effect of reputation gap on price premium in online auctions, *Strategic Management Journal*, 32(4): 447–456; V. P. Rindova, A. P. Petkova, & S. Kotha, 2007, Standing out: How firms in emerging markets build reputation, *Strategic Organization*, 5: 31–70; J. Shamsie, 2003, The context of dominance: An industry-driven framework for exploiting reputation, *Strategic Management Journal*, 24: 199–215.

104. D. D. Bergh & P. Gibbons, 2011, The stock market reaction to the hiring of management consultants: A signalling theory approach, *Journal of Management Studies*, 48(3): 544–567; P. W. Roberts & G. R. Dowling, 2003, Corporate reputation and sustained superior financial performance, *Strategic Management Journal*, 24: 1077–1093.

105. W. J. Ferrier, K. G. Smith, & C. M. Grimm, 1999, The role of competitive actions in market share erosion and industry dethronement: A study of industry leaders and challengers, *Academy of Management Journal*, 42: 372–388.

106. R. Karlgaard, 2011, Transitions: Michael reinvents Dell, *Forbes*, http://www.forbes.com, May 9.

107. Smith, Grimm, & Gannon, *Dynamics of Competitive Strategy*.

108. P. Li, 2010. Toward a learning-based view of internationalization: The accelerated trajectories of cross-border learning for latecomers, *Journal of International Management*, 16(1): 43–59; L. Li, L. Zhang, & B. Arys, 2008, The turtle–hare story revisited: Social capital and resource accumulation for firms from emerging economies, *Asia Pacific Journal of Management*, 25: 251–275.

109. A. Karnani & B. Wernerfelt, 1985, Multiple point competition, *Strategic Management Journal*, 6: 87–97.

110. L. Kwanghui, H. Chesbrough, & R. Yi, 2010, Open innovation and patterns of R&D competition, *International Journal of Technology Management*, 52(3/4): 295–321; Smith, Ferrier, & Ndofor, Competitive dynamics research, 330.

111. P. Burrows, 2011, Empire-building at Akamai, *Bloomberg Businessweek*, http://www.businessweek.com, February 14.

112. Lee, Venkatraman, Tanriverdi, & Iyer, Complementarity-based hypercompetition in the software industry; S. L. Newbert, 2007, Empirical research on the resource-based view of the firm: An assessment and suggestions for future research, *Strategic Management Journal*, 28: 121–146; G. McNamara, P. M. Vaaler, & C. Devers, 2003, Same as it ever was: The search for evidence of increasing hypercompetition, *Strategic Management Journal*, 24: 261–278.

113. C. Giachetti & G. Marchi, 2010, Evolution of firms' product strategy over the life cycle of technology-based industries: A case study of the global mobile phone industry, 1980–2009, *Business History*, 52(7): 1123–1150.

114. J. R. Williams, 1992, How sustainable is your competitive advantage? *California Management Review*, 34(3): 29–51.

115. B. Pinkham, J. Picken, & G. Dess, 2010, Creating value in the modern organization: The role of leveraging technology, *Organizational Dynamics*, 39(3): 226–239; J. A. Lamberg, H. Tikkanen, & T. Nokelainen, 2009, Competitive dynamics, strategic consistency and organizational survival, *Strategic Management Journal*, 30: 45–60.

116. R. A. D'Aveni, G. Dagnino, & K. G. Smith, 2010, The age of temporary advantage, *Strategic Management Journal*, 31(13): 1371–1385; N. Pangarkar & J. R. Lie, 2004, The impact of market cycle on the performance of Singapore acquirers, *Strategic Management Journal*, 25: 1209–1216.

117. T. Randall, 2011, Merck's risky bet on research. *Bloomberg Businessweek*, April 25, 25-26.

118. G. Pacheco-de-Almeida, 2010, Erosion, time compression, and self-displacement of leaders in hypercompetitive environments, *Strategic Management Journal*, 31(13): 1498–1526.

119. 2003, How fast is your company? *Fast Company*, June, 18.

120. F. Hermelo & R. Vassolo, 2010, Institutional development and hypercompetition in emerging economies, *Strategic Management Journal*, 31(13): 1457–1473; D. P. Forbes, 2007, Reconsidering the strategic implications of decision comprehensiveness, *Academy of Management Review*, 32: 361–376; T. Talaulicar, J. Grundei, & A. V. Werder, 2005, Strategic decision making in startups: The effect of top management team organization and processes on speed and comprehensiveness, *Journal of Business Venturing*, 20: 519–541.

121. C. Hall & D. Lundberg, 2010, Competitive knowledge and strategy in high velocity environments, *IUP Journal of Knowledge Management*, 8(1/2): 7–17; A. H. Ang, 2008, Competitive intensity and collaboration: Impact on firm growth across technological environments, *Strategic Management Journal*, 29: 1057–1075; M. Song, C. Droge, S. Hanvanich, & R. Calantone, 2005, Marketing and technology resource complementarity: An analysis of their interaction effect in two environmental contexts, *Strategic Management Journal*, 26: 259–276.

122. G. Clarkson & P. Toh, 2010, 'Keep out' signs: The role of deterrence in the competition for resources, *Strategic Management Journal*, 31(11): 1202–1225.

123. S. F. Turner, W. Mitchell, & R. A. Bettis, 2010, Responding to rivals and complements: How market concentration shapes generational product innovation strategy, *Organization Science*, 21(4): 854–872.

124. M. Useem, 2010, Four lessons in adaptive leadership, *Harvard Business Review*, 88(11): 86–90.

125. M. Kumar, 2011, Are joint ventures positive sum games? The relative effects of cooperative and noncooperative behavior, *Strategic Management Journal*, 32(1): 32–54; D. Li, L. Eden, M. A. Hitt, & R. D. Ireland, 2008, Friends, acquaintances or strangers? Partner selection in R&D alliances, *Academy of Management Journal*, 51: 315–334; D. Gerwin, 2004, Coordinating new product development in strategic alliances, *Academy of Management Review*, 29: 241–257.

126. F. Zirpoli & M. C. Becker, 2011, What happens when you outsource too much?, *MIT Sloan Management Review*, 52(2): 59–64; K. Coucke & L. Sleuwaegen, 2008, Offshoring as a survival strategy: Evidence from manufacturing firms in Belgium, *Journal of International Business Studies*, 39: 1261–1277.

127. Turner, Mitchell, & Bettis, Responding to rivals and complements; P. Carbonell & A. I. Rodriguez, 2006, The impact of

market characteristics and innovation speed on perceptions of positional advantage and new product performance, *International Journal of Research in Marketing*, 23(1): 1–12; R. Sanchez, 1995, Strategic flexibility in production competition, *Strategic Management Journal,* 16 (Special Issue): 9–26.

128. V. Kumar, F. Jones, R. Venkatesan, & R. Leone, 2011, Is market orientation a source of sustainable competitive advantage or simply the cost of competing?, *Journal of Marketing*, 75(1): 16–30; R. Adner & D. Levinthal, 2008, Doing versus seeing: Acts of exploitation and perceptions of exploration, *Strategic Entrepreneurship Journal*, 2: 43–52.

129. C. Edwards, 2011, Technology: Fighting for 3D survival, *Bloomberg Businessweek*, April 25, 38–40.

130. L. Josephs, 2011, Candy lovers face bitter Easter, *Wall Street Journal*, February 18, C10.

CHAPTER 6
Corporate-Level Strategy

Studying this chapter should provide you with the strategic management knowledge needed to:

1. Define corporate-level strategy and discuss its purpose.

2. Describe different levels of diversification with different corporate-level strategies.

3. Explain three primary reasons firms diversify.

4. Describe how firms can create value by using a related diversification strategy.

5. Explain the two ways value can be created with an unrelated diversification strategy.

6. Discuss the incentives and resources that encourage diversification.

7. Describe motives that can encourage managers to overdiversify a firm.

GENERAL ELECTRIC: THE QUINTESSENTIAL DIVERSIFIED FIRM

It would almost be easier to list the industries in which General Electric (GE) does not compete than to list those in which it sells products. GE competes in 16 different industries: appliances, aviation, consumer electronics, electrical distribution, energy, entertainment, finance, gas, health care, lighting, locomotives, oil, software, water, weapons, and wind turbines. As one can see from this list, these industries are quite diverse. Yet, there are similarities among several of them. In fact, GE's businesses are grouped in four divisions: GE Capital, GE Energy, GE Technology Infrastructure, and GE Home & Business Solutions. In recent years, more than 50 percent of GE's annual revenue has come from its financial services businesses. Thus, it could be labeled a services company with a strong industrial component. In 2011 (based on 2010 data), GE was ranked the sixth largest corporation in the *Fortune* 500. It is the only company that was listed in the initial Dow Jones Industrial Average in 1896 that remains on it today. For the last 119 years, GE has achieved an average annual increase in its stock value of 5.8 percent.

These data suggest that GE has an impressive history and has experienced a significant amount of success. It is one of the few widely diversified firms to achieve such success. GE is a highly influential global corporation. Its CEO, Jeffrey Immelt, was selected by President Obama to chair an advisory group on economic and job creation concerns. However, GE has experienced some "bumps in the road" along the way. This is to be expected because it is difficult to manage a large, widely diversified set of businesses.

Langrock/Zenit/laif/Redux

These General Electric wind turbines in France each produce 1.5 megawatts of energy.

For example, it has been criticized for its control over media it owns, such as NBC. GE has restricted NBC reporters from reporting on certain content that is critical of GE. Additionally, in the past GE was criticized for the poor environmental records of some of its businesses. Finally, it had reductions in stock value during the first decade of the twenty-first century.

GE has bounced back from these problems. It has worked hard to overcome and correct its environmental problems. Today, it is a major player in the "clean energy" industry, such as wind turbines and solar power. GE is also beginning to experience strong growth from its investments in emerging economies such China and Brazil. In both of these countries, GE has made major business investments working with local partners and has developed R&D centers as well. A common strategy to achieve growth (and diversification) for GE over the years has been mergers and acquisitions. For example, in 2011, GE acquired a French company, Converteam, for $3.2 billion. This company will provide support equipment for GE's wind turbine business. In 2010 and in the first few months of 2011, GE spent more than $11 billion on acquisitions to add to its repertoire of energy businesses.

© Nicholas Monu/iStockphoto.com

STRATEGY RIGHT NOW

Learn more about NBC's media bias.

www.cengagebrain.com

Sources: General Electric, 2011, *Wikipedia*, http://en.wikipedia.org, May 15; C. Loomis, 2011, The really, really, really long-term record for GE, *Fortune*, http://www.fortune.com, May 14; T. Woody, 2011, GE's new ecomagination chief: Green tech innovation goes global, *Forbes*, http://www.forbes.com, May 3; S. Pearson, 2011, GE targets Latin America for growth, *Financial Times*, http://www.ft.com, May 1; E. Crooks, 2011, GE says growth outlook is very strong, *Financial Times*, http://www.ft.com, April 28; B. Sechler, 2011, GE plan will tap solar power, *Wall Street Journal*, http://online.wsj.com, April 8; T. Zeller, 2011, GE to buy French company for $3.2 billion, *The New York Times*, http://dealbook.nytimes.com, March 29; R. Layne, 2011, General Electric agrees to buy Converteam for $3.2 billion, *Bloomberg Businessweek*, http://www.businessweek.com, March 29; General Electric plans to invest $2 billion in China, *Bloomberg Businessweek*, 2010, http://www.businessweek.com, November 9; D. Zax, 2010, GE and Siemens outpacing wind pioneers, becoming clean energy's new oligopoly, *Fast company*, http://www.fastcompany.com, November 2.

Our discussions of business-level strategies (Chapter 4) and the competitive rivalry and competitive dynamics associated with them (Chapter 5) have concentrated on firms competing in a single industry or product market.[1] In this chapter, we introduce you to corporate-level strategies, which are strategies firms use to *diversify* their operations from a single business competing in a single market into several product markets—most commonly, into several businesses. Thus, a **corporate-level strategy** specifies actions a firm takes to gain a competitive advantage by selecting and managing a group of different businesses competing in different product markets. Corporate-level strategies help companies to select new strategic positions—positions that are expected to increase the firm's value.[2] As explained in the Opening Case, General Electric competes in 16 widely diverse industries.

As is the case with GE, firms use corporate-level strategies as a means to grow revenues and profits, but there can be different strategic intents in addition to growth. Firms can pursue defensive or offensive strategies that realize growth but have different strategic intents. Firms can also pursue market development by moving into different geographic markets (this approach will be discussed in Chapter 8). Firms can acquire competitors (horizontal integration) or buy a supplier or customer (vertical integration). These strategies will be discussed in Chapter 7. The basic corporate strategy, the topic of this chapter, focuses on diversification.

The decision to take actions to pursue growth is never a risk-free choice for firms. Indeed, as the Opening Case explored, GE experienced difficulty in its media businesses, especially NBC, and its environmental record suffered. In one case, it tried to control NBC too much, trying to protect the firm. In so doing, it created questions about the objectivity of NBC's reporting. Its environmental record likely suffered because of the lack of adequate oversight and the strong interest in producing returns for the shareholders. Effective firms carefully evaluate their growth options (including the different corporate-level strategies) before committing firm resources to any of them.[3]

Because the diversified firm operates in several different and unique product markets and likely in several businesses, it forms two types of strategies: corporate-level (or company-wide) and business-level (or competitive).[4] Corporate-level strategy is concerned with two key issues: in what product markets and businesses the firm should compete and how corporate headquarters should manage those businesses.[5] For the diversified corporation, a business-level strategy (see Chapter 4) must be selected for each of the businesses in which the firm has decided to compete. In this regard, each of GE's product divisions uses different business-level strategies; while most focus on differentiation, its consumer electronics business has products that compete in market niches to include some that are intended to serve the average income consumer. Thus, cost must also be an issue along with some level of quality.

As is the case with a business-level strategy, a corporate-level strategy is expected to help the firm earn above-average returns by creating value.[6] Some suggest that few corporate-level strategies actually create value.[7] As the Opening Case indicates, realizing value through a corporate strategy can be achieved but it is challenging to do so. In fact, GE is one of the few widely diversified and large firms that has been successful over time.

A **corporate-level strategy** specifies actions a firm takes to gain a competitive advantage by selecting and managing a group of different businesses competing in different product markets.

Evidence suggests that a corporate-level strategy's value is ultimately determined by the degree to which "the businesses in the portfolio are worth more under the management of the company than they would be under any other ownership."[8] Thus, an effective corporate-level strategy creates, across all of a firm's businesses, aggregate returns that exceed what those returns would be without the strategy[9] and contributes to the firm's strategic competitiveness and its ability to earn above-average returns.[10]

Product diversification, a primary form of corporate-level strategies, concerns the scope of the markets and industries in which the firm competes as well as "how managers buy, create and sell different businesses to match skills and strengths with opportunities presented to the firm."[11] Successful diversification is expected to reduce variability in the firm's profitability as earnings are generated from different businesses.[12] Diversification can also provide firms with the flexibility to shift their investments to markets where the greatest returns are possible rather than being dependent on only one or a few markets.[13] Because firms incur development and monitoring costs when diversifying, the ideal portfolio of businesses balances diversification's costs and benefits. CEOs and their top-management teams are responsible for determining the best portfolio for their company.[14]

We begin this chapter by examining different levels of diversification (from low to high). After describing the different reasons firms diversify their operations, we focus on two types of related diversification (related diversification signifies a moderate to high level of diversification for the firm). When properly used, these strategies help create value in the diversified firm, either through the sharing of resources (the related constrained strategy) or the transferring of core competencies across the firm's different businesses (the related linked strategy). We then discuss unrelated diversification, which is another corporate-level strategy that can create value. The chapter then shifts to the topic of incentives and resources that may stimulate diversification which is value neutral. However, managerial motives to diversify, the final topic in the chapter, can actually destroy some of the firm's value.

Levels of Diversification

Diversified firms vary according to their level of diversification and the connections between and among their businesses. Figure 6.1 lists and defines five categories of businesses according to increasing levels of diversification. The single- and dominant-business categories denote relatively low levels of diversification; more fully diversified firms are classified into related and unrelated categories. A firm is related through its diversification when its businesses share several links; for example, businesses may share products (goods or services), technologies, or distribution channels. The more links among businesses, the more "constrained" is the relatedness of diversification. "Unrelated" refers to the absence of direct links between businesses.

Low Levels of Diversification

A firm pursuing a low level of diversification uses either a single- or a dominant-business, corporate-level diversification strategy. A *single-business diversification strategy* is a corporate-level strategy wherein the firm generates 95 percent or more of its sales revenue from its core business area.[15] For example, Wm. Wrigley Jr. Company, the world's largest producer of chewing and bubble gums, historically used a single-business strategy while operating in relatively few product markets. Wrigley's trademark chewing gum brands include Spearmint, Doublemint, and Juicy Fruit, although the firm produces other products as well. Sugar-free Extra, which currently holds the largest share of the U.S. chewing gum market, was introduced in 1984.

© Nicholas Monu/iStockphoto.com

STRATEGY RIGHT NOW

Find out more about GE's diversification strategy.

www.cengagebrain .com

Figure 6.1 Levels and Types of Diversification

Low Levels of Diversification		
Single business:	95% or more of revenue comes from a single business.	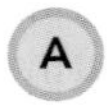
Dominant business:	Between 70% and 95% of revenue comes from a single business.	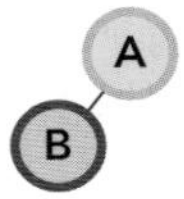
Moderate to High Levels of Diversification		
Related constrained:	Less than 70% of revenue comes from the dominant business, and all businesses share product, technological, and distribution linkages.	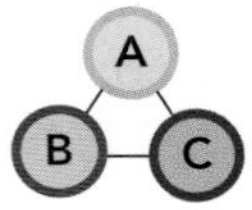
Related linked (mixed related and unrelated):	Less than 70% of revenue comes from the dominant business, and there are only limited links between businesses.	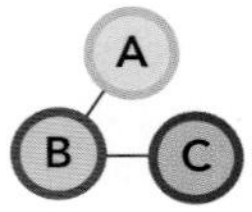
Very High Levels of Diversification		
Unrelated:	Less than 70% of revenue comes from the dominant business, and there are no common links between businesses.	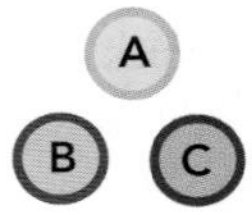

Source: Adapted from R. P. Rumelt, 1974, *Strategy, Structure and Economic Performance*, Boston: Harvard Business School.

In 2005, Wrigley shifted from its traditional focused strategy when it acquired the confectionary assets of Kraft Foods Inc., including the well-known brands Life Savers and Altoids. As Wrigley expanded, it may have intended to use the dominant-business strategy with the diversification of its product lines beyond gum; however, Wrigley was acquired in 2008 by Mars, a privately held global confection company (the maker of Snickers and M&Ms).[16]

With the *dominant-business diversification strategy,* the firm generates between 70 and 95 percent of its total revenue within a single business area. United Parcel Service (UPS) uses this strategy. Recently UPS generated 60 percent of its revenue from its U.S. package delivery business and 22 percent from its international package business, with the remaining 18 percent coming from the firm's non-package business.[17] Though the U.S. package delivery business currently generates the largest percentage of UPS's sales revenue, the firm anticipates that in the future its other two businesses will account for the majority of revenue growth. This expectation suggests that UPS may become more diversified, both in terms of its goods and services and in the number of countries in which those goods and services are offered.

Firms that focus on one or very few businesses and markets can earn positive returns, because they develop capabilities useful for these markets and can provide superior service to their customers. Additionally, there are fewer challenges in managing one or a very small set of businesses, allowing them to gain economies of scale and efficiently use their resources.[18] Family-owned and controlled businesses are commonly less diversified. They prefer the focus because the family's reputation is related closely to that of the business. Thus, family members prefer to provide quality goods and services which a focused strategy better allows.[19]

STRATEGIC FOCUS

RELATEDNESS AMONG BUSINESS BEARS FRUIT AT THE PUBLICIS GROUPE

The Publicis Groupe uses a related constrained diversified strategy with three major groups of businesses, each in a highly related but unique market area: advertising, media, and digital.

Publicis is the third largest communications company in the world. It is a leader in digital communications, the second largest global media business, and the global leader in digital operations. Furthermore, it is the world leader in health care communications. Publicis's financial performance in 2010 outpaced analysts' expectations. It achieved an organic growth rate of 8.3 percent in revenues over 2009, and an increase in its profits of 31 percent.

Publicis invested early in digital technology and in emerging markets. Both decisions are paying off today. The digital revolution has changed advertising. In fact, digital technology now allows the customization of a message to a specific customer (or customer type) at a specific point in time. This is significantly different from ads targeted for a mass audience. Publicis Digital business provides the tools for use by its advertising businesses, thereby sharing resources and capabilities. Because emerging economies are largely driving the economic growth globally, Publicis plans to increase its investments and business in the largest emerging markets such as China and Brazil. In fact, the firm expects that revenues from these high-growth regions will represent 30 percent of the firm's total revenues in the near future.

In support of its continuing related diversification efforts, in 2011 Publicis developed a new performance marketing agency called Performics France. It will also launch this service internationally. The agency offers the Publicis Webformance toolkit to companies, allowing them to make the most effective use of online advertising, e-commerce, and mobile communications. The agency helps firms learn how to best use Google and Facebook platforms. This agency will especially target small and medium-sized businesses.

An example of the value being created at Publicis is shown by the fact that General Motors shifted its advertising account for Chevrolet from a firm that had it for 96 years to Publicis in late 2010. This change represented a major coup for Publicis. The firm's strong global presence, especially in China, a market of considerable importance to GM, and its strong digital capabilities helped Publicis win the account. The future looks to be bright, indeed, for Publicis.

HENNY RAY ABRAMS/AFP/Getty Images

Publicis Groupe S.A., a French company which provides international media, advertising, and communications services, celebrated its listing on the New York Stock Exchange with Chairman and CEO Maurice Levy ringing the opening bell.

Sources: Groupe profile, 2011, Publicis Groupe, http://www.publicisgroupe .com, May 30; Publicis Groupe, 2011, Wikipedia, http://en.wikipedia.org, March 4; S. Kimberly, 2011, Publicis targets small businesses with new offering, *Campaign*, http://www.campaignlive.co.uk, February 21; E. Hall, 2011, Publicis reports 31% profit growth in 2010 after turnaround in North America, *AdvertisingAge*, http://adage.com, February 10; T. Bradshaw, 2011, Strong finish to 2011 for Publicis ad agencies, *Financial Times*, http://www.ft.com, February 10; R. Bender, 2011, Strategy bears fruit at Publicis, *Wall Street Journal*, http://online.wsj.com, February 10; D. Sacks, 2010, The future of advertising, *Fast Company*, http://www.fastcompany.com, November 17; T. Bradshaw, 2010, Publicis sees rapid rebound in ad spending, *Financial Times*, http://www.ft.com, October 21; S. Elliott, 2010, Era ends as Chevrolet account drives off to Publicis, *The New York Times*, http://mediadecoder.blogs.nytimes.com, April 23.

Moderate and High Levels of Diversification

A firm generating more than 30 percent of its revenue outside a dominant business and whose businesses are related to each other in some manner uses a related diversification corporate-level strategy. When the links between the diversified firm's businesses are rather direct, a *related constrained diversification strategy* is being used. Campbell Soup, Procter & Gamble, and Merck & Company all use a related constrained strategy, as do some large cable companies. With a related constrained strategy, a firm shares resources and activities between its businesses.

Clearly, the Publicis Groupe uses a related constrained strategy, deriving value from the potential synergy across its various groups, especially the digital capabilities in its advertising business. Given its recent performance, the related constrained strategy has created value for Publicis customers and its shareholders.

The diversified company with a portfolio of businesses that have only a few links between them is called a mixed related and unrelated firm and is using the *related linked diversification strategy* (see Figure 6.1). As displayed in the Opening Case, GE uses this corporate-level diversification strategy. Compared with related constrained firms, related linked firms share fewer resources and assets between their businesses, concentrating instead on transferring knowledge and core competencies between the businesses. GE has four strategic business units (see Chapter 11 for a definition of SBUs) it calls "divisions," each composed of related businesses. There are no relationships among the strategic business units, only within them. As with firms using each type of diversification strategy, companies implementing the related linked strategy constantly adjust the mix in their portfolio of businesses as well as make decisions about how to manage these businesses.[20] Managing a diversified firm such as GE is highly challenging, but GE appears to have been well managed over the years given its success.

A highly diversified firm that has no relationships between its businesses follows an *unrelated diversification strategy*. United Technologies, Textron, Samsung, and Hutchison Whampoa Limited (HWL) are examples of firms using this type of corporate-level strategy. Commonly, firms using this strategy are called *conglomerates*. HWL is a leading international corporation with five core businesses: ports and related services; property and hotels; retail; energy, infrastructure, investments and others; and telecommunications. These businesses are not related to each other, and the firm makes no efforts to share activities or to transfer core competencies between or among them. Each of these five businesses is quite large; for example, the retailing arm of the retail and manufacturing business has more than 9,300 stores in 33 countries. Groceries, cosmetics, electronics, wine, and airline tickets are some of the product categories featured in these stores. This firm's size and diversity suggest the challenge of successfully managing the unrelated diversification strategy. However, Hutchison's CEO Li Ka-shing has been successful at not only making smart acquisitions, but also at divesting businesses with good timing.[21]

Reasons for Diversification

A firm uses a corporate-level diversification strategy for a variety of reasons (see Table 6.1). Typically, a diversification strategy is used to increase the firm's value by improving its overall performance. Value is created either through related diversification or through unrelated diversification when the strategy allows a company's businesses to increase revenues or reduce costs while implementing their business-level strategies.

Other reasons for using a diversification strategy may have nothing to do with increasing the firm's value; in fact, diversification can have neutral effects or even reduce

Table 6.1 Reasons for Diversification

Value-Creating Diversification
■ Economies of scope (related diversification)
• Sharing activities
• Transferring core competencies
■ Market power (related diversification)
• Blocking competitors through multipoint competition
• Vertical integration
■ Financial economies (unrelated diversification)
• Efficient internal capital allocation
• Business restructuring
Value-Neutral Diversification
■ Antitrust regulation
■ Tax laws
■ Low performance
■ Uncertain future cash flows
■ Risk reduction for firm
■ Tangible resources
■ Intangible resources
Value-Reducing Diversification
■ Diversifying managerial employment risk
■ Increasing managerial compensation

a firm's value. Value-neutral reasons for diversification include a desire to match and thereby neutralize a competitor's market power (such as to neutralize another firm's advantage by acquiring a similar distribution outlet). Decisions to expand a firm's portfolio of businesses to reduce managerial risk can have a negative effect on the firm's value. Greater amounts of diversification reduce managerial risk in that if one of the businesses in a diversified firm fails, the top executive of that business does not risk total failure by the corporation. As such, this reduces the top executives' employment risk. In addition, because diversification can increase a firm's size and thus managerial compensation, managers have motives to diversify a firm to a level that reduces its value.[22] Diversification rationales that may have a neutral or negative effect on the firm's value are discussed later in the chapter.

Operational relatedness and corporate relatedness are two ways diversification strategies can create value (see Figure 6.2). Studies of these independent relatedness dimensions show the importance of resources and key competencies.[23] The figure's vertical dimension depicts opportunities to share operational activities between businesses (operational relatedness) while the horizontal dimension suggests opportunities for transferring corporate-level core competencies (corporate relatedness). The firm with a strong capability in managing operational synergy, especially in sharing assets between its businesses, falls in the upper left quadrant, which also represents vertical sharing of assets through vertical integration. The lower right quadrant represents a highly developed corporate capability for transferring one or more core competencies across businesses.

Figure 6.2 Value-Creating Diversification Strategies: Operational and Corporate Relatedness

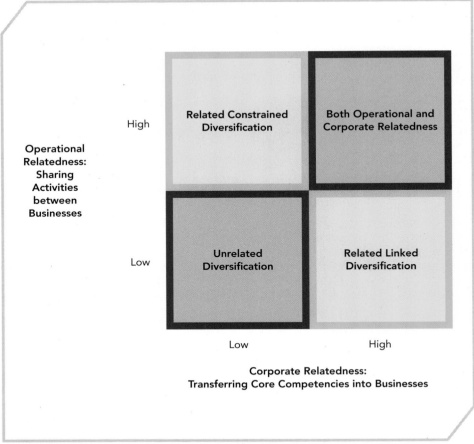

© 2013 Cengage Learning.

This capability is located primarily in the corporate headquarters office. Unrelated diversification is also illustrated in Figure 6.2 in the lower left quadrant. Financial economies (discussed later), rather than either operational or corporate relatedness, are the source of value creation for firms using the unrelated diversification strategy.

Value-Creating Diversification: Related Constrained and Related Linked Diversification

Economies of scope are cost savings that the firm creates by successfully sharing some of its resources and capabilities or transferring one or more corporate-level core competencies that were developed in one of its businesses to another of its businesses.

With the related diversification corporate-level strategy, the firm builds upon or extends its resources and capabilities to build a competitive advantage by creating value for customers.[24] The company using the related diversification strategy wants to develop and exploit economies of scope between its businesses.[25] Available to companies operating in multiple product markets or industries,[26] economies of scope are cost savings that the firm creates by successfully sharing some of its resources and capabilities or transferring one or more corporate-level core competencies that were developed in one of its businesses to another of its businesses.

As illustrated in Figure 6.2, firms seek to create value from economies of scope through two basic kinds of operational economies: sharing activities (operational relatedness) and transferring corporate-level core competencies (corporate relatedness). The difference between sharing activities and transferring competencies is based on how separate resources are jointly used to create economies of scope. To create economies of scope tangible resources, such as plant and equipment or other business-unit physical assets, often must be shared. Less tangible resources, such as manufacturing know-how and technological capabilities, can also be shared.[27] However, know-how transferred between separate activities with no physical or tangible resource involved is a transfer of a corporate-level core competence, not an operational sharing of activities.[28]

Operational Relatedness: Sharing Activities

Firms can create operational relatedness by sharing either a primary activity (such as inventory delivery systems) or a support activity (such as purchasing practices)—see Chapter 3's discussion of the value chain. Firms using the related constrained diversification strategy share activities in order to create value. Procter & Gamble (P&G) uses this corporate-level strategy. P&G's paper towel business and baby diaper business both use paper products as a primary input to the manufacturing process. The firm's paper production plant produces inputs for both businesses and is an example of a shared activity. In addition, because they both produce consumer products, these two businesses are likely to share distribution channels and sales networks.

Activity sharing is also risky because ties among a firm's businesses create links between outcomes. For instance, if demand for one business's product is reduced, it may not generate sufficient revenues to cover the fixed costs required to operate the shared facilities. These types of organizational difficulties can reduce activity-sharing success. Additionally, activity sharing requires careful coordination between the businesses involved. The coordination challenges must be managed effectively for the appropriate sharing of activities.[29]

Although activity sharing across businesses is not risk-free, research shows that it can create value. For example, studies of acquisitions of firms in the same industry (horizontal acquisitions), such as the banking industry and software, found that sharing resources and activities and thereby creating economies of scope contributed to post-acquisition increases in performance and higher returns to shareholders.[30] Additionally, firms that sold off related units in which resource sharing was a possible source of economies of scope have been found to produce lower returns than those that sold off businesses unrelated to the firm's core business.[31] Still other research discovered that firms with closely related businesses have lower risk.[32] These results suggest that gaining economies of scope by sharing activities across a firm's businesses may be important in reducing risk and in creating value. Further, more attractive results are obtained through activity sharing when a strong corporate headquarters office facilitates it.[33]

Corporate Relatedness: Transferring of Core Competencies

Over time, the firm's intangible resources, such as its know-how, become the foundation of core competencies. Corporate-level core competencies are complex sets of resources and capabilities that link different businesses, primarily through managerial and technological knowledge, experience, and expertise.[34] Firms seeking to create value through corporate relatedness use the related linked diversification strategy as exemplified by GE.

In at least two ways, the related linked diversification strategy helps firms to create value.[35] First, because the expense of developing a core competence has already been incurred in one of the firm's businesses, transferring this competence to a second

Corporate-level core competencies are complex sets of resources and capabilities that link different businesses, primarily through managerial and technological knowledge, experience, and expertise.

Virgin Group Ltd's reach spans airlines, cosmetics, music, drinks, mobile phones, and health clubs, like the one pictured here.

Kevin Wheal / Alamy

business eliminates the need for that business to allocate resources to develop it. Such is the case at Hewlett-Packard (HP), where the firm transferred its competence in ink printers to high-end copiers. Rather than the standard laser printing technology in most high-end copiers, HP is using ink-based technology. One manager liked the product because, as he noted, "We are able to do a lot better quality at less price."[36] This capability gives HP the opportunity to sell more ink products and create higher profit margins.

Resource intangibility is a second source of value creation through corporate relatedness. Intangible resources are difficult for competitors to understand and imitate. Because of this difficulty, the unit receiving a transferred corporate-level competence often gains an immediate competitive advantage over its rivals.[37]

A number of firms have successfully transferred one or more corporate-level core competencies across their businesses. Virgin Group Ltd. transfers its marketing core competence across airlines, cosmetics, music, drinks, mobile phones, health clubs, and a number of other businesses.[38] Honda has developed and transferred its competence in engine design and manufacturing among its businesses making products such as motorcycles, lawnmowers, and cars and trucks. Company officials state that Honda is a major manufacturer of engines and is focused on providing products for all forms of human mobility.[39]

One way managers facilitate the transfer of corporate-level core competencies is by moving key people into new management positions.[40] However, the manager of an older business may be reluctant to transfer key people who have accumulated knowledge and experience critical to the business's success. Thus, managers with the ability to facilitate the transfer of a core competence may come at a premium, or the key people involved may not want to transfer. Additionally, the top-level managers from the transferring business may not want the competencies transferred to a new business to fulfill the firm's diversification objectives.[41] Research also suggests too much dependence on outsourcing can lower the usefulness of core competencies and thereby reduce their useful transferability to other business units in the diversified firm.[42]

Market Power

Firms using a related diversification strategy may gain market power when successfully using a related constrained or related linked strategy. **Market power** exists when a firm is able to sell its products above the existing competitive level or to reduce the costs of its primary and support activities below the competitive level, or both.[43] Mars' acquisition of the Wrigley assets was part of its related constrained diversification strategy and added market share to the Mars/Wrigley integrated firm, as it realized 14.4 percent of the market share. This catapulted Mars/Wrigley above Cadbury and Nestle, which had 10.1 and 7.7 percent of the market share, respectively, at the time and left Hershey with only 5.5 percent of the market.[44]

In addition to efforts to gain scale as a means of increasing market power, as Mars did when it acquired Wrigley, firms can create market power through multipoint competition and vertical integration. **Multipoint competition** exists when two or more diversified firms simultaneously compete in the same product areas or geographic markets.[45] The actions taken by UPS and FedEx in two markets, overnight delivery and ground shipping, illustrate multipoint competition. UPS has moved into overnight delivery, FedEx's stronghold; FedEx has been buying trucking and ground shipping assets to move into ground shipping, UPS's stronghold. Moreover, geographic competition for markets increases. The strongest shipping company in Europe is DHL. All three competitors (UPS, FedEx, and DHL) are moving into large foreign markets to either gain a stake or to expand their existing share. If one of these firms successfully gains strong positions in several markets while competing against its rivals, its market power may increase. Interestingly, DHL had to exit the U.S. market because it was too difficult to compete against UPS and FedEx, which are dominant in the United States.

Some firms using a related diversification strategy engage in vertical integration to gain market power. **Vertical integration** exists when a company produces its own inputs (backward integration) or owns its own source of output distribution (forward integration). In some instances, firms partially integrate their operations, producing and selling their products by using company businesses as well as outside sources.[46]

Vertical integration is commonly used in the firm's core business to gain market power over rivals. Market power is gained as the firm develops the ability to save on its operations, avoid market costs, improve product quality, possibly protect its technology from imitation by rivals, and potentially exploit underlying capabilities to handle special resources (e.g., sophisticated chemicals or technologies).[47] Market power also is created when firms have strong ties between their assets for which no market prices exist. Establishing a market price would result in high search and transaction costs, so firms seek to vertically integrate rather than remain separate businesses.[48]

Vertical integration has its limitations. For example, an outside supplier may produce the product at a lower cost. As a result, internal transactions from vertical integration may be expensive and reduce profitability relative to competitors.[49] Also, bureaucratic costs can be present with vertical integration.[50] Because vertical integration can require substantial investments in specific technologies, it may reduce the firm's flexibility, especially when technology changes quickly. Finally, changes in demand create capacity balance and coordination problems. If one business is building a part for another internal business but achieving economies of scale requires the first division to manufacture quantities that are beyond the capacity of the internal buyer to absorb, it would be necessary to sell the parts outside the firm as well as to the internal business. Thus, although vertical integration can create value, especially through market power over competitors, it is not without risks and costs.[51]

As noted in the Strategic Focus, Google is diversifying into new markets that allow it to engage in multipoint competition. For example, Google is competing with Microsoft and Apple now in several markets. All of its competitors know that Google is a formidable rival with significant resources to invest in the competition. As such, the competitors have reacted, some with substantive actions and others in less positive ways. For example, Apple acquired Siri, a small voice search firm, to help it compete with Google's search business.[52] As noted in the Strategic Focus, Microsoft filed a complaint with the EU about potential antitrust violations by Google. Yahoo! has undertaken advertising that criticizes Google, and Facebook hired a public relations firm to plant negative stories in the press about Google.[53] Some of Google's diversification moves represent a form of vertical integration because the new business areas build on the company's substantial search business (forward integration).

Although Google appears to be increasing its vertical integration, many manufacturing firms have been reducing vertical integration as a means of gaining market power.[54] In fact, deintegration is the focus of most manufacturing firms, such as Intel and Dell, and even some large auto companies, such as Ford and General Motors, as they develop independent supplier networks.[55] Flextronics, an electronics contract manufacturer, represents a new breed of large contract manufacturers that is helping to foster this revolution in supply-chain management.[56] Such firms often manage their customers' entire product lines and offer services ranging from inventory management to delivery and after-sales service.

Vertical integration exists when a company produces its own inputs (backward integration) or owns its own source of output distribution (forward integration).

STRATEGIC FOCUS

THE ECONOMIC POWER OF GOOGLE AND THE COMPETITIVE DERIVATIVES

Google dominates the Internet search engine business and as a result has substantial market power. In fact, approximately 96 percent of its current annual revenue is derived from advertising on this medium. In fact, given Google's search engine advertising 2010 revenue of $29.32 billion, a considerable amount of revenue comes from Google's (approximately $29.15 billion in 2010). Google also has significant cash reserves and invests heavily in R&D. For example, its R&D expenditures in 2010 were approximately 12.6 percent of revenues, a considerable amount especially for a service firm. At the end of 2010, Google also had about $35 billion in cash holdings. The R&D and cash provide opportunities for the firm to diversify into new markets, which is an obvious goal. In fact, in recent times, Google has been diversifying partly through acquisitions (using its cash reserves) and through internal development (e.g., R&D).

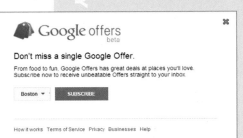

Google Offers competes with Groupon and other special deal sites.

In fact, Google is diversifying in several ways that extend the services it provides. Commonly, the services are partly related to the current ones offered, but some under consideration could lead the firm toward a related link type of diversification strategy. Some of the new services create multipoint competition with prominent competitors (e.g., Microsoft, Facebook), and some appear to represent a form of vertical integration. For example, Google is developing a subscription service for publishers and consumers that will represent a "plug and play." Google managers are negotiating with the National Basketball Association, movie studios, and celebrities for features on its video platform. Google appears to be developing YouTube to operate like a network in that it presents a variety of topics such as entertainment, news and politics, and sports.

Because of Google's new market entries in recent years, it has "locked horns" with such substantial competitors as Microsoft (e.g., office software, browsers, smartphones, Internet access, and e-mail), Apple (e.g., search services, smartphones), Netflix (movie distribution), Yahoo! and AOL (media sites, news), and Facebook (social media). All of these competitors watch Google's moves closely and often react with moves of their own. Microsoft has perhaps been the most vocal and engaged in the strongest responses. In fact, Microsoft filed a complaint with the EU claiming that Google violated antitrust laws/regulations. Of course, such reactions by Microsoft are interesting in that it has itself been the target of claims that the firm engaged in anticompetition practices.

Google recently increased its competition with Apple by introducing mobile applications run on devices powered by its Android software. Consumers can install the mobile apps through an Internet browser instead of on their devices. Google is also reportedly developing its own "Groupon knockoff" in which special deals (coupons) are offered to customers for local businesses products. This competes with Groupon but also eBay and Amazon to a degree.

Google is a competitor that even huge and resourceful corporations have learned to respect and fear.

Find out more about Google's Android software.

www.cengagebrain.com

Sources: B. Ortutay, 2011, Facebook-Google rivalry intensifies with PR fiasco, *MSNBC*, http://www.msnbc.com, May 13; B. Rigby & F. Y. Chee, 2011, Microsoft files EU competition complaint vs. Google, *Reuters*, http://www.reuters.com, March 31; D. Carr, 2011, The evolving mission of Google, *The New York Times*, http://www.nytimes.com, March 20; Google ratchets up Apple rivalry with Android market, Honeycomb for tablets, 2011, *Los Angeles Times*, http://www.latimesblogs.latimes.com, February 2; R. Orricchio, 2011, Reports: Google launching Groupon knockoff, *Inc.*, http://www.inc.com, January 21; J. Brodkin, 2010, The 10 bloodiest battles Microsoft and Google fought in 2010, *Network World*, http://www.networkworld.com, December 15; D. Nosowitz, 2010, Apple buys voice search Siri, aiming squarely at Google, April 29.

Simultaneous Operational Relatedness and Corporate Relatedness

As Figure 6.2 suggests, some firms simultaneously seek operational and corporate relatedness to create economies of scope.[57] The ability to simultaneously create economies of scope by sharing activities (operational relatedness) and transferring core competencies (corporate relatedness) is difficult for competitors to understand and learn how to imitate. However, if the cost of realizing both types of relatedness is not offset by the benefits created, the result is diseconomies because the cost of organization and incentive structure is very expensive.[58]

Walt Disney Co. uses a related diversification strategy to simultaneously create economies of scope through operational and corporate relatedness. Within the firm's Studio Entertainment business, for example, Disney can gain economies of scope by sharing activities among its different movie distribution companies such as Touchstone Pictures, Hollywood Pictures, and Dimension Films. Broad and deep knowledge about its customers is a capability on which Disney relies to develop corporate-level core competencies in terms of advertising and marketing. With these competencies, Disney is able to create economies of scope through corporate relatedness as it cross-sells products that are highlighted in its movies through the distribution channels that are part of its Parks and Resorts and Consumer Products businesses. Thus, characters created in movies become figures that are marketed through Disney's retail stores (which are part of the Consumer Products business). In addition, themes established in movies become the source of new rides in the firm's theme parks, which are part of the Parks and Resorts business and provide themes for clothing and other retail business products.[59]

Thus, Walt Disney Co. has been able to successfully use related diversification as a corporate-level strategy through which it creates economies of scope by sharing some activities and by transferring core competencies. However, it can be difficult for investors to actually observe the value created by a firm (such as Walt Disney Co.) as it shares activities and transfers core competencies. For this reason, the value of the assets of a firm using a diversification strategy to create economies of scope often is discounted by investors.

Unrelated Diversification

Firms do not seek either operational relatedness or corporate relatedness when using the unrelated diversification corporate-level strategy. An unrelated diversification strategy (see Figure 6.2) can create value through two types of financial economies. **Financial economies** are cost savings realized through improved allocations of financial resources based on investments inside or outside the firm.[60]

Efficient internal capital allocations can lead to financial economies. Efficient internal capital allocations reduce risk among the firm's businesses—for example, by leading to the development of a portfolio of businesses with different risk profiles. The second type of financial economy concerns the restructuring of acquired assets. Here, the diversified firm buys another company, restructures that company's assets in ways that allow it to operate more profitably, and then sells the company for a profit in the external market.[61] Next, we discuss the two types of financial economies in greater detail.

Efficient Internal Capital Market Allocation

In a market economy, capital markets are thought to efficiently allocate capital. Efficiency results as investors take equity positions (ownership) with high expected future cash-flow values. Capital is also allocated through debt as shareholders and debt holders try to improve the value of their investments by taking stakes in businesses with high growth and profitability prospects.

Financial economies are cost savings realized through improved allocations of financial resources based on investments inside or outside the firm.

In large diversified firms, the corporate headquarters office distributes capital to its businesses to create value for the overall corporation. The nature of these distributions may generate gains from internal capital market allocations that exceed the gains that would accrue to shareholders as a result of capital being allocated by the external capital market.[62] Because those in a firm's corporate headquarters generally have access to detailed and accurate information regarding the actual and prospective performance of the company's portfolio of businesses, they have the best information to make capital distribution decisions.

Compared with corporate office personnel, external investors have relatively limited access to internal information and can only estimate the performances of individual businesses as well as their future prospects. Moreover, although businesses seeking capital must provide information to potential suppliers (such as banks or insurance companies), firms with internal capital markets may have at least two informational advantages. First, information provided to capital markets through annual reports and other sources may not include negative information, instead emphasizing positive prospects and outcomes. External sources of capital have limited ability to understand the operational dynamics of large organizations. Even external shareholders who have access to information have no guarantee of full and complete disclosure.[63] Second, although a firm must disseminate information, that information also becomes simultaneously available to the firm's current and potential competitors. With insights gained by studying such information, competitors might attempt to duplicate a firm's value-creating strategy. Thus, an ability to efficiently allocate capital through an internal market may help the firm protect the competitive advantages it develops while using its corporate-level strategy as well as its various business-unit–level strategies.

If intervention from outside the firm is required to make corrections to capital allocations, only significant changes are possible, such as forcing the firm into bankruptcy or changing the top management team. Alternatively, in an internal capital market, the corporate headquarters office can fine-tune its corrections, such as choosing to adjust managerial incentives or suggesting strategic changes in one of the firm's businesses.[64] Thus, capital can be allocated according to more specific criteria than is possible with external market allocations. Because it has less accurate information, the external capital market may fail to allocate resources adequately to high-potential investments. The corporate headquarters office of a diversified company can more effectively perform such tasks as disciplining underperforming management teams through resource allocations.[65] GE (discussed in the Opening Case) has done an exceptionally good job of allocating capital across its many businesses. Although a related linked firm, it differentially allocates capital across its four major strategic business units. GE Capital has produced the greatest returns for GE over the last few decades (until the latest financial crisis) and thus has received a healthy amount of capital from internal allocations.

Large, highly diversified businesses often face what is known as the "conglomerate discount." This discount results from analysts not knowing how to value a vast array of large businesses with complex financial reports. To overcome this discount, many unrelated diversified or industrial conglomerates have sought to establish a brand for the parent company. For instance, United Technologies initiated a brand development approach with the slogan "United Technologies. You can see everything from here." United Technologies suggested that its earnings multiple (PE ratio) compared to its stock price is only average even though its performance has been better than other conglomerates in its group. It is hoping that the "umbrella" brand advertisement will raise its PE to a level comparable to its competitors.[66] In another attempt to sway investors on the value of a large diversified company, United Technologies CEO Louis Chenevert stated that "... our future success depends on our ability to innovate—to find new and better ways to serve our customers. And, our ability to innovate relies on our ability to leverage the power of diverse inputs."[67]

In spite of the challenges associated with it, a number of corporations continue to use the unrelated diversification strategy, especially in Europe and in emerging markets. Siemens, for example, is a large German conglomerate with a highly diversified approach. Its former CEO argued that "When you are in an up-cycle and the capital markets have plenty of opportunities to invest in single-industry companies … investors savor those opportunities. But when things change pure plays go down faster than you can look."[68] In economic downturns, diversification can help some companies improve future performance.[69]

Siemens, headquartered in Germany, utilizes a highly diversified approach.

The Achilles' heel for firms using the unrelated diversification strategy in a developed economy is that competitors can imitate financial economies more easily than they can replicate the value gained from the economies of scope developed through operational relatedness and corporate relatedness. This issue is less of a problem in emerging economies, where the absence of a "soft infrastructure" (including effective financial intermediaries, sound regulations, and contract laws) supports and encourages use of the unrelated diversification strategy.[70] In fact, in emerging economies such as those in Korea, India, and Chile, research has shown that diversification increases the performance of firms affiliated with large diversified business groups.[71]

Restructuring of Assets

Financial economies can also be created when firms learn how to create value by buying, restructuring, and then selling the restructured companies' assets in the external market.[72] As in the real estate business, buying assets at low prices, restructuring them, and selling them at a price that exceeds their cost generates a positive return on the firm's invested capital.

Unrelated diversified companies that pursue this strategy try to create financial economies by acquiring and restructuring other companies' assets but it involves significant trade-offs. For example, Danaher's success requires a focus on mature manufacturing businesses because of the uncertainty of demand for high-technology products.[73] In high-technology businesses, resource allocation decisions are highly complex, often creating information-processing overload on the small corporate headquarters offices that are common in unrelated diversified firms. High-technology businesses are often human-resource dependent; these people can leave or demand higher pay and thus appropriate or deplete the value of an acquired firm.[74]

Buying and then restructuring service-based assets so they can be profitably sold in the external market is also difficult. Sales in such instances are often a product of close personal relationships between a client and the representative of the firm being restructured. Thus, for both high-technology firms and service-based companies, relatively few tangible assets can be restructured to create value and sell profitably. It is difficult to restructure intangible assets such as human capital and effective relationships that have evolved over time between buyers (customers) and sellers (firm personnel). Care must be taken in an economic downturn to restructure and buy and sell at appropriate times. A downturn can present opportunities but also some risks. Ideally, executives will follow a strategy of buying businesses when prices are lower, such as in the midst of a recession, and selling them at late stages in an expansion.[75]

Value-Neutral Diversification: Incentives and Resources

The objectives firms seek when using related diversification and unrelated diversification strategies all have the potential to help the firm create value by using a corporate-level strategy. However, these strategies, as well as single- and dominant-business diversification strategies, are sometimes used with value-neutral rather than value-creating objectives in mind. As we discuss next, different incentives to diversify sometimes exist, and the quality of the firm's resources may permit only diversification that is value neutral rather than value creating.

Incentives to Diversify

Incentives to diversify come from both the external environment and a firm's internal environment. External incentives include antitrust regulations and tax laws. Internal incentives include low performance, uncertain future cash flows, and the pursuit of synergy and reduction of risk for the firm.

Antitrust Regulation and Tax Laws

Government antitrust policies and tax laws provided incentives for U.S. firms to diversify in the 1960s and 1970s.[76] Antitrust laws prohibiting mergers that created increased market power (via either vertical or horizontal integration) were stringently enforced during that period.[77] Merger activity that produced conglomerate diversification was encouraged primarily by the Celler-Kefauver Antimerger Act (1950), which discouraged horizontal and vertical mergers. As a result, many of the mergers during the 1960s and 1970s were "conglomerate" in character, involving companies pursuing different lines of business. Between 1973 and 1977, 79.1 percent of all mergers were conglomerate in nature.[78]

During the 1980s, antitrust enforcement lessened, resulting in more and larger horizontal mergers (acquisitions of target firms in the same line of business, such as a merger between two oil companies).[79] In addition, investment bankers became more open to the kinds of mergers facilitated by regulation changes; as a consequence, takeovers increased to unprecedented numbers.[80] The conglomerates, or highly diversified firms, of the 1960s and 1970s became more "focused" in the 1980s and early 1990s as merger constraints were relaxed and restructuring was implemented.[81]

In the late 1990s and early 2000s, antitrust concerns emerged again with the large volume of mergers and acquisitions (see Chapter 7).[82] Mergers are now receiving more scrutiny than they did in the 1980s and through the early 1990s.[83]

The tax effects of diversification stem not only from corporate tax changes, but also from individual tax rates. Some companies (especially mature ones) generate more cash from their operations than they can reinvest profitably. Some argue that *free cash flows* (liquid financial assets for which investments in current businesses are no longer economically viable) should be redistributed to shareholders as dividends.[84] However, in the 1960s and 1970s, dividends were taxed more heavily than were capital gains. As a result, before 1980, shareholders preferred that firms use free cash flows to buy and build companies in high-performance industries. If the firm's stock value appreciated over the long term, shareholders might receive a better return on those funds than if the funds had been redistributed as dividends, because returns from stock sales would be taxed more lightly than would dividends.

Under the 1986 Tax Reform Act, however, the top individual ordinary income tax rate was reduced from 50 to 28 percent, and the special capital gains tax was changed to treat capital gains as ordinary income. These changes created an incentive for shareholders to stop encouraging firms to retain funds for purposes of diversification. These tax law changes also influenced an increase in divestitures of unrelated business units after 1984. Thus, while individual tax rates for capital gains and dividends created a shareholder incentive to increase diversification before 1986, they encouraged lower diversification after 1986, unless it was funded by tax-deductible debt. The elimination of personal interest deductions, as well as the lower attractiveness of retained earnings to shareholders, could prompt the use of more leverage by firms (interest expenses charged to firms are tax deductible).

Corporate tax laws also affect diversification. Acquisitions typically increase a firm's depreciable asset allowances. Increased depreciation (a non-cash-flow expense) produces lower taxable income, thereby providing an additional incentive for acquisitions. Before 1986, acquisitions may have been the most attractive means for securing tax benefits,[85] but the 1986 Tax Reform Act diminished some of the corporate tax advantages of diversification.[86] More recent changes recommended by the Financial Accounting Standards Board eliminated the "pooling of interests" method to account for the acquired firm's assets and it also eliminated the write-off for research and development in process, and thus reduced some of the incentives to make acquisitions, especially acquisitions in related high-technology industries (these changes are discussed further in Chapter 7).[87]

Although federal regulations were partially loosened in the 1980s and then retightened in the late 1990s, a number of industries experienced increased merger activity due to industry-specific deregulation, including banking, telecommunications, oil and gas, and electric utilities. For instance, in banking the Garns–St. Germain Deposit Institutions Act of 1982 (GDIA) and the Competitive Equality Banking Act of 1987 (CEBA) reshaped the acquisition frequency in banking by relaxing the regulations that limited interstate bank acquisitions.[88] Regulation changes have also affected convergence between media and telecommunications industries, which has allowed a number of mergers, such as the successive Time Warner and AOL mergers. The Federal Communications Commission (FCC) made a highly contested ruling "allowing broadcasters to own TV stations that reach 45 percent of U.S. households (up from 35 percent), own three stations in the largest markets (up from two), and own a TV station and newspaper in the same town."[89] Thus, regulatory changes such as the ones we have described create incentives or disincentives for diversification. Interestingly, European antitrust laws have historically been more strict regarding horizontal mergers than those in the United States, but more recently have become similar.[90]

Low Performance

Some research shows that low returns are related to greater levels of diversification.[91] If "high performance eliminates the need for greater diversification,"[92] then low performance may provide an incentive for diversification. In 2005, eBay acquired Skype for $3.1 billion in hopes that it would create synergies and improve communication between buyers and sellers. However, within three years, eBay decided to sell Skype because it has failed to increase cash flow for its core e-commerce business and the expected synergies were not realized. In 2011, eBay sold Skype to Microsoft for $8.5 billion. Although analysts thought the premium paid by Microsoft may have been too high, one review in the *Financial Times* suggested that Skype could play a prominent role in Microsoft's multimedia strategy. Thus, the potential synergies between Skype and Microsoft may be greater than those with eBay.[93] The poor performance may be because of errors made by top managers (such as eBay's original acquisition of Skype), and thus lead to divestitures similar to eBay's action.[94]

Research evidence and the experience of a number of firms suggest that an overall curvilinear relationship, as illustrated in Figure 6.3, may exist between diversification and performance.[95] Although low performance can be an incentive to diversify, firms that are more broadly diversified compared to their competitors may have overall lower performance.

Figure 6.3 The Curvilinear Relationship between Diversification and Performance

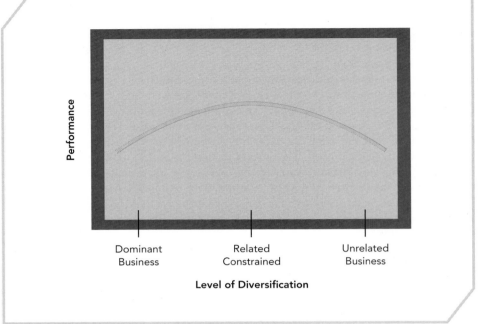

© 2013 Cengage Learning.

Uncertain Future Cash Flows

As a firm's product line matures or is threatened, diversification may be an important defensive strategy.[96] Small firms and companies in mature or maturing industries sometimes find it necessary to diversify for long-term survival.[97] For example, music retailers began to diversify as CD sales started to decline. By the end of 2009, CD sales had declined by about 50 percent from their peak. Best Buy started to sell musical instruments in 2008 in response to the decline in CD sales. The musical instrument industry accumulated sales revenues of $5.9 billion in 2009. Best Buy continues to sell music CDs but adds other products to make up for the loss in revenue from CDs.[98]

Diversifying into other product markets or into other businesses can reduce the uncertainty about a firm's future cash flows. Merck decided to expand into the biosimilars business (production of drugs that are similar to approved drugs) in hopes of stimulating its prescription drug business due to lower expected results as many of its drug patents expire.[99] Thus, in 2009 it purchased Insmed's portfolio of follow-on biologics for $130 million. It will carry out the development of biologics that prevent infections in cancer patients receiving chemotherapy. One such drug, INS-19, is in late-stage trials, while INS-20 is in early-stage development.[100]

Synergy and Firm Risk Reduction

Diversified firms pursuing economies of scope often have investments that are too inflexible to realize synergy between business units. As a result, a number of problems may arise. **Synergy** exists when the value created by business units working together exceeds the value that those same units create working independently. But as a firm increases its relatedness between business units, it also increases its risk of corporate failure, because synergy produces joint interdependence between businesses that constrains the firm's flexibility to respond. This threat may force two basic decisions.

First, the firm may reduce its level of technological change by operating in environments that are more certain. This behavior may make the firm risk averse and thus uninterested in pursuing new product lines that have potential but are not proven.

Synergy exists when the value created by business units working together exceeds the value that those same units create working independently.

Alternatively, the firm may constrain its level of activity sharing and forgo potential benefits of synergy. Either or both decisions may lead to further diversification.[101] The former likely leads to related diversification into industries in which more certainty exists.[102] The latter may produce additional, but unrelated, diversification. Research suggests that a firm using a related diversification strategy is more careful in bidding for new businesses, whereas a firm pursuing an unrelated diversification strategy may be more likely to overprice its bid, because an unrelated bidder is less likely to have full information about the acquired firm.[103] However, firms using either a related or an unrelated diversification strategy must understand the consequences of paying large premiums.[104] In the situation with eBay, former CEO Meg Whitman received heavy criticism for paying such a high price for Skype, especially when the firm did not realize the synergies it was seeking. Alternatively, it sold Skype six years later at 175 percent of the price at which eBay purchased the business. The question now is whether Microsoft paid too high a premium to achieve positive returns from the acquisition of Skype.

Resources and Diversification

As already discussed, firms may have several value-neutral incentives as well as value-creating incentives (such as the ability to create economies of scope) to diversify. However, even when incentives to diversify exist, a firm must have the types and levels of resources and capabilities needed to successfully use a corporate-level diversification strategy.[105] Although both tangible and intangible resources facilitate diversification, they vary in their ability to create value. Indeed, the degree to which resources are valuable, rare, difficult to imitate, and nonsubstitutable (see Chapter 3) influences a firm's ability to create value through diversification. For instance, free cash flows are a tangible financial resource that may be used to diversify the firm. However, compared with diversification that is grounded in intangible resources, diversification based on financial resources only is more visible to competitors and thus more imitable and less likely to create value on a long-term basis.[106] Tangible resources usually include the plant and equipment necessary to produce a product and tend to be less-flexible assets. Any excess capacity often can be used only for closely related products, especially those requiring highly similar manufacturing technologies. For example, large computer makers such as Dell and Hewlett-Packard have underestimated the demand for tablet computers, especially Apple's iPad. Apple developed the iPad and may expect it to eventually replace the personal computer (PC). In fact, H-P's and Dell's sales of their PCs have been declining since the introduction of the iPad. Apple expects to sell 70 million iPads in 2011 and analysts projects sales of the iPad to reach 246 million in 2014. HP and Dell likely need to diversify their product lines.[107]

Excess capacity of other tangible resources, such as a sales force, can be used to diversify more easily. Again, excess capacity in a sales force is more effective with related diversification, because it may be utilized to sell similar products. The sales force would be more knowledgeable about related-product characteristics, customers, and distribution channels.[108] Tangible resources may create resource interrelationships in production, marketing, procurement, and technology, defined earlier as activity sharing. Intangible resources are more flexible than tangible physical assets in facilitating diversification. Although the sharing of tangible resources may induce diversification, intangible resources such as tacit knowledge could encourage even more diversification.[109]

Sometimes, however, the benefits expected from using resources to diversify the firm for either value-creating or value-neutral reasons are not gained.[110] For example, Sara Lee executives found that they could not realize synergy between elements of its diversified portfolio, and subsequently shed businesses accounting for 40 percent of company revenue to focus on food and food-related products and more readily achieve synergy.[111]

Value-Reducing Diversification: Managerial Motives to Diversify

Managerial motives to diversify can exist independent of value-neutral reasons (i.e., incentives and resources) and value-creating reasons (e.g., economies of scope). The desire for increased compensation and reduced managerial risk are two motives for top-level executives to diversify their firm beyond value-creating and value-neutral levels.[112] In slightly different words, top-level executives may diversify a firm in order to diversify their own employment risk, as long as profitability does not suffer excessively.[113]

Diversification provides additional benefits to top-level managers that shareholders do not enjoy. Research evidence shows that diversification and firm size are highly correlated, and as firm size increases, so does executive compensation.[114] Because large firms are complex, difficult-to-manage organizations, top-level managers commonly receive substantial levels of compensation to lead them.[115] Greater levels of diversification can increase a firm's complexity, resulting in still more compensation for executives to lead an increasingly diversified organization. Governance mechanisms, such as the board of directors, monitoring by owners, executive compensation practices, and the market for corporate control, may limit managerial tendencies to overdiversify. These mechanisms are discussed in more detail in Chapter 10.

In some instances, though, a firm's governance mechanisms may not be strong, resulting in a situation in which executives may diversify the firm to the point that it fails to earn even average returns.[116] The loss of adequate internal governance may result in poor relative performance, thereby triggering a threat of takeover. Although takeovers may improve efficiency by replacing ineffective managerial teams, managers may avoid takeovers through defensive tactics, such as "poison pills," or may reduce their own exposure with "golden parachute" agreements.[117] Therefore, an external governance threat, although restraining managers, does not flawlessly control managerial motives for diversification.[118]

Most large publicly held firms are profitable because the managers leading them are positive stewards of firm resources, and many of their strategic actions, including those related to selecting a corporate-level diversification strategy, contribute to the firm's success.[119] As mentioned, governance mechanisms should be designed to deal with exceptions to the managerial norms of making decisions and taking actions that will increase the firm's ability to earn above-average returns. Thus, it is overly pessimistic to assume that managers usually act in their own self-interest as opposed to their firm's interest.[120]

Top-level executives' diversification decisions may also be held in check by concerns for their reputation. If a positive reputation facilitates development and use of managerial power, a poor reputation may reduce it. Likewise, a strong external market for managerial talent may deter managers from pursuing inappropriate diversification.[121] In addition, a diversified firm may police other firms by acquiring those that are poorly managed in order to restructure its own asset base. Knowing that their firms could be acquired if they are not managed successfully encourages executives to use value-creating, diversification strategies.

As shown in Figure 6.4, the level of diversification that can be expected to have the greatest positive effect on performance is based partly on how the interaction of resources, managerial motives, and incentives affects the adoption of particular diversification strategies. As indicated earlier, the greater the incentives and the more flexible the resources, the higher the level of expected diversification. Financial resources (the most flexible) should have a stronger relationship to the extent of diversification than either tangible or intangible resources. Tangible resources (the most inflexible) are useful primarily for related diversification.

As discussed in this chapter, firms can create more value by effectively using diversification strategies. However, diversification must be kept in check by corporate governance (see Chapter 10). Appropriate strategy implementation tools, such as organizational structures, are also important (see Chapter 11).

We have described corporate-level strategies in this chapter. In the next chapter, we discuss mergers and acquisitions as prominent means for firms to diversify and to grow profitably. These trends toward more diversification through acquisitions, which have been partially reversed due to restructuring (see Chapter 7), indicate that learning has taken place regarding corporate-level diversification strategies.[122] Accordingly, firms that diversify should do so cautiously, choosing to focus on relatively few, rather than many, businesses. In fact, research suggests that although unrelated diversification has decreased, related diversification has increased, possibly due to the restructuring that continued into the 1990s and early twenty-first century. This sequence of diversification followed by restructuring is now taking place in Europe and other places such as Korea, mirroring actions of firms in the United States and the United Kingdom.[123] Firms can improve their strategic competitiveness when they pursue a level of diversification that is appropriate for their resources (especially financial resources) and core competencies and the opportunities and threats in their country's institutional and competitive environments.[124]

Figure 6.4 Summary Model of the Relationship between Diversification and Firm Performance

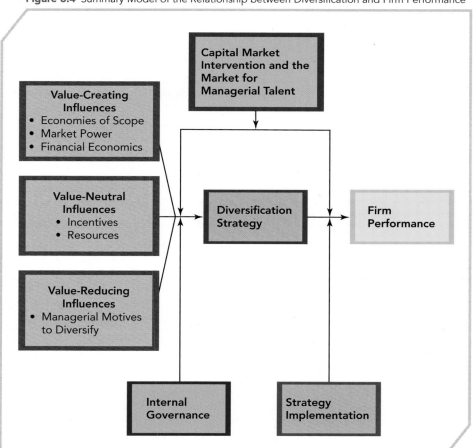

Source: Adapted from R. E. Hoskisson & M.A. Hitt, 1990, Antecedents and performance outcomes of diversification: A review and critique of theoretical perspectives, *Journal of Management*, 16: 498.

SUMMARY

- The primary reason a firm uses a corporate-level strategy to become more diversified is to create additional value. Using a single- or dominant-business corporate-level strategy may be preferable to seeking a more diversified strategy, unless a corporation can develop economies of scope or financial economies between businesses, or unless it can obtain market power through additional levels of diversification. Economies of scope and market power are the main sources of value creation when the firm diversifies by using a corporate-level strategy with moderate to high levels of diversification.

- The related diversification corporate-level strategy helps the firm create value by sharing activities or transferring competencies between different businesses in the company's portfolio.

- Sharing activities usually involves sharing tangible resources between businesses. Transferring core competencies involves transferring core competencies developed in one business to another business. It also may involve transferring competencies between the corporate headquarters office and a business unit.

- Sharing activities is usually associated with the related constrained diversification corporate-level strategy. Activity sharing is costly to implement and coordinate, may create unequal benefits for the divisions involved in the sharing, and can lead to fewer managerial risk-taking behaviors.

- Transferring core competencies is often associated with related linked (or mixed related and unrelated)

diversification, although firms pursuing both sharing activities and transferring core competencies can also use the related linked strategy.

- Efficiently allocating resources or restructuring a target firm's assets and placing them under rigorous financial controls are two ways to accomplish successful unrelated diversification. Firms using the unrelated diversification strategy focus on creating financial economies to generate value.

- Diversification is sometimes pursued for value-neutral reasons. Incentives from tax and antitrust government policies, performance disappointments, or uncertainties about future cash flow are examples of value-neutral reasons that firms may choose to become more diversified.

- Managerial motives to diversify (including to increase compensation) can lead to overdiversification and a subsequent reduction in a firm's ability to create value. Evidence suggests, however, that many top-level executives seek to be good stewards of the firm's assets and avoid diversifying the firm in ways that destroy value.

- Managers need to pay attention to their firm's internal organization and its external environment when making decisions about the optimum level of diversification for their company. Of course, internal resources are important determinants of the direction that diversification should take. However, conditions in the firm's external environment may facilitate additional levels of diversification, as might unexpected threats from competitors.

REVIEW QUESTIONS

1. What is corporate-level strategy and why is it important?

2. What are the different levels of diversification firms can pursue by using different corporate-level strategies?

3. What are three reasons firms choose to diversify their operations?

4. How do firms create value when using a related diversification strategy?

5. What are the two ways to obtain financial economies when using an unrelated diversification strategy?

6. What incentives and resources encourage diversification?

7. What motives might encourage managers to overdiversify their firm?

EXPERIENTIAL EXERCISES

EXERCISE 1: WHAT'S MY CORPORATE-LEVEL STRATEGY AND HOW DID I GET THIS WAY?

Your text defines corporate-level strategy as "actions a firm takes to gain a competitive advantage by selecting and managing a group of different businesses competing in different product markets." However, these actions are dynamic and longitudinal—they evolve over time. How did General Electric or Ford Motor Company or IBM arrive at the corporate-level strategies they use today, and what are those strategies?

Part One

Form teams of four or five students and select a publicly traded firm, preferably one that has been in existence for a few decades. A comprehensive listing of all U.S. publicly traded firms may be found at the Investor Guide Web site (http://www.investorguide.com/stock list.php) as well as links to each firm's homepage and other financial data. You will also want to access the firm's SEC filings, which could be available at your library or through the Securities and Exchange Commission's Web site at http://www.sec.gov/edgar.shtml.

Part Two

Complete a poster that can be displayed in class. Your poster should represent the firm and its evolution as far back in its history as you can get on one poster. The goal is to highlight the firm's beginnings, its acquisitions and divestiture activity, and its movement from one corporate-level strategy to another. You will need to do some extensive research on the firm to identify common linkages between operating units.

Be prepared to answer the following questions:

■ How has the firm's corporate-level strategy evolved over time?
■ What is the current corporate-level strategy and what links, if any, exist between operating units?

■ Critique the current corporate-level strategy (e.g., too much diversification, too little, just right, and why).

EXERCISE 2: HOW DOES THE FIRM'S PORTFOLIO STACK UP?

The Boston Consulting Group (BCG) product portfolio matrix has been around for decades and was introduced by the BCG as a way for firms to understand the priorities that should be given to various segments within their mix of businesses. It is based on a matrix with two vertices: firm market share and projected market growth rate:

Each firm therefore can categorize its business units as follows:

■ Stars: High growth and high market share. These business units generate large amounts of cash but also use large amounts of cash. These are often the focus of the firm's priorities as this segment has a potentially bright future.
■ Cash cows: Low market growth coupled with high market share. Profits and cash generated are high, need for new cash is low. Provides a foundation for the firm from which it can launch new initiatives.
■ Dogs: Low market growth and low market share. This is usually a situation the firms seek to avoid. These units are quite often the target of a turnaround plan or liquidation effort.
■ Question marks: High market growth but low market share. It is difficult to say what the firm should do in this quadrant and creates a need to move strategically because of high demands on cash due to market needs yet low cash returns because of the low firm market share.

Using this matrix to analyze a firm's corporate-level strategy or the way in which it rewards and prioritizes its business units has come under some criticism. For one, market share is not the only way in which a firm should view success or potential success; second, market growth is not the only indicator for the attractiveness of a market; and third, sometimes "dogs" can earn as much cash as "cows."

Part One

Select a publicly traded firm that has a diversified corporate-level strategy. The more unrelated the segments, the better.

Part Two

Analyze the firm utilizing the BCG matrix. In order to do this, you will need to develop market share ratings for each operating unit and assess the overall market attractiveness for that segment.

VIDEO CASE

THE ROAD TO DIVERSIFICATION
Barry Diller/Senior Executive/IAC

Barry Diller, once the chairman and CEO of Paramount Pictures and Fox and intrigued by interactive commerce, purchased QVC only to lose it in other business acquisition attempts, particularly his bid to purchase Paramount. Losing the bid to own Paramount as well as other organizations, Barry Diller purchased QVC competitor HSN and began an interactive conglomerate from financial services to matchmaking services such as match.com. Along the way, Diller discovered that his many businesses related to one another and united all his brands under one corporate headquarters. Barry Diller, driven by vision and the ability to grasp new and difficult concepts, insists that IAC/InterActiveCorp is a brand-by-brand endless multiproduct company similar to Procter & Gamble.

Be prepared to discuss the following concepts and questions in class:

Concepts

- Corporate-level strategy
- Levels of diversification
- Value-creating diversification
- Operational and corporate relatedness
- Related and unrelated diversification
- Motivations to overdiversify

Questions

1. Describe Diller's corporate-level strategy.
2. Describe IAC's level of diversification.
3. What do you think was Diller's reason to diversify?
4. Is Diller's approach value-creating diversification? Why or why not?
5. Explain how IAC businesses and brands are related. Do they have related diversification?
6. Is Diller in a position to overdiversify?

NOTES

1. M. E. Porter, 1980, *Competitive Strategy*, New York: The Free Press, xvi.

2. M. D. R. Chari, S. Devaraj, & P. David, 2008, The impact of information technology investments and diversification strategies on firm performance, *Management Science*, 54: 224–234; A. Pehrsson, 2006, Business relatedness and performance: A study of managerial perceptions, *Strategic Management Journal*, 27: 265–282.

3. A. O'Connell, 2009, Lego CEO Jørgen Vig Knudstorp on leading through survival and growth, *Harvard Business Review*, 87(1): 1–2.

4. M. E. Porter, 1987, From competitive advantage to corporate strategy, *Harvard Business Review*, 65(3): 43–59.

5. Ibid.; M. E. Raynor, 2007, What is corporate strategy, really? *Ivey Business Journal*, 71(8): 1–3.

6. W. P. Wan, R. E. Hoskisson, J. C. Short, & D. W. Yiu, 2011, Resource-based theory and corporate diversification: Accomplishments and opportunities, *Journal of Management*, in press; A. A. Calart & J. E. Ricart, 2007, Corporate strategy: An agent-based approach, *European Management Review*, 4: 107–120.

7. K. Lee, M. W. Peng, & K. Lee, 2008, From diversification premium to diversification discount during institutional transitions, *Journal of World Business*, 43(1): 47–65; M. Ammann & M. Verhofen, 2006, The conglomerate discount: A new explanation based on credit risk, *International Journal of Theoretical & Applied Finance*, 9(8): 1201–1214; S. A. Mansi & D. M. Reeb, 2002, Corporate diversification: What gets discounted? *Journal of Finance*, 57: 2167–2183.

8. A. Campbell, M. Goold, & M. Alexander, 1995, Corporate strategy: The question for parenting advantage, *Harvard Business Review*, 73(2): 120–132.

9. D. Collis, D. Young, & M. Goold, 2007, The size, structure, and performance of corporate headquarters, *Strategic Management Journal*, 28: 283–405; M. Goold & A. Campbell, 2002, Parenting in complex structures, *Long Range Planning*, 35(3): 219–243; T. H. Brush, P. Bromiley, & M. Hendrickx, 1999, The relative influence of industry and corporation on business segment performance: An alternative estimate, *Strategic Management Journal*, 20: 519–547.

10. H. Chesbrough, 2007, The market for innovation: Implications for corporate strategy, *California Management Review*, 49(3): 45–66; D. Miller, 2006, Technological diversity, related diversification performance, *Strategic Management Journal*, 27: 601–619; D. J. Miller, 2004, Firms' technological resources and the performance effects of diversification: A longitudinal study, *Strategic Management Journal*, 25: 1097–1119.

11. D. D. Bergh, 2001, Diversification strategy research at a crossroads: Established, emerging and anticipated paths, in M. A. Hitt, R. E. Freeman, & J. S. Harrison (eds.), *Handbook of Strategic Management*, Oxford, UK: Blackwell Publishers, 363–383.

12. H. C. Wang & J. B. Barney, 2006, Employee incentives to make firm-specific investments: Implications for resource-based theories of corporate diversification, *Academy of Management Journal*, 31: 466–476.

13. K. Z. Zhou & F. Wu, 2010, Technological capability, strategic flexibility and product innovation, *Strategic Management Journal*, 31: 547–561.

14. J. J. Marcel, 2009, Why top management team characteristics matter when employing a chief operating officer: A strategic contingency perspective, *Strategic Management Journal*, 30(6): 647–658; A. J. Ward, M. J. Lankau, A. C. Amason, J. A. Sonnenfeld, & B. R. Agle, 2007, Improving the performance of top management teams, *MIT Sloan Management Review*, 48(3): 85–90.

15. R. P. Rumelt, *Strategy, Structure, and Economic Performance*, Boston: Harvard Business School, 1974; L. Wrigley, 1970, *Divisional Autonomy and Diversification* (Ph.D. dissertation), Harvard Business School.

16. P. Gogoi, N. Arndt, & J. Crown, 2008, A bittersweet deal for Wrigley: Selling the family business wasn't William Wrigley Jr.'s plan, but the Mars offer was too good to refuse, *BusinessWeek*, May 12, 34.

17. 2011, United Parcel Service 2010 Annual Report, http://www.ups.com, May 30.

18. R. Rumelt, 2011, *Good Strategy/Bad Strategy: The Difference and Why it Matters*, New York: Crown Business Publishing.

19. L. R. Gomez-Mejia, M. Makri, & M. L. Kintana, 2010. Diversification decisions in family controlled firms, *Journal of Management Studies*, 47: 223–252.

20. J. L. Stimpert, I. M. Duhaime, & J. Chesney, 2010, Learning to manage a large diversified firm, *Journal of Leadership and Organizational Studies*, 17: 411–425.

21. 2011, Hutchison Whampoa Limited Annual Report, http://www.hutchison-whampoa.com/eng/investor/annual/annual.htm#ar10, May 30.

22. J. E. Core & W. R. Guay, 2010, Is CEO pay too high and are incentives too low? A wealth-based contracting framework, *Academy of Management Perspectives,* 24 (1): 5–19; I. Filatotchev & D. Allcock, 2010, Corporate governance and executive remuneration: A contingency framework, *Academy of Management Perspectives,* 24 (1): 20–33; M. A. Williams, T. B. Michael, & E. R. Waller, 2008, Managerial incentives and acquisitions: A survey of the literature. *Managerial Finance,* 34(5): 328–341.

23. D. G. Sirmon, M. A. Hitt, R. D. Ireland, & B. A. Gilbert, 2011, Resource orchestration to create competitive advantage: Breadth, depth and life cycle effects, *Journal of Management,* in press; D. J. Miller, M. J. Fern, & L. B. Cardinal, 2007, The use of knowledge for technological innovation within diversified firms, *Academy of Management Journal,* 50: 308–326.

24. R. A. D'Aveni, G. B. Dagnino, & K. G. Smith, 2010. The age of temporary advantage, *Strategic Management Journal,* 31: 1371–1385; H. Tanriverdi & C.-H. Lee, 2008, Within-industry diversification and firm performance in the presence of network externalities: Evidence from the software industry, *Academy of Management Journal,* 51(2): 381–397.

25. M. E. Graebner, K. M. Eisenhardt, & P. T. Roundy, 2010, Success and failure of technology acquisitions: Lessons for buyers and sellers, *Academy of Management Perspectives,* 24(3): 73–92; M. D. R. Chari, S. Devaraj, & P. David, 2008, The impact of information technology investments and diversification strategies on firm performance, *Management Science,* 54(1): 224–234.

26. M. E. Porter, 1985, *Competitive Advantage,* New York: Free Press, 328.

27. M. Makri, M. A. Hitt, & P. J. Lane, 2010, Complementary technologies, knowledge relatedness and invention outcomes in high technology mergers and acquisitions, *Strategic Management Journal,* 31: 602–628.

28. N. Shin, 2009, Information technology and diversification: How their relationship affects firm performance. *International Journal of E-Collaboration,* 5(1): 69–83; D. Miller, 2006, Technological diversity, related diversification, and firm performance, *Strategic Management Journal,* 27: 601–619.

29. Y. M. Zhou, 2011, Synergy, coordination costs, and diversification choices, *Strategic Management Journal,* 32: 624–639.

30. Ibid.; Tanriverdi & Lee, Within-industry diversification and firm performance in the presence of network externalities: Evidence from the software industry; P. Puranam & K. Srikanth, 2007, What they know vs. what they do: How acquirers

leverage technology acquisitions, *Strategic Management Journal,* 28: 805–825.

31. D. D. Bergh, 1995, Size and relatedness of units sold: An agency theory and resource-based perspective, *Strategic Management Journal,* 16: 221–239.

32. M. Lubatkin & S. Chatterjee, 1994, Extending modern portfolio theory into the domain of corporate diversification: Does it apply? *Academy of Management Journal,* 37: 109–136.

33. E. Dooms & A. A. Van Oijen, 2008, The balance between tailoring and standardizing control, *European Management Review,* 5(4): 245–252; T. Kono, 1999, A strong head office makes a strong company, *Long Range Planning,* 32(2): 225.

34. I.-C. Hsu & Y.-S. Wang, 2008, A model of intraorganizational knowledge sharing: Development and initial test. *Journal of Global Information Management,* 16(3): 45–73; Puranam & Srikanth, What they know vs. what they do; F. T. Rothaermel, M. A. Hitt, & L. A. Jobe, 2006, Balancing vertical integration and strategic outsourcing: Effects on product portfolio, product success, and firm performance, *Strategic Management Journal,* 27: 1033–1056.

35. A. Rodríguez-Duarte, F. D. Sandulli, B. Minguela-Rata, & J. I. López-Sánchez, 2007, The endogenous relationship between innovation and diversification, and the impact of technological resources on the form of diversification, *Research Policy,* 36: 652–664; L. Capron & N. Pistre, 2002, When do acquirers earn abnormal returns? *Strategic Management Journal,* 23: 781–794.

36. C. Lawton, 2007, H-P begins push into high-end copiers, *Wall Street Journal,* April 24, B3.

37. Miller, Fern, & Cardinal, The use of knowledge for technological innovation within diversified firms; J. W. Spencer, 2003, Firms' knowledge-sharing strategies in the global innovation system: Empirical evidence from the flat panel display industry, *Strategic Management Journal,* 24: 217–233.

38. J. Thottam, 2008, Branson's flight plan, *Time,* April 28, 40.

39. 2011, Honda operations, Honda Motor Company, http://www.honda.com, May 30.

40. L. C. Thang, C. Rowley, T. Quang, & M. Warner, 2007, To what extent can management practices be transferred between countries?: The case of human resource management in Vietnam, *Journal of World Business,* 42(1): 113–127; G. Stalk Jr., 2005, Rotate the core, *Harvard Business Review,* 83(3): 18–19.

41. J. A. Martin & K. M. Eisenhardt, 2010, Rewiring: Cross-business unit collaborations in multibusiness organizations, *Academy of Management Journal,* 53: 265–301.

42. S. Gupta, A. Woodside, C. Dubelaar, & D. Bradmore, 2009, Diffusing knowledge-

based core competencies for leveraging innovation strategies: Modeling outsourcing to knowledge process organizations (KPOs) in pharmaceutical networks, *Industrial Marketing Management,* 38(2): 219–227.

43. A. Pehrsson, 2010, Business-relatedness and the strategy of moderations: Impacts on foreign subsidiary performance, *Journal of Strategy and Management,* 3: 110–133; S. Chatterjee & J. Singh, 1999, Are trade-offs inherent in diversification moves? A simultaneous model for type of diversification and mode of expansion decisions, *Management Science,* 45: 25–41.

44. J. Wiggins, 2008, Mars' move for Wrigley leaves rivals trailing, *Financial Times,* April 29, 24.

45. L. Fuentelsaz & J. Gomez, 2006, Multipoint competition, strategic similarity and entry into geographic markets, *Strategic Management Journal,* 27: 477–499; J. Gimeno & C. Y. Woo, 1999, Multimarket contact, economies of scope, and firm performance, *Academy of Management Journal,* 42: 239–259.

46. T. A. Shervani, G. Frazier, & G. Challagalla, 2007, The moderating influence of firm market power on the transaction cost economics model: An empirical test in a forward channel integration context, *Strategic Management Journal,* 28: 635–652; R. Gulati, P. R. Lawrence, & P. Puranam, 2005, Adaptation in vertical relationships: Beyond incentive conflict, *Strategic Management Journal,* 26: 415–440.

47. L. Diestre & N. Rajagopalan, 2011, An environmental perspective on diversification: The effects of chemical relatedness and regulatory sanctions, *Academy of Management Journal,* 54: 97–115; P. Broedner, S. Kinkel, & G. Lay, 2009, Productivity effects of outsourcing: New evidence on the strategic importance of vertical integration decisions, *International Journal of Operations & Production Management,* 29(2): 127–150.

48. R. Carter & G. M. Hodgson, 2006, The impact of empirical tests of transaction cost economics on the debate on the nature of the firm, *Strategic Management Journal,* 27: 461–476; O. E. Williamson, 1996, Economics and organization: A primer, *California Management Review,* 38(2): 131–146.

49. S. Novak & S. Stern, 2008, How does outsourcing affect performance dynamics? Evidence from the automobile industry, *Management Science,* 54(12): 1963–1979.

50. E. Rawley, 2010, Diversification, coordination costs and organizational rigidity: Evidence from microdata, *Strategic Management Journal,* 31: 873–891.

51. C. Wolter & F. M. Veloso, 2008, The effects of innovation on vertical structure: Perspectives on transaction costs and competences, *Academy of Management Review,* 33(3): 586–605; M. G. Jacobides, 2005, Industry change through vertical

disintegration: How and why markets emerged in mortgage banking, *Academy of Management Journal*, 48: 465–498.

52. D. Nosowitz, 2010, Apple buys voice search startup Siri, aiming squarely at Google, *Fast Company*, http://www .fastcompany.com, April 29.

53. B. Ortutay, 2011, Facebook-Google rivalry intensifies with PR fiasco, *MSNBC*, http:// www.msnbc.com, May 13; D. Nosowitz, 2010, Yahoo slams Google in new, ill-conceived ads, *Fast Company*, http:// www.fastcompany.com, May 6.

54. L. R. Kopczak & M. E. Johnson, 2003, The supply-chain management effect, *MIT Sloan Management Review*, 3: 27–34; K. R. Harrigan, 2001, Strategic flexibility in the old and new economies, in M. A. Hitt, R. E. Freeman, & J. S. Harrison (eds.), *Handbook of Strategic Management*, Oxford, UK: Blackwell Publishers, 97–123.

55. T. Hutzschenreuter & F. Gröne, 2009, Changing vertical integration strategies under pressure from foreign competition: The case of U.S. and German multinationals, *Journal of Management Studies*, 46(2): 269–307.

56. 2011, Flextronics International Ltd., http:// www.flextronics.com, May 31.

57. K. M. Eisenhardt & D. C. Galunic, 2000, Coevolving: At last, a way to make synergies work, *Harvard Business Review*, 78(1): 91–111.

58. P. David, J. P. O'Brien, T. Yoshikawa, & A. Delios, 2010, Do shareholders or stakeholders appropriate the rents from corporate diversification? The influence of ownership structure, *Academy of Management Journal*, 53: 636–654; J. A. Nickerson & T. R. Zenger, 2008, Envy, comparison costs, and the economic theory of the firm, *Strategic Management Journal*, 13: 1429–1449.

59. 2011, Corporate information, Walt Disney company, http://corporate.disney.go.com, June 1; L Greene, 2009, Adult nostalgia for childhood brands, *Financial Times*. http://www.ft.com, February 14; M. Marr, 2007, The magic kingdom looks to hit the road, *Wall Street Journal*, http://www.wsj .com, February 8.

60. D. Lee & R. Madhaven, 2010, Divestiture and firm performance: a meta-analysis, *Journal of Management*, 36: 1345–1371; D. W. Ng, 2007, A modern resource based approach to unrelated diversification. *Journal of Management Studies*, 44(8): 1481–1502; D. D. Bergh, 1997, Predicting divestiture of unrelated acquisitions: An integrative model of ex ante conditions, *Strategic Management Journal*, 18: 715–731.

61. Porter, *Competitive Advantage*.

62. S. Lee, K. Park, H. H. Shin, 2009, Disappearing internal capital markets: Evidence from diversified business groups in Korea. *Journal of Banking & Finance*, 33(2): 326–334; D. Collis, D. Young, & M. Goold, 2007, The size, structure, and performance of corporate headquarters, *Strategic Management Journal*, 28: 283–405; O. E. Williamson, 1975, *Markets*

and *Hierarchies: Analysis and Antitrust Implications*, New York: Macmillan Free Press.

63. R. Aggarwal & N. A. Kyaw, 2009, International variations in transparency and capital structure: Evidence from European firms. *Journal of International Financial Management & Accounting*, 20(1): 1–34; R. J. Indjejikian, 2007, Discussion of accounting information, disclosure, and the cost of capital, *Journal of Accounting Research*, 45(2): 421–426.

64. A. Capezio, J. Shields, & M. O'Donnell, 2011, Too good to be true: Board structural independence as a moderator of CEO pay-for-performance, *Journal of Management Studies*, 48: 487–513.

65. A. Mackey, 2008, The effect of CEOs on firm performance, *Strategic Management Journal*, 29(12): 1357–1367; Dooms & Van Oijen, The balance between tailoring and standardizing control; D. Miller, R. Eisenstat, & N. Foote, 2002, Strategy from the inside out: Building capability-creating organizations, *California Management Review*, 44(3): 37–54; M. E. Raynor & J. L. Bower, 2001, Lead from the center: How to manage divisions dynamically, *Harvard Business Review*, 79(5): 92–100.

66. P. Engardio & M. Arndt, 2007, What price reputation: Many savvy companies are starting to realize that a good name can be their most important asset— and actually boost the stock price, *BusinessWeek*, July 8, 70–79; J. Lunsford & B. Steinberg, 2006, Conglomerates' conundrum, *Wall Street Journal*, B1, B7.

67. L. Chenevert, 2011, NCCJ Annual Human Relations Award Acceptance Speech, United Technologies, http://www.utc.com/ News/Executive+Speeches, June 1.

68. F. Guerrera, 2007, Siemens chief makes the case for conglomerates, *Financial Times*, http://www.ft.com, February 5.

69. B. Quint, 2009, Companies deal with tough times through diversification, *Information Today*, 26(3): 7–8.

70. S. L. Sun, X. Zhoa, & H. Yang, 2010, Executive compensation in Asia: A critical review, *Asia Pacific Journal of Management*, 27: 775–802; A. Delios, D. Xu, & P. W. Beamish, 2008, Within-country product diversification and foreign subsidiary performance, *Journal of International Business Studies*, 39(4): 706–724; M. W. Peng, & A. Delios, 2006, What determines the scope of the firm over time and around the world? An Asia Pacific perspective, *Asia Pacific Journal of Management*, 23: 385–405.

71. Lee, Park, Shin, Disappearing internal capital markets: Evidence from diversified business groups in Korea; A. Chakrabarti, K. Singh, & I. Mahmood, 2006, Diversification and performance: Evidence from East Asian firms, *Strategic Management Journal*, 28: 101–120; T. Khanna & K. Palepu, 2000, Is group affiliation profitable in emerging markets? An analysis of diversified Indian business groups, *Journal of Finance*, 55: 867–892; T. Khanna & K. Palepu, 2000, The future

of business groups in emerging markets: Long-run evidence from Chile, *Academy of Management Journal*, 43: 268–285.

72. D. D. Bergh, R. A. Johnson, & R. L. Dewitt, 2008, Restructuring through spin-off or sell-off: Transforming information asymmetries into financial gain, *Strategic Management Journal*, 29(2): 133–148; C. Decker & M. Mellewigt, 2007, Thirty years after Michael E. Porter: What do we know about business exit? *Academy of Management Perspectives*, 2: 41–55; S. J. Chang & H. Singh, 1999, The impact of entry and resource fit on modes of exit by multibusiness firms, *Strategic Management Journal*, 20: 1019–1035.

73. 2011, Danaher, http://www.danaher.com, June 1.

74. R. Coff, 2003, Bidding wars over R&D-intensive firms: Knowledge, opportunism, and the market for corporate control, *Academy of Management Journal*, 46: 74–85.

75. P. Navarro, 2009, Recession-proofing your organization, *MIT Sloan Management Review*, 50(3): 45–51.

76. M. Lubatkin, H. Merchant, & M. Srinivasan, 1997, Merger strategies and shareholder value during times of relaxed antitrust enforcement: The case of large mergers during the 1980s, *Journal of Management*, 23: 61–81.

77. D. P. Champlin & J. T. Knoedler, 1999, Restructuring by design? Government's complicity in corporate restructuring, *Journal of Economic Issues*, 33(1): 41–57.

78. R. M. Scherer & D. Ross, 1990, *Industrial Market Structure and Economic Performance*, Boston: Houghton Mifflin.

79. A. Shleifer & R. W. Vishny, 1994, Takeovers in the 1960s and 1980s: Evidence and implications, in R. P. Rumelt, D. E. Schendel, & D. J. Teece (eds.), *Fundamental Issues in Strategy*, Boston: Harvard Business School Press, 403–422.

80. S. Chatterjee, J. S. Harrison, & D. D. Bergh, 2003, Failed takeover attempts, corporate governance and refocusing, *Strategic Management Journal*, 24: 87–96; Lubatkin, Merchant, & Srinivasan, Merger strategies and shareholder value; D. J. Ravenscraft & R. M. Scherer, 1987, *Mergers, Sell-Offs and Economic Efficiency*, Washington, DC: Brookings Institution, 22.

81. D. A. Zalewski, 2001, Corporate takeovers, fairness, and public policy, *Journal of Economic Issues*, 35: 431–437; P. L. Zweig, J. P. Kline, S. A. Forest, & K. Gudridge, 1995, The case against mergers, *BusinessWeek*, October 30, 122–130; J. R. Williams, B. L. Paez, & L. Sanders, 1988, Conglomerates revisited, *Strategic Management Journal*, 9: 403–414.

82. E. J. Lopez, 2001, New anti-merger theories: A critique, *Cato Journal*, 20: 359–378; 1998, The trustbusters' new tools, *The Economist*, May 2, 62–64.

83. R. Croyle & P. Kager, 2002, Giving mergers a head start, *Harvard Business Review*, 80(10): 20–21.

84. M. C. Jensen, 1986, Agency costs of free cash flow, corporate finance, and takeovers, *American Economic Review*, 76: 323–329.

85. R. Gilson, M. Scholes, & M. Wolfson, 1988, Taxation and the dynamics of corporate control: The uncertain case for tax motivated acquisitions, in J. C. Coffee, L. Lowenstein, & S. Rose-Ackerman (eds.), *Knights, Raiders, and Targets: The Impact of the Hostile Takeover*, New York: Oxford University Press, 271–299.

86. C. Steindel, 1986, Tax reform and the merger and acquisition market: The repeal of the general utilities, *Federal Reserve Bank of New York Quarterly Review*, 11(3): 31–35.

87. M. A. Hitt, J. S. Harrison, & R. D. Ireland 2001, *Mergers and Acquisitions: A Guide to Creating Value for Stakeholders*, New York: Oxford University Press.

88. J. Haleblian; J.-Y. Kim, & N. Rajagopalan, 2006, The influence of acquisition experience and performance on acquisition behavior: Evidence from the U.S. commercial banking industry, *Academy of Management Journal*, 49: 357–370.

89. D. B. Wilkerson & R. Britt, 2003, It's showtime for media deals: Radio lessons fuel debate over control of TV, newspapers, *MarketWatch*, http://www.marketwatch.com, May 30.

90. M. T. Brouwer, 2008, Horizontal mergers and efficiencies; theory and antitrust practice, *European Journal of Law and Economics*, 26(1): 11–26.

91. T. Afza, C. Slahudin, & M. S. Nazir, 2008, Diversification and corporate performance: An evaluation of Pakistani firms, *South Asian Journal of Management*, 15(3): 7–18; J. M. Shaver, 2006, A paradox of synergy: Contagion and capacity effects in mergers and acquisitions, *Academy of Management Journal*, 31: 962–976; C. Park, 2002, The effects of prior performance on the choice between related and unrelated acquisitions: Implications for the performance consequences of diversification strategy, *Journal of Management Studies*, 39: 1003–1019.

92. Rumelt, *Strategy, Structure and Economic Performance*, 125.

93. M. Palmer & T. Bradshaw, 2011, Skype can be the "glue" in Microsoft's multimedia strategy, *Financial times*, http://blogs.ft.com, May 14.

94. K. Shimizu & M. A. Hitt, 2011, Errors at the top of the hierarchy, in D.A. Hofmann & M. Friese (eds.), *Errors in Organizations*, New York: Routledge.

95. L. E. Palich, L. B. Cardinal, & C. C. Miller, 2000, Curvilinearity in the diversification-performance linkage: An examination of over three decades of research, *Strategic Management Journal*, 21: 155–174.

96. D. G. Sirmon, M. A. Hitt, & R. D. Ireland, 2007, Managing firm resources in dynamic environments to create value: Looking inside the black box, *Academy of Management Review*, 32: 273–292;

A. E. Bernardo & B. Chowdhry, 2002, Resources, real options, and corporate strategy, *Journal of Financial Economics*, 63: 211–234.

97. W. H. Tsai, Y. C. Kuo, J.-H. Hung, 2009, Corporate diversification and CEO turnover in family businesses: Self-entrenchment or risk reduction? *Small Business Economics*, 32(1): 57–76; N. W. C. Harper & S. P. Viguerie, 2002, Are you too focused? *McKinsey Quarterly*, Mid-Summer, 29–38; J. C. Sandvig & L. Coakley, 1998, Best practices in small firm diversification, *Business Horizons*, 41(3): 33–40.

98. J. Plambeck, 2010, As CD sales wane, music retailers diversify, *The New York Times*, http://www.nytimes.com, May 30.

99. L. Jarvis, 2008, Pharma strategies: Merck launches into the biosimilars business, *Chemical & Engineering News*, December, 86(50): 7.

100. J. Carroll, 2009, Merck acquires bio-similars in $130M pact, *Fierce Biotech*, http://www.fiercebiotech.com, February 12.

101. T. B. Folta & J. P. O'Brien, 2008, Determinants of firm-specific thresholds in acquisition decisions, *Managerial and Decision Economics*, 29(2/3): 209–225.

102. N. M. Kay & A. Diamantopoulos, 1987, Uncertainty and synergy: Towards a formal model of corporate strategy, *Managerial and Decision Economics*, 8: 121–130.

103. R. W. Coff, 1999, How buyers cope with uncertainty when acquiring firms in knowledge-intensive industries: Caveat emptor, *Organization Science*, 10: 144–161.

104. P. B. Carroll & C. Muim 2008, 7 ways to fail big, *Harvard Business Review*, 86(9): 82–91.

105. D. G. Sirmon, S. Gove, & M. A. Hitt, 2008, Resource management in dyadic competitive rivalry: The effects of resource bundling and deployment, *Academy of Management Journal*, 51(5): 919–935; S. J. Chatterjee & B. Wernerfelt, 1991, The link between resources and type of diversification: Theory and evidence, *Strategic Management Journal*, 12: 33–48.

106. E. N. K. Lim, S. S. Das, & A. Das, 2009, Diversification strategy, capital structure, and the Asian financial crisis (1997–1998): Evidence from Singapore firms, *Strategic Management Journal*, 30(6): 577–594; W. Keuslein, 2003, The Ebitda folly, *Forbes*, March 17, 165–167.

107. A. Ricadela & D. Bass, 2011, Apple iPad's "buzz saw" success cuts PC sales at HP, Dell, *Bloomberg Businessweek*, http://www.businessweek.com, May 18.

108. L. Capron & J. Hull 1999, Redeployment of brands, sales forces, and general marketing management expertise following horizontal acquisitions: A resource-based view, *Journal of Marketing*, 63(2): 41–54.

109. M. V. S. Kumar, 2009, The relationship between product and international diversification: The effects of short-run constraints and endogeneity. *Strategic Management Journal*, 30(1): 99–116;

C. B. Malone & L. C. Rose, 2006. Intangible assets and firm diversification, *International Journal of Managerial Finance*, 2(2): 136–153.

110. C. Moschieri, 2011, The implementation and structuring of divestitures: The unit's perspective, *Strategic Management Journal*, 32: 368–401; K. Shimizu & M. A. Hitt, 2005, What constrains or facilitates divestitures of formerly acquired firms? The effects of organizational inertia, *Journal of Management*, 31: 50–72.

111. D. Cimilluca & J. Jargon, 2009, Corporate news: Sara Lee weighs sale of European business, *Wall Street Journal*, March 13, B3; J. Jargon & J. Vuocolo, 2007, Sara Lee CEO challenged on antitakeover defenses, *Wall Street Journal*, May 11, B4.

112. A. J. Nyberg, I. S. Fulmer, B. Gerhart, & M. A. Carpenter, 2010, Agency theory revisited: CEO return, and shareholder interest alignment, *Academy of Management Journal*, 53: 1029–1049; M. A. Williams, T. B. Michael, & E. R. Waller, 2008, Managerial incentives and acquisitions: A survey of the literature, *Managerial Finance*, 34(5): 328–341; J. G. Combs & M. S. Skill, 2003, Managerialist and human capital explanation for key executive pay premiums: A contingency perspective, *Academy of Management Journal*, 46: 63–73.

113. L. L. Lan & L. Heracleous, 2010, Rethinking agency theory: The view from law, *Academy of Management Review*, 35: 294–314; R. E. Hoskisson, M. W. Castleton, & M. C. Withers, 2009, Complementarity in monitoring and bonding: More intense monitoring leads to higher executive compensation, *Academy of Management Perspectives*, 23(2): 57–74.

114. Geiger & Cashen, Organizational size and CEO compensation; J. J. Cordeiro & R. Veliyath, 2003, Beyond pay for performance: A panel study of the determinants of CEO compensation, *American Business Review*, 21(1): 56–66; Wright, Kroll, & Elenkov, Acquisition returns, increase in firm size, and chief executive officer compensation; S. R. Gray & A. A. Cannella Jr., 1997, The role of risk in executive compensation, *Journal of Management*, 23: 517–540.

115. Y. Deutsch, T. Keil, & T. Laamanen, 2011, A dual agency view of board compensation: The joint effects of outside director and CEO options on firm risk, *Strategic Management Journal*, 32: 212–227; R. Bliss & R. Rosen, 2001, CEO compensation and bank mergers, *Journal of Financial Economics*, 1: 107–138.

116. A. J. Wowak & D. C. Hambrick, 2010, A model of person-pay interaction: How executives vary in their responses to compensation arrangements, *Strategic Management Journal*, 31: 803–821; J. Bogle, 2008, Reflections on CEO compensation, *Academy of Management Perspectives*, 22(2): 21–25; J. J. Janney, 2002, Eat or get eaten? How equity ownership and diversification shape CEO

risk-taking, *Academy of Management Executive*, 14(4): 157–158.

117. M. Kahan & E. B. Rock, 2002, How I learned to stop worrying and love the pill: Adaptive responses to takeover law, *University of Chicago Law Review*, 69(3): 871–915.

118. R. C. Anderson, T. W. Bates, J. M. Bizjak, & M. L. Lemmon, 2000, Corporate governance and firm diversification, *Financial Management*, 29(1): 5–22; J. D. Westphal, 1998, Board games: How CEOs adapt to increases in structural board independence from management, *Administrative Science Quarterly*, 43: 511–537; J. K. Seward & J. P. Walsh, 1996, The governance and control of voluntary corporate spin-offs, *Strategic Management Journal*, 17: 25–39; J. P. Walsh & J. K. Seward, 1990, On the efficiency of internal and external corporate control mechanisms, *Academy of Management Review*, 15: 421–458.

119. S. M. Campbell, A. J. Ward, J. A. Sonnenfeld, & B. R. Agle, 2008, Relational ties that bind: Leader-follower relationship dimensions and charismatic attribution, *Leadership Quarterly*, 19(5): 556–568; M. Wiersema, 2002, Holes at the top: Why CEO firings backfire, *Harvard Business Review*, 80(12): 70–77.

120. D. Allcock & I. Filatotchev, 2010, Executive incentive schemes in initial public offerings: The effects of multiple-agency conflicts and corporate governance, *Journal of Management*, 36: 663–686; J. M. Bizjak, M. L. Lemmon, & L. Naveen, 2008, Does the use of peer groups contribute to higher pay and less efficient compensation? *Journal of Financial Economics*, 90(2): 152–168; N. Wasserman, 2006, Stewards, agents, and the founder discount: Executive compensation in new ventures, *Academy of Management Journal*, 49: 960–976.

121. E. F. Fama, 1980, Agency problems and the theory of the firm, *Journal of Political Economy*, 88: 288–307.

122. M. Y. Brannen & M. F. Peterson, 2009, Merging without alienating: Interventions promoting cross-cultural organizational integration and their limitations, *Journal of International Business Studies*, 40(3): 468–489; M. L. A. Hayward, 2002, When do firms learn from their acquisition experience? Evidence from 1990–1995, *Strategic Management Journal*, 23: 21–39.

123. R. E. Hoskisson, R. A. Johnson, L. Tihanyi, & R. E. White, 2005, Diversified business groups and corporate refocusing in emerging economies, *Journal of Management*, 31: 941–965.

124. C. N. Chung & X. Luo, 2008, Institutional logics or agency costs: The influence of corporate governance models on business group restructuring in emerging economies, *Organization Science*, 19(5): 766–784; Chakrabarti, Singh, & Mahmood, Diversification and performance: Evidence from East Asian firms; W. P. Wan & R. E. Hoskisson, 2003, Home country environments, corporate diversification strategies, and firm performance, *Academy of Management Journal*, 46: 27–45.

CHAPTER 7

Merger and Acquisition Strategies

Studying this chapter should provide you with the strategic management knowledge needed to:

1. Explain the popularity of merger and acquisition strategies in firms competing in the global economy.

2. Discuss reasons why firms use an acquisition strategy to achieve strategic competitiveness.

3. Describe seven problems that work against achieving success when using an acquisition strategy.

4. Name and describe the attributes of effective acquisitions.

5. Define the restructuring strategy and distinguish among its common forms.

6. Explain the short- and long-term outcomes of the different types of restructuring strategies.

TECHNOLOGY GIANTS' ACQUISITION STRATEGIES AND THEIR OUTCOMES

When Microsoft announced that it would acquire Skype Global S.à.r.l., the leading Internet telecommunications company, for $8.5 billion, there were both positive and negative attributions about the deal in the media. Using Skype telecommunication software, family, friends, and colleagues can call free with messaging, voice, and video services. Additionally, at a very low cost, they can call landlines or mobiles virtually worldwide. Skype also recently introduced group videos, allowing groups of more than two to communicate more effectively whenever they are apart.

Skype has an interesting history. It was purchased by eBay in September 2005 as a way to bolster its Internet auction site through better communications. However, the service did not function as strategically designed, and in November 2009 eBay sold the service in a spin-off to an investment group led by Silver Lake, a private equity firm. During the 18 months of Silver Lake's leadership, calling minutes increased by 150 percent and there was significant growth in the overall number of users. Silver Lake recruited an outstanding senior management team who facilitated this growth.

Skype was founded in 2003 and based in Luxembourg. Because it was founded and headquartered outside the United States, Microsoft was able to use cash that was not repatriated into the United States to pay for the deal. In so doing, it avoided paying U.S. income tax. Those who have complained about the price that Microsoft paid suggest that they should have done it earlier because eBay sold 18 months ago for just

Recently, Microsoft acquired Skype Global for $8.5 billion.

Blend Images/Ariel Skelley/Jupiter Images

$2.75 billion to Silver Lake. However, under its new leadership, Skype gained 145 million new customers per month. As such, the $8.5 billion represents a cost of $14.70 per customer. Comparatively, when Skype was bought by eBay in 2005, eBay paid $45.60 per user. Although Skype's acquisition price went up, its price per user has gone down relative to its previous purchase. Previously, Microsoft invested in Facebook when it had only 100 million users, which worked out to $1.50 per user, at an overall price of $15 billion. The view is positive about Microsoft's investment in Facebook. Comparatively, Microsoft paid less than eBay for Skype, and its eBay investment also seems very favorable.

Whether Microsoft will be able to utilize the service and integrate it into its focus on business customers relative to the consumer focus of Skype remains to be seen. The second challenge is whether Microsoft will be able to incorporate the Skype service into its various devices and software platforms. A high priority will be to integrate Skype with Windows for smartphones. This is an effort to compete with Apple's iPhone and Google's Android operating systems. There is also a defensive rationale: "If Microsoft did not buy Skype it may end up in the hands of a competitor such as Google who might be able to use it to strengthen its ecosystem at the expense of Microsoft."

Google also has been pursuing an acquisition strategy, although Google's approach is usually to acquire earlier-stage companies than Microsoft's deal to acquire Skype. Google purchased YouTube for $1.6 billion in 2006, just 20 months after YouTube's founders registered the YouTube.com domain name. Its monthly audience has mushroomed from 344 to 500 million unique users. Much of their efforts have translated into "more and more money." In another acquisition, Google paid $3.2 billion for DoubleClick, Inc. With DoubleClick, Google's goal was to move from search advertising to the much larger market of display ads. DoubleClick's expertise was in producing graphical ads that appear on tops and sides of Web pages. After the acquisition of DoubleClick, Google's stock price soared. Its display ad sales brought in $2.5 billion annually as of October 2010. Additionally, although Google had offered $4 billion for Groupon, which produces daily promotion ads in large communities around the world, its offer was rejected. Groupon is considering an initial public offering (IPO) instead.

Facebook has a somewhat different approach to acquisitions. It recently bought Snaptu. Snaptu provides application software for services such as Facebook, Twitter, and LinkedIn, which allows these services to be featured on phones. Facebook has made 11 acquisitions since 2007; however, almost none of the acquired companies' services have survived as independent businesses. Their Web sites are often shut down, and the human capital, the employees and software engineers, become Facebook employees. Because Facebook is not a publicly traded company, it is difficult to tell how well these acquired companies have been integrated into Facebook. It is apparent, though, that the employees are utilized to improve Facebook's capabilities and develop new businesses. Online social networks, such as Facebook, have caused Procter & Gamble (P&G) to reallocate their advertising resources away from television and to more digital formats. Through advertising on Facebook, Amazon has become one of the top 10 retailers for Pampers (a P&G diaper brand). Online commerce is thus moving into a consumer-oriented retail phase, of which many companies such as Facebook and Amazon are seeking to take advantage. Acquisitions are a quick way to move into the space that these tech giants see evolving, such as Microsoft seeking to broaden its communication base, Google expanding beyond search to experiment with new models of advertising, and Facebook's attempts to learn from the human capital that they are able to acquire.

Sources: T. Bradshaw, 2011, Skype users expect more ads under Microsoft, *Financial Times*, May 12, 18; T. Bradshaw, N. Palmer, & R. Waters, 2011, Knocking at the door of tech heaven, *Financial Times*, March 11, 23; T. Catan & A. Efrati, 2011, Google, U.S. near accord on travel deal, *Wall Street Journal*, April 8, B1–B2; A. Efrati, 2011, Google cranks M&A machine, *Wall Street Journal*, March 5, B1, B4; J. Gapper, 2011, Microsoft must narrow its outlook, *Financial Times*, May 12, 11; K. MacFadyen, 2011, The digital revolution 2.0, *Mergers and Acquisitions*, 46(2): 14; D. MacMillan, 2011, Going after online plane-ticket buyers, *Bloomberg Businessweek*, www.businessweek .com, May 9; J. Neff, 2011, P&G's commerce chief sees blurring of sales, marketing, *Advertising Age*, April 11, 8; D. Sacks, 2011, Blown away, *Fast Company*, February, 58–62, 64–65, 104; B. Stone, 2011, Is DoubleClick clicking for Google?, *Bloomberg Businessweek*, March 14, 38–39; N. Wingfield, 2011, Microsoft dials up change – CEO Ballmer defends hefty $8.5 billion price tag for Internet-phone firm Skype, *Wall Street Journal*, May 11, A1.

Learn more about Microsoft's acquisition of Skype.

www.cengagebrain .com

We examined corporate-level strategy in Chapter 6, focusing on types and levels of product diversification strategies that firms derive from their core competencies to create competitive advantages and value for stakeholders. As noted in that chapter, diversification allows a firm to create value by productively using excess resources.[1] In this chapter, we explore merger and acquisition strategies. Firms throughout the world use these strategies, often in concert with diversification strategies, to become more diversified. As noted in the Opening Case, merger and acquisition strategies remain popular as a source of firm growth and, hopefully, of above-average returns.

Most corporations are very familiar with merger and acquisition strategies. For example, the latter half of the twentieth century found major companies using these strategies to grow and to deal with the competitive challenges in their domestic markets as well as those emerging from global competitors. Today, smaller firms also use merger and acquisition strategies to grow in their existing markets and to enter new markets.[2]

Not unexpectedly, some mergers and acquisitions fail to reach their promise.[3] Accordingly, explaining how firms can successfully use merger and acquisition strategies to create stakeholder value[4] is a key purpose of this chapter. To do this, we first explain the continuing popularity of merger and acquisition strategies as a choice firms evaluate when seeking growth and strategic competitiveness. As part of this explanation, we describe the differences between mergers, acquisitions, and takeovers. We next discuss specific reasons firms choose to use acquisition strategies and some of the problems organizations may encounter when implementing them. We then describe the characteristics associated with effective acquisitions before closing the chapter with a discussion of different types of restructuring strategies. Restructuring strategies are commonly used to correct or deal with the results of ineffective mergers and acquisitions.

The Popularity of Merger and Acquisition Strategies

Merger and acquisition (M&A) strategies have been popular among U.S. firms for many years. Some believe that these strategies played a central role in the restructuring of U.S. businesses during the 1980s and 1990s and that they continue generating these types of benefits in the twenty-first century.[5]

Although popular, and appropriately so, as a means of growth with the potential to lead to strategic competitiveness, it is important to emphasize that changing conditions in the external environment influence the type of M&A activity firms pursue. During the recent financial crisis, tightening credit markets made it more difficult for firms to complete "megadeals" (those costing $10 billion or more). However, the flow of deals picked up in 2011 in the United States, where "first-quarter deal volume rose a healthy 45 percent to $290.8 billion, compared with $200.6 billion" in 2010; "Europe saw a volume increase in the quarter, though not by as much as in the U.S., as worries over the health of government finances in the region lingered."[6] Additionally, a relatively weak currency, such as the U.S. dollar, increases the interest of firms from other nations with a strong currency to pursue cross-border acquisitions in the country where the currency is weaker.[7]

In the final analysis, firms use merger and acquisition strategies to improve their ability to create more value for all stakeholders, including shareholders. As suggested by Figure 1.1, this reasoning applies equally to all of the other strategies (e.g., business-level, corporate-level, international, and cooperative) a firm may formulate and then implement.

However, evidence suggests that using merger and acquisition strategies in ways that consistently create value is challenging. This is particularly true for acquiring firms in that some research results indicate that shareholders of acquired firms often earn above-average returns from acquisitions, while shareholders of acquiring firms typically earn returns that are close to zero.[8] Moreover, in approximately two-thirds of all acquisitions, the acquiring firm's stock price falls immediately after the intended transaction is announced. This negative response reflects investors' skepticism about the likelihood that the acquirer will be able to achieve the synergies required to justify the premium.[9] Premiums can sometimes appear to be excessive, as in the acquisition of National Semiconductor by Texas Instruments. One analyst suggested that the 85 percent premium "indicated the level of confidence TI execs have in both the purchase and the ability to rapidly boost the flagging growth rate of National's product sales."[10] Obviously, creating the amount of value required to account for this type of premium is not going to be easy. Overall then, those leading firms that are using merger and acquisition strategies must recognize that creating more value for their stakeholders by doing so is indeed difficult.[11]

Mergers, Acquisitions, and Takeovers: What Are the Differences?

A merger is a strategy through which two firms agree to integrate their operations on a relatively coequal basis. Recently, United and Continental Airlines received government approval of their proposed "merger of equals." "The new carrier, which will operate under the United name but with the Continental livery, logo and colors, arguably will

A **merger** is a strategy through which two firms agree to integrate their operations on a relatively coequal basis.

be the most balanced U.S. major airline in terms of regions served, mix of domestic and international flying, and hub geography."[12]

Even though the transaction between United and Continental appears to be a merger, the reality is that few true mergers actually take place. The main reason for this is that one party to the transaction is usually dominant in regard to various characteristics such as market share, size, or value of assets. Interestingly, although United is the larger carrier, Jeff Smisek, CEO of Continental, will serve as CEO of the combined firm.

An **acquisition** is a strategy through which one firm buys a controlling, or 100 percent, interest in another firm with the intent of making the acquired firm a subsidiary business within its portfolio. After completing the transaction, the management of the acquired firm reports to the management of the acquiring firm.

Although most of the mergers that are completed are friendly in nature, acquisitions can be friendly or unfriendly. A **takeover** is a special type of acquisition wherein the target firm does not solicit the acquiring firm's bid; thus, takeovers are unfriendly acquisitions. For example, in March 2011, Valeant Pharmaceuticals proposed a hostile takeover of Cephalon, which was not approved by Cephalon's board. Valeant was focused on obtaining rights to a drug that Cephalon was producing for narcolepsy, a disorder that causes excessive sleepiness. The drug, Provigil, was soon to lose its patent rights and would become a target of generic drugmakers. Because Valeant's offer was rejected by Cephalon's board, Valeant sought to vote out the board of directors of Cephalon. The deal ultimately fell apart, however, when Teva Pharmaceuticals struck a $6.8 billion friendly deal with Cephalon a few weeks later, forcing Valeant to withdraw its lower offer.[13]

Research evidence reveals that "pre-announcement returns" of hostile takeovers "are largely anticipated and associated with a significant increase in the bidder's and target's share prices."[14] This evidence provides a rationale why some firms are willing to pursue buying another company even when that firm is not interested in being bought. Often, determining the price the acquiring firm is willing to pay to "take over" the target firm is the core issue in these transactions. In Valeant Pharmaceuticals' takeover attempt of Cephalon, Valeant's offer was $5.8 billion, or $73 a share, and represented a 24.5 percent premium. However, as noted above, Cephalon was purchased by Teva for $6.8 billion, or $81.50 a share, a premium of 39 percent.

On a comparative basis, acquisitions are more common than mergers and takeovers. Accordingly, we focus the remainder of this chapter's discussion on acquisitions.

Reasons for Acquisitions

In this section, we discuss reasons firms decide to acquire another company. Although each reason can provide a legitimate rationale, acquisitions are not always as successful as the involved parties want them to be. Later in the chapter, we examine problems firms may encounter when seeking growth and strategic competitiveness through acquisitions.

Increased Market Power

Achieving greater market power is a primary reason for acquisitions.[15] Defined in Chapter 6, *market power* exists when a firm is able to sell its goods or services above competitive levels or when the costs of its primary or support activities are lower than those of its competitors. Market power usually is derived from the size of the firm and its resources and capabilities to compete in the marketplace;[16] it is also affected by the firm's share of the market. Therefore, most acquisitions that are designed to achieve greater market power entail buying a competitor, a supplier, a distributor, or a business in a highly related industry to allow the exercise of a core competence and to gain competitive advantage in the acquiring firm's primary market.

An **acquisition** is a strategy through which one firm buys a controlling, or 100 percent, interest in another firm with the intent of making the acquired firm a subsidiary business within its portfolio.

A **takeover** is a special type of acquisition wherein the target firm does not solicit the acquiring firm's bid; thus, takeovers are unfriendly acquisitions.

If a firm achieves enough market power, it can become a market leader, which is the goal of many firms. For example, in March 2011, AT&T made a surprising announcement that it was acquiring T-Mobile USA from Deutsche Telekom AG for $39 billion. This acquisition would put AT&T in the lead market share position of wireless service providers in the United States. Sprint was surprised because they were seeking to make a deal with T-Mobile as well. It remains to be seen whether the U. S. government will approve the acquisition; many experts suggest that the second and fourth largest providers face a "rocky path to approval and at a minimum will require large divestitures." Not only would AT&T's customers increase by a third, but the cell towers and wireless spectrum that T-Mobile provides would largely resolve congestion problems that have given AT&T a bad name.[17]

Next, we discuss how firms use horizontal, vertical, and related types of acquisitions to increase their market power.

AT&T Chairman and CEO Randall Stephenson and Deutsche Telekom Chairman and CEO Rene Obermann meet after announcing AT&T's $39 billion acquisition of T-Mobile USA.

Horizontal Acquisitions

The acquisition of a company competing in the same industry as the acquiring firm is a *horizontal acquisition.* Horizontal acquisitions increase a firm's market power by exploiting cost-based and revenue-based synergies.[18] For instance, the AT&T and T-Mobile acquisition noted above brings together two large players that would comprise the largest wireless carrier in the United States, surpassing the size of Verizon Wireless, a joint venture between Verizon and Vodaphone.

Research suggests that horizontal acquisitions result in higher performance when the firms have similar characteristics,[19] such as strategy, managerial styles, and resource allocation patterns. Similarities in these characteristics, as well as previous alliance management experience, support efforts to integrate the acquiring and the acquired firm. Horizontal acquisitions are often most effective when the acquiring firm integrates the acquired firm's assets with its own assets, but only after evaluating and divesting excess capacity and assets that do not complement the newly combined firm's core competencies.[20]

Vertical Acquisitions

A *vertical acquisition* refers to a firm acquiring a supplier or distributor of one or more of its goods or services.[21] Through a vertical acquisition, the newly formed firm controls additional parts of the value chain (see Chapters 3 and 6),[22] which is how vertical acquisitions lead to increased market power.

Larry Ellison, CEO of Oracle Corporation, has been pursuing many acquisitions of other software firms, most of which were horizontal acquisitions. However, he has also orchestrated vertical acquisitions. For example, Oracle acquired Sun Microsystems, a computer hardware producer (backward vertical integration), in 2010. With the deal Sun also gained significant software expertise that is important for developing cloud computing expertise (see Strategic Focus in Chapter 5). Oracle has also made vertical acquisitions of producers in particular markets that facilitate distribution into industries in which it does not have a strong presence; for example, Oracle "got into healthcare through its purchase of Relsys, a maker of analytics applications for the life sciences industry."[23]

MARK DYE/NEWSCAST/Landov

Related Acquisitions

Acquiring a firm in a highly related industry is called a *related acquisition*. Through a related acquisition, firms seek to create value through the synergy that can be generated by integrating some of their resources and capabilities. For example, Amazon has been acquiring a set of related businesses to build its retail services beyond books, music, DVDs, and appliances. It recently acquired an online entertainment business, LOVEFiLM International, known as the Netflix of Europe, at a price of $555 million. This is an important move for Amazon as DVD sales make up about 20 percent of its revenues, and online video delivery is likely to displace much of this revenue in the future.[24]

Horizontal, vertical, and related acquisitions that firms complete to increase their market power are subject to regulatory review as well as to analysis by financial markets.[25] For example, as noted earlier, the acquisition of T-Mobile by AT&T is sure to receive scrutiny by the Federal Trade Commission and Antitrust Division of the Justice Department, which approves proposed mergers.[26] Thus, firms seeking growth and market power through acquisitions must understand the political/legal segment of the general environment (see Chapter 2) in order to successfully use an acquisition strategy.

Overcoming Entry Barriers

Barriers to entry (introduced in Chapter 2) are factors associated with a market or with the firms currently operating in it that increase the expense and difficulty new firms encounter when trying to enter that particular market. For example, well-established competitors may have economies of scale in the manufacture or service of their products. In addition, enduring relationships with customers often create product loyalties that are difficult for new entrants to overcome. When facing differentiated products, new entrants typically must spend considerable resources to advertise their products and may find it necessary to sell below competitors' prices to entice new customers.

Facing the entry barriers that economies of scale and differentiated products create, a new entrant may find acquiring an established company to be more effective than entering the market as a competitor offering a product that is unfamiliar to current buyers. In fact, the higher the barriers to market entry, the greater the probability that a firm will acquire an existing firm to overcome them.

As this discussion suggests, a key advantage of using an acquisition strategy to overcome entry barriers is that the acquiring firm gains immediate access to a market. This advantage can be particularly attractive for firms seeking to overcome entry barriers associated with entering international markets.[27] Large multinational corporations from developed economies seek to enter emerging economies such as Brazil, Russia, India, and China (BRIC) because they are among the fastest-growing economies in the world.[28] As discussed next, completing a cross-border acquisition of a local target allows a firm to quickly enter fast-growing economies such as these.

Cross-Border Acquisitions

Acquisitions made between companies with headquarters in different countries are called *cross-border acquisitions*.[29] The purchase of U.K. carmakers Jaguar and Land Rover by India's Tata Motors is an example of a cross-border acquisition.

There are other interesting changes taking place in terms of cross-border acquisition activity. Historically, North American and European companies were the most active acquirers of companies outside their domestic markets. However, the current global competitive landscape is one in which firms from other nations may use an acquisition strategy more frequently than do their counterparts in North America and Europe. In this regard, Chinese companies, in particular, are well positioned for cross-border acquisitions. Chinese corporations are well capitalized with strong balance sheets and cash reserves, and they have learned from their past failures, as indicated in the Strategic Focus.[30] In the Strategic Focus, we also describe recent cross-border acquisitions by some Indian and Brazilian companies and how their approaches differ. As you will see, many of the deals cited are horizontal acquisitions through which the acquiring companies seek to increase their market power.

S T R A T E G I C **F O C U S**

CROSS-BORDER ACQUISITIONS BY FIRMS FROM EMERGING ECONOMIES: LEVERAGE RESOURCES TO GAIN A LARGER GLOBAL FOOTPRINT AND MARKET POWER

Historically, large multinational firms from North America and Europe have pursued international acquisitions in emerging and developing countries in order to establish stronger economies of scale for domestic brands as well as provide opportunities for sourcing of scarce resources. Although the Spanish economy is in the doldrums, Spanish firms have used this strategy relatively recently to expand, first into Latin America and then into other European countries. Telefónica and Banco Santander are Spanish companies that have extended their reach, especially through cross-border acquisitions. For instance, Telefónica is now the world's fifth largest telecommunication provider in terms of revenue, and Santander is the fourth largest bank on the same metric and has become Latin America's largest retail bank.

Like many Spanish firms, many emerging economy firms are seeking to build a global footprint through acquisitions. For example, after China was accepted into the World Trade Organization in 2000, many Chinese cross-border mergers and acquisitions were attempted. However, many Chinese companies who made cross-border acquisitions saw

© Shutterstock

In today's business climate, many emerging economies are seeking to create a global footprint by acquiring international counterparts.

them end in failure in their first attempts. In 2003, there was $1.6 billion spent on acquisitions, which swelled to $18.2 billion by 2006. However, TLC Corporation's acquisition of France's Thomson Electronics, SAIC's takeover of South Korea's SsangYong Motor Company, Ping An's investment in the Belgium-Dutch financial services group Fortis, and Ningbo Bird's strategic partnership with France's Sajan ended in stunning failures, where the Chinese either pulled out or had to sell off much of their acquired assets. The Chinese, however, have learned from their mistakes. Instead of buying global brands, sales networks, and goodwill in branded products, they are now mainly trying to acquire concrete assets such as mineral deposits, state of the art technologies, or R&D facilities. This strategy was encouraged by the government after pulling back from the failed acquisitions just mentioned. As the economy around the world depreciated assets and as the RMB (China's currency) appreciated relative to developed economies, the strategy focused on hard assets because it made better investing sense rather than seeking to buy established branded products, in which they did not always have managerial capability to realize successful performance. This was signaled by the third largest PC maker, Lenovo (acquired from IBM), after HP and Dell, was taken over by Taiwan's Acer Computer as Lenovo slipped to fourth in worldwide market share.

Another major emerging market, India, is pursuing cross-border acquisitions as well. To highlight the difference between M&A activity of Chinese versus Indian firms, focusing on acquisitions in the agricultural input sector is illustrative. China National Chemical Corporation (ChemChina) and United Phosphorus (UPL) have different strategies in expanding globally and securing supplies. Both countries have major food consumption needs because of their large populations. ChemChina is mostly a state-owned firm, and therefore has the backing of the government in terms of its capital endowment. As such, ChemChina is quite aggressive in its consolidation activity through acquisition. It acquired the Israeli company, Makhteshim Agan Industries, the world's largest maker of generic pesticides, for $2.4 billion in January 2010. UPL, on the other hand, purchased a fungicide business from DuPont using a much smaller acquisition approach. UPL is very careful in terms of its valuation. One analyst was quoted as saying, "They never acquire something unless it meets their criteria for a 3- to 4-year payback period." If the valuations are not in their favor, they won't make the acquisition. India recorded 554 cross-border deals worth $54.9 billion, which equals 80 percent of the total share of 2010 deals. As noted by Ernst & Young, there were 13 deals worth over $1 billion each, with only two such deals recorded in 2009. In 2010, 263 were outbound FDI deals worth $32.4 billion. This represents 47 percent of the 2010 flow of deals, whereas these were only six percent of such deals in 2009.

Brazil is another country with a large emerging economy whose companies have significant acquisition activity. In 2010, Marfrig, a Brazilian meat packer, acquired Keystone Foods for $1.25 billion. Keystone is a top supplier to American fast food chains such as Subway and McDonald's. JBS, now the world's largest meat packer, bought Pilgrim's Pride for $800 million as well as Swift for $1.4 billion. Both of these firms are meat packing operations, which gives JBS a significant exposure in the United States. These acquisitions in large part were made possible by Brazil's national development bank (BNDES), which supports Brazilian firms in developing their international operations. Petrobras, the government-owned oil monopoly, bought a significant interest in Devon Energy's stake in the Gulf of Mexico's Cascade field. Banco do Brasil, a large mostly government-owned Brazilian bank, received a license to open branch banks across the United States and has also begun acquisitions by acquiring a small, Florida-based lender, EuroBank. Banco do Brasil has a presence in 23 countries besides Brazil.

Although acquisitions allow emerging market economies to enter foreign developed country markets as well as industries outside their domestic market, such acquisitions come at a price. The research suggests that emerging economy firms pay a higher premium than other firms. Perhaps these firms feel they have to pay this premium in order to win the deal and persuade regulators that they are not a threat, especially in industries which domestic politics indicate are strategic. For instance, Potash Corporation, a large agro-input firm in Canada, was sought by BHP Billiton, an Australian natural resources firm. However, the deal was quashed by regulatory analysts because it was seen by the Canadian government as a "strategic industry" for their agricultural needs. Much of the research suggests that government ownership leads firms to overpay and that the overpayment reduces value for minority shareholders (nongovernment shareholders). However, much of the deal activity is driven by large reserves in the domestic emerging economies because their currencies have been appreciating relative to the U.S. dollar and the Euro. Many of these acquisitions are also becoming less focused on infrastructure development and more on consumer market acquisitions because the firms can not only extend their power into developed companies, but they can restore technology into their own domestic market, where a large middle class is emerging with consumers having more buying power. It is expected that this trend of acquisitions from emerging economy to developed economy will continue. In 2010, for example, 16 percent of the deals in the United States were from emerging economy participants.

Sources: A. Alves & G. Parra-Bernal, 2011, Update 1-Banco do Brasil may pursue acquisitions in the U.S., *Reuters*, http://www.reuters.com, April 25; R. Buchanan, 2011, Burst of M&A activity keeps bankers busy, *Latin Trade*, January, 57–59; R. Dwyer, 2011, Cross-border M&A: LatAm companies go deal hunting, *EuroMoney*, http://www.euromoney.com, March; O. Hope, W. Thomas, & D. Vyas, 2011, A cost of pride: Why do firms from developing countries bid higher?, *Journal of International Business Studies*, 42(1): 128–151; A. Lobov, 2011, ChemChina and UPL vary routes in M&A race, *AsiaMoney*, http://www.AsiaMoney.com, February 8; R. Samora, 2011, Update 3-JBS says BNDES to nearly double stake to 31 pct, *Reuters*, http://www.reuters.com, May 18; M. Turner, 2011, Emerging markets M&A surges, *Wall Street Journal*, http://www.wsj.com, May 19; P. J. Williamson & A. P. Raman, 2011, How China reset its global acquisition agenda, *Harvard Business Review*, 89(4): 109–114; J. Zhang, C. Zhou, & H. Ebbers, 2011, Completion of Chinese overseas acquisitions: Institutional perspectives and evidence, *International Business Review*, 20(2): 226–238; D. Gross, 2010, Say Bom Dia to Brazilian Business, *Newsweek*, http://www.newsweek.com, June 18; S. Malhotra, Z. PengCheng, & W. Locander, 2010, Impact of host-country corruption on U.S. and Chinese cross-border acquisitions, *Thunderbird International Business Review*, 52(6): 491–507.

As noted in the Strategic Focus, firms headquartered in India are also completing more cross-border acquisitions than in the past. The weak U.S. dollar and more favorable government policies toward cross-border acquisitions are supporting Indian companies' desire to rapidly become more global, although in some cases they are more careful than other emerging market counterparts, such as those found in China.[31] In addition to rapid market entry, Indian companies typically seek access to product innovation capabilities and new brands and distribution channels when acquiring firms outside their domestic market.

Firms using an acquisition strategy to complete cross-border acquisitions should understand that these transactions are not risk free. For example, firms seeking to acquire companies in China must recognize that China remains a challenging environment for foreign investors. Political and legal obstacles make acquisitions in China risky and difficult.[32] Due diligence is problematic as well because corporate governance and transparency of financial statements are often obscure. Thus, firms must carefully study the risks as well as the potential benefits when contemplating cross-border acquisitions.

Learn more about how mergers and acquisitions are handled internationally, specifically in South Africa.

www.cengagebrain.com

Cost of New Product Development and Increased Speed to Market

Developing new products internally and successfully introducing them into the marketplace often requires significant investment of a firm's resources, including time, making it difficult to quickly earn a profitable return.[33] Because an estimated 88 percent of innovations fail to achieve adequate returns, firm managers are also concerned with achieving adequate returns from the capital invested to develop and commercialize new products. Potentially contributing to these less-than-desirable rates of return is the successful imitation of approximately 60 percent of innovations within four years after the patents are obtained. These types of outcomes may lead managers to perceive internal product development as a high-risk activity.[34]

Acquisitions are another means a firm can use to gain access to new products and to current products that are new to the firm. Compared with internal product development processes, acquisitions provide more predictable returns as well as faster market entry. Returns are more predictable because the performance of the acquired firm's products can be assessed prior to completing the acquisition.[35,36]

Medtronic is the world's largest medical device maker with $15.8 billion in sales. While most pharmaceutical firms invent many of their products internally, most of Medtronic's products are acquired from surgeons or other outside inventors. Research confirms that it can be a good strategy to buy early stage products, especially if you have strong R&D capability, even though there is risk and uncertainty in doing so.[37]

A number of pharmaceutical firms use an acquisition strategy besides internal development because of the cost of new product development. Acquisitions can enable firms to enter markets quickly and to increase the predictability of returns on their investments. This strategy is exemplified by Teva Pharmaceuticals' friendly acquisition of Cephalon noted earlier in the chapter.

Lower Risk Compared to Developing New Products

Because the outcomes of an acquisition can be estimated more easily and accurately than the outcomes of an internal product development process, managers may view acquisitions as being less risky.[38] However, firms should exercise caution when using acquisitions to reduce their risks relative to the risks the firm incurs when developing new products internally. Indeed, even though research suggests acquisition strategies are a common means of avoiding risky internal ventures (and therefore risky R&D investments), acquisitions may also become a substitute for innovation. Accordingly, acquisitions should always be strategic rather than defensive in nature. Thus, Teva's acquisition of Cephalon should be driven by strategic factors (e.g., cost and revenue synergies) instead of by defensive reasons (e.g., to gain sales revenue in the short term that will compensate for the revenue that will be lost when Lipitor goes off patent). Moreover, Teva should not reduce its emphasis on increasing the productivity from its R&D expenditures as a result of acquiring Cephalon.

Increased Diversification

Acquisitions are also used to diversify firms. Based on experience and the insights resulting from it, firms typically find it easier to develop and introduce new products in markets they are currently serving. In contrast, it is difficult for companies to develop products that differ from their current lines for markets in which they lack experience.[39] Thus, it is relatively uncommon for a firm to develop new products internally to diversify its product lines.[40]

For example, Xerox purchased Affiliated Computer Services, an outsourcing firm, to bolster its services business. Xerox is seen primarily as a hardware technology company, selling document management equipment. However, over time, Xerox has sought to diversify into helping firms to manage business processes and technology services. As such, through this acquisition it seeks to have more and more of its business in the technology service sector. Ursula Burns, who became CEO of Xerox in 2009, indicated that Xerox is helping firms to focus on their real business while Xerox "takes care of the document-intensive business processes behind the scenes."[41]

Acquisition strategies can be used to support use of both unrelated and related diversification strategies (see Chapter 6).[42] For example, United Technologies Corp. (UTC) uses acquisitions as the foundation for implementing its unrelated diversification strategy. Since the mid-1970s it has been building a portfolio of stable and noncyclical businesses, including Otis Elevator Co. (elevators, escalators, and moving walkways) and Carrier Corporation (heating and air conditioning systems) in order to reduce its dependence on the volatile aerospace industry. Pratt & Whitney (aircraft engines),

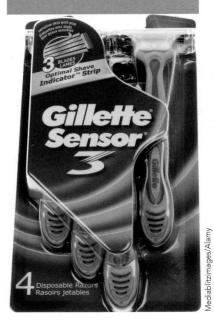

When P&G acquired Gillette, it gained a stronger foothold in the men's razor segment.

Hamilton Sundstrand (aerospace and industrial systems), Sikorsky (helicopters), UTC Fire & Security (fire safety and security products and services), and UTC Power (fuel cells and power systems) are the other businesses in which UTC competes as a result of using its acquisition strategy. While each business UTC acquires manufactures industrial and/or commercial products, many have a relatively low focus on technology (e.g., elevators, air conditioners, and security systems).[43]

In contrast to UTC, Cisco Systems pursues related acquisitions. Historically, these acquisitions have helped the firm build its network components business that is focused on producing network backbone hardware. In 2009, however, Cisco purchased IronPort Systems Inc., a company focused on producing security software for networks. This acquisition helped Cisco diversify its operations beyond its original expertise in network hardware and network management software into network security software. More recent acquisitions have focused on software to facilitate video conferences (the Tandberg acquisition)[44] and helping client firms manage cloud computing applications (the newScale acquisition).[45]

Firms using acquisition strategies should be aware that, in general, the more related the acquired firm is to the acquiring firm, the greater is the probability the acquisition will be successful.[46] Thus, horizontal acquisitions and related acquisitions tend to contribute more to the firm's strategic competitiveness than do acquisitions of companies operating in product markets that are quite different from those in which the acquiring firm competes, although complementary acquisitions in different industries can help expand a firm's capabilities.[47]

Reshaping the Firm's Competitive Scope

As discussed in Chapter 2, the intensity of competitive rivalry is an industry characteristic that affects the firm's profitability.[48] To reduce the negative effect of an intense rivalry on their financial performance, firms may use acquisitions to lessen their dependence on one or more products or markets. Reducing a company's dependence on specific markets shapes the firm's competitive scope.

Each time UTC enters a new business (such as UTC Power, the firm's latest business segment), the corporation reshapes its competitive scope. In a more subtle manner, P&G's acquisition of Gillette reshaped its competitive scope by giving P&G a stronger presence in some products for whom men are the target market. Xerox's purchase of Affiliated Computer Services likewise has reshaped Xerox's competitive scope to focus more on services, and Cisco has become more focused on software through its latest acquisitions. Thus, using an acquisition strategy reshaped the competitive scope of each of these firms.

Learning and Developing New Capabilities

Firms sometimes complete acquisitions to gain access to capabilities they lack. For example, acquisitions may be used to acquire a special technological capability. Research shows that firms can broaden their knowledge base and reduce inertia through acquisitions.[49] For example, research suggests that firms increase the potential of their capabilities when they acquire diverse talent through cross-border acquisitions.[50] Of course, firms are better able to learn these capabilities if they share some similar properties with the firm's current capabilities. Thus, firms should seek to acquire companies with different but related and complementary capabilities in order to build their own knowledge base.[51]

A number of large pharmaceutical firms are acquiring the ability to create "large molecule" drugs, also known as biological drugs, by buying biotechnology firms. Thus, these firms are seeking access to both the pipeline of possible drugs and the capabilities that these firms have to produce them. Such capabilities are important for large pharmaceutical firms because these biological drugs are more difficult to duplicate by chemistry alone (the historical basis on which most pharmaceutical firms have expertise). Biotech firms are focused on DNA research and have a biology base rather than a chemistry base. As an example, Sanofi-Aventis acquired Genzyme for $20 billion. Sanofi's hope is that the biotech company (Genzyme) will help it keep rare-disease drugs in the pipeline without losing sales to more generic competition (those drugs that have lost patent protection). It is critical in an acquisition such as this that Sanofi keep experimental drug projects moving forward, and this requires that science-based and research-oriented employees stay in the merged firm. Sanofi hopes to transfer Genzyme's expertise in genetics and biomarkers back to Sanofi. Such biomarkers "are biological substances in the body that help show the body is responding to disease and medication."[52] If the acquisition is successful, there is added competitive advantage. Biological drugs must clear more regulatory barriers or hurdles which, when accomplished, add more to the advantage the acquiring firm develops through such acquisitions.

Problems in Achieving Acquisition Success

Acquisition strategies based on reasons described in this chapter can increase strategic competitiveness and help firms earn above-average returns. However, even when pursued for value-creating reasons, acquisition strategies are not problem-free. Reasons for the use of acquisition strategies and potential problems with such strategies are shown in Figure 7.1.

Figure 7.1 Reasons for Acquisitions and Problems in Achieving Success

© 2013 Cengage Learning.

Research suggests that perhaps 20 percent of all mergers and acquisitions are successful, approximately 60 percent produce disappointing results, and the remaining 20 percent are clear failures; evidence on technology acquisitions reports even higher failure rates.[53] In general, though, companies appear to be increasing their ability to effectively use acquisition strategies. One analyst suggests that "Accenture research and subsequent work with clients show that half of large corporate mergers create at least marginal returns—an improvement from a decade ago, when many studies concluded that as many as three-quarters of all mergers destroyed shareholder value as measured two years after the merger announcement."[54] Greater acquisition success accrues to firms able to (1) select the "right" target, (2) avoid paying too high a premium (doing appropriate due diligence), and (3) effectively integrate the operations of the acquiring and target firms.[55] In addition, retaining the target firm's human capital, as illustrated by

Facebook's approach described in the opening case, is foundational to efforts by employees of the acquiring firm to fully understand the target firm's operations and the capabilities on which those operations are based.[56] The Sanofi-Aventis acquisition of Genzyme noted above is an example of the importance of retaining the right employees. As shown in Figure 7.1, several problems may prevent successful acquisitions.

Integration Difficulties

The importance of a successful integration should not be underestimated.[57] As suggested by a researcher studying the process, "Managerial practice and academic writings show that the post-acquisition integration phase is probably the single most important determinant of shareholder value creation (and equally of value destruction) in mergers and acquisitions."[58]

Although critical to acquisition success, firms should recognize that integrating two companies following an acquisition can be quite difficult. Melding two corporate cultures, linking different financial and control systems, building effective working relationships (particularly when management styles differ), and resolving problems regarding the status of the newly acquired firm's executives are examples of integration challenges firms often face.[59]

Integration is complex and involves a large number of activities, which if overlooked can lead to significant difficulties.[60] For example, when United Parcel Service (UPS) acquired Mail Boxes Etc., a large retail shipping chain, it appeared to be a merger that would generate benefits for both firms. The problem is that most of the Mail Boxes Etc. outlets were owned by franchisees. Following the merger, the franchisees lost the ability to deal with other shipping companies such as FedEx, which reduced their competitiveness. Furthermore, franchisees complained that UPS often built company-owned shipping stores close by franchisee outlets of Mail Boxes Etc. Additionally, a culture clash evolved between the free-wheeling entrepreneurs who owned the franchises of Mail Boxes Etc. and the efficiency-oriented corporate approach of the UPS operation, which focused on managing a large fleet of trucks and an information system to efficiently pick up and deliver packages. Also, Mail Boxes Etc. was focused on retail traffic, whereas UPS was focused more on the logistics of wholesale pickup and delivery. Although 87 percent of Mail Boxes Etc. franchisees decided to rebrand under the UPS name, many formed an owner's group and even filed suit against UPS in regard to the unfavorable nature of the franchisee contract.[61]

Inadequate Evaluation of Target

Due diligence is a process through which a potential acquirer evaluates a target firm for acquisition. In an effective due-diligence process, hundreds of items are examined in areas as diverse as the financing for the intended transaction, differences in cultures between the acquiring and target firm, tax consequences of the transaction, and actions that would be necessary to successfully meld the two workforces. Due diligence is commonly performed by investment bankers such as Deutsche Bank, Goldman Sachs, and Morgan Stanley, as well as accountants, lawyers, and management consultants specializing in that activity, although firms actively pursuing acquisitions may form their own internal due-diligence team. Although due diligence often focuses on evaluating the accuracy of the financial position and accounting standards used (a financial audit), due diligence also needs to examine the quality of the strategic fit and the ability of the acquiring firm to effectively integrate the target to realize the potential gains from the deal.[62]

The failure to complete an effective due-diligence process may easily result in the acquiring firm paying an excessive premium for the target company. Interestingly, research shows that in times of high or increasing stock prices due diligence is relaxed; firms often overpay during these periods and long-run performance of the newly formed firm suffers.[63] Research also shows that without due diligence, "the purchase price is

This group of experts begins the laborious due diligence process.

David Young-Wolff/PhotoEdit

driven by the pricing of other 'comparable' acquisitions rather than by a rigorous assessment of where, when, and how management can drive real performance gains. [In these cases], the price paid may have little to do with achievable value."[64]

In addition, firms sometimes allow themselves to enter a "bidding war" for a target, even though they realize that their current bids exceed the parameters identified through due diligence. Earlier, we mentioned Valeant Pharmaceutical's bid for Cephalon at 24 percent versus the winning bid by Teva at a 30 percent premium. We cannot be sure that Teva overpaid, but the point is that rather than enter a bidding war, firms should only extend bids that are consistent with the results of their due-diligence process. It could be that Cephalon will provide Teva with a new platform for growth and over time this deal will look cheap, but the key is doing a strategic analysis along with rational due diligence so that both the strategic fit and financials make sense.[65]

Large or Extraordinary Debt

To finance a number of acquisitions completed during the 1980s and 1990s, some companies significantly increased their levels of debt. A financial innovation called junk bonds helped make this possible. *Junk bonds* are a financing option through which risky acquisitions are financed with money (debt) that provides a large potential return to lenders (bondholders). Because junk bonds are unsecured obligations that are not tied to specific assets for collateral, interest rates for these high-risk debt instruments sometimes reached between 18 and 20 percent during the 1980s.[66] Some prominent financial economists viewed debt as a means to discipline managers, causing them to act in the shareholders' best interests.[67] Managers holding this view are less concerned about the amount of debt their firm assumes when acquiring other companies.

Junk bonds are now used less frequently to finance acquisitions, and the conviction that debt disciplines managers is less strong.[68] Nonetheless, firms sometimes still take on what turns out to be too much debt when acquiring companies. Caterpillar, Inc., betting on a long-term boom and global demand for mining equipment, purchased Bucyrus International, Inc., a maker of mining equipment, for $7.6 billion in 2011. Rapid growth in emerging economies such as China, India, Brazil, and other developing economies over the next decade will push demand for coal, copper, iron ore, and "everything that comes out of the ground."[69] Caterpillar paid a 32 percent premium for Bucyrus. Furthermore, Bucyrus bought Terex Corp. for $1.3 billion in February 2010. Bucyrus's debt, because of previous acquisitions, is significant and will force Caterpillar not only to issue new stock but absorb this additional debt. As noted earlier, firms often pay rich premiums and possibly "overpay," partly because they have to take on additional debt. This has happened before—Bucyrus went through a leveraged buyout and had to file for bankruptcy in the mid-1990s because it took on more debt than it could handle at the time. Because of the assumption of debt for this deal, the price tag increased from $7.6 to $8.6 billion. As such, this is a significant increase in the premium noted earlier because of the assumption of debt.[70] Thus, firms using an acquisition strategy must be certain that their purchases do not create a debt load that overpowers the company's ability to remain solvent.

Inability to Achieve Synergy

Derived from *synergos,* a Greek word that means "working together," *synergy* exists when the value created by units working together exceeds the value those units could create working independently (see Chapter 6). That is, synergy exists when assets are worth more when used in conjunction with each other than when they are used separately. For shareholders, synergy generates gains in their wealth that they could not duplicate or exceed through their own portfolio diversification decisions.[71] Synergy is created by the efficiencies derived from economies of scale and economies of scope and by sharing resources (e.g., human capital and knowledge) across the businesses in the merged firm.[72]

A firm develops a competitive advantage through an acquisition strategy only when a transaction generates private synergy. *Private synergy* is created when combining and integrating the acquiring and acquired firms' assets, yield capabilities, and core competencies that could not be developed by combining and integrating either firm's assets with another company. Private synergy is possible when firms' assets are complementary in unique ways; that is, the unique type of asset complementarity is not possible by combining either company's assets with another firm's assets.[73] Because of its uniqueness, private synergy is difficult for competitors to understand and imitate. However, private synergy is difficult to create.

A firm's ability to account for costs that are necessary to create anticipated revenue- and cost-based synergies affects its efforts to create private synergy. Firms experience several expenses when trying to create private synergy through acquisitions. Called transaction costs, these expenses are incurred when firms use acquisition strategies to create synergy.[74] Transaction costs may be direct or indirect. Direct costs include legal fees and charges from investment bankers who complete due diligence for the acquiring firm. Indirect costs include managerial time to evaluate target firms and then to complete negotiations, as well as the loss of key managers and employees following an acquisition.[75] Firms tend to underestimate the sum of indirect costs when the value of the synergy that may be created by combining and integrating the acquired firm's assets with the acquiring firm's assets is calculated.

Too Much Diversification

As explained in Chapter 6, diversification strategies can lead to strategic competitiveness and above-average returns. In general, firms using related diversification strategies outperform those employing unrelated diversification strategies. However, conglomerates formed by using an unrelated diversification strategy also can be successful, as demonstrated by United Technologies Corp.

At some point, however, firms can become overdiversified. The level at which overdiversification occurs varies across companies because each firm has different capabilities to manage diversification. Recall from Chapter 6 that related diversification requires more information processing than does unrelated diversification. Because of this additional information processing, related diversified firms become overdiversified with a smaller number of business units than do firms using an unrelated diversification strategy.[76] Regardless of the type of diversification strategy implemented, however, overdiversification leads to a decline in performance, after which business units are often divested.[77] Commonly, such divestments, which tend to reshape a firm's competitive scope, are part of a firm's restructuring strategy. (We discuss the strategy in greater detail later in the chapter.)

Even when a firm is not overdiversified, a high level of diversification can have a negative effect on its long-term performance. For example, the scope created by additional amounts of diversification often causes managers to rely on financial rather than strategic controls to evaluate business units' performance (we define and explain financial and strategic controls in Chapters 11 and 12). Top-level executives often rely on financial controls to assess the performance of business units when they do not have a rich understanding of business units' objectives and strategies. Using financial controls, such as return on investment (ROI), causes individual business-unit managers to focus on short-term outcomes at the expense of long-term investments. When long-term investments are reduced to increase short-term profits, a firm's overall strategic competitiveness may be harmed.[78]

Another problem resulting from too much diversification is the tendency for acquisitions to become substitutes for innovation. As we noted earlier, pharmaceutical firms such as Teva Pharmaceutical must be aware of this tendency as they acquire other firms to gain access to their products and capabilities. Typically, managers have no interest in acquisitions substituting for internal R&D efforts and the innovative outcomes that they can produce. However, a reinforcing cycle evolves. Costs associated with acquisitions may result in fewer allocations to activities, such as R&D, that are linked to innovation. Without adequate support, a firm's innovation skills begin to atrophy. Without internal innovation skills, the only option available to a firm to gain access to innovation is to complete still more acquisitions. Evidence suggests that a firm using acquisitions as a substitute for internal innovations eventually encounters performance problems.[79]

Managers Overly Focused on Acquisitions

Typically, a considerable amount of managerial time and energy is required for acquisition strategies to be used successfully. Activities with which managers become involved include (1) searching for viable acquisition candidates, (2) completing effective due-diligence processes, (3) preparing for negotiations, and (4) managing the integration process after completing the acquisition.

Top-level managers do not personally gather all of the data and information required to make acquisitions. However, these executives do make critical decisions on the firms to be targeted, the nature of the negotiations, and so forth. Company experiences show that participating in and overseeing the activities required for making acquisitions can divert managerial attention from other matters that are necessary for long-term competitive success, such as identifying and taking advantage of other opportunities and interacting with important external stakeholders.[80]

Both theory and research suggest that managers can become overly involved in the process of making acquisitions.[81] One observer suggested, "Some executives can become preoccupied with making deals—and the thrill of selecting, chasing and seizing a target."[82] The overinvolvement can be surmounted by learning from mistakes and by not having too much agreement in the boardroom. Dissent is helpful to make sure that all sides of a question are considered (see Chapter 10).[83] When failure does occur, leaders may be tempted to blame the failure on others and on unforeseen circumstances rather than on their excessive involvement in the acquisition process.

The acquisitions strategy of Citigroup is a case in point. In 1998, Citigroup's CEO John Reed in a merger between Citicorp and Travelers Group (CEO Sanford I. Weill) set out to cross-sell financial services to the same customer and thereby reduce sales costs. Weill ultimately became the CEO. To accomplish this goal, the merged firm focused on a set of acquisitions including insurance and private equity investing beyond traditional banking services. However, as noted by one commentator, "More than once, ambitious executives, such as Sanford Weill of Citigroup fame, have assembled 'financial supermarkets,' and thinking that customers' needs for credit cards, checking accounts, wealth management services, insurance, and stock brokerage could be furnished most efficiently and effectively by the same company. Those efforts have failed, over and over again. Each function fulfills a different job that arises at a different point in a customer's life, so a single source for all of them holds no advantage."[84] As outlined in the Strategic Focus, Vikram Pandit, the CEO who took over after Charles Prince at Citigroup, was forced to sell off a lot of those peripheral financial service businesses.

STRATEGIC FOCUS

THE ACQUISITIONS AND MERGERS TO FORM CITIGROUP: DIVESTITURES ASSOCIATED WITH THE FAILED CONCEPT OF THE FINANCIAL SUPERMARKET

Citigroup was formed through a $76 billion merger between Travelers Group and Citicorp in 1998. Sanford I. Weill (Travelers) and John S. Reed (Citicorp), the two CEOs at the time, expected that Congress would soon pass legislation overturning the Glass-Steagall Act, which kept banking and insurance businesses separate. They foresaw developing "the financial supermarket," serving every financial need of consumers and businesses. In 2002, with a significant downturn in Citigroup's stock price, Well retired. Through a search process, Charles Prince became the CEO of Citigroup in 2003. Vikram Pandit became the CEO of Citigroup just before the 2008 recession. In the midst of the recession, there was severe criticism of the "financial supermarket" concept, and many businesses were scheduled for sale as Citigroup restructured its operations to focus on more traditional consumer banking and investment banking focused on institutional and business clients. In fact, a part of Travelers Group had already been spun off in 2002 because it was harming Citigroup's earnings. As part of this more recent restructuring program, Pandit orchestrated a division of Citigroup's assets into two large camps, one focused on the traditional businesses as noted and another, called Citi Holdings, consisting of businesses that were up for sale as part of the restructuring effort.

Manuel Balce Ceneta/AP Photos

State Street Corporation, Morgan Stanley, Citigroup, and Wells Fargo CEOs testify on Capitol Hill in Washington before the House Financial Services Committee.

On December 31, 2010, Citigroup announced that it had sold both its Discover Financial Services and its student loan corporation, which capped $31 billion in the last quarter of 2010. Citi Holdings' CEO Michael Corbat, a former Salomon Brothers executive, said Citigroup wanted to "get these assets out the door" but that it "is not a distress seller." Besides the $31 billion in the final quarter, $168 billion of combined assets had already been sold in 2009. This included the 51 percent stake that Citigroup held in the Smith Barney brokerage in a joint venture with Morgan Stanley. Another business that has not totally been sold is CitiFinancial, which focuses on providing commercial credit to subprime borrowers. Another approach it used was to do a spin-off of Primerica, the company with most of Citigroup's insurance holdings, through an IPO in combination with Warburg Pincus LLC (a private equity partnership), although Citigroup maintained $7 billion in insurance assets because they generate steady cash flows.

Citigroup has also sold some of its private equity assets, even though these assets are part of its investment bank group. The Citigroup private equity operation manages many other businesses that are not in financial services. Some of these assets are in partnership with other private equity firms such as CVC Capital Partners Ltd.

Although part of the divestiture activity can be accounted for because of the financial crisis, another part is due to the media attention that Citigroup received from taking $45 billion in bailout funds from the U.S. government at the peak of the crisis to stave off possible bankruptcy. With this receipt of additional capital came tighter regulations that ultimately required re-separation of consumer banking and investment banking. Furthermore, Citigroup's every move was scrutinized by both the government and the media. Ultimately, Citigroup paid back the funds to the U.S. government but is still focused on restructuring its businesses in order to not only focus on "core areas" in banking but also to meet new, stricter regulatory requirements.

ETHICS • ETHICS • ETHICS • ETHICS • ETHICS • ETHICS

At the height of the crisis, bankers' salaries, including that of CEO Pandit, received significant scrutiny. Given the significant media attention and government criticism, Pandit requested that the board reduce his salary to $1 a year until Citigroup's performance improved; however, the board had already set his salary at $1.75 million. The board thought his work was done well but had to justify the $10 million in restricted stock that he received in 2011. To realize this incentive, he has to meet certain income targets as well as manage the ongoing organizational restructuring and staffing goals.

In summary, through the history of Citigroup one can see that pursuing a concept that creates a firm that is overly diversified relative to its core businesses, too large to manage effectively, and too diversified such that it lacks the synergy to cross-sell products leads to significant devaluation for stockholders, especially during a financial crisis when multiple problems are revealed simultaneously. This was certainly the case for Citigroup during the crisis, and as such, it had to restructure itself into a much smaller, though global, business financial service firm. Although Citigroup is still involved in many financial services sectors, those that will remain after the refocusing of Citi Holdings is complete will be much more solidly focused on its main businesses, consumer and investment banking. However, it may be that due to the increased financial regulation that its profits from trading will not be as great; because the opportunities for financial service firms will be scrutinized more intensely by the media and government officials, it is likely that less trading risk will be undertaken.

Sources: 2011, Brand in the news: Egg, *Marketing*, March 9, 7; 2011, Citi to sell its Egg credit card portfolio to Barclays Bank plc, http://www.citigroup.com, March 1; J. Hughes, 2011, The short view, *Financial Times*, April 20, 17; M. Rieker, 2011, Citigroup sets big retention award for CEO Pandit, *Wall Street Journal*, http://www.wsj.com, May 18; 2010, Citicorp redux, *Economist*, August 14, 63; D. McDonald, 2010, Catching up with Jamie Dimon, *Fortune*, November 1, 20; L. Moyer & D. Fisher, 2010, Too big to thrive? *Forbes*, May 24, 24; R. Smith, 2010, Citigroup's yard sales slows its turnaround. Bank, under Pandit, toils to sell off unwanted assets, *Wall Street Journal*, March 25, C1; R. Smith & R. Sidel, 2010, Citi sheds its student-loan business, *Wall Street Journal*, September 18, B3; M. Rieker, 2010, Citigroup divestiture progress of Citi Holdings stays strong, http://www.advfn.com, February 1.

STRATEGY RIGHT NOW

Learn more about Discover Financial Services' acquisitions.

www.cengagebrain.com

Too Large

Most acquisitions create a larger firm, which should help increase its economies of scale. These economies can then lead to more efficient operations—for example, two sales organizations can be integrated using fewer sales representatives because such sales personnel can sell the products of both firms (particularly if the products of the acquiring and target firms are highly related).[85] As illustrated by the Strategic Focus on Citigroup, size can also increase the complexity of the management challenge and create diseconomies of scope; that is, not enough economic benefit to outweigh the costs of managing the more complex organization created through acquisitions. This was also the case of the failed merger between DaimlerChrysler and Mitsubishi; it became too costly to integrate the operations of Mitsubishi to derive the necessary benefits of economies of scale in the merged firm.[86]

Many firms seek increases in size because of the potential economies of scale and enhanced market power (discussed earlier). At some level, the additional costs required to manage the larger firm will exceed the benefits of the economies of scale and additional market power. The complexities generated by the larger size often lead managers to implement more bureaucratic controls to manage the combined firm's operations. *Bureaucratic controls* are formalized supervisory and behavioral rules and policies designed to ensure consistency of decisions and actions across different units of a firm. However, through time, formalized controls often lead to relatively rigid and standardized managerial behavior.[87] Certainly, in the long run, the diminished flexibility that accompanies rigid and standardized managerial behavior may produce less innovation. Because of innovation's importance to competitive success, the bureaucratic controls resulting from a large organization (i.e., built by acquisitions) can have a detrimental effect on performance. For this reason, Cisco announced an internal restructuring to reduce bureaucracy after its numerous acquisitions; "it will dispense with most of a network of internal councils and associated boards that have been criticized for adding layers of bureaucracy and wasting managers' time."[88] As one analyst noted, "Striving for size per se is not necessarily going to make a company more successful. In fact, a strategy in which acquisitions are undertaken as a substitute for organic growth has a bad track record in terms of adding value."[89]

Effective Acquisitions

Earlier in the chapter, we noted that acquisition strategies do not always lead to above-average returns for the acquiring firm's shareholders.[90] Nonetheless, some companies are able to create value when using an acquisition strategy.[91] The probability of success increases when the firm's actions are consistent with the "attributes of successful acquisitions" shown in Table 7.1.

Cisco Systems appears to pay close attention to Table 7.1's attributes when using its acquisition strategy. In fact, Cisco is admired for its ability to complete successful acquisitions and integrate them quickly, although as noted this has created a larger firm.[92] A number of other network companies pursued acquisitions to build up their ability to sell into the network equipment binge, but only Cisco retained much of its value in the post-bubble era. Many firms, such as Lucent, Nortel, and Ericsson, teetered on the edge of bankruptcy after the dot-com bubble burst. When it makes an acquisition, "Cisco has gone much further in its thinking about integration. Not only is retention important, but Cisco also works to minimize the distractions caused by an acquisition. This is important, because the speed of change is so great that if the target firm's product development teams are distracted, they will be slowed, contributing to

Table 7.1 Attributes of Successful Acquisitions

Attributes	Results
1. Acquired firm has assets or resources that are complementary to the acquiring firm's core business	1. High probability of synergy and competitive advantage by maintaining strengths
2. Acquisition is friendly	2. Faster and more effective integration and possibly lower premiums
3. Acquiring firm conducts effective due diligence to select target firms and evaluate the target firm's health (financial, cultural, and human resources)	3. Firms with strongest complementarities are acquired and overpayment is avoided
4. Acquiring firm has financial slack (cash or a favorable debt position)	4. Financing (debt or equity) is easier and less costly to obtain
5. Merged firm maintains low to moderate debt position	5. Lower financing cost, lower risk (e.g., of bankruptcy), and avoidance of trade-offs that are associated with high debt
6. Acquiring firm has sustained and consistent emphasis on R&D and innovation	6. Maintain long-term competitive advantage in markets
7. Acquiring firm manages change well and is flexible and adaptable	7. Faster and more effective integration facilitates achievement of synergy

acquisition failure. So, integration must be rapid and reassuring."[93] For example, Cisco facilitates acquired employees' transitions to their new organization through a link on its Web site called "Cisco Acquisition Connection." This Web site has been specifically designed for newly acquired employees and provides up-to-date materials tailored to their new jobs.[94]

Results from a research study shed light on the differences between unsuccessful and successful acquisition strategies and suggest that a pattern of actions improves the probability of acquisition success.[95] The study shows that when the target firm's assets are complementary to the acquired firm's assets, an acquisition is more successful. With complementary assets, the integration of two firms' operations has a higher probability of creating synergy. In fact, integrating two firms with complementary assets frequently produces unique capabilities and core competencies. With complementary assets, the acquiring firm can maintain its focus on core businesses and leverage the complementary assets and capabilities from the acquired firm. In effective acquisitions, targets are often selected and "groomed" by establishing a working relationship prior to the acquisition.[96] As discussed in Chapter 9, strategic alliances are sometimes used to test the feasibility of a future merger or acquisition between the involved firms.[97]

The study's results also show that friendly acquisitions facilitate integration of the firms involved in an acquisition. Through friendly acquisitions, firms work together to find ways to integrate their operations to create synergy.[98] In hostile takeovers, animosity often results between the two top-management teams, a condition that in turn affects working relationships in the newly created firm. As a result, more key personnel in the acquired firm may be lost, and those who remain may resist the changes necessary to integrate the two firms.[99] With effort, cultural clashes can be overcome, and fewer key managers and employees will become discouraged and leave.[100]

Additionally, effective due-diligence processes involving the deliberate and careful selection of target firms and an evaluation of the relative health of those firms (financial health, cultural fit, and the value of human resources) contribute to successful acquisitions.[101] Financial slack in the form of debt equity or cash, in both the acquiring and acquired firms, also frequently contributes to acquisition success. Even though financial slack provides access to financing for the acquisition, it is still important to maintain a low or moderate level of debt after the acquisition to keep debt costs low. When substantial debt was used to finance the acquisition, companies with successful acquisitions reduced the debt quickly, partly by selling off assets from the acquired firm, especially noncomplementary or poorly performing assets. For these firms, debt costs do not prevent long-term investments such as R&D, and managerial discretion in the use of cash flow is relatively flexible.

Another attribute of successful acquisition strategies is an emphasis on innovation, as demonstrated by continuing investments in R&D activities.[102] Significant R&D investments show a strong managerial commitment to innovation, a characteristic that is increasingly important to overall competitiveness in the global economy as well as to acquisition success.

Flexibility and adaptability are the final two attributes of successful acquisitions. When executives of both the acquiring and the target firms have experience in managing change and learning from acquisitions, they will be more skilled at adapting their capabilities to new environments.[103] As a result, they will be more adept at integrating the two organizations, which is particularly important when firms have different organizational cultures.

As we have learned, firms use an acquisition strategy to grow and achieve strategic competitiveness. Sometimes, though, the actual results of an acquisition strategy fall short of the projected results. When this happens, firms consider using restructuring strategies.

Restructuring

Restructuring is a strategy through which a firm changes its set of businesses or its financial structure.[104] Restructuring is a global phenomenon.[105] From the 1970s into the 2000s, divesting businesses from company portfolios and downsizing accounted for a large percentage of firms' restructuring strategies. Commonly, firms focus on a fewer number of products and markets following restructuring. The words of an executive describe this typical outcome: "Focus on your core business, but don't be distracted, let other people buy assets that aren't right for you."[106]

Although restructuring strategies are generally used to deal with acquisitions that are not reaching expectations, firms sometimes use these strategies because of changes they have detected in their external environment.[107] For example, opportunities sometimes surface in a firm's external environment that a diversified firm can pursue because of the capabilities it has formed by integrating firms' operations. In such cases, restructuring may be appropriate to position the firm to create more value for stakeholders, given the environmental changes.[108] This seems to be the case with the restructuring of Citigroup noted in the Strategic Focus.

As discussed next, firms use three types of restructuring strategies: downsizing, downscoping, and leveraged buyouts.

Downsizing

Downsizing is a reduction in the number of a firm's employees and, sometimes, in the number of its operating units, but it may or may not change the composition of businesses in the company's portfolio. Thus, downsizing is an intentional proactive management strategy whereas "decline is an environmental or organizational phenomenon that occurs involuntarily and results in erosion of an organization's resource base."[109] Downsizing is often a part of acquisitions that fail to create the value anticipated when the transaction was completed. Downsizing is often used when the acquiring firm paid too high of a premium to acquire the target firm.[110] Once thought to be an indicator of organizational decline, downsizing is now recognized as a legitimate restructuring strategy.

Reducing the number of employees and/or the firm's scope in terms of products produced and markets served occurs in firms to enhance the value being created as a result of completing an acquisition. When integrating the operations of the acquired firm and the acquiring firm, managers may not at first appropriately downsize. This is understandable in that "no one likes to lay people off or close facilities."[111] However, downsizing may be necessary because acquisitions often create a situation in which the newly formed firm has duplicate organizational functions such as sales, manufacturing, distribution, human resource management, and so forth. Failing to downsize appropriately may lead to too many employees doing the same work and prevent the new firm from realizing the cost synergies it anticipated. Managers should remember that as a strategy, downsizing will be far more effective when they consistently use human resource practices that ensure procedural justice and fairness in downsizing decisions.[112]

Downscoping

Downscoping refers to divestiture, spin-off, or some other means of eliminating businesses that are unrelated to a firm's core businesses. Downscoping has a more positive effect on firm performance than does downsizing[113] because firms commonly find that downscoping causes them to refocus on their core business.[114] Managerial effectiveness increases because the firm has become less diversified, allowing the top management team to better understand and manage the remaining businesses.[115] Interestingly, sometimes the divested unit can also take advantage of unforeseen opportunities not recognized while under the leadership of the parent firm.[116]

Restructuring is a strategy through which a firm changes its set of businesses or its financial structure.

Firms often use the downscoping and the downsizing strategies simultaneously. In Citigroup's restructuring (see the Strategic Focus) it has used both downscoping and downsizing, as have many large financial institutions in the recession.[117] However, when doing this, firms need to avoid layoffs of key employees, as such layoffs might lead to a loss of one or more core competencies. Instead, a firm that is simultaneously downscoping and downsizing becomes smaller by reducing the diversity of businesses in its portfolio.[118]

In general, U.S. firms use downscoping as a restructuring strategy more frequently than do European companies—in fact, the trend in Europe, Latin America, and Asia has been to build conglomerates. In Latin America, these conglomerates are called *grupos*. Many Asian and Latin American conglomerates have begun to adopt Western corporate strategies in recent years and have been refocusing on their core businesses. This downscoping has occurred simultaneously with increasing globalization and with more open markets that have greatly enhanced competition. By downscoping, these firms have been able to focus on their core businesses and improve their competitiveness.[119]

Leveraged Buyouts

A *leveraged buyout* (LBO) is a restructuring strategy whereby a party (typically a private equity firm) buys all of a firm's assets in order to take the firm private. Once the transaction is completed, the company's stock is no longer traded publicly. Traditionally, leveraged buyouts were used as a restructuring strategy to correct for managerial mistakes or because the firm's managers were making decisions that primarily served their own interests rather than those of shareholders.[120] However, some firms use buyouts to build firm resources and expand rather than simply restructure distressed assets.[121]

After a firm is taken over by a private equity firm, such acquired firms are free to do "add-on" or "role-up" acquisitions to build the businesses from the base platform of a single acquisition. For example, Roark Capital Partners, a private equity firm, launched Focus Brands in 2004 through acquiring Cinnabon and Seattle's Best Coffee International, niche franchise food service concepts, from AFC Enterprises. "Carvel, an existing portfolio company, was rolled into the platform and subsequent acquisitions included Schlotzky's, Moe's Southwest Grill and most recently, Auntie Anne's."[122]

However, significant amounts of debt are commonly incurred to finance a buyout; hence the term *leveraged* buyout. To support debt payments and to downscope the company to concentrate on the firm's core businesses, the new owners may immediately sell a number of assets.[123] It is not uncommon for those buying a firm through an LBO to restructure the firm to the point that it can be sold at a profit within a five- to eight-year period.

Management buyouts (MBOs), employee buyouts (EBOs), and whole-firm buyouts, in which one company or partnership purchases an entire company instead of a part of it, are the three types of LBOs. In part because of managerial incentives, MBOs, more so than EBOs and whole-firm buyouts, have been found to lead to downscoping, increased strategic focus, and improved performance.[124] Research shows that management buyouts can lead to greater entrepreneurial activity and growth.[125] As such, buyouts can represent a form of firm rebirth to facilitate entrepreneurial efforts and stimulate strategic growth and productivity.[126]

Restructuring Outcomes

The short- and long-term outcomes associated with the three restructuring strategies are shown in Figure 7.2. As indicated, downsizing typically does not lead to higher firm performance.[127] In fact, some research results show that downsizing contributes to lower returns for both U.S. and Japanese firms. The stock markets in the firms' respective nations evaluated downsizing negatively, believing that it would have long-term negative effects on the firms' efforts to achieve strategic competitiveness. Investors also seem to

Figure 7.2 Restructuring and Outcomes

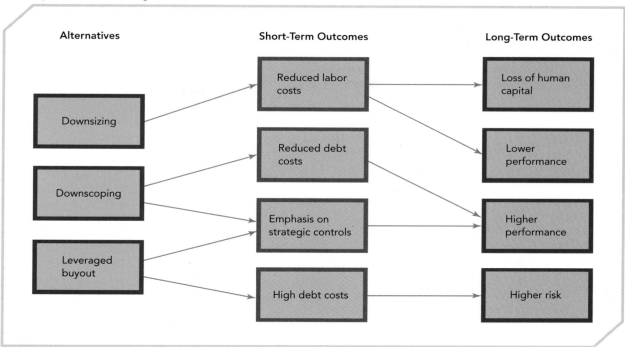

© 2013 Cengage Learning.

conclude that downsizing occurs as a consequence of other problems in a company.[128] This assumption may be caused by a firm's diminished corporate reputation when a major downsizing is announced.[129]

The loss of human capital is another potential problem of downsizing (see Figure 7.2). Losing employees with many years of experience with the firm represents a major loss of knowledge. As noted in Chapter 3, knowledge is vital to competitive success in the global economy. Research also suggests that such loss of human capital can also spill over into dissatisfaction of customers.[130] Thus, in general, research evidence and corporate experience suggest that downsizing may be of more tactical (or short-term) value than strategic (or long-term) value,[131] meaning that firms should exercise caution when restructuring through downsizing.

Downscoping generally leads to more positive outcomes in both the short and long term than does downsizing or a leveraged buyout. Downscoping's desirable long-term outcome of higher performance is a product of reduced debt costs and the emphasis on strategic controls derived from concentrating on the firm's core businesses. In so doing, the refocused firm should be able to increase its ability to compete.[132]

Although whole-firm LBOs have been hailed as a significant innovation in the financial restructuring of firms, they can involve negative trade-offs.[133] First, the resulting large debt increases the firm's financial risk, as is evidenced by the number of companies that filed for bankruptcy in the 1990s after executing a whole-firm LBO. Sometimes, the intent of the owners to increase the efficiency of the bought-out firm and then sell it within five to eight years creates a short-term and risk-averse managerial focus.[134] As a result, these firms may fail to invest adequately in R&D or take other major actions designed to maintain or improve the company's core competence.[135] Research also suggests that in firms with an entrepreneurial mind-set, buyouts can lead to greater innovation, especially if the debt load is not too great.[136] However, because buyouts more often result in significant debt, most LBOs have been completed in mature industries where stable cash flows are possible.

SUMMARY

- Although the number of mergers and acquisitions completed declined in 2008 and 2009, largely because of the global financial crisis, merger and acquisition strategies became more frequent in 2010 and 2011, as a path to firm growth and earning strategic competitiveness. Globalization and deregulation of multiple industries in many economies are two of the factors making mergers and acquisitions attractive to large corporations and small firms.

- Firms use acquisition strategies to (1) increase market power, (2) overcome entry barriers to new markets or regions, (3) avoid the costs of developing new products and increase the speed of new market entries, (4) reduce the risk of entering a new business, (5) become more diversified, (6) reshape their competitive scope by developing a different portfolio of businesses, and (7) enhance their learning as the foundation for developing new capabilities.

- Among the problems associated with using an acquisition strategy are (1) the difficulty of effectively integrating the firms involved, (2) incorrectly evaluating the target firm's value, (3) creating debt loads that preclude adequate long-term investments (e.g., R&D), (4) overestimating the potential for synergy, (5) creating a firm that is too diversified, (6) creating an internal environment in which managers devote increasing amounts of their time and energy to analyzing and completing the acquisition, and (7) developing a combined firm that is too large, necessitating extensive use of bureaucratic, rather than strategic, controls.

- Effective acquisitions have the following characteristics: (1) the acquiring and target firms have complementary resources that are the foundation for developing new capabilities; (2) the acquisition is friendly, thereby facilitating integration of the firms' resources; (3) the target firm is selected and purchased based on thorough due diligence;

(4) the acquiring and target firms have considerable slack in the form of cash or debt capacity; (5) the newly formed firm maintains a low or moderate level of debt by selling off portions of the acquired firm or some of the acquiring firm's poorly performing units; (6) the acquiring and acquired firms have experience in terms of adapting to change; and (7) R&D and innovation are emphasized in the new firm.

- Restructuring is used to improve a firm's performance by correcting for problems created by ineffective management. Restructuring by downsizing involves reducing the number of employees and hierarchical levels in the firm. Although it can lead to short-term cost reductions, they may be realized at the expense of long-term success, because of the loss of valuable human resources (and knowledge) and overall corporate reputation.

- The goal of restructuring through downscoping is to reduce the firm's level of diversification. Often, the firm divests unrelated businesses to achieve this goal. Eliminating unrelated businesses makes it easier for the firm and its top-level managers to refocus on the core businesses.

- Through an LBO, a firm is purchased so that it can become a private entity. LBOs usually are financed largely through debt. Management buyouts (MBOs), employee buyouts (EBOs), and whole-firm LBOs are the three types of LBOs. Because they provide clear managerial incentives, MBOs have been the most successful of the three. Often, the intent of a buyout is to improve efficiency and performance to the point where the firm can be sold successfully within five to eight years.

- Commonly, restructuring's primary goal is gaining or reestablishing effective strategic control of the firm. Of the three restructuring strategies, downscoping is aligned most closely with establishing and using strategic controls and usually improves performance more on a comparative basis.

REVIEW QUESTIONS

1. Why are merger and acquisition strategies popular in many firms competing in the global economy?

2. What reasons account for firms' decisions to use acquisition strategies as a means to achieving strategic competitiveness?

3. What are the seven primary problems that affect a firm's efforts to successfully use an acquisition strategy?

4. What are the attributes associated with a successful acquisition strategy?

5. What is the restructuring strategy, and what are its common forms?

6. What are the short- and long-term outcomes associated with the different restructuring strategies?

EXPERIENTIAL EXERCISES

EXERCISE 1: HOW DID THE DEAL WORK OUT?:

The text argues that mergers and acquisitions are a popular strategy for businesses both in the United States and across borders. However, returns for acquiring firms do not always live up to expectations. This exercise seeks to address this notion by analyzing, pre- and post hoc, the results of actual acquisitions. By looking at the notifications of a deal beforehand, categorizing that deal, and then following it for a year, you will be able to learn about actual deals and their implications for strategists.

Working in teams, identify a merger or acquisition that was completed in the last few years. This may be a cross-border acquisition or a U.S.–centered one. A couple of possible sources for this information are Reuters's online M&A section or Yahoo! Finance's U.S. Mergers and Acquisitions Calendar. Each team must get their M&A choice approved in advance so as to avoid duplicates.

To complete this assignment, you should be prepared to answer the following questions:

1. Describe the environment for this arrangement at the time it was completed. Using concepts discussed in the text, focus on management's representation to shareholders, the industry environment, and the overall rationale for the deal.

2. Did the acquirer pay a premium for the target firm? If so, how much? In addition, search for investor comments regarding the wisdom of this agreement. Attempt to identify how the market reacted at the announcement of the deal (LexisNexis typically provides an article that will address this issue).

3. Describe the merger or acquisition going forward. Use the concepts from the text such as, but not limited to:

   a. The reason for the merger or acquisition (i.e., market power, overcoming entry barriers, etc.)

   b. Were there problems in achieving acquisition success?

   c. Would you categorize this deal as successful as of the time of your research, and give the reasons why or why not.

Plan on presenting your findings to the class in a 10- to 15-minute presentation. Organize the presentation as if you were updating the shareholders of the newly combined firm.

EXERCISE 2: WHY RESTRUCTURE?

According to your text, "Restructuring is a strategy through which a firm changes its set of businesses or its financial structure." One way in which to analyze a firm's restructuring is to look at the spin-offs that have occurred over time. According to Investopedia.com, a spin-off occurs when an independent company is created through the sale or distribution of new shares from an existing firm. This is a divestiture. Firms often do this to streamline operations by selling noncore or nonproducing assets. Often after a period of acquisition activity firms find themselves with divisions that do not fit their corporate-level strategy.

A search of the Bloomberg database reveals that between 2006 and halfway through 2011 there were 32 spin-offs originated by firms in the S&P 500. A listing of those firms is below.

Announce Date	Target Name	Seller Name	Announced Value (millions of dollars)
1/13/2006	Covidien PLC	Tyco International Ltd.	$21,360.97
1/13/2006	TE Connectivity Ltd.	Tyco International Ltd.	19,009.29
6/28/2006	Spectra Energy Corp.	Duke Energy Corp.	17,260.03
8/2/2006	Broadridge Financial Solutions Inc.	Automatic Data Processing Inc.	2,897.29
12/19/2006	Discover Financial Services	Morgan Stanley	15,785.78
1/8/2007	Teradata Corp.	NCR Corp.	4,638.43
1/31/2007	Kraft Foods Inc.	Altria Group Inc.	45,532.27
2/1/2007	WABCO Holdings Inc.	Trane Inc.	3,504.92
2/26/2007	Forestar Group Inc.	Temple-Inland Inc.	838.40
2/26/2007	Guaranty Financial Group Inc.	Temple-Inland Inc.	578.09
2/26/2007	KBR Inc.	Halliburton Co.	N/A
4/3/2007	Metavante Technologies Inc.	Marshall & Ilsley Corp.	N/A
5/18/2007	Patriot Coal Corp.	Peabody Energy Corp.	940.64
7/12/2007	PharMerica Corp.	AmerisourceBergen Corp.	290.73

(continued)

Announce Date	Target Name	Seller Name	Announced Value (millions of dollars)
8/29/2007	Philip Morris International Inc.	Altria Group Inc.	$107,649.85
10/16/2007	Scripps Networks Interactive Inc.	EW Scripps Co.	5,215.49
10/25/2007	Total System Services Inc.	Synovus Financial Corp.	4,403.50
11/5/2007	Ticketmaster Entertainment Inc.	IAC/InterActiveCorp.	1,155.89
11/5/2007	Interval Leisure Group Inc.	IAC/InterActiveCorp.	694.36
11/5/2007	HSN Inc.	IAC/InterActiveCorp.	632.16
11/5/2007	Tree.com Inc.	IAC/InterActiveCorp.	74.13
2/13/2008	Lender Processing Services Inc.	Fidelity National Information Services Inc.	2,970.64
3/26/2008	Motorola Mobility Holdings Inc.	Motorola Solutions Inc.	8,317.87
5/21/2008	Time Warner Cable Inc.	Time Warner Inc.	39,558.03
9/29/2008	CareFusion Corp.	Cardinal Health Inc.	3,330.66
3/31/2009	Aviat Networks Inc.	Harris Corp.	146.72
5/13/2009	Frontier Communications Corp.	Verizon Communications Inc.	N/A
5/28/2009	AOL Inc.	Time Warner Inc.	2,512.42
11/16/2009	Mead Johnson Nutrition Co.	Bristol-Myers Squibb Co.	N/A
5/18/2010	QEP Resources Inc.	Questar Corp.	5,398.14
1/13/2011	Marathon Petroleum Corp.	Marathon Oil Corp.	13,889.90
3/15/2011	Huntington Ingalls Industries Inc.	Northrop Grumman Corp.	3,415.93

Your team's challenge is to find out why any one of these transactions occurred. You may choose any transaction above with the approval of the instructor.

You should be prepared to answer the following questions:

1. Categorize the spin-off as downscoping, downsizing, or a leveraged buyout.

2. Read the management and analyst reports. What was the rationale given for implementing the spin-off?

3. Describe the spin-off in terms of ownership. Did the parent retain equity post-spin-off and did this ownership change over time (look at a year or two after the completion date if possible)?

4. What happened to the stock price of the parent company at the time of the spin-off announcement? How did the stock price change when the transaction was completed? Why do you think these changes occurred?

5. What has happened to the spun-off company? Has it been successful since the transaction was completed?

6. Overall, summarize the spin-off in terms of the parent company. Compare your thoughts with the information presented in Figure 7.2 in the text (Restructuring and Outcomes), in terms of short- and long-term consequences.

Be prepared to defend your observations and conclusions in class.

VIDEO CASE

THE POWER OF A MERGER: SOUTHWEST

Southwest, long recognized for its discount airfares and its targeting of the price-conscious consumer, has combined forces with another discount carrier—AirTran. AirTran asserts that with such a merger the potential exists for the expansion of discount airfares in the industry. In an industry where profit motive is high, consolidation is not uncommon even among major airlines, but the air traveler still sees fewer seats and higher prices. While major carriers reap billions, particularly in add-on fees,

Southwest continues to press the competition by refraining from excessive fees.

Be prepared to discuss the following concepts and questions in class:

Concepts
- Mergers
- Acquisitions
- Restructuring

Questions

1. What would make the arrangement between Southwest and AirTran a merger and not an acquisition?

2. What were the reasons that Southwest and AirTran had for merging? What approach(es) did these companies use?

3. What would cause the Southwest/AirTran merger not to be successful?

4. What strategies would you recommend to Southwest should it need to restructure?

NOTES

1. D. J. Teece, 2010, Alfred Chandler and "capabilities" theories of strategy and management, *Industrial and Corporate Change*, 19: 297–316; M. L. McDonald, J. D. Westphal, & M. E. Graebner, 2008, What do they know? The effects of outside director acquisition experience on firm acquisition performance, *Strategic Management Journal*, 29: 1155–1177.

2. H. R. Greve, 2011, Positional rigidity: Low performance and resource acquisition in large and small firms, *Strategic Management Journal*, 32(1): 103–114; J. Wiklund & D. A. Shepherd, 2009, The effectiveness of alliances and acquisitions; The role of resource combination activities, *Entrepreneurship Theory and Practice*, 33: 193–212.

3. M. A. Hitt, D. King, H. Krishnan, M. Makri, M. Schijven, K. Shimizu, & H. Zhu, 2009, Mergers and acquisitions: Overcoming pitfalls, building synergy and creating value, *Business Horizons*, 52(6): 523–529.

4. C. M. Christensen, R. Alton, C. Rising, & A. Waldeck, 2011, The new M&A playbook, *Harvard Business Review*, 89(3): 48–57; G. M. McNamara, J. Haleblian, & B. J. Dykes, 2008, The performance implications of participating in an acquisition wave: Early mover advantages, bandwagon effects, and the moderating influence of industry characteristics and acquirer tactics, *Academy of Management Journal*, 51: 113–130; M. A. Hitt, J. S. Harrison, & R. D. Ireland, 2001, *Mergers and Acquisitions: A Guide to Creating Value for Stakeholders*, New York: Oxford University Press.

5. R. Dobbs & V. Tortorici, 2007, Cool heads will bring in the best deals; Boardroom discipline is vital if the M&A boom is to benefit shareholders, *Financial Times*, February 28, 6.

6. G. Chon, A. Das, & D. Cimilluca, 2011, Urge to merge not seen fading, *Wall Street Journal*, April 1, C11.

7. G. J. Georgopoulos, 2008, Cross-border mergers and acquisitions: Does the exchange rate matter? Some evidence for Canada, *Canadian Journal of Economics*, 41(2): 450–474.

8. M. Cornett, B. Tanyeri, & H. Tehranian, 2011, The effect of merger anticipation on bidder and target firm announcement period returns, *Journal of Corporate Finance*, 17(3): 595–611; J. J. Reuer, 2005, Avoiding lemons in M&A deals, *MIT Sloan Management Review*, 46(3): 15–17.

9. M. Baker, X. Pan, & J. Wurgler, 2009, The psychology of pricing in mergers and acquisitions, working paper: http://www.papers.ssrn.com/so13/papers.cfm?abstract_id=1364152; K. Cool & M. Van de Laar, 2006, The performance of acquisitive companies in the U.S., in L. Renneboog (ed.), *Advances in Corporate Finance and Asset Pricing*, Amsterdam, Netherlands: Elsevier Science, 77–105.

10. B. Ojo, 2011, TI-National deal a smart use of cash, *Electronic Engineering Times*, April 18, 10–11.

11. V. Ambrosini, C. Bowman, & R. Schoenberg, 2011, Should acquiring firms pursue more than one value creation strategy? An empirical test of acquisition performance, *British Journal of Management*, 22(1): 173–185; K. J. Martijn Cremers, V. B. Nair, & K. John, 2009, Takeovers and the cross-section of returns, *Review of Financial Studies*, 22: 1409–1445.

12. P. Flint, 2010, Merger of equals, *Air Transport World*, June, 47–49.

13. J. D. Rockoff, 2011, After long pursuit, Teva wins Cephalon, *Wall Street Journal*, May 3, B1.

14. M. Martynova & L. Renneboog, 2011, The performance of the European market for corporate control: Evidence from the fifth takeover wave, *European Financial Management*, 17(2): 208–259; S. Sudarsanam & A. A. Mahate, 2006, Are friendly acquisitions too bad for shareholders and managers? Long-term value creation and top management turnover in hostile and friendly acquirers, *British Journal of Management: Supplement*, 17(1): S7–S30.

15. S. Bhattacharyya & A. Nain, 2011, Horizontal acquisitions and buying power: A product market analysis, *Journal of Financial Economics*, 99(1): 97–115; E. Akdogu, 2009, Gaining a competitive edge through acquisitions: Evidence from the telecommunications industry, *Journal of Corporate Finance*, 15: 99–112; E. Devos, P.-R. Kadapakkam, & S. Krishnamurthy, 2009, How do mergers create value? A comparison of taxes, market power, and efficiency improvements as explanations for synergies, *Review of Financial Studies*, 22: 1179–1211.

16. T. Hamza, 2011, Determinants of short-term value creation for the bidder: Evidence from France, *Journal of Management & Governance*, 15(2): 157–186; J. Haleblian, C. E. Devers, G. McNamara, M. A. Carpenter, & R. B. Davison, 2009, Taking stock of what we know about mergers and acquisitions: A review and research agenda, *Journal of Management*, 35: 469–502.

17. M. Peers, 2011, AT&T sprints ahead of T-Mobile, *Wall Street Journal*, March 21, C10.

18. K. E. Meyer, S. Estrin, S. K. Bhaumik, & M. W. Peng, 2009, Institutions, resources, and entry strategies in emerging economies, *Strategic Management Journal*, 30: 61–80; D. K. Oler, J. S. Harrison, & M. R. Allen, 2008, The danger of misinterpreting short-window event study findings in strategic management research: An empirical illustration using horizontal acquisitions, *Strategic Organization*, 6: 151–184.

19. M. Zollo & J. J. Reuer, 2010, Experience spillovers across corporate development activities, *Organization Science*, 21(6): 1195–1212; C. E. Fee & S. Thomas, 2004, Sources of gains in horizontal mergers: Evidence from customer, supplier, and rival firms, *Journal of Financial Economics*, 74: 423–460.

20. T. Ushijima, 2009, R&D intensity and acquisition and divestiture of corporate assets: Evidence from Japan, *Journal of Economics and Business*, 61(5): 415–433; L. Capron, W. Mitchell, & A. Swaminathan, 2001, Asset divestiture following horizontal acquisitions: A dynamic view, *Strategic Management Journal*, 22: 817–844.

21. H. Li & M. Tang, 2010, Vertical integration and innovative performance: The effects of external knowledge sourcing modes, *Technovation*, 30(7/8): 401–410; B. Gulbrandsen, K. Sandvik, & S. A. Haugland, 2009, Antecedents of vertical integration: Transaction cost economics and resource-based explanations, *Journal of Purchasing and Supply Management*, 15: 89–102; F. T. Rothaermel, M. A. Hitt, & L. A. Jobe, 2006, Balancing vertical integration and strategic outsourcing: Effects on product portfolio, product success, and firm performance, *Strategic Management Journal*, 27: 1033–1056.

22. M. F. Guillén & E. García-Canal, 2010, How to conquer new markets with old skills, *Harvard Business Review*, 88(11): 118–122; A. Parmigiani, 2007, Why do firms both make and buy? An investigation of concurrent sourcing, *Strategic Management Journal*, 28: 285–311.

23. K. MacFadyen, 2010, Strategic buyer of the year: Shrewd Larry, *Mergers & Acquisitions Report*, 23(14): 19.

24. K. MacFadyen, 2011, Amazon buys Netflix rival, *Mergers & Acquisitions Report*, 24(4): 7.

25. J. W. Brock & N. P. Obst, 2009, Market concentration, economic welfare, and antitrust policy, *Journal of Industry, Competition and Trade*, 9: 65–75; M. T. Brouwer, 2008, Horizontal mergers and efficiencies: Theory and antitrust practice, *European Journal of Law and Economics*, 26: 11–26.

26. E. Ante & A. Scatz, 2011, T-Mobile deal faces antitrust barriers, *Wall Street Journal*, March 21, B1.

27. P. Zhu, V. Jog, & I. Otchere, 2011, Partial acquisitions in emerging markets: A test of the strategic market entry and corporate control hypotheses, *Journal of Corporate Finance*, 17(2): 288–305; K. E. Meyer, M. Wright, & S. Pruthi, 2009, Managing knowledge in foreign entry strategies: A resource-based analysis, *Strategic Management Journal*, 30: 557–574.

28. C. Y. Tseng, 2009, Technological innovation in the BRIC economies, *Research-Technology Management*, 52: 29–35; S. McGee, 2007, Seeking value in BRICs, *Barron's*, July 9, L10–L11.

29. K. Boeh, 2011, Contracting costs and information asymmetry reduction in cross-border M&A, *Journal of Management Studies*, 48(3): 568–590; R. Chakrabarti, N. Jayaraman, & S. Mukherjee, 2009, Mars-Venus marriages: Culture and cross-border M&A, *Journal of International Business Studies*, 40: 216–237.

30. P. J. Williamson & A. P. Raman, 2011, How China reset its global acquisition agenda, *Harvard Business Review*, 89(4): 109–114; E. Zabinski, D. Freeman, & X. Jian, 2009, Navigating the challenges of cross-border M&A, *The Deal Magazine*, http://www.thedeal.com, May 29.

31. A. Lobov, 2011, ChemChina and UPL vary routes in M&A race, *AsiaMoney*, http://www.AsiaMoney.com, February 8.

32. Y. W. Chin, 2011, M&A under China's Anti-Monopoly Law, *Business Law Today*, 19(7): 1–5; J. Chapman & W. Xu, 2008, Ten strategies for successful cross-border acquisitions in China, *Nixon Peabody LLP Special Report, Mergers & Acquisitions*, September, 30–35.

33. G. K. Lee & M. B. Lieberman, 2010, Acquisition vs. internal development as modes of market entry, *Strategic Management Journal*, 31(2): 140–158; C. Homburg & M. Bucerius, 2006, Is speed of integration really a success factor of mergers and acquisitions? An analysis of the role of internal and external relatedness, *Strategic Management Journal*, 27: 347–367.

34. H. K. Ellonen, P. Wilstrom, & A. Jantunen, 2009, Linking dynamic-capability portfolios and innovation outcomes, *Technovation* 29: 753–762; M. Song & C. A. De Benedetto, 2008, Supplier's involvement

and success of radical new product development in new ventures, *Journal of Operations Management*, 26: 1–22; S. Karim, 2006, Modularity in organizational structure: The reconfiguration of internally developed and acquired business units, *Strategic Management Journal*, 27: 799–823.

35. M. Makri, M. A. Hitt, & P. J. Lane, 2010, Complementary technologies, knowledge relatedness, and invention outcomes in high technology M&As, *Strategic Management Journal*, 31: 602–628; R. E. Hoskisson & L. W. Busenitz, 2002, Market uncertainty and learning distance in corporate entrepreneurship entry mode choice, in M. A. Hitt, R. D. Ireland, S. M. Camp, & D. L. Sexton (eds.), *Strategic Entrepreneurship: Creating a New Mindset*, Oxford, U.K.: Blackwell Publishers, 151–172; M. A. Hitt, R. E. Hoskisson, R. A. Johnson, & D. D. Moesel, 1996, The market for corporate control and firm innovation, *Academy of Management Journal*, 39: 1084–1119.

36. M. Herper, 2010. Medtronic's bionic battle, *Forbes*, http://forbes.com, December 12.

37. S. Ransbotham & S. Mitra, 2010, Target age and the acquisition of innovation in high-technology industries, *Management Science*, 56(11): 2076–2093.

38. W. P. Wan & D. W. Yiu, 2009, From crisis to opportunity: Environmental jolt, corporate acquisitions, and firm performance, *Strategic Management Journal*, 30: 791–801; G. Ahuja & R. Katila, 2001, Technological acquisitions and the innovation performance of acquiring firms: A longitudinal study, *Strategic Management Journal*, 22: 197–220.

39. X. Dean, Z. Changhui, & P. H. Phan, 2010, A real options perspective on sequential acquisitions in China, *Journal of International Business Studies*, 41(1): 166–174; F. Damanpour, R. M. Walker, & C. N. Avellaneda, 2009, Combinative effects of innovation types and organizational performance: A longitudinal study of service organizations, *Journal of Management Studies*, 46: 650–675.

40. U. Zander & L. Zander, 2010, Opening the grey box: Social communities, knowledge and culture in acquisitions, *Journal of International Business Studies*, 41(1): 27–37; F. Vermeulen, 2005, How acquisitions can revitalize companies, *MIT Sloan Management Review*, 46(4): 45–51; M. A. Hitt, R. E. Hoskisson, R. D. Ireland, & J. S. Harrison, 1991, Effects of acquisitions on R&D inputs and outputs, *Academy of Management Journal*, 34: 693–706.

41. G. Colvin, 2010, Ursula Burns, *Fortune*, May 3, 96–102.

42. H. Prechel, T. Morris, T. Woods, & R. Walden, 2008, Corporate diversification revisited: The political-legal environment, the multilayer-subsidiary form, and mergers and acquisitions, *The Sociological Quarterly*, 49: 849–878; C. E. Helfat &

K. M. Eisenhardt, 2004, Inter-temporal economies of scope, organizational modularity, and the dynamics of diversification, *Strategic Management Journal*, 25: 1217–1232.

43. E. Crooks, 2011, United Technologies seeks emerging market expansion, *Financial Times*, April 28, 15.

44. R. Myers, 2011, Cisco's Tandberg acquisition: Ready on day one, *CFO*, January/February, 57.

45. C. Tamika, 2011, Cisco Buys newScale, *Mergers & Acquisitions Report*, 24(16): 35.

46. Makri, Hitt, & Lane, Complementary technologies, knowledge relatedness, and invention outcomes in high technology M&As; T. Laamanen & T. Keil, 2008, Performance of serial acquirers: Toward an acquisition program perspective, *Strategic Management Journal*, 29: 663–672.

47. Lee & Lieberman, Acquisition vs. internal development as modes of market entry; J. Anand & H. Singh, 1997, Asset redeployment, acquisitions and corporate strategy in declining industries, *Strategic Management Journal*, 18 (Special Issue): 99–118.

48. Bhattacharyya & Nain, Horizontal acquisitions and buying power; T. Yu, M. Subramaniam, & A. A. Cannella, Jr., 2009, Rivalry deterrence in international markets: Contingencies governing the mutual forbearance hypothesis, *Academy of Management Journal*, 52: 127–147; D. G. Sirmon, S. Gove, & M. A. Hitt, 2008, Resource management in dyadic competitive rivalry: The effects of resource bundling and deployment, *Academy of Management Journal*, 51: 919–933.

49. M. Zollo & J. J. Reuer, 2010, Experience spillovers across corporate development activities, *Organization Science*, 21(6): 1195–1212; P. Puranam & K. Srikanth, 2007, What they know vs. what they do: How acquirers leverage technology acquisitions, *Strategic Management Journal*, 28: 805–825.

50. B. Park & P. N. Ghauri, 2011, Key factors affecting acquisition of technological capabilities from foreign acquiring firms by small and medium-sized local firms, *Journal of World Business*, 46(1): 116–125; S. A. Zahra & J. C. Hayton, 2008, The effect of international venturing on firm performance: The moderating influence of absorptive capacity, *Journal of Business Venturing*, 23: 195–220.

51. Makri, Hitt, & Lane, Complementary technologies, knowledge relatedness, and invention outcomes in high technology mergers and acquisitions; J. S. Harrison, M. A. Hitt, R. E. Hoskisson, & R. D. Ireland, 2001, Resource complementarity in business combinations: Extending the logic to organizational alliances, *Journal of Management*, 27: 679–690.

52. J. Whalen, 2011, Sanofi offers bonuses to retain Genzyme scientists, *Wall Street Journal*, http://www.wsj.com, April 28.

53. M. E. Graebner, K. M. Eisenhardt, & P. T. Roundy, 2010, Success and failure

in technology acquisitions: Lessons for buyers and sellers, *Academy of Management Perspectives*, 24(3), 73–92; J. A. Schmidt, 2002, Business perspective on mergers and acquisitions, in J. A. Schmidt (ed.), *Making Mergers Work*, Alexandria, VA: Society for Human Resource Management, 23–46.

54. T. Herd, 2010, M&A success beating the odds, *Bloomberg Businessweek*, http://www.businessweek.com, June 23.

55. M. Cording, P. Christmann, & D. R. King, 2008, Reducing causal ambiguity in acquisition integration: Intermediate goals as mediators of integration decisions and acquisition performance, *Academy of Management Journal*, 51: 744–767.

56. D. S. Siegel & K. L. Simons, 2010, Assessing the effects of mergers and acquisitions on firm performance, plant productivity, and workers: New evidence from matched employer-employee data, *Strategic Management Journal*, 31(8): 903–916; N. Kumar, 2009, How emerging giants are rewriting the rules of M&A, *Harvard Business Review*, 87(5): 115–121; M. C. Sturman, 2008, The value of human capital specificity versus transferability, *Journal of Management*, 34: 290–316.

57. M. Marks & P. Mirvis, 2011, Merge ahead: A research agenda to increase merger and acquisition success, *Journal of Business & Psychology* 26(2): 161–168; K. M. Ellis, T. H. Reus, & B. T. Lamont, 2009, The effects of procedural and informational justice in the integration of related acquisitions, *Strategic Management Journal*, 30: 137–161.

58. M. Zollo, 1999, M&A—The challenge of learning to integrate: Mastering strategy (part eleven), *Financial Times*, December 6, 14–15.

59. E. Clark & M. Geppert. 2011, Subsidiary integration as identity construction and institution building: A political sensemaking approach, *Journal of Management Studies* 48(2): 395–416; H. G. Barkema & M. Schijven, 2008, Toward unlocking the full potential of acquisitions: The role of organizational restructuring, *Academy of Management Journal*, 51: 696–722; J. Harrison, 2007, Why integration success eludes many buyers, *Mergers and Acquisitions*, 42(3):18–20.

60. A. E. Rafferty & S. L. D. Restburg, 2010, The impact of change process and context on change reactions and turnover during a merger. *Journal of Management*, 36: 1309–1338.

61. R. Gibson, 2006, Package deal; UPS's purchase of Mail Boxes Etc. looked great on paper. Then came the culture clash, *Wall Street Journal*, May 8, R13.

62. J. DiPietro, 2010, Responsible acquisitions yield growth, *Financial Executive*, 26(10): 16–19.

63. T. B. Folta & J. P. O'Brien, 2008, Determinants of firm-specific thresholds in acquisition decisions, *Managerial and Decision Economics*, 29: 209–225;

R. J. Rosen, 2006, Merger momentum and investor sentiment: The stock market reaction to merger announcements, *Journal of Business*, 79: 987–1017.

64. A. Rappaport & M. L. Sirower, 1999, Stock or cash? The trade-offs for buyers and sellers in mergers and acquisitions, *Harvard Business Review*, 77(6): 149.

65. Christensen, Alton, Rising, & Waldeck, The new M&A playbook.

66. G. Yago, 1991, *Junk Bonds: How High Yield Securities Restructured Corporate America*, New York: Oxford University Press, 146–148.

67. M. C. Jensen, 1986, Agency costs of free cash flow, corporate finance, and takeovers, *American Economic Review*, 76: 323–329.

68. S. Guo, E. S. Hotchkiss, & W. Song, 2011, Do buyouts (still) create value?, *Journal of Finance*, 66(2): 479–517.

69. J. R. Hagerty & B. Tita, 2010, Caterpillar digs deeper in mining, *Wall Street Journal*, November 16, B1.

70. K. Geressy-Nilsen, 2011, Merger financing drives busy day in corporate debt issues, *Wall Street Journal*, http://www.wsj.com, May 24.

71. S. W. Bauguess, S. B. Moeller, F. P. Schlingemann, & C. J. Zutter, 2009, Ownership structure and target returns, *Journal of Corporate Finance*, 15: 48–65; H. Donker & S. Zahir, 2008, Takeovers, corporate control, and return to target shareholders, *International Journal of Corporate Governance*, 1: 106–134.

72. Y. M. Zhou, 2011, Synergy, coordination costs, and diversification choices, *Strategic Management Journal*, 32: 624–639; A. B. Sorescu, R. K. Chandy, & J. C. Prabhu, 2007, Why some acquisitions do better than others: Product capital as a driver of long-term stock returns, *Journal of Marketing Research*, 44(1): 57–72; T. Saxton & M. Dollinger, 2004, Target reputation and appropriability: Picking and deploying resources in acquisitions, *Journal of Management*, 30: 123–147.

73. J. B. Barney, 1988, Returns to bidding firms in mergers and acquisitions: Reconsidering the relatedness hypothesis, *Strategic Management Journal*, 9 (Special Issue): 71–78.

74. O. E. Williamson, 1999, Strategy research: Governance and competence perspectives, *Strategic Management Journal*, 20: 1087–1108.

75. M. Cleary, K. Hartnett, & K. Dubuque, 2011, Road map to efficient merger integration, *American Banker*, March 22, 9; S. Chatterjee, 2007, Why is synergy so difficult in mergers of related businesses? *Strategy & Leadership*, 35(2): 46–52.

76. E. Rawley, 2010, Diversification, coordination costs and organizational rigidity: Evidence from microdata, *Strategic Management Journal*, 31: 873–891; C. W. L. Hill & R. E. Hoskisson, 1987, Strategy and structure in the multiproduct firm, *Academy of Management Review*, 12: 331–341.

77. W. P. Wan, R. E. Hoskisson, J. C. Short, & D. W. Yiu, 2011, Resource-based theory and corporate diversification: Accomplishments and opportunities, *Journal of Management*, in press; M. L. A. Hayward & K. Shimizu, 2006, De-commitment to losing strategic action: Evidence from the divestiture of poorly performing acquisitions, *Strategic Management Journal*, 27: 541–557; R. A. Johnson, R. E. Hoskisson, & M. A. Hitt, 1993, Board of director involvement in restructuring: The effects of board versus managerial controls and characteristics, *Strategic Management Journal*, 14 (Special Issue): 33–50; C. C. Markides, 1992, Consequences of corporate refocusing: Ex ante evidence, *Academy of Management Journal*, 35: 398–412.

78. P. David, J. P. O'Brien, T. Yoshikawa, & A. Delios, 2010, Do shareholders or stakeholders appropriate the rents from corporate diversification? The influence of ownership structure, *Academy of Management Journal*, 53: 636–654; D. Marginso & L. McAulay, 2008, Exploring the debate on short-termism: A theoretical and empirical analysis, *Strategic Management Journal*, 29: 273–292; R. E. Hoskisson & R. A. Johnson, 1992, Corporate restructuring and strategic change: The effect on diversification strategy and R&D intensity, *Strategic Management Journal*, 13: 625–634.

79. J. L. Stimpert, I. M. Duhaime, & J. Chesney, 2010, Learning to manage a large diversified firm, *Journal of Leadership and Organizational Studies*, 17: 411–425; T. Keil, M. V. J. Maula, H. Schildt, & S. A. Zahra, 2008, The effect of governance modes and relatedness of external business development activities on innovative performance, *Strategic Management Journal*, 29: 895–907; K. H. Tsai & J. C. Wang, 2008, External technology acquisition and firm performance: A longitudinal study, *Journal of Business Venturing*, 23: 91–112.

80. A. Kacperczyk, 2009, With greater power comes greater responsibility? Takeover protection and corporate attention to stakeholders, *Strategic Management Journal*, 30: 261–285; L. H. Lin, 2009, Mergers and acquisitions, alliances and technology development: An empirical study of the global auto industry, *International Journal of Technology Management*, 48: 295–307; M. L. Barnett, 2008, An attention-based view of real options reasoning, *Academy of Management Review*, 33: 606–628.

81. J. A. Martin & K. J. Davis, 2010, Learning or hubris? Why CEOs create less value in successive acquisitions, *Academy of Management Perspectives*, 24(1): 79–81; M. L. A. Hayward & D. C. Hambrick, 1997, Explaining the premiums paid for large acquisitions: Evidence of CEO hubris, *Administrative Science Quarterly*, 42: 103–127; R. Roll, 1986, The hubris

hypothesis of corporate takeovers, *Journal of Business*, 59: 197–216.

82. F. Vermeulen, 2007, Business insight (a special report): Bad deals: Eight warning signs that an acquisition may not pay off, *Wall Street Journal*, April 28, R10.

83. L. A. Nemanich & D. Vera, 2009, Transformational leadership and ambidexterity in the context of an acquisition, *The Leadership Quarterly*, 20: 19–33.

84. Christensen, Alton, Rising, & Waldeck, The new M&A playbook.

85. V. Swaminathan, F. Murshed, & J. Hulland, 2008, Value creation following merger and acquisition announcements: The role of strategic emphasis alignment, *Journal of Marketing Research*, 45: 33–47.

86. J. Begley & T. Donnelly, 2011, The DaimlerChrysler Mitsubishi merger: A study in failure, *International Journal of Automotive Technology and Management*, 11(1): 36–48.

87. H. Greve, 2011, Positional rigidity: Low performance and resource acquisition in large and small firms, *Strategic Management Journal*, 32(1): 103–114.

88. D. Clark & S. Tibken, 2011, Corporate news: Cisco to reduce its bureaucracy, *Wall Street Journal*, May 6, B4.

89. Vermeulen, Business insight (a special report): Bad deals: Eight warning signs that an acquisition may not pay off.

90. M. Cording, P. Christmann, & C. Weigelt, 2010, Measuring theoretically complex constructs: The case of acquisition performance, *Strategic Organization*, 8(1): 11–41; H. G. Barkema & M. Schijven, 2008, How do firms learn to make acquisitions? A review of past research and an agenda for the future, *Journal of Management*, 34: 594–634.

91. S. Chatterjee, 2009, The keys to successful acquisition programmes, *Long Range Planning*, 42: 137–163; C. M. Sanchez & S. R. Goldberg, 2009, Strategic M&As: Stronger in tough times? *Journal of Corporate Accounting & Finance*, 20: 3–7; C. Duncan & M. Mtar, 2006, Determinants of international acquisition success: Lessons from FirstGroup in North America, *European Management Journal*, 24: 396–410.

92. R. Myers, 2011, Integration Acceleration, *CFO*, 27(1): 52–57.

93. D. Mayer & M. Kenney, 2004, Economic action does not take place in a vacuum: Understanding Cisco's acquisition and development strategy, *Industry and Innovation*, 11(4): 299–325.

94. 2011, Cisco acquisition connection, http://www.cisco.com, June 9.

95. M. A. Hitt, R. D. Ireland, J. S. Harrison, & A. Best, 1998, Attributes of successful and unsuccessful acquisitions of U.S. firms, *British Journal of Management*, 9: 91–114.

96. Zollo & Reuer, Experience spillovers across corporate development activities; K. Uhlenbruck, M. A. Hitt, & M. Semadeni, 2006, Market value effects of acquisitions involving Internet firms: A resource-based

analysis, *Strategic Management Journal*, 27: 899–913.

97. A. Zaheer, E. Hernandez, & S. Banerjee, 2010, Prior alliances with targets and acquisition performance in knowledge-intensive industries, *Organization Science*, 21: 1072–1094; P. Porrini, 2004, Can a previous alliance between an acquirer and a target affect acquisition performance? *Journal of Management*, 30: 545–562.

98. D. K. Ellis, T. Reus, & B. Lamont, 2009, The effects of procedural and informational justice in the integration of related acquisitions, *Strategic Management Journal*, 30(2): 137–161; R. J. Aiello & M. D. Watkins, 2000, The fine art of friendly acquisition, *Harvard Business Review*, 78(6): 100–107.

99. J. Haleblian, C. Devers, G. McNamara, M. Carpenter, & R. Davidson, 2009, Mergers and acquisitions: A review of research on the antecedents, consequences, and process of acquisitions, *Journal of Management*, 35: 469–502; D. D. Bergh, 2001, Executive retention and acquisition outcomes: A test of opposing views on the influence of organizational tenure, *Journal of Management*, 27: 603–622; J. P. Walsh, 1989, Doing a deal: Merger and acquisition negotiations and their impact upon target company top management turnover, *Strategic Management Journal*, 10: 307–322.

100. D. A. Waldman & M. Javidan, 2009, Alternative forms of charismatic leadership in the integration of mergers and acquisitions, *The Leadership Quarterly*, 20: 130–142; F. J. Froese, Y. S. Pak, & L. C. Chong, 2008, Managing the human side of cross-border acquisitions in South Korea, *Journal of World Business*, 43: 97–108.

101. K. Marmenout, 2010, Employee sensemaking in mergers: How deal characteristics shape employee attitudes, *Journal of Applied Behavioral Science*, 46(3): 329–359; M. E. Graebner, 2009, Caveat venditor: Trust asymmetries in acquisitions of entrepreneurial firms, *Academy of Management Journal*, 52: 435–472; N. J. Morrison, G. Kinley, & K. L. Ficery, 2008, Merger deal breakers: When operational due diligence exposes risk, *Journal of Business Strategy*, 29: 23–28.

102. J. Jwu-Rong, H. Chen-Jui, & L. Hsieh-Lung, 2010, A matching approach to M&A, R&D, and patents: Evidence from Taiwan's listed companies, *International Journal of Electronic Business Management*, 8(3): 273–280.

103. J. M. Shaver & J. M. Mezias, 2009, Diseconomies of managing in acquisitions: Evidence from civil lawsuits, *Organization Science*, 20: 206–222; M. L. McDonald, J. D. Westphal, & M. E. Graebner, What do they know? The effects of outside director acquisition experience on firm acquisition performance, *Strategic Management Journal*, 29: 1155–1177.

104. D. Lee & R. Madhaven, 2010, Divestiture and firm performance: A meta-analysis,

Journal of Management, 36: 1345–1371; D. D. Bergh & E. N.-K. Lim, 2008, Learning how to restructure: Absorptive capacity and improvisational views of restructuring actions and performance, *Strategic Management Journal*, 29: 593–616.

105. Y. Zhou, X. Li, & J. Svejnar, 2011, Subsidiary divestiture and acquisition in a financial crisis: Operational focus, financial constraints, and ownership, *Journal of Corporate Finance*, 17(2): 272–287; Y. G. Suh & E. Howard, 2009, Restructuring retailing in Korea: The case of Samsung-Tesco, *Asia Pacific Business Review*, 15: 29–40; Z. Wu & A. Delios, 2009, The emergence of portfolio restructuring in Japan, *Management International Review*, 49: 313–335.

106. S. Thurm, 2008, Who are the best CEOs of 2008?, *Wall Street Journal Online*, http://www.wsj.com, December 15.

107. L. Diestre & N. Rajagopalan, 2011, An environmental perspective on diversification: The effects of chemical relatedness and regulatory sanctions, *Academy of Management Journal*, 54: 97–115.

108. J. L. Morrow, Jr., D. G. Sirmon, M. A. Hitt, & T. R. Holcomb, 2007, Creating value in the face of declining performance: Firm strategies and organizational recovery, *Strategic Management Journal*, 28: 271–283; J. L. Morrow, Jr., R. A. Johnson, & L. W. Busenitz, 2004, The effects of cost and asset retrenchment on firm performance: The overlooked role of a firm's competitive environment, *Journal of Management*, 30: 189–208.

109. G. J. Castrogiovanni & G. D. Bruton, 2000, Business turnaround processes following acquisitions: Reconsidering the role of retrenchment, *Journal of Business Research*, 48: 25–34; W. McKinley, J. Zhao, & K. G. Rust, 2000, A sociocognitive interpretation of organizational downsizing, *Academy of Management Review*, 25: 227–243.

110. J. D. Evans & F. Hefner, 2009, Business ethics and the decision to adopt golden parachute contracts: Empirical evidence of concern for all stakeholders, *Journal of Business Ethics*, 86: 65–79; H. A. Krishnan, M. A. Hitt, & D. Park, 2007, Acquisition premiums, subsequent workforce reductions and post-acquisition performance, *Journal of Management*, 44: 709–732.

111. K. McFarland, 2008, Four mistakes leaders make when downsizing, *BusinessWeek Online*, http://www.businessweek.com, October 24.

112. R. Iverson & C. Zatzick, 2011, The effects of downsizing on labor productivity: The value of showing consideration for employees' morale and welfare in high-performance work systems, *Human Resource Management*, 50(1): 29–43; C. O. Trevor & A. J. Nyberg, 2008, Keeping your headcount when all about you are losing theirs: Downsizing,

voluntary turnover rates, and the moderating role of HR practices, *Academy of Management Journal*, 51: 259–276.

113. Bergh & Lim, Learning how to restructure; R. E. Hoskisson & M. A. Hitt, 1994, *Downscoping: How to Tame the Diversified Firm*, New York: Oxford University Press.

114. A. T. Nicolai, A. Schulz, & T. W. Thomas, 2010, What Wall Street wants – exploring the role of security analysts in the evolution and spread of management concepts, *Journal of Management Studies*, 47(1): 162–189; L. Dranikoff, T. Koller, & A. Schneider, 2002, Divestiture: Strategy's missing link, *Harvard Business Review*, 80(5): 74–83.

115. R. E. Hoskisson & M. A. Hitt, 1990, Antecedents and performance outcomes of diversification: A review and critique of theoretical perspectives, *Journal of Management*, 16: 461–509.

116. C. Moschieri, 2011, The implementation and structuring of divestitures: The unit's perspective, *Strategic Management Journal*, 32: 368-401.

117. 2010, Citi to shrink its consumer-lending unit, *American Banker*, June 2, 16.

118. A. Kambil, 2008, What is your recession playbook? *Journal of Business Strategy*, 29: 50–52; M. Rajand & M. Forsyth, 2002, Hostile bidders, long-term performance, and restructuring methods: Evidence from the UK, *American Business Review*, 20: 71–81.

119. D. Hillier, P. McColgan, & S. Werema, 2008, Asset sales and firm strategy: An analysis of divestitures by UK companies, *European Journal of Finance*, 15: 71–87; R. E. Hoskisson, R. A. Johnson, L. Tihanyi, & R. E. White, 2005, Diversified business groups and corporate refocusing in emerging economies, *Journal of Management*, 31: 941–965.

120. S. N. Kaplan & P. Stromberg, 2009, Leveraged buyouts and private equity, *Journal of Economic Perspectives*, 23: 121–146; C. Moschieri & J. Mair, 2008, Research on corporate divestures: A synthesis, *Journal of Management & Organization*, 14: 399–422.

121. J. Mair & C. Moschieri, 2006, Unbundling frees business for take off, *Financial Times*, October 19, 2.

122. T. Cody & K. MacFadyen, 2011, Tuck-in deals were an easy answer to the credit shortfall; the challenge will be the ensuing integration efforts, *Mergers & Acquisitions: The Dealermaker's Journal*, 46(2): 16–56.

123. K. H. Wruck, 2009, Private equity, corporate governance, and the reinvention of the market for corporate control, *Journal of Applied Corporate Finance*, 20: 8–21; M. F. Wiersema & J. P. Liebeskind, 1995, The effects of leveraged buyouts on corporate growth and diversification in large firms, *Strategic Management Journal*, 16: 447–460.

124. R. Harris, D. S. Siegel, & M. Wright, 2005, Assessing the impact of management buyouts on economic efficiency: Plant-level evidence from the United Kingdom, *Review of Economics and Statistics*, 87: 148–153; A. Seth & J. Easterwood, 1995, Strategic redirection in large management buyouts: The evidence from post-buyout restructuring activity, *Strategic Management Journal*, 14: 251–274; P. H. Phan & C. W. L. Hill, 1995, Organizational restructuring and economic performance in leveraged buyouts: An ex-post study, *Academy of Management Journal*, 38: 704–739.

125. M. Meuleman, K. Amess, M. Wright, & L. Scholes, 2009, Agency, strategic entrepreneurship, and the performance of private equity-backed buyouts, *Entrepreneurship Theory and Practice*, 33: 213–239; C. M. Daily, P. P. McDougall, J. G. Covin, & D. R. Dalton, 2002, Governance and strategic leadership in entrepreneurial firms, *Journal of Management*, 3: 387–412.

126. Siegel & Simons, Assessing the effects of mergers and acquisitions on firm performance, plant productivity, and workers; W. Kiechel III, 2007, Private equity's long view, *Harvard Business Review*, 85(8): 18–20; M. Wright, R. E. Hoskisson, & L. W. Busenitz, 2001, Firm rebirth: Buyouts as facilitators of strategic growth and entrepreneurship, *Academy of Management Executive*, 15(1): 111–125.

127. E. G. Love & M. Kraatz, 2009, Character, conformity, or the bottom line? How and why downsizing affected corporate reputation, *Academy of Management Journal*, 52: 314–335; J. P. Guthrie & D. K. Datta, 2008, Dumb and dumber: The impact of downsizing on firm performance as moderated by industry conditions, *Organization Science*, 19: 108–123.

128. H. A. Krishnan & D. Park, 2002, The impact of work force reduction on subsequent performance in major mergers and acquisitions: An exploratory study, *Journal of Business Research*, 55(4): 285–292; P. M. Lee, 1997, A comparative analysis of layoff announcements and stock price reactions in the United States and Japan, *Strategic Management Journal*, 18: 879–894.

129. D. J. Flanagan & K. C. O'Shaughnessy, 2005, The effect of layoffs on firm reputation, *Journal of Management*, 31: 445–163.

130. P. Williams, K. M. Sajid, & N. Earl, 2011, Customer dissatisfaction and defection: The hidden costs of downsizing, *Industrial Marketing Management*, 40(3): 405–413.

131. P. Galagan, 2010, The biggest losers: The perils of extreme downsizing, *T+D*, November, 27–29; D. S. DeRue, J. R. Hollenbeck, M. D. Johnson, D. R. Ilgen, & D. K. Jundt, 2008, How different team downsizing approaches influence team-level adaptation and performance, *Academy of Management Journal*, 51: 182–196; C. D. Zatzick & R. D. Iverson, 2006, High-involvement management and workforce reduction: Competitive advantage or disadvantage? *Academy of Management Journal*, 49: 999–1015.

132. Moschieri, The implementation and structuring of divestitures; K. Shimizu & M. A. Hitt, 2005, What constrains or facilitates divestitures of formerly acquired firms? The effects of organizational inertia, *Journal of Management*, 31: 50–72.

133. D. T. Brown, C. E. Fee, & S. E. Thomas, 2009, Financial leverage and bargaining power with suppliers: Evidence from leveraged buyouts, *Journal of Corporate Finance*, 15: 196–211; S. Toms & M. Wright, 2005, Divergence and convergence within Anglo-American corporate governance systems: Evidence from the US and UK, 1950–2000, *Business History*, 47(2): 267–295.

134. S. B. Rodrigues & J. Child, 2010, Private equity, the minimalist organization and the quality of employment relations, *Human Relations*, 63(9): 1321–1342; G. Wood & M. Wright, 2009, Private equity: A review and synthesis, *International Journal of Management Reviews*, 11: 361–380; A.-L. Le Nadant & F. Perdreau, 2006, Financial profile of leveraged buy-out targets: Some French evidence, *Review of Accounting and Finance*, (4): 370–392.

135. M. Goergen, N. O'Sullivan, & G. Wood, 2011, Private equity takeovers and employment in the UK: Some empirical evidence, *Corporate Governance: An International Review*, 19(3): 259–275; G. D. Bruton, J. K. Keels, & E. L. Scifres, 2002, Corporate restructuring and performance: An agency perspective on the complete buyout cycle, *Journal of Business Research*, 55: 709–724; W. F. Long & D. J. Ravenscraft, 1993, LBOs, debt, and R&D intensity, *Strategic Management Journal*, 14 (Special Issue): 119–135.

136. S. A. Zahra, 1995, Corporate entrepreneurship and financial performance: The case of management leveraged buyouts, *Journal of Business Venturing*, 10: 225–248.

CHAPTER 8

International Strategy

Studying this chapter should provide you with the strategic management knowledge needed to:

1. Explain incentives that can influence firms to use an international strategy.

2. Identify three basic benefits firms achieve by successfully implementing an international strategy.

3. Explore the determinants of national advantage as the basis for international business-level strategies.

4. Describe the three international corporate-level strategies.

5. Discuss environmental trends affecting the choice of international strategies, particularly international corporate-level strategies.

6. Explain the five modes firms use to enter international markets.

7. Discuss the two major risks of using international strategies.

8. Discuss the strategic competitiveness outcomes associated with international strategies particularly with an international diversification strategy.

9. Explain two important issues firms should have knowledge about when using international strategies.

INTERNATIONAL STRATEGY: CRITICAL TO STARBUCKS' FUTURE SUCCESS

With a mission "to inspire and nurture the human spirit—one person, one cup and one neighborhood at a time," Starbucks launched its operations in 1971; today, Starbucks is one of the world's most recognized brand names. Saying that it offers "...the finest coffees in the world, grown, prepared and served by the finest people," Starbucks has over 17,000 stores (about half of the stores are company owned with the other half being licensed) with locations in more than 50 countries. While its operations in the United States remain important, global growth is a key objective for Starbucks. Based on a belief that profitable growth will result from embracing the global marketplace, the firm wants to grow substantially outside of North America, especially in China and India, markets it believes have significant potential for the firm. In fact, Starbucks believes that China may one day be second only to the United States in terms of sales revenue generated. Embracing the global marketplace is also important to Starbucks because it currently commands less than 1 percent of the global coffee market, suggesting there are significant growth opportunities available.

Of course seeking growth in China is not isolated to Starbucks. The size of China's consumer and commercial markets entices a number of companies from around the world to find ways to successfully use an international strategy as the foundation for competitive success there. In the words of Starbucks' CEO Howard Schulz: "There is a gold-rush mentality by every western brand known to mankind rushing into China." However, only firms that successfully implement an international strategy that is appropriate for China have the potential to succeed there.

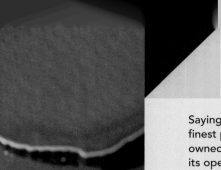

TAO Images Limited/Alamy

This Chinese Starbucks location merges the traditional architecture of Shikumen houses while maintaining the signature Starbucks' signage.

As we noted in Chapter 4's Opening Case, Starbucks now has over 400 locations on mainland China, with plans to increase this number to 1,500 by 2015. Starbucks uses an international differentiation business-level strategy and a transnational international corporate-level strategy in its efforts to succeed in China. (We discuss both of these strategies in this chapter.) There are several capabilities that are the foundation on which these strategies were selected and are being implemented. Brand strength, superior customer service, convenient locations, and product innovation are examples of capabilities (that are also core competencies for the firm) on which Starbucks relies to implement its international strategies. Starbucks' international differentiation strategy finds the firm offering unique products and experiences to customers, for which they are willing to pay a premium price. The transnational strategy is one through which Starbucks uses its core competencies to standardize its operations to gain global efficiencies while decentralizing decision-making responsibilities to local units in China so that some products can be customized to meet local consumers' unique needs. The firm captures the essence of its transnational strategy by saying that while competing in China it continues "to stay true to (its) brand while finding fresh ways to be locally relevant..." Efforts to consolidate control of its mainland China operations for the purpose of ensuring a consistent brand image throughout the country while simultaneously seeking to introduce localized products in South China also demonstrate the implementation of the transnational strategy.

Explore Starbuck's expansion in China.

www.cengagebrain
.com

© Nicholas Monu/iStockphoto.com

Sources: A. Booker, 2011, To caffeinate China, Starbucks takes a page from Burberry's playbook, *Forbes.com*, http://www.forbes.com, June 9; M. Townsend & L. Patton, 2011, Starbucks CEO says Japan disruption tempered by chain's size, *Bloomberg Businessweek*, http://www.businessweek.com, March 30; H. Yousuf, 2011, Emerging markets are hot: Place your bets, *CNNMoney*, http://www.cnnmoney.com, February 1; 2011, Starbucks, *Standard and Poor's Stock Report*, http://www.standardandpoors.com, June 10; Treflis team, 2011, China takes Starbucks to next level, *Forbes.com*, http://www.forbes.com, May 13; 2011, Starbucks Corporation, 2010 Annual Report, http://www.starbucks.com, March 10; 2011, Starbucks reinvents the customer experience in the prestigious Carrousel du Louvre, http://www.starbucks.com, January 11; 2010, Starbucks outlines strategy for accelerating profitable global growth, http://www.starbucks.com, March 24.

In Chapter 4's opening case, we described how Starbucks changed the nature of coffee drinking in the United States. We also discussed actions the firm is taking to recover from the downturn it experienced in 2008. Extending this earlier discussion, our description of Starbucks' competitive actions in this chapter's Opening Case highlights the increasing importance of international markets for this firm. However, being able to effectively compete in countries and regions outside a firm's domestic market is increasingly important to firms of all types, not just Starbucks. One reason for this is that the effects of globalization continue reducing the number of industrial and consumer markets in which only domestic firms can compete successfully. In place of what historically were relatively stable and predictable domestic markets, firms across the globe find they are now competing in globally oriented industries—industries in which firms must compete in all world markets where a consumer or commercial good or service is sold in order to be competitive.[1] Unlike domestic markets, global markets are relatively unstable and unpredictable.

The purpose of this chapter is to discuss how international strategies can be a source of strategic competitiveness for firms competing in global markets. To do this, we examine a number of topics (see Figure 8.1). After describing factors or incentives that influence firms to identify international opportunities, we discuss three basic benefits that can accrue to firms that successfully use international strategies. We then turn our attention to the international strategies available to firms. Specifically, we examine both

Figure 8.1 Opportunities and Outcomes of International Strategy

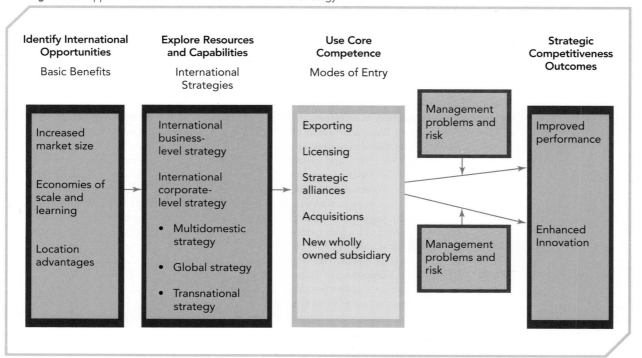

Source: © Copyrighted 2011 by Michael A. Hitt, R. Duane Ireland, and Robert E. Hoskisson

international business-level strategies and international corporate-level strategies. The five modes of entry firms consider when deciding how to enter international markets as a foundation for implementing their chosen international strategies are then considered. Firms encounter economic and political risks when using international strategies. These risks must be effectively managed if the firm is to achieve the strategic competitiveness outcomes of improved performance and enhanced innovation. After discussing the outcomes firms seek when using international strategies, the chapter closes with mention of two cautions about international strategy that should be kept in mind.

Identifying International Opportunities

An **international strategy** is a strategy through which the firm sells its goods or services outside its domestic market.[2] In some instances, firms using an international strategy become quite diversified geographically as they compete in numerous countries or regions outside their domestic market. This is the case for Starbucks in that it competes in over 50 countries. In other cases, firms experience less geographic or international diversification in that they only compete in a small number of markets outside their "home" market.

There are incentives for firms to use an international strategy and to diversify their operations geographically; and they can gain three basic benefits when they successfully do so.[3] We show international strategy's incentives and benefits in Figure 8.2.

Figure 8.2 Incentives and Basic Benefits of International Strategy

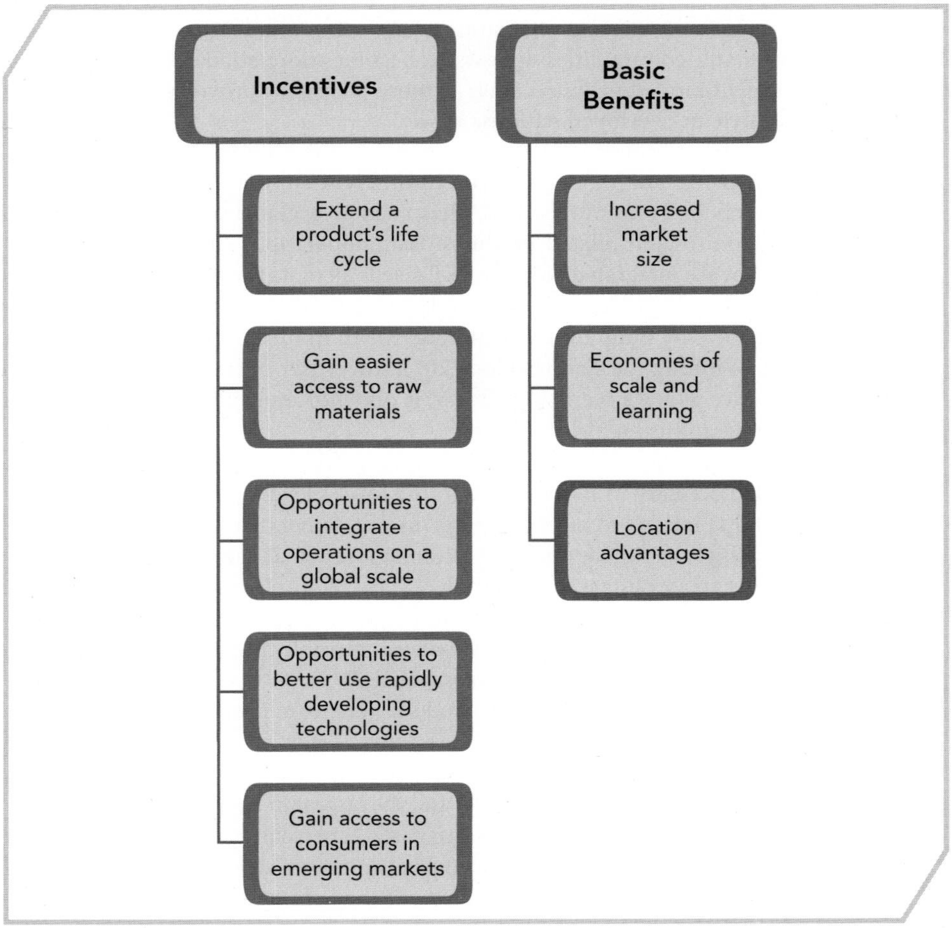

Source: © Copyrighted 2011 by Michael A. Hitt, R. Duane Ireland, and Robert E. Hoskisson

An **international strategy** is a strategy through which the firm sells its goods or services outside its domestic market.

Incentives to Use International Strategy

Raymond Vernon expressed the classic rationale for an international strategy.[4] He suggested that typically a firm discovers an innovation in its home-country market, especially in advanced economies such as those in Germany, France, Japan, Sweden, Canada, and the United States. Often demand for the product then develops in other countries, causing a firm to export products from its domestic operations to fulfill that demand. Continuing increases in demand can subsequently justify a firm's decision to establish operations outside of its domestic base. As Vernon noted, taking these actions in the form of international strategy has the potential to help a firm extend the life cycle of its product(s).

Gaining access to needed and potentially scarce resources is another reason firms use an international strategy. Key supplies of raw material—especially minerals and energy—are critical to firms' efforts in some industries to manufacture their products. Of course energy and mining companies have operations throughout the world to gain access to the raw materials they in turn sell to manufacturers requiring those resources. Rio Tinto is a leading international mining group. Operating as a global organization, the firm indicates that "most of (its) assets are in Australia and North America, but that (the firm) also operates in Europe, South America, Asia and Africa." Rio Tinto extracts the raw materials it sells from various sources including "open pit and underground mines, mills, refineries and smelters…"[5] In other industries where labor costs account for a significant portion of a company's expenses, firms may choose to establish facilities in other countries to gain access to less expensive labor. Clothing and electronics manufacturers are examples of firms pursuing an international strategy for this reason.

Increased pressure to integrate operations on a global scale is another factor influencing firms to pursue an international strategy. As nations industrialize, the demand for some products and commodities appears to become more similar. This borderless demand for globally branded products such as those Starbucks provides may be due to similarities in lifestyle in developed nations.

Increases in global communications also facilitate the ability of people in different countries to visualize and model lifestyles in different cultures.[6] With over 127,000 employees and stores in 41 countries, IKEA has become a global retail brand selling a wide variety of furniture and related products. Using operations (including marketing and advertising) that are integrated globally, IKEA sells all of its furniture in components that can be packaged in flat packs and assembled by consumers after purchase. This business model allows for easy shipping and handling, which in turn facilitates development of a global brand. Winning the Cannes Lions 2011 Advertiser of the Year Award for its "creative and effective global advertising efforts" is one indicator of IKEA's effectiveness at integrating its operations on a global basis.[7]

In an increasing number of industries, technology drives globalization because the economies of scale necessary to reduce costs to the lowest level often require an investment greater than that needed to meet domestic market demand. Moreover, in emerging markets the increasingly rapid adoption of technologies such as the Internet and mobile applications permits greater integration of trade, capital, culture, and labor. In this sense, technologies are the foundation for efforts to bind together disparate markets and operations across the world. International strategy makes it possible for firms to use technologies to organize their operations into a seamless whole.[8]

The potential of large demand for goods and services from people in emerging markets such as China and India is another strong incentive for firms to use an international strategy.[9] This is the case for French-based Carrefour Group. This firm is the world's second-largest retailer (behind only Walmart) and the largest in Europe. Carrefour operates four main grocery stores formats—hypermarkets, supermarkets, hard discount, and convenience stores.[10] Recently, Carrefour acquired minority stakes in three mainland Chinese retailers to strengthen its presence there, as the firm sees this market as critical to its growth plans.[11]

Even though India, another emerging market economy, differs from Western countries in many respects, including culture, politics, and the precepts of its economic system, it also offers a huge potential market and its government is becoming more supportive of foreign direct investment.[12] However, differences among Chinese, Indian, and Western-style economies and cultures make the successful use of an international strategy challenging. In particular, firms seeking to meet customer demands in emerging markets must learn how to manage an array of political and economic risks,[13] such as those we discuss later in the chapter.

We've now discussed incentives that influence firms to use international strategies. Firms derive three basic benefits by successfully using international strategies: (1) increased market size; (2) increased economies of scale and learning; and (3) development of a competitive advantage through location (e.g., access to low-cost labor, critical resources, or customers). These benefits will be examined here in terms of both their costs (such as higher coordination expenses and limited access to knowledge about host country political influences)[14] and their challenges.

Three Basic Benefits of International Strategy

As noted, effectively using one or more international strategies can result in three basic benefits for the firm. These benefits facilitate the firm's effort to achieve strategic competitiveness (see Figure 8.1) when using an international strategy.

Increased Market Size

Firms can expand the size of their potential market—sometimes dramatically—by using an international strategy to establish stronger positions in markets outside their domestic market. As noted, access to additional consumers is a key reason Carrefour sees China as a major source of growth.

Takeda, a large Japanese pharmaceutical company, recently acquired Swiss drug maker Nycomed for $13.7 billon. Buying Nycomed makes Takeda a major player in European markets. More significantly, the acquisition broadens Takeda's distribution capability in emerging markets "at a time when pharmaceutical firms world-wide are wrestling with the impact on revenue from the expiration of patents." In fact, the Nycomed deal will increase Takeda's sales in China about fourfold.[15] Along with Starbucks, Carrefour and Takeda are two additional companies relying on international strategy as the path to increased market size in China.

Firms such as Starbucks, Carrefour, and Takeda understand that effectively managing different consumer tastes and practices linked to cultural values or traditions in different markets is challenging. Nonetheless, they accept this challenge because of the potential to enhance the firm's performance. Other firms accept the challenge of successfully implementing an international strategy largely because of limited growth opportunities in their domestic market. This appears to be at least partly the case for major competitors Coca-Cola and PepsiCo, firms that have not been able to generate significant growth in their U.S. domestic (and North America) markets for some time. Indeed, most of these firms' growth is occurring in international markets. These two firms approach international growth somewhat differently. PepsiCo, the world's largest snack-food maker as a result of its Frito-Lay division, relies "on chip sales overseas to make up for slower beverage sales volumes in North America."[16] Less diversified than PepsiCo in terms of products but not in terms of geography, Coca-Cola is the world's largest producer of soft drink concentrates and syrups and the world's largest producer of juice and juice-related products. Selling its products in more than 200 countries, Coca-Cola derives only approximately 32 percent of its revenue from sales in North America, suggesting that the firm's international strategies are critical to its efforts to be competitively successful and that it does not rely on sales in North America as the cornerstone of its efforts to outperform PepsiCo, its chief rival.[17]

An international market's overall size also has the potential to affect the degree of benefit a firm can accrue as a result of using an international strategy. In general, larger international markets offer higher potential returns and thus pose less risk for the firm choosing to invest in those markets. Relatedly, the strength of the science base of the international markets in which a firm may compete is important in that scientific knowledge and the human capital needed to use that knowledge can facilitate efforts to more effectively sell and/or produce products that create value for customers.[18]

Economies of Scale and Learning

By expanding the number of markets in which they compete, firms may be able to enjoy economies of scale, particularly in their manufacturing operations. More broadly, firms able to standardize the processes used to produce, sell, distribute, and service their products across country borders enhance their ability to learn how to continuously reduce costs while hopefully increasing the value their products create for customers. For example, rivals Airbus SAS and Boeing have multiple manufacturing facilities and outsource some activities to firms located throughout the world, partly for the purpose of developing economies of scale as a source of being able to create value for customers.

Economies of scale are critical in a number of settings in addition to the airline manufacturing industry. Automobile manufacturers certainly seek economies of scale as a benefit of their international strategies. Competing in markets throughout the world, Ford Motor Company "is counting on rapid growth in Asia to fuel a dramatic expansion of sales and boost profits over the next several years..."[19] Overall, Ford seeks to increase the annual number of products it sells outside of North America to 8 million units by the end of 2015 (up from about 5.3 million sold internationally in 2010). Ford is using a global corporate-level international strategy to reach this objective (this strategy is discussed later in the chapter). Demonstrating the use of this international strategy is the fact that Ford is now run as a single global business developing cars and trucks that can be built and sold throughout the world. By 2015, the firm intends for about 75 percent of all the vehicles it sells globally to be variants of five basic sets of manufacturing platforms. "The company is counting on these platforms to cut costs by increasing economies of scale."[20] Using these five platforms and the relatively small number of product variants they allow the firm to produce, Ford intends to increase the number of products it sells in China from 5 to 15 and in India to from 5 to 8.

Firms may also be able to exploit core competencies in international markets through resource and knowledge sharing between units and network partners across country borders.[21] By sharing resources and knowledge in this manner, firms can learn how to create synergy, which in turn can help each firm learn how to produce higher-quality products at a lower cost. This may be the case for the members of the International Aero Engines (IAE) consortium: Pratt & Whitney, Rolls Royce, Japanese Aero Engines, and MTU Aero. Relying on their members' joint capabilities and core competencies, IAE recently developed an innovative PurePower geared turbofan engine platform. One version of this engine is in some of Airbus' new A320neo aircraft, which the consortium sees as a positive reaction to its innovation.[22]

Working in multiple international markets also provides firms with new learning opportunities,[23] perhaps even in terms of research and development activities. Increasing the firm's R&D ability can contribute to its efforts to enhance innovation, which is critical to both short- and long-term success. However, research

Pratt & Whitney, part of the International Aero Engines (IAE) consortium, maximizes its and other members' core competencies to produce state of the art engines and other technologically advanced products.

testing/Shutterstock.com

results suggest that to take advantage of international R&D investments, firms need to already have a strong R&D system in place to absorb knowledge resulting from effective R&D activities.[24]

Location Advantages

Locating facilities in markets outside their domestic market can sometimes help firms reduce costs. This benefit of an international strategy accrues to the firm when its facilities in international locations provide easier access to lower-cost labor, energy, and other natural resources. Other location advantages include access to critical supplies and to customers. Once positioned favorably with an attractive location, firms must manage their facilities effectively to gain the full benefit of a location advantage.[25]

A firm's costs, particularly those dealing with manufacturing and distribution, as well as the nature of international customers' needs, affect the degree of benefit it can capture through a location advantage.[26] Cultural influences may also affect location advantages and disadvantages. International business transactions are less difficult for a firm to complete when there is a strong match among the cultures with which the firm is involved while implementing its international strategy.[27] Finally, physical distances influence firms' location choices as well as how to manage facilities in the chosen locations.[28]

International Strategies

Firms choose to use one or both basic types of international strategy: business-level international strategy and corporate-level international strategy. At the business level, firms select from among the generic strategies of cost leadership, differentiation, focused cost leadership, focused differentiation, and integrated cost leadership/differentiation. At the corporate level, multidomestic, global, and transnational international strategies (the transnational is a combination of the multidomestic and global strategies) are considered. To contribute to the firm's efforts to achieve strategic competitiveness in the form of improved performance and enhanced innovation (see Figure 8.1), each international strategy the firm uses must be based on one or more core competencies.[29]

International Business-Level Strategy

Firms considering the use of any international strategy first develop domestic-market strategies (at the business level and at the corporate level if the firm has diversified at the product level). One reason this is important is that the firm may be able to use some of the capabilities and core competencies it has developed in its domestic market as the foundation for competitive success in international markets.[30] However, research results indicate that the value created by relying on capabilities and core competencies developed in domestic markets as a source of success in international markets diminishes as a firm's geographic diversity increases.[31]

As we know from our discussion of competitive dynamics in Chapter 5, firms do not select and then use strategies in isolation of market realities. In the case of international strategies, conditions in a firm's domestic market affect the degree to which the firm can build on capabilities and core competencies it established in that market to create capabilities and core competencies in international markets. The reason for this is grounded in Michael Porter's analysis of why some nations are more competitive than other nations and why and how some industries within nations are more competitive relative to those industries in other nations. Porter's core argument is that conditions or factors in a firm's home base—that is, in its domestic market—either hinder the firm's efforts to use an international business-level strategy for the purpose of establishing a competitive advantage in international markets or support those efforts. Porter identifies four factors as determinants of a national advantage that some countries possess (see Figure 8.3).[32] Interactions among these four factors influence a firm's choice of international business-level strategy.

Figure 8.3 Determinants of National Advantage

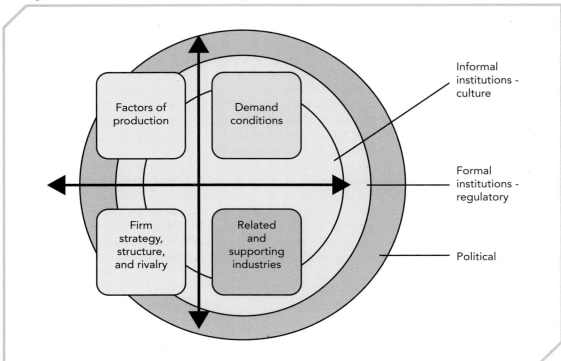

Source: © Copyrighted 2011 by Michael A. Hitt, R. Duane Ireland, and Robert E. Hoskisson.

The first determinant of national advantage is factors of production. This determinant refers to the inputs necessary for a firm to compete in any industry. Labor, land, natural resources, capital, and infrastructure (such as transportation, postal, and communication systems) are examples of such inputs. There are basic factors (for example, natural and labor resources) and advanced factors (such as digital communication systems and a highly educated workforce). Other production factors are generalized (highway systems and the supply of debt capital) and specialized (skilled personnel in a specific industry, such as the workers in a port that specialize in handling bulk chemicals). If a country possesses advanced and specialized production factors, it is likely to serve an industry well by spawning strong home-country competitors that also can be successful global competitors.

Ironically, countries often develop advanced and specialized factors because they lack critical basic resources. For example, some Asian countries, such as South Korea, lack abundant natural resources but have a workforce with a strong work ethic, a large number of engineers, and systems of large firms to create an expertise in manufacturing. Similarly, Germany developed a strong chemical industry, partially because Hoechst and BASF spent years creating a synthetic indigo dye to reduce their dependence on imports, unlike Britain, whose colonies provided large supplies of natural indigo.[33]

The second factor or determinant of national advantage, demand conditions, is characterized by the nature and size of customers' needs in the home market for the products firms competing in an industry produce. Meeting the demand generated by a large number of customers creates conditions through which a firm can develop scale-efficient facilities and refine the capabilities, and perhaps core competencies, required to use those facilities. Once refined, the probability that the capabilities and core competencies will benefit the firm as it diversifies geographically increases.

This may be the case for some Chinese manufacturing companies that have spent years building their businesses in China and developing economies of scale and scale efficient facilities in the process of doing so. Today, many of these firms hope to be able to rely on these facilities and the capabilities and core competencies they have developed to use those facilities to become "global players," capable of using international business-level strategies to profitably sell their products in multiple international markets.[34]

The third factor in Porter's model of the determinants of national advantage is related and supporting industries. Italy has become the leader in the shoe industry because of related and supporting industries. For example, a well-established leather-processing industry provides the leather needed to construct shoes and related products. Also, many people travel to Italy to purchase leather goods, providing support in distribution. Supporting industries in leather-working machinery and design services also contribute to the success of the shoe industry. In fact, the design services industry supports its own related industries, such as ski boots, fashion apparel, and furniture. In Japan, cameras and copiers are related industries. Similarly, it is argued that the creative resources associated with "popular cartoons such as Manga and the animation sector along with technological knowledge from the consumer electronics industry facilitated the emergence of a successful video game industry in Japan."[35] In a like manner, Germany is known for the quality of its machine tools, and Eastern Belgium is known for skilled manufacturing (supporting and related industries are important in these two settings too).[36]

Firm strategy, structure, and rivalry make up the final determinant of national advantage and also foster the growth of certain industries. The types of strategy, structure, and rivalry among firms vary greatly from nation to nation. The excellent technical training system in Germany fosters a strong emphasis on continuous product and process improvements. In Japan, unusual cooperative and competitive systems facilitate the cross-functional management of complex assembly operations. In Italy, the national pride of the country's designers spawns strong industries not only in shoes but also sports cars, fashion apparel, and furniture. In the United States, competition among computer manufacturers and software producers contributes to further development of these industries.

The four determinants of national advantage (see Figure 8.3) emphasize the structural characteristics of a specific economy that contribute to some degree to national advantage and that influence the firm's selection of an international business-level strategy. Individual governments' policies also affect the nature of the determinants as well as how firms compete within the boundaries governing bodies establish and enforce within a particular economy.[37] While studying their external environment (see Chapter 2), firms considering the possibility of using an international strategy need to gather information and data that will allow them to understand the effects of governmental policies and their enforcement on their nation's ability to establish advantage relative to other nations as well as the relative degree of competitiveness on a global basis of the industry in which firms might compete on a global scale.

Those leading companies should recognize that a firm based in a country with a national competitive advantage is not guaranteed success as it implements its chosen international business-level strategy. The actual strategic choices managers make may be the most compelling reasons for success or failure as firms diversify geographically. Accordingly, the factors illustrated in Figure 8.3 are likely to produce the foundation for a firm's competitive advantages only when it develops and implements an appropriate international business-level strategy that takes advantage of distinct country factors. Thus, these distinct country factors should be thoroughly considered when making a decision about the international business-level strategy the firm will use. In a competitive rivalry sense, the firm will then make continuous adjustments to its international business-level strategy in light of the nature of competition it encounters in different international markets and in light of customers' needs. Lexus, for example, does not have the share of the luxury car market in China that it desires. Accordingly, Toyota (Lexus' manufacturer) is adjusting how it implements its international differentiation business-level strategy in China to better serve customers. The firm is doing this by "turning to the feature that cemented its early success in the United States: extreme customer service.

Showroom amenities such as cappuccino machines, Wi-Fi, Lego tables for the kids, and airport shuttles for busy executives dropping off their cars for servicing are examples of the services now being offered to customers in China."[38] Time will tell if this adjustment to Lexus' strategy in China will lead to the success the firm desires.

International Corporate-Level Strategy

A firm's international business-level strategy is also based at least partially on its international corporate-level strategy. Some international corporate-level strategies give individual country units the authority to develop their own business-level strategies, while others dictate the business-level strategies in order to standardize the firm's products and sharing of resources across countries.[39]

International corporate-level strategy focuses on the scope of a firm's operations through geographic diversification.[40] International corporate-level strategy is required when the firm operates in multiple industries that are located in multiple countries or regions (e.g., Southeast Asia or the European Union) and in which they sell multiple products. The headquarters unit guides the strategy, although as noted, business- or country-level managers can have substantial strategic input depending on the type of international corporate-level strategy the firm uses. We show the three international corporate-level strategies in Figure 8.4. As shown, the international corporate-level strategies vary in terms of two dimensions—the need for global integration and the need for local responsiveness.

Multidomestic Strategy

A **multidomestic strategy** is an international strategy in which strategic and operating decisions are decentralized to the strategic business units in individual countries or regions for the purpose of allowing each unit the opportunity to tailor products to the

> A **multidomestic strategy** is an international strategy in which strategic and operating decisions are decentralized to the strategic business units in individual countries or regions for the purpose of allowing each unit the opportunity to tailor products to the local market.

Figure 8.4 International Corporate-Level Strategies

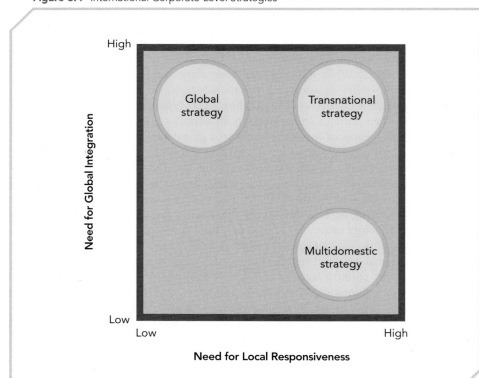

local market.[41] With this strategy, the firm's need for local responsiveness is high while its need for global integration is low. Influencing these needs is the firm's belief that consumer needs and desires, industry conditions (e.g., the number and type of competitors), political and legal structures, and social norms vary by country. Thus, a multidomestic strategy focuses on competition within each country in that market needs are thought to be segmented by country boundaries. To meet the specific needs and preferences of local customers, country or regional managers have the autonomy to customize the firm's products. Therefore, these strategies should maximize a firm's competitive response to the idiosyncratic requirements of each market.[42] The multidomestic strategy is most appropriate for use when the differences between the markets a firm serves and the customers in them are significant.

The use of multidomestic strategies usually expands the firm's local market share because the firm can pay attention to the local clientele's needs. However, using a multidomestic strategy results in less knowledge sharing for the corporation as a whole because of the differences across markets, decentralization, and the different international business-level strategies employed by local units.[43] Moreover, multidomestic strategies do not allow the development of economies of scale and thus can be more costly.

Unilever is a large European consumer products company selling products in over 180 countries. The firm has more than 400 global brands that are grouped into three business units—foods, home care, and personal care. Historically, Unilever has used a highly decentralized approach for the purpose of managing its global brands. This approach allows regional managers considerable autonomy to adapt the characteristics of specific products to satisfy the unique needs of customers in different markets. However, more recently, Unilever has sought to increase the coordination between its independent subsidiaries in order to establish an even stronger global brand presence.[44] As such, Unilever may be transitioning from a multidomestic strategy to a transnational strategy.

Global Strategy

A global strategy is an international strategy in which a firm's home office determines the strategies business units are to use in each country or region.[45] This strategy indicates that the firm has a high need for global integration and a low need for local responsiveness. These needs indicate that compared to a multidomestic strategy, a global strategy seeks greater levels of standardization of products across country markets. The firm using a global strategy seeks to develop economies of scale as it produces the same or virtually the same products for distribution to customers throughout the world who are assumed to have similar needs. The global strategy offers greater opportunities to take innovations developed at the corporate level or in one market and apply them in other markets.[46] Improvements in global accounting and financial reporting standards facilitate use of this strategy.[47] A global strategy is most effective for us when the differences between markets and the customers the firm is serving are insignificant.

Efficient operations are required to successfully implement a global strategy. Increasing the efficiency of a firm's international operations mandates resource sharing and greater coordination and cooperation across market boundaries. Centralized decision making as designed by headquarters details how resources are to be shared and coordinated across markets. Research results suggest that the outcomes a firm achieves by using a global strategy become more desirable when the strategy is used in areas where regional integration among countries is occurring.[48]

CEMEX is a global building materials company that uses the international strategy. CEMEX is the world's leading supplier of ready-mix concrete and one of the world's largest producers of white Portland cement. CEMEX sells to customers in more than 50 countries in multiple regions, including the Americas, Europe, Africa, the Middle East, and Asia. With annual sales of more than $14 billion, the firm employs more than 47,000 people.

To implement its global strategy, CEMEX has centralized a number of its activities. The Shared Services Model is a recent example of how this firm centralizes operations in

A global strategy is an international strategy in which a firm's home office determines the strategies business units are to use in each country or region.

order to gain scale economies, among other benefits. According to company documents, this model "converges, centralizes, and streamlines back-office services—such as human resources and payroll, information technology, and transactional and financial services—for our operations across regions."[49] In essence, the Shared Services Model integrates and centralizes some support functions from the firm's value chain (see Chapter 3). This integration and centralization brings about the types of benefits sought by firms when using a global strategy. Significant cost savings, increases in the productivity of the involved support functions, the fostering of economies of scale, and the freeing up of resources to enable an improved focus on core tasks are examples of the benefits CEMEX is accruing by using its Shared Services Model.

Because of increasing global competition and the need to simultaneously be cost efficient and produce differentiated products, the number of firms using a transnational international corporate-level strategy is increasing.

Transnational Strategy

A **transnational strategy** is an international strategy through which the firm seeks to achieve both global efficiency and local responsiveness. With this strategy, the firm has strong needs for both global integration and local responsiveness. As noted in the Opening Case, Starbucks is using the transnational strategy to pursue profitable growth in international markets. For example, in China Starbucks is trying to standardize its operations (global integration) while it simultaneously decentralizes some decision-making responsibility to local levels so products can be made to meet customers' unique needs (local responsiveness). Chai tea lattes, green tea black sesame frappuccinos, and back bean muffins are examples of products Starbucks has adapted to meet local tastes in China.[50]

Realizing the twin goals of global integration and local responsiveness is difficult in that global integration requires close global coordination while local responsiveness requires local flexibility. "Flexible coordination"—building a shared vision and individual commitment through an integrated network—is required to implement the transnational strategy. Such integrated networks allow a firm to manage its connections with customers, suppliers, partners, and other parties more efficiently rather than using arm's-length transactions.[51] The transnational strategy is difficult to use because of its conflicting goals (see Chapter 11 for more on the implementation of this and other corporate-level international strategies). On the positive side, effectively implementing a transnational strategy often produces higher performance than does implementing either the multidomestic or global strategies.[52]

Transnational strategies are becoming increasingly necessary to successfully compete in international markets. Reasons for this include the fact that continuing increases in the number of viable global competitors challenge firms to reduce their costs. Simultaneously, the increasing sophistication of markets with greater information flows made possible largely by the diffusion of the Internet and the desire for specialized products to meet consumers' unique needs pressures firms to differentiate their products in local markets. Differences in culture and institutional environments also require firms to adapt their products and approaches to local environments. However, some argue that transnational strategies are not required to successfully compete in international markets. Those holding this view suggest that most multinational firms try to compete at the regional level (e.g., the European Union) rather than at the country level. To the degree this is the case, the need for the firm to simultaneously offer relatively unique products that are adapted to local markets and to produce those products at lower costs permitted by developing scale economies is reduced.[53]

Next we discuss trends in the global environment that are affecting the choices firms make when deciding which international corporate-level strategies to use and in which international markets to compete.

A **transnational strategy** is an international strategy through which the firm seeks to achieve both global efficiency and local responsiveness.

Environmental Trends

Although the transnational strategy is difficult to implement, an emphasis on global efficiency is increasing as more industries and the companies competing within them encounter intensified global competition. Magnifying the scope of this issue is the fact that, simultaneously, firms are experiencing demands for local adaptations of their products. These demands can be from customers (for products to satisfy their tastes and preferences) and from governing bodies (for products to satisfy a country's regulations). In addition, most multinational firms desire coordination and sharing of resources across country markets to hold down costs, as illustrated by the CEMEX example.[54]

Because of these conditions, some large multinational firms with diverse products use a multidomestic strategy with certain product lines and a global strategy with others when diversifying geographically. Many multinational firms may require this type of flexibility if they are to be strategically competitive, in part due to trends that change over time.

Liability of foreignness and regionalization are two important trends influencing a firm's choice and use of international strategies, particularly international corporate-level strategies. We discuss these trends next.

Liability of Foreignness

The dramatic success of Japanese firms such as Toyota and Sony in the United States and other international markets in the 1980s was a powerful jolt to U.S. managers and awakened them to the importance of international competition and the fact that many markets were rapidly becoming globalized. In the twenty-first century, Brazil, Russia, India, and China (BRIC) represent major international market opportunities for firms from many countries, including the United States, Japan, Korea, and members of the European Union.[55] However, even if foreign markets seem attractive, as appears to be the case with the BRIC countries, there are legitimate concerns for firms considering entering these markets. This is the *liability of foreignness*,[56] a set of costs associated with various issues firms face when entering foreign markets, including unfamiliar operating environments; economic, administrative, and cultural differences; and the challenges of coordination over distances.[57] Four types of distances commonly associated with liability of foreignness are cultural, administrative, geographic, and economic.[58]

Walt Disney Company's experience while opening theme parks in foreign countries demonstrates the liability of foreignness. For example, Disney suffered "lawsuits in France, at Disneyland Paris, because of the lack of fit between its transferred personnel policies and the French employees charged to enact them."[59] Disney executives learned from this experience in building the firm's theme park in Hong Kong as the company "went out of its way to tailor the park to local tastes."[60] Thus, as with Walt Disney Company, firms thinking about using an international strategy to enter foreign markets must be aware of the four types of distances they'll encounter when

Disney executives learned from their mistakes with Disneyland Paris when entering other foreign markets, such as Hong Kong.

Chad Ehlers/Alamy

doing so and determine actions to take to reduce the potentially negative effects associated with those distances.

Regionalization

Regionalization is a second global environmental trend influencing a firm's choice and use of international strategies. This trend is becoming prominent largely because where a firm chooses to compete can affect its strategic competitiveness.[61] As a result, the firm considering using international strategies must decide if it should enter individual country markets or if it would be better served by competing in one or more regional markets rather than in individual country markets.

Currently, the global international strategy is used less frequently. It remains difficult to successfully implement even when the firm uses Internet-based strategies.[62] In addition, the amount of competition vying for a limited amount of resources and customers can limit firms' focus to a specific region rather than on country-specific markets that are located in multiple parts of the world. A regional focus allows firms to marshal their resources to compete effectively rather than spreading their limited resources across multiple country-specific international markets.[63]

However, a firm that competes in industries where the international markets differ greatly (in which it must employ a multidomestic strategy) may wish to narrow its focus to a particular region of the world. In so doing, it can better understand the cultures, legal and social norms, and other factors that are important for effective competition in those markets. For example, a firm may focus on Far East markets only rather than competing simultaneously in the Middle East, Europe, and the Far East. Or the firm may choose a region of the world where the markets are more similar and some coordination and sharing of resources would be possible. In this way, the firm may be able not only to better understand the markets in which it competes, but also to achieve some economies, even though it may have to employ a multidomestic strategy. For instance, research suggests that most large retailers are better at focusing on a particular region rather than being truly global.[64] Firms commonly focus much of their international market entries on countries adjacent to their home country, which might be referred to as their home region.[65]

Countries that develop trade agreements to increase the economic power of their regions may promote regional strategies. The European Union (EU) and South America's Organization of American States (OAS) are country associations that developed trade agreements to promote the flow of trade across country boundaries within their respective regions.[66] Many European firms acquire and integrate their businesses in Europe to better coordinate pan-European brands as the EU creates more unity in European markets. With this process likely to continue as new countries are added to the agreement, some international firms may prefer to focus on regions rather than multiple country markets when entering international markets.

The North American Free Trade Agreement (NAFTA), signed by the United States, Canada, and Mexico, facilitates free trade across country borders in North America. NAFTA loosens restrictions on international strategies within this region and provides greater opportunity for regional international strategies.[67]

Most firms enter regional markets sequentially, beginning in markets with which they are more familiar. They also introduce their largest and strongest lines of business into these markets first, followed by other product lines once the initial efforts are deemed successful. The additional product lines typically are introduced in the original investment location.[68] However, research also suggests that the size of the market and industry characteristics can influence this decision.[69]

After selecting its business- and corporate-level international strategies, the firm determines how it will enter the international markets in which it has chosen to compete. We turn to this topic next.

Choice of International Entry Mode

Five modes of entry into international markets are available to firms. We show these entry modes and their characteristics in Figure 8.5. Each means of market entry has its advantages and disadvantages, suggesting that the choice of entry mode can affect the degree of success the firm achieves by implementing an international strategy. Large firms competing in multiple markets commonly use more than one and may use all five entry modes.

Exporting

For many firms, exporting is the initial mode of entry used.[70] *Exporting* is an entry mode through which the firm sends products it produces in its domestic market to international

Figure 8.5 Modes of Entry and Their Characteristics

Type of Entry	Characteristics
Exporting	High cost, low control
Licensing	Low cost, low risk, little control, low returns
Strategic alliances	Shared costs, shared resources, shared risks, problems of integration (e.g., two corporate cultures)
Acquisitions	Quick access to new markets, high costs, complex negotiations, problems of merging with domestic operations
New wholly owned subsidiary	Complex, often costly, time consuming, high risk, maximum control, potential above-average returns

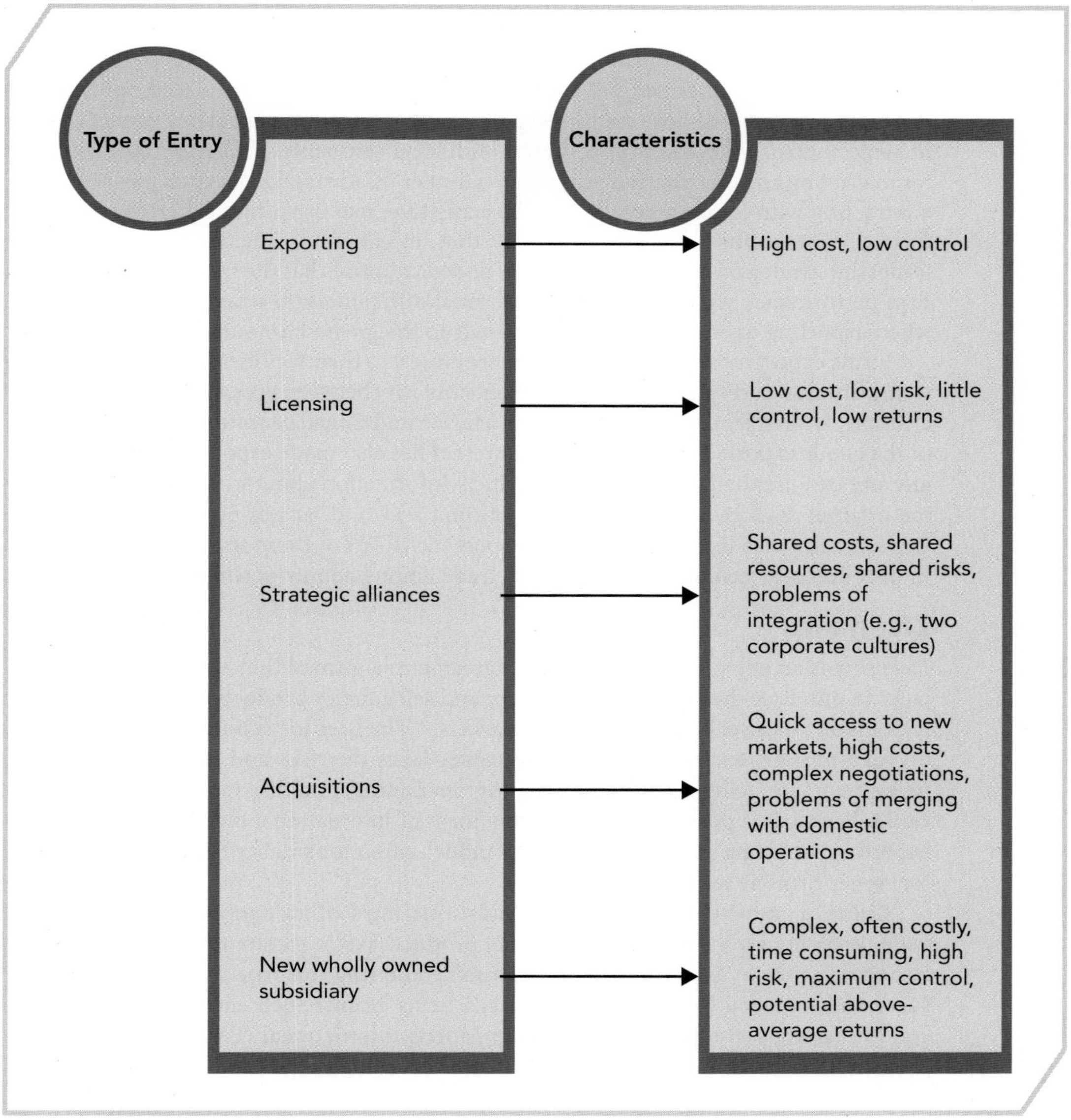

Source: © Copyrighted 2011 by Michael A. Hitt, R. Duane Ireland, and Robert E. Hoskisson

markets. Western Forms Inc., a manufacturing firm based in Kansas City, Missouri, is successfully using exporting as an entry mode. Employing approximately 200 employees, Western Forms makes aluminum-forming systems for concrete buildings. In 2010, the U.S. International Trade Administration recognized Western Forms for its exporting achievement as demonstrated by millions of dollars of new sales in India. In recognizing this firm, an official said that "Western Forms is a great example of a firm that has and continues to diversify internationally to better weather the ups and downs of its industry and the global economy."[71] Western Forms' selection of exporting as the way of entering international markets is not surprising in that exporting is a popular entry mode choice for small businesses.

The number of small U.S. firms using an international strategy is increasing, with some predicting that up to 50 percent of small U.S. firms will be involved in international trade by 2018, most of them through export.[72] By exporting, firms avoid the expense of establishing operations in host countries (that is, in countries outside their home country) in which they have chosen to compete. However, firms must establish some means of marketing and distributing their products when exporting. Usually, contracts are formed with host-country firms to handle these activities. Potentially high transportation costs to export products to international markets and the expense of tariffs placed on the firm's products as a result of host countries' policies are examples of exporting costs. The loss of some control when the firm contracts with local companies located in host countries for marketing and distribution purposes is another disadvantage of exporting. Moreover, contracting with local companies can be expensive, making it harder for the exporting firm to earn profits.[73] Evidence suggests that, in general, using an international cost leadership strategy when exporting to developed countries has the most positive effect on firm performance while using an international differentiation strategy with larger scale when exporting to emerging economies leads to the greatest amount of success.[74]

Firms export mostly to countries that are closest to their facilities because of the lower transportation costs and the usually greater similarity between geographic neighbors. For example, United States' NAFTA partners Mexico and Canada account for more than half of the goods exported from Texas. The Internet has also made exporting easier. Firms of any size can use the Internet to access critical information about foreign markets, examine a target market, research the competition, and find lists of potential customers.[75] Governments also use the Internet to support the efforts of those applying for export and import licenses, facilitating international trade among countries while doing so.

Licensing

Licensing is an entry mode in which an agreement is formed that allows a foreign company to purchase the right to manufacture and sell a firm's products within a host country's market or a set of host countries' markets.[76] The licensor is normally paid a royalty on each unit produced and sold. The licensee takes the risks and makes the monetary investments in facilities for manufacturing, marketing, and distributing products. As a result, licensing is possibly the least costly form of international diversification. As with exporting, licensing is an attractive entry mode option for smaller firms, and potentially for newer firms as well.[77]

China, a country accounting for almost one-third of all cigarettes smoked worldwide, is obviously a huge market for this product. U.S. cigarette firms want to have a strong presence in China but have had trouble entering this market, largely because of successful lobbying by state-owned tobacco firms against such entry. Because of these conditions, cigarette manufacturer Philip Morris International (PMI) had an incentive to form a deal with these state-owned firms. Accordingly, PMI and the China National Tobacco Corporation (CNTC) completed a licensing agreement at the end of 2005. This agreement provides CNTC access to the most famous brand in the world, Marlboro.[78] Because it is a licensing agreement rather than a foreign direct investment by PMI, China maintains control of distribution. However, the Chinese state-owned tobacco monopoly, as part of the agreement, also gets to have PMI's help in distributing its own brands in select foreign markets. The result of this distribution approach for Chinese cigarettes is uncertain though. An analyst made the following observation about this distribution arrangement: "The question is whether it can pluck three cigarette brands—RGD, Harmony and Dubliss—from relative obscurity and elevate them to an international, or at least regional, presence."[79]

Another potential benefit of licensing as an entry mode is the possibility of earning greater returns from product innovations by selling the firm's innovations in international markets as well as in the domestic market.[80] Edu-Science, a Hong-Kong manufacturer of educational toys that have a base in science, is doing this through its recent multiyear licensing agreement with *Scientific American* magazine. *Scientific American*, founded in 1845 and the oldest continuously published magazine in the United States, remains an important science publication. The agreement calls for Edu-Science to produce a *Scientific American*-branded toy line ranging from "Science Fair Projects" to "How Things Work Today." Using some of its existing innovative products in addition to others the firm may develop, the Edu-Science toys that will be part of the *Scientific American* brand are to be "distributed internationally and to all retail channels."[81]

Licensing also has disadvantages. For example, once a firm licenses its product or brand to another party, it has little control over selling and distribution. Developing licensing agreements that protect the interests of both parties while supporting the relationship embedded within an agreement helps deal with this potential disadvantage.[82] In addition, licensing provides the least potential returns because returns must be shared between the licensor and the licensee. Another disadvantage is that the international firm may learn the technology of the party with whom it formed an agreement and then produce and sell a similar competitive product after the licensing agreement expires. Komatsu, for example, first licensed much of its technology from International Harvester, Bucyrus-Erie, and Cummins Engine to compete against Caterpillar in the earthmoving equipment business. Komatsu then dropped these licenses and developed its own products using the technology it had gained from the U.S. companies.[83] Because of potential disadvantages such as those we have discussed, the parties to a licensing arrangement should formally finalize an agreement only after they are convinced that both parties' best interests are protected.

Strategic Alliances

Increasingly popular as an entry mode among firms using international strategies,[84] a *strategic alliance* finds a firm collaborating with another company in a different setting in order to enter one or more international markets.[85] Firms share the risks and the resources required to enter international markets when using strategic alliances.[86] Moreover, because partners bring their unique resources together for the purpose of working collaboratively, strategic alliances can facilitate developing new capabilities and possibly core competencies that may contribute to the firm's strategic competitiveness.[87] Indeed, developing and learning how to use new capabilities and/or competencies (particularly those related to technology) is often a key purpose for which firms use strategic alliances as an entry mode.[88] Firms should be aware that establishing trust between partners is critical for developing and managing technology-based capabilities while using strategic alliances.[89]

French-based Limagrain is the fourth largest seed company in the world through its subsidiary Vilmorin & Cie. An international agricultural cooperative group specializing in field seeds, vegetable seeds, and cereal products, part of Limagrain's strategy calls for it to enter additional international markets. Limagrain is using strategic alliances as an entry mode. Recently the firm formed a strategic alliance with the Brazilian seed company Sementes Guerra in Brazil. Corn is the focus of the alliance between these companies. Guerra is a family-owned company engaged in seed research, the production of corn, wheat, and soybeans, and the distribution of those products to farmers in Brazil and neighboring countries. Commenting about the purpose of this alliance, a Limagrain official suggested that, "Our investment in research, combined with Guerra's knowledge of the Brazilian market and its commercial network, will extend the range of varieties (of seeds and corn) proposed to farmers."[90]

Not all alliances formed for the purpose of entering international markets are successful.[91] Incompatible partners and conflict between the partners are primary reasons for failure when firms use strategic alliances as an entry mode. Another issue here is that international strategic alliances are especially difficult to manage. Trust is an important aspect of alliances and must be carefully managed. The degree of trust between partners strongly influences alliance success. The probability of alliance success increases as the amount of trust between partners expands. Efforts to build trust are affected by at least four fundamental issues: the initial condition of the relationship, the negotiation process to arrive at an agreement, partner interactions, and external events.[92] Trust is also influenced by the country cultures involved in the alliance.[93] Firms should be aware of these issues when trying to appropriately manage trust.

Research has shown that equity-based alliances over which a firm has more control are more likely to produce positive returns.[94] (We discuss equity-based and other types of strategic alliances in Chapter 9.) However, if trust is required to develop new capabilities through an alliance, equity positions can serve as a barrier to the necessary relationship building. If conflict in a strategic alliance formed as an entry mode is not manageable, using acquisitions to enter international markets may be a better option.[95]

Acquisitions

When a firm acquires another company to enter an international market, it has completed a cross-border acquisition. Specifically, a *cross-border acquisition* is an entry mode through which a firm from one country acquires a stake in or purchases all of a firm located in another country.

As free trade expands in global markets, firms throughout the world are completing a larger number of cross-border acquisitions. The ability of cross-border acquisitions to provide rapid access to new markets is a key reason for their growth. In fact, of the five entry modes, acquisitions often are the quickest means for firms to enter international markets.[96]

Today, there is a broad range of cross-border acquisitions being completed by a diverse set of companies. Increasingly, Chinese companies are acquiring firms in other nations as a means of entering international markets. LDK Solar Co., with headquarters in Hi-Tech Industrial Park, Xinyu City, Jiangxi Province in the People's Republic of China, is a leading vertically integrated manufacturer of photovoltaic products as well as a leading manufacturer of solar wafers in terms of capacity. This firm recently acquired 70 percent of U.S.-based Solar Power Inc. (SPI), which too is a vertically integrated photovoltaic solar developer. In commenting about this transaction, LDK Solar's CEO said, "This transaction … expands our downstream vertical integration opportunities and provides LDK Solar and SPI the opportunity to jointly explore opening manufacturing operations in the U.S. to further enhance SPI's competitive advantage in North America."[97] Thus, the expectation is that both firms will benefit from this transaction.

JA Solar is another Chinese company involved with solar power that is using cross-border acquisitions as an entry mode. One of the world's largest manufacturers of high-performance solar cells and solar power products, JA Solar acquired 100 percent of Silver Age Holdings, "a British Virgin Islands company that owns 100 percent of Solar Silicon Valley Electronic Science and Technology Co., Ltd."[98] A JA Solar official commented about the expected benefits of this acquisition: "By boosting JA Solar's internal wafer capacity through this acquisition, we expect to achieve greater economies of scale and improve the company's profitability."[99]

Interestingly, firms use cross-border acquisitions less frequently to enter markets where corruption affects business transactions and, hence, the use of international strategies. Firms' preference is to use joint ventures to enter markets in which corruption is an issue rather than using acquisitions. (Discussed fully in Chapter 9, a joint venture is a type of strategic alliance in which two or more firms create a legally independent company and share their resources and capabilities to operate it.) However, these ventures fail more often, although this is less frequently the case for firms experienced with entering "corrupt" markets. When acquisitions are made in such countries, acquirers commonly pay smaller premiums to buy firms in different markets.[100]

Although increasingly popular, acquisitions as an entry mode are not without costs, nor are they easy to successfully complete and operate. Cross-border acquisitions carry some of the disadvantages of domestic acquisitions (see Chapter 7). In addition, they often require debt financing to complete, which carries an extra cost. Another issue for firms to consider is that negotiations for cross-border acquisitions can be exceedingly complex and are generally more complicated than are the negotiations associated with domestic acquisitions. Dealing with the legal and regulatory requirements in the target firm's country and obtaining appropriate information to negotiate an agreement are also frequent problems. Finally, the merging of the new firm into the acquiring firm is often more complex than is the case with domestic acquisitions. The firm completing the cross-border acquisition must deal not only with different corporate cultures, but also with potentially different social cultures and practices.[101] These differences make integrating the two firms after the acquisition more challenging; it is difficult to capture the potential synergy when integration is slowed or stymied because of cultural differences.[102] Therefore, while cross-border acquisitions are popular as an entry mode primarily because they provide rapid access to new markets, firms considering this option should be fully aware of the costs and risks associated with using it.

New Wholly Owned Subsidiary

A greenfield venture is an entry mode through which a firm invests directly in another country or market by establishing a new wholly owned subsidiary. The process of creating a greenfield venture is often complex and potentially costly, but this entry mode affords maximum control to the firm and has the greatest amount of potential to contribute to the firm's strategic competitiveness as it implements international strategies. This potential is especially true for firms with strong intangible capabilities that might be leveraged through a greenfield venture.[103] Moreover, having additional control over its operations in a foreign market is especially advantageous when the firm has proprietary technology.

Research also suggests that "wholly owned subsidiaries and expatriate staff are preferred" in service industries where "close contacts with end customers" and "high levels of professional skills, specialized know-how, and customization" are required.[104] Other research suggests that as investments, greenfield ventures are used more prominently when the firm's business relies significantly on the quality of its capital-intensive manufacturing facilities. In contrast, cross-border acquisitions are more likely to be used as an entry mode when a firm's operations are human capital intensive—for example, if a strong local union and high cultural distance would cause difficulty in transferring knowledge to a host nation through a greenfield venture.[105]

The risks associated with greenfield ventures are significant in that the costs of establishing a new business operation in a new country or market can be substantial. To support the operations of a newly established operation in a foreign country, the firm may have to acquire knowledge and expertise about the new market by hiring either host-country nationals, possibly from competitors, or through consultants, which can be costly. This new knowledge and expertise often is necessary to facilitate the building of new facilities, establishing distribution networks, and learning how to implement marketing strategies that can lead to competitive success in the new market.[106] Importantly, while taking these actions the firm maintains control over the technology, marketing, and distribution of its products. Research also suggests that when the country risk is high, firms prefer to enter with joint ventures instead of greenfield investments. However, if

A **greenfield venture** is an entry mode through which a firm invests directly in another country or market by establishing a new wholly owned subsidiary.

firms have previous experience in a country, they prefer to use a wholly owned greenfield venture rather than a joint venture.[107]

The globalization of the air cargo industry has implications for companies such as UPS and FedEx. The impact of this globalization is especially pertinent to China and the Asia Pacific region. China's air cargo market is expected to grow 11 percent per year through 2023. Accordingly, UPS and FedEx opened new hub operations in Shanghai and Guangzhou, respectively. These hubs supported the firms' distribution and logistics business during the Olympics in Beijing. These investments are wholly owned because these firms need to maintain the integrity of their IT and logistics systems in order to maximize efficiency. Greenfield ventures also help these two firms maintain the proprietary nature of their systems.[108]

Dynamics of Mode of Entry

Several factors affect the firm's choice about how to enter international markets. Market entry is often achieved initially through exporting, which requires no foreign manufacturing expertise and investment only in distribution. Licensing can facilitate the product improvements necessary to enter foreign markets, as in the Komatsu example. Strategic alliances are a popular entry mode because they allow a firm to connect with an experienced partner already in the market. Partly because of this, geographically diversifying firms often use alliances in uncertain situations, such as an emerging economy where there is significant risk (e.g., Venezuela and Columbia).[109] However, if intellectual property rights in the emerging economy are not well protected, the number of firms in the industry is growing fast, and the need for global integration is high, other entry modes such as a joint venture (see Chapter 9) or a wholly owned subsidiary are preferred.[110] In the final analysis though, all three modes—export, licensing, and strategic alliance—can be effective means of initially entering new markets and for developing a presence in those markets.

Acquisitions, greenfield ventures, and sometimes joint ventures are used when firms want to establish a strong presence in an international market. Aerospace firms Airbus and Boeing have used joint ventures, especially in large markets, to facilitate entry, while military equipment firms such as Thales SA have used acquisitions to build a global presence. Japanese auto manufacturer Toyota has established a presence in the United States through both greenfield ventures and joint ventures. Because of Toyota's highly efficient manufacturing processes, the firm wants to maintain control over manufacturing when possible. To date, Toyota has established manufacturing facilities in over 20 countries. Demonstrating the importance of greenfield ventures and joint ventures to Toyota's international diversification strategy is the fact that the firm opened its first new manufacturing plant in Japan in over 20 years in 2011.[111] Both acquisitions and greenfield ventures are likely to come at later stages in the development of a firm's international strategies.

Thus, to enter a global market, a firm selects the entry mode that is best suited to the situation at hand. In some instances, the various options will be followed sequentially, beginning with exporting and ending with greenfield ventures. In other cases, the firm may use several, but not all, of the different entry modes, each in different markets. The decision regarding which entry mode to use is primarily a result of the industry's competitive conditions, the country's situation and government policies, and the firm's unique set of resources, capabilities, and core competencies.

Walmart Stores Inc.'s operations are divided into three divisions—Walmart USA, Sam's Club, and Walmart International. Through Walmart International, this firm is diversified geographically and uses several entry modes to enter the international markets it serves. We discuss Walmart International's operations and its entry modes in the Strategic Focus. Of course, Walmart uses the international cost leadership business-level strategy and, historically at least, has used the global strategy as its international corporate-level strategy.

© Nicholas Monu/iStockphoto.com

Explore Walmart's international growth strategy.

www.cengagebrain .com

STRATEGIC FOCUS

WALMART INTERNATIONAL: USING MULTIPLE PATHS TO ENTER INTERNATIONAL MARKETS

Walmart's size and scope have become legendary since the firm was started in Rogers, Arkansas in 1962. The company now serves more than 200 million customers weekly through its roughly 9,300 retail units operating in 15 countries under a total of 60 banners (Asda [United Kingdom] and Seiyu [Japan] are two of Walmart's banners). Walmart's fiscal year 2010 sales exceeded $405 billion; the firm employs 2.1 million people on a worldwide basis.

In 1991, Walmart entered Mexico. This was the firm's first foray into international markets. Today, Walmart International (WMI), one of three Walmart divisions that was formed in 1993, is important to the firm's continuing growth. Commenting about this importance, the firm's executive vice president and chief financial officer recently stated that "We're stepping up growth in our international operations to take advantage of growing economies and opportunities in emerging markets such as China and Brazil."

Generating sales in excess of $115 billion in 2010, WMI accounts for more than 25 percent of Walmart's total sales; importantly, WMI's sales revenue is increasing approximately 20 percent per year. Typically, Walmart relies on its distribution, warehousing, logistics, and data management core competencies that were developed in its domestic (U.S.) market as the foundation for entering international markets.

Walmart uses several entry modes to enter international markets. A joint venture with Mexico-based Cifra for the purpose of establishing a Sam's Club in Mexico City was its first international entry. Thus, Walmart did not use exporting as its first entry mode, demonstrating the fact that firms do not necessarily use the five entry modes sequentially. Walmart acquired a majority interest in Cifra in 1997 and officially changed the Cifra name to Walmart de Mexico in 2000. Today, Walmart operates close to 1,800 retail units in Mexico. In many ways, Mexico remains Walmart's most successful entry into international markets.

Pierre BESSARD/REA/Redux

Walmart operates close to 1,800 retail units in Mexico like the one pictured here.

Walmart's most common entry modes are acquisitions and joint ventures. For example, Walmart Canada was founded in 1994 when Walmart acquired the Canadian Woolco chain of 122 stores from Woolworth Canada. To enter Honduras, Walmart bought a 33 percent interest in Central American Retail Holding Company in 2005. Initially, Walmart entered Argentina by establishing a Sam's Club as a new wholly owned subsidiary in 1995. In 2007, Walmart enhanced its position in Argentina when it acquired three Auchan stores. Also in 2007, Walmart entered India through a joint venture with Bharti Enterprises. Operating as a joint venture, Bharti Walmart Pvt. Ltd. intends to open 20 additional cash-and-carry stores in India by the end of 2012. Recently, Walmart acquired a minority stake in the holding company of Yihaodian, a fast-growing e-commerce company in China. Yihaodian has achieved a strong position in online grocery sales. This firm provides next-day delivery of purchased items to customers at what it believes are competitive prices.

As our discussion shows, over time, Walmart has used joint ventures, acquisitions, and new wholly owned subsidiaries to enter international markets. In each instance, Walmart selects the entry mode that is most appropriate to the international market it wishes to enter based on the conditions (e.g., governmental policies and regulations) characterizing each market. But as is true for all firms, successfully implementing international strategies once it has entered an international market can be a challenge. Recently, China accused Walmart

STRATEGY RIGHT NOW

© Nicholas Monu/iStockphoto.com

Learn more about Sam's Club in Mexico.

www.cengagebrain
.com

(as well as Carrefour) of "price gouging and misleading consumers by advertising false discounts on goods sold in their stores." More broadly, New York City pension funds asked Walmart to do more than require its vendors "to publish annual reports detailing working conditions in their factories." Walmart indicated that it intends to positively respond to these matters as well as others that might surface as it implements its international strategies.

Sources: S. Clifford, 2011, Wal-Mart is being pressed to disclose how global suppliers treat workers, *The New York Times*, http://www.nytimes.com, May 30; A. D'Innocenzio, 2011, Wal-Mart unveils tiny Walmart Express in Arkansas, *NewsVine*, http://www.newsvine.com, June 3; N. Gulati, 2011, Bharti Wal-Mart to expand, *Wall Street Journal*, http://www.wsj.com, May 24; 2011, About Us, Wal-Mart Stores Inc. home page, http://www.walmart.com, July 7; 2011, China accuses Wal-Mart of "deceptive prices," *CNNMoney.com*, http://www.cnnmoney.com, January 26; 2010, Walmart updates growth plans, Wal-Mart Stores home page, http://www.walmart.com, October 22.

Risks in an International Environment

International strategies are risky, particularly those that would cause a firm to become substantially more diversified in terms of geographic markets served. Political and economic risks cannot be ignored by firms using international strategies (see specific examples of political and economic risks in Figure 8.6).

Political Risks

Political risks "denote the probability of disruption of the operations of multinational enterprises by political forces or events whether they occur in host countries, home country, or result from changes in the international environment."[112] Possible disruptions to a firm's operations when seeking to implement its international strategy create numerous problems, including uncertainty created by government regulation, the existence of many, possibly conflicting, legal authorities or corruption, and the

Figure 8.6 Risks in the International Environment

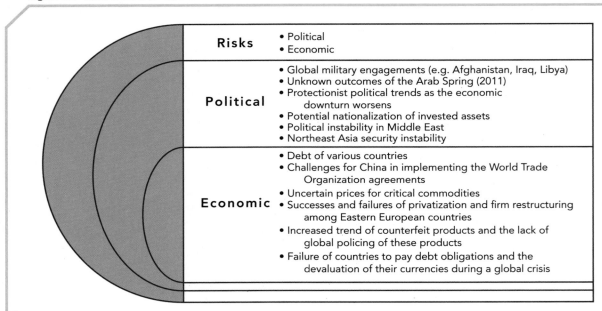

Risks	• Political • Economic
Political	• Global military engagements (e.g. Afghanistan, Iraq, Libya) • Unknown outcomes of the Arab Spring (2011) • Protectionist political trends as the economic downturn worsens • Potential nationalization of invested assets • Political instability in Middle East • Northeast Asia security instability
Economic	• Debt of various countries • Challenges for China in implementing the World Trade Organization agreements • Uncertain prices for critical commodities • Successes and failures of privatization and firm restructuring among Eastern European countries • Increased trend of counterfeit products and the lack of global policing of these products • Failure of countries to pay debt obligations and the devaluation of their currencies during a global crisis

Source: © Copyrighted 2011 by Michael A. Hitt, R. Duane Ireland, and Robert E. Hoskisson.

potential nationalization of private assets.[113] Firms investing in other countries when implementing their international strategy may have concerns about the stability of the national government and the effects of unrest and government instability on their investments or assets.[114] To deal with these concerns, firms should conduct a political risk analysis of the countries or regions they may enter using one of the five entry modes. Through political risk analysis, the firm examines potential sources and factors of noncommercial disruptions of their foreign investments and the operations flowing from them.[115]

Russia has experienced a relatively high level of institutional instability in the years following its revolutionary transition to a more democratic government. Decentralized political control and frequent changes in policies created chaos for many, but especially for those in the business landscape. In an effort to regain more central control and reduce the chaos, Russian leaders took actions such as prosecuting powerful private firm executives, seeking to gain state control of firm assets, and not approving some foreign acquisitions of Russian businesses. The initial institutional instability, followed by the actions of the central government, caused some firms to delay or avoid significant foreign direct investment in Russia. Although leaders in Russia have tried to reassure potential investors about their property rights, prior actions, the fact that other laws (e.g., environmental and employee laws) are weak, and commonplace government corruption make firms leery of investing in Russia.[116]

Economic Risks

Economic risks include fundamental weaknesses in a country or region's economy with the potential to cause adverse effects on firms' efforts to successfully implement their international strategies. As illustrated in the example of Russian institutional instability and property rights, political risks and economic risks are interdependent. If firms cannot protect their intellectual property, they are highly unlikely to use a means of entering a foreign market that involves significant and direct investments. Therefore, countries need to create, sustain, and enforce strong intellectual property rights in order to attract foreign direct investment.

Another economic risk is the perceived security risk of a foreign firm acquiring firms that have key natural resources or firms that may be considered strategic in regard to intellectual property. For instance, many Chinese firms have been buying natural resource firms in Australia and Latin America as well as manufacturing assets in the United States. This has made the governments of the key resource firms nervous about such strategic assets falling under the control of state-owned Chinese firms.[117] Terrorism has also been of concern. Indonesia has difficulty competing for investment against China and India, countries that are viewed as having fewer security risks.

As noted earlier, the differences and fluctuations in the value of currencies is among the foremost economic risks of using an international strategy.[118] This is especially true as the level of the firm's geographic diversification increases to the point where the firm is trading in a large number of currencies. The value of the dollar relative to other currencies determines the value of the international assets and earnings of U.S. firms; for example, an increase in the value of the U.S. dollar can reduce the value of U.S. multinational firms' international assets and earnings in other countries. Furthermore, the value of different currencies can at times dramatically affect a firm's competitiveness in global markets because of its effect on the prices of goods manufactured in different countries.[119] An increase in the value of the dollar can harm U.S. firms' exports to international markets because of the price differential of the products. Thus, government oversight and control of economic and financial capital in a country affect not only local economic activity, but also foreign investments in the country. Certainly, the significant political and policy changes in Eastern Europe since the early 1990s have stimulated much more FDI there.[120]

Strategic Competitiveness Outcomes

As previously discussed, international strategies can result in three basic benefits (increased market size, economies of scale and learning, and location advantages) for firms. These basic benefits are gained when the firm successfully manages political and economic risks while implementing its international strategies; in turn, these benefits are critical to the firm's efforts to achieve strategic competitiveness (as measured by improved performance and enhanced innovation—see Figure 8.1).

Overall, the degree to which firms achieve strategic competitiveness through international strategies is expanded or increased when they successfully implement an international diversification strategy. As an extension or elaboration of international strategy, an international diversification strategy is a strategy through which a firm expands the sales of its goods or services across the borders of global regions and countries into a potentially large number of geographic locations or markets. Instead of entering one or just a few markets, the international diversification strategy finds firms using international business-level and international corporate-level strategies for the purpose of entering multiple regions and markets in order to sell their products.

An **international diversification strategy** is a strategy through which a firm expands the sales of its goods or services across the borders of global regions and countries into a potentially large number of geographic locations or markets.

International Diversification and Returns

Evidence suggests numerous reasons for firms to use an international diversification strategy,[121] meaning that international diversification should be related positively to firms' performance as measured by the returns it earns on its investments. Research has shown that as international diversification increases, a firm's returns decrease initially but then increase quickly as it learns how to manage the increased geographic diversification it has created.[122] In fact, the stock market is particularly sensitive to investments in international markets. Firms that are broadly diversified into multiple international markets usually achieve the most positive stock returns, especially when they diversify geographically into core business areas.[123]

Japan's Asahi Group Holdings Ltd. seeks to become one of the world's top 10 food and beverage companies. It touts alcoholic beverages, soft drinks, infant formula, dietary supplements, freeze dried soups, and candy in its portfolio.

david pearson/Alamy

Many factors contribute to the positive effects of international diversification, such as private versus government ownership, potential economies of scale and experience, location advantages, increased market size, and the opportunity to stabilize returns. The stabilization of returns helps reduce a firm's overall risk.[124] Large, well-established firms and entrepreneurial ventures can both achieve these positive outcomes by successfully implementing an international diversification strategy.

Based in Japan, Asahi Group Holdings Ltd. seeks to become one of the world's top 10 food and beverage companies "by focusing overseas making use of a M&A war chest valued at $4.9 billion in the period up to fiscal 2012."[125] Using the acquisition mode of entry, Asahi is currently implementing an international diversification strategy as it acquires a number of companies in foreign markets. Recently, Asahi acquired all or part of companies in Australia, New Zealand, and China and plans to acquire companies in other markets in the years to come for the purpose of expanding its geographic scope, strengthening its product portfolio, and gaining economies of scale, particularly in supply chain management.

Enhanced Innovation

In Chapter 1, we indicated that developing new technology is at the heart of strategic competitiveness. As noted in our discussion of the determinants of national advantage (see Figure 8.3), a nation's competitiveness depends, in part, on the capacity of its industries to innovate. Eventually and inevitably, competitors outperform firms that fail to innovate. Therefore, the only way for individual nations and individual firms to sustain a competitive advantage is to upgrade it continually through innovation.[126]

An international diversification strategy and the geographic diversification it brings about create the potential for firms to achieve greater returns on their innovations (through larger or more numerous markets) while reducing the often substantial risks of R&D investments. Additionally, international diversification may be necessary to generate the resources required to sustain a large-scale R&D operation. An environment of rapid technological obsolescence makes it difficult to invest in new technology and the capital-intensive operations necessary to compete in such an environment. Firms operating solely in domestic markets may find such investments difficult because of the length of time required to recoup the original investment. However, diversifying into a number of international markets improves a firm's ability to appropriate additional returns from innovation before competitors can overcome the initial competitive advantage created by the innovation. In addition, firms moving into international markets are exposed to new products and processes. If they learn about those products and processes and integrate this knowledge into their operations, further innovation can be developed. To incorporate the learning into their own R&D processes, firms must manage those processes effectively in order to absorb and use the new knowledge to create further innovations.[127] For a number of reasons then, international strategies and certainly an international diversification strategy provide incentives for firms to innovate.[128]

The relationship among international geographic diversification, innovation, and returns is complex. Some level of performance is necessary to provide the resources the firm needs to diversify geographically; in turn, geographic diversification provides incentives and resources to invest in R&D. Effective R&D should enhance the firm's returns, which then provide more resources for continued geographic diversification and investment in R&D. Of course, the returns generated from these relationships increase through effective managerial practices. Evidence suggests that more culturally diverse top management teams often have a greater knowledge of international markets and their idiosyncrasies, but their orientation to expand internationally can be affected by the nature of their compensation.[129] Moreover, managing the business units of a geographically diverse multinational firm requires skill, not only in managing a decentralized set of businesses, but also coordinating diverse points of view emerging from businesses located in different countries and regions. Firms able to do this increase the likelihood of outperforming their rivals.[130]

The Challenge of International Strategies

Effectively using international strategies creates basic benefits and contributes to the firm's strategic competitiveness. However, for several reasons, attaining these positive outcomes is difficult.

Complexity of Managing International Strategies

Pursuing international strategies, particularly an international diversification strategy, typically leads to growth in a firm's size and the complexity of its operations. In turn, larger size and greater operational complexity make a firm more difficult to manage. At some point, size and complexity either cause firms to become virtually unmanageable or increase the cost of their management beyond the value using international strategies creates. Different cultures and institutional practices (such as those associated with governmental agencies) that are part of the countries in which a firm competes when using an international strategy also can create difficulties.[131]

Toyota's experiences over the past few years appear to demonstrate the relationship between firm size and managerial complexity. Toyota became the world's largest car manufacturer at the end of 2008, surpassing General Motors (GM had been the largest auto manufacturer for 77 years). As always is the case though, larger size makes a firm harder to manage successfully. In spite of its legendary focus on and reputation for quality, Toyota experienced product quality problems, particularly in the all-important U.S. market, over the past few years and after becoming the world's largest manufacturer. Perhaps the increased difficulty of managing a larger firm contributed to Toyota's product quality problems. However, Toyota seems to be recovering from these difficulties and continues seeking additional growth through its international strategy. Saying that "India is an integral part of (the firm's) global growth strategy," Toyota recently introduced the Etios Liva as a competitor in India's small car market.[132]

Interestingly, Volkswagen-Porsche has replaced Toyota as the world's largest car and truck manufacturer. Highly diversified, this company's portfolio of passenger cars includes Audi, Bentley, Bugatti, Lamborghini, SEAT, and Skoda in addition to Porsche and VW. Time will tell if this firm is now of a size and complexity level that will make it difficult to successfully manage its international strategies.

Limits to International Expansion

Learning how to effectively manage an international strategy improves the likelihood of achieving positive outcomes such as enhanced performance. However, at some point the degree of geographic and (possibly) product diversification the firm's international strategies bring about causes the returns from using the strategies to level off and eventually become negative.[133]

There are several reasons that explain the limits to the positive effects of the diversification associated with international strategies. First, greater geographic dispersion across country borders increases the costs of coordination between units and the distribution of products. Second, trade barriers, logistical costs, cultural diversity, and other differences by country (e.g., access to raw materials and different employee skill levels) greatly complicate the implementation of an international strategy.

Institutional and cultural factors can be strong barriers to the transfer of a firm's core competencies from one market to another. Marketing programs often have to be redesigned and new distribution networks established when firms expand into new markets. In addition, firms may encounter different labor costs and capital expenses. In general, it becomes increasingly difficult to effectively implement, manage, and control a firm's international operations with increases in geographic diversity.

The amount of diversification in a firm's international operations that can be managed varies from company to company and is affected by managers' abilities to deal with ambiguity and complexity. The problems of central coordination and integration are mitigated if the firm's international operations find it competing in friendly countries that are geographically close and have cultures similar to its own country's culture. In that case, the firm is likely to encounter fewer trade barriers, the laws and customs are better understood, and the product is easier to adapt to local markets.[134] For example, U.S. firms may find it less difficult to expand their operations into Mexico, Canada, and Western European countries than into Asian countries.

Relationships between the firm using an international strategy and the governments in the countries in which the firm is competing can also be constraining.[135] The reason for this is that the differences in host countries' governmental policies and practices can be substantial, creating a need for the focal firm to learn how to manage what can be a large set of different enforcement policies and practices. At some point, the differences create too many problems for the firm to be successful. Using strategic alliances is another way firms can deal with this limiting factor. Partnering with companies in different countries allows the focal firm to rely on its partner to help deal with local laws, rules, regulations, and customs. But these partnerships are not risk free and managing them tends to be difficult.[136]

Known initially as the Qingdao Refrigerator Company, Haier Group is a Chinese company that started selling products in 1999 under the Haier name in international markets. Prior to doing so, the firm became a dominant competitor in its domestic Chinese markets and is using some of its domestic capabilities and core competencies to support its objective of establishing Haier as a global brand. We discuss these efforts in the Strategic Focus.

STRATEGIC FOCUS

HAIER GROUP: A STORY OF PRODUCT AND GEOGRAPHIC DIVERSIFICATION

Based in Qingdao, China, Haier Group is a company with a significant amount of product and geographic diversification. In terms of product diversification, the firm's portfolio includes a broad array of products such as white goods home appliances (refrigerators, washing machines, freezers, televisions, DVD players, and so forth) and communication and information products (mobile phones and computers), among many others. Serving customers in Europe, South Asia, Asia-Pacific, the Middle East, and North America and in individual countries such as China demonstrates the company's extensive geographic diversification. Haier America, which is the North American division of Haier Group, was established in 1999 as a wholly owned subsidiary. Today, Haier Group holds the largest share of the world's market for major appliances.

Relying initially on techniques such as total quality management, Haier established a strong brand name for its refrigerators in China, its domestic market. Reliability and product quality were core competencies that allowed the firm to become China's leading manufacturing of refrigerators. The firm then diversified into related appliances such as dishwashers, freezers, and microwaves and was able to expand its reputation for producing reliable, high-quality products. As is true for many firms, Haier concluded that geographic diversification in addition to the product diversification it had already experienced were critical to the firm's continuing growth efforts. Today, product quality, reliability, and a strong customer focus are the core competencies developed in its domestic market on which Haier relies as the foundation for its international strategies.

When still known as the Qingdao Refrigerator Co., the firm exported refrigerators to Germany, its first international market. A more significant exporting effort was launched in 1992 when the firm exported larger numbers of refrigerators to Indonesia. To further diversify geographically, Haier has also used joint ventures and greenfield ventures. Over time, the firm has produced and sold its products through joint ventures in countries such as Indonesia, Malaysia, Yugoslavia, and Bangladesh and by establishing wholly owned subsidiaries in regions including North America. Thus, this firm has used several entry modes to enter international markets.

Using the multidomestic international corporate-level strategy, Haier wants to build a global brand name for its products. To some observers, reaching this objective could be

AP Photos/Jing wei

China's Haier Group was a major advertiser at the 2008 Beijing Olympic Games.

difficult in that "effective brand building is (an) obvious weakness" for a number of Chinese companies. Moreover, some believe that "Many Chinese companies cling to centralized managerial methods that are ill-suited to businesses aspiring to operate across multiple time zones and cultures." Given this concern about managerial practices, the decision to use a multidomestic strategy may serve the Haier Group well. The choice of this strategy is but one decision Haier has taken to support its efforts to build a global brand as it competes in a number of international markets. The following comments identify other actions Haier is taking to build a global brand: "Haier has distinguished itself among Chinese companies in efforts to build a global brand. Its leading market share in white goods has been underpinned by advertising and marketing campaigns with the National Basketball Association (NBA) in the U.S. and sponsorship of the Beijing Olympics." The recent decision to restructure Haier America into three stand-alone business units—air conditioning, white goods, and digital products—may allow the focus needed to concentrate on specific customers to emphasize the quality and reliability associated with Haier's various products. If successful, establishing this knowledge with customer groups would be instrumental in making Haier a strong global brand name.

Sources: J. R. Hagerty & B. Tita, 2011, China isn't golden for Whirlpool, *Wall Street Journal*, http://www.wsj.com, April 28; M.-J. Shen, 2011, Haier's "sun" rising in the Olympic year, *Inspired Living*, http://www.english-for-chinese.com, June 20; M.-J. Shen, 2011, Haier Group's expansion dilemma, *Inspired Living*, http://www.english-for-chinese.com, May 6; K. Taylor, 2011, Getting China ready to go abroad, *Wall Street Journal*, http://www.wsj.com, May 19; Bloomberg News, 2011, China's manufacturing grows at slowest pace in six months, *Bloomberg Businessweek*, http://www.businessweek.com, March 1.

SUMMARY

- The use of international strategies is increasing. Multiple factors and conditions are influencing the increasing use of these strategies, including opportunities to (1) extend a product's life cycle, (2) gain access to critical raw materials, sometimes including relatively inexpensive labor, (3) integrate a firm's operations on a global scale to better serve customers in different countries, (4) better serve customers whose needs appear to be more alike today as a result of global communications' media and the Internet's capabilities to inform, and (5) meet increasing demand for goods and services that is surfacing in emerging markets.

- When used effectively, international strategies yield three basic benefits: increased market size, economies of scale and learning, and location advantages. Firms use international business-level and international corporate-level strategies to geographically diversify their operations.

- International business-level strategies are usually grounded in one or more home-country advantages. Research suggests that there are four determinants of national advantage: factors of production; demand conditions; related and supporting industries; and patterns of firm strategy, structure, and rivalry.

- There are three types of international corporate-level strategies. A multidomestic strategy focuses on competition within each country in which the firm competes. Firms using a multidomestic strategy decentralize strategic and operating

decisions to the business units operating in each country, so that each unit can tailor its products to local conditions. A global strategy assumes more standardization of products across country boundaries; therefore, a competitive strategy is centralized and controlled by the home office. Commonly, large multinational firms, particularly those with multiple diverse products being sold in many different markets, use a multidomestic strategy with some product lines and a global strategy with others.

- A transnational strategy seeks to integrate characteristics of both multidomestic and global strategies for the purpose of being able to simultaneously emphasize local responsiveness and global integration.

- Two global environmental trends—liability of foreignness and regionalization—are influencing firms' choices of international strategies as well as their implementation. Liability of foreignness challenges firms to recognize that four types of distance between their domestic market and international markets affect how they compete. Some firms choose to concentrate their international strategies on regions (e.g., the EU and NAFTA) rather than on individual country markets.

- Firms can use one or more of five entry modes to enter international markets. Exporting, licensing, strategic alliances, acquisitions, and new wholly owned subsidiaries, often referred to as greenfield ventures, are the five entry modes. Most firms begin with exporting or licensing, because of their lower costs and risks, but later they might use strategic alliances and acquisitions as well. The most expensive and risky means of entering a new international market is establishing a new wholly owned subsidiary. On the other hand, such subsidiaries provide the advantages of maximum control by the firm and, if successful, the greatest returns. Large, geographically diversified firms such as Walmart use most or all five entry modes when implementing international strategies.

■ Firms encounter a number of risks when implementing international strategies. The two major categories of risks firms need to understand and address when diversifying geographically through international strategies are political risks (risks concerned with the probability a firm's operations will be disrupted by political forces or events, whether they occur in the firm's domestic market or in the markets the firm has entered to implement its international strategies) and economic risks (risks resulting from fundamental weaknesses in a country's or a region's economy with the potential to adversely affect a firm's ability to implement its international strategies).

■ Successful use of international strategies (especially an international diversification strategy) contributes to a firm's strategic competitiveness in the form of improved performance and enhanced innovation. International diversification facilitates innovation in a firm because it provides a larger market to gain greater and faster returns from investments in innovation. In addition, international diversification may generate the resources necessary to sustain a large-scale R&D program.

■ In general, international diversification is related to above-average returns, but this assumes that the diversification is effectively implemented and that the firm's international operations are well managed. International diversification provides greater economies of scope and learning which, along with greater innovation, help produce above-average returns.

■ Several issues or conditions affect a firm's use of international strategies to pursue strategic competitiveness. Some limits also constrain the ability to manage international expansion effectively. International diversification increases coordination and distribution costs, and management problems are exacerbated by trade barriers, logistical costs, and cultural diversity, among other factors.

REVIEW QUESTIONS

1. What incentives influence firms to use international strategies?

2. What are the three basic benefits firms can achieve by successfully using an international strategy?

3. What four factors are determinants of national advantage and serve as a basis for international business-level strategies?

4. What are the three international corporate-level strategies? What are the advantages and disadvantages associated with these individual strategies?

5. What are some global environmental trends affecting the choice of international strategies, particularly international corporate-level strategies?

6. What five entry modes do firms consider as paths to use to enter international markets? What is the typical sequence in which firms use these entry modes?

7. What are political risks and what are economic risks? How should firms approach dealing with these risks?

8. What are the strategic competitiveness outcomes firms can reach through international strategies, and particularly through an international diversification strategy?

9. What are two important issues that can potentially affect a firm's ability to successfully use international strategies?

EXPERIENTIAL EXERCISES

EXERCISE 1: McDONALD'S: GLOBAL, MULTIDOMESTIC, OR TRANSNATIONAL STRATEGY?

McDonald's is one of the world's best-known brands: The company has approximately 32,000 restaurants located in more than 117 countries, and serves 58 million customers *every day*. McDonald's opened its first international restaurant in Japan in 1971. Its "golden arches" are featured prominently in two former bastions of communism: Pushkin Square in Moscow and Tiananmen Square in Beijing, China.

What strategy has McDonald's used to achieve such visibility? For this exercise, each group will be asked to conduct some

background research on the firm and then make a brief presentation to identify the international strategy (i.e., global, multidomestic, or transnational) that McDonald's is implementing.

Individual

Search the Internet to find examples of menu variations in different countries. How much do menu items for a McDonald's restaurant in the United States differ from those in McDonald's located outside the United States?

Groups

Review the characteristics of global, multidomestic, and transnational strategies. Conduct additional research to assess the strategy that best describes the one McDonald's is using. Prepare a flip chart with a single page of bullet points to explain your reasoning.

Whole Class

Each group should have five to seven minutes to explain its reasoning. Following a Q&A for each group, each class member should vote for his or her respective strategy choice.

EXERCISE 2: WHERE NEXT?

In this exercise, you are to consider your team to be a consultant to a multinational fast food restaurant company that is trying to increase its international exposure in the coming years. As you recall from the chapter, an international strategy is one in which "the firm sells its goods or services outside its domestic market." The choices to do so are varied and include exporting, licensing, alliance, acquisition, or creating a new wholly owned subsidiary. The reasons are just as varied as the entry modes.

To identify a suitable candidate for analysis, consult research databases such as Datamonitor or Business Source Complete. For example, Jack in the Box operates over 2,700 units but they are all in the United States, which provides advantages as well as disadvantages. Compare this with McDonald's, the world's largest food-service retailing chain, with 32,737 restaurants operating in 117 countries as of 2011. You will also find SWOT (strengths, weaknesses, opportunities, threats) analysis on companies through databases such as those mentioned above.

Your consulting firm has been retained by the fast-food retailer to investigate the feasibility of expanding internationally. You should be prepared to address the following questions:

1. Which international location(s) seem to fit best based on your research?

2. Which entry mode seems the most reasonable for the firms to use?

3. What macro environmental and industry trends support your recommendations? Economic characteristics include gross national product, wages, unemployment, and inflation. Trend analysis of these data (e.g., are wages rising or falling, rate of change in wages, etc.) is preferable to single point-in-time snapshots.

4. What country risks seem most problematic?

The following additional Internet resources may be useful in your research:

- The Library of Congress has a collection of country studies.
- BBC News offers country profiles.
- The Economist Intelligence Unit (http://www.eiu.com) offers country profiles.
- Both the United Nations and International Monetary Fund provide statistics and research reports.
- The CIA World Factbook has profiles of different regions.
- The Global Entrepreneurship Monitor provides reports with detailed information about economic conditions and social aspects for a number of countries.
- Links can be found at http://www.countryrisk.com to a number of resources that assess both political and economic risk for individual countries.
- For U.S. data, see http://www.census.gov.

Be prepared to discuss and defend your recommendations in class.

VIDEO CASE

THE LURE OF AN INTERNATIONAL STRATEGY: INDIA/MOHANDAS PAI/CEO/INFOSYS

India, home to low-cost living and resources, has become a technology mecca that maintains the second-largest software industry in the world. The country has managed to amass the presence of big-name international companies and create a few of its own, such as InfoSys. Mohandas Pai, CEO of InfoSys, has stated that the key to luring foreign investors and workers is to create companies on par with any in the West. InfoSys, which is similar to a resort spa, continues to offer more experience and opportunity for many young Americans from U.S. colleges and has grown from 500 employees to 50,000 in 12 years.

Be prepared to discuss the following concepts and questions in class:

Concepts

- International strategy
- Business-level strategy
- Corporate-level strategy
- National advantage

Questions

1. What international strategy incentives does India offer to a foreign investor? What limitations exist in India for companies desiring international expansion?
2. What benefits does InfoSys receive from its international strategy?
3. How does India's national advantage(s) influence its business-level strategy?
4. What corporate-level strategy is used by InfoSys and why?

NOTES

1. J. H. Dyer & W. Chu, 2011, The determinants of trust in supplier-automaker relationships in the U.S., Japan, and Korea, *Journal of International Business Studies*, 42: 10–27; M. J. Nieto & A. Rodriguez, 2011, Offshoring of R&D: Looking abroad to improve innovation performance, *Journal of International Business Studies*, 42: 345–361.

2. E. Golovko & G. Valentini, 2011, Exploring the complementarity between innovation and export for SMEs' growth, *Journal of International Business Studies*, 42: 362–380; H. Berry, M. F. Guillen, & N. Zhou, 2010, An institutional approach to cross-national distance, *Journal of International Business Studies* 41: 1460–1480; M. A. Hitt, L. Tihanyi, T. Miller, & B. Connelly, 2006, International diversification: Antecedents, outcomes and moderators, *Journal of Management*, 32: 831–867.

3. M. F. Wiersema & H. P. Bowen, 2011, The relationship between international diversification and firm performance: Why it remains a puzzle, *Global Strategy Journal*, 1: 152–170.

4. R. Vernon, 1996, International investment and international trade in the product cycle, *Quarterly Journal of Economics*, 80: 190–207.

5. 2011, Our strategy, Rio Tinto homepage, http://www.riotinto.com, June 20.

6. E. Ko, C. R. Taylor, H. Sung, J. Lee, U. Wagner, D. Martin-Consuega Navarro, & F. Wang, 2011, Global marketing segmentation usefulness in the sportswear industry, *Journal of Business Research*, in press.

7. J. R. Thomas, 2011, IKEA's international marketing recognized at Cannes Lions 2011, *Integrated Marketing News*, http://www.mktgnews.wordpress.com, May 17.

8. 2011, The globalization index 2010, Ernst & Young, http://www.wy.com, January.

9. A. Cuervo-Cazurra & M. E. Genc, 2011, Obligating, pressuring, and supporting dimensions of the environment and the non-market advantages of developing-country multinational companies, *Journal of Management Studies*, 48: 441–455; K. E. Meyer, R. Mudambi, & R. Nanula, 2011, Multinational enterprises and local contexts: The opportunities and challenges of multiple embeddedness, *Journal of Management Studies*, 48: 235–252; F. Fortanier & R. van Tulder, 2009, Internationalization trajectories—a cross country comparison: Are large Chinese and Indian companies different? *Industrial and Corporate Change*, 18: 223–247.

10. 2011, Our group, Carrefour Group homepage, http://www.carrefour.com, June 10.

11. M. Colchester, 2011, Carrefour documents remain sealed, *Wall Street Journal*, http://www.wsj.com, June 24.

12. T. R. Annamalai & A. Deshmukh, 2011, Venture capital and private equity in India: An analysis of investments and exits, *Journal of Indian Business Research*, 3: 6–21; P. Zheng, 2009, A comparison of FDI determinants in China and India, *Thunderbird International Business Review*, 51: 263–279.

13. P. Sharma, 2011, Country of origin effects in developed and emerging markets: Exploring the contrasting roles of materialism and value consciousness, *Journal of International Business Studies*, 42: 285–306; S. Athreye & S. Kapur, 2009, Introduction: The internationalization of Chinese and Indian firms—trends, motivations and strategy, *Industrial and Corporate Change*, 18: 209–221.

14. M. Carney, E. R. Gedajlovic, P. M. A. R. Heugens, M. van Essen, & J. van Oosterhout, 2011, Business group affiliation, performance, context, and strategy: A meta-analysis, *Academy of Management Journal*, 54: 437-460; B. Elango, 2009, Minimizing effects of "liability of foreignness": Response strategies of foreign firm in the United States, *Journal of World Business*, 44: 51–62.

15. K. Inagaki & J. Osawa, 2011, Takeda, Toshiba make $16 billion M&A push, *Wall Street Journal*, http://www.wsj.com, May 20; K. Iagaki, 2011, Takeda buys Nycomed for $14 billion, *Wall Street Journal*, http://www.wsj.com, May 20.

16. D. Stanford, 2011, PepsiCo first-quarter sales rise 27%; profit beats estimate, *Bloomberg.com*, http://www.bloomberg.com, April 28.

17. 2011, Coca-Cola Company, *Standard and Poor's Stock Report*, http://www.standardandpoors.com, June 12.

18. S. B. Choi, S. H. Lee, & C. Williams, 2011, Ownership and firm innovation in transition economy: Evidence from China, *Research Policy*, 40: 441–452; S. Shimizutani & Y. Todo, 2008, What determines overseas R&D activities? The case of Japanese multinational firms, *Research Policy*, 37: 530–544.

19. N. E. Boudette, 2011, Ford forecasts sharp gains from Asian sales, *Wall Street Journal*, http://www.wsj.com, June 8.

20. Ibid.

21. L. Nachum & S. Song, 2011, The MNE as a portfolio: Interdependencies in MNE growth trajectory, *Journal of International Business Studies*, 42: 381–405.

22. J. Podsada, 2011, Pratt & Whitney jumps to fast start at Paris air show, *Courant.com*, http://www.courant.com, June 20.

23. G. Qian, T. A. Khoury, M. W. Peng, & Z. Qian, 2010, The performance implications of intra- and inter-regional geographic diversification, *Strategic Management Journal*, 31: 1018–1030; H. Zou & P. N. Ghauri, 2009, Learning through international acquisitions: The process of knowledge acquisition in China, *Management International Review*, 48: 207–226.

24. Y. Zhang, H. Li, Y. Li, & L.-A. Zhou, 2010, FDI spillovers in an emerging market: The role of foreign firms' country origin diversity and domestic firms' absorptive capacity, *Strategic Management Journal*, 31: 969–989; J. Song & J. Shin, 2008, The paradox of technological capabilities: A study of knowledge sourcing from host countries of overseas R&D operations, *Journal of International Business Studies*, 39: 291–303.

25. H. Hoang & F. T. Rothaermel, 2010, Leveraging internal and external experience: Exploration, exploitation, and R&D project performance, *Strategic Management Journal*, 31: 734–758; D. Strutton, 2009, Horseshoes, global supply chains, and an emerging Chinese threat: Creating remedies one idea at a time, *Business Horizons*, 52(1): 31–43.

26. A. Gambardella & M. S. Giarratana, 2010, Localized knowledge spillovers and skill-based performance, *Strategic Entrepreneurship Journal*, 4: 323–339; A. M. Rugman & A. Verbeke, 2009, A new perspective on the regional and global strategies of multinational services firms, *Management International Review*, 48: 397–411.

27. G. L. F. Holburn & B. A. Zelner, 2010, Political capabilities, policy risk and international investment strategy: Evidence from the global electric power generation industry, *Strategic Management Journal*, 31: 1290–1315; R. Chakrabarti, Gupta-Mukherjee, & N. Jayaraman, 2009, Mars-Venus marriages: Culture and cross-border M&A, *Journal of International Business Studies*, 40: 216–236.

28. B. T. McCann & G. Vroom, 2010, Pricing response to entry and agglomeration effects, *Strategic Management Journal*, 31: 284–305; C. C. J. M. Millar & C. J. Choi, 2009, Worker identity, the liability of foreignness, the exclusion of local managers and unionism: A conceptual analysis, *Journal of Organizational Change Management*, 21: 460–470.

29. P. Kappen, 2011, Competence-creating overlaps and subsidiary technological evolution in the multinational corporation, *Research Policy*, 40: 673–686; R. Morck, B. Yeung, & M. Zhao, 2008, Perspectives on China's outward foreign direct investment, *Journal of International Business Studies*, 39: 337–350; J. Gimeno, R. E. Hoskisson, B. D. Beal, & W. P. Wan, 2005, Explaining the clustering of international expansion moves: A critical test in the U.S. telecommunications

industry, *Academy of Management Journal*, 48: 297–319.

30. A. Cuervo-Cazurra & M. Gene, 2008, Transforming disadvantages into advantages: Developing-country MNEs in the least developed countries, *Journal of International Business Studies*, 39: 957–979; M. A. Hitt, L. Bierman, K. Uhlenbruck, & K. Shimizu, 2006, The importance of resources in the internationalization of professional service firms: The good, the bad and the ugly, *Academy of Management Journal*, 49: 1137–1157.

31. A. Arino, 2011, Building the global enterprise: Strategic assembly, *Global Strategy Journal*, 1: 47–49; P. Dastidar, 2009, International corporate diversification and performance: Does firm self-selection matter? *Journal of International Business Studies*, 40: 71–85.

32. M. E. Porter, 1990, *The Competitive Advantage of Nations*, New York: The Free Press.

33. Ibid., 84.

34. K. Taylor, 2011, Getting China ready to go abroad, *Wall Street Journal*, http://www.wsj.com, May 19.

35. C. Storz, 2008, Dynamics in innovation systems: Evidence from Japan's game software industry, *Research Policy*, 37: 1480–1491.

36. 2011, New building blocks for jobs and economic growth, Global competition and collaboration conference, Georgetown University, May 16 and 17.

37. J. Nishimura & H. Okamuro, 2011, Subsidy and networking: The effects of direct and indirect support programs of the cluster policy, *Research Policy*, 40: 714–727; S. Sheng, K. Z. Zhou, & J. J. Li, 2011, The effects of business and political ties on firm performance: Evidence from China, *Journal of Marketing*, 75: 1–15.

38. M. Kitamura, A. Ohnsman, & Y. Hagiwara, 2011, Why Lexus doesn't lead the pack in China, *Bloomberg Businessweek*, April 3, 32–33.

39. J. M. Shaver, 2011, The benefits of geographic sales diversification: How exporting facilitates capital investment, *Strategic Management Journal*, 32: 1046–1060.

40. L. Diestre & N. Rajagopalan, 2011, An environmental perspective on diversification: The effects of chemical relatedness and regulatory sanctions, *Academy of Management Journal*, 54: 97–115.

41. S. A. Appelbaum, M. Roy, & T. Gilliland, 2011, Globalization of performance appraisals: Theory and applications, *Management Decision*, 49: 570–585; D. A. Ralson, D. H. Holt, R. H. Terpstra, & Y. K. Cheng, 2008, The impact of national culture and economic ideology on managerial work values: A study of the United States, Russia, Japan, and China, *Journal of International Business Studies*, 39: 8–26.

42. S. Zaheer & L. Nachum, 2011, Sense of place: From location resources to MNE locational capital, *Global Strategy Journal*, 1: 96–108; N. Guimaraes-Costs & M. P. E. Cunha, 2009, Foreign locals: A liminal perspective of international managers, *Organizational Dynamics*, 38: 158–166.

43. J.-S. Chen & A. S. Lovvorn, 2011, The speed of knowledge transfer within multinational enterprises: The role of social capital, *International Journal of Commerce and Management*, 21: 46–62; H. Kasper, M. Lehrer, J. Muhlbacher, & B. Muller, 2009, Integration-responsiveness and knowledge-management perspectives on the MNC: A typology and field study of cross-site knowledge-sharing practices, *Journal of Leadership & Organizational Studies*, 15: 287–303.

44. 2011, Unilever global, Unilever homepage, http://www.unilever.com, June 25; J. Neff, 2008, Unilever's CMO finally gets down to business, *Advertising Age*, July 11.

45. M. P. Koza, S. Tallman, & A. Ataay, 2011, The strategic assembly of global firms: A microstructural analysis of local learning and global adaptation, *Global Strategy Journal*, 1: 27–46; P. J. Buckley, 2009, The impact of the global factory on economic development, *Journal of World Business*, 44: 131–143.

46. A. Zaheer & E. Hernandez, 2011, The geographic scope of the MNC and its alliance portfolio: Resolving the paradox of distance, *Global Strategy Journal*, 1: 109–126.

47. L. Hail, C. Leuz, & P. Wysocki, 2010, Global accounting convergence and the potential adoption of IFRS by the U.S. (part II): Political factors and future scenarios for U.S. accounting standards, *Accounting Horizons*, 24: 567–581; R. G. Barker, 2003, Trend: Global accounting is coming, *Harvard Business Review*, 81(4): 24–25.

48. L. H. Shi, C. White, S. Zou, & S. T. Cavusgil, 2010, Global account management strategies: Drivers and outcomes, *Journal of International Business Studies*, 41: 620–638; M. Demirbag & E. Tatoglu, 2009, Competitive strategy choices of Turkish manufacturing firms in European Union, *Journal of Management Development*, 27: 727–743.

49. 2010, Building a stronger foundation, 2010 Annual Report, http://www.cemex.com, December.

50. Treflis team, 2011, China takes Starbucks to next level, *Forbes.com*, http://www.forbes.com, May 13.

51. R. Greenwood, S. Fairclough, T. Morris, & M. Boussebaa, 2010, The organizational design of transnational professional service firms, *Organizational Dynamics*, 39: 173–183.

52. C. Stehr, 2010, Globalisation strategy for small and medium-sized enterprises, *International Journal of Entrepreneurship and Innovation Management*, 12: 375–391; A. M. Rugman & A. Verbeke, 2008, A regional solution to the strategy and structure of multinationals, *European Management Journal*, 26: 305–313.

53. 2010, Regional resilience: Theoretical and empirical perspectives, *Cambridge Journal of Regions, Economy and Society*, 3–10; Rugman & Verbeke, A regional solution to the strategy and structure of multinationals.

54. M. W. Peng & Y. Jiang, 2010, Institutions behind family ownership and control in large firms, *Journal of Management Studies*, 47: 253–273; A. M. Rugman & A. Verbeke, 2003, Extending the theory of the multinational enterprise: Internationalization and strategic management perspectives, *Journal of International Business Studies*, 34: 125–137.

55. D. Klonowski, 2011, Private equity in emerging markets: Stacking up the BRICs, *Journal of Private Equity*, 14: 24–37.

56. J. Alcacer & W. Chung, 2011, Benefiting from location: Knowledge seeking, *Global Strategy Journal*, 1: 132–134.

57. K. Goodall & J. Roberts, 2003, Only connect: Teamwork in the multinational, *Journal of World Business*, 38: 150–164.

58. P. Ghemawat, 2001, Distance still matters, *Harvard Business Review*, 79(8): 137–145.

59. N. Y. Brannen, 2004, When Mickey loses face: Recontextualization, semantic fit and semiotics of foreignness, *Academy of Management Review*, 29: 593–616.

60. M. Schuman, 2006, Disney's Hong Kong headache, *Time*, http://www.time.com, May 8.

61. J. Cantwell & Y. Zhang, 2011, Innovation and location in the multinational firm, *International Journal of Technology Management*, 54: 116–132; C. H. Oh & A. M. Rugman, 2007, Regional multinationals and the Korean cosmetics industry, *Asia Pacific Journal of Management*, 24: 27–42.

62. K. Ito & E. L. Rose, 2010, The implicit return on domestic and international sales: An empirical analysis of U.S. and Japanese firms, *Journal of International Business Studies*, 41: 1074–1089; A. M. Rugman & A. Vergeke, 2007, Liabilities of foreignness and the use of firm-level versus country-level data: A response to Dunning et al. (2007), *Journal of International Business Studies*, 38: 200–205.

63. E. R. Banalieva, M. D. Santoro, & R. J. Jiang, 2011, Home region focus and technical efficiency of multinational enterprises: The moderating role of regional integration, *Management International Review*, in press; S. R. Miller & L. Eden, 2006, Local density and foreign subsidiary performance, *Academy of Management Journal*, 49: 341–355.

64. A. M. Rugman & S. Girod, 2003, Retail multinationals and globalization: The evidence is regional, *European Management Journal*, 21: 24–37.,

65. D. E. Westney, 2006, Review of the regional multinationals: MNEs and global strategic management (book review),

Journal of International Business Studies, 37: 445–449.

66. R. D. Ludema, 2002, Increasing returns, multinationals and geography of preferential trade agreements, *Journal of International Economics*, 56: 329–358.

67. M. Aspinwall, 2009, NAFTA-ization: Regionalization and domestic political adjustment in the North American economic area, *Journal of Common Market Studies*, 47: 1–24.

68. D. Zu & O. Shenar, 2002, Institutional distance and the multinational enterprise, *Academy of Management Review*, 27: 608–618.

69. A. Ojala, 2008, Entry in a psychically distant market: Finnish small and medium-sized software firms in Japan, *European Management Journal*, 26: 135–144.

70. J. M. Shaver, 2011 (see reference 39); C. A. Cinquetti, 2009, Multinationals and exports in a large and protected developing country, *Review of International Economics*, 16: 904–918.

71. 2011, Kansas City firm recognized for excellence in exporting, *International Trade Administration*, http://trade.gov, February 4.

72. M. Bandyk, 2008, Now even small firms can go global, *U.S. News & World Report*, March 10, 52.

73. B. Cassiman & E. Golovko, 2010, Innovation and internationalization through exports, *Journal of International Business Studies*, 42: 56–75.

74. M. Hughes, S. L. Martin, R. E. Morgan, & M. J. Robson, 2010, Realizing product-market advantage in high-technology international new ventures: The mediating role of ambidextrous innovation, *Journal of International Marketing*, 18: 1–21; S. Shankar, C. Ormiston, N. Bloch, & R. Shaus, 2008, How to win in emerging markets, *MIT Sloan Management Review*, 49(3): 19–23.

75. P. Ganotakis & J. H. Love, 2011, R&D, product innovation, and exporting: Evidence from UK new technology-based firms, *Oxford Economic Papers*, 63: 279–306; M. Gabrielsson & P. Gabrielsson, 2011, Internet-based sales channel strategies of born global firms, *International Business Review*, 20: 88–99.

76. P. S. Aulakh, M. Jiang, & Y. Pan, 2010, International technology licensing: Monopoly rents transaction costs and exclusive rights, *Journal of International Business Studies*, 41: 587–605; R. Bird & D. R. Cahoy, 2008, The impact of compulsory licensing on foreign direct investment: A collective bargaining approach, *American Business Law Journal*, 45: 283–330.

77. M. S. Giarratana & S. Torrisi, 2010, Foreign entry and survival in a knowledge-intensive market: Emerging economy countries' international linkages, technology competences, and firm experience, *Strategic Entrepreneurship Journal*, 4: 85–104; U. Lichtenthaler, 2008,

Externally commercializing technology assets: An examination of different process stages, *Journal of Business Venturing*, 23: 445–464.

78. N. Byrnes & F. Balfour, 2009, Philip Morris unbound, *BusinessWeek*, May 4, 38–42.

79. N. Zamiska, J. Ye, & V. O'Connell, 2008, Chinese cigarettes to go global, *Wall Street Journal*, http://www.wsj.com, January 30.

80. E. Dechenaux, J. Thursby, & M. Thursby, 2011, Inventor moral hazard in university licensing: The role of contracts, *Research Policy*, 40: 94–104; S. Hagaoka, 2009, Does strong patent protection facilitate international technology transfer? Some evidence from licensing contrasts of Japanese firms, *Journal of Technology Transfer*, 34: 128–144.

81. 2011, Edu-Science (H.K.) Limited, About us, Edu-Science homepage, http://www.edu-science.com.hk, June 23; 2011, Stone America announces licensing agreement between *Scientific American* and Edu-Science, *Scientific American* homepage, June 6; E. A. Reid, 2011, Stone America announces licensing agreement for new science toys, *Toybook.com*, http://www.toybook.com, June 7.

82. U. Lichtenthaler, 2011, The evolution of technology licensing management: Identifying five strategic approaches, *R&D Management*, 41: 173–189; M. Fiedler & I. M. Welpe, 2010, Antecedents of cooperative commercialisation strategies of nanotechnology firms, *Research Policy*, 39: 400–410.

83. C. A. Barlett & S. Rangan, 1992, Komatsu Limited, in C. A. Bartlett & S. Ghoshal (eds.), Ireland, 1992, *Transnational Management: Text, Cases and Readings in Cross-Border Management*, Homewood, IL: Irwin, 311–326.

84. C. Schwens, J. J. Eiche, & R. Kabst, 2011, The moderating impact of informal institutional distance and formal institutional risk on SME entry mode choice, *Journal of Management Business Studies*, 48: 330–351; H. K. Steensma, J. Q. Barden, C. Dhanaraj, M. Lyles, & L. Tihanyi, 2008, The evolution and internationalization of international joint ventures in a transitioning economy, *Journal of International Business Studies*, 39: 491–507.

85. S. Prashantham & S. Young, 2011, Post-entry speed of international new ventures, *Entrepreneurship Theory and Practice*, 35: 275–292.

86. D. Morschett, H. Schramm-Klein, & B. Swoboda, 2010, Decades of research on market entry modes: What do we really know about external antecedents of entry mode choice? *Journal of International Management*, 16: 60–77; J. S. Harrison, M. A. Hitt, R. E. Hoskisson, & R. D. Ireland, 2001, Resource complementarity in business combinations: Extending the logic to organization alliances, *Journal of Management*, 27: 679–690.

87. R. A. D'Aveni, G. B. Dagnino, & K. G. Smith, 2010, The age of temporary advantage, *Strategic Management Journal*, 31: 1371–1385; M. A. Hitt, D. Ahlstrom, M. T. Dacin, E. Levitas, & L. Svobodina, 2004, The institutional effects on strategic alliance partner selection in transition economies: China versus Russia, *Organization Science*, 15: 173–185.

88. R. A. Corredoira & L. Rosenkopf, 2010, Should auld acquaintance be forgot? The reverse transfer of knowledge through mobility ties, *Strategic Management Journal*, 31: 159–181; T. Chi & A. Seth, 2009, A dynamic model of the choice of mode for exploiting complementary capabilities, *Journal of International Business Studies*, 40: 365–387; E. W. K. Tsang, 2002, Acquiring knowledge by foreign partners for international joint ventures in a transition economy: Learning-by-doing and learning myopia, *Strategic Management Journal*, 23: 835–854.

89. D. E. Boyd & R. E. Spekman, 2010, The licensing of market development rights within technology alliances: A shareholder value perspective, *Journal of Product Innovation Management*, 27: 593–605; M. J. Robson, C. S. Katsikeas, & D. C. Bello, 2008, Drivers and performance outcomes of trust in international strategic alliances: The role of organizational complexity, *Organization Science*, 19: 647–668; S. Zaheer & A. Zaheer, 2007, Trust across borders, *Journal of International Business Studies*, 38: 21–29.

90. 2011, Limagrain signs strategic alliance to enter Brazilian corn market, *Great Lakes Hybrids*, http://www.greatlakeshybrids.com, February 14.

91. C. Schwens, J. Eiche, & R. Kabst, 2011, The moderating impact of informal institutional distance and formal institutional risk on SME entry mode choice, *Journal of Management Studies*, 48: 330–351; M. H. Ogasavara & Y. Hoshino, 2009, The effects of entry strategy and interfirm trust on the survival of Japanese manufacturing subsidiaries in Brazil, *Asian Business & Management*, 7: 353–380; M. W. Peng & O. Shenkar, 2002, Joint venture dissolution as corporate divorce, *Academy of Management Executive*, 16(2): 92–105.

92. Y. Luo, O. Shekar, & H. Gurnani, 2008, Control-cooperation interfaces in global strategic alliances: A situational typology and strategic responses, *Journal of International Business Studies*, 39: 428–453.

93. T. K. Das, 2010, Interpartner sensemaking in strategic alliances: Managing cultural differences and internal tensions, *Management Decision*, 48: 17–36; X. Lin & C. L. Wang, 2008, Enforcement and performance: The role of ownership, legalism and trust in international joint

ventures, *Journal of World Business*, 43: 340–351.

94. B. B. Nielsen, 2010, Strategic fit, contractual, and procedural governance in alliances, *Journal of Business Research*, 63: 682–689; D. Li, L. Eden, M. A. Hitt, & R. D. Ireland, 2008, Friends, acquaintances and stranger? Partner selection in R&D alliances, *Academy of Management Journal*, 51: 315–334.

95. S.-F. S. Chen, 2010, A general TCE model of international business institutions; market failure and reciprocity, *Journal of International Business Studies*, 41: 935–959; J. Wiklund & D. A. Shepherd, 2009, The effectiveness of alliances and acquisitions: The role of resource combination activities, *Entrepreneurship Theory and Practice*, 33: 193–212.

96. Z. Huang, X. Han, F. Roche, & J. Cassidy, 2011, The dilemma facing strategic choice of entry mode, *Global Business Review*, 12: 181–192; A. Boateng, W. Qian, & Y. Tianle, 2008, Cross-border M&As by Chinese firms: An analysis of strategic motives and performance, *Thunderbird International Business Review*, 50: 259–270; M. A. Hitt & V. Pisano, 2003, The cross-border merger and acquisition strategy, *Management Research*, 1: 133–144.

97. 2011, LK Solar finalizes acquisition of 70% of Solar Power Inc., LDK Solar homepage, http://www.ldksolar.com, March 31.

98. 2011, *Market Watch*, JA Solar to acquire wafer producer Solar Silicon Valley, http://www.marketwatch.com, July 1.

99. Ibid.

100. S. Malhotra, P.-C. Zhu, & W. Locander, 2010, Impact of host-country corruption on U.S. and Chinese cross-border acquisitions, *Thunderbird International Business Review*, 52: 491–507; P. X. Meschi, 2009, Government corruption and foreign stakes in international joint ventures in emerging economies, *Asia Pacific Journal of Management*, 26: 241–261.

101. R. Balsvik & S. A. Haller, 2011, Foreign firms and host-country productivity: Does the entry mode matter? *Oxford Economic Papers*, 63: 158–186.

102. D. R. Denison, B. Adkins, & A. Guidroz, 2011, Managing cultural integration in cross-border mergers and acquisitions, in W. H. Mobley, 2011, M. Li, & Y. Wang (eds.), *Advances in Global Leadership*, Vol. 6, Bingley, UK: Emerald Publishing Group, 95–115; S. F. S. Chen, 2008, The motives for international acquisitions: Capability procurements, strategic considerations, and the role of ownership structures, *Journal of International Business Studies*, 39: 454–471.

103. Y. Fang, G.-L. F. Jiang, S. Makino, & P. W. Beamish, 2010, Multinational firm knowledge, use of expatriates, and foreign subsidiary performance, *Journal of Management Studies*, 47: 27–54; H. Raff, M. Ryan, & F. Stahler, 2009, The choice of market entry mode: Greenfield

investment, M&A and joint venture, *International Review of Economics & Finance*, 18(1): 3–10.

104. C. Bouquet, L. Hebert, & A. Delios, 2004, Foreign expansion in service industries: Separability and human capital intensity, *Journal of Business Research*, 57: 35–46.

105. C. Schwens, J. Eiche, & R. Kabst, 2011, The moderating impact of informal institutional distance and formal institutional risk on SME entry mode choice, *Journal of Management Studies*, 48: 330–351; K. F. Meyer, S. Estrin, S., Bhaumik, & M. W. Peng, 2009, Institutions, resources, and entry strategies in emerging economics, *Strategic Management Journal*, 30: 61–80.

106. K. D. Brouthers & D. Dikova, 2010, Acquisitions and real options: The Greenfield alternative, *Journal of Management Studies*, 47: 1048–1071; K. F. Meyer, M. Wright, & S. Pruthi, 2009, Managing knowledge in foreign entry strategies: A resource-based analysis, *Strategic Management Journal*, 30: 557–574.

107. Y. Parke & B. Sternquist, 2008, The global retailer's strategic proposition and choice of entry mode, *International Journal of Retail & Distribution Management*; 36: 281–299.

108. 2009, FedEx moves its Asia-Pacific hub to China, *China Daily*, http://www.chinadaily.com, February 7; A. Roth, 2008, Beijing Olympics 2008: UPS markets its delivery for China only: Company transports gear from the Games, *Wall Street Journal* (Europe), August 11, 29.

109. J. Anand, R. Oriani, & R. S. Vassolo, 2010, Alliance activity as a dynamic capability in the face of a discontinuous technological change, *Organization Science*, 21: 1213–1232; R. Farzad, 2007, Extreme investing: Inside Colombia, *BusinessWeek*, May 28, 50–58.

110. A. M. Rugman, 2010, Reconciling internalization theory and the eclectic paradigm, *Multinational Business Review*, 18: 1–12; J. Che & G. Facchini, 2009, Cultural differences, insecure property rights and the mode of entry decision, *Economic Theory*, 38: 465–484.

111. A. Peterson, 2011, Toyota opens first new Japanese plant in 20 years, *Motor Trend*, http://www.motortrend.com, February 18.

112. C. Giersch, 2011, Political risk and political due diligence, *Global Risk Affairs*, http://www.globalriskaffairs.com, March 4.

113. J. Li & Y. Tang, 2010, CEO hubris and firm risk taking in China: The moderating role of managerial discretion, *Academy of Management Journal*, 53: 45–68; I. Alon & T. T. Herbert, 2009, A stranger in a strange land: Micro political risk and the multinational firm, *Business Horizons*, 52: 127–137; P. Rodriguez, K. Uhlenbruck, & L. Eden, 2003, Government corruption and the entry strategies of multinationals, *Academy of Management Review*, 30: 383–396.

114. O. Branzei & S. Abdelnour, 2010, Another day, another dollar: Enterprise resilience under terrorism in developing countries, *Journal of International Business Studies*, 41: 804–825; F. Wu, 2009, Singapore's sovereign wealth funds: The political risk of overseas investment, *World Economics*, 9(3): 97–122; P. S. Ring, G. A. Bigley, T. D'aunno, & T. Khanna, 2005, Perspectives on how governments matter, *Academy of Management Review*, 30: 308–320.

115. Giersch, Political risk and political due diligence.

116. M. D. Hanous & A. Prazdnichnyky, 2011, The Russia competitiveness report 2011, *World Economic Forum*, January; A. Kouznetsov, 2009, Entry modes employed by multinational manufacturing enterprises and review of factors that affect entry mode choices in Russia, *The Business Review*, 10: 316–323.

117. G. Fornes & A. Butt-Philip, 2011, Chinese MNEs and Latin America: A review, *International Journal of Emerging Markets*, 6: 98–117; S. Globerman & D. Shapiro, 2009, Economic and strategic considerations surrounding Chinese FDI in the United States, *Asia Pacific Journal of Management*, 26: 163–183.

118. C. R. Goddard, 2011, Risky business: Financial-sector liberalization and China, *Thunderbird International Business Review*, 53: 469–482; I. G. Kawaller, 2009, Hedging currency exposures by multinationals: Things to consider, *Journal of Applied Finance*, 18: 92–98.

119. C. C. Chung, S.-H. Lee, P. W. Beamish, & T. Ksobe, 2010, Subsidiary expansion/contraction during times of economic crisis, *Journal of International Business Studies*, 41: 500–516.

120. V. Monatiriotis & R. Alegria, 2011, Origin of FDI and intra-industry domestic spillovers: The case of Greek and European FDI in Bulgaria, *Review of Development Economics*, 15: 326–339; N. Bandelj, 2009, The global economy as instituted process: The case of Central and Eastern Europe, *American Sociological Review*, 74: 128–149; L. Tihanyi & W. H. Hegarty, 2007, Political interests and the emergence of commercial banking in transition economies, *Journal of Management Studies*, 44: 789–813.

121. P. David, J. P. O'Brien, T. Yoshikawa, & A. Delios, 2010, Do shareholders or stakeholders appropriate the rents from corporate diversification? The influence of ownership structure, *Academy of Management Journal*, 53: 636–654; M. F. Wiersma & H. P. Bowen, 2008, Corporate international diversification: The impact of foreign competition, industry globalization and product diversification, *Strategic Management Journal*, 29: 115–132.

122. L. Li, 2007, Multinationality and performance: A synthetic review and

research agenda, *International Journal of Management Reviews*, 9: 117–139; J. A. Doukas & O. B. Kan, 2006, Does global diversification destroy firm value? *Journal of International Business Studies*, 37: 352–371.

123. S. E. Christophe & H. Lee, 2005, What matters about internationalization: A market-based assessment, *Journal of Business Research*, 58: 636–643.

124. T. J. Andersen, 2011, The risk implications of multinational enterprise, *International Journal of Organizational Analysis*, 19: 49–70; H. Zou & M. B. Adams, 2009, Corporate ownership, equity risk ad returns in the People's Republic of China, *Journal of International Business Studies*, 39: 1149–1168.

125. H. Kachi, 2011, Asahi expands global acquisitions, *Wall Street Journal*, http://www.wsj.com, July 4.

126. A. Y. Lewin, S. Massini, & C. Peeters, 2011, Microfoundations of internal and external absorptive capacity routines, *Organization Science*, 22; J. Penner-Hahn & J. M. Shaver, 2005, Does international research and development increase patent outcome? An analysis of Japanese pharmaceutical firms, *Strategic Management Journal*, 26: 121–140.

127. H. A. Ndofor, D. G. Sirmon, & X. He, 2011, Firm resources, competitive actions and performance: Investigating a mediated model with evidence from the in-vitro diagnostics industry, *Strategic Management Journal*, 32: 81–98; 640–657; B. Ambos & B. B. Schlegelmilch, 2007, Innovation and control in the multinational firm: A comparison of political and contingency approaches,

Strategic Management Journal, 28: 473–486.

128. G. R. G. Benito, R. Lunnan & S. Tomassen, 2011, Distant encounters of the third kind: Multinational companies locating divisional headquarters abroad, *Journal of Management Studies*, 48: 373–394; M. A. Hitt, L. Tihanyi, T. Miller, & B. Connelly, 2006, International diversification: Antecedents, outcomes, and moderators, *Journal of Management*, 32: 831–867.

129. D. Holtbrugge & A. T. Mohr, 2011, Subsidiary interdependencies and international human resource management practices in German MNCs, *Management International Review*, 51: 93–115; E. Matta & P. W. Beamish, 2008, The accentuated CEO career horizon problem: Evidence from international acquisitions, *Strategic Management Journal*, 29: 683–700.

130. I. Filatotchev & M. Wright, 2010, Agency perspectives on corporate governance of multinational enterprises, *Journal of Management Studies*, 47: 471–486; H. L. Sirkin, J. W. Hemerling, & A. K. Bhattacharya, 2009, Globality: Challenger companies are radically redefining the competitive landscape, *Strategy & Leadership*, 36(6): 36-41.

131. D. Dikova, P. R. Sahib, & A. van Witteloostuijn, 2010, Cross-border acquisition abandonment and completion: The effect of institutional differences and organizational learning in the international business service industry, 1981–2001, *Journal of International Business Studies*, 41: 223–245; C. Crossland & D. C. Hambrick, 2007, How national systems differ in their constraints on corporate executives: A study of CEO

effects in three countries, *Strategic Management Journal*, 28: 767–789.

132. N. Gulati & A. Choudhury, 2011, Toyota enters India's small car market, *Wall Street Journal*, http://www.wsj.com, June 28.

133. Wiersema & Bowen, The relationship between international diversification and firm performance; C.-F. Wang, L.-Y. Chen, & S.-C. Change, 2011, International diversification and the market value of new product introduction, *Journal of International Management*, in press.

134. L. Berchicci, A. King, & C. L. Tucci, 2011, Does the apple always fall close to the tree? The geographical proximity choice of spin-outs, *Strategic Entrepreneurship Journal*, 5: 120–136; A. Ojala, 2008, Entry in a psychically distant market: Finnish small and medium-sized software firms in Japan, *European Management Journal*, 26: 135–144.

135. B. L. Connelly, R. E. Hoskisson, L. Tihanyi, & S. T. Certo, 2010, Ownership as a form of corporate governance, *Journal of Management Studies*, 47: 1561–1589; M. L. L. Lam, 2009, Beyond credibility of doing business in China: Strategies for improving corporate citizenship of foreign multinational enterprises in China, *Journal of Business Ethics*, 87: 137–146.

136. E. Fang & S. Zou, 2010, The effects of absorptive capacity and joint learning on the instability of international joint ventures in emerging economies, *Journal of International Business Studies*, 41: 906–924; D. Lavie & S. Miller, 2009, Alliance portfolio internationalization and firm performance, *Organization Science*, 19: 623–646.

CHAPTER 9

Cooperative Strategy

Studying this chapter should provide you with the strategic management knowledge needed to:

1. Define cooperative strategies and explain why firms use them.

2. Define and discuss the three major types of strategic alliances.

3. Name the business-level cooperative strategies and describe their use.

4. Discuss the use of corporate-level cooperative strategies in diversified firms.

5. Understand the importance of cross-border strategic alliances as an international cooperative strategy.

6. Explain cooperative strategies' risks.

7. Describe two approaches used to manage cooperative strategies.

THE RENAULT-NISSAN ALLIANCE: COLLABORATING TO SUCCEED

March 27, 1999—this is the day the alliance between French-based Renault and Japan-based Nissan was formally launched. At the time the alliance was formed, each of these firms lacked the size necessary to develop economies of scale and economies of scope that were critical to efforts to succeed in the 1990s and beyond in the global automobile market. The alliance the two companies formed finds them holding ownership stakes in each other; the larger of the two companies, Renault has a 44.3 percent stake in Nissan while Nissan has a 15 percent stake in Renault. Brazilian-born Carlos Ghosn serves as CEO for both companies. Three values guide this corporate-level synergistic alliance (we discuss this type of alliance later in the chapter): (1) *Trust* (work fairly, impartially and professionally), (2) *Respect* (honor commitments, liabilities, and responsibilities), and (3) *Transparency* (be open, frank, and clear).

The Renault-Nissan alliance is recognized for its success. The firms' decision to establish Renault-Nissan B.V., which is a strategic management company that is responsible for creating common strategies for the companies and for facilitating and managing synergies resulting from combining some of the firms' respective resources, capabilities, and core competencies, is a key reason for the alliance's success. Also supporting the management of this alliance is a number of committees with members from each company. These individuals are expected to do everything possible to integrate the firms' resource portfolios for the purpose of creating products customers will value and that will contribute to the firms' profitability.

Cooperative strategies such as the one formed at the corporate level between Renault and Nissan are increasingly important to firms; but firms form many types of cooperative relationships in addition to corporate-level ones. Moreover, an individual firm's set of cooperative relationships can be complicated, as the Nissan and Renault alliance demonstrates. In addition to their corporate-level alliance, Renault and Nissan have each formed horizontal complementary strategic alliances at the business-unit level with other companies. (We discuss several types of business-unit level alliances in the chapter.) For example, Nissan and Mitsubishi Motors Corporation formed a joint venture (called NMKV Co., Ltd.) to produce minicars for the Japanese market. The cars are to be introduced in 2012 and are being manufactured in a facility the venture built in Thailand. This venture was formed for the purpose of uniting "the strengths of Nissan and Mitsubishi in the areas of vehicle engineering, development and parts sourcing, as part of an overall strategy to bring new minicar products to market." Additionally, the firms are discussing the possibility of using this relationship for the purposing of collaborating to develop electric vehicles as well. Ghosn sees electric vehicles as a pillar to future strategies for both companies.

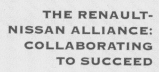

Danny Gys/PhotoShot, Inc.

The successful Renault-Nissan alliance is built upon three standards—trust, respect, and transparency.

© Nicholas Monu/IStockphoto.com

Read more about Tata Motors competitive strategy.

www.cengagebrain .com

Renault has a cooperative relationship with Bajaj Auto Ltd. of India that is intended to produce a minicar that will compete against Tata Motors' (headquartered in India) Nano, currently the world's cheapest car at $US 3,158 for the base model. This partnership has yet to reach the level of success the partners seek. Additionally, Renault recently terminated a partnership with India's Mahindra & Mahindra Ltd. because the sales in India resulting from this joint venture's operations were disappointing.

As these examples demonstrate, the cooperative relationship between Renault and Nissan is complicated. Indeed, CEO Ghosn has noted that he is challenged to lead these firms in ways that allow each company to maintain its separate identify while benefitting from their collaboration.

Sources: L. Denning, 2011, Long and winding road for electric vehicles, *Wall Street Journal*, http://www.wsj .com, July 2; N. Gulati, 2011, Renault India: Low-cost small car unlikely in 2012, *Wall Street Journal*, http:// www.wsj.com, June 8; E. Loveday, 2011, Nissan, Mitsubishi establish NMKV minicar joint venture for possible city car EV, *Autoblog*, http//www.green.autoblog.com, June 22; E. Niedermeyer, 2011, Renault-Nissan rethinking their relationship, *The Truth About Cars*, http://www.thetruthaboutcars.com, February 25; D. Pearson & S. Moffett, 2011, Renault electric vehicle program hits delay, *Wall Street Journal*, http://www.wsj.com, July 7; Y. Takahashi, 2011, Nissan CEO still holds a top spot in pay, *Wall Street Journal*, http://www.wsj.com, June 30; Y. Takahashi & C. Dawson, 2011, Nissan revs up to win bigger share, *Wall Street Journal*, http://www.wsj.com, June 28.

As explained in the Opening Case, Renault and Nissan have formed a corporate-level cooperative strategy as a means of improving each firm's performance. Additionally, each company is independently using a number of cooperative strategies at the business-unit level with the same objective in mind—to improve the performance of the individual firms. In all of these instances, Renault and Nissan, as is the case for all companies, are trying to use their resources and capabilities in ways that will create the greatest amount of value for stakeholders.[1]

Forming a cooperative strategy like the one between Renault and Nissan, or between other global automobile companies (for example, Fiat SpA and Chrysler Group),[2] has the potential to be a viable engine of firm growth.[3] Specifically, a **cooperative strategy** is a means by which firms collaborate for the purpose of working together to achieve a shared objective.[4] Cooperating with other firms is a strategy firms use to create value for a customer that it likely could not create by itself. For example, in describing a Fiat-designed and developed compact car that Chrysler will build and sell in the United States under its own name, an auto industry analyst said that a product such as this is "why the two auto makers . . . have a relationship."[5]

Firms also try to create competitive advantages when using a cooperative strategy. A competitive advantage developed through a cooperative strategy often is called a *collaborative* or *relational* advantage,[6] denoting that the relationship that develops among collaborating partners is commonly the basis on which a competitive advantage is built. Importantly, successful use of cooperative strategies finds a firm outperforming its rivals in terms of strategic competitiveness and above-average returns,[7] often because they've been able to form a competitive advantage.

We examine several topics in this chapter. First, we define and offer examples of different strategic alliances as primary types of cooperative strategies. We focus on strategic alliances because firms use them more frequently than other types of cooperative relationships. Next, we discuss the extensive use of cooperative strategies in the global economy and reasons for that use. In succession, we describe business-level, corporate-level, international, and network cooperative strategies. The chapter closes with a discussion of the risks of using cooperative strategies as well as how effectively managing the strategies can reduce those risks.

A **cooperative strategy** is a means by which firms collaborate for the purpose of working together to achieve a shared objective.

Strategic Alliances as a Primary Type of Cooperative Strategy

A **strategic alliance** is a cooperative strategy in which firms combine some of their resources and capabilities for the purpose of creating a competitive advantage.[8] Strategic alliances involve firms with some degree of exchange and sharing of resources and capabilities to co-develop, sell, and service goods or services.[9] In addition, firms use strategic alliances to leverage their existing resources and capabilities while working with partners to develop additional resources and capabilities as the foundation for new competitive advantages.[10] To be certain, the reality today is that "strategic alliances have become a cornerstone of many firms' competitive strategy."[11] This means that for many firms, and particularly for large global competitors, strategic alliances are potentially many in number but are always important to efforts to outperform competitors.

Consider the case of BMW Group. Focusing exclusively on premium products, this firm uses an international focused differentiation business-level strategy (see Chapter 8) to sell its cars, trucks, and motorcycles in multiple geographic regions. According to the company's CEO, this firm relies in part on a host of strategic alliances "to further shape (BMW's) future, which involves topics such as technology leadership."[12] Among BMW Group's current alliances are (1) a purchasing cooperation with Daimler AG, (2) a joint venture with the SGL Group to produce carbon fibers (SGL Group is one of the world's leading producers of carbon-based products), and (3) a joint venture with PSA Peugeot Citroen (BMW Peugeot Citroen Electrification) to produce four-cylinder engines and hybrid components.

Before describing three types of major strategic alliances and reasons for their use, we need to note that for all cooperative strategies, success is more likely when partners behave cooperatively. Actively solving problems, being trustworthy, and consistently pursuing ways to combine partners' resources and capabilities to create value are examples of cooperative behavior known to contribute to alliance success.[13] Recall that *trust*, *respect*, and *transparency* are three core values on which the Renault-Nissan corporate-level cooperative strategy is based. Perhaps these values are instrumental to the success that is credited to this cooperative relationship.

Types of Major Strategic Alliances

Joint ventures, equity strategic alliances, and nonequity strategic alliances are the three major types of strategic alliances firms use. The ownership arrangement is a key difference among these alliances.

A **joint venture** is a strategic alliance in which two or more firms create a legally independent company to share some of their resources and capabilities for the purpose of developing a competitive advantage. Some evidence suggests that recent economic difficulties have increased the attractiveness of this type of strategic alliance: "Joint ventures have become a more prevalent way for companies to gain access to new capabilities, products, and geographies since the start of the most recent economic downturn."[14] Often formed to improve a firm's ability to compete in uncertain competitive environments, such as those associated with economic downturns,[15] joint ventures are effective in establishing long-term relationships and in transferring tacit knowledge. Because it can't be codified, tacit knowledge, which is increasingly critical to firms' efforts to develop core competencies, is learned through experiences such as those taking place when people from partner firms work together in a joint venture.[16] Overall, a joint venture may be the optimal type of cooperative arrangement when firms need to combine their resources and capabilities to create a competitive advantage that is substantially different from any they possess individually and when the partners intend to enter highly uncertain, hypercompetitive markets.

A **strategic alliance** is a cooperative strategy in which firms combine some of their resources and capabilities for the purpose of creating a competitive advantage.

A **joint venture** is a strategic alliance in which two or more firms create a legally independent company to share some of their resources and capabilities for the purpose of developing a competitive advantage.

Typically, partners in a joint venture own equal percentages and contribute equally to the venture's operations. When established in 1999, Germany's Siemens AG and Japan's Fujitsu Ltd. each owned 50 percent of the joint venture Fujitsu Siemens Computers B.V. Based in Maarssen, The Netherlands, this collaboration was the last major European-based computer manufacturer. This joint venture was established so Fujitsu and Siemens could combine primarily their technology-based resources and capabilities to compete in an uncertain market (computer manufacturing). On April 1, 2009 though, this company became Fujitsu Technology Solutions after Fujitsu bought Siemens' share of the joint venture. As this outcome suggests, joint ventures are not necessarily permanent in nature. There are different reasons for the lack of permanence including dissatisfaction by one or all parties with the partnership's outcomes or changes in the strategic direction one or more partners wish to pursue. As you will see by reading the Strategic Focus, the agreement reached to end the joint venture was very amicable and served the emerging interests of Fujitsu and Siemens.

STRATEGIC FOCUS

FUJITSU SIEMENS COMPUTERS B.V.— THE BEGINNING AND THE END

The personal computer (PC) market has long been dynamic and challenging. In 1999, Fujitsu and Siemens formed a joint venture as a means of successfully dealing with the challenges associated with the PC market. This venture, Fujitsu Siemens Computers (FSC), was a legally independent company that the two partners owned equally (50 percent each). This company was formed by combining Fujitsu Computers Limited (at the time, the European computer business of Fujitsu Limited) and the Computer Systems business in Europe, the Middle East, and Africa of Siemens AG. Immediately then, FSC had a strong presence in key markets across the EMEA region (Europe, the Middle East, and Africa). Producing and selling a wide variety of products such as desktops, laptops, high-end servers and mainframes, storage devices, and peripherals in over 170 countries, FSC also focused on "green" computers and was recognized as an innovator in terms of its green manufacturing processes.

When forming the collaboration, the partners concluded that integrating their technological capabilities was critical to the venture's success. In addition to integrating actual technologies, the partners agreed to find ways to transfer tacit knowledge and skills through which the technologies could be used for the purpose of creating value for customers.

Notebooks are produced in a Fujitsu Siemens Computer factory located in Augsburg, Germany.

a11/ZUMA Press/Newscom

FSC achieved a reasonable degree of success, although as can be the case for firms competing in hypercompetitive markets, there were times when the venture's performance trailed what its partners expected. Overall though the partners were pleased with FSC's performance, as suggested by the following comments from a Fujitsu spokesperson: "In just a decade, the company has established a leading position in the EMEA market for IT infrastructure, earning a reputation for quality and innovation in the server, PC, and data storage fields." The fact that the joint venture lasted for approximately 10 years is another indicator of its success.

Formally, FSC was dissolved when Fujitsu acquired Siemens' 50 percent of the joint venture as of April 1, 2009. Siemens indicated that it agreed to sell its FSC stake so the company could focus on "the strategic sectors Energy, Industry and Healthcare." For Siemens, exiting its partnership with Fujitsu was a product of the decision to restructure (see Chapter 7) its portfolio of businesses. After buying out its partner, Fujitsu formed Fujitsu Technology Solutions (FTS) as one of its strategic business units. According to company documents, FTS is "the leading European IT infrastructure provider with a presence in all key markets in Europe, the Middle East and Africa, plus India, serving large-, medium- and small-sized companies as well as consumers." For Fujitsu, owning all of its former joint venture with Siemens supported the firm's global growth strategy. In the words of a Fujitsu official: "Fully integrating Fujitsu Siemens Computers into the Fujitsu Group fits perfectly into our global growth strategy. We're inheriting a strong customer base in EMEA and an R&D capability that can support our global products development . . ."

Although the joint venture known as FSC was dissolved, Fujitsu and Siemens announced at that time that the companies would continue collaborating "in various fields of technology" in the years to come. Thus, as a joint venture, FSC helped the partnering firms reach objectives for a period of time; but the venture was dissolved when the partners made independent decisions about their business portfolios.

Sources: 2011, About Fujitsu Technology Solutions, Fujitsu homepage, http://www.fujitsu.com, July 12; 2011, Management direction, Fujitsu homepage, http://www.fujitsu.com, July 12; Siemens to sell PC stake to Fujitsu, *ITPro*, http://www.itpro.co.uk, November 4; R. Harding, 2008, Fujitsu to take over Siemens' IT stake, *FT.com*, http://www.ft.com, November 5; 2007, Fujitsu Siemens Computers and EMC Corporation expand alliance, Fujitsu homepage, http://www.fujitsu.com, March 14.

An **equity strategic alliance** is an alliance in which two or more firms own different percentages of the company they have formed by combining some of their resources and capabilities for the purpose of creating a competitive advantage. Many foreign direct investments, such as those companies from multiple countries are making in China, are completed through equity strategic alliances.[17]

Recently, Japanese telecom operator NTT DoCoMo Inc. and Chinese Internet search operator Baidu Inc. established an equity strategic alliance in China to distribute games and other mobile-phone content. Baidu will own 80 percent of this collaboration with DoCoMo holding the remaining 20 percent. Content such as Japanese games, animation, and comic books are to be distributed in China, where "demand for mobile phone content is expected to surge in the coming years."[18] This collaborative arrangement contributes to DoCoMo's efforts to increase its presence in international markets and to Baidu's desire to generate additional revenues outside its core online search advertising business.

A **nonequity strategic alliance** is an alliance in which two or more firms develop a contractual relationship to share some of their resources and capabilities for the purpose of creating a competitive advantage.[19] In this type of alliance, firms do not establish a separate independent company and therefore do not take equity positions. For this reason, nonequity strategic alliances are less formal, demand fewer partner commitments than do joint ventures and equity strategic alliances, and generally do not foster an intimate relationship between partners; nonetheless, research evidence indicates that they can create value for the involved firms.[20] The relative informality and lower commitment levels characterizing nonequity strategic alliances make them unsuitable for complex projects where success requires effective transfers of tacit knowledge between partners.[21] Licensing agreements, distribution agreements, and supply contracts are examples of nonequity strategic alliances.

A number of technology-based firms form nonequity strategic alliances. Hewlett-Packard (HP) actively uses this type of cooperative strategy to license some of its intellectual property. Xerox formed a six-year relationship with HCL Technologies. This nonequity alliance will find HCL handling disaster recovery, data center hosting and migration, virtualization, and consolidation tasks across Xerox's data centers in North America and Europe. Describing the reason for this alliance, Xerox's chief information officer said that "Data center environments are the heart of our business operations and we look to partner with companies that can manage our centers and take them to the next level."[22]

Commonly, outsourcing commitments are specified in the form of a nonequity strategic alliance. (Discussed in Chapter 3, *outsourcing* is the purchase of a value-chain

© Nicholas Monu/iStockphoto.com

STRATEGY RIGHT NOW

Explore the strategic alliance between HP and Healthways, Inc.

www.cengagebrain.com

A **equity strategic alliance** is an alliance in which two or more firms own different percentages of the company they have formed by combining some of their resources and capabilities for the purpose of creating a competitive advantage.

A **nonequity strategic alliance** is an alliance in which two or more firms develop a contractual relationship to share some of their resources and capabilities for the purpose of creating a competitive advantage.

activity, or a support function activity from another firm.) Dell Inc. and most other computer firms outsource most or all of their production of laptop computers and often form nonequity strategic alliances to detail the nature of the relationship with firms to whom they outsource. Interestingly, many of these firms that outsource introduce modularity that prevents the contracting partner or outsourcee from gaining too much knowledge or from sharing certain aspects of the business the outsourcing firm does not want revealed.[23]

Reasons Firms Develop Strategic Alliances

Cooperative strategies are an integral part of the competitive landscape and are quite important to many companies and even to educational institutions. In fact, many firms are cooperating with educational institutions to help commercialize ideas flowing from basic research projects completed at universities.[24] In for-profit organizations, many executives believe that strategic alliances are central to their firm's growth and success.[25] The fact that alliances can account for up to 25 percent or more of a firm's sales revenue demonstrates their importance. Also highlighting alliances' importance is the fact that in some settings, such as the global airline industry, competition is increasingly between large alliances rather than between large companies.[26]

Among other benefits, strategic alliances allow partners to create value that they couldn't develop by acting independently and to enter markets more quickly and with greater market penetration possibilities.[27] For example, Japanese trading house Itochu Corp. recently acquired a 20 percent stake in a Colombian coal-mining operation owned by Drummond Company Inc. As comments from the company indicate, Itochu formed this joint venture for the purpose of quickly expanding its market size. "Itochu said the investment in the operations, with production of about 25 million tons per year, is a 'key step' in plans to more than double its equity share in global mining operations. Itochu is targeting access to more than 20 million metric tons of coal per year by 2015, compared with 8 million metric tons currently."[28]

Another reason to form strategic alliances is that most (if not all) firms lack the full set of resources and capabilities needed to reach their objectives, which indicates that partnering with others will increase the probability of reaching firm-specific performance objectives. This may be especially true for small businesses—ones in which capital is scarce. Given constrained resources, small firms can collaborate for a number of purposes, including those of reaching new customers and broadening the distribution of their products without adding significantly to their cost structures.[29]

Unique competitive conditions characterize slow-cycle, fast-cycle, and standard-cycle markets.[30] We discussed these three market types in Chapter 5 while examining competitive rivalry and competitive dynamics. These unique conditions find firms using strategic alliances to reach objectives that differ slightly by market type (see Figure 9.1).

Slow-cycle markets are markets where the firm's competitive advantages are shielded from imitation for relatively long periods of time and where imitation is costly. These markets are close to monopolistic conditions. Railroads and, historically, telecommunications, utilities, and financial services are industries characterized as slow-cycle markets. In *fast-cycle markets,* the firm's competitive advantages are not shielded from imitation, preventing their long-term sustainability. Competitive advantages are moderately shielded from imitation in *standard-cycle markets,* typically allowing them to be sustained for a longer period of time than in fast-cycle market situations, but for a shorter period of time than in slow-cycle markets.

Slow-Cycle Markets
Firms in slow-cycle markets often use strategic alliances to enter restricted markets or to establish franchises in new markets. For example, because of consolidating acquisitions, the American steel industry has two remaining major players: U.S. Steel and Nucor. To improve their ability to compete successfully in the global steel market, these companies are forming cooperative relationships. They have formed strategic alliances in Europe and Asia and are invested in ventures in South America and Australia.

Figure 9.1 Reasons for Strategic Alliances by Market Type

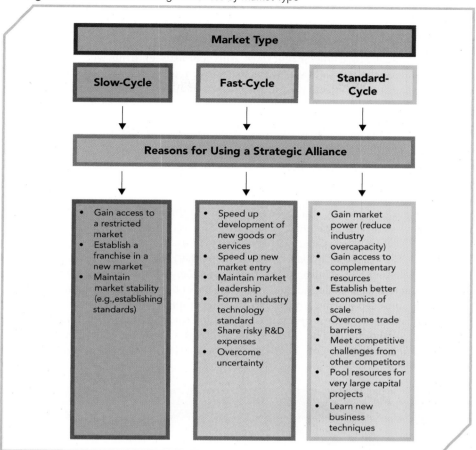

Source: © Copyrighted 2011 by Michael A. Hitt, R. Duane Ireland, and Robert E. Hoskisson.

One of Nucor's alliances with a firm outside its U.S. domestic market is its joint venture with Italian-based Duferco Group's subsidiary Duferdofin. Each firm has a 50 percent ownership of the venture, called Duferdofin–Nucor S.r.l. Through this collaboration, the firms are producing steel joists and beams in Italy and then selling them in Europe and North Africa. The resources and capabilities contributed by each partner are suggested by the following comment from Nucor's CEO: "(This venture) combines Nucor's world-recognized know-how in the efficient production of structural shapes with Duferdofin's strong management team and strategic locations in Italy."[31] On the domestic front, Nucor recently formed a long-term strategic alliance with Truswal Systems Corporation, "a leading supplier of engineered products and state of the art software for the building components industry." The purpose of this collaboration is the development of proprietary design, engineering, and layout software.[32] The expectation is that the Truswal alliance will facilitate Nucor's efforts to successfully compete in the global light gauge steel framing market.

Slow-cycle markets are becoming rare in the twenty-first century competitive landscape for several reasons, including the privatization of industries and economies, the rapid expansion of the Internet's capabilities for quick dissemination of information, and the speed with which advancing technologies make quickly imitating even complex products possible.[33] Firms competing in slow-cycle markets, including steel manufacturers, should recognize the future likelihood that they'll encounter situations in which their competitive advantages become partially sustainable (in the instance of a standard-cycle market) or unsustainable (in the case of a fast-cycle market). Cooperative strategies can help firms transition from relatively sheltered markets to more competitive ones.[34]

Fast-Cycle Markets

Fast-cycle markets are unstable, unpredictable, and complex; in a word, hypercompeti-tive.[35] Combined, these conditions virtually preclude establishing long-lasting competitive advantages, forcing firms to constantly seek sources of new competitive advantages while creating value by using current ones. Alliances between firms with current excess resources and capabilities and those with promising capabilities help companies compete in fast-cycle markets to effectively transition from the present to the future and to gain rapid entry into new markets. As such a "collaboration mindset" is paramount.[36]

The entertainment business is fast becoming a new digital marketplace as television content is now available on the Web. This has led the entertainment business into a fast-cycle market where collaboration is important not only to succeed but to survive. Many of the firms that have digital video content have also sought to make a profit through digital music and have had difficulties in profiting from their earlier ventures. To address issues such as these, GE's NBC Universal and News Corporation formed Hulu.com in 2007. Walt Disney Company joined this equity strategic alliance in 2009 (private equity investor Providence Equity Partners also has a stake in this alliance.) This Web-based cooperative relationship is an alliance between firms that are direct competitors. To support Hulu, ABC (owned by Disney) makes much of its content available on the Hulu site as do the other content providers including NBC Universal. As digital video content moves onto the Web, it will be interesting to see the evolution of competition and cooperation between these firms.[37]

Telecommunications and software firms also compete in fast-cycle markets and use strategic alliances as a means of doing so. Microsoft and Nokia recently formed a comprehensive collaboration. The firms' CEOs issued the following statement describing the agreed-upon arrangement: "Our two companies (have) plans for a broad strategic

STRATEGIC FOCUS

MICROSOFT AND NOKIA FORM A PARTNERSHIP TO SHAPE THE FUTURE

"Today, the battle is moving from one of mobile devices to one of mobile ecosystems, and our strengths here are complementary. Ecosystems thrive when they reach scale, when they are fueled by energy and innovation, and when they provide benefits and value to each person or company who participates. This is what we are creating; this is our vision; this is the work we are driving from this day forward." Articulated jointly by Stephen Elop, CEO of Nokia, and Steve Ballmer, Microsoft's CEO, these statements describe the comprehensive strategic alliance these firms announced in February 2011. The fact that several hundred pages were developed to specify the scope of the alliance and to detail each party's responsibilities demonstrates this collaboration's comprehensiveness and potentially its complexity.

Essentially, the strategic alliance between these firms calls for Nokia to transition its smartphone portfolio to Microsoft's Windows phone platform. Additionally, there is a wide range of ways these firms will collaborate to complete this transition and to form a mobile ecosystem. For example, Microsoft's Bing will power Nokia's search services across all of its devices and services, Microsoft's development tools are to be used to create applications that will run on Nokia Windows Phones, and the firms will collaborate to design and execute joint marketing activities. The market's immediate reaction to this collaboration was negative, as Nokia's

Nokia's "N8" smartphone will run exclusively on Microsoft's Windows phone platform. Some say this is a risky move for Nokia.

AP Photos/Winfried Rothermel/DAPD

market value declined 5.7 billion euros ($7.7 billion) in the first two days following announcement of the alliance. A reason for this immediate reaction could be the risk some analysts believe Nokia is accepting by adopting the Windows Phone platform as its primary smartphone strategy.

Firms competing in fast-cycle markets experience a great deal of uncertainty, change, and dynamism. Being able to set a new industry standard in a fast-cycle market has the potential to be the foundation for a firm's ability to deal successfully with these industry conditions and to outperform its rivals while doing so. In the instance of this alliance, the firms seek to use their complementary resources to build and sustain an ecosystem in the mobile communications space. In essence, "a business ecosystem's scope is the set of positive sum relationships (symbiosis) between actors who work together around a core technology platform" such as Microsoft Windows "that induces a synergy between MS Windows compatible companies delivering hardware, software, services, etc." Customers, markets, products, processes, organizations, stakeholders, and governments are an ecosystem's actors. The idea of an ecosystem is that actors will share a key technology platform as the primary source of how they can flourish in this intertwined, networked environment. Using their strategic alliance to form a mobile ecosystem, Microsoft and Nokia believe they will be able "to deliver ground-breaking enterprise solutions for mobile productivity" while competing in and possibly disrupting the competitive patterns in what is a fast-cycle market.

As is true for all cooperative strategies, the success of the comprehensive alliance between Microsoft and Nokia is not assured. Some analysts believe that going forward Nokia's R&D activities need to create more value than now seems to be the case, customers' uncertainty about the viability and appropriateness of adopting a Windows-based smartphone strategy must be overcome, and the degree to which this alliance may help the partners (particularly Nokia) develop a product for the fast-growing tablet-based computer market must be monitored. Additionally, the firms' ability to collaborate as the basis for developing a viable mobile ecosystem is an open question.

© Nicholas Monu/iStockphoto.com

Learn more about Microsoft's collaborative culture.

www.cengagebrain.com

Sources: 2011, Business ecosystem, ProvenModels, http://www.provenmodels.com, July 20; G. A. Fowler & I. Sherr, 2011, Nokia CEO defends shift to Microsoft software, *Wall Street Journal*, http://www.wsj.com, June 1; A. Moen, 2011, Nokia posts strong earnings, *Wall Street Journal*, http://www.wsj.com, April 21; H. Plumridge, 2011, Nokia may need a little help from its friends, *Wall Street Journal*, http://www.wsj.com, June 14; M. Srivastava & D. ben-Aaron, 2011, Nokia rethinks R&D spending, *Bloomberg Businessweek*, http://www.businessweek.com, February 14; 2011, Nokia and Microsoft announce plants for a broad strategic partnership to build a new global mobile ecosystem, Microsoft homepage, http://www.microsoft.com, February 11; 2011, Our mission, Microsoft homepage, http://www.microsoft.com, July 12; 2011, Microsoft Corp, *Standard & Poor's Stock Reports*, http://www.standardandpoors.com, July 9.

partnership that combines the respective strengths of our companies and builds a new global mobile ecosystem. The partnership increases our scale, which will result in significant benefits for consumers, developers, mobile operators and businesses around the world. We both are incredibly excited about the journey we are on together."[38] As we discuss in the Strategic Focus, the alliance Microsoft and Nokia have formed demonstrates use of a collaborative mind-set as the foundation for the firms' efforts to develop new products and perhaps form an industry technology standard as well (see Table 9.1).

Standard-Cycle Markets

In standard-cycle markets, alliances are more likely to be made by partners that have complementary resources and capabilities. The alliances formed by airline companies are an example of standard-cycle market alliances.

When initially established decades ago, these alliances were intended to allow firms to share their complementary resources and capabilities to make it easier for passengers to fly between secondary cities in the United States and Europe. Today, airline alliances are mostly global in nature and are formed primarily so members can gain marketing clout, have opportunities to reduce costs, and have access to additional international routes.[39] Of these reasons, international expansion by having access to more international routes is the most important in that these routes are the path to increased revenues and potential profits. To support efforts to control costs, alliance members jointly purchase some items and share facilities when possible, such as passenger gates, customer service centers, and airport passenger lounges. For passengers, airline alliances "offer simpler ticketing and smoother connections on intercontinental trips as well as the chance to earn and redeem frequent-flier miles on other member carriers."[40]

There are three major airline alliances operating today. Star Alliance is the largest with 27 members. With 12 members, OneWorld Alliance is the smallest while the 13-member SkyTeam Alliance has one more member. Given the geographic areas where markets are growing, these global alliances are adding partners from Asia. For example, in recent years, China Southern Airlines joined the SkyTeam alliance and Air China was added to the Star Alliance.

In addition to the three major alliances, a host of other alliances exist among airline carriers. For example, ANA (All Nippon Airways) and Deutsche Lufthansa AG are both members of the Star Alliance. However, these firms decided to launch a joint venture at the end of 2011 for the purpose of combining their resources to serve routes between Japan and Europe. Sharing revenue, coordinating flight schedules, and working together on joint product sales are examples of how the firms' resources and capabilities are to be shared through the joint venture.[41] Similarly, Singapore Airlines, a member of Star Alliance, and Virgin Australia announced plans for a wide-ranging alliance. Under the alliance, Singapore Airlines would have access to Virgin Australia's routes to New Zealand and the U.S. West Coast. At the same time, Virgin Australia was planning to complete alliances with Air New Zealand and Etihad Airways PJSC, based in Abu Dhabi.[42] In general, most airline alliances such as the ones we've described are formed to help firms gain economies of scale and meet competitive challenges (see Figure 9.1).

Business-Level Cooperative Strategy

A **business-level cooperative strategy** is a strategy through which firms combine some of their resources and capabilities for the purpose of creating a competitive advantage by competing in one or more product markets. As discussed in Chapter 4, business-level strategy details what the firm intends to do to gain a competitive advantage in specific product markets. Thus, the firm forms a business-level cooperative strategy when it believes that combining some of its resources and capabilities with those of one or more partners will create competitive advantages that it can't create by itself and will lead to success in a specific product market. We list the four business-level cooperative strategies in Figure 9.2.

Complementary Strategic Alliances

Complementary strategic alliances are business-level alliances in which firms share some of their resources and capabilities in complementary ways for the purpose of creating a competitive advantage.[43] Vertical and horizontal are the two types of complementary strategic alliances (see Figure 9.2).

Vertical Complementary Strategic Alliance

In a *vertical complementary strategic alliance,* firms share some of their resources and capabilities from different stages of the value chain for the purpose of creating a competitive advantage (see Figure 9.3).[44] Oftentimes, vertical complementary alliances are formed to adapt to environmental changes;[45] sometimes the changes represent an opportunity for partnering firms to innovate while adapting.[46]

Operating with four segments (EA Games, EA Sports, The Sims, and EA Casual Entertainment), Electronic Arts (EA) develops, markets, publishes, and distributes video game software, mobile games, and online interactive games in over 35 countries, meaning that the firm is geographically diversified as well as diversified with its product lines.

A **business-level cooperative strategy** is a strategy through which firms combine some of their resources and capabilities for the purpose of creating a competitive advantage by competing in one or more product markets.

Complementary strategic alliances are business-level alliances in which firms share some of their resources and capabilities in complementary ways for the purpose of creating a competitive advantage.

Figure 9.2 Business-Level Cooperative Strategies

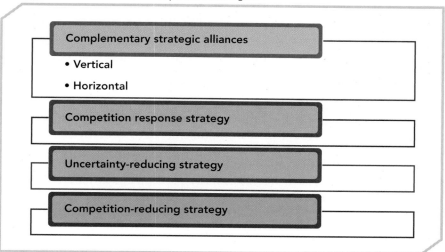

Source: © Copyrighted 2011 by Michael A. Hitt, R. Duane Ireland, and Robert E. Hoskisson.

Figure 9.3 Vertical and Horizontal Complementary Strategic Alliances

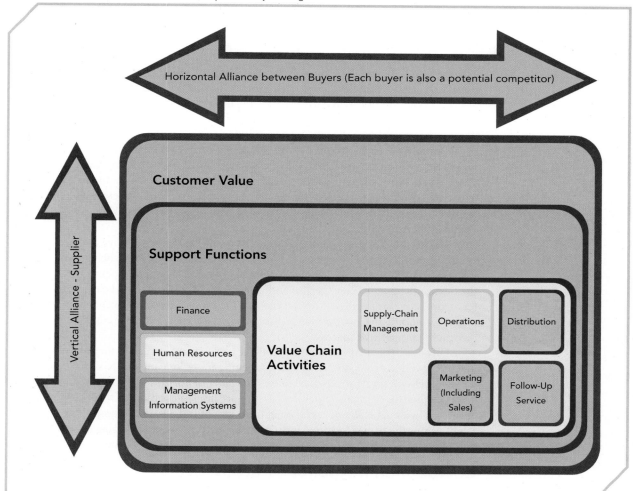

Source: © Copyrighted 2011 by Michael A. Hitt, R. Duane Ireland, and Robert E. Hoskisson.

Vertical strategic alliances are a key part of how EA competes, including the ones the firm has formed with Nintendo and Hasbro. EA produces software and games for Nintendo's Wii game console through the alliance it has with that firm. Through the alliance with Hasbro, EA offers *MONOPOLY Millionaires* on Facebook. An EA executive describes the firm's alliance with Hasbro in this manner: "We strive to continually re-imagine Hasbro brands digitally in creative ways and *MONOPOLY Millionaires* is no exception. We're bringing the world's favorite game brand into the new era of social gaming, offering an accessible and enjoyable experience for Facebook users worldwide."[47]

Sometimes, private–public sector vertical collaborations are formed, such as the alliance Novartis AG and the World Health Organization (WHO) developed in 2001. The purpose of the 10-year alliance was to battle malaria in developing countries. The agreement called for Novartis to provide one of its drugs, Coartem, at an average price of USD $1.57 per treatment for adults and at a substantially discounted price for children, who are most vulnerable to malaria. Using the distribution part of the value chain, the WHO evaluated requests for Coartem and then distributed the drug through government agencies of malaria-endemic countries.

The terms of the original alliance between Novartis and the WHO expired in May 2011. At that time though, Norvartis announced that because of its long-term commitment to battling malaria, it would "continue to provide Coartem to public health systems in developing countries on the same terms as before."[48]

Horizontal Complementary Strategic Alliance

A *horizontal complementary strategic alliance* is an alliance in which firms share some of their resources and capabilities from the same stage (or stages) of the value chain for the purpose of creating a competitive advantage. Commonly, firms use complementary strategic alliances to focus on joint long-term product development and distribution opportunities.[49] As noted previously, Hulu (http://www.hulu.com) is a joint Web site that GE's NBC Universal, News Corporation, and Walt Disney Company formed for the purpose of distributing video content. Through this equity strategic alliance, the alliance's partners provide content (one stage of the value chain) to Hulu for distribution (another part of the value chain).

Pharmaceutical companies form a number of horizontal alliances. For example, as health care reform takes place in the United States, large pharmaceutical firms are seeking relationships with generic drug producers. Pfizer recently formed an alliance with Santaris Pharma A/S to develop and commercialize RNA-targeted medicines using Santaris Pharma A/S's locked nucleic acid (LNA) drug platform. (Santaris is a clinical-stage biopharmaceutical company.)[50]

Novartis AG's orientation to collaborations reflects the perspective of many pharmaceutical manufacturers. Supporting Norvartis' collaborations is the belief that "the path for scientific breakthrough to successful pharmaceutical brand depends on mobilizing the best global resources, expertise and experience."[51] Thus as noted earlier in the chapter, cooperative strategies are used largely so firms (such as pharmaceutical manufacturers) can combine the "world's best" resources, capabilities, and core competencies in the pursuit of competitive success.

Many horizontal complementary strategic alliances are formed in the automobile manufacturing industry. As discussed in the Opening Case, Renault and Nissan formed a corporate-level synergistic strategic alliance. A number of horizontal complementary strategic alliances the two firms have developed support implementation of their corporate-level alliance. The Renault alliance with Bajaj Auto Ltd. of India is an example of the horizontal relationships the firm is forming. Even more broadly, cooperative strategies of all types are instrumental to automobile manufacturers' efforts to successfully compete globally.

Competition Response Strategy

As discussed in Chapter 5, competitors initiate competitive actions to attack rivals and launch competitive responses to their competitors' actions. Strategic alliances can be used at the business level to respond to competitors' attacks. Because they can be difficult to reverse and expensive to operate, strategic alliances are primarily formed to take strategic rather than tactical actions and to respond to competitors' actions in a like manner.

Even during the downtown the U.S. housing market has experienced over the past few years, the Washington D.C. area remains fairly strong. As a result, this area is attractive to builders and land and community developers. In fact, investors are buying land parcels to develop and homebuilders are building houses throughout the area. In response to this increased level of activity, homebuilder NVR Inc. has formed a joint venture with an affiliate of investment bank Morgan Stanley to purchase a large land portfolio in the suburbs of the U.S. capital. Specifically, the partners intend to buy 5,600 home sites in nine master-planned communities in the Virginia suburbs. Analysts feel that this partnership demonstrates that the two parties are confident that the D.C. market will remain attractive and that their collaboration is one through which they will be able to compete successfully against strong competitors in the D.C. market.[52]

Uncertainty-Reducing Strategy

Firms sometimes use business-level strategic alliances to hedge against risk and uncertainty, especially in fast-cycle markets.[53] These strategies are also used where uncertainty exists, such as in entering new product markets and especially those of emerging economies.

As large global auto firms manufacture more hybrid vehicles, there is insufficient industry capacity to meet the demand for the type of batteries used in these vehicles. In turn, the lack of a sufficient supply of electric batteries creates uncertainty for automobile manufacturers. To reduce this uncertainty, auto firms are forming alliances. For example, Volkswagen has formed an agreement with Samuel Electric and Toshiba Corp. of Japan to manufacture lithium-ion batteries used in hybrid vehicles.[54] Renault-Nissan established a joint venture with the French government in 2009 to make batteries. However, this venture was dissolved in mid-2011 because the "French government will no longer help finance the battery plant as had originally been planned."[55]

Competition-Reducing Strategy

Used to reduce competition, collusive strategies differ from strategic alliances in that collusive strategies are often an illegal type of cooperative strategy. Explicit collusion and tacit collusion are the two types of collusive strategies.

Explicit collusion exists when two or more firms negotiate directly to jointly agree about the amount to produce as well as the prices for what is produced.[56] Explicit collusion strategies are illegal in the United States and most developed economies (except in regulated industries). Accordingly, companies choosing to use explicit collusion as a strategy should recognize that competitors and regulatory bodies might challenge the acceptability of their competitive actions.

Tacit collusion exists when several firms in an industry indirectly coordinate their production and pricing decisions by observing each other's competitive actions and responses.[57] Tacit collusion results in production output that is below fully competitive levels and above fully competitive prices. Unlike explicit collusion, firms engaging in tacit collusion do not directly negotiate output and pricing decisions. However, research suggests that joint ventures or cooperation between two firms can lead to less competition in other markets in which both firms operate.[58]

Tacit collusion tends to be used as a competition-reducing business-level strategy in industries with a high degree of concentration, such as the airline and breakfast cereal industries. Research in the airline industry suggests that tacit collusion reduces service quality and on-time performance.[59] Firms in these industries recognize their interdependence, which means that their competitive actions and responses significantly affect competitors' behavior toward them. Understanding this interdependence and carefully observing competitors can lead to tacit collusion.

Four firms, Kellogg Company, General Mills Inc., Ralcorp Holdings Inc., and Quaker Foods North America, account for as much as 80 percent of sales volume in the ready-to-eat segment of the U.S. cereal market. Kellogg is the producer of many cereal favorites such as Corn Flakes, Fruit Loops, and Raisin Bran.

Richard Levine/Alamy

Over time, four firms—Kellogg Company (producers of Kellogg's Corn Flakes, Fruit Loops, etc.), General Mills Inc. (Cheerios, Charms, etc.), Ralcorp Holdings Inc. (Shredded Wheat, Post Raisin, etc.), and Quaker Foods North America, a part of PepsiCo (Quaker Oatmeal, Cap'n Crunch, etc.)—have accounted for as much as 80 percent of sales volume in the ready-to-eat segment of the U.S. cereal market.[60] Some believe that this high degree of concentration results in prices to consumers that substantially exceed the costs companies incur to produce and sell their products. If prices are above the competitive level in this industry, it may be a possibility that the dominant firms use a tacit collusion cooperative strategy.

Discussed in Chapter 6, *mutual forbearance* is a form of tacit collusion in which firms do not take competitive actions against rivals they meet in multiple markets. Rivals learn a great deal about each other when engaging in multimarket competition, including how to deter the effects of their rivals' competitive attacks and responses. Given what they know about each other as competitors, firms choose not to engage in what could be destructive competition in multiple product markets.[61]

In general, governments in free-market economies seek to determine how rivals can form cooperative strategies for the purpose of increasing their competitiveness without violating established regulations about competition.[62] However, this task is challenging when evaluating collusive strategies, particularly tacit ones. For example, the regulation of pharmaceutical and biotech firms who collaborate to meet global competition might lead to too much price fixing, meaning that regulation is required to make sure that the balance is "right" (though sometimes the regulation gets in the way of efficient markets).[63] In turn, individual companies must analyze the effect of a competition-reducing strategy on their performance and competitiveness and decide if pursuing such a strategy is an overall facilitator of their competitive success.

Assessing Business-Level Cooperative Strategies

Firms use business-level cooperative strategies to develop competitive advantages that can contribute to successful positions in individual product markets. Evidence suggests that complementary business-level strategic alliances, especially vertical ones, have the greatest probability of creating a competitive advantage and possibly even a sustainable one.[64] Horizontal complementary alliances are sometimes difficult to maintain because often they are formed between firms that compete against each other at the same time they are cooperating. Renault and Nissan still compete against each other with some of their products while collaborating to produce and sell other products. In a case such as this, partnering firms may feel a "push" toward and a "pull" from alliances. Airline firms, for example, want to compete aggressively against others serving their markets and target customers. However, the need to develop scale economies and to share resources and capabilities (such as scheduling systems) dictates that alliances be formed so the firms can compete by using cooperative actions and responses while they simultaneously compete against one another through competitive actions and responses. The challenge in these instances is for each firm to find ways to create the greatest amount of value from both their competitive and cooperative actions. It seems that Nissan and Renault may have learned how to achieve this balance.

Although strategic alliances designed to respond to competition and to reduce uncertainty can also create competitive advantages, these advantages often are more temporary than those developed through complementary (both vertical and horizontal) alliances. The primary reason for this is that complementary alliances have a stronger focus on creating value than do competition-reducing and uncertainty-reducing alliances, which are formed to respond to competitors' actions or reduce uncertainty rather than to attack competitors.

Of the four business-level cooperative strategies, the competition-reducing strategy has the lowest probability of creating a competitive advantage. For example, research suggests that firms following a foreign direct investment strategy using alliances as a follow-the-leader imitation approach may not have strong strategic or learning goals. Thus, such investment could be attributable to tacit collusion among the participating firms rather than trying to develop a competitive advantage (which should be the core objective).

Corporate-Level Cooperative Strategy

A **corporate-level cooperative strategy** is a strategy through which a firm collaborates with one or more companies for the purpose of expanding its operations. The alliance between Itochu Corp. and Drummond Company mentioned earlier will "allow Itochu to diversify its coal assets to a new geographic region and grow its trading activities."[65] As such this is a corporate-level cooperative strategy between these two firms. Diversifying alliances, synergistic alliances, and franchising are the most commonly used corporate-level cooperative strategies (see Figure 9.4).

Firms use diversifying and synergistic alliances to improve their performance by diversifying their operations through a means other than or in addition to internal organic growth or a merger or acquisition.[66] When a firm seeks to diversify into markets in which the host nation's government prevents mergers and acquisitions, alliances become an especially appropriate option. Corporate-level strategic alliances are also attractive compared with mergers and particularly acquisitions, because they require fewer resource commitments[67] and permit greater flexibility in terms of efforts to diversify partners' operations.[68] An alliance can be used as a way to determine whether the partners might benefit from a future merger or acquisition between them. This "testing" process often characterizes alliances formed to combine firms' unique technological resources and capabilities.[69]

Figure 9.4 Corporate-Level Cooperative Strategies

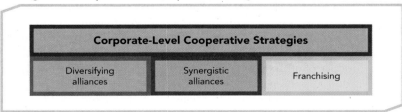

Source: © Copyrighted 2011 by Michael A. Hitt, R. Duane Ireland, and Robert E. Hoskisson.

corporate-level cooperative strategy is a strategy through which a firm collaborates with one or more companies for the purpose of expanding its operations.

Diversifying Strategic Alliance

A **diversifying strategic alliance** is a strategy in which firms share some of their resources and capabilities to engage in product and/or geographic diversification. The agreement between Itochu and Drummond is a diversifying strategic alliance.

The spread of high-speed wireless networks and devices with global positioning chips and the popularity of Web site applications running on various companies' smartphones indicate that consumers are more frequently and intensely accessing mobile information. Equipped with this knowledge, Alcatel-Lucent entered the market through mobile advertising, which will allow a cell phone carrier to alert customers about the location of a favorite store or the closest ATM.[70] The partners are pursuing this alliance with 1020 Placecast, a California-based developer of cell phone online ads associated with user locations. Hyatt, FedEx, and Avis are especially interested in using the service. The ads will also include a link to coupons or other promotions. Recently, Alcatel-Lucent and Millicom Ghana Ltd. "under the brand of Tigo, one of Ghana's leading mobile network operators, (formed) a partnership to introduce the first permission- and preference-based mobile advertising service in Ghana."[71] Through this partnership, Tigo's customers are able to receive targeted promotions on their phones. Overall, these networks are trying to gain a share of the profits that would normally be out of their reach through revenue-sharing models with companies that are advertising as well as the ad-producing service companies.

Synergistic Strategic Alliance

A **synergistic strategic alliance** is a strategy in which firms share some of their resources and capabilities to create economies of scope. Similar to the business-level horizontal complementary strategic alliance, synergistic strategic alliances create synergy across multiple functions or multiple businesses between partner firms. The Renault-Nissan collaboration we discussed in the Opening Case is a synergistic strategic alliance in that among other outcomes, the firms seek to create economies of scope by sharing their resources and capabilities to develop manufacturing platforms that can be used to produce cars that will be either a Renault or a Nissan. The cooperative arrangement between Fiat and Chrysler is also a synergistic alliance. As noted earlier, Chrysler will produce a Fiat-designed and developed compact car in its Belvidere, Illinois facility. Reflecting the complexity of synergistic alliances and their "twin" horizontal complementary alliances at the business-unit level is the fact that Fiat used the same underpinnings for what will be a car carrying the Dodge brand that it uses to produce the Alfa Romeo Giulietta.[72] (Alfa Romeo is a part of Fiat SpA.) Without economies of scope such as those Fiat seeks by using the same underpinnings for a car carrying the Dodge brand and the Alfa Romeo brand, the probability of success with a synergistic alliance is substantially reduced.

Franchising

Franchising is a strategy in which a firm (the franchisor) uses a franchise as a contractual relationship to describe and control the sharing of its resources and capabilities with its partners (the franchisees).[73] A *franchise* is a "contractual agreement between two legally independent companies whereby the franchisor grants the right to the franchisee to sell the franchisor's product or do business under its trademarks in a given location for a specified period of time."[74] Often, success is determined in these strategic alliances by how well the franchisor can replicate its success across multiple partners in a cost-effective way.[75]

Franchising is a popular strategy. Recent estimates are that in the United States alone, the gross domestic product of all franchised businesses is approximately $1.2 trillion (this is about one-third of all sales generated in the United States) and that there are more than 828,000 individual franchise store locations employing a total of 18 million people.[76] Already frequently used in developed nations, franchising is also expected to account for significant portions of growth in emerging economies in the twenty-first century.[77] As with diversifying and synergistic strategic alliances, franchising is an

diversifying strategic alliance is a strategy in which firms share some of their resources and capabilities to engage in product and/or geographic diversification.

A **synergistic strategic alliance** is a strategy in which firms share some of their resources and capabilities to create economies of scope.

Franchising is a strategy in which a firm (the franchisor) uses a franchise as a contractual relationship to describe and control the sharing of its resources and capabilities with its partners (the franchisees).

alternative to pursuing growth through mergers and acquisitions. McDonald's, Hilton International, Marriott International, Mrs. Fields Cookies, Subway, and Ace Hardware are well-known examples of firms using the franchising corporate-level cooperative strategy.

Franchising is a particularly attractive strategy to use in fragmented industries, such as retailing, hotels and motels, and commercial printing. In fragmented industries, a large number of small and medium-sized firms compete as rivals; however, no firm or small set of firms has a dominant share, making it possible for a company to gain a large market share by consolidating independent companies through the contractual relationships that are a part of a franchise agreement.

In the most successful franchising strategy, the partners (the franchisor and the franchisees) work closely together.[78] A primary responsibility of the franchisor is to develop programs to transfer to the franchisees the knowledge and skills that are needed to successfully compete at the local level.[79] In return, franchisees should provide feedback to the franchisor regarding how their units could become more effective and efficient.[80] Working cooperatively, the franchisor and its franchisees find ways to strengthen the core company's brand name, which is often the most important competitive advantage for franchisees operating in their local markets.[81]

Assessing Corporate-Level Cooperative Strategies

Costs are incurred to implement each type of cooperative strategy.[82] Compared with their business-level counterparts, corporate-level cooperative strategies commonly are broader in scope and more complex, making them relatively more challenging and costly to use.

Pat Canova/Alamy

This Ace Hardware store in High Springs, Florida is a franchisee.

In spite of these costs, firms can create competitive advantages and value for customers by effectively using corporate-level cooperative strategies.[83] Internalizing successful alliance experiences makes it more likely that the strategy will attain the desired advantages. In other words, those involved with forming and using corporate-level cooperative strategies can also use them to develop useful knowledge about how to succeed in the future. To gain maximum value from this knowledge, firms should organize it and verify that it is always properly distributed to those involved with forming and using alliances.

We explain in Chapter 6 that firms answer two questions when dealing with corporate-level strategy—in which businesses and product markets will the firm choose to compete and how will those businesses be managed? These questions are also answered as firms form corporate-level cooperative strategies. Thus, firms able to develop corporate-level cooperative strategies and manage them in ways that are valuable, rare, imperfectly imitable, and nonsubstitutable (see Chapter 3) develop a competitive advantage that is in addition to advantages gained through the activities completed to implement individual cooperative strategies. (Later in the chapter, we further describe alliance management as another potential competitive advantage.)

International Cooperative Strategy

The new competitive landscape finds firms using cross-border transactions for several purposes. In Chapter 7, we discussed cross-border acquisitions, actions through which a company located in one country acquires a firm located in a different country. In

Chapter 8, we described how firms use cross-border acquisitions as a way of entering international markets. Here in Chapter 9, we examine cross-border strategic alliances as a type of international cooperative strategy. Thus, firms engage in cross-border activities to achieve several related objectives.

A **cross-border strategic alliance** is a strategy in which firms with headquarters in different countries decide to combine some of their resources and capabilities for the purpose of creating a competitive advantage. Taking place in virtually all industries, the number of cross-border alliances firms are completing continues to increase.[84] These alliances too are sometimes formed instead of mergers and acquisitions, which can be riskier. Even though cross-border alliances can themselves be complex and hard to manage,[85] they have the potential to help firms use some of their resources and capabilities to create value in locations outside their home market.

Limited domestic growth opportunities and foreign government economic policies are key reasons firms use cross-border alliances. As discussed in Chapter 8, local ownership is an important national policy objective in some nations. In India and China, for example, governmental policies reflect a strong preference to license local companies. Thus, in some countries, the full range of entry mode choices we described in Chapter 8 may not be available to firms seeking to geographically diversify into a number of international markets. Indeed, investment by foreign firms in these instances may be allowed only through a partnership with a local firm, such as in a cross-border alliance. Important too is the fact that strategic alliances with local partners can help firms overcome certain liabilities of moving into a foreign country, including those related to a lack of knowledge of the local culture or institutional norms.[86] A cross-border strategic alliance can also help foreign partners from an operational perspective, because the local partner has significantly more information about factors contributing to competitive success such as local markets, sources of capital, legal procedures, and politics.[87] Interestingly, research results suggest that firms with foreign operations have longer survival rates than domestic-only firms, although this is reduced if there are competition problems between foreign subsidiaries.[88]

As a result of two major global trends—increasing fuel costs and tougher environmental regulations—airlines are deeply interested in flying planes that are powered by more fuel-efficient engines. Manufacturers of airplane engines are responding to this strong customer interest and are pushing "the frontiers of technology by building lighter plans and borrowing essential engine-design advances from the auto industry, like automatic transmissions."[89] To build these engines, manufacturers are forming strategic alliances, many of which are cross-border alliances. For example, Volvo Aero, which is a wholly owned subsidiary of Sweden's AB Volvo, and U.S.-based Pratt & Whitney (which is one of United Technology's strategic business units) formed a cross-border strategic alliance to collaborate on the new PW1100G engine, an engine that "is a part of Pratt & Whitney's Next Generation Product Family of engines which contain geared turbofan technology."[90] Through this collaboration—which is not the first between these two firms—Volvo Aero will design and manufacture two components that are critical to Pratt & Whitney's new engine. As we noted in Chapter 8 this engine initially is being designed for use in the A320neo family, which is an updated version of the Airbus A320. "The engine is expected to reduce fuel consumption, carbon dioxide and nitric oxide emissions, and noise, as well as lowering running and operating costs significantly."[91]

In general then, cross-border strategic alliances are more complex and risky than are domestic strategic alliances, especially when used in emerging economies. However, the fact that firms competing internationally tend to outperform domestic-only competitors suggests the importance of learning how to geographically diversify into international markets. Compared with mergers and acquisitions, cross-border alliances may be a better way to learn this process, especially in the early stages of a firm's geographic diversification efforts.

A **cross-border strategic alliance** is a strategy in which firms with headquarters in different countries decide to combine some of their resources and capabilities for the purpose of creating a competitive advantage.

Network Cooperative Strategy

In addition to forming their own alliances with individual companies, an increasing number of firms are collaborating in multiple networks.[92] A **network cooperative strategy** is a strategy wherein several firms agree to form multiple partnerships for the purpose of achieving shared objectives.

Through its Global Partner Network, Cisco has formed alliances with a host of individual companies including IBM, Microsoft, Accenture, Emerson, Fujitsu, Intel, and Nokia. According to Cisco, partnering allows a firm to "drive growth and differentiate (its) business by extending (its) capabilities to meet customer requirements."[93] Demonstrating the complexity of network cooperative strategies is the fact that Cisco also competes against a number of the firms with whom it has formed cooperative agreements. For example, Cisco is competing against IBM as it now sells and services servers. Although a new business line for Cisco, sales revenue for Cisco's servers exceeded $900 million in 2010.[94] At the same time, Cisco and IBM's alliance is very active as the firms seek to help customers "maximize (their) business results by uniting IBM's vast industry, business process and implementation expertise with Cisco's world-class unified communications and networking technologies."[95] Overall, in spite of their complexity as the IBM/Cisco example shows, firms are using network cooperative strategies more extensively as a way of creating value for customers by offering many goods and services in many geographic (domestic and international) markets.

Singapore's fusionopolis complex represents the collaboration of physical sciences and engineering to tackle global science and technology challenges.

A network cooperative strategy is particularly effective when it is formed by geographically clustered firms,[96] as in California's Silicon Valley (where "the culture of Silicon Valley encourages collaborative webs"[97]) and Singapore's Biopolis (in the biomedical sciences) and the new fusionopolis (collaborations in "physical sciences and engineering to tackle global science and technology challenges").[98] Effective social relationships and interactions among partners while sharing their resources and capabilities make it more likely that a network cooperative strategy will be successful,[99] as does having a productive *strategic center firm* (we discuss strategic center firms in detail in Chapter 11). Firms involved in networks gain information and knowledge from multiple sources. They can use these heterogeneous knowledge sets to produce more and better innovation. As a result, firms involved in networks of alliances tend to be more innovative.[100] However, there are disadvantages to participating in networks as a firm can be locked into its partnerships, precluding the development of alliances with others. In certain network configurations, such as Japanese *keiretsus,* firms in a network are expected to help other firms in that network whenever support is required. Such expectations can become a burden and negatively affect the focal firm's performance over time.[101]

Alliance Network Types

An important advantage of a network cooperative strategy is that firms gain access to their partners' other partners. Having access to multiple collaborations increases the likelihood that additional competitive advantages will be formed as the set of shared resources and capabilities expands.[102] In turn, being able to develop new capabilities further stimulates product innovations that are critical to strategic competitiveness in the global economy.

A **network cooperative strategy** is a strategy wherein several firms agree to form multiple partnerships for the purpose of achieving shared objectives.

The set of strategic alliance partnerships firms develop when using a network cooperative strategy is called an *alliance network.* Companies' alliance networks vary by industry characteristics. A *stable alliance network* is formed in mature industries where demand is relatively constant and predictable. Through a stable alliance network, firms try to extend their competitive advantages to other settings while continuing to profit from operations in their core, relatively mature industry. Thus, stable networks are built primarily to *exploit* the economies (scale and/or scope) that exist between the partners such as in the airline industry.[103]

Dynamic alliance networks are used in industries characterized by frequent product innovations and short product life cycles.[104] For instance, the pace of innovation in the information technology (IT) industry (as well as other fast-cycle market industries) is too fast for any one company to be successful across time if it only competes independently. Another example is the movie industry, an industry in which firms participate in a number of networks for the purpose of producing and distributing movies.[105] In dynamic alliance networks, partners typically *explore* new ideas and possibilities with the potential to lead to product innovations, entries to new markets, and the development of new markets.[106] Often large firms in industries such as software and pharmaceuticals create networks of relationships with smaller entrepreneurial startup firms in their search for innovation-based outcomes.[107] An important outcome for small firms successfully partnering with larger firms in an alliance network is the credibility they build by being associated with their larger collaborators.[108]

Competitive Risks with Cooperative Strategies

Stated simply, many cooperative strategies fail. In fact, evidence shows that two-thirds of cooperative strategies have serious problems in their first two years and that as many as 50 percent of them fail. This failure rate suggests that even when the partnership has potential complementarities and synergies, alliance success is elusive.[109] Although failure is undesirable, it can be a valuable learning experience, meaning that firms should carefully study a cooperative strategy's failure to gain insights with respect to how to form and manage future cooperative arrangements.[110] We show prominent cooperative strategy risks in Figure 9.5.

Figure 9.5 Managing Competitive Risks in Cooperative Strategies

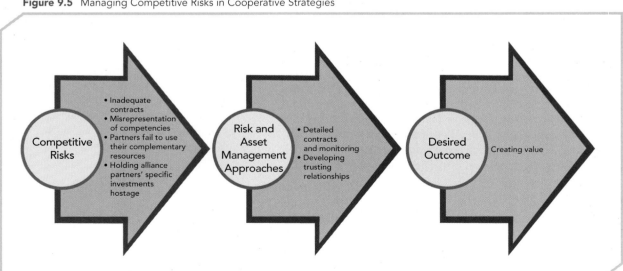

One cooperative strategy risk is that a firm may act in a way that its partner thinks is opportunistic. Amylin Pharmaceuticals seems to believe that this is the case with Eli Lilly & Co., its partner in an alliance formed in 2002. Developing and commercializing the type 2 diabetes drug exenatide, which is sold as a twice-daily injection under the brand Byetta, is a major outcome of this alliance. However, Lilly's recently signed agreement with another firm for the purpose of jointly developing and commercializing several diabetes drugs—including Tradjenta, a drug the U.S. Food and Drug Administration has approved—is creating a situation in which Amylin seems to have concluded that Lilly is acting opportunistically. Because of this, Amylin has filed a lawsuit against Lilly, "alleging (that) Lilly's recent diabetes venture with Boehringer Ingelheim GmbH breaches the terms of Lilly's older partnership with Amylin to market other drugs for the disease."[111]

In general, opportunistic behaviors surface either when formal contracts fail to prevent them or when an alliance is based on a false perception of partner trustworthiness. Not infrequently, the opportunistic firm wants to acquire as much of its partner's tacit knowledge as it can.[112] Full awareness of what a partner wants in a cooperative strategy reduces the likelihood that a firm will suffer from another's opportunistic actions.[113]

Some cooperative strategies fail when it is discovered that a firm has misrepresented the competencies it can bring to the partnership. This risk is more common when the partner's contribution is grounded in some of its intangible assets. Superior knowledge of local conditions is an example of an intangible asset that partners often fail to deliver. An effective way to deal with this risk may be to ask the partner to provide evidence that it does possess the resources and capabilities (even when they are largely intangible) it will share in the cooperative strategy.[114]

A firm's failure to make available to its partners the resources and capabilities (such as the most sophisticated technologies) that it committed to the cooperative strategy is a third risk. For example, the effectiveness of a recently-formed collaboration between BP Plc and OAO Rosneft is dependent on each firm contributing some of its seismic and drilling-related resources and capabilities as the foundation for efforts to develop three blocks in Russia's Arctic Ocean. A failure by either partner to contribute needed resources and capabilities to this alliance has the potential to diminish the likelihood of success. This particular risk surfaces most commonly when firms form an international cooperative strategy, especially in emerging economies.[115] In these instances, different cultures and languages can cause misinterpretations of contractual terms or trust-based expectations.

A final risk is that one firm may make investments that are specific to the alliance while its partner does not. For example, the firm might commit resources and capabilities to develop manufacturing equipment that can be used only to produce items coming from the alliance. If the partner isn't also making alliance-specific investments, the firm is at a relative disadvantage in terms of returns earned from the alliance compared with investments made to earn the returns.

Managing Cooperative Strategies

Cooperative strategies are an important means of firm growth and enhanced performance, but these strategies are difficult to effectively manage. Because the ability to effectively manage cooperative strategies is unevenly distributed across organizations in general, assigning managerial responsibility for a firm's cooperative strategies to a high-level executive or to a team improves the likelihood that the strategies will be well managed. In turn, being able to successfully manage cooperative strategies can itself be a competitive advantage.[116]

Those responsible for managing the firm's cooperative strategies should take the actions necessary to coordinate activities, categorize knowledge learned from previous experiences, and make certain that what the firm knows about how to effectively form and use cooperative strategies is in the hands of the right people at the right time. Firms must also learn how to manage both the tangible and intangible assets (such as knowledge) that are involved with a cooperative arrangement. Too often, partners concentrate on managing tangible assets at the expense of taking action to also manage a cooperative relationship's intangible assets.[117]

Cost minimization and opportunity maximization are the two primary approaches firms use to manage cooperative strategies[118] (see Figure 9.5). In the *cost-minimization* approach, the firm develops formal contracts with its partners. These contracts specify how the cooperative strategy is to be monitored and how partner behavior is to be controlled. The alliance between BP Plc and OAO Rosneft, through which the firms will develop three blocks in Russia's Arctic Ocean to search for oil, is managed largely through contracts.[119] Remember from the discussion of the Microsoft/Nokia alliance in the Strategic Focus that hundreds of pages were developed to specify each party's responsibilities and commitments to the collaboration. Thus it appears that at least at the outset, the cost-minimization approach is being used to manage this alliance. The goal of the cost-minimization approach is to minimize the cooperative strategy's cost and to prevent opportunistic behavior by a partner.

Maximizing a partnership's value-creating opportunities is the focus of the *opportunity-maximization* approach. In this case, partners are prepared to take advantage of unexpected opportunities to learn from each other and to explore additional marketplace possibilities. Less formal contracts, with fewer constraints on partners' behaviors, make it possible for partners to explore how their resources and capabilities can be shared in multiple value-creating ways. This is the approach Renault and Nissan use to manage their collaborative relationship. The values of *trust*, *respect*, and *transparency* on which this alliance is based facilitate use of the opportunity-maximization management approach.

Firms can successfully use both approaches to manage cooperative strategies. However, the costs to monitor the cooperative strategy are greater with cost minimization, in that writing detailed contracts and using extensive monitoring mechanisms is expensive, even though the approach is intended to reduce alliance costs. Although monitoring systems may prevent partners from acting in their own best interests, they also often preclude positive responses to new opportunities that surface to productively use alliance partners' resources and capabilities. Thus, formal contracts and extensive monitoring systems tend to stifle partners' efforts to gain maximum value from their participation in a cooperative strategy and require significant resources to be put into place and used.[120]

The relative lack of detail and formality that is a part of the contract developed when using the opportunity-maximization approach means that firms need to trust that each party will act in the partnership's best interests. The psychological state of *trust* in the context of cooperative arrangements is the belief that a firm will not do anything to exploit its partner's vulnerabilities even if it has an opportunity to do so. When partners trust each other, there is less need to write detailed formal contracts to specify each firm's alliance behaviors[121] and the cooperative relationship tends to be more stable.[122]

On a relative basis, trust tends to be more difficult to establish in international cooperative strategies compared with domestic ones. Differences in trade policies, cultures, laws, and politics that are part of cross-border alliances account for the increased difficulty. When trust exists, monitoring costs are reduced and opportunities to create value are maximized. Essentially, in these cases, the firms have built social capital.[123] Renault and Nissan have built social capital through their alliance by building their relationship on the mutual trust between the partners as well as their adherence to operating within the framework of agreed-upon confidentiality rules.[124]

Research showing that trust between partners increases the likelihood of success when using alliances highlights the benefits of the opportunity-maximization approach to managing cooperative strategies. Trust may also be the most efficient way to influence and control alliance partners' behaviors. Research indicates that trust can be a capability that is valuable, rare, imperfectly imitable, and often nonsubstitutable.[125] Thus, firms known to be trustworthy can have a competitive advantage in terms of how they develop and use cooperative strategies. Increasing the importance of trust in alliances is the fact that it is not possible to specify all operational details of a cooperative strategy in a formal contract. As such, being confident that its partner can be trusted reduces the firm's concern about the inability to contractually control all alliance details.

S U M M A R Y

- A cooperative strategy is one through which firms work together to achieve a shared objective. Strategic alliances, where firms combine some of their resources and capabilities for the purpose of creating a competitive advantage, are the primary form of cooperative strategies. Joint ventures (where firms create and own equal shares of a new venture), equity strategic alliances (where firms own different shares of a newly created venture), and nonequity strategic alliances (where firms cooperate through a contractual relationship) are the three major types of strategic alliances. Outsourcing, discussed in Chapter 3, commonly occurs as firms form nonequity strategic alliances.

- Collusive strategies are the second type of cooperative strategies (with strategic alliances being the other). In many economies, explicit collusive strategies are illegal unless sanctioned by government policies. Increasing globalization has led to fewer government-sanctioned situations of explicit collusion. Tacit collusion, also called mutual forbearance, is a cooperative strategy through which firms tacitly cooperate to reduce industry output below the potential competitive output level, thereby raising prices above the competitive level.

- The reasons firms use cooperative strategies vary by slow-cycle, fast-cycle, and standard-cycle market conditions. To enter restricted markets (slow cycle), to move quickly from one competitive advantage to another (fast cycle), and to gain market power (standard cycle) are among the reasons firms choose to use cooperative strategies.

- Four business-level cooperative strategies are used to help the firm improve its performance in individual product markets: (1) Through vertical and horizontal complementary alliances, companies combine some of their resources and capabilities to create value in different parts (vertical) or the same parts (horizontal) of the value chain. (2) Competition response strategies are formed to respond to competitors' actions, especially strategic actions. (3) Uncertainty-reducing strategies are used to hedge against the risks created by the conditions of uncertain competitive environments (such as new product markets). (4) Competition-reducing strategies are used to avoid excessive competition while the firm marshals its resources and capabilities to improve its strategic competitiveness. Complementary alliances have the highest probability of helping a firm form a competitive advantage; competition-reducing alliances have the lowest probability.

- Firms use corporate-level cooperative strategies to engage in product and/or geographic diversification. Through diversifying strategic alliances, firms agree to share some of their resources and capabilities to enter new markets or produce new products. Synergistic alliances are ones where firms share some of their resources and capabilities to develop economies of scope. Synergistic alliances are similar to business-level horizontal complementary alliances where firms try to develop operational synergy, except that synergistic alliances are used to develop synergy at the corporate level. Franchising is a corporate-level cooperative strategy where the franchisor uses a franchise as a contractual relationship to specify how resources and capabilities will be shared with franchisees.

- As an international cooperative strategy, a cross-border strategic alliance is used for several reasons, including the performance superiority of firms competing in markets outside their domestic market and governmental restrictions on a firm's efforts to grow through mergers and acquisitions. Commonly, cross-border strategic alliances are riskier than their domestic counterparts, particularly when partners aren't fully aware of each other's purpose for participating in the partnership.

- In a network cooperative strategy, several firms agree to form multiple partnerships to achieve shared objectives. A firm's opportunity to gain access "to its partner's other partnerships" is a primary benefit of a network cooperative strategy. Network cooperative strategies are used to form either a stable alliance network or a dynamic alliance network. Used in mature industries, stable networks are used to extend competitive advantages into new areas. In rapidly changing environments where frequent product innovations occur, dynamic networks are used primarily as a tool of innovation.

- Cooperative strategies aren't risk free. If a contract is not developed appropriately, or if a partner misrepresents its competencies or fails to make them available, failure is likely. Furthermore, a firm may be held hostage through asset-specific investments made in conjunction with a partner, which may be exploited.

- Trust is an increasingly important aspect of successful cooperative strategies. Firms place high value on opportunities to partner with companies known for their trustworthiness. When trust exists, a cooperative strategy is managed to maximize the pursuit of opportunities between partners. Without trust, formal contracts and extensive monitoring systems are used to manage cooperative strategies. In this case, the interest is "cost minimization" rather than "opportunity maximization."

REVIEW QUESTIONS

1. What is the definition of cooperative strategy, and why is this strategy important to firms competing in the twenty-first century competitive landscape?

2. What is a strategic alliance? What are the three major types of strategic alliances firms form for the purpose of developing a competitive advantage?

3. What are the four business-level cooperative strategies? What are the key differences among them?

4. What are the three corporate-level cooperative strategies? How do firms use each of these strategies for the purpose of creating a competitive advantage?

5. Why do firms use cross-border strategic alliances?

6. What risks are firms likely to experience as they use cooperative strategies?

7. What are the differences between the cost-minimization approach and the opportunity-maximization approach to managing cooperative strategies?

EXPERIENTIAL EXERCISES

EXERCISE 1: WHAT IS IT—TV, INTERNET, OR BOTH?

Hulu (http://www.hulu.com) is a Web site and cooperative alliance that offers commercially supported content of TV (video on demand) shows through the Internet. The name is derived from a Chinese word that means "holder of precious things." The alliance has many different partners that are related in interesting ways and that are from very different market types.

Working in groups, answer the following questions:

1. Describe the alliance partners. Characterize the market type as slow, fast, or standard cycle.

2. Characterize the type of strategic alliance Hulu has become.

3. In what type of market is Hulu competing?

4. Why did this alliance form? List some competitive pressures that made this alliance a necessity for its partners.

5. What does the future hold for this alliance?

EXERCISE 2: AIRLINES AND ALLIANCES

According to your text, a *strategic alliance* "is a partnership between firms whereby their resources and capabilities are combined to create a competitive advantage." So what is in an alliance for an airline company such as United, American, or British Airways? In this exercise, your instructor will assign one of the three main alliances (OneWorld, Star, or SkyTeam) and your teams will be requested to investigate the alliance and be prepared to discuss the following issues:

1. In general, why do airlines form an alliance with one another (particularly internationally) rather than expanding by acquisition?

2. What is the history of the alliance to which you were assigned?

3. Describe the main benefits that airlines hope to gain through membership. What is the competitive advantage of your particular alliance, if you find there is one?

4. Categorize the alliance in terms of the three types of strategic alliance. Also describe the cooperative strategy of a member firm in relation to its business-level and corporate-level strategy.

5. Think through issues of the future of airline alliances. If you were the CEO of a major U.S. airline, what might worry you about in your particular alliance, if anything?

VIDEO CASE

A PARTNERSHIP WITH A COOPERATIVE TWIST: MICROSOFT AND YAHOO!

In its infancy, the Microsoft/Yahoo! partnership brought a cloud of layoff and market concerns, but the priority was to compete against Google for control of the Internet search market. Media and analysts predicted benefits to partners and consumers over the long term. Yahoo! remains an independent company with control of its user interface, while Microsoft added strength to its browser and gained a greater share of Internet advertising, which all provide an alternative to the Internet search market. Statistics show that Google has 65 percent of the Internet search market, with Yahoo! at 20 percent and Microsoft at 10 percent.

Be prepared to discuss the following concepts and questions in class:

Concepts

- Cooperative strategy
- Strategic alliance
- Business-level cooperative strategies
- Corporate-level cooperative strategies

Questions

1. What kind of competitive advantage is created through the Microsoft/Yahoo! cooperative strategy?
2. What kind of strategic alliance has occurred between Microsoft and Yahoo!? Explain your answer. For what reasons do you think they developed such an alliance?
3. Now that Microsoft and Yahoo! have partnered, what business-level cooperative strategies do you think we can expect? Why?
4. What corporate-level cooperative strategies do you think we can expect? Why?

NOTES

1. J. Sydow & G. Schreyoegg, 2011, Organizing for fluidity? Dilemmas of new organizational forms, *Organization Science*, 21: 1251–1262; D. Lavie, 2009, Capturing value from alliance portfolios, *Organizational Dynamics*, 38(1): 26–36; J. L. Morrow, Jr., D. G. Sirmon, M. A. Hitt, & T. R. Holcomb, 2007, Creating value in the face of declining performance: Firm strategies and organizational recovery, *Strategic Management Journal*, 28: 271–283.
2. J. Bennett, 2011, Dodge will test Fiat alliance, *Wall Street Journal*, http://www.wsj.com, June 25.
3. B. Cuellar-Fernandez, Y. Fuertes-Callen, & J. A. Lainez-Gadea, 2011, The impact of strategic alliances on the market value of telecommunications firms, *Journal of High Technology-Management Research* 22: 1–13; T. W. Tong, J. J. Reuer, & M. W. Peng, 2008, International joint ventures and the value of growth options, *Academy of Management Journal*, 51: 1014-1049.
4. H. Yang, Z. Lin, & Y. Lin, 2010, A multilevel framework of firm boundaries: Firm characteristics, dyadic differences, and network attributes, *Strategic Management Journal*, 31: 237–261; H. Ness, 2009, Governance, negotiations, and alliances dynamics: Explaining the evolution of relational practice, *Journal of Management Studies*, 46: 451–480.
5. Bennett, Dodge will test Fiat alliance.
6. J. H. Dyer & W. Chu, 2011, The determinants of trust in supplier–automaker relationships in the US, Japan, and Korea, *Journal of International Business Studies*, 42: 10–27; R. Lunnan & S. A. Haugland, 2008, Predicting and measuring alliance performance: A multi-dimensional analysis, *Strategic Management Journal*, 29: 545–556.
7. R. J. Jiang, Q. T. Tao, & M. D. Santoro, 2010, Alliance portfolio diversity and firm performance, *Strategic Management Journal*, 31: 1136–1144; M. J. Chen, 2008, Reconceptualizing the competition cooperation relationship: A transparadox perspective, *Journal of Management Inquiry*, 17: 288–304.
8. Y. Chao, 2011, Decision-making biases in the alliance life cycle: Implications for alliance failure, *Management Decision*, 49: 350–364; C. E. Ybarra & T. A. Turk, 2009, The evolution of trust in information technology alliances, *Journal of High Technology Management Research*, 20: 62–74; R. D. Ireland, M. A. Hitt, & D. Vaidyanath, 2002, Alliance management as a source of competitive advantage, *Journal of Management*, 28: 413–446.
9. F. Lumineau, M. Frechet, & D. Puthod, 2011, An organizational learning perspective on the contracting process, *Strategic Organization*, 9: 8–32; M. A. Schilling, 2009, Understanding the alliance data, *Strategic Management Journal*, 30: 233–260.
10. L. Nachum & S. Song, 2011, The MNE as a portfolio: Interdependencies in MNE growth trajectory, *Journal of International Business Studies*, 42: 381–405; S. Lahiri & B. L. Kedia, 2009, The effects of internal resources and partnership quality on firm performance: An examination of Indian BPO providers, *Journal of International Management*, 15: 209–222.
11. K. H. Heimeriks & G. Duysters, 2007, Alliance capability as a mediator between experience and alliance performance: An empirical investigation into the alliance capability development process, *Journal of Management Studies* 44: 25–49.
12. 2011, Statement and charts by Dr. Norbert Reithofer at annual accounts press conference 2011, *BMW Blog*, http://www.bmwblog.com, March 15.
13. B. D. Carlson, G. L. Frankwick, & K. J. Cuiskey, 2011, A framework for understanding new product alliance success, *Journal of Marketing Theory and Practice*, 19: 7–26; K. H. Heimeriks, E. Klijn, & J. J. Reuer, 2009, Building capabilities for alliance portfolios, *Long Range Planning*, 42: 96–114.
14. T. Herd, 2010, Joint ventures: Creating value against the odds, *Bloomberg Businessweek*, http://www.businessweek.com, November 2.
15. M. S. Jiang, R. Chu, & Y. Pan, 2011, Anticipated duration of international joint ventures, *Journal of International Management*, 17: 175–183; X. Lin & C. L. Wang, 2008, Enforcement and performance: The role of ownership, legalism and trust in international joint ventures, *Journal of World Business*, 43: 340-351.
16. D. Tan & K. E. Meyer, 2011, Country-of-origin and industry FDI agglomeration of foreign investors in an emerging economy, *Journal of International Business Studies*, 42: 504–520; F. Evangelista & L. N. Hau, 2008, Organizational context and knowledge acquisition in IJVs: An empirical study, *Journal of World Business*, 44: 63–73.
17. Z. Huang, X. Han, F. Roche, & J. Cassidy, 2011, The dilemma facing strategic choice of entry mode: Multinational hotels in China, *Global Business Review*, 12: 181–192; J. Xia, J. Tan, & D. Tan, 2008, Mimetic entry and bandwagon effect: The rise and decline of international equity joint venture in China, *Strategic Management Journal*, 29: 195–217.
18. J. Osawa, 2011, Baidu, NTT DoCoMo to set up JV in China, *Wall Street Journal*, http://www.wsj.com, July 8.
19. T. Das & N. Rahman, 2010, Determinants of partner opportunism in strategic alliances: A conceptual framework, *Journal of Business Psychology*, 25: 55–74; Y. Wang & S. Nicholas, 2007, The formation and evolution of nonequity strategic alliances in China, *Asia Pacific Journal of Management*, 24: 131–150.
20. J. J. Reuer, E. Klijn, F. A. J. van den Bosch, & H. W. Volberda, 2011, Bringing corporate governance to international joint ventures, *Global Strategy Journal*, 1: 54–66; N. Garcia-Casarejos, N. Alcalde-Fradejas, & M. Espitia-Escuer, 2009, Staying close to the core: Lessons of studying the cost of unrelated alliances in Spanish banking, *Long-Range Planning*, 42: 194–215.
21. J. Schweitzer & S. P. Gudergan, 2011, Contractual complexity, governance and organisational form in alliances, *International Journal of Strategic Business Alliances*, 2: 26–40; C. Weigelt, 2009, The impact of outsourcing new technologies on integrative capabilities

and performance, *Strategic Management Journal*, 30: 595–616.

22. 2009, Xerox signs six-year deal with India's HCL, *BusinessWeek*, April 6.

23. F. Zirpoli & M. C. Becker, 2011, The limits of design and engineering outsourcing: Performance integration and the unfulfilled promise of modularity, *R&D Management*, 41: 21–43; D. Campagnolo & A. Camuffo, 2010, The concept of modularity in management studies: A literature review, *International Journal of Management Review*, 12: 259–283; A. Tiwana, 2008, Does interfirm modularity complement ignorance? A field study of software outsourcing alliances, *Strategic Management Journal*, 29: 1241–1252.

24. R. Ponds, F. van Oort, & K. Frenken, 2010, Innovation, spillovers and university-industry collaboration: An extended knowledge production function approach, *Journal of Economic Geography*, 10: 231–255; A. L. Sherwood & J. G. Covin 2008, Knowledge acquisition in university-industry alliances: An empirical investigation from a learning theory perspective, *Journal of Product Innovation Management*, 25: 162–179.

25. J. Kim, 2011, Alliance governance and technological performance: Some evidence from biotechnology alliances, *Industrial and Corporate Change*, 20: 969-990; P. Beamish & N. Lupton, 2009, Managing joint ventures, *Academy of Management Perspectives*, 23(2): 75–94.

26. U. Wassmer, 2010, Alliance portfolios: A review and research agenda, *Journal of Management*, 38: 141–171; R. Flores-Fillo, 2009, Allied alliances: Parallel or complementary? *Applied Economic Letters*, 16: 585–590; S. G. Lazzarini, 2007, The impact of membership in competing alliance constellations: Evidence on the operational performance of global airlines, *Strategic Management Journal*, 28: 345–367.

27. D. Lavie, P. Haunschild, & P. Khanna, 2011, Organizational differences, relational mechanisms, and alliance performance, *Strategic Management Journal*, in press; H. Yang, Z. Lin, & Y. Lin, 2010, A multilevel framework of firm boundaries: Firm characteristics, dyadic differences, and network attributes, *Strategic Management Journal*, 31: 237–261.

28. K. Maxwell, 2011, Itochu buys stake in Colombian coal operation, *Wall Street Journal*, http://www.wsj.com, June 16.

29. M. Mehta, 2010, Using a joint venture to expand, *Bloomberg Businessweek*, http://www.businessweek.com, October 8.

30. J. R. Williams, 1998, *Renewable Advantage: Crafting Strategy through Economic Time*, New York: Free Press.

31. 2009, Nucor acquires 50% of Duferdofin – Nucor S.r.l., Nucor homepage, http://www.nucor.com, July 8.

32. 2011, Nucor announces strategic alliance with Truswal; Partnership to develop leading software for light gauge steel framing, Nucor homepage, http://www.nucor.com, January 25.

33. P. Savetpanuvong, U. Tanlamai, & C. Lursinsap, 2011, Sustaining innovation in information technology entrepreneurship with a sufficiency economy philosophy, *International Journal of Innovation Science*, 3(2): 69–82.

34. H. Ouyang, 2010, Imitator-to-innovator S curve and chasms, *Thunderbird International Business Review*, 52: 31–44; H. K. Steensma, J. Q. Barden, C. Dhanaraj, M. Lyles, & L. Tihanyi, 2008, The evolution and internationalization of international joint ventures in a transitioning economy, *Journal of International Business Studies*, 39: 491–507.

35. B. Bowonder, A. Dabal, S. Kumar, & A. Shirodkar, 2010, Innovation strategies for creating competitive advantage, *Research-Technology Management*, 53(3): 19–32; K. M. Eisenhardt, 2002, Has strategy changed? *MIT Sloan Management Review*, 43(2): 88–91.

36. P.-H. Soh, 2010, Network patterns and competitive advantage before the emergence of a dominant design, *Strategic Management Journal*, 31: 438–461; S. Lahiri, L. Perez-Nordtvedt, & R. W. Renn, 2008, Will the new competitive landscape cause your firm's decline? It depends on your mindset, *Business Horizons*, 51: 311–320.

37. 2011, About us, Hulu homepage, http://www.hulu.com, July 12; S. Schechner & E. Holmes, 2009, Disney teams up with other networks online, buying stake in Hulu site, *Wall Street Journal*, May 1, B1.

38. S. Elop & S. Ballmer, 2011, Open letter from CEO Stephen Elop, Nokia and CEO Steve Ballmer, Microsoft, Nokia Conversations, Nokia homepage, http://www.nokia.com, February 11.

39. A.-P. de Man, N. Roijakkers, & H. de Graauw, 2010, Managing dynamics through robust alliance governance structures: The case of KLM and Northwest Airlines, *European Management Journal*, 28: 171–181; C. Czipura & D. R. Jolly, 2007, Global airline alliances: Sparking profitability for a troubled industry, *Journal of Business Strategy*, 28(2): 57–64.

40. S. Stellin, 2011, The clout of air alliances, *New York Times*, http://www.nytimes.com, May 2.

41. K. Niththyananthan, 2011, Lufthansa, ANA get antitrust clearance, *Wall Street Journal*, http://www.wsj.com, June 1.

42. G. Raghuvanshi & C. Koons, 2011, Virgin Australia, Singapore Airlines seek alliance, *Wall Street Journal*, http://www.wsj.com, June 7.

43. W. Shi & J. E. Prescott, 2011, Sequence patterns of firms' acquisition and alliance behavior and their performance implications, *Journal of Management Studies*, 48: 1044-1070; S. G. Lazzarini, D. P. Claro, & L. F. Mesquita, 2008, Buyer-supplier and supplier-supplier alliances: Do they reinforce or undermine one another? *Journal of Management Studies*, 45: 561–584.

44. S. M. Mudambi & S. Tallman, 2010, Make, buy or ally? Theoretical perspectives on knowledge process outsourcing through alliances, *Journal of Management Studies*, 47: 1434–1456.

45. M. Meuleman, A. Lockett, S. Manigart, & M. Wright, 2010, Partner selection decisions in interfirm collaborations: The paradox of relational embeddedness, *Journal of Management Studies*, 47: 995–1019; Y. Yan, D. Ding, & S. Mak, 2009, The impact of business investment on capability exploitation and organizational control in international strategic alliances, *Journal of Change Management*, 9(1): 49–65.

46. J. Zhang & C. Baden-Fuller, 2010, The influence of technological knowledge base and organizational structure on technology collaboration, *Journal of Management Studies*, 47: 679–704; J. Wiklund & D. A. Shepherd, 2009, The effectiveness of alliances and acquisitions: The role of resource combination activities, *Entrepreneurship Theory and Practice*, 31: 193–212.

47. 2011, *MONOPOLY Millionaires*, a free-to-play social gaming version of the world's favorite family game brand, now available on Facebook from Electronic Arts, *Reuters*, http://www.reuters.com, February 16.

48. 2011, The Novartis malaria initiative: Lessons from a dramatic decade, Novartis homepage, July 17.

49. D. H. Hus & S. Wakeman, 2011, Resource benefits and learning costs in strategic alliances, University of Pennsylvania, working paper, March; M. Makri, M. A. Hitt, & P. J. Lane, 2010, Complementary technologies, knowledge relatedness, and invention outcomes in high technology mergers and acquisitions, *Strategic Management Journal*, 31: 602–628.

50. 2011, Santaris Pharma A/S announces expanded worldwide strategic alliance with Pfizer, Santaris Pharma homepage, http://www.santaris.com, January 4.

51. 2011, Collaborations, Novartis homepage, http://www.novartis.com, July 17.

52. R. Whelan, 2011, Morgan Stanley and NVR Inc. pay $180 million for large Washington land portfolio, *Wall Street Journal*, http://www.wsj.com, July 7.

53. C. Lopez-Duarte & M. M. Vidal-Suarez, 2010, External uncertainty and entry mode choice: Cultural distance, political risk and language diversity, *International Business Review*, 19: 575–588; J. J. Reuer & T. W. Tong, 2005, Real options in international joint ventures, *Journal of Management*, 31: 403–423.

54. C. Rauwald & N. Shirouzu, 2009, Volkswagen eyes China venture, *Wall Street Journal*, May 27, B4.

55. D. Pearson & S. Moffett, 2011, Renault electric vehicle program hits delay, *Wall Street Journal*, http://www.wsj.com, July 7.

56. M. Escrihuela-Villar, 2011, On collusion and industry size, *Annals of Economics and Finance*, 12(1): 31–40; L. Tesfatsion, 2007, Agents come to bits: Toward a

constructive comprehensive taxonomy of economic entities, *Journal of Economic Behavior & Organization*, 63: 333–346.

57. Y. Lu & J. Wright, 2010, Tacit collusion with price-matching punishments, *International Journal of Industrial Organization*, 28: 298–306.

58. R. W. Cooper & T. W. Ross, 2009, Sustaining cooperation with joint ventures, *Journal of Law Economics and Organization*, 25(1): 31–54.

59. J. T. Prince & D. H. Simon. 2009, Multi-market contact and service quality: Evidence from on-time performance in the U.S. airline industry, *Academy of Management Journal*, 52: 336–354.

60. N. Panteva, 2011, IBISWorld Industry Report 31123: Cereal production in the US, January.

61. Z. Guedri & J. McGuire, 2011, Multimarket competition, mobility barriers, and firm performance *Journal of Management Studies*, 48: 857–890.

62. P. Massey & M. McDowell, 2010, Joint dominance and tacit collusion: Some implications for competition and regulatory policy, *European Competition Journal*, 6: 427–444.

63. J. D. Rockoff, 2009, Drug CEOs switch tactics on reform: Pharmaceutical companies join health-care overhaul hoping to influence where costs are cut, *Wall Street Journal*, May 27, B1, B2.

64. B. Nielsen, 2010, Strategic fit, contractual, and procedural governance in alliances, *Journal of Business Research*, 63: 682–689; P. Dussauge, B. Garrette, & W. Mitchell, 2004, Asymmetric performances: The market share impact of scale and link alliances in the global auto industry, *Strategic Management Journal*, 25: 701–711.

65. Maxwell, Itochu buys stake in Colombian coal operation.

66. C. Haeussler, 2011, The determinants of commercialization strategy: Idiosyncrasies in British and German biotechnology, *Entrepreneurship Theory and Practice*, 35: 653–681.

67. P. Ritala & H.-K. Ellonen, 2010, Competitive advantage in interfirm cooperation: Old and new explanations, *Competitiveness Review*, 20: 367–383; L. H. Lin, 2009, Mergers and acquisitions, alliances and technology development: An empirical study of the global auto industry, *International Journal of Technology Management*, 48: 295–307.

68. J. Anand, R. Oriani, & R. S. Vassolo, 2010, Alliance activity as a dynamic capability in the face of a discontinuous technological change, *Organization Science*, 21: 1213–1232; J. Li, C. Dhanaraj, & R. L. Shockley, 2008, Joint venture evolution: Extending the real options approach, *Managerial and Decision Economics*, 29: 317–336.

69. V. Moatti, 2009, Learning to expand or expanding to learn? The role of imitation and experience in the choice among several expansion modes, *European Management Journal*, 27: 36–46.

70. S. Silver & E. Steel, 2009, Alcatel gets into mobile ads; Service will target cell phone users based on location, *Wall Street Journal*, May 21, B9.

71. 2011, Tigo and Alcatel-Lucent personalized mobile advertising to millions of subscribers in Ghana, Alcatel-Lucent homepage, http://www.alcatel-lucent.com, February 16.

72. R. Hutton, 2010, 2010 Alfa Romeo Giulietta—first drive review, *Car and Driver*, http://www.caranddriver.com, April.

73. J. G. Combs, D. J. Ketchen, Jr., C. L. Shook, & J. C. Short, 2011, Antecedents and consequences of franchising: Past accomplishments and future challenges, *Journal of Management*, 37: 99–126; A. M. Doherty, 2009, Market and partner selection processes in international retail franchising, *Journal of Business Research*, 62: 528–534.

74. F. Lafontaine, 1999, Myths and strengths of franchising, "Mastering Strategy" (Part Nine), *Financial Times*, November 22, 8–10.

75. D. Grewal, G. R. Iyer, R. G. Javalgi, & L. Radulovich, 2011, Franchise partnership and international expansion: A conceptual framework and research propositions, *Entrepreneurship Theory and Practice*, 35: 533–557; A. M. Hayashi, 2008, How to replicate success, *MIT Sloan Management Review*, 49(3): 6–7.

76. 2011, Building local businesses one opportunity at a time, International Franchise Association, http://www.buildingopportunity.com, July 12.

77. G. M. Kistruck, J. W. Webb, C. J. Sutter, & R. D. Ireland, 2011, Microfranchising in base-of-the-pyramid markets: Institutional challenges and adaptations to the franchise model, *Entrepreneurship Theory and Practice*, 35: 503–531.

78. J. McDonnell, A. Geatson, & C.-H. Huang, 2011, Investigating relationships between relationship quality, customer loyalty and cooperation: An empirical study of convenience stores' franchise chain systems, *Asia Pacific Journal of Marketing and Logistics*, 23: 367–385.

79. T. M. Nisar, 2011, Intellectual property securitization and growth capital in retail franchising, *Journal of Retailing*, in press; A. K. Paswan & C. M. Wittman, 2009, Knowledge management and franchise systems, *Industrial Marketing Management*, 38: 173–180.

80. W. R. Meek, B. Davis-Sramek, M. S. Baucus & R. N. Germain, 2011, Commitment in franchising: The role of collaborative communication and a franchisee's propensity to leave, *Entrepreneurship Theory and Practice*, 35: 559–581.

81. T. W. K. Leslie & L. S. McNeill, 2010, Towards a conceptual model for franchise perceptual equity, *Journal of Brand Management*, 18: 21–33; B. Arrunada, L. Vazquez, & G. Zanarone, 2009, Institutional constraints n organizations: The case of Spanish car dealerships, *Managerial and Decision Economics*, 30: 15–26.

82. M. J. Nieto & A. Rodriguez, 2011, Offshoring of R&D: Looking abroad to improve innovation performance, *Journal of International Business Studies*, 42: 345–361; A. Tiwana, 2008, Does technological modularity substitute for control? A study of alliance performance in software outsourcing, *Strategic Management Journal*, 29: 769–780.

83. E. Levitas & M. A. McFadyen, 2009, Managing liquidity in research-intensive firms: Signaling and cash flow effects of patents and alliance activities, *Strategic Management Journal*, 30: 659–678.

84. L. D. Qiu, 2010, Cross-border mergers and strategic alliances, *European Economic Review*, 54: 818–831; H. Ren, B. Gray, & H. Kim, 2009, Performance of international joint ventures: What factors really make a difference and how? *Journal of Management*, 35: 805–832.

85. Y. Yan, D. Ding, & S. Mak, 2009, The impact of business investment on capability exploitation and organizational control in international strategic alliances, *Journal of Change Management*, 9(1): 49–65.

86. A. Zaheer & E. Hernandez, 2011, The geographic scope of the MNC and its alliance portfolio: Resolving the paradox of distance, *Global Strategy Journal*, 1: 109–126; B. Elango, 2009, Minimizing effects of "liability of foreignness:" Response strategies of foreign firms in the United States, *Journal of World Business*, 44(1): 51–62.

87. M. Meuleman & M. Wright, 2011, Cross-border private equity syndication: Institutional context and learning, *Journal of Business Venturing*, 26: 35–48; T. J. Wilkinson, A. R. Thomas, & J. M. Hawes, 2009, Managing relationships with Chinese joint venture partners, *Journal of Global Marketing*, 22(2): 109–120.

88. D. Kronborg & S. Thomsen, 2009, Foreign ownership and long-term survival, *Strategic Management Journal*, 30: 207–220.

89. S. Mayerowitz, 2011, Airlines making speed to boost fuel efficiency, *Houston Chronicle*, http://www.chron.com, July 8.

90. 2011, Volvo Aero global, Volvo Aero homepage, http://www.volvoaero.com, July 15.

91. Ibid.

92. D. Lavie, 2009, Capturing value from alliance portfolios, *Organizational Dynamics*, 38(1): 26–36; D. Lavie, C. Lechner, & H. Singh, 2007, The performance implications of timing of entry and involvement in multipartner alliances, *Academy of Management Journal*, 49: 569–604.

93. 2011, Partner with Cisco, Cisco homepage, http://www.cisco.com, July 15.

94. S. Higginbotham, 2011, Amid gloom, Cisco's servers approaching a $1B business, Gigacom.com, http://www.gigacom.com, May 12.

95. 2011, Strategic alliance—IBM, Cisco homepage, http://www.cisco.com, July 15.

96. A. T. Arkan & M. A. Schilling, 2011, Structure and governance in industrial districts: Implications for competitive advantage, *Journal of Management Studies*, 48: 772–803; K. Atkins, J. Chen, V. S. A. Kumar, M. Macauley, & A. Marathe, 2009, Locational market power in network constrained markets, *Journal of Economic Behavior & Organization*, 70: 416–430.

97. K. Sawyer, 2007, Strength in webs, *The Conference Board*, July/August, 9–11.

98. C. Yarbrough, 2008, Singapore to open Fusionopolis, *Research Technology Management*, 51: 4–5.

99. J. Wincent, S. Anokhin, D. Ortqvist, & E. Autio, 2010, Quality meets structure: Generalized reciprocity and firm-level advantage in strategic networks, *Journal of Management Studies*, 47: 597–624; D. Lavie, 2007, Alliance portfolios and firm performance: A study of value creation and appropriation in the U.S. software industry, *Strategic Management Journal*, 28: 1187–1212.

100. A. M. Joshi & A. Nerkar, 2011, When do strategic alliances inhibit innovation by firms? Evidence from patent pools in the global optical disc industry, *Strategic Management Journal*, 38: in press; R. Cowan & N. Jonard, 2009, Knowledge portfolios and the organization of innovation networks, *Academy of Management Review*, 34: 320–342.

101. J. P. MacDuffie, 2011, Inter-organizational trust and the dynamics of distrust, *Journal of International Business Studies*, 42: 35–47; H. Kim, R. E. Hoskisson, & W. P. Wan, 2004, Power, dependence, diversification strategy and performance in keiretsu member firms, *Strategic Management Journal*, 25: 613–636.

102. A. V. Shipilov, 2009, Firm scope experience, historic multimarket contact with partners, centrality, and the relationship between structural holes and performance, *Organization Science*, 20: 85–106.

103. P.-H. Soh, 2010, Network patterns and competitive advantage before the emergence of a dominant design, *Strategic Management Journal*, 31: 438–461.

104. G. Soda, 2011, The management of firms' alliance network positioning: Implications for innovation, *European Management Journal*, in press; T. Kiessling & M. Harvey, 2008, Globalisation of internal venture capital opportunities in developing small and medium enterprises' relationships, *International Journal of Entrepreneurship and Innovation Management*, 8: 233–253; V. Shankar & B. L. Bayus, 2003, Network effects and competition: An empirical analysis of the home video game industry, *Strategic Management Journal*, 24: 375–384.

105. J. J. Ebbers & N. M. Wijnberg, 2010, Disentangling the effects of reputation and network position on the evolution of alliance networks, *Strategic Organization*, 8: 255–275; A. Schwab & A. S. Miner, 2008, Learning in hybrid-project systems: The effects of project performance on repeated collaboration, *Academy of Management Journal*, 51: 1117–1149.

106. A. Capaldo & A. M. Petruzzelli, 2011, In search of alliance-level relational capabilities: Balancing innovation, value creation, and appropriability in R&D alliances, *Scandinavian Journal of Management*, in press; A. E. Leiponen, 2008, Competing through cooperation: The organization of standard setting in wireless telecommunications, *Management Science*, 54: 1904–1919.

107. D. Somaya, Y. Kim, & N. S. Vonortas, 2011, Exclusivity in licensing alliances: Using hostages to support technology commercialization, *Strategic Management Journal*, 32: 159–186; P. Puranam & K. Srikanth, 2007, What they know vs. what they do: How acquirers leverage technology acquisitions, *Strategic Management Journal*, 28: 805–825.

108. M. J. Nieto & L. Santamaria, 2010, Technological collaboration: Bridging the innovation gap between small and large firms, *Journal of Small Business Management*, 48: 44–69; P. Ozcan & K. M. Eisenhardt, 2009, Origin of alliance portfolios: Entrepreneurs network strategies, and firm performance, *Academy of Management Journal*, 52: 246–279.

109. H. R. Greve, J. A. C. Baum, H. Mitsuhashi, & T. J. Rowley, 2010, Built to last but falling apart: Cohesion, friction, and withdrawal from interfirm alliances, *Academy of Management Journal*, 53: 302–322; M. Rod, 2009, A model for the effective management of joint ventures: A case study approach, *International Journal of Management*, 26(10): 3–17.

110. G. Vasudeva & J. Anand, 2011, Unpacking absorptive capacity: A study of knowledge utilization from alliance portfolios, *Academy of Management Journal*, 54: 611–623; J.-Y. Kim & A. S. Miner, 2007, Vicarious learning from the failures and near-failures of others: Evidence from the U.S. Commercial banking industry, *Academy of Management Journal*, 49: 687–714.

111. P. Loftus, 2011, Amylin sues Eli Lilly over diabetes pact, *Wall Street Journal*, http://www.wsj.com, May 16.

112. R. Agarwal, D. Audretsch, & M. B. Sarkar, 2010, Knowledge spillovers and strategic entrepreneurship, *Strategic Entrepreneurship Journal*, 4: 271–283; Y. Li, Y. Liu, & H. Wu, 2008, Transformational offshore outsourcing: Empirical evidence from alliances in China, *Journal of Operations Management*, 26: 257–274.

113. T. K. Das, 2011, Regulatory focus and opportunism in the alliance development process, *Journal of Management*, 37: 682–708; J. Connell & R. Voola, 2007, Strategic alliances and knowledge sharing: Synergies or silos? *Journal of Knowledge Management*, 11: 52–66.

114. M. S. Giarratana & S. Torrisi, 2010, Foreign entry and survival in a knowledge-intensive market: Emerging economy countries' international linkages, technology competencies, and firm experience, *Strategic Entrepreneurship Journal*, 4: 85–104; M. G. Sarkar, P. S. Aulakh, & A. Madhok, 2009, Process capabilities and value generation in alliance portfolios, *Organization Science*, 20: 583–600.

115. F. Lumineau, M. Frechet, & D. Puthod, 2011, An organizational learning perspective on the contracting process, *Strategic Organization*, 9: 8–32; P.-X. Meschi, 2009, Government corruption and foreign stakes in international joint ventures in emerging economies, *Asia Pacific Journal of Management*, 26: 241–261.

116. D. G. Sirmon, M. A. Hitt, R. D. Ireland, & B. A. Gilbert, 2011, Resource orchestration to create competitive advantage: Breadth, depth, and life cycle effects, *Journal of Management*, in press; M. H. Hansen, R. E. Hoskisson, & J. B. Barney, 2008, Competitive advantage in alliance governance: Resolving the opportunism minimization-gain maximization paradox, *Managerial and Decision Economics*, 29: 191–208.

117. C. C. Chung & P. W. Beamish, 2010, The trap of continual ownership change in international equity joint ventures, *Organization Science*, 21: 995–1015.

118. Mudambi & Tallman, Make, buy or ally?; Hansen, Hoskisson, & Barney, Competitive advantage in alliance governance: Resolving the opportunism minimization-gain maximization paradox.

119. W. Kennedy & A. Shiryaevskaya, 2011, BO agrees Rosneft share swap to form global strategic alliance, *Bloomberg Businessweek*, http://www.businessweek.com, January 14.

120. R. P. Lee & J. L. Johnson, 2010, Managing multiple facets of risk in new product alliances, *Decision Sciences*, 41: 271–300; L. Poppo, K. Z. Zhou, & S. Ryu, 2008, Alternative origins to interorganizational trust: An interdependence perspective on the shadow of the past and the shadow of the future, *Organization Science*, 19: 39–56.

121. J. J. Li, L. Poppo, & K. Z. Zhou, 2010, Relational mechanisms, formal contracts, and local knowledge acquisition by international subsidiaries, *Strategic Management Journal*, 31: 349–370; K. Langfield-Smith, 2008, The relations between transactional characteristics trust and risk in the start-up phrase of a collaborative alliance, *Management Accounting Research*, 19: 344–364.

122. H. C. Dekker & A. Van den Abbeele, 2010, Organizational learning and interfirm control: The effects of partner search and prior exchange experience, *Organization Science*, 21: 1233–1250;

T. K. Das & R. Kumar, 2009, Interpartner harmony in strategic alliances: Managing commitment and forbearance, *International Journal of Strategic Business Alliances*, 1(1): 24–52.

123. G. Dokko & L. Rosenkopf, 2010, Social capital for hire? Mobility of technical professionals and firm influence in wireless standards committees, *Organization Science*, 21: 677–695; J. W. Rottman, 2008, Successful knowledge transfer within offshore supplier networks: A case study exploring social capital in strategic alliances, *Journal of Information Technology*, 23(10): 31–43.

124. 2011, The principles of the alliance, Renault homepage, http://www.renault.com, July 13.

125. C. C. Phelps, 2010, A longitudinal study of the influence of alliance network structure and composition on firm exploratory innovation, *Academy of Management Journal*, 53: 890–913; C. E. Ybarra & T. A. Turck, 2009, The evolution of trust in information technology alliances, *Journal of High Technology Management Research*, 20(10): 62–74.

PART 3
Strategic Actions: Strategy Implementation

10. Corporate Governance, 292

11. Organizational Structure and Controls, 324

12. Strategic Leadership, 360

13. Strategic Entrepreneurship, 390

© Ryan McVay / Getty Images

CHAPTER 10

Corporate Governance

Studying this chapter should provide you with the strategic management knowledge needed to:

1. Define corporate governance and explain why it is used to monitor and control top-level managers' decisions.

2. Explain why ownership is largely separated from managerial control in organizations.

3. Define an agency relationship and managerial opportunism and describe their strategic implications.

4. Explain the use of three internal governance mechanisms to monitor and control managers' decisions.

5. Discuss the types of compensation top-level managers receive and their effects on managerial decisions.

6. Describe how the external corporate governance mechanism—the market for corporate control—restrains top-level managers' decisions.

7. Discuss the nature and use of corporate governance in international settings, especially in Germany, Japan, and China.

8. Describe how corporate governance fosters the making of ethical decisions by a firm's top-level managers.

© Ryan McVay/Getty Images

CORPORATE GOVERNANCE: WHAT IS ALL THE FUSS ABOUT?

"Pay for top brass gushes higher." "Meeting a timeline is not the driving force for the search; finding the right (CEO) candidate is." "The approach a company takes to governance ... can create or destroy real value."

Appearing in business publications, these statements deal with slightly different but related issues. What the statements have in common is that each deals with corporate governance. Defined formally in the first part of this chapter, corporate governance is concerned with various activities, including those intended to (1) strengthen the effectiveness of a company's board of directors, (2) verify the transparency of a firm's operations, (3) enhance accountability to shareholders, (4) effectively incentivize executives, and in an overall sense, (5) maximize the firm's ability to create value for stakeholders and especially for shareholders. Thus, at a core level, corporate governance deals with the actions a firm should take as a result of top-level managers' decisions and verifying that the intended actions do take place.

In this chapter, we explore the set of issues and subsequent actions that are central to corporate governance. One of these issues is the set of responsibilities assigned to a firm's board of directors. For example, a board is expected to verify that the firm has a viable CEO succession plan in place at all times. Apple Inc.'s board recently used that firm's succession plan to appoint Tim Cook as CEO following Steve Jobs' resignation. Cook had been serving as Apple's Chief Operating Officer and had been with the firm for a total of 13 years at the time of his appointment as CEO. Selecting the CEO and working with that individual and her/his top-management team to form a firm's strategy are other important board of directors' responsibilities.

AP Photo/Paul Sakuma, file

Apple Inc.'s board used the firm's succession plan to replace Steve Jobs, the firm's co-founder and CEO. Selecting the CEO and working with that individual to formulate a winning strategy is a vital responsibility for a board of directors.

Given recent criticisms, boards' actions in nations throughout the world are being more carefully scrutinized and regulated. In the United Kingdom, directors are now required to stand for re-election annually. Additionally, a new principle in the United Kingdom "is that members of the board should be selected on merit, against objective criteria, and with due regard for the benefits of diversity including gender diversity." In the United States, the fact that after being fired by their firm, a number of CEOs still remain as members of other firms' boards of directors is drawing close attention.

Corporate governance is also important to nations. Accordingly, "India plans to soon seek parliament's approval for a new companies' bill that would replace some of the archaic laws and help boost investors' confidence as the South Asian nation stresses on sprucing its corporate governance image." The Chinese government apparently is assessing actions to take to deal with conclusions drawn by ratings agencies such as Moody's Investors Services and Fitch Ratings. This suggests that corporate governance is weak in many Chinese firms and that there is concern about the validity and reliability of some auditors' work and the quality of companies' financial statements.

As these examples suggest, the reason there is a "fuss" about corporate governance is that these activities are critical to a nation's efforts to signal to the global community that its business-related infrastructure is consistent with global standards for transparency and to the ability of individual firms in countries throughout the world to achieve strategic

© Nicholas Monu/iStockphoto.com

Find out more about Apple's corporate governance policies.

www.cengagebrain
.com

competitiveness. From the perspective of individual companies and certainly those head-quartered in developed economies, the following statements describe corporate governance's importance: "Corporate governance issues rise and fall in prominence; but certain fundamentals remain constant. Directors should stay focused on creating long-term value for shareholders, using performance-related pay to attract and retain senior management and exercising sound business judgment to evaluate opportunities and manage risk. Communication with key shareholders remains an important element of corporate governance; companies and investors alike would do well to remember that they have nothing to lose and everything to gain by working tougher to create lasting corporate success."

Sources: S. Chaturvedi, 2011, India aims to seek Parliament OK for companies' bill, *Wall Street Journal*, http://www.wsj.com, July 6; D. Clark & J. S. Lublin, 2011, CEO hunt at AMD drags on, *Wall Street Journal*, http://www.wsj.com, July 22; Y. I. Kane, J. S. Lublin, & N. Wingfield, 2011, Some Apple directors ponder CEO succession, *Wall Street Journal*, http://www.wsj.com, July 19; D. A. Katz, Focus in 2011 will remain on executive compensation, Harvard Law School forum on corporate governance and financial regulation, http://www.blogs.la.harvard.edu, January 16; J. S. Lublin, 2011, Staying on boards after humble exit, *Wall Street Journal*, http://www.wsj.com, June 6; K. O'Keeffe, 2011, Fitch sees risk in China accounting standards, *Wall Street Journal*, http://www.wsj.com, July 18; K. O'Keeffe, 2011, Moody's raises some "red flags" in China, *Wall Street Journal*, http://www.wsj.com, July 12; R. L. Martin, 2011, The trouble with directors, *The Conference Board Review*, Summer, 37–39; D. Prossner 2010, U. K. has new corporate governance code, *Bloomberg Businessweek*, http://www.businessweek.com, May 28.

As the Opening Case suggests, corporate governance involves a number of activities dealing with how firms operate and, at a broader level, the type of infrastructure individual nations develop as the framework within which companies compete. Given that we are concerned with the strategic management process firms use, our focus in this chapter is on corporate governance in companies rather than on governance-related issues affecting individual nations (although we do also address governance at the level of nations as well).

Comprehensive in scope and complex in nature, corporate governance is a responsibility that challenges firms and their leaders. Successfully dealing with this challenge is important, as evidence suggests that corporate governance is critical to firms' success; because of this, governance is an increasingly important part of the strategic management process.[1] For example, if the board makes the wrong decisions in selecting, governing, and compensating the firm's CEO as its key strategic leader, the shareholders and the firm suffer. When CEOs are motivated to act in the best interests of the firm—in particular, the shareholders—the company's value should increase. Additionally, effective succession plans and appropriate monitoring and direction-setting efforts by the board of directors contribute positively to a firm's performance.

Corporate governance is the set of mechanisms used to manage the relationship among stakeholders and to determine and control the strategic direction and performance of organizations.[2] At its core, corporate governance is concerned with identifying ways to ensure that decisions (especially strategic decisions) are made effectively and that they facilitate a firm's efforts to achieve strategic competitiveness.[3] Governance can also be thought of as a means to establish and maintain harmony between parties (the firm's owners and its top-level managers) whose interests may conflict.

In modern corporations—especially those in nations with "Westernized" infrastructures and business practices such as the United States and the United Kingdom—ensuring that top-level managers' interests are aligned with other stakeholders' interests, particularly those of shareholders, is a primary objective of corporate governance. Thus, corporate governance involves oversight in areas where owners, managers, and members of boards of directors may have conflicts of interest. Processes used to elect members of the firm's board of directors, the general supervision of CEO pay and more focused supervision of director pay, and the corporation's overall strategic direction are examples of areas in which oversight is sought.[4] Because corporate governance is an ongoing process concerned with how a firm is to be managed, its nature evolves in light of types of never-ending changes in a firm's external environment that we discussed in Chapter 2.

Corporate governance is the set of mechanisms used to manage the relationships among stakeholders and to determine and control the strategic direction and performance of organizations.

The recent emphasis on corporate governance that is occurring across the globe stems mainly from the apparent failure of corporate governance mechanisms to adequately monitor and control top-level managers' decisions during recent times. In turn, undesired or unacceptable consequences resulting from using corporate governance mechanisms cause changes to these mechanisms, especially to the board of directors as a means of governance. A second and more positive reason for this interest comes from evidence that a well-functioning corporate governance system can create a competitive advantage for an individual firm.[5]

As noted earlier, corporate governance is of concern to nations as well as to individual firms.[6] Although corporate governance reflects company standards, it also collectively reflects the societal standards of nations.[7] Commenting about governance-related changes being made in Singapore, an official noted that, "Good corporate governance plays an important role in ensuring the effective functioning of Singapore's capital markets."[8] Ensuring the independence of board members and practices a board should follow to exercise effective oversight of a firm's internal control efforts are examples of recent changes to governance standards being applied in Singapore. Efforts such as these are important in that research shows that how nations choose to govern their corporations does affect firms' investment decisions. In other words, firms seek to invest in nations with national governance standards that are acceptable to them.[9] This is particularly the case when firms consider the possibility of geographically expanding into emerging markets.

In the chapter's first section, we describe the relationship on which the modern corporation is built—namely, the relationship between owners and managers. We use the majority of the chapter to explain various mechanisms owners use to govern managers and to ensure that they comply with their responsibility to satisfy stakeholders' needs, especially those of shareholders.

Three internal governance mechanisms and a single external one are used in the modern corporation. The three internal governance mechanisms we describe in this chapter are (1) ownership concentration, represented by types of shareholders and their different incentives to monitor managers; (2) the board of directors; and (3) executive compensation. We then consider the market for corporate control, an external corporate governance mechanism. Essentially, this market is a set of potential owners seeking to acquire undervalued firms and earn above-average returns on their investments by replacing ineffective top-level management teams.[10] The chapter's focus then shifts to the issue of international corporate governance. We briefly describe governance approaches used in German, Japanese, and Chinese firms. In part, this discussion suggests that the structures used to govern global companies competing in both developed and emerging economies are becoming more, rather than less, similar. Closing our analysis of corporate governance is a consideration of the need for these control mechanisms to encourage and support ethical behavior in organizations.

Separation of Ownership and Managerial Control

Historically, U.S. firms were managed by founder-owners and their descendants. In these cases, corporate ownership and control resided in the same persons. As firms grew larger, "the managerial revolution led to a separation of ownership and control in most large corporations, where control of the firm shifted from entrepreneurs to professional managers while ownership became dispersed among thousands of unorganized stockholders who were removed from the day-to-day management of the firm."[11] These changes created the modern public corporation, which is based on the efficient separation of ownership and managerial control. Supporting the separation is a basic legal premise suggesting that the primary objective of a firm's activities is to increase the corporation's profit and, thereby, the owners' (shareholders') financial gains.[12]

The separation of ownership and managerial control allows shareholders to purchase stock, which entitles them to income (residual returns) from the firm's operations after paying expenses. This right, however, requires that shareholders take a risk that the firm's expenses may exceed its revenues. To manage this investment risk, shareholders maintain a diversified portfolio by investing in several companies to reduce their overall risk.[13] The poor performance or failure of any one firm in which they invest has less overall effect on the value of the entire portfolio of investments. Thus, shareholders specialize in managing their investment risk.

Commonly, those managing small firms also own a significant percentage of the firm. In such instances, there is less separation between ownership and managerial control. Moreover, in a large number of family-owned firms, ownership and managerial control are not separated at all. Research shows that family-owned firms perform better when a member of the family is the CEO than when the CEO is an outsider.[14]

In many regions outside the United States, such as in Latin America, Asia, and some European countries, family-owned firms dominate the competitive landscape.[15] The primary purpose of most of these firms is to increase the family's wealth, which explains why a family CEO often is better than an outside CEO. Family ownership is also significant in U.S. companies in that at least one-third of the S&P 500 firms have substantial family ownership, holding on average about 18 percent of a firm's equity.[16]

Family-controlled firms face at least two critical issues related to corporate governance. First, as they grow, they may not have access to all of the skills needed to effectively manage the firm and maximize returns for the family. Thus, outsiders may be required to facilitate growth. Also, as they grow, they may need to seek outside capital and thus give up some of the ownership. In these cases, protecting the minority owners' rights becomes important.[17] To avoid these potential problems, when family firms grow and become more complex, their owner-managers may contract with managerial specialists. These managers make major decisions in the owners' firm and are compensated on the basis of their decision-making skills. Research suggests that firms in which families own enough equity to have influence without major control tend to make the best strategic decisions.[18]

Without owner (shareholder) specialization in risk bearing and management specialization in decision making, a firm may be limited by its owners' abilities to simultaneously manage it and make effective strategic decisions relative to risk. Thus, the separation and specialization of ownership (risk bearing) and managerial control (decision making) should produce the highest returns for the firm's owners.

Agency Relationships

The separation between owners and managers creates an agency relationship. An **agency relationship** exists when one or more persons (the principal or principals) hire another person or persons (the agent or agents) as decision-making specialists to perform a service.[19] Thus, an agency relationship exists when one party delegates decision-making responsibility to a second party for compensation (see Figure 10.1).

In addition to shareholders and top-level managers, other examples of agency relationships are consultants and clients and insured and insurer. Moreover, within organizations, an agency relationship exists between managers and their employees, as well as between top-level managers and the firm's owners.[20] However, in this chapter we focus on the agency relationship between the firm's owners (the principals) and top-level managers (the principals' agents) because these managers are responsible for formulating and implementing the firm's strategies, which have major effects on firm performance.[21]

The separation between ownership and managerial control can be problematic. Research evidence documents a variety of agency problems in the modern corporation.[22] Problems can surface because the principal and the agent have different interests

An **agency relationship** exists when one or more persons (the principal or principals) hire another person or persons (the agent or agents) as decision-making specialists to perform a service.

Figure 10.1 An Agency Relationship

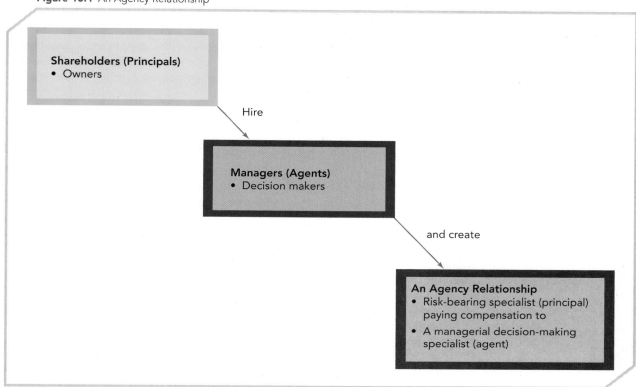

and goals or because shareholders lack direct control of large publicly traded corporations. Problems also surface when an agent makes decisions that result in pursuing goals that conflict with those of the principals. Thus, the separation of ownership and control potentially allows divergent interests (between principals and agents) to occur, which can lead to managerial opportunism.

Managerial opportunism is the seeking of self-interest with guile (i.e., cunning or deceit).[23] Opportunism is both an attitude (e.g., an inclination) and a set of behaviors (i.e., specific acts of self-interest).[24] Principals do not know beforehand which agents will or will not act opportunistically. A top-level manager's reputation is an imperfect predictor; moreover, opportunistic behavior cannot be observed until it has occurred. Thus, principals establish governance and control mechanisms to prevent agents from acting opportunistically, even though only a few are likely to do so. Interestingly, research suggests that when CEOs feel constrained by governance mechanisms, they are more likely to seek external advice that in turn helps them make better strategic decisions.[25]

The agency relationship suggests that any time principals delegate decision-making responsibilities to agents, the opportunity for conflicts of interest exists. Top-level managers, for example, may make strategic decisions that maximize their personal welfare and minimize their personal risk.[26] Decisions such as these prevent maximizing shareholder wealth. Decisions regarding product diversification demonstrate this situation.

Product Diversification as an Example of an Agency Problem

As explained in Chapter 6, a corporate-level strategy to diversify the firm's product lines can enhance a firm's strategic competitiveness and increase its returns, both of which serve the interests of all stakeholders and certainly shareholders and top-level managers. However, product diversification can create two benefits for top-level managers that

Managerial opportunism is the seeking of self-interest with guile (i.e., cunning or deceit).

shareholders do not enjoy, meaning that they may prefer product diversification more than shareholders do.[27]

The fact that product diversification usually increases the size of a firm and that size is positively related to executive compensation is the first of the two benefits of additional diversification that may accrue to top-level managers. Diversification also increases the complexity of managing a firm and its network of businesses, possibly requiring additional managerial pay because of this complexity.[28] Thus, increased product diversification provides an opportunity for top-level managers to increase their compensation.[29]

The second potential benefit is that product diversification and the resulting diversification of the firm's portfolio of businesses can reduce top-level managers' employment risk. *Managerial employment risk* is the risk of job loss, loss of compensation, and loss of managerial reputation.[30] These risks are reduced with increased diversification, because a firm and its upper-level managers are less vulnerable to the reduction in demand associated with a single or limited number of product lines or businesses. Events occurring at Kellogg Co. demonstrate these issues.

In 2001, Kellogg was almost entirely focused on breakfast cereal when it suffered its first-ever market share leadership loss to General Mills, Inc. Shortly thereafter, long-time Kellogg employee Carlos Gutierrez became Kellogg's CEO. Under his leadership, the firm embarked on a new strategy to overcome its poor performance. A business writer described some of the details of Gutierrez's strategy as follows: "To drive sales, Gutierrez unveiled such novel products as Special K snack bars, bought cookie maker Keebler Co., and ramped up Kellogg's health-foods presence by snapping up Worthington Foods Inc., a maker of soy and vegetarian products, and cereal maker Kashi. He pushed net earnings up 77 percent, to $890.6 million, from 1998 to 2004, as sales rose 42 percent, to $9.6 billion."[31]

Today, as it pursues its vision "to be the food company of choice," Kellogg operates manufacturing facilities in 18 countries and sells its diversified product lines in more than 180 countries. Kellogg indicates that it "is the world's leading producer of cereal and a leading producer of convenience foods, including cookies, crackers, toaster pastries, cereal bars, fruit-flavored snacks, frozen waffles and veggie foods."[32] As this set of products suggests and as indicated by the number of countries in which the firm sells what it produces, Kellogg's diversification continues increasing in terms of products and geography. However, the increased diversification involves highly related businesses through which Kellogg creates synergy as a foundation for competitive success. As Kellogg became more diversified in terms of products and geography, the risk of job loss for former CEO Gutierrez and his successors David Mackay and current CEO John Bryant was also reduced. Importantly, research results suggest that related diversification such as Kellogg pursued can enhance a firm's profitability.[33]

Free cash flow is the source of another potential agency problem. Calculated as operating cash flow minus capital expenditures, free cash flow represents the cash remaining after the firm has invested in all projects that have positive net present value within its current businesses.[34] Top-level managers may decide to invest free cash flow in product lines that are not associated with the firm's current lines of business to increase the firm's degree of diversification. However, when managers use free cash flow to diversify the firm in ways that do not have a strong possibility of creating additional value for stakeholders and certainly for shareholders, the firm is overdiversified. Overdiversification is an example of self-serving and opportunistic managerial behavior. In contrast to managers, shareholders may prefer that free cash flow be distributed to them as dividends, so they can control how the cash is invested.[35]

In Figure 10.2, Curve *S* shows shareholders' optimal level of diversification. As the firm's owners, shareholders seek the level of diversification that reduces the risk of the firm's total failure while simultaneously increasing its value by developing economies of scale and scope (see Chapter 6). Of the four corporate-level diversification strategies shown in Figure 10.2, shareholders likely prefer the diversified position noted by point *A* on Curve *S*—a position that is located between the dominant business and

Figure 10.2 Manager and Shareholder Risk and Diversification

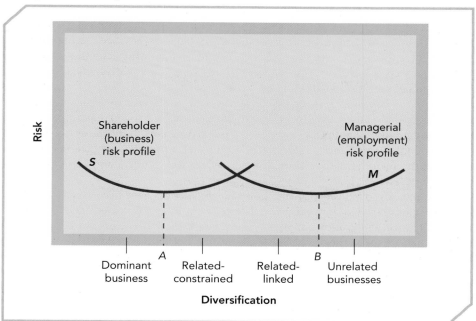

related-constrained diversification strategies. Of course, the optimum level of diversification owners seek varies from firm to firm.[36] Factors that affect shareholders' preferences include the firm's primary industry, the intensity of rivalry among competitors in that industry, and the top management team's experience with implementing diversification strategies and its effects on other firm strategies, such as its entry into international markets.[37]

As is the case for principals, top-level managers—as agents—also seek an optimal level of diversification. Declining performance resulting from too much diversification increases the probability that external investors (representing the market for corporate control) will purchase a substantial percentage of or the entire firm for the purpose of controlling it. If a firm is acquired, the employment risk for its top-level managers increases significantly. Furthermore, these managers' employment opportunities in the external managerial labor market (discussed in Chapter 12) are affected negatively by a firm's poor performance. Therefore, top-level managers prefer that the firms they lead be diversified. However, their preference is that the firm's diversification falls short of the point at which it increases their employment risk and reduces their employment opportunities.[38] Curve *M* in Figure 10.2 shows that top-level managers prefer higher levels of product diversification than do shareholders. Top-level managers might find the optimal level of diversification as shown by point *B* on Curve *M*.

In general, shareholders prefer riskier strategies and more focused diversification. Shareholders reduce their risk by holding a diversified portfolio of investments. Alternatively, managers cannot balance their employment risk by working for a diverse portfolio of firms; therefore, managers may prefer a level of diversification that maximizes firm size and their compensation while also reducing their employment risk. Product diversification, therefore, is a potential agency problem that could result in principals incurring costs to control their agents' behaviors.

Agency Costs and Governance Mechanisms

The potential conflict between shareholders and top-level managers shown in Figure 10.2, coupled with the fact that principals cannot easily predict which managers might act opportunistically, demonstrates why principals establish governance mechanisms. However, the firm incurs costs when it uses one or more governance mechanisms. Agency costs are the sum of incentive costs, monitoring costs, enforcement costs, and individual financial losses incurred by principals because governance mechanisms cannot guarantee total compliance by the agent. Because monitoring activities taking place within a firm is difficult, the principals' agency costs are larger in diversified firms given the additional complexity of diversification.[39]

In general, managerial interests may prevail when governance mechanisms are weak and as such, ineffective; this is exemplified in situations where managers have a significant amount of autonomy to make strategic decisions. If, however, the board of directors controls managerial autonomy, or if other strong governance mechanisms are used, the firm's strategies should better reflect stakeholders and certainly shareholders' interests.

More recently, observers of firms' governance practices have been concerned about more egregious behavior beyond mere ineffective corporate strategies, such as that discovered at Enron and WorldCom. Partly in response to these behaviors, the U.S. Congress enacted the Sarbanes-Oxley (SOX) Act in 2002 and passed the Dodd-Frank Wall Street Reform and Consumer Protection Act (Dodd-Frank) in mid-2010.

Because of these two acts, corporate governance mechanisms should receive greater scrutiny.[40] While the implementation of SOX has been controversial to some, most believe that its use has led to generally positive outcomes in terms of protecting stakeholders and certainly shareholders' interests. For example, Section 404 of SOX, which prescribes significant transparency improvement on internal controls associated with accounting and auditing, has arguably improved the internal auditing scrutiny (and thereby trust) in firms' financial reporting. Moreover, research suggests that internal controls associated with Section 404 increase shareholder value.[41] Nonetheless, some argue that the Act, especially Section 404, creates excessive costs for firms. In addition, a decrease in foreign firms listing on U.S. stock exchanges occurred at the same time as listing on foreign exchanges increased. In part, this shift may be because of the costs SOX generates for firms seeking to list on U.S. exchanges.

Although the details of its implementation remain incomplete, Dodd-Frank is recognized as the most sweeping set of financial regulatory reforms in the United States since the Great Depression. The Act is intended to align financial institutions' actions with society's interests. Dodd-Frank includes provisions related to the categories of consumer protection, systemic risk oversight, executive compensation, and capital requirements for banks. Some legal analysts offer the following description of the Act's provisions: "(Dodd-Frank) creates a Financial Stability Oversight Council headed by the Treasury Secretary, establishes a new system for liquidation of certain financial companies, provides for a new framework to regulate derivatives, establishes new corporate governance requirements, and regulates credit rating agencies and securitizations. The Act also establishes a new consumer protection bureau and provides for extensive consumer protection in financial services."[42]

More intensive application of governance mechanisms as mandated by legislation such as Sarbanes-Oxley and Dodd-Frank affects firms' choice of strategies. For example, more intense governance might find firms choosing to pursue fewer risky projects, possibly decreasing shareholder wealth as a result. In considering how some provisions associated with Dodd-Frank that deal with banks might be put into practice, a U.S. federal regulator said, "To put it plainly, my view is that we are in danger of trying to squeeze too much risk and complexity out of banking."[43] As this comment suggests, determining governance practices that strike an appropriate balance between protecting stakeholders' interests and allowing firms to implement strategies with some degree of risk is difficult.

Next, we explain the effects of the three internal governance mechanisms on managerial decisions regarding the firm's strategies.

Agency costs are the sum of incentive costs, monitoring costs, enforcement costs, and individual financial losses incurred by principals because governance mechanisms cannot guarantee total compliance by the agent.

Ownership Concentration

Ownership concentration is defined by the number of large-block shareholders and the total percentage of the firm's shares they own. Large-block shareholders typically own at least 5 percent of a company's issued shares. Ownership concentration as a governance mechanism has received considerable interest because large-block shareholders are increasingly active in their demands that firms adopt effective governance mechanisms to control managerial decisions so that they will best represent owners' interests.[44] In recent years, the number of individuals who are large-block shareholders has declined. Institutional owners have replaced individuals as large-block shareholders.

In general, diffuse ownership (a large number of shareholders with small holdings and few, if any, large-block shareholders) produces weak monitoring of managers' decisions. One reason for this is that diffuse ownership makes it difficult for owners to effectively coordinate their actions. As noted earlier, diversification beyond the shareholders' optimum level can result from ineffective monitoring of managers' decisions. Higher levels of monitoring could encourage managers to avoid strategic decisions that harm shareholder value, such as too much diversification. Research evidence suggests that ownership concentration is associated with lower levels of firm product diversification.[45] Thus, with high degrees of ownership concentration, the probability is greater that managers' decisions will be designed to maximize shareholder value.[46]

As noted, ownership concentration influences decisions made about the strategies a firm will use and the value created by their use. In general, but not in every case, ownership concentration's influence on strategies and firm performance is positive. For example, when large-block shareholders have a high degree of wealth, they have power relative to minority shareholders to appropriate the firm's wealth; this is particularly the case when they are in managerial positions. Excessive appropriation at the expense of minority shareholders is somewhat common in countries such as Korea where minority shareholder rights are not as protected as they are in the United States.[47] The importance of boards of directors to mitigate excessive appropriation of minority shareholder value has been found in firms with strong family ownership wherein family members have incentives to appropriate shareholder wealth, especially in the second generation after the founder has departed.[48]

The Increasing Influence of Institutional Owners

A classic work published in the 1930s argued that a separation of ownership and control had come to characterize the "modern" corporation.[49] This change occurred primarily because growth prevented founders-owners from maintaining their dual positions in what were increasingly complex companies. More recently, another shift has occurred: Ownership of many modern corporations is now concentrated in the hands of institutional investors rather than individual shareholders.[50]

Institutional owners are financial institutions such as mutual funds and pension funds that control large-block shareholder positions. Because of their prominent ownership positions, institutional owners, as large-block shareholders, have the potential to be a powerful governance mechanism. In 2009, estimates were that institutional owners held roughly 51 percent of all U.S. corporate equity and close to 73 percent of the equity among the 1,000 largest U.S. companies.[51] Recent commentary suggests the importance of pension funds to an entire economy: "Pension funds are critical drivers of growth and economic activity in the United States because they are one of the only significant sources of long-term, patient capital."[52]

These percentages suggest that as investors, institutional owners have both the size and the incentive to discipline ineffective top-level managers and that they can significantly influence a firm's choice of strategies and strategic decisions.[53] Research evidence indicates that institutional and other large-block shareholders are becoming

---

Ownership concentration is defined by the number of large-block shareholders and the total percentage of the firm's shares they own.

Large-block shareholders typically own at least 5 percent of a company's issued shares.

Institutional owners are financial institutions such as mutual funds and pension funds that control large-block shareholder positions.

CalPERS, the largest U.S. public pension fund, is headquartered in Sacramento.

REUTERS/Max Whittaker

more active in their efforts to influence a corporation's strategic decisions, unless they have a business relationship with the firm. Initially, these shareholder activists and institutional investors concentrated on the performance and accountability of CEOs and contributed to the dismissal of a number of them. Activists often target the actions of boards more directly via proxy vote proposals that are intended to give shareholders more decision rights because they believe board processes have been ineffective.[54] A rule approved by the U.S. Securities and Exchange Commission allowing large shareholders (owning 1 to 5 percent of a company's stock) to nominate up to 25 percent of a company's board of directors may enhance shareholders' decision rights.[55]

Established in 1932, CalPERS is a large institutional owner providing retirement and health coverage to more than 1.6 million California public employees, retirees, and their families. In 2011, CalPERS was the largest public employee pension fund in the United States. The recent economic crisis resulted in the fund encountering a loss of 24 percent of its invested assets in 2009, though by mid-2011 much of that loss had been recovered.[56]

As a large institutional owner, CalPERS is thought to aggressively promote governance decisions and actions that it believes will enhance shareholder value in companies in which it invests. One action CalPERS takes is to annually develop its Shareowner/Corporate Engagement Program to engage "underperforming public stock companies through private contacts and proxy actions rather than by posting a public 'name-and-shame' List."[57] Previously, CalPERS published a Focus List of companies it felt demonstrated very poor governance practices. Commenting about the change to its new program, the president of the CalPERS board noted that "The Focus List has served us well by calling public attention to some of the worst market players, but the time has come for a more effective approach."[58] Regardless of the actions taken, CalPERS is recognized as an effective steward of shareholders' best interests when interacting with companies in which it has invested.

To date, research suggests that institutional activism may not have a strong direct effect on firm performance but may indirectly influence a targeted firm's strategic decisions, including those concerned with international diversification and innovation. Thus, to some degree at least, institutional activism has the potential to discipline managers and to enhance the likelihood of a firm taking future actions that are in shareholders' best interests.[59]

Board of Directors

The **board of directors** is a group of elected individuals whose primary responsibility is to act in the owners' best interests by formally monitoring and controlling the firm's top-level managers.

Shareholders elect the members of a firm's board of directors. The **board of directors** is a group of elected individuals whose primary responsibility is to act in the owners' best interests by formally monitoring and controlling the firm's top-level managers.[60] Those elected to a firm's board of directors are expected to oversee managers and to ensure that the corporation operates in ways that will best serve stakeholders' interests, and particularly the owners' interests. Helping board members reach their expected objectives are their powers to direct the affairs of the organization and reward and discipline top-level managers.

Though important to all shareholders, a firm's individual shareholders with small ownership percentages are very dependent on the board of directors to represent their interests. Unfortunately, evidence suggests that boards have not been highly effective in monitoring and controlling top-level managers' decisions and subsequent actions.[61] Because of their relatively ineffective performance and in light of the recent financial crisis, boards are experiencing increasing pressure from shareholders, lawmakers, and regulators to become more forceful in their oversight role to prevent top-level managers from acting in their own best interests. Moreover, in addition to their monitoring role, board members increasingly are expected to provide resources to the firms they serve. These resources include their personal knowledge and expertise and their relationships with a wide variety of organizations.[62]

Generally, board members (often called directors) are classified into one of three groups (see Table 10.1). *Insiders* are active top-level managers in the company who are elected to the board because they are a source of information about the firm's day-to-day operations.[63] *Related outsiders* have some relationship with the firm, contractual or otherwise, that may create questions about their independence; but, these individuals are not involved with the corporation's day-to-day activities. *Outsiders* provide independent counsel to the firm and may hold top-level managerial positions in other companies or may have been elected to the board prior to the beginning of the current CEO's tenure.[64]

Historically, inside managers dominated a firm's board of directors. A widely accepted view is that a board with a significant percentage of its membership from the firm's top-level managers provides relatively weak monitoring and control of managerial decisions.[65] With weak board monitoring, managers sometimes use their power to select and compensate directors and exploit their personal ties with them. In response to the SEC's proposal to require audit committees to be composed of outside directors, in 1984 the New York Stock Exchange implemented a rule requiring outside directors to head the audit committee. Subsequently, other rules required that independent outsider directors lead important committees such as the compensation committee and the nomination committee.[66] These other requirements were instituted after the Sarbanes-Oxley Act was passed, and policies of the New York Stock Exchange now require companies to maintain boards of directors that are composed of a majority of outside independent directors and to maintain full independent audit committees. Thus, additional scrutiny of corporate governance practices is resulting in a significant amount of attention being devoted to finding ways to encourage boards to take actions that fully represent shareholders' best interests.

Critics advocate reforms to ensure that independent outside directors are a significant majority of a board's total membership; research suggests this has been accomplished.[67] However, others argue that having outside directors is not enough to resolve the problems in that CEO power can strongly influence a board's decision. One proposal to reduce the power of the CEO is to separate the chair's role and the CEO's role on the board so that the same person does not hold both positions.[68] A situation in which an individual holds both the CEO and chair of the board title is called *CEO duality*. Yet,

Table 10.1 Classification of Board of Directors' Members

Insiders
- The firm's CEO and other top-level managers

Related outsiders
- Individuals not involved with the firm's day-to-day operations, but who have a relationship with the company

Outsiders
- Individuals who are independent of the firm in terms of day-to-day operations and other relationships

having a board that actively monitors top-level managers' decisions and actions does not ensure high performance. The value that the directors bring to the company also influences the outcomes. For example, boards with members having significant relevant experience and knowledge are the most likely to help the firm formulate and implement effective strategies.[69]

Alternatively, having a large number of outside board members can also create some problems. For example, because outsiders typically do not have contact with the firm's day-to-day operations and do not have ready access to detailed information about managers and their skills, they lack the insights required to fully and effectively evaluate their decisions and initiatives.[70] Outsiders can, however, obtain valuable information through frequent interactions with inside board members and during board meetings to enhance their understanding of managers and their decisions.

Because they work with and lead the firm daily, insiders have access to information that facilitates forming and implementing appropriate strategies. Accordingly, some evidence suggests that boards with a critical mass of insiders typically are better informed about intended strategic initiatives, the reasons for the initiatives, and the outcomes expected from pursuing them.[71] Without this type of information, outsider-dominated boards may emphasize financial, as opposed to strategic, controls to gather performance information to evaluate managers' and business units' performances. A virtually exclusive reliance on financial evaluations shifts risk to top-level managers who, in turn, may make decisions to maximize their interests and reduce their employment risk. Reducing investments in R&D, further diversifying the firm, and pursuing higher levels of compensation are some of the results of managers' actions to reach the financial goals set by outsider-dominated boards.[72] Additionally, boards can make mistakes in CEO succession decisions because of the lack of important information about candidates as well as the firm's specific needs. Overall, knowledgeable and balanced boards are likely to be the most effective over time.[73]

Executive Director of the United Nations World Food Programme, Josette Sheeran, Co-Chair of the Bill & Melinda Gates Foundation, Melinda Gates, World Health Organization (WHO) General-Director Margaret Chan, U2 pop group lead singer Bono, Chairman of the Board and Chief Executive Officer (CEO) of The Coca-Cola Company, Muhtar A. Kent, and President and Chief Executive Officer of Novo Nordisk, Lars Sorensen attend a session entitled "Raising Healthy Children" at the World Economic Forum. Often, individuals sit on multiple boards at a time.

WEF/Photoshot/Newscom

Enhancing the Effectiveness of the Board of Directors

Because of the importance of boards of directors in corporate governance and as a result of increased scrutiny from shareholders—in particular, large institutional investors—the performances of individual board members and of entire boards are being evaluated more formally and with greater intensity.[74] The demand for greater accountability and improved performance is stimulating many boards to voluntarily make changes. Among these changes are (1) increases in the diversity of the backgrounds of board members (e.g., a greater number of directors from public service, academic, and scientific settings; a greater percentage of ethnic minorities and women; and members from different countries on boards of U.S. firms), (2) the strengthening of internal management and accounting control systems, (3) establishing and consistently using formal processes to evaluate the board's performance, (4) modifying the compensation of directors, especially reducing or eliminating stock options as a part of their package, and (5) creating the "lead director" role[75] that has strong powers with regard to the board agenda and oversight of nonmanagement board member activities.

An increase in the board's involvement with a firm's strategic decision-making processes creates the need for effective collaboration between board members and top-level managers. Some argue that improving the processes used by boards to make decisions and monitor managers and firm outcomes is important for board effectiveness.[76] Moreover, because of the increased pressure from owners and the potential conflict among board members, procedures are necessary to help boards function effectively while seeking to discharge their responsibilities.

Increasingly, outside directors are being required to own significant equity stakes as a prerequisite to holding a board seat. In fact, some research suggests that firms perform better if outside directors have such a stake; the trend is toward higher pay for directors with more stock ownership, but with fewer stock options.[77] However, other research suggests that too much ownership can lead to lower independence for board members.[78] In addition, other research suggests that diverse boards help firms make more effective strategic decisions and perform better over time.[79] Although questions remain about whether more independent and diverse boards enhance board effectiveness, the trends for greater independence and increasing diversity among board members are likely to continue.

Executive Compensation

The compensation of top-level managers, and especially of CEOs, generates a great deal of interest and strongly held opinions. Some believe that top-management team members and certainly CEOs have a great deal of responsibility for a firm's performance and that they should be rewarded accordingly.[80] Others conclude that these individuals (and again, especially CEOs) are greatly overpaid and that their compensation is not as strongly related to firm performance as should be the case.[81] One of the three internal governance mechanisms seeks to deal with these issues. Specifically, **executive compensation** is a governance mechanism that seeks to align the interests of managers and owners through salaries, bonuses, and long-term incentives, such as stock awards and options.[82]

Long-term incentive plans (typically involving stock options and stock awards) are an increasingly important part of compensation packages for top-level managers, especially those leading U.S. firms. Theoretically, using long-term incentives facilitates the firm's efforts (through the board of directors' pay-related decisions) to avoid potential agency problems by linking managerial compensation to the wealth of common shareholders.[83] Effectively designed long-term incentive plans have the potential to prevent large-block stockholders (e.g., institutional investors) from pressing for changes in the composition of the board of directors and the top-management team in that they assume that when exercised, the plans will ensure that top-level managers will act in shareholders' best interests. Additionally, shareholders typically assume that top-level managers' pay and the firm's performance are more properly aligned when outsiders are the dominant block of a board's membership. Research results suggesting that fraudulent behavior can be associated with stock option incentives, such as earnings manipulation,[84] demonstrate the importance of the firm's board of directors (as a governance mechanism) actively monitoring the use of executive compensation as a governance mechanism.

Effectively using executive compensation as a governance mechanism is particularly challenging for firms implementing international strategies. For example, the interests of the owners of multinational corporations may be best served by less uniformity in the firm's foreign subsidiaries' compensation plans.[85] Developing an array of unique compensation plans requires additional monitoring, potentially increasing the firm's agency costs. Importantly, pay levels vary by regions of the world. For example, managerial pay is highest in the United States and much lower in Asia. Historically, compensation for top-level managers has been lower in India partly because many of the largest firms have

Executive compensation is a governance mechanism that seeks to align the interests of managers and owners through salaries, bonuses, and long-term incentives such as stock awards and options.

strong family ownership and control.[86] Also, acquiring firms in other countries increases the complexity associated with a board of directors' efforts to use executive compensation as an effective internal corporate governance mechanism.[87]

The Effectiveness of Executive Compensation

As an internal governance mechanism, executive compensation—especially long-term incentive compensation—is complicated, for several reasons. First, the strategic decisions top-level managers make are complex and nonroutine, meaning that direct supervision (even by the firm's board of directors) is likely to be ineffective as a means of judging the quality of their decisions. The result is a tendency to link top-level managers' compensation to outcomes the board can easily evaluate, such as the firm's financial performance. This leads to a second issue in that, typically, the effects of top-level managers' decisions are stronger on the firm's long-term than its short-term performance. This reality makes it difficult to assess the effects of their decisions on a regular basis such as annually. Third, a number of other factors affect a firm's performance besides top-level managerial decisions and behavior. Unpredictable changes in segments (economic, demographic, political/legal, etc.) in the firm's general environment (see Chapter 2) make it difficult to separate out the effects of top-level managers' decisions and the effects (both positive and negative) of changes in the firm's external environment on the firm's performance.

Properly designed and used incentive compensation plans for top-level managers may increase the value of a firm in line with shareholder expectations, but such plans are subject to managerial manipulation.[88] Additionally, annual bonuses may provide incentives to pursue short-run objectives at the expense of the firm's long-term interests. Although long-term, performance-based incentives may reduce the temptation to under-invest in the short run, they increase executive exposure to risks associated with uncontrollable events, such as market fluctuations and industry decline. The longer term the focus of incentive compensation, the greater are the long-term risks top-level managers bear. Also, because long-term incentives tie a manager's overall wealth to the firm in a way that is inflexible, such incentives and ownership may not be valued as highly by a manager as by outside investors who have the opportunity to diversify their wealth in a number of other financial investments.[89] Thus, firms may have to overcompensate for managers using long-term incentives.

Even though some stock option-based compensation plans are well designed with option strike prices substantially higher than current stock prices, some have been developed for the primary purpose of giving executives more compensation. Research of stock option repricing where the strike price value of the option has been lowered from its original position suggests that action is taken more frequently in high-risk situations.[90] However, repricing also happens when firm performance is poor, to restore the incentive effect for the option. Evidence also suggests that politics are often involved, which has resulted in "option backdating."[91] While this evidence shows that no internal governance mechanism is perfect, some compensation plans accomplish their purpose. For example, recent research suggests that long-term pay designed to encourage managers to be environmentally friendly has been linked to higher success in preventing pollution.[92]

The Strategic Focus summarizes some issues regarding executive compensation. As the discussion suggests, this internal governance mechanism is likely to continue receiving a great deal of scrutiny in the years to come. One of these issues is the degree to which executive compensation practices promote a long-term versus a short-term focus on the part of CEOs.

When designed properly and used effectively, each of the three internal governance mechanisms can contribute positively to the firm operating in ways that best serve stakeholders and especially shareholders' interests. By the same token, because none of the three mechanisms are perfect in design or execution, the market for corporate control, an external governance mechanism, is sometimes needed.

Learn more about "Say on Pay" initiatives.

www.cengagebrain .com

© Nicholas Monu/iStockphoto.com

STRATEGIC FOCUS

EXECUTIVE COMPENSATION: WHAT ARE SOME OF THE ISSUES AND WHAT MIGHT THE FUTURE HOLD?

CEO pay remains a topic of interest to multiple parties including shareholders, boards of directors, government regulators, and citizens of many countries. Increasingly, this intense interest is spreading to other members of top-management teams seeing increases in pay, such as chief financial officers (CFOs). In 2010 in the United States, CFO pay varied widely from $600,000 to more than $60 million, with five CFOs receiving over $20 million in compensation. Governance observers suggest that additional responsibilities mandated to CFOs by legislation such as Sarbanes-Oxley contribute to enhancements of compensation plans for these individuals.

Average compensation for the CEOs of large corporations in the United States was noticeably higher in 2010 compared to 2009: "The median value of salaries, bonuses and long-term incentive awards for CEOs of 350 major companies surged 10.7 percent to $9.27 million" in 2010. Simultaneously, the stock market's performance improved during the same year, as shown by the 13 percent increase in the value of the S&P 500 index.

Many believe that CEO pay is too high. A recent survey of a broad range of people (teachers, laborers, students, doctors, community leaders, and others) revealed that 77 percent believe that CEOs are paid too much. However, this must be placed in the context of the CEO's job-related expectations. In other words, are CEOs overpaid relative to what is expected of them?

As we know, as an agent for the firm's shareholders (the principals), the CEO is to lead the firm by making decisions that are in the owners' best interests. The consensus from a corporate governance perspective is that agents need to serve shareholders' long-term interests more so than their short-term interests. This is a potential issue—are CEOs rewarded primarily for short-term performance rather than for the firm's long-term performance? Walt Disney Company CEO Robert Iger believes that this is indeed the case in that "there is too much emphasis in his and other CEOs' pay packages on short-term stock results, and he urges compensation committees to rethink their approach." Thus a governance issue is that boards of directors need to verify that the CEO and other top-management team members are receiving compensation plans framed around the shareholders' long-term, not short-term, interests.

REUTERS/Jim Ruymen

Viacom Inc. Co-President and CBS chairman, Leslie Moonves, was recently one of the top five highest paid U.S. CEOs.

A potentially more significant governance issue relative to executive compensation is the possibility that CEO pay is not tied to the firm's short- or long-term performance. Following extensive analyses of significant amounts of data, well-known compensation consultant Graf Crystal recently reported that "no matter how (you) parse the numbers, (there is) no relationship between shareholder returns and CEO compensation." These findings caused Crystal to conclude that companies simply are not paying CEOs for the performance the firm delivers under their direction. If Crystal's conclusion is shown by additional research to be valid and reliable, boards of directors are challenged to develop and then use executive compensation plans with a higher probability of aligning agents and principals' long-term interests.

Ideas about how executive compensation could be more effectively structured for the purpose of aligning agents, and principals' interests are being offered. For example, "Crystal recommends awarding stock options with a strike price that's the average of the last 90 days

Read more about Viacom Inc.'s CEO compensation plans.

www.cengagebrain.com

and can't be exercised for five years to avoid 'opportunistic' pricing. He also suggests reducing bonuses if incentive targets aren't met." From a regulatory perspective, one of the provisions of Dodd-Frank, called "say for pay," allows shareholders to approve the compensation upper-level executives are to receive. Supporters believe that this provision can "empower shareholders and curb (executive) pay." Additional recommendations include large-block shareholders accepting full responsibility for evaluating CEO and company performance instead of relying on third parties to complete those evaluations and increasing the transparency of boards of directors' decisions and actions. Given the interest in executive compensation, there is little doubt that many additional recommendations regarding how to best use this governance mechanism will be offered in the years to come.

Sources: 2011, Live chat: The rise in executive pay, *Wall Street Journal*, http://www.wsj.com, May 9; A. Ignatius, 2011, CEO pay is up! Is that good? *HBR.org*, http://www.hbr.org, July-August; J. Holzer, 2011, A 'yes' in say on pay, *Wall Street Journal*, http://www.wsj.com, July 8; B. Philbin, 2011, Greenhill CEO sees lower pay costs, *Wall Street Journal*, http://www.wsj.com, July 20; J. Silver-Greenberg & A. Leondis, 2010, How much is a CEO worth? *Bloomberg Businessweek*, http://www.businessweek.com, May 6.

Market for Corporate Control

The **market for corporate control** is an external governance mechanism that is active when a firm's internal governance mechanisms fail.[93] The market for corporate control is composed of individuals and firms that buy ownership positions in or purchase all of potentially undervalued corporations typically for the purpose of forming new divisions in established companies or merging two previously separate firms. Because the top-level managers are assumed to be responsible for the undervalued firm's poor performance, they are usually replaced. An effective market for corporate control ensures that ineffective and/or opportunistic top-level managers are disciplined.[94]

Commonly, target firm managers and board members are sensitive about takeover bids emanating from the market for corporate control in that being a target suggests that they have been ineffective with efforts to fulfill their responsibilities. For top-level managers, a board's decision to accept an acquiring firm's offer typically finds them losing their jobs in that the acquirer usually wants different people to lead the firm. At the same time, rejection of an offer also increases the risk of job loss for top-level managers because the pressure from the board and shareholders for them to improve the firm's performance becomes substantial.[95]

A hedge fund is a fund that can pursue many different investment strategies such as taking long and short positions, using arbitrage, and buying and selling undervalued securities for the purpose of maximizing investors' returns. Growing at roughly 20 percent annually, hedge funds are estimated to be a $1 trillion industry in the United States alone.[96] Given investors' increasing desire to hold underperforming funds and their managers accountable, hedge funds are becoming increasingly active in the market for corporate control.[97]

In general, activist pension funds (as institutional investors and as an internal governance mechanism) are reactive in nature, taking actions when they conclude that a firm is underperforming. In contrast, activist hedge funds (as part of the market for corporate control) are proactive, "identifying a firm whose performance could be improved and then investing in it."[98] This means that "hedge funds are better at identifying undervalued companies, locating potential acquirers for them, and removing opposition to a takeover."[99]

In mid-2011, investor Carl Icahn made a bid to purchase Clorox Co. In announcing his bid, Icahn criticized Clorox's top-level managers for what he believed was the firm's underperformance relative to its potential. In leveling this criticism he was essentially saying that the firm's internal governance mechanisms had failed. Clorox's board

The **market for corporate control** is an external governance mechanism that is active when a firm's internal governance mechanisms fail.

rejected the initial bid of $76.50 per share as well as Icahn's subsequent bid of $80 per share, indicating that both bids undervalued the firm's true worth.[100]

The situation between Icahn and Clorox demonstrates the possibility that the firm may have been underperforming and, as such, that the market for corporate control should be active to discipline managers and to represent shareholders' best interests. The situation also demonstrates another possibility that research results indicates can happen—namely, that as a governance mechanism, investors sometimes use the market for corporate control to take an ownership position in firms that are performing well.[101] A study of active corporate raiders in the 1980s showed that takeover attempts often were focused on above-average performance firms in an industry,[102] suggesting that the market for corporate control too is an imperfect governance mechanism.[103]

In summary, the market for corporate control may appear to be a blunt instrument for corporate governance; nonetheless, this governance mechanism does have the potential to represent shareholders' best interests. Accordingly, top-level managers want to lead their firms in ways that make disciplining by activists outside the company unnecessary and/or inappropriate.

There are a number of defense tactics top-level managers can choose to use to fend off a takeover attempt. Managers leading a target firm that is performing well are almost certain to use tactics to thwart the takeover attempt. Even in instances when the target firm is underperforming its peers, managers might use defense tactics to protect their own interests. In general, managers' use of defense tactics is thought to be self-serving in nature.

Managerial Defense Tactics

In the majority of cases, hostile takeovers are the principal means by which the market for corporate control is activated. A *hostile takeover* is an acquisition of a target company by an acquiring firm that is accomplished "not by coming to an agreement with the target company's management but by going directly to the company's shareholders or fighting to replace management in order to get the acquisition approved."[104] Firms targeted for a hostile takeover may use multiple defense tactics to fend off the takeover attempt. The increased use of the market for corporate control has enhanced the sophistication and variety of managerial defense tactics that are used in takeovers.

Because the market for corporate control tends to increase risk for managers, managerial pay may be augmented indirectly through golden parachutes (wherein a CEO can receive up to three years' salary if his or her firm is taken over). Golden parachutes, similar to most other defense tactics, are controversial. Another takeover defense strategy is traditionally known as a "poison pill." This strategy usually allows shareholders (other than the acquirer) to convert "shareholders' rights" into a large number of common shares if an individual or company acquires more than a set amount of the target firm's stock (typically 10 to 20 percent). Increasing the total number of outstanding shares dilutes the potential acquirer's existing stake, meaning that to maintain or expand its ownership position the potential acquirer must buy additional shares at premium prices. The additional purchases increase the potential acquirer's costs. Some firms amend the corporate charter so board member elections are staggered, resulting in only one third of members being up for reelection each year. Research shows that this results in managerial entrenchment and reduced vulnerability to hostile takeovers.[105] Additional takeover defense strategies beyond those discussed here are presented in Table 10.2.

Most institutional investors oppose the use of defense tactics. TIAA-CREF and CalPERS have taken actions to have several firms' poison pills eliminated. Many institutional investors also oppose severance packages (golden parachutes), and the opposition is increasing significantly in Europe as well.[106] However, an advantage to severance packages is that they may encourage top-level managers to accept takeover bids with the potential to best serve shareholders' interest.[107] Alternatively, research results show that using takeover defenses reduces the amount of pressure managers feel to seek short-term

Table 10.2 Hostile Takeover Defense Strategies

Defense strategy	Success as a strategy	Effects on shareholder wealth
Capital structure change Dilution of the target firm's stock, making it more costly for an acquiring firm to continue purchasing the target's shares. Employee stock option plans (ESOPs), recapitalization, issuance of additional debt, and share buybacks are actions associated with this strategy.	Medium	Inconclusive
Corporate charter amendment An amendment to the target firm's charter for the purpose of staggering the elections of members to its board of directors so that all are not elected during the same year. This change to the firm's charter prevents a potential acquirer from installing a completely new board in a single year.	Very low	Negative
Golden parachute A lump-sum payment of cash that is given to one or more top-level managers when the firm is acquired in a takeover bid.	Low	Negligible
Greenmail The repurchase of the target firm's shares of stock that were obtained by the acquiring firm at a premium in exchange for an agreement that the acquirer will no longer target the company for takeover.	Medium	Negative
Litigation Lawsuits that help the target firm stall hostile takeover attempts. Antitrust charges and inadequate disclosure are examples of the grounds on which the target firm could file.	Low	Positive
Poison pill An action the target firm takes to make its stock less attractive to a potential acquirer.	High	Positive
Standstill agreement A contract between the target firm and the potential acquirer specifying that the acquirer will not purchase additional shares of the target firm for a specified period of time in exchange for a fee paid by the target firm.	Low	Negative

Sources: R. Campbell, C. Ghosh, M. Petrova, & C. F. Sirmans, 2011, Corporate governance and performance in the market for corporate control: The case of REITS, *Journal of Real Estate Finance & Economics*, 42: 451–480; M. Ryngaert & R. Schlten, 2010, Have changing takeover defense rules and strategies entrenched management and damaged shareholders? The case of defeated takeover bids, *Journal of Corporate Finance*, 16: 16–37; M. Ruiz-Mallorqui & D. J. Santana-Martin, 2009, Ultimate institutional owner and takeover defenses in the controlling versus minority shareholders context, *Corporate Governance: An International Review*, 17: 238–254; J. A. Pearce II & R. B. Robinson, Jr., 2004, Hostile takeover defenses that maximize shareholder wealth, *Business Horizons*, 47(5): 15–24.

performance gains, resulting in them concentrating on developing strategies with a longer time horizon and a high probability of serving stakeholders' interests. When they do this, the firm's market value increases, rewarding shareholders as a result of doing so.[108]

An awareness on the parts of top-level managers about the existence of external investors in the form of individuals (e.g., Carl Icahn) and groups (e.g., hedge funds) often positively influences them to align their interests with those of the firm's stakeholders, especially the shareholders. Moreover, when active as an external governance mechanism, the market for corporate control has brought about significant changes in many firms' strategies and, when used appropriately, has served shareholders' interests. Next, we describe international governance practices to explain how they differ across regions and countries.

International Corporate Governance

Corporate governance is an increasingly important issue in economies around the world, including emerging economies. Globalization in trade, investments, and equity markets increases the potential value of firms throughout the world using similar mechanisms to govern corporate activities. Moreover, because of globalization, major companies want to attract foreign investment. For this to happen, foreign investors must be confident that adequate corporate governance mechanisms are in place to protect their investments.

Although globalization is stimulating an increase in the intensity of efforts to improve corporate governance and potentially to reduce the variation in regions and nations' governance systems,[109] the reality remains that different nations do have different governance systems in place. Recognizing and understanding differences in various countries' governance systems as well as changes taking place within those systems improves the likelihood a firm will be able to compete successfully in the international markets it chooses to enter. Next, to highlight the general issues of differences and changes taking place in governance systems, we discuss corporate governance practices in two developed economies—Germany and Japan—and in China, a developing economy.

Corporate Governance in Germany and Japan

In many private German firms, the owner and manager may be the same individual. In these instances, agency problems are not present.[110] Even in publicly traded German corporations, a single shareholder is often dominant. Thus, the concentration of ownership is an important means of corporate governance in Germany, as it is in the United States.[111]

Historically, banks occupied the center of the German corporate governance system. This is the case in other European countries as well, such as Italy and France. As lenders, banks become major shareholders when companies they financed seek funding on the stock market or default on loans. Although the stakes are usually less than 10 percent, banks can hold a single ownership position up to but not exceeding 15 percent of the bank's capital. Although shareholders can tell banks how to vote their ownership position, they generally do not do so. The banks monitor and control managers, both as lenders and as shareholders, by electing representatives to supervisory boards.

German firms with more than 2,000 employees are required to have a two-tiered board structure that places the responsibility for monitoring and controlling managerial (or supervisory) decisions and actions in the hands of a separate group.[112] All the functions of strategy and management are the responsibility of the management board (the Vorstand); however, appointment to the Vorstand is the responsibility of the supervisory tier (the Aufsichtsrat). Employees, union members, and shareholders appoint members to the Aufsichtsrat. Proponents of the German structure suggest that it helps prevent corporate wrongdoing and rash decisions by "dictatorial CEOs." However, critics maintain that it slows decision making and often ties a CEO's hands. The corporate governance practices in Germany make it difficult to restructure companies as quickly as can be done in the United States. Because of the role of local government (through the board structure) and the power of banks in Germany's corporate governance structure, private shareholders rarely have major ownership positions in German firms. Large institutional investors, such as pension funds and insurance companies, are also relatively insignificant owners of corporate stock. Thus, at least historically, German executives generally have not been dedicated to maximizing shareholder wealth to the degree that is the case for top-level managers in the United Kingdom and the United States.[113]

However, corporate governance practices used in Germany are changing. A manifestation of these changes is that a number of German firms are beginning to gravitate toward U.S. governance mechanisms. Recent research suggests that the traditional system in Germany produced some agency costs because of a lack of external ownership power. Interestingly, German firms with listings on U.S. stock exchanges have increasingly adopted executive stock option compensation as a long-term incentive pay policy.[114]

The concepts of obligation, family, and consensus affect attitudes toward corporate governance in Japan. In Japan, an obligation "may be to return a service for one rendered or it may derive from a more general relationship, for example, to one's family or old alumni, or one's company (or Ministry), or the country. This sense of particular obligation is common elsewhere but it feels stronger in Japan."[115] As part of a company family, individuals are members of a unit that envelops their lives; families command

Nomura Securities is headquartered in Tokyo, Japan. Japan has a bank-based financial and corporate governance structure.

the attention and allegiance of parties throughout corporations. Moreover, a *keiretsu* (a group of firms tied together by cross-shareholdings) is more than an economic concept; it, too, is a family. Some believe, though, that extensive cross-shareholdings impede the type of structural change that is needed to improve the nation's corporate governance practices.[116] Consensus, another important influence in Japanese corporate governance, calls for the expenditure of significant amounts of energy to win the hearts and minds of people whenever possible, as opposed to top-level managers issuing edicts.[117] Consensus is highly valued, even when it results in a slow and cumbersome decision-making process.

As in Germany, banks in Japan have an important role in financing and monitoring large public firms.[118] Because it owns the largest share of stocks and holds the largest amount of debt, the main bank has the closest relationship with a firm's top-level managers. The main bank provides financial advice to the firm and also closely monitors managers. Thus, Japan has a bank-based financial and corporate governance structure whereas the United States has a market-based financial and governance structure.[119]

Aside from lending money, a Japanese bank can hold up to 5 percent of a firm's total stock; a group of related financial institutions can hold up to 40 percent. In many cases, main-bank relationships are part of a horizontal keiretsu. A keiretsu firm usually owns less than 2 percent of any other member firm; however, each company typically has a stake of that size in every firm in the keiretsu. As a result, somewhere between 30 and 90 percent of a firm is owned by other members of the keiretsu. Thus, a keiretsu is a system of relationship investments.

Japan's corporate governance practices are changing. For example, because of Japanese banks' continuing development as economic organizations, their role in the monitoring and control of managerial behavior and firm outcomes is less significant than in the past.[120] Also, deregulation in the financial sector has reduced the cost of mounting hostile takeovers.[121] As such, deregulation facilitated additional activity in Japan's market for corporate control, which was nonexistent in past years. Interestingly, however, recent research shows that CEOs of both public and private companies in Japan receive similar levels of compensation and their compensation is tied closely to observable performance goals.[122]

Corporate Governance in China

"China has a unique and large, socialist, market-oriented economy. The government has done much to improve the corporate governance of listed companies."[123] These comments denote the fact that corporate governance practices in China are changing and that the country is experiencing increasing privatization of businesses and the development of equity markets. However, the stock markets in China remain young and underdeveloped. In their early years, these markets were weak because of significant insider trading, but with stronger governance these markets have improved.[124]

There has been a gradual decline in China in the equity held in state-owned enterprises and the number and percentage of private firms have grown, but the state still relies on direct and/or indirect controls to influence the strategies firms use. In terms of long-term success, these conditions may affect firms' performances in that research shows that firms with higher state ownership tend to have lower market value and more volatility in that value across time. This is because of agency conflicts in the firms and because the executives do not seek to maximize shareholder returns given that they must also seek to satisfy social goals placed on them by the government.[125] This suggests a potential conflict between the principals, particularly the state owner and the private equity owners of the state-owned enterprises.[126]

Some evidence suggests that corporate governance in China may be tilting toward the Western model. For example, China YCT International (a firm specializing in producing and selling Gingko nutraceutical health products) is strengthening its corporate governance. To this end, the firm has established an audit committee within its board of directors, appointed three new independent directors, and more openly speaks about serving investors' needs.[127] In addition, recent research shows that with increasing frequency, the compensation of top-level executives in Chinese companies is closely related to prior and current financial performance of their firm.[128]

In spite of these changes and as suggested in the Opening Case, much work remains if the governance of Chinese companies is to meet international and Western standards. For example, after analyzing governance practices in multiple Chinese companies in mid-2011, Fitch Ratings concluded that, "Allegations of fraud and accounting irregularities at Chinese companies are likely to continue for at least the near term and the accusations may hamper the firms' access to funds regardless of the claims' merit."[129] This warning from Fitch highlights the fact that changing a nation's governance systems is a complicated task that will encounter problems as well as successes while seeking progress. Thus, corporate governance in Chinese companies continues evolving and likely will for some time to come as parties (e.g., the Chinese government and those seeking further movement toward free-market economies) interact to form governance mechanisms that are best for their nation, business firms, and citizens.

Governance Mechanisms and Ethical Behavior

The three internal and one external governance mechanisms are designed to ensure that the agents of the firm's owners—the corporation's top-level managers—make strategic decisions that best serve the interests of all stakeholders. In the United States, shareholders are commonly recognized as the company's most significant stakeholders. Increasingly though, top-level managers are expected to lead their firms in ways that will also serve the needs of product market stakeholders (e.g., customers, suppliers, and host communities) and organizational stakeholders (e.g., managerial and nonmanagerial employees).[130] Therefore, the firm's actions and the outcomes flowing from them should result in at least minimal satisfaction of the interests of all stakeholders. Without at least minimal satisfaction of its interests, a dissatisfied stakeholder will withdraw its support from the firm and provide it to another (e.g., customers will purchase products from a supplier offering an acceptable substitute).

Some believe that the internal corporate governance mechanisms designed and used by ethically responsible companies increase the likelihood the firm will be able to at least minimally satisfy all stakeholders' interests.[131] Scandals at companies such as Enron, WorldCom, HealthSouth, and Satyam (a large information technology company based in India), among others, illustrate the negative effects of poor ethical behavior on a firm's efforts to satisfy stakeholders. The issue of ethical behavior by top-level managers as a foundation for best serving stakeholders' interests is being taken seriously in countries throughout the word.[132] In India, the former managing director of Mumbai-based DB Realty and officials from mobile-phone operators Unitech and Reliance ADA Group all face charges of unethical behavior while leading their companies.[133]

The decisions and actions of the board of directors can be an effective deterrent to unethical behaviors by top-level managers. Indeed, evidence suggests that the most effective boards set boundaries for their firms' business ethics and values.[134] Once the

STRATEGIC FOCUS

THE MANY FACETS OF CORPORATE GOVERNANCE: RIO TINTO'S EXPERIENCES

"Integrity delivered through good governance. Successful operation of our business requires good governance, whether it be complying with legal requirements or engaging with our stakeholders to understand their expectations in relation to our business." These comments from Rio Tinto suggest that the company is fully committed to designing and using governance practices that, among other outcomes, will align agents and principals' interests. The values of accountability, respect, teamwork, and integrity facilitate effective implementation of the firm's governance practices.

Perhaps the firm's size and complexity increase the difficulty associated with achieving effective corporate governance. Rio Tinto is a leading international mining group that is widely diversified in terms of products (focusing on copper, diamonds, gold, industrial materials, titanium dioxide, borates, talc, and salt and iron ore) and geography (operating in over 40 countries). Being a dual listed company is a strong indicator of the firm's complexity. Formally, the firm is known as Rio Tinto Group, which is a combination of Rio Tinto plc, a London-listed public company headquartered in the United Kingdom, and Rio Tinto Limited, which is listed on the Australian Stock Exchange.

Regardless of the reasons, Rio Tinto's governance has been challenged. In 2000, large-block pension funds supported union-backed resolutions requesting the appointment of a single independent non-executive deputy chairman and the adoption of the International Labour Organisation's conventions concerning human rights conditions and practices at worksites. Responding to other pressures, Rio Tinto's CEO indicated in 2002 that the firm would resume reviewing its business and governance practices following a five-year absence of formally doing so.

Rio Tinto Chairman, Jan du Plessis, and CEO, Tom Albanese, hold a press conference in 2010. The company has recently reaffirmed its commitment to transparent corporate governance.

EPA/Photoshot

More recently, concerns have been expressed about executive compensation practices. A business writer expressed these concerns as follows: "Rio Tinto is facing a fresh row over pay after one of its largest investors criticized the mining giant for handing bosses generous reward for hitting 'unchallenging' targets." The statement captures large-block institutional owner Standard Life Investments' (the firm's fifth largest shareholder) position in that this investor concluded that Rio Tinto's top-level managers could receive significant rewards by achieving goals that were not challenging and in the shareholders' best interests. The fact that a regulation was passed in Australia (and might pass in New Zealand as well) giving shareholders the power to force the "re-election of an entire board if they think executives are being paid too much" suggests that actions will be forthcoming from Rio Tinto's board to develop compensation plans that challenge executives as a foundation for driving superior growth and profitability for the firm's owners.

On the other hand, Rio Tinto is being acknowledged for strengthening its governance practices for the purpose of better supporting "whistleblowers." One reason to strengthen such practices is that some believe that "Australian whistleblower-protection laws are about the worst in the English-speaking world." Another reason is that four of Rio's Shanghai-based employees were recently found guilty of accepting bribes. "Speak-Out" is Rio Tinto's governance program, which it has enlarged and strengthened to

ETHICS • ETHICS • ETHICS • ETHICS • ETHICS • ETHIC

ensure compliance by all managers and employees with the firm's expectations regarding ethical behavior.

As these examples demonstrate, effective corporate governance can be challenging for multinational companies with significant amounts of product and geographic diversification. Rio Tinto is aware of this reality and seeks to establish and use strong corporate governance practices. As part of its corporate governance standards manual, the firm notes that "Rio Tinto is committed to high standards of corporate governance for which the directors are accountable to shareholders." The manual also stipulates that "The role of the board is to provide Rio Tinto with good governance and strategic direction." Thus, Rio Tinto formally supports and seeks governance practices that are consistent with generally accepted expectations regarding effective corporate governance mechanisms.

Sources: 2011, Investors in Oz get big say on execs' pay, *The New Zealand Herald*, http://www.nzherald.co.nz; 2011, Sustainable development, Rio Tinto homepage, http://www.riotinto.com, August 1; T. Boreham, 2011, Blow the whistle and be damned, *Weekend Australian*, http://www.theaustralian.com.au, April 1; M. Chambers, 2011, Rio's $657m Guinea payment faces scrutiny, *Weekend Australian*, http://www.theaustralian.com.au, May 21; O. Shah, 2011, Rio faces pay revolt from major investor, *The Australian*, http://www.theaustralian.com.au, April 18; O. Shah, 2011, Shareholder rebels on Rio Tinto pay, *The Sunday Times*, http://www.sundaytimes.com, April 17; 2007, Corporate governance standards, Rio Tinto homepage, http://www.riotinto.com, February.

boundaries for ethical behavior are determined and likely formalized in a code of ethics, the board's ethics-based expectations must be clearly communicated to the firm's top-level managers and to other stakeholders (e.g., customers and suppliers) with whom interactions are necessary for the firm to produce and sell its products. Moreover, as agents of the firm's owners, top-level managers must understand that the board, acting as an internal governance mechanism, will hold them fully accountable for developing and supporting an organizational culture in which only ethical behaviors are permitted. As explained in Chapter 12, CEOs can be positive role models for improved ethical behavior.

Through effective governance that results from well-designed internal mechanisms and the appropriate use of the market for corporate control as an external mechanism, top-level managers, working with others, are able to help their firm select and use strategies with a high probability of resulting in strategic competitiveness and earning above-average returns. While some firms' governance mechanisms are ineffective, other companies are recognized for the quality of their governance activities.

World Finance evaluates the corporate governance practices of companies throughout the world. For 2011, some of this group's "Best Corporate Governance Awards" by country were given to Royal Bank of Canada (Canada), Vestas Wind Systems A/S (Denmark), BSF AG (Germany), Empresas ICA (Mexico), and Cisco Systems (United States). These awards are determined by analyzing a number of issues concerned with corporate governance, such as board accountability and financial disclosure, executive compensation, shareholder rights, ownership base, takeover provisions, corporate behavior, and overall responsibility exhibited by the company.[135]

As the discussion in this chapter suggests, corporate governance mechanisms are a vital, yet imperfect, part of firms' efforts to select and successfully use strategies. And as we discuss in the Strategic Focus about Rio Tinto, firms are involved with a wide range of different kinds of issues when dealing with corporate governance. The effectiveness of this firm's governance has been challenged from time to time, even though Rio Tinto seeks to establish and use effective governance mechanisms.

SUMMARY

- Corporate governance is a relationship among stakeholders that is used to determine a firm's direction and control its performance. How firms monitor and control top-level managers' decisions and actions affects the implementation of strategies. Effective governance that aligns managers' decisions with shareholders' interests can help produce a competitive advantage for the firm.

- Three internal governance mechanisms are used in the modern corporation: (1) ownership concentration, (2) the board of directors, and (3) executive compensation. The market for corporate control is an external governance mechanism influencing managers' decisions and the outcomes resulting from them.

- Ownership is separated from control in the modern corporation. Owners (principals) hire managers (agents) to make decisions that maximize the firm's value. As risk-bearing specialists, owners diversify their risk by investing in multiple corporations with different risk profiles. Owners expect their agents (the firm's top-level managers, who are decision-making specialists) to make decisions that will help to maximize the value of their firm. Thus, modern corporations are characterized by an agency relationship that is created when one party (the firm's owners) hires and pays another party (top-level managers) to use its decision-making skills.

- Separation of ownership and control creates an agency problem when an agent pursues goals that conflict with the principals' goals. Principals establish and use governance mechanisms to control this problem.

- Ownership concentration is based on the number of large-block shareholders and the percentage of shares they own. With significant ownership percentages, such as those held by large mutual funds and pension funds, institutional investors often are able to influence top-level managers' strategic decisions and actions. Thus, unlike diffuse ownership, which tends to result in relatively weak monitoring and control of managerial decisions, concentrated ownership produces more active and effective monitoring. Institutional investors are a powerful force in corporate America and actively use their positions of concentrated ownership to force managers and boards of directors to make decisions that best serve shareholders' interests.

- In the United States and the United Kingdom, a firm's board of directors, composed of insiders, related outsiders, and outsiders, is a governance mechanism expected to represent shareholders' interests. The percentage of outside directors on many boards now exceeds the percentage of inside directors. Through implementation of the SOX Act, outsiders are expected to be more independent of a firm's

top-level managers compared with directors selected from inside the firm. New rules imposed by the U.S. Securities and Exchange Commission to allow owners with large stakes to propose new directors are likely to change the balance even more in favor of outside and independent directors. Although their precise nature is unknown, additional governance-related regulations will flow from Dodd-Frank as well.

- Executive compensation is a highly visible and often criticized governance mechanism. Salary, bonuses, and long-term incentives are used for the purpose of aligning managers' and shareholders' interests. A firm's board of directors is responsible for determining the effectiveness of the firm's executive compensation system. An effective system elicits managerial decisions that are in shareholders' best interests.

- In general, evidence suggests that shareholders and boards of directors have become more vigilant in controlling managerial decisions. Nonetheless, these mechanisms are imperfect and sometimes insufficient. When the internal mechanisms fail, the market for corporate control—as an external governance mechanism—becomes important. Although it too is imperfect, the market for corporate control has been effective in causing corporations to combat inefficient diversification and to implement more effective strategic decisions.

- Corporate governance structures used in Germany, Japan, and China differ from each other and from the structure used in the United States. Historically, the U.S. governance structure focused on maximizing shareholder value. In Germany, employees, as a stakeholder group, take a more prominent role in governance. By contrast, until recently, Japanese shareholders played virtually no role in monitoring and controlling top-level managers. However, Japanese firms are now being challenged by "activist" shareholders. In China, the central government still plays a major role in corporate governance practices. Internationally, all these systems are becoming increasingly similar, as are many governance systems both in developed countries, such as France and Spain, and in transitional economies, such as Russia and India.

- Effective governance mechanisms ensure that the interests of all stakeholders are served. Thus, strategic competitiveness results when firms are governed in ways that permit at least minimal satisfaction of capital market stakeholders (e.g., shareholders), product market stakeholders (e.g., customers and suppliers), and organizational stakeholders (managerial and nonmanagerial employees; see Chapter 2). Moreover, effective governance produces ethical behavior in the formulation and implementation of strategies.

REVIEW QUESTIONS

1. What is corporate governance? What factors account for the considerable amount of attention corporate governance receives from several parties, including shareholder activists, business press writers, and academic scholars? Why is governance necessary to control managers' decisions?

2. What is meant by the statement that ownership is separated from managerial control in the corporation? Why does this separation exist?

3. What is an agency relationship? What is managerial opportunism? What assumptions do owners of corporations make about managers as agents?

4. How is each of the three internal governance mechanisms—ownership concentration, boards of directors, and executive compensation—used to align the interests of managerial agents with those of the firm's owners?

5. What trends exist regarding executive compensation? What is the effect of the increased use of long-term incentives on top-level managers' strategic decisions?

6. What is the market for corporate control? What conditions generally cause this external governance mechanism to become active? How does this mechanism constrain top-level managers' decisions and actions?

7. What is the nature of corporate governance in Germany, Japan, and China?

8. How can corporate governance foster ethical decisions and behaviors on the part of managers as agents?

EXPERIENTIAL EXERCISES

EXERCISE 1: WHO PAYS BETTER AT THE TOP: THE MOST- OR LEAST-ADMIRED COMPANY?

According to your text, "*executive compensation* is a governance mechanism that seeks to align the interests of managers and owners through salaries, bonuses, and long-term incentives such as stock awards and options." The key to the compensation structure for a firm is to achieve a balance that both enhances short-term financial performance and also preserves the firm's competitive advantage to allow it to achieve long-term competitive success.

Fortune magazine annually publishes its list of most admired companies in the United States. The magazine also publishes its least-admired list of companies. They are ranked in nine different categories, including social responsibility, financial soundness, and innovation.

So who pays better; most admired or least admired?

Part One

Each team should pick a pair of companies—one from *Fortune's* most admired list and one from *Fortune's* least admired. The teams should pick two companies that come from the same comparison list, such as one of the most admired and one of the least admired in innovation. There are nine comparison categories so choose the category your team finds most interesting (your instructor may pick these for you). You will note that some of the firms on the *Fortune* list are foreign-owned entities. While a foreign-owned firm will make for interesting comparison, make sure you are able to gather appropriate data for that firm.

Part Two

Present to the class a description of what you find. In particular, be able to discuss the following topics for each firm.

1. CEO compensation and that of the top 5 executives.

2. The governance structure and any relationships between directors that might hinder objectivity.

3. CEO tenure and that of the members of the firm's top-management team.

4. Compensation plan structure—stock, fixed pay, other perks.

5. Conclusions you might draw from looking at the two firms side by side.

6. Each firm's performance versus the general market it is in, such as the S&P 500. Look short term and long term.

7. The way in which *Fortune* creates its lists. What are the rules?

EXERCISE 2: GOVERNANCE: DOES IT MATTER COMPETITIVELY?

Governance mechanisms are effective when they meet the needs of all stakeholders. Governance mechanisms are also a key way in which to ensure that strategic decisions are made effectively. As a potential employee, how would you go about investigating a firm's governance structure, and would that investigation weigh in your decision to become an employee? Identify a firm that you currently would like to join or one that you just find interesting. Working individually, research the following aspects of your target firm:

- Find a copy of the firm's most recent proxy statement and 10-K. Proxy statements are sent to shareholders prior to each year's annual meeting and contain detailed information about the company's governance and issues on which a shareholder vote might be held. Proxy statements are typically available from a firm's Web site (look for an "Investors" submenu). You can also access proxy statements and other government filings such as the 10-K from the SEC's EDGAR database (http://www.sec.gov/edgar.shtml). Alongside the proxy you should also be able to access the firm's annual report. Here you will find information concerning performance, governance, and the firm's outlook, among other matters.

■ Identify one of the firm's main competitors for comparison. You can find one of the firm's main competitors by using company analysis tools such as Datamonitor.

Some of the topics that you should examine include:

■ Compensation plans (for both the CEO and board members; be sure to look for difference between fixed and incentive compensation)

■ Board composition (e.g., board size, insiders and outsiders, interlocking directorates, functional experience, how many active CEOs, how many retired CEOs, what is the demographic makeup, and age diversity)

■ Committees (e.g., how many, composition, compensation)

■ Stock ownership by officers and directors—identify beneficial ownership from stock owned (you will need to look through the notes of the ownership tables to comprehend this)

■ Ownership concentration—how much of the firm's outstanding stock is owned by institutions, individuals, insiders? How

many large-block shareholders are there (5 percent or more owners)?

■ Does the firm utilize a duality structure for the CEO and chair of the board?

■ Is there a lead director who is not an officer of the company?

■ Activities by activist shareholders regarding corporate governance issues of concern

■ Are there any managerial defense tactics employed by the firm? For example, what does it take for a shareholder proposal to come to a vote and be adopted?

■ What is the firm's code of conduct?

Prepare a report summarizing the results of your findings that compares your target firm and its competitor side by side. Your memo should include the following topics:

■ Summarize the key aspects of the firms' governance mechanisms.

■ Create a single graph covering the last 10-year historical stock performance for both companies. If applicable, find a representative index to compare both with, such as S&P or NASDAQ.

■ Highlight key differences between your target firm and its competitor.

■ Based on your review of the firm's governance, did you change your opinion of the firm's desirability as an employer? Why or why not? How does the target firm compare to the main competitor you identified?

V I D E O   C A S E

KNOWLEDGE BRINGS CORPORATE GOVERNANCE: WHISTLEBLOWING/STAFFORD GENERAL HOSPITAL

Emphasizing targets rather than proper care, Stafford General Hospital created a culture that discouraged complaints and resulted in high mortality rates. The public campaigns of family members and relatives to vocalize their knowledge of Stafford's failures in basic nursing care stimulated government investigations, which revealed doctor and nurse knowledge of the hospital's poor care and how their concerns were ignored. While whistleblower provisions were already in place, this investigation and new leadership has made quality of care a primary concern along with monetary commitments to staff, facilities, and training, and a "no blame whistleblowing policy" to bring poor practices out in the open.

Be prepared to discuss the following concepts and questions in class:

Concepts
■ Corporate governance
■ Agency relationship

■ Market for corporate control
■ International corporate governance

Questions

1. What corporate governance mechanisms failed at Stafford General Hospital?

2. Were there possibilities of agency problems within Stafford? Why or why not? Could managerial opportunism be an issue?

3. Can the Trust Foundation for Stafford be effective as a market for corporate control?

4. What role do you think the corporate governance structure of the United Kingdom played in the problems at Stafford?

5. How do you think the situation at Stafford will impact international corporate governance?

NOTES

1. D. R. Dalton & C. M. Dalton, 2011, Integration of micro and macro studies in governance research: CEO duality, board composition, and financial performance, *Journal of Management*, 37: 404–411; B. W. Heineman, Jr., 2009, Redefining the CEO role. *BusinessWeek*, http://www.businessweek.com, April 16.

2. A. P. Cowen & J. J. Marcel, 2011, Damaged goods: Board decisions to dismiss reputationally compromised directors, *Academy of Management Journal*, 54: 509–527; I. Okhmatovskiy & R. J. David, 2011, Setting your own standards: Internal corporate governance codes as a response to institutional pressure, *Organization Science*, in press.

3. G. D. Bruton, I. Filatotchev, S. Chahine, & M. Wright, 2010, Governance, ownership structure, and performance of IPO firms: The impact of different types of private equity investors and institutional environments, *Strategic Management Journal*, 31: 491–509; M. A. Rutherford, A. K. Buchholtz, & J. A. Brown, 2007, Examining the relationships between monitoring and incentives in corporate governance, *Journal of Management Studies*, 44: 414–430.

4. A. T. Arikan & M. A. Schilling, 2011, Structure and governance in industrial districts: Implications for competitive advantage, *Journal of Management Studies*, 48: 772–803; D. R. Dalton, M. A. Hitt, S. T. Certo, & C. M. Dalton, 2008, The fundamental agency problem and its mitigation: Independence, equity and the market for corporate control, in J. P. Walsh and A. P. Brief (eds.), *The Academy of Management Annals*, New York: Lawrence Erlbaum Associates, 1–64; E. F. Fama & M. C. Jensen, 1983, Separation of ownership and control, *Journal of Law and Economics*, 26: 301–325.

5. R. V. Aguilera, 2011, Interorganizational governance and global strategy, *Global Strategy Journal*, 1: 90–95; J. S. Harrison, D. A. Bosse, & R. A. Phillips, 2010, Managing for stakeholders, stakeholder utility functions, and competitive advantage, *Strategic Management Journal*, 31: 58–74.

6. T. J. Boulton, S. B. Smart, & C. J. Zutter, 2010, IPO underpricing and international corporate governance, *Journal of International Business Studies*, 41: 206–222; X. Giroud & H. M. Mueller, 2010, Does corporate governance matter in competitive industries? *Journal of Financial Economics*, 95: 312–331.

7. W. Judge, 2010, Corporate governance mechanisms throughout the world, *Corporate Governance: An International Review*, 18: 159–160; R. E. Hoskisson, D. Yiu, & H. Kim, 2004, Corporate governance systems: Effects of capital and labor market congruency on corporate innovation and global competitiveness, *Journal of High Technology Management*, 15: 293–315.

8. A. Tan, 2011, Singapore proposes corporate governance changes to shield image, *Bloomberg Businessweek*, http://www.businessweek.com, June 14.

9. W. Kim, T. Sung, & S.-J. Wei, 2011, Does corporate governance risk at home affect investment choice abroad? *Journal of International Economics*, in press; X. Lour, C. N. Chung, & M. Sobczak, 2009, How do corporate governance model differences affect foreign direct investment in emerging economies? *Journal of International Business Studies*, 40: 444–467.

10. S. Boivie, D. Lange, M. L. McDonald, & J. D. Westphal, 2011, Me or we: The effects of CEO organizational identification on agency costs, *Academy of Management Journal*, 54: 551–576; M. A. Hitt, R. E. Hoskisson, R. A. Johnson, & D. D. Moesel, 1996, The market for corporate control and firm innovation, *Academy of Management Journal*, 45: 697–716.

11. G. E. Davis & T. A. Thompson, 1994, A social movement perspective on corporate control, *Administrative Science Quarterly*, 39: 141–173.

12. V. V. Acharya, S. C. Myers, & R. G. Rajan, 2011, The internal governance of firms, *Journal of Finance*, 66: 689–720; R. Bricker & N. Chandar, 2000, Where Berle and Means went wrong: A reassessment of capital market agency and financial reporting, *Accounting, Organizations, and Society*, 25: 529–554.

13. A. M. Colpan, T. Yoshikawa, T. Hikino, & E. G. Del Brio, 2011, Shareholder heterogeneity and conflicting goals: Strategic investments in the Japanese electronics industry, *Journal of Management Studies*, 48: 591–618; R. M. Wiseman & L. R. Gomez-Mejia, 1999, A behavioral agency model of managerial risk taking, *Academy of Management Review*, 23: 133–153.

14. A. Minichilli, G. Corbetta, & I. C. MacMillan, 2010, Top management teams in family-controlled companies: 'Familiness', 'faultlines', and their impact on financial performance, *Journal of Management Studies*, 47: 205–222; T. Zellweger, 2007, Time horizon, costs of equity capital, and generic investment strategies of firms, *Family Business Review*, 20(1): 1–15.

15. M. W. Peng & Y. Jiang, 2010, Institutions behind family ownership and control in large firms, *Journal of Management Studies*, 47: 253–273.

16. R. C. Anderson & D. M. Reeb, 2004, Board composition: Balancing family influence in S&P 500 firms, *Administrative Science Quarterly*, 49: 209–237.

17. E.-T. Chen & J. Nowland, 2010, Optimal board monitoring in family-owned companies: Evidence from Asia, *Corporate Governance: An International Review*, 18: 3–17; M. Santiago-Castro & C. J. Brown, 2007, Ownership structure and minority rights: A Latin American view, *Journal of Economics and Business*, 59: 430–442.

18. D. G. Sirmon, J.-L. Arregle, M. A. Hitt, & J. W. Webb, 2008, Strategic responses to the threat of imitation, *Entrepreneurship Theory and Practice*, 32: 979–998.

19. J. O. Okpara, 2011, Corporate governance in a developing economy: Barriers, issues, and implications for firms, *Corporate Governance*, 11: 184–199; G. Dushnitsky & Z. Shapira, 2010, Entrepreneurial finance meets organizational reality: Comparing investment practices and performance of corporate and independent venture capitalists, *Strategic Management Journal*, 31: 990–1017.

20. S. Machold, M. Huse, A. Minichilli, & M. Nordqvist, 2011, Board leadership and strategy involvement in small firms: A team production approach, *Corporate Governance: An International Review*, 19: 368–383.

21. T. Yoshikawa, A. A. Rasheed, & E. B. Del Brio, 2010, The impact of firm strategy and foreign ownership on executive bonus compensation in Japanese firms, *Journal of Business Research*, 63: 1254–1260; A. Mackey, 2008, The effects of CEOs on firm performance, *Strategic Management Journal*, 29: 1357–1367.

22. L. L. Lan & L. Heracleous, 2010, Rethinking agency theory: The view from law, *Academy of Management Review*, 35: 294–314; Dalton, Hitt, Certo, & Dalton, 2008, The fundamental agency problem and its mitigation: Independence, equity and the market for corporate control.

23. K. Vafai, 2010, Opportunism in organizations, *Journal of Law, Economics, and Organization*, 26: 158–181; O. E. Williamson, 1996, *The Mechanisms of Governance*, New York: Oxford University Press, 6.

24. F. Lumineau & D. Malhotra, 2011, Shadow of the contract: How contract structure shapes interfirm dispute resolution, *Strategic Management Journal*, 32: 532–555; B. E. Ashforth, D. A. Gioia, S. L. Robinnson, & L. K. Trevino, 2008, Reviewing organizational corruption, *Academy of Management Review*, 33: 670–684.

25. M. L. McDonald, P. Khanna, & J. D. Westphal, 2008, Getting them to think outside the circle: Corporate governance CEOs' external advice networks, and firm performance, *Academy of Management Journal*, 51: 453–475.

26. L. Weber & K. J. Mayer, 2011, Designing effective contracts: Exploring the influence of framing and expectations, *Academy of Management Review*, 36: 53–75; Fama, Agency problems and the theory of the firm.

27. E. Levitas, V. L. Barker, III, & M. Ahsan, 2011, Top manager ownership levels and incentive alignment in inventively active firms, *Journal of Strategy and Management*, 4: 116–135; P. Jiraporn, Y. S. Kim, W. N. Davidson, & M. Singh, 2006, Corporate governance, shareholder rights and firm diversification: An empirical analysis, *Journal of Banking & Finance*, 30: 947–963.

28. I. K. El Medi & S. Sebout, 2011, Corporate diversification and earnings management, *Review of Accounting and Finance*, 10: 176–196; P. David, J. P. O'Brien, T. Yoshikawa, &. A. Delios, 2010, Do shareholders or stakeholders appropriate the rents from corporate diversification? The influence of ownership structure, *Academy of Management Journal*, 53: 636–654; G. P. Baker & B. J. Hall, 2004, CEO incentives and firm size, *Journal of Labor Economics*, 22: 767–798.

29. S. W. Geiger & L. H. Cashen, 2007, Organizational size and CEO compensation: The moderating effect of diversification in downscoping organizations, *Journal of Managerial Issues*, 9: 233–252.

30. M. Larraza-Kintana, L. R. Gomez-Mejia, & R. M. Wiseman, 2011, Compensation framing and the risk-taking behavior of the CEO: Testing the influence of alternative reference points, *Management Research: The Journal of the Iberoamerican Academy of Management*, 9: 32–55; J. Li & Y. Tanng, 2010, CEO hubris and firm risk taking in China: The moderating role of managerial discretion, *Academy of Management Journal*, 53: 45–68; S. Rajgopal, T. Shevlin, & V. Zamaora, 2006, CEOs' outside employment opportunities and the lack of relative performance evaluation in compensation contracts, *Journal of Finance*, 61: 1813–1844.

31. J. Weber, 2007, The accidental CEO (well, not really): Kellogg needed a new boss, fast. Here's how it groomed insider David Mackay, *BusinessWeek*, April 23, 65.

32. 2011, Our Company, Kellogg homepage, http://www.kellogg.com, July 26.

33. M. F. Wiersema & H. P. Bowen, 2011, The relationship between international diversification and firm performance: Why it remains a puzzle, *Global Strategy Journal*, 1: 152–170; M. Ganco & R. Agarwal, 2009, Performance differentials between diversifying entrants and entrepreneurial start-ups: A complexity approach, *Academy of Management Review*, 34: 228–252.

34. M. S. Jensen, 1986, Agency costs of free cash flow, corporate finance, and takeovers, *American Economic Review*, 76: 323–329.

35. R. E. Meyer & M. A. Hollerer, 2010, Meaning structures in a contested issue field: A topographic map of shareholder value in Austria, *Academy of Management Journal*, 53: 1241–1262; A. V. Douglas, 2007, Managerial opportunism and proportional corporate payout policies, *Managerial Finance*, 33(1): 26–42; M. Jensen & E. Zajac, 2004, Corporate elites and corporate strategy: How demographic preferences and structural position shape the scope of the firm, *Strategic Management Journal*, 25: 507–524.

36. W. Wagner, 2010, Diversification at financial institutions and systemic crises, *Journal of Financial Intermediation*, 19: 373–386; Y. Zhang & J. Gimeno, 2010, Earnings pressure and competitive behavior: Evidence from the U.S. electricity industry, *Academy of Management Journal*, 53: 743–768.

37. J. Azar, 2011, Diversification, shareholder value maximization, and competition: A trilemma? Working paper, Princeton University, March 20; M. V. S. Kumar, 2009, The relationship between product and international diversification: The effects of short-run constraints and endogeneity, *Strategic Management Journal*, 30: 99–116.

38. A. Milidonis & K. Stathopoulos, 2011, Managerial incentives, conservatism, and debt, Working paper, http://ssrn.com/abstract=1879186, July 5; D. D. Bergh, R. A. Johnson, & R.-L. Dewitt, 2008, Restructuring through spin-off or sell-off: Transforming information asymmetries into financial gain, *Strategic Management Journal*, 29: 133–148.

39. R. Duchin, 2010, Cash holdings and corporate diversification, *Journal of Finance*, 65: 955–992; E. Rawley, 2010, Diversification, coordination costs, and organizational rigidity: Evidence from microdata, *Strategic Management Journal*, 31: 873–891; T. K. Berry, J. M. Bizjak, M. L. Lemmon, & L. Naveen, 2006, Organizational complexity and CEO labor markets: Evidence from diversified firms, *Journal of Corporate Finance*, 12: 797–817.

40. M. Hossain, S. Mitra, Z. Rezaee, & B. Sarath, 2011, Corporate governance and earnings management in the pre- and post-Sarbanes-Oxley act regimes: Evidence from implicated option backdating firms, *Journal of Accounting Auditing & Finance*, 28: 279–315; V. Chhaochharia & Y. Grinstein, 2007, Corporate governance and firm value: The impact of the 2002 governance rules, *Journal of Finance*, 62: 1789–1825.

41. Z. Singer & H. You, 2011, The effect of Section 404 of the Sarbanes-Oxley act on earnings quality, *Journal of Accounting and Finance*, 26: 556–589; D. Reilly, 2006, Checks on internal controls pay off, *Wall Street Journal*, August 10, C3.

42. 2010, The Dodd-Frank Act: Financial reform update index, Faegre & Benson, http://www.faegre.com, September 7.

43. B. Appelmaum, 2011, Dodd-Frank supporters clash with currency chief, *The New York Times*, http://www.nytimes.com, July 23.

44. M. Goranova, R. Dhanwadkar, & P. Brandes, 2010, Owners on both sides of the deal: Mergers and acquisitions and overlapping institutional ownership, *Strategic Management Journal*, 31: 1114–1135; F. Navissi & V. Naiker, 2006, Institutional ownership and corporate value, *Managerial Finance*, 32: 247–256.

45. B. L. Connelly, R. E. Hoskisson, L. Tihanyi, & S. T. Certo, 2010, Ownership as a form of corporate governance, *Journal of Management Studies*, 47: 1561–1589; M. Singh, I. Mathur, & K. C. Gleason, 2004, Governance and performance implications of diversification strategies: Evidence from large U.S. firms, *Financial Review*, 39: 489–526.

46. J. Wu, D. Xu, & P. H. Phan, 2011, The effects of ownership concentration and corporate debt on corporate divestitures in Chinese listed firms, *Asia Pacific Journal of Management*, 28: 95–114; G. Iannotta, G. Nocera, & A. Sironi, 2007, Ownership structure, risk and performance in the European banking industry, *Journal of Banking & Finance*, 31: 2127–2149.

47. M. Fackler, 2008, South Korea faces question of corporate control, *The New York Times*, http://nytimescom, April 24.

48. D. Miller, I. Le Breton-Miller, & R. H. Lester, 2011, Family and lone founder ownership and strategic behavior: Social context, identity, and institutional logics, *Journal of Management Studies*, 48: 1–25; B. Villalonga & R. Amit, 2006, How do family ownership, control and management affect firm value? *Journal of Financial Economics*, 80: 385–417.

49. A. Berle & G. Means, 1932, *The Modern Corporation and Private Property*, New York: Macmillan.

50. R. A. Johnson, K. Schnatterly, S. G. Johnson, & S.-C. Chiu, 2010, Institutional investors and institutional environment: A comparative analysis and review, *Journal of Management Studies*, 47: 1590–1613; M. Gietzmann, 2006, Disclosure of timely and forward-looking statements and strategic management of major institutional ownership, *Long Range Planning*, 39: 409–427.

51. 2011, Urge investors to vote all their proxies, Investment News, http://www.investmentnews.com, May 22.

52. D. Marchick, 2011, Testimony of David Marchick—The power of pensions: Building a strong middle class and a strong economy, The Carlyle Group homepage, http://www.carlyle.com, July 12.

53. J. Chou, L. Ng, V. Sibilkov, & Q. Wang, 2011, Product market competition and corporate governance, *Review of Development Finance*, 1: 114–130; S. D. Chowdhury & E. Z. Wang, 2009, Institutional activism types and CEO compensation: A time-series analysis of

large Canadian corporations, *Journal of Management*, 35: 5–36; D. K. Datta & P. Herrmann, 2009, Ownership structure and CEO compensation: Implications for the choice of foreign market entry modes, *Journal of International Business Studies*, 40: 321–338.

54. Y. Ertimur, F. Ferri, & S. R. Stubben, 2010, Board of directors' responsiveness to shareholders: Evidence from shareholder proposals, *Journal of Corporate Finance*, 16: 53–72; T. W. Briggs, 2007, Corporate governance and the new hedge fund activism: An empirical analysis, *Journal of Corporation Law*, 32: 681–723.

55. D. Brewster, 2009, U.S. investors get to nominate boards, *Financial Times*, http://www.ft.com, May 20.

56. 2011, Largest public pension fund thrives after crisis, National Public Radio, http://www.npr.org, May 6.

57. 2010, CalPERS adopts new plan for engaging underperforming portfolio companies, CalPERS homepage, http://www.calpers.ca.gov, November 15.

58. Ibid.

59. M. Hadani, M. Goranova, & R. Khan, 2011, Institutional investors, shareholder activism, and earnings management, *Journal of Business Research*, in press; S. M. Jacoby, 2007, Principles and agents: CalPERS and corporate governance in Japan, *Corporate Governance*, 15: 5–15; L. Tihanyi, R. A. Johnson, R. E. Hoskisson, & M. A. Hitt, 2003, Institutional ownership differences and international diversification: The effects of boards of directors and technological opportunity, *Academy of Management Journal*, 46: 195–211.

60. O. Faleye, R. Hoitash, & U. Hoitash, 2011, The costs of intense board monitoring, *Journal of Financial Economics*, 101: 160–181; L. Bonazzi & S. M. N. Islam, 2007, Agency theory and corporate governance: A study of the effectiveness of boards in their monitoring of the CEO, *Journal of Modeling in Management*, 2(1): 7–23.

61. C. M. Dalton & D. R. Dalton 2006, Corporate governance best practices: The proof is in the process, *Journal of Business Strategy*, 27(4): 5–7; R. V. Aguilera, 2005, Corporate governance and director accountability: An institutional comparative perspective, *British Journal of Management*, 16(S1): S39–S53.

62. T. Dalziel, R. J. Gentry & M. Bowerman, 2011, An integrated agency-resource dependence view of the influence of directors' human and relational capital on firms' R&D spending, *Journal of Management Studies*, 48: 1217–1242; R. H. Lester, A. Hillman, A. Zardkoohi, & A. A. Cannella, 2008, Former government officials as outside directors: The role of human and social capital, *Academy of Management Journal*, 51: 999–1013; M. L. McDonald, J. D. Westphal, & M. E. Graebner, 2008, What do they know? The effects of outside director acquisition experience on firm acquisition

performance, *Strategic Management Journal*, 29: 1155–1177.

63. O. Faleye, 2011, CEO directors, executive incentives, and corporate strategic initiatives, *Journal of Financial Research*, 34: 241–277; C. S. Tuggle, D. G. Sirmon, C. R. Reutzel, & L. Bierman, 2010, Commanding board of director attention: Investigating how organizational performance and CEO duality affect board members' attention to monitoring, *Strategic Management Journal*, 31: 946–968.

64. S. Chahine, I. Filatotchev, & S. A. Zahra, 2011, Building perceived quality of founder-involved IPO firms: Founders' effects on board selection and stock market performance, *Entrepreneurship Theory and Practice*, 35: 319–335; Y. Ertimur, F. Ferri, & S. R. Stubben, 2010, Board of directors' responsiveness to shareholders: Evidence from shareholder proposals, *Journal of Corporate Finance*, 16: 53–72.

65. M. A. Valenti, R. Luce, & C. Mayfield, 2011, The effects of firm performance on corporate governance, *Management Research Review*, 34: 266–283; D. Reeb & A. Upadhyay, 2010, Subordinate board structures, *Journal of Corporate Finance*, 16: 469–486.

66. A. K. Gore, S. Matsunaga, & P. C Yeung, 2011, The role of technical expertise in firm governance structure: Evidence from chief financial officer contractual incentives, *Strategic Management Journal*, 32: 771–786; R. Duchin, J. G. Matsusaka, & O. Ozbas, 2010, *Journal of Financial Economics*, 96: 195–214.

67. R. C. Anderson, D. M. Reeb, A. Upadhyay, & W. Zhao, 2011, The economics of director heterogeneity, *Financial Management*, 40: 5–38; S. K. Lee & L. R. Carlson, 2007, The changing board of directors: Board independence in S&P 500 firms, *Journal of Organizational Culture, Communication and Conflict*, 11(1): 31–41.

68. S. Crainer, 2011, Changing direction: One person can make a difference, *Business Strategy Review*, 22: 10–16; M. Z. Islam, 2011, Board-CEO-chair relationship, Working paper, http://ssrn.com/abstract=1861386; R. C. Pozen, 2006, Before you split that CEO/chair, *Harvard Business Review* 84(4): 26–28.

69. M. Huse, R. E. Hoskisson, A. Zattoni, & R. Vigano, 2011, New perspectives on board research: Changing the research agenda, *Journal of Management and Governance*, 15(1): 5–28; M. Kroll, B. A. Walters, & P. Wright, 2008, Board vigilance, director experience and corporate outcomes, *Strategic Management Journal*, 29: 363–382.

70. A. Agrawal & M. A. Chen, 2011, Boardroom brawls: An empirical analysis of disputes involving directors, http://ssrn.com/abstracts=1362143; J. Roberts, T. McNulty, & P. Stiles, 2005, Beyond agency conceptions of the work of

the non-executive director: Creating accountability in the boardroom, *British Journal of Management*, 16(S1): S5–S26.

71. S. Muthusamy, P. A. Bobinski, & D. Jawahar, 2011, Toward a strategic role for employees in corporate governance, *Strategic Change*, 20: 127–138; Y. Zhang & N. Rajagopalan, 2010, Once an outsider, always an outsider? CEO origin, strategic change, and firm performance *Strategic Management Journal*, 31: 334–346.

72. B. Baysinger & R. E. Hoskisson, 1990, The composition of boards of directors and strategic control: Effects on corporate strategy, *Academy of Management Review*, 15: 72–87.

73. G. A. Ballinger & J. J. Marcel, 2010, The use of an interim CEO during succession episodes and firm performance, *Strategic Management Journal*, 31: 262–283; Y. Zhang, 2008, Information asymmetry and the dismissal of newly appointed CEOs: An empirical investigation, *Strategic Management Journal*, 29: 859–872.

74. C. Shropshire, 2010, The role of the interlocking director and board receptivity in the diffusion of practices, *Academy of Management Review*, 35: 246–264; E. E. Lawler III & D. L. Finegold, 2005, The changing face of corporate boards, *MIT Sloan Management Review*, 46(2): 67–70.

75. D. Carey, J. J. Keller, & M. Patsalos-Fox, 2010, How to choose the right nonexecutive board leader, *McKinsey Quarterly*, May.

76. D. Northcott & J. Smith, 2011, Managing performance at the top: A balanced scorecard for boards of directors, *Journal of Accounting & Organizational Change*, 7: 33–56; L. Erakovic & J. Overall, 2010, Opening the 'black box': Challenging traditional governance theorems, *Journal of Management & Organization*, 16: 250–265.

77. I. Okhmatovskiy & R. J. David, 2011, Setting your own standards: Internal corporate governance codes as a response to institutional pressure, *Organization Science*, 1–22; J. L. Koors, 2006, Director pay: A work in progress, *The Corporate Governance Advisor*, 14(5): 14–31.

78. Y. Deutsch, T. Keil, & T. Laamanen, 2007, Decision making in acquisitions: The effect of outside directors' compensation on acquisition patterns, *Journal of Management*, 33: 30–56.

79. F. A. Gul, B. Srinidhi, & A. C. Ng, 2011, Does board gender diversity improve the informativeness of stock prices? *Journal of Accounting and Economics*, 51: 314–338; D. A. Matsa & A. R. Miller, 2011, Chipping at the glass ceiling: Gender spillovers in corporate leadership, http://ssrn.com/abstract=1709462; A. J. Hillman, C. Shropshire, & A. A. Cannella, Jr., 2007, Organizational predictors of women on corporate boards, *Academy of Management Journal*, 50: 941–952.

80. M. J. Conyon, J. E. Core, & W. R. Guay, 2011, Are U.S. CEOs paid more than U.K. CEOs? Inferences from risk-adjusted pay, *Review of Financial Studies*, 24: 402–438; S. N. Kaplan, 2008, Are U.S. CEOs overpaid? *Academy of Management Perspectives*, 22(2): 5–20.

81. E. A. Fong, V. F. Misangyi, Jr., & H. L. Tosi, 2010, The effect of CEO pay deviations on CEO withdrawal, firm size, and firm profits, *Strategic Management Journal*, 31: 629–651; J. P. Walsh, 2009, Are U.S. CEOs overpaid? A partial response to Kaplan, *Academy of Management Perspectives*, 23(1): 73–75; J. P. Walsh, 2008, CEO compensation and the responsibilities of the business scholar to society, *Academy of Management Perspectives*, 22(3): 26–33.

82. M. A. Geletkanycz & B. K. Boyd, 2011, CEO outside directorships and firm performance: A reconciliation of agency and embeddedness views, *Academy of Management Journal*, 54: 335–352; K. Rehbein, 2007, Explaining CEO compensation: How do talent, governance, and markets fit in? *Academy of Management Perspectives*, 21(1): 75–77; J. S. Miller, R. M. Wiseman, & L. R. Gomez-Mejia, 2002, The fit between CEO compensation design and firm risk, *Academy of Management Journal*, 45: 745–756.

83. D. Souder & J. M. Shaver, 2010, Constraints and incentives for making long horizon corporate investments, *Strategic Management Journal*, 31: 1316–1336; M. Larraza-Kintana, R. M. Wiseman, L. R. Gomez-Mejia, & T. M. Welborne, 2007, Disentangling compensation and employment risks using the behavioral agency model, *Strategic Management Journal*, 28: 1001–1019.

84. E. A. Fong, 2010, Relative CEO underpayment and CEO behavior towards R&D spending, *Journal of Management Studies*, 47: 1095–1122; X. Zhang, K. M. Bartol, K. G. Smith, M. D. Pfarrer, & D. M. Khanin, 2008, CEOs on the edge: Earnings manipulations and stock-based incentive misalignment, *Academy of Management Journal*, 51: 241–258; J. P. O'Connor, R. L. Priem, J. E. Coombs, & K. M. Gilley, 2006, Do CEO stock options prevent or promote fraudulent financial reporting? *Academy of Management Journal*, 49: 483–500.

85. Y. Du, M. Deloof, & A Jorissen, 2011, Active boards of directors in foreign subsidiaries, *Corporate Governance: An International Review*, 19: 153–168; J. J. Reuer, E. Klijn, F. A. J. van den Bosch, & H. W. Volberda, 2011, Bringing corporate governance to international joint ventures, *Global Strategy Journal*, 1: 54–66; K. Roth & S. O'Donnell, 1996, Foreign subsidiary compensation: An agency theory perspective, *Academy of Management Journal*, 39: 678–703.

86. B. Balasubramanian, B. S. Black, & V. Khanna, 2010, The relation between firm-level corporate governance and market value: A study of India, University of Michigan working paper series; A. Ghosh, 2006, Determination of executive compensation in an emerging economy: Evidence from India, *Emerging Markets, Finance & Trade*, 42(3): 66–90.

87. M. Ederhof, 2011, Incentive compensation and promotion-based incentives of mid-level managers: Evidence from a multinational corporation, *The Accounting Review*, 86: 131–154; C. L. Staples, 2007, Board globalization in the world's largest TNCs 1993–2005, *Corporate Governance*, 15: 311–332.

88. Y. Deutsch, T. Keil, & T. Laamanen, 2011, A dual agency view of board compensation: The joint effects of outside director and CEO stock options on firm risk, *Strategic Management Journal*, 32: 212–227; P. Kalyta, 2009, Compensation transparency and managerial opportunism: A study of supplemental retirement plans, *Strategic Management Journal*, 30: 405–423.

89. L. K. Meulbroek, 2001, The efficiency of equity-linked compensation: Understanding the full cost of awarding executive stock options, *Financial Management*, 30(2): 5–44.

90. Z. Dong, C. Wang, & F. Xie, 2010, Do executive stock options induce excessive risk taking? *Journal of Banking & Finance*, 34: 2518–2529; C. E. Devers, R. M. Wiseman, & R. M. Holmes, Jr., 2007, The effects of endowment and loss aversion in managerial stock option valuation, *Academy of Management Journal*, 50: 191–208.

91. D. Anginer, M. P. Narayanan, C. A. Schipani, & H. N. Seyhun, 2011, Should size matter when regulating firms? Implications from backdating of executive options, Ross School of Business working paper; T. G. Pollock, H. M. Fischer, & J. B. Wade, 2002, The role of politics in reprising executive options, *Academy of Management Journal*, 45: 1172–1182.

92. P. Berrone & L. R. Gomez-Mejia, 2009, Environmental performance and executive compensation: An integrated agency-institutional perspective, *Academy of Management Journal*, 52: 103–126.

93. V. V. Acharya, S. C. Myers, & R. G. Rajan, 2011, The internal governance of firms, *Journal of Finance*, 66: 689–720; R. Sinha, 2006, Regulation: The market for corporate control and corporate governance, *Global Finance Journal*, 16: 264–282.

94. T. Yoshikawa & A. A. Rasheed, 2010, Family control and ownership monitoring in family-controlled firms in Japan, *Journal of Management Studies*, 47: 274–295; D. N. Iyer & K. D. Miller, 2008, Performance feedback, slack, and the timing of acquisitions, *Academy of Management Journal*, 51: 808–822; R. W. Masulis, C. Wang, & F. Xie, 2007, Corporate governance and acquirer returns, *Journal of Finance*, 62: 1851–1889.

95. E. M. Fich, J. Cai, & A. L. Tran, 2011, Stock option grants to target CEOs during private merger negotiations, *Journal of Financial Economics*, 101: 413–430;

J. A. Krug & W. Shill, 2008, The big exit: Executive churn in the wake of M&As, *Journal of Business Strategy*, 29(4): 15–21.

96. 2011, What is a hedge fund? Magnum Funds, http://www.magnum.com, July 28.

97. N. M. Boyson & R. M. Mooradian, 2011, Corporate governance and hedge fund activism, *Review of Derivatives Research*, 169–204; L. A. Bebchuk & M. S. Weisbach, 2010, The state of corporate governance research, *Review of Financial Studies*, 23: 939–961; T. W. Briggs, 2007, Corporate governance and a new hedge fund activism, *Empirical Analysis*, 32: 681–723.

98. S. Bainbridge, 2011, Hedge funds as activist investors, *ProfessorBainbridge.com*, http://www.professorbainbridge.com, March 21.

99. R. Greenwood, 2007, The hedge fund as activist, HBR Working knowledge, http://www.hbrworkingknowledge.com, August 22.

100. E. Byron, G. Zuckerman, & G. Chon, 2011, Icahn raises his bid for Clorox to $80 a share, *Wall Street Journal*, http://www.wsj.com, July 21; P. Ziobro, 2011, Clorox board rejects Icahn bid, *Wall Street Journal*, http://www.wsj.com, July 26.

101. M. L. Humphery-Jenner & R. G. Powell, 2011, Firm size takeover profitability, and the effectiveness of the market for corporate control: Does the absence of anti-takeover provisions make a difference? *Journal of Corporate Finance*, 17: 418–437; K. Ruckman, 2009, Technology sourcing acquisitions: What they mean for innovation potential, *Journal of Strategy and Management*, 2: 56–75.

102. J. P. Walsh & R. Kosnik, 1993, Corporate raiders and their disciplinary role in the market for corporate control, *Academy of Management Journal*, 36: 671–700.

103. R. Bauer, P. Eichholtz, & N. Kok, 2010, Corporate governance and performance: The REIT effect, *Real Estate Economics*, 38: 1–29; J. Haleblian, C. E. Devers, G. McNamara, M. A. Carpenter, & R. B. Davison, 2009, Taking stock of what we know about mergers and acquisitions: A review and research agenda, *Journal of Management*, 35: 469–502.

104. 2011, Hostile takeover, *Investopedia*, http://www.investopedia.com, July 28.

105. P. Jiraporn & Y. Liu, 2011, Staggered boards, accounting discretion and firm value, *Applied Financial Economics*, 21: 271–285; O. Faleye, 2007, Classified boards, firm value, and managerial entrenchment, *Journal of Financial Economics*, 83: 501–529.

106. T. Sokoly, 2011, The effects of antitakeover provisions on acquisition targets, *Journal of Corporate Finance*, 17: 612–627; M. Martynova & L. Renneboog, 2010, A corporate governance index: Convergence and diversity of national corporate governance regulations, http://ssrn.com/abstract=1557627; 2007, Leaders: Pay slips; management in Europe, *Economist*, June 23, 14.

107. J. A. Pearce II & R. B. Robinson, Jr., 2004, Hostile takeover defenses that maximize

shareholder wealth, *Business Horizons* 47(5): 15–24.

108. A. Kacperzyk, 2009, With greater power comes greater responsibility? Takeover protection and corporate attention to stakeholders, *Strategic Management Journal*, 30: 261–285.

109. I. Haxhi & H. Ees, 2010, Explaining diversity in the worldwide diffusion of codes of good governance, *Journal of International Business Studies*, 41: 710–726; P. Witt, 2004, The competition of international corporate governance systems—a German perspective, *Management International Review*, 44: 309–333.

110. J. Block & F. Spiegel, 2011, Family firms and regional innovation activity: Evidence from the German Mittelstand, http://ssrn .com/abstract=1745362.

111. S. K. Bhaumik & A. Gregoriou, 2010, 'Family' ownership, tunneling and earnings management: A review of the literature, *Journal of Economic Surveys*, 24: 705–730; A. Tuschke & W. G. Sanders, 2003, Antecedents and consequences of corporate governance reform: The case of Germany, *Strategic Management Journal*, 24: 631–649; J. Edwards & M. Nibler, 2000, Corporate governance in Germany: The role of banks and ownership concentration, *Economic Policy*, 31: 237–268.

112. D. Hillier, J. Pinadado, V. de Queiroz, & C. de la Torre, 2010, The impact of country-level corporate governance on research and development, *Journal of International Business Studies*, 42: 76–98; P. C. Fiss, 2006, Social influence effects and managerial compensation evidence from Germany, *Strategic Management Journal*, 27: 1013–1031.

113. J. T. Addison & C. Schnabel, 2011, Worker directors: A German product that did not export? *Industrial Relations: A Journal of Economy and Society*, 50: 354–374; P. C. Fiss & E. J. Zajac, 2004, The diffusion of ideas over contested terrain: The (non)adoption of a shareholder value orientation among German firms, *Administrative Science Quarterly*, 49: 501–534.

114. A. Chizema, 2010, Early and late adoption of American-style executive pay in Germany: Governance and institutions, *Journal of World Business*, 45: 9–18; W. G. Sanders & A. C. Tuschke, 2007, The adoption of the institutionally contested organizational practices: The emergence of stock option pay in Germany, *Academy of Management Journal*, 50: 33–56.

115. J. P. Charkha, 1994, *Keeping Good Companies: A Study of Corporate Governance in Five Countries*, New York: Oxford University Press, 70.

116. 2010, Japan: Principles of corporate governance, *eStandardsForum*, http://www.estandardsforum.org, May.

117. D. R. Adhikari & K. Hirasawa, 2010, Emerging scenarios of Japanese corporate management, *Asia-Pacific Journal of Business Administration*, 2: 114–132;

M. A. Hitt, H. Lee, & E. Yucel, 2002, The importance of social capital to the management of multinational enterprises: Relational networks among Asian and Western firms, *Asia Pacific Journal of Management*, 19: 353–372.

118. W. P. Wan, D. W. Yiu, R. E. Hoskisson, & H. Kim, 2008, The performance implications of relationship banking during macroeconomic expansion and contraction: A study of Japanese banks' social relationships and overseas expansion, *Journal of International Business Studies*, 39: 406–427.

119. P. M. Lee & H. M. O'Neill, 2003, Ownership structures and R&D investments of U.S. and Japanese firms: Agency and stewardship perspectives, *Academy of Management Journal*, 46: 212–225.

120. X. Wu & J. Yao, 2011, Understanding the rise and decline of the Japanese main bank system: The changing effects of bank rent extraction, *Journal of Banking & Finance*, in press; I. S. Dinc, 2006, Monitoring the monitors: The corporate governance in Japanese banks and their real estate lending in the 1980s, *Journal of Business*, 79: 3057–3081.

121. K. Kubo & T. Saito, 2011, The effect of mergers on employment and wages: Evidence from Japan, *Journal of the Japanese and International Economics*, in press; N. Isagawa, 2007, A theory of unwinding of cross-shareholding under managerial entrenchment, *Journal of Financial Research*, 30: 163–179.

122. J. M. Ramseyer, M. Nakazato, & E. B. Rasmusen, 2009, Public and private firm compensation: Evidence from Japanese tax returns, *Harvard Law and Economics* discussion paper, February 1.

123. J. Yang, J. Chi, & M. Young, 2011, A review of corporate governance in China, *Asian-Pacific Economic Literature*, 25: 15–28.

124. H. Berkman, R. A. Cole, & L. J. Fu, 2010, Political connections and minority-shareholder protection: Evidence from securities-market regulation in China, *Journal of Financial and Quantitative Analysis*, 45: 1391–1417; S. R. Miller, D. Li, E. Eden, & M. A. Hitt, 2008, Insider trading and the valuation of international strategic alliances in emerging stock markets, *Journal of International Business Studies*, 39: 102–117.

125. J. Chi, Q. Sun, & M. Young, 2011, Performance and characteristics of acquiring firms in the Chinese stock markets, *Emerging Markets Review*, 12: 152–170; Y.-L. Cheung, P. Jiang, P. Limpaphayom, & T. Lu, 2010, Corporate governance in China: A step forward, *European Financial Management*, 16: 94–123; H. Zou & M. B. Adams, 2008, Corporate ownership, equity risk and returns in the People's Republic in China, *Journal of International Business Studies*, 39:1149–1168.

126. S. Globerman, M. W. Peng, & D. M. Shapiro, 2011, Corporate governance and Asian companies, *Asia Pacific Journal of Management*, 28: 1–14; Y. Su, D. Xu, & P. H. Phan, 2008, Principal-principal conflict in the governance of the Chinese public corporation, *Management and Organization Review*, 4: 17–38.

127. 2009, China YTC International strengthens corporate governance with establishment of audit committee and appointments of three new independent directors, YTI homepage, http://www.yctgroup.com.

128. P. Adithipyangkul, I. Alon, & T. Zhang, 2011, Executive perks: Compensation and corporate performance in China, *Asia Pacific Journal of Management*, 28: 401–425; T. Buck, X. Lui, & R. Skovoroda, 2008, Top executives' pay and firm performance in China, *Journal of International Business Studies*, 39: 833–850.

129. 2011, Allegations against Chinese cos to continue, affect funding—Fitch, *Reuters*, http://www.reuters.com, July 17.

130. S. Muthusamy, P. A. Bobinski, & D. Jawahar, 2011, Toward a strategic role for employees in corporate governance, *Strategic Change*, 20: 127–138; T. Tse, 2011, Shareholder and stakeholder theory: After the financial crisis, *Qualitative Research in Financial Markets*, 3(1): 51–63; C. Shropshire & A. J. Hillman, 2007, A longitudinal study of significant change in stakeholder management, *Business & Society*, 46(1): 63–87.

131. R. A. G. Monks & N. Minow, 2011, *Corporate governance*, 5th ed., New York: John Wiley & Sons.

132. S. P. Deshpande, J. Joseph, & X. Shu, 2011, Ethical climate and managerial success in China, *Journal of Business Ethics*, 99: 527–534; D. L. Gold & J. W. Dienhart, 2007, Business ethics in the corporate governance era: Domestic and international trends in transparency, regulation, and corporate governance, *Business and Society Review*, 112: 163–170.

133. M. Srivastava, 2011, India's powerful can't escape jail, *Bloomberg Businessweek*, June 13–19, 13–14.

134. A. P. Cowan & J. J. Marcel, 2011, Damaged goods: Board decisions to dismiss reputationally compromised directors, *Academy of Management Journal*, 54: 509–527; J. R. Knapp, T. Dalziel, & M. W. Lewis, 2011, Governing top managers: Board control, social categorization, and their unintended influence on discretionary behaviors, *Corporate Governance: An International Review* 19: 295–310; R. V. Aguilera, D. E. Rupp, C. A. Williams, & J. Ganapathi, 2007, Putting the S back in corporate social responsibility: A multilevel theory of social change in organizations, *Academy of Management Review*, 32: 836–863.

135. 2011, 2011 corporate governance awards, *World Finance*, http://www.worldfinance .com, March 14.

CHAPTER 11

Organizational Structure and Controls

Studying this chapter should provide you with the strategic management knowledge needed to:

1. Define organizational structure and controls and discuss the difference between strategic and financial controls.

2. Describe the relationship between strategy and structure.

3. Discuss the functional structures used to implement business-level strategies.

4. Explain the use of three versions of the multidivisional (M-form) structure to implement different diversification strategies.

5. Discuss the organizational structures used to implement three international strategies.

6. Define strategic networks and discuss how strategic center firms implement such networks at the business, corporate, and international levels.

© Ryan McVay/Getty Images

ANOTHER ONE BITES THE DUST: BORDERS DECLARES BANKRUPTCY

Continuing the saga from Chapter 1, Borders, one of the original superstore chains, declared bankruptcy in 2011 with debts of $1.293 billion and assets of $1.275 billion. Borders was founded in 1971 in Ann Arbor, Michigan. It had an innovative inventory system, made certain that employees were knowledgeable about books, and offered espresso (before Starbucks became popular). Its inventory system was popular and the Borders brothers licensed it and simultaneously began to expand the Borders' store locations. In 1991 they sold the relatively small bookstore chain and inventory system to Kmart. At the time, Borders was performing well but Kmart was just beginning its decline. This led to Borders being spun off with an initial public offering (IPO) in 1995. This change worked for a while as Borders started to expand and take market share from independent book retailers.

However, Borders began making mistakes. Partly in reaction to Amazon.com's success in selling books in the Internet, Borders launched a major growth initiative into international markets. This diversification reduced Borders' focus on the largest and most lucrative book retailing market in the United States. It seemed unable to structure its operations in ways that allowed it to manage the different businesses in each country and market effectively. Eventually, the international strategy failed and its stores in the United States became vulnerable to competition because they no longer were operated as they were at one time. In fact, one analyst described Borders as changing "from a place that celebrated books to a place that warehoused them."

It also seemed that Borders developed an insular management structure that was impervious to the changes in the market. For example, when competitors such as Barnes & Noble developed the capability to sell online, Borders signed an agreement with Amazon

This London Borders Bookstore shuttered its doors in 2011.

to handle its Internet sales. This was a boon to Amazon but a disaster for Borders because it sent customers and business to a major competitor. It was obviously a way to save money because of the required investment in technology and human capital with that specialized knowledge, but it was a very poor decision. The lack of technological expertise in Borders was astounding. Upon a visit to a Borders store in Madison, Wisconsin, one writer was surprised to learn that it had no Internet connection (and this was in 2007). All external communications had to be channeled through the company headquarters in Ann Arbor. This suggests that the firm was highly centralized, which largely disallows flexibility at the local level to respond to unique needs in the community. The lack of technology expertise was evident in Borders' lack of adaptation to the market's demand for e-books. It was the last major book retailer to enter this market segment and then sold e-book readers developed by others (e.g., Sony's e-book reader).

Because of the centralized and insular structure leading to further poor strategic decisions, Borders ended up with a large number of unprofitable stores, perhaps as many as 275 out of a little more than 600 stores. It had already closed 264 stores in 2008–2010. It had significant debt still on the books from its failed foray into international markets. In an attempt to increase its stock price to help shareholders and encourage investors, top executives decided to borrow money and use it to buy back stock. However, this increased debt to exceptionally high levels. In 1998, Borders stock price reached its highest level at $41.75. In March 2011 after declaring bankruptcy, its stock price was 23 cents per share.

Learn more about Amazon.com's success in online sales.

www.cengagebrain .com

Borders had incredibly bad management, especially at the higher levels of the firm. In addition, it was unable to correct these problems because of an inadequate structure and a focus on financial engineering (financial controls), both of which crippled its ability to respond effectively to changes in the marketplace and to implement its strategies (e.g., international strategy) effectively.

Sources: B. Rochelle, 2011, Lehman, Borders, Blockbuster, Innkeepers, Javo: Bankruptcy, Bloomberg *Business-week*, http://www.businessweek.com, May 2; C. Caldwell, 2011, A fate written in the stores, *Financial Times*, http://www.ft.com, March 4; I. Sidhu, 2011, Limit your options, limit your horizons: A lesson from Borders' bankruptcy, *Forbes*, http://www.forbes.com, February 18; 2011, Borders bankruptcy: What went wrong, *Wall Street Journal*, http://www.wsj.com, February 16; M. Frazier, 2011, The three lessons of the Borders bankruptcy, *Forbes*, http://www.forbes.com, February 2; J. Raznick, 2011, In-depth analysis: Can Borders survive? *Forbes*, http://www.forbes.com, January 27; P. Osnos, 2011, What went wrong at Borders? *The Atlantic*, http://www .theatlantic.com, January 11, 2011.

As we explained in Chapter 4, all firms use one or more business-level strategies. In Chapters 6–9, we discuss other strategies firms may choose to use (corporate-level, international, and cooperative). After they are selected, strategies must be implemented effectively to make them work. Organizational structure and controls, this chapter's topic, provide the framework within which strategies are implemented and used in both for-profit organizations and not-for-profit agencies.[1] However, as we explain, separate structures and controls are required to successfully implement different strategies. In all organizations, top-level managers have the final responsibility for ensuring that the firm has matched each of its strategies with the appropriate organizational structure and that both change when necessary. Thus, the CEO of Borders (actually there were several during the years of its decline) is responsible for changing its organizational structure to effectively implement its business- or corporate-level strategy. The match or degree of fit between strategy and structure influences the firm's attempts to earn above-average returns.[2] Thus, the ability to select an appropriate strategy and match it with the appropriate structure is an important characteristic of effective strategic leadership.[3] Borders employed some ineffective (i.e., wrong) strategies and also did a very poor job of implementing the strategies chosen. First, its decision to enter international markets likely failed because of poor implementation and management of the international operations. The wrong strategies were employed regarding the use of technologies in sales and type of material provided. Having a centralized structure in which Internet connections were disallowed for individual stores (as late as 2007), requiring instead that all communications flow through the central office, was an obvious manifestation of Borders' problems. Strategic management scholar Richard Rumelt sums up the problems of Borders in his statement that "… weakly managed organizations tend to become less organized and focused."[4]

This chapter opens with an introduction to organizational structure and controls. We then provide more details about the need for the firm's strategy and structure to be properly matched. Affecting firms' efforts to match strategy and structure is their influence on each other.[5] As we discuss, strategy has a more important influence on structure, although once in place, structure influences strategy.[6] Next, we describe the relationship between growth and structural change successful firms experience. We then discuss the different organizational structures firms use to implement separate business-level, corporate-level, international, and cooperative strategies. A series of figures highlights the different structures firms match with strategies. Across time and based on their experiences, organizations, especially large and complex ones, customize these general structures to meet their unique needs.[7] Typically, the firm tries to form a structure that is complex enough to facilitate use of its strategies but simple enough for all parties to understand and implement.[8] When strategies become more diversified, a firm must adjust its structure to deal with the increased complexity.

Organizational Structure and Controls

Research shows that organizational structure and the controls that are a part of the structure affect firm performance.[9] In particular, evidence suggests that performance declines when the firm's strategy is not matched with the most appropriate structure and controls.[10] Even though mismatches between strategy and structure do occur, research indicates that managers try to act rationally when forming or changing their firm's structure.[11] His record of success at General Electric (GE) suggests that CEO Jeffrey Immelt pays close attention to the need to make certain that strategy and structure remain matched, as evidenced by restructuring alignments in GE Capital, GE's financial service group, during the economic downturn.[12]

Organizational Structure

Organizational structure specifies the firm's formal reporting relationships, procedures, controls, and authority and decision-making processes.[13] Developing an organizational structure that effectively supports the firm's strategy is difficult, especially because of the uncertainty (or unpredictable variation[14]) about cause-effect relationships in the global economy's rapidly changing and dynamic competitive environments.[15] When a structure's elements (e.g., reporting relationships, procedures, etc.) are properly aligned with one another, the structure facilitates effective use of the firm's strategies.[16] Thus, organizational structure is a critical component of effective strategy implementation processes.[17]

A firm's structure specifies the work to be done and how to do it, given the firm's strategy or strategies. Thus, organizational structure influences how managers work and the decisions resulting from that work. Supporting the implementation of strategies, structure is concerned with processes used to complete organizational tasks.[18] Having the right structure and process is important. For example, many product-oriented firms have been moving to develop service businesses associated with those products. As we learned in Chapter 6, this strategy has been used by GE. However, research suggests that developing a separate division for such services in product-oriented companies, rather than managing the service business within the product divisions, leads to additional growth and profitability in the service business. GE developed a separate division for its financial services businesses and this helped facilitate GE's growth over the last two decades. [19]

Effective structures provide the stability a firm needs to successfully implement its strategies and maintain its current competitive advantages while simultaneously providing the flexibility to develop advantages it will need in the future.[20] *Structural stability* provides the capacity the firm requires to consistently and predictably manage its daily work routines[21] while *structural flexibility* provides the opportunity to explore competitive possibilities and then allocate resources to activities that will shape the competitive advantages the firm will need to be successful in the future.[22] An effectively flexible organizational structure allows the firm to *exploit* current competitive advantages while *developing* new ones that can potentially be used in the future.[23] Alternatively, an ineffective structure that is inflexible may drive good employees away because of frustration and an inability to complete their work in the best way possible. As such it can lead to a loss of knowledge by the firm, sometimes referred to as a knowledge spillover, which benefits competitors.[24]

Modifications to the firm's current strategy or selection of a new strategy call for changes to its organizational structure. However, research shows that once in place, organizational inertia often inhibits efforts to change structure, even when the firm's performance suggests that it is time to do so.[25] In his pioneering work, Alfred Chandler found that organizations change their structures when inefficiencies force them to.[26] Chandler's contributions to our understanding of organizational structure and its

Organizational structure specifies the firm's formal reporting relationships, procedures, controls, and authority and decision-making processes.

relationship to strategies and performance are quite significant. Indeed, some believe that Chandler's emphasis on "organizational structure so transformed the field of business history that some call the period before Chandler's work was published 'B.C.,' meaning 'before Chandler.'"[27]

Firms seem to prefer the structural status quo and its familiar working relationships until the firm's performance declines to the point where change is absolutely necessary.[28] For example, necessity is obviously the case for General Motors given that it went into bankruptcy to force the required restructuring.[29] As noted in the Opening Case, after bankruptcy, Borders is now restructuring. However, there are concerns that it may not survive or perhaps another company will purchase the firm's remaining assets and put them to more effective use.

Top-level managers often hesitate to conclude that the firm's structure (or its strategy, for that matter) is the problem, because doing so suggests that their previous choices were not the best ones. Because of these inertial tendencies, structural change is often induced instead by actions from stakeholders (e.g., those from the capital market and customers—see Chapter 2) who are no longer willing to tolerate the firm's performance. This happened at Borders, for example. Evidence shows that appropriate timing of structural change happens when top-level managers recognize that a current organizational structure no longer provides the coordination and direction needed for the firm to successfully implement its strategies.[30] Interestingly, many organizational changes take place in an economic downturn, as was the case with the recent one, apparently because poor performance reveals organizational weaknesses. As we discuss next, effective organizational controls help managers recognize when it is time to adjust the firm's structure.

Organizational Controls

Organizational controls are an important aspect of structure.[31] **Organizational controls** guide the use of strategy, indicate how to compare actual results with expected results, and suggest corrective actions to take when the difference is unacceptable. When fewer differences separate actual from expected outcomes, the organization's controls are more effective.[32] It is difficult for the company to successfully exploit its competitive advantages without effective organizational controls.[33] Properly designed organizational controls provide clear insights regarding behaviors that enhance firm performance.[34] Firms use both strategic controls and financial controls to support the implementation and use of their strategies.

Strategic controls are largely subjective criteria intended to verify that the firm is using appropriate strategies for the conditions in the external environment and the company's competitive advantages. Thus, strategic controls are concerned with examining the fit between what the firm *might do* (as suggested by opportunities in its external environment) and what it *can do* (as indicated by its competitive advantages). Effective strategic controls help the firm understand what it takes to be successful.[35] Strategic controls demand rich communications between managers responsible for using them to judge the firm's performance and those with primary responsibility for implementing the firm's strategies (such as middle and first-level managers). These frequent exchanges are both formal and informal in nature.[36]

Strategic controls are also used to evaluate the degree to which the firm focuses on the requirements to implement its strategies. For a business-level strategy, for example, the strategic controls are used to study primary and support activities (see Tables 3.6 and 3.7, on page 000) to verify that the critical activities are being emphasized and properly executed. In fact, Nokia failed to employ effective strategic controls and is now fighting for survival as a result.[37] With related corporate-level strategies, strategic controls are used by corporate strategic leaders to verify the sharing of appropriate strategic factors such as knowledge, markets, and technologies across businesses. To effectively use strategic controls when evaluating related diversification strategies, headquarter executives must

Organizational controls guide the use of strategy, indicate how to compare actual results with expected results, and suggest corrective actions to take when the difference is unacceptable.

Strategic controls are largely subjective criteria intended to verify that the firm is using appropriate strategies for the conditions in the external environment and the company's competitive advantages.

have a deep understanding of each unit's business-level strategy.[38] As we described in the Opening Case, Borders' significant strategic problems likely stemmed at least partly from the ineffective use of strategic controls.

Financial controls are largely objective criteria used to measure the firm's performance against previously established quantitative standards. Accounting-based measures such as return on investment (ROI) and return on assets (ROA) as well as market-based measures such as economic value added are examples of financial controls. Partly because strategic controls are difficult to use with extensive diversification,[39] financial controls are emphasized to evaluate the performance of the firm using the unrelated diversification strategy. The unrelated diversification strategy's focus on financial outcomes (see Chapter 6) requires using standardized financial controls to compare performances between business units and associated managers.[40]

When using financial controls, firms evaluate their current performance against previous outcomes as well as against competitors' performance and industry averages. In the global economy, technological advances are being used to develop highly sophisticated financial controls, making it possible for firms to more thoroughly analyze their performance results, and to assure compliance with regulations. Companies such as Oracle and SAP sell software tools that automate processes firms use to meet the financial reporting requirements specified by the Sarbanes-Oxley Act. As noted in Chapter 10, this act requires a firm's principal executive and financial officers to certify corporate financial and related information in quarterly and annual reports submitted to the Securities and Exchange Commission. These companies will likely develop software to help the financial services industry deal with the newest federal regulations on banking.

Both strategic and financial controls are important aspects of each organizational structure, and as we noted previously, any structure's effectiveness is determined by using a combination of strategic and financial controls. However, the relative use of controls varies by type of strategy. For example, companies and business units of large diversified firms using the cost leadership strategy emphasize financial controls (such as quantitative cost goals), while companies and business units using the differentiation strategy emphasize strategic controls (such as subjective measures of the effectiveness of product development teams).[41] As previously explained, a corporation-wide emphasis on sharing among business units (as called for by related diversification strategies) results in an emphasis on strategic controls, while financial controls are emphasized for strategies in which activities or capabilities are not shared (e.g., in an unrelated diversification strategy).

As firms consider controls, the important point is to properly balance the use of strategic and financial controls. Indeed, overemphasizing one at the expense of the other can lead to performance declines. According to Michael Dell, an overemphasis on financial controls to produce attractive short-term results contributed to performance difficulties at Dell Inc. In addressing this issue, Dell said the following: "The company was too focused on the short term, and the balance of priorities was way too leaning toward things that deliver short-term results."[42] Executives at Dell have now achieved a more appropriate emphasis on the long term as well as the short term due a reemphasis on strategic controls, continuing its focus on recapturing market share and leadership in the PC market.

SAP, headquartered in Walldorf, Germany, sells software that helps firms with accounting and financial planning.

Financial controls are largely objective criteria used to measure the firm's performance against previously established quantitative standards.

Relationships between Strategy and Structure

Strategy and structure have a reciprocal relationship.[43] This relationship highlights the interconnectedness between strategy formulation (Chapters 4, 6–9) and strategy implementation (Chapters 10–13). In general, this reciprocal relationship finds structure flowing from or following selection of the firm's strategy. Once in place though, structure can influence current strategic actions as well as choices about future strategies. Consider, for example, the possible influences of Borders' structure and control system in influencing its strategy as illustrated in the Opening Case. The financial engineering in which it engaged by buying its own stock led to higher debt. This suggests that Borders' managers likely used strong financial controls to try to pay the heavy debt costs. The centralized structure did not provide information from local stores that might have been useful in changing its technology strategy much sooner than it did. The general nature of the strategy/structure relationship means that changes to the firm's strategy create the need to change how the organization completes its work.

Alternatively because structure likely influences strategy by constraining the potential alternatives considered, firms must be vigilant in their efforts to verify how their structure not only affects implementation of chosen strategies, but also the limits the structure places on future strategies to be considered. Research shows, however, that "strategy has a much more important influence on structure than the reverse."[44]

Regardless of the strength of the reciprocal relationships between strategy and structure, those choosing the firm's strategy and structure should be committed to matching each strategy with a structure that provides the stability needed to use current competitive advantages as well as the flexibility required to develop future advantages. Therefore, when changing strategies, the firm should simultaneously consider the structure that will be needed to support use of the new strategy; properly matching strategy and structure can create a competitive advantage.[45]

Evolutionary Patterns of Strategy and Organizational Structure

Research suggests that most firms experience a certain pattern of relationships between strategy and structure. Chandler[46] found that firms tend to grow in somewhat predictable patterns: "first by volume, then by geography, then integration (vertical, horizontal), and finally through product/business diversification"[47] (see Figure 11.1). Chandler interpreted his findings as an indication that firms' growth patterns determine their structural form.

As shown in Figure 11.1, sales growth creates coordination and control problems the existing organizational structure cannot efficiently handle. Organizational growth creates the opportunity for the firm to change its strategy to try to become even more successful. However, the existing structure's formal reporting relationships, procedures, controls, and authority and decision-making processes lack the sophistication required to support using the new strategy.[48] A new structure is needed to help decision makers gain access to the knowledge and understanding required to effectively integrate and coordinate actions to implement the new strategy.[49]

Firms choose from among three major types of organizational structures—simple, functional, and multidivisional—to implement strategies. Across time, successful firms

Figure 11.1 Strategy and Structure Growth Pattern

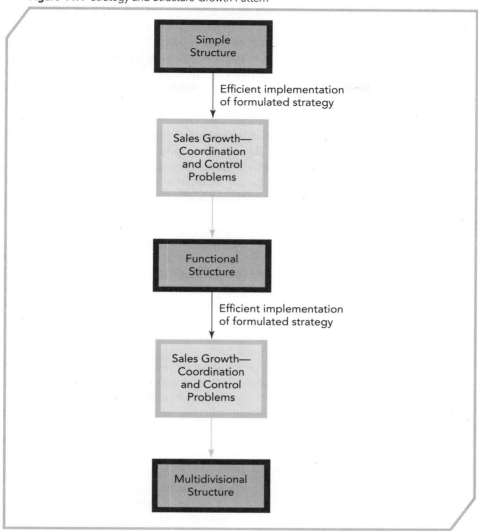

© 2013 Cengage Learning.

move from the simple to the functional to the multidivisional structure to support changes in their growth strategies.[50]

Simple Structure

The **simple structure** is a structure in which the owner-manager makes all major decisions and monitors all activities while the staff serves as an extension of the manager's supervisory authority.[51] Typically, the owner-manager actively works in the business on a daily basis. Informal relationships, few rules, limited task specialization, and unsophisticated information systems characterize this structure. Frequent and informal communications between the owner-manager and employees make coordinating the work to be done relatively easy. The simple structure is matched with focus strategies and business-level strategies, as firms implementing these strategies commonly compete by offering a single product line in a single geographic market. Local restaurants, repair businesses, and other specialized enterprises are examples of firms using the simple structure.

The **simple structure** is a structure in which the owner-manager makes all major decisions and monitors all activities while the staff serves as an extension of the manager's supervisory authority.

As the small firm grows larger and becomes more complex, managerial and structural challenges emerge. For example, the amount of competitively relevant information requiring analysis substantially increases, placing significant pressure on the owner-manager. Additional growth and success may cause the firm to change its strategy. Even if the strategy remains the same, the firm's larger size dictates the need for more sophisticated workflows and integrating mechanisms. At this evolutionary point, firms tend to move from the simple structure to a functional organizational structure.[52]

Functional Structure

The **functional structure** consists of a chief executive officer and a limited corporate staff, with functional line managers in dominant organizational areas such as production, accounting, marketing, R&D, engineering, and human resources.[53] This structure allows for functional specialization,[54] thereby facilitating active sharing of knowledge within each functional area. Knowledge sharing facilitates career paths as well as professional development of functional specialists. However, a functional orientation can negatively affect communication and coordination among those representing different organizational functions. For this reason, the CEO must verify that the decisions and actions of individual business functions promote the entire firm rather than a single function. The functional structure supports implementing business-level strategies and some corporate-level strategies (e.g., single or dominant business) with low levels of diversification. When changing from a simple to a functional structure, firms want to avoid introducing value-destroying bureaucratic procedures such as failing to promote innovation and creativity.[55]

This executive heads up a productive brainstorming meeting with a team of functional line managers.

Benis Arapovic/Shutterstock.Com

Multidivisional Structure

With continuing growth and success, firms often consider greater levels of diversification. Successfully using a diversification strategy requires analyzing substantially greater amounts of data and information when the firm offers the same products in different markets (market or geographic diversification) or offers different products in several markets (product diversification). In addition, trying to manage high levels of diversification through functional structures creates serious coordination and control problems,[56] a fact that commonly leads to a new structural form.[57]

The **multidivisional (M-form) structure** consists of a corporate office and operating divisions, each operating division representing a separate business or profit center in which the top corporate officer delegates responsibilities for day-to-day operations and business-unit strategy to division managers. Each division represents a distinct, self-contained business with its own functional hierarchy.[58] As initially designed, the M-form was thought to have three major benefits: "(1) it enabled corporate officers to more accurately monitor the performance of each business, which simplified the problem of control; (2) it facilitated comparisons between divisions, which improved the resource allocation process; and (3) it stimulated managers of poorly performing divisions to look for ways of improving performance."[59] Active monitoring of performance through the M-form increases the likelihood that decisions made by managers heading individual units will be in stakeholders' best interests. Because diversification is a dominant corporate-level strategy used in the global economy, the M-form is a widely adopted organizational structure.[60]

The **functional structure** consists of a chief executive officer and a limited corporate staff, with functional line managers in dominant organizational areas such as production, accounting, marketing, R&D, engineering, and human resources.

The **multidivisional (M-form) structure** consists of a corporate office and operating divisions, each operating division representing a separate business or profit center in which the top corporate officer delegates responsibilities for day-to-day operations and business-unit strategy to division managers.

Used to support implementation of related and unrelated diversification strategies, the M-form helps firms successfully manage diversification's many demands.[61] Chandler viewed the M-form as an innovative response to coordination and control problems that surfaced during the 1920s in the functional structures then used by large firms such as DuPont and General Motors.[62] Research shows that the M-form is appropriate when the firm grows through diversification.[63] Partly because of its value to diversified corporations, some consider the multidivisional structure to be one of the twentieth century's most significant organizational innovations.[64]

No one organizational structure (simple, functional, or multidivisional) is inherently superior to the others.[65] Peter Drucker says the following about this matter: "There is no one right organization. . . . Rather the task . . . is to select the organization for the particular task and mission at hand."[66] This statement suggests that the firm must select a structure that is "right" for successfully using the chosen strategy. Because no single structure is optimal in all instances, managers concentrate on developing proper matches between strategies and organizational structures rather than searching for an "optimal" structure. We now describe the strategy/structure matches that evidence shows positively contribute to firm performance.

Matches between Business-Level Strategies and the Functional Structure

Firms use different forms of the functional organizational structure to support implementing the cost leadership, differentiation, and integrated cost leadership/differentiation strategies. The differences in these forms are accounted for primarily by different uses of three important structural characteristics: *specialization* (concerned with the type and number of jobs required to complete work[67]), *centralization* (the degree to which decision-making authority is retained at higher managerial levels[68]), and *formalization* (the degree to which formal rules and procedures govern work[69]).

Using the Functional Structure to Implement the Cost Leadership Strategy

Firms using the cost leadership strategy sell large quantities of standardized products to an industry's typical customer. Firms using this strategy need a structure and capabilities that allow them to achieve efficiencies and produce their goods at costs lower than those of competitors.[70] Simple reporting relationships, few layers in the decision-making and authority structure, a centralized corporate staff, and a strong focus on process improvements through the manufacturing function rather than the development of new products by emphasizing product R&D help to achieve the efficiencies and thus characterize the cost leadership form of the functional structure[71] (see Figure 11.2). This structure contributes to the emergence of a low-cost culture—a culture in which employees constantly try to find ways to reduce the costs incurred to complete their work.[72] They can do this through the development of a product architecture that is simple and easy to manufacture, as well as through the development of efficient processes to produce the goods.[73]

In terms of centralization, decision-making authority is centralized in a staff function to maintain a cost-reducing emphasis within each organizational function (engineering, marketing, etc.). While encouraging continuous cost reductions, the centralized staff also verifies that further cuts in costs in one function won't adversely affect the productivity levels in other functions.[74]

Jobs are highly specialized in the cost leadership functional structure; work is divided into homogeneous subgroups. Organizational functions are the most common subgroup, although work is sometimes batched on the basis of products produced or clients served. Specializing in their work allows employees to increase their efficiency, resulting in reduced costs. Guiding individuals' work in this structure are highly formalized rules and procedures, which often emanate from the centralized staff.

Figure 11.2 Functional Structure for Implementing a Cost Leadership Strategy

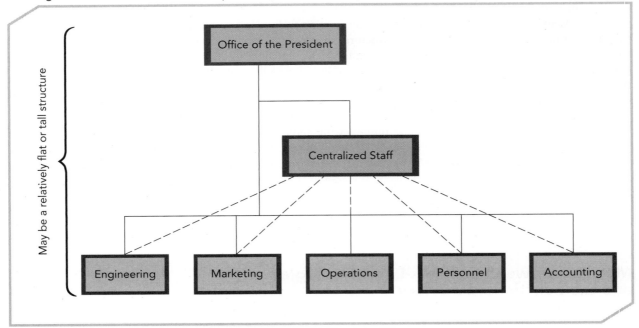

Notes:
- Operations is the main function
- Process engineering is emphasized rather than new product R&D
- Relatively large centralized staff coordinates functions
- Formalized procedures allow for emergence of a low-cost culture
- Overall structure is mechanistic; job roles are highly structured

Walmart Stores Inc. uses the functional structure to implement cost leadership strategies in each of its three segments (Walmart Stores, Sam's Clubs, and International Division). In the Walmart Stores segment (which generates the largest share of the firm's total sales), the cost leadership strategy is used in the firm's Supercenter, Discount, and Neighborhood Market retailing formats.[75] The stated purpose of Walmart from the beginning has been "saving people money to help them live better."[76] Although the slogan is new, Walmart continues using the functional organizational structure in its divisions to drive costs lower. As discussed in Chapter 4, competitors' efforts to duplicate the success of Walmart's cost leadership strategies have generally failed, partly because of the effective strategy/structure matches in each of the firm's segments.

Using the Functional Structure to Implement the Differentiation Strategy

Firms using the differentiation strategy produce products that customers hopefully perceive as being different in ways that create value for them. With this strategy, the firm wants to sell nonstandardized products to customers with unique needs. Relatively complex and flexible reporting relationships, frequent use of cross-functional product development teams, and a strong focus on marketing and product R&D rather than manufacturing and process R&D (as with the cost leadership form of the functional structure) characterize the differentiation form of the functional structure (see Figure 11.3). From this structure emerges a development-oriented culture in which employees try to find ways to further differentiate current products and to develop new, highly differentiated products.[77]

Continuous product innovation demands that people throughout the firm interpret and take action based on information that is often ambiguous, incomplete, and

Figure 11.3 Functional Structure for Implementing a Differentiation Strategy

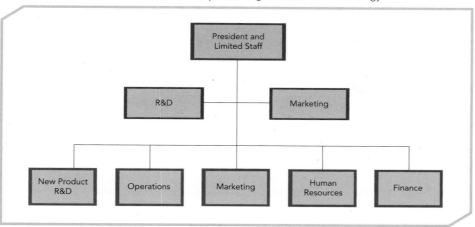

Notes:
- Marketing is the main function for keeping track of new product ideas
- New product R&D is emphasized
- Most functions are decentralized, but R&D and marketing may have centralized staffs that work closely with each other
- Formalization is limited so that new product ideas can emerge easily and change is more readily accomplished
- Overall structure is organic; job roles are less structured

uncertain. Following a strong focus on the external environment to identify new opportunities, employees often gather this information from people outside the firm (e.g., customers and suppliers). Commonly, rapid responses to the possibilities indicated by the collected information are necessary, suggesting the need for decentralized decision-making responsibility and authority. It also requires building a strong technological capability and strategic flexibility, which allow the organization to take advantage of opportunities created by changes in the market.[78] To support the creativity needed and the continuous pursuit of new sources of differentiation and new products, jobs in this structure are not highly specialized. This lack of specialization means that workers have a relatively large number of tasks in their job descriptions. Few formal rules and procedures also characterize this structure. Low formalization, decentralization of decision-making authority and responsibility, and low specialization of work tasks combine to create a structure in which people interact frequently to exchange ideas about how to further differentiate current products while developing ideas for new products that can be crisply differentiated.

Under Armour has used a differentiation strategy and matching structure to create success in the sports apparel market. Under Armour's objective is to create improved athletic performance through innovative design, testing, and marketing, especially to professional athletes and teams, and translate that perception to the broader market. With a strong match between strategy and structure, it has successfully created innovative sports performance products and challenged Nike and other sports apparel competitors.[79]

Using the Functional Structure to Implement the Integrated Cost Leadership/ Differentiation Strategy

Firms using the integrated cost leadership/differentiation strategy sell products that create value because of their relatively low cost and reasonable sources of differentiation. The cost of these products is low "relative" to the cost leader's prices while their differentiation is "reasonable" when compared with the clearly unique features of the differentiator's products.

Although challenging to implement, the integrated cost leadership/differentiation strategy is used frequently in the global economy. The challenge of using this strategy is due largely to the fact that different primary and support activities (see Chapter 3) are emphasized when using the cost leadership and differentiation strategies. To achieve the cost leadership position, production and process engineering need to be emphasized, with infrequent product changes. To achieve a differentiated position, marketing and new product R&D need to be emphasized while production and process engineering are not. Thus, effective use of the integrated strategy depends on the firm's successful combination of activities intended to reduce costs with activities intended to create additional differentiation features. As a result, the integrated form of the functional structure must have decision-making patterns that are partially centralized and partially decentralized. Additionally, jobs are semi-specialized, and rules and procedures call for some formal and some informal job behavior. All of this requires a measure of flexibility to emphasize one or the other set of functions at any given time.[80]

Matches between Corporate-Level Strategies and the Multidivisional Structure

As explained earlier, Chandler's research shows that the firm's continuing success leads to product or market diversification or both.[81] The firm's level of diversification is a function of decisions about the number and type of businesses in which it will compete as well as how it will manage the businesses (see Chapter 6). Geared to managing individual organizational functions, increasing diversification eventually creates information processing, coordination, and control problems that the functional structure cannot handle. Thus, using a diversification strategy requires the firm to change from the functional structure to the multidivisional structure to develop an appropriate strategy/structure match.

As defined in Figure 6.1, corporate-level strategies have different degrees of product and market diversification. The demands created by different levels of diversification highlight the need for a unique organizational structure to effectively implement each strategy (see Figure 11.4).

Cisco must use a differentiation strategy in order to compete in its several high technology product market segments. However, given the presence of major competitors in those markets, such as Hewlett-Packard and Huawei, and its loss of market share in its core market of routers, Cisco must also be sensitive to costs. Thus, the horizontal structure can be useful to integrate the two disparate dimensions of structure needed to implement Cisco's integrated cost leadership-differentiation strategy. In addition, Cisco needs to coordinate several related product units, and the horizontal structure should facilitate this cooperation. Therefore, Cisco's approach is similar to the cooperative M-form structure, discussed next.

Figure 11.4 Three Variations of the Multidivisional Structure

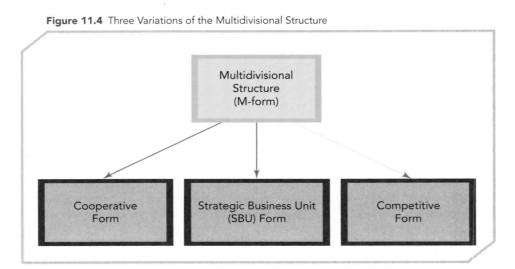

S T R A T E G I C F O C U S

CISCO: COOPERATION TO THE EXTREME AND BACK

A few years ago, Cisco's CEO, John T. Chambers, announced major changes in the structure of the firm. The intent of the changes was to promote greater coordination, integration, and cooperation across the major units in the organization. Essentially, the new structure involved a large number of cross-functional councils responsible for making key decisions regarding the allocation of resources to units and projects. The hope was for this structure to facilitate Cisco's move into a significant number of consumer product market segments, such as health care. Actually, the new structure entailed three levels of teams with the councils at the highest level. Below them were a larger number of management boards. In all, the company had 59 different teams. The hope for these interdisciplinary teams was to increase the speed and ability for execution of their assigned tasks.

Unfortunately, the teams did not create the outcomes desired. In fact, they harmed the focus in the organization and reduced the firm's ability to move quickly and to execute. Some managers inside the organization suggest that it created chaos with managers often attending several meetings of different teams each day, spending hours trying to reach decisions. It not only slowed the decision-making and implementation processes but also made accountability for decisions less clear. Many managers were frustrated because they had to petition councils/boards for departmental budgets, and they felt they had less control of these units. Because this structure created a culture of frustration, Cisco lost a number of its top managers and other key professionals.

The new structure caused Cisco to "take its eye off" of its most critical and lucrative market for routers. As a result, it started to lose market share to major competitors such as Hewlett-Packard, Huawei Technologies, and Juniper Networks. In fact, Cisco's market share in routers declined from 68 percent to 55 percent. The loss of market share and key human capital produced lower confidence among analysts and investors, resulting in a declining stock price. Chambers had to make changes and did so. In 2011, he announced a significant reduction in the number of councils and boards. Now, the firm will have three cross-functional councils, down from nine, and 15 management boards, down from 42. Thus, Cisco is still trying to achieve coordination and collaboration but in a more efficient manner, with a greater balance between the vertical and horizontal structures. In addition, Chambers also announced that the firm would focus anew on core routing, switching and ser-

Danny Moloshok/REUTERS

Cisco, maker of FlipCam, announced that it has decided to discontinue manufacturing and supporting this product. It made this decision so it can focus on its revised structure.

vices, collaboration, data center virtualization, architectures, and video. It will streamline its sales, services, and engineering operations and reorganize its worldwide field operations into three geographic regions: Americas (United States, Canada, and Latin America), EMEA (Europe, Middle East, and Africa), and Asia Pacific (including Japan and Greater China). In order to help the firm focus, it closed the Flip Camera business it had acquired only a few years earlier.

Thus, although the CEO tried to move away from the "silo" structure that often creates inertia and slow or little change, he too heavily emphasized the horizontal structure and thereby created chaos. Hopefully, the new structure will gain the benefits of both without the negative outcomes (inertia or chaos).

Sources: J. Galante, 2011, Cisco's Chambers ditches sales target amid strategy change, *Bloomberg Businessweek*, http://www.bloomberg.com, May 14; S. Mitra, 2011, Is Cisco's restructuring too little, too late? http://www.sramanamitra .com, May 13; G. Burkett, 2011, Cisco's restructuring begins, *Money*, http://money.msn.com, May 12; R. M. Kanter, 2011, Cisco and a cautionary tale about teams, *Harvard Business Review*, http://blogs.hbr.org, May 9; J. Duffy, 2011, Cisco's 3 biggest weaknesses, Amnet, http://www.amnet.com, May 6; J. Mann, 2011, Cisco reshuffle to simplify management, *Financial Times*, http://blogs.ft.com, May 5; M. Rosoff, 2011, Cisco's crazy management structure wasn't working, so Chambers is changing it, *Business Insider*, http://www.businessinsider.com, May 5; J. Duffy, 2011, Cisco restructures, streamlines operations, *Network World*, http://www.networkworld.com, May 5; S. Hall, 2011, Will Cisco restructuring stem talent exodus? ITBusinessEdge, http://www.itbusinessedge.com, May 5; J. Rogers, 2011, Cisco streamlines ... again, *The Street*, http://www.thestreet.com, May 5; T. Poletti, 2011, Cisco should ditch committee structure, Market Watch, http://www.marketwatch.com, April 14; D. Parkayastha, 2010, Cisco's organizational structure and its collabora- tive approach to decision making, http://www.icmrindia.org/casestudies.

Explore Hewlett-Packard's competitive strategy.
www.cengagebrain .com

> The **cooperative form** is an M-form structure in which horizontal integration is used to bring about interdivisional cooperation.

Using the Cooperative Form of the Multidivisional Structure to Implement the Related Constrained Strategy

The **cooperative form** is an M-form structure in which horizontal integration is used to bring about interdivisional cooperation. Divisions in a firm using the related constrained diversification strategy commonly are formed around products, markets, or both. In Figure 11.5, we use product divisions as part of the representation of the cooperative form of the multidivisional structure, although market divisions could be used instead of or in addition to product divisions to develop the figure.

Figure 11.5 Cooperative Form of the Multidivisional Structure for Implementing a Related Constrained Strategy

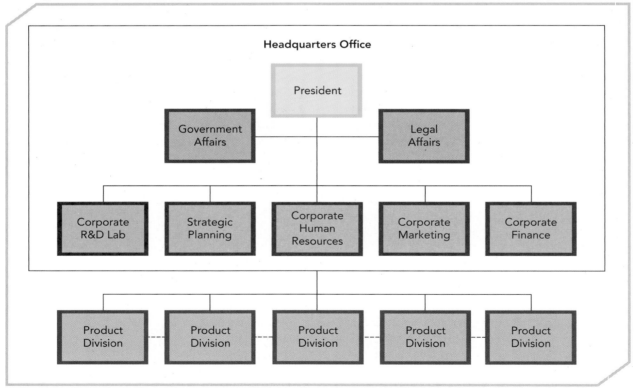

Notes:
• Structural integration devices create tight links among all divisions
• Corporate office emphasizes centralized strategic planning, human resources, and marketing to foster cooperation between divisions
• R&D is likely to be centralized
• Rewards are subjective and tend to emphasize overall corporate performance in addition to divisional performance
• Culture emphasizes cooperative sharing

Using this structure, Cisco has implemented the related constrained strategy as described in the Strategic Focus. Cisco tried to enter 30 consumer markets related to its core businesses. This required implementation of the cooperative M-form and Cisco tried to manage it with significant decentralization among the various business units to foster cooperation and synergy. However, there were too many markets, and the horizontal teams designed to foster collaboration and coordination across related businesses created significant challenges. In the end, there was not enough vertical structure to provide oversight and avoid the chaos created by the multiple cross-functional teams and management boards. Thus, Cisco has streamlined its set of businesses and balanced its vertical and horizontal structure to mirror the more common form of the cooperative structure. Interestingly, research suggests that informal ties may be even more important than formal coordination devices in achieving cooperation.[82]

Sharing divisional competencies facilitates the corporation's efforts to develop economies of scope. As explained in Chapter 6, economies of scope (cost savings resulting from the sharing of competencies developed in one division with another division) are linked with successful use of the related constrained strategy. Interdivisional sharing of competencies depends on cooperation, suggesting the use of the cooperative form of the multidivisional structure.[83] Cisco's new structure and processes hopefully will accomplish this.

The cooperative structure uses different characteristics of structure (centralization, standardization, and formalization) as integrating mechanisms to facilitate interdivisional cooperation. Frequent, direct contact between division managers, another integrating mechanism, encourages and supports cooperation and the sharing of knowledge, capabilities, or other resources that could be used to create new advantages.[84] Sometimes, liaison roles are established in each division to reduce the time division managers spend integrating and coordinating their unit's work with the work occurring in other divisions. Temporary teams or task forces may be formed around projects whose success depends on sharing competencies that are embedded within several divisions. Cisco uses these devices for gaining collaboration and coordination between units, as described in the Strategic Focus. Formal integration departments might be established in firms frequently using temporary teams or task forces.

Ultimately, a matrix organization may evolve in firms implementing the related constrained strategy. A *matrix organization* is an organizational structure in which there is a dual structure combining both functional specialization and business product or project specialization.[85] Although complicated, an effective matrix structure can lead to improved coordination among a firm's divisions.[86]

The success of the cooperative multidivisional structure is significantly affected by how well divisions process information. However, because cooperation among divisions implies a loss of managerial autonomy, division managers may not readily commit themselves to the type of integrative information-processing activities that this structure demands. Moreover, coordination among divisions sometimes results in an unequal flow of positive outcomes to divisional managers. In other words, when managerial rewards are based at least in part on the performance of individual divisions, the manager of the division that is able to benefit the most by the sharing of corporate competencies might be viewed as receiving relative gains at others' expense. Strategic controls are important in these instances, as divisional managers' performance can be evaluated at least partly on the basis of how well they have facilitated interdivisional cooperative efforts. In addition, using reward systems that emphasize overall company performance, besides outcomes achieved by individual divisions, helps overcome problems associated with the cooperative form. Still, the costs of coordination and inertia in organizations limit the amount of related diversification attempted (i.e., they constrain the economies of scope that can be created).[87]

© Nicholas Monu/iStockphoto.com

Explore the implications of Cisco's restructuring.

www.cengagebrain.com

Using the Strategic Business Unit Form of the Multidivisional Structure to Implement the Related Linked Strategy

Firms with fewer links or less constrained links among their divisions use the related linked diversification strategy. The strategic business unit form of the multidivisional structure supports implementation of this strategy. The strategic business unit (SBU) form is an M-form structure consisting of three levels: corporate headquarters, strategic business units (SBUs), and SBU divisions (see Figure 11.6). The SBU structure is used by large firms and can be complex, given associated organization size and product and market diversity.

The divisions within each SBU are related in terms of shared products or markets or both, but the divisions of one SBU have little in common with the divisions of the other SBUs. Divisions within each SBU share product or market competencies to develop economies of scope and possibly economies of scale. The integrating mechanisms used by the divisions in this structure can be equally well used by the divisions within the individual strategic business units that are part of the SBU form of the multidivisional structure. In this structure, each SBU is a profit center that is controlled and evaluated by the headquarters office. Although both financial and strategic controls are important, on a relative basis financial controls are vital to headquarters' evaluation of each SBU; strategic controls are critical when the heads of SBUs evaluate their divisions' performances. Strategic controls are also critical to the headquarters' efforts to determine whether the company has formed an effective

> The **strategic business unit (SBU) form** is an M-form consisting of three levels: corporate headquarters, strategic business units (SBUs), and SBU divisions.

Figure 11.6 SBU Form of the Multidivisional Structure for Implementing a Related Linked Strategy

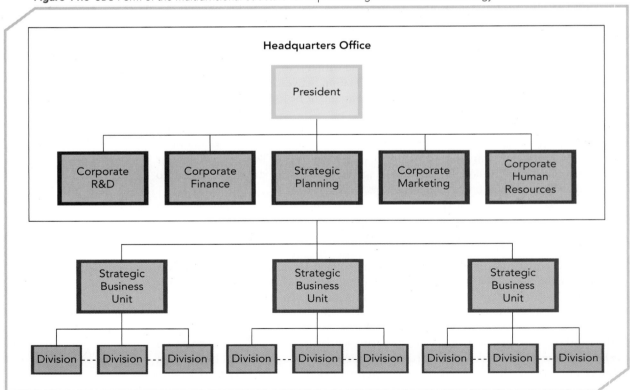

Notes:
- Structural integration among divisions within SBUs, but independence across SBUs
- Strategic planning may be the most prominent function in headquarters for managing the strategic planning approval process of SBUs for the president
- Each SBU may have its own budget for staff to foster integration
- Corporate headquarters staff members serve as consultants to SBUs and divisions, rather than having direct input to product strategy, as in the cooperative form

portfolio of businesses and whether those businesses are being successfully managed. Therefore, there is need for strategic structures that promote exploration to identify new products and markets, but also for actions that exploit the current product lines and markets.[88]

Sears Holdings changed to the SBU form in 2008 by dividing into five strategic business units (with multiple divisions as parts of each SBU): brands, real estate, support, online, and store operations.[89] This allowed for related businesses to work together (such as Sears and K-Mart, which merged in 2005) to focus on their distinct customer sets, but also provided for better control for headquarters in order to evaluate performance of each strategic business unit and division within the SBU. The annual sales revenues for Sears declined for five straight years starting in 2006. In 2007, Sears' stock price reached its highest level in recent years ($143.78/share) but declined to $61.76 early in 2010. At the time, this price was well below the average S&P price of $110.53 and the retail industry average price of $115.96.[90] Therefore, change in structure was likely designed to improve the firm's overall performance but thus far it has not done so. The SBU structure is difficult to implement.

Sharing competencies among units within an SBU is an important characteristic of the SBU form of the multidivisional structure (see the notes to Figure 11.6). A drawback to the SBU structure is that multifaceted businesses often have difficulties in communicating this complex business model to stockholders.[91] Furthermore, if coordination between SBUs is needed, problems can arise because the SBU structure, similar to the competitive form discussed next, does not readily foster cooperation across SBUs.

Using the Competitive Form of the Multidivisional Structure to Implement the Unrelated Diversification Strategy

Firms using the unrelated diversification strategy want to create value through efficient internal capital allocations or by restructuring, buying, and selling businesses.[92] The competitive form of the multidivisional structure supports implementation of this strategy.

The competitive form is an M-form structure characterized by complete independence among the firm's divisions which compete for corporate resources (see Figure 11.7). Unlike the divisions included in the cooperative structure, divisions that are part of the competitive structure do not share common corporate strengths. Because strengths are not shared, integrating devices are not developed for use by the divisions included in the competitive structure.

The efficient internal capital market that is the foundation for using the unrelated diversification strategy requires organizational arrangements emphasizing divisional competition rather than cooperation.[93] Three benefits are expected from the internal competition. First, internal competition creates flexibility (e.g., corporate headquarters can have divisions working on different technologies and projects to identify those with the greatest potential). Resources can then be allocated to the division appearing to have the most potential to fuel the entire firm's success. Second, internal competition challenges the status quo and inertia, because division heads know that future resource allocations are a product of excellent current performance as well as superior positioning in terms of future performance. Last, internal competition motivates effort in that the challenge

> The **competitive form** is an M-form structure characterized by complete independence among the firm's divisions which compete for corporate resources.

Tim Boyle/Getty Images

This Kmart store reopened as a Sears Essentials Store. This merger was part of Sears Holdings' goal of dividing into five strategic business units: brands, real estate, support, online, and store operations.

Figure 11.7 Competitive Form of the Multidivisional Structure for Implementing an Unrelated Strategy

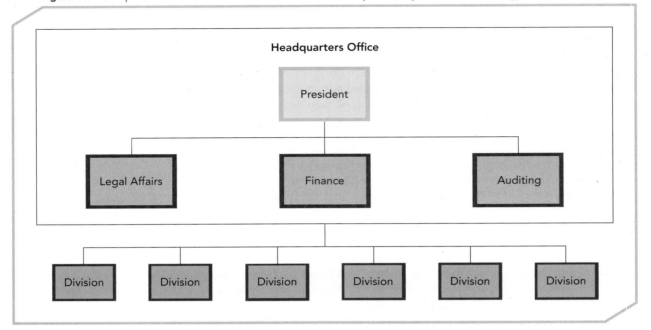

Notes:
- Corporate headquarters has a small staff
- Finance and auditing are the most prominent functions in the headquarters office to manage cash flow and assure the accuracy of performance data coming from divisions
- The legal affairs function becomes important when the firm acquires or divests assets
- Divisions are independent and separate for financial evaluation purposes
- Divisions retain strategic control, but cash is managed by the corporate office
- Divisions compete for corporate resources

of competing against internal peers can be as great as the challenge of competing against external rivals.[94] In this structure, organizational controls (primarily financial controls) are used to emphasize and support internal competition among separate divisions and as the basis for allocating corporate capital based on divisions' performances.

Table 11.1 Characteristics of the Structures Necessary to Implement the Related Constrained, Related Linked, and Unrelated Diversification Strategies

Structural Characteristics	Overall Structural Form		
	Cooperative M-Form (Related Constrained Strategy)[a]	SBU M-Form (Related Linked Strategy)[a]	Competitive M-Form (Unrelated Diversification Strategy)[a]
Centralization of operations	Centralized at corporate office	Partially centralized (in SBUs)	Decentralized to divisions
Use of integration mechanisms	Extensive	Moderate	Nonexistent
Divisional performance evaluation	Emphasizes subjective (strategic) criteria	Uses a mixture of subjective (strategic) and objective (financial) criteria	Emphasizes objective (financial) criteria
Divisional incentive compensation	Linked to overall corporate performance	Mixed linkage to corporate, SBU, and divisional performance	Linked to divisional performance

[a]Strategy implemented with structural form.

Textron Inc., a large "multi-industry" company, seeks "to identify, research, select, acquire and integrate companies, and has developed a set of rigorous criteria to guide decision making." Textron continuously looks "to enhance and reshape its portfolio by divesting non-core assets and acquiring branded businesses in attractive industries with substantial long-term growth potential." Textron operates four independent businesses—Bell Helicopter (31 percent of revenue), Cessna Aircraft (24 percent), Textron Systems (19 percent), Finance (2 percent), and Industrial (24 percent). The firm uses return on invested capital (ROIC) as a way to evaluate the contribution of its diversified set of businesses as they compete internally for resources.[95]

To emphasize competitiveness among divisions, the headquarters office maintains an arm's-length relationship with them, intervening in divisional affairs only to audit operations and discipline managers whose divisions perform poorly. In emphasizing competition between divisions, the headquarters office relies on strategic controls to set rate-of-return targets and financial controls to monitor divisional performance relative to those targets. The headquarters office then allocates cash flow on a competitive basis, rather than automatically returning cash to the division that produced it. Thus, the focus of the headquarters' work is on performance appraisal, resource allocation, and long-range planning to verify that the firm's portfolio of businesses will lead to financial success.[96]

The three major forms of the multidivisional structure should each be paired with a particular corporate-level strategy. Table 11.1 shows these structures' characteristics. Differences exist in the degree of centralization, the focus of the performance evaluation, the horizontal structures (integrating mechanisms), and the incentive compensation schemes. The most centralized and most costly structural form is the cooperative structure. The least centralized, with the lowest bureaucratic costs, is the competitive structure. The SBU structure requires partial centralization and involves some of the mechanisms necessary to implement the relatedness between divisions. Also, the divisional incentive compensation awards are allocated according to both SBUs and corporate performance.

The Strategic Focus on the LG Company suggests that it is operating like a holding company and appears to be using a competitive multidivisional structure. The different units are operating in significantly different industries. LG Electronics, one of the companies in the LG Company portfolio, has several businesses operating in different consumer products businesses. LG Company issued financial controls to govern and evaluate the different corporations in its portfolio. The replacing of the CEO of LG Electronics after only two quarters of losses suggests a heavy emphasis on financial criteria in performance evaluations.

Matches between International Strategies and Worldwide Structure

As explained in Chapter 8, international strategies are becoming increasingly important for long-term competitive success[97] in what continues to become an increasingly borderless global economy.[98] Among other benefits, international strategies allow the firm to search for new markets, resources, core competencies, and technologies as part of its efforts to outperform competitors.[99]

As with business-level and corporate-level strategies, unique organizational structures are necessary to successfully implement the different international strategies.[100] Forming proper matches between international strategies and organizational structures facilitates the firm's efforts to effectively coordinate and control its global operations. More importantly, research findings confirm the validity of the international strategy/structure matches we discuss here.[101]

STRATEGIC FOCUS

EVALUATING PERFORMANCE IN A LARGE CONGLOMERATE: LG COMPANY

The LG Company is a large conglomerate headquartered in Korea that has manufacturing corporations operating in such industries as electronics, chemicals, household goods and health care, life sciences, and oil. The two largest corporations in the group are LG Chemicals and LG Electronics. LG Electronics received a lot of coverage in the media in 2010 and 2011 because its CEO was replaced and a competitor filed a major complaint with the U.S. Commerce Department accusing LG of selling its refrigerators in the U.S. market at a price that was lower than it cost to produce them. How did the electronics business reach this state of affairs?

LG Electronics performed reasonably well in 2009 despite the global economic problems. It had good increases in sales revenue in each of its five major divisions and was profitable. However, in the fourth quarter of 2010 and the first quarter of 2011, LG Electronics suffered losses and the CEO was replaced. This shows that the LG Company was strongly emphasizing financial criteria to evaluate the performance of its business portfolio. The problems, however, ran deeper than two unprofitable quarters. The Mobile Communications Division had projected an increase in sales for 2010 but it did not materialize. In fact, its third quarter share of the global mobile phone market declined from 10.3 percent in 2009 to 6.6 percent in 2010. Its 2010 sales were almost 17 percent below what the firm projected. The firm also experienced slow demand for flat-screen televisions. Thus, it experienced declines in its revenues and profits even though some divisions performed well (e.g., LG's Home Appliance Division).

Smart Refrigerator with THINQ™

David Becker/Getty Images

The LG Smart Refrigerator, a product in LG's Home Appliance Division, helped the firm achieve increases in sales revenue, while its Mobile Communications Division did not contribute to the sales increases.

Perhaps because of pressure to enhance the financial picture for the overall electronics business, it sold refrigerators at an exceptionally low price in the U.S. market. Whirlpool filed a complaint suggesting that the Korean government had provided subsidies to both LG and Samsung allowing them to sell products at below the cost of production. Of course, Whirlpool argued that this represented unfair competition. The U.S. International Trade Commission ruled in favor of Whirlpool. As demonstrated, use of strong financial controls even in a competitive multidivisional structure, such as used by LG Company, can produce some unintended consequences. Executives may try to take short-term actions to shore up the overall financial picture that are not in the long-term best interests of the company.

Sources: 2011, LG Electronics contests finding by U.S. trade panel, Yahoo! Finance, http://www.yahoo.com, May 13; J. Yang, 2011, LG Electronics posts unexpected loss on phones, televisions, *Bloomberg Businessweek*, http://www.bloomberg.com, April 27; J. A. Lee, 2011, LG Electronics swings to loss, *Wall Street Journal Online*, http://www.online.wsj.com, April 27; J. R. Hagerty & B. Tita, 2011, Whirlpool accuses Samsung, LG of 'dumping' refrigerators, *Wall Street Journal Online*, http://www.online.wsj.com, March 31; 2011, LG Electronics, Wikipedia, http://www.wikipedia.org, March 30; 2011, LG Corporation, Answers.com, http://www.answers.com, March 30; A. Shah, 2010, LG CEO quits over poor performance, CIO, http://www.cio.co.uk, September 10; J. Kendrick, 2010, LG CEO resigns over poor smartphone performance, Gigaom, http://gigaom.com, September 17.

Using the Worldwide Geographic Area Structure to Implement the Multidomestic Strategy

The *multidomestic strategy* decentralizes the firm's strategic and operating decisions to business units in each country so that product characteristics can be tailored to local preferences. Firms using this strategy try to isolate themselves from global competitive forces by establishing protected market positions or by competing in industry segments that are most affected by differences among local countries. The worldwide geographic area structure is used to implement this strategy. The worldwide geographic area structure emphasizes national interests and facilitates the firm's efforts to satisfy local differences (see Figure 11.8).

Although the U.S. automobile industry is doing poorly in global markets, on a relative basis Ford of Europe is doing better than other auto firms in Europe within the same middle market segment strategy. This is due to the fact that Ford implemented the worldwide geographic area structure more than a decade ago to give local European managers more autonomy to manage their operations. One analysis called Ford "the most efficient volume carmaker in Europe."[102] Furthermore, Ford has an efficient set of designs matched responsively to the European market. Ford has kept costs down by partnering with European automakers such as Fiat and France's PSA Peugeot Citroen on chassis and engine production. Using the multidomestic strategy requires little coordination between different country markets, meaning that integrating mechanisms among divisions around the world are not needed. Coordination among units in a firm's worldwide geographic area structure is often informal. As mentioned earlier, this may be the most effective form of cooperation.

The multidomestic strategy/worldwide geographic area structure match evolved as a natural outgrowth of the multicultural European marketplace. Friends and family

Figure 11.8 Worldwide Geographic Area Structure for Implementing a Multidomestic Strategy

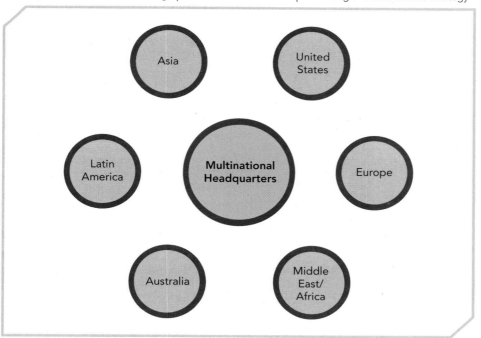

Notes:
- The perimeter circles indicate decentralization of operations
- Emphasis is on differentiation by local demand to fit an area or country culture
- Corporate headquarters coordinates financial resources among independent subsidiaries
- The organization is like a decentralized federation

The worldwide geographic area structure emphasizes national interests and facilitates the firm's efforts to satisfy local differences.

members of the main business who were sent as expatriates into foreign countries to develop the independent country subsidiary often used this structure for the main business. The relationship to corporate headquarters by divisions took place through informal communication among "family members."[103]

A key disadvantage of the multidomestic strategy/worldwide geographic area structure match is the inability to create strong global efficiency. With an increasing emphasis on lower-cost products in international markets, the need to pursue worldwide economies of scale has also increased. These changes foster use of the global strategy and its structural match, the worldwide product divisional structure.

Using the Worldwide Product Divisional Structure to Implement the Global Strategy

With the corporation's home office dictating competitive strategy, the *global strategy* is one through which the firm offers standardized products across country markets. The firm's success depends on its ability to develop economies of scope and economies of scale on a global level. Decisions to outsource or maintain integrated subsidiaries may in part depend on the country risk and institutional environment in which the firm is entering.[104]

The worldwide product divisional structure supports use of the global strategy. In the **worldwide product divisional structure**, decision-making authority is centralized in the worldwide division headquarters to coordinate and integrate decisions and actions among divisional business units (see Figure 11.9). This structure is often used in rapidly growing firms seeking to manage their diversified product lines effectively. Avon Products, Inc. is an example of a firm using the worldwide product divisional structure.

In the **worldwide product divisional structure**, decision-making authority is centralized in the worldwide division headquarters to coordinate and integrate decisions and actions among divisional business units.

Figure 11.9 Worldwide Product Divisional Structure for Implementing a Global Strategy

Notes:
- The "headquarters" circle indicates centralization to coordinate information flow among worldwide products
- Corporate headquarters uses many intercoordination devices to facilitate global economies of scale and scope
- Corporate headquarters also allocates financial resources in a cooperative way
- The organization is like a centralized federation

Avon is a global brand leader in products for women such as lipsticks, fragrances, and anti-aging skin care. Committed to "empowering women all over the world since 1886," Avon relies on product innovation to be a first-mover in its markets. For years, Avon used the multidomestic strategy. However, the firm's growth came to a screeching halt in 2006. Contributing to this decline were simultaneous stumbles in sales revenues in emerging markets (e.g., Russia and Central Europe), the United States, and Mexico. To cope with its problems, the firm changed to a global strategy and to the worldwide product divisional structure to support its use. Commenting on this change, CEO Andrea Jung noted that, "Previously, Avon managers from Poland to Mexico ran their own plants, developed new products, and created their own ads, often relying as much on gut as numbers."[105]

Today, Avon is organized around product divisions including Avon Color, the firm's "flagship global color cosmetics brand, which offers a variety of color cosmetics products, including foundations, powders, lip, eye, and nail products," Skincare, Bath & Body, Hair Care, Wellness, and Fragrance. The analysis of these product divisions' performances is conducted by individuals in the firm's New York headquarters. One of the purposes of changing strategy and structure is for Avon to control its costs and gain additional scale economies as paths to performance improvements. Avon announced the success of this restructuring program and vowed to cut costs even further; the original program was "expected to result in annual savings of about $430 million by 2011–12," while the additional changes were expected to achieve "another $450 million expected to be saved beginning in 2010."[106] The results are staring to pay off as Avon's financial performance in 2011 is much better than 2010. In the first quarter of 2011 net operating profit is 29 percent higher than in the previous year, and earnings per share were more than three times those achieved in the first quarter of 2010.[107]

Integrating mechanisms are important in the effective use of the worldwide product divisional structure. Direct contact between managers, liaison roles between departments, and both temporary task forces and permanent teams are examples of these mechanisms. One researcher describes the use of these mechanisms in the worldwide structure: "There is extensive and formal use of task forces and operating committees to supplement communication and coordination of worldwide operations."[108] The disadvantages of the global strategy/worldwide structure combination are the difficulty involved with coordinating decisions and actions across country borders and the inability to quickly respond to local needs and preferences.

To deal with these types of disadvantages, Avon has approximately 6.5 million local salespeople in 100 countries who are committed to the organization and who help the company to become locally responsive. Another solution is to develop a regional approach in addition to the product focus, which might be similar to the combination structure discussed next.[109]

Using the Combination Structure to Implement the Transnational Strategy

The *transnational strategy* calls for the firm to combine the multidomestic strategy's local responsiveness with the global strategy's efficiency. Firms using this strategy are trying to gain the advantages of both local responsiveness and global efficiency.[110] The combination structure is used to implement the transnational strategy. The **combination structure** is a structure drawing characteristics and mechanisms from both the worldwide geographic area structure and the worldwide product divisional structure. The transnational strategy is often implemented through two possible combination structures: a global matrix structure and a hybrid global design.[111]

The global matrix design brings together both local market and product expertise into teams that develop and respond to the global marketplace. The global matrix design (the basic matrix structure was defined earlier) promotes flexibility in designing products and responding to customer needs. However, it has severe limitations in that it places employees in a position of being accountable to more than one manager. At any

The **combination structure** is a structure drawing characteristics and mechanisms from both the worldwide geographic area structure and the worldwide product divisional structure.

given time, an employee may be a member of several functional or product group teams. Relationships that evolve from multiple memberships can make it difficult for employees to be simultaneously loyal to all of them. Although the matrix places authority in the hands of managers who are most able to use it, it creates problems in regard to corporate reporting relationships that are so complex and vague that it is difficult and time-consuming to receive approval for major decisions.

We illustrate the hybrid structure in Figure 11.10. In this design, some divisions are oriented toward products while others are oriented toward market areas. Thus, in cases when the geographic area is more important, the division managers are area-oriented. In other divisions where worldwide product coordination and efficiencies are more important, the division manager is more product-oriented.

The fit between the multidomestic strategy and the worldwide geographic area structure and between the global strategy and the worldwide product divisional structure is apparent. However, when a firm wants to implement the multidomestic and global strategies simultaneously through a combination structure, the appropriate integrating mechanisms are less obvious. The structure used to implement the transnational strategy must be simultaneously centralized and decentralized; integrated and nonintegrated; formalized and nonformalized.

IKEA has done a good job of balancing these organization aspects in implementing the transnational strategy.[112] IKEA is a global furniture retailer with more than 300 outlets in 39 countries and regions. IKEA focuses on lowering its costs and understanding its customers' needs, especially younger customers. It has been able to manage these seemingly opposite characteristics through its structure and management process. It has also been able to encourage its employees to understand the effects of cultural and geographic diversity on firm operations. The positive results from this are evident in the more than 600 million visitors to IKEA stores.[113] IKEA's system also has internal network attributes, which are discussed next in regard to external interorganizational networks.

Matches between Cooperative Strategies and Network Structures

As discussed in Chapter 9, a network strategy exists when partners form several alliances in order to improve the performance of the alliance network itself through cooperative endeavors.[114] The greater levels of environmental complexity and uncertainty facing

Figure 11.10 Hybrid Form of the Combination Structure for Implementing a Transnational Strategy

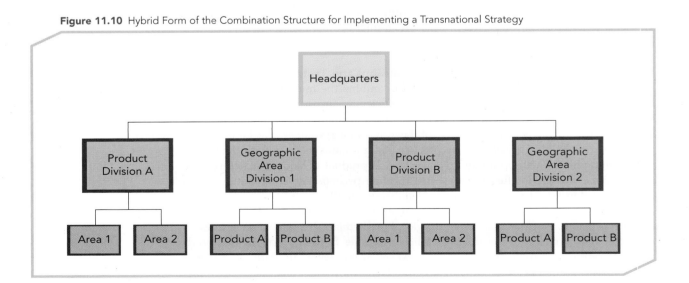

companies in today's competitive environment are causing more firms to use cooperative strategies such as strategic alliances and joint ventures.[115]

The breadth and scope of firms' operations in the global economy create many opportunities for firms to cooperate.[116] In fact, a firm can develop cooperative relationships with many of its stakeholders, including customers, suppliers, and competitors. When a firm becomes involved with combinations of cooperative relationships, it is part of a strategic network, or what others call an alliance constellation or portfolio.[117]

A *strategic network* is a group of firms that has been formed to create value by participating in multiple cooperative arrangements. An effective strategic network facilitates discovering opportunities beyond those identified by individual network participants. A strategic network can be a source of competitive advantage for its members when its operations create value that is difficult for competitors to duplicate and that network members can't create by themselves.[118] Strategic networks are used to implement business-level, corporate-level, and international cooperative strategies.

Commonly, a strategic network is a loose federation of partners participating in the network's operations on a flexible basis. At the core or center of the strategic network, the *strategic center firm* is the one around which the network's cooperative relationships revolve (see Figure 11.11).

Because of its central position, the strategic center firm is the foundation for the strategic network's structure. Concerned with various aspects of organizational structure, such as formal reporting relationships and procedures, the strategic center firm manages what are often complex, cooperative interactions among network partners. To perform the tasks discussed next, the strategic center firm must make sure that incentives for participating in the network are aligned so that network firms continue to have a reason to remain connected[119] The strategic center firm is engaged in four primary tasks as it manages the strategic network and controls its operations:[120]

Strategic outsourcing. The strategic center firm outsources and partners with more firms than other network members. At the same time, the strategic center firm requires

Figure 11.11 A Strategic Network

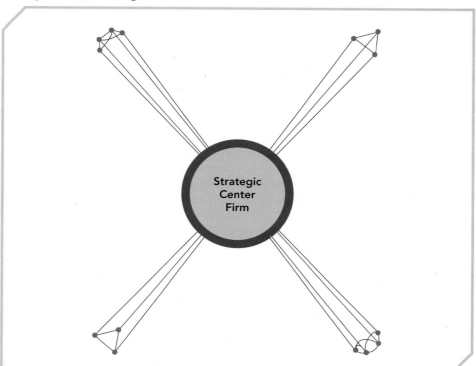

network partners to be more than contractors. Members are expected to find opportunities for the network to create value through its cooperative work.

Competencies. To increase network effectiveness, the strategic center firm seeks ways to support each member's efforts to develop core competencies with the potential of benefiting the network.

Technology. The strategic center firm is responsible for managing the development and sharing of technology-based ideas among network members. The structural requirement that members submit formal reports detailing the technology-oriented outcomes of their efforts to the strategic center firm facilitates this activity.[121]

Race to learn. The strategic center firm emphasizes that the principal dimensions of competition are between value chains and between networks of value chains. Because of this interconnection, the strategic network is only as strong as its weakest value-chain link. With its centralized decision-making authority and responsibility, the strategic center firm guides participants in efforts to form network-specific competitive advantages. The need for each participant to have capabilities that can be the foundation for the network's competitive advantages encourages friendly rivalry among participants seeking to develop the skills needed to quickly form new capabilities that create value for the network.[122]

Interestingly, strategic networks are being used more frequently, partly because of the ability of a strategic center firm to execute a strategy that effectively and efficiently links partner firms. Improved information systems and communication capabilities (e.g., the Internet) make such networks possible.

Implementing Business-Level Cooperative Strategies

As noted in Chapter 9, the two types of business-level complementary alliances are vertical and horizontal. Firms with competencies in different stages of the value chain form a vertical alliance to cooperatively integrate their different, but complementary, skills. Firms combining their competencies to create value in the same stage of the value chain are using a horizontal alliance. Vertical complementary strategic alliances such as those developed by Toyota Motor Company are formed more frequently than horizontal alliances.[123]

A strategic network of vertical relationships such as the network in Japan between Toyota and its suppliers often involves a number of implementation issues.[124] First, the strategic center firm encourages subcontractors to modernize their facilities and provides them with technical and financial assistance to do so, if necessary. Second, the strategic center firm reduces its transaction costs by promoting longer-term contracts with subcontractors, so that supplier-partners increase their long-term productivity. This approach is diametrically opposed to that of continually negotiating short-term contracts based on unit pricing. Third, the strategic center firm enables engineers in upstream companies (suppliers) to have better communication with those companies with whom it has contracts for services. As a result, suppliers and the strategic center firm become more interdependent and less independent.

The lean production system (a vertical complementary strategic alliance) pioneered by Toyota and others has been diffused throughout the global auto industry.[125] In vertical complementary strategic alliances, such as the one between Toyota and its suppliers, the strategic center firm is obvious, as is the structure that firm establishes. However, the same is not always true with horizontal complementary strategic alliances where firms try to create value in the same part of the value chain For example, airline alliances are commonly formed to create value in the marketing and sales primary activity segment of the value chain (see Table 3.6). Because air carriers commonly participate in multiple horizontal complementary alliances such as the Star Alliance between Lufthansa, United (and originally Continental before its merger with United), US Airways, Thai, Air Canada, SAS, and others, it is difficult to determine the strategic center firm. Moreover, participating in several alliances can cause firms to question partners' true loyalties and intentions. Also, if rivals band together in too many collaborative activities, one or more governments may suspect the possibility of illegal collusive activities. For these reasons, horizontal complementary alliances are used less often and less successfully than their vertical counterpart, although there are examples of success, for instance, among auto and aircraft manufacturers.

Implementing Corporate-Level Cooperative Strategies

Corporate-level cooperative strategies (such as franchising) are used to facilitate product and market diversification. As a cooperative strategy, franchising allows the firm to use its competencies to extend or diversify its product or market reach, but without completing a merger or an acquisition.[126] Research suggests that knowledge embedded in corporate-level cooperative strategies facilitates synergy.[127] For example, McDonald's Corporation pursues a franchising strategy, emphasizing a limited value-priced menu in more than 100 countries. The McDonald's franchising system is a strategic network. McDonald's headquarters serves as the strategic center firm for the network's franchisees. The headquarters office uses strategic and financial controls to verify that the franchisees' operations create the greatest value for the entire network.

An important strategic control issue for McDonald's is the location of its franchisee units. Because it believes that its greatest expansion opportunities are outside the United States, the firm has decided to continue expanding in countries such as China and India, where it often needs to adjust its menu according to the local culture. For example, "McDonald's adapts its restaurants in India to local tastes; in a nation that is predominantly Hindu and reveres the cow, beef isn't on the menu, for instance, replaced by chicken burgers and vegetable patties."[128] As the strategic center firm around the globe for its restaurants, McDonald's is devoting the majority of its capital expenditures to develop units in non–U.S. markets.

Implementing International Cooperative Strategies

Strategic networks formed to implement international cooperative strategies result in firms competing in several countries.[129] Differences among countries' regulatory environments increase the challenge of managing international networks and verifying that at a minimum, the network's operations comply with all legal requirements.[130]

Distributed strategic networks are the organizational structure used to manage international cooperative strategies. As shown in Figure 11.12, several regional strategic center firms are included in the distributed network to manage partner firms' multiple cooperative arrangements.[131] The structure used to implement the international cooperative strategy is complex and demands careful attention to be used successfully.

Figure 11.12 A Distributed Strategic Network

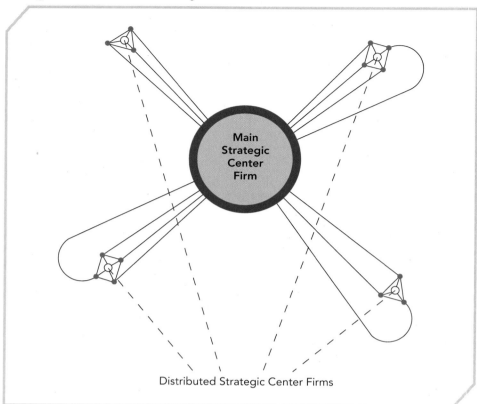

Distributed Strategic Center Firms

SUMMARY

■ Organizational structure specifies the firm's formal report-ing relationships, procedures, controls, and authority and decision-making processes. Essentially, organizational struc-ture details the work to be done in a firm and how that work is to be accomplished. Organizational controls guide the use of strategy, indicate how to compare actual and expected results, and suggest actions to take to improve performance when it falls below expectations. A proper match between strategy and structure can lead to a competitive advantage.

■ Strategic controls (largely subjective criteria) and financial controls (largely objective criteria) are the two types of organizational controls used to implement a strategy. Both controls are critical, although their degree of emphasis varies based on individual matches between strategy and structure.

■ Strategy and structure influence each other; overall though, strategy has a stronger influence on structure. Research indicates that firms tend to change structure when declin-ing performance forces them to do so. Effective managers anticipate the need for structural change and quickly modify structure to better accommodate the firm's strategy when evidence calls for that action.

■ The functional structure is used to implement business-level strategies. The cost leadership strategy requires a centralized functional structure—one in which manufacturing efficiency and process engineering are emphasized. The differentiation strategy's functional structure decentralizes implementation-related decisions, especially those concerned with marketing, to those involved with individual organizational functions. Focus strategies, often used in small firms, require a simple structure until such time that the firm diversifies in terms of products and/or markets.

■ Unique combinations of different forms of the multidivisional structure are matched with different corporate-level diver-sification strategies to properly implement these strategies. The cooperative M-form, used to implement the related con-strained corporate-level strategy, has a centralized corporate office and extensive integrating mechanisms. Divisional incentives are linked to overall corporate performance to foster cooperation among divisions. The related linked SBU M-form structure establishes separate profit centers within the diversified firm. Each profit center or SBU may have divisions offering similar products, but the SBUs are often unrelated to each other. The competitive M-form structure, used to implement the unrelated diversification strategy, is highly decentralized, lacks integrating mechanisms, and utilizes objective financial criteria to evaluate each unit's performance.

■ The multidomestic strategy, implemented through the worldwide geographic area structure, emphasizes decentralization and locates all functional activities in the host country or geographic area. The worldwide product divisional structure is used to implement the global strategy. This structure is centralized in order to coordinate and integrate different functions' activities so as to gain global economies of scope and economies of scale. Decision-making authority is centralized in the firm's worldwide division headquarters.

■ The transnational strategy—a strategy through which the firm seeks the local responsiveness of the multidomestic strategy and the global efficiency of the global strategy—is

implemented through the combination structure. Because it must be simultaneously centralized and decentralized, integrated and nonintegrated, and formalized and nonformalized, the combination structure is difficult to organize and successfully manage. However, two structural designs are suggested: the matrix and the hybrid structure with both geographic and product-oriented divisions.

■ Increasingly important to competitive success, cooperative strategies are implemented through organizational structures framed around strategic networks. Strategic center firms play a critical role in managing strategic networks. Business-level strategies are often employed in vertical and horizontal alliance networks. Corporate-level cooperative strategies are used to pursue product and market diversification. Franchising is one type of corporate strategy that uses a strategic network to implement this strategy. This is also true for international cooperative strategies, where distributed networks are often used.

REVIEW QUESTIONS

1. What is organizational structure and what are organizational controls? What are the differences between strategic controls and financial controls? What is the importance of these differences?

2. What does it mean to say that strategy and structure have a reciprocal relationship?

3. What are the characteristics of the functional structures used to implement the cost leadership, differentiation, integrated cost leadership/differentiation, and focused business-level strategies?

4. What are the differences among the three versions of the multidivisional (M-form) organizational structures that are

used to implement the related constrained, the related linked, and the unrelated corporate-level diversification strategies?

5. What organizational structures are used to implement the multidomestic, global, and transnational international strategies?

6. What is a strategic network? What is a strategic center firm? How is a strategic center used in business-level, corporate-level, and international cooperative strategies?

EXPERIENTIAL EXERCISES

EXERCISE 1: ORGANIZATIONAL STRUCTURE AND BUSINESS-LEVEL STRATEGY

The purpose of this exercise is to apply the concepts introduced in this chapter to live examples of business-level strategies and to examples of how various firms actually structure their organizations to compete. Your instructor will assign teams of students a business-level strategy, such as differentiation or cost leadership. After you have your category assigned, identify a firm that exemplifies this strategy and pictorially draw out its corporate structure. You will need to present the results of your investigation by comparing your firm's organizational chart with that in your text identified for your particular business-level strategy

(see Figure 11.3 labeled "Functional Structure for Implementing a Differentiation [or Cost Leadership] Strategy).

Be prepared to address the following issues:

1. Describe your firm's business-level strategy. Why do you consider it to be a cost leader or a differentiator?

2. What is the mission statement and/or vision statement of this firm? Are there specific goals that you can identify that this firm is targeting?

3. Using the text examples for a functional structure, how does your firm differ, if it does?

4. Summarize your conclusions. Does your team believe that this firm is structured appropriately, considering its goals for the future?

EXERCISE 2: IS STRUCTURE CONTAGIOUS?

Form two teams to analyze and recommend changes (if any) regarding pairs of competitors. Are these competitors, such as Walgreen and CVS, structured similarly or differently? How do their strategies and board structure compare?

Part One

Select a pair of competitors. You have wide latitude in this choice, such as large publicly held companies (i.e., Walgreens/ CVS; Whole Foods/Kroger; American Airlines/Delta Airlines; Cooper Industries/Danaher; Loews/Home Depot; to name a few). Another option is to select two competitors that reside in your town that may be small to medium-sized firms. The important thing is that the firms should be competitors and roughly comparable in size.

Part Two

Research the firms and be prepared to address the following issues:

- Describe the strategies of the two firms—differences and similarities.
- Present the two firms' organizational structures and note differences and similarities.
- Does structure follow strategy as Chandler argues?
- Are the boards of directors structured similarly between the pair as far as committees, meetings, and titles?
- Which one of these companies would you most likely desire to work for, all else being equal?

Be prepared to discuss your findings in a PowerPoint presentation to the class.

VIDEO CASE

A MATCH FOR ORGANIZATIONAL STRUCTURE AND CONTROL—GM BANKRUPTCY

Emerging from bankruptcy, GM's commitment to smaller more fuel-efficient cars has resulted in a move from a GM corporation to a smaller GM company. Selling-off and phasing-out brands along with changing logos are steps toward a new GM. With the Obama administration's desire for a complete overhaul of GM's structure, the U.S. Treasury became the company's biggest stockholder while American taxpayers had greater than 60 percent ownership in the new company. New management teams representing stability and design appear to set the stage for a match point.

BE PREPARED TO DISCUSS THE FOLLOWING CONCEPTS AND QUESTIONS IN CLASS:

Concepts

- Organizational structure
- Organizational controls
- Strategic controls
- Strategy and structure relationships

Questions

1. Is GM's organizational structure aligned with its strategies? If so, why? If not, what is needed?
2. What organizational controls do you think were lacking in the old GM? What organizational controls are needed in the new GM?
3. What specific strategic controls do you believe are key to GM's future success? Should GM's value chain change?
4. Recognizing GM's current state, how do you see the new GM strategy and structure relationship? How do you see it evolving?

NOTES

1. K. M. Eisenhardt, N. R. Furr, & C. B. Bingham, 2010, Microfoundations of performance: Balancing efficiency and flexibility in dynamic environments, *Organization Science*, 21: 1263–1273; P. Jarzabkowski, 2008, Shaping strategy as a structuration process, *Academy of Management Journal*, 51(4): 621–650; S. Kumar, S. Kant, & T. L. Amburgey, 2007, Public agencies and collaborative management approaches, *Administration & Society*, 39: 569–610.
2. R. Gulati & P. Puranam, 2009, Renewal through reorganization: The value of inconsistencies between formal and informal organization, *Organization Science*, 20(2): 422–440; R. E. Miles & C. C. Snow, 1978, *Organizational Strategy, Structure and Process,* New York: McGraw-Hill.
3. S. T. Hannah & P. B. Lester, 2009, A multilevel approach to building and leading learning organizations, *Leadership Quarterly*, 20(1): 34–48; E. M. Olson, S. F. Slater, & G. T. M. Hult, 2007, The importance of structure and process to strategy implementation, *Business Horizons*, 48(1): 47–54; D. N. Sull & C. Spinosa, 2007, Promise-based management, *Harvard Business Review*, 85(4):79–86.

4. R. Rumelt, 2011, *Good Strategy/Bad Strategy: The Difference and Why It Matters*, NY: Crown Publishing Company.
5. R. Ireland, J. Covin, & D. Kuratko, 2009, Conceptualizing corporate entrepreneurship strategy, *Entrepreneurship Theory and Practice*, 33(1): 19–46; T. Amburgey & T. Dacin, 1994, As the left foot follows the right? The dynamics of strategic and structural change, *Academy of Management Journal*, 37: 1427–1452.
6. L. F. Monteiro, N. Arvidsson, & J. Birkinshaw, 2008, Knowledge flows within multinational corporations: Explaining

subsidiary isolation and its performance implications, *Organization Science*, 19(1): 90–107; P. Ghemawat, 2007, Managing differences: The central challenge of global strategy, *Harvard Business Review*, 85(3): 59–68; B. Keats & H. O'Neill, 2001, Organizational structure: Looking through a strategy lens, in M. A. Hitt, R. E. Freeman, & J. S. Harrison (eds.), *Handbook of Strategic Management*, Oxford, UK: Blackwell Publishers, 520–542.

7. R. E. Hoskisson, C. W. L. Hill, & H. Kim, 1993, The multidivisional structure: Organizational fossil or source of value? *Journal of Management*, 19: 269–298.

8. Jarzabkowski, Shaping strategy as a structuration process; E. M. Olson, S. F. Slater, G. Tomas, & G. T. M. Hult, 2005, The performance implications of fit among business strategy, marketing organization structure, and strategic behavior, *Journal of Marketing*, 69(3): 49–65.

9. T. Burns & G. M. Stalker, 1961, The *Management of Innovation*, London: Tavistok; P. R. Lawrence & J. W. Lorsch, 1967, *Organization and Environment*, Homewood, IL: Richard D. Irwin; J. Woodward, 1965, *Industrial Organization: Theory and Practice*, London: Oxford University Press.

10. A. M. Rugman & A. Verbeke, 2008, A regional solution to the strategy and structure of multinationals, *European Management Journal*, 26(5): 305–313; H. Kim, R. E. Hoskisson, L. Tihanyi, & J. Hong, 2004, Evolution and restructuring of diversified business groups in emerging markets: The lessons from chaebols in Korea, *Asia Pacific Journal of Management*, 21: 25–48.

11. R. Kathuria, M. P. Joshi, & S. J. Porth, 2007, Organizational alignment and performance: Past, present and future, *Management Decision*, 45: 503–517.

12. B. Sechler, 2008, Corporate news: General Electric's reorganization resurrects GE Capital, *Wall Street Journal*, August 1, B3.

13. R. Greenwood & D. Miller, 2010, Tackling design anew: Getting back to the heart of organization theory, *Academy of Management Perspectives*, 24(4): 78–88; A. Tempel & P. Walgenbach, 2007, Global standardization of organizational forms and management practices: What new institutionalism and the business-systems approach can learn from each other, *Journal of Management Studies*, 44: 1–24; Keats & O'Neill, Organizational structure, 533.

14. T. Yu, M. S. Insead, & R. H. Lester, 2008, Misery loves company: The spread of negative impacts resulting from an organizational crisis, *Academy of Management Review*, 33(2): 452–472; R. L. Priem, L. G. Love, & M. A. Shaffer, 2002, Executives' perceptions of uncertainty sources: A numerical taxonomy and underlying dimensions, *Journal of Management*, 28: 725–746.

15. A. N. Shub & P. W. Stonebraker, 2009, The human impact on supply chains: Evaluating the importance of "soft" areas on integration and performance, *Supply Chain Management*, 14(1): 31–40; S. K. Ethiraj & D. Levinthal, 2004, Bounded rationality and the search for organizational architecture: An evolutionary perspective on the design of organizations and their evolvability, *Administrative Science Quarterly*, 49: 404–437.

16. R. Khadem, 2008, Alignment and follow-up: Steps to strategy execution, *Journal of Business Strategy*, 29(6): 29–35; J. G. Covin, D. P. Slevin, & M. B. Heeley, 2001, Strategic decision making in an intuitive vs. technocratic mode: Structural and environmental consideration, *Journal of Business Research*, 52: 51–67.

17. J. R. Maxwell, 2008, Work system design to improve the economic performance of the firm, *Business Process Management Journal*, 14(3): 432–446; E. M. Olson, S. F. Slater, & G. T. M. Hult, 2005, The importance of structure and process to strategy implementation, *Business Horizons*, 48(1): 47–54.

18. P. Legerer, T. Pfeiffer, G. Schneider, & J. Wagner, 2009, Organizational structure and managerial decisions, *International Journal of the Economics of Business*, 16(2): 147–159; C. B. Dobni & G. Luffman, 2003, Determining the scope and impact of market orientation profiles on strategy implementation and performance, *Strategic Management Journal*, 24: 577–585.

19. H. Gebauer & F. Putz, 2009, Organizational structures for the service business in product-oriented companies, *International Journal of Services Technology and Management*, 11(1): 64–81; M. Hammer, 2007, The process audit, *Harvard Business Review*, 85(4): 111–123.

20. R. D. Ireland & J. W. Webb, 2007, Strategic entrepreneurship: Creating competitive advantage through streams of innovation, *Business Horizons*, 50: 49–59; T. J. Andersen, 2004, Integrating decentralized strategy making and strategic planning processes in dynamic environments, *Journal of Management Studies*, 41: 1271–1299.

21. J. Rivkin & N. Siggelkow, 2003, Balancing search and stability: Interdependencies among elements of organizational design, *Management Science*, 49: 290–321; G. A. Bigley & K. H. Roberts, 2001, The incident command system: High-reliability organizing for complex and volatile task environments, *Academy of Management Journal*, 44: 1281–1299.

22. Monteiro, Arvidsson, & Birkinshaw, Knowledge flows within multinational corporations; S. Nadkarni & V. K. Narayanan, 2007, Strategic schemas, strategic flexibility, and firm performance: The moderating role of industry clockspeed, *Strategic Management Journal*, 28: 243–270; K. D. Miller & A. T. Arikan, 2004, Technology search investments: Evolutionary, option reasoning, and option pricing approaches, *Strategic Management Journal*, 25: 473–485.

23. S. Raisch & J. Birkinshaw, 2008, Organizational ambidexterity: Antecedents, outcomes, and moderators, *Journal of Management* 34: 375–409; C. Zook, 2007, Finding your next core business, *Harvard Business Review*, 85(4): 66–75.

24. R. Agarwal, D. Audretsch, & M. B. Sarkar, 2010, Knowledge spillovers and strategic entrepreneurship, *Strategic Entrepreneurship Journal*, 4: 271–283; J. Woolley, 2010, Technology emergence through entrepreneurship across multiple industries, *Strategic Entrepreneurship Journal*, 4: 1–21.

25. Rumelt, *Good Strategy/Bad Strategy*; B. W. Keats & M. A. Hitt, 1988, A causal model of linkages among environmental dimensions, macroorganizational characteristics, and performance, *Academy of Management Journal*, 31: 570–598.

26. A. Chandler, 1962, *Strategy and Structure*, Cambridge, MA: MIT Press.

27. D. Martin, 2007, Alfred D. Chandler, Jr., a business historian, dies at 88, *New York Times Online*, http://www.nytimes.com, May 12.

28. R. E. Hoskisson, R. A. Johnson, L. Tihanyi, & R. E. White, 2005, Diversified business groups and corporate refocusing in emerging economies, *Journal of Management*, 31: 941–965; J. D. Day, E. Lawson, & K. Leslie, 2003, When reorganization works, *The McKinsey Quarterly*, (2): 20–29.

29. B. Simon, 2009, Restructuring chief sees benefits in GM's maligned culture, *Financial Times*, July 4, 16.

30. S. K. Ethiraj, 2007, Allocation of inventive effort in complex product systems, *Strategic Management Journal*, 28: 563–584.

31. A. M. Kleinbaum & M. L. Tushman, 2008, Managing corporate social networks, *Harvard Business Review*, 86(7): 26–27; A. Weibel, 2007, Formal control and trustworthiness, *Group & Organization Management*, 32: 500–517; P. K. Mills & G. R. Ungson, 2003, Reassessing the limits of structural empowerment: Organizational constitution and trust as controls, *Academy of Management Review*, 28: 143–153.

32. C. Rowe, J. G. Birnberg, & M. D. Shields, 2008, Effects of organizational process change on responsibility accounting and managers' revelations of private knowledge, *Accounting, Organizations and Society*, 33(2/3): 164–198; M. Santala & P. Parvinen, 2007, From strategic fit to customer fit, *Management Decision*, 45: 582–601.

33. P. Greve, S. Nielsen, & W. Ruigrok, 2009, Transcending borders with international top management teams: A study of European financial multinational corporations, *European Management Journal*, 27(3): 213–224; T. Galpin, R. Hilpirt, & B. Evans, 2007, The

connected enterprise: Beyond division of labor, *Journal of Business Strategy*, 28(2): 38–47.

34. M. A. Hitt, K. T. Haynes, & R. Serpa, 2010. Strategic leadership for the 21st century, *Business Horizons*, 53: 437–444; M. A. Desai, 2008, The finance function in a global corporation, *Harvard Business Review*, 86(7): 108–112.

35. I. Filatotchev, J. Stephan, & B. Jindra, 2008, Ownership structure, strategic controls and export intensity of foreign-invested firms in transition economies, *Journal of International Business Studies*, 39(7): 1133–1148; G. J. M. Braam & E. J. Nijssen, 2004, Performance effects of using the balanced scorecard: A note on the Dutch experience, *Long Range Planning*, 37: 335–349.

36. J. Kratzer, H. G. Gemünden, & C. Lettl, 2008, Balancing creativity and time efficiency in multi-team R&D projects: The alignment of formal and informal networks, *R&D Management*, 38(5): 538–549; D. F. Kuratko, R. D. Ireland, & J. S. Hornsby, 2004, Corporate entrepreneurship behavior among managers: A review of theory, research, and practice, in J. A. Katz & D. A. Shepherd (eds.), *Advances in Entrepreneurship: Firm Emergence and Growth: Corporate Entrepreneurship*, Oxford, UK: Elsevier Publishing, 7–45.

37. P. Burrows, 2011, Elop's fable, *Bloomberg Businessweek*, June 6: 56–61; Y. Doz & M. Kosonen, 2008, The dynamics of strategic agility: Nokia's rollercoaster experience, *California Management Review*, 50(3): 95–118.

38. Y. Liu & T. Ravichandran, 2008, A comprehensive investigation on the relationship between information technology investments and firm diversification, *Information Technology and Management*, 9(3): 169–180; K. L. Turner & M. V. Makhija, 2006, The role of organizational controls in managing knowledge, *Academy of Management Review*, 31: 197–217; M. A. Hitt, R. E. Hoskisson, R. A. Johnson, & D. D. Moesel, 1996, The market for corporate control and firm innovation, *Academy of Management Journal*, 39: 1084–1119.

39. Desai, The finance function in a global corporation; M. A. Hitt, L. Tihanyi, T. Miller, & B. Connelly, 2006, International diversification: Antecedents, outcomes, and moderators, *Journal of Management*, 32: 831–867; R. E. Hoskisson & M. A. Hitt, 1988, Strategic control and relative R&D investment in multiproduct firms, *Strategic Management Journal*, 9: 605–621.

40. S. Lee, K. Park, & H. H. Shin, 2009, Disappearing internal capital markets: Evidence from diversified business groups in Korea, *Journal of Banking & Finance*, 33(2): 326–334; D. Collis, D. Young, & M. Goold, 2007, The size, structure, and performance of corporate headquarters, *Strategic Management Journal*, 28: 383–405.

41. X. S. Y. Spencer, T. A. Joiner, & S. Salmon, 2009, Differentiation strategy, performance measurement systems and organizational performance: Evidence from Australia, *International Journal of Business*, 14(1): 83–103; K. Chaharbaghi, 2007, The problematic of strategy: A way of seeing is also a way of not seeing, *Management Decision*, 45: 327–339; J. B. Barney, 2002, *Gaining and Sustaining Competitive Advantage*, 2nd ed., Upper Saddle River, NJ: Prentice Hall.

42. S. Lohr, 2007, Can Michael Dell refocus his namesake? *New York Times Online*, http://www.nytimes.com, September 9.

43. Gebauer & Putz, 2009, Organizational structures for the service business in product-oriented companies; X. Yin & E. J. Zajac, 2004, The strategy/governance structure fit relationship: Theory and evidence in franchising arrangements, *Strategic Management Journal*, 25: 365–383.

44. Keats & O'Neill, Organizational structure, 531.

45. K. M. Green, J. G. Covin, & D. P. Slevin, 2008, Exploring the relationship between strategic reactiveness and entrepreneurial orientation: The role of structure-style fit. *Journal of Business Venturing*, 23(3): 356; Olson, Slater, & Hult, The importance of structure and process to strategy implementation; D. Miller & J. O. Whitney, 1999, Beyond strategy: Configuration as a pillar of competitive advantage, *Business Horizons*, 42(3): 5–17.

46. Chandler, Strategy and Structure.

47. Keats & O'Neill, Organizational structure, 524.

48. W. P. Wan, R. E. Hoskisson, J. C. Short & D. W. Yiu, 2011, Resource-based theory and corporate diversification: Accomplishments and opportunities, *Journal of Management*, in press; E. Rawley, 2010, Diversification, coordination costs and organizational rigidity: Evidence from microdata, *Strategic Management Journal*, 31: 883–891.

49. J. W. Yoo, R. Reed, S. J. Shin, & D. J. Lemak, 2009, Strategic choice and performance in late movers: Influence of the top management team's external ties, *Journal of Management Studies*, 46(2): 308–335; S. Karim & W. Mitchell, 2004, Innovating through acquisition and internal development: A quarter-century of boundary evolution at Johnson & Johnson, *Long Range Planning*, 37: 525–547.

50. I. Daizadeh, 2006, Using intellectual property to map the organizational evolution of firms: Tracing a biotechnology company from startup to bureaucracy to a multidivisional firm, *Journal of Commercial Biotechnology*, 13: 28–36.

51. C. Levicki, 1999, *The Interactive Strategy Workout*, 2nd ed., London: Prentice Hall.

52. E. E. Entin, F. J. Diedrich, & B. Rubineau, 2003, Adaptive communication patterns in different organizational structures, *Human Factors and Ergonomics Society Annual Meeting Proceedings*, 405–409; H. M. O'Neill, R. W. Pouder, & A. K. Buchholtz, 1998, Patterns in the diffusion of strategies across organizations: Insights from the innovation diffusion literature, *Academy of Management Review*, 23: 98–114.

53. 2011, Organizational structure, *Wikipedia*, http://en.wikipedia.org; Spencer, Joiner, & Salmon, Differentiation strategy, performance measurement systems and organizational performance.

54. Keats & O'Neill, Organizational structure, 539.

55. C. M. Christensen, S. P. Kaufman, & W. C. Shih, 2008, Innovation killers, *Harvard Business Review: Special HBS Centennial Issue*, 86(1): 98–105; J. Welch & S. Welch, 2006, Growing up but staying young, *BusinessWeek*, December 11, 112.

56. O. E. Williamson, 1975, Markets and Hierarchies: Analysis and Anti-Trust Implications, New York: The Free Press.

57. S. H. Mialon, 2008, Efficient horizontal mergers: The effects of internal capital reallocation and organizational form, *International Journal of Industrial Organization*, 26(4): 861–877; Chandler, *Strategy and Structure*.

58. R. Inderst, H. M. Muller, & K. Warneryd, 2007, Distributional conflict in organizations, *European Economic Review*, 51: 385–402; J. Greco, 1999, Alfred P. Sloan Jr. (1875–1966): The original organizational man, *Journal of Business Strategy*, 20(5): 30–31.

59. Hoskisson, Hill, & Kim, The multidivisional structure, 269–298.

60. Mialon, Efficient horizontal mergers: The effects of internal capital reallocation and organizational form; H. Zhou, 2005, Market structure and organizational form, *Southern Economic Journal*, 71: 705–719; W. G. Rowe & P. M. Wright, 1997, Related and unrelated diversification and their effect on human resource management controls, *Strategic Management Journal*, 18: 329–338.

61. C. E. Helfat & K. M. Eisenhardt, 2004, Inter-temporal economies of scope, organizational modularity, and the dynamics of diversification, *Strategic Management Journal*, 25: 1217–1232; A. D. Chandler, 1994, The functions of the HQ unit in the multibusiness firm, in R. P. Rumelt, D. E. Schendel, & D. J. Teece (eds.), *Fundamental Issues in Strategy*, Cambridge, MA: Harvard Business School Press, 327.

62. O. E. Williamson, 1994, Strategizing, economizing, and economic organization, in R. P. Rumelt, D. E. Schendel, & D. J. Teece (eds.), *Fundamental Issues in Strategy*, Cambridge, MA: Harvard Business School Press, 361–401.

63. Hoskisson, Hill, & Kim, The multidivisional structure: Organizational fossil or source of value?

64. O. E. Williamson, 1985, The Economic Institutions of Capitalism: Firms, Markets, and Relational Contracting, New York: Macmillan.

65. Keats & O'Neill, Organizational structure, 532.

66. M. F. Wolff, 1999, In the organization of the future, competitive advantage will be inspired, *Research Technology Management*, 42(4): 2–4.

67. R. H. Hall, 1996, *Organizations: Structures, Processes, and Outcomes*, 6th ed., Englewood Cliffs, NJ: Prentice Hall, 13; S. Baiman, D. F. Larcker, & M. V. Rajan, 1995, Organizational design for business units, *Journal of Accounting Research*, 33: 205–229.

68. L. G. Love, R. L. Priem, & G. T. Lumpkin, 2002, Explicitly articulated strategy and firm performance under alternative levels of centralization, *Journal of Management*, 28: 611–627.

69. Hall, *Organizations*, 64–75.

70. D. G. Sirmon, M. A. Hitt, R. D. Ireland, & B. A. Gilbert, 2011, Resource orchestration to create competitive advantage: Breadth, depth and life cycle effects, *Journal of Management*, in press.

71. Barney, Gaining and Sustaining Competitive Advantage, 257.

72. H. Karandikar & S. Nidamarthi, 2007, Implementing a platform strategy for a systems business via standardization, *Journal of Manufacturing Technology Management*, 18: 267–280.

73. H. Wang & C. Kimble, 2010, Low-cost strategy through product architecture: Lessons from China, *Journal of Business Strategy*, 31(3): 12–20.

74. Olson, Slater, Tomas, & Hult, The performance implications of fit.

75. 2007, Wal-Mart Stores, Inc, *New York Times Online*, http://www.nytimes.com, July 21.

76. Our purpose, 2011, Walmart Corporate, http://www.walmartstores.com, June 13.

77. Sirmon, Hitt, Ireland, & Gilbert, Resource orchestration to create competitive advantage; Olson, Slater, Tomas, & Hult, The performance implications of fit.

78. K. Z. Zhou & F. Wu, 2010, Technological capability, strategic flexibility and product innovation, *Strategic Management Journal*, 31: 547–561.

79. Mission, 2011, Under Armour, http://www.underarmour.com, June 14; T. Heath, 2008, In pursuit of innovation at Under Armour: Founder Kevin Plank says Super Bowl commercial has generated "buzz," *Washington Post*, February 25, D03.

80. Sirmon, Hitt, Ireland, & Gilbert, Resource orchestration to create competitive advantage.

81. Chandler, Strategy and Structure.

82. O. N. Rank, G. L. Robins, & P. E. Pattison, 2010, Structural logic of intraorganizational networks, *Organization Science*, 21: 745–764.

83. Y. M. Zhou, 2011, Synergy, coordination costs, and diversification choices, *Strategic Management Journal*, 32: 624–639; C. C. Markides & P. J. Williamson, 1996, Corporate diversification and organizational structure: A resource-based view, *Academy of Management Journal*,

39: 340–367; C. W. L. Hill, M. A. Hitt, & R. E. Hoskisson, 1992, Cooperative versus competitive structures in related and unrelated diversified firms, *Organization Science*, 3: 501–521.

84. Sirmon, Hitt, Ireland, & Gilbert, Resource orchestration to create competitive advantage; M. Makri, M. A. Hitt, & P. J. Lane, 2010, Complementary technologies, knowledge relatedness and invention outcomes in high technology mergers and acquisitions, *Strategic Management Journal*, 31: 602–628.

85. S. H. Appelbaum, D. Nadeau, & M. Cyr, 2008, Performance evaluation in a matrix organization: A case study (part two), *Industrial and Commercial Training*, 40(6): 295–299.

86. S. H. Appelbaum, D. Nadeau, & M. Cyr, 2009, Performance evaluation in a matrix organization: A case study (part three), *Industrial and Commercial Training*, 41(1): 9–14; M. Goold & A. Campbell, 2003, Structured networks: Towards the well designed matrix, *Long Range Planning*, 36(5): 427–439.

87. E. Rawley, 2010, Diversification, coordination costs, and organizational rigidity: Evidence from microdata, *Strategic Management Journal*, 31: 873–891.

88. C. Fang, J. Lee, & M. A. Schilling, 2010, Balancing exploration and exploitation through structural design: The isolation of subgroups and organizational learning, *Organization Science*, 21: 625–642.

89. P. Eavis, 2008, The pain at Sears grows, *Wall Street Journal Online*, http://www.wsj.com, May 30.

90. General information, 2011, Sears holdings, http://www.sears.com.

91. N. M. Schmid & I. Walter, 2009, Do financial conglomerates create or destroy economic value? *Journal of Financial Intermediation*, 18(2): 193–216; P. A. Argenti, R. A. Howell, & K. A. Beck, 2005, The strategic communication imperative, *MIT Sloan Management Review*, 46(3): 84–89.

92. M. F. Wiersema & H. P. Bowen, 2008, Corporate diversification: The impact of foreign competition, industry globalization, and product diversification, *Strategic Management Journal*, 29: 115–132; R. E. Hoskisson & M. A. Hitt, 1990, Antecedents and performance outcomes of diversification: A review and critique of theoretical perspectives, *Journal of Management*, 16: 461–509.

93. Hill, Hitt, & Hoskisson, Cooperative versus competitive structures, 512.

94. Lee, Park, & Shin, Disappearing internal capital markets: Evidence from diversified business groups in Korea; J. Birkinshaw, 2001, Strategies for managing internal competition, *California Management Review*, 44(1): 21–38.

95. Textron 2010 Annual Report, Textron, June 18; 2009, Vision and strategy, http://www.textron.com, July 16.

96. M. Maremont, 2004, Leadership; more can be more: Is the conglomerate a

dinosaur from a bygone era? The answer is no—with a caveat, *Wall Street Journal*, October 24, R4; T. R. Eisenmann & J. L. Bower, 2000, The entrepreneurial M-form: Strategic integration in global media firms, *Organization Science*, 11: 348–355.

97. R. M. Holmes, T. Miller, M. A. Hitt, & M. P. Salmador, 2011, The interrelationships among informal institutions, formal institutions and inward foreign direct investment, *Journal of Management*, in press; T. Yu & A. A. Cannella, Jr., 2007, Rivalry between multinational enterprises: An event history approach, *Academy of Management Journal*, 50: 665–686; S. E. Christophe & H. Lee, 2005, What matters about internationalization: A market-based assessment, *Journal of Business Research*, 58: 636–643.

98. M. A. Hitt, K. T. Haynes, & R. Serpa, 2010, Strategic leadership for the 21st century, *Business Horizons*, 53: 437–444; M. Mandel, 2007, Globalization vs. immigration reform, *BusinessWeek*, June 4, 40.

99. T. M. Begley & D. P. Boyd, 2003, The need for a corporate global mind-set, *MIT Sloan Management Review*, 44(2): 25–32; Tallman, Global strategic management, 467.

100. G. R. G. Benito, R. Lunnan, & S. Tomassen, 2011, Distant encounters of the third kind: Multinational companies locating divisional headquarters abroad, *Journal of Management Studies*, 48: 373–394; T. Kostova & K. Roth, 2003, Social capital in multinational corporations and a micro-macro model of its formation, *Academy of Management Review*, 28: 297–317.

101. J. Jermias & L. Gani, 2005, Ownership structure, contingent-fit, and business-unit performance: A research model and evidence, *International Journal of Accounting*, 40: 65–85; J. Wolf & W. G. Egelhoff, 2002, A reexamination and extension of international strategy-structure theory, *Strategic Management Journal*, 23: 181–189.

102. J. Ewing, 2009, A magic moment for Ford of Europe, *BusinessWeek*, July 6, 48–49.

103. C. A. Bartlett & S. Ghoshal, 1989, *Managing Across Borders: The Transnational Solution*, Boston: Harvard Business School Press.

104. Holmes, Miller, Hitt, & Salmador, The interrelationships among informal institutions, formal institutions and inward foreign direct investment; G. M. Kistruck & P. W. Beamish, 2010, The interplay of form, structure, and embeddedness in social intrapreneurship, *Entrepreneurship Theory & Practice*, 34: 735–761; S. Feinberg & A. Gupta, 2009, MNC subsidiaries and country risk: Internalization as a safeguard against weak external institutions, *Academy of Management Journal*, 52(2): 381–399.

105. N. Byrnes, 2007, Avon: More than cosmetic changes, *BusinessWeek*, March 12, 62–63.

106. K. Nolan, 2009, Corporate news: Avon unveils new cost cuts, *Wall Street Journal*, February 20, B2.

107. 10-Q Quarterly Report, 2011, Avon Products, Inc., May 3.

108. Malnight, Emerging structural patterns, 197.

109. Rugman & Verbeke, A regional solution to the strategy and structure of multinationals.

110. M. P. Koza, S. Tallman, & A. Ataay, 2011, The strategic assembly of global firms: A microstructural analysis of local learning and global adaptation, *Global Strategy Journal*, 1: 27–46.

111. B. Connelly, M. A. Hitt, A. DeNisi, & R. D. Ireland, 2007, Expatriates and corporate-level international strategy: Governing with the knowledge contract, *Management Decision*, 45: 564–581.

112. M. E. Lloyd, 2009, IKEA sees opportunity in slump, *Wall Street Journal Online*, http://online.wsj.com, February 17; E. Baraldi, 2008, Strategy in industrial networks: Experiences from IKEA, *California Management Review*, 50(4): 99–126.

113. Welcome to IKEA.com, 2011, http://www .ikea.com, June 18.

114. T. Saebi, 2011, *Successfully Managing Alliance Portfolios: An Alliance Capability View*, Maastricht: University of Maastricht; D. Lavie, 2009, Capturing value from alliance portfolios, *Organizational Dynamics*, 38(1): 26–36.

115. V. A. Aggarwal, N. Siggelkow, & H. Singh, 2011, Governing collaborative activity: Interdependence and the impact of coordination and exploration, *Strategic Management Journal*, 32: 705–730; J. Li, C. Zhou, & E. J. Zajac, 2009, Control, collaboration, and productivity in international joint ventures: Theory and evidence, *Strategic Management Journal*, 30: 865–884; Y. Luo, 2007, Are joint venture partners more opportunistic in a more volatile environment? *Strategic Management Journal*, 28: 39–60.

116. D. Li, L. E. Eden, M. A. Hitt, & R. D. Ireland, 2008, Friends, acquaintances, or strangers? Partner selection in R&D alliances, *Academy of Management Journal*, 51(2): 315–334.

117. J. Wincent, S. Anokhin, D. Ortqvist, & E. Autio, 2010, Quality meets structure: Generalized reciprocity and firm-level advantage in strategic networks, *Journal of Management Studies*, 47: 597–624; Lavie, Capturing value from alliance portfolios.

118. T. P. Moliterno & D. M. Mahoney, 2011, Network theory of organization: A multilevel approach, *Journal of Management*, 37: 443–467; V. Moatti, 2009, Learning to expand or expanding to learn? The role of imitation and experience in the choice among several expansion modes, *European Management Journal*, 27(1): 36–46.

119. A. T. Arikan & M. A. Schilling, 2011, Structure and governance of industrial districts: Implications for competitive advantage, *Journal of Management Studies*, 48: 772–803; J. Wiklund & D. A. Shepherd, 2009, The effectiveness of alliances and acquisitions: The role of resource combination activities, *Theory and Practice*, 31(1): 193–212; R. D. Ireland & J. W. Webb, 2007, A multi-theoretic perspective on trust and power in strategic supply chains, *Journal of Operations Management*, 25: 482–497.

120. S. Harrison, 1998, *Japanese Technology and Innovation Management*, Northampton, MA: Edward Elgar.

121. J. Bae, F. C. Wezel, & J. Koo, 2011, Cross-cutting ties, organizational density and new firm formation in the U.S. biotech industry, 1994–98, *Academy of Management Journal*, 54: 295–311; J. Zhang & C. Baden-Fuller, 2010, The influence of technological knowledge base and organizational structure on technological collaboration, *Journal of Management Studies*, 47: 679–704; M. H. Hansen, R. E. Hoskisson, & J. B. Barney, 2008, Competitive advantage in alliance governance: Resolving the opportunism minimization-gain maximization paradox, *Managerial and Decision Economics*, 29: 191–208.

122. H. Hoang & F. T. Rothaermel, 2010, Leveraging internal and external experience: Exploration, exploitation and R&D project performance, *Strategic Management Journal*, 31: 734–758; G. Lorenzoni & C. Baden-Fuller, 1995, Creating a strategic center to manage a web of partners, *California Management Review*, 37(3): 146–163.

123. A. C. Inkpen, 2008, Knowledge transfer and international joint ventures: The case of NUMMI and General Motors, *Strategic Management Journal*, 29(4): 447–453; T. A. Stewart & A. P. Raman, 2007, Lessons from Toyota's long drive, *Harvard Business Review*, 85(7/8): 74–83; J. H. Dyer & K. Nobeoka, 2000, Creating and managing a high-performance knowledge-sharing network: The Toyota case, *Strategic Management Journal*, 21: 345–367.

124. L. F. Mesquita, J. An, & J. H. Brush, 2008, Comparing the resource-based and relational views: Knowledge transfer and spillover in vertical alliances, *Strategic Management Journal*, 29: 913–941: M. Kotabe, X. Martin, & H. Domoto, 2003, Gaining from vertical partnerships: Knowledge transfer, relationship duration and supplier performance improvement in the U.S. and Japanese automotive industries, *Strategic Management Journal*, 24: 293–316.

125. S. G. Lazzarini, D. P. Claro, & L. F. Mesquita, 2008, Buyer-supplier and supplier-supplier alliances: Do they reinforce or undermine one another? *Journal of Management Studies*, 45(3): 561–584; P. Dussauge, B. Garrette, & W. Mitchell, 2004, Asymmetric performance: The market share impact of scale and link alliances in the global auto industry, *Strategic Management Journal*, 25: 701–711.

126. A. M. Hayashi, 2008, How to replicate success. *MIT Sloan Management Review*, 49(3): 6–7; M. Tuunanen & F. Hoy, 2007, Franchising: Multifaceted form of entrepreneurship, *International Journal of Entrepreneurship and Small Business*, 4: 52–67.

127. A. Zaheer, R. Gozubuyuk, & H. Milanov, 2010, It's the connections: The network perspective in interorganizational research, *Academy of Management Perspectives*, 24 (1): 62–77; J. Li, C. Dhanaraj, & R. L. Shockley, 2008, Joint venture evolution: Extending the real options approach, *Managerial and Decision Economics*, 29(4): 317–336.

128. E. Bellman, 2009, Corporate news: McDonald's plans expansion in India, *Wall Street Journal*, June 30, B4.

129. T. W. Tong, J. J. Reuer, & M. W. Peng, 2008. International joint ventures and the value of growth options, *Academy of Management Journal*, 51: 1014–1029; P. H. Andersen & P. R. Christensen, 2005, Bridges over troubled water: Suppliers as connective nodes in global supply networks, *Journal of Business Research*, 58: 1261–1273; C. Jones, W. S. Hesterly, & S. P. Borgatti, 1997, A general theory of network governance: Exchange conditions and social mechanisms, *Academy of Management Review*, 22: 911–945.

130. M. W. Hansen, T. Pedersen, & B. Petersen, 2009, MNC strategies and linkage effects in developing countries, *Journal of World Business*, 44(2):121–139; A. Goerzen, 2005, Managing alliance networks: Emerging practices of multinational corporations, *Academy of Management Executive*, 19(2): 94–107.

131. C. C. Phelps, 2010, A longitudinal study of the influence of alliance network structure and composition on the firm exploratory innovation, *Academy of Management Journal*, 53: 890–913; L. H. Lin, 2009, Mergers and acquisitions, alliances and technology development: An empirical study of the global auto industry, *International Journal of Technology Management*, 48(3): 295–307.

CHAPTER 12

Strategic Leadership

Studying this chapter should provide you with the strategic management knowledge needed to:

1. Define strategic leadership and describe top-level managers' importance.

2. Explain what top management teams are and how they affect firm performance.

3. Describe the managerial succession process using internal and external managerial labor markets.

4. Discuss the value of strategic leadership in determining the firm's strategic direction.

5. Describe the importance of strategic leaders in managing the firm's resources.

6. Define organizational culture and explain what must be done to sustain an effective culture.

7. Explain what strategic leaders can do to establish and emphasize ethical practices.

8. Discuss the importance and use of organizational controls.

© Ryan McVay/Getty Images

SUCCESSION AT HP: CAN THE NEW CEO SAVE THE COMPANY'S SOUL?

Mark Hurd, the former CEO at HP, left under a controversial cloud. Hurd was efficiency oriented and had made the company money by tightly controlling costs, but HP's culture of innovation suffered under his leadership. Thus, when he departed because of allegations of misusing his position, the new CEO had the opportunity to "reboot" the company and its culture. Former SAP CEO Leo Apotheker was named as HP's CEO to succeed Hurd. He was described by one HP board member as a strategic thinker with a passion for technology. It was also suggested that he had a record of promoting technological innovation, just what many believed HP needed. However, some also questioned his selection because he lost his position as CEO of SAP after only seven months on the job (although he was co-CEO for almost two years prior to holding the position alone).

Apotheker began his work by talking to employees, customers, and analysts to understand the company and its strategic position. He made a decision popular with employees to restore several of the pay cuts made by Hurd in the previous year. Over the next several months, he made several other moves, including replacing a number of top managers and changing the reporting structure of some positions. The changes were in line with the new strategy he developed to focus HP on the development of new software in line with cloud computing. Given that HP has been a major hardware company (e.g., the largest manufacturer of personal computers), this represents a significant change in direction for the company. Apotheker claims that his strategy will be evolutionary and will feed HP's core businesses but many question this outcome. In addition, he intends to employ a disciplined acquisition strategy that

Leo Apotheker, former CEO of HP.

will allow the firm to purchase new capabilities. In fact, this may be required to make the moves into software and cloud computing successful, given that HP has lost its culture of innovation. It is very difficult to rebuild an innovation culture and capability.

Apotheker was hired as CEO in the fall of 2010, but by the summer of 2011 he was on the hot seat because HP announced a reduction in its profit target (the second time the target was reduced during Apotheker's short tenure) and the price of the firm's shares of stock declined. Thus, he was facing criticism for his new strategy in the face of declining company performance. Some investors were questioning Apotheker's leadership. Unfortunately, the market is merciless and expects strong performance. This expectation exists even though a major strategic change along with a new structure and key management personnel in new jobs take time to produce fruitful results. Thus, a major requirement for Apotheker and all strategic leaders is to convince constituents of the efficacy of their strategy and changes so that he or she will be given enough time to bring them to fruition. Information leaked that Apotheker was considering layoffs to reduce costs and increase profits. Unfortunately such actions have a short-term focus and are unlikely to help the firm reclaim an innovation culture. And, because of these problems, Apotheker was replaced by the board with Meg Whitman in September 2011.

Read more about SAP's leadership.

www.cengagebrain .com

Sources: A. Ricadela, 2011, Apotheker revamps HP management, *Bloomberg Businessweek*, http://www .businessweek.com, June 14; A. Hesseldahl, 2011, HP CEO Leo Apotheker says he won't ship TouchPad till it's perfect, *All Things Digital*, http://www.allthingsd.com, June 1; B. Worthen, 2011, H-P's chief in hot seat, *Wall Street Journal Online*, http://www.online.wsj.com, May 18; M. Rosoff, 2011, HP's CEO Leo Apotheker reveals his master plan, *Business Insider*, http://www.businessinsider.com, March 14; R. I. Sutton, 2011, Hope for HP's culture, *Fast Company*, http://www.fastcompany.com, March 11; A. Ricadela, 2011, Apotheker seeks to save HP's 'lost soul' with software growth, *Bloomberg Businessweek*, http://www.businessweek.com, March 9; J. Yarrow, 2010, HP employees rejoice as new CEO returns pay to previous levels, *Business Insider*, http://www.businessinsider .com, November 22; 2010, HP board faces new doubts after CEO pick, *CBSNews*, http://www.cbsnews.com, October 1; M. G. Siegler, 2010, HP names former SAP CEO Leo Apotheker as new CEO/President; Ray Lane as chairman, *TechCrunch*, http://www.techcrunch.com, September 30.

As the Opening Case implies, strategic leaders' work is demanding, challenging, and requires balancing short-term performance with long-term goals. Regardless of how long (or short) they remain in their positions, strategic leaders (and most prominently CEOs) can make a major difference in how a firm performs.[1] If a strategic leader can create a strategic vision for the firm using forward thinking, she may be able to energize the firm's human capital and achieve positive outcomes. However, the challenge of strategic leadership is significant. For example, replacing Mark Hurd as CEO of HP was difficult, even though HP likely needed new leadership at the time. Although Apotheker's strategy to refocus on HP's innovation culture appeared to have value, making these changes while simultaneously maintaining short-term performance proved to be highly challenging. Thus HP's Board named Meg Whitman to replace Apotheker as the CEO.

A major message in this chapter is that effective strategic leadership is the foundation for successfully using the strategic management process. As is implied in Figure 1.1 (on page 5), strategic leaders guide the firm in ways that result in forming a vision and mission (see Chapter 1). Often, this guidance finds leaders thinking of ways to create goals that stretch everyone in the organization to improve performance.[2] Moreover, strategic leaders facilitate the development of appropriate strategic actions and determine how to implement them. As we show in Figure 12.1, these actions are the path to strategic competitiveness and above-average returns.[3]

We begin this chapter with a definition of strategic leadership; we then discuss its importance as a potential source of competitive advantage as well as effective strategic leadership styles. Next, we examine top management teams and their effects on innovation, strategic change, and firm performance. Following this discussion, we analyze the internal and external managerial labor markets from which strategic leaders are selected. Closing the chapter are descriptions of the five key components of effective strategic leadership: determining a strategic direction, effectively managing the firm's resource portfolio (which includes exploiting and maintaining core competencies along with developing human capital and social capital), sustaining an effective organizational culture, emphasizing ethical practices, and establishing balanced organizational controls.

Strategic Leadership and Style

Strategic leadership is the ability to anticipate, envision, maintain flexibility, and empower others to create strategic change as necessary. Multifunctional in nature, strategic leadership involves managing through others, managing an entire enterprise rather than a functional subunit, and coping with change that continues to increase in the global economy. Because of the global economy's complexity, strategic leaders must learn how to effectively influence human behavior, often in uncertain environments. By word or by personal example, and through their ability to envision the future, effective strategic leaders meaningfully influence the behaviors, thoughts, and feelings of those with whom they work.[4]

The ability to attract and then manage human capital may be the most critical of the strategic leader's skills,[5] especially because the lack of talented human capital constrains

Strategic leadership is the ability to anticipate, envision, maintain flexibility, and empower others to create strategic change as necessary.

Figure 12.1 Strategic Leadership and the Strategic Management Process

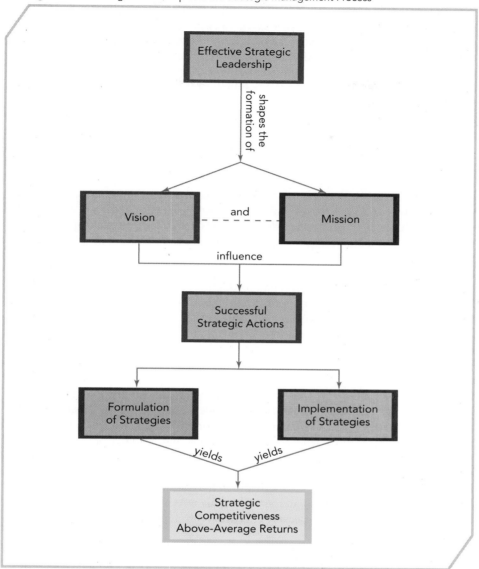

firm growth. Increasingly, leaders throughout the global economy possess or are developing this skill. Some believe, for example, that leaders now surfacing in Chinese companies understand the rules of competition in market-based economies and are leading in ways that will develop their firm's human capital.[6]

In the twenty-first century, intellectual capital that the firm's human capital possesses, including the ability to manage knowledge and create and commercialize innovation, affects a strategic leader's success.[7] Effective strategic leaders also establish the context through which stakeholders (such as employees, customers, and suppliers) can perform at peak efficiency.[8] Being able to demonstrate these skills is important, given that the crux of strategic leadership is the ability to manage the firm's operations effectively and sustain high performance over time.[9]

A firm's ability to achieve a competitive advantage and earn above-average returns is compromised when strategic leaders fail to respond appropriately and quickly to changes in the complex global competitive environment. The inability to respond or to identify the need for change in the competitive environment is one of the reasons some CEOs fail. Although Mark Hurd was replaced as CEO of HP for questionable practices, his replacement felt that HP's former innovation culture needed to be revived in order to respond effectively to the rapidly changing technology environment (described in the Opening Case). The new HP CEO implied that HP had not kept pace with technology development or its competitors. Therefore, strategic leaders must learn how to deal with diverse and complex environmental situations. Individual judgment is an important part of learning about and analyzing the firm's competitive environment.[10] In particular, effective strategic leaders build strong ties with external stakeholders to gain access to information and advice on the events in the external environment.[11]

The primary responsibility for effective strategic leadership rests at the top, in particular with the CEO. Other commonly recognized strategic leaders include members of the board of directors, the top management team, and divisional general managers. In truth, any individual with responsibility for the performance of human capital and/or a part of the firm (e.g., a production unit) is a strategic leader. Regardless of their title and organizational function, strategic leaders have substantial decision-making responsibilities that cannot be delegated.[12] Strategic leadership is a complex but critical form of leadership. Strategies cannot be formulated and implemented for the purpose of achieving above-average returns without effective strategic leaders.[13]

The styles used to provide leadership often affect the productivity of those being led. Transformational leadership is the most effective strategic leadership style. This style entails motivating followers to exceed the expectations others have of them, to continuously enrich their capabilities, and to place the interests of the organization above their own.[14] Transformational leaders develop and communicate a vision for the organization and formulate a strategy to achieve the vision. They make followers aware of the need to achieve valued organizational outcomes and encourage them to continuously strive for higher levels of achievement. These types of leaders have a high degree of integrity (Ray Kroc, founder of McDonald's, was a strategic leader valued for his high degree of integrity)[15] and character. Speaking about character, one CEO said the following: "Leaders are shaped and defined by character. Leaders inspire and enable others to do excellent work and realize their potential. As a result, they build successful, enduring organizations."[16] Additionally, transformational leaders have emotional intelligence. Emotionally intelligent leaders understand themselves well, have strong motivation, are empathetic with others, and have effective interpersonal skills.[17] As a result of these characteristics, transformational leaders are especially effective in promoting and nurturing innovation in firms.[18]

The Role of Top-Level Managers

Top-level managers play a critical role in that they are charged to make certain their firm is able to effectively formulate and implement strategies.[19] Top-level managers' strategic decisions influence how the firm is designed and goals will be achieved. Thus, a critical element of organizational success is having a top management team with superior managerial skills.[20]

Managers often use their discretion (or latitude for action) when making strategic decisions, including those concerned with effectively implementing strategies.[21] Managerial discretion differs significantly across industries. The primary factors that determine the amount of decision-making discretion held by a manager (especially a top-level manager) are (1) external environmental sources such as the industry structure, the rate of market growth in the firm's primary industry, and the degree to which products can be differentiated; (2) characteristics of the organization, including its size, age, resources, and culture; and (3) characteristics of the manager, including commitment to the firm and its strategic outcomes, tolerance for ambiguity, skills in working with different people, and aspiration levels (see Figure 12.2). Because strategic leaders' decisions are intended to help the firm gain a competitive advantage, how managers exercise discretion when determining appropriate strategic actions is critical to the firm's success.[22]

In addition to determining new strategic initiatives, top-level managers develop a firm's organizational structure and reward systems. Top executives also have a major effect on a firm's culture. Evidence suggests that managers' values are critical in shaping a firm's cultural values.[23] Accordingly, top-level managers have an important effect on organizational activities and performance.[24] Because of the challenges top executives face, they often are more effective when they operate as top management teams.

Top Management Teams

In most firms, the complexity of challenges and the need for substantial amounts of information and knowledge require strategic leadership by a team of executives. Using a team to make strategic decisions also helps to avoid another potential problem when these decisions are made by the CEO alone: managerial hubris. Research evidence shows that when CEOs begin to believe glowing press accounts and to feel that they are unlikely to make errors, they are more likely to make poor strategic decisions.[25] Top executives

Figure 12.2 Factors Affecting Managerial Discretion

Source: Adapted from S. Finkelstein & D. C. Hambrick, 1996, *Strategic Leadership: Top Executives and Their Effects on Organizations*, St. Paul, MN: West Publishing Company.

need to have self-confidence but must guard against allowing it to become arrogance and a false belief in their own invincibility.[26] To guard against CEO overconfidence and poor strategic decisions, firms often use the top management team to consider strategic opportunities and problems and to make strategic decisions. The **top management team** is composed of the key individuals who are responsible for selecting and implementing the firm's strategies. Typically, the top management team includes the officers of the corporation, defined by the title of vice president and above or by service as a member of the board of directors.[27] The quality of the strategic decisions made by a top management team affects the firm's ability to innovate and engage in effective strategic change.[28]

Top Management Team, Firm Performance, and Strategic Change

The job of top-level executives is complex and requires a broad knowledge of the firm's operations, as well as the three key parts of the firm's external environment—the general, industry, and competitor environments, as discussed in Chapter 2. Therefore, firms try to form a top management team with knowledge and expertise needed to operate the internal organization, yet that also can deal with all the firm's stakeholders as well as its competitors.[29] To have these characteristics normally requires a heterogeneous top management team. A **heterogeneous top management team** is composed of individuals with different functional backgrounds, experience, and education.

Members of a heterogeneous top management team benefit from discussing the different perspectives advanced by team members.[30] In many cases, these discussions increase the quality of the team's decisions, especially when a synthesis emerges within the team after evaluating the diverse perspectives.[31] The net benefit of such actions by heterogeneous teams has been positive in terms of market share and above-average returns. Research shows that more heterogeneity among top management team members promotes debate, which often leads to better strategic decisions. In turn, better strategic decisions produce higher firm performance.[32]

It is also important for top management team members to function cohesively. In general, the more heterogeneous and larger the top management team is, the more difficult it is for the team to effectively implement strategies.[33] Comprehensive and long-term strategic plans can be inhibited by communication difficulties among top executives who have different backgrounds and different cognitive skills.[34] Alternatively, communication among diverse top management team members can be facilitated through electronic communications, sometimes reducing the barriers before face-to-face meetings.[35] However, a group of top executives with diverse backgrounds may inhibit the process of decision making if it is not effectively managed. In these cases, top management teams may fail to comprehensively examine threats and opportunities, leading to a suboptimal strategic decision. Thus, the CEO must attempt to achieve behavioral integration among the team members.[36]

Having members with substantive expertise in the firm's core functions and businesses is also important to a top management team's effectiveness.[37] In a high-technology industry, it may be critical for a firm's top management team members to have R&D expertise, particularly when growth strategies are being implemented. Yet their eventual effect on strategic decisions depends not only on their expertise and the way the team is managed but also on the context in which they make the decisions (the governance structure, incentive compensation, etc.).[38]

The characteristics of top management teams and even the personalities of the CEO and other team members are related to innovation and strategic change.[39] For example, more heterogeneous top management teams are positively associated with innovation and strategic change. The heterogeneity may force the team or some of its members to "think outside of the box" and thus be more creative in making decisions.[40]

Therefore, firms that need to change their strategies are more likely to do so if they have top management teams with diverse backgrounds and expertise. When a new CEO is hired from outside the industry, the probability of strategic change is greater than

The **top management team** is composed of the key individuals who are responsible for selecting and implementing the firm's strategies.

A **heterogeneous top management team** is composed of individuals with different functional backgrounds, experience, and education.

if the new CEO is from inside the firm or inside the industry.[41] Also, there can some-times be significant change if the new CEO is from outside the firm but from within the industry. The Opening Case suggests that HP's new CEO, who had experience at SAP, is making major changes in the direction of HP. Although hiring a new CEO from outside the industry adds diversity to the team, the top management team must be managed effectively to use the diversity in a positive way. Thus, to successfully create strategic change, the CEO should exercise transformational leadership to shape the new capabilities needed for implementation of the change.[42] A top management team with various areas of expertise is more likely to identify environmental changes (opportuni-ties and threats) or changes within the firm, suggesting the need for a different strategic direction.

In the current competitive environment, an understanding of international markets is vital. However, recent research suggests that only about 15 percent of the top execu-tives in *Fortune* 500 firms have global leadership expertise.[43] Executives generally gain this knowledge by working in one of the firm's international subsidiaries but can also gain some knowledge by working with international alliance partners.[44]

The CEO and Top Management Team Power

As noted in Chapter 10, the board of directors is an important governance mechanism for monitoring a firm's strategic direction and for representing stakeholders' interests, especially those of shareholders.[45] In fact, higher performance normally is achieved when the board of directors is more directly involved in shaping a firm's strategic direction.[46]

Boards of directors, however, may find it difficult to direct the strategic actions of powerful CEOs and top management teams.[47] Often, a powerful CEO appoints a number of sympathetic outside members to the board or may have inside board members who are also on the top management team and report to her or him.[48] In either case, the CEO may significantly influence the board's actions. Thus, the amount of discretion a CEO has in making strategic decisions is related to the board of directors and how it chooses to oversee the actions of the CEO and the top management team.[49]

CEOs and top management team members can achieve power in other ways. A CEO who also holds the position of chairperson of the board usually has more power than the CEO who does not.[50] Some analysts and corporate "watchdogs" criticize the practice of CEO duality (when the CEO and the chairperson of the board are the same) because it can lead to poor performance and slow response to change, partly because the board engages in less monitoring of the CEO's decisions and actions.[51]

Although it varies across industries, CEO duality occurs most commonly in larger firms. Increased shareholder activism, however, has brought CEO duality under scrutiny and attack in both U.S. and European firms. As reported in Chapter 10, an independ-ent board leadership structure in which the same person did not hold the positions of CEO and chair is commonly believed to enhance a board's ability to monitor top-level managers' decisions and actions, particularly with respect to financial performance.[52] On the other hand, if a CEO acts as a steward, holding the dual roles facilitates effective decisions and actions. In these instances, the increased effectiveness gained through CEO duality accrues from the individual who wants to perform effectively and desires to be the best possible steward of the firm's assets. Because of this person's positive orientation and actions, extra governance and the coordination costs resulting from an independent board leadership structure would be unnecessary.[53]

Top management team members and CEOs who have long tenure—on the team and in the organization—have a greater influence on board decisions. CEOs with greater influence may take actions in their own best interests, the outcomes of which increase their compensation from the company.[54] As reported in Chapter 10, many people are angry about excessive top executive compensation, especially during poor economic times when others are losing their jobs because of ineffective strategic decisions made by the same managers.

In general, long tenure is thought to constrain the breadth of an executive's knowledge base. Some evidence suggests that with the limited perspectives associated with a restricted knowledge base, long-tenured top executives typically develop fewer alternatives to evaluate in making strategic decisions.[55] However, long-tenured managers also may be able to exercise more effective strategic control, thereby obviating the need for board members' involvement because effective strategic control generally produces higher performance.[56] Intriguingly, recent findings suggest that "the liabilities of short tenure … appear to exceed the advantages, while the advantages of long tenure—firm-specific human and social capital, knowledge, and power—seem to outweigh the disadvantages of rigidity and maintaining the status quo."[57] Overall then the relationship between CEO tenure and firm performance is complex, indicating that to strengthen the firm, boards of directors should develop an effective relationship with the top management team.

In summary, the relative degrees of power held by the board and top management team members should be examined in light of an individual firm's situation. For example, the abundance of resources in a firm's external environment and the volatility of that environment may affect the ideal balance of power between the board and the top management teams. Moreover, a volatile and uncertain environment may create a situation where a powerful CEO is needed to move quickly, but a diverse top management team may create less cohesion among team members and prevent or stall necessary strategic actions. With effective working relationships, boards, CEOs, and other top management team members have the foundation required to select arrangements with the highest probability of best serving stakeholders' interests.[58]

> An **internal managerial labor market** consists of a firm's opportunities for managerial positions and the qualified employees within that firm.

Managerial Succession

The choice of top executives—especially CEOs—is a critical decision with important implications for the firm's performance.[59] Many companies use leadership screening systems to identify individuals with managerial and strategic leadership potential as well as to determine the criteria individuals should satisfy to be candidates for the CEO position.[60]

The most effective of these systems assesses people within the firm and gains valuable information about the capabilities of other companies' managers, particularly their strategic leaders.[61] Based on the results of these assessments, training and development programs are provided for current individuals in an attempt to preselect and shape the skills of people who may become tomorrow's leaders. Because of the quality of its programs, General Electric "is famous for developing leaders who are dedicated to turning imaginative ideas into leading products and services."[62] However, there are many companies that do not have succession plans for their top executives. For example, a recent survey found that 43 percent of the largest public companies in the United States had no formal succession plan for their CEOs. Of those companies with plans, only about 20 percent were satisfied with their succession processes.[63]

> An **external managerial labor market** is the collection of managerial career opportunities and the qualified people who are external to the organization in which the opportunities exist.

Organizations select managers and strategic leaders from two types of managerial labor markets—internal and external.[64] An **internal managerial labor market** consists of a firm's opportunities for managerial positions and the qualified employees within that firm. An **external managerial labor market** is the collection of

This CEO assesses candidates to take the helm upon his retirement. Succession plans are vital to a firm's long-term success.

Luis Louro/Alamy

managerial career opportunities and the qualified people who are external to the organization in which the opportunities exist.

Several benefits are thought to accrue to a firm when the internal labor market is used to select an insider as the new CEO. Because of their experience with the firm and the industry environment in which it competes, insiders are familiar with company products, markets, technologies, and operating procedures. Also, internal hiring produces lower turnover among existing personnel, many of whom possess valuable firm-specific knowledge. When the firm is performing well, internal succession is favored to sustain high performance. It is assumed that hiring from inside keeps the important knowledge necessary to sustain performance.

Results of work completed by management consultant Jim Collins support the value of using the internal labor market when selecting a CEO. Collins found that high-performing firms almost always appoint an insider to be the new CEO. He argues that bringing in a well-known outsider, whom he refers to as a "white knight," is a recipe for mediocrity.[65] For example, given the phenomenal success of General Electric (GE) during Jack Welch's tenure as CEO and the firm's highly effective management and leadership development programs, insider Jeffrey Immelt was chosen to succeed Welch. However, shareholders have become disgruntled because GE's stock values have decreased in recent years; GE has suffered along with many other firms in the global economic crisis. Thus, GE under Immelt's leadership is not experiencing the returns achieved by his predecessor.

Employees commonly prefer the internal managerial labor market when selecting top management team members and a new CEO. In the past, companies have also had a preference for insiders to fill top-level management positions because of a desire for continuity and a continuing commitment to the firm's current vision, mission, and chosen strategies.[66] For example, Campbell Soup Company has had relatively stable leadership with only 12 CEOs since it was founded in 1869. This represents a CEO succession about every 12 years on average. And, the firm implemented a CEO succession in 2011 with the naming of insider Denise Morrison. Unfortunately, analysts are concerned about the lack of growth in the company and the firm's stock price declined by approximately 8 percent when Morrison was announced as the new CEO. Analysts believed that major changes are required and that an insider is unlikely to make those changes.[67]

Because of a changing competitive landscape and varying levels of performance, an increasing number of boards of directors are turning to outsiders to succeed CEOs. A firm often has valid reasons to select an outsider as its new CEO. In some situations, long tenure with a firm may reduce strategic leaders' level of commitment to pursue innovation. Given innovation's importance to firm success (see Chapter 13), this hesitation could be a liability for a strategic leader. In Figure 12.3, we show how the composition of the top management team and the CEO succession (managerial labor market) interact to affect strategy. For example, when the top management team is homogeneous (its members have similar functional experiences and educational backgrounds) and a new CEO is selected from inside the firm, the firm's current strategy is unlikely to change. Alternatively, when a new CEO is selected from outside the firm and the top management team is heterogeneous, the probability is high that strategy will change. When the new CEO is from inside the firm and a heterogeneous top management team is in place, the strategy may not change, but innovation is likely to continue. An external CEO succession with a homogeneous team creates a more ambiguous situation. Furthermore, outside CEOs who lead moderate change often achieve increases in performance, but high strategic change by outsiders frequently leads to declines in performance.[68]

When firms do not have a formal managerial succession plan, they sometimes will appoint an interim CEO until a new CEO is identified and in place.[69] The advantage of using an interim CEO is that it allows adequate time to do a thorough search to find the best candidate. Most interim CEOs perform the basic functions and keep the organization operating; however, they rarely will make major strategic decisions. Therefore, interim CEOs are generally only used when the CEO departs unexpectedly and abruptly.

Figure 12.3 Effects of CEO Succession and Top Management Team Composition on Strategy

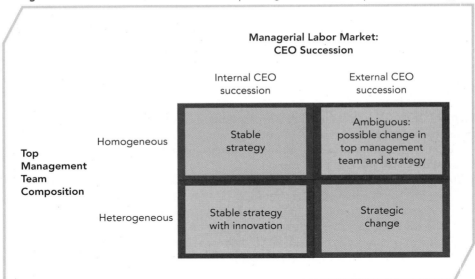

© 2013 Cengage Learning.

Succession plans are very important to maintain the desired course for the firm when there is a change in the CEO. Yet, the Strategic Focus suggests that only slightly more than one-third of the companies are prepared for a succession of the CEO. Because of the importance of the CEO position and the influence CEOs have on the firm's stock price (e.g., Steve Jobs at Apple), investors have been placing increasing pressure on boards to develop formal succession plans for the top management positions. As noted in the Strategic Focus, formal succession plans often call for the use of external executive search firms (sometimes referred to as headhunters). Research suggests that executive search firms primarily target executives in large, reputable, and high-performing firms but these firms also identify the executives to target, largely based on their job title instead of known capabilities or individual performance. The executives who agree to be candidates in the search frequently have less tenure and experience and hold positions in less successful firms.[70] Therefore, executive search firms may not always provide the best pool of candidates.

Including talent from all parts of both the internal and external labor markets increases the likelihood that the firm will be able to form an effective top-management team. Evidence suggests that women are a qualified source of talent as strategic leaders that have been somewhat overlooked. In light of the success of a growing number of female executives, the foundation for change may be established. Trailblazers such as Catherine Elizabeth Hughes (the first African-American woman to head a firm that was publicly traded on a U.S. stock exchange), Muriel Siebert (the first woman to purchase a seat on the New York Stock Exchange), and publisher Judith Regan have made important contributions as strategic leaders. Recent years have produced several prominent female CEOs, such as Anne Mulcahy (Xerox Corporation), Meg Whitman (eBay and HP), and Andrea Jung (Avon Products). As noted in the following Strategic Focus, perhaps the next CEO of IBM will be a woman (Virginia Rometty).

Managerial talent is critical to a firm's success, and one area in which managerial talent is crucial is in the integration of an acquired firm into the acquiring business. In fact, the top management team of an acquired firm is vital to a successful integration process because they play a critical role in helping the change be implemented and accepted by the acquired firm's employees.[71] However, it is common for there to be major turnover among the top management team of acquired firms. Sometimes it occurs because the acquiring firm unwisely replaces them. In other cases, the managers depart voluntarily

STRATEGIC FOCUS

CAN HIGHLY SUCCESSFUL LEADERS BE REPLACED SUCCESSFULLY? THE IMPORTANCE OF SUCCESSION PLANNING

Can the replacement for Steve Jobs, the highly successful former CEO of Apple, Tim Cook, be equally successful? It will be very difficult to do so. In fact, the stock market does not seem to think so. When Steve Jobs announced his retirement and the new CEO, the price of Apple's stock declined. Likewise, can IBM's successful CEO, Sam Palmisano, be replaced successfully. Because IBM's CEOs have a tradition of retiring when they are 60, Palmisano is expected to retire in 2012. There are several potential successors but the most likely is Virginia Rometty, who heads IBM's sales unit.

Investor groups pressured Apple's board to develop a formal succession plan for Steve Jobs because in 2011 he was on his third medical leave. This caused considerable angst among investors. The board did not want to name formal successors because the members wanted Jobs back and also believed that he was very important to Apple's success. Jobs turned 56 in 2011 but his age was not the concern; it was his illnesses that created worry. Despite his third leave of absence, Jobs proclaimed that he would participate in all major strategic decisions. Even the laborers' union pushed Apple for a succession plan. The delay in communicating a succession plan coupled with Jobs eventual resignation as CEO did not inspire confidence among the various groups concerned about the loss of Jobs.

Alternatively, IBM seems to be in much better position for a smooth transition of CEOs. There are at least three candidates for the CEO position when vacated by Palmisano. They are Rometty, mentioned earlier; Michael Daniels, head of the Global Services unit; and Rodney Adkins, senior vice president of hardware. All three have demonstrated their capabilities with strong performances in their respective units. In addition, Palmisano has established a strong plan of action through 2015. For example, the plan calls for generating 30 percent of IBM's total annual revenue from emerging markets by 2015. The plan also calls for $7 billion in annual cloud revenue and $16 billion in annual business analytics revenue within the same time period. As such, the next CEO only needs to continue efforts already launched.

Interestingly, CEO turnover among the 2,500 largest public companies in the world declined in 2010. However, this is clouded by the fact that more emerging market firms (including many from China) have been added to the list and they have low turnover among their CEOs. Therefore, there is still considerable CEO turnover in North American and European firms. As such, they have a greater need for succession planning. Selecting successors for the CEO and other officer positions is the responsibility of the board of directors. Boards have come under increasing pressure to develop formal succession plans, especially for the CEO position. However, recent surveys suggest that only about 35 percent of them are prepared for a departure of their CEO. Most formal plans begin with the purposeful development of internal candidates. The better plans also have preparations to replace the CEO in emergency situations (e.g., the CEO dies unexpectedly). Many formal plans call for the use of executive search firms, assuming that external searches are implemented.

Baker Hughes has a formal succession plan. In accordance with the plan, it announced in 2011 that its current CEO and chairman, Chad Deaton, would undertake the new role of executive chairman

This photo of Steve Jobs was taken in 2009 right after Jobs returned from his first medical leave. His ailing health put investors on high alert.

Robert Galbraith/Reuters/Landov

SUSTAINABILITY • SUSTAINABILITY

STRATEGY RIGHT NOW

Learn more about IBM's succession of leadership.

www.cengagebrain.com

and that Martin Craighead would become president and chief executive officer. Likewise, Howard Stringer, CEO of Sony, has been grooming four potential successors. In 2011, he promoted one of them, Kazuo Hirai, to be his top manager reporting directly to him. Thus, it appears that Sony has also chosen its CEO successor.

Sources: M. Yasu, 2011, 'Charming' Hirai promoted; Sony's Stringer plans succession, *Bloomberg Businessweek*, http://www.businessweek.com, June 16; L. Dignan, 2011, As centennial looms, IBM CEO succession talk perks up, *ZDNet*, http://www.zdnet.com/blog, June 13; J. Moran & J. Cohn, 2011, Why companies are so bad at CEO succession planning, *Business Insider*, http://www.businessinsider.com, May 31; B. Worthen & J. S. Lublin, 2011, Executives churn at HP, *Wall Street Journal Online*, http://www.online.wsj.com, May 26; 2011, 2010 CEO turnover falls sharply, finds Booz & company CEO succession study, *Business Intelligence*, http://www.bi-me.com, May 17; R. Waters, 2011, The mystery surrounding HP's services business, *Financial Times*, http://www.ft.com, May 17; G. Fiaharty & A. A. Reznichenko, 2011, Baker Hughes announces CEO succession plan, *PR Newswire*, http://www.prnewswire.com, April 28; A. Satariano, 2011, Apple challenged by investors on Jobs succession planning, *Bloomberg Businessweek*, http://www.businessweek.com, February 23; 2011, Understanding CEO succession, *NACD*, http://blog.nacdonline.org.

to seek other top management positions. Research shows that high turnover among the acquired firm's top managers often produces poor performance and perhaps even leads to a failed acquisition.[72] Therefore, acquiring firms should work hard to avoid successions during the integration process and thereafter.

Key Strategic Leadership Actions

Certain actions characterize effective strategic leadership; we present the most important ones in Figure 12.4. Many of the actions interact with each other. For example, managing the firm's resources effectively includes developing human capital[73] and contributes to establishing a strategic direction, fostering an effective culture, exploiting core competencies, using effective organizational control systems, and establishing ethical practices. The most effective strategic leaders create viable options in making decisions regarding each of the key strategic leadership actions.[74]

Determining Strategic Direction

Determining strategic direction involves specifying the vision and the strategy to achieve this vision over time.[75] The strategic direction is framed within the context of the conditions (i.e., opportunities and threats) strategic leaders expect their firm to face in roughly the next three to five years.

STRATEGY RIGHT NOW

Read more about succession planning and its importance for a successful firm.

www.cengagebrain.com

The ideal long-term strategic direction has two parts: a core ideology and an envisioned future. The core ideology motivates employees through the company's heritage, but the envisioned future encourages employees to stretch beyond their expectations of accomplishment and requires significant change and progress to be realized.[76] The envisioned future serves as a guide to many aspects of a firm's strategy implementation process, including motivation, leadership, employee empowerment, and organizational design. The strategic direction could include such actions as entering new international markets and developing a set of new suppliers to add to the firm's value chain.[77]

Most changes in strategic direction are difficult to design and implement; however, CEO Jeffrey Immelt had an even greater challenge at GE. GE performed exceptionally well under Jack Welch's leadership. Although change was necessary because the competitive landscape had shifted significantly, stakeholders accustomed to Jack Welch and high performance had problems accepting Immelt's changes (e.g., changes to the firm's corporate-level strategy and structure). As explained in the Strategic Focus, it is difficult following successful leaders such as Jack Welch, Steve Jobs (Apple), and Sam Palmisano (IBM). Additionally, information regarding the firm's strategic direction must be consistently and clearly communicated to all affected parties.[78]

Determining strategic direction involves specifying the vision and the strategy to achieve this vision over time.

Figure 12.4 Exercise of Effective Strategic Leadership

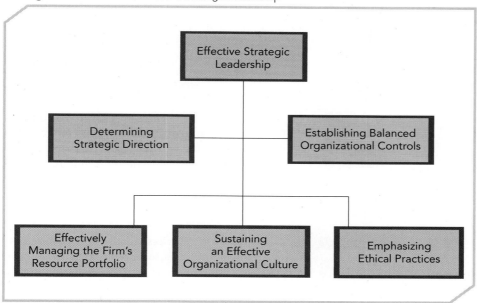

© 2013 Cengage Learning.

Some strategic leaders, however, may not choose the best strategy for the firm to follow given its competitive environment. For example, some executives are committed to the status quo. This risk-averse stance is common in firms that have performed well in the past and for CEOs who have been in their jobs for extended periods of time.[79] Research also suggests that some CEOs are erratic or even ambivalent in their choices of strategic direction, especially when their competitive environment is turbulent and it is difficult to identify the best strategy.[80] Of course, these behaviors are unlikely to produce high performance and may then lead to CEO turnover. Interestingly, research has found that incentive compensation in the form of stock options encourages talented executives to select the best strategies and thus achieve the highest performance. However, the same incentives used with less talented executives produce lower performance.[81]

A charismatic CEO may foster stakeholders' commitment to a new vision and strategic direction. Nonetheless, it is important not to lose sight of the organization's strengths and weaknesses when making changes required by a new strategic direction. The firm must take advantage of resource strengths and overcome or avoid actions requiring capabilities in areas where the firm is weak.[82] To do this requires that top managers develop the capability to analyze complex conditions and understand the interrelationships that exist in order to design the most effective strategy.[83] In the current global competitive landscape, top managers also need to be ambicultural. In other words, they need to be able to identify the best managerial and strategic practices regardless of their cultural origin and meld them to create the best strategic approach for their firm wherever they operate across the globe.[84] The goal is to pursue the firm's short-term need to adjust to a new vision and strategic direction while maintaining its long-term survivability by effectively managing its portfolio of resources.

Effectively Managing the Firm's Resource Portfolio

Effectively managing the firm's portfolio of resources may be the most important strategic leadership task. The firm's resources are categorized as financial capital, human capital, social capital, and organizational capital (including organizational culture).[85]

Clearly, financial capital is critical to organizational success; strategic leaders understand this reality.[86] However, the most effective strategic leaders recognize the equivalent importance of managing each remaining type of resource as well as managing the

Leadership groups perform many tasks, such as budgeting for effective training programs for its staff.

Yuri Arcurs/Shutterstock.com

integration of resources (e.g., using financial capital to provide training opportunities to enhance the capabilities embedded in human capital). Most importantly, effective strategic leaders manage the firm's resource portfolio by organizing the resources into capabilities, structuring the firm to facilitate using those capabilities, and choosing strategies through which the capabilities are successfully leveraged to create value for customers.[87] Exploiting and maintaining core competencies and developing and retaining the firm's human and social capital are actions taken to reach these important objectives.

Exploiting and Maintaining Core Competencies

Examined in Chapters 1 and 3, *core competencies* are capabilities that serve as a source of competitive advantage for a firm over its rivals. Typically, core competencies relate to an organization's functional skills, such as manufacturing, finance, marketing, and research and development. Strategic leaders must verify that the firm's competencies are emphasized when implementing strategies. Intel, for example, has core competencies of *competitive agility* (an ability to act in a variety of competitively relevant ways) and *competitive speed* (an ability to act quickly when facing environmental and competitive pressures).[88] Capabilities are developed over time as firms learn from their actions and enhance their knowledge about specific actions needed. For example, through repeated interactions, some firms have formed a capability allowing them to fully understand customers' needs as they change.[89] Firms with capabilities in R&D that develop into core competencies are rewarded by the market because of the critical nature of innovation in many industries.[90] To continuously develop current competencies and build new ones, firms create a *dynamic capability*.[91]

Given the need for transformation, GM's newest CEO, Dan Akerson, is investing to build new capabilities in technology development and in marketing, especially in customer service. His intent is to develop these into the new core competencies of GM.[92] Using the dynamic capability described earlier, firms must continuously develop and, when appropriate, change their core competencies to outperform rivals. If they have a competence that provides an advantage, competitors will eventually imitate that competence and reduce or eliminate the firm's competitive advantage. Additionally, firms must guard against the competence becoming a liability, thereby preventing change.

As we discuss next, human capital is critical to a firm's success. One reason it's so critical is that human capital is the resource through which core competencies are developed and used.

Developing Human Capital and Social Capital

Human capital refers to the knowledge and skills of a firm's entire workforce. From the perspective of human capital, employees are viewed as a capital resource requiring continuous investment.[93]

Investments made to acquire and develop high-quality human capital are productive, in that much of the development of U.S. industry can be attributed to the effectiveness of its human resources. This fact suggests that "as the dynamics of competition accelerate, people are perhaps the only truly sustainable source of competitive advantage."[94] In all types of organizations—large and small, new and established, and so forth—human capital's increasing importance suggests a significant role for the firm's human resource management activities.[95] As a support activity (see Chapter 3), human resource

Human capital refers to the knowledge and skills of a firm's entire workforce.

management practices facilitate people's efforts to successfully select and especially to use the firm's strategies.[96]

Effective training and development programs increase the probability of individuals becoming successful strategic leaders.[97] These programs are increasingly linked to firm success as knowledge becomes more integral to gaining and sustaining a competitive advantage.[98] Additionally, such programs build knowledge and skills, inculcate a common set of core values, and offer a systematic view of the organization, thus promoting the firm's vision and organizational cohesion.

Effective training and development programs also contribute positively to the firm's efforts to form core competencies.[99] Furthermore, they help strategic leaders improve skills that are critical to completing other tasks associated with effective strategic leadership, such as determining the firm's strategic direction, exploiting and maintaining the firm's core competencies, and developing an organizational culture that supports ethical practices. Thus, building human capital is vital to the effective execution of strategic leadership. Indeed, some argue that the world's "best companies are realizing that no matter what business they're in, their real business is building leaders."[100]

wavebreakmedia ltd/Shutterstock.com

A firm can never invest too much capital to ensure its workforce is happy, motivated, and successful.

When human capital investments are successful, the result is a workforce capable of learning continuously. Continuous learning and leveraging the firm's expanding knowledge base are linked with strategic success.[101]

Learning also can preclude making errors. Strategic leaders tend to learn more from their failures than their successes because they sometimes make the wrong attributions for the successes.[102] For example, the effectiveness of certain approaches and knowledge can be context specific. Thus, some "best practices" may not work well in all situations. We know that using teams to make decisions can be effective, but sometimes it is better for leaders to make decisions alone, especially when the decisions must be made and implemented quickly (e.g., in crisis situations).[103] As such, effective strategic leaders recognize the importance of learning from success *and* from failure.

Learning and building knowledge are important for creating innovation in firms.[104] Innovation leads to competitive advantage. Overall, firms that create and maintain greater knowledge usually achieve and maintain competitive advantages. However, as noted with core competencies, strategic leaders must guard against allowing high levels of knowledge in one area to lead to myopia and overlooking knowledge development opportunities in other important areas of the business.

When facing challenging conditions, firms sometimes decide to lay off some of their human capital. Strategic leaders must recognize though that layoffs can result in a significant loss of the knowledge possessed by the firm's human capital. Research shows that moderate-sized layoffs may improve firm performance, but large layoffs produce stronger performance downturns in firms because of the loss of human capital.[105] Although it is also not uncommon for restructuring firms to reduce their expenditures on or investments in training and development programs, restructuring may actually be an important time to increase investments in these programs. The reason for increased focus on training and development is that restructuring firms have less slack and cannot absorb as many errors; moreover, the employees who remain after layoffs may find themselves in positions without all the skills or knowledge they need to perform the required tasks effectively.

Viewing employees as a resource to be maximized rather than as a cost to be minimized facilitates successful implementation of a firm's strategies, as does the strategic leader's ability to approach layoffs in a manner that employees believe is fair and equitable. A critical issue for employees is the fairness in the layoffs and how they are treated in their jobs, especially relative to their peers.[106]

Social capital involves relationships inside and outside the firm that help the firm accomplish tasks and create value for customers and shareholders.[107] Social capital is a critical asset for a firm. Inside the firm, employees and units must cooperate to get the work done. In multinational organizations, employees often must cooperate across country boundaries on activities such as R&D to achieve performance objectives (e.g., developing new products).[108]

External social capital is increasingly critical to firm success. The reason for this is that few if any companies have all of the resources they need to successfully compete against their rivals. Firms can use cooperative strategies such as strategic alliances (see Chapter 9) to develop social capital. Social capital can be built in strategic alliances as firms share complementary resources. Resource sharing must be effectively managed, though, to ensure that the partner trusts the firm and is willing to share the desired resources.[109] This social capital has many benefits. For example, firms with strong social capital are able to be more ambidextrous; that is, they can develop or have access to multiple capabilities providing them with the flexibility to take advantage of opportunities identified and to respond to significant challenges encountered.[110]

Research evidence suggests that the success of many types of firms may partially depend on social capital. Large multinational firms often must establish alliances in order to enter new foreign markets. Likewise, entrepreneurial firms often must establish alliances to gain access to resources, venture capital, or other types of resources (e.g., special expertise that the entrepreneurial firm cannot afford to maintain in-house).[111] Retaining quality human capital and maintaining strong internal social capital can be affected strongly by the firm's culture.

Sustaining an Effective Organizational Culture

In Chapter 1, we defined organizational culture as a complex set of ideologies, symbols, and core values that are shared throughout the firm and influence the way business is conducted. Evidence suggests that a firm can develop core competencies in terms of both the capabilities it possesses and the way the capabilities are leveraged when implementing strategies to produce desired outcomes. In other words, because the organizational culture influences how the firm conducts its business and helps regulate and control employees' behavior, it can be a source of competitive advantage.[112] Given its importance, it may be that a vibrant organizational culture is the most valuable competitive differentiator for business organizations. Thus, shaping the context within which the firm formulates and implements its strategies—that is, shaping the organizational culture—is an essential strategic leadership action.[113]

Entrepreneurial Mind-Set

Especially in large organizations, an organizational culture often encourages (or discourages) strategic leaders from pursuing (or not pursuing) entrepreneurial opportunities.[114] This issue is important because entrepreneurial opportunities are a vital source of growth and innovation.[115] Therefore, a key role of strategic leaders is to encourage and promote innovation by pursuing entrepreneurial opportunities.[116]

One way to encourage innovation is to invest in opportunities as real options—that is, invest in an opportunity in order to provide the potential option of taking advantage of the opportunity at some point in the future.[117] For example, a firm might buy a piece of land to have the option to build on it at some time in the future should the company need more space and should that location increase in value to the company. Firms might enter strategic alliances for similar reasons. In this instance, a firm might form an alliance to have the option of acquiring the partner later or of building a stronger relationship with it (e.g., developing a joint new venture).[118]

In Chapter 13, we describe how large firms use strategic entrepreneurship to pursue entrepreneurial opportunities and to gain first-mover advantages. Small and medium-sized firms also rely on strategic entrepreneurship when trying to develop innovations as

Social capital involves relationships inside and outside the firm that help the firm accomplish tasks and create value for customers and shareholders.

An **organizational culture** consists of a complex set of ideologies, symbols, and core values that are shared throughout the firm and influence the way business is conducted.

the foundation for profitable growth. In firms of all sizes, strategic entrepreneurship is more likely to be successful when employees have an entrepreneurial mind-set.[119]

Five dimensions characterize a firm's entrepreneurial mind-set: autonomy, innovativeness, risk taking, proactiveness, and competitive aggressiveness.[120] In combination, these dimensions influence the actions a firm takes to be innovative and launch new ventures.

Autonomy, the first of an entrepreneurial orientation's five dimensions, allows employees to take actions that are free of organizational constraints and permits individuals and groups to be self-directed. The second dimension, *innovativeness,* "reflects a firm's tendency to engage in and support new ideas, novelty, experimentation, and creative processes that may result in new products, services, or technological processes."[121] Cultures with a tendency toward innovativeness encourage employees to think beyond existing knowledge, technologies, and parameters to find creative ways to add value. *Risk taking* reflects a willingness by employees and their firm to accept risks when pursuing entrepreneurial opportunities. Assuming significant levels of debt and allocating large amounts of other resources (e.g., people) to projects that may not be completed are examples of these risks. The fourth dimension of an entrepreneurial orientation, *proactiveness,* describes a firm's ability to be a market leader rather than a follower. Proactive organizational cultures constantly use processes to anticipate future market needs and to satisfy them before competitors learn how to do so. Finally, *competitive aggressiveness* is a firm's propensity to take actions that allow it to consistently and substantially outperform its rivals.[122]

Changing the Organizational Culture and Restructuring

Changing a firm's organizational culture is more difficult than maintaining it; however, effective strategic leaders recognize when change is needed. Incremental changes to the firm's culture typically are used to implement strategies.[123] More significant and sometimes even radical changes to organizational culture support selecting strategies that differ from those the firm has implemented historically. Regardless of the reasons for change, shaping and reinforcing a new culture requires effective communication and problem solving, along with selecting the right people (those who have the values desired for the organization), engaging in effective performance appraisals (establishing goals and measuring individual performance toward goals that fit in with the new core values), and using appropriate reward systems (rewarding the desired behaviors that reflect the new core values).[124] As noted in the Opening Case, the new CEO at HP is trying to recapture the firm's soul.

Evidence suggests that cultural changes succeed only when the firm's CEO, other key top management team members, and middle-level managers actively support them.[125] To effect change, middle-level managers in particular need to be highly disciplined to energize the culture and foster alignment with the strategic vision.[126] In addition, managers must be sensitive to the effects of other major strategic changes on organizational culture. For example, major downsizings can have negative effects on an organization's culture, especially if they are not implemented in accordance with the dominant organizational values.[127]

Emphasizing Ethical Practices

The effectiveness of processes used to implement the firm's strategies increases when they are based on ethical practices. Ethical companies encourage and enable people at all organizational levels to act ethically when doing what is necessary to implement strategies. In turn, ethical practices and the judgment on which they are based create "social capital" in the organization, increasing the "goodwill available to individuals and groups" in the organization.[128] Alternatively, when unethical practices evolve in an organization, they may become acceptable to many managers and employees.[129] One study found that in these circumstances, managers were particularly likely to engage in unethical practices to meet their goals when current efforts to meet them were insufficient.[130]

To properly influence employees' judgment and behavior, ethical practices must shape the firm's decision-making process and must be an integral part of organizational culture. In fact, research evidence suggests that a value-based culture is the most effective means of ensuring that employees comply with the firm's ethical requirements.[131] As we explained in Chapter 10, managers may act opportunistically, making decisions that are in their own best interests but not in the firm's best interests when facing lax expectations regarding ethical behavior. In other words, managers acting opportunistically take advantage of their positions, making decisions that benefit themselves to the detriment of the firm's stakeholders.[132] But strategic leaders are most likely to integrate ethical values into their decisions when the company has explicit ethics codes, the code is integrated into the business through extensive ethics training, and shareholders expect ethical behavior.[133]

Firms should employ ethical strategic leaders—leaders who include ethical practices as part of their strategic direction for the firm, who desire to do the right thing, and for whom honesty, trust, and integrity are important.[134] Strategic leaders who consistently display these qualities inspire employees as they work with others to develop and support an organizational culture in which ethical practices are the expected behavioral norms.[135]

Strategic leaders can take several actions to develop an ethical organizational culture. Examples of these actions include (1) establishing and communicating specific goals to describe the firm's ethical standards (e.g., developing and disseminating a code of conduct); (2) continuously revising and updating the code of conduct, based on inputs from people throughout the firm and from other stakeholders (e.g., customers and suppliers); (3) disseminating the code of conduct to all stakeholders to inform them of the firm's ethical standards and practices; (4) developing and implementing methods and procedures to use in achieving the firm's ethical standards (e.g., using internal auditing practices that are consistent with the standards); (5) creating and using explicit reward systems that recognize acts of courage (e.g., rewarding those who use proper channels and procedures to report observed wrongdoings); and (6) creating a work environment in which all people are treated with dignity.[136] The effectiveness of these actions increases when they are taken simultaneously and thereby are mutually supportive. When strategic leaders and others throughout the firm fail to take actions such as these—perhaps because an ethical culture has not been created—problems are likely to occur.

As explained in the Strategic Focus, Alibaba experienced a significant problem with the fraud it discovered. The problem was made more serious because it was purposefully facilitated by some of its own employees, suggesting that the company was unable to prevent the unethical practices. Alibaba dealt with this perception by taking forceful actions in the resignations of its CEO and COO. Furthermore, it repaid those customers who lost money due to the fraud. And, it instituted new practices trying to ensure these problems do not reoccur. Hopefully, the firm's actions will restore the trust in Alibaba's practices so important to all firms but especially to e-commerce firms. As we discuss next, formal organizational controls can help prevent further problems and reinforce better ethical practices.

Establishing Balanced Organizational Controls

Organizational controls are basic to a capitalistic system and have long been viewed as an important part of strategy implementation processes.[137] Controls are necessary to help ensure that firms achieve their desired outcomes.[138] Defined as the "formal, information-based ... procedures used by managers to maintain or alter patterns in organizational activities," controls help strategic leaders build credibility, demonstrate the value of strategies to the firm's stakeholders, and promote and support strategic change.[139] Most critically, controls provide the parameters for implementing strategies as well as the corrective actions to be taken when implementation-related adjustments are required. For example, Alibaba exercised control to identify and eliminate the fraud. Furthermore, it developed additional controls to prevent such actions from occurring again.

S T R A T E G I C F O C U S

ETHICS · ETHICS · ETHICS · ETHICS · ETHICS · ETHICS · ETHICS ·

THE KEY TO E-COMMERCE IS TRUST: FRAUD AT ALIBABA

Jack Ma, founder of Alibaba, once said that the key to the success of e-commerce in China is trust. He was likely correct, and his firm garnered a fair amount of trust as it became the largest Internet company in China. In fact, Alibaba.com's IPO on the Hong Kong stock exchange produced $1.7 billion—the second largest Internet IPO behind only Google. Alibaba accounts for 80 percent of all e-commerce in China, with gross sales volume of almost $60 billion in 2010. Alibaba has 57 million registered users globally and about 14 million of them are registered on its English language network.

Despite its success and Ma's emphasis on trust and values, he announced in February that an internal investigation found fraudulent practices within the company. Essentially, approximately 2,300 sellers who pay Alibaba to sell their goods and services on its site defrauded customers (e.g., obtaining payments but never providing the goods to the buyers). These sellers received assistance from about 100 of the more than 5,000 sales associates employed by Alibaba. Overall, the sales amounted to approximately $6 million, only a small amount of Alibaba's total business. However, all of the buyers defrauded were from outside of China, the primary set of customers targeted by Alibaba for China's companies. Ma and Alibaba acted swiftly and forcefully when the investigation conclusively showed fraud. Alibaba's CEO, David Wei, and COO, Elvis Lee, both resigned accepting blame for the unethical practices, even though they were not directly involved in the activities. In addition, Deng Kangming, chief of human resources, was demoted. These actions suggest the seriousness with which the firm judges these problems. Jonathan Lu, CEO of Taobao, another major company in the Alibaba group, was named CEO of Alibaba.com. Eventually, Chinese police arrested 36 individuals for the Alibaba.com fraudulent activity.

Ju Huanzong Xinhua News Agency/Newscom

In early 2011, Alibaba discovered that nearly 2,300 of its sales personnel had defrauded customers. The company is now working double time to regain the trust of its e-commerce customers.

Now, Alibaba must work hard to reestablish the trust that Ma feels is so important for an e-commerce company. It is establishing practices to guard against further fraudulent activities. Furthermore, it is identifying the customers defrauded and repaying them the money that they lost in the transactions. The fraud is likely to slow Alibaba's growth but most analysts suggest that the problems will be experienced only in the short term if the company takes the proper actions. Hopefully the firm can avoid such problems in the future.

Sources: 2011, Chinese police arrest 36 in Alibaba.com fraud sting, *Reuters*, http://www.reuters.com, June 30; T. Orlik, 2011, Alibaba's most valuable treasure still in the cave, *Wall Street Journal Online*, http://www.online.wsj.com, March 18; T. Culpan, 2011, Alibaba's chief Lu wants to 'fix mistakes, prevent detours', *Bloomberg Businessweek*, http://www.businessweek.com, February 24; B. Powell, 2011, Why Alibaba's CEO had to go, *Fortune*, http://tech.fortune.cnn.com, February 22; K. Hille, 2011, Alibaba chiefs quit after fraud cases, *Financial Times*, February 22, p. 18; D. Barboza, 2011, 2 executives quit Alibaba.com amid fraud inquiry, *The New York Times*, http://www.nytimes.com, February 21.

In this chapter, we focus on two organizational controls—strategic and financial—that were introduced in Chapter 11. Strategic and financial controls are important because strategic leaders, especially those at the top of the organization, are responsible for their development and effective use.

As we explained in Chapter 11, financial control focuses on short-term financial outcomes. In contrast, strategic control focuses on the *content* of strategic actions rather than their *outcomes*. Some strategic actions can be correct but still result in poor financial outcomes because of external conditions such as an economic recession, unexpected domestic or foreign government actions, or natural disasters. Therefore, emphasizing financial controls often produces more short-term and risk-averse managerial decisions, because financial outcomes may be caused by events beyond managers' direct control. Alternatively, strategic control encourages lower-level managers to make decisions that incorporate moderate and acceptable levels of risk because outcomes are shared among the business-level executives making strategic proposals and the corporate-level executives evaluating them.

The challenge for strategic leaders is to achieve an appropriate balance of financial and strategic controls so that firm performance improves. The Balanced Scorecard is a tool that helps strategic leaders to evaluate the effectiveness of the controls used.

The Balanced Scorecard

The balanced scorecard is a framework firms can use to evaluate whether they have achieved the appropriate balance among the strategic and financial controls to attain the desired level of firm performance.[140] This technique is most appropriate for use in evaluating business-level strategies; however, it can also be used with the other strategies firms implement (e.g., corporate level, international, and cooperative).

The underlying premise of the balanced scorecard is that firms jeopardize their future performance when financial controls are emphasized at the expense of strategic controls.[141] This occurs because financial controls provide feedback about outcomes achieved from past actions, but do not communicate the drivers of future performance.[142] Thus, an overemphasis on financial controls may promote managerial behavior that sacrifices the firm's long-term, value-creating potential for short-term performance gains.[143] An appropriate balance of strategic controls and financial controls, rather than an overemphasis on either, allows firms to achieve higher levels of performance.

Four perspectives are integrated to form the balanced scorecard framework: *financial* (concerned with growth, profitability, and risk from the shareholders' perspective), *customer* (concerned with the amount of value customers perceive was created by the firm's products), *internal business processes* (with a focus on the priorities for various business processes that create customer and shareholder satisfaction), and *learning and growth* (concerned with the firm's effort to create a climate that supports change, innovation, and growth). Thus, using the balanced scorecard framework allows the firm to understand how it responds to shareholders (financial perspective), how customers view it (customer perspective), the processes it must emphasize to successfully use its competitive advantage (internal perspective), and what it can do to improve its performance in order to grow (learning and growth perspective).[144] Generally speaking, strategic controls tend to be emphasized when the firm assesses its performance relative to the learning and growth perspective, whereas financial controls are emphasized when assessing performance in terms of the financial perspective.

Firms use different criteria to measure their standing relative to the scorecard's four perspectives. We show sample criteria in Figure 12.5. The firm should select the number of criteria that will allow it to have both a strategic understanding and a financial understanding of its performance without becoming immersed in too many details.[145] For example, we know from research that a firm's innovation, quality of its goods and services, growth of its sales, and its profitability are all interrelated.[146]

Strategic leaders play an important role in determining a proper balance between strategic controls and financial controls, whether they are in single-business firms or large diversified firms. A proper balance between controls is important, in that "wealth creation for organizations where strategic leadership is exercised is possible because these leaders make appropriate investments for future viability [through strategic control], while maintaining an appropriate level of financial stability in the present [through financial control]."[147] In fact, most corporate restructuring is designed to refocus the firm

The **balanced scorecard** is a framework firms can use to verify that they have established both strategic and financial controls to assess their performance.

Figure 12.5 Strategic Controls and Financial Controls in a Balanced Scorecard Framework

Perspectives	Criteria
Financial	• Cash flow • Return on equity • Return on assets
Customer	• Assessment of ability to anticipate customers' needs • Effectiveness of customer service practices • Percentage of repeat business • Quality of communications with customers
Internal Business Processes	• Asset utilization improvements • Improvements in employee morale • Changes in turnover rates
Learning and Growth	• Improvements in innovation ability • Number of new products compared to competitors • Increases in employees' skills

on its core businesses, thereby allowing top executives to reestablish strategic control of their separate business units.[148]

Successfully using strategic control frequently is integrated with appropriate autonomy for the various subunits so that they can gain a competitive advantage in their respective markets.[149] Strategic control can be used to promote the sharing of both tangible and intangible resources among interdependent businesses within a firm's portfolio. In addition, the autonomy provided allows the flexibility necessary to take advantage of specific marketplace opportunities. As a result, strategic leadership promotes simultaneous use of strategic control and autonomy.[150]

The balanced scorecard is being used by car manufacturer Porsche. After this manufacturer of sought-after sports cars regained its market-leading position, it implemented a balanced scorecard approach in an effort to maintain this position. In particular, Porsche used the balanced scorecard to promote learning and continuously improve the business. For example, knowledge was collected from all Porsche dealerships throughout the world. The instrument used to collect the information was referred to as "Porsche Key Performance Indicators." The fact that Porsche is now the world's most profitable automaker suggests the value the firm gained and is gaining by using the balanced scorecard as a foundation for simultaneously emphasizing strategic and financial controls.[151]

As we have explained, strategic leaders are critical to a firm's ability to successfully use all parts of the strategic management process. As described in the Strategic Focus, Jack Ma and his new CEO of Alibaba, Jonathan Lu, are acting as strategic leaders to achieve the appropriate balance of strategic and financial controls to create positive outcomes for all of a firm's stakeholders.

SUMMARY

- Effective strategic leadership is a prerequisite to successfully using the strategic management process. Strategic leadership entails the ability to anticipate events, envision possibilities, maintain flexibility, and empower others to create strategic change.

- Top-level managers are an important resource for firms to develop and exploit competitive advantages. In addition, when they and their work are valuable, rare, imperfectly imitable, and nonsubstitutable, strategic leaders are also a source of competitive advantage.

- The top management team is composed of key managers who play a critical role in selecting and implementing the firm's strategies. Generally, they are officers of the corporation and/or members of the board of directors.

- The top management team's characteristics, a firm's strategies, and its performance are all interrelated. For example, a top management team with significant marketing and R&D knowledge positively contributes to the firm's use of a growth strategy. Overall, having diverse skills increases most top management teams' effectiveness.

- Typically, performance improves when the board of directors is involved in shaping a firm's strategic direction. However, when the CEO has a great deal of power, the board may be less involved in decisions about strategy formulation and implementation. By appointing people to the board and simultaneously serving as CEO and chair of the board, CEOs increase their power.

- In managerial succession, strategic leaders are selected from either the internal or the external managerial labor market. Because of their effect on firm performance, selection of strategic leaders has implications for a firm's effectiveness. There are a variety of reasons that companies select the firm's strategic leaders from either internal or external sources. In most instances, the internal market is used to select the CEO; but the number of outsiders chosen is increasing. Outsiders often are selected to initiate major changes in strategy.

- Effective strategic leadership has five major components: determining the firm's strategic direction, effectively managing the firm's resource portfolio (including exploiting and maintaining core competencies and managing human capital and social capital), sustaining an effective organizational culture, emphasizing ethical practices, and establishing balanced organizational controls.

- Strategic leaders must develop the firm's strategic direction. The strategic direction specifies the image and character the firm wants to develop over time. To form the strategic direction, strategic leaders evaluate the conditions (e.g., opportunities and threats in the external environment) they expect their firm to face over the next three to five years.

- Strategic leaders must ensure that their firm exploits its core competencies, which are used to produce and deliver products that create value for customers, when implementing its strategies. In related diversified and large firms in particular, core competencies are exploited by sharing them across units and products.

- The ability to manage the firm's resource portfolio and manage the processes used to effectively implement the firm's strategy are critical elements of strategic leadership. Managing the resource portfolio includes integrating resources to create capabilities and leveraging those capabilities through strategies to build competitive advantages. Human capital and social capital are perhaps the most important resources.

- As a part of managing the firm's resources, strategic leaders must develop a firm's human capital. Effective strategic leaders view human capital as a resource to be maximized—not as a cost to be minimized. Such leaders develop and use programs designed to train current and future strategic leaders to build the skills needed to nurture the rest of the firm's human capital.

- Effective strategic leaders build and maintain internal and external social capital. Internal social capital promotes cooperation and coordination within and across units in the firm. External social capital provides access to resources the firm needs to compete effectively.

- Shaping the firm's culture is a central task of effective strategic leadership. An appropriate organizational culture encourages the development of an entrepreneurial orientation among employees and an ability to change the culture as necessary.

- In ethical organizations, employees are encouraged to exercise ethical judgment and to always act ethically. Improved ethical practices foster social capital. Setting specific goals to meet the firm's ethical standards, using a code of conduct, rewarding ethical behaviors, and creating a work environment where all people are treated with dignity are actions that facilitate and support ethical behavior.

- Developing and using balanced organizational controls are the final components of effective strategic leadership. The balanced scorecard is a tool that measures the effectiveness of the firm's strategic and financial controls. An effective balance between strategic and financial controls allows for flexible use of core competencies, but within the parameters of the firm's financial position.

REVIEW QUESTIONS

1. What is strategic leadership? In what ways are top executives considered important resources for an organization?

2. What is a top management team, and how does it affect a firm's performance and its abilities to innovate and design and implement effective strategic changes?

3. How important are the internal and external managerial labor markets for the managerial succession process?

4. What is the effect of strategic leadership on determining the firm's strategic direction?

5. How do strategic leaders effectively manage their firm's resource portfolio to exploit its core competencies and leverage the human capital and social capital to achieve a competitive advantage?

6. What is organizational culture? What must strategic leaders do to develop and sustain an effective organizational culture?

7. As a strategic leader, what actions could you take to establish and emphasize ethical practices in your firm?

8. What are organizational controls? Why are strategic controls and financial controls important aspects of the strategic management process?

EXPERIENTIAL EXERCISES

EXERCISE 1: THE CEO AND TOP MANAGEMENT TEAM

Chapter 10 discussed corporate governance and the fiduciary role that the board plays in overseeing the affairs of the company. The composition of the top management team is critical in assessing the strategic direction of a firm. It is not uncommon for a powerful CEO and top management team to thwart the desires of the board. There are various ways in which a CEO may become powerful; it may be the result of equity ownership, tenure, expertise, or by appointing sympathetic board members, etc. This exercise will allow you to assess the power of a CEO and his or her team and develop your thoughts regarding their relationship to the board.

Part One

Identify with your team the firm you would like to analyze. Pick a company that is publicly traded so that you have adequate information about the executives.

Part Two

Explore the power relationship between the CEO and his top management team (TMT) and the board. You should at a minimum be able to address the following points:

1. CEO tenure

2. TMT tenure

3. TMT relationships to the CEO (i.e., were they hired by the CEO or his predecessor?)

4. Board member tenure and structure (i.e., does the board structure possess a lead independent director, is CEO duality present?)

5. Describe the CEO and his TMT in terms of experience and networks. For example, do they sit on other firms' boards of directors, are there any overlaps with their employer's board?

6. What conclusions do you reach regarding the power relationship between the CEO and the board?

Be prepared to discuss this utilizing a PowerPoint presentation of your findings and conclusions.

EXERCISE 2: STRATEGIC LEADERSHIP IS TOUGH!

Your text defines strategic leadership as "the ability to anticipate, envision, maintain flexibility, and empower others... ." Accordingly, this exercise combines the practical elements of leadership in an experiential exercise. You are asked to replicate leaders and followers in the attainment of a defined goal.

Divide the class into teams of 3 to 5 individuals. Each team should choose a leader (and by that decision, who will be the followers). It is important to choose wisely. The classroom instructor will then assign the task to be completed.

Students should be prepared to debrief the rest of the class when the assignment is completed. Your instructor will guide this discussion.

VIDEO CASE

AN EXAMPLE OF STRATEGIC LEADERSHIP: MEG WHITMAN/CEO/EBAY

Meg Whitman, head of eBay, is considered a pioneer at creating a global marketplace and at inciting an e-commerce revolution. Whitman attributes her female characteristics as being effective in the eBay environment. Despite the real and difficult sacrifices and the guilt of not spending as much time with her children, she attributes her drive to keep going to her love and satisfaction for helping to continue the next chapter of eBay. Despite having trade-offs between home and work, Whitman contends she would do it all over again. Today, eBay has more than 10 million registered users, produces $224 million in annual revenue, and has an actual income of $10.8 million.

Be prepared to discuss the following concepts and questions in class:

Concepts

- Strategic leadership
- Top management team
- Human capital
- Social capital
- Organizational culture

Questions

1. In what ways did Meg Whitman's characteristics provided strategic leadership at eBay?
2. How is Meg Whitman appropriate for a top management team?
3. What do you think would be Whitman's approach to human capital?
4. How important is social capital to the success of eBay?
5. With Meg Whitman at the helm, describe eBay's organizational culture. Is there evidence of an entrepreneurial mind-set?

NOTES

1. A. Mackey, 2008, The effect of CEOs on firm performance, *Strategic Management Journal*, 29: 1357–1367.

2. A. Bryant, 2011, Distilling the wisdom of CEOs, *The New York Times*, http://www.nytimes.com, April 16; E. F. Goldman, 2007, Strategic thinking at the top, *MIT Sloan Management Review*, 48(4): 75–81.

3. M. A. Hitt, K. T. Haynes, & R. Serpa, 2010, Strategic leadership for the 21st century, *Business Horizons*, 53: 437–444; R. D. Ireland & M. A. Hitt, 2005, Achieving and maintaining strategic competitiveness in the 21st century: The role of strategic leadership, *Academy of Management Executive*, 19: 63–77.

4. J. P. Kotter, 2007, Leading change: Why transformation efforts fail, *Harvard Business Review*, 85(1): 96–103.

5. M. A. Hitt, C. Miller, & A. Colella, 2011, *Organizational Behavior*, 3rd ed., Hoboken, NJ: John Wiley & Sons; R. E. Ployhart & T. P. Moliterno, 2011, Emergence of the human capital resource: A multilevel model, *Academy of Management Review*, 36: 127–150.

6. D. Roberts & C.-C. Tschang, 2007, China's rising leaders, *BusinessWeek*, October 1, 33–35.

7. J. Zhang, P.-H. Soh, & P.-K. Wong, 2010, Entrepreneurial resource acquisition through indirect ties: Compensatory effects of prior knowledge, *Journal of Management*, 36: 511–536; A. S. DeNisi, M. A. Hitt, & S. E. Jackson, 2003, The knowledge-based approach to sustainable competitive advantage, in S. E. Jackson, M. A. Hitt, & A. S. DeNisi (eds.), *Managing Knowledge for Sustained Competitive Advantage*, San Francisco: Jossey-Bass, 3–33.

8. L. Bossidy, 2007, What your leader expects of you: And what you should expect in return, *Harvard Business Review*, 85(4): 58–65; J. E. Post, L. E. Preston, & S. Sachs, 2002, Managing the extended enterprise: The new stakeholder view, *California Management Review*, 45(1): 6–28.

9. A. McKee & D. Massimilian, 2007, Resonant leadership: A new kind of leadership for the digital age, *Journal of Business Strategy*, 27(5): 45–49.

10. Z. Simsek, C. Heavy, & K. L. Veiga, 2010, The impact of CEO core self evaluation on the firm's entrepreneurial orientation, *Strategic Management Journal*, 31: 110–119; E. Baraldi, R. Brennan, D. Harrison, A. Tunisini, & J. Zolkiewski, 2007, Strategic thinking and the IMP approach: A comparative analysis, *Industrial Marketing Management*, 36: 879–894.

11. K. M. Ismail & D. L. Ford, 2010, Organizational leadership in central Asia and the caucasus: Research considerations and directions, *Asia Pacific Journal of Management*, 27: 321–340; M. L. McDonald, P. Khanna, & J. D. Westphal, 2008, Getting them to think outside the circle: Corporate governance, CEOs' external advice networks and firm performance, *Academy of Management Journal*, 51: 453–475.

12. R. A. Burgelman & A. S. Grove, 2007, Let chaos reign, then rein in chaos— repeatedly: Managing strategic dynamics for corporate longevity, *Strategic Management Journal*, 28: 965–979.

13. T. R. Holcomb, R. M. Holmes, & B. L. Connelly, 2009, Making the most of what you have: Managerial ability as a source of resource value creation, *Strategic Management Journal*, 30: 457–485.

14. B. M. Galvin, P. Balkundi, & D. A. Waldman, 2010, Spreading the word: The role of surrogates in charismatic leadership processes, *Academy of Management Review*, 35: 477–494; A. E. Colbert, A. L. Kristof-Brown, B. H. Bradley, & M. R. Barrick, 2008, CEO transformational leadership: The role of goal importance congruence in top management teams, *Academy of Management Journal*, 51: 81–96.

15. T. G. Buchholz, 2007, The Kroc legacy at McDonald's, *The Conference Review Board*, July/August, 14–15.

16. H. S. Givray, 2007, When CEOs aren't leaders, *BusinessWeek*, September 3, 102.

17. D. Goleman, 2004, What makes a leader? *Harvard Business Review*, 82(1): 82–91.

18. Y. Ling, Z. Simsek, M. H. Lubatkin, & J. F. Veiga, 2008, Transformational leadership's role in promoting corporate entrepreneurship: Examining the CEO-TMT interface, *Academy of Management Journal*, 51: 557–576.

19. J. L. Morrow, Jr., D. G. Sirmon, M. A. Hitt, & T. R. Holcomb, 2007, Creating value in the face of declining performance: Firm strategies and organizational recovery, *Strategic Management Journal*, 28: 271–283; R. Castanias & C. Helfat, 2001, The managerial rents model: Theory and empirical analysis, *Journal of Management*, 27: 661–678.

20. L. S. Tsui-Auch & G. Mollering, 2010, Wary managers: Unfavorable environments, perceived vulnerability, and the development of trust in foreign enterprises in China, *Journal of International Business Studies*, 41: 1016–1035; M. Beer & R. Eisenstat, 2000, The silent killers of strategy implementation

and learning, *Sloan Management Review*, 41(4): 29–40.

21. A. M. L. Raes, M. G. Heijlties, U. Glunk, & R. A. Roe, 2011, The interface of the top management team and middle managers: A process model, *Academy of Management Review*, 36: 102–126; V. Santos & T. Garcia, 2007, The complexity of the organizational renewal decision: The management role, *Leadership & Organization Development Journal*, 28: 336–355;.

22. D. G. Sirmon, J.-L. Arregle, M. A. Hitt, & J. W. Webb, 2008, The role of family influence in firms' strategic responses to threat of imitation, *Entrepreneurship Theory and Practice*, 32: 979–998; Y. L. Doz & M. Kosonen, 2007, The new deal at the top, *Harvard Business Review*, 85(6): 98–104.

23. A. S. Tsui, Z-X. Zhang, H. Wang, K. R. Xin, & J. B. Wu, 2006, Unpacking the relationship between CEO leadership behavior and organizational culture, *The Leadership Quarterly*, 17: 113–137; J. A. Petrick & J. F. Quinn, 2001, The challenge of leadership accountability for integrity capacity as a strategic asset, *Journal of Business Ethics*, 34: 331–343.

24. M. S. Wood & M. D. Michalsin, 2010, Entrepreneurial drive in the top management team: Effects on strategic choice and firm performance, *Journal of Leadership and Organizational Studies*, 17: 222–239; D. G. Sirmon, S. Gove, & M. A. Hitt, 2008, Resource management in dyadic competitive rivalry: The effects of resource bundling and deployment, *Academy of Management Journal*, 51: 918–935.

25. J. Li & Y. Tang, 2010, CEO hubris and firm risk taking in China: The moderating role of managerial discretion, *Academy of Management Journal*, 53: 45–68; M. L. A. Hayward, V. P. Rindova, & T. G. Pollock, 2004, Believing one's own press: The causes and consequences of CEO celebrity, *Strategic Management Journal*, 25: 637–653.

26. Simsek, Heavy, & Veiga, The impact of CEO core self evaluation on the firm's entrepreneurial orientation; K. M. Hmieleski & R. A. Baron, 2008, When does entrepreneurial self-efficacy enhance versus reduce firm performance? *Strategic Entrepreneurship Journal*, 2: 57–72.

27. A. M. L. Raes, U. Glunk, M. G. Heijitjes, & R. A. Roe, 2007, Top management team and middle managers, *Small Group Research*, 38: 360–386; I. Goll, R. Sambharya, & L. Tucci, 2001, Top management team composition, corporate ideology, and firm performance, *Management International Review*, 41(2): 109–129.

28. J. Bunderson, 2003, Team member functional background and involvement in management teams: Direct effects and the moderating role of power and centralization, *Academy of Management Journal*, 46: 458–474; L. Markoczy, 2001, Consensus formation during strategic

change, *Strategic Management Journal*, 22: 1013–1031.

29. V. Souitaris & B. M. M. Maestro, 2010, Polychronicity in top management teams: The impact on strategic decision processes and performance in new technology ventures, *Strategic Management Journal*, 31: 652–678.

30. Y. Ling & F. W. Kellermans, 2010, The effects of family firm specific sources of TMT diversity: The moderating role of information exchange frequency, *Journal of Management Studies*, 47: 322–344; R. Rico, E. Molleman, M. Sanchez-Manzanares, & G. S. Van der Vegt, 2007, The effects of diversity faultlines and team task autonomy on decision quality and social integration, *Journal of Management*, 33: 111–132.

31. A. Srivastava, K. M. Bartol, & E. A. Locke, 2006, Empowering leadership in management teams: Effects on knowledge sharing, efficacy, and performance, *Academy of Management Journal*, 49: 1239–1251; D. Knight, C. L. Pearce, K. G. Smith, J. D. Olian, H. P. Sims, K. A. Smith, & P. Flood, 1999, Top management team diversity, group process, and strategic consensus, *Strategic Management Journal*, 20: 446–465.

32. T. Buyl, C. Boone, W. Hendricks, & P. Matthyssens, 2011, Top management team functional diversity and firm performance: The moderating role of CEO characteristics, *Journal of Management Studies*, 48: 151–177; B. J. Olson, S. Parayitam, & Y. Bao, 2007, Strategic decision making: The effects of cognitive diversity, conflict, and trust on decision outcomes, *Journal of Management*, 33: 196–222.

33. S. Finkelstein, D. C. Hambrick, & A. A. Cannella, Jr., 2008, *Strategic Leadership: Top Executives and Their Effects on Organizations*, New York: Oxford University Press.

34. A. Minichilli, G. Corbetta, & I. C. Macmillan, 2010, Top management teams in family-controlled companies: 'Familiness', 'faultlines', and their impact on financial performance, *Journal of Management Studies*, 47: 205–222; J. J. Marcel, 2009, Why top management team characteristics matter when employing a chief operating officer: A strategic contingency perspective, *Strategic Management Journal*, 30: 647–658.

35. B. J. Avolio & S. S. Kahai, 2002, Adding the "e" to e-leadership: How it may impact your leadership, *Organizational Dynamics*, 31: 325–338.

36. Z. Simsek, J. F. Veiga, M. L. Lubatkin, & R. H. Dino, 2005, Modeling the multilevel determinants of top management team behavioral integration, *Academy of Management Journal*, 48: 69–84.

37. A. A. Cannella, J. H. Park, & H. U. Lee, 2008, Top management team functional background diversity and firm performance: Examining the roles of team member collocation and environmental uncertainty, *Academy of Management Journal*, 51: 768–784.

38. A. S. Cui, R. J. Calantone, & D. A. Griffith, 2011, Strategic change and termination of interfirm partnerships, *Strategic Management Journal*, 32: 402–423; M. Jensen & E. J. Zajac, 2004, Corporate elites and corporate strategy: How demographic preferences and structural position shape the scope of the firm, *Strategic Management Journal*, 25: 507–524.

39. S. Nadkarni & P. Hermann, 2010, CEO personality, strategic flexibility and firm performance: The case of the Indian business process outsourcing industry, *Academy of Management Journal*, 53: 1050–1073; W. B. Werther, 2003, Strategic change and leader-follower alignment, *Organizational Dynamics*, 32: 32–45.

40. H. Li & J. Li, 2009, Top management team conflict and entrepreneurial strategy making in China, *Asia Pacific Journal of Management*, 26: 263–283; S. C. Parker, 2009, Can cognitive biases explain venture team homophily? *Strategic Entrepreneurship Journal*, 3: 67–83.

41. Y. Zhang & N. Rajagopalan, 2003, Explaining the new CEO origin: Firm versus industry antecedents, *Academy of Management Journal*, 46: 327–338.

42. I. Barreto, 2010, Dynamic capabilities: A review of the past research and an agenda for the future, *Journal of Management*, 36: 256–280; T. Dvir, D. Eden, B. J. Avolio, & B. Shamir, 2002, Impact of transformational leadership on follower development and performance: A field experiment, *Academy of Management Journal*, 45: 735–744.

43. J. P. Muczyk & D. T. Holt, 2008, Toward a cultural contingency model of leadership, *Journal of Leadership and Organizational Studies*, 14: 277–286.

44. C. Bouquet, A. Morrison, & J. Birkinshaw, 2009, International attention and multinational enterprise performance, *Journal of International Business Studies*, 40: 108–131; H. U. Lee & J. H. Park, 2008, The influence of top management team international exposure on international alliance formation, *Journal of Management Studies*, 45: 961–981.

45. K. T. Haynes & A. Hillman, 2010, The effect of board capital and CEO power on strategic change, *Strategic Management Journal*, 31: 1145–1163; C. Thomas, D. Kidd, & C. Fernandez-Araoz, 2007, Are you underutilizing your board? *MIT Sloan Management Review*, 48(2): 71–76.

46. M. L. McDonald & J. D. Westphal, 2010, A little help here? Board control, CEO identification with the corporate elite, and strategic help provided to CEOs at other firms, *Academy of Management Journal*, 53: 343–370; L. Tihanyi, R. A. Johnson, R. E. Hoskisson, & M. A. Hitt, 2003, Institutional ownership and international diversification: The effects of boards of directors and technological opportunity, *Academy of Management Journal*, 46: 195–211.

47. S. Wu, X. Quan, & L. Xu, 2011, CEO power, disclosure quality and the

variability in firm performance, *Nankai Business Review International*, 2: 79–97; B. R. Golden & E. J. Zajac, 2001, When will boards influence strategy? Inclination times power equals strategic change, *Strategic Management Journal*, 22: 1087–1111.

48. M. Carpenter & J. Westphal, 2001, Strategic context of external network ties: Examining the impact of director appointments on board involvement in strategic decision making, *Academy of Management Journal*, 44: 639–660.

49. M. A. Abebe, A. Angriawan, & Y. Lui, 2011, CEO power and organizational turnaround in declining firms: Does environment play a role? *Journal of Leadership and Organizational Studies*, 18: 260–273; M. A. Rutherford & A. K. Buchholtz, 2007, Investigating the relationship between board characteristics and board information, *Corporate Governance: An International Review*, 15: 576–584.

50. X. Huafang & Y. Jianguo, 2007, Ownership structure, board composition and corporate voluntary disclosure: Evidence from listed companies in China, *Managerial Auditing Journal*, 22: 604–619.

51. C. S. Tuggle, D. G. Sirmon, C. R. Reutzel, & L. Bierman, 2010, Commanding board of director attention: Investigating how organizational performance and CEO duality affect board members' attention to monitoring, *Strategic Management Journal*, 32: 640-657; J. Coles & W. Hesterly, 2000, Independence of the chairman and board composition: Firm choices and shareholder value, *Journal of Management*, 26: 195–214.

52. C. M. Daily & D. R. Dalton, 1995, CEO and director turnover in failing firms: An illusion of change? *Strategic Management Journal*, 16: 393–400.

53. D. Miller, I. LeBreton-Miller, & B. Scholnick, 2008, Stewardship vs. stagnation: An empirical comparison of small family and non-family businesses, *Journal of Management Studies*, 51: 51–78; J. H. Davis, F. D. Schoorman, & L. Donaldson, 1997, Toward a stewardship theory of management, *Academy of Management Review*, 22: 20–47.

54. G. Van der Laan, 2010, CEO pay as a reflection of power or performance: An empirical test for The Netherlands, 2002–2006, *Journal of Strategy and Management*, 3: 157–173; P. Kalyta, 2009, Compensation transparency and managerial opportunism: A study of supplemental retirement plans, *Strategic Management Journal*, 30: 405–423.

55. E. Matta & P. W. Beamish, 2008, The accentuated CEO career horizon problem: Evidence from international acquisitions, *Strategic Management Journal*, 29: 683–700; N. Rajagopalan & D. Datta, 1996, CEO characteristics: Does industry matter? *Academy of Management Journal*, 39: 197–215.

56. R. A. Johnson, R. E. Hoskisson, & M. A. Hitt, 1993, Board involvement in restructuring: The effect of board versus managerial controls and characteristics, *Strategic Management Journal*, 14 (Special Issue): 33–50.

57. Z. Simsek, 2007, CEO tenure and organizational performance: An intervening model, *Strategic Management Journal*, 28: 653–662.

58. M. Schneider, 2002, A stakeholder model of organizational leadership, *Organization Science*, 13: 209–220.

59. M. Sorcher & J. Brant, 2002, Are you picking the right leaders? *Harvard Business Review*, 80(2): 78–85; D. A. Waldman, G. G. Ramirez, R. J. House, & P. Puranam, 2001, Does leadership matter? CEO leadership attributes and profitability under conditions of perceived environmental uncertainty, *Academy of Management Journal*, 44: 134–143.

60. J. Werdigier, 2007, UBS not willing to talk about departure of chief, *New York Times Online*, http://www.nytimes.com, July 7.

61. W. Shen & A. A. Cannella, 2002, Revisiting the performance consequences of CEO succession: The impacts of successor type, postsuccession senior executive turnover, and departing CEO tenure, *Academy of Management Journal*, 45: 717–734.

62. D. Ulrich & N. Smallwood, 2007, Building a leadership brand, *Harvard Business Review*, 85(7/8): 93–100.

63. Y. Zhang & N. Rajagopalan, 2010, CEO succession planning: Finally at the center stage of the boardroom. *Business Horizons*, 53: 455–462.

64. G. A. Ballinger & F. D. Schoorman, 2007, Individual reactions to leadership succession in workgroups, *Academy of Management Review*, 32: 116–136; R. E. Hoskisson, D. Yiu, & H. Kim, 2000, Capital and labor market congruence and corporate governance: Effects on corporate innovation and global competitiveness, in S. S. Cohen & G. Boyd (eds.), *Corporate Governance and Globalization*, Northampton, MA: Edward Elgar, 129–154.

65. M. Hurlbert, 2005, Lo! A white knight! So why isn't the market cheering? *New York Times Online*, http://www.nytimes.com, March 27.

66. W. Shen & A. A. Cannella, 2003, Will succession planning increase shareholder wealth? Evidence from investor reactions to relay CEO successions, *Strategic Management Journal*, 24: 191–198.

67. D. Brady & M. Boyle, 2011, Recipe for a CEO, *Bloomberg Businessweek*, June 27, 60–66.

68. Y. Zhang & N. Rajagopalan, 2010, Once an outsider, always an outsider? CEO origin, strategic change and firm performance, *Strategic Management Journal*, 31: 334–346.

69. G. A. Ballinger & J. J. Marcel, 2010, The use of an interim CEO during succession episodes and firm performance, *Strategic Management Journal*, 31: 262–283.

70. M. Hamari, 2010, Who gets headhunted—and who gets ahead? The impact of search firms on executive careers, *Academy of Management Perspectives*, 24(4): 46–59.

71. T. Kiessling, M. Harvey, & J. T. Heames, 2008, Operational changes to the acquired firm's top management team and subsequent organizational performance, *Journal of Leadership and Organizational Studies*, 14: 287–302.

72. J. A. Krug & W. Shill, 2008, The big exit: Executive churn in the wake of M&As, *Journal of Business Strategy*, 29(4): 15–21.

73. R. Mahsud, G. Yukl, & G. E. Prussia, 2011, Human capital, efficiency, and innovative adaptation as strategic determinants of firm performance, *Journal of Leadership and Organizational Studies*, 18: 229–246.

74. J. O'Toole & E. E. Lawler, Jr., 2006, The choices managers make—or don't make, *The Conference Board*, September/October, 24–29.

75. S. Nadkarni & P. S. Barr, 2008, Environmental context, managerial cognition, and strategic action: An integrated view, *Strategic Management Journal*, 29: 1395–1427; M. A. Hitt, B. W. Keats, & E. Yucel, 2003, Strategic leadership in global business organizations, in W. H. Mobley & P. W. Dorfman (eds.), *Advances in Global Leadership*, Oxford, UK: Elsevier Science, Ltd., 9–35.

76. I. M. Levin, 2000, Vision revisited, *Journal of Applied Behavioral Science*, 36: 91–107.

77. E. Verwaal, H. Commandeur, & W. Verbeke, 2009, Value creation and value claiming in strategic outsourcing decisions: A resource contingency perspective, *Journal of Management*, 35: 420–444; S. R. Miller, D. E. Thomas, L. Eden, & M. Hitt, 2008, Knee deep in the big muddy: The survival of emerging market firms in developed markets, *Management International Review*, 48: 645–666.

78. J. Welch & S. Welch, 2007, When to talk, when to balk, *BusinessWeek*, April 30, 102.

79. P. L. McClelland, X. Ling, & V. L. Barker, 2010, CEO commitment to the status quo: Replication and extension using content analysis, *Journal of Management*, 36: 1251–1277.

80. J. R. Mitchell, D. A. Shepherd, & M. P. Sharfman, 2011, Erratic strategic decisions: when and why managers are inconsistent in strategic decision making, *Strategic Management Journal*, 32: 683–704; N. Plambeck & K. Weber, 2010, When the glass is half full and half empty: CEOs' ambivalent interpretations of strategic issues, *Strategic Management Journal*, 31: 689–710.

81. A. J. Wowak & D. C. Hambrick, 2010, A model of person-pay interaction: How executives vary in their response to compensation arrangements, *Strategic Management Journal*, 31: 803–821.

82. D. G. Sirmon, M. A. Hitt, J.-L. Arregle, & J. T. Campbell, 2010, The dynamic interplay of capability strengths and weaknesses: Investigating the bases of temporary advantage, *Strategic Management Journal*, 31: 1386–1409.

83. M. S. Gary & R. E. Wood, 2011, Metal models, decision rules and performance heterogeneity, *Strategic Management Journal*, 32: 569–594.

84. M.-J. Chen & D. Miller, 2010, West meets east: Toward an ambicultural approach to management, *Academy of Management Perspectives*, 24: 17–24.

85. J. Kraaijenbrink, J.-C. Spender, & A. J. Groen, 2010, The resource-based view: A review and assessment of its critiques, *Journal of Management*, 36: 349–372; J. Barney & A. M. Arikan, 2001, The resource-based view: Origins and implications, in M. A. Hitt, R. E. Freeman, & J. S. Harrison (eds.), *Handbook of Strategic Management*, Oxford, UK: Blackwell Publishers, 124–188.

86. E. T. Prince, 2005, The fiscal behavior of CEOs, *Managerial Economics*, 46(3): 23–26.

87. H. A. Ndofor, D. G. Sirmon & X. He, 2011, Firm resources, competitive actions and performance: Investigating a mediated model with evidence from the in-vitro diagnostics industry, *Strategic Management Journal*, 32: 640–657; Holcomb, Holmes, & Connelly, Making the most of what you have; Sirmon, Gove, & Hitt, Resource management in dyadic competitive rivalry.

88. R. A. Burgelman, 2001, *Strategy Is Destiny: How Strategy-Making Shapes a Company's Future*, New York: The Free Press.

89. M. Gruber, F. Heineman, M. Brettel, & S. Hungeling, 2010, Configurations of resources and capabilities and their performance implications: An exploratory study of technology ventures, *Strategic Management Journal*, 31: 1337–1356; D. J. Ketchen, Jr., G. T. M. Hult, & S. F. Slater, 2007, Toward greater understanding of market orientation and the resource-based view, *Strategic Management Journal*, 28: 961–964.

90. E. Daneels, 2011, Trying to become a different type of company: Dynamic capability at Smith Corona, *Strategic Management Journal*, 32: 1–31; S. K. Ethiraj, 2007, Allocation of inventive effort in complex product systems, *Strategic Management Journal*, 28: 563–584.

91. S. E. A. Dixon, K. E. Meyer, & M. Day, 2010, Stages of organizational transformation in transition economies: A dynamic capabilities approach, *Journal of Management Studies*, 47: 416–436.

92. B. Simon, 2011, GM's new chief executive in reshuffle, *Financial Times*, http://www.ft.com, January 20.

93. R. E. Ployhart, C. H. Van Idderkinge, & W. J. MacKenzie, 2011, Acquiring and developing human capital in service contexts: The interconnectedness of human capital resources, *Academy of Management Journal*, 54: 353–368; N. W. Hatch & J. H. Dyer, 2004, Human capital and learning as a source of sustainable competitive advantage, *Strategic Management Journal*, 25: 1155–1178.

94. M. A. Hitt, L. Bierman, K. Uhlenbruck, & K. Shimizu, 2006, The importance of resources in the internationalization of professional service firms: The good, the bad and the ugly, *Academy of Management Journal*, 49: 1137–1157; M. A. Hitt, L. Bierman, K. Shimizu, & R. Kochhar, 2001, Direct and moderating effects of human capital on strategy and performance in professional service firms: A resource-based perspective, *Academy of Management Journal*, 44: 13–28.

95. S. E. Jackson, M. A. Hitt, & A. S. DeNisi (eds.), 2003, *Managing Knowledge for Sustained Competitive Advantage: Designing Strategies for Effective Human Resource Management*, Oxford, UK: Elsevier Science, Ltd.

96. B. E. Becker & M. A. Huselid, 2007, Strategic human resources management: Where do we go from here? *Journal of Management*, 32: 898–925.

97. R. E. Ployhart, 2007, Staffing in the 21st century: New challenges and strategic opportunities, *Journal of Management*, 32: 868–897.

98. J. Pfeffer, 2010, Building sustainable organizations: The human factor, *Academy of Management Perspectives*, 24(1): 34–45; R. A. Noe, J. A. Colquitt, M. J. Simmering, & S. A. Alvarez, 2003, Knowledge management: Developing intellectual and social capital, in S. E. Jackson, M. A. Hitt, & A. S. DeNisi (eds.), 2003, *Managing Knowledge for Sustained Competitive Advantage: Designing Strategies for Effective Human Resource Management*, Oxford, UK: Elsevier Science, Ltd., 209–242.

99. G. P. Hollenbeck & M. W. McCall Jr., 2003, Competence, not competencies: Making global executive development work, in W. H. Mobley & P. W. Dorfman (eds.), *Advances in Global Leadership*, Oxford, UK: Elsevier Science, Ltd., 101–119.

100. G. Colvin, 2007, Leader machines, *Fortune*, October 1, 100–106.

101. T. R. Holcomb, R. D. Ireland, R. M. Holmes, & M. A. Hitt, 2009, Architecture of entrepreneurial learning: Exploring the link among heuristics, knowledge, and action, *Entrepreneurship, Theory & Practice*, 33: 173–198; J. S. Bunderson & K. M. Sutcliffe, 2003, Management team learning orientation and business unit performance, *Journal of Applied Psychology*, 88: 552–560.

102. R. J. Thomas, 2009, The leadership lessons of crucible experiences, *Journal of Business Strategy*, 30(1): 21–26; J. D. Bragger, D. A. Hantula, D. Bragger, J. Kirnan, & E. Kutcher, 2003, When success breeds failure: History, hysteresis, and delayed exit decisions, *Journal of Applied Psychology*, 88: 6–14.

103. Hitt, Miller, & Colella, *Organizational Behavior*.

104. A. Carmeli & B. Azeroual, 2009, How relational capital and knowledge combination capability enhance the performance of work units in a high technology industry, *Strategic Entrepreneurship Journal*, 3: 85–103; J. W. Spencer, 2003, Firms' knowledge-sharing strategies in the global innovation system: Empirical evidence from the flat-panel display industry, *Strategic Management Journal*, 24: 217–233.

105. R. D. Nixon, M. A. Hitt, H. Lee, & E. Jeong, 2004, Market reactions to corporate announcements of downsizing actions and implementation strategies, *Strategic Management Journal*, 25: 1121–1129.

106. T. Simons & Q. Roberson, 2003, Why managers should care about fairness: The effects of aggregate justice perceptions on organizational outcomes, *Journal of Applied Psychology*, 88: 432–443; M. L. Ambrose & R. Cropanzano, 2003, A longitudinal analysis of organizational fairness: An examination of reactions to tenure and promotion decisions, *Journal of Applied Psychology*, 88: 266–275.

107. C.-L. Luk, O. H. M. Yau, L. Y. M. Sin, A. C. B. Tse, R. P. M. Chow, & J. S. Y. Lee, 2008, The effects of social capital and organizational innovativeness in different institutional contexts, *Journal of International Business Studies*, 39: 589–612; P. S. Adler & S. W. Kwon, 2002, Social capital: Prospects for a new concept, *Academy of Management Review*, 27: 17–40.

108. J. J. Li, L. Poppo, & K. Z. Zhou, 2008, Do managerial ties in China always produce value? Competition, uncertainty, and domestic vs. foreign firms, *Strategic Management Journal*, 29: 383–400; S. Gao, K. Xu, & J. Yang, 2008, Managerial ties, Absorptive capacity & innovation, *Asia Pacific Journal of Management*, 25: 395–412.

109. P. Ozcan & K. M. Eisenhardt, 2009, Origin of alliance portfolios: Entrepreneurs, network strategies, and firm performance, *Academy of Management Journal*, 52: 246–279; W. H. Hoffmann, 2007, Strategies for managing a portfolio of alliances, *Strategic Management Journal*, 28: 827–856.

110. Q. Cao, Z. Simsek, & H. Zhang, 2010, Modelling the joint impact of the CEO and the TMT on organizational ambidexterity, *Journal of Management Studies*, 47: 1272–1296; A. S. Alexiev, J. J. P. Jansen, F. A. J. Van den Bosch. & H. W. Volberda, 2010, Top management team advice seeking and exploratory innovation: The moderating role of TMT heterogeneity, *Journal of Management Studies*, 47: 1343–1364.

111. F. X. Molina-Morales & M. T. Martinez-Fernandez, 2010, Social networks: Effects of social capital on firm innovation, *Journal of Small Business Management*, 48: 258–279; H. E. Aldrich & P. H. Kim 2007, Small worlds, infinite possibilities? How social networks affect entrepreneurial team formation and search, *Strategic Entrepreneurship Journal*, 1: 147–165.

112. A. Klein, 2011, Corporate culture: Its value as a resource for competitive advantage, *Journal of Business Strategy*, 32(2): 21–28; J. B. Barney, 1986, Organizational

388

culture: Can it be a source of sustained competitive advantage? *Academy of Management Review*, 11: 656–665.

113. E. F. Goldman & A. Casey, 2010, Building a culture that encourages strategic thinking, *Journal of Leadership and Organizational Studies*, 17: 119–128; V. Govindarajan & A. K. Gupta, 2001, Building an effective global business team, *Sloan Management Review*, 42(4): 63–71.

114. R. D. Ireland, J. G. Covin, & D. F. Kuratko, 2009, Conceptualizing corporate entrepreneurship strategy, *Entrepreneurship Theory and Practice*, 33(1): 19–46; D. F. Kuratko, R. D. Ireland, & J. S. Hornsby, 2001, Improving firm performance through entrepreneurial actions: Acordia's corporate entrepreneurship strategy, *Academy of Management Executive*, 15(4): 60–71.

115. J. H. Dyer, H. B. Gregersen, & C. Christensen, 2008, Entrepreneur behaviors, opportunity recognition and the origins of innovative ventures, *Strategic Entrepreneurship Journal*, 2: 317–338; R. D. Ireland & J. W. Webb, 2007, Strategic entrepreneurship: Creating competitive advantage through streams of innovation, *Business Horizons*, 50: 49–49.

116. S. A. Alvarez & J. B. Barney, 2008, Opportunities, organizations and entrepreneurship, *Strategic Entrepreneurship Journal*, 2: 171–174; D. S. Elenkov, W. Judge, & P. Wright, 2005, Strategic leadership and executive innovation influence: An international multi-cluster comparative study, *Strategic Management Journal*, 26: 665–682.

117. R. E. Hoskisson, M. A. Hitt, R. D. Ireland, & J. S. Harrison, 2008, *Competing for Advantage*, 2nd ed., Thomson Publishing; R. G. McGrath, W. J. Ferrier, & A. L. Mendelow, 2004, Real options as engines of choice and heterogeneity, *Academy of Management Review*, 29: 86–101.

118. Y. Luo, 2008, Structuring interorganizational cooperation: The role of economic integration in strategic alliances, *Strategic Management Journal*, 29: 617–637; R. S. Vassolo, J. Anand, & T. B. Folta, 2004, Non-additivity in portfolios of exploration activities: A real options analysis of equity alliances in biotechnology, *Strategic Management Journal*, 25: 1045–1061.

119. M. A. Hitt, R. D. Ireland, D. G. Sirmon, & C. A. Trahms, 2011, Strategic entrepreneurship: Creating value for individuals, organizations and society, *Academy of Management Perspectives*, 25(2): 57–75; P. G. Kein, 2008, Opportunity discovery, entrepreneurial action and economic organization, *Strategic Entrepreneurship Journal*, 2: 175–190.

120. G. T. Lumpkin & G. G. Dess, 1996, Clarifying the entrepreneurial orientation construct and linking it to performance, *Academy of Management Review*, 21: 135–172; R. G. McGrath & I. MacMillan,

2000, *The Entrepreneurial Mindset*, Boston: Harvard Business School Press.

121. Lumpkin & Dess, Clarifying the entrepreneurial orientation construct, 142.

122. Ibid., 137.

123. D. D. Bergh, R. A. Johnson, & R. Dewitt, 2008, Restructuring through spinoff or sell-off: Transforming information asymmetries into financial gain, *Strategic Management Journal*, 29: 133–148; P. Pyoria, 2007, Informal organizational culture: The foundation of knowledge workers' performance, *Journal of Knowledge Management*, 11(3): 16–30.

124. M. Kuenzi & M. Schminke, 2009, Assembling fragments into a lens: A review, critique, and proposed research agenda for the organizational work climate literature, *Journal of Management*, 35: 634–717; C. M. Christensen & S. D. Anthony, 2007, Put investors in their place, *BusinessWeek*, May 28, 10.

125. J. Kotter, 2011, Corporate culture: Whose job is it? *Forbes*, http://blog .forbes.com/johnkotter, February 17; J. S. Hornsby, D. F. Kuratko, & S. A. Zahra, 2002, Middle managers' perception of the internal environment for corporate entrepreneurship: Assessing a measurement scale, *Journal of Business Venturing*, 17: 253–273.

126. D. F. Kuratko, R. D. Ireland, J. G. Covin, & J. S. Hornsby, 2005, A model of middle-level managers' entrepreneurial behavior, *Entrepreneurship Theory and Practice*, 29: 699–716.

127. E. G. Love & M. Kraatz, 2009, Character, conformity, or the bottom line? How and why downsizing affected corporate reputation, *Academy of Management Journal*, 52: 314–335.

128. Adler & Kwon, Social capital.

129. J. Pinto, C. R. Leana, & F. K. Pil, 2008, Corrupt organizations or organizations of corrupt individuals? Two types of organization-level corruption, *Academy of Management Review*, 33: 685–709.

130. M. E. Scheitzer, L. Ordonez, & M. Hoegl, 2004, Goal setting as a motivator of unethical behavior, *Academy of Management Journal*, 47: 422–432.

131. D. C. Kayes, D. Stirling, & T. M. Nielsen, 2007, Building organizational integrity, *Business Horizons*, 50: 61–70; L. K. Trevino, G. R. Weaver, D. G. Toffler, & B. Ley, 1999, Managing ethics and legal compliance: What works and what hurts, *California Management Review*, 41(2): 131–151.

132. X. Zhang, K. M. Bartol, K. G. Smith, M. D. Pfaffer, & D. M. Khanin, 2008, CEOs on the edge: Earnings manipulation and stock-based incentive misalignment, *Academy of Management Journal*, 51: 241–258; M. A. Hitt & J. D. Collins, 2007, Business ethics, strategic decision making, and firm performance, *Business Horizons*, 50: 353–357.

133. J. M. Stevens, H. K. Steensma, D. A. Harrison, & P. L. Cochran, 2005, Symbolic or substantive document? Influence of ethics codes on financial executives'

decisions, *Strategic Management Journal*, 26: 181–195.

134. Y. Zhang & M. F. Wiersema, 2009, Stock market reaction to CEO certification: The signaling role of CEO background, *Strategic Management Journal*, 30: 693–710; C. Driscoll & M. McKee, 2007, Restoring a culture of ethical and spiritual values: A role for leader storytelling, *Journal of Business Ethics*, 73: 205–217.

135. R. Rumelt, 2011, *Good Strategy/Bad Strategy*, New York: Crowne Business; C. Caldwell & L. A. Hayes, 2007, Leadership, trustworthiness, and the mediating lens, *Journal of Management Development*, 26: 261–281.

136. B. E. Ashforth, D. A. Gioia, S. L. Robinson, & L. K. Trevino, 2008, Re-viewing organizational corruption, *Academy of Management Review*, 33: 670–684; M. Schminke, A. Arnaud, & M. Kuenzi, 2007, The power of ethical work climates, *Organizational Dynamics*, 36: 171–186; L. B. Ncube & M. H. Wasburn, 2006, Strategic collaboration for ethical leadership: A mentoring framework for business and organizational decision making, *Journal of Leadership & Organizational Studies*, 13: 77–92.

137. A. Weibel, 2007, Formal control and trustworthiness, *Group & Organization Management*, 32: 500–517; G. Redding, 2002, The capitalistic business system of China and its rationale, *Asia Pacific Journal of Management*, 19: 221–249.

138. B. D. Rostker, R. S. Leonard, O. Younassi, M. V. Arena, & J. Riposo, 2009, Cost controls: How the government can get more bag for its buck, *Rand Review*, http://www.rand.org/publications/ randreview/issues/spring2009; A. C. Costa, 2007, Trust and control interrelations, *Group & Organization Management*, 32: 392–406.

139. Control (management), 2011, *Wikipedia*, http://en.wikipedia.org/wiki/control, July 6; M. D. Shields, F. J. Deng, & Y. Kato, 2000, The design and effects of control systems: Tests of direct- and indirect-effects models, *Accounting, Organizations and Society*, 25: 185–202.

140. R. S. Kaplan & D. P. Norton, 2009, The balanced scorecard: Measures that drive performance (HBR OnPoint Enhanced Edition), *Harvard Business Review*, Boston, MA, March; R. S. Kaplan & D. P. Norton, 2001, The strategy-focused organization, *Strategy & Leadership*, 29(3): 41–42.

141. B. E. Becker, M. A. Huselid, & D. Ulrich, 2001, *The HR Scorecard: Linking People, Strategy, and Performance*, Boston: Harvard Business School Press, 21.

142. Kaplan & Norton, The strategy-focused organization.

143. R. S. Kaplan & D. P. Norton, 2001, Transforming the balanced scorecard from performance measurement to strategic management: Part I, *Accounting Horizons*, 15(1): 87–104.

144. Balanced scorecard, 2011, *Wikipedia*, http://en.wikipedia.org/wiki/control, July 6; R. S. Kaplan & D. P. Norton, 1992, The

balanced scorecard—measures that drive performance, *Harvard Business Review*, 70(1): 71–79.

145. M. A. Mische, 2001, *Strategic Renewal: Becoming a High-Performance Organization*, Upper Saddle River, NJ: Prentice Hall, 181.

146. H. J. Cho & V. Pucik, 2005, Relationship between innovativeness, quality, growth, profitability and market value, *Strategic Management Journal*, 26: 555–575.

147. G. Rowe, 2001, Creating wealth in organizations: The role of strategic leadership, *Academy of Management Executive*, 15(1): 81–94.

148. R. E. Hoskisson, R. A. Johnson, D. Yiu, & W. P. Wan, 2001, Restructuring strategies of diversified business groups: Differences associated with country institutional environments, in M. A. Hitt, R. E. Freeman, & J. S. Harrison (eds.), *Handbook of Strategic Management*, Oxford, UK: Blackwell Publishers, 433–463.

149. J. Birkinshaw & N. Hood, 2001, Unleash innovation in foreign subsidiaries, *Harvard Business Review*, 79(3): 131–137.

150. Hitt, Haynes, & Serpa, Strategic leadership for the 21st century; Ireland & Hitt, Achieving and maintaining strategic competitiveness.

151. Balanced scorecard, 2011, *Maxi-Pedia*, http://www.maxipedia.com/balanced+scorecard+method+what+is; G. Edmondson, 2007, Pedal to the metal at Porsche, *BusinessWeek*, September 3, 68; J. D. Gunkel & G. Probst, 2003, Implementation of the balanced scorecard as a means of corporate learning: The Porsche case, European Case Clearing House: Cranfield, UK.

CHAPTER 13

Strategic Entrepreneurship

Studying this chapter should provide you with the strategic management knowledge needed to:

1. Define strategic entrepreneurship and corporate entrepreneurship.

2. Define entrepreneurship and entrepreneurial opportunities and explain their importance.

3. Define invention, innovation, and imitation, and describe the relationship among them.

4. Describe entrepreneurs and the entrepreneurial mind-set.

5. Explain international entrepreneurship and its importance.

6. Describe how firms internally develop innovations.

7. Explain how firms use cooperative strategies to innovate.

8. Describe how firms use acquisitions as a means of innovation.

9. Explain how strategic entrepreneurship helps firms create value.

© Ryan McVay/Getty Images

OPEN INNOVATION: COMBINING EXTERNAL TECHNOLOGIES AND IDEAS WITH INTERNAL R&D CAPABILITIES

Fast Company has labeled Apple, Twitter, Facebook, Nissan, Groupon, Google, Dawning Information Industry, Netflix, Zynga, and Epocrates as the world's 10 most innovative companies in 2011. Continuous innovation is the engine that drives these highly successful companies. It is an especially potent competitive weapon during tough economic times, allowing such firms to redefine the marketplace when others are not pursuing continuous innovation. Henry Chesbrough and others have conceived of firm innovation systems as potentially open rather than closed. Historically, firms have sought to keep their innovation systems inside the firm (closed systems) so as not to expose their key innovations to potential competitors. Likewise, open innovation and change are occurring when a firm finds that a good idea is not commercially viable, given a firm's present strategy; rather than shelving the idea, commercialization can take place through licenses, spin-offs, and joint ventures through entities outside the boundaries of the firm.

Procter & Gamble (P&G), one of the acknowledged global industry leaders in consumer product innovation, has implemented the concept of open innovation. P&G launched its "Connect & Develop" program in 2001. It was launched by then CEO A. G. Lafley. Lafley's goal was to have 50 percent of P&G's new products come from partnerships with entities, customers, suppliers, other firms, inventors, and universities, all outside the boundaries of the firm. It realized that goal four years later with 60 percent of new products coming through ideas external to the firm using a co-creation process. For example, Tide Total Care, a premium version of its Tide detergent, was ranked number two on the top 10 non-food products list in 2009.

Mike Ehrmann/WireImage/Getty Images

Nike teamed with Apple to create the Nike+iPod, which combines the Nike Air Zoom Moire and the Apple iPod to communicate with each other via the Nike+iPod kit, using a sensor in the shoe to communicate wirelessly with the iPod to relay information from the shoe, such as distance, pace, time running, and calories burned.

This product was developed through Sweden's Lund University along with two small chemical companies as partners. Its new product innovations even include the Glad brand plastic bag joint venture with Clorox, a historical rival. It also has food product joint ventures with ConAgra and General Mills. It has a goal of $3 billion in annual sales by 2015, up from its current $1 billion, through new products with outside partners. It currently has 25 percent of its revenues generated through outside open innovation partnerships and hopes to have 60 percent of total revenue generated in the future.

Other companies have used the open innovation approach as well. Nike worked with Apple to develop a sensor that can transmit data from inside the shoe to the runner's iPod or iPhone. Little Swimmers Sun Care is an adhesive sticker that parents put on a child to alert parents to the risk of sunburn. The sticker changes color as the child becomes exposed to too much ultraviolet light, which leads to sunburn. The sticker includes an ultraviolet-sensitive material developed and marketed in a partnership between Kimberly-Clark and SunHealth Solutions. Aquafresh White Trays is a tooth-whitening strip developed through a partnership between GlaxoSmithKline and Oratech. Finally, S'mores is a product combining Kraft graham cracker biscuits and marshmallows in partnership with Hershey, a U.S. chocolate maker. S'mores are usually a mixture of hot marshmallows that melt the chocolate between two graham crackers and are a popular treat when sitting around a campfire.

There are at least three paths to scout external opportunities to arrive at open innovation solutions. One approach engages current and potential customers to better capture unarticulated needs and jointly shape new products and services, striving to be the first to market with a new offering. Stanley Black & Decker, Inc.'s DeWalt division, a maker of power tools for professionals, regularly scouts construction sites, observes construction crews in action, and also tests new product ideas in the field. Others pursue breakthrough technology ideas and focus on incremental changes to solve unarticulated customer problems with a new technology. Siemens A.G. spends five percent of its overall R&D budget to develop detailed technological road maps within each individual business unit to pursue this technology-driven strategy. Finally, there are companies that continuously monitor customers and competitors, making incremental changes as a "fast follower" of a proven concept. However, each of these externally oriented strategies requires activities and processes that match the particular approach for aligning a company's external open innovation approach with its business strategy. Research suggests that "a scatter shot approach" to open innovation will not be successful. It is important to establish a systematic process for capturing external ideas, bringing them in and developing them, and commercializing the golden ideas that surface.

It is important that the firm have senior level executive involvement championing the program organizationally. A dedicated innovation office with associated funds is also critical for success. Establishing focal external relationships with outside partners, whether it be universities, other companies, independent investors, or consumers, is important for developing systematic processes to surface and vet ideas. A firm must also have agreed-upon intellectual property (IP) policies that allow for proper licensing of ideas and establishment of appropriate relationships with external partners. Having the right culture to promote open innovation may be challenging for companies, especially those that pursue technology as a driver, because this is where the "not-invented-here" syndrome can be a challenge. Having appropriate processes and tools such as the Connect & Develop program of Procter & Gamble is essential.

In this chapter we illustrate how internal innovation approaches as well as alliance and acquisition approaches can help a firm profit in establishing new entrepreneurial ventures. All of these concepts are appropriate in an open innovation approach to entrepreneurial activities. These will all be discussed, in turn, as essential pieces of strategic entrepreneurship in this chapter.

Sources: 2011, The world's most innovative companies 2011, *Fast Company*, http://www.fastcompany.com, February 16; M. Bianchi, A. Cavaliere, D. Chiaroni, F. Frattini, & V. Chiesa, 2011, Organisational modes for open innovation in the bio-pharmaceutical industry: An exploratory analysis, *Technovation*, 31(1): 22–33; S. Billings, 2011, Open source: The art of creative collaboration, *Marketing*, April 13, 33–37; J. Birkinshaw, C. Bouquet, & J.-L. Barsoux, 2011, The 5 myths of innovation, *MIT Sloan Management Review*, 52(2): 43–50; H. Chesbrough, 2011, Bringing open innovation to services, *MIT Sloan Management Review*, 52(2): 85–90; E. K. R. E. Huizingh, 2011, Open innovation: State of the art and future perspectives, *Technovation*, 31: 2–9; B. Jaruzelski & R. Holman, 2011, The three paths to open innovation, *Strategy+Business*, http://www.strategy-business.com, May 23; A. L. Porter & N. C. Newman, 2011, Mining external R&D, *Technovation*, 31: 171–176; J. Birchall, 2010, Open innovation powers growth, *Financial Times*, December 28, 10; F. Rothaermel & A. Hess, 2010, Innovation strategies combined, *MIT Sloan Management Review*, 51(3): 13–15.

Read more about the innovative culture at Netflix.

www.cengagebrain .com

© Nicholas Monu/iStockphoto.com

In Chapter 1, we indicated that *organizational culture* refers to the complex set of ideologies, symbols, and core values that are shared throughout the firm and that influence how the firm conducts business. Thus, culture is the social energy that drives—or fails to drive—the organization. The Opening Case describes the open innovation process by which firms such as Procter & Gamble (P&G) view innovation as an open rather than a closed system. Increasingly, a firm's ability to engage in innovation not only inside the firm but through outside parties makes the difference in gaining and maintaining a competitive advantage and achieving performance targets.[1]

P&G is clearly an entrepreneurial and innovative company. P&G is a leading consumer products company because it consistently produces innovations. From reading this chapter, you will understand that P&G's ability to innovate shows that it successfully practices strategic entrepreneurship.

Strategic entrepreneurship is taking entrepreneurial actions using a strategic perspective. In this process, the firm tries to find opportunities in its external environment that it can try to exploit through innovations. Identifying opportunities to exploit through innovations is the *entrepreneurship* dimension of strategic entrepreneurship, while determining the best way to manage the firm's innovation efforts is the *strategic* dimension. Thus, firms engaging in strategic entrepreneurship integrate their actions to find opportunities and to successfully innovate in order to pursue them.[2] In the twenty-first-century competitive landscape, firm survival and success depend on a firm's ability to continuously find new opportunities and quickly produce innovations to pursue them.[3]

To examine strategic entrepreneurship, we consider several topics in this chapter. First, we examine entrepreneurship and innovation in a strategic context. Definitions of entrepreneurship, entrepreneurial opportunities, and entrepreneurs as those who engage in entrepreneurship to pursue entrepreneurial opportunities are presented. We then describe international entrepreneurship, a phenomenon reflecting the increased use of entrepreneurship in economies throughout the world. After this discussion, the chapter shifts to descriptions of the three ways firms innovate. Internally, firms innovate through either autonomous or induced strategic behavior. We then describe actions firms take to implement the innovations resulting from those two types of strategic behaviors.

In addition to innovating within the firm, firms can develop innovations by using cooperative strategies, such as strategic alliances, and by acquiring other companies to gain access to their innovations and innovative capabilities.[4] Most large, complex firms use all three methods to innovate as illustrated in the Opening Case by P&G. The chapter closes with summary comments about how firms use strategic entrepreneurship to create value and earn above-average returns.

As emphasized in this chapter, innovation and entrepreneurship are vital for young and old and for large and small firms, for service companies as well as manufacturing firms, and for high-technology ventures.[5] In the global competitive landscape, the long-term success of new ventures and established firms is a function of their ability to meld entrepreneurship with strategic management.[6]

A major portion of the material in this chapter is on innovation and entrepreneurship within established organizations. This phenomenon is called **corporate entrepreneurship**, which is the use or application of entrepreneurship within an established firm.[7] Corporate entrepreneurship has become critical to the survival and success of established organizations.[8] Indeed, established firms use entrepreneurship to strengthen their performance and to enhance growth opportunities.[9] Of course, innovation and entrepreneurship play a critical role in the degree of success achieved by startup entrepreneurial ventures as well. Much of the content examined in this chapter is equally important in entrepreneurial ventures (sometimes called "startups") and established organizations.[10]

© Nicholas Monu/iStockphoto.com

Find out more about complex and exciting world of intrapreneurship.

www.cengagebrain .com

Strategic entrepreneurship is taking entrepreneurial actions using a strategic perspective.

Corporate entrepreneurship is the use or application of entrepreneurship within an established firm.

Entrepreneurship is the process by which individuals, teams, or organizations identify and pursue entrepreneurial opportunities without being immediately constrained by the resources they currently control.

Entrepreneurship and Entrepreneurial Opportunities

Entrepreneurship is the process by which individuals, teams, or organizations identify and pursue entrepreneurial opportunities without being immediately constrained by the resources they currently control.[11] **Entrepreneurial opportunities** are conditions in which new goods or services can satisfy a need in the market. These opportunities exist because of competitive imperfections in markets and among the factors

Entrepreneurial opportunities are conditions in which new goods or services can satisfy a need in the market.

Two business partners research potential locations while finalizing their business plan.

Konstantin Chagin/Shutterstock.com

of production used to produce them or because they were independently developed by entrepreneurs.[12] Entrepreneurial opportunities come in many forms such as the chance to develop and sell a new product and the chance to sell an existing product in a new market.[13] Firms should be receptive to pursuing entrepreneurial opportunities whenever and wherever they may surface.[14]

As these two definitions suggest, the essence of entrepreneurship is to identify and exploit entrepreneurial opportunities—that is, opportunities others do not see or for which they do not recognize the commercial potential—and manage risks appropriately as they arise.[15] As a process, entrepreneurship results in the "creative destruction" of existing products (goods or services) or methods of producing them and replaces them with new products and production methods.[16] Thus, firms engaging in entrepreneurship place high value on individual innovations as well as the ability to continuously innovate across time.[17]

We study entrepreneurship at the level of the individual firm. However, evidence suggests that entrepreneurship is the economic engine driving many nations' economies in the global competitive landscape.[18] Thus entrepreneurship and the innovation it spawns are important for companies competing in the global economy and for countries seeking to stimulate economic climates with the potential to enhance the living standard of their citizens. A study conducted by the Boston Consulting Group and the Small Business Division of Intuit found that 10 million people in the United States were considering starting a new business. About one-third of those who do will expand into international markets. The study suggested that by 2017 the number of entrepreneurs will increase, and the entrepreneurs will be younger and include more women and immigrants. Thus, even though the importance of entrepreneurship continues to grow, the "face" of those who start new ventures is also changing.[19]

Innovation

Peter Drucker argued that "innovation is the specific function of entrepreneurship, whether in an existing business, a public service institution, or a new venture started by a lone individual."[20] Moreover, Drucker suggested that innovation is "the means by which the entrepreneur either creates new wealth-producing resources or endows existing resources with enhanced potential for creating wealth."[21] Thus, entrepreneurship and the innovation resulting from it are critically important for all firms. The realities of competition in the competitive landscape of the twenty-first century suggest that to be market leaders, companies must regularly develop innovative products desired by customers. This means that innovation should be an intrinsic part of virtually all of a firm's activities.[22]

Innovation is a key outcome firms seek through entrepreneurship and is often the source of competitive success, especially in turbulent, highly competitive environments.[23] For example, research results show that firms competing in global industries that invest more in innovation also achieve the highest returns.[24] In fact, investors often react positively to the introduction of a new product, thereby increasing the price of a firm's stock. Furthermore, "innovation may be required to maintain or achieve competitive parity, much less a competitive advantage in many global markets."[25] Investing in the development of new technologies can increase the performance of firms that operate in different but related product markets (refer to the discussion of related diversification in Chapter 6). In this way, the innovations can be used in multiple markets, and return on the investments is earned more quickly.[26]

In his classic work, Schumpeter argued that firms engage in three types of innovative activities.[27] **Invention** is the act of creating or developing a new product or process. **Innovation** is the process of creating a commercial product from an invention. Innovation begins after an invention is chosen for development.[28] Thus, an invention brings something new into being, while an innovation brings something new into use. Accordingly, technical criteria are used to determine the success of an invention, whereas commercial criteria are used to determine the success of an innovation.[29] Finally, **imitation** is the adoption of a similar innovation by different firms. Imitation usually leads to product or process standardization, and products based on imitation often are offered at lower prices, but without as many features. Entrepreneurship is critical to innovative activity in that it acts as the linchpin between invention and innovation.[30]

In the United States in particular, innovation is the most critical of the three types of innovative activities. Many companies are able to create ideas that lead to inventions, but commercializing those inventions has, at times, proved difficult.[31] This difficulty is suggested by the fact that approximately 80 percent of R&D occurs in large firms, but these same firms produce fewer than 50 percent of the patents.[32] Patents are a strategic asset and the ability to regularly produce them can be an important source of competitive advantage, especially when a firm intends to commercialize the invention and when the firm competes in a knowledge-intensive industry (e.g., pharmaceuticals).[33]

Entrepreneurs

Entrepreneurs are individuals, acting independently or as part of an organization, who perceive an entrepreneurial opportunity and then take risks to develop an innovation to exploit it. Entrepreneurs can be found throughout an organization—from top-level managers to those working to produce a firm's goods or services. Entrepreneurs are found throughout Amazon, for example. Many Amazon employees must devote at least a portion of their time developing innovations. Entrepreneurs tend to demonstrate several characteristics: they are highly motivated, willing to take responsibility for their projects, self-confident, and often optimistic.[34] In addition, entrepreneurs tend to be passionate and emotional about the value and importance of their innovation-based ideas.[35] They are able to deal with uncertainty and are more alert to opportunities than others.[36] Interestingly, recent research found that genetic factors partly influence people to engage in entrepreneurship.[37] To be successful, entrepreneurs often need to have good social skills and to plan exceptionally well (e.g., to obtain venture capital).[38] Entrepreneurship entails much hard work to be successful, but it can also be highly satisfying. As noted by Mary Kay Ash, founder of Mary Kay Cosmetics, "It is far better to be exhausted from success than to be rested from failure."[39]

Evidence suggests that successful entrepreneurs have an entrepreneurial mind-set. The person with an **entrepreneurial mind-set** values uncertainty in the marketplace and seeks to continuously identify opportunities with the potential to lead to important innovations.[40] Because it has the potential to lead to continuous innovations, an individual's entrepreneurial mind-set can be a source of competitive advantage for a firm.[41] Entrepreneurial mind-sets are fostered and supported when knowledge is readily available throughout a firm. Indeed, research has shown that units within firms are more innovative when they have access to new knowledge.[42] Transferring knowledge, however, can be difficult, often because the receiving party must have adequate absorptive capacity (or the ability) to learn the knowledge.[43] Learning requires that the new knowledge be linked to the existing knowledge. Thus, managers need to develop the capabilities of their

Invention is the act of creating or developing a new product or process.

Innovation is the process of creating a commercial product from an invention.

Imitation is the adoption of a similar innovation by different firms.

Entrepreneurs are individuals, acting independently or as part of an organization, who perceive an entrepreneurial opportunity and then take risks to develop an innovation to exploit it.

The person with an **entrepreneurial mind-set** values uncertainty in the marketplace and seeks to continuously identify opportunities with the potential to lead to important innovations.

human capital to build on their current knowledge base while incrementally expanding that knowledge.[44]

Some companies are known for their entrepreneurial culture. For example, in 2011 Apple was ranked as the most innovative company for the seventh year in a row by *Fast Company* magazine. The remainder of the top 10 most innovative companies were Twitter, Facebook, Nissan, Groupon, Google, Dawning Information Industry, Netflix, Zynga, and Epocrates.[45] Yet, there are other companies known as the antithesis of innovation. For example, GM was known for sacrificing innovation for profits. Of course, this approach eventually led to GM's bankruptcy.[46] However, often such failures can lead to improvement; GM's product lines are doing much better after it emerged from bankruptcy.[47]

International Entrepreneurship

International entrepreneurship is a process in which firms creatively discover and exploit opportunities that are outside their domestic markets in order to develop a competitive advantage.[48] As the practices suggested by this definition show, entrepreneurship is a global phenomenon.[49] As noted earlier, approximately one-third of new ventures move into international markets early in their life cycle. Most large established companies have significant foreign operations and often start new ventures in domestic and international markets. Large multinational companies, for example, generate approximately 54 percent of their sales outside their domestic market, and more than 50 percent of their employees work outside of the company's home country.[50]

A key reason that entrepreneurship has become a global phenomenon is that, in general, internationalization leads to improved firm performance.[51] Nonetheless, decision makers should recognize that the decision to internationalize exposes their firms to various risks, including those of unstable foreign currencies, problems with market efficiencies, insufficient infrastructures to support businesses, and limitations on market size.[52] Thus, the decision to engage in international entrepreneurship should be a product of careful analysis.

Even though entrepreneurship is a global phenomenon, the rate of entrepreneurship differs across countries.[53] A study of 43 countries found that the percentage of adults involved in entrepreneurial activity ranged from a high of more than 45 percent in Bolivia to a low of approximately 4.4 percent in Russia. The United States had a rate of almost 19 percent. Importantly, this study also found a strong positive relationship between the rate of entrepreneurial activity and economic development in a country.[54]

> **International entrepreneurship** is a process in which firms creatively discover and exploit opportunities that are outside their domestic markets in order to develop a competitive advantage.

Culture is one of the reasons for the differences in rates of entrepreneurship among different countries. The research suggests that a balance between individual initiative and a spirit of cooperation and group ownership of innovation is needed to encourage entrepreneurial behavior. For firms to be entrepreneurial, they must provide appropriate autonomy and incentives for individual initiative to surface, but also promote cooperation and group ownership of an innovation if it is to be implemented successfully. Thus, international entrepreneurship often requires teams of people with unique skills and resources, especially in cultures that highly value

Entrepreneurship is a global phenomenon, with one-third of new ventures moving into international territories.

pop_jop/iStockphoto.com

individualism or collectivism. In addition to a balance of values for individual initiative and cooperative behaviors, firms must build the capabilities to be innovative and acquire the resources needed to support innovative activities.[55]

The level of investment outside of the home country made by young ventures is also an important dimension of international entrepreneurship. In fact, with increasing globalization, a greater number of new ventures have been "born global."[56] Research has shown that new ventures that enter international markets increase their learning of new technological knowledge and thereby enhance their performance.[57]

The probability of entering international markets increases when the firm has top executives with international experience, which increases the likelihood of the firm successfully competing in those markets.[58] Because of the learning and economies of scale and scope afforded by operating in international markets, both young and established internationally diversified firms often are stronger competitors in their domestic market as well. Additionally, as research has shown, internationally diversified firms are generally more innovative.[59]

The ability of firms to gain and sustain a competitive advantage may be based partly or largely on the capability to produce innovations. Thus, we next discuss different types of innovations.

Internal Innovation

In established organizations, most innovation comes from efforts in research and development (R&D). Effective R&D often leads to firms filing for patents to protect their innovative work. Increasingly, successful R&D results from integrating the skills available in the global workforce. Thus, the ability to have a competitive advantage based on innovation is more likely to accrue to firms capable of integrating the talent of human capital from countries around the world.[60]

Increasingly, it seems possible that in the twenty-first-century competitive landscape, R&D may be the most critical factor in gaining and sustaining a competitive advantage in some industries, such as pharmaceuticals. Larger, established firms, certainly those competing globally, often try to use their R&D labs to create disruptive new technologies and products. Being able to innovate in this manner can create a competitive advantage for firms in many industries.[61] Although critical to long-term corporate success, the outcomes of R&D investments are uncertain and often not achieved in the short term, meaning that patience is required as firms evaluate the outcomes of their R&D efforts.[62]

Incremental and Radical Innovation

Firms produce two types of internal innovations—incremental and radical innovations—when using their R&D activities. As illustrated in the Strategic Focus on 3M, most innovations are *incremental*—that is, they build on existing knowledge bases and provide small improvements in the current product lines. Incremental innovations are evolutionary and linear in nature.[63] "The markets for incremental innovations are well-defined, product characteristics are well understood, profit margins tend to be lower, production technologies are efficient, and competition is primarily on the basis of price."[64] Adding a different kind of whitening agent to a soap detergent is an example of an incremental innovation, as are improvements in televisions over the last few decades. Companies launch far more incremental innovations than radical innovations because they are cheaper, easier and faster to produce, and involve less risk, although even incremental innovation can be risky if it creates too much change for the organization to absorb.[65]

STRATEGIC FOCUS

ENTREPRENEURSHIP • ENTREPRENEURSHIP • ENTREPRENEURSHIP

3M HAS A CULTURE FOCUSED ON CREATING INNOVATION

3M, historically known as Minnesota Mining and Manufacturing Co., has developed a range of practices to promote "out-of-the-box" thinking to foster innovation. George Buckley, the current chairman and CEO of 3M, wants to increase the effectiveness of the inventive culture at 3M. Under the former CEO, James McNerney, a former executive at GE, 3M became more streamlined; 8,000 people were laid off, and Six Sigma management techniques popularized by GE were emphasized. The Six Sigma method seeks to improve efficiency of processes, curb waste, and reduce product defects. Although this brought discipline and focus in regard to execution, outside analysts suggested that the efficiency gains came at a price—a reduced focus on the creative process. One engineer at a lab suggested "it's really tough to schedule invention."

The company traditionally had a goal of generating 30 percent of its revenue from new product introductions in the past five years. By 2005, when McNerney left to run Boeing, the percentage was down to 21 percent. Buckley, comparatively, has been an outspoken champion of the research labs. Each of 3M's six major business units has its own research lab which is product-focused, while the corporate research staff works on core technologies that are shared by all the businesses. 3M employs 6,500 of its 75,000 employees in R&D jobs. 3M's six business units are focused on consumer and office products (including Post-it, Scotch, and Scotch-Brite, among other brands), display and graphics (including display enhancement films, reflective materials, eye-catching graphics, and projection systems), electro-communications (including components that facilitate electrical power, high-performance electronic devices, and speedy and dependable telecommunication networks), health care business (including medical and oral care products and drug delivery and health information systems), industrial and transportation (including tapes, abrasives, adhesives, special materials, and filtration

George Buckley, CEO and board chairman of 3M, and Japan's Sumitomo 3M president Jesse Singh (right) attend the opening of the company's temporary "3M store" to show off new product concepts in Tokyo's fashion district of Harajuku.

Kazuhiro Nogi/AFP/Getty Images/Newscom

systems sold to a diverse set of markets from automotive to aerospace to renewable energy), and safety, security, and protection services (including products that improve the safety, security, and productivity of people, facilities, and systems around the world).

To improve innovation processes in each of these businesses, the R&D people are expected to spend 15 percent of their time on new ideas. To increase the incentive for people to invent inside, 3M awards annual Genesis grants worth as much as $100,000 to scientists to foster research on unconventional ideas. However, the focus has "never been about inventing the Next Big Thing. It's about inventing hundreds and hundreds of Next Small Things, year after year." Buckley provides an example, Cubitron II, "an industrial abrasive that cuts faster, lasts longer, sharpens itself, and requires less elbow grease than any other abrasive on the market." This is a traditional business focused on the construction industry; the historical name for this abrasive is called sandpaper: "little things like grains of sand that add up to big business, that is 3M."

Not only does 3M focus on incremental innovation on existing products, it also develops internal cooperative relationships between businesses. For instance, the Cubitron II (sandpaper) example came from a combination of the abrasives division, optical systems division (for the shape technology), the tape divisions (for the coatings), and corporate research (for math modeling and fracture analysis). In total, seven different technologies were used to create the product, only two of which came from the abrasives division itself.

Although 3M's research efforts are primarily focused on product line extensions using internal and external collaborations, it does have a new ventures division called 3M New Ventures, which focuses on acquiring minority shares in innovative and fast-growing, small to medium-sized companies around the world. The 3M New Ventures organization seeks top-notch technology platforms with outstanding innovative technologies with highly-scaled business models. The support offered by 3M can be attractive to entrepreneurs around the world because of 3M's extensive research capabilities as well as a complementary manufacturing and sales network to help attract up-and-coming entrepreneurs when they want to scale up.

Although 3M is focused, as noted above, on developing incremental technology improvements using incentives for internal innovation at all levels, it also uses collaborative approaches within the company between divisions. It gets ideas through collaborating with outside partners such as customers and university researchers with ideas related to 3M products. 3M has 30 customer technology centers around the world where technical and marketing employees meet with customers and expose them to 3M technology platforms. Additionally, as noted, it seeks to invest in startup companies that have products related to its main businesses and can create scalable new platforms for innovative new products in each of its business areas. Although historically 3M has sought to do organic or internal innovation, it has now created a system that is more open to collaboration with inside and outside stakeholders such as customers and new startups guided by entrepreneurs that have scalable businesses. In this way, it is more likely to overcome the "not invented here" syndrome, which is the downside of internal innovation systems.

Sources: 2011, 3M Businesses, http://www.3M.com/3Mbusinesses, Accessed on June 17; 2011, 3M wins best innovator award for corporate venturing, *Business Wire*, http://www.BusinessWire.com, June 9; B. Jaruzelski, R. Holman, & E. Baker, 2011, 3M's open innovation, *Strategy + Business*, http://www.strategy-business.com, May 30; 2011, B. Schneider & K. B. Paul, In the company we trust, *HRMagazine*, January, 40–43; M. Gunther, M. Adamo, & B. Feldman, 2010, 3M's innovation revival, *Fortune*, http://www.fortune.com, September 27; J. R. Hagerty, 2010, 3M brings along the basics as it balances new and old, *Wall Street Journal*, November 11, B1–B2; M. Hosea, 2010, 3M Digital strategy: 'I want to rewire 3M for the future,' *Marketing Week*, November 25, 45.

Explore 3M New Ventures Organization.
www.cengagebrain.com

In contrast to incremental innovations, *radical innovations* usually provide significant technological breakthroughs and create new knowledge. Radical innovations, which are revolutionary and nonlinear in nature, typically use new technologies to serve newly created markets. The development of the original personal computer (PC) was a radical innovation at the time. Reinventing the computer by developing a "radically new computer-brain chip" (e.g., with the capability to process a trillion calculations per second) is an example of a radical innovation. Obviously, such a radical innovation would seem to have the capacity to revolutionize the tasks computers could perform. Perhaps some of the new products to be produced by the joint venture between Intel and Nokia integrating smartphones and computers will be considered to be radical innovations.

Because they establish new functionalities for users, radical innovations have strong potential to lead to significant growth in revenue and profits. For example, Toyota's innovation, embodied in the Prius, "the first mass-produced hybrid-electric car," changed the industry in this segment.[66] Developing new processes is a critical part of producing radical innovations. Both types of innovations can create value, meaning that firms should determine when it is appropriate to emphasize either incremental or radical innovation. However, radical innovations have the potential to contribute more significantly to a firm's efforts to earn above-average returns, although they may be more risky.

Radical innovations are rare because of the difficulty and risk involved in developing them. The value of the technology and the market opportunities are highly uncertain.[67] Because radical innovation creates new knowledge and uses only some or little of a firm's current product or technological knowledge, creativity is required. However, creativity does not produce something from nothing. Rather, creativity discovers, combines, or synthesizes current knowledge, often from diverse areas.[68] This knowledge is then used to develop new products that can be used in an entrepreneurial manner to move into new markets, capture new customers, and gain access to new resources.[69] Such innovations are often developed in separate business units that start internal ventures.[70]

Internally developed incremental and radical innovations result from deliberate efforts. These deliberate efforts are called *internal corporate venturing*, which is the set of activities firms use to develop internal inventions and especially innovations.[71] As shown in Figure 13.1, autonomous and induced strategic behaviors are the two types of internal corporate venturing. Each venturing type facilitates incremental and radical innovations. However, a larger number of radical innovations spring from autonomous strategic behavior while the greatest percentage of incremental innovations come from induced strategic behavior.

Autonomous Strategic Behavior

Autonomous strategic behavior is a bottom-up process in which product champions pursue new ideas, often through a political process, by means of which they develop and coordinate the commercialization of a new good or service until it achieves success in the marketplace.[72] A *product champion* is an organizational member with an entrepreneurial vision of a new good or service who seeks to create support for its commercialization. Product champions play critical roles in moving innovations forward. Indeed, in many corporations, "Champions are widely acknowledged as pivotal to innovation speed and success."[73] Champions are vital to sell the ideas to others in the organization so that the innovations will be commercialized. Commonly, product champions use their social capital to develop informal networks within the firm. As progress is made, these networks become more formal as a means of pushing an innovation to the point of successful commercialization.[74] Internal innovations springing from autonomous strategic behavior frequently differ from the firm's current strategy,

Figure 13.1 Model of Internal Corporate Venturing

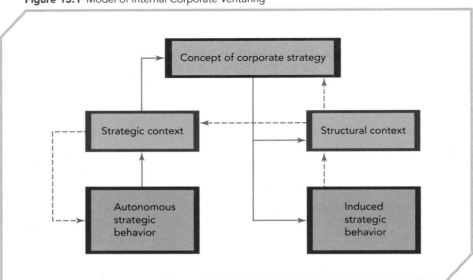

Source: Adapted from R. A. Burgelman, 1983, A model of the interactions of strategic behavior, corporate context, and the concept of strategy, *Academy of Management Review*, 8:65.

taking it into new markets and perhaps new ways of creating value for customers and other stakeholders.

Autonomous strategic behavior is based on a firm's wellspring of knowledge and resources that are the sources of the firm's innovation. Thus, a firm's technological capabilities and competencies are the basis for new products and processes.[75] As described in the Strategic Focus, 3M uses autonomous strategic behavior extensively to identify new technologies and products that can better serve its customers. Similarly, the iPod likely resulted from autonomous strategic behavior at Apple, though the development of the iPhone was more the result of induced strategic behavior discussed in the next section.

Changing the concept of corporate-level strategy through autonomous strategic behavior results when a product is championed within strategic and structural contexts (see Figure 13.1). Such a transformation occurred with the development of the iPod and introduction of iTunes at Apple. The strategic context is the process used to arrive at strategic decisions (often requiring political processes to gain acceptance). The best firms keep changing their strategic context and strategies because of the continuous changes in the current competitive landscape. Thus, some believe that the most competitively successful firms reinvent their industry or develop a completely new one across time as they compete with current and future rivals.[76]

To be effective, an autonomous process for developing new products requires that new knowledge be continuously diffused throughout the firm. In particular, the diffusion of tacit knowledge is important for development of more effective new products.[77] Interestingly, some of the processes important for the promotion of autonomous new product development behavior vary by the environment and country in which a firm operates. For example, the Japanese culture is high on uncertainty avoidance. As such, research has found that Japanese firms are more likely to engage in autonomous behaviors under conditions of low uncertainty because they prefer stability.[78]

3M's diverse portfolio is broken into six business units: consumer and office products, display and graphics, electro-communications, health care business, industrial and transportation, and safety, security, and protection services.

Adrian Brown/Sipa Press/Newscom

Induced Strategic Behavior

The second of the two forms of internal corporate venturing, induced strategic behavior, is a top-down process whereby the firm's current strategy and structure foster innovations that are closely associated with that strategy and structure.[79] In this form of venturing, the strategy in place is filtered through a matching structural hierarchy. In essence, induced strategic behavior results in internal innovations that are highly consistent with the firm's current strategy. Thus, the top management team plays a key role in induced strategic behavior, suggesting that the composition and the effectiveness of the team are important.[80]

In the Strategic Focus on 3M, a new abrasive, Cubitron II, was an example of innovation created through cooperative relationships between 3M business units. The technology came not only from the abrasives division but from the optical systems and coatings and tape divisions. Furthermore, the math modeling and fracture analysis units of the corporate research center were also involved in this internal cooperative venture to create this excellent product. Because 3M spends $1 billion annually internally in R&D, it supports ideas like this plus facilitates cooperative relations between the corporate office and the business units to create innovation. As such, the Cubitron II is an example of an induced innovation process.[81]

Implementing Internal Innovations

An entrepreneurial mind-set is required to be innovative and to develop successful internal corporate ventures. Because of environmental and market uncertainty, individuals and firms must be willing to take risks to commercialize innovations. Although they must continuously attempt to identify opportunities, they must also select and pursue the best opportunities and do so with discipline. Employing an entrepreneurial mind-set entails not only developing new products and markets but also execution in order to do these things effectively. Often, firms provide incentives to managers to be entrepreneurial and to commercialize innovations.[82]

Having processes and structures in place through which a firm can successfully implement the outcomes of internal corporate ventures and commercialize the innovations is critical. Indeed, as the Strategic Focus on 3M illustrates, the successful introduction of innovations into the marketplace reflects implementation effectiveness. In the context of internal corporate ventures, managers must allocate resources, coordinate activities, communicate with many different parties in the organization, and make a series of decisions to convert the innovations resulting from either autonomous or induced strategic behaviors into successful market entries.[83] As we describe in Chapter 11, organizational structures are the sets of formal relationships that support processes managers use to commercialize innovations.

Effective integration of the various functions involved in innovation processes—from engineering to manufacturing and, ultimately, market distribution—is required to implement the incremental and radical innovations resulting from internal corporate ventures.[84] Increasingly, product development teams are being used to integrate the activities associated with different organizational functions. Such integration involves coordinating and applying the knowledge and skills of different functional areas in order to maximize innovation.[85] Teams must help to make decisions as to which projects should be commercialized and which ones should end. Although ending a project is difficult, sometimes because of emotional commitments to innovation-based projects, effective teams recognize when conditions change such that the innovation cannot create value as originally anticipated.

Cross-Functional Product Development Teams

Cross-functional teams facilitate efforts to integrate activities associated with different organizational functions, such as design, manufacturing, and marketing. These teams may also include representatives from major suppliers because they can facilitate the firm's innovation processes.[86] In addition, new product development processes can be completed more quickly and the products more easily commercialized when cross-functional teams work effectively.[87] Using cross-functional teams, product development stages are grouped into parallel or overlapping processes to allow the firm to tailor its product development efforts to its unique core competencies and to the needs of the market.

Horizontal organizational structures support the use of cross-functional teams in their efforts to integrate innovation-based activities across organizational functions.[88] Therefore, instead of being designed around vertical hierarchical functions or departments, the organization is built around core horizontal processes that are used to produce and manage innovations. Some of the core horizontal processes that are critical to innovation efforts are formal; they may be defined and documented as procedures and practices. More commonly, however, these processes are informal. Such informal processes are critical to successful innovations and are supported properly through horizontal organizational structures more so than through vertical organizational structures.

Two primary barriers that may prevent the successful use of cross-functional teams as a means of integrating organizational functions are independent frames of reference of team members and organizational politics.[89] Team members working within a distinct specialization (e.g., a particular organizational function) may have an independent frame of reference typically based on common backgrounds and experiences. They are likely to use the same decision criteria to evaluate issues such as product development efforts as they do within their functional units. Research suggests that functional departments vary along four dimensions: time orientation, interpersonal orientation, goal orientation, and formality of structure.[90] Thus, individuals from different functional departments having different orientations on these dimensions can be expected to perceive product development activities in different ways. For example, a design engineer may consider the characteristics that make a product functional and workable to be the most important of the product's characteristics. Alternatively, a person from the marketing function may judge characteristics that satisfy customer needs to be most important. These different orientations can create barriers to effective communication across functions and even produce conflict in the team at times.[91]

Organizational politics is the second potential barrier to effective integration in cross-functional teams. In some organizations, considerable political activity may center on allocating resources to different functions. Inter-unit conflict may result from aggressive competition for resources among those representing different organizational functions. This dysfunctional conflict between functions creates a barrier to their integration.[92] Methods must be found to achieve cross-functional integration without excessive political conflict and without changing the basic structural characteristics necessary for task specialization and efficiency.

Facilitating Integration and Innovation

Shared values and effective leadership are important for achieving cross-functional integration and implementing innovation.[93] Highly effective shared values are framed around the firm's vision and mission and become the glue that promotes integration between functional units. Thus, the firm's culture promotes unity and internal innovation.[94]

Strategic leadership is also highly important for achieving cross-functional integration and promoting innovation. Leaders set the goals and allocate resources. The goals include integrated development and commercialization of new goods and services. Effective strategic leaders also ensure a high-quality communication system to facilitate cross-functional integration. A critical benefit of effective communication is the sharing of knowledge among team members. Effective communication thus helps create synergy and gains team members' commitment to an innovation throughout the organization. Shared values and leadership practices shape the communication systems that are formed to support the development and commercialization of new products.[95]

Creating Value from Internal Innovation

The model in Figure 13.2 shows how firms can create value from the internal corporate venturing processes they use to develop and commercialize new goods and services. An entrepreneurial mind-set is necessary so that managers and employees will consistently try to identify entrepreneurial opportunities the firm can pursue by developing new goods and services and new markets. Cross-functional teams are important for promoting integrated new product design ideas and commitment to their subsequent implementation. Effective leadership and shared values promote integration and vision for innovation and commitment to it. The end result for the firm is the creation of value for the customers and shareholders by developing and commercializing new products.[96] We should acknowledge that not all entrepreneurial efforts succeed, even with effective management. Sometimes managers must exit the market as well to avoid value decline.[97]

In the next two sections, we discuss the other ways firms innovate—by using cooperative strategies and by acquiring companies with potential to create innovation.

Figure 13.2 Creating Value through Internal Innovation Processes

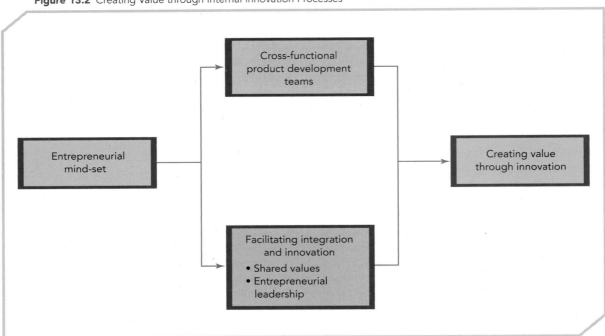

Innovation through Cooperative Strategies

Virtually all firms lack the breadth and depth of resources (e.g., human capital and social capital) in their R&D activities needed to internally develop a sufficient number of innovations to meet the needs of the market and remain competitive. As indicated in the Opening Case, firms must be open to using external resources to help produce innovations.[98] Alliances with other firms can contribute to innovations in several ways. First, they provide information on new business opportunities and how to exploit them.[99] In other instances, firms use cooperative strategies to align what they believe are complementary assets with the potential to lead to future innovations. In fact, research suggests that such innovation will lead to "breakthroughs" and new product classes more often than other modes.[100]

The rapidly changing technologies of the twenty-first-century competitive landscape, globalization, and the need to innovate at world-class levels are primary influences on firms' decisions to innovate by cooperating with other companies. Indeed, some believe that because of these conditions, firms are becoming increasingly dependent on cooperative strategies as a path to successful competition in the global economy.[101] Even venerable old firms such as P&G and 3M have learned that they need help to create innovations necessary to be competitive in a twenty-first-century environment. As noted in the Opening Case, P&G produces Glad brand plastic bags in joint venture with Clorox.[102]

Both entrepreneurial firms and established firms use cooperative strategies (e.g., strategic alliances and joint ventures) to innovate. An entrepreneurial firm, for example, may seek investment capital as well as established firms' distribution capabilities to successfully introduce one of its innovative products to the market.[103] Alternatively, more-established companies may need new technological knowledge and can gain access to it by forming a cooperative strategy with entrepreneurial ventures.[104] Alliances between large pharmaceutical firms and biotechnology companies increasingly have been formed to integrate the knowledge and resources of both to develop new products and bring them to market.[105]

Because of the importance of strategic alliances, particularly in the development of new technology and in commercializing innovations, firms are beginning to build networks of alliances that represent a form of social capital to them.[106] Building social capital in the form of relationships with other firms provides access to the knowledge and other resources necessary to develop innovations.[107] Knowledge from these alliances helps firms develop new capabilities.[108] Some firms seek other companies to participate in their internal new product development processes. It is not uncommon, for example, for firms to have supplier or customer representatives on their cross-functional innovation teams because of the importance of their input to ensure quality materials for any new product developed.[109]

However, alliances formed for the purpose of innovation are not without risks. In addition to conflict that is natural when firms try to work together to reach a mutual goal, cooperative strategy participants also take a risk that a partner will appropriate a firm's technology or knowledge and use it to enhance its own competitive abilities.[110] To prevent or at least minimize this risk, firms, particularly new ventures, need to select their partners carefully. The ideal partnership is one in which the firms have complementary skills as well as compatible strategic goals.[111] However, because companies are operating in a network of firms and thus may be participating in multiple alliances simultaneously, they encounter challenges in managing the alliances. Research has shown that firms can become involved in too many alliances, which can harm rather than facilitate their innovation capabilities.[112] Thus, effectively managing a cooperative strategy to produce innovation is critical.

As explained in the Strategic Focus, social networking Internet sites have become highly popular with the general public and with professionals as well. Furthermore, entrepreneurs have begun to use them in ways to facilitate their businesses. These sites provide many opportunities for businesses and especially for gaining access to ideas and information. Therefore, they can facilitate innovation. Firms can use them to identify unique product ideas, do market research, and access new markets and new customers. As the Strategic Focus illustrates, they are also being used to facilitate innovation communities such as application development for iPhone and Android smartphones. As a result, the social networking sites are highly valuable business mechanisms.

Innovation through Acquisitions

Firms sometimes acquire companies to gain access to their innovations and to their innovative capabilities. One reason companies make these acquisitions is that the capital market values growth; acquisitions provide a means to rapidly extend one or more product lines and increase the firm's revenues.[113] Acquisitions pursued for this reason should, nonetheless, have a strategic rationale. For example, several large pharmaceutical firms have made acquisitions in recent years for several reasons, such as enhancing growth. However, a primary reason for acquisitions in this industry has been to acquire innovation—new drugs that can be commercialized. In this way companies strengthen their new product pipeline. For example, as noted in Chapter 7, Teva Pharmaceuticals recently purchased Cephalon after outbidding Valeant Pharmaceuticals. Cephalon produces a medication for narcolepsy, a sleep disorder that causes excessive sleepiness, allowing Teva to expand into this remedy area.[114]

Similar to internal corporate venturing and strategic alliances, acquisitions are not a risk-free approach to innovating. A key risk of acquisitions is that a firm may substitute an ability to buy innovations for an ability to produce innovations internally. In support of this contention, research shows that firms engaging in acquisitions introduce fewer new products into the market.[115] This substitution may take place because firms lose

TECHNOLOGY • TECHNOLOGY • TECHNOLOGY • TECH

SOCIAL NETWORKING WEB SITES FACILITATE INNOVATION: APPLICATION SOFTWARE INNOVATION

Social networks are one of the major innovations in the first decade of the twenty-first century. Perhaps the most popular and important social networking Internet sites are Facebook, Twitter, LinkedIn, and MySpace. For example, Facebook, which has more than 600 million users and was recently valued at $50 billion, is gaining competitive muscle and beginning to disrupt established Internet companies such as Yahoo! and Google. It is now competing with Google and Microsoft for top engineering talent. Chief operating officer Sheryl Sandberg said, "We think every industry is going to be rebuilt around social engagement." In just two years, Facebook's share of online display ads has risen from 2.9 percent to 13.6 percent of the U.S. market share, reaching $8.88 billion in 2010. Facebook's share of this ad revenue was between $1.9 and $2 billion in 2010. Many are doing online shopping through the Facebook portal, and its electronic payments are beginning to rival those of eBay Inc.'s PayPal.

Michel Gaillard/Rea/Redux Michel Gaillard/Rea/Redux

Facebook executives are encouraging developers to write code on the HTML5 platform, which is compatible with Apple's iOS (operating system) and Google's Android system.

As a social network site it has become popular to facilitate connections between game developers and application developers for Apple's iPhone and iPad, as well as for Google's Android platform. Also, Facebook executives are encouraging developers to write Facebook apps using a relatively new technology standard called HTML5. Facebook is using HTML5 to enhance its own mobile offering used on iPhones and Android phones. The HTML5 platform is compatible with Apple's iOS operating system and Google's Android system. As such, the Facebook applications can be written for browser users in different operating systems without completely rewriting the code for each system. Furthermore, Facebook is popular for software developers because it can help such developers gain greater visibility among social network peers and companies who are using their software. However, Facebook is far from being a dominant player in the mobile area because many of its software utilities are currently only on Facebook's Web site without mobile phone applications.

Besides being used for application software development networking, social networking sites are also being used to identify potential new employees and to make all types of professional and business contacts. They provide access to new ideas and information that can be useful for solving problems and even for making strategic decisions. The access to information and ideas makes these sites excellent sources in the innovation process. For example, the use of cross-functional teams and incorporating suppliers and customers to facilitate the development of new products has been valuable because of the integration of diverse ideas incorporating multiple and important perspectives. However, social networking sites provide access to many more diverse perspectives and ideas and can be used for these functions as well. In addition, the opportunity to perform virtual market tests with a large sample from the market exists with these sites. Finally, social networking sites provide the opportunity to identify new and different markets for existing and new product ideas. Therefore, if managed properly, they could be highly valuable in the innovation process, from the identification of new product ideas through market research, and to reach many new potential customers.

Sources: G. A. Fowler & Y. I. Kane, 2011, Digital media: Facebook seeks bigger role in software for mobile apps, *Wall Street Journal*, June 17, B5; G. A. Fowler, 2011, Facebook's web of frenemies, *Wall Street Journal*, February 15, B1; B. Stone, 2011, Why Facebook needs Sheryl Sandberg, *Bloomberg Businessweek*, http://www.businessweek.com, May 16; Q. Hardy, 2011, Adobe is watching every click, *Forbes*, http://www.forbes.com, April 11; J. Hempel, 2011, Trouble @ Twitter, *Fortune*, May 2, 66; J. Light, 2011, Managing & Careers – Theory & Practice: At mature techs, a young vibe – H-P, IBM, Microsoft pour on the charm to compete for talent with start-ups, *Wall Street Journal*, June 13, B7; B. Remneland-Wikhamn, J. Ljungberg, N. Bergquist, & J. Kuschel, 2011, Open innovation, generativity and the supplier as peer: The case of iPhone and Android, *International Journal of Innovation Management*, 15(1): 205–230; Q. Hardy, 2010, Google's Android attack, *Forbes*, http://forbes.com, December 20.

strategic control and focus instead on financial control of their original and, especially, of their acquired business units. Yet, careful selection of companies to acquire—ones with complementary science and technology knowledge—can enhance innovation if the knowledge acquired is used effectively.[116]

We note in Chapter 7 that companies can also learn new capabilities from firms they acquire. Thus, firms may gain capabilities to produce innovation from an acquired company. Additionally, firms that emphasize innovation and carefully select companies for acquisition that also emphasize innovation are likely to remain innovative.[117] Likewise, firms must manage well the integration of the acquired firm's technical capabilities so that they remain productive and continue to produce innovation after the acquired firm is merged into the acquiring firm.[118] Cisco has been highly successful with the integration of acquired technology firms. Cisco managers take great care not to lose key personnel in the acquired firm, realizing they are the source of many innovations.

This chapter closes with an assessment of how strategic entrepreneurship helps firms create value for stakeholders through its operations.

Creating Value through Strategic Entrepreneurship

Newer entrepreneurial firms often are more effective than larger established firms in the identification of entrepreneurial opportunities.[119] As a consequence, entrepreneurial ventures often produce more radical innovations than do their larger, more established counterparts. Entrepreneurial ventures' strategic flexibility and willingness to take risks at least partially account for their ability to identify opportunities and then develop radical innovations to exploit them.

Alternatively, larger and well-established firms often have more resources and capabilities to exploit identified opportunities.[120] Younger, entrepreneurial firms generally excel in the opportunity-seeking dimension of strategic entrepreneurship while more established firms generally excel in the advantage-seeking dimension. However, to compete effectively in the twenty-first-century competitive landscape, firms must not only identify and exploit opportunities but do so while achieving and sustaining a competitive advantage.[121] Thus, on a relative basis, newer entrepreneurial firms must learn how to gain a competitive advantage (advantage-seeking behaviors), and older, more established firms must relearn how to identify entrepreneurial opportunities (opportunity-seeking skills).

In some large organizations, action is being taken to deal with these matters. For example, an increasing number of widely known, large firms, including Williams-Sonoma, Inc., Wendy's International, AstraZeneca, and Choice Hotels, have created a new, top-level managerial position commonly called president or executive vice president of emerging brands. The essential responsibility of people holding these positions is to find entrepreneurial opportunities for their firms. If a decision is made to pursue one or more of the identified opportunities, this person also leads the analysis to determine whether the innovations should be internally developed, pursued through a cooperative venture, or acquired. The objective is to help firms develop successful incremental and radical innovations.

To be entrepreneurial, firms must develop an entrepreneurial mind-set among their managers and employees. Managers must emphasize the management of their resources, particularly human capital and social capital.[122] The importance of knowledge to identify and exploit opportunities as well as to gain and sustain a competitive advantage suggests that firms must have strong human capital.[123] Social capital is critical for access to complementary resources from partners in order to compete effectively in domestic and international markets.[124]

Many entrepreneurial opportunities continue to surface in international markets, a reality that is contributing to firms' willingness to engage in international entrepreneurship. By entering global markets that are new to them, firms can learn new technologies and management practices and diffuse this knowledge throughout the entire enterprise. Furthermore, the knowledge firms gain can contribute to their innovations. Research has shown that firms operating in international markets tend to be more innovative.[125] Entrepreneurial ventures and large firms now regularly enter international markets. Both types of firms must also be innovative to compete effectively. Thus, by developing resources (human and social capital), taking advantage of opportunities in domestic and international markets, and using the resources and knowledge gained in these markets to be innovative, firms achieve competitive advantages. In so doing, they create value for their customers and shareholders.

Firms practicing strategic entrepreneurship contribute to a country's economic development. In fact, some countries have made dramatic economic progress by changing the institutional rules for businesses operating in the country. This approach could be construed as a form of institutional entrepreneurship. Likewise, firms that seek to establish their technology as a standard, also representing institutional entrepreneurship, are engaging in strategic entrepreneurship because creating a standard produces a competitive advantage for the firm.[126]

Research shows that because of its economic importance and individual motives, entrepreneurial activity is increasing around the globe. Furthermore, more women are becoming entrepreneurs because of the economic opportunity entrepreneurship provides and the individual independence it affords. The Kauffman Foundation, which promotes entrepreneurship, reports that women "launch 40 percent of all private companies."[127] In the United States, for example, women are the nation's fastest-growing group of entrepreneurs.[128] In future years, entrepreneurial activity may increase the wealth of less-affluent countries and continue to contribute to the economic development of the more-affluent countries. Regardless, the entrepreneurial ventures and large, established firms that choose to practice strategic entrepreneurship are likely to be the winners in the twenty-first century.[129]

After identifying opportunities, entrepreneurs must develop capabilities that will become the basis of their firm's core competencies and competitive advantages. The process of identifying opportunities is entrepreneurial, but this activity alone is not sufficient to create maximum wealth or even to survive over time. As we learned in Chapter 3, to successfully exploit opportunities, a firm must develop capabilities that are valuable, rare, difficult to imitate, and nonsubstitutable. When capabilities satisfy these four criteria, the firm has one or more competitive advantages to exploit the identified opportunities (as described in Chapter 3). Without a competitive advantage, the firm's success will be only temporary (as explained in Chapter 1). An innovation may be valuable and rare early in its life, if a market perspective is used in its development. However, competitive actions must be taken to introduce the new product to the market and protect its position in the market against competitors to gain a competitive advantage.[130] These actions combined represent strategic entrepreneurship.

SUMMARY

- Strategic entrepreneurship is taking entrepreneurial actions using a strategic perspective. Firms engaging in strategic entrepreneurship simultaneously engage in opportunity-seeking and advantage-seeking behaviors. The purpose is to continuously find new opportunities and quickly develop innovations to exploit them.

- Entrepreneurship is a process used by individuals, teams, and organizations to identify entrepreneurial opportunities without being immediately constrained by the resources they control. Corporate entrepreneurship is the application of entrepreneurship (including the identification of entrepreneurial opportunities) within ongoing, established organizations. Entrepreneurial opportunities are conditions in which new goods or services can satisfy a need in the market. Increasingly, entrepreneurship positively contributes to individual firms' performance and stimulates growth in countries' economies.

- Firms engage in three types of innovative activities: (1) invention, which is the act of creating a new good or process, (2) innovation, or the process of creating a commercial product from an invention, and (3) imitation, which is the adoption of similar innovations by different firms. Invention brings something new into being while innovation brings something new into use.

- Entrepreneurs see or envision entrepreneurial opportunities and then take actions to develop innovations to exploit them. The most successful entrepreneurs (whether they are establishing their own venture or are working in an ongoing organization) have an entrepreneurial mind-set, which is an orientation that values the potential opportunities available because of marketplace uncertainties.

- International entrepreneurship, or the process of identifying and exploiting entrepreneurial opportunities outside the firm's domestic markets, is important to firms around the globe. Evidence suggests that firms capable of effectively engaging in international entrepreneurship outperform those competing only in their domestic markets.

- Three basic approaches are used to produce innovation: (1) internal innovation, which involves R&D and forming internal corporate ventures, (2) cooperative strategies such as strategic alliances, and (3) acquisitions. Autonomous strategic behavior and induced strategic behavior are the two forms of internal corporate venturing. Autonomous strategic behavior is a bottom-up process through which a product champion facilitates the commercialization of an innovative good or service. Induced strategic behavior is a top-down process in which a firm's current strategy and structure facilitate the development and implementation of product or process innovations. Thus, induced strategic behavior is driven by the organization's current corporate strategy and structure while autonomous strategic behavior can result in a change to the firm's current strategy and structure arrangements.

- Firms create two types of innovations—incremental and radical—through internal innovation that takes place in the form of autonomous strategic behavior or induced strategic behavior. Overall, firms produce more incremental innovations, but radical innovations have a higher probability of significantly increasing sales revenue and profits. Cross-functional integration is often vital to a firm's efforts to develop and implement internal corporate venturing activities and to commercialize the resulting innovation. The cross-functional teams now commonly include representatives from external organizations such as suppliers. Additionally, integration and innovation can be facilitated by developing shared values and effectively using strategic leadership.

- To gain access to the specialized knowledge commonly required to innovate in the complex global economy, firms may form a cooperative relationship such as a strategic alliance with other companies, some of which may be competitors.

- Acquisitions are another means firms use to obtain innovation. Innovation can be acquired through direct acquisition, or firms can learn new capabilities from an acquisition, thereby enriching their internal innovation abilities.

- The practice of strategic entrepreneurship by all types of firms, large and small, new and more established, creates value for all stakeholders, especially for shareholders and customers. Strategic entrepreneurship also contributes to the economic development of countries.

REVIEW QUESTIONS

1. What is strategic entrepreneurship? What is corporate entrepreneurship?

2. What is entrepreneurship, and what are entrepreneurial opportunities? Why are they important for firms competing in the twenty-first-century competitive landscape?

3. What are invention, innovation, and imitation? How are these concepts interrelated?

4. What is an entrepreneur, and what is an entrepreneurial mind-set?

5. What is international entrepreneurship? Why is it important?

6. How do firms develop innovations internally?

7. How do firms use cooperative strategies to innovate and to have access to innovative capabilities?

8. How does a firm acquire other companies to increase the number of innovations it produces and improve its capability to produce innovations?

9. How does strategic entrepreneurship help firms to create value?

EXPERIENTIAL EXERCISES

EXERCISE 1: IS CORPORATE ENTREPRENEURSHIP DIFFERENT FROM STARTUP ENTREPRENEURSHIP?

Your text argues that corporate entrepreneurship is "the use or application of entrepreneurship within an established firm." In this exercise you will form groups and examine what you believe to be the major differences between becoming a startup entrepreneur and doing entrepreneurship within a corporation with existing businesses. Each group will be called upon to describe what it perceives to be the main differences. Think in terms of careers, risks, and money, and anything else your group finds important.

EXERCISE 2: THE SOCIAL NATURE OF ENTREPRENEURSHIP

Entrepreneurship is said to be as much about social connections and networks as it is about the fundamentals of running a new venture. The relationships that an entrepreneur can count on are also key resources of financial capital, human capital, mentoring, and legal advice.

A popular blog covering social media and Web 2.0 recently identified what it considered to be the top 10 social networks for entrepreneurs (Online-Education.net 2011). One of their bloggers took a stab at creating a top 10 list, identified as follows:

1. LinkedIn
2. The Funded
3. PartnerUp
4. Young Entrepreneur
5. Startup Nation
6. Go BIG Network
7. Biznik
8. Perfect Business
9. Cofounder
10. Entrepreneur Connect

In teams pick one social network from the list, or another you might favor (your instructor will ensure that there is a unique choice for each team). Spend some time on this network's Web site reading the posts to get a feel for the types of information presented. Prepare a 10-minute presentation to the class on your network site and be sure to address the following, at a minimum:

1. Provide an overview of the site—what it is used for, how popular it is, features, types of conversations, etc.

2. What is unique about this site and why does it attract followers? What technologies are enabled here—RSS, Twitter, etc.?

3. Describe the target audience for this Web site. Who would use it and what types of information are available to entrepreneurs?

4. How do you think this site maintains its presence? Does it support itself with ad revenue, corporate sponsors, not-for-profit sponsors, or by some other means?

5. Would this site be useful for corporate entrepreneurs as well as startup entrepreneurs? If so, how?

VIDEO CASE

A NEW ENTREPRENEUR ON THE BLOCK: SARA BLAKELY, FOUNDER AND ENTREPRENEUR/ SPANX

SPANX, creating a slimming/invisible underlayer garment, surfaced about 10 years ago. Sara Blakely, founder and entrepreneur, confronted with the male-dominated manufacturing of women's shapewear, was able to offer a female-oriented solution. With shapewear as an expanding segment in a newly competitive market, Blakely designs a wide range of SPANX products by placing herself in the position of a customer. Currently, SPANX records more than $150 million a year in sales.

Be prepared to discuss the following concepts and questions in class:

Concepts

- Strategic entrepreneurship
- Corporate entrepreneurship
- Entrepreneurial opportunities
- Innovation
- Entrepreneurial mind-set
- International entrepreneurship

Questions

1. Is there evidence in the account of Sara Blakely that strategic entrepreneurship exists?

2. Does Sara Blakely set the stage for corporate entrepreneurship?

3. What entrepreneurial opportunities do you see ahead for Sara Blakely?

4. How would you classify the SPANX innovation? What advantages and risks are associated with the SPANX innovation?

5. Is Sara Blakely an entrepreneur with an entrepreneurial mind-set?

6. Should Sara Blakely pursue international entrepreneurship? Why or why not? What concerns might she have?

NOTES

1. M. Gruber, F. Heinemann, M. Brettel, & S. Hungeling, 2010, Configurations of resources and capabilities and their performance implications: An exploratory study on technology ventures: *Strategic Management Journal*, 31(12): 1337–1356; S. Sato, 2009, Beyond good: Great innovations through design, *Journal of Business Strategy*, 30(2/3): 40–49.

2. M. A. Hitt, R. D. Ireland, D. G. Sirmon, & C. A. Trahms, 2011, Strategic entrepreneurship: Creating value for individuals, organizations, and society, *Academy of Management Perspectives*, 25(2): 57–75; R. D. Ireland & J. W. Webb, 2007, Strategic entrepreneurship: Creating competitive advantage through streams of innovation, *Business Horizons*, 50(4): 49–59; M. A. Hitt, R. D. Ireland, S. M. Camp, & D. L. Sexton, 2001, Strategic entrepreneurship: Entrepreneurial strategies for wealth creation, *Strategic Management Journal*, 22 (Special Issue): 479–491.

3. C. Williams & S. Lee, 2011, Entrepreneurial contexts and knowledge coordination within the multinational corporation, *Journal of World Business*, 46(2): 253–264; R. Durand, O. Bruyaka, & V. Mangematin, 2008, Do science and money go together? The case of the French biotech industry, *Strategic Management Journal*, 29: 1281–1299; R. K. Sinha & C. H. Noble, 2008, The adoption of radical manufacturing technologies and firm survival, *Strategic Management Journal*, 29: 943–962.

4. M. Bogers, 2011. The open innovation paradox: Knowledge sharing and protection in R&D collaborations, *European Journal of Innovation Management*, 14(1): 93–117; E. Levitas & M. A. McFadyen, 2009, Managing liquidity in research-intensive firms: Signaling and cash flow effects of patents and alliance activities, *Strategic Management Journal*, 30: 659–678.

5. A. Spithoven, B. Clarysse, & M. Knockaert, 2011, Building absorptive capacity to organise inbound open innovation in traditional industries, *Technovation*, 31(1): 10–21; J. L. Morrow, D. G. Sirmon, M. A. Hitt, & T. R. Holcomb, 2007, Creating value in the face of declining performance: Firm strategies and organizational recovery, *Strategic Management Journal*, 28: 271–283.

6. R. Lee, 2010, Extending the environment-strategy-performance framework: The roles of multinational corporation network strength, market responsiveness, and product innovation, *Journal of International Marketing*, 18(4): 58–73; D. F. Kuratko, 2007, Entrepreneurial leadership in the 21st century, *Journal of Leadership and Organizational Studies*, 13(4): 1–11; R. D. Ireland, M. A. Hitt, & D. G. Sirmon, 2003, A model of strategic entrepreneurship: The construct and its dimensions, *Journal of Management*, 29: 963–989.

7. D. Kelley, 2011. Sustainable corporate entrepreneurship: Evolving and connecting with the organization, *Business Horizons*, 54(1): 73–83; B. R. Barringer & R. D. Ireland, 2008, *Entrepreneurship: Successfully Launching New Ventures*, Upper Saddle River, NJ: Pearson Prentice Hall, 5.

8. T. C. Sebora, T. Theerapatvong, & S. M. Lee, 2010, Corporate entrepreneurship in the face of changing competition, *Journal of Organizational Change Management*, 23(4): 453–470; M. H. Morris, S. Coombes, & M. Schindehutte, 2007, Antecedents and outcomes of entrepreneurial and market orientations in a non-profit context: Theoretical and empirical insights, *Journal of Leadership and Organizational Studies*, 13(4): 12–39.

9. S. Ahmad & R. G. Schroeder, 2010, Knowledge management through technology strategy: Implications for competitiveness, *Journal of Manufacturing Technology Management*, 22(1): 6–24; J. Uotila, M. Maula, T. Keil, & S. A. Zahra, 2009, Exploration, exploitation and financial performance: Analysis of S&P 500 corporations, *Strategic Management Journal*, 30: 221–231.

10. D. Benson & R. H. Ziedonis, 2010, Corporate venture capital and the returns to acquiring portfolio companies, *Journal of Financial Economics*, 98(3): 478–499; B. A. Gilbert, P. P. McDougall, & D. B. Audretsch, 2006, New venture growth: A review and extension, *Journal of Management*, 32: 926–950.

11. D. Grégoire, D. P. S. Barr, & D. A. Shepherd, 2010, Cognitive processes of opportunity recognition: The role of structural alignment, *Organization Science*, 21(2): 413–431; Barringer & Ireland, *Entrepreneurship*; S. A. Zahra, H. J. Sapienza, & P. Davidsson, 2006, Entrepreneurship and dynamic capabilities: A review, model and research agenda, *Journal of Management Studies*, 43: 917–955.

12. I. P. Vaghely & P.-A. Julien, 2010, Are opportunities recognized or constructed? An information perspective on entrepreneurial opportunity identification, *Journal of Business Venturing*, 25: 73–86; S. A. Alvarez & J. B. Barney, 2008, Opportunities, organizations and entrepreneurship, *Strategic Entrepreneurship Journal*, 2: 265–267.

13. J. M. Shulman, R. K. Cox, & T. T. Stallkamp, 2011, The strategic entrepreneurial growth model, *Competitiveness Review*, 21(1): 29–46; P. G. Klein, 2008, Opportunity discovery, entrepreneurial action and economic organization, *Strategic Entrepreneurship Journal*, 2: 175–190; W. Kuemmerle, 2005, The entrepreneur's path to global expansion, *MIT Sloan Management Review*, 46(2): 42–49.

14. B. Chakravorti, 2010, Finding competitive advantage in adversity, *Harvard Business Review*, 88(11): 102–108; R. K. Mitchell, J. R. Mitchell, & J. B. Smith, 2008, Inside opportunity formation: Enterprise failure, cognition and the creation of opportunities, *Strategic Entrepreneurship Journal*, 2: 225–242.

15. C. G. Gilbert & M. J. Eyring, 2010, Beating the odds when you launch a new venture, *Harvard Business Review*, 88(5): 92–98; S. A. Zahra, 2008, The virtuous cycle of discovery and creation of entrepreneurial opportunities, *Strategic Entrepreneurship Journal*, 2: 243–257.

16. J. Schumpeter, 1934, *The Theory of Economic Development*, Cambridge, MA: Harvard University Press.

17. M. Hughes, S. Martin, R. Morgan, & M. Robson, 2010, Realizing product-market advantage in high-technology international new ventures: The mediating role of ambidextrous innovation, *Journal of International Marketing*, 18(4): 1–21; J. H. Dyer, H. B. Gregersen, & C. Christensen, 2008, Entrepreneur behaviors and the origins of innovative ventures, *Strategic Entrepreneurship Journal*, 2: 317–338.

18. H. Mayer, 2010, Catching up: The role of state science and technology policy in open innovation, *Economic Development Quarterly*, 24(3): 195–209; W. J. Baumol, R. E. Litan, & C. J. Schramm, 2007, *Good Capitalism, Bad Capitalism, and the Economics of Growth and Prosperity*, New Haven: Yale University Press.

19. K. E. Klein, 2007, The face of entrepreneurship in 2017, *BusinessWeek*, http://www.businessweek.com, January 31.

20. P. F. Drucker, 1998, The discipline of innovation, *Harvard Business Review*, 76(6): 149–157.

21. Ibid.

22. B. R. Bhardwaj, Sushil, & K. Momaya, 2011, Drivers and enablers of corporate entrepreneurship: Case of a software giant from India, *Journal of Management Development*, 30(2): 187–205; A. Leiponen, 2008, Control of intellectual assets in client relationships: Implications for innovation, *Strategic Management Journal*, 29: 1371–1394.

23. G. F. Alberti, S. Sciascia, C. Tripodi, & F. Visconti, 2011, The entrepreneurial growth of firms located in clusters: A cross-case study, *International Journal of Technology Management*, 54(1): 53–79; F. F. Suarez & G. Lanzolla, 2007, The role of environmental dynamics in building a first mover advantage theory, *Academy of Management Review*, 32: 377–392.

24. M. J. Leiblein & T. L. Madsen, 2009, Unbundling competitive heterogeneity:

Incentive structures and capability influences on technological innovation, *Strategic Management Journal*, 30: 711–735; R. Price, 1996, Technology and strategic advantage, *California Management Review*, 38(3): 38–56.

25. M. A. Hitt, R. D. Nixon, R. E. Hoskisson, & R. Kochhar, 1999, Corporate entrepreneurship and cross-functional fertilization: Activation, process and disintegration of a new product design team, *Entrepreneurship: Theory and Practice*, 23(3): 145–167.

26. M. Makri, M. A. Hitt, & P. J. Lane, 2010, Complementary technologies, knowledge relatedness, and invention outcomes in high technology M&As, *Strategic Management Journal*, 31: 602–628; R. Oriani & M. Sobero, 2008, Uncertainty and the market valuation of R&D within a real options logic, *Strategic Management Journal*, 29: 343–361.

27. Schumpeter, *The Theory of Economic Development*.

28. L. Jiang, J. Tan, & M. Thursby, 2011, Incumbent firm invention in emerging fields: Evidence from the semiconductor industry, *Strategic Management Journal*, 32(1), 55–75; R. Katila & S. Shane, 2005, When does lack of resources make new firms innovative? *Academy of Management Journal*, 48: 814–829.

29. P. Sharma & J. L. Chrisman, 1999, Toward a reconciliation of the definitional issues in the field of corporate entrepreneurship, *Entrepreneurship: Theory and Practice*, 23(3): 11–27; R. A. Burgelman & L. R. Sayles, 1986, *Inside Corporate Innovation: Strategy, Structure, and Managerial Skills*, New York: Free Press.

30. M. W. Johnson, 2011, Making innovation matter. *Bloomberg Businessweek*, http://www.businessweek.com, March 3; D. G. Sirmon, J.-L. Arregle, M. A. Hitt, & J. W. Webb, 2008, The role of family influence in firms' strategic responses to the threat of imitation, *Entrepreneurship Theory and Practice*, 32: 979–998.

31. S. F. Latham & M. Braun, 2009, Managerial risk, innovation and organizational decline, *Journal of Management*, 35: 258–281.

32. R. E. Hoskisson & L. W. Busenitz, 2002, Market uncertainty and learning distance in corporate entrepreneurship entry mode choice, in M. A. Hitt, R. D. Ireland, S. M. Camp, & D. L. Sexton (eds.), *Strategic Entrepreneurship: Creating a New Mindset*, Oxford, UK: Blackwell Publishers, 151–172.

33. S. Moon, 2011, How does the management of research impact the disclosure of knowledge? Evidence from scientific publications and patenting behavior, *Economics of Innovation & New Technology*, 20(1): 1–32; S. Thornhill, 2006, Knowledge, innovation, and firm performance in high- and low-technology regimes, *Journal of Business Venturing*, 21: 687–703.

34. D. Ucbasaran, P. Westhead, M. Wright, & M. Flores, 2010, The nature of entrepreneurial experience, business failure and comparative optimism, *Journal of Business Venturing*, 25(6): 541–555; K. M. Hmieleski & R. A. Baron, 2009, Entrepreneurs' optimism and new venture performance: A social cognitive perspective, *Academy of Management Journal*, 52: 473–488.

35. M.-D. Foo, 2011, Emotions and entrepreneurial opportunity evaluation, *Entrepreneurship: Theory & Practice*, 35(2): 375–393; M. S. Cardon, J. Wincent, J. Singh, & M. Drovsek, 2009, The nature and experience of entrepreneurial passion, *Academy of Management Review*, 34: 511–532.

36. P. Westhead, D. Ucbasaran, & M. Wright, 2009, Information search and opportunity identification, *International Small Business Journal*, 27(6): 659–680; J. O. Fiet, 2007, A prescriptive analysis of search and discovery, *Journal of Management Studies*, 44: 592–611.

37. N. Nicolaou, S. Shane, L. Cherkas, & T. D. Spector, 2009, Opportunity recognition and the tendency to be an entrepreneur: A bivariate genetics perspective, *Organizational Behavior & Human Decision Processes*, 110(2): 108–117; N. Nicolaou, S. Shane, L. Cherkas, & T. D. Spector, 2008, The influence of sensation seeking in the heritability of entrepreneurship, *Strategic Entrepreneurship Journal*, 2: 7–21.

38. D. De Clercq, X. Castañer, & I. Belausteguigoitia, 2011, Entrepreneurial initiative selling within organizations: Towards a more comprehensive motivational framework, *Journal of Management Studies*, 48(6) (Special Issue): 1269–1290; X. P. Chen, X. Yao, & S. Kowtha, 2009, Entrepreneur passion and preparedness in business plan presentations: A persuasion analysis of venture capitalists' funding decisions, *Academy of Management Journal*, 52: 199–214.

39. S. Allen, 2009, Entrepreneurs: Quotations from famous entrepreneurs on entrepreneurship, *About.com*, http://entrepreneurs.about.com, June 13.

40. W. Stam & T. Elfring, 2008, Entrepreneurial orientation and new venture performance: The moderating role of intra- and extraindustry social capital, *Academy of Management Journal*, 51: 97–111; R. A. Baron, 2006, Opportunity recognition as pattern recognition: How entrepreneurs "connect the dots" to identify new business opportunities, *Academy of Management Perspectives*, 20(1): 104–119; R. G. McGrath & I. MacMillan, 2000, *The Entrepreneurial Mindset*, Boston, MA: Harvard Business School Press.

41. R. D. Ireland, M. A. Hitt, & J. W. Webb, 2005, Entrepreneurial alliances and networks, in O. Shenkar and J. J. Reuer (eds.), *Handbook of Strategic Alliances*, Thousand Oaks, CA: Sage Publications, 333–352; T. M. Begley & D. P. Boyd, 2003, The need for a corporate global mind-set, *MIT Sloan Management Review*, 44(2): 25–32.

42. W. Tsai, 2001, Knowledge transfer in intraorganizational networks: Effects of network position and absorptive capacity on business unit innovation and performance, *Academy of Management Journal*, 44: 996–1004.

43. S. A. Zahra & G. George, 2002, Absorptive capacity: A review, reconceptualization, and extension, *Academy of Management Review*, 27:185–203.

44. M. A. Hitt, L. Bierman, K. Uhlenbruck, & K. Shimizu, 2006, The importance of resources in the internationalization of professional service firms: The good, the bad and the ugly, *Academy of Management Journal*, 49: 1137–1157; M. A. Hitt, L. Bierman, K. Shimizu, & R. Kochhar, 2001, Direct and moderating effects of human capital on strategy and performance in professional service firms, *Academy of Management Journal*, 44: 13–28.

45. 2011, The world's most innovative companies 2011, *Fast Company*, http://www.fastcompany.com, February 16.

46. M. Maynard, 2008, At G. M., innovation sacrificed to profits, *New York Times Online*, http://www.nytimes.com, December 6; 2008, Creativity and innovation driving business—Innovation index, *BusinessWeek/ Boston Consulting Group*, http://www.creativityandinnovationblogspot.com, April 22.

47. K. Linebaugh, M. Dolan, M. Ramsey, & S. Terlep, 2011, Detroit keeps its cool as gas prices heat up, *Wall Street Journal*, January 5, B1-B2.

48. P. Ellis, 2011, Social ties and international entrepreneurship: Opportunities and constraints affecting firm internationalization, *Journal of International Business Studies*, 42(1): 99–127; M. M. Keupp & O. Gassman, 2009, The past and future of international entrepreneurship: A review and suggestions for developing the field, *Journal of Management*, 35: 600–633.

49. C. Williams & S. H. Lee, 2011, Political heterarchy and dispersed entrepreneurship in the MNC, *Journal of Management Studies*, 48(6): 1243–1268; H. J. Sapienza, E. Autio, G. George, & S. A. Zahra, 2006, A capabilities perspective on the effects of early internationalization on firm survival and growth, *Academy of Management Review*, 31: 914–933.

50. M. Musteen, J. Francis, & D. Datta, 2010, The influence of international networks on internationalization speed and performance: A study of Czech SMEs, *Journal of World Business*, 45(3): 197–205; M. Javidan, R. M. Steers, & M. A. Hitt, 2007, *The Global Mindset*, Amsterdam: Elsevier Ltd.

51. S. A. Fernhaber, B. A. Gilbert, & P. P. McDougal, 2008, International entrepreneurship and geographic location: An empirical examination of new venture internationalization, *Journal*

of International Business Studies, 39: 267–290; Hitt, Bierman, Uhlenbruck, & Shimizu, The importance of resources in the internationalization of professional service firms.

52. J. A. LiPuma, 2011, Internationalization and the IPO performance of new ventures, *Journal of Business Research*, forthcoming; H. Ren, B. Gray, & K. Kim, 2009, Performance of international joint ventures: What factors really make a difference and how? *Journal of Management*, 35: 805–832.

53. J. Tang, 2010, How entrepreneurs discover opportunities in China: An institutional view, *Asia Pacific Journal of Management*, 27(3): 461–479; P. Cappelli, H. Singh, J. Singh, & M. Useem, 2010, The India way: Lessons for the U.S., *Academy of Management Perspectives*, 24(2): 6–24.

54. N. Bosma, Z. J. Acs, E. Autio, A. Conduras, & J. Levie, 2009, *Global Entrepreneurship Monitor: 2008 Executive Report*, Global Entrepreneurship Research Consortium, http://www.gemconsortium .org, June 23.

55. U. Stephan & L. M. Uhlaner, 2010, Performance-based vs. socially supportive culture: A cross-cultural study of descriptive norms and entrepreneurship, *Journal of International Business Studies*, 41: 1347–1364; R. A. Baron & J. Tang, 2009, Entrepreneurs' social skills and new venture performance: Mediating mechanisms and cultural generality, *Journal of Management*, 35: 282–306; D. W. Yiu, C. M. Lau, & G. D. Bruton, 2007, International venturing by emerging economy firms: The effects of firm capabilities, home country networks, and corporate entrepreneurship, *Journal of International Business Studies*, 38: 519–540.

56. D. Kim, C. Basu, G. M. Naidu, & E. Cavusgil, 2011, The innovativeness of Born-Globals and customer orientation: Learning from Indian Born-Globals, *Journal of Business Research*, 64(8): 879–886.

57. Ibid.; S. A. Zahra, R. D. Ireland, & M. A. Hitt, 2000, International expansion by new venture firms: International diversity, mode of market entry, technological learning and performance, *Academy of Management Journal*, 43: 925–950.

58. D. J. McCarthy, S. M. Puffer, & S. V. Darda, 2010, Convergence in entrepreneurial leadership style: Evidence from Russia, *California Management Review*, 52(4): 48–72; H. U. Lee & J. H. Park, 2008, The influence of top management team international exposure on international alliance formation, *Journal of Management Studies*, 45: 961–981; H. G. Barkema & O. Chvyrkov, 2007, Does top management team diversity promote or hamper foreign expansion? *Strategic Management Journal*, 28: 663–680.

59. M. Mors, 2010, Innovation in a global consulting firm: When the problem is too much diversity, *Strategic Management Journal*, 31(8): 841–872; L. Carvalho, 2010, Innovation propensity of multinational firms in the service sector, *Journal of Transnational Management*, 15(1): 26–45.

60. A. Teixeira & N. Fortuna, 2010, Human capital, R&D, trade, and long-run productivity: Testing the technological absorption hypothesis for the Portuguese economy, 1960–2001, *Research Policy*, 39(3): 335–350; J. Song & J. Shin, 2008, The paradox of technological capabilities: A study of knowledge sourcing from host countries of overseas R&D operations, *Journal of International Business Studies*, 39: 291–303.

61. M. H. Morris, D. F. Kuratko, & J. G. Covin, 2011, *Corporate Entrepreneurship and Innovation*, 3rd ed. Mason, OH: Cengage/ Thomson South-Western; W. Chung & S. Yeaple, 2008, International knowledge sourcing: Evidence from U.S. firms expanding abroad, *Strategic Management Journal*, 29: 1207–1224; J. Santos, Y. Doz, & P. Williamson, 2004, Is your innovation process global? *MIT Sloan Management Review*, 45(4): 31–37.

62. L. A. Bettencourt & S. L. Bettencourt, 2011, Innovating on the cheap, *Harvard Business Review*, 89(6): 88–94; Y.-S. Su, E. W. K. Tsang, & M. W. Peng, 2009, How do internal capabilities and external partnerships affect innovativeness? *Asia Pacific Journal of Management*, 26: 309–331.

63. L. Jiang, J. Tan, & M. Thursby, 2011, Incumbent firm invention in emerging fields: Evidence from the semiconductor industry, *Strategic Management Journal*, 32(1): 55–75; F. K. Pil & S. K. Cohen, 2006, Modularity: Implications for imitation, innovation, and sustained advantage, *Academy of Management Review*, 31: 995–1011.

64. 2005, Radical and incremental innovation styles, *Strategies 2 innovate*, http://www .strategies2innovate.com, July 12.

65. D. McKendrick & J. Wade, 2010, Frequent incremental change, organizational size, and mortality in high-technology competition, *Industrial and Corporate Change*, 19(3): 613–639.

66. T. Magnusson & C. Berggren, 2011, Entering an era of ferment—radical vs incrementalist strategies in automotive power train development, *Technology Analysis & Strategic Management*, 23(3): 313–330; 2005, Getting an edge on innovation, *BusinessWeek*, March 21, 124.

67. B. Buisson & P. Silberzahn, 2010, Blue Ocean or fast-second innovation? A four-breakthrough model to explain successful market domination, *International Journal of Innovation Management*, 14(3): 359–378; A. J. Chatterji, 2009, Spawned with a silver spoon? Entrepreneurial performance and innovation in the medical device industry, *Strategic Management Journal*, 30: 185–206.

68. P. Scott, P. Gibbons, & J. Coughlan, 2010, Developing subsidiary contribution to the MNC—Subsidiary entrepreneurship and strategy creativity, *Journal of International Management*, 16(4): 328–339; C. E. Shalley & J. E. Perry-Smith, 2008, The emergence of team creative cognition: The role of diverse outside ties, socio-cognitive network centrality, and team evolution, *Strategic Entrepreneurship Journal*, 2: 1, 23–41.

69. J. M. Oldroyd & R. Gulaty, 2010, A learning perspective on intraorganizational knowledge spill-ins, *Strategic Entrepreneurship Journal*, 4(4): 356–372; K. G. Smith & D. Di Gregorio, 2002, Bisociation, discovery, and the role of entrepreneurial action, in M. A. Hitt, R. D. Ireland, S. M. Camp, & D. L. Sexton (eds.), *Strategic Entrepreneurship: Creating a New Mindset*, Oxford, UK: Blackwell Publishers, 129–150.

70. J. M. Shulman, R. A. K. Cox, & T. T. Stallkamp, 2011, The strategic entrepreneurial growth model, *Competitiveness Review*, 21(1): 29–46; S. A. Hill, M. V. J. Maula, J. M. Birkinshaw, & G. C. Murray, 2009, Transferability of the venture capital model to the corporate context: Implications for the performance of corporate venture units, *Strategic Entrepreneurship Journal*, 3: 3–27; Hoskisson & Busenitz, Market uncertainty and learning distance.

71. A. Sahaym, H. K. Steensma, & J. Q. Barden, 2010, The influence of R&D investment on the use of corporate venture capital: An industry-level analysis, *Journal of Business Venturing*, 25(4): 376–388; Hill, Maula, Birkinshaw, & Murray, Transferability of the venture capital model to the corporate context; R. A. Burgelman, 1995, *Strategic Management of Technology and Innovation*, Boston: Irwin.

72. A. Shabana, 2010, Focusing on intrapreneurship: An employee's centered approach, *Advances in Management*, 3(12): 32–37.

73. J. M. Howell, 2005, The right stuff: Identifying and developing effective champions of innovation, *Academy of Management Executive*, 19(2): 108–119.

74. D. Kelley & H. Lee, 2010, Managing innovation champions: The impact of project characteristics on the direct manager role, *Journal of Product Innovation Management*, 27(7): 1007–1019; M. D. Hutt & T. W. Speh, 2009, *Business Marketing Management: B2B*, 10th ed., Mason, OH: Cengage South-Western.

75. R. M. Yam, W. Lo, E. Y. Tang, & A. W. Lau, 2011, Analysis of sources of innovation, technological innovation capabilities, and performance: An empirical study of Hong Kong manufacturing industries, *Research Policy*, 40(3): 391–402; S. K. Ethiraj, 2007, Allocation of inventive effort in complex product systems, *Strategic Management Journal*, 28: 563–584; M. A. Hitt, R. D. Ireland, & H. Lee, 2000, Technological learning, knowledge management, firm growth and performance, *Journal of Engineering and Technology Management*, 17: 231–246.

76. A. M. Subramanian, K. Chai, & S. Mu, 2011, Capability reconfiguration of incumbent firms: Nintendo in the video game industry, *Technovation*, 31(5/6): 228–239; V. Gaba & A. D. Meyer, 2008, Crossing the organizational species barrier: How venture capital practices infiltrated the information technology sector, *Academy of Management Journal*, 51: 976–998; H. W. Chesbrough, 2002, Making sense of corporate venture capital, *Harvard Business Review*, 80(3): 90–99.

77. M. Subramaniam & N. Venkatraman, 2001, Determinants of transnational new product development capability: Testing the influence of transferring and deploying tacit overseas knowledge, *Strategic Management Journal*, 22: 359–378.

78. C. Webster & A. White, 2010, Exploring the national and organizational cultural mix in service firms, *Journal of the Academy of Marketing Science*, 38(6): 691–703; M. Song & M. M. Montoya-Weiss, 2001, The effect of perceived technological uncertainty on Japanese new product development, *Academy of Management Journal*, 44: 61–80.

79. C. Williams & S. H. Lee, 2011, Entrepreneurial context and knowledge coordination within the multinational corporation, *Journal of World Business*, 46(2): 253–264; B. Ambos & B. B. Schegelmilch, 2007, Innovation and control in the multinational firm: A comparison of political and contingency approaches, *Strategic Management Journal*, 28: 473–486.

80. Bhardwaj, Sushil, & Momaya, Drivers and enablers of corporate entrepreneurship; H. Li & J. Li, 2009, Top management team conflict and entrepreneurial strategy in China, *Asia Pacific Journal of Management*, 26: 263–283; S. C. Parker, 2009, Can cognitive biases explain venture team homophily?, *Strategic Entrepreneurship Journal*, 3: 67–83.

81. J. R. Hagerty, 2010, 3M brings along the basics as it balances new and old, *Wall Street Journal*, November 1, B1.

82. J. R. Blasi & D. L. Kruse, 2010, Shared capitalism at work: Employee ownership, profit and gain sharing, and broad-based stock options, *Journal of Employee Ownership Law & Finance*, 22(3): 43–79; M. Makri, P. J. Lane, & L. R. Gomez-Mejia, 2006, CEO incentives, innovation and performance in technology-intensive firms: A reconciliation of outcome and behavior-based incentive schemes, *Strategic Management Journal*, 27: 1057–1080.

83. P. L. Drnevich & A. P. Kriauciunas, 2011, Clarifying the conditions and limits of the contributions of ordinary and dynamic capabilities to relative firm performance, *Strategic Management Journal*, 32: 254–279; C. Zhou & J. Li, 2008, Product innovation in emerging market-based international joint ventures: An organizational ecology perspective, *Journal of International Business Studies*, 39: 1114–1132; E. Danneels, 2007, The process of technological competence

84. C. Nakata & S. Im, 2010, Spurring cross-functional integration for higher new product performance: A group effectiveness perspective, *Journal of Product Innovation Management*, 27(4): 554–571; F. T. Rothaermel & W. Boeker, 2008, Old technology meets new technology: Complementarities, similarities and alliance formation, *Strategic Management Journal*, 29: 47–77; L. Yu, 2002, Marketers and engineers: Why can't we just get along? *MIT Sloan Management Review*, 43(1): 13.

85. R. Slotegraaf & K. Atuahene-Gima, 2011, Product development team stability and new product advantage: The role of decision-making processes, *Journal of Marketing*, 75(1): 96–108; R. Cowan & N. Jonard, 2009, Knowledge portfolios and the organization of innovation networks, *Academy of Management Review*, 34: 320–342; A. Somech, 2006, The effects of leadership style and team process on performance and innovation in functionally heterogeneous teams, *Journal of Management*, 32: 132–157.

86. M. Brettel, F. Heinemann, A. Engelen, & S. Neubauer, 2011, Cross-functional integration of R&D, marketing, and manufacturing in radical and incremental product innovations and its effects on project effectiveness and efficiency, *Journal of Product Innovation Management*, 28(2): 251–269; A. Azadegan, K. J. Dooley, P. L. Carter, & J. R. Carter, 2008, Supplier innovativeness and the role of interorganizational learning in enhancing manufacturer capabilities, *Journal of Supply Chain Management*, 44(4): 14–34.

87. G. Gemser & M. M. Leenders, 2011, Managing cross-functional cooperation for new product development success, *Long Range Planning*, 44(1): 26–41; B. Fischer & A. Boynton, 2005, Virtuoso teams, *Harvard Business Review*, 83(7): 116–123.

88. Hitt, Nixon, Hoskisson, & Kochhar, Corporate entrepreneurship.

89. Hitt, Nixon, Hoskisson, & Kochhar, Corporate entrepreneurship.

90. R. Oliva & N. Watson, 2011, Cross-functional alignment in supply chain planning: A case study of sales and operations planning, *Journal of Operations Management*, 29(5): 434–448; A. C. Amason, 1996, Distinguishing the effects of functional and dysfunctional conflict on strategic decision making: Resolving a paradox for top management teams, *Academy of Management Journal*, 39: 123–148.

91. D. Clercq, B. Menguc, & S. Auh, 2009, Unpacking the relationship between an innovation strategy and firm performance: The role of task conflict and political activity, *Journal of Business Research*, 62(11): 1046–1053; M. A. Cronin & L. R. Weingart, 2007, Representational gaps, information processing, and conflict in functionally heterogeneous teams,

Academy of Management Review, 32: 761–773.

92. Hitt, Nixon, Hoskisson, & Kochhar, Corporate entrepreneurship.

93. H. Ernst, W. D. Hoyer, & C. Rübsaamen, 2010, Sales, marketing, and research-and-development cooperation across new product development stages: Implications for success, *Journal of Marketing*, 74(5): 80–92; V. Ambrosini, N. Collier, & M. Jenkins, 2009, A configurational approach to the dynamics of firm-level knowledge, *Journal of Strategy and Management*, 2: 4–30.

94. Gary Hamel, 2000, *Leading the Revolution*, Boston: Harvard Business School Press.

95. L. Z. Song & M. Song, 2010, The role of information technologies in enhancing R&D–marketing integration: An empirical investigation, *Journal of Product Innovation Management*, 27(3): 382–401; P. H. Kim, K. T. Dirks, & C. D. Cooper, 2009, The repair of trust: A dynamic bilateral perspective and multilevel conceptualization, *Academy of Management Review*, 34: 401–422.

96. S. Sarin & G. O'Connor, 2009, First among equals: The effect of team leader characteristics on the internal dynamics of cross-functional product development teams, *Journal of Product Innovation Management*, 26(2): 188; N. Stieglitz & L. Heine, 2007, Innovations and the role of complementarities in a strategic theory of the firm, *Strategic Management Journal*, 28: 1–15.

97. K. Wennberg, J. Wiklund, D. R. DeTienne, & M. S. Cardon, 2010, Reconceptualizing entrepreneurial exit: Divergent exit routes and their drivers, *Journal of Business Venturing*, 25(4): 361–375; M. B. Sarkar, R. Echambadi, R. Agarwal, & B. Sen, 2006, The effect of the innovative environment on exit of entrepreneurial firms, *Strategic Management Journal*, 27: 519–539.

98. S. Billings, 2011, Open source: The art of creative collaboration, *Marketing*, April 13, 33–37; T. Keil, M. Maula, H. Schildt, & S. A. Zahra, 2008, The effect of governance modes and relatedness of external business development activities on innovative performance, *Strategic Management Journal*, 29: 895–907.

99. S. Terjesen, P. C. Patel, & J. G. Covin, 2011, Alliance diversity, environmental context and the value of manufacturing capabilities among new high technology ventures, *Journal of Operations Management*, 29(1/2): 105–115; P. Ozcan & K. M. Eisenhardt, 2009, Origin of alliance portfolios: Entrepreneurs, network strategies, and firm performance, *Academy of Management Journal*, 52: 246–279; A. Tiwana & M. Keil, 2007, Does peripheral knowledge complement control? An empirical test in technology outsourcing alliances, *Strategic Management Journal*, 28: 623–634.

100. D. Dunlap-Hinkler, M. Kotabe, & R. Mudambi, 2010, A story of

breakthrough versus incremental innovation: Corporate entrepreneurship in the global pharmaceutical industry, *Strategic Entrepreneurship Journal*, 4(2): 106–127; K. B. Whittington, J. Owen-Smith, & W. W. Powell, 2009, Networks, propinquity, and innovation in knowledge-intensive industries, *Administrative Science Quarterly*, 54: 90–122; C. Dhanaraj & A. Parkhe, 2006, Orchestrating innovation networks, *Academy of Management Review*, 31: 659–669.

101. Y. Zheng, J. Liu, & G. George, 2010, The dynamic impact of innovative capability and inter-firm network on firm valuation: A longitudinal study of biotechnology start-ups, *Journal of Business Venturing*, 25(6): 593–609; D. Li, L. Eden, M. A. Hitt, & R. D. Ireland, 2008, Friends, acquaintances, or strangers? Partner selection in R&D alliances, *Academy of Management Journal*, 51: 315–334; F. T. Rothaermel, M. A. Hitt, & L. A. Jobe, 2006, Balancing vertical integration and strategic outsourcing: Effects on product portfolio, product success and firm performance, *Strategic Management Journal*, 27: 1033–1056.

102. J. Birchall, 2010, Open innovation powers growth, *Financial Times*, December 28, 10.

103. J. T. Eckhardt & S. A. Shane, 2011, Industry changes in technology and complementary assets and the creation of high-growth firms, *Journal of Business Venturing*, 26(4): 412–430; A. C. Cooper, 2002, Networks, alliances and entrepreneurship, in M. A. Hitt, R. D. Ireland, S. M. Camp, & D. L. Sexton (eds.), *Strategic Entrepreneurship: Creating a New Mindset*, Oxford, UK: Blackwell Publishers, 204–222.

104. G. Dushnitsky & D. Lavie, 2010, How alliance formation shapes corporate venture capital investment in the software industry: A resource-based perspective, *Strategic Entrepreneurship Journal*, 4(1): 22–48; B. S. Teng, 2007, Corporate entrepreneurship activities through strategic alliances: A resource-based approach toward competitive advantage, *Journal of Management Studies*, 44: 119–142; S. A. Alvarez & J. B. Barney, 2001, How entrepreneurial firms can benefit from alliances with large partners, *Academy of Management Executive*, 15(1): 139–148.

105. H. Ernst, U. Lichtenthaler, & C. Vogt, 2011, The impact of accumulating and reactivating technological experience on R&D alliance performance, *Journal of Management Studies*, 48(6): 1194–1216; F. T. Rothaermel, 2001, Incumbent's advantage through exploiting complementary assets via interfirm cooperation, *Strategic Management Journal*, 22 (Special Issue): 687–699.

106. J. Baum, R. Cowan, & N. Jonard, 2010, Network-independent partner selection and the evolution of innovation networks, *Management Science*, 56(11): 2094–2110; B. R. Koka & J. E. Prescott, 2008,

Designing alliance networks: The influence of network position, environmental change and strategy on firm performance, *Strategic Management Journal*, 29: 639–661.

107. E. Fang, 2011, The effect of strategic alliance knowledge complementarity on new product innovativeness in China, *Organization Science*, 22(1): 158–172; C. L. Luk, O. H. M. Yau, L. Y. M. Sin, A. C. B. Tse, R. P. M. Chow, & J. S. Y. Lee, 2008, The effects of social capital and organizational innovativeness in different institutional contexts, *Journal of International Business Studies*, 39: 589–612.

108. L. Zhou, B. Barnes, & Y. Lu, 2010, Entrepreneurial proclivity, capability upgrading and performance advantage of newness among international new ventures, *Journal of International Business Studies*, 41(5): 882–905; A. Tiwana, 2008, Do bridging ties complement strong ties? An empirical examination of alliance ambidexterity, *Strategic Management Journal*, 29: 251–272.

109. A. Azadegan, 2011, Benefiting from supplier operational innovativeness: The influence of supplier evaluations and absorptive capacity, *Journal of Supply Chain Management*, 47(2): 49–64; Azadegan, Dooley, Carter, & Carter, Supplier innovativeness and the role of interorganizational learning in enhancing manufacturer capabilities; A. Takeishi, 2001, Bridging inter- and intra-firm boundaries: Management of supplier involvement in automobile product development, *Strategic Management Journal*, 22: 403–433.

110. B. Lokshin, J. Hagedoorn, & W. Letterie, 2011, The bumpy road of technology partnerships: Understanding causes and consequences of partnership and mal-functioning, *Research Policy*, 40(2): 297–308; R. H. Shah & V. Swaminathan, 2008, Factors influencing partner selection in strategic alliances: The moderating role of alliance context, *Strategic Management Journal*, 29: 471–494; Li, Eden, Hitt, & Ireland, Friends, acquaintances, or strangers?; R. D. Ireland, M. A. Hitt, & D. Vaidyanath, 2002, Strategic alliances as a pathway to competitive success, *Journal of Management*, 28: 413–446.

111. Fang, The effect of strategic alliance knowledge complementarity on new product innovativeness in China; M. A. Hitt, M. T. Dacin, E. Levitas, J. L. Arregle, & A. Borza, 2000, Partner selection in emerging and developed market contexts: Resource-based and organizational learning perspectives, *Academy of Management Journal*, 43: 449–467.

112. G. Duysters & B. Lokshin, 2011, Determinants of alliance portfolio complexity and its effect on innovative performance of companies, *Journal of Product Innovation Management*, 28(4): 570–585; J. J. Reuer, M. Zollo, & H. Singh, 2002, Post-formation dynamics in strategic

alliances, *Strategic Management Journal*, 23: 135–151.

113. C. M. Christensen, R. Alton, C. Rising, & A. Waldeck, 2011, The new M&A playbook, *Harvard Business Review*, 89(3): 48–57; M. A. Hitt, D. King, H. Krishnan, M. Makri, M. Schijven, K. Shimizu, & H. Zhu, 2009, Mergers and acquisitions: Overcoming pitfalls, building synergy and creating value, *Business Horizons*, 52(6): 523–529; H. G. Barkema & M. Schijven, 2008, Toward unlocking the full potential of acquisitions: The role of organizational restructuring, *Academy of Management Journal*, 51: 696–722.

114. J. D. Rockoff, 2011, After long pursuit, Teva wins Cephalon, *Wall Street Journal*, May 3, B1.

115. P. Desyllas & A. Hughes, 2010, Do high technology acquirers become more innovative? *Research Policy*, 39(8): 1105–1121; M. A. Hitt, R. E. Hoskisson, R. A. Johnson, & D. D. Moesel, 1996, The market for corporate control and firm innovation, *Academy of Management Journal*, 39: 1084–1119.

116. M. Makri, M. A. Hitt, & P. J. Lane, 2010, Complementary technologies, knowledge relatedness, and invention outcomes in high technology M&As, *Strategic Management Journal*, 31: 602–628.

117. M. E. Graebner, K. M. Eisenhardt, & P. T. Roundy, 2010, Success and failure in technology acquisitions: Lessons for buyers and sellers, *Academy of Management Perspectives*, 24(3): 73–92; P. Puranam & K. Srikanth, 2007, What they know vs. what they do: How acquirers leverage technology acquisitions, *Strategic Management Journal*, 28: 805–825; M. A. Hitt, J. S. Harrison, & R. D. Ireland, 2001, *Mergers and Acquisitions: A Guide to Creating Value for Stakeholders*, New York: Oxford University Press.

118. A. E. Rafferty & S. L. D. Restburg, 2010, The impact of change process and context on change reactions and turnover during a merger, *Journal of Management*, 36: 1309–1338; M. Cording, P. Christman, & D. King, 2008, Reducing causal ambiguity in acquisition integration: Intermediate goals as mediators of integration decisions and acquisition performance, *Academy of Management Journal*, 51: 744–767.

119. D. Elfenbein & B. Hamilton, 2010, The small firm effect and the entrepreneurial spawning of scientists and engineers, *Management Science*, 56(4): 659–681; Ireland, Hitt, & Sirmon, A model of strategic entrepreneurship.

120. S. Ransbotham & S. Mitra, 2010, Target age and the acquisition of innovation in high-technology industries, *Management Science*, 56(11): 2076–2093; A. Afuah, 2009, *Strategic Innovation: New Game Strategies for Competitive Advantage*, New York: Routledge.

121. H. Greve, 2011, Positional rigidity: Low performance and resource acquisition in large and small firms, *Strategic Management Journal*, 32(1): 103–114;

Hitt, Ireland, Camp, & Sexton, Strategic entrepreneurship.

122. M. Gruber, F. Heinemann, M. Brettel, & S. Hungeling, 2010, Configurations of resources and capabilities and their performance implications: An exploratory study on technology ventures, *Strategic Management Journal*, 31(12): 1337–1356; D. G. Sirmon, M. A. Hitt, & R. D. Ireland, 2007, Managing firm resources in dynamic environments to create value: Looking inside the black box, *Academy of Management Review*, 32: 273–292.

123. F. Rothaermel & A. Hess, 2010, Innovation strategies combined, *MIT Sloan Management Review*, 51(3): 13–15; D. G. Sirmon, S. Gove, & M. A. Hitt, 2008, Resource management in dyadic competitive rivalry: The effects of resource bundling and deployment, *Academy of Management Journal*, 51: 918–935.

124. S. Paruchuri, 2010, Intraorganizational networks, interorganizational networks, and the impact of central inventors: A longitudinal study of pharmaceutical firms, *Organization Science*, 21(1): 63–80; Tiwana, Do bridging ties complement strong ties?

125. Kim, Basu, Naidu, & Cavusgil, The innovativeness of Born-Globals and customer orientation; K. Asakawa & A. Som, 2008, Internationalization of R&D in China and India: Conventional wisdom versus reality, *Asia Pacific Journal of Management*, 25: 375–394; M. A. Hitt, R. E. Hoskisson, & H. Kim, 1997, International diversification: Effects on innovation and firm performance in product diversified firms, *Academy of Management Journal*, 40: 767–798.

126. L. P. Kyrgidou & M. Hughes, 2010, Strategic entrepreneurship: Origins, core elements and research directions, *European Business Review*, 22(1): 43–63; Baumol, Litan, & Schramm, *Good Capitalism, Bad Capitalism*; R. Garud, S. Jain, & A. Kumaraswamy, 2002, Institutional entrepreneurship in the sponsorship of common technological standards: The case of Sun Microsystems and JAVA, *Academy of Management Journal*, 45: 196–214.

127. K. E. Klein, 2011, Business plan contest: Where are the women? *Bloomberg Businessweek*, http://www.businessweek.com, February 10; B. Batjargal, A. Tsui, M. A. Hitt, J. L. Arregle, T. Miller, & J. Webb, 2009, How relationships matter: Women and men entrepreneurs' social networks and new venture success across cultures, paper presented at the Academy of Management Conference, Chicago, August.

128. J. D. Jardins, 2005, I am woman (I think), *Fast Company*, May, 25–26.

129. Hitt, Ireland, Camp, & Sexton, Strategic entrepreneurship.

130. D. G. Sirmon & M. A. Hitt, 2009, Contingencies within dynamic managerial capabilities: Interdependent effects of resource investment and deployment on firm performance, *Strategic Management Journal*, 30: 1375–1394.

PART 4
Cases

CASE STUDIES

CASE 1
Adobe Systems
Incorporated, 2

CASE 2
Apple Inc.: Keeping the
"i" in "Innovation", 16

CASE 3
AT&T: Another Century
of Innovation?, 40

CASE 4
Finding the Best Buy, 57

CASE 5
Chipotle: The Challenges
of Integrity, 71

CASE 6
Coinstar: A Sleeping
Giant Awakens, 88

CASE 7
Domino's Pizza: A Case
Study in Organizational
Evolution, 99

CASE 8
Dr Pepper Snapple
Group 2011: Fighting
to Prosper in a Highly
Competitive Market, 115

CASE 9
Ford Motor Company,
Staying "Ford
Tough", 127

CASE 10
Google, 155

CASE 11
Developing Global
Teams to Meet
Twenty-First Century
Challenges at W. L. Gore
& Associates, 172

CASE 12
Herman Miller: A Case
of Reinvention and
Renewal, 184

CASE 13
Luck Companies: Igniting
Human Potential, 196

CASE 14
McDonald's: From Big
Mac to P'tit Plaisir, 207

CASE 15
CIBC Mellon: Managing
a Cross-Border Joint
Venture, 219

CASE 16
MGM Resorts
International, 231

CASE 17
Microsoft Corp., 251

CASE 18
The Movie Exhibition
Industry: 2011, 266

CASE 19
Navistar: Can It Keep
On Truckin'?, 277

CASE 20
Netflix, 300

CASE 21
Porsche, 317

CASE 22
Rite Aid Corporation, 327

CASE 23
Reynolds American
Inc., 339

CASE 24
The Entrepreneurs at
Twitter: Building a Brand,
a Social Tool or a Tech
Powerhouse?, 352

CASE 25
The Ultimate Fighting
Championship and
Cultural Viability, 359

CASE 26
Under Armour:
Working to Stay on
Top of Its Game, 370

CASE 27
Union Pacific
Corporation, 383

CASE 28
Valeant Pharmaceuticals
International, Inc., 400

CASE 29
Victory: The New
American Motorcycle
Celebrates Its First
Decade on the Road, 419

CASE 30
Zipcar: The Future of
Transportation?, 437

McVay/Getty Images

Case Title	Manu-facturing	Service	Consumer Goods	Food/Retail	High Technology	Internet	Transportation/Communication	International Perspective	Social/Ethical Issues	Industry Perspective
Adobe		●	●		●	●				●
Apple	●		●		●					●
AT&T		●			●		●			●
Best Buy		●	●	●						●
Chipotle Mexican Grill		●		●					●	
Coinstar (Redbox)							●			
Domino's Pizza		●	●	●				●		●
Dr Pepper Snapple Group	●			●					●	●
Ford	●		●				●	●		●
Google		●			●	●	●	●		
Gore	●		●					●	●	●
Herman Miller	●		●	●				●		
Luck Company	●						●	●		●
McDonald's		●		●				●	●	●
Mellon		●		●						●
MGM		●		●				●		●
Microsoft	●	●			●	●				●
Movie Exhibition Industry		●								●
Navistar	●						●			●
Netflix		●	●		●		●			●
Porsche	●						●	●		
Rite Aid		●	●	●						●
RJ Reynolds	●			●					●	●
Twitter		●			●		●	●		
Ultimate Fighting		●							●	●
Under Armour	●			●	●					●
Union Pacific		●					●		●	●
Valeant	●							●		●
Victory	●						●			●
Zipcar		●				●	●		●	●

Case Title	Chapters												
	1	2	3	4	5	6	7	8	9	10	11	12	13
Adobe		●			●	●	●						
Apple			●	●	●				●				●
AT&T				●	●	●			●		●		●
Best Buy				●	●	●	●		●	●			
Chipotle Mexican Grill		●	●	●	●					●	●	●	
Coinstar (Redbox)	●					●			●		●	●	●
Domino's Pizza		●	●	●	●						●		●
Dr Pepper Snapple Group	●	●	●	●		●	●				●	●	
Ford	●	●		●	●			●				●	●
Google		●	●	●	●	●		●	●			●	●
Gore		●	●	●		●				●		●	
Herman Miller		●	●								●	●	
Luck Company			●		●				●	●	●	●	
McDonald's	●	●		●				●		●			
Mellon									●	●	●	●	●
MGM		●		●	●	●	●	●	●			●	
Microsoft			●		●	●	●		●		●	●	
Movie Exhibition Industry		●		●	●								
Navistar		●			●	●	●	●				●	
Netflix		●	●	●	●				●			●	●
Porsche		●		●	●	●			●	●			
Rite Aid		●		●	●	●	●				●		
RJ Reynolds		●		●		●	●					●	
Twitter				●	●						●	●	●
Ultimate Fighting	●	●	●									●	
Under Armour				●	●			●			●		
Union Pacific	●	●										●	
Valeant		●	●			●	●					●	●
Victory				●		●							●
Zipcar		●	●	●								●	●

What to Expect from In-Class Case Discussions

As you will learn, classroom discussions of cases differ significantly from lectures. The case method calls for your instructor to guide the discussion and to solicit alternative views as a way of encouraging your active participation when analyzing a case. When alternative views are not forthcoming, your instructor might take a position just to challenge you and your peers to respond thoughtfully as a way of generating still additional alternatives. Often, instructors will evaluate your work in terms of both the quantity and the quality of your contributions to in-class case discussions. The in-class discussions are important in that you can derive significant benefit by having your ideas and recommendations examined against those of your peers and by responding to thoughtful challenges by other class members and/or the instructor.

During case discussions, your instructor will likely listen, question, and probe to extend the analysis of case issues. In the course of these actions, your peers and/or your instructor may challenge an individual's views and the validity of alternative perspectives that have been expressed. These challenges are offered in a constructive manner; their intent is to help all parties involved with analyzing a case develop their analytical and communication skills. Developing these skills is important in that they will serve you well when working for all types of organizations. Commonly, instructors will encourage you and your peers to be innovative and original when developing and presenting ideas. Over the course of an individual discussion, you are likely to form a more complex view of the case as a result of listening to and thinking about the diverse inputs offered by your peers and instructor. Among other benefits, experience with multiple case discussions will increase your knowledge of the advantages and disadvantages of group decision-making processes.

Both your peers and instructor will value comments that contribute to identifying problems as well as solutions to them. To offer relevant contributions, you are encouraged to think independently and, through discussions with your peers outside of class, to refine your thinking. We also encourage you to avoid using "I think," "I believe," and "I feel" to discuss your inputs to a case analysis process. Instead, consider using a less emotion laden phrase, such as "My analysis shows…." This highlights the logical nature of the approach you have taken to analyze a case. When preparing for an in-class case discussion, you should plan to use the case data to explain your assessment of the situation. Assume that your peers and instructor are familiar with the basic facts included in the case. In addition, it is good practice to prepare notes regarding your analysis of case facts before class discussions and use them when explaining your perspectives. Effective notes signal to classmates and the instructor that you are prepared to engage in a thorough discussion of a case. Moreover, comprehensive and detailed notes eliminate the need for you to memorize the facts and figures needed to successfully discuss a case.

The case analysis process described above will help prepare you effectively to discuss a case during class meetings. Using this process results in consideration of the issues required to identify a focal firm's problems and to propose strategic actions through which the firm can increase the probability it will outperform its rivals. In some instances, your instructor may ask you to prepare either an oral or a written analysis of a particular case. Typically, such an assignment demands even more thorough study and analysis of the case contents. At your instructor's discretion, oral and written analyses may be completed by individuals or by groups of three or more people. The information and insights gained by completing the six steps shown in Table 1 often are of value when developing an oral or a written analysis. However, when preparing an oral or written presentation, you must consider the overall framework in which your information and inputs will be presented. Such a framework is the focus of the next section.

Preparing an Oral/Written Case Presentation

Experience shows that two types of thinking (analysis and synthesis) are necessary to develop an effective oral or written presentation (see Exhibit 1). In the analysis stage, you should first analyze the general external environmental issues affecting the firm. Next, your environmental analysis should focus on the particular industry (or industries, in the case of a diversified company) in which a firm operates. Finally, you should examine companies against which the focal firm competes. By studying the three levels of the external environment (general, industry, and competitor), you will be able to identify a firm's opportunities and threats. Following the external environmental analysis is the analysis of the firm's internal organization. This analysis provides the insights needed to identify the firm's strengths and weaknesses.

As noted in Exhibit 1, you must then change the focus from analysis to synthesis. Specifically, you must synthesize information gained from your analysis of the firm's external environment and internal organization. Synthesizing information allows you to generate alternatives that can resolve the significant problems or challenges facing the focal firm. Once you identify a best alternative, from an evaluation based on predetermined criteria and goals, you must explore implementation actions.

In Table 2, we outline the sections that should be included in either an oral or a written presentation: strategic profile and case analysis purpose, situation analysis, statements of strengths/weaknesses and opportunities/threats, strategy formulation, and strategy implementation. These sections are described in the following discussion. Familiarity with the contents of your book's thirteen chapters is helpful because the general outline for an oral or a written presentation shown in Table 2 is based on an understanding of the strategic management process detailed in those chapters. We follow the discussions of the parts of Table 2 with a few comments about the "process" to use to present the results of your case analysis in either a written or oral format.

Strategic Profile and Case Analysis Purpose

You will use the strategic profile to briefly present the critical facts from the case that have affected the focal firm's historical strategic direction and performance. The case facts should not be restated in the profile; rather, these comments should show how the critical facts lead to a particular focus for your analysis. This primary focus should be emphasized in this section's conclusion. In addition, this section should state important assumptions about case facts on which your analyses are based.

Table 1 An Effective Case Analysis Process

Step 1: Gaining Familiarity	a. In general—determine who, what, how, where, and when (the critical facts of the case). b. In detail—identify the places, persons, activities, and contexts of the situation. c. Recognize the degree of certainty/uncertainty of acquired information.
Step 2: Recognizing Symptoms	a. List all indicators (including stated "problems") that something is not as expected or as desired. b. Ensure that symptoms are not assumed to be the problem (symptoms should lead to identification of the problem).
Step 3: Identifying Goals	a. Identify critical statements by major parties (for example, people, groups, the work unit, and so on). b. List all goals of the major parties that exist or can be reasonably inferred.
Step 4: Conducting the Analysis	a. Decide which ideas, models, and theories seem useful. b. Apply these conceptual tools to the situation. c. As new information is revealed, cycle back to substeps a and b.
Step 5: Making the Diagnosis	a. Identify predicaments (goal inconsistencies). b. Identify problems (discrepancies between goals and performance). c. Prioritize predicaments/problems regarding timing, importance, and so on.
Step 6: Doing the Action Planning	a. Specify and prioritize the criteria used to choose action alternatives. b. Discover or invent feasible action alternatives. c. Examine the probable consequences of action alternatives. d. Select a course of action. e. Design an implementation plan/schedule. f. Create a plan for assessing the action to be implemented.

Source: C. C. Lundberg and C. Enz, 1993, A framework for student case preparation, Case Research Journal, 13 (Summer): 144. Reprinted by permission of NACRA, North American Case Research Association.

Exhibit 1 Types of Thinking in Case Preparation: Analysis and Synthesis

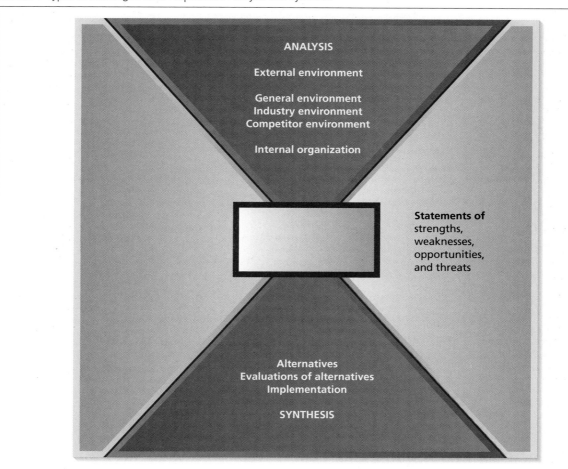

ANALYSIS

External environment

General environment
Industry environment
Competitor environment

Internal organization

Statements of strengths, weaknesses, opportunities, and threats

Alternatives
Evaluations of alternatives
Implementation

SYNTHESIS

Situation Analysis

As shown in Table 2, a general starting place for completing a situation analysis is the general environment.

General Environmental Analysis. Your analysis of the general environment should focus on trends in the six segments of the general environment (see Table 3). Many of the segment issues shown in Table 3 for the six segments are explained more fully in Chapter 2 of your book. The objective you should have in evaluating these trends is to be able to *predict* the segments that you expect to have the most significant influence on your focal firm over the next several years (say three to five years) and to explain your reasoning for your predictions.

Industry Analysis. Porter's five force model is a useful tool for analyzing the industry (or industries) in which your firm competes. We explain how to use this tool in Chapter 2. In this part of your analysis, you want to determine the attractiveness of an industry (or a seg-

Table 2 General Outline for an Oral or Written Presentation

I. Strategic Profile and Case Analysis Purpose

II. Situation Analysis
 A. General environmental analysis
 B. Industry analysis
 C. Competitor analysis
 D. Internal analysis

III. Identification of Environmental Opportunities and Threats and Firm Strengths and Weaknesses (SWOT Analysis)

IV. Strategy Formulation
 A. Strategic alternatives
 B. Alternative evaluation
 C. Alternative choice

V. Strategic Alternative Implementation
 A. Action items
 B. Action plan

ment of an industry) in which your firm is competing. As attractiveness increases, so does the possibility your firm will be able to earn profits by using its chosen

Table 3 Sample General Environmental Categories

Technological Trends
- Information technology continues to become cheaper with more practical applications
- Database technology enables organization of complex data and distribution of information
- Telecommunications technology and networks increasingly provide fast transmission of all sources of data, including voice, written communications, and video information
- Computerized design and manufacturing technologies continue to facilitate quality and flexibility

Demographic Trends
- Regional changes in population due to migration
- Changing ethnic composition of the population
- Aging of the population
- Aging of the "baby boom" generation

Economic Trends
- Interest rates
- Inflation rates
- Savings rates
- Exchange rates
- Trade deficits
- Budget deficits

Political/Legal Trends
- Antitrust enforcement
- Tax policy changes
- Environmental protection laws
- Extent of regulation/deregulation
- Privatizing state monopolies
- State-owned industries

Sociocultural Trends
- Women in the workforce
- Awareness of health and fitness issues
- Concern for the environment
- Concern for customers

Global Trends
- Currency exchange rates
- Free-trade agreements
- Trade deficits

strategies. After evaluating the power of the five forces relative to your firm, you should make a judgment as to *how* attractive the industry is in which your firm is competing.

Competitor Analysis. Firms also need to *analyze* each of their primary competitors. This analysis should identify competitors' current strategies, strategic intent, strategic mission, capabilities, core competencies, and a competitive response profile (see Chapter 2). This information is useful to the focal firm in formulating an appropriate strategy and in predicting competitors' probable responses. Sources that can be used to gather information about an industry and companies with whom the focal firm competes are listed in Appendix I. Included in this list is a wide range of publications, such as periodicals, newspapers, bibliographies, directories of companies, industry ratios, forecasts, rankings/ratings, and other valuable statistics.

Internal Analysis. Assessing a firm's strengths and weaknesses through a value chain analysis facilitates moving from the external environment to the internal organization. Analysis of the primary and support activities of the value chain provides opportunities to understand how external environmental trends affect the specific activities of a firm. Such analysis helps highlight strengths and weaknesses (see Chapter 3 for an explanation and use of the value chain).

For purposes of preparing an oral or a written presentation, it is important to note that strengths are internal resources and capabilities that have the potential to be core competencies. Weaknesses, on the other hand, are internal resources and capabilities that have the potential to place a firm at a competitive disadvantage relative to its rivals. Thus, some of a firm's resources and capabilities are strengths; others are weaknesses.

When evaluating the internal characteristics of the firm, your analysis of the functional activities emphasized is critical. For instance, if the strategy of the firm is primarily technology driven, it is important to evaluate the firm's R&D activities. If the strategy is market driven, marketing functional activities are of paramount importance. If a firm has financial difficulties, critical financial ratios would require careful evaluation. In fact, because of the importance of financial health, most cases require financial analyses. Appendix II lists and operationally defines several common financial ratios. Included are tables describing profitability, liquidity, leverage, activity, and shareholders' return ratios. Leadership, organizational culture, structure, and control systems are other characteristics of firms you should examine to fully understand the "internal" part of your firm.

Identification of Environmental Opportunities and Threats and Firm Strengths and Weaknesses (SWOT Analysis).

The outcome of the situation analysis is the identification of a firm's strengths and weaknesses and its environmental threats and opportunities. The next step requires that you *analyze* the strengths and weaknesses and the opportunities and threats for configurations that benefit or do not benefit your firm's efforts to perform well. Case analysts and organizational strategists as well seek to match a firm's strengths with its opportunities. In addition, strengths are chosen to prevent any serious environmental threat from negatively affecting the firm's performance. The key objective of conducting a SWOT analysis is to determine how to position the firm so it can take advantage of opportunities, while simultaneously avoiding or minimizing environmental threats. Results from a SWOT analysis yield valuable insights into the selection of a firm's strategies. The analysis of a case should not be overemphasized relative to the synthesis of results gained from your analytical efforts. There may be a temptation to spend most of your oral or written case analysis on results from the analysis. It is important, however, that you make an equal effort to develop and evaluate alternatives and to design implementation of the chosen strategy.

Strategy Formulation—Strategic Alternatives, Alternative Evaluation, and Alternative Choice.

Developing alternatives is often one of the most difficult steps in preparing an oral or a written presentation. Developing three to four alternative strategies is common (see Chapter 4 for business-level strategy alternatives and Chapter 6 for corporate-level strategy alternatives). Each alternative should be feasible (i.e., it should match the firm's strengths, capabilities, and especially core competencies), and feasibility should be demonstrated. In addition, you should show how each alternative takes advantage of the environmental opportunity or avoids/buffers against environmental threats. Developing

carefully thought out alternatives requires synthesis of your analyses' results and creates greater credibility in oral and written case presentations.

Once you develop strong alternatives, you must evaluate the set to choose the best one. Your choice should be defensible and provide benefits over the other alternatives. Thus, it is important that both alternative development and evaluation of alternatives be thorough. The choice of the best alternative should be explained and defended.

Strategic Alternative Implementation–Action Items and Action Plan.

After selecting the most appropriate strategy (that is, the strategy with the highest probability of helping your firm in its efforts to earn profits), implementation issues require attention. Effective synthesis is important to ensure that you have considered and evaluated all critical implementation issues. Issues you might consider include the structural changes necessary to implement the new strategy. In addition, leadership changes and new controls or incentives may be necessary to implement strategic actions. The implementation actions you recommend should be explicit and thoroughly explained. Occasionally, careful evaluation of implementation actions may show the strategy to be less favorable than you thought originally. A strategy is only as good as the firm's ability to implement it.

Process Issues.

You should ensure that your presentation (either oral or written) has logical consistency throughout. For example, if your presentation identifies one purpose, but your analysis focuses on issues that differ from the stated purpose, the logical inconsistency will be apparent. Likewise, your alternatives should flow from the configuration of strengths, weaknesses, opportunities, and threats you identified by analyzing your firm's external environment and internal organization.

Thoroughness and clarity also are critical to an effective presentation. Thoroughness is represented by the comprehensiveness of the analysis and alternative generation. Furthermore, clarity in the results of the analyses, selection of the best alternative strategy, and design of implementation actions are important. For example, your statement of the strengths and weaknesses should flow clearly and logically from your analysis of your firm's internal organization.

Presentations (oral or written) that show logical consistency, thoroughness, and clarity of purpose, effective analyses, and feasible recommendations (strategy and implementation) are more effective and are likely to be more positively received by your instructor and peers. Furthermore, developing the skills necessary to make such presentations will enhance your future job performance and career success.

Appendix I Sources for Industry and Competitor Analyses

Abstracts and Indexes	
Periodicals	ABI/Inform Business Periodicals Index InfoTrac Custom Journals InfoTrac Custom Newspapers InfoTrac OneFile EBSCO Business Source Premiere Lexis/Nexis Academic Public Affairs Information Service Bulletin (PAIS) Reader's Guide to Periodical Literature
Newspapers	NewsBank—Foreign Broadcast Information NewsBank-Global NewsBank New York Times Index Wall Street Journal Index Wall Street Journal/Barron's Index Washington Post Index
Bibliographies	Encyclopedia of Business Information Sources
Directories	
Companies—General	America's Corporate Families and International Affiliates Hoover's Online: The Business Network www.hoovers.com/free D&B Million Dollar Directory (databases: http://www.dnbmdd.com) Standard & Poor's Corporation Records Standard & Poor's Register of Corporations, Directors, and Executives (http://www.netadvantage.standardandpoors.com for all of Standard & Poor's) Ward's Business Directory of Largest U.S. Companies
Companies—International	America's Corporate Families and International Affiliates Business Asia Business China Business Eastern Europe Business Europe Business International Business International Money Report Business Latin America Directory of American Firms Operating in Foreign Countries Directory of Foreign Firms Operating in the United States Hoover's Handbook of World Business International Directory of Company Histories Mergent's International Manual Mergent Online (http://www.fisonline.com—for "Business and Financial Information Connection to the World") Who Owns Whom
Companies—Manufacturers	Thomas Register of American Manufacturers U.S. Office of Management and Budget, Executive Office of the President, Standard Industrial Classification Manual U.S. Manufacturer's Directory, Manufacturing & Distribution, USA
Companies—Private	D&B Million Dollar Directory Ward's Business Directory of Largest U.S. Companies

(Continued)

Appendix I Sources for Industry and Competitor Analyses (*Continued*)

Abstracts and Indexes

Companies—Public	Annual Reports and 10-K Reports
	Disclosure (corporate reports) *Q-File*
	Securities and Exchange Commission Filings & Forms (EDGAR)
	    http://www.sec.gov/edgar.shtml
	Mergent's Manuals:
	
	  • *Mergent's Bank and Finance Manual*
	  • *Mergent's Industrial Manual*
	  • *Mergent's International Manual*
	  • *Mergent's Municipal and Government Manual*
	  • *Mergent's OTC Industrial Manual*
	  • *Mergent's OTC Unlisted Manual*
	  • *Mergent's Public Utility Manual*
	  • *Mergent's Transportation Manual*
	
	Standard & Poor's Corporation, *Standard Corporation Descriptions:*
	    http://www.netadvantage.standardandpoors.com
	
	  • *Standard & Poor's Analyst Handbook*
	  • *Standard & Poor's Industry Surveys*
	  • *Standard & Poor's Statistical Service*

Companies—Subsidiaries and Affiliates	*America's Corporate Families and International Affiliates* *Ward's Directory* *Who Owns Whom* *Mergent's Industry Review* *Standard & Poor's Analyst's Handbook* *Standard & Poor's Industry Surveys* (2 volumes) U.S. Department of Commerce, *U.S. Industrial Outlook*
Industry Ratios	Dun & Bradstreet, *Industry Norms and Key Business Ratios* *RMA's Annual Statement Studies* *Troy Almanac of Business and Industrial Financial Ratios*
Industry Forecasts	International Trade Administration, *U.S. Industry & Trade Outlook*

Rankings & Ratings	Annual Report on American Industry in *Forbes*
	    Business Rankings Annual
	Mergent's Industry Review http://www.worldcatlibraries.org
	Standard & Poor's Industry Report Service http://www.netadvantage
	    .standardandpoors.com
	Value Line Investment Survey
	Ward's Business Directory of Largest U.S. Companies

Statistics	*American Statistics Index (ASI)* Bureau of the Census, U.S. Department of
	    Commerce, *Economic Census Publications*
	Bureau of the Census, U.S. Department of Commerce, *Statistical Abstract of the*
	    United States
	Bureau of Economic Analysis, U.S. Department of Commerce, *Survey of Current*
	    Business
	Internal Revenue Service, U.S. Treasury Department, *Statistics of Income:*
	    Corporation Income Tax Returns
	Statistical Reference Index (SRI)

Appendix II Financial Analysis in Case Studies

Table A-1 Profitability Ratios

Ratio	Formula	What It Shows
1. Return on total assets	$$\frac{\text{Profits after taxes}}{\text{Total assets}}$$ or $$\frac{\text{Profits after taxes} + \text{Interest}}{\text{Total assets}}$$	The net return on total investments of the firm or The return on both creditors' and shareholders' investments
2. Return on stockholders' equity (or return on net worth)	$$\frac{\text{Profits after taxes}}{\text{Total stockholders' equity}}$$	How profitably the company is utilizing shareholders' funds
3. Return on common equity	$$\frac{\text{Profits after taxes} - \text{Preferred stock dividends}}{\text{Total stockholders' equity} - \text{Par value of preferred stock}}$$	The net return to common stockholders
4. Operating profit margin (or return on sales)	$$\frac{\text{Profits before taxes and before interest}}{\text{Sales}}$$	The firm's profitability from regular operations
5. Net profit margin (or net return on sales)	$$\frac{\text{Profits after taxes}}{\text{Sales}}$$	The firm's net profit as a percentage of total sales

Table A-2 Liquidity Ratios

Ratio	Formula	What It Shows
1. Current ratio	$$\frac{\text{Current assets}}{\text{Current liabilities}}$$	The firm's ability to meet its current financial liabilities
2. Quick ratio (or acid-test ratio)	$$\frac{\text{Current assets} - \text{Inventory}}{\text{Current liabilities}}$$	The firm's ability to pay off short-term obligations without relying on sales of inventory
3. Inventory to net working capital	$$\frac{\text{Inventory}}{\text{Current assets} - \text{Current liabilities}}$$	The extent to which the firm's working capital is tied up in inventory

Table A-3 Leverage Ratios

Ratio	Formula	What It Shows
1. Debt-to-assets	$$\frac{\text{Total debt}}{\text{Total assets}}$$	Total borrowed funds as a percentage of total assets
2. Debt-to-equity	$$\frac{\text{Total debt}}{\text{Total shareholders' equity}}$$	Borrowed funds versus the funds provided by shareholders
3. Long-term debt-to-equity	$$\frac{\text{Long-term debt}}{\text{Total shareholders' equity}}$$	Leverage used by the firm
4. Times-interest-earned (or coverage ratio)	$$\frac{\text{Profits before interest and taxes}}{\text{Total interest charges}}$$	The firm's ability to meet all interest payments
5. Fixed charge coverage	$$\frac{\text{Profits before taxes and interest} + \text{Lease obligations}}{\text{Total interest charges} + \text{Lease obligations}}$$	The firm's ability to meet all fixed-charge obligations including lease payments

Table A-4 Activity Ratios

Ratio	Formula	What It Shows
1. Inventory turnover	$\dfrac{\text{Sales}}{\text{Inventory of finished goods}}$	The effectiveness of the firm in employing inventory
2. Fixed-assets turnover	$\dfrac{\text{Sales}}{\text{Fixed assets}}$	The effectiveness of the firm in utilizing plant and equipment
3. Total assets turnover	$\dfrac{\text{Sales}}{\text{Total assets}}$	The effectiveness of the firm in utilizing total assets
4. Accounts receivable turnover	$\dfrac{\text{Annual credit sales}}{\text{Accounts receivable}}$	How many times the total receivables have been collected during the accounting period
5. Average collecting period	$\dfrac{\text{Accounts receivable}}{\text{Average daily sales}}$	The average length of time the firm waits to collect payment after sales

Table A-5 Shareholders' Return Ratios

Ratio	Formula	What It Shows
1. Dividend yield on common stock	$\dfrac{\text{Annual dividend per share}}{\text{Current market price per share}}$	A measure of return to common stockholders in the form of dividends
2. Price-earnings ratio	$\dfrac{\text{Current market price per share}}{\text{After-tax earnings per share}}$	An indication of market perception of the firm; usually, the faster-growing or less risky firms tend to have higher PE ratios than the slower-growing or more risky firms
3. Dividend payout ratio	$\dfrac{\text{Annual dividends per share}}{\text{After-tax earnings per share}}$	An indication of dividends paid out as a percentage of profits
4. Cash flow per share	$\dfrac{\text{After-tax profits + Depreciation}}{\text{Number of common shares outstanding}}$	A measure of total cash per share available for use by the firm

Justin Martin, Aditya Mittal, Michelle Richard, N. Dominic Taboada
Texas A&M University

Introduction

Adobe Systems Inc. is a $17 billion dollar NASDAQ 100 software company with one of the most diversified product lines in the multimedia design world. Over nearly 30 years of leading edge software development, Adobe has built a successful portfolio of design related software packages that has been supplemented by products secured in Adobe's quite strategic mergers and acquisitions. Many of Adobe's products are considered prestigious, industry-standard tools in their respective fields of use. Representing the diversity of its offerings, its portfolio also contains several software platforms with outputs consumed near daily by virtually every user of computers and handheld devices worldwide. Even the name of one of its products—the legendary Photoshop—has become a verb in popular lexicon meaning, "to alter, using an image editing application."[1]

As self described in its fiscal year 2010 10-K, Adobe offers a wide range of products used for "managing, delivering, optimizing, and engaging with compelling content" across a wide variety of media.[2] In essence, Adobe offers a variety of mostly high-end multimedia design software packages to amateurs and professionals alike in fields including video editing, desktop publishing, and graphic design, among others. Some of its product lines have become so ubiquitous that the licensing of the proprietary software rights is an increasingly important source of additional revenue for the company.

Because Adobe is an authoritative first mover with many of its product lines, it generally avoids attracting much competition; in fact, it could be argued that some of its products have no accessible substitute whatsoever. At the end of 2005, Adobe acquired its most direct multimedia design competitor, Macromedia, thereby expanding its product portfolio significantly, but more importantly, procuring—and in some cases, quickly discontinuing—products that provided the only serious competitive threats to portions of Adobe's portfolio.[3]

Although several companies offer one or perhaps two products that compete directly with Adobe products, no other multimedia software development firm can claim the hegemony Adobe currently enjoys.

The main constituents of Adobe's product portfolio have always been multimedia design software packages. Assuming the status of industry leader early it its life with programs like Illustrator, Photoshop, and Acrobat, Adobe has continued to expand its product portfolio to encompass additional digital media formats including sound, video, web design, and animation. In addition, it has augmented its portfolio with online services that provide additional functionality to its software products, file formats for the delivery of online media content, and software packages that allow for the behind-the-scenes management of its web-based publishing products. Although most of Adobe's products are geared toward professional design use and accordingly priced at a relative premium, many are widely used by educational institutions, home computer users, and general businesses.

More recently, Adobe has diversified its portfolio with products and services that lie outside its traditional multimedia focus. It has developed products to improve general business functionality including videoconference calling software and online marketing packages. Via its acquisition of Omniture in 2009, Adobe now also offers web analytics and optimization services to businesses that rely upon a large and well-organized online presence.[4]

Adobe maintains a notably high level of software *re*development, in most cases releasing upgraded versions of its flagship products every one to two years. Adobe products are supplemented by extensive product support networks and services with similar interfaces that increase user friendliness and attractiveness. Because Adobe's industry leadership status extends past software packages to data and content delivery formats, Adobe governs entire product ecosystems and provides the means to create, market, and mass distribute across a wide variety of media platforms.

However, some industry observers have accused Adobe of taking advantage of its leadership position by releasing expensive and slow-to-load updates[5] offering only marginal added functionality.[6] Adobe has been further criticized for its pricing policies in international markets where retail consumers often pay up to twice as much as their US counterparts. Finally, its Flash platform for online streaming video development and delivery, recognized as an industry standard, has been—perhaps unfairly—criticized for having security flaws and stability issues.[7]

The Latest Trends… for now

There are several trends in the industry with the potential to affect Adobe. Perhaps most apparent is the increasing online dependence of modern corporations. As more companies take advantage of the massive economies of scope and scale that can be leveraged from the information technology of the Internet, it will become increasingly difficult for a business to succeed without some sort of online presence.[8] Furthermore, companies are becoming more interconnected and forging relationships with an ever-increasing number of stakeholders. In their efforts to satisfy the incessant shareholder desire for sustained growth, companies are also expanding their multinational operations. This global trend of increased economic interdependence serves to intensify the modern firms' reliance on online information technology to maintain a smooth flow of operations.

On a more personal level, the Internet has also become a more important factor in the life of the modern individual. A major socio-cultural trend related to Adobe's operations is the move toward greater consumption of online content among younger generations. As the first generations of Americans who grew up with the Internet as a major part of their lives now enter adulthood, the volume of online media being consumed is rising rapidly. Traditional news media such as newspapers and magazines are ceding their erstwhile dominance to the online consumption of news articles and opinion commentary in formats ranging from amateur opinion blogs to full blown online renditions of old standards like the Wall Street Journal. Television shows and movies can now be delivered immediately and in high definition via streaming video. The pages of out-of-print textbooks can be digitally thumbed through. Even music can be consumed in popular venues like Pandora's online radio or YouTube's music videos. As the populace continues to consume increasingly greater quantities of media from the Internet, the market and opportunity for digital content will grow along with it.

Several tangential factors may influence Adobe's operations as well. Economically, the world—especially Adobe's primary market, the US—has purportedly now seen the bottom of a serious financial crisis and economic recession. Although Adobe products (see Exhibit 1 for a complete list) are essential to production in certain industries, home users with tightened budgets are certain to continue to postpone their consumption of high-end software upgrades.[9] As a consequence, Adobe may face increased efforts of consumers to pirate (i.e., acquire unauthorized copies of) its products. Adobe's products have always been popular targets of pirating, perhaps due to their relatively high prices and excellent reputations. In the past, Adobe has cited the level of piracy to justify in part its pricing policy and continues to introduce increasingly stringent controls against the unauthorized installation and use of its software packages. Nevertheless, corporate software developers are routinely outperformed by the software piracy community, a group that is responsible for depressing software development profits across all sectors of the economy and roundly considered a plague on the industry.

In addition to the diminished state of the world economy, the poor fiscal condition of Adobe's state of incorporation, California, may affect its operations. To analysts, California's budget deficit and spending obligations appear unsustainable. This uncertainty about the stability of California's economic future injects a measure of risk into Adobe's operating environment.[10]

The emergent albeit, at present, minor technological trend whose longevity has yet to be demonstrated but may affect Adobe is the recent foray into three-dimensional film and video. The opportunity for Adobe to position itself as the market leader in three-dimensional video formats is tempered by the threat of three-dimensional video failing to become a significant source of media consumption. Although Adobe has historically established itself as a market leader in media creation and editing software, the tenuous acceptance to date of three-dimensional video may temper Adobe's desire to expand into the market. On the other hand, excessive caution could preclude Adobe from the pioneering advantages that have served to establish its products as industry standard trade tools in the past.[11]

Finally, the popular trend toward digital content applies not only to a younger demographic of content consumers but content *creators* as well. The emerging generations have, for the first time, grown up with computers and its artists are likely to express themselves outside the traditional media of, among others, film, printed text, or paint. In time, the majority share of the media creation market will likely bear the imprint of Adobe's

Exhibit 1 Adobe Products

A-D	E-O	P-Z
Acrobat X Pro	eLearning Suite 2.5	PageMaker® 7.0
Acrobat X Standard	Encore® CS5	Photoshop CS5
Acrobat X Suite	ExportPDF	Photoshop CS5 Extended
Acrobat.com	Fireworks® CS5	Photoshop Elements 9
After Effects®	Flash Access®	Photoshop Elements 9 and Adobe Premiere® Elements 9
Adobe® AIR®	Flash Builder® 4.5	Photoshop Lightroom 3
Adobe Audition® CS5.5	Flash Catalyst™ CS5.5	Photoshop.com
Authorware® 7	Flash Media Live Encoder	Adobe Premiere Elements 9
BrowserLab	Flash Media Playback	Adobe Premiere Express
Business Catalyst®	Flash Media Server	Adobe Premiere Pro CS5.5
Adobe Captivate® 5.5	Flash Media Server on Amazon Web Services™	Presenter 7
Central Pro Output Server	Flash Platform Services	Adobe Publish
Adobe Connect™	Adobe® Flash® Player	Reader® X
ColdFusion 9	Flash Professional CS5.5	Adobe Recommendations
ColdFusion Builder 2	Flash Video Streaming Services	RoboHelp® 9
Content Server 4	Flex® 4.5	RoboHelp Server 9
Contribute® CS5	Font Folio® 11	Scene7®
CS Live	Adobe FormsCentral	Adobe SearchCenter
CS Review	FrameMaker®10	Shockwave® Player
CreatePDF	FrameMaker Server 10	SendNow
Creative Suite 5.5 Design Premium	FreeHand® MX	SiteCatalyst®
Creative Suite 5.5 Design Standard	Adobe Genesis™	Adobe SiteSearch™
Creative Suite 5.5 Web Premium	HTTP Dynamic Streaming	Soundbooth® CS5
Creative Suite 5.5 Master Collection	Illustrator® CS5	Story
Creative Suite 5.5 Production Premium	InContext Editing	Adobe Survey
CQ5 Digital Asset Management	InCopy® CS5.5	Technical Communication Suite 3.0
CQ5 Marketing Campaign Management	InDesign CS5.5	Test&Target™
CQ5 Mobile	InDesign CS5.5 Server	Type products
CQ5 Social Collaboration	Adobe Insight	Visual Communicator® 3
CQ5 Web Content Management	JRun™ 4	Adobe Web Fonts
CRX	Kuler®	Web Output Pak
Digital Editions	LiveCycle Enterprise Suite 2	
Digital Publishing Suite	Adobe Merchandising	
Director® 11.5	Adobe OnLocation™ CS5	
Adobe Discover™	Output Designer	
Distiller Server 8	Output Pak for mySAP.com	
Dreamweaver CS5.5	Ovation®	

Source: http://www.adobe.com

wide ranging suite of creative and development products, thus providing sustainable streams of revenue as the artistic professions progressively transition to digital media formats.

Clearly, however, the most significant trend in terms of Adobe's exposure is the growing need for modern businesses to have a well-developed online presence. As businesses increasingly recognize the inherent value of integrated information technology systems and a stream-lined online presence, Adobe's recent and well-timed diversifications into online analytics and business optimization services have provided an attractive avenue for growth. The greater technological trend toward online business allows Adobe to leverage its existing directions into online business services: a direction providing *massive* opportunities for sustained growth. On the other side of the coin however, the rapid growth of online business services markets also presents somewhat of a threat to Adobe's long recognized position as a market leader. If Adobe is not able to cope with the scale of the demand, existing and new competitors may capture valuable market share.[12] Furthermore, the rapid rate of change associated with the online environment—especially as related to media and data exchange platforms and file encoding formats—presents another threat to Adobe's bid for domination of the online business optimization market. Stubborn adherence to unpopular data formats can result in significant losses. Adobe must carefully consider the strategic landscape before fully committing to unproven platforms.

In summary, the increasing consumption of online and offline digital content in popular culture will continue to impact Adobe's future. The opportunities afforded Adobe by the proliferation of digital media are obvious; however, as for its forays into the business optimization markets, Adobe must remain cognizant of the threat posed by the new market entrants inevitable to any massive market expansion. Choosing to rest on its market leadership laurels would be a fatal error as failing to provide continued innovation and product development may leave the door open for other firms to enter into markets traditionally dominated by Adobe's products and formats.

Adobe's Culture

Adobe's commitment to innovation is as strong today as it was when founded in 1982. Over the years, Adobe has set the standard for communication and collaboration via its pioneering software and technologies. Adobe was founded on four core values that serve as the corner-stone of the organization and continue to be instilled in every employee. Those values include *authenticity, excellence, innovation,* and *involvement.* "The values shape everything we do, from how we develop and market our products to how we serve our customers, employees, and communities," states current Adobe CEO, Shantanu Narvayen.[13] Adobe is committed to operating with integrity and treating others with respect. In addition, Adobe seeks exceptional quality not only in every product produced, but in each employee as well. "Good is not good enough" at Adobe.[14] Ideas come from

everywhere in the organization as it strives to be creative and introduce innovative business solutions. These ideas come from the people: customers, partners, employees, and community alike. The "people are [Adobe's] greatest asset."[15] These values have created a "culture of creativity and innovation" that has led Adobe to become a leader in the software industry.[16]

From co-founder, John Warnock,

We have a saying around Adobe that the antibodies will kill off any new idea. Companies build antibodies. They build resistance to change. They get comfort zones where they want to work, and employees don't want to try something new for fear that they are going to fail. So they reject ideas. One of the hardest things about keeping a company innovative is killing off the antibodies and forcing change.[17]

Employees and Organization

Adobe takes great pride in its employees. Adobe believes "that the growth and success of [its] business is directly linked to the growth and performance of [its] employees."[18] Thus, Adobe is committed to finding the best managers, engineers, programmers, etc. Operating in a constantly evolving industry where the first mover advantage is critical, Adobe relies on its intellectual assets to recognize and solve the next big problem before its competitors. When Adobe was founded, PostScript was its competitive advantage. Invented by Warnock, PostScript opened the door for Adobe into the software industry.[19] No other firm in the industry knew how to solve what Adobe called the "font problem." To keep this technology from becoming public knowledge, Adobe did not apply for a patent. Adobe sustained this competitive advantage for seven years—a phenomenal achievement in the tech industry—and had moved on to other technological breakthroughs before its competitors had even solved the first problem. Because the product life cycle of innovations in the software industry is short lived, Adobe has always recognized the importance of hiring the best of the best to remain at the forefront of innovation. In short, Adobe understands that the competitive advantage of a product is not sustainable, but the competitive advantage of a top-notch employee is.[20]

Adobe services a wide variety of consumers, from large corporations such as FedEx and Sony to the individual computer user. To meet the demands of each customer group, Adobe has established six different product/services businesses that operate in 34 different countries and support over one trillion user interactions each quarter.[21] With a CEO at the top of the organization and every business segment represented by a Senior Vice President, the strategy and structure of Adobe are oriented to support its product and services segments.

Market Segments

Exhibit 2 provides details of the six reportable products and services business established by Adobe as they entered fiscal year 2011: *Digital Media Solutions, Creative and Interactive Solutions, Knowledge Worker, Enterprise, Omniture,* and *Print and Publishing.* Each division is a proven success. In fact, Adobe's revenues in 2010 were $3.8 billion (balance sheet and income statement provided in Exhibits 3A and 3B respectively). Reported in fiscal year 2010 as a single segment, its most profitable segment, Creative Solutions (now split into Digital Media Solutions and Creative and Interactive Solutions), brought in 54 percent of Adobe's total revenues (Exhibit 4 shows revenue by segment) with the other segments accounting for the remaining 46 percent of revenues.[22]

Geographically, Adobe has a presence that spans the globe.[23] Its largest customer base is in the US (see Exhibit 5 for customers by geographic areas) and responsible for 44 percent of total revenues.[24] As noted in Exhibit 5, emerging markets (i.e., Europe, Middle East, and Africa) contribute 31 percent of Adobe revenues. While the growth potential in emerging markets is extremely high, to capitalize on them, Adobe will have to adopt marketing strategies and product options that adapt its approaches to these developing markets' needs.

Product History

To stay at the forefront of developing technology in a rapidly changing industry, Adobe has taken on the challenge of identifying and solving customer needs before its competitors. Adobe targets a large consumer segment that includes many different industries and professions, all with similar problems due to the growing reliance on technology. The very first unmet need recognized by Adobe was the inability of creative professionals to translate text and images as seen on a computer screen into a printed format.

In 1982, John Warnock and Chuck Geschke co-founded Adobe Systems Incorporated and, by 1990, had introduced Adobe Postscript, Adobe Illustrator, and Adobe Photoshop to the world.[25] These software innovations changed the face of the design industry by upgrading the quality and increasing the complexity of images that could be printed, used for video, or posted to the web. As computers and technology advanced, a new customer need became apparent—the need

Exhibit 2 Adobe's Products and Services Business Segments

1. *Creative and Interactive Solutions* – The Creative and Interactive Solutions segment focuses on the needs of professional customers, as well as web and application developers. The Creative Suite family of products is used by creative professionals to create printed and on-line information people see, read, and interact with every day, including newspapers, magazines, Web sites, Rich Internet Applications (RIAs), catalogs, advertisements, brochures, product documentation, books, memos, reports, and banners. Its tools are also used to create and enhance content, including video, animation and mobile content, that is created by multimedia, film, television, audio and video producers who work in advertising, web design, music, entertainment, corporate and marketing communications, product design, user interface design, sales training, printing, architecture and fine arts.

2. *Digital Media Solutions* – The Digital Media Solutions segment contains professional imaging and video products. Its offerings extend from desktop tools, to smartphone and tablet applications, to cloud-based SaaS capabilities, to real-time rich media solutions that give business users the control to upload, manage, enhance, and publish content with minimal information technology (IT) support.

3. *Knowledge Worker* – As part of the Digital Enterprise Solutions focus, the Knowledge Worker segment addresses the needs of the knowledge worker customer. Knowledge workers include a range of job functions, such as accountants, attorneys, architects, educators, engineers, graphic designers, insurance underwriters, and stock analysts. The Acrobat.com service provides centralized online file sharing and storage capabilities, as well as simple portable document format (PDF) creation, an online word processor, spreadsheet, and personal web conferencing services with Adobe ConnectNow.

4. *Enterprise* – As the second part of the Digital Enterprise Solutions focus, the Enterprise business segment addresses the needs of large enterprises and governments. The customer experience management (CEM) platform enables customers to not only reach their constituents through new communication channels, such as mobile and social, but also to provide common infrastructure across customer touch points and processes in an enterprise.

5. *Omniture* – The Omniture business unit provides web analytics and online business optimization products, solutions and services, delivered through the Omniture line of products and the Adobe Online Marketing Suite. Customers use Omniture products and services to manage and optimize online, offline, digital and multi-channel business initiatives. Customers who use Omniture solutions include marketing professionals, web content editors, web analysts, and web production managers.

6. *Print and Publishing* – The Print and Publishing business segment contains products and services that address diverse market opportunities, including e-Learning solutions, technical document publishing, web application development, and high-end printing.

Source: Reuters.com. Profile: Adobe Systems Inc (ADBE.O). http://www.reuters.com

Exhibit 3A Balance Sheet

ADOBE SYSTEMS INCORPORATED CONSOLIDATED BALANCE SHEETS	December 3, 2010	November 27, 2009
	(In thousands, except par value)	
ASSETS		
Current assets:		
Cash and cash equivalents	$ 749,891	$ 999,487
Short-term investments	1,718,124	904,986
Trade receivables, net of allowances for doubtful accounts of $15,233 and $15,225, respectively	554,328	410,879
Deferred income taxes	83,247	77,417
Prepaid expenses and other current assets	110,460	80,855
Total current assets	3,216,050	2,473,624
Property and equipment, net	448,881	388,132
Goodwill	3,641,844	3,494,589
Purchased and other intangibles, net	457,263	527,388
Investment in lease receivable	207,239	207,239
Other assets	169,871	191,265
Total assets	$ 8,141,148	$7,282,237
LIABILITIES AND STOCKHOLDERS' EQUITY		
Current liabilities:		
Trade payables	$ 52,432	$ 58,904
Accrued expenses	564,275	419,646
Capital lease obligations, current	8,799	—
Accrued restructuring	8,119	37,793
Income taxes payable	53,715	46,634
Deferred revenue	380,748	281,576
Total current liabilities	1,068,088	844,553
Long-term liabilities:		
Debt and capital lease obligations, non-current	1,513,662	1,000,000
Deferred revenue	48,929	36,717
Accrued restructuring	8,254	6,921
Income taxes payable	164,713	223,528
Deferred income taxes	103,098	252,486
Other liabilities	42,017	27,464
Total liabilities	2,948,761	2,391,669
Commitments and contingencies		
Stockholders' equity:		
Preferred stock, $0.0001 par value; 2,000 shares authorized; none issued	—	—
Common stock, $0.0001 par value; 900,000 shares authorized; 600,834 shares issued; 501,897 and 522,657 shares outstanding, respectively	61	61
Additional paid-in-capital	2,458,278	2,390,061
Retained earnings	5,980,914	5,299,914
Accumulated other comprehensive income	17,428	24,446
Treasury stock, at cost (98,937 and 78,177 shares, respectively), net of re-issuances	(3,264,294)	(2,823,914)
Total stockholders' equity	5,192,387	4,890,568
Total liabilities and stockholders' equity	$ 8,141,148	$7,282,237

Exhibit 3B Income Statement

ADOBE SYSTEMS INCORPORATED CONSOLIDATED STATEMENTS OF INCOME	Years Ended		
	December 3, 2010	November 27, 2009	November 28, 2008
	(In thousands, except per share data)		
Revenue:			
Products	$3,159,161	$2,684,789	$3,354,554
Subscription	386,805	74,602	41,988
Services and support	254,034	186,462	183,347
Total revenue	3,800,000	2,945,853	3,579,889
Cost of revenue:			
Products	127,453	180,611	243,180
Subscription	195,595	48,286	23,209
Services and support	80,454	67,835	96,241
Total cost of revenue	403,502	296,732	362,630
Gross profit	3,396,498	2,649,121	3,217,259
Operating expenses:			
Research and development	680,332	565,141	662,057
Sales and marketing	1,244,197	981,903	1,089,341
General and administrative	383,499	298,749	337,291
Restructuring charges	23,266	41,260	32,053
Amortization of purchased intangibles and incomplete technology	72,130	71,555	68,246
Total operating expenses	2,403,424	1,958,608	2,188,988
Operating income	993,074	690,513	1,028,271
Non-operating income (expense):			
Interest and other income (expense), net	13,139	31,380	43,847
Interest expense	(56,952)	(3,407)	(10,019)
Investment gains (losses), net	(6,110)	(16,966)	16,409
Total non-operating income (expense), net	(49,923)	11,007	50,237
Income before income taxes	943,151	701,520	1,078,508
Provision for income taxes	168,471	315,012	206,694
Net income	$ 774,680	$ 386,508	$ 871,814
Basic net income per share	$ 1.49	$ 0.74	$ 1.62
Shares used to compute basic income per share	519,045	524,470	539,373
Diluted net income per share	$ 1.47	$ 0.73	$ 1.59
Shares used to compute diluted income per share	525,824	530,610	548,553

Source: http://www.sec.gov/Archives

Exhibit 4 Sales by Product Segment*

	Adobe Systems Incorporated Sales by Product Segment						
Fiscal Year 2010	Creative Solutions	Knowledge Worker	Enterprise	Omniture	Platform	Print & Publishing	Total
Revenues	$2,056,546	$654,327	$355,046	$360,564	$178,906	$194,611	$3,800,000
Cost of revenue	120,744	20,266	61,726	179,461	9,991	11,314	403,502
Gross profit	$1,935,802	$634,061	$293,320	$181,103	$168,915	$183,297	$3,396,498
Gross profit as a percentage of revenue	94%	97%	83%	50%	94%	94%	89%
Revenues as a percentage of total revenues	54%	17%	9%	10%	5%	5%	100%

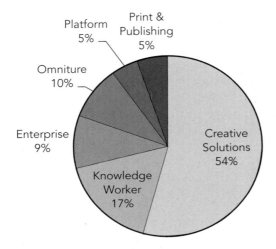

*Product and Services segments for FY 2011 have changed to include Creative and Interactive Solutions (formerly included in Creative Solutions), Digital Media Solutions (formerly included in Creative Solutions), Knowledge Worker, Enterprise, Omniture, Print and Publishing. Additionally, the Platform reporting segment was absorbed by the new Creative and Interactive Solutions segment.

Source: http://www.sec.gov/Archives

to share content across various operating systems. These operating systems were, at times, incompatible; therefore, Adobe introduced the Portable Document Format, more commonly known as the PDF. The PDF allowed people to share documents and collaborate with one another even when working on incompatible operating systems.

As the technology industry continued to grow, so too did consumers' dependence on the Internet. Static HTML pages hindered end-user activities and the fluid integration required to do business. Adobe's acquisition of competitor Macromedia in 2005 brought two programs essential to the development of interactive web pages into the Adobe stable: Dreamweaver and Flash.[26] Currently, Adobe is focused on integrating enterprise technologies and researching rich media solutions to solve business problems. Adobe's Flash Platform—including Flash Player and Adobe Air—

has been created to enhance Internet applications that offer competitive advantages and efficiencies to businesses.[27]

The Industry

As one of the largest software companies in the world, Adobe offers a variety of products and solutions in content authoring, online marketing, and customer experience management. While its customer base encompasses users in multiple industries like publishing, financial services, government, education, and advertising, among others, it is able to articulate and employ a simple, unified company mission: "Revolutionizing how the world engages with ideas and information."[28]

Adobe has a history of innovation beginning at its inception, be it in revolutionizing desktop

Exhibit 5 Sales by Geographic Region

Adobe Systems Incorporated Sales by Geographic Segment		
Revenue	**2010**	
United States	1,665,714	44%
Other Americas	193,309	5%
EMEA*	$1,168,217	31%
Asia	$ 772,760	20%
Revenue	$3,800,000	100%

*Europe, Middle East, and Africa

Sales by Geographic Segment

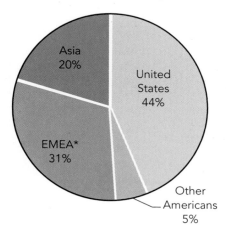

Source: http://www.sec.gov/Archives

publication via Adobe Postscript or, more recently, in revolutionizing rich Internet applications via its Adobe Flash platform. As such, Adobe's innovation strategy gives it an edge that makes it difficult for new entrants to replicate its formula for success.[29]

Furthermore, Adobe has successfully imbued within its customers a strong sense of brand loyalty by promising an efficient, useful, effortless, meaningful, and immersive experience.[30] Its strong brand identity and loyalty of users poses another big challenge to potential competitors.

Adobe enjoys a global presence, with more than half of its revenues coming from outside the US. Its Adobe AIR software has a market penetration of over 300 million, Adobe Flash Player is installed on over 98 percent of Internet enabled desktops, and an astounding 90 percent plus of creative professionals have Adobe Photoshop software on their desktops.[31]

Adobe's pricing of its premium products, including Photoshop and Dreamweaver, has generated some resentment among users not only in the US but,

because these already pricy products are even more expensive in the UK and Europe, overseas as well. Adobe's senior marketing manager attributes Adobe's pricing disparities to the significantly higher per unit cost of doing business in the UK and Europe.[34] In response to Adobe's high prices, consumers everywhere have sought comparable yet less expensive or, in some cases, free products. Some examples of such substitutions include using Gimp (i.e., free photo retouching software) instead of CS5, Kompozer (i.e., a web authoring system) instead of Dreamweaver, Inkscape (i.e., an open-source vector graphics editor) in lieu of Adobe Illustrator, and Foxit Reader rather than Adobe Reader. Furthermore, the rapid advent of cloud computing and web applications presents the increasing threat of low cost, highly responsive, pay-only-as-you-use software.

In Adobe's context, competitors like IBM, Microsoft, Oracle, and Quark all offer competitive solutions at competitive prices to the same market that Adobe targets. (See Exhibit 6 for comparative financial data and outcomes for Adobe's competitors.)[32,33] With technology being commoditized, there is little room for differentiation and squeezing out profits has become increasingly difficult, leading to intense rivalries in the industry in which Adobe operates. Consumers are well informed and quick to respond to attractive prices and features, increasing the likelihood of software switching. Nevertheless, Adobe has sustained itself in the competitive marketplace owing to its proactive approach to innovation and an engaging customer experience. While Adobe differentiates its products through creativity, it also makes strategic decisions such as mitigating competition by acquiring rival firms. As mentioned earlier, by acquiring its former competitor Macromedia in 2005, Adobe was able to enter the market of animation tools and pit itself squarely against another competitor—Microsoft.

Microsoft

Microsoft partnered with Adobe to use its Flash content on social media sites like YouTube and MySpace; however, after launching its own line of cheaper design tools (i.e., Microsoft Expression Studio), Microsoft began competing directly with two of Adobe's flagship products: Photoshop and Illustrator.[35] With the soaring popularity of Rich Interactive Applications (RIA), Microsoft and Adobe continue to find themselves competing with similar products (e.g., Microsoft's Silverlight and Adobe's Flash) in the same target market.

However, Microsoft, with its core competencies in operating systems and desktop software, is a relative

Exhibit 6 Financial Data and Outcomes of Adobe and Competitors

Key Statistics					
	ADBE	**ORCL**	**IBM**	**AAPL**	**MSFT**
	ADOBE SYSTEMS INC	**ORACLE CORP**	**INT'L BUSINESS MACHINES**	**APPLE INC**	**MICROSOFT CORP**
Sector	Info Tech	Info Tech	Info Tech	Info Tech	Info Tech
Industry	Software	Software	IT Services	Computers	Software
Market Cap	$17.08B	$170.19B	$202.37B	$305.73B	$210.73B
% of Institutional Ownership	83.60%	57.86%	59.28%	68.90%	58.16%
EPS (TTM)	$1.71	$1.50	$11.52	$17.91	$2.35
EPS Growth (TTM vs Prior TTM)	151.47%	34.82%	15.68%	74.90%	29.83%
Dividend Yield (Annualized)	-- / --	0.24% / 0.70%	2.60% / 1.56%	-- / --	0.64% / 2.52%
BETA (1 Yr Annualized)	0.15	0.46	1.56	4.21	0.06
Total Revenue	$3.97B	$34.35B	$99.87B	$76.28B	$66.69B
Revenue Growth	31.50%	42.09%	4.30%	63.32%	13.63%
Price Performance (Last 4 wks)	7.88%	11.12%	6.62%	-0.97%	2.30%
Price Performance (Last 52 wks)	1.50%	31.71%	27.24%	32.36%	-17.28%

Dividends					
	ADBE	**ORCL**	**IBM**	**AAPL**	**MSFT**
	ADOBE SYSTEMS INC	**ORACLE CORP**	**INT'L BUSINESS MACHINES**	**APPLE INC**	**MICROSOFT CORP**
Dividend (Most Recent Quarter)	—	$0.06	$0.65	—	$0.16
Annualized Dividend	—	$0.24	$2.60	—	$0.64
Dividend Yield (Annualized)	—	0.70%	1.56%	—	2.52%
Dividend Ex-Date	—	4/11/2011	2/8/2011	—	5/17/2011
Dividend Growth					
1-Yr Average	—	20.00%	18.18%	—	23.08%
5-Yr Average	—	--	26.58%	—	12.20%
Payout Ratio (TTM)	—	13.07%	21.39%	—	23.01%

Growth					
	ADBE	**ORCL**	**IBM**	**AAPL**	**MSFT**
	ADOBE SYSTEMS INC	**ORACLE CORP**	**INT'L BUSINESS MACHINES**	**APPLE INC**	**MICROSOFT CORP**
EPS Growth					
Last Qtr vs. Same Qtr Prior Yr	91.67%	78.26%	16.43%	75.20%	4.05%
TTM vs. Prior TTM	151.47%	34.82%	15.68%	74.90%	29.83%
Last 5 Yrs	4.32%	17.08%	18.60%	57.56%	13.40%
Projected EPS Growth					
Next Yr vs. This Yr	13.90%	10.14%	10.63%	16.20%	8.24%
Next 5 Yrs	14.14%	15.18%	10.93%	20.78%	10.28%
Revenue Growth					
TTM vs. Prior TTM	31.50%	42.09%	4.30%	63.32%	13.63%
Last 5 Yrs	14.08%	17.85%	1.85%	36.17%	9.45%
Cash Flow Growth					
TTM	0.13%	0.19%	0.06%	0.17%	0.03%
Last 5 Yrs	9.26%	20.48%	8.33%	58.36%	10.11%

(Continued)

Exhibit 6 Financial Data and Outcomes of Adobe and Competitors (*Continued*)

Profit Margins					
	ADBE	**ORCL**	**IBM**	**AAPL**	**MSFT**
	ADOBE SYSTEMS INC	**ORACLE CORP**	**INT'L BUSINESS MACHINES**	**APPLE INC**	**MICROSOFT CORP**
Gross Margin					
Most Recent Qtr	94.98%	78.07%	53.74%	39.84%	79.10%
TTM	95.07%	76.46%	51.47%	40.30%	83.31%
EBITD Margin (TTM)	35.79%	42.21%	23.57%	29.71%	43.71%
Operating Margin					
Most Recent Qtr	29.42%	35.48%	23.54%	29.27%	40.92%
TTM	28.48%	34.01%	18.73%	28.17%	39.56%
Pretax Margin					
Most Recent Qtr	27.84%	32.24%	23.96%	29.78%	42.59%
TTM	26.78%	30.34%	19.74%	28.51%	40.62%

Returns					
	ADBE	**ORCL**	**IBM**	**AAPL**	**MSFT**
	ADOBE SYSTEMS INC	**ORACLE CORP**	**INT'L BUSINESS MACHINES**	**APPLE INC**	**MICROSOFT CORP**
Return on Sales					
Most Recent Qtr	22.83%	24.14%	18.12%	22.45%	33.25%
TTM	22.23%	22.42%	14.85%	21.81%	30.84%
Return on Equity (TTM)	16.90%	23.00%	67.14%	35.99%	43.92%
Return on Assets (TTM)	10.89%	11.77%	13.82%	23.46%	23.18%
Return on Investment (TTM)	12.92%	15.49%	30.00%	33.00%	37.06%
Return on Capital (TTM)	2.42%	−0.64%	0.88%	−73.09%	−2.99%

Debt					
	ADBE	**ORCL**	**IBM**	**AAPL**	**MSFT**
	ADOBE SYSTEMS INC	**ORACLE CORP**	**INT'L BUSINESS MACHINES**	**APPLE INC**	**MICROSOFT CORP**
Long Term Debt/Equity					
Most Recent Qtr	27.86%	40.29%	94.79%	0.00%	19.95%
TTM	28.90%	41.68%	97.39%	0.00%	14.96%
Total Debt/Assets					
Most Recent Qtr	18.30%	21.80%	25.23%	0.00%	10.48%
Last Fiscal Year	18.70%	23.80%	25.23%	0.00%	6.90%
Total Debt/Equity					
Most Recent Qtr	28.02%	40.29%	124.20%	0.00%	19.95%
Last Fiscal Year	29.15%	37.37%	94.79%	0.00%	10.70%
Current Ratio (TTM)	3.28%	2.31%	1.26%	2.13%	2.23%
Payout Ratio (TTM)	—	13.07%	21.39%	—	23.01%

TTM = Trailing Twelve Months

Quark is not included in this analysis because it is a privately owned company.

Source: http://eresearch.fidelity.com

amateur when compared to Adobe's years of experience in the multimedia design industry. To truly compete with Adobe, Microsoft would have to strengthen its hold on the design industry by hiring and cultivating additional professional designers.

Both Microsoft and Adobe are exploring the concept of *hybrid technology,* which combines the power of desktop with web style multimedia.[36] Again, Adobe holds the upper hand with hybrid applications that can run on many types of operating systems, as opposed to Microsoft products that are limited to developing outputs that run exclusively on Windows-based PCs.

While Microsoft and Adobe have largely been competitors thus far, many believe that in the face of the future business landscape the only recourse for the two is to collaborate—particularly in light of Apple's recent coup in the mobile phone market. It is speculated that if Microsoft acquired Adobe, both would be in a better position to fend off the aggressive growth of Apple.[37]

IBM

Currently, enterprise marketing management software has a market worth of $2.5 billion with market expansion expected to double in size annually for the foreseeable future.[38] As expected, many companies, including IBM and Adobe, are working to strengthen their positions in this business domain. To this end, IBM acquired Unica (an enterprise marketing software company), Coremetrics (a leader in web analytics), and Sterling Commerce (a business-to-business commerce solutions provider).

Adobe has followed suit. Expanding beyond its niche graphic design market, Adobe is now vying to be a marketing department's digital command center of sorts. Adobe's acquisition of Omniture (a web analytics solution provider) and Day Software (a web content management provider) represent two significant steps in this direction.

While IBM is focused on cross- and multi-channel enterprise marketing management, Adobe has an eye on web experience management. Despite this fact, IBM's Coremetrics web analytics technologies and Unica's interactive marketing software are in direct competition with Adobe's Omniture and Day Software CQ5 platforms, respectively.

Quark

Adobe's creative and interactive solutions compete directly with those provided by Quark. For example, Adobe's InDesign product and Quark Xpress go head-to-head in the desktop publishing market. However, Quark enjoys several advantages including an established industry infrastructure built around the use of its XPress product in print shops and service bureaus

and the development of third-party plug-in products. Furthermore, there are significant infrastructure conversion, training, software, and hardware procurement costs involved should Quark customers choose to switch to Adobe InDesign.

Despite these barriers, Adobe continues to increase its InDesign market share owing to its innovative product offering, strong brand identity, and improved integration with other products in its creative suite.

Apple, Corel, and other Original Equipment Manufacturers (OEMs)

Adobe faces stiff competition in digital imaging solutions from several companies including Apple, Corel, Sony, Google, and ArcSoft, among others. Adobe's biggest name products in this category include Adobe Photoshop, Adobe Photoshop Lightroom, Adobe Photoshop Elements, and Adobe After Effects. Adobe Photoshop and Photoshop Lightroom compete directly with Apple's Aperture product and Corel. Adobe Photoshop is able to compete favorably in this area owing to high brand awareness among digital imaging customers and positive recommendations of market influencers. Even so, Apple integrates its digital imaging features with its operating system, thus diminishing Adobe's share in the Apple market. Following a bundling strategy similar to Apple, OEMs of smartphones, tablets, cameras, and other hardware (e.g., Dell, Canon, HP, etc.) try to differentiate their products by including free digital imaging software.

Recently, Adobe has found itself in the middle of a technological culture war of sorts centered on its Flash content. Because Flash is the most ubiquitous format for online video content, Adobe has been able to comfortably rely upon the online advertising industry's burgeoning exploration of video advertising to drive the collection of licensing fees and, perhaps more importantly, stimulate direct sales of its Flash animation software. Although Flash Player, necessary to view Flash content, is offered to the public free of change, the software used to *create* Flash content is an important component of Adobe's software sales.

Perhaps in response to the market leadership status of Flash content, both the format and Flash Player have been criticized by a number of voices in the tech community. The blog MarxSoftware questions Adobe's continued commitment to the closed source development of its player.[39] Jakob Nielsen of useit.com suggests that the overuse of Flash on the web actually detracts from a web site's general usability.[40]

However, the greatest blow came from Apple's recently retired CEO, Steve Jobs, who has been particularly harsh in his criticism of Flash content. In a public letter published in April 2010, Jobs claimed that Adobe's Flash Player had been singled out by computer security firm Symantec for having one of the worst security records in 2009.[41] In addition, Apple recently made the decision to stop offering Flash security updates to users of computers running its OSX operating system.[42] In fact, since the introduction of the first model of Apple's groundbreaking iPhone, Flash content has not been allowed on Apple's handheld devices or spin-offs such as the iPad.[45]

Adobe responded to Jobs' open letter by asserting that Symantec had actually found Flash Player to have the second *fewest* vulnerabilities of any Internet browser or content plug-in it had tested.[43] Nevertheless, Adobe's response did not enjoy the media exposure of Jobs' initial open letter and Apple has not yet publically retracted Jobs' statement. As Jobs is seen as a visionary by many both within and outside the tech industry, Adobe risks further damage to its reputation if it does not mount a decisively successful public relations campaign to counteract Jobs' claims.

Primary Challenges

The market in which Adobe operates is as highly competitive as it is dynamic. As technologies evolve and customer needs change, first rate exploration and innovation will be crucial to the survival of Adobe. To date, and despite the existence of several cost free alternatives in its industry, Adobe has maintained its market leadership position (see Exhibit 7).[44] Adobe's existing network of locked in enterprise and business customers and the positive perception users have of its products have contributed significantly to its success. Still, as Adobe's competitors continue to incorporate superior performance in their lower priced (or even free of charge) products, it will be imperative that Adobe outshine its competitors with trailblazing improvements that, like the PDF when introduced, anticipate future needs and desires. Without this innovation, more and more cost sensitive customers will start exploring alternatives to Adobe products.

Licensing revenue has become an increasingly important contributor to Adobe's bottom line, and Adobe depends on the continued market share dominance of Flash content to maintain and grow licensing revenues. Notably, market share for Apple computers has been increasing dramatically and, as of the beginning of 2011, Apple claimed third place status in computer sales.[45] Because Jobs no longer allows the pre-installation of Flash on Apple computers, Adobe has to rely on Apple consumers to download Flash Player from its web site of their own accord. Because of this, maintaining communication with Apple computer users via an authentic and transparent response to Jobs' criticisms is essential.

In addition to the growth of Apple's PC market share, Adobe also has to contend with the extremely rapid growth of the mobile broadband computing industry, which FCC Chairman Julius Genachowski called "the fastest growing computer platform in history" during a speech in 2011.[46] The introduction of this radically different computing platform has provided opportunities for market entrants to develop new technologies that could threaten Adobe's hegemony. Adobe will have to prove again its penchant for forward thinking or risk missing out on this newest opportunity to define the industry standard for another new market.

Exhibit 7 Adobe Compared to Industry Average

Industry Average			
	ADBE	Industry Average	Percentile in Industry
Market Capitalization	$17.08B	$12.44B	98th
Beta (1 Year Annualized)	0.11	1.14	82nd
EPS (Adjusted, 02/28/2011 TTM)	$1.71	$1.55	95th
Current Consensus EPS Estimate	$0.51	—	—
EPS Growth (TTM vs. Prior TTM)	151.47%	43.75%	89th
P/E (TTM) AS OF 04/15/2011	20.18	35.13	56th
Dividend Yield (Annual) —	—	1.53%	—
Total Revenue (TTM) AS OF 02/28/2011	$3.97B	$26.63B	97th
Revenue Growth (TTM vs Prior TTM)	31.50%	19.91%	82nd
Shares Outstanding	504M	3,407M	95th

Source: http://eresearch.fidelity.com

Conclusion

Historically, Adobe Systems has focused on the creation of multimedia and creativity software products; however, through exploration, innovation, and exploitation, the company has evolved into a broad-based Internet application and software developer.

Co-founded in 1982 by John Warnock and Chuck Geschke in California, Adobe has grown to become a global industry leader. The development of the PDF, Photoshop, Flash, and other innovations have made Adobe products commonplace in homes and businesses around the world. The brand recognition associated with Adobe is admirable, as is brand loyalty. The products themselves generally carry with them a prestigious and reliable reputation.

While Adobe is known as an innovative company, it does not hesitate to expand its horizons through acquisitions and strategic alliances (e.g., Omniture and Macromedia) as well. Adobe is considered a powerful first mover in the tech industry, a fact that enhances the prestige Adobe holds.

While not entirely without, Adobe enjoys a very limited number of competitors with product and service lines that closely mirror its own. Even so, Adobe faces both short- and long-term challenges. As the technological trend for online business grows, so does the scale of demand Adobe will be required to meet. The company will need to manage explosive growth without sacrificing its positive company culture and reputation for meeting the needs of consumers by delivering quality services and products.

NOTES

1. Definition: photoshop. (2010). *Dictionary.com*. http://dictionary.reference.com/browse/photoshop
2. Adobe Systems Incorporated: Form 10-K. Page 3. (2010, Dec 3). *sec.gov*. http://www.sec.gov/Archives/edgar/data/796343/000079634311000003/form_10k.htm
3. Adobe completes acquisition of macromedia. (2005, Dec 5). *Adobe.com*. http://www.adobe.com/aboutadobe/pressroom/pressreleases/pdfs/200512/120505AdobeAcquiresMacromedia.pdf
4. Omniture acquisition: Frequently asked questions. (2009, Oct 26). *Omniture.com*. http://www.omniture.com/en/company/adobe_faq
5. LePage, R. (2007, Nov 15). Bruce Chizen's legacy. *Macworld.com*. http://www.macworld.com/article/61059/2007/11/chizen.html
6. Hawkins, A. (2009, Feb 9). Is the Adobe CS4 Suite worth the upgrade? *Pixel Clever.com*. http://www.pixelclever.com/is-adobe-cs4-worth-upgrade
7. Jobs, S. (2010, Apr). Thoughts on Flash. *Apple.com*. http://www.apple.com/hotnews/thoughts-on-flash/
8. Hoskisson, R., Hitt, M., Ireland, R. D., & Harrison, J. (2008). *Competing for Advantage*. Second Ed. Mason, OH: Thomson Higher Education. Page 5.
9. Adobe Systems Incorporated: Form 10-K. *op. cit*. Page 123.
10. The trouble with half and half. (2011, 24 Mar). *Economist.com*. http://www.economist.com/node/18441049?story_id=18441049
11. Hoskisson, R., Hitt, M., Ireland, R. D., & Harrison, J. *op. cit*. Pages 166–168.
12. Hoskisson, R., Hitt, M., Ireland, R. D., & Harrison, J. *op. cit*. Pages 80–84.
13. Adobe Systems Incorporated. (2011). Core Values. *Adobe.com*. http://www.adobe.com/aboutadobe/careeropp/core_values.html
14. *Ibid*.
15. *Ibid*.
16. Adobe Systems Incorporated (2011, Mar). Adobe fast facts. *Adobe.com*. http://www.adobe.com/aboutadobe/pressroom/pdfs/Adobe_Fast_Facts_3_2011.pdf
17. Adobe co-founder John Warnock on the competitive advantages of aesthetics and the 'right' technology. (2010, Jan 20). *Knowledge@Wharton*. http://knowledge.wharton.upenn.edu/article.cfm?articleid=2418
18. Adobe Systems Incorporated. (2011). Involved Managers. *Adobe.com*. http://www.adobe.com/aboutadobe/careeropp/involved_managers.html
19. Adobe co-founder John Warnock on the competitive advantages of aesthetics and the 'right' technology. *op.cit*.
20. Hoskisson, R., Hitt, M., Ireland, R. D., & Harrison, J. *op. cit*. Page 103.
21. Adobe Systems Incorporated. (2010, Mar). Adobe fast facts. *op. cit*.
22. Adobe Systems Incorporated: Form 10-K. *op. cit*. Page 124.
23. Hoskisson, R., Hitt, M., Ireland, R. D., & Harrison, J. *op. cit*. Page 279.
24. Adobe Systems Incorporated: Form 10-K. *op. cit*. Page 125.
25. Adobe Systems Incorporated. (2010, Apr). Corporate Overview. *Adobe.com*. http://www.adobe.com/aboutadobe/pressroom/pdfs/profile.pdf
26. LePage, R. *op. cit*.
27. Hoskisson, R., Hitt, M., Ireland, R. D., & Harrison, J. *op. cit*. Page 2.
28. Adobe Systems Incorporated. (2010, Apr). Professional development. *Adobe.com*. http://www.adobe.com/aboutadobe/careeropp/development.html
29. Hoskisson, R., Hitt, M., Ireland, R. D., & Harrison, J. *op. cit*. Pages 146-147.
30. Adobe corporate brand guidelines. (2010, Oct 25). *Adobe.com*. http://brandcenterdl.adobe.com/Corpmktg/Brandmktg/Campaign_Assets/guidelines/corporate/corporate_brand_guidelines.pdf
31. Adobe Systems Incorporated: Form 10-K. *op. cit*. Page 125.
32. Fidelity Research (2011, Apr). Stock research center. *Fidelity.com*. http://eresearch.fidelity.com/eresearch/landing.jhtml
33. Morningstar Research (2011, Apr). Stock research. *Morningstar.com*. http://www.morningstar.com/Cover/Stocks.html
34. Adobe Systems Incorporated. (2010, Apr). Adobe discussion forum. *Adobe.com*. http://forums.adobe.com/message/2732506
35. Mintz, J. (2007, Apr 16). Microsoft, Adobe competition heats up. *MSNBC.com*. http://www.msnbc.msn.com/id/18142087/ns/technology_and_sciencetech_and_gadgets/
36. *Ibid*.
37. Bilton, N. (2010, Oct 7). What did Microsoft and Adobe chiefs talk about? *New York Times*. http://bits.blogs.nytimes.com/2010/10/07/microsoft-and-adobe-chiefs-meet-to-discuss-partnerships/
38. Brinker, S. (2010, Aug 15). Adobe, IBM and the big business of marketing software. *Chief Marketing Technologist*. http://www.chiefmartec.com/2010/08/adobe-ibm-and-the-big-business-of-marketing-software.html
39. Marx, D. (2008, Jul 31). Flex/Flash criticisms addressed. *MarxSoftware.com*. http://marxsoftware.blogspot.com/2008/07/flexflash-critcisms-addressed.html

40. Nielsen, J. (2000, Oct 29). Flash – 99% Bad. *useIt.com*. http://www.useit.com/alertbox/20001029.html

41. Jobs, S. *op. cit.*

42. Keizer, G. (2010, Oct 22). Apple dumps flash from Mac OS X. *ComputerWorld.com*. http://www.computerworld.com/s/article/9192699/Apple_dumps_Flash_from_Mac_OS_X?taxonomyId=123&pageNumber=1

43. Adobe Systems Incorporated. (2011). The truth about Flash. *Adobe.com*. http://www.adobe.com/choice/flash.html

44. Fidelity Research. *op. cit.*

45. McDougall, P. (2011, Jan 27). iPad fuels 241% growth in Apple's market share. *InformationWeek.com*. http://www.informationweek.com/news/hardware/mac/229100377

46. FCC Chairman says spectrum crunch requires action now on broadband. (2011, Apr 12). *Radio-Info.com*. http://www.radio-info.com/news/fcc-chairman-says-spectrum-crunch-requires-action-now-on-broadband

Apple Inc.: Keeping the "i" in "Innovation"

Robin Chapman, Robert E. Hoskisson, Gail Christian

Arizona State University

As one of the most well-known and respected companies in the world, Apple Inc. was one of the few companies to emerge from the recession stronger than ever. By spring 2011, Apple had an array of impressive products including the iPad, iPhone, iPod shuffle, iPod nano, iPod touch, iPod classic, Apple TV, MacBook, MacBook Pro, MacBook Air, Mac mini, iMac, and MacPro.[1] Apple was also the only company to maintain its status as No. 1 for innovativeness on *Fortune's* list of the World's Most Admired Companies in both pre-recession 2007 and post-recession 2011. In addition, Apple was named the World's Most Admired Company overall in 2011 by *Fortune*, a position it has held since 2008.[2] In March 2011, *Fast Company* also named Apple its Most Innovative Company. According to editor Robert Safian, "In putting together this month's special package on the 2011 Most Innovative Companies, we really had no choice: Apple had to be No. 1."[3] With net sales (in millions) of $37,491, $42,905, and $65,225 in 2008, 2009, and 2010, respectively, Apple's stream of innovative products supported Steve Jobs' philosophy that if you make something "really great, then everybody will want to use it"[4] (see Exhibit 1).

Although Apple started in 1976 as a computer business, much of Apple's success has been attributed to its music- and video-related products and the iPhone. According to Steve Jobs, Apple's charismatic former CEO and co-founder, "This will go down in history as a turning point for the music industry. This is landmark stuff. I can't overestimate it!"[5] Jobs was referring to the April 2003 debut of Apple's iTunes Online Music Store, the first legal online music service to have agreements with the five major record labels at that time. Although initially available only to Macintosh users, iTunes sold more than 1 million songs by the end of its first week in operation. Not only did iTunes change the nature of the music industry, it also added greatly to Apple's revenues by way of promoting the purchase of the iPod—a portable digital music device that could store downloaded iTunes songs. As Apple quickly became known as a company that made innovative consumer electronics products instead of just a company that made computers, it changed its name in 2007 from "Apple Computer" to "Apple Inc." Jobs said, "The Mac, iPod, Apple TV and iPhone. Only one of those is a computer. So we're changing the name."[6]

Apple's focus on innovation has helped it maintain a competitive advantage and marketing prowess over other industry players that have historically been much stronger than Apple.[3] However, Apple must continue to beat the competition on a number of levels. iTunes faces stiff competition from new and existing online music and video download services. The iPod, iPad, Apple TV, and iPhone all face the threat of lower-priced rivals and possible substitutes.

Then, on January 17, 2011, Apple was faced with an additional challenge when Steve Jobs handed control of the company to chief operating officer Timothy D. Cook, with the announcement of another medical leave.[7] This would be his third medical leave in less than six years. For the time, Jobs retained the title of CEO, but Cook handled day-to-day operations at the company. Jobs did not share his reason for leaving the company or tell his employees when he might return.[8] Diagnosed with a rare form of pancreatic cancer in 2004, Jobs took an undisclosed leave of absence that year for treatment. In 2009 he took a six-month leave to undergo a liver transplant at the Methodist University Hospital Transplant Institute in Memphis. Although these absences did not interrupt Apple's run of successes, with Jobs' August 24, 2011 announcement that he is retiring, the new question becomes, "What happens to a modern company whose innovations and inspirations are so closely tied to the vision of one leader when that leader's influence is in decline?"[9]

To understand how Apple became a leader in innovation and how closely Steve Jobs is associated with Apple and its many achievements, it is necessary to first examine Apple's history.

Exhibit 1 Apple Inc. Selected Financial Data

	(In millions, except share amounts which are reflected in thousands and per share amounts)				
	2010	**2009**	**2008**	**2007**	**2006**
Net sales	$ 65,225	$ 42,905	$ 37,491	$ 24,578	$ 19,315
Net income	$ 14,013	$ 8,235	$ 6,119	$ 3,495	$ 1,989
Earnings per common share:					
Basic	$ 15.41	$ 9.22	$ 6.94	$ 4.04	$ 2.36
Diluted	$ 15.15	$ 9.08	$ 6.78	$ 3.93	$ 2.27
Cash dividends declared per common share	$ 0	$ 0	$ 0	$ 0	$ 0
Shares used in computing earnings per share:					
Basic	909,461	893,016	881,592	864,595	844,058
Diluted	924,712	907,005	902,139	889,292	877,526
Total cash, cash equivalents and marketable securities	$ 51,011	$ 33,992	$ 24,490	$ 15,386	$ 10,110
Total assets	$ 75,183	$ 47,501	$ 36,171	$ 24,878	$ 17,205
Total long-term obligations (a)	$ 5,531	$ 3,502	$ 1,745	$ 687	$ 395
Total liabilities	$ 27,392	$ 15,861	$ 13,874	$ 10,347	$ 7,221
Total shareholders' equity	$ 47,791	$ 31,640	$ 22,297	$ 14,531	$ 9,984

(a) The Company did not have any long-term debt during the five years ended September 25, 2010. Long-term obligations excludes non-current deferred revenue.

Source: Apple Inc. Annual Report 2010.

Early Company History

On April 1, 1976, Steve Jobs and Stephen Wozniak began the partnership that would eventually become Apple Computer. Both electronics gurus, Jobs and Wozniak had known each other since high school and had worked together previously on other projects.[10] In early 1976, Wozniak had been working on combining video monitors with computers. His idea was to invent a user-friendly computer that ordinary consumers could buy. Wozniak, who worked for Hewlett-Packard (HP) at the time, decided to approach his employer with his idea. HP, however, did not see a future for personal computers (PCs) and soundly rebuffed him. At that point, Steve Jobs told his friend Wozniak that they should go into business together and sell computers themselves.[11]

Their first computer, the Apple I, was built in Jobs' parents' garage. Known as a "kit computer," the original Apple consisted merely of a circuit board and did not even have an exterior casing. It was intended to be sold to hobbyists only. Jobs called the computer an "Apple" in honor of his days working at an orchard while seeking enlightenment—and because neither he nor Wozniak could come up with a better name.[12] The Apple I received mixed responses from hobbyists, and the duo decided it was time to expand the market for personal computers by building a more attractive and useful machine, the Apple II[13] (see Exhibit 2).

Growth

After taking on new partners to fund expansion plans, the company officially became Apple Computer, Inc., in early 1977.[14] Within months, the recapitalized company introduced the Apple II, the first computer to come with a sleek plastic casing and color graphics.[15] Annual sales increased dramatically to $10 million, and the company began to grow quickly in size, adding thousands of employees.[16] On December 12, 1980, Apple became a public company. On the first day of trading, its share price increased from an initial $22 offering to $29.[17] By the end of the year, Apple reached $100 million in annual sales.[18] The fledgling company, however, soon faced some experienced competition.

In 1981, IBM released its first personal computer. IBM's sheer size ensured its domination of the young PC market. Steve Jobs realized that Apple would have to move fast in order to remain a viable company. Over the next few years, the company released several new computer models, most notably the Apple III and the Lisa. Neither of these models sold particularly well.

In 1983, Jobs recruited Pepsi-Cola CEO John Sculley as Apple's president and CEO. Jobs hoped that this change would bring more structure and organization to the young company.[19] Apple's biggest computer achievement, the Macintosh (Mac), was released. After initially opposing it, Jobs had personally taken on the task of developing the Mac, which became the

Exhibit 2 Select Apple Product Releases

1976	Apple I
1977	Apple II
1980	Apple III
1983	Lisa
1984	Macintosh Graphical User Interface (GUI)
1986	Macintosh Plus
1987	Macintosh II
1991	Macintosh Quadra PowerBook 100
1994	PowerMac 6100
1997	PowerBook G3
1998	iMac
1999	iBook
2001	iTunes iDVD iPod
2003	iLife suite iTunes 4 (online music store w/200,000 downloadable songs)
2004	iPod Mini eMac iPod (Click Wheel) iPod (U2 Special Edition) iPod Photo
2005	iPod Shuffle iPod nano iPod color iPod with video
2006	MacBook Mac mini
2007	Apple TV iPhone
2008	iPhone 3G iPod classic (120 GB)
2009	iPhone 3GS
2010	iPhone 4 iPad
2011	iPad 2

Source: http://www.apple-history.com.

first PC featuring a graphical interface and a mouse for navigation. Apple first presented the now-famous Macintosh computer with a riveting January 1984 Super Bowl commercial. The memorable commercial featured an Orwellian 1984 world filled with stoic human zombies, all watching a large-screen image of "Big Brother." A young woman rushes into the room and dramatically destroys the screen. Apple used this 1984 imagery to depict IBM's computer dominance being destroyed by the new Macintosh.[20] With features that made the Mac easy to use for publishing and a marketing strategy that concentrated on universities, the new computer

sold very well, pushing Apple's fiscal 1984 sales to an unprecedented $1.5 billion.[21]

Shake-Up

By 1985, however, Jobs and Sculley began to disagree over the direction they wanted the company to take. After Jobs' attempt to remove Sculley failed, Jobs left Apple in May to start his own new business, NeXT Computers. Meanwhile, Microsoft benefited from Apple's poor negotiation of a contract that cleared the way for successive versions of the Windows operating system to use graphical user interface (GUI) technology similar to that of the Mac. With this agreement, "Apple had effectively lost exclusive rights to its interface design."[22]

In 1990, Microsoft released Windows 3.0, the first universal software that could run on nearly every PC regardless of the manufacturer. Although Apple's worldwide sales had reached $7 billion by 1992, Apple soon found itself fighting an uphill battle against the movement toward standardized software. More and more businesses and consumers wanted compatible operating systems, but the Macintosh still ran exclusively on Mac OS, a system not available to other computers. By 1993, Apple's board of directors replaced Sculley as CEO. Apple moved through two CEOs over the next five years.

During this time, Apple partnered with IBM and Motorola to produce the PowerPC chip to run the company's new line of PowerMacs, allowing it to outperform computers powered by Intel microprocessors.[23] Despite this and Apple's attempts to reorganize, losses mounted in 1996 and 1997. In December 1996, Apple acquired NeXT with the plan of using its technology as the basis for a new operating system. After being gone for more than a decade, Jobs returned to the company he had co-founded with Wozniak.

Jobs' Return

One of the first problems Steve Jobs moved to fix was the ongoing dispute between Apple and Microsoft over the Windows graphical user interface (GUI). Microsoft not only paid an undisclosed amount to Apple, but also made its Office 98 suite compatible with Macintoshes.[24] Jobs then proceeded to change the company's sales strategy in 1997 to encompass direct sales—both online and by phone. In a flurry of product releases, Apple introduced the new generation of PowerMacs, PowerBooks, and the highly anticipated iMac and iBook, which were less expensive computers aimed at the low-end computer market. After an entire year without showing a profit, the first quarter of 1998 began three years of profitable quarters for Apple.[25]

Exhibit 3 iPod Products

iPod shuffle	iPod nano	iPod classic	iPod touch
The incredibly small, wearable music player has buttons, and VoiceOver tells you the song or playlist you're listening to. **Learn more**	Multi-Touch comes to the smaller, lighter iPod nano, along with features like a built-in FM radio, pedometer, clip, and more. **Learn more**	With 160GB of storage for music, video, and photos, iPod classic is the take-everything everywhere iPod. **Learn more**	Have more fun than ever with FaceTime,* Retina display, HD video recording, and the powerful A4 chip. **Learn more**
Capability			
Music, audiobooks, podcasts	Music, audiobooks, podcasts, photos, FM radio, pedometer, Nike + iPod support**	Music, movies, TV shows, videos, audiobooks, podcasts, photos	Music, movies, TV shows, videos, games, applications, ebooks, audiobooks, podcasts, photos, Safari web browser, email, Maps, FaceTime,* HD video recording and editing, Nike + iPod support built in
Battery life***			
Audio playback Up to 15 hours	**Audio playback** Up to 24 hours	**Audio playback** Up to 36 hours **Video Playback** Up to 6 hours	**Audio playback** Up to 40 hours **Video playback** Up to 7 hours
Colors			
⬤⬤⬤⬤⬤	⬤⬤⬤⬤⬤⬤ Apple Store Exclusive color ⬤ (PRODUCT)^{RED}	⬤⬤	⬤
Includes			
Earphones, iPod shuffle USB Cable	Earphones, USB cable	Earphones, dock adapter, USB cable	Earphones, USB cable
Capacity and price****			
2GB **$49**	8GB **$149** 16GB **$179** A portion of the proceeds from every ⬤ (PRODUCT)^{RED} purchase will go to the Global Fund to fight AIDS in Africa.	160GB **$249**	8GB **$229** 32GB **$299** 64GB **$399**
Size			
1.14 x 1.24 x 0.34 inches (29 x 31.6 x 8.7 mm) including clip	1.48 x 1.61 x 0.35 inches (37.5 x 40.9 x 8.78 mm) including clip	4.1 x 2.4 x 0.41 inches (103.5 x 61.8 x 10.5 mm)	4.4 x 2.3 x 0.28 inches (111 x 58.9 x 7.2 mm)
Weight			
0.44 ounce (12.5 grams)	0.74 ounces (21.1 grams)	4.9 ounces (140 grams)	3.56 ounces (101 grams)

(Continued)

Exhibit 3 iPod Products (*Continued*)

iPod shuffle	**iPod** nano	**iPod** classic	**iPod** touch
Charge time			
About 3 hours (2-hour fast charge to 80%)	About 3 hours (1.5-hour fast charge to 80%)	About 4 hours (2-hour fast charge to 80%)	About 4 hours (2-hour fast charge to 80%)
Display			
	1.54-inch (diagonal) color Multi-Touch display	2.5-inch (diagonal) color LCD with LED backlight	3.5-inch (diagonal) widescreen Multi-Touch display
Navigation			
Clickable controls with VoiceOver button	Multi-Touch display	Click Wheel	Multi-Touch display
Ports			
iPod shuffle USB cable	Dock connector, stereo minijack	Dock connector, stereo minijack	Dock connector, stereo minijack
Connectivity			
iPod shuffle USB cable	USB through dock connector; audio through headphone jack	USB through dock connector; component and composite video through dock connector (with AV cables, sold separately); audio through headphone jack	USB through dock connector; component and composite video through dock connector (with AV cables, sold separately); audio through headphone jack
Wireless			
			802.11b/g/n Wi-Fi (802.11n 2.4GHz only), Nike + iPod support built in, Maps location-based service, Bluetooth 2.1 + EDR
Audio support			
AAC (8 to 320 Kbps), Protected AAC (from iTunes Store), MP3 (8 to 320 Kbps), MP3 VBR, Audible (formats 2, 3, 4, Audible Enhanced Audio, AAX, and AAX+), Apple Lossless, AIFF, and WAV	Audio formats supported: AAC (8 to 320 Kbps), Protected AAC (from iTunes Store), HE-AAC, MP3 (8 to 320 Kbps), MP3 VBR, Audible (formats 2, 3, 4, Audible Enhanced Audio, AAX, and AAX+), Apple Lossless, AIFF, and WAV	AAC (8 to 320 Kbps), Protected AAC (from iTunes Store), MP3 (16 to 320 Kbps), MP3 VBR, Audible (formats 2, 3, and 4), Apple Lossless, WAV, and AIFF	Audio formats supported: AAC (8 to 320 Kbps), Protected AAC (from iTunes Store), HE-AAC, MP3 (8 to 320 Kbps), MP3 VBR, Audible (formats 2, 3, 4, Audible Enhanced Audio, AAX, and AAX+), Apple Lossless, AIFF, and WAV
Photo support			
	Syncs iPod-viewable photos in JPEG, BMP, GIF, TIFF, PSD (Mac only), and PNG formats	Syncs iPod-viewable photos in JPEG, BMP, GIF, TIFF, PSD (Mac only), and PNG formats	Syncs iPod-viewable photos in JPEG, BMP, GIF, TIFF, PSD (Mac only), and PNG formats

(*Continued*)

Exhibit 3 iPod Products (*Continued*)

iPod shuffle	iPod nano	iPod classic	iPod touch
Video support			
		H.264 video, up to 1.5 Mbps, 640 by 480 pixels, 30 frames per second, Low-Complexity version of the H.264 Baseline Profile with AAC-LC audio up to 160 Kbps, 48kHz, stereo audio in .m4v, .mp4, and .mov file formats; H.264 video, up to 2.5 Mbps, 640 by 480 pixels, 30 frames per second, Baseline Profile up to Level 3.0 with AAC-LC audio up to 160 Kbps, 48kHz, stereo audio in .m4v, .mp4, and .mov file formats; MPEG-4 video, up to 2.5 Mbps, 640 by 480 pixels, 30 frames per second, Simple Profile with AAC-LC audio up to 160 Kbps, 48kHz, stereo audio in .m4v, .mp4, and .mov file formats	H.264 video up to 720p, 30 frames per second, Main Profile level 3.1 with AAC-LC audio up to 160 Kbps, 48kHz, stereo audio in .m4v, .mp4, and .mov file formats; MPEG-4 video, up to 2.5 Mbps, 640 by 480 pixels, 30 frames per second, Simple Profile with AAC-LC audio up to 160 Kbps per channel, 48kHz, stereo audio in .m4v, .mp4, and .mov file formats; Motion JPEG (M-JPEG) up to 35 Mbps, 1280 by 720 pixels, 30 frames per second, audio in ulaw, PCM stereo audio in .avi file format

More Information

- * FaceTime requires fourth-generation iPod touch or iPhone 4 and a Wi-Fi connection for both caller and recipient.
- ** Sold separately.
- *** Rechargeable batteries have a limited number of charge cycles and may eventually need to be replaced (see www.apple.com/support/ipod/service/battery). Battery life and number of charge cycles vary by use and settings. See www.apple.com/batteries for more information.
- ****1GB = 1 billion bytes; actual formatted capacity less.
- Available on iTunes. Title availability subject to change.

Source: Apple, Inc. Annual Report 2010.

Jobs stated that he wanted to transform the company by making the Mac "the hub of [the consumers'] digital lifestyle." To do this, Apple introduced iLife in 2002, a software suite including applications such as iPhoto, iMovie, iTunes, and eventually the iPod. With the advent of Napster and peer-to-peer music sharing, Apple saw a way to capitalize on the emerging trend of cheap music downloads by creating a legal online music distribution network. iTunes would be the key to exploiting this market. Once downloaded by way of iTunes, music could then be transferred only to an iPod (due to encryption). With iTunes, Apple revolutionized the distribution of music and hoped to do the same with the distribution of movies on demand. Similar strategies were planned for the iPhone in the mobile or smartphone industry segments and for Apple TV in the mobile media and set-top box industry segments.

iTunes: Apple's Online Music Store

Apple ventured into the market of legal downloads with the introduction of its iTunes Music Store.[26] By 2011, the iTunes Store provided customers in 23 countries with music, movies, HDTV shows, apps, games, podcasts, audiobooks, and ways to connect with artists and friends via Ping (Apple's own social network for music). iTunes offers downloads at a specified price without requiring a subscription or monthly fees.[27] Originally offered exclusively on Apple's own Mac, iTunes can now be installed on PCs, iPhones, iPods, iPads, and Apple TV.[28] In addition, the iTunes Store provides customers with recommendations from fellow fans, celebrity playlists, recommendations from iTunes based on previous purchases, a free single of the week, and the option of subscribing to iTunes newsletters.

iTunes offers its users a selection of more than 13 million songs, with new songs continually added[29] from just about every genre of music. Users can perform a search by type of music, artist name, or title of track or album. Each song available can be previewed without making a purchase. The purchase prices are $0.69, $0.99, or $1.29. Through iTunes U, users can download lectures, discussions, language lessons, and other opportunities for learning for free from leading universities, museums, and other institutions.

Once songs are downloaded, they are stored as a digital music library. As this collection grows, this list of songs can be arranged in many different ways. Songs can be arranged by personal rating, artist, or genre. This feature allows for a customizable playlist. In addition, the iTunes Store includes Apple's App Store and iBookstore. Gift certificates are also available in different denominations and can be sent electronically.

As previously mentioned, in its first week of existence, the number of downloads from iTunes surpassed the 1 million mark. This feat is amazing considering that at the time of iTunes' introduction, the download service was available only for the Mac, and less than 5 percent of US computer users had Macs. When iTunes became available for use on the PC, sales increased even more rapidly. iTunes PC downloads reached the 1 million mark in three days, less than half the time it took for the Mac version. But the success of iTunes is not measured in number of downloads sold per day or week, as it is also used as a means to boost the sales of iPods, iPhones, iPads, and Apple TVs.

iTunes, iPod, iPhone, iPad, and Apple TV

iTunes and iPod
For music lovers, the iPod is the greatest invention since the Sony Walkman. There are currently four different iPod styles: the iPod shuffle, iPod classic, iPod nano, and iPod touch. iPod owners can purchase accessories such as armbands, radio remotes, and universal docks to make using the iPod even more enjoyable. While others seek to simply duplicate the complementary and innovative relationships between iPod and iTunes, Apple continues to innovate with new products such as the iPad and updated versions of existing products such as the iPhone and Apple TV.[30]

iPhone
In the first quarter of 2007, Apple launched its "revolutionary" product, the iPhone. The iPhone combined three concepts popular with consumers: a mobile phone, a wide-screen iPod, and an Internet communication device. Apple bragged that its iPhone had "an entirely new user interface based on a large multi-touch display and pioneering software" that users could control with just their fingers.[31] Apple sold 1 million iPhones within three months of making this product available to consumers.

As other companies tried to create products comparable to the iPhone, Apple was busy creating innovative features to make the iPhone more powerful, easier to use, and more appealing to users. In 2010, the iPhone surpassed personal computers as Apple's largest product line with the iPhone and related products representing 39 percent of its revenues that year.[32] By December 2010, sales of the iPhone had grown by 87 percent year-over-year, outpacing the growth in the global smartphone market of 70 percent year-over-year[33] (see Exhibit 4).

The iPhone 4 was introduced in 2010, with new features including the A4 processor, video calling, high-definition video recording and editing, two cameras (one in front facing the user and one on the back), and the ability to multitask (run third-party applications, or "apps," and switch between them instantly without slowing performance or draining the battery). In addition, the App Store on iTunes offered more than 350,000 mobile apps for downloading, many of which were free. Apple referred to the iPhone 4 as "the biggest thing to happen to iPhone since iPhone."[34]

The next "biggest thing" is the iPhone 5, which is rumored to be scheduled for launch sometime between late 2011 and early 2012. The launches of the iPhone 3G, 3GS, and 4 were announced in this manner. As the anticipation builds for the new product, speculations about new features include a curved metal-clad back, which would look similar to the original iPhone, and a larger four-inch screen.[35]

Apple TV
In addition to the iPhone, Apple introduced the Apple TV in 2007. With this product, Apple intended to revolutionize the Internet video industry, as it did with the music download industry. Users could download movies and TV shows via the iTunes online service or via YouTube as well as view digital photos and home videos.[36] Some negative hype claimed that the Apple TV would be a flop just like the Apple III and the Power Mac Cube. Some of the features that made the first edition unpopular included the following:

- Users were not able to download a movie from iTunes directly to their TVs; they had to download it to their computers first.
- It required an HDTV, but the movies that could be downloaded were of such low resolution that the picture looked fuzzy and old-fashioned.
- It had no DVD drive.

Exhibit 4 Apple Inc. Net Sales by Product

Information regarding net sales by product for the three years ended September 25, 2010, is as follows (in millions):	2010	2009	2008
Desktops (a)	$ 6,201	$ 4,324	$ 5,622
Portables (b)	11,278	9,535	8,732
Total Mac net sales	17,479	13,859	14,354
iPod	8,274	8,091	9,153
Other music related products and services (c)	4,948	4,036	3,340
iPhone and related products and services (d)	25,179	13,033	6,742
iPad and related products and services (e)	4,958	0	0
Peripherals and other hardware (f)	1,814	1,475	1,694
Software, service and other net sales (g)	2,573	2,411	2,208
Total net sales	$65,225	$42,905	$37,491

(a) Includes iMac, Mac mini, Mac Pro and Xserve product lines.

(b) Includes MacBook, MacBook Air and MacBook Pro product lines.

(c) Includes iTunes Store sales, iPod services, and Apple-branded and third-party iPod accessories.

(d) Includes revenue recognized from iPhone sales, carrier agreements, services, and Apple-branded and third- party iPhone accessories.

(e) Includes revenue recognized from iPad sales, services and Apple-branded and third-party iPad accessories.

(f) Includes sales of displays, wireless connectivity and networking solutions, and other hardware accessories.

(g) Includes sales of Apple-branded operating system and application software, third-party software, Mac and Internet services.

Source: Apple Inc. Annual Report 2010.

Steve Jobs announced at the Macworld Conference & Expo in January 2008 that the upgraded version of Apple TV would allow owners to order movies directly from the TV rather than having to download them to their computers.[37] Jobs said, "Apple TV was designed to be an accessory for iTunes and your computer. It was not what people wanted. We learned what people wanted was movies, movies, movies."[38]

By 2011, Apple had redesigned Apple TV with a focus on providing the kind of entertainment that would appeal to the masses. Smaller in size by 80 percent, it had a built-in power supply, was energy efficient, and stayed cool without a fan. Everything (movies, TV shows, photos, and music) streamed wirelessly to Apple TV. Features included instant access to SD and HD movies, often on the same day they came out on DVD; instant TV show rentals; direct access to a Netflix account from an HDTV; access to Internet content such as YouTube videos, HD podcasts, Flickr photos, and MobileMe galleries; and access to an iTunes library. In addition, with a free remote app from the App Store, the Apple TV could be controlled by an iPhone, iPad, or iPod touch. With AirPlay, music, photos, and videos could be streamed from an iPhone, iPad, and iPod touch to Apple TV. At a price of $99, the future of the new Apple TV looked promising.[39]

iPad

Tablets had been around for approximately 20 years before the iPad was introduced in 2010, but the new Apple iPad had many more innovative features and capabilities than any of its predecessors. The iPad was considered a completely new portable computing model, and from the beginning, Apple wanted to show consumers that it was more than just a "newfangled tablet"; it was a new approach to mobile computing and a great productivity device.[40]

The iPad had a touchscreen display that measured approximately 10 inches, and a number of functions such as games, music, videos, accessing the Internet, checking e-mail, and serving as an e-reader for books, magazines, and newspapers.[41] A mobile keyboard and keyboard dock allowed users to do work on it similar to a laptop. The iBook's application for purchasing and storing e-books was also introduced.[42] In addition, Apple used its own processor for the device.

Although some analysts were skeptical in the beginning about who the target customer was for this new tablet, it was eventually concluded that "the customer is everyone who likes cool technology."[43] The iPad was named Best Tablet on *PCWorld* magazine's list of the Best Products of 2010, and sales of the iPad soared to approximately $5 billion the first year.[44] Apple sold 300,000 devices on the first day.[45]

Amid much hype and anticipation, the iPad 2 was launched in March 2011. It was thinner than the original iPad and offered upgrades such as a new AF chip that provided faster graphics processing and general performance; dual cameras for video chat, HD video recording, and stills; an improved design incorporating internal magnets for the Smart Cover accessory; 3G versions available on AT&T and Verizon Wireless; improved AirPlay features; and the ability to support HDMI output via an optional adapter.[46] The iPad 2 was named Editor's Choice for tablets by *PCWorld* and was widely considered the benchmark tablet to beat, with a "top-notch seamless design paired with a robust app store."[47]

One key component that must be in place to have good media content for the iPod, iPhone, Apple TV, and iPad products is the relationship that Apple has with each of its media and phone service suppliers.

Service Suppliers

iTunes

By 2007, iTunes had agreements with all four major record labels (the now merged Sony BMG, as well as EMI, Universal, and Warner Bros.) as well as more than 200 independent labels. These agreements allowed iTunes to sell the music owned by these labels and pay the record label each time a song was downloaded. This deal was considered a reseller agreement, meaning that Apple was not licensing content from these labels, but rather buying it wholesale and reselling it to consumers.[48] Apple was allowed to keep its share, while the portion the label received was divided among many parties including artists, producers, and publishers. Labels earned approximately 70 cents per song sold on iTunes. This figure may seem small, but it was still greater than losing money to the millions of illegal downloads that nearly crippled the music industry at that time.

The revenues for record labels dropped in 2006 and 2007 due to tough market conditions, and Apple introduced a strategy to help increase revenues by at least a small percentage. It contracted with EMI to make its entire catalog available to iTunes' users in two formats: the traditional download option, which included the FairPlay digital rights management (DRM) software and DRM-free versions. The DRM software limited the number of times a song could be copied, which decreased the quality of the song. The DRM-free versions would deliver greater quality music but would require a higher price tag. iTunes started the DRM-free songs at $1.29 per song versus the traditional $0.99 per song.

DRM software was developed to protect music from unlimited copying and piracy. After the DRM restrictions were removed from the EMI songs, the industry was able to obtain hard data on how removing DRM restrictions from legally purchased music affected piracy. According to Bill Rosenplatt, DRM specialist and president of GiantSteps Media Technology Strategies, "The statistics show that there's no effect on piracy."[49] Since DRM did not discourage piracy, it was soon considered to be simply a nuisance to the user.[50] Record companies that were previously extremely cautious about selling their music on iTunes became extremely interested in obtaining access to iTunes' millions of customers. In January 2009, Apple announced that all four major music labels (Universal Music Group, Sony BMG, Warner Music Group, and EMI) and thousands of independent labels would offer music in iTunes Plus, which was Apple's DRM-free format.[51] In addition, companies such as Amazon and Netflix that compete with Apple in the sales of music and videos have taken advantage of Apple's customer base by offering applications for their products and services for use on Apple devices through the App Store.

The App Store

The App Store, opened in 2008, offers software applications for the iPhone, iPod touch, and iPad that are created by third-party software developers. The number of apps available surpassed 100,000 by the end of 2009, and by spring 2011 there were more than 350,000 apps available. Many apps are free to users, others cost relatively small amounts, and thousands of new apps are added monthly. The App Store has been a significant source of revenue for Apple, which charges a fee of 30 percent of the sales of third-party apps.[52]

On February 15, 2011, Apple announced a new subscription plan for "all publishers of content-based apps on the App Store, including magazines, newspapers, video, music, etc."[53] Publishers have the ability to determine subscriptions to be weekly, monthly, bimonthly, quarterly, biannual, or annual. The subscription is paid at the time the customer places the order and subscriptions are managed through the user's iTunes account. Personal information provided by customers through the App Store is sent to the publisher and is subject to the publisher's privacy policy, not Apple's.[54]

Apple will use the same billing system currently used for apps and in-app purchases for the subscription service, which means Apple will charge publishers 30 percent of the revenue. Publishers, however, can waive fees for existing subscribers and can advertise and sell subscriptions outside the App Store on company Web sites. In these cases, customer information is not exchanged through Apple and, as stated by Steve Jobs, "the publisher keeps 100 percent [of the profits] and Apple earns nothing."[55] Subscriptions purchased outside of the app must also be made available within the app at the same or lower price.[56]

Under the new plan, publishers will no longer have the ability to use the application to send users outside of the app to purchase content or subscriptions. For example, Amazon will be required to change its Kindle app, which sends users to a "mobile version of the Kindle Store Web site" for purchases.[57] Other services, including Netflix, Rhapsody, Spotify, and Hulu Plus, will also lose 30 percent of in-app subscription sales, which could lead to higher prices for customers. Since Apple continues to dominate the smartphone and fast-growing tablet markets, switching to a different platform such as Android does not currently appear feasible.[58]

Most magazine publishers have balked at the idea of giving up 30 percent of their profits to Apple and have chosen to sell single issues of selected titles instead. However, on April 11, 2011, Bloomberg L.P. agreed to the new terms and *Bloomberg Businessweek* subscriptions became available on the iTunes Store.[59] In return for the 30 percent of each subscription sold on iTunes, the publisher will gain access to the readers who purchased iPads in 2010 (14.8 million potential subscribers) and to the 40 to 50 million (or more) who are anticipated to purchase an iPad or iPad 2 in 2011.[60]

Following is the *Wall Street Journal* list of publishers who have and have not agreed to Apple's terms as of April 11, 2011:[61]

Have agreed:

- *Bloomberg Businessweek*: $2.99 per month
- *Elle*: $2.99 per month or $18.00 per year
- *Popular Science*: $14.99 per year
- *Maxim*: N/A

Have not agreed:

- Time Inc., publisher of *Time, Fortune, People, Sports Illustrated*, and others.
- Condé Nast, publisher of *Vogue, The New Yorker, Vanity Fair*, and others.
- Hearst Corp., publisher of *Esquire, Cosmopolitan, Harper's Bazaar*, and others.

Some publishers are waiting to see if the terms of the new plan will be modified before accepting, and all publishers are waiting to see if the terms can be improved. According to Philippe Guelton, executive vice president/chief operating officer at Hachette Filipacchi Media US (publisher of Elle), "This is a work in progress. I don't think this is something that is set in stone either for us or for Apple. I'd rather work with them to improve it over time than just sit on the sidelines."[62]

Apple TV

Apple did not have an easy time finalizing contracts with movie studios that would allow Apple to sell movies on iTunes for use on the iPod and Apple TV. Not only were the studios concerned about losing significant revenues from the sales of DVDs and Blu-ray discs, but some studios urged Apple to require a watermark on digital video for it to play on its devices. Their concern was heightened given the pirating experienced in the music download business. One movie studio executive said, "Our position is, if you want our content, you have to protect our business." Apple, however, responded that it trusted its consumers not to play pirated movies.[63]

The limited number of movie downloads available on iTunes would significantly diminish the success of Apple TV. Thus, Apple's CEO was persistent in his negotiations with the movie studios. Jobs announced at the Macworld Expo in 2008 that Apple had reached agreement with the following major studios: Twentieth Century Fox, The Walt Disney Studios, Warner Bros., Paramount, Sony Pictures Entertainment, MGM, Lionsgate, and New Line Cinema.[64] Despite NBC's issues with Apple concerning TV shows, Universal Pictures (owned by NBC and General Electric) agreed to allow Apple to rent its movies via iTunes.

The original supplier agreement between Apple and the movie studios was that new movies would not be available for rent until 30 days after the DVD was distributed. Within a 24-hour period, customers would be able to watch a film as many times as they wanted once the movie was started. Movies that were downloaded but not started would not be available for viewing after 30 days.[65]

By 2011, thousands of releases from every major Hollywood studio, along with select TV shows from all the networks, were available on iTunes for rent or purchase in standard or high definition and were available for streaming on Macs or PCs, iPhones, iPads, iPod touch, or television via Apple TV.[66]

iPhone

Cingular was selected as the exclusive wireless carrier for the iPhone because, according to Steve Jobs, Cingular was the best and most popular carrier in the US.[67] Together, these companies developed the Visual Voicemail feature that allowed users to listen to selected voicemails rather than having to listen to all messages in succession. After the agreement was made between Cingular and Apple and the iPhone was introduced, Cingular was acquired by AT&T and iPhone owners were required to sign a two-year service agreement with AT&T.[68] After numerous complaints that AT&T was the only service provider available to iPhone users in the US, Apple made its iPhone available through Verizon Wireless in February 2011.[69]

International service providers for iPhone include China Unicom, Deutsch Telekom, and O2. The iPhone was distributed in approximately 90 countries through 166 carriers worldwide in 2010.[70]

Hardware

Apple is not usually forthcoming with information about its hardware suppliers. Major electronics companies consider their supply chain operations to be trade secrets. However, a disassembled 2008 iPhone revealed that the microprocessor chip was supplied by Samsung; Philips, Texas Instruments, and Linear Technology all played a role in providing the batteries, and many other companies provided chips that were central to the camera, display, and motion sensor.[71]

In 2011, industry analysts estimated that Apple obtained approximately 35 percent of its lightweight flash memory chips used in its iPhones and iPads from Toshiba, and the remaining 65 percent from South Korea.[72]

The possibility of disruptions in the supply chain because of natural disasters that occur overseas is one of the potential risks facing all companies that operate in the global market. On March 11, 2011, the same day that the iPad 2 became available for sale, northern Japan was devastated by an 8.9 magnitude earthquake that set off a tsunami. During the aftermath in Tokyo, trains and phones were down, all hotels were booked, and roads were closed or jammed with traffic. Apple store and corporate employees were allowed to stay overnight at Apple stores. As the senior store managers had stocked break rooms with food and beverages after the first earthquake hit, employees asked and were allowed to have their family members stay at the stores as well. The heads of Apple International HR and of Japan Retail were in Japan that week; they also spent the night at Apple stores.[73] In addition, Apple created a donation page, a special iTunes link in its iTunes store, where people could easily donate to the Red Cross to benefit Japan.[74]

After the earthquake, analysts attempted to gauge the effects that would be felt by Apple, as shipping times for the iPad 2 went from three to five days to four to five weeks. In the two weeks following the earthquake, Apple's stock fell more than 5 percent.[75]

iSupply Research's Andrew Rassweiler identified five key Apple product components that were produced in Japan: NAND flash memory from Toshiba, DRAM (dynamic random access memory) from Elpida Memory Inc., an electronic compass from AKM Semiconductor, the touchscreen overlay glass from Asahi Glass Co., and the system battery from Apple Japan Inc.[76] According to Rassweiler, Apple would be able to obtain the NAND and DRAM from other companies, such as Samsung and Micron, but the battery compass and glass would

be more difficult to obtain elsewhere. Analyst Gene Munster with Piper Jaffray pointed out that Apple was probably in a better position than its competitors as it tends to buy components in large pre-payment deals that guarantee supply and pricing.[77]

Many suppliers have expressed frustration in working with Apple because Steve Jobs has been very clear on his vision for his products and has a reputation for being controlling. Maintaining good supplier relationships and keeping enough control to provide the quality of products expected of Apple is a balance that Apple will have to maintain to stay ahead of its competitors.

Competitors

iTunes

Since the October 2003 launch of iTunes.com for Windows, Apple has faced a multitude of competitors. During the late 1990s, the emergence of music sharing came about with Napster, a freeware program offering free downloads using peer-to-peer transfers. Peer-to-peer transfers allow users to connect directly with other users without the need for a central point of management.[78] However, due to legal proceedings, Napster and other competitors have become subscription services.

Napster. In May 1999, 19-year-old Shawn Fanning created Napster while a student at Northeastern University. The name "Napster" came from the Internet "handle" he had used as a programmer. He created a type of software that allowed music fans anywhere to "share" MP3s in one forum. During the first year of service, Napster was obtaining more than 250,000 new users a week while maintaining a free service.[79] This software creation led to the ever-growing controversy of the availability of MP3s on the Internet. Music sharing exploded in the late 1990s, and Napster's servers were overloaded with millions of requests a day for media downloads. Music artists considered this new "sharing" forum to be a continuous copyright violation. Fanning soon became the target of music industry animosity.

During 2000, Napster was in and out of court and was finally slated to shut down on July 26, 2000, though that decision was reversed two days later.[80] In 2001, Konrad Hilbers, a 38-year-old German, became CEO of the rapidly declining music file-sharing site. In June 2001, Napster had more than 26 million users, but growth was declining fast, going from 6.3 billion to 2.2 billion minutes used a day. On March 7, 2002, Napster closed its servers while opting to implement a fee-based service to comply with the federal judge's decision. On June 3, 2002, Napster filed for Chapter 11 bankruptcy in an effort to secure court-ordered protection from creditors. This move was part of the overall financial restructuring strategy of Bertelsmann AG, which was proceeding with its takeover of the once popular file-sharing system. By July 2003, Roxio, Inc., had acquired Napster and eventually relaunched Napster 2.0 as a successful, legal, fee-based service.[81]

Through restructuring and quality legal representation, Napster finally has a legal base that is expected to stand. In 2011, Napster's library was made up of more than 12 million songs. Members have unlimited access to the library for $5 to $10 (includes mobile access) per month. Napster now accommodates the use of its software for connected computers, iPhone, iPod, iPod touch, Android, BlackBerry, compatible TV, Blu-ray players, and other compatible home audio products.[82]

Kazaa. Sharman Networks Limited was founded in January 2002 as a private limited company that developed and marketed Internet applications, including Kazaa Media Desktop and Kazaa Plus. Sharman Networks earned revenue by soliciting companies to advertise on its software. Users that preferred ad-free use of the software were able to purchase an upgrade, Kazaa Plus, for $29.95. This upgrade also allowed for greater search capabilities and more download sources.[83]

Being Australian-based, the company avoided legal intervention in allowing the file sharing, but in 2005, the Federal Court of Australia ruled that Kazaa had knowingly allowed users to illegally download copyrighted songs. The company was charged to change its software to prohibit copyrighted music or videos from being shared.[84] Kazaa's owners agreed to pay the four major record labels (Universal Music, Sony BMG, EMI, and Warner Music) $100 million.[85]

Kazaa Media Desktop was a program rumored to be littered with spyware and ad-based programs that would "infect" consumer systems; thus many users became wary of accessing Kazaa's site.[86]

By 2011, Kazaa had become a subscription-based online digital music service owned by Internet marketing firm Atrinsic, offering unlimited plays and downloads, playlists, and music from all popular genres. Users could share playlists, rate and review their favorite artists, albums, songs, and playlists, "shout out" to people they would like to contact, and "follow" people they liked by following Kazaa on Facebook, Twitter, and MySpace. Ringtones for smartphones were also available through Kazaa.[87]

In March 2011, shares of Atrinsic more than doubled after the announcement was made that subscribers would be able to access Kazaa on iPads, iPhones, and Android-based devices by streaming it from Kazaa's Web site. This move was in response to Apple's recently announced plan to charge 30 percent on all revenue from the sale of online subscriptions through the App Store.[88]

RealNetworks, Inc. Through its RealPlayer Music Store, RealNetworks sought a price war with Apple by dropping its prices to $0.49 per song and $4.99 per album as compared to Apple's price of $0.99 and $9.99, respectively. Analysts indicated that RealNetworks was pricing below the cost of purchasing the music from the record companies, and eventually it did increase its price to $0.99 per song; however, it still offers select songs for $0.49 a track. As part of its battle to reduce Apple's market share, RealNetworks launched Harmony, which allowed RealNetworks users to translate songs purchased from RealPlayer Music Store into a format that could be played on an iPod and on Microsoft formats.[89]

RealPlayer is a RealNetworks medium through which it competes in the video-on-demand market. Video can be downloaded from any Web site to an iPod, PC, or DVD. With the RealPlayer video converter, users are able to convert many types of video files into the MP3 format needed for use on a computer, mobile phone, or portable device. Downloaded videos can be converted for playback on an iPod or iPhone. Video files can also be converted to audio files.[90] Digital media can be transferred to mobile devices from PCs and smartphones. RealPlayer customers can subscribe to its SuperPass membership that combines the benefits of RealPlayer and the RealPlayer Music Store. The $14.99 monthly fee provides subscribers with 10 music downloads per month, one game to keep per month, premium video feeds, RealPlayerPlus (with added features such as three times faster video downloads and the ability to create professional music CDs), and free antivirus and Internet security software.[91]

In August 2003, RealNetworks purchased the digital music service Rhapsody, and in 2007, formed Rhapsody America in a joint venture with MTV Networks. This company was spun off in 2010 as Rhapsody International. By 2011, Rhapsody continued to operate as an online music subscription service, providing over 10 million songs for $10 per month. Apps were made available for iPhone, iPod touch, Android, and BlackBerry.[92]

Walmart. Walmart launched its own online music store. It is currently the number two music retailer in the nation behind Apple. Walmart offers music in MP3 format at price points of $0.64, $0.94, and $1.24 per song, with many albums offered at $7.00 or less.[93]

Amazon. Amazon offers more than 15 million songs and albums that can be played on any Android device, PC, or Mac. Customers must have an Amazon account to purchase music from the Amazon MP3 store. Digital music purchases can be downloaded directly onto a player using the Amazon MP3 Downloader for Windows Media Player or iTunes, downloaded to a Mac or PC, or saved to Amazon's online storage service, Amazon Cloud Drive. The Amazon MP3 Store is only available to customers in the US who have a credit or debit card issued by a US bank with a US billing address. In addition, customers must be physically located in the US at the time of purchase.[94]

Apple TV

By 2011, the video-on-demand business had become so lucrative that it had attracted a myriad of competitors. Among the many competitors offering movies and/or TV shows for free, rent, or purchase via downloading or streaming were cable television service providers such as Cox Communications and Time Warner, television networks such as HBO, satellite TV providers such as DISH Network and DIRECTV, online distributors with or without subscription services such as Apple's iTunes, Netflix, Vudu, and CinemaNow, electronics retailers such as Walmart (Vudu) and Best Buy (CinemaNow), online retailers such as Amazon, and movie studios such as Disney and Warner Brothers. In addition, companies that manufactured viewing devices such as HD TVs, DVD and Blu-Ray disc players, gaming consoles, computers, smartphones, MP3 players, and other portable handheld devices offered software that was preloaded.

Following are some of Apple TV's and iTunes' competitors.

Amazon Unbox. The Amazon Unbox Video Player was introduced in 2006. Users download videos or TV shows from Amazon Instant Video to the Amazon Unbox Player or Windows Media Player. The Unbox Video Player is not compatible with Mac or Linux computers, and downloaded videos cannot be transferred to iPods.[95]

In addition, Amazon sells a wide variety of Amazon Instant Video compatible devices such as the Logitech Revue Companion Box, the Roku HD Streaming Player, TiVo TCD746320 Premiere DVR, along with compatible HDTVs from Vizio, Samsung, and Panasonic and Blu-ray disc players from Sony and Panasonic. There are more than 90,000 movies and TV shows available for instant viewing through Amazon Instant Video.[96]

CinemaNow. This company seemed to be ahead of the game, entering the video download market in 1999. It was the first to offer pay-per-view movies from the major Hollywood studios, the first to offer download-to-own services, and the first distributor of burn-to-DVD movies. It is headquartered in Marina Del Rey, California, and its library consists of more than 10,000 movie titles, television programs, music concerts, and shorts.[97]

Movie rentals, memberships and downloads for purchase are available from popular movie companies such as Disney, MGM, 20th Century Fox, and Miramax. Its service also offers streaming video and HD downloads that are compatible with Windows mobile-based portable media centers. A "Burn to DVD" section has recently been added that allows users to burn selected titles to be played on DVD players.[98]

The monthly membership fee is $29.95 and includes adult content videos, news and concert downloads, and access to approximately 1,400 free videos. It does not include unlimited access to Hollywood "hit" movies, which are offered on a pay-per-movie basis. Movie rentals range in price from $1.99 to $3.99 each, with unlimited access for 24 hours after the movie is started.[99] Although the downloads are compatible with Microsoft products, CinemaNow services are not available for Apple products or through Internet browsers other than Internet Explorer.

In 2011, CinemaNow received the number one ranking by TopTenREVIEWS.com for movie download service providers for its variety and availability of movie selections and ease of use of the service.[100] CinemaNow is owned by Sonic Solutions, which has Best Buy as a shareholder.[101]

Disney. Movies from the Disney Studios library are available at the Disney Movies Online Web site to "buy, rent and watch instantly."[102] "Watch instantly" means that customers can stream movies to any computer with an Internet connection at any time. Movies that are purchased or rented are stored in the customer's online movie library and do not require downloading to a computer; they can be accessed immediately by logging into Disney Movies Online.[103] Currently, Disney Movies cannot be accessed through most portable video devices and work best on a dedicated computer.[104]

In 2009, Disney acquired a 30 percent stake in Hulu, the digital content distribution service. Disney also distributes films and TV shows through Apple's iTunes store. Steve Jobs is Disney's largest individual stockholder, having acquired a 7 percent holding when Disney purchased Pixar.[105]

Netflix. Netflix subscribers (numbering more than 20 million by 2011) can stream an unlimited number of movies and TV shows per month to their PCs or TVs, unconstrained by hourly limits, for a monthly fee with plans starting at $7.99 per month.[106] DVD rentals are also available for delivery through the US Postal Service from distribution centers located in major cities in the US. Currently Netflix plans to invest heavily in streaming content and possible agreements with pay TV channels and networks such as HBO. Netflix also plans to expand its online streaming service internationally. Netflix gained many new subscribers during the recession as people stayed home to save money and looked for inexpensive sources of entertainment.[107]

Walmart. In December 2006, Walmart entered the movie download segment of the entertainment industry, but only a year later, it exited the business because it had not caught on with consumers. Raul Vasquez, Walmart's CEO for walmart.com, stated that the download service was an experiment. "We want to understand what the customers want. And I think what we learned is that the initial experience of buying and downloading content needs to be better. We thought it was going to be easier for the customer to understand."

Then, in 2010, Walmart decided to re-enter the lucrative and increasingly popular online video business by purchasing the movie download service Vudu. According to Walmart Vice-Chairman Eduardo Castro-Wright, the Vudu purchase would "provide customers with unprecedented access to home entertainment options as they migrate to a digital environment."[108]

Vudu, headquartered in Santa Clara, California, entered the video-on-demand market in April 2007. Vudu's original black box connected to the TV and Internet, and the built-in hard drive gave users the option of viewing 5,000 movie titles instantly. The box was priced at $400. The service had no monthly service charge, but the rental cost was $2 to $4 per movie. As such, Vudu claimed to be the cure-all for the movie rental business; it saved customers from running back and forth to the video store or waiting for the movie to come in the mail from Netflix or Blockbuster; it offered more movie titles than video-on-demand providers; and it was more functional than Internet download services because it did not require a PC. Similar to Vudu's competitors, once a movie was downloaded, it had to be viewed within 24 hours.[109]

Offered on Walmart's Web site, Vudu services are available in the US only and can be used on devices from LG, Mitsubishi Electric, Vizio, Samsung, Viore, Panasonic, Sharp, Sony PlayStation, Philips, Sanyo, Toshiba, Magnavox, and RCA. There is no monthly subscription fee or contract and there are no late fees. New releases are available the same day they come out on DVD, and titles are available at $2 for two nights. Walmart also offers Vudu-enabled devices for sale, including HDTVs, Blu-ray disc players, PS3 consoles, and home theater systems. Through the acquisition of Vudu, Walmart also hoped to increase hardware sales.[110]

Warner Brothers. A new venue offering video for rent or purchase was announced by Warner Brothers on March 8, 2011. Shares of Netflix stock fell $11.95 to $195.45 after Warner Brothers announced that it would offer videos through social network Facebook, which has more than 500 million active users.[111]

Time Warner had previously expressed the opinion that the $7.99 per month streaming service offered by Netflix devalued movies and TV shows. Using Facebook, users would be able to click a "rent" icon and pay with $3 in Facebook Credits. Facebook would get a share of the sales when credits were used. According to Jefferies & Co. analyst Youssef H. Squali, "The $3 rental appears to preserve the value of content in studios' eyes." He added that other studios may follow Warner Brothers, considering Facebook's large customer base and the potential to make a profit from a-la-carte rentals.[112] Videos will be available for viewing on all devices that offer Facebook, including Apple products.[113]

However, according to Goldman, Sachs & Co. analyst James Mitchell, the Warner Brothers service is not an immediate threat to Netflix as it currently offers only pay-per-view, is not available at a centralized storefront, and cannot be easily viewed on larger-screen televisions.[114]

iPhone

When the iPhone was introduced in 2007, it revolutionized the cell phone business. The iPhone became the benchmark that other manufacturers rushed to imitate. The competition is fierce, with numerous contenders struggling for market share. Several companies that manufacture the iPhone's competitors follow.

Motorola. Motorola has been a long-time leader in mobile phone sales in the United States. However, since Apple's iPhone and Research In Motion's (RIM) BlackBerry began to gain ground, the leader fell hard and fast. Motorola's RAZR phone lost its popularity and its smartphone made in partnership with Microsoft, the Motorola Q, did not perform as expected. Motorola announced in January 2008 that it was seeking alternatives for its handset business, most likely a divestiture.[115]

In 2008, Motorola sold 100 million phones, but in 2009 it sold only 55 million, a 45 percent decrease. By 2010, sales rebounded with its introduction of 22 new phone models. By the end of the third quarter of 2010, its Mobile Devices segment was profitable for the first time in three years.[116]

In January 2011, Motorola spun off its smartphone business into the stand-alone company, Motorola Mobility. After the spinoff, Motorola was renamed Motorola Solutions. Motorola Mobility took over the mobile devices, wireless accessories, set-top boxes, and video distribution systems products. Motorola Mobility operates in 40 countries, and has major facilities in Brazil, China, Taiwan, and the US.[117]

Motorola's Milestone XT720 was the first smartphone running Google's Android 2.1 operating system to offer the Xenon flash for use in taking pictures and shooting videos. The Xenon flash was more powerful than the usual LED illumination, allowing flash pictures to be taken at lower light levels and greater distances. Additional features include GPS navigation, FM radio, and a 3.5-millimeter audio jack.[118]

The Motorola Droid X was also considered one of the top smartphones introduced in summer 2010. With a 4.3-inch WVGA 854-by-480-resolution display and a few third-party video apps preinstalled, the Droid X could also be used as a portable video player.[119]

Research In Motion. The BlackBerry, created by Research In Motion (RIM), has been a popular product among corporate consumers who mainly needed e-mail service and a calendar. To stay in the competitive game, however, RIM added features to make its product more appealing to users who want fun features in addition to the features that aid in their work.[120]

In an effort to compete with Apple's popular App Store, in 2010 RIM introduced a similar mobile software store named BlackBerry App World. Software tools and games could be purchased that would appeal to users and add functionality to their phones. RIM sells BlackBerry products to customers in approximately 170 countries. Its largest market is the US, with approximately 60 percent of sales, followed by Canada and the United Kingdom.[121]

RIM's BlackBerry Bold 9800, re-named the Blackberry Torch 9800, was the first device to offer the Blackberry OS 6 operating system. The new OS provided an improved browser, enhanced multimedia experience, and improved user interface; however, the display and processor were not upgraded and the phone did not compare well with many of the other smartphones. This was also RIM's first slider phone, with a touchscreen, full QWERTY keyboard, and track pad. Originally anticipated to be a viable competitor for the iPhone 4, the phone's features and performance fell short of analysts' predictions.[122] However, BlackBerry has many loyal fans and RIM continues to be a strong contender in the smartphone market with its 2011 product lineup.

HTC. Established in 1997, HTC is a Taiwanese company that partners with Microsoft for its Windows Mobile operating system. Other strategic partners include Intel, QUALCOMM, and Texas Instruments in the US. Currently HTC offers smartphones using the Windows Mobile operating system or the Google Android software operating system. Many of HTC's products are self-branded, but some carry HTC's subsidiary Dopod's name. Dopod International is a mobile phone vendor in China and other Asian markets. Other products are re-branded using the names of partnering mobile operators such as T-Mobile, AT&T, Verizon, and Sprint.[123] HTC also partners with five leading operators in Europe.[124]

HTC offered three phones that were considered competitors for the iPhone 4: the HTC Incredible using the Android 2.1 operating system and offered by Verizon, the HTC Evo 4G using the Android 2.1 operating system and offered by Sprint, and the HTC HD2 using the Windows Mobile 6.5 operating system and offered by T-Mobile.[125]

By 2011, Google, Apple, and RIM were the main competitors in the smartphone arena. According to data from Nielsen, Google's Android operating system was the most popular in the US with 29 percent of market share. Apple's iOS and RIM's BlackBerry OS tied with 27 percent each.[126] The remainder of the market share was divided among Microsoft's Windows Mobile and Windows Phone 7 combined at 10 percent, HP's Palm WebOS at 4 percent, and Nokia's Symbian at 2 percent.[127]

Apple and RIM, which make their own devices with their own operating systems, continue to dominate the market for devices with their 27 percent market share each. Third-place HTC garnered approximately 12 percent share with the Android operating system and 7 percent with Microsoft's mobile OS. Motorola and Samsung followed.[128]

iPod

MP3 players are available in a wide range of sizes and colors, and offer a variety of features. The "one-size-fits-all" MP3 player does not exist, as some consumers want a small player for use at the gym, while others need a tablet-sized player with wide-screen video playback.[129] Manufacturers continue to add new features to their players in an effort to set them apart from the competition, and the resulting variety of players and features offered can be confusing. Features to be considered include color screens, photo viewing and video playback capabilities, radio, wireless capability, music recording, data storage, personal information management, sound-tweaking options, advanced playback features, and battery type and life.[130]

Not surprisingly, iPods are among the most popular MP3 players on the market. The current leader is the iPod touch 2010 (32GB), which is ranked first and was Editor's Choice on CNET Reviews' (reviews.cnet.com) Best 5 MP3 Players list.[131] This is the fourth-generation iPod touch, with photo and video capture, FaceTime video chat, a high-resolution Retina display, and a GameCenter that allows social gaming with other iOS devices. It is also *PCWorld* magazine's Editor's Choice MP3 player.[132] Competitors include the Zune HD

(32GB), the SanDisk Sansa Clip+ (4GB), and the Sony X-Series Walkman (16GB).

Also appearing on reviews.cnet.com's Best 5 MP3 Players list is the sixth-generation iPod Nano 2010 (8GB). This model is almost less than half the size of the previous versions, and includes unique features such as Genius Mixes (preselected compilations of songs from the user's iTunes library), Genius playlists, FM radio with pause and replay capability, and a pedometer.[133]

iPad

The iPad 2 became available for purchase in the US on Friday, March 11, 2011. It was scheduled to hit stores Friday afternoon, but those who couldn't wait until then to own one of the new devices could purchase one online beginning at 2:00 AM.[134] To emphasize the importance of the iPad to Apple, Steve Jobs emerged from medical leave to introduce the new version to bloggers and Apple enthusiasts. On March 25, the iPad 2 went on sale in 26 other markets including Mexico and New Zealand, as well as Spain and other European countries.[135]

The newly released iPad 2 easily dominated its competitors, according to tests conducted by *Consumer Reports*. In a test that evaluated devices using 17 different criteria, the iPad 2 was rated "excellent" in nearly every category, in particular, "touch-screen responsiveness, versatility, portability, screen glare, and ease of use."[136] *Consumer Reports* electronics editor Paul Reed said, "So far, Apple is leading the tablet market in both quality and price, which is unusual for a company whose products are usually premium priced. However, it's likely we'll see more competitive pricing in tablets as other models begin to hit the market."[137] Technology analysts also view the iPad 2 as the top contender in the tablet market.

The Motorola Xoom is the only tablet considered to be in the same league with the iPad or the iPad 2. The Xoom was the first tablet to feature Google's tablet-centric Android 3.0 (called "Honeycomb") operating system. Samsung's Galaxy Tab ranked third behind the iPad 2 and the Xoom.[138]

Technology analysts at Gartner Research predict that Apple will continue to dominate the tablet market through 2015. iPad sales in 2011 are forecast at 48 million compared to approximately 13.9 million tablets that use Google's Android operating system. Analyst Carolina Milanese said, "Many [tablet vendors] are making the same mistake that was made in the first response wave to the iPhone, as they are prioritizing hardware features over applications, services and overall user experience. Tablets will be much more dependent on the latter than smartphones have been, and the sooner vendors realize that, the better chance they have to compete head-to-head with Apple."[139] Much of Apple's continued success and dominance over the competition has been due to the ingenuity of its marketing efforts.

Marketing

Apple's marketing endeavors have earned it awards, product sales, and a devoted base of customers, both new and old. Apple has won accolades for its marketing abilities and its focus on innovation. It has been hailed as one of the best marketers by many different sources and has had a reputation over the years of being a brand that can gain customers through its well-thought-out and carefully executed marketing strategies.

Marketing has been one of Apple's strengths; however, staying on top of the game has become more difficult as Apple develops a broader range of products for the mainstream customer rather than just the "tech-savvy fanatics" in fields such as education and design.[140] "The customer base is now more diverse, including students and mainstream consumers, and it's harder to satisfy as a whole," says Lopo L. Rego, a marketing professor at the University of Iowa.[141] Business leaders today have a daunting job in balancing shareholder demands and running a successful company. Businesses want to market new products aggressively to try and ensure their products' success. Apple heavily promoted the iPhone when it was introduced in July 2007. Customer and investor expectations, due to Apple's reputation, boosted the stock price.

Apple garnered major success for iPod and iTunes by way of strategic partnerships with other well-known brands. Apple created marketing agreements with Volkswagen of America, Burton Snowboards, Nike, and Starbucks. By affiliating itself with different brands, Apple gained consumer confidence as well as exposure through marketing partner advertisements.

Marketing Plan

A marketing plan begins with design of the product.[142] In an industry of low profit margins and cost cutting, Apple takes a different approach to the design of its products. While competitors do everything they can to keep costs down, Apple does what it can to make its product different. Its former CEO, Steve Jobs, has been called "a legend for his design sense."[143] Even employees of one of Apple's biggest competitors, Microsoft, recognized Apple's dominance in the design of eye-catching products; the employees created a mock promotion for the iPod had it been created by Microsoft and circulated the video on YouTube.[144]

The typical Apple ad has been called "arresting in its minimalism, culturally resonating, and stunning enough to stop people in their tracks on probably the most crowded stretch of New York City."[145] Apple's advertising focuses more on a lifestyle instead of a product, and has helped create a cult-like loyalty among Apple enthusiasts. Customers are made to feel as if purchasing an Apple product "got them into a hip global family."[146] Apple spent $501 million on global advertising in 2009, and in 2010 it received *Advertising Age*'s first "Marketer of the Decade" award. *Adweek* also named Apple's "Get a Mac" and "Silhouettes" campaigns as the best of the decade in their respective categories.[147]

As stated in a *USA Today* article, "Apple's arsenal of attention-getting tools holds lessons for any company: design cool, innovative products. Have a streamlined product line. Invest in memorable ads. Work your customer base to make customers feel special and create word-of-mouth agents. Most important: keep the world and media surprised, to generate gobs of attention."[148]

Apple continues its history of memorable ads with the new 30-second television ad for the new iPad 2 that debuted on April 9, 2011. A narrator speaks over understated piano music, "This is what we believe… Technology alone is not enough. Faster, thinner, lighter; those are all good things. But when technology gets out of the way, everything becomes more delightful, even magical. That's when you leap forward. That's when you end up with something like this…"[149]

Steve Jobs is considered essential to the public relations and promotional aspect of Apple. As CEO, he maintained relationships with the media and was called the "public face and champion of the brand."[150] He was an expert when it came to talking with the press, maintaining relationships with magazine editors, and continually creating new relationships.[151] Because of his dynamic, high-energy personality, he usually held a new idea that he was energetic about and was always ready and willing to share the idea to gain exposure.

Jobs also took action in response to customer feedback to show that he was listening and concerned. For example, three months after the iPhone was available in stores, Apple cut the price of this product by one-third. This was a strategic move to increase demand and meet sales goals; it was not the result of a faulty product. Consumers who had purchased the iPhone in the first three months for the higher price expressed great dissatisfaction. Jobs responded by promising these consumers a $100 Apple store credit.[152]

In addition to online marketing and sales, Apple products are offered through its retail stores. Apple has opened more than 300 retail stores located in the US and approximately 80 stores in other countries. At the time that Apple opened its first retail store in 2001, analysts predicted that Apple would report huge losses and shut the store within two years. At the time, no computer manufacturer had proven profitable in running its own branded store.[153] However, Apple's retail stores contributed an estimated $2.4 billion and $1.7 billion in 2010 and 2009, respectively, representing 15 to 16 percent of its profits during the past two years (see Exhibit 5).[154] Apple's philosophy behind the stores is brand exposure. Apple believes that the more people can touch an Apple product and see what it can do with their own eyes, the greater the potential market share.[155] In addition, the stores provide free group workshops, personal training, and personal assistance for Apple customers.[156]

Apple offers a One-to-One program for an annual fee of $99 (available only at the time of purchase of a new Mac from the Apple Retail Store or the Apple Online Store);[157] subscribers can attend a tutorial session with an Apple expert for one hour once a week for one year. Apple customers can also consult with the staff at the "Genius Bar" by appointment. The Genius Bar is where Apple product users meet face-to-face with Apple's "geniuses" for answers to technical questions and for problem troubleshooting. In addition, customers wanting to purchase a new computer or other equipment can schedule an appointment with a shopping assistant who helps ensure that the customer selects the right equipment for his or her needs. "Apple has become the new gathering place," said Steven Addis, chief executive of Addis Creson, a brand strategy and design firm in Berkeley. "You can't help but get caught up with it when you first walk in."[158]

Going Global

Stephen Kobrin, a Wharton multinational management professor, explained in a recent interview that high-tech companies that are driven by technology that demands they expand into many countries simultaneously are "born global." He clarifies by further stating, "Companies that are born global tend to have high-tech products that immediately find acceptance in many different cultures and societies."[159]

Apple certainly meets Professor Kobrin's specifications for a company that was "born global," with reportable operating segments consisting of the Americas (North and South America), Europe (European countries), the Middle East, Africa, Japan, Asia-Pacific (Australia and Asia but not Japan), and the retail segment operating Apple-owned stores in the US and international markets.[160] At the end of fiscal year 2010, the Americas was the leading segment in sales ($24.5 billion) and operating income ($7.6 billion), followed by Europe with net sales of $18.7 billion and operating income of $7.5 billion.[161] Additional information on Apple's operating segments can be found in Exhibit 5.

Exhibit 5 Apple Summary Information by Operating Segment

Summary information by operating segment for the three years ended September 25, 2010 is as follows (in millions):	2010	2009	2008
Americas:			
Net sales	$24,498	$18,981	$16,552
Operating income	$ 7,590	$ 6,658	$ 4,901
Depreciation, amortization and accretion	$ 12	$ 12	$ 10
Segment assets (a)	$ 2,809	$ 1,896	$ 1,693
Europe:			
Net sales	$18,692	$11,810	$ 9,233
Operating income	$ 7,524	$ 4,296	$ 3,022
Depreciation, amortization and accretion	$ 9	$ 7	$ 6
Segment assets	$ 1,926	$ 1,352	$ 1,069
Japan:			
Net sales	$ 3,981	$ 2,279	$ 1,728
Operating income	$ 1,846	$ 961	$ 549
Depreciation, amortization and accretion	$ 3	$ 2	$ 2
Segment assets	$ 991	$ 483	$ 272
Asia-Pacific:			
Net sales	$ 8,256	$ 3,179	$ 2,686
Operating income	$ 3,647	$ 1,100	$ 748
Depreciation, amortization and accretion	$ 3	$ 3	$ 3
Segment assets	$ 1,622	$ 529	$ 390
Retail:			
Net sales	$ 9,798	$ 6,656	$ 7,292
Operating income	$ 2,364	$ 1,677	$ 1,661
Depreciation, amortization and accretion (b)	$ 163	$ 146	$ 108
Segment assets (b)	$ 1,829	$ 1,344	$ 1,139

(a) The Americas asset figures do not include fixed assets held in the U.S. Such fixed assets are not allocated specifically to the Americas segment and are included in the corporate and Retail assets figures below.

(b) Retail segment depreciation and asset figures reflect the cost and related depreciation of its retail stores and related infrastructure.

Source: Apple Inc. Annual Report 2010.

Apple, Innovation, and Steve Jobs

Steve Jobs led Apple on an unprecedented run of successful products and services that disrupted the music, mobile phone, media, and video game industries. Following ExxonMobil, Apple is now the second-most highly valued company in the world. On January 19, 2011, it announced a record-breaking profit of $6 billion in the first quarter of fiscal year 2011, which ended on December 25, 2010. This surpassed its previous high by 40 percent.[162] With more than 50,000 employees and a market capitalization of more than $300 billion, Apple has no debt and enough cash on hand to "buy any country it wants"[163] (see Exhibits 6, 7, and 8).

Much of Apple's success has been attributed to Jobs. With a unique ability to visualize innovative product designs and predict what people would like to have, Jobs was known to be obsessive about process and detail. He kept Apple focused on just a few products that had the potential for high return. He routinely sent products back to the lab, and insisted that Apple must build the best products, period. No product hit the market unless it met his exacting standards.[164]

Jobs will be difficult to replace—no other person at Apple has had the experience of founding the company, being asked to leave the company, and returning years later to save it from bankruptcy. Jobs is self-taught. He attended Reed College for a while, but dropped out after he became bored with his classes. Although he was not

Exhibit 6 Apple Inc. Consolidated Statements of Operations

CONSOLIDATED STATEMENTS OF OPERATIONS (In millions, except share amounts which are reflected in thousands and per share amounts)			
Three years ended September 25, 2810	**2010**	**2009**	**2008**
Net sales	$ 65,225	$ 42,905	$ 37,491
Cost of sales	39,541	25,683	24,294
Gross margin	25,684	17,222	13,197
Operating expenses:			
Research and development	1,782	1,333	1,109
Selling, general and administrative	5,517	4,149	3,761
Total operating expenses	7,299	5,482	4,870
Operating income	18,385	11,740	8,327
Other income and expense	155	326	620
Income before provision for income taxes	18,540	12,066	8,947
Provision for income taxes	4,527	3,831	2,828
Net income	$ 14,013	$ 8,235	$ 6,119
Earnings per common share:			
Basic	$ 15.41	$ 9.22	$ 6.94
Diluted	$ 15.15	$ 9.08	$ 6.78
Shares used in computing earnings per share:			
Basic	909,461	893,016	881,592
Diluted	924,712	907,005	902,139

Source: Apple Inc. Annual Report 2010.

trained in product design, he managed what could be the best design shop in the world. He does not have an M.B.A. degree, yet he is considered to be one of the world's leading business strategists. His marketing, communications, and salesmanship skills are unsurpassed.[165] Some analysts and other "Apple watchers" say that one of the best strategic moves Jobs made as CEO was to surround himself with extraordinary people.[166]

Apple has a reputation for hiring the best, most talented people in their disciplines. As a result, Apple has a team of highly skilled specialists with an operating system that more closely resembles a startup instead of an established company that nurtures and grooms seasoned executives to take over the CEO spot. One of Apple's specialists is former COO Tim Cook, who was selected by Jobs to be Apple's next CEO. Cook, a veteran of both IBM and Compaq, is known to be "an operations genius, adept at cutting costs while delivering complex products on time and coping with staggering growth."[167] Also, Cook successfully led the company during Jobs' three previous absences, one of which occurred in some of the worst months of the recession. However, during all his medical leaves, Jobs remained involved in all major strategic decisions; thus Cook will now be completely tested in the CEO role.

Thus, a nagging question on the minds of many analysts, Apple enthusiasts, employees, and shareholders is, "Will Apple survive without Steve Jobs?"

There is no doubt that Apple will carry on now that Jobs has officially retired. It has products in the pipeline for at least two years, maybe three, according to Barclays Capital analyst Ben Reitzes. He added, "They are on autopilot to a degree, at least in terms of the big picture."[168] There are additional indicators that Apple will continue to thrive.

Sales of the iPhone and iPad are surging: 16.24 million iPhones were sold in the fourth quarter of 2010. This represents an 86 percent growth over the same quarter a year ago. With the iPhone 4 recently made available on Verizon and the iPhone 5 anticipated later in 2011, analysts believe it is reasonable to expect that Apple will sell between 25 and 30 million iPhones in 2011. In addition, 7.33 million iPads were sold during the same quarter, up 70 percent from the 4.9 million sold in the previous quarter.[169] Though iPod sales decreased 7 percent for the quarter, they still sold 19.45 million of them. iPod sales could increase after Apple introduces its cloud streaming service later in 2011. Apple sold 13 million Macs, a 23 percent increase over the previous year.[170]

Exhibit 7 Apple Inc. Consolidated Balance Sheets

CONSOLIDATED BALANCE SHEETS (In millions, except share amounts)		
ASSETS:	**September 25, 2011**	**September 26, 2009**
Current assets:		
Cash and cash equivalents	$11,261	$ 5,263
Short-term marketable securities	14,359	18,201
Accounts receivable, less allowances of $55 and $52, respectively	5,510	3,361
Inventories	1,051	455
Deferred tax assets	1,636	1,135
Vendor non-trade receivables	4,414	1,696
Other current assets	3,447	1,444
Total current assets	41,678	31,555
Long-term marketable securities	25,391	10,528
Property, plant and equipment, net	4,768	2,954
Goodwill	741	206
Acquired intangible assets, net	342	247
Other assets	2,263	2,011
Total assets	$75,183	$47,501
LIABILITIES AND SHAREHOLDERS' EQUITY:		
Current liabilities:		
Accounts payable	$12,015	$ 5,601
Accrued expenses	5,723	3,852
Deferred revenue	2,984	2,053
Total current liabilities	20,722	11,506
Deferred revenue – non-current	1,139	853
Other non-current liabilities	5,531	3,502
Total liabilities	27,392	15,861
Commitments and contingencies		
Shareholders' equity:		
Common stock, no par value; 1,800,000,000 shares authorized; 915,970,050 and 899,805,500 shares issued and outstanding, respectively	10,668	8,210
Retained earnings	37,169	23,353
Accumulated other comprehensive (loss)/income	(46)	77
Total shareholders' equity	47,791	31,640
Total liabilities and shareholders' equity	$75,183	$47,501

Source: Apple Inc. Annual Report 2010.

Finally, as long as Jobs retained the CEO title, morale at Apple remained high. However, all will be watching Tim Cook and his team. Kaufman Brothers analyst Shaw Wu said to Reuters that Jobs' role is "important, but at the same time, as the company continues to execute, it becomes more secondary. The way Steve thinks, his methodology, his sense of style: frankly, a lot of it has been ingrained into the Apple culture."[171]

Although Apple will continue to face challenges as the company adjusts to operating without Steve Jobs, most analysts are confident that Apple will survive the loss. The coming months and years, as products flow through the pipeline, will tell if they are right or wrong.

Exhibit 8 Apple Inc. Consolidated Statements of Cash Flows

CONSOLIDATED STATEMENTS OF CASH FLOWS (In millions)			
Three years ended September 25,2010	**2010**	**2009**	**2008**
Cash and cash equivalents, beginning of the year	$ 5,263	$ 11,875	$ 9,352
Operating activities:			
Net income	14,013	8,235	6,119
Adjustments to reconcile net income to cash generated by operating activities:			
Depreciation, amortization and accretion	1,027	734	496
Stock-based compensation expense	879	710	516
Deferred income tax expense	1,440	1,040	398
Loss on disposition of property, plant and equipment	24	26	22
Changes in operating assets and liabilities:			
Accounts receivable, net	(2.142)	(939)	(785)
Inventories	(596)	54	(163)
Vendor non-trade receivables	(2,718)	586	110
Other current assets	(1,514)	163	(384)
Other assets	(120)	(902)	289
Accounts payable	6,307	92	596
Deferred revenue	1,217	521	718
Other liabilities	778	(161)	1,664
Cash generated by operating activities	18,595	10,159	9,596
Investing activities:			
Purchases of marketable securities	(57,793)	(46,724)	(22,965)
Proceeds from maturities of marketable securities	24,930	19,790	11,804
Proceeds from sales of marketable securities	21,788	10,888	4,439
Purchases of other long-term investments	(18)	(101)	(38)
Payments made in connection with business acquisitions, net of cash acquired	(638)	0	(220)
Payments for acquisition of property, plant and equipment	(2,005)	(1,144)	(1,091)
Payments for acquisition of intangible assets	(116)	(69)	(108)
Other	(2)	(74)	(10)
Cash used in investing activities	(13,854)	(17,434)	(8,189)
Financing activities:			
Proceeds from issuance of common stock	912	475	483
Excess tax benefits from stock-based compensation	751	270	757
Taxes paid related to net share settlement of equity awards	(406)	(82)	(124)
Cash generated by financing activities	1,257	663	1,116
Increase/(decrease) in cash and cash equivalents	5,998	(6,612)	2,523
Cash and cash equivalents, end of the year	$ 11,261	$ 5,263	$ 11,875
Supplemental cash flow disclosure: Cash paid for income taxes, net	$ 2,697	$ 2,997	$ 1,267

Source: Apple Inc. Annual Report 2010.

NOTES

1. http://store.apple.com/us?mco-NzcIMjVlwNQ.
2. G. Colvin, 2011, The world's most admired companies, *Fortune*, vol. 163, no. 4, March 21.
3. R. Safian, 2011, Letter from the editor, *Fast Company*, March, 17.
4. B. Morris, 2008, What makes Apple golden, *Fortune*, March 3.
5. D. Leonard, 2003, Songs in the key of Steve, *Fortune*, April 28.
6. M. Honan, 2009, Apple drops 'Computer' from name, Macworld, Macworld Expo, January 9, http://www.macworld.com/article/54770/2007/01/applename.html.
7. B. Stone and P. Burrows, 2011, The essence of Apple, *Bloomberg Businessweek*, January 24, 6.
8. Ibid.
9. Ibid.
10. R. E. Hoskisson, 2007, Strategic Focus: Apple: Using innovation to create technology trends and maintain competitive advantage, Hitt, Ireland, & Hoskisson, *Strategic Management: Competitiveness and Globalization*, 8th edition, South-Western Cengage Learning: Mason, OH.
11. Apple history, http://www.apple-history.com/frames.
12. Ibid.
13. L. Kimmel, 1998, Apple Computer, Inc.: A history, http://www.geocities.com/Athens/3682/applehistory.html.
14. Ibid.
15. http://apple-history.com.
16. Apple Computer history weblog, http://apple.computerhistory.org.
17. L. Kimmel, 1998, Apple Computer, Inc.: A history.
18. Apple Computer history weblog.
19. http://apple-history.com.
20. Ibid.
21. Apple Computer history weblog.
22. http://apple-history.com.
23. Ibid.
24. Ibid.
25. Ibid.
26. http://www.apple.com/itunes.
27. 2010 Apple Inc. annual report.
28. http://www.apple.com/itunes/what-is/
29. Ibid.
30. R. E. Hoskisson, Strategic Focus: Apple.
31. 2007, Apple reinvents the phone with iPhone, Apple Inc. press release, htttp://www.apple.com/pr/library/2007/01/09iphone.html,January 9.
32. 2011, Apple Inc., Hoover's company reports.
33. A. Zaky, 2011, Why Apple investors shouldn't sweat Android, *Fortune*, April 11, http://tech.fortune.cnn.com/2011/04/11/why-apple-investors-shouldnt-sweat-android/.
34. http://www.apple.com/phone/features/.
35. C. Ziberg, 2011, iPhone 5 Available by June 20?, *Motley Fool on MSNBC*, http://www.msnbc.msn.com/id/42183093/ns/business-motley_fool/
36. 2007, In three months, iPhone sales top a million, *New York Times*, http://www.nytimes.com, September 11.
37. M. Quinn & D. C. Chmielewski, 2008, Studios join Apple's movie rental service, *Los Angeles Times*, http://www.latimes.com, January 16.
38. C. Edwards, 2008, Jobs appeals to the crowd, *BusinessWeek*, January 15.
39. http://theapple.tv/history-of-apple-tv/.
40. T. Bajarin, 2010, How the iPad will change mobile computing, February 1, *PCMag*, http://www.pcmag.com/article2/0,2817,2358602,00.asp.
41. 2011, Apple Inc., Hoover's company reports.
42. T. Bajarin, 2010, How the iPad will change mobile computing, February 1, *PCMag*, http://www.pcmag.com/article2/0,2817,2358602,00.asp.
43. E. Griffin, 2010, Best products of 2010, *PCMag*, November 19, http://www.pcmag.com/article2/0,2817,2372799,00.asp.
44. 2011, Apple Inc., Hoover's company reports.
45. 2011, iPad 2 sales start with pre-dawn online orders, Associated Press, March 11, http://www.abc15.com/dpp/news/science_tech/ipad-2-sales-to-start-with-pre-dawn-online-orders
46. T. Gideon, 2011, Apple iPad 2 (Wi-Fi + 3G), *PCWorld*, March 9, http://www.pcmag.com/article2/0,2817,2381687,00.asp.
47. T. Gideon, 2011, How to buy the best tablet, *PCWorld*, March 31, http://www.pcmag.com/article2/0,2817,2382821,00.asp.
48. W. Cohen, www.rollingstone.com/news/newsarticle.asp?nid =18075.
49. T. Anderson, 2008, How Apple is changing DRM, *The Guardian*, May 15.
50. Ibid.
51. http://www.apple.com/pr/library/2009/01/06itunes.html.
52. 2011, Apple Inc., Hoover's company reports.
53. 2011, Apple launches subscriptions on the App Store, February 15, 2011, http://www.apple.com/pr/library/2011/02/15appstore.html.
54. B. Slattery, 2011, Apple subscription plan launched, *PCWorld*, February 15, http://www.pcworld.com/article/219702/apple_launches_app_store_subscriptions.html.
55. Ibid.
56. Ibid.
57. Ibid.
58. Ibid.
59. P. Elmer-DeWitt, 2011, iPad mags: Another publisher blinks, *Fortune*, April 11, http://tech.fortune.cnn.com/2011/04/11/ipad-mags-another-publisher-blinks/
60. Ibid.
61. Ibid.
62. N. Ives, 2011, Why Elle, Nylon and Pop Sci said yes to Apple's iPad subscription terms, *AdAgeMEDIAWORKS*, February 16, http://adage.com/article/mediaworks/elle-nylon-pop-sci-accepted-ipad-subscription-plan/148920/.
63. D. C. Chmielewski & M. Quinn, 2007, Technology; Movie studios fear the sequel to iPod; They see risk that new Apple TV signals effort to control distribution, *Los Angeles Times*, June 11, C1.38.
64. 2008, Apple premieres iTunes movie rentals with all major film studios, Apple press release, www.apple.com/pr/library, January 15.
65. Ibid.
66. http://www.apple.com/itunes/whats-on/#movies.
67. 2007, Apple chooses Cingular as exclusive U.S. carrier for its revolutionary iPhone, Apple Inc. press release, www.apple.com/pr/library/2007/01/09cingular.html, January 9.
68. 2008, http://www.apple.com/iphone.
69. http://www.apple.com/pr/library/2011/02/02iphone.html.
70. 2011, Apple Inc., Hoover's company reports.
71. A. Hesseldahl, 2007, Take the iPhone apart, *BusinessWeek*, http://www.businessweek.com, July 2.
72. C. Bruemmer, 2011, Electronic manufacturer supply chain hit by Japan earthquake-tsunami, http://www.toptenwholesale.com/news/electronic-manufacturer-supply-chain-hit-by-japan-earthquake-tsunami-3984.html.
73. K. Rose, 2011, Apple Japan goes the extra mile in earthquake's aftermath, *MacDailyNews*, March 15, http://macdailynews.com/2011/03/15/applejapan-goes-the-extra-mile-in-earchquake-aftermath/.
74. C. White, 2011, Apple & Microsoft take different approaches to Japan relief, *Mashable*, March 13, http://mashable.com/2011/03/13/apple-microsoft-japan/.
75. D. Goldman, 2011, Apple's iPad 2 supply concerns mount, *CNNMoney*, March 23, http://money.cnn.com/2011/03/23/technology/apple_ipad_japan_supply_chain_concerns/index.html.
76. P. Elmer-DeWitt, 2011, Japan supplied 5 key iPad parts, *Fortune*, March 18, http://tech.fortune.cnn.com/2011/03/18/5-key-ipad-parts-that-came-from-japan/?section=magazines_fortune.
77. Ibid.
78. 2001, Napster's history, http://w3.uwyo.edu/~pz/nap2.htm.

79. 2001, The history of the Napster struggle, http://www .theneworleanschannel.com/news/457209/detail.html.

80. 2003, Napster 2.0 to launch by Christmas, http://www.roxio.com/ en/company/news/archive/prelease030728.jhtml.

81. Ibid.

82. http://www.napster.com.

83. J. Ketola, 2003, Kazaa Plus service launched, http://www.afterdawn .com, August.

84. 2008, Wikipedia, http://en.wikipedia.org/wiki/kazaa.

85. Ibid.

86. 2003, Kazaa Usage Map, http://tools.waglo.com/kazaa.

87. http://www.kazaa.com/#/about.

88. S. I. Ahmed, 2011, Atrinsic says Kazaa users can stream music on phones, Reuters, March 7, http://www.reuters.com/ article/2011/03/07/us-atrinsic-shares-jdUSTRE72657320110307.

89. N. Wingfield, 2004, Price war in online music, *Wall Street Journal*, http://www.wsj.com, August 17.

90. http://www.real.com/realplayer/convert-video.

91. http://www.real.com/realplayer/player-plus.

92. http://www.rhapsody.com/-discover.

93. http://mp3.walmart.com/store/home.

94. http://www.amazon.com/go/help/customer/display.html/ref-hp _mp3store_gettingstarted/.

95. http://www.amazon.com/gp/video/ontv/player.

96. http://www.amazon.com/go/video/ontv/ref-sv_atv_2.

97. 2008, CinemaNow Inc., *BusinessWeek*, http://investing .businessweek.com, March 14; 2008, http://www.cinemanow.com; 2008, Wikipedia, http://en.wikipedia.org; A. Gonsalves, 2007, *InformationWeek*, http://www.informationweek.com, July 18.

98. 2011, CinemaNow, TopTenREVIEWS.com, http://movie-download -review.toptenreviews.com/cinemanow-review.html.

99. Ibid.

100. Ibid.

101. O. Kharif, 2010, Wal-Mart picks up digital VUDU, *Bloomberg Businessweek*, February 22, http://www.businessweek.com/ technology/content/feb2010/tc20100222_235241.html.

102. http://disneymoviesonline.go.com/movies.

103. Ibid.

104. Ibid.

105. 2011, The Walt Disney Company, Hoover's company reports.

106. 2011, Netflix, Hoover's company reports.

107. Ibid.

108. O. Kharif, 2010, Wal-Mart picks up digital VUDU, *Bloomberg Businessweek*, February 22, http://www.businessweek.com/ technology/content/feb2010/tc20100222_235241.html.

109. D. Pogue, 2007, High-speed video store in the living room, *The New York Times*, http://www.nytimes.com, September 6.

110. http://www.walmart.com/cp/vudu/1066144.

111. C. Edwards, B. Womack, & A. Sherman, 2011, Netflix falls as Warner Bros. offers Facebook movies, *Bloomberg*, http://www .bloomberg.com/news/2011-03-08/netflix-falls-as-warner-bros -starts-offering-movies-on-facebook.html.

112. Ibid.

113. Ibid.

114. Ibid.

115. J. Goldman, 2008, Motorola hangs up on handsets, http://www .cnbc.com, January 31; A. Hasseldahl, 2008, Blackberry vs. iPhone: Who wins? *BusinessWeek*, http://www.articles.moneycentral.msn .com, January 3.

116. 2011, Motorola Mobility Holdings, Inc., Hoover's company reports.

117. Ibid.

118. M. Ricknas, 2010, Motorola announces flashy Android phone, *PCWorld*, June 7, http://www.pcworld.com/article/198/159/ motorola_announces_flashy_android_phone.html.

119. G. Miles, 2010, Motorola Droid X: The best of the Droids, *PCWorld*, June 23, http://www.pcworld.com/article/199747/motorola_droid _is_the_best_of _the_droids.html.

120. J. Goldman, 2008, iPhone vs. Blackberry: Apple launches new software, http://www.cnbc.com, March 6.

121. 2011, Research in Motion Limited, Hoover's company reports.

122. B. Cha, 2010, The RIM BlackBerry Torch 9800, *CNET Reviews*, October 12, http://reviews.cnet.com/blackberry-torch -review#reviewPage1.

123. 2011, HTC Corporation, Hoover's company reports.

124. http://www.htc.com/www/about_htc.aspx

125. D. Ionescu, 2010, Apple iPhone 4 vs. The Rest of the Smartphone Pack, *PCWorld*, June 7, http://www.pcworld.com/article/198214/ apple_iphone_4_vs_the_rest_of_the_smartphone_pack.html.

126. L. Whitney, 2011, Android is No. 1 OS, but Apple, RIM rule devices, *CNET Reviews*, March 4, http://reviews.cnet.com/8301 -19736_7-20039240-251.html.

127. Ibid.

128. Ibid.

129. D. Bell, 2010, Best 5 MP3 players, *CNET Reviews*, December 22, http://reviews.cnet.com/best-mp3-players/?tag=contentMain ;contentAux.

130. 2009, MP3 player buying guide, *CNET Reviews*, December 2, http://reviews.cnet.com/2719-7964_7-272-3.html?tag=page;page.

131. D. Bell, 2010, Best 5 MP3 players, *CNET Reviews*, December 22, http://reviews.cnet.com/best-mp3-players/?tag=contentMain ;contentAux.

132. 2010, Apple iPod touch (4th Generation with Camera), September 7, http://www.pcmag.com/article2/0,2817,2179701,00.asp.

133. D. Bell, 2010, Best 5 MP3 players, *CNET Reviews*, December 22, http://reviews.cnet.com/best-mp3-players/?tag=contentMain ;contentAux.

134. 2011, iPad 2 sales start with pre-dawn online orders, Associated Press, March 11, http://www.abc15.com/dpp/news/science_tech/ ipad-2-sales-to-start-with-pre-dawn-online-orders.

135. Ibid.

136. B. Reed, 2011, iPad Rivals not up to snuff, says *Consumer Reports*, NetworkWorld, *PCWorld*, April 5, http://www.pcworld.com/ businesscenter/article/224315/ipad_rivals_not_up_to_snuff_says_ consumer_reports.html.

137. Ibid.

138. Ibid.

139. G. Keizer, 2011, Apple will dominate tablet market through 2015, says Gartner, Computerworld, *PCWorld*, April 11, http://www .pcworld.com/businesscenter/article/224865/apple_will_dominate _tablet_market_through_2015_says_gartner.html.

140. 2007, A bruise or two on Apple's reputation, *BusinessWeek*, http:// www.businessweek.com, October 22.

141. Ibid.

142. J. Quelch, 2007, How marketing hype hurt Boeing and Apple, *Harvard Business*, http://discussionleader.hbsp.com, November 2.

143. L. Gomes, 2006, Above all else, rivals of Apple mostly need some design mojo, *Wall Street Journal*, May 24, B1.

144. Ibid.

145. R. Goldbert, 2011, Selling the Apple lifestyle: What makes the ads work, http://minyanville.com, March 22, http://www .minyanville.com/special-features/articles/apple-ad-best-ad-copy -apple/3/22/2011/id/33115.

146. Ibid.

147. Ibid.

148. J. Graham, 2007, Apple buffs marketing savvy to a high shine, *USA Today*, http://www.usatoday.com, March 3.

149. P. Elmer-DeWitt, 2011, iPad ad as mission statement, *Fortune*, http://tech.fortune.cnn.com/2011/04/03/ipad-ad-as-mission -statement/#more-56374.

150. Cuneo, Apple transcends as lifestyle brand.

151. Ibid.

152. 2007, In 3 months, iPhone sales top a million.

153. R. Stross, 2007, Apple's lesson for Sony's stores: Just connect, *The New York Times*, http://www.nytimes.com, May 27.

154. 2010, Apple Inc. annual report.

155. Cuneo, Apple transcends as lifestyle brand.

156. http://www.apple.com/findouthow/retail/.

157. http://www.apple.com/retail/onetoone/

158. Ibid.

159. 2007, What makes a global leader? India knowledge at Wharton, http://knowledge.wharton.upenn.edu/india, October 4.

160. 2010, Apple Inc. annual report.

161. Ibid.

162. B. Stone and P. Burrows, 2011, The essence of Apple, *Bloomberg Businessweek*, January 24, 6.

163. A. Corn, 2011, Apple prepares for its next act: Time to officially appoint Cook as CEO, *Seeking Alpha*, April 12, http://seekingalpha .com/article/263025-apple-prepares-for-its-next-act-time-to -officially-appoint-cook-as-ceo.

164. P. Elmer-DeWitt, 2011, Thinking the unthinkable: Apple without Steve Jobs, *Fortune*, January 17, http://tech.fortune.cnn .com/2011/01/17thinking-the-unthinkable-apple-without-steve-jobs/.

165. D. Lyons, 2011, Facing a Jobs-Less Apple, *Newsweek*, January 23, http://www.newsweek.com/2011/01/23/facing-a-jobs-less-apple.html.

166. Ibid.

167. P. Elmer-DeWitt, 2011, Thinking the unthinkable: Apple without Steve Jobs, *Fortune*, January 17, http://tech.fortune.cnn .com/2011/01/17thinking-the-unthinkable-apple-without -steve-jobs/.

168. B. Stone & P. Burrows, 2011, The essence of Apple, *Bloomberg Businessweek*, January 24, 6.

169. C. Boulton, 2011, Enterprise mobility: Apple without Steve Jobs will do just fine: 10 reasons why, *eWeek.com*, January 20, http://www .eweek.com/c/a/Mobile-and-Wireless-Apple-Without-Steve-Jobs -Will-Do-Just-Fine-10-Reasons-Why-205563/.

170. Ibid.

171. Ibid.

AT&T: Another Century of Innovation?

Ryan Christensen, Andrew Folkert, Ryan Goodnight, Christina Moore, Philippe Thiam

Texas A&M University

Randall L. Stephenson, Chairman of the Board, President, and CEO of AT&T, was appointed to his position in 2007. Stephenson began his career with AT&T in 1982 and worked his way up through the company in high-level finance, marketing, and operational positions. He was present for the Bell System divestiture of 1984, the growth of computers and the Internet in the 90s, the massive restructuring into three separate companies in 1995, and the legendary leadership of Ed Whitacre, whom he replaced.

Today, Stephenson faces many challenges of his own. First and foremost are limitations to the capacity of wireless traffic demands required by the iPhone. AT&T is handling up to half the wireless traffic because of iPhone data requirements. Relatedly, is the loss of AT&T's iPhone exclusivity agreement with Apple as Verizon became another outlet for iPhone sales and service in early 2011. The legacy provider of phone service is also facing substitution as more users switch from wire service to newer technology solutions such as mobile and Voice over Internet Protocol (VoIP) services. AT&T has upgraded its service to meet these needs by offering its U-verse video service. Of course, with this service it competes with other phone companies, as well as cable and satellite providers. These and many other challenges will be reviewed in this case.

Company History[1]

From the beginning, AT&T has been a leader in innovation, always on the cutting edge of the markets. When Alexander Graham Bell started the company that would later become AT&T in 1876, no one could have predicted the future of telecommunications. By 1892, the American Telephone and Telegraph Company (AT&T) had established its first long distance line connecting Chicago and New York. AT&T weathered its first competitive threat in the 1890s when Bell's second patent expired and over 6,000 new companies flooded the market over a ten-year period. This fostered a culture of rapid innovation and led to the development of the loading coil, making longer telephone lines possible and keeping AT&T, if not ahead of, at least even with the collective competition. In 1915, AT&T opened the first transcontinental telephone line, connecting phones across the continental US. Just twelve years later, transatlantic telephone service from the US to London was in operation. That same year, AT&T presented the very first television broadcast, a live moving image of President Herbert Hoover. Bell Telephone Laboratories, Inc. was established in 1925 as the research and development subsidiary of AT&T and, leaping forward to 1971, researchers at Bell created the computer operating system that would later become the underlying language of the Internet.

As testimony to its research-focused strategy, seven AT&T employees have won Nobel Prizes over the course of the company's existence. The first was awarded in 1937 for the experimental confirmation of the wave nature of the electron and the most recent in 2009 for the invention of the CCD sensor—an imaging semiconductor circuit.[2]

Throughout its history, AT&T has negotiated a sometimes tenuous but often fortuitous agreement with the US government and its regulation of monopolies[3]. In 1913, AT&T settled its first federal anti-trust suit. The resulting Kingsbury Commitment essentially established AT&T as a government sanctioned monopoly. In 1956, AT&T came to an agreement with the US Justice Department that restricted AT&T's activities to those involving the national telephone system and special projects for the government and ended a seven-year antitrust suit. The year 1982 brought an end to an eight-year anti-trust suit with AT&T agreeing to divest itself of its local telephone operations and the Justice Department agreeing in exchange to lift some of the restrictions on AT&T's activities. With the divestiture of AT&T and seven regional Bell operating companies (RBOCs), the old Bell System ceased to exist in 1984. AT&T was allowed to retain only its long distance operations while the seven "Baby Bells" provided local telephone service to customers within their regions. The Federal Communications Commission (FCC) began Equal Access carrier selection, which led to full competition in the long distance telephone market. After enjoying most of the century without competitive threat, this forced AT&T to reduce its rates by more than 40 percent over the next six years.

The rapid growth of technology in the 90s brought about a series of mergers and acquisitions sought in AT&T's attempt to take advantage of the synergies between computers and communication. AT&T acquired computer maker, NCR Corporation, in 1991.[4] In 1993, AT&T acquired McCaw Cellular Communications, Inc.,[5] renaming it AT&T Wireless. The company underwent a major restructuring in 1995 that broke it into three separate operating companies: a services company (AT&T), a computer company (NCR), and a products and systems company (Lucent). President Bill Clinton signed the Telecommunications Act into law in 1996. As the first rewriting of US communications law since 1934, the act promoted competition in the industry and provided a plan for the elimination of legal and regulatory barriers.[6] AT&T then went on to acquire the second largest cable company in the US, TCI,[7] in 1998, and MediaOne in 2000.[8] Another restructuring, announced in 2000, eventually resulted in the divestiture of AT&T's broadband business to Comcast in 2002.[9] In 2005, AT&T Corp. merged with SBC Communications, Inc., one of the seven RBOCs, to become AT&T, Inc. In 2006, the US antitrust authorities approved the merger of AT&T, Inc. and BellSouth Corp., another legacy RBOC. This $86 billion merger made AT&T the largest telecommunications company in the US.[10]

Financial Performance

AT&T has organized its business into the following four operating segments: wireless, wireline, advertising solutions, and other subsidiaries. Despite declines in revenue from its traditional segments in recent years,[i] AT&T has experienced overall steady revenue growth as its wireless segment has grown.[11] (See Exhibit 1 for historical revenue sources by segment and Exhibit 2 for consolidated financial data.)

---

[i]Due to changes in AT&T's "method of recognizing actuarial gains and losses for pension and other post-retirement benefits for all benefit plans" in January 2011, the 2010 Annual Report reports significantly altered revenues for YE 2008 and moderately altered revenues for 2006, 2007, and 2009 as compared to previous annual reports.

Wireless Division Performance

AT&T's wireless business revenue has increased at a steady rate nearly equal to its declines in wireline. This business segment accounts for just over 43 percent of the $124 billion in consolidated revenue reported in 2010. From 2007 (the first full year of results following the merger of AT&T and BellSouth) to 2010, wireless revenue rose to $53.5 billion from $38.6 billion. This is the only business segment of AT&T to see consistent growth, thanks in large part to the 3G network and AT&T's agreement with Apple as the exclusive provider of the iPhone.

Wireline Division Performance

AT&T's wireline segment divides into two broad product lines. Voice products comprise the traditional local and long distance services for businesses, government, and consumers. Revenues from the voice product line decreased about 30.6 percent from year-end 2007 through year-end 2010. Total voice revenues have decreased by $12.5 billion over that same period as consumers have switched from traditional phones to mobile phones. Wireline's data products line is comprised of Internet access, video services, and certain business services offered by the company. With the addition of U-verse television service, revenue for wireline data revenue has experienced modest growth, equaling just over $4 billion during the same period.

Directory Services Performance

With the exception of a slight uptick in 2008, directory business revenue has declined for several years. With the continued growth of Internet search engines and other online directories, demand for print directory advertising has decreased. Overall, directory services revenue for 2010 represented only 3.2 percent of consolidated revenues.

Other Services Performance

Segment operating revenues decreased 8.4 percent in 2010 compared to 2008 due to lower revenues from operator services, payphones, and other business services.

Industry Comparison

AT&T's largest, most similar competitor is Verizon Communications, Inc. AT&T and Verizon operate primarily in the US and have similar service offerings in the wireless and wireline arenas, including video services over their respective fiber optics networks. Aside from the 1.2 percent downtick reported at year-end 2010, Verizon has experienced healthy growth in consolidated revenues. In addition, Verizon's shares have consistently outperformed telecom industry stock

Exhibit 1 AT&T Revenue Source by Segment, 2007 to 2010

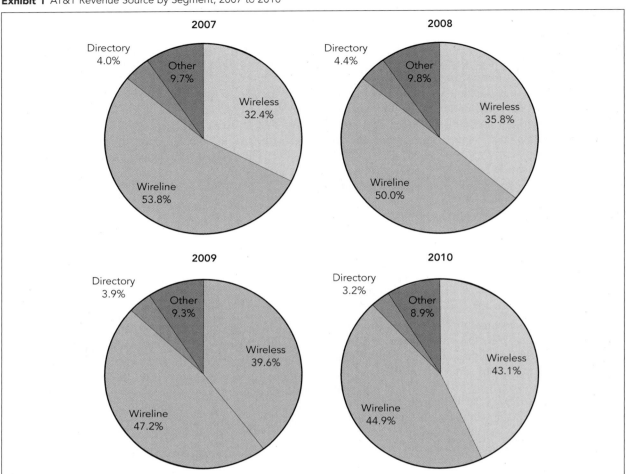

Sources: Data adapted from http://www.att.com

indices since 2006 (refer to Exhibit 3A) while AT&T returns have dipped below industry returns beginning in 2008 (refer to Exhibit 3B).

Wireless Industry Comparison

AT&T ranks a close second to Verizon in the US in number of wireless subscribers (see Exhibit 4). Average service revenue per user (ARPU) is an industry metric to gauge operator financial performance. Due to intense industry competition, ARPU has declined slightly even with the advent of wireless data services. Verizon's ARPU fell 1.6 percent in 2009[12] while AT&T's ARPU remained fairly constant from 2008 numbers.[13] T-Mobile's ARPU dropped 8.1 percent[14] while Sprint's ARPU stayed constant over the past year.[15]

Wireline Industry Comparison

While competition in wireline services is relatively fragmented, Verizon and AT&T are dominant players with a combined market share of 53.9 percent.[16] Wireline

services accounted for 47 percent and 42.7 percent of consolidated revenues for AT&T and Verizon, respectively. Both companies have experienced declining wireline segment revenues as consumers continue to shift to wireless services for their communication needs. AT&T and Verizon also offer video services over their fiber optics networks (AT&T's U-verse and Verizon's FiOS). Segment operating profit margins were 12.1 percent[17] and 4.3 percent[18] for AT&T and Verizon, respectively.

The Telecommunications Industry

During much of the twentieth century, the US telecommunications industry was dominated by a large number of regional companies with limited product offerings. Following the inventions of the Internet and wireless communication, these major players began expanding their services and pursuing large acquisitions. It is now argued that no other industry

Exhibit 2 AT&T Historical Financial Performance

Selected Financial and Operating Data Dollars in millions except per share amounts					
At December 31 or for the year ended:	2010	2009[1]	2008[1]	2007[1]	2006[1,2]
		As Adjusted			
Financial Data					
Operating revenues	$124,280	$122,513	$123,443	$118,322	$ 62,518
Operating expenses	$104,707	$101,513	$125,133	$ 89,181	$ 44,521
Operating income (loss)	$ 19,573	$ 21,000	$ (1,690)	$ 29,141	$ 17,997
Interest expense	$ 2,994	$ 3,368	$ 3,369	$ 3,460	$ 1,800
Equity in net income of affiliates	$ 762	$ 734	$ 819	$ 692	$ 2,043
Other income (expense) – net	$ 897	$ 152	$ (332)	$ 814	$ 398
Income tax expense (benefit)	$ (1,162)	$ 6,091	$ (2,210)	$ 9,917	$ 6,088
Net Income (Loss)	$ 20,179	$ 12,447	$ (2,364)	$ 17,228	$ 12,547
Less: Net Income Attributable to Noncontrolling Interest	$ (315)	$ (309)	$ (261)	$ (196)	$ (5)
Net Income (Loss) Attributable to AT&T	$ 19,864	$ 12,138	$ (2,625)	$ 17,032	$ 12,542
Earnings (Loss) Per Common Share: **Net Income (Loss) Attributable to AT&T**	$ 3.36	$ 2.06	$ (0.44)	$ 2.78	$ 3.23
Earnings (Loss) Per Common Share – Assuming Dilution: **Net Income (Loss) Attributable to AT&T**	$ 3.35	$ 2.05	$ (0.44)	$ 2.76	$ 3.22
Total assets	$ 268,488	$268,312	$264,700	$274,951	$270,118
Long-term debt	$ 58,971	$ 64,720	$ 60,872	$ 57,253	$ 50,062
Total debt	$ 66,167	$ 72,081	$ 74,990	$ 64,112	$ 59,795
Construction and capital expenditures	$ 20,302	$ 17,294	$ 20,290	$ 17,831	$ 8,337
Dividends declared per common share	$ 1.69	$ 1.65	$ 1.61	$ 1.47	$ 1.35
Book value per common share	$ 18.94	$ 17.28	$ 16.35	$ 19.07	$ 18.52
Ratio of earnings to fixed charges[6]	4.52	4.42	—	6.95	8.67
Debt ratio	37.1%	41.4%	43.8%	35.7%	34.1%
Weighted average common shares outstanding (000,000)	5,913	5,900	5,927	6,127	3,882
Weighted average common shares outstanding with dilution (000,000)	5,938	5,924	5,958	6,170	3,902
End of period common shares outstanding (000,000)	5,911	5,902	5,893	6,044	6,239
Operating Data					
Wireless connections (000)[3]	95,536	85,120	77,009	70,052	60,962
In-region network access lines in service (000)	43,678	49,392	55,610	61,582	66,469
Broadband connections (000)[4,5]	17,755	17,254	16,265	14,802	12,170
Number of employees	266.590	282,720	302,660	309,050	304,180

[1]Financial data for 2006 – 2009 has been adjusted to reflect our voluntary change in accounting for pension and postretirement benefits. See Note 1 to consolidated financial statements.

[2]Our 2006 Income statement amounts reflect results from BellSouth Corporation (BellSouth) and AT&T Mobility LLC (AT&T Mobility), formerly Cingular Wireless LLC, for the two days following the December 29, 2006 acquisition. Our 2006 balance sheet and end-of-year metrics include 100% of BellSouth and AT&T Mobility. Prior to the December 29, 2006 BellSouth acquisition, AT&T Mobility was a joint venture in which we owned 60% and was accounted for under the equity method.

[3]The number presented represents 100% of AT&T Mobility cellular/PCS customers.

[4]Broadband connections include in-region DSL lines, in-region U-verse High Speed Internet access, satellite broadband and 3G LaptopConnect cards.

[5]Prior-period amounts restated to conform to current period reporting methodology.

[6]Earnings were not sufficient to cover fixed charges in 2008, the deficit was $943.

Source: http://www.att.com

(Continued)

Exhibit 2 AT&T Historical Financial Performance (*Continued*)

Consolidated Statements of Income Dollars in millions except per share amounts	2010	2009	2008
		As Adjusted	
Operating Revenues			
Wireless service	$ 53,510	$ 48,563	$ 44,249
Voice	28,315	32,324	37,322
Data	27,479	25,561	24,416
Directory	3,935	4,724	5,416
Other	11,041	11,341	12,040
Total operating revenues	124,280	122,513	123,443
Operating Expenses			
Cost of services and sales (exclusive of depreciation and amortization shown separately below)	52,263	50,571	56,688
Selling, general and administrative	33,065	31,427	40,772
Depreciation and amortization	19,379	19,515	19,673
Total operating expenses	104,707	101,513	125,133
Operating Income (Loss)	19,573	21,000	(1,690)
Other Income (Expense)			
Interest expense	(2,994)	(3,368)	(3,369)
Equity in net income of affiliates	762	734	819
Other income (expense) – net	897	152	(332)
Total other income (expense)	(1,335)	(2,482)	(2,882)
Income (Loss) from Continuing Operations Before Income Taxes	18,238	18,518	(4,572)
Income tax (benefit) expense	(1,162)	6,091	(2,210)
Income (Loss) from Continuing Operations	19,400	12,427	(2,362)
Income (Loss) from Discontinued Operations, net of tax	779	20	(2)
Net Income (Loss)	20,179	12,447	(2,364)
Less: Net Income Attributable to Noncontrolling Interest	(315)	(309)	(261)
Net Income (Loss) Attributable to AT&T	$ 19,864	$ 12,138	$ (2,625)
Basic Earnings (Loss) Per Share from Continuing Operations Attributable to AT&T	$ 3.23	$ 2.06	$ (0.44)
Basic earnings per share discontinued Operations Attributable to AT&T	0.13	—	—
Basic Earnings (Loss) Per Share Attributable to AT&T	$ 3.36	$ 2.06	$ (0.44)
Diluted Earnings (Loss) Per Share from Continuing Operations Attributable to AT&T	$ 3.22	$ 2.05	$ (0.44)
Diluted Earnings Per Share from Discontinued Operations Attributable to AT&T	0.13	—	—
Diluted Earnings (Loss) Per Share Attributable to AT&T	$ 3.35	$ 2.05	$ (0.44)

The accompanying notes are an integral part of the consolidated financial statements.

Source: http://www.att.com

(*Continued*)

Exhibit 2 AT&T Historical Financial Performance (*Continued*)

Consolidated Balance Sheets
Dollars in millions except per share amounts

	December 31,	
	2010	**2009**
ASSETS	**As Adjusted**	
Current Assets		
Cash and cash equivalents	$ 1,437	$ 3,741
Accounts receivable - net of allowances for doubtful accounts of $957 and $1,202	13,610	14,845
Prepaid expenses	1,458	1,562
Deferred income taxes	1,170	1,247
Other current assets	2,276	3,792
Total current assets	19,951	25,187
Property, Plant and Equipment - Net	103,196	99,519
Goodwill	73,601	72,702
Licenses	50,372	48,741
Customer Lists and Relationships - Net	4,708	7,393
Other Intangible Assets - Net	5,440	5,494
Investments in Equity Affiliates	4,515	2,921
Other Assets	6,705	6,275
Total Assets	$268,488	$268,312
LIABILITIES AND STOCKHOLDERS' EQUITY		
Current Liabilities		
Debt maturing within one year	$ 7,196	$ 7,361
Accounts payable and accrued liabilities	20,055	21,260
Advanced billing and customer deposits	4,086	4,170
Accrued taxes	72	1,681
Dividends payable	2,542	2,479
Total current liabilities	33,951	36,951
Long-Term Debt	58,971	64,720
Deferred Credits and Other Noncurrent Liabilities		
Deferred income taxes	22,070	23,579
Post employment benefit obligation	28,803	27,847
Other noncurrent liabilities	12,743	13,226
Total deferred credits and other noncurrent liabilities	63,616	64,652
STOCKHOLDERS' EQUITY		
Common stock ($I par value. 14,000,000,000 authorized at December 31, 2010 and 2009: issued 6,495,231,088 at December 31, 2010 and 2009)	6,495	6,495
Additional paid-in capital	91,731	91,707
Retained earnings	31,792	21,944
Treasury stock (584,144,220 at December 31, 2010, and 593,300,187 at December 31, 2009, at cost)	(21,083)	(21,260)
Accumulated other comprehensive income	2,712	2,678
Noncontrolling interest	303	425
Total stockholders' equity	111,950	101,989
Total Liabilities and Stockholders' Equity	$268,488	$268,312

The accompanying notes are an integral part of the consolidated financial statements.

Source: http://www.att.com

Exhibit 3A Verizon Stock Price Performance

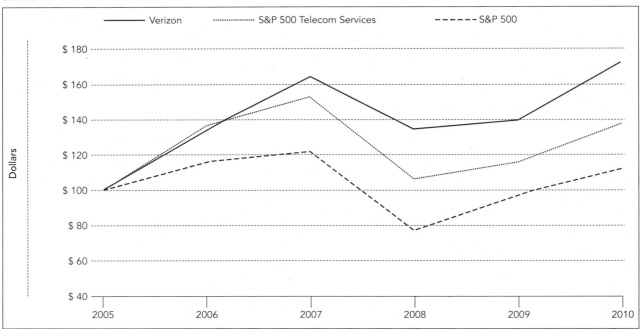

Source: Verizon Communications 2010 Annual Report. Verizon.com. http://www22.verizon.com

Exhibit 3B AT&T Stock Price Performance

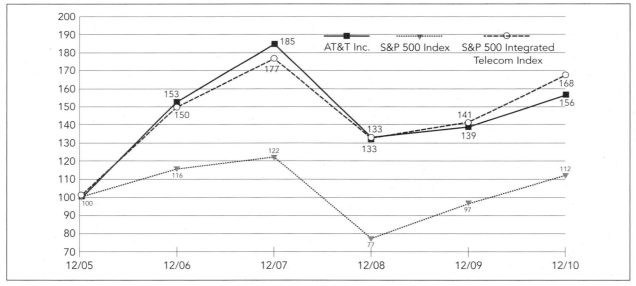

Source: http://www.att.com

touches more areas of technology related business than telecommunications. In addition to facilitating communications around the world, the telecom industry has also exploded into one of the largest sectors of employment. With annual revenues of $1.2 trillion in the US, over 1 million people work in telecommunications.[19] Despite this intense growth, the industry has not been immune to the challenges imposed by changing market conditions. Whereas people traditionally relied on landline phones for personal use, the portability and affordability of cellular devices has shifted customers away from conventional wired technology. For many of the companies offering both wired and wireless communications, this has significantly shifted where

Exhibit 4 US Wireless Industry Subscribers

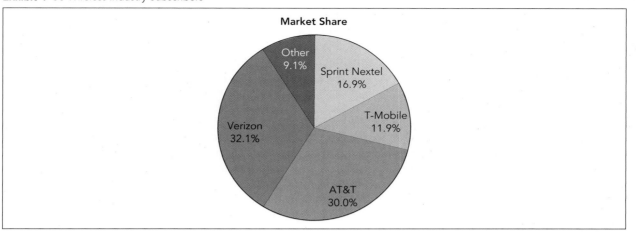

Source: Data adapted from Wireless Telecommunications Bureau of the Federal Communications Commission. (2010, May 20). 14th Mobile Wireless Competition Report. http://wireless.fcc.gov

corporate earnings are generated. Additionally, the move to wireless technologies has put pressure on providers from the perspective of network infrastructures. With a limited amount of wireless bandwidth shared by all customers, telecommunications companies are being forced to add additional cellular towers and improve existing hardware in an effort to enhance coverage.[20] Advances in cellular phone technology over the past few years have made handheld Internet access possible and, in conjunction with device improvements, there have been advances in network technology. These new networks, such as the widely known 3G and now 4G networks, are in great demand and telecommunications companies are struggling to expand quickly enough to keep up with consumer demand.[21] In general, telecom companies face constant customer scrutiny over their ability to keep up with customer bandwidth demands.[22] These market pressures will only continue to worsen as new wireless devices and uses for those devices join the already crowded networks.

Paralleling the advances in wireless communications has been the continued development of cable and broadband services. To take advantage of increasingly faster data transfer rates, many cable providers are pressuring telecommunications companies to expand into their markets. With optimal data transfer rates, not only can customers receive their Internet and television programming through cable and broadband lines, but advances in VoIP technology make cabled rather than landline phones possible. This advancement consolidates two products, and two providers, into one—a fact the cable companies are pursuing with enthusiasm. As for entertainment, while satellite television appeared to be the future of programming in the late 90s, fiber optic lines have made it possible to stream television

through the Internet—a trend that is quickly gaining momentum.[23] While the telecommunications industry could perhaps be considered "recession hardy," the budgetary constraints and slowed growth as a result of the global recession do not make meeting unabating consumer demands any easier.

Wireless Expansion into a Global Market

Beginning around the turn of this century, the telecommunications industry saw a dramatic change in the competitive landscape. Many governments around the world recognized the importance of capitalistic competition and began deregulating their previously nationalized telecommunications infrastructures.[24] Among many other changes, this brought about rapid wireless expansion into markets that were previously unreachable. Since 2003, there has been compounded annual growth of 23.2 percent in the worldwide cellular market that in 2010 translated into a world market penetration of 59.3 percent. Recognizing the opportunity for further global expansion, companies have worked feverishly to develop inexpensive phones to make available to the world's poorest populations. These efforts have produced amazing results, and it is estimated that by 2012 over 5.5 billion people will be wireless subscribers.[25] To handle this growth, telecom companies are doubling down on their efforts to develop infrastructures to support these new subscribers. By 2015, it is expected that annual global capital expenditures on wireless network infrastructures will reach $224.5 billion.[26] As the rate of new subscribers begins to fall due to market saturation, these expenditures are expected to drop; however, maintenance and network upgrade costs will continue far into the future.

Introduction of the "Smart Phone"

While the first "smart phone" was arguably developed by IBM as early as 1992, this class of devices didn't reach a wide market until the introduction of the BlackBerry by Research In Motion (RIM) in 2002.[27] The differentiating feature of a smart phone is its ability to run multiple operations in addition to calling and text including wireless web browsing, contact organization, music storage, etc. For the first few years, the majority of smart phone users were business executives and technology enthusiasts: the high cost and complex design of smart phones made them unattractive to the typical cellular customer. However, this trend turned on a dime in 2007 when Apple released the iPhone with AT&T. While several telecommunications companies were capable of servicing the iPhone, Apple chose AT&T because of its ability to work secretly on the design in the early stages of development. The iPhone, which now harnesses the high data rates of a 3G network, was originally released on the slower, yet more developed, GSM EDGE platform.[28] This decision was made in anticipation of the strain a wide number of new users would place on the network. Since its release, the iPhone has sold several million units and has changed the industry standard for cellular devices. Companies such as RIM, Palm, Samsung, and even Google have responded to this new demand by releasing smart phones of their own. What has ensued is an exclusivity war between the major telecom companies as the never-ending battle to lure subscribers away from competitors is provided new weaponry.

Smart phones have not only changed the selling points of providers, but have also changed the way cellular customers interact with their communications devices. When cell phones were first developed, they were designed solely as a means of making phone calls. As such, networks were designed to handle only this type of usage. The iPhone and other smart phones have changed user expectations and it is now assumed that phones will consolidate many functions into a single device. For example, Google's Android smart phone operating system not only places phone calls, but users can take a picture of a product's UPC bar code using the phone's camera and then access the Internet to identify what other nearby locations may carry that product at a lower price. This and other utilities like it were not anticipated when the first cell phone towers were developed and began going up around the world and today, those infrastructures are struggling to handle these new sources of traffic. As these newer devices continue to push the technological limits of the Internet, bandwidth demands will steadily increase, creating increased network strain and customer frustration well into our immediate future.

The Fight over Net Neutrality

One of the most significant issues involving the telecommunications industry today is the concept of net neutrality. At its core, the net neutrality debate is about how access to the Internet should be facilitated. Those in favor of net neutrality say that maintaining the status quo grants broadband providers the ability to "block, speed up, or slow down web content based on its source, ownership, or destination."[29] Net neutrality proponents argue that, in accordance with the founding principles of the Internet, no user should have any restrictions placed on who, what, where, when, how, or why (barring illegal activities) they communicate (i.e., receive or transmit data) with others on the Internet. The telecommunications industry, in general, is opposed to net neutrality and counters by stating that net neutrality regulations provide a solution to a problem that doesn't exist.[30]

And yet, despite their dismissal of consumer concerns, from the perspective of the telecommunications industry, the proposition of net neutrality has many implications. While the argument is typically pitted as one regarding freedom of information, it is actually more of a battle between the major telecom companies and giant content providers such as eBay, Google, and Amazon.[31] Currently, content providers do not pay to utilize the telecom industry's infrastructure to transmit data to end users—even if the amount of bandwidth required to do so happens to be much higher than average. If the net neutrality rules go into effect, service providers will lose the ability to monitor (purportedly the precursor to determining who and how much to charge) how much bandwidth each content provider and user requires. As an example of the potential issues of unmonitored bandwidth usage and from the perspective of the telecom industry, if thousands of users in New York suddenly decided to stream a Knicks basketball game, existing infrastructures may not be able to handle the increased load and could collapse.

In an effort to solve this eventuality, two solutions have been proposed. First, to drastically increase the amount of bandwidth available—an unreasonable proposition considering the telecom industry is already struggling to keep ahead of this challenge. Second, begin charging high bandwidth content providers for access to the infrastructure of the telecoms. As one might imagine, content providers are opposed to this idea and telecom companies are in favor.[32] While many argue that with net neutrality rules in place, the telecom industry could lose its ability to adapt to the changing market conditions and would then be locked into a business model that could prove unprofitable as the Internet evolves, it could also prove true that without net neutrality, providers and users will find alternative means to communicate, thus cutting telecoms out of the picture entirely.

Demand for Lower Wireless Rates

American society has become notorious for its rampant consumerism and fancy cellular devices top many "must have" lists.[33] This demand has put immense pressure on AT&T, Verizon, T-Mobile, and Sprint—the four largest wireless telecommunications companies servicing the US. With over 85 million subscribers in North America, AT&T is currently held in second place by number one Verizon for the title of largest wireless telecom company in the US. To stave off price-sensitive customers switching providers, the major telecoms have tried to increase network switching costs by creating contract plans that entice subscribers to commit to a single network for several years in exchange for a deeply discounted phone and periodic phone upgrades. As data plans and more technologically advanced phones become the norm, wireless providers have begun to increase the price of these contracts. Recognizing growing customer discontent, several new telecommunications companies have entered the market with a new business model. Rather than offering significant discounts on phones in exchange for locking customers into a long-term contract, providers such as Cricket Wireless and MetroPCS offer pre-paid and month-to-month plans at competitive rates. Because MetroPCS and Cricket Wireless do not have the infrastructures to support massive subscriber bases, most of the larger telecoms such as AT&T do not consider these new entrants to be viable threats. Even so, AT&T and Verizon have shifted the focus of their advertising to the breadth and strength of their networks and away from price points where they cannot compete with the new business model.

Expanding Coverage in the Future

Despite the fact that telecommunications companies continually invest in additional network infrastructure, the demand for better service far outpaces the progress being made. One of the major reasons that companies such as AT&T and Verizon struggle to keep their networks in prime operating condition is the bureaucracy surrounding the integration of new technology.[34] Lobbying groups operating at all levels—from local communities all the way up to Capitol Hill—put immense pressure on Congress to limit the amount of expansion that can occur at any given time. This activity severely hinders the ability of telecoms to act in the best interest of themselves and their customers and is part of the reason for the sluggish networks in the US. Looking forward, AT&T and other major telecom companies will have to commit significant resources and work closely with technology developers to advance the status of the North American communications infrastructure.

Strategies Used

AT&T has reinvented itself a number of times in its hundred-plus year history. By merging with SBC Communications in 2005 and BellSouth in 2006, the company reaffirmed its status as a dominant telecommunications services company in the US. AT&T also recognizes the advantages of diversification and has pursued opportunities in media, primarily as a content provider. The company's annual report states: "We plan to offer new services that combine our traditional wireless and wireline services, thereby making our customers' lives more convenient and productive and fostering competition and further innovation in the communications and entertainment industry."[35]

Recognizing the importance of customer loyalty, AT&T's management has established a broad mission that centers on its customers. Traditional distinctions between telephone services, online computing, and even television have been effectively blurred as the company seeks to bring a variety of easy-to-use content to each user. To achieve this, AT&T has organized its business into four operating segments: wireless, wireline, advertising solutions, and other subsidiaries.

Product and Services[36]

Wireless. AT&T's wireless subsidiary, AT&T Mobility, provides mobile telecommunications services to 95.5 million customers. The company's subscriber base includes consumers, businesses, and government users. For its consumer segments, the company offers voice services on both a prepaid and postpaid basis under a variety of plans and price points. Postpaid plans vary with respect to price and feature options such as minutes available, time of day or week usage, number of users, and even international dialing. AT&T also offers postpaid multiple-line plans specifically targeting families under its FamilyTalk brand: FamilyTalk plans start at $60 for two lines with each additional line costing $10. The high-end US and Canada FamilyTalk plan is priced at $320 a month and features free calls to all family members. For simplicity, the company's postpaid voice plan offerings provide nationwide long distance to all. Individual plans range from $40 to $220 and offer packages of up to 6,000 minutes per month for calls to the US and Canada. Postpaid plans generally require either a one- or two-year contract, and offer a discounted device as an incentive. For the budget-conscious or non-committal customer, AT&T offers prepaid mobile voice services through its GoPhone brand. The company's mobile voice service covers the vast majority of the continental US as well as parts of Alaska, Hawaii, Puerto Rico, and the US Virgin Islands.

AT&T also provides wireless data services to its customers. Subscribers can access AT&T's data services via smart phones, notebooks, or emerging devices such as netbooks, tablets, and eReaders. The company's wireless data devices include the popular Apple iPhone, which AT&T was the exclusive US network for until February 2011 when Verizon entered the iPhone market. AT&T provides a variety of data plans including plans that provide unlimited data access.

In the past, the company had offered voice and data services using Global System for Mobile Communication (GSM), General Packet Radio Services (GPRS), and Enhanced Data Rates for GSM Evolution. Recently, however, AT&T has expanded its third-generation (3G) Universal Mobile Telecommunications System (UMTS) network coverage to include most major cities in the US. Because 3G network coverage provides faster data transmission speeds, customers can more easily take advantage of new features on their mobile devices. Because AT&T has chosen to adopt technologies that are compatible with the vast majority of wireless carriers in the world it is able to offer worldwide coverage to its traveling customers via roaming agreements with wireless carriers in other countries.

Wireline.[37] Wireline communications represent AT&T's legacy product offering. With this technology, the company provides voice, data, and other services to customers in the US and internationally. AT&T's US wireline business covers 22 continental states.

Voice services include local and long distance telephone connections for business users, consumers, and government users. In addition to these connections, AT&T's wireline voice services segment includes the sales of calling cards, 1-800 services, and teleconferencing. The company also sells access to its wireline network to other carriers on a wholesale basis. As of December 31, 2010, wireline services accounted for approximately 49 percent of AT&T's total operating revenues. The company derives voice revenues from value-added features such as caller ID, call waiting, and voicemail. Consumer voice plans offer a variety of options to customers including per-minute rates and unlimited long distance plans—each with their own specific price points.

AT&T's wired consumer data services include Internet access, equipment sales, and its newest product, U-verse. U-verse represents AT&T's fiber-to-the-premises (FTTP) offering for very high-speed video and data services. This fiber optic network competes directly with Verizon's FIOS. The company also includes its VoIP products in the data services business. With respect to business and government users, the company offers switched and dedicated transport, network integration, dedicated Internet services, and enterprise networking

services. Other services provided under the wireline services product line include outsourcing, security, and satellite video offerings.

Advertising Solutions. AT&T publishes both White and Yellow Pages directories that generate advertising revenue for the company. The print directory operation is primarily limited to AT&T's 22 wireline states. In addition, AT&T offers an online directory and local search service through its advertising solutions business.

Other. AT&T offers services through its business integration software and services subsidiary, Sterling, as well as operator services.

Key Marketing Approaches
The AT&T brand is the centerpiece of the company's marketing strategies. Because the AT&T brand represented a rich history of innovation in the telecommunications industry and a tradition of quality service in the American marketplace,[38] following the 2006 merger of BellSouth and AT&T, Inc., the AT&T brand was adopted across all company businesses. The company launched a massive advertising campaign that included a refreshed AT&T logo and new slogan.[39]

Around the world, our customers recognize the AT&T brand for meaningful innovation, a commitment to customer service, high quality and exceptional reliability. AT&T, BellSouth and Cingular are now one company, and going to market with our services under one brand is the right thing to do.[40]

ED WHITACRE
THEN-CHAIRMAN AND CEO, AT&T

Since the merger, AT&T has maintained a strong advertising presence in print, television, and Internet media. As naming rights sponsor of the 18,000-seat AT&T Center in San Antonio, TX, the company receives further brand exposure through nationally televised professional basketball games. Maintaining a nationally recognized brand name helps the company market its services to a variety of customers.

AT&T effectively targets all customer segments with a portfolio of highly diversified communications products and services. Products span numerous price points and give customers myriad options with respect to features. The company offers flexibility through various offerings such as prepaid mobile telephone and its well-known rollover feature that allows customers to keep unused mobile minutes indefinitely. While recent revenue growth has predominantly come from wireless, AT&T maintains its large footprint in wireline and directory advertising for those customers that perceive such services as value-added. The company's slogan, "Your World. Delivered." symbolizes its goal of delivering limitless content to its customers in a convenient and productivity-enhancing manner. AT&T has effectively created a one-stop shop for its customers through its complementary wireless and wireline product offerings.[41]

With respect to its distribution network, AT&T uses a variety of channels, particularly with its wireless consumer business. AT&T operates its network of branded stores throughout the US in shopping centers and other high-traffic retail locations. The company also sells its products and services through independent retail shops and, for customers who prefer to shop online, AT&T's Web site is another possible destination.

Strategic Context and Organizational Structure

AT&T has sought a moderate level of relatedness across its business units that provide products and services exclusively in telecommunications and media. AT&T has maintained these links principally through its one-brand marketing approach and its operations business unit. As an example of these shared activities, customers are able to purchase a variety of services such as home and wireless phones while managing their accounts all through the company's Web site.

Organizational Structure.[42] AT&T has an organizational structure that is aligned with the company's broad market profiles. Mobility and consumer markets, business solutions, and diversified businesses are separate business units, each reporting to a business unit CEO. Additionally, the company's structure includes a dedicated operations company (led by its own CEO) responsible for maintaining the infrastructure supporting each of the market-based units. Finally, senior officers assume responsibility for corporate-level support activities such as marketing, human resources, and strategy development.

Business Unit and Cooperative Strategies. Consistent with the shared brand name, all business units are positioned as higher quality services for which the company is able to command a price premium over the competition. To maintain its competitive advantage, AT&T spent an average of $934 million over the last three years on research and development activities.[43] As such, AT&T typically charges higher prices than T-Mobile and Sprint for wireless services. However, the company's pricing is generally aligned with that of Verizon.

In the wireless space, AT&T adopts technologies that are compatible with the vast majority of wireless networks in the world.[44] Accordingly, the company boasts of offering its traveling customers cellular service in over 220 countries through roaming agreements with other carriers.[45] Additionally, technology compatibility affords users some flexibility with respect to choosing their wireless devices. Customers can even use a non-AT&T device on the company's network as long as they subscribe to a voice or data plan. Chief competitors Verizon and Sprint, both of which use an alternative technology for their wireless service, cannot offer their users the same breadth of geographic coverage with a single device or the same degree of device flexibility.

AT&T's diverse device portfolio includes the wildly successful Apple iPhone. The iPhone, and AT&T's exclusive distribution contract from launch in June 2007 until February 2011, was arguably what fueled the phenomenal growth of AT&T's wireless segment. As for its other products, one reason AT&T is able to provide differentiated devices is its adoption of wireless technologies that are shared with many carriers around the world. Due to the larger market, manufacturers seem more willing to supply their best phones to GSM and UMTS carriers as opposed to CDMA or other less prominent standards.

AT&T also offers service bundles to customers with various communications needs. For example, the company offers "quadruple play" bundles that include home telephone, wireless, television, and Internet access. As customers perceive value in the convenience of bundled services, AT&T can lock in customers that would otherwise have to obtain this array of services from more than one carrier.

It follows from the company's strategy that the legacy wireline business remains a key component of its business. While wireline voice has experienced significant revenue decline with the advent of wireless technology, AT&T has kept its 22-state wireline business intact and continues to provide a full spectrum of voice, data, and video services. Importantly, AT&T has not slowed innovation and adoption of new technologies for its wireline business. The company has invested heavily in expanding its fiber optics network across its 22-state region to offer high-speed Internet access and streaming video services to its customers.

AT&T has entered into several partnerships to enhance its position as a multi-disciplinary player in the telecommunications and media industries. The most visible of these alliances was AT&T's exclusive US distribution agreement with Apple. The agreement allowed the company to be the sole carrier of the iPhone from its launch in mid-2007 until February 2011—a coup that significantly hindered competitors' ability to attract trendsetters and Apple enthusiasts to their networks. Another important strategic partnership is the one AT&T formed with DIRECTV that provides satellite television services to customers in the US. AT&T arranged to market DIRECTV's digital television service to its customers.

Lastly, AT&T negotiated to become the exclusive wireless provider for customers on 130 cruise ships.[46]

AT&T has also formed equity strategic alliances with companies as part of its international strategy. AT&T has share holdings in Telmex, America Movil, and Telmex International through consortiums that have voting control of the companies. The total book value of those investments was $4.5 billion as of December 31, 2010. Exhibit 5 provides a brief description of the nature of these investees.[47] Through these equity investments, AT&T has derived a steady stream of income for its shareholders. More importantly, however, the company is strategically allied with telecom companies in emerging markets where telecommunications services are fast growing, especially in the wireless space where penetration rates remain relatively low.[48] These investments are consistent with AT&T's bet that future growth will primarily come from wireless services.

In addition, AT&T's management team is aggressively pursuing growth in the wireless and wireline data services arenas in the US. A series of acquisitions—including Cellular One, Centennial, Wayport, and Qualcomm—following the mega-merger of AT&T and BellSouth in 2006 added wireless subscribers and spectrum to the company's business. Despite what many consider to be a near-saturated US market, the number of AT&T's wireless subscribers swelled from 60.9 million at the end of 2006 to 95.5 million[49] at the end of 2010.[50] As previously mentioned, AT&T is investing in network upgrades to cover most major cities in wireless technology in calendar year 2011. The company is also expanding its fiber optics network-based Internet access and video services under the U-verse brand. U-verse is an important growth area where management is expected to focus its efforts in the future. AT&T management believes these services will further differentiate the company as a full-service telecommunications and media firm.

Finally, AT&T is using the presence of strong industry regulation to protect its business interests. For example, the firm has challenged Google's recent foray in telecom services through VoIP technology. AT&T involved the FCC in determining whether Google's Google Voice service should be considered a traditional telephone service offering and thereby fall under the purview of the FCC and be subject to certain fees.[51] With these efforts, AT&T appears to be attempting to level the playing field with its competitors by selectively using powers associated with regulatory bodies in the industries with which it is affiliated.

Supply Chain

AT&T maintains certain parts of its value chain in house and outsources other parts. In the operations arena, network equipment manufacturers are key suppliers for AT&T's wireless network. Similarly, transmission line constructors are crucial for AT&T's wireline businesses. The level of involvement of outside companies can vary and may be as simple as providing copper wire or as complex as the installation of cell phone towers. AT&T has spent an average of $18.9 billion a year on construction and capital expenditures over the period spanning 2007–2010.[52] This amount of capital expenditure highlights the importance of the buying side of the value chain. Alcatel-Lucent and Ericsson are the two network equipment suppliers for AT&T's current 3G network and AT&T has leveraged those existing relationships by selecting both suppliers for the construction of its next generation wireless network.[53] Ericsson is also a key supplier for AT&T's wireline business.[54] With extensive relationships with large suppliers, AT&T is able to take advantage of economies of scale by outsourcing certain operations to the firms that dominate the global network equipment industry. While the company's internal research and development

Exhibit 5 Description of AT&T Equity Investments

Company Name	AT&T Equity Interest (%)	Fair Value of AT&T Equity Interest (in millions)	Description
Telefonos de Mexico, S.A. de C.V. (Telmex)	9.8	$1,492	Mexico's national telecommunications provider of fixed-line telephone services. The company had approximately 18 million access lines in service and revenues of 124 billion pesos in 2008.[55]
America Movil S.A. de C.V.	8.8	$6,741	Mexico-based wireless provider with investments in the US and Latin America. Largest wireless provider in Latin America with 183 million subscribers and 2008 operating revenues of 141 billion pesos.[56]
Telmex Internacional S.A. de C.V.	9.9	$1,597	Latin America and Yellow Pages operations spun off from Telmex in December 2007. The company had operating revenues of 76 billion Pesos in 2008.[57]

Source: AT&T, Inc. Annual Report on Form 10-K for the year ended December 31, 2009. http://www.att.com

activities have primarily supported the wireline business,[58] wireless technologies such as GSM, UMTS, and Long Term Evolution (LTE) were developed by others and are generally widely adopted in the industry.

On the sales and marketing side of the value chain, AT&T again uses a combination of outsourcing and in-house activities to reach customers. The company's wireless plans and devices are available through company stores and third-party resellers alike.

Company Leadership

Edward "Ed" E. Whitacre, Jr. joined AT&T in 1963 as a facility engineer. He became chairman and chief executive in 1990 when the company was known as Southwestern Bell Telephone Co. Since then, he presided over numerous acquisitions, including the $67 billion purchase of BellSouth. In this position, he led the company's transformation into the nation's largest service provider of wireless, broadband, and telephone service.[59] AT&T's new headquarters building in Dallas was dubbed "Whitacre Tower" in honor of his 44 years at the company, 17 of which were spent as chairman and CEO. Upon his retirement in 2007, Whitacre was one of the longest-serving CEOs in the country. When asked about future competition, Whitacre responded, "Our big competition in the future is with the cable companies. Verizon's going to be a player, and certainly I want to compete. And I want our shareowners to do better than anyone else."[60] He also described the firm's strategy in terms of customers and competition.

It's still about scale and scope. It's about owning the assets that connect customers. The assets that probably can't be duplicated except maybe by the cable companies. We have that, Verizon has that, BellSouth has some of that. The cable companies have it. It's the numbers of customers you can get to. So it's scale and scope.[61]

As noted in the introduction, Randall L. Stephenson succeeded Ed Whitacre as chairman, CEO, and president of AT&T in 2007. Stephenson has worked for AT&T since 1982 and moved into this position from his previous post as COO. According to Stephenson, "One of the issues AT&T faces is the large amount of wireless traffic the iPhone generates." He stated that AT&T is carrying half of the nation's wireless data traffic. He added that carriers will eventually move to a "variable pricing model," and that it was inevitable that heavy users should pay more than low users. "Emerging market products such as an electronic reader already follow the variable model."[62] Randall Stephenson is just two years into his tenure as CEO of AT&T, but he faces challenges that have been decades in the making. Among them:

Remaking AT&T amid the steady decline of its landline business, future-proofing business as our appetites for bandwidth grow, competing with the likes of Comcast (CMCSA) in the cable TV market and fending off the proponents of Net neutrality, who don't care much for the idea of a two-tiered Internet.[63]

Current CFO Richard "Rick" G. Lindner has been with AT&T since 1986. He has played a key role in many strategic decisions by providing the necessary financial analyses. The most recent example is the U-verse endeavor. In an interview, Lindner discussed the growth of U-verse and his future predictions for the financial stability of the company.

Our expectation for U-verse is to continue to, market permitting, grow at the kind of rates you've seen us grow over the last four to five quarters. In just about all U-verse markets, penetration tends to increase at one percentage point per month.

In 2010, AT&T expects to deliver "stable consolidated revenue," Lindner said, and pointed to some improvement in business sector trends. However, he added, "Frankly I think the economy is still fragile at this point in time."

AT&T's success can be attributed to the keen ability of its leaders, past and present, to evaluate the market, analyze the competition, assess the external environment, and make strategic decisions that consistently lead to growth and development.

Strategic Challenges

AT&T's global reach and multiple divisions provide for a complex set of strategic challenges for its strategic leaders, encompassing various areas of the company and AT&T as a whole. AT&T's challenges are exacerbated by changing consumer preferences and the continuous stream of new technologies brought to the marketplace. AT&T's task is to determine how to deal with divisional and firm-wide challenges to maximize returns in the coming years.

Firm-Wide Challenges
Transforming Traditional Revenue Streams.
AT&T's legacy business is its wireline division. However, because of technological innovation in the last decade, this traditional revenue stream has experienced declines as more users switch to newer technology solutions such as mobile and VoIP services. AT&T continues to grapple with how to market these newer services and has recently filed a request with the FCC to start phasing out copper landlines. As evidence of the dramatic change in usage patterns, AT&T stated that "over 25 percent of Americans have dropped their landline service entirely" with a rate of over 700,000 landlines cancelled every month.[64]

Many of these users have been switching to VoIP services and AT&T must determine how to compete in Internet services without cannibalizing its existing cell phone business. Complicating this issue are government regulations concerning phone service availability to low-income and rural populations. Indeed, current regulation mandates that phone service be provided to all Americans and newer services will either not have the reach or not be affordable for this minority.[65]

Service Quality. The company must also deal with negative customer perceptions concerning customer and phone service quality. The National Customer Service Ranking released in May 2011 ranked AT&T last among the top four wireless service providers, third (behind Qwest and Cox) for fixed line telephone service, and third again (behind Verizon and DirectTV) for subscription television service.[63] While AT&T has made a conscious effort to address customer service complaints, there does not appear to be much of an impact on overall customer satisfaction, as survey results have not showed any noticeable improvement. This represents a serious challenge for the firm as the impact of low customer service scores in the wireless arena could spread to other parts of AT&T's business.

Wireless Division

AT&T struggles with negative customer perceptions of cellular phone service quality. Verizon has taken advantage of the public's perception by launching an aggressive marketing campaign targeted against AT&T. Recent Verizon advertisements have labeled AT&T as "lacking in 3G coverage," referring to AT&T's high-speed wireless network used by smart phone users. AT&T has responded with advertisements that focus mainly on defending the company from these allegations rather than emphasizing the areas where the company is competitive: data plans delivered over the high-speed 3G network are the crux of the wireless division's profits.

Saturated US Markets. With cell phones already in the pockets and purses of approximately 91 percent of Americans, wireless carriers face the reality of a saturated US marketplace.[67] Indeed, subscriber growth is now expected to come from poaching customers from competing networks. This market saturation in AT&T's fastest growing segment has led to Wall Street's diminishing

expectations of future growth for the company. AT&T and Verizon have been two of the lowest performing stocks in the Dow Jones Industrial Average index.[68]

Loss of iPhone Exclusivity. AT&T has managed to retain (and even add) many wireless subscribers over the last three years because of its exclusive contract to distribute Apple's iPhone in the US. The iPhone provided an advantage through initial buzz and Apple's evolutionary upgrades strategy. However, with Verizon's entry into this market in February 2011, AT&T has lost a major competitive advantage and may be vulnerable to customer defections.[69]

Wireline Division

Video Strategy. AT&T has been able to operate U-verse (over 3 million subscribers at the end of 2010) as a "video service" subject to federal oversight and as such, outside the jurisdiction of state and local cable laws.[70] Many municipalities and cable companies are challenging AT&T's position and claiming that U-verse should be classified as a traditional cable service subject to state and local regulatory oversight. These legal challenges have hampered AT&T's rollout efforts in several areas. Depending on the outcome of these legal and regulatory issues, AT&T could be required to offer U-verse in significantly different ways, which could have adverse affects on the company's cost structure and AT&T's strategy for its wireline business.

Increasing Internet Functionality. As consumers become more technologically savvy, it will be increasingly difficult to find and maintain a user base in the cabled television realm, especially as Internet-based entertainment becomes more readily available. Nearly 800,000 US households have already discontinued their cable service and switched to watching TV on Internet mediums such as Apple, Inc.'s iTunes Store and Hulu.[71]

Overall, these challenges are complex and appropriate decisions will be required to maintain AT&T's trajectory and growth in the years to come. The executive leadership of AT&T will have to make key resource allocations once the decisions are made and execute their strategic changes well in the face of an ever changing external environment.

NOTES

1. Milestones in AT&T History. (n.d.). *AT&T.com*. http://www.corp.att.com/history/milestones.html

2. The Nobel Prizes. (n.d.). *Nobel Prize.org*. http://nobelprize.org/nobel_prizes/

3. Thierer, A. D. (Fall 1994). Unnatural monopoly: Critical moments in the development of the Bell system monopoly. *The Cato Journal*, 14(2). http://www.cato.org/pubs/journal/cjv14n2-6.html

4. Shapiro, E. (1991, May 7). AT&T buying computer maker in stock deal worth $7.4 billion. *New York Times*. http://www.nytimes.com/1991/05/07/business/at-t-buying-computer-maker-in-stock-deal-worth-7.4-billion.html?pagewanted=all&src=pm

5. Young, J. S. (1998, Jun 22). Craig McCaw -- The Wireless Wizard of Oz. *Forbes.com*. http://www.forbes.com/1998/06/22/feat.html

6. Telecommunications Act of 1996. (last reviewed/updated 2008, Nov 15). *FCC.gov*. http://transition.fcc.gov/telecom.html

7. AT&T completes the acquisition of TCI. (1999, Mar 10). *New York Times*. http://www.nytimes.com/1999/03/10/business/at-t-completes-the-acquisition-of-tci.html

8. Labaton, S. (2000, Jun 6). AT&T's acquisition of MediaOne wins approval by FCC. *New York Times*. http://www.nytimes.com/2000/06/06/business/at-t-s-acquisition-of-mediaone-wins-approval-by-fcc.html

9. AT&T Inc. 10-K – Filed Period 12/31/01. *ATT.com*. http://phx.corporate-ir.net/phoenix.zhtml?c=113088&p=irol-sec&secCat01.4_rs=81&secCat01.4_rc=10&control_selectgroup=Annual%20Filings

10. Vorman, J. (2006, Dec 29). AT&T closes $86 billion BellSouth deal. *Reuters*. http://www.reuters.com/article/ousiv/idUSWBT00636120070102 .

11. AT&T Inc. 2010 Annual Report. *ATT.com*. http://www.att.com/Common/about_us/annual_report/pdfs/ATT2010_Full.pdf

12. Verizon Communications 2009 Annual Report. *Verizon.com*. http://www.annualreports.com/HostedData/AnnualReports/PDFArchive/vz2009.pdf

13. AT&T Inc. 2009 Annual Report. *ATT.com*. http://www.att.com/Common/about_us/annual_report/pdfs/ATT2009_Full.pdf

14. The 2009 financial year. *Deutsche Telekom*. http://www.download-telekom.de/dt/StaticPage/82/04/80/deutsche_telekom_annual_report_2009_820480.pdf

15. Sprint Nextel Corporation Form 10-K for fiscal year ended Dec 31, 2009. *Sprint.com*. http://phx.corporate-ir.net/External.File?item=UGFyZW50SUQ9MzY1NzB8Q2hpbGRJRD0tMXxUeXBlPTM=&t=1

16. Wired Telecommunications Carriers. (2011, May 6). *IBISWorld.com*. http://.ibisworld.com/industry/default.aspx?indid=1268

17. AT&T Inc. 2010 Annual Report. *op. cit.*

18. Verizon Communications 2010 Annual Report. *Verizon.com*. http://www22.verizon.com/investor/investor-consump/groups/public/documents/investorrelation/2010_annualreport_quicklinks.pdf

19. Introduction to the Telecommunications Industry. (n.d.). *Plunkett Research, Ltd.* http:// www.plunkettresearch.com/Industries/Telecommunications/Telecommunicationstrends/tabid/95/Default.aspx

20. San Miguel, R. (2009, Oct 8). FCC Chair Warns of Wireless Gridlock. *TechNewsWorld.com*. http://www.technewsworld.com/story/68328.html?wlc=1305992918

21. Koskey, A. (2010, Mar 18). Towers of Cell Power. *San Francisco Examiner*. http://www.sfexaminer.com/local/Towers-of-cell-power-88273702.html

22. Kharif, O. & Thomson, A. (2010, Apr 1). AT&T may find iPad downloads exert bigger-than-anticipated network strain. *Bloomberg*. http://www.bloomberg.com/apps/news?pid=20601204&sid=aeh.Ql1MFc7Y

23. Hoag, D. (2010, Feb 17). The future of high-speed internet with fiber optics. *Ezine @rticles*. http://ezinearticles.com/?The-Future-of-High-Speed-Internet-With-Fiber-Optics&id=3778733

24. Smith, C. S. (1996, Sep 16). Opening lines; China's grudging nod toward deregulation has prompted a flurry of joint ventures between foreign and local firms. *Wall Street Journal*. http://www.faqs.org/abstracts/Business-general/Opening-lines-Chinas-grudging-nod-toward-deregulation-has-prompted-a-flurry-of-joint-ventures-betwee.html

25. Introduction to the Telecommunications Industry. *op. cit.*

26. Global Telecom Industry Capex to Touch $224 Billion by 2015. (2010, Mar 23). *LiveMint.com*. http://www.livemint.com/2010/03/23155240/Global-telecom-industry-capex.html

27. Martin, J. P. (2009, Mar 12). A short history of the smartphone. *Ezine @rticles*. http://ezinearticles.com/?A-Short-History-of-the-Smartphone&id=2093670

28. Pogue, D. (2007, Jan 11). The ultimate iPhone frequently asked questions. *The New York Times*. http://pogue.blogs.nytimes.com/2007/01/11/the-ultimate-iphone-frequently-asked-questions/

29. Pieklo, J. (2009, Oct 22). Save the Internet. *Care2 Make a Difference*. http://www.care2.com/causes/politics/blog/save-the-internet/

30. Malkin, M. (2010, Dec 22). Internet access is not a 'civil right'. *NewsBusters.org*. http://www.newsbusters.org/blogs/michelle-malkin/2010/12/22/internet-access-not-civil-right

31. Frequently Asked Questions. (n.d.). *Save The Internet/FAQ*. http://www.savetheinternet.com/faq

32. *Ibid.*

33. Desire, Not Necessity, Drives Spending. (2002). *USA Today*. http://findarticles.com/p/articles/mi_m1272/is_2687_131/ai_90870877/

34. New Cell Phone Towers Are Not The Answer. (2010, Feb 11). *Deadzones*. http://www.deadzones.com/2010/02/new-cell-phone-towers-are-not-answer.html

35. AT&T Inc. 2009 Annual Report. *op. cit.*

36. AT&T Inc. 2010 Annual Report. *op. cit.*

37. *Ibid.*

38. Belson, K. (2006, Jul 21). AT&T bets its brand is more than nostalgia. *New York Times*. http://www.nytimes.com/2006/07/21/business/21adco.html?_r=1&oref=slogin

39. Sampey, K. (2006, Jan 9). How AT&T, Intel decided to ring in the new year. *ADWEEK.com*. http://www.adweek.com/news/advertising/how-att-intel-decided-ring-new-year-83415

40. Cingular is now the new AT&T. (2007, Jan 12). *ATT.com*. http://www.att.com/gen/press-room?pid=4800&cdvn=news&newsarticleid=23308&mapcode=corporate|consumer

41. Searcey, D. (2007, Jan 12). Bye, Cingular, in AT&T rebranding. *Wall Street Journal*. http://proquest.umi.com.ezproxy.rice.edu/pqdweb?index=0&did=1193079251&SrchMode=1&sid=1&Fmt=3&VInst=PROD&VType=PQD&RQT=309&VName=PQD&TS=1306721170&clientId=480

42. AT&T Inc. 2009 Annual Report. *op. cit.*

43. *Ibid.*

44. Wired Telecommunications Carriers. *op. cit.*

45. Global Reach. (n.d.). *ATT.com*. http://www.att.com/gen/investor-relations?pid=5711

46. *Ibid.*

47. AT&T Inc. 2009 Annual Report. *op. cit.*

48. Erwin C. (2010, Oct 11). Report: Cell phone use soars in Latin America. *The Latin Americanist*. http://ourlatinamerica.blogspot.com/2010/10/report-cell-phone-use-soars-in-latin.html

49. AT&T Selects LTE Equipment Suppliers. (2010, Feb 10). *ATT.com*. http://www.att.com/gen/press-room?pid=4800&cdvn=news&newsarticleid=30493&mapcode=wireless-networks-general|financial

50. AT&T Names Ericsson as Key Supplier for Future Wireline Business. (2009, Sep 7). *Ericsson.com*. http://www.ericsson.com/news/1339721

51. *Ibid.*

52. AT&T Inc. 2009 Annual Report. *op. cit.*

53. Tse, T. M. (2007, Apr 28). Long-Serving AT&T Chief to Leave with Huge Payout. *Washington Post*. http://www.washingtonpost.com/wp-dyn/content/article/2007/04/27/AR2007042702276.html

54. Ante, S. E. & Crocket, R. O. (2005, Nov 7). Rewired and Ready for Combat. *Bloomberg Businessweek*. http://www.businessweek.com/magazine/content/05_45/b3958089.htm

55. Telefonos de Mexico, S.A.B. de C.V. Annual Report on Form 20-F for the Year Ended Dec 31, 2008. http://www.telmex.com/mx/corporativo/salaPrensa_ComPrensa2009_090529-ev.185.html`

56. America Movil, S.A.B. de C.V. Annual Report on Form 20-F for the Year Ended Dec 31, 2008. http://www.americamovil.com/amx/en/cm/news/2009/2009_06_30_eng.pdf

57. Telmex Internacional S.A.B. de C.V. Annual Report on Form 20-F for the Year Ended Dec 31, 2008. http://www.telmexinternacional.com/assets/docs/20-F2008TelmexInternacional.pdf

58. AT&T Inc. 2010 Annual Report. *op. cit.*

59. Wireless Telecommunications Carriers. *op. cit.*

60. *Ibid.*

61. *Ibid.*

62. Slivka, E. (2010, Mar 2). AT&T CEO Randall Stephenson Speaks About iPhone and iPad. *MacRumors*. http://www.macrumors.com/2010/03/02/atandt-ceo-randall-stephenson-speaks-about-iphone-and-ipad/

63. Paczkaowski, J. (2009, May 27). AT&T CEO Randall Stephenson: "Wireless is the Priority of This Business." *All Things D*. http://d7.allthingsd.com/20090527/randall-stephenson/

64. Duncan, G. (2009, Dec 31). AT&T Looks to Leave Landlines Behind. *Digital Trends*. http://www.digitaltrends.com/computing/att-looks-to-leave-landlines-behind/

65. *Ibid.*

66. May 2011 and historical ACSI scores. (2011, May 17). *The American Customer Satisfaction Index.* http://www.theacsi.org/index.php?option=com_content&view=article&id=205:acsi-scores-may&catid=14&Itemid=261

67. Wireless Telecommunications Carriers. *op. cit.*

68. La Monica, P. R. (2010, Apr 1). Verizon vs. AT&T: They're both losers. *CNNMoney.* http://money.cnn.com/2010/04/01/markets/thebuzz/index.htm

69. Sarno, D. (2009, Jul 15). Analyst sees dimming future for AT&T wireless if Verizon gets iPhone. *Los Angeles Times.* http://latimesblogs.latimes.com/technology/2009/07/analyst-sees-dimming-future-for-att-wireless-if-verizon-gets-iphone.html

70. AT&T Inc. 2010 Annual Report. *op. cit.*

71. Patterson, B. (2010, Apr 13). Nearly 800,000 US TV households 'cut the cord,' report says. *Yahoo! News.* http://news.yahoo.com/s/ytech_gadg/ytech_gadg_tc1598

John Arcenas, Heather Covill, Aaron Kramer, Bret Linton, Michael Moon, Cindy Thimmesch, Steve Weber
Arizona State University

Introduction

In the battle to become the largest consumer electronics retailer in the US, some might say that Best Buy is up by a few rounds. Beginning as a single location car and home stereo store in 1966, Best Buy has grown into a massive firm with 1,400 stores in North America and over 2,600 stores in Europe and China.[1] As recently as 2007, Best Buy was seen as the team to beat, boasting a strong lead in market share over its competitors, large and consistent profits, healthy stock returns, and a global expansion strategy. In accomplishing this feat, Best Buy brought down its biggest competitors—Circuit City and CompUSA.[2]

With CompUSA out of the way (at least temporarily) in 2007, the economic recession and the ensuing reduction in consumer discretionary spending added the last bit of leverage needed to topple Circuit City in 2009.[3] This allowed Best Buy to emerge as the clear champion of the large format consumer electronics retail segment; a position many consider prophetic of future success. However, whether the downfall of its competitors is the result of Best Buy's superiority or simply the inevitable demise of a retail model that is becoming obsolete remains to be seen.

Unfortunately for Best Buy, recent results suggest that the latter might be the case. As shown in Exhibit 1, Best Buy's recent stock returns have been consistently below those of the S&P retailing group as well as those of the S&P 500.[4] In addition, revenue growth slowed to a miniscule 1.6 percent over the course of fiscal year 2011.[i] While the recession can be blamed at least in part for this reversal of fortunes, more of the blame likely lies with the presence of new competitors in the industry including the better diversified Walmart and Costco, additional "go straight to the source" Apple stores, and the monster of online retail—Amazon

.com. In fact, Amazon's stock price increase is a near mirror image of Best Buy's stock price decline.[5] Likewise, these new competitors have been gaining market share in the consumer electronics segment while Best Buy has been losing it.[6] The threat of these new entrants is particularly ominous in that they are quite different from Best Buy in terms of their structure, focus, and features that customers find attractive. For example, it is not uncommon for a customer to browse Best Buy for a particular product, use Amazon's app on their smartphone to scan the barcode, and then purchase the product from Amazon at a better price while still in Best Buy—a scenario that has led to a new—and painful—nickname for Best Buy—"Amazon's showroom."[7]

History

In 1966, Richard Schulze, disgruntled that his suggestions for improvement weren't being taken seriously, quit his family's electronics distribution business and, together with a partner, started his Minnesota-based home and car stereo store called "Sound of Music." The firm grew through acquisitions and the opening of new stores and hit the million-dollar revenue mark by 1970. During the 70s, Schulze's company experienced significant financial success, allowing him to expand the chain and buy out his partner. Even early in his managerial career, Schulze showed an uncanny ability to adjust to market trends and seek out profitable opportunities. For example, his position on a school board gave him insight into the fact that the customer pool of 15- to 18-year-old males (his target demographic) was shrinking. Consequently, he adjusted his business approach by diversifying into appliances and video equipment with the goal of targeting the expanding demographic of older and wealthier customers emerging in the 80s. As another example, when a tornado destroyed one of his stores but left the inventory largely unharmed, Schulze held a "no

[i] Best Buy's fiscal year 2011 closed on February 26, 2011.

Exhibit 1 Comparison of 5 Year Cumulative Total Return among Best Buy Co, Inc., the S&P 500, and the S&P Retailing Group

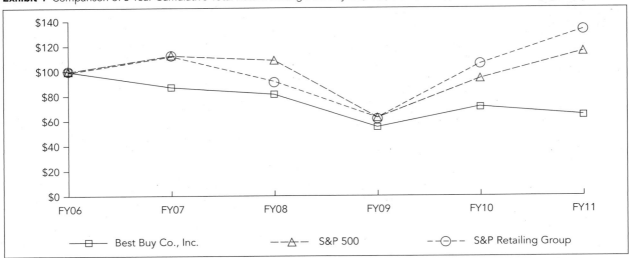

Source: Best Buy Co. Inc. Form 10-K For fiscal year ended February 26, 2011. *sec.gov.* [Online] May 17, 2011. [Cited: May 17, 2011]. http://www.sec.gov

frills" parking lot sale with reduced prices. This approach was so successful that in 1983, Schulze reorganized the business into a superstore format under the "Best Buy" brand name and in 1985, took the new company public.[8]

As Best Buy continued to evolve, the sales approach used in the superstores changed from that of a specialty electronics retailer with highly knowledgeable commissioned sales staff, to a mass merchandiser with a larger variety of products, discounted prices, and a more dispersed and non-commissioned sales force.[9] Although customers seemed to appreciate the increased variety and did not seem to mind the reduction in sales assistance, some suppliers were skeptical of the superstore concept and, for a time, pulled some of their products from Best Buy's shelves.[10] Since the introduction of the superstore, Best Buy has refined the concept to allow for moderate levels of customer service, balanced with displays and product groupings designed to allow customers to shop for many items without extensive assistance.[11]

This moderated approach was successful and prompted the brand to expand rapidly throughout the US between 1989 and 1995—opening 47 new stores in 1995 alone. However, Best Buy's rapid expansion brought with it high debt levels and low profit margins that eventually forced the firm to slow its expansion and reconsider some of its low-cost strategy. This setback notwithstanding, Best Buy began to expand again in 1999, opening new superstores in additional regions of the US and launching a separate subsidiary—BestBuy.com—to claim its stake to the online market.[12]

If Best Buy experienced rapid growth in the last 34 years of the twentieth century, it was paltry compared to the meteoric rise it experienced during the decade beginning in 2000. Growth came through

organic means (opening new store locations), new ventures within the firm (Best Buy Mobile stores), and both domestic and overseas acquisitions.[13] Domestic acquisitions included Magnolia Hi-fi (a chain of 13 high-end stereo electronics stores) in 2000, the Musicland Group (comprised of over 1,300 Sam Goody, Suncoast Video, and Media Play stores) in 2001, Pacific Sales Kitchen and Bath Centers (a chain of home appliance and remodeling stores) in 2006, and Napster (an online music download website) in 2008.[14] Also domestically, the firm acquired Geek Squad (an omnibus computer/electronics installation, repair, and support service) in 2003 to offer after-purchase support services to customers, and Speakeasy (a provider of broadband voice, data, and IT services to small businesses) in 2008.[15]

International acquisitions were even more extensive starting with Future Shop (the largest electronics retailer in Canada) in 2002.[16] Next up, Best Buy acquired 75 percent of Five Star Appliance (a major Chinese appliance and electronics retailer) in 2007, and scooped up the remaining 25 percent in 2009.[17] In 2009, Best Buy formed Best Buy Europe and entered a 50/50 joint venture in Europe with Carphone Warehouse, a company that included over 2,400 stores and, not coincidentally, had acted as a consultant when Best Buy opened its US mobile stores two years earlier. These acquisitions were all followed by the opening of Best Buy superstores in their respective markets of Canada, China, and Europe. Best Buy also opened superstores in Mexico in 2009 and Turkey in 2010.[18]

Not all of Best Buy's expansions were successful, however. Due to poor performance, the firm closed almost 100 Musicland Group stores in early 2003, and sold all remaining Musicland assets later that year.[19] Best Buy's Speakeasy acquisition ultimately did not provide the strategic advantages Best Buy had expected, and was sold in 2011. Due to the lethal combination of non-existent brand equity and cultural mismatch, the Best Buy branded stores in Turkey and China also performed poorly, resulting in the decision to close (or in the case of China, convert to Five Star branded stores) those locations in 2011 and 2012 respectively.[20]

Managerial changes at Best Buy have been infrequent over the course of the firm's history and because most of the changes that have occurred have been internal leadership promotions, managerial succession has had little impact on Best Buy's overall strategy. Dick Schulze led the company from its founding in 1966 until he resigned from the CEO position in 2002 and continues to be a driving force as Chairman of the Board. Upon Schulze's retirement from CEO, Brad Anderson, who had been serving as the firm's vice chairman, took over the position and worked as the company's CEO until 2009 when he retired. Brian Dunn, who started his career with Best Buy working as a sales associate over 25 years ago, accepted the CEO position in 2009.[21]

Industry

Suppliers

Due to the variety of products Best Buy offers, the firm maintains relationships with hundreds of suppliers. Even so, in 2010 Best Buy purchased almost 65 percent of its products from just 20 suppliers with 5 of those suppliers (Apple, HP, Samsung, Sony, and Toshiba) providing almost 40 percent of its merchandise.[22] Although there are no signs of supply disruption from any of these major companies, supplier firms themselves are evolving. In the past, major electronics producers like Sony would sell only to specialty electronics retailers like Best Buy or Circuit City. Today, the major electronics suppliers are increasingly allowing their products to be sold by warehouse clubs and online distributors. As suppliers extend the scope of their distribution, Best Buy loses the exclusivity it once enjoyed.[23] Compounding this problem is the fact that major supplier firms like Apple are integrating forward and distributing their products through websites and bricks-and-mortar stores.[24]

As Best Buy has increased its emphasis on cell phone sales through the Best Buy Mobile store-within-a-store format, the major cell phone carriers are becoming more important as suppliers than in the past.[25] However, because the cell phone business is becoming increasingly concentrated and commoditized, the cut for middle-man distributors is dwindling. In the end, vendors such as Best Buy may find it too difficult to achieve profit margins sufficient to continue this foray.[26]

Customers

Like many firms that focus on retail sales, Best Buy's customers represent a broad array with no single customer profile accounting for a significant portion of overall sales.[27] Nevertheless, in its effort to meet each customer in an efficient manner, Best Buy has worked to understand its customers better. As an example, the firm has recently worked to increase its offerings to business customers—training designated staff to provide consultation services to business purchasers as well as showcasing products specifically designed for business applications.[28]

Of course, technological trends have important implications for firms in the consumer electronics industry. The increased use of the Internet provides businesses with multiple challenges and opportunities, both in terms of the range of products offered as well as new ways to conduct business and access customers. The trend toward a decrease of retail prices in the consumer electronics industry combined with an increase in market saturation could become problematic for firms.[29] Additionally, the smartphone and tablet trend toward the consolidation of functions (i.e. computing, messaging, phone calls, GPS navigation, games, camera, etc.) will influence not only the demand for these products, but the products they replace as well.

The increasing rate at which technology is changing offers firms in this industry an endless supply of new products, but carries with it the threat of being caught with unsold stock that is newly obsolete or simply suddenly unpopular. To offset this particular risk, firms with the ability to bring products to an international market could benefit from economies of scale. In addition, offering products considered by advanced markets as obsolete to secondary and tertiary markets would extend the shelf life of a product and give sellers the opportunity to move products from inventory that could not otherwise be sold. International access to inexpensive labor and production facilities also affords firms in the industry the opportunity to consider backward integration in terms of developing their own "house brand" products with lower financial risk than would be the case without international options.

Specifically in regard to the US, the aging population suggests the need to offer products and use marketing approaches that appeal to older customers. Likewise, the increased ethnic diversity of the population, the staying power of the dual career family, and the subsequent increase in the purchasing power of women mark opportunities to provide and market electronic products to consumer groups beyond the typical white-middle-aged-male segment. Also, stagnating population growth in the US and expanding international populations and economies fuel opportunities in international expansion—opportunities that come however with the threat of increased competition from international firms.[30]

The economic downturn and tightening of credit late in the most recent decade resulted in decreased growth for several consumer electronics firms and likely contributed to the demise of Best Buy competitors such as Circuit City and CompUSA. In general, firms selling lower-end electronic products are thought to benefit from this trend while those selling cutting-edge technologies are expected to suffer. Clearly, the speed and extent of economic recovery will influence future growth opportunities. Recent indicators suggest that personal income is on the rise in the US, a change that will likely increase the demand for luxury, high-end, and discretionary products once again.[31] However, recession induced trends such as increased financial prudence could at least temporarily delay this effect. Responses to the recession that influence inflation and trade balances internationally—and by extension, exchange rates—will affect the viability of international expansion.

With increased competition in the consumer electronics industry coming from online retailers, the political/legal segment is becoming increasingly important to firms like Best Buy. This is because when a company operates even a single bricks-and-mortar retail outlet in a US state, all sales made within that state, both in-store and online, are subject to sales tax.[32] Alternatively, if a firm does not have a "physical presence" in a state, they do not have to charge its online customers sales tax. The issue up for debate is whether distribution centers fall within the definition of "physical presence" with online retailers threatening to pull distribution centers— and the jobs they provide—from any state that says it is so. With retail locations in the majority of US states, Best Buy would like to see state legislators level the playing field by clearing up the definition to explicitly include these distribution centers.[33]

Competitors

The industry in which Best Buy operates is in an unprecedented state of flux. The recession finished the job of eliminating weak competitors in the specialty consumer electronics store segment that started years earlier with the advent of the Internet and mass-market merchandisers. With the elimination of Best Buy's traditional head-to-head competitors (i.e., those like Circuit City and CompUSA that sold the same products and used the same format), Best Buy is left to compete primarily against unfamiliar rivals on unknown terrain. The strategies and tactics used by competitors coming from the online retail, warehouse club, and mass market approaches differ from those traditionally used by bricks-and-mortar electronics stores. Major competitors

in the "new" consumer electronics industry and their effects on industry competition are discussed below.

Amazon.com. Jeff Bezos developed the idea for Amazon.com in 1990 when he was struck by the goodness-of-fit of book selling via online marketing because of the need for precise and automated inventory controls in each. Over the next four years, he developed the idea for his new company and launched the online bookstore in 1995. Sales grew rapidly and the company went public in 1997. Realizing the potential based on its unprecedented success, in 1998, Bezos contracted with AOL and Netscape to increase Amazon's visibility to Internet users, and later that year, Amazon added music, video, electronics, and toy segments to its product offerings.[34]

Since its inception, Amazon has continued to grow— sometimes through its own ventures including the development of Endless.com, Amazon's online shoe store, its own e-reader device, the Kindle, and the addition of media downloading services including music, TV shows, and movies—but oftentimes through acquisitions of online retail firms. Each representing a product market niche, the firms Amazon has acquired offer a range of products and services including audio books (audible.com), to pet care (pets.com), and groceries (homegrocer.com). Acquisition of a European version of Netflix suggests that Amazon may be considering entry into the mail-delivered DVD rental business in the US. While most acquisitions serve to extend Amazon's reach into markets it can effectively and efficiently supply, some come with additional benefits as well. For example, Amazon's acquisition of Zappos.com not only increased its presence in the online shoe market but also made it possible for Amazon to integrate some of Zappo's customer service skills into its main operation.[35]

Not one to be behind the curve, Amazon quickly capitalized on the smartphone trend as a way to sell new products and attract new business. Early in 2011, Amazon went into direct competition with Google's App Marketplace with the launch of its Appstore for Android. Amazon's site allows customers to "test drive" an app before purchasing, carries ad supported free apps, and has a "premium-app-a-day" giveaway to increase market share and encourage customers to regularly check back with the site.[36] In a major coup and as mentioned previously, Amazon's new shopping app allows smartphone users to say the name of a product or take a picture of its cover art or bar code (presumably in a store) and receive instant information on the price of the product at Amazon—as well as the opportunity to make the purchase.[37]

There are two factors central to Amazon's successful bid as a consumer electronics retailer. First, its operating expenses are lower than those typical of a bricks-and-mortar operation with less than average lease obligations, payroll, insurance, utilities, and the like.[38] Because of these cost savings, Amazon has been able to engage in price wars to increase market share and profits. Second and as previously discussed, because Amazon does not have physical retail locations, it is able to sell its products without sales tax in most locations, giving it an automatic price advantage of several percent over bricks-and-mortar competitors in most states.[39] As might be expected, Amazon's operating results—even in the midst of a recession—have been impressive. The firm has averaged 32 percent annual revenue growth between fiscal years 2008 and 2010 and, with growth of almost 40 percent during the last year, this growth is accelerating. During this same three-year period, the firm's net profit margin remained stable at 3.37 percent.[40] These results support investors' optimism for Amazon's future and account for the 33 percent increase in its stock price.[41]

Walmart. Sam Walton opened a five-and-dime store as a franchisee in 1945. After the franchise owners dismissed his idea of opening discount stores in small towns, he and his brother Bud opened their first Walmart store in 1962. The firm grew quickly and is now the largest retailer in the world. Although most of its sales come from Walmart and Sam's Club stores in the US, Walmart's international division is growing rapidly and has established its presence in Canada, Mexico, Europe, and Asia.[42]

Walmart stores epitomize the "big box" model of retail. The firm operates stores that range from large to gigantic with product offerings designed to meet most of the needs of the average consumer. While the mega retailer officially falls within the "Discount and Variety Retail" industry, depending on location, its major product offerings may include groceries, pharmacy goods, gasoline, clothing, furnishings, music and video entertainment, software, office products, sporting goods, toys, consumer electronics, and appliances. Additionally, the firm has a significant online presence, has dabbled in online music downloads, and is considering a video downloading venture.[43]

Walmart uses its unmatched economies of scale and scope, considerable bargaining power with suppliers, as well as well-developed logistical competencies to offer a broad range of merchandise at prices that competing firms have a hard time matching.[44] While Walmart does not classify itself as an electronics retailer, it is second in electronics sales only to Best Buy—and gaining. It is important to note however that most of Walmart's electronics sales come from lower-end audio/video products where margins tend to be lower.[45]

Similar to most businesses considered in economic terms to carry inferior products, Walmart fared well during the recession. While revenue growth was modest and stable from fiscal year 2008 to 2011 at 3.65 percent per year, the firm's net profit margin steadily increased from 3.3 percent in 2009 to 3.89 percent in 2011.[46]

Costco. The firm known today as Costco Wholesale resulted from the merger of Price Club and Costco Wholesale in 1993. Price Club was founded by Sol Price in 1975, and the original Costco was founded by Jeffrey Brotman, a former executive VP of Price Club, in 1983. The merger of the two firms and its subsequent growth in the US, Canada, Mexico, Europe, and Asia makes Costco Wholesale the largest wholesale club in the world. Though Costco locations offer limited variety within each product type, the scope of its product offerings is wide and includes fresh foods and groceries, household items, clothing, jewelry, pharmacy, office supplies, tools, automotive supplies, consumer electronics, furniture, insurance, payroll and travel services, and even car sales.[47]

Costco offers products that are of a slightly higher quality compared to other mass-market merchandisers, often contracting with upscale brands for large quantities of a certain product. These products may then be sold under the original brand name (or a version of it) or, alternatively, rebranded and sold under Costco's Kirkland Signature store brand that, as store brands go, has come to have an upscale image. Costco is able to offer low prices by almost exclusively stocking items that sell quickly, allowing it to take a smaller margin on each item while continuing to provide exceptional value to its customers and maintaining a high level of profitability.[48]

As is the case with Walmart, consumer electronics is only a portion of Costco's business. Best Buy attempts to maintain an edge over discounters like Costco by offering superior service, a bigger selection, and cutting-edge technologies. However, with the recent economic downturn, consumers have been more reticent to jump into buying the newest technologies, making Costco's "garden variety" offerings and low prices quite appealing. The firm has also made some progress on the service front. While its departmental service remains limited, the addition of its "Concierge" program—offering after-sale technical assistance via telephone and a free second year warranty—is beginning to encroach on benefits typically dominated by specialty retailers.[49] In addition, Costco has begun to develop relationships with premium suppliers like Sony, allowing it to sell higher-end products that were once distributed only by specialty electronics retailers.[50]

Despite its discounted pricing, Costco's reputation for higher product quality backfired during the economic recession as many customers returned to their "bare bones" purchasing habits. This likely explains Costco's 6.57 percent three-year revenue growth average compared to its five-year average of 8.05 percent. Nevertheless, Costco's traditionally low net profit margin has been stable with a 1.65 percent average between 2007 and 2010.[51]

Radio Shack. In 1963, Charles Tandy purchased a financially distressed electronics parts distributor named Radio Shack to add to his investment portfolio. Within ten years, the Radio Shack portion of his portfolio accounted for 50 percent of sales and 80 percent of earnings. Between 1973 and 2010, the firm undertook multiple acquisitions and divestitures in industries as diverse as furniture, trucking, and consumer credit, but the small format Radio Shack branded store remained at the center of business.[52]

Radio Shack's primary industry is consumer electronics. Despite offering a small variety of traditional consumer electronics including televisions, DVD players, stereo equipment, MP3 players, navigation systems, electronic toys, etc., the company is most well known for its selection of batteries, electronic parts, and components—a market niche that has not been intruded upon by its larger competitors. However, Radio Shack has lost market share of traditional consumer electronics to Best Buy in recent years and its specialty electronics and components business has not been profitable enough to carry the chain. In response to this difficulty, Radio Shack (or "The Shack" as it is trying to rebrand itself) shifted its emphasis to the sales of cell phones and wireless contracts for three major carriers—a shift that resulted in a significant financial turnaround for the firm.[53] However, major cell phone companies have reduced the profitability of the cell phone brokering business and this will cut into Radio Shack's profits and growth beginning immediately.[54]

At this point, Radio Shack's operating results still tell a story of recovery. Revenue growth in 2010 was 4.6 percent compared to an average of 1.7 percent for the three years prior and −2.52 percent for the five years prior. Net profit margins also increased markedly after Radio Shack's emphatic switch to mobile phone and contract sales, averaging 4.88 percent for the four years since refocusing, compared to a net profit margin of 1.54 percent for the year before the change.[55] However, net profit margins have stagnated at recent levels (4.61 percent for YTD 2011) and have nowhere to go but down as the cell phone business becomes increasingly less profitable.

The Big Picture

Reporting Segments

Best Buy's operations are divided into two main segments. The domestic segment accounts for the bulk

of Best Buy's revenues ($37.1 billion of $50.3 billion in 2011), and is made up of Best Buy branded big box stores, a number of Best Buy Mobile, Geek Squad, Pacific Sales, and Magnolia Audio Video stores, as well as the Napster brand. The international segment is made up of relatively fewer Best Buy stores and an eclectic mix of appliance, electronic, and cell phone store brands Best Buy has acquired in its forays into international markets. This division accounts for $13.1 billion of 2011 revenue.

Both the domestic and international divisions generate revenue through sales in six main categories: consumer electronics (televisions, home theater systems, and DVD players), home office (computers and cell phones), entertainment (DVDs, Blu-ray discs, and video game software), appliances (refrigerators, washing machines, and vacuums), services (installation, repair, and support), and other (non-core items such as food and beverage). As shown in Exhibit 2, consumer electronics and home office products account for the bulk of sales in both divisions while entertainment makes up a significant portion of sales (14 percent) in the domestic division, and the appliances and services segments make up a significant portion of sales (9 percent each) in the international division.[56]

Retail Formats

Best Buy Big Box Stores. These large format stores account for the bulk of the firm's domestic operations and are beginning to become more prevalent abroad. The stores are designed to be one-stop shops that meet all of the consumer electronics and home appliance needs of its customers. These stores offer a wide variety of brands and models in each of the product segments listed above including premium brands (such as Sony, Apple, and Samsung in the consumer electronics segment) as well as lower-cost brands (such as LG), and more recently, low-cost store brands (such as Insignia). In addition, many Best Buy stores now offer the Best Buy Mobile store-within-a-store feature and access to Geek Squad services, with plans to outfit the remaining stores with these services as well.[57]

Best Buy's big box stores have been profitable in the US, Canada (where Best Buy also operates Future Shop large format stores—giving the illusion of competition), and Mexico. In its original plans with European joint venture partner Carphone Warehouse, Best Buy announced it would open its first stores in 2009 and "a hundred or so" big box stores in the UK (later re-estimated at 80) and 200 across Europe within four to five years.[58] After opening its first location a year late in 2010, Best Buy Europe CEO Scott Wheway speculated it would have another nine stores open within the year.[59] As of the mid-year mark in 2011, Best Buy Europe had managed to open ten locations in the UK and was going

Exhibit 2 Best Buy Business Segment Performance (in millions)

	2011	2010	2009
Revenue			
Domestic	$37,186	$37,314	$35,070
International	13,086	12,380	9,945
Total revenue	$50,272	$49,694	$45,015
Percentage of revenue, by revenue category			
Domestic:			
Consumer electronics	37%	39%	39%
Home office	37%	34%	31%
Entertainment	14%	16%	19%
Appliances	5%	4%	5%
Services	6%	6%	6%
Other	1%	1%	< 1%
Total	100%	100%	100%
International:			
Consumer electronics	21%	20%	26%
Home office	55%	53%	45%
Entertainment	6%	7%	9%
Appliances	9%	8%	10%
Services	9%	12%	10%
Other	<1%	<1%	<1%
Total	100%	100%	100%

Source: Best Buy Co. Inc. Form 10-K For fiscal year ended February 26, 2011. *sec.gov.* [Online] May 17, 2011. [Cited: May 17, 2011]. http://www.sec.gov

back to the drawing board with Carphone Warehouse to review their plans.[60] Best Buy has had difficulty in other international locations as well. The Best Buy branded big box stores in China have not proven to be as profitable as those run under the acquired Five Star brand, and Best Buy is currently working to reformat its Best Buy stores into Five Star locations. Additionally, the Best Buy store in Turkey has been unprofitable and will be closed this year.[61] Closer to home, with no large format competitors left in existence, the size of some of Best Buy's big box stores may be superfluous as, having a showroom four times the size the nearest competitor may be less profitable than being only two or three times their size.

Geek Squad. Best Buy acquired Geek Squad in 2003 and integrated the firm and its concept within its big box stores. This branch of Best Buy offers after-sale services including installation, repair, and technical support.[62] Examples of specific services offered include home theater and surround sound setup, flat screen television mounting, wireless network setup, virus and spyware removal, and the installation of aftermarket electronic equipment such as GPS and remote starters in cars.[63]

Though the services Best Buy sells through the Geek Squad make up a relatively small portion of revenue, the percentage is consistently increasing and the profit margin earned on Geek Squad services is higher than the firm average.[64]

Best Buy Mobile. These stores focus on selling cellular phones and small computing devices and their associated service plans and accessories. Best Buy Mobile stores can be found within all domestic and Canadian big box locations and, in increasing numbers, as stand-alone "small box" stores.[65] It offers cell phones from all major brands including Apple, Motorola, LG, and Samsung running on all major platforms (i.e., iOS, Android, Blackberry, and Windows), and sells service contracts with all major providers such as Verizon, AT&T, T-Mobile, and Sprint as well as contract-free phones through Boost Mobile, Virgin Mobile, and MetroPCS.[66] As with Geek Squad, Best Buy Mobile operations have provided a financial cushion for the firm in what could have been a very difficult time. For example, although Best Buy comparable store sales experienced a five percent slump in December 2010, the decrease would have been 15 percent if not for the addition of Best Buy Mobile sales.[67]

Bestbuy.com. In recent years, Bestbuy.com, the firm's online channel, has become more integrated with the in-store experience. Most of the same products offered in the big box stores are available through the online channel, as well as many additional products.[68] Driving customers to the site, Bestbuy.com attempts to outdo other online retailers by providing superior assistance to customers making purchases. For example, the site provides 24/7 human customer assistance, user forums, professional and customer reviews, and optional in-store pickup. The website's value to Best Buy extends beyond the revenue produced by sales. In fact, it has been estimated that regardless of whether they eventually purchase products from the website or a bricks-and-mortar store, 60 percent of Best Buy customers begin their research and shopping on the Best Buy website.[69]

The Carphone Warehouse. Unlike the domestic division's big box format stores, most of the stores making up the Best Buy Europe portion of the international division are either Carphone Warehouse or Phone House branded "small box" stores. Not coincidentally, these stores are similar to Best Buy Mobile stores, offering cell phones, service contracts, and small computing devices with a large percentage of their revenue derived from the sales of device insurance. (A team of consultants from Carphone Warehouse helped develop the Best Buy Mobile plan.) Many of the stores also offer Geek Squad services that focus mainly on the repair of consumer-owned devices.[70] Best Buy Europe is a 50 percent owner in the over 1400 Carphone Warehouse and Phone House stores in Europe.

Five Star Appliances. Prior to its acquisition by Best Buy in 2007, the Jiangsu Five Star Appliance Company was one of the largest retailers of consumer electronics and appliances in China.[71] Best Buy's reasoning for the acquisition was two-fold. First, it offered a quick way to move into and gain a foothold in the lucrative and growing consumer electronics market in China and second, it was seen as an opportunity to get an inside perspective of selling electronics in China from a successful firm. With the exception of entertainment media, the large format Five Star stores offer a similar mix of products to Best Buy stores in the US. Overall, Best Buy's Five Star branded stores have done well, even during the recession, and Best Buy plans to open 10 to 15 additional stores in the coming year.[72] The importance of the Five Star stores is seen when their success is juxtaposed against the lack-luster performance of the soon-to-be-closed/re-branded Best Buy stores in China. With similar product offerings and overhead expenses, this disparity of outcomes can only be explained by the fact that Five Star was developed by individuals who understood the culture, while Best Buy stores and operating procedures were largely imported from abroad.

Past and Current Strategies

Before Best Buy's bricks-and-mortar competitors shut down it was clear that, considering how easy it was to drive to a competitor's location, no firm targeting the broad consumer electronics market would be successful if it charged too high a premium over its competitors. Because of this, Best Buy was forced to find ways to reduce its costs to remain competitive. While Best Buy's size and purchasing power was and is an important factor in keeping costs down, former CEO Brad Anderson admitted that the firm did not develop its own approaches to reducing costs. Instead, Best Buy observed companies like Walmart and Target and then acted as a "fast follower" to implement new ideas and efficiencies in ways suited to Best Buy's operations.[73] Through copying the successful approaches to logistical issues of stores like Walmart and Target[74] and building relationships with its network of suppliers,[75] Best Buy is able to quickly and accurately distribute its products to stores and customers worldwide.

Although cost efficiencies have been important to Best Buy, to avoid falling into a "commodity hell" where all competition in the industry is based on price, the firm has had to develop other reasons for Best Buy to be a shopper's first stop. According to Ranjay Gulati of Harvard Business School, Best Buy has done this by doing a better job than its competitors at looking at the electronics industry through the eyes of a customer. In other words, instead of telling customers what they *should* want next, Best Buy works to understand both the technology as well as its customers' needs, wants, and tendencies so it may then provide technological solutions that not only match, but actually work for the consumer.[76] In addition, rather than simply presenting a display model and a stack of boxes containing the product, Best Buy is highly adept at anticipating all of the needs a consumer may have in association with a particular purchase. These needs may include help with product comparison and selection, home delivery and setup, training, accessories, service, etc. To meet these needs, Best Buy has developed well thought out and communicated processes, structures, displays, and services.[77]

As an extension of this proficiency and even before the recent narrowing of the field in the big box segment of the consumer electronics industry, Best Buy had a reputation for providing superior sales assistance for a big box retailer. Today, with its main competitors a warehouse chain offering essentially no sales assistance, a website that discourages person-to-person customer service contact, and an oversized grocery store with extremely limited specialized support staff, it would seem that Best Buy has the potential to not only retain, but extend, this lead. Disappointingly, however, a recent consumer survey revealed that customers perceived Best Buy's service as only average, placing Best Buy flat even with Amazon and only slightly ahead of Costco and Walmart. While the customer service expectations of a consumer entering a Best Buy are likely higher than when entering a Costco or Walmart, Best Buy cannot lower the bar to those levels simply because CompUSA and Circuit City are no longer around.[78]

Best Buy refers to its overarching plan for its future as the "Connected World" strategy. Best Buy defines this approach as follows: "Broadly defined, our Connected World strategy is based on the goal to demystify and humanize technology to help customers get the most out of the rapidly expanding role that technology plays in their lives."[79] Major objectives associated with this goal include growing the Bestbuy.com web presence to capitalize on online opportunities, expanding the Best Buy Mobile segment in the US, utilizing its size and scale to improve returns in international markets, and increasing its presence at a reduced cost by increasingly relying on stores with a smaller footprint.[80] As a positive indication of the potential of its international expansion, compared to many firms that experience a high failure rate in their foreign acquisitions, the vast majority of Best Buy's acquisitions of foreign electronics companies have been profitable.[81] This suggests that the firm knows how to bring the benefits of Best Buy's scale and experience to its acquired firms without requiring conformity in areas that could dilute the location specific strategies that made the acquired firm desirable in the first place.

While Best Buy has standardized many of its processes across its big box stores to create economies of scale and reduce operating costs, as illustrated by its management of acquisitions, Best Buy remains flexible in many novel ways including its understanding of the benefits attached to supporting entrepreneurial innovations initiated at the store level. For example, noticing the large Brazilian population near a Manhattan store, store managers hired Portuguese-speaking staff to better serve that population segment and brokered a deal with a Brazilian cruise company to bring tourists to Best Buy as a stop on their trip.[82] With a company culture that values the ability to recognize opportunity and spearhead this type of initiative, Best Buy is more likely to develop company policies that allow it to compete successfully with small local competitors both domestically and abroad.

As for innovation beyond the big box model most often associated with Best Buy, the rapid financial success of the new Best Buy Mobile stores in the US and Canada, as well as the ongoing profitable growth of the Carphone Warehouse stores in Europe suggest that Best Buy has the capabilities necessary to compete in this market. Furthermore, the speed with which Best Buy Mobile stores in North America went from non-existent to successful suggests that Best Buy may be particularly adept at adapting knowledge gained in one locale to another.

Financial Results

The above strategies have resulted in the financial outcomes examined in this section. Despite a 1.16 percent increase in gross revenue, Best Buy's fiscal year 2011 net income dropped 3 percent (see Exhibits 3A and 3B for and overview of BBY financial performance). A key component of Best Buy's decreasing net income was an increase in selling, general, and administrative (SG&A) expenses. From 2010 to 2011, SG&A increased $452 million, or 4.4 percent, and followed its 2009 to 2010 increase of over 10 percent. Clearly, Best Buy did not adjust its fixed costs when revenue growth went into decline.[83] Although its increased expenses were well masked by gains in other segments, the economic downturn and changes in the competitive nature of the industry have affected Best Buy. While its average revenue growth over the last five years was 10.26 percent, it slowed to 7.9 percent in the last three years, and became downright sluggish in fiscal year 2011 at 1.16 percent.

Best Buy's domestic sales contribute 74 percent of total gross revenues—$37.2 billion compared to $13.1 billion from the international segment (see again, Exhibit 2). In the international segment, Best Buy's primary regions are Europe with 10.9 percent of total revenue ($5.5 billion), Canada with 10.8 percent ($5.4 billion), and China with 3.9 percent ($1.9 billion) (Exhibit 4). Beyond these three, the total of all other foreign sales contribute the remaining .03 percent ($155 million) of total revenue. Historical financial reports demonstrate that revenue growth as a percentage of sales is greatest in the international segment of the firm; from 2007 to 2010, international gross revenue increased an average of 15 percent per year as opposed to less than 6 percent in the domestic segment.[84]

Looking at the product categories that Best Buy sells, consumer electronics comprise 37 percent of US sales (down from 39 percent in the previous fiscal year) and 21 percent of international sales (up from 20 percent) (Exhibit 2). Home office equipment was the largest component in foreign sales at 55 percent, which was a 2 percent increase from prior year sales. In the US, home office equipment accounted for 37 percent of sales, up 3 percent from the previous year. In total, the remaining categories of entertainment, appliances, services, and other made up 26 percent of US sales (down 1 percent as a group) and 24 percent of international sales (down 3 percent).[85]

Exhibit 3A Best Buy Income Statement (in millions)

Fiscal Years Ended	$ in millions, except per share amounts		
	February 26, 2011	February 27, 2010	February 28, 2009
Revenue	$50,272	$49,694	$45,015
Cost of goods sold	37,611	37,534	34,017
Restructuring charges — cost of goods sold	24	—	—
Gross profit	12,637	12,160	10,998
Selling, general and administrative expenses	10,325	9,873	8,984
Restructuring charges	198	52	78
Goodwill and tradename impairment	—	—	66
Operating income	2,114	2,235	1,870
Other income (expense)			
Investment income and other	51	54	35
Investment impairment	—	—	(111)
Interest expense	(87)	(94)	(94)
Earnings before income tax expense and equity in income of affiliates	2,078	2,195	1,700
Income tax expense	714	802	674
Equity in income of affiliates	2	1	7
Net earnings including noncontrolling interests	1,366	1,394	1,033
Net earnings attributable to noncontrolling interests	(89)	(77)	(30)
Net earnings attributable to Best Buy Co., Inc.	$ 1,277	$ 1,317	$ 1,003
Earnings per share attributable to Best Buy Co., Inc.			
Basic	$ 3.14	$ 3.16	$ 2.43
Diluted	$ 3.08	$ 3.10	$ 2.39
Weighted-average common shares outstanding (in millions)			
Basic	406.1	416.8	412.5
Diluted	416.5	427.5	422.9

Source: Best Buy Co. Inc. Form 10-K For fiscal year ended February 26, 2011. *sec.gov.* [Online] May 17, 2011. [Cited: May 17, 2011]. http://www.sec.gov

Exhibit 3B Best Buy Consolidated Balance Sheet (in millions)

	February 26, 2011	February 27, 2010
Assets		
Current Assets		
Cash and cash equivalents	$ 1,103	$ 1,826
Short-term investments	22	90
Receivables	2,348	2,020
Merchandise inventories	5,897	5,486
Other current assets	1,103	1,144
Total current assets	10,473	10,566
Property and Equipment		
Land and buildings	766	757
Leasehold improvements	2,318	2,154
Fixtures and equipment	4,701	4,447
Property under capital lease	120	95
	7,905	7,453
Less accumulated depreciation	4,082	3,383
Net property and equipment	3,823	4,070

(Continued)

Exhibit 3B Best Buy Consolidated Balance Sheet (in millions) (*Continued*)

	February 26, 2011	February 27, 2010
Goodwill	2,454	2,452
Tradenames, Net	133	159
Customer Relationships, Net	203	279
Equity and Other Investments	328	324
Other Assets	435	452
Total Assets	**$17,849**	**$18,302**
Liabilities and Equity		
Current Liabilities		
Accounts payable	$ 4,894	$ 5,276
Unredeemed gift card liabilities	474	463
Accrued compensation & related expenses	570	544
Accrued liabilities	1,471	1,681
Accrued income taxes	256	316
Short-term debt	557	663
Current portion of long-term debt	441	35
Total current liabilities	8,663	8,978
Long-Term Liabilities	1,183	1,256
Long-Term Debt	711	1,104
Contingencies and Commitments		
Equity		
Best Buy Co., Inc. Shareholders' Equity		
Common stock, $0.10 par value: Authorized — 1.0 billion shares; Issued and outstanding — 392,590,000 and 418,815,000 shares, respectively	39	42
Additional paid-in capital	18	441
Retained earnings	6,372	5,797
Accumulated other comprehensive income	173	40
Total BB Co., Inc. shareholders' equity	6,602	6,320
Noncontrolling interests	690	644
Total equity	7,292	6,964
Total Liabilities and Equity	**$17,849**	**$18,302**

Source: Best Buy Co. Inc. Form 10-K For fiscal year ended February 26, 2011. *sec.gov*. [Online] May 17, 2011. [Cited: May 17, 2011]. http://www.sec.gov

When compared to its competitors, Best Buy's gross profit margin of 25.14 percent is only slightly less than Walmart's 25.26 percent and better than Amazon's 22.37 percent. It is in the net profit margin that Best Buy's challenges surface. At 2.54 percent, Best Buy is markedly lower that Walmart and Amazon at 3.88 percent and 2.85 percent respectively. Providing further comparison, the market standards in the gross and net profit margin categories are 30.36 percent and 3.87 percent respectively.[86]

Strategic Leaders

The strategic leaders responsible for the financial results discussed are described in this section. Best Buy's ownership is made up of 65 percent institutional and mutual fund owners, 19 percent insiders and large-block shareholders, with the remaining shares held by various investors. The largest institutional stockholder of Best Buy (FMR LLC) and the largest mutual fund stockholder (American Funds) collectively own more than 10 percent of Best Buy thus providing a solid governance mechanism. The largest individual stockholder is Richard Schulze, founder and current Chairman of the Board.[87]

External members and insiders represent 71 percent and 29 percent of Best Buy's comparatively heterogeneous Board of Directors, respectively. The key insiders on the Board of Directors include Richard Schulze (Founder and Chairman of the Board), Brian

Exhibit 4 Foreign and Domestic Sales Distribution (in millions)

Net sales to customers	2011	2010	2009
US	$37,186	$37,315	$35,070
Europe	5,511	5,591	3,205
Canada	5,468	5,065	5,174
China	1,952	1,677	1,558
Other	155	46	8
Total revenue	$50,272	$49,694	$45,015
Long-lived assets			
US	$ 2,741	$ 2,960	$ 3,155
Europe	438	464	439
Canada	474	462	408
China	147	152	161
Other	23	32	11
Total long-lived assets	$ 3,823	$ 4,070	$ 4,174

Source: Best Buy Co. Inc. Form 10-K For fiscal year ended February 26, 2011. *sec.gov.* [Online] May 17, 2011. [Cited: May 17, 2011]. http://www.sec.gov

Dunn (CEO), and Elliot Kaplan (Director of Finance & Investment Policy Committee). Additional key insiders on the Board include Jianguo Wang (Chairman of subsidiary Jiangsu Five Star Appliance), Kathy Higgins (Independent Director of Best Buy since November 1999), Ronald James (Independent Director of Best Buy since May 2004), and Rogelio Rebolledo (Director of Best Buy since August 2006). Key outsiders on the Board include Hatim Tyabji (Bytemobile), Gerard Vittecoq (Caterpillar), Lisa Caputo (Citigroup), Matthew Paull (KapStone Paper and Packaging), Sanjay Khosla (Kraft Foods), and George Mikan III (UnitedHealth Group).[88]

Best Buy's key strategic decision makers include Richard Schulze (Founder and Chairman of the Board), Brian Dunn (CEO), James Meuhlbauer (CFO), and Andrew Harrison (Best Buy Europe CEO).[89]

Richard Schulze received technical training in electronics from the US Air Force and founded the company in 1966. He took Best Buy public in 1985 and held the position of CEO for the following 19 years. Aside from Best Buy, Schulze is a member of several Boards including St. Thomas Business School, National Entrepreneurs of the Year Institute, and Pentair, Inc. Schulze's marketing and entrepreneurial spirit was instrumental in Best Buy growing into the largest US electronics retailer. Currently Chairman of the Board, Schulze's main responsibilities include long-term strategic planning and the development of leaders within the company. Schulze's total compensation for the year 2010 was $165,000.[90]

Brian Dunn has been with Best Buy for 26 years, working his way up from Store Manger to become CEO in 2009. In addition to his position at Best Buy, Dunn

also serves on the Board of Directors for Dick's Sporting Goods and is a member of the Board of the Consumer Electronics Association. Dunn's total compensation for the year 2010 was $10.2 million.[91]

James Meuhlbauer was hired as CFO in 2008 after serving as interim CFO in 2007. He came to Best Buy after 10 years with Pillsbury where he was a Vice President and Controller. Meuhlbauer has extensive experience in audit/compliance having worked as a consultant and full time employee of several law firms. Meuhlbauer's total compensation for the year 2010 was $2.95 million.[92]

Andrew Harrison was named CEO of Best Buy Europe in February 2011 amidst a suddenly unstable time within the Carphone Warehouse/Best Buy joint venture during which it lost several key leaders including Best Buy Europe's head of online services, its branded operations chief, marketing director,[93] CEO, and Carphone's senior insight manager.[94] Originally hired in 1995 by Carphone Warehouse as its Strategy Manager, Harrison became Carphone's Commercial Director in 1998 and CEO in 2001. Harrison had been previously appointed COO of Best Buy Europe in July 2010 in addition to his CEO position with Carphone Warehouse and The Phone House.

Challenges

Best Buy's strategic leaders begin the second decade of the 21st century facing several key strategic challenges. From its beginnings as a single retail outlet, it has grown to become the largest big box chain in the consumer electronics industry. Through its 45-year life, the company has successfully navigated changes in technology, customer needs, and the industry environment in general to remain profitable but to continue to do so will require its leadership to make important strategic decisions. An increased intensity of competition in an evolved and less familiar form is exerting pressure on Best Buy's bottom line. The retail industry in general has embraced the online delivery of products—a development that places weighty competitive pressure on retailers that continue to bear the costs associated with maintaining bricks-and-mortar stores. As the products that Best Buy traditionally sells become increasingly commoditized and profit margins are reduced, the firm will need to find new ways to achieve profitability in the industry—or will need to find a new industry in which to compete. Will Best Buy try to continue to set itself apart through its product line and customer service? Will it try to find a way to reduce costs substantially enough to "slug it out" with online competitors? Can its strategic leaders formulate a strategy to do both?

At face value, Best Buy's "Connected World Strategy" appears to be a reasonable approach to answering these questions. A closer and more critical analysis of the firm's own description of how it will execute this strategy, however, raises concern. When parsed for meaning, this strategy seems to center on customer facing goals. However, whether these goals can be achieved via the operational objectives and physical alterations (i.e., non customer facing goals) discussed earlier remains to be seen.

Combining these questions leads to one main query that the firm's leadership will need to answer: Given the realities of the new industry environment, how can Best Buy best develop, combine, and exploit its capabilities and competencies to form a sustainable competitive advantage? Best Buy's continued growth, profitability, relevance, and, in fact, survival will likely depend on the ability of its leaders to find concrete and effective answers to this question.

NOTES

1. Best Buy Co., Inc. Profile. *Hoovers A D&B Company.* [Online] May 15, 2011. [Cited: May 15, 2011]. http://subscriber.hoovers .com.ezproxy1.lib.asu.edu /H/company360/companyPDFReport .pdf?companyId=10209000000000

2. White, B. Best Buy's CEO tells secret of success. *BloggingStocks. com.* [Online] Apr 19, 2007. [Cited: May 15, 2011]. http://www .bloggingstocks.com/2007/04/19/best-buys-ceo-a-qanda-with-the -industry/

3. Tennant, D. Why Circuit City tanked. *ComputerWorld.* [Online] Jan 16, 2009. [Cited: Aug 9, 2011]. http://blogs.computerworld.com/ why_circuit_city_tanked

4. Best Buy Co. Inc. Form 10-K for fiscal year ended February 26, 2011. *sec.gov.* [Online] May 17, 2011. [Cited: May 17, 2011]. http:// www.sec.gov/Archives/edgar/data/764478/000104746911004045/ a2203505z10-k.htm

5. Best Buy (BBY): Amazon's (AMZN) Showroom? *Haaretz Daily.* [Online] Mar 25, 2011. [Cited: May 17, 2011]. http://www .haaretzdaily.com/best-buy-bby-amazon%e2%80%99s-amzn -showroom/

6. Jannarone, J. Forecast for Best Buy: worst is yet to come. *The Wall Street Journal.* [Online] Mar 4, 2011. [Cited: May 17, 2011]. http://online.wsj.com/article/SB10001424052748703300904576178 740814079726.html

7. Best Buy (BBY): Amazon's (AMZN) Showroom? *op. cit.*

8. Best Buy Co., Inc. Profile. *op. cit.*

9. Best Buy Co. Inc. Form 10-K for fiscal year ended February 26, 2011. *op. cit.*

10. Best Buy Co., Inc. Profile. *op. cit.*

11. Best Buy Co. Inc. Form 10-K for fiscal year ended February 26, 2011. o *op. cit.*

12. Best Buy Co., Inc. Profile. *op. cit.*

13. Best Buy Co. Inc. Form 10-K for fiscal year ended February 26, 2011. *op. cit.*

14. Best Buy Co., Inc. Profile. *op. cit.*

15. Best Buy Co. Inc. Form 10-K for fiscal year ended February 26, 2011. *op. cit.*

16. *Ibid.*

17. Best Buy Co., Inc. Profile. *op. cit.*

18. Best Buy Co. Inc. Form 10-K for fiscal year ended February 26, 2011. *op. cit.*

19. Best Buy Co., Inc. Profile. *op. cit.*

20. Best Buy Co. Inc. Form 10-K for fiscal year ended February 26, 2011. *op. cit.*

21. Best Buy Co., Inc. Profile. *op. cit.*

22. Best Buy Co. Inc. Form 10-K for fiscal year ended February 26, 2011. *op. cit.*

23. Jannarone, J. *op. cit.*

24. Martin, S. How apple stores rewrote the rules of retailing. *usatoday .com.* [Online] May 18, 2011. [Cited: May 18, 2011]. http://www .usatoday.com/tech/news/2011-05-18-apple-retail-stores_n .htm?csp=34tech

25. Best Buy Co. Inc. Form 10-K for fiscal year ended February 26, 2011. *op. cit.*

26. Barrett, B. What would Best Buy do with Radio Shack? *gizmodo .com.* [Online] Mar 26, 2010. [Cited: May 18, 2011]. http://gizmodo .com/5502922/what-would-best-buy-do-with-radio-shack

27. Best Buy Co. Inc. Form 10-K for fiscal year ended February 26, 2011. *op. cit.*

28. *Ibid.*

29. Consumer electronics & appliance retail. *Hoovers, A D&B Company.* [Online] May 20, 2011. [Cited: May 20, 2011]. http:// subscriber.hoovers.com.ezproxy1.lib.asu.edu/H/industry360/ overview.html?industryId=1526

30. Harvey, C. Amazon distribution centers in Arizona face tax quandary. *Phoenix Business Journal.* [Online] May 13, 2011. [Cited: May 18, 2011]. http://www.bizjournals.com/phoenix/print -edition/2011/05/13/amazon-distribution-centers-face-tax.html

31. Consumer electronics & appliance retail. *op. cit.*

32. Manjoo, F. Every day's a tax holiday; How Amazon.com undersells Best Buy, the Apple store, and almost everybody else. *slate.com.* [Online] Nov 19, 2010. [Cited: May 18, 2011]. http://www.slate .com/id/2275552/

33. Harvey, C. *op. cit.*

34. Amazon.com Inc. Profile. *Hoovers: A D&B Company.* [Online] May 17, 2011. [Cited: May 17, 2011]. http://subscriber.hoovers .com.ezproxy1.lib.asu.edu/H/company360/companyPDFReport .pdf?companyId=51493000000000

35. *Ibid.*

36. Kincaid, J. Amazon's android app store launches: test drive apps directly from your browser. *techcrunch.com.* [Online] Mar 22, 2011. [Cited: May 18, 2011]. http://techcrunch.com/2011/03/22/amazon -android-app-store-3/

37. Carmody, T. Amazon's price check might be perfect smartphone shopping app. *Wired.com.* [Online] Nov 23, 2010. [Cited: May 18, 2011]. http://www.wired.com/gadgetlab/2010/11/amazons-price -check-might-be-perfect-smartphone-shopping-app/

38. Best Buy Co., Inc. Profile. *op. cit.*

39. Jannarone, J. *op. cit.*

40. Amazon.com Inc. Profile. *op. cit.*

41. Best Buy (BBY): Amazon's (AMZN) Showroom? *op. cit.*

42. Walmart Stores Inc. Profile. *Hoovers: A D&B Company.* [Online] May 17, 2011. [Cited: May 17, 2011]. http://subscriber.hoovers .com.ezproxy1.lib.asu.edu /H/company360/companyPDFReport .pdf?companyId=11600000000000

43. *Ibid.*

44. R. E. Hoskisson, M. A. Hitt, R. D. Ireland, & J. S. Harrison. *Competing For Advantage,* Second Edition. Mason, Ohio : South-Western Cengage Learning, 2008

45. Best Buy gives up market share to Walmart. *RetailerDaily .com.* [Online] Jun 4, 2009. [Cited: May 17, 2011]. http://www .retailerdaily.com/entry /41621/best-buy-market-share-wal-mart/

46. Walmart Stores Inc. Profile. *op. cit.*

47. Costco Wholesale Corporation Profile. *Hoovers: A D&B Company.* [Online] May 17, 2011. [Cited: May 17, 2011]. http:// subscriber.hoovers.com. ezproxy1.lib.asu.edu/H/company360/ companyPDFReport.pdf?companyId=17060000000000

48. Trefis Team. Costco just can't beat Best Buy in electronics, stock price headed south. *Forbes.com*. [Online] Dec 23, 2010. [Cited: May 18, 2011]. http://blogs.forbes. com/greatspeculations/2010/12/23/costco-just-cant-beat-best-buy-in-electronics-stock-price-headed-south/

49. Costo.com. Costco concierge services: technical support. *costco.com*. [Online] [Cited: May 19, 2011]. http://www.costco.com/Service/FeaturePage.aspx?ProductNo=11217032

50. Jannarone, J. *op. cit.*

51. Costco Wholesale Corporation Profile. *op. cit.*

52. RadioShack Corporation Inc. Profile. *Hoovers: A D&B Company*. [Online] May 17, 2011. [Cited: May 17, 2011]. http://subscriber.hoovers.com.ezproxy1. lib.asu.edu/H/company360/companyPDFReport.pdf?companyId=11441000000000

53. *Ibid.*

54. Barrett, B. *op. cit.*

55. RadioShack Corporation Inc. Profile. *op. cit.*

56. Best Buy Co. Inc. Form 10-K for fiscal year ended February 26, 2011. *op. cit.*

57. *Ibid.*

58. Felsted, A. Best Buy Europe strategy under review. *Financial Times*. [Online] Jun 12, 2011. [Cited: Aug 10, 2011] http://www.ft.com/intl/cms/s/0/b210f042-9524-11e0-a648-00144feab49a.html

59. Felsted, A. Best Buy Europe opens first British store. *Financial Times*. [Online] Apr 26, 2010. [Cited: Aug 10, 2011]. http://www.ft.com/cms/s/0/d11b5316-515e-11df-bed9-00144feab49a.html#axzz1UbmqVaZ3

60. Felsted, A. Best Buy Europe strategy under review. *op. cit.*

61. Best Buy Co. Inc. Form 10-K for fiscal year ended February 26, 2011. *op. cit.*

62. *Ibid.*

63. The Geek Squad: How may we assist you? *geeksquad.com*. [Online] 2011. [Cited: May 20, 2011]. http://www.geeksquad.com/

64. Best Buy Co. Inc. Form 10-K for fiscal year ended February 26, 2011. *op. cit.*

65. *Ibid.*

66. Best Buy Mobile Magazine. *bestbuymobile.com*. [Online] 2011. [Cited: May 20, 2011]. http://www.bestbuymobile.com/

67. Pinkerton, J. Dealer Profile: Best Buy Mobile gains traction. *Dealerscope*. [Online] Feb 23, 2011. [Cited: May 20, 2011]. http://www.dealerscope.com/article/best-buy-seeks-capitalize-new-devices-faster-networks/1

68. Best Buy Co. Inc. Form 10-K for fiscal year ended February 26, 2011. *op. cit.*

69. BestBuy.com provides value and a stress-free shopping experience for cyber monday and throughout the season. *Business Wire*. [Online] Dec 1, 2008. [Cited: May 18, 2011]. http://login.ezproxy1.lib.asu.edu/login?url=http://search.proquest.com/?url=http://search.proquest.com/docview/444355815?accountid=4485

70. Best Buy Co. Inc. Form 10-K for fiscal year ended February 26, 2011. *op. cit.*

71. Best Buy Co., Inc. Profile. *op. cit.*

72. Best Buy Co. Inc. Form 10-K for fiscal year ended February 26, 2011. *op. cit.*

73. Boyle, M. Q&A with Best Buy CEO Brad Anderson. *CNN Money*. [Online] Apr 18, 2007. [Cited: May 29, 2011]. http://money.cnn.com/magazines/fortune/fortune_archive/2007/04/30/8405481/index.htm

74. *Ibid.*

75. Best Buy Co. Inc. Form 10-K for fiscal year ended February 26, 2011. *op. cit.*

76. Gulati, R. Inside Best Buy's customer-centric strategy. *Harvard Business Review*. [Online] Apr 12, 2010. [Cited: May 18, 2011]. http://blogs.hbr.org/hbsfaculty/2010/04/inside-best-buys-customer-cent.html

77. Best Buy Co. Inc. Form 10-K for fiscal year ended February 26, 2011. *op. cit.*

78. Consumer Reports. Best electronics. *Consumer Reports*. Dec 1, 2010, pp. 20-22

79. Best Buy Co. Inc. Form 10-K for fiscal year ended February 26, 2011. *op. cit.*

80. *Ibid.*

81. *Ibid.*

82. Boyle, M. *op. cit.*

83. Best Buy Co. Inc. Form 10-K for fiscal year ended February 26, 2011. *op. cit.*

84. *Ibid.*

85. *Ibid.*

86. Best Buy Co., Inc. Profile. *op. cit.*

87. Best Buy CO., Inc. Major Holders. *Yahoo Finance*. [Online] 2011. [Cited: May 18, 2011]. http://finance.yahoo.com/q/mh?s=BBY+Major+Holders

88. Best Buy Co Inc. *Bloomberg.com*. [Online] 2011. [Cited: May 18, 2011]. http://investing.businessweek.com/research/stocks/people/people.asp?ticker=BBY:US

89. *Ibid.*

90. *Ibid.*

91. *Ibid.*

92. *Ibid.*

93. Baker, R. Best Buy UK marketing director exits. *MarketingWeek*. [Online] Feb 7, 2011. [Cited: Aug 8, 2011]. http://www.marketingweek.co.uk/sectors/retail/best-buy-uk-marketing-director-exits/3023163.article

94. Johnson, B. Carphone Warehouse retail insight chief jumps ship. *MarketingWeek*. [Online] Mar 14, 2011. [Cited: Aug 8, 2011]. http://www.marketingweek.co.uk/disciplines/data-strategy/carphone-warehouse-retail-insight-chief-jumps-ship/3024424.article

Chipotle: The Challenges of Integrity

Ryan Ruud, Jennifer Lee, Garrett Borges, Monica Bethke, Ron Bomkamp, Preston Jensen
Arizona State University

"FRESH IS NOT ENOUGH ANYMORE."
STEVE ELLS
CHIPOTLE CO-CEO, FOUNDER, AND CHAIR

Introduction

Chipotle Mexican Grill (NYSE: CMG) has experienced great success satisfying the desire of consumers for a quick-serve restaurant that doesn't sacrifice quality for speed. Known in the food industry as a "fast-casual" restaurant, Chipotle is part of the fastest growing segment of the restaurant industry.[1] With annual revenues pushing $2 billion and a stock price that doubled in 2010, Chipotle's steady growth and strong financial statements make it highly attractive to investors (see Exhibits 1–3). Chipotle achieves customer satisfaction while maintaining a unique vision that has committed the company to "finding the very best ingredients raised with respect for the animals, the environment, and the farmers."[2] Coupled with a deceptively simple menu that allows for over 60,000 different burrito combinations alone, interactive ordering so customers can personalize their experience and meal, and a reasonable price—it's no wonder Chipotle restaurants are full of happy customers and that the company has grown to nearly 1,100 locations in only 17 years.

History

At an age when most of his peer group was still watching cartoons, Steve Ells was a dedicated fan of Julia Childs' cooking show on PBS. After earning a bachelors degree in art history from the University of Colorado at Boulder, Ells began his formal cooking education at the Culinary Institute of America in New York. Following his graduation in 1990 and while working in San Francisco, Ells acquired a taste for the large, made-to-order burritos found at the many taquerias in the city.[3]

Deciding he could shake up the traditional Mexican made-to-order burrito by adding gourmet ingredients, the dream of Chipotle Mexican Grill was born.

With an $80,000 loan and an $85,000 investment from his father, Ells opened the first Chipotle restaurant in Denver, Colorado in 1993. Quickly ditching the traditional back-of-the-house kitchen, Ells brought customers and staff together with an open kitchen design that increased efficiency and gave customers more control over their food orders. While the menu and food ordering process was simple, Ells put his culinary education to work to imbue his burrito meats and other ingredients with gourmet flavor and panache.[4] Chipotle's original menu and ordering system was designed to offer only a few meal options (burritos and crispy or soft tacos), a manageable number of ingredient options (16), but thousands of flavor combinations. While its menu has remained primarily unchanged from the original, sensible additions like tortilla-free burrito bowls and salads for diet-conscious consumers keep Chipotle current with consumer trends.[5]

The original Chipotle was an instant success and Ells was able to repay his father nearly a month after opening. With a subsequent $1.5 million investment from his father and a $1.5 million private stock offering, Ells opened two more locations in 1995 and another five in 1996.[6] Chipotle had found its as yet unnamed niche market between fast food and casual dining—fast-casual.

Ells quickly discovered that raising capital for expansion took him away from what he enjoyed most—the day-to-day business. Solving this problem, Ells established a board of investors. Interested in continued expansion but with limited capital, Chipotle's board sent an unsolicited business plan to the McDonald's Corporation. Following a year of negotiations, in 1998, McDonald's ventured into unchartered territory, purchasing its first minority stake in a restaurant chain. As a result of this new partnership, Ells had significant

Exhibit 1 Income Statement

Period Ending	Dec 31, 2010	Dec 31, 2009	Dec 31, 2008
Total Revenue	1,835,922	1,518,417	1,331,968
Cost of Revenue	1,143,613	965,317	1,045,041
Gross Profit	692,309	553,100	286,927
Operating Expenses			
Research Development	—	—	—
Selling General and Administrative	321,494	273,730	89,155
Non Recurring	7,767	8,401	20,963
Others	68,921	61,308	52,770
Total Operating Expenses	—	—	—
Operating Income or Loss	287,831	203,705	124,039
Income from Continuing Operations			
Total Other Income/Expenses Net	(4,797)	(5,031)	3,469
Earnings Before Interest And Taxes	289,330	204,630	127,508
Interest Expense	269	405	302
Income Before Tax	289,061	204,225	127,206
Income Tax Expense	110,080	77,380	49,004
Minority Interest	—	—	—
Net Income From Continuing Ops	178,981	126,845	78,202
Non-recurring Events			
Discontinued Operations	—	—	—
Extraordinary Items	—	—	—
Effect Of Accounting Changes	—	—	—
Other Items	—	—	—
Net Income	178,981	125,845	78,202

Source: Chipotle Mexican Grill, Inc. (CMG) Financials at Yahoo! Finance.

Exhibit 2 Balance Sheet

Period Ending	Dec 31, 2010	Dec 31, 2009	Dec 31, 2008
Assets			
Current Assets			
Cash And Cash Equivalents	224,838	219,566	88,044
Short Term Investments	124,766	50,000	99,990
Net Receivables	33,503	7,897	6,485
Inventory	7,098	5,614	4,789
Other Current Assets	16,016	14,377	11,764
Total Current Assets	406,221	297,454	211,072
Long Term Investments	—	—	—
Property Plant and Equipment	679,881	636,411	585,899
Goodwill	21,939	21,939	21,939
Intangible Assets	—	—	—
Accumulated Amortization	—	—	—
Other Assets	16,564	5,701	6,075
Deferred Long Term Asset Charges	—	—	—
Total Assets	1,121,605	961,505	824,985

Globe: © Jan Rysavy/iStockphoto.com

(Continued)

Exhibit 2 Balance Sheet (*Continued*)

Period Ending	Dec 31, 2010	Dec 31, 2009	Dec 31, 2008
Liabilities			
Current Liabilities			
Accounts Payable	122,933	102,057	76,706
Short/Current Long Term Debt	—	—	—
Other Current Liabilities	121	96	82
Total Current Liabilities	**123,054**	**102,153**	**76,788**
Long Term Debt	—	—	—
Other Liabilities	13,486	10,633	8,735
Deferred Long Term Liability Charges	174,192	145,258	116,872
Minority Interest	—	—	—
Negative Goodwill	—	—	—
Total Liabilities	**310,732**	**258,044**	**202,395**
Stockholders' Equity			
Misc Stocks Options Warrants	—	—	—
Redeemable Preferred Stock	—	—	—
Preferred Stock	—	—	—
Common Stock	340	335	329
Retained Earnings	456,514	277,533	150,688
Treasury Stock	(240,618)	(114,316)	(30,227)
Capital Surplus	594,331	539,880	501,993
Other Stockholder Equity	606	29	(193)
Total Stockholder Equity	**810,873**	**703,461**	**622,590**
Net Tangible Assets	**788,934**	**681,522**	**600,651**

Source: Chipotle Mexican Grill, Inc. (CMG) Financials at Yahoo! Finance.

Exhibit 3 Statement of Cash Flow

Period Ending	Dec 31, 2010	Dec 31, 2009	Dec 31, 2008
Net Income	**178,981**	**126,845**	**76,202**
Operating Activities, Cash Flows Provided By or Used In			
Depreciation	68,921	61,308	52,770
Adjustments To Net Income	69,792	59,169	34,181
Changes In Accounts Receivables	743	875	1,290
Changes In Liabilities	13,361	38,160	28,711
Changes In Inventories	1,481	825	(457)
Changes In Other Operating Activities	10,588	2,239	3,810
Total Cash Flow From Operating Activities	**289,191**	**260,673**	**198,507**
Investing Activities, Cash Flows Provided By or Used In			
Capital Expenditures	(113,215)	(117,198)	(152,101)
Investments	(76,666)	49,990	(79,990)
Other Cash flows from Investing Activities	—	—	—
Total Cash Flows From Investing Activities	**(189,881)**	**(67,208)**	**(232,091)**

(*Continued*)

Exhibit 3 Statement of Cash Flow (*Continued*)

Period Ending	Dec 31, 2010	Dec 31, 2009	Dec 31, 2008
Financing Activities, Cash Flows Provided By or Used In			
Dividends Paid	—	—	—
Sale Purchase of Stock	(108,952)	(72,296)	(29,756)
Net Borrowings	—	—	(76)
Other Cash Flows from Financing Activities	(96)	(82)	284
Total Cash Flows From Financing Activities	**(94,522)**	**(61,943)**	**(29,548)**
Effect Of Exchange Rate Changes	484	—	—
Change In Cash and Cash Equivalents	**5,272**	**131,522**	**(63,132)**

Source: Chipotle Mexican Grill, Inc. (CMG) Financials at Yahoo! Finance.

capital at his disposal. By 1999, Chipotle had expanded to 37 restaurants nationally and increased its revenues from $13 million in 1997 to $31 million in 1999.[7] Chipotle's success eventually led McDonald's to increase its stake in the company to a majority shareholder.

It was after reading *The Art of Eating* by Edward Behr in 1999 that Ells' *Food with Integrity* mission came into being.[8] Chipotle's newfound commitment to organic and sustainable ingredients began with pork in 2000 and, while the increased cost of ingredients was passed along to its customers, Chipotle's revenues continued to rise.[9] Clearly, Chipotle's customers were willing to pay a little more for quality ingredients and seemed interested in helping Chipotle realize its vision of reducing the environmental impact of its restaurants. Encouraged, Ells didn't stop with pork: naturally raised chicken was introduced in 2002, followed by beef in 2007. Ells' *Food with Integrity* philosophy soon reached beyond its ingredients: "It is the philosophy that guides every decision we make at Chipotle." As an example, Chipotle began to focus on reducing its impact on the environment by constructing sustainable restaurants—receiving the first platinum certification in the Leadership in Energy and Environmental Design (LEED) rating system ever awarded to a restaurant at a recent store opening.[10]

Over time, Ells' commitment to his *Food with Integrity* philosophy led him to reevaluate Chipotle's relationship with McDonald's and, soon after the company went public in 2006, it split from McDonald's. Over the seven-year relationship, McDonald's invested $360 million in Chipotle and, in the end, had earned $1.5 billion.[11] Chipotle's public offering and split from McDonald's did not slow Chipotle's success as evidenced by a compound annual growth rate of revenue (CAGR) of 19.6 percent for 2005 through 2010.

Chipotle's international expansion began in Toronto in 2008. A London location soon followed in 2010, and Chipotle has now set its sights on Paris and Munich.[12] While international expansion may bring new challenges to Ells' *Food with Integrity* mission, Ells is optimistic explaining,

In many ways, the food culture in Europe matches our priorities much more closely than in the US, and I think we'll be able to source beautiful ingredients from local and sustainable sources ... and establish sustainable supply chains elsewhere as we look at other European markets.[13]

Food Fight

Chipotle continuously faces fierce competition. Chipotle's niche, which relies heavily on its unique focus on taste and organics, has helped thwart the advances of some competitors. However, having already blazed the path, sourcing and offering quality ingredients is now a relatively simple model for any competitor to copy. An increasing number of fast food and fast-casual restaurants are now using fresh and quality ingredients and marketing themselves as such. In addition, there is the simple pressure of rival chains that have the means and are moving quickly to expand both domestically and internationally.

What is Fast-Casual?

Broadly, Chipotle competes in the restaurant industry with its primary competitors in the fast-casual restaurant segment.[14] As a new segment, fast-casual remains loosely defined in the industry but is generally agreed to have higher average tickets, more upscale fare, as well as better décor and atmosphere than quick-serve (fast-food) restaurants. Additionally, many argue that to be considered fast-casual, a restaurant cannot offer table or drive-through service.[15]

The Evolution of Fast Food—and *Devolution* of Full-Service

As a member of the fastest growing restaurant segment, Chipotle has no shortage of competitors. Even fast food chains—accustomed to modifying their formats with upgraded décor and new menu offerings—are beginning to compete with fast-casual restaurants.[16] As fast food chains make these modifications, they have the potential to undercut Chipotle's price and create value that attracts Chipotle customers. With both full-service restaurant chains and quick-service chains entering the market, competition is on the rise. Demonstrating this flexibility, several of Chipotle's competitors—including Qdoba and Pei Wei—are owned by companies that previously only operated restaurants in other segments.

The Evolution of Fast-Casual

New concepts also threaten to dilute the marketplace. Fast-casual is currently dominated by bakery-style restaurants like Panera Bread and ethnic formats like Chipotle. In 2010, Mexican food became the largest food category within the fast-casual segment, surpassing bakery for the first time. Even so, "Better Burgers" captured the fastest growing menu category for 2010 with 16.1 percent growth.[17] While offering a different type of food, new concepts have the potential to unseat Chipotle's reign as the hip place to eat. In the attempt to glom onto some of Chipotle's success, Chipotle imitators have emerged in the market. "Many fast-casual startups describe themselves as the 'Chipotle of [fill in blank].'"[18] Examples include Piada Italian Street Food, the "Chipotle of Italian" in Columbus, OH; Cava Mezze Grill, the "Chipotle of Greek" in Washington DC; and Hello Pasta, the "Chipotle of Pasta" in New York.[19] Even Chipotle itself is testing the ability to imitate its own success with its new Asian food concept—ShopHouse.

An additional threat to Chipotle comes from current competitors within the fast-casual segment revamping their existing formats to more closely replicate Chipotle's offerings. For example, Baja Fresh—a fast-casual restaurant with Mexican food menu offerings—is similar to Chipotle in several ways including fresh ingredients, custom prepared food, and open kitchens. However, Baja Fresh prepares its food made-to-order on grills creating a delay of several minutes between the time a customer orders their food at the counter and the time they actually receive their food. To better compete with Chipotle, Baja Fresh is redesigning select restaurants to its new Baja Fresh Express concept with fewer menu offerings and an assembly line style ordering process similar to Chipotle. It has also invested in new

technology such as tortilla grills that reduce warming time from 2 minutes to only 25 seconds.[20]

Within the fast-casual segment, Chipotle faces numerous local and regional competitors including many privately owned and publicly held companies. In 2010, three of Chipotle's most successful publicly held competitors were Panera Bread, Qdoba, and Pei Wei (see Exhibit 4 for a comparison of select financial data).

Panera Bread. Formed in 1998, Panera Bread is Chipotle's largest competitor with annual sales in 2010 of $1.54 billion. Panera operates 1,453 bakery-style restaurants in 40 states, the District of Columbia, and Canada. It is comprised of both company owned restaurants (662) and franchise locations (791). Panera Bread touts a philosophy it calls "Concept Essence." Concept Essence is embodied by the quality artisan bread anchoring its menu, the warm, comfortable environment of its restaurants, and the relationships it builds with customers through passion and expertise.[21]

Panera Bread strives to deliver quality food that customers perceive as a value. Its menu includes "baked goods, made to order sandwiches on freshly baked breads, hearty, unique soups and sides, fresh, hand tossed salads, and custom roasted coffees." To provide a consistent namesake product, Panera relies on a dough production system to supply each restaurant with fresh dough daily. Additionally, it transports fresh tuna, cream cheese, and other products from distribution centers up to 500 miles to its restaurants. Panera also continuously looks to update its menu by adding new, high quality items. Examples of this in 2010 included its Cuban Chicken Panini and All Natural Steak Chili with Cornbread Crumbles.[22] Panera also added steaks to its menu and Panini grills to its restaurants in 2010.

With a combination of company owned and franchised restaurants, Panera is able to rely primarily on cash generated from operations to fund new company owned locations while maximizing expansion through new franchises. Despite ready access to credit, Panera incurred no debt when funding expansion in 2010.[23]

Exhibit 4 Key Competitor Data

Company	Annual Sales (in thousands)	2010 Same Store Sales Growth	Number of Restaurants	Marketing Expenses (in thousands)	States / Countries Outside US	Company Owned	Franchise
Chipotle	$1,835,922	9.4%	1,092	25,703	39 / 2	100%	—
Panera Bread[1]	$1,542,489	7.5%	1,453	27,400	41 / 1	46%	54%
Qdoba[2]	$ 168,424	2.8%	510	5,053[3]	44 / 0	34%	66%
Pei Wei[4]	$ 310,131	n/a	168	n/a	22 / 0	100%	—

[1]From Panera Bread 2010 Annual Report to Stockholders.

[2]From JBX 2010 10-K. Other financial data from: Top 50 Special Report, *QSR* Magazine.

[3]Marketing expense estimated at 3 percent of revenue as JBX does not report advertising expenses by business segment.

[4]From P.F. Chang's Inc. 2010 10-K.

With a portion of franchisee payments dedicated to this expense, Panera Bread markets itself in a variety of ways. The focus of all Panera Bread marketing is to build brand image and strengthen relationships with its customers to drive repeat sales. As an example, in 2010, Panera launched its customer loyalty program—MyPanera—that rewards repeat customers with bonuses and gifts such as a free bakery item.[24]

To maximize sales opportunities, Panera Bread serves breakfast, lunch, and dinner. A catering business currently in development is a key component in its growth plan. Driven by investments in its sales force and training programs, catering sales increased by 26 percent in 2010. According to President and CEO William Moreton, "We believe that continued development of our off premise solutions provides us with an opportunity for significant growth in the future."[25]

Qdoba Mexican Grill. With approximately half the restaurant locations of Chipotle, Qdoba Mexican Grill operates 188 company owned restaurants and 337 franchised locations throughout the US and generated $168.4 million in revenue in 2010.[26] Founded in 1995, Qdoba operates as a wholly owned subsidiary of Jack in the Box Company (JBX). Similar to Chipotle, Qdoba serves traditional Mexican food prepared to the customers' liking. Fresh guacamole, slow simmered beans, slow roasted shredded beef and pork, and flame grilled chicken and steak are all key components of a Qdoba burrito. JBX has successfully expanded Qdoba Mexican Grill into 43 states and the District of Columbia by offering hand-crafted, top-quality food prepared on open grills in front of waiting customers.[27] Qdoba also offers healthy and less filling options including its Mexican Lettuce Wraps that were added to the menu in 2010.[28] Bringing its food to locations other than its restaurants, Qdoba provides catering for groups up to 500, offering several options including fully staffed hot taco, nacho, and burrito bars.

Qdoba franchises are largely responsible for its growth. In 2010, 21 of the 36 restaurant openings were franchise owned. Franchising offers several advantages for JBX. Franchisees pay an up-front fee of $30,000 and royalty fees that are typically five percent of gross revenues. JBX is able to use this income to offset the startup costs associated with opening a company owned restaurant. Franchisees also pay up to two percent of gross revenue to JBX in marketing fees and are required to spend a minimum of two percent on local advertising. Franchisees are eligible for rebates on portions of these fees if applied to the opening of a new restaurant, thus encouraging additional growth.[29] Because franchise locations do not require the same level of support as company owned restaurants, JBX enjoys lower corporate overhead than it would were all Qdoba locations company owned.

While franchise locations of all industries are sometimes perceived to lack the quality of a tightly monitored company owned store, JBX has highly developed systems to ensure consistent operations across all restaurants. For example, its "farm to fork" quality assurance program "combines employee training, testing by suppliers, documented restaurant practices, and detailed attention to product quality at every stage of the food preparation cycle." Additionally, while only 45 percent of Qdoba restaurants utilize the JBX purchasing and supply chain systems, all restaurants are required to exclusively use JBX quality control approved suppliers.[30] JBX expects to open 50 to 60 new Qdoba Mexican Grill restaurants in 2011.

Pei Wei. Pei Wei, owned by P.F. Chang's China Bistro, Inc., opened its first restaurant in 2000, and is another strong competitor in the fast-casual segment. In 2010, the 168 Pei Wei locations in 22 states produced $310 million in revenue.[31]

P.F. Chang's also operates full-service restaurants of the same name. Its strategy for Pei Wei is "to serve freshly prepared, wok seared, contemporary, pan-Asian cuisine in a relaxed, warm environment, with friendly, attentive counter service and take-out flexibility." P.F. Chang's believes that, by providing both a full-service offering as well as a fast-casual option, it gains brand loyalty.[32]

In addition to its standard fare, Pei Wei includes Limited Time Offers (LTOs) on its menu three to four times per year. Pei Wei typically keeps these dishes on the menu for a 12-week cycle. Pei Wei's LTOs keep its menu fresh by providing new dishes to customers. Examples of LTOs offered in 2010 were the Thai Mango Chicken and Japanese Chile Beef Ramen. Pei Wei also offers a limited alcohol selection that accounts for one to two percent of sales revenue each year. With take-out orders responsible for approximately 40 percent of total sales, Pei Wei offers online ordering to facilitate customers that don't want to wait.[33]

P.F. Chang's utilizes a cooperative network of suppliers called Distribution Market Advantage to supply all its restaurant locations. For its Asian-specific ingredients, P.F. Chang's relies on a single supplier and uses its size to negotiate reduced rates. Aside from the economies of scale it enjoys with this supplier, quality is more easily controlled with a single source.[34]

P.F. Chang's relies heavily on positive customer experiences to drive positive word-of-mouth for its Pei Wei locations. While it has utilized traditional media advertisement in the past, it is generally on a very limited basis. Despite launching a loyalty program for its P.F. Chang's customers, Pei Wei customers have not yet been offered their own nor are they included in P.F. Chang's program.

To deliver the desired experience to customers, prospective Pei Wei managers must complete a nine-week manager training program that concludes with a certification process validating the manager candidates have achieved proficiency in both culinary and overall operational skills. Hourly employees receive a full week of training and, similar to managers, are required to pass a certification process specific to their respective positions before being allowed to serve customers.[35]

P.F. Chang's has announced plans to open between six and eight new Pei Wei restaurants in 2011.[36]

Chipotle's Plate...and What's on It

Chipotle targets customers seeking high-quality food ingredients from a source that is faster and/or less expensive than a full-service restaurant. Chipotle also focuses on the "customer experience" to build a strong following and develop better branding. Initiatives to develop employees and maintain a strong workforce have also contributed to Chipotle's success.

What's for Dinner?

Chipotle's *Food with Integrity* philosophy sets it apart from its competitors by creating a unique taste that is difficult to imitate. Its great tasting food develops customer loyalty, which helps to increase patronage by positive word-of-mouth. In connection with this philosophy is the dependence Chipotle has on organic farmers to supply its restaurants with the necessary ingredients. Chipotle's use of a network of farmers keeps a heavy concentration from developing on any one supplier, which helps to minimize—but not eliminate—the risk of supply outages.

Chipotle restaurants receive ingredients from 22 independently owned and operated regional distribution centers. However, Chipotle first approves all farmers the distributors use on its behalf. Distributors have little bargaining power as Chipotle selects farmers based on "quality specifications, and [distributors] purchase within pricing guidelines and protocols [Chipotle has] established with the suppliers."[37] Chipotle prefers to work with farms that are family owned and operated. They partner with suppliers like Niman Ranch (a network of independent ranchers),[38] Meister Cheese Company (local Wisconsin farmers and founders of the Animal Friendly Family Farms program),[39] and The Chef's Garden (a grower of artisanal produce straight "from Earth to Table").[40] Chipotle is the largest restaurant buyer of locally grown produce and the only national restaurant chain to expand its commitment to the use of local products year after year.[41]

Chipotle is highly dependent on the success of its suppliers because, without them, it cannot meet its *Food with Integrity* goals. When Chipotle started working with the Niman Ranch network to increase supply over a decade ago, the network had only 50 farms; as of 2010, Niman Ranch now represents over 500 farms and, not surprisingly, Chipotle is its largest customer.[42] Even so, Chipotle continues to encounter challenges in sourcing ingredients that meet its high standards in the quantities it requires. As a result of supplier shortages, it has not yet fully met its goals for 100 percent naturally raised meat, pasture raised dairy, antibiotic free chicken, or organic beans as,[43] even when Chipotle has a sustainable supplier, the supplier may experience shortages thus leaving some restaurants without key ingredients.

Because it takes longer to identify and develop supplier relationships, it costs more to establish them. This results in "higher costs and other risks associated with purchasing naturally raised or sustainably grown ingredients." Additionally, because Chipotle depends on a smaller number of suppliers, it is more difficult to replace or substitute a supplier, resulting in serious interruptions to the supply chain.[44]

The cost of sourcing its high quality ingredients results in a higher cost for Chipotle customers. The restaurant attempts to reduce other operating costs by using a centralized purchasing department that works with local suppliers and regional distributors to help reduce transportation costs.[45] Fortunately, having previously partnered with McDonald's, Chipotle has been able to leverage many of the supply chain management capabilities of its former owner.

Despite the challenges and costs incurred by using only suppliers who pass the test of producing naturally raised meats and organic foods, Chipotle's *Food with Integrity* has been successful and it is evident that customers are willing to pay a premium for better tasting food.

On what is unfortunately the negative side of being a highly visible proponent of environmental and ethical causes, Chipotle faces sharp criticism any time its actions appear out-of-step with social causes. For example, the company did not initially agree when People for the Ethical Treatment of Animals (PETA) called for the use of poultry suppliers using controlled atmosphere killing (CAK)—a purportedly less cruel method of slaughter whereby a bird's oxygen in slowly replaced with other gases. Arguing there were an insufficient number of suppliers using CAK to meet its needs, after heavy petitioning and a shareholder resolution, Chipotle relented and agreed to give preference to suppliers using CAK.[46] Additionally, in Florida, despite putting the proposed wage increases in escrow while attempting to determine if farm workers would in fact receive the money, Chipotle came under fire from the Coalition of Immokalee Workers for its failure to act to improve wages and conditions of Florida farm workers.[47] After months of protests and negative publicity, Chipotle completed its negotiations and paid the higher wages. As a leader in ethical business practices and self designated member of the global community, Chipotle will continue to be a target for activists should it not respond as promptly as the activists deem it should or, even worse, should it disagree with a popular—irrespective of its validity—initiative.

Who's Hungry?

The fast-casual segment draws customers in search of better quality food than fast food and "something hipper, faster, and cheaper than full service."[48] Chipotle satisfies those customer needs by providing fresh, quick, customizable food that is prepared in front of customers while they wait.[49] The chain has a wide appeal, mainly serving adults between the ages of 18 and 49.[50] Chipotle has among the highest customer ratings in the fast-casual and fast food segments (see Exhibit 5A for 2010 Zagat ratings). The J.D. Power and Associates 2010 US Restaurant Satisfaction Study asked consumers in ten markets to rate their top choices based on price, environment, meal, and service. Chipotle placed among the top three in nine of the ten markets—more than any other fast-casual restaurant (see Exhibit 5B).[51] A study in the *International Journal of Hospitality Management* showed that customer satisfaction is a good predictor of customer purchase intentions; "High levels of customer satisfaction decreases the perceived benefits of service provider switches, thereby increasing customer repurchase intentions."[52]

Even when the company had shared ownership with McDonald's, Chipotle always ran its business autonomously without significant involvement from its parent. As a result, many of the initial concepts that made the restaurant successful continue today. One of its founding concepts was to sell to the customer that Chipotle was a hip place to eat. In alignment with Ells' approach to food, Chipotle's restaurant design mentality was to use simple materials without significant fabrication to create something extraordinary. Chipotle designs individual restaurants to fit into their distinctive environments. While each restaurant typically has a sleek, modern feel with plenty of exposed wood and steel, Chipotle believes this foundation creates an "appealing, eclectic atmosphere."[53]

Chipotle prides itself on being unique in the industry due to its *Food with Integrity* philosophy and offerings. Indeed, as a competitor analysis shows, dishes made fresh-to-order with fresh ingredients—like those from Chipotle—appeal to the fast-casual segment.[54] Chipotle believes that sustainably raised products make its food taste better, which, in turn, gives it a competitive advantage. Nevertheless, there is some uncertainty surrounding to what extent sustainable ingredients are at the forefront of its customers' minds. In an in-house ethnography study, the Chief Marketing Officer found that customers don't necessarily return to Chipotle because of

…the fact that we spend a lot of time and effort on making all of our food as sustainably and naturally raised as possible. We all assumed that that was a big driving factor. Even people who were coming to Chipotle for a long time, they appreciate it, but it's not the reason they are coming in. They just love the way the food tastes. That was a little bit of a surprise to us.[55]

However, others believe that naturally raised ingredients set Chipotle apart and lend to its customer growth.[56] Either way, customers will continue to patronize Chipotle for the great taste and, whether intentionally or not, in doing so, lend their support to the sustainability cause. In the meantime, Chipotle remains hopeful that sales will be driven even further as customers become increasingly aware of where its food is sourced.

Exhibit 5A The 2010 Zagat Fast-Food Survey

	Top Food Large Chain (up to 5,000 locations)	Best Value	Best Grilled Chicken
1	In-N-Out Burger	McDonald's	Chick-fil-A
2	Papa Murphy's	Panera Bread	KFC
3	Chick-fil-A	**Chipotle**	El Pollo Loco
4	Five Guys	Taco Bell	Panera Bread
5	**Chipotle**	Chick-fil-A	**Chipotle**

Definitions	
Fast-Food Chain	National restaurant chain offering burgers, chicken, or other main-course items but no table service
Large Chain	Fast-food chain with up to 5,000 locations
Food	Quality of menu items
Best	Cited most often as being the best for a particular menu item
Top	Highest Zagat rating for food, facilities, or service among all chains in a particular category

Survey does not have a separate category between fast food and full-service, fast-casual included within fast food category.

National survey of 6,500 diners.

Source: http://www.zagat.com

Exhibit 5B J.D. Power and Associates 2010 US Restaurant Satisfaction Study: Top Three Quick-Service Restaurant Brands in Overall Customer Satisfaction by Market

Market	Rank	Brand
Atlanta	1	Chick-fil-A
	2	**Chipotle Mexican Grill**
	3	Jason's Deli
Boston	1	**Chipotle Mexican Grill**
	2	Panera Bread
	3	Uno Chicago Grill
Chicago	1	Culver's
	2	**Chipotle Mexican Grill (tie)**
	2	Jersey Mike's Subs (tie)
Houston	1	Chick-fil-A
	2	Papa John's
	3	Jason's Deli
Los Angeles / Riverside / Ventura County, CA	1	In-N-Out Burger
	2	Chick-fil-A
	3	**Chipotle Mexican Grill**
Minneapolis-St. Paul	1	Papa Murphy's Take N Bake Pizza
	2	Panera Bread
	3	**Chipotle Mexican Grill**
New York / Northern New Jersey	1	Panera Bread
	2	Sonic America's Drive-In
	3	**Chipotle Mexican Grill**
Phoenix	1	In-N-Out Burger
	2	Chick-fil-A
	3	**Chipotle Mexican Grill**
San Francisco Bay Area, CA	1	In-N-Out Burger
	2	**Chipotle Mexican Grill**
	3	Baja Fresh
Washington DC	1	Chick-fil-A
	2	**Chipotle Mexican Grill**
	3	Panera Bread

Source: J.D. Power and Associates 2010 U.S. Restaurant Satisfaction Study[SM]. Charts and graphs extracted from this press release must be accompanied by a statement identifying J.D. Power and Associates as the publisher and the J.D. Power and Associates 2010 U.S. Restaurant Satisfaction Study[SM] as the source. Rankings are based on numerical scores, and not necessarily on statistical significance. No advertising or other promotional use can be made of the information in this release or J.D. Power and Associates study results without the express prior written consent of J.D. Power and Associates.

While Chipotle should be applauded for its efforts to source healthful foods, an important but often-unconsidered fact remains—just because the ingredients of a meal are environmentally sound does not make the meal healthy. Even as Chipotle offers quality and sustainable ingredients, its menu options can be packed full of calories. As an example, the general rule of thumb dictates that a healthy adult should consume 1,800 to 2,000 calories—including 60 grams of fat and 2,400 milligrams of sodium—a day. However, an average Chipotle burrito can contain 900 to 1,000 calories, 50 grams of fat, and 2,300 mg of sodium.[57] While Chipotle offers healthier options in the form of its burrito bowls and salads and allows customers to easily customize a meal depending on their health needs, it might need to consider increased disclosure of nutritional information regarding its ingredients.

Despite all the societal good and tasty reasons to eat at Chipotle, food costs for the restaurant industry have increased across the board making it increasingly difficult to further delay price hikes that could alienate customers living on dwindling budgets. In February 2011, domestic wholesale food prices were reported to have risen 3.9 percent since January 2010, with global increases of 37 percent for the same period.[58] In its 2010 Annual Report, Chipotle acknowledged that increases in critical menu items could "adversely affect [its] operating results" or force it to suspend an item from the menu temporarily, which could "negatively impact restaurant traffic and comparable restaurant sales."[59] While Chipotle implemented price increases in the Pacific region, it had no immediate plans to pass increases to other Chipotle customers before assessing customer resistance and the size and timing of inflation in Q3 2011.[60] Analysts, however, warn that delaying price increases will result in a continued impact on margins and, more likely than not, make a more aggressive price increase necessary. Chipotle's last significant increase in Q4 2008 "was followed by several quarters of same store traffic declines."[61] Key competitors like Panera Bread and Pei Wei have already bitten the bullet and increased menu prices in Q4 2010 to mitigate higher commodity costs.[62,63]

Who's Serving?

Chipotle views its approach to employees as central to its success. Monty Moran, the company's co-CEO, states,

The single best way to improve operations is to make sure that restaurant managers are the best they can be and that they have the company's full support. The restaurant manager position is more important than my job and Ells' job. It's key to how a customer experiences our food every day.[64]

In the early days of the restaurant, Chipotle operated using a standard hierarchy: staff employees reported to a restaurant manager, who reported to a regional manager, who reported to company directors, who reported to the President. However, as Chipotle promoted managers to higher positions and they left their restaurants, Chipotle discovered the flaw inherent to its structure. "We promoted our best managers, those who had the best effect on customers, the best food, the cleanest restaurants, and the best crew," said Moran.[65] To combat this issue, Chipotle launched the "Restaurateur Program" in 2006. This program was designed to encourage good managers to make a career of the position by developing staff and increasing store revenue. The incentives for doing so included large bonuses that allowed good managers to earn as much or more than their supervisors. As Moran put it, "It's truly entrepreneurial, and it puts the manager in a position that is as close to ownership as possible without being an owner."[66]

With incentives for good managers to remain in their positions, staff turnover decreased due to consistency in the workplace and because staff development was a key driver to a manager's bonus. Moran believes that managers who are promoted from within are four times less likely to leave than those hired from outside. "We're rewarded by the fact that once they become managers, they're fiercely loyal and they know this company better than anyone else."[67]

Expanding this view to the next level, Chipotle also wanted its employees to be innovative and carry an entrepreneurial mindset. Marketing Director Jim Adams is known for telling candidates interviewing for corporate positions that "the way to fit in at Chipotle is to be creative and independent."[68] Chipotle empowers its employees and shows this by entrusting them to prepare its food as a chef would in a restaurant. Employees are paid an amount higher than minimum wage and everyone has access to health care benefits. Ells believes that by allowing his employees certain freedoms and self-empowerment, morale improves, creating a positive work environment that, ultimately, has a positive effect on the customer experience.

Creating a notable impact on the culture and community of particular Chipotle locations, in recent years, the US Immigration and Customs Enforcement (ICE) shifted its focus from undocumented individuals and began instead to target employers that hire undocumented workers.[69] Restaurants in particular were admonished to reduce their use (and thus the demand for) illegal workers and encouraged to carefully examine hiring practices.[70] For Chipotle, ICE audits of its restaurants resulted in about 500 firings of illegal workers in Minnesota, Virginia, and Washington DC with investigations continuing in Los Angeles and Atlanta.[71] These raids were not only embarrassing to its reputation, but also carried fines and resulted in higher costs. Because all Chipotle locations are company owned, ultimately, Chipotle is responsible for each restaurant meeting federal hiring regulations. Chipotle acknowledged the firings created a temporary increase to its labor costs as it hired and trained new employees. Chipotle also understands that, without franchisees to share the costs, it shoulders considerable more risk than many of its competitors.[72]

Who's Selling?

Leveraging its customer loyalty, Chipotle encourages fan interaction and uses social media to connect with seasoned and prospective customers alike. Chipotle has a much larger Facebook following compared to its top rivals—1.3 million "likes" compared to 513,000 for Panera Bread, 102,000 for Pei Wei, and 92,000 for Qdoba Mexican Grill.[73] Chipotle fans both on and offline provide valuable word-of-mouth marketing for the company and drive the majority of first time visits to Chipotle. Media consulting firms affirm that when people hear a recommendation from a friend or stranger "they'll probably believe it since the tipster has nothing to gain. Chipotle so far has got it nailed. You have people evangelizing the brand because they love it."[74]

As new restaurants open and the company works to attract new customers, a common marketing tactic is to offer free burritos to neighboring businesses and residents.[75] Although expensive, Chipotle believes the brand awareness created outweighs the cost involved. According to Adams, "When you take this idea that your best marketing tool is the restaurant and the experience customers have in it, then the object is, of course, to drive people in so they can experience it."[76]

Chipotle also participates in charity fundraisers to help build the brand. In fact, the company has a dedicated group of marketing personnel specifically charged with working with charities, schools, and other organizations to set up events thus driving more customers into its restaurants. While learning about Chipotle's unique approach to high-quality ingredients from sustainable resources is an incentive to some, customer positive word-of-mouth continues to be Chipotle's best form of free advertising. Marketing Director Adams notes that the company spends less than 2 percent of revenues on advertising, while its competitors spend between 3 and 5 percent.[77]

Keeping It in the Family

Chipotle owns and operates all of its restaurants and has determined it will not sell franchises. Because management places such a strong emphasis on the importance of the restaurant manager, it has determined that having a direct say in who is managing individual restaurants is to its advantage.

With Chipotle's plan to expand both domestically and internationally, the company faces both organizational and cultural challenges. Organizationally, Chipotle is a simple structure with a single corporate office in Denver overseeing all of its restaurants. This creates issues with management and effective communication, as well as understanding local and cultural differences as they open new locations.

Domestically, Chipotle will be challenged to continue to find "A" locations given its vast geographic footprint. In 2010, there were 1,092 Chipotle restaurants in the US.[78] Chipotle operates in 39 states, with California, Ohio, Texas, Colorado, and Illinois being the largest markets (Exhibit 6). The company plans to expand significantly over the next three years, including the opening of 135 to 145 stores in 2011.[79] With the majority of openings in 2011 scheduled to occur in the second half of the year, the inconsistent pace could result in reduced oversight of construction projects, which could result in higher than expected costs. Additionally, in current markets, new stores could cannibalize sales from existing stores. Finally, approximately 30 percent of the new stores will be opened using its A-Model format.[80] This model has a smaller footprint and initially produced a slightly lower volume than the traditional Chipotle format.[81]

International expansion poses its own unique brand challenges. The primary issue with expanding into new and unfamiliar territory is the risk of the product not being accepted by local consumers. Consumer tastes and discretionary spending habits are different from those in the US: international customers may not understand or even appreciate Chipotle's *Food with* *Integrity* philosophy due to their country's unique cultural or economic circumstances. At the end of 2010, Chipotle had only three international locations (one in the UK and two in Canada).[82] Chipotle's management expertise in the US may lead it to make international business decisions that, while appropriate in the US, may not be acceptable overseas. In addition, the company may not be equipped from an information systems or structural standpoint to support international operations properly.

The Cooks in the Kitchen

"It's not often that graduates of the Culinary Institute of America set out to make the burrito into a culinary experience."[83] His father was proud that Ells was well on his way to becoming a chef when working at Stars in San Francisco. So, when Ells borrowed money from him just three years out of school at the age of 28 to open the first Chipotle in Denver, most of Ells' friends, family, and acquaintances were skeptical. Ells remembered, "Everyone told me that [Chipotle] was a bad name to use, because no one knew what it was or could pronounce it. And now everyone knows what it is."[84] Ells attended Boulder High School, the University of Colorado at Boulder, and the Culinary Institute of America in Hyde Park, New York, graduating in 1990. Ells continues to be Chipotle's visionary leader and currently serves as co-CEO and Chairman of the Board.[85]

Alongside Ells as Chipotle's business leader is co-CEO Montgomery F. (Monty) Moran. As the former CEO of the Denver law firm Messner & Reeves, LLC and general counsel of Chipotle, Moran was appointed to co-CEO in 2009 after serving as President and COO of Chipotle since March 2005. His experience as general counsel and COO of the business positions him for success in his current role. Moran holds a bachelors degree in communications from the University of Colorado and a J.D. from Pepperdine University.[86]

Also key to the future success of the company is Chief Development Officer since February 2010, Robert Blessing. Blessing opened the first Chipotle in the Northeast region after coming to Chipotle in 1999 as a regional director. From 2005 to 2008, Blessing's role expanded to include the entire Northeast and Central regions. As Chipotle's Restaurant Support Officer from 2008 to 2010, he provided field support for marketing and oversaw five regional directors and purchasing. Prior to Chipotle, Blessing held executive leadership roles at Vie de France Retail and Restaurant Bakery, Franchise Management Corporation (an Arby's franchisee), and Thompson Hospitality (a contract food service company).[87]

Exhibit 6 Chipotle Restaurant Locations

As of December 31, 2010, Chipotle operated 1,084 restaurants			
Alabama	3	Nevada	11
Arizona	41	New Hampshire	2
California	165	New Jersey	17
Colorado	71	New York	50
Connecticut	3	North Carolina	12
Delaware	1	Ohio	123
District of Columbia	8	Oklahoma	6
Florida	58	Oregon	12
Georgia	13	Pennsylvania	24
Illinois	78	Rhode Island	3
Indiana	14	South Carolina	2
Iowa	2	Tennessee	5
Kansas	17	Texas	93
Kentucky	8	Utah	4
Maine	1	Virginia	52
Maryland	40	Washington	12
Massachusetts	23	Wisconsin	12
Michigan	12	Wyoming	1
Minnesota	51	United Kingdom	1
Missouri	24	Canada	2
Nebraska	7		

Source: 2010 Chipotle Annual Report & Proxy Statement.

Cilantro, Lime, and Other Shades of Green

Chipotle has achieved unprecedented financial results over the past six years (see Exhibit 7 for total company revenue growth) due in large part to both rapid new store expansion and same store sales (SSS) growth. CAGR over this period was 19.6 percent with Chipotle building new stores at an average rate of 126 per year. Chipotle was able to drive SSS at existing units by, among other things, building brand awareness, promoting *Food with Integrity*, maintaining a simplistic approach to its menu, and embracing social media. At the unit level, economics remain highly attractive. Chipotle earns restaurant level revenue of $1.84 million and cash flow of $0.49 million (26.7 percent of revenues). Approximate investment cost per unit is $0.80 million, which results in an ROI of 61.8 percent (see Exhibit 8).[88]

Exhibit 7 Total Company Revenue

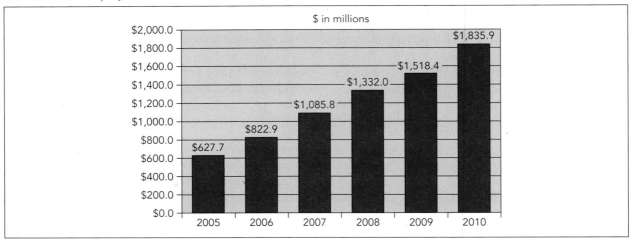

Source: Chipotle Mexican Grill, Raymond James 32nd Annual Institutional Investors Conference, March 8, 2011 (PDF presentation).

Exhibit 8 Average Unit Volume / Unit Economic Model

	$ in thousands
Average trailing 12-month sales	$1,840
Restaurant level cash flow	$ 491
Restaurant level operating margin %	26.7%
Approximate investment cost	$ 795
ROI %	61.8%

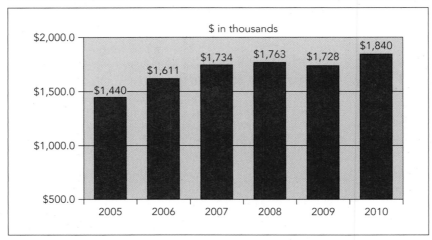

Source: Chipotle Mexican Grill, Raymond James 32nd Annual Institutional Investors Conference, March 8, 2011 (PDF presentation).

As a whole, Chipotle generated $179 million of net income on revenues of $1,836 million for fiscal year 2010. Its three international stores contributed only nominally to the overall performance of the company. Revenues increased 20.9 percent as a result of 129 new store openings during the year and a 9.4 percent increase in SSS.[89] The increase in SSS was mainly the result of an uptick in traffic, as opposed to increases in average ticket sales. Chipotle's SSS have significantly outpaced the industry over the last six years (see Exhibit 9 for historical SSS and traffic trends by industry segment). The company's stock was rewarded for 2010 results with notably better performance relative to broader markets. Chipotle stock gained 141 percent (vs. 13 percent for the S&P).[90]

First quarter 2011 results built off a strong 2010. Total company revenue was up 24.3 percent, SSS increased 12.4 percent, and net income gained 22.7 percent. Similar to fiscal year 2010, the SSS increase was driven primarily from traffic since pricing increased only 0.7 percent. Twelve new restaurants opened during this period.[91] As for the balance of its profit and loss statement, Chipotle maintained its focus on prime costs, otherwise known as cost of goods sold and labor. Prime costs are traditionally the two biggest operating expenses

incurred by restaurant chains and, for fast-casual restaurants, typically consume 60 percent of revenues or more (see Exhibit 10). Chipotle's prime costs in first quarter 2011 were 100 basis points higher than fourth quarter 2010, of which 60 basis points were attributable to higher tomato and produce costs. Chipotle continuously monitors food and beverage costs—not surprising considering recent commodity pressures resulting from higher fuel prices, droughts, etc. (see Exhibit 11). Commodity costs are even more relevant for the company given its *Food with Integrity* mission that inherently limits the number of available suppliers. Other costs experiencing pressure in the first quarter 2011 were labor (due to the previously mentioned immigration raids) and operating costs as a result of increased promotional and marketing expenses.[92]

Yet, relative to its competition, Chipotle continues to outperform. Panera Bread is considered by many as a leader in the fast-casual segment of the restaurant industry. As compared to Panera, Chipotle has 2.5 times the market capitalization, close to 1.5 times the EBITDA, and almost 2.0 times EV/EBITDA (see Exhibit 12). Both companies have very strong balance sheets with no bank debt. Chipotle recently notified Bank of America it was cancelling its revolving line of credit because of

Exhibit 9 Same-Store Sales and Traffic

Historically, SSS at QSRs are more consistent than FSR SSS, particularly for sandwich and chicken chains. During the downturn, QSRs (including snack and fast casual) experienced six quarters (3Q08-4Q09) of SSS decline, while FSRs (including fine dining) declined for 10 consecutive quarters (4Q07-1Q10). Both QSRs and FSRs are on similar recovery trajectories, rising 4.1% and 3.8%, respectively, in 4Q10.

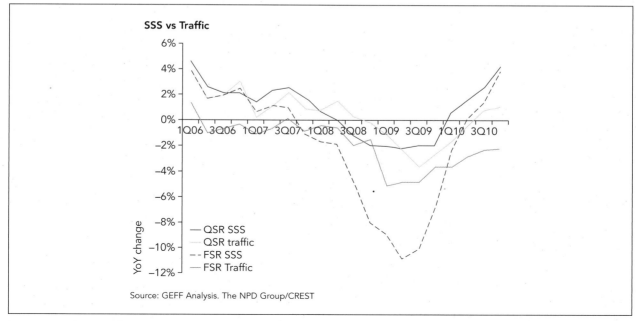

Source: GEFF Analysis. The NPD Group/CREST

Note: Fast-casual restaurant chains such as Chipotle are captured within the segment QSR, or quick-serve restaurants.

Source: GE Capital, Franchise Finance 2011 Chain Restaurant Industry Review.

Exhibit 10 Components of the Restaurant Dollar

Menu Price Increases & Components of the Restaurant Dollar	QSR			FSR[1]		
	2008	2009	2010	2008	2009	2010
PPI – food mfg	**9.6%**	**−2.5%**	**3.5%**	**9.6%**	**−2.5%**	**3.5%**
Employment cost index	3.6	2.2	1.7	4.0	3.2	3.7
Food & beverage spend (% of sales)	30.4	31.9	31.9[2]	33.1	31.8	31.8[2]
Labor spend (% of sales)	28.6	29.4	29.4[2]	33.5	33.2	33.2[2]
Occupancy, operating & o/head spend (% of sales)	29.2	29.9	29.9[2]	27.7	30.6	30.6[2]
% of net income before tax	9.7	5.9	5.9[2]	3.6	3.5	3.5[2]
Menu price increase to maintain margin:						
Food costs	2.9	−0.8	1.1	3.2	−0.8	−0.8
Labor costs	1.0	0.7	0.5	1.3	1.1	1.2
Total menu price increase to maintain margin	**4.0%**	**−0.1%**	**1.6%**	**4.6%**	**0.3%**	**0.4%**
Menu price increase (CPI FAFH FSR)	—	—	—	4.0	2.8	1.3
Menu price increase (CPI FAFH QSR)	4.9	4.2	0.9	—	—	—
Available for occ, operating & o/head costs: or improvement of income before tax	0.9%	4.3%	−0.7%	−0.5%	2.5%	0.9%

[1]Avg check $l5-$24.99

[2]Preliminary calculations based on NRA/Deloitte 2010 Restaurant Industry Operations Report. Source: BLS, Deloitte, NRA.

Note: fast-casual restaurant chains such as Chipotle are captured within the segment QSR, or quick-serve restaurants.

Source: GE Capital, Franchise Finance 2011 Chain Restaurant Industry Review.

Exhibit 11 Select Commodity Prices

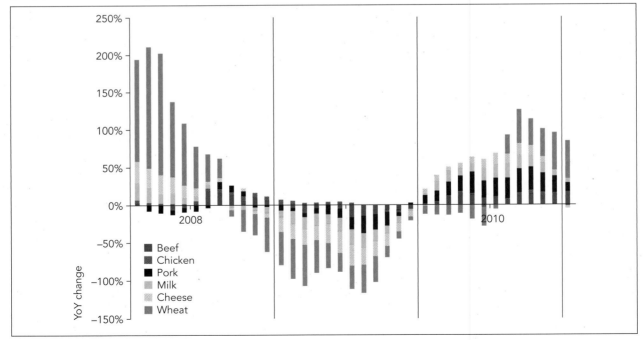

Source: GE Capital, Franchise Finance 2011 Chain Restaurant Industry Review.

non-usage. The restaurant chain will continue to fund new store development with cash on hand and cash flow from operations.

Chipotle also faces the issue of decelerating SSS growth in 2011 and beyond. SSS directly affects overall sales growth and will continue to be a critical factor affecting profit growth—a strong evaluation metric for investors.[93] Given the state of the economy in general and the restaurant industry in particular, Chipotle's SSS performance has been unprecedented. In the long

Exhibit 12 Restaurant Valuation EV/EBITDA

(as of the close on 04/20/11)	Rating(1)	Price	Share O/S	Market Cap	Total Debt	Cash & Equivalents	Enterprise Value	Calendar EBITDA 2010	2011E	2012E	EV/Calendar EBITDA 2010	2011E	2012E
Quick-Service													
DPZ	N	$ 18.38	62.1	1,141	1,452	133	2,460	252	263	268	9.8X	9.4X	9.2X
JACK	U	$ 20.80	52.9	1,100	373	17	1,457	261	217	247	5.6	6.7	5.9
MCD	B	$ 78.40	1,068.3	83,794	11,505	2,387	92,912	8,756	9,423	9,919	10,6	9.9	9.4
SONC	U	$ 9.23	61.9	571	538	38	1,071	125	125	128	8.6	8.6	8.4
WEN	N	$ 4.75	418.4	1,987	1,572	514	3,046	397	406	449	7.7	7.5	6.8
YUM	B	$ 51.55	488.0	25,156	3,588	1,426	27,318	2,410	2,749	3,050	11.3	9.9	9.0
Average											8.9X	8.7X	8.1X
Casual Dining													
CAKE	B	$ 30.60	60.6	1,853	52	82	1,824	200	214	232	9.1X	3.5X	7.9X
EAT	U	$ 25.52	92.1	2,351	536	114	2,772	343	362	382	8.1	7.7	7.3
DRI	B	$ 48.46	140.0	6,784	1,603	90	8,298	1,007	1,103	1,206	8.2	7.5	6.9
PFCB	U	$ 46.30	23.0	1,065	3	71	997	143	150	164	7.0	6.7	6.1
RRGB	U	$ 28.06	15.7	441	159	18	581	75	81	94	7.7	7.2	6.2
RT	N	$ 11.00	652	718	291	8	1,000	144	144	152	6.9	6.9	6.6
Average											7.9X	7.4X	6.8X
Family Dining													
CBRL	B	$ 51.00	23.9	1,220	577	63	1,734	235	248	270	7.4X	7.0X	6.4X
Specialty													
CMG	N	$288.10	31.7	9,133	4	350	8,788	363	417	491	24.2X	21.1 X	17.9X
PNRA	N	$123.38	30.1	3,713	0	229	3,483	254	295	322	13.7	11.8	10.8
SBUX	N	$ 36.89	766.7	26,284	549	2,051	26,782	2,111	2,262	2,603	12.7	11.8	10.3
Average											16.9X	14.9X	13.0X

Source: FactSet Research Systems Inc.; Reuters; Thomson Financial; BofA Merrill Lynch Global Research estimates (1) Ratings: B=Buy N=Neutral U=Underperform

Source: GE Capital, Franchise Finance 2011 Chain Restaurant Industry Review.

term however, Chipotle's current growth rate is not sustainable.

Top management's guidance for profitability is mid-single digit SSS growth for the full 2011 fiscal year.[94] Assuming Chipotle does not alter its prices in the short term, declining traffic rates would result in a lower level of comp sales increases or even flat sales. If Chipotle's overall traffic rates decline, analysts will likely point to one or a combination of four main causes: 1) an aging store base, 2) decreased marketing expenditures, 3) increased competition in the quick-serve, fast-casual, and/or casual dining segments, and/or 4) sales cannibalization due to new store openings.

Looking forward, the market will keep a close eye on SSS, specifically the rate at which it may decelerate in 2011 and beyond. Just as important, Wall Street will be focused on how 2010 store openings season after their honeymoon periods end as well as how 2011 store openings perform. Also, maintaining or increasing

margins will be important, especially cost of goods sold and labor line items.

Next on the Menu...

With the high level of growth Chipotle has realized thus far, there are many challenges related to organizational structure and personnel that could affect Chipotle maintaining or improving its performance as the company continues to expand. Chipotle's approach of embracing environmental consciousness—rather unique to chains in the restaurant industry—causes additional challenges for Chipotle and its supply chain, distribution operations, and plans for growth. Nevertheless, to date, the loyalty of and word-of-mouth marketing provided by its customers have helped Chipotle's revenues grow thus keeping shareholders happy and funding Chipotle's environmental agendas.

Steve Ells and the Chipotle team are dedicated to the company and its vision for the future. In Ells' discussion of first quarter 2011 results with staff and shareholders, he reinforced the company's commitment.

I remain confident that our performance is rooted in our long-term vision to change the way people think about and eat fast food...This focused approach makes us unique in the restaurant industry, and continues to differentiate Chipotle in significant ways.[95]

It is clear that Ells feels the path Chipotle is on has made possible its high market share and continued growth. So far, Chipotle has maintained the success of its current locations and, based on this model, has significant growth plans for additional locations. With its potential for additional financial and market share growth, how the company reacts to and handles these opportunities will determine its future.

NOTES

1. Fast casual restaurant growth continues to outpace rest of industry, finds Technomic. (2011, May 16). *PR Newswire*. Retrieved May 22, 2011, from http://www.prnewswire.com/news-releases/fast-casual -restaurant-growth-continues-to-outpace-rest-of-industry-finds -technomic-121892343.html
2. What is food with integrity? *Chipotle.com*. Retrieved May 28, 2011, from http://www.chipotle.com/en-US/fwi/fwi.aspx
3. Chipotle Mexican Grill, Inc. *Funding Universe*. Retrieved Apr 28, 2011, from http://www.fundinguniverse.com/company-histories/ Chipotle-Mexican-Grill-Inc-Company-History.html
4. *Ibid.*
5. Corporate Profile. *Chipotle.com*. Retrieved Apr 29, 2011, from http://ir.chipotle.com/phoenix.zhtml?c=194775&p=irol -homeprofile&t=&id=&
6. *Ibid.*
7. *Ibid.*
8. What is food with integrity? *op. cit.*
9. Chipotle Mexican Grill, Inc. *Funding Universe. op. cit.*
10. Chipotle earns the first LEED-Platinum Certification awarded to a restaurant. (2009, Jul 9). *Greener Buildings*. Retrieved May 28, 2011, from http://www.greenbiz.com/news/2009/07/09/ chipotle-earns-first-leed-platinum-certification-awarded-restaurant
11. Heffernan, M. (2010, Sep 14). Chipotle Grill's secret ingredient: Obsession. *BNet – The CBS Interactive Business Network*. Retrieved May 19, 2011, from http://www.bnet.com/blog/business-strategy/ chipotle-grills-secret-ingredient-obsession/106?tag=mantle _skin;content
12. Chipotle finalizes London location. (2009, Nov 17). *Chipotle.com*. Retrieved May 12, 2011, from http://ir.chipotle.com/phoenix .zhtml?c=194775&p=irol-newsArticle&ID=1356314&highlight=
13. *Ibid.*
14. Chipotle: 2010 Annual Report & Proxy Statement. *Chipotle.com*. http://phx.corporate-ir.net/External.File?item=UGFyZW50SUQ9NDI xMjg4fENoaWxkSUQ9NDM4OTQzfFR5cGU9MQ==&t=1
15. What exactly is fast casual? (2008, Jan). *Franchise Times*. Retrieved May 18, 2011, from http://www.franchisetimes.com/content/story .php?article=00643
16. Fast casual restaurant growth continues to outpace rest of industry, finds Technomic. *op. cit.*
17. *Ibid.*
18. The next Chipotle? Emerging fast-causal players vie to repeat success of highly regarded burrito brand. (Mar 7, 2011). *Nation's Restaurant News*. Retrieved May 12, 2011, from http://goliath .ecnext.com/coms2/gi_0198-737151/The-next-Chipotle-Emerging -fast.html
19. *Ibid.*
20. Jennings, L. (2008, Oct 12). Baja Fresh adapts Chipotle order style with 'speedline' interactive revamping. *Nation's Restaurant News*. Retrieved May 22, 2011, from http:// www.nrn.com/article/baja-fresh-adapts-chipotle-order-style -%E2%80%98speedline%E2%80%99-interactive-revamping
21. Panera Bread Company: 2010 Annual Report to Stockholders. (2011, Apr 18). *Panera Bread.com*. Retrieved May 18, 2011, from http://www.panerabread.com/pdf/ar-2010.pdf
22. *Ibid.*
23. *Ibid.*
24. *Ibid.*
25. *Ibid.*
26. Jack in the Box, Inc. Form 10-K, as amended for the fiscal year ended Oct 3, 2010. jackinthebox.com. Retrieved May 14, 2011, from http://phx.corporate-ir.net/External.File?item=UGFyZW50SUQ 9Nzc0MDV8Q2hpbGRGRJRD0tMXxUeXBlPTM=&t=1.
27. Our philosophy. *Qdoba.com*. Retrieved May 18, 2011, from http:// www.qdoba.com/Philosophy.aspx
28. Killifer, V. (2011, Mar 17). FastCasual.com releases top 100 movers & shakers. *Fast Casual.com*. Retrieved May 19, 2011, from http:// www.fastcasual.com/article/180020/FastCasual-com-releases-Top -100-Movers-Shakers
29. Jack in the Box, Inc. Form 10-K as amended for the fiscal year ended Oct 3, 2010. *op. cit.*
30. *Ibid.*
31. PFCB P.F. Chang's China Bistro, Inc. 2010 Annual Report. Retrieved May 14, 2011, from http://phx.corporate-ir.net/External.File?item =UGFyZW50SUQ9NDE3NzY0fENoaWxkSUQ9NDMwNDk3fFR5cGU 9MQ==&t=1
32. *Ibid.*
33. *Ibid.*
34. *Ibid.*
35. *Ibid.*
36. *Ibid.*
37. Chipotle: 2010 Annual Report & Proxy Statement. *op. cit.*
38. Farmers strike gold. (2011, Mar). *The Gold Burrito Digest, Vol. I*. Retrieved May 19, 2011, from http://www.chipotle.com/en-US/ chipotle_story/gold_ingredients/downloads/TheGoldBurritoDigest -vol1.pdf
39. Profiles in farming: World's best cheese also most friendly. (2011, Mar). *The Gold Burrito Digest, Vol. I*. Retrieved May 19, 2011, from http://www.chipotle.com/en-US/chipotle_story/gold_ingredients/ downloads/TheGoldBurritoDigest-vol1.pdf
40. Gourmet garden of eatin' found in Ohio. (2011, Apr). *The Gold Burrito Digest, Vol. 2*. Retrieved May 19, 2011, from http://www .chipotle.com/en-US/chipotle_story/gold_ingredients/downloads/ TheGoldBurritoDigest-vol2.pdf
41. Chipotle remains largest restaurant buyer of locally grown produce. (2010, May 18). *Chipotle.com*. Retrieved May 19, 2011, from http://phx.corporate-ir.net/phoenix.zhtml?c=194775&p=irol -newsArticle&ID=1428368&highlight=
42. Farmers strike gold. *op. cit.*
43. What is food with integrity? *op. cit.*
44. Chipotle: 2010 Annual Report & Proxy Statement. *op. cit.*
45. *Ibid.*
46. Chipotle bows to PETA's demands on chicken suppliers. (2008, Mar 13). *Nation's Restaurant News*. Retrieved May 24, 2011, from http://www.nrn.com/article/chipotle-bows-peta%E2%80%99s -demands-chicken-suppliers
47. Glover, K. (2009, Sep 10). Chipotle agrees to raise tomato wages (finally). *BNet – The CBS Interactive Business Network*. Retrieved May 19, 2011, from http://www.bnet.com/blog/food/chipotle -agrees-to-raise-tomato-wages-finally/979

48. Rowe, M. (2009, Apr 1). Why fast casual kicks butt. *Restaurant Hospitality*. Retrieved May 18, 2011 from http://restaurant -hospitality.com/features/why-fast-casual-0409/

49. Personal Interview with Chipotle mid-day shift supervisor, Javier Ramirez, in Glendale, CA on May 20, 2011.

50. Lepore, M. (2011, Mar 31). The amazing story of Chipotle. *Business Insider*. Retrieved May 20, 2011, from http://www.businessinsider .com/the-chipotle-story-2011-3?op=1

51. Melnick, J. Local heroes top golden arches. *QSR Magazine*. Retrieved May 13, 2011, from http://www2.qsrmagazine.com/ articles/exclusives/0810/customer-1.phtml

52. Ryu, K., Han, H,, & Kim, T-H. 2007. The relationships among overall quick-casual restaurant image, perceived value, customer satisfaction, and behavioral intentions. *International Journal of Hospitality Management, 27*(3) 459-469.

53. Chipotle: 2010 Annual Report & Proxy Statement. *op. cit.*

54. Hendrickson, B. (2010, Nov 15). Mintel offers up insights, trends for fast-casual segment. *The Food Channel*. Retrieved on May 20, 2011, from http://www.foodchannel.com/articles/article/mintel -offers-insights-trends-fast-casual-segment/

55. Wong, E. (2009, Feb 13). Chipotle CMO wants the whole enchilada. *Adweek*. Retrieved May 18, 2011, from http://www .adweek.com/news/advertising-branding/chipotle-cmo-wants -whole-enchilada-105272

56. Tice, C. (2010, Jun 29). How Chipotle got to 1,000 restaurants. *BNet – The CBS Interactive Business Network*. Retrieved May 19, 2011, from http://www.bnet.com/blog/retail-stores/how-chipotle -got-to-1000-restaurants/769?tag=content;drawer-container

57. Fong, B. (2010, Jun 10). Chipotle Grill nutrition information. *Livestrong.com*. Retrieved May 14, 2011, from http://www .livestrong.com/article/145382-chipotle-grill-nutrition-information/

58. Severson, K. (2011, Apr 23). Behind the rising cost of food. *The New York Times*. Retrieved May 14, 2011, from http://www .nytimes.com/2011/04/24/weekinreview/24food.html

59. Chipotle: 2010 Annual Report & Proxy Statement. *op. cit.*

60. Chipotle Mexican Grill's CEO discusses Q1 2011 results- earnings call transcript. (2011, Apr 20). *Seeking Alpha*. Retrieved May 12, 2011, from http://seekingalpha.com/article/264620-chipotle -mexican-grill-s-ceo-discusses-q1-2011-results-earnings -call-transcript

61. Buckley, J. (2011, Feb 11). Great 4Q but downgrade to neutral. *docstoc.com*. Retrieved May 24, 2011, from http://www.docstoc .com/docs/71361885/?key=YjQyOTAzYjUt&pass=NWNjYi00MWU3

62. Ruggless, R. (2011, Feb 10). Panera sales, profit surge in 4Q. *Nation's Restaurant News*. Retrieved May 14, 2011, from http:// www.nrn.com/article/panera-sales-profit-surge-4q

63. Ruggless, R. (2011, Feb 16). P.F. Chang's 4Q profit rises. *Nation's Restaurant News*. Retrieved May 14, 2011, from http://www.nrn .com/article/pf-changs-4q-profit-rises

64. Warren, C. (2006, May/Jun). Chipotle's fresh mission. *NYSE Magazine*. Retrieved May 21, 2011, from http://www.nyse.com/ pdfs/NYSE_MAY_JUNE_06_Chipotle.pdf

65. *Ibid.*

66. *Ibid.*

67. *Ibid.*

68. *Ibid.*

69. Baertlein, L. (2011, May 4). Federal agents widen Chipotle immigration probe. *Reuters*. Retrieved May 14, 2011, from http://www.reuters.com/article/2011/05/04/us-chipotle -idUSTRE74307S20110504

70. Jennings, L. (2011, Feb 8). Chipotle: Immigration crack down has been 'eye opening.' *Nation's Restaurant News*. Retrieved May 14, 2011, from http://www.nrn.com/article/chipotle-immigration-crack -down-eye-opening

71. Baertlein, L. *op. cit.*

72. Chipotle: 2010 Annual Report & Proxy Statement. *op. cit.*

73. Facebook pages of Chipotle, Panera Bread, Qdoba Mexican Grill, and Pei Wei. Retrieved May 16, 2011, from http://www.facebook .com/chipotle, http://www.facebook.com/panerabread, http://www .facebook.com/QdobaMexicanGrill, http://www.facebook.com/ peiwei

74. Arndt, M. (2007, Mar 12). Burrito buzz—and so few ads. *Business Week*. Retrieved May 20, 2011, from http://www.businessweek .com/print/magazine/content/07_11/b4025088.htm?chan-gl

75. Personal Interview. *op. cit.*

76. Warren, C. (2006, May/Jun). *op. cit.*

77. *Ibid.*

78. Chipotle: 2010 Annual Report & Proxy Statement. *op. cit.*

79. Chipotle Mexican Grill, Inc.: 4Q10 solid: '11 comp and cost reversion. (2011, Feb 11). *Barclays Capital*. Retrieved May 24, 2011, from http://box407.bluehost.com/pipermail/research _avantefg.com/attachments/20110211/9c62acaa/attachment-0003 .pdf

80. Buckley, J. (2011, Feb 11). *op. cit.*

81. Chipotle Mexican Grill's CEO discusses Q1 2011 results- earnings call transcript. *op. cit.*

82. Chipotle Mexican Grill Inc. 2009 Form 10-K and 2010 Form 10-K. Retrieved May 14, 2011, http://www.sec.gov/cgi-bin/browse-edgar ?action=getcompany&CIK=0001058090&type=10-K&dateb=&own er=exclude&count=40

83. Dizon, K. (2004, Apr 6). A moment with … Steve Ells, Chipotle boss. Retrieved May 12, 2011, from http://www.seattlepi .com/lifestyle/food/article/A-moment-with-Steve-Ells-Chipotle -boss-1141563.php

84. *Ibid.*

85. Steve Ells: Chairman of the Board and Co-Chief Executive Officer. *Forbes.com*. Retrieved May 12, 2011, from http://people.forbes .com/profile/steve-ells/19160

86. Montgomery F. (Monty) Moran: Director and Co-Chief Executive Officer. *Forbes.com*. Retrieved May 12, 2011, from http://people .forbes.com/profile/montgomery-f-monty-moran/19166

87. Robert (Bob) N. Blessing: Chief Development Officer. *Forbes.com*. Retrieved May 12, 2011, from http://people.forbes.com/profile/ robert-bob-n-blessing/19162

88. Chipotle Mexican Grill. (2011, Mar 8). Raymond James 32nd Annual Institutional Investors Conference presentation. PDF.

89. Chipotle Mexican Grill. (2011, May 11). Baird 2011 Growth Stock Conference presentation. PDF.

90. Chipotle Mexican Grill, Inc.: 4Q10 solid: '11 comp and cost reversion. *op. cit.*

91. Chipotle Mexican Grill, Inc. announces first quarter 2011 results. (2011, Apr 20). *Chipotle.com*. Retrieved May 14, 2011, from http://ir.chipotle.com/phoenix.zhtml?c=194775&p=irol -newsArticle&ID=1552867&highlight=

92. Chipotle Mexican Grill, Inc.: 4Q10 solid: '11 comp and cost reversion. *op. cit.*

93. *Ibid.*

94. Chipotle: 2010 Annual Report & Proxy Statement. *op. cit.*

95. Chipotle Mexican Grill's CEO discusses Q1 2011 results-earnings call transcript. *op. cit.*

Coinstar: A Sleeping Giant Awakens

Martin Burns, Jason Parker, Erin Baldinger, Chet Wall

Arizona State University

One billion rentals is an incredible milestone as Redbox has quickly become the local video store for millions of consumers nationwide. Our popularity is a testament to our consumers' loyalty and our steadfast commitment to making movie rentals affordable and convenient for our consumers.

> MITCH LOWE
> REDBOX PRESIDENT, SEPTEMBER 5, 2010

Introduction

After nearly twenty years of plodding diligently along, it has been a busy time for Coinstar. Within a three-year period beginning in 2008, Coinstar expanded through its acquisition of Redbox, changed its CEO, shuffled executive management, and sold off three of its four differentiated lines of business. In addition, it amassed over $350 million in debt that is now convertible, maturing, or subject to a spread higher than the current bank market would dictate and representing over 30 percent of assets. Despite its growing pains while searching for a long-term strategic identity, Coinstar was also able to increase consolidated revenue by $382.5 million (or 58.8 percent) in 2009 and $403.8 million (or 39.1 percent) in 2010.[1]

Coinstar's recent growth was primarily fueled by revenue generated by Redbox—a DVD rental kiosk business with almost 31,000 retail locations. Consumers made penny wise by the recession flocked to Redbox in search of cheap entertainment in the form of $1 per day DVD rentals. The popularity of Redbox helped Coinstar nearly double revenues to $1 billion and made it a Wall Street darling with its stock trading as high as $60 a share.[2]

As of 2011, Coinstar consisted of two primary lines of business—coin-counting kiosks and Redbox kiosks—and had many decisions to make as it continued to compete in these segments. From developing future product lines, to becoming more streamlined, to restructuring its balance sheet to fund expansion and support long-term sustainable returns to shareholders, Coinstar leaders had a few late nights ahead.

More Than Just a Jar of Chump Change... *Lots* More

As have so many iconic American entrepreneurial enterprises, Coinstar's humble beginnings were born and bred on a college campus. Coinstar was founded by Jens Molbak in 1991 and officially, and literally, began turning a dollar after Molbak installed his first coin-counting machines in four San Francisco grocery stores in 1992. The immediate success of those first four machines prompted aggressive expansion plans and, under the leadership of Molbak, the company went public in 1997. By 2002, Coinstar had installed its 10,000th machine and processed more than $4.5 billion worth of coins and, despite not having turned a profit yet, was valued at an estimated $130 million.[3] In a rather mind-boggling feat, by 2001, Coinstar machines were collecting and returning into circulation more coins annually than those being produced by the US Mint. In fact, in 2002, the US Mint began reducing its workforce and by 2010, it was producing less than one third of the average number of coins it had produced annually over the last 30 years,[4] a fact nearly wholly attributed to Coinstar.

In an effort to diversify its revenue stream, Coinstar invested in four primary subsidiaries in the early to mid 2000s: a money transfer business called GroupEx, an electronic payments service, an entertainment business consisting of gumball machines and crane games, and Redbox. While the former three of these businesses had combined revenues of over $261 million in 2008, by 2010, revenues had plunged to $104 million. Having already initiated an evaluation of its product lines, business segments, and corporate structure in 2008, by 2010,

Exhibit 1 Segment Revenues

Coin Revenues				DVD Revenues			
2005	**2006**	$ change 05 to 06	% change 05 to 06	**2005**	**2006**	$ change 05 to 06	% change 05 to 06
220.7	261.0	**40.3**	**18.3%**	239.0	273.4	**34.4**	**14.4%**
	2007	$ change 06 to 07	% change 06 to 07		**2007**	$ change 06 to 07	% change 06 to 07
	307.4	**46.4**	**17.8%**		238.9	**-34.5**	**-12.6%**
	2008	$ change 07 to 08	% change 07 to 08		**2008**	$ change 07 to 08	% change 07 to 08
	261.3	**-46.1**	**-15.0%**		388.5	**149.6**	**62.6%**
	2009	$ change 08 to 09	% change 08 to 09		**2009**	$ change 08 to 09	% change 08 to 09
	259.1	**-2.2**	**-0.8%**		773.5	**385.0**	**99.1%**
	2010	$ change 09 to 10	% change 09 to 10		**2010**	$ change 09 to 10	% change 09 to 10
	276.3	**17.2**	**6.6%**		1160.1	**386.6**	**50.0%**
Cumulative		$ change 05 to 10	% change 05 to 10	**Cumulative**		$ change 05 to 10	% change 05 to 10
	276.3	**55.6**	**25.2%**		1160.1	**921.1**	**385.4%**
e-payment revenue included with Coin				Inclusive of all "entertainment" revenue			

Source: Data taken from 2007, 2008, 2009, 2010 Coinstar 10-K

Coinstar made the decision to divest all but Redbox thus demonstrating its commitment to its two primary business segments—Redbox and Coinstar kiosks (see Exhibit 1).

Redbox Division

With more than 27,000 locations nationwide, Redbox is the fun, fast, easy way to rent the latest new release movies for just $1 a night for DVD rentals and $1.50 a night for Blu-ray Disc rentals. The network of bright red Redbox kiosks are located at leading grocery stores, mass merchant retailers, drugstores, restaurants, and convenience stores nationwide. Featuring up to 200 titles and 630 movies, Redbox is a fully automated video rental store contained in 12-square feet of retail space.[5]

McDonald's, the popular fast food chain, created Redbox in 2002 as a way to generate revenue by renting DVDs at its restaurant locations. In 2005, McDonalds entered into a joint venture with Coinstar, spinning Redbox off into its own corporation and giving Coinstar a 47 percent ownership stake with future ownership options. On January 1, 2008, Coinstar increased its Redbox ownership as allowed by its operating agreement to 51 percent and, in February 2009, Coinstar acquired the remaining shares of Redbox.[6] With a combination of stock and cash, the total transaction cost Coinstar an estimated $176 million.[7]

After two years of test piloting at more than 5,000 kiosks, in 2011, Coinstar introduced video game rentals to more than 21,000 of its 31,000 Redbox kiosks. With its sole remaining bricks-and-mortar competitor Blockbuster already reduced through store closings to a whisper of its former self, Coinstar has targeted expansion to include an additional 14,000 Redbox kiosks nationwide—adding to the four kiosks it has already placed within a five-minute drive of every Blockbuster location.[8] In response to the increasing popularity of streaming video and to compete with its other major rival—Netflix—Redbox CEO Mitch Lowe confirmed that plans were in the works for Redbox to offer a video streaming subscription service.[9]

Coin Business

Coinstar's coin-counting kiosks have been a steady source of revenue and the foundation of the company since its inception. As of 2011, Coinstar operated 18,900 coin-counting kiosks in the US, Canada, the UK, and Ireland.[10] Jens Molbak, a second year MBA student at Stanford, came up with the idea while staring at a jar of loose change on his desk. He later rolled the questions of 'what do people do with their loose change?' and 'exactly how much loose change is out of circulation?' into a graduate research project. What he discovered after surveying 1,500 consumers confirmed his own sentiment that it was a hassle to roll the coins and cash them in. What surprised him however was, based on what people were telling him, the astronomical dollar amount of coins he estimated to be sitting in jars just like his, across the nation.

Coinstar estimates that the average consumer touches about $600 in change every year and has between $30 and $50 worth of change sitting out of circulation at home. That amounts to about $144 billion in annual coin flow, with more than $7 billion in change sitting idle across the nation.[11]

Central to Coinstar's success are the original five patents Coinstar holds for its coin-counting machine technologies. The machine counts unsorted change poured in by a customer at a rate of 600 coins per minute—separating the coins from common debris, lint, and other random tidbits sometimes found in coin jars. When the sorting is done, the machine provides a voucher for the total amount counted less the Coinstar processing fee. Customers then exchange their voucher for cash at the retail location hosting the machine. Because the alternative is to do it themselves, Coinstar customers offered little resistance to its recent processing fee price increase from 8.9 percent to 9.8 percent of gross. The fee increase was expected to raise same store growth by at least 5 percent.[12] One year later, Coinstar reported a decrease of over 640,000 transactions across its fleet of machines. Despite this however, the fee increase ensured positive growth of same-store revenue of 5.3 percent (see Exhibit 2).

As a new alternative to paying the processing fee, customers may instead choose to receive a fully funded (i.e., no processing fee deducted) gift card or eCertificate in lieu of cash.[13] Additionally, Coinstar customers can now also opt to have a Coinstar Account whereby users can track their coin redemptions online, make charitable donations to large partner charities, and receive exclusive offers via e-mail.

New Ventures

With the divestiture of its three other product lines, starting in 2011, Coinstar will be reporting a new segment called New Ventures. Per Coinstar's SEC filings, in the past, the company reported the segment under the Redbox and Coin segments. Currently, the segment is mostly involved in what is referred to as "Coffee and Chirp" businesses, along with other trial kiosk concepts.

The Coffee kiosks can dispense a "real brewed" cup of coffee, designed by the person who developed the Starbucks stands that are commonly found in grocery stores. The Chirp kiosks will sell ladies merchandise to women shopping at grocery stores, with an inventory that will be completely replaced each week. Other ideas include a kiosk called Gizmo selling small high-value electronic gadgets and consumer goods, Face Cube which is a photo booth connected to the Internet, and a partnership with ecoATM which is a kiosk that recycles old cell phones.[14]

All the kiosk concepts replicate the existing service model whereby kiosks are updated weekly and designed to attract specific demographics in particular locations. Coinstar is able to leverage its existing infrastructure to deliver more goods to more people in what holds the potential to be a one-stop shop. Coinstar has trademarked the term "4th Wall," which is "a merchandising strategy based on the variety of front-of-store businesses and including coin conversion, pay-as-you-go products/services, DVD rental, money transfer, and coffee kiosks"[15]—and Coinstar's plan for future growth.

A Strong Collective of Expertise

Jens Molbak founded and served as the CEO of Coinstar from 1991 until February 2000 when he retired at age 39. At that time, Daniel Gerrity, Coinstar's President and COO, assumed the role of CEO, serving for only nine months before turning in his own resignation. Succeeding Gerrity was David Cole who served as CEO from 2000 to 2009. Currently serving as CEO and member of the Board of Directors is Paul Davis.[16]

Paul Davis, Chief Executive Officer

Paul Davis came to Coinstar as the COO in April 2008 and assumed the role of CEO and Director of the Board in April 2009.[17] Before joining Coinstar, Davis held a variety of sales and executive management positions with Kettle Foods, Barilla America, Starbucks North America, PepsiCo's Frito-Lay Canada, and Procter and Gamble. Davis holds a bachelor's degree from the University of Central Missouri.[18]

Gregg Kaplan, President and Chief Operating Officer

Gregg Kaplan was hired by Coinstar from Redbox as President and COO in April 2009 upon the promotion of Paul Davis.[19] Kaplan started with Redbox as part of McDonald's strategy and development team, becoming

Exhibit 2 Same Store Sales Growth

DVD Kiosk Same Store Sales			
	Q1	Q2	Q3	Q4
2010	21.0%	3.5%	17.2%	12.5%
2009	35.0%	33.0%	26.0%	21.0%
2008	37.4%	63.2%	40.6%	64.3%

Coin Kiosk Same Store Sales			
	Q1	Q2	Q3	Q4
2010	0.5%	7.9%	7.9%	—
2009	-5.0%	-4.3%	-5.4%	-3.9%
2008	-0.2%	-3.2%	-1.8%	-5.0%

Source: Data taken from 2010 Coinstar 10-K

Redbox CEO in 2005 when it became a separate company. In his almost seven years with Redbox, he grew the business from its first kiosk to over 14,000—from a team of five employees to over 1,200. Before McDonald's, Kaplan worked with Internet start-ups and as an investment banker. Kaplan holds a bachelor's in philosophy from the University of Michigan and an MBA from Harvard Business School.

J. Scott Di Valerio, Chief Financial Officer

Scott Di Valerio came on board with Coinstar in March 2010 as CFO.[20] With prior work experience at Lenovo, Microsoft, and Mindwave Software, Di Valerio also leads Coinstar's corporate IT functions. Other experience includes time spent with Walt Disney and Pricewaterhouse Coopers. Di Valerio holds a bachelor's in business administration from the University of San Diego and is a Certified Public Accountant.[21]

Mitch Lowe, President, Redbox

Like Kaplan, Mitch Lowe started his career with Redbox as part of the McDonald's team tasked with its development.[22] After splitting from McDonald's in 2005, Lowe was hired by Redbox as the COO and named President in 2009. Prior to McDonald's he held the Chairman and Director positions of the Video Software Dealers Association and was a Founding Executive of Netflix.

Mike Skinner, President, Coin

Mike Skinner was hired by Coinstar at the end of 2004 and held various senior management roles prior to his promotion to President of Coin in 2009.[23] Prior to Coinstar, Skinner had amassed over 30 years of experience with companies including National Beverage, PIA Merchandising, and Impli Media. Skinner received his bachelor's in business administration from Oregon State.[24]

Setting the Tone

The majority of Coinstar sales and operations are in the US with no formal plans for significant international expansion. Generally, the US population is growing larger through longer life expectancy due to medical advancements and an increase in immigration. Always considered a "melting pot," the US is becoming an even more diverse society than before, a fact that is already significantly affecting the current and future target audiences businesses are identifying. Collectively, these trends continue to expand the consumer market of the US.

The US economy officially endured a recessionary contraction from December 2007 through June 2009. However, because the primary driver of the recovery has been loose monetary and fiscal government policies, the economy remains weak. Additionally, the US budget deficit remains at a record high, raising concerns about the long-term creditworthiness of the US government and diluting the value of the US dollar in global markets. To Coinstar's advantage however, this weakened economy makes low-priced goods and services (i.e. Redbox) very attractive to consumers and a prolonged recovery could bode well for low-cost goods and services providers as consumers remain wary of spending beyond their means.

As it affects mostly the Redbox division, physical DVD sales are expected to drop $4.6 billion from 2009 to 2014 due to technological advances such as video streaming over the Internet and the variety of viewing portals available including televisions, computers, phones, tablets, and music players. General improvement of Internet data transmission speeds and data storage advancements continue to be a key factor in this development.

Taking a Toll

Coinstar's Redbox division has more competitors than its Coin division including Netflix, Vudu (owned by Walmart), AppleTV, and recently Amazon.com. In any discussion of the industry, it is important to also note that, while movie studios have historically relied upon distribution contracts and royalties for post-production revenue, recent technological advancements have simplified electronic distribution—a fact the studios could leverage at any time to not only maximize their revenue streams, but pocket any advertising dollars generated by their Internet portals. Coinstar's Coin division's most notable competitors include Global Payment Technology (GPT) as well as the installation of free coin-counting machines and the daily cashiering operations of bricks-and-mortar banks.

Redbox DVD Segment Competition

Blockbuster / DISH. The success of Redbox has caught the attention of many companies and, despite its bankruptcy and seeming demise, the most notable of these is Blockbuster. Seeing the opportunity the kiosk market offers, Blockbuster launched its own kiosk network with 600 kiosks as of year-end 2010 and plans to install another 4,000 outlets in the future.[25] With Blockbuster's brand recognition, sentimental appeal, and newfound resources via its new owner, DISH Network, it cannot be counted out of the running just yet.[26]

Netflix. With 20 million subscribers, Netflix offers a formidable challenge to Coinstar's Redbox division. While Netflix and Redbox both serve the consumer in search of recent releases, Netflix has also amassed a large collection of special interest (foreign, independent, and hard-to-find) movies and a large audience of subscribers interested in this content. Netflix reported $2.16 billion in annual revenue in 2010—a 29 percent increase from 2009 following a 22 percent increase from 2008. Because Netflix is a flat-rate service, barring rate increases, revenue increases are the result of additional subscribers.[27] Netflix subscribers have two subscription options: for $7.99 per month, subscribers can stream an unlimited number of movies and television shows or, with a $2.00 upgrade, they can also choose to receive DVDs at home via mail in as few as two business days.[28]

The number of Netflix subscribers continues to grow unabated (see Exhibit 3). Netflix believes that by continually improving the customer experience, it will continue to add subscribers. By increasing its number of subscribers, Netflix has greater leverage when negotiating with studios and is able to obtain more content. Netflix's subscription growth enables additional investments in research and development to improve services thus leading back to the start of the cycle—subscriber growth.

Walmart's Vudu. Founded in 2004, Vudu entered the video-on-demand market in April 2007. Like Netflix, Vudu allows viewers to watch movies via the Internet by streaming them to a home television, Sony Playstation, DVD player, or laptop. However, unlike Netflix, viewers only pay for what they watch—currently $2 for two nights of access. Also, Vudu allows consumers to stream more movies in HD and offers customers the ability to

stream movies the same day they are released.[29] Redbox and Netflix on the other hand each require 28 days from the day of release before being able to offer the physical DVD, and delivery via streaming can take significantly longer if available at all.

Walmart acquired Vudu in 2010 because it provided the opportunity and means to enter the streaming market and begin to offset its anticipated future losses in the sales of DVD and Blu-ray as these formats become obsolete. Vudu currently has licensing agreements to distribute 16,000 separate titles.[30] Vudu's main selling point however was not only its licensing agreements, but also its unique digital technology that demonstrates a real expertise in the Internet streaming business.

AppleTV. Apple has not ignored the growth potential in streaming movies and television shows and has developed its own device—AppleTV ($99)—onto which users can stream content. The niche of AppleTV is that it co-promotes iTunes as well as allows access to recently released television shows.[31] In an effort to expand the reach of this product, Apple recently negotiated a partnership with Netflix that provides AppleTV owners with access to Netflix's catalog. The alliance gives Netflix users the ability to watch instantly released movies via streaming. Apple gains because its owners are notoriously loyal and AppleTV drives traffic to iTunes for streaming video.

Amazon.com. Amazon.com, a publicly held corporation based in Seattle, entered into the streaming media market in February 2011. Its streaming offering, Amazon Prime, allows users to stream unlimited amounts of data over its network for an annual fee of $79. Currently, the free unlimited streaming videos are limited to late 90s

Exhibit 3 Netflix Subscribers

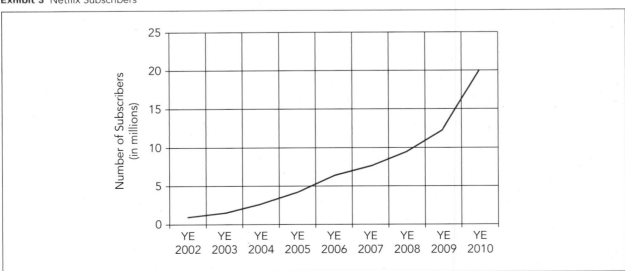

Source: Data taken from 2005, 2010 Netflix 10-K

and early 2000s movies as well as some television shows. It is estimated that Amazon currently offers just over 5,000 free (with annual membership fee) titles. In addition to access to streaming content, Amazon Prime also offers unlimited free two-day shipping on any order placed on its website, as well as one-day shipping for an upgrade fee of $3.99 per shipment. Though its streaming services are new, Amazon.com has offered the shipping discounts as part of its Amazon Prime membership since 2005. The company is currently offering new Amazon Prime members a monthlong trial of its services at no cost.[32]

Accessibility to Amazon's movie database is currently only available through Samsung, Vizio, Sony, and Panasonic Internet connectable HD televisions and Blu-Ray players as well as TiVo and Roku set-top boxes and DVRs. As the newest player in the streaming market, Amazon's movie and television show selection is not of the same size or quality of Netflix. Even so, the company is actively working to expand its library to include additional popular titles in the near future.[33]

Coin Segment Competitors

Global Payment Technologies. Global Payment Technologies (GPT) is a worldwide leader in the design and manufacture of currency handling equipment used in payment systems, tickets, gaming, and vending machines. Its core competency is its combined hardware and software that allows companies to offer secure and reliable currency handling and recordkeeping.

GPT's customers are companies and not individuals. One of its largest typical customers is a bank as the sensors in its equipment allow for the verification of bank notes. With a global presence in over 50 countries, GPT's equipment has the ability to reject counterfeit bank notes while accepting 99 percent of genuine currency.[34]

Financially, GPT has been struggling with annual revenues of $10.98 million and a negative net income of −$3.97 million. Despite projected growth of 22 percent, GPT will need to improve its profit margins to obtain favorable funding for future innovations and expansions.

Banks. An increasing number of banks have begun to install coin-counting machines as a value-added convenience for their customers—including 400 banks that have contracted with Coinstar for its machines, rebranded with the bank logo.[35] In some areas of the US, regional banks have begun offering full price coin redemptions in the form of a no upfront fee gift card. Having free coin-counting services has been a way to attract more customers to banks. For non-customers, many of these regional banks charge a 6 percent service fee.[36]

Customers

Customers of Redbox are credit or debit card holding individuals that want to watch movies without the hassle of being tied down to a contract or subscription. Customers can rent movies by either reserving a specific movie online to pick up at a nearby kiosk, or by simply selecting and renting a movie at a local kiosk without a reservation. Redbox customers are primarily in search of comedies and action movies and, with a flat rate of $1 per night, overwhelmingly state "good price" as their reason for patronizing Redbox. Additionally, some 45 percent of customers take advantage of the fact they can return a rented DVD to any Redbox kiosk,[37] resolving an oft-mentioned complaint of Blockbuster customers and making Redbox a very appealing service for travelers.[38] As an impetus to adding electronic download and streaming options, in a recent survey of its Redbox customers, Coinstar found that 65 percent were already familiar with downloading content (as compared to 52 percent of the general population).[39]

Quite simply, customers of Coinstar coin kiosks are those that have excess loose change and a desire to trade it in for coupons, paper money, or gift cards.

Spreading the Word

Coinstar's overall success stems from its sales and marketing efforts and strong relationships with retailers contracted to provide space for both Coin and DVD kiosks, with Walmart, Walgreens, and Kroger accounting for 19.6 percent, 13.7 percent, and 10.6 percent, respectively.[40] These relationships have enabled the rapid growth of Coinstar and, in particular, its Redbox DVD segment. Contracts with retailers vary but typically last three to five years for both Coin and DVD kiosks and include a percentage of sales for the host retailer. Contracts are customized based on the potential and success of a location.

While Coin kiosks are less affected, Redbox experiences seasonality in its DVD rentals due to cyclical lifestyle and movie release patterns as well as the introduction of new television series.[41] DVD rental income is higher in summer months when children are out of school and many television series are on hiatus for the summer travel months. Revenues then typically drop in September and October due to the start of the school year and the resumption of fall television programming.

In 2010, Coinstar's marketing expenditures totaled $14.7 million—an 80 percent increase over 2009. Those increased marketing dollars were utilized for national programs such as radio advertising, search engine marketing, and social media outlets for the Redbox segment[42] (see Exhibits 4 and 5).

Exhibit 4 Marketing Expenses

	Year Ended December 31,		Change	
	2010	**2009**	**$**	**%**
DVD Services	$ 14,726.00	$ 8,212.00	$ 6,514.00	79.3%
Coin Services	$ 9,092.00	$ 7,242.00	$ 1,850.00	25.5%
Share-based payment expense	$ 18.00	$ 25.00	$ (7.00)	-28.0%
Total	$ 23,836.00	$ 15,479.00	$ 8,357.00	54.0%

(dollars in thousands)

	2009	**2008**	**$**	**%**
DVD Services	$ 8,212.00	$ 7,018.00	$ 1,194.00	17.0%
Coin Services	$ 7,242.00	$ 7,682.00	$ (440.00)	-5.7%
Share-based payment expense	$ 25.00	$ 50.00	$ (25.00)	-50.0%
Total	$ 15,479.00	$ 14,750.00	$ 729.00	4.9%

(dollars in thousands)

Source: 2010 Coinstar 10-K

Exhibit 5 Marketing Expenses as a Percentage of Revenue

	2008	2009	2010
DVD Services	1.8%	1.1%	1.3%
Coin Services	2.9%	2.8%	3.3%
Total	**2.3%**	**1.5%**	**1.7%**

Source: 2010 Coinstar 10-K

Making It All Possible

Redbox kiosks are stocked with DVDs that it purchases from licensed distributors, including movie studios. However, recognizing its phenomenal appeal and success, studios are very concerned that Redbox is hurting their DVD sales—the studio's primary source of revenue after a movie leaves the theatre—which dropped 13 percent in the fourth quarter of 2008 and was projected to keep falling.[43] With Redbox kiosks in so many convenient locations, fewer customers are willing to drive to spend $20 per DVD when they can rent it for only $1. However, because Redbox continues to grow and each kiosk continues to generate an average of $50,000 per year in revenue, the studios have not been willing to pull Redbox's access to content knowing that this distribution network exposes more people to their movies thus translating into more revenue. Even though it has not yet been done in the US, the possibility remains for studios to decide to distribute content themselves if its supply contracts become less fruitful as well as to better protect themselves from piracy.

Coinstar depends on strong relationships with movie studios to build its Redbox DVD inventory. Redbox has established its DVD inventory by entering into licensing agreements with movie companies such as Paramount, Universal Studios, 20th Century Fox, Warner, Lionsgate Films, SBHE Scan Based Trading Corporation, as well as wholesale distributors.[44] Inventory management is a delicate balancing act for Redbox as each kiosk has a fixed amount of DVD storage within each unit. For this reason, correctly choosing the DVD titles and quantities that will generate business at any particular location is critical as Redbox strives to meet optimal availability levels for its customers.

As an example of when this did *not* work out, in the fourth quarter of 2010, Redbox purchased too many copies of certain new release DVD titles, forcing the premature removal of older titles from its kiosks. Consequently, there was a negative impact on revenues and gross margins due to removing these older titles too early.[45]

Coinstar's dependence on its relationships with movie studios caused a disadvantage for Redbox when, in exchange for reduced rates on its purchases, it entered into a licensing agreement with Warner, Universal Studios, and 20th Century Fox in 2010 agreeing to delay the availability of new releases until 28 days after the DVDs were available for sale. The majority of competing movie providers however remain able to offer the content the same day as DVD release. This new "delayed rental window" creates a negative impact on Redbox business as, by the time Redbox can offer a new release, many customers have seen it via a competitor.[46] DVD rental has indirect competitors—including video on demand, digital downloads, and video streaming—that are all a major threat to the future of Redbox. Even so, Redbox still has a pricing advantage: with rentals priced at $1 a night, Redbox maintains a strong foothold in today's movie rental business. Nevertheless, with DVDs going the way of VHS, Coinstar must invest in some long-term strategic planning if it intends to keep this segment alive.[47]

Coinstar places its coin-counting machines primarily in supermarkets and other retail locations. While the strategic location of a kiosk determines its success, the provider of the location benefits as well through a share of the kiosk's revenue and as, more often than not, customers spend their exchanged money at that same location.

At year-end 2010, Coinstar employed 2,585 people, 1,718 of whom were field service employees, throughout the US and internationally. However, Coinstar outsources many functions to third parties including kiosk manufacturing, coin pickup and processing, and kiosk servicing and repairs. Because these functions are outsourced, Coinstar depends on its relationships with these suppliers, without whom it could not continue to provide exceptional customer service, nor expand.[48]

Coinstar's investment in research and development and technological advances is evident through the number of patents the company holds related to its kiosks. Its kiosk technology is central to the Coin and Redbox segments. Collectively, Coinstar holds 100 patents in the US and international markets, 90 of which are related to its self-service coin-counting machines, including patents for machine networking, fraud avoidance, and voucher authentication. The remaining 10 patents held are related to the Redbox DVD business and include kiosk security and inventory management technologies.[49] Additional patents are pending.

Income Statement

Coinstar's healthy increases in revenue are due in large part to its increases in capital expenditures associated with adding 8,700 new DVD kiosks in 2009 and another 7,800 in 2010 coupled with increased marketing expenditures over the past few years (see Exhibit 6). Aggregate marketing expenditures have increased from approximately $15.5 million in 2009 to $23.8 million in 2010 with the majority of the increase due to marketing of the DVD business.[50]

Where revenue growth is driven almost solely by the DVD business, margins are a different scenario. The Coin margin has consistently outperformed the DVD operating margin—33.9 percent compared to 16.6 percent in 2010. This is primarily due to the expenses associated

Exhibit 6 Income Statement Analysis

DVD Segment			
Periods/Months Covered Statement Date	**Historical Unqualified**		
	12/31/2008	**12/31/2009**	**12/31/2010**
Number of DVD Kiosks	13,700	22,400	30,200
Revenue ($)	$388,453	$773,511	$1,160,110
Revenue Growth (%)	379.0%	99.1%	50.0%
Operating Income ($)	$ 50,169	$101,908	$ 192,563
Operating Income as a % of Revenue	12.9%	13.2%	16.6%
Direct Operating Expenses ($)	$276,262	$583,926	$ 855,642
Marketing Expenditures	$ 7,018	$ 8,212	$ 14,726
COIN Segment			
Periods/Months Covered Statement Date	**Historical Unqualified**		
	12/31/2008	**12/31/2009**	**12/31/2010**
Number of Coin Kiosks	18,400	19,200	18,900
Revenue ($)	$261,626	$259,112	$276,311
Revenue Growth (%)	4.1%	-1.0%	6.6%
Operating Income ($)	$104,395	$101,601	$ 93,652
Operating Income as a % of Revenue	39.9%	39.2%	33.9%
Direct Operating Expenses ($)	$130,260	$130,196	$137,339
Marketing Expenditures	$ 7,682	$ 7,242	$ 9,092
OVERALL			
Net Income ($)	$ 14,112	$ 53,643	$ 51,008
Net Profit Margin (%)	1.55%	4.69%	3.55%

Source: 2010 Coinstar 10-K

with the DVD contracts, maintenance of DVD inventory levels, and marketing expenditures whereas research and development expenditures that have not been capitalized remain approximately proportionate to sales. Though margins have remained disproportional between the Redbox and Coin segments, Redbox was the primary driver of Coinstar's net profit in 2010 of $51 million.[51]

Balance Sheet

The Coinstar balance sheet is best characterized as one surrounded with uncertainty regarding what the optimal capital structure would be going forward to maximize shareholder wealth as well as maintain strong future financial performance (see Exhibit 7). At year-end 2010, Coinstar showed a $400 million revolving credit facility that will mature in 2012 as well as senior convertible notes outstanding in the amount of $173.1 million. In addition, Coinstar's Board authorized additional share repurchases up to $74.5 million bringing the total authorized to $134.1 million. In 2010, it had repurchased $55.8 million in shares leaving $78.3 million authorized as of December 31, 2010.[52]

Cash flow leverage for 2010, as measured by total debt to EBITDA, showed marked improvement over

2009 from 2.39x to 1.44x. This is due to the coupled effect of aggressive debt pay down fueled by increased cash flows.

Cash Flow

EBITDA growth year over year has been driven by the aforementioned net profit and revenue increases (see Exhibit 8). However, much of this cash flow was used in 2010 to pay down debt as well as expand property and equipment assets. The majority of this property and equipment increase was due to additional kiosk installations as demonstrated by the $170.8 million spent in 2010 and the $148.5 spent in 2009.[53]

Forward Thinking

Without question, Coinstar faces more than a few serious issues. First and foremost is the likelihood that DVDs will soon be considered obsolete. Over the past few years, many Redbox competitors have implemented robust networks of streaming applications into their distribution channels. For example, Netflix distributes its streaming media through Internet enabled televisions, DVD players, gaming consoles, and more. In 2010, Netflix management predicted that the majority of its

Exhibit 7 Balance Sheet Analysis

Period/Months Covered ($-000's)	Historical Unqualified	Historical Unqualified	Historical Unqualified	Historical Unqualified
Statement Date	12/31/2007	12/31/2008	12/31/2009	12/31/2010
Periods/Months Covered	12	12	12	12
Working Capital	104,724	(16,317)	16,106	(255,223)
Quick Ratio	1.25	0.64	0.68	0.33
Current Ratio	1.53	0.96	1.04	0.6
Total Liabilities	272,651	351,370	468,957	397,487
Total Net Worth	305,130	320,028	412,391	443,122
Tot Liab/TNW	0.89	1.10	1.14	0.90
Adj Tot Debt/Adj. Cap.	0.55	0.59	0.57	0.61
Total Debt / EBITDA	2.19	2.22	2.39	1.44

Source: 2010 Coinstar 10-K

Exhibit 8 Cash Flow Analysis

Period/Months Covered ($-000's)	Historical Unqualified	Historical Unqualified	Historical Unqualified	Historical Unqualified
Statement Date	12/31/2007	12/31/2008	12/31/2009	12/31/2010
Base Cash Flow (EBITDA)	124,431	158,320	196,245	275,578
Cash Provided By Oper. Activities	58,066	169,670	123,890	315,619
Cash Used by Investing Activities	(99,273)	(168,881)	(148,105)	(143,087)
Cash Provided (used) by Fin. Activities	58,285	4,646	41,939	(122,046)

Source: 2010 Coinstar 10-K

customer consumption would be through its streaming channels rather than its traditional mail based distribution system.[54] Netflix continues to see tremendous growth as indicated in its share price, revenues, and profit margin due to its continued push toward streaming.[55]

And while the industry's push toward streaming just follows the natural path of technological development, what prevents movie studios from taking over the entire lifecycle of their products? Aside from the risk of drawing the ire of customers accustomed to finding movies at a 'one stop shop' and the fact that to do so most effectively a studio would need to acquire an established movie distribution company, it only makes sense that they consider this option. To prevent this, Coinstar must determine if it is doing everything possible to keep its relationships with movie and television studios *co*-dependent, and not just dependent.

Another recent industry eye opener was the closure of over 500 Blockbuster locations and its subsequent purchase out of bankruptcy by DISH Network.[56] This can be seen as a positive in that it creates more customers for Redbox as traditional bricks-and-mortar customers move to the convenience of Redbox. However, Blockbuster's demise can also be seen as a negative in the sense that the traditional movie rental industry is on a downward trend.

Coinstar also faces questions regarding what its optimal capital structure should be going forward to maximize shareholder wealth as well as maintain strong future financial performance. As of 2010, Coinstar had its revolving credit facility maturing in 2012, the share buyback program, as well as senior convertible notes. As the company's expansion reached an inflection point in 2010 with a 10 percent decline in Redbox installations in 2010 and another 20 percent decline projected in 2011, would a larger share buyback program signal to investors that Coinstar believes its stock is undervalued and its business model has sustainable long-term growth potential?[57]

There are several implications when deciding on a capital structure including the cost of capital, the effects of ratings agencies, the key financial ratios affected and, perhaps most importantly, the combined effects these decisions have on shareholders. Going into this, one thing is certain: some serious decisions surrounding the capital layout of Coinstar will be made in the near future that will have long-term implications on Coinstar's share price and sustainability. The question is, what is the most advantageous capital structure to achieve the long-term prosperity associated with these short-term capital structure decisions?

This is the optimal time for Coinstar to consider capital structure alternatives as well as overall strategies going forward. When looking toward refinancing its existing debt, lenders and market investors will become more and more concerned with these strategies. Technology is, without a doubt, fast moving and, going forward, Coinstar's current distribution method is questionable at best.

And what does the future hold for its New Ventures segment? In many cases, diversification is a wise move if ones main business is threatened. However, with a host of other failed products introduced in its attempt to take over the fourth wall of supermarkets and the like, does Coinstar have the demographics research power to make profitable product placements or will it simply employ an "it worked here, let's try it there" methodology?

Finally, Coinstar has announced its intention to grow its namesake segment by 1 to 5 percent year over year by making improvements to its coin kiosks and additional marketing. Considering the recessionary climate, it seems odd that the Coin segment experienced *declines* in revenue in 2008 and 2009. In view of the number of Americans making every dollar count, were customers just holding back everything they could in reserve and temporarily unwilling to part with their loose change? With a margin that outperforms the DVD segment two to one, how to make this segment more functional is a critical challenge.

NOTES

1. Coinstar, Inc. Form 10-K for the fiscal year ended December 31, 2010. *SEC.gov.* http://www.sec.gov/Archives/edgar/data/941604/000119312511029330/d10k.htm
2. Baker, M. S. Redbox: Coinstar's red-hot growth machine. Nov 2010. *Seattle Business.* http://www.seattlebusinessmag.com/article/redbox-coinstar%E2%80%99s-red-hot-growth-machine
3. Coinstar installs 10,000th machine; Supermarkets continue to add service to satisfy growing customer demand. 27 Jun 2002. *Business Wire.*
4. Appelbaum, B. Yes, coins too. 7 July 2011. *New York Times.* http://economix.blogs.nytimes.com/2011/07/07/yes-coins-too/
5. Media Center. Facts About Redbox. *Redbox.* http://www.redbox.com/facts
6. Coinstar, Inc. Form 10-K for the fiscal year ended December 31, 2009. *SEC.gov.* http://www.sec.gov/Archives/edgar/data/941604/000119312510037612/d10k.htm
7. Ali, R. DVD kiosk firm Redbox bought out by Coinstar for up to $176 million; McDonald's paid out. 13 Feb 2009. *PaidContent.org.* http://paidcontent.org/article/419-dvd-kiosk-firm-redbox-bought-out-by-coinstar-for-up-to-176-million-mcdo/
8. Murphy, M. UPDATE: Coinstar 1Q profit jumps on Redbox revenue; Year view raised. 28 Apr 2011. *Wall Street Journal.* http://online.wsj.com/article/BT-CO-20110428-727091.html
9. Pepitone, J. Redbox plans to take on Netflix with video streaming service. 17 Feb 2011. *CNN Money.* http://money.cnn.com/2011/02/17/technology/redbox_streaming/index.htm

10. Coinstar, Inc. Form 10-K for the fiscal year ended December 31, 2010. *op.cit.*

11. Murphy, M. *op.cit.*

12. Seitz, P. Coinstar raising fees for its coin-counting machines. 11 Feb 2010. *Click – IBD's Technology Blog.* http://blogs.investors.com/click/index.php/home/60-tech/1118-coinstar-raising-fees-for-its-coin-counting-machines

13. Coin to Card. *Coinstar.* http://www.coinstar.com/FreeCoinCounting

14. Hachman, M. Redbox parent trialling 'Gizmo' EBay-in-a-kiosk concept. 17 Feb 2011. *PC Magazine.* http://www.pcmag.com/article2/0,2817,2380549,00.asp

15. Marching Orders. *Coinstar.* http://www.coinstarinc.com/us/WebDocs/A3-2-1

16. Senior Management. *Coinstar.* http://phx.corporate-ir.net/phoenix.zhtml?c=92448&p=irol-govmanage

17. *Ibid.*

18. Paul Davis Profile. *Forbes.* http://people.forbes.com/profile/paul-davis/21014

19. Senior Management. *op.cit.*

20. *Ibid.*

21. Executive profile: J. Scott Di Valerio. *Bloomberg BusinessWeek.* http://investing.businessweek.com/research/stocks/people/person.asp?personId=22509296&ticker=CSTR:US&previousCapId=26674&previousTitle=COINSTAR%20INC

22. Senior Management. *op.cit.*

23. *Ibid.*

24. Mike Skinner. *Linked In.* http://www.linkedin.com/pub/mike-skinner/28/44/864

25. Chmielewski, D. C. Redbox's $1 vending-machine video rentals worry studios. 30 Mar 2009. *Los Angeles Times.* http://articles.latimes.com/2009/mar/30/business/fi-cotown-redbox30

26. Spector, M. and Checkler, J. Dish wins blockbuster. 7 Apr 2011. *Wall Street Journal Online.* http://wsj.com

27. Netflix, Inc. Form 10-K for the fiscal year ended December 31, 2010. *SEC.gov.* http://www.sec.gov/Archives/edgar/data/1065280/000119312511040217/d10k.htm

28. Unlimited TV Episodes and movies instantly over the Internet! *Netflix.* https://www.netflix.com/

29. Stambor, Z. Wal-Mart to buy a movie-streaming company. 23 Feb 2010. *Internet Retailer.* http://www.internetretailer.com/2010/02/23/wal-mart-to-buy-a-movie-streaming-company

30. *Ibid.*

31. Chapman, R. and Hoskisson, R. E. 2007 "Apple Computer, INC.: Maintaining the Music Business While Introducing IPhone and Apple TV"

32. *Amazon.com.* www.amazon.com

33. *Ibid.*

34. Global Payment Technologies. *GPT World.* http://www.gptworld.com/GPT.htm

35. Carrns, A. Banks where you can still count your change. 2 Jun 2011. *New York Times.* http://bucks.blogs.nytimes.com/2011/06/02/banks-where-you-can-still-count-your-change/

36. Coin to Card. *op.cit.*

37. Lowe, M. Coinstar, Inc. Analyst Day. 16 Feb 2011. http://phx.corporate-ir.net/External.File?item=UGFyZW50SUQ9MzY1Mjc4M3xDaGlsZElEPTQxNDU3MXxUeXBlPTI=&t=1

38. Dixon, E. Redbox customers get more rental freedom and lower cost than Blockbuster and Netflix. 13 May 2011. *newStaar MEDIA* .http://newstaar.com/redbox-customers-get-more-rental-freedom-and-lower-cost-than-blockbuster-and-netflix/353361/

39. Gruenwedel, E. Redbox eyeing catalog rentals. 16 Nov 2010. *Home Media Magazine.* http://www.homemediamagazine.com/redbox/redbox-eying-catalog-rentals-21162

40. Coinstar, Inc. Form 10-K for the fiscal year ended December 31, 2010. *op.cit.*

41. *Ibid.*

42. *Ibid.*

43. Chmielewski, D. C. *op.cit.*

44. Coinstar, Inc. Form 10-K for the fiscal year ended December 31, 2010. *op.cit.*

45. *Ibid.*

46. *Ibid.*

47. Fontevecchia, A. Coinstar sinking but cheap movies are a lifeboat. 14 Jan 2011. *Forbes.com.* http://www.forbes.com/2011/01/14/coinstear-redbox-netflix-markets-equities-video.html

48. Coinstar, Inc. Form 10-K for the fiscal year ended December 31, 2010. *op.cit.*

49. *Ibid.*

50. *Ibid.*

51. *Ibid.*

52. *Ibid.*

53. *Ibid.*

54. Netflix, Inc. Form 10-Q for the nine months ended September 30, 2010. *SEC.gov.* http://www.sec.gov/Archives/edgar/data/1065280/000119312510235785/d10q.htm

55. Netflix, Inc. Form 10-K for the fiscal year ended December 31, 2010. *op.cit.*

56. Strott, E. Blockbuster to close 500 stores. 25 Feb 2010. *MSN Money.* http://money.msn.com/market-news/post.aspx?post=00000065-0000-0000-bf4d-190000000000&_blg=310

57. Mahaney, M. S. Netflix Inc (NFLX) Q1:11 "Cheat sheet" and preview. Rep. Citigroup Global Markets. 21 Apr 2011

Ryan McVay/Getty Images

John Bradley, Eric Friedman, Eric Jeanes, Edward Novotny, Kelly Schuler

Arizona State University

Tina Borja

Rice University

Introduction

Historically, Domino's Pizza has been a strong player in both the domestic US and international out-of-home pizza marketplaces. With more than 9,300 locations in 65 countries, Domino's is the number two pizza restaurant behind Pizza Hut and number one in the pizza delivery segment with market share numbers approaching 20 percent.[1] (See Exhibit 1 for a ranking of the top 50 pizzeria brands in 2009 by sales.) In recent years, however, Domino's has come under consumer fire and, although masked by international revenue growth of 13.2 percent for the same period, the company posted a 16.3 percent decrease in domestic revenue from year-end 2005 through year-end 2009. While the economic recession could certainly be blamed at least in part for its lagging financial performance,[2] Domino's knew that this dip was more than just an economic indicator.

In fact, the news reaching the executive suite indicated that Domino's was suffering from a negative reputation in the marketplace. Central to consumer complaints was that Domino's served low quality pizza with inferior ingredients that lacked taste. Coupled with the fact that consumers continue to become more and more educated about obesity and diet related health concerns and it was clear—Domino's had to act.

To stay competitive, Domino's addressed both the taste deficiency complaints and the growing preference for fresh products by introducing a re-formulated pizza recipe in late 2009. To do so and in a move *Advertising Age* called "one of the riskiest marketing campaigns of all time," Domino's launched the "Oh yes we did" campaign.[3] The campaign quite frankly and very publicly admitted the shortcomings of its previous recipe with TV commercials showing focus group participants on hidden camera complaining that Domino's pizza "tastes like cardboard." The commercials continue by showing the first dejected and then resolved-to-do-better Domino's test kitchen chefs. Throughout the campaign, Domino's encouraged formerly dissatisfied customers to try their new pizza, even airing "live footage" of test kitchen chefs surprising the same disgruntled focus group participants seen in previous commercials at home to deliver a re-formulated recipe pizza for them to try and, not surprisingly, endorse.[4] With a full money-back guarantee, Domino's hoped to drive sales by recouping lost customers and gaining new customers with their candid and fresh approach.

In addition to re-formulating its pizza recipe and in advance of launching its risky advertising campaign, Domino's also began a careful expansion of its menu. In 2008, Domino's launched Oven Baked Sandwiches, effectively growing its customer base and lunchtime revenues.[5] The public was introduced in 2009 to BreadBowl Pastas, American Legends pizzas, and Chocolate Lava Crunch Cakes and, in 2011, Domino's delivered boneless chicken and wings and—via the marketing campaign for its newest menu items—"Tate," the secluded chicken chef within a pizza company[6] (a sympathetic fellow if there ever was one). As hoped, these additions to its traditional "pizza only" menu brought not only new customers, but new head-to-head competitors as well—most notably, Subway.[7]

Its recent challenges aside, Domino's has spent years carving out a significant niche for itself in its ordering and delivery processes, providing streamlined online ordering and, in 2010, bringing its e-commerce efforts in-house to respond more quickly to the changing capabilities of technology.[8] Since its first "30-minutes or it's free" guarantee in 1973 (abandoned in 1993 due to the liabilities incurred by the accidents of rushing delivery drivers),[9] Domino's has been known to deliver pizza fast. The "Total Satisfaction Guarantee" launched

Exhibit 1 Top 50 US Pizzerias Based on 2009 Sales

Rank	Chain Name	2009 U.S. Sales (×1,000)	2008 U.S. Sales (×1,000)	% Change
1	Pizza Hut	5,000,000	5,500,000	−9.1
2	**Domino's Pizza**	**3,030,779***	**3,037,703***	**−0.2**
3	Papa John's	2,057,267	2,034,047	1.1
4	Little Caesars	1,130,000*	1,055,000*	7.1
5	Papa Murphy's Take 'N' Bake Pizza	630,000	585,000	7.7
6	CiCi's Pizza	573,000	585,000	−2.1
7	Sbarro	517,083*	545,323*	−5.2
8	Chuck E. Cheese's	437,900*	441,600*	−0.8
9	Round Table Pizza	390,000*	420,000*	−7.1
10	Godfather's Pizza	331,500*	333,300*	−0.5
11	Hungry Howie's Pizza & Subs	275,000*	279,000*	−1.4
12	Fox's Pizza Den	187,500*	195,000*	−3.8
13	Donatos Pizza	185,000*	177,000	4.5
14	Peter Piper Pizza	166,000*	164,000*	1.2
15	Mazzio's Italian Eatery	154,000*	155,600	−1.0
16	Papa Gino's Pizzeria	151,000*	153,000	−1.3
17	Jets Pizza	149,604	132,200*	13.2
18	Gatti's Pizza	140,878	150,075	−6.1
19	Pizza Pro	132,000*	132,600*	−0.5
20	Pizza Inn	122,176	132,013	−7.5
21	Villa Fresh Italian Kitchen	112,000*	109,000*	2.8
22	Pizza Ranch	109,537	101,390	8.0
23	Marco's Pizza	102,433	92,938	10.2
24	Rosati's Pizza	100,000*	95,000*	5.3
25	Wolfgang Puck Express	93,500*	88,600*	5.5
26	Ledo Pizza	82,000	76,000*	7.9
27	Greek's Pizzeria	79,000*	73,000*	8.2
28	Mountain Mike's Pizza	75,000*	76,000*	−1.3
29	Imo's Pizza	69,000*	74,000*	−6.8
30	Shakey's Pizza Parlors	65,400	60,500*	8.1
31	Me-N-Ed's Pizzeria	59,000*	61,500*	−4.1
32	RedBrick Pizza	58,000*	57,000*	1.8
33	Bellacino's Pizza & Grinders	57,000*	63,000*	−9.5
34	Famous Famiglia	56,000	47,000*	19.1
35	Monicals Pizza	55,186	54,000	2.2
36	Simple Simon's Pizza	55,000*	54,000*	1.9
37	Zpizza	55,000*	49,000*	12.2
38	Pizza Factory	51,500*	55,500*	−7.2
39	Vocelli Pizza	51,000*	56,500	−9.7
40	Straw Hat Pizza	43,855	40,000	9.6

*Estimate

(*Continued*)

Rank	Chain Name	2009 U.S. Sales (x1.000)	2008 U.S. Sales (×1,000)	% Change
41	East of Chicago Pizza	43,500*	50,000*	−13.0
42	Happy Joe's Pizza & Ice Cream	41,000	43,600	−6.0
43	Pizza Patron	38,000	31,000	22.6
44	Extreme Pizza	37,000	33,500	10.4
45	Monkey Joe's	37,000	27,500	34.5
46	CPK ASAP	32,390	31,705	2.2
47	Stevi B's The Ultimate Pizza Buffet	31,500	28,000	12.5
48	Pizza Boli's	30,600	30,300	1.0
49	Nancy's Pizza	29,500	32,000	−7.8
50	Mr. Jim's Pizza	29,000	30,300	−4.3

Source: *PMQ Pizza Magazine* http://pmq.com

in 1993 has since been a cornerstone of the brand and states, "If for any reason you are dissatisfied with your Domino's Pizza dining experience, we will re-make your pizza or refund your money."[10] A major key for Domino's moving forward will be proving to customers that it can maintain its exceptional delivery reputation without sacrificing its new higher standards and diversity of food.

The financial metrics through year-end 2010 show significant gains for Domino's as a result of its new market position and advertising with across-the-board (i.e., including domestic store locations for the first time since negligible growth of less than 1 percent in 2007) annual same store sales up a respectable 9.9 percent.[11] Nevertheless, still new Domino's CEO Patrick Doyle has a challenging road ahead. Between rising food and gasoline costs, unemployment rates and diminished disposable income, the fluctuating value of the dollar, as well as the growing selection and quality of convenient and affordable frozen pizza, there are a host of issues to address beyond taste and reputation as he attempts to maintain, and possibly improve, Domino's position in the pizza industry.[12] (Exhibits 2 and 3 provide selected financial data for Domino's Pizza.)

Company History

The story of Domino's began in December 1960 when brothers Tom and James Monaghan borrowed $900 to buy DomiNick's, a small pizzeria in Ypsilanti, Michigan.[13] Not too long after, James traded his share of the business to Tom for a used Volkswagen Beetle.[14] In 1965, sole proprietor Tom changed the business name to Domino's.[15]

As luck would have it, two particularly busy and short-staffed days prompted Monaghan to implement a "simple menu" concept that eliminated subs and specialty

pizzas to temporarily scale back the workload and thus provide better service. Upon review and to Monaghan's surprise, both profits and sales rose on these two days, leading Monaghan to permanently adopt the simple menu and thus creating a philosophical foundation that would serve Domino's for the next 30 years. The limited menu featured one crust type, eleven topping options, and one drink—Coca Cola—the only non-pizza item on the menu. In doing so, Monaghan stuck to his founding principles to provide quality pizza and great customer service.[16]

Expansion ramped up starting in the late 60s with the popular new business model of franchising. Recognizing a captive and hungry audience, Monaghan decided to expand onto college campuses across the Midwest and had five franchise locations by 1968. During this time, Monaghan was also spending a lot of time on the road observing the competition and taking what he could learn from them back home. When faced with a problem no one else had solved, Monaghan improvised and innovated to make Domino's better, for example, using a meat grinder to not only shred cheese but also mix dough nine times faster than a standard mixer.[17]

In 1973, Domino's introduced its first "delivery guarantee," promising delivery within "a half hour or a half dollar off" and also founded The College of Pizzarology to train potential franchisees.[18] The 70s held several other highlights for Domino's including the introduction of the belt-driven pizza oven, the decentralization of operations, a new logo, and several acquisitions—all of which led to company growth.[19, 20]

This momentum continued into the 80s as Domino's opened its first international locations in 1983 in Winnipeg, Canada and Brisbane, Australia.[21] Domino's "added an average of nearly 500 stores each year through the decade," opening its 5,000th store in January 1989. Other significant developments included the addition

Exhibit 2 Domino's 2010 Financial Highlights

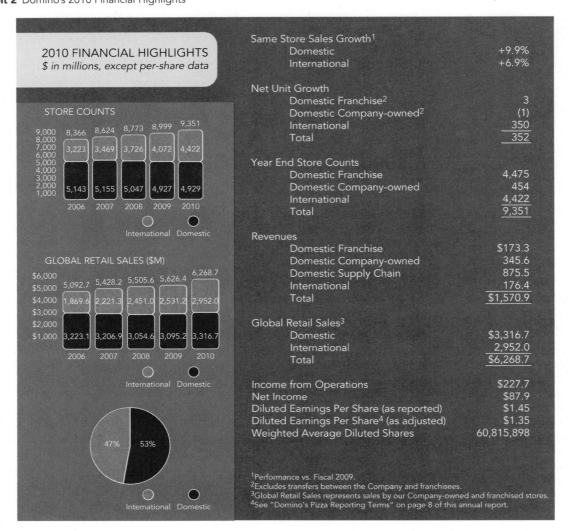

2010 FINANCIAL HIGHLIGHTS
$ in millions, except per-share data

STORE COUNTS

	2006	2007	2008	2009	2010
Total	8,366	8,624	8,773	8,999	9,351
International	3,223	3,469	3,726	4,072	4,422
Domestic	5,143	5,155	5,047	4,927	4,929

International Domestic

GLOBAL RETAIL SALES ($M)

	2006	2007	2008	2009	2010
Total	5,092.7	5,428.2	5,505.6	5,626.4	6,268.7
International	1,869.6	2,221.3	2,451.0	2,531.2	2,952.0
Domestic	3,223.1	3,206.9	3,054.6	3,095.2	3,316.7

International Domestic

47% 53%

International Domestic

Same Store Sales Growth[1]	
Domestic	+9.9%
International	+6.9%
Net Unit Growth	
Domestic Franchise[2]	3
Domestic Company-owned[2]	(1)
International	350
Total	352
Year End Store Counts	
Domestic Franchise	4,475
Domestic Company-owned	454
International	4,422
Total	9,351
Revenues	
Domestic Franchise	$173.3
Domestic Company-owned	345.6
Domestic Supply Chain	875.5
International	176.4
Total	$1,570.9
Global Retail Sales[3]	
Domestic	$3,316.7
International	2,952.0
Total	$6,268.7
Income from Operations	$227.7
Net Income	$87.9
Diluted Earnings Per Share (as reported)	$1.45
Diluted Earnings Per Share[4] (as adjusted)	$1.35
Weighted Average Diluted Shares	60,815,898

[1]Performance vs. Fiscal 2009.
[2]Excludes transfers between the Company and franchisees.
[3]Global Retail Sales represents sales by our Company-owned and franchised stores.
[4]See "Domino's Pizza Reporting Terms" on page 8 of this annual report.

Source: *Domino's Pizza, Inc. 2010 Annual Report.* https://materials.proxyvote.com

of the deep pan pizza to the Domino's menu that helped Domino's achieve $1.44 billion in sales in 1987.[22]

Perhaps the largest development of the 80s however was at the organizational level with the addition of Don Vlcek. Domino's hired Vlcek to take over the commissary—an operation of regionalized locations that produce and distribute ingredients and supplies. Vlcek streamlined the commissaries and would take the best practices of one commissary and apply them to all. "Once Vlcek had taken care of the basics, in one eight-month period he opened a new commissary a month, all with state-of-the-art equipment."[23]

During the 90s, Domino's continued to make sweeping changes. The company introduced breadsticks to the menu, its "first national non-pizza item," and

buffalo wings. In 1996, Domino's debuted its website and achieved system-wide sales of $2.8 billion. Other changes included the introduction of the Heat Wave bag and, after a series of accidents involving drivers rushing to meet their deadlines, the elimination of its 30-minute delivery guarantee.[24, 25]

Ready to move on, in 1998, Monaghan sold a controlling 93 percent stake in Domino's to Bain Capital, a Boston-based private equity investment firm, for about $1 billion and the assumption of approximately $50 million in debt.[26] With that, David Brandon assumed the reins as CEO.[27]

Domino's pushed forward through the early 2000s, relocating several stores to increase visibility and profits.[28] Although effective, these efforts were not

Exhibit 3 Domino's Financial Report

(dollars in millions, except per share data)	Fiscal year ended				
	December 31, 2006	December 30, 2007	December 28, 2008	January 3, 2010	January 2, 2011
Income statement data:					
Revenues:					
Domestic Company-owned stores	$ 393.4	$ 394.6	$ 357.7	$ 335.8	$ 345.6
Domestic franchise	157.7	158.1	153.9	157.8	173.3
Domestic stores	551.1	552.6	511.6	493.6	519.0
Domestic supply chain	762.8	783.3	771.1	763.7	875.5
International	123.4	126.9	142.4	146.8	176.4
Total revenues	1,437.3	1,462.9	1,425.1	1,404.1	1,570.9
Cost of sales	1,052.8	1,084.0	1,061.9	1,017.1	1,132.3
Operating margin	384.5	378.9	363.3	387.0	438.6
General and administrative expense	170.3	184.9	168.2	197.5	210.9
Income from operations	214.2	193.9	195.0	189.5	227.7
Interest income	1.2	5.3	2.7	0.7	0.2
Interest expense	(55.0)	(130.4)	(114.9)	(110.9)	(96.8)
Other	—	(13.3)	—	56.3	7.8
Income before provision for income taxes	160.4	55.6	82.9	135.5	138.9
Provision for income taxes	54.2	17.7	28.9	55.8	51.0
Net income	$ 106.2	$ 37.9	$ 54.0	$ 79.7	$ 87.9
Earnings per share:					
Common stock – basic	$ 1.68	$ 0.61	$ 0.93	$ 1.39	$ 1.50
Common stock – diluted	1.65	0.59	0.93	1.38	1.45
Dividends declared per share	$ 0.48	$ 13.50	$ —	$ —	$ —
Balance sheet data (at end of period):					
Cash and cash equivalents	$ 38.2	$ 11.3	$ 45.4	$ 42.4	$ 47.9
Restricted cash and cash equivalents	—	81.0	78.9	91.1	85.5
Working capital	11.1	(29.6)	25.8	(31.9)	33.4
Total assets	380.2	473.2	463.8	453.8	460.8
Total long-term debt	740.1	1,704.8	1,704.4	1,522.5	1,451.3
Total debt	741.6	1,720.1	1,704.8	1,572.8	1,452.2
Total stockholders' deficit	(564.9)	(1,450.1)	(1,424.6)	(1,321.0)	(1,210.7)

Source: Domino's Pizza, Inc. 2010 Annual Report. https://materials.proxyvote.com

enough to maintain the company's position and in 2004, Domino's began trading common stock on the NYSE under the ticker symbol DPZ.[29] Domino's experienced moderate success, won some industry awards, introduced new menu items, and improved its overall financial position throughout the rest of the decade but, financially, the chain was still floundering. Through the new interconnected online world, Domino's customers began to share their dissatisfaction with Domino's products in a new and more vocal manner. Customers believed that Domino's pizza lacked taste and quality ingredients and reported receiving poor quality delivery pizzas. Marketing Chief Russell Weiner commented,

"We weren't winning against everyone on taste." In a 2009 survey of consumer taste preferences among national chains by research firm Brand Keys, Domino's tied with Chuck E. Cheese's for last place.[30] Luckily, monumental change was right around the corner.

In response to consumer feedback, Domino's introduced a brand new pizza recipe to the US market on December 27, 2009.[31] This new and improved pizza offered an entirely redesigned crust recipe, fresh ingredients, a new sauce, and real shredded cheese.[32] "The best defense is a good offense," said Russell Weiner. The advertising and PR campaign was aggressive and included the launch of a new website—pizzaturnaround.com—where social media links allowed consumers to comment on Domino's new recipes. The campaign also featured television ads showing extremely critical consumers trying the new recipe for the first time and, at times, poking fun at the old Domino's pizza recipe.[33]

In January 2010, J. Patrick Doyle, former President of Domino's USA, succeeded David Brandon as CEO[34] and in March 2010, Domino's opened its 9,000th location.[35]

Domino's Business Segments

Three business segments drive the sales and growth of Domino's: domestic stores, domestic supply chain services, and international. These business segments are supported by the Domino's World Resource Center in Ann Arbor, Michigan, which provides accounting, marketing, legal, franchise development, human resources support, and more.

Within the domestic stores segment are 454 company-owned stores and 4,475 franchise stores.[36] Franchise stores are operated by entrepreneurs, each of whom own and operate an average of four locations.[37]

The domestic supply chain services segment consists of dough manufacturing and supply chain centers—or commissaries—that produce fresh dough on a daily basis and purchase, receive, store, and deliver pizza-related food and products to all company-owned stores and 99 percent of domestic franchise stores. The domestic supply chain segment operates 16 regional dough manufacturing and food supply chain centers with each regional center serving approximately 300 stores. In addition, this segment runs one thin crust manufacturing center, one supply chain center for equipment and other operational dry goods supplies, and one vegetable processing supply chain center.[38]

Of publicly traded restaurant brands, Domino's is the fourth largest international business.[39] The international segment oversees Domino's network of 4,422 international franchise stores located throughout the world. The international segment also manufactures dough and distributes food and supplies (albeit in a limited number of international markets) via six company-owned dough manufacturing and supply chain centers. The principal source of revenue from international operations comes from royalty payments generated by retail sales and supply chain center sales to franchisees.[40]

Marketplace

There are a number of companies that present Domino's with significant competitive rivalry—a number that will do nothing but rise as Domino's increases its menu offerings to appeal to a larger demographic. At its core, however, pizza remains a very popular product—appealing to a wide demographic of Americans that consider restaurants an essential part of their lifestyle. Even in the throes of the most recent economic recession, according to the National Restaurant Association, 45 percent of adults say that restaurants are a major part of their lifestyle and they will continue to frequent their favorite restaurants. A survey of 795 adults completed by Rasmussen Reports in April 2011 revealed that 40 percent of Americans eat pizza at least once per month with adults ages 30 to 49 the most frequent consumers. Married adults and parents are more likely to use takeout than adults that are unmarried and/or without children.[41] (Exhibit 4 provides US consumer pizza-eating frequency statistics.)

The pizza segment of the food industry represents 11.7 percent of all restaurants and accounts for more than 10 percent of all food service sales. Between June 2008 and June 2009, the US pizza industry recorded nearly $37 billion in sales and the first quarter of 2010 showed an increase in pizza sales from 2009.[42] So, while the threat of substitute products within the pizza industry remains high, pizza is an integral part of American culture and shows no sign of exiting the market. (See Exhibit 5 for US pizza sales by vendor.)

Domino's Competitors

While Domino's has numerous competitors both large and small, its most significant chain competitors are Pizza Hut (Yum! Brands), Papa John's, and Little Caesars. In addition, the majority of Domino's locations also compete with various smaller, locally owned pizza restaurants as well as other fast-casual and delivery restaurants outside the pizza industry. (Exhibit 6 illustrates the number of US pizza stores by vendor.)

Exhibit 4 US Consumption of Pizza

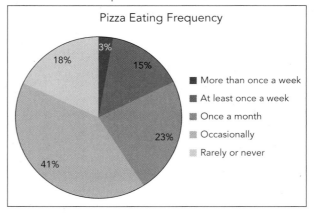

Source: Rasmussen Reports http://www.rasmussenreports.com

Exhibit 5 US Pizza Sales for 2009

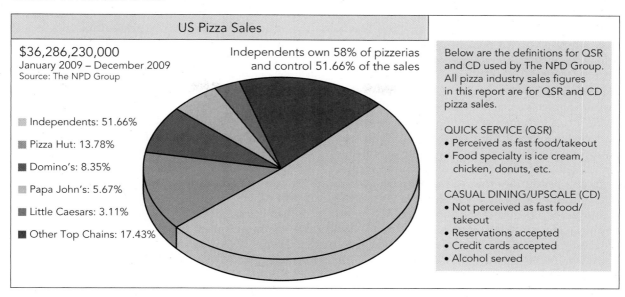

US Pizza Sales

$36,286,230,000
January 2009 – December 2009
Source: The NPD Group

Independents own 58% of pizzerias
and control 51.66% of the sales

Below are the definitions for QSR and CD used by The NPD Group. All pizza industry sales figures in this report are for QSR and CD pizza sales.

- Independents: 51.66%
- Pizza Hut: 13.78%
- Domino's: 8.35%
- Papa John's: 5.67%
- Little Caesars: 3.11%
- Other Top Chains: 17.43%

QUICK SERVICE (QSR)
- Perceived as fast food/takeout
- Food specialty is ice cream, chicken, donuts, etc.

CASUAL DINING/UPSCALE (CD)
- Not perceived as fast food/takeout
- Reservations accepted
- Credit cards accepted
- Alcohol served

Source: *PMQ Pizza Magazine* http://pmq.com

Exhibit 6 US Pizza Store Count

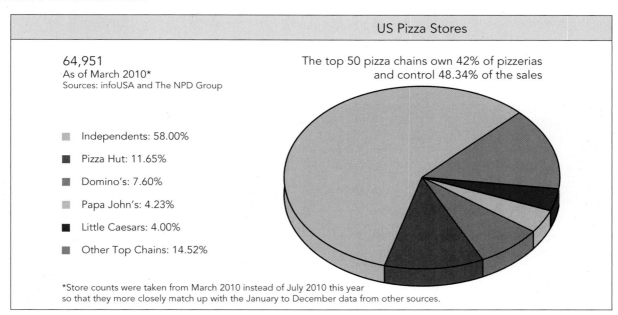

US Pizza Stores

64,951
As of March 2010*
Sources: infoUSA and The NPD Group

The top 50 pizza chains own 42% of pizzerias
and control 48.34% of the sales

- Independents: 58.00%
- Pizza Hut: 11.65%
- Domino's: 7.60%
- Papa John's: 4.23%
- Little Caesars: 4.00%
- Other Top Chains: 14.52%

*Store counts were taken from March 2010 instead of July 2010 this year
so that they more closely match up with the January to December data from other sources.

Source: *PMQ Pizza Magazine* http://pmq.com

Pizza Hut

Yum! Brands operates and licenses five restaurant chains—KFC, Taco Bell, Long John Silver's, A&W Restaurants, and Pizza Hut—Domino's fiercest competitor. Only two years older than Domino's, Pizza Hut has locations in 95 countries with over 13,000 store locations in total. It focuses on a variety of "ready-to-eat pizza products" that customers can customize with an assortment of toppings tailored to local tastes and culture. Pizza Hut serves a variety of products ranging from specialty pizzas to pasta, sandwiches, and chicken wings—a product also offered via over 3,000 WingStreet locations (a Yum! Brands subsidiary).[43]

As a part of Yum! Brands, Pizza Hut's financial information is consolidated along with Yum! Brands' other holdings. In 2010, Yum! reported a 4.7 percent increase in revenues over 2009. Operating profits and net income were also up over 2009 by 11.3 and 8.1 percent respectively. Same store sales for Pizza Hut in the US increased by 8.8 percent in the same period, matching its 2008 figures and recouping the losses seen in 2009.[44] (Limited financial data for Yum! Brands is found in Exhibit 7.)

While Domino's remains the leader in the US delivery segment, Pizza Hut maintains the top spot in the US pizza segment with a 13.78 percent market share as of December 2009.[45] Pizza Hut has been able to capitalize on the changing demographics and consumers focused on getting a decent meal fast through its quick serve locations. Despite slipping a few places in 2010, Pizza Hut enjoys a formidable reputation as the only quick serve pizza company on the Interbrand "100 Best Global Brands" list,[46] providing Pizza Hut sufficient negotiating power when entering new markets, especially in China, a new focus for the brand.

Pizza Hut's goal moving forward is to become known not as a pizza restaurant, but as a "pizza, pasta, and wings" brand. To complete the transformation, Pizza Hut is working to make its menu items more competitively priced (as seen in its "$10 any way you want it" promotion), improving service times, and focusing on great customer service (via its "Heart of the Hut" program).[47] Yum! Brands also hopes to lower administrative costs and provide a steady stream of franchise revenue by adding more Pizza Hut franchisees, thus effectively diluting its company-owned to franchise ratio. Lastly, to help gain market share throughout the world, Pizza Hut is focusing its expansion plans on China, one of the world's rapidly growing marketplaces.

Papa John's

Papa John's is the world's third ranked pizza delivery and carryout restaurant behind Pizza Hut and Domino's. Papa John's owns and franchises 3,646 restaurants (612 company-owned, 3,034 franchised) in all 50 states and 32 countries worldwide. Papa John's was founded in 1984 by John Schnatter on the premise that if you make the best pizza and price it competitively, you can sell it.[48] Papa John's major products include pizza, breadsticks, cheesesticks, chicken strips, wings, dessert items, and beverages for delivery or carryout.

Papa John's operates through six segments: domestic restaurants, domestic commissaries (quality control centers), domestic franchising, international operations, variable interest entities, and "all other" business units.[49] The domestic restaurant segment focuses on operations of corporate-owned locations as well as pizza and side-item product sales. The domestic commissary segment houses operations including dough production locations and product distribution centers. The domestic

Exhibit 7 Selected Financial Data: Yum! Brands

(In millions, except for per share amounts)			
Year-end	2010	2009	%B/(W) change
Company Sales	$ 9,783	$ 9,413	4
Franchise and License Fees and Income	$ 1,560	$ 1,423	10
Total Revenues	$11,343	$10,836	5
Operating Profit	$ 1,769	$ 1,590	11
Net Income - Yum! Brands, Inc.	$ 1,158	$ 1,071	8
Diluted Earnings Per Common Share before Special Items[a]	$ 2.53	$ 2.17	17
Special Items Earnings Per Common Share[a]	$ (0.15)	$ 0.05	NM
Reported Diluted Earnings Per Common Share	$ 2.38	$ 2.22	7
Cash Flows Provided by Operating Activities	$ 1,968	$ 1,404	40

(a) See page 29 of our 2010 Form 10-K for further discussion of Special Items.

Average US Sales per System Unit[a]						
(In thousands)						
Year-end	2010	2009	2008	2007	2006	5-year growth[b]
KFC	$ 933	$ 960	$ 967	$ 994	$ 977	—
Pizza Hut	855	786	854	825	794	1%
Taco Bell	1,288	1,255	1,265	1,147	1,178	2%

(a) Excludes license units.

(b) Compounded annual growth rate.

Source: http://www.yum.com

franchising segment is dedicated to franchise sales and support. International operations support Papa John's locations outside the US. Variable interest entities includes all entities from which Papa John's is not a primary beneficiary and includes BIBP, "a third-party entity formed by franchisees for the sole purpose of reducing cheese price volatility to domestic system-wide restaurants through fiscal 2010." Lastly, the all other business segment includes revenue-earning divisions such as printing, risk management, information systems, and related operational services.[50]

By 1999, Papa John's had opened its 2,000th store and took over the number three spot in the US market from Little Caesars. But in the early 2000s, Papa John's hit the wall. By putting the brakes on its expansion plans, closing underperforming stores, adding chicken strips and specialty pizzas to its menu, and hiring Nigel Travis in 2005 to take over as president and CEO, Papa John's braced itself for a bumpy ride through the sluggish economy.[51]

As of December 2009, Papa John's accounted for 5.67 percent of the pizza sales in the US. The economic recession caused another dip in revenues for year-end 2009; however, year-end 2010 numbers show a return to 2008 figures.[52] In an effort to re-energize its brand during this period, Papa John's invested heavily in advertising, becoming the official pizza sponsor for the NFL and also signing on to sponsor three upcoming Super Bowls.[53] In addition, Papa John's launched a highly successfully promotion for consumers to create the next Papa John's specialty pizza to be added to its menu.[54] (Exhibit 8 provides selected financial data for Papa John's.)

Exhibit 8 Selected Financial Data 2010: Papa John's

(In thousands, except per share data)	Year Ended				
Income Statement Data	Dec. 26, 2010 52 weeks	Dec. 27, 2009 52 weeks	Dec. 28, 2008 52 weeks	Dec. 30, 2007 52 weeks	Dec. 31, 2006 53 weeks
Domestic revenues:					
Company-owned restaurant sales	$ 503,272	$ 503,818	$ 533,255	$ 504,330	$447,938
Franchise royalties	68,358	61,012	59,704	55,283	56,374
Franchise and development fees	340	519	1,600	4,758	2,597
Commissary sales	454,506	417,689	431,650	401,081	415,392
Other sales	51,951	54,045	61,415	61,820	50,505
International revenues:					
Royalties and franchise and development fees	14,808	13,244	12,868	10,314	7,551
Restaurant and commissary sales	33,162	28,223	25,849	20,860	15,658
Total revenues	1,126,397	1,078,550	1,126,341	1,058,446	996,015
Operating income	86,744	95,218	65,486	53,072	99,446
Investment income	875	629	848	1,446	1,682
Interest expense	(5,338)	(5,653)	(7,536)	(7,465)	(3,480)
Income from continuing operations before income taxes	82,281	90,194	58,798	47,053	97,648
Income tax expense	26,856	28,985	19,980	13,293	33,171
Income from continuing operations, including noncontrolling interests	55,425	61,209	38,818	33,760	64,477
Income attributable to noncontrolling interests	(3,485)	(3,756)	(2,022)	(1,025)	(1,491)
Income from continuing operations, net of noncontrolling interests	51,940	57,453	36,796	32,735	62,986
Income from discontinued operations, net of tax	—	—	—	—	389
Net income	$ 51,940	$ 57,453	$ 36,796	$ 32,735	$ 63,375
Basic earnings per common share:					
Income from continuing operations, net of noncontrolling interests	$ 1.97	$ 2.07	$ 1.31	$ 1.10	$ 1.95

(Continued)

Exhibit 8 Selected Financial Data 2010: Papa John's *(Continued)*

(In thousands, except per share data)					
	Year Ended (1)				
Income Statement Data	**Dec. 26, 2010** 52 weeks	**Dec. 27, 2009** 52 weeks	**Dec. 28, 2008** 52 weeks	**Dec. 30, 2007** 52 weeks	**Dec. 31, 2006** 53 weeks
Income from discontinued operations, net of tax	—	—	—	—	0.01
Basic earnings per common share	$ 1.97	$ 2.07	$ 1.31	$ 1.10	$ 1.96
Earning per common share – assuming dilution:					
Income from continuing operations, net of noncontrolling interests	$ 196	$ 2.06	$ 1.30	$ 1.09	$ 1.91
Income from discontinued operations, net of tax	—	—	—	—	0.01
Earnings per common share - assuming dilution	$ 1.96	$ 2.06	$ 1.30	$ 1.09	$ 1.92
Basic weighted average shares outstanding	26,328	27,738	28,124	29,666	32,312
Diluted weighted average shares outstanding	26,468	27,909	28,264	30,017	33,046
Balance sheet data					
Total assets	$415,941	$393,726	$385,464	$400,885	$379,056
Total debt	99,017	99,050	130,654	142,706	97,036
Total stockholders' equity	207,200	185,037	138,238	134,938	152,395

Source: http://files.shareholder.com

Little Caesars

Family-owned Little Caesars Enterprises, Inc., a subsidiary of Illitch Holdings, owns and franchises over 2,600 units in the US and 11 other countries. As a subsidiary of a family-owned company, Little Caesars is not required to publish its individual financial information. As of March 2010, Little Caesars owned 4 percent of the US pizza store locations and was a major competitor of Domino's despite its lack of delivery service.[55] In addition, according to Technomic Inc., Little Caesars was the fastest growing pizza restaurant chain in the US in 2009.[56]

Approximately 80 percent of Little Caesars locations are franchises with many stores located in strip malls or other popular shopping areas. Little Caesars offers a variety of pizzas and other specialty items including crazy bread and sauce, cheese bread, Caesar dips, and churros. In addition, it also offers party catering service.

Little Caesars is known for its two-for-one "Pizza! Pizza!" marketing campaign that started in 1971 and became a permanent fixture in 1975. Little Caesars has topped a host of "Best Pizza Value in America" lists for years and years in a row and, despite some setbacks in the 90s as Papa John's climbed the pizza ladder, continues to offer some hard-to-beat competition.[57]

Domino's Strategic Approach

As described, several major nationwide and international brand names (not to mention the local and individual pizza shops too numerous to describe here) vie for the top spots in the pizza delivery and carryout markets. These companies compete to varying degrees on taste and price with the general trend of pizza as a low-cost commodity in lower-income neighborhoods and near college campuses, and becoming increasingly higher-cost and specialty in more affluent neighborhoods.

Generally, Domino's selects locations that benefit its core strategy of carryout and delivery as it does not accommodate customers looking to dine on premises. In fact, the majority of locations usually have no more than three seats for customers waiting for a pizza—a clear indicator of its heavy emphasis on delivery. Logistically speaking, Domino's is designed to deliver pizza. Providing the support to do so is its domestic supply chain. (Exhibit 9 shows the origin of pizzas eaten in the US.)

Domino's prides itself on its consistency and logistical operations that keep overhead costs down and provide a less expensive pizza. Supply centers are responsible for producing pizza dough that is then shipped to each franchise location. To optimize pizza delivery speeds, one of Domino's strategies is to provide "routing strategies to reduce the frequency of late deliveries and help stores meet the rush with necessary product inventory."[58] Domino's also cross trains its drivers[i] so if there is not a delivery waiting, the driver is able to be productive in the store by "arranging store coolers according to

---

[i]Because delivery drivers are generally paid less than minimum wage (due to tips), this practice does not come without controversy.

Exhibit 9 Where Americans Get Their Pizza

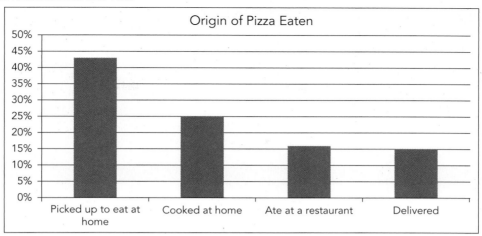

Source: Rasmussen Reports http://www.rasmussenreports.com

product usage dates and to service stores by answering questions, assisting with set-up, taking phone messages and even mopping up floors."[59]

Prior to the launch of its new ad campaign in December 2009, Domino's was generally considered the cost leader in the market. As described earlier, for much of its history, Domino's business strategy centered around offering a single product—pizza —through company-owned stores and franchises in as many neighborhoods as possible. Traditionally, expansion took the form of stores opening near college campuses, locations notorious for a special affection for low-cost pizza. According to the Pizza Magazine Power Report,[60] as of November 2009, 8.35 percent of the pizzas sold in the US were from Domino's. The only chain with a larger percentage of sales was Pizza Hut at 13.78 percent of sales.[ii] Domino's most direct competitor for the cost leadership position in the market is Little Caesars Pizza. As a byproduct of its cost leadership strategy however, Domino's developed a reputation for poor quality pizza that was often ridiculed as the worst tasting pizza in the industry. From 2005 to 2009, Domino's market share fell more than 2 percent, from 10.62 to 8.35 percent.[61] (Exhibits 10a and 10b provide market share information for US pizza restaurants.)

As noted in the introduction, in an effort to reverse this downward spiral, Domino's instituted major changes in 2009. Previously, Domino's had structured its entire business around producing an adequate product for as low a price as possible. Today, Domino's is focused on a more palatable menu that speaks to more than just the budget-conscious mentality. Domino's

"Oh yes we did" campaign repositioned the brand to better compete with the quality of Pizza Hut and the "Better Ingredients, Better Pizza" strategy of Papa John's. This strategic shift started back in 2007 with a reexamination of its business processes and product offerings. Domino's turned its attention to improving the taste of its key product—pizza—and began adding herbs and butter to its crust. Domino's also added side dishes, desserts, and even new entrees to its menu to better match competitors in the "better taste" segment of the pizza delivery market and expand overall product offerings. Part of this early strategy included an advertising campaign that directly matched Domino's sandwiches against a Subway-like chain, using then CEO David Brandon as the spokesperson. Even so, by the time its newest business-level strategy was adopted by Domino's in December 2009, its market share by sales had dropped to 8.35 percent.[62]

Financial Results

As seen in Exhibit 2, Domino's sales distribution is 53 percent domestic and 47 percent international.[63] In 2010, Domino's saw retail sales of $3.316 billion domestically and $2.952 billion internationally.[64] Other than a negligible uptick in fiscal year 2007, Domino's total revenue has been in a steady decline since peaking in fiscal year 2005 with the fall of deeper domestic declines softened by overall growth internationally. Nevertheless, following its marketing and public relations blitz, not only did fiscal year 2010 revenues show a healthy return, but cost of sales decreased by 3.25 percent between fiscal year 2008 and fiscal year 2010, tempering the concerns of many investors that product expansion and enhancement would lead to lower profits.

[ii]Independent pizzerias comprised the largest single block of pizza sales for the same period with 58%.

Exhibit 10a US Pizza Sales Distribution: 2005 to 2009

	YE 2005 ($)	YE 2006 ($)	YE 2007 ($)	As of July 2009 ($)	YE 2009 ($)
Pizza Hut	17.06	16.01	13.85	14.46	13.78
Papa John's	5.82	6.09	5.34	5.55	5.67
Domino's	10.62	10.02	8.68	8.29	8.35
Little Caesars	2.5	2.58	2.47	2.88	3.11
Independent	49.47	50.21	53.03	50.98	51.66
Other Top Chains	14.52	15.09	16.63	17.93	17.43

Source: PMQ Industry Reports. Pizza Power Reports 2006, 2007, 2008, 2009, 2010. http://pmq.com

Exhibit 10b US Pizza Store Distribution: 2005 to 2009

	YE 2005 (%)	YE 2006 (%)	YE 2007 (%)	As of July 2009 (%)	YE 2009 (%)
Pizza Hut	10.9	10.13	9.77	11.2	11.65
Papa John's	3.75	3.57	3.61	4.13	4.23
Domino's	7.34	6.92	6.72	7.47	7.6
Little Caesars	2.72	2.72	2.82	3.7	4
Independent	64.81	66.51	65	58.78	58
Other Top Chains	10.48	10.12	12.05	14.72	14.52

Source: PMQ Industry Reports. Pizza Power Reports 2006, 2007, 2008, 2009, 2010. http://pmq.com

Revenue declines aside, due to interest, repurchasing of stock, and other financial implications, after a 65 percent fall from 2006 to 2007, net income increased over the last four years. Net income was $37.9 million in 2007, $54.0 million in 2008, $79.8 million in 2009, and $87.9 million in 2010—annual increases of 42.5 percent, 47.7 percent, and 10.25 percent respectively.[65] Furthermore, Domino's has been able to reduce its total debt over the past four years, from $1.72 billion in 2007 to $1.45 billion in 2010.[66]

While two of Domino's main competitors, Pizza Hut and Little Caesars, are privately held companies without public financial statements, Domino's can certainly be compared to its publicly held competitor—Papa John's. As noted in Exhibit 11, Domino's compares favorably to Papa John's. For 2010, Domino's had higher revenue ($1.55 billion compared to $1.14 billion), higher net income ($87.36 million compared to $51.61 million), and a lower P/E ratio (10.19 compared to 13.68) than Papa John's.[67] Furthermore, by comparing Exhibits 3 and 8, Domino's had a higher total revenue and net income in each of the past five years compared to Papa John's.[68] Despite the rosy picture this paints, in 2010, Domino's had approximately 9,300 stores worldwide while Papa John's had less than half that number with 3,600 stores worldwide.[69] Considering that Domino's has 5,600 more stores, it is not surprising Domino's has higher total revenue and higher net income. In fact, when viewed on a revenue per store basis for 2010, Domino's produced [$1.571 billion/9300 =]

$170,000 in revenue per store, while Papa John's produced almost double the revenue per store at [$1.126 billion/3600 =] $313,000.[70] While profitable, in order for Domino's to provide exceptional value to its shareholders, it must create more revenue per store.

Domino's Leadership

Much of what Domino's is today is due to the strategic leadership of David Brandon, the current Chairman of the Board and former CEO and President from 1999-2010. Under Brandon's leadership, Domino's worked hard to innovate products and expand its brand scope, introducing—and at times abandoning—new menu growth vehicles. In reference to the development of new menu offerings, Brandon exhibited his managerial discretion saying, "We don't put anything on the menu unless we test it and find a consumer demand. We also balance those things with the items that fit our operational platform."[71]

Prior to the current "Oh yes we did" advertising campaign, Domino's had primarily focused on being the delivery leader in the industry. Under Brandon, the dominant campaign had been "Get the door, it's Domino's" which spoke to a key competitive advantage of Domino's—efficiency.

As a leader, Brandon tended toward inclusive management techniques, empowering others to create strategic change and gathering feedback directly from his employees through multiple programs such as

Exhibit 11 Domino's Pizza Inc., Direct Competitor Comparison

Direct Competitor Comparison					
	Dominos'	**Little Caesars**	**Papa John's**	**Pizza Hut**	**Industry**
Market Cap	891.61M	N/A	673.71 M	N/A	203.70M
Employees	10,200	N/A	16,000	N/A	2.80K
Qtrly Rev Growth (yoy)	14.80%	N/A	6.50%	N/A	9.30%
Revenue (ttm)	1.55B	N/A	1.14B	N/A	348.04M
Gross Margin (ttm)	27.77%	N/A	31.07%	N/A	24.77%
EBITDA (ttm)	253.50M	N/A	133.05M	N/A	40.88M
Operating Margin (ttm)	14.45%	N/A	8.73%	N/A	6.00%
Net Income (ttm)	87.36M	N/A	51.61M	N/A	N/A
EPS (ttm)	1.46	N/A	1.91	N/A	0.43
P/E (ttm)	10.19	N/A	13.68	N/A	16.95
PEG (5 yr expected)	1.14	N/A	1.46	N/A	1.33
P/S (ttm)	0.57	N/A	0.58	N/A	0.71

Source: Yahoo Finance http://finance.yahoo.com

"What's Up, Domino's?" described as "a large forum for employees to listen to management, communicate their own ideas, and ask questions." Another program, "Lunch with Dave," was a monthly meeting where 12 Domino's employees, randomly selected by computer, were invited to have lunch with Brandon. Brandon describes the lunches as forums where "I listen to the things they'd like me to know about what's happening out there in our company, right and wrong." As one might imagine, he reported, "I learn a lot from that."[72]

Despite appearing as the company spokesperson in a number of television advertisements and garnering a good deal of personal attention, Brandon showed no tendencies toward hubris that would prevent him from making effective strategic decisions. In a series of lectures that Brandon conducted with a group called "Leadership Center by Les50ns," Brandon spoke at length about his management style. Speaking specifically to his style, he said, "If I walk into a room of my most trusted advisers, and 100 percent of them feel one way and I feel the other, it's an easy decision to make."[73]

One of the keys of the I/O economic model is the idea that "economic performance is determined by a firm's general, industry, and competitor environment and by how well the firm implements the strategy dictated by those environments."[74] Brandon described two key philosophies that support this thinking. Upon his arrival at Domino's in 1999, Brandon saw that key performance metrics and benchmarking took place against same-store sales from the previous periods, either quarters or years. While Brandon saw value in

this, he recognized the necessity to be cognizant of not only internal comparisons, but how Domino's fared versus the industry as well. Even in times of prosperity, Brandon intoned,

One of the things I do over and over and over again, is reinforce the concept that we have to get better, even during times of tremendous success. A big part of it is against who and how you benchmark yourself. We not only had to look at what our past results were, but we had to look at the world around us, look at our competitors. I wanted us to look at the best in class and hold ourselves accountable for that particular level of performance.[75]

Another one of David Brandon's strategic strengths was in his approach to managing human capital. In "Competing for Advantage," Hoskisson et al. state, "The crux of strategic leadership is the ability to manage the firm's operations and employees effectively in order to sustain high performance over time."[76] To support this, Brandon operated under the philosophy that you must "adapt your leadership style for each individual and find out how people want to be treated and treat them that way."[77] By focusing on the fact that all people are different and respond differently to situations and personalities, Brandon established a one size does *not* fit all leadership style.

To support his belief in the importance of human capital, Brandon emphasized the need for employees to remain flexible and prepared to support the ever-changing and immensely competitive food industry. Borrowing from his days as a college football player at the University of Michigan under legendary coach

Bo Schembechler, Brandon preached the necessity of preparedness with his employees through the practice of "Sudden Change." Brandon felt that all too often change had a negative connotation and that, through practice and preparation, this could be reversed.

"Employees were programmed to believe that when this very negative situation occurred, rather than responding negatively, we would actually see it as an opportunity, and get excited about it and anticipate it in a way that we knew we were going to be successful."[78] Brandon wanted to emphasize that not only can change be positive but, if anticipated appropriately, it can also serve as a tremendous competitive advantage. "If organizations believe that change is good, when you are confronted with change, particularly change that is challenging, a great organization is going to be ready for that: anticipate that and see it as an opportunity."[79]

Leading an organization as large as Domino's often requires its leaders to make very difficult decisions, both in times of prosperity and in times of hardship. Being ultimately responsible to stakeholders requires that the leader ensure the organization is well positioned for economic success. When Brandon arrived at Domino's in 1999 amid a strong financial period for the company, he found what he described as "a lot of fat" or excess human resources that, if excised, would provide the opportunity for greater financial gains. To remedy that situation, Brandon acted decisively and proactively. "What I did was I anticipated that, at some point, life was going to get tougher and I wanted to learn from my past experiences and be ready. So, at the end of a record year, my first as CEO, we restructured the company. We did a significant number of job reductions, because it was the right thing to do. Don't wait until you are at the edge of the cliff to do the right thing."[80] Brandon's rather unconventional approach supports his philosophy.

The best way to take the risks associated with change is during the time when business is great. The organization will be more resilient, there will be more resources available to invest in that process and make it happen successfully. You'll have more focus and attention on managing that process more carefully than when you are in a crisis-management mode. Human nature is to mortgage the problem until that point in the future when you have no other choice, and I think a lot of leaders embrace that, but it's a mistake.[81]

From enacting change in an instant, to making tough and often unpopular decisions, Brandon remained ardent in providing the strategic direction for Domino's. The CEO's job is to be "the chief architect of strategic direction . . . and obtain input from many people inside and outside the organization."[82]

Brandon, the architect of the "Oh yes we did" campaign that has proven so central to Domino's current culture, stepped down as CEO in early 2010 yet remains the Chairman of the Board and an integral voice in the Domino's organization. Brandon's successor, Patrick Doyle, immediately assumed the role of CEO and, despite some initial misgivings, continued to support the campaign. In an interview with Bloomberg Businessweek in April 2010, Doyle stated,

It wasn't a hard choice to change the pizza. But it was absolutely a calculated risk to advertise it this way. There was no Plan B. If it didn't work, there was no going back. You can't say your old pizza was bad and this new pizza is great and expect to go back to the old formula if people don't like it. My initial reaction to the campaign was "Wow, that's incredibly blunt." The more I digested the idea, the more comfortable I got. This new pizza was dramatically different. It tasted better—there was no question. We knew all we had to do was get people to try it.[83]

Strategic Challenges Facing Domino's

To remain an industry leader and perpetuate the current trend of success, Domino's must be prepared to handle a wealth of challenges facing nearly all channels of its business. From the constantly changing needs to the methods of communication with the customer to how Domino's innovates, reacts, and adapts to the market—there are many key determinants for future success.

As described, a major challenge facing the pizza industry relates to the demographic changes in the market. With obesity levels at record highs and the subsequent increased awareness and emphasis on health consciousness, the pizza industry as a whole must be prepared to make shifts in the quality and origin of the food it provides. Currently, organic foods is the fastest-growing sector of the American food marketplace with sales increasing 17 to 20 percent per year since 2004 (as compared to increased sales of non-organic, conventional food at only 2 percent).[84] However, this shift to organics comes with a significant cost as estimates show that "organic food is typically 20 to 100 percent more expensive than a conventional counterpart."[85] Domino's will face increasing pressure from the marketplace in the upcoming years to find a balance between the changing demands of consumers for healthier alternatives and the significantly increased costs associated with doing so. Ultimately, the question for Domino's will become whether it wants to maintain its position as a low-cost provider or shift its focus to a more health-conscious approach with a higher price tag.

Whether shifting to an organic product approach or remaining conventional, Domino's must also determine what product offerings are needed to keep pace with the changing tastes of the market. While Domino's has recently shown a strong willingness and ability to offer new products, ongoing decisions about not only what to add, but what to remove from the menu will need to be made using customer research and market trend analysis. While its core product will undoubtedly remain pizza long into the future, the ingredients used as well as the complementary products offered will become increasingly important to meet the changing needs of the consumer.

As Domino's has very successfully carved out the niche as the leader in delivery, the company must be able to adapt and capitalize on the ever-changing ways that customers communicate with businesses. To date, Domino's has adapted well, offering online ordering and an iPhone application to allow customers to place their orders without having to call to a specific location.[86] While these new ordering methods are adequate for the current marketplace, technology trends are changing at an incredible pace and Domino's must continually optimize its systems and commit the resources necessary to keep up with the latest tech trends.

Ordering aside, customers now interact with their chosen brands in entirely new ways and Domino's must determine how to be and stay relevant in the tech world of social media. Domino's currently has a strong social media presence with over 1.2 million Facebook Fans[87] and over 20,000 followers on Twitter.[88] The primary focus points of these interactions include customer service, promotions, and loyalty benefits. To continue to capitalize on this, Domino's must remain focused on interacting and evolving with its loyal customers. Doing so will not only increase retention and grow incremental sales, but will help Domino's anticipate tomorrow's best and most cost-effective use of these media vehicles.

From market shifts in eating habits to increased consumer expectations regarding brand communication, the road to sustained success for Domino's is paved with what any other organization would consider to be potholes, but that a company brought up under the tutelage of David Brandon might consider opportunities. Even so, CEO Patrick Doyle, along with the legions of franchisees and stakeholders whose livelihoods depend on the economic success of Domino's, will face countless challenges in their efforts to maintain and expand upon Domino's favorable position in the market.

NOTES

1. Domino's Pizza, Inc. *Hoovers.com*.
2. Schwartz, N. D. The economy looks a lot like pizza. *New York Times*. 6 Jan 2008. http://www.nytimes.com/2008/01/06/business/06maker.html
3. Klaassen, A. Domino's talks radical authenticity. *Advertising Age*. 28 Oct 2010. http://adage.com/article/special-report-ideaconference/domino-s-talks-radical-authenticity/146782/
4. http://www.youtube.com/user/dominosvids
5. Domino's Pizza Delivers New Line of Oven Baked Sandwiches Nationwide. *Domino's Investor Relations - Press Release*. 21 Feb 2011. http://phx.corporate-ir.net/phoenix.zhtml?c=135383&p=irol-newsArticle&ID=1188128&highlight
6. Domino's Pizza Continues Its Reinvention by Revamping New Chicken: Domino's to share story as told by the chicken chef himself. *Domino's Investor Relations - Press Release*. 21 Feb 2011. http://phx.corporate-ir.net/phoenix.zhtml?c=135383&p=irol-newsArticle&ID=1530876&highlight=
7. Domino's 'Jared' promo targets sandwich market. *Nation's Restaurant News*. 20 Aug 2008. http://www.nrn.com/article/dominopercentE2percent80percent99s-wants-jareds-try-new-sandwiches
8. Domino's Pizza, Inc. 2010 Annual Report. Page 3. *Dominosbiz.com* .https://materials.proxyvote.com/Approved/25754A/20110314/AR_81862/HTML2/dominos_pizza-ar2010_0006.htm
9. Jury award spurs Domino's to drop deadly policy. *Georgia Trial Lawyers Association*. http://www.gtla.org/GA/index.cfm?event=showPage&pg=DropDeadPolicy
10. About Domino's Pizza: History. *Dominosbiz.com*. http://www.dominosbiz.com/Biz-Public-EN/Site+Content/Secondary/About+Dominos/History/
11. Domino's Pizza Announces 2010 Financial Results. *Domino's Investor Relations - Financial Results*. 1 Mar 2011. http://phx.corporate-ir.net/phoenix.zhtml?c=135383&p=irol-newsArticle&ID=1534134&highlight=
12. Domino's Pizza, Inc. 2010 Annual Report. *op. cit*. Pages 16, 17.
13. Domino's Pizza, Inc: Company Profile. *Reference for Business*. http://www.referenceforbusiness.com/history2/60/Domino-s-Pizza-Inc.html
14. The History of Domino's Pizza. *Recipe Pizza*. http://www.recipepizza.com/the_history_of_dominos_pizza.htm
15. Domino's Pizza, Inc: Company Profile. *op. cit*.
16. Domino's, Inc. *Funding Universe*. http://www.fundinguniverse.com/company-histories/Dominos-Inc-Company-History.html
17. *Ibid*.
18. Domino's Pizza, Inc: Company Profile. *op. cit*.
19. *Ibid*.
20. The History of Domino's Pizza. *op. cit*.
21. Domino's, Inc. *Funding Universe*. *op. cit*.
22. Domino's Pizza, Inc. *International Directory of Company Histories*. http://www.encyclopedia.com/topic/Dominos_Pizza_Inc.aspx
23. Domino's Pizza, Inc: Company Profile. *op. cit*.
24. About Domino's Pizza: History. *op. cit*.
25. Janofsky, M. Domino's ends fast-pizza pledge after big award to crash victim. *New York Times*. 22 Dec 1993. http://www.nytimes.com/1993/12/22/business/domino-s-ends-fast-pizza-pledge-after-big-award-to-crash-victim.html
26. Company News; Domino's Pizza founder to retire and sell a stake. *New York Times*. 26 Sep 1998. http://www.nytimes.com/1998/09/26/business/company-news-domino-s-pizza-founder-to-retire-and-sell-a-stake.html?src=pm
27. Zuber, A. Domino's CEO search over, taps Brandon to lead chain. *Nation's Restaurant News*. 22 Mar 1999. http://findarticles.com/p/articles/mi_m3190/is_12_33/ai_54289857/
28. Domino's, Inc. *Funding Universe*. *op. cit*.
29. Domino's Pizza, Inc. *NYSE Euronext*. http://www.nyse.com/about/listed/dpz_news.html
30. Brand Keys. Press. http://www.brandkeys.com/news/press/Slicepercent203711percent20BK.pdf

31. Horovitz, B. Domino's Pizza delivers change in its core pizza recipe. *USA Today*. 16 Dec 2009. http://www.usatoday.com/money/industries/food/2009-12-16-dominos16_ST_N.htm

32. Kuban, A. Chain Reaction: Domino's new pizza recipe – what does it taste like? *Slice*. http://slice.seriouseats.com/archives/2009/12/how-does-dominos-new-pizza-recipe-taste-what-is-it-like.html

33. Horovitz, B. *op. cit.*

34. Domino's Chairman & CEO David A. Brandon Transitioning to Non-Executive Chairman; J. Patrick Doyle to be Named CEO. *Domino's Investor Relations - Press Release*. 5 Jan 2010. http://phx.corporate-ir.net/phoenix.zhtml?c=135383&p=irol-newsArticle&ID=1370618&highlight=

35. Domino's opens 9000th store. *PR Newswire*. http://www.prnewswire.com/news-releases/dominos-pizza-opens-9000th-store-87373007.html

36. Domino's Pizza, Inc. 2010 Annual Report. *op. cit.* Page 7.

37. Domino's Pizza, Inc. 2010 Annual Report. *op. cit.* Page 9.

38. Domino's Pizza Inc. (DPZ). *Reuters*. http://www.reuters.com/finance/stocks/companyProfile?symbol=DPZ

39. Domino's Pizza, Inc. 2010 Annual Report. *op. cit.* Page 5.

40. Domino's Pizza, Inc. 2010 Annual Report. *op. cit.* Page 7.

41. Pizza Hut, Papa John's are tops among American pizza-eaters. *Rasmussen Reports*. 15 Apr 2011. http://www.rasmussenreports.com/public_content/lifestyle/general_lifestyle/april_2011/pizza_hut_papa_john_s_are_tops_among_american_pizza_eaters

42. Pizza Franchise Industry Report 2010. *Franchise Direct*. http://www.franchisedirect.com/foodfranchises/pizzafranchises/pizzafranchiseindustryreport2010/80/275

43. Yum! Brands: Our Brands. http://www.yum.com/company/ourbrands.asp

44. Yum! Brands, Inc: Company Overview. *DataMonitor*.

45. 2010 Pizza Power Report. *Pizza Magazine Quarterly*. http://pmq.com/digital/201009/56.html

46. Interbrand Releases 11th Annual Ranking of the 100 'Best Global Brands.' *Sys-Con Media*. 15 Sep 2010. http://www.sys-con.com/node/1535061

47. Yum! Brands 2009 Annual Customer Mania Report. Page 10. http://www.yum.com/investors/annualreport/09annualreport/pdf/2009AnnualReport.pdf

48. Papa John's International, Inc. *Funding Universe*. http://www.fundinguniverse.com/company-histories/Papa-Johns-International-Inc-Company-History.html

49. Papa John's 2010 Annual Report 10-K. Pages 1-2. *Papa John's Investor Relations*. http://files.shareholder.com/downloads/PZZA/1259918080x0x453082/69A638FF-89A3-48B5-A141-B816620D3E5F/PZZA_2010_Annual_Report.pdf

50. Papa John's 2010 Annual Report 10-K. *op. cit.* Pages 5, 88.

51. Papa John's International, Inc. *Funding Universe. op. cit.*

52. Papa John's 2010 Annual Report 10-K. *op. cit.* Page 89.

53. Papa John's Takes the Field as Official Pizza Sponsor of the NFL and Super Bowl XLIV. *Papa John's Press Release*. 12 Jan 2010. http://ir.papajohns.com/releasedetail.cfm?ReleaseID=437003

54. Papa's Specialty Pizza Challenge. *PapaJohns.com*. http://www.papajohns.com/pizzachallenge/index.shtm

55. Papa John's International, Inc. *Hoovers.com*.

56. Business models and market leaders. *Franchise Direct*. http://www.franchisedirect.com/foodfranchises/pizzafranchises/pizzaindustryreportbusinessmodelsandmarketleaders/80/276

57. History of Little Caesar Enterprises, Inc. *Reference for Business*. http://www.referenceforbusiness.com/history2/62/Little-Caesar-Enterprises-Inc.html

58. Picklesimer, D. Correspondence with Larry Manning, Marketplace Relations and Communications, Domino's Pizza. Distribution information handout. 22 Nov 2010.

59. *Ibid.*

60. 2010 Pizza Power Report. *op. cit.*

61. PMQ Industry Reports. Pizza Power Reports 2006, 2007, 2008, 2009, 2010. *Pizza Magazine Quarterly*. http://pmq.com/industryreports.php

62. 2010 Pizza Power Report. *op. cit.*

63. Domino's Pizza, Inc. 2010 Annual Report. *op. cit.* Page 2.

64. *Ibid.*

65. Domino's Pizza, Inc. 2010 Annual Report. *op. cit.* Page 26.

66. Domino's Pizza, Inc. 2010 Annual Report. *op. cit.* Page 21.

67. Domino's Pizza, Inc. (DPZ). Direct Competitor Comparison. *Yahoo! Finance*. http://finance.yahoo.com/q/co?s=DPZ+Competitors

68. Papa John's 2010 Annual Report 10-K. *op. cit.* Page 33.

69. *Ibid.*

70. *Ibid.*

71. Cassano, E. Domino effect. *Smart Business Detroit*. 30 Aug 2006. http://www.sbnonline.com/2006/08/domino-effect-how-david-brandon-keeps-domino-x2019-s-pizza-at-the-top-of-its-industry/

72. *Ibid.*

73. Brandon, D. Make the Tough Call, Then Act. *LMMatters LES50NS*. http://lmmatters.fiftylessons.com/products_services/lessons/?browse=company&initial=D&company=Domino's+Pizza

74. Hoskisson, R. E., Hitt, M. A., Ireland, R. D. 2003. *Competing for Advantage*. Thomson South-Western: Mason, OH.

75. Brandon, D. If You're Not Getting Better, You're Getting Worse. *LMMatters LES50NS*. http://lmmatters.fiftylessons.com/products_services/lessons/?browse=company&initial=D&company=Domino's+Pizza

76. Hoskisson, R. E., Hitt, M. A., Ireland, R. D. *op. cit.*

77. Brandon, D. Adapt Your Leadership Style for Each Individual. *LMMatters LES50NS*. http://lmmatters.fiftylessons.com/products_services/lessons/?browse=company&initial=D&company=Domino's+Pizza

78. Brandon, D. Change is Good. *LMMatters LES50NS*. http://lmmatters.fiftylessons.com/products_services/lessons/?browse=company&initial=D&company=Domino's+Pizza

79. *Ibid.*

80. Brandon, D. Make Painful Changes in Good Times, Not Bad. *LMMatters LES50NS*. http://lmmatters.fiftylessons.com/products_services/lessons/?browse=company&initial=D&company=Domino's+Pizza

81. Brandon, D. Make the Tough Call, Then Act. *op. cit.*

82. *Ibid.*

83. (as told to) Brady, D. Domino's CEO J. Patrick Doyle. *Bloomberg Businessweek*. 29 Apr 2010. http://www.businessweek.com/magazine/content/10_19/b4177084249824.htm

84. Hansen, N. Organic food sales see healthy growth. *CNBC TV*. 3 Dec 2004. http://www.msnbc.msn.com/id/6638417/ns/business-cnbc_tv/

85. *Ibid.*

86. NEW Domino's iPhone App. *Dominos.com*. http://www.dominos.com.au/corporate/inside/iphoneapp.aspx

87. http://www.facebook.com/#!/Dominos

88. http://twitter.com/#!/dominos

Ryan McVay/Getty Images

Joseph S. Harrison

University of Richmond

Larry Young, President and CEO of Dr Pepper Snapple Group, Inc. (NYSE: DPS) seemed to be on a roll. Named 2010 Beverage Executive of the Year by *Beverage Industry* magazine, he led the company through three very difficult economic years since it separated from the London-based food and beverage giant Cadbury Schweppes. Reflecting on that time, he chuckled, "There couldn't have been a worse year to go public."[1] Triggered by the collapse of mortgage-backed securities, the recession froze credit markets and led to unprecedented commodities prices. In spite of adverse economic conditions and fierce competition, the company managed to obtain modest growth in sales in 2010.

Perhaps most satisfying of all was the recent turnaround of the Snapple brand, which had been struggling for many years.[2] Sales volume for the brand grew 10 percent in 2010, fueled by new products, packages, and distribution. In addition, Dr Pepper, Canada Dry, Crush, Mott's, and Hawaiian Punch all experienced increases in demand. A healthy cash flow allowed the company to reduce its debt, increase dividends, and repurchase shares. A question remained as to whether the company was simply taking advantage of some fairly obvious opportunities that it could not pursue when it was owned by Cadbury Schweppes, or whether this number three firm could actually begin to prosper in an industry dominated by two of the strongest brands in the world. After all, although DPS sales were up almost 2 percent in 2010, profits were lower than in 2009. In comparison, Coca-Cola Company experienced revenue growth in 2010 of 13.3 percent, with operating income increasing by 2.7 percent. During the same time period, PepsiCo had revenue growth of 33.8 percent and growth in operating profit of 3.6 percent.

The Dr Pepper Snapple Story

The original Dr Pepper soft drink was invented in 1885 by a young pharmacist named Charles Alderton. At the time, Alderton was working at Morrison's Old Corner Drug Store in Waco, Texas, which served carbonated soft drinks from a soda fountain. Using that resource, Alderton began to experiment with his own recipes and soon discovered that one particular drink, referred to as "the Waco," was gaining popularity among his customers. As demand grew, Alderton and Morrison brought in a third partner to help with the manufacturing and bottling of the soft drink. The partner was Robert S. Lazenby, owner of the Circle "A" Ginger Ale Company. Alderton left the business shortly thereafter, but Morrison and Lazenby continued, eventually forming what would come to be known as the Dr Pepper Company, named after a friend of Morrison. The company was introduced to the general public in 1904 at the World's Fair Exposition in St. Louis.[3]

From its humble beginnings in Morrison's Old Corner Drug Store, the company Morrison and Lazenby started has become one of the largest beverage manufacturers in North America. DPS's current product portfolio is closely tied to the history of mergers and acquisitions of its one-time parent company, Cadbury Schweppes plc (Cadbury Schweppes). Cadbury Schweppes emerged in 1969 from the merger of Cadbury plc, a British confectionary and a soft drink company, and Schweppes, an international beverage brand. In the three decades that followed, Cadbury Schweppes gained the third largest share of the beverage market in North America through strategic acquisitions. Some notable acquisitions included the Duffy-Mott Company (later known as Mott's), Canada Dry, Sunkist, Crush, and Sun Drop in the 1980s. In 1993, the company bought the A&W brands Squirt and Vernors as well as its signature root beer and cream soda

This case is intended for classroom use and is not intended to illustrate good or bad management practices. I would like to acknowledge the helpful assistance of Dr. Jeffrey S. Harrison in preparing this case. I am also grateful to the Robins School of Business at the University of Richmond for providing me with the resources I used to research this company and its competitive environment.

flavors. Cadbury finally purchased Dr Pepper/Seven UP, Inc., in 1995, an acquisition that brought Dr Pepper, 7UP, IBC Root Beer, and the Welch's soft drink line into the company portfolio.[4]

In 2000, Cadbury Schweppes acquired the Snapple Beverage Group (Snapple). Snapple had previously been part of a failed acquisition by Quaker in 1994. The acquisition was intended to help Quaker strengthen its beverage division, which at the time included Gatorade. However, after failing to successfully integrate the contrasting corporate cultures, in 1997 Snapple was acquired by Triarc Companies, an investment company with a history of purchasing struggling assets.[5] It was from Triarc that Cadbury Schweppes ultimately acquired Snapple.

Three years after acquiring Snapple, Cadbury Schweppes combined its four North American beverage companies—Dr Pepper/Seven UP, Snapple, Mott's, and Bebidas Mexico—into Cadbury Schweppes Americas Beverages (CSAB). By 2006, CSAB had developed a common vision, business strategy, and management structure and established its own bottling and distribution network. In May 2008, under the direction of Larry Young, CSAB officially spun off from Cadbury's confectionary manufacturing division and became known as Dr Pepper/Snapple Group, Inc.[6]

Today, DPS manufactures, markets, and distributes over 50 brands of carbonated soft drinks, juices, mixers, teas, and other beverages. In addition to Dr Pepper and Snapple brand drinks, DPS products include Mott's juices, 7UP, A&W, RC Cola, Squirt, Sunkist soda, Canada Dry, Schweppes, Hawaiian Punch, Yoo-Hoo, and other well-known beverages.[7] It has a market share of over 40 percent in the non-cola carbonated soft drink category.

The Company

Dr Pepper Snapple Group, Inc. is a major beverage company with an integrated business model including brand ownership, bottling, and distribution of nonalcoholic beverages in the United States, Canada, and Mexico. The company's portfolio includes dozens of brands of flavored (non-cola) carbonated soft drinks and noncarbonated beverages like mixers, juice drinks, and ready-to-drink teas and juices. Since the spin-off of Cadbury in May 2008, the company has established itself as the top non-cola carbonated soft drink company in the United States, and has maintained the number three spot in the broader beverage industry in North America.[8]

The Management Team

Current DPS management includes seasoned professionals with decades of experience in the food and beverage industry. Most notable in the organization are

president and CEO Larry Young, chief financial officer Martin Ellen, and President of Packaged Beverages Rodger L. Collins.[9]

President and CEO: Larry Young. Larry Young has been president and CEO of the company since October 2007 and led the separation of DPS from Cadbury in 2008. Before coming to the company, Young worked for more than 25 years in the PepsiCo system, where he began as a truck driver and worked his way up to president and CEO of Pepsi-Cola General Bottlers. In 2005, he joined the Dr Pepper/Seven UP Bottling Group, again as president and CEO. Young finally joined Cadbury Schweppes in April 2006 when it acquired Dr Pepper/Seven Up.

Chief Financial Officer: Martin Ellen. Martin (Marty) Ellen joined DPS in April 2010. He has 25 years of experience as chief financial officer in companies in the manufacturing, franchising, distribution, and service industries. His previous appointment was at Snap-on Inc., a manufacturer and marketer of professional tools, equipment, and software. His beverage industry experience took place at Whitman Corporation, owner of Pepsi-Cola General Bottlers, where he helped realign and expand Pepsi bottling territories in the United States and Europe.

President of Packaged Beverages: Rodger L. Collins. Rodger Collins has been affiliated with the bottling group of Dr Pepper Snapple or its predecessors for more than 30 years, having survived numerous acquisitions, restructurings, and the spin-off of DPS from Cadbury Schweppes. In his current role, he manages a coast-to-coast sales force and fleet with responsibility for direct-to-store delivery and warehouse distribution.

Board of Directors

As a publicly traded company, DPS management is directed by a board of directors chaired by Wayne Sanders, who served as Chairman and CEO of Kimberly-Clark Corporation until retiring in 2003.[10] As stated in the company's Corporate Governance Guidelines, the board's responsibility is to manage the business affairs of the company, including regular evaluation of strategic direction, policies and procedures, and top management. It must ensure that the company's managers act in the best interests of the company and its stockholders and maintain a high level of ethical conduct.[11] In addition to Chairman Sanders, there are eight more members of the board of directors, including John Adams, formerly of Trinity Industries and Texas Commercial Bank; Terence Martin, former senior vice president and CFO of Quaker Oats; and DPS CEO Larry Young[12] (for full information on directors, see Exhibit 1).

Exhibit 1 Board of Directors

Wayne R. Sanders, Chairman

Mr. Sanders has served as a director since May 2008 and is chairman of the board of directors and chairman of the nominating and corporate governance committee. Mr. Sanders served as the chairman and the chief executive officer of Kimberly-Clark Corporation from 1992 until his retirement in 2003. Mr. Sanders currently serves on the boards of directors of Texas Instruments Inc. and Belo Corp. He previously served on the board of directors of Adolph Coors Company. Mr. Sanders is also a National Trustee and Governor of the Boys & Girls Club of America and was a member of the Marquette University Board of Trustees from 1992 to 2007, serving as chairman from 2001 to 2003.

Larry D. Young, President, Chief Executive Officer, and Director

Larry Young is president and chief executive officer for Dr Pepper Snapple Group, Inc., one of the world's leading beverage companies. Mr. Young was named president and chief executive officer in October 2007 after serving as president and chief operating officer for the company's Bottling Group division, and led the spin-off of Dr Pepper Snapple Group from Cadbury Schweppes plc in May 2008. Mr. Young joined the company in April 2006 through its full acquisition of Dr Pepper/Seven Up Bottling Group, where he was president and CEO since 2005. As head of operations, he played a central role in helping to create a new business model for a fully integrated beverage company. In his 30-year career, Mr. Young has been involved with producing and selling virtually every type of beverage in the Americas and across Europe and Russia. He served more than 25 years in the Pepsi system, most recently with PepsiAmericas and before that with Pepsi-Cola General Bottlers, where he began on a route truck and worked his way to president and chief operating officer.

John L. Adams, Director

Mr. Adams has served as a director since May 2008. Mr. Adams served as Executive Vice President of Trinity Industries, Inc. from January 1999 to June 2005 and held the position of Vice Chairman from July 2005 to March 2007. Prior to joining Trinity Industries, Mr. Adams spent 25 years in various positions with Texas Commerce Bank, N.A. and its successor, Chase Bank of Texas, National Association. From 1997 to 1998, he served as Chairman and Chief Executive Officer of Chase Bank of Texas. Mr. Adams currently serves on the boards of directors of Trinity Industries, Inc. and Group 1 Automotive, Inc., where he has served as chairman since April 2005. He previously served on the boards of directors of American Express Bank Ltd. and Phillips Gas Company.

Terence D. Martin, Director

Mr. Martin has served as a director since May 2008 and serves as chairman of the audit committee. Mr. Martin served as Senior Vice President and Chief Financial Officer of Quaker Oats Company from 1998 until his retirement in 2001. From 1995 to 1998, he was Executive Vice President and Chief Financial Officer of General Signal Corporation. Mr. Martin was Chief Financial Officer and Member of the Executive Committee of American Cyanamid Company from 1991 to 1995 and served as Treasurer from 1988 to 1991. Since 2002, Mr. Martin has served on the board of directors of Del Monte Foods Company and currently serves as the chairman of its audit committee.

Pamela H. Patsley, Director

Ms. Patsley has served as a director since May 2008. Ms. Patsley served as Senior Executive Vice President of First Data Corporation from March 2000 to October 2007 and President of First Data International from May 2002 to October 2007. She retired from those positions in October 2007. From 1991 to 2000, she served as President and Chief Executive Officer of Paymentech, Inc., prior to its acquisition by First Data. Ms. Patsley also previously served as Chief Financial Officer of First USA, Inc. Ms. Patsley currently serves on the boards of directors of Molson Coors Brewing Company and Texas Instruments Incorporated, and she is the chair of the audit committee of Texas Instruments Incorporated.

Ronald G. Rogers, Director

Mr. Rogers has served as a director since May 2008. Mr. Rogers served in various positions with Bank of Montreal between 1972 and 2007. From 2002 to 2007, he served as Deputy Chair, Enterprise Risk & Portfolio Management, BMO Financial Group; and from 1994 to 2002 he served as Vice Chairman, Personal & Commercial Client Group. Prior to 1994, Mr. Rogers held various executive vice president positions at Bank of Montreal.

Jack L. Stahl, Director

Mr. Stahl has served as a director since May 2008 and serves as chairman of the compensation committee. Mr. Stahl served as Chief Executive Officer and President of Revlon, Inc. from February 2002 until his retirement in September 2006. From February 2000 to March 2001, he served as President and Chief Operating Officer of The Coca-Cola Company and previously served as Chief Financial Officer and Senior Vice President of The Coca-Cola Company's North America Group and Senior Vice President of The Coca-Cola Company's Americas Group. Mr. Stahl currently serves on the board of directors of Schering-Plough Corporation.

M. Anne Szostak, Director

Ms. Szostak has served as a director since May 2008. Since June 2004, Ms. Szostak has served as President and Chief Executive Officer of Szostak Partners LLC, a consulting firm that advises executive officers on strategic and human resource issues. From 1998 until her retirement in 2004, she served as Executive Vice President and Corporate Director–Human Resources and Diversity of FleetBoston Financial Corporation. She also served as Chairman and Chief Executive Officer of Fleet Bank–Rhode Island from 2001 to 2003. Ms. Szostak currently is a director of Belo Corp., ChoicePoint, Inc., Tupperware Brands Corporation, and Spherion Corporation, where she serves as chair of the compensation committee.

Mike Weinstein, Director

Mr. Weinstein was elected as a director in February 2009. Mr. Weinstein is a co-founder of INOV8, which specializes in developing and commercializing innovative beverage products, such as the HYDRIVE energy drink. Mr. Weinstein served as president and chief operating officer of A&W Brands, Inc. in the early 1990s and later as chief executive officer of Snapple Beverage Group, which was acquired by Cadbury Schweppes in 2000. During his career, he also has overseen such brands as RC Cola, Squirt, Mistic, Stewart's, and Vernors and has led global innovation and business development teams. Mr. Weinstein was named to *Beverage World* magazine's Hall of Fame in 2000 and received *Beverage Digest*'s prestigious "Visionary Award" in 2004.

Company Strategies

Since it was spun off from Cadbury Schweppes, DPS management has concentrated a great deal of time and attention on strategy development and implementation. Through focused strategic development, management has sought to establish the firm as a leader in the higher margin segments of the nonalcoholic beverage industry.

Consistent with this strategic direction, management has established six specific strategies:

- Build and enhance leading brands.
- Focus on opportunities in high-growth and high-margin categories.
- Increase presence in high-margin channels and packages.
- Leverage the firm's integrated business model.
- Strengthen the firm's distribution channels through acquisitions.
- Improve operating efficiency.

While most of the strategies are centered on internal development, management is attempting to broaden the firm's market through continued acquisition activity and contractual agreements with other organizations.[13] Whether internally or externally focused, however, the key to implementing each of these strategies has been a focus on marketing (for a detailed explanation of DPS strategies, see Exhibit 2).

Marketing

Shortly after DPS demerged from Cadbury, the economy in the United States began to struggle and discretionary spending was constricted. As a result, sales in the industry tanked, leading many companies to drastically cut marketing budgets. In contrast to the mainstream reaction, DPS intensified its focus on marketing and advertising. This decision was based on an analysis of the early 1980s recession conducted by Nielson, a major marketing research company and a partner of DPS. The analysis looked at brands across multiple consumer categories in 1983 and 1984, and found that the most successful brands all pursued a common strategy—continued investment in core brands. Consequently, DPS dramatically increased its marketing budget for its core brands and focused its marketing money on brand development, availability, and advertising.[14]

Brand Development. Despite slow sales in the overall non-cola carbonated soft drink market, many top managers within the company believe that flavored soft drinks showed room for growth. As Young put it, they

Exhibit 2 Strategy

THE KEY ELEMENTS OF OUR BUSINESS STRATEGY ARE TO:
Build and Enhance Leading Brands. We use an ongoing process of market and consumer analysis to identify key brands that we believe have the greatest potential for profitable sales growth. We intend to continue to invest most heavily in these key brands to drive profitable and sustainable growth by strengthening consumer awareness, developing innovative products and brand extensions to take advantage of evolving consumer trends, improving distribution, and increasing promotional effectiveness.
Focus on Opportunities in High-Growth and High-Margin Categories. We are focused on driving growth in our business in selected profitable and emerging categories. These categories include ready-to-drink teas, energy drinks, and other functional beverages. We also intend to capitalize on opportunities in these categories through brand extensions, new product launches, and selective acquisitions of brand and distribution rights.
Increase Presence in High-Margin Channels and Packages. We are focused on improving our product presence in high-margin channels, such as convenience stores, vending machines, and small independent retail outlets, primarily by increased selling activity and investments in coolers and other cold drink equipment. We also intend to increase demand for high-margin products like single-serve packages for many of our key brands through increased promotional activity and innovation.
Leverage Our Integrated Business Model. We believe our integrated brand ownership, bottling, and distribution business model provides opportunities for net sales and profit growth through the alignment of the economic interests of our brand ownership and our bottling and distribution businesses. We intend to leverage our integrated business model to reduce costs by creating greater geographic manufacturing and distribution coverage and to be more flexible and responsive to the changing needs of our large retail customers by coordinating sales, service, distribution, promotions, and product launches.
Strengthen Our Route-to-Market through Acquisitions. The acquisition and creation of our Bottling Group is part of our longer-term initiative to strengthen the route-to-market for our products. We believe additional acquisitions of regional bottling companies will broaden our geographic coverage and enhance coordination with our large retail customers.
Improve Operating Efficiency. We believe our recently announced restructuring will reduce our selling, general, and administrative expenses and improve our operating efficiency. In addition, the integration of recent acquisitions into our Bottling Group has created the opportunity to improve our manufacturing, warehousing, and distribution operations.

Source: 2011, Strategy, http://investor.drpeppersnapple.com

believe that while consumers are growing tired of colas, flavored soft drinks are the "sweet spot" in the industry. By developing its flavored brands like Dr Pepper, Sunkist, and A&W, DPS believes it has the potential to gain market share over its rivals.[15]

DPS has made a number of changes to its soft drink brands, including the addition of a new Green Tea Ginger Ale to the Canada Dry line, the extension of a 7UP line with added antioxidants, an updated recipe for A&W Root Beer that includes aged vanilla, and the development of Dr Pepper Cherry for consumers who prefer a lighter tasting Dr Pepper.[16] In addition to soft drink development, the company seeks to recover lost distribution in its line of healthier flavored water and energy drinks. For example, it invested in Hydrive Energy LLC, a small energy drink maker, and created Snapple Antioxidant water to compensate for the loss of Vitaminwater to Coca-Cola.[17] Also, DPS created Venom, a new energy drink to recover losses from two previous brands.[18]

More than just adding and investing in new product line extensions, DPS also refocused its efforts related to existing products. The most dramatic change occurred within its Snapple brand, which had been struggling before separating from Cadbury. In the third quarter of 2008, Snapple sales had fallen 10 percent, contributing greatly to the company's 31 percent drop in profits for that quarter.[19] In response to the drop in sales in 2008, DPS changed everything about the product—its packaging and look, taste, and the marketing thrust associated with the brand. Snapple presented new formulations for its teas to increase consumer interest, and began to focus on the product's health benefits. DPS also started distributing Snapple juices and lemonades in sleek 16-ounce glass bottles with labels indicating their health benefits.[20] These and other changes paid off, as sales of Snapple actually increased in 2010, in spite of a poor economic climate.

Increasing Advertising and Availability. Despite the company's strong history of brand development, many of its brands, such as Mott's, A&W, and Canada Dry, had not received any serious advertising investment since the end of the 1990s.[21] Beyond developing the brands, the company recognized the need to increase its efforts in advertising and distribution. Marketing Chief Jim Trebilcock explained the strategy:

We have, in our portfolio, a host of brands that are very trusted, high-quality brands and at times like these, we believe if we invest in them…we can make a pretty significant impact on our business moving forward and actually strengthen and position ourselves for consistent growth when we come out of this economic downturn.[22]

Most notable among the changes in advertising was the use of celebrities, a strategy that had worked for Snapple in the late 1980s and early 1990s.[23] In connection with Dr Pepper, DPS's most heavily supported brand, the company launched a television commercial campaign including celebrities like the rapper/producer Dr. Dre and Gene Simmons of the rock band Kiss. In the commercials, the celebrities endorse Dr Pepper by referring to its superior taste and flavor and then simply stating, "Trust me, I'm a doctor."

In addition to television commercials, DPS also began to target specific demographic segments through online viral marketing. In 2009, for example, the entire budget for Sunkist was allocated to a viral campaign targeted towards teenagers and 20 percent of the budget for Dr Pepper was allocated to Internet advertising. Although this was a fairly significant change compared to earlier DPS marketing strategies, management believed that reaching out through the Internet would help the company connect to its markets in a more relevant way.[24]

To supplement the increase in advertising, DPS also focused more attention on distribution. One of the major methods for increasing distribution was by investing in coolers, vending machines, and fast-food fountains containing DPS products. In 2008, DPS added 31,000 fountain placements in fast-food restaurants throughout the United States. In 2009, the company announced that it would add its products to 14,000 McDonald's franchises in order to increase its availability in that chain from 60 to 100 percent. In that same year, the company also outlined a strategy that would add 175,000 coolers (units in which soft drinks are stored and kept cool) and vending machines throughout the country over a five-year period.[25] Again, Trebilcock commented on the strategy:

If you have people drinking your products at work, at play, when they go into the grocery store, they're going to buy that product and take it home with them. So we put a very strong focus on what we like to refer to as our lower per-cap markets. We beefed up our marketing there, we've made sure we were closing distribution voids, placing cold drink equipment. Our fountain/foodservice team has done an excellent job of getting Dr Pepper and some of the other brands on the fountain equipment.[26]

Other major investments in distribution came in the form of joint ventures with proven distributers that significantly increased the availability of particular soft drink brands. For example, agreements with Pepsi Bottling Group in New York and PepsiAmericas in Minnesota more than doubled the availability of Crush, making it the second best-selling orange-flavored soft drink behind Sunkist, which DPS also owns.[27] Also, in 2010, DPS signed a $715 million deal that gives Coke the rights to distribute Dr Pepper and Canada Dry in the US.[28]

Operations

DPS is headquartered in Plano, Texas, and employs approximately 20,000 people throughout North America and the Caribbean. It operates 24 production plants and more than 200 distribution centers in those areas.[29] Almost all beverage concentrates are produced in a plant in St. Louis, Missouri. The business model includes both company-owned direct-store-delivery (DSD) distribution networks and third-party distribution. Within the model, approximately 40 percent of the company's volume is distributed through company-owned networks; another 40 percent through third-party distributers in the Coca-Cola, Pepsi-Cola, and independent bottler systems; and the remainder split between warehouse direct and food-service distributors.[30]

All of the internal DSD distribution is carried out by railroad and truck, operating on a hub-and-spoke supply chain system with major distribution centers in key areas. The hub-and-spoke system is set up to provide manufacturing capabilities in all five major US regions—northeast, southeast, midwest, southwest, and western. It allows for orders to be filled closer to customers, increasing customer service and controlling transportation costs. As stated by Joe Rowland, senior vice president and business unit general manager for the central and southeast regions, DPS has "the ultimate goal of providing better service to the customer, because that will translate to sales."[31]

A good example of DPS's operations is its largest hub, which is based in Northlake, Illinois and distributes to Chicago and its surrounding areas. The facility is about one million square feet in size and employs 1,250 people, of which 750 work on site and the rest in the field. On-site operations consist of nine manufacturing lines, including plastic bottle, can, and hot-fill glass lines for DSD distribution, and a bag-in-box line for soda fountains at food-service locations. Most of the lines are versatile, allowing for variations in batches, but some also have unique capabilities. For example, Line 1 produces cold-fill glass and plastic bottles, while the Snapple line produces hot-fill products. The Northlake facility produces about 220,000 cases of product a day that are stored in the company's 25-dock warehouse until they are loaded onto one of the 150 trucks owned by the facility.[32] In addition to line manufacturing, the facility utilizes a quality assurance program to check for both internal specifications and external requirements. DPS works closely with external auditors, such as the American Institute of Bakers, to ensure that manufacturing and other processes conform to product requirements.

To facilitate business operations, DPS makes use of highly integrated information systems and networks. Prior to 2008, Cadbury Schweppes supplied all IT support and staffing for DPS. Since the separation, the company has developed completely independent IT operations, with primary hosting based in Toronto, Canada, and two primary vendors for application support and maintenance outsourced to India.[33]

Under the leadership of Marty Ellen, CFO, the company has embarked on a program it calls Rapid Continuous Improvement (RCI). According to Ellen, "RCI is about excelling at delivering customer value and improving productivity by eliminating all non-value-adding activities, thereby enhancing growth opportunities."[34] The company is examining its supply chain, including innovation, manufacturing, marketing, distribution, and administration, and looking for ways to increase efficiency, consistent with Six Sigma improvement methods.

Financial Performance

Overall, DPS's financial performance since the spin-off has exceeded analysts' expectations. While many of the company's brands experienced moderate to high growth in 2010, sales of Sunkist, 7UP, and A&W declined, leading to overall company sales of $5.6 billion, up about 2 percent from 2009. Even so, in spite of the sales increase and measures the company took to increase efficiency, profits were down approximately 5 percent from the prior year. Nevertheless, the company experienced a huge loss in 2008, and the economy was very challenging in 2009 and 2010, so financial performance should be considered in its appropriate context (for detailed financial statements, see Exhibit 3). The company experienced large increases in cash flow from operations during 2010 and used the additional cash to increase dividends, pay down debt, and buy back common stock.

The Industry

The Dr Pepper Snapple Group (DPS) competes in the US beverage manufacturing and bottling industry (NAICS: 42119). The industry is made up of about 3,000 companies, including manufacturers, bottlers, and distributers of nonalcoholic beverages. Despite the vast number of companies in the industry, revenues are highly concentrated. Over 90 percent of the combined $70 billion in annual revenues are generated by the three largest companies—Coca-Cola, PepsiCo, and DPS—and their subsidiaries. Carbonated soft drinks, including colas and other flavors, bottled waters, juices, and a variety of syrups and mixes, are this industry's major products.[35]

Beverage Consumers and Market Trends

The beverage manufacturing and bottling industry is greatly influenced by economic and other market trends associated with consumers. Factors such as

Exhibit 3 Financial Statements for Dr. Pepper Snapple Group

DR PEPPER SNAPPLE GROUP, INC. CONSOLIDATED STATEMENTS OF OPERATIONS For the Years Ended December 31, 2010, 2009, and 2008	For the Year Ended December 31		
	2010	2009	2008
	(In millions of dollars, except per share data)		
Net sales	$5,636	$5,531	$5,710
Cost of sales	2,243	2,234	2,590
Gross profit	3,393	3,297	3,120
Selling, general, and administrative expenses	2,233	2,135	2,075
Depreciation and amortization	127	117	113
Impairment of goodwill and intangible assets	—	—	1,039
Restructuring costs	—	—	57
Other operating expense (income), net	8	(40)	4
Income (loss) from operations	1,025	1,085	(168)
Interest expense	128	243	257
Interest income	(3)	(4)	(32)
Loss on early extinguishment of debt	100	—	—
Other income, net	(21)	(22)	(18)
Income (loss) before provision for income taxes and equity in earnings of unconsolidated subsidiaries	821	868	(375)
Provision for income taxes	294	315	(61)
Income (loss) before equity in earnings of unconsolidated subsidiaries	527	553	(314)
Equity in earnings of unconsolidated subsidiaries, net of tax	1	2	2
Net income (loss)	$ 528	$ 555	$ (312)
Earnings (loss) per common share:			
Basic	2.19	2.18	(1.23)
Diluted	2.17	2.17	(1.23)
Weighted average common shares outstanding:			
Basic	240.4	254.2	254.0
Diluted	242.6	255.2	254.0
Cash dividends declared per common share	0.90	0.15	—

DR PEPPER SNAPPLE GROUP, INC. CONSOLIDATED BALANCE SHEETS As of December 31, 2010 and 2009	December 31, 2010	December 31, 2009
	(In millions except share and per share data)	
ASSETS		
Current assets:		
Cash and cash equivalents	$ 315	$ 280
Accounts receivable:		
Trade, net	536	540
Other	35	32
Inventories	244	262
Deferred tax assets	57	53
Prepaid expenses and other current assets	122	112
Total current assets	1,309	1,279
Property, plant and equipment, net	1,168	1,109

(Continued)

Exhibit 3 Financial Statements for Dr. Pepper Snapple Group (*Continued*)

DR PEPPER SNAPPLE GROUP, INC. CONSOLIDATED BALANCE SHEETS As of December 31, 2010, and 2009	December 31, 2010	December 31, 2009
	(In millions except share and per share data)	
ASSETS		
Investments in unconsolidated subsidiaries	11	9
Goodwill	2,984	2,983
Other intangible assets, net	2,691	2,702
Other non-current assets	552	543
Non-current deferred tax assets	144	151
Total assets	$8,859	$8,776
LIABILITIES AND STOCKHOLDERS' EQUITY		
Current liabilities:		
Accounts payable and accrued expenses	$ 851	$ 850
Deferred revenue	65	—
Current portion of long-term obligations	404	—
Income taxes payable	18	4
Total current liabilities	1,338	854
Long-term obligations	1,687	2,960
Non-current deferred tax liabilities	1,083	1,038
Non-current deferred revenue	1,515	—
Other non-current liabilities	777	737
Total liabilities	6,400	5,589
Commitments and contingencies		
Stockholders' equity:		
Preferred stock, $.01 par value, 15,000,000 shares authorized, no shares issued	—	—
Common stock, $.01 par value, 800,000,000 shares authorized, 223,936,156 and 254,109,047 shares issued and outstanding for 2010 and 2009, respectively	2	3
Additional paid-in capital	2,085	3,156
Retained earnings	400	87
Accumulated other comprehensive loss	(28)	(59)
Total stockholders' equity	2,459	3,187
Total liabilities and stockholders' equity	$8,859	$8,776

DR PEPPER SNAPPLE GROUP, INC. SEGMENT RESULTS For the Years Ended December 31, 2010 and 2009	For the Year Ended December 31	
	2010	2009
Net sales		
Beverage concentrates	$1,156	$1,063
Packaged beverages	4,098	4,111
Latin America beverages	382	357
Net sales	$5,636	$5,531
Segment operating profit (SOP)		
Beverage concentrates	$ 745	$ 683
Packaged beverages	536	573

(*Continued*)

Exhibit 3 Financial Statements for Dr. Pepper Snapple Group (*Continued*)

DR PEPPER SNAPPLE GROUP, INC. SEGMENT RESULTS For the Years Ended December 31, 2010 and 2009	For the Year Ended December 31	
	2010	**2009**
Segment operating profit (SOP)		
Latin America beverages	40	54
Total SOP	1,321	1,310
Unallocated corporate costs	288	265
Other operating expense (income), net	8	(40)
Income (loss) from operations	$1,025	$1,085
Interest expense, net	125	239
Loss on early extinguishment of debt	100	—
Other income, net	(21)	(22)
Income (loss) before provision for income taxes and equity in earnings of unconsolidated subsidiaries	$ 821	$ 868

Source: Dr Pepper Snapple Group, Inc. 2010 Report 10-K

economic stability, seasonality, commodities prices, and consumer tastes and preferences are of great importance to beverage company managers who develop and implement strategies partly for the purpose of successfully dealing with changes in the industry.

Perhaps the most significant factor influencing food and beverage companies is economic stability. Since carbonated soft drinks are a discretionary item, sales are considerably impacted by weakness in the economy. Between 2008 and 2010, the economy was the major problem facing beverage companies like DPS, Coke, and Pepsi. Intensified by the inefficiency and failure of the securities market, the United States found itself in one of the worst recessions in history. As unemployment rates increased and the credit markets froze, consumers significantly reduced spending. Discretionary spending as a percentage of total consumer spending dropped below 16 percent, its lowest level in over 50 years.[36]

As discretionary spending decreased, consumers turned from flavored drinks and colas to less expensive alternatives, including tap water. DPS CEO Larry Young explained the phenomenon, "Even though the majority of Americans are still working, the fear factor that has gripped the nation is having a significant impact on consumer psychology." As a result, Young suggested that shoppers were actively seeking out good deals and making decisions based on "product satisfaction and price."[37]

Along with influencing consumer confidence, the recession significantly increased commodity prices. Specific to the beverage industry, the prices for aluminum, natural gas, resins, corn, pulp, and other commodities all increased. These commodities are used to produce beverages and, exert a considerable amount of pressure

on industry margins. For instance, the price of sugar on the US commodity market rose from under 12 cents per pound in 2007 to 37 cents per pound in October 2010.[38]

Several other consumer trends influence the beverage manufacture and bottling industry. Factors such as changes in demographics, health concerns, preferences, changes in lifestyle, and seasonality all influence marketing and distribution methods. An increased concern about health and wellness is one of the most significant trends affecting the beverage industry. As consumers continue to reduce caloric intake and look for products richer in vitamins, the less-healthy sectors of the beverage industry are expected to shrink.[39] As soft drink sales decline, however, demand for healthier alternatives such as low or no calorie soft drinks and noncarbonated drinks such as sports drinks, ready-to-drink teas, and flavored and regular bottled water are projected to grow.[40] Through 2013, sales of bottled water were projected to grow by 9 percent, ready-to-drink teas by 24 percent, and flavored and functional waters by 71 percent.[41]

Additional consumer trends of significance to the industry are seasonality and changing demographics. Relative to seasonality, beverage sales tend to be higher during the summer months and holidays. Sales are slower during the winter months and fluctuate somewhat with the weather. With regard to demographics, the most significant changes in the United States have to do with the prevalence of aging Baby Boomers and growth in the Hispanic population.[42]

Market Channels

Although the final consumer drives demand for the beverage industry, beverage companies' direct customers are bottlers/distributers and retailers. Building strong relationships with these customers is an important part of succeeding in the beverage industry.

Bottling and distribution companies buy beverage concentrates from beverage brand companies, from which they manufacture, bottle, and distribute finished beverages. Additionally, bottlers manufacture and distribute syrups and mixes used in soda fountains for the food-service industry. Major beverage bottling companies include Coca-Cola Enterprises, PepsiAmericas, the Pepsi Bottling Group, and the Dr Pepper Snapple Bottling Group. For DPS, a substantial portion of net sales in beverage concentrates is generated through bottlers not owned by the company. As much as two-thirds of DPS volume in concentrates is sold to third-party bottlers. Some of these are owned by competitors such as PepsiCo and Coke. In 2010, 71 percent of Dr Pepper's sales volume was generated through distribution of its products through Coca-Cola- and PepsiCo-affiliated bottlers.[43] Productive relationships with these bottlers are possible because of the strength and position of the Dr Pepper brand.

Retail companies buy finished beverages from distributers for mass merchandise and sale to the final consumer. Recent trends in the industry have caused many retailers to consolidate, resulting in a smaller number of large, sophisticated retailers with greater buying power. Major retailers tied to the beverage industry include Walmart, Target, Kroger, SuperValu, and Safeway. In addition to these retailers, beverage manufacturers also depend on food-service customers that buy syrups for fountain drinks. Major food-service companies include McDonald's, Burger King, and Yum! Brands, which includes KFC, Pizza Hut, and Taco Bell.[44]

The Competition

The beverage manufacturing and bottling industry is highly competitive and constantly shifting to respond to changes in consumer tastes and preferences. Competitive position is most effectively attained through brand recognition and based on factors such as price, quality, taste, selection, and availability. Major competitors in the manufacturing segment include the Coca-Cola Company (Coke), PepsiCo, Inc. (Pepsi), Nestlé, S.A., and Kraft Foods, Inc. Major competitors in the bottling and distribution segment include Coca-Cola Enterprises, Pepsi Bottling Group, and numerous smaller bottlers and distributors.[45]

Relative to the competition, DPS is the third largest beverage business in North America, behind Coke and Pepsi, which collectively account for 63 percent of the sales in the industry.[46] According to analysts, part of the reason that DPS is so much smaller than its competitors in the United States can be attributed to the spin-off of DPS from Cadbury in 2008. Taking advantage of the company's position post spin-off, Coke and Pepsi had a significant head start on acquiring healthier juices, teas, and enhanced waters. Analysts suggest that DPS had insufficient resources at the time to maintain pace with competing acquisitions.[47]

Aside from its problems gaining overall market share in the United States, DPS has also had difficulty competing internationally. The company generates about 89 percent of its revenues in the US market, 80 percent of which come from carbonated soft drinks. In comparison, Coke collects about 74 percent of its sales outside of North America, and Pepsi generates over 40 percent of its sales internationally. Still, DPS management has expressed an intention to maintain its focus on North America.[48]

In general, while DPS has strong brands and distribution, the company has struggled to compete head-to-head with industry leaders Coke and Pepsi. Based in Atlanta, Georgia, the Coca-Cola Company (Coke) is the largest manufacturer, distributer, and marketer of nonalcoholic beverage concentrates and syrups in the world. Coke markets four of the world's top five carbonated soft drinks—Coca-Cola, named the world's most valuable brand, Diet Coke, Fanta, and Sprite. Coke also owns and licenses nearly 500 other brands including diet and light beverages, enhanced waters, juice drinks, teas, coffees, and sports and energy drinks. Coke is primarily a brand owner and manufacturer, selling its concentrates and syrups to bottling and canning companies, fountain wholesalers and retailers, and distributers.[49]

As outlined on its company website, the three-phase mission of Coke is "to refresh the world, to inspire moments of optimism and happiness, and to create value and make a difference."[50] Consistent with its mission statement, Coke maintains an international focus, marketing and distributing its products in over 200 countries.[51] To facilitate its international focus, Coke spends a significant amount of capital on technological development and marketing. For example, Coke introduced a new fountain beverage machine that used "micro-dosing" technology to dispense over 120 beverages from one machine. The machine takes up the same space as the eight-valve machine currently being used by food-service businesses.[52] International sales, technology development, and marketing have made Coke one of the most widely recognized and profitable companies in the world (for selected financial data on the Coca-Cola Company, see Exhibit 4).

PepsiCo, Inc., another major DPS competitor, is based in North Carolina and is a global leader in beverage, snack, and food manufacture and distribution. Pepsi is divided into three major business units—PepsiCo Americas Foods, PepsiCo Americas Beverages, and PepsiCo International. These business units manufacture, market, and sell a variety of convenient,

Exhibit 4 Selected Competitor Financial Data (in millions)

COCA-COLA COMPANY AND SUBSIDIARIES			
Year Ended December 31	2010	2009	2008
Net operating revenues	$35,119	$30,990	$31,944
Cost of goods sold	12,693	11,088	11,374
Selling, general and administrative expenses	13,158	11,358	11,774
Other operating charges	819	313	350
Operating income	8,449	8,231	8,446
Net income after taxes	11,809	6,824	5,807
Total current assets	21,579	17,551	12,176
Total assets	72,921	48,671	40,519
Total current liabilities	18,508	13,721	12,988
Total long-term debt and other liabilities	23,096	9,604	7,059
Total equity	31,317	25,346	20,472
PEPSICO, INC.			
Fiscal Years Ended December 25, 26 and 27	2010	2009	2008
Net operating revenues	$57,838	$43,232	$43,251
Cost of goods sold	26,575	20,099	20,351
Selling, general, and administrative expenses	22,814	15,026	15,877
Amortization of intangible assets	117	63	64
Operating profit	8,332	8,044	6,959
Net income after taxes	6,320	5,946	5,142
Total current assets	17,569	12,571	10,806
Total assets	68,153	39,848	35,994
Total current liabilities	15,892	8,756	8,787
Total long-term debt and other liabilities	30,785	13,650	14,625
Total equity	21,476	17,442	12,582

Note: Much of the difference between operating income and net income in 2010 is attributable to a gain from reclassifying the value of the company's previous investment in a business it acquired during the year. The acquisition is also reflected by the large increase in total assets in 2010.

Sources: Coca-Cola Company 2009 and 2010 Report 10-K; PepsiCo, Inc. 2009 and 2010 Annual Reports.

salty, sweet, and grain-based snacks, carbonated soft drinks, noncarbonated beverages, and other foods in approximately 200 countries. Some of the company's key brands include Pepsi, Pepsi One, Diet Pepsi, Mug, Mountain Dew, Sierra Mist, Frito-Lay, Doritos, Cheetos, Tostitos, Sunchips, SoBe and SoBe Lifewater, Propel, Quaker, and Tropicana. Pepsi also holds the trademarks for many valuable products, including Lipton, Starbucks, Dole, and Ocean Spray.[53]

Pepsi's goal is to be the world's best consumer products company in convenient foods and beverages. The company seeks to accomplish its goal by producing "financial rewards to investors as we provide opportunities for growth and enrichment to our employees, our business partners and the communities in which we operate." An important part of Pepsi's mission statement is its socially responsible approach, concentrating on improving all aspects of the world in which it operates—the environment, societies, and economies.[54] The company puts its vision into action through meeting consumer needs, environmental stewardship initiatives, societal benefits, employee support and organizational programs, and operations that increase shareholder value.[55]

As is the case for Coca-Cola, Pepsi's strategies maintain an international focus and include improvements in product development and marketing. The company has recently made significant changes to packaging, redesigning Pepsi brand products, Sierra Mist, and others. Additionally, Pepsi introduced a new advertising campaign that put a modern twist on the "Pepsi Generation" campaign used in the 1960s. The campaign combined footage from the old advertisements with current images to express the new tagline, "Every Generation Refreshes the World." [56] By focusing on social responsibility and diversifying its brand and product portfolio, Pepsi has become one of the most successful global food and beverage companies in history (for selected financial data on the PepsiCo, Inc., see Exhibit 4).

Possible Future Actions

Moving into 2011, Larry Young had many decisions to make. While he was pleased by the performance of many of the company's individual brands, Young knew the firm had to cut costs in order to improve profit margins. However, DPS could not afford to make any cuts that would damage its strong brands or alienate consumers. Furthermore, DPS's rivals, Coke and PepsiCo, were experiencing much higher performance levels than DPS and were not going to stand still. How can DPS continue to grow at levels that will satisfy shareholders? To what extent should acquisitions, joint ventures, licensing agreements, and/or internal growth tactics be pursued? Should DPS diversify into other product markets? What other growth options are available to the company? Should any products or brands be divested? Young had a great deal to think about.

NOTES

1. S. Theodore, 2009, DPS puts the flavor back in CSDs, *Beverage Industry*, July 15, 16–18.
2. K. E. Grace, 2009, Dr Pepper profit rises but Snapple business continues to suffer, *The Wall Street Journal*, May 14, B10.
3. M. Bellis, 2009, The history of Dr Pepper, *About.com*, http://inventors.about.com/library/inventors/bldrpepper.htm, November 27.
4. 2009, Company history, Dr Pepper Snapple Group, http://investor.drpeppersnapple.com/index.cfm?pagesect=history, November 22.
5. J. Deighton, 2003, *Snapple*, Boston: Harvard Business Publishing.
6. 2009, Company history, Dr Pepper Snapple Group, *op. cit.*
7. *Ibid.*
8. Dr Pepper Snapple Group, Inc. Annual Report 2010.
9. 2011, Leadership team, Dr Pepper Snapple Group, http://investor.drpeppersnapple.com/management.cfm, March 3
10. 2009, Board of Directors, Dr Pepper Snapple Group, http://investor.drpeppersnapple.com/directors.cfm, March 3.
11. 2009, Corporate governance guidelines, Dr Pepper Snapple Group, http://files.shareholder.com/downloads/DPSG/783586250x0x274076/72e046bf-1115-42c0-bcad-677a33841a9b/DPS_WebDoc_5432.pdf, December 14.
12. 2009, Board of Directors, Dr Pepper Snapple Group, *op. cit.*
13. 2009, Strategy, Dr Pepper Snapple Group, http://investor.drpeppersnapple.com/index.cfm?pagesect=strategy, December 14.
14. N. Zmuda, 2009, Dr Pepper ups marketing spend, readies for growth, *Advertising Age*, 80(16), May 4, 18.
15. P. Ziobro, 2010, Dr Pepper sees sticky prices sweetening profits, *Wall Street Journal*, December 28, B1.
16. S. Theodore, *op. cit.*
17. B. Mckay, 2008, Dr Pepper gets stake in energy drink, *The Wall Street Journal*, July 25, B11.
18. S. Theodore, *op. cit.*
19. 2008, A snappier look for Snapple, *Progressive Grocer*, http://www.progressivegrocer.com/progressivegrocer/content_display/features/beverage/e3i87155f066147ca396666a26fc9517c42, November 28, April 7.
20. *Ibid.*
21. N. Zmuda, 2009, *op. cit.*
22. *Ibid*, 18.
23. J. Deighton, *Snapple. op. cit.*
24. N. Zmuda, 2009, *op. cit.*
25. S. Theodore, *op. cit.*
26. *Ibid*, 17.
27. S. Theodore, *op. cit.*
28. 2010, FTC approves Coke's bottler deal, *Wall Street Journal Online Edition*, http://search.proquest.com/docview/755056266?accountid=14731, September 27.
29. 2009, Company history, Dr Pepper Snapple Group, *op. cit.*
30. S. Theodore, *op. cit.*
31. S. Scott, 2009, Plant focus: Plant transitions to a DPS hub, *Beverage Industry*, July 15, 100(7), 20–22.
32. *Ibid.*
33. Dr Pepper Snapple Group, Inc. 2009 Annual Report
34. Dr Pepper Snapple Group, Inc. 2010 Annual Report, 10.
35. 2009, Industry profile: Beverage manufacture and bottling, *First Research Online*, http://newman.richmond.edu:2541/industry.aspx?chapter=0&pid=164, November 27.
36. B. McKay & K. E. Grace, 2009, Dr Pepper's outlook juiced by value drinks. *The Wall Street Journal*, March 27, B3.
37. *Ibid.*
38. T. Graves & E. Y. Kwon, 2009, *Industry Surveys: Foods & Nonalcoholic Beverages*, New York: Standard & Poor's.
39. J. Rivkin, 2009, Refreshingly healthy, *Contract Manufacturing & Packaging*. August 24, 12–14.
40. Dr Pepper Snapple Group, Inc. 2009 Annual Report
41. J. Rivkin, 2009, *op. cit.*
42. Dr Pepper Snapple Group, Inc. 2009 Annual Report
43. Dr Pepper Snapple Group, Inc. 2010 Annual Report, 6.
44. Dr Pepper Snapple Group, Inc. 2009 Annual Report
45. *Ibid.*
46. Dr Pepper Snapple Group, Inc. 2010 Annual Report, 8.
47. E. Ody, 2008. Dr Pepper: Strong brand, cheap stock, *Kiplinger.com*, http://www.kiplinger.com/columns/picks/archive/2008/pick0521.htm.
48. *Ibid.*
49. Coca-Cola Company 2009 Annual Report
50. 2009, Our company: Mission, vision & values, Coca-Cola Company, http://www.thecoca-colacompany.com/ourcompany/mission_vision_values.html, December 15.
51. S. Theodore, 2009, Category focus: 2009 soft drink report, *Beverage Industry*, 100(3), March 15, 16–22.
52. *Ibid.*
53. PepsiCo, Inc. 2010 Annual Report
54. 2009, Company: Our mission and vision, PepsiCo, Inc., http://www.pepsico.com/Company/Our-Mission-and-Vision.html, December 15.
55. PepsiCo, Inc. 2009 Annual Report
56. S. Theodore, 2009, Category focus, 20. *op. cit.*

Ford Motor Company: Staying "Ford Tough"

Jeff Andress, Melodie Bolin, Dennis Horton, Cody Kleven, Mike McCullar, Hollon Stevens
Arizona State University

Robin Chapman, Gail Christian

Introduction

During the financial crisis, the future of Ford Motor Company was hanging in the balance, and no one was certain how to save the once-great company. Question after question without any easy answers . . . How much longer could Ford survive with large losses? Would it have to sell assets or financially restructure? Could it cut enough costs, and where should it cut? Would union leaders realize the situation, and how much would they be willing to help? When would Chinese competitors enter the US market? How could Ford develop its product offerings to adjust for higher fuel costs? How could Ford improve its product offerings to reverse or at least stop its market share losses? How much more market share would it lose?

The magnitude of the situation was overwhelming. To overcome these challenges, it seemed Ford would have to restructure every aspect of its business. It would require improved product offerings with cutting-edge design and high quality; improved operations with more flexibility and lower costs; and improved marketing with better brand image and customer interest. Ford was at a crossroads, and the road ahead remained shrouded in uncertainty.

History

Ford Motor Company has gone through many evolutions since its humble beginnings on June 16, 1903. Engineer and entrepreneur Henry Ford began the corporation (now synonymous with the assembly line, Industrial Revolution, and the "American Dream") with 11 business associates and $28,000 in capital. Its first car, the Model A, debuted in Detroit amid offerings from 87 other car manufacturing companies in the US.[1] At that time, cars were considered luxury items that only the wealthy could afford. However, Henry Ford believed these vehicles had the potential to transform society, and with the right manufacturing techniques, they could be made affordable to the general public.

I will build a car for the great multitude . . . large enough for the family, but small enough for the individual to run and care for. It will be constructed of the best materials, by the best men to be hired, and after the simplest designs that modern engineering can devise. It will be so low in price that no man making a good salary will be unable to own one – and enjoy with his family the blessing of hours of pleasure in God's great open spaces.[2]

The Model T debuted on August 12, 1908. The first moving conveyor belt was introduced at Ford's Highland Park plant in 1914, followed in 1917 by the construction of the Rouge plant, envisioned by Ford as "an all-in-one manufacturing complex, where the processing of raw materials, parts, and final automobiles could happen efficiently in a single place."[3] In 1914, Ford produced 308,162 cars, more than all other US automakers combined. Production of the Model T increased from 20,277 vehicles at $780 each in 1910 to 585,388 at $360 each in 1916.[4] The increase in sales and decrease in price was primarily the result of production and supply chain efficiencies related to the implementation of the assembly line manufacturing process and Ford's vertically integrated supply chain.

Henry Ford believed he could manage the entire supply chain more efficiently within his own organization. As Ford expanded, the following process developed:

- Ford employees mined iron ore from Ford-owned pits.
- Ore was transported on Ford ships and tractors.
- The ore was unloaded using Ford cranes.
- Ford steel mills processed the iron ore to make steel plate from which Ford factories built the Model T.[5]

Ford was known to boast that iron ore unloaded at his Rouge plant became the steel components of a Ford vehicle rolling off the assembly line within 48 hours.[6]

Ford also understood that the mass production process would create more jobs that, in turn, would create more people able to afford the lower priced vehicles produced by his company, and he wanted to make certain that Ford employees would be able to afford the vehicles they helped produce. In 1914, he more than doubled the existing minimum wage per day to $5. Ford viewed the high wage he paid to Ford employees as a "profit-sharing" program.

In 1919, following a dispute with other Ford stockholders, Henry, his wife Clara, and son Edsel purchased all outstanding shares for $105,820,894 and made Ford Motor Company a family-owned business. Outside ownership of company stock would not be allowed again until 1956.[7] For many years, the company and the man were inseparable—the public image of the company focused on the personality of its charismatic leader. Having begun the international expansion of the company, at the height of operations, Ford Motor Company operated or sold products in more than 30 countries, including Indonesia, China, Brazil, Egypt, and much of Europe.[8]

Henry's son Edsel joined the company in 1915, assuming responsibility for the business side of the company (sales, purchasing, advertising, and much of the day-to-day business operations), leaving Henry free to focus on engineering and production. In 1919, Edsel became president of the company, but Henry remained actively involved. Edsel believed that, in addition to its functionality, the auto could be stylish and beautiful and he pushed for aesthetic improvements of the Model T, convincing Henry that the Model T should be available in a variety of colors, despite Henry's famous statement, "You can have any color, as long as it's black."[9] Other innovations credited to Edsel include the installation of hydraulic brakes, production of a six-cylinder engine in addition to the V-8, and the development of safety glass. In 1922, Ford bought the Lincoln Motor Company, and the Mercury brand debuted in 1938 allowing Ford to enter the medium price market, an area that would benefit from the shift to higher-priced vehicles.[10]

Ford Motor Company continued to operate with minimal leadership problems until the death of Edsel Ford in 1943 from cancer. Intense dissension about who should succeed Edsel continued until Henry Ford, at the age of 79, returned from retirement to lead the company. It was widely believed that Henry had never recovered fully from the death of his son Edsel, and in 1945, he resigned at age 82. In his letter of resignation, he recommended that Edsel's oldest son, Henry Ford II, become his successor.[11]

By the time Henry Ford II took over, Ford's US market share had slipped to number three, behind General Motors (GM) and Chrysler. As the nation struggled to recover from World War II, Henry II hired a group of ten young former US Army Air Force officers to create a sophisticated management system including accounting and financial controls. The group eventually became known as the "Whiz Kids" and included financial disciplinarians J. Edward "Ed" Lundy, Arjay R. Miller, and Robert S. McNamara, who eventually became Secretary of Defense in the John F. Kennedy administration. The Whiz Kids are credited with bringing "quantitative analysis and the science of modern management to Ford Motor Company."[12] Under Henry II's leadership and with the help of the Whiz Kids, Ford recaptured the number two position in 1950.

In 1956, Ford Motor Company went public, offering 10.2 million shares of Ford stock for sale to the public in what was considered at the time the largest stock issue ever offered. Henry II retained his position as president and CEO and was instrumental in the establishment of Ford Motor Company of Europe in 1967 and the consolidation of its US, Canadian, and Mexican operations into its North American Automotive Operations in 1971 (more than 20 years prior to the North American Free Trade Agreement). He is credited with revitalizing Ford with modern engineering, manufacturing, assembly, and distribution facilities in the US and 22 foreign countries. Henry Ford II served as president from 1945 until 1960, CEO from 1945 until 1979, chairman of the board of directors from 1960 until 1980, and chairman of the finance committee from 1980 until his death in 1987.[13]

The 70s and early 80s were turbulent times in the US automotive industry. Gas prices quadrupled over the span of a few months in the early 70s when the Middle Eastern OPEC nations halted exports to the US and other western nations. Although the embargo lasted only a year, it created conservation awareness within US consumers. Vehicle manufacturers were required to increase the fuel efficiency of their products and the US Big Three automotive manufacturers (Ford, GM, and Chrysler), which manufactured larger, heavier, less fuel efficient vehicles, saw sales decline while sales of Japanese imports (Toyota, Honda, and Nissan), which met the new fuel efficiency standards, increased.[14] Ford responded in the 80s by cutting its workforce and closing plants.

Ford's rebound started with the 1988 introduction of the Ford Taurus and Mercury Sable, the popularity of which enabled Ford to increase its share of the US auto market to 22%—its largest in ten years. In the late 80s, Ford began to diversify its product offerings with the hope of expanding profits and worldwide sales by purchasing luxury European brands such as Aston Martin and Jaguar. In 1997, Ford began making a minibus line in China, beating General Motors in the race to produce vehicles for the Chinese market. In 1998, William Clay Ford, Jr. (Bill Ford), the great-grandson of company founder Henry Ford, became chairman of the board, and Jacques A. Nasser, with 31 years of experience with Ford, took over the CEO position in early 1999. Ford purchased the Swedish automaker Volvo in 1999 and formed the Premier Automotive Group (PAG) that would eventually include the European brands Aston Martin, Jaguar, Volvo, and Land Rover.[15]

In 2000, Ford spun off its automotive systems supplier Visteon (formerly Ford Automotive Products Operation) as an independent company and purchased Land Rover from BMW to increase its European presence. In July 2001, Nasser, who had acquired the nickname "Jacques the Knife" as a result of his cost cutting efforts including extensive cuts in personnel, resigned from the company. Bill Ford took over the CEO seat, marking the first time since the departure of Henry Ford II in 1979 that a Ford family member held the reins.[16]

Ford had not yet fully recovered from the extensive recall of Firestone tires (used as original equipment on Ford Explorers) that cost Ford approximately $2.1 billion to replace when September 11, 2001 arrived. The terrorist attacks on American soil extracted a heavy toll with Ford suffering net losses totaling $692 million. Also in 2001, Ford recalled approximately 300,000 cars, including the 1995-96 Ford Contour and Mercury Mystique sedans for possible fire danger from engine overheating problems. In August 2001, Ford announced it would eliminate 4,500 to 5,000 of its salaried employees (approximately 10 percent) using early retirement incentives and, shortly afterward, combined its car and truck engineering groups. In early 2002, Ford announced further cost-cutting measures, including the closure of three North American assembly plants, 35,000 worldwide job cuts (22,000 in North America), and the discontinuation of four vehicle models—Ford Escort, Mercury Villager, Mercury Cougar, and Lincoln Continental.[17]

According to the annual National Automobile Dealers Association (NADA) DATA report, US franchised new car and light truck dealers recorded their third strongest year on record in 2005, selling more than 16.94 million vehicles (up from 16.86 million in 2004). Sales were driven primarily by incentives including cash rebates, attractive financing rates, lease options, and enhanced dealership services. Light trucks outsold cars for the fifth consecutive year and represented 54.8 percent of total new vehicle sales in 2005. Large domestic sedans and crossover utility vehicles led the sales increases, which grew 31 percent and 14 percent, respectively. Small car sales were up by a mere 0.8 percent.[18] Although Ford reported earnings of $2 billion in 2005, this amount represented a 42 percent decline from its 2004 profit of $3.5 billion. It was the third straight year that Ford reported a profit; however, gains from international sales in Europe, Asia, and other areas were offset by a $1.6 billion loss in North American operations as the US auto industry went into decline[19] (see Exhibit 1 for Ford's historical income).

In January 2006, Ford announced plans to cut 25,000 to 30,000 hourly jobs, 12 percent of management positions, and close 14 facilities by 2012 as part of a massive restructuring plan (called "The Way Forward") designed to reverse the $1.6 billion loss. The cuts represented 20 to 25 percent of its 122,000 remaining North American workforce. Making the announcement, Bill Ford said, "These cuts are a painful last resort, and I'm deeply mindful of their impact. In the long run, we will create far more stable and secure jobs. We all have to change and we all have to sacrifice, but I believe this is the path to winning."[20] As anticipated, United Auto Workers president Ron Gettelfinger and vice president Gerald

Exhibit 1 Ford Motor Company Historical Income

Year	Revenue ($ M)	Net Income ($ M)	Net Profit Margin	Employees
Dec 2010	128,954	6,561	5.09%	164,000
Dec 2009	118,308	2,717	2.30%	198,000
Dec 2008	146,277	(14,672)	—	213,000
Dec 2007	172,455	(2,723)	—	246,000
Dec 2006	160,123	(12,613)	—	283,000
Dec 2005	177,089	2,275	1.28%	300,000
Dec 2004	171,652	3,487	2.03%	324,864
Dec 2003	164,196	759	0.46%	327,531
Dec 2002	163,420	22	0.01%	350,321
Dec 2001	162,412	(5,453)	—	354,431

Source: Data gathered from Hoover's Company Reports, The Ford Motor Company, www.hoovers.com and http://corporate.ford.com/investors/reports-financial-information/annual-reports

Bantom said the news was "extremely disappointing," and that Ford should focus on gaining market share instead of aligning production capacity with shrinking demand for the company's vehicles.[21]

Ford was not the only US automobile manufacturer experiencing difficulty in 2006. GM and Chrysler also faced decreasing product demand, increased competition from foreign manufacturers such as Toyota, Nissan, and Honda, and increased spending on high union wages, healthcare, and retiree benefits (known as "legacy costs") that their non-unionized foreign competitors did not have. With rising gas prices, demand shifted away from trucks and sport utility vehicles (SUVs) produced by US manufacturers to more fuel-efficient cars and car-based crossover vehicles, both strengths of Toyota and the other Asian competitors.[22] Toyota passed Ford in July 2006 to become the second largest auto company behind GM in the US in terms of vehicle sales, and Honda outsold Chrysler for the first time.[23]

Ford officials realized their business model was outdated and in September 2006, made announcements of further cuts, including an additional 10,000 white-collar jobs. The company would also offer early retirement and buyout packages to 75,000 hourly workers. The new cuts would reduce the total North American workforce approximately 29 percent from 130,000 to 92,000 by the end of 2008. Ford would also close two more plants, bringing the total to 16 since the January announcement, and cease production of minivans. The new goal was to cut $5 billion in annual operating costs in 2006 and introduce new products that would be more appealing to consumers on a faster production schedule. Mark Fields, Ford's president of the Americas, said, "We're dealing with the world as it is – not as it was ten years ago."[24] Ford's market share had declined steadily from about 26 percent in the early 90s, and it conceded in the announcement that it was ready to accept a smaller share of the market while focusing less on volume and more on profitable sales. With new products and quality improvements, Ford planned for a market share of 14 to 15 percent going forward. New CEO Alan Mulally, who had joined the company the week prior to the announcement, said, "The most important thing we do is to size our company and our capacity to the current demand and, on top of that, to continue to invest in the products and services—the cars and trucks—that the customers really, really want."[25]

While Bill Ford had led Ford Motor Company to three straight years of profitability, this period was followed by a sharp decrease in profits and a $1.44 billion loss in the first half of 2006.[26] This motivated him to remove himself from the CEO position and search for a new CEO from outside the industry.

In September 2006, Alan Mulally of Boeing Corporation was selected as the next CEO. Mulally demonstrated the leadership skills Henry Ford had established many years ago as critical to success and stood out as a qualified successor. Additionally, he came from a "metal-bending business . . . that is buffeted by global competition, has a unionized workforce, and is subject to complex regulation and rapidly changing technologies"[27] that was similar in many ways to auto manufacturing. Designing new airplane models takes years, so Mulally was aware it would take time to improve Ford's 2006 product lineup. The decision to hire Alan Mulally would be a major turning point in the history of Ford Motor Company.

While Ford posted a seemingly insurmountable loss of $12.6 billion in 2006, Mulally made a prophetic decision that would enable Ford to survive and remain independent during the worst new-vehicle market in almost 30 years. Although the US economy was healthy at the time, Ford raised $23.6 billion in loans by using many of its North American assets as collateral, including the Ford logo. According to Mulally, the money would provide Ford with a "cushion to protect for a recession or other unexpected event."[28]

Under Mulally, Ford expanded its plans to increase profitability by "improving its cost structure, introducing new products, strengthening its balance sheet, and operating as a single global team."[29] To focus on its core US brands, Ford began to divest the foreign brands in the PAG and eventually decreased its stake in Mazda to approximately three percent.[30] (Ford had held an ownership stake in Mazda since it purchased a 25 percent share in 1979.) Ford's emphasis on quality resulted in five segment winners in the 2007 Initial Quality Survey by J.D. Power and Associates—more than any other manufacturer that year. All operations were profitable in 2007, except North America, and Ford fell to the number three position in the US vehicle market for the first time since the Great Depression, behind GM and Toyota. Ford also reached an agreement with the United Auto Workers Union. The new four-year collective bargaining agreement contained provisions for reduced retiree healthcare costs, more competitive wages and benefits, and improved operational flexibility. Also in 2007, Ford appointed the auto industry's first senior executive dedicated to sustainability and formed the Transformation Advisory Council, a group of "nationally known thought leaders from outside Ford" to provide guidance about future technologies and global trends. This group would meet several times each year with Ford executives with the goal of making Ford a leader in sustainability.[31]

With the global economic downturn well underway, by the end of 2008, US auto sales had dropped 37 percent compared to 2007, amounting to approximately 400,000 fewer vehicles sold that year. Toyota had passed GM as the world's largest automaker in terms of vehicles sold. Suffering from the effects of the financial crisis and the global economic recession, Ford, GM, and Chrysler CEOs went to Washington, DC, to ask the US government for a $34 billion bailout. They argued that the effects of the auto industry were so far reaching that if their companies went out of business, at least three million layoffs would result within one year, sending the US economy even further into recession. At the time, the US auto industry employed approximately 850,000 workers in manufacturing and 1.8 million in dealerships.[32] Raw materials producers, parts manufacturers, and other suppliers would also be affected if the US automakers went bankrupt.

Many lawmakers were irritated with the CEOs because they had flown to Washington on private jets to request the bailout funds and were not prepared to discuss their plans for using the money thus, despite the grim picture the CEOs painted, the original request was rejected. The automakers were instructed to prepare and be ready to defend business plans proving that, upon receiving the bailout money, they would be able to generate positive cash flows, thus ensuring they could repay the government loans. The automakers drafted business plans and the CEOs returned to Washington—this time driving hybrid vehicles.[33]

In January 2009, the government used $24.9 of the $700 billion bailout fund (originally designated to buy mortgage-backed securities that were in danger of defaulting from banks) to bail out GM and Chrysler. In addition, the Presidential Task Force on the Auto Industry was formed to oversee the financial and operational restructuring of GM and Chrysler. Ford had asked for a $9 billion line of credit. Although Ford lost $14.7 billion in 2008 (the highest loss in its 105-year history), because of the decision to mortgage Ford's assets in 2006, ultimately, Ford did not need or receive any government bailout funds.[34] As there had been intense opposition by US taxpayers to the bailout of the automakers, Ford's exemption from the bailout caused its popularity among the American public to soar, winning new customers and improving its reputation.

Back on the car making side of business, Mulally's focus on product quality won accolades for Ford in March 2009 when *Consumer Reports* recommended 70 percent of Ford's vehicles, compared with only 19 percent of GM's and none of Chrysler's.[35] Ford reported a profit of $2.7 billion for 2009, its first in four years, after the record $14.7 billion loss in 2008 (see Exhibit 1). The profit was made possible in part by cost cuts and layoffs, to the extent that Ford's hourly workforce at the end of 2009 was less than half of what it had been five years before at the end of 2004. The company continued to produce new vehicles and market their fuel efficiency heavily.[36]

New vehicle sales in 2009 received support from the federal government when US President Barack Obama signed the "Cash for Clunkers" bill into law in June. The intent was to modernize America's vehicles on the road and "accelerate national economic recovery."[37] This program, officially named the Car Allowance Rebate System (CARS), offered $3,500 to $4,500 to people who traded in qualifying used vehicles for new ones with higher fuel efficiency and less harmful effects on the environment. The trade-ins had to be less than 25 years old with fuel economy of 18 miles per gallon or less and had to be sent to salvage. The Bush administration had introduced a similar program in 1992 as a "market-based approach to environmental policy."[38]

In 2010, US vehicle sales increased 11 percent. Ford passed Toyota to regain the number two position in terms of vehicles sold in the US with sales of 1.97 million vehicles, an increase of 17 percent from 2009. GM was first in terms of US vehicle sales, with 2.22 million vehicles sold. Toyota recalled more than 8 million vehicles worldwide in 2010 primarily due to unintended acceleration flaws. Its total number of vehicles sold in the US was 1.76 million.[39] Ford's total sales increased 15.2 percent despite the sale of Volvo to China's Zhejiang Geely Holding in March and the closure of the Mercury brand in the fall. Ford had originally paid $6.45 billion for Volvo in 1999, but sold it to Geely for $1.8 billion after struggling for years to make it profitable.[40]

For the first time since 1993, Ford's market share increased for the second consecutive year in 2010 and in February, Ford outsold GM for the first time in more than 50 years (with the exception of several months in 1998 when the GM workers were on strike).[41] At the end of 2010, Ford was the best-selling automaker in Canada for the first time in more than 50 years and sales increased by 32 percent in China and 168 percent in India.[42] Also in 2010, the Fusion became the first Ford sedan to sell more than 200,000 units in one year since 2004,[43] and global sales of the latest generation model Fiesta, available on five continents, surpassed one million.[44] In addition, the 2011 Fiesta became the first car in its segment (lower small market, or B-market, according to Ward's segmentation) to earn top crash-test ratings in all three of the world's largest auto markets that perform safety testing—the US, China, and Europe.[45] In 2010, Ford sold approximately 5,524,000 vehicles at wholesale throughout the world and had a net income of $6.6 billion.[46]

The summer of 2011 has been called the "best summer in years for Detroit carmakers" by *The Detroit News*. Ford, GM, and Chrysler claimed 50.1 percent of the US auto market in June. When a massive earthquake and tsunami hit Japan in March 2011, Japanese automakers and parts suppliers experienced major disruptions in their operations and announced that production would probably not reach normal levels until fall. Toyota,

Honda, and Nissan were all forced to stop production at some of their plants while damages were assessed, resulting in inventory and parts shortages during the first half of the year. In addition, the Detroit Three were producing vehicles that more closely matched consumer needs—vehicles that were smaller, more stylish, and more fuel-efficient. The Chevrolet Cruze became the best-selling car in the US in June, beating the Toyota Camry, Honda Civic, and Honda Accord. Chrysler's Jeep Grand Cherokee and Ford's new version of the Explorer (a more fuel-efficient crossover vehicle compared with the previous SUV version) were also successful. The popularity of these domestic products seemed to indicate that they had emerged from restructuring with some best-in-class vehicles.[47]

Today, Ford Motor Company operates in four business segments in the automotive sector: Ford North America, Ford South America, Ford Europe, and Ford Asia Pacific Africa. Ford's finance unit, Ford Motor Credit, is one of the leading automotive finance companies in the US. In 2011, Ford ranked tenth on *Fortune Magazine's* Fortune 500 list of America's largest companies, after capturing eighth place in 2010.[48]

Ford's accomplishments were made possible primarily through the vision and insight of its executive leadership team.

Strategic Leadership

When Bill Ford made the decision to step down as president and CEO of Ford in 2006, the company was facing recalls, global recessions, and high gas prices. Sales of trucks and SUVs had slowed, and consumers considered its lineup of cars old and stale. Bill Ford said, "We strayed from what got us to the top of the mountain, and it cost us greatly." He decided to ask for help from the board of directors. Ford said,

At the time, I was chairman, I was CEO, I was COO and I was president. I was wearing all the hats. And they said, 'Well, what do you need? Are you looking for a CEO or a COO?' I said, 'I really don't much care. What I want is the right person.[49]

Although Bill Ford determined that the right person was Alan Mulally, the reaction inside the company ranged from suspicion to outrage. Automotive companies frequently hired executives from each other, but the industry was resistant to outsiders, especially at the highest level. The management team was upset, especially those who would have liked to be considered for the position. When questioned about the decision, Bill Ford said that the company needed a fresh perspective. Ford knew that the company had a history of rejecting outsiders and was determined to provide all the assistance and

advice Mulally needed. In a meeting with Mulally prior to his acceptance of the CEO position, Ford told him that his biggest challenge would be breaking down silos, specifically the operating regions around the world that were more interested in defending their turf than working together.[50]

When Alan Mulally arrived at Ford, he discovered for himself that one of Ford's major problems was the lack of global synergy. All groups and brands were working independently as separate businesses. He was surprised that prior to his arrival the plan had been "to operate our eight Fords"[51] (one separate business for each of Ford's brands).

Mulally implemented weekly meetings with Ford's management team, during which each business head would present his results and forecasts. At the first meeting, Mulally was stunned by the lack of transparency within the company. "Why don't all the pieces add up for the total corporate financials?" he asked. One manager responded, "We don't share everything." He said that Ford executives ran their units without meshing with other divisions and sometimes held back information. The following week all executives brought complete figures. According to Mulally, "Data can set you free…You can't manage a secret."[52]

Ford's leadership team was reorganized in 2007, positions were streamlined, and some people were promoted to head unified global organizations. All product development operations worldwide would report to one person, Group Vice President of Global Product Development, Derrick Kuzak. Purchasing, manufacturing, quality, communications, and other functions were also given a global structure. James Farley, Jr. (a 22-year veteran of Toyota) became Group Vice President of Marketing and Communications (later renamed Global Marketing, Sales, and Service) and Sue Cischke was named Senior Vice President of Sustainability, Environment, and Safety Engineering.[53] Although the top management team has been restructured several times since 2007, these executives remain in their positions (see Exhibit 2 for a list of Ford's executive officers).

Alan Mulally

Alan Mulally was named CEO and president of Ford Motor Company in September 2006. He is also a member of the board of directors. Prior to joining Ford, Mulally was an executive vice president at Boeing as well as the president and CEO of Boeing Commercial Airlines. Mulally has received many accolades throughout his career and has been recognized numerous times for his contributions and industry leadership with awards including "Businessperson of the Year" by the readers of *Fortune* magazine, "Industry Leader of the Year" by *Automotive News*, one of "The World's Most

Exhibit 2 Ford Motor Company Executive Officer Group

William Clay Ford, Jr. Executive Chairman and Chairman of the Board	**Susan M. Cischke** Group Vice President – Sustainability, Environment and Safety Engineering	**J C Mays** Group Vice President and Chief Creative Officer – Design
Alan R. Mulally President and Chief Executive Officer	**James D. Farley, Jr.** Group Vice President – Global Marketing, Sales and Service	**Stephen T. Odell** Group Vice President, Chairman and Chief Executive Officer, Ford of Europe
Michael E. Bannister Executive Vice President – Chairman and Chief Executive Officer, Ford Motor Credit Company	**Felicia J. Fields** Group Vice President – Human Resources and Corporate Services	**Ziad S. Ojakli** Group Vice President – Government and Community Relations
Lewis W. K. Booth Executive Vice President and Chief Financial Officer	**Bennie W. Fowler** Group Vice President – Quality	**Robert L. Shanks** Vice President and Controller
Mark Fields Executive Vice President – President, The Americas	**Joseph R. Hinrichs** Group Vice President – President, Asia Pacific and Africa	**Nicholas J. Smither** Group Vice President – Information Technology
John Fleming Executive Vice President – Global Manufacturing and Labor Affairs	**Derrick M. Kuzak** Group Vice President – Global Product Development	
Tony Brown Group Vice President – Purchasing	**David G. Leitch** Group Vice President and General Counsel	

Source: The Ford Motor Company Annual Report 2010.

Influential People" by *TIME* magazine, "Chief Executive of the Year" by *Chief Executive* magazine, and one of "The Best Leaders" by *Business Week* magazine. He also received the Automotive Executive of the Year Award, the Edison Achievement Award, and was inducted into the Kansas Business Hall of Fame.[54]

In June 2011, Mulally was named "2011 Chief Executive of the Year" by *CEO Magazine*. According to James Turley, chairman and CEO of Ernst & Young and a member of the 2011 selection committee,

The foresight he showed throughout the process, the courage he showed in making some tough decisions on popular brands, the global mindset he showed and above all, the statesmanship he showed when two major competitors were on the public dole shows he was thinking for the good of the country as well as his company and industry.[55]

Previous winners include Bill Gates, Jack Welch, Michael Dell, and Herb Kelleher. Prior to his tenure at Ford, Mulally was perhaps best known for his efforts to streamline Boeing's production system and the associated transformation of the company's commercial aircraft product line.[56]

Today, Mulally is credited with not only turning around Boeing's commercial aircraft division, but also downsizing and restructuring Ford's global operation, revamping Ford's product lineup, unifying the branches of the organization under the ONE Ford plan, and restoring Ford Motor Company to profitability. His progress at Ford was described by Robert Djurovic, executive director of the Automotive Executive of the

Year Award program, when Mulally was presented with the award on April 13, 2011.

Alan Mulally shows such clear confidence in his company, its people, its products, and its brand. With his leadership and conviction, Ford Motor Company stood apart from its competitors by standing on its own two feet. And the US consumer—inspired by his quiet confidence and strong belief that Ford Motor Company could manage its own recovery without taxpayers' hard-earned dollars— got behind him, cheered him on, and bought Ford cars.[57]

William Clay Ford, Jr.

The current executive chairman of Ford Motor Company is William (Bill) Clay Ford, Jr. Bill Ford has been a member of the board since 1988, and was elected to the office of chairman on January 1, 1999. He is also the chair of the board's Finance Committee and a member of the Sustainability Committee (formerly the Environmental and Public Policy Committee). Bill Ford also served as CEO from October 2001 to September 2006. As CEO, Bill Ford led the company to three straight years of profitability, after experiencing a $5.5 billion loss in 2001, by focusing on improving quality, lowering costs, and delivering new products that satisfied customers.[58]

On his step back from CEO to executive chairman, Bill Ford said in an interview with journalist Keith Naughton of *Newsweek*, "I've always said that titles are not important to me. This company has been part of my life since the day I was born and will be until the day I die. What's important is getting this company headed in the right direction."[59] Bill Ford continues to work with Alan Mulally to focus on the future of Ford Motor Company and the strategies that will move it successfully into the future. He is quoted as saying, "The ongoing success of Ford Motor Company is my life's work. We want to have an even greater impact in our next 100 years than we did in our first 100."[60]

Board of Directors

Ford Motor Company's board of directors is comprised of 15 extremely diverse members representing different corporate and personal backgrounds, ranging from a professor of physics to individuals with careers in consulting, banking, and auditing. Three of the directors are members of the Ford family and six have served on the board of directors for more than ten years (see Exhibit 3 for a listing of board members). Despite the myriad of backgrounds presented in Ford's board of directors, past decisions have shown that the Ford family retains most of the decision-making power and influence, along with approximately 42 percent of the voting stock in the company.

To maintain profitability and competitiveness, Alan Mulally, Bill Ford, and the executive leadership team constantly monitor current and emerging trends in the US and international auto markets.

Trends in the US Auto Market

Dealership Consolidation

In 2005, the US auto market was saturated with dealerships and the demand for US-manufactured vehicles was declining rapidly. Ford consolidated dealerships and by the end of 2010, reduced the number of retail outlets from almost 4,400 to 3,424. GM and Chrysler reduced their dealer ranks by more than 2,200 dealers in bankruptcy reorganization. GM reduced its number of dealers from 5,969 before the 2009 bankruptcy to approximately 4,500, and Chrysler reduced its number of dealers by 789, from 3,100 to 2,311 in February 2011.[61]

Most of Ford's cuts were from larger metropolitan markets and the elimination of the Mercury brand. Ford has indicated it may also eventually cut approximately 35 percent of its Lincoln dealerships. After a meeting with Lincoln dealers in October 2010, Mark Fields, Ford's president of the Americas, said, "In the top 130 markets, our vision is to substantially reduce the number of dealers to become competitive…We need to make sure our dealers are competitive in their throughput so they can provide the experience our customers expect."[62]

Customers

Auto manufacturers sell their cars to a distribution network of dealerships that then sell to fleet customers

Exhibit 3 Ford Motor Company Board of Directors*

Name	Title	Principal Occupation	Director Since
Stephen G. Butler	Director	Retired Chairman and CEO, KPMG, LLP	2004
Kimberly A. Casiano	Director	President, Kimberly Casiano & Associates, Inc.	2003
Anthony F. Earley, Jr.	Director	Chairman and CEO, DTE Energy	2009
Edsel B. Ford II	Director	Director and Consultant, Ford Motor Company	1988
William Clay Ford, Jr.	Chairman	Executive Chairman and Chairman of the Board of Directors, Ford Motor Company	1988
Richard A. Gephardt	Director	President and CEO, Gephardt Group	2009
James H. Hance, Jr.	Director	Senior Advisor to the Carlyle Group	2010
Irvine O. Hockaday, Jr.	Director	Retired President and CEO, Hallmark Cards, Inc.	1987
Richard A. Manoogian	Director	Chairman of the Board, Masco Corporation	2001
Ellen R. Marram	Director	President, The Barnegat Group, LLC	1988
Alan Mulally	Director	President and CEO, Ford Motor Company	2006
Homer A. Neal	Director	Director, ATLAS Project, Professor of Physics, Interim President Emeritus and VP for Research Emeritus, University of Michigan	1997
Gerald L. Shaheen	Director	Retired Group President, Caterpillar	2007
John L. Thornton	Director	Professor and Director, Global Leadership Program, Tsinghua University	1996
William Clay Ford	Director Emeritus	Director Emeritus, The Ford Motor Company	2001

Source: 2011, The Ford Motor Company Corporate Web site, http://corporate.ford.com

* Data compiled as of October, 2010.

(including commercial fleet customers), daily rental car companies, leasing companies, and governments, in addition to the general public. Almost all Ford vehicles and parts are marketed through independently owned dealerships.

Although the auto manufacturers sell to the dealerships, they must be aware of all the factors that can influence the decision to purchase a vehicle, including slowing economic growth (state of the economy), geopolitical events, the cost of purchasing and operating a vehicle, the availability and cost of credit, and fuel. Each manufacturer's share of the market is influenced by how its products are perceived by the customer in comparison to other manufacturers based on such factors as price, quality, styling, reliability, safety, fuel efficiency, effect on the environment (sustainability), functionality, and reputation.[63]

Today's consumers are more technology-savvy than ever before and with the vast amount of information available on the Internet they have access to an almost unlimited amount of information to compare products to determine the vehicles that meet their needs. Many well-informed consumers choose to shop and negotiate pricing between dealerships, while others prefer to not negotiate price at all, choosing instead to purchase vehicles from companies such as CarMax that sell used vehicles at fixed "no-haggle" prices.[64]

In the past, the car buying experience was considered unpleasant by many customers, particularly those who did not like to negotiate. Stereotypical salesmen used hard sell tactics and showed little consideration for customers. The main focus of many salesmen was to make the sale and earn their commission, with no thought given to creating a positive experience for the customer so s/he would return to the dealership for future purchases of vehicles and/or services. Because profit margins are generally larger on used vehicles and on the sales of products and services after the purchase of a new vehicle (such as maintenance and light repair, collision repair, vehicle accessories, and extended service contracts), the most successful dealerships strive for 100 percent service absorption. In this manner, income generated by the parts and service departments covers the operating expenses of the dealership, making income from the lower-margin sales of new vehicles pure profit.

Historically, US manufacturers paid little attention to customer feedback regarding their preferences on vehicle styles and features, and little attention to feedback from their dealers. Instead, a "push" system of distribution was used, in which a manufacturer's representative would call on dealers to determine what vehicles the dealerships would order. Frequently, dealers had to accept a number of vehicles that were not considered popular or desirable by their customers if they wanted to receive vehicles that were. Manufacturers produced the vehicles, then "pushed" the vehicles to the dealers who, in turn, "pushed" them to their customers.

As US manufacturers lost market share to their Asian competitors, they realized the need to revise their business plans to place a much higher priority on customer satisfaction, thus creating customers for life. Their production and distribution processes changed from "push" to "pull" and became driven by market forces such as customer demand and preferences.

Many of the new models target specific customer segments, such as the Ford Fiesta and Chevrolet Sonic minicar that target Generation Y buyers. The auto industry targets younger first-time buyers hoping to keep them as customers as they get older. In addition, according to TrueCar.com's lead analyst Jesse Toprak, "Generation Y buyers are very important to automakers because they help set trends, from popularizing social media sites such as Facebook or Twitter or technologies such as the iPhone and iPod."[65] In July 2011, TrueCar.com released study results indicating that while turning away from the larger manufacturers such as Toyota and Honda, younger buyers still prefer Asian brands to the US manufacturers. Scion was the number one preference, followed by Mitsubishi, Mazda, Nissan, Volkswagen, Kia, Hyundai, Honda, Toyota, and Subaru. The highest-ranking domestic manufacturer, Chrysler, didn't show up until number 12.[66]

Ford and its competitors are seeking to significantly increase their customer bases through international expansion.

Globalization

As the demand for vehicles fell in the US, automakers took steps to increase their presence in international markets, particularly emerging markets such as China and India. Vehicle sales in China rose 46 percent in 2009, ousting the US as the world's largest auto market. Sales of passenger cars, buses, and trucks rose to 13.6 million with Chinese auto sales expected to reach 35 million by 2020, according to J.D. Power and Associates.[67]

US automakers can enter international markets through joint ventures or partnerships with domestic companies, with these partners sometimes collaborating on other international projects as well. Partnerships and joint ventures can be beneficial as each partner can capitalize on the strengths of the other. Ford has participated in joint ventures with companies in China, Germany, Mexico, Taiwan, Turkey, and Vietnam, among others.[68] GM and its Chinese partner, Shanghai Automotive Industry Corporation (SAIC), have collaborated on a number of successful joint ventures in China and, in early 2011, announced plans to launch a vehicle designed to rival the Maruti Alto and other vehicles in

India.[69] The Maruti Alto has been one of India's largest selling cars with average monthly sales of approximately 30,000 vehicles. GM has been slow to enter the Indian market, and Tim Lee, GM international operations president, said that SAIC would play a "major role" in the development and launch of new products in India. "The frugal element (in vehicle design and production) is added by SAIC, while GM helps with its branding, distribution set-up, and existing products."[70] As the world's sixth-largest auto market, India is poised to increase its ranking to third-largest market after China and the US for vehicle sales by 2020 with expected sales of approximately 11 million.[71]

Ford currently has approximately three percent of the Indian market and, in June 2011, announced plans to launch eight new vehicles by 2015, with at least five to six small cars included. Ford also plans to expand its sales and service network to more than 200 outlets by the end of 2011, and plans to triple its number of dealerships by 2016. Ford has one manufacturing plant in India that produces the Ford Figo hatchback, and is in discussion with the Gujarat state government to establish a second plant.[72]

Ford has been slow to enter the Chinese market and currently has only a 2.6 percent market share. While Mulally's attention was focused on fixing Ford in the US, GM was working to gain a 10 percent share of the Chinese market. According to IHS Automotive analyst Michael Robinet, "Asia has been a sore point for Ford for years. GM had so much success in emerging Asia, and Ford was always following along like a baby brother."[73] In June 2011, Mulally announced a major global expansion plan that included spending $1.6 billion in China to build four factories, including an assembly plant and an engine factory in Chongqing. He also announced intentions to triple Ford's product lineup in China to 15 models by 2015. Ford is currently opening approximately two new showrooms per week, and plans to double its distribution network by 2016. Ford's success in China will depend on its new vehicle lineup with new models that share mechanical underpinnings (platforms) worldwide. By using a standardized platform, Ford should be able to reduce operating costs and Mulally believes Ford will be able to offer many models in China profitably for less than $14,500. Currently, approximately 70 percent of all models sold in China are at that price or lower.[74]

Despite these plans, auto sales in China have slowed and actually fell in April 2011. Even with its new models, Ford will still have gaps in its product lineup. It does not yet have a tiny car to compete with India's $2,500 Nano from Tata Motors and does not have a contender for China's fast-growing luxury car market. Lincoln is receiving a makeover but will not be ready for sale outside the US for several years. Even so, Chinese consumers have not been enthusiastic about GM's Cadillac brand, instead preferring Volkswagen's Audi and BMWs. Ford has had sluggish sales in other emerging markets as well, ranking number four in Brazil and number five in Russia, with less than half the sales of GM in each market.[75]

Mulally's new global expansion plan amounts to a 50 percent increase in global sales for Ford and, if successful, would mean that approximately half of Ford's revenues would come from international operations, up from approximately 20 percent currently. It is considered by many analysts to be very ambitious, even for Mulally. According to Jefferies analyst Peter Nesvold, "This is a very dramatic transformation. If they can pull this off, this is a new Ford."[76]

Sustainability

The increasing global focus on sustainability and need to develop alternative power sources for vehicles has significantly influenced the automotive industry and auto manufacturers' efforts to increase their share of both the global and domestic markets. The world population is rapidly increasing and with it, the demand for fuel, thus leading to higher gasoline prices and an increasing impact on the environment.

Ford has produced an annual Sustainability Report since 1999 to offer the public a comprehensive view of the company's progress on environmental, economic, and social issues such as improving fuel economy and safety, decreasing greenhouse gas emissions and water use, and operational sustainability.[77]

Electric/gasoline-powered hybrid vehicles are the most widely used alternative power vehicles today, and several companies offer fully electric vehicles as well. The Chevrolet Volt, *Motor Trend's* 2011 Car of the Year, is an electric car that can use gasoline to create its own electricity and extend its range. The battery is charged by plugging into a standard 120-volt household outlet.[78] The Volt competes with the Nissan Leaf, a pure electric vehicle with a range of approximately 75 miles between charges. Many plug-in models are in the development process and will be available soon in the US from companies including Ford, Toyota, Honda, and Mitsubishi.[79]

One alternative fuel currently used by automakers is a biofuel, or "farm fuel," E85—a corn-based fuel composed of a blend of 85 percent ethanol (a form of alcohol) and 15 percent gasoline. E85 provides about 25 percent less energy than traditional gasoline, but advocates argue that it will reduce US dependence on foreign oil and develop a domestic industry that supports farmers.[80] Since it is plant based, it is a renewable energy source. However, opponents contend that large amounts of farmland and labor are required to make ethanol from corn, and using significant amounts for fuel could limit the amount available for food, thus driving up prices.

Hydrogen fuel cell vehicles (FCVs) are still in the early stages of development, but have the potential to reduce US dependence on foreign oil significantly and lower emissions that cause climate change. FCVs look like ordinary vehicles, but contain technologically advanced components such as a fuel cell stack that converts hydrogen gas stored onboard with oxygen from the air into electricity to run the electric motor that propels the vehicle. A storage tank stores hydrogen gas compressed at extremely high pressure to increase driving range and a power control unit governs the flow of electricity. FCVs emit only heat and water (steam) from their tailpipes. Manufacturers are currently working to solve issues involving safe onboard hydrogen storage, high vehicle cost, fuel cell durability and reliability, how to deliver hydrogen to consumers, and public acceptance of the dependability and safety of the vehicles.[81]

Rules and regulations on vehicle mileage and emissions standards are established by the federal government. Recently the Obama administration and the auto manufacturers were in negotiations over new standards that could reduce global warming emissions by millions of tons per year and decrease oil imports by billions of barrels during the life of the program. Proposed regulations would require new US cars and trucks to reach an average of as much as 56.2 miles per gallon by 2025 with increases in fuel efficiency of nearly five percent per year for cars from 2017 to 2025.[82] This would place US fuel efficiency at the same level as Europe, China, and Japan.

The automakers requested that the government phase in the standard gradually and wanted assurance that the government would help build the charging stations needed for electric and plug-in hybrid-electric vehicles. The manufacturers agreed that the standard could be achieved, but they expressed concern that US consumers would not accept the smaller, lighter, and, in some cases, more expensive vehicles. Gloria Bergquist, vice president for public affairs at the Alliance of Automobile Manufacturers (the leading industry lobby in Washington), said, "We can build these vehicles. The question is, will consumers buy them?" The manufacturers also warned that it would cost billions of dollars for development.[83] After talks with the automakers, the Obama administration eased the requirements to 54.5 mpg, with a 3.5 percent per year increase in fuel efficiency for light trucks through 2021, but kept the requirement for passenger cars at five percent. By July 28, 2011, Ford, GM, Chrysler, and Toyota had indicated they would support the proposal, but Mazda, Volkswagen AG, and Daimler AG indicated they would probably not, claiming that the guidelines gave unfair benefits to full-size pickup trucks, a staple

in the product lineup of the Detroit Three, and placed the major increases on passenger cars. The formal proposal is scheduled to be disclosed by September 30, 2011, and the final ruling should be made by the end of July 2012.[84]

Ford has already invested billions of dollars in the research and development of new fuel-efficient products in response to consumer demands. Currently, the company has 12 vehicles with best-in-class fuel economy and 4 models with at least 40 mpg.[85] According to the J.D. Power 2011 Automotive Performance, Execution, and Layout (APEAL) study, all of Ford's newer retail vehicles earned fuel efficiency ratings that were above their segment averages. Eight vehicles ranked in the top three in their respective segments, including the Fiesta, Explorer, and F-150 trucks. The F-150 is the only large pickup that received an award for both Initial Quality and APEAL in 2011.[86] The APEAL study is an annual survey that asks consumers to rate the performance, execution, and layout of their new vehicle after three months of ownership. Ford posted the highest scores of the Detroit automakers and outperformed Toyota and Honda as well. Lincoln scored higher than any other domestic luxury brand.[87]

US Auto Industry Competitive Market

Recovery from the global economic recession has been slow and in 2010, dealers faced challenges including low disposable income among consumers and the discontinuation of several brands including Mercury, Saturn, and Pontiac. This led to the closure of 760 franchised dealerships in 2010. In 2011, the earthquake in Japan disrupted production and rising gas prices again affected consumer demand. The demand for small cars and crossover vehicles rose, leading to an overall increase in new vehicle sales of 26.6 percent and 14.8 percent in used vehicle sales. One positive result of the Japanese earthquake was lower inventory of vehicles in dealerships, which meant it cost less for dealerships to finance their inventories. Paul Taylor, chief economist for the National Automobile Dealers Association, said,

Despite challenges such as higher gasoline prices and generally slow economic growth, dealers have managed to increase sales while keeping their expenses low. As production ramps up in July and lenders increase their loan volume, we can expect to see continued growth in both sales and profits.[88]

In June 2011, sales for the Detroit automakers increased their combined market share to just over 50 percent while leading Japanese manufacturers continued to report sales declines. Compared with March 2011 when the earthquake struck Japan, Nissan's US vehicle inventories were down 7.3 percent, Toyota's were down 39.5 percent, and Honda's were 47.2 percent lower, according to auto research firm Edmunds.com. While Nissan had larger US dealer inventories than its Japanese competitors, Toyota and Honda continued to work to restore production at their Japanese and overseas plants. They do not expect that US dealership inventory levels will return to normal until fall 2011.[89]

At the end of 2010, Ford had 16.7 percent of US sales, an increase from 15.5 percent of US sales in 2009 and 15 percent in 2008.[90] At the end of the second quarter 2011, Ford had 18.4 percent of the total US market, compared with GM (20.4 percent), Chrysler LLC (11.4 percent), Toyota (10.5 percent), Honda (8.0 percent), and Nissan (6.8 percent). Hyundai and Kia have also increased their presence in the US market with 5.6 percent and 4.3 percent of the US market, respectively[91] (see Exhibit 4).

Exhibit 4 Sales and Share of Total US Automotive Market by Manufacturer as of June 2011

	SALES			YTD SALES			% MARKET SHARE			
	June 2011	June 2010	% Chg	2011	2010	% Chg	June 2011	June 2010	YTD 2011	YTD 2010
General Motors	**215,335**	**194,716**	**10.6**	**1,261,610**	**1,076,993**	**17.1**	**20.4**	**19.8**	**19.9**	**19.2**
Total Cars	95,416	74,918	27.4	533,825	424,207	25.8	9.1	7.6	8.4	7.6
Total Light Trucks	119,919	119,798	0.1	727,785	652,786	11.5	11.4	12.2	11.5	11.6
Ford Motors	**193,415**	**170,695**	**13.3**	**1,069,736**	**953,146**	**12.2**	**18.4**	**17.4**	**16.9**	**17.0**
Total Cars	73,116	62,519	17.0	399,937	354,882	12.7	6.9	6.4	6.3	6.3
Total Light Trucks	120,299	108,176	11.2	669,799	598,264	12.0	11.4	11.0	10.6	10.7
Chrysler LLC	**120,394**	**92,482**	**30.2**	**639,932**	**527,219**	**21.4**	**11.4**	**9.4**	**10.1**	**9.4**
Total Cars	31,659	30,065	5.3	163,570	157,849	3.6	3.0	3.1	2.6	2.8
Total Light Trucks	88,735	62,417	42.2	476,362	369,370	29.0	8.4	6.3	7.5	6.6
Toyota USA	**110,937**	**140,604**	**−21.1**	**812,788**	**846,542**	**−4.0**	**10.5**	**14.3**	**12.8**	**15.1**
Total Cars	56,558	78,448	−27.9	443,550	472,214	−6.1	5.4	8.0	7.0	8.4
Total Light Trucks	54,379	62,156	−12.5	369,238	374,328	−1.4	5.2	6.3	5.8	6.7
American Honda	**83,892**	**106,627**	**−21.3**	**607,442**	**593,909**	**2.3**	**8.0**	**10.8**	**9.6**	**10.6**
Total Cars	44,261	62,229	−28.9	338,715	347,499	−2.5	4.2	6.3	5.3	6.2
Total Light Trucks	39,631	44,398	−10.7	268,727	246,410	9.1	3.8	4.5	4.2	4.4
Nissan NA	**71,941**	**64,570**	**11.4**	**504,973**	**440,332**	**14.7**	**6.8**	**6.6**	**8.0**	**7.8**
Total Cars	46,726	42,674	9.5	341,367	299,909	13.8	4.4	4.3	5.4	5.3
Total Light Trucks	25,215	21,896	15.2	163,606	140,423	16.5	2.4	2.2	2.6	2.5
Hyundai America	**59,209**	**51,205**	**15.6**	**322,797**	**255,782**	**26.2**	**5.6**	**5.2**	**5.1**	**4.6**
Total Cars	45,840	39,628	15.7	260,274	188,363	38.2	4.4	4.0	4.1	3.4
Total Light Trucks	13,369	11,577	15.5	62,523	67,419	−7.3	1.3	1.2	1.0	1.2
Mazda America	**19,307**	**18,238**	**5.9**	**122,379**	**115,719**	**5.8**	**1.8**	**1.9**	**1.9**	**2.1**
Total Cars	12,233	12,651	−3.3	78,120	78,417	−0.4	1.2	1.3	1.2	1.4
Total Light Trucks	7,074	5,587	26.6	44,259	37,302	18.7	0.7	0.6	0.7	0.7
Mitsubishi NA	**8,299**	**4,198**	**97.7**	**44,115**	**26,490**	**66.5**	**0.8**	**0.4**	**0.7**	**0.5**
Total Cars	4,367	3,099	40.9	26,042	18,243	42.8	0.4	0.3	0.4	0.3
Total Light Trucks	3,932	1,099	257.8	18,073	8,247	119.1	0.4	0.1	0.3	0.1
Kia America	**45,044**	**31,906**	**41.2**	**245,104**	**170,069**	**44.1**	**4.3**	**3.2**	**3.9**	**3.0**
Total Cars	28,558	16,793	70.1	146,561	91,884	59.5	2.7	1.7	2.3	1.6
Total Light Trucks	16,486	15,113	9.1	98,543	78,185	26.0	1.6	1.5	1.6	1.4
Subaru America	**19,794**	**21,601**	**−8.4**	**132,049**	**125,960**	**4.8**	**1.9**	**2.2**	**2.1**	**2.2**
Total Cars	14,148	13,819	2.4	93,633	81,714	14.6	1.3	1.4	1.5	1.5
Total Light Trucks	5,646	7,782	−27.4	38,416	44,246	−13.2	0.5	0.8	0.6	0.8

(Continued)

Exhibit 4 Sales and Share of Total US Automotive Market by Manufacturer as of June 2011 (*Continued*)

	SALES			YTD SALES			% MARKET SHARE			
	June 2011	June 2010	% Chg	2011	2010	% Chg	June 2011	June 2010	YTD 2011	YTD 2010
American Suzuki	2,278	2,035	11.9	13,402	11,549	16.0	0.2	0.2	0.2	0.2
Total Cars	552	718	−23.1	3,746	2,420	54.8	0.1	0.1	0.1	...
Total Light Trucks	1,726	1,317	31.1	9,656	9,129	5.8	0.2	0.1	0.2	0.2
Mercedes-Benz	22,563	18,997	18.8	118,021	106,972	10.3	2.1	1.9	1.9	1.9
Total Cars	12,845	13,022	−1.4	71,738	68,649	4.5	1.2	1.3	1.1	1.2
Total Light Trucks	9,718	5,975	62.6	46,283	38,323	20.8	0.9	0.6	0.7	0.7
Saab	323	216	49.5	3,436	1,346	155.3	...	...	0.1	...
Total Cars	323	209	54.5	3,436	1,259	172.9	...	...	0.1	...
Total Light Trucks	...	7	...	...	87	...	...	...	...	...
Volvo	7,100	4,995	42.1	36,303	28,206	28.7	0.7	0.5	0.6	0.5
Total Cars	4,202	2,412	74.2	21,178	14,848	42.6	0.4	0.2	0.3	0.3
Total Light Trucks	2,898	2,583	12.2	15,125	13,358	13.2	0.3	0.3	0.2	0.2
VW America	28,444	21,051	35.1	154,124	126,012	22.3	2.7	2.1	2.4	2.2
Total Cars	24,463	17,535	39.5	130,836	105,501	24.0	2.3	1.8	2.1	1.9
Total Light Trucks	3,981	3,516	13.2	23,288	20,511	13.5	0.4	0.4	0.4	0.4
Audi America	10,051	8,601	16.9	55,909	48,440	15.4	1.0	0.9	0.9	0.9
Total Cars	7,479	5,981	25.0	40,060	35,348	13.3	0.7	0.6	0.6	0.6
Total Light Trucks	2,572	2,620	−1.8	15,849	13,092	21.1	0.2	0.3	0.3	0.2
BMW NA	21,637	19,182	12.8	113,705	100,632	13.0	2.1	1.9	1.8	1.8
Total Cars	15,474	14,490	6.8	82,338	78,423	5.0	1.5	1.5	1.3	1.4
Total Light Trucks	6,163	4,692	31.4	31,367	22,209	41.2	0.6	0.5	0.5	0.4
Porsche NA	2,546	2,141	18.9	15,542	10,984	41.5	0.2	0.2	0.2	0.2
Total Cars	1,537	1,645	−6.6	8,665	8,379	3.4	0.1	0.2	0.1	0.1
Total Light Trucks	1,009	496	103.4	6,877	2,605	164.0	0.1	0.1	0.1	...
All Others	10,386	9,066	14.6	56,507	44,239	27.7	0.1	0.2	0.1	0.1
Total Cars	7234	5276	15.3	39215	29275	34.0				
Total Light Trucks	3152	2790	13.0	17292	14964	15.6				
TOTAL CAR	527,344	499,743	5.5	3,229,498	2,862,764	12.8	50.1	50.8	51.0	51.0
TOTAL TRUCK	525,904	483,995	8.7	3,103,068	2,751,258	12.8	49.9	49.2	49.0	49.0
TOTAL LIGHT VEHICLE SALES	1,053,248	983,738	7.1	6,332,566	5,614,022	12.8	100.0	100.0	100.0	100.0
Selling Days	26	25	...	152	151	...	...	...	...	...

Source: www.motorintelligence.com via The Wall Street Journal Market Data Center, Auto Sales, http://online.wsj.com

To keep increasing its market share, Ford must continue to monitor the actions of its competitors.

Chrysler Group LLC

In 1920, the Maxwell Motor Car Company went into receivership and former Buick president and General Motors vice president Walter Chrysler was hired to reorganize the company. He became president in 1923 and took over the company in 1925, renaming it after himself. Chrysler became known as one of the US Big Three automakers, surpassing Ford as number two in 1933, but slipping back to third place by 1950. During the OPEC embargo in the 70s, Chrysler continued to make large cars in spite of quadrupled gas prices, giving little attention to changes in consumer demand. Faced with bankruptcy, $1.5 billion in federal loan guarantees were obtained from the federal government and in 1978, Lee Iacocca, a former president of Ford, joined the company as CEO. By 1983 and seven years ahead of schedule, Chrysler had repaid all guaranteed loans and in 1984, Chrysler introduced the first minivan. During an economic downturn in 1992, Iacocca resigned. In 1998, Daimler-Benz acquired Chrysler for an estimated $37 billion in, what was at the time, the largest takeover of a

US firm by a foreign buyer. It spent the next eight years as part of the DaimlerChrysler organization.[92]

At year-end 2006, DaimlerChrysler employed approximately 360,000 people and sold almost 4.7 million vehicles (both passenger and commercial) to consumers in 200 different countries.[93] Similar to the financial struggles experienced by Ford and GM, DaimlerChrysler announced a $1.2 billion loss in 2006, a 9 percent decrease in sales, and a 0.5 percent decrease in market share to 13.5 percent.[94] Ultimately, the merger had not proven to be beneficial for Daimler and, in August 2007, the majority interest of Chrysler was divested to a private equity group, Cerberus Capital Management, for $7.4 billion. Former Home Depot executive Robert Nardelli became CEO and Thomas LaSorda was named vice chairman and president.

As the global economic recession and financial crisis accelerated in 2008, Chrysler implemented cost-cutting measures such as reducing the number of dealerships through consolidation, requesting a five percent cost reduction from non-production parts suppliers, and spinning off its Walter P. Chrysler Museum into a not-for-profit organization. In 2009, Chrysler went through Chapter 11 bankruptcy reorganization and continued to operate with loans from the federal government. On May 14, 2009, Chrysler terminated franchise agreements with 789 dealerships (approximately 25 percent of Chrysler's dealer network) to lower distribution costs and increase profitability of its remaining dealers.[95]

In June 2009, Chrysler entered a partnership giving Fiat, S.p.A. a 20 percent stake in Chrysler as it emerged from bankruptcy. Fiat's Sergio Marchionne became CEO and C. Robert Kidder became chairman of the board of directors. In 2010, Chrysler posted net revenues of $41.9 billion and launched 16 all new or "significantly refreshed" vehicles. US vehicle sales rose 17 percent compared with 2009 and market share improved from 8.8 percent to 9.2 percent.[96] By April 2011, Fiat had increased its stake to 30 percent, and on May 19, 2011, Chrysler announced a $7.5 billion refinancing plan that included paying off the US government loans and a further increase of Fiat's stake in Chrysler.[97]

By the end of July 2011, Fiat owned a controlling stake of 53.5 percent of Chrysler. Fiat's stake is expected to increase to 58.5 percent later in 2011, and Marchionne has indicated that he intends to raise it even higher.[98] Joe Phillippi of AutoTrends Consulting Inc., said, "This is going to be one company one way or another, so it makes sense to announce these changes now. People need to know who is in charge."[99] In early July, Marchionne told reporters in Zurich, "We'll be a single company in terms of leadership pretty quickly."[100] Then, on July 28, Marchionne announced the new structure and management team. Marchionne,

CEO of both Fiat S.p.A and Chrysler Group LLC, will remain in charge of both automakers in North America under a new Group Executive Council. The council will be responsible for running both day-to-day business and establishing a unified strategy for both Fiat and Chrysler. In addition to Marchionne, the council includes 16 executives from Fiat and six from Chrysler. Marchionne stated, "We have now reached the right moment to step on the accelerator of the Fiat-Chrysler integration. We recognize in these leaders the future of Fiat-Chrysler as an efficient, multi-national competitor in a global automotive marketplace."[101]

Fiat provided technology, platforms, and power trains for smaller and mid-size cars that Chrysler needed. Today Chrysler products include the Chrysler, Jeep, Dodge, and Ram brand vehicles, along with MoPar parts and accessories. Chrysler products are sold in more than 120 countries worldwide. It also manufactures and sells the Fiat 500 in North America.[102]

In line with its competitors, Chrysler has also invested in the development of more fuel-efficient technologies and has focused its efforts on reducing fuel consumption and emissions, vehicle energy demand, engines, transmissions, axles, and alternatively fueled powertrains including flex-fuel, compressed natural gas, hybrid, and fully electric vehicles. In 2010, Chrysler introduced the Pentastar V-6 engine designed to increase fuel efficiency by seven percent over previous engines. A small, fuel-efficient engine from Fiat was introduced with the December 2010 production launch of the Fiat 500: a 1.4 liter four-cylinder Fiat Fully Integrated Robotized Engine (FIRE) that incorporates Fiat's MultiAir technology. This engine will provide an up to 7.5 percent improvement in fuel economy and CO_2 emissions, while enhancing vehicle performance. The MultiAir technology will be adapted for use in future Chrysler engines, and a fully electric version of the Fiat 500 is slated for introduction to the US market in 2012.[103]

General Motors

Believing that manufacturers could benefit if they joined together, William Durant, who had purchased the failing Buick Motors in 1904, founded General Motors 1908. He bought 17 additional companies including Oldsmobile, Cadillac, and Pontiac by 1910, and formed a company with racecar driver Louis Chevrolet in 1915.[104]

Alfred Sloan, president of GM from 1923 to 1937, is credited with building GM into a corporate behemoth. Unlike Ford, which at the time offered cars only in black, GM offered a range of models and colors and by 1927, was established as the industry leader. GM continued to prosper until the Japanese automakers entered the market in the 70s. In 1984, GM established a joint venture with Toyota forming the New United Motor Manufacturing

Inc. (NUMMI) to explore whether Toyota's manufacturing processes would be successful in the US and, in 1990, launched the Saturn brand.[105] In 1999, GM spun off its auto parts manufacturing company, Delphi, and in 2000, company president Rick Wagoner took over as CEO. Despite workforce reductions since 2000 of over 40 percent, on November 21, 2005, GM announced plant closings and additional workforce reductions that would result in an annual reduction of expenses of $7 billion and a 30 percent reduction in capacity.[106]

In 2007, fighting for healthcare for retirees, the UAW called for a strike against GM. This was the first nationwide strike against GM in more than 35 years. The strike lasted two days and resulted in a deal that created a $50 billion independent health care trust (with GM providing most of the funding). Later in 2007, GM reported an annual loss of $38.7 billion, the largest annual loss in the history of the automotive industry. The company then offered buyouts to as many as 74,000 hourly workers in the US with approximately 35,000 workers accepting the buyout terms (about one-third of GM's hourly workforce). In addition, GM cut seven percent (approximately 25,000 jobs) of its white-collar workers.[107]

GM lost approximately $32 billion in 2008 and by the time it returned to Washington in 2009 to present its business plan, GM reported that it might not have enough funds to survive another month without government assistance.[108]

In mid-2009, GM ended its brief government-supervised bankruptcy reorganization and emerged from Chapter 11 with fewer brands, less debt, and fewer operating costs. The US government owned approximately 60 percent of GM at that time. GM withdrew from the NUMMI joint venture with Toyota and continued to divest brands. Saturn was discontinued after a plan to sell it to Penske Automotive Group failed.[109]

In November 2010, GM raised $20.1 billion in the biggest initial public offering (IPO) in US history. Shares were priced at the top of the proposed range as a result of investor demand, which indicated an increase in investor confidence that GM would be able to move beyond its taxpayer-funded bankruptcy.[110] The US Treasury sold 358 million shares to reduce its ownership in GM to slightly less than 37 percent of the company.[111] By July 2011, the US government still owned approximately 26 percent of GM but had managed to recover $23.1 billion of the $49.5 billion in bailout funds that GM had received.[112]

GM currently employs approximately 209,000 people and manufactures its cars and trucks in 31 countries.[113] Its annual sales in 2010 amounted to $135 billion.[114] By mid 2011, GM and its strategic partners produced, sold, and serviced the Buick, Cadillac, Chevrolet (Chevy), GMC, Daewoo, Holden, Isuzu, Jiefang, Opel, Vauxhall, and Wuling brands. Its largest national market was China, followed by the US, Brazil, the United Kingdom, Germany, Canada, and Russia.[115]

GM manufactures the Chevrolet Volt, an "all-electrically driven" vehicle with a range of up to 379 miles. The Volt is powered by the Voltec propulsion system consisting of a 16-kWh lithium-ion battery pack and electric drive unit that gives the Volt a pure electric range between 25 and 50 miles. Its four-cylinder 1.4 L gasoline-powered engine extends the range of the vehicle an additional 344 miles on a full tank of fuel. The engine operates the vehicle's electric drive system until it can be plugged in and recharged or refueled. Electric-only vehicles, unlike the Volt, can't be operated when recharging.[116] GM also offers five hybrid vehicles: Chevrolet Tahoe, Chevrolet Silverado, GMC Yukon, GMC Sierra, and Cadillac Escalade. Seventeen vehicle models from all four US brands can run on E85 (a fuel blend of 85 percent ethanol and 15 percent gasoline), and hydrogen fuel cell vehicles are being tested.[117]

GM won accolades in 2011 when the Chevy Cruze compact model became the best-selling passenger car in the US in June, surpassing traditional leaders Toyota Camry and Honda Civic. This was the first time in years that a US manufacturer won top honor in the passenger car category. The Cruze was the third best-selling vehicle overall, behind Ford's F-Series and Chevy Silverado trucks. Although the Japanese manufacturers were still suffering from the effects of the massive earthquake and tsunami in March, this indicates that GM is making significant progress with the design of its small cars. Alan Batey, US vice president of Chevrolet Sales and Service, remarked, "Chevrolet's investment in advanced engine technology is reflected in the increased popularity of our four-cylinder models. These technologies offer the performance and refinement drivers expect from Chevy in smaller engines that deliver the fuel efficiency they want."[118]

Toyota

Japanese automaker Toyota Motor Company has made tremendous strides in increasing market share and sales volume in the North American automotive market since its first vehicle, the Toyopet Crown, was introduced. Although the Crown was underpowered for the US market, the Corona (1965) and Corolla (1968) models became highly popular. In 1989, the Lexus line was launched in the US. In 1997, the Prius—the first mass-produced hybrid (electric- and gas-powered) vehicle—was introduced. In 2008, worldwide Prius sales exceeded 1 million vehicles, and in 2010, exceeded 2 million.[119] The success of Toyota and the other Japanese manufacturers in the US led to the change in the "Big Three" moniker; Ford, GM, and Chrysler instead became the "Detroit Three."[120]

Although Toyota passed GM in 2008 to become the world's largest auto manufacturer, it also posted its first operating loss in more than 70 years in 2009, with global sales falling four percent.[121] Faced with the economic downturn and financial crisis, Toyota saw its revenue decrease approximately 20 percent in 2009 over 2008, but the declines lessened in 2010 with only a seven percent decrease in vehicle sales.[122]

Historically, Toyota's appeal has been based on its vehicle lineup, quality, safety ratings, and resale value. Toyota offers a diverse vehicle lineup that includes subcompacts, luxury, and sports vehicles, SUVs, trucks, minivans, and buses. Its vehicles are produced with either internal combustion engines or hybrid engines. Popular models include the Camry, Corolla, Land Cruiser, and luxury Lexus line.[123]

In late 2009 and 2010, Toyota faced record recalls for unintended acceleration problems in the Prius model. From fall 2009 through spring 2011, Toyota recalled nearly 10 million vehicles worldwide (approximately 5 million in the US) for defective gas pedals, faulty floor mats, flawed fuel pump wiring, and problems with braking software.[124] In June 2011, Toyota said it would recall 105,784 early model Prius cars to repair a fault with the steering and gearbox—52,000 of those units were in the US. On June 29, 2011, Toyota announced another recall of 45,500 Highlander Hybrids and 36,700 Lexus RX 400h SUVs in the US due to inadequately soldered transistors. The company also recalled 11,164 units in Japan and 15,000 in Europe.[125]

Toyota suffered another setback in 2009 when GM withdrew from their joint venture in California, NUMMI. NUMMI's California plant terminated almost 5,000 workers and was closed in spring 2010 with operations moved to plants in Canada and Texas. However, approximately one month later, Tesla, which manufactures luxury electric vehicles, purchased the NUMMI plant. At the closing of Tesla's IPO in mid-2010, Toyota invested $50 million in Tesla stock and the companies agreed to cooperate on the development of electric parts, production systems, and vehicles. They agreed on a new $60 million deal in fall 2010 and Tesla agreed to develop the power train for an electric version of Toyota's popular RAV4 SUV.[126]

Toyota's largest markets include North America (approximately 30 percent of sales), Europe, China, and Asia. Like its competitors, one of Toyota's major goals is to increase its presence in China.[127]

Additional Competitive Threats

Even though factors such as capital requirements, economies of scale, need for distribution channels, and threat of retaliation make it unlikely for a new entrant to emerge from within the US, history has shown that new entrants can succeed in the US market. Asian automakers such as Toyota and Honda successfully entered and established themselves as key players in the market. More recently, Kia and Hyundai have made significant progress in the US. Automakers already established in foreign countries have been able to gain a foothold by exporting to the US and targeting a niche market. Once they have established a reputation and distribution channels, they are then able to expand into the broader market. After reaching an economic scale, they typically establish production within the US. Chinese and Indian auto manufacturers will likely provide the next wave of foreign entrants into the US market.

Regardless of whether a company is an established auto manufacturer or new to the market, maintaining efficient supply chain operations and good relationships with suppliers is imperative to achieving success and profitability.

Suppliers

The auto industry obtains resources from a wide array of firms globally. Although the number of suppliers has dropped since the recession, some of the survivors are growing and beginning to diversify. Louis Green, president of the Michigan Minority Supplier Development Council, called the survivors "highly competitive." He also stated that the surviving suppliers' customers were sometimes surprised by how competitive they are. For example, SET Enterprises, Inc., a firm that processes steel, expects to generate revenues of $300 million in 2011, up from $222 million in 2010. Prior to the recession there were 1,600 companies affiliated with the Michigan Minority Supplier Development Council, but that number had fallen to 1,132 by spring 2011.[128]

Many suppliers rely heavily on the auto industry for a large percentage of their revenue. For example, Gentex Corp. supplies high-end rearview mirrors and realizes 98 percent of its sales from the auto industry.[129] Some of these suppliers went out of business during the economic downturn and decline of the US auto industry, and more were hurt by the March earthquake in Japan. Large diversified suppliers such as BASF and Dow Chemical supply plastics, foams, paint, and other basic materials to the auto industry as well as many other industries. Although these large suppliers are diversified with many products in many industries, the automotive industry is still a significant customer, especially for specific divisions within the large firms.

It is extremely important for auto manufacturers to develop and maintain strong relationships with their suppliers to gain access to their best technologies and receive priority order fulfillment in case of material or product shortages. According to Ford's purchasing chief, Tony Brown, the increased pressure on suppliers as Japanese manufacturers' rebound from the March earthquake will not have an impact on Ford's production. In an interview with *Automotive News*, Brown said that Ford has not deviated from its production plan established at the beginning of 2011—to produce 13 to 13.5 million units for the US market in 2011 and 14 to 14.5 million units for the European market. Under Ford's Executive Business and Technology Review (EBTR) program (developed in 2006), Ford senior purchasing leaders and their engineering counterparts meet regularly with key suppliers to share Ford's strategies in great detail. In prior years, Ford was among the last to be offered new technology and struggled to get new technology to the market—but this has changed under the EBTR program. For example, Ford was able to offer features on the Focus including self-parking technology and blind spot detection that were first-to-market features for the compact car segment[130] (see Exhibit 5 for segment volume information).

In 2005, Ford reduced its number of suppliers to create the Aligned Business Framework (ABF) and entered into long-term agreements with select strategic global suppliers. This diverse group of suppliers continues to play a key role in Ford's global sourcing plans, helping to improve Ford quality and lower development and production costs.[131] By 2011, Ford had 102 ABF suppliers including Robert Bosch LLC, Continental AG, Faurecia, GETRAG FORD Transmissions, Johnson Controls, Lear Corp, TRW Automotive, Tenneco, Ford's spun off parts supplier Visteon, and GM's spun off supplier Delphi.[132] Visteon's US operations filed for bankruptcy in 2009 and emerged from Chapter 11 protection in 2010. Although it is considered by analysts to be recovering, it is also considered a "takeover candidate" for another auto parts supplier wanting to increase its presence in Asia. Visteon owns a 50 percent stake in Yanfeng Visteon Automotive Trim Systems, a Chinese supplier of interiors and seating, and 70 percent of South Korean Halla Climate, a maker of vehicle air conditioning systems. In 2010, sales to Ford Motor Company accounted for 25 percent of Visteon's revenues.[133]

Delphi emerged from bankruptcy reorganization in 2009 as Delphi Electronics and Safety, operating under the umbrella of Delphi Automotive. Delphi, which introduced the in-dash car radio (1936), the AM/FM radio (1963), cruise control (1963), and production air bags (1973), celebrated its 75th anniversary in June 2011. With new products entering the market, company president Jeff Owens is optimistic about the future and expects that Delphi will produce more than 1 billion products by the end of 2019 and reach revenues of $6 billion by 2020.[134]

Ford's efficient management of its supply chain is an important part of its corporate strategy.

Exhibit 5 Vehicle Segment Totals Ranked by June 2011 US Unit Sales

	June 2011	% Chg from June' 10	YTD 2011	% Chg from YTD 2010
CARS	527,344	5.5	3,229,498	12.8
Midsize	251,987	3.2	1,565,058	11.0
Small	194,771	15.3	1,179,250	21.0
Luxury	73,854	−5.1	440,361	2.1
Large	6,732	−22.3	44,829	−4.7
LIGHT-DUTY TRUCKS	525,904	8.7	3,103,068	12.8
Pickup	150,783	9.2	825,730	10.8
Cross-over	200,206	4.0	1,268,119	9.5
Minivan	61,867	−0.7	362,432	9.5
Midsize SUV	62,220	41.9	364,367	46.6
Large SUV	18,751	−14.7	110,324	−8.7
Small SUV	19,579	31.9	102,014	23.3
Luxury SUV	12,498	20.0	70,082	6.7
Total SUV/Cross-over	313,254	10.4	1,914,906	14.3
Total SUV	113,048	24.1	646,787	24.9
Total Cross-over	200,206	4.0	1,268,119	9.5

Source: www.motorintelligence.com via The Wall Street Journal Market Data Center, Auto Sales, http://online.wsj.com

Corporate Strategy

When Alan Mulally took over as President and CEO of Ford, he was faced with nearly insurmountable management and operational problems resulting from the lack of both unity and communication within such a large global organization. On his first day at his new job, Mulally found an executive parking lot filled with Jaguars, Land Rovers, and Aston Martins. Mulally said, "There wasn't one Ford in the parking lot. I thought 'Oh-oh.'" The key issue was clear. If Ford executives wouldn't drive Fords, who would?[135] In response, Mulally developed the ONE Ford business transformation plan designed to create a leaner, more efficient global enterprise and return the company to profitability.

The ONE Ford plan focuses on four priorities that have remained virtually unchanged since the plan's original implementation in 2007:

1. Aggressively restructure to operate profitably at the current demand and the changing model mix.
2. Accelerate the development of high quality, fuel-efficient, safe new products that customers want and value.
3. Finance the plan and improve the balance sheet.
4. Work together as one team to leverage Ford's global assets.[136]

The ONE Ford plan enabled Alan Mulally to unite the numerous entities of the global organization and streamline operations. Ford has consolidated dealerships, closed plants, reduced its workforce, reduced its supplier base, sold or shut down unprofitable brands, cut its debt, developed products and technologies that consumers want and value, and recently announced an aggressive plan to increase its presence in global markets, particularly in India and China. Since its inception, all Ford employees have been given and are expected to carry a 2″ by 3″ laminated card with the description of the ONE Ford plan and its mission: "ONE Ford. ONE Team. ONE Plan. ONE Goal."[137] (see Exhibit 6 for a complete description of the ONE Ford mission).

According to Mulally,

We achieved great success as we rebuilt our company in extremely challenging economic conditions. Now we are eager to show the world what a revitalized Ford Motor Company can accomplish in a growing global economy. We are one team with one plan and one goal: to continue serving our global customers with a full family of best-in-class products and delivering profitable growth for all associated with Ford.[138]

Product Design, Research, and Development

When Alan Mulally became CEO of Ford in 2006, the company had 97 models. "It was absolutely clear that we had to simplify Ford dramatically," he stated.[139] Some models were eliminated by the sale of the PAG brands and the discontinuation of the Mercury brand, but in fall 2010, Mulally said that Ford would reduce its lineup even further to as few as 20 models. According to Mulally, "Fewer brands means you can put more focus into improving the quality of engineering."[140] Component specifications for each product were simplified and standardized to reduce costs and improve quality. For example, by fall 2010, the Fiesta model, with approximately ten variations worldwide, had standardized an average of 65 percent of its parts.[141]

Ford's current vehicle lineup includes cars, hybrids and electric vehicles, crossovers, SUVs, trucks, commercial trucks, and commercial vans. The Ford F-Series pickup truck was the best-selling truck in America in 2010 for the 34th year in a row and the best-selling vehicle (car or truck) for the 29th year in a row and continues to dominate its segment. The E-Series was America's best-selling full-size van for the 31st year in a row[142] (see Exhibit 7 for a list of the best-selling vehicles in June 2011).

Exhibit 6 One Ford

ONE FORD	
ONE TEAM • ONE PLAN • ONE GOAL	
ONE FORD: ONE Ford expands on the company's four-point business plan for achieving success globally. It encourages focus, teamwork, and a single global approach, aligning employee efforts toward a common definition of success and optimizing their collective strengths worldwide. The elements of ONE Ford are:	**ONE PLAN:** The company's four-point plan consists of balancing our cost structure with our revenue and market share; accelerating development of new vehicles that customers want and value; financing our plan and rebuilding our balance sheet; and working together to leverage our resources around the world.
ONE TEAM: ONE Ford emphasizes the importance of working together as one team to achieve automotive leadership, which is measured by the satisfaction of our customers, employees, and essential business partners, such as our dealers, investors, suppliers, unions/councils, and communities.	**ONE GOAL:** The goal of ONE Ford is to create an exciting and viable company with profitable growth for all.

Source: The Ford Motor Company Annual Report 2010.

Exhibit 7 Top 20 Vehicle Sales for June 2011

	Jun 2011	% Chg from Jun '10	YTD 2011	% Chg from YTD 2010
FORD F-SERIES PICK UP	49,618	6.7	264,079	9.9
Chevrolet Silverado PU	32,579	5.1	182,785	9.6
Chevrolet Cruze	24,896	n/a	122,972	n/a
Chevrolet Malibu	23,737	14.6	122,783	13.4
FORD ESCAPE	22,274	43.3	122,607	23.9
FORD FOCUS	21,385	41.2	98,024	9.2
Toyota Camry / Solara	21,375	−24.8	147,469	−4.4
Dodge Ram PU	21,362	34.7	111,898	31.8
FORD FUSION	20,808	13.0	131,686	18.4
Hyundai Elantra	19,992	40.3	103,301	79.5
Nissan Altima	19,534	22.7	131,842	17.6
Toyota Corolla / Matrix	18,872	−13.7	136,747	−2.7
Hyundai Sonata	18,644	4.9	115,014	28.9
Chevrolet Equinox	17,954	56.3	95,838	43.1
Honda Civic	17,485	−34.0	127,571	−4.5
Volkswagen Jetta	17,105	88.3	91,751	66.0
Chevrolet Impala	16,325	13.0	103,644	15.8
Honda Accord	15,712	−37.0	127,105	−13.9
Honda CR-V	15,493	−3.4	110,916	27.7
GMC Sierra PU	12,377	8.2	67,598	21.6

Source: www.motorintelligence.com via The Wall Street Journal Market Data Center, Auto Sales, http://online.wsj.com

Ford is "reenergizing" its Lincoln brand as a world-class luxury brand with compelling vehicles and consumer experience. Its current product lineup includes the Lincoln MKZ Hybrid—the most fuel-efficient luxury sedan in the US with an EPA-certified 41 mpg city rating. Ford will introduce an additional seven all-new or refreshed vehicles within the next three years.[143]

Ford launched 24 new or redesigned vehicles in 2010 in key markets around the world, including the redesigned Ford Explorer, Ford Edge, and Lincoln MKX, and all-new Ford Fiesta in North America; a redesigned Ford C-MAX and new Ford Grand C-MAX in Europe; and the new Ford Figo in India. The introduction of new products continued in 2011 with the launch of the new global Ford Focus in North America, Europe, and Asia Pacific Africa. The Ford Focus Electric is scheduled for launch later in 2011 and the new global Ford Ranger small pickup truck is scheduled for introduction in 2011 in Asia Pacific Africa and Europe.[144]

Ford has invested $135 million within the past year to design, engineer, and manufacture key components for its hybrid, plug-in hybrid, and battery electric vehicles. This investment brought battery and hybrid transmission production in-house and created more than 220 jobs in Michigan. By spring 2012, Ford anticipates it will be manufacturing more hybrid transmissions in North America than any other auto manufacturer or supplier. The new transmission will replace a unit currently made in Japan and used in Ford and Lincoln hybrid vehicles and will provide improved performance over the Japanese manufactured unit.[145]

In July 2011, Ford signed an agreement with Azure Dynamics Corp. to install plug-in hybrid powertrains in the F-Series Super Duty trucks. The F-350, F-450, and F-550 trucks will be retrofitted with Azure's hybrid-electric drive trains beginning with the F-550 in early 2013. The F-Series Super Duty represents approximately half of the 100,000 commercial cabs and chassis produced and sold in the US annually. Ford partnered with Azure previously to manufacture the Transit Connect Electric and the 450 Balance Hybrid Electric Step Van and Shuttle Bus.[146]

Ford is also preparing a 1.0-liter, three-cylinder EcoBoost engine touted to be the smallest engine Ford has ever built. (Ford's EcoBoost engines are gasoline engines that can deliver up to 20 percent better fuel economy and up to 15 percent fewer CO_2 emissions by combining direct fuel injection and turbo charging.) Ford claims it will offer output comparable to a normally aspirated 1.6-liter four-cylinder engine and will be available globally in Ford's smaller cars. A specific timeline has not been announced, but a 2012 or 2013 launch is rumored.[147] Ford will also add an in-house designed eight-speed automatic transmission. This will allow Ford to keep pace with premium carmakers such as Mercedes-Benz and BMW. According to Ford's vice president of Global Product Development Derrick Kuzak, "Today, we have the freshest powertrain lineup in the industry. And there is plenty more coming."[148]

In spring 2011, Ford made a 3.5-liter direct-injection turbocharged EcoBoost V6 engine available in its popular F-150 series trucks and, for the first time since 1985, F-150 pickups with V6 engines (including both naturally aspirated and EcoBoost V6 engines) outsold those with V8 engines. Consumer demand has been so great that production has not been able to keep up and Ford's two engine plants in Ohio were put on overtime production to fulfill demand.[149]

Ford introduced Transit Connect commercial vans, a highly popular series in Europe, to fleet customers in 2009. The Transit Connect vans are powered by lithium ion batteries and in July 2011, New York City joined Boston, Chicago, and Philadelphia on the list of major cities that have approved the Transit Connect Taxi for use. According to Mark Fields, Ford president of The Americas,

For decades, Ford has been synonymous with New York City taxis, and we are pleased residents and tourists now will benefit from our next-generation vehicle. We have Transit Connect Taxis in service across the country, and people tell us they love its spaciousness and its fuel efficiency.[150]

Ford has also invested heavily in the development of premium technology to better serve its customers. Ford Work Solutions is a collection of affordable technologies that provide connectivity, flexibility, visibility, and security for truck and van customers. It features an in-dash computer that provides high-speed internet access and wireless accessories including a printer, Tool Link (an asset tracking system for customers to maintain real-time inventory of tools and equipment in the vehicle), Crew Chief (a telematics and diagnostics system to inform fleet managers of their fleets' locations and maintenance needs), and Cable Lock (a security system to secure large tools or equipment in the cargo area).[151]

SYNC—an integrated communication and entertainment system that allows voice-activated control—was introduced in 2007. SYNC with MyFord Touch combines SYNC connectivity with over 10,000 first-level voice commands, a full-color eight-inch touch screen, and two 4.2 inch LCD screens that make vehicle functions, settings, and information easily accessible through voice commands, steering wheel controls, or a tap of the touch screen. Additional products include SYNC AppLink, SYNC with Traffic, Directions and Information, SYNC 911 Assist, SYNC Destinations, and SYNC Wi-Fi Mobile Hot Spot.[152]

Ford also continues to focus on safety innovations such as inflatable seat belts and Curve Control—technology that rapidly reduces engine torque and applies four-wheel braking to slow the vehicle by up to 10 mph per second when it senses a driver is entering a curve too quickly—both of which were introduced on the new 2011 Explorer. Curve Control is standard on the 2011 Explorer and will be available on 90 percent of Ford's North American crossovers, SUVs, trucks, and vans by 2015.[153] Additional global driver-assist features include the Blind Spot Information System, Active Park Assist, and Adaptive Cruise Control. The next suite of new safety features and driver assistance technologies are currently offered in Europe. These features include Speed Limiter, Torque Vectoring Control, Lane Departure Warning, Lane Keeping Aid, Active City Stop, Traffic Sign Recognition System, Driver Alert, All-Seat Beltminder, and Power Child Locks.[154]

Ford is in the process of developing "intelligent vehicle technology" that will allow vehicles to communicate with each other through Wi-Fi to reduce accidents and traffic congestion. These research and development efforts were highlighted at the "Forward with Ford" event held in June 2011, a conference exploring the linkage of Ford vehicles and technologies to global consumer trends. According to a National Highway Traffic Safety Administration (NHTSA) analysis in 2010, such vehicle-to-vehicle systems could potentially affect 79 percent of all vehicle target crashes, 81 percent of all light-vehicle target crashes, and 71 percent of all heavy-truck target crashes each year.[155]

To generate public interest and awareness of its innovative products and features, Ford continually updates its marketing strategies.

Branding and Marketing Strategies

Under Mulally's guidance, Ford sold the PAG brands (Aston Martin in 2007, Jaguar and Land Rover in 2008, and Volvo in 2010) and reduced its ownership share in Mazda. In 2010, it discontinued the Mercury brand

and gave dealers permission to sell their remaining new Mercury vehicles under the used vehicle category. Currently, Ford is focused on building its two remaining brands—Ford and Lincoln. Historically, the Ford brand included light trucks and cars targeted at the more price-conscious consumers; Lincoln targeted higher-end consumers and the defunct Mercury brand aimed to fill the gap between the upper-end Lincoln and the lower-end Ford. However, the Ford brand now offers a product mix that appeals to both the price-conscious and middle market consumers, thus eliminating the need for Mercury.

In recent years, Ford has been very successful in its marketing and advertising efforts. It has "leveraged the 'digital' mindset of today's consumers" and capitalized on a renewed sense of patriotism and national pride.[156] The company reaches consumers through traditional venues such as newspaper, radio, and television advertising, as well as through social media venues including Facebook, Twitter, LinkedIn, and YouTube. Ford also sponsors the popular television reality show American Idol, and is a title sponsor of the "World's Toughest Endurance Event"—the Ironman Triathlon series leading to the Ford Ironman World Championship.[157]

Ford builds rapport with consumers through authenticity in its communications. Ford's Swap Your Ride campaign took place recently in 2010 and 2011. Although the offer did not extend to Ford's higher-end offerings (hybrid vehicles or the Shelby GT500, for example), consumers were given the opportunity to exchange their competitive-make vehicles for a new Ford to drive for one week. According to Nielsen Automotive statistics, Swap Your Ride ads were 48 percent more memorable than ads for average sales events.[158] Candid feedback from consumers who participated in the Swap Your Ride event was then included in Ford's media advertising. According to Matt VanDyke, Ford's director of US Marketing Communications,

We've found that challenging people's perceptions head-on is the best way to change their minds about Ford. We're tapping real people, allowing them to experience our vehicles for themselves and then capturing their enthusiasm for the products. We're telling the Ford story through the eyes of the people who matter most – real consumers.[159]

Thanks to Ford's innovative product designs, technology, and performance, "It's very cool to see people react the way they do," VanDyke added, "When they get into a Ford for the first time, they're really surprised with the fuel efficiency, performance, and great technology. That's been a consistent reaction to our entire lineup."[160]

Ford recently announced it would venture into racing education for motorsports, a move designed to attract the millennial demographic (18 to 29 year olds). The Octane Academy will be led by Ford motorsport superstars Ken Block, Brian Deegan, Tanner Foust, and Vaughn Gittin, Jr. Each will take a turn hosting one of four "action sports fantasy camps" and will help design the courses. The first class is scheduled to begin in November 2011 and will be taught by off-road truck racer Deegan. The Octane Academy is only offered to those in the millennial age group and the vehicles used will all be Fords. Each four-day camp will end with a competition with the winner receiving a Ford vehicle specially designed by Block, Deegan, Foust, and Gittin.[161]

Ford connects with teenage drivers and their parents by offering the Driving Skills for Life program—a program designed to encourage teens to learn driving skills and techniques that will make them safer, more competent drivers. Driving Skills for Life was established in 2003 by Ford along with the Governors Highway Safety Association and a panel of safety experts. The program includes an interactive online learning experience, video and educational curriculum, and hands-on safe driving demonstrations held across the country. Driving Skills for Life focuses on four key skills believed by safety experts to be significant in preventing crashes, injuries, and fatalities: hazard recognition, vehicle handling, space management, and speed management. Ford's team of professional instructors offer ride-and-drive events for schools across the US where teens are allowed to drive modified Ford vehicles, specially designed to simulate road hazards and hazardous driving conditions, with professional drivers at their sides.[162]

Under Alan Mulally's leadership, Ford has developed a highly competitive product line with a positive brand image. Its desirable products and successful marketing strategies have contributed to its success in the highly competitive auto industry.

The success of Ford's corporate strategy is evident by its financial results.

Financial Condition

In 2010, Ford had an annual net income of $6.6 billion, an increase of $3.8 billion over 2009. Every region was profitable, led by a strong performance in North America. Ford was also able to reduce its debt by 43 percent, or $14.5 billion. In March 2011, Ford reduced its automotive debt by another $3 billion[163] (see Exhibits 8 and 9 for Ford's fiscal year 2010 financial information).

Ford reported strong progress in the first quarter of 2011, with net income of $2.6 billion, a $466 million increase over the first quarter of 2010. Total company

Exhibit 8 Ford Motor Company Selected Financial Data

On January 1, 2010, we adopted the new accounting standard regarding consolidation of VIEs. We have applied the standard retrospectively to periods covered in this Report, and present prior-year financial statement data on a basis that is revised for the application of this standard. The following table sets forth selected financial data for each of the last five years (dollar amounts in millions, except for per share amounts).

SUMMARY OF OPERATIONS	2010	2009	2008	2007	2006
Total Company					
Sales and revenues	$ 128,954	$ 116,283	$ 143,584	$ 168,884	$ 156,711
Income/(Loss) before income taxes	$ 7,149	$ 2,600	$ (14,805)	$ (4,286)	$ (15,400)
Provision for/(Benefit from) income taxes	592	(113)	(62)	(1,467)	(2,880)
Income/(Loss) from continuing operations	6,557	2,712	(14,833)	(2,819)	(12,610)
Income/(Loss) from discontinued operations	—	5	9	41	16
Income/(Loss) before cumulative effects of changes in accounting principles	6,557	2,717	(14,824)	(2,778)	(12,594)
Cumulative effects of changes in accounting principles	—	—	—	—	(7)
Net income/(loss)	6,557	2,717	(14,824)	(2,778)	(12,601)
Less: Income/(Loss) attributable to noncontrolling interests	(4)	—	(58)	17	16
Net income/(Loss) attributable to Ford Motor Company	$ 6, 561	$ 2,717	$ (14,766)	$ (2,795)	$ (12,617)
Automotive Sector					
Sales	$ 119,280	$ 103,868	$ 127,635	$ 152,691	$ 141,727
Operating income (loss)	5,789	(3.352)	(9,976)	(4,979)	(18.518)
Income/(Loss) before income taxes	4,146	785	(12,314)	(5,510)	(17,456)
Financial Services Sector					
Revenues	$ 9,674	$ 12,415	$ 15,949	$ 16,193	$ 14,984
Income/(Loss) before income taxes	3,003	1,814	(2,581)	1,224	1,966
Amounts Per Share Attributable to Ford Motor Company Common and Class B Stock Basic:					
Income/(Loss) from continuing operations	$ 1.90	$ 0.91	$ (6.50)	$ (1.43)	$ (6.73)
Income/(Loss) from discontinued operations	—	—	—	0.02	0.01
Cumulative effects of change in accounting principles	—	—	—	—	—
Net income/(loss)	$ 190	$ 0.91	$ (6.50)	$ (1.41)	$ (6.72)
Diluted:					
Income/(Loss) from continuing operations	$ 1.66	$ 0.86	$ (6.50)	$ (1.43)	$ (6.73)
Income/(Loss) from discontinued operations	—	—	—	0.02	0.01
Cumulative effects of change in accounting principles	—	—	—	—	—
Net income/(loss)	$ 1,66	$ 0.86	$ (6.50)	$ (1.41)	$ (6.72)
Cash dividends	$ —	$ —	$ —	$ —	$ 0.25
Common Stock price range (NYSE Composite Intraday)					
High	$ 17.42	$ 10.37	$ 8.79	$ 9.70	$ 9.48
Low	9.75	1.50	1.01	6.65	6.06
Average number of shares of Ford Common and Class B Stock outstanding (in millions)	3,449	2,992	2,273	1,979	1,879

Source: The Ford Motor Company Annual Report 2010.

revenue was $33.1 billion, up $5 billion from the first quarter of 2010. According to Alan Mulally,

Our team delivered a great quarter, with solid growth and improvements in all regions. We continue to acceler-ate our One Ford plan around the world, delivering on our commitments to serve our global customers with a full family of best-in-class vehicles and deliver profitable growth for all, despite uncertain economic conditions.[164]

Exhibit 9 Ford Motor Company and Subsidiaries Consolidated Balance Sheet (in millions)

	December 31, 2010	December 31, 2009
ASSETS		
Cash and cash equivalents	$ 14,805	$ 20,894
Marketable securities	20,765	21,387
Finance receivables, net	70,070	75,892
Other receivables, net	7,388	7,194
Net investment in operating leases	11,675	17,270
Inventories	5,917	5,041
Equity in net assets of affiliated companies	2,569	2,367
Net property	23,179	22,637
Deferred income taxes	2,003	3,479
Net intangible assets	102	165
Assets of held-for-sale operations	—	7,618
Other assets	6,214	8,096
Total assets	$164,687	$192,040
LIABILITIES		
Payables	$ 16,362	$ 14,301
Accrued liabilities and deferred revenue	43.844	46,144
Debt	103,988	131,635
Deferred income taxes	1,135	2,421
Liabilities of held-for-sale operations	—	5,321
Total liabilities	165,329	199,822
EQUITY		
Capital stock		
Common Stock, par value $0.01 per share (3,707 million shares issued of 6 billion authorized)	37	33
Class B Stock, par value $0.01 per share (71 million shares issued of 530 million authorized)	1	1
Capital in excess of par value of stock	20,803	16,786
Accumulated other comprehensive income/(loss)	(14,313)	(10,864)
Treasury stock	(163)	(177)
Retained earnings/(Accumulated deficit)	(7,038)	(13,599)
Total equity/(deficit) attributable to Ford Motor Company	(673)	(7,820)
Equity/(Deficit) attributable to noncontrolling interests	31	38
Total equity/(deficit)	(642)	(7,782)
Total liabilities and equity	$164,687	$192,040

The following table includes assets to be used to settle liabilities of the consolidated VIEs. These assets and liabilities are included in the consolidated balance sheet above. See Note 13 for additional information on our VIEs.

	December 31, 2010	December 31, 2009
ASSETS		
Cash and cash equivalents	$ 4,062	$ 4,922
Marketable securities	—	—
Finance receivables, net	50,473	57,353
Other receivables, net	13	34
Net investment in operating leases	6,121	10,246
Inventories	19	106
Net property	31	154

(Continued)

Exhibit 9 Ford Motor Company and Subsidiaries Consolidated Balance Sheet (in millions) (*Continued*)

	December 31, 2010	December 31, 2009
Deferred income taxes	—	—
Other assets.	28	56
LIABILITIES		
Payables	16	23
Accrued liabilities and deferred revenue	222	560
Debt	40,247	46,167

Source: The Ford Motor Company Annual Report 2010.

In the second quarter of 2011, Ford reported net income of $2.4 billion, a $201 million decrease from second quarter 2010. However, total company revenue was $35.5 billion, up $4.2 billion from second quarter 2010.[165] Ford Chief Financial Officer Lewis Booth said that it was not the easiest of quarters for Ford. Although some vehicle production had been lost in Asia Pacific because of the Japanese tsunami, the amount was lower than anticipated and Ford did not lose any significant production anywhere else in the world. Ford's outlook for US sales in 2011 has been dropped to 13 million vehicles, from 13.5 million predicted earlier in the year. Booth also said that Ford's second quarter profit had been hindered by higher commodity costs related mostly to higher oil prices. In addition, prices for plastics, steel, aluminum, copper, and precious metals increased and affected Ford's profit margins.[166]

Regardless of Ford's financial success and turnaround over the past two years, there are still numerous obstacles on the road ahead.

Challenges

New entrants to the US auto market will eventually come from China and India, among others. Although Chinese manufacturers including Brilliance, Geely, Great Wall, and BYD Auto have displayed vehicles at the Detroit and Los Angeles auto shows, no vehicles have entered the US market. Currently, BYD claims that its plug-in hybrid will be introduced in the US in spring 2012. If this does happen, it is not anticipated to be a significant threat as hybrids and electric vehicles currently represent only 2.2 percent of global sales.[167] Even so, the Chinese and Indian vehicles will enter the US eventually, and Ford must be prepared.

As the population increases, roads and highways become more congested. Many urban areas are developing or enhancing public transportation systems such as light rail systems and subways, as well as increasing bus routes and schedules. Other alternative transportation methods include trolleys, Dial-A-Ride (a door-to-door shared ride service), taxis, bicycles, and walking. It is possible that personal mobility will become a service in the future, with more people choosing to use public transportation or a car-sharing program, such as Zipcar. This would significantly decrease consumer demand for vehicles.

Although the UAW made concessions to the US automakers to help them through the industry downturn, it is probable that the union will want to take back those concessions now that the automakers have returned to profitability. UAW president Bob King, who took over from Ron Gettelfinger in 2010, has told automakers that they need to share their newfound profits with workers, and the workers need to trade wage increases for profit sharing. The Detroit automakers have indicated they welcome this approach and industry analysts believe it makes sense. However, many workers share the opinion of Ford worker Gary Walkowicz, who told the *Detroit News* "A lot of people feel like we need some guaranteed money. People are looking to get back a lot of the things we gave up."[168]

In addition, Alan Mulally's $25.6 million and Bill Ford's $25.2 million pay packages received in 2010 practically guarantee that wage increases will be a key issue in union negotiations with Ford.[169] Wage increases and greater benefits for workers would lead to increased operating costs that would once again reduce the competitiveness of US manufacturers with their foreign rivals. Currently, Ford spends approximately $58 per hour for wages and benefits to UAW members—$8 more than the average labor costs at the primarily non-union US factories of foreign competitors such as Hyundai, and more than domestic competitors Chrysler and GM. Chrysler reports labor costs of approximately $50 per hour and GM estimates hourly labor costs at $56. As part of the bankruptcy restructuring, the UAW made agreements with GM and Chrysler to not strike during the 2011 contract negotiations. However, Ford has no such protection and could face the threat of a strike.[170] King has also indicated that that the UAW wants a seat on Ford's board of directors.[171] Talks between the UAW and Ford began on July 29, 2011 and continued as of this writing.

Within a six month period in early 2011, Ford made a series of recalls and, as a result, its quality ratings slipped. Approximately 1.4 million F-150 pickup trucks were recalled worldwide for airbags that could unexpectedly deploy,[172] and approximately 25,000 Ford Rangers and

9,100 Ford Edge, F-Series trucks, and Lincoln MKX vehicles were recalled for electrical problems that could cause vehicle fires.[173] Given the number of recent recalls, it is not surprising that Ford has fallen in the J.D. Power and Associates 2011 US Initial Quality Study—a survey that tracks vehicle problems reported within the first 90 days of ownership. Ford, which ranked fifth and was the highest mass-market brand in the 2010 Initial Quality Study, fell to 23, and Lincoln fell from eighth place in 2010 to 17.[174] (See Exhibit 10 for the 2011 survey listings.)

When Alan Mulally announced Ford's plan to increase worldwide sales 50 percent to eight million vehicles annually by 2015, Wall Street analysts were skeptical, investors were worried, and in the two weeks following the announcement in June 2011, shares fell to their lowest level in 2011, to $12.65, down 23 percent since January 1. In particular, analysts and investors were concerned that Ford was expanding too late, after growth in China had already started to slow. Although some analysts are supportive of Mulally's plan, many analysts and investors are taking a wait-and-see approach.[175]

Although 65-year-old Alan Mulally has said he is not going to rush to leave Ford as long as he's having "fun," insiders have indicated there is much speculation about who might eventually replace Mulally and when. Although Bill Ford has indicated he would like to keep Mulally in his current position until he reaches the age of 80, it is a certainty that Mulally will eventually leave Ford.[176] Given the numerous challenges facing the auto industry and the current global economic environment, Ford's ability to survive without him at this point is viewed by many as questionable.

Conclusion

As UAW president Bob King explained, the success that Ford, GM, and Chrysler now enjoy is relative. The Detroit Three still face formidable foreign competition, including potential new entrants from China and India. In addition, the economy remains weak and vehicle sales in the US and Europe remain well below their historic highs.[177] In addition, if the US government is unable to reach an agreement on whether to raise the debt ceiling and defaults, many types of interest rates could rise, making it more difficult for businesses and consumers to borrow money.[178]

Successful innovation in manufacturing processes, product design, marketing approach, and business structure were all attained under Alan Mulally's leadership. Ford Motor Company returned to profitability after the global economic crisis and differentiated itself as the only major US automaker that did not require a government bailout. Today, Ford is faced with challenges that include intense domestic and international competition, pressure to maintain quality standards while bringing new, innovative, energy-efficient products to market,

Exhibit 10 J.D. Power and Associates 2011 US Initial Quality Study* 2011 Ranking/Problems per 100 Vehicles

Brand	Score
Lexus	73
Honda	86
Acura	89
Mercedes-Benz	94
Mazda	100
Porsche	100
Toyota	101
Infiniti	102
Cadillac	103
GMC	104
Industry Average	107
Hyundai	108
Subaru	108
BMW	109
Chevrolet	109
Volvo	109
Chrysler	110
LINCOLN	**111**
Audi	113
Kia	113
Buick	114
Jaguar	114
Ram	114
FORD	**116**
Nissan	117
Jeep	122
Land Rover	123
Scion	123
MINI	131
Volkswagen	131
Mitsubishi	133
Suzuki	136
Dodge	137

*Study released June 23, 2011

Source: *The Automotive News,* June 23, 2011. http://www.autonews.com

the threat of a UAW strike if contract negotiations reach a stalemate, and decreased analyst and stockholder confidence after Mulally's announcement of Ford's bold international expansion plan. However, Alan Mulally's reputation is untarnished and his leadership abilities are confirmed by successful turnarounds at both Boeing and Ford. Although Mulally has a proven track record, it will be interesting to see if he can continue to manage Ford and maneuver around the significant obstacles ahead.

NOTES

1. About Ford / Innovator, Industrialist, Outdoorsman: Henry Ford Started it All. *Ford Motor Company*. http://corporate.ford.com/about-ford/heritage/people/650-henry-ford

2. G. Botelho. 10 Aug 2004. The car that changed the world. *CNN US*. http://articles.cnn.com/2004-08-06/us/model.t_1_henry-ford-model-ts-business-model?_s=PM:US

3. *Ibid.*

4. Ford Motor Car Company History / Birth of the Ford Model T. *Ford Motor History*. http://www.fordmotorhistory.com/history/model-t.php

5. J. Hershauer. 30 Aug 2010. What is a Dealership? Sustainable Dealership Management, Arizona State University.

6. *Ibid.*

7. Ford Motor Company. *Hoovers*. www.hoovers.com

8. About Ford / Innovator, Industrialist, Outdoorsman: Henry Ford Started it All. *op. cit.*

9. About Ford / Edsel Ford Brought Design and Elegance to Ford Motor Company Vehicles. *Ford Motor Company*. http://corporate.ford.com/about-ford/heritage/people/edselford/652-edsel-ford

10. *Ibid.*

11. About Ford / Innovator, Industrialist, Outdoorsman: Henry Ford Started it All. *op. cit.*

12. About Ford / "Whiz Kids" Brought Financial Expertise and Modern Management to Ford Motor Company. *Ford Motor Company*. http://corporate.ford.com/about-ford/heritage/people/whizkids/659-whiz-kids

13. About Ford / Henry Ford II Led the Company Into Prosperity and Strengthened its Global Presence. *Ford Motor Company*. http://corporate.ford.com/about-ford/heritage/people/henryfordii/654-henry-ford-ii

14. 1970s Oil Crisis. *Recession.org*. http://recession.org/history/1970s-oil-crisis

15. Ford Motor Company. *Hoovers*. *op. cit.*

16. Ford chief Jacques Nasser ousted. 30 Oct 2001. *BBC News*. http://news.bbc.co.uk/2/hi/business/1627300.stm

17. Ford Motor Company. *Hoovers*. *op. cit.*

18. Annual NADA DATA Report: 2005 Auto Sales Third Strongest on Record. 17 May 2005. *NADA.org*. http://www.nada.org/MediaCenter/News+Releases/2006/NADAData+5-17-2006.htm

19. Ford announces job cuts, plans to close 14 facilities. 23 Jan 2006. *Vidette Online / Illinois State University*. http://www.videtteonline.com/index.php?option-com_content&view=article&id=15782:ford-announces-job-cuts--plans-to-close-14-facilities&catid=67:newsarchive&Itemid-53

20. *Ibid.*

21. *Ibid.*

22. Ford's plan: Cut operating costs by $5 billion. 15 Sep 2006. *CNBC*. http://www.cnbc.com/id/14831365/

23. M. Maynard and F. Warner. Toyota passes Ford in US vehicle sales. 2 Aug 2006. *The New York Times*. http://www.nytimes.com/2006/08/02/business/worldbusiness/02iht-auto.2363745.html

24. *Ibid.*

25. Ford's plan: Cut operating costs by $5 billion. *op. cit.*

26. R. Jones. 6 Sep 2006. Ford makes bold move, but is it enough? *MSNBC.com*. http://www.msnbc.msn.com/id/14687037/

27. D. Levin. 7 Sep 2006. Mulally's hire by Ford may be too late. *Bloomberg*. http://www.bloomberg.com/apps/news?pid=newsarchive&refer=columnist_levin&sid=acFj5T8M1jEo#share

28. Business Day / Ford Motor Company. *The New York Times*. Accessed 7 Jun 2011. http://topics.nytimes.com/top/news/business/companies/ford_motor-company/index.html

29. Progress and Priorities / Ford Motor Company 2007 Annual Report. *Ford Motor Company.com*. http://corporate.ford.com/doc/2007_ar.pdf

30. Ford Motor Company. *Hoovers*. *op. cit.*

31. Progress and Priorities / Ford Motor Company 2007 Annual Report. *op. cit.*

32. K. Amadeo. 22 May 2011. The Auto Bailout. *About.com / US Economy*. http://useconomy.about.com/od/criticalissues/a/auto_bailout.htm

33. L. Montgomery and K. Marr. 5 Dec 2008. Lawmakers still not sold on auto rescue. *The Washington Post*. http://www.washingtonpost.com/wp-dyn/content/article/2008/12/04/AR2008120401541.html

34. D. Kiley. 5 Mar 2009. Alan Mulally: The outsider at Ford. *Bloomberg Businessweek*. http://www.businessweek.com/magazine/content/09_11/b4123038630999.htm

35. *Ibid.*

36. N. Bunkley. 28 Jan 2010. Ford profit comes as Toyota hits a bump. *New York Times*. http://www.nytimes.com/2010/01/29/business/29ford.html

37. D. Welch. 1 Jul 2009. The 'Cash for Clunkers' law looks like a lemon. *Bloomberg Businessweek*. http://www.businessweek.com/magazine/content/09_28/b4139000349712.htm?cha=top+news_special+report+--+auto+bailout+2009

38. Car allowance rebate system (Cash for Clunkers). 20 Aug 2009. *New York Times* http://topics.nytimes.com/topics/reference/timestopics/subjects/c/cash_for_clunkers/index.html

39. D. Welch. 4 Jan 2011. Toyota still under "Clouds," falls behind Ford as US auto sales increase. *Bloomberg Businessweek*. http://www.bloomberg.com/news/2011-01-04/gm-december-total-u-s-sales-up-7-5-est-up-4-3-.html

40. D. Pierson. 29 Mar 2010. Ford sells Volvo to China's Geely auto group for $1.8 billion. *Los Angeles Times*. http://articles.latimes.com/2010/mar/29/business/la-fi-ford-volvo29-2010mar29

41. *Ibid.*

42. ONE Ford / Ford Motor Company / 2010 Annual Report. *Ford Motor Company.com*. http://corporate.ford.com/doc/ir_2010_annual_report.pdf

43. E. Mayne. 28 Feb 2011. Ford Fiesta invading C-Segment. *WardsAuto.com*. http://www.wardsauto.com/ar/ford_fiesta_invading_110228/

44. European Ford Fiesta Sales Hit 850,000 Since Launch Despite Continuing Market Weakness. 14 Oct 2010. *Ford Motor Company News Center*. http://www.corporate.ford.com/news-center/news/press-releases/press-releases-detail/pr-european-ford-fiesta-sales-hit-33402

45. Sustainability Report 2010/11. *Ford Motor Company.com*. http://corporate.ford.com/microsites/sustainability-report-2010-11/default

46. Ford Reports 2010 Full Year Net Income of $6.6 Billion; Fourth Quarter Net Income of $190 Million. 28 Jan 2011. *Ford Motor Company News Center*. http://www.corporate.ford.com/news-center/news/press-releases/press-releases-detail/pr-ford-reports-2010-full-year-net-33916

47. A. Priddle. 30 Jul 2011. Hits, misses as summer auto sales sizzle. *Detroit News*. http://www.detnews.com/article/20110730/AUTO01/107300358/1148/?source=nletter-auto

48. Fortune 500 2011. *CNN Money*. http://money.cnn.com/magazines/fortune/fortune500/2011/index.html

49. P. LeBeau. 11 Nov 2010. How Ford got back on the fast track to success. *CNBC TV on msnbc.com*. http://www.msnbc.msn.com/id/40010150/ns/business-cnbc_tv/t/how-ford-got-back-fast-track-success/

50. D. Kiley. 5 Mar 2009. Alan Mulally: The outsider at Ford. *op. cit.*

51. M. Langley. 22 Dec 2006. Inside CEO Mulally's radical overhaul of Ford. *Wall Street Journal via Pittsburgh Post Gazette*. http://www.post-gazette.com/pg/06356/748288-185.stm#ixzz1RTM39rey

52. *Ibid.*

53. Progress and Priorities / Ford Motor Company 2007 Annual Report. *op. cit.*

54. Alan Mulally. *Media.Ford.com*. http://media.ford.com/article_display.cfm?article_id=24203

55. M. Wayland. 27 Jun 2011. Ford CEO Alan Mulally named '2011 Chief Executive of the Year' by his peers. *mlive.com*. http://www.mlive.com/auto/index.ssf/2011/06/ford_ceo_alan_mulally_named_20_1.html

56. Alan Mulally. *Media.Ford.com*. http://media.ford.com/article_display.cfm?article_id=24203

57. Ford Motor Company's Alan R. Mulally to Receive 2011 Automotive Executive of the Year Award. 13 Apr 2011. *Automotive Executive of the Year*. http://www.autoexecoftheyear.com

58. William Clay Ford Jr. *Media.Ford.com*. http://media.ford.com/article_display.cfm?article_id=93

59. New top man at Ford. 6 Sep 2006. *Car Keys*. http://www.carkeys.co.uk/news/new-top-man-ford

60. William Clay Ford Jr. *op. cit.*

61. K. Naughton. 4 Feb 2011. Ford cut 3.6% of US dealers in 2010 while share rose. *Bloomberg*. http://www.bloomberg.com/news/2011-02-04/ford-eliminated-3-6-of-u-s-dealers-in-2010-while-adding-share.html

62. *Ibid.*

63. ONE Ford / Ford Motor Company / 2010 Annual Report. *op. cit.*

64. About CarMax / A Better Way to Buy Cars. *CarMax.com*. http://www.carmax.com/enus/company-info/about-us.html

65. P. A. Eisenstein. 7 Jul 2011. Detroit makers still struggling to win young buyers, but there are some surprises among the brands Millennials want most. *Detroit Bureau*. http://www.thedetroitbureau.com/2011/07/detroit-makers-still-struggling-to-win-young-buyers/

66. *Ibid.*

67. *Ibid.*

68. Ford Motor Company. *Hoovers. op. cit.*

69. P. Doval. 28 Jan 2011. GM plans rival to Alto with Chinese partner. *Times of India*. http://www.timesofindia.indiatimes.com/business/india-business/GM-plans-rival-to-Alto-with-Chinese-partner/articleshow/7375411.cms

70. *Ibid.*

71. D. Seetharaman. 14 Jun 2011. India to be No. 3 auto market by 2020 – J.D. Power. *Reuters*. http://in.reuters.com/article/2011/06/13/idINIndia-57675920110613

72. Ford India to treble dealership network by 2016 to support launches in Indian car market. 18 Jul 2011. *RushLane*. http://www.rushlane.com/ford-india-to-treble-dealership-network-by-2016-to-support-launches-in-indian-car-market-1217402.html

73. K. Naughton. 27 Jun – 3 Jul 2011. Can Alan Mulally take Ford's show on the road? *Bloomberg Businessweek*. p. 21.

74. *Ibid.*

75. *Ibid.*

76. *Ibid.*

77. Ford releases its 12th Annual Sustainability Report. 15 Jun 2011. *The Auto Channel*. http://www.theautochannel.com/news/2011/06/15/536938-greening-blue-oval-ford-releases-its-12th-annual-sustainability-report.html

78. The First Ever Prius Plug-In Hybrid. *Toyota*. http://touch.toyota.com/prius-plug-in/

79. P. Lienert. 6 Jul 2011. Leaf passes Volt in first-falf sales. *Edmunds Inside Line*. www.insideline.com/nissan/leaf/leaf-passes-volt-in-first-half-sales.html

80. R. Vartabedian. Jun 2006. E85 getting attention. *Energy Refuge.com*. http://www.energyrefuge.com/archives/e85_getting_attention.htm

81. Fuel Cell Vehicles. *US Department of Energy*. www.fueleconomy.gov/feg/fuelcell.shtml

82. J. M. Broder. 3 Jul 2011. Carmakers and White House haggling over mileage. *New York Times*. http://www.nytimes.com/2011/07/04/business/energy-environment/04mileage.html

83. *Ibid.*

84. D. Shepardson. 28 Jul 2011. Big 3 agree to new mpg rules. *Detroit News*. http://www.detnews.com/article/20110728/AUTO01/107280347/1148/?source-nletter-autos

85. Ford releases its 12th Annual Sustainability Report. *op. cit.*

86. J.D. Power: Ford's Quality Vehicles Earn High APEAL Rankings from Customers for Fuel Efficiency. 27 Jul 2011. *Media.Ford.com*. http://media.ford.com/article_display.cfm?article_id=34967

87. B. G. Hoffman. 28 Jul 2011. Ford leads Big 3 in J.D. Power customer satisfaction survey. *Detroit News*. http://www.detnews.com/article/20110728/AUTO01/107280363/?source=nletter-auto

88. Dealer profits up despite challenges. 23 Jun 2011. *Automotive Digest*. http://www.automotivedigest.com/content/displayArticle.aspx?a=80937

89. C. Tierney. 2 Jul 2011. June sees Detroit 3 pick up market share from struggling rivals. *Detroit News*. http://detnews.com/article/20110702/AUTO01/107020338/June-sees-Detroit-3-pick-up-market-share-from-struggling-rivals

90. K. Naughton. 4 Feb 2011. *op. cit.*

91. Auto Sales / Overview Charts. *Wall Street Journal / Market Data Center*. http://online.wsj.com/mdc/public/page/2_3022-autosales.html

92. M. Maynard. 1 May 2009. Chrysler: A short history. *New York Times / Dealb%k*. http://dealbook.nytimes.com/2009/05/01/chrysler-a-short-history/

93. 2006, DaimlerChrysler: Corporate profile, http://www.daimlerchrysler.com

94. 2007, The road ahead for the US auto industry, Office of Aerospace and Automotive Industries International Trade Administration, US Department of Commerce, April.

95. D. Kiley. 14 May 2009. It's official: Chrysler to close 789 dealers. *Bloomberg Businessweek*. http://www.businessweek.com/autos/autobeat/archives/2009/05/its_official_ch_1.html?chan=top+news_special+report+--+auto+bailout+2009_special+report+---+-auto+bailout-2009

96. About Us. *Chrysler Group LLC*. http://www.chryslergroupllc.com/EN-US/COMPANY/Pages/Aboutus.aspx

97. Chrysler details plans to pay back US, Canada. 19 May 2011. *Business on msnbc.com*. http://www.msnbc.msn.com/id/43094346/ns/business/t/chrysler-details-plan-pay-back-us-canada/

98. Fiat execs dominate Marchionne's unified Fiat-Chrysler management team. 28 Jul 2011. *Automotive News*. http://www.autonews.com/apps/pbcs.dll/article?AID=/20110728/OEM/110729845/1179

99. B. Hoffman. 19 Jul 2011. Fiat, Chrysler CEO moving quickly toward merger, globalization. *Detroit News*. http://www.detnews.com/article/20110719/AUTO01/107190338/1148/?source=nletter-auto

100. *Ibid.*

101. J. Bennett and L. Moloney. 28 Jul 2011. Fiat names new executive team. *Wall Street Journal*. http://online.wsj.com/article/SB10001424053111904800304576474321855693648.html?mod=googlenews_wsj

102. About Us. Chrysler Group LLC. op. cit.

103. *Ibid.*

104. General Motors Company. *Hoovers*. www.hoovers.com

105. *Ibid.*

106. 2006, The road ahead for the US auto industry, Office of Aerospace and Automotive Industries International Trade Administration, US Department of Commerce, April.

107. General Motors Company. *Hoovers. op. cit.*

108. L. Montgomery and K. Marr. 5 Dec 2008. *op. cit.*

109. General Motors Company. *Hoovers. op. cit.*

110. C. Baldwin and S. Kim. 17 Nov 2010. GM IPO raises $20.1 billion. *Reuters*. http://www.reuters.com/article/2010/11/17/us-gm-ipo-idUSTRE6AB43H20101117

111. S. Gelsi. 18 Nov 2010. GM's IPO drives off the lot with premium. *MarketWatch*. http://www.marketwatch.com/story/gms-ipo-drives-off-the-lot-with-a-pop-2010-11-18

112. D. Shepardson. 26 Jul 2011. General Motors touts resurgence with new ads. *Detroit News*. http://www.detnews.com/article/20110726/AUTO01/107260340/1148/?source=nletter-auto

113. Company: About GM. *General Motors*. http://www.gm.com/company/aboutGM.html

114. General Motors Company. *Hoovers. op. cit.*

115. Company: About GM. *op. cit.*

116. Chevrolet Volt – 2011 / Vehicle Highlights. *Media.GM.com*. http://media.gm.com/media/us/en/chevrolet/vehicles/volt/2011.html

117. Innovation: Environment / Greener Vehicles. *General Motors*. http://www.gm.com/vision/greener_vehicles.html

118. J. Oosting. 7 Jul 2011. It's a hit! Chevrolet Cruze the best-selling car in US for June as Toyota Camry sales slow. *mlive.com*. http://www.mlive.com/auto/index.ssf/2011/07/its_a_hit_chevrolet_cruze_the.html

119. Toyota Motor Corporation. *Hoovers*. www.hoovers.com

120. A. Taylor III. 7 Mar 2007. America's best car company: Toyota has become a red, white, and blue role model. How? By understanding Americans better than Detroit does. *Fortune.* http://money.cnn .com/magazines/fortune/fortune_archive/2007/03/19/8402324/ index.htm

121. 2011, Toyota passes GM as world's largest automaker. 21 Jan 2009. *US News and World Report.* http://usnews .rankingsandreviews.com/cars-trucks/daily-news/090121-Toyota -Passes-GM-as-World-s-Largest-Automaker/

122. Toyota Motor Corporation. *Hoovers. op. cit.*

123. Toyota Motor Corporation. *Hoovers. op. cit.*

124. *Ibid.*

125. Toyota recalls 82,200 hybrid SUVs in US. 29 Jun 2011. *Forbes.* http:// billionaires.forbes.com/article/07nMeLVeWj9wI?q=Lexus+RX+400h

126. Toyota Motor Corporation. *Hoovers. op. cit.*

127. *Ibid.*

128. D. Sedgwick. 12 Jul 2011. Minority supplier SET Enterprises thrives, diversifies after recession. *Crain's Detroit Business.* http://www .crainsdetroit.com/article/20110712/FREE/110719986/minority -supplier-set-enterprises-thrives-diversifies-after-recession

129. SEC Filings. *Gentex Corporation.* http://ir.gentex.com/easyir/edgr .do?easyirid=4364F5BCCFF04FC6

130. J. Stein, C. Child and D. Sedgwick. 18 Jul 2011. Ford purchaser: We'll deliver on production plan. *Featured Car.* http://www .featuredcar.com/archives/27362

131. Ford, Key Suppliers Roll Out Innovative Business Model. 29 Sep 2005. *Media.Ford.com.* http://media.ford.com/article_display .cfm?article_id=21677

132. Ford Suppliers Add 5,500 Jobs to Support Global Launch of All-New Ford Focus. 25 Feb 2011. *Media.Ford.com.* http://media.ford .com/article_display.cfm?article_id=34148

133. D. Seetharaman. 27 Jun 2011. Visteon seen as possible takeover target: analyst. *Reuters.* http://www.reuters.com/ article/2011/06/27/us-visteon-takeover-idUSTRE75Q5VL20110627

134. D. Human. 10 Jun 2011. Delphi celebrates 75 years. *Indiana Economic Digest.* http://www.indianaeconomicdigest.net/main .asp?SectionID=31&SubSectionID=135&ArticleID=60376

135. S. Finlay. 14 Apr 2011. New boss recalls arriving at Ford to find no Fords parked in lot. *Wardsauto.com.* http://blog.wardsauto.com/ sfinlay/2011/04/14/new-boss-recalls-arriving-at-ford-to-find-no -fords-parked-in-lot

136. ONE Ford / Ford Motor Company / 2010 Annual Report. *op. cit.*

137. S. Finlay. 14 Apr 2011. *op. cit.*

138. *Ibid.*

139. S. Rothwell. 27 Sep 2010. Ford may cut lineup to as few as 20 models, CEO Says. *Bloomberg Businessweek.* http://www .businessweek.com/news/2010-09-27/ford-may-cut-lineup-to-as -few-as-20-models-ceo-says.html

140. *Ibid.*

141. *Ibid.*

142. ONE Ford / Ford Motor Company / 2010 Annual Report. *op. cit.*

143. *Ibid.*

144. *Ibid.*

145. G. Migliore. 2 Jun 2011. Ford to make three-cylinder EcoBoost engine, eight-speed transmission. *Autoweek.* http://www .autoweek.com/article/20110602/CARNEWS/110609986

146. J. Lichterman. 28 Jul 2011. Ford teams with Azure for hybrid F-Series Super Duty trucks. *Automotive News.* http://www .autonews.com/apps/pbcs.dll/article?AID=/20110728/ OEM05/110729849/1492

147. G. Migliore. 2 Jun 2011. *op. cit.*

148. *Ibid.*

149. J. Lareau. 25 Jul 2011. V6s now trump V8s in Ford F-150. *Autoweek.* http://www.autoweek.com/article/20110725/ CARNEWS/110729928

150. New York City Approves Ford Transit Connect Taxi for Use; Versatile Cabs to Start Hitting Streets in Late Summer. 21 Jul 2011. *Ford Motor Company News Center.* http://corporate.ford.com/ news-center/news/press-releases/press-releases-detail/pr-new -york-city-approves-ford-34944

151. *Ibid.*

152. *Ibid.*

153. *Ibid.*

154. *Ibid.*

155. Ford showcasing vehicle-to-vehicle communication for crash avoidance; potential for leveraging WiFi and smartphones to extend quickly the number of participating vehicles. 19 Jul 2011. *Green Car Congress.* http://www.greencarcongress.com/2011/07/ fordv2v-20110719.html

156. R. Grillo. 1 Feb 2011. Ford: A sound marketing strategy to deliver long-term growth. *Seeking Alpha.* http://seekingalpha.com/ article/249957-ford-a-sound-marketing-strategy-to-deliver-long -term-growth

157. Ford joins world's toughest endurance event as Ironman Triathlon title sponsor. 7 Jul 2010. *Ironman.com.* http://ironman.com/ ironstuff/ironlife/ford#axzz1SWAtnCZA

158. Ford's 'Swap Your Ride' Ad Campaign Proves a Real Eye-Opener for Consumers. 5 Apr 2011. *Media.Ford.com.* http://media.ford .com/article_display.cfm?article_id=34341

159. *Ibid.*

160. *Ibid.*

161. E. Chu. 29 Jul 2011. Ford launches Octane Academy. *ESPN Action Sports.* http://sports.espn.go.com/action/news/ story?id=6784656

162. Ford Driving Skills for Life. *Driving Skills for Life.* https://www .drivingskillsforlife.com/index.php

163. *Ibid.*

164. Ford Reports $2.6 billion 2011 First Quarter Net Income as One Ford Plan Continues Strong Progress. 26 Apr 2011. *Media.Ford .com.* http://media.ford.com/article_display.cfm?article_id=34463

165. Ford Earns $2.4 Billion Net Income in Second Quarter 2011; Strengthens Foundation for Continued Global Growth. 26 Jul 2011. *Media.Ford.com.* http://media.ford.com/article_display .cfm?article_id=34932

166. B. Wodall. 26 Jul 2011. Ford profits despite economy, rising costs. *Reuters.* http://www.reuters.com/article/2011/07/26/us-ford -idUSTRE76P20Y20110726

167. K. Belson. 18 Feb 2011. Where are the Chinese cars? *New York Times.* http://www.nytimes.com/2011/02/20/ automobiles/20CHINA.html

168. B. Hoffman. 18 Jul 2011. UAW chief endorses profit sharing. *Detroit News.* http://www.detnews.com/article/20110718/ AUTO01/107180342/1148/?source-nletter-auto

169. Ford CEO Alan Mulally got $26.5 million pay package. 1 Apr 2011. *Cleveland.com.* http://www.cleveland.com/business/index .ssf/2011/04/ford_ceo_alan_mulally_got_265.html

170. T. Higgins. 25 Jul 2011. UAW President says labor costs to stay similar at GM, Ford and Chrysler. *Bloomberg.* http://www .bloomberg.com/news/2011-07-25/uaw-says-labor-costs-to-stay v-similar-at-gm-ford-and-chrysler.html

171. C. Trudell. 29 Jul 2011. UAW wants a board seat at Ford, President Bob King says. *Bloomberg.* http://www.bloomberg.com/ news/2011-07-29/uaw-wants-a-board-seat-at-ford-president-Bob -King-says.html

172. J. Crawley and B. Woodall. 14 Apr 2011. Ford expands recall to more than 1.4 million F-150s. *Reuters.* http://www.reuters.com/ article/2011/04/14/us-ford-recall-idUSTRE73D81V20110414

173. R. Smith. 3 Mar 2011. Ford recalls 2011 Ford Edge, F-Series and Lincoln MKS. *USNews.* http://usnews.rankingsandreviews.com/cars -trucks/daily-news/110303-Ford-Recalls-2011-Ford-Edge-F-Series -and-Lincoln-MKX/

174. J. Snyder. 23 Jun 2011. Ford scores tumble, Toyota rebounds in initial quality survey. *Auto Week.* http://www.autoweek.com/ article/20110623/CARNEWS/110629937

175. K. Naughton. *op. cit.*

176. P. Eisenstein. 22 Jul 2011. Stack of potential suitors line up at Ford for life after Mulally. *Autoblog.com.* http://www.autoblog .com/2011/07/22/stack-of-potential-suitors-line-up-at-ford-for-life -after-mulall/

177. B. Hoffman. 18 Jul 2011. *op. cit.*

178. L. Opsitnik. 29 Jul 2011. Car shoppers could pay more if US defaults. *USNews.* http://usnews.rankingsandreviews.com/cars -trucks/best-cars-blog/2011/07/Car_Shoppers_Could_Pay_More _if_US_Defaults/

Benjamin Archer, Jessica Dunphy, Steven Carter, Ioana Ludwick, Mitchel Nosack, Aatif Qadeer
Arizona State University

Introduction

How does one define Google? Ironically, you can Google the answer. Currently, the top two results for the Google search "define:Google" are from Princeton's WorldNet. edu Web site:

■ (v) search the Internet (for information) using the Google search engine; "He googled the woman he had met at the party"; "My children are googling all day."
■ (n) a widely used search engine that uses text-matching techniques to find web pages that are important and relevant to a user's search.[1]

With less than thirteen years under its belt, Google has evolved from a graduate school project to join the ranks of Kleenex, Xerox, and Q-tip as a genericized word known throughout the world as a synonym for "Internet search." Host to 70 percent of the worldwide Internet search market, it should come as no surprise that one's Google page ranking is the yardstick against which most Internet companies are measured.

This success is due to Google consistently utilizing its competencies to challenge the strategies of the world's leading technological innovators. This is a notable accomplishment considering the current global economic crisis crippling the economies of even developed nations and further emphasizes the codependent relationship of technology and globalization. When weighing the 2009 financial performances of Google's competitors against each other as well as the market as a whole, Google has not only managed to hold its own, but to also take first place in the overall per share data and growth categories and take second place in overall profitability. Taken as a whole, its 2009 figures demonstrate that Google is giving its competitors a run for their money and their market share.

According to *New York Times* writer, John Markoff, Google's competitive advantage is in its ability to "leverage the power of free."[2] Add to that the idea that Google's "innovations don't stop at the desktop"[3] and a way to define Google begins to emerge. Although its search and advertising services are still the heart and soul of Google, its desire to bring the world to within the reach of every consumer has initiated its move into Apps (applications) and mobile features and turned Google into an "inventor."[4] As Google ventures further into the growth phase of its life cycle and diversifies its business into new segments, the prominent challenges it faces include:

■ Identifying the optimal mix of resources and capabilities needed to manage the growth of the Android mobile operating system
■ The need for strategic action to handle the escalating situation in China without removing itself from that market
■ Responding appropriately to amplified concerns over privacy to minimize the impact of those concerns on future operations

Google's History

In 1996, Stanford students Larry Page and Sergey Brin created a web search engine called BackRub, later changed to Google (an intentional misspelling of googol, a word representing a number starting with a "1" and followed by one hundred zeros),[5] and put into motion a series of events leading to the creation of what is now the world's most used Web site.[6]

In 1998, Google incorporated and received its first investor funding of $100,000.[7] In the midst of the dot-com boom, new web startups were common and an informal but hardworking business style was almost universal. Google fit into this world quite naturally, hiring its first company chef in 1999 with only 40 employees.

Unlike most other web startups of the late 90s, however, and thanks to its advertising revenues, Google was able to maintain its profitability when the dot-com bubble later burst.[8]

In 2001, Google named Eric Schmidt Chairman of the Board of Directors and CEO. Co-founder Larry Page explained why Schmidt was a natural choice: "Eric is widely acknowledged as a brilliant technologist and savvy business leader. These qualities, combined with his entrepreneurial spirit, fit with Google's culture, making Eric the perfect addition to our board of directors."[9]

Also in 2001, Google made its first major foray into diversification when it purchased Deja.com, an acquisition that evolved to become Google Groups.[10] Over the years, many other acquisitions followed, including Blogger (web blogging software), Picasa (a photo sharing Web site with photo editing software), Keyhole (satellite imagery software that became Google Earth and Google Maps), Writely (online document editing, to become Google Docs), and YouTube (video sharing), to name just a few.[11] These acquisitions enabled Google to leverage its capabilities in new ways and built the Google brand from one of a simple search engine company with a small set of leaders to the massive web enterprise it is today. In its present stage of development, Google has four major areas of focus: web search, advertising, apps, and mobile.

Web Search

"Search is how Google began, and it's at the heart of what we do today."[12]

Google's web search functionality is an indispensable feature of the Internet and recognized by Google as essential to its business. Programmers and engineers work constantly to make search results and page rankings as relevant as possible, devoting more time to it than any other Google product.[13] Search is available in over 130 languages and Google owns over 160 localized country/regional domains.[14]

Advertising

"You can make money without doing evil."[15]

Advertising sales accounted for approximately 97 percent of Google's total revenues in 2008 and 2009.[16] Balancing the necessity of ad revenue with consumers' distaste for ads, Google makes a concerted effort to keep ads unobtrusive, clearly marked as advertisements, and relevant to the end user's needs. For instance, searching for business schools will produce advertisements for online business schools and MBA school rankings. Similarly, advertisements in Gmail are based on the content of a user's sent and received email. A user who emails friends about a Las Vegas getaway

would likely see advertisements on Gmail for Las Vegas hotels and shows. Because users are more likely to find the ads relevant, click-through rates increase and advertisers receive a higher return on their investment.

Apps

"We built Google Apps from the ground up for today's connected world."[17]

Google Apps is a suite of cloud computing tools comprised of many of the products of Google's acquisitions as well as a great deal of internal development. There are many systems within Google Apps, including:

- Gmail—Gmail changed the world of online email. At a time when most free email providers offered 10 MB of storage or less, Google announced free email with a 1 GB (and growing) storage limit. In addition, Gmail has advanced spam-filtering techniques that significantly reduce the amount of junk mail reaching a user's inbox. (Exhibit 1 illustrates the amount of spam Gmail users report receiving.)

- Google Docs—A suite of online editing tools encompassing word processing, spreadsheets, presentations, drawings, and forms. Generally, Google Docs is less feature-rich than full desktop applications such as Microsoft Office and Apple iWork; however, it offers the essential (and therefore most used) features of each application. Google Docs is available for use by anyone on any computer with a web browser. Easily the most attractive feature of Google Docs is users' ability to share documents with anyone with an email address, thus allowing for simultaneous live editing by multiple users.

- Google Calendar—An online calendar system that allows for online and mobile access, synchronization to many applications and mobile devices, event reminders via email and SMS, and easy calendar sharing with friends and coworkers.

- Other Google Apps include Orkut (social networking), Picasa (photo editing, cataloging, and sharing), Reader (RSS/news feed reader), Sites (Web site creation), SketchUp (computer-aided design and 3D modeling), Talk (instant messaging with voice and webcam chat), and YouTube (video sharing).

Mobile

"You don't need to be at your desk to need an answer."[18]

Mobile computing is widely regarded as the future of the Internet and Google embraced mobile technology from the start. Google has mobile search and mapping apps as well as other apps including YouTube and Buzz for many smartphones.

Exhibit 1 Gmail Spam Rates

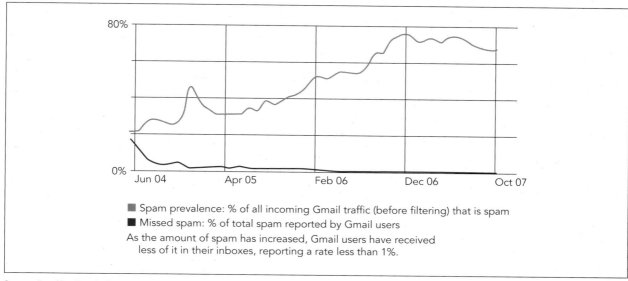

■ Spam prevalence: % of all incoming Gmail traffic (before filtering) that is spam
■ Missed spam: % of total spam reported by Gmail users
As the amount of spam has increased, Gmail users have received
less of it in their inboxes, reporting a rate less than 1%.

Source: Gmail by Google. http://www.google.com

Google's largest contribution to the mobile world however was leading in the creation of the Open Handset Alliance (OHA): a collection of 71 technology and mobile companies responsible for creating the first full, open-source, and freely available mobile phone operating system called Android. Android is also a player in the growing world of portable tablet computing, competing with Apple's iPad.

Strategic Leadership

Google would not exist as it does today if not for the work of its leaders. Google's 2009 annual report states, "Our future success depends in a large part upon the continued service of key members of our senior management team. In particular, our CEO, Eric Schmidt, and our founders, Larry Page and Sergey Brin, are critical to the overall management of Google as well as the development of our technology, our culture, and our strategic direction."[19] Since 2005, all three executives have been offered a market-competitive annual salary and each year they decline, instead receiving an annual base salary of $1.[20] Of course, their equity in the company is worth a very large sum. Despite differing titles, the triumvirate share responsibility for determining strategy and running Google.

Dr. Eric Schmidt: Chairman of the Board and CEO
Schmidt joined Google in 2001 as Chairman of the Board of Directors and Google quickly named him CEO. His prior experience included CEO/Chairman of Novell Inc., Chief Technology Officer for Sun Microsystems, and researcher at Xerox's Palo Alto Research Center—the birthplace of much of modern computing, including graphical user interfaces for personal computers (PCs).[21]

Schmidt also served on the board of directors of Apple from 2006 until 2009 at which point he resigned due to increased conflict of interest as Google and Apple began to compete head-to-head in more business segments with the introductions of Android and Chrome OS.[22] Schmidt is one of 21 members of the President's Council of Advisors on Science and Technology (PCAST), an "advisory group of the nation's leading scientists and engineers who directly advise the President and the Executive Office of the President."[23]

Larry Page: President of Products
Co-founder Larry Page was Google's first CEO and served until 2001 when he became President of Products. His father, a computer science professor at Michigan State University, exposed Page to computers at a very young age thus seeding a passion that never let go. He holds a bachelor's degree in computer engineering, a master's degree in computer science and, during his Ph.D. studies at Stanford, met Sergey Brin and developed Google's prototype, BackRub.[24]

Sergey Brin: President of Technology
Similar to Page's upbringing with computers, co-founder Sergey Brin's father and grandfather were both mathematicians. Born in Moscow, he came to the US at a young age and later double-majored and graduated with honors as an undergraduate in mathematics and computer science. He also holds a master's degree in computer science from Stanford.

Brin and Page are seldom mentioned individually and are often called the "Google guys." To those that know them, it seems that since the BackRub project began they have been inseparable. Withdrawing prior to completing the program, Stanford considers both Brin and Page to be "on leave" from their Ph.D. studies , placing what some might deem "their future" on hold.

The World of Google

Overview of Industry

The competitive industries that Google operates in cannot be classified by using only one or two NAICS (North American Industry Classification System) or SIC (Standard Industrial Classification) codes: its diversified portfolio spans a wide array of products and services all revolving around the opportunities brought on by the advent of the Internet. Similarly, it would be extremely shortsighted to discuss only the aspects of Google's strategy related to its most notable offerings—Web Search and Advertising.

For these reasons, an "overview of Google's industry" is better achieved by an examination of the key competitors Google faces across the spectrum of its offerings. Those competitors include Yahoo!, Microsoft, and Apple. These companies are diversified to include several industries with the common goal of each company to provide innovative products and services that provide consumers with the ability to access, disseminate, create, and use computer data.

To fully appreciate the intensity of the rivalry that exists to provide innovative capabilities to consumers between the four key players identified, the following is a discussion—including historical background information and 2009 financial performance data—of Google's competitors.

Yahoo! Inc. In 1994, Jerry Wang and David Flo, Stanford University students, created Yahoo! when they developed "an Internet bookmark list and directory of interesting sites."[25] (If this sounds familiar, remember that just two years later, Google was started by two Stanford students

as well.) In 2000, Yahoo! formed a partnership that allowed Google to power Yahoo!'s organic results thus effectively introducing "their largest competitor to the world," making Google "a household name" and, in the process, cutting its own throat.[26, 27]

Within five years, Google was outperforming Yahoo! and by 2009, had captured 70 percent of the search engine market share.[28] Yahoo! ended 2009 with a market capitalization value of $21.4 billion, sales of $6.5 billion, and net income of $598 million: 14 percent, 27 percent, and 9 percent of Google's respective key figures. (Exhibits 2 and 3 provide segment performance and expenditures information for Yahoo!.)

Yahoo!'s vision is "to be the center of people's online lives by delivering personally relevant, meaningful Internet experiences." The company focuses on four categories that offer Yahoo! users the opportunity to turn the Internet into a unique and personal online portal by displaying specific content, pages, and applications chosen by the user. These categories include:[29]

- Integrated Consumer Experiences—contains the personalized Yahoo! Home Page, MyYahoo!, Yahoo! Toolbar, Yahoo! Local, and Connected TV
- Applications (Communications and Communities)—includes Yahoo! Mail, Yahoo! Messenger, Yahoo! Groups, Yahoo! Answers, and Flickr
- Search—Yahoo!'s proprietary search technology via Yahoo! Search
- Media Products & Solutions—home to Yahoo! News, Yahoo! Finance, Yahoo! Sports, Yahoo! Entertainment & Lifestyles (including Yahoo! Movies, Yahoo! Music, Yahoo! TV, omg!, Yahoo! Games, and Shine), Yahoo! Health, Yahoo! Tech, Yahoo! Education, Yahoo! Weather, Yahoo! Shopping, Yahoo! Travel, Yahoo! Real Estate, Yahoo! HotJobs, Yahoo! Personals, Yahoo! Autos, and Yahoo! Small Business

Exhibit 2 Yahoo! 2009 10-K Filing Data

YAHOO! Inc. Year Ended December 31,					
SALES BY OPERATING SEGMENT (in millions)	**2007**	**2008**	**% Change from 2007**	**2009**	**% Change from 2008**
Marketing services:					
Owned and Operated sites	3,670	4,046	**10%**	3,553	−12%
Affiliate sites	2,419	2,270	**−6%**	2,121	−7%
Marketing services	6,088	6,316	**4%**	5,674	−10%
Fees	881	892	**1%**	787	−12%
Total Sales $	**6,969**	**7,209**	**3%**	**6,460**	−10%
SALES BY MAJOR GEOGRAPHIC AREAS (in millions)	**2007**	**2008**	**% Change from 2007**	**2009**	**% Change from 2008**
United States	4,724	5,182	**10%**	4,714	−9%
International	2,245	2,026	**−10%**	1,746	−14%
Total Sales $	**6,969**	**7,209**	**3%**	**6,460**	−10%

(Continued)

Exhibit 2 Yahoo! 2009 10-K Filing Data (*Continued*)

YAHOO! Inc. *Year Ended December 31,*					
SALES BY OPERATING SEGMENT **(in % of Total Sales)**	**2007**	**2008**	**% Change from 2007**	**2009**	**% Change from 2008**
Marketing services:					
Owned and Operated sites	53%	56%	3%	55%	−1%
Affiliate sites	35%	31%	−3%	33%	1%
Marketing services	87%	88%	0%	88%	0%
Fees	13%	12%	0%	12%	0%
Total Sales %	**100%**	**100%**	**0%**	**100%**	**0%**
SALES BY MAJOR GEOGRAPHIC AREAS **(in % of Total Sales)**	**2007**	**2008**	**% Change from 2007**	**2009**	**% Change from 2008**
United States	68%	72%	4%	73%	1%
International	32%	28%	−4%	27%	−1%
Total Sales %	**100%**	**100%**	**0%**	**100%**	**0%**

Source: Securities and Exchange Commission

Exhibit 3 Yahoo! Expenses: 2007 to 2009

YAHOO!			
(*In millions, except percentages*)	**2007**	**2008**	**2009**
Research and development expenses	$1,084	$1,222	$1,210
as a Percentage of Sales	16%	17%	19%
Sales and marketing expenses	$1,610	$1,563	$1,245
as a Percentage of Sales	23%	22%	19%
General and administrative expenses	$ 633	$ 705	$ 580
as a Percentage of Sales	9%	10%	9%

Source: Securities and Exchange Commission

With the near impossible task of catching up to Google, in the summer of 2009, Yahoo! partnered with Microsoft to provide worldwide sales support for premium search advertisers in exchange for Microsoft's platform technology services. In the short term, Yahoo! stands to profit from the agreement, receiving 88 percent of net revenues generated. However, by handing Microsoft an exclusive 10-year license to its core search technology as well as permission to integrate this technology into its existing web search platforms, only time will tell whether, in its determination to beat Google, Yahoo! has once again helped a competitor more than it helped itself.[30]

Microsoft Corp. In December 1974, Bill Gates and high school friend Paul Allen were introduced to the world's first PC—the Altair 8800—via a *Popular Electronics* magazine article. Recognizing the potential and given the green light from its developer, Gates and Allen went to work developing BASIC, the programming language for the Altair. They named their company Micro Soft, which they subsequently trademarked as Microsoft in November of 1976.[31]

By 1978, Microsoft's revenues surpassed the $1 million mark and in 1980, Bill Gates recruited his old friend from Harvard, Steve Ballmer, as Microsoft's first business manager. This led to the licensing of MS-DOS in 1980 and the incorporation of Microsoft in 1981. By the end of 1983, the company was well on its way to earning hundreds of millions of dollars. As if that weren't enough, in 1985, Microsoft permanently changed the face of the PC industry with its release of Microsoft Windows.[32]

Today, Microsoft is "the worldwide leader in software, services, and solutions that help people and businesses realize their full potential."[33] Its corporate strategy revolves around the following five business segments with each segment responsible for the development and marketing of all products within its segment:

■ Windows and Windows Live—products include all versions of Windows 7, Windows Vista, Windows XP Home, and Windows Live
■ Server and Tools—server software, software developer tools, services, and solutions including Windows Server OS, Windows Azure, Microsoft SQL Server, SQL Azure, Visual Studio, Silverlight, System Center products, Biz Talk Server, Microsoft Consulting Services, and Premier product support services

- Online Services—including Bing, Microsoft adCenter, MSN, and Atlas online tools for advertisers and publishers
- Microsoft Business—product line includes Microsoft Office, Microsoft SharePoint, Microsoft Dynamics ERP and CRM, and Microsoft Office Web Apps
- Entertainment and Devices—the only division also responsible for the production of its products, this segment offers Xbox 360 console and games, Xbox LIVE, Windows Phone, Windows Embedded device OS, Zune, Mediaroom, Windows Automotive, as well as branded hardware products including mice, keyboards, etc.[34]

With subsidiaries in 109 countries and 2009 figures that include a market capitalization value of $235.2 billion, sales of $58.4 billion, and net income of $14.6 billion (165 percent, 243 percent, and 219 percent of Google's respective key figures), it is apparent that Microsoft is an enormous presence in the technology industry across all operating segments and—with product offerings in four of its five segments (Server and Tools excepted) that directly rival Google offerings—an enormous competitor of Google. (See Exhibit 4 for an income statement as well as a financial summary by segment for Microsoft.)

Exhibit 4 Microsoft 2009 10-K Filing Data

MICROSOFT Corp. Year Ended June 30,					
SALES BY OPERATING SEGMENT (In millions)	2007	2008	% Change from 2007	2009	% Change from 2008
Client	14,779	16,472	11%	14,414	−12%
Server and Tools	11,117	13,121	18%	14,135	8%
Online Services Business	2,434	3,190	31%	3,088	−3%
Microsoft Business Division	16,478	18,935	15%	18,902	0%
Entertainment and Devices Division	6,136	8,213	34%	7,753	−6%
Unallocated and other	178	489	175%	145	−70%
Total Sales $	**51,122**	**60,420**	**18%**	**58,437**	**−3%**
SALES BY MAJOR GEOGRAPHIC AREAS (In millions)	2007	2008	% Change from 2007	2009	% Change from 2008
United States	$ 31,346	$ 35,928	15%	33,052	−8%
Other countries	19,776	24,492	24%	25,385	4%
Total Sales $	**$51,122**	**$60,420**	**18%**	**58,437**	**−3%**

MICROSOFT Corp Year Ended June 30,					
SALES BY OPERATING SEGMENT (in % of Total Sales)	2007	2008	% Change from 2007	2009	% Change from 2008
Client	29%	27%	−2%	25%	−3%
Server and Tools	22%	22%	0%	24%	2%
Online Services Business	5%	5%	1%	5%	0%
Microsoft Business Division	32%	31%	−1%	32%	1%
Entertainment and Devices Division	12%	14%	2%	13%	0%
Unallocated and other	0%	1%	0%	0%	−1%
Total Sales %	**100%**	**100%**	**0%**	**100%**	**0%**
SALES BY MAJOR GEOGRAPHIC AREAS (in % of Total Sales)	2007	2008	% Change from 2007	2009	% Change from 2008
United States	61%	59%	−2%	57%	−3%
Other countries	39%	41%	2%	43%	3%
Total Sales %	**100%**	**100%**	**0%**	**100%**	**0%**

Source: Securities and Exchange Commission

Apple Inc. Apple Inc.'s founders, Steve Wozniak, Steve Jobs, and Ron Wayne were reading the same magazines as Bill Gates and Paul Allen in early 1975 and founded Apple Computer Company in April 1976.[35] Taking the hardware rather than software approach of Microsoft, Apple has been defined by a very volatile history of industry highs and lows and, despite their different strategies, has been largely shaped by its lifelong competition with Microsoft.

The leadership presence of Jobs, who was ousted from the company in 1985 and returned in 1997, is the undeniable driving force behind Apple's most recent and longest lasting resurgence. Jobs envisioned the future market of several important product lines that would utilize the Mac as the "hub of [the consumer's] digital lifestyle."[36] Jobs realized his vision with breakthrough products that drive the company's financial success today including iTunes, the iPod, and the iPhone.

Apple bases its operations primarily on geographic segments rather than individual subsidiaries: users' ability to access customized language pages on its Web site by choosing from approximately 105 different countries/regions illustrates Apple's worldwide presence.[37] Apple's business strategy revolves around its commitment "to bringing the best personal computing, mobile communication, portable digital music, and video experience to consumers, students, educators, businesses, and government agencies through its inno-vative hardware, software, peripherals, services, and Internet offerings."[38] Its product offerings are broken out between Mac and iPod with subcategories defined as follows:[39]

- Mac Desktops—products include iMac, Mac mini, Mac Pro, and Xserve
- Mac Portables—including the MacBook, MacBook Air, and MacBook Pro product lines
- Music related products and services—inclusive of iTunes Store sales, iPod services, as well as Apple-branded and third-party iPod accessories
- iPhone and related products and services—comprised of handset sales, carrier agreements, and both Apple-branded and third-party iPhone accessories
- Peripherals and other hardware—display sales, wireless connectivity, networking solutions, and other hardware accessories
- Software, service, and other sales—sales of Apple-branded operating systems and application software, third-party software, AppleCare, and Internet services

As of the end of September 2009, Apple's financial performance placed it second to Microsoft with a market capitalization value of $220.5 billion, sales of $36.5 billion, and net income of $5.7 billion—143 percent, 152 percent, and 85 percent of Google's respective key figures (see Exhibit 5 for Apple's sales broken out by operating segments and geography).

Exhibit 5 Apple 2009 10-K Filing Data

APPLE Inc. *Year Ended September 26,*						
SALES BY OPERATING SEGMENT (in millions)	2007	2008	% Change from 2007	2009	% Change from 2008
Desktops	4,020	5,603	39%	4,308	−23%
Portables	6,294	8,673	38%	9,472	9%
Total Mac net sales	10,314	14,276	**38%**	13,780	**−3%**
iPod	8,305	9,153	**10%**	8,091	**−12%**
Other music related products and services	2,496	3,340	**34%**	4,036	**21%**
iPhone and related products and services	123	1,844	**1399%**	6,754	**266%**
Peripherals and other hardware	1,260	1,659	**32%**	1,470	**−11%**
Software, service and other sales	1,508	2,207	**46%**	2,406	**9%**
Total net sales	24,006	32,479	**35%**	36,537	**12%**
SALES BY MAJOR GEOGRAPHIC AREAS (in millions)	2007	2008	% Change from 2007	2009	% Change from 2008
Americas net sales	11,596	14,573	**26%**	16,142	**11%**
Europe net sales	5,460	7,622	**40%**	9,365	**23%**
Japan net sales	1,082	1,509	**39%**	1,831	**21%**
Retail net sales	4,115	6,315	**53%**	6,574	**−4%**
Other Segments net sales	1,753	2,460	**40%**	2,625	**7%**
Total net sales	24,006	32,479	**35%**	36,537	**12%**

(Continued)

Exhibit 5 Apple 2009 10-K Filing Data (*Continued*)

APPLE Inc. *Year Ended September 26,*					
SALES BY OPERATING SEGMENT **(in % of Total Sales)**	**2007**	**2008**	**% Change from 2007**	**2009**	**% Change from 2008**
Desktops	17%	17%	0%	12%	−5%
Portables	26%	27%	1%	26%	−1%
Total Mac net sales	43%	44%	1%	38%	−6%
iPod	35%	28%	−7%	22%	−6%
Other music related products and services	10%	10%	0%	11%	1%
iPhone and related products and services	1%	6%	5%	18%	12%
Peripherals and other hardware	5%	5%	0%	4%	−1%
Software, service and other sales	6%	7%	1%	7%	0%
Total Sales %	**100%**	**100%**	**0%**	**100%**	**0%**
SALES BY MAJOR GEOGRAPHIC AREAS **(in % of Total Sales)**	**2007**	**2008**	**% Change from 2007**	**2009**	**% Change from 2008**
Americas net sales	48%	45%	−3%	44%	−1%
Europe net sales	23%	23%	0%	26%	3%
Japan net sales	5%	5%	0%	5%	0%
Retail net sales	17%	19%	2%	18%	−1%
Other Segments net sales	7%	8%	1%	7%	−1%
Total Sales %	**100%**	**100%**	**0%**	**100%**	**0%**

Source: Securities and Exchange Commission

On May 26, 2010, *The New York Times* reported that, "Wall Street has called the end of an era and the beginning of the next one: The most important technology product no longer sits on your desk but rather fits in your hand. Apple Passes Microsoft as No. 1 in Tech."[40] Three quarters of the way into its 2010 fiscal year, Apple's posted market capitalization increased from $220.5 billion to $222.12 billion while, one month shy of the end of its fiscal year, Microsoft's market capitalization value fell from $235.2 billion to $219.18 billion.[41] And with that, the apple upset the cart.[42]

Firm-Specific Industry Highlights

All four firms are Internet-related technological frontrunners. To succeed in an industry where obsolescence can occur with the click of a mouse, innovation is the key not only to survival, but to success as well.[43] To stay ahead of the competition, research and development as well as the ability to market and sell products and services is vital.

To tackle the first of these requirements, Google spends the majority of its operating expense dollars on research and development. As for the second, anyone that looks at the source of its revenue can determine that Google is in the business of advertising. Coupled with the fact that its products and services are virtual—thus limiting its cost of sales by reducing labor, production, warehousing, and distribution costs—it is not necessary for Google to spend a significant amount on sales and marketing (see Exhibit 6 for an overview of Google's expenses).

On the other hand, because Microsoft sells physical goods in addition to its virtual offerings as well as the fact it must now defend its market position, Microsoft spends

Exhibit 6 Google Expenses: 2007 to 2009

GOOGLE			
(in millions, except percentages)	**2007**	**2008**	**2009**
Research and development expenses	$2,120	$2,793	$2,843
as a Percentage of Sales	13%	12.8%	12%
Sales and marketing expenses	$1,461	$1,946	$1,984
as a Percentage of Sales	8.8%	8.9%	8.4%
General and administrative expenses	$1,279	$1,803	$1,667
as a Percentage of Sales	7.7%	8.3%	7%

Source: Securities and Exchange Commission

Exhibit 7 Microsoft Expenses: 2007 to 2009

MICROSOFT			
(In millions, except percentages)	**2007**	**2008**	**2009**
Research and development expenses	$ 7,121	$ 8,164	$ 9,010
as a Percentage of Sales	14%	14%	15%
Sales and marketing expenses	$11,541	$13,260	$12,879
as a Percentage of Sales	23%	22%	22%
General and administrative expenses	$ 3,329	$ 5,127	$ 3,700
as a Percentage of Sales	7%	8%	6%

Source: Securities and Exchange Commission

heavily on both sales and marketing (see Exhibit 7). Because Microsoft largely relies on the success and widespread use of its Windows and Office products and makes only incremental innovations, it has to work harder to sell new products and services. However, as Google moves into Microsoft's software market with Google Apps, rather than defend this heavily fortified position, Microsoft is instead looking to take a bite out of Google's online search market and feels its partnership with Yahoo! is the means to achieve this goal.

Despite having no physical goods, Yahoo!'s research and development, marketing, and sales expenditures have largely mirrored those of Microsoft rather than that of Google. In recent years, Yahoo! has made incremental increases to its research and development budget that are nearly directly offset by decreases to its sales and marketing budget, a shift made possible by their partnership with Microsoft.

As has been its strategy and style from the beginning, Apple's approach and a possible key to its success lies in its ability to market itself through a "digital lifestyle" that touts its products as highly desirable, premium offerings as well as "a culture of secrecy, marketing capability, brand image, and Steve Jobs."[44] Validating the secrecy aspect and as seen in Exhibit 8, Apple does not differentiate its sales and marketing costs from its general and administrative expenses. Adding to the mystique,

viewed as a percentage of sales, Apple's research and development expenses consistently run an average of 10 percent *less* than that of its competitors. In true Apple form, instead of providing insight, Apple's financial disclosures seem to create more questions.

Together, these four companies illustrate varying degrees of diversification, but each remains under the related technology umbrellas of computing applications and use of the Internet. Associated technological trends necessary to remain competitive are explored next.

The Global Impact of Technology

In the Internet Age, ever-changing technology rules the domain. As recently as just two decades ago, the Internet was in the "early adopters" stage with the average consumer experiencing personal computing for the first time.[45] By the end of 2009, there were 1.8 billion Internet users worldwide with an impressive 40 percent of those users residents of undeveloped or third world nations.[46] As the exponential pace of technological advancement continues to render yesterday's innovations obsolete, companies competing in an industry relying on the Internet will find that, without the proper investment in infrastructure, no amount of innovation will keep them ahead of the competition. The technologies necessary to ensure the viability of a firm in this industry include server hardware, storage, and bandwidth.

Exhibit 8 Apple Expenses: 2007 to 2009

APPLE			
(In millions, except percentages)	**2007**	**2008**	**2009**
Research and development expenses	$782	1,109	1,333
as a Percentage of Sales	3%	3%	4%
Sales and marketing expenses [(1)]	—	—	—
as a Percentage of Sales	—	—	—
General and administrative expenses	2,963	$3,761	$4,149
as a Percentage of Sales	12%	12%	11%

[(1)] Included as "Selling Expense" in the "General and administrative expenses" line

Source: Securities and Exchange Commission

Server Hardware. Many companies offer server hardware including HP, Dell, IBM, and Sun. Platform compatibility and comparable specifications make server hardware a commodity to large businesses. Interestingly, Google does not purchase servers but instead, builds its own. The Gartner Group, an information technology research and advisory firm, estimated in 2006 that Google has become the fourth largest server manufacturer in the world saying, "They are building an enormous computing resource on a scale that is almost unimaginable."[47]

Storage. For most large-scale web companies, storage space is a significant investment. Most companies use large storage arrays: single devices that hold many high-performance drives that generally include redundancy to handle drive failures. These devices, and the drivers inside them, come at a cost significantly higher than standard desktop computer storage. As with server hardware, Google does not follow the norm, instead adopting a low-price, high-redundancy model where individual drives are very inexpensive and are expected to fail.[48] Exact details of Google's configurations, however, are a closely held trade secret.

Bandwidth. Transferring data over the Internet has a cost, in the form of bandwidth. Internet service providers (ISPs) generally charge based on the amount of data transferred; however, information on how much very large firms pay for bandwidth is tightly controlled. It is widely suspected that Google pays very little for bandwidth due to its large-scale purchases of "dark fiber"—fiber optic cable laid in the dot-com heyday but since left unused.[49]

To say that Google's entire basis for operations depends upon the Internet's existence and functionality is not an exaggeration. Additionally, with advertising providing 97 percent of Google's revenues and with approximately 47 percent of that revenue attributed to US sales (see Exhibit 9), it is no surprise that Google aspires to "change the competitive landscape of broadband America."[50] To do so, it is focusing its capital resources into the development of "ultra-fast fiber networks it plans to start rolling out in the near future."[51]

In addition to the fixed fiber optic connection challenges, the demand for wireless connectivity presents a completely separate host of issues. Between year-end 2008 and year-end 2009, the amount of data transfers that occurred via mobile computing grew an astounding 158 percent. The growth within this segment has been so significant over the past five years that mobile providers are struggling to catch up and expectations are that the growth of this segment's bandwidth needs will outpace that of desktop computing within the very near future. The introduction of appealing mobile computing devices such as Android-based devices, the iPhone, iPad, and connected iPods, have wireless providers rethinking the flat-rate plans—initially offered to entice wary users—that dominate this segment. Google's entry into this market has already caused one of the world's largest mobile operators, Telefonica, to consider charging Google and "other big Internet firms" for access to its network. With mobile data traffic expected to increase to 39 times its present rate within the next five years, network providers are seeking ways to monetize this segment and, consequently, the cost of doing business for Internet-based companies, including Google, will rise.[52]

The sum of 4.6 billion worldwide mobile subscriptions and 1.8 billion worldwide Internet users equals what one computer scientist at the University of California in Berkeley coined to be "the industrial revolution of data."[53] With increases in mobile computing, the demand for digital global storage has outpaced supply since 2007. This fact makes the discussions of cloud computing—virtual data warehouses with enormous capacity that store data via the Internet—that upstaged Office 2010 at its own launch party a bit more understandable.[54]

According to data provided by Euromonitor International, despite the global financial crisis that created economic volatility in virtually all markets and defined the economic climate for the past three years,[55] since 2004, the number of worldwide Internet users has increased 93 percent with the majority of that growth happening in emerging markets, particularly in the Middle East/Africa and Asia Pacific geographic regions. According to Millward Brown Optimor, a consultancy that issues annual reports aimed at measuring the intangible value of brand names to the companies that own them, as of April 2010, Google, Apple, and Microsoft were in three of the top four spots.[56] With the growing relevance of consumers and Internet users in emerging markets, global macroeconomic factors can affect these companies almost as much as the changes in technology previously discussed.

Strategies Used

Google's competitive environment is extremely complicated as it is involves different industries and markets, each with its own set of competitors and challenges. As briefly discussed previously, Google's main areas of focus are Search, Advertising, Apps, and Mobile.

Exhibit 9 Google 2009 10-K SEC Filing Data

GOOGLE Inc. Year Ended December 31,					
SALES BY OPERATING SEGMENT (in millions)	**2007**	**2008**	**% Change from 2007**	**2009**	**% Change from 2008**
Advertising revenues:					
Google web sites	$10,625	$14,414	36%	$15,722	9%
Google Network web sites	5,788	6,715	16%	7,166	7%
Total advertising revenues	16,413	21,129	29%	22,889	8%
Licensing and other revenues	181	667	268%	762	14%
Total Sales $	**16,594**	**21,796**	**31%**	**23,651**	**9%**
SALES BY MAJOR GEOGRAPHIC AREAS (in millions)	**2007**	**2008**	**% Change from 2007**	**2009**	**% Change from 2008**
United States	8,698	10,636	22%	11,194	5%
United Kingdom	2,531	3,038	20%	2,986	−2%
Rest of the world	5,365	8,122	51%	9,471	17%
Total Sales $	**16,594**	**21,796**	**31%**	**23,651**	**9%**
GOOGLE Inc. Year Ended December 31,					
SALES BY OPERATING SEGMENT (in % of Total Sales)	**2007**	**2008**	**% Change from 2007**	**2009**	**% Change from 2008**
Advertising revenues:					
Google web sites	64%	66%	2%	66%	0%
Google Network web sites	35%	31%	−4%	30%	−1%
Total advertising revenues	99%	97%	−2%	97%	0%
Licensing and other revenues	1%	3%	2%	3%	0%
Total Sales %	**100%**	**100%**	**0%**	**100%**	**0%**
SALES BY MAJOR GEOGRAPHIC AREAS (in % of Total Sales)	**2007**	**2008**	**% Change from 2007**	**2009**	**% Change from 2008**
United States	52%	49%	−4%	47%	−1%
United Kingdom	15%	14%	−1%	13%	−1%
Rest of the world	32%	37%	5%	40%	3%
Total Sales %	**100%**	**100%**	**0%**	**100%**	**0%**

Source: Securities and Exchange Commission

Search

Page and Brin's original data indexing algorithms were the start of Google's success and Google's search capabilities have only gotten better as the two continue their pursuit of the most perfectly intuitive Internet search. In the words of Larry Page: "The perfect search engine would understand exactly what you mean and give back exactly what you want. When the dot-com boom exploded and competitors spent millions on marketing campaigns to "build brand," Google focused instead on quietly building a better search engine."[57,58]

Google adopted several key areas of search comprehensiveness and relevance in which it seeks continuous advancements: objectivity, global access, ease of use, pertinent and useful commercial information, multiple access platforms, and improving the web.[59] As Google grew, it increased its capital expenditures to target these key areas and others including satellite imaging. The effect of this spending resulted in a solid infrastructure, better products, increased traffic, appeal for advertisers, and what is most likely a standard unreachable by competitors.[60]

Advertising

With its single overarching strategy in advertising sales to deliver cost-effective, targeted, relevant ads that are useful to the end user, advertising dollars provide 97 percent of Google's revenue. In the Google world, "Ads are information and complement search results."[61]

AdWords and AdSense are the two main advertising products of Google. AdWords allows advertisers to target their ads to user searches for specific topics and/or geographic regions. This provides advertisers with a very targeted, cost-effective, and successful method of advertising and provides users with ads that are relevant to where they are and what they are interested in at that moment. To get on board, advertising customers bid in an auction format to have their ads appear next to search results for certain keywords.[62] Google's second advertising product, AdSense, allows Web site owners to share in the revenue generated by click-through traffic from Google ads placed on their site that are targeted to users based on the content of their site. AdSense has become an easy and common way for companies and individuals to generate revenue through their Web sites.

When an advertiser pays Google to show you an ad, Google believes you have the right to know and that it has an ethical responsibility to tell you. Because of this, Google differentiates ads from other content with a "sponsored links" or "Ads by Google" label. In addition, ad placements are not available for sale inside search results and advertisers cannot pay a premium for a higher ranking inside a search. These strategies benefit the user greatly as ads do not clutter actual search results. Google also makes tracking advertising more measureable and efficient for advertisers by offering tools like Google Analytics, Website Optimizer, Insights for Search, and Ad Planner.

Apps

Google Apps, including Gmail and YouTube, exist to improve the web for users and provide another avenue for advertising. Google offers apps like Gmail free for personal and educational use, with a nominal fee for business use, to offer additional functionality to users, improve their web experience, and ultimately, to generate goodwill for Google. While some apps do not contain ads (such as Google Docs and Picasa), several of them do. Gmail, for instance, serves up context-relevant ads based on the content of recent emails.

Google recently launched the Google Apps Marketplace, similar to the Android Market except specifically for web applications that integrate seamlessly with other Google Apps. The Marketplace is the first viable platform for cloud computing from third parties. This works well for increasing utilization of the Google Apps platform because, in the words of Google, "we certainly can't and won't do it all, and there are hundreds of business applications for which we have no particular

expertise."[63] Bringing third parties in strategically fills this gap and offers more functionality without dedicating Google's resources to creating applications outside its expertise.[64] Google collects 20 percent of the revenue generated by the third-party applications without spending any additional resources of its own. In exchange, app developers are integrated with Google products that are a core part of many users' lives and gain access to a huge audience. Due to the immense computing power offered by Google and low costs for both parties, this approach is virtually limitless.

Cloud computing is the centerpiece of Google's 2010 strategy. Schmidt told CNBC, "It's a new model. You basically put all your information on servers and you have fast networks and lots of different kinds of PCs and mobile phones that can use the applications . . . it's a powerful model and it's where the industry is going. It is the centerpiece of our 2010 strategy."[65]

What is Google's cloud? It's a network made of, by some estimates, one million inexpensive servers, each not much more powerful than the PCs in our homes. This network stores huge amounts of data including multiple mirrors, or copies, of the World Wide Web. This makes search faster, helping find answers to billions of queries in a fraction of a second. However, unlike many traditional supercomputers, Google's system doesn't get old. When an individual server dies, usually after about three years, a newer and faster one replaces it. This means the cloud regenerates its computing power and capacity as it grows.[66]

Mobile

Google's strategy in the mobile market has been a remarkable success as evidenced by the rapid growth in Android-enabled handsets in the past year. There are two main components to Google's mobile strategy: free, rich feature offerings and distribution of the operating system to handset manufacturers for free or, as explained later, less than free. [67]

Android has made a dramatic push in market share by matching and often surpassing competitors' features. Apple's iPhone 3G offers a touch screen, accelerometer, app store, GPS, compass, video camera, and voice recognition.[68] The Motorola Droid, a flagship Android device competing with the iPhone, offers all of these same features plus a QWERTY keyboard and multitasking.[69]

Apple recently announced that the iPhone would not support Adobe Flash, a major component of rich media on the Internet. Android, however, has announced that its next software upgrade will support not only Flash, but more advanced Microsoft Exchange features as well.[70,71] In what may be Android's most "killer app," turn-by-turn GPS navigation is also available free through Google Maps. Turn-by-turn navigation has historically required access to proprietary databases maintained by GPS companies; however, Google makes it available free on Android (immediately causing stocks for GPS companies Garmin and TomTom to drop 16 percent and 21 percent, respectively).

Android is an open-source operating system meaning it is free for anyone to use and modify as needed. If that was not reason enough for handset and tablet manufacturers to use it, Google also shares advertising revenues with manufacturers using Google's Apps pack. In other words, instead of paying licensing fees for phone operating systems, manufacturers are instead paid to use Android. This "less-than-free" business model is a new concept in the mobile device world and will likely change the game significantly.[72]

Strategic Challenges

To help summarize, three major challenges in Google's immediate future are examined (these may not be exhaustive as its competitive landscape is continually evolving): managing the growth of Android, handling the escalating situation in China, and responding to the increasing customer concerns over privacy.

Android

Android is the name of the mobile phone operating system developed by the OHA, a movement led by Google to create a standard, open-source, free platform for mobile devices. Android was developed to compete directly with Apple's iPhone and Microsoft Windows Mobile. Google, like Apple, has an online mobile application store where users can purchase third-party software.

Open Handset Alliance (OHA). In late 2007, Google led in the creation of the OHA, an alliance originally formed by an impressive 65 member companies (now more than 80) that all agreed to the development and endorsement of a standard mobile device platform called Android. OHA member companies continue to represent a wide range of industries including mobile device manufacturers like Motorola and HTC, service providers such as T-Mobile and Sprint Nextel, semiconductor companies including Intel and NVidia, software companies such as Accenture and Wind River, and commercialization companies including eBay and NXP.[73]

The "first joint project" of the OHA was to create Android, which "was built from the ground up with the explicit goal to be the first open, complete, and free platform created specifically for mobile devices."[74]

Android has enjoyed unprecedented growth in the mobile arena. Gartner trends as of Q1 2010 showed that Android device shipments increased to 9.6 percent of smartphones, compared to just 1.6 percent in Q1 2009.[75] In fact, by year-end 2010, Android had catapulted to the number two spot on Gartner's worldwide smartphone sales to end users by operating system statistics laying stake to 22.7% of market share.

While Apple has very stringent controls on the software available for sale in the iPhone App Store, offering applications for sale in Google's Android Market requires no prior approval. Google also has far fewer controls on allowable software, provided they do not violate the Android Developer Distribution Agreement.

Launched in October 2008, the number of apps available via Android Market has experienced exponential growth, surpassing the 200,000 mark by year-end 2010.

Android's Strategic Challenges. Strategically, the mobile market may be very important to Google. How can Google help sustain Android's growth in the market? What is the best way for Google to monetize mobile computing? What can Google do to make Android-based handsets a "must-have" over the iPhone, BlackBerry, and Nokia systems? With the exponential growth of wireless computing, how can Google appease wireless providers?

China

In December 2009, Google and about 20 other companies were the targets of a highly sophisticated attack dubbed "Operation Aurora."[76] As a major market, this event had serious implications for Google and changed the way it does business in China.

The Golden Shield Project and Operation Aurora. With more than 1.3 billion citizens, China is an ideal target for global expansion of products and services for many companies—Google included. However, inherent social fears and an autocratic form of government led by the Communist Party of China (CPC) prevent the easy access of foreign companies.

Billed as the Golden Shield Project (and also known as The Great Firewall of China), and affecting many of Google's offerings, in 2003, China announced that foreign media companies must seek prior approval before distributing pictures, graphics, and news.[77] This project was a censoring mechanism utilized by the Chinese government to monitor, track, and at times block access to subversive material. Prompted when the Chinese government recognized that access to YouTube provided viewers with sexually explicit and politically subversive material (such as video footage of the 1989 protests and government backed massacre in Tiananmen Square), it evolved into a much broader level of control that ultimately prevented Chinese citizens from accessing all of Google's applications.

Investigative research conducted by Google found that not only did the attacks originate in China with the primary goal to access Gmail accounts of Chinese human rights activists,[78] but that the attacks were so sophisticated—utilizing highly advanced levels of encryption to avoid detection—that most concluded the Chinese government was involved.[79] In the end, Google determined that Aurora accessed only two Gmail accounts; however, the ongoing investigation has revealed that dozens of advocates for human rights in China using Gmail in the US, China, and Europe have been hacked by phishing scams or malware intrusions.[80]

In response to the network intrusions and the Chinese government's mandated censorship, Google decided it would not seek approval of its content from the Chinese government and instead now redirects all user attempts to access google.cn (Google China) to the uncensored google.com.hk (Google Hong Kong).

Baidu. In addition to its political/social struggle with the Chinese government, China is the home of one of Google's main regional competitors: Baidu. In 2008, Comscore data showed Baidu had passed Google to become the most popular country-specific search engine—and Baidu offers much more than just search.[81] In addition to its e-commerce market and online payment business, the Baidu Union ad network claims more than 1 billion ad impressions daily.[82] Baidu has been the main beneficiary of the explosive growth of the Internet in China. Currently, Baidu has nearly 70 percent of the market share in China: a number that has been growing 30 to 40 percent each year. Google China has approximately 20 percent market share and has experienced several execution setbacks in the past few years.[83] If Google chooses to pull out of China because of government controls, China will be left with just one major Internet search engine. Unfortunately, this would likely slow the development of the Internet in China. According to Yu Yang, a chief executive at Analysis International, a Beijing research firm, "The whole industry will become worse. Without competition with Google, Baidu has no motivation to innovate."[84] Baidu achieved the top spot in China due to its keen understanding of local tastes and its willingness to cooperate with government censorship. In three months time, Baidu stock climbed from ~$52 to ~$76[85] and some analysts speculate that Google's inability to catch Baidu may be one reason it is considering pulling out of China.[86]

Strategic Challenges in China. Should Google stand by its "don't be evil" and "the need for information crosses all borders" philosophies and continue to provide uncensored content to China?[87] Alternatively, does the additional market share make it worth the risk of exploiting the loopholes afforded by the Internet? Or will Google's OHA partners' concern about the potential of Google's position disrupting relationships with major Chinese cellular phone service providers force Google to play nice?

Privacy

As the Internet and its use grows, concern over online privacy has extended beyond that of the passing thought of a solitary programmer and into fodder for public speculation and conversation. The press has recently targeted the popular social networking site Facebook for exploiting access to user data and has criticized Google for eavesdropping on Internet traffic from wireless hotspots. Users are starting to take online privacy much more seriously, a fact that spells challenges for the company that knows more about most Internet users than any other.

Each time it is used, Google's search engine saves personal information surrounding the user's areas of interests using a system of tracking cookies. In addition, email content (Gmail), personal and business schedules (Google Calendar), favorite destinations searches (Google Latitude), viewing habits (YouTube), voicemail (Google Voice), online business and personal collaborations (Google Docs), Photos (Picasa), and even favorite books (Google Books) are also available to Google.[88] The fact that Google even possesses such data makes it a ripe target for attacks such as Project Aurora.

History has shown us that information leaks, data system attacks, and data spills happen. In 2006, AOL inadvertently released the search activity of 658,000 users quickly sending a shockwave of concern throughout its customer base and negatively affecting its membership and reputation.[89]

Social networking site Facebook, the world's second most popular Web site (after Google),[90] has fueled the fire of privacy concerns by exhibiting repeated disregard for user privacy. Information like photos and status updates that were originally private have become publicly available, user data is being shared with third parties without explicit approval, changing the default privacy settings is complicated and cumbersome, and completely deleting a Facebook account is notoriously difficult.[91] As a result, Facebook has become a lightning rod for privacy concerns, a trend that is now turning its eye toward Google.

While Google has had relatively few major privacy violations, there is a great deal of "what if?" speculation regarding what could happen when one company is responsible for so much private data. The most notable privacy issues caused by Google include Google Buzz and Wi-Fi eavesdropping.

Google Buzz. Google launched its new social networking service, Google Buzz, to compete directly with Facebook and, blending the worlds of private email and public social communication, Google fully integrated its new app with users' Gmail accounts. However, in a much-criticized and quickly reversed decision, unless users opted out, Google had made the default setting of Google Buzz to publicly display all of a user's Gmail contacts thus triggering an immediate outcry from privacy experts and resulting in Google's revision of the settings.[92]

Wi-Fi Eavesdropping. Thinking it could kill two birds with one stone, when Google sent its Street View vehicles out to take 360-degree photographs of streets around the world, it also tasked them with indexing and cataloging the wireless networks within range of their routes. In doing so however, they were also saving whatever users were doing on those wireless networks at the time: approximately 600 GB of data per network. Google announced that it was not aware its Street View vehicles were capturing the data and Alan Eustace, Senior VP of Engineering and Research, wrote, "We are acutely aware that we failed badly here."[93]

Strategic Challenges for Privacy. Moving forward, under increased scrutiny of privacy, how can Google maintain the trust of the Internet-using public—without which it would be impossible to continue its current business practices?

Conclusion

All things considered, Google has come a long way from its simple beginnings as a grad school project to becoming a defining icon of the culture of the Internet age. While Google has competition in each industry it serves, its main cross-industry competition comes from the giants of the digital age: Apple, Microsoft, and Yahoo!

Despite the fact that Google is in an excellent position technologically, financially, and culturally, there are still real challenges looming on the horizon. These challenges take the form of growth for its mobile platform, a rapidly worsening situation in China, and an increased focus on user privacy that, unaddressed, could threaten Google's status.

Faced with a rapidly changing world and a constantly moving technological landscape, Google's strategy of providing excellent services to end users at no cost has won many computing hearts and minds. However, with a thoroughly undiversified revenue stream, it is wise to continue to innovate, keep its ear to the ground, and not rest solely on its current strong base.

NOTES

1. Google Inc. Google Search Results. *Google.* [Online] Accessed Jun 2010. http://www.google.com/search?sourceid=chrome&ie=UTF-8&q=define:google
2. Markoff, J. Yahoo deal is big, but is it the next big thing? *Silicon Valley Memo.* [Online] *The New York Times,* Feb 3, 2008. http://www.nytimes.com/2008/02/03/technology/03valley.html?pagewanted=1&_r=1&ei=5087&em&en=d1049203ae0dc529&ex=1202187600
3. Google Inc. Technology Overview. *Corporate Information.* [Online] Accessed May 2010. http://www.google.com/intl/en/corporate/tech.html
4. Hansell, S. and Markoff, J. A search engine that's becoming an inventor. *The New York Times-Technology.* [Online] Jul 3, 2006. http://www.nytimes.com/2006/07/03/technology/03google.html?ei=5088&en=11ad7f241098c6e2&ex=1309579200&adxnnl=1&partner=rssnyt&emc=rss&adxnnlx=1151888719-NxrsEO+lzRvSa28feeFzfw&pagewanted=all&pagewanted=all
5. Google Inc. Google History. *Corporate Information.* [Online] Accessed May 2010. http://www.google.com/corporate/history.html
6. Alexa The Web Information Company. Top Sites. *Alexa The Web Information Company.* [Online] Accessed May 2010. http://www.alexa.com/topsites
7. Google Inc. Google History. *op. cit.*
8. Google Inc. Investor Relations. *2009 SEC Filings Archive.* [Online] Accessed Feb 2010. http://investor.google.com/documents/2009_google_annual_report.html
9. Google Inc. Dr. Eric Schmidt Joins Google's Board of Directors as Chairman. *Press Center.* [Online] Mar 26, 2001. http://www.google.com/press/pressrel/chairman.html
10. Google Inc. Google History. *op. cit.*
11. Wikipedia. List of acquisitions by Google. *Wikipedia, the free encyclopedia.* [Online] Accessed May 2010. http://en.wikipedia.org/wiki/List_of_acquisitions_by_Google
12. Google Inc. Overview. *Corporate Information.* [Online] Accessed May 2010. http://www.google.com/intl/en/corporate/
13. *Ibid.*
14. Google Inc. Translated Search. *Language Tools.* [Online] Accessed May 2010. http://www.google.com/language_tools?hl=en
15. Google Inc. Our Philosophy. *Corporate Information.* [Online] Accessed May 2010. http://www.google.com/intl/en/corporate/tenthings.html
16. Google Inc. Investor Relations. *2009 SEC Filings Archive. op. cit.*
17. Google Inc. Our Philosophy. *op. cit.*
18. *Ibid.*
19. Google Inc. Investor Relations. *2009 SEC Filings Archive. op. cit.*
20. Google Inc. Investor Relations. *2010 SEC Filings Archive.* [Online] Accessed May 2010. http://investor.google.com/documents/2010_google_proxy_statement.html
21. Google Inc. Management Team. *Corporate Information.* [Online] Accessed May 2010. http://www.google.com/intl/en/corporate/execs.html
22. Apple Inc. Dr. Eric Schmidt Resigns from Apple's Board of Directors. *Press Release.* [Online] Aug 3, 2009. http://www.apple.com/pr/library/2009/08/03bod.html

23. The White House. About PCAST. *Office of Science and Technology Policy*. [Online] Apr 27, 2009. http://www.whitehouse.gov/administration/eop/ostp/pcast/about

24. Google Inc. Management Team. *Corporate Information. op. cit.*

25. Baker, L. Timeline of search engine history. *Search Engine Journal*. [Online] Sep 15, 2009. http://www.searchenginejournal.com/search-engine-history/13152/

26. Tate, R. An instant history of Yahoo. *Valleywag*. [Online] Dec 10, 2008. http://gawker.com/#!5106940/an-instant-history-of-yahoo

27. Baker, L. *op. cit.*

28. Singer, R. Yahoo and Microsoft join search forces. *WIRED*. [Online] Feb 18, 2010. http://www.wired.com/epicenter/2010/02/yahoo-microsoft-search/

29. Yahoo! Inc. Investor Relations. *SEC Filings*. [Online] Accessed Feb 2010. http://files.shareholder.com/downloads/YHOO/1204918651x0xS1193125-09-41172/1011006/filing.pdf

30. Singer, R. *op. cit.*

31. BBC. Timeline: Bill Gates and Microsoft. *BBC News*. [Online] Jun 18, 2008. http://news.bbc.co.uk/2/hi/business/7457191.stm

32. *Ibid.*

33. Microsoft Corp. Facts About Microsoft. *Microsoft News Center*. [Online] Accessed May 2010. http://www.microsoft.com/presspass/inside_ms.mspx

34. Microsoft. Investor Relations. *Microsoft SEC Filings*. [Online] Accessed Jul 2010. http://shareholder.api.edgar-online.com/efx_dll/edgarpro.dll?FetchFilingRTF1?sessionid=Bng6HtJ6viJK2bN&ID=7382799&PageBreakStyleID=2

35. Mesa, A. F. Apple History Timeline. *Apple Museum*. [Online] Oct 1998. http://applemuseum.bott.org/sections/history.html

36. Chapman, R. and Hoskisson, R. E. 2008. Apple Computer, Inc.: Maintaining the Music Business while Introducing iPhone and Apple TV. In R. D. Ireland, R. E. Hoskisson and M. A. Hitt (eds.) *Understanding Business Strategy: Concepts & Cases*. Cengage Learning: Mason, OH.

37. Apple, Inc. Choose your country or region. *Apple Inc. Corporate Website*. [Online] Accessed May 2010. http://www.apple.com/choose-your-country/

38. Apple, Inc. Investor Relations. *SEC Filings*. [Online] Accessed May 2010. https://www.apple.com/investor/

39. *Ibid.*

40. Helft, M. and Vance, A. Apple passes Microsoft as no. 1 in tech. *The New York Times*. [Online] May 26, 2010. http://www.nytimes.com/2010/05/27/technology/27apple.html

41. *Ibid.*

42. Using English. Idiom: Don't upset the apple cart. *UsingEnglish.com*. [Online] Accessed Mar 2011. http://www.usingenglish.com/reference/idioms/don't+upset+the+applecart.html

43. Chapman, R. and Hoskisson, R. E. 2008. *op. cit.*

44. *Ibid.*

45. Ulmer, D. J. and ISSU. What's beyond information. *Beyond the Information Age*. [Online] Jan 3, 2007. http://www.vias.org/beyinfoage/beyinfoage_06_03.html

46. The World Bank. Number of Internet Users by Region, 2000 and 2007. [Online] Accessed Mar 2011. http://web.worldbank.org/WBSITE/EXTERNAL/TOPICS/EXTINFORMATIONANDCOMMUNICATIONANDTECHNOLOGIES/EXTIC4D/0,,contentMDK:22229812~menuPK:6202960~pagePK:64168445~piPK:64168309~theSitePK:5870636,00.html

47. Hansell, S. and Markoff, J. *op. cit.*

48. Mellor, C. Google's storage strategy. *TechWorld*. [Online] Apr 6, 2004. http://features.techworld.com/storage/467/googles-storage-strategy/

49. The Economist. World Wide Wait: The faster the Internet becomes, the slower it loads pages. *Science & Technology*. [Online] Feb 12, 2010. http://www.economist.com/node/15523761

50. The Economist. Googlenet: A cure for America's lame and costly broadband. *Science & Technology*. [Online] Apr 1, 2010. http://www.economist.com/node/15841658

51. *Ibid.*

52. The Economist. Breaking up: Will the rapid growth in data traffic overwhelm wireless networks? *Business & Finance*. [Online] Feb 11, 2010. http://www.economist.com/node/15498399

53. The Economist. Data, data everywhere: Information has gone from scarce to superabundant. *A special report on managing information*. [Online] Feb 25, 2010. http://www.economist.com/node/15557443

54. The Economist. Office politics: Microsoft bids to keep its grip on corporate computing against Google's challenge. *Business & Finance*. [Online] May 13, 2010. http://www.economist.com/node/16113333

55. Brookings. Collection of Articles. *Global Financial Crisis*. [Online] Accessed May 2010. http://www.brookings.edu/topics/global-financial-crisis.aspx

56. The Economist. The world turned upside down. *A special report on innovation in emerging markets*. [Online] Apr 15, 2010. http://www.economist.com/node/15879369

57. Google Inc. Our Philosophy. *op. cit.*

58. Google Inc. Investor Relations. *2009 SEC Filings Archive. op. cit.*

59. *Ibid.*

60. The Financial Times. Google. *LEX Column*. Mar 31, 2006. page 16.

61. Google Inc. About Google Ads. *AdWords*. [Online] 2010. http://www.google.com/adwords/aboutgoogleads/#utm_source=about_page_en-us&utm_medium=about_page_promo&utm_campaign=en]%%2029

62. Google Inc. Investor Relations. *2009 SEC Filings Archive. op. cit.*

63. Google Inc. Open for Business: the Google Apps Marketplace. *The Official Google Blog*. [Online] Mar 9, 2010. http://googleblog.blogspot.com/2010/03/open-for-business-google-apps.html

64. Google Inc. Investor Relations. *2009 SEC Filings Archive. op. cit.*

65. Brodie, L. CEO Eric Schmidt Reveals 'Centerpiece' of Google's 2010 Strategy. *CNBC*. [Online] Dec 3, 2009. http://www.cnbc.com/id/34264616/CEO_Eric_Schmidt_Reveals_Centerpiece_Of_Google_s_2010_Strategy

66. Google Inc. Top ten advantages of Google's cloud. *Google Apps for Business*. [Online] Accessed Mar 2011. http://www.google.com/apps/intl/en/business/cloud.html

67. Gurley, B. Google redefines disruption: The "less than free" business model. *abovethecrowd.com*. [Online] Oct 29, 2009. http://abovethecrowd.com/2009/10/29/google-redefines-disruption-the-%E2%80%9Cless-than-free%E2%80%9D-business-model/

68. Apple Inc. Apple Introduces the New iPhone 3G. *Press Release*. [Online] Jun 9, 2008. http://www.apple.com/pr/library/2008/06/09iphone.html

69. Motorola. DROID by Motorola. *Mobile Phones*. [Online] Accessed May 2010. http://www.motorola.com/Consumers/US-EN/Consumer-Product-and-Services/Mobile-Phones/ci.Motorola-DROID-US-EN.alt

70. Adobe Systems Incorporated. Adobe Flash Player 10.1 beta for Android (2.2) FroYo now available. *Adobe Labs*. [Online] May 20, 2010. http://blogs.adobe.com/labs/archives/2010/05/adobe_flash_pla_4.html

71. Android Developers. Android 2.2 Platform Highlights. *ANDROID developers*. [Online] Accessed May 2010. http://developer.android.com/sdk/android-2.2-highlights.html

72. Gurley, B. *op.cit.*

73. Open Handset Alliance. Members. *Alliance*. [Online] Accessed May 2010. http://www.openhandsetalliance.com/oha_members.html

74. Open Handset Alliance. Overview. *Alliance*. [Online] Accessed May 2010. http://www.openhandsetalliance.com/oha_overview.html

75. Gartner. Gartner says worldwide mobile phone sales grew 17 percent in first quarter 2010. *Press Releases*. [Online] May 19, 2010. http://www.gartner.com/it/page.jsp?id=1372013

76. De, P. Google hack attack (Operation Aurora): What we know. *Techie Buzz* . [Online] Jan 15, 2010. http://techie-buzz.com/tech-news/google-hack-attack-operation-aurora.html

77. Anderson, N. Do Google and YouTube have ethical responsibility for their video services? *ARS Technica*. [Online] Nov 27, 2006. http://arstechnica.com/news.ars/post/20061127-8289.html

78. Drummond, D. A new approach to China. *The Official Google Blog*. [Online] Jan 12, 2010. http://googleblog.blogspot.com/2010/01/new-approach-to-china.html

79. De, P. *op. cit.*

80. Drummond, D. *op. cit.*

81. Farley, S. Baidu vs. Google: Who's the #1 country-specific search engine? *Seeking Alpha*. [Online] Sep 22, 2008. http://seekingalpha.com/article/96785-baidu-vs-google-who-s-the-1-country-specific-search-engine

82. *Ibid.*

83. The Wall Street Transcript. With 70% Chinese market share, Baidu greatly outperforms Google. *TWST.com*. [Online] May 24, 2010. http://www.twst.com/yagoo/Wang4.html

84. Barboza, D. Baidu's gain from departure could be China's loss. *New York Times*. [Online] Jan 13, 2010. http://www.nytimes.com/2010/01/14/technology/companies/14baidu.html

85. Yahoo! Finance. Baidu, Inc. (BIDU). *Historical Prices*. [Online] Accessed May 2010. http://finance.yahoo.com/q/hp?s=BIDU+Historical+Prices

86. Barboza, D. *op. cit.*

87. Google Inc. Our Philosophy. *op. cit.*

88. Mitchell, R. What Google knows about you. *Computerworld*. [Online] May 11, 2009. http://www.computerworld.com/s/article/337791/What_Google_Knows_About_You

89. Singel, R. FAQ: AOL's search gaffe and you. *WIRED*. [Online] Aug 11, 2006. www.wired.com/politics/security/news/2006/08/71579

90. Alexa The Web Information Company. *op. cit.*

91. Yoder, D. Top ten reasons you should quit facebook. *GIZMODO*. [Online] May 3, 2010. http://gizmodo.com/5530178/top-ten-reasons-you-should-quit-facebook

92. Carlson, N. How Google went into "code red" and saved Google Buzz. *Business Insider SAI*. [Online] Feb 16, 2010. http://www.businessinsider.com/how-google-went-into-code-red-and-saved-google-buzz-2010-2

93. Yahoo! Finance. Google grabs personal info off of Wi-Fi networks. *News*. [Online] May 14, 2010. http://finance.yahoo.com/news/Google-grabs-personal-info-apf-2162289993.html?x=0

Developing Global Teams to Meet Twenty-First Century Challenges at W. L. Gore & Associates

Frank Shipper

Franklin P. Perdue School of Business, Salisbury University

Charles C. Manz

Isenberg School of Management, University of Massachusetts Amherst

Greg L. Stewart

Tippie College of Business, University of Iowa

In 2008, W. L. Gore & Associates celebrated its 50th year in business. During the first four decades of its existence, Gore became famous for its products and for its use of business teams located in a single facility. To facilitate the development of teams, corporate facilities were kept to 200 associates or fewer. Due to the challenges of a global marketplace, business teams are no longer in a single facility; in fact, they are now often spread over three continents. Gore products are sold on six continents and used on all seven, as well as under the ocean and in space. The challenge of having a successful global presence requires virtual teams to enable a high degree of coordination in the development, production, and marketing of products to customers across the world. As previously, teams are defined primarily by product, but no longer by facility. Team members are now separated by thousands of miles, multiple time zones, and a variety of languages and cultures. Growth and globalization present significant challenges for W. L. Gore as it strives to maintain a family-like, entrepreneurial culture. According to Terri Kelly, the president of Gore and a 25-year associate,[i]

In the early days, our business was largely conducted at the local level. There were global operations, but most relationships were built regionally, and most decisions were made regionally. That picture has evolved dramatically over the last 20 years, as businesses can no longer be defined by brick and mortar. Today, most of our teams are spread across regions and continents. Therefore, the decision-making process is much more global and virtual in nature, and there's a growing need to build strong relationships across geographical boundaries. The globalization of our business has been one of the biggest changes I've seen in the last 25 years.

Elements of the culture at Gore are captured in Exhibit 1. The core belief in the need to take the long-term view in business situations and to make and keep commitments drives cooperation among individuals and small teams. This is supported by key practices that replace the traditional, hierarchical structure with flexible relationships and a sense that all workers are in the same boat. The ultimate focus is on empowering talented associates to deliver highly innovative products.

Despite substantial growth, the core values have not changed at Gore. The "objective" of the company, "To make money and have fun," set forth by the founder Wilbert (Bill) Gore is still part of the Gore culture. Associates around the world are asked to follow the company's four guiding principles:

1. Try to be fair.
2. Encourage, help, and allow other associates to grow in knowledge, skill, and scope of activity and responsibility.

---

[i]Throughout this case, the word associate is used because Gore always uses the word associate instead of employee. In fact, the case writers were told that the term *associates* evolved early in the company's history because it expressed the belief that everyone had a stake in the success of the enterprise.

Many sources were helpful in providing material for this case, most particularly associates at Gore who generously shared their time and viewpoints about the company to help ensure that the case accurately reflected the company's practices and culture. They provided many resources, including internal documents and stories of their personal experiences. Copyrighted © 2009 by the case authors.

Exhibit 1 W. L. Gore & Associates' Culture

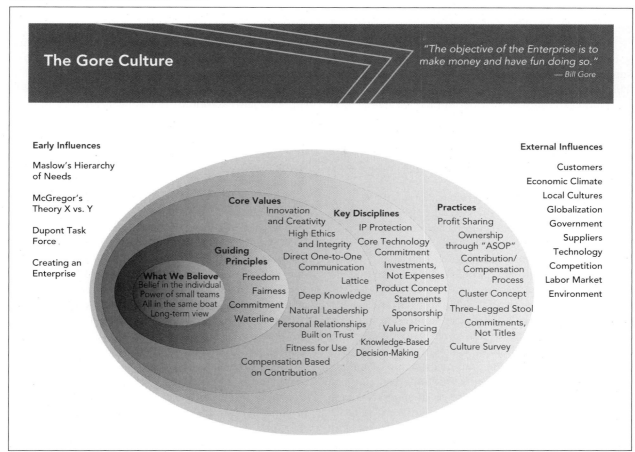

The Gore Culture

"The objective of the Enterprise is to make money and have fun doing so."
— Bill Gore

Early Influences

Maslow's Hierarchy of Needs

McGregor's Theory X vs. Y

Dupont Task Force

Creating an Enterprise

External Influences

Customers
Economic Climate
Local Cultures
Globalization
Government
Suppliers
Technology
Competition
Labor Market
Environment

Core Values
Innovation and Creativity
High Ethics and Integrity
Direct One-to-One Communication
Lattice
Deep Knowledge
Natural Leadership
Personal Relationships Built on Trust
Fitness for Use
Compensation Based on Contribution

Guiding Principles
Freedom
Fairness
Commitment
Waterline

What We Believe
Belief in the individual
Power of small teams
All in the same boat
Long-term view

Key Disciplines
IP Protection
Core Technology Commitment
Investments, Not Expenses
Product Concept Statements
Sponsorship
Value Pricing
Knowledge-Based Decision-Making

Practices
Profit Sharing
Ownership through "ASOP"
Contribution/ Compensation Process
Cluster Concept
Three-Legged Stool
Commitments, Not Titles
Culture Survey

3. Make your own commitments, and keep them.

4. Consult with other associates before taking actions that may be "below the waterline."

The four principles are referred to as *fairness, freedom, commitment,* and *waterline.* The waterline principle is drawn from an analogy to ships. If someone pokes a hole in a boat above the waterline, the boat will be in relatively little real danger. If, however, someone pokes a hole below the waterline, the boat is in immediate danger of sinking. The expectation is that "waterline" issues will be discussed across teams, plants, and continents as appropriate before those decisions are made. This principle is still emphasized even though team members who need to share in the decision-making process are now spread across the globe.

Commitment is spoken of frequently at Gore. The commitment principle's primary emphasis is on the freedom Gore's associates have to make their own commitments, rather than having others assign them to projects or tasks. But, commitment may also be viewed as a mutual commitment between associates and the enterprise. Associates worldwide commit to make contributions to the company's success. In return, the company is committed to providing a challenging, opportunity-rich work environment that is responsive to associate needs and concerns.

Background

Gore was formed by Wilbert L. "Bill" Gore and his wife in 1958. The idea for the business sprang from Bill's personal, technical, and organizational experiences at E. I. du Pont de Nemours & Co. and, in particular, his involvement in the characterization of a chemical compound with unique properties. The compound, called polytetrafluorethylene (PTFE), is now marketed by DuPont under the Teflon brand name. Bill saw a wide variety of potential applications for this unique new material and when DuPont showed little interest in pursuing most of them directly, he decided to form his own company and start pursuing the concepts himself. Thus, Gore became one of DuPont's first customers for this new material.

Since then, Gore has evolved into a global enterprise with annual revenues of more than $2.5 billion, supported by more than 8,500 associates worldwide. This placed Gore at No. 180 on *Forbes* magazine's 2008 list of the 500 largest private companies in the US. The enterprise's unique, and now famous, culture and leadership practices have helped make Gore one of only a select few companies to appear on all of the US "100 Best Companies to Work For" rankings since it was introduced in 1984.

Bill Gore was born in Meridian, Idaho, in 1912. By age six, according to his own account, he was an avid hiker in Utah. Later, at a church camp in 1935, he met Genevieve, his future wife. In their eyes, the marriage was a partnership; he would make breakfast and Vieve, as everyone called her, would make lunch. Their partnership lasted a lifetime.

Bill Gore attended the University of Utah and earned a bachelor of science in chemical engineering in 1933, and a master of science in physical chemistry in 1935. He began his professional career at American Smelting and Refining in 1936, moved to Remington Arms, a DuPont subsidiary, in 1941, and then to DuPont's headquarters in 1945. He held positions as research supervisor and head of operations research. While at DuPont, he felt a sense of excited commitment, personal fulfillment, and self-direction while working with a task force to develop applications for PTFE.

Having followed the development of the electronics industry, he felt that PTFE had ideal insulating characteristics for use with such equipment. He tried many ways to make a PTFE-coated ribbon cable without success until a breakthrough in his home basement laboratory. One night, while Bill was explaining the problem to his 19-year-old son, Bob, the young Gore saw some PTFE sealant tape and asked his father, "Why don't you try this tape?" Bill explained that everyone knew that you could not bond PTFE to itself. After Bob went to bed, however, Bill remained in the basement lab and proceeded to try what conventional wisdom said could not be done. At about 5:00 AM Bill woke up Bob, waving a small piece of cable around and saying excitedly, "It works, it works!" The following night father and son returned to the basement lab to make ribbon cable insulated with PTFE. Because the idea came from Bob, the patent for the cable was issued in his name.

After a while, Bill Gore came to realize that DuPont wanted to remain a supplier of raw materials for industrial buyers and not a manufacturer of high-tech products for end-use markets. Bill and Vieve began discussing the possibility of starting their own insulated

wire and cable business. On January 1, 1958, their wedding anniversary, they founded Gore. The basement of their home served as their first facility. After finishing breakfast, Vieve turned to her husband of 23 years and said, "Well, let's clear up the dishes, go downstairs, and get to work."

When Bill Gore (a 45-year-old with five children to support) left DuPont, he put aside a career of 17 years and a good, secure salary. To finance the first two years of their new business, he and Vieve mortgaged their house and took $4,000 from savings. All their friends cautioned them against taking on such a big financial risk.

The first few years were challenging. Some of the young company's associates accepted stock in the company in lieu of salary. Family members who came to help with the business lived in the home as well. At one point, 11 associates were living and working under one roof. One afternoon, while sifting PTFE powder, Vieve received a call from the City of Denver's water department. The caller wanted to ask some technical questions about the ribbon cable and asked for the product manager. Vieve explained that he was not in at the moment (Bill and two other key associates were out of town). The caller asked next for the sales manager and then for the president. Vieve explained that "they" were also not in. The caller finally shouted, "What kind of company is this anyway?!" With a little diplomacy the Gores were eventually able to secure an order from Denver's water department for around $100,000. This order put the company over the start-up hump and onto a profitable footing. Sales began to take off.

During the decades that followed, Gore developed a number of new products derived from PTFE, the best-known of which is GORE-TEX® fabric. The development of GORE-TEX® fabric, one of hundreds of new products that followed a key discovery by Bob Gore, is an example of the power of innovation. In 1969, Gore's Wire and Cable Division was facing increased competition. Bill Gore began to look for a way to expand PTFE: "I figured out that if we could ever unfold those molecules, get them to stretch out straight, we'd have a tremendous new kind of material." The new PTFE material would have more volume per pound of raw material with no adverse effect on performance. Thus, fabricating costs would be reduced and profit margins increased. Bob Gore took on the project; he heated rods of PTFE to various temperatures and then slowly stretched them. However, regardless of the temperature or how carefully he stretched them, the rods broke. Working alone late one night after countless failures, Bob in frustration stretched one of the rods violently. To his surprise, it did not break. He tried it again and again with the same results. The next morning, Bill Gore recalled, "Bob wanted to surprise me so he took a rod and stretched it slowly. Naturally, it broke. Then he pretended to get mad. He grabbed another rod and said, 'Oh, the hell with this,' and gave it a pull. It didn't break—he'd done it." The new arrangement of molecules not only changed the Wire and Cable Division, but led to the development of GORE-TEX® fabric and many other products.

In 1986, Bill Gore died while backpacking in the Wind River Mountains of Wyoming. Vieve Gore continued to be involved actively in the company and served on the board of directors until her death at 91 in 2005.

Gore has had only four presidents in its 50-year history. Bill Gore served as the president from the enterprise's founding in 1958 until 1976. At that point, his son Bob became president and CEO. Bob has been an active member of the firm from the time of its founding, most recently as chairman of the board of directors. He served as president until 2000, when Chuck Carroll was selected as the third president. In 2005, Terri Kelly succeeded him. As with all the presidents after Bill Gore, she is a long-time employee. She had been with Gore for 22 years before becoming president.

The Gore family established a unique culture that continues to be an inspiration for associates. For example, Dave Gioconda, a current product specialist, recounted meeting Bob Gore for the first time—an experience that reinforced Gore's egalitarian culture:

Two weeks after I joined Gore, I traveled to Phoenix for training… I told the guy next to me on the plane where I worked, and he said, "I work for Gore, too." "No kidding?" I asked. "Where do you work?" He said, "Oh, I work over at the Cherry Hill plant"….

I spent two and a half hours on this plane having a conversation with this gentleman who described himself as a technologist and shared some of his experiences. As I got out of the plane, I shook his hand and said, "I'm Dave Gioconda, nice to meet you." He replied, "Oh, I'm Bob Gore." That experience has had a profound influence on the decisions that I make.

Due to the leadership of Bill, Vieve, Bob and many others, Gore was selected as one of the US "100 Best Companies to Work For" in 2009 by *Fortune* magazine for the twelfth consecutive year. In addition, Gore was included in all three *100 Best Companies to Work For in America* books (1984, 1985, and 1993). It is one of only a select few companies to appear on all 15 lists. Gore has also been selected as one of the best companies to work for in France, Germany, Italy, Spain, Sweden, and the United Kingdom.

As a privately held company, Gore does not make its financial results public. It does share, however, financial results with all associates on a monthly basis. In 2008, *Fortune* magazine reported that Gore sales grew just over 7 percent in 2006, the latest year for which data were available.

Competitive Strategy at W. L. Gore

For product management, Gore is divided now into four divisions—Electronics, Fabrics, Industrial, and Medical. The Electronic Products Division (EPD) develops and manufactures high-performance cables and assemblies as well as specialty materials for electronic devices. The Fabrics Division develops and provides fabric to the outdoor clothing industry as well as the military, law enforcement, and fire protection industries. Gore fabrics marketed under the GORE-TEX®, WINDSTOPPER®, CROSSTECH®, and GORE® CHEMPAK® brands provide the wearer protection while remaining comfortable. The Industrial Products Division (IPD) makes filtration, sealant, and other products. These products meet diverse contamination and process challenges in many industries. The Gore Medical Products Division (MPD) provides products such as synthetic vascular grafts, interventional devices, endovascular stent-grafts, surgical patches for hernia repair, and sutures for use in vascular surgery, cardiac surgery, general surgery, and oral procedures. Although they are recognized as separate divisions, they frequently work together.

Since its four divisions serve different industries, Gore can be viewed as a diversified conglomerate. Bob Winterling, a financial associate, described how the four divisions work together financially as follows:

The thing I love about Gore is that we have four very diverse divisions. During my time here, I've noticed that when one or two divisions are down, you always have one, two, or three that are up. I call them cylinders. Sometimes all four cylinders are working really well; not all the time though. Normally it's two or three, but that's the luxury that we have. When one is down—it's good to know that another is up.

At the end of 2007, all four divisions were performing well. Having four diversified divisions not only protects against swings in any one industry, but also provides multiple investment opportunities. Entering 2008, Gore was investing in a large number of areas, with the heaviest area of investment in the Medical Products Division. This was a conscious choice, as these opportunities were judged the largest intersection between Gore's unique capabilities and some very large, attractive market needs. As Brad Jones, an enterprise leader, said, "All opportunities aren't created equal, and there's an awful lot of opportunity that's screaming for resources in the medical environment." At the same time, the leadership at Gore scrutinizes large investments so those in what Brad Jones refers to as "big burn" projects are not made unless there is a reasonable expectation of a payoff.

Developing Quality Products by Creating and Protecting Core Technology

The competitive objective of Gore is to use core technology derived from PTFE and ePTFE to create highly differentiated and unique products. In every product line, the goal is not to produce the lowest cost goods but rather to create the highest quality goods that meet and exceed the needs of customers. Of course, Gore works hard to maintain competitive pricing, but the source of competitive advantage is clearly quality and differentiation. Gore is a company built on technological innovations.

Leaders at Gore often refer to a three-legged stool to explain how they integrate operations. As shown in Exhibit 2, the three legs of the stool are technology, manufacturing, and sales. For each product, the legs of the stool are tied together by a product specialist. For instance, a product specialist might coordinate efforts to design, make, and sell a vascular graft. Another product specialist coordinates efforts related to the creation and marketing of fabric for use in winter parkas. Support functions such as human resources (HR), IT, and finance also help tie together various aspects of technology, manufacturing, and sales.

Gore's Fabrics Division practices cooperative marketing with the users of its fabrics. In most cases, Gore does not make the finished goods from its fabrics; rather, it supplies the fabrics to manufacturers such as North Face, Marmot, L. L. Bean, Salomon, Adidas, and Puma. On each garment is a tag indicating that it was made using GORE-TEX® fabric. According to a former president of Cotton Inc., Gore is a leader in secondary branding. For example, a salesman in a golf pro shop related how he initially tried to explain that

he had GORE-TEX® fabric rain suits made by various manufacturers. After realizing his customers did not care who manufactured it, only that it was made from GORE-TEX® fabric, he gave up and just led the customers to the GORE-TEX® fabric rain suits.

Because of its commitment to producing superior goods, Gore emphasizes product integrity. For example, Gore supplies only certified and licensed manufacturers with its fabrics. Gore maintains "rain-rooms" in which to test new garment designs. Shoes with GORE-TEX® fabric in them will be flexed in water approximately 300,000 times to ensure they are waterproof.

Yet, even when all preventive measures fail, Gore stands behind its products regardless of who the manufacturer is and even if the defect is cosmetic in nature. Susan Bartley, a manufacturing associate, recounted a recent recall:

A cosmetic flaw, not a fitness-for-use flaw, was found in finished garments, so we (Gore) bought back the garments from the manufacturer because we didn't want those garments out on the market.

Such recalls due to either cosmetic or fitness-for-use flaws happen infrequently. One associate estimated that the last one happened 10 years before the most recent one.

Gore's Fabrics sales and marketing associates believe positive buyer experiences with one GORE-TEX® product (for instance, a ski parka) carry over to purchases of other GORE-TEX® products (gloves, pants, rain suits, boots, and jackets). Also, they believe that positive experiences with Gore products are shared among customers and potential customers and lead to more sales.

The sharing and enhancing of knowledge is seen as key to the development of current and future products. Great emphasis is placed on sharing knowledge. According to Terri Kelly,

There's a real willingness and openness to share knowledge. That's something I experienced 25 years ago, and it's not changed today. This is a healthy thing. We want to make sure folks understand the need to connect more dots in the lattice.

Associates make a conscious effort to share technical knowledge. For example, a core leadership team consisting of eight technical associates meets every other month, reviews each other's plans, and looks for connections across upcoming products. According to Jack Kramer, an enterprise leader, "We put a lot of effort into trying to make sure that we connect informally and formally across a lot of boundaries." One way associates connect formally to share knowledge is through monthly technical meetings. At the monthly meetings, scientists and engineers from different divisions present information to other associates and colleagues. Attended

Exhibit 2 Coordinating Technology, Manufacturing, and Sales at Gore

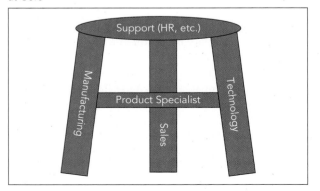

regularly by most technical associates in the area, these presentations are often described as "passionate" and "exciting."

Even though Gore shares knowledge within the organization, much of its highly technical know-how must be protected for competitive reasons. In a global environment, protection of specialized knowledge is a challenge. Some of Gore's technology is protected by patents. In fact, some of its products are protected by an umbrella of patents. Normally, under US law, patents expire 20 years from the earliest claimed filing date. Thus, the original patents have expired on GORE-TEX® fabric and some other products. Globally, patent procedures, protection, and enforcement vary. Both products and the processes are patentable. To protect its knowledge base, Gore has sought and been granted more than 2,000 patents worldwide in all areas in which it competes, including electronics, medical devices, and polymer processing. However, patents can sometimes be difficult or expensive to enforce, especially globally. Therefore some of the technology is protected internally. Such knowledge is commonly referred to as proprietary.

Within Gore, proprietary knowledge is shared on a need-to-know basis. Associates are encouraged to closely guard such information. This principle can lead to some awkward moments. Terri Kelly was visiting Shenzhen, China and was curious about a new laminate that was being commercialized. The development engineer leader kept dodging her questions. Finally he smiled, and he said, "Now, Terri. Do you have a need to know?"

As Terri retold the incident, "He played back exactly what he was supposed to, which is don't share with someone, even if it's a CEO, something that they have no need to know." She laughed and said, "You're right. I'm just being nosy."

Terri continued, "And everyone's—I could see the look in their eyes—thinking, 'Is he going to get fired?' He had taken a great personal risk, certainly for that local culture. We laughed, and we joked and for the next week, it became the running joke." Through stories like this, the culture is shared with others in Gore.

The sharing and enhancing of its technology have brought recognition from many sources. From the United Kingdom, Gore received the Pollution Abatement Technology Award in 1989, and the Prince Philip Award for Polymers in the Service of Mankind in 1985. In addition, Gore received or shared in receiving the prestigious Plunkett Award from DuPont—for innovative uses of DuPont fluoropolymers—nine times between 1988 and 2006. Bill and Vieve Gore, as well as Bob Gore, received numerous honors for both their business and technical leadership.

Continuing Globalization and Deliberate Growth

Ever since the company was founded, Gore has recognized the need for globalization. Gore established its first international venture in 1964, only six years after its founding. By 2008, it had facilities in two dozen countries and manufacturing facilities in six countries distributed across four continents (see Exhibit 3). Two examples of Gore's global reach are that it is the dominant supplier of artificial vascular grafts to the global medical community and that the majority of Gore's Fabrics Division sales are generated overseas.

In addition to globalization, Gore has a strategy of continued growth. Growth is expected to come from two sources. One source includes the innovative ideas contributed by Gore associates. The Gore culture is designed to foster such innovation and allow ideas to be energetically pursued, developed, and evaluated. These ideas lead to new products and processes. Within Gore, this form of growth is referred to as organic. Gore encourages both new products and extensions of existing products. To support innovation, all associates are encouraged to ask for and receive raw material to try out their ideas. Through this process, multiple products have come from unexpected areas. For example, the idea for dental floss came from the Industrial and not the Medical Division. Two associates who were fabricating space suits took to flossing their teeth with scraps. Thus, Gore's highly successful dental floss, GLIDE® floss, was born. GORE™ RIDE ON® bike cables came from a couple of passionate mountain bikers in the Medical Division. ELIXIR® guitar strings also came from the Medical Division from an associate who was also a musician. Due to Gore's track record of developing innovative products, Fast Company magazine called it "pound for pound, the most innovative company in America."

A second but much less significant source of growth comes from external acquisitions. Gore evaluates opportunities to acquire technologies and even companies based on whether they offer a unique capability that could complement an existing, successful business. The leadership at Gore considers this strategy a way to stack the probability deck in its favor by moving into market spaces its associates already know very well. To facilitate this growth strategy, Gore has a few associates who evaluate acquisition opportunities at the enterprise level. They do not do this in isolation, but in concert with leaders within each division.

By a multi-billion dollar corporate standard, the acquisitions made by Gore are small. To date, the largest company acquired employed approximately 100 people. Another attribute of these acquisitions is that no stock swap occurs. Since Gore is a privately held company, stock swaps are not an option. Acquisitions are made with cash.

Exhibit 3 Locations of Gore's Global Facilities

W. L. Gore & Associates — Worldwide Locations

© 2009 W. L. Gore & Associates, Inc.

A clear issue to any acquisition that Gore considers is cultural compatibility. Gore will consider the leadership style in an acquired company. According to Brad Jones, "If you're acquiring a couple patents and maybe an inventor, that's not a big issue. Although, if he's a prima donna inventor, it will be an issue." When acquiring a company, the culture that made it successful is closely examined. Issues regarding integrating the acquired company's culture with Gore's, and whether Gore's culture will add value to the acquired company, are just two of many cultural considerations. Gore wants to be able to expand by buying complementary organizations and their associated technologies, but not at the expense of its culture of 50 years.

Occasionally, Gore must divest itself of a product. One example is GLIDE® dental floss. The product, developed by Gore, was well received by consumers due to its smooth texture, shred resistance, and ability to slide easily between teeth. To meet demand when the product took off, leaders were processing credit cards, human resource associates

and accountants were out on the manufacturing floor packaging GLIDE® floss, and everybody else in the facility pitched in to make sure that the product got out the door. One associate observed that by rolling up their sleeves and pitching in, leaders built credibility with other associates.

Not long after its introduction, mint flavor GLIDE® floss became the top selling dental floss. That attracted the attention of the traditional dental floss manufacturers. Eventually, Procter & Gamble (P&G) and Gore reached an agreement whereby P&G bought the rights to market GLIDE® floss, while Gore continued to manufacture it.

Gore made this agreement with the understanding that no one would be laid off. The announcement of the agreement was made to the entire GLIDE® floss team on a Thursday. It did come as a shock to some. By Monday, however, the same team was working on a transition plan. Associates that were no longer needed in the manufacturing or selling of GLIDE® floss were absorbed into other fast-growing Gore businesses. In addition, everybody in the enterprise received a share of the profit from the P&G purchase.

Leadership at Gore

Competitive strategy at Gore is supported by a unique approach to leadership. Many people step forward and take on a variety of leadership roles, but these roles are not part of a hierarchical structure and traditional authority is not vested in the roles. Leadership is a dynamic and fluid process where leaders are defined by "followership." Future leaders emerge because they gain credibility with other associates. Gore refers to this process as "Natural Leadership." Credibility is gained by demonstrating special knowledge, skill, or experience that advances a business objective or series of successes, and involves others in significant decisions.

Associates step forward to lead when they have the expertise to do so. Within Gore, this practice is referred to as *knowledge-based decision-making*. Based on this practice decisions are "…made by the most knowledgeable person, not the person in charge," according to Terri Kelly. This form of decision making flows naturally from the four guiding principles established by Bill Gore.

Leadership responsibilities can take many forms at Gore. In an internal memo, Bill Gore described the following kinds of leaders and their roles:

1. *The Associate who is recognized by a team as having a special knowledge, or experience* (for example, this could be a chemist, computer expert, machine operator, salesman, engineer, lawyer). This kind of leader gives the team *guidance in a special area.*
2. *The Associate the team looks to for coordination of individual activities in order to achieve the agreed upon objectives of the team.* The role of this leader is to persuade team members to *make the commitments* necessary for success (commitment seeker).
3. *The Associate who proposes necessary objectives and activities and seeks agreement and team consensus on objectives.* This leader is perceived by the team membership as having a good grasp of how the objectives of the team fit in with the broader objectives of the enterprise. This kind of leader is often also a "commitment seeking" leader.
4. *The leader who, in consultation with other sponsors, evaluates the relative contribution of team members and reports these contribution evaluations to a compensation committee.* This leader may also participate in the compensation committee on relative contribution and pay and *reports changes in compensation* to individual Associates. This leader is then also a compensation sponsor.
5. *The leader who coordinates the research, manufacturing, and marketing of one product type within a business,* interacting with team leaders and individual Associates who have commitments to the product type. These leaders are usually called product specialists. They are respected for their knowledge and dedication to their products.
6. *Plant leaders* who help coordinate activities of people within a plant.
7. *Business leaders* who help coordinate activities of people in a business.
8. *Functional leaders* who help coordinate activities of people in a "functional" area.
9. *Corporate leaders* who help coordinate activities of people in different businesses and functions and who try to promote communication and cooperation among all Associates.
10. *Intrapreneuring Associates who organize new teams* for new businesses, new products, new processes, new devices, new marketing efforts, or new or better methods of all kinds. These leaders invite other Associates to "sign up" for their project.

Developing a Unique and Flexible Leadership Structure

The leadership structure that works at Gore may have the world's shortest organizational pyramid for a company of its size. Gore is a company largely without titles, hierarchical organization charts, or any other conventional structural arrangement typically employed by enterprises with billions of dollars in sales revenues and thousands of employees.

There are few positions at Gore with formal titles presented to the public. Due to laws of incorporation, the company has a president, Terri Kelly, who also functions as CEO. Terri is one of four members of the cross-functional Enterprise Leadership Team, the team responsible for the overall health and growth of the enterprise.

The real key to the egalitarian culture of Gore is the use of a unique lattice rather than a hierarchical structure. The features of Gore's lattice structure include the following:

1. Direct lines of communication—person to person— with no intermediary.
2. No fixed or assigned authority.
3. Sponsors, not bosses.
4. Natural leadership as evidenced by the willingness of others to follow.
5. Objectives set by those who must "make them happen."
6. Tasks and functions organized through commitments.

The lattice structure, as described by the people at Gore, is complex and depends on interpersonal interactions, self-commitment to group-known responsibilities, natural leadership, and group-imposed discipline. According to Bill Gore, "Every successful organization has an underground lattice. It's where the news spreads like lightning, where people can go around the organization to get things done."

One potential disadvantage of such a lattice structure could be a lack of quick response times and decisive action. Gore associates say adamantly that this is not the case, and they distinguish between two types of decisions. First, for time-critical decisions, they maintain that the lattice structure is faster in response than traditional structures because interaction is not hampered by bureaucracy. The leader who has responsibility assembles a knowledge-based team to examine and resolve the issue. The team members can be recruited by the leader from any area of the company if their expertise is needed. Once the issue is resolved, the team ceases to exist and its members return to their respective areas. Associate Bob Winterling asserted, "We have no trouble making crisis decisions, and we do it very swiftly and very quickly."

The other response is for critical issues that may have a significant impact on the enterprise's long-term operations. Associates will admit that such decisions can sometimes take a little longer than they would like. Chrissy Lyness, another financial associate, stated,

We get the buy-in up front instead of creating and implementing the solution and putting something out there that doesn't work for everybody. That can be frustrating to new associates, because they're used to a few people putting their heads together, saying, "This is what we're going to do. This is a solution." That's not the way it works at Gore.

Here, you spend a lot of time at the beginning of the decision-making process gaining feedback, so that when you come out of that process, you have something that's going to work, and the implementation is actually pretty easy.

The associates at Gore believe that time spent in the beginning, tapping into the best ideas and gaining consensus, pays in the implementation. They believe that authoritarian decision making may save time initially, but the quality of the decision will not be as good as one made by consensus. In addition, they believe that authoritarian decisions will take longer to implement than those made by consensus.

The egalitarian culture is supported also informally. For example, all associates are referred to and addressed by their first names. This is as true for the president as for any other associate.

Gore's leaders believe that its unique structure and culture have proven to be significant contributors to associate satisfaction and retention. *Fortune* magazine reports a turnover rate of 5 percent for Gore. In addition, it reports 19,108 applicants for 276 new jobs in 2008. In other words, it is harder to get a job a Gore than to get accepted at an elite university.

Global Human Resource Practices

The competitive strategy of using cutting-edge technology, empowered teams, and collaborative leadership to create high-quality goods is supported by a number of innovative HR practices, globally. Many HR initiatives are designed to support the concept that all associates are stakeholders in the enterprise and have a shared responsibility for its success. Parking lots have no reserved parking spaces for leaders. Dining areas—only one in each plant—are set up as focal points for associate interaction. As an associate in Arizona explained, "The design is no accident. The lunchroom in Flagstaff has a fireplace in the middle. We want people to like to be here." The location of a plant is also no accident. Sites are selected on the basis of transportation access, nearby universities, beautiful surroundings, and climate appeal. To preserve the natural beauty of the site on which a production facility was built in 1982, Vieve Gore insisted that the large trees be preserved, much to the dismay of the construction crews. The Arizona associate explained the company's emphasis on selecting attractive plant sites, stating, "Expanding is not costly in the long run. Losses are what you make happen by stymieing people and putting them into a box." Such initiatives are practiced at Gore facilities worldwide.

Getting the Right People on Board

Gore receives numerous applicants for every position. Initially, job applicants at Gore are screened by personnel specialists. Each candidate who passes the initial screening is interviewed by a group of associates from the team with which the person will work. Finally, personnel specialists contact multiple references before issuing a job offer. Recruitment is described by Donna Frey, leader of the global HR function and one of four members of the Enterprise Leadership Team (ELT), as a two-way process. She explained:

Our recruiting process is very much about us getting to know the applicants and them getting to know us. We are very open and honest about who we are, the kind of organization we have, the kind of commitments we want and whether or not we think that the applicant's values are aligned with ours. Applicants talk to a number of people that they'll be working directly with if hired. We work very hard in the recruiting process to really build a relationship, get to know people and make sure that we're bringing people in who are going to fit this enterprise.

When someone is hired at Gore, an experienced associate makes a commitment to be the applicant's sponsor. The sponsor's role is to take a personal interest in the new associate's contributions, interests, and goals, acting as both a coach and an advocate. The sponsor tracks the new associate's progress, offers help and encouragement, points out weaknesses and suggests ways to correct them, and concentrates on how the associate can better make use of his or her strengths. Sponsoring is not a short-term commitment. When individuals are hired initially, they are likely to have a sponsor in their immediate work area. As associates' commitments change or grow, it is normal for them to change sponsors, or in some cases add a second sponsor. For instance, if they move to a new job in another area of the company, they may gain a sponsor there and then decide whether to keep their former sponsor or not. Because sponsorship is built on the personal relationship between two people, the relationship most often continues even if the official sponsorship role does not.

New associates are expected to focus on building relationships during the first three to six months of their careers. Donna Frey described the first months for a new associate at Gore as follows:

When new associates join the enterprise, they participate in an orientation program. Then, each new associate works with a starting sponsor to get acclimated and begin building relationships within Gore. The starting sponsor provides the new hire with a list of key associates he/she should meet with during the next few months.

We encourage the new hire to meet with these associates one-on-one. It's not a phone conversation, but a chance to sit down with them face-to-face and get to know them.

This process helps demonstrate the importance of relationships. When you're hiring really good people, they want to have quick wins and make contributions, and building relationships without a clear goal can be difficult. Often, new associates will say, "I don't feel like I'm contributing. I've spent three months just getting to know people." However, after a year they begin to realize how important this process was.

To ensure that new associates are not overwhelmed by what is probably their first experience in a non-hierarchical organization, Gore has a two-day orientation program it calls "Building on the Best." New associates are brought together with other new associates after two or three months to participate in the program, which addresses many of Gore's key concepts, who Gore is, and how the enterprise works. The program includes group activities and interactive presentations given by leaders and other longtime associates.

Helping Associates Build and Maintain Relationships

Gore recognizes the need to maintain initial relationships, continuously develop new ones, and cement ongoing relationships. One way this is fostered is through its digital voice exchange called Gorecom. According to Terri Kelly, "Gorecom is the preferred media if you want a quick response." An oral culture is fostered because it encourages direct communication.

To further foster the oral culture, team members and leaders are expected to meet face-to-face regularly. For team members and especially leaders, this can mean lots of travel. As one technical associate joked, "Probably, in the last 12 years, I spent 3 years traveling internationally, a couple weeks at a time."

Another way that Gore facilitates the development of teams and individuals is through training. An associate in Newark noted that Gore "works with associates who want to develop themselves and their talents." Associates are offered a variety of in-house training opportunities, not only in technical and engineering areas but also in leadership development. In addition, the company has established cooperative education programs with universities and other outside providers.

In many ways, Gore can feel like an extended family for its associates and the communities in which they live. Based on their own interests and initiatives, associates give back to their communities through schools, sports clubs, universities, and other local organizations. Recently, Gore has encouraged their US associates' community outreach activities by providing up to eight hours of paid time off for such efforts. Through this program, associates worked nearly 7,800 hours at non-profits in Gore's last fiscal year. In reality, Gore associates volunteer much more of their personal time. The associates individually or in teams decide what to commit their time to.

Rewarding Associates for Contributions

Compensation at Gore has both short- and long-term equity sharing components. Its compensation goal is to ensure internal fairness and external competitiveness. To ensure fairness, associates are asked to rank their team members each year in order of contribution to the enterprise. In addition, team members are asked to comment on their rationale for the ranking, as well as on particular strengths or potential areas of improvement for the associates. To ensure competitiveness, each year Gore benchmarks its associates' pay against a variety of functions and roles with that of peers at other companies.

Gore also uses profit sharing as a form of short-term compensation. Profits remaining after business requirements are met are distributed among associates as profit sharing. Profit shares are distributed when established financial goals are reached. Every month the business results are reviewed with associates, and they know whether they are on track to meet forecasts. The first profit sharing occurred in 1960, only two years after the founding of the company.

Beyond short-term equity sharing, Gore has an associates' stock ownership program (ASOP). Each year Gore contributes up to 12 percent of pay to an account that purchases Gore stock for associates with more than one year of service. Associates become 100 percent vested and have ownership of the account after three years of service. Gore also has a 401(K) plan. Gore contributes of up to 3 percent of pay to each associate's personal investment account. Associates are eligible after one month of service and are 100 percent vested immediately.

Yet another area where Gore's practices differ from traditional practices at other organizations is in how the majority of its force is compensated. They are paid not on commission, but with salary, stock through ASOP, and profit sharing with all the other associates.[ii] When a sales associate was asked to explain this practice, he responded as follows:

The people who are just concerned with making their sales numbers in other companies usually struggle when they come to Gore. We encourage folks to help others. For example, when we hire new sales associates, we ask experienced sales associates to take some time to help get them acclimated to Gore and how we do things. In other companies where I've worked, that would have been seen as something that would detract from your potential to make your number, so you probably wouldn't be asked to do such a thing.

In other words, they see individual sales commissions as detracting from mentoring and sharing what is at the core of the Gore culture.

The entire package of compensation extends beyond direct monetary payments. As with most companies, associates receive a range of benefits, such as medical and dental insurance. Another benefit extended to associates is onsite childcare. In addition, in *Fortune* magazine's 2008 story about Gore being one of the "100 Best Companies to Work For," onsite fitness centers are listed as a benefit. Gore does have such benefits, but they are not driven from the top-down. Gore supports multiple wellness programs, but there is no single enterprise-wide program. In keeping with Gore's principles and philosophy, Gore looks for an associate or a group of associates to initiate a program. For example,

in the Fabrics Division an associate who is a committed runner will champion a lunchtime group. Gore will then support such activities with fitness centers, softball fields, volleyball courts, and running trails. Pockets of associates all over Gore pursue these and other wellness activities.

GORE™ RIDE ON® Bike Cables: An Example of Strategy, Leadership, and HR in Action

A good example of strategy, leadership, and effective talent deployment is illustrated by the development of a product called GORE™ RIDE ON® bike cables. Initially, the cables were derailleur and brake cables for trail bikes. They were developed by a group of trail bike enthusiasts at the medical facilities in Flagstaff, Arizona in the 90s. When the trail bike market declined, the product was withdrawn from the market. In 2006, a group of young engineers went to Jack Kramer, a technical leader at Gore, and said that they wanted to learn what it takes to develop a new product by reviving the cables. His response was, "You need someone who has some experience before you go off and try to do that."

One of the young engineers approached Lois Mabon, a product specialist who had about 16 years of experience at Gore and worked in the same facility, and asked her to be the group's coach. Lois went back to Jack and talked to him. He was still not sold on the idea, but he allowed Lois to find out what had happened to the bike cables and explore with the group what it would take to bring a new product to market. Within Gore, associates are encourage to set aside "dabble time." Dabble time is when people have the freedom to develop new products and evaluate their viability. After some exploration of what happened to the cables, Lois led a group that made a presentation to Jack and some others in the company and, even though they still were not sure, they said, "All right, keep working on it."

After about nine or ten months of exploring the possibility, a team of excited and passionate associates developed a set of GORE™ RIDE ON® products. In their exploration, the team learned that the road bike market is larger than the trail bike market and there was potentially a product for the racing market as well.

A presentation, referred to within Gore as a "Real-Win-Worth" presentation, was prepared and presented to the IPD leadership team. Real-Win-Worth is a rigorous discipline that Gore uses to help hone in on the most promising new opportunities. Three issues must be addressed in Real-Win-Worth: Is the idea real, can Gore win in the market, and is it worth pursuing? After listening and questioning the presenters, the IPD leadership team responded, "You know what? You do have some really good ideas. Let's do a market study on it and see if the market is interested."

[ii]Gore's ASOP is similar legally to an employee stock ownership plan (ESOP). Again, Gore simply has never allowed the word employee in any of its documentation. The ASOP and profit sharing will be explained in more detail later.

Samples of the new product were made and taken to 200 top bike stores across the US. They were handed out to the store owners and in turn, the store owners were asked to fill out a survey. The survey focused on three questions: Is this a product you would buy, is it a product you would recommend to your customers, and how would you compare this to the other products out in the industry?

An analysis of the surveys showed that 65 to 75 percent of all respondents would either definitely buy the product or were interested in it. Based on these results, the team concluded that people would want to buy the product.

With that data in hand, another presentation was made to the IPD leadership team in August 2006. The response was, "Okay, go launch it." The product team had 12 months to improve the mountain bike cables, develop the new road bike cables, redesign the packaging and logo, set up production, and do everything else associated with a new product introduction.

Every Gore division was involved in producing the cables. The product was overseen by a team in IPD. The GORE BIKE WEAR™ products team in the Fabrics Division served as the sales team. The MPD made a component that goes in it and the EPD coated the cables.

In September 2007, the product was officially launched at two bike shows. The first was the Euro-Bike on Labor Day and the other was the Interbike show held in Las Vegas. The top 100 GORE BIKE WEAR™ product customers and shops were invited to these shows. In fewer than three months, Gore had sold approximately 8,000 pairs of cables. In addition, Gore had teamed with one of the top shifter manufacturers to co-market its products with the shift manufacturer using the Gore cables in its best-selling shifter line, introduced in November 2007.

Facing the Future Together

Associates believe that Gore's unique organizational culture will allow the company to continue maximizing individual potential while cultivating an environment where creativity can flourish. Gore's unique culture results from an unwavering commitment to the use of cutting-edge technology to develop high-quality products. This strategy is carried out through a unique approach to leadership and HR management. The record of success is demonstrated not only by high financial profitability, but also the creation of a highly desirable workplace. Nevertheless, success in the past cannot be seen as assurance of success in the future. As Brad Jones of the Enterprise Leadership Team said:

Twenty or thirty years ago, markets in different parts of the world were still somewhat distinct and isolated from one another. At that time, we could have pretty much the entire global business team for a particular market niche located in a building. Today, as our markets become more global in nature, we are increasingly seeing the need to support our customers with global virtual teams. How do our paradigms and practices have to change to accommodate those changing realities? Those are active discussions that apply across these many different businesses.

The answer of how Gore will evolve to meet these challenges is not something that will be decided by an isolated CEO or an elite group of executives. Critical decisions, those below the waterline, have never been made that way and there is no expectation that this will change.

Herman Miller: A Case of Reinvention and Renewal

Frank Shipper, Stephen B. Adams

Franklin B. Perdue School of Business, Salisbury University

Karen P. Manz

Author and Researcher

Charles C. Manz

Isenberg School of Management, University of Massachusetts Amherst

At first glance, Herman Miller would appear to be only a $1.3 billion manufacturer of office furniture. Since De Pree became president over 90 years ago, however, Herman Miller has also been known for its innovation in products and processes.[i] It is one of only four organizations—and the only non–high technology one—selected for *Fortune* magazine's "100 Best Companies to Work For" and "Most Admired Companies," and *Fast Company* magazine's "Most Innovative Companies" in both 2008 and 2010. The three high tech organizations selected were Microsoft, Cisco, and Google; not the usual company for a firm in a mature industry and definitely not for an office furniture company. Ever since De Pree became president, Herman Miller has followed a different path from most firms: one distinctively marked by reinvention and renewal.

This path has served it well. Early in its history, it survived the Great Depression and since then, multiple recessions. In the early part of the twenty-first century, it recovered from the dot-com bust. As it enters 2010, Herman Miller once again faces a turbulent economy. Will this path allow it to flourish once again?

Background

Herman Miller's roots go back to 1905 and the Star Furniture Company, a manufacturer of traditional style bedroom suites in Zeeland, Michigan. In 1909, it was renamed Michigan Star Furniture Company and hired Dirk Jan (D. J.) De Pree as a clerk. By 1919, De Pree was president. Four year later, De Pree convinced his father-in-law, Herman Miller, to purchase the majority of shares and, in recognition of his support, De Pree renamed the company Herman Miller Furniture Company.[ii]

In 1927, De Pree committed to treating "all workers as individuals with special talents and potential." This occurred after he visited the family of a millwright who had died unexpectedly. At the visit, the widow read some poetry. De Pree asked the widow who the poet was and was surprised to learn it was the millwright. This led him to wonder whether the millwright was a person who wrote poetry or a poet who was also a millwright. This story is part of the cultural folklore at Herman Miller that perpetuates the value of respect for all employees and fuels the quest to tap the diversity of gifts and skills held by all.

In 1930, the country was in the Great Depression and, along with the rest of the nation, Herman Miller was in financial trouble. De Pree was looking for a way to save the company. At the same time, Gilbert Rhode, a designer from New York, approached De Pree and asked for the opportunity to create a bedroom suite design for a fee of $1000. When De Pree reacted negatively to the fee, Gilbert Rhode suggested an alternative payment

---

[i] Corporate titles such as president and chief executive officer are not capitalized in this case because they are not capitalized in company documents.

[ii] In Herman Miller, people including the De Prees are referred to by their first or nick names or in combination with their surnames, but hardly ever by their titles or surnames alone.

Many sources were helpful in providing material for this case, most particularly employees at Herman Miller who generously shared their time and viewpoints about the company to help ensure that the case accurately reflected the company's practices and culture. They provided many resources, including internal documents and stories of their personal experiences.

plan, 3 percent royalty on the furniture sold, to which De Pree agreed, figuring he had nothing to lose.

A few weeks later, De Pree received the first designs from Rhode. Again, he reacted negatively. He "thought that they looked as if they had been done for a manual training school and told him so." Gilbert Rhode explained in a letter his design philosophy—first, "utter simplicity: no surface enrichment, no carvings, no moldings," and second, "furniture should be anonymous. People are important, not furniture. Furniture should be useful." Rhode's designs were antithetical to traditional designs, but De Pree saw their merits and thus set Herman Miller on a course of designing and selling furniture that reflected a way of life.

In 1942, Herman Miller produced its first office furniture—a Gilbert Rhode design referred to as the Executive Office Group. When Rhode died two years later, De Pree began a search for a new design leader. Based largely on an article in *Life* magazine, he hired George Nelson as Herman Miller's first design director.

In 1946, Charles and Ray Eames, designers based in Los Angeles, were hired to design furniture. In the same year, Charles Eames designs were featured in the first one-man furniture exhibit at New York's Museum of Modern Art. Some of his designs are now part of the museum's permanent collection.

In 1950, Herman Miller, under the guidance of Dr. Carl Frost, a Michigan State University professor, was the first company in Michigan to implement a Scanlon Plan. Underlying the Scanlon Plan are "principles of equity and justice for everyone in the company . . ." Two major functional elements of Scanlon Plans are the use of committees for sharing ideas on improvements and a structure for sharing increased profitability. The relationship between Dr. Frost and Herman Miller continued for at least four decades.

During the 50s, Herman Miller introduced a number of new furniture designs including those by Alexander Girard, Charles and Ray Eames, and George Nelson. Specifically, the first molded fiberglass chairs were introduced and the Eames lounge chair and ottoman debuted on NBC's *Home* show with Arlene Francis, a precursor to the *Today Show* (Exhibit 1). Also in the 50s, Herman Miller began its first forays overseas, selling its products in the European market.

In 1962, and after over 40 years as president, D. J. De Pree became chairman of the board and his son, Hugh De Pree, stepped up to become president and CEO.

During the 60s, many new designs were introduced for both home and the workplace. The most notable design was the Action Office System, the world's first open-plan modular office arrangement of movable panels and attachments. By the end of the 60s, Herman Miller had formed a subsidiary in England with sales and marketing responsibilities throughout England and the Scandinavian countries. Also, it had established dealers in South and Central Americas, Australia, Canada, Europe, Africa, the Near East, and Japan.

In 1970, Herman Miller went public and made its first stock offering. The stock certificate was designed by the Eames Office staff. In 1971, it entered the health/science market, and in 1976, the Ergon chair, its first design based on scientific observation and ergonomic principles, was introduced. In 1979, in conjunction with the University of Michigan, it established the Facility Management Institute that established the profession of facility management. Also, in the 70s, Herman Miller continued to expand overseas and introduce new designs.

Exhibit 1 Eames Lounge Chair and Ottoman

Source: http://hermanmiller.com/DotCom/jsp/aboutUs/newsDetail.jsp?navId=194&topicId=49&newsId=408

Globe: © Jan Rysavy/iStockphoto.com

By 1977, over half of Herman Miller's 2,500 employees worked outside the production area. In addition, employees worked at multiple US and overseas locations. Thus, the Scanlon Plan needed an overhaul since it had originally been designed for a production workforce. As a result, in 1978, an ad hoc committee of 54 employees from nearly every segment of the company was elected to examine the need for changes and make recommendations. By January 1979, the committee had developed a final draft. The plan established a new organizational structure based on work teams, caucuses, and councils. All employees were given the opportunity of small group settings to discuss it. On January 26, 1979, 96 percent of the employees voted to accept the new plan.

After 18 years, Hugh De Pree stepped down, and Max De Pree, Hugh's younger brother, became chairman and CEO in 1980. In 1981, Herman Miller took a major initiative to become more efficient and environmentally friendly. Its Energy Center generated both electric and steam power to run its million-square-foot facility by burning waste.

In 1983, Herman Miller established a plan whereby all employees became shareholders. This initiative occurred approximately 10 years before congressional incentives fueled ESOP (Employee Stock Ownership Plan) growth.

In 1984, the Equa chair, a second chair based on ergonomic principles, was introduced along with many other designs in the 80s. In 1987, the first non-family member, Dick Ruch, became CEO.

By the end of the decade, the Equa chair was recognized as a "Design of the Decade" by *TIME* magazine. Also, in 1989, Herman Miller established its Environmental Quality Action Team created to "coordinate environmental programs worldwide and involve as many employees as possible."

In 1990, Herman Miller was a founding member of the Tropical Forest Foundation and the only furniture manufacturer to belong. That same year, it discontinued using endangered rosewood in its award-winning Eames lounge chair and ottoman, and substituted cherry and walnut from sustainable sources. It also became a founding member of the US Green Building Council in 1994. Some of the buildings at Herman Miller have been used to establish Leadership in Energy & Environmental Design (LEED) standards. Because of its environmental efforts, Herman Miller received awards from *Fortune* magazine and the National Wildlife Federation in the 90s.

Also in the 90s, Herman Miller again introduced some groundbreaking designs. In 1994, it introduced the Aeron chair and almost immediately, it was added to the New York Museum of Modern Art's permanent Design Collection (Exhibit 2). In 1999, the Aeron chair won "Design of the Decade" from *Business Week* and the Industrial Designers Society of America.

Exhibit 2 Aeron Chair

Source: http://hermanmiller.com/DotCom/jsp/designResources/imgSearchResults.jsp?prodId=8

In 1992, J. Kermit Campbell became Herman Miller's fifth CEO and president. He was the first person from outside the company to hold either position. At the time of Campbell's resignation in 1995, the industry was in a slump, sales were approximately $1 billion, and Herman Miller was being restructured. Mike Volkema had been with Meridian, a company Herman Miller acquired in 1990, for seven years. So, with approximately 12 years of experience between Herman Miller and Meridian and at the age of 39, Mike Volkema became CEO.

In 1994, Herman Miller for the Home was launched to focus on the residential market. It reintroduced some of its modern classic designs from the 40s, 50s, and 60s as well as new designs. In 1998, hmhome.com was set up to tap this market.

Additional marketing initiatives were taken to focus on small and mid-size businesses. A network of 180 retailers was established to focus on small businesses and a 3D computer design program was made available to mid-size customers. In addition, order entry was digitally linked among Herman Miller, suppliers, distributors, and customers to expedite orders and improve accuracy.

The 2000s

The 2000s started off spectacularly with record profits and sales in 2000 and 2001. An Employee Stock Option Plan (ESOP) was offered in July 2000, and the Eames molded plywood chair was selected as a "Design of the Century" by *TIME* magazine. Sales had more than doubled in the six years that Mike Volkema had been CEO.

Then, the dot-com bubble burst and September 11, 2001 brought the US to a standstill. Sales dropped 34 percent from $2.2 billion in 2001 to $1.5 billion in 2002. In the same years, profits dropped from $144.1 million to losses of $56.0 million. In an interview for *Fast Company* magazine in 2007, Volkema said, "One night I went to bed a genius and woke up the town idiot."

Although sales continued to fall in 2003, Herman Miller returned to profitability. To do so, Herman Miller had to drop its long-held tradition of lifelong employment; approximately 38 Percent of its workforce was laid off. One entire plant in Georgia was closed. Mike Volkema and Brian Walker, then president of Herman Miller North America, met with all the workers to tell them what was happening and why it had to be done. One of the workers being laid off was so moved by their presentation that she told them she felt sorry for them having to personally lay off workers. To replace the tradition of lifelong employment, Volkema, with input from many, developed "the new social contract." He explains it as follows:

We are a commercial enterprise, and the customer has to be on center stage, so we have to first figure out whether your gifts and talents have a match with the needs and wants of this commercial enterprise. If they don't, then we want to wish you the best, but we do need to tell you that I don't have a job for you right now.

As part of the implementation of the social contract, benefits such as educational reimbursement and 401K plans were redesigned to be more portable. This was done to decrease the cost of changing jobs for employees whose gifts and talents no longer matched customer needs.

In 2003, Brian Walker became president and, when Volkema became chairman of the board in 2004, Walker stepped in as CEO. Sales and profits began to climb from 2003 to 2008. In 2008, even though sales were not at an all-time high, profits were. Just as things were looking up, Herman Miller was hit by the recession of 2009. Sales dropped 19 percent from $2.0 billion in 2008 to $1.6 billion in 2009. In the same years profits dropped from $152 million to $68 million. In March, Mark Schurman, director of External Communications at Herman Miller, predicted that the changes made to recover from the 2001 to 2003 recession would help it weather the 2007 to 2009 recession.

Herman Miller Entering 2010

Herman Miller has codified its long practiced organizational values and has published them on its Web site on a page entitled "What We Believe." These beliefs are intended as a basis for uniting all employees, building relationships, and contributing to communities. Those beliefs as stated in 2005, and remaining in effect in 2010, are as follows:

- **Curiosity and Exploration**: These are two of our greatest strengths. They lie behind our heritage of research-driven design. How do we keep our curiosity? By respecting and encouraging risk, and by practicing forgiveness. You can't be curious and infallible. In one sense, if you never make a mistake, you're not exploring new ideas often enough. Everybody makes mistakes: we ought to celebrate honest mistakes, learn from them, and move on.

- **Engagement**: For us, it is about being owners—actively committed to the life of this community called Herman Miller, sharing in its success and risk. Stock ownership is an important ingredient, but it's not enough. The strength and the payoff really come when engaged people own problems, solutions, and behavior. Acknowledge responsibility, choose to step forward and be counted. Care about this community and make a difference in it.

- **Performance**: Performance is required for leadership. We want to be leaders, so we are committed to performing at the highest level possible. Performance isn't a choice. It's up to everybody at Herman Miller to perform at his or her best. Our own high performance—however we measure it—enriches our lives as employees, delights our customers, and creates real value for our shareholders.

- **Inclusiveness**: To succeed as a company, we must include all the expressions of human talent and potential that society offers. We value the whole person and everything each of us has to offer, obvious or not so obvious. We believe that every person should have the chance to realize his or her potential regardless of color, gender, age, sexual orientation, educational background, weight, height, family status, skill level—the list goes on and on. When we are truly inclusive, we go beyond toleration to understanding all the qualities that make people who they are, that make us unique, and most important, that unite us.

- **Design**: Design for us is a way of looking at the world and how it works—or doesn't. It is a method for getting something done, for solving a problem. To design a solution, rather than simply devising one, requires research, thought, sometimes starting over, listening, and humility. Sometimes design results in memorable occasions, timeless chairs, or really fun parties. Design isn't just the way something looks; it isn't just the way something works, either.

- **Foundations**: The past can be a tricky thing—an anchor or a sail, a tether or a launching pad. We value and respect our past without being ruled by it. The stories, people, and experiences in Herman Miller's past form a unique foundation. Our past teaches us about design, human compassion, leadership, risk taking, seeking out change and working together.

From that foundation, we can move forward together with a common language, a set of owned beliefs and understandings. We value our rich legacy more for what it shows us we might become than as a picture of what we've been.

- **A Better World**: This is at the heart of Herman Miller and the real reason why many of us come to work every day. We contribute to a better world by pursuing sustainability and environmental wisdom. Environmental advocacy is part of our heritage and a responsibility we gladly bear for future generations. We reach for a better world by giving time and money to our communities and causes outside the company; through becoming a good corporate citizen worldwide; and even in the (not so) simple act of adding beauty to the world. By participating in the effort, we lift our spirits and the spirits of those around us.

- **Transparency**: Transparency begins with letting people see how decisions are made and owning the decisions we make. So when you make a decision, own it. Confidentiality has a place at Herman Miller, but if you can't tell anybody about a decision you've made, you've probably made a poor choice. Without transparency, it's impossible to have trust and integrity. Without trust and integrity, it's impossible to be transparent.

All employees are expected to live these values. In a description of the current processes that follow, numerous examples of these values in action can be found.

Management

Mike Volkema is currently the chairman of the board, and Brian Walker is the president and chief executive officer. Walker's compensation was listed by *Bloomberg Businessweek* as $668,685. Compensation for CEOs at four competitors was listed by *Bloomberg Businessweek* to range from $792,000 to $1,100,000. Walker and four other top executives at Herman Miller took a 10 percent pay cut in January 2009, and took another 10 percent pay cut along with all salaried workers in March 2009. Production workers were placed on a nine days in two weeks work schedule effectively cutting their pay by 10 percent as well. That the executives would take a pay cut before all others and twice as much is just one way human compassion is practiced at Herman Miller.

By Securities and Exchange Commission (SEC) regulations, a publicly traded company must have a board of directors. By corporate policy, the majority of the 14 members of the board must be independent. To be judged an independent, the individual as a minimum must meet the NASDAQ National Market requirements for independent directors (NASDAQ Stock Market Rule 4200). In addition, the individual must not have any "other material relationship with the company or its affiliates or with any executive officer of the company or

his or her affiliates." Moreover, any "transaction between the Company and any executive officer or director of the Company (including that person's spouse, children, stepchildren, parents, stepparents, siblings, parents-in-law, children-in-law, siblings-in-law, and persons sharing the same residence) must be disclosed to the Board of Directors and is subject to the approval of the Board of Directors or the Nominating and Governance Committee unless the proposed transaction is part of a general program available to all directors or employees equally under an existing policy or is a purchase of Company products consistent with the price and terms of other transactions of similar size with other purchasers." Furthermore, "It is the policy of the Board that all directors, consistent with their responsibilities to the stockholders of the company as a whole, hold an equity interest in the company. Toward this end, the Board requires that each director will have an equity interest after one year on the Board, and within five years the Board encourages the directors to have shares of common stock of the company with a value of at least three times the amount of the annual retainer paid to each director." In other words, board members are held to standards consistent with the corporate beliefs and its ESOP program.

Although Herman Miller has departments, the most frequently referenced work unit is a team. Paul Murray, director of Environmental Health and Safety explains their relationship as follows:

At Herman Miller, "team" has just been the term that has been used since the Scanlon Plan and the De Prees brought that into Herman Miller. And so I think that's why we use that almost exclusively. The department—as a department, we help facilitate the other teams. And so they aren't just department driven.

Teams are often cross functional. Membership on a team is based on ability to contribute to that team. As Gabe Wing, Design for the Environment Lead Chemical Engineer, describes it,

You grab the appropriate representative who can best help your team achieve its goal. It doesn't seem to be driven based on title. It's based on who has the ability to help us drive our initiatives towards our goal.

Teams are often based on product development. When that product has been developed, the members of that team are redistributed to new projects. New projects can come from any level in the organization. At Herman Miller, leadership is shared. One way this is done is through Herman Miller's concept of "talking up and down the ladder." Workers at all levels are encouraged to present new ideas. As Rudy Bartels, Environmental Specialist, says,

If they try something, they know that they have folks there that will help them and be there for them. And by doing that, either—whether that requires a presence of one of us or an email or just to say, "Yeah, I think that's a great idea." That's how a lot . . . in the organization works.

Because workers feel empowered, new managers can run into some behaviors that may startle them. As Paul Murray recalls,

I can remember my first day on the job. I took my safety glasses off . . . and an employee stepped forward and said, "Get your safety glasses back on." At [Company X, Company Y],[iii] there was no way they would have ever talked to a supervisor like that, much less their supervisor's manager. It's a fun journey when the workforce is that empowered.

The beliefs are also reinforced through the Employee Gifts Committee and Environmental Quality Action Team. True to its practice of shared leadership, the Employee Gifts Committee distributes funds and other resources based on employee involvement. As Jay Link, manager of Corporate Giving, explains, the program works as follows:

. . . our first priority is to honor organizations where our employees are involved. We believe that it's important that we engender kind of a giving spirit in our employees, so if we know they're involved in organizations, which is going to be where we have a manufacturing presence, then our giving kind of comes alongside organizations that they're involved with. So that's our first priority.

In addition, all employees can work 16 paid hours a year with the charitable organization of their choice. Herman Miller sets goals for the number of employee volunteer hours contributed annually to its communities. Progress toward meeting those goals is reported to the CEO.

The Environmental Affairs Team is responsible for such areas as solid waste recycling and designing products from sustainable resources. It was formed in 1988 with the authorization of Max De Pree. One major success that it has had is in the reduction of solid waste taken to the landfill. In 1991, Herman Miller was sending 41 million pounds of waste to the landfill. By 1994, it was down to 24 million pounds and by 2008, it was reduced to 3.6 million pounds. Such improvements are not only environmentally friendly, but cost effective as well.

Herman Miller's beliefs are carried over to the family and community as well. Gabe Wing related how, "I've got the worst lawn in my neighborhood. That's because I don't spread pesticides on it, and I don't put fertilizer down." He went on to say how his wife and he had to make a difficult decision the summer of 2009 because

Herman Miller has a policy "to avoid PVC (polyvinyl chloride) wherever possible." In restoring their home, they chose fiber cement board over PVC siding even though it was considerably more costly. Gabe went on to say, "Seven years ago, I didn't really think about it."

Rudy Bartels is involved in a youth soccer association. As is typical, every year, it needs to raise money to buy uniforms. Among other fundraisers, Rudy spearheaded collecting newspapers and aluminum cans. As he tells it, "When I speak they'll say, 'Yeah, that's Rudy. He's Herman Miller. You should know, we're gonna have to do this.'"

These beliefs carry over to all functional areas of the business. Some of them are clearly beneficial and some of them are simply the way Herman Miller has chosen to conduct its business.

Marketing

Herman Miller products are sold internationally through wholly owned subsidiaries in various countries including Canada, France, Germany, Italy, Japan, Mexico, Australia, Singapore, China, India, and the Netherlands. Its products are offered through independent dealerships and its customer base is spread over 100 countries.

Herman Miller uses "green marketing" to sell its products. For example, the Mirra Chair with PostureFit Technology introduced in 2003, was developed from its inception to be environmentally friendly (cradle-to-cradle principles). Mirra chairs are made of 45 percent recycled materials, and 96 percent of its materials are recyclable. In addition, it is assembled using 100 percent renewable energy. Builders that use Herman Miller products in their buildings can earn points toward LEED certification. In addition, Herman Miller engages in cooperative advertising with strategic partners. For example, some Hilton Garden Inn rooms are equipped with Herman Miller's Mirra chairs (Exhibit 3). On the desk in the room is a card explaining how to adjust the chair for comfort as well as a Hilton Garden Inn Web site where the chair can be purchased (Exhibit 3).

Production/Operations

Herman Miller is globally positioned in terms of manufacturing operations. In the US, its manufacturing operations are located in Michigan, Georgia, and Washington State. In Europe, it has a considerable manufacturing presence in the UK, its largest market outside the US. In Asia, it has manufacturing operations in Ningbo, China.

Herman Miller manufactures products using a system of lean manufacturing techniques collectively referred to as the Herman Miller Performance System (HMPS) (Exhibit 4). It strives to maintain efficiencies and cost savings by minimizing the amount of inventory on hand through a "just in time" process. Some suppliers

---

[iii]The names of the two Fortune 500 companies were deleted by the authors.

Exhibit 3 An Example of Cooperative Advertising

Source: Courtesy of Hilton Garden Inn.

deliver parts to Herman Miller production facilities five or six times per day.

Production is order driven with direct materials and components purchased as needed to meet demand. The standard lead time (time needed for production) for the majority of its products is 10 to 20 days. As a result, its inventory turnover rate is high. These combined factors cause inventory levels to appear relatively low in relation to sales volume. A key element of its manufacturing strategy is to limit fixed production costs by outsourcing component parts from strategic suppliers. This strategy has allowed it to increase the variable nature of its cost structure while retaining proprietary control over those production processes that Herman Miller believes provide a competitive advantage. Because of this strategy, manufacturing operations are largely assembly based.

The success of the HMPS was the result of much hard work. For example, in 1996, the Integrated Metals Technology (IMT) subsidiary was not doing well. IMT supplies pedestals to its parent company, Herman Miller. IMTs prices were high, lead times were long, and quality was in the 70 percent range. The leadership of the subsidiary decided to hire the consulting arm of Toyota,

Toyota Supplier Support Center (TSSC). Significant improvements were made by inquiring, analyzing, and "enlisting the help and ideas of everyone." As a result, quality defects in parts per million decreased from approximately 9,000 in 2000 to 1,500 in 2006. Concurrently, on-time shipments improved from 80 percent to 100 percent and safety incidents per 100 employees dropped from 10 to 3 per year.

The organizational values mentioned earlier were incorporated into the design of The Greenhouse, Herman Miller's main production facility in Michigan. From its inception, the building was designed to be environmentally friendly. For example, it takes advantage of natural light and landscaping. Native plants are grown without the use of fertilizers, pesticides, or irrigation. After the facility opened, aggressive paper wasps found the design to their liking. Employees and guests were stung—frequently. In keeping with Herman Miller beliefs, an environmentally sound solution was sought. Through research, it was learned that honeybees and paper wasps are incompatible. Therefore, 600,000 honeybees and their 12 hives were co-located on the property. The wasps soon left. Two unanticipated benefits are enjoyed to this day: due to pollination by the bees, the area around the facility blooms

Exhibit 4 The Herman Miller Production System

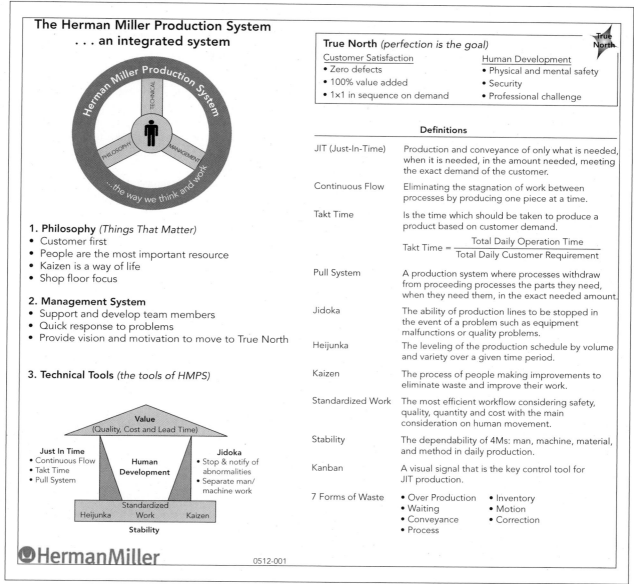

The Herman Miller Production System
. . . an integrated system

True North *(perfection is the goal)*

Customer Satisfaction
- Zero defects
- 100% value added
- 1×1 in sequence on demand

Human Development
- Physical and mental safety
- Security
- Professional challenge

1. Philosophy *(Things That Matter)*
- Customer first
- People are the most important resource
- Kaizen is a way of life
- Shop floor focus

2. Management System
- Support and develop team members
- Quick response to problems
- Provide vision and motivation to move to True North

3. Technical Tools *(the tools of HMPS)*

Definitions	
JIT (Just-In-Time)	Production and conveyance of only what is needed, when it is needed, in the amount needed, meeting the exact demand of the customer.
Continuous Flow	Eliminating the stagnation of work between processes by producing one piece at a time.
Takt Time	Is the time which should be taken to produce a product based on customer demand. $$\text{Takt Time} = \frac{\text{Total Daily Operation Time}}{\text{Total Daily Customer Requirement}}$$
Pull System	A production system where processes withdraw from proceeding processes the parts they need, when they need them, in the exact needed amount.
Jidoka	The ability of production lines to be stopped in the event of a problem such as equipment malfunctions or quality problems.
Heijunka	The leveling of the production schedule by volume and variety over a given time period.
Kaizen	The process of people making improvements to eliminate waste and improve their work.
Standardized Work	The most efficient workflow considering safety, quality, quantity and cost with the main consideration on human movement.
Stability	The dependability of 4Ms: man, machine, material, and method in daily production.
Kanban	A visual signal that is the key control tool for JIT production.
7 Forms of Waste	• Over Production • Inventory • Waiting • Motion • Conveyance • Correction • Process

HermanMiller

0512-001

Source: Courtesy of Hilton Garden Inn.

with wildflowers and a large amount of honey is produced. Guests to the home office are given a four-ounce bottle of the honey to symbolize its corporate beliefs.

Human Resource Management

Human resource management is considered a strength for Herman Miller. It is routinely listed on *Fortune* magazine's "100 Best Companies to Work For," including 2010. Herman Miller has approximately 278 applicants for every job opening. In the 2009 downturn, Herman Miller cut its workforce by more than 15 percent, reduced pay of the remaining workforce by at least 10 percent, and suspended company sponsored 401(k) contributions. Despite this, employees praised management for

"handling the downturn with class and doing what is best for the collective whole" according to *Fortune* magazine's February 8, 2010 issue. *Fortune* also estimated voluntary turnover to be less than 2 percent. On June 1, 2010, the 10 percent time-and-pay cuts implemented in the spring of 2009 were reversed due to Herman Miller's quick turnaround.

Herman Miller practices "Business as Unusual" as pointed out many years ago by Hugh De Pree, former president, and it appears to pay off in both good and tough times. Herman Miller shares the gains as well as the pains with its employees—especially in regard to compensation.

Pay is geared to company performance and takes many forms at Herman Miller. As in other companies, all employees receive a base pay. In addition, all employees participate in a profit-sharing program whereby employees receive stock based on the company's annual financial performance. Employees are immediately enrolled in this plan upon joining Herman Miller and immediately vested. Profit sharing is based on corporate performance because, as one employee explained:

The problem we see is you get to situations where project X corporately had a greater opportunity for the entirety of the business, but it was difficult to tell these folks that they needed to sacrifice in order to support the entirety of the business when they were being compensated specifically on their portion of the business. So you would get into some turf situations. So we ended up moving to a broader corporate EVA (Economic Value Added) compensation to prevent those types of turf battles.

The company offers an Employee Stock Purchase Plan (ESPP) through payroll deductions at a 15 percent discount from the market price. Also, all employees are offered a 401(k) and receive a 50 percent match for the first 6 percent of their salaries that the employee contributes. Again, employees are immediately eligible to participate in this plan upon joining Herman Miller and immediately vested. (The company match was suspended in 2009 due to the recession.) Through the profit sharing and the ESPP, the employees own approximately 8 percent of the outstanding stock.

Furthermore, all employees are offered a retirement income plan whereby the company deposits into an account 4 percent of compensation on which interest is paid quarterly. Employees are immediately eligible to participate in this plan upon joining Herman Miller, but are required to participate for five years before being vested. Additionally, a length of service bonus is paid after five years of employment. Finally, the company pays a universal annual bonus to all employees based on the company's performance against Economic Value Added (EVA) objectives. EVA is a calculation of the company's net operating profits, after tax, minus a fee for the cost of shareholder capital. This is in addition to the other compensation programs, including profit sharing, with the same calculation used to determine both employee and executive bonus potential.

Thus, pay takes a number of forms at Herman Miller, but most forms are at least partially, if not wholly, contingent on corporate performance. One employee summed up pay as follows, "You can dip into Herman Miller's pocket several times based on the performance of the company."

Other benefits also take many forms at Herman Miller. Employees are given a range of benefits as they are in many organizations. Some are, however, quite different from those found in other organizations, such

as a $100 rebate on a bike purchase. It is justified as "part of our comprehensive program designed for a better world around you." Other benefits that Herman Miller provides that are identified by the company as "unique" are:

- 100 percent tuition reimbursement
- Flexible schedules: job sharing, compressed work-week, and telecommuting options
- Concierge services—from directions, dry cleaning, greeting cards, or a meal to take home—these services make it easier for employees to balance work and home life
- Employee product purchase discounts
- On-site services including massage therapy, cafeterias, banking, health services, fitness center, fitness classes, and personal trainers

Herman Miller, in keeping with its beliefs, offers extensive wellness benefits including fitness facilities or subsidized gym memberships, health services, employee assistance programs, wellness programs/classes, and health risk assessments. The other benefits that are offered that most large organizations also offer include health insurance, dental insurance, vision care plan, prescription plan, flexible spending accounts, short and long term disability, life insurance, accidental death and disability insurance, and critical illness/personal accident/long-term care. All benefits are available also to domestic partners. When appropriate, Herman Miller promotes people within the organization. Education and training are seen as key to preparing employees to take on new responsibilities. For example, Rudy Bartels as well as multiple vice presidents began their careers at Herman Miller on the production floor.

Three other benefits are unique to Herman Miller. First, every family that has or adopts a child receives a Herman Miller rocking chair. Second, every employee that retires after 25 years with the company and is 55 years or older receives an Eames lounge chair. Third, Herman Miller has no executive retreat, but it does have an employee retreat, The Marigold Lodge on Lake Michigan. This retreat is available to employees for corporate related events, such as retirement parties and other celebrations, and in some instances includes invited family and guests.

Finance

During normal economic times, financial management at Herman Miller would be considered conservative. Through 2006, its leverage ratio was below the industry average and its times interested earned ratio was over twice the industry average. Due to the drop in business, the debt to equity ratio rose precipitously from 1.18 in 2006 to 47.66 in 2008. To improve this ratio, over

Table 1 Consolidated Balance Sheets

(In millions, except share and per share data)	May 29, 2010	May 30, 2009	May 31, 2008	June 2, 2007	June 3, 2006
ASSETS					
Current Assets:					
Cash and cash equivalents	$134.8	$192.9	$155.4	$ 76.4	$106.8
Short-term investments (Note 1)	—	—	15.7	15.9	15.2
Marketable securities	12.1	11.3	—	—	—
Accounts receivable	144.7	148.9	209.0	188.1	173.2
Less allowances in each year	4.4	7.3	5.6	4.9	5.0
Inventories, net	57.9	37.3	55.1	56.0	47.1
Prepaid expenses and other	45.2	60.5	58.0	48.3	47.9
Total Current Assets	**394.7**	**450.9**	**493.2**	**384.7**	**390.2**
Property and Equipment:					
Land and improvements	19.4	18.8	19.0	18.9	20.9
Buildings and improvements	147.6	137.4	139.4	137.2	139.1
Machinery and equipment	546.4	552.0	547.4	543.3	523.8
Construction in progress	10.7	9.8	17.4	17.6	23.5
	724.1	718.0	723.2	717.0	707.3
Less: accumulated depreciation	(548.9)	(538.8)	(526.9)	(520.4)	(504.0)
Net Property and Equipment	**175.2**	**179.2**	**196.3**	**196.6**	**203.3**
Goodwill and indefinite-lived intangibles	132.6	72.7	40.2	39.1	39.1
Other amortizable intangibles, net	25.0	11.3	—	—	—
Other assets	43.1	53.2	53.5	45.8	35.4
Total Assets	**$770.6**	**$767.3**	**$783.2**	**$666.2**	**$668.0**
LIABILITIES AND SHAREHOLDERS' EQUITY					
Current Liabilities:					
Unfunded checks	4.3	3.9	8.5	7.4	6.5
Current maturities of long-term debt	100.0	75.0	—	3.0	3.0
Accounts payable	96.3	79.1	117.9	110.5	112.3
Accrued liabilities	112.4	124.2	184.1	163.6	177.6
Total Current Liabilities	**313.0**	**282.2**	**310.5**	**284.5**	**299.4**
Long-term debt, less current maturities	201.2	302.4	375.5	173.2	175.8
Other liabilities	176.3	174.7	73.8	52.9	54.2
Total Liabilities	**690.5**	**759.3**	**759.8**	**510.6**	**529.4**
Minority Interest	—	—	—	0.3	0.2
Shareholders' Equity:					
Preferred stock, no par value (10,000,000 shares authorized, none issued)	—	—	—	—	—
Common stock, $0.20 par value (240,000,000 shares authorized, 57,002,733 and 53,826,061 shares issued and outstanding in 2010 and 2009, respectively)	11.4	10.8	11.1	12.6	13.2
Additional paid-in capital	55.9	5.9	—	—	—
Retained earnings	152.4	129.2	76.7	197.8	192.2
Accumulated other comprehensive loss	(136.2)	(134.1)	(60.1)	(51.6)	(63.3)
Key executive deferred compensation	(3.4)	(3.8)	(4.3)	(3.5)	(3.7)
Total Shareholders' Equity	**80.1**	**8.0**	**23.4**	**155.3**	**138.4**
Total Liabilities and Shareholders' Equity	**$770.6**	**$767.3**	**$783.2**	**$666.2**	**$668.0**

Table 2 Consolidated Statement of Operations

(In millions, except per share data)	May 29, 2010	May 30, 2009	May 31, 2008	June 2, 2007	June 3, 2006
Net sales	$1,318.8	$1,630.0	$2,012.1	$1,918.9	$1,737.2
Cost of sales	890.3	1,102.3	1,313.4	1,273.0	1,162.4
Gross margin	428.5	527.7	698.7	645.9	574.8
Operating Expenses:					
Selling, general, and administrative	317.7	330.8	395.8	395.8	371.7
Restructuring expenses	16.7	28.4	5.1	—	—
Design and research	40.5	45.7	51.2	52.0	45.4
Total operating expenses	374.9	404.9	452.1	447.8	417.1
Operating earnings	53.6	122.8	246.6	198.1	157.7
Other Expenses (Income):					
Interest expense	21.7	25.6	18.8	13.7	14.0
Interest and other investment income	(4.6)	(2.6)	(3.8)	(4.1)	(4.9)
Other, net	1.7	0.9	1.2	1.5	1.0
Net other expenses	18.8	23.9	16.2	11.1	10.1
Earnings before income taxes and minority interest	34.8	98.9	230.4	187.0	147.6
Income tax expense	6.5	31.0	78.2	57.9	47.7
Minority interest, net of income tax	—	(0.1)	(0.1)	—	0.7
Net Earnings	$ 28.3	$ 68.0	$ 152.3	$ 129.1	$ 99.2
Earnings per share - basic	$ .51	$ 1.26	$ 2.58	$ 2.01	$ 1.46
Earnings per share - diluted	$ .43	$ 1.25	$ 2.56	$ 1.98	$ 1.45

Source: Herman Miller 10-Ks

3 million shares were sold in fiscal year 2009.[iv] In the four previous fiscal years, Herman Miller had been repurchasing shares. The debt to equity ratio was reduced to 3.81 by the end of 2009. To improve short-term assets, dividends per share were cut by approximately 70 percent and capital expenditures were reduced to zero in 2009 (financial statements for years 2006–2010 can be found in Tables 1 and 2).

For fiscal year 2008, 15 percent of Herman Miller's revenues and 10 percent of its profits were from non–North American countries. In 2007, non–North American countries had accounted for 16.5 percent of revenues and approximately 20 percent of Herman Miller's profits.

Financially, Herman Miller holds true to its beliefs. Even in downturns, it invests in research and development; in fact, during the dot-com downturn, it devoted tens of millions of dollars. Inside Herman Miller, this investment project was code named "Purple." In the December 19, 2007 issue of *Fast Company* magazine, Clayton Christensen, Harvard Business School professor and author of *The Innovator's Dilemma,* commented on this project and is quoted as saying, "Barely one out of 1,000 companies would do

what they did. It was a daring bet in terms of increasing spending for the sake of tomorrow while cutting back to survive today."

Accessories Team: An Example of Herman Miller's Strategy, Leadership, and Beliefs in Action

The Accessories Team was an outgrowth of project "Purple." One of the goals of this project was to stretch beyond the normal business boundaries. Office accessories is one area Herman Miller has not been historically involved in, even though it is a big part of what the independent dealers sell. According to Mark Schurman, director of External Communications at Herman Miller, once the idea was identified, "Robyn was tapped to put together a team to really explore this as a product segment that we could get more involved with."

In 2006, Robyn Hofmeyer established the team by recruiting Larry Kallio to be the head engineer and Wayne Baxter to lead sales and marketing. Together, they assembled a flexible team to launch a new product in 16 months. They recruited people with different disciplines needed to support that goal. Over the next two years, they remained a group of six. People would join the team as needed and, when the team would get through that particular phase or piece of work, they would move on to different roles within the company. During its first

[iv]Herman Miller's fiscal year ends on May 30th of the following calendar year.

eight months, the team met twice a week for half a day. Twenty months later, it met only once a week.

The group acts with a fair amount of autonomy, but it does not want complete autonomy because, "We don't want to be out there completely on our own because we have such awesome resources here at Herman Miller," Robyn explained. The group reaches out to other areas in the company when different disciplines are needed for a particular product, and taps people that can allocate some of their time to support it.

Wayne describes the team as follows:

We all seem to have a very strong voice regarding almost any topic; it's actually quite fun and quite dynamic. We all have kind of our roles on the team, but I think other than maybe true engineering, we've all kind of tapped into other roles and still filled in to help each other as much as we could.

Another member of the accessories team describes decision making as follows:

If we wanted to debate and research and get very scientific, we would not be sitting here talking about the things that we've done, we'd still be researching them. In a sense, we rely upon our gut a lot, which I think is, at the end of the day just fine because we have enough experience. We're not experts, but we're also willing to take risks and we're also willing to evolve.

Thus, leadership and decision making is shared both within the team and across the organization. Ideas and other contributions to the success of the team are accepted from all sources.

What is known as the "Thrive Collection" has grown out of this process. The name was chosen to indicate the focus on the individual and the idea of personal comfort, control, and ergonomic health. Products included in the collection are the Ardea® Personal Light, the Leaf® Personal Light, Flo® Monitor Arm, and C2® Climate Control. All were designed to improve individual working environments. Continuing Herman Miller's tradition of innovative design, the Ardea light earned both Gold and Silver honors from the International Design Excellence Awards (IDEA) in June 2010.

The Industry

Office equipment is an economically volatile industry and the office furniture segment of the industry was hit hard by the recession. Sales were expected to drop by 26.5 percent from 2008 to 2009; Herman Miller's sales dropped 19 percent. Herman Miller's stock market value of $1.09 billion at the end of 2009 represented 7.3 percent of the total stock market value of the industry identified by Standard & Poor's Research Insight as Office Services & Supplies. According to Hoover's, Herman Miller's top three competitors are Haworth, Steelcase, and HNI.

The industry has been impacted by a couple of trends. First, telecommuting has decreased the need for large companies to provide office equipment for all employees. Some companies such as Oracle have a substantial percentage of their employees telecommuting and the majority of Jet Blue reservation clerks telecommute. Second, more employees spend more hours in front of computer screens than ever before. Due to this trend, the need for ergonomically correct office furniture has increased. Such furniture helps decrease fatigue and reduce the incidence of injuries such as carpal tunnel syndrome.

As with most industries, the cost of raw materials and competition from overseas has had an impact. However, these trends tend to affect the low-cost producers more than the high-quality producers.

The Future

In a June 24, 2010, press release, Herman Miller's CEO, Brian Walker, stated,

One of the hallmarks of our company's history has been the ability to emerge from challenging periods with transformational products and processes. I believe our commitment to new products and market development over the past two years has put us in a position to do this once again. Throughout this period, we remained focused on maintaining near-term profitability while at the same time investing for the future. The award-winning new products we introduced last week at the NeoCon tradeshow are a testament to that focus, and I am incredibly proud of the collective spirit it has taken at Herman Miller to make this happen.

Questions to Address: Will the strategies that have made Herman Miller an outstanding and award winning company continue to provide it with the ability to reinvent and renew itself? Will disruptive global, economic, and competitive forces compel it to change its business model?

Robley Wood, Jr., Wallace Stettinius, Robert S. Kelley, Thomas K. Quinton

Virginia Commonwealth University

In the spring of 2011, Mr. Charlie Luck, IV, was sitting in his office preparing his notes and readying himself to meet with his Senior Leadership Team. As he went through his notes, he began thinking about his years as CEO of family owned Luck Companies. He had become President and COO in 1995, and CEO in 1999, succeeding his father. A 1983 graduate of the Virginia Military Institute, Charlie followed up his degree in Civil Engineering with a three-year career as a professional racecar driver on the NASCAR circuit. At the end of 1986, he put his racing helmet aside and returned home to begin work as a full-time employee of Luck Companies.

As a teenager, Charlie worked summers at the quarries doing various jobs such as repairing machinery and driving trucks. Growing up around the quarries gave Charlie a good sense of the business from the bottom up, but both he and his father thought it was necessary for him to have extensive experience in all aspects and levels of the business if he was to succeed his father as CEO. His father wanted him to not only earn the position, but earn the respect of the company's associates as well. If Charlie did not prove capable, his father would not promote him.

Thus, in early 1987, Charlie began working full time in the quarries and other departments—systematically moving through supervisory and mid-management positions for the next eight years. This kind of training had many benefits—among them, learning various aspects of the business, developing managerial skills, and building relationships. Throughout the test, Charlie learned not only the importance of having a sound and innovative business strategy, but also the role that values and culture—the same values and culture that Charlie would later find were the catalyst to the company's past success—play in executing business strategies.

After eight years of on-the-job training, his father decided that Charlie was ready to run the company. Thus, in 1995, Charlie was promoted to President and in 1999, CEO.

By the time Charlie was appointed CEO, the company, driven by the business acumen and values of his father and grandfather, already had a long history of success in the aggregate business in Virginia. Luck Companies had been operated over the years in a very thoughtful, measured manner, accumulating little or no debt while maintaining a solid but not rapid growth rate. The company's operations were all in Virginia and, like many small businesses, had a "top-down" management style. Over the years, the aggregates industry had experienced little consolidation and was primarily comprised of family-owned businesses. Built on a "we care" attitude that emphasized integrity and treating people right, Luck Companies was a leader in customer service. By the late 90s, Luck Stone was also known as a technology leader and was ranked as one of the top 15 crushed-stone producers in the US.

The new millennium brought with it growing consolidation in the industry and fiercer competition. There was tremendous expansion in the markets and Luck Companies grew faster, got bigger, and increased debt to finance the growth. By the mid 90s, Charlie and his leadership team realized that the top-down management style at Luck Companies was not ideal for meeting the needs of customers or employees. After much deliberation, they determined that management decisions needed to be made closer to the customer. The organization was decentralized and associate duties and responsibilities were changed to better handle the growing complexity of sales opportunities.

Despite its growth, Charlie recognized his was a mature industry and therefore, he needed to diversify. Recognizing the increasing uniqueness of each business unit, Luck Company's leadership chose to separate the company into four businesses with distinct brand identities. The vision throughout the strategic planning process was for each new business to meet the unique needs of its particular marketplace, resulting in specific strategies, brands, and business plans for each.

Thinking back to the success of his father and grandfather, Charlie wondered what the future held for Luck Companies. At this point, he was challenging his management team to operate the company in a manner that not only advanced the company financially, but also positively impacted the lives of its customers and associates. He was convinced that the company was well positioned to become even more successful in the future.

Luck Companies and Industry Overview

Luck Stone, founded in 1923 by Charles Luck, Jr., is the largest privately owned aggregate supply company in the US. Over the last century, the Luck family turned a single quarry on the west end of Richmond, Virginia, into one of the top 20 largest producers of aggregate in the US. Luck Companies operates under four separate business units or SBUs: Luck Stone, Charles Luck (runs the Charles Luck Stone Center retail operations), Luck Development Partners, and Har-Tru. Although the Luck Companies business portfolio is diversified into four SBUs, all business units operate under Luck Companies' values-based leadership system.

Luck Stone

Luck Stone, the largest business unit of Luck Companies, operates fifteen crushed stone plants and three distribution yards in Virginia, and one sand and gravel operation in North Carolina. Luck Stone supplies a wide range of crushed stone, sand, gravel, and specialty stone—collectively called aggregate. The aggregates industry is broken down into two main production segments: crushed stone and sand and gravel. Although Luck Stone primarily mines and sells crushed stone, 10 years ago, it began producing sand and gravel as well. Due to the various sources, weights, sizes, and shipping costs associated with aggregates, the industry is defined

geographically and significantly fragmented with 1,600 companies operating 4,000 quarries in the US.[1] Luck Stone's operations are located in the Mid-Atlantic region of the US—Virginia in particular.

Aggregates are mined from various quarries and serve as inputs for the construction industry. The prosperity of the aggregate industry is directly correlated to the growth and economic stability of the construction industry, consisting of both private and public construction and further broken down into residential and nonresidential construction segments. Private residential and nonresidential construction spending in the US during 2010 was roughly $239 billion and $262 billion, respectively. Public residential and nonresidential construction spending in the US during 2010 was roughly $9 billion and $293 billion, respectively.[2] While private construction accounts for the majority of construction spending, historically it has been highly volatile. This volatility has had a crippling impact on the aggregate industry during the recent recession. The public segment, primarily funded by local, state, and federal government organizations, is considerably more stable than the private segment.

In 2006, Luck Stone sold 27 million tons of aggregate yielding a market share of roughly 30 percent in Virginia. By 2009, Luck Stone's volume sales had fallen to 11.7 million tons of aggregate yielding a market share of roughly 23 percent in Virginia. However, even with the significant decrease in aggregate sales, Luck Stone remains the most profitable business unit of Luck Companies and contributes more than 80 percent of total enterprise net sales. In 2008, Luck Stone was the 16th largest producer of construction aggregate in the US and the 12th largest producer of crushed stone in the US.[3,4] Luck Stone's largest competitors, Vulcan Materials and Martin Marietta Materials, were also hit hard by the recession; however, they remain in first and second place respectively for construction aggregate production in the US. Vulcan Materials, the industry leader with 10 percent US market share, had net sales of $2.5 billion in 2009, a significant decrease from its 2006 net sales of $3.0 billion.[5] Vulcan Materials and Martin Marietta Materials both operate with an overall cost leadership business strategy, while Luck Stone utilizes a business strategy based on superior customer service and logistical excellence. In 2010, Luck Stone controlled roughly 25 percent of the market for aggregate in Virginia.

Charles Luck Stone Center

In 1976, Luck Stone opened its first retail showroom for architectural stone adjacent to its corporate offices. The retail showroom concept was widely praised as unique in the stone industry. The official name of this business unit was the Architectural Stone Division of Luck Stone. In 1993, Mark Fernandes became VP of the Architectural Stone Division. When Charlie Luck was appointed CEO in 1995, he directed Fernandes to develop a five-year strategic plan that focused on expansion. By the end of the 90s, the Architectural Stone Division was operating six Architectural Stone Centers.

In 2000, a second five-year strategic plan was developed with a strategic focus on product innovation. The Architectural Stone Division sought differentiation through new product offerings and began sourcing stone internationally. During this period, the Architectural Stone Division experienced increasing levels of competition from other contractor stone yards as well as big-box retailers such as Home Depot and Lowe's. The management of the Architectural Stone Division knew that further differentiation was necessary to remain profitable.

In 2007, the Architectural Stone Division went through a significant rebranding and name change to Charlie Luck Stone Center. The strategic rebranding shifted the brand from a contractor stone yard to an upscale, design-oriented architectural stone center. The new brand focuses on a market of design savvy, affluent homebuyers. Unfortunately, over the past ten years, Charles Luck Stone Center sales have been 82 percent correlated with housing starts and the recent housing crisis significantly reduced Charles Luck Stone Center sales. However, management reported that for the last few years, this division has experienced the best cash returns on capital of any of the Luck Company business units.

In the early 2000s, the Architectural Stone Division supplied granite countertops and interior surfaces to Home Depot. However, Home Depot became over-saturated with lower-end products and demanded lower prices from the Architectural Stone Division. It was at this point that the division rebranded and shifted its strategy to concentrate only on high-end stone sales and ceased to be one of Home Depot's suppliers. Home Depot contracted a new supplier who was willing to meet its low price demands but was unable to deliver on its order promises. Home Depot subsequently fired this new supplier and asked the Charles Luck Stone Center to return as a supplier. However, the Charles Luck Stone Center management was no longer interested in supplying stone to big-box retailers. Even so, they agreed to supply Home Depot for 120 days while it looked for a new supplier. This decision was driven by the values of Luck Companies to always treat each customer right even if doing so does not fit with its long-term strategies.

Luck Development Partners

Luck Development Partners was founded in 1993 to realize the development potential of the real estate held by Luck Companies. Each quarry owned by Luck Companies needs nearly 500 acres to operate efficiently. Location is vital to the aggregate industry for the aforementioned reasons and serves as one of the largest competitive advantages in this industry. Similarly, the land development industry is highly dependent on location and proximity to population hubs. However, the life of a quarry is limited to the amount of aggregate reserves in the ground. The long-range sustainable use of the land comes in the form of innovative real estate practices. Developing these land assets allows Luck Companies to reap alternative revenue from its land holdings. Luck Development Partners creates unique places by integrating and highlighting natural, historical, and environmental elements into its project designs.

Har-Tru

Har-Tru is a global leader in tennis court surfacing and accessories. Har-Tru was originally Lee Tennis Court Products and was founded in the 50s by engineer Robert Lee. In 1997, Lee Tennis Court Products was acquired by longtime partner and supplier, Luck Companies. Two years after the acquisition, Luck Companies acquired Lee Tennis Court Products' largest competitor, ISP Tennis Products. Shortly after, Luck Companies acquired the manufacturing assets of the original Har-Tru material provider and, finally, bought the Har-Tru brand name.

Currently Har-Tru maintains between 85 and 90 percent of the US market share for clay tennis courts. The main competition to the clay tennis court market comes from companies building non-traditional tennis courts with clay substitutes. While it is the leader in its industry, Har-Tru is the smallest business unit of Luck Companies and in 2009, contributed about 6 percent to total enterprise net sales.

History

The Founders Years: 1923 to 1964

Luck Stone acquired its first quarry, Sunnyside Granite Company, Inc., in Richmond, Virginia, in 1923. First year sales were $22,212 for "chips" and "dust." These sales were fueled by the C. S. Luck Construction Company, owned by Charles Samuel Luck, the great grandfather of Luck Companies current CEO. In 1925, the quarry employed 23 men and the first available production records show sales of 94,000 tons of stone at an average price of $1.40/ton for the year 1928.

During the 30s, Luck Stone acquired four more quarries in Virginia. One of the quarries purchased was the Boscobel quarry located about 20 miles from the center of Richmond in Manakin-Sabot, Virginia; where the company's headquarters is now located. The Boscobel quarry has been in operation since the 1880s and production records for 1931 show it produced 130,151 tons of stone with net sales of $138,065. In 1938, Luck Stone purchased Fairfax Quarries Inc. for $17,500. This quarry became one of its most successful due to the growth in Northern Virginia and its proximity to Washington DC.

In the 40s, the US involvement in World War II caused major production problems for Luck Stone. By 1942, there was a freeze on all state road contracts, a slowdown in the construction industry, and labor shortages for nearly all domestic companies. All of Luck Stone's quarries were forced to minimize operations with production coming to a virtual halt in 1943 and 1944. The Boscobel quarry was able to continue operations on a reduced scale, selling exclusively to the US government for military base construction in the greater Hampton Roads area. In 1949, the property for a new (and still operational) quarry near Charlottesville was purchased for $43,500 from the Thomas Jefferson Memorial Commission.

Land for its first quarry in the Shenandoah Valley region was purchased in 1950 for $35,000. The land was located in Augusta County and in 1957, final approvals were received to operate the quarry. The Augusta Quarry is no longer owned by Luck Companies but is still operational, producing limestone that is rich in calcium.

In 1961, Luck Stone acquired a quarry in Farmville, Virginia that it never operated. Luck Stone subsequently sold the property in 2005. In 1964, it purchased a quarry near Greenville, Virginia that ceased production in 1967.

Expansion—the Charles S. Luck, III Years: 1965 to 1992

After spending summers working in the quarries, Charles Luck, III, Charlie's father, joined the company in 1957 after his graduation from the Virginia Military Institute and two years of active service in the US Air Force. He became President of Luck Stone in 1965, succeeding his father, Charles S. Luck Jr., who became Chairman of the Board.

When Charles took over in 1965, sales were approximately two million tons of crushed stone per year. When he passed the baton to his son in 1995, annual tonnage of crushed stone had grown to almost 15 million tons per year. The company had expanded to 14 crushed stone operations including one in North Carolina. In Virginia, quarries were purchased or developed and became operational under the Luck Stone name in Goochland County (1965), Loudon County (1971), Green County (land purchased in 1982, quarry

operational in 1984), Powhatan County (land purchased in 1984, quarry operational in 1985), Fauquier County (land purchased in 1987, quarry operational in 1988), Louisa County (land leased and limited production started in 1989), Leesburg (1993), and King William County (1996).

The oil crisis and recession of 1973 produced skyrocketing energy prices, high inflation, and a major lull in the construction industry. Luck Stone's management used this time to begin an initiative to bring energy savings, cost cutting, and efficiency improvements to its operations. Despite the depth of the recession and the need to reduce expenses, no employees were laid off.

Following the recession of 1973, management looked for opportunities for diversification to help lessen the impact of the cyclical nature of the construction industry. As a result, the Architectural Stone Division was started in 1977 and its first stone center opened the next year in Goochland, Virginia.

Under the leadership of Charles, the company established itself as an industry leader in technology and innovation. In 1977, employees of Luck Stone designed and built the first totally automated lime plant in the aggregates industry in Augusta County, Virginia. The plant was designed to run unattended with sensors that would shut down the plant if a problem was detected. In 1987, Luck Stone's engineering team designed and built segmentation and automation systems that would allow a plant to produce crushed stone 24 hours a day. Through his years as president and CEO of Luck Companies, Charles grew the company significantly, created a culture focused on people, and brought the company to the forefront of innovation.

The Early Charles Luck IV Years: 1995 to 2003

In 1995, Charles Luck IV (Charlie) was named President of Luck Companies, and his father, Charles, became Chairman and CEO. At that point, the company employed approximately 400 associates, produced over 12 million tons of crushed stone, and was known for its "WE CARE" culture. In addition, Luck Stone had established a nationally recognized safety program that became a model for the industry.

Charlie describes his early years as CEO as follows:

I really did not fully understand the company at first. I knew that decision making was centralized and we never shared our profit and loss data with our people in the field. I started sharing revenue, cost data, and profitability numbers with our field managers and I also decentralized our management structure. To begin the development of our management team, I sent our officers to executive business programs and we produced our first five-year strategic plan for the years 1995–2000.

Charlie describes his experience for the first five years as:

1. Learning to see the business in totality from a general management perspective. Up until that point, he had only seen it from operational and functional perspectives. He found that being CEO required a very different way of thinking about the business.
2. Building his management team while dealing with a generational management succession of his father's team. The existing senior managers were steeped in the quarry business and some found it very challenging to respond quickly to the demands of a rapidly growing business or think of ways to diversify.
3. Restructuring the business to reflect its increasing complexity and size with an emphasis on decentralizing operations.
4. Learning to manage the numbers in terms of growth and profit.
5. Creating a strategic management process with the first five-year plan.
6. Realizing that, in a less centralized environment, an overall plan with clear goals and objectives is essential to tie the parts into a coherent whole.

Between 1995 and 2006, the company set new profit and volume records every year. In 2003, it employed 830 associates and produced over 21 million tons of crushed stone. It had diversified into tennis courts, land development, and stone centers. By 2005, the company had almost 1200 employees. This tripling of associates led to numerous promotions and hiring new talent from outside the company. Acquisitions of companies and quarries also provided a steady stream of new associates. This period was in stark contrast to the very deliberate and measured growth cultivated by Charlie's father and grandfather.

The year 2002 was truly remarkable for the company with record sales yet again. Three more Virginia quarries were purchased (Culpeper, Spotsylvania, and Bull Run) and work was finished on a new North Carolina based quarry that was to produce roofing granules for a 3M factory in North Carolina. The North Carolina quarry entered 2003 ready to produce almost two million tons a year for 3M's facility and the local market.

However, despite record sales and rapid growth, not everyone shared in Charlie's enthusiasm. In 2000, George Fox—a key associate who had been with the company for a couple of decades—told Charlie he felt that Luck Stone was losing its way. He said there were many people making decisions in ways that he did not believe were aligned with the traditional values the company had held for decades. Charlie recalls:

During this same period of time, we had grown our executive leadership group and I was observing that, although we were getting record financial results, we were not working together as effectively as we could or should as a team. Often, there were the "meetings after the meetings" where issues were being discussed that could have, and should have, been resolved and settled in the first meeting.

I felt like we had a team that could be so much more effective in leading our company if we worked together in a high-performing, constructive, but challenging and respectful way where we completed meetings all on the same page. To help us improve, Jay Coffman, VP of Human Resources and I hired a management consultant who was recommended to us by Caterpillar executives in Peoria, Illinois. The management consultants began meeting with us once a quarter for two days. He met with all the leadership team members for about 18 months. During this period, we learned that our values and leadership journey started with ourselves. We realized that we needed to look at our own personal leadership as it pertained to issues in the company.

The Values Journey—Vision 2010—Phase I: 2003–2007

Beginning in early 2003, the leadership team met to decide what values would define the company. The leadership team did not realize that this endeavor would result in a values-based leadership journey that would dramatically transform the organization.

During this period, officers also began what was coined "Tools Training." Tools Training was built on various forms of insight testing that ultimately taught the officers to understand themselves and others in order to make a difference. In one of these private meetings, Charlie came to the realization that the Values Journey had to start with him:

For two hours I sat in front of the group, while the team filled flip chart pages with comments about what they did and didn't like about my leadership. They then covered the walls with all the pages. At this particular time, I found the negative observations to be painful and I did not see them as gifts but rather as attacks on me. There was a side of me that was extremely upset and mad but I also knew that I had to do something different. Upon returning to Richmond, I talked with my father about this experience. He asked me about the feedback and I told him it was the same thing he had been telling me for the past nine years. He then asked me what I was going to do about it and I promised him that I was not going to quit and that I was going to work as hard as I possibly could to be a better leader for our company and for our people. This was clearly a pivotal point that forced me to look in the mirror and figure out how I could be a better leader at Luck Companies.

After a year of these periodic meetings and Tools Trainings, other associates began to notice a difference in the officers. At the end of this 18-month period, the values that would lead the company were agreed upon:

- Integrity: Earning the trust and respect of others.
- Commitment: Building the long-term success of associates, customers, and community.
- Leadership: Achieving legendary performance.
- Creativity: Fostering an environment where ideas and innovation add value.

These values emphasized the importance of performance but went beyond that to describe the behaviors required to do the right things. Charlie believed strongly that a values-driven culture was the way to achieve even better outcomes and performance. Examples of outcomes included:

- Improved customer loyalty and key account retention through integrity and commitment to anyone the company came into contact with.
- Increased product innovation by focusing on and embracing creativity throughout the company.
- Better efficiency and safety through an unwavering commitment to a best-in-class safety program.
- Acquisition advantages by gaining respect as an industry leader for operating with integrity as a core value in everyday operations.

In 2004, after a year and a half of deciding what values would define Luck Companies, Charlie and the senior team decided it was time to unveil the Values Journey and Vision 2010 to the entire company. A series of departmental meetings were held where Charlie gave the speech that would change the company forever. In his speech, Charlie told the employees that he was no longer worried about just making money but instead, how that money was being made. Many associates were shocked at Charlie's newfound Vision 2010, "To be the Model of a Values-Based Organization."

The next task was to embed this newfound vision throughout the company. It was important that these values did not become superficial posters merely hung on a wall to collect dust. Charlie and the senior team knew that to truly achieve the vision, the values would have to reach the deepest depths of the company and become ingrained in each and every associate. Every associate would be held accountable to these values and through this accountability, the vision would ignite potential in the associates to not only become better employees, but better individuals holistically. To ensure the values were embraced and carried out by every associate, a unique and intense process costing thousands of working hours and millions of dollars was developed to embed and operationalize Vision 2010. Below is an overview of the steps taken to drive the vision:

- **The Monthly Values Program:** A year-long program starting with top associates in groups of 40 providing the same tools training the officers had received.
- **Established the First Ritual:** Any and every meeting would start with 10 to 15 minutes of sharing values stories.
- **Restructured the annual associate performance reviews (APRs):** APRs built around values and behaviors, and encompassing two sections—what and how.
- **Insights Study:** Every employee given an insights study to learn about themselves.
- **New Values Curriculum:** This new curriculum was built around values, insights, and supporting tools.
- **Introduced Walking the Talk Awards:** Associates submitted names of coworkers acting out the values (top five received a prize).
- **Hired and embedded site specific HR personnel:** Assigned to work in the field and teach and train the new values.
- **Quarterly Values Program:** Attended by all associates.
- **Implemented a Mentoring Program:** Started with officers mentoring five senior leaders each for a year. Senior leaders then mentored the associates beneath them.
- **Employee Interview Process Overhaul:** Managers began to ask values-based behavior questions of interviewees.
- **New Officer Incentive Plan:** Self-development as measured by 360 assessments changed to account for 33 percent of officer bonuses.

In 2005, Mark Barth was appointed the Director of Values. Others were also appointed as dedicated associates in the Values Journey and Vision 2010. At the time, Luck Companies was allocating between one to two million dollars to Vision 2010 per year. However, institutionalizing the values model as the business grew was no easy feat. A number of managers could not or did not want to adapt to a more values-oriented leadership style, preferring to strictly emphasize the importance of performance and/or other variables not aligned with the values identified. Some seasoned associates were unable to see the benefit of incorporating values into their leadership style and the behaviors of some senior leaders conflicted with the values the Senior Leadership Team was promoting. Some left and others were asked to leave.

It took three years, but by 2006, the Values Journey was gaining traction and people were truly acting differently and adopting the values. Associates were approaching Charlie at company events to tell him how the values not only benefited their work life, but their personal and family life as well.

The Values Journey—Vision 2020—Phase II: 2007–2008

At 46 years of age, Charlie was thinking even more deeply at a personal level about what life was about. He had seen 15 years of annual financial records and the Values Journey was working. Yet, somehow it didn't seem to be enough. He was beginning to think there had to be a bigger purpose in life. Charlie joined his wife's brother, Kyle Petty, on his an annual charity ride across the country with a large group of friends. Out in the west, Charlie was riding due east directly into the sunrise. He had been riding for about an hour at 100 miles per hour when he looked over to his right at hundreds of migrant workers picking strawberries. He asked, "Why wasn't I born into a family of migrant workers?" He remembered something his mother had told him when he was a young child, "To whom much is given, much is expected."

Charlie returned from his cross-country trip and, seeing his name on trusts and wills, began to think about his own children. He traveled to a Family Office consultant in Chicago to look into starting a Family Office for the Luck Family. When he arrived, the consultant asked Charlie about his company. He told her about his Values Journey and his thoughts about a larger purpose in life. They began to talk about this larger purpose and her curiosity grew. She asked about the lives that the company had touched and the progress that the Values Journey had made. He told her stories of associates coming up and telling him how they have a better relationship with their children, with their parents, and with themselves. She stopped him and asked, "How often does a company get the chance to touch the lives of three generations?"

He realized that he and his company had the opportunity and ability to positively impact the lives of more people than he originally thought. Five years of the Values Journey had made a positive impact on the company overall, but there was still more to be done to create a company that could touch the lives of everyone. He realized that the higher purpose he sought was for his company to enrich the lives of the people it touched—from employees to customers to suppliers to the community. He and his top associates began to research literature and others' experiences about doing good as the best path to doing well. They realized that the model would be built on leadership; values-based leadership would serve as the means to spread their values more effectively throughout the company and in turn, the lives of the people the company touched. From here, Vision 2020 was created, "To be recognized as one of the top five values-based leadership organizations in the world."

The values-based leadership model development process began in the spring of 2007. Another consulting firm was brought in to help facilitate the design and assessment process. A small team of cross-functional leaders from the four business units was selected to build the framework and behavioral components of the model. This team was led internally by two senior leaders, John Pullen, VP of Strategy and Real Estate, and Jay Coffman, VP of Human Resources. The development team was given the assignment to align the mission, values, and Charlie's 2010 Vision into a practical and inspiring model that included the essential behaviors required for success as a leader at Luck Companies. The model would also provide a framework for ongoing selection and development of company leaders, content for leadership training, and behavioral standards for performance management. The process used to build the leadership model contained the following steps.

- **Step 1:** Planning session (s) to understand expectations and deliverables of the project.
- **Step 2:** The facilitation of design meetings with cross-functional leaders to create the initial draft of the leadership model.
- **Step 3:** Online content validation with the entire leadership population to refine and generate Values-Based Leadership acceptance.
- **Step 4:** Recalibration of the model to include feedback from the content validation process.
- **Step 5:** Senior leadership team validation and blessing.
- **Step 6:** Final balancing of the model.
- **Step 7:** An initial 360 assessment of top leaders to test the model.

Steps 1–6 took approximately ten months. The framework of the model was designed to:

- Advance the values-based culture of Luck Companies.
- Build exceptional experiences with our customers and constituencies.
- Drive differentiated growth.

At the end of 2007, both the CFO and VP of Human Resources announced their retirements in 2008 and 2009 respectively. These pending retirements gave Charlie the opportunity to examine the structure of his senior leadership team to ensure that the proper infrastructure would be in place to drive future growth.

New Strategic Leadership Team

There were several key changes to the senior leadership structure. First, Charlie decided to add a Chief Growth Officer position to the team. John Pullen was appointed to this position and tasked with the responsibility of driving differentiated growth and financial results across the enterprise. Each business unit would report directly to John. The other key change was the creation of a Chief Leadership Officer who would be responsible for the overall strategic and tactical support of the acquisition, development, and retention of high-performing talent. This position would have direct accountability for working with other senior leaders to bring the leadership model to life. Mark Fernandes, once president of Charles Luck and Har-Tru, was selected as the Chief Leadership Officer (see Exhibit 1). In short, Charlie's intention for these positions was to manage and achieve, in parallel, best-in-class financial performance and organization-wide values alignment.

Another key change to the leadership structure was the addition of a Chief Family Officer. Wanda Ortwine was appointed to this unique position and tasked with the job of developing the leadership and competencies of Charlie's family in preparation for the future, handling family investments, estate planning, and serving on the Strategic Leadership Team to transform the organization in alignment with the mission.

After contributing over 20 years of service to the organization, Jim Parker retired and was replaced Roy Goodman who was given the titles of Chief Financial Officer and Vice President of Finance for Luck Companies. Prior to joining Luck Companies, Roy had been the CFO for RealNetworks, a high growth technology company located in Seattle, Washington.

The organizational changes were announced in the spring of 2008, and an orderly two-year transition plan was put into place. However, three unexpected events occurred during the 2008/2009 timeframe; the US entered a deep recession, the president of the aggregate division, who had a record of excellent performance, was asked to leave the company due to a misalignment with the organization's values, and Charlie became seriously ill. These events put Step 7, the final step of testing the new leadership model, on hold as the company worked to regain traction.

Reduction in Force: 2008

Charlie said that in 2008, the "financials fell to pieces." The recession was hitting all aspects of the stone industry hard and demand for some of its products had been eroding since 2006. The company had expanded to almost 1,200 associates in 2008, but it was obvious to the leadership team that sales were not returning anytime soon and it did not have the revenues necessary to support such a large workforce.

In September 2008, things got so bad that the federal government had to save several large US corporations. Charlie commented, "We then knew that 2009 was going to be worse than 2008." Management had already taken typical expense reduction steps such as a hiring freeze, delaying equipment purchases, and cutting non-essential expenses. However, they now realized that the recession was unlike others they had experienced and they were going to have to take more drastic measures.

Exhibit 1: New Luck Companies Organizational Chart

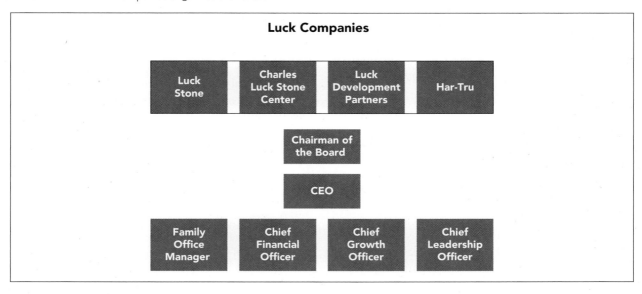

In the end, they concluded that it would be better to operate with 125 fewer associates than negatively affect everyone. This decision was especially difficult for the managers of a company that had never had a reduction in force in its entire history and was known for treating its employees like family.

Once the decision was made, Charlie and his leadership team discussed the type of company and associates they wanted to have once the recession was over. They decided not to use seniority to guide them in their decisions about who would no longer be an employee of the company, but instead revisited their core values. A generous separation package was prepared for each departing employee that "stretched the company." In an attempt to slow down the inevitable rumor mill and ensure that every employee had exactly the same information, a video was prepared that explained in great detail why the reduction was necessary and it was shown to every employee on Tuesday, November 11, 2008. On Wednesday, November 12, 2008 and Thursday, November 13, 2008, managers met with the employees that had to be let go.

Commenting on the reduction, Charlie said, "We wanted our employees to say, 'It's an awful thing to do, but you did it better than anybody else.' We wanted our people to say, 'This is how a values-based company does this.'"

To aid employees after the reduction in force, Luck Companies leased a building and turned it into an Employee Relocation Center. There, they helped employees write resumes and cover letters and find new employment. As a testament to the reputation, culture, and values of Luck Companies, many other companies reached out, eager to accept Luck Companies' ex-employees as new hires.

In March 2009, Charlie fell ill. At first, he believed that he had contracted the flu virus and would be back to work soon. However, the illness worsened and Charlie became bed-ridden with disabling fatigue for nearly 20 hours a day. The doctors were unable to diagnose his illness. During this time, Charlie thought a lot about the life he had lived and what else could be done to fulfill his purpose. After two long months, he began to improve and returned to work.

The Values Journey Continues— Phase III: 2009 to Present

In the fall of 2009, Charlie returned to an organization that was struggling because of the recession. The two prior years of Charlie's life had a significant impact on the way he wanted to continue to run the company. After nearly dying, Charlie decided Vision 2020 was too far in the future and not significant enough to achieve his goals for the company. He rewrote the vision with an even higher purpose and shortened the time span by five years. The new mission was coined Mission 2015 and now states "We will ignite human potential around the world and positively impact the lives of others through values-based leadership."

He presented the mission to Mark Fernandes, Chief Leadership Officer, and tasked him with making it operational. Mark knew that it would not be easy to drive such a lofty mission at a time when the company had fewer financial resources and fewer associates and was operating in markets that were in a recession. Despite these negative circumstances, Mark and rest of the leadership team believed in the mission and worked to develop a new values-based leadership model that would make it happen. To guide them in this development, the senior team members relied on the company's "Core Ideology and Beliefs" as well as the "Values-Based Leadership Value Proposition" presented below:

Core Ideology and Beliefs:

"We believe all people are born with the extraordinary potential to make a positive difference in the world. We believe making a difference is a choice, a conscious choice that begins with our own self-awareness and alignment. Values-based leaders consistently make this choice then insure others to do the same, positively impacting the lives of those around them."

Values-Based Leadership Value Proposition:

"At Luck Companies we believe doing good (making a difference) is the best path to doing well (business performance); and values-based leadership is how we do good and why we do well."

During this same time, Charlie put Step 7 into effect and had the senior leadership team collectively go through a robust 360 assessment process where each leader received feedback on how their behavior was aligned with the model. After the 360 assessment, the leaders went through an intense period of values development and behavioral management training to accomplish Mission 2015. After 12 months of preparation, it was time for the four businesses to undergo an intense 5-year strategic planning process to drive the mission and the company through 2015. By late 2010, the organization had completed all of the strategic planning for the business units. The key initiatives for 2011 through 2015 are listed below:

Luck Stone

1. Management will make a concerted effort to grow reserves in the core crushed stone business. Reserves expansion is a complex process that can take years to complete, often involving multiple public hearings.

2. Implement a new business model called the "customer-inspired strategy." This model calls for employees of Luck Stone to operate the company in such a way that it becomes a partner with the customer. Every effort will be made to fully understand the logistics of the customer's business and to improve the customer experience.

3. Salespeople will go mobile using iPads and other mobile devices so they may quickly access pricing and product information when meeting with potential customers.

4. Further develop the fast-growing Hampton Roads, Virginia market, a market entered in 2008 through an acquisition from Florida Rock Company. This acquisition includes, for the first time in the company's history, a water transportation business.

5. Finally, continue working to turn used quarries in Northern Virginia into water reservoirs. The first Luck Stone quarry to be used as a reservoir is expected to be operational in Loudoun County, Virginia, in 2017.

Har-Tru

In 2010, Luck Companies rebranded Lee Tennis Court Products and officially changed the name to Har-Tru. However, this significant rebranding was far more than just a corporate brand name change. Anderson McNeill, former VP of Reebok International and a brand expert, was appointed as president of both Har-Tru and Charles Luck. Anderson repositioned the brand from a tennis supply company to a true sports brand. Har-Tru Sports is now a global sports company with its roots in the tennis industry. The new brand is positioned to drive a cult following similar to sports brands such as Nike and Under Armor. Anderson describes the shift as, "moving from a comfort brand to a brand of strength; developing champions is a real position of strength." The following are the 2011 through 2015 high-level strategies for Har-Tru:

1. Focus on developing youth tennis players into champions as well as promoting the sport among youth to drive longevity.

2. Diversify product offerings to encompass more aspects of the sport.

3. Heavily promote Har-Tru with social and interactive media.

4. Expand internationally and grow sales in China.

5. Research and develop a larger variety of clay surface colors.

Charles Luck (Charles Luck Stone Center)

The key initiatives for the Charles Luck Stone Center brand and division for 2011 through 2015 are to:

1. **Expand Our Reach:** Focus on growth in major urban areas with less expensive studios in leased storefront, outside sales representatives, and strategic alliances.

2. **Increase Relevance:** Build the brand into a nationally recognized architectural stone designer and supplier.

3. **Improve Performance:** Change Charles Luck into a performance driven business, as opposed to an operations driven business. For the first time in the history of Luck Companies, Charles Luck is implementing an incentive-based sales program and basing 50 percent of Charles Luck sales associates' compensation on commission.

4. **Add Real Value:** Implement the new mission of Charles Luck that now reads, "Always add 'real' value to our customer, their business, and the clients they serve."

Luck Development Partners

When the economy turns, there are plans for Luck Development Partners to build a new community on the banks of the Ni River in Spotsylvania County, Virginia. This will be the largest project ever undertaken by Luck Development Partners and will encompass 300 acres of land that is currently a light industrial business park called River Run. Luck Development Partners plans to build 900,000 square feet of commercial space, 90,000 square feet of retail space, and 950 housing units. It will be a sustainable, mixed-use community with an environmentally responsible infrastructure. The team in charge of this project envisions a place where people can live, work, and play with minimum automobile use.

Senior Leadership Team Meeting

As Charlie sat at his desk, as proud as he was of the past performance record, he knew that his focus had to be on the future. He was very aware that the outlook for the economy was still poor and that the housing market had not come out of its depression. Despite these negative forces, he knew he had the senior leadership structure, senior leadership team, and strategies in place to drive the company.

He thoroughly reviewed the reports detailing the status of the company and each of its four businesses. As always, he gave particular attention to the data from the Luck Stone division that continued to produce over 80 percent of the firm's total sales. Direct comparisons with Vulcan Materials and Martin Marietta showed that all three firms had sales growth in 2010 but that Luck Stone was growing 7 percent faster than either of its two key competitors. He also noted with pride that its employee safety record was much better than the industry average and that bad debt write-offs as a percent of sales were only 0.003 percent, near the lowest in the history of the company.

Charlie gathered his notes and walked down the hall to the main conference room, "Natural Bridge." Charlie was excited to hear his teams' views on how to drive Mission 2015 and the financial performance of the company. He was particularly excited about further developing the Values Journey and demonstrating to a wider audience the impact it had on people's lives and corporate performance.

NOTES

1. US Geological Survey, 2011, Mineral commodity summaries 2011: Reston, VA, US Geological Survey
2. US Census Bureau, 2011, Annual value of construction put in place 2002–2010: Washington, DC, Government Printing Office
3. US Geological Survey, 2011, Directory of principal construction aggregates producers in the US in 2008: Reston VA, US Geological Survey
4. US Geological Survey, 2011, Directory of principal crushed stone producers in the US in 2008: Reston VA, US Geological Survey
5. Vulcan Materials, 2010, December 31, Form 10-K

Ryan McVay/Getty Images

Sam DeMarie, Pam Manhart, Charles B. Shrader
Iowa State University

Introduction[1, 2, 3]

Jim Skinner, CEO of McDonald's Corporation, sat in his office and reflected on his company's recent experiences. The firm had overcome many obstacles in its quest to be viewed as a valued business partner in each of its operating regions. The future looked bright.

Was it only a few short years ago that McDonald's had been the focus of demonstrations and sometimes violent protests? McDonald's had doggedly used its tried and true business practice of standardization to create a consistent customer experience throughout the world. This allowed the company to become the world's largest fast-food restaurant business. Yet somehow this previously sound business strategy had unintentionally led the company to become an icon for much of what was wrong with global business. Those were challenging times, and rebuilding the global brand of McDonald's had required significant changes.

As Skinner considered his company's situation, the phone rang. It was Cindy Goody, director of nutrition for the company. Goody told Skinner about a troubling commercial she had just finished watching on US television. In the commercial the iconic golden arches appear shackled over the feet of a dead man with the caption "I was lovin' it." A hamburger is clutched in his hand, and a woman weeps over his body. Goody knew this was exactly the type of thing she and Skinner thought they had defeated. The commercial, developed by the nonprofit group, Physicians' Committee for Responsible Medicine, was the latest in a series of attempts to blame fast-food consumption for increasing rates of heart disease and obesity. Frustrated but resolute, Goody knew the company was now committed to providing balanced menu choices for customers, and that many of its menu items were healthy while being reasonably priced. She felt confident that the company's new menu reflected traditional American tastes but also incorporated foods from around the world. The new, more expansive menu now included everything from one-dollar burgers and snack wraps to moderately priced salads and was appealing to an ever-widening range of customers.

Goody was instrumental in developing the healthier and more international menu over the past few years. Her work entailed traveling the world for menu ideas, infusing the menu with healthier items, and hiring a company chef, Dan Coudreaut. Coudreaut, or Chef Dan as he was known in the company, was a graduate of the Culinary Institute of America and former head chef of the Four Seasons Resort in Dallas, Texas. Chef Dan held the title of Director of Culinary Innovation at McDonald's and supervised a staff of 16 that evaluated as many as 1,800 potential new menu ideas each year. Goody realized Chef Dan's operation had breathed valuable life into the old traditional burger and fries menu and had helped the company grow during the recession.

Goody and Skinner considered the company's recent performance. The new dollar menu was a success. The new salads and healthier menu options were appealing to a wider range of customers. Net income for September 2010 increased 12 percent on a 5 percent increase in sales. McDonald's competitors Wendy's and Burger King were struggling with their menus, experiencing low growth, and dealing with the possibility of being acquired. With foreign demand for McDonald's at an all-time high, nearly 65 percent of McDonald's sales now came from overseas. McDonald's was rated by the *Wall Street Journal* in the top five of the Dow 30 with the largest overseas revenue.

Skinner told Goody that they would have to keep in close touch over the next few months. In a comforting tone he said, "Don't worry, we are on the right track." This seemed to mollify Goody and they hung up, but in the back of his mind, Skinner started to mull things over. Was McDonald's current performance merely a natural response of increased demand for low-priced fast food during the slow economy? Should the firm continue developing its menu with the multicultural approach to which McDonalds attributed its recent success, or go back to a simpler and more standardized set of options? Could the company retain its long-standing burger and fries menu and simultaneously be at the forefront of healthy eating? Should the firm worry about health? How should the company continue to grow internationally? Was the business environment changing again and if so, would these changes affect McDonalds in its efforts to achieve strategic competitiveness?

Company History

McDonald Brothers[4]

Brothers Mac and Dick McDonald opened their first restaurant in California in 1940. It was built during the carhop craze and attracted a limited market of teenagers. Plagued with the common problems of the carhop business—labor intensive work, high turnover, waitresses dating customers, silverware theft, and grounds strewn with litter—the brothers decided to try a new business approach: self-serve. Barbeque and other items were removed to simplify the menu and eliminate the need for silverware. An all male crew was hired, each of whom was trained to perform a single task, which was enabled by the new limited menu. It was in 1954 that the brothers' newly designed operation caught the attention of Ray Kroc, who was to become the founder of McDonald's Corporation. Kroc was selling multi-mixers used for mixing multiple shakes at once. Because of the large volume each five-spindle unit could process, Kroc seldom had large sales. After selling 10 separate machines to the McDonald brothers, he went to San Bernardino to personally investigate the situation. He immediately saw the potential for expansion and negotiated to become the brothers' franchising agent.

Ray Kroc[4]

The 50s was an era marked by the rapid growth of franchises. Kroc's multi-mixer business had exposed him to sizable franchises like Dairy Queen and Tastee Freeze. From this experience, he concluded that the way for a corporation to make money was to ensure that its franchisees made money. The widespread practice at the time was to charge considerable franchising fees, sell territory rights, and require store operators to purchase equipment and supplies from the corporation at cripplingly high margins. This caused many franchisees to cut corners to earn a profit, which hurt the reputation of other franchisees. Kroc saw this as detrimental to the corporation overall. This conclusion became legendary due to Kroc's perpetual insistence that every McDonald's store conform to the corporate tradition. He believed that lack of orthodoxy would not only damage the brand image, but would result in operational inefficiencies as well. He created standardized menus, foolproof production processes, common suppliers,

consistent training, unwavering cleanliness directives, and required a minimum advertising budget to ensure the longevity of both the corporation and the franchisee. McDonald's Corporation provided a business model to the entrepreneur and in return earned royalties based upon the success of that formula. Kroc opened his first store in 1955 in suburban Chicago and in 1961, bought the company for $2.7 million. In 1985, when McDonald's launched its initial public stock offering, Kroc's share of the firm was valued at $32 million.

Marketing[4, 5]

Early on, teenagers were McDonald's primary customers; however, Kroc's objective was to target the larger, more profitable family market. Accordingly, promotions such as Happy Meals were aimed at children so that they would appeal to their parents to go to McDonald's. Newspaper ads featuring Rockwellesque paintings were provided by McDonald's Corporation to franchisees for use in their local media. The Yellow Pages and newspaper ads were the most common advertising medium in the 50s; but, these ads were ineffective in terms of reaching kids. Ronald McDonald was created and broadcast during children's shows when spots were cheaper. Creating this company "spokesperson" and using it during children's shows flew in the face of convention during a time when television advertising was never used by restaurants. This approach proved successful, though, and contributed to a rapid increase in sales of roughly 30 percent. By 1985, McDonald's had the largest and most powerful promotional budget of any brand.

The company was also considered a pioneer when it advertised during the first Super Bowl. At the time, devoting heavy expenditures to television advertising during the game was unproven; as such, it was also reasonably inexpensive. In 1967, it was estimated that 60 million viewers tuned in to the championship game and advertising ran about $80,000 for a 60-second spot. Super Bowl ads have since become a phenomenon and McDonald's 1993 Super Bowl ad, called "The Showdown" and featuring Michael Jordan and Larry Bird, is today regarded as one of the top Super Bowl ads of all time.

McDonald's Operations

Standardization[4]

One of McDonald's greatest concepts has been its strict adherence to operating standards, known as QSC&V (quality, service, cleanliness, and value). Because of standardization, customers initially were and today still are certain of the experience they will receive, regardless of the McDonald's location they visit. Thus, a Big Mac is sure to be the same in Chicago as in Cheyenne. Quality is reliable. Service is always fast and courteous. Stores and restrooms are clean at every location. Uniformity has allowed for greater cost control through greater economies of scale that in turn allow McDonald's to maintain low prices. Value is also maintained through price controls. Customers pay the same amount in each store they visit. QSC&V are consistent company wide to protect the brand image, so that no single franchisee can damage the reputation of units located in other markets.

Supplier Relationships[4]

For McDonalds, supplier relationships are a key component in its efforts to control costs. To this end, the firm has traditionally maintained very strong relationships with a small handful of suppliers. Each supplier's processes are scrutinized for compliance to McDonald's standardized procedures. For example, each burger must weigh the same and have identical proportions of beef to fat to facilitate the automated cooking process. Unique clamshell style griddles were developed to cook both sides at once and create a perfectly cooked burger in as little time as possible. A non-standard burger would either be under- or overcooked. The process is designed to be error-free by eliminating variation. Suppliers with proven process controls are rewarded with McDonald's exclusive business and volumes that almost guarantee profits.

As a result, suppliers willingly share their expertise with the company. Suppliers create unique process designs knowing their efforts will be rewarded by the company. In addition, they are confident their loyalty will be rewarded. The exclusive nature of the supplier relationship fosters a partnering of ideas. For example, a supplier solved the challenge of producing a consistent French fry. McDonald's had experimented with various temperatures and cooking times but still experienced unpredictable results. Inconsistency in the potato supply chain complicated matters. The pioneering supplier found a potato that could be obtained year round and environmentally controlled the storage process to regulate the conversion of starch into sugar.

Although it was a franchisee who thought of the filet of fish, a supplier found a way to successfully make the filets. Originally, filets were sliced, battered, and fried by hand in each restaurant. Availability issues led to the use of various types of fish, thus the filet patties lacked uniformity. The filleting process was too lengthy and varied to replicate in the necessary mass volumes. A supplier determined how to obtain significant volumes of a single type of fish, and developed the process to repeatedly create a consistent filet size and shape suitable for standardized cooking at all restaurant locations. As a result, company store managers were able to outsource much of the labor to suppliers.

Menu[4, 6, 7]

The menu has traditionally been one of the most tightly controlled aspects of McDonald's business operations.

Too many menu variations can create several problems including disruptions in the supply chain, inconsistent quality, increased expenses due to inefficiencies, and uncertainty in consumers' minds. Pricing is also strictly restrained to manage demand and maintain fairness between franchisees. Exhibit 1 details major menu developments over the years.

Global Expansion[4, 8, 9]

To continue growing and as a foundation for competitive success, McDonald's transported its business strategies to other countries (see Exhibit 2 for a timeline of McDonald's global expansions). To enter new markets, McDonald's utilized the formula that had proven so successful over the years. The strategy in entering foreign markets was "one world, one taste." In this regard, the firm was committed to the standardized formula that was the bedrock of its success. The goal was to offer American food at a reasonable price. "One world, one taste" was reinforced by the decision to begin expansion with English-speaking countries that were more accepting of America. American businessmen and tourists frequented company restaurants for a familiar taste of home while overseas. The company was selling American culture.

McDonald's top management believed: "If we incorporate their food we lose our identity," but the company underestimated the impact of its restaurants on the cultures of the host countries. This made the company vulnerable to much resentment. The original "American" appeal eventually wore off and concerns grew regarding fatty diets. Scares over mad cow disease and a growing anti-American sentiment strengthened the negative image of McDonald's as a global "powerhouse" in terms of food. Attacks and protests directed at the company increased.

Additionally, there were operational problems with executing this standardized approach. The company was growing and the infrastructure necessary to support the restaurants was not in place. Careful scrutiny and supervision had been the key to success, but many overseas operations were joint ventures and difficult to supervise. Foreign operations often didn't have the qualified suppliers that were the key to standardization. As a result, overseas locations were less profitable on average than their domestic counterparts.

Broadening Global Appeal[4, 10, 11, 12, 13, 14, 15]

In 2003, management adopted a strategy called "Plan to Win" that shifted emphasis from increasing the number of store locations to improving existing locations. Rather than promoting what American customers expected,

Exhibit 1 McDonald's Menu Over the Years

Year	US Menu Change	Status	Comments
1948	Menu reduced to support drive-thru	Repeatedly	
1949	French fries replace potato chips	Current	
1949	Shakes	Current	
1963	Hula Burger	Flop	Catholic abstinence on Friday.
1964	Filet O Fish	Current	Catholic abstinence on Friday.
1968	Big Mac	Current	
1973	Quarter Pounder & Quarter Pounder w/Cheese	Current	
1975	Egg McMuffin	Current	
1979	Happy Meals	Current	
1980	Chicken McNuggets	Current	
1981	McRib	Off/On	Barbeque sauce. 1981, 1994, 2005; farewell tours 2006, 2007, 2008; available again in 2011.
1985	McDLT	Flop	Hot burger, separate cool tomato and lettuce. Too expensive.
1987	Salads	Continuous Revisions	
1989	McPizza, Lasagna, Spaghetti	Flop	Attempts for supper. Preparation took too long.
1991	Big N Tasty Sandwich (revamped McDLT)	Current	
1991	McLean Deluxe	Flop	91 percent fat free. Attempt to "lean" menu. Dry.
1992	McJordan	Flop	Bacon and barbeque sauce.
1996	Arch Deluxe	Flop	Attempt towards adult tastes. Too distant from McFamily tradition.
2002	McAfrica	Flop	Massive famine in Africa, considered an insensitive campaign.
2003	Premium Salads	Current	
2003	Dollar Menu	Current	Key sales driver. Drives customer traffic.
2004	Phase out supersize	Current	Simplify menu. Support balanced choices.
2006	Snack Wrap	Current	
2009	McCafe	Current	

Source: http://en.wikipedia.org/wiki/List_of_countries_with_McDonald%27sproducts

Exhibit 2 International Expansion Timeline

Year	Markets Entered
1967	Canada, Puerto Rico
1970	Virgin Isles, Costa Rica
1971	Guam, Japan, Netherlands, Panama, Germany, Australia
1972	France, El Salvador
1973	Sweden
1974	Guatemala, England
1975	Hong Kong, Bahamas
1976	New Zealand, Switzerland
1977	Ireland, Austria
1978	Belgium
1979	Brazil, Singapore
1981	Spain, Denmark, Philippines
1982	Malaysia
1983	Norway
1984	Andorra, Wales, Finland

(Continued)

Exhibit 2 International Expansion Timeline (*Continued*)

Year	Markets Entered
1985	Thailand, Aruba, Luxembourg, Venezuela, Italy, Mexico
1986	Cuba, Turkey, Argentina
1987	Macau, Scotland
1988	Serbia, South Korea, Hungary
1990	Soviet Union, China, Chile
1991	Indonesia, Portugal, Greece, Uruguay, Martinique
1992	Czechoslovakia, Guadeloupe, Poland, Monaco, Brunei, Morocco
1993	Marianas, Iceland, Slovenia, Saudi Arabia
1994	Botswana, Kuwait, New Caledonia, Oman, Egypt, Bulgaria, Bahrain, Latvia, United Arab Emirates
1995	Estonia, Romania, Malta, Columbia, Slovakia, South Africa, Qatar, Honduras, Saint Martin
1996	Croatia, Samoa, Fiji Islands, Liechtenstein, Lithuania, Cyprus, India, Peru, Jordan, Paraguay, Dominican Republic, French Polynesia, Belarus
1997	Ukraine, Yemen, Republic of Macedonia, Ecuador, Reunion, Isle of Man, Suriname
1998	Moldova, Nicaragua, Lebanon, Pakistan, Sri Lanka
1999	Georgia, San Marino, Gibraltar, Azerbaijan
2000	French Guiana
2001	Mauritius
2003	Kazakhstan, Mayotte
2004	Montenegro
2006	Algeria, Kenya, Iraq

Source: http://www.sec.gov/cgi-bin/srch-edgar; http://en.wikipedia.org/wiki/List_of_countries_with_McDonald%27s_franchises

McDonald's attempted to become more relevant to local and regional preferences.

To begin, the company started utilizing local suppliers. McDonald's incented local suppliers to upgrade their operations, and some US suppliers built plants overseas to serve stores in foreign markets. Regional distribution centers were established as the foundation for distributing indigenous foods to multiple stores within a region and to support more customized menus.

The company encouraged regional experimentation with the menu to align with local tastes. When McDonald's experienced success with a menu item in one region, it would then leverage that experience in other regions. One example of this was *McCafe*—an upscale coffee concept that originated in Germany. Ultimately, this concept was instrumental to the turnaround of US stores. Another was the P'tit Plaisir, a line of mini-size snack foods developed in France that is now served in 12 different countries.

The company also took purposeful actions aimed at becoming a valued member of its local communities. For example, McDonald's in France hosted an open door community event after one of its stores was destroyed by a protestor. This strategy is now used in other countries as well and offers customers the opportunity to tour the kitchen and meet executives and suppliers. Finally, stores were redesigned to be more modern, comfortable, and amenable to overseas expectations. The new fast-food idea was to encourage patrons to linger and relax—to be a destination, not just a drive-thru. Ambiance and comfort were improved with upholstered vinyl chairs, tables of various sizes and shapes, subdued lighting, and décor appropriate to local customs. Individual franchisees have created some very unique designs. Outlets and free Wi-Fi for customers to work on laptops while eating have also been added.

Multidomestic Strategies

Skinner felt the company needed to become more connected to a global customer base. Over time, this resulted in significant variance in strategic actions in different countries. The examples that follow highlight key variations in country-level strategies.

France[16, 17, 18, 19, 20, 21]

In France, McDonald's was fondly referred to as McDo, pronounced McDough. After the rebrand, France became McDonald's second most profitable market in the world. As mentioned earlier, McDonald's was not always well received in France; in fact, the company often was the focus of protests, sometimes resulting in violence. The company's French leadership redesigned the brand so it would not be seen as an American company subverting the French culture of high cuisine. The company touts, "Yes, we were born in the US, but we are made in France." McDonald's now features premium ingredients, 75 percent local sources, eco-friendly stores, and nutrition content significantly better than the country's traditional choices featuring high fat cheeses and potatoes soaked in duck fat. McDonald's was also an active participant in the premier agricultural show, Salon de l'Agriculture, which features premium, locally-sourced foods.

The new menu in France offers many choices not familiar in the US such as the P'tit Plaisir (mini snack foods), Little Mozza (tomato and mozzarella salad), Croques Monsieurs (grilled ham and cheese), and Jambon Beurre (ham and butter on a crusty baguette). In addition, stand-alone *McCafes* carry traditional French sweets such as macaroons, fruit tarts, and flan, and serve beverages in ceramic mugs.

Although 70 percent of Americans traditionally order food to go, dining is a particularly social event in France. People are likely to come in groups and spend more money, but expect to dine in, linger, and have at least two courses. McDonald's prospered in France by positioning its restaurants as primarily takeout, offering quality options without the time commitment. This strategy delivers a direct cost benefit to the consumer; traditional restaurants are required to tax patrons at a rate of 19.6 percent, while McDonald's is only required to tax patrons 5.5 percent. This makes inexpensive food even more reasonable in a sluggish economy with high unemployment.

Germany[22, 23, 24, 25]

Early on, McDonald's located its German restaurants on properties owned by German brewers to facilitate the selling of local beers. While this feature attracted a bar crowd, it deterred the families McDonald's preferred. Local management understood the German market to be very price sensitive so they increased beer prices and developed a coffee bar. This later evolved into the concept known as *McCafe*.

With the recent addition of more locations, McDonald's has become the most popular restaurant brand to Germans aged 12 to 18. This is due in part to the firm's commercials starring Heidi Klum, a German supermodel. Her ads combat the obesity image associated with McDonald's. In addition, stores are simply decorated and focus on the essentials typical of German design. Most stores feature televisions tuned to the McDonald's German Network, a very popular in-store television network. It carries branding, entertainment, leisure content, and advertising.

Germany is considered one of the most environmentally conscious countries in the world. Sensitive to this, a typical German McDonald's store converts used oil into biodiesel fuel, buys solar-powered air conditioners, and uses refrigerators that operate without harmful chlorofluorocarbons. McDonald's also developed a prototype store that uses 25 percent less energy. Staff patrol the grounds for garbage and the firm displays anti-litter slogans on trash cans. To reduce waste, wrappers are made from 72 percent recycled paper while other disposables such as tray liners, napkins, and toilet paper are made from 100 percent recycled content. The firm even redesigned McFlurry lids to save, of all things, hedgehogs.[i]

McDonald's also improved its local sourcing in Germany. In response to government pressure, McDonald's started adding locally raised, organic beef to its patties.

McDonald's marketing executives also identified a German fascination with Mexican culture and a love of that culture's spicy foods. Accordingly, McDonald's Germany added Los Scharfos (fried cottage cheese and jalapeno snack), El Pikanted (beef patty, pita, and picante sauce), and a big bacon burger topped with jalapenos. The popular Mexican food items were tied to a promotion that used Facebook and YouTube to allow patrons to enter a sweepstakes.

Russia[26, 27, 28, 29, 30, 31]

After 14 years of negotiations that began at a meeting during the Canadian Olympics, McDonald's was allowed to enter the former Soviet Union market. Despite being a very challenging economy that prompted many other international businesses to leave, McDonald's did not retreat. Because there were few individuals with the resources necessary to become franchisees, one of the keys to McDonald's early success was participating in a 51 percent joint venture with the Moscow City Council.

Historically, Russians had difficulty obtaining permission to leave the country. Thus, patronizing an American company in Russia became a cheap and easy way to get a glimpse of the US. In addition, McDonald's was an attractive alternative to the poor service consumers were accustomed to, as quite often they had to stand in line for hours for food at other vendors. Fast food had very little competition because restaurants for the average citizen were rare. Most traditional restaurants were very fancy and exclusively targeted the rich. Remarkably, the fast-food diet was not an issue. Due to basic food scarcity, McDonald's instead got complaints that the fat content in the mayonnaise was not high enough. The menu in Russia was augmented with simple foods unique to local tastes such as cabbage pie and kvass (alcohol from fermented brown bread).

The average family income level in Russia also worked in McDonald's favor. While McDonald's was sometimes criticized in the US for low wages, Russians were very happy with McDonald's jobs. Each new store opening created approximately 100 new jobs. Most families were poor and very few owned cars, so McDonald's didn't

---

[i]Apparently, hedgehogs have a sweet tooth and would stick their heads in the hole on the lid of a discarded McFlurry and often not be able to pull it back out. This sometimes resulted in the animal starving to death. The new lid with a smaller hole prevents the hedgehog from sticking its head inside.

need drive-thru windows. Store owners alternatively developed walk-up windows.

In Russia there was little infrastructure and few suppliers. Out of necessity, McDonald's chose to build their *McComplex* food processing facility while developing a domestic supplier network. When McDonald's started in Russia, the state of affairs was in such infancy that, for instance, there wasn't machinery available to mass harvest potatoes in the necessary volumes. Additionally, health and safety standards lagged. After significant contributions to the food service, processing, agriculture, and business industries, today 80 percent of supplies are sourced domestically. It is estimated that the McDonald's supply chain network alone created over 100,000 new jobs in Russia.

Currency management was another new challenge to which McDonald's had to adapt. Rubles were not always easily convertible, but McDonald's stores only accepted rubles, the local currency, to make it easy for the local public to spend their money. Because of the difficulty in converting the rubles back to dollars and the difficulty obtaining loans, McDonald's strategy was to buy local real estate to spend the rubles, then charge rent from those properties and collect in hard currency. This gave the company money to import the supplies it couldn't source locally. The approach has paid off. McDonald's early real estate investments have appreciated about 40 percent and land is now almost impossible to acquire today. Consequently, as competitors attempted to enter the market, they were faced with exorbitant rents.

China[32, 33, 34, 35]

The Chinese market was also challenging for McDonald's in terms of real estate. McDonald's US site selection is calculated down to a science and emphasizes the suburbs because that is where most American families spend their time. Generally speaking, McDonald's found China's inner cities were less deteriorated than US inner cities, and made them the primary target markets. McDonald's also decided that the best way to expand was to build groups of stores simultaneously, thereby achieving economies of scale in construction, sourcing, training, and distribution. The firm secured locations in growing areas that would become prime real estate in the future. Similar to the experience in Russia, the firm took the risk to buy low and have that presence when property prices started to appreciate.

In contrast to Russia, China was experiencing tremendous economic growth and consequently, more and more Chinese were driving cars. New drivers seemed to enjoy driving everywhere possible. McDonald's was the first fast-food provider to offer a drive-up lane in China, and the concept proved very popular. Trying to further take advantage of the growing car ownership

in China, McDonald's closed a deal with the Chinese state-owned oil company allowing the company to open stores at its gas stations.

The Chinese tend to not dine out nearly as often as Americans. However, when they do dine out, they are typically not looking for their traditional cuisine, but something more novel. Going to McDonald's provides the opportunity to experience the outside world to which China has only recently become open. In China, McDonald's food is expensive for the average citizen, so the firm's pricing is tiered by district based on the income of local consumers.

The American experience offered by McDonald's is a popular dining choice; therefore, the traditional Western-style menu is still the basis of McDonald's Chinese menu. Even so, the Chinese menu does have some unique selections. In the Chinese culture, beef is associated with strength and energy, so China is home to the "Mega Mac" with four beef patties. The new quarter pounder in China had cucumbers instead of pickles. There are also inexpensive, traditional Chinese choices on the menu such as a corn cup, a pork sandwich, and seafood and vegetable soups.

During traditional festivals, people tend to gravitate toward conventional Chinese restaurants. McDonald's hoped to reverse this tendency by celebrating Chinese national holidays as well. Given this objective, the firm decorates stores with cultural emblems of Fu (happiness), magpies, and twin fishes' symbols, to recognize and show respect for Chinese traditions and culture.

Food safety is a major issue for McDonald's in China. McDonald's relies heavily on suppliers to minimize service time in the store, but safe food handling practices were not common. To remedy this, the firm held Chinese suppliers to the same high standards as US suppliers and frequently dropped in unannounced for inspections. McDonald's worked hard to establish local supply chain networks in order to be less vulnerable to restrictive governmental trade policies.

Australia[22, 36, 37, 38, 39, 40, 41, 42]

McDonald's in Australia is often called "Maccas." McDonald's emphasizes premium Angus beef and has positioned itself as a high-end fast-food outlet. They call this approach "masstige," prestige for the masses, premium but affordable. The beef McDonald's uses in Australia is 100 percent Angus and locally sourced. Two of the more popular sandwich choices are the grand Angus and the mighty Angus. Quality is important and Australia's internationally recognized livestock identification system provides strong traceability and safety in terms of quality control. There has been such a strong interest in healthy menu choices in Australia that McDonald's has offered as many as 16 products on its "light choice" menu, nine of which are approved by the Australian National Heart Foundation. Even the French fries in Australia have been altered to adapt to local regulations and do not contain wheat or milk. McDonald's officials indicate that the firm worked for a full year to develop products in ways that would result in approval by the National Heart Foundation.

Environmental concerns have been very important in Australia as well. McDonald's efforts in this area include changing from foam to paper packaging, increasing the recycled content of paper products, comprehensive waste recovery, and composting. The firm encourages suppliers to reduce their environmental impact as well. For example, all coffee is certified sustainable by the rainforest alliance. A McDonald's team is working with the marine stewardship council on fish-farming sustainability. Additionally, McDonald's has helped its carton board supplier work supportively with the forestry stewardship council.

The company has exhibited a strong commitment to employees in Australia. Casual employees have the same 12-month parental leave as full-time employees. Wages are above the federal minimum. In 2001, McDonald's was voted the employer of choice for women and identified by Institute Australia as a "Best Company to Work For" in 2008.

Japan[36, 43, 44, 45, 46]

McDonald's has found the Japanese market to be challenging and dynamic. The firm's early marketing strategy emphasized the appeal of US style products. This approach was successful at first, but has recently experienced difficulties. McDonald's initially used a low-price strategy that was not well received in Japan. Although the market is very price sensitive, it is also susceptible to fashion and trends. In response, promotions have been used to appeal to the younger generation. For example, various mega-burgers have been offered for a limited time only. The company also used a creative and bold strategy to tout the future release of a "top secret" sandwich. A select few high-profile stores were temporarily closed and re-opened with the top-secret burger—the Big Mac, which was not available at other McDonald's restaurants in Japan. One of the few items unique to Japan to consistently remain on the menu is the teriyaki burger.

The company targets the youth market segment as having the highest profit potential and, in doing so, competes directly with Japanese convenience stores. The company also now emphasizes coffee sales to leverage its large pricing advantage over Starbucks and appeal to price-sensitive consumers.

One of the keys to future growth is to eliminate the competition by converting convenience store locations into McDonald's restaurants. Locations McDonald's has targeted include train stations and other busy sites with heavy traffic throughout all hours of the day.

Because of relatively fewer natural resources, the Japanese have not required local sourcing as much as other countries. Superior imports are considered acceptable. Thus, McDonald's has formed key partnerships to create viable supply chains. For example, beef is not domestically produced but comes from Australia.

India[47, 48]

India is the world's most populous democracy and the third largest economy in Asia, just behind China and Japan. Given this, it is no surprise that McDonald's was one of the first American fast-food chains to enter the Indian market, with its first restaurant established in New Delhi in 1996. McDonald's franchises, while not as widespread as in other parts of Asia and the Pacific Rim, are now found in many parts of India. In June 2009, the company announced expansion plans for 40 new restaurants across India, increasing the total number of Indian locations to over 200. The current franchise growth rate is higher in India than any other Asian country. Entry is typically accomplished through the use of joint ventures with Indian firms.

Initially, McDonald's experienced difficulty in India due to environmentalists and animal welfare activists. Religious and anti-Western sentiment also presented challenges to the company. Over 40 percent of the Indian population is vegetarian. Out of respect for the local religion and culture, McDonald's serves no beef or pork products in India. Instead, McDonald's developed a special line of vegetable, fish, and chicken sandwiches. The company developed both vegetarian and nonvegetarian menus with separate kitchens and service crews. McDonald's also offers kitchen and restaurant tours to assure customers the staffs are separate.

Seventy-five percent of the McDonald's menu is localized for India. This represents a much larger portion of the total menu than for other Asian countries. The *Chicken Maharaja Mac*, two grilled chicken patties with smoke-flavored mayonnaise, cheddar cheese, and vegetables, has become one of the most successful choices on the localized menu. The popularity of the chicken nuggets and sandwiches caused some restaurants to run out of supplies. The high demand for this sandwich has led the company to also offer it in a lamb version.

McDonald's continues to reach out to local communities to improve its image. It has engaged in partnerships with Indian communities to support schools, gardens, and parks. The company has also made donations to the Bhuj, Gujarat, and Latur earthquake relief efforts.

Brazil[49, 50, 51]

McDonald's in Brazil is among the most popular fast-food restaurants in a country that loves fast food. At first, growth proceeded quickly and franchises were often opened too close to existing outlets, sometimes causing franchisees to sue the company. The owners' concerns were cannibalization of existing stores' sales and growing without consideration of the areas served by existing locations. Some Brazilian store owners also complained about the extremely high rents charged by the company.

Over time, McDonald's developed several social initiatives to improve its image and to better fit the Brazilian environment. One was the McHappy Day (McDia Feliz) partnership with the Ronald McDonald Institute that raised approximately 38 million Brazilian real ($21 million) for the purpose of treating teenagers and children who have cancer. Other community-oriented activities include training courses, clothing and book donations, and rehabilitation of green areas in Brazilian communities.

McDonald's eventually chose a strategy in Brazil that was somewhat unique for the company. In 2007, McDonald's sold its businesses in Brazil and 13 other Latin American countries, totaling almost 1,600 restaurants, to a licensee organization. This arrangement allows McDonald's to receive royalties in Brazil rather than operating sales and rents. The licensee group has agreed to pay monthly royalties at a rate of 5 percent of gross sales as well as grow the business by paying fees for opening new restaurants and committing funds to improve existing ones. McDonald's has a 20-year royalty and fee agreement with the licensee group.

Current Situation

With continuing growth, the magnitude of McDonald's impact on national and world culture has become increasingly significant. The presence of the golden arches is often seen as evidence of American hegemony. It has become the quintessential example of efficiency, standardization, and bureaucracy.

Because of its size and influence, McDonald's has received more than its share of public attention, both positive and negative. The company has high brand exposure, a large dependence on natural resources, and a considerable impact on the environment. McDonald's operations require a significant amount of packaging materials, and it is no secret that McDonald's can generate a great strain on the infrastructure everywhere it operates. McDonald's began to experience increasingly frequent incidents of violence and vandalism because the firm was a symbol of Western culture. To combat this international backlash, McDonald's engaged in a series of socially responsible activities.

Corporate Responsibility[52, 53, 54]

Kathleen Bannan, manager of corporate social responsibility for McDonald's, emphasized six general areas in terms of corporate responsibility: community, employment experience, environmental responsibility, governance and ethics, nutrition and well-being, and a sustainable supply chain. Bannan implemented a strategy that allowed the company to consider more social and environmental issues in the areas where it did business. As part of this strategy, the company identified a set of key performance indicators centered on sustainability concepts. For example, in the supply chain area, the company charted the worldwide percentage of firms that affirm the Code of Conduct created for McDonald's suppliers. The firm also set goals and standards in the areas of animal welfare and packaging. In terms of employment, McDonald's charted employee development, internal promotions, and advancement opportunities for women. In addition, community philanthropic activities and in-restaurant nutritional information were supported worldwide. The firm tracks improvement relative to the above stated goals areas on an annual basis.

McDonald's also entered into several productive relationships with non-governmental organizations (NGOs). The company works actively with NGOs in an attempt to improve and better track the effects of its operations on both suppliers and customers. Packaging, for example, has been a huge environmental issue. In conjunction with Environmental Defense in Europe, the company developed an alternative to polystyrene packaging called the "clamshell," a cardboard container that keeps the food warm but is not as environmentally harmful as polystyrene.

The large industrial cattle operations needed to supply the company have a sizeable environmental footprint as well. McDonald's has also worked with NGOs and suppliers to better understand the firm's impacts on water pollution, waste management, and soil erosion. As part of its collaborations, the company has engaged in pilot projects with beef suppliers in an attempt to establish sustainability goals and metrics. The result has been improved environmental practices that in turn provide both defense against criticism and support of the company brand. McDonald's has required beef suppliers to document that their cattle do not have mad cow disease and it has asked its chicken suppliers to reduce antibiotic use.

Through a process called "anticipatory issues management" the company identified a potential problem—the batteries included with some Happy Meal toys contained mercury. The batteries never became a big public relations problem for McDonald's because the company proactively identified the risk and eliminated all mercury batteries from the toys.

Together with Unilever, Coca-Cola, the United National Environment Program, and Greenpeace, McDonald's created a natural refrigerant program that explored alternatives to ozone-depleting chemicals. This program, called "Refrigerants Naturally," won an Environmental Protection Agency award in 2005.

In 2009, the company developed an interactive software program named EcoProgress that enables its restaurants to reduce energy consumption by up to 11 percent. McDonald's also pioneered improvements in water management through its storm water retention tank program. The goals of this program are to save on water use not only in the restaurants, but in communities as well. Additionally, McDonald's has started programs for transforming its used cooking oil into biodiesel fuels and has installed electric vehicle charging stations at restaurants in certain locations. The firm has also partnered with the Japanese government to offer discounts to citizens who register to participate in CO_2 emission reduction programs.

Conclusion

As Skinner reflected on the past and how McDonald's had systematically used its standardized business practices to create a consistent customer experience, he realized how this aspect of McDonald's approach to business contributed to the success the firm enjoyed, including becoming the largest fast-food restaurant in the world. But the old McDonald's existed in a stable world that changed very slowly. CEO Skinner now felt as though the world that his firm competed in was changing daily, and in significant ways. McDonald's current multidomestic strategy, including its unique and customized approaches to each country, allowed it to respond more quickly to this dynamic environment. New socially responsible initiatives would help maintain the company's reputation abroad. Still, Skinner knew he was going to have to continually rethink his strategy for company growth. In this regard, a major question lingered, "What is our next move going to be?" Skinner knew, these were indeed challenging times and continual effort would be required for McDonald's to compete successfully throughout what was a rapidly changing world and competitive environment. While the firm's recent financial results were positive (see Exhibit 3), continuing to perform in this manner would challenge the firm, its managers, and employees.

Exhibit 3 Selected Financial Data for McDonald's Corporation

Revenue (values in millions)	2009	2008	2007	2006	2005	2004
United States	$ 7,943.8	$ 8,078.3	$ 7,905.5	$ 7,464.1	$ 6,955.1	$ 6,525.6
Europe	9,273.8	9,922.9	8,926.2	7,637.7	7,071.8	6,736.3
APMEA	4,337.0	4,230.8	3,598.9	3,053.5	2,815.8	2,721.3
Other Countries & Corporate	1,190.1	1,290.4	2,356.0	2,739.9	2,274.6	2,610.8
Total Revenue	22,744.7	23,522.4	22,786.6	20,895.2	19,117.3	18,594.0
Cost of Revenue	13,952.9	14,883.2	14,881.4	13,963.2	12,940.0	12,690.6
Gross Profit	8,791.8	8,639.2	7,905.2	6,932.0	6,177.3	5,903.4
Selling & Administrative Expenses	2,234.2	2,355.5	2,367.0	2,295.7	2,118.4	1,939.1
Impairment and Other Charges	(61.1)	6.0	1,670.3	134.2	(28.4)	281.4
Other Operating Expenses	(222.3)	(165.2)	(11.1)	69.1	103.3	145.0
Operating Income	6,841.0	6,442.9	3,879.0	4,433.0	3,984.0	3,537.9
Interest Income (Expense)	473.2	522.6	410.1	401.9	356.2	358.4
Gain (Loss) on Sale of Assets	(94.9)	(160.1)	0	0	0	0
Other, Net	(24.3)	(77.6)	(103.2)	(123.3)	(32.4)	(21.2)
Income Before Taxes	6,487.0	6,158.0	3,572.1	4,154.4	3,660.2	3,200.7
Income Tax	1,936.0	1,844.8	1,237.1	1,288.3	1,082.6	923.2
Income After Tax	4,551.0	4,313.2	2,335.0	2,866.1	2,577.6	2,277.5
Total Extraordinary Items	0	0	60.1	678.1	24.6	1.0
Net Income	4,551.0	4,313.2	2,395.1	3,544.2	2,602.2	2,278.5

(Continued)

Exhibit 3 Selected Financial Data for McDonald's Corporation (*Continued*)

Balance Sheet (values *in millions*)	2009	2008	2007	2006	2005	2004
Assets						
Cash and Short-Term Investments	$ 1,796.0	$ 2,063.4	$ 1,981.3	$ 2,128.1	$ 4,260.6	$ 1,379.8
Total Receivables, Net	1,060.4	931.2	1,053.8	806.9	793.9	745.5
Total Inventory	106.2	111.5	125.3	112.4	144.3	147.5
Prepaid Expenses	453.7	411.5	421.5	318.6	640.2	585.0
Other Current Assets, Total	0	0	0	1,826.2	380.0	0
Total Current Assets	3,416.3	3,517.6	3,581.9	5,192.2	6,219.0	2,857.8
Property, Plant, Equipment Total—Net	21,531.5	20,254.5	20,984.7	1,9438.1	19,573.3	20,703.1
Goodwill, Net	2,425.2	2,237.4	2,301.3	2,073.6	1,924.4	1,828.3
Intangibles, Net	0	0	0	0	0	0
Long-Term Investments	1,212.7	1,222.3	1,156.4	1,035.4	1,035.4	1,109.9
Note Receivable—Long Term	0	0	0	0	0	0
Other Long-Term Assets, Total	1,639.2	1,229.7	1,367.4	1,235.2	1,236.7	1,338.4
Other Assets, Total	0	0	0	0	0	0
Total Assets	30,224.9	28,461.5	2,9391.7	28,974.5	29,988.8	27,837.5
Liabilities and Shareholders' Equity						
Accounts Payable	636.0	620.4	624.1	668.7	678.0	714.3
Payable Accrued	0	0	0	0	0	0
Accrued Expenses	1,854.8	1,633.0	1,635.3	1,459.5	1,316.6	1,367.6
Notes Payable/Short-Term Debt	0	0	1,126.6	0	544	0
Current Portion of LT Debt/Capital Leases	18.1	31.8	864.5	17.7	658.5	862.2
Other Current Liabilities, Total	479.8	252.7	248.0	805.7	910.6	576.4
Total Current Liabilities	2,988.7	2,537.9	4,498.5	2,951.6	4,107.7	3,520.5
Total Long-Term Debt	10,560.3	10,186.0	7,310.0	8,389.9	8,934.3	8,357.3
Deferred Income Tax	1,278.9	944.9	960.9	1,076.3	949.2	781.5
Minority Interest	0	0	0	0	0	0
Other Liabilities, Total	1,363.1	1,410.1	1,342.5	1,098.4	851.5	976.7
Total Liabilities, Total	16,191.0	15,078.9	14,111.9	13,516.2	14,842.7	13,636.0
Redeemable Preferred Stock	0	0	0	0	0	0
Preferred Stock—Nonredeemable, Net	0	0	0	0	0	0
Common Stock	16.6	16.6	16.6	16.6	16.6	16.6
Additional Paid-In Capital	4,853.9	4,600.2	4,226.7	3,445.0	2,720.2	2,186.0
Retained Earnings (Accumulated Deficit)	31,270.8	28,953.9	26,461.5	25,845.6	23,516.0	21,755.8
Treasury Stock: Common	(22,854.8)	(20,289.4)	(16,762.4)	(13,552.2)	(10,373.6)	(9,578.1)
ESOP Debt Guarantee	(134.6)	0	0	0	0	(82.8)
Other Equity, Total	882.0	101.3	1,337.4	(296.7)	(733.1)	(96.0)
Total Equity	14,033.9	13,382.6	15,279.8	15,458.3	15,146.1	14,201.5
Total Liabilities & Shareholders' Equity	30,224.9	28,461.5	29,391.7	28,974.5	29,988.8	27,837.5
Total Common Shares Outstanding	1,076.7	1,115.3	1,165.3	1,203.7	1,263.2	1,269.9
Total Preferred Shares Outstanding	0	0	0	0	0	0

Source: http://www.sec.gov/cgi-bin/srch-edgar

NOTES

1. J. Lehart, 2010, Divided by a two-track economy, *Wall Street Journal*, Sep 8.
2. J. Jargon & G. Chon, 2010, Burger King's latest pickle, *Wall Street Journal*, Sep 9.
3. J. Cloud & O. Brook, 2010, McDonald's has a Chef?, *TIME*, Feb 22.
4. J. F. Love, 1986, *McDonald's Behind the Arches*. New York: Bantam Books.
5. J. Alder, Super Bowl I, *About.com*.
6. List of McDonald's products, *Mc*.
7. Creating new foods: The product developer's guide, *New Zealand Institute of Food Science and Technology Inc.*
8. L. Lewis, 2003, Japan's fast food funk, *J@pan Inc*, May.
9. T. Royle, 2000, *Working for McDonald's in Europe*. Routledge.
10. T. Howard, 1993, Local strategies edging out 'assembly-line' menus, *Nation's Restaurant News*, Jul 19.
11. R. Tomkins, 1997, When the chips are down: McDonald's strategy of opening more restaurants to compensate for falling US market share has backfired, *Financial Times (London edition)*, Jul 16.
12. McDonald's Corporation, *Funding Universe*.
13. http://www1.mcdonalds.com/college/pdfs/Calculate_College_Credits.pdf
14. McDonald's College Credit Connection, *McDonald's corporate website*.
15. R. Frost, 2005, Local success on a global scale, *Brand Channel*, May 2.
16. A. Shanahan, 2008, Why did France fall in love with McDonald's? *Guardian*, Jul 23.
17. J. Gershman, 2007, McDonald's takes Paris, *New York Sun*, Jul 2.
18. L. Schiffren, 2009, McDonald's in France, *National Review Online*, Jul 1.
19. N. Audi, 2009, France, land of epicures, gets taste for McDonald's, *New York Times*, Oct 25.
20. A. Chalupa, 2009, France's shocking love affair with McDonald's, *Daily Finance*, Oct 6.
21. M. Steinberger, 2009, How McDonald's conquered France, *Slate*, Jun 25.
22. When it comes to sustainable packaging and waste, less is more, *McDonald's corporate website*.
23. 2001, McDonald's using more organic meat in Germany—brief article, *Eurofood*, Aug 30.
24. 2009, McDonald's uses Facebook, MMS with German promotion, *Burger Business*, Oct 8.
25. J. S. Baskin, 2009, Branding and sustainability... In Germany McDonald's changes arches logo color to green, *Social Media Today*, Dec 3.
26. 2007, As burgers boom in Russia, McDonald's touts discipline, *Drovers Cattle Network*, Oct 16.
27. A. Blackman, 1990, Moscow's Big Mak attack, *TIME*, Feb 5.
28. K. Keeton, 2009, McDonald's walk up window in Russia!, *Russian Photos from Russia!*, Mar 24.
29. E. E. Arvedlund, 2005, McDonald's commands a real estate empire in Russia, *New York Times*, Mar 16.
30. 2011, Capitalist triumph, *National Post*, Jan 30.
31. 2010, McDonald's celebrates 20th anniversary in Russia, *Marketwire*, Feb 1.
32. E. B. Colby, 2006, McDonald's expands in China, *Sun-Times* does its part, *Columbia Journalism Review*, Oct 4.
33. 2004, KFC and McDonald's—a model of blended culture, *China Daily*, Jun 1.
34. W. Griffith, 2008, McDonald's has a big appetite for China, *MSNBC*, Aug 15.
35. L. Jie, 2008, McDonald's growing in China, *China Daily*, Sep 8.
36. Mezzio, 2007, McDonald's Australia: History, *Everything 2*, Apr 10.
37. 2009, McDonald's Japan sells with Aus NLIS, *Western Farmer-Stockman*, Apr 8.
38. C. Alarcon, 2007, McDonald's gets tick of approval, *B&T*, Feb 19.
39. 2002 Award Sponsor — McDonald's, *Australian Government: Equal Opportunity for Women in the Workplace Agency*.
40. Gary, 2008, McDonald's Australia (or, long live the king), *Everything Everywhere*, May 31.
41. 2006, McDonald's Australia French fries free of wheat and milk, *Medical News Today*, Feb 21.
42. I. Drake, 2009, McDonald's Australia gets boost from Angus burgers, *Australian Food News*, Sep 21.
43. 2005, McDonald's Japan: One chain's recovery from stagnant sales, *NPD Group*, May.
44. J. Smerd, 2006, McDonald's Japan no longer serving up forced retirement, *Workforce*, Sep 5.
45. 2007, Recipe for success: Revamping the corporate menu at McDonald's Japan, *Japan Society*, Jan 11.
46. K. Worsley, 2009, McDonald's betting on coffee for profit growth?, *Japan Economy News and Blog*, Nov 3.
47. A. Rangnekar, McDonald's India launch.
48. E. Bellman, 2009, McDonald's to expand in India, *Wall Street Journal*, Jun 30.
49. L. Luxner, 2002, Golden arches over Brazil, *Latin CEO*, Mar-Apr.
50. McDonald's 2009 Annual Report, *McDonald's corporate website*.
51. Z. Shahan, 2009, McDonald's going green?, *Matter Network*, Aug 20.
52. K. Bannan, How serious is McDonald's about sustainability?, *McDonald's corporate website blog*.
53. D. C. Esty and A. S. Winston, 2009, *Green to Gold: How Smart Companies use Environmental Strategy to Innovate, Create Value, and Build Competitive Advantage*. Hoboken, NJ: John Wiley Publishers.
54. http://www.mcdonalds.ca/pdfs/history_final.pdf

Paul Beamish

Richard Ivey School of Business

The University of Western Ontario

IVEY

Richard Ivey School of Business
The University of Western Ontario

Thomas MacMillan leaned back in his chair and glanced out of his office window down onto Bay Street, the epicenter of the Canadian financial industry. During his 10-year tenure as president and CEO of CIBC Mellon, MacMillan had presided over the dramatic growth of the jointly owned, Toronto-based asset servicing business of CIBC and The Bank of New York Mellon Corporation (BNY Mellon). However, now it was an overcast day in mid-September 2008 and MacMillan had a front-row seat to witness the onset of the worst financial crisis since the Great Depression.

CIBC Mellon was facing this oncoming global financial storm with a solid balance sheet and was secure in the knowledge that both of its parents were also well capitalized. However, the well-publicized impending collapse of several long-standing financial titans threatened to impact all players in the financial services industry worldwide. Despite the fact that joint ventures (JVs) were uncommon in the financial sector, MacMillan believed that the CIBC Mellon JV was uniquely positioned to withstand the fallout associated with the financial crisis and that it would be able to weather the most significant risks facing the JV—execution risk and the potential exodus of assets and clients who were panicked by the wider financial pandemonium. MacMillan and his team recognized that it would be critical for the JV to continue to deliver a high level of client service and to avoid any major operational missteps.

MacMillan's moment of introspection was interrupted by a knock on the door. He was scheduled to meet with three members of the company's executive management committee, Paul Marchand, Mark Hemingway and James Slater, to discuss two pressing issues facing the JV. First, they needed to discuss how to best manage any risks confronting the JV as a consequence of the financial crisis. Given the massive size and global reach of the largest financial service giants, and the likelihood that some of these behemoths might now be teetering on the edge of bankruptcy, CIBC Mellon, like other players in the financial services industry, would be forced to move adeptly to protect its operations from any potential exposure to the larger players' fates. While the systems, structure and culture that prevailed at CIBC Mellon served as evidence of MacMillan and his team's diligent efforts over the past 10 years to focus on risk management and to foster a culture of synergistic cooperation, the question remained—how could the policies and practices developed during the past decade be leveraged to sustain the JV through the broader financial crisis? Second, the four men were scheduled to continue discussions regarding options for refining CIBC Mellon's strategic focus, so that the JV could emerge from the financial meltdown on even stronger footing. Notwithstanding the immediate urgency of the financial crisis, the JV's management team recognized the need to continue to manage the business with a view towards future growth.

Professor Paul Beamish wrote this case with the assistance of Michael Sartor solely to provide material for class discussion. The authors do not intend to illustrate either effective or ineffective handling of a managerial situation. The authors may have disguised certain names and other identifying information to protect confidentiality.

Background

The Asset Servicing / Global Custody Business

When the JV was conceived in 1996, its principal emphasis was on asset servicing—the global custody business—which was generally viewed as "a dull business, with dull services, in a dull little corner of the financial services sector." Asset servicing delivers securities-related administrative services to support the investment processes and goals of clients. Such services include global custody, securities lending, cash management, multicurrency accounting and reporting, global performance measurement and analytics, transition management, commission recapture and foreign exchange. Clients include pension plans, investment managers, mutual funds, insurance companies, and global financial institutions. The fees charged to provide such administrative services would typically be much less than one half of one per cent of the value of the asset being supported.

In 1996, CIBC was one of the big five Schedule 1 (domestic) banks in Canada. At that time, it had an average custodial operation, with approximately 14 competitors, principally trust companies and the security departments of the major banks. CIBC had $100 billion in custody assets and a handful of clients. Its technology platform was poor and needed significant investment. It had three choices to make:

1. Invest—the problem there was that it would have had to invest a lot of money ($300, $400, $500 million)—to come up with a world-class custodial system. It was concerned that the revenue potential from the Canadian marketplace would not have resulted in it receiving adequate returns for its investment.
2. Exit the business—as a lot of companies in Canada subsequently did.
3. Form a joint venture if it could find the right partner. CIBC believed there was the potential of creating a good, viable Canadian-based business, but it needed a partner.

In 1996, Pittsburgh-based Mellon Bank had a Schedule II (Canadian bank which was a subsidiary of a foreign bank) banking operation in Canada, which MacMillan ran. Its Canadian custody market share was about one per cent—specifically one client, Cdn$8 billion in assets under administration, which was being administered out of Boston. However, Mellon had a world-class technology platform, had scale (in a scale business) and was committed to growing its market share but was having difficulty breaking into the Canadian marketplace. It knew it would be a difficult

and slow process to get established in Canada by setting up a greenfield operation.

CIBC approached several potential partners, but it was Mellon's technology and people that impressed it the most. CIBC had a Canadian presence and a client base, but no technology and its service was average. Mellon had great technology, products and services, but no presence in Canada and few clients in the country. And it was receptive to CIBC's overtures. It seemed the ideal circumstance for the birth of a joint venture—a great fit. Both parties needed each other and there was very little overlap. The opportunity to create a world-class Canadian asset servicing company—when not many existed in Canada at the time—was too enticing to pass up for both organizations. CIBC Mellon was the first significant JV for either parent.

Given the relative rarity of JVs in the financial services sector, the two sole shareholders in the proposed JV (CIBC and BNY Mellon) devoted a considerable amount of thought and planning during 1996 to the design and structure of the entity. A significant volume of legal agreements was negotiated to establish the parameters that would govern the relationship between the two shareholders. Buried within the reams of legal documents were provisions drafted to prohibit each of the shareholder parents from competing against the JV; to detail the limitations surrounding the JV's use of the parent shareholders' trademarks and other intellectual property; to outline the basis upon which each parent would provide services to the JV, including, in the case of BNY Mellon, the basis upon which it would provide and "Canadianize" its technology for the JV; and to require each of the shareholders to utilize the JV as a supplier of asset servicing and global custody services.

One of the most critical governance clauses pertained to voting rights. Under the JV's shareholder agreement, each of the parties would enjoy a 50 per cent vote on every issue. In effect, this eliminated the need to vote on any issue—only consensus could yield a decision and the JV managers needed to secure the approval of both shareholders before taking any major issues to the board. Accordingly, at the outset MacMillan and his team recognized that in order for the JV to execute on its mission both strategically and operationally, it would be critical for the two shareholders, their employees and the JV's employees to develop an acute understanding and respect for the unique capabilities that each shareholder brought to the JV. MacMillan acknowledged that "the governance processes developed for this JV effectively facilitated our ability to leverage the expertise of each shareholder." While both parties were strong players in the credit markets, BNY Mellon had a strong understanding of credit in the global custody market and enjoyed a strong reputation with federal regulators in the United States. CIBC, on the other hand, had a strong understanding of credit in the Canadian marketplace and was known for its strong global trading platform (CIBC World Markets).

Equally important were provisions pertaining to risk management. The shareholders agreed to the formation and to the membership on the JV's Asset & Liability Committee (ALCO). ALCO was tasked with the responsibility of overseeing the formulation of risk management policies and asset investment policies associated with the JV's treasury and securities lending activities—principal activities under which financial services firms could become exposed to credit risk and market risk. This pivotal committee was populated by senior management from CIBC, BNY Mellon and the JV itself. MacMillan acknowledged that both shareholders had sought to structure the JV to develop a discrete, low-risk business and that risk tolerance would be maintained in the parents' businesses. As such, the JV only engaged in very conservative transactions and did not engage in proprietary trading. Appropriately managing risk necessitated clear and constant communication in order to ensure that the JV was aligned with its shareholders. It also effectively positioned the JV's management team to tap into the knowledge assets and accumulated experience of two major financial institutions.

When formed at the end of 1996, the JV had fewer than 200 employees, $110 billion in assets under administration, a market share of less than 10 per cent and revenues of about $25 million. However, over the next decade, the business grew dramatically. In 1997, it acquired the Canada Trust custody business. In 1999, it acquired the Bank of Montreal custody business, in 2002, the TD Bank third-party custody business, and in 2006, it was awarded the IG/Mackenzie custody business. By 2006, there were 1,400 employees and 1,140 custody clients. At this point, the asset servicing business offered a wide and integrated range of products and services from custody to risk management which could be grouped into two broad categories—core asset servicing functions and capital markets functions (see Exhibit 1). Historically, each of these two categories of business functions contributed approximately 50 per cent of the profits generated by the JV's asset servicing business. While the core asset servicing business functions supplied a stream of recurring-fee revenue to the JV, the income stream generated by the capital markets functions could be more volatile, depending upon the state of the capital markets. The global

securities lending component of the capital markets functions involved acting as an agent in facilitating the lending of debt and equities from the JV's clients to other clients, who were typically brokers. While they did not disclose to CIBC Mellon why they were undertaking any particular loan, it could be expected that the brokers that borrowed the assets from CIBC Mellon would utilize the assets both for their own proprietary trading and to loan to the brokers' clients, sometimes including hedge funds that pursued short positions in equities. Short positions were established by traders who sold equities that they did not currently own. In essence, short sales involved selling borrowed equity assets. Consistent with regulatory requirements and its low-risk culture, CIBC Mellon routinely secured the loans that it extended to its broker clients by requiring the borrowers to pledge high-quality assets in excess of the value of the underlying loans as collateral. Exhibit 2 illustrates the interactions that occurred between external parties and CIBC Mellon's securities lending service.

By 2007, assets under administration for the JV's asset servicing business exceeded $800 billion, and were growing. The JV had become the second-largest asset servicing business in Canada, with a market share over 30 per cent. It was settling 15,000 transactions each day. Total revenues for CIBC Mellon exceeded $350 million, and healthy quarterly dividends were being paid to each partner.

The Stock Transfer and Corporate Trust Businesses

In 1997, the JV entered the trust services business through CIBC's purchase of a 50 per cent interest in Mellon's R-M Trust Company. The purchase was undertaken because the JV required a trust company as a deposit-taker for its asset servicing business and because R-M also had established stock transfer and corporate trust businesses. Through this business, Canadian companies that issued securities that traded on major stock exchanges relied on CIBC Mellon to manage administrative duties like security holder record keeping, securities transfers, investor communication, dividend payments and employee plan administration. The JV also acted as a corporate trustee for its trust clients' assets. In its corporate trustee role, the JV acted as indenture trustee for a number of series of asset-backed commercial paper (ABCP). ABCPs were typically short-term commercial paper investments that were collateralized by other financial assets which were characterized by very low risk. As of 2006, the JV had 1,200 trust clients. CIBC Mellon did not borrow or lend any securities in connection with this line of business.

In a November 2006 speech to the Financial Services Institute, MacMillan was asked to reflect on both the reasons he felt many joint ventures failed (see Exhibit 3) and the reasons why CIBC Mellon had been so successful.

Let me start with the one main reason that towers over all of them: our people. They are amazing and we have together somehow created an atmosphere where we can all thrive. Our people are our big differentiator. This can happen in any company. It has happened in our JV. We have succeeded because:

■ *The original business plan made sense.*

CIBC Mellon is profitable, growing, with good returns because the original business rationale was solid. It wasn't two "lousy" businesses coming together. Outstanding Mellon technology and service was introduced into Canada relatively quickly through a JV that had CIBC in its name and made an immediate positive market impact.

■ *The parents receive benefit from the JV itself in the form of dividends but also from outside of the JV.*

Both parents make significant FX revenues for their own books from JV clients. We help Mellon win global custody bids, we help CIBC win additional banking business that is often tied to asset servicing, for example cash management. We contribute to the building of strong client relationships for both parents. Mellon gets to appropriately allocate costs to the joint venture connected with their technology spend—and this spend is significantly larger than what they could otherwise afford because of the JV.

■ *Both parents cooperate.*

I see it at every board meeting—they respect and appreciate the contribution of the others; work collaboratively to make the JV a success. Despite the historical, jurisdictional and managerial differences, we've managed to put these differences to the side to make the JV work. And when there are differences of opinion (and frankly there's not that many) they work it out; and both organizations complement each other: CIBC defers to Mellon's expertise in the global custody business; Mellon defers to CIBC's knowledge/expertise relative to Canadian business and banking. I think it helps that both banks had a good solid friendship for many decades prior to the formation of the JV. They were (and are) comfortable with each other. They don't really compete against each other in any major business lines. Canadians are generally comfortable working with Americans and vice versa. Both parents' head offices are in the same time zone.

■ *Commitment of the parents.*

They have from the very beginning wanted to see the JV succeed and grow and they spent time making this happen. When more capital was required for acquisitions (the asset servicing business of Canada Trust, BMO, TD)—both parents were there. Early on in our history we had teething pains (our level of client service was not what it is today)—the parents didn't waiver and constructively helped us overcome issues and push on.

■ *The JV has effectively leveraged the strength of both parents.*

Mellon has 50 per cent ownership, but we benefit 100 per cent from their ongoing technology spend—over US$200 million a year. On a stand-alone basis, we couldn't afford US$200 million each year for technology in support of asset servicing business. This is an enormous plus for us.

From CIBC, we consistently leverage their client banking relationships to win new business for CIBC Mellon. We also leverage governance standards and risk management practices from both partners.

■ *And finally—our company is well managed.*

We have a strong board composed of mature, competent executives who can speak for their organizations. There has been minimal board turnover and when it has happened the transitions have been smooth. My lead board members from both organizations have been there since day one.

But equally important, I am blessed with an extremely strong executive management team. This team gets direction from the board and we run with it. They are also very skillful at working with both shareholders to ensure that all interests are balanced and satisfied and the strengths of both parents are fully realized. This is a skill requirement unique to joint ventures. For example:

- *Leveraging technology development at Mellon and sales development at both parents.*
- *Working with both parents' risk, audit and compliance.*
- *It is a skill to unleash the power of our parents without being overwhelmed by them.*

And while we are proactive in leveraging the strengths of our shareholders, we never forget we are a stand-alone organization that needs to be managed effectively. We have developed a strong internal culture quite independent of our parents, including our own strategy, brand, vision and core values. And we've shown enormous skills in initiating and successfully concluding major acquisitions at critical times.

■ *We have also been a little bit lucky.*

The markets have been generally favourable the last 10 years. There has been tremendous growth in the mutual fund industry, a major sector for us. There has been an accelerating trend to globalization of the capital markets, including increased complexity of financial instruments, and heightened requirements for reporting and transparency and real time information. These all play to our strengths. Not all of this was anticipated back in 1996. Over the past 10 years, we've had a good tailwind. You are better to be lucky than good, but we have been good.

2007–2008: From Tailwind to Headwind

The growth that had characterized the global financial sector up until 2006 began to materially change in 2007. A rapid series of problems began to either emerge or become more widely acknowledged. Fundamental differences that existed between the Canadian and U.S. banking sectors posed a unique set of concerns for financial institutions with operations on both sides of the border. Discrepancies in consumer debt and equity levels, divergent banking regulations and differences in the structure of each country's mortgage security industry comprised some of the most significant concerns.

The Canadian Financial Sector[i]

Canada as a whole was entering the crisis with a strong balance sheet and economic position. Consumers had lower debt and more savings than in the United States.

Mortgages were originated and held by Canadian banks, not packaged up and sold as securities. Canadian mortgages were generally five years or less, and mortgage interest was not tax deductible in Canada, so homebuyers were not encouraged to buy beyond their means. There were no 40-year terms, and buyers had to be able to have a down payment. Canadian Banks could not lend more than 80 per cent of the value of a house without mortgage insurance from the Canada Mortgage and Housing Corporation.

Canadian banks were large, stable and sophisticated national entities (an oligopoly). With branches across the country and often in other countries, Canadian bank risk was dispersed. Canadian bankers tended to be more risk-averse than their U.S. and international counterparts. Canadian banks were required to maintain a tier one capital ratio of seven per cent and generally exceeded it. They had to cap overall leverage at 20× capital.

Canadian banks were regulated by a single piece of legislation, the Bank Act, which was reviewed every five years, and one national body, the Office of the Superintendant of Financial Institutions (OSFI). OSFI had broad oversight—there was no "shadow banking system" that fell outside the regulations. Canada also had strong monetary policy set by the Bank of Canada and the Department of Finance.

In Canada, most investment banks were owned by commercial banks, providing them with access to capital during a crisis.

The U.S. Financial Sector

Despite the close geographic proximity, the nature of the United States banking and mortgage industry differed significantly from the system that prevailed in Canada.

Decades ago, the U.S. government launched two agencies to promote home ownership in the United States—the Federal National Mortgage Association ("Fannie Mae") and the Federal Home Loan Mortgage Corporation ("Freddie Mac"). These agencies were designed to increase the availability of funds for originating mortgages and to encourage the emergence of a secondary market for mortgages. Subsequently, mortgages could be traded without the involvement of either the original borrower or the original lender.

In the 1990s, to further encourage home ownership in the United States, policymakers lowered the amount of equity that homebuyers were required to invest in the purchase of a home. As a consequence of this policy shift, borrowers who were previously unable to secure a mortgage were able to enter the housing market. Further, the overall degree of leverage in the U.S. housing market increased substantially and a housing bubble emerged as homeowners began to speculate by moving into more expensive homes.

The coincident emergence of three financial innovations in the United States—interest-only mortgages, asset securitizations and credit default swaps—ultimately set the stage for the perfect storm that had converged over the U.S. financial system by 2007.

Unlike self-amortizing mortgages in which the mortgage principal was retired through regular payments of principal and interest over the life of a mortgage, interest-only mortgages were mortgages in which the borrower was given the opportunity to pay only the interest portion of a regularly scheduled mortgage payment. Interest-only mortgages were designed to open home ownership to low-income earners who demonstrated enhanced future earning potential, at which point their mortgage would be converted into a self-amortizing mortgage. Interest-only mortgages benefitted these low-income

[i]This section is from "You Can Take It to the Bank," *Ivey inTouch Magazine*, Fall 2009, p. 14.

homeowners by facilitating their entry into the housing market through payments which were lower than the payments under a self-amortizing mortgage. However, the emergence of interest-only mortgages also contributed to speculation in the housing market, as some investors purchased homes, made the interest payments while waiting for the value of their homes to increase and then sold the homes, paying back the mortgage principal with the proceeds from the home sale and pocketing the surplus.

Asset securitization involved aggregating a series of future cash flows into a security which was then sold to investors. Mortgage-backed securities (MBSs) were a type of asset securitization in which the underlying asset backing the security was a mortgage which generated cash flows from the interest payments. A securitization was a structured finance product that was originally designed to distribute risk. In fact, when conceived, MBSs were regarded as low-risk investments because they were backed by mortgages and mortgage defaults were relatively rare occurrences.

Credit default swaps (CDSs) resembled insurance policies in the sense that one party paid a series of cash flows to a counter-party in exchange for the promise that the counter-party would reimburse the payer if the underlying asset defaulted. A significant portion of the market for CDSs was built around MBSs. Investors in asset-backed securities such as MBSs regularly insured their investments by purchasing CDSs. The premium revenue stream associated with a CDS on an MBS was considered particularly attractive due to the low level of perceived risk, again due to the relatively rare occurrence of mortgage defaults. Despite their resemblance to insurance policies, CDSs were traded as contracts in the derivatives markets and were free from insurance industry regulations. Consequently, the relative ease with which CDSs could be issued, coupled with the fact that it was not necessary to own the underlying asset in order to purchase a CDS, effectively fueled speculative behaviour in the CDS market.

Two phenomena associated with these three financial innovations further compromised the precarious foundation upon which the U.S. banking and mortgage industry was perched—subprime mortgages and individual compensation systems prevailing in the financial sector. While mortgages issued to creditworthy borrowers were known as prime mortgages, subprime mortgages were issued to borrowers with poor credit. MBSs based on subprime mortgages became particularly attractive investment vehicles due to their high returns and low levels of perceived risk (due to the assumption that widespread mortgage defaults were highly unlikely). At the same time, mortgage originators

and derivative traders were being compensated on the volume of mortgages originated and derivatives sold (MBSs and CDSs). Increased trading volumes in these assets were fueled by the fact that compensation was rarely adjusted to the riskiness of either the borrower or the underlying asset.

By 2007, the robust growth in U.S. home prices slowed dramatically. As home prices began to decline, the value of mortgages began to exceed the market value of many homes. A flood of mortgage defaults ensued to the point that mortgage-backed securities began to decline in value. The complex nature of these securities further undermined their value. Given that it was not possible to link an MBS to specific properties, investors could not evaluate the risk of default on specific MBSs and, therefore, were unable to ascertain market values for these MBSs. The secondary market for mortgages was near collapse.

The difficulty associated with valuing these securities proved to be particularly problematic for financial institutions that owned the devalued MBSs and for financial institutions facing insurance-like claims on the CDSs they had written on the bet that widespread mortgage defaults would never occur. Consequently, these financial institutions were required to raise more capital to shore up their capital ratios. However, the increasing pervasiveness of uncertainty effectively turned off the taps in both credit and capital markets, making the task of raising capital almost impossible.

As the cost of capital skyrocketed and credit stopped flowing in the United States, financial institutions began to fail. Several "runs on the bank" were triggered in which customers lined up to fully withdraw their deposits. In June 2008, panicked customers of IndyMac Bank in the United States withdrew $1.5 billion in deposits (approximately 7.5 per cent of total bank deposits). Similarly, over the course of ten days in September 2008, customers withdrew more than $16 billion from Washington Mutual Bank (totaling nine per cent of total bank deposits). The uncertainty spilled over U.S. borders, triggering bank runs and failures overseas as well. Most notable was the bank run and subsequent failure of the U.K.–based Northern Rock bank, which was subsequently nationalized, in part, to subdue the panic.

Conclusion

The Challenge of Refining the Future Direction of the Joint Venture

As early as the summer of 2007, credit spreads for certain financial companies and instruments widened dramatically. In Canada, the marketplace for ABCP began to show signs of stress. The JV's ALCO

Committee, on the recommendation of CIBC Mellon's risk management group, and leveraging the respective credit market specialties of both shareholders, directed the JV to refrain from using any of CIBC Mellon's treasury or client funds (the latter in the form of cash collateral for securities lending transactions) to purchase non-bank-owned ABCP. Eventually, in August 2007, the $30 billion market for non-bank-owned ABCP essentially froze. The looming financial crisis did not portend a quick or strong recovery in the credit markets, particularly in the ABCP market.

MacMillan and his team suspected that the future growth potential for the stock transfer and corporate trust business segments was more limited than it was for the asset servicing business. Notwithstanding the onset of the financial crisis, MacMillan debated whether the JV should retain or divest these business lines in order to focus more intensely on the asset servicing business for which the JV was formed.

The Challenge of Avoiding Major Operational Missteps

The brewing financial storm became fodder for the media and it started to rattle financial markets. Despite the fact that there were reasons to believe that the impending financial crisis might not be as bad in Canada as it was likely to be in the United States and elsewhere, numerous challenges remained. Not least of these was the fact that the crisis would likely bring out the worst in many long-term business relationships. As liquidity was tightening, many financial sector lenders, borrowers and partners alike were putting aside years, even decades, of cooperation in order to ensure their own survival. This was in contrast to the approach adopted by CIBC Mellon in the months leading up to and during the crisis. It retained its long-standing practice of emphasizing very extensive communication with its clients and its shareholders, ensuring shared understanding of issues, including having representatives from both parents on ALCO and maintaining transparency.

By mid-September 2008, the most significant risks facing CIBC Mellon were credit risk, operational risk and market risk, as well as the potential exodus of assets and clients who were panicked by the wider financial chaos. MacMillan and his team recognized that it would be critical for the JV to continue to deliver a high level of client service and to avoid any major operational missteps. A key challenge facing the JV pertained to efforts to remain loyal to both long-time and newer business clients, while not exposing the JV to excessive risk in the context of an increasingly volatile market. While CIBC Mellon's global securities lending operations had extended considerable credit to some of the now more precariously perched financial giants, the JV was comfortable that these loans were adequately collateralized. Nevertheless, in order to ensure that the loaned assets were not subsumed into any debtors' possible bankruptcy proceedings, the JV would need to execute against legal agreements with rigour, to preserve its legal rights, including, if necessary, taking possession of collateral assets and then liquidating these assets in an increasingly turbulent market. Critical decisions were faced by MacMillan, Marchand, Hemingway and Slater, ranging from short-run decisions such as how to determine when to call in credit extended to some of the JV's global securities lending clients and how to liquidate any collateral that the JV was forced to take into possession, to longer-run decisions surrounding how to manage the JV's relationships with its solvent clients, so as to stem any risk of client or asset flight.

MacMillan closed the door to his office. Notwithstanding the 110 years of collective experience between MacMillan, Marchand, Hemingway and Slater, the four men recognized that the markets were headed for uncharted waters. MacMillan opened the meeting, reminding the group, "Gentlemen, now more than ever, we need to leverage our JV's administrative heritage, the guidance of our shareholders and the respective strengths of the parents to move through these unprecedented times..."

Exhibit 1 CIBC Mellon Asset Servicing Business Functions

CORE ASSET SERVICING BUSINESS FUNCTIONS:
The following eight functions constituted the core asset servicing business functions:
CUSTODY The CIBC Mellon custody system is a real-time, multicurrency processor of security and currency movement for the institutional trust/custody business. It maintains automated interfaces to/from depositories and subcustodians, supporting trade affirms/confirmation, trade instructions, settlement confirmations, cash instructions and cash and security position status.
TRADE PROCESSING & SETTLEMENT Trades entering the custody system are auto-matched and confirmed to CDS (*Canadian Depository for Securities*) and its U.S. equivalent, DTC (*Depository Trust Company*). Discrepancies are flagged, reported to the client and updated with fail codes. If matched, trades automatically settle on the settlement date and the clients' securities and cash positions are updated. Each day, the service team validates the CDS Daily Settled Trades Report against the settled transactions in the system. CIBC Mellon offers contractual settlement of buys, sells and maturities for issues publicly traded on recognized exchanges in 47 countries. All other markets across all asset classes and registration locations, including physical delivery of securities, settle on the actual settlement date.

(Continued)

Exhibit 1 CIBC Mellon Asset Servicing Business Functions (*Continued*)

CORE ASSET SERVICING BUSINESS FUNCTIONS:

ACCOUNTING The CIBC Mellon accounting system integrates both Canadian and international securities on a single platform. This trade date, multicurrency system reflects cash movements on the actual settlement date and security transactions on the trade date. Integrated with its custody system, the accounting system manages derivative investments and accommodates both pending trades and income accruals.

SAFEKEEPING CIBC Mellon provides a secure facility for the safekeeping of stocks, bonds, notes and other securities—in both physical and book-based environments. It ensures assets are held securely and recorded accurately in its custody system. These two objectives are accomplished by performing an annual depository risk assessment along with regular reconciliation of physical vault and depository positions.

CORPORATE ACTIONS CIBC Mellon has a Corporate Actions Security Capture and Delivery Engine (Cascade) to keep it informed on all relevant announcements, while providing clients and their investment managers with instant access to information. It provides notification within hours of receipt of notice, with immediate encumbrance of position on receipt of response, and instant settlement on receipt of payment. Its online, real-time mandatory and voluntary corporate action and class action notifications enable clients to respond to events quickly. The most comprehensive sources of corporate action information for Canadian, U.S. and international markets are used, comparing vendor data to ensure accuracy and timely notification is provided to clients.

INCOME COLLECTION The system automatically accrues for all interest and dividend income for each security, providing the amount in local currency prior to the payable date. A contractual income policy for dividends, interest and maturities is offered in which CIBC Mellon guarantees to pay income on the day it is due; amounts are credited to client accounts regardless of receipt of payment. In non-contractual markets, income is credited upon actual receipt of funds. Assets must be held in the depository or registered in CIBC Mellon's name or its agent's nominee name. The funds are credited in local currency on the pay-date, unless otherwise specified.

ONLINE REPORTING Workbench offers a wide array of browser-based information capabilities allowing customers to effectively manage, evaluate and report on their individual or consolidated portfolios. The key features range from access to market news and analysis to a fully-secured virtual meeting place to performance analytics and monthly statements. Workbench cash availability and forecast reports are updated in real-time during business hours and also include custody share reports, pending trades, transaction settlements, corporate action notifications and cash balance projections of portfolios. The reporting feature, Workbench Express, facilitates the automatic distribution of reports to a designated printer, a local network drive, an e-mail account or an FTP server, all without manual intervention.

PERFORMANCE & RISK ANALYTICS (P&RA) This unit provides performance measurement, attribution, and investment analysis services to over 1,800 institutional investors in 50 countries and is responsible for US$8.2 trillion in assets under measurement. In Canada, it has 151 clients using performance measurement services and products. Its suite of value-added products and services includes tools for performance measurement, portfolio analytics and universe comparison. Its performance measurement systems are fully integrated with CIBC Mellon's systems.

CAPITAL MARKETS FUNCTIONS:

The following two functions constituted the asset servicing business's capital markets functions:

FOREIGN EXCHANGE CIBC Mellon executes foreign exchange (FX) transactions through the trading desk of one of its corporate parents. From the perspective of the counterparty to the transaction, CIBC or BNY Mellon deals as principal directly with its clients. Only one step is required to execute a trade and instruct for settlement, reducing operational risks and duplication of tasks. CIBC Mellon has neither a principal nor broker role in the transaction but acts simply as a service provider. It facilitates the transactions required to support clients' global trading activity, providing a complex FX trading solution from initiation and execution to settlement and reporting.

GLOBAL SECURITIES LENDING The company delivers client-tailored solutions to the 120 institutional clients participating in its in-house program. Beneficial owners for whom securities are lent include pension funds, government agencies, insurance companies, mutual funds, asset managers and pooled funds. The focus is on the strategic development of new products and services to enhance client revenue performance, with a commitment to product collateral and risk management. Global One is used—the lending system of choice for more than 70 financial institutions in over 20 countries—designed by top market participants.

Source: Company materials.

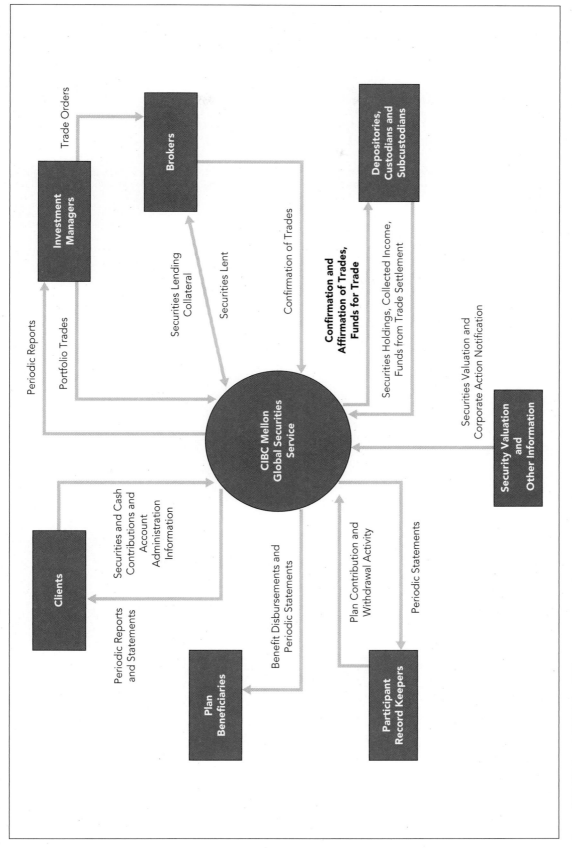

Exhibit 2 The Interactions Between External Parties and CIBC Mellon's Global Securities Service

Investment Managers

Brokers

Depositories, Custodians and Subcustodians

Trade Orders

Periodic Reports

Portfolio Trades

Securities Lending Collateral

Securities Lent

Confirmation of Trades

Confirmation and Affirmation of Trades, Funds for Trade

Securities Holdings, Collected Income, Funds from Trade Settlement

Securities Valuation and Corporate Action Notification

CIBC Mellon Global Securities Service

Security Valuation and Other Information

Clients

Securities and Cash Contributions and Account Administration Information

Periodic Reports and Statements

Benefit Disbursements and Periodic Statements

Plan Contribution and Withdrawal Activity

Periodic Statements

Plan Beneficiaries

Participant Record Keepers

Source: CICA 5970 Report, CIBC Mellon, 2009.

Exhibit 3 Top General Reasons for Joint Venture Failures

1. The rationale for setting up the JV wasn't a good one—Two lousy businesses put together will not make one good business. Two lousy businesses put together give you one big lousy business. Double the fun! At the core there has to be a good business proposition that creates adequate returns to the shareholding partners. It helps when the founding partners each bring something special to the joint venture that the other doesn't have.
2. Insufficient planning—Parties need to agree up front to a comprehensive plan outlining the business transaction, which includes governance, dispute resolution, ownership of intellectual property, how each party will contribute to the JV (whether it's money, expertise, technology, etc.). It's also very important to identify and agree on exit arrangements. Parameters of any business transaction will change. You need to agree to how the exit occurs, up front.
3. Inadequate capitalization—Starting out, each partner must commit a set amount of capital that is adequate enough to get the business off the ground. Also, both partners need to agree on how they will fund additional capital calls.
4. Lack of leadership—This may be the most important factor of all. If you don't have strong leadership, you are going to fail. In any business, you always need outstanding leadership, but never more so than on the board of a joint venture and within the JV itself.
5. Lack of commitment—Poor performance by the JV can result in one or both parties getting disinterested quickly. Results do count. But even if the JV is successful, things can happen to one of the parents quite unrelated to what is happening at the JV that will lead to a lack of commitment. For example, one parent can get into operational difficulties which will cause them to take their eye off the JV ball or even force them to exit the JV. Or, one of the parents can have a perfectly legitimate change in strategy that results in the joint venture no longer being core to them.
6. Cultural differences and differences of opinion emerge between the two partners. There is definitely a JV mindset—it's different working with another partner than just on your own. You have to sometimes temper your own culture to accommodate a quite different culture or approval of your partner to the benefit of the JV. Some companies are good at it, and some aren't.

Source: Tom MacMillan, November 2006.

Exhibit 4 Organization Chart of Senior Officers of CIBC Mellon as of September 2008

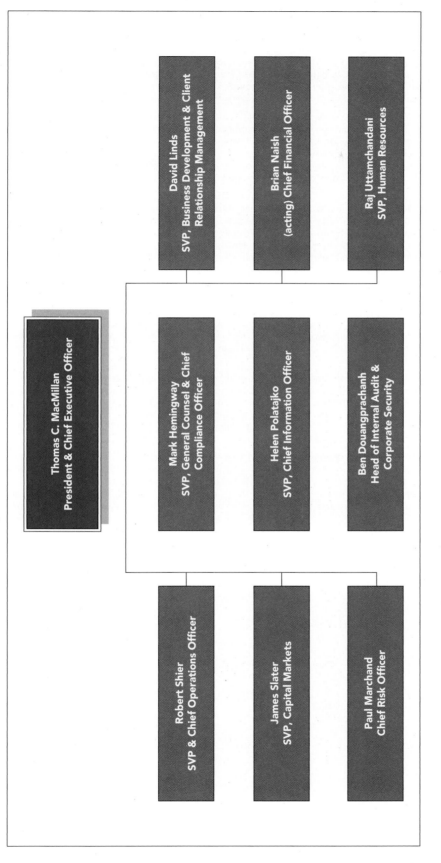

Exhibit 5 Brief Bios of Select Senior Officers

Thomas C. MacMillan was president and chief executive officer of CIBC Mellon. He had 35 years of extensive experience in the financial services industry in both Canada and the United States. From 1994-1998, he was chairman, president and chief executive officer of Mellon Bank Canada. Mr. MacMillan was instrumental in the formation of the CIBC Mellon joint venture, and previously held various senior positions with the Bank of Montreal, Chase Manhattan Bank of Canada and Montreal Trust. A native of Toronto, Mr. MacMillan received a bachelor's degree from Princeton University and a master's degree from the London School of Economics and Political Science. He also had significant board experience in both the private and not-for-profit sectors.

Mark R. Hemingway was senior vice president, general counsel and chief compliance officer, and a member of the company's executive management committee. He was responsible for the legal, compliance, corporate secretarial and privacy functions at CIBC Mellon. Mr. Hemingway had 20 years of experience in the legal profession. Prior to joining CIBC Mellon, he held general counsel and corporate secretary positions in a number of large Canadian companies, and was previously a litigation lawyer at Torys. He received his law degree from Queen's University and his master of laws degree from Cambridge University. He articled at the Supreme Court of Canada.

James E. R. Slater was senior vice president, capital markets, and a member of the company's executive management committee. Mr. Slater had overall leadership responsibility for CIBC Mellon's capital markets function, which included global securities lending, treasury and cash management. Mr. Slater's accountabilities also included providing strategic client service engagement in relation to his trading and financial markets responsibilities. He also chaired the company's asset liability committee. Mr. Slater had 20 years of experience in the financial services industry with CIBC World Markets and CIBC Mellon. While at CIBC World Markets, he was part of the team charged with the formation of CIBC Mellon.

C. Paul Marchand was the head of risk management. He joined CIBC Mellon in 2002, after 35 years with a major Canadian bank. At CIBC Mellon, he was responsible for designing and overseeing the company's Risk Management frameworks and programs for both CIBC Mellon Trust Company and CIBC Mellon Global Securities Services Company. His mandate included bringing together comprehensive oversight and reporting of all risk issues affecting CIBC Mellon including credit, market and operational risks up to and including the boards of directors and joint venture partners. He also served as the enterprises' chief compliance officer and chief anti-money laundering officer from 2002 to 2006. Marchand held a bachelor of commerce degree from McGill University.

David S. Linds was senior vice president, business development and client relationship management, and a member of the company's executive management committee. Mr. Linds also oversaw the company's product management and client integration solutions group, which was responsible for ensuring existing and future development of products and services as well as client reporting needs of institutional clients for asset servicing and ancillary services. Mr. Linds had more than 25 years of experience in the financial services industry, including 18 years with CIBC World Markets and CIBC Mellon. While at CIBC World Markets, he was part of the team charged with the formation of CIBC Mellon.

Robert M. Shier was senior vice president and chief operations officer, and a member of the company's executive management committee. Mr. Shier was responsible for CIBC Mellon's operational divisions, including client and investment management services, asset servicing, investment fund accounting for the CIBC Mellon Global Securities Services Company and investor services, stock transfer and employee plan administration for CIBC Mellon Trust Company. He joined CIBC Mellon in 1997, and had more than 25 years of operational experience in financial services including brokerage, banking, asset servicing and transfer agency services.

Scott Currence, Greg Giordano, Greg Jennings, Katie Punske, Peter Ocko, Ryan Smart
W. P. Carey School of Business, Arizona State University

Tina Borja
Rice University

Introduction

MGM Resorts International (MGM) is a *Fortune* 500 company traded on the NYSE in the complex and unpredictable industry of gaming and hospitality. MGM is one of the leading global hospitality companies with a portfolio of 15 wholly owned resorts and gaming properties located in Nevada, Mississippi, and Michigan and 50 percent stakes in four additional properties in the US and China (Exhibit 1). With approximately 45,000 full time employees, the company has an enterprise value of $18.09 billion and 2010 revenues of more than $6 billion (Exhibit 2). It is the third largest revenue generating company in its industry. MGM believes its success is due to its reputation for delivering high quality gaming and luxury services and believes its hospitality and entertainment venues are the best in the business.[1]

Previously thought to be a recession-proof industry, gaming was not only hit harder than expected by the most recent economic recession, but is on a slower than predicted road to recovery. Nevertheless, many leading analysts view MGM as a worthwhile long-term investment. In fact, within the MGM conglomerate, Mandalay Bay, Bellagio, and MGM Las Vegas experienced double-digit EBITDA growth in 2010 and were projected to grow even more in 2011.[2]

Yet, despite its isolated wins and the subtle optimism in the financial community toward the gaming industry as a whole, MGM faces significant concerns. At $12.1 billion, MGM carries one of the heaviest debt burdens and shows the largest net operating losses in the industry year over year since 2007—posting losses in excess of $1 billion for both 2009 and 2010[3] (Exhibit 3). Domestically, MGM has debt obligations maturing in 2013 and 2014. Internationally, MGM is working to offset a weak dollar with new growth ventures in China and Vietnam and has experienced higher than anticipated returns from its Macau (China) property. While its competitors are experiencing similar difficulties and achievements domestically and abroad, MGM also faces market share erosion as its competitors put capital toward enhancing their images against the MGM brand with more frequency and ease.

Adding to its challenges and central to its recent lack of flexibility is MGM's ill-timed massive undertaking—CityCenter. Construction began on this 68-acre, $9 billion joint venture on the Las Vegas Strip (The Strip) in 2006 when American businesses could still reasonably turn a blind eye to the brewing implosion of the banking and credit markets and the subsequent withdrawal of the common consumer from the gaming and hospitality markets. While MGM cannot be blamed for the timing of this bit of bad luck, it had to weather the storm and now must deal with the damage rendered.

In a nutshell, MGM is at a crossroads that could provide the opportunity for a timely strategic evaluation; it needs to reevaluate its identity within the industry and seek opportunities that enable long-term sustainability. The company and its directors must analyze its tangible and intangible assets and determine if and where they fit within the vision for the company. Most pressing however is whether MGM should downsize to cut its losses and how to stop the flow of market share to its competitors.

Firm History

Part 1: The Beginning

The group of properties that comprise what is now known as MGM Resorts International began in the 60s under the leadership of Kirk Kerkorian. Kerkorian, a pilot and the owner of a small charter airline that

Exhibit 1 MGM Resorts International Current Holdings

Locale	Name	Opened / Acquired	Stake*
Las Vegas Strip	MGM Grand Las Vegas	opened 1993	
	New York-New York	opened 1997	
	The Mirage	acquired in 2000 / Wynn	
	Bellagio		
	Monte Carlo		
	Mandalay Bay		
	Luxor	acquired in 2005 / Mandalay Resort Group	
	Excalibur		
	Circus Circus Las Vegas		
	CityCenter	opened 2009	50%
Las Vegas Suburb	Gold Strike Jean	acquired in 2005 / Mandalay Resort Group	
	Railroad Pass Henderson		
Reno, NV	Circus Circus Reno	acquired in 2005 / Mandalay Resort Group	
	Silver Legacy		50%
Detroit, MI	MGM Grand Detroit	opened 1999	
Biloxi, MS	Beau Rivage	acquired in 2000 / Wynn	
Elgin, IL	Grand Victoria	acquired in 2005 / Mandalay Resort Group	50%
Tunica, MS	Gold Strike Tunica	acquired in 2005 / Mandalay Resort Group	
Macau SAR, China	MGM Grand Macau	opened 2007	51%

Source: 2011 MGM Resorts International History, UNLV Center for Gaming Research and MGM Resorts International 2010 10-k

Exhibit 2 MGM Resorts International Annual Income Statement

	Historical MGM Income Statement (Summarized)					
	Fiscal Year Ending December 31,					
	2005	2006	2007	2008	2009	2010
Total Revenue	6,128.8	7,176.0	7,691.6	7,208.8	5,978.6	6,019.2
Cost of Revenue	3,316.9	3,715.1	4,027.6	4,034.4	3,539.3	3,757.5
Gross Profit	2,812.0	3,460.9	3,664.1	3,174.4	2,439.3	2,261.7
SG&A, Total	1,036.2	1,367.1	1,604.7	1,420.4	1,312.1	1,257.3
D&A, Total	560.6	629.6	700.3	778.2	689.3	633.4
Operating Income	1,215.2	1,464.1	1,359.0	975.7	437.9	371.0
EBITDA	1,803.3	2,118.1	2,059.4	1,754.0	1,127.2	1,004.4
Net Interest (Expense)/Income	(628.7)	(749.2)	(691.1)	(609.3)	(775.4)	(1,113.6)
Other, Net	137.6	223.0	207.8	78.8	(124.5)	(173.1)
EBT Excl. Unusual Items	724.0	938.0	875.7	445.2	(462.0)	(915.7)
Merger & Restructuring Charges	0.1	(1.0)	0.0	0.0	0.0	0.0
Impairment of Goodwill	0.0	0.0	0.0	(1,179.8)	0.0	0.0
Gain (Loss) on Sale of Investments	0.0	0.0	0.0	0.0	(1,131.6)	(1,422.6)
Gain (Loss) on Sale of Assets (One Time)	0.0	(3.8)	8.3	25.0	187.4	0.0
Other Unusual Items, Total	(57.0)	44.8	1,274.4	40.6	(606.5)	122.3
EBT Incl. Unusual Items	667.1	977.9	2,158.4	(669.0)	(2,012.6)	(2,216.0)
Income Tax Expense	231.7	341.9	757.9	186.3	(720.9)	(778.6)
Earnings from Cont. Ops.	435.4	636.0	1,400.5	(855.3)	(1,291.7)	(1,437.4)
Discontinued Operations	7.9	12.3	183.9	0.0	0.0	0.0
Net Income	443.3	648.3	1,584.4	(855.3)	(1,291.7)	(1,437.4)

Source: Capital IQ. MGM Resorts International. Retrieved May 5, 2011 from www.capitaliq.com

Globe: © Jan Rysavy/iStockphoto.com

Exhibit 3 MGM Resorts International Annual Balance Sheet

	Historical MGM Balance Sheet (Summarized)					
	Fiscal Year Ending December 31,					
	2005	2006	2007	2008	2009	2010
Cash	377.9	452.9	416.1	295.6	2,056.2	499.0
Total Receivables	352.7	381.5	412.9	368.1	753.0	497.9
Inventory	111.8	118.5	126.9	111.5	101.8	96.4
Prepaid Expenses	110.6	124.4	106.4	155.7	104.0	252.2
Other Current Assets	65.5	437.4	63.5	602.1	38.5	110.1
Total Current Assets	**1,018.6**	**1,514.8**	**1,125.8**	**1,533.0**	**3,053.5**	**1,455.6**
Net PP&E	16,541.7	17,241.9	16,870.9	16,289.2	15,070.0	14,554.4
Long-Term Investments	931.2	1,092.3	2,482.7	4,642.9	3,611.8	1,923.2
Goodwill	1,314.6	1,300.7	1,262.9	86.4	86.4	86.4
Other Intangibles	377.5	367.2	362.1	347.2	344.3	342.8
Other Assets	516.0	629.4	623.2	376.1	352.4	598.7
Total Assets	**20,699.4**	**22,146.2**	**22,727.7**	**23,274.7**	**22,518.2**	**18,961.0**
Accounts Payable	156.4	182.2	220.5	142.7	173.7	167.1
Accrued Expenses	950.9	956.2	934.7	856.7	794.2	785.7
Other Current Liabilities	427.3	509.8	569.5	955.6	335.9	292.0
Total Current Liabilities (excl. ST Debt)	**1,534.6**	**1,648.1**	**1,724.7**	**1,955.0**	**1,303.8**	**1,244.7**
Total Debt	12,355.4	12,994.9	11,175.2	13,464.2	14,055.9	12,050.4
Other Liabilities	3,574.3	3,653.7	3,767.1	3,881.2	3,288.1	2,667.3
Total Liabilities	**17,464.3**	**18,296.7**	**16,667.0**	**19,300.4**	**18,647.8**	**15,962.5**
Common Stock	3,235.1	3,849.5	6,060.7	3,974.4	3,870.4	2,998.5
Total Equity	3,235.1	3,849.5	6,060.7	3,974.4	3,870.4	2,998.5
Total Liabilities & Equity	**20,699.4**	**22,146.2**	**22,727.7**	**23,274.7**	**22,518.2**	**18,961.0**

Source: Capital IQ. MGM Resorts International. Retrieved May 5, 2011 from www.capitaliq.com

ferried gamblers from Los Angeles to Las Vegas, began to purchase, lease, sell, and build properties, such as The Flamingo and The International, through his Leisure International Company. In 1971, and soon after opening the world's largest hotel at the time, Paradise Road, Kerkorian sold Leisure International to Hilton Hotels. The following year, Kerkorian began to build another hotel-casino on The Strip that would open in 1973 as the MGM Grand Las Vegas. With 2,100 rooms, the MGM Grand Las Vegas allowed Kerkorian to reclaim the bragging rights as owner of the world's largest hotel. In 1986, Kerkorian sold the MGM Grand Las Vegas and the MGM Grand Reno to Bally's (both renamed Bally's after their purchase) and, later that year, incorporated MGM Grand. The late 80s and early 90s held several ventures for Kerkorian and MGM including the start of MGM Grand Air, a new charter airline, and the opening of the new 5,005 room MGM Grand—making Kerkorian, once again, owner of the largest hotel in the world.[4]

Part 2: The Growth Years 1995–2007

In the mid 90s, MGM riveted its attention to the booming real-estate market. Not only did it acquire property and facilities on The Strip, but also in South Africa and Australia. Between 1995 and 1997, MGM opened New York-New York on The Strip and MGM Grand Australia in Darwin, and agreed to manage four casinos in South Africa. Looking to expand further, MGM acquired Primadonna Resorts in 1999. Later that year, MGM Grand Detroit opened in a temporary facility and 'The Mansions,' high-end luxury suites at MGM Grand Las Vegas, were introduced.[5] From 1995 to 2000, net revenues grew 327 percent—from $722 million to $3.08 billion.[6,7]

This growth trend continued into the early 2000s with the $6.4 billion acquisition of Steve Wynn's Mirage Resorts. This acquisition included Golden Nugget, Monte Carlo (50 percent), Mirage, and Bellagio on The Strip as well as other regional locations including Beau Rivage in Biloxi, Mississippi. With the acquisition of

Mirage Resorts, MGM Grand Inc. was renamed MGM Mirage. In 2005, MGM made another large purchase acquiring Mandalay Resort Group for $7.9 billion and its 16 locations including Luxor, Mandalay Bay, and Circus Circus on The Strip. The acquisitions of the Mirage and Mandalay holdings incurred large debt transactions of $2 billion[8] and $2.5 billion,[9] respectively.

In 2006, MGM announced its focus on extending the MGM brand into the development of its hospitality subsidiary, MGM Hospitality, responsible for sourcing both gaming and non-gaming investment and management opportunities. Concurrently, the company opened the Grand Macau in China. Divestments of multiple properties played a major role in accumulating nearly $1 billion in capital during this same period.[10] By the end of 2007, total revenue had increased 7.2 percent and net income was an astonishing $1.58 billion. However, within only 15 months of its 2007 banner year, MGM's stock prices would plummet from $99.75/share to less than $2.00/share (Exhibit 4).

Part 3: Economic Downturn 2008 Forward

In 2006, MGM had begun construction in Las Vegas on the largest private development project in US history—CityCenter: a multi-use gaming, condominium, hotel, convention, and retail outlet development. It was CityCenter that would bring MGM to the brink of bankruptcy in 2009.

With many industries beginning to feel the strain of the weakening economy beginning in 2008, the majority of industry experts continued to contend the gaming industry was recession proof. But when called on its bluff, The Strip—overbuilt and significantly funded by MGM's growth investments—showed its hand. In 2008, MGM reacted by folding its $5 billion Atlantic City project and selling its Treasure Island Resort and Casino for approximately $775 million.[11] The $7 billion CityCenter project budget quickly ballooned to over $9 billion and MGM had to be bailed out by its joint venture partner—Dubai World.[12] To avoid negative credit/stock ratings and continue operations, MGM needed to generate cash; however, it was in too deep on a number of projects and had no choice but to stick it out and see them to completion. CityCenter opened in December 2009—unfortunately, to less than stellar fanfare. Stock prices fell hard and fast with impending negative quarterly profit earnings. MGM reported a net loss of $856 million in 2008 and $1.3 billion in 2009 and saw its stock price hit an all-time low on March 6, 2009 of $1.81/share.[13]

Exhibit 4 MGM Resorts International Stock Price Change

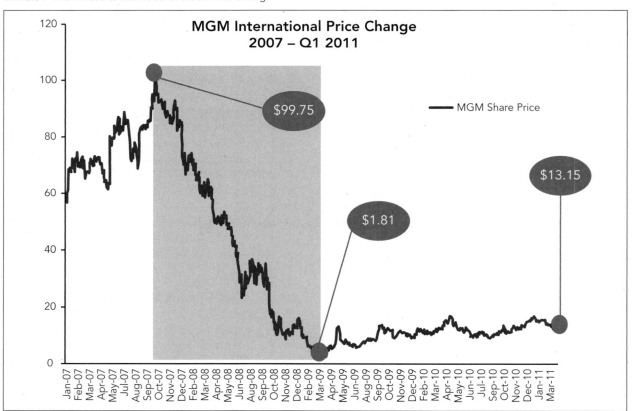

Source: Capital IQ. MGM Resorts International. Retrieved May 5, 2011 from www.capitaliq.com

Looking at this period in retrospect in April 2011, Chief Financial Officer Dan D'Arrigo explained it this way:

We were faced with many challenges over a 24-month period. We were focused on getting to the finish line with CityCenter and then shoring up our own finances and liquidity as it pertains to MGM Resorts. We were able to do a lot of things during that time, however, that a lot of companies could not do, including raising capital and improving our liquidity. What gets lost often is the fact that this company raised over $7 billion in liquidity during some of the darkest financial times when capital markets were closed. Bond markets were closed and there was no lending going on at all. . . . One thing became crystal clear to us. We weren't effectively leveraging who we are and who we were as an entity.[14]

On June 15, 2010, the company officially changed its name to MGM Resorts International based on CEO Jim Murren and the board of directors' hopes of better aligning the MGM brand with its international intentions.[15] Although 2010 ended with a net loss of $1.43 billion, many industry analysts believed that, based on its fourth quarter 2010 results, MGM was on track for a return to prosperity—albeit in ten years or more. While operations contributed positive cash flows of $499 million in 2010, analysts expressed short-term concerns that this was the result of a period of underinvestment in its properties due to high debt burdens. In addition, some analysts forecasted negative cash flows in 2011— further limiting MGM's financial flexibility.[16,17]

To the surprise of most, when MGM released its 2011 first quarter earnings in May 2011, MGM reported increases to revenue of 3 percent and EBITDA of 15 percent. Even though a net loss of $90 million was reported, it was $7 million less than the loss reported in the same quarter the previous year. All told, the announcement was considered by many a healthy progression compared to the previous few years. Additionally, signs of a spring thaw began to pop up in the form of improved room occupancy as well as a rebound of the heavily relied upon Las Vegas convention market. A major bright spot were the increased revenues from overseas markets with MGM Grand Macau continuing to show improvements, again reinforcing optimism around MGM.[18]

Future expectations for MGM are mixed. Despite being the third largest company in its industry, MGM has the lowest profits. Earnings estimates by top analysts show modest sales increases of 3 percent to 5 percent expected in 2011 and 2012 with year over year earnings estimated between −0.3 and −0.6 percent.[19] Already factored into their estimates, on April 13, 2011 MGM announced it would take a 51 percent ownership stake in the MGM Grand Macau.[20] Along with the potential

sale of the Atlantic City Borgata, this ownership stake should result in positive liquidity of approximately $311 million.[21] In the meantime, management has been able to retain large assets and continue construction on properties yet to be completed. One of these properties is the MGM Grand Ho Tram in Vietnam scheduled to open in 2013. This $4.2 billion multifunctional entertainment site is located near Ho Chi Minh City near the South China Sea and features 1,100 luxury rooms[22] (Exhibit 5).

The Pit Bosses

MGM is a premier luxury resort and entertainment conglomerate. Many companies have portfolios similar to MGM and compete in various geographic markets with a variety of casino sizes and target markets (Exhibit 6). MGM's primary competitors are Las Vegas Sands, Wynn Resorts, Penn National, Boyd Gaming, and Caesars Entertainment (Exhibits 7 and 8). As MGM consolidated its energies and efforts to survive the economic recession amidst its massive development of CityCenter, each of these competitors staked a claim to a piece of MGM's market share.

Las Vegas Sands

Las Vegas Sands (LVS) is a gaming and convention company with properties and resorts in Nevada, Pennsylvania, Macau, and Singapore and the second highest revenues in the industry. Incorporated in 1988, LVS owns and operates The Strip's very popular Venetian and Palazzo. LVS reports an enterprise value of $38.6 billion with revenues in 2010 of $6.9 billion (up over 50 percent from 2009) and over 34,000 employees on payroll.[23] While LVS experienced net losses in 2008 and 2009 of $164 million and $355 million respectively, the company rebounded in 2010 to turn a profit of $599 million with an 8.75 percent profit margin.[24] Like many of its competitors, LVS came through the recession by suspending operations that did not have the potential to quickly turn a profit. On a less optimistic note, in March 2011, LVS was subpoenaed in a joint SEC and Department of Justice investigation stemming from allegations made by fired CEO of Sands China, Steve Jacobs, that he was instructed to engage in illegal activities including bribery of foreign officials.[25] Despite this and the cautious expectations for the industry overall, LVS's first quarter 2011 results were much more favorable than predicted with operating income reported at $299 million—making LVS, at least for the moment, leader of the pack.[26]

Wynn Resorts Ltd

Founded in 2002, Wynn Resorts (Wynn) primarily owns and operates Wynn Las Vegas and Encore at Wynn Las Vegas on The Strip. Additionally, the company

Exhibit 5 MGM Resorts International Timeline

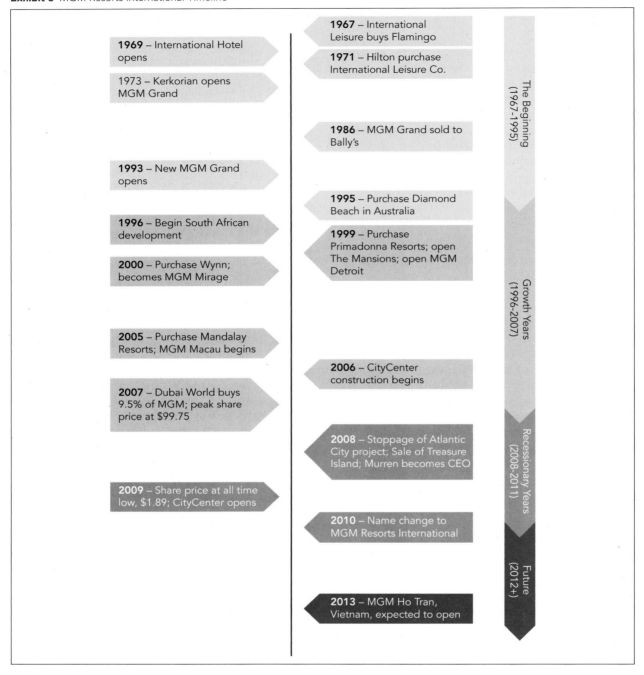

Source: 2011 MGM Resorts International History, UNLV Center for Gaming Research

operates two casinos in Macau that opened in 2006 and 2010.[27] Wynn hotels and casinos are considered preeminent luxury destinations. By 2010, and with only three properties, Wynn had developed an enterprise value of $19 billion with over 16,000 employees. Wynn's 2010 revenue exceeded $4.5 billion with a reported profit of $307 million and a profit margin of 6.77 percent. With ongoing pressure to outperform its competitors in the upper-end luxury gaming market, Wynn has successfully managed its finances by borrowing money to clear its balance sheet and delever itself by generating cash from new operations.[28] For example, Wynn created a new alliance with PokerStar, a popular online gaming poker business, to establish a new environment promoting safe online poker play. Furthermore, Wynn has closely managed its budgets on new investments. As

Exhibit 6 Penn, Wynn, LVS, MGM, Caesars, and Boyd Diversity of US Locations by State

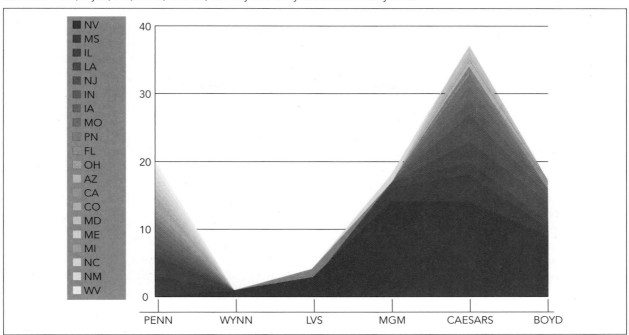

Legend: NV, MS, IL, LA, NJ, IN, IA, MO, PN, FL, OH, AZ, CA, CO, MD, ME, MI, NC, NM, WV

Categories: PENN, WYNN, LVS, MGM, CAESARS, BOYD

Sources: Corresponding corporation 10-k filings for year end 2010

Exhibit 7 Caesars, LVS, MGM, Wynn, Penn, and Boyd Side by Side Comparison

	Caesars	LVS	MGM	Wynn	Penn	Boyd
Employees	50,000	34,000	45,000	16,405	15,636	21,300
Enterprise Value (in B)	n/a	$40.70	$19.37	$22.19	$5.37	$4.07
Net Revenues* (in B)	$8.82	$7.63	$6.07	$4.54	$2.53	$2.29
Net Revenue per Employee (in T)	$176,400	$224,412	$134,889	$276,745	$161,806	$107,512
Net Income* (in M)	($843,10)	$664.52	($143,000)	$306.94	($49.96)	($1.65)
Net Income per Employee (in T)	($16,862)	$19,545	($31,778)	$18,710	($3,195)	($77)
Profit Margin*	−9.56%	8.71%	−23.58%	6.77%	−1.74%	−0.07%
Total Debt** (in B)	$18.29	$10.10	$12.08	$3.18	$2.15	$3.43
Debt as a % of Revenue	207%	132%	199%	70%	85%	150%

Source: Yahoo Finance and corresponding corporation 10-k filings.

* for period 04/01/2010 through 03/31/2011

** as of 3/31/2011

part of its 2009 efficiency initiatives, the construction of its casino in Macau that opened in 2010 came in $125 million under budget.[29]

Trends in 2011 show its first quarter earnings were primarily driven by its holdings in Macau. Table game holds allowed Wynn to achieve an increase in EBITDA of over 70 percent in the first quarter 2011. With net income reported at $173.4 million, in April, the board announced a cash dividend of $0.50/share.[30]

Penn National
Founded in Pennsylvania at the Penn National Race Course, Penn National Gaming Inc. (Penn) began business in 1972 and went public in May 1994.[31] Penn owns

and operates 19 casinos and racetracks in 16 different states and is primarily an acquisition-based company of mid-size casinos. Penn employs 16,000 people and has over 27,000 gaming machines. Penn's enterprise value in 2010 was $4.91 billion with $2.5 billion in revenue and net income amounting to $47 million. Penn's first quarter EBITDA for 2011 increased by 19.7 percent to $178 million primarily due to new acquisitions and openings in West Virginia and Pennsylvania.[32]

Boyd Gaming Corporation
Boyd Gaming (Boyd) was founded in 1975 by Sam Boyd and taken public in 1988. Over the next thirty years, it acquired 16 gaming properties in six different

states. Boyd's company vision states it is "a billion-dollar company that retains the philosophy of a family-owned business, focused on creating long-term, sustainable growth for our shareholders. This philosophy defines and separates us from the competition, making us unique in our industry."[33] In 2010, Boyd had an enterprise value of $4.1 billion with revenues of $2.2 billion and a net loss of $1.65 billion. In the first quarter of 2011, Boyd sustained a $3.5 million loss and a 36 percent increase in expenses.[34] Furthermore, Boyd announced on May 16, 2011, that The Sahara, a presence on The Strip for nearly 60 years, was officially closing its doors.[35]

Caesars Entertainment Corporation (formerly Harrah's)

Caesars Entertainment Corporation (Caesars) is considered the "largest and most diverse casino company in the world" with operations under the Harrah's, Horseshoe, and Caesars names.[36] Founded and headquartered in 1998 in Las Vegas, Caesars has over 50,000 employees and is the number one revenue generator in the industry. On January 28, 2008, Apollo Global Management, LLC and TPG Capital, LP, both private equity firms, acquired Caesars and assumed its debt load of $13.4 billion in an all-cash transaction valued at $30.7 billion. As a result of this acquisition, Caesars stock is no longer publicly traded and complete financial data for direct industry comparison is not available. In 2010, Caesars had net revenues of $8.8 billion with a loss of $831 million.[37] Caesars strives to abide by the following philosophy: "We concentrate on building loyalty and value for our customers, employees, business partners, and communities by being the most service-oriented, technology-driven, geographically-diversified company in gaming."[38]

Although Caesars fourth quarter 2010 EBITDA increased by 3 percent, net revenue decreased 0.4 percent. Las Vegas occupancy at Caesars properties increased 440 basis points with continued growth on The Strip.[39] While 2011 showed modest growth—albeit with declining revenues—and after winning a court ruling to proceed, Caesars planned to move ahead with a new 27,000 seat sports arena on The Strip.[40]

A Tale of Two Cultures

In a review of the US based hospitality/gaming industry, two distinct customer geographies must be addressed— the US and China—each of which drives significant revenue for the sector.

The United States

Within the US, populations are both aging and migrating away from Eastern and Midwestern urban areas.[41] By 2030, one in five Americans will be over the age of 65. Sunbelt states such as Florida, Nevada, and Texas have all seen significant gains in both population and new business. Despite a post-9/11 slowdown owing to tighter immigration restrictions, over 1 million legal immigrants have arrived each year since 2005—numbers that will help replace and support the retiring baby-boomer workforce.[42]

The recent collapse and subsequent federal resuscitation of many major US banks has put a significant strain on the nation's economy. Americans fortunate enough to have a job are now putting what little disposable and discretionary income they have toward delayed expenditures and reducing debts incurred during this period (Exhibit 9). With more than 25 percent of the

Exhibit 8 MGM, LVS, Wynn, Penn, and Boyd 2010 Income Statements

	Fiscal Year Ending December 31, 2010				
	MGM	LVS	Wynn	Penn	Boyd
Total Revenue	6,019.2	6,853.2	4,184.7	2,459.1	2,140.9
Growth Over Prior Year	0.68%	50.19%	37.40%	3.79%	30.46%
Gross Profit	2,261.7	2,980.2	2,897.9	994.2	805.3
Margin %	37.57%	43.49%	69.25%	40.43%	37.62%
EBITDA	1,004.4	1,971.5	1,056.0	582.8	379.8
Margin %	16.69%	28.77%	25.24%	23.70%	17.74%
EBIT	371.0	1,235.2	650.5	370.4	180.5
Margin %	6.16%	18.02%	15.54%	15.06%	8.43%
Earnings from Cont. Ops.	(1,437.4)	781.6	316.6	(61.7)	18.7
Margin %	−23.88%	11.40%	7.57%	−2.51%	0.87%
Net Income	(1,437.4)	599.4	160.1	(59.5)	10.3
Margin %	−23.88%	8.75%	3.83%	−2.42%	0.48%
Diluted EPS Excl. Extra Items	(3.19)	0.51	1.29	(0.76)	0.12

Source: Capital IQ. MGM Resorts International. Retrieved May 5, 2011 from www.capitaliq.com

Exhibit 9 Consumer Spending Trends

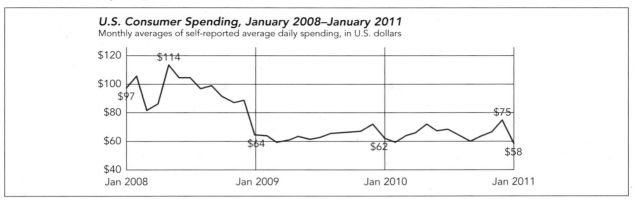

U.S. Consumer Spending, January 2008–January 2011
Monthly averages of self-reported average daily spending, in U.S. dollars

Source: Gallup Poll. Consumer Spending. Accessed April 30, 2011

two fastest growing demographic segments in the US—Blacks and Hispanics—living at or below the poverty rate,[43] entitlement programs funded by the increasingly poorer federal and state governments—both of which have seen tax revenues drop significantly over the last three years—are stretched to the limit.[44]

With the faltering economy the central focus of American discourse, local governments and populations have begun to move away from the traditional moral questions surrounding casino development of "Should we?" and toward "How can we?" (Exhibit 10). State legislatures in Pennsylvania,[45] Michigan,[46] Indiana,

Exhibit 10 US Casino Facilities

State	# of Commercial Casinos	Land-based Casinos	Riverboat or Dockside Casinos	Racetrack Casinos	Racetrack Casinos[1]	Indian Casinos	Non-casino Slot Device Locations
NV	256	X				X	X
SD	34	X[2]				X	X
CO	32	X				X	
MS	30	X	X			X	
LA	18	X	X		w/ table games	X	X
IN	13	X	X		w/ table games		
MO	12		X			X	
NJ	11	X					
PE	10	X		X			
IL	9		X				
NY	8				X	X	
FL	5			X		X	
NM	5			X		X	
WV	5	X			w/ table games		X
DE	3				w/ table games		
MI	3	X				X	
OK	2			X		X	
RI	2				X		
KS	1	X[3]				X	
MD	1	X[4]		X			
ME	1				X		
OH	TBD						

[1]with publicly run video lottery terminals and slots
[2]maximum bet $100
[3]state owned
[4]slots only

(Continued)

Exhibit 10 US Casino Facilities *(Continued)*

States with Indian Casinos Only
AK
AL
AZ
CA
CT
ID
MN
MT
NC
ND
NE
OR
TX
WA
WI
WY

States with No Commercial or Indian Casinos
AR
GA
HI
KY
MA
NH
SC
TN
UT
VA
VT

Source: American Gaming Association - Industry Resources. http://www.americangaming.org

Illinois, and Mississippi have seen regional casinos thrive—generating revenue and providing jobs for constituents (Exhibit 11).[47] The trend continues with Ohio casinos set to begin operations in 2012 and expected to contribute in excess of $500 million per year to state coffers.[48] Of course, Nevada continues to be a force as well with casinos the largest employers in the state, a powerful lobby in the American Gaming Association, and the vocal advocacy of the Senate majority leader, Harry Reid.[49]

Las Vegas continues to occupy a unique place in American consciousness. Having been dubbed "Sin City," it serves as a multifaceted escape. Its marketing campaign tagline "What happens here, stays here"[50] signifies the break from normal life it provides. The industry is now attempting to spread this feeling to casinos across the country to capitalize on the American demand for instant gratification by providing levers to pull and dice to roll. Once considered a diversion of the less virtuous, many factors are purported to contribute to the less contentious acceptance of the world of casinos, gaming, and gambling. Among others, these include declining religious affiliations, a sharp jump in teen pregnancies,[51] a rise in prescription narcotics use, and the displacement of the traditional family by cohabitating (both opposite and same gender) and single parents[52]—all considered indicators of changing socio-cultural values in the US.[53] Topped off with a mind numbing news cycle and the tacit acceptance of the wholesale erosion of privacy, the fact that casinos

are no longer associated with moral or lifestyle choices but instead viewed as yet another form of entertainment is unsurprising (Exhibit 12).

While public gaming corporations in the US are subject to the same transparency regulations of the SEC as any other US corporation, their forays into China have created issues. Most notably are potential Foreign Corrupt Practices Act (FCPA) violations by LVS[54] and MGM's difficulties in New Jersey given its dealings with a questionable Chinese investment partner.[55]

China

As one of the oldest cultures in the world, China has a rich history and tradition of gambling that extends back thousands of years. Interestingly, the oft-envisioned demand of the Chinese government for social order may in fact be what perpetuates the habit and obsession with gambling held by so many of its citizens. Deprived of many freedoms, Chinese have a measurable external locus of control—in other words, they "believe that luck, destiny, chance and powerful others control their lives more than themselves."[56] Seemingly contraindicated, this, in combination with proper deference to superstitions, leads to a higher illusion of control—and thus, increased risk taking, often, at games of chance. Measuring one's karma or virtue in this manner may also explain the large percentage of Chinese that gamble not for the money, but for camaraderie and entertainment. In 2010, nearly 25 million people visited the tiny 11 square mile coastal region of Macau with 88 percent

Exhibit 11 MGM Resorts International: Presence in Top 20 US Casino Markets by Revenue

Rank	Casino Market	2010 Annual Revenues	% of MGM Attention
1	Las Vegas Strip (NV)	$ 5.777 billion	55.9%
2	Atlantic City (NJ)	$ 3.573 billion	
3	Chicagoland (IN/IL)	$ 2.057 billion	2.9%
4	Connecticut	$ 1.385 billion	
5	Detroit (MI)	$ 1.378 billion	5.9%
6	St. Louis (MO/IL)	$ 1.086 billion	
7	Tunica/Lula (MS)	$926.92 million	5.9%
8	Biloxi (MS)	$830.86 million	5.9%
9	Philadelphia (PA)	$816.31 million	
10	Shreveport (LA)	$764.92 million	
11	Boulder Strip (NV)	$757.03 million	
12	Kansas City/St. Joseph (MO)	$753.44 million	
13	Reno/Sparks (NV)	$684.05 million	8.8%
14	Lawrenceburg/Rising Sun/Belterra (IN)	$676.17 million	
15	New Orleans (LA)	$640.94 million	
16	Lake Charles (LA)	$639.13 million	
17	Black Hawk (CO)	$625.17 million	
18	Yonkers (NY)	$582.23 million	
19	Pittsburgh/Meadow Lands (PA)	$531.80 million	
20	Downtown Vegas (NV)	$493.39 million	
n/r	Vegas suburbs – Henderson/Jean		11.8%
n/a	Macau		2.9%

% of MGM Attention calculated based on number of locations in area as a percentage of total MGM locations – partial ownership/joint ventures credited as .5 location.

Source: http://www.americangaming.org

Exhibit 12 Las Vegas Visitor Demographics

	2010 %
GENDER	
Male	50%
Female	50
MARITAL STATUS	
Married	79
Single	14
Separated/Divorced	5
Widowed	2
EMPLOYMENT	
Employed	66
Unemployed	2
Student	3
Retired	27
Homemaker	3
EDUCATION	
High school or less	23
Some college	24
College graduate	48
Trade/vocational school	5

	2010 %
ETHNICITY	
White	86%
African American/Black	5
Asian/Asian American	3
Hispanic/Latino	6
Other	1
HOUSEHOLD INCOME	
Less than $20,000	1
$20,000 to $39,999	7
$40,000 to $59,999	17
$60,000 to $79,999	24
$80,000 to $99,999	16
$100,000 or more	24
Not sure/no answer	10
VISITOR ORIGIN	
U.S.A.	**82**
Eastern states	6
Southern states	11
Midwestern states	12

(Continued)

Exhibit 12 Las Vegas Visitor Demographics (*Continued*)

	2010 %
AGE	
21 to 29	10
30 to 39	19
40 to 49	23
50 to 59	19
60 to 64	9
65 or older	20
MEAN	49.2

	2010 %
Western states	**54**
California	**30**
Southern California	26
Northern California	4
Arizona	7
Other Western states	16
No ZIP code given	0
Foreign	**18**

Source: Year End Summary 2010–Only Vegas–Retrieved from http://www.lvcva.com

of those visitors coming from China, Hong Kong, and Taiwan.[57] Unlike Las Vegas, however, nearly 55 percent of Macau visitors are "day trippers"—visitors that arrive and leave without spending money on accommodations.

China is predicted to reach the same proportion of 1 in 5 citizens over the age of 65 ten years after the US, in 2040.[58] However, by today's population rates, that will equal 267.9 million seniors in China as compared to only 62.4 million in the US.[59] Complicating the issue of its aging population will be a marked shortage of working age Chinese (as a result of China's 1979 one child policy) to replace and support its aging population. Unlike the US, immigration has not, and likely will not, replenish China's youth.[60]

Even so, at present and in contrast to the US, urban incomes in China rose tenfold between 1991 and 2009[61] making China's middle class alone the same size as the entire US population.[62] In addition to being newly affluent, China's new middle class, at least for now, is able to both spend and save simultaneously.[63]

Despite being illegal in China, there is no shortage of opportunities for those living in China to gamble. From a friendly round of mah jong with the neighbors to roaming card games to cruise ships in Hong Kong and Singapore that take passengers to international waters and set anchor, gambling has and will continue to be an integral part of Chinese culture. Officially, casino operations are restricted to the former Portuguese colony of Macau where a tenuous balance of private interests, criminal elements, and regional government are all now being more closely watched by Beijing.[64] While a lucrative source of income for the Chinese government, many are beginning to express concern about the reasoning of officials that, because gambling is illegal, it is not possible that any of its citizens would have a gambling addiction; therefore, because it could not be a problem, no gambling addiction education, intervention, or rehabilitation is required or offered.

The Dealers

In the casino/hotel realm, there are two distinct supplier lines inbound to properties: hospitality related supplies, including everything from food to sheets to soap, and casino/gaming specific supplies with slot machines to electronic poker to craps tables and thousands upon thousands of decks of cards. For all their consumable and durable products, the resort casinos have a large contingent of eager suppliers to choose from for anything from mattresses and poker chips to staff uniforms and bottled water.[65] The cost of ultra luxury products or furnishings may still be relatively high, but with fewer buyers in the market and the promise to consider a long-term relationship, casinos are often able to leverage their size and sustainability as a customer to squeeze the margins of a supplier. In fact, in this high-profile market, even elite manufacturers of branded goods can find themselves competing for "shelf space" inside a hotel or casino. "Even top tier brands are not concerned about pricing power when a casino comes calling," says Carleen Jorgensen, Managing Director of Brand and Consumer Marketing at Burson Marsteller. ". . .via partnership or other arrangement, they will find their way in before a competitor does to get exposure."[66]

On the other hand, casino specific suppliers face a tough battle. International Game Technology, better known as IGT, is the most successful maker of slots and electronic gaming machines and does well with its highly diversified offering of branded machines.[67] However, IGT has faced not only antitrust complaints from rival slotmaker Bally Technologies,[68] but battles with WMS Industries, another game manufacturer, and others in casino operations and security as well.[69] Due to this lack of industry solidarity, the major casinos in Las Vegas and Macau hold the winning hand.

Specialized assets such as the exclusive rights to a high demand show, popular entertainer, or even a celebrity chef are significantly more expensive on relative terms but, compared to the revenue they can generate, represent a small portion of total expenses and can pay off in spades.[70]

The Players

Hotel/casinos derive revenue from two distinct customer bases: conventions, purchased with corporate dollars, and leisure travelers not affiliated with an event or meeting.[71] Although trade shows, associations, and corporations have traditionally paid a premium to meet in Las Vegas, the recession allowed what was left of these customers to extract substantial discounts from hotel/casinos.[72] With alternatives to Vegas cropping up across the country, corporate pricing power now extends not only to pitting hotel/casinos against one another to host events, but to one geographic destination as compared to another as well. Jill Goldner, head of travel and meeting services for Sketchers USA, said that while Las Vegas was historically a lead candidate for major events, other locations, fueled by municipal and state government incentives, are offering loss-leading hospitality and exhibition packages to secure long-term deals.[73] Although conventions account for less than 20 percent of Las Vegas business, they are a rich and essential overall piece of the pie given their spending patterns, and their relative absence has seated bargaining power squarely with consumers.[74]

In addition to discounts for corporate travelers, former Jefferies casino analyst and LVS consultant Larry Klatzkin said that the occupancy and utilization hole left by fewer conventions has created a several-year buying power opportunity for leisure travelers who, of late, have been staying in hotels and dining at locations that would normally be well outside their normal price range. While temporary, the bargaining power of the leisure traveler is likely to remain for several more years. To the hotel/casino owner, however, leisure travelers are next to no help at all as they are less likely to deliver revenue to on-site entertainment venues or high-end dining, preferring to go off site to less expensive options.[75] Needless to say, with luxury properties at rock bottom, losses at lower-tier properties have been pushed even further.

Despite the bargaining power of individual buyers, rising airfares and travel costs have enhanced the popularity of the newly coined "staycation" whereby potential vacationers enjoy time off closer to their physical home.[76] Additionally, unlike the Chinese gaming demographic that has the cash flow to spend without having to forego saving, Americans are now more carefully deciding what to do with their smaller cash streams.

The Wild Card

Aside from the fact that the capital requirements just to construct, let alone operate a casino are daunting, the US hotel/casino market is currently saturated with rooms and gaming space and it is estimated to be several years before this capacity is absorbed.[77] In addition, with the era of cheap money likely ending,[78] a new entrant would have significant difficulty securing financing for a competitive project and, in the market today, would have to operate with untenable discounts. Even were these challenges surmounted, creating a destination unique enough to lure away the deeply loyal customers of other resorts is unlikely.

The existing major gaming concerns also hold the advantage when it comes to attracting top shows and performers. Furthermore, gaming companies must secure premium advertising channels and retail tenants.[79] Here, the issue is not of a store refusing to carry a product, but a new entrant's ability to secure desirable partners in the absence of a significant value-driving brand. With those partners only interested in extending reach at prime destinations, the well-established relationships built by MGM, Wynn, Caesars, and others will not be easily unseated. These barriers are furthered by government policies and dynamics where, within an already heavily regulated structure where long cultivated personal relationships are critical, the major players are already well ensconced with the American Gaming Association speaking for them.

Finally, according to an industry insider, retaliation from the major players would be "brutal."[80] The overall collection of resources, systems, political power, and financial power concentrated in the hands of the top hotel/casinos would make it nearly impossible for a new operator to succeed. Often cited is the experience of the Sahara: upon its assumption of the Sahara, novice operator SBE, an owner/operator of hotels and nightclubs in Los Angeles, was unprepared to compete directly with other mid-market offerings and failed to establish a strong brand strategy, even as it looked to redevelop. The result was a quick shuttering of the historic Las Vegas casino in May 2011.[81]

Forbidden in the US, Internet gambling—what would otherwise be a strategic bypass of these various challenges—is not an option.

Playing a Player

The rivalry among the largest hotel/casinos has been fueled by desperate attempts to stay economically viable in a difficult time. Pre-recession, the rivalry assumed the form of "bigger is better" with MGM, LVS, Wynn, Caesars, and Boyd each attempting to top one another with more extravagant showpiece casinos (Borgata, CityCenter, etc.) and serial acquisitions spurred by vibrant and seemingly unlimited debt markets. Currently, each is battling to attract US visitors to Las Vegas with a handful attempting to simultaneously pursue the lucrative Macau market and yet another mix concentrating on burgeoning regional markets such as Pennsylvania and Ohio.[82] However, the attention paid to Macau and regional locations is diminishing the pot in Las Vegas.[83] UBS analyst and portfolio manager Robert McCarthy calls the sector "the most competitive besides tech, with bigger egos and bigger bankrolls. . . . Share of wallet is only so much, and even loyal customers are subject to relentless entreaties for their limited money."[84] Users of high-end casino features such as restaurants, spas, and golf courses spend a greater total percentage of money gambling, so each casino is determined to keep them on site to capture those bets.[85] The intensity of the rivalry is so great, leaders taunt each other by name when poaching convention business. Though their balance sheets look different, most of MGM's competitors are equally balanced across customer segments (value, mid-market, and luxury) with Sands and Wynn going toe-to-toe with MGM in Macau—and understandably so as, in February 2010 alone, Macau casinos generated $1.68 billion+[86] and the local government is highly motivated to move infrastructure projects along to deliver additional visitors.[87] Industry growth overall has been notably slowed in Las Vegas by the recession; however, domestic gaming-focused destinations and Asian properties are thriving.

Winner Takes All

As with many industries, the hotel and gaming industry suffered a direct hit during the most recent recessionary period with consumer discretionary spending—the primary sales driver for the industry—dropping 43 percent from December 2007 through January 2011.[88] After record revenues of $7.7 billion in 2007,[89] MGM realized a net reduction of 16.5 percent to $6.0 billion in net sales from the fiscal years ending 2007 to 2010.[90] During this same period, direct competitors LVS and Wynn *increased* net sales via casino openings by 132 percent and 56 percent, respectively.[91, 92] MGM saw a 3.3 percent increase in its 2011 first quarter year over year revenue—from $1.457 billion to $1.505 billion.[93] This increase was primarily derived from non-casino revenues (room, food and beverage, entertainment, and retail). The 3.3 percent increase is lackluster, however, compared to that of competitors with average increases seen by Boyd, Penn, Wynn, and LVS in this period at 36.4 percent (Exhibit 13).

Exhibit 13 Industry Ratios

	MGM	LVS	Wynn	Penn	Boyd	MGM Ranking (Out of 5)
Profitability						
Return on assets	1.1%	3.7%	5.7%	5.0%	2.2%	5
Return on capital	1.4%	4.2%	6.5%	5.6%	2.6%	5
Return on equity	(41.9%)	9.9%	11.4%	(3.4%)	1.5%	5
Margin						
Gross Margin %	37.6%	43.5%	69.2%	40.4%	37.6%	5
SG&A Margin %	20.8%	12.2%	9.3%	16.7%	19.5%	5
EBITDA Margin %	16.7%	28.8%	25.2%	23.7%	17.7%	5
Net Income Margin %	−23.9%	8.7%	3.8%	−2.4%	0.5%	5
Liquidity						
Current Ratio	1.2x	1.6x	1.8x	0.7x	0.5x	3
Quick Ratio	0.8x	1.4x	1.6x	0.4x	0.3x	3
Leverage						
Debt to Equity	401.9%	120.2%	138.2%	123.7%	247.0%	5
Debt to Capital	80.1%	54.6%	58.0%	55.3%	71.2%	5
Liabilities/Assets	84.2%	59.9%	64.3%	60.2%	75.3%	5
Other						
Capex as a % of Revenue	3.4%	29.5%	6.8%	14.8%	4.1%	5
Q1 2011 YoY Revenue Improvement	3.3%	38.7%	58.3%	12.6%	36.1%	5
Q1 2011 Stock Performance	−11.4%	−8.1%	22.5%	5.4%	−11.6%	4
Full Year 2010, unless otherwise noted						

Source: Capital IQ. MGM Resorts International. Retrieved May 5, 2011 from www.capitaliq.com

In 2010, MGM's casinos contributed 36.7 percent of overall gross revenue ($2.443 billion), down from 39.4 percent ($2.618 billion) in 2009. This reduction was primarily driven by a 13 percent decrease in revenue from table games. Non-casino revenue saw a slight improvement in 2010, increasing its portion of gross revenue from 60.6 percent, or $4.026 billion, to 63.3 percent, or $4.210 billion.[94]

From 2007 to 2010, with immense pressure on top-line revenues, MGM gross margins incurred a 1,006 basis point decline, from 47.6 percent to 37.6 percent.[95] At 37.6 percent, this 2010 gross margin is well below those of LVS (43.5 percent) and Wynn (69.3 percent). However, recent cost savings strategies, along with the introduction of M-Life—a customer rewards program—have proven favorable to gross margin performance, providing 64 basis points of gross margin improvement and moving MGM from 36.9 percent in the first quarter of 2010 to 37.5 percent for the same period in 2011.[96]

In 2010, three properties—Bellagio, MGM Grand Las Vegas, and MGM Grand Detroit—contributed over 67 percent of operating income (before corporate expenses).[97] MGM Macau showed the greatest increase in profitability jumping from $24.6 million in 2009 to $129.6 million in 2010.

Like revenues, MGM's peak earnings occurred in 2007, with earnings from continuing operations of $1.4 billion, and earnings per share (EPS) of $4.70.[98] During the subsequent recessionary years, earnings fell 200 percent to −$1.4 billion in 2010. EPS followed, falling $7.89, to −$3.19. Competitors LVS and Wynn did not see this large decrease in profitability. In fact, LVS had an increase of over $650 million in earnings from 2007 to 2010 and an EPS increase of 55 percent, from $0.33 to $0.51.[99] Wynn also increased its earnings by over $120 million; however, its EPS declined 28 percent from $1.80 to $1.29.[100]

From December 2007 to March 2011, MGM share prices fell 84 percent, from $84.02 to $13.15.[101] Over the same period, LVS share prices fell only 59 percent, from $103.05 to $42.22 (Exhibit 14). Wynn has actually provided shareholders with a 30.8 percent increase in share price from year ending 2007 to first quarter ending 2011. Looking at only the first quarter of 2011, MGM shares have declined 11.4 percent. This decline is second within the industry only to Boyd, with an 11.6 percent share price decline. LVS, Penn, and Wynn all outperformed MGM providing returns of −8.1 percent, 5.4 percent, and 22.5 percent, respectively.

With the majority of MGM's revenue cash based, operating cash flows are significant.[102] Because of the capital intensive nature of the industry, these significant operating cash flows provide the necessary capacity to fund reinvestment requirements throughout the company, repay debt financing, and provide excess cash for future needs. MGM's poorest operating cash flow performance in the last decade occurred in 2010 with $504 million in operating cash—a 59.1 percent reduction from its 2006 high of $1.232 billion (Exhibit 15).

Exhibit 14 MGM Resorts International vs. Peers 2011

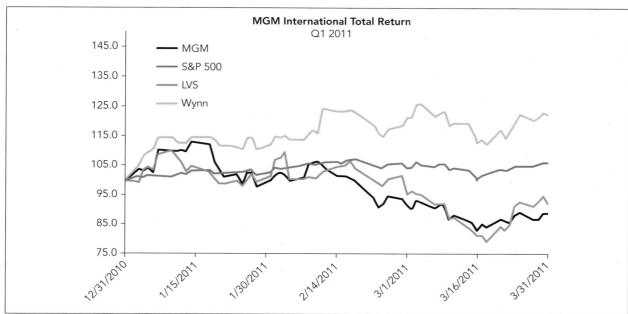

Source: Capital IQ. MGM Resorts International. Retrieved May 5, 2011 from www.capitaliq.com

Exhibit 15 MGM Resorts International Annual Cash Flows

	Historical MGM Cash Flows (Summarized)					
	Fiscal Year Ending December 31,					
	2005	2006	2007	2008	2009	2010
Net Income	443.3	648.3	1,584.4	(855.3)	(1,291.7)	(1,437.4)
D & A, Total	588.1	653.9	700.3	778.2	689.3	633.4
Amortization of Deferred Charges	5.8	(3.1)	4.3	10.6	50.9	88.0
Other Non-Cash Items, Total	189.8	124.8	(1,351.9)	1,306.3	1,568.8	1,021.1
Change in Net Operating Assets	(44.1)	(191.9)	57.2	(486.9)	(429.3)	198.9
Cash Flow from Operations	**1,182.8**	**1,232.0**	**994.4**	**753.0**	**587.9**	**504.0**
Capital Expenditure	(719.1)	(1,758.8)	(2,917.4)	(781.8)	(136.9)	(207.5)
Sale of P, P&E	7.8	11.4	47.6	86.0	22.3	77.6
Cash Acquisitions	(4,421.0)	0.0	0.0	0.0	0.0	0.0
Divestitures	0.0	0.0	0.0	0.0	746.3	0.0
Other Investing Activities	(170.5)	105.0	3,079.1	(1,285.7)	(962.0)	(456.2)
Cash Flow from Investing	**(5,302.8)**	**(1,642.4)**	**209.3**	**(1,981.4)**	**(330.3)**	**(586.1)**
Total Cash Dividends Paid	0.0	0.0	0.0	0.0	0.0	0.0
Issue/(Retire) of Debt	4,196.2	662.4	(1,804.5)	2,389.8	497.8	(1,872.7)
Issue/(Retire) of Common Equity	(71.6)	(157.8)	463.8	(1,240.9)	3,356.7	588.5
Financing Cash Flow Items	(61.8)	5.5	100.2	(26.9)	(2,365.7)	(190.9)
Cash Flow from Financing Activities	**4,062.8**	**510.0**	**(1,240.5)**	**1,122.1**	**1,488.8**	**(1,475.2)**
Foreign Exchange Effects	0.0	0.0	0.0	0.0	0.0	0.0
Miscellaneous Cash Flow Adjustment	0.0	(24.5)	0.0	(14.2)	14.2	0.0
Change in Cash	**(57.2)**	**75.0**	**(36.8)**	**(120.5)**	**1,760.6**	**(1,557.2)**

Source: Capital IQ. MGM Resorts International. Retrieved May 5, 2011 from www.capitaliq.com

Other competitors did not have this level of operational cash flow degradation over the same period, 2006 to 2010; Boyd decreased 32.0 percent, from $419.5 million to $285.1 million;[103] Wynn increased 339.1 percent, from $240.8 million to $1.057 billion;[104] and LVS increased operating cash flows by $2.067 billion, from −$196.7 million in 2006 to $1.87 billion in 2010.[105] With the high level of capital within the industry, a high level of expenditures is necessary to either maintain or revitalize assets. MGM is behind the industry in terms of reinvestment into its business, spending only 3.4 percent of sales in 2010 on capital expenditures.[106] This compares to 4.1 percent, 6.8 percent, and 29.5 percent in 2010 for Boyd, Wynn, and LVS, respectively. Certain industry analysts view MGM's low level of reinvestment in 2010 as a threat to the quality of the MGM portfolio.[107]

Carrying a high level of debt is indicative of a capital-intensive industry. In the early to mid 2000s, debt was cheap at rates of ~4.3 percent, relative to highs in the 80s of ~15 percent to 16 percent.[108] MGM took advantage of these rates during the pre-recessionary years, undertaking projects such as CityCenter and purchases including Mandalay Resort Group. With debt as its primary funding source, however, MGM was highly leveraged

with net debt to EBITDA nearly doubling from 5.9x in 2006, to 11.5x in 2010.[109] The extent of MGM's leverage far exceeds that of its competitors at 8.8x, 3.6x, 3.4x, and 1.9x, for Boyd, LVS, Penn, and Wynn respectively. MGM considered and then ruled out selling locations from its portfolio. This was fortunate as the locations with the highest likelihood of sale (Detroit and Biloxi) ultimately proved to be the most accretive and cash flow generating businesses for MGM.[110] Instead, over the course of 2010 and start of 2011, MGM refinanced its debt, thus supplying sufficient liquidity through 2012 and into 2013.[111]

How It's Been Done

After its growth and acquisition period in the 90s and early 2000s, MGM was able to market its stable of holdings as "the finest assembly of resort brands in the hospitality industry."[112] Within the MGM portfolio are products and services that appeal to customers on both the high and value ends of the customer spectrum. Properties such as Bellagio offer exclusive products including world class restaurants and shopping, salon and spa treatments, limousine service, art collections, and full concierge services for its guests.[113] Targeting a different market segment, Circus Circus, for example, offers more value-oriented products and services such as a pizzeria and access to Dollar Rent-a-Car.[114] Because MGM's target markets vary, it aligns primary and secondary products and services to meet the particular needs of its customers and guests.

One of MGM's primary objectives is to operate all its properties with an emphasis on delivering excellent customer service. With guest and concierge services, MGM employees are available to fulfill just about any guest request. MGM's commitment to recruit, train, and retain well-qualified, motivated employees who provide superior and friendly customer service is evident in the exemplary service provided throughout the organization.[115]

Complimenting its service activities are MGM's marketing and sales activities. MGM offers unique, "must-see" entertainment attractions, communicated through distinctive and memorable promotional programs.[116] To encourage customer loyalty, MGM introduced its M Life Players Club at all wholly owned properties in 2010. M Life is a customer rewards club with a tiered point system. Customers earn points for purchases as well as gaming activity and can redeem those points for food, concerts, or other unique experiences.[117] Additional aspects of M Life include MGM's ability to personalize marketing, for example, "If a guest attends a Madonna concert, he or she might receive an offer to attend an upcoming Lady Gaga show."[118]

With its large-scale projects like CityCenter and MGM Macau, MGM has attempted to both solidify its place in Las Vegas and simultaneously expand its reach into a high growth international market. While these projects could provide unparalleled returns, their timing and costs have stressed the financial capacity and flexibility of MGM. In its 2011 first quarter earnings call, CEO Jim Murren confirmed that debt reduction and necessary renovations and upgrades are at the top of the priority list.[119] This continuous reinvestment through capital improvements plays a significant role in customers' perceived value as any visible degradation of properties or services signals lower quality and less value.

Leaders and Headings

Although Kirk Kerkorian is widely acknowledged as the Vegas visionary that helped build the modern MGM, in reality, he was more of a facilitator than a leader.[120] Kerkorian's April 2011 retirement "Director Emeritus" status leaves Jim Murren, the current Chairman and CEO, to navigate MGM (Exhibit 16). Beyond reducing its significant leverage, MGM Resorts International has a makeover to complete.

First and foremost is the question of whether MGM is properly managing its portfolio of properties. Should the company seek to shed underperforming assets or those that do not fit well into the organization post-recession? Is MGM well represented enough in

Exhibit 16 MGM Resorts International Executive Officers

Name	Age	Position	Year Started with MGM
James J. Murren	49	Chairman, CEO, President and Director	1998
Robert H. Baldwin	60	Chief Design and Construction Officer and Director	2000
William J. Hornbuckle	53	Chief Marketing Officer	1998
Corey I. Sanders	47	Chief Operating Officer	1997
Daniel J. D'Arrigo	42	Executive VP, CFO and Treasurer	2000
Phyllis A. James	58	Executive VP & Special Counsel—Litigation and Chief Diversity Officer	2002
Aldo Manzini	47	Executive VP and Chief Administrative Officer	2007
John McManus	43	Executive VP, General Counsel and Secretary	2001
William M. Scott IV	50	Executive VP—Corporate Strategy and Special Counsel	2009
Robert C. Selwood	55	Executive VP and Chief Accounting Officer	2000
Rick Arpin	38	Senior VP—Corporate Controller	2002
Alan Feldman	52	Senior VP—Public Affairs	2000
James A. Freeman	42	Senior VP—Capital Markets and Strategy	2010
Shawn T. Sani	45	Senior VP—Taxes	2002
Average Age	**48.6**	**Average Tenure at MGM through 2010**	**9.1 years**

Source: MGM Resorts International 10-k filing for year ended 2010

high growth areas? Are there acquisitions, even in an ambiguous economic landscape, that make sense considering the impending transformations of the domestic and Asian demographic markets?

Second, where can MGM most quickly make up the biggest differences between itself and its competitors? Are there experts or practices in complementary industries that could deliver systems that would be unique—and profitable—given the current circumstances of the hospitality and gaming industry?

Away from home, given the forecasts and development in Asia, what is the right model for MGM internationally? Has MGM given enough consideration to the end goals of its Asian customer or is it simply charging ahead with a "Las Vegas approach"?

And finally, does the ceremonial exit of its figurehead mark the end of an era or simply make MGM an open target? Do its partnerships with Dubai World and Pansy Ho—relationships that provide fiscal security and a capacity for growth it could not achieve independently—signal weakness and sully its reputation in the eyes of its customers and, if so, ultimately, is it worth it?

NOTES

1. MGM Resorts International: Company Overview. *MGM Resorts .com*. Retrieved Apr 27, 2011, from http://mgmresorts.com/company/company-overview.aspx
2. MGM Investment Research. (2011, Apr). *Goldman Sachs*.
3. MGM Resorts International. Form 10-K for the fiscal year ended December 31, 2010. Retrieved from http://www.sec.gov/Archives/edgar/data/789570/000095012311019786/p18354e10vk.htm
4. 2011 MGM Resorts International History. UNLV Center for Gaming Research. Retrieved Apr 26, 2011, from http://gaming.unlv.edu/abstract/fin_mgm.html
5. *Ibid.*
6. MGM Grand Inc. Form 10-K for the fiscal year ended December 31, 1995. Retrieved from http://www.sec.gov/Archives/edgar/data/789570/0000898430-96-001054.txt
7. MGM Mirage. Form 10-K for the fiscal year ended December 31, 2000. Retrieved from http://www.sec.gov/Archives/edgar/data/789570/000091205701008574/a2040243z10-k405.htm
8. S. Warner. (2000, Mar 7). MGM Grand to buy Mirage. *Philly .com*. Retrieved from http://articles.philly.com/2000-03-07/news/25605294_1_mirage-shares-joseph-coccimiglio-gaming-industry
9. Associated Press. (2005, Apr 26). MGM Mirage and Mandalay Bay finish merger. *MSNBC*. Retrieved from http://www.msnbc.msn.com/id/7634660/ns/business-us_business/t/mgm-mirage-mandalay-resort-finish-merger/
10. MGM Resorts International. Form 10-K for the fiscal year ended December 31, 2007. Retrieved from http://www.sec.gov/Archives/edgar/data/789570/000095015308000421/p75046e10vk.htm
11. 2011 MGM Resorts International History. *op. cit.*
12. CityCenter News. (page last updated 2010, Nov 14). *Vegas Today and Tomorrow*. Retrieved from http://www.vegastodayandtomorrow.com/citycenter.htm
13. MGM Resorts International – Historical Prices. *Yahoo! Finance*. Retrieved from http://www.google.com/finance/historical?cid=21913&startdate=Mar+1%2C+2009&enddate=Mar+30%2C+2009&num=30
14. R. Gros. (2011, Apr 26). The World View. *Global Gaming Business*. Vol 10. No. 5 May 2011. Retrieved from http://ggbmagazine.com/issue-printer/vol-10-no-5-may-2011
15. K. Benston. (2010, Oct 29). Casino companies change names to elevate image. *Las Vegas Sun*. Retrieved from http://www.lasvegassun.com/news/2010/jun/15/mgm-mirage-changes-name-now-mgm-resorts-international
16. A. Salzman. (2011, Apr 26). Blog: Sell MGM on "Mountain of Debt," Mediocre Growth Prospects: Credit Suisse. *Barrons*. Retrieved from http://blogs.barrons.com
17. J. Simkins, J. Longstreet, & L. Buzik. (2011, Apr 26). Lion Taming. Company Update: MGM Resorts *International*. *Credit Suisse Equity Research*.
18. Better. . .and gaining momentum in Las Vegas; Raising estimates. (2011, May 4). *BMO Capital Markets*.
19. CNNMoney. 2011. Retrieved from http://money.cnn.com/magazines/fortune/fortune500/2010/Industries
20. S. Green. MGM resorts confirms 1.5B China IPO. May 2011. Retrieved from http://www.vegasinc.com/news/2011/may/16/mgm-resorts-confirms-15-billion-china-ipo/
21. H. Stutz. (2011, Apr 23). MGM Resorts to gain majority ownership of MGM Grand Macau. *Las Vegas Journal-Review*. Retrieved from http://www.lvjr.com
22. Asian Coast Development. May 2011. Retrieved from http://www.asiancoastdevelopment.com/mgm-grand-ho-tram.php
23. Las Vegas Sands. Form 10-K for the fiscal year ended December 31, 2010. Retrieved from http://investor.lasvegassands.com/annuals.cfm
24. Yahoo! Finance. Las Vegas Sands. 2011. Retrieved from http://finance.yahoo.com/q/ks?s=LVS+Key+Statistics
25. R. Olsen. (2011, Mar). Las Vegas Sands reveals SEC probe. *Forbes.com*. Retrieved from http://blogs.forbes.com/robertolsen/2011/03/02/las-vegas-sands-reveals-sec-probe-into-macau-business/
26. Reuters. Las Vegas Sands Reported Earnings Reports. Q1 2011. Retrieved from http://www.reuters.com/article/2011/05/03/idUS245170+03-May-2011+MW20110503
27. Wynn Las Vegas. 2011. Retrieved from http://www.wynnlasvegas.com/
28. Wynn Resorts Ltd. (WYNN): Key Statistics. *Yahoo! Finance*. Retrieved from http://finance.yahoo.com/q/ks?s=WYNN+Key+Statistics
29. Gaming Market Overview. (2011, Apr). The Forest for the Trees. *Bank of America/Merrill Lynch*.
30. *Ibid.*
31. Company History. *Penn National Gaming, Inc.* Retrieved from http://www.pngaming.com/main/comphist.shtml
32. Penn National Gaming Inc. (PENN): Profile. *Yahoo! Finance*. Retrieved from http://finance.yahoo.com/q/pr?s=PENN+Profile
33. Mission and Vision. *Boyd Gaming*. Retrieved from http://www.boydgaming.com/about-boyd/mission-and-vision
34. Boyd Gaming records first quarter loss. (2011, May 3). *Travel Pulse*. Retrieved from http://www.travelpulse.com/boyd-gaming-reports-firstquarter-loss-of-35-million.html
35. R. Raynaldy. (2011, May 16). End of an era as Vegas casino closes. *China Daily*. Retrieved from http://www.chinadaily.com.cn/cndy/2011-05/16/content_12514185.htm
36. Gaming Market Overview. (2011, Apr). The Forest for the Trees. *Bank of America/Merrill Lynch*.
37. Caesars Entertainment Corporation. Form 10-K for the fiscal year ended December 31, 2010. http://www.sec.gov/Archives/edgar/data/858339/000119312511056393/d10k.htm

38. Company Overview. *Caesars Entertainment*. Retrieved from http://www.caesarswindsor.com/corporate/index.html

39. Caesars Entertainment reports results for first quarter 2011. (2011, May 10). Retrieved from http://phx.corporate-ir.net/External.File?item=UGFyZW50SUQ9OTI5ODF8Q2hpbGRJRD0tMXxUeXBlIPTM=&t=1

40. C. Ryan. (2011, May 9). Caesars Entertainment wins legal battle over proposed Strip arena. *Las Vegas Sun*. Retrieved from http://www.lasvegassun.com/news/2011/may/09/caesars-entertainment-wins-legal-battle-over-propo/

41. S. Ohlemmacher. (2006, Mar 15). Americans moving out of cities. *Daily Herald*. Retrieved from http://www.heraldextra.com/business/article_bae509c4-4084-5bba-9718-be9496a4dbdb.html

42. L. Shrestha & E. Heisler. (2011, Mar 31). The changing demographic profile of the US. *Congressional Research Service*. Retrieved from http://www.fas.org/sgp/crs/misc/RL32701.pdf

43. US Population Projections: 2005-2050. (2008, Feb 11). *Pew Hispanic Center*. Retrieved from http://pewhispanic.org/reports/report.php?ReportID=85

44. M. Cooper. (2010, Feb 22). Recession tightens grip on state tax revenues. *The New York Times*. Retrieved from http://www.nytimes.com/2010/02/23/us/23states.html

45. P. Cunningham. (2011, May 5). PA tax revenue from casinos higher than Nevada. *WFMZ News*. Retrieved from http://www.wfmz.com/berksnews/27796204/detail.html

46. J. Trop. (2011, May 5). Michigan casino revenue growth beats average. *The Detroit News*. http://webcache.googleusercontent.com/search?q=cache:AsMerROA2SEJ:www.detroitnews.com/apps/pbcs.dll/article%3FAID%3D/20110505/BIZ/105050341/%26template%3Dartiphone+%22Michigan+casino+revenue+growth+beats+average%22+trop&cd=1&hl=en&ct=clnk&gl=us&source=www.google.com

47. M. Perez. (2011, May 22). Gambling association says casino revenue stabilized. *Sun Herald*. Retrieved from http://www.responsiblegambling.org/articles/Gaming_association_says.pdf

48. Ohio Casino Information. Retrieved on May 16, 2011, from http://www.ohiocasinoinfo.com/index.html

49. M. Isikoff. (2010, Dec 8). Reids 'Net betting bill would benefit his casino backers. *MSNBC – politics.com*. Retrieved from http://politics.newsvine.com/_news/2010/12/08/5614339-reids-net-betting-bill-would-benefit-his-casino-backers

50. T. Audi. (2009, May 13). Vegas tries luck with old slogan. *The Wall Street Journal*. Retrieved from http://online.wsj.com/article/SB124217791927013441.html#articleTabs%3Dcomments

51. R. Stein. (2010, Jan 26). Rise in teenage pregnancy rate spurs new debate on arresting it. *The Washington Post*. Retrieved from http://www.washingtonpost.com/wp-dyn/content/article/2010/01/25/AR2010012503957.html

52. D. Cohn. (2011, Apr 8). New facts about families – Recent findings on family meals, cohabitation and divorce. *Pew Research Publications*. Retrieved from http://pewresearch.org/pubs/1959/family-meals-cohabitation-divorce-new-findings-contradict-conventional-wisdom

53. Online pharmacies: Internet tied to rise in drug use. (2011, May 15). *Huff Post – Health*. Retrieved from http://www.huffingtonpost.com/2011/05/16/online-pharmacies-interne_n_862088.html

54. A. Lin. Las Vegas Sands FCPA investigation spotlights Macau lawyer, profession. (2011, Mar 11). *Law.com*. Retrieved from http://www.law.com/jsp/article.jsp?id=1202485625524&Las_Vegas_Sands_FCPA_Investigation_Spotlights_Macau_Lawyer_Profession&slreturn=1&hbxlogin=1#

55. B. Jinks. (2010, Mar 18). MGM partner Ho is 'unsuitable," gambling agency says. Retrieved from http://www.bloomberg.com/apps/news?pid=newsarchive&sid=aqZga1sai1Lg

56. D. Lam. (2009, Sep 9). Unlocking the world of Chinese gambling. *Global Gaming Business*. Retrieved from http://ggbmagazine.com/issue/vol-8-no-9-september-2009/article/unlocking-the-world-of-chinese-gambling

57. Macau: Gambling capital of the world. *Companies Asia*. Retrieved from http://companies.asia/2011/01/29/macau-gambling-capital-of-the-world/

58. China population by age groups. *Starmass Dream Co*. Retrieved from http://www.starmass.com/china_review/demographic_data/population_by_age_group.htm

59. S. Ohlemmacher. *op. cit.*

60. L. Shrestha & E. Heisler. *op. cit.*

61. Annual disposable income per capita for urban households. *Starmass Dream Co*. Retrieved from http://www.starmass.com/china_review/living_index/chinese_disposable_income.htm

62. D. Farrell, U. Gersch, & E. Stephenson. (2006, Jun). The value of Chinas emerging middle class. *The McKinsey Quarterly*. http://www.mckinseyquarterly.com/The_value_of_Chinas_emerging_middle_class_1798

63. T. McHenry. Former Deputy General Council. MGM Resorts International. Telephone interview, April 29, 2011.

64. Ollie. (2010, Mar 9). China government to clean up crime in Macau after Beijing Olympics. *Macau.com*. Retrieved from http://www.a2zmacau.com/1289/china-government-to-clean-up-crime-in-macau-after-beijing-olympics/

65. N. Mark. EVP Operations. SBE. Personal Interview, May 16, 2011.

66. C. Jorgensen. Managing Director of Brand Marketing. Burson Marsteller. Personal interview, May 20, 2011.

67. International game technology (IGT). Casino Vendors.com. Retrieved on http://www.casinovendors.com/vendor/international-game-technology-igt/

68. H. Stutz. (2009, Aug 6). Lawsuits say IGT made false claims. *Casino City Times*. Retrieved from http://www.casinocitytimes.com/article/lawsuits-say-igt-made-false-claims-57263

69. WMS Industries Inc. (NYSE: WMS). *International Guild of Hospitality & Restaurant Managers*. http://www.hospitalityguild.com/Financial/Casinos/WMS.htm

70. T. McHenry. *op. cit.*

71. J. Goldner. Head of Travel and Meeting Services. Sketchers, USA. Telephone interview, May 20, 2011.

72. L. Benston. (2011, May 4). MGM's Jim Murren: 'Recovery has finally arrived.' *Vegas Inc*. http://www.vegasinc.com/news/2011/may/04/mgms-jim-murren-recovery-has-finally-arrived/

73. J. Goldner. *op. cit.*

74. T. O'Reiley. (2011, Apr 8). Las Vegas visitor count hurt by convention change. *Las Vegas Review Journal*. Retrieved from http://www.lvrj.com/business/las-vegas-visitor-count-rises-1-percent-over-last-february-119487069.html

75. L. Klatzkin. Former Jefferies Casino analyst and current LVS Consultant. Telephone interview, May 5, 2001.

76. P. Suciu. (2011, May 17). Staycation or USAcation for this summer? CNBC.com. http://mob.cnbc.com/special_reports/0/content/42785061/1

77. S. Hand. (2011, Feb 24). Slow recovery taking hold in Las Vegas: Moody's. Retrieved from http://www.reuters.com/article/2011/02/24/us-economy-nevada-las-vegas-idUSTRE71N62720110224

78. B. Baden. (2011, Mar 15). What happens after QE2 ends? *US News and World Report*. http://money.usnews.com/money/personal-finance/mutual-funds/articles/2011/03/15/what-happens-after-qe2-ends

79. L. Klatzkin. *op. cit.*

80. T. McHenry. *op. cit.*

81. N. Mark. *op. cit.*

82. A. Finnegan. (2010, Feb 17). Gaming execs: Competition could spur creativity in Las Vegas. *Las Vegas Sun*. http://www.lasvegassun.com/news/2010/nov/17/gaming-execs-competition-could-spur-creativity-las/

83. Macau's gaming operators concerned about competition from Singapore. (2010, Jul 21). Macau News. http://www.macaunews.com.mo/index.php?option=com_content&task=view&id=510&Itemid=45

84. W. S. Ruehl. (1996). Competition, Casino Spending, and Use of Casino Amenities *Journal of Travel Research*. 34(3), 57–62.

85. *Ibid.*

86. Macau casinos continue to crush the competition. (2010, Mar 7). *Casino News Authority*. http://webcache.googleusercontent.com/search?q=cache:DSRjHWFoN9cJ:casinonewsauthority.com/macau-casinos-continue-to-crush-the-competition/112280/+%22Macau+Casinos+Continue+to+Crush+the+Competition%22&cd=1&hl=en&ct=clnk&gl=us&source=www.google.com

87. Y. Mei Hui & K. Chen. (2010, Jun 21). Regional Industry Focus: Macau Gaming. *DBS Group Research Equity*. Retrieved from

https://www.dbsvresearch.com/research%5CDBS%5Cresearch.nsf/%28vwAllDocs%29/2E6C2AA9EEF532A04825776700300558/$FILE/0621Macau%20Gaming%20Sector.pdf

88. D. Jacobe. (2011, Feb 10). US consumers self-reported spending down in January. *Gallup*. Retrieved May 10, 2011 from http://www.gallup.com/poll/146060/consumers-self-reported-spending-down-january.aspx

89. MGM Resorts International. Form 10-K for the fiscal year ended December 31, 2007. *op. cit.*

90. MGM Resorts International. Form 10-K for the fiscal year ended December 31, 2010. *op. cit.*

91. S. Green. *op. cit.*

92. Wynn Resorts, Limited. Form 10-K for the fiscal year ended December 31, 2010. Retrieved from http://www.sec.gov/Archives/edgar/data/1174922/000119312511050547/d10k.htm

93. MGM Resorts International. Form 10-K for the fiscal year ended December 31, 2010. *op. cit.*

94. *Ibid.*

95. *Ibid.*

96. MGM Resorts International Q1 2011 earnings call transcript. (2011, May 4). *Morningstar*. Retrieved from http://www.morningstar.com/earnings/25423704-mgm-mirage-inc-mgm-q1-2011.aspx

97. MGM Resorts International. Form 10-K for the fiscal year ended December 31, 2010. *op. cit.*

98. W. S. Ruehl. (1996). Competition, Casino Spending, and Use of Casino Amenities *Journal of Travel Research*. 34(3), 57-62.

99. S. Green. *op. cit.*

100. Macau casinos continue to crush the competition. *op. cit.*

101. Stock Price Quotes. *Capital IQ*. Retrieved from http://www.capitaliq.com

102. MGM Resorts International. Form 10-K for the fiscal year ended December 31, 2010. *op. cit.*

103. Boyd Gaming Corporation. Form 10-K for the fiscal year ended December 31, 2010. Retrieved from http://www.sec.gov/Archives/edgar/data/906553/000144530511000424/byd10k2010.htm

104. Macau casinos continue to crush the competition. *op. cit.*

105. S. Green. *op. cit.*

106. MGM Resorts International. Form 10-K for the fiscal year ended December 31, 2010. *op. cit.*

107. K. Benston. (2010, Oct 29). Casino companies change names to elevate image. *Las Vegas Sun*. Retrieved from http://www.lasvegassun.com/news/2010/jun/15/mgm-mirage-changes-name-now-mgm-resorts-international

108. Selected interest rates (daily) – H.15. *Federal Reserve*. Retrieved from http://www.federalreserve.gov/releases/h15/data.htm

109. MGM Resorts International. Form 10-K for the fiscal year ended December 31, 2010. *op. cit.*

110. R. Gros. (2011, Apr 26). The World View. *Global Gaming Business. Vol 10. No. 5 May 2011*. Retrieved from http://ggbmagazine.com/issue-printer/vol-10-no-5-may-2011

111. Wynn Resorts, Limited. Form 10-K for the fiscal year ended December 31, 2010. *op. cit.*

112. MGM Resorts International. Form 10-K for the fiscal year ended December 31, 2010. *op. cit.*

113. Bellagio. Overview. 2011 Retrieved from http://www.bellagio.com/

114. Circus Circus. 2011. Overview. Retrieved from http://www.circuscircus.com/

115. MGM Resorts International. Form 10-K for the fiscal year ended December 31, 2010. *op. cit.*

116. *Ibid.*

117. Welcome to M Life. Retrieved from https://www.mlife.com/default.aspx

118. A. Finnegan. (2011, Jan 11). MGM launches M Life rewards program, will track nongaming spending. *Las Vegas Sun*. Retrieved from http://www.lasvegassun.com/news/2011/jan/11/mgm-resorts-launches-m-life-rewards-program-will-t/

119. Y. Mei Hui & K. Chen. *op. cit.*

120. T. McHenry, *op. cit.*

Rene Hatch, Nicholas Mau, John Gibson, Chris Scheich, Van Visweswaran, Melinda Wasinger
Arizona State University

Tina Borja
Rice University

Wall Street has called the end of an era and the beginning of the next one: The most important technology product no longer sits on your desk but rather fits in your hand.[1]

THE NEW YORK TIMES, MAY 26, 2010

Microsoft is arguably one of the biggest names in the technology industry, dominating the software and operating systems markets for more than three decades. The success of its initial public offering (IPO) in 1986 was unprecedented with its stock rising from $25 to $85 in less than a year and reportedly making about 12,000 of its employees virtually instant millionaires.[2] Aside from its entrepreneurial leadership, Microsoft's success is most often attributed not to its creation of innovative products, but rather to its strategic business practices of integrating products and building partner relationships.

And yet despite its unbroken domination of a notoriously fast-paced and fickle industry, the summer of 2010 may have marked the end of the Microsoft era as Apple usurped the title of world's most valuable technology company from Microsoft when Wall Street valued Apple at $222.12 billion and Microsoft at $219.18 billion.[3] As indicated by this shift, even though Microsoft continues to dominate the enterprise (business) market, it has started to lose ground to competitors in the consumer (individual) market. According to the *New York Times*, Apple's recent accomplishment "heralded an important cultural shift: consumer tastes have overtaken the needs of business as the leading force shaping technology."[4]

As always, the technology industry changes rapidly and, of late, Microsoft has lagged behind its competitors in the introduction of modern technologies such as tablets, gaming, mobile, and media. Equally damning, the products it has offered are often judged outdated by the time they reach market. Despite the fact that PC sales still dwarf sales of modern technologies, Microsoft would seem to have been caught asleep at the wheel in regard to where the industry is heading. The rapid growth in smartphone technology coupled with businesses leveraging consumer products (such as smartphones and tablets) to increase employee productivity and communication led to smartphone sales growing five times faster than PC sales in 2010.[5,6]

Making things even more difficult, in the past, Microsoft was able to attract and retain some of the most brilliant technological minds in the world; its human capital was a major asset and one of the main reasons Microsoft is number one in the software industry today. However, even with an overall attrition rate relatively low for the industry, Microsoft is losing many of its creative resources to the competition and, in the past year, many top executives—Chris Liddell (CFO), Robbie Bach (Entertainment Head), J Allard (Device Design Leader), Stephen Elop (Business Division Chief), and Ray Ozzie (Bill Gates' successor as Chief Software Architect)—have retired or left for other companies as well.[7] Mark Lucovsky, named one of Microsoft's 16 Distinguished Engineers, left for Google in 2004 citing in his blog even then that Microsoft's size and inability to act quickly led to his departure—a complaint the ensuing years have done nothing to assuage.[8] Employee concerns such as wage and benefit reductions despite high profits, bureaucratic management that stifles creativity, and poor stock performance now regularly surface through media interviews, court testimony, and personal blogs.[9]

It would appear that what was once considered a radical upstart has somehow become the lumbering establishment to eschew.

Product History

Microsoft was established in 1975 when long-time friends Bill Gates and Paul Allen saw the Altair 8800 microcomputer featured in the January 1975 issue of *Popular Electronics*. They quickly recognized the beginning of a new market and immediately contacted Altair with an offer to provide software for what was the world's first PC.[10] After getting the green light from Altair, Gates dropped out of Harvard and Allen quit his job as a programmer at Honeywell to work around the clock to develop BASIC for the Altair 8800.[11]

Microsoft was able to gain an early foothold in the growing computer industry by striking an exclusive agreement with IBM in the early 80s to provide BASIC software and MS-DOS operating systems on all IBM PCs while retaining the right to sell these products to IBM's competitors. At the time of the agreement, Microsoft didn't even have a system to sell, but Gates didn't let that stop them from closing the deal. Microsoft quickly acquired an existing operating system from another company, rewrote it, and marketed it as MS-DOS. This strategic move made Microsoft a powerhouse as PCs rapidly outsold the competition and eventually dominated the computer market.[12]

In 1983, Microsoft replaced the MS-DOS operating system with Windows to compete with Macintosh's Apple computer interface. This early version of Windows was a graphical user interface that eliminated the necessity of DOS prompt commands.[13] Seven years later, Microsoft released a new and highly enhanced version—Windows 3.0—that sold more than one million copies in four months. The coupling of Windows on the less expensive PC meant consumers could have the ease of operation of the Macintosh at a much lower cost.[14] Microsoft's pairing of Windows with PCs established its business model as the high-volume, low-cost software provider of choice and, once again, Microsoft's strategic relationship with IBM would lead it to dominate the market.

On the software front, Microsoft began releasing its office products in the mid 80s beginning with Microsoft Works, a program that combined features found in typical office applications such as a word processor, database, and spreadsheet. Microsoft Office—a bundle of applications including Word and Excel—was introduced in 1989.[15] In less than two years, Microsoft Office represented more than half of Microsoft's total office applications sales.[16] In 1994 alone, over seven million units of Microsoft Office were sold, making it the number one product in its category.[17]

Doing its part to usher in the age of the Internet, in 1995, Microsoft released Internet Explorer, a technology providing Internet browsing, email, and multi-media features. Microsoft returned to its strategy of bundling software with its release of Internet Explorer 3.0 in 1996. The Internet Explorer bundle included Internet Mail and News, Address Book, NetMeeting, and Windows Media Player. While other browsers charged for their products, Microsoft included the Internet Explorer bundle free with Windows.[18] By 2002, Internet Explorer dominated the market with 96 percent market share.[19,20]

Despite the success of Internet Explorer, the Internet brought rapid changes to the software market; new competitors started to appear and the emergence of cloud-based computing poses a serious threat to software "sold in a box."[21] In an effort to enter the lucrative search engine and ad market, Microsoft made an unsuccessful attempt to acquire Yahoo! for $47.5 billion in 2008. Instead, in June 2009, Microsoft introduced its own search engine—Bing.[22] At present, Microsoft's Bing is third in the search engine rankings, holding 11.5 percent of market share compared to Google's 66.3 percent and Yahoo!'s 16.5 percent as of October 2010 (see Exhibit 1).

Recognizing the potential of the gaming market, Microsoft launched its Xbox gaming console in 2001. Xbox Live—an Internet multi-player gaming service—followed in 2002 and by 2010, had reached 23 million subscribers.[23] Kinect, a motion-based gaming accessory for Xbox designed to compete directly with the Wii and PlayStation Move, sold a record 2.5 million units in less than a month when released in late 2010 and continues to post strong sales.[24]

In June 2010, after years of little to no improvement to its antiquated mobile operating system, Microsoft belatedly introduced the Kin to compete in the rapidly growing smartphone market. However, due to low sales, Microsoft pulled Kin from the market after just two months.[25] Attributing its failure to poor security and a missed target demographic, Microsoft launched Windows Phone 7 in October 2010; that too has fallen short, but remains on the market.[26] While the phone is still relatively new, its problems and slow start out of

Exhibit 1 Summary of Search Engine Market Share

Core Search Entity	Explicit Core Search Share (%)		
	Sep-10	Oct-10	Point Change
Total Explicit Core Search	*100.0%*	*100.0%*	*N/A*
Google Sites	66.1%	66.3%	0.2
Yahoo! Sites	16.7%	16.5%	−0.2
Microsoft Sites	11.2%	11.5%	0.3
Ask Network	3.7%	3.6%	−0.1
AOL LLC Network	2.3%	2.1%	−0.2
excludes contextually driven searches that do not reflect specific user intent to interact with the search results			

Source: Data gathered at comScore.com, accessed Nov 2010

the gate have made it difficult for Microsoft to alter the growing perception of consumers that Microsoft is nothing more than a fair substitute to the new technology of its competitors.

The House That Bill Built

Organizational Structure

In 2005, Steve Ballmer, Microsoft's President and CEO, re-organized Microsoft's structure in an effort to "align our business groups in a way that will enhance decision making and speed of execution." Three new divisions—Products and Services, Business, and Entertainment and Devices—were added and Ray Ozzie, Microsoft's new Chief Software Architect, was tapped to oversee them.[27]

Despite the reorganization, many analysts didn't think Ballmer had gone far enough and called on him to take more drastic measures. Additionally, analysts and employees were echoing one another in their suggestion that Microsoft's size and structure was impeding its ability to innovate and compete. In 2010, Goldman Sachs officially downgraded Microsoft's rating from

"buy" to "neutral" and recommended that the company split its enterprise and consumer businesses. Justifying their decision, Goldman Sachs analyst Sarah Friar wrote, "In our view the intrinsic value of the shares cannot be realized if the status quo remains intact." She continued by saying, "In addition, we have increased caution near term on a more elongated PC refresh cycle, combined with the newer threat of notebook cannibalization from tablets, where Windows does not yet have a presence."[28] Ballmer continues to vehemently disagree with the analysts' recommendations and has stated that Microsoft will not divide its business.[29]

According to a Microsoft employee who preferred to remain anonymous due to a non-disclosure agreement, "From an internal point of view, Microsoft's biggest issues are: bureaucracy due to size, multiple strategies that can sometimes conflict, and same people [with the] same ideas."[30]

Business Divisions

Microsoft's corporate structure is divided into five business divisions, each with its own unique blend of often overlapping competitors (see Exhibit 2).

Exhibit 2 Summary of Business Segments by Product/Competition/Consumer

Products and Services	Key Competitors	Consumers
Windows and Windows Live		
Windows OS: **Windows 7** (including Home Basic, Home Premium, Professional, Ultimate, Enterprise, and Starter Edition); **Windows Vista** (including Home Basic, Home Premium, Ultimate, Business, Enterprise and Starter Edition); and **Windows XP Home**	Apple OS; Google OS; Linux Apple, Google, Mozilla, and Opera Software Company offer software that competes with Internet Explorer, a component of Windows.	OEMs (80%); Enterprise; Consumer
Windows Live suite of applications and web services	Google and Yahoo!	Enterprise; Consumer
Microsoft Business Division		
Microsoft Office; **Microsoft SharePoint;** **Microsoft Office Web Apps** (online companions to Microsoft Word, Excel, PowerPoint and OneNote)	Adobe; Apple; Corel; Google; IBM; Novell; Oracle; Red Hat; Zoho **OpenOffice.org** (project providing a freely downloadable cross-platform application that has been adapted by various commercial software vendors—including IBM, Novell, Oracle, and Red Hat—to sell under their brands)	Enterprise (80%); Consumer
Microsoft Dynamics ERP and **CRM**	Infor and Sage for small businesses Oracle and SAP for large businesses Salesforce.com on demand	Enterprise
Server and Tools Division		
Windows Server OS; Windows Azure; Microsoft SQL Server; SQL Azure; Visual Studio; Silverlight; System Center products; Biz Talk Server; Microsoft Consulting Services; Premier product support services; and other products and services.	Hewlett-Packard; IBM; Oracle (all offer their own versions of the Unix OS preinstalled on server hardware)	Enterprise; OEMs

(Continued)

Exhibit 2 Summary of Business Segments by Product/Competition/Consumer (*Continued*)

Products and Services	Key Competitors	Consumers
Online Services Division		
Bing; Microsoft adCenter; MSN; Atlas (all online tools for advertisers & publishers)	Google and Yahoo!	Merchants; Consumer
Entertainment and Devices Division		
Xbox 360 console and games; **Xbox LIVE**	Sony; Nintendo; various game developers	Consumer
Windows Phone	Apple; Google; Nokia; Openwave Systems; Palm; QUALCOMM; Research In Motion; Symbian	Consumer
Embedded device OS	IBM; Intel; versions of embeddable Linux	Consumer
Zune	Apple; other media device manufacturers	Consumer
Mediaroom	Various competitors providing elements of an Internet protocol television delivery platform	Consumer
Numerous consumer software and hardware products (such as Mac Office, mice, keyboards)	Various computer and hardware manufacturers, many of which are partners	Consumer

Source: Microsoft 2010 Annual Report

Windows and Windows Live Division (aka Windows Division). The main products of the Windows Division are Windows operating systems (OS), Windows Live, and Internet Explorer. This division accounted for almost half of Microsoft's total operating income for fiscal year 2010 (see Exhibit 3).

Microsoft's primary OS competitors are Mac OS X (Apple) and Linux (a free, open source OS collaboration mainly used in servers) with, as of November 2010, 11.6 and .52 percent market share, respectively.[31] Because 80 percent of Windows Division products are distributed through original equipment manufacturers, sales of both Windows and Internet Explorer depend heavily on the strength of the PC market.[32] With demand for new mobile devices such as smartphones and tablets growing rapidly, many believe these devices could take a large piece of the PC market, and with it, Windows Division revenue. In addition, Internet Explorer faces multiple competitors including Google, Mozilla, and Apple's Safari. Microsoft faces an uphill battle as recent studies

Exhibit 3 Revenue and Operating Income by Business Segment

Year End June 30	2010	2009	2008
Revenue (in millions)			
Windows & Windows Live Division	$17,788	$14,690	$16,815
Server and Tools	14,878	14,276	13,217
Online Services Division	2,198	2,110	2,164
Microsoft Business Division	18,909	18,864	18,904
Entertainment and Devices Division	8,114	8,035	8,502
Unallocated and other	597	462	818
Consolidated	$62,484	$58,437	$60,420
Operating Income (Loss) (in millions)			
Windows & Windows Live Division	$12,089	$ 9,569	$11,876
Server and Tools	4,990	4,638	3,845
Online Services Division	(2,436)	(1,760)	(619)
Microsoft Business Division	11,664	11,454	11,681
Entertainment and Devices Division	589	(3)	314
Reconciling amounts	(2,798)	(3,535)	(4,826)
Consolidated	$24,098	$20,363	$22,271

Source: Microsoft 2010 Annual Report

show that, for the first time, consumers are turning away from Internet Explorer to alternative browsers (see Exhibit 4).[33]

Business Division. Microsoft's Business Division is the second largest source of revenue for Microsoft (see again, Exhibit 3). The Business Division's main products include Microsoft Office, Sharepoint, Dynamics ERP and CRM, and Office Web Apps. Despite the diversity of these offerings, Microsoft Office is the powerhouse of this division, accounting for more than 90 percent of its sales.[34] Microsoft Office has overshadowed its competition and steadily captured 94 percent of market share for several years running.[35] According to Microsoft, Office has 500 million users and is installed on more than 81 percent of enterprise PCs. Google Docs—an online, cloud-based alternative to Office—is its nearest competitor, claiming 4 percent of businesses and 25 million users after less than four years on the market.[36] Google Docs charges $50 annually per user for businesses but is offered free of charge to personal users. Microsoft Office 2010 on the other hand ranges from a one-time fee of $119 to $499 per license (an amount paid again upon the release and purchase of subsequent versions) depending on the bundle configuration purchased.[37] As web-based software grows in popularity with the emergence of cloud computing, the number of competitors and intensity of competition could seriously damage Microsoft's software dominance.[38] Richard Williams, an analyst with Cross Research, says, "Google is not the threat that it will be once the 'virtual desktop' becomes a no-brainer. That's the time Microsoft really has to worry about."[39]

Server and Tools. The Server and Tools Division at Microsoft provides software, tools, and services designed for enterprise systems and IT professionals and

Exhibit 4 Top Browser Share Trend: May 2009 to February 2011

Month	Internet Explorer	Firefox	Chrome	Safari	Opera	Other
May 2009	68.10%	22.75%	2.18%	3.70%	2.06%	1.21%
Aug 2009	66.97%	22.98%	2.84%	4.07%	2.04%	1.10%
Nov 2009	63.62%	24.72%	3.93%	4.36%	2.31%	1.06%
Feb 2010	61.58%	24.23%	5.61%	4.45%	2.35%	1.77%
May 2010	59.75%	24.32%	7.04%	4.77%	2.43%	1.69%
Aug 2010	60.48%	22.90%	7.50%	5.15%	2.36%	1.61%
Nov 2010	58.44%	22.76%	9.26%	5.55%	2.20%	1.79%
Feb 2011	56.77%	21.74%	10.93%	6.36%	2.15%	2.06%

Source: Data gathered at http://marketshare.hitslink.com/

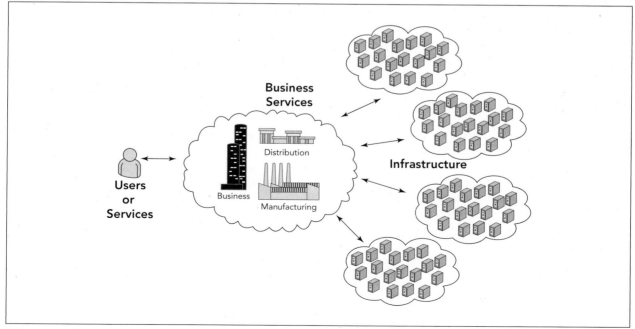

developers. This segment is the third largest contributor to Microsoft's operating income with $4,990 million in 2010 (see again, Exhibit 3). Annual licensing agreements contribute about 50 percent of the division's annual revenue. Approximately 30 percent of the remaining revenue is from transactional licensing agreements, original equipment manufacturers, and retail sales, with the remaining 20 percent coming from enterprise services.[40] Due to the complexity of the products and services in this division, Microsoft has many different competitors. For example, Windows Server OS includes various services and tools such as Internet Information Services (IIS) and SQL Server, each with unique competitors such as Sun and Oracle, known for their web servers and database management systems, respectively.

Online Services Division. The Online Services Division, which includes Microsoft's search engine and online advertising platform, Bing, posted a loss from operations for fiscal year 2010 of $2,436 million. This was mainly due to an agreement penned with Yahoo! in 2009 to provide the algorithmic and search platform for Yahoo! Web sites.[41] Under the pact, Yahoo! keeps 88 percent of the search-generated ad revenue for the first five years, decreasing incrementally thereafter.[42] This strategic partnership was formed as a line of attack on Google's 65 percent stronghold on the search engine market (see again, Exhibit 1). Although Microsoft posted a short-term loss due to the Yahoo! agreement, it anticipates the alliance will have future benefits. As an indication of this, even though Online Services is Microsoft's smallest division, Bing has gotten the attention of its top rival with Google turning the tables to take a page from Microsoft's playbook— Google is letting Microsoft experiment with Bing and then pilfering its most popular features for its own site.[43] According to an interview with Google's CEO Eric Schmidt, he considers Bing his number one competitor. "Bing is a well-run, highly competitive search engine."[44]

Entertainment and Devices Division. The Entertainment and Devices Division offerings include the Xbox platform, Windows Phone, and Zune digital music platform. The products in these markets have very rapid lifecycles with new products/technology continually entering the consumer market. For example, gaming and entertainment consoles have a lifecycle of only 5 to 10 years and competition is fierce with an emphasis on price and innovation.[45] Nintendo and Sony are the most prominent competitors for the Xbox platform with Sony's PlayStation 3 steadily taking market share from both Nintendo and Microsoft, resulting in

a 3.9 percent decline year after year to 22.68 percent for Xbox.[46] Microsoft is hoping that strong sales from the 2010 Kinect-for-Xbox release may help make up lost ground.

Even less optimistically, however, the Entertainment and Devices Division hasn't been successful with its non-gaming products. Zune, a digital media player marketed to rival Apple's iPod, failed to make even a small dent in iPod's huge market share, resulting in many stores removing it from their inventory. Similarly, the poor sales performances of the Kin and Windows Phone do not bode well for Microsoft's future in the smartphone industry. Lackluster phone sales and Microsoft's failure to introduce a tablet or slate device have left many analysts wondering if Microsoft can compete in this fast-paced and "hip" consumer market. Microsoft's now former Chief Software Architect, Ray Ozzie, commented on his blog about Microsoft's poor performance in these markets saying, "Our early and clear vision notwithstanding, [competitors'] execution has surpassed our own in mobile experiences, in the seamless fusion of hardware and software and services, and in social networking and myriad new forms of Internet-centric social interaction."[47]

More Glitches in the System

Sales and Manufacturing. Microsoft's customer base is vast, ranging from individual consumers for its Entertainment and Devices and Online Services divisions to companies and original equipment manufacturers for its Windows, Business, and Server and Tools divisions (see again, Exhibit 2). Historically, Microsoft's products and services were geared toward the enterprise market. However, while businesses may have outfitted their employees with electronic products in the past, increasingly, companies are allowing employees to use personal devices at and for work. Unfortunately for Microsoft, a growing number of these devices are Macs, iPads, iPhones, and Android smartphones. Microsoft is now attempting to capture more of the consumer market with products such as Bing, Windows Phone, and the Xbox platform as it recognizes that its command of the enterprise market may be at risk if it cannot gain the attention of personal consumers.[48]

While the Entertainment and Devices Division utilizes third-party manufacturers for the majority of the software and hardware components of its products, Microsoft's other divisions develop the bulk of their products in-house. Microsoft uses multiple vendors for its outsourced manufacturing needs and maintains volume discount contracts with an assortment of vendors for raw materials, supplies, and components for all of its divisions.[49]

Litigation. With intellectual property claims part and parcel to the industry coupled with its aggressive business practices, Microsoft has found itself in the defendant's seat for a plethora of lawsuits in its 35-year history. Its first foray at the federal level was in 1991 when the Federal Trade Commission opened its investigation of Microsoft and IBM for limiting competitiveness with the installation of Microsoft Windows OS on IBM PCs. Over the next decade, Microsoft faced many lawsuits for its aggressive and exclusionary behaviors and practices. In 1998, the US Justice Department filed an antitrust lawsuit against Microsoft for demanding that PC manufacturers bundle Internet Explorer with their hardware products in order to obtain Windows. As a result, in 2000, Microsoft was ordered by a judgment to break up into two companies; however, a federal appeals court reversed the decision in 2001.[50] In 2003, the European Union found Microsoft guilty of monopolistic practices and continues to investigate Microsoft today, filing additional cases in recent years.[51,52] According to Microsoft insiders, this antitrust scrutiny has defined Microsoft as we know it today. Mary Jo Foley, longtime Microsoft analyst, said, "In speaking with several Microsoft insiders, antitrust suits and oversight were mentioned, time and again, as having changed irrevocably the course of the company."[53]

Above and beyond the antitrust lawsuits it faced for monopolistic practices, Microsoft has had to mount a legal defense more times than it probably cares to remember. The following are just a few examples.

- In 1988, Apple sued Microsoft for copyright infringement claiming that Windows OS had stolen the "look and feel" of the Macintosh OS; the case was dismissed after four years.[54]
- Again, Apple sued Microsoft in 1995 for stealing several thousand programming lines of its QuickTime software; the case was settled with an undisclosed payoff estimated to be between $500 million to $2 billion.[55]
- Spyglass won an $8 million settlement against Microsoft for deception after licensing its browser to Microsoft for a percentage of sales. Spyglass was unable to profit from the deal because Microsoft turned the browser into Internet Explorer and bundled it with Windows at no cost to the consumer.[56]

For fiscal year 2010, Microsoft had accrued about $1 billion in other liabilities and $236 million in long-term liabilities for contingent legal matters.[57] Again, Mary Jo Foley: "Microsoft brass know that every product development and marketing decision Microsoft makes for the rest of the time it is in existence will be scrutinized for possible lawsuit opportunities."[58]

The Human Factor. As previously mentioned, Microsoft has recently lost several talented employees to its competitors. Many analysts and employees have expressed concern that Microsoft has gotten too big and cumbersome to adapt quickly enough to changes in the fast-paced technology industry. "Every time Bill [Gates] and Steve [Ballmer] made a change to be more like other big companies, we lost a little bit of what made Microsoft special," says a former Microsoft VP.[59] Microsoft may have a tough time attracting top talent to a company "that is not a leader in a number of key, hot markets."[60]

A second factor causing dissatisfaction among employees is the widening compensation gap between employees and executives. In 2005 and with a $56 billion cash reserve, Microsoft implemented a new executive incentive plan that would pay each of its 120 VPs a salary of one million while the remaining workforce would continue to be paid market rates.[61] Around the same time, Microsoft announced reductions to employee benefits such as increased prescription co-pays and reduced stock options. The reduced benefits and flat stock performance negatively affected employee morale and made the once unthinkable idea of trading teams not only reasonable, but unsurprising.[62]

The Cloud with the Silver Lining?

The technology market stands on the verge of a major market shift with the increase in cloud computing. Although there are many definitions of cloud computing, essentially, it is online software and data retention services. Online software eliminates the need for individuals and businesses to buy individual or site licenses or install software. Data can be stored and, if desired, easily shared "on the cloud" rather than taking up space on a hard driver or server. Most often, cloud computing is available via a subscription-based or pay-per-use fee structure and is anticipated to have a large impact on the software industry in the near future. Chris Capossela, Sr. VP for Microsoft, predicts, "In five years, half of all Exchange mailboxes will be in the cloud, and 100 percent of Office users will be using at least some cloud features."[63] Steve Ballmer is betting on the cloud becoming the new frontier and estimates it will become a $3.3 trillion industry;[64] thus Microsoft is investing heavily in its cloud computing platform. According to its 2010 Annual Report,

In fiscal 2010, Microsoft invested $8.7 billion in research and development, with most of that devoted to cloud technologies. Today, roughly 70 percent of Microsoft's 40,000 engineers work on cloud-related products and services, and in fiscal 2011 that number will grow to nearly 90 percent.[65]

Perhaps unbeknownst to many users, Microsoft has many cloud applications already in use including Windows Live Hotmail and Windows Live Messenger with more than 300 million users, Xbox Live with 25 million subscribers, and online versions of Microsoft Office 2010 and SharePoint.[66] It has also delivered new cloud computing platform innovations including Windows Azure and SQL Azure. Windows Azure is an enterprise cloud platform that delivers "power, cooling, and automation technologies to create datacenter efficiency" and SQL Azure is a database management system.[67]

One of the biggest concerns for cloud platform customers is security and control issues with public cloud services. In November 2010, Microsoft VP Brad Anderson announced its private cloud offerings will "fulfill the need at the infrastructure level while providing a clear migration path to cloud services at the platform level."[68] However, the potential for new competitors to enter the cloud applications market is substantial and will continue to grow as the technology matures and reaches consumer acceptance. At present, the frontrunners for cloud platform services include Amazon Web Service, Google AppEngine, and Force.com from SalesForce.com.[69]

Key Competitors

Although every Microsoft division has competition, as a whole, Microsoft's key competitors are Google and Apple. Google competes in four of Microsoft's five divisions and Apple competes in three.

Google

Google is a global company providing Internet search, online advertising, and cloud computing technology. More than 97 percent of its 2009 revenues came from its online advertising program that allows businesses to place targeted advertisements on Google Web sites.[70] While its user base is primarily consumer, it is attempting to gain enterprise market share with its cloud computing platform. Google's growth strategy includes multiple corporate acquisitions and, cited with possible anti-competitive behavior, Google has recently drawn the attention of the Federal Trade Commission.[71]

The corporate culture at Google is notoriously informal, making it an intensely popular employer for the new generation of computing innovators and keeping Google in *Fortune* magazine's "Top Five Companies to Work For" list for four years in a row.[72] Google is heavily focused on creative innovation and encourages its engineers to spend 20 percent of their time working on great ideas they may have that don't necessarily fall within their usual job description.[73]

Apple

Apple's core products are consumer electronics (iPhone, iPad, and iPod), PCs (Macintosh), and software (Mac OS X and iTunes media browser).[74] Part of Apple's more recent strategy has been in creating an "entertainment hub" that revolves around its iTunes Store. Apple's iTunes Store is an online music, application, and e-book store that makes it easy for Apple product users to purchase and manage media content.[75] iTunes was the first entertainment hub of its kind and a critical factor in the success of Apple's electronic products. Apple markets primarily to consumers and, with 300 locations in 10 countries, its retail stores provide unprecedented sales, training, and maintenance support.[76] Apple has established an avid and devoted customer base and was named the "Most Admired Company in the World" by *Fortune* magazine in 2008, 2009, and 2010.[77] Almost 60 percent of Apple's 2010 revenue came from consumer electronics sales with 27 percent from sales of PCs.[78]

Looking at Microsoft's Source Code

For the last few decades, Microsoft has been the high-volume, low-cost software and services provider of the computer industry. Microsoft's strategy has involved several facets including innovation through strategic acquisitions and alliances, coordinated internal development, and a strong distribution channel.

Integrated Innovation

"Integrated Innovation" is a phrase coined by Bill Gates to describe Microsoft's strategy of designing products built on the same technologies to make the features of all products compatible with one another. This strategy gave Microsoft an advantage because competitors could not easily integrate their products with Microsoft products. Microsoft also used this concept to promote new products by bundling them with established products to promote usage.[79]

A great as it may sound, Gates' integrated innovation strategy has its issues as well. Due to the dependencies the mandate of integration creates, the development process of new products is slowed. Coordinating products forces design teams to schedule time to work together and can complicate the design. Additionally, and often thwarting its original intent, integration forces developers to spend more time updating existing products rather than creating new ones, thus negating the "innovation" part of the phrase.[80] Finally, it is important to remember that it was in the successful pursuit of this concept that Microsoft was eventually led to its monopolistic business practices and antitrust woes.

Antitrust suits and coordination difficulties aside, by incorporating this strategy Microsoft was able to embed its products (specifically Windows and Office) into corporate culture, making it difficult for competitors to steal market share. However, it appears that Google is positioning itself to gain some of the enterprise market share with its recent new product announcements. In November 2010, Google VP Linus Upson boldly predicted, "Sixty percent of Windows PCs in business could be replaced with machines running [Google's] forthcoming Chrome OS."[81] In addition, Google is offering free downloadable software that will connect Microsoft Office products to Google's cloud in an attempt to entice consumers who are reluctant to change their software.[82]

Strategic Relationships

One of the main strengths leading to Microsoft's success has been the ability of its leaders to develop strategic relationships with critical partners from IBM to Yahoo! to Apple. Examples of this success range from exclusive software agreements to product development partnerships to gaining rights to display the Microsoft logo on original equipment manufacturer hardware. Many times, it has been these partnership agreements that have catapulted Microsoft's growth even more so than its products.

In the process, however, Microsoft has earned somewhat of a cutthroat reputation as a partner or ally. As evidenced by the volume of lawsuits for patent and copyright infringement and anticompetitive behavior, many firms that have entered into partnerships with Microsoft have later accused the company of stealing their intellectual property. As an example, internal documents subpoenaed for an unrelated lawsuit revealed that Microsoft violated nondisclosure agreements by using business plans from Go Corporation to develop PenWindows—a competing product—and then influenced Intel to reduce its investment in Go.[83] In addition, Stac Electronics was awarded a $120 million settlement after it accused Microsoft of stealing its data compression code and using it in MS-DOS 6.[84]

Despite its reputation, Microsoft continues to be able to forge beneficial business relationships. Using but a drop in the bucket to provide some examples, at present, Microsoft has signed on in the smartphone market with Nokia;[85] in a cloud computing partnership using Windows Azure with Dell, HP, ebay, and Fujitsu;[86] with Gorillaz—the self-proclaimed "world's greatest animated band" and indie-culture icon—to promote the release of Internet Explorer 9;[87] and even the North Carolina Public School System where Microsoft Learning will launch a Microsoft IT Academy Program within every public high school in the state to provide students with real-world technology skills as well as the training and curriculum necessary for teachers to do so.[88] Time will tell if the only reason Microsoft is able to negotiate its alliances is simply because, as the dominant player in all things computer, other companies are too afraid to say no. If so, Microsoft may find itself at an all too unfamiliar disadvantage before long.

Acquisitions

Even though many consider Microsoft to be a leader of innovation, upon closer inspection one finds that many of Microsoft's products and services have been either acquired or modified from the innovations of its competitors.[89] As examples, QDOS was purchased from Seattle Computer Products and then modified and sold to IBM as MS-DOS, Apple accused Microsoft of stealing the "look and feel" of Macintosh when developing Windows, and Internet Explorer originated from a browser developed by Spyglass. In the case of Microsoft, it would seem it wasn't the innovation of its products that made it an industry leader but instead its strategy of aligning itself "at the center of the entire PC industry."[90]

Product Development and Distribution

According to Microsoft's 2010 Annual Report,

Our model for growth is based on our ability to initiate and embrace disruptive technology trends, to enter new markets, both in terms of geographies and product areas, and to drive broad adoption of the products and services we develop and market. Increasingly, we are taking a global approach to innovation.[91]

Even though the majority of its research and development activities are conducted at its corporate location in Washington State, Microsoft also maintains research and development facilities around the world to remain competitive in the global market.[92]

Microsoft serves a worldwide customer base and maintains offices in more than 100 countries.[93] To customize its products for its geographically diverse customers, Microsoft has regional operations centers in Ireland (serving Europe, Africa, and the Middle East), Singapore (serving the Asia Pacific region), and in the US (serving North, South, and Latin Americas) and routinely localizes its products to allow for differences in languages and conventions.[94] Approximately 42 percent of revenue earned for fiscal 2010 originated outside the US (see Exhibit 5).

Microsoft distributes and markets its products and services through original equipment manufacturers, distributors, retailers, and online. The majority of Microsoft's software, including Windows and Office, is licensed to original equipment manufacturers for distribution as pre-installed software on new PCs.

Exhibit 5 Revenue by Major Geographic Region

(in millions)			
Year End June 30	2010	2009	2008
US(a)	$36,173	$33,052	$35,928
Other countries	26,311	25,385	24,492
Total	$62,484	$58,437	$60,420

(a)Includes shipments to customers in the US and licensing to certain OEMs and multinational organizations.

Source: Microsoft 2010 Annual Report

Microsoft has agreements with almost all of the multinational original equipment manufacturers including HP, Lenovo, Dell, Acer, and others. Most businesses purchase licenses in volume through large account resellers, distributors, value-added resellers, original equipment manufacturers, or retailers. Microsoft also sells directly to large organizations through enterprise agreements. If not already pre-installed on their computers, individual consumers primarily purchase Microsoft products through retail outlets such as Best Buy, Walmart, and Target. In keeping with Apple's model, Microsoft recently announced it would open a limited number of retail stores to better connect with consumers and learn about their product preferences and buying habits (see Exhibit 6).[95] Microsoft is also expanding the portfolio of products and services it markets and distributes online as part of its cloud computing solution.[96]

Financial Results

Despite its seemingly myriad difficulties, fiscal 2010 was a record-breaking year for Microsoft with a 7 percent increase in revenue over fiscal 2009, reaching $62.5 billion. Efficiency also increased as operating income of $24.1 billion exceeded the previous year by 18 percent. Diluted earnings per share jumped 30 percent to $2.10 while Microsoft distributed almost $16 billion to shareholders through stock buybacks and dividends (see Exhibits 7A and 7B).

Microsoft's strong financial performance in 2010 is primarily attributable to healthy sales of the new Windows 7 and the recovering global PC market. Over the last few years, the PC market declined as companies delayed IT purchases due to the unfavorable economic conditions. Microsoft has steadily increased its revenue over the past 10 years with the exception of 2009 and yet, after climbing 61,000 percent since its IPO in 1986 to reach its peak in 2001, its stock has since remained relatively flat and key competitors have repeatedly outperformed Microsoft over the last five years (see Exhibits 8A and 8B).

The Code Writers

Bill Gates

If there is one prominent and defining trait of Bill Gates it would be his competitive nature and desire to win at almost any cost. This characteristic was evident from the

Exhibit 6 Microsoft Retail Store Locations

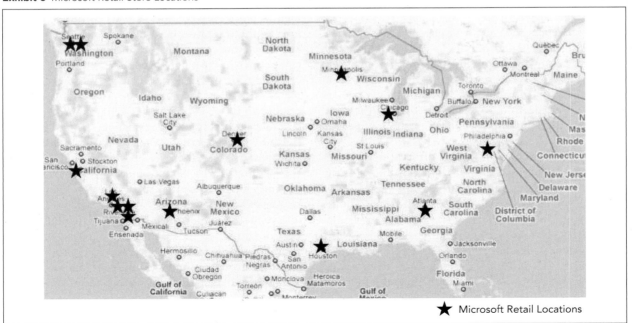

Source: Data from Microsoft Web site – information accessed September 2011

Exhibit 7A Financial Highlights: 2006 to 2010

(in millions, except per share data)					
Year Ended June 30	2010	2009	2008	2007	2006
Revenue	$62,484	$58,437	$60,420	$51,122	$44,282
Operating income	$24,098	$20,363	$22,271[c]	$18,438	$16,380
Net income	$18,760	$14,569	$17,681[c]	$14,065	$12,599
Diluted earnings per share	$ 2.10	$ 1.62	$ 1.87	$ 1.42	$ 1.20
Cash dividends declared per share	$ 0.52	$ 0.52	$ 0.44	$ 0.40	$ 0.35
Cash and cash equivalents and short-term investments	$36,788	$31,447	$23,662	$23,411	$34,161
Total assets	$86,113	$77,888	$72,793	$63,171	$69,597
Long-term obligations	$13,791[a]	$11,296[b]	$ 6,621	$ 8,320	$ 7,051
Stockholders' equity	$46,175	$39,558	$36,286	$31,097	$40,104

[a]Includes $1.25 billion of convertible debt securities issued in June 2010 and $3.75 billion of debt securities issued in May 2009.

[b]Includes $3.75 billion of debt securities issued in May 2009.

[c]Includes charge of $1.4 billion (€899 million) related to the fine imposed by the European Commission in February 2008.

Source: Microsoft 2010 Annual Report

Exhibit 7B Financial Results with Percentage Change: 2008 to 2010

(in millions)	2010	2009	2008	% Change 2010 vs. 2009	% Change 2009 vs. 2008
Revenue	$62,484	$ 58,437	$ 60,420	7%	−3%
Operating income	$24,098	$ 20,363	$ 22,271	18%	−9%
Diluted earnings per share	$ 2.10	$ 1.62	$ 1.87	30%	−13%

Source: Microsoft 2010 Annual Report

start with negotiating a 64 percent share in Microsoft from co-founder Paul Allen one of Gates' first big victories.[97] This story illustrates how Gates eventually became the richest man in the world.

His competitive nature was visible in his aggressive leadership style as well, continually pushing his staff to achieve more. He was known for calling employees on weekends and evenings if they weren't in the office to ask, "Why aren't you working?" He also held very tight financial control, many times reviewing executive expense statements himself and flying coach for years after making his first million.[98] Many former employees go so far as to describe his management style as "bullying" or confrontational.[99]

Gates always sought the upper hand in his business dealings and partnerships and, as a result, has been accused of strong-arm tactics on more than one occasion. Bob Kutnick, a former executive of AST Research, recalled, ". . . a letter from Microsoft stating that they would give us a better price on DOS if we would take DESQview [a direct competitor] out of the box."[100] Ultimately, Gates was a farsighted and shrewd businessman, singlehandedly developing many of the strategic relationships in Microsoft's history. Philippe

Kahn, a technology innovator, described Bill Gates in 1987: "He has everyone—even enemies like IBM, Apple, Tandy, and Compaq—believing he's their biggest ally. Of course, he's the one that's the biggest winner."[101]

When asked to explain Microsoft's success, Gates responded, "Our original vision." From his book, *The Road Ahead,* "We glimpsed what lay beyond that Intel 8080 chip, and then acted on it. We asked, 'What if computing were nearly free?' We believed there would be computers everywhere."[102]

In 2006, Bill Gates relinquished his day-to-day supervisory role at Microsoft to devote his time to the Bill and Melinda Gates Foundation. In doing so, he passed the baton of Chief Software Architect to Ray Ozzie, then the Chief Technical Officer.

Even today, it is difficult to think of Microsoft without the face of Bill Gates popping up. He was the original visionary of Microsoft, the primary architect of its product strategy, and even the face of Microsoft, appearing in ads for the company. Despite that Gates no longer has a role in Microsoft's daily operations, he retains the Chairman's seat on the Board of Directors and remains the largest shareholder, owning 7 percent of outstanding shares with a market value of $15 billion.[103]

Exhibit 8A Microsoft Historical Stock Performance

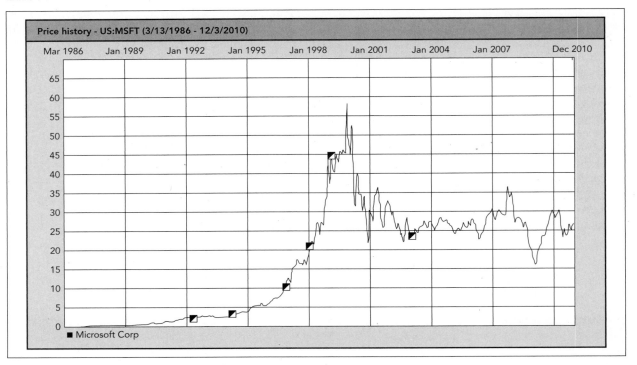

◢ Stock Split

Source: MoneyCentral.MSN.com Historical Charts

Exhibit 8B Microsoft vs. Major Competitors 5 Year Stock Performance

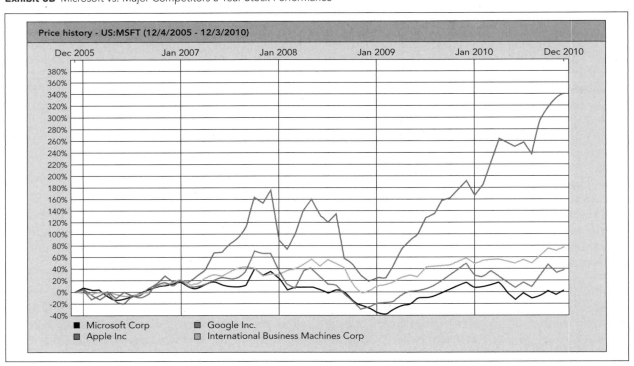

◢ Stock Split

Source: MoneyCentral.MSN.com Historical Charts

Steve Ballmer

Steve Ballmer first met Bill Gates at Harvard when they lived in the same dorm and became friends. When Gates needed help running Microsoft, he turned to Ballmer who joined Microsoft in 1980 as the business manager and Microsoft's 30th employee.[104] Ballmer was officially named President and CEO in 2000 so Gates could concentrate on the technological vision as Microsoft's first Chief Software Architect. The transition of power caused tension between Gates and Ballmer with Ballmer reportedly stating, "[Once Gates leaves] I'm not going to need him for anything. That's the principle. Use him, yes, need him, no."[105]

Despite the friction, the management styles of Ballmer and Gates complement each other, Ballmer as the outgoing sales and marketing guru and Gates as the technical guy.[106] Ballmer is known for his imposing personality, "bombastic style," explosive temper, and unbridled enthusiasm for all things Microsoft.[107] Microsoft analyst Mary Jo Foley sums up the duo saying, "[Ballmer] was always the foil to Gates. Gates is such a serious, plodding, methodical guy and Ballmer knew that to be part of the dynamic duo with Bill, he needed to be the opposite."[108]

Even with record revenues in 2010, Ballmer has received lukewarm reviews from Microsoft employees and the Board of Directors. In a recent employee survey, Ballmer received only a 51 percent approval rating for his performance as CEO[109] and, according to the annual proxy filing with the SEC, the Board of Directors awarded only 50 percent of his potential bonus, citing "the unsuccessful launch of the Kin phone, loss of market share in the company's mobile phone business, and the need for the Company to pursue innovations to take advantage of new form factors."[110] Wall Street has also shown its concern over Ballmer's leadership:

Some on Wall Street have been calling for his head for years. Since Ballmer took the reins as CEO from Bill Gates in 2000, Microsoft's stock has been nearly cut in half. Despite this year's strong financial performance and impressive sales of Windows 7, Office 2010 and cloud products for corporate customers, Microsoft's stock has gotten hammered, falling 20 percent.[111]

A Missing Link

Before starting his career at Microsoft in 2005 as a Chief Technical Officer, Ray Ozzie was best known for his development of Lotus Notes and considered "one of the world's best programmers."[112] Shortly after joining Microsoft, Ozzie wrote a well publicized seven page internal memo titled The Internet Services Disruption that detailed the changing technology market and encouraged Microsoft to focus on emerging markets such as cloud computing. "We must respond quickly and decisively. It's clear that if we fail to do so, our business as we know it is at risk."[113]

When Gates stepped down from the role in 2006, Ozzie assumed the official position of Chief Software Architect and unofficial position as technology visionary for Microsoft. Ozzie was primarily responsible for Microsoft's commitment to cloud computing and developed the plan for the Azure platform.[114] In October 2010, Ballmer announced that Ozzie was leaving Microsoft and that the position of Chief Software Architect would not be filled. Ballmer gave no reason for Ozzie's departure and did not explain why the position would remain unfilled.[115]

The Future of Microsoft

Microsoft has had phenomenal success as a software giant, mainly due to the continued success of its flagship products—Microsoft Office and Microsoft Windows. However, Microsoft is at a crossroads: the technology market is shifting toward a service model and cloud computing; consumers have emerged to influence new technology trends much more so than in the past; and Microsoft is no longer the "employer of choice" for young technology talent nor the hip, agile company it was in the 80s and 90s when it dominated the industry. With more than 89,000 employees, many speculate that Microsoft has gotten too big and bloated to adapt to the changing marketplace. "In this age, the race really is to the swift. You cannot afford to be an hour late or a dollar short," says Laura DiDio, principal analyst at Information Technology Intelligence Consulting (ITIC). "Now the biggest question is: Can [Microsoft] make it in the 21st century and compete with Google and Apple?"[116]

With the departure of Gates and now Ozzie, the unofficial role of technology visionary for Microsoft remains unfilled. It will be up to Ballmer to determine who will guide Microsoft's technology innovation: will he hire new blood to lead Microsoft into the next generation, will he promote internally and maintain the current direction, or will he assume the role himself even though this has not been his strength in the past? "There is general criticism that Steve's [Ballmer] not as visionary as Bill Gates, but his role is not to replace Bill," Neil MacDonald, lead Microsoft market analyst at Gartner, pointed out. "Steve's job is not to have the overall overriding vision; it's more about execution."[117] Even so, it would appear that Microsoft is about to find out if Steve Ballmer really does not need Bill Gates.

NOTES

1. Helft, M. and Vance, A. "Apple Passes Microsoft as No. 1 in Tech," *The New York Times,* May 26, 2010; http://www.nytimes .com/2010/05/27/technology/27apple.html?_r=2

2. Funding Universe "Microsoft Corporation," http://www .fundinguniverse.com/company-histories/Microsoft-Corporation -Company-History.html (accessed Dec 2010).

3. Helft, M. *op. cit.*

4. The New York Times: Business: Companies, "Microsoft Corporation," updated Aug 2, 2010; http://topics.nytimes.com/top/ news/business/companies/microsoft_corporation/index.html

5. *Ibid.*

6. Goldman, D. "Microsoft is a Dying Consumer Brand," *CNN Money,* Oct 28, 2010; http://money.cnn.com/2010/10/27/technology/ microsoft_pdc.index.htm?cnn=yes&hpt=T2

7. *Ibid.*

8. Greene, J. "Troubling Exits at Microsoft," *BusinessWeek,* Sep 26, 2005; http://www.businessweek.com/magazine/content/05_39/ b3952001.htm

9. *Ibid.*

10. Byrne, J. "How Microsoft Became Microsoft," *Business Insider,* Sep 21, 2010; http://www.businessinsider.com/how-did-microsoft -become-microsoft-2010-9

11. Gates, B. with Myhrvold, N and Rinearson, P.; The Road Ahead (New York: Viking, 1995) 17–18.

12. Wallace, J. and Erickson, J.; Hard Drive: Bill Gates and the Making of the Microsoft Empire (Harper Business, 1992) 189–90.

13. The New York Times: Business: Companies, *op. cit.*

14. Wallace, J. *op. cit.*

15. Montalbano, E. "Forrester: Microsoft Office in No Danger from Competitors," *PCWorld,* Jun 4, 2009; http://www.pcworld.com/ businesscenter/article/166123/forrester_microsoft_office_in_no _danger_from_competitors.html

16. The History of Computing Project, "Microsoft Company Timeline," http://www.thocp.net/companies/microsoft/microsoft_company.htm (accessed Dec 2010).

17. *Ibid.*

18. Microsoft, "Windows History: Internet Explorer History," http:// www.microsoft.com/windows/WinHistoryIE.mspx (accessed Nov 2010).

19. "Browser Stats," *The Counter.com,* http://www.thecounter.com/ stats/2002/December/browser.php (accessed Feb 2011).

20. Business and Company Resource Center, "Web Browser Shares, 2002," Telecomworldwire, August 2, 2002, from StatMarket. Market Share Reporter 2004. Gale Group, 2003. Reproduced in Business and Company Resource Center. Farmington Hills, Mich.: Gale Group, June 2002. http://galenet.galegroup.com.ezproxy.rice .edu/servlet/BCRC (accessed Feb 2011).

21. The New York Times: Business: Companies, op.cit.

22. *Ibid.*

23. Whitten, M. "An Open Letter from Xbox Live General Manager Marc Whitten," Feb 5, 2010; http://www.xbox.com/en-US/Press/ archive/2010/0205-whittenletter

24. Parr, B. "Is It Time to Call the Xbox Kinect a Hit?," *CNN,* Nov 30, 2010; http://edition.cnn.com/2010/TECH/gaming.gadgets/11/30/ kinect.hit.mashable/index.html?hpt=Sbin

25. The New York Times: Business: Companies, *op. cit.*

26. Gruman, G. "Windows Phone 7: Why it's a Disaster for Microsoft," *InfoWorld,* Nov 12, 2010; http://www.infoworld.com/d/mobilize/ windows-phone-7-even-bigger-disaster-i-thought-912?page=0,1

27. Noguchi, Y. "Microsoft Remakes Corporate Structure," *The Washington Post,* Sep 21, 2005; http://www.washingtonpost.com/ wp-dyn/content/article/2005/09/20/AR2005092001768.html

28. *Ibid.*

29. *Ibid.*

30. Anonymous Microsoft employee, interviewed on Dec 5, 2010.

31. "Operating Systems Market Share," *StatOwl,* (accessed Dec 2010); http://www.statowl.com/operating_system_market_share_trend .php?1=1&timeframe=custom|2008-09|2010-10&interval=month&chart _id=13&fltr_br=&fltr_os=&fltr_se=&fltr_cn=&timeframe=last_6

32. "Microsoft 2010 Annual Report," *Microsoft;* http://www.microsoft .com/investor/reports/ar10/10k_fr_dis.html

33. Goldman, D. *op. cit.*

34. "Microsoft 2010 Annual Report," *op. cit.*

35. Rigby, B. and Oreskovic, A. "Microsoft Corp Updates Office, Vies Online with Google," *Reuters,* May 11, 2010; http://www.reuters .com/article/idUSTRE64A6JM20100511

36. *Ibid.*

37. *Ibid.*

38. Microsoft 2010 10K, http://cid-4910e8dd2e872bb2.office.live.com/ view.aspx/FY2010/Microsoft percent202010 percent2010K.docx

39. Rigby, B. *op. cit.*

40. "Microsoft 2010 Annual Report," *op. cit.*

41. *Ibid.*

42. Lohr, S. "Skepticism Greets Microsoft-Yahoo Agreement," *The Boston Globe,* Jul 30, 2009; http://www.boston.com/business/ technology/articles/2009/07/30/skepticism_greets_microsoft _yahoo_agreement/

43. Pian Chan, S. "Q&A with Steve Ballmer on Mobile, Search and Facebook," *The Seattle Times,* Sep 28, 2010; http://seattletimes .nwsource.com/html/microsoftpri0/2013016876_steveballmerqa .html

44. *Ibid.*

45. "Microsoft 2010 Annual Report," *op. cit.*

46. Storm, G. "Home Console Market Share 2010," *Gameolosophy,* Jun 1, 2010; http://gameolosophy.com/consoles/wii/home-console -market-share-2010-may-22nd/

47. Goldman, D. *op. cit.*

48. Goldman, D. *op. cit.*

49. "Microsoft 2010 Annual Report," *op. cit.*

50. "US v. Microsoft: Timeline," *Wired,* Nov 4, 2002; http://www.wired .com/techbiz/it/news/2002/11/35212

51. Fried, I. "EU closes in on Microsoft Penalty," *CNET News.com,* Aug 6, 2003; http://news.cnet.com/2100-1016_3-5060463.html

52. "Microsoft is Accused by EU Again," *BBC News Mobile,* Jan 17, 2009; http://news.bbc.co.uk/2/hi/business/7834792.stm

53. Foley, M.; Microsoft 2.0, Kindle Version (Wiley Publishing, 2008) 335–39.

54. Every, D. "Have You Ever Heard of VFW?" *Mackido,* 1999; http:// www.mackido.com/History/History_VfW.html

55. *Ibid.*

56. Mercurio, M. "Microsoft's $8 Million Goodbye to Spyglass," *BusinessWeek,* Jan 22, 2010; http://www.businessweek.com/ bwdaily/dnflash/january/new0122d.htm

57. "Microsoft 2010 Annual Report," *op. cit.*

58. Foley, M. *op. cit.,* 362–63.

59. Greene, J. *op. cit.*

60. Foley, M. *op. cit.,* 362–63.

61. Greene, J. *op. cit.*

62. *Ibid.*

63. Fitzgerald, M. "Steve Ballmer's Cloud Computing Ambitions for Microsoft," *Fast Company,* Nov 1, 2010; http://www.fastcompany .com/magazine/130/microsoft-puts-its-head-in-the-cloud.html

64. "Steve Ballmer: Cloud Computing," *Microsoft News Center,* Mar 4, 2010; http://www.microsoft.com/presspass/exec/steve/2010/ 03-04cloud.mspx

65. "Microsoft 2010 Annual Report," *op. cit.*

66. *Ibid.*

67. *Ibid.*

68. Thurrott, P. "Microsoft Expands Enterprise Cloud Offerings, Offers Private Cloud Solutions," *Windows IT Pro,* Nov 9, 2010; http://www.windowsitpro.com/article/paul-thurrotts-wininfo/ Microsoft-Expands-Enterprise-Cloud-Offerings-Offers-Private -Cloud-Solutions.aspx

69. Ferrill, P. "How Microsoft's Azure Stacks up Against Cloud Competitors," *DevX.com,* Jul 2, 2010; http://www.devx.com/ enterprise/Article/45095

70. Google Inc. 2009 10K; http://markets.financialcontent.com/stocks/ quote/filings/quarterly?Symbol=GOOG

71. Foremski, T. "Google will have to Rethink its Acquisition Strategy," *ZDNet,* Mar 12, 2010; http://www.zdnet.com/blog/foremski/google-will-have-to-rethink-its-acquisition-strategy/1244

72. "100 Best Companies to Work For - 2010," *Fortune Magazine*; http://money.cnn.com/magazines/fortune/bestcompanies/2010/full_list/

73. Mediratta, B. "The Google Way, Give Engineers Room," *The New York Times,* Oct 21, 2010; http://www.nytimes.com/2007/10/21/jobs/21pre.html

74. Apple Inc. 2010 10K; https://www.apple.com/investor/

75. Yoffle, D. and Kim, R. "Apple Inc. in 2010," Harvard Business School Case Study 9-710-467, Sep 1, 2010

76. "Apple Retail Store," *Apple.com,* (accessed Dec 2010); http://www.apple.com/retail/storelist/

77. "World's Most Admired Companies - 2010," *Fortune Magazine*; http://money.cnn.com/magazines/fortune/mostadmired/2010/snapshots/670.html

78. Apple Inc. 2010 10K *op. cit.*

79. "Agile Innovation to Speed Development," *Directions on Microsoft,* Aug 28, 2006; http://www.directionsonmicrosoft.com/sample/DOMIS/update/2006/10oct/1006aitsd.htm

80. Greene, J. *op. cit.*

81. Cunningham, A. "Chrome OS Could Replace 60 percent of Windows PCs, Says Google Exec," *Windows 7 News,* Nov 27, 2010; http://www.windows7news.com/2010/11/27/chrome-os-replace-60-windows-pcs-google-exec/

82. Eluvangal, S. "King of Consumer, Google has its Eyes on the Enterprise," *Daily News and Analysis,* Nov 26, 2010; http://www.dnaindia.com/money/report_king-of-consumer-google-has-its-eyes-on-the-enterprise_1472458

83. Markoff, J. "Newly Released Documents Shed Light on Microsoft Tactics," *The New York Times,* Mar 24, 2004; http://www.nytimes.com/2004/03/24/business/newly-released-documents-shed-light-on-the-tactics-used-by-microsoft.html

84. Fisher, L. "Microsoft Loses Case on Patent," *The New York Times,* Feb 24, 1994; http://query.nytimes.com/gst/fullpage.html?res=9C03E2D6113BF937A15751C0A962958260

85. Elop, S. and Ballmer, S. "Open Letter from CEO Stephen Elop, Nokia and CEO Steve Ballmer, Microsoft," *Nokia Conversations, The Official Nokia Blog,* Feb 11, 2011; http://conversations.nokia.com/2011/02/11/open-letter-from-ceo-stephen-elop-nokia-and-ceo-steve-ballmer-microsoft/

86. Huang, G. "Dell, eBay, HP Use Microsoft Cloud," *Seattle Post Intelligencer,* 12 July 2010, http://www.seattlepi.com/xconomy/423260_xconomy92477.html

87. "Microsoft and Gorillaz come together to launch Internet Explorer 9 Beta," *EMI Music,* 16 Sep 2010; http://www.emimusic.com/news/2010/microsoft-and-gorillaz-come-together-to-launch-internet-explorer-9-beta/

88. "NCDPI and Microsoft Announce Partnership," *Public Schools of North Carolina News Releases 2010-11*; http://www.ncpublicschools.org/newsroom/news/2010-11/20101115-01

89. The New York Times: Business: Companies, *op. cit.*

90. Byrne, J. *op. cit.*

91. "Microsoft 2010 Annual Report," *op. cit.*

92. *Ibid.*

93. Microsoft 2010 10K *op. cit.*

94. "Microsoft 2010 Annual Report," *op. cit.*

95. Wingfield, N. "Microsoft to Open Stores, Hires Retail Hand," *The Wall Street Journal,* Feb 13, 2009; http://online.wsj.com/article/SB123448293075579777.html

96. "Microsoft 2010 Annual Report," *op. cit.*

97. Cringely, R. "The New Bill Gates," *PBS.org,* Nov 23, 2000; http://www.pbs.org/cringely/pulpit/2000/pulpit_20001123_000672.html

98. Manes, S. and Andrews, P.; Gates: How Microsoft's Mogul Reinvented an Industry (Doubleday, 1993) 298–99.

99. "Microsoft Memories," *Tom Evslin blog,* (accessed Dec 2010); http://blog.tomevslin.com/2007/05/microsoft_memor.html

100. Manes, S. *op. cit.,* 351.

101. Manes, S. *op. cit.,* 356.

102. Gates, B. *op. cit.,* 18.

103. "Ownership: MSFT," MoneyCentral.msn.com, (accessed Dec 2010); http://moneycentral.msn.com/ownership?Holding=5 percent25+Ownership&Symbol=US percent3AMSFT

104. Gates, B. *op. cit.,* 43.

105. Guth, R. "Gates-Ballmer Clash Shaped Microsoft's Coming Handover," *Wall Street Journal,* Jun 5, 2008; http://online.wsj.com/article/SB121261241035146237.html?mod=googlenews_wsj&apl=y&r=125394

106. "Ballmer Becomes Lone Voice at Microsoft's Helm," *The Economic Times,* Jun 30, 2008; http://economictimes.indiatimes.com/Infotech/Software/Ballmer_becomes_lone_voice_at_Microsofts_helm/articleshow/3178425.cms

107. Johnson, B. "Loyalty is his Number One Strength," *Guardian.co.uk,* Jun 27, 2008; http://www.guardian.co.uk/business/2008/jun/27/microsoft.microsoft

108. "Ballmer Becomes Lone Voice at Microsoft's Helm," *op. cit.*

109. Goldman, D. "Employees Love Microsoft – But Not Ballmer," *CNN Money,* Oct 6, 2010; http://money.cnn.com/2010/10/06/technology/microsoft_employee_survey/

110. Fiscal Year 2010 Proxy Statement for Microsoft Corporation; http://www.microsoft.com/investor/InvestorServices/InvestorInfo/default.aspx

111. Goldman, D. *op. cit.*

112. Vance, A. "Microsoft's Top Software Architect, A Cloud Computing Advocate, Quits," *The New York Times,* Oct 18, 2010; http://www.nytimes.com/2010/10/19/technology/19soft.html?_r=1&src=busln

113. *Ibid.*

114. *Ibid.*

115. *Ibid.*

116. Goldman, D. *op. cit.*

117. Adhikari, Richard "Ballmer: Windows 7 Tablet Will Have Its Day," *E-Commerce Times,* Jul 30, 2010; http://www.ecommercetimes.com/story/70523.html?wlc=1291483844

Steve Gove, David Thornblad
Virginia Tech

Brett P. Matherne
Loyola University of New Orleans

The Motion Picture Industry Value Chain

The motion picture industry value chain consists of three stages: studio production, distribution, and—the primary focus here—exhibition. All stages of the value chain are undergoing consolidation.

Studio Production

The studios produce the lifeblood of the industry, the films that are its content. The top six studios produce just 20 percent of all films, but this 20 percent is responsible for over 80 percent of domestic box office receipts (Exhibit 1). Studios are increasingly part of larger corporations, managed as any other profit center. Managing a studio is a challenge as investments are large and a successful formula elusive. Profitability swings wildly. The cost of bringing a typical feature to market exceeds $100 million, up 25 percent in five years.[1] Typically, one-third of costs are marketing expenses.

Studios know their core audience: 12- to 24-year-olds. This group purchases nearly 40 percent of theater tickets. Half are "frequent moviegoers" attending at least one movie per month. Profits are driven by the studios' ability to satisfy this fickle audience. In 2008, two films targeting the core market and based on two successful comic book characters met with wildly different fates.[2] Paramount's successful *Iron Man* was produced for $140 million and grossed $318 million at the domestic box office. On the other hand, Warner Bros. *Speed Racer*, produced for $120 million and released the following weekend, was a flop, grossing just $44 million.

Exhibit 1 Market Share of Film Production 2000–2010

Distributor	2010				2005				2000			
	Rank	Market Share	Total Gross	# Movies	Rank	Market Share	Total Gross	# Movies	Rank	Market Share	Total Gross	# Movies
Warner Bros.	1	18.2%	$ 1,924	27	1	15.6%	$1,377	19	3	11.9%	$ 905	22
Paramount	2	16.2%	$ 1,715	15	6	9.4%	$ 832	12	4	10.4%	$ 791	12
20th Century Fox	3	14.0%	$ 1,482	17	2	15.3%	$1,354	18	6	9.5%	$ 723	13
Disney/Buena Vista	4	13.8%	$ 1,456	14	4	10.4%	$ 922	17	1	15.5%	$1,176	21
Sony/Columbia	5	12.1%	$ 1,283	18	5	10.4%	$ 918	24	7	9.0%	$ 682	29
Universal	6	8.3%	$ 882	15	3	11.4%	$1,010	19	2	14.1%	$1,069	13
Total for leading 6		82.6%	$ 8,742	106		72.5%	$6,413	109		70.4%	$5,346	110
Industry Total			$10,565	529			$8,840	547			$7,661	478
As % of Industry			82.7%	20.0%			72.5%	19.9%			69.8%	23.0%

Source: Data retrieved from Boxofficemojo.com.

Demographic trends are not favorable for the industry. The US population will increase 17 percent by 2025, an increase of 54 million people (Exhibit 2). But the number of 12- to 24-year-olds is expected to increase only nine percent, just four million more potential viewers. Based on current theaters and screens, this is an increase of fewer than 700 additional viewers per theater, roughly 100 per screen.

Distribution

Distributors are the intermediaries between the studios and exhibitors. Distribution entails all steps following a film's artistic completion including marketing, logistics, and administration. Exhibitors negotiate a percentage of gross by the studio or purchase rights to films and profit from the box office receipts. Distributors select and market films to exhibitors, seeking to maximize potential attendees. Distributors coordinate the manufacture and distribution of the film to exhibitors. They also handle collections, audits of attendees, and other administrative tasks. There are over 300 active distributors, but much is done by a few major firms, including divisions of studios. Pixar,

for example, coproduced *Finding Nemo* with Disney and distribution was conducted by Disney's Buena Vista.

Exhibition

Studios historically sought full vertical integration through theater ownership, allowing greater control over audiences and capturing exhibition profits. A common practice was for the studios to use their theater ownership to reduce competition by not showing pictures produced by rivals. This ended in 1948 with the Supreme Court's ruling against the studios in *US v. Paramount Pictures*. Theaters were soon divested, leaving studios and exhibitors to negotiate film access and rental.

Theaters are classified according to the number of screens at one location (Exhibit 3). Single-screen theaters were the standard from the introduction of film through the 80s. They have since rapidly declined in number, replaced by theater complexes. These include miniplexes (two to seven screens), multiplexes (8 to 15 screens), and megaplexes (16 or more screens). The number of theaters decreased more than 20 percent between 2000 and 2010, but the number of screens increased due

Exhibit 2 Population Trend Among 14–17 and 18–24 Age Groups (millions)

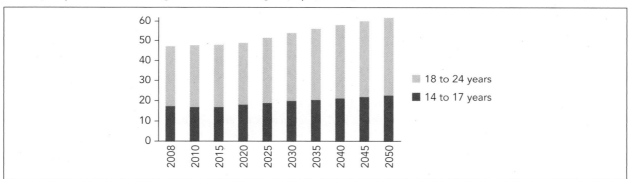

Source: US Census.

Exhibit 3 Number of Theaters by Complex Size

	2000	2005	2010	Change		
				2000 to 2005	2005 to 2010	2000 to 2010
Single Screens	2,368	1,723	1,610	−27%	−7%	−32%
Miniplexes (2–7 Screens)	3,170	2,381	1,884	−25%	−21%	−41%
Multiplexes (8–15 Screens)	1,478	1,599	1,683	8%	5%	14%
Megaplexes (16+ Screens)	405	558	645	38%	16%	59%
Total	7,421	6,260	5,817	−16%	−7%	−22%

Sources: Author estimates based on data from Entertainment Industry, 2007 & 2009 Motion Picture Association of America reports, and Mintel Report "Movie Theaters - US - February 2008."

Exhibit 4 Exhibition Market Leaders: 2009

Company	Theater Brands	# US Theater Locations	# US Screens	Avg. Screens per Theater
Regal	Regal, United Artists, Edwards	548	6,768	12.4
AMC	AMC, Loews	297	4,513	15.2
Cinemark	Cinemark, Century	294	3,830	13.0
Carmike	Carmike	244	2,277	9.3
Total for leading four		1,383	17,388	12.6
Industry total		6,039	39,717	6.6

Source: SEC Filings & Author estimates.

to growth in megaplexes. Over 10 percent of theaters are now megaplexes and the number of screens is at a historically high level of 39,717.[3] Many analysts argue the industry has overbuilt and too many theaters and screens exist to make the business profitable.

The Lead Actors

Declining ticket sales and the increased costs associated with developing megaplexes began a wave of consolidation among exhibitors. Four companies now dominate the industry: Regal, AMC, Cinemark, and Carmike (Exhibit 4). These companies—operating 1,383 theaters in the country (just 23 percent)—control 43 percent of screens. This market share provides these exhibitors with negotiating power for access to films, prices for films and concessions, and greater access to revenues from national advertisers.

There is little differentiation in the offerings of the major theater exhibitors—prices within markets differ little, the same movies are shown at the same times, and the food and services are nearly identical. Competition between theaters often comes down to distance from home, convenience of parking, and proximity to restaurants. Innovations by one theater chain are quickly adopted by others. The chains serve different geographic markets and do so in different ways.[4] Regal focuses on midsize markets using multiplexes and megaplexes. In 2009, Regal's average ticket price of $8.15 was the highest among the leaders (Exhibit 5). AMC concentrates on urban areas with megaplexes and on the large population centers such as those in California, Florida, and Texas. Cinemark serves smaller markets, operating as the sole theater chain in over 80 percent of its markets. Cinemark's average ticket price of $5.46 was the lowest of the majors. Carmike concentrates on small to midsized markets, targeting populations of less than 100,000 that have few other entertainment options. Carmike's average ticket price in 2009 was $6.56 but at $3.21, their average concession revenue per patron is the highest among the majors.

The differing approaches of these companies are reflected in the cost of fixed assets per screen. These costs result from decisions about how to serve customers, such as the level of technology and finish of the theater—digital projection and marble floors cost more than traditional projectors and a carpeted lobby.[5] Despite multi and megaplex facilities, Regal's cost per screen is the highest at $430,000. Carmike's, the rural operator, is the lowest at just $206,000. Cinemark is in the middle at $367,000. Costs for AMC are expected to be near or to exceed that of Regal.

The Business of Exhibition

There are three primary sources of revenue for exhibitors: concessions, advertising, and box office receipts. Managers have low discretion: their ability to influence revenues and expenses is limited. Operating margins among exhibitors average a slim 10 percent. This is before significant expenses such as facility and labor costs. The result is marginal or negative net income. Overall, the business of exhibitors is best described as loss leadership on movies: the firms make money selling concessions and selling ads that are shown to patrons who are drawn by the movie.

Concessions

Moviegoers frequently lament the high prices for concessions. In 2009, concessions averaged 30 percent of exhibitor revenues. Direct costs are less than 15 percent of selling price, making concessions the largest source of exhibitor profit. These are influenced by three factors: attendance, pricing, and material costs. The most important is attendance: more attendees leads to greater concession sales. The $3.75 price point for the large soda is not by accident, but rather the result of market research and profit maximization calculation. Costs are influenced by purchase volume, with larger chains able to negotiate better prices on everything from popcorn and soda pop to cups and napkins.

Advertising

Exhibitors also generate revenue through preshow advertising. Though this constitutes just 5 percent of revenues, it is highly profitable. Mintel reports that advertising revenues among exhibitors are expected to

Exhibit 5 Average Movie Ticket Price, 1980 to 2010

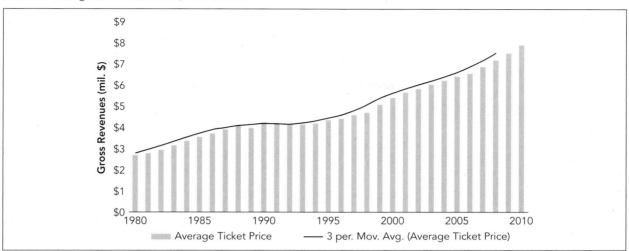

Source: Data retrieved from Boxofficemojo.com.

increase at an annual rate of 10 percent over the coming decade despite audiences' disapproval.[6] Balancing the revenues from ads with audience tolerance is an ongoing struggle for exhibitors, though not a new one. In the early 70s, one industry executive argued:

It is not a policy of our corporation to use commercial advertising for income on our screen. We are selling the public one item—a particular motion picture—and to use the screen for other purposes detracts from this item.[7]

Box Office Revenues

Ticket sales constitute two-thirds of exhibition business revenues but yield little or no profit. Historically, the power imbalance between studios and exhibitors yielded rental contracts that returned as much as 90 percent of box office revenue to the studios during the initial weeks of a film's release. The split is now closer to 55/45 for large chains. Still, it is common for an exhibitor's portion of ticket revenues to not cover operational costs fully. The record-setting revenues at the box office have been the result of increases in ticket prices that have flowed back to the studios and help cover exhibitors' facilities and debt load.

From 2005 to 2009, ticket price increases averaged 3.8 percent per year (Exhibit 6). While these increases set records, an even greater opportunity materialized with the resurgence of 3D. Prior to 2009, a $1 to $2 "surcharge" was installed to cover glasses, license fees paid to 3D equipment providers, and to studios in higher rental rates. Following the success of *Avatar*, exhibitors saw the opportunity to use the surcharge as an alternative to ticket price increases. The 3D premium now reaches $3 to $5; for IMAX it is $4 to $7. Price increases

in March 2010 by AMC, Regal, and Cinemark averaged 8.3 percent nationally on 3D movies, rising from $13.60 to $14.73.[8] In some markets, 3D prices jumped 20 percent.[9]

Recent increases in exhibitor revenues are attributed almost entirely to 3D. In 2005, the box office for 3D was just $40 million. By 2009, it had risen to $1.14 billion or 11 percent of all revenues. From 2008 to 2009, 3D receipts grew 375 percent, whereas revenues for non-3D grew less than 1 percent.[10] In addition, these figures may actually under-represent the actual demand for 3D as the rapid expansion in the number of 3D films produced created a bottleneck for the 3D screen space available.[11] Longer runs on 3D screens will likely increase the proportion of revenues from 3D. However, Paul Dergarabedian of Hollywood.com cautions that the ticket price increases are not sustainable.

It's what we call a recession-resistant business. Times get tough and people go to the movies because it's the one thing they see as a relative bargain. The minute they cease to see it that way, it's not good for the industry.[12]

AMC may have, intentionally or not, stumbled onto a price cap when several of their New York theaters hit $20 per ticket for *Shrek* in IMAX 3D at several locations. Amidst a public outcry and unwanted media attention, the chain apologized, citing a pricing error, and reduced prices to $17 and $19. This situation suggests there is indeed a cap on the willingness to pay for even this "special" viewing experience. The backlash may make it difficult to raise prices in the near future; any cap on ticket prices is a serious cause for concern for exhibitors as it has been the primary way to increase revenues.

Exhibit 6 Change in Average Ticket Price, 1980 to 2010

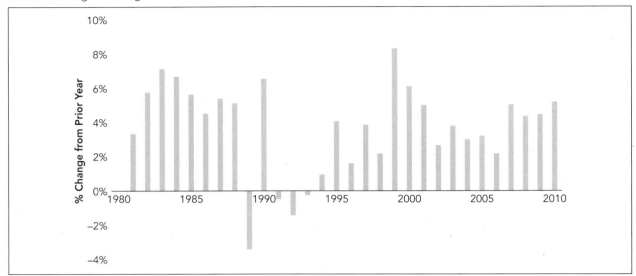

Source: Data retrieved from Boxofficemojo.com.

The evidence is mixed that 3D is having a positive impact on exhibitors' bottom lines. This suggests either that the benefits have yet to accrue to exhibitors or are being appropriated by studios. The National Association of Theater Owners (NATO) estimates the savings of digital over film as $1 billion annually[13] due to lower production costs of master reels and prints, elimination of shipping, etc. They argue these cost savings will largely accrue to distributors.

By all accounts, revenues per admission have increased, but these are split with studios. At Regal, for example, film rental and advertising costs as a percent of revenues dropped slightly, to 53.3 percent from 54.2 percent for the second quarter 2010 compared to the same period in 2009. Similarly, Carmike's exhibition costs declined slightly as a percent of revenue, from 57.6 percent to 56.8 percent, but other theater operating costs grew from 59.6 percent to 62.9 percent of admissions revenue. In each of these cases, the data reflect substantial increases in ticket prices—and 3D surcharges began in spring 2010. This suggests studios are appropriating a large portion of the revenue increases.

At Regal, this holds true for operating profits as a percent of revenues, which decreased from 12.2 percent in the second quarter 2009 to 9.0 percent in the same quarter in 2010. For Carmike, the net effect was operating income declining significantly, from 8.8 percent of total revenue to 4.1 percent. The overall picture appears similar for Cinemark. Operating income as a percentage of revenues for second quarter 2010 declined from the levels in the same period in 2009, dropping from 14.6 percent to 14.4 percent. While limited to just the first comparative quarter when most price increases and

surcharges went into effect, these trends suggest that, despite substantial investments in digital and 3D, exhibitors may not be able to capitalize on them.

Overall, the exhibitor has limited control over both revenues and profits. Box office receipts are the bulk of revenues, but yield few profits. Attendance allows for profitable sales of concessions and advertisements, but there are significant caps on the volume of concession sales per person, and selling prices seem to have reached a maximum. Advertising remains an attractive avenue for revenues and profits, but audiences loathe it.

The Process of Exhibition

The fundamentals of film exhibition changed little from the introduction of motion pictures to well into the 90s. Historically, each theater received a shipment of physical canisters containing a "release print" from the distributor. Making these prints requires $20,000–$30,000 in up-front costs and $1,000–$1,500 for each print. Thus, a modern major motion picture opening on 2,500 screens simultaneously requires $2.50 to $3.75 million in print costs. This expense is borne by the studios, but paid for by movie attendees. Each release print is actually several reels of 35-mm film that are manually loaded onto projector reels, sequenced, and queued for display by a projector operator. The film passes through a projector that shines intense light through the film, projecting the image through a lens used to focus the image on the screen. A typical projection system costs $50,000 with one needed for each screen.

In the late 90s, the industry began converting to digital distribution, a format that is now becoming economically viable. Digital cinema involves a high resolution (4096×2160) digitized image projected onto the screen. The cost of a digital projection system is considerable, averaging $75,000 per screen. 3D capability can add an additional $25,000. However, the cost for a digital release print is far lower than traditional film; but these cost savings most directly benefit the studio while, in the meantime, exhibitors pay to convert their theaters. Nevertheless, the number of digital theaters is expanding rapidly. In 2004, there were fewer than 100 in the US. At the end of 2007, 4,702 digital screens had been installed, and by 2009, there were 7,736.

Financing these investments was a significant issue for exhibitors due to the total costs and their weak balance sheets. Two financing avenues were taken by the major theater chains. Forming an agreement with Christie Digital Systems, Carmike went solo with a lease-service approach. Under its 10-year agreement, digital and digital 3D systems are installed with an up-front cost of $800 per screen. Christie provides equipment service and maintenance amounting to $2,340 per screen annually. This arrangement effectively puts both the risk and upside with Carmike as fixed costs are increased. Revenues beyond these fixed costs benefit Carmike. Alternately, AMC, Cinemark, and Regal financed the transition through the Digital Cinema Implementation Partners (DCIP) partnership, securing $660 million in financing to convert nearly 14,000 or over 90 percent of their screens. Each company pays a $5,000 to $10,000 per screen conversion charge and subsequent royalty fees of approximately $0.50 per admission. Conversion of screens ranges from 1,000 screens for Regal to 1,500 for Cinemark.

By the end of 2009, 1,000 screens were being converted to digital every six months. Carmike had converted over 90 percent of its screens to digital. The DCIP firms on average had converted approximately 25 percent of their screens. Plans are in place for the nearly complete conversion to digital among the leading four exhibitors.

To the audience, the most visible aspect of the digital transition is 3D, which went mainstream in 2010. In 2005, just 192 digital 3D capable screens were installed. By 2007, that number more than tripled to 600, reaching 3,378 by the end of 2009. Twenty-two percent of Carmike's screens are 3D capable. The DCIP partners have on average 10 percent of their screens as 3D capable with plans to grow that number to approximately 25 percent. In 2010, 3D screens were responsible for approximately one-third of all box office admissions, generating roughly 40 to 50 percent of all revenues. A study by the International 3D Society reported 3D is responsible for the majority of opening weekend revenues.[14] Of *Avatar's* $77 million opening weekend, 82 percent was from 3D; for *Alice in Wonderland*, it was 70 percent.

Still, some argue that 3D may be a novelty. The appeal of 3D varies by film, with action and animated as the leading genres. The long-term trend appears to be downward, to what threshold no one knows (Exhibit 7). "Because the pricing of 3D tickets is now so high, people are becoming more selective about what they see in 3D," said Rich Greenfield, media analyst for BTIG.[15] A focus on 3D may result in more action movies and fewer comedies and dramas, further alienating the non-core audience for movies.[16]

The Theater Experience

While the industry touts the ongoing transition to digital projection and the latest 3D as the draw for the box office, the allure may be more fundamental. Moviegoers describe the attraction of going to the theater as an "experience" based on: (1) the giant theater screen, (2) the opportunity to be out of the house, (3) not having to wait to see a particular movie on home video, (4) the experience of watching movies with a theatrical sound system, and (5) as a location option for dating.[17]

The ability of theaters to provide these benefits beyond what audiences can achieve at home appears to be diminishing. Of the reasons that people go to the movies, only the place aspects—the opportunity to be out of house and as a place for dating—seem immune from substitution. Few teenagers want movie and popcorn with their date at home with mom and dad.

The overall "experience" currently offered by theaters falls short for many. Marketing research firm Mintel reports the reasons for not attending theaters more frequently are largely the result of declining experience. Specific factors include the overall cost, at-home viewing options, interruptions (such as cell phones in the theater), rude patrons, the overall hassle, and ads prior to the show.[18] Patrons report general dismay with the theater experience. A recent *Wall Street Journal* article reported on interruptions ranging from the intrusion of sound tracks in adjacent theaters to cell phones. "The interruptions capped a night of movie going already marred by out-of-order ticketing kiosks and a parade of preshow ads so long that, upon seeing the Coca-Cola polar bears on screen, one customer grumbled: 'This is obscene.'"[19] Recounting bad experiences is a lively topic for bloggers. A typical comment:

I say it has gotten worse. I hate paying $9.00 for a ticket and the movie is 90–100 minutes long, people talking on the cell phone, the people who work at the theaters look like they are bored, and when you ask them a question, the answer is very rude. I worked as an usher in the late 60s and we had to wear uniforms and white gloves on Friday and Saturday nights, those days are long gone.[20]

A trip to the local cinemaplex can be an eye-opening event for industry insiders. In 2005, Toby Emmerich, New Line Cinema's head of production,

Exhibit 7 Percentage of Opening Weekend Sales from 3D

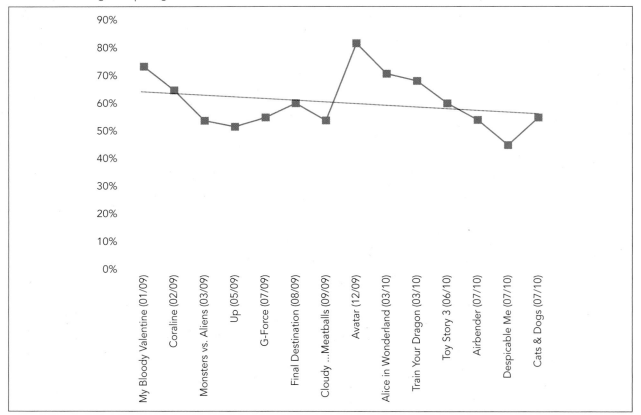

Source: Data retrieved from Boxofficemojo.com.

faced a not-so-common choice: attending *War of the Worlds* in a theater or in a screening room at actor Jim Carrey's house. Said Emmerich in an *LA Times* article

I love seeing a movie with a big crowd, but I had no idea how many obnoxious ads I'd have to endure—it really drove me crazy. After sitting through about 15 minutes of ads, I turned to my wife and said, "Maybe we should've gone to Jim Carrey's house after all." [21]

The unique value proposition offered by movie theaters' large screens, the long wait for DVD release, and advantages of theatrical sound systems also appear to be fading. Increasingly larger television sets, DVD content, and the adoption of high definition (HD) technology are all eroding these advantages. One blogger posts, "Whereas the electronics industry has been innovating to create immersive experiences from the comfort of our own home, the US theater industry has been dragging their feet." [22]

Home Viewing Technology

Many home television sets are increasingly large HD sets coupled with inexpensive yet impressive audio systems. In 1997, the screen size of the average television was just 23 inches. Currently, almost all television manufacturers sell LCD televisions with screens 36 inches or larger. [23] Because set size is measured as the diagonal screen size, increases in viewable area are greater than the measurement suggests; in fact, the viewing area of sets doubled from 250 inches[2] to 550 inches[2].

The Federal Communications Commission (FCC) requirement that all broadcasters convert to digital broadcasts by 2009 is widely credited with starting a consumer movement to upgrade televisions. Since the 50s, television transmissions were formatted as 480 interlaced vertical lines (480i) of resolution. The new digital format is HD, providing up to 1080 vertical lines of resolution (1080p). [24] Three-quarters of all televisions sold since 2006 are HD capable.

As LCD technology became the standard for both computer and television screens, manufacturing costs declined. Wholesale prices for televisions fell 65 percent from the late 90s. [25] In 2006, the average television retailed for $29 per diagonal inch of set size. This is expected to decrease to $22 within five years. [26] Consumers, however, are actually spending more on every television, consistently electing to purchase larger sets to achieve a better viewing experience. Sharp, a leading manufacturer of televisions, predicts that by 2015 the average screen will reach 60 inches.[27]

Large-screen televisions, DVD players, and audio and speaker components are commonly packaged as low-cost home theaters. The average DVD player now costs just $72[28] and HD DVD players are beginning to penetrate the market. Retail price wars during the 2008 Christmas season led to HD Blu-Ray players dropping below $200. These home theater systems offer a movie experience that rivals many theaters, all for $1,000–$2,000. Says Mike Gabriel, Sharp's head of marketing and communications, "People can now expect a home cinema experience from their TV. Technology that was once associated with the rich and famous is now accessible to homes across the country."[29]

Content Expansion

Sales of DVDs have aided the expansion of home theaters and profited the studios. DVD sales have been a primary source of studio profits for more than a decade, but fell precipitously, down 13.3 percent in 2009 on top of an 8.4 percent decline in 2008.[30] At $8.5 billion, 2009's DVD sales equaled 2001 levels; total revenues from DVD sales dropped below that of box office receipts in the US for the first time since 2000.[31] This decline in DVD sales is due in part to the expanded availability of rentals and pay-per-view, and is at least partially attributable to the studios.

Rentals also serve this market. Netflix grew revenues 85 percent from 2006 to 2009, and it is actively expanding into online streaming. Coinstar's Redbox had over 12,000 rental kiosks offering $1/night rentals through partnerships with McDonald's (which is also an investor in the company), Walmart, Walgreens, and other retailers even *before* adding kiosks to half of 7-Eleven's national locations.[32]

Studios are responding by trying to spur DVD and pay-per-view fees through shorter release windows, actions seemingly incompatible and inconsistent with the drive to increase theater attendance. In 2000, the average window between theatrical release and DVD sales was 5 months, 16 days. In 2009, it was 4 months, 11 days—a 20 percent reduction.[33] Studios are eager to accelerate DVD revenue streams and capitalize on initial marketing expenditures. Arguing in favor of a reduced window, Bob Iger, CEO of Disney, said, "The problem with waiting these days is that we're dealing with a much more competitive marketplace than ever before—there are more choices that people have."[34] Theaters may fear complete disintermediation.

The accelerated DVD release of *Alice in Wonderland* in the US (just 88 days after opening and while the film remained in theaters) created great concern among film exhibitors. Exhibitors fear shorter windows deter attendance (Exhibit 8). US theater owners and major Hollywood studios reached an agreement wherein the studios will be able to release one or two movies each year on an accelerated schedule, cutting a month off the traditional four-month DVD release window.[35] The *Wall Street Journal* reports,

Theaters have benefited recently from a boom in box-office receipts, even as studios have suffered from a steep decline in DVD sales. Adjusting the windows is an attempt to maintain the health of both camps, which depend on one another.[36]

Exhibit 8 *Alice in Wonderland*: Weekly Domestic Box Office Gross

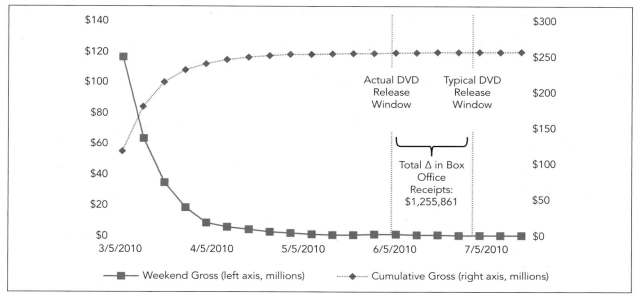

Source: Data retrieved from Boxofficemojo.com.

Hollywood is also seeking to expand direct-to-viewer delivery, avoiding the DVD and capturing revenues directly. Studios won regulatory approval to temporarily block analog outputs on viewers' electronics during pay-per-view movies. While controls for digital outputs are features that are built into modern electronics, viewers with analog equipment could record pay-per-view movies if the regulatory block failed. Studios considered this loophole a security issue. Allowing temporary blockage paves the way for studios to pursue short release windows, offering "premium" pay-per-view opportunities prior to DVD release.

Overall, studios are increasingly seeking to overcome their own lost profits through increased DVD sales and alternative channels to serve the home audience directly. Both are detrimental to exhibitors.

Recession Effects

Beyond the previous attendance drivers mentioned, there is a more ominous one: recession. There has been a long-standing effect between economic recession and depression and movie attendance: as the economy declines, attendance increases. As early as 1911, one observer described movies as a "door of escape, for a few cents, from the realities of life."[37] During the depression of the 30s, movie theaters were described as "an acre of seats in a garden of dreams."[38] The recession of 2008 saw rapid increases in gas prices, stock market declines, and significant layoffs. One summer movie patron commented, "There's not a whole lot you can do for $10 anymore."[39]

The recession of 2008 saw attendance increase 10 to 15 percent over 2007. The air-conditioned comfort of a dark theater and the latest Hollywood release offered a break not just from the summer heat, but from reality. "It's escapism, absolutely. It's probably a subconscious thing, and people don't realize it. But there's just so much going on, with people trying to pay their mortgages and get by. It's an escape for a couple of hours."[40] However, attendance for 2009 overall was down 4.1 percent. The Motion Picture Association of America (MPAA) routinely touts movies as bargain entertainment. Four tickets to a movie costs under $27 compared to $141 for an amusement park or $261 for a pro football game.[41] This comparison, however, may no longer be relevant as the true substitute may be a home theater and an existing cable subscription.

Possible Alternative Business Models

Under the studio-based film exhibition model, unchanged since the 30s, exhibitors have just two alternative revenue streams: advertising and concessions. Both appear limited in opportunities for increasing revenues and profits.

Advertising, while increasing in amount, threatens to alienate customers. While a 2007 Arbitron survey indicated 63 percent of those 12 and older report they "do not mind the ads they put on before the movie begins,"[42] other viewers loathe them. Even the industry struggles with the issue. Bob Pisano, president of the MPAA, calls increased advertising or higher concession prices "mutually assured destruction" for both exhibitors and the studios. They "try moviegoers' patience" he argues, "leading them to stay home and rent or, worse, illegally download a film."[43]

While ticket prices quadrupled, per capita spending on concessions has only doubled since the 70s.[44] Theater chains have expanded food offerings, some to the point of rivaling mall food courts. The NATO estimates that over 400 theaters now have on-site restaurant or bar service. These theaters appear at odds with the primary demographic market for movies. While the average moviegoer is the teen to 20-something, these theaters seek 35- to 50-year-olds. AMC is experimenting with an in-theater food model to serve this market. Gold Class Cinemas adds a service approach with 40-seat theaters more akin to club lounges than auditoriums, and offers full food and wine service. Tickets, $20–$25 per person, are purchased not from a ticket booth but from a concierge. Food sales average near $20 per person. Some also offer valet parking and childcare to lure customers.[45] Rob Goldberg, Gold Class Cinema's COO, explains this is part of the appeal saying, "We don't get the teenage crowd."[46]

Keeping patrons coming to the theater and increasing profitability may require a dramatic change for exhibitors. The investment in digital distribution and projection increases both visual quality and operational flexibility, serving as a classic "enabling technology" and opening the door for alternative content. New York Metropolitan Opera's *Live in HD* is an alternative content leader, now entering its fifth season. The series offers opera to audiences where it may not be available locally. Featuring 12 performances on Saturday afternoons, the series is broadcast to more than 500 HD-equipped theaters. Exhibitors continue to experiment with alternative content, mostly for individual sporting events where exhibitors must compete directly with home viewing. Says Jeremy Devine, marketing VP for a Dallas-based theater chain showing the NBA All-Star Game, "I don't care how good your buddy's system is, this is a 52-foot screen. And it's in 3D."[47]

Despite the potential for alternative content, virtually all admissions continue to be for studio movies. The evidence suggests continued problems with profitability under this studio-dominated model. The surge in revenues from 3D does not appear to be increasing profitability.

While exhibitors are, with the exception of Cinemark, predominantly US based, studios are increasingly focusing their attention on the international market where growth is highest. While US revenues grew 20 percent from 2005 to 2009, international revenues grew 35 percent.[48] Internationally, both attendance and receipts are growing.[49] Studios' proportional revenues are also further shifting toward international. In 2005, box office receipts totaled $23 billion with $14 billion (60 percent) international. By 2009, that increased to two-thirds of the $30 billion total.[50] There appear to be opportunities to increase revenues from increased attendance and ticket price increases. In India, for example, last year's 3.3 billion attendees paid an average of just $0.50.[51] In just that market at current growth rates, the annual volume increase in attendance equals total current US annual admissions.[52] Among leading US exhibitors, Cinemark has the largest international presence with 130 theaters (1,066 screens) in Mexico and seven in central and South American countries.

Raising the Exhibition Curtain in 2011 and Beyond

Despite a continuing recession, the end of the 2010 season saw an alarming statistic: summer admissions declined 3 percent from 2009 levels, resulting in a decline in both admissions and revenues (Exhibit 9). The increased costs of going to the theater may be causing audiences to be more selective in the movies they choose to see. Perhaps the escapism of the movies is bumping into a reality of empty wallets. Higher prices are "a very dangerous situation for the movie industry," says Dergarabedian,

When is too much too much? The demand has been huge, but theater owners should not just think that they can charge whatever they want, because there is a point when people will literally just stop coming because they can't afford it.[53]

Others explain the decline as a lack of content. Even with expectedly high revenues from big-budget movies, no sleeper hits emerged.

Fitch Ratings summarized the long-term situation:

[R]evenues and profitability of movie theatres could be increasingly challenged by factors that are largely out of managements' control... [T]he significant degree of operating leverage means that cash flow can be meaningfully affected by moderate top-line declines. These factors and financial policy decisions will remain the main drivers of credit quality over the longer term.[54]

What can exhibitors do to improve their performance? To reverse the downward trends in attendance? To improve their profitability at a time when the studios, relying on the box office more than ever, are increasingly looking internationally?

Exhibit 9 Domestic Tickets Sold & Box Office Gross 1980 to 2010

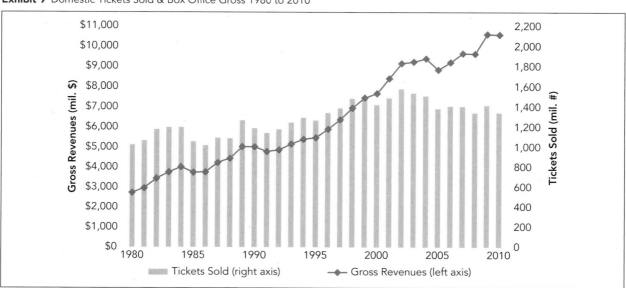

Source: Data retrieved from Boxofficemojo.com/yearly.

NOTES

1. MPAA 2007 Entertainment Industry Market Statistics.
2. All data on these two films from *www.BoxOfficeMojo.com*.
3. Developed by author from: Entertainment Industry, 2009 Report Motion Picture Association of America.
4. Data on the firms, screen sizes, location, from websites and SEC filings.
5. All data is from SEC filings, based on net property, plant, and equipment reported in 2007 balance sheet and the number of screens.
6. Mintel, Movie Theaters - US - February 2008 - Segment Performance - Cinema Advertising.
7. S. H. Durwood, 2002, The Exhibitors (1972), in G. A. Waller (ed.), *Moviegoing in America: A Sourcebook in the History of Film Exhibition*, Malden, MA: Blackwell Publishers Ltd, 279–281.
8. Reuters, 2010, US movie ticket sales strong despite price hike, *Reuters News*, April 6.
9. L. A. E. Schuker & E. Smith, 2010, Higher prices make box-office debut, *Wall Street Journal*, March 25, B1, B5.
10. Motion Picture Association of America, 2009, *Theatrical Market Statistics: 2009*: Motion Picture Association of America.
11. *Ibid.*
12. C. Muther, 2010, Prices for 3-D movies flyaway with 'Dragon', *Boston Globe*, March 27, B1.
13. National Association of Theater Owners, 2010, Talking Points: Digital Cinema. *www.natoonline.org*
14. International 3D Society, 2010, 3D movie fans expand box office says international 3D society study.
15. L. A. E. Schuker, 2010, A 2-D 'Eclipse' stakes its claim in 3-D world, *Wall Street Journal*, July 6, B1, B2.
16. 2010, The box office strikes back, *The Economist*, May 6.
17. Mintel Report, Movie Theaters - US - February 2008 - Reasons to go to Movies over Watching a DVD.
18. Mintel Report, Movie Theaters - US - February 2008 - Reasons why Attendance is not Higher.
19. K. Kelly, B. Orwall, & P. Sanders, 2005, The multiplex under siege, *Wall Street Journal*, December 24, P1.
20. Blog comment on Cinema Treasures, Over the past ten years, the movie theater experience has..., http://cinematreasures.org/polls/22/, December 11, 2008.
21. P. Goldstein, 2005, Now playing: A glut of ads, *Los Angeles Times*, July 12 E-1, http://articles.latimes.com/2005/jul/12/entertainment/et-goldstein12 (accessed December 5, 2008).
22. 2008, Designs of the week: The movie theater experience, November 23, http://www.sramanamitra.com/2008/11/23/designs-of-the-week-the-movie-theater-experience/ (accessed December 11, 2008).
23. DuBravac, 2007.
24. *Ibid.*
25. *Ibid.*
26. B. Keefe, 2008, Prices on flat-screen TVs expected to keep falling, *The Atlanta Journal-Constitution*, March 15.
27. 2008, Source: Average TV size up to 60-inch by 2015 says Sharp, *TechDigest*, December 11, http://www.techdigest.tv/2008/01/average_tv_size.html
28. MPAA 2007 *op. cit.*
29. 2008, Source: *op. cit.*
30. 2009, National Association of Theater Owners, ShoWest 2010 Talking Points, http://www.natoonline.org
31. L. A. E. Schuker & E. Smith, 2010, Hollywood eyes shortcut to TV, *Wall Street Journal*, May 22.
32. 2009, Convenient entertainment; 7-Eleven rolls out Redbox® $1 per night new release DVD rentals, *Business Wire*, January 5.
33. National Association of Theater Owners, 2010, *Average Video Announcement and Video Release Windows*.
34. E. Smith & L. A. E. Schuker, 2010, Studios unlock DVD release dates, *Wall Street Journal*, February 12.
35. *Ibid.*
36. *Ibid.*
37. M. H. Vorse, 2002, Some picture show audiences (1911), in G. A. Waller (ed.), *Moviegoing in America: A Sourcebook in the History of Film Exhibition*, Malden, MA: Blackwell Publishers Ltd, 50–53.
38. K. H. Fuller, 2002, You can have the strand in your own town": The struggle between urban and small-town exhibition in the picture palace era, in G. A. Waller (ed.), *Moviegoing in America*, 88–98.
39. J. Woestendiek & C. Kaltenbach, 2008, $10 is small price for a big escape: Movie box office figures are flourishing despite, or because of, economic worries, *Baltimore Sun*, July 8.
40. *Ibid.*
41. MPAA 2007 *op cit.*
42. C. Brodesser-Akner, 2008, What popcorn prices mean for movies; ethanol and rising costs of paper eat into sales that subsidize tickets, *Advertising Age*, May 19.
43. *Ibid.*
44. *Ibid.*
45. J. Russell, 2009, Winning ticket? Cinemas hope high-end services pack 'em in, *Los Angeles Business Journal*, November 2.
46. R. Ruggless, 2009, Dinner and a movie: One hot ticket for operators, *Nation's Restaurant News*, 43(41).
47. M. T. Moore, 2009, Moving beyond movies, *USA Today*, February 9, 3A.
48. Motion Picture Association of America, 2009, *op cit.*
49. 2010, The box office strikes back, *op cit.*
50. *Ibid.*
51. A. Thakur, 2009, India dominates world of films, *The Times of India*, July 29.
52. *Ibid.*
53. D. B. Wood & G. Goodale, 2010, Want to see a 3D movie? Ticket prices go up 20 percent, *The Christian Science Monitor*, March 26.
54. 2009, Fitch: High debt levels reduce flexibility for US movie exhibitors in 2009, *Business Wire*, January 27.

Ryan McVay/Getty Images

Johanna Gunther, Andy Jackson, Heather Lassourreille, Bertrand Maillet, Corey Martin, K. C. Procter
Arizona State University

Tina Borja
Rice University

"One step at a time, the hardest one first."
LIFELONG MOTTO OF CYRUS MCCORMICK
INVENTOR OF THE REAPER[1]

Navistar International Corporation (NAV) is a $12 billion company with a rich 180-year history. The company has morphed over the years from a farm equipment giant to a company deeply anchored in the truck, bus, and diesel engine markets. However, with 67 percent of its 2010 sales tied up in North American truck sales, Navistar has been a victim of the declining economy that has led to fewer goods shipped and consequently, a delay in fleet upgrades.[2] While truck demand bottomed out in early 2010 to a 50-year low, Navistar, at least in the short term, has emerged triumphant, taking market share, improving profitability, and investing in technology and complementary businesses.[3]

In addition to the time, energy, and money spent guarding against the economic storm, stricter regulations of engine emissions across the globe have led to increased research and development and production costs. However, rather than fight the system and public sentiment, Navistar is using these stiffer regulations to leverage its culture of innovation to raise the bar. In fact, Navistar stands alone in the industry with its dramatically different emissions compliance solution. According to Navistar president and CEO, Daniel Ustian,

The biggest differentiator has been our ability to meet the 2010 US emissions standard with no additional after treatment. By taking responsibility for emissions compliance in cylinder, we're eliminating the added weight and driver training required by our competitors.[4]

With volatility in the heavy-duty truck market, the growth of Navistar's military business has been a great stabilizer. In four short years, Navistar has built a $2 billion business primarily around the conversions of commercial platforms.[5] Due to a shift in government spending priorities from combat vehicles to more high-tech surveillance and reconnaissance equipment,[6] Navistar experienced a decline in military sales in 2010 but is working to balance this shift through diversification and contracts with other US friendly countries.[7]

Navistar is determined to control its own destiny and become less reliant on system suppliers. With targeted investments and acquisitions, Navistar is "offering key technologies designed to work perfectly in sync."[8] That means better performance with lower integration and production costs.

And yet, despite its recent success and apparent investment in the future, the question remains whether Navistar can emerge from its position as a North American player primarily anchored in the trucking market and transform into a global force reminiscent of its glory days when the company was known throughout the world as International Harvester.

History

In 1831, Cyrus McCormick invented the first mechanical reaper, revolutionizing how grain was harvested and liberating the American farmer. At the beginning of the twentieth century, McCormick Harvesting Machine Company became International Harvester, an industrial powerhouse that, at its peak, reached close to 100,000 employees with over 48 manufacturing facilities.[9] Now, McCormick's company bears the name *Navistar International* and is credited with an integral role in America's agricultural and industrial development.

The Early Years

After perfecting his reaper, McCormick moved west and opened a factory in Chicago.[10] McCormick was not just a technological innovator, but also a pioneer in the world of marketing. By the time of his death in 1884, McCormick had introduced forward thinking loyalty programs like installment plans, written guarantees, and factory-trained repairmen.[11]

With an investment from banker J. P. Morgan, in 1902, the company merged with Deering Harvester and several smaller companies to form International Harvester. It wasn't long before International Harvester controlled over 85 percent of all US-based harvester production.[12] In 1905, International Harvester went global when its first overseas plant opened in Sweden.[13]

By 1907, International Harvester had entered both the tractor industry and had developed what was the precursor to the truck—the Auto Buggy.[14] By 1910, International Harvester had sales well in excess of $100 million with annual tractor and truck production at 1,400 and 1,300 units respectively. The Farmall, the first all-purpose tractor, was introduced in 1924 and International Harvester began making heavy trucks in 1928. By 1937, International Harvester was the largest manufacturer of both medium- and heavy-duty trucks in the US.[15]

Post WWII and the Decline

International Harvester came out of WWII overextended, underfinanced, and the victim of increased competition and a sharp decline in market share. By 1955, it was producing more trucks than farm equipment and by 1958, had lost its agricultural equipment lead to John Deere. Ford took the lead in medium-duty truck sales in the 60s just as International Harvester's construction equipment business began to decline dramatically.[16] By 1980, International Harvester was at the brink of bankruptcy. To salvage what it could, International Harvester sold its construction equipment division in 1982 and, in 1985, the company not only sold the division that had started it all—the agricultural equipment business—but its highly recognized International Harvester name as well.[17] With only six North American plants left in operation (down from 48 international locations), 85 percent of employees were let go.[18]

The New Formative Years

In 1986, the company adopted a new name, a new look, and a new attitude and Navistar International, with an overhauled focus on the medium- and heavy-duty truck markets, was born. Navistar aggressively redesigned 85 percent of its truck product line by 1987 and introduced a new state of the art nine-speed heavy-truck transmission in 1989. Navistar saw a spike in demand for heavy trucks in 1992 and 1993 that resulted in a 33 percent increase in Navistar's retail deliveries. In 1994, Navistar raised the bar once again, unveiling a new clean-burning engine for vans and trucks that led to increased share in the diesel engine market.[19] The popularity of this new diesel engine also indirectly launched Navistar into the lead of the bus chassis market. To round out its bus portfolio, the company purchased one-third of American Transportation Corporation (AmTran) in 1991 and the remaining two-thirds in 1995. In 2002, AmTran was re-branded as Integrated Coach (IC) and to this day is the leader in the international bus market.[20]

Intense competition in the heavy-truck market led to declining sales in 1996,[21] but Navistar countered with a major truck redesign. With the new truck line launch, its focus on plant operations and product simplification, a stable economy, and problems in the railroad industry due to deregulation, consolidation, and aging capital, Navistar doubled its revenues in 1998.[22]

A Decade of Expansion, Diversification, and Innovation

In 2000, Navistar's leaders recognized that well over 70 percent of its business was based in the North American market. As a countermeasure, Navistar created International Truck and Engine Corporation and began to move its engine business to a newly formed subsidiary—International Engine Corporation—thus initiating its plans for global expansion.[23] The company then opened a plant in Mexico and invested in a 50 percent ownership of Maxion Motores—the largest producer of diesel engines in South America. In 2001, Navistar and Ford announced their Blue Diamond joint venture and began manufacturing trucks in Mexico.[24] In 2004, Navistar continued its global expansion via a joint venture with Mahindra & Mahindra Limited that gave Navistar access to the quickly growing truck market in India.[25] In 2006, the company's MaxxForce engine, initially built to meet US emissions standards, was modified for use in Brazil and Mexico, and intermediate plans to expand into China, India, and Russia were made.[26] In 2008, Navistar expanded its bus leadership position by establishing a joint venture with Camiones y Motores International de Mexico, the Mexico-based subsidiary of Navistar, and San Marino Ônibus e Implementos LTDA, a Brazilian builder of bus bodies.[27] Initially, the new venture served Mexico and South America with both mid-size and minibus models distributed under the Integrated Coach (IC) brand.[28] The venture quickly expanded into the US and Canada with plans for future expansion into other world markets.[29]

Along with recognizing the need for increased geographic diversity, Navistar leaders also identified the need for a more diverse type of customer. In late 2003, the company formed an operating unit for the sole purpose of establishing business with the US government.[30] By April 2004, Navistar had secured a contract for more than 1,700 medium-duty trucks for the US Postal Service.[31] Navistar also emerged as the prime supplier of mine-resistant ambush-protected (MRAP) armored vehicles for the US military, with orders for 12,900 vehicles between 2007 and 2009 that generated several billion dollars in revenue over the period.[32] Navistar further diversified its customer base in 2009 with the $47 million acquisition of recreational vehicle manufacturer Monaco RV. This acquisition enhances Navistar by expanding its diesel and RV chassis business along with providing increased manufacturing capacity in the US.[33]

Navistar's corporate culture of innovation has launched industry-leading technology and driven its success over the past ten years. In 2005, the company introduced a small fleet of first-in-class diesel-electric hybrid utility trucks that won accolades following real world trials. To build on this green technology further, Navistar unveiled its best-in-class energy efficient International ProStar and LoneStar long-haul trucks in 2007 to the US, Canada, and Mexico and planned to expand further via modified versions in South America and other world markets.[34] However, Navistar raised the innovation bar to an entirely new level in 2009 when it purchased a stake in Amminex, a Danish technology company and owner of a proprietary technology that reduces exhaust gas to levels that meet many of the new regulatory emission requirements.[35] As the only company in its industry that can eliminate NOx

inside the engine, thus dispensing with the usual 200 to 300 pounds of additional equipment and weight on the truck, Navistar has changed the game.[36]

Competitive Situation

Navistar International Corporation is active across four market segments: trucks (including medium- and heavy-duty trucks and buses) accounting for 63.1 percent of 2009 revenues; diesel engines (for Navistar and other manufacturers) claiming 23.3 percent of 2009 revenues; engine parts bringing in 18.8 percent in 2009; and financial services (for both Navistar and other truck manufacturers) at 3.0 percent of 2009 revenues.[37]

With such broad market segments, the list of Navistar's competitors is extensive and includes PACCAR, AB Volvo, Daimler Group, MAN Engines and Components, Scania Group, Cummins Engines,[38] BAE Services, Oshkosh Corporation, Commercial Vehicle Group, Miller Industries, and Force Protection among others. Identification of key competitors in primary or essential market segments narrows this list to PACCAR, AB Volvo, and Daimler Group across the truck, bus, and engine segments;[39] Cummins in the engine segment;[40] and BAE Services and Oshkosh Corporation in the military segment[41,42] (Exhibit 1).

PACCAR Inc.

Located in Bellevue, Washington, PACCAR is most similar in overall size and market segmentation to Navistar. Founded in 1905 by William Pigott, Sr., PACCAR has been led for four generations by the Pigott family. PACCAR's primary market segments are nearly identical to Navistar's and include trucks and buses, engines, parts, and financial services. PACCAR manufactures and distributes a

Exhibit 1 Industry Comparison

	2010 Revenues	2009 Revenues	% Change	2010 Market Share North American	2010 Market Share Europe	% of Sales North America	% of Sales Europe	% of Sales Asia	% of Sales Other
Navistar	$ 12.15	$ 11.57	5%						
PACCAR	$ 10.29	$ 8.10	27.2%	24.10%	15.10%	50%			
Daimler Group	$130.60	$105.46	24.0%						
AB Volvo	$ 39.45	$ 32.66	21.0%			18%	39%	25%	18%
Cummins	$ 13.23	$ 10.80	23.0%			36%			64%
BAE Systems	$ 34.76	$ 34.14	1.8%			72%			
Oshkosh	$ 9.84	$ 5.25	87.0%						

*all figures are in billions of U.S. Dollars

Sources: Compiled by authors from data found in the respective 2010 Annual Reports of Navistar, PACCAR, Daimler Group, AB Volvo, Cummins, Inc., BAE Systems, and Oshkosh Corporation.

variety of brand names to different geographic segments: Kenworth in North America and Australia, Peterbilt in the US and Canada, and DAF in Europe with distribution to Asia, Africa, and North America as well.[43]

PACCAR is not only a major player in the North American truck market, holding a 24.1 percent market share, but also maintains a noteworthy 15.1 percent market share in Europe.[44] Its first global acquisition, Foden in the UK in 1981, launched PACCAR into the European market and was solidified with its subsequent acquisitions of DAF in the Netherlands in 1996 and Leyland trucks in England in 1998. Currently, PACCAR's dealer network includes 100 countries with 1,800 locations and it is rapidly expanding in the Asian market.[45]

Net sales and revenues for 2010 were $10.29 billion—a welcome 27.2 percent increase over 2009 after a 46 percent drop in 2008.[46] The 2010 increase is primarily attributed to an additional 18,000 truck deliveries and increased sales of after-market parts. Though this figure remains at less than half of the units sold in 2006,[47] first quarter earnings for 2011 were up 183.0 percent over first quarter 2010.[48] Generally, 89.7 percent of sales revenue at PACCAR is attributed to its trucks and parts segments[49] with 50 percent of total revenues generated outside the US (Exhibit 2).[50]

PACCAR has a reputation for producing high quality products and takes great pride in its technologically advanced systems achieved through centrally managed functional teams such as purchasing, finance, and design.[51] Its commitments to the environment and the communities in which it does business are clearly represented on its Web site and in its philanthropic ventures in education and the arts.[52]

Volvo Group

Based in Sweden, AB Volvo produced its first car in 1927, its first truck in 1928, and its first bus in 1934, before expanding into aircraft engines in the 40s.[53] Through acquisitions, divisional growth, and the sale of its car division in 1999, Volvo has narrowed its primary market segments to the production of trucks (63 percent of net sales), construction equipment (20 percent), and buses (8 percent), with aircraft and marine engines (Aero and Penta) and financial services providing the balance (9 percent) (Exhibits 3A, B, and C).[54] Acquisitions such as Renault (including Mack Trucks) in 2001, Nissan Diesel in 2007, and a majority ownership of Lingong in China, vastly increased Volvo's global diversity and presence.[55,56] Volvo now has more than 1,000 dealers in 180 countries with facilities in 19 countries.[57]

Exhibit 2 PACCAR: Selected Financial Data

	2010	2009	2008	2007	2006
			(millions except per share data)		
Truck and Other Net Sales and Revenues	$ 9,325.1	$7,076.7	$13,709.6	$14,030.4	$15,503.3
Financial Services Revenues	967.8	1,009.8	1,262.9	1,191.3	950.8
Total Revenues	$10,292.9	$8,086.5	$14,972.5	$15,221.7	$16,454.1
Net Income	$ 457.6	$ 111.9	$ 1,017.9	$ 1,227.3	$ 1,496.0
Net Income Per Share:					
Basic	1.25	.31	2.79	3.31	3.99
Diluted	1.25	.31	2.78	3.29	3.97
Cash Dividends Declared Per Share	.69	.54	.82	1.65	1.84
Total Assets:					
Truck and Other	6,355.9	6,137.7	6,219.4	6,599.9	6,296.2
Financial Services	7,878.2	8,431.3	10,030.4	10,710.3	9,811.2
Truck and Other Long-Term Debt	173.5	172.3	19.3	23.6	20.2
Financial Services Debt	5,102.5	5,900.5	7,465.5	7,852.2	7,259.8
Stockholders' Equity	5,357.8	5,103.7	4,846.7	5,013.1	4,456.2
Ratio of Earnings to Fixed Charges	4.07x	1.57x	4.58x	5.36x	7.78x

Source: http://www.paccar.com

Exhibit 3A Volvo Trucks

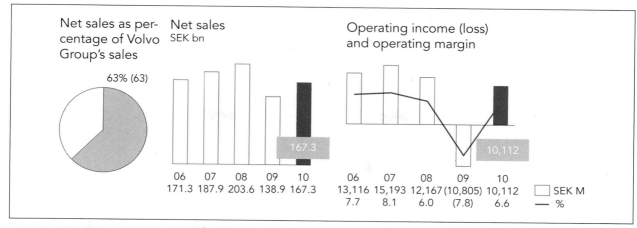

Deliveries by market		
Trucks	**2009**	**2010**
Europe	49,145	65,503
North America	17,574	24,282
South America	12,587	21,483
Asia	34,800	53,833
Other markets	13,575	14,888
Total	**127,681**	**179,989**

Net Sales by market		
Trucks, SEK M	**2009**	**2010**
Europe	65,874	69,606
North America	21,563	26,901
South America	12,490	21,680
Asia	26,943	35,231
Other markets	12,069	13,888
Total	**138,940**	**167,305**

Source: http://www3.volvo.com

Exhibit 3B Volvo Buses

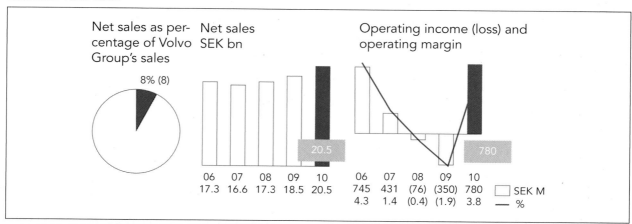

Deliveries by market		
Buses	**2009**	**2010**
Europe	3,164	2,395
North America	1,539	2,092
South America	690	1,174
Asia	3,839	3,477
Other markets	625	1,091
Total	**9,857**	**10,229**

Net Sales by market		
Buses, SEK M	**2009**	**2010**
Europe	7,707	6,242
North America	5,673	7,200
South America	1,235	1,737
Asia	2,749	3,299
Other markets	1,101	2,038
Total	**18,465**	**20,516**

Source: http://www3.volvo.com

Exhibit 3C Volvo: Financial Services

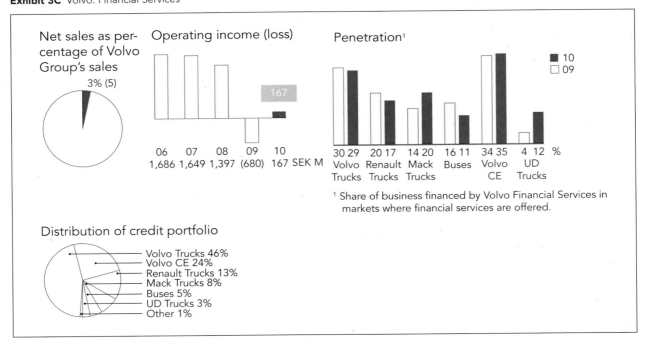

¹ Share of business financed by Volvo Financial Services in markets where financial services are offered.

Source: http://www.3.volvo.com

Net revenues in 2010 for Volvo Group were $39.45 billion,ⁱ a 21 percent increase over 2009 net revenues. Though all market segments (except Aero, down 1 percent) showed increased revenue, construction equipment posted the largest gains with a 51 percent increase followed by trucks, up by 20 percent. Geographically, Volvo relies heavily on the European market with 39 percent of 2010 sales located there, though its market share in the heavy- and medium-duty truck segments has remained nearly stagnant. Secondary geographic markets include Asia with 25 percent of sales (increasing market share in China; decreasing share in Japan) and North America at 18 percent[58] with increased market share in recent years.[59]

Since its founding, Volvo has maintained that, "safety is and must be the basic principle in all design work,"[60] with additional consideration to quality and durability.[61] This translates into Volvo's corporate values of quality, safety, and environmental care that, despite a decentralized structure, serve as the base for all Volvo's brands.[62,63] All business units benefit from universal processes and strengths including "economies of scale, logistics, and business services,"[64] while maintaining a customer focus.[65]

Daimler Group

The founders of the Daimler Group invented the automobile in 1886.[66] Through a succession of acquisitions and expansions, this German-based global giant now does business in five primary market segments.[67] Financials for fiscal year 2010 divide these segments into: Mercedes-Benz cars, Daimler trucks, Mercedes-Benz vans, Daimler buses, and financial services (Exhibits 4A, B, and C).[68]

The Daimler Group manufactures and distributes globally under numerous brands. Excluding the passenger car segment, these include Mercedes-Benz (trucks, buses, and vans), Freightliner Trucks, Orion, Mitsubishi Fuso, and Thomas Built Buses, among others.[69] Net revenue across all divisions for 2010 was $130.6 billion,ⁱⁱ up 24 percent from 2009.[70] Excluding the substantial volume of Mercedes-Benz cars, Daimler produced 618,605 units—a 35.2 percent increase over 2009.[71]

Daimler's Web site and 2010 Annual Report heavily leverage nostalgia for the original founders' innovation of the automobile,[72,73] using it as the basis for the company's value statement, "What We Stand For: As the pioneers of automotive manufacture, we consider it both an incentive and an obligation to continue our tradition of groundbreaking technologies and high-quality products."[74] In fact, their 2010 Annual Report is titled "Innovation From Tradition."[75] This vision is reinforced by continual increases to its research and development budget, up 16 percent in 2010 from 2009. Although Western Europe and North America still

ⁱconverted from 264.7 SEK billion at 12/31/10 exchange rate

ⁱⁱconverted from €97.8 billion at 12/31/10 exchange rate

Exhibit 4A Daimler: Key Figures and Ratios

(in millions of EUR)	Fiscal Year 2010	2009	Change
Unit Sales (in units)	1,895,432	1,551,291	+22%
Revenue	97,761	78,924	+24%
EBIT	7,274	−1,513	—
Net Profit (loss), Group	4,674	−2,644	—
Profit (loss) attributable to shareholders of Daimler AG	4,498	−2,640	—
Depreciation and amortization (including amortization on capitalized development costs, excluding depreciation on leased assets)	3,364	3,264	+3%
R&D expenditure total	4,849	4,181	+16%
Expensed R&D costs	3,476	2,896	+20%
Capitalized development costs	1,373	1,285	+7%
Amortization on capitalized development costs	719	647	+11%
Capital expenditure (Property, plant & equipment)	3,653	2,423	+51%

Source: http://www.daimler.com

Exhibit 4B Daimler: Unit Sales

(in units)	Fiscal Year 2010	2009	Change
Mercedes-Benz Cars*	1,276,827	1,093,905	+17%
Daimler Trucks	355,263	259,328	+37%
Mercedes-Benz Vans	224,224	165,576	+35%
Daimler Buses	39,118	32,482	+20%
Daimler Group*	1,895,432	1,551,291	+22%

*Including Mitsubishi vehicles manufactured and/or sold in South Africa.

Source: http://www.daimler.com

Exhibit 4C Daimler: Revenue

(in millions of EUR)	Fiscal Year 2010	2009	Change
Mercedes-Benz Cars	53,426	41,318	+29%
Daimler Trucks	24,024	18,360	+31%
Mercedes-Benz Vans	7,812	6,215	+26%
Daimler Buses	4,558	4,238	+8%
Daimler Financial Services	12,788	11,996	+7%
Reconciliation	−4,847	−3,203	−51%
Daimler Group	97,761	78,924	+24%

Source: http://www.daimler.com

account for most of Daimler's sales, there is an increased effort to establish the Daimler brands in foreign markets through joint ventures.[76]

Cummins, Inc.

Although Cummins does not compete with Navistar in multiple market segments, as Navistar's primary competitor in the engine market—supplying engines to PACCAR, Volvo, Daimler, Ford, and even Navistar—it merits exploration.[77,78] Based in Indiana, Cummins was founded in 1919 as an engine company and has since expanded into four business units: engines, power generation, components, and distribution.[79] Cummins began its global expansion in the 50s when it opened a facility in Scotland. By the end of the 60s, it had aggressively expanded into 98 countries.[80] Early expansion into China, Brazil, and India and subsequent expansion has brought the company into 190 countries with 5,200 dealer locations today. Indicative of its global presence, 2010 sales from outside of the US were 64 percent—up from 52 percent in 2009.[81]

In 2009, Cummins held 38 and 37 percent market share of the North American market in heavy- and medium-duty truck engines, respectively.[82] While sales in 2010 were up 23 percent over 2009,[83] it did not make up for its significant losses (-27 percent) in 2008 to 2009 due to economic conditions[84] (see Exhibit 5). This reduction in sales led to workforce reductions of 15 percent as well as salary cuts at the director and officer levels.[85]

Cummins is focused on "innovation, persistence, and commitment to community."[86] Being the "first to market the best products" and "partnering with customers" are part of the company's mission statement.[87] These ideals are clearly supported not only by its sizeable investments in new technologies designed to meet new emissions

Exhibit 5 Cummins: Engine Segment Data

| In millions | Years ended December 31, | | | Favorable/(Unfavorable) | | | |
| | | | | 2010 vs. 2009 | | 2009 vs. 2008 | |
	2010	2009	2008	Amount	Percent	Amount	Percent
External sales	$6,594	$5,582	$7,432	$1,012	18%	$(1,850)	(25)%
Intersegment sales	1,294	823	1,378	471	57%	(555)	(40)%
Total sales	7,888	6,405	8,810	1,483	23%	(2,405)	(27)%
Depreciation and amortization	171	185	180	14	8%	(5)	(3)%
Research, development and engineering expenses	263	241	286	(22)	(9)%	45	16%
Equity, royalty and interest income from investees	161	54	99	107	NM	(45)	(45)%
Interest income	12	3	10	9	NM	(7)	(70)%
Segment EBIT	809	252	535	557	NM	(283)	(53)%

	2010	2009	2008	Percentage Points	Percentage Points
Segment EBIT as a percentage of total sales	10.3%	3.9%	6.1%	6.4	(2.2)

Engine segment sales by market were as follows:

| In millions | Years ended December 31, | | | Favorable/(Unfavorable) | | | |
| | | | | 2010 vs. 2009 | | 2009 vs. 2008 | |
	2010	2009	2008	Amount	Percent	Amount	percent
Heavy-duty truck	$1,503	$1,996	$2,308	$ (493)	(25)%	$ (312)	(14)%
Medium-duty truck and bus	1,435	1,232	1,550	203	16%	(318)	(21)%
Light-duty automotive and RV	1,022	688	804	334	49%	(116)	(14)%
Total on-highway	3,960	3,916	4,662	44	1%	(746)	(16)%
Industrial	2,889	1,821	3,029	1,068	59%	(1,208)	(40)%
Stationary power	1,039	668	1,119	371	56%	(451)	(40)%
Total sales	$7,888	$6,405	$8,810	$1,483	23%	$(2,405)	(27)%

Unit shipments by engine classification (including unit shipments to Power Generation) were as follows:

| | Years ended December 31, | | | Favorable/(Unfavorable) | | | |
| | | | | 2010 vs. 2009 | | 2009 vs. 2008 | |
	2010	2009	2008	Amount	Percent	Amount	Percent
Midrange	368,900	269,200	418,300	99,700	37%	(149,100)	(36)%
Heavy-duty	61,200	85,900	108,300	(24,700)	(29)%	(22,400)	(21)%
High-horsepower	18,500	13,400	20,600	5,100	38%	(7,200)	(35)%
Total unit shipments	448,600	368,500	547,200	80,100	22%	(178,700)	(33)%

Source: http://www.sec.gov/Archives

standards ($310 million in 2009) and expansion into emerging markets,[88] but also through its newly adopted principle to "Lead in Critical Technologies."[89]

BAE Systems

BAE Systems primarily provides systems and support services for military customers. The London based company is one of Europe's largest defense contractors[90] providing military combat,[91] artillery, and engineering vehicles[92] and competes with Navistar in this market. Operating worldwide in markets from North America to Europe to the Middle East, BAE has been heavily impacted by reduced government defense spending and has countered this reduction by expanding further into emerging markets.[93]

In 2010, BAE Systems net sales revenue across all divisions was $34.76 million,[iii] a 1.8 percent increase over 2009. Its land and armaments division accounted for 26 percent of total sales revenue, a 12 percent decrease from 2009 (Exhibit 6).[94] A recent civil settlement with the US government as well as previously imposed restrictions on BAE applications due to ethics issues regarding arms sales have also impacted BAE as half

of its sales revenues have historically originated in the US.[95] Because of its questionable reputation and despite a recent restructuring of its ethical standards,[96] the US Department of Justice continues to require an ethics monitor as a contingency of doing business.[97]

Oshkosh Corp

Oshkosh Corporation was founded in 1917 as Wisconsin Duplex Auto Company and has expanded through the years to include manufacturing facilities across North America, Europe, Australia, and China, producing brand names such as Oshkosh, JLG, Jerr-Dan, and others. Oshkosh specializes in military and specialty vehicles, such as fire engines, and competes with Navistar in the military vehicle segment.[98]

Primarily due to its defense market segment, sales revenue at Oshkosh increased 87 percent in 2010 to reach $9.8 billion.[99] Net sales revenue for defense totaled $7.2 billion, a 177 percent increase over 2009 figures.[100] Despite a global presence, 72 percent of Oshkosh's sales revenue comes from the US government (Exhibit 7).[101]

Oshkosh has made 15 strategic acquisitions since 1996. Oshkosh maintains strict, self-imposed guidelines for acquisitions including requirements for product diversification, operational synergies, or premium

---

[iii]converted from £22.4 million at 12/31/10 exchange rate

Exhibit 6 BAE: Five Year Financial Summary

Income statement[1,2,3]	2010 £m	2009 £m	2008 £m	2007 £m	2006 £m
Continuing operations					
Sales including Group's share of equity accounted investments					
Electronics, Intelligence & Support	5,653	5,637	4,459	3,916	4,007
Land & Armaments	5,930	6,738	6,407	3,538	2,115
Programmes & Support	6,680	6,298	4,638	5,327	4,615
International	4,534	3,828	2,926	3,009	3,102
HQ & Other Businesses	278	254	235	243	295
Intra-operating group sales	(683)	(765)	(529)	(673)	(695)
	22,392	21,990	18,136	15,360	13,439
Underlying EBITA[4]					
Electronics, Intelligence & Support	668	575	506	437	429
Land & Armaments	604	604	566	324	168
Programmes & Support	529	670	491	456	331
International	478	419	417	403	387
HQ & Other Businesses	(65)	(71)	(101)	(203)	(146)
	2,214	2,197	1,879	1,417	1,169
Profit on disposal of businesses	1	68	238	40	13
Pension curtailment gains	2	261	—	—	—
Regulatory penalties	(18)	(278)	—	—	—
Uplift on acquired inventories	—	—	—	(12)	—
EBITA[5]	2,199	2,248	2,117	1,445	1,182

(Continued)

Exhibit 6 BAE: Five Year Financial Summary (*Continued*)

Income statement[1,2,3]	2010 £m	2009 £m	2008 £m	2007 £m	2006 £m
Amortisation and impairment of intangible assets	(517)	(1,259)	(303)	(297)	(139)
Finance costs including share of equity accounted investments	(194)	(698)	701	93	(174)
Profit before taxation	1,488	291	2,515	1,241	869
Taxation expense including share of equity accounted investments	(461)	(352)	(636)	(366)	(243)
Profit/(loss) for the year - continuing operations	1,027	(61)	1,879	875	626
Profit/(loss) for the year - discontinued operations	54	16	(111)	47	1,013
Profit/(loss) for the year	1,081	(45)	1,768	922	1,639

Balance sheet	2010 £m	2009[6] £rn	2008 £m	2007 £m	2006 £m
Intangible assets	11,216	11,306	12,306	9,559	7,595
Property, plant and equipment, and investment property	2,848	2,663	2,558	1,887	1,869
Non-current investments	798	852	1,040	787	678
Inventories	644	887	926	701	395
Assets held in Trust	261	227	—	—	—
Payables (excluding cash on customers' account) less receivables	(6,159)	(6,918)	(5,866)	(5,373)	(4,298)
Other financial assets and liabilities	(10)	(45)	240	52	6
Retirement benefit obligations	(3,456)	(4,679)	(3,365)	(1,629)	(2,499)
Provisions	(1,077)	(929)	(845)	(809)	(695)
Net tax	580	896	256	63	648
Net (debt)/cash (as defined by the Group)	(242)	403	39	700	435
Disposal groups held for sale	—	—	—	64	—
Non-controlling interests	(71)	(72)	(55)	(36)	(17)
Total equity attributable to equity holders of the parent	5,332	4,591	7,234	5,966	4,117

Movement in net (debt)/cash (as defined by the Group)	2010 £m	2009 £m	2008 £m	2007 £m	2006 £m
Cash inflow from operating activities	1,535	2,232	2,009	2,162	778
Net capital expenditure[7]	(364)	(489)	(503)	(262)	(141)
Dividends received from equity investments	71	77		78	145
Assets Contributed to Trust	(25)	(225)	—	—	—
Cash held for charitable contribution to Tanzania	(30)	—	—	—	—
Operating business cash flow	1,187	1,595	1,595	1,978	782
Acquisitions and disposals	(88)	(254)	(1,038)	(2,112)	1,330
Interest	(173)	(186)	(98)	(65)	(207)
Tax and dividends	(958)	(889)	(750)	(509)	(431)
(Purchase)/issue of equity shares	(520)	(20)	(27)	603	(71)
Preference share conversion	—	—	—	245	6
Exchange movements	(20)	262	(374)	36	323
Other movements[8]	(80)	(132)	5	57	(11)
Net (decrease)/increase in net funds	(652)	376	(687)	233	1,721
Movement in cash on customers' account	7	(12)	26	32	(9)
Movement in net (debt)/cash (as defined by the Group)	(645)	364	(661)	265	1,712
Opening net cash/(debt) (as defined by the Group)	403	39	700	435	(1,277)
Closing net (debt)/cash (as defined by the Group)	(242)	403	39	700	435

(Continued)

ERRATA SHEET

Credit Line Correction for: Strategic Management, 10th Edition

Hitt, Ireland, and Hoskisson

ISBN: 9781111825874 Concepts and Cases: Competitiveness and Globalization

ISBN: 9781133495253 Instructor's Edition: Strategic Management

ISBN: 9781133495239 Strategic Management: Concepts: Competitiveness and Globalization

Figure 4.1 Southwest Airlines Activity System

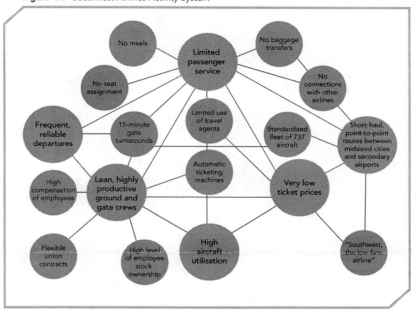

subsidiary, United Airlines' United Shuttle, Delta's Song, and Continental Airlines' Continental Lite). Hindsight shows that these competitors offered low prices to customers, but weren't able to operate at costs close to those of Southwest or to provide customers with any notable sources of differentiation, such as a unique experience while in the air. The key to Southwest's success has been its ability to continuously reduce its costs while providing customers with *acceptable* levels of differentiation such as an engaging culture. Firms using the cost leadership strategy must understand that in terms of sources of differentiation that accompany the cost leader's product, the customer defines *acceptable*. Fit among activities is a key to the sustainability of competitive advantage for all firms, including Southwest Airlines. Strategic fit among the many activities is critical for competitive advantage. It is more difficult for a competitor to match a configuration of integrated activities than to imitate a particular activity such as sales promotion, or a process technology.[49]

Types of Business-Level Strategies

Firms choose from among five business-level strategies to establish and defend their desired strategic position against competitors: *cost leadership, differentiation, focused cost leadership, focused differentiation,* and *integrated cost leadership/differentiation* (see Figure 4.2). Each business-level strategy helps the firm to establish and exploit a particular *competitive advantage* within a particular *competitive scope.* How firms integrate the activities they perform within each different business-level strategy demonstrates how they differ from one another.[50] For example, firms have different activity maps, and thus, a Southwest Airlines activity map differs from those of competitors JetBlue, Continental, American Airlines, and so forth. Superior integration of activities increases the likelihood of being able to gain an advantage over competitors and to earn above-average returns.

Part Two

Complete a poster that can be displayed in class. Your poster should represent the firm and its evolution as far back in its history as you can get on one poster. The goal is to highlight the firm's beginnings, its acquisitions and divestiture activity, and its movement from one corporate-level strategy to another. You will need to do some extensive research on the firm to identify common linkages between operating units.

Be prepared to answer the following questions:

- How has the firm's corporate-level strategy evolved over time?
- What is the current corporate-level strategy and what links, if any, exist between operating units?

- Critique the current corporate-level strategy (e.g., too much diversification, too little, just right, and why).

EXERCISE 2: HOW DOES THE FIRM'S PORTFOLIO STACK UP?

The Boston Consulting Group (BCG) product portfolio matrix has been around for decades and was introduced by the BCG as a way for firms to understand the priorities that should be given to various segments within their mix of businesses. It is based on a matrix with two vertices: firm market share and projected market growth rate:

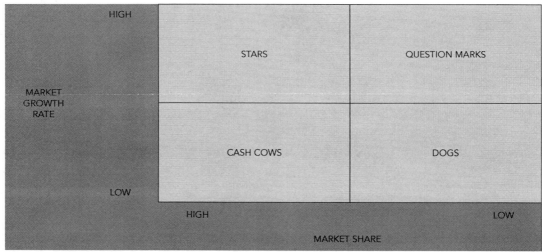

© 2012 Boston Consulting Group.

Each firm therefore can categorize its business units as follows:

- Stars: High growth and high market share. These business units generate large amounts of cash but also use large amounts of cash. These are often the focus of the firm's priorities as this segment has a potentially bright future.
- Cash cows: Low market growth coupled with high market share. Profits and cash generated are high, need for new cash is low. Provides a foundation for the firm from which it can launch new initiatives.
- Dogs: Low market growth and low market share. This is usually a situation the firms seek to avoid. These units are quite often the target of a turnaround plan or liquidation effort.
- Question marks: High market growth but low market share. It is difficult to say what the firm should do in this quadrant and creates a need to move strategically because of high demands on cash due to market needs yet low cash returns because of the low firm market share.

Using this matrix to analyze a firm's corporate-level strategy or the way in which it rewards and prioritizes its business units has come under some criticism. For one, market share is not the only way in which a firm should view success or potential success; second, market growth is not the only indicator for the attractiveness of a market; and third, sometimes "dogs" can earn as much cash as "cows."

Part One

Select a publicly traded firm that has a diversified corporate-level strategy. The more unrelated the segments, the better.

Part Two

Analyze the firm utilizing the BCG matrix. In order to do this, you will need to develop market share ratings for each operating unit and assess the overall market attractiveness for that segment.

Exhibit 6 BAE: Five Year Financial Summary (*Continued*)

Other information	2010	2009	2008	2007	2006
Continuing operations					
Basic earnings/(loss) per share - total (pence)	28.9	(2.3)	52.7	25.2	19.3
Basic earnings per share - underlying[9] (pence)	40.8	40.1	36.8	29.4	22.9
Order book including the Group's share of equity accounted investments (£bn)	39.7	46.3	45.7	37.9	30.9
Including discontinued operations					
Dividend per ordinary share (pence)	17.5	16.0	14.5	12.8	11.3
Number of employees, excluding share of employees of equity accounted investments, at year end	92,000	98,000	94,000	88,000	79,000
Capital expenditure including leased assets (£m)	437	522	552	341	538

[1] For the year ended 31 December 2006, Airbus SAS is presented as a discontinued operation.

[2] For the year ended 31 December 2006, the operating group information has been restated to reflect changes made to the Group's organisational structure.

[3] For the years ended 31 December 2006 to 2010, Saab AB is presented as a discontinued operation.

[4] Earnings before amortisation and impairment of intangible assets, finance costs and taxation expense (EBITA) excluding non-recurring items. From 2006 to 2008, non-recurring items are profit on disposal of businesses and uplift on acquired inventories. In 2009 end 2010, non-recurring items are profit on disposal of businesses, pension curtailment gains and regulatory penalties.

[5] Earnings before amortisation and impairment of intangible assets, finance costs and taxation expense.

[6] Restated following finalisation of the fair values recognised on acquisition of the 45% shareholding in BVT Surface Fleet Limited (see note 29).

[7] Includes expenditure on property, plant and equipment, investment property, intangible assets and other investments, and equity accounted investment funding.

[8] Other movements include cash flows from matured derivative financial instruments, cash collateral and other non-cash movements (see page 172).

[9] Earnings excluding amortisation and impairment of intangible assets, non-cash finance movements on pensions and financial derivatives, and non-recurring items. From 2006 to 2008, nonrecurring items are profit on disposal of businesses and uplift on acquired inventories. In 2009 and 2010, non-recurring items are profit on disposal of businesses, pension curtailment gains and regulatory penalties.

Source: http://ar2010.baesystems.com

Exhibit 7 Oshkosh: Three Year Segment Summary

	Fiscal Year Ended September 30,		
	2010	2009	2008
Net sales			
Defense	$ 7,161.7	$2,594.8	$1,891.9
Access equipment	3,011.9	1,225.5	3,212.6
Fire & emergency	916.0	1,042.3	1,009.4
Commercial	622.1	590.0	835.1
Intersegment eliminations	(1,869.3)	(199.5)	(71.3)
Consolidated	$ 9,842.4	$5,253.1	$6,877.7

The following table presents net sales by geographic region based on product shipment destination (in millions):

	Fiscal Year Ended September 30,		
	2010	2009	2008
Net sales			
United States	$8,882.6	$4,487.1	$4,997.2
Other North America	111.0	89.7	180.6
Europe, Africa and the Middle East	508.6	468.6	1,283.5
Rest of the world	340.2	207.7	416.4
Consolidated	$9,842.4	$5,253.1	$6,877.7

Source: http://www.sec.gov/Archives

market share positions. Oshkosh is also committed to investing in innovation and providing quality products and services.[102]

Making Navistar's Work Possible

In 2010, Navistar embraced a new philosophy of "controlling our destiny."[103] In working to demonstrate this philosophy, Navistar is decreasing its reliance on suppliers.[104] This ideal extends across many facets of Navistar's production including the engine business, providing emissions solutions (including the development of proprietary technologies), and the valve business.[105] Through its acquisitions—including Pure Power Technologies (an emissions solutions company) and Holley Performance Products (to acquire proprietary valve technology),[106]—Navistar is not only reducing its reliance on suppliers, but also gaining valuable technology. Navistar has also received considerable attention for its new engine line—MaxxForce. Success with the MaxxForce will not only reduce Navistar's dependence on Cummins (its primary engine supplier), but will put Navistar in competition with Cummins in the engine segment.[107]

In the past, Navistar has run the risk of late delivery of products when suppliers were unable to meet their orders. Concern in the industry is that if demand returns to the market too quickly, supplier lag will create a shortage of materials thus forcing suppliers to choose which customers to satisfy first. In cases such as Alison Transmissions and Dana Holding Corporation—both near monopolies in their own markets—Navistar makes great efforts to develop and maintain good relationships to ensure its products are delivered first. Navistar also makes every attempt to establish long-term purchasing contracts with suppliers to minimize the effects of fluctuations in material costs on overall product costs.[108]

Key Customers

Navistar serves a variety of customers including fleet dealers, government entities, original equipment manufacturers (OEMs), internal brand customers, and dealerships.[109]

The truck segment—including buses and military sales—primarily serves large fleet dealers,[110] large bus providers, and national governments. Navistar's engine business serves not only internal customers by providing engines and components for Navistar's multiple brands of truck, bus, and other heavy equipment, but also external customers by supplying multiple OEMS, primarily in North and South America, including Ford Motor, one of Navistar's largest customers.[111] In 2010, government and defense sales were made in over 26 countries—though primarily in the UK and the US.[112]

Both the parts and financial services (including retail, wholesale, and lease financing) segments serve not only current Navistar customers as support services

to the primary manufacturing business, but also other truck manufacturers.[113]

Navistar enjoys a high level of customer loyalty, winning the J.D. Power and Associates 2010 US Heavy-Duty Truck Customer Satisfaction Award.[114] Its "International Advantage" program is free and offers customers money saving tips, discounts on parts and services, a *Trail Magazine* subscription, monthly e-newsletter, toll-free phone support, and an online portal featuring Navistar's "Ask the Expert" feature.[115] In 2010, Navistar introduced its Customer Parts Recovery program whereby it provides cash or credit to customers returning new, unused parts. Customers that purchase a predetermined amount of parts over a set period of time can eventually receive full credit for their returns.[116]

If Not By Land. . .

For those customers that need to move product, there are essentially four ways to get it there. Depending on the origination point and destination, a combination of transport options is often necessary. Aside from trucking, the three alternatives include rail, sea, and air. While rail is less expensive and more fuel-efficient—factors that have led to increased market share recently—it is not convenient to every origination or destination point.[117] If a company needs to send product further, faster, air cargo guarantees both for a premium.[118] Finally, like air cargo, maritime shipping also goes further, but certainly not faster.

Fortunately, no matter the primary transport choice, at some point, a medium- or heavy-duty truck is likely to run a leg in the relay. While those in the trucking industry may prefer to run the entire race alone, trucking has shared the road with these other transport providers for a very long time.

Sharing the Road

It takes more than money to get into the truck and engine manufacturing business—know-how, connections, and customers to build economies of scale are equally essential.[119] The newest competitors most often come from smaller companies that "go global."[120] For example, Swedish-based Scania, a $12.0 billion company,[iv] operates in 100 countries,[121] has sizable market share in the South American truck market, and is already active in the engine segment in the US.[122] MAN Engines & Components, based in Germany, is one of Europe's largest truck and engine manufacturers with net sales in 2010 of $19.4 billion.[123] Poised for growth, MAN has announced to its shareholders the need for further globalization and "sustained growth," though BRIC nations (Brazil, Russia, India, and China) are its current target. With current production

---

[iv]converted from 80,109 SEK billion at 12/31/10 exchange rate

sites in Mexico and Brazil, however, extension into the North American market may not be far off.[124]

Rocky Roads

The global economy, though improved, remains uncertain and everything from fluctuating interest rates, foreign exchange rate instability, increased raw materials cost, and rising fuel prices can adversely affect Navistar's business. Being located in and with a large market share of the US, Navistar is especially sensitive to fluctuations within the domestic economy, including stringent lending guidelines. Despite evidence of a recovery and the anticipated strength of the market through 2011, continued volatility in the truck market is expected.[125]

As if the economic stressors weren't enough to deal with, increasingly stringent engine emissions regulations imposed by both the US Environmental Protection Agency (EPA, effective in 2010) and the European Union (Euro VI, effective 2013) require all OEMs to significantly reduce particle and nitrogen emissions to meet new standards. Significant research and development investments (an estimated €8 billion across Europe)[126] will be required to meet these new regulations.[127,128] Given the increasingly environmentally conscious society, it is anticipated that additional regulations pertaining to emissions will be imposed in the future.[129]

We are in a position to witness an interesting face-off posed by the two best answers to emissions presented by engine technology: specifically, EGR (Exhaust Gas Recirculation) versus SCR (Selective Catalytic Reduction). Navistar's election to utilize the innovative EGR technology versus the industry's more universally embraced SCR solution is a calculated risk. Parallels can be drawn to the Beta versus VHS debate; however, unlike knowing that VHS reigned supreme (until the advent of the DVD anyway), the winning emissions design has yet to be determined. Proven and significant advantages of EGR technology include lighter and smaller component weight and size, decreased operator maintenance, and increased fuel economy. As nothing is without faults however, its main disadvantages include reduced horsepower and the need to re-engineer the engine. An additional consideration is the speculation that the future of the trucking industry will be determined by technology that will include eco-friendly design and engines, higher fuel efficiency, alternative fuel sources, and lighter body materials.[130]

Mapping a Route

Navistar offers great products at competitive costs. For example, the MaxxForce® ADVANCED EGR technology developed to meet the 2010 US EPA emission requirements handles both of the byproducts of the diesel engine operation targeted for reduction by re-circulating cooled diesel exhaust back into the engine. Doing so reduces emissions "in cylinder" before final emission.[131] Despite doubts regarding its trucks' fuel economy,[132] Navistar consistently extols the advantages of its EGR technology (Exhibit 8).

Two quotes stress the commitment with which Navistar is offering customers its EGR technology. According to Eric Tech, president of Navistar Engine Group, "…Navistar continues to seek innovative products which differentiate us from the marketplace, while others embrace the status quo."[133] For Jim Hebe, senior VP for North American sales, "It's a culture, part of the [Navistar] corporate strategy to be different if it benefits the customer."[134]

Navistar had long been "only a medium-duty company" relying on Cummins to supply its heavy-duty engines.[135] To implement EGR, Navistar used a blend of internal capabilities, partnerships, and acquisitions with its first order of business to create three new heavy-duty engines—the MaxxForce 11, 13, and 15 (liters). To do so, it not only leveraged internal know-how from its medium-duty engine experts, but also built strategic partnerships with other truck and engine manufacturers: first with MAN to develop the MaxxForce 11 and 13 and later with Caterpillar for the MaxxForce 15. The goal of these partnerships was to exploit the strengths of each company to create value for all parties. BNet reporter Mike

Exhibit 8 EGR Advantages/SCR Disadvantages

EGR *(Exhaust Gas Recirculation)*	SCR *(Selective Catalytic Reduction)*
■ Burden of compliance rests on manufacturer	■ Burden of compliance rests on operator (e.g., system maintenance)
■ Unchanged driver interface reducing vehicle complexity	■ Driver interface requires additional audible and visual indicators
■ Vehicle packaging and payload superiority	■ Requires additional tanks, exhaust components, and electrical control systems
■ Diagnostic requirements unchanged	
■ Lower operating cost	
■ Neutral price	■ Additional cost: additional fluid, time, and payload
■ Neutral fuel economy	

Source: Ray, R. (n.d.). Navistar Engine Group Presentation: 2010 Engine Emissions. http://www.faptflorida.org

Brezonick said, "The new engine will be an interesting mix between Caterpillar and Navistar technologies, with Cat supplying the muscle and Navistar the brains."[136]

In addition to banking on EGR, Navistar is also pursuing other opportunities to deliver future "state-of-the-art, customer-focused solutions." In early 2011, Navistar reached an agreement with EcoMotors International that involves the future commercialization of a revolutionary new engine design.[137] Moreover, Navistar offers products utilizing the three main green energies: electric, hybrid, and natural gas. Here again, Navistar is developing select partnerships to achieve a broad offering using a design by Modec of Great Britain to produce the eStar, "the company's first fully-electric cargo van,"[138] Eaton Corp.'s electric-drive system in combination with a MaxxForce-DT for its DuraStar hybrid, and Emissions Solutions to convert its DT-466 to natural gas for its WorkStar natural gas-fired vocational truck.[139] As Eric Tech said, "This approach is consistent with our strategy to leverage what we have and what others have built in order to bring better products to our customers."[140]

According to Jim Hebe, Navistar is "fully convinced that natural gas will play a big part in transportation in America." As such, it already offers additional engines converted to natural gas technology. MaxxForce 11 and 13 are currently available and natural gas versions of models 9 and 10 will roll out soon. Then, "all but Navistar's smaller MF 7 V-8 diesel will have natural gas versions."[141]

Navistar develops great products but not without leveraging economies of scale to keep them affordable. Eric Tech gives the following example of the innovative approach his engineering team is taking:

They determined that the EGR cooler on the MaxxForce 13 doesn't have enough heat rejection for the MaxxForce 15, so they had to figure out how they were going to get around that problem. They looked at our parts bin and saw we have a 7.6 L DT engine that, like all of our engines, also has an EGR cooler. They did the math and they literally took two DT EGR coolers and packaged it as a twin EGR cooler for the MaxxForce 15.[142]

Not one to rely simply on new products, Navistar actively pursues new customers as well. In negotiating contracts with the US government, it managed to create a new business and product line while leveraging its existing core capabilities—engines and trucks. Navistar CEO Daniel Ustian explains:

Commercial trucks and diesel engines—that's what we do. We already have trucks. No new design. We already have engines. No new design. We have a $3 billion business run by 40 people. Tell me who in the world has got that?[143]

Thanks to Navistar's platform system, most truck and engine models are "similar enough in their manufacturing process that the incremental cost for each of our facilities to build every unit we design is small enough to make a flexible manufacturing strategy cost effective and appropriate."[144] This allows each plant to produce a wide, if not complete, selection of Navistar's portfolio. Additionally, Navistar is committed to lean manufacturing and distribution techniques and recently consolidated its truck and engine research development activities to its new Lisle, Illinois World Headquarters.[145]

Finally, Navistar is also working to achieve "profitable growth in areas [they] haven't played in"[146] including not only new products or new business segments as discussed, but also new geographies. While, Navistar is present in Mexico, Canada, Brazil, Argentina, and South Africa, the company is now focusing on high growth markets. Since 2005, Navistar has signed two joint venture agreements with Mahindra & Mahindra Ltd. of India and today, Mahindra Navistar manufactures diesel engines, commercial trucks, as well as buses in India.[147] Also, as part of their 2009 strategic alliance, Navistar and Caterpillar launched a 50/50 joint venture called NC2. Their goal is to "develop, manufacture, and distribute commercial trucks in regions outside of North America and India, with an initial focus on Australia, Brazil, China, Russia, South Africa, and Turkey."[148]

Financials

Over the past several years, Navistar has seen significant fluctuations in revenue and net income. Navistar realized its largest net income in the last five years in 2009, despite it being the lowest truck market in 50 years, due in part to increased military sales of $2.8 billion (Exhibit 9).[149]

Total assets have decreased by 24 percent over the past five years mostly due to a 68 percent reduction in receivables and a 53 percent reduction in long-term assets, with a corresponding 23 percent reduction in total liabilities due mostly to a 37 percent reduction in long-term debt over the same trailing five years. Going forward Navistar is continuing to focus on balance sheet activity by putting heavy attention to cash management (Exhibits 10A-E).[150]

Compared to its competitors and the industry, Navistar's financial metrics consistently fall in line with the industry average, lagging slightly behind just a few competitors with regard to profitability measures, but slightly ahead on liquidity measures. Navistar had a 2010 gross profit margin of 19.9 percent and a net profit margin of 1.6 percent compared to the industry mean of 22.2 percent and 1.6 percent. BAE and PACCAR lead the list of competitors with gross profit margins of 55.2 and 20.1 percent, respectively; and net profit margins of 5.0 and 5.1 percent, respectively. The same holds true with return on assets with Navistar at 2.2 percent and the industry mean at 1.9 percent while BAE and PACCAR again lead the pack at 4.3 and 4.0 percent respectively.

Exhibit 9 Navistar: Five-Year Summary of Units Invoiced, Revenue, and Net Income

	2006	2007	2008	2009	2010
Units Invoiced	155,400	113,600 (−41,800)	102,200 (−11,400)	76,800 (−25,400)	86,900 (+10,100)
Revenue	$ 14,200	$ 12,295 (−1,905)	$ 14,724 (+2,429)	$ 11,569 (−3,155)	$ 12,145 (+576)
Net Income	$ 301	$ 120 (−181)	$ 134 (+14)	$ 320 (+186)	$ 223 (−97)

Sources: 2007 Annual Report to Shareholders. http://files.shareholder.com/downloads/NAV/1296127258x0x213905/97C07844-AC05-4F6A-A58C-FE982490BC77/Navistar_2007_Annual_Report.pdf; 2009 Annual Report to Shareholders http://files.shareholder.com/downloads/NAV/1296127258x0x343731/CC261514-F641-456B-83C9-5AF0DB1FAEC6/NAV_2009_Annual_Report_Final.pdf; 2010 Annual Report to Shareholders http://files.shareholder.com/downloads/NAV/1296127258x0x429697/5255C71D-0E9E-493E-8B7D-BE1D110B0EC8/NIC_2010_-_10-K.pdf

Exhibit 10A Navistar: Five-Year Summary of Selected Financial and Statistical Data

As of and for the Years Ended October 31, (in millions, except per share data)	2010	2009	2008	2007	2006
RESULTS OF OPERATIONS DATA					
Sales and revenues, net	$12,145	$11,569	$14,724	$12,295	$14,200
Income (loss) before extraordinary gain	267	322	134	(120)	301
Extraordinary gain, net of tax	—	23	—	—	—
Net income (loss)	267	345	134	(120)	301
Less: Net income attributable to non-controlling interest	44	25	—	—	—
Net income (loss) attributable to Navistar International Corporation	$ 223	$ 320	$ 134	$ (120)	$ 301
Basic earnings (loss) per share:					
Income (loss) attributable to Navistar International Corporation before extraordinary gain	$ 3.11	$ 4.18	$ 1.89	$ (1.70)	$ 4.29
Extraordinary gain, net of tax	—	0.33	—	—	—
Net income (loss) attributable to Navistar International Corporation	$ 3.11	$ 4.51	$ 1.89	$ (1.70)	$ 4.29
Diluted earnings (loss) per share:					
Income (loss) attributable to Navistar International Corporation before extraordinary gain	$ 3.05	$ 4.14	$ 1.82	$ (1.70)	$ 4.12
Weighted average number of shares outstanding:					
Basic	71.7	71.0	70.7	70.3	70.3
Diluted	73.2	71.8	73.2	70.3	74.5
BALANCE SHEET DATA					
Total assets	$ 9,730	$10,028	$10,390	$11,448	$12,830
Long-term debt:(A)					
Manufacturing operations	1,841	1,670	1,639	1,665	1,946
Financial services operations	2,397	2,486	3,770	4,418	4,809
Total long-term debt	$ 4,238	$ 4,156	$ 5,409	$ 6,083	$ 6,755
Redeemable equity securities	8	13	143	140	—

(A) Exclusive of current portion of long-term debt.

Source: Navistar International Corporation 10-K filing for fiscal year ended October 31, 2010. http://www.sec.gov/Archives

Exhibit 10B Navistar: Consolidated Statements of Operations

	For the Years Ended October 31,		
(in millions, except per share data)	**2010**	**2009**	**2008**
Sales and revenues			
Sales of manufactured products, net	$11,926	$11,300	$14,399
Finance revenues	219	269	325
Sales and revenues, net	12,145	11,569	14,724
Costs and expenses			
Costs of products sold	9,741	9,366	11,942
Restructuring charges	(15)	59	—
Impairment of property and equipment	—	31	358
Selling, general and administrative expenses	1,406	1,344	1,437
Engineering and product development costs	464	433	384
Interest expense	253	251	469
Other (income) expenses, net	(44)	(228)	14
Total costs and expenses	11,805	11,256	14,604
Equity in (loss) income of non-consolidated affiliates	(50)	46	71
Income before income tax and extraordinary gain	290	359	191
Income tax expense	23	37	57
Income before extraordinary gain	267	322	134
Extraordinary gain, net of tax	—	23	—
Net income	267	345	134
Less: Net income attributable to non-controlling interests	44	25	—
Net income attributable to Navistar International Corporation	$ 223	$ 320	$ 134
Basic earnings per share:			
Income attributable to Navistar International Corporation before extraordinary gain	$ 3.11	$ 4.18	$ 1.89
Extraordinary gain, net of tax	—	0.33	—
Net income attributable to Navistar International Corporation	$ 3.11	$ 4.51	$ 1.89
Diluted earnings per share:			
Income attributable to Navistar International Corporation before extraordinary gain	$ 3.05	$ 4.14	$ 1.82
Extraordinary gain, net of tax	—	0.32	—
Net income attributable to Navistar International Corporation	$ 3.05	$ 4.46	$ 1.82
Weighted average shares outstanding			
Basic	71.7	71.0	70.7
Diluted	73.2	71.8	73.2

Source: Navistar International Corporation 10-K filing for fiscal year ended October 31, 2010. http://www.sec.gov/Archives

Exhibit 10C Navistar: Consolidated Balance Sheets

	As of October 31,	
	2010	**2009**
(in millions, except per share data)		**(Revised)[A]**
ASSETS		
Current assets		
Cash and cash equivalents	$ 585	$ 1,212
Marketable securities	586	—

(Continued)

Exhibit 10C Navistar: Consolidated Balance Sheets (*Continued*)

	As of October 31,	
	2010	**2009**
(in millions, except per share data)		**(Revised)(A)**
Trade and other receivables, net	987	855
Finance receivables, net	1,770	1,706
Inventories	1,568	1,666
Deferred taxes, net	83	107
Other current assets	256	202
Total current assets	5,835	5,748
Restricted cash and cash equivalents	180	485
Trade and other receivables, net	44	26
Finance receivables, net	1,145	1,498
Investments in and advances to non-consolidated affiliates	103	62
Property and equipment, net	1,442	1,467
Goodwill	324	318
Intangible assets, net	262	264
Deferred taxes, net	63	57
Other noncurrent assets	332	103
Total assets	**$ 9,730**	**$10,028**
LIABILITIES, REDEEMABLE EQUITY SECURITIES AND STOCKHOLDERS' DEFICIT		
Liabilities		
Current liabilities		
Notes payable and current maturities of long-term debt	$ 632	$ 1,136
Accounts payable	1,827	1,872
Other current liabilities	1,130	1,177
Total current liabilities	3,589	4,185
Long-term debt	4,238	4,156
Postretirement benefits liabilities	2,097	2,595
Deferred taxes, net	142	142
Other noncurrent liabilities	588	624
Total liabilities	10,654	11,702
Redeemable equity securities	8	13
Stockholders' deficit		
Series D convertible junior preference stock	4	4
Common stock ($0.10 par value per share, 110.0 shares authorized, 75.4 shares issued at both dates)	7	7
Additional paid in capital	2,206	2,181
Accumulated deficit	(1,878)	(2,101)
Accumulated other comprehensive loss	(1,196)	(1,690)
Common stock held in treasury, at cost (3.6 and 4.7 shares, at the respective dates)	(124)	(149)
Total stockholders' deficit attributable to Navistar International Corp	(981)	(1,748)
Stockholders' equity attributable to non-controlling interest	49	61
Total stockholders' deficit	(932)	(1,687)
Total liabilities, redeemable equity securities, and stockholders' deficit	**$ 9,730**	**$10,028**

(A) Revised; See Note 1, Summary of significant accounting policies

Source: Navistar International Corporation 10-K filing for fiscal year ended October 31, 2010. http://www.sec.gov/Archives

Exhibit 10D Navistar: Consolidated Statements of Cash Flows

(in millions)	For the Years Ended October 31,		
	2010	**2009**	**2008**
Cash flows from operating activities			
Net income	**$ 267**	$ 345	$ 134
Adjustments to reconcile net income to cash provided by operating activities:			
Depreciation and amortization	**265**	288	329
Depreciation of equipment leased to others	**51**	56	64
Deferred taxes	**17**	(18)	56
Impairment of property and equipment, goodwill, and intangible assets	**—**	41	372
Amortization of debt issuance costs	**38**	16	15
Stock-based compensation	**24**	16	15
Provision for doubtful accounts	**29**	50	65
Equity in loss/income of affiliated companies, net of dividends	**55**	13	14
Other non-cash operating activities	**61**	54	49
Changes in operating assets and liabilities, exclusive of the effects of businesses acquired and disposed:			
Trade and other receivables	**(136)**	197	(352)
Finance receivables	**546**	391	614
Inventories	**122**	135	(221)
Accounts payable	**(72)**	(204)	339
Other assets and liabilities	**(160)**	(142)	(373)
Net cash provided by operating activities	**1,107**	1,238	1,120
Cash flows from investing activities			
Purchases of marketable securities	**(1,876)**	(382)	(42)
Sales or maturities of marketable securities	**1,290**	384	46
Net change in restricted cash and cash equivalents	**515**	71	(143)
Capital expenditures	**(234)**	(151)	(176)
Purchase of equipment leased to others	**(45)**	(46)	(39)
Proceeds from sales of property and equipment	**23**	6	20
Investments in and advances to non-consolidated affiliates	**(97)**	(44)	(17)
Proceeds from sales of affiliates	**7**	10	20
Business acquisitions, net of escrow received	**(2)**	(60)	—
Acquisition of intangibles	**(15)**	—	—
Other investing activities	**—**	—	(2)
Net cash used in investing activities	**(434)**	(212)	(333)
Cash flows from financing activities			
Proceeds from issuance of securitized debt	**1,460**	349	1,076
Principal payments on securitized debt	**(1,579)**	(1,191)	(1,725)
Proceeds from issuance of non-securitized debt	**687**	1,868	104
Principal payments on non-securitized debt	**(883)**	(1793)	(64)
Net increase (decrease) in notes and debt outstanding under revolving credit facilities	**(866)**	159	(18)
Principal payments under financing arrangements and capital lease obligations	**(62)**	(42)	(67)
Debt issuance costs	**(35)**	(40)	(11)
Stock repurchases	**—**	(29)	—
Call options and warrants, net	**—**	(38)	—

(Continued)

Exhibit 10D Navistar: Consolidated Statements of Cash Flows (*Continued*)

(in millions)	For the Years Ended October 31,		
	2010	2009	2008
Proceeds from exercise of stock options	35	13	29
Dividends paid to non-controlling interest	(57)	(20)	—
Net cash used in financing activities	(1,300)	(764)	(676)
Effect of exchange rate changes on cash and cash equivalents	—	9	(27)
Increase (decrease) in cash and cash equivalents	(627)	271	84
Increase in cash and equivalents upon consolidation of Blue Diamond Parts and Blue Diamond Truck	—	80	—
Cash and cash equivalents at beginning of the year	1,212	861	777
Cash and cash equivalents at end of the year	$ 585	$ 1,212	$ 861

Source: Navistar International Corporation 10-K filing for fiscal year ended October 31, 2010. http://www.sec.gov/Archives

Exhibit 10E Navistar: Segment Data

(in millions, except % change)	2010	2009	Change	% Change
Truck segment sales - U.S. and Canada	$7,393	$6,807	$ 586	9
Truck segment sales - ROW	814	490	324	66
Total Truck segment sales, net	$8,207	$7,297	$ 910	12
Truck segment profit	$ 424	$ 147	$ 277	188

(in millions, except % change)	2010	2009	Change	% Change
Engine segment sales - U.S. and Canada	$1,611	$1,836	$(225)	(12)
Engine segment sales - ROW	1,375	854	521	61
Total Engine segment sales, net	$2,986	$2,690	$ 296	11
Engine segment profit(A)	$ 51	$ 253	$(202)	(80)

(in millions, except % change)	2010	2009	Change	% Change
Parts segment sales - U.S. and Canada	$1,718	$2,038	$(320)	(16)
Parts segment sales - ROW	167	135	32	24
Total Parts segment sales, net	$1,885	$2,173	$(288)	(13)
Parts segment profit	$ 266	$ 436	$(170)	(39)

(in millions, except % change)	2010	2009	Change	% Change
Financial Services segment revenues - U.S. and Canada(B)	$ 254	$ 268	$ (14)	(5)
Financial Services segment revenues - ROW	55	80	(25)	(31)
Total Financial Services segment revenues, net	$ 309	$ 348	$ (39)	(11)
Financial Services segment profit	$ 95	$ 40	$ 55	138

(A) Included in Engine segment profit for 2009 was income of $160 million from the Ford Settlement, net of related charges.
(B) Our Financial Services segment does not have Canadian operations or revenues.

Source: Navistar International Corporation 10-K filing for fiscal year ended October 31, 2010. http://www.sec.gov/Archives

Leadership

Daniel C. Ustian, Chairman of the Board, President, and CEO

Daniel Ustian was hired by Navistar in 1973 and initially served in various roles in both manufacturing and finance. He has remained in high-level leadership since being promoted to the head of Engine and Foundry in 1993. He served other roles before being named CEO in 2003 including Chief Operating Officer in 2002.[151] During that time he was "participating in the development of the company's future strategic direction with a particular emphasis on growth initiatives"[152] Ustian attended DePaul University and earned his bachelor's in business administration in 1972.[153]

As CEO, Ustian has navigated Navistar quite well, though countless decisions will still need to be made to guarantee Navistar's survival in the industry. Ustian is a particularly good fit as the company's leader with his background as an insider and is notably capable of articulating Navistar's overall vision by painting an engaging picture for his audiences of where the company has been and where it needs to go.[154] He has successfully led the company in growth through acquisitions, partnerships, and collaborations designed to utilize each firm's abilities and products for mutual benefit.[155] As the *Wall Street Journal* reported, "Ustian's intense focus on operational excellence encouraged several breakthrough technologies that drove product capability and increased sales."[156] Moving toward the future, Ustian must continue to think and act strategically and creatively for Navistar to achieve its 2015 goal of $20 billion in revenue.[157]

Andrew J. Cederoth, Executive VP and CFO

A. J. Cederoth joined Navistar in 1990, working in finance departments and different areas of the company including a stint as the strategic planning manager of the Engine Division. He moved to the corporate level in 1999[158] and was promoted to the executive management level as VP and Treasurer in 2001. In 2006, Cederoth took on a lead financial role for the Engine Division as VP and CFO. After CFO Terry Endsley passed away in April 2009,[159] he was appointed Executive VP and CFO in September 2009.[160] Cederoth attended the University of Illinois for his undergraduate degree, a BA in economics and mathematics, and graduated with his MBA from DePaul University in 1990.[161]

With his cross-divisional experience, Cederoth has a solid understanding of Navistar. As CEO Daniel Ustian explains, "A. J. has the hands-on experience and the strong financial leadership skills necessary to help support the growth of the company's current business and drive future growth on a global basis."[162] Taking over just as the economy came to a standstill, Cederoth made tough decisions in an environment of plummeting new truck sales and an aging fleet.[163] As he sees it, "2010 has been the year for us to move our products with their emissions strategy and to improve our cost structure." Understanding that every venture will not make money right away, Cederoth is poised to be a major asset as the company moves forward. On the subject of global ventures and expansions he says, "By 2011, we expect this business to be at break even, and this business offers the potential to be a significant revenue opportunity and earnings opportunity as we expand our strategy."[164] Cederoth is a key and welcome decision maker that brings experience and a solid financial foundation to Navistar's new ventures and future.

Jack Allen, North American Truck Group President

Jack Allen started with Navistar in 1981 and has served in various roles over the years. He headed up Navistar's joint venture with Ford and its Blue Diamond Truck Company and was instrumental in setting record sales in 2003 while heading the parts division.[165] Despite the seeming confines of his current title, Allen has a track record of establishing successful global relationships, having worked with both the acquisition of a Brazilian engine company as well as Navistar's partnership with the German company, MAN AG.[166] In his current position, he is involved in and must answer to the decisions on US EPA standards and Navistar's solution-of-choice: EGR. Publically, Allen maintains, "We didn't make this decision lightly…we're confident that our solution is what customers will want."[167] Allen also is closely involved with the electronic vehicle productions on the Monaco lines and, because of his position and experience, is most often Navistar's spokesperson for activities there.[168] Overall, Allen has had extensive experience with many different lines of the business and will likely prove to be an important executive on the team.

William H. Osborne, VP of Custom Products

Navistar's newest executive leader is Bill Osborne, though he is familiar with the company, having served since 2009 on the Board of Directors.[169] Before joining Navistar, Osborne served as President and CEO at Federal Signal Corporation, Ford of Canada, and Ford of Australia.[170] Osborne recalled, "Ford of Canada gained market share for the first time after ten years of erosion, sales increased eight percent, and the business recorded record profits."[171] Between 1977 and 1990 and prior to his experience at Ford, he worked at both Chrysler and General Motors.[172] He received both a bachelor's and master's degree in engineering from Kettering University and Wayne State University respectively. Osborne also attended the University of Chicago to earn his MBA.[173]

While Osborne is just beginning his journey with Navistar, with the outside experience he brings to the company, he fulfills an important role as a well-connected innovator within the custom products division. Daniel Ustian explained, "Bill has unique insights into our company. His manufacturing and automotive experience and expertise will be of great value to Navistar as we continue to diversify and expand globally into new marketplaces."[174]

What Will Keep Navistar Truckin'?

While Navistar has come a long way since the early 80s, as a player in a changing industry, there is no time to rest on its laurels or stop to enjoy the rewards of its hard work. Not to mention the fact that there are still a few trouble spots in the company to address.

First and foremost is Navistar's dependence on the North American economy. With US sales representing nearly 80 percent of annual revenue in the latter half of the decade and the early 2010 50-year low in the industry, should Ustian more aggressively explore foreign opportunities for Navistar beyond the Western hemisphere? With PACCAR performing strongly in Europe and Volvo AB's domination in Asia, should Navistar pursue other less or untapped markets—or should Navistar bring the fight to their front door?

Second, while strategic acquisitions have provided Navistar with proprietary technology and the opportunity to swim against the tide as the sole manufacturer committed to EGR technology, will customers go for it or will they just stick with what they know? To what extent should Navistar develop plans should its EGR be rejected and, more importantly, what should those plans include?

Third, what can and should Navistar do to stay one step ahead of what are expected to be ongoing and increasingly stringent emissions regulations? How much should be invested in research and development to discover the next innovation and get ahead of anticipated government regulation? Would the acquisition of, or a joint venture with, a biotech firm researching alternate fuels add stakeholder value?

Finally, is Navistar doing everything it can to protect its home turf? As discussed earlier, the most likely source of new trucking companies is from smaller firms taking their products to the global market. Despite millions of dollars spent on advertising to encourage the behavior, US consumers are not particularly loyal to US firms and will likely have no qualms about changing if courted by a foreign firm offering comparable products for less money, or worse, better products at a comparable or fair price. Are Navistar's loyalty programs enough to keep its customers or, given the circumstances, would old Cyrus McCormick be offering more?

NOTES

1. Casson, H. N. *Cyrus Hall McCormick: His Life and Work*, (Washington DC: Beard Books, 2001/10)
2. Cramer, J. Mar 10, 2011. CEO Interview with Daniel Ustian, CEO Navistar Corp. *MadMoneyRecap*. http://www.madmoneyrecap .com/madmoney_nightlyrecap_110310_5.htm
3. 2010 Annual Report to Shareholders. *Navistar.com*. http://files.shareholder.com/downloads/ NAV/1296127258x0x429697/5255C71D-0E9E-493E-8B7D -BE1D110B0EC8/NIC_2010_-_10-K.pdf
4. *Ibid.*
5. Navistar International. (n.d.). *Wikipedia.* http://en.wikipedia.org/ wiki/Navistar
6. Navistar International Corporation Overview. (n.d.). *Hoovers.* http:// www.hoovers.com/company/Navistar_International_Corporation/ rrfjyi-1.html
7. Navistar International. *op. cit.*
8. *Ibid.*
9. Durr, K., Sullivan, L. (2007). *International Harvester, McCormick, Navistar: Milestones in the Company that Helped Build America.* Portland, OR: Graphic Arts Center Publishing Company.
10. Inside Navistar: History. (n.d.). *Navistar.* http://www.navistar.com/ Navistar/Inside+Navistar/History
11. Navistar International Corporation Overview. *op. cit.*
12. Inside Navistar: History. *op. cit.*
13. Navistar International Corporation Overview. *op. cit.*
14. Inside Navistar: History. *op. cit.*
15. Navistar International Corporation Overview. *op. cit.*
16. *Ibid.*
17. Navistar International. *op. cit.*
18. Navistar International Corporation Overview. *op. cit.*
19. *Ibid.*
20. Navistar International. *op. cit.*
21. Engel, C. (1998). Competition Drives the Trucking Industry. *Monthly Labor Review.* 121: 4.
22. Navistar International Corporation Overview. *op. cit.*
23. Inside Navistar: History. *op. cit.*
24. Navistar International Corporation Overview. *op. cit.*
25. Navistar International. *op. cit.*
26. Navistar International Corporation Overview. *op. cit.*
27. Media. Sep 4, 2008. San Marino Plan Global Integrated Commercial Bus Joint Venture. *Navistar.com.* http://de.media .navistar.com/index.php?s=43&item=184
28. Navistar International. *op. cit.*
29. Media. Sep 4, 2008. *op. cit.*
30. Navistar International. *op. cit.*
31. Inside Navistar: History. *op. cit.*
32. Navistar International. *op. cit.*
33. Business Wire. Jun 4, 2009. Navistar Affiliate Completes Purchase of Certain Monaco Coach Assets. *Navistar.com.* http://ir.navistar .com/releasedetail.cfm?releaseid=388148
34. Inside Navistar: History. *op. cit.*
35. Navistar International Corporation Overview. *op. cit.*
36. Business Wire. Dec 31, 2009. Navistar Looks to the Future to Extend Technology Leadership Strategy. http://ir.navistar.com/ releasedetail.cfm?releaseid=431581
37. Navistar International (NAV). (n.d.). *WikiInvest.com.* http://www .wikinvest.com/stock/Navistar_International_(NAV)
38. Navistar management interview with Shayne Gibbons, VP of Finance Custom Products; Kevin Sadowski, Financial Planning and Analysis; John Miller, VP Finance and CFO. May 11, 2011.
39. Noealt Corporate Services. Feb 1, 2011. Navistar International Corporation Business Snapshot & SWOT Analysis. *MarketResearch .com.* http://www.marketresearch.com/vendors/viewvendor .asp?vendorid=3747
40. Navistar management interview *op. cit.*
41. GlobalData. Apr 2011. NAV – Financial and Strategic SWOT Analysis Review. *GlobalData.com.* http://www .globalcompanyintelligence.com/GCIReports.aspx?search=1
42. Standard & Poor's, Apr 23, 2011, Quantitative Stock Report - Navistar Intl, p 3.
43. Get to know PACCAR. (n.d.). *PACCAR.* http://www.paccar.com/ company/get_to_know.asp
44. PACCAR 2010 Annual Report, p 4. (n.d.). *PACCAR.* http://www .paccar.com/investors/annual_reports/PACCAR-AR-2010.pdf
45. Get to know PACCAR. *op. cit.*
46. 282. Paccar. (n.d.). Fortune 500 2010 Top 1000 American Companies. *CNN Money.* http://money.cnn.com/magazines/ fortune/fortune500/2010/snapshots/318.html
47. PACCAR 2010 Annual Report, exhibit 13, p 24. *op. cit.*
48. Apr 19, 2011. PACCAR Announces Improved First Quarter Revenues and Earnings. *PACCAR.* http://www.paccar.com/ NewsReleases/article_news.asp?file=2664
49. PACCAR 2010 Annual Report, p 3. *op. cit.*
50. Get to know PACCAR. *op. cit.*

51. PACCAR 2010 Annual Report, p 3. *op. cit.*
52. Get to know PACCAR. *op. cit.*
53. Volvo Group Global: Our History. (n.d.). *Volvo.* http://www
     .volvogroup.com/group/global/en-gb/volvo%20group/history/
     pages/history.aspx
54. The Volvo Group 2010 (Annual Report), p iii, 5. (n.d.). *Volvo.* http://
     www3.volvo.com/investors/finrep/ar10/ar_2010_eng.pdf
55. Volvo Group Global: Volvo 80 Years. (n.d.). *Volvo.* http://www
     .volvogroup.com/group/global/en-gb/volvo%20group/history/
     volvo_80years/Pages/volvo_80-years.aspx
56. AB Volvo Overview. (n.d.). *Hoovers.com.* http://www.hoovers.com/
     company/AB_Volvo/crxhci-1.html
57. Volvo Group Global: Our History. *op. cit.*
58. The Volvo Group 2010 (Annual Report), p 5. *op. cit.*
59. The Volvo Group 2010 (Annual Report), p 29. *op. cit.*
60. Volvo Group Global: Safety as a Corporate Value. (n.d.). *Volvo.*
     http://www.volvogroup.com/group/global/en-gb/volvo%20
     group/ourvalues/safety/pages/safety.aspx
61. Volvo Group Global: OurValues. (n.d.). *Volvo.* http://www
     .volvogroup.com/group/global/en-gb/volvo%20group/ourvalues/
     pages/volvovalues.aspx
62. The Volvo Group 2010 (Annual Report), p 10. *op. cit.*
63. Volvo Group Global: The Volvo Way, p 15. Aug 2009. *Volvo.* http://
     www.volvogroup.com/SiteCollectionDocuments/VGHQ/Volvo%20
     Group/Volvo%20Group/Our%20values/volvo_way_eng.pdf
64. Volvo Group Global: The Volvo Way, p 21. *op. cit.*
65. Volvo Group Global: The Volvo Way, p 10–11. *op cit*
66. Company. (n.d.). *Daimler.* http://www.daimler.com/company
67. Business Units. (n.d.). *Daimler.* http://www.daimler.com/company/
     business-units
68. Daimler Fact Sheet for Q4 2010 and Full Year 2010, p 5, 7. Mar 2,
     2011. *Daimler.* http://www.daimler.com/Projects/c2c/channel/
     documents/1979737_Daimler_Q4___FY_2010_Fact_Sheet.pdf
69. Brands & Products. (n.d.). *Daimler.* http://www.daimler.com/
     brands-and-products
70. Daimler Annual Report 2010. *Daimler.com.* http://www.daimler
     .com/Projects/c2c/channel/documents/1985489_Daimler_Annual
     _Report_2010.pdf
71. Daimler Fact Sheet for Q4 2010 and Full Year 2010, p 5. *op. cit.*
72. Company. (n.d.). *Daimler. op. cit.*
73. Daimler Annual Report 2010. *op. cit.*
74. What We Stand For. (n.d.). *Daimler.* http://www.daimler.com/
     company/what-we-stand-for
75. Daimler Annual Report 2010. *op. cit.*
76. Daimler AG (DDAIF). (n.d.). *WikiInvest.com.* http://www.wikinvest
     .com/stock/Daimler_AG_(DDAIF)
77. Cummins, Inc. Form 10-K for fiscal year ended Dec 31,
     2009. *Cummins.* http://media.corporate-ir.net/media_files/
     irol/11/112916/2009_10K.pdf
78. Navistar management interview *op. cit.*
79. About Cummins. (n.d.). *Cummins.* http://regions.cummins.com/
     regions/la/AboutCummins/index.jsp?menuId=0
80. Company Background. (n.d.). *Cummins.* http://www.cummins.com/
     cmi/navigationAction.do?nodeId=3&siteId=1&nodeName=In+W
     ords&menuId=1000
81. Cummins Inc (CMI). 10-K. Filed on 2-24-2011. Filed period 12-31-
     2010. *Cummins.* http://phx.corporate-ir.net/External.File?item=
     UGFyZW50SUQ9NDI3MDk0fENoaWxkSUQ9NDQzMjE0fFR5cG
     U9MQ==&t=1
82. Cummins (CMI). (n.d.). *WikiInvest.com.* http://www.wikinvest.com/
     wiki/Cummins
83. Cummins Inc (CMI). 10-K. *op. cit.*
84. Cummins, Inc. Form 10-K for fiscal year ended Dec 31, 2009,
     p 32. *Cummins.* http://media.corporate-ir.net/media_files/
     irol/11/112916/2009_10K.pdf
85. Message From The Chairman. (n.d.). *Cummins.* http://www
     .cummins.com/cmi/navigationAction.do?nodeId=5&siteId=1&nod
     eName=Message+from+the+Chairman&menuId=1002
86. Company Background. (n.d.). *Cummins. op. cit.*
87. Our Vision, Mission and Values. (n.d.). *Cummins.* http://www.cummins
     .com/cmi/navigationAction.do?nodeId=6&siteId=1&nodeName=Our
     +Vision+Mission+and+Values&menuId=1000
88. Investor Overview. (n.d.). *Cummins.* http://phx.corporate-ir.net/
     phoenix.zhtml?c=112916&p=irol-IRHome
89. Our New Strategic Principle. (n.d.). *Cummins.* http://
     www.cummins.com/cmi/navigationAction.do?nodeId=
     82&siteId=1&nodeName=Our+new+strategic+principle&men
     uId=1050
90. Reuters. May 17, 2011. BAE Systems to pay $79M fine for breach
     of US military export rules. *guardian.co.uk.* http://www.guardian
     .co.uk/business/2011/may/17/bae-to-pay-79m-dollar-fine-to-us
91. Land & Armaments. (n.d.). *BAE Systems.* http://www.baesystems
     .com/Businesses/LandArmaments/
92. BAE Systems: Five Year Summary. (n.d.). *BAE Systems.* http://
     bae-systems-investor-relations.production.investis.com/financial
     -information/five-year-summary.aspx
93. BAE Systems (LON: BA). (n.d.). *WikiInvest.com.* http://www
     .wikinvest.com/wiki/Bae_systems
94. BAE Systems: Five Year Summary. *op. cit.*
95. Reuters. May 17, 2011. *op. cit.*
96. O'Connell, D. Nov 1, 2009. Nimrod crash puts BAE Systems ethics
     under fire again. *The Sunday Times.* http://business.timesonline
     .co.uk/tol/business/industry_sectors/engineering/article6898106
     .ece
97. Atkinson, D. Feb 6, 2010. US Imposes ethics watchdog on
     BAE. *Daily Mail Online.* http://www.dailymail.co.uk/money/
     article-1248994/US-imposes-ethics-watchdog-BAE.html
98. About Oshkosh: Company Profile. (n.d.). *Oshkosh Corporation.*
     http://www.oshkoshcorporation.com/about/company_profile.cfm
99. Oshkosh 2010 Annual Report, p 42. *Oshkosh.* http://thomson
     .mobular.net/thomson/7/3146/4373/
100. Oshkosh 2010 Annual Report, p 32. *op. cit.*
101. Oshkosh 2010 Annual Report, p 24. *op. cit.*
102. About Oshkosh: Company Profile. *op. cit.*
103. Navistar - Jefferies 6th Annual Global Industrials and A&D
     Conference, p 3. Aug 10, 2010. *Navistar.com.* http://files
     .shareholder.com/downloads/NAV/1296115525x0x394849/
     c36ca606-038a-4ba8-a69b-3556e1c50374/NAVISTAR
     -Jefferies%20081010-final.pdf
104. Navistar management interview *op. cit.*
105. GlobalData. *op. cit.*
106. Business Wire. Jan 19, 2010. Navistar's Pure Power Technologies
     Acquires Holley EGR Valve Technology. *Navistar.com.* http://
     ir.navistar.com/releasedetail.cfm?releaseid=438382
107. GlobalData. *op. cit.*
108. Navistar management interview *op. cit.*
109. 2010 Annual Report to Shareholders. *Navistar.com. op. cit.*
110. Navistar management interview *op. cit.*
111. *Ibid.*
112. 2010 Annual Report to Shareholders. *Navistar.com. op. cit.*
113. Navistar International (NAV). *op. cit.*
114. Press Release. July 1, 2010. International ranks highest in vocational
     truck segment and in dealer service among Class 8 customers. *J.D.
     Power and Associates.* http://businesscenter.jdpower.com/news/
     pressrelease.aspx?ID=2010102
115. International Advantage. (n.d.). *InternationalTrucks.com.* https://
     www.internationaltrucks.com/IAdvantage/
116. Media. Jan 12, 2010. Navistar launches Customer Parts Recovery
     (CPR) program offering cash for customers' obsolete and
     surplus parts. *Navistar.com.* http://media.navistar.com/index
     .php?s=43&item=348
117. Zacks Equity Research. May 20, 2011. US Railroad Industry Outlook
     – May 2011. *Zacks.com.* http://www.zacks.com/stock/news/53717/
     US+Railroad+Industry+Outlook+-+May+2011
118. World Air Cargo Forecast 2010–2011, p 2. (n.d.). *Boeing.com.*
     http://www.boeing.com/commercial/cargo/wacf.pdf
119. Hoskisson, R., Hitt, M., Ireland, R. D., Harrison, J. 2008. *Competing
     for Advantage.* Mason, OH: South-Western, p 80–82.
120. Noealt Corporate Services.
121. Company Overview. (n.d.). *Scania.com.* http://www.scania.com/
     investor-relations/company-overview/
122. Annual Report 2010 Scania, p 23. *op. cit.*
123. Key MAN SE Financials. (n.d.). *Hoovers.com.* http://www.hoovers
     .com/company/MAN_SE/srrjif-1-1njea5.html

124. MAN Diesel and Turbo Annual Report 2010. *MANDieselTurbo .com*. http://mandieselturbo.com/files/news/filesof587/MAN%20 Diesel%20&%20Turbo%20Annual%20Report%202010.pdf

125. J.P. Morgan. Jun 16, 2011. May Truck Data, p.1 https:// www.chase.com/online/commercial-bank/document/ NewsLetterTruckData.pdf

126. Noealt Corporate Services. *op. cit.*

127. Daimler Annual Report 2010, p 109. *op. cit.*

128. The Volvo Group 2010 (Annual Report), p 28. *op. cit.*

129. 2010 Annual Report to Shareholders. *Navistar.com. op. cit.*

130. Noealt Corporate Services. *op. cit.*

131. MaxxForce® Advanced EGR FAQ. (n.d.). *Navistar.com.* http://www.navistar.com/StaticFiles/navistardotcom/pdf/ Advanced+EGR+FAQ.pdf

132. Dow Jones News Service. Jan 31, 2011. Navistar Expects Traction from Engine Strategy in 2011. *Heavy Duty Manufacturers Association.* http://www.hdma.org/Main-Menu/HDMA -Publications/Diesel-Download/January-31-2011/Navistar -Expects-Traction-from-Engine-Strategy-in-2011.html

133. PR Newswire. Feb 22, 2011. EcoMotors International's Opposed-Piston, Opposed-Cylinder Engine Promises to Revolutionize Commercial Vehicle Design with Powerful, Lightweight, Fuel Efficient, Low Emissions Engines. *EcoMotors International.* http:// www.ecomotors.com/ecomotors-internationals-opposed-piston -opposed-cylinder-engine-promises-revolutionize-commercial-ve

134. Cox, D. Mar 31, 2011. Navistar's Jim Hebe: There's a strategy in being different 'if it benefits the customer.' *The Trucker.com.* http://www.thetrucker.com/News/Stories/2011/3/31/ NavistarsJimHebeTheresastrategyinbeing differentifitbenefitsthecustomer.aspx

135. Dow Jones News Service. Jan 31, 2011. *op. cit.*

136. Brezonik, M. Sticking to the familiar formula: MaxxForce 15 development continues Navistar's strategy of leveraging its own capabilities and scale with that of partners. *Diesel Progress North American Edition.* Jul 2009.

137. PR Newswire. Feb 22, 2011. *op. cit.*

138. Loveday, E. May 15, 2010, Navistar begins commercial production of eStar electric cargo van, first four going to FedEx. *AutoBlogGreen.com.* http://green.autoblog.com/2010/05/15/ navistar-begins-commercial-production-of-estar-electric-cargo-va/

139. Berg, T. Mar 10, 2011. Navistar Offers Electric, Hybrid and Natural Gas Power, Hebe Notes. *Trucking Info.* http://www.truckinginfo .com/news/news-detail.asp?news_id=73188

140. Brezonik, M. Sticking to the familiar formula: *op. cit.*

141. *Ibid.*

142. *Ibid.*

143. Gray, S. Jun 13, 2008. Navistar's Military Maneuver Pays Off. *Business Week.* http://www.businessweek.com/investor/content/ jun2008/pi20080613_982797.htm

144. Nov/Dec 2009. Blurring the Lines: Truck Manufacturing Strategy Comes to Life in North America. *Navistar.com.* www.negotiations .navistar.com/pdf/ManufacturingStrategyNovDec2009.pdf

145. Navistar Fact Book, 2010, p 1. *Navistar.com.* http://ir.navistar .com/common/download/download.cfm?companyid= NAV&fileid=318973&filekey=cbade9a7-cafa-4898-a18f -efea693b88b9&filename=NAV-Fact_Book-2008.pdf

146. *Ibid.*

147. Business Wire. Nov 2, 2007. Navistar Affiliate Enters JV with Mahindra & Mahindra to Manufacture Diesel Engines in India. *Navistar.com.* http://ir.navistar.com/releasedetail .cfm?releaseid=272900

148. Business Wire. Mar 24, 2010. Navistar Continues to Build for the Future. *Navistar.com.* http://ir.navistar.com/releasedetail .cfm?ReleaseID=454492

149. 2009 Annual Report to Shareholders, p 24. *Navistar.com. op. cit.*

150. Interview with Corey Martin, Financial Analyst at International Truck and Engine. May, 2011.

151. Daniel C. Ustian. (n.d.). *Forbes.* http://people.forbes.com/profile/ daniel-c-ustian/54644

152. Daniel C. Ustian. (n.d.). *The Wall Street Journal.* http://topics.wsj .com/person/U/daniel-ustian/1118

153. Daniel C. Ustian. (n.d.). Management Bios. *Navistar.com.* http:// www.navistar.com/Navistar/Inside+Navistar/Management+Bios

154. Navistar management interview *op. cit.*

155. Daniel C. Ustian. (n.d.). Management Bios. *op. cit.*

156. Daniel C. Ustian. (n.d.). *The Wall Street Journal. op. cit.*

157. Daniel C. Ustian. (n.d.). Management Bios. *op. cit.*

158. Andrew J. (A. J.) Cederoth. (n.d.). Management Bios. *Navistar .com.* http://www.navistar.com/Navistar/Inside+Navistar/ Management+Bios

159. Business Wire. Apr 15, 2009. Navistar Mourns Passing of CFO Terry M. Endsley; A.J. Cederoth Continues Day-to-Day Finance Role. *Reuters.* http://www.reuters.com/article/2009/04/15/ idUS174115+15-Apr-2009+BW20090415

160. A. J. Cederoth. (n.d.). *Forbes.* http://people.forbes.com/profile/ a-j-cederoth/128867

161. Andrew J. (A. J.) Cederoth. (n.d.). Management Bios. *op. cit.*

162. Oct 1, 2009. Navistar taps Cederoth as new CFO. *Truckinginfo .com.* http://www.truckinginfo.com/operations/news-detail .asp?news_id=67983&news_category_id=7

163. Navistar management interview *op. cit.*

164. Navistar International Corp Q3 2010 Earnings Call Transcript. Sep 8, 2010. *Morningstar.com.* http://www.morningstar.com/earn-0/ earnings--17408888-navistar-international-corp-nav-q3-2010.aspx .shtml?pindex=5

165. Business Wire. Jan 15, 2004. Navistar International Corporation Shifts Two Senior Officers. *Navistar.com.* http://nav.client .shareholder.com/releasedetail.cfm?ReleaseID=126646

166. Jack Allen. (n.d.). Management Bios. *Navistar.com.* http://www .navistar.com/Navistar/Inside+Navistar/Management+Bios

167. Zeller, T., Mayersohn, N. Apr 4, 2011. To Cut Smog, Navistar Blazes Risky Path of Its Own. *The New York Times.* http://www .nytimes.com/2011/04/05/business/energy-environment/05truck .html

168. Odendahl, M. Mar 29, 2010. Navistar FedEx show electric vehicle to be built in Wakarusa. *Indiana Economic Digest.* http://www .indianabusinessnews.com/main.asp?SectionID=31&SubSectionID =135&ArticleID=53475&TM=31299.55

169. May 3, 2011. Navistar names new VP of custom products division. *Truck News.* http://www.trucknews.com/issues/story .aspx?aid=1000409374

170. William H. Osborne. (n.d.). *Forbes.* http://people.forbes.com/ profile/william-h-osborne/120868

171. William H. Osborne. (n.d.). *Black Profiles.* http://www .blackentrepreneurprofile.com/profile-full/article/william-h -osborne/

172. William H. Osborne. (n.d.). *Forbes. op. cit.*

173. May 3, 2011. William H. Osborne to Head Navistar's Expansionary Businesses. *Navistar.com.* http://media.navistar.com/index .php?s=43&item=486

174. May 3, 2011. Navistar names new VP of custom products division. *op. cit.*

Ryan McVay/Getty Images

Vincent Cholewa, Lori Dreager, Greg Grilliot, Sze Yuin Lee, Drew Wallace, Sean Wright

Arizona State University

Well, let's separate the market into two phases. One is the phase of DVD, which peaks in five to 10 years and lasts for 20 to 30 years. Then there is the phase of Internet delivery, which peaks 20 or 30 years from now and lasts for 100 years.[1]

REED HASTINGS
FOUNDER AND CEO OF NETFLIX, FEBRUARY 2005

Introduction

In late April 2010, Reed Hastings, Founder and CEO of Netflix, announced that his company had exceeded expectations by achieving outstanding first quarter results. The company, which Hastings co-founded in 1997, had grown its subscriber base by 35 percent in the course of one year (Q1-2009 to Q1-2010) to nearly 14 million subscribers. Within the same period, revenue grew by 25 percent to $493.7 million and net income by 44 percent to $32.3 million.[2] By all accounts, the company had come out of the "great recession" in fine form and the market rewarded Netflix as measured by an increase of almost 300 percent in the value of a share of its stock to an all-time high of $119.50 by the time of the earnings announcement.[3]

However, in spite of the outstanding results, there was still cause for concern at the publicly traded company's Los Gatos, California headquarters. The subscription DVD rental company had just heard that its delivery partner, the US Postal Service (USPS), was considering stopping Saturday delivery as a way to hopefully staunch its financial losses.[4] With this change and the certitude of continued USPS postage rate increases, Netflix knew it could soon be forced to either raise prices or disappoint customers with slower DVD delivery—and neither was appealing.

Additionally, because of the proliferation of video content available via Internet-connected consumer electronic devices, the Netflix subscriber consumption model was changing. According to Netflix, 55 percent of its subscribers streamed their movies and TV episodes rather than waiting for DVDs in the mail during Q1-2010.[5] This indicated that the subscriber consumption model was fully engaged in a significant change; unfortunately, this also meant that a new breed of competitor—such as Amazon VOD (video on demand), Hulu, and Apple TV—were entering the fray alongside Netflix's historical competitors, Blockbuster and Redbox.

On the supplier side of the business, the major Hollywood studios and content providers were lining up to protect their most valuable revenue stream—DVD sales. In an effort to maximize those sales, Warner Brothers negotiated an agreement with Netflix in January 2010 that required Netflix to delay its rental of new releases until 28 days after the DVDs on-sale date in exchange for lower rates on the DVDs Netflix purchased for its rental stock. However, because 75 percent of DVD sales occur within the first four weeks of availability, many saw Warner Brothers as the key winner in this deal as the more customers that felt compelled to purchase the DVD in lieu of waiting 28 days, the fewer customers there would be in the potential rental pool later.[6] If other studios followed Warner's model, consumers could become disenchanted with the late availability of content in the Netflix library and seek other sources.

Netflix knew that, in the face of increased competition and free video available on the Internet, it must somehow maintain the relevance of the firm's brand in the minds of consumers. Consumers in this market are loyal to content and sensitive to price, meaning that if Netflix failed to continue providing timely and reasonably priced new releases via mail order and streaming service, due to the relatively low barriers of entry in the streaming arena, someone else would (Exhibit 1 provides a visual illustration of video-streaming trends).

Exhibit 1 Video-Streaming Trend

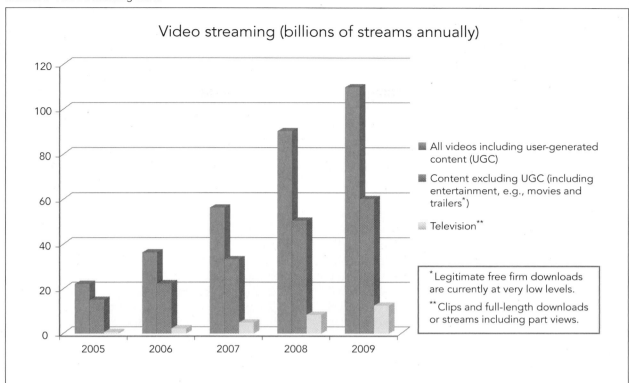

Video streaming (billions of streams annually)

Legend:
- All videos including user-generated content (UGC)
- Content excluding UGC (including entertainment, e.g., movies and trailers*)
- Television**

*Legitimate free firm downloads are currently at very low levels.

**Clips and full-length downloads or streams including part views.

Source: Future source estimates from selected Web analytics (Accustream, Nielsen, Comscore, INS/The Conference Board).

Company History

Reed Hastings and Marc Randolph, proven veteran "new technology" entrepreneurs, founded Netflix in 1997 in Scotts Valley, California, together with Mitch Lowe.[i,7] Hastings came up with the idea for a rent-by-mail video business after he was forced to pay a $40 late fee for an overdue in-store copy of *Apollo 13*. Investing $2.5 million from the sale of his former company—Pure Atria Software—Netflix was born.[8]

Early Phase & IPO

Netflix launched its Web site on April 14, 1998, and thus positioned itself to take advantage of the new DVD technology that Hastings and Randolph believed would eventually replace VHS as the preferred playback format. In the early years, there were only a few companies—such as Magic Disc, DVD Express, and Reel.com—competing in the rent-by-mail DVD industry. To promote its brand, Netflix provided a free rental coupon to consumers that purchased Toshiba, Sony, and Pioneer DVD players or select Hewlett-Packard PCs and Apple computers. Also in 1998, with a deal

widely publicized in the media, Netflix boosted its brand recognition by selling Bill Clinton's grand jury testimony in the Monica Lewinsky scandal for two cents plus shipping. To preempt the rise of a formidable competitor while in its nascency, Netflix called an early truce with Amazon and ended that firm's foray into DVD sales after agreeing to forward customers interested in purchasing DVDs to Amazon in exchange for Amazon promoting Netflix for rentals on its heavily trafficked Web site.

To the delight of consumers perpetually disappointed to find new releases out of stock at their local bricks-and-mortar video rental stores, Netflix's Web site guaranteed that all DVD titles would be in stock and delivered quickly and directly to customers' doorsteps via the USPS. Initially, Netflix offered a 7-day pay-per-rental model at a cost of $4 per DVD plus $2 postage with applicable late fees. In September 1999, Netflix introduced its monthly subscription plan—the Marquee Program—charging $15.95 per month and allowing four (later cut to three) DVD rentals per shipment, unlimited non-concurrent shipments, with no due dates or late fees. With 97 percent of business driven through the Marquee Program within four months of its offering, Netflix dropped its per rental fee model in early 2000. "The new program was

---

[i]Mitch Lowe, who helped found Netflix and bring it to IPO, is now president of Redbox Automated Retail, LLC, one of Netflix's main competitors today.

Globe: © Jan Rysavy/iStockphoto.com

possible because the company had achieved economies of scale, with 10,000 orders processed each day by its own proprietary software system," said Hastings.[9] In July 1999, Hastings secured $30 million in financing to help build and market the Netflix brand to consumers and maintain its rapid dominance of the rent-by-mail DVD industry.

Netflix signed revenue sharing agreements with movie studios including Warner Home Video, Columbia Tri-Star, DreamWorks, and Artisan in exchange for lower prices on bulk DVD purchases. In addition to stocking the more mainstream selections, Netflix also found great success renting lesser-known and hard-to-find independent and foreign films. In February 2002, Netflix reached its goal of 500,000 customers and completed its initial public offering (IPO), selling 5.5 million shares of common stock and raising $82.5 million in equity. Despite the unprofitable revenue stream of Netflix's early years, the firm enjoyed steady growth in its customer base and opened 10 regional distribution centers in different metro areas of the US to increase the number of customers receiving next-day DVD deliveries.

Aggressive Growth and Earning a Profit

By 2002, Netflix had signed revenue sharing agreements with an unprecedented 50 film distributors. Growing consumer demand for DVD rentals brought competition from firms such as Blockbuster and Walmart, with both starting their own online DVD rental services and Walmart undercutting Netflix's subscription price by more than a dollar. As a result, Netflix's cancellation rate began to climb and its stock price dropped by 50 percent. Rather than lowering its price, in response, Netflix opened a dozen additional distribution centers around the US, thus improving its service for thousands of customers. Conceding the win, Walmart ended its DVD rental services and entered instead into a promotional deal with Netflix in 2005.[10] Blockbuster, on the other hand, engaged in a monthly subscription price war with Netflix, eventually settling on a price structure identical to Netflix only to be undercut when Netflix lowered the prices of its two most popular subscription plans by one dollar.[11] Despite the competition, Netflix managed to double its subscriber base and reach one million subscribers by February 2003. In addition, Netflix reported its first profitable quarter by June of the same year. After achieving its first profit, Netflix continued to grow and fend off an increasing number of competitors.[12] As a value-added service and to give the firm an edge in competing with new entrants, Netflix developed, patented, and maintained an extensive personalized video recommendation system based on user rentals, ratings, and reviews.

In addition to the challenges of direct competition from other firms, on a separate front, Netflix faced ongoing legal issues. For example, in 2005, Netflix opted to settle a class action suit alleging the firm did not "provide unlimited DVD rentals and one day delivery as promised in its marketing materials," by giving the plaintiffs a free one-month upgrade in their service.[13] Despite the increased competition and incessant legal issues during this period, Netflix continued to increase its customer base and not only turn a profit, but continue to.

Dawn of the Digital Age

In 2000, Netflix shifted its goal from DVD rentals to streaming video with Hastings stating, "What Netflix is about is owning a transition stage as rental converts to video on demand."[14] Foreseeing that "DVD is not a hundred-year format," Hastings introduced online content streaming that allowed subscribers to watch movies and TV shows on their PCs at no additional cost. Despite the fact that its initial library of titles was limited, they came from studios such as NBC Universal, Sony Pictures, 20th Century Fox, Paramount Pictures, and Warner Brothers and thus comprised a respectable opening library of titles.[15] By 2009, Netflix's streaming library had grown eightfold, offered titles in HD 720-progressive format, and compatibility to include PCs, Macs, TVs, Blu-Ray players, TiVo, Roku, Microsoft Xbox 360, and Sony's Playstation 3.[16,17] Further improvements to the firm's proprietary movie recommendation software, Saturday shipping, and automated distribution centers allowed Netflix to acquire one million new subscribers in Q4-2009 alone. In early 2010, Netflix further increased its compatibility by offering its streaming services via Apple's iPad and Nintendo's Wii.[18,19] Netflix's early start in the subscription DVD rental industry, strong distribution capabilities, and loyal customers keep it the industry leader and make it an e-commerce success story in an ever-changing business landscape.[20]

Remember When VHS and Betamax Were Awesome?

According to Dave Hoffman, content planning and analysis manager at Netflix, "Our business model went from dead, to streaming is cool but all the money is made on DVDs, to wow, we're actually delivering great content and people are paying for it instead of going to Blockbuster." These sentiments describe the general landscape of the digital video-streaming marketplace as competition continues to intensify.

Technology plays a major factor in the new media world as barriers to entry in the digital world are limited to non-existent. This technological transformation coupled with increased consumer demand for digital content delivery has forced companies like Blockbuster to shut down bricks-and-mortar locations and develop platforms that mimic Netflix and allow customers to order online and/or stream content.[21] The Diffusion Group, a market research company, projects revenue from Internet video to TV to grow from $1 billion in 2009 to $5.7 billion in 2014. Companies like Netflix will reap enhanced consumer loyalty from devices such as Blu-Ray players and video game consoles equipped to stream content. As a partial result of streaming deals with several consumer electronics device manufacturers, Netflix saw its subscriber base increase by 35 percent from Q1-2009 to Q1-2010. The key for any player in this marketplace is to win the digital fight and the major advantages a company can develop are being first to market, having the best content, and scaling benefits. Technological threats include illegal downloads and Internet hackers. The growth Netflix has experienced since its inception has obviously attracted hackers to manipulate the company. For example, Netflix tracks how long a user streams each downloaded video; nevertheless, a hacker admitted to getting around this so Netflix would not know he was able to watch more than a few minutes of a film.[22]

Demographic trends such as increased world population (6.1 billion in 2000 to 7.2 billion in 2015[23]) present opportunities to Netflix as it currently only operates in the US. In 2009, there were 384 million Internet users in China[24] and 81 million Internet users in India.[25] Expanding into these countries and others across the globe has the potential to give Netflix a competitive advantage, especially since ailing Blockbuster plans to focus on its North American market and will potentially pull out of 17 countries worldwide. Netflix could tap into these markets; however, the firm must consider the costs to expand (i.e., distribution centers if it chooses to mail DVDs, a new department at corporate HQ for the international segment, etc.), prepare for barriers to entry across borders, as well as learn the nuances of negotiating agreements with foreign film studios.

With little governmental regulation over delivery of streaming content, the biggest legal barrier for Netflix is gaining rights from movie studios to obtain first-run content sooner. In their attempt to avoid cannibalization and maximize DVD sales, currently, Warner Brothers, 20th Century Fox, and Universal Studios[26] have a 28-day delay on Netflix obtaining newly released DVDs. Premium subscriptions (and the increased revenue they generate) are the key to a content provider being first-to-market with original content; however, from the studios' perspective, doing so will require remuneration for their loss of DVD sales. Whether content suppliers

and content providers can reach this type of agreement has yet to be seen.

An Open Casting Call

When Netflix diversified its DVD-by-mail distribution model to include streaming content over the Internet, it became the first to offer subscribers two delivery options for one low monthly price.[27] While the market for Internet delivered video content is still in its formative stages[28] and competition is expected to build, the overall market for in-home entertainment video is very competitive, largely because consumers can subscribe to multiple providers simultaneously or shift their spending from one provider to another with ease.[29] As an example, consumers can subscribe to cable, rent a DVD from Redbox, buy a DVD from Walmart, download a movie from Apple iTunes, view a television program on Hulu.com, and subscribe to Netflix all within the same period (Exhibit 2 provides a side-by-side comparison of DVD rental company products and services). Currently, Netflix is the main provider in the subscription segment, but the firm faces competition from Blockbuster and Redbox in this space.[30]

Blockbuster Inc.

Blockbuster's objective is to remain the world's largest video rental chain. Blockbuster operates more than 6,500 company-owned or franchised stores in 17 countries with 62 percent of those stores located in the US. Annually, the chain as a whole rents more than 1 billion videos, DVDs, and video games. In addition to in-store rentals and purchases—and putting it in direct competition with Netflix and, to some degree, Redbox—customers can watch a rented or purchased instant download via "Blockbuster Online."

Recently, Blockbuster has closed hundreds of stores and has plans to divest its foreign operations to focus on its North American business in its effort to move toward a digital future and stay afloat. At present, Blockbuster carries $1 billion in debt and is accelerating its store-closing schedule: shutting down 20 percent of its stores and reducing the footprint of 250 stores by the end of 2010. To assist in transitioning from a store-based distribution system to a multi-channel approach involving mail, vending, and digital download options, in January 2009, Blockbuster created an executive position to lead its digital entertainment division. In addition, Blockbuster has partnered with Samsung Electronics America to allow owners of Samsung's next generation of high-definition TVs to rent Blockbuster DVDs with the press of a button using their high-speed Internet connection. Blockbuster also provides VOD service through alliances with TiVo and is following Redbox's

Exhibit 2 Comparison of Online DVD Rental Services

	Netflix	Blockbuster Online	iTunes	Green Cine	DVD Avenue	Cinema Now	Cafe DVD
Lowest Monthly Price	$7.99	$9.99	$3.99	$9.95	$9.99	$3.99	$14.95
Cost of Instant Viewing per Month							
One Movie	$7.99	$8.99	$3.99	N/A	N/A	$3.99	N/A
10 Movies	$7.99	$39.99	$39.99	N/A	N/A	$39.99	N/A
50 Movies	$7.99	$199.50	$199.50	N/A	N/A	$199.50	N/A
100 Movies	$7.99	$399.00	$399.00	N/A	N/A	$399.00	N/A
Membership Features							
By mail	✔	✔	✔	✔	✔	✔	✔
Watch instantly (stream)	✔	✔	✔			✔	
Free Trial	✔	✔					
Unlimited per month DVD rental or TV	✔	✔	✔	✔	✔	✔	
No due dates and free two-way shipping	✔	✔		✔	✔		
No late fees	✔	✔	✔	✔	✔		
Library	100,000	95,000		30,000	25,000		60,000
Avg delivery time (in days)	Mail 1–2/ Instant	Mail 1–2/ Instant	Instant only	Mail only 1–4	Mail only 1–2	Instant only	Mail only 1–4
Accessibility							
Watch with TV	✔	✔	✔	✔	✔	✔	✔
Access/watch with PC	✔	✔	✔	✔	✔	✔	✔
Access by mail	✔	✔		✔	✔		✔
Instant access on Wii	✔						
Instant access on PS3 or Xbox 360	✔					✔	
Instant access on iPad, iPhone, or iPod Touch	✔		✔				
Instant access on Roku	✔						
Access with Internet TV	✔						
In-Store Exchanges		✔					

Source: Adapted from http://dvd-rental-review.toptenreviews.com

lead with Blockbuster Express branded DVD kiosks for video rentals in supermarkets, convenience stores, and other retail locations in a deal with ATM manufacturer, NCR. This partnership got a boost in late 2009 when NCR acquired DVDPlay, a West Coast based kiosk DVD rental company with about 1,500 kiosks already in place. The NCR purchase boosted the number of installed kiosks to about 3,800 by the end of 2009 with Blockbuster/NCR planning to install an additional 6,200, or 10,000 total, kiosks. In 2007, Blockbuster acquired Movielink, an online movie-downloading company owned by major Hollywood studios, to explore alternative distribution channels[31,32] and in 2009, Blockbuster announced a partnership with digital media firm, Sonic Solutions. The two companies have been working together to offer VOD for PCs, cell phones, TVs connected to the Internet, and other electronic devices and plan to have streaming and progressive download options available when the service launches.

Redbox Automated Retail, LLC (Redbox)

Redbox, founded in 2003, is owned by Coinstar and its President, Mitch Lowe, was formerly Netflix's VP of business development. Redbox offers an alternative in an industry dominated by Netflix and Blockbuster: it places automated red kiosks at selected McDonald's, supermarkets, and convenience stores where any customer with a credit or debit card can rent movies for $1 per day. For added convenience, customers can reserve movies online, then pick the movie up at the selected kiosk, and return movies to any Redbox machine—all without a membership. Each kiosk holds more than 700 discs with 200 titles and the fast-growing company owns and operates 22,000 kiosks nationwide—a number projected to more than double by 2012.[33,34]

The latest recession spurred an increased use of Redbox, which recently generated four million card swipes in one month. In July 2009, Netflix rightly declared that Redbox and its convenient kiosks would be its number one competitor by the end of the year. Redbox's $1 rentals have been disruptive not only to its DVD rental rivals, but to Hollywood as well. Studios are torn between supplying Redbox with cheap wholesale discs and trying to starve it by keeping the selections late and/or limited in the hopes of preserving their more lucrative DVD sales to consumers. So far, 20th Century Fox and Universal Pictures are in favor of not distributing newer titles to Redbox; however, in July 2009, Sony Pictures signed a five-year supply deal with the company. In August 2009, Redbox filed suit against 20th Century Fox after it requested that Redbox delay renting DVDs of its films until 30 days after their public release date. Redbox then filed similar suits against Universal (and its 45-day wait) and Warner Home Video (with a 28-day delay).[35,36,37]

Everyone Else

In the long run, Netflix's stiffest challenge will be the growing demand for digital movie rentals provided by Internet and cable companies. These providers are subdivided into the VOD segment (including Apple's iTunes, Amazon.com, and CinemaNow), the ad-supported segment (Hulu.com, Google's YouTube, and the newly introduced Google TV), and the subscription segment (Blockbuster Online).[38]

Other indirect competitors include video package providers with pay-per-view and VOD content. For example, cable providers such as Time Warner and Comcast; direct satellite providers such as DIRECTV and Echostar; and telecommunications providers such as AT&T and Verizon. Entertainment video stores selling DVDs such as Best Buy, Walmart, and Amazon.com also compete against Netflix indirectly.[39]

An as yet entirely new dimension to the market that Netflix may have to deal with is the possibility of content providers taking on the responsibility of the digital distribution of their own content. Potential entrants to this market range from the actual studios that create and own the rights to the content, to illegal digital distributors. Within this range and, again, because of the low barriers to entry, are a multitude of content provider permutations. Suppliers with significant capital at their disposal could afford to assume complete control over the timing of the physical and digital distribution of their content in an attempt to maximize their profit. This supplier power would mean that, as a middleman distributor, Netflix could experience a compromised revenue stream and be unable to maintain pace with the cost of licensing content.[40] Sony or Disney, for instance, could generate and distribute their own content exclusively through their own streaming service. At the same time, the content would most likely be available to savvy consumers via the Internet for free. To maintain an advantage, Netflix must ensure high streaming quality and easy access so initial consumer experiences are successful. Additionally, Netflix must generate early brand identity in the streaming video content delivery method by leveraging its DVD rental subscriptions and "giving away" its video-streaming library.[41]

Content Providers

Netflix operates in a challenging industry due to the fact that content suppliers—television and movie studios—wield significant influence: a fact that renders Netflix untouchable in one respect and vulnerable in another. The line of demarcation that separates Netflix's defenses and vulnerabilities is the video content delivery method. Netflix constantly assesses its position in the industry from both the DVD rental perspective as well as the streaming video perspective. That said, the DVD rental method will deteriorate significantly over the next two decades and shift to streaming video. This change will transfer the upper hand to content suppliers because the relatively low barriers to entry into the streaming video market will create countless distributors from which suppliers may choose.[42]

Because Netflix dominates the DVD rental segment, this is where it leverages its distribution expertise to generate significant revenue for the firm and the movie studios. Aside from the fact that the rental of a physical DVD will soon be a thing of the past, at this point, the threat of competition on this side of the industry is low due to the relatively high barriers to entry. These barriers include the establishment of multiple physical distribution centers to ensure quick delivery, considerable capital to acquire enough reasonably priced DVDs to ensure demand for new releases is met, and favorable bulk postage rates. Netflix utilizes the sheer size of its subscriber/customer base to create economies of scale that are difficult to imitate, yielding a potentially sustainable competitive advantage for the firm.[43]

As for the streaming video segment however, a number of factors leave Netflix exposed to potential competitive disadvantages. For example, because the studios that supply content currently generate a significant portion of their revenue from DVD sales, they will continue to be reluctant to allow immediate streaming rights to any provider and will demand increasingly higher licensing fees.[44] This reluctance to provide streaming rights coupled with the proliferation of illegal video pirating and downloads occurring while movies are still in theatres means studios will continue to leverage the early demand for their products to garner the maximum licensing fees.[45] This will impact Netflix's bottom line as the firm bids against other streaming video providers and acquisition fees begin to trend up as a result.[46]

As demand for streaming video content accelerates, DVD rental demand will diminish. As previously mentioned, because consumers are loyal to content and not to particular distributors, Netflix may be hard pressed to convince consumers to view content from its service as opposed to one of the other many new choices available now and expected to appear.[47] The low barriers to entry into the market have the potential to fuel an explosive growth of content distributors all vying to satisfy the convenience and instant gratification cravings of consumers. For a distributor to provide desirable content in terms of price and quality as demanded by consumers, it must first negotiate content licensing with suppliers—suppliers with a wide array of streaming distribution options. With forecasts estimating that "Internet video alone will account for 57 percent of all consumer Internet traffic in 2014" and strong demand for their content, movie studios in particular will enjoy a strong position in all negotiations.[48]

Who Decides?

With both physical and streaming video demand forecast to increase significantly, consumers will gravitate to simple-to-use services that provide the content they seek. Today, Netflix definitely provides value to its customers by quickly delivering DVDs to their mailboxes. This convenience cannot be underestimated, particularly because the most valuable resources of consumers today—time and money—are expected to remain constrained. For Netflix's long-term survival, its transition to streaming content satisfies both of these consumer value propositions. However, while Netflix's early insertion into the streaming market will pay dividends in terms of embedding its brand in consumer consciousness, with the continued proliferation of electronic devices with Internet video capabilities and the anticipated expansion of content distributors, in the end, consumers' choices among competitors will determine the winners among those competing in these markets. With low switching costs, consumers will leverage the Internet's inherent capabilities to find

the video they seek at precisely the moment they want to view it. Wisely, even Netflix itself makes it easy for consumers to switch their subscription plans or suspend their service at any time via its Web site. An example of this is the recent trend of customers signing up for the lowest priced unlimited DVD-by-mail subscription plan with unlimited streaming video availability and content. This trend is interesting because it signals a toggle in consumers' awareness of Netflix's streaming video capabilities—an awareness that will, ultimately, impact Netflix's bottom line.

Another impact on the bottom line is the price Netflix will eventually have to pay to license and distribute content. Netflix's position as a middleman distributor is useful for the DVD rental portion of its business because, at present, suppliers rely on Netflix to generate a portion of their revenue. However, this doesn't mean the supplier doesn't have any power because, as demand for video increases, Netflix must continue to provide the latest and most popular releases in a timely manner and studios can charge a premium for Netflix to be able to do so.

Yet another pivotal facet of the Netflix rental distribution model is the firm's reliance on the USPS and broadband Internet providers. The USPS continues to raise postage rates in an attempt to combat revenue losses caused by a decrease in overall volume as a result of the growth of electronic mail, digital downloading, and e-commerce. In addition to the ongoing cost increases of the USPS are the eventual charges that consumers will have to pay for the volume of content they download via their broadband Internet connections.[49] This increased cost to the consumer will most likely result in consumers demanding lower subscription fees from providers such as Netflix. Without some concession, the consumer would likely seek less expensive or even free providers of video content via the Internet, an outcome that could wring out a majority of Netflix's profits.

Although Netflix does not face a significant threat from substitute forms of visual entertainment such as reading, live entertainment, or visiting a museum, the firm must recognize an industry-wide lack of brand loyalty and the real threat of consumers switching to substitute content providers that offer a compelling enough quality and cost combination. For example, switching costs are relatively non-existent because customers pay for their subscriptions on a month-to-month basis and can suspend, alter, and reinstate their subscriptions at will.[50] Although the demand for video is increasing, there is a physical limit to the amount of time the average consumer can realistically view video, currently estimated at an average of five hours a day. To gain market share, Netflix has partnered with hardware providers to make it easy for consumers to connect and subscribe to its service.[51]

Recently, this convenience appears to have helped grow Netflix subscriptions to more than 13 million.[52] The main driver of this is the connection convenience provided by Netflix's partnerships with gaming console manufacturers that allow the Wi-Fi enabled devices to stream Netflix to the consumer's TV via the console. This is a significant transformation of the living room to a center of on demand entertainment enabled by the ability to connect the TV to the Internet. This transformation will be further spurred by the introduction of Internet-enabled TVs.[53]

Behind the Scenes

Netflix has positioned itself as a cost leader with a variety of products and services. The company's Q1-2010 earnings report illustrates this point:

Our core strategy is to grow a large subscription business consisting of streaming and DVD-by-mail content. By combining streaming and DVD as part of the Netflix subscription, we are able to offer subscribers a uniquely compelling selection of movies for one low monthly price. We believe this creates a competitive advantage as compared to a streaming only subscription service.[54]

From the cost perspective, Netflix appeals to price sensitive consumers who are not willing to pay more to either purchase a DVD or view content "à la carte" as with VOD or download. As a result of the company's substantial monthly subscriber revenue, Netflix is able to differentiate itself from other content providers with of its extensive catalogue, proprietary recommendation system, outstanding customer service, and near constant innovation.

How Netflix Works

Netflix subscribers are able to select, receive, and watch/ stream content in an unlimited "all you can eat" manner for as little as $8.99 per month.[55] The process starts when Netflix subscribers interface with a simple Web-portal that allows them to build a 'queue,' or list, of DVDs and digital streaming content they wish to view in the future. Building a queue can be done by browsing a diverse set of pre-selected category lists such as 'New Releases' and 'Critics Picks' or by viewing the customized 'Movies You'll ♥' link to access titles matched to the user via an algorithm based on their past viewing history.[56] After the subscriber has created a queue, Netflix then either sends a DVD to them via the USPS in the company's signature red mailing envelope or, if preferred and offered, makes it available for immediate download via a broadband Internet connection. In the case of DVDs, the subscriber is able to keep the title as long as they wish without a late fee before returning it using the postage pre-paid, red envelope provided by Netflix.

Delivering DVDs to Subscribers

A large part of Netflix's large-scale, quick growth is due to its innovative logistics system that allows it to deliver DVDs by mail to "more than 97 percent of customers in one business day."[57] To do this, Netflix operates 58 warehouses across the country and ships over two million discs from its inventory six days a week. With the exception of Sunday morning, each day at a Netflix warehouse begins at 3:00 am when a truck leaves to pick up boxes of returned DVDs from the post office. When the truck returns, the boxes are unloaded and employees "rip open each envelope, toss it, pull the disc from its sleeve, check that the title matches the sleeve, inspect the disc for cracks or scratches, inspect the sleeve for stains or marks, clean the disc with a quick circular motion on a towel pulled tight across a square block of wood, insert the disc into its sleeve, and file the disc." Netflix expects line workers to perform this task "a minimum of 650 times per hour." Inspected DVDs are then checked back into inventory by a machine that scans sleeve barcodes, at a rate of up to 30,000 DVDs per hour. Following this step, workers run the entire warehouse inventory through a similar scanning and sorting station to separate out the DVDs scheduled to ship to subscribers that day. They then send the separated DVDs to a stuffing machine that seals the discs into envelopes and prints delivery labels with a laser.[58] In recent years, Netflix has moved to automate 60 percent of its processes and the resulting efficiency improvements have led to a 17 percent lower cost per shipment. For example, at one time, only 600 DVDs could be inserted into mailers per hour: this rate is now more than 4,000 DVDs per hour.[59]

The entire process is finished by 5:00 pm, when the delivery truck departs for the post office. Netflix is extremely tight lipped about its quality targets for DVD delivery, but failure rates are thought to be "far less than a quarter of one percent."[60] If true, Netflix has achieved a six-sigma level process in distribution of DVDs.

Streaming Content to Subscribers

With the emergence of higher capacity broadband Internet connections, advances in audio- and video-streaming technology, and the development of compression/decompression (codec) software, in 2007, Netflix released its "View Instantly" offering allowing subscribers to stream data to their home PC.[61] In streaming, the codecs "discard unnecessary data, lower the overall [screen] resolution and take other steps to make the file smaller"[62] so it may be more quickly and easily transmitted to the user. Additionally, "playing the streaming file discards the data as you watch. A full copy of the file never exists on your computer, so you can't save it for later."[63]

Netflix is now pursuing several alternative methods for delivering streaming content.[64] Subscribers are currently able to stream content from Netflix using "Microsoft's Xbox 360, Sony's PS3 game consoles, and Nintendo's Wii console; Blu-ray disc players from Samsung, LG, and Insignia; Internet TVs from LG, Sony, and VIZIO; the Roku digital video player and TiVo digital video recorders; and Apple's iPad tablet."[65] By embedding its streaming technology on a wide variety of devices, Netflix has the advantage of not requiring consumers to purchase a dedicated set-top box to stream content.[66]

Because each of these devices require a unique set of codecs and a complex "always-on" infrastructure, in recent months Netflix has chosen Amazon Web Services (AWS) "to run a variety of mission-critical, customer-facing and backend applications."[67] By stepping into Amazon's cloud computing infrastructure, Netflix hopes to "utilize vast numbers of servers to transcode and store TV episodes and movies into new formats quickly, and AWS pay-as-you-go pricing ensures that Netflix pays only for resources used."[68] As a result of this set of technological innovations, in Q1-2010, more than 55 percent of Netflix subscribers streamed at least 15 minutes of content from the site.[69]

Marketing and Sales

To attract new subscribers, Netflix uses a variety of on and offline advertising including Web-based banner ads, paid Web-based search listings, print advertising, and direct mail promotions.[70] To encourage potential new subscribers, Netflix offers a no-obligation first month of free service; additionally, the firm has a convenient tool on its Web site that allows current subscribers to invite their friends to join. As streaming has gained momentum, Netflix has even given current subscribers a 10 percent discount in the first month after they stream content using a device such as Nintendo's Wii.[71]

Customer Service and Company Culture

According to independent researcher Foresee Results, since 2005, Netflix has placed first in 90 percent of polls measuring e-commerce customer satisfaction. Other indices, such as the American Customer Satisfaction Index (ACSI), also rank Netflix first as compared to other e-retail Web sites.[72] Under his tenure, Hastings has ensured that Netflix isn't considered mediocre, as was the case at his first start-up company, Pure Software. Says Hastings of that experience, "We went from being a heat-filled, everybody-wants-to-be-here place to a dronish, when-does-the-day-end sausage factory. We got more bureaucratic as we grew."[73] Upon starting Netflix, recruiting, rewarding, and retaining the best talent has been Hastings answer to this. He expects extremely high performance with the average employee doing the job of three to four people and he rewards them for it by providing extremely attractive compensation packages, choice in how they are paid (cash vs. stock ratio), and unlimited vacation time. With this culture, there is nowhere to hide and average performers are provided with a generous severance package as an incentive to walk away. Hastings ensures the company hires the most talented from its pool of candidates by telling recruiters, "Money is no object."[74] In 2006, he successfully applied this strategy to capitalize on intellectual resources external to Netflix by holding a contest with a $1 million prize open to the worldwide public that challenged individuals or teams to come up with an at least 10 percent more accurate algorithm to predict consumer movie preferences. Netflix received 44,014 valid submissions from 5,169 individuals and teams with, ultimately, two teams achieving the 10 percent improvement goal sought by Hastings.[75] In 2009, Hastings awarded the $1 million prize to the first team to submit and, despite subsequent litigation alleging violation of privacy laws, its success has prompted Hastings to explore similar contest ideas with $1 million prizes.[76]

At the Box Office

According to the firm's 2010 annual report, Netflix's revenue, which is substantially derived from monthly subscription fees, increased in 2009 by $305.7 million compared to 2008 and another $492.4 in 2010 compared to 2009 (see Exhibit 3A for Netflix revenue for these periods). This increase is attributed to increased consumer awareness of the compelling value of streaming video and DVD-by-mail for one low price as well as the other benefits Netflix offers. This subscriber growth, which has been highly correlated with Netflix's earnings growth trend over the past 11 years, appears to be sustainable even with higher customer attrition as the firm is able to offset those losses with new customer acquisitions or reactivations. However, revenue per subscriber declined primarily due to the growing popularity of Netflix's lower priced plans and reduced marketing spending[77] (Exhibit 3B shows financial data per subscriber). This financial outcome could be by design as the company has been using its margins to develop its digital streaming platform: a strategy that results in limited near-term incremental monetization opportunity, such as not declaring or paying any cash dividends presently or in the foreseeable future (see Exhibit 3C).[78]

Netflix's main source of liquidity has been cash from operations. In 2009, however, long-term debt financing was added as part of its source of liquidity as it issued a $200 million aggregate principal amount of senior notes that are due in November 2017. This resulted in Netflix posting much higher debt ratios relative to the industry

Exhibit 3A Netflix: Consolidated Statements of Operations (in thousands, except per share data)

	Year ended December 31		
	2010	2009	2008
Revenues	$2,162,625	$1,670,269	$1,364,661
Cost of revenues:			
Subscription	1,154,109	909,461	761,133
Fulfillment expenses	203,246	169,810	149,101
Total cost of revenues	1,357,355	1,079,271	910,234
Gross profit	805,270	590,998	454,427
Operating expenses:			
Technology and development	163,329	114,542	89,873
Marketing	293,839	237,744	199,713
General and administrative	70,555	51,333	49,662
Gain on disposal of DVDs	(6,094)	(4,560)	(6,327)
Total operating expenses	521,629	399,059	332,921
Operating income	283,641	191,939	121,506
Other income (expense):			
Interest expense	(19,629)	(6,475)	(2,458)
Interest and other income	3,684	6,728	12,452
Income before income taxes	267,696	192,192	131,500
Provision for income taxes	106,843	76,332	48,474
Net income	$ 160,853	$ 115,860	$ 83,026
Net income per share:			
Basic	$ 3.06	$ 2.05	$ 1.36
Diluted	$ 2.96	$ 1.98	$ 1.32
Weighted-average common shares outstanding:			
Basic	52,529	56,560	60,961
Diluted	54,304	58,416	62,836

Source: Netflix 10-K filing for year ended December 31, 2010. SEC.gov.

median. Nevertheless, its profitability and operation ratios outperformed the industry revealing Netflix's strong position (Exhibit 3D shows financial ratios as compared to the industry). Additionally, with higher cash balance growth rates, Netflix's primary use of cash has involved financing its stock repurchase program, delivery expenses, content acquisitions, as well as capital expenditures related to information technology and automated equipment for operations, marketing, and fulfillment, thereby leading to an increased assets growth rate and a significantly decreased liability growth rate over the past three years. Judging from Netflix's resource investments/allocations and its financial ratios against overall industry performance, Netflix is transitioning well into a hybrid model while becoming a better funded company than its competitors (Exhibits 4A, 4B, 4C, and 4D provide financial data in comparison to Netflix competitors).

Key Strategic Leaders

Reed Hastings—Founder, Chairman, and CEO

Reed Hastings received a BA in mathematics from Bowdoin College in 1983 and a master's in computer science from Stanford University in 1988. Hastings founded Pure Software in 1991 at the age of 31. In 1997, Pure Atria Software was acquired by Rational Software for $700 million and Hastings began to work on his new idea—Netflix.[79,80] He launched the subscription service for Netflix in 1999 that grew to one million subscribers in less than four years. Ten years after its founding, Netflix had a total of 12.3 million subscribers. Due to Hastings's vision and tremendous success, he was added to *TIME* magazine's "*TIME* 100" list that included the most influential global citizens in 2005. In 2007, he was appointed to Microsoft's Board of Directors and later that year was inducted to the Video Business Hall of Fame.[81]

Exhibit 3B Netflix: Annual Revenue by Subscriber

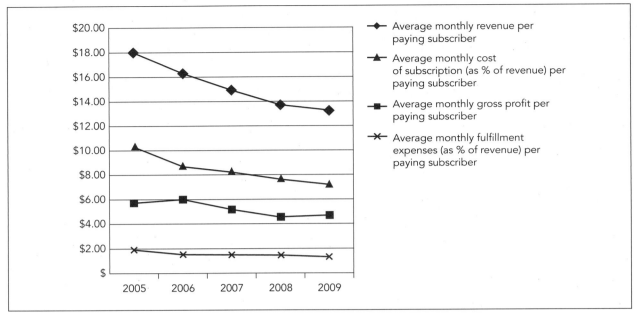

Data		Year ended December 31			
	2005	**2006**	**2007**	**2008**	**2009**
Revenues ($ thousands)	682,213	996,660	1,205,340	1,364,661	1,670,269
Gross Profit ($ thousands)	217,663	369,675	419,172	454,427	590,998
Other Data:					
Average number of paying subscribers	3,169	5,083	6718	8,268	10,464

(Percentages)		Year ended December 31			
	2005	**2006**	**2007**	**2008**	**2009**
Revenues	100.0%	100.0%	100.0%	100.0%	$682,213
Cost of Revenues:					
Subscription	57.7%	53.4%	55.1%	55.8%	54.4%
Fulfillment Expenses	10.6%	9.5%	10.1%	10.9%	10.2%
Total Cost of Revenues	68.3%	62.9%	65.2%	66.7%	64.6%

(Calculations)		Year ended December 31			
	2005	**2006**	**2007**	**2008**	**2009**
Average monthly revenue per paying subscriber	$17.94	$16.34	$14.95	$13.75	$13.30
Average monthly gross profit per paying subscriber	$5.72	$6.06	$5.20	$4.58	$4.71
Average monthly cost of subscription (as % of revenue) per paying subscriber	$10.35	$8.73	$8.24	$7.67	$7.24
Average monthly fulfillment expenses (as % of revenue) per paying subscriber	$1.90	$1.55	$1.51	$1.50	$1.36

Source: Raw data retrieved from Netflix 10-K filings for years ending 2005 to 2009. SEC.gov.

Exhibit 3C Netflix: Consolidated Statements of Cash Flows (in thousands)

	Year Ended December 31,		
	2009	2008	2007
Cash flows from operating activities:			
Net income	$ 115,860	$ 83,026	$ 66,608
Adjustments to reconcile net income to net cash provided by operating activities:			
Depreciation of property, equipment and intangibles	38,044	32,454	22,219
Amortization of content library	219,490	209,757	203,415
Amortization of discounts and premiums on investments	607	625	24
Amortization of debt issuance costs	1,124	—	—
Stock-based compensation expense	12,618	12,264	11,976
Excess tax benefits from stock-based compensation	(12,683)	(5,220)	(26,248)
Loss (gain) on disposal of property and equipment	254	101	142
Gain on sale of short-term investments	(1,509)	(3,130)	(687)
Gain on disposal of DVDs	(7,637)	(13,350)	(14,637)
Gain on sale of investment in business	(1,783)	—	—
Deferred taxes	6,328	(5,905)	(893)
Changes in operating assets and liabilities:			
Prepaid expenses and other current assets	(11,001)	(4,181)	(3,893)
Content library	(64,217)	(48,290)	(34,821)
Accounts payable	(2,256)	7,111	16,555
Accrued expenses	13,169	(1,824)	32,809
Deferred revenue	16,970	11,462	1,987
Other assets and liabilities	1,685	9,137	2,868
Net cash provided by operating activities	325,063	284,037	277,424
Cash flows from investing activities:			
Purchases of short-term investments	(228,000)	(256,959)	(405,340)
Proceeds from sale of short-term investments	166,706	304,163	200,832
Proceeds from maturities of short-term investments	35,673	3,170	—
Purchases of property and equipment	(45,932)	(43,790)	(44,256)
Acquisition of intangible asset	(200)	(1,062)	(550)
Acquisitions of content library	(193,044)	(162,849)	(208,647)
Proceeds from sale of DVDs	11,164	18,368	21,640
Investment in business	—	(6,000)	—
Proceeds from sale of investment in business	7,483	—	—
Other assets	71	(1)	297
Net cash used in investing activities	(246,079)	(144,960)	(436,024)
Cash flows from financing activities:			
Principal payments of lease financing obligations	(1,158)	(823)	(390)
Proceeds from issuance of common stock	35,274	18,872	9,609
Excess tax benefits from stock-based compensation	12,683	5,220	26,248
Borrowings on line of credit, net of issuance costs	18,978	—	—
Payments on line of credit	(20,000)	—	—
Proceeds from issuance of debt, net of issuance costs	193,917	—	—
Repurchases of common stock	(324,335)	(199,904)	(99,858)
Net cash used by financing activities	(84,641)	(176,635)	(64,391)
Net decrease in cash and cash equivalents	(5,657)	(37,558)	(222,991)
Cash and cash equivalents, beginning of year	139,881	177,439	400,430
Cash and cash equivalents, end of year	$134,224	$139,881	$177,439
Supplemental disclosure:			
Income taxes paid	$ 58,770	$ 40,494	$ 15,775
Interest paid	3,878	2,458	1,188

Source: Netflix 10-K filing for year ended December 31, 2010. SEC.gov.

Exhibit 3D Selected Financial Data: Financial Ratios

	Company	Industry Median
Profitability		
Gross profit margin	36.31%	24.42%
Net profit margin	7.11%	2.14%
Return on equity	51.00%	14.00%
Return on assets	19.70%	5.90%
Operations		
Inventory turnover	20.3	9.8
Days cost of goods sold in inventory	18.0	37.0
Asset Turnover	2.8	2.7
Financial		
Current ratio	1.82	1.36
Quick ratio	1.4	0.9
Leverage ratio*	3.41	2.71
Total debt/equity*	1.00	0.12
Interest coverage	20.43	46.85
Per Share Data ($)		
Revenue per share*	31.09	37.8
Cash flow per share	5.88	3.65
Working capital per share	3.53	3.4
Long-term debt per share*	4.53	0.51

*Ratio worse than industry performance.
Source: Data for exhibit retrieved from Morningstar, Inc.

Exhibit 4A Blockbuster: Statement of Operations

	Year Ended Jan 2, 2011
Revenues:	
Rental revenues	$1,816.0
Merchandise sales	296.4
Other revenues	44.1
	2,156.5
Cost of sales:	
Cost of rental revenues	655.9
Cost of merchandise sold	228.9
	884.8
Gross profit	1,271.7
Operating expenses:	
General and administrative	1,233.1
Advertising	50.6
Depreciation and intangible amortization	85.0
Impairment of long-lived assets	22.2
	1,390.9
Operating income (loss)	(119.2)
Interest (expense) income, net	(93.5)
Other items, net	(3.1)

(Continued)

Revenues:	
Income (loss) before reorganization items and income taxes	(215.8)
Reorganization items, net	(9.7)
Provision for income taxes	(2.2)
Equity in income (loss) of non-debtor subsidiaries, net of tax	(20.9)
Income (loss) from continuing operations	(248.6)
Income (loss) from discontinued operations, net of tax	(19.4)
Net income (loss)	$ (268.0)

Source: Blockbuster 10-K filing for year ended January 2, 2011. SEC.gov.

Exhibit 4B Amazon: Consolidated Statements of Operations (in millions, except per share data)

	Year Ended December 31		
	2010	2009	2008
Net sales	$34,204	$24,509	$19,166
Operating expenses			
Cost of sales	26,561	18,978	14,896
Fulfillment	2,898	2,052	1,658
Marketing	1,029	680	482
Technology and content	1,734	1,240	1,033
General and administrative	470	328	279
Other operating expense (income), net	106	102	(24)
Total operating expenses	32,798	23,380	18,324
Income from operations	1,406	1,129	842
Interest income	51	37	83
Interest expense	(39)	(34)	(71)
Other income (expense), net	79	29	47
Total non-operating income (expense)	91	32	59
Income before income taxes	1,497	1,161	901
Provision for income taxes	(352)	(253)	(247)

Source: Amazon 10-K filing for year ended December 31, 2010. SEC.gov.

Exhibit 4C Walmart: Percentage of Segment Net Sales

	January 31,	
STRATEGIC MERCHANDISE UNITS	2011	2010
Grocery	54%	53%
Entertainment	12%	13%
Hardlines	11%	11%
Health and wellness	11%	10%
Apparel	7%	8%
Home	5%	5%
Total	100%	100%

Source: Walmart 10-K filing for year ended January 31, 2011. SEC.gov.

Exhibit 4D Walmart: Consolidated Results of Operations

	Fiscal Years Ended January 31		
	2011	**2010**	**2009**
Net sales[1]	$418,952	$405,132	$401,087
Percentage change from comparable period	3.4%	1.0%	7.3%
Total U.S. calendar comparable store and club sales	−0.6%	−0.8%	3.5%
Gross profit margin as a percentage of sales	24.7%	24.9%	24.2%
Operating income[1]	$ 25,542	$ 24,002	$ 22,767
Operating income as a percentage of net sales	6.1%	5.9%	5.7%
Income from continuing operations[1]	$ 15,959	$ 14,962	$ 13,734
Unit counts	8,970	8,459	7,909
Retail square feet[2]	984,949	952,237	918,044

[1]Dollar amounts in millions.

[2]Amounts in thousands.

Source: Walmart 10-K filing for year ended January 31, 2011. SEC.gov.

In March 2010, Hastings was recognized by *Barron's* when he was placed on its annual "30 Most Respected CEOs" list. His ability to consistently defy odds and position Netflix as the leader in the DVD rental and video-streaming business while competitors such as Blockbuster close the doors of their bricks-and-mortar establishments is what qualifies Hastings to stand among the likes of Steve Jobs of Apple, Larry Ellison of Oracle, and Warren Buffett of Berkshire Hathaway.[82] Hastings prefers to use a functional structure with specialized functions such as marketing, operations, talent, and content to support implementation of the firm's strategy (Exhibit 5 shows the executive level of the Netflix organization chart).

Andrew Rendich—Chief Service and DVD Operations Officer

Andrew Rendich holds computer science and computer engineering degrees from the Rochester Institute of Technology and Alfred State and had over eight years experience in software development and engineering management before joining Netflix in 1999. Before his promotion to VP of operations in 2007, Rendich was VP of systems development where he played a key role in furthering the automation of Netflix's DVD delivery service: work that ultimately reduced errors and lowered costs. Daily DVD shipments have multiplied from a few thousand to more than two million under Rendich's leadership. As chief service and operations officer, Rendich is in charge of Netflix's relationship with the USPS and thus pivotal to one of the key challenges Netflix faces today: USPS's possible elimination of Saturday delivery service.[83]

Ted Sarandos—Chief Content Officer

Ted Sarandos has more than 25 years of experience in the home entertainment industry. He managed a retail video

Exhibit 5 Netflix Organizational Chart

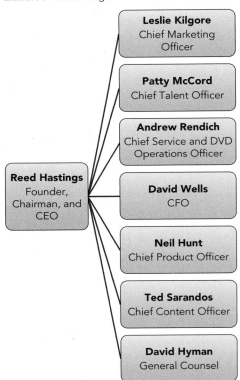

Source: Information taken August 2011 from http://ir.netflix.com/management.cfm.

chain from 1983 until 1988 and was the director of sales and operations for video distributor ETD. Just prior to joining Netflix in 2000, he served as VP of product and merchandising for Video City where he negotiated the industry's first DVD revenue sharing agreement. With the recent agreement between Warner Brothers and Netflix, Sarandos's prior experience has been and will continue to be instrumental to Netflix's success in this sector. As chief content officer, Sarandos oversees 75 employees in the Beverly Hills office and manages Netflix's relationships with studios, producers, and the like in his pursuit of content acquisitions. Sarandos has grown Netflix's DVD library from 2,000 to 100,000 titles and helped launch the video-streaming business with over 17,000 TV shows and movies available for download.[84] In 2008, he helped cut a deal with STARZ to stream Disney and Sony films, a move that put him under the scrutiny of Hollywood studios as he works to position Netflix for the future.

How to Set a Sail to Catch the Wind

After the Q1-2010 financial results announcement, Hastings stated,

It is clear that our performance, and the overall appeal of the Netflix service, is being driven by subscribers watching instantly. On that score, we reached a milestone in the quarter as more than half of all members—55 percent and growing—enjoyed movies and TV episodes streamed from Netflix over the Internet.[85]

As Netflix positions itself for the future, the relevance of streaming video is apparent. With a streaming video content library of only 17,000 titles[86] (compared to over 100,000 DVD titles), will Sarandos be able to successfully convince movie studios that Netflix is the best medium for their streaming content? Will Hastings and Sarandos be able to complete a deal with the studios that allows Netflix to retain its low-cost subscription model? Also, how will the 28-day delay negotiated between Netflix and Warner Brothers, 20th Century Fox, and Universal affect Netflix subscriptions; will subscribers jump ship and go elsewhere to watch their movies sooner; will Netflix lose subscribers to competitors such as Hulu and Vudu? How will Netflix prevent subscriber defection and retain its current customer base? Will Netflix be able to maintain its foundation of successful innovation and maintain its competitive advantages?

Streaming video is likely to assuage the desire for instant gratification that mail delivery does not, but what about subscribers who have not made the shift to streaming video? How will Rendich overcome the obstacle of possible elimination of Saturday mail delivery? Can Netflix offer customers an alternative such as the kiosk model currently implemented by Redbox and Blockbuster Express? How will Netflix maintain profits in the face of increased competition and costs? Also, as Blockbuster continues to decline, would a move into the international arena be wise considering Netflix has yet to tap into that market? If Netflix grows internationally, will illegal downloads become a bigger issue with Netflix opening the floodgates to more subscribers across the globe? Without question, these are key issues that Hastings and his executive team will need to address in the coming years if Netflix is to remain a viable and strong competitor in the DVD rental and video-streaming business.

NOTES

1. Hastings, R. 2 Feb 2005. What is Netflix's Greatest Threat? (Interviewed by Motley Fool Staff). http://www.fool.com/investing/high-growth/2005/02/02/what-is-netflixs-greatest-threat.aspx
2. Netflix, Inc. 2010. Form-10Q Quarterly Report. *SEC.gov.* Accessed 17 May 2010. http://www.sec.gov/Archives/edgar/data/1065280/000119312510095215/d10q.htm
3. Netflix Stock Quotation and History. *Yahoo Finance.* Accessed 31 May 2010. http://finance.yahoo.com/q?s=NFLX
4. Epstein, E. 3 Mar 2010. Netflix is the big loser in Postal Service changes. *The Big Money.* http://www.msnbc.msn.com/id/36100708/ns/business-the_big_money
5. Netflix, Inc. 2010. Form-10Q Quarterly Report. *op. cit.*
6. Grover, R., Satariano, A., and Levy, R. 29 Dec 2009. Netflix vs. the Hollywood Studios. *Bloomberg Businessweek.* http://www.businessweek.com/magazine/content/10_02/b4162054151330.htm
7. Goodrich, C. 2010. Executive Bio: Mitch Lowe. Redbox Press Room. *Redbox Corporate Web site.* Accessed 27 May 2010. http://redboxpressroom.com/index.html
8. Company History Index. 2010. Netflix, Inc. Company Profile, Information, Business Description, History, Background Information on Netflix, Inc. *Reference for Business.* Accessed 16 May 2010. http://www.referenceforbusiness.com/history2/81/Netflix-Inc.html
9. *Ibid.*
10. Fisher, K. 19 June 2005. Netflix sees a bright future, sans Amazon competition. *Ars Techina.* http://arstechnica.com/old/content/2005/06/5011.ars
11. Price War: Netflix Drops Price of Two Plans by $1. 24 Jul 2007. *HackingNetflix.com.* http://www.hackingnetflix.com/2007/07/price-war-netfl.html
12. Company History Index. 2010. *op. cit.*
13. Netflix Class Action Lawsuit Settlement. 1 Nov 2005. *HackingNetflix.com.* http://www.hackingnetflix.com/2005/11/netflix_class_a.html
14. Company History Index. 2010. *op. cit.*
15. Helft, M. 16 Jan 2007. Netflix to Deliver Movies to the PC. *New York Times.* http://www.nytimes.com/2007/01/16/technology/16netflix.html?pagewanted=1&ei=5088&en=71618d2092f5b372&ex=1326603600&partner=rssnyt&emc=rss
16. Netflix, Inc. 2008. Form-10K Annual Report. *SEC.gov.* Accessed 14 May 2010. http://www.sec.gov/Archives/edgar/data/1065280/000119312509037430/d10k.htm
17. Captain, S. 10 Dec 2008. Netflix Goes HD. *Popular Science.* http://www.popsci.com/entertainment-amp-gaming/article/2008-12/netflix-goes-hd
18. Netflix, Inc. 2009. Form-10K Annual Report. *SEC.gov.* Accessed 14 May 2010. http://www.sec.gov/Archives/edgar/data/1065280/000119312510036181/d10k.htm
19. Truta, F. 1 Apr 2010. Netflix iPad App Confirmed at Debut, Video Streaming Available Instantly. *Softpedia.* http://news.softpedia.com/news/Netflix-iPad-App-Confirmed-at-Debut-Video-Streaming-Available-Instantly-139003.shtml
20. Company History Index. 2010. *op. cit.*

21. DVD-by-Mail Isn't Going Away. 10 Mar 2010. *Canaccord Adams.* http://www.streetinsider.com/New+Coverage/Canaccord+Adams+Initiates+Coverage+on+Netflix+(NFLX)+with+a+Buy 3B+DVD-by-Mail+Isnt+Going+Away/5426194.html

22. Demerjian, D. 15 Mar 2007. Rise of the Netflix Hackers. *Wired.com.* http://www.wired.com/science/discoveries/news/2007/03/72963#ixzz0pN0kT0kV

23. Hoskisson, R. 2008. Howard Shultz: Differentiation. Strategic Management: Module 2 Strategic Analysis, Strategy. W.P Carey School of Business, Arizona Board of Regents. http://content.wpcareyonline.com

24. Miniwatts Marketing Group. 2010. China: Internet Usage Stats and Population Report. *Internet World Stats.* http://www.internetworldstats.com/asia/cn.htm

25. Miniwatts Marketing Group. 2010. India: Internet Usage Stats and Population Report. *Internet World Stats.* http://www.internetworldstats.com/asia/cn.htm

26. Schiffman, B. 9 Apr 2010. Netflix renews DVD Deals with 20th Century Fox, Universal. *Daily Finance.* http://www.dailyfinance.com/story/company-news/new-release-dvds-delayed-for-netflix-in-20th-century-fox-univer/19433042/

27. Flynn, L. J. 3 Jun 2002. Two Challenges for Netflix Founder. *The New York Times.* http://www.nytimes.com/2002/06/03/technology/03FLIX.html

28. Dogan, E. 9 May 2009. Experience as the competitive advantage – Netflix case. *NextLeap.net.* http://nextleap.net/index.php/2009/05/09/experience-as-the-competitive-advantage-netflix-case

29. Netflix, Inc., 2009, Form-10K Annual Report. *op. cit.*

30. Rath, J., Chang, W. T., Delleo, D. 1 Apr 2010. New Media: Over-the-top Video/TV. *Canaccord Adams, Equity Research.* http://www.investorvillage.com/groups.asp?mb=13685&mn=6725&pt=msg&mid=8960957

31. Blockbuster Inc. Overview. *Hoover's.* Accessed 18 May 2010. http://premium.hoovers.com/subscribe/co/overview.xhtml?ID=ffffrftrxxfcksxkct

32. Articles about Blockbuster Inc. various dates. *The New York Times.* http://topics.nytimes.com/top/news/business/companies/blockbuster_inc/index.html?scp=1&sq=blockbuster 20digital 20future&st=cse

33. Redbox Automated Retail, LLC. Overview. *Hoover's.* Accessed 18 May 2010. http://premium.hoovers.com/subscribe/co/overview.xhtml?ID=ffrhxttfrkhjcrjfs

34. Redbox's Vending Machines Are Giving Netflix Competition. 21 Jun 2009. *The New York Times.* http://www.nytimes.com/2009/06/22/business/media/22redbox.html

35. Barnes, B. 6 Sep 2009. Movie Studios See a Threat in Growth of Redbox. *The New York Times.* http://www.nytimes.com/2009/09/07/business/media/07redbox.html?_r=1&ref=technology

36. Barnes, B. 1 Oct 2009. The March of the Redbox Litigation. *The New York Times.* http://mediadecoder.blogs.nytimes.com/2009/10/01/the-march-of-the-redbox-litigation/

37. Boorstin, J. 22 Apr 2010. Redbox, Universal, 20th Century Fox End Lawsuits in DVD Deal. *CNBC Media Money.* http://www.cnbc.com/id/36721603/Redbox_Universal_20th_Century_Fox_End_Lawsuits_in_DVD_Deal

38. Netflix, Inc. 2009. Form-10K Annual Report. *op. cit.*

39. *Ibid.*

40. Cuban, M. 28 May 2010. Netflix and the Future of the Entertainment Business. *blog maverick.* http://blogmaverick.com/2010/05/28/netflix-and-the-future-of-the-entertainment-business/

41. *Ibid.*

42. Wingfield, N. 23 Jun 2009. Netflix Boss Plots Life After the DVD. *WSJ Online.* http://online.wsj.com/article/SB124570665631638633.html

43. Ockham Research. 28 Jan 2010. Netflix: Rental Dominance on Display. *Wall Street Pit.* http://wallstreetpit.com/15602-netflix-rental-dominance-on-display

44. Disney May Raise Costs for Netflix. 2 Feb 2010. *Trefis.* http://www.trefis.com/articles/10668/disney-may-raise-costs-for-netflix/2010-02-02

45. Cuban, M. 28 May 2010. *op. cit.*

46. Jahnke, R. 25 Jul 2006. Netflix Releases Lower Outlook. *Briefing.com.* http://www.briefing.com/GeneralContent/Active/ArticlePopup/ArticlePopup.aspx?SiteName=InvestorPopUp&ArticleId=NS20060725101451HeadlineHits

47. Sandoval, G. 29 Jan 2010. Amazon May Again be Mulling Netflix Buy. *CNET News.* http://news.cnet.com/digital-media/?keyword=The+Wall+Street+Journal

48. Cisco. 2 Jun 2010. Cisco Visual Networking Index: Forecast and Methodology, 2009-2014. *Cisco.com.* http://www.cisco.com/en/US/solutions/collateral/ns341/ns525/ns537/ns705/ns827/white_paper_c11-481360_ns827_Networking_Solutions_White_Paper.html

49. Goldman, D. 13 May 2010. Armageddon, Brought to You by the FCC. *money.cnn.com.* http://money.cnn.com/2010/05/13/technology/net_neutrality/index.htm

50. Netflix Investor Relations Brochure. *Netflix Corporate Web site.* Accessed 31 May 2010. http://ir.netflix.com/

51. Reardon, M. 27 Apr 2010. Verizon Adds More Net Content to Fios. *CNET News.* http://news.cnet.com/wireless/?keyword=Netflix

52. Netflix Investor Relations Brochure. *op. cit.*

53. Robuck, M. 9 Sep 2009. Hulu Spurs Growth of Internet TV. *CEDMagazine.com.* http://www.cedmagazine.com/News-Report-Hulu-growth-Internet-TV-090909.aspx

54. Netflix, Inc. 2010. Form-10Q Quarterly Report. *op. cit.*

55. *Ibid.*

56. Hesseldahl, A. 21 Sep 2009. Video Interview with Reed Hastings. *Vimeo.* http://vimeo.com/6683186.

57. Netflix Investor Relations Brochure. *op. cit.*

58. Borrelli, C. 4 Aug 2009. How Netflix gets your movies to your mailbox so fast. *Chicago Tribune.* http://www.chicagotribune.com/entertainment/chi-0804-netflixaug04,0,6424990.story

59. Netflix Management. *Netflix Corporate Web site.* Accessed 22 May 2010. http://www.netflix.com/MediaCenter?id=5380#rhastings

60. Borrelli, C. *op. cit.*

61. Wilson, T. V. 2010. How Streaming Video and Audio Work. *HowStuffWorks.* http://computer.howstuffworks.com/internet/basics/streaming-video-and-audio.htm

62. *Ibid.*

63. *Ibid.*

64. DVD-by-Mail Isn't Going Away. *op. cit.*

65. Netflix Investor Relations Brochure. *op. cit.*

66. DVD-by-Mail Isn't Going Away. *op. cit.*

67. Amazon News Releases: Netflix Selects Amazon Web Services to Power Mission-Critical Technology Infrastructure. *Amazon Corporate Web site.* 7 May 2010. http://phx.corporate-ir.net/phoenix.zhtml?c=176060&p=irol-newsArticle&ID=1423977&highlight=

68. *Ibid.*

69. Netflix, Inc. 2010. Form-10Q Quarterly Report. *op. cit.*

70. *Ibid.*

71. Netflix Investor Relations Brochure. *op. cit.*

72. Netflix Management. *op. cit.*

73. Conlin, M. 13 Sep 2007. Netflix: Recruiting and Retaining the Best Talent. *Bloomberg Businessweek.* http://www.businessweek.com/managing/content/sep2007/ca20070913_564868.htm

74. *Ibid.*

75. Netflix Prize Leaderboard. *Netflix Corporate Web site.* Accessed 16 Mar 2011. http://www.netflixprize.com//leaderboard

76. Hesseldahl, A. *op. cit.*

77. Netflix, Inc. 2009. Form-10K Annual Report. *op. cit.*

78. *Ibid.*

79. Hastings, R. 17 Dec 2006. (As told by Zipkin, A.) Office Space: The Boss; Out of Africa, Onto the Web. *The New York Times.* http://query.nytimes.com/gst/fullpage.html?res=9B0CE2D91231F934A25751C1A9609C8B63

80. Company History Index. 2010. *op. cit.*

81. Netflix Management. *op. cit.*

82. The Best CEOs. 29 Mar 2010. *Barrons.com.* http://online.barrons.com/article/SB126964409156568321.html

83. Netflix Management. *op. cit.*

84. *Ibid.*

85. Netflix Press Release: Netflix Announces Q1 2010 Financial Result. Apr 2010. *Netflix Corporate Web site.* http://netflix.mediaroom.com/index.php?s=43&item=355

86. Grover, R., Satariano, A., and Levy, R. *op. cit.*

Brandon Boatcallie, Austin Chase, Bobby Salehi, Ivo Skrisovsky, Alfredo Volio

Texas A&M University

I couldn't find the sports car of my dreams, so I built it myself.

FERDINAND PORSCHE

Introduction

After over 100 years as an independent and highly successful car maker, in 2008, Porsche fell victim to the financial crisis when it failed to secure the capital needed to acquire a controlling stake in VW Auto Group (VW). During a reverse takeover in 2010, Porsche was forced to hand over its keys to VW. Subsequently, VW management, eager to use Porsche's expertise to assist other brands under the VW umbrella, began moving Porsche executives into key roles with other automotive brands.

As part of the Porsche corporate restructuring initiative, VW appointed former Audi executive Matthias Mueller as Porsche's new CEO. Mueller had considerable experience with VW—the world's third largest automobile manufacturer controlling the Audi, Bentley, Bugatti, Lamborghini, Scania, Seat, Skoda, VW, and now Porsche brands. Mueller's mission was straightforward: integrate Porsche into the VW family, extend the Porsche product line, and increase production.

However, because of Porsche's successful track record, there were many things to consider in the transition of Porsche. Should Porsche diversify and extend its product line while expanding production? How could Porsche effectively combat possible brand dilution? Should Porsche acknowledge the trade-offs and focus on its pure play products—sports cars? How would the market react to multiple sports cars offerings from Audi, Lamborghini, and Porsche?

History

Ferdinand Porsche, the engineering genius and founder of Porsche, began carving his name in car history early on. In 1900, at the age of 25, Ferdinand introduced the world to not only the first hybrid (petrol/electric) vehicle but an all-wheel-drive racecar as well. This splashy introduction was merely the beginning of Porsche's unprecedented success.[1]

Ferdinand had what seemed to be the perfect ratio of brains to passion when it came to designing sports cars. The German citizen, born and educated in the Czech town of Liberec, not only engineered but also raced his own models. In 1910, an Austro-Daimler sports car of his design won the prestigious Prince Henry Trials—with Ferdinand behind the wheel.

On April 25, 1931, Ferdinand Porsche opened an office for "engineering and consultation on engine and vehicle design" in Stuttgart, Germany. The company, Dr. Ing. h.c. F. Porsche KG, did not have to wait long for contracts to build vehicles for German manufacturers such as Auto Union, Zündapp, NSU, and Wanderer. In perhaps a bit of irony, Ferdinand's company designed and sent into mass production the "Ur Beetle"—the first VW "Bug" and the basis for a design that has not lost its appeal some 75 years later. Ferdinand clearly possessed the ability to anticipate and envision the future, maintain organizational flexibility, and empower others to create one of the world's most valuable car brands. He was a racecar driver at heart, an engineer by trade, and employed his entrepreneurial spirit on a daily basis in a growing company that proudly carried his name. Ferdinand's son, known by all as Ferry, began running the company in 1946 and, upon his father's death in 1951 and with his own son at his side, officially took the wheel.

Without question, Porsche was a powerhouse in racing, collecting victories in virtually all major racing events throughout the world including the Can-Am racing series, Paris-Dakar Rally, Pharaoh's Rally, Rally Monte Carlo, 24 Hours of Le Mans, and the World Championship of Makes. On the consumer side, in 1964, Porsche began producing what would become its most famous sports car—the 911. Throughout the 70s and 80s, the 911 (and variations of) kept Porsche in the black.

In its efforts to provide variety in both design and price, in 1996, Porsche introduced the Boxster. The Boxster was the first mid-engine production sports car Porsche had ever manufactured and a big hit—selling as many in its first year as the entire 911 line-up combined. In 2002, Porsche surprised many purists by presenting a sports-utility vehicle—the Cayenne. Once again, Porsche's newest offering outsold all other models in its first two years. In 2005, the Cayman was launched as a hard-top version of the successful Boxster and Porsche once again surprised the automotive world in 2010 by introducing the first four-door Porsche sedan ever—the Panamera.

By 2011, the company produced five models with a combined total of 40 different trim levels. This increased diversification brought higher shareholder returns—one of Porsche's main objectives.

Economic and Political Challenges

As it was for most automakers, the economic climate beginning in 2007 was challenging for Porsche. Oil prices were at record highs, topping $100 a barrel. For every ten cents that gasoline prices rose, approximately 1,000 trucking companies went bankrupt.[2] The global economy struggled to step out of the deepest recession the US and Europe had experienced in decades. Consumers were extremely price sensitive and unemployment in the US hovered around 10 percent. Of particular concern to Porsche were gasoline prices: as a sports car manufacturer, it was fighting the stereotype of a gas-guzzling automobile segment.

Consequently, Porsche re-engineered many of its offerings to provide (relatively) higher gasoline efficiency. For example, the 911 Turbo had an EPA estimate of 18 miles per gallon (mpg) throughout most of the 90s; however, the 2010 estimate was 24 to 25 mpg (depending on cylinders and auto/manual) and, as a bonus, came with roughly 75 percent more horsepower. In addition, the highly sought after Carrera (a 911 variation) offered 24 to 27 mpg, the Boxster 26 to 29 mpg, and even the four-wheel drive SUV Cayenne boasted 22 to 23 mpg.[3] Unaccustomed to trailing the pack, Porsche rekindled its hybrid roots by engineering a hybrid Cayenne and Panamera S with mpg ratings of 25 and 35, respectively.[4]

And yet, even with Porsche's efforts toward fuel efficiency, US government actions have put even more pressure on the Bavarian carmaker. Under the direction of President Obama, the National Highway Traffic Safety Administration and the EPA increased the mpg requirements for all cars in the US through an old emissions policy known as Corporate Average Fuel Economy (CAFE). In the past, CAFE had levied small fines on carmakers with mpg ratings that didn't meet specified regulations and Porsche and other high-performance

car makers simply absorbed the relatively minor fee. However, the 2009 legislation imposes not only a significantly higher mpg requirement, but a significantly higher penalty as well: CAFE mandates that, by 2020, automobile manufacturers and importers must have an average mpg rating of 39 for cars and 30 for trucks or pay $35,700 for each individual car in violation.[5] Upon passage, Porsche commented that if the 2020 CAFE policies are enforced, it simply won't be able to sell cars in the US.[6]

On a more positive note, economic support for Porsche is strong in its German homeland. Germany is the third largest exporter in the world.[7] Union workers are protected by strong labor laws and wide support, and approximately 93 percent of the German workforce is unionized.[8] Manufacturing employees constitute approximately 30 percent of the nation's workforce.[9] Though Germany has not been immune to the global recession, Porsche has continued to enjoy a supportive manufacturing infrastructure.

Industry Characteristics

The sports car industry faced its share of economic woes throughout the latter half of the 20th century with many sports car makers experiencing fatal cash flows. Lamborghini declared bankruptcy in 1978. It was later revived and sold to Chrysler only to then be sold to the Suharto family in 1994 and sold again to Audi in 1998.[10] In that same year Bentley, Bugatti, and Audi (and thus Lamborghini) were acquired by VW. Aston Martin, which had sold a controlling share to Ford in 1987, was bought outright by Ford in 1994 and then sold again in 2007.[11] Jaguar was also bought and sold by Ford in 1990 and 2007, respectively. Getting out of the gate even earlier, Fiat acquired Ferrari in 1969, Alfa Romeo in 1986, and Maserati in 1993.[12] Even so, through it all, Porsche managed to not only stay independent but, more importantly, financially buoyant.

Porsche competes in a market segment where relatively few can compete. Manufacturing a car of any caliber—no less the caliber of Porsche—requires sizeable capital investments. Additionally, the engineering expertise required to design a car capable of competing with Lamborghini, Ferrari, Aston Martin, Porsche, and others keeps all but the truly intent from entering the field.

Though there seem to be several *supercar*[i] options like the McLaren MP4, Ferrari FXX, and Ferrari Enzo that cost more than $500,000, consumers have few

---

[i]A *supercar* is typically an exotic or rare sports care whose performance is highly superlative to contemporary sports cars (Supercars/Exotic Cars. *TopSpeed.com*. http://www.topspeed.com/cars/supercars-exotic-cars/ke177.html).

alternatives—if any—for a mid to low $100,000 car like the Porsche 911 Turbo—particularly one that boasts near supercar performance. Companies including BMW, Nissan, and GM have each produced one or two cars comparable in price and performance to the Porsche line, but their offerings do not present the prestige or variety of Porsche's emblem or full lineup.[13]

Sports car enthusiasts are few and fickle; trend conscious buyers are inherent to luxury and high-end markets. That means Porsche must constantly innovate to keep up with trends. As evidenced by the short lifetimes of independent sports car manufacturers over the last 30 years, surviving in this type of a market is extremely challenging. Despite this, Porsche's greatest challenge would appear to lie in the impending CAFE regulations—regulations that could spell an end to Porsche sales in its number one market, the US.[14]

Global Trend Toward Emerging Economies

Many automotive firms have sought international exposure to increase their market share. In 2010, Porsche sold 14 percent of its volume in Germany and over 26 percent of its volume in the US. Given the possibility of CAFE regulation enforcement, Porsche has been diversifying its international scope. China, for example, has become an area of extraordinary expansion for Porsche, accounting for approximately 15.6 percent of overall sales (see Exhibits 1A and 1B). Current management believes China will be the largest consumer segment for Porsche within two or three years.[15] To encourage this new market, Porsche has even begun building race tracks for Porsche drivers on the mainland of China. Depending on this level and pace of expansion in China is not without risk, however. The Chinese government has increased scrutiny of foreign operations within its borders and firms investing in China face uncertainty when dealing with the undervalued yuan.[16] Yet, with plans to allow a gradual increase in value of local currency and boasting the most rapid economic growth of any country at the time, China has too much potential as an export market to ignore.

Typically, in a capital-intensive industry, efficient international expansion of production yields greater economies of scale and increases market penetration. Other automakers, such as VW and GM, employ a transnational strategy by modifying current models according to the demands in international regions. Porsche, however, employs a global strategy whereby it offers the same models for the whole world. This lower risk trade-off helps protect the Porsche brand from international dilution and enables Porsche to remain consistent with regard to costs in its strategy forged in Germany.

Porsche has always expanded to international markets exclusively through exportation—a less expensive option as compared to greenfield ventures or establishing new bases of operation. Inherent to multinational expansion are increasingly complex economic and political risks. Porsche's strategy hedges against such

Exhibit 1A Units Sold per Multi-Geographic Market: 2009 to 2010

Multi-Geographic Markets	FY 2009	FY 2010	Change 2009 to 2010
United States	18,958	22,181	17.0%
China	7,708	13,254	72.0%
Germany	12,506	11,911	−4.8%
Other European Countries	6,749	8,407	24.6%
Middle East/Africa	5,941	6,275	5.6%
United Kingdom	4,926	6,157	25.0%
Italy	3,930	3,655	−7.0%
Japan	2,915	2,775	−4.8%
France	2,010	2,432	21.0%
Canada	1,622	1,823	12.4%
Asia Pacific	1,116	1,660	48.7%
Latin America (excluding Brazil)	2,123	1,441	−32.1%
Russia	1,278	1,302	1.9%
Australia/New Zealand	1,076	1,148	6.7%
Brazil	n/a	781	n/a
Total	72,858	85,202	16.9%

Source: Data adapted from http://quote.morningstar.com

Exhibit 1B Percentage of Sales per Multi-Geographic Market: 2009 to 2010

Multi-Geographic Markets	% of Sales 2009	% of Sales 2010
United States	26.0%	26.0%
China	10.6%	15.6%
Germany	17.2%	14.0%
Other European Countries	9.3%	9.9%
Middle East/Africa	8.2%	7.4%
United Kingdom	6.8%	7.2%
Italy	5.4%	4.3%
Japan	4.0%	3.3%
France	2.8%	2.9%
Canada	2.2%	2.1%
Asia Pacific	1.5%	1.9%
Latin America (excluding Brazil)	2.9%	1.7%
Russia	1.8%	1.5%
Australia/New Zealand	1.5%	1.3%
Brazil	n/a	0.9%

Source: Data adapted from http://quote.morningstar.com

complexity by focusing solely on exportation rather than manufacturing expansion, acquisition, and licensing. With the exception of its contract with Valmet in Austria for the Boxster/Cayman, Porsche produces all of its cars within its labor union dominated, Bavarian borders.

Product Quality

Porsche. There is no substitute.

> **TOM CRUISE**
> **RISKY BUSINESS, 1983**

High-performance sports cars are generally high-maintenance, low-reliability vehicles. To consistently perform as intended, most sports cars need frequent and expensive attention and maintenance. In March 2010, J. D. Power and Associates ranked Porsche as providing the best long-term reliability of any brand in the US.[17] What makes this designation truly exceptional is that the comparison was not made solely within the high-performance sports car segment, but was extended to all automobile lines including sedans, SUVs, trucks, etc., offered by such reputable brands as Toyota, Ford, BMW, and Honda: truly an extraordinary accomplishment for any vehicle within any segment, but even more so for one within the notoriously temperamental high-performance sports car segment. Additionally, J. D. Power and Associates market researchers hailed the Porsche production plant in Stuttgart as "the best car factory in the world."[18]

Innovation

Porsche largely generates innovative technologies through its racing programs. According to Porsche Motorsports, Porsche "is the most successful manufacturer by far in the history of international sports car racing."[19] With over 50 years of racing experience, Porsche has accumulated a wealth of technological expertise and employs some of the brightest engineering minds in the world. Porsche has consistently developed class-leading technologies that competitors find difficult to imitate. For example, the seven-gear Porsche Doppelkupplung (PDK) system allows drivers to shift between gears without interrupting the flow of power. The Porsche Torque Vectoring (PTV) system can sense the vehicle steering angle and speed, accelerator pedal position, yaw rate, and vehicle speed to vary the torque distribution to rear wheels to ensure more predictable and stable vehicle maneuvers at all speeds. Ceramic composites are utilized in various vehicle components, such as brakes and clutch plates, to provide lightweight, durable performance.[20] The technology Porsche has developed—and continues to develop—produces exceptionally reliable performance at comparatively low prices.

Porsche Strategic Partners

Clearly, depending on racecar technology for the lion's share of innovation can serve a car maker well in many ways. Nevertheless, Porsche is neither above nor hesitant to develop strategic alliances as needed when particular technologies are not within its immediate grasp. Whether through its highly selective paid internship program[21] or alliances formed with other automakers to receive a crash course in hybrid technology,[22] Porsche has forged partnerships to keep its business on the cutting edge.

In one of its more forward-thinking moves, in 1999, Porsche bought a 49 percent interest in Miseschke Hofmann und Partner (MHP), a specialty IT technology and process improvement group and SAP (Systems, Applications, and Products in Data Processing) Implementation and Service Partner. Initially, the venture was an equity strategic alliance in which MHP subcontracted to consult and improve Porsche processes. This vertical complementary alliance helped Porsche learn new business techniques and technologies. Subsequently, Porsche bought a controlling interest of MHP (74.8 percent) and MHP served as the exclusive provider of IT improvements and process engineering for Porsche[23] while continuing to serve outside clients—mostly in the automotive industry. In 2001, SAP AG named MHP as the first Special Expertise Partner SAP for the automotive category. MHP was also rated SAP Silver Partner Service and SAP Channel Partner Gold. MHP's contributions to the Porsche manufacturing process allow several manufacturing advantages, including the ability to produce the Cayenne, Carrera GT, and Panamera at the same plant and on the same line in Leipzig, Germany.[24]

Porsche also engages in alliances not requiring equity ownership. Concurrent with its launch of the Boxster in 1996, Porsche announced it would sub-contract production to a non-German manufacturer for the first time. With Porsche building the engines and various other components in its main factory in Zuffenhausen, the state-owned Finnish manufacturer—Valmet—produced the majority of the Boxster line, adding production of the Cayman in 2005. In 2008, and with the Cayman/Boxster production contract set to expire in 2012, Valmet announced it would begin production on the Fisker Karma plug-in hybrid sports car beginning in 2012.[25] Porsche's Deputy Chairman, Holger P. Haerter, confirmed the Valmet contract would end in 2012, and announced that Magna Steyr Fahrzeugtechnik (MSF) of Graz, Austria would take over production of the Boxster and Cayman.[26] A year later, Porsche paid MSF an undisclosed sum to cancel the contract and it is now expected that production will move to the factories of bankrupt Karmann Ghia—now the property of VW.[27]

Diversification: SUVs and Sedans

While the Porsche brand name and product quality never wavered, in the mid to late 90s it became clear that customer preferences were changing. Particularly in the US—Porsche's biggest export market—the SUV began to dominate the road. Porsche had to decide if it would continue focusing on its traditional two-door sports car models or further diversify its product line by offering new models that departed from the historic Porsche image. Purists argued that extending the product line would dilute the Porsche brand name and ultimately destroy the distinct Porsche image. Others argued that economic growth made it worth the risk, as existing product sales were flat. In the end, Porsche decided to extend its product line to include a SUV—the Cayenne. Despite the radical departure from its niche, the 2002 introduction of the Cayenne was extremely profitable and helped fuel Porsche's growth for several years. As for its reception in the auto world,

On one level it is the world's best 4x4, on another it is the cynical exploitation of a glorious brand that risks long-term damage to that brand's very identity in the pursuit of easy money... So I applaud the extraordinary Cayenne and wish it every success while at the same time still wishing, in part at least, that it had never been built.[28]

Having weathered the stigma of introducing a SUV, in 2009, Porsche offered another first: the four-door Panamera sedan. With global economic tensions increasing in 2008 and 2009, consumer tastes for Porsche's traditional high-performance two-door models flattened. Nevertheless, sales of the Panamera and Cayenne models grew significantly.

Loyalty

When Porsche decided to enter the SUV market with its luxury Cayenne model, it surprised the auto industry by locating its new assembly plant in Leipzig, Germany. Many observers believed Porsche should locate the plant in either central or eastern Europe where labor costs were very low, or even perhaps in the US (as had Mercedes and BMW) where it could be close to its major market. The critical issue driving Porsche's Leipzig plant decision appeared to be the primacy of Porsche's strategy of quality, craftsmanship, and engineering excellence. Ultimately, maintaining brand image (while, paradoxically, simultaneously upsetting that brand image) was much more important to Porsche than saving on labor costs—especially when assembly costs comprise only a small portion of overall vehicle cost.[29] In the end, Porsche emphasized design, research and technology development, and marketing to maintain its reputation for a commitment to excellence.[30]

In North America, Porsche aficionados tend to be college-educated men between 36 to 55 years of age with an annual gross income in excess of $380,000 per year. They value innovation and independence and are often senior executives, medical professionals, and entrepreneurs.[31] This customer segment buys Porsche because of its innovative features, exceptional styling, and European origin.

Introduction of new features and innovative technology by BMW, Mercedes, and Lexus prompted Porsche to implement lean production practices. However, because Porsche produces a limited number of models, its switch to lean production practices was somewhat easier than that of its competitors. In addition, Porsche engineers have been able to keep vehicle performance and handling of their vehicles at the forefront of the sports car segment. As a result, Porsche has enjoyed record sales and profit (see Exhibits 2A and 2B). In early 2010,

with only a handful of focused car-making companies remaining, Porsche led the pack.

The Prestigious Competition

The sports car manufacturing segment faces a complicated, competitive environment. Changing industry dynamics frequently present Porsche's management team with rigorous obstacles to overcome. Porsche offers several product lines of sports cars available in many geographic markets. Porsche focuses on quality and not quantity and as a result and fully 80 years after its founding, Porsche only offers five different car models: the Boxster, the Cayman, the 911, the Panamera, and the Cayenne.

Exhibit 2A Income Statement of Porsche Automobil Holding SE

€ Million	2009/10	2008/09
Revenue	0	5
Other operating income	641	52,790
Personnel expenses	−18	−77
Other operating expenses	−631	−55,407
Income from investments	9,850	2,992
Interest result	−851	−746
Income from ordinary activities	**8,991**	**−443**
Taxes	0	−553
Profit/loss after tax	**8,991**	**−996**
Withdrawals from retained earnings	0	1,004
Transfer to retained earnings	−4,495	0
Net profit available for distribution	**4,496**	**8**

Source: Data adapted from http://quote.morningstar.com

Exhibit 2B Balance Sheet of Porsche Automobil Holding SE

€ Million	July 31, 2010	July 31, 2009
Assets		
Financial assets	24,771	24,838
Receivables	4,348	2,703
Other receivables and assets	230	1,202
Cash and cash equivalents	887	2,164
Prepaid expenses	53	263
Equity and liabilities	**30,289**	**31,170**
Equity	16,977	7,993
Provisions	1,572	3,371
Liabilities to banks	7,000	10,561
Other liabilities	4,740	9,245
	30,289	**31,170**

Source: Data adapted from http://quote.morningstar.com

Two of Porsche's three most recent additions, the Cayenne and Panamera models introduced in 2002 and 2009 respectively, compete mainly with other *prestige brands*.[ii] The Cayenne is offered in four different models ranging from the stock Cayenne to the Cayenne Turbo S. Its main competitors are the BMW X6 M, Mercedes-Benz ML63 AMG, and Audi Q7, among others.[32] The BMW X6 M is slightly faster than the Cayenne Turbo S with a 0–60 of 4.0 compared to 4.1 for the Porsche.[33] The Mercedes-Benz ML63 AMG is less expensive than the Cayenne but slower with a 0–60 of 4.6 seconds. The Audi Q7 is the slowest of the pack but has more interior space and torque than the Mercedes.[34] Each model has distinct advantages and disadvantages when compared to the Cayenne, making it a very competitive arena.

The Panamera is offered in seven different models ranging from stock to the Turbo S. The Panamera was introduced in 2009 to compete against the BMW M5, Mercedes-Benz S65 AMG, and Audi S8, among others.[35] The BMW M5 is a sporty luxury sedan but significantly slower than the Panamera Turbo S with a 0–60 of 4.4 compared to 4.0 for the Porsche. However, only the M5 offers a standard gear box. The Mercedes S65 AMG offers the smoothest ride of the four and garners higher rankings on spaciousness and comfort. The Audi S8 is again the slowest of the group but offers exceptional interior quality. The Panamera competes directly against these models and has been touted to be the fastest luxury sedan in the world.[36]

The Boxster and Cayman are also relatively recent additions to the company's offerings. The Boxster was first introduced as a roadster in 1996, the same year BMW launched James Bond's Z3. The Cayman was launched ten years later, in 2006, as a coupé derived from Porsche's second-generation Boxster convertible. Today, the Boxster is offered in four different models: Boxster, Boxster S, Boxster Black Edition, and Boxster Spyder. The Cayman is only offered in three different models: Cayman, Cayman S, and Cayman R. These Boxster and Cayman models compete against the BMW Z4, Mercedes-Benz SLK models, and Audi TT, among others.[37] The Z4 is considered to have a more luxurious angle when compared to the Boxster or Cayman. The Mercedes offering in this roadster class has significantly less horsepower and fewer sport options. Overall, the Boxster and Cayman models compete well against their competitors, most notably in reliability as, in 2010, the Boxster was rated the most reliable car, regardless of model, in the world[38] (see Exhibit 3).

Porsche's fifth and most recognized offering is the iconic Porsche 911. The 911 was introduced in 1963 and boasted an air-cooled rear-engine design, independent rear suspension, and a swing axle pioneered by Porsche. Over its almost 50-year lifetime, the 911 had undergone continuous development, though the basic concept had remained mostly unchanged. Among its many awards, the 911 ranked fifth in the 1999 international poll for the Car of the Century award. Today, the 911 is offered in over 20 stock models. Most models are variations of the Carrera, Targa, Turbo, Black Edition, or GT. The Porsche 911 competes with the Ferrari Enzo, Aston Martin V12 Vanquish, Lamborghini Murcielago, and Bentley Continental GT, among others.[39] These super-cars offer outstanding performance but are extremely expensive with price tags in the range of $250,000 to $400,000. Porsche on the other hand has been able to produce equal performance and prestige, yet at more affordable prices ranging from $130,000 to $145,000 for the Turbo trims and up to $245,000 for the GT2 RS. In addition to the supercars, the 911 competes against the BMW M6, Mercedes-Benz SL-Class, and Audi R8, among others. These competitors have similar brand prestige as Porsche but lack in some aspects of sport performance. Furthermore, the 911 faces competition from less prestigious brands that deliver comparable performance. The Nissan GT-R and Dodge Viper, for example, both boast excellent performance figures and lower price tags than the 911 but lack the pedigree of the Porsche line.[40]

The price range and performance varies greatly among the five model lines and their respective trim levels. Boxster, Cayman, and 911 models target sports car enthusiasts, whereas Panamera and Cayenne target luxury vehicle and SUV market segments, respectively. Each model not only meets but with additional sports performance, exceeds the standards of their respective automobile class. In addition to the five production models, Porsche also manufactures track-ready race-cars. Taken together, Porsche's model offerings provide a wide selection for many needs and different stages of life.

Influence of the Volkswagen Group

In 2010, VW employed about 400,000 employees, operated 62 production facilities worldwide, produced 200 different vehicle models at a rate of 30,000 vehicles per day, and was active in more than 150 countries. VW consists of two main divisions: the automotive division (VW Group) and the financial services division. The automotive division is comprised of 10 different automotive brands: VW passenger cars, Audi, Skoda, SEAT,

---

[ii]*Prestige brands* are well established as status symbols, represent the highest form of craftsmanship, and command a loyal consumer following that is not affected by trends (*Roumeliotis, J.D. (2011, February 10). Defining luxury brands: Business. WCW Insight.* http://www.whitefieldconsulting.com/wordpress/?p=7350).

Exhibit 3 Porsche Awards and Accolades

Year	Car Type	Awards
2011	911	*AutoPacific* Best Sportscar—Vehicle Satisfaction Awards (VSA)
2011	911	*Car and Driver* Editor's Choice
2010	Boxster	*Car and Driver* Best Handling Car in America
2010	Boxster/Cayman	*Car and Driver* Editor's Choice
2010	918 Spyder	*Edmunds.com* Insideline Most Wanted
2010	Cayenne	*Motor Trend* SUV of the Year
2010	Panamera	*About.com Cars*—Best New Cars of 2010
2010	Panamera	*Car and Driver* Editor's Choice
2010	Porsche Brand	*Kelly Blue Book* Brand Image Awards—Coolest Brand
2010	Porsche Brand	*J.D. Power and Associates* #1: Initial Quality Survey
2010	Porsche Brand	*Auto Pacific* Ideal Vehicle Awards (IVA) #1
2010	Porsche Brand	*J.D. Power and Associates* APEAL Study—#1
2009	Panamera	*Bloomberg* Car of the Year
2009	Cayman	*Motor Trend* Best Drivers Car
2009	911	*Automobile Magazine's* All-Stars Award
2009	911	*Robb Report* Best of the Best
2008	Boxster/Cayman	*Car and Driver Magazine's* 10 Best Cars Sold in America
2008	911	*Edmunds Editors'* Most Wanted Award
2008	Porsche Brand	*Luxury Institute's* Top Luxury Automotive *Brand*
2008	Porsche Brand	*J.D. Power* 1st in Initial Quality Survey
2007	Porsche Brand	*J.D. Power and Associates* APEAL Study—#1
2007	Boxster/Cayman	*J.D. Power and Associates* Best Premium Sports Cars
2007	Boxster/Cayman	*Car and Driver's* "Ten Best"

Source: Data adapted from http://quote.morningstar.com

Bentley, VW commercial vehicles, Scania, Bugatti, Lamborghini, and Porsche. Each brand within the automotive division is led by a brand CEO and Board of Management. The financial services division is the largest automotive financial services provider in Europe and offers dealer and customer financing, leasing, banking activities, insurance activities, and fleet management.

At the corporate level, VW is charged with becoming the "leading automotive group globally." VW's Strategy 2018 sets forth the roadmap to achieve this goal using its unrivaled distribution capabilities, best-in-class manufacturing and technology, and superior quality. Best practices are leveraged across brands, and purchasing, production, and distribution synergies develop as brands work together.

While the VW brands compete in a number of consumer markets and segments, VW's flexible engineering design and architecture processes allow its brands to share compatible components to customize vehicles and meet regional customer preferences. To promote local customization, production facilities are located in various markets including China, Russia, the Slovak Republic, the Ukraine, Kazakhstan, Spain, France, the US, Brazil, and Argentina.

The Porsche brand will play a key role within the VW family in various global markets. VW's executive team plans to fully integrate the Porsche brand into the group by the end of 2011 via a multi-stage transaction. It is expected that Porsche will contribute to the group synergy and help other group brands improve in innovation, manufacturing, and quality by sharing technology, research and development, components, and platforms. Product line extensions are planned to produce new Porsche vehicles that will meet emerging customer demands in various markets. Production goals are aimed at increasing Porsche production from 80,000 units to 150,000 units annually within five years. VW's distribution network will be leveraged to introduce the Porsche brand into new markets.[41]

Overview of Strategic Challenges

VW's Strategy 2018 calls for the company to become "the most successful and fascinating automaker by 2018." Over the past 15 years, VW Group has acquired more than half a dozen brands including Porsche, Lamborghini, and Bentley. Porsche will help VW achieve its goals by sharing its technology with other VW brands, increasing production, and diversifying the Porsche product line. For example, VW has already announced its plans for Porsche to launch the Cajun (pronounced CAY-OON) a smaller, more fuel-efficient version of the Cayenne SUV. Also, rumors have been circulating that an even smaller version of the Boxster will begin production by 2013. VW has seen the success of Porsche's recent diversification and is looking for an even broader offering.

However, Porsche has traditionally been a top-tier sports car company, producing variations of the legendary 911 platform. Its newest product offerings—the Cayenne and Panamera—were the hands-down sportiest options within their respective segments. For example, the Panamera Turbo S was the fastest sedan in the world after less than two years of production. Further extension of the sedan or SUV lines could lead to performance dilution.

By complying with VW's Strategy 2018, the Porsche brand would evolve from a focused approach to a broader brand of car segments. Porsche would no longer solely focus on its traditional target customer but would instead be forced to appeal to multiple consumer segments. As such, Porsche faces the risk of diluting its brand, alienating its customer base, and potentially destroying its competitive advantage.

NOTES

1. Milestones – Porsche History. *Porsche.com*. http://www.porsche .com/usa/aboutporsche/porschehistory/milestones/
2. Hoskisson, R. E., Hitt, M. A., and Ireland, R. D. (2008). *Competing for Advantage*. Mason, OH: Thomson South-Western.
3. Find a Car. *FuelEconomy.gov*. http://www.fueleconomy.gov/feg/ findacar.htm
4. Welsh, J. (2011, Feb 16). Is the Panamera hybrid the most fuel-efficient Porsche ever? *The Wall Street Journal*. http://blogs.wsj .com/drivers-seat/2011/02/16/is-the-panamera-hybrid-the-most-fuel-efficient-porsche-ever/
5. Allen, M., and Javers, E. (2009, May 18). Obama announces new fuel standards. *Politico.com*. http://www.politico.com/news/ stories/0509/22650.html
6. Schmitt, B. (2010, Feb 22). Obama will take away your Porsche. *TheTruthAboutCars.com* http://www.thetruthaboutcars .com/2010/02/obama-will-take-away-your-porsche/
7. The World Factbook. *CIA.com*. https://www.cia.gov/library/ publications/the-world-factbook/geos/gm.html
8. German labor unions. *Photius.com*. http://www.photius.com/ countries/germany/government/germany_government_labor_ unions.html
9. Germany trade, Germany exports, Germany imports. *EconomyWatch.com*. http://www.economywatch.com/world_ economy/germany/export-import.html
10. Ferruccio Lamborghini. *LamboWeb.com*. http://www.lamboweb .com/History.htm
11. History Timeline. *AstonMartin.com* http://site.astonmartin.com/ eng/thecompany/historytimeline
12. Ferrari S.p.A. *FundingUniverse.com*. http://www.fundinguniverse .com/company-histories/Ferrari-SpA-Company-History.html
13. Porsche enjoyes unsurpassed prestige in US. (2006, May 5). *Porsche.com*. http://www.porsche.com/usa/aboutporsche/ pressreleases/pag/?pool=international-de&id=2006-05-05
14. Porsche Annual Report 2009/2010. *Porsche-se.com*. http://www. porsche-se.com/pho/en/investorrelations/mandatorypublications/ annualreport-09-10/download/
15. Elliott, H. (2011, Jan 13). Porsche plans small 'cajun' SUV, new sports car under Boxster. http://blogs.forbes.com/ hannahelliott/2011/01/13/porsche-plans-small-cajun-suv-new-sports-car-under-boxster/
16. Batson, A., and Fong, M. (2006, Aug 30). China hits foreign investors with new hurdles. *Wall Street Journal via Pittsburgh Post-Gazette.com*. http://www.post-gazette.com/ pg/06242/717522-28.stm
17. J.D. Power vehicle dependability study: Porsche ranked number 1. (2010, Mar 18). *Porsche.com*. http://www21.porsche.com/usa/ aboutporsche/pressreleases/pcna/?lang=none&pool=internatio nal-de&id=2010-03-18-2
18. J. D. Power and Associates names Porsche 911 the most reliable sports car. (2011, Mar 22). *OnEightTurbo.com*. http://www. oneighturbo.com/porsche/j-d-power-and-associates-names-porsche-911-the-most-reliable-sports-car/#more-16557
19. Motorsports. *Porsche.com*. http://press.porsche.com/motorsport/
20. Technology Glossary. *Porsche.com*. http://www.porsche.com/usa/ aboutporsche/porschetechnologyglossary/
21. Harryson, S., and Lorange, P. (2005, Dec). Bringing the college inside. *Harvard Business Review*. http://hbr.org/2005/12/bringing-the-college-inside/ar/1
22. World's automakers embracing hybrid vehicles. (2005, Sep 14). *Autos on msnbc.com*. http://www.msnbc.msn.com/id/9338664/ns/ business-autos/t/worlds-automakers-embracing-hybrid-vehicles/
23. Porsche subsidiary MHP enjoys strong turnover growth once again. (2008, Oct 9). *Porsche.com*. http://www.porsche.com/ international/aboutporsche/pressreleases/archive2008/ quarter4/?pool=international-de&id=2008-10-09
24. Company. *Mieschke Hofmann und Partner (MHP) – the process supplier.de*. http://www.mhp.de/ Company.10+M5519f187cad.0.html#/tabs-6)
25. Abuelsamid, S. (2010, May 27). Report: Fisker Karma full production delayed to February 2011. *Green.Autoblog.com*. http://green .autoblog.com/2010/05/27/fisker-karma-full-production-delayed-to-february-2011/)
26. Valmet Automotive's current assembly contract with Porsche to come to an end in 2012. (2008, Jun 26). *Valmet-Automotive.com*. http://www.valmet-automotive.com/automotive/bulletin.nsf/PEBD /8BEA6EBAD367D2C5C2257474003900DF?opendocument
27. Schmitt, B. (2009, Dec 18). Porsche to Magna: Take the money and run. *TheTruthAboutCars.com*. http://www.thetruthaboutcars .com/2009/12/porsche-to-magna-take-the-money-and-run/
28. Frankel, A. (2002, Nov 17). Porsche Cayenne. *The Sunday Times*. http://www.timesonline.co.uk/tol/driving/new_car_reviews/ article823701.ece
29. Contemporary Strategy Analysis (6th edition) – Notes and suggestions on self-study questions. (2007, Jun 18).

http://higheredbcs.wiley.com/legacy/college/grant/1405163097/self_study_ans/ch14.pdf

30. Stonehouse, G., Campbell, D., Hamill, J., and Purdie, T. (2000). *Global and Transnational Business: Strategy and Management.* New York: John Wiley & Sons.

31. Statistics and demographic information. (2006, Feb 7). *Renntech – Porsche Technical Forum.* http://www.renntech.org/forums/topic/7991-statistics-and-demographic-information/

32. Porsche Cayenne. *Autos.MSN.com.* http://autos.msn.com/research/vip/default.aspx?make=Porsche&model=Cayenne

33. Swan, T. (2009, Dec). X5 M vs. Grand Cherokee SRT8, Range Rover Sport Supercharged, Cayenne Turbo S – comparison tests. *CarAndDriver.com.* http://www.caranddriver.com/reviews/comparisons/09q4/x5_m_vs._grand_cherokee_srt8_range_rover_sport_supercharged_cayenne_turbo_s_-comparison_tests/2009_porsche_cayenne_turbo_s_page_4

34. Audi Q7 V12 TDI vs ML 63 AMG 2010 models. (2010, May 27). *VCART.com.* http://www.vcar7.com/2010/05/audi-q7-v12-tdi-vs-ml-63-amg-2010-models/

35. 2011 Porsche Panamera. *Autos.MSN.com.* http://autos.msn.com/research/vip/overview.aspx?year=2011&make=Porsche&model=Panamera&trimid=113069

36. Larry. (2011, Apr 21). The fastest production sedan in the world featured at 2011 New York Auto Show: 2011 Porsche Panamera Turbo S. *AutomotiveAddicts.com.* http://www.automotiveaddicts.com/19312/fastest-production-sedan-2011-new-york-auto-show-2011-porsche-panamera-turbo-s

37. 2011 Porsche Cayman. *Autos.MSN.com.* http://autos.msn.com/research/vip/overview.aspx?year=2011&make=Porsche&model=Cayman&trimid=113134

38. Davis, B. (2010, Oct 28). Porsche Boxster rated most reliable car by Consumer Reports' results. *CarAdvice.com.* http://www.caradvice.com.au/89609/porsche-boxster-rated-most-reliable-car-by-consumer-reports-results/

39. 2003 Porsche 911. *Autos.MSN.com.* http://autos.msn.com/research/vip/overview.aspx?year=2003&make=Porsche&model=911

40. 2011 Porsche 911. *Autos.MSN.com* http://autos.msn.com/research/vip/overview.aspx?year=2011&make=Porsche&model=911&trimid=113124

41. Volkswagen Group – Factbook 2011. *VolkswagenAG.com.* http://www.volkswagenag.com/vwag/vwcorp/info_center/en/publications/2011/04/Factbook_2011.-bin.acq/qual-BinaryStorageItem.Single.File/Factbook%202011.pdf

Ryan McVay/Getty Images

Doug Bernstein, Walther Del Orbe, Shara Fessler, Christian Fischer, Mike Kreger, Tyler Whitlow

Arizona State University

Rite Aid Corporation is a pharmacy retailer that opened its first store in the early 60s. Today, it is the third largest drugstore retailer in the US, with Walgreens and CVS as its primary competitors. In addition to providing pharmacy services, Rite Aid also offers over-the-counter drugs, household and personal care items, convenience foods, nutritional supplements, and photofinishing services. There are roughly 4,800 Rite Aid locations in 31 states, with an especially strong presence on the east and west coasts. Rite Aid (RAD) is a publically traded company on the New York Stock Exchange with annual revenues exceeding $25 billion.[1]

The retail pharmacy industry is highly competitive. CVS and Walgreens have more than 14,000 retail locations in aggregate nationwide. Individually, the two companies have a market capitalization that dwarfs Rite Aid Corporation four times over.[2] Marketplace challenges have plagued Rite Aid since it entered the industry almost 50 years ago and, in the last two decades, Rite Aid has struggled with issues such as Medicare fraud, executive malfeasance, human resource and quality control issues, and company accounting scandals. As a result, stock price dropped from $50 a share in 1999 to less than $1 barely ten years later. Adding to its woes, Rite Aid acquired the Brooks/Eckerd drugstores in 2007 and saddled themselves with billions of dollars in debt and hundreds of underperforming stores. The recent recession has also affected Rite Aid as sources of credit have dried up, leaving it with challenges managing its debt. As the US economy labors in the grasp of recession, Rite Aid faces inconsistent store sales, fierce industry competition, continuing employee relations problems, and debt issues from the Brooks/Eckerd acquisition.

Rite Aid History

1962–1986

Rite Aid was born out of repealed federal legislation in 1962 concerning fixed minimum retail pricing on products in the retail industry. To capitalize on the legislative changes that promoted a more competitive marketplace, Alex Grass, Rite Aid's founder and future CEO, opened the first Rite Aid discount drugstore in 1962 in Scranton, PA under the name Thrif D Discount Center. The company expanded very quickly and by 1965, had opened five more locations in the Northeast. Rite Aid Corporation became official in 1968 with the company's first public offering on the American Stock Exchange followed quickly by a move to the New York Stock Exchange in 1970.[3]

Through multiple acquisitions of many smaller regional chains across the Northeast, Rite Aid grew to over 267 stores in 10 states within a matter of only a decade. Not even the Middle East oil embargo and slow economic growth from the persistent recession of the mid to late 70s could slow the company's momentum. By 1981, the company had become the third largest retail pharmacy chain in the nation and, in 1983, surpassed the $1 billion sales mark.[4]

1987–1997

Rite Aid's growth continued throughout the 80s and early 90s, culminating in 1995 with the acquisition of 224 Perry Drug Stores in Michigan, bringing its total number of stores to over 3,000. With a strong market presence on the East Coast, the company decided to expand its services to the west through the acquisition of Thrifty PayLess Holdings, Inc. in 1996. This 1,000 store acquisition, along with the acquisition of two large firms on the Gulf Coast, provided the company with a strong market presence nationwide.[5] By March 1997, Rite Aid was operating 3,623 retail drugstores nationwide.[6]

1998–2002

In 1998, Rite Aid diversified within the health care industry through the acquisition of one of the leading pharmacy benefits management companies in the US— PCS Health Systems, Inc. A pharmacy benefits manager is a company contracted by managed care organizations, self-insured companies, and government programs to manage pharmacy network management, drug utilization review, outcomes management, and disease management with the goal to decrease overall health care costs.[7] While Rite Aid later sold the holding to Advance Paradigm in an effort to reduce bad debt,[8] it is noteworthy that Rite Aid explored the strategy of diversified growth by acquisition. Rite Aid did manage to create successful strategic partnerships with General Nutrition Companies, Inc., better known simply as GNC, and drugstore.com to increase market presence and reach across various distribution channels within the health care industry.

Despite the impetus of increased revenue and profits, Rite Aid's continued expansion and growth came at a cost to the company as its aggressive strategy overextended its financial capabilities. By 1999, Rite Aid was carrying nearly $6.7 billion in debt on its balance sheets. Much of this is attributable to the 1996 acquisition of Thrifty PayLess Holdings. Many of Thrifty's buildings were old and outdated and major renovation projects were implemented to get the stores up to company standards. In addition, allegations of accounting fraud surfaced and brought about a large-scale investigation that eventually led to a reduction in earnings of $500 million.[9]

Mary Sammons, who joined Rite Aid as COO, guided Rite Aid's strategy from 1999 until 2010. At the time she joined Rite Aid, energies were divided between managing the quest for growth by acquisition and recovering from managerial errors as a result of both unethical behavior and just poor management. Sammons and her boss, Robert Miller (CEO), were faced with reviving a company that many expected to fail.

The new leadership focused on the basics—creating a positive culture, stricter financial controls, and streamlining the company's operations. The aggressive growth plan was temporarily halted and many underperforming facilities were closed or sold. The new leadership also implemented a competitive pricing plan on many of the company's top selling products to attract customers and increase sales in an attempt to combat the company's ballooning debt.[10]

2003–Present

The first few years of the new century continued to be tough for Rite Aid. A $200 million class action suit brought about by shareholders and the indictments of many former Rite Aid executives exemplify its difficulties. The resulting press coverage and bad public relations had a negative effect on employee morale, the financial impact of former mismanagement persisted, and the company's debt continued to increase.

Despite this, the new leadership remained steadfast as additional underperforming stores were divested and strict financial controls became the norm across all business units. These efforts led to a significant turnaround; in one year, the company cut its net losses by 86.4 percent from $827.7 million in 2002 to $112.1 million in 2003. By the third quarter of 2004, the company was back in the black with net income of $22.5 million for the quarter.[11]

After putting Rite Aid back on firm financial ground, Sammons spearheaded the decision to acquire nearly 1,850 stores of the Brooks/Eckerd chain at a cost of over $3 billion.[12] Although it brought Rite Aid closer to Walgreens and CVS, the issues the acquisition brought mirrored many of the same issues faced when the company purchased Thrifty PayLess Holdings in 1996, and the company found itself dealing yet again with nearly unmanageable debt and run-down stores. The acquisition carried over $2 billion in outstanding debt as well as many underperforming facilities. The result was a 2008 loss of $1.1 billion followed in 2009 with a $2.9 billion loss.[13] Rite Aid stock plummeted to under $1 from previous highs in 1999 around $50. On June 23, 2010, COO John Standley succeeded then CEO Mary Sammons.[14]

Pharmaceutical Retail Industry

The pharmaceutical retail industry is the main distribution channel for pharmaceutical products. Although the pharmaceutical industry is one of the most profitable businesses in the world,[15] the retail sector of this market, including Rite Aid and categorized as "Food and Drug Stores," ranked as only the 37th most profitable industry in the US for 2009 with a return on revenue of only 1.5 percent.[16]

In 2001, with prescription profitability on the decline among pharmaceutical retailers, the emphasis within the drugstore business model shifted to "front-end" merchandising. Drugstores, similar to gas stations and convenience stores, began to increasingly drive profits by diversifying their product offerings to include nonprescription products—otherwise known as front-end merchandise—such as gum and mints at the pharmacy counter, chocolate near photo finishing services, and impulse-buy items at checkout.[17]

Pricing

Today, prescription items are a low-margin product for pharmacy retailers because of how the industry is structured. Pharmacy prices are dictated by the US pharmacy distribution and reimbursement system, which affects the pharmacy chain or retailer, manufacturers, wholesalers, third-party payers, and in the end, customers. In general, pharmacies receive reimbursements for prescriptions sold based on negotiated rates or contract pricing from third-party payers such as insurance companies, pharmacy benefits managers, government agencies, private employers, or any other managed care providers. Based on the payer type, pharmacies receive a different rate of reimbursement and payment terms. (Exhibit 1 provides a detailed flowchart of the pharmacy reimbursement system.)

The newest of these facilitators are the pharmacy benefits managers, which were integrated into the reimbursement cycle as a means to reduce prescription drug costs. Pharmacy benefits managers are primarily funded by two major parts of the distribution and reimbursement system: manufacturers and third-party payers. Manufacturers provide pharmacy benefits managers with rebates and incentives to have their formularies—a list of medicines they manufacture—added as accepted drugs. Over 70 percent of all prescription benefits are managed by pharmacy benefits managers, an important fact to manufacturers because it results in increased sales of their products.[18]

Third-party payers—insurance carriers, HMOs, and government as the provider of Medicare and Medicaid—contract with pharmacy benefits managers as well so they can receive below market pricing.

This is advantageous to the third-party payers because it reduces the overall cost of prescription services, thus lowering the overall cost of health care. To make up the difference of the discounts provided to third-party payers, pharmacy benefits managers provide pharmacies with lower reimbursements. The difference between these two values—called the "spread"—is a significant revenue stream for pharmacy benefits managers.[19]

Current pricing information is vital to retail pharmacies. First Data Bank and MediSpan, two companies that work with drug manufacturers and third-party payers on a regular basis, maintain the most up-to-date databases of pricing metrics and drug information. Pharmacies pay a subscription fee to access these databases to ensure their pharmacy billing software has the latest pricing updates and reimbursement rates available in order to ensure they charge their customers the proper amount for prescriptions filled. Accurate pricing information is critical as the average profit margin for pharmacy-related sales averages a scant 2 to 4 percent.[20]

Because of these pricing controls, many retail pharmacies maintain numerous wholesaler relationships. Retailers will purchase the majority of their products from a primary supplier, thus enabling them to receive rebate and

Exhibit 1 Pharmacy Reimbursements

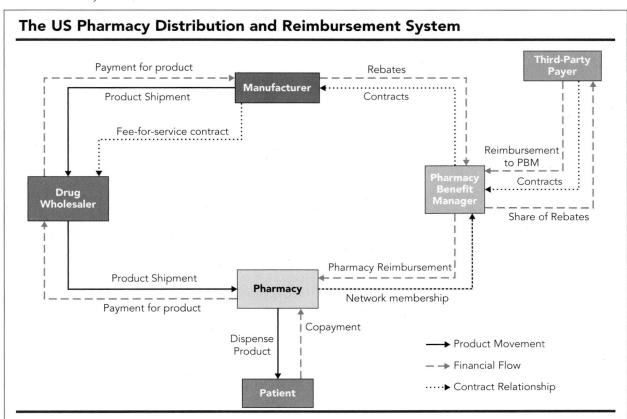

Source: http://www.pembrokeconsulting.com

pricing incentives based on their contract compliance levels for the various drug groups (i.e., brand, generic, OTC, etc.). However, many pharmacies maintain supplemental relationships with other wholesalers for price shopping capabilities and leverage when contract renewal with their primary vendor occurs. Thin drug margins mean front-end sales via private label branding, zone pricing, as well as other value-added services such as immunizations and specialty services are essential to profitability.

End Users

Retail pharmacies serve a variety of customers—most of whom live in the immediate vicinity of the store—with various health care and general merchandising needs. In 2009, over 4.5 billion prescriptions were filled in the US, accounting for $300.3 billion in total sales.[21] The average number of prescriptions filled per person in 2009 was 12.6,[22] the majority of which were likely filled by consumers over the age of 60. These numbers are predicted to steadily grow over the next several years due to the growing population of older consumers from the baby boomer generation as well as health care reform through the Patient Protection and Affordability Care Act. The new health care laws are estimated to expand coverage to more than 40 million previously uninsured customers. Both factors will combine to provide a larger customer base and additional opportunities for growth.[23]

While these factors may seem promising, there are also several challenges ahead for the industry. There has been a substantial rise in the number of prescriptions left unfilled by consumers. Influenced by both abandonment and denials, 14.4 percent of all new commercial plan prescriptions were unfilled in 2009. The sluggish economy is partially responsible for these rising numbers as consumers are increasingly price conscious and spending their income on essentials as opposed to maintenance medications. For customers continuing to fill their prescriptions, they are offsetting the cost of prescription drugs by requesting generics, soliciting samples from their physician, splitting pills and/or buying from other resources such as the Internet, discount stores, or bulk purchasing.[24]

Manufacturers

Pharmaceutical manufacturing is the third highest net profit industry in the US with net profits of 19.3 percent in 2008.[25] The supply chain for these manufacturers is as follows: wholesalers purchase 64 percent of finished goods for redistribution, 30 percent are distributed directly to retail pharmacy chains, and the remaining supply is sold to hospitals and mail-order pharmacy services.[26]

Competition for the major players in pharmaceutical manufacturing such as Pfizer and Merck has become fierce as more and more generic manufacturers and small role players enter the competitive space. Patents on many

financially successful drugs like Ambien and Prevacid have expired and others such as Lipitor and Plavix are on the verge of expiration. This creates intense generic competition and smaller margins. On average, generic equivalents are 50 percent less expensive than their brand name counterparts.[27] Development costs for new drugs average $500 to $800 million for commercial use in the US, with only one out of every 50,000 receiving FDA approval.[28] Manufacturers must concentrate on the profitability of each successful drug as patents last a maximum of only 20 years.[29] Adding fuel to the fire, stricter FDA regulations for obtaining new patents and the lack of new discoveries resulting from R&D efforts have many manufacturers concerned about future financial stability.

Manufacturers are consistently pressured by other influential sources as well. With pharmacy benefits managers and both state and federal legislatures continuing to push for better pricing for consumers and reduced reimbursement rates, the bottom line of manufacturers continues to be eaten away.

Wholesalers

Pharmaceutical manufacturers distribute their products to four main channels: wholesalers, retailers, hospitals, and mail-order pharmacies. While brand name drugs contribute 61 percent of total revenue for wholesalers, approximately 56 percent of gross profits are derived from generic drug sales.[30] (Exhibit 2 details revenue and gross profits from brand name and generic drugs.)

Wholesalers dominate the distribution line, accounting for 64 percent of manufacturer sales and, while there are numerous wholesalers in the pharmaceutical industry, AmeriSource Bergen, Cardinal Health, and McKesson—the three largest drug wholesalers in the US and otherwise known as the "Big Three"—collectively account for 95 percent of those manufacturer to wholesaler sales in what is estimated to be a quarter-trillion dollar market. Although some retailers and end users have direct links to manufacturers, it is estimated that nearly four out of every five drugs sold pass through the supply chain of the Big Three. This strong market position enables them to leverage their buying power with the manufacturers that, in turn, are becoming more reluctant to deal directly with smaller wholesalers and end users; in many cases, they redirect those customers to the Big Three for product. Because of the lock these wholesalers have on the sell and buy sides of pharmaceutical distribution, regulators are fearful of an oligopoly occurring in the future. The Federal Trade Commission's Bureau of Competition notes that 90 percent of market control shared between a few companies becomes a concern because of the potential for a monopoly to occur.[31]

Pharmaceutical wholesalers move product to the customer via five main retailing channels: independent

Exhibit 2 Revenue and Gross Profits from Brand-Name and Generic Drugs

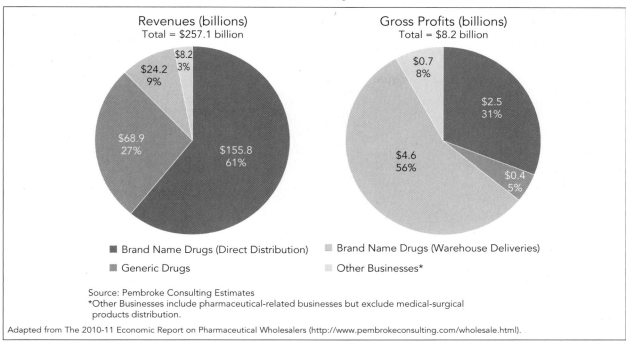

Source: Pembroke Consulting Estimates
*Other Businesses include pharmaceutical-related businesses but exclude medical-surgical
products distribution.

Adapted from The 2010-11 Economic Report on Pharmaceutical Wholesalers (http://www.pembrokeconsulting.com/wholesale.html).

Source: http://www.drugchannels.net

pharmacies, chain pharmacies, mass merchants with pharmacies, supermarkets with pharmacies, and mail-order pharmacies.[32]

Retailers

In 2009, chain pharmacies were responsible for 40.5 percent or $109 billion of the retail pharmacy market sales of $268.9 billon. Leading up to these 2009 figures, retail pharmacy revenue had been trending up since 2007 with sales of $101.19 billion growing to $104.20 billion in 2008.[33] Over 40,000 pharmacies[34] make up the chain pharmacy channel with nearly 70 percent of those pharmacies owned by Walgreens, CVS, or Rite Aid. (Exhibit 3 shows the market share of drugstore chains and non-drugstore chains.)

Mail-order pharmacies are the second largest retailers with a market share of 22.8 percent of total retail pharmacy sales in 2009. This format seems to be increasingly appealing to consumers as there has been significant

revenue growth in this retail group: 5.5 percent from 2007 to 2008, and 10.7 percent from 2008 to 2009. The growth in mail-order pharmacies puts competitive pressure on chain pharmacies as more and more prescriptions are filled through this outlet. Even though revenue has grown in both channels, market share for chain drugstores declined by one-half percent from 2008 to 2009.[35]

Supermarkets, mass merchants, and independent pharmacies in aggregate make up about 37 percent of the market for retail pharmacy sales.[36] The top providers in the supermarket format are Safeway and Kroger. The largest competitors in the mass merchant sector are Walmart, Target, and Kmart, with Walmart's market share twice that of Target and Kmart combined. (See Exhibit 4 for a break down of market share of the entire pharmacy retail industry for the US.)

The business models of supermarkets and mass merchants differ from that of drugstore chains where the

Exhibit 3 Market Share of Drugstore Chains and Non-drugstore Chains

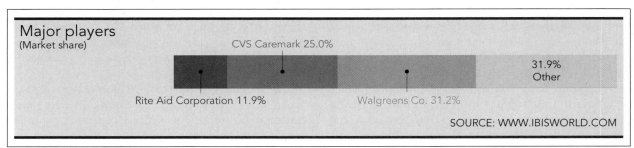

Source: http://www.wikinvest.com

Exhibit 4 Market Share of Entire Pharmacy Retail Industry for the US

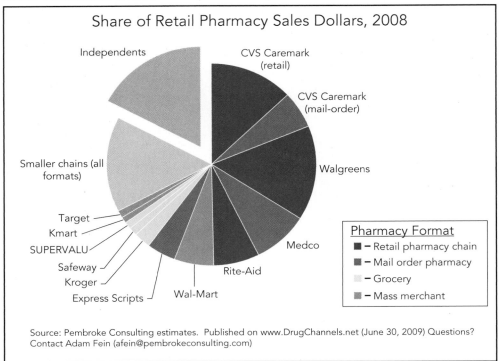

Source: Pembroke Consulting estimates. Published on www.DrugChannels.net (June 30, 2009) Questions? Contact Adam Fein (afein@pembrokeconsulting.com)

Source: http://www.drugchannels.net

pharmacy and store are financially one and the same. Instead, supermarkets and mass merchants have pharmacy services provided within the store but grocery and pharmacy services are financially independent from one another.

Market share for the top pharmacy chains is expected to steadily grow over the next several years as pharmacy services in grocery and independent channels experience eroding profit margins.[37]

Competitive Landscape

Walgreens Corporation

Founded in 1901, Charles Walgreen, a Chicago pharmacist, wanted to provide his pharmacy customers with high quality drugs at low prices. Initially, Walgreen bought his products from other manufacturers, but by the 20s, Walgreen was manufacturing his own line of popular drug products. Unlike many of its competitors, the Walgreens chain expanded without the help of acquisitions until 2006, when it acquired several competitors in attractive markets including Happy Harry's, Farmacias El Amal, and Duane Reade.

Walgreens has a rich and well-documented history of innovation carried out through decades of strong family leadership. In 1933, Charles Walgreen advanced drugstore layouts by testing new lighting techniques, colors, and advanced fixture designs. Charles Walgreen Jr.

took the helm in 1939 and continued in his father's footsteps by changing to self-service instead of clerk-service stores and filling prescriptions in child-resistant bottles. In 1969, Charles Walgreen III took over as President. During his tenure, the first Intercom computers were installed to—using satellite technology—connect all Walgreens pharmacy departments. He also expedited the checkout process by installing point-of-sale scanning and drive-through pharmacies. Walgreens continued to demonstrate its understanding of the importance of technology when, in 1997, it integrated Intercom Plus into all stores to further speed up the prescription filling process and allow for better patient consulting.

In 1999, the Walgreen family legacy ended and L. Daniel Jorndt took over as chairperson. In the past decade, Walgreens Corp. has continued to improve and innovate, providing a comprehensive Web site with access to Mayo Clinic health information and becoming the first drugstore chain to offer labels in multiple languages.[38] Today, there are over 7,500 Walgreens across the US supporting specialty pharmacy, health care clinic services, home infusion services, as well as drugstore pharmacy needs.[39]

As stated in Walgreens' 2010 investor relations packet,[40] Walgreens' core goal is "being America's most trusted and convenient provider of consumer goods and services, and pharmacy, health, and wellness solutions." Walgreens lists its core strengths as:

- Best store network in America (convenience)— 75 percent of Americans live within 5 miles of a Walgreens location
- Customer Service—Walgreens is currently focused on renovating 5,500 stores and expanding product lines to include fresh foods and other customer demanded products
- Operational Efficiency—Walgreens is undergoing an internal efficiency initiative expected to help the company improve operating costs[41]

CVS Caremark Corporation

CVS is the second largest chain drugstore operator in the US, reaching 41 states and Puerto Rico. Stanley and Sidney Goldstein and Ralph Hoagland established Customer Value Stores (CVS) in 1964. In 1969, Melville Corporation purchased CVS. Over the next four decades, it acquired over a dozen other major drugstore chains resulting in over 7,000 pharmacy stores today. In addition to expansion via acquisition, CVS also expanded internally by opening small health and beauty aid stores in shopping malls.[42]

In its 2009 investor relations packet, CVS states that one of its top strategies is taking an integrated approach to the health care market.[43] CVS continues to diversify its operation by now offering mail-order pharmacy and in-store clinic services, and further securing its business by merging with a pharmacy benefits manager—Caremark Rx, Inc. In 2007, Caremark was the premier integrated pharmacy services provider for the nation. The merger of CVS's pharmacy retail chains with Caremark's services has allowed CVS to gain unprecedented leverage over suppliers.[44]

The mail-order pharmacy has become a significant part of CVS's prescription revenues, making up almost one third of all CVS prescription revenue sales in 2010. In addition, clinic services are provided in over 500 CVS stores nationwide under the MinuteClinic brand name. Because of its diversified business model, CVS is recognized as the leading specialty pharmacy, retail clinic operator, and prescription provider,[45] accounting for approximately 20 percent of all pharmacy retail prescription revenues for 2010. (Details of the retail pharmacy market share by prescription revenue for 2010 can be found in Exhibit 5.)

Medco Health Solutions, Inc.

Medco Health Solutions, the largest pharmacy benefits manager and mail-order pharmacy in the US, became

Exhibit 5 Retail Pharmacy Market Share by Prescription Revenue: 2010

Largest US Pharmacies Ranked by Total Prescription Revenues, 2010				
Company	Stock Ticker	Estimated 2010 Prescription Revenues* (billions)	Share of Prescription Revenues	Primary Dispensing Format
CVS Caremark Corporation	CVS			
• Retail Pharmacy		$39.0	14.1%	Chain drugstore
• Pharmacy Services**		$16.7	6.0%	Mail-order pharmacy
Walgreens Company	WAG	$44.9	16.2%	Chain drugstore
Medco Health Solutions, Inc.	MHS	$24.5	8.8%	Mail-order pharmacy
Rite Aid Corporation	RAD	$17.1	6.2%	Chain drugstore
Wal-Mart Stores, Inc.***	WMT	$17.1	6.2%	Mass merchant with pharmacy
Express Scripts, Inc.	ESRX	$13.2	4.8%	Mail-order pharmacy
The Kroger Company	KR	$7.1	2.6%	Supermarket with pharmacy
Safeway, Inc.	SWY	$4.0	1.4%	Supermarket with pharmacy
Target Corporation	TGT	$3.0	1.1%	Mass merchant with pharmacy
SUPERVALU Inc.	SVU	$2.5	0.9%	Supermarket with pharmacy
Kmart Corporation	SHLD	$2.4	0.9%	Mass merchant with pharmacy
All other chains and specialty	n/a	$39.1	14.2%	various
Independent Pharmacies	n/a	$46.4	16.7%	Independent drugstores
Total		$277.2	100.0%	

Totals may not sum due to rounding.

* Includes revenues from retail, specialty, mail-order, and institutional pharmacies.

** Includes 90-day claims filled in CVS retail pharmacies under the Maintenance Choice program.

*** Includes Walmart and Sam's Club stores

Source: http://www.pembrokeconsulting.com

a publicly traded company in 2003.[46,47] According to a 2010 report of the largest US pharmacies based on prescription revenues, Medco has 8.8 percent of the market share. This places Medco as the third largest pharmacy retailer behind CVS Caremark and Walgreens, and just ahead of Rite Aid. Medco also has an international presence in Sweden, the Netherlands, and the UK and recently formed a joint venture with Celesio AG, a leading provider in pharmaceutical and health care services in Europe.[48]

Originally a pharmacy benefits manager, Medco has made great strides to move beyond this traditional role to be at the forefront of industry knowledge, technology, and innovation, and in introducing proprietary new products and services.[49] Because of its highly integrated business model, Medco is able to offer low prescription drug costs through pharmacy benefit modeling; this includes designing affordable drug programs between plans and enrollees. Medco is also able to leverage its pharmacy networks and buying power to provide the best price option of pharmaceuticals to the customer. Medco is one of the largest purchasers of generic drugs in the nation and its network of retail pharmacies, mail-order pharmacies, and specialty pharmacies all work together to find the best solutions for Medco clients.[50]

Walmart

Launched by Bud and Sam Walton, Walmart started as a discount store in 1962 and was incorporated in 1969.[51] It ranks first in market share of the mass merchants offering pharmacy services as measured by prescription revenues: an amount equivalent to that of Rite Aid's market share at 6.2 percent (see Exhibit 5). Walmart is considered the largest retailer in the US, earning over $400 billion in revenue for 2009, and has a strong global presence with 24 percent of its earnings coming from international sales. Almost half of Walmart's US revenue is supported by grocery sales with entertainment goods contributing 13 percent, followed by hardline items (hardware, housewares, automotive, electronics, sporting goods, health and beauty aids, or toys) at 12 percent.[52]

Walmart added pharmacies to its retail locations in 2006,[53] offering $4 prescriptions or a 90-day supply for $10.[54] Walmart achieves these prices by importing generic medications from overseas manufacturers.[55] Industry analysts suspect that Walmart uses its prescription prices as a loss leader to attract new customers and maintain repeat customers.[56] In 2007, Walmart supported its pharmacy efforts as a founding member of Better Health Care Together; a coalition of business, labor, government, and non-profit leaders dedicated to "achieving a new American health care system by 2012."[57]

The Kroger Company

Kroger enjoys the largest market share in the supermarket channel with 2.6 percent of total prescription revenues in the pharmaceutical retail industry (Exhibit 5). Kroger is the largest grocery retailer in the US[58] and operates under three formats: multi-department stores, price impact warehouse stores, and marketplace stores. Marketplace stores are the only format to include pharmacy services. Other than groceries and a pharmacy department, these establishments also offer general merchandise such as outdoor living items, electronics, home goods, and toys.[59]

Recent Trends

Crossing the Border

Rising health care costs have become a politically charged topic in the face of new health care reform legislation. The uncertainties associated with health care reform are causing patients to search for low-cost alternatives outside traditional retail outlets. These alternatives include Internet-based prescription drug sales as well as purchasing less regulated and thus less expensive prescription drugs from other countries. For example, 93 percent of the top 100 branded prescription drugs in Canada and the US are an average of 43 percent less expensive in Canada than in the US.[60] In a 2003 survey, while only 7 percent of respondents said they had purchased prescription drugs from another country, 48 percent indicated they would not hesitate to go outside the US to buy prescription drugs in the future.[61]

Mail-Order Pharmacies

Mail-order pharmacies have experienced significant growth in the past several years and this trend is expected to continue as more health care and insurance companies push to save money on prescription services and overall health care costs. The growth in patients utilizing these services has risen as well. According to IMS, a leading "pharmaceutical intelligence" company, mail-order prescriptions have steadily increased over the past few years, rising from 222.9 million prescriptions in 2005 to 237.5 million prescriptions in 2009. Mail-order pharmacies are considered more efficient due to economies of scale[62] and have lower overhead costs than the traditional bricks-and-mortar pharmacy as they have fewer staff and rely heavily on automation and computers to enhance their daily fill capabilities.

Discussing the efficiencies of mail-order pharmacies, Assistant Professor David A. Mays from the University of Maryland said, "I bet they can fill 10,000 prescriptions a day with fewer errors than a neighborhood pharmacist with 100 a day and the phone ringing and people coming to the counter, mail-order is done by bar coding and quadruple-checked."[63] Mail-order pharmacies provide a convenient and cost saving option for patients who take medications on a regular basis. The pharmacies' ability to buy and dispense in bulk quantities allows providers to offer discounts to patients utilizing these services.

This puts many retail pharmacies at a disadvantage because they cannot match the cost savings that mail-order pharmacies provide to consumers. Retail owners are concerned about the future of the industry as many companies are moving toward mandating the use of mail-order services for maintenance medications: medications that happen to constitute 50 to 60 percent of all prescriptions filled for many retail pharmacies.[64]

Generic Drugs

Consumers are increasingly requesting cheaper, generic drugs from their physicians and pharmacies. Over half of physicians say they frequently talk with patients about the out-of-pocket costs of medicines they prescribe with 62 percent saying they switch patients to less expensive drugs and 58 percent saying they give patients free office samples. Almost 80 percent of FDA-approved drugs have a generic equivalent. In 2008, 22 percent of total prescription drug sales and 72 percent of total prescriptions dispensed were generic medicines. Generic sales grew 8 percent from 2005 to 2006. Six of today's best selling medications are expected to lose their patents in 2011 and 2012, and will face stiff generic competition. While total drug sales may decline as a result, the competition from generic drugs will likely bring down costs for patients.[65]

Jobs Trends

A shortage of pharmacists has recently improved; however, the US Bureau of Health Professions predicts that future shortages will be worse than before. Factors contributing to the anticipated shortage include increasing demand for prescription drugs and pharmacists spending more time on patient counseling.[66] The bureau estimates there are 8,000 unfilled pharmacist positions at present and predict a shortage of 150,000 pharmacists by 2020. Such a drastic shortage of professionals critical to Rite Aid's core competencies will certainly affect customer service.

Medical Services

Walk-in clinics located in drugstore chains, mass merchants, and supermarkets are a growing trend. These clinics offer customers basic health services such as minor injuries, illness, school, sports, and camp physicals, and routine vaccines.

In-store clinics began to appear around the turn of the century and the concept has spread rapidly since.

According to the Convenient Care Association, an industry trade group based in Philadelphia, there are currently more than 600 clinics located in retail venues across the country. The association estimates that by 2012, there could be as many as 6,000 clinics.

The clinics have expanded in large part because, especially for the now more than 47 million uninsured in the US, they serve as a convenient and affordable alternative to a doctor's office or hospital visit. Services performed at an in-store clinic cost about $60, though prices vary by clinic and service. For example, at CVS Pharmacy, services range between $49 and $59 per visit or, if insured, the amount of a co-pay.

Of the drugstore retailers, CVS and Walgreens dominate the in-store health clinic market. CVS is the industry leader with more than 500 in-store clinics in 26 states under its MinuteClinic brand.[67] Walgreens manages over 350 Take Care clinics in 18 states across the nation.[68] Walmart, the world's largest retailer, is playing catch up after RediClinic shut down its 78 locations.[69] Taking a different tack this second time around, Walmart is leasing space in its stores to "independent local hospitals or health systems that the community already knows and trusts."[70] It currently operates 117 in-store clinics within Walmarts in 26 states.[71]

Rite Aid's Strategy and Challenges

Improving the pharmacy is paramount to bringing customers into the store, and offering economical front-end products allows the company to be more profitable. Rite Aid is currently developing its own private brand of products to be sold in its stores under the brand name "Simplify." Also, by means of a licensing agreement with Sav-A-Lot stores, it is test marketing a new grocery store/pharmacy concept in 10 stores in South Carolina.[72]

Rite Aid has also implemented several loyalty programs including Wellness+, a program designed to attract and keep shoppers. Additionally, the Gift of Savings program for the 2010 holiday season allowed customers to earn cash back on purchases (up to $25) between Thanksgiving and Christmas Eve.[73]

Although several strategies have been implemented in an effort to repair Rite Aid's failing business, fourth quarter earnings from 2010 show Rite Aid continues to underperform. Same-store sales were down 1.5 percent from the third quarter and the income from operations did not cover even 10 percent of the $140 million interest expense from its $6.2 billion debt. (Exhibit 6 provides selected fiscal year financial data for Rite Aid from 2006 through 2010.) Rite Aid is also in a desperate position now, competing against Walmart for market share, and

Exhibit 6 Selected Financial Data for Rite Aid through Fiscal Year 2010

	Fiscal Year Ended				
	February 27, 2010 (52 weeks)	February 28, 2009 (52 weeks)	March 1, 2008 (52 weeks)	March 3, 2007 (52 weeks)	March 4, 2006 (53 weeks)
	(Dollars in thousands, except per share amounts)				
Summary of Operations:					
Revenues[1]	$ 25,669,117	$ 26,289,268	$ 24,326,846	$ 17,399,383	$ 17,163,044
Costs and expense: Cost of goods sold[2]	18,845,027	19,253,616	17,689,272	12,710,609	12,491,642
Selling, general and administrative expenses[3][4]	6,603,372	6,985,367	6,366,137	4,338,462	4,275,098
Goodwill impairment charge	—	1,810,223	—	—	—
Lease termination and impairment charges	208,017	293,743	86,166	49,317	68,692
Interest expense	515,763	477,627	449,596	275,219	277,017
Loss on debt modifications and retirements, net	993	39,905	12,900	18,662	9,186
(Gain) loss on sale of assets and investments, net	(24,137)	11,581	(3,726)	(11,139)	(6,463)
Total costs and expenses	26,149,035	28,872,062	24,600,345	17,381,130	17,115,172
(Loss) income before income taxes	(479,918)	(2,582,794)	(273,499)	18,253	47,872
Income tax expense (benefit)[5]	26,758	329,257	802,701	(11,609)	(1,228,136)
Net (loss) income from continuing operations	(506,676)	(2,912,051)	(1,076,200)	29,862	1,276,008
Loss from discontinued operations, net of gain on disposal and income tax benefit	—	(3,369)	(2,790)	(3,036)	(3,002)
Net (loss) income	$ (506,676)	$ (2,915,420)	$ (1,078,990)	$ 26,826	$ 1,273,006
Basic and diluted (loss) income per share: Basic (loss) income per share	$ (0.59)	$ (3.49)	$ (1.54)	$ (0.01)	$ 2.36
Diluted (loss) income per share	$ (0.59)	$ (3.49)	$ (1.54)	$ (0.01)	$ 1.89
Year-End Financial Position: Working capital	$ 2,332,976	$ 2,062,505	$ 2,123,855	$ 1,363,063	$ 741,488
Property, plant and equipment, net	2,293,153	2,587,356	2,873,009	1,743,104	1,717,022
Total assets	8,049,911	8,326,540	11,488,023	7,091,024	6,988,371
Total debt	6,370,899	6,011,709	5,985,524	3,100,288	3,051,446
Stockholders' (deficit) equity	(1,673,551)	(1,199,652)	1,711,185	1,662,846	1,606,921
Other Data:					
Cash flows (used in) provided by:					
Operating activities	(325,063)	359,910	79,368	309,145	417,165
Investing activities	(120,486)	(346,358)	(2,933,744)	(312,780)	(231,084)
Financing activities	397,108	(17,279)	2,903,990	33,716	(272,835)
Capital expenditures	193,630	541,346	740,375	363,728	341,349
Basic weighted average shares	880,843,000	840,812,000	723,923,000	524,460,000	523,938,000
Diluted weighted average shares	880,843,000	840,812,000	723,923,000	524,460,000	676,666,000
Number of retail drugstores	4,780	4,901	5,059	3,333	3,323
Number of associates	97,500	103,000	112,800	69,700	70,200

[1]Revenues for the fiscal years 2007 and 2006 have been adjusted by $108,336 and $107,924 respectively for the effect of discontinued operations.
[2]Cost of goods sold for the fiscal years 2007 and 2006 have been adjusted by $80,988 and $80,218 respectively for the effect of discontinued operations.
[3]Selling, general and administrative expenses for the fiscal years 2007 and 2006 have been adjusted by $32,019 and $32,323 respectively for the effect of discontinued operations.
[4]Includes stock-based compensation expense. Stock based compensation expense for the fiscal years 2010, 2009, 2008 and 2007 was determined using the fair value method set forth in ASC 718, "Compensation—Stock Compensation." Stock-based compensation expense for the fiscal year ended March 4, 2006 was determined using the fair value method set forth in the former SFAS No. 123, "Accounting for Stock-Based Compensation."
[5]Income tax benefit for the fiscal years 2007 and 2006 has been adjusted by $1,635 and $1,616 respectively for the effect of discontinued operations.

Source: Rite Aid Corporation, 2010 Annual Report; please note also that selected financial data for March 1, 2008 includes Brooks Eckerd results of operations for the 39-week period ended March 1, 2008.

lacking the capital needed for improvements to over 4,800 stores. Aside from battling with tough competitors, Rite Aid faces the ongoing challenges of rising health care expenses for its employees, contract raises, and payroll, as well as the current and building challenges of a slow economy, a decreasing number of new generics, and a shrinking pharmacist candidate pool.[74]

As the incoming CEO, John Standley has a list of issues to consider and tackle. With a share price less than

$1, he will be under pressure from all sides to continue Mary Sammons' work at "Rite-ing" the ship. He must figure out how to staunch Rite Aid's massive financial losses, resuscitate or excise its most recent acquisitions, and relieve the doubts of employees and stakeholders. Will having risen before from the depths of not only near bankruptcy, but scandal and mismanagement as well, serve to Rite Aid's advantage, or could this latest round of setbacks serve the fatal blow?

NOTES

1. History. *Rite Aid corporate site*. http://www.riteaid.com/company/about/history.jsf. Accessed Nov 2010.
2. RAD, WAG, CVS. *Morningstar*. http://www.morningstar.com/. Accessed Nov 2010.
3. History. *Rite Aid corporate site. op. cit.*
4. *Ibid.*
5. *Ibid.*
6. Rite Aid 1996 10-K Report. *SEC.gov*. http://www.sec.gov/Archives/edgar/data/84129/0000893220-97-001091.txt. Accessed Nov 2010.
7. Definition of pharmacy benefit manager. *Med Terms.com*. http://www.medterms.com/script/main/art.asp?articlekey=24243. Accessed Mar 2011.
8. Rite Aid Corporation Business Information: Profile and History. *JRank*. http://companies.jrank.org/pages/3569/Rite-Aid-Corporation.html. Accessed Nov 2010.
9. *Ibid.*
10. *Ibid.*
11. *Ibid.*
12. Rite Aid Makes Move for Eckerd, Brooks. *CNNMoney.com*. 24 Aug 2006. http://money.cnn.com/2006/08/24/news/companies/riteaid/index.htm
13. Rite Aid Reports Loss, Plans Store Closings. *The Providence Journal*. 29 Apr 2009. http://www.projo.com/news/content/bz_riteaid03_04-03-09_RRDTVKG_v7.2fcc195.html
14. History. *Rite Aid corporate site. op. cit.*
15. Global 500, 2009 – Top industries: Most profitable. *Fortune*. http://money.cnn.com/magazines/fortune/global500/2009/performers/industries/profits/. Accessed Dec 2010.
16. *Ibid.*
17. Selling One More Thing. *NACDS/American Greetings Research Council*. 2002. http://www.nacds.org/user-assets/pdfs/2009/publications/selling_one.pdf
18. Richardson, J. Pharmacy Benefit Managers: The Basics and an Industry Overview. *Federal Trade Commission*. 26 Jun 2003. http://www.ftc.gov/ogc/healthcarehearings/docs/030626richardson.pdf
19. Pharmacy Benefit Manager Information Source. *RxMail*. http://www.rxmail.com/page1/page1.html, Accessed Dec 2010.
20. Rite Aid (RAD). *wikinvest*. http://www.wikinvest.com/stock/Rite_Aid_(RAD). Accessed Nov 2010.
21. Berkot, B. US Prescription Drug Sales Hit $300 Billion in 2009. *Reuters*. 1 Apr 2010. http://www.reuters.com/article/idUSTRE6303CU20100401
22. Prescription Drug Trends. *The Henry J. Kaiser Family Foundation*. http://www.kff.org/rxdrugs/upload/3057-08.pdf. Accessed Dec 2010.
23. Kimberly, J., Pauly, M., Grande, D. and David, G. (2010) Rx for the Pharmaceutical Industry: Focus on Innovation, Not Marketing. *ArabicKnowledge@Wharton*. http://knowledge.wharton.upenn.edu/arabic/article.cfm?articleid=1170
24. Prescription Drug Trends. *op. cit.*
25. *Ibid.*
26. Cook, A., Somers, J. and Christensen, J. "Prescription Drug Pricing." 30 Jan 2009. *National Health Policy Forum*. http://www.nhpf.org/library/handouts/Cook.slides_01-30-09.pdf
27. Five-Year Prescription: Dozens of Drugs Go Generic. *ABC News*. Aired 9 Aug 2007. http://abcnews.go.com/Health/Drugs/story?id=3464643&page=1

28. FDA & Drug Evaluations. *Lymphomation.org*. http://www.lymphomation.org/fda.htm. Accessed Feb 2010.
29. Karst, K. R. Patent Expiration, Pediatric Exclusivity, and Generic Drug Approval. *FDA Law Blog*. 18 Aug 2010. http://www.fdalawblog.net/fda_law_blog_hyman_phelps/2010/08/patent-expiration-pediatric-exclusivity-and-generic-drug-approval-some-interesting-tensions-between-.html
30. Fein, A. Wholesaler Profits: Brand vs. Generic Drugs. *DrugChannels.net*. 3 Jun 2010. http://www.drugchannels.net/2010/06/wholesaler-profits-brand-vs-generic.html
31. Britt, R. Growing Share of 'Big Three' Gets Federal Attention. *The Wall Street Journal: MarketWatch*. 30 May 2007. http://www.marketwatch.com/story/growing-share-of-big-three-drug-wholesalers-gets-attention
32. Fein, A. New Data on Pharmacy Industry Market Share. *DrugChannels.net*. 4 Aug 2010. http://www.drugchannels.net/2010/08/new-data-on-pharmacy-industry-market.html
33. 2009 Community Pharmacy Results. *NACDS*. http://www.nacds.org/user-assets/pdfs/2010/publications/2009Results.pdf. Accessed Dec 2010.
34. Pharmacies: Improving Health, Reducing Costs. *NACDS*. http://www.nacds.org/user-assets/pdfs/2010/PrinciplesOfHealthcare2010.pdf. Accessed Nov 2010.
35. 2009 Community Pharmacy Results. *op. cit.*
36. *Ibid.*
37. Fein, A. 2008 Pharmacy Market Share Data. *DrugChannels.net*. 30 Jun 2009. http://www.drugchannels.net/2009/06/2008-pharmacy-market-share-data.html
38. Our Past. *Walgreens corporate site*. http://www.walgreens.com/marketing/about/history/default.html. Accessed Dec 2010.
39. Walgreen Company WAG. *Morningstar*. http://quote.morningstar.com/stock/s.aspx?t=WAG. Accessed Dec 2010.
40. 2010 Annual Report Walgreens. *Walgreens Investor Relations*. http://files.shareholder.com/downloads/WAG/1063038696x0x415505/1D8F76D6-DBFF-4936-8168-A67ECF0488DF/WALGREEN_2010_ANNUAL_Lo.pdf. Accessed Dec 2010.
41. *Ibid.*
42. History. *CVS Caremark corporate site*. http://info.cvscaremark.com/our-company/history. Accessed Dec 2010.
43. CVS Caremark 2009 Annual Report. *CVS Caremark Investor Relations*. http://phx.corporate-ir.net/External.File?item=UGFyZW50SUQ9MzkwNjJ8Q2hpbGRJRD0tMXxUeXBlPTM=&t=1. Accessed Dec 2010.
44. CVS Caremark Corporation CVS. *Morningstar*. http://quote.morningstar.com/stock/s.aspx?t=CVS&culture=en-US&region=USA&r=185297&byrefresh=yes. Accessed Dec 2010.
45. CVS Caremark Facts. *CVS Caremark corporate site*. http://info.cvscaremark.com/our-company/cvs-caremark-facts. Accessed Dec 2010.
46. Company overview. *Medco Health Solutions, Inc. corporate site*. http://phx.corporateir.net/phoenix.zhtml?c=131268&p=irol-homeProfile. Accessed Dec 2010.
47. Medco Health Solutions Inc. MHS. *Morningstar*. http://quote.morningstar.com/stock/s.aspx?t=MHS&culture=en-US&region=USA&r=980855&byrefresh=yes. Accessed Dec 2010.

48. Company overview. *op. cit.*

49. Who we are. *Medco Health Solutions, Inc. corporate site.* http://www.medcohealth.com/medco/corporate/home.jsp?ltSess=y&articleID=CorpWhoWeAre. Accessed Dec 2010.

50. Our products and services. *Medco Health Solutions, Inc. corporate site.* http://www.medcohealth.com/medco/corporate/home.jsp?BV_SessionID=@@@@1517241199.1291738920-mm462480632738@@@@&BV_EngineID=ccglademekggjglcfklcgffdghfdfil.0&articleID=CorpWhatWe Offer. Accessed Dec 2010.

51. History. *Walmart corporate site.* http://walmartstores.com/AboutUs/297.aspx. Accessed Dec 2010.

52. Wal-Mart Stores Inc. WMT. *Morningstar.* http://quote.morningstar.com/stock/s.aspx?t=WMT&culture=en-US&region=USA&r=1258&byrefresh=yes. Accessed Dec 2010.

53. History Timeline. *Walmart corporate site.* http://walmartstores.com/AboutUs/7603.aspx. Accessed Dec 2010.

54. Pharmacy. *Walmart corporate site.* http://www.walmart.com/cp/4-Prescriptions-Program/%20http://www.walmart.com/cp/1078664. Accessed Dec 2010.

55. Norman, A. India: Wal-Mart's Drug Connection. *Huffington Post.* 21 Jun 2008. http://www.huffingtonpost.com/al-norman/india-wal-marts-drug-conn_b_108466.html. Accessed Jun 2010.

56. Wal-Mart Cuts Prices of Generic Drugs as Competitors Follow Suit. PBS Newshour. Aired 22 Sep 2006. http://www.pbs.org/newshour/bb/health/july-dec06/walmart_09-22.html. Accessed Sep 2010.

57. AT&T, Baker Center, Center for American Progress, CED, CWA, Intel, Kelly Services, SEIU and Wal-Mart Launch "Better Health Care Together" Campaign. *Walmart corporate site.* 7 Feb 2007. http://walmartstores.com/pressroom/news/6253.aspx

58. Kroger Company KR. *Morningstar.* http://quote.morningstar.com/stock/s.aspx?t=KR&culture=en-US&region=USA&r=651069&byrefresh=yes. Accessed Dec 2010.

59. About Kroger Co. *Yahoo! Finance.* http://biz.yahoo.com/cc/7/118917.html. Accessed Dec 2010.

60. Skinner, B.J. Canada's Drug Price Paradox. *Fraser Institute.* 23 Feb 2005. http://www.fraserinstitute.org/publicationdisplay.aspx?id=12864&terms=%22canada%27s+drug+price+paradox%22

61. Greenspan, R. Web Swallows Chunk of Prescription Sales. *ClickZMarketing Network.* 19 Nov 2003. http://www.clickz.com/showPage.html?page=3111481

62. Stock, S. Patients, Pharmacies Adapt to Drugs by Mail. *newsobserver.com.* 11 Apr 2010. http://www.newsobserver.com/2010/04/11/430578/patients-pharmacies-adapt-to-drugs.html

63. Lawrence, J. Does Mail-Order Pharmacy Really Deliver the Goods? *Managed Care Magazine.* Jun 1988. http://www.managedcaremag.com/archives/9806/9806.backlash.shtml

64. Stock, S. *op. cit.*

65. Prescription Drug Trends. *op. cit.*

66. Frederick, J. Retirement, Part-time Allure Spell Rising Pharmacist Shortages. *Drug Store News.* 26 Jun 2006. http://findarticles.com/p/articles/mi_m3374/is_8_28/ai_n26701136/

67. Our History. *MinuteClinic CVS Caremark corporate site.* http://www.minuteclinic.com/about/history.aspx. Accessed Mar 2011.

68. Take Care Clinic. *Take Care Clinic Walgreens corporate site.* http://takecarehealth.com/. Accessed Dec 2010.

69. Freudenheim, M. Wal-Mart Begins to Rebuild Health Clinic Business. *New York Times.* 11 May 2009. http://www.nytimes.com/2009/05/12/business/12clinicside.html

70. Clinics. *Walmart corporate site.* http://walmartstores.com/healthWellness/7613.aspx. Accessed Mar 2011.

71. Clinic Locations. *Walmart corporate site.* http://i.walmart.com/i/if/hmp/fusion/Clinic_Locations.pdf. Accessed Mar 2011.

72. Birchall, J. Rite Aid to Test New Store Format. *Financial Times.* 7 Sep 2010. http://www.ft.com/cms/s/0/72fce77c-bac7-11df-9e1d-00144feab49a.html#axzz1FqdnY1H1

73. Harkreader, E. Just in Time for Black Friday. *Business Wire.* 23 Nov 2010. http://www.businesswire.com/news/home/20101123005932/en/Time-Black-Friday-Rite-Aid-Helps-Holiday

74. Thompson, S. Rite Aid (NYSE: RAD): Disappointing 4th Quarter Struggling To Keep Up. *Americas News Online.* 26 Nov 2010. http://www.americasnewsonline.com/rite-aid-nyse-rad-disappointing-4th-quarter-struggling-to-keep-up-911/

Reynolds American Inc.

Corky Whipple, John Justice, Patricia Gainer, Christopher Johnson, Irene Alvidrez

Arizona State University

Introduction

Every year, 443,000 people in the US die from health issues arising from cigarette smoking or exposure to secondhand smoke.[1] Scientists and health researchers alike have been adamant for years about the harmful effects of smoking cigarettes and many experts state bluntly that tobacco products kill their users. These statistics and criticisms certainly paint a grim picture for the tobacco industry; yet every day, the CEO of Reynolds American Incorporated (herein referred to as RAI), Daniel Delen, must assess these conditions and successfully manage an organization devoted to selling tobacco products.

While the history of smoking goes as far back as anyone can remember and across every border of the world, the cigarette and tobacco market in the US has changed dramatically over the years. Carefully marketed, cigarette manufacturers captured the once-closeted female customer in the early- to mid-nineteenth century and cinema made both the on- and off-screen smoking of movie stars—and thus impressionable average Americans—de rigueur.[2]

However, as the suppliers to what was once a very open and highly advertised leisure activity, tobacco firms began to feel the squeeze of tightening restrictions in the latter half of the century. The first major mandate affecting business came down in 1965 with the Federal Cigarette Labeling and Advertising Act requiring manufacturers to place the Surgeon General's Warning—"Caution: Cigarette Smoking May Be Hazardous to Your Health"—on every pack of cigarettes. With cigarette advertising banned from radio and television as of January 1, 1971, cigarette manufacturers were left to rely primarily on billboards and print advertising—venues that, as of 1972, were required to carry health warnings as well. In the first federal restriction of smoking in public places, in 1973, the Civil Aeronautics Board required that non-smoking sections be created on all airlines, subsequently providing the first tangible division of smokers from non-smokers and

enlightening non-smokers to the idea of advocating for smoke-free spaces. In response to the rash of litigation by non-smokers as well as smatterings of successful local legislation, the Clean Indoor Air Act was passed in 1985, prohibiting smoking in government facilities, museums, and office buildings, and started a landslide of similar measures at state and local levels. Back in the friendly skies, by 1988, smoking on flights shorter than two hours was prohibited and on January 1, 1990, all smoking on interstate buses and domestic flights of less than six hours was banned.

Legislation designed to warn the general public about the dangers of tobacco products and curb underage use has continued with the Master Settlement Act of 1998, the FDA Trafficking Act of 2009, the Prevent All Cigarette Trafficking Act of 2010, and most recently, the Family Smoking Prevention and Tobacco Control Act that went into effect on June 22, 2010.[3] The restrictions in place today seriously handicap the tobacco industry from employing the typical avenues used to promote and sell products and yet, while the percentage of cigarette smokers in 1965 was more than double what it is today, there has only been about a 5 percent decline in smokers since 1990 (Exhibit 1). Even so, tobacco firms will continue to rely heavily on product development, marketing techniques, and increased health standards to stay competitive in this environment.

Despite the mounting roadblocks, RAI is steadfast in its business model. R.J. Reynolds Tobacco, the largest division of RAI, ranks as the second largest tobacco company in the US cigarette market (Exhibit 2). Reinforcement of its brand sustainability comes from its smokeless tobacco holding, American Snuff Company, with top products Grizzly and Kodiak. RAI has positioned itself to harvest growth through an increased presence in the smokeless tobacco market, investing $71 million in research and development toward this end.

RAI considers itself the provider of the highest quality products and an innovative leader in the tobacco industry. The firm is divided into three core business units:

Exhibit 1 Current Cigarette Smoking in Persons 18 and Older by Sex, Selected Years, 1965–2008

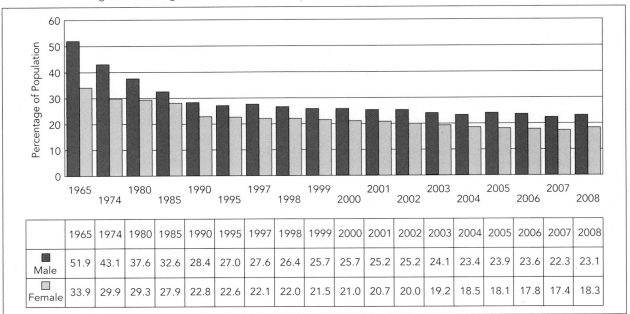

	1965	1974	1980	1985	1990	1995	1997	1998	1999	2000	2001	2002	2003	2004	2005	2006	2007	2008
■ Male	51.9	43.1	37.6	32.6	28.4	27.0	27.6	26.4	25.7	25.7	25.2	25.2	24.1	23.4	23.9	23.6	22.3	23.1
□ Female	33.9	29.9	29.3	27.9	22.8	22.6	22.1	22.0	21.5	21.0	20.7	20.0	19.2	18.5	18.1	17.8	17.4	18.3

Source: Centers for Disease Control and Prevention. National Center for Health Statistics. National Health Interview Survey, 1965–2008. Analysis by the American Lung Association, Research and Program Services Division using SPSS and SUDAAN software.

Notes:

(1) A current smoker is a person who has smoked at least 100 cigarettes and who now smokes. In 1992, the definition of a current smoker was modified to include persons who smoked every day or some days.

(2) Because these estimates are based on a sample, they may differ from figures that would be obtained from a census of the population. Each data point reported is an estimate of the true population value and subject to sampling variability.

Source: American Lung Association publication, Trends in Tobacco Use. http://www.lungusa.org

Exhibit 2 US Cigarette Market Share

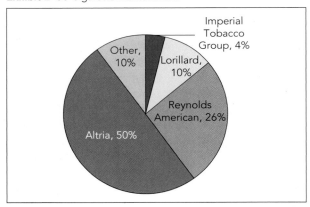

Source: Distribution percentages for chart taken from Blashill, Graham. 2008. Implementing our strategy in the USA. Accessed 20 May 2011. http://www.imperial-tobacco.com

R.J. Reynolds Tobacco Company (RJR), American Snuff Company, and Santa Fe Natural Tobacco. Due to the size of Santa Fe Natural Tobacco, RAI incorporates the financial data from that unit into its "All Other Business" segment. RJR's revenue contributes approximately 85 percent of RAI's total sales with American Snuff, the second

largest segment, depositing approximately ten percent of the firm's total revenue, and All Other Business accounting for the remaining five percent of revenue in the company's portfolio.

Despite perpetually bleak sales forecasts, RAI has been strong financially, reporting overall net sales of $8.17 billion in 2010—up from $8.02 billion in 2009. Demonstrating the flexibility necessary for the firm to cut costs if the need arises, RAI boasts a gross margin of nearly 50 percent. Further growth indicators include a year-over-year 15 percent return on equity increase, indicating increased profitability and a competitive return on assets when compared to similar companies within the tobacco industry.

Company History

Early Years

RAI, founded as and by R.J. Reynolds in 1875, is a US held corporation headquartered in Winston-Salem, North Carolina. It is principally engaged in manufacturing tobacco related products such as cigarettes, smokeless tobacco, additive free tobacco, and cigars, with nicotine replacement therapy products offered in certain markets. Having its start in chewing tobacco, in the early 1900s,

RJR correctly anticipated the smoking tobacco market would grow.[4] By the mid 1920s, RJR was one of the most profitable corporations in the world. Incremental changes followed with the introduction of menthol, tips, and cellophane packaging. In the 60s, embracing the intermittently successful conglomerate merger trend, RJR began diversifying into food and other non-tobacco businesses and became the well known firm—RJR Nabisco.[5]

After its poor response following the market crash of 1987, CEO F. Ross Johnson put the company in play and became involved in one of the most infamous leveraged buyouts of its time.[6,7] In the end, Kohlberg, Kravis Roberts & Co. (KKR), a large private equity firm, won control of the company, turning it private. Even so, RJR began active trading again in the early 90s with KKR fully divesting itself by 1995.

With increasing pressure to eliminate the marketing of tobacco products to children, and after the American Medical Association established that children were attracted to ads featuring him, in 1997, RJR withdrew its advertising cartoon character, Joe the Camel. In 1999, RJR was spun off from R.J. Nabisco with then CEO Steven F. Goldstone explaining, "Cookies and cigarettes do not share distribution or marketing or even the same sales force. They are very, very different businesses."[8]

Mid-2000s to Current

After several acquisitions and joint ventures, including the addition of Santa Fe Natural and Brown and Williamson (B&W), RJR's parent company—RAI—was created in 2004. The organization's reportable subsidiaries include R.J. Reynolds Tobacco Company (RJR) and American Snuff. The Santa Fe Natural Tobacco Company, Inc.

and Niconovum AB (nicotine replacements products) subsidiaries are reported as "All Other" within the company's financial statements. RAI focuses on the US market with any foreign sales occurring via its B&W affiliates.

As the second largest tobacco company in the US, RJR produces, markets, and sells Camel, Pall Mall, Doral, Kool, Winston, and Salem—six of the ten best-selling cigarette brands in the US as of December 2010.[9] RJR also produces Camel Snus and Camel Dissolvables, two types of smoke-free tobacco seeing increased use across markets. Camel Crush, a menthol selectable cigarette, and Camel Sticks, Strips, and Orbs (the dissolvable products), are considered innovative products in the industry.[10] RJR divides its cigarette product line into three segments: *growth, support,* and *non-support.* Growth brands are supported by strong marketing for future growth, while support brands receive limited marketing funds but are relied upon for long-term sustainability. Non-support brands continue to be manufactured and distributed based on consumer demand (see Exhibit 3 for RAI holdings and products). Camel and Pall Mall account for RJR's growth brands and are responsible for approximately 55 percent of RJR's cigarette sales.[11] The company sells its cigarettes primarily to distributors, wholesalers, retail chains, and other direct customers.[12]

The US cigarette market is forecast to decline approximately four percent in 2011, similar to the decline seen in 2010. RJR's revenue is approximately 85 percent of RAI's total sales and accounts for approximately 28 percent of the overall industry market.[13]

The American Snuff segment, approximately ten percent of RAI's revenue, is experiencing high single digit growth annually.[14] It is the second largest smokeless tobacco product manufacturer in the US, consisting of

Exhibit 3 RAI Holdings and Products

Reynolds American Inc.									
RJ Reynolds Tobacco Company (85%)					American Snuff Co, LLC (10%)			All Other (5%)	
Cigarettes			Smoke Free		Snuff	Non Snuff		Santa Fe Natural Tobacco Co, Inc.	Niconovum AB
Growth	Support	Non-Support	Camel Snus*	Camel Dissolvables*		Cigars	Loose Tobacco		
• Camel • Pall Mall	• Winston • Kool • Salem • Capri • Doral • Misty	• Carlton • Eclipse • GPC • Lucky Strike • Monarch • More • Now • Private-Label • Tareyton • Vantage	• Robust • Winterchill	• Orbs • Strips • Sticks	• Grizzly* • Kodiak* • Levi Garret • Hawken	• Winchester • Captain Black	• Bugler	• American Spirit • Dunhill • State Express 555	

*Additional growth brands

Source: Information compiled using http://www.rjrt.com/whoweare.aspx.

the moist-snuff brands—Grizzly and Kodiak. American Snuff was acquired in 2006 for $3.5 billion (known at the time of its sale as Conwood) and considered a key strategic move for RAI as its purchase provided entry into the smokeless tobacco business.[15] The American Snuff segment holds approximately 31 percent of its target market but competition in this segment is high. RAI attributes increases in this segment to Grizzly's lid redesign and strong product value.[16]

The premium Santa Fe cigarette brands (Dunhill, State Express 555, and the no additive Natural American Spirit), in addition to the Niconovum business, account for RAI's remaining five percent in revenue. Santa Fe, though small, delivered double-digit growth in 2010 on earnings and volume.[17] While some analysts see RAI's customers as an older demographic,[18] Santa Fe branding could act as an entry to a younger, premium customer base.

Delen, President and CEO since March 2011, has continued the business strategy of outgoing CEO, Susan Ivey. Ivey, a 30-year veteran of the industry and the former CEO of B&W assumed the CEO position when RAI was created in 2004. During this transition, RAI separated the Chairman of the Board from the CEO. RAI has de-emphasized private label brands to reduce complexity, increased prices, continued other factory and operating improvements (such as an ERP system), and remains committed to achieving an 80 percent payout target that will go hand in hand with a very hefty dividend of about 5.4 percent. As an industry less susceptible to market risk with a beta of .68, RAI is making it attractive for shareholders to care about supporting this $22.9 billion entity in its future ventures.[19]

The Black Sheep of America

While a lagging economy presents grave concerns to many industries, compared to the other challenges of the tobacco industry, it is likely the least of its worries. Easily usurping the majority of the time and attention of RAI executives are federal regulations and ongoing litigation. On June 22, 2009, the US government passed the Family Smoking Prevention and Tobacco Control Act. Most notably, this act significantly increases taxes on the sale of tobacco products and grants the US Food and Drug Administration (FDA) unprecedented control over the manufacture, sale, marketing, and packaging of tobacco products. Among other things, this act requires tobacco companies to disclose ingredients used in manufacturing including nicotine yield, limits flavor additives such as menthol and wintergreen, and places further restrictions on smoking in public places and advertisements (including no logos or ads on t-shirts, caps, or other apparel).[20] Were these restrictions not challenging enough for a company attempting to advertise, private industry has

also taken the initiative to ban advertisements of cigarette products. Microsoft and Google both have policies banning tobacco promotion on their advertising networks and the Motion Picture Association of America threatens filmmakers making movies that depict gratuitous smoking with higher ratings that exclude admission to children and teens without a parent.

Altria Group

Altria Group, incorporated in Virginia in 1985, is the holding company for Philip Morris USA and UST and includes US Smokeless Tobacco Company LLC (USSTC). Cigarettes and smokeless products accounted for almost 95 percent of total income for Altria Group in 2010, with approximately 82 percent from cigarettes and 12 percent from smokeless products. Altria focuses on promoting brand equity, anticipating and responding to consumer preferences, competing in lower-priced markets, and enhancing margins through cost savings or price increases.[21]

Philip Morris USA is the largest tobacco company in the US. Its most popular brand, Marlboro, has been the leading cigarette brand in the US for over 30 years and accounts for 87 percent of Philip Morris' cigarette sales volume. Overall, Philip Morris products claim 49.8 percent of the total US cigarette market.[22]

Altria acquired USSTC, the leader in the smokeless tobacco market as determined by retail share, on January 6, 2009. Copenhagen and Skoal are the most notable brands offered by USSTC and combined, the two account for 83 percent of total smokeless tobacco volume within the company. Copenhagen retains 25.6 percent of the US retail market share while Skoal accounts for 22.4 percent. With all its smokeless tobacco products, USSTC controls over 55 percent of total US market share.[23]

Lorillard Tobacco Company

Lorillard Tobacco Company was founded in 1760, making it the oldest continuously operating tobacco company in the US. With corporate offices located in Greensboro, North Carolina, Lorillard ranks as the third largest cigarette manufacturer in the US. In a similar fashion to RAI, Lorillard sold all major trademarks outside the US in 1977 and now produces cigarettes exclusively for the premium and discount segments of the US market. Lorillard's primary brand, Newport, accounts for roughly 90 percent of total company sales. Additional brands include Kent, True, Maverick, and Old Gold among many others. The Newport brand alone owns almost 11 percent of domestic market share, with Newport's menthol product holding a strong 35 percent share within the menthol segment. As a company, Lorillard reported earnings of $1.725 billion in 2010.[24]

Lorillard relies on in-store price reduction programs to promote the sale of its products. According to CEO Murray Kessler, Lorillard's long-term growth depends on the strength of the Newport brand. Despite a FDA report stating that the "removal of menthol cigarettes from the marketplace would benefit public health in the US," Lorillard is committed to the protection and growth of its core menthol cigarette business. Lorillard also directs its focus to enhancing internal capabilities to control operational costs as well as marketing efforts designed to penetrate strategic US markets.[25]

The Disappearing Smoker?

Consumers in the US spent about $90 billion on tobacco products in 2006 with roughly $84 billion of that total spent on cigarettes and $3 billion on smokeless tobacco.[26] At that time, 23.6 percent of the adult (18 or older) American public actively smoked and 25.8 percent of the youth population smoked.[27] Interestingly, the consumer base outside the US does not face the volume reduction challenges faced here; however, RAI has limited itself to the US market, so this is a unique disadvantage it faces compared to several of its competitors—especially Philip Morris.[28]

Consumers recognize the financial and health constraints that tobacco use imposes. During 2000–2004, consumers suffered an estimated $193 billion in health-related losses due to the effects of tobacco consumption. These additional medical costs contribute to an average of $10.47 per pack, on top of already soaring prices.[29] With the lagging economic pressures, increased awareness of the effects of tobacco use, and the burdensome cost to the consumer, the trend away from smoking is likely to continue.

Perhaps making the biggest impact to the decline in smokers, however, is the social stigma of being a smoker—particularly a smoker amongst friends and family that have quit. With increasing restrictions on where one can smoke, smokers report feeling increasingly harassed and ostracized. A person is 67 percent less likely to smoke if they have a spouse that quit smoking. In addition, smoking is disproportionately becoming a habit of the lower classes—the less educated, the less wealthy, and individuals with mental illness and/or addiction issues. The fact that smoking within the more elite circles is becoming increasingly taboo has prompted many smokers to quit rather than risk trying to rub elbows only to find a cold shoulder.[30]

However, while smoking has been cut in half since 1965, the decline in adult smokers has stalled at just above 20 percent for several years. While the decline is credited to several socio-cultural factors including a fall in the social acceptability of smoking, increased awareness campaigns regarding the health concerns related to tobacco use, and increased pressure from anti-tobacco organizations, there is no clear evidence to explain the apparent limits of the efficacy of these efforts.[31]

Tobacco Producers

Tobacco growers worldwide supply the industry with tobacco. The largest supplies come from China, Brazil, the US, and Zimbabwe. In almost all tobacco producing countries, the government influences the production and trade of tobacco. This influence typically extends to supply management and subsidies aimed at maintaining stable prices. Tobacco is a significantly more profitable crop when compared to others, thus providing developing countries with the opportunity to trade internationally with substantial margins. For example, in Zimbabwe, tobacco is nearly seven times more profitable than the next best crop.[32]

Tobacco growers have organized to protect their interests and leverage their collective voice with both national and international organizations. In the US, one such group is the US Tobacco Cooperative, which exists "to enhance the livelihood of [its] members…"[33] Internationally, member countries have organized the International Tobacco Growers' Association. Like other cooperatives, this group is focused on sharing information between tobacco growers, creating strategies to stabilize supply and prices, and protecting the legitimate interests of tobacco growers.[34]

The Smoking Gun—Nicotine, or Rather the Smoke?

Two separate issues face smokers trying to quit. The first is kicking the habit of smoking—the places and times that a smoker ritualistically has a cigarette—and the second is kicking the physical addiction to nicotine. With the majority of smoking related health issues tied directly to smoking and not nicotine, it would seem a fairly simple proposition to replace the nicotine delivery method to something less lethal than smoking, thus curing every smoker.

New advances in technology for nicotine delivery support this trend away from using tobacco products. Products such as nicotine patches and chewing gums have been in use over the last decade as an alternative to tobacco use. Prescription medications have been created and, in recent years, the advent of the electronic cigarette, or e-cigarette, has provided smokers with an experience similar to smoking purportedly without the harmful effects associated with burning tobacco. And, as mentioned previously, new sticks, strips, and orbs packed with nicotine are hitting the marketplace. All of these products have siphoned away profits from tobacco companies as smokers work harder at conforming to societal expectations, saving money, improving their health, or all of the above.

And yet despite these advances, the fact remains that 74 percent of smokers report they have tried and failed to quit. One important factor in the ability to quit seems to lie in the age that smoking starts. Smokers that pick up the habit after the age of 21 are far more likely to quit successfully—a factor that has not escaped the notice of tobacco companies and likely drove the underage-directed marketing that received considerable attention in the latter part of the last century.

Getting to the Top

With 86 percent of its revenue coming from its RJR segment, the dominant business of RAI is cigarettes. American Snuff contributes eight percent of all revenue, while All Other Business contributes the final six percent.[35] Because of this revenue split, RAI strives to maximize the profitability and market share growth of RJR while simultaneously nurturing growth within American Snuff. RAI uses the profits associated with the All Other Business to fund the promotion and growth of its two primary segments. Similar to other corporations with this type of structure, RAI makes decisions, allocates resources, and assesses the performance of each segment individually. In addition, RAI has a subsidiary, RAI Services Company, that provides support functions such as legal services, information management, and human resources. By keeping each segment operating independently with support functions provided via a subsidiary, RAI is able to choose which segments receive greater resources and growth efforts.[36]

RAI's goal is to strengthen individual brand identity and in doing so, persuade consumers to switch from whichever competitor's brand they may currently be buying. The marketing necessary to do so demands that RAI keep a constant surveillance on changes in customer behaviors and values. To increase its market share, RAI has split its products into two main categories: *price-value* and *premium*. The price-value brands are targeted to the price-conscious consumer, while premium brands are targeted to quality conscious consumer segments. While American Snuff bases its diversification almost entirely on this two party consumer system, RJR goes a step further. Within its price-value and premium product segments, RJR has developed brands aimed at smaller consumer segments.

RJR's Misty brand is a good example of this strategy. It is packaged and promoted to specifically appeal to middle-class women. This type of segment-specific packaging and promotion is an effective tool for RJR's smaller brands. RJR's flagship brand, Camel, is pack-

aged, promoted, and advertised in a more neutral, all-encompassing manner, thus ensuring its appeal to the largest market possible. These types of segment-specific products allow RAI to maximize its market potential.

RAI is able to maintain lower costs through a variety of activities and practices. Unlike a corporation dedicated solely to providing the lowest cost products of its industry, RAI's variety of products allows them to price products effectively to maximize market share. The fact that RAI owns all of the manufacturing facilities for RJR and American Snuff products helps control prices. This vertical integration allows them to monitor raw material and production costs, and price its products accordingly. Additionally, to protect itself against competitors that may attempt to take market share through cost cutting, RAI has established various discount opportunities for retailers. By discounting at the retail level—wherein RAI makes payments to retailers to reduce the price paid by the consumer—RAI is able to keep its products priced competitively to ensure maximum market share.[37] This type of pricing structure is especially important in industries with such intense rivalry. While its manufacturing price controls help with long-term pricing, only these real time, customer-level pricing strategies ensure that RAI can react to competitors' attacks on market share via pricing.

Ensuring Stockholder Support

Another corporate strength for RAI can be seen in its commitment to offer rising dividends, high yields, and steady earnings when it comes to its stock.

The S&P 500 tobacco index of four stocks—Altria Group Inc., Lorillard Inc., Philip Morris International Inc., and Reynolds American Inc.—has gained 121 percent over the past five years to the end of March (2011), after factoring in dividends. Over the same period, the S&P 500 has risen a mere 14 percent.[38]

For a corporation to grow and reach its optimum level of success, it must have outside investors purchase stock in the company. Public perception of tobacco companies and the products they offer leave some potential investors with a moral dilemma when it comes to investing. To counteract this, RAI leans on its strong financial record to recruit new and additional investments (Exhibit 4). It is important that RAI show strong returns and rising dividends to keep the faith of prospective and current stockholders. Due to the amount of legislation and litigation affecting tobacco companies, these large returns protect

Exhibit 4 RAI Financial Results

	Ratio	Formula	Results				Meaning
			2007	2008	2009	2010	
Profitability Ratios	Gross Margin	(Revenue − COGS)/ Revenue × 100	45.0%	45.0%	46.7%	46.9%	Represents the percent of total sales revenue a company realizes after recognizing COGS. The higher the percentage, the more revenue the company retains on each dollar of sales.
	Return on Equity	Net Income/ Shareholder's Equity	17.5%	21.5%	14.8%	17.1%	Measures how much profit a company is generating using funds invested by shareholders and is a key indicator of company growth.
	Return on Assets	Net Income/Total Assets	7.0%	7.4%	5.3%	6.5%	Indicates how well a company is using its assets to generate earnings.
	Net Profit Margin	(Net Income/ Revenue)	14.5%	15.1%	11.4%	13.0%	Calculates how much of each dollar earned is translated into profits.
Liquidity Ratio	Current Ratio	Current Assets Current Liabilities	1.3	1.3	1.3	1.1	Provides a measure of a company's ability to repay short-term borrowings with short-term assets such as cash and receivables.
Leverage Ratios	Debt to Equity	Total Liabilities/ Shareholder's Equity	60.5%	75.1%	68.3%	63.0%	Calculates the proportion of equity and debt a company is using to finance capital expenditures.
	Debt to Assets	Total Debt/Total Assets	59.9%	65.6%	63.9%	61.9%	Measures financial risk by calculating the percentage of a company's assets financed by debt.
Activity Ratios	Inventory Turnover	Net Sales/Inventory	4.1	4.2	3.7	4.3	Measures how many times a company's inventory is sold and replenished.
	Collection Ratio	Accounts Receivable/ (Revenue/365)	3.0	3.5	4.7	5.0	Calculates average number of days it takes a company to collect on receivables.
	Asset Turnover	Revenue/Total Assets	48.4%	48.7%	46.7%	50.1%	Represents the amount of sales generated for every dollar in assets.
Shareholder's Return Ratio	Equity Multiplier	Assets/Shareholder's Equity	2.5	2.9	2.8	2.6	Provides a measure of financial leverage and provides insight on the portion of ROE resulting from debt.

Sources: Reynolds American, Inc. Form 10-K for the fiscal year ended 12/31/2007. Form 10-K for the fiscal year ended 12/31/2008. Form 10-K for the fiscal year ended 12/31/2009. Form 10-K for the fiscal year ended 12/31/2010. Accessed 23 Feb 2011. http://www.reynoldsamerican.com/sec.cfm?DocType=Annual&Year=

RAI from having its stock price fall due to fears about the future health of the company. However, for these strong returns and the benefits they cause to continue, RAI must continue to grow. RAI's main efforts to grow overall sales and brand market share are conducted through marketing.[39]

Modern Marketing

The Master Settlement Act of 1998 changed the way tobacco companies were allowed to advertise and market their products greatly. This act focused on the perceived ability of tobacco providers to target advertising toward children. The highlights of this act included the banning of cartoons in tobacco advertisements, restricting brand-name sponsorship for events with significant youth audiences, and the banning of outdoor advertising.[40]

This act led to drastic advertising and promotional changes within RAI. In anticipation of the act, Joe the Camel, a popular advertising caricature associated with the Camel brand, was preemptively pulled from all advertising and promotional campaigns on July 12, 1997.[41] Additionally, RAI changed its overall approach to advertising and promotion. Blocked from using standard advertising avenues, RAI began utilizing direct mail, advertisements in newspapers and magazines not restricted by federal, state, and local law, and a renewed and expanded presence at organized adult events and venues.[42] Due to the intense competition between tobacco companies and despite the extensive restrictions on marketing and promotions, cigarette companies still managed to spend $12.4 billion on advertising and promotional expenses in the US in 2006—more than double their expenditures in 1997. Where RAI had once used marketing to target new (i.e. younger) users, its new strategy was to strengthen brand image, build brand awareness and loyalty, and recruit adult consumers of competing brands to RJR and American Snuff brands.[43]

Growth, Support, and Non-Support Brands.

To effectively employ its marketing approach of strong brand image, awareness, and loyalty, as well as entice other brand users to its products, RAI divides its products into different operational groups.[44] While its brands fall under the premium or price-value product lines when it comes to the type of customer being targeted, RAI uses the terms *growth, support,* and *non-support* brands when it comes to its promotional strategies.

Growth brands include Pall Mall cigarettes, Grizzly and Kodiak moist snuff, and its flagship brand, Camel. The goal of these brands is long-term market share and growth in profits. RAI's commitment to the growth of American Snuff is evidenced by the fact that both of its major brands, Kodiak and Grizzly, are seen as growth brands by RAI. In addition, the modern smoke-free products, such as Camel Snus and Camel Dissolvables, marketed under the Camel brand, are targeted for long-term market share growth. While all of the brands under the growth umbrella receive a large amount of promotional funding, the majority of these resources are earmarked to promote Camel products.[45]

Support brands are managed for long-term sustainability and profitability. These brands include Winston, Kool, Capri, Salem, Doral, and Misty and receive little to no promotional or advertising support. Together, these products form a solid platform of sustainable growth and profits for RAI, with essentially no funds allotted or necessary for their promotion or growth.

Non-support brands are all other products under the RAI umbrella. The goal of these products is short-term profitability. These short-term profits are then used in the promotion and advertising of growth products. This system of grouping brands by marketing strategy has allowed RAI to defend its market share in the ultra-competitive tobacco industry, while also funding the initiatives necessary to steal market share away from the competition.[46]

The House That Reynolds Built

American Snuff has manufacturing facilities in Tennessee, North Carolina, and Kentucky. American Snuff owns all three facilities and began capacity upgrades and expansions in 2009.[47] RJR owns its manufacturing facilities as well and has recently consolidated completely to its Tobaccoville, North Carolina location. Total product capacity for RJR is estimated at 160 billion cigarettes per year.[48] As a result of this consolidation, RAI is seen as benefiting financially from economies of scale.[49]

Research and development has traditionally been performed at the RJR facility where scientists and engineers focus on developing new products, new packaging models, harm reduction technologies, and FDA compliance. However, RAI is relocating the research and development segment to a new facility to further consolidate research and development efforts across all business segments. RAI's research and development expenses were $71 million, $68 million, and $59 million in 2010, 2009, and 2008, respectively. Increases primarily reflect the development of harm reduction and smoke-free products for RJR.[50]

Financial Results

In 2010, RAI reported net sales of $8.6 million—a 1.6 percent increase over the reported $8.4 million in sales in 2009 (Exhibits 5A and 5B). This is important given that key competitors within the tobacco industry indicated significant decreases in 2010 net sales. Much of this growth can be attributed to increased sales within the

Exhibit 5A RAI: Consolidated Statements of Income

(Dollars in Millions, Except Per Share Amts)	For the Years Ended December 31,		
	2010	2009	2008
Net sales[1]	$8,170	$8,015	$8,377
Net sales, related party	381	404	468
Net sales	8,551	8,419	8,845
Costs and expenses:			
Cost of products sold[1][2][3][4]	4,544	4,485	4,863
SG&A	1,493	1,508	1,500
Amortization expense	25	28	22
Asset impairment and exit charges	38	—	—
Trademark impairment charges	6	567	318
Goodwill impairment charge	26	—	—
Restructuring charge	—	56	90
Operating income	2,419	1,775	2,052
Interest and debt expense	232	251	275
Interest income	(12)	(19)	(60)
Gain on termination of joint venture	—	—	(328)
Other expense, net	7	9	37
Income from continuing operations before income taxes	2,192	1,534	2,128
Provision for income taxes	863	572	790
Income from continuing operations	1,329	962	1,338
Losses from disc operations, net of tax	(216)	—	—
Net income	$1,113	$ 962	$1,338
Basic income per share:[5]			
Income from continuing operations	$ 2.28	$ 1.65	$ 2.28
Losses from discontinued operations	(0.37)	—	—
Net income	$ 1.91	$ 1.65	$ 2.28
Diluted income per share:			
Income from continuing operations	$ 2.27	$ 1.65	$ 2.28
Losses from discontinued operations	(0.37)	—	—
Net income	$ 1.9	$ 1.65	$ 2.28
Dividends declared per share	$ 1.84	$ 1.73	$ 1.7

[1]Excludes excise taxes of $4,340 M, $3,927 M, and $1,890 M for the years ended December 31, 2010, 2009 and 2008, respectively.

[2]Includes Master Settlement Agreement, referred to as MSA, and other state settlement agreements with the states of Mississippi, Florida, Texas, and Minnesota, together with the MSA collectively referred to as the State Settlement Agreements, expense of $2,496 M, $2,540 M, and $2,703 M for the years ended December 31, 2010, 2009 and 2008, respectively.

[3]Includes federal tobacco quota buyout expenses of $243 M, $240 M, and $249 M for the years ended December 31, 2010, 2009 and 2008, respectively.

[4]Includes US Food and Drug Administration user fees of $75 M and $22 M for the years ended December 31, 2010 and 2009, respectively.

[5]All per share amounts have been retroactively adjusted to reflect the November 15, 2010, two-for-one stock split.

Source: Reynolds American, Inc. Form 10-K for the fiscal year ended 12/31/10. Accessed 23 Feb 2011. http://www.reynoldsamerican.com

Exhibit 5B RAI: Consolidated Balance Sheet

(Dollars in Millions)	December 31, 2010	December 31, 2009
Assets		
Current assets:		
Cash and cash equivalents	$ 2,195	$ 2,723
Accounts receivable	118	109
Accounts receivable, related party	48	96
Notes receivable	34	36
Other receivables	10	15
Inventories	1,055	1,219
Deferred income taxes, net	946	956
Prepaid expenses and other	195	341
Assets held for sale	201	—
Total current assets	4,802	5,495
Property, plant and equipment, at cost:		
Land and land improvements	89	88
Buildings and leasehold improvements	656	661
Machinery and equipment	1,700	1,759
Construction-in-process	157	87
Total property, plant and equipment	2,602	2,595
Less accumulated depreciation	1,600	1,570
Property, plant and equipment, net	1,002	1,025
Trademarks and other intangible assets, net of accumulated amortization (2010 — $672; 2009 — $647)	2,675	2,718
Goodwill	8,010	8,185
Other assets and deferred charges	589	586
	$17,078	$18,009
Liabilities and shareholders' equity		
Current liabilities:		
Accounts payable	$ 179	$ 196
Tobacco settlement accruals	2,589	2,611
Due to related party	4	3
Deferred revenue, related party	53	57
Current maturities of long-term debt	400	300
Other current liabilities	1,147	1,173
Total current liabilities	4,372	4,340
Long-term debt (less current maturities)	3,701	4,136
Deferred income taxes, net	518	441
Long-term retirement benefits (less current portion)	1,668	2,218
Other noncurrent liabilities	309	376
Commitments and contingencies:		
Shareholders' equity:		
Common stock (shares issued: 2010 — 583,043,872; 2009 — 582,848,102)	—	—
Paid-in capital	8,535	8,498
Accumulated deficit	(547)	(579)
Accumulated other comprehensive loss — (Defined benefit pension and post-retirement plans: 2010 — $(1,446) and 2009 — $(1,376), net of tax)	(1,478)	(1,421)
Total shareholders' equity	6,510	6,498
	$17,078	$18,009

Source: Reynolds American, Inc. Form 10-K for the fiscal year ended 12/31/10. Accessed 23 Feb 2011. http://www.reynoldsamerican.com

Exhibit 6 American Snuff Brand Financials

(millions of cans)	For the 12 Months Ending December 31,		
	2010	2009	2008
KODIAK	47.5	47.8	51
GRIZZLY	325.3	304.6	279.6
OTHER	4.5	4.1	4.5
TOTAL MOIST SNUFF SALES	$377.3	$356.5	$335.2

Source: Reynolds American, Inc. Form 10-K for the fiscal year ended 12/31/10. Accessed 23 Feb 2011. http://www.reynoldsamerican.com

American Snuff business segment as RJR only realized a 0.2 percent increase in net sales from 2009 (Exhibit 6). RAI 2010 net profit mirrored net sales increases, reflecting a 1.6 percent increase over 2009.[51]

Leadership

RAI key executive officers include Daniel (Daan) M. Delen and Thomas R. Adams. Delen became President and CEO of RAI on March 1, 2011. Delen previously served as President and CEO of reporting segment RJR from 2007 to 2010 and served as Chairman of the Board of RJR from 2008 to 2010, yielding a total of four years active experience with RAI.[52] Prior to retirement in 2011, Susan M. Ivey preceded Delen, having served as President and CEO of RAI for seven years.

Thomas Adams has served as Executive Vice President and CFO of RAI since January 2008. Adams' prior experience with RAI dates back to 2005 and includes leadership roles such as Senior Vice President, Chief Accounting Office, Senior Vice President of Business Processes, and Controller.

Board of Directors

The RAI Board of Directors is made up of 12 Board members, each serving a three-year term and divided into classes I, II, and III. Each class represents a year of staggered term end dates. Board members include a mix of inside and outside directors that help promote industry knowledge while fostering a greater degree of Board independence. Board committees are crucial to the ongoing monitoring of top executives and as such, RAI's Board of Directors has established the following three standing committees: *Audit and Finance, Compensation and Leadership Development,* and *Corporate Governance and Nominating.*

The current Chairman of the Board, Thomas C. Wainert, stepped into the role in November 2010. Relevant industry qualifications include having previously served as a Director of both RAI and RJR. Wainert has also held the CEO position in public and privately held firms. The Board of Directors meets a minimum of five times during an annual calendar year with meeting agendas developed by the Chairman, the CEO, and the Secretary of the Company. Board members may also provide recommendations for additional agenda items as deemed necessary. Finally, all Board members retain open access to RAI's senior management.

RAI's top executives, serving as agents on behalf of shareholders, share a combined total of over 150 years of direct experience with RAI and the tobacco industry (Exhibit 7). This provides RAI with an extensive amount of knowledge from which to leverage decision making. RAI has established proper checks and balances of executives by incorporating formal evaluations of leadership, including an evaluation of the CEO by the Compensation and Leadership Development Committee. Additionally, the Governance Committee monitors Board membership to ensure a diversity of perspectives, skill sets, and superior business and professional experience are represented. The Governance Committee also conducts an annual evaluation of the Board's performance. These control mechanisms counter managerial opportunism (i.e. pursuit of non-approved product diversification) and provide assurance to stakeholders by ensuring decisions are made with the best interests of RAI in mind. Further evidence of sound internal controls are exhibited by executive Sarbanes-Oxley assertions within RAI's audited financial statements.

Maintaining Momentum

Analysis of the tobacco industry reveals tremendous pressure and key challenges facing the market—and RAI is no exception. Specific to the firm, these obstacles include a growing competitive base, slow economic recovery from the recession, severely tightened government regulation, and substantial societal obstacles. RAI faces intense strategic challenges as a result of this. Challenges such as product mix, differentiation factors, pricing, research and development investment, successful product placement, and marketing must all be addressed.

Exhibit 7 RAI Leadership

Name	Title	Years at RAI
Nicholas Bumbacco	President of Santa Fe (All Other Business, RAI)	5
Lisa J. Caldwell	Executive VP and Human Resources Officer	10
Robert H. Dunham	Senior VP – Public Affairs	6
Daniel A. Fawley	Senior VP and Treasurer	11
Jeffrey S. Gentry	Executive VP – Operations and Chief Scientific Officer, RJR Tobacco	24
Andrew D. Gilchrist	President and Chief Commercial Officer, RJR Tobacco	6
Martin L. Holton III	Executive VP, General Counsel and Assistant Secretary, RAI	6
J. Brice O'Brien	Executive VP – Consumer Marketing, RJR Tobacco	15
Tommy J. Payne	President of Niconovum USA, Inc.	22
Frederick W. Smothers	Senior VP and Chief Accounting Officer, RAI	8
Randall M. (Mick) Spach	President of American Snuff Co.	9
Robert D. Stowe	Executive VP – Trade Marketing, RJR Tobacco	6
E. Kenan Whitehurst	Senior VP – Strategy and Business Development, RAI	22

Sources: Raw data provided by Reynolds American, Inc. Form 10-K for the fiscal year ended 12/31/10. Accessed 23 Feb 2011. http://www.reynoldsamerican.com

The tobacco industry is subject to a wide range of laws and regulations regarding the marketing, sale, taxation, and use of tobacco products imposed by local, state, federal, and foreign governments. One example of such regulation is the Family Smoking Prevention and Tobacco Control Act.

The health conscious consumer also presents stiff resistance to RAI. From increased scientific studies and research on the influence of tobacco to innumerable anti-smoking groups, the obstacles are significant.

With heavy consideration given to these encumbrances, the management team of RAI must develop a very focused strategy to overcome these obstacles. Despite some difficult societal economic hardships, RAI has demonstrated consistent financial results. Considering the challenges within the industry, RAI's approach to sustainability across its brands must be continued. With firm strategic initiatives and strong management leadership, RAI will continue to be a powerful company, capable of long-term success.

NOTES

1. Centers for Disease Control and Prevention. 22 Feb 2011. *The Tobacco Use Epidemic Can Be Stopped.* Accessed 19 May 2011. http://www.cdc.gov/chronicdisease/resources/publications/aag/osh.htm

2. *Smoke: A Global History of Smoking.* (2004). Edited by Sander L. Gilman and Zhou Xun. London: Reaktion Books.

3. US Food and Drug Administration. *Frequently Asked Questions: Protecting Kids from Tobacco.* Accessed 28 Jun 2011. http://www.fda.gov/TobaccoProducts/ProtectingKidsfromTobacco/RegsRestrictingSale/ucm204589.htm#ACT

4. Reynolds American Fact Sheet. Accessed 19 May 2011. http://files.shareholder.com/downloads/RAI/0x0x278558/d3bee8ad-b2bb-47f6-9a2a-df9f1bee8182/FactSheet.pdf

5. Reynolds American, Inc. Form 10-K for the fiscal year ended 12/31/10. Accessed 23 Feb 2011. http://www.reynoldsamerican.com/secfiling.cfm?filingID=950123-11-16932

6. F. Ross Johnson. Wikipedia search results. Accessed 24 May 2011. http://en.wikipedia.org/wiki/F._Ross_Johnson

7. RJR Nabisco. Wikipedia search results. Accessed 24 May 2011. http://en.wikipedia.org/wiki/RJR_Nabisco

8. Funding Universe. *R. J. Reynolds Tobacco Holdings, Inc.* Accessed 26 Apr 2011. http://www.fundinguniverse.com/company-histories/RJ-Reynolds-Tobacco-Holdings-Inc-Company-History.html

9. Reynolds American, Inc. Form 10-K for the fiscal year ended 12/31/10. *op. cit.*

10. Gorham, P., CFA; Morningstar Investment Research Center - Reynolds American, Inc. RAI Thesis 04-25-2011 http://library.morningstar.com/stocknet/MorningstarAnalysis.aspx?Country=USA&Symbol=RAI

11. Reynolds American, Inc. Form 10-K for the fiscal year ended 12/31/10. *op. cit.*

12. Reynolds American CEO discusses Q4 2010 results - Earnings call transcript. 3 Feb 2011. Accessed 26 Apr 2011. http://seekingalpha.com/article/250625-reynolds-american-ceo-discusses-q4-2010-results-earnings-call-transcript

13. *Ibid.*

14. Gorham, P., CFA; *op. cit.*

15. RJ Reynolds Buys Conwood; Are Altria and UST Next? (RAI, UST, MO). 27 Apr 2006. Accessed 26 May 2011. http://seekingalpha.com/article/9643-rj-reynolds-buys-conwood-are-altria-and-ust-next-rai-ust-mo.

16. Reynolds American CEO discusses Q4 2010 results - Earnings call transcript. *op. cit.*

17. *Ibid.*

18. Gorham, P, CFA; *op. cit.*

19. Google Finance. *Reynolds American, Inc.* Accessed 26 May 2011. http://www.google.com/finance?q=rai

20. Reynolds American, Inc. Form 10-K for the fiscal year ended 12/31/10. *op. cit.*

21. Altria Group, Inc. 2010 Annual Report. Accessed 25 Feb 2011. http://phx.corporate-ir.net/External.File?item=UGFyZW50SUQ9ODg4Nzl8Q2hpbGRJRD0tMXxUeXBlPTM=&t=1

22. *Ibid.*

23. *Ibid.*

24. Lorillard 2010 Annual Report. Accessed 24 Feb 2011. http://phx .corporate-ir.net/External.File?item=UGFyZW50SUQ9ODg0OTB8 Q2hpbGRJRD0tMXxUeXBlPTM=&t=1

25. *Ibid.*

26. Centers for Disease Control and Prevention. *Economic Facts About US Tobacco Production and Use.* Accessed 23 May 2011. http://www .cdc.gov/tobacco/data_statistics/fact_sheets/economics/econ_facts/

27. World Health Organization. 2002. *Tobacco Atlas.* Accessed 23 May 2011. http://www.who.int/tobacco/resources/publications/ tobacco_atlas/en/index.html

28. Gorham, P., CFA; *op. cit.*

29. Centers for Disease Control and Prevention. *Economic Facts About US Tobacco Production and Use. op. cit.*

30. Springen, K. 21 May 2008. *Modern Outcasts.* http://www .newsweek.com/2008/05/20/modern-outcasts.html

31. Saad, L. 26 Aug 2010. *Adult Smoking Ranges from 13% to 31% Across US States.* Gallup. Accessed 24 Jun 2011. http://www.gallup .com/poll/142694/Adult-Smoking-Ranges-Across-States.aspx

32. Economic and Social Development Department. 2003. Food and Agricultural Organization of the United Nations. *Issues in the Global Tobacco Economy.* Accessed 25 May 2011. http://www.fao .org/DOCREP/006/Y4997E/Y4997E00.HTM

33. US Tobacco Cooperative. *Mission Statement.* Accessed 25 May 2011. http://www.ustobaccofarmer.com/mission.htm

34. International Tobacco Grower's Association. *Who We Are and What We Do.* Accessed 25 May 2011. http://www.tobaccoleaf.org/ conteudos/default.asp?ID=7&IDP=2&P=2

35. Reynolds American, Inc. Form 10-K for the fiscal year ended 12/31/2007. Form 10-K for the fiscal year ended 12/31/2008. Form 10-K for the fiscal year ended 12/31/2009. Form 10-K

36. for the fiscal year ended 12/31/2010. Accessed 23 Feb 2011. http://www.cleanlungs.com/settlement/leaves.html

Ibid.

37. Seeking Alpha. *Company Description, Reynolds American Inc. (RAI).* Accessed 20 May 2011. http://seekingalpha.com/symbol/rai/ description

38. Berman, D. 18 Apr 2011. *They call it the evil weed, but returns sure are good.* The Globe and Mail (Canada) via Tobacco.org. Accessed 18 Apr 2011. http://www.tobacco.org/news/318587 .html

39. *Ibid.*

40. Wilson, J. J. March 1999. *Summary of the Attorneys General Master Tobacco Settlement.* Accessed 22 Feb 2011. http:// academic.udayton.edu/health/syllabi/tobacco/summary.htm

41. Joe the Camel. Wikipedia search results. Accessed 21 May 2011. http://en.wikipedia.org/wiki/R._J._Reynolds_Tobacco _Company#Joe_Camel

42. Reynolds American, Inc. Form 10-K for the fiscal year ended 12/31/2007. *op. cit.*

43. Berman, D. *op. cit.*

44. Seeking Alpha. *op. cit.*

45. *Ibid.*

46. Reynolds American, Inc. Form 10-K for the fiscal year ended 12/31/2007. *op. cit.*

47. Seeking Alpha. *op. cit.*

48. Reynolds American, Inc. Form 10-K for the fiscal year ended 12/31/10. *op. cit.*

49. Gorham, P., CFA; *op. cit.*

50. Reynolds American, Inc. Form 10-K for the fiscal year ended 12/31/10. *op. cit.*

51. *Ibid.*

52. *Ibid.*

The Entrepreneurs at Twitter: Building a Brand, a Social Tool or a Tech Powerhouse?[1]

Ryan McVay/Getty Images

Ken Mark, Simon Parker

Richard Ivey School of Business

The University of Western Ontario

IVEY

Richard Ivey School of Business
The University of Western Ontario

Introduction

On April 9, 2011, a technology analyst working for a large Canadian bank was looking at Twitter as part of her analysis for an industry note on emerging technologies. Twitter is a micro-blogging service that allows subscribers to send "tweets" of 140 characters or less to their "followers." It is regarded as one of the hottest technology companies since Google and Facebook, and been cited as being an influential factor in socio-political events such as Senator Barack Obama's U.S. presidential campaign, as well as in political protests in Iran, and the uprisings in Egypt and Algeria in 2011.

But Twitter's user numbers had fallen to 24 million by the end of 2009 after having peaked at 29 million in mid-2009. About half of Twitter's user base came from the United States.[2] The analyst wondered whether the drop in users was a blip or whether it signalled that Twitter needed to revisit its marketing strategy. After all, the service had attained its current level of popularity based on referrals, extensive (and free) media coverage, and the fact that it employed an open source platform, which encouraged the development of third-party applications by others.

Although Twitter's user numbers have continued to grow steadily, rising from 29 million in mid-2009 to nearly 200 million by March 2011, the company is still some way from making a profit.[3] Furthermore, despite receiving $200 million in its latest round of venture capital financing in December 2010, valuing the company at approximately $3.7 billion by February 2011, its business model and strategy remain opaque. It was true that 2010 witnessed some revenue-raising initiatives, including "promoted tweets" (whereby companies advertise their products based on keyword matching); but it was equally clear that Twitter had barely begun to commercially exploit its large and rapidly growing user base. The analyst also wondered about the implications of the ongoing changes in the top management team, which were taking on something of a "revolving door" character.

There continued to be much speculation over what the company would eventually adopt as a moneymaking business model, but Twitter was silent on specifics. Speaking about Twitter's business model, Ray Valdes, an analyst with Gartner Inc. commented:

They have a dilemma. On the one hand, they need a robust revenue model. But they are also aware their perceived value is that they have a lot of potential. The moment they say one thing about their revenue model, whatever they choose will have a few limitations and risk associated with it. And that will diminish their perceived value.[4]

Twitter had an ambitious goal of reaching one billion users and earning more than $1 billion in net income by 2013. The analyst wondered what steps the company needed to take to achieve those targets in three years.

Company—Origins

Twitter founder's Evan Williams's early background hinted at the entrepreneurial path he would take. As a teenager growing up in Nebraska, he preferred the mental challenge of coming up with great business ideas to the physical demands of hunting or farming. Bored with university, he did not focus on a major and dropped out without completing his degree. He moved from job to job, pursuing entrepreneurial ideas on the side, but he struggled to follow through on any of his early projects, discarding them as soon as a more alluring idea emerged. "It was turning into a constant pattern," recalled Williams.[5]

Looking to restart his career in 1996, Williams took a marketing job in Marin County before progressing to writing software code for large companies such as Intel and Hewlett-Packard. "For the first time, I learned what it was like to work in an office and have a normal career. To be in real meetings. I also learned that I did not want to do that," added Williams.[6]

In August 1999, several years before Twitter was founded, Williams and his friends were working as IT contractors on web projects during the day and thinking about their own Internet startup on the side. While in the midst of creating what they believed would be a much-sought after technology, they veered off-course on a whim, and ended up creating a landmark service that allowed Internet users to disseminate information to others, in real-time. With just a handful of employees, the company raised a small amount of venture capital and started releasing new versions of technology for free in order to build traction with users. As they reached a million users, competitors started to emerge. Less than four years after it started, the company had not yet generated any significant revenue and was not close to turning a profit. Even so, Google offered to buy it in exchange for stock, and Williams accepted the offer.

That company was Pyra Labs, the firm behind the blog creation tool Blogger.com, which was started in August 1999 and sold to Google in 2003. One of the business partners working on Blogger.com was Christopher Isaac "Biz" Stone, a fellow programmer whom Williams had met online. Stone had dropped out of college, lured by the prospect of designing book covers at Little, Brown Book Group. Soon after, he learned to write software code and design websites.[7]

Despite the fact that Pyra Labs had a willing buyer in Google, some observers were skeptical of the deal. Danny Sullivan of Search Engine Watch, for example,

in an article entitled "Google Buys Blogging Company – But Why?" speculated that "one chief reason Google has done this is for ad distribution reasons,"[8] which implied that Blogger.com, on its own, would not be profitable.

Williams stayed with Google until October 2004, and then launched a podcasting firm named Odeo, Inc. Podcasting—a play on the words "iPod" and "broadcasting"—i.e., the practice of recording and releasing digital media files via the web.

With just five people working from a walk-up apartment in San Francisco, Odeo's objective was to build a profitable company by building an "all-in-one system that makes it possible for someone with no more equipment than a telephone to produce podcasts," and "for users to assemble custom playlists of audio files and copy them directly onto MP3 audio players."[9] Williams commented: "Odeo aims to enable this new distribution channel and medium by creating the best one-source solution for finding, subscribing to, and publishing audio content."[10]

Once again, many observers were skeptical. A journalist commented in the *New York Times*:

The question for Odeo, and for the many other entrepreneurial efforts almost certain to come, is whether there is any money to be made from podcasting. Recall that the dot-com boom was full of start-ups betting on one or another notion of the Web's potential. But for every felicitous pairing like Google and keyword searching, there were dozens of broken marriages like Pets.com and online dog food sales.[11]

Williams was undeterred as he saw huge potential in the podcasting industry. His excitement about the Odeo project and his belief that podcasting would become the next great technological medium convinced him to stay put on this particular path.[12]

Soon after Odeo shipped its major product, Odeo Studio, deep-pocketed competitors such as Apple, Inc. started to enter the market. In early 2006, faced with poor prospects for the company's future, Odeo's board of directors requested that Odeo revamp its strategy. It was during this period that one of Odeo's employees, an engineer called Jack Dorsey, presented an idea to the team that was based around a service that would enable users carrying standard cellular phones to update small groups of people on their current situation by pressing a few buttons and tapping out a message. The key insight was that users would not need to enter the address of each recipient separately, every single time a message was to be sent. All the user had to do was enter a short numerical code before beginning the message. Odeo decided to adopt Dorsey's idea, initially for internal usage. At first, Odeo's team members kept the testing of the service close – no one affiliated with a large firm was allowed to participate in the test. By the spring of 2006, "Twttr Beta" was launched.

But Odeo's board was hard pressed to see the relevance of Twttr Beta and chose to conserve cash by trimming headcount. Six employees had their contracts terminated. Even so, on the midst of this turmoil, Twttr. com was made available to the public.

In an attempt to put more focus on this new project, Stone, Williams, Dorsey and their team set up Obvious Corp. in October 2006 to acquire the Twttr project. The URL www.twitter.com was acquired and the team rebranded the service.

Twitter: How It Works

Twitter can be described as an easy-to-use, micro-blogging application, instant messenger or social presence notifier.[13] It is essentially a broadcasting system that allows users to transmit short bursts of information to lots of strangers as well as to friends. Twitter is built on open source software and allows users to send and receive messages to a mailing list of recipients ("followers") in real-time. Followers log on to Twitter and add themselves to an author's list of followers. To send a message to their list of followers, authors type in 140-character messages ("Tweets") via Twitter's website, by SMS (short message service) from cell phones, through an IM (instant messaging) client, through an RSS (really simple syndication) feed, or through third-party webtools. Authors can restrict their subscription lists to selected subscribers, or they can leave it open, which allows anyone to sign up to read their Tweets.

The original product name or codename for the service was "twttr," inspired by Flickr and the fact that American SMS short codes were five characters. From a technology perspective, Twitter is a web interface created using an "open source web application framework" called Ruby on Rails,[14] and using Starling as the primary message queue server.[15] Cell phone users can tweet using SMS, typing in one of five short telephone numbers—known as short codes—used to address SMS messages. There are short codes for the United States, Canada, India and New Zealand and an Isle of Man-based number for international use.

The developers initially experimented with "10958" as a short code, but they later changed it to "40404"[16] for "ease of use and memorability."[17] Dorsey explained why the name "twitter" was chosen:

The working name was just "Stat us" for a while. It actually didn't have a name. We were trying to name it, and mobile was a big aspect of the product early on. . . . We liked the SMS aspect, and how you could update from anywhere and receive from anywhere.

We wanted to capture that in the name—we wanted to capture that feeling: the physical sensation that you're buzzing your friend's pocket. It's like buzzing all over the world. So we did a bunch of name-storming, and we came up with the word "twitch," because the phone kind of vibrates when it moves. But twitch is not a good product name because it doesn't bring up the right imagery. So we looked in the dictionary for words around it, and we came across the word "twitter" and it was just perfect. The definition was "a short burst of inconsequential information," and "chirps from birds." And that's exactly what the product was.[18]

Twitter is not a proprietary technology, as it offers the option of integrating other applications or web services with Twitter via an application programming interface (API).[19] APIs, which allow third-party software developers to build programs to interface with Twitter's data, were introduced by Twitter in September 2006.

An observer described how Twitter differed from online chat forums:

We've all chatted online before – reserved our handle, entered a chatroom, and started messaging away. Well, there are two problems with chat in that form. First, the chatroom is (usually) filled with strangers, and second, you must be logged into the chatroom to have access to messages. Twitter is essentially a net-based chatroom filled with your friends.[20]

Twitter also differs from Facebook, which has rapidly become the world's largest social networking site, counting over 600 million users worldwide by January 2011.[21] Facebook users can communicate with each other only by mutual consent, whereas anyone can log into Twitter and sign up to view any public tweets they like. Another difference between the two tools is that Facebook allows people to exchange videos and photos, whereas Twitter remains essentially text-based. For this reason, Stone has said that he sees a greater affinity between Twitter and Google than with Facebook, describing his business as an "information company."

Promoting the Service

For the first six months of Twitter's existence, the company relied on its original users to become "personal evangelists" for the service.

By April 2007, Twitter.com was spun out of Obvious Corp. as its own company. A big break for the new Twitter came in March 2007, in Austin, at the South by Southwest festival. There, participants were able to see their tweets flash across television screens in real time. The number of tweets tripled to 60,000 per day, as participants talked about the service and the bloggers in attendance wrote about it.

Williams and his team were pleasantly surprised that their service was a hit. Referring to Twitter, he stated: "It took us a while to figure that it was a big deal."

Stone added: "I found myself watching groups of people twittering each other to coordinate their actions—which bar to go to, which speech to attend—and it was like seeing a flock of birds in motion."[22]

Building on the success at South by Southwest, Twitter added new features to its product such as RSS feeds and integration with IM. Each feature that was added boosted the number of users and usage per user.[23]

Over the next year and a half, Twitter's service was mentioned numerous times in the media. In addition, adoption of the service by new users came as a result of word-of-mouth promotion. As Twitter added employees, its founders marvelled at the growing complexity of the organization. Stone stated: "We've never had a company that grew past 15 to 20 people. We're kind of excited about that."[24] The rapid growth of Twitter brought its own problems, however, with several server crashes raising questions about the reliability of the service. More recently, these problems have been largely ironed out.

Organizations began to take note of Twitter's potential to reach out to a more technologically savvy audience. The service was especially valuable to small companies, with limited budgets, looking to gain recognition in the marketplace. With Twitter, these small firms could reach out and provide updates to a growing list of followers. Within larger organizations, there was the potential for managers to update and coordinate groups of employees. However, managers were aware of the downside as well—employees could be spending unnecessary amounts of time on the service.

Twitter gained in usage during the 2008 U.S. presidential campaign and was cited as a key tool during the 2008 attacks in Mumbai, India. During the Iranian presidential election, the popularity of Twitter as a tool used by protesters grew; participants relied on the service to coordinate their movements and to send message to the world outside Iran. Reliance on the service grew to such a point that Twitter delayed a 90-minute maintenance shutdown following a request from the U.S. State Department to keep the service available for the Iranian protesters.[25] Since 2009, Twitter has constantly been in the news. There were publicity stunts initiated by users, such as Ashton Kutcher's challenge to CNN in a "Twitter popularity contest,"[26] and a Twitter name charity auction for "@drew," which attracted a US$1 million bid from comedian Drew Carey if he reached one million followers by the end of 2009.[27] And Twitter has continued to play an important role politically, for example during the "Arab Spring" uprisings in early 2011 in Tunisia and Egypt.

Venture Capital Invests in Twitter

Seeking to capitalize on what seemed to be the next Google or Facebook, investors injected a total of $155 million into Twitter in 2009. Some investors in Twitter included Institutional Venture Partners, Benchmarks Capital, Union Square Ventures, Spark Capital, Digital Garage, Bezos Expeditions and Insight Venture Partners, among others. This round of financing, completed at the end of September 2009, valued the company at US$1 billion. Following on from this, in December 2010, another $200 million of venture capital was injected into Twitter, valuing the company at about $3.7 billion by February 2011.[28] The valuation of Twitter has risen further since then, to as much as $10 billion, fueled by rumours that the company could be bought by Facebook or Google.[29] That is despite Evan Williams and Dick Costolo, the company's CEO, repeatedly insisting that Twitter is not for sale.

Twitter's founders wanted to ensure that they had enough funds to continue building the company and supporting the millions of users who were using the service. Williams stated: "It was important to us that we find investment partners who share our vision for building a company of enduring value. Twitter's journey has just begun, and we are committed to building the best product, technology and company possible."[30]

David Garrity, principal of GVA Research LLC, stated: "It's interesting to see, almost 10 years since we had the first Internet bubble, that we've now got billion-dollar valuations on companies that haven't defined how they're going to monetize their traffic. It would be nice to see how the company is going to, one, generate revenues, and two, generate profits."[31]

Ellen Siminoff, a former Yahoo! Inc. executive who co-founded the education Web site Shmoop University Inc., disagreed, saying: "Where you have audiences, you will make money."[32]

Todd Chaffee, a Twitter board member and general partner at Institutional Venture Partners, one of Twitter's investors, suggested that e-commerce was an avenue the company could explore:

Commerce-based search businesses monetize extremely well, and if someone says, "What treadmill should I buy?" then you, as the treadmill company, want to be there. As people use Twitter to get trusted recommendations from friends and followers on what to buy, e-commerce navigation and payments will certainly play a role in Twitter monetization. Over time, Twitter will develop filters to help users manage and classify their tweet streams into useful categories, such as tweets from friends, family, celebrities, news organizations, charities.[33]

Co-founder Stone suggested that Twitter would begin adding services for businesses to generate fees in the fourth quarter of 2009. At a Twitter management team meeting in April 2009, the team discussed licensing tweets to partners: "We can give people stuff for free, but not forever."[34] This was followed in April 2010 by a public announcement that Twitter would launch "promoted tweets." Promoted tweets allow advertisers to insert themselves in the stream of real-time conversations on Twitter, based on their relevance to the subject matter being discussed. Several companies signed up to advertise in this way, including Best Buy, Virgin America, Starbucks and Bravo.

A range of other opportunities beckon for Twitter. A role model might be Skype, an Internet telephone service that offers users "free and great value" calls. Skype has gained in popularity by offering users free Internet calls, and has now started to charge fees for certain connections while retaining free Skype-to-Skype calls. Skype has gained a critical mass of users and sold itself to eBay in 2005 for US$2.6 billion in up-front cash and eBay stock, and performance-based options.[35] By 2009, Skype was thought to be generating approximately US$600 million a year in revenues. That year, eBay changed its strategy, selling a controlling stake in Skype in a deal that valued the service at US$2.75 billion in 2009.

Twitter's Business Model—Still in Question

Documents uncovered by hackers and posted on TechCrunch, with Twitter's (reluctant) approval, revealed, among other things, that Twitter was aiming to be more than just a micro-blogging service. It was aiming at one billion users by 2013—a "user" as being "a unique individual having a conscious twitter experience in a given week."[36] The types of revenue models being talked about were still very broad: business-to-business services; e-commerce, especially retailing recommended products; and advertising. Twitter also expected to employ 5,200 people by 2013 (from 450 people by March 2011) and earn $1.1 billion on revenues of US$1.54 billion,[37] $4 million in revenues by the end of 2009, and $62 million by the end of 2010 (see Exhibit 1). Twitter, according to reports, had exceeded its 2009 revenue target by signing a non-exclusive deal with Google and Microsoft to provide these companies' search engines with access to real-time Twitter feeds. Based on an estimated value of $25 million in revenue from Microsoft and from other search deals, Twitter could have turned profitable in 2009.[38] Actual 2010 outcomes have been estimated to be $45 million in revenue, with a probable loss; the latest projections are of $100 million-$110 million in revenues in 2011.[39]

The technology analyst wondered how the company planned to ramp up revenues and profits to more than

$1 billion by 2013. For a better idea of which path the firm was likely to take, the analyst referred back to an internal Twitter document that talked about how the firm perceived and defined itself. In addition, the document described, in point form, how Twitter wanted to differentiate itself from its closest competitors, Facebook and Google (see Exhibit 2).

The analyst suspected that Twitter would be eventually pressured by its investors to deliver a return on investment, even though Twitter's founders did not seem to have an urgent need to develop a financial plan as they believed they had patient investors. Recognizing that the company had cash in the bank, Stone stated: "We are enamored with the idea of going all the way." Williams added: "We want to have as large an impact as possible."[40]

But even as the team was trying to find ways to generate revenues, Williams revealed to a journalist that he was already thinking of his next "big" idea—how to revolutionize e-mail.[41] For his part, Dorsey (let go as CEO in 2008) was pursuing a side-venture called Square, which sought to enable everyone to accept credit card payments for online commerce.

What Will Twitter's Future Look Like?

Despite the continuing growth in the number of users, not all has been well at Twitter. First, Twitter continues to suffer from high abandonment rates among users, being as high as 40 percent.[42] Second, there has been organizational turbulence. For example, Jack Dorsey was replaced as CEO in 2008 by Evan Williams, with Dorsey becoming chairman. Two years later, Williams was replaced by former COO Dick Costolo, with Williams focusing on product strategy. In March 2011 Dorsey returned to Twitter full-time to lead product development. Rumours abound about the working relationships between Dorsey and Williams.

Third, competitors had started to emerge, offering functionality that was unavailable from Twitter. For example, Friendfeed allowed users to send text messages as well as import information from their blogs, Flickr photos, and YouTube videos. Identi.ca, another micro-blogging service, made its source code freely available, allowing users to create their own micro-blogging service. Present.ly, which was designed specifically for businesses, allows companies to create their own micro-blogging network on its service and separate users into groups.[43]

In an attempt to win market share in this growing space, larger, more established companies have rolled out free services as well. In 2008, Facebook attempted to purchase Twitter for $500 million in Facebook stock,

357

Case 24: The Entrepreneurs at Twitter: Building a Brand, a Social Tool, or a Tech Powerhouse?

but Twitter's management team rejected the offer. After these takeover talks were abandoned, Facebook introduced several Twitter-like changes to its service, including updating users' home pages to allow them to provide real-time updates to friends. Facebook also gave more visibility to its pages for celebrities and other high-profile figures and lifted the ceiling on the maximum number of online fans they could have on the site.

Finally, in early February 2010, Google launched a Twitter competitor called "Google Buzz," which, among other things, allowed users to post updates in real time by using their mobile phones.[44] Google earned the bulk of its income from selling advertising and made no money from Google Buzz. Twitter aimed to enlist developers in creating applications for its service by highlighting its open source philosophy. In February 2010, Twitter launched a directory of all the open source projects on which Twitter employees were working or contributing.[45]

The technology analyst sat down at her desk and sifted through the rest of the news reports on Twitter. She switched on her computer and started to write down some conclusions about Twitter's potential impact and the challenges the firm could face as it tried to fend off other firms encroaching on its space. She wanted to make an educated guess at what the company's service represented to users, its likely business strategy, and how it planned to survive in the long-run.

Exhibit 1 Twitter's Forecast Financials as Posted on TechCrunch

	2009				2010			
	Q1	Q2	Q3	Q4	Q1	Q2	Q3	Q4
Users in millions	8	12	16	25	35	48	72	100
Revenue	$0	$0	$400,000	$4,000,000	$8,000,000	$17,000,000	$53,000,000	$62,000,000
Total Yearly				$4,400,000				$140,000,000
Number of Employees	30	45	60	78	120	197	275	345
				Target: 65				Target: 500
People Costs	$1,050,000	$1,575,000	$2,100,000	$2,730,000	$4,200,000	$6,895,000	$9,625,000	$12,075,000
Organization Costs	$2,030,000	$3,045,000	$4,060,000	$6,343,750	$8,881,250	$12,180,000	$18,270,00 0	$25,375,000
Gross Margin	$43,950,000	$39,330,000	$33,570,000	$28,496,250	$23,415,000	$21,340,000	$46,445,000	$70,995,000
Net Earnings	$28,567,500	$25,564,500	$21,820,500	$18,522,563	$15,219,750	$13,871,000	$30,189,250	$46,146,750

Exhibit 2 What's Twitter, the Company?

- Facebook – social network
- Google – search engine
- Twitter is for discovering and sharing what is happening right now (Do other people describe Twitter in this way?)
- Twitter is the most varied communication network.
- Twitter introduced a new form of communication to the world.
- Twitter is an index to my friends' thoughts and I subscribe to that.
- The way to find out what's happening
- The way to share what's happening
- Google is "old news"

Source: http://www.techcrunch.com/2009/07/16/twitters-internal-strategy-laid-bare-to-be-the-pulse-of-the-planet/, accessed March 2, 2010.

NOTES

1. This case has been written on the basis of published sources only. Consequently, the interpretation and perspectives presented in this case are not necessarily those of Twitter or any of its employees.

2. http://www.cnn.com/2010/TECH/01/26/has.twitter.peaked/index.html?hpt=C1, accessed March 5, 2010.

3. Nicholas Carlson, "Twitter Valued At $7.8 Billion In Private Market Auction," *Business Insider via San Francisco Chronicle*, March 4, 2011,Hearst,http://www.sfgate.com/cgi-bin/article.cgi?f=/g/a/2011/03/04/businessinsider-twitter-valued-at-78-billion-in-privatemarket-auction-2011-3.DTL, accessed March 26, 2011.

4. http://www.marketwatch.com/story/teens-arent-into-twitter-but-they-love-facebook-2010-02-09?reflink=MW_news_stmp, accessed February 9, 2010.

5. http://online.wsj.com/article/SB124000817787330413.html, accessed March 2, 2010.

6. Ibid.

7. Ibid.

8. http://searchenginewatch.com/2165221, accessed October 15, 2009 and http://www.blogger.com/about, accessed October 15, 2009.

9. http://www.nytimes.com/2005/02/25/technology/25podcast.html?_r=1, accessed July 15, 2009.

10. http://evhead.com/2005/02/how-odeo-happened.asp, accessed July 15, 2009.

11. http://www.nytimes.com/2005/02/25/technology/25podcast.html?_r=1, accessed July15, 2009.

12. http://evhead.com/2005/02/how-odeo-happened.asp, accessed July 15, 2009.

13. http://dev.aol.com/article/2007/04/definitive-guide-to-twitter, accessed November 15, 2009.

14. http://www.techcrunch.com/2008/05/01/twitter-said-to-be-abandoning-ruby-on-rails/, accessed November 15, 2009.

15. http://www.artima.com/scalazine/articles/twitter_on_scala.html, accessed November 23, 2009.

16. "40404" is the U.S. short code.

17. Dom Sagolla, (2009-01-30). "How Twitter Was Born," 140 Characters, http://www.140characters.com/2009/01/30/howtwitter-was-born/, accessed June 25, 2009.

18. David Sano, (2009-02-18), "Twitter creator Jack Dorsey illuminates the site's founding document," *Los Angeles Times*, http://latimesblogs.latimes.com/technology/2009/02/twitter-creator.html, accessed September 15, 2009.

19. http://apiwiki.twitter.com/Things-Every-Developer-Should-Know, accessed November 15, 2009.

20. http://dev.aol.com/article/2007/04/definitive-guide-to-twitter, accessed November 15, 2009.

21. "Goldman To clients: Facebook Has 600 Million Users," MSNBC, January 5, 2011. http://www.msnbc.msn.com/id/40929239/ns/technology_and_science-tech_and_gadgets/, accessed January 15, 2011.

22. http://online.wsj.com/article/SB124000817787330413.html, accessed March 2, 2010.

23. http://www.140characters.com/2009/01/30/how-twitter-was-born/, accessed Mary 2, 2010.

24. http://online.wsj.com/article/SB124000817787330413.html, accessed March 2, 2010.

25. Andrew LaVallee, (2009-06-15). "Web Users in Iran Reach Overseas for Proxies," *The Wall Street Journal*, http://blogs.wsj.com/digits/2009/06/15/web-users-in-iran-reach-overseas-for-proxies/, accessed June 16, 2009; and Mike Musgrove, (2009-06-17), "Twitter Is a Player In Iran's Drama," *The Washington Post*, http://www.washingtonpost.com/wp-dyn/content/article/2009/06/16/AR2009061603391.html?hpid=topnews, accessed July 09, 2009.

26. http://www.cnn.com/2009/TECH/04/15/ashton.cnn.twitter.battle/index.html

27. http://mashable.com/2009/10/07/drew-carey-twitter-bid/, accessed October 15, 2009.

28. Nicholas Carlson, "Twitter Valued At $7.8 Billion In Private Market Auction," *Business Insider via San Francisco Chronicle*, March 4, 2011, Hearst, http://www.sfgate.com/cgi-bin/article.cgi?f=/g/a/2011/03/04/businessinsider-twitter-valued-at-78-billion-in-private-market-auction-2011-3.DTL, accessed March 26, 2011.

29. http://www.telegraph.co.uk/technology/twitter/8315851/Twitter-could-be-bought-by-Facebook-or-Google.html, accessed April 16, 2011.

30. http://blog.twitter.com/2009/09/new-twitter-funding.html

31. http://www.bloomberg.com/apps/news?pid=20601087&sid=aPAHFu.jBrhM

32. http://www.bloomberg.com/apps/news?pid=20601087&sid=aPAHFu.jBrhM

33. http://bits.blogs.nytimes.com/2009/06/19/twitter-plans-to-offer-shopping-advice-and-easy-purchasing/

34. http://www.techcrunch.com/2009/07/16/twitters-internal-strategy-laid-bare-to-be-the-pulse-of-the-planet/

35. http://about.skype.com/2005/09/ebay_to_acquire_skype.html, accessed March 2, 2010.

36. http://www.techcrunch.com/2009/07/16/twitters-internal-strategy-laid-bare-to-be-the-pulse-of-the-planet/, March 2, 2010.

37. Adapted from http://www.techcrunch.com/2009/07/15/twitters-financial-forecast-shows-first-revenue-in-q3-1-billion-users-in2013/.

38. http://www.marketwatch.com/story/teens-arent-into-twitter-but-they-love-facebook-2010-02-09?reflink=MW_news_stmp, accessed February 9, 2010.

39. Nicholas Carlson, Nicholas, "Twitter Valued At $7.8 Billion In Private Market Auction," *Business Insider via San Francisco Chronicle*, March 4, 2011, Hearst, http://www.sfgate.com/cgi-bin/article.cgi?f=/g/a/2011/03/04/businessinsider-twitter-valued-at-78-billion-in-private-market-auction-2011-3.DTL, accessed March 26, 2011.

40. http://online.wsj.com/article/SB124000817787330413.html, accessed March 2, 2010.

41. Ibid.

42. Stefanie Hoffman, "Twitter Quitters Outnumber Those Who Stay, Report Finds," United Business Media, April 29, 2009, http://www.crn.com/security/217200834;jsessionid=0AQSMPNH52QRQQSNDLOSKHSCJUNN2JVN, accessed April 29, 2009

43. http://news.cnet.com/8301-17939_109-10120401-2.html, accessed February 9, 2010.

44. http://news.cnet.com/8301-30684_3-10449662-265.html, accessed February 9, 2010.

45. http://techcrunch.com/2010/02/16/twitter-open-source/, accessed March 2, 2010.

Ryan McVay/Getty Images

Tara L. Ceranic

Richard Ivey School of Business

The University of Western Ontario

Richard Ivey School of Business
The University of Western Ontario

Lorenzo Fertitta, chief executive officer (CEO) and co-owner of the Ultimate Fighting Championship (UFC), walked into the empty Acer Arena in Sydney, Australia, sat down next to the Octagon in which the fights take place, and thought about how far the UFC had come in only a few short years. From an unsanctioned mêlée to a regulated sport, mixed martial arts (MMA) grew immensely in popularity in the United States, and the Australian fanbase was also clearly excited for the pay-per-view (PPV) event that was about to take place. The Acer Arena would soon be filled with more than 17,000 screaming fans waiting to see live fights in the Octagon. UFC 110 (Nogueira versus Velasquez) sold out in record time and the Australian fans could not wait, but would the rest of the world be this open to the UFC?

After an incredibly successful event in Australia, Fertitta had a lot to think about on his long flight back to Las Vegas. Should he pursue other international locales for similar live pay-per-view events? Could the UFC find success and support for this type of combat-based entertainment in other areas of the world? Would different cultures be willing to accept the sport or would there simply be too much of a cultural gap between various audiences? In other words, was the UFC a culturally viable business venture in new locations around the globe? Fertitta needed to consider a great deal of information in order to determine his course of action.

The History of the Ultimate Fighting Championship

Mixed martial arts had existed since the original Olympic Games in Athens. The sport was originally called *pankration,* a word that combines two Greek words: *pan,* meaning "all," and *kratos,* meaning "powers."[1] Opponents used a combination of Hellenic boxing and wrestling and fought using any and all of their abilities until one participant was knocked unconscious or raised his hand to signal defeat.[2]

The popularity of *pankration* declined over the years as other combat sports developed in different areas of the world; the West favoured wrestling and the East saw a rise in the popularity of more traditional martial arts.[3] In the 1930s, a form of MMA called *vale tudo* (meaning "anything goes") rose to prominence in Brazil. *Vale tudo* matches were shown on television and took place in martial arts studios. The sport eventually made its way to the United States thanks to Rorion Gracie. Gracie was a member of the renowned Gracie jiu-jitsu family, often thought of as the founders of MMA in Brazil and a significant influence on the transmission of MMA to the United States.

MMA's popularity developed steadily over the years and in 1993 the UFC was founded by Rorion Gracie, Art Davie and Bob Meyrowitz, president of Semaphore Entertainment Group (SEG), a corporation that specialized in arranging live PPV sporting events.[4] Considering the variety of martial arts forms and varied techniques within each (see Exhibit 1), the founders of the UFC wanted to determine which was ultimately superior. They began pitting opponents of different styles against one another in a no-holds-barred tournament in order to find "the Ultimate Fighting Champion." The early marketing of the UFC "unapologetically peddled the burlesque of violence, the rage, the blood, even the chance of death."[5]

This marketing approach caused many to question the organization and ethics of such a sport. The first six UFC events had no time limits, no weight classes, no mandatory safety equipment and very few rules. Observers assumed that "You'd have to have a death wish—or at least be a little unhinged—to put yourself in that arena."[6] These initial tournaments drew a great deal of negative attention as well as supportive fans. Many claimed that it was too violent; Senator John McCain, an avid boxing fan, famously remarked that the UFC was "barbaric," "not a sport" and likened it to "human cockfighting."[7]

McCain spearheaded a campaign to ban the UFC: he wrote letters advocating his views on the sport to the governors of all 50 states and many agreed that the sport was too violent.[8] Mayors across the country held press conferences and announced that Ultimate Fighting was not welcome in their towns; as a result, the UFC was banned in New York State and lawsuits blocked it in other areas as well.[9] "The thirty-six member-states in the Association of Boxing Commissions unanimously agreed to ban no-holds-barred fights"[10] and the Nevada Athletic Commission would not sanction UFC bouts. UFC sponsorship was rejected on particular television stations that had previously only denied advertisements for the Ku Klux Klan,[11] and many venues would not rent their facilities to the organization.[12] UFC's PPV options also faced difficulty when, in 1997, John McCain employed the power of the Federal Communications Commission (FCC), of which he was a member, and pressured cable companies to remove UFC events from their offerings.[13] Dana White, UFC president, voiced his opinion: "Just to be totally clear: you could order porn on pay-per-view no problem," but UFC was not allowed.[14]

Faced with pressure from many sources, Davie and Gracie sold their shares in UFC in 1995, leaving Meyrowitz alone at the helm of SEG. In 2001, with mounting legal fees and difficulties at every turn, the final original owner of the UFC decided to cut his losses and sell the organization.

Zuffa, LLC

When brothers Frank and Lorenzo Fertitta purchased the UFC for US$2 million in January 2001, they also established Zuffa, LLC.[15] In Italian, the word *zuffa* means "to fight": the brothers decided this would be an apt name for the sports management company they founded in Las Vegas.[16] Initially, the Fertittas seemingly acquired little more than "a trademark, some unpaid bills and a few fighters' contracts."[17] The purchase appeared to be more of a fun diversion than a business, as the brothers' original ownership contract included the following dispute-resolution clause: "In order to resolve a deadlock among [board] members, Frank and Lorenzo shall engage in a jiu-jitsu match."[18]

Although sometimes viewed as an overnight success after its purchase by the Fertittas, the UFC "continued to bleed money, with losses approaching $40 million in 2004."[19] At one point, the Fertittas considered selling to avoid losing their family's investments, but the only buyer offered $4 million and they decided to carry on and attempt to expand the organization instead.[20]

Frank Fertitta

In addition to his involvement with Zuffa, in 2011 Frank Fertitta was the chief executive officer and chairman of the board for Station Casinos, the casino operation founded by his father. Frank attended the University of Southern California where he obtained a bachelor's degree in Arts and Sciences. He held various positions within Station Casinos such as general manager and chief operating officer. Due to his involvement with Station Casinos, Frank held a privileged gaming license in Nevada[21] and, along with his brother, made Station Casinos into the fifth-largest gaming company in the United States.

Lorenzo Fertitta

In 2011, Lorenzo Fertitta was the CEO of Zuffa, LLC. Lorenzo obtained a bachelor's degree in Business Administration from the University of San Diego and an MBA from the Stern School of Business at New York University. In 1993, he worked as an executive at Fertitta Enterprises, a private financial services organization, and dealt primarily with managing investment portfolios consisting of various marketable securities and properties. Lorenzo also held a privileged gaming license in Nevada and was involved as an active member on the board of directors for Station Casinos.

Lorenzo appreciated MMA as a sport and, due to his business education, he knew how to make it appeal to a larger audience. In 2008, Lorenzo stepped down as an active member of the board for Station Casinos and became full-time CEO of Zuffa to increase his involvement with the UFC.

Dana White

Dana White was born in Manchester, Connecticut, but attended high school in Las Vegas where he met the Fertitta brothers. He studied at the University of Massachusetts for two years, but dropped out to pursue his passion: boxing. He stated that he loved boxing for its lack of pretension:

Two guys. One winner. One loser. . . . No spin. The rich guys didn't have an advantage, no matter how many roman numerals came after their name or what kind of car they had parked outside.[22]

Moving from job to job, White continued to train as an amateur boxer until 1992 when he decided that his career as a fighter was not promising enough to continue. He settled in Las Vegas, created a sports management company (Dana White Enterprises), and opened three gyms where he trained boxers.

White's connections through Dana White Enterprises led him to meet two emerging MMA fighters: Tito Ortiz and Chuck Liddell.[23] While managing Oritz, White was introduced to his former manager, Bob Meyerwitz, president of Semaphore Entertainment Group, then owner of the UFC.[24] Meyerwitz told White that the struggling UFC was searching for a buyer and White quickly contacted Frank and Lorenzo Fertitta.

After the purchase by the Fertittas, White was named president of the UFC.[25] According to Zuffa management, White was not only the face of the organization, but part of the UFC brand. A popular figure with the public, White had more than 1.1 million followers on Twitter in early 2011, 125,000 followers subscribed to his YouTube videos and he was even nominated as one of Time Magazine's 100 most influential people of 2010.

Regulation of UFC

After the purchase of the UFC, Zuffa's first priority was legitimizing MMA as a sport. They intended to clean up the image created by the company's former owners, marketing the UFC not as a fight to the death competition, but rather, as "an incredible sport with amazing athletes."[26]

Their vision relied on ensuring that the UFC was organized, regulated and controlled.[27] According to Bruce Buffer, announcer for all UFC events, "sanctioning provides a legitimization for the sport," and the Zuffa team was determined to have a sport that was regulated and legitimized.[28]

In order to legalize the sport so that it could reach a wider audience, Zuffa asked states to regulate MMA. Much like boxing, MMA needed government regulations and specific rules that all fighters followed within the Octagon. Requesting regulation was rarely done, and Zuffa had to invest a great deal of time and money to get the process underway. Zuffa created a department devoted to regulatory issues, and its executive vice-president and general counsel, Lawrence Epstein, hired additional regulatory consultants. Through these efforts, Zuffa streamlined the process of being regulated. Rather than starting from scratch in every state, Zuffa representatives presented each state with the plan for regulation that had worked in other states.

A large part of this regulatory process focused on the fact that Zuffa established rules for the Octagon (see Exhibits 2 and 3). Based partially on the rules of boxing, bouts were no longer untimed and weight classes were established. Due to these regulations, a five-year study (2002–2007) of injury trends in sanctioned MMA fights found that there were no critical injuries to any of the fighters involved in the study, and that the most common injuries were lacerations and upper extremity injuries.[29] The authors determined that "injury rates in regulated professional MMA competition [were] similar to other combat sports; the overall risk of critical sports-related injury appear[ed] low."[30]

As of January 2011, MMA was regulated in almost every U.S. state with the exception of Connecticut, Vermont and New York. With the regulation of MMA came approval from some surprising sources: in 2007, John McCain was quoted as saying that the UFC "have cleaned up the sport to the point, at least in my view, where it is not human cockfighting anymore."[31]

Zuffa Acquisitions

In addition to the purchase of UFC, Zuffa also acquired three large former competitors. In March of 2011, Zuffa purchased Strikeforce, formerly their largest competitor. Strikeforce began as a kickboxing organization in 1985, but became involved with MMA in 2006. It signed several popular fighters[32] and was the only organization that staged female bouts. Its events were not PPV and were available on Showtime and CBS, depending on the event. After the purchase, Dana White commented that, "Strikeforce [was] going to continue to run business as usual."[33] This included keeping Strikeforce management in place and fulfilling all Strikeforce contracts.

World Extreme Cagefighting (WEC) was founded in 2001 and focused on lighter weight classes; Zuffa purchased WEC in October 2006, and combined the organizations by including the WEC weight classes in UFC bouts in October 2010. White commented on this acquisition: "It's time, as we continue to grow globally—we're doing enough fights to fold this thing into the UFC."[34]

Pride Fighting Championships (Pride FC) was founded in Japan in 1997, and held more than 60 extremely popular MMA events.[35] In May 2007, Zuffa purchased Pride FC from Dream Stage Entertainment in Tokyo with the initial agreement that the organizations would remain legally independent entities with separate management. In October 2007, however, after senior Pride FC management refused to submit to background investigations, they were let go and Zuffa's management took control of the organization. As of March 2011, Zuffa was utilizing Pride FC's valuable library of MMA content on Spike TV's broadcast, *The Best of Pride Fighting Championships.*

Viewer Demographics

The primary viewing demographic of the UFC was thought to be men aged 18 to 34[36]; however, the organization purported to market to everyone. According to Lorenzo Fertitta, the UFC attempted to be family friendly and, although it did not necessarily target children, it ensured that its broadcasts were censored. Swearing was removed from televised events and the "UFC Octagon Girls" wore what the organization described as "athletic attire" rather than bikinis.[37]

Zuffa also made attempts to broaden the reach of the UFC, especially with African-American and Hispanic audiences. White insisted, "I don't care what color you are or what language you speak, we're all human beings and fighting is in our DNA."[38] This sentiment seemed to resonate with the fighters as well. Shonie "Mr. International" Carter was an African-American fighter and former Marine who began fighting in the UFC in 2000. He commented:

I don't see myself as a racial athlete, so fans don't see me as one either. I don't care if you're black, white, green, or blue. I'm gonna hit you the same way: hard and frequently. I'm going to kick you, choke you, and manipulate your joints. Then I'm gonna shake your hand and buy you a drink, because I respect you for getting in that cage![39]

Many popular fighters came from African-American and Hispanic communities,[40] and Zuffa wanted to increase their viewership within these demographics. It attempted to reach these groups by partnering with musical artists that were popular with African-American and Hispanic audiences, such as 50 Cent and LL Cool J.[41] According to White:

Originally, when the sports [media] wouldn't cover us, Hollywood did. Entertainers always want to be athletes, and athletes want to be entertainers. All the stuff we're doing with 50 Cent is giving us exposure because he's reaching out to his fans and letting them know what he's doing.[42]

For example, UFC 91 (2008) promoted a new 50 Cent single and premiered the music video—which starred several UFC fighters—during the event.

Furthermore, in March 2010, the first-ever UFC PPV (UFC 111) event was presented entirely in Spanish.[43] Announcers Troy Santiago and Victor Davila welcomed fans to the event, provided commentary and conducted interviews inside the Octagon for Hispanic fans all over the United States and Mexico. In October 2010 (UFC 121), Cain Velazquez, a Mexican-American heavyweight fighter, became the UFC Heavyweight Champion, which further increased UFC's exposure to the Spanish-speaking audience.

Marketing

Zuffa reached out to UFC fans in a variety of ways (see Exhibit 4). Its primary outlet was PPV events; however, between 2001 and 2008, attendance at UFC events rose by 400 percent.[44] These events occurred between 12 to 14 times per year and were the largest revenue generator for the organization.[45] With word of mouth and rapidly increasing popularity, PPV purchases took the growth of the company to the next level. In 2008, UFC generated an estimated 5,000,000 PPV purchases; in fact, UFC PPV numbers rivaled and often surpassed those of other combat sports such as boxing and professional wrestling (see Exhibit 5).

In order to reach an even larger audience, Zuffa designed a reality-based television program called *The Ultimate Fighter* (TUF). The winner of each season earned a six-figure contract as a fighter with the UFC. The show aired on Spike TV and helped propel the sport further into mainstream consciousness: "In just one season of television, TUF had done what 10 years of lobbying could not do: it had legitimized mixed martial arts."[46] With consistently high ratings, TUF became a major hit, showing fighters before, during and after their bouts in the Octagon. Zuffa also used its partnership with Spike TV to help create shows that centered primarily on upcoming PPV events. The UFC Countdown show focused on the fighters in the main event as well as the two fighters paired in the co-main event, highlighting their training camps and personal lives with the aim of gaining new viewers for the PPVersus.

Zuffa developed an assortment of other marketing outlets that collectively promoted its PPV events. In

2009, a highly successful video game, *UFC Undisputed*, was launched. The game was so popular that a new version was created and launched in 2010. Zuffa utilized the video game to promote upcoming PPV events by changing the writing on the mat (floor) of the Octagon in the game: players saw a different message depending on the upcoming PPV event.

UFC merchandise was another successful aspect of generating revenue. Zuffa focused on the distribution of clothing online and in sporting goods stores. The organization developed action figures of prominent fighters that were distributed as collectibles; only select fighters were released at a given time. The UFC also opened three gyms in California that focused primarily on MMA training to those interested in learning more about the sport; a UFC magazine debuted in August 2009 as well.

Popular social media applications were also a way for Zuffa to promote the UFC. Management and fighters utilized Twitter, Facebook and iPhone applications to keep fans up to date on the latest news of the UFC and its fighters. The interaction between fighters and fans via these applications increased brand awareness and dedication. According to Zuffa management, if it were possible, it would encourage its fighters to "tweet" between rounds from the Octagon.[47] Managers encouraged fighters to post video blogs in order to spark interest in upcoming fights and White published his own video blogs before fights.

The pre-fight weigh-ins were used as another tool to gain the interest of fans. These weigh-ins were broadcast live on the UFC website so that fans could log on and become part of the fight atmosphere. Preliminary PPV fights were also aired on Spike TV. The organization selected two or three fights to broadcast an hour before the fight aired: this allowed for last-minute anticipation surrounding the fights and drew PPV purchases from viewers who might not have planned to purchase originally.

Previous Internationalization of Sports

In the past, other American-based sports management organizations had made the choice to enter into international markets. This was a difficult transition for any organization to make, but the cultural components embedded in sports made it exceptionally challenging in some cases. Some sports were met with a great deal of success abroad, while others were forced to retire permanently from the international scene.

Baseball

Perhaps the sport with the greatest amount of success related to internationalization was baseball. Major League Baseball (MLB) drew players from around the world,[48] and countries such as the Dominican Republic, Cuba, China, Japan, Venezuela, Puerto Rico and Panama adopted the sport as part of their cultures. Many MLB teams had internationally based camps and academies that developed local talent. Competition for entrance to these training camps was fierce: in some of these countries, economic distress was common and baseball was viewed as a rare opportunity to achieve wealth and success in the United States.

National Football League (NFL)

In the early 1980s, British television station Channel 4 played a weekly American football highlight show that garnered surprisingly high ratings.[49] The number of British viewers of the program steadily increased and, in 1991, the NFL founded the World League of American football (WLAF), a professional American football organization slated to play games in North America, Europe and Asia.[50] The league had teams from across Europe[51] and for several years it drew large crowds everywhere they played. However, the league was inconsistent: there were constant league name changes, season-long hiatuses and a roster of teams that changed from season to season which caused the international interest in American football to dwindle. In June 2007, NFL Europa (formerly WLAF) officially ceased operations.[52] Even without the presence of NFL Europa, fans of American football still existed in the United Kingdom. Due to their interest, the Super Bowl continued to be broadcast on British television, and London hosted an NFL game every year since 2007.

Boxing

Important boxing matches typically took place within the United States; however, on the first two occasions that popular American boxers participated in bouts abroad, the response was enormous. The first event was the *Rumble in the Jungle* fight, held in Zaire (Democratic Republic of the Congo) on October 30, 1974. It pitted then heavyweight champion George Foreman against Muhammad Ali. A year later, the *Thrilla in Manila* match took place in the Philippines on October 1, 1975, featuring Muhammad Ali and Joe Frazier fighting for the Heavyweight Boxing Champion of the World title. Although internationalization was not built into the framework of boxing, these two events became key components of the sport's history. Both bouts were consistently included not only in lists of top boxing matches, but also in records of the best sporting events in general. The decision to internationalize for particular fights brought the sport worldwide recognition and made its fighters household names across the globe.

UFC Internationalization

Since 1996 (San Juan, Puerto Rico: UFC 9), the UFC has been holding international events. However, beginning in 2008, the organization began to increase its international presence with events in Canada (UFC 115, 124), the United Kingdom (UFC 95, 120), Australia (UFC 110, 127) and Germany (UFC 99, 122) to name a few. Fertitta was at the forefront of the UFC's international expansion. Zuffa established television deals to bring the UFC to a multitude of locations around the world. In 2011, UFC programming reached more than 416 million households worldwide via 12 channels in Europe, nine channels in Asia, two in Australia, four in South America and three channels in the Middle East and North Africa.[53] Additionally, in September 2010, the UFC reached a deal with FOX Sports en Latinoamerica to broadcast programming to Argentina, Chile, Colombia, Ecuador, Paraguay, Peru, Uruguay and Venezuela.[54]

In January 2010, Zuffa sold a 10 percent stake of the UFC to an Abu Dhabi–based live events company called Flash Entertainment.[55] Flash was a wholly owned subsidiary of the Government of the Emirate of Abu Dhabi, and ties to Flash allowed the UFC to penetrate new markets. Zuffa management hoped that this relationship would provide the UFC with more exposure in the Middle East and throughout Asia.[56]

Potential International UFC Markets

With successful live PPV events in several international locations, Zuffa needed to assess the cultural viability of entering into further new markets abroad. Without a thorough understanding of where the UFC would be culturally acceptable, the financial viability of the venture would be in jeopardy. At the top of the company's list of possibilities were some areas of the world quite unlike those in which the UFC was already popular. In order to evaluate the viability of the UFC in these locations, Zuffa needed to consider the fundamental cultural elements of each locale.

China

China's growing gross domestic product (GDP),[57] along with its 1.3 billion inhabitants, made it an appealing market for business organizations, but many companies discovered that tapping into the Chinese market presented unique obstacles. The cultural differences often proved challenging for American companies, as Chinese business etiquette was quite different from that of the United States. As a single-party state, the ruling Communist Party of China further complicated entrance into the Chinese market for international representatives. In China, "political control [was] dependent on economic growth, and economic growth require[d] the modernization of information technologies, which in turn ha[d] the potential to undermine political control."[58]

Chinese culture was often described as being collectivist, meaning that individual needs were typically given lower priority than the needs of a community (family, work, team, etc.). There was strong emphasis on traditional Chinese values of trust and patience in business relations, though inequality of power and wealth existed within society, particularly within business organizations.[59] The Chinese were said to have an attitude of perseverance and a different attitude toward time because they viewed trust and patience as crucial components to any business agreement.[60] Members of Chinese culture were unwilling to enter into business dealings without an established relationship, and completing business agreements in China could take up to four times as long as elsewhere.[61]

In the past, Chinese consumers were often wary of outside cultural influences.[62] One exception to this was the Chinese athlete Yao Ming, an international basketball sensation. Ming's connection to China fostered the popularity of basketball within the nation. However, the growth of the Chinese economy created an urban middle class that had the potential to instigate a cultural shift in favour of non-Chinese brands. These individuals were demanding Western luxury goods and had a significant amount of expendable income.[63] Considering the rich history of martial arts in China, Zuffa speculated that the new middle class may be persuaded to take an interest in the UFC and its merchandise as a way to combine their culture with their developing consumerism. As of January 2011, the UFC did not have any signed or up-and-coming Chinese fighters to forge this relationship.

Beginning in January 2010, UFC events were available via live stream on Sohu.com, China's equivalent to Yahoo Sports.[64] Sohu was the official partner of the NBA, ESPN, Adidas and Sports Illustrated in China, which made it a good fit for the UFC.[65] Sohu Sports did not have its own web page or area for the UFC; instead, UFC coverage was combined with pages on the Chinese martial arts Kungfu and Sanda. To combat this lack of coverage, Zuffa established a Chinese-language UFC website and an office in China in July 2010.

India

Like China, India was a rapidly developing area of the world, with a 2010 GDP growth rate of 8.6 percent and a population of more than one billion; also similar to China, this large population was incredibly economically diverse. Indian culture was often perceived as being very open to new ideas and having fewer rules and regulations than many other countries in the area, which allowed for the development of an entrepreneurial spirit.[66]

Wrestling was very popular in India. Many Indians engaged in and watched traditional wrestling, known as Kushti, in which fighters grappled in a clay or dirt pit using judo and jiu-jitsu technique. Professional wrestling had a significant following in India as well: in 1996, The Great Khali became the first Indian professional wrestler to be signed by World Wrestling Entertainment (WWE).[67] Due to his size (over seven feet tall), fame as Mr. India (1995 and 1996) and appearance in Hollywood and Bollywood films, The Great Khali had many fans in India and around the world.

In contrast, many Indians had not been exposed to MMA, and the UFC did not have a presence in India as of January 2011. Nevertheless, there seemed to be budding interest in MMA as a sport. Fights took place across India, and a business called Tigers Gym called itself the "home of mixed martial arts in India."[68] A 2009 story from Indian news network IBN reported that some Indians viewed MMA as second only to cricket as a sport that could provide the opportunity for Indian athletes to become professionals.[69] As of early 2011, there were no Indian fighters in the UFC, yet India had a rich tradition of martial arts practice and hand-to-hand combat as sport.

South Korea

South Korea's economy grew rapidly since the 1960s, and the country was so industrialized that it was thought to be "the most wired nation on the planet."[70] Although its population was less than 50 million, South Korea was a G-20 major economy, a member of the Organization for Economic Co-operation and Development (OECD), ranked 12th in the world in purchasing power parity[71] and was a fully functioning modern democracy.[72] In December 2010, the United States finalized a trade deal with South Korea that was estimated to bring approximately US$10 million dollars of American exports to the country.[73] South Korea's president Lee Myung-bak said that "[t]he accord is significant because it lays the groundwork for a 'win-win' relationship by reflecting the national interests of Korea and the United States in a balanced manner."[74]

South Korea had an inflexible labour market and had faced previous economic challenges, fostering a cultural preference for security rather than uncertainty.[75] Making business connections in South Korea was a process similar to doing so in China: it was imperative to have personal connections. Third-party introductions were crucial to beginning new business ventures.[76]

Martial arts had been popular in South Korea for more than 2,000 years and were cited as one of the most recognizable cultural aspects of the country.[77] Taekwondo began as a military training technique but had gone on to become the national sport of South Korea and was instituted as an Olympic sport in 2000. It was widely practiced around the world and had been called the "world's most popular martial art."[78] In addition to taekwondo, Koreans practiced the martial art of hapkido, which combined the use of weapons with more traditional martial arts defenses such as kicks and punches.

Since 2008, South Korea had a major representative in the UFC: Dong Hyum Kim, a welterweight from Busan, fought six UFC bouts with a combined record of 13 wins, zero losses, one draw and one no-contest. Chan Sung Jung, "The Korean Zombie," was slated to make his UFC debut in 2011, representing Po-Hang, South Korea. In addition to having fighters in the UFC, South Korea was home to two budding MMA promotion organizations: Spirit MC and Road Fighting Championship, both of which seemed to be having success despite previous South Korean MMA events being plagued with difficulties.[79] South Korea was also home to numerous gyms that trained elite MMA fighters.

The cultures of China, India and South Korea were each unique, yet shared some common traits. In order for the UFC to broaden its reach globally, the organization had to determine if the cultural profiles of these countries were suitable for the expansion of the sport.

Thoughts for the Flight

After watching the successful events in Australia, Lorenzo settled into his seat on the flight back to Las Vegas. He had the next 20 hours to contemplate the next steps for the UFC. Considering the history of the UFC and the challenges that cultural differences presented to sports-related organizations abroad, could he make a case for the UFC's cultural viability in these potential international markets? Should he move forward with pursuing these international locales for live PPV events, or was it best to continue holding events where there was already a large fanbase?

Exhibit 1 Types of Martial Arts Used in Mixed Martial Arts

	Origin	Main components(s)	Meaning/nickname
Boxing	Greece	Punching	Sweet science
Jiu-Jitsu	India, China, Japan, Brazil (BJJ)	Chokeholds, joint locks	Gentle art
Capoeira	Brazil	Acrobatics, feints, leg sweeps, takedowns	Wild grass cut short
Grappling	Greece	Clinches, submissions, takedowns	
Hapkido	Korea	Joint locks, kicks, punches	Way of coordinating energy
Karate	Japan	Elbow strikes, kicks, knee strikes, locks, punches	Empty hand
Muay Thai	Thailand	Elbow strikes, kicks, knee strikes, locks, punches	Art of eight limbs
Sambo	Russia	Leg locks, submissions, throwing	Self-defense without weapons
Sumo	Japan	Pushing, pulling, sweeping, tugging	To mutually rush at
Taekwondo	Korea	Kicks, punches	The art of the foot and the fist
Wrestling	Greece	Joint locks, pins, takedowns, throws	

Exhibit 2 UFC Bout Fouls

1. Butting with the head.
2. Eye gouging of any kind.
3. Biting.
4. Hair pulling.
5. Fish hooking.
6. Groin attacks of any kind.
7. Putting a finger into any orifice or into any cut or laceration on an opponent.
8. Small joint manipulation.
9. Striking to the spine or the back of the head.
10. Striking downward using the point of the elbow.
11. Throat strikes of any kind, including, without limitation, grabbing the trachea.
12. Clawing, pinching or twisting the flesh.
13. Grabbing the clavicle.
14. Kicking the head of a grounded opponent.
15. Kneeing the head of a grounded opponent.
16. Stomping a grounded opponent.
17. Kicking to the kidney with the heel.
18. Spiking an opponent to the canvas on his head or neck.
19. Throwing an opponent out of the ring or fenced area.
20. Holding the shorts or gloves of an opponent.
21. Spitting at an opponent.
22. Engaging in an unsportsmanlike conduct that causes an injury to an opponent.
23. Holding the ropes or the fence.
24. Using abusive language in the ring or fenced area.
25. Attacking an opponent on or during the break.
26. Attacking an opponent who is under the care of the referee.
27. Attacking an opponent after the bell has sounded the end of the period of unarmed combat.
28. Flagrantly disregarding the instructions of the referee.
29. Timidity, including, without limitation, avoiding contact with an opponent, intentionally or consistently dropping the mouthpiece or faking an injury.
30. Interference by the corner.
31. Throwing in the towel during competition.

Source: UFC.com, ND (original document extraction), www.ufc.com/about/Rules, accessed September 25, 2010.

Exhibit 3 Ways to Win

1. Submission by:

    Physical tap out, verbal tap out.

2. Technical knockout by the referee stopping the contest.

3. Decision via the scorecards, including:

    Unanimous decision [all judges pick the same fighter as the winner].

    Split decision [One judge picks one fighter, the other two judges pick the other fighter].

    Majority decision [Two of three judges pick the same fighter as the winner, the final judge says the fight was a draw].

    Draw, including:

    > Unanimous draw,
    > Majority draw,
    > Split draw.

4. Technical decision.

5. Technical draw.

6. Disqualification.

7. Forfeit.

8. No contest.

Source: UFC.com, ND (original document extraction), www.ufc.com/about/Rules, accessed September 25, 2010.

Exhibit 4 UFC'S Brand Control

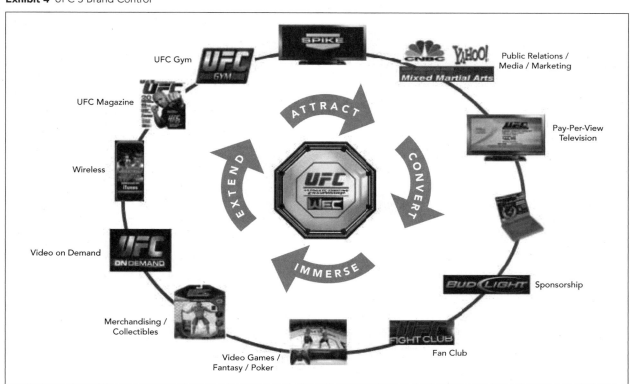

Source: K. Hendrick, "UFC," PowerPoint presentation courtesy of Zuffa, LLC., 2009.

Exhibit 5 Top PPV Purchases 2009

1. **UFC 100:** Brock Lesnar versus Frank Mir, July 11, 1.6 million
2. **Boxing:** Manny Pacquiao versus Miguel Cotto, Nov. 14, 1.25 million
3. **Boxing:** Floyd Mayweather Jr. versus Juan Manuel Marquez, Sept. 19, 1.05 millon
4. **UFC 94:** Georges St. Pierre versus B.J. Penn, Jan. 31, 920,000 buys
5. **UFC 101:** Penn versus Kenny Florian/Anderson Silva versus Forrest Griffin, Aug. 8, 850,000
6. **Boxing:** Pacquiao versus Ricky Hatton, May 2, 825,000
7. **UFC 107:** Penn versus Diego Sanchez, Dec. 12, 650,000
8. **UFC 97:** Silva versus Thales Leites/Chuck Liddell versus Mauricio Rua, April 18, 650,000
9. **UFC 99:** Lyoto Machida versus Rashad Evans/Matt Hughes versus Matt Serra, May 23, 635,000
10. **Wrestling:** WWE WrestleMania 25, April 5, 582,000 buys

Source: Dave Meltzer, "UFC remains king of PPV hill," Yahoo! Sports, February 15, 2010, http://sports.yahoo.com/mma/news?slug=dm-ppvbiz021510, accessed December 5, 2010 (original document extraction).

NOTES

1. Donald F. Walter Jr., "Mixed Martial Arts: Ultimate Sport, or Ultimately Illegal?" *GrappleArts*, 2003, www.grapplearts.com/Mixed-Martial-Arts-1.htm, accessed December 4, 2010.
2. Ibid.
3. Ibid.
4. Ibid.
5. L. Jon Wertheim, *Blood in the Cage: Mixed Martial Arts, Pat Miletich, and the Furious Rise of the UFC*, Mariner Books, Boston, MA, 2009, p. 95.
6. Sam Sheridan, *A Fighter's Heart: One Man's Journey Through the World of Fighting*, Grove Press, New York, 2007, p. 333.
7. MMA conspiracy theorists suggested that, as a longtime boxing fan, McCain saw UFC as a threat to his favorite sport and that this spurred his comments (Wertheim, 2009, 97).
8. David Plotz, "Fight Clubbed," *Slate*, November 17, 1999, www.slate.com/id/46344, accessed December 5, 2010.
9. L. Jon Wertheim, *Blood in the Cage: Mixed Martial Arts, Pat Miletich, and the Furious Rise of the UFC*, Mariner Books, Boston, MA, 2009, p. 95.
10. Ibid, 94.
11. David Plotz, "Fight Clubbed," *Slate*, November 17, 1999, www.slate.com/id/46344, accessed December 5, 2010.
12. Ibid.
13. L. Jon Wertheim, *Blood in the Cage: Mixed Martial Arts, Pat Miletich, and the Furious Rise of the UFC*, Mariner Books, Boston, MA, 2009, p. 95.
14. Ibid, 139.
15. Daniel Schorn, "Mixed Martial Arts: A New Kind Of Fight," *CBS News*, July 29, 2007, www.cbsnews.com/stories/2006/12/08/60minutes/main2241525_page2.shtml, accessed September 25, 2010.
16. Donald F. Walter Jr., "Mixed-Martial Arts: Ultimate Sport, or Ultimately Illegal?," *GrappleArts*, 2003, www.grapplearts.com/Mixed-Martial Arts-1.htm, accessed December 4, 2010.
17. L. Jon Wertheim, *Blood in the Cage: Mixed Martial Arts, Pat Miletich, and the Furious Rise of the UFC*, Mariner Books, Boston, MA, 2009, p. 145.
18. Ibid, 145.
19. Ibid, 151.
20. Ibid, 145.
21. A privileged gaming license means that the Fertittas have gone through an extensive investigation by the Nevada Gaming Control Board that assessed their personal and financial histories. This license holds the Fertittas to a high standard of behaviour, and the license can be revoked should they engage in any illegal activities. The license also means that the Fertittas must be sure that UFC activities are all above board so as not to impact the standing of Station Casino's license.

22. L. Jon Wertheim, *Blood in the Cage: Mixed Martial Arts, Pat Miletich, and the Furious Rise of the UFC*, Mariner Books, Boston, MA, 2009, p. 141.
23. In January 2011, Liddell was named executive vice-president of Business Development for UFC.
24. E. Carmichael, "How Dana White Launched the UFC," *YoungEntrepreneur.com*, October 14, 2008, www.youngentrepreneur.com/blog/uncategorized-blog/how-dana-white-launched-the-ufc/, accessed January 17, 2011.
25. At the time, White owned 10 per cent and the Fertitta brothers owned 90 per cent.
26. Steve Cooper, "Meet UFC President Dana White," *Entrepreneur.com*, June 21, 2007, www.entrepreneur.com/startingabusiness/successstories/article180692.html, accessed December 5, 2010.
27. http://www.ufc.com/about/History, ND accessed October 12, 2008.
28. Donald F. Walter Jr., "Mixed Martial Arts: Ultimate Sport, or Ultimately Illegal?," *GrappleArts*, 2003, www.grapplearts.com/Mixed-Martial-Arts-1.htm, accessed December 4, 2010.
29. Ka Ming Ngai, Frederick Levy, Edbert B. Hsu, "Injury Trends in Sanctioned Mixed Martial Arts Competition: A Five-Year Review 2002–2007," *British Journal of Sports Medicine*, 42 (2008), pp. 686–689.
30. Ibid, 686.
31. Michael David Smith, "UFC President Dana White: 'I Consider John McCain the Guy Who Started the UFC,'" *MMAFighting.com*, June 22, 2008, www.mmafighting.com/2008/06/22/ufc-president-dana-white-i-consider-john-mccain-theguy-who-st/, accessed December 4, 2010.
32. Fedor Emelianenko, Alistair Overeem, Andrei Arlovski and Cung Le, for example.
33. Staff, "UFC Purchases Strikeforce; UFC Boss Says Organizations to Operate Independently," MMAjunkie.com, March 12, 2011, http://mmajunkie.com/news/22807/ufc-purchases-strikeforce.mma, accessed March 30, 2011.
34. Ken Pishna, "UFC-WEC Merger: UFC's Major Announcement," *MMAWeekly.com*, October 28, 2010, http://mmaweekly.com/ufc-announcement-ufc-and-wec-merger-mma, accessed December 4, 2010.
35. Pride FC holds the record for the largest live MMA audience of more than 70,000 people at the Pride and K-1 coproduction, Shockwave/Dynamite, held in August 2002 (Ivan Trembow, "UFC 68 breaks North American attendance record," MMAWeekly.com, March 15, 2007, http://mmaweekly.com/ufc-68-breaks-north-american-attendance-record-2, accessed September 25, 2010.
36. According to Tony Ponturo, Anheuser-Busch vice-president of global media and sports marketing, its research shows 76 per cent of male beer drinkers between the ages of 21-27 are fans of the UFC (David Sweet, "How upstart UFC crushed its competition,"

MSNBC, November 5, 2008, www.msnbc.msn.com/id/27562254, accessed on December 5, 2010.).

37. Personal communication, 2009.

38. George Willis, "UFC out to attract the African American market," ESPN.com, December 26, 2008, http://sports.espn.go.com/extra/mma/news/story?id=3792904, accessed on December 5, 2010.

39. L. Jon Wertheim, *Blood in the Cage: Mixed Martial Arts, Pat Miletich, and the Furious Rise of the UFC*, Mariner Books, Boston, MA, 2009, p. 163.

40. Rashad Evans, Quinton "Rampage" Jackson, Kimbo Slice, Tito Ortiz, Diego Sanchez, Miguel Torres and Cain Velasquez, to name only a few.

41. George Willis, "UFC out to attract the African-American market," *ESPN.com*, December 26, 2008, http://sports.espn.go.com/extra/mma/news/story?id=3792904, accessed September 25, 2010.

42. Ibid.

43. This event was also broadcast in French for the Canadian audience.

44. HR&A Advisors, "Economic Impacts of the Ultimate Fighting Championship," Prepared for Zuffa, LLC, 2009.

45. "Ultimate Fighting Championship," *UFC.com*, http://www.ufc.com/about/History.accessed October 15, 2009.

46. L. Jon Wertheim, *Blood in the Cage: Mixed Martial Arts, Pat Miletich, and the Furious Rise of the UFC*, Mariner Books, Boston, MA, 2009, p. 189.

47. Personal communication, 2009.

48. Approximately 30 per cent of the players in the Major Leagues are from outside of the United States (*U.S. Department of State* "The Internationalization of Baseball," March 3, 2009, www.america.gov/st/texttransenglish/2009/March/20080414085218opnativel0.8558161.html, accessed on September 25, 2010.).

49. Elie Ofek, David B. Godes and Peter Wickersham, "NFL UK," *Harvard Business Publishing, Cambridge*, MA, 2010.

50. Paul Johns, "History of NFL Europe," OurSportsCentral.com, March 3, 2000, www.oursportscentral.com/services/releases/?id=2707565, accessed on September 12, 2010.

51. Germany, England, Scotland, The Netherlands.

52. Martin Gough, "NFL move marks end of an era," *BBC*, June 30, 2007, www.bbc.co.uk/dna/606/A24302044, accessed September 12, 2010.

53. K. Hendrick, "UFC," PowerPoint presentation courtesy of Zuffa, LLC, 2009.

54. John Paul Vill, "Dana White: UFC will Officially Broadcast in en Latinoamérica," *FightingInsider.com*, September 26, 2010, www.fightinginsider.com/2010/09/26/dana-whiteufc-will-officially-broadcast-in-en-latinoamerica/, accessed December 4, 2010.

55. The new ownership split: Frank Fertitta, 40.5 per cent; Lorenzo Fertitta, 40.5 per cent; Flash, 10 per cent; Dana White, nine per cent.

56. Jonathan Snowden, "The Fertitta Files: The UFC Eyes China as Next Break Through Market," *BloodyElbow.com*, June 9, 2010, www.bloodyelbow.com/2010/6/9/1506620/thefertitta-files-the-ufc-eyes, accessed December 4, 2010.

57. As of June 2010, the GDP growth rate for China was 11.9 per cent.

58. Greg Walton, "Executive Summary," *China's Golden Shield: Corporations and the Development of Surveillance Technology in the People's Republic of China*, International Centre for Human Rights and Democratic Development, 2001, p. 5.

59. Eric Yee, "Doing Chinese Business Based On Hofstede," @rticles.com, http://ezinearticles.com/?Doing-ChineseBusiness-Based-On-Hofstede&id=797967, accessed December 4, 2010.

60. Geert Hofstede, *Culture's Consequences: Comparing Values, Behaviors, Institutions, and Organizations Across Nations*, 2nd ed., Sage Publications, Thousand Oaks, CA, 2001.

61. Eric Yee, "Doing Chinese Business Based On Hofstede," @rticles.com, http://ezinearticles.com/?Doing-Chinese-Business-Based-On-Hofstede&id=797967, accessed December 4, 2010.

62. Jonathan Snowden, "The Fertitta Files: The UFC Eyes China as Next Break Through Market," BloodyElbow.com, June 9, 2010, www.bloodyelbow.com/2010/6/9/1506620/thefertitta-files-the-ufc-eyes, accessed December 4, 2010.

63. Diana Farrell, Ulrich A. Gersch and Elizabeth Stephenson, "The value of China's emerging middle class," *McKinseyQuarterly.com*, June 2006, www.mckinseyquarterly.com/The_value_of_Chinas_emerging_middle_class_1798, accessed December 5, 2010.

64. Jonathan Snowden, "The Fertitta Files: The UFC Eyes China as Next Break Through Market," BloodyElbow.com, June 9, 2010, www.bloodyelbow.com/2010/6/9/1506620/the-fertitta-files-the-ufc-eyes, accessed December 4, 2010.

65. Thomas Gerbasi, "China next on White's hit list," UFC.com, February 5, 2010, http://www.ufc.com/news/China-next-onWhites-hit-list-landmark deal-with-Sohu, accessed March 3, 2010.

66. Geert Hofstede, *Culture's Consequences: Comparing Values, Behaviors, Institutions, and Organizations Across Nations*, 2nd ed., Sage Publications, Thousand Oaks, CA, 2001.

67. "The Great Khali," *WWE.com*, www.wwe.com/superstars/raw/thegreatkhali/bio/, accessed January 6, 2010.

68. www.tigersgym.com, accessed December 4, 2010.

69. Michael David Smith, "A Look at MMA in India," *MMAFighting.com*, February 26, 2009, www.mmafighting.com/2009/02/26/a-look-at-mma-in-india/, accessed December 5, 2010.

70. www.pbs.org/frontlineworld/stories/south_korea802/, accessed December 5, 2010.

71. According to the OECD, "Purchasing Power Parities (PPPs) are currency conversion rates that both convert to a common currency and equalize the purchasing power of different currencies. In other words, they eliminate the differences in price levels between countries in the process of conversion" (OECD, "Purchasing Power Parities (PPP)," OECD.org, 2010, www.oecd.org/department/0,3355,en_2649_34357_1_1_1_1,00.html, accessed December 5, 2010.

72. "The World Factbook: Korea, South," Central Intelligence Agency (CIA), March 16, 2011, www.cia.gov/library/publications/the-world-factbook/geos/ks.html, accessed December 5, 2010.

73. "Background note: South Korea," U.S. Department of State, December 10, 2010, www.state.gov/r/pa/ei/bgn/2800.htm, accessed December 5, 2010.

74. Associated Press (AP), "Obama: S. Korean trade deal will help U.S. economy," *MSNBC*, December 4, 2010, www.msnbc.msn.com/id/40497926/ns/business-world_business/, accessed December 5, 2010.

75. Geert Hofstede, *Culture's Consequences: Comparing Values, Behaviors, Institutions, and Organizations Across Nations*, 2nd ed., Sage Publications, Thousand Oaks, CA, 2001.

76. "South Korea: Language, Culture, Customs and Etiquette," Kwintessential.co.uk, www.kwintessential.co.uk/resources/global-etiquette/south-korea-country-profile.html, accessed December 5, 2010.

77. "Korean Martial Arts," *KoreaOrbit.com*, www.koreaorbit.com/korea-culture/korean-martial-arts.html, accessed December 5, 2010.

78. Yeon Hwan Park and Jon Gerrard, *Tae Kwon Do: The Ultimate Reference Guide to the World's Most Popular Martial Art*, Checkmark Books, New York, NY, 1989.

79. For example, in 2005 lax regulations lead to Korea's first recorded MMA death; in 2009, all of the fighters under new MMA promotion company refused to fight due to non-payment and forced the cancellation of the show; two larger international promoters, K-1 and Dream, both backed out of events due to poor ticket sales and attendance (Chris Nelson "Road Less Traveled: Korea's Newest MMA Promotion Takes a Different Path," *Bloodyelbow.com*, October 18, 2010, www.bloodyelbow.com/2010/10/18/1759020/road-less-traveled-koreas-newest-mma-promotion-takes-a-different-path, accessed December 5, 2010).

*Mark Brewer, Brandi Chauvin, Eric Mitchell, Eric Partington, Mark Radel,
Don Riddle, Yinghong (Sara) Song, Robin Chapman, Gail Christian*

Arizona State University

Countless people each year try to come up with a "million dollar" idea. Many believe that it requires an "unfathomable" idea, but sometimes going back to the basics is the key. That's what allowed Kevin Plank, the founder of Under Armour, to achieve success. The simple impetus was to make a superior T-shirt and nothing more. It all began in 1996 when the former University of Maryland football player wished he had an undershirt that would help control the temperature of his body during a workout and not just get soggy as it soaked up his sweat. He wanted a shirt that could enhance performance rather than detract from it. As a result, Plank created a synthetic shirt made of high-tech material cut for a snug fit and designed to feel like a second skin.

Today, the technology behind Under Armour's diverse product lines for men, women, and youth is complex, but the message is simple: wear HeatGear when it's hot, ColdGear when it's cold, and AllSeasonGear between the extremes. Three fit types are available within each line: compression (tight fit), fitted (athletic fit), and loose (relaxed fit).[1] Under Armour's mission is "to make all athletes better through passion, science, and the relentless pursuit of innovation. Every Under Armour product is doing something for you; it's making you better."[2]

Under Armour's stated goal is to be "a leading developer, marketer, and distributor of branded performance products." It has successfully penetrated the sports apparel market by using the image and influence of domestic and international professional teams, collegiate teams, Olympians, and individuals. Utilizing broad-based, frequently free endorsements, and well-received publicity, Under Armour has also reached the markets of regular athletes, active outdoor enthusiasts, elite tactical professionals, and active lifestyle consumers.

Under Armour quickly become a leader in the sports apparel industry and with its widespread popularity among top-name athletes, sports programs, and teams, and today, it is arguably Nike's greatest competitor. Its "arrival" in the industry is further evidenced by a five-year compound annual growth rate of 30.5 percent and an enormous increase in operating income, from $77 million in 2008 to $112 million in 2010.[3] As of 2010, Under Armour had $1.06 billion in sales revenue, a far cry from its first year's revenue in 1996 of $17,000 (see Exhibit 1).[4]

Under Armour products are sold worldwide, with the company's headquarters located in the US (Baltimore, Maryland), European headquarters in the Netherlands, and support offices in Hong Kong and Guangzhou, China. Primary sales are achieved through wholesale distribution and licensing to distributors. Products are offered through the company's Web site and catalog, retailers (including more than 23,000 sporting goods stores worldwide),[5] and company stores in the US, Europe, Japan, Canada, South Africa, Australia, and New Zealand. Through the Under Armour Affiliate Program, Under Armour also allows approved Web sites to link to its Web site to offer Under Armour products. Commissions are paid on every click-through sale.[6] The majority of Under Armour's sales are from North America (Canada and the US) (see Exhibits 2 and 3).[7]

Under Armour operates in a highly competitive industry in which the dominant players have a significant breadth of market, making it difficult for any new company to find an entry point. The main competitors have had many years to advertise their brands and establish distribution channels, marketing agreements, and recognition. Thus, the battle for Under Armour was more akin to a marathoner hitting the wall than it was to a seventh inning stretch. Even so, Under Armour succeeded in breaking into this mature market and is no longer simply an amateur player in the sports apparel arena. The question is: "How does this company stay on top of its game?"

Case 26: Under Armour: Working to Stay on Top of Its Game

Exhibit 1 Under Armour Consolidated Statement of Income 2008 to 2010

Under Armour, Inc. and Subsidiaries Consolidated Statements of Income (In thousands, except per share amounts)	Year Ended December 31		
	2010	2009	2008
Net revenues	$1,063,927	$856,411	$725,244
Cost of goods sold	533,420	446,286	372,203
Gross profit	530,507	410,125	353,041
Operating expenses			
Selling, general and administrative expenses	418,152	324,852	276,116
Income from operations	112,355	85,273	76,925
Interest expense, net	(2,258)	(2,344)	(850)
Other income (expense), net	(1,178)	(511)	(6,175)
Income before income taxes	108,119	82,418	69,900
Provision for income taxes	40,442	35,633	31,671
Net income	$68,477	$46,785	$38,229
Net income available per common share			
Basic	$1.35	$0.94	$0.78
Diluted	$1.34	$0.92	$0.76
Weighted average common shares outstanding			
Basic	50,798	49,848	49,086
Diluted	51,282	50,650	50,342

Source: Under Armour Annual Report 2010.

Exhibit 2 Geographic Diversity

Location	Use
Baltimore, MD	Corporate headquarters
Amsterdam, The Netherlands	European headquarters
Glen Burnie, MD	Distribution facilities, 17,000-square-foot quick-turn, Special Make-Up Shop manufacturing facility, and 6,000-square-foot Factory House store
Denver, CO	Sales office
Ontario, Canada	Sales office
Guangzhou, China	Quality assurance & sourcing for footwear
Hong Kong	Quality assurance & sourcing for apparel
Various	Retail store space

Source: Under Armour Annual Report 2010.

Exhibit 3 Net Revenue by Geographic Region

(In thousands)	Year Ended December 31		
	2010	2009	2008
North America (Canada and US)	$997,816	$808,020	$692,388
Other Foreign Countries*	66,111	48,391	32,856
Total net revenues	$1,063,927	$856,411	$725,244

*Latin America, Europe, the Middle East, Africa and Asia. These operating segments did not meet the quantitative thresholds for individual disclosure as reportable segments and were combined into "Other Foreign Countries."

Source: Under Armour Annual Report 2010.

Globe: © Jan Rysavy/iStockphoto.com

History of Under Armour

As previously mentioned, when Kevin Plank was a football player, he grew tired of having to change the damp, heavy T-shirt under his jersey, so he set out to create a unique product that would meet the needs of athletes. His laboratory was his grandmother's basement in Maryland. After many prototypes, Plank created his first shirt; it was a shiny, tight shirt made of high-tech fibers that wicked away moisture and kept athletes cool, dry, and feeling "light." Plank's shirts truly did regulate athletes' body temperatures, lending to improved performance.[8]

Starting Small

Plank believed that he could make a profitable apparel business with his advanced feature shirts, so he used $20,000 of his savings and put $40,000 onto his credit cards to launch Under Armour.[9] Success was initially slow in coming, but after Plank made his first big sale to Georgia Tech University,[10] Under Armour grew rapidly.

At the end of its first year of operations, Under Armour had five lines of clothing made for every climate, and the company's operations were moved out of Plank's grandmother's basement and into a manufacturing warehouse in Maryland.

Growing into a Recognized Brand

By the late 90s, Under Armour had achieved national recognition. By 1998, it was the official supplier of performance apparel to NFL Europe. In 1999, it signed a contract to feature Under Armour in Warner Brothers movies. By 2000, only four years since its founding, Under Armour had become a globally recognized brand and was supplying performance apparel to the National Football League, National Hockey League, Major League Baseball, USA Baseball, and the US ski team as well as other professional leagues abroad.[11]

As of 2005, Under Armour was supplying over 100 NCAA Division I-A football programs and 30 NFL teams, but it was still looking for other areas to branch into within the performance apparel industry. Consequently, Under Armour introduced a loose-fit clothing line and added women's clothing to its product line.[12] Also in 2005, the company went public, seeking to sell as much as $100 million in shares of common stock. Ben Sturner, president of Leverage Sports Agency, a New York–based sports marketing firm, said, "Under Armour is no longer an up-and-coming brand. [It] [has] positioned [itself] as a real player in the industry and in the eyes of consumers in only a few years' time."[13]

During 2006, Under Armour increased its marketing initiatives by opening company owned retail and outlet stores. Plank recognized that, "You can't be a world-class athletic brand without the ability to outfit the athlete head to toe,"[14] so Under Armour developed athletic footwear. As of the first quarter of 2008, Under Armour had 43 percent of the total US performance apparel business sold through sporting goods stores, versus 32 percent for Nike and 5.1 percent for Adidas.[15]

By 2010, Under Armour had become the official outfitter of the athletic teams at Auburn University (the 2011 BCS National Champions), Boston College, Texas Tech University, the University of Maryland, the University of South Florida, and the University of South Carolina.[16] It was also the official outfitter for the football teams at the University of Utah and the University of Hawaii among others, supplying them with uniforms, sideline apparel, and fan gear. It has been an official supplier of footwear to the National Football League (NFL) since 2006, and signed an agreement to become an official supplier of gloves beginning in 2011 and combined training apparel beginning in 2012. Also in 2010, Under Armour became the official performance footwear supplier for Major League Baseball and signed a new five-year contract with the NFL for on-field glove and footwear rights, and to remain the NFL Scouting Combine's exclusive title sponsor. International customers include European soccer and rugby teams, including the Hannover 96 football club and the Welsh Rugby Union. It is also an official supplier of performance apparel to Hockey Canada.[17]

In 2010, Under Armour reached an important milestone—it met and surpassed $1 billion in sales, a 24 percent increase over 2009. Its goal for 2011 is to increase revenues by approximately 25 percent. Introducing new items, entering new product categories such as basketball in 2010, heavy marketing and promotion, and the expansion of its wholesale distribution have contributed to Under Armour's rapid growth and helped build its reputation for providing quality performance products.[18]

A marketing consultant said, "Under Armour is identified with performance the way Starbucks is identified with better coffee, and that is a huge advantage in entering new categories."[19] Plank attributes the company's success to the fact that "[it] ha[s] grown and reinforced [its] brand name and image through sales to athletes and teams at all levels, from youth to professional, as well as through sales to consumers with active lifestyles around the globe."[20]

Current Product and Sales Profile

Geographic Distribution

Approximately 94 percent of Under Armour's sales in 2010 were in North America (the US and Canada), with the remaining 6 percent split among international markets (Latin America, Europe, the Middle East, Africa, and Asia) (see Exhibit 3). Net revenues in Western Europe were primarily from Austria, France,

Germany, Ireland, and the UK. Net revenues in other foreign countries were from partnerships and third-party distributors, primarily in Australia, Italy, Greece, New Zealand, Panama, Scandinavia, and Spain, along with license revenues from a Japanese licensee, Dome Corporation, which has exclusive rights to distribute Under Armour products in Japan.[21] The international expansion plan received new emphasis in 2006 with the opening of a European headquarters in Amsterdam. In an effort to increase the geographic diversity of sales, this headquarters was opened to manage sales and distribution channels, and additional experienced industry talent was brought on board (see Exhibit 2). However, in 2010 Under Armour halted efforts to expand the existing business to focus specifically on reinventing its footwear lines.[22]

Product Segment Distribution

Under Armour's sales results are divided into apparel, footwear, accessories, and licensed products (see Exhibits 4 and 5). Apparel dominated in 2010 with 80.2 percent of total sales. Under Armour's non-apparel product segments made up the remaining 19.8 percent of sales: footwear (12.0 percent), accessories (4.1 percent), and licensed products (3.7 percent). The footwear product, launched in the fourth quarter of 2006, initially only offered baseball, softball, and lacrosse cleats designed for high performance through a highly breathable and lightweight design. The footwear line now includes shoes for golf, football, running, and cross-training. In 2010, Under Armour introduced basketball footwear, a product category historically dominated by Nike, with approximately 96 percent of the lucrative $2.5 billion market.[23] As previously mentioned, Under Armour also became the official performance footwear supplier for Major League Baseball, and signed a contract with the NFL for on-field glove and footwear rights and to be the title sponsor of the NFL Scouting Combines.[24] Under Armour's accessories category is developed and managed directly by Under Armour. Primary accessories products

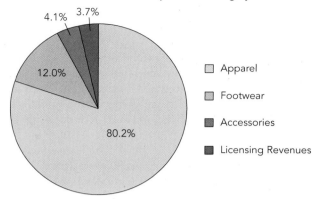

Exhibit 5 2010 Net Revenues by Product Category

- Apparel
- Footwear
- Accessories
- Licensing Revenues

Source: Under Armour Annual Report 2010.

include performance gloves for football, baseball, running, and golf aligned to the HeatGear and ColdGear product lines with unique performance features.

Under Armour also licenses its brand name to independent manufacturers for other miscellaneous products such as bags, socks, headwear, team uniforms, eyewear, watches, and custom-molded mouth guards. The company works directly with multiple licensees throughout the product development process to ensure the products are aligned with its brand and quality expectations, and also has relationships with several licensees for the distribution of its products to college bookstores and golf pro shops. Under Armour has recently developed its own headwear and bags that will be sold exclusively by Under Armour instead of its licensees as of 2011.[25]

Approximately 73 percent of Under Armour's 2010 sales were generated through its wholesale business. Customers include Cabela's, the Army and Air Force Exchange, Dick's Sporting Goods, and the Sports Authority. Combined, Dick's Sporting Goods and the Sports Authority provided nearly 27 percent of Under Armour's 2010 revenue. The addition of 20 company owned retail stores contributed to an increase of about 57 percent in direct-to-consumer sales. By the end of

Exhibit 4 Net Revenues by Product Category

(In thousands)	Year Ended December 31		
	2010	2009	2008
Apparel	$853,493	$651,779	$578,887
Footwear	127,175	136,224	84,848
Accessories	43,882	35,077	31,547
Total net sales	1,024,550	823,080	695,282
License revenues	39,377	33,331	29,962
Total net revenues	$1,063,927	$856,411	$725,244

Source: Under Armour Annual Report 2010.

2010, Under Armour operated approximately 55 of its own Factory House and specialty stores.[26]

Seasonality

There has been a continuing trend for Under Armour's sales to increase in the third and fourth quarters of each year, aligning with the football and basketball seasons and the traditional holiday gift-giving season in the US, in addition to the seasonality of Under Armour's higher priced ColdGear line.[27]

Operations and Distributions/Distributors

Under Armour possesses an efficient operations and distribution network. As with any corporation, this requires a blend of physical location metrics and strategic qualities. By leveraging its licensing partners, Under Armour can provide a wider range of branded products to its customers. This broader range of products adds value by reinforcing the brand and generating revenue without being required to organically develop capabilities in these adjacent product categories. Through keen selection and effective partner relationships, Under Armour has developed unique products that its consumers value.

For the first 10 years of its existence, the company was able to sustain operations by using "off the shelf" software programs, but after it went public in 2006, Under Armour invested in a new SAP system. This system has been essential to the company's ability to add products to its list of offerings and it has allowed Under Armour to manage a more diverse inventory and to ship directly to distributors.[28]

Prior to 2010, Under Armour did not have a patent on any of the materials[29] used in its products. Therefore, it had to be cautious in its licensing agreements so companies did not steal its know-how and introduce their own versions. Under Armour filed several patent applications in 2010 for certain products and designs that offered "a unique utility or function," and indicated that it planned to protect its inventions and designs by filing more applications in the future as its business grows and more innovations are made.[30] Though the majority of materials and technology used to create its products were not exclusive, by implementing an effective corporate strategy, Under Armour has been able to fashion itself as a profitable business and remain a key player among competitors.

Major Competitors

There is intense competition in the athletic apparel industry with companies of various sizes employing different strategies to attract consumers to their products and brand. The athletic apparel industry is so diverse that some smaller companies may choose to target a specific area such as yoga, whereas the larger companies try to capture the whole market. The larger companies continuously up the competition by spending large amounts of money on product innovation, advertising, and sponsorships. Under Armour's three largest competitors in the industry are Nike, Adidas, and Columbia Sportswear.[31] There are also smaller competitors such as SportHill that have the potential to become larger threats.

Nike

Nike was founded in 1964 by a University of Oregon track star, Phil Knight. Knight saw the need for better running shoes and began selling shoes imported from Asia out of the trunk of his car. By 1972, he severed his strained relationships with suppliers abroad and developed his first shoe branded as Nike, after the Greek goddess of victory. Over time, Nike became known as a high-quality, innovative product that consumers and athletes wanted to wear and were willing to pay a premium price to own.

By 1980, Nike had captured 50 percent of the athletic shoe market and began expanding into other areas through acquisitions and product innovation. In 2000, Nike launched a line of athletic electronics that included MP3 players, heart monitors, and two-way radios, and signed golfer Tiger Woods to a five-year endorsement contract.[32] It acquired Converse in 2003, keeping the Converse name and operating it as a separate unit.

Nike produces four main product segments (footwear, apparel, equipment, and accessory products).[33] Almost all of Nike's products are manufactured by independent contractors in China, Vietnam, Indonesia, Thailand, India, Malaysia, Sri Lanka, Turkey, Cambodia, Taiwan, Argentina, Brazil, and Mexico among other countries. Nike is the world leader in athletic footwear and apparel, grossing $19 billion in fiscal year 2010. It sells products for every sport and climate and strives to be the best in every segment. Nike advertises its brand through high-priced endorsement deals, media advertising, event sponsorships, partnerships, and alliances. Its products are sold to retail accounts through Nike-owned retail stores, online, and through independent distributors and licensees in more than 170 countries.[34] With more than 36,000 employees worldwide, Nike is an industry leader that is continually striving to stay ahead of the competition. Co-founder and legendary track coach Bill Bowerman's words continue to inspire employees, "If you have a body, you are an athlete."[35]

Adidas

Adidas, combined with Reebok (through an acquisition), is the second largest athletic apparel manufacturer in the world. Adidas was founded in 1924 in Germany by Adolf Dassler and is headquartered in Herzogenaurach. Dassler created the first running shoe made by hand without electricity in his mother's kitchen. Dassler's big break came in 1954 when the German soccer team defeated Hungary in the World Cup while wearing Adidas cleats. From that point forward, Adidas was the industry leader in soccer shoes and apparel.[36]

Changes in leadership during the late 80s led Adidas to branch out into other markets, but it struggled to find its niche. Through acquisitions and better management, it was back on track by the mid-90s. Adidas acquired three smaller companies: TaylorMade, Salomon Group, and Maxfli. These acquisitions gave it access to the golf and winter sports market segments. In 2006, it purchased athletic apparel and equipment giant Reebok for approximately $3.8 billion,[37] making it the second largest athletic apparel manufacturer in the world. In 2008, the TaylorMade-Adidas golf subsidiary divested the Maxfli brand and acquired golf apparel and accessories maker Ashworth. Also in 2008, Adidas purchased US-based Textronics, which specialized in wearable sensors. Today, the Adidas product line includes footwear, apparel, and accessories for basketball, football, running, soccer, fitness, golf, hockey, and outdoor adventure, along with sportswear and high fashion products. Adidas operates globally with 44,362 employees[38] worldwide, approximately 170 subsidiaries,[39] and a reported $15.9 billion in revenue in 2010.[40]

Columbia Sportswear

Columbia Sportswear Company started in the 30s as a family owned and operated hat company in Portland, Oregon. Tired of working with inadequate suppliers, founder Paul Lamfrom decided to manufacturer his own products. Columbia quickly gained a reputation for its innovative, high-quality products.[41]

Columbia's introduction of waterproof, breathable fabrics triggered the growth it has experienced since the 80s from a small family owned business to a billion dollar, publicly traded company that is still controlled by the Boyle family, which has approximately 63 percent of the company's shares. Lamfrom's daughter, Gertrude Boyle, continues to oversee company operations in her role as chair, and her son, Timothy Boyle, is company president, CEO, and director.[42] Columbia continues to grow thanks to its innovative product development and the acquisitions of Sorel, Mountain Hardware, Pacific Trail, and Montrail. These acquisitions enabled the company to branch out into other market segments.

Columbia Sportswear is now the top US skiwear seller and one of the largest sellers of outdoor apparel, specializing in skiwear and snowboard gear, as well as hunting, fishing, hiking, camping, and casual wear. Columbia began its e-commerce operations in 2009 in the US and announced plans to expand to Canadian and European markets by fall 2011. In 2010, approximately 40 percent of its sales came from outside the US.

Columbia currently operates 7,500 retail stores in more than 100 countries and has 3,626 employees worldwide. In 2010, Columbia posted net sales of $1.48 billion.[43]

SportHill

SportHill was founded in 1985 by yet another University of Oregon track star who saw the need for cold weather track gear. Jim Hill, a five-time All-American and World Championship competitor, discovered that the cotton sweats and nylon shorts he had worn at home in Virginia were not suitable for Oregon's cold, rainy climate.[44] While running and racing in Europe, he searched for athletic clothing that would be more appropriate for use in Oregon. His athletic apparel design concept merged the best American fabrics with European style to make unique athletic apparel designed for use in any climate and for any sport. SportHill utilizes the expertise of elite athletes to perfect its design and innovate new products. It is well known for quality, comfort, and reliability. The 3SP® fabric developed by Hill is marketed on SportHill's Web site as "the fastest drying fabric in the world" and has been used by the Canadian National and Olympic Cross Country Ski Teams since 1994.[45]

SportHill's clothing can be found globally in most major retail stores and can be purchased online. The success of SportHill is apparent in the number of sponsorships it has, including many Olympic athletes and collegiate running teams; however, it is a privately held company so financial information is not available.

Under Armour's Leaders

Under Armour's success and rapid growth may seem unbelievable at first, but it's no accident. Plank's drive to keep trying, even during difficult times when it seemed the company might never flourish, made it possible. In the beginning, when customers would request products that Plank had not created, he would respond, "Of course we make that!" and then immediately go to work with suppliers and contractors to deliver on his promise. Two such examples include when the equipment manager for the Atlanta Falcons wanted long-sleeve Under Armour shirts, and when the equipment manager for Arizona State wanted clothing for cold weather.[46]

"He's one of the hardest workers I've known in my life," says Plank's mother.[47] Plank's humble beginnings give him valuable insight into his business. He knows every aspect of it because at one time, he actually did the work himself. Many of his first employees were his college classmates and teammates and many of them still play important roles in management. His brother, J. Scott Plank, joined the company in 2000 and now serves as executive vice president of business development (see Exhibit 6).

Exhibit 6 Under Armour Executive Team

Kevin A. Plank
President, Chief Executive Officer and Chairman of the Board
Kevin A. Plank is the founder of Under Armour and has served as Chief Executive Officer (CEO) and Chairman of the Board of Directors since 1996 and as President from 1996 to July 2008 and again since August 2010. Mr. Plank also serves on the Board of Directors of the National Football Foundation and College Hall of Fame, Inc. and is a member of the Board of Trustees of the University of Maryland College Park Foundation.

Wayne A. Marino
Chief Operating Officer
Wayne A. Marino has been Chief Operating Officer (COO) since March 2008. Prior to that, he served as Executive Vice President (VP) and CFO from March 2006 to February 2008, as Senior VP and CFO from February 2005 to February 2006, and as VP and CFO from January 2004 to January 2005. Prior to joining Under Armour, Mr. Marino served as CFO of Nautica Enterprises, Inc. from 2000 to 2003 and CFO of Hartstrings Inc. from 1998 to 2000. Prior there to, Mr. Marino served in a variety of capacities, including Divisional CFO, for Polo Ralph Lauren Corporation.

Brad Dickerson
Chief Financial Officer
Brad Dickerson has been CFO since March 2008. Prior to that, he served as VP of Accounting and Finance from February 2006 to February 2008, and Corporate Controller from July 2004 to February 2006. Prior to joining Under Armour, Mr. Dickerson served as CFO of Macquarie Aviation North America from January 2003 to July 2004 and in various capacities for Network Building & Consulting from 1994 to 2003, including CFO from 1998 to 2003.

Kip J. Fulks
Executive Vice President of Product
Kip J. Fulks has been Executive VP of Product since January 2011. Prior to that, he served as Senior VP of Outdoor and Innovation from March 2008 to December 2010, as Senior VP of Outdoor from October 2007 to February 2008, as Senior VP of Sourcing, Quality Assurance, and Product Development from March 2006 to September 2007, and VP of Sourcing and Quality Assurance from 1997 to February 2006.

Gene McCarthy
Senior Vice President of Footwear
Gene McCarthy has been Senior VP of Footwear since August 2009. Prior to joining Under Armour, he served as Co-President of the Timberland brand from December 2007 to July 2009, President of its Authentic Youth Division from February 2007 to November 2007, and Group VP of Product and Design from April 2006 to January 2007. Prior thereto, Mr. McCarthy served as Senior VP of Product and Design for Reebok International from July 2003 to November 2005 and in a variety of capacities for Nike from 1982 to 2003, including Global Director of Sales and Retail Marketing for Brand Jordan, from 1999 to 2003.

J. Scott Plank
Executive Vice President of Business Development
Scott Plank has been Executive VP of Business Development since August 2009, focusing on domestic and international business development opportunities. Prior to that, he served as Senior VP of Retail from March 2006 to July 2009 with responsibility for retail outlets, specialty stores, and e-commerce, as Chief Administrative Officer from January 2004 to February 2006, and VP of Finance from 2000 to 2003 with operational and strategic responsibilities. Mr. Plank was a director of Under Armour, Inc. from 2001 until July 2005. Mr. Plank is the brother of Kevin A. Plank, CEO and Chairman of the Board of Directors.

John S. Rogers
Vice President/General Manager of E-commerce
John Rogers has been VP/General Manager of Global E-commerce since May 2010. Prior to joining Under Armour, he served in a variety of capacities for The Orvis Company, Inc., including VP of Multi-Channel Marketing and General Manager of the UK Division from 2006 to April 2010, Director of Multi-Channel Marketing from 2004 to 2006, and Director of E-commerce Marketing from 2000 to 2004. Prior thereto, Mr. Rogers served as Director of Branding for Toysmart.com, a Walt Disney company, from 1999 to 2000 and Director of Global Brands for Hasbro, from 1994 to 1999.

Dan J. Sawall
Vice President of Retail
Dan J. Sawall has been VP of Retail since February 2010. Prior to joining Under Armour, he served as Senior VP and General Merchandise Manager of Golfsmith from August 2009 to January 2010, General Manager for US Nike Factory Stores from February 2007 to April 2009, an independent marketing and business consultant from January 2003 to January 2007, VP and General Merchandise Manager for the d.e.m.o. division of Pacific Sunwear from July 2000 to May 2002, and General Merchandise Manager, Retail Stores for Guess? from 1998 to 2000. He began his career as a buyer for Federated Department Stores and then worked as a buyer and in various management capacities, including Divisional Merchandising Manager, for 15 years for Dillard's Department Stores.

(Continued)

Exhibit 6 Under Armour Executive Team (*Continued*)

> **Henry B. Stafford**
> **Senior Vice President of Apparel**
> Henry Stafford has been Senior VP of Apparel since June 2010. Prior to joining Under Armour, he worked with American Eagle Outfitters as Senior VP and Chief Merchandising Officer of the AE Brand from April 2007 to May 2010, General Merchandise Manager and Senior VP of Men's and AE Canadian Division from April 2005 to March 2007, and General Merchandise Manager and VP of Men's from September 2003 to March 2005. Prior thereto, Mr. Stafford served in a variety of capacities for Old Navy from 1998 to 2003, including Divisional Merchandising Manager for Men's Tops from 2001 to 2003, and served as a buyer for Abercrombie and Fitch from 1996 to 1998.

Source: Under Armour Web site, http://investor.underarmour.com/company/managementTeam.cfm, May 2011.

In the early days, Plank spent five months driving round-trip from Baltimore to Moundsville at least twice a week to help Ella Mae Holmes produce and ship Under Armour products. He left Baltimore at 4AM, arrived in Moundsville at about 8AM, and worked with Holmes and her boyfriend throughout the day. At 8PM, Plank would take his shipment to the local FedEx office and drive four hours back to Baltimore.[48]

Plank effectively uses his athletic experience and connections to help Under Armour's marketing and sales teams earn new business. In the athletic world, he is considered by his customers to be "one of them" rather than the CEO of a very profitable business. It frequently takes competitors years to develop a loyal customer, but Under Armour has been able to quickly earn loyalty after a customer has had one or two good experiences with a purchase. Most of the sports teams feel that Plank is truly helping them by providing a better product and not simply trying to sell his brand. Plank embraces and nurtures this connection respectfully and gracefully. He regularly seeks feedback regarding existing products and the need for new products. Plank has served as CEO and chairman of the board since the company was founded in 1996. In addition, he served as president from 1996 to July 2008, and again took over the responsibilities of president in August 2010. He is also Under Armour's largest shareholder, controlling approximately 75 percent of the company's voting shares.[49]

Under Armour's executive team represents a significant degree of industry expertise. For example, Chief Operating Officer (COO) Wayne A. Marino's prior positions include Chief Financial Officer (CFO) of Nautica Enterprises, Inc. and Divisional CFO of Polo Ralph Lauren Corporation. Senior Vice President of Footwear Gene McCarthy served as Co-President of the Timberland brand, Senior Vice President of Product and Design for Reebok International, and Global Director of Sales and Retail Marketing of Brand Jordan for Nike. Vice President of Retail Dan J. Sawall has held leadership positions with Golfsmith, Nike, Pacific Sunwear, Guess, and Dillard's Department Stores, and Henry B. Stafford, Senior Vice President of Apparel has worked for such well-known companies as American Eagle Outfitters, Old Navy, and Abercrombie and Fitch (see Exhibit 6).

Management Style

Having been part of a sports team, Plank manages his company with a unique, team-driven style.

Under Armour is one team and my job is to help ensure we operate and execute as one team. Because there's a lot of noise and clutter surrounding our brand, I try to simplify our story and objectives for the team to help keep everyone running on the same wavelength and working towards the same goal: to become the world's number one performance athletic brand.[50]

To remind him of his critical role every day, Plank has written on a whiteboard in his office four things that define his job: (1) make a great product, (2) tell a great story about the product, (3) service the business, and (4) build a great team. Every morning when he arrives at the office and every evening before he leaves, he looks at the board. Plank said, "If I don't work toward those things, I'm not doing my job. . . You can overcomplicate your job . . . It's important that you don't allow the clutter to grow too loud [. . .] and distract you from your mission."[51]

Under Armour's Business Strategies

Since its inception in 1996, Under Armour's leaders have worked to achieve the company's vision of becoming the world's leading performance athletic apparel brand. Under Armour attains physical differentiation through the value chain activities of technological development and procurement. As CEO Kevin Plank stated, "The key driver is to offer products that are better than what is currently in the market, best in class."[52] Additionally, Under Armour has hundreds of professional athletes that not only volunteer to wear Under Armour gear, but actually want to wear it. Most budding stars or weekend recreational athletes want to wear the gear the pros wear. Plank focused on maintaining differentiation from Nike, and has used "authenticity" as his guiding principle to grow and advertise the brand. In the past, Under Armour has identified itself with team sports, rather than individual sports and fashion. "Everything we do is centered on performance . . . we aren't ever going to develop products to fill up a sales table," said Plank. Specifically, Under Armour maintained the philosophy that it would never use cotton to produce its clothing.[53]

However, by 2011 Under Armour recognized that to retain its current customers while attracting new ones, it would have to find new ways to keep its products fresh. Talent was recruited from top US fashion design schools, and Under Armour began to take more fashion risks in an effort to modernize its vision.[54] In 2009 and 2010, new members were added to Under Armour's executive team to bring a new level of knowledge and expertise in the apparel industry (see Exhibit 6).

Analysts have said that Under Armour would need to make its products attractive to customers outside the locker room to effectively compete against the Nike, Reebok, and Converse brands. According to research firm NPD Group, almost 80 percent of activewear is worn for non-sports activities. SportsOneSource has found that more than 85 percent of athletic footwear is used for activities that are different from the sport for which they were originally developed. Matt Powell, an analyst with SportsOneSource, stated, "I think there is a glass ceiling on how big the true athletic business can be."[55] However, change is accompanied by risk, and analysts and sports marketing experts believe that Under Armour will need to find a balance between being fashionable while retaining its credibility with serious athletes.[56]

According to Under Armour executives, the increasing fashion focus is aligned with its strategy to stay ahead of the competition, and emphasize that performance is still the "number 1 goal." For example, Under Armour introduced its first cotton garment in 2011, a T-shirt with the same moisture-wicking ability of the original line.[57] According to Plank,

We never hated cotton. We hated that cotton never performed.[58] This is truly one of the most exciting product releases in the history of Under Armour, as Charged Cotton is the ultimate marriage of innovation and performance. It has long been our mission to make all athletes better, and that's exactly what we've done with one of nature's most beloved materials.[59]

Noreen Naroo-Pucci, senior creative director of women's and youth apparel, said, "Ultimately, we will never compromise the performance aspect of what we offer," and a mass email was sent to customers with the subject "Sure, Our Accessories Look Good . . . But They Also Perform."[60]

In June 2011, during "Investor Day" at company headquarters, Plank told shareholders and analysts that Under Armour planned to double its growth in the next three years to more than $2 billion. According to Plank, principal drivers of the increase would be apparel sales and direct-to-consumer business (including e-commerce and sales from company owned retail stores).[61] Prices would also be raised on some products to offset the increasing cost of materials.

Several executives made presentations at the event that included limited information on new products and business ventures that were in the planning process. New products such as water-repellent "hoodies" (hooded sweatshirts) were announced, along with plans to introduce yoga pants and new sports bras in an effort to expand the women's clothing line. A new line of shirts and shorts using coldblack technology, fabric designed to better absorb the sun's ultraviolet and infrared rays to prevent the wearer from getting hot as quickly, was also announced. These products are designed to appeal to golfers and people who perform many of their outdoor activities in the sun. A line of underwear with the same moisture-wicking capabilities as its outerwear is scheduled for introduction in spring 2012. Senior Vice President of Apparel Henry Stafford said, "Innovation is core to our DNA. It is the engine to our growth."[62] Additional plans included remodeling stores, opening new stores, updating fixtures, adding floor space at some retailers (including Dick's Sporting Goods and Sports Authority), and the launch of a new Web site to drive online shopping.[63]

Plans were also announced to introduce the first of Under Armour's revamped footwear line and in October 2011, the Charge RC was made available to the public. Footwear sales had dropped 7 percent in 2010, to $127.2 million,[64] as several models did not sell as well as Under Armour anticipated. Executives commented that they did not expect footwear to impact revenue until 2013. Plank said that it was important for the company to take the necessary time to develop the footwear line, and added, "This doesn't mean that we don't get it and don't know footwear."[65] Several years ago, Plank told investors that Under Armour's goal was to eventually make footwear a greater profit driver for the company than its apparel lines. To date, the company has not deviated from this path. According to Plank, "We will win in footwear. It's not ego talking. It's what I see. We have great belief in what footwear will do for this company."[66]

In pursuit of this goal, a new marketing campaign for the footwear line, "Footsteps," launched during the 2011 back-to-school sales season.

Marketing

Under Armour's marketing strength has been twofold. First, its products have been so effective that professional athletes have wanted to use them. Second, Under Armour became a master of product placement in movies, TV shows, and video games. Under Armour has typically spent approximately 13 percent of its annual net income on marketing[67] and prior to 2011, an in-house marketing and promotions department designed and produced most of Under Armour's marketing campaigns.[68]

Even so, Plank believes that word-of-mouth advertising is the most effective method. Plank has said, "We always build a product for the athlete's needs. The customer is willing to pay the price because the Under Armour product has value in it. Without value, our product is just an expensive T-shirt. But we have the technology in the fabric [and] the design and the features satisfy what the athlete needs.[69] Our model is getting to the athletes—supplying them with great product that helps them perform better."[70]

Athletes are a valuable marketing resource that allow products to be seen in use on the field, providing exposure to a number of consumers through the Internet, television, magazines, and at live sporting events.[71] The company signed a five-year partnership agreement in April 2009 with Cal Ripken, Jr., a retired professional baseball player, to be its official uniform representative. Under Armour believed this was a great opportunity because Ripken was previously partnered with Nike.[72] Other established athletes who have sponsorship agreements with Under Armour include professional baseball players Ryan Zimmerman and Jose Reyes, professional football players Tom Brady and Vernon Davis, triathlon champion Chris "Macca" McCormack, US Women's National Soccer Team players Heather Mitts and Lauren Cheney, US Olympic swimmer Michael Phelps, US Olympic and professional volleyball player Nicole Branaugh, and professional golfer Hunter Mahan.[73] Under Armour also seeks to identify the next generation of star athletes, such as Milwaukee Bucks, point guard Brandon Jennings and skier Lindsey Vonn, and sign them to multiyear endorsement contracts.[74]

The company has reached out to capture much of the youth sports industry by sponsoring recreational teams and major youth tournaments, including American Youth Football (a football organization that promotes the development of youth), the Under Armour All-America high school football and lacrosse games, and the Under Armour Senior Bowl (an annual competition among the top seniors in high school football). Under Armour is also the presenting sponsor for the 2010 NFL Scouting Combine.

Under Armour reaches nearly 35,000 young baseball players annually through its partnership with Ripken Baseball to outfit Ripken Baseball participants, and as the title sponsor for all 25 of the Ripken youth baseball tournaments. Under Armour partners with the Baseball Factory to outfit the top high school baseball athletes in the US and the company serves as the title sponsor for

nationally recognized baseball teams and tournaments[75] (see Exhibit 7).

Under Armour has initiated other sponsorships to help get its name out to the public such as the Baltimore Marathon, which is now named the Under Armour Marathon. In an effort to boost its women's clothing line, Under Armour sponsored the women's US field hockey team and some of the US women's softball and volleyball athletes during the 2008 Olympic Games.[76] Under Armour also bought its first Super Bowl commercial in 2008.

Specifically, Under Armour seeks to sponsor events that will "drive awareness and brand authenticity from a grassroots level."[77] The company has entered an agreement with IMG Academies for the development of a unique and comprehensive athletic training platform. Under Armour believes that this training platform will establish a global measurement standard for sports performance, health, and fitness. In 2010, Under Armour hosted more than 50 combines, camps, and clinics for a variety of sports at regional sites across the US for both male and female athletes.[78]

In 2010, Under Armour's original "rally cry" was brought back with the "Protect This House, I Will" global marketing campaign. This campaign featured some of the world's most popular and exciting young athletes, including Mixed Martial Arts champion Georges St. Pierre, NBA star Brandon Jennings, and Olympic gold medalists Lindsey Vonn and Michael Phelps.[79]

However, in 2011, Under Armour selected Optimum Sports, a unit of Omnicom Media Group, to manage its media account. This is the first time Under Armour has used an outside agency for media planning and buying. It is responsible for the media placement of Under Armour's new TV, print, and digital campaigns for its new and re-engineered footwear line that launched during the 2011 back-to-school sales season. Steve Battista,

Exhibit 7 Sponsorship and Other Marketing Commitments

(In thousands)	December 31 2010
2011	$ 43,506
2012	39,251
2013	32,764
2014	29,731
2015	18,894
2016 and thereafter	3,483
Total future minimum sponsorship and other marketing payments	$167,629

Source: Under Armour Annual Report 2010.

Under Armour's Senior Vice President of Brands, said, "We believe Optimum is the ideal partner in helping us expand upon the strong foundation we have built with our current marketing efforts."[80] Optimum Sports Managing Director Tom McGovern commented,

I don't think there's anyone in the industry that hasn't been amazed at the speed and effectiveness with which the Under Armour team has established its brand with consumers, leagues, teams, and athletes. We're looking forward to helping them build on this success as they continue to grow their product line and brand reach.[81]

Other well-known brands that are clients of Optimum Sports include Gatorade, State Farm, Callaway, and Pepsi.[82] The amount Under Armour has agreed to pay Optimum Sports has not been disclosed.

Strategic Challenges

There are numerous challenges facing Under Armour as it strives to achieve its goal of doubling growth within the next three years. These challenges include effective management of its rapid growth and competition from major rivals such as Nike and Adidas. Although Under Armour has earned a reputation as a leading innovator of performance apparel, the sporting goods industry is highly competitive. The growth potential and strong profit margins in the performance apparel category make it attractive to other companies, and others in the industry have developed similar performance enhancing products.

Although analysts are optimistic about Under Armour's continued growth, they believe its entry into new product categories such as footwear will be particularly challenging. The launch of the football and baseball cleats in 2006 and 2007 was successful; however, there was a mixed response to its introduction of cross-training footwear in 2008 and running shoes in 2009. Sell-throughs and reorders were weaker than anticipated. Morningstar analysts expressed the opinion that Under Armour had attempted to grow too fast, and some of the shoe styles were "under-engineered" for their price range.[83] While customers have been willing to pay a premium price for Under Armour's apparel based on its reputation for producing a quality product that will enhance performance, this brand loyalty has not followed with its footwear line.

Although Under Armour has dedicated a large amount of resources to reinvent its footwear line, there are a number of well-entrenched competitors, including Saucony, that specialize in running shoes. Some have a high degree of brand loyalty, similar to Nike in basketball. Some, including Nike, Adidas, and Mizuno, have advantages of scope and scale, and an extensive global presence. These competitors no longer regard Under Armour as a minor player as its growth and success have been widely recognized, and some competitors have taken steps in direct response to Under Armour. Nike, in particular, has spent a significant amount of time and money to revamp its performance apparel line. In addition, analysts believe that Nike purposely targeted Under Armour by launching new basketball shoes at the same time Under Armour was attempting to introduce its first basketball footwear at the end of 2010.[84]

Under Armour is still relatively small in size and financial strength compared to its major competitors, Nike and Adidas. As it has shifted focus from domestic and international expansion of the business to reinventing its footwear line, expanding its product portfolio could have a dilutive effect on merchandise margins. Footwear generates lower margins than Under Armour's technologically advanced performance apparel, and the decision to offer more fashionable products will be risky. There will be increased product development and marketing costs. In addition, the introduction of cotton products will most likely divert sales from Under Armour's other products. As Under Armour modifies its strategy by expanding its portfolio with products that are similar to competitors (footwear, cotton products, and more fashionable products), it risks diluting its brand image that "every Under Armour product is doing something for you: it's making you better."[85] It is essential that Under Armour maintain its brand image, as consumers will not pay premium prices for a brand name if they believe the products do not provide premium quality and performance.

Additional risk factors include the lack of proprietary product rights and intellectual property rights in foreign countries, and a heavy reliance on third-party suppliers and manufacturers that could adversely affect the long-term sustainability of the firm. "The intellectual property rights in much of the technology, materials, and processes used to manufacture our products are often owned or controlled by our suppliers."[86] The company's ability to obtain patent protection for its products has historically been limited; however, several patent applications were filed in 2010, and the number is expected to grow as the business grows.[87]

Intangible assets such as trademarks are very important to the Under Armour brand, as are licensing arrangements and other legal agreements. The intellectual property rights laws and regulations of countries in the global market vary dramatically and Under Armour relies heavily on suppliers and manufacturers outside the US. In fact, 70 to 75 percent of the fabrics used in its products come from only eight suppliers, lending to Under Armour's weak position relative to its suppliers. Additionally, some of its supplies are commodities and thus are subject to price fluctuations; for example, petroleum-based materials are used in Under Armour's products and the petroleum industry has experienced significant swings in price and relative availability in recent months and years.[88]

There are many questions and issues that Kevin Plank and his executive leadership team must consider as the company moves forward. The reinvention and recent introduction of the footwear line will be risky, along with the new product offerings. What steps can be taken to ensure that these products meet the standards of quality and performance set by Under Armour's performance apparel products? Will Under Armour be able to accurately predict changing consumer fashion trends and preferences? If a product fails, what steps can be taken to lessen the impact on Under Armour's brand image? Was it wise to hire a media development company from outside when the in-house marketing team has been so successful with prior campaigns? Should Under Armour dedicate such extensive resources to the footwear line, to the point of slowing business expansion? Does Under Armour possess appropriate supplier relationships and have an understanding of the inher-

ent economic impacts on raw materials? If not, how will Under Armour acquire or develop these capabilities? What capabilities should Under Armour develop to ensure international success? What barriers to entry exist in additional markets, and is licensing or some other method the best approach? Is the correct management team in place to lead the company's international expansion efforts when the company is ready to make expansion of the business the top priority?

Analysts believe that the demand for Under Armour's apparel products remains strong, and predict 30 percent wholesale apparel growth in 2011 and 25 percent growth in footwear sales.[89] There are opportunities for extended growth over the next several years in women's, youth, and international apparel categories in particular. Despite intense competition from its larger rivals, Under Armour's future appears positive, and company founder, CEO and chairman of the board Kevin Plank agrees. According to Plank, "Our trip is still just getting started and we remain humble and hungry as this next part of the journey begins."[90]

NOTES

1. 2010, Under Armour Annual Report.
2. http://www.uabiz.com/company/about.cfm
3. 2010, Under Armour Annual Report.
4. 2010, Under Armour Annual Report.
5. 2011, Hoover's Company Reports, Under Armour, Inc.
6. http://www.underarmour.com/shop/us/en/affiliate-home.
7. 2010, Under Armour Annual Report.
8. 2008, Five questions with Under Armour CEO, Kevin Plank, *Sports Business Journal*, http://www.sportsbusinessconferences.com/sss-pov/entries/2008/five-questions-with-kevin-plank, Aug 15.
9. *Ibid.*
10. S. Lyster, 2008, The history of Under Armour—A mastermind for performance apparel, http://www.ezinearticles.com, Dec 4.
11. 2008, Under Armour performance apparel, *Funding Universe*, http://www.fundinguniverse.com, Dec 4.
12. *Ibid.*
13. D. Rovell, 2005, Under Armour could offer up to $100 million in stock, http://sports.espn.go.com, Aug 26.
14. S. N. Mehta, 2009, Under Armour reboots: The sports apparel maker is sprinting into footwear—and trying to take on Nike—with the help of software and science, *Fortune*, http://www.money.cnn.com, Mar 5.
15. D. Kiley, 2008, Under Armour steps into footwear field: Sports apparel maker set to do battle with Nike and Adidas, *BusinessWeek*, http://www.businessweek.com, Jan 31.
16. 2010, Under Armour Annual Report.
17. *Ibid.*
18. 2011, Hoover's Company Reports, Under Armour.
19. D. Kiley, 2008, *op. cit.*
20. 2008, Under Armour 10-K 2007 Annual Report, http://www.underarmour.com/annuals.cfm, Feb.
21. 2011, Hoover's Company Reports, Under Armour.
22. R. Sharrow, 2011, Under Armour CEO Plank: 'We will win in footwear', *Baltimore Business Journal*, May 3, http://www.bizjournals.com/baltimore/news/2011/05/03/under-armour-ceo-plank-we-will-win.html?page=all.

23. Trefis Team, 2011, Under Armour Imposing on Nike's Turn, But is Still Far From a Serious Threat, *NASDAQ*, Feb 10, http://community.nasdaq.com/News/2011/-02/under-armour-imposing-on-nikes-turf-but-is-still-far-from-a-serious-threat.aspx?storyid-57146.
24. 2010, Under Armour Annual Report.
25. *Ibid.*
26. 2011, Hoover's Company Reports, Under Armour.
27. 2010, Under Armour Annual Report.
28. S. N. Mehta, 2009, *op. cit.*
29. D. Kiley, 2008, *op. cit.*
30. *Ibid.*
31. 2011, Hoover's Company Reports, Under Armour.
32. 2011, Hoover's Company Reports, NIKE, Inc.
33. 2010, NIKE, Inc. Annual Report.
34. *Ibid.*
35. http://www.nikebiz.com/company_overview/.
36. 2008, Adidas group history, Adidas Group, http://www.adidas-group.com/en/overview/history/default.asp. Dec 4.
37. 2010, Hoover's Company Reports, Adidas.
38. http://investing.businessweek.com/research/stocks/private/snapshot.asp?privcapid=92816.
39. http://www.adidas-group.com/en/pressroom/factsheets/Group/default/aspx.
40. 2011, Hoover's Company Reports, Adidas.
41. 2008, Columbia Sportswear, *Funding Universe*, http://www.fundinguniverse.com/company-histories/Columbia-Sportswear-Company-Company-History1.html, Dec 4.
42. 2011, Hoover's Company Reports, Columbia Sportswear Company.
43. *Ibid.*
44. http://www.sporthill.com/aboutus.php.
45. *Ibid.*
46. M. Hyman, 2003, How I did it: Kevin Plank: For the founder of apparel-maker Under Armour, entrepreneurship is 99% perspiration and 1% polyester, *Inc.*, http://www.inc.com, Dec.

47. S. Graham, 2004, Kevin Plank's drive makes Under Armour an industry overachiever, *Sports Business Journal*, http://www.sportsbusinessjournal.com/article/36213, Jan 19.
48. *Ibid.*
49. 2011, Hoover's Company Reports, Under Armour.
50. 2008, Five questions with Under Armour CEO, Kevin Plank. *op. cit.*
51. 2008, How do you define your job? *Business Management Daily*, http://www.businessmanagementdaily.com, Nov 8.
52. T. Heath, 2008, In pursuit of innovation at Under Armour: Founder Kevin Plank says Super Bowl commercial has generated "buzz," *Washington Post*, Feb 25, D03.
53. D. Kiley, 2008, *op. cit.*
54. A. K. Walker, 2011, Focus on Fashion: Under Armour looking to broaden appeal, *Baltimore Sun*, May 31, http://www.baltimoresun.com/business/bs-bz-under-armour-fashion-20110531,0,7618345.story.
55. *Ibid.*
56. *Ibid.*
57. *Ibid.*
58. R. Sharrow, 2011, *op. cit.*
59. 2011, Under Armour launches groundbreaking performance cotton collection, *PR Newswire*, Jan 27, http://www.prnewswire.com/news-releases/under-armour-launches-groundbreaking-performance-cotton-collection-114716364.html.
60. *Ibid.*
61. A. K. Walker, 2011, Plank: Under Armour plans to double growth in next three years, *Baltimore Sun*, Jun 9, http://www.baltimoresun.com/business/bs-bz-under-armour-investors-20110609,0,7055046.story.
62. *Ibid.*
63. 2011, Under Armour stock gives back early gains, *Associated Press*, Jun 10, CBS moneywatch.com, http://moneywatch.bnet.com/investing/news/under-armour/stock-gives-back-early-gains/6245641.
64. N. O'Leary, 2011, Under Armour taps Optimum Sports: Omnicom unit will handle media, *ADWEEK*, Jun 6, http://www.adweek.com/news/advertising-branding/under-armour-taps-optimum-sports-132279.
65. A. K. Walker, 2011, Plank: Under Armour plans to double growth in next three years, *op. cit.*
66. R. Sharrow, 2011, *op. cit.*
67. 2011, Hoover's Company Reports, Under Armour.
68. 2010, Under Armour Annual Report.
69. 2007, I am, Video interview with Kevin Plank, *CNBC*, http://www.cnbc.com/id/25191722, Sep 11.
70. M. Hyman, 2003, *op. cit.*
71. *Ibid.*
72. R. Sharrow, 2009, Under Armour, Ripken Baseball swing for fences with sportswear pact, *Baltimore Business Journal*, http://www.baltimore.bizjournals.com, Apr 22.
73. *Ibid.*
74. 2011, Hoover's Company Reports, Under Armour.
75. 2010, Under Armour Annual Report.
76. R. Sharrow, 2008, Under Armour entering an Olympic contest of its own, *Baltimore Business Journal*, http://www.baltimore.bizjournals.com, Aug 1.
77. 2010, Under Armour Annual Report.
78. *Ibid.*
79. *Ibid.*
80. E. Wendell, 2011, Under Armour Taps Optimum Sports to Manage Media and Sponsorships, *Yahoo! News (PRWEB)*, Jun 6, http://news.yahoo.com/s/prweb/20110606/bs_prweb/prweb8535033.
81. *Ibid.*
82. *Ibid.*
83. *Ibid.*
84. P. Swinand, 2011, Under Armour, Inc. Analyst Report, Morningstar Investment Research Center, May 9, http://library.morningstar.com.ezproxy1.lib.asu.edu/stocknet/MorningstarAnalysis.aspx?Country-USA&Symbol-UA.
85. http://www.uabiz.com/company/about.cfm
86. 2010, Under Armour Annual Report.
87. *Ibid.*
88. *Ibid.*
89. P. Swinand, 2011, *op. cit.*
90. 2010, Under Armour Annual Report.

Jeffrey Cope, John Deegan, Jason Landry, Sriram Rajagopal, Adam Ward

Texas A&M University

Introduction

Founded in 1862, Union Pacific Railroad Company (UNP) provides rail transportation services throughout the Southern and Western US, as well as Mexico and Western Canada. It has over 30,000 route miles linking ports on the Pacific and Gulf coasts to cities throughout the Midwest and Western US. UNP also owns gateways in Chicago, Alberta, and northern Mexico, allowing for the dispersion of goods outside its geographic footprint. The company transports everything from agricultural products to automobiles to chemicals as well as petroleum and other energy commodities. Bulk commodities are the "golden goose" of the railroad industry because they must be shipped in massive quantities, are prohibitively heavy, and provide a repetitive stream of business. For these reasons, railroad companies are extremely active in areas of highly concentrated agricultural and coal mines.

Though the rail shipping industry has many players, four companies dominate the competitive landscape—UNP, Burlington Northern Santa Fe (BNSF), Norfolk Southern (NS), and CSX—and collectively, they provide the greatest share of rail transport in the US. While UNP is the largest of these companies, BNSF is a very close second and poses a great threat to UNP's market share (see Exhibit 1 for a comparison of these four railroads.) To maintain and expand its position as the market leader among Class I[i] railroads, it is important for UNP to develop a creative, long-term strategy.

The Landscape on Which the Rail Runs

Conditions in the environment affect how UNP operates. While the segments of this environment affect other firms within both the railroad and broader transportation

[i]Railroad companies are classified as I, II, or III based on annual operating revenue with Class I railroads the largest.

industry similarly, ongoing and in-depth analysis is necessary for firms to identify opportunities and threats facing the industry collectively and the firm specifically.

The 2010 US census reveals interesting population changes in the areas in which UNP operates. Population in the US increased 9.7 percent between 2000 and 2010 and, although every census region saw a significant increase in population, the South and West represented the regions with the greatest increases—gains of 14.3 and 13.8 percent respectively.[1] The twenty-three states where UNP operates (UNP states) saw average population increases of 11.9 percent from 2000 to 2010, outpacing overall US growth by 2.2 percent. Geographically, UNP serves two-thirds of the US; however, this only includes 48.6 percent of the population—an increase of almost one percent from 2000 (see Exhibit 2 for a complete population breakdown by region and state). UNP state are simply less dense. On average, the US boasts 87.4 people per square mile while UNP states average 72.2 people per square mile. While the overall population density change over the last decade saw an increase of about 9.7 percent more people per square mile, UNP states increased 9.8 percent (Exhibit 3).

Drivers of Rail Industry Growth

The rail industry in the US is experiencing a rebirth primarily due to rising fuel prices and a renewed appreciation in the business community for the fuel efficiency of shipping by rail. During the economic recession beginning in 2007, railroads experienced a surge in revenue due to fuel surcharges and attractive shipping prices compared to other transportation modes. However, as the recession further deepened in 2009 and fuel prices declined, railroads were hit with a 22.3 percent decrease in revenues. In 2010, railroad revenues bounced back by 14.6 percent as fuel prices again climbed and the consumer returned.[2]

Exhibit 1 Comparisons of Four Largest Class I Railroads in the US

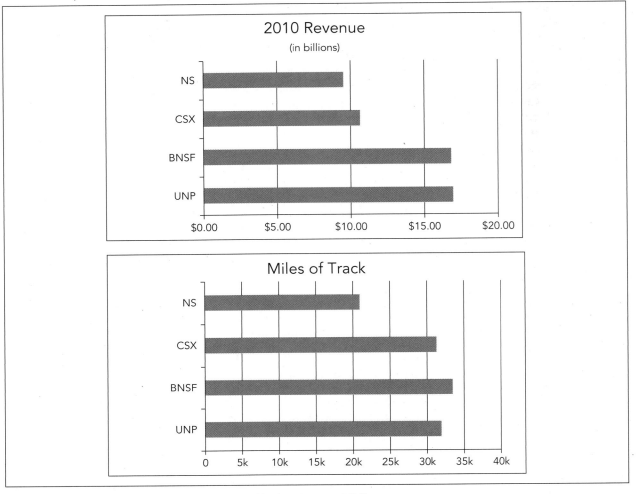

Source: Data provided by Rail Transportation in the US. IBIS World Industry Report and 10-K reports.

Exhibit 2 US Population Changes

Population Change By Region				
Region	2000	2010	2010 Change	2010 % Change
Northeast	53,594,378	55,317,240	1,722,862	3.2%
Midwest	64,392,776	66,927,001	2,534,225	3.9%
South	100,236,820	114,555,744	14,318,924	14.3%
West	63,197,932	71,945,553	8,747,621	13.8%
Total US Population	**281,421,906**	**308,745,538**	**27,323,632**	**9.7%**

Population Changes in UNP States				
State	2000	2010	2010 Change	2010 % Change
Arizona	5,130,632	6,392,017	1,261,385	24.6%
Arkansas	2,673,403	2,915,918	242,518	9.1%
California	33,871,648	37,253,956	3,382,308	10.0%
Colorado	4,301,261	5,029,196	727,935	16.9%

(Continued)

Exhibit 2 US Population Changes (*Continued*)

State	2000	2010	2010 Change	2010 % Change
Idaho	1,293,953	1,567,582	273,629	21.1%
Illinois	12,419,293	12,830,632	411,339	3.3%
Iowa	2,926,324	3,046,355	120,031	4.1%
Kansas	2,688,418	2,853,118	164,700	6.1%
Louisiana	4,468,976	4,533,372	64,396	1.4%
Minnesota	4,919,479	5,303,925	384,446	7.8%
Missouri	5,595,211	5,988,927	393,716	7.0%
Montana	902,195	989,415	87,220	9.7%
Nebraska	1,711,263	1,826,341	115,078	6.7%
Nevada	1,998,257	2,700,551	702,294	35.1%
New Mexico	1,819,046	2,059,179	240,133	13.2%
Oklahoma	3,450,654	3,751,351	300,697	8.7%
Oregon	3,421,399	3,831,074	409,675	12.0%
Tennessee	5,689,283	6,346,105	656,822	11.5%
Texas	20,851,820	25,145,561	4,293,741	20.6%
Utah	2,233,169	2,763,885	530,716	23.8%
Washington	5,894,121	6,724,540	830,419	14.1%
Wisconsin	5,363,675	5,686,986	323,311	6.0%
Wyoming	493,782	563,626	69,844	14.1%
TOTAL US Population Served by Union Pacific	**134,117,259**	**150,103,612**	**15,986,353**	**11.9%**

Percent of US Population Served by Union Pacific (2000)	**47.7%**
Percent of US Population Served by Union Pacific (2010)	**48.6%**
Population Served Increase	**0.96%**
Overall US Population Growth	**9.7%**
Overall US Population Served by Union Pacific Growth	**11.9%**

Source: Data provided by US Census Bureau. Accessed on 4/11/2011. http://2010.census.gov/

The Context of Rail Companies' Operations

The railroad industry is heavily regulated both locally and federally. The Federal Railroad Administration (FRA) is the US Department of Transportation (US DOT) agency tasked with the oversight, promulgation, and enforcement of rail safety in the US.[3] It is one of ten agencies focused on *intermodal transportation*—freight transport requiring multiple modes of transportation within a single shipment (maritime, truck, rail, air, and/or barge).

The US Environmental Protection Agency (US EPA) focuses on reducing the amount of pollution emitted from, among other things, locomotives. It is particularly concerned with large amounts of nitrogen oxides and particulate matter as they contribute to public health concerns.[4] Further environmental regulation at the state and local levels also exist, including a litany of laws from the Clean Air Act to the Comprehensive Environmental Response, Compensation, and Liability Act.

Railroad employment relations are not without heavy regulation via unionization. The United Transportation Union (UTU) represents employees from every Class I railroad including UNP.[5] The Railway Labor Act of 1926 sets guidelines for resolving disputes between railroads and employees to ensure interstate commerce continues uninterrupted and the collective bargaining rights of railroad employees are preserved.[6] An independent agency within the executive branch of the federal government, the Railroad Retirement Board (RRB) is tasked with providing unemployment, sickness, and retirement benefits to US railroad workers and their families.[7] The RRB performs functions similar to the Social Security Administration and state unemployment offices with the primary difference being that railroad employers are required to pay a higher percentage into the RRB fund.

In the wake of the terrorist attacks of September 11, 2001, railroads began to work closely with several

Exhibit 3 US Population Density*

Population Density* of States Where Union Pacific Operates							
State	2000	2010	2000 Density	2010 Density	2010 % Change	2000 Rank	2010 Rank
United States	281,421,906	308,745,538	79.7	87.4	9.66%		
Arizona	5,130,632	6,392,017	45.2	56.3	24.56%	38	35
Arkansas	2,673,400	2,915,918	51.4	56	8.95%	36	36
California	33,871,648	37,253,956	217.4	239.1	9.98%	14	13
Colorado	4,301,261	5,029,196	41.5	48.5	16.87%	39	39
Idaho	1,293,953	1,567,582	15.7	19	21.02%	46	46
Illinois	12,419,293	12,830,632	223.7	231.1	3.31%	13	14
Iowa	2,926,324	3,046,355	52.4	54.5	4.01%	35	38
Kansas	2,688,418	2,853,118	32.9	34.9	6.08%	42	42
Louisiana	4,468,976	4,533,372	103.4	104.9	1.45%	24	26
Minnesota	4,919,479	5,303,925	61.8	66.6	7.77%	33	33
Missouri	5,595,211	5,988,927	81.4	87.1	7.00%	29	30
Montana	902,195	989,415	6.2	6.8	9.68%	50	50
Nebraska	1,711,263	1,826,341	22.3	23.8	6.73%	44	45
Nevada	1,998,257	2,700,551	18.2	24.6	35.16%	45	44
New Mexico	1,819,046	2,059,179	15	17	13.33%	47	47
Oklahoma	3,450,654	3,751,351	50.3	54.7	8.75%	37	37
Oregon	3,421,399	3,831,074	35.6	39.9	12.08%	41	41
Tennessee	5,689,283	6,346,105	138	153.9	11.52%	21	21
Texas	20,851,820	25,145,561	79.8	96.3	20.68%	30	28
Utah	2,233,169	2,763,885	27.2	33.6	23.53%	43	43
Washington	5,894,121	6,724,540	88.7	101.2	14.09%	27	27
Wisconsin	5,363,675	5,686,986	99	105	6.06%	26	25
Wyoming	493,782	563,626	5.1	5.8	13.73%	51	51
TOTAL Density Change of States Served by Union Pacific	134,117,259	150,103,612	65.75	72.20	9.81%		
US Population Density Change	9.66%						
Population Density Change Within States Served by Union Pacific	9.81%						

* Density expressed as people per square mile. Density ranking expressed as most dense (1) to least dense (52)

Source: Data provided by US Census Bureau. Accessed on 4/11/2011. http://2010.census.gov/

state and federal agencies (Department of Homeland Security, the National Joint Terrorism Task Force, and the US Customs and Border Protection) to ensure the safety and protection of physical rail and the people and shipments that run on those rails. These efforts continue today.

Worldwide, people are becoming increasingly concerned with environmental protection of the planet. The increased social awareness of the damage carbon emissions wreak on the environment provides a powerful marketing tool for the railroad industry.[8] However, clients moving massive amounts of freight are still at least slightly more concerned about their bottom lines[9]—a fact that provides significant benefits to railroads when fuel prices are high as savvy customers/shippers often choose to not only lower their transportation costs by using rail, but also exploit their more environmentally sound decisions via marketing.[10]

With the recent increase in profits, railroad companies are investing in more fuel-efficient locomotives.[11]

High-speed rail may also greatly affect the freight industry with improved rail infrastructure, upgraded locomotives, increased capacity for railroads and trucking companies, and cost sharing benefits between freight and passenger trains.[12] Some experts believe high-speed rail will impact the freight industry in the same way the interstate highway system did, provided cooperation between freight and passenger rail operators is possible and safety in a high-speed environment is attainable.

The railroad industry in the US is defined by a low level of globalization as US railroads are owned primarily by domestic firms. Railroad industry revenues are largely generated from domestic operations even though many have operations inside Canada and one operates in Mexico.[13] However, factors outside the US—including the economic environments of Mexico, Canada, and China specifically, and additional foreign trade through western US ports indirectly—affect UNP nevertheless. The North American Free Trade Agreement (NAFTA) greatly increased surface transportation between Mexico, Canada, and the US yet, to date, the trucking industry appears to be the bigger beneficiary of this trend.[14] On the other hand, rail operators in the Western US benefit significantly from Chinese and other Asian imports as shipments brought to port on the Pacific Coast and shipped overland to the East Coast enjoy a 38 percent reduction in transport time compared to shipping through the Panama Canal to an East Coast port.[15]

The Inside Track

Class I railroads consist of eight large carriers that offer nearly identical services and attempt to differentiate based on the geography they serve and the number of shipments that originate and terminate within their miles of track. In 2003, the leading states for total rail tonnage originated included Wyoming, Illinois, West Virginia, Pennsylvania, and Kentucky. The leading states by tonnage terminated included Texas, Illinois, Florida, Ohio, and California.[16]

Industry analysts describe the Class I railroad industry as having economies of density: long hauls, large amounts of cargo, and reduced interchanges of traffic.[17] Since the creation of the doublestack rail car and the innovation of distributed powertrain operations (DPS), there has been increasing demand for long-haul and intermodal shipping. Doublestack cars allow railroads to carry double the freight per car length, allowing for more dense and thus more profitable hauls. However, economies of scale are not achieved through increased tonnage alone. The invention of DPS has allowed railroads to increase the number of rail cars per shipment, thus consuming less fuel per car while simultaneously reducing the cycle times of shipments. The top four players are expected to account for 78.3 percent of industry

revenue in 2011. This high concentration indicates the dominance of Class I operators and their extensive and efficient operations.[18]

The railroad industry is not an attractive industry for new entrants. Considerable capital is required to develop the necessary system infrastructure of rail networks, cars, locomotives, and new technologies. For example, between 1980 and 2009, Class I railroads spent $460 billion on infrastructure, equipment maintenance, and upgrades.[19] Rail lines are very expensive to construct and construction must be coordinated within an already active, complicated, and congested system. Line expansions must be connected with hubs and spokes of existing systems and to do so requires the cooperation of competitors.[20] These high capital investment costs combined with fierce competition from a highly concentrated field of four well-established, large players contribute to these barriers.[21]

Rail customers include industrial product manufacturers, intermodal transport companies, as well as agricultural, automotive, chemical, and energy firms. Large customers in the energy and intermodal segments often leverage their size for price concessions, a practice referred to as *countervailing*.[22] Customers are considered to have significant buying power due to the high concentration of revenues coming from certain industries, such as coal and intermodal transport, which accounted for 22 and 17 percent of rail transport revenue in 2010, respectively.[23] Intermodal traffic is increasing dramatically in the US—domestic intermodal traffic rose 11.7 percent in 2010, but UNP only garnered a 4 percent increase.[24] Shipping customers will pay more for the convenience and environmental benefits achieved through intermodal transport, yet intermodal capacity still lags globally.[25]

Switching costs have diminished in recent years due to the innovation of the Interline Settlement System (ISS) and Rate EDI Network (REN)—industry-wide standards of computerized data management that administer revenue sharing among railroads when goods are shipped on more than one line, as is often the case, as well as rapid billing and dispute resolution within the industry. In addition to ISS and REN, a system called Railinc that expedites service and tracking between carriers is widely used. While these new technologies make it easier to use multiple carriers, existing industry competitors often sign lengthy service contracts with their customers to discourage changing carriers. Switching costs may increase further with the growing trend of carriers to provide integrated logistics services and door-to-door delivery. This trend is expected to grow in the US, among shipping, freight forwarding, and road transport companies.[26]

In 2011, it is estimated that 22.6 percent of industry revenue will be spent on purchases. The primary purchase made by the rail transportation industry is fuel. Fortunately for industry operators, much of this cost is passed on to clients through fuel surcharges. As of 2006, fuel surcharges have been correlated to the actual cost of fuel for specific shipments. Consequently, the proportion of revenue required for purchases fluctuates with the cost of fuel and while revenue increases with the cost of fuel via surcharges, the potential profit gains are lost in the additional expense incurred.[27]

A trend forming in the industry is the move toward more cooperative relationships. "Our customers [railroads] are now showing signs of willingness to share the internal details of capital and maintenance budgets that are allowing us to make long-term decisions to meet capacity demands," says Georgetown Rail Equipment Company President and CEO, Wiggie Shell. Shell goes on to say, "There appears to be an emerging spirit of cooperation that never existed before between railroads and supplier contractors."[28]

The relationship between railroad and government is long-standing. One of the more significant government actions in recent years affecting railroad carriers was the passing of the Staggers Rail Act of 1980. Reforms within the Staggers Act included greater flexibility in pricing without close regulatory restraint, increased independence from collective rate-making procedures in rail pricing and service offers, permission to negotiate contract rates, and easier entry into and exit from rail markets.[29]

The Rail Safety and Improvement Act of 2008 (RSIA) mandated widespread installation of Positive Train Control (PTC) by 2015 and affects almost every railroad. PTC technology prevents train-to-train collisions and other types of accidents. Additionally, the RSIA revised its hours of service rules for specific railroad employees, imposed passenger service requirements, and expanded several safety-related issues with increased fines for violations.[30] UNP plans to spend $250 million on PTC in 2011 alone.[31]

The Surface Transportation Board (STB) is the successor agency to the Interstate Commerce Commission under the US DOT. The STB is a decision independent economic regulatory agency tasked with resolving railroad rate and service disputes and overseeing railroad mergers.[32] In addition, the STB affects the railroad industry through common carrier service of regulated traffic and freight car compensation as well as the transfer, extension, and abandonment of rail lines. Recently, the STB launched exploratory proceedings on whether to expand rail regulation and several bills introduced within the US Senate in 2011 could provide additional authority to the STB that would include new antitrust provisions.[33]

Of particular note for this industry is that, under federal law, railroads have a "common carrier obligation" to not only transport hazardous materials, but to bear the financial liabilities of doing so as well.[34] As part of the FRA, rail carriers are required to conduct an analysis prior to transporting hazardous materials to establish an appropriate route that enhances the safety and security of those living in areas where the materials may travel.[35]

Railroad Crossings

Trucking Industry

Possibly the most significant competitors of UNP are not railroads at all. The railroad industry is part of the larger land freight transportation strategic group that includes pipelines and trucking companies along with Class I railroads. Trucking accounts for more than 85 percent of freight shipments (by volume) in the US and the trucking industry holds several competitive advantages over rail.[36] Perhaps the most significant of these advantages is that trucking is faster; it takes only 60 hours for a truck, driven by a team, to drive from New York to Los Angeles.[37] In response to this advantage, UNP and CSX entered into a strategic alliance in 2003 to provide 63-hour coast-to-coast freight transport. While their ability to ally to diminish this advantage is commendable, the advantages of over-the-road delivery don't stop there. Trucks are not restricted to existing rail networks and can travel all over cities to make door-to-door deliveries. And finally, the roads trucking companies rely on are financed by federal, state, and local governments whereas railroads have to finance and construct their rail networks themselves.

Class I Railroads

The Class I railroad group is a broad category and represents an array of rail companies that vary greatly in size, scope, and resources. In 2006, the American Association of Railroads classified companies with annual revenues in excess of $346.8 million dollars as Class I.[38] To illustrate the significant differences in Class I carriers, UNP, the largest railroad operating in North America, had revenues of $15.5 billion in 2006, a number 44 times greater than the smallest Class I railroad. There are eight Class I railroads operating in North America but the top four players will likely account for 78.3 percent of all group revenues in 2011. As stated earlier, the four major players in Class I are BNSF, UNP, CSX, and NS and all compete fiercely on price, transit time, and reliability.[39] Several major product industries represent the highly sought after customers of these Class I railroads—industrial, agricultural food, consumer goods, chemicals, and coal. All Class I railroads exhibit a great deal of resource similarity.

Burlington Northern-Santa Fe Corporation (BNSF). Largely due to the similar geographic territory each covers, BNSF and UNP are major competitors. With the vast majority of their business happening west of the Mississippi River, BNSF and UNP account for 24.5

percent and 24.6 percent of Class I railroad revenues, respectively. One of the most active areas of competition between these two firms is the Southern Powder River Basin of Wyoming. A large amount of coal—the bread and butter of the railroad industry—is produced in this relatively small area of the western US and both BNSF and UNP are strongly represented in the region. Making its organizational structure unique in the top four, in 2010, BNSF became a wholly owned subsidiary of Berkshire Hathaway and its shares are no longer publicly traded.[40]

CSX Corporation. CSX Corporation is the largest railroad operating east of the Mississippi River with what little geographic overlap it has with UNP mostly occurring around Chicago and New Orleans. In 2003, UNP and CSX entered into a strategic alliance to provide 63-hour coast-to-coast freight transport, effectively removing a historical advantage of the trucking industry.[41]

In 2010, CSX accounted for 15.4 percent of market share among Class I railroads; coal shipments accounted for a high percentage of CSX's revenue and freight volume, 30 percent and 27 percent respectively.[42] The company has a high degree of market dependence on the coal industry, especially in West Virginia.

Norfolk Southern (NS). Norfolk Southern is the main competitor of CSX. The two railroads operate in the same area of the US (east of the Mississippi River) and depend greatly on the same products (in 2010, 24.5 percent of NS revenue was derived from coal). However, compared to CSX, NS is a smaller, more diversified company. It has subsidiaries operating in natural resources, land development, and telecommunications.[43] This is likely a revenue growth strategy employed by NS in response to its position as the fourth largest player in a well staked out industry.

Looking Inside UNP

Some of UNP's largest and most notable resources are its financial assets, which have grown in each of the past five years. In 2010, UNP reported $16.9 billion in revenue—up 20 percent from 2009. An excess of $1.4 billion was recorded as free cash flows. At year end, UNP had more than $43 billion in total assets.[44]

Employees

Another important resource for UNP is its highly trained, professional workforce. UNP employs nearly 43,000 people and trains them extensively to maintain UNP's quality standards.[45] UNP designed its Educational Assistance Program to encourage full-time, regular staff employees to enroll in job or career related courses, thus increasing their value within the company. In addition, UNP offers several other programs to improve

the quality of its workforce including its Management Development Program, Leadership Development Program, Field Management Training Program, and Operations Management Program.[46]

Tracks and Rail Equipment

UNP's rail network includes 31,953 route miles. Of this, it owns 26,083 miles and the remaining are operated through trackage rights and leases. Apart from this, it includes 6,596 miles of other main lines, 3,118 miles of passing lines and turnouts, and 9,006 miles of switching and classification yard lines. In total, UNP controls 50,673 miles of tracks in the US. Its trackage distribution and mileage is similar to that of BNSF. UNP has recently invested $1.7 billion in new tracks to reduce fuel consumption, transportation, and idling times.[47]

Rail equipment includes locomotives, railcars, heavy maintenance equipment, as well as machinery and vehicles for maintenance, transportation of crews, and other activities (see Exhibit 4 for complete breakdown of rail equipment infrastructure).[48]

Facilities

UNP operates multiple dispatching centers that coordinate locomotive movement, manage traffic and crews, and coordinate interchanges with other railroads. The Harriman Dispatching Center in Omaha, NE is UNP's primary dispatching facility, with 900 employees.[49]

Intermodal terminals handle containers that can be transported using multiple modes of transport. UNP manages major intermodal terminals in Los Angeles, Memphis, Wilmington, Chicago, Dallas, and San Antonio.[50] UNP is currently in the midst of a $2.6 billion dollar infrastructure upgrade[51] and will begin construction of a new $500 million intermodal facility in New Mexico this year.[52] However, the company still lacks sufficient intermodal capacity in key areas like Texas, California, and Illinois, and requires more miles of double track in Southern California where 26 percent of its shipments originate.[53]

Classification yards are used to sort the rail carriages for separation and transportation of goods. UNP operates multiple such yards. The Bailey Yard in North Platte, Nebraska is the largest of this type in the world.[54]

Technology

With a railroad's large asset base and heavy reliance on transaction-based processes, new technologies can be scaled upward immediately to deliver strong financial returns. UNP employs a CAD III (Computer Aided Dispatching) system to provide managers with real-time information regarding train and locomotive location and status and assists them in making decisions to improve both utilization and on-time performance.[55]

Exhibit 4 Rail Equipment Details

Locomotives	Owned	Leased	Total	Average Age (yrs.)
Multiple purpose	4,935	2,628	7,563	15.9
Switching	431	26	457	31.5
Other	95	59	154	25
Total locomotives	**5,461**	**2,713**	**8,174**	**N/A**

Freight cars	Owned	Leased	Total	Average Age (yrs.)
Covered hoppers	12,123	18,252	30,375	28.7
Open hoppers	11,854	4,351	16,205	31.2
Gondolas	6,500	6,190	12,690	28.1
Boxcars	5,702	1,857	7,559	28
Refrigerated cars	2,584	4,331	6,915	22.6
Flat cars	2,885	664	3,549	33.3
Other	104	456	560	N/A
Total freight cars	**41,752**	**36,101**	**77,853**	**N/A**

Highway revenue equipment	Owned	Leased	Total	Average Age (yrs.)
Containers	9,401	39,234	48,635	5.2
Chassis	2,669	23,210	25,879	7.3
Total highway revenue equipment	**12,070**	**62,444**	**74,514**	**N/A**

Source: Union Pacific Corporation Form 10-K for the fiscal year ended Dec 31, 2010.

Competing on a Daily Basis

UNP links 23 states in the western two-thirds of the US. It has the largest track network in the industry and serves many of the fastest growing cities in the US. Its freight comes from a diverse range of industries including agriculture, automotive, chemical, energy, industrial, and intermodal,[56] providing it with protection from cyclical business fluctuations.

UNP connects with Canada's rail systems and is the only railroad serving all six major gateways to Mexico, making it North America's premier rail franchise.[57]

The rail freight industry is extremely fuel efficient when compared to its major competitor—the trucking industry. Rising fuel prices are proving to be a competitive advantage to the rail freight industry as more freight is being pushed off the roads and onto rails.[58]

Due to high barriers of entry, railroad companies typically face more competition from alternate modes of transport rather than from other railroads. Depending on the specific market, deregulated motor carriers and other railroads, as well as river barges, ships, and pipelines in certain markets, may exert pressure on price and service levels.[59] Additionally, advanced, high service truck lines offering expedited delivery using a subsidized infrastructure affect the market for non-bulk, time-sensitive freight.

UNP's primary rail competitor in the Western region of the US is BNSF Railway. Other Class I railroads, numerous regional railroads, and motor carriers also operate in the same territories served by UNP.[60]

Rising demand for coal in developing countries coupled with the drop in demand for coal within the US could increasingly drive this major revenue source to seaports—especially for mines located near the coasts.

To remain competitive, UNP and other railroads must continue to develop and implement operating efficiencies to improve productivity and expedite delivery. It must also continually focus on the addition of new track, double tracking of existing routes, new routes, and fuel-efficient locomotives to better leverage the fuel efficiency advantage of rail over trucking.[61]

UNP's Culture

UNP emphasizes high ethical standards, corporate citizenship, and a commitment to safety. The dynamics of this industry expose many of its employees to time away from home, fluctuating work schedules, and safety challenges. UNP addresses these challenges through actively promoting a work culture that values people and relationships. UNP supports employee health through its HealthTrack initiative and its emphasis on preventative measures. UNP believes that a healthy workplace leads to a healthy life; thus it has invested in policies and infrastructure to address many industry specific needs including better on-the-job sleeping facilities, stress management, and workload flexibility. Additionally, UNP emphasizes safety through its Total Safety Culture initiative, focuses on risk reduction, and works to improve and standardize best practices. Due to these measures, UNP has achieved record-breaking reductions in injuries. UNP also continues to make environmental stewardship a priority as evidenced by its energy-efficient locomotives and offices.[62]

UNP's vision is one of stable growth achieved with a clearly charted path, hard work, and good decisions. UNP actively seeks input from its employees and clearly communicates its expectations to provide employees with a clear understanding of their role in creating a successful future for UNP. Teamwork is actively encouraged as an efficient approach to reach common goals, improve safety, and increase customer satisfaction.[63]

UNP's Leaders

UNP has a moderately heterogeneous top management team. Having worked in a variety of management positions within UNP since 1978, James Young, UNP's CEO, has deep industry and company insight. UNP's Executive VPs—Lance Fritz, John Koraleski, and Robert Knight—have extensive industry and company experience as well. Collectively, they bring a healthy mix of finance, safety, operations, marketing, labor relations, energy, and automotive experience to the table—most of it acquired in the railroad industry.[64] While the absence of "fresh blood" and the insights it can bring could be viewed as a negative in many industries, because of the unique culture, life cycle, and requirements of railroads, extensive industry knowledge is essential for top management to maintain a steady, long-term strategy.

Twelve members led by the CEO comprise the UNP board and represent various realms of business and position including education, energy, law, military, investment management, banking, and strategy. This diversification allows UNP to explore future growth and contributions to society with the informed guidance of its board. The board believes that CEO duality is not an issue and that unified leadership fosters clear accountability, effective decision making, and better oversight of and focus on corporate strategy and strategic initiatives. The board does, however, appoint an independent director to ensure a balance of power.[65]

Linking Up UNP's Parts

UNP started as a highly centralized organization; however, as it grew, difficulties with scheduling and route planning emerged. To overcome this issue, UNP moved to empower regional divisions. Today, regional managers make operational decisions related to scheduling and routing within their territories. UNP has subdivided these regions into service units and further divided each of these service units into subdivisions based on a track network of mainlines and branch lines.[66] This structure has helped the firm improve customer satisfaction, operational excellence, responsiveness, accountability, and

flexibility. Given that the organization plans to expand into serving new industries and is in a position to recruit additional business due to increasing oil prices, this decentralized structure provides the firm with strategic flexibility. Specifically, this decentralized structure helps UNP leverage its regional know-how, capabilities, and stakeholder relationships to respond more rapidly to local needs and improve its competitive advantage.

Staying on Track

Several challenges currently face UNP and its response to these challenges will significantly affect the overall health and position of the company in the future. Many of these problems will require creative, far-reaching solutions and not a small amount of capital expenditure.

Consistency of Shipping Volume

As evidenced by wildly variable revenues from 2007 to 2010, recent volatility in the price of oil and the overall health of the economy has led to significant variance in UNP's total shipments over the last several years (Exhibit 5). The high price of oil in 2008 forced many companies to transition their shipments from trucking to rail to take advantage of the fuel efficiencies enjoyed by railroad shipping. However, later that year, the financial crisis hastened an overall decrease in shipping volume—a problem exacerbated, from UNP's perspective, by plummeting oil prices, making shipping by truck economical once again.

Necessary Infrastructure Improvements

The railroad industry is a capital-intensive industry that requires a great deal of plant, property, and equipment (PPE) expenditures merely to maintain the status quo. UNP is facing a situation where significant capital outlays beyond infrastructure maintenance will be required. Expenditures on the PTC system, new intermodal ramps, and additional miles of double track will easily cost several billion dollars and UNP must find a cost-effective way to raise this capital.

Door-to-Door Industry Trend

One of the major changes underway in the shipping industry is the customers' desire for "one stop shopping" when it comes to coordinating the delivery of their products.[67] Manufacturers at home and abroad want to deal with integrated shipping companies that can pick up goods at a factory anywhere in the world and carry them all the way to their final destination. Meeting this customer need will require that a company have access to all modes of shipping: boat, rail, air, and truck. UNP has a litany of financial resources, logistics expertise, and a significant history of mergers and acquisitions that would allow it to enter the marketplace and acquire trucking

Exhibit 5 Union Pacific Railroad – Financial Performance

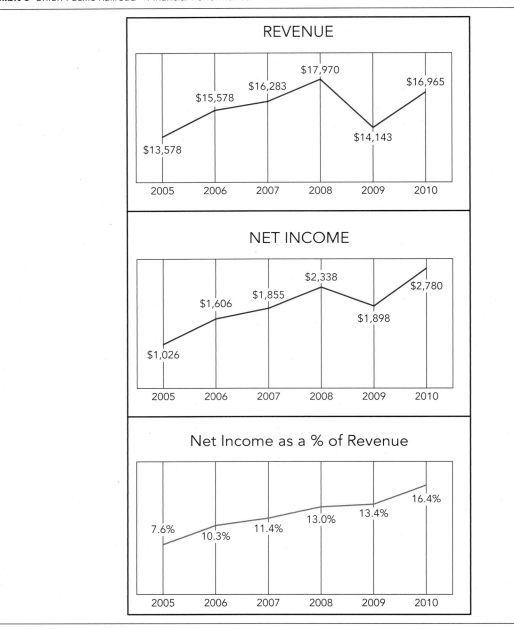

Source: Data adapted from Rail Transportation in the US. *IBIS World Industry Report.*

and shipping companies to complement its rail shipping services. Should they choose to compete at this level, whether UNP chooses joint ventures or full on horizontal integration, a large source of new capital will be required.

UNP'S Track Record

UNP has great need for an increase of capital in the coming years to meet the demands of the market. There will be significant spending for the government required safety system—PTC—and additional track.

Further, should UNP choose to pursue it, a long-term strategy of horizontal integration would require large cash flows for strategic purchases. To facilitate these investments, UNP will need to raise roughly nine billion dollars in the capital markets. To determine the most beneficial means of raising this capital, it is necessary to compare the current position of both UNP and its direct public competitors (see Exhibits 6-11).[ii] These

[ii]As a privately held corporation, financial statements for BNSF are not available.

Exhibit 6 Union Pacific Consolidated Statements of Income

Consolidated Statements of Income (USD $)	12 Months Ended		
In Millions, except Per Share data	Dec. 31, 2010	Dec. 31, 2009	Dec. 31, 2008
Operating revenues [Abstract]			
Freight revenues	$16,069	$13,373	$17,118
Other revenues	896	770	852
Total operating revenues	16,965	14,143	17,970
Operating expenses [Abstract]			
Compensation and benefits	4,314	4,063	4,457
Fuel	2,486	1,763	3,983
Purchased services and materials	1,836	1,644	1,928
Depreciation	1,487	1,427	1,366
Equipment and other rents	1,142	1,180	1,326
Other	719	687	840
Total operating expenses	11,984	10,764	13,900
Operating income	4,981	3,379	4,070
Other income	54	195	92
Interest expense	(602)	(600)	(511)
Income before income taxes	4,433	2,974	3,651
Income taxes	(1,653)	(1,084)	(1,316)
Net income	$ 2,780	$ 1,890	$ 2,335
Share and Per Share [Abstract]			
Earnings per share - basic	$5.58	$3.76	$4.57
Earnings per share - diluted	$5.53	$3.74	$4.53
Weighted average number of shares - basic	498.2	503	510.6
Weighted average number of shares - diluted	502.9	505.8	515
Dividends declared per share	$ 1.31	$ 1.08	$ 0.98

Source: Union Pacific Corporation Form 10-K for the fiscal year ended Dec 31, 2010.

Exhibit 7 Union Pacific Consolidated Statements of Financial Position

Consolidated Statements of Financial Position (USD $)	12 Months Ended	
In Millions	Dec. 31, 2010	Dec. 31, 2009
Current assets [Abstract]		
Cash and cash equivalents	$1,086	$1,850
Accounts receivable, net	1,184	666
Materials and supplies	534	475
Current deferred income taxes	261	339
Other current assets	367	350
Total current assets	3,432	3,680
Investments	1,137	1,036
Net properties	38,253	37,202
Other assets	266	266
Total assets	43,088	42,184

(Continued)

Exhibit 7 Union Pacific Consolidated Statements of Financial Position (*Continued*)

| Consolidated Statements of Financial Position (USD $) | 12 Months Ended | |
In Millions	Dec. 31, 2010	Dec. 31, 2009
Current liabilities [Abstract]		
Accounts payable and other current liabilities	2,713	2,470
Debt due within one year	239	212
Total current liabilities	2,952	2,682
Debt due after one year	9,003	9,636
Deferred income taxes	11,557	11,044
Other long-term liabilities	1,813	2,021
Commitments and contingencies		
Total liabilities	25,325	25,383
Common shareholders' equity [Abstract]		
Common shares, $2.50 par value, 800,000,000 authorized; 553,931,181 and 553,497,981 issued; 491,565,880 and 505,039,952 outstanding, respectively	1,385	1,384
Paid-in-surplus	3,985	3,968
Retained earnings	17,154	15,027
Treasury stock	(4,027)	(2,924)
Accumulated other comprehensive loss	(734)	(654)
Total common shareholders' equity	17,763	16,801
Total liabilities and common shareholders' equity	$43,088	$42,184

Source: Union Pacific Corporation Form 10-K for the fiscal year ended Dec 31, 2010.

Exhibit 8 Norfolk Southern Consolidated Statements of Income

| Consolidated Statements of Income (USD$) | 12 Months Ended | | |
In Millions, except Per Share data	Dec. 31, 2010	Dec. 31, 2009	Dec. 31, 2008
Consolidated Statements of Income			
Railway operating revenues	$9,516	$7,969	$10,661
Railway operating expenses:			
Compensation and benefits	2,708	2,401	2,684
Purchased services and rents	1,477	1,403	1,599
Fuel	1,079	725	1,638
Depreciation	819	837	804
Materials and other	757	641	852
Total railway operating expenses	6,840	6,007	7,577
Income from railway operations	2,676	1,962	3,084
Other income - net	153	127	110
Interest expense on debt	462	467	444
Income before income taxes	2,367	1,622	2,750
Provision for income taxes	871	588	1,034
Net income	$1,496	$1,034	$ 1,716
Per share amounts:			
Basic	$ 4.06	$ 2.79	$ 4.58
Diluted	$ 4.00	$ 2.76	$ 4.52

Source: Norfolk Southern Corporation Form 10-K for the fiscal year ended Dec 31, 2010.

Exhibit 9 Norfolk Southern Consolidated Balance Sheets

Consolidated Balance Sheets (USD $) In Millions	Dec. 31, 2010	Dec. 31, 2009
Assets		
Cash and cash equivalents	$ 827	$ 996
Short-term investments	283	90
Accounts receivable - net	807	766
Materials and supplies	169	164
Deferred income taxes	145	142
Other current assets	240	88
Total current assets	2,471	2,246
Investments	2,193	2,164
Properties less accumulated depreciation	23,231	22,643
Other assets	304	316
Total assets	28,199	27,369
Liabilities and stockholders' equity		
Accounts payable	1,181	974
Short-term debt	100	100
Income and other taxes	199	109
Other current liabilities	244	232
Current maturities of long-term debt	358	374
Total current liabilities	2,082	1,789
Long-term debt	6,567	6,679
Other liabilities	1,793	1,801
Deferred income taxes	7,088	6,747
Total liabilities	17,530	17,016
Stockholders' equity:		
Common stock $1.00 per share par value, 1,350,000,000 shares authorized; outstanding 357,362,604 and 369,019,990 shares, respectively, net of treasury shares	358	370
Additional paid-in capital	1,892	1,809
Accumulated other comprehensive loss	(805)	(853)
Retained income	9,224	9,027
Total stockholders' equity	10,669	10,353
Total liabilities and stockholders' equity	$28,199	$27,369

Source: Norfolk Southern Corporation Form 10-K for the fiscal year ended Dec 31, 2010.

Exhibit 10 CSX Consolidated Income Statements

Consolidated Income Stmts (USD $)	12 Months Ended		
In Millions, except Share data in Thousands, unless otherwise specified	Dec. 31, 2010	Dec. 25, 2009	Dec. 26, 2008
Income Statement [Abstract]			
Revenue	$10,636	$9,041[1]	$11,255[1]
Expense			
Labor and Fringe	2,957	2,629[1]	2,955[1]
Materials, Supplies and Other	2,075	1,999[1]	2,407[1]
Fuel	1,212	849[1]	1,817[1]
Depreciation	947	903[1]	900[1]
Equipment and Other Rents	374	391[1]	425[1]
Total Expense	7,565	6,771[1]	8,504[1]
Operating Income	3,071	2,270[1]	2,751[1]
Interest Expense	−557	−558[1]	-519[1]
Other Income - Net	32	34[1]	100[1]
Earnings from Continuing Operations Before Income Taxes	2,546	1,746[1]	2,332[1]
Income Tax Expense	−983	−618[1]	−847[1]
Earnings from Continuing Operations	1,563	1,128[1]	1,485[1]
Discontinued Operations	0	15[1]	−130[1]
Net Earnings	$ 1,563[2]	$1,143[1], [2]	$ 1,355[1], [2]
Net Earnings Per Share, Basic			
Continuing Operations (in $ per share)	$ 4.1	$ 2.88[1]	$ 3.71[1]
Discontinued Operations (in $ per share)	$ 0	$ 0.04[1]	$ (0.32)[1]
Net Earnings (in $ per share)	$ 4.1	$ 2.92[1]	$ 3.39[1]
Net Earnings Per Share, Assuming Dilution			
Continuing Operations (in $ per share)	$ 4.06	$ 2.85[1]	$ 3.64[1]
Discontinued Operations (in $ per share)	$ 0	$ 0.04[1]	$ (0.32)[1]
Net Earnings (in $ per share)	$ 4.06	$ 2.89[1]	$ 3.32[1]
Average Common Shares Outstanding (Thousands) (in shares)	381,108	392,127[1]	400,740[1]
Average Common Shares Outstanding, Assuming Dilution (Thousands) (in shares)	384,509	395,686[1]	408,620[1]
Cash Dividends Paid Per Common Share (in $ per share)	$ 0.98	$ 0.88[1]	$ 0.77[1]

[1]Certain amounts have been adjusted for the retrospective change in accounting policy for rail grinding.

[2]CSX follows a 52/53 week fiscal reporting calendar which allows every year to consistently end on a Friday. Fiscal years 2010, 2009, 2008 and 2007 ended on December 31, 2010, December 25, 2009, December 26, 2008 and December 28, 2007.

Source: CSX Corp Form 10-K for the fiscal year ended Dec 31, 2010.

statements show that UNP has a significant advantage in both ROA (6.52 percent) and Operating ROA (11.68 percent). UNP also outpaces competitors in return on invested capital (11.58 percent). These factors lead UNP to have a much larger net operating income (Exhibit 12). The financials indicate that UNP is more efficient with both assets and invested capital.

The capital markets consider the rail industry a fairly safe investment because of the relatively steady cash flows generated by operations. The industry has very low costs for the debt markets and UNP could obtain a very advantageous rate if it were to issue long-term bonds. However, when raising such a large amount of capital, it is first necessary to determine the effect each financing choice would have on the capital structure of the firm. This is determined by the weighted average cost of capital (WACC). The current WACC for UNP is 10.05 percent and is largely in line with the industry.

Case 27: Union Pacific Corporation

Exhibit 11 CSX Consolidated Balance Sheets

Consolidated Balance Sheets (USD $)	Dec. 31, 2010	Dec. 25, 2009
In Millions		
Current Assets		
Cash and Cash Equivalents	$ 1,292	$ 1,029
Short-term Investments	54	61[1]
Accounts Receivable - Net	993	995[1]
Materials and Supplies	218	203[1]
Deferred Income Taxes	192	158[1]
Other Current Assets	106	124[1]
Total Current Assets	2,855	2,570[1]
Properties	32,065	30,907[1]
Accumulated Depreciation	(8,266)	(7,843)[1]
Properties - Net	23,799	23,064[1]
Investment in Conrail	673	650[1]
Affiliates and Other Companies	461	438[1]
Other Long-term Assets	353	165[1]
Total Assets	28,141	26,887[1]
Current Liabilities		
Accounts Payable	1,046	967[1]
Labor and Fringe Benefits Payable	520	383[1]
Casualty, Environmental and Other Reserves	176	190[1]
Current Maturities of Long-term Debt	613	113[1]
Income and Other Taxes Payable	85	112[1]
Other Current Liabilities	97	100[1]
Total Current Liabilities	2,537	1,865[1]
Casualty, Environmental and Other Reserves	502	547[1]
Long-term Debt	8,051	7,895[1]
Deferred Income Taxes	7,053	6,528[1]
Other Long-term Liabilities	1,298	1,284[1]
Total Liabilities	19,441	18,119[1]
Common Stock, $1 Par Value	370	393[1]
Other Capital	0	80[1]
Retained Earnings	9,087	9,090[1]
Accumulated Other Comprehensive Loss	(771)	(809)[1]
Noncontrolling Minority Interest	14	14[1]
Total Shareholders' Equity	8,700[2]	8,768[1],[2]
Total Liabilities and Shareholders' Equity	$28,141	$26,887[1]

[1]Certain amounts have been adjusted for the retrospective change in accounting policy for rail grinding.

[2]CSX follows a 52/53 week fiscal reporting calendar which allows every year to consistently end on a Friday. Fiscal years 2010, 2009, 2008 and 2007 ended on Dec 31, 2010, Dec 25, 2009, Dec 26, 2008 and Dec 28, 2007.

Source: CSX Corp Form 10-K for the fiscal year ended Dec 31, 2010.

Were bonds to be issued, the advantage of the company would increase nearly two times. In addition, the added debt would increase the cost of that debt and consequently the required return demanded by equity investors.

The View from the Caboose

Despite its magnitude, until a driver is stuck at a train crossing, the railroad industry tends to operate just below the consciousness of most Americans. As the

Exhibit 12: UNP's Net Operating Income

	UNP Equity	CSX Equity	NSC Equity
Operating ROA	11.68	11.16	9.63
ROA	6.52	5.68	5.38
ROIC	11.58	7.98	7.11
NOPAT	3140.66	1900.30	1696.30

most essential building block in the early expansion of this nation—once a cultural staple and the subject of folklore—the significance of the service it provides as well as the uncharted potential it holds is too often overlooked or, at best, considered only as an after-thought. To regain its stronghold, UNP and other rail-roads must continue to develop and implement operating efficiencies to improve productivity and expedite delivery. It must also focus on adding new track, building new routes, and employing increasingly more fuel-efficient locomotives to better leverage its fuel efficiency advantage over trucking. Finally, its humble workhorse mindset notwithstanding, UNP should not hesitate to toot its own horn now and again just to remind us all of the job they do.

NOTES

1. Mackun, P., Wilson, S. (Mar 2011). Population Distribution and Change: 2000 to 2010. *US Census Bureau*. Accessed 11 Apr 2011 at http://www.census.gov/prod/cen2010/briefs/c2010br-01.pdf
2. Culbert, K. (Mar 2011). Rail Transportation in the US. *IBIS World Industry Report*.
3. About the FRA. *Federal Railroad Administration*. Accessed 11 Apr 2011 at http://www.fra.dot.gov/Pages/2.shtml
4. Nonroad Engines, Equipment, and Vehicles: Locomotives. (6 Jan 2011). *US Environmental Protection Agency*. Accessed 11 Apr 2011 at http://www.epa.gov/otaq/locomotives.htm
5. About UTU: The United Transportation Union. *United Transportation Union*. Accessed 22 Apr 2011 at http://www.utu.org/worksite/about2.htm
6. About the FRA. *op. cit.*
7. US Railroad Retirement Board: An Agency Overview. (Jan 2011). *US Railroad Retirement Board*. Accessed 12 Apr 2011 at http://www.rrb.gov/opa/agency_overview.asp
8. Culbert, K. *op. cit.*
9. The GfK Roper Yale Survey on Environmental Issues. (Summer 2008). *Yale University*. Accessed 22 Apr 2011 at http://environment.yale.edu/climate/files/GfK%20Roper%20Yale%20Survey%20-%20Summer%202008%20FINAL.pdf
10. Culbert, K. *op. cit.*
11. *Ibid.*
12. Aadnesen, C. 10 Ways High-Speed Rail Will Impact the Freight Industry. *Journal of Commerce*. Accessed 22 Apr 2011 at http://www.joc.com/2010/10-ways-high-speed-rail-will-impact-freight-industry
13. Culbert, K. *op. cit.*
14. 2010 Surface Trade with Canada and Mexico Rose from 2009, Remains Lower than 2008. (17 Mar 2011). *RITA, Bureau of Transportation Statistics*. Accessed 22 Apr 2011 at http://www.bts.gov/press_releases/2011/bts016_11/html/bts016_11.html
15. Culbert, K. *op. cit.*
16. *Ibid.*
17. Schoech, P.E., Swanson, J. A. (2010). Patterns of Productivity Growth for US Class I Railroads: An Examination of Pre- and Post-Deregulation Determinants. *lrca.com*. Accessed 26 Apr 2011 at http://www.lrca.com/topics/Schoech_Swanson_Patterns_of_Productivity_Growth_for_US_Class_I_Railroads.pdf
18. Culbert, K. *op. cit.*
19. Gale. "Railroads-Line-Haul Operating." *Cengage Learning* (2011).
20. Culbert, K. *op. cit.*
21. Schoech, P.E., Swanson, J. A. *op. cit.*
22. Culbert, K. *op. cit.*
23. Gale. *op. cit.*
24. Terreri, A. (2 Jan 2011). Intermodal Rail Gains Momentum. *World Trade 100*. Accessed 20 Apr 2011 at http://www.worldtradewt100.com/articles/87269-intermodal-rail-gains-momentum?WT.rss_f=Ground&WT.rss_a=Intermodal+Rail+Gains+Momentum&WT.rss_ev=a
25. Brett, D. (1 Dec 2010). Shippers Will Pay More to Go Intermodal. *IFW*. Accessed 20 Apr 2011 at http://www.ifw-net.com/freightpubs/ifw/article.htm?artid=20017830386&src=rss
26. Gale. *op. cit.*
27. Culbert, K. *op. cit.*
28. Miller, L. S. (2 Feb 2011). Productivity's Big Payoff. *Railway Age*. Accessed 20 Apr 2011 at http://www.railwayage.com/in-this-issue/productivity-s-big-payoff-february-2011.html
29. Derthick, M., Quirk, P. J. (1985). *The Politics of Deregulation*. Washington, DC: Brookings Institution.
30. Public Law 110-432-Oct 15, 2008: Federal Rail Safety Improvements. *US Government Printing Office*. Accessed 20 Apr 2011 at http://www.gpo.gov/fdsys/pkg/PLAW-110publ432/pdf/PLAW-110publ432.pdf
31. Union Pacific Corporation Form 10-K for the fiscal year ended Dec 31, 2010. *sec.gov*. Accessed 16 Apr at http://www.sec.gov/Archives/edgar/data/100885/000119312511024531/d10k.htm
32. About STB: Overview. *Surface Transportation Board*. Accessed 14 Apr 2011 at http://www.stb.dot.gov/stb/about/overview.html
33. Union Pacific Corporation Form 10-K for the fiscal year ended Dec 31, 2010. *op. cit.*
34. *Ibid.*
35. About the FRA. *op. cit.*
36. Terreri, A. *op. cit.*
37. Culbert, K. *op. cit.*
38. Class I Railroad Statistics. (15 Jan 2008). *Association of American Railroads-Policy and Economics Department*. Accessed 20 Apr 2011 at http://www.aar.org/AboutAAR/~/media/AAR/Common/Statistics.ashx
39. Culbert, K. *op. cit.*
40. *Ibid.*
41. *Ibid.*
42. *Ibid.*
43. *Ibid.*
44. Union Pacific Corporation Form 10-K for the fiscal year ended Dec 31, 2010. *op. cit.*
45. *Ibid.*
46. Working at Union Pacific. *Union Pacific*. Accessed 26 Apr 2011 at http://www.unionpacific.jobs/careers/working/index.shtml
47. Union Pacific Corporation Form 10-K for the fiscal year ended Dec 31, 2010. *op. cit.*
48. *Ibid.*

49. *Ibid.*
50. *Ibid.*
51. Hunt, A. (6 Oct 2010). Union Pacific Railroad to Recommence Double-Track Project on Railroad's Historic Sunset Route. *Union Pacific.* Accessed 25 Apr 2011 at http://www.uprr.com/newsinfo/releases/service/2010/1006_sunset.shtml
52. Newly minted New Mexico law paves way for UP intermodal facility. (6 Apr 2011). *Progressive Railroading.* Accessed 25 Apr 2011 at http://www.progressiverailroading.com/news/article/Newly-minted-New-Mexico-law-paves-way-for-UP-intermodal-facility--26236
53. Hunt, A. *op. cit.*
54. Union Pacific Corporation Form 10-K for the fiscal year ended Dec 31, 2010. *op. cit.*
55. Union Pacific Railroad: Overview. *Union Pacific.* Accessed 26 Apr 2011 at http://www.up.com/investors/factbooks/factbook99/uprrhigh99.pdf
56. Union Pacific Corporation Form 10-K for the fiscal year ended Dec 31, 2010. *op. cit.*
57. *Ibid.*
58. Culbert, K. *op. cit.*
59. *Ibid.*
60. *Ibid.*
61. *Ibid.*
62. Safety. *Union Pacific.* Accessed 26 Apr 2011 at http://www.unionpacific.jobs/careers/working/culture/safety.shtml
63. Company Culture. *Union Pacific.* Accessed 26 Apr 2011 at http://www.unionpacific.jobs/careers/working/culture/index.shtml
64. Executive Profiles. *Union Pacific.* Accessed 26 Apr 2011 at http://www.uprr.com/aboutup/exec/index.shtml
65. Corporate Governance. *Union Pacific.* Accessed 26 Apr 2011 at http://www.up.com/investors/governance/index.shtml
66. *Ibid.*
67. Culbert, K. *op. cit.*

Jason Arnold, Kari Froehlich, Mat McBride, Stanley Parker, Ann Utterback, Robin Chapman, Gail Christian

Arizona State University

Introduction

Valeant Pharmaceuticals International, Inc. promotes itself as a multinational specialty pharmaceutical company with a diverse product portfolio focusing on branded pharmaceuticals, branded and unbranded generics, and over-the-counter (OTC) products specializing in neurology and dermatology.[1] Product sales focus on North America, Central Europe, Mexico, Brazil, and Australia, with manufacturing sites in Canada, Brazil, Poland, and Mexico.[2]

In his 2006 message to shareholders, Timothy C. Tyson, then president and CEO, reflected, "In many ways, 2006 was a life-changing year for Valeant Pharmaceuticals. It was a challenging year—one that certainly stretched us and tested our resolve."[3] That was the year that Valeant lost its chairman, Robert W. O'Leary, to cancer. Valeant would face a new set of challenges in the fall of 2010, when it merged with Canada's Biovail Corporation. Although Valeant eventually recovered from the loss of chairman Robert W. O'Leary, would it be able to overcome the challenges of the merger and strategically position itself to capture a significant portion of the global pharmaceutical market that was expected to reach $1.1 trillion by 2014?[4]

Although we give a brief history of Valeant here, this case focuses on the Biovail merger and Valeant's neurology division. This division manufactures and markets products to treat Parkinson's disease (PD), epilepsy, migraines, depression, chronic pain, Huntington's disease, and myasthenia gravis. A central question is whether Valeant will be able to capitalize on an aging population's growing demand for its new epilepsy drug, retigabine, and its other products. Also, due to significant restructuring efforts occurring before and resulting from the merger, an important question is whether the changes will yield the benefits promised to shareholders and enable the firm to compete more effectively. The answers to these questions and others will influence Valeant's future success.

History

Valeant Pharmaceuticals was founded in 1960 by Milan Panic, a Yugoslav defector. The company started in California and was originally called International Chemical & Nuclear Corp. (ICN). Panic ran the company for 43 years.[5] Initially, the company's primary business involved chemical and drug sales, but it grew through acquisitions of small drug companies. In 1963, the company launched its IPO.[6]

In 1970, ICN scientists discovered ribavirin, and in 1985, it received US Food and Drug Administration (FDA) approval for the drug to be used as a treatment for lung infections in children. As a blockbuster drug, ribavirin powered ICN's growth and reputation for decades.[7] In later years, Panic directed ICN to promote ribavirin as a treatment for AIDS and hepatitis C.[8] During the 70s, ribavirin failed to qualify for FDA approval as a stand-alone hepatitis C drug. However, in the 90s, ribavirin did receive FDA approval to be used in combination with Schering-Plough's interferon drug to treat hepatitis C. The licensing of ribavirin's patent to Schering-Plough was lucrative and led to a similar interferon/ribavirin royalty-generating agreement with Roche Pharmaceuticals.[9]

The year 2002 was a watershed one in ICN's history. That year, Panic was paid $63.5 million, which included $33 million in bonuses, and other senior executives received bonuses of $15 million.[10] A shareholder proxy fight over excessive executive compensation resulted in

The authors thank Professors Robert E. White and Robert E. Hoskisson for their support and under whose direction the case was developed. The authors do not intend to illustrate either effective or ineffective handling of a managerial situation. The case solely provides material for class discussion. Reprinted by permission.

the replacement of Panic, the entire board of directors, and most senior management.[11] In the summer of 2006, Panic reached a settlement with the company to return $20 million of his 2002 annual bonus.[12]

In 2003, ICN changed its name to Valeant Pharmaceuticals International and relisted its stock symbol on the New York Stock Exchange as VRX. The name change signified Valeant's new strategic focus and emphasized its core principles and values. This change was made in conjunction with restructuring. Valeant's restructuring efforts focused on the following activities: centralization of global purchasing activities to leverage buying power on a global basis;[13] rationalization of Valeant's manufacturing network; and restructuring of debt, resulting in a longer maturity structure and decreasing the effective interest rate.[14] These activities allowed Valeant to raise cash for its 2004 and 2005 acquisitions.[15] Valeant expanded its specialty neurology platform by acquiring Amarin Pharmaceuticals, Inc., Xcel Pharmaceuticals, and Tasmar (a neurology drug).[16]

In 2004, Valeant improved its financial outlook by purchasing and redeeming its 6.5 percent convertible subordinated notes.[17] However, it experienced a financial reversal when the FDA approved a generic version of ribavirin. At its peak, ribavirin royalties comprised a quarter of all sales; but in 2009, after the generic version appeared on the market, it only accounted for 6 percent of revenues (see Exhibit 1). In 2010, this revenue stream would diminish further when generic drug competition entered the Japanese and European markets.[18]

In 2006, Valeant announced another strategic restructuring program intended to reduce costs, grow earnings, and focus research and development (R&D) resources on late-stage pipeline drugs. To accomplish these goals, Valeant reduced headcount[19] and sold its manufacturing facility in Poland, its discovery and preclinical assets, and its cancer and HIV drug development programs.[20] These actions produced cost savings of $30 million during 2006, and an estimated $50 million annually thereafter.

Also in 2006, Valeant obtained FDA permission to market and launch two drugs in the US: the cannabinoid drug Cesamet® (used to treat nausea and vomiting associated with cancer chemotherapy) and Zelapar® to treat PD. It also acquired the hepatitis C drug Infergen® from Intermune.

In the beginning of 2007, Valeant sold its manufacturing plants in Switzerland and Puerto Rico. Then, in late 2007, it sold Infergen® because it had not met growth and profitability expectations.[21] Also in 2007, Valeant initiated a study of retigabine for pain associated with postherpetic neuralgia, and a Phase 2b clinical study of taribavirin for treatment of chronic hepatitis C.[22]

In 2008, the company experienced some significant changes in structure and strategic direction as it went through another change in leadership; J. Michael Pearson became the new chairman and CEO. In March 2008, Valeant announced a companywide restructuring plan to reduce the company's focus to two therapeutic classes (dermatology and neurology) and five geographic areas (the US, Canada, Australia/New Zealand, Mexico/Brazil, and Central Europe). The business infrastructure was adjusted to support this strategy. Nonstrategic products and regional operations that did not meet growth and profitability expectations were divested or discontinued. Infergen® rights, Asian assets (including subsidiaries, branch offices, and commercial rights in Singapore, the Philippines, Thailand, Indonesia, Vietnam, Taiwan, Korea, China, Hong Kong, Malaysia, and Macau), product rights in Japan, subsidiaries in Argentina and Uruguay, and business operations located in Western and Eastern Europe, the Middle East, and Africa (known as the "WEEMEA" business) were sold.[23] Under Pearson, Valeant's growth strategy focused on "small buys and diversified drugs, avoiding too much reliance on a single drug."[24] Valeant continued its strategy of growth through acquisitions with Coria Laboratories, Ltd. (a privately held US specialty pharmaceutical company focused on dermatology products), DermaTech Pty Ltd (an Australian specialty pharmaceutical company focused on dermatology products marketed in Australia), and Dow Pharmaceutical Sciences, Inc. (a privately held dermatology company that specialized in the development of topical products).[25] According to Pearson, "Dermatology, we think, is a very attractive area for us to continue to grow as a smaller company. Skin drugs carry less development risks and don't require a big sales force in order for Valeant to compete with larger players."[26] In addition, it successfully completed the retigabine Phase III epilepsy program and announced a worldwide license and collaboration agreement with GlaxoSmithKline (GSK) for the development and commercialization of retigabine.[27]

As part of the 2008 restructuring plan, Valeant also cut its R&D budget by half. Such a move is generally considered unwise in the pharmaceutical industry, as profitability depends heavily on the development of new drugs.[28] Valeant decided to use the funds resulting from the budget cut for acquisitions and stock buybacks, in addition to paying off debt. Research was considered so

Exhibit 1 Ribavirin Royalty Revenues

	Revenue ($ millions)	Percent of Total Revenue
2009	46.7	6
2008	59.4	9
2007	67.2	10
2006	81.2	9
2005	91.6	11

Source: Valeant 2007 Annual Report and Valeant 2009 Annual Report, http://www.valeant.com.

Globe: © Jan Rysavy/iStockphoto.com

risky, it was best left to small biotechnology companies that Valeant could later buy if they were successful.[29] Robert Ingram, Valeant's lead director (now chairman of the board) and vice chairman of pharmaceuticals at GSK, believed that R&D "is a high-risk bet, and the fact is we fail more often than we succeed. Rather than invest in a high-risk bet, we will be smart through acquisition and licensing."[30] The strategy appeared to pay off as Valeant shares increased 60 percent on the New York Stock Exchange during 2008.[31]

More acquisitions followed in 2009, including EMO-FARM sp. z o.o. (a privately held Polish company specializing in gel-based OTC and cosmetic products), Tecnofarma S.A. de C.V. (a Mexican generic company), Private Formula Holdings International Pty Limited (a privately held company in Australia engaged in product development and sales and marketing of premium skincare products mostly in Australia), and Laboratoire Dr. Renaud (a privately held cosmeceutical company located in Canada). The year 2009 was also when the FDA accepted the New Drug Application (NDA) filing for retigabine.[32] As external R&D expenses for taribavirin were $2.3 million in 2009 and $8.5 million in 2008, Valeant chose to stop further independent development of taribavirin and seek potential partners for the program.[33]

In 2010, Valeant acquired three Brazilian companies (Instituto Terapeutico Delta Ltda, Bunker Industria Farmaceutica Ltda, and a branded generics/OTC company), along with Vital Science Corp. in Canada and Aton Pharma, Inc., located in Lawrenceville, New Jersey. Aton, a specialty pharmaceutical company, focused on ophthalmology and "orphan drugs" that are used to treat rare medical conditions.[34] The Aton acquisition was considered a significant enhancement to Valeant's neurology and other products as it had both an in-line business and a development pipeline that mainly consisted of orphan drugs.[35] In addition, Valeant entered into collaboration with Spear Pharmaceuticals. In June 2010, Valeant announced plans to merge with the Canadian pharmaceutical company Biovail and, on September 28, 2010, Valeant Pharmaceuticals International and Biovail Corporation completed the merger to form one company.[36]

The Merger

Although the merger was officially announced in June 2010, Valeant and Biovail Corporation, one of Canada's largest pharmaceutical companies, had been independently considering a business combination or transaction with the other for several years. Management of each company was generally familiar with the other's businesses, and in early 2008, when Valeant implemented its new strategy focused on shifting investment from R&D to acquiring small in-line undervalued products and companies, it also considered a transformational business combination to apply the new strategy to a larger asset base with the goal of increasing shareholder value. It identified Biovail as a future potential transaction partner. In August 2009, Pearson contacted William M. Wells, CEO of Biovail, to discuss a transaction involving a Valeant neurological product, based on Biovail's primary focus on specialty neurology. Discussions continued throughout 2009 and in January 2010, shifted to a potential merger. In June 2010, the board of directors of each company approved the finalized agreement, and on June 21, Valeant and Biovail issued a joint press release announcing the merger[37] (see Exhibit 2).

Exhibit 2 Valeant Pharmaceuticals International Merger Plan

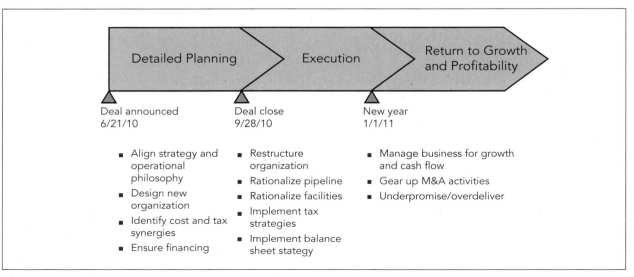

The deal, a reverse merger worth approximately $3.2 billion, would allow Biovail to acquire Valeant. Biovail shareholders would own 50.5 percent of the combined company and Valeant shareholders would own 49.5 percent.[38] The combined company would be listed on both the Toronto Stock Exchange and the New York Stock Exchange. Just prior to the merger, Valeant shareholders would receive a one-time special dividend of $16.77 per share, and would receive 1.7809 shares of Biovail common stock in exchange for each share of Valeant stock owned. Biovail shareholders would continue to own their existing common shares. The transaction was intended to qualify as a tax-exempt reorganization for Valeant shareholders.[39] After the merger in November 2010, Valeant declared a special one-time dividend of $1.00 per common share, as outlined in the merger agreement. The company stated that it did not anticipate paying dividends in the future. The board also established a Special Dividend Reinvestment Plan in which shareholders could elect to reinvest the special dividend in additional common shares. This plan would automatically terminate after payment of the dividend.[40]

Under terms of the merger, the name of the combined company would be Valeant Pharmaceuticals International, Inc., and it would be headquartered in Mississauga, Ontario, Canada, where corporate income taxes were 18 percent federal and 14 percent provincial, as opposed to a location in the US where the corporate tax rate was 35 to 40 percent with a state tax rate of approximately 8 percent.[41] Pearson would become CEO and Wells would serve as nonexecutive chairman of the board of directors.[42] The initial composition of the board of directors would be 11 directors including five representatives from Valeant, five representatives from Biovail, and one additional resident Canadian director who would be selected through a search process, chosen by Valeant and subject to the approval of Biovail.[43] Biovail's corporate structure would be retained.

The merger was considered a positive move by both companies. Biovail CEO William Wells said that Biovail had always planned to add a second therapeutic area, along with international markets, once it had established a position in specialty neurology, and it had been acquiring products in various stages of development in that area for the past few years. According to Wells, "With this deal, we have accomplished that in one fell swoop. We've achieved with this deal what I only hoped we'd be able to do in ten years."[44] Additional benefits of the merger included:[45]

- a larger, more globally diversified company with a broader and better diversified range of products, a deeper drug development pipeline and an expanded presence in North America and internationally;

- the combination of two well known and respected specialty pharmaceutical companies to create a superior combined specialty pharmaceutical company;
- the expected market capitalization, strong balance sheet, free cash flow, liquidity, and capital structure of the combined company;
- the belief that the combined company could achieve approximately $175 million in annual operational cost savings (synergy benefits) by the second year of operations, coming from reductions in general and administrative expenses, R&D consolidation, and sales and marketing;
- Valeant's and Biovail's product lines and geographic markets were complementary and did not present significant areas of overlap;
- additional revenue growth opportunities presented by the expanded product offerings and stable cash flows from legacy products anticipated to support future growth with limited patent exposure with respect to the existing portfolio of products;
- the combination of two strong senior management teams;
- the combined company would be able to operate under Biovail's existing corporate structure.

Valeant and Biovail would have to obtain governmental and regulatory approvals prior to closing the merger. Notifications were required by the FTC and the Antitrust Division of the Department of Justice, and a mandatory pre-merger waiting period had to be observed. The merger was not notifiable under the Competition Act in Canada. A pre-merger notification was required in Poland under the Competition and Consumer Protection Act and in Mexico under the Federal Economic Competition Law.[46] All approvals were obtained successfully, and on September 27, 2010, the shareholders of Valeant Pharmaceuticals International and Biovail Corporation voted in favor of combining the two companies.[47]

After the merger, Pearson began a new restructuring plan for the combined company. Valeant targeted 1,100 jobs (approximately 25 percent of the combined workforce) that were considered redundant for elimination. By January 2011, approximately 500 employees had received notification[48] (see Exhibit 3). Valeant also eliminated eight or nine R&D programs to focus on its strategy of growth through acquisitions of small companies rather than creating new products in house. "What we try to do is find these things, most of these companies no one's ever heard of and we like that," said Pearson. "We try to buy them inexpensively. Our average price since I've been here is 1.8 times sales." Pearson also said that the company would like to make at least five acquisitions in 2011.[49] By October 2011, Valeant was in negotiations for Afexa Life Sciences, Kaunas, Ortho Dermatologics, and Dermik.

Exhibit 3 Valeant Pharmaceuticals International, Inc., US and Canada Personnel Reductions

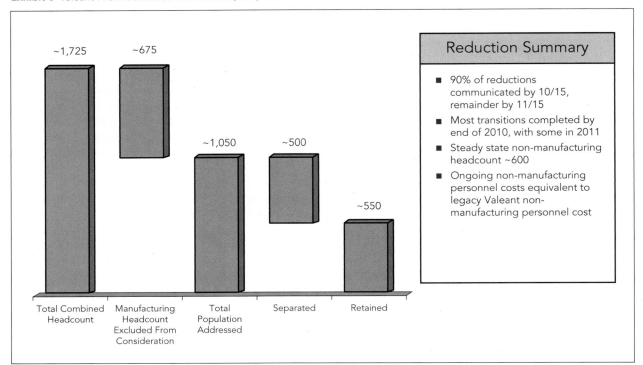

Source: Valeant Pharmaceuticals International, Inc., Third Quarter Earnings Call, Nov 4, 2010.

On February 1, 2011, Valeant announced an agreement for Valeant to acquire PharmaSwiss S.A., a privately owned pharmaceutical company based in Zug, Switzerland specializing in branded generics and OTC pharmaceuticals. Valeant agreed to pay approximately 350 million euros for the company. PharmaSwiss has a product portfolio in seven therapeutic areas and operations in 19 countries throughout Central and Eastern Europe including Poland, Hungary, the Czech Republic, and Serbia. It also has operations in Greece and Israel.[50] On February 3, 2011, Valeant launched an offering of $650 million aggregate principal amount of 6.75 percent senior unsecured notes due 2021. Proceeds from the offering would be used to finance the PharmaSwiss acquisition and the acquisition of all US and Canadian rights to nonophthalmic topical formulations of Zovirax (an antiviral drug) from GSK, along with associated fees and expenses, and for general corporate purposes.[51] The acquisition of PharmaSwiss was expected to close in the first or second quarter of 2011. According to Pearson,

This acquisition of PharmaSwiss solidifies our position as a leading pharmaceutical company in Central and Eastern Europe. PharmaSwiss has an attractive partnering strategy as well as a complementary branded generics and OTC product portfolio that will strengthen our presence in the region.[52]

CEO Pearson, formerly with McKinsey & Company, had the leadership skills and abilities required to lead Valeant through the merger process and into its next phase of development efficiently and effectively.

Leadership

In 2002, because of shareholder disgruntlement, Robert W. O'Leary replaced Panic as the new CEO and chairman of the board. O'Leary was well respected in the health care industry, having served as CEO of six different companies in 28 years prior to joining Valeant. He specialized in managing difficult restructuring circumstances. His job was to undertake a complete strategic restructuring of Valeant. The goal was to create a leaner company that emphasized the specialty pharmaceutical business. In pursuit of this goal, noncore businesses not fitting with future strategic growth plans were divested. The divestiture process began by eliminating all operations in Russia and Eastern Europe and the raw materials businesses in Central Europe. The biomedical division, North American photonics business, personal radiation dosimetry division, and Circe unit were also immediately divested. The company's real estate holdings in Costa Mesa, California, were sold in 2006, and the headquarters moved to a new, leased campus in Aliso Viejo, California.[53]

O'Leary formed a new management team with the majority of his senior personnel recruits remaining in place for many years. The change in the composition of the board of directors was dramatic. Nearly all of the new board members were not employed by the company and had no previous consulting or other business relationship with Valeant. A primary goal of the new board was to institute new corporate governance initiatives to make the board independent and transparent.[54] O'Leary remained with the company until his death from cancer in 2006.[55]

In January 2005, Timothy C. Tyson took over as Valeant's CEO when O'Leary became too sick to manage the firm on a daily basis. Tyson had been hired as the president and COO. Before coming to Valeant, Tyson was president of global manufacturing and supply for GSK, the third-largest pharmaceutical company in the US at that time. The connection to GSK is noteworthy because, at the time, many members of senior management were alumni of that company. This influx of GSK alumni in management helped to accelerate needed culture changes, many derived from GSK.

In February 2008, Tyson resigned as CEO and J. Michael Pearson was selected as the successor. Pearson was head of McKinsey & Company's global pharmaceutical practice and head of its mid-Atlantic region. Pearson held various positions at McKinsey during his 23-year career, including membership on McKinsey's board of directors.[56] At McKinsey, Pearson worked with leading CEOs to develop and implement major turnarounds, acquisitions, and corporate strategy. Pearson was already providing advice and guidance to Valeant prior to Tyson's departure.

Pearson's pay package, in sharp contrast to Panic's, was developed by G. Mason Morfit, chairman of Valeant's board compensation committee. Morfit was also a partner of Value-Act Capital, an "activist hedge fund" with a 22 percent stake in Valeant, which made it Valeant's largest stockholder.[57] The pay package focused on giving Pearson incentives to increase long-term value for investors and was considered unusual for a public company. Morfit explained to Pearson and the other finalists for the CEO position that he preferred the private equity model for executive compensation "because it aligns management's incentives with those of the investor." He later recalled, "Nobody was scared off."[58] This drew national attention and praise from compensation critics.[59] Pearson was awarded $18.1 million in equity but was also required to buy at least $3 million in stock and would not receive routine annual equity grants. He would not be allowed to sell most restricted shares or exercise stock options for two years after they vested and would only get to keep certain restricted shares if Valeant's share price increased by at least 15 percent per year through February 2011. Pearson actually purchased $5 million in Valeant shares.[60] Pearson and the board of directors then adopted the same approach for new senior executives. They were required to buy large amounts of company stock, which limited candidates to "affluent risk takers." According to Pearson, already successful people were willing to take less guaranteed pay up front.[61]

Although this pay plan model was not a guarantee of success, from the end of the 2009 fiscal year to May 2010, Valeant's shares were up 40 percent with a market value of approximately $3.5 billion and a first-quarter adjusted profit of $52.8 million (up 39 percent from the previous year). Valeant also posted a 40 percent gain in 2009.[62] According to analyst David Amsellem of Piper Jaffray & Co., "It is time for us to concede that the run in the stock is no fluke and that investors are likely to view this management team with increasing confidence given its execution over the past one to two years."[63]

After the merger, Pearson became the CEO of the combined company, Valeant Pharmaceuticals International, Inc. He agreed to waive the accelerated vesting of the equity awards he would have been entitled to in association with the merger. A significant portion of his future compensation would be in the form of equity in the company and would be contingent on the performance of the company's common shares.[64]

Although Pearson has continued in his role as CEO of the combined company, William Wells resigned from his position as nonexecutive chairman in December 2010. One week after Wells' resignation, CFO Peggy Mulligan also resigned. Although the reasons for both resignations were stated as "to pursue other interests," analysts said that old Valeant personnel had dominated the combined company, and the changes were viewed as part of the new direction and strategy of the new company.[65] Philip W. Loberg, Valeant's former senior vice president and corporate controller, was appointed Interim CFO replacing Mulligan,[66] and Valeant's Lead Independent Director, Robert A. Ingram, was appointed as Chairman of the Board of Directors[67] (see Exhibit 4). Pearson and Valeant's management team continue to work together to help Valeant reach its potential in providing products that offer relief to customers and generate revenue.

Product Overview

As noted in the introduction, this case focuses on the neurology division—a division that develops products to treat PD, epilepsy, migraines, and other central nervous system disorders.

Exhibit 4 Valeant Pharmaceuticals International, Inc. Leadership

Board of Directors	
Robert A. Ingram	Chairman General Partner, Hatteras Venture Partners Formerly Lead Director of the Valeant board of directors
J. Michael Pearson	CEO, Valeant Pharmaceuticals International, Inc. Formerly Chairman of the Valeant board of directors and CEO of Valeant
Kate Stevenson	Corporate Director
Lloyd Segal	Equity Partner, Persistence Capital Partners Formerly a member of the Biovail board of directors
Norma A. Provencio	President and Owner, Provencio Advisory Services Inc. Formerly a member of the Valeant board of directors
Robert N. Power	Corporate Director Formerly a member of the Biovail board of directors
G. Mason Morfit	Partner, ValueAct Capital Formerly a member of the Valeant board of directors
Dr. Laurence Paul	Founding Principal, Laurel Crown Capital LLC Formerly a member of the Biovail board of directors
Michael R. Van Every	Retired Partner of Price Waterhouse Coopers LLP Formerly Chairman of the Audit Committee of the Biovail board of directors
Theo Melas-Kyriazi	Chief Financial Officer, Levitronix LLC Formerly a member of the Valeant board of directors
Senior Management	
J. Michael Pearson	CEO, Valeant Pharmaceuticals International, Inc. Formerly Chairman of the Valeant board of directors and CEO of Valeant
Philip W. Loberg	Executive Vice President and Chief Financial Officer Formerly Senior Vice President, Group Financial Controller for Valeant
Robert Chai-Onn	Executive Vice President, General Counsel and Corporate Secretary Formerly Vice President, Assistant General Counsel, of Valeant
Mark Durham	Senior Vice President, Human Resources Formerly Senior Vice President, Human Resources of Biovail Corp.
Rajiv De Silva	President, Valeant Pharmaceuticals International, Inc. and COO, Specialty Pharmaceuticals Formerly COO of Specialty Pharmaceuticals for Valeant
Richard K. Masterson	President of Biovail Laboratories International in Barbados, a wholly owned subsidiary of Valeant Pharmaceuticals, International

Source: 2011, Valeant Pharmaceuticals, www.valeant.com.

Parkinson's Disease

Parkinson's disease (PD), a disorder characterized by slow movement, rigidity, and tremor, affects more than one million Americans.[68] Most people are diagnosed with PD in the later years of life. It is estimated that four to six million people around the world currently have PD. Approximately 50,000 to 60,000 new cases are diagnosed each year.[69] As the US population ages and lives longer, PD is expected to "rise astronomically in the coming decades."[70] Valeant's PD drugs include Zelapar® and Tasmar®. Both products are approved for use as an adjunctive treatment with levadopa/carbidopa (l-dopa), a product every patient with PD eventually takes.

Valeant obtained Zelapar® through the acquisition of Xcel Pharmaceuticals. Zelapar® offers patients the ease of once-daily dosing, as compared to other medications used to treat PD that require multiple dosages each day.[71] Two other products that compete in the same market are Teva's Azilect® and the generic drug selegiline.

Tasmar® is a COMT-inhibitor.[72] It is used as a last resort option in the pharmaceutical treatment algorithm since it has a "black box" warning that requires patients to monitor their liver functions on a biweekly basis. Tasmar® was initially launched in 1997 by Roche Pharmaceuticals but, due to three patient deaths in 1998, it stopped promoting it. Valeant acquired the product in May 2004 in an effort to expand its presence in the neurology market.[73] The only other COMT-inhibitor on the market is Novartis's Comtan®.

Epilepsy

Approximately three million Americans live with epilepsy, a disorder caused by the hyperactivity of electrical charges in the brain, and "approximately 200,000 new cases of seizures and epilepsy occur each year."[74] However, an estimated 30 percent of patients with epilepsy do not find sufficient relief with current drugs. Analysts forecast that the annual sales of epilepsy medications will range from $200 million to $800 million in 2011.[75]

Valeant's Diastat® Acudial™ is the only FDA-approved medication for at-home acute seizure control; as such, it does not have any direct competitors. However, as a rectal gel, the delivery system is unattractive to patients,[76] and Valeant is developing a new delivery system where the drug would be administered intranasally.

Retigabine, referred to as ezogabine in the US, is a neuronal potassium channel blocker that is a possible treatment for adult partial-onset seizures in combination with other antiepileptic products. It is also used for postherpetic neuralgia pain.[77] In December 2010, retigabine received preliminary approval from the Swiss Agency for Therapeutic Products, Swissmedic, and in January 2011, Valeant and GSK announced that the European Medicines Agency's Committee for Medicinal Products for Human Use (CHMP) recommended marketing authorization for retigabine.[78] In the US, retigabine's NDA is under review by the FDA. Until the NDA has been approved by the FDA, retigabine cannot be commercialized in the US.[79]

Migraines

Migraines affect 28 million Americans and are characterized by severe headaches with side effects including nausea, vomiting, and sensitivity to light and/or sound. Migranal® is Valeant's migraine medication and the only product available in its medication class. Migranal® is administered intranasally, a distinct advantage for patients experiencing nausea or vomiting. Valeant gained the rights to Migranal® through its acquisition of Xcel.

Myasthenia Gravis

Myasthenia gravis is a rare disease that affects only 13,600 Americans. It is a neuromuscular disorder that affects the body's voluntary muscles. It is often characterized by a drooping eyelid or loss of facial movement. Unfortunately, the low incidence of myasthenia gravis provides little financial incentive for pharmaceutical companies to invest in drug development. Mestinon® is Valeant's approved, but not promoted, drug for myasthenia gravis.

Additional Products

As a result of the merger, Valeant added the following key neurology products to its portfolio: Wellbutrin® XL for depression, Ultram® ER for chronic pain management, Xenazine® for the reduction of involuntary movements caused by Huntington's disease, and Ativan® for the treatment of anxiety disorders.[80]

Valeant also has products in its development pipeline. These products include retigabine (for treating epilepsy and pain), taribavirin (for chronic hepatitis C), and several dermatology drugs for treating rosacea, acne, and dermatological fungus. Valeant plans to expand its pipeline with the addition of new compounds and product extensions through company and product acquisitions[81] (see Exhibit 5).

To remain competitive and achieve its vision of becoming the "leading specialty pharmaceutical company in the world,"[82] Valeant needs to be aware of its competitors and their products.

Competitive Environment

In the US, approximately 1,500 companies compete in the pharmaceutical market estimated to be worth $200 billion annually. Revenue market share is highly consolidated with 80 percent of the market driven by the top 50 companies. Global pharmaceutical market growth is predicted to reach $880 billion in 2011.[83] Market consolidation is further highlighted by the recent acquisition trend, whereby drug manufacturers gain R&D capability by acquiring smaller firms.[84] Valeant's neurology division competitors can be narrowed to a few key companies: Teva Pharmaceutical Industries Ltd., UCB S.A., and H. Lundbeck (see Exhibit 6 for comparative information on Valeant and its competitors).

Teva Pharmaceutical Industries Ltd.

Teva endeavors to introduce generic versions of branded products as early as possible following pate' expiration. To support this strategy, Teva acti' reviews current patents for opportunities to legitim challenge patent duration. It also enters into a' to share product development and litigati and maintains the lowest R&D investmer

Exhibit 5 Valeant Pharmaceuticals International, Inc. Product Development Pipeline

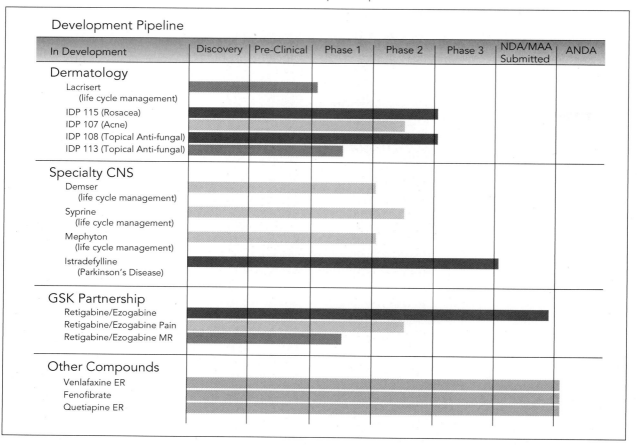

Source: Valeant Pharmaceuticals International, Inc. website, http://www.valeant.com, January 2011.

the central nervous system product category. Teva's Azilect® (offered through a collaborative agreement with H. Lundbeck) competes with Valeant's Zelapar® product for the treatment of PD. In 2009, Teva had $13.9 billion in sales.[85,86]

UCB

UCB's vision is to develop a leadership position in severe disease categories to deliver superior long-run returns to shareholders. It aspires to connect with patients to understand their pain points, and to connect sciences, specifically "biology and chemistry in a unique way to target proteins which are currently undruggable."

UCB has nine products in the R&D pipeline to address epilepsy, migraine prophylaxis, multiple sclerosis, fibromyalgia, restless legs syndrome, and PD.[88] Sales of central nervous system (CNS) products accounted for 41 percent of its 2009 net sales of 2.7 billion euros.[89] Consistent with its strategy, UCB maintains more than 0 partnerships to gain access to specific R&D expertise

within the value chain. For example, it has alliances with Sanofi-Aventis and Amgen.[87]

H. Lundbeck A/S

H. Lundbeck focuses primarily on developing medicine for the treatment of CNS diseases. Main products include Cipralex® (marketed as Lexapro® in the US) for depression and anxiety disorders, Ebixa® for Alzheimer's disease, and Azilect® for the treatment of PD (offered through a collaborative agreement with Teva). Approximately 20 percent of its annual revenue ($2.6 billion in 2009) is spent on R&D.[90]

Company and Product Acquisitions

Valeant uses its acquisition strategy as a resource allocation methodology as well as to manage the competitive environment. These acquisitions also establish future products in the pipeline, such as retigabine. Valeant's acquisitions have allowed it to overcome barriers to

Exhibit 6 Valeant Pharmaceuticals International, Inc. Competitive Landscape

KEY NUMBERS	Valeant Pharm.	Lundbeck	Teva Pharm.	UCB		
Annual Sales ($ mil.)	820.4	2,647.7	13,899.0	4,170.6		
Employees	1,311	5,733	35,089	9,324		
Market Cap ($ mil.)	11,696.6	—	52,210.1	—		
PROFITABILITY	Valeant Pharm.	Lundbeck	Teva Pharm.	UCB	Industry Median	Market Median[1]
Gross Profit Margin	73.15%	80.40%	56.11%	64.78%	57.16%	28.77%
Pre-Tax Profit Margin	(6.01%)	22.29%	21.32%	23.20%	11.22%	8.48%
Net Profit Margin	(11.46%)	16.68%	18.96%	17.63%	(0.48%)	5.53%
Return on Equity	(3.1%)	22.9%	14.4%	12.2%	(0.5%)	10.1%
Return on Assets	(1.6%)	13.4%	8.1%	5.5%	(0.2%)	1.5%
Return on Invested Capital	(1.6%)	22.9%	10.8%	12.2%	(0.3%)	4.4%
VALUATION	Valeant Pharm.	Lundbeck	Teva Pharm.	UCB	Industry Median	Market Median
Price/Sales Ratio	6.86	1.50	3.29	1.65	3.06	—
Price/Earnings Ratio	(59.88)	8.98	17.36	9.66	50.00	—
Price/Book Ratio	2.19	2.05	2.41	1.09	2.99	—
Price/Cash Flow Ratio	15.87	5.52	12.79	16.29	16.72	—
OPERATIONS	Valeant Pharm.	Lundbeck	Teva Pharm.	UCB	Industry Median	Market Median
Days of Sales Outstanding	117.06	52.09	116.73	—	78.04	34.66
Inventory Turnover	0.8	1.9	1.9	2.7	2.5	8.1
Days Cost of Goods Sold in Inventory	442	195	196	137	144	45
Asset Turnover	0.1	0.8	0.4	0.3	0.5	0.3
Net Receivables Turnover Flow	3.1	7.0	3.1	—	4.7	10.5
Effective Tax Rate	—	25.2%	10.0%	24.9%	—	37.9%
FINANCIAL	Valeant Pharm.	Lundbeck	Teva Pharm.	UCB	Industry Median	Market Median
Current Ratio	1.36	1.36	1.60	0.87	2.05	1.33
Quick Ratio	0.9	—	1.0	—	1.4	1.2
Leverage Ratio	1.53	1.95	1.76	2.06	1.92	7.13
Total Debt/Equity	0.29	0.30	0.29	0.51	0.42	1.37
Interest Coverage	(0.31)	15.98	15.25	4.05	4.75	17.33
PER SHARE DATA	Valeant Pharm.	Lundbeck	Teva Pharm.	UCB	Industry Median	Market Median
Revenue Per Share	5.68	75.34	16.95	15.87	7.87	—
Dividends Per Share	0.37	2.21	0.62	0.92	0.47	0.25
Cash Flow Per Share	2.46	20.45	4.36	1.61	1.44	—
Working Capital Per Share	0.31	8.25	4.85	(1.46)	2.86	—
Long-Term Debt Per Share	1.27	—	4.61	—	2.65	—
Book Value Per Share	17.83	54.90	23.15	24.09	8.06	—
Total Assets Per Share	6.89	87.33	36.12	49.74	13.69	—

(Cor

Exhibit 6 Valeant Pharmaceuticals International, Inc. Competitive Landscape Valeant Pharmaceuticals International, Inc. and Top Competitors (*Continued*)

GROWTH	Valeant Pharm.	Lundbeck	Teva Pharm.	UCB	Industry Median	Market Median
12-Month Revenue Growth	8.4%	21.9%	25.4%	(19.2%)	14.7%	31.9%
12-Month Net Income Growth	(11.7%)	32.9%	215.0%	1,095.3%	—	(27.7%)
12-Month EPS Growth	(11.2%)	33.5%	185.9%	1,095.7%	—	(50.0%)
12-Month Dividend Growth	(57.0%)	(10.2%)	17.5%	0.0%	(9.7%)	—
36-Month Revenue Growth	(8.5%)	14.2%	18.2%	4.9%	18.1%	14.3%
36-Month Net Income Growth	(4.7%)	21.9%	54.2%	11.9%	84.5%	(5.6%)
36-Month EPS Growth	(5.1%)	25.0%	47.8%	3.0%	—	(14.7%)
36-Month Dividend Growth	8.9%	—	23.7%	—	13.1%	—

[1]Public companies trading on the NYSE, ASE, and NASDAQ.

© 2011 Morningstar, Inc. Financial Data provided by MORNINGSTAR. Hoover's Company Reports 2011, Valeant Pharmaceuticals International, Inc.

market entry and quickly provide new products; it has also potentially reduced the number of competitors.

In addition to its acquisition strategy, Valeant seeks opportunities to outsource some of the secondary operations so it can focus on key operations.

Outsourcing

In an effort to capitalize on core competencies, pharmaceutical companies are moving toward areas of specialty, specifically in R&D, manufacturing, or sales and marketing. In turn, they outsource other functions.

Valeant and other companies rely heavily on their outsourcing partners for a number of reasons including to reduce the time it takes to bring a drug to market through enhanced R&D or manufacturing processes; to increase patient enrollment in clinical trials; to optimize the drug's promotion; or to capitalize on human labor, whether involving scientists, marketing, or sales personnel. The FDA enforces stringent regulations on quality manufacturing and ethical promotions therefore, pharmaceutical companies must consider quality, compliance, and reputation ahead of contract flexibility and price when selecting outsourcing partners to help them meet the demands of key customers.[91]

Key Customers

Companies in the pharmaceutical industry typically focus on four customer groups: physicians, pharmacy benefit managers (PBMs), patients, and pharmacies.

Physicians

Valeant specifically targets neurologists and primary care providers. According to an interview with Dr. Joseph Sirven, a neurologist at the Mayo Clinic in Scottsdale, Arizona, physicians utilize several methods to learn about a product and its use in clinical practice. They study product-specific articles published in peer-reviewed journals, paying close attention to the efficacy and safety outcomes, the number of subjects enrolled, the journal in which the study was published, and the physicians who conducted the trial. The volume of clinical trials available and the long-term safety data reported on a particular product also carry significant weight. Sales and marketing efforts, a product's cost, availability of insurance coverage, and physician habit all influence a physician's decision-making process.[92]

Pharmacy Benefit Managers (PBMs)

PBMs are companies that manage the prescription pharmaceutical benefits for managed care companies, employers, and government programs. Approximately 95 percent of all drug formularies (lists of medications that are usually covered under a particular health care plan) are managed by a PBM.[93] The role of a PBM is to determine the drugs that will be placed on a formulary, a tier status for the drugs, restrictions, and copays. They also make suggestions to physicians and patients regarding disease-state management.

Pharmaceutical companies negotiate contracts with PBMs to get their products on formularies, offering discounts to get preferred status. A drug with preferred status is easier for physicians to prescribe and more affordable for patients. Some formularies place "prior authorizations" on certain products, requiring physicians to justify why they requested the medication. Products without prior authorization requirements have a better chance of being prescribed because they eliminate the need for extra paperwork and patient wait-time.[94]

Patients

Many patients take an active role in their health care. These proactive patients search the Internet to find product- and disease-specific websites and often ask their physicians about the products they see advertised on television and in magazines. They also attend support groups and seek out local foundations to learn more about available therapies, costs, symptomatic benefits, and physicians' recommendations regarding the prescriptions they take.

Pharmacists

Pharmaceutical companies must work with distributors to ensure pharmacies have ample stock to fill prescriptions. Companies must also provide pharmacists with educational tools regarding the drugs and their indications, as they influence patients' medication regimens. If pharmacists are not educated on the role a product plays in disease management, they may provide information that negatively influences the patients' desires to fill the prescription and could perhaps harm patients.

Customer needs and desires are significantly affected by the general environment. Therefore, Valeant must analyze the trends and adjust its strategies accordingly.

Trends Influencing Pharmaceutical Companies

Technological advancements, demographic changes, cultural tendencies, and various governmental policies all create added pressures to the pharmaceutical industry.

Technology

Technology provides the means to increase the speed and efficiency of pharmaceutical companies in bringing a product to market. Companies are moving toward electronic collaboration software such as the EMC Documentum enterprise compliance platform to reduce costs, provide faster solution delivery times, and improve the ability to quickly retrieve information.[95] Because information changes quickly, books such as encyclopedias are considered outdated even as they are printed. With information constantly updated, scientists and pharmaceutical companies are finding it hard to keep up.[96]

According to the World Health Organization (WHO), "chronic conditions are projected to be the leading cause of disability throughout the world by the year 2020; if not successfully prevented and managed, they will become the most expensive problems faced by our health care systems."[97] Technological advances in equipment aid in early detection and will help keep rising health costs in check.

Aging Population and Lifestyle

Life expectancy in the US is increasing due to advances in medicine and technology as well as improved access to health care. Life expectancy at birth and at 65 years has steadily increased for both genders. "The US population age 65 and over is expected to double in size within the next 25 years."[98] According to the WHO, "Neurological disorders ranging from migraines to epilepsy and dementia affect up to one billion people worldwide and the toll will rise as populations' age."[99] These factors will increase the need for drugs. Moreover, a study conducted by the US Government Accountability Office found that the cost of prescription medications increased by almost 25 percent from 1997 to 2002.[100] With the trend only worsening, the entire health care industry needs a better way to manage its rising costs.

Many adults try alternative treatments rather than pharmaceuticals as an answer to health-related issues. Complementary and alternative medicine (CAM) include a variety of techniques including prayer, massage therapy, yoga, herbal remedies, breathing techniques, meditation, and altering one's diet. Another option is surgery, especially for many neurological conditions, with a goal of offering patients improved symptomatic benefits.[101] However, this alternative is not without risk; deep brain stimulation is associated with potential side effects such as panic attacks, brain hemorrhages, infection, mood changes, delirium, movement disorders, lightheadedness, insomnia, speech problems, and suicide.[102]

On the other hand, for the members of society not pursuing alternative cures, prescription drug use is increasing. Many patients believe that pills can cure just about anything. From diet pills to ADHD pills, the majority of Americans are becoming more medicated. Greg Critser, author of *Generation RX: How Prescription Drugs Are Altering American Lives, Minds and Bodies*, discusses how "the average number of prescriptions per person in 1993 was seven, but that had risen to 11 by 2000, and 12 in 2004."[103]

Prescription drug abuse is on the rise, particularly among teens. In the US, for example, "Abuse of prescription pain killers now ranks second—only behind marijuana—as the nation's most prevalent illegal drug problem."[104] The President's National Drug Control Strategy 2010 outlines the extent of prescription drug abuse in the US and federal programs designed to address the problem.[105]

Regulation

The US government's role in the pharmaceutical industry is highlighted by the FDA and the associated hurdles that companies must clear to safely take a drug to mark These hurdles represent an expensive, time-consur process that increases the cost of drugs. The prob' that many consumers view the high cost for presc as greed on the part of pharmaceutical compan'

Statistics show that "R&D costs in the dr are among the highest with only three out of ' drugs producing revenues that match or exceed average R&D costs."[106] These factors, in addition to other government restrictions such as "stem cell research limitations and US visa policies,"[107] are a leading cause in the trend of offshore pharmaceutical R&D processes.[108]

The Health Insurance Portability and Accountability Act of 1996 (HIPAA) has significantly affected the pharmaceutical industry's marketing strategies. Patient Health Information (PHI) must be removed from all records before pharmaceutical companies can use it to gather marketing data. This restriction directly affects mail advertising campaigns. Additionally, it limits the number of individuals who qualify for clinical studies, as pharmaceutical companies must now work with covered providers to obtain patient authorization of medical records.[109]

The Prescription Drug Marketing Act (PDMA) was created by the FDA to monitor prescription drugs. PDMA requires pharmaceutical companies to perform annual audits of drug samples in addition to monitoring the storage of the drug sample. The goal is to "assure that the drug samples are free of contamination, deterioration, and adulteration."[110]

The FDA also has a Division of Drug Marketing, Advertising, and Communications (DDMAC). It ensures that "information contained in prescription drug promotional materials is not false or misleading."[111] The DDMAC has a list of firm guidelines that pharmaceutical companies must follow when publishing all communications, including commercials. If the DDMAC decides to ban this mode of advertising, pharmaceutical companies will need to find other effective means of advertising their products. The DDMAC also administers the FDA's educational outreach program, the "Bad Ad" program, designed to educate health care providers on ways they can assist the FDA to ensure that prescription drug advertising and promotion is truthful and straightforward. It also provides them with an easy way to report misleading prescription drug promotion.[112]

Medicare Part D, a program to assist Medicare beneficiaries pay for their prescription drugs, has resulted in more US consumers choosing generic drugs. Medicare Part D has a gap (known as the "Donut Hole") such that Medicare beneficiaries must pay for drugs out-of-pocket when they reach a certain benefit limit and do not qualify for the next tier in the prescription drug structure. The increased out-of-pocket expenses has caused more patients to shift their use of branded products to the cheaper generic products.[113] However, in 2011, efforts began to close the Donut Hole. People who reach the Donut Hole in 2011 will receive a 50 percent discount on brand-name formulary drugs and a 7 percent discount on all generic formulary medications.[114]

Retail pharmacies such as Walmart offer $4 generic prescription options.[115] Because of its size, Walmart and similar large retail pharmacies further contribute to the increased generic drug awareness and usage.[116] Therefore, to keep its products in the preferred category, Valeant works hard to employ effective and creative marketing strategies.

Marketing

Valeant sells its products through its direct sales forces in Canada and the US and through marketing partnerships.[117] Valeant develops marketing materials for its sales force to use in interactions with key customers. They, however, must ensure that the marketing pieces are medically accurate and compliant with the DDMAC. They also provide prescription samples. Samples allow physicians to gauge whether a medication is well tolerated and efficacious before patients purchase a prescription. Valeant also generates press releases and special interest stories, and develops advertising for medical journals, websites, email opt-ins, pharmacy fax blasts, and physician and patient direct mailings.

Related to its direct marketing efforts, Valeant provides funding and educational materials for peer-to-peer and pharmacy educational programs. These programs are divided into two segments: (1) medical education, continuing medical education, grand rounds, and unrestricted educational grants (Valeant provides funding for these programs, but in no way influences the content); and (2) promotional programs, including peer-to-peer programs, roundtable discussions, and pharmacy educational events. Valeant drives the content that is approved through the regulatory and legal departments.

Additionally, Valeant supports national foundations including the Epilepsy Foundation, Michael J. Fox Foundation, National PD Foundation, and American PD Foundation. Valeant provides these foundations with educational resources and financial support to promote research in different therapeutic areas.

Valeant employees also attend professional society meetings and trade shows to display product information and to gain information on the changing pharmaceutical environment.[118]

Patients who are financially disadvantaged can apply for free medicine through the Valeant Patient Assistance Program. It is available to legal residents of the US who do not have a medical insurance plan that covers prescription drug costs and/or do not have funding from government or private programs for medicine.[119]

Financial Results

With the two companies expected to be fully integrated by the middle of 2011 and a $250 million savings resulting from the merger anticipated the same year, Valeant gave strong forecasts for fourth quarter 2010 and fiscal year 2011:[120]

Fourth Quarter 2010

- 44 to 48 cents profit per share
- $510 to $520 million in revenue

Fiscal Year 2011

- $2.25 to $2.50 profit per share
- $2.1 to $2.3 billion in total revenue
- $850 to $950 million in sales of neurologic drugs and other products
- $480 to $515 million in US sales of dermatology products
- $285 to $305 million in revenue from Canada and Australia
- $225 to $245 million in sales of branded generic drugs in Central Europe

- $260 to $285 million in sales of branded generic drugs in Latin America (see Exhibit 7)

In 2009, Valeant posted $820 million in annual revenue with a gross profit margin of 74.56 percent, which was above both the industry median of 57.16 and market median of 28.77 percent (see Exhibits 8, 9, 10, and 11).

Analysts believe that the combined company will benefit from greater scale, tax benefits, and stable cash flows and anticipate that Valeant will meet its earnings forecasts. Pearson's recommendation that the executive management team should not receive bonuses if Valeant fails to meet its targeted earnings per share also gained analysts' approval, and they liked that he waived the accelerated vesting of his equity awards because of the merger.[121] Analysts support Valeant's acquisition strategy and subsequent savings on R&D expenses and expect that Valeant will be able to generate compound annual growth of 17 percent until 2019.[122]

Exhibit 7 Valeant Pharmaceuticals International Segment Information 2007 through 2009

	Year Ended December 31		
Revenues	**2009**	**2008**	**2007**
Specialty pharm product sales	$403,865	$ 303,723	$326,682
Specialty pharm service and alliance revenue	73,028	4,374	19,200
Branded generics—Europe product sales	151,650	152,804	125,070
Branded generics—Latin America product sales	155,246	136,638	151,299
Alliances (ribavirin royalties only)	46,672	59,438	67,252
Consolidated revenues	$830,461	$ 656,977	$689,503
Operating Income (Loss)			
Specialty pharm	$165,920	$ 3,778	$ 14,846
Branded generics—Europe	37,650	45,262	41,908
Branded generics—Latin America	55,300	25,751	36,218
	258,870	74,791	92,972
Alliances	46,672	59,438	67,252
Corporate	(56,290)	(60,127)	(74,724)
Subtotal	249,252	74,102	85,500
Special charges and credits including acquired in-process research and development	(6,351)	(186,300)	—
Restructuring, asset impairments, dispositions and acquisition-related costs	(10,068)	(21,295)	(27,675)
Consolidated segment operating income (loss)	232,833	(133,493)	57,825
Interest income	4,321	17,129	17,584
Interest expense	(43,571)	(45,385)	(56,923)
Gain (loss) on early extinguishment of debt	7,221	(12,994)	
Other income (expense), net including translation and exchange	(1,455)	2,063	1,6
Income (loss) from continuing operations before income taxes	$199,349	$(172,680)	$ 2(

Source: Valeant Pharmaceuticals International 2009 Annual Report.

Exhibit 8 Valeant Pharmaceuticals International, Inc. Selected Financial Data

	Year Ended December 31				
	2009	**2008**	**2007**	**2006**	**2005**
	(In thousands except per share data)				
Revenues:					
Product sales	$ 710,761	$ 593,165	$603,051	$603,810	$ 546,429
Service revenue	22,389	—	—	—	—
Alliance revenue	97,311	63,812	86,452	81,242	91,646
Total revenues	830,461	656,977	689,503	685,052	638,075
Income (loss) from continuing operations before income taxes	199,349	(172,680)	20,145	3,522	(92,838)
Provision (benefit) for income taxes	(58,270)	34,688	13,535	36,577	67,034
Income (loss) from continuing operations	257,619	(207,368)	6,610	(33,055)	(159,872)
Income (loss) from discontinued operations, net of tax	6,125	166,548	(26,796)	(37,332)	(40,468)
Net income (loss)	263,744	(40,820)	(20,186)	(70,387)	(200,340)
Less: Net income attributable to noncontrolling interest	3	7	2	3	287
Net income (loss) attributable to Valeant	$ 263,741	$ (40,827)	$(20,188)	$(70,390)	$(200,627)
Basic income (loss) per share attributable to Valeant:					
Income (loss) from continuing operations attributable to Valeant	$ 3.15	$ (2.37)	$ 0.07	$ (0.35)	$ (1.74)
Income (loss) from discontinued operations attributable to Valeant	0.07	1.90	(0.29)	(0.40)	(0.45)
Net income (loss) per share attributable to Valeant	$ 3.22	$ (0.47)	$ (0.22)	$ (0.75)	$ (2.19)
Diluted income (loss) per share attributable to Valeant:					
Income (loss) from continuing operations attributable to Valeant	$ 3.07	$ (2.37)	$ 0.07	$ (0.35)	$ (1.74)
Income (loss) from discontinued operations attributable to Valeant	0.07	1.90	(0.28)	(0.40)	(0.45)
Net income (loss) per share attributable to Valeant	$ 3.14	$ (0.47)	$ (0.21)	$ (0.75)	$ (2.19)
Dividends declared per share of common stock	$ —	$ —	$ —	$ 0.24	$ 0.23

Source: SEC.gov http://www.sec.gov/Archives

Exhibit 9 Valeant Pharmaceuticals International Inc. Balance Sheet 2005–2009

	As of December 31				
	2009	**2008**	**2007**	**2006**	**2005**
	(In thousands)				
Balance Sheet Data:					
Cash and cash equivalents	$ 68,080	$ 199,582	$ 287,728	$ 311,012	$ 208,397
Working capital	125,079	175,450	412,272	348,402	220,447
Net assets of discontinued operations	—	—	272,047	282,251	307,096
Total assets	1,305,479	1,185,932	1,492,321	1,503,386	1,512,740
Total debt	600,589	398,802	716,821	698,502	681,606
Stockholders' equity	371,179	251,748	479,571	509,857	527,843

Source: SEC.gov http://sec.gov/Archives

Exhibit 10 Valeant Pharmaceuticals International, Inc. Cash Flow Statement

	2009	2008	2007
	(In thousands)		
Cash flows from operating activities:			
Net income (loss)	$ 263,744	$ (40,820)	$(20,186)
Income (loss) from discontinued operations	6,125	166,548	(26,796)
Income (loss) from continuing operations	257,619	(207,368)	6,610
Adjustments to reconcile income (loss) from continuing operations to net cash provided by operating activities in continuing operations:			
Depreciation and amortization	86,381	66,480	71,634
Provision for losses on accounts receivable and inventory	2,911	21,665	6,488
Stock compensation expense	16,121	5,064	12,419
Excess tax deduction from stock options exercised	(1,735)	(12,303)	—
Translation and exchange (gains) losses, net	1,019	(2,063)	(1,659)
Impairment charges and other non-cash items	14,966	9,242	30,035
Payments of accreted interest on long-term debt	(35,338)	(6,115)	
Acquired in-process research and development	—	186,300	—
Deferred income taxes	(97,653)	(23,663)	18,122
(Gain) loss on extinguishment of debt	(7,221)	954	—
Change in assets and liabilities, net of effects of acquisitions:			
Accounts receivable	1,508	11,038	23,440
Inventories	(13,193)	(22,369)	7,609
Prepaid expenses and other assets	2,885	9,517	(7,839)
Trade payables and accrued liabilities	6,144	49,111	(9,768)
Income taxes	1,297	32,842	(57,350)
Other liabilities	(49,390)	82,323	824
Cash flow from operating activities in continuing operations	186,321	200,655	100,565
Cash flow from operating activities in discontinued operations	(2,768)	9,759	(8,044)
Net cash provided by operating activities	183,553	210,414	92,521
Cash flows from investing activities:			
Capital expenditures	(20,047)	(16,575)	(29,140)
Proceeds from sale of assets	760	971	38,627
Proceeds from sale of businesses	3,342	48,575	2,453
Proceeds from investments	135,937	200,802	35,248
Purchase of investments	(129,089)	(155,653)	(72,518)
Acquisition of businesses, license rights, and product lines	(328,442)	(355,303)	(22,520)
Cash flow from investing activities in continuing operations	(337,539)	(277,183)	(47,850)
Cash flow from investing activities in discontinued operations	(4,941)	447,101	8,508
Net cash (used in) provided by investing activities	(342,480)	169,918	(39,342)
Cash flows from financing activities:			
Payments on long-term debt and notes payable	(151,718)	(323,804)	(3,494)
Proceeds from issuance of long-term debt and notes payable	348,982	118	1,799
Stock option exercises and employee stock purchases	40,387	49,054	15,288
Payments of employee withholding taxes related to equity awards	(7,099)	—	
Excess tax deduction from stock options exercised	1,735	12,303	
Purchase of treasury stock	(202,378)	(206,517)	(9?
Cash flow from financing activities in continuing operations	29,909	(468,846)	
Cash flow from financing activities in discontinued operations	—	(43)	

Exhibit 10 Valeant Pharmaceuticals International, Inc. Cash Flow Statement (*Continued*)

Net cash provided by (used in) financing activities	29,909	(468,889)	(93,317)
Effect of exchange rate changes on cash and cash equivalents	(2,484)	(21,226)	23,924
Net decrease in cash and cash equivalents	(131,502)	(109,783)	(16,214)
Cash and cash equivalents at beginning of period	199,582	309,365	325,579
Cash and cash equivalents at end of period	68,080	199,582	309,365
Cash and cash equivalents classified as part of discontinued operations	—	—	(21,637)
Cash and cash equivalents of continuing operations	$ 68,080	$ 199,582	$287,728

Source: SEC.gov http://www.sec.gov

Exhibit 11 Valeant Pharmaceuticals International, Inc. Key Ratios

Valuation	
P/E (TTM)	—
Price to Revenue (TTM)	12.06
Price to Cash Flow (TTM)	166.54
Price to Book (MRQ)	2.05
Per Share	
Revenue/Share (TTM)	5.66
EPS Fully Diluted (TTM)	−.62
Dividend/Share (TTM)	.38
Book Value/Share (MRQ)	18.13
Cash Flow/Share (TTM)	.41
Cash (MRQ)	2.03
Profitability	
Operating Margin (TTM) (%)	−.94
Net Profit Margin (TTM) (%)	−11.46
Gross Margin (TTM) (%)	72.50
Growth	
5-Year Annual Growth (%)	−1.28
5-Year Annual Revenue Growth Rate (%)	−1.37
5-Year Annual Dividend Growth Rate (%)	—
5-Year EPS Growth (%)	1.45
Financial Strength	
Quick Ratio (MRQ)	1.19
Current Ratio (MRQ)	1.54
LT Debt to Equity (MRQ) (%)	58.21
Total Debt to Equity (MRQ) (%)	60.48
Management Effectiveness	
Return on Equity (TTM) (%)	−3.13
Return on Assets (TTM) (%)	−1.58
Return on Investment (TTM) (%)	−1.72
Efficiency	
Asset Turnover (TTM)	.14
Inventory Turnover (TTM)	1.32

*TTM (Trailing 12 Months) refers to the most recently completed 12-month period, ending on the last day of the most recent month. Above data refer to the 12-month period ending Dec 2010.

Source: Valeant Pharmaceuticals International, Inc. company website, http://www.valeant.com, Jan 2011.

Strategic Direction

Before resigning, Tyson outlined to shareholders his strategy as follows:

Our strategic focus will be to aggressively acquire, develop and commercialize new products. Through strategic acquisitions, growth in our promoted brands, and continued management of expenses, we expect to make further progress toward our goal of creating long-term value for our stockholders.... We have talented and experienced professionals, good products and a sound business strategy. The management team continues to be committed to delivering on its promises.[123]

Tyson's successor, J. Michael Pearson, appears to have been successful in the application and further development of Tyson's acquisition strategy. However, there are many challenges and opportunities ahead. For example, pharmaceutical sales in emerging markets are anticipated to increase by 14 to 17 percent through 2014, led by China and Brazil, compared with a 3 to 6 percent growth rate in developed markets, according to IMS Health.[124] Some Western companies such as Eli Lilly and Novartis, have already made long-term investments in manufacturing facilities and partnerships with local Chinese firms. Pfizer has announced plans to pursue a 6 percent market share in China within three years.[125] Although Brazil is one of Valeant's target markets and it has a manufacturing facility there, was the March 2008 sale of Valeant's Asian assets to Invida Pharmaceutical Holdings Pte. Ltd.[126] a decision that Pearson will eventually regret? Is the February 2011 purchase of PharmaSwiss an indication that Pearson is considering further expansion of Valeant's geographic scope?

Will the strategy outlined here combined with the current restructuring efforts resulting from the merge be substantiated in the marketplace or will the strategy need to be further refined? Where Pearson invests the combined company's financial, intellectual, and other resources will be critical to the firm's success in delivering long-term value to shareholders.

NOTES

1. 2011, Valeant Pharmaceuticals International, Inc., http://www.valeant.com.
2. *Ibid.*
3. 2007, Valeant, http://www.valeant.com.
4. B. Berkrot, 2010, Global drug sales to top $1 trillion in 2014-IMS, *Reuters*, Apr 20, http://www.reuters.com.
5. *Ibid.*
6. 2007, Valeant, Hoovers, www.hoovers.com/valeant/—ID__10763—/freeukco-factsheet.xhtml.
7. 2001, Valeant Pharmaceuticals, ICN to maximize shareholder value, *SEC Online*, http://www.secinfo.com/dRY7g.45z.htm, Apr 6.
8. 1985, Ribavirin vs. AIDS, *Fortune*, Jan 21, 11.
9. 2007, Valeant, *Research & Markets*, http://www.researchandmarkets.com/reportinfo. asp?report_id=222850.
10. M. Cecil, 2000, ICN is frozen with panic against heartland, *Mergers & Acquisitions*, Jul 31, 42.
11. 2002, Where is ICN Pharmaceuticals Incorporated? Labor productivity and financial competitiveness benchmarks published, *Market Wire*, http://findarticles.com/p/articles/mi_pwwi/is_200204/ai_mark09040884, Apr.
12. 2007, *BusinessWeek*, http://investing.businessweek.com/research/stocks/snapshot/snapshot.asp?capId=92852.
13. V. Reed, 2007, Valeant refocuses, strategy questioned; where's Blockbuster?
14. 2002, Panic gone, new ICN team finds finances in disarray, *Los Angeles Business Journal*, Jul 29, 28.
15. 2003, ICN, International Directory of Company Histories, http://www.fundinguniverse.com/company-histories/ICN-Pharmaceuticals-Inc-Company-History.html.
16. V. Reed, 2007, *op. cit.*
17. 2007, Valeant, http://www.valeant.com/aboutValeant/seniorManagementDetail. jspf?objectId=20.
18. 2007, Valeant, *Hoovers.com*, http://www.valeant.com/—ID__10763—/free-co-factsheet.xhtml.
19. K. McCormack, 1999, Foolish love, ICN, *Smartmoney.com*, www.smartmoney.com/stockscreen/index.cfm?story=19990922intro, Sep 22.
20. 2006, Valeant sells development programs, *FierceBiotech.com*, http://www. fiercebiotech.com/tags/valeant-pharmaceuticals, Dec 21.
21. 2007, Valeant Pharma hits new low on downgrade, *BusinessWeek*, http://www. businessweek.com/ap/financialnews/D8SNT41G0.htm, Nov 5.
22. *Ibid.*
23. 2009, Valeant Pharmaceuticals International, Annual Report.
24. V. Reed, 2010, Valeant's cost cutting, small buys find favor with Wall Street, *Orange County Business Journal*, May 23.
25. 2009, Valeant Pharmaceuticals International, *op cit.*
26. V. Reed, 2010, *op. cit.*
27. 2010, Retigabine NDA accepted for filing, *PRNewswire-First Call*, Dec 30, http://www.drugs.com/nda/retigabine_091230.html.
28. J. Rockoff, 2009, Drug firm leaves R&D to others – Valeant Pharmaceuticals prefers to forgo the risk, grow through acquisitions, *Wall Street Journal*, March 2, B6.
29. *Ibid.*
30. *Ibid.*
31. *Ibid.*
32. 2011, Valeant Pharmaceuticals, *op cit.*
33. 2009, Valeant Pharmaceuticals International, *op cit.*
34. V. Reed, 2010, *op. cit.*
35. 2010, Aton Pharma, Inc., http://www.atonrx.com/press/18/pdf.
36. *Ibid.*
37. 2010, Biovail Corporation S-4/A Registration of Securities Issued in Business Combination Transactions, Aug 18.
38. S. Stovall, 2010, Valeant, Biovail agree to merge, *Wall Street Journal*, Jun 21.
39. *Ibid.*
40. 2010, Valeant Pharmaceuticals International, Inc. declares special dividend and plans to create a special dividend reinvestment plan, *Reuters*, http://www.reuters.com/finance/stocks/keyDevelopments?sy mbol=VRX&pn=2, Nov 4.
41. P. Sacha, 2010, Why Canada's corporate tax policy is paying off in spades, *Divestor*, Canadian Finance, Economics and Securities Analysis, http://divestor.com/2010/06/21/why-canadas-corporate-tax-policy-ispaying-off-in-spades, Jun 21.
42. 2010, Biovail Corporation *op. cit.*
43. *Ibid.*
44. A. Georgiades, 2010, Biovail says Valeant deal rockets company into the future, *Wall Street Journal Online*, http://onlinewsj.com/article/SB10001424052748704895204575320350568757726.html, Jun 21.
45. 2010, Biovail Corporation S-4/A *op. cit.*
46. *Ibid.*
47. 2011, Valeant Pharmaceuticals, *op cit.*
48. S. Freeman, 2011, Valeant Pharmaceuticals lays off 500 employees in merger with Biovail, *The Canadian Press*, Jan 12.
49. *Ibid.*
50. 2011, Valeant Pharmaceuticals to acquire PharmaSwiss S.A., *PR Newswire Association LLC*, http://corporate.lexisnexis.com/news/marketing. branding/cat300001_doc1351234472.html, Feb 1.
51. 2011, Valeant Pharmaceuticals International, Inc. announces pricing of senior notes, *Reuters*, http://www.reuters.com/finance/stocks/keyDevelopments?symbol=VRX, Feb 3.
52. 2011, Valeant Pharmaceuticals to acquire PharmaSwiss S.A., *op. cit.*
53. M. Herper, 2002, ICN shareholders win. Now what? *Forbes.com*, http://www.forbes. com/2002/05/30/0530icn.html, May 30.
54. 2004, Valeant Annual Report 2003, *Valeant.com*, http://www.valeant.com.
55. 2003, ICN, *International Directory of Company Histories*, http://www.fundinguniverse.com/company-histories/ICN-Pharmaceuticals-Inc-Company-History.html.
56. 2010, J. Michael Pearson executive profile, *Forbes*, http://people.forbes.com/profile/j-michael-pearson/83598.
57. J. Lublin, 2009, Valeant CEO's pay package draws praise as a model, *Wall Street Journal*, Aug 24, B4.
58. *Ibid.*
59. *Ibid.*
60. *Ibid.*
61. *Ibid.*
62. V. Reed, 2010, *op. cit.*
63. *Ibid.*
64. 2010, Biovail Corporation *op. cit.*
65. 2010, Update1 – Valeant searches for new CFO, shares slide, *Reuters*, Dec 20.
66. *Ibid.*
67. 2010, Valeant Pharmaceuticals International, Inc. announces appointment of Robert A. Ingram as chairman, *Reuters*, http://www.reuters. com/finance/stocks/keyDevelopments?symbol=VRX, Dec 13.
68. 2006, Ten frequently asked questions about Parkinson's Disease, *Parkinson's Disease Foundation*, http://www.pdf.org/Publications/factsheets/PDF_Fact_Sheet_ 1.0_Final.pdf, Nov 25.
69. 2011, Parkinson's Disease (PD) overview, National Parkinson Foundation, http://www.parkinson.org/parkinson-s-disease.aspx.
70. 2006, Statistics on Parkinson's Disease, http://www.medopedia. com/parkinsons/statistics, Nov 26.
71. 2007, http://www.valeant.com/products/neurology/index.jsp, Nov 27.
72. Catechol-O-methyltransferase (COMT) inhibitors are a new class drugs that provide an alternate therapeutic option to patients Parkinson's disease. They are most useful for "wearing-off" dose deterioration) motor fluctuations and are used in com with levodopa; C. Waters & A. Constantino, 2001, The u COMT inhibitors in older patients, *Geriatric Times* 2(2)

73. 2004, Valeant Pharmaceuticals acquires rights to Tasmar®, http://www.valeant.com mediaCenter/newsArticle/newsArticle. jspf?objectId=393, Nov 26.

74. 2011, Epilepsy and seizure statistics, about epilepsy & seizures, Epilepsy Foundation, http://www.epilepsyfoundation.org/about/ statistics.cfm.

75. 2010, FDA declines to OK Glaxo epilepsy drug for now, *Reuters*, http://www.reuters.com/article/idUSTRE6B06HI20101201, Dec.1.

76. Diastat® Acudial™ is a gel that is administered through the rectum.

77. Postherpetic neuralgia (post-her-PET-ic noo-RAL-jah) is a complication of shingles. It is a painful condition affecting the nerve fibers and skin such that patients feel sharp jabbing, burning, or deep aching pain, itching, and numbness, headaches, or extreme sensitivity to touch and temperature; 2008, *Mayo Clinic*, http:// www.mayoclinic.com/health/postherpetic-neuralgia/; 2007, Valeant R&D portfolio, http://www.valeant.com/researchAndDevelopment/ pipeline/retigabine.jspf, Nov 26.

78. 2011, Regulatory update – GSK and Valeant receive positive opinion in Europe from the CHMP for Trobalt (Retigabine), *PRNewswire*, Jan 21.

79. 2010, Retigabine NDA accepted for filing, *PRNewswire-First Call*, http://www.drugs.com/nda/retigabine_091230.html, Dec 30.

80. 2011, Valeant Pharmaceuticals, *op cit.*

81. *Ibid.*

82. *Ibid.*

83. G. Gatyas, 2010, IMS Health forecasts global pharmaceutical market growth of 5–7 percent in 2011, reaching $880 billion, http:// www.imshealth.com, Oct 6.

84. 2007, Hoover's, http://premium.hoovers.com.ezproxy1.lib.asu.edu/ subscribe/ind/fr/profile/basic.xhtml?ID=108.

85. 2008, Teva Pharmaceutical Industries Ltd. 2007 Annual Report, http://www.tevapharm.com, Feb.

86. 2011, Hoover's Company Reports, Teva Pharmaceutical Industries Limited.

87. 2008, UCB 2007 Annual Report, http://www.ucb-group.com/ investor_relations/financials/index.asp.

88. 2011, UCB company web site, http://www.ucb.com/about-ucb/ facts/sales.

89. *Ibid.*

90. 2011, Hoover's Company Reports, H. Lundbeck A/S.

91. K. Richards, 2004, Outsourcing: The pharmaceutical industry's strategy of choice for managing risk and rapid change, http://www. touchbriefings.com/pdf/890/PT04_richards.pdf, Nov 22.

92. J. Sirven, 2007, personal interview, Nov 21.

93. AIS, *A Guide to Drug Cost Management Strategies,* 2002; PCMA, 2001.

94. J. Richardson, 2003, PBMs: The basics and an industry overview, http://www.ftc. gov/ogc/healthcarehearings/ docs/030626richardson.pdf, Nov 25.

95. C. Sprague, 2007, Speeding time to market and ensuring regulatory compliance with business process and content management integration, http://www.ngpharma.com/pastissue/ article.asp?art=270061&issue=201, Nov 26.

96. J. Carroll, 2006, 10 major health care/pharmaceutical trends, http:// www.jimcarroll. com/weblog/archives/000757.html, Nov 26.

97. 2002, Integrating prevention into health care, http://www.who.int/ mediacentre/factsheets/fs172/en/index.html, Nov 25.

98. 2007, *US Census Bureau*, http://www.census.gov/Press-Release/ www/releases/archives/aging_population/006544.html, Nov 27.

99. S. Nebehay, 2007, Neurological disorders affect one billion people—WHO, *Reuters*, http://www.reuters.com/article/latestCrisis/ idUSL27230278, Nov 25.

100. 2005, Prescription drugs: Price trends for frequently used brand and generic drugs from 2000 through 2004, *United States Government Accountability Office*, http://www.gao.gov/new.items/ d05779.pdf, Nov 23.

101. 2004, Questions and answers about Activa Parkinson's control therapy, *Medtronic*, http://www.medtronic.com/neuro/parkinsons/ activa_qa2.html#9, Nov 23.

102. Mayo Clinic Staff, 2006, Deep brain stimulation: An experimental depression treatment, *Mayo Clinic*, http://www.mayoclinic.com/ health/deep-brainstimulation/MH00114, Nov 25.

103. M. Kakutani, 2005, Generation RX: How prescription drugs are altering American lives, minds and bodies, http://www.iht.com/ articles/2005/10/02/features/booklun.php, Nov 26.

104. M. Lombardi, 2007, Raising awareness of "Generation Rx," http:// www.cbsnews. com/blogs/2007/11/29/couricandco/entry3553088. shtml, Nov 29.

105. 2010, National Drug Control Strategy, Office of National Drug Control Policy, http://www.whitehousedrugpolicy.gov/policy/ndcs. html.

106. 2004, Offshore outsourcing of pharmaceutical R&D.

107. Visa policies are an issue for pharmaceutical companies because they are not able to hire and retain knowledge from foreign human capital.

108. J. Carroll, 2006, *op. cit.*

109. S. Salam, 2002, HIPAA: Impact on the pharmaceutical industry, http://www. pharmabiz.com/article/detnews.asp?articleid=11394&s ectionid=46, Nov 23.

110. 2006, Inventories and audits for Prescription Drug Marketing Act (PDMA) Compliance, *Global Compliance*, http://www .globalcompliance.com/prescriptiondrug-marketing-actpdma.html, Nov 27.

111. 2007, Division of Drug Marketing, Advertising, and Communications, *US Food and Drug Administration*, http://www .fda.gov/cder/ddmac, Nov 22.

112. 2011, Truthful Prescription Drug Advertising and Promotion (Bad Ad Program), *US Food and Drug Administration*, http://www .fad/gov/Drugs/GuidanceComplainceRegulatoryInformation/ Surveillance?DrugMarketingAd vertisingandCommunications/ ucm209384/htm

113. S. Saul, 2007, Patient money: Strategies to avoid Medicare's big hole, *The New York Times*, http://www.nytimes.com/2007/11/24/ health/policy/24donut. html?ref=todayspaper, Nov 26.

114. 2011, How does this Donut Hole really work?, Q1Medicare.com, http://www.q1medicare.com/PartD-MoreOnTheDonutHolesOrCoverageGap.php.

115. 2007, Considerations for generic drug use in the elderly, *Pharmacy Times*, http://www.pharmacytimes.com/issues/ articles/2007-01_4286.asp, Nov 27.

116. J. Frederick, 2007, Medicare Part D driving up generic dispensing, *BET Research Center*, http://findarticles.com/p/articles/mi_m3374/ is_3_29/ai_n19020244, Nov 23.

117. 2011, Hoover's Company Reports, Valeant Pharmaceuticals International, Inc.

118. C. North, personal interview.

119. 2011, Valeant Pharmaceuticals, *op cit.*

120. 2011, Valeant Pharma soars on 4Q and 2011 forecasts, *Bloomberg Businessweek*, Jan 6, http://www.businessweek.com/ap/ financialnews/D9KJ2B001.htm.

121. 2011, M. Venu, Valeant Pharmaceuticals International, Inc. analyst report, *Morningstar Investment Research Center*, http://library.morningstar.com.ezproxy1.lib.asu.edu/stocknet/ MorningstarAnalysis.aspx?Country=USA&Sym bol=VRX&Custid- &CLogin=&CType=&CName=.

122. *Ibid.*

123. 2007, Valeant, *op cit.*

124. B. Berkrot, 2010, *op. cit.*

125. M. Rimes, 2010, Big Pharma's challenge: figuring out China, *Fortune*, http://money.cnn.com/2010/09/23/news/international/ big_pharma_china.fortune/index.htm, Sep 23.

126. 2009, Valeant Pharmaceuticals International Annual Report.

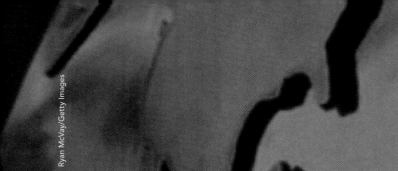

Michelle L. Stotts, Charles B. Shrader, Samuel M. DeMarie

Iowa State University

Now that we are in our 10th year and have a fairly complete line of premium cruiser and touring motorcycles, it is clear what we stand for, and who we appeal to most. Victory stands for class-leading quality, innovation, and style. Victory is American and new—always looking forward. We are all about the future of American motorcycles.

—MARK BLACKWELL, VICTORY VICE PRESIDENT[1]

Mark Blackwell, vice president in charge of Victory Motorcycles at Polaris Industries, glanced up at company headquarters in Medina, Minnesota as he pulled his gleaming cruiser into the parking lot. Having won the national 500cc motocross championship and been inducted into the American Motorcycle Association's Hall of Fame, Blackwell was an accomplished rider himself and so he knew firsthand that his company's bikes had come pretty far since they were first introduced to the riding public in 1998. With the development of the new Vision, a luxury touring bike, and the steady release of aggressively styled cruisers, the company had continually innovated throughout its first decade in business. Yet Blackwell couldn't help pondering the recurring questions facing Victory Motorcycles and Polaris. He wondered if the initial decision to diversify into heavyweight motorcycles was the right road to take. He realized Polaris took a big risk by moving into motorcycles and going up against the recognized powerhouses in the industry. He questioned if Victory could continue successfully competing against the Japanese giants, new, energetic, and innovative motorcycle companies, and its closest rival—Harley-Davidson.

Victory began making motorcycles in 1998. From 1998 to 2006, Polaris invested over $100 million in motorcycle development, and by 2006, the division was profitable for the first time. Victory's sales were $113 million, 7 percent of company sales for that year[2] (see Exhibit 1). In 2009, Victory Motorcycles celebrated its first decade in the motorcycle business, but a global recession led to poor sales, corporate restructuring, and company-wide layoffs. In that year Polaris, Victory's parent company, announced a new "on-road" vehicle division of which Victory would be part. Mike Jonikas was appointed vice president of the new division and Blackwell as vice president of Polaris's present and future motorcycle business.[3] Both Jonikas and Blackwell reported directly to Polaris's chief operating officer (COO), Bennett Morgan (see Exhibit 2).

Jonikas and Blackwell knew Victory needed to maintain a high level of quality engineering throughout its production processes. If Victory was to be a successful brand with high demand, it needed to meet customer expectations and not fall behind in terms of innovation like its main heavyweight competitor, Harley-Davidson. Victory mangers also needed to consider whether it was a good decision to limit sales of Victory motorcycles to Polaris dealerships. The intent was to monitor quality, but was Victory simultaneously losing potential business?

After 10 years, Victory could still call itself a new motorcycle brand. The challenge was how to continue to innovate and grow in a difficult market segment. The need to examine the motorcycle division's strategy seemed imperative.

Polaris Industries, Inc.

Polaris Industries, Inc. designs, engineers, and manufactures snowmobiles, all-terrain recreational and utility vehicles (ATVs), motorcycles, personal watercraft (PWC), on- and off-road vehicles, and low-emission vehicles; and markets them, together with related replacement parts, garments, and accessories (PG&A), through dealers and distributors principally located in the US, Canada, and Europe.[4] Garment and accessory items include helmets, boots, T-shirts, sweat pants, touring luggage, and trailers.[5] The company is widely known as the world's largest manufacturer of snowmobiles, one of the biggest makers of ATVs and PWC in (see Exhibit 3).

Exhibit 1 Victory Sales (dollars in millions)

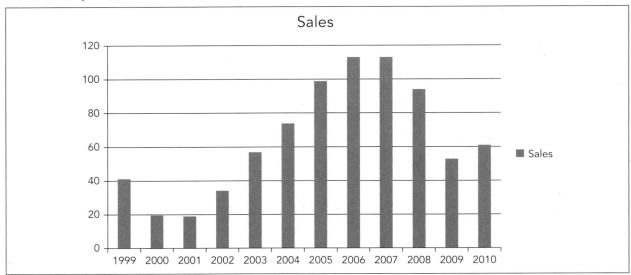

Sources: Polaris Industries 2009, 2006, 2003, and 2000 annual reports. Polaris Industries 2010 10K Q1, Q2, and Q3 quarterly reports.

In 1954, Polaris produced its first snowmobile under co-founder and former CEO Alan Hetteen. Textron, Inc. bought Polaris from its original Roseau, Minnesota

Exhibit 2 Polaris Industries: Top Management

Scott W. Wine	Chief Executive Officer
Bennett J. Morgan	President and COO
Todd M. Balan	VP – Corporate Development
Mark E. Blackwell	VP – Victory Motorcycles
Stacy L. Bogart	VP – General Counsel and Corporate Secretary
John B. Corness	VP – Human Resources
Michael D. Dougherty	VP – Global New Market Development
William C. Fisher	VP – Chief Information Officer
Matthew J. Homan	VP – Off-Road Vehicles
Michael P. Jonikas	VP – On-Road Vehicles, Sales & Marketing
Michael W. Malone	VP – Finance and CFO

Source: Polaris Industries Web site, http://phx.corporate-ir.net

ownership group in 1968.[7] In 1981, Textron, Inc. sold the Polaris division to a group of private investors led by W. Hall Wendel Jr., a Textron division head.[8]

The snowmobile business kept the Roseau, Minnesota, plant busy six months out of the year, but company managers wanted to figure out how to fill the other six months. They extensively surveyed the Polaris snowmobiler customer base, and decided in 1985 to diversify and produce ATVs. The company once again diversified by manufacturing PWC in 1992, and eventually became a world leader in both ATV and PWC production and sales. In 1987, Polaris became a publicly traded company.[9]

To facilitate its operations, Polaris both leases and owns extensive property (see Exhibit 4). Within the upper Midwest of the US, Polaris owns:[10]

■ Minneapolis, MN—130,000-square-foot headquarters and warehouse.
■ Roseau, MN—635,000-square-foot facility on 100 acres for principal engineering and manufacturing. This is where the company was founded in the 50s.

Exhibit 3 Polaris: Percent Sales Mix by Product, 1998–2009

	2009	2008	2007	2006	2005	2004	2003	2002	2001	2000	1999	1998
Off-road vehicles	65%	67%	67%	67%	66%	66%	65%	62%	56%	59%	59%	57%
Snowmobiles	12%	10%	10%	10%	14%	16%	14%	19%	25%	22%	28%	32%
Personal watercraft							3%	4%	4%	5%	4%	4%
On-road vehicles/motorcycles	3%	5%	6%	7%	5%	4%	4%	2%	1%	1%	4%	1%
Parts, garments, and accessories	20%	18%	17%	16%	15%	14%	14%	13%	14%	13%		
International											5%	6%

Sources: 1999, 2003, and 2009 annual reports.

Exhibit 4 Polaris Properties

Location		Facility Type/Use	Leased/Owned	Square Footage
US	California — Ontario	Wholegoods Distribution	Leased	112,000
	Iowa — Spirit Lake	Wholegoods Manufacturing	Owned	258,000
	Iowa — Spirit Lake	Warehouse	Leased	90,000
	Iowa — Spencer	Wholegoods Distribution	Leased	45,000
	Minnesota — Medina	Headquarters	Owned	130,000
	Minnesota — Roseau	Wholegoods Manufacturing/R&D	Owned	635,000
	Minnesota — Roseau	Injection Molding Manufacturing	Owned	76,800
	Minnesota — Roseau	Warehouse (various locations)	Leased	39,600
	Minnesota — Wyoming	Research and Development Facility	Owned	127,000
	Minnesota — Eagan	Wholegoods Distribution	Leased	35,000
	Minnesota — Brooklyn Park	Wholegoods Distribution	Leased	25,000
	New York — E. Syracuse	Wholegoods Distribution	Leased	40,000
	South Dakota — Vermillion	Distribution Center	Owned	385,000
	Tennessee — Nashville	Wholegoods Distribution	Leased	37,500
	Texas — Irving	Wholegoods Distribution	Leased	46,300
	Washington — Tacoma	Wholegoods Distribution	Leased	15,000
	Wisconsin — Osceola	Component Parts Manufacturing	Owned	188,800
	Wisconsin — Osceola	Engine Manufacturing	Owned	97,000
International	Australia — Ballarat, Victoria	Office and Distribution facility	Leased	9,200
	Australia — Melbourne	Retail store	Leased	9,600
	Canada — Winnipeg, Manitoba	Office and Distribution facility	Leased	31,000
	France — Passy	Office and Distribution facility	Leased	10,000
	Germany — Griesheim	Office and Distribution facility	Leased	3,200
	Norway — Askim	Office and Distribution facility	Leased	10,800
	Spain — Barcelona	Office and Distribution facility	Leased	4,300
	Sweden — Ostersund	Office and Distribution facility	Leased	14,300
	UK — Birmingham	Office and Distribution facility	Leased	6,500

Source: Polaris 2009 10K report, 14

Polaris broke ground on a 77,000-square-foot plastic injection molding facility at this site.

- Wyoming, MN—127,000-square-foot R&D facility.
- Osceola, WI—189,000 square feet on 38 acres for a fabricating facility and 97,000 square feet for engines.
- Spirit Lake, IA—258,000 square feet on 24 acres to assemble PWCs, certain ATV models, and motorcycles.
- Vermillion, SD—385,000 square feet on 50 acres for a PG&A distribution center.

As a result of its diversification, Polaris was able to manufacture products all year. Snowmobile manufacturing took place in the spring through late autumn or early winter and PWC were manufactured during the fall, winter, and spring months. Polaris has had the ability to manufacture ATVs year-round since May 1993. ATV production starts in late autumn and continues through early autumn of the following year.[11]

Because of the seasonality of the Polaris products and associated production cycles, total employment levels vary throughout the year. Approximately 3,000 individuals are employed by the company. Polaris employees have not been represented by a union since July 1982. The company announced layoffs in its Osceola, Wisconsin, plant in early 2011 due to the recession.[12]

Expansion into Motorcycles[13,14]

Matt Parks joined Polaris in 1987 as a distri... manager hired to develop the dealer net... California, Nevada, and Arizona. He was n...

product manager in 1992 and earned a spot at the company's headquarters. W. Hall Wendel Jr. asked him to do research on prospective acquisitions or expansions. Parks, with the additional title of general manager of new products, considered such things as go-karts, golf carts, lawn-and-garden products, chainsaws, and even Hula Hoops by investigating the various industries in terms of competition, size, level of service, and new trends. Parks and others studied the off-road motorcycle market when two dirt bike companies were put up for sale. Then, a European motorcycle company asked to distribute its bikes through Polaris. Parks recalls,

That sparked a study of the motorcycle business that uncovered signs of a promising market. Along with the dirt bike research, we did a quick study of the street bike business at that time, and we were kind of interested. We thought, "You know, this makes some sense."[15]

In 1993, Polaris distributed over 300,000 surveys through the company's *Spirit* magazine distributed to Polaris vehicle owners to measure readers' interest in buying a wide variety of products from Polaris. "Motorcycling did really, really well [in the survey]," said Parks.[16] The survey results were personally interesting to Parks since he was a lifetime motorcycle rider and owned several motorcycles, including a '74 Norton, '66 and '91 BMWs, a '77 Harley XLCR, and an '81 Ducati. Motorcycles also caught the interest of Wendel, who at the time owned a Harley-Davidson.

In pursuing the possibility of motorcycle production, "Victory" became the project's confidential code name. Parks came up with the name because it was a nonsensical name with positive connotations. "It's 'V' for victory. It's nostalgic; it has World War II connotations."[17]

Parks and Bob Nygaard, Snowmobile Division general manager, proceeded with investigating the motorcycle production possibility by hiring two outside firms to assist them in conducting further confidential research on motorcycles. They chose McKinsey and Company, one of the largest and most prestigious consulting firms in the world, and Jerry Stahl, an advertising executive who was very familiar with recreational motorsports and the motorcycle business. Stahl also had experience with Harley-Davidson's advertising campaigns. From May through August 1993, Parks and Nygaard assessed the Polaris infrastructure, including the company's sales force, dealer network, service and warranty operation, and parts and accessories division. They also looked at Polaris's current customers to see what types of activities they were interested in and whether they would buy a motorcycle from Polaris. Polaris analysts and consultants reviewed statistics from the Motorcycle Industry Council (MIC) of the location, displacement, and types of bikes sold in the industry.

The research showed there was industry capacity for another manufacturer in the cruiser business. The research also revealed that Polaris dealers would like to have on-road motorcycles to sell. Consultants believed that a functionally superior cruiser built in America could find competitive space between Harley-Davidson and the Japanese producers. "We focused in on Harley and the Japanese manufacturers and said to ourselves, 'Is Harley vulnerable from any standpoint?' We thought that their costs were high," Nygaard said.

We thought that, based on re-engineering the Harley bike, we could build it for less money. We felt that customers were waiting too long to take delivery of their Harleys, and they (Harley-Davidson) were vulnerable from that standpoint. We could get to market with a bike that we could make money, and the heavy cruiser end of it was certainly what we wanted to target because that's where the (sales) numbers were, and that's where the (profit) margin was. It was the best fit for us, in that the Japanese were vulnerable there. They really hadn't been able to tackle Harley, because it might look like a Harley, but the real rider knew that it wasn't an American-made bike from an American manufacturer. We were close (at the time) to being in the domestic engine business, and we could build our own US engine, and that gave us a major leg up on the Japanese. We were an American company.[18]

"The result of the study was, believe it or not, yes, there was a tremendous opportunity in the motorcycle market," Parks said. "It's not the off-road motorcycle market; it's the on-road motorcycle market, and the entry point, the best entry point, would be in the cruiser market."[19] Cruisers were defined as stripped-down versions of heavyweight touring bikes that were intended for leisurely travel. Research showed that many cruiser owners immediately replaced many components, such as brakes, seats, wheels, vibration-adsorption devices, frame stiffeners, and intake systems on their brand-new motorcycles. This was interpreted as an opportunity to fulfill demand created by undershot customers in the market.

Polaris had over 44 years of experience producing recreational vehicles. It had the engineering talent and production capabilities to design and produce distinctly different vehicle lines—snowmobiles, ATVs, and PWC—and produce its own engines for many of those vehicles. Parks said the study showed "the manufacturing capabilities and technological know-how required to produce cruisers seemed within Polaris' grasp."[20] "My biggest concern was: Let me sell against price, let me sell against features and benefits, let me sell against more advertising, and I can find ways to do that," Nygaard said. "Help me to sell against the lifestyle, with loyalty that is as passionate as I've ever seen on any product

(Harley-Davidson). To sell against an image is very, very difficult, and that was my biggest concern."[21] In August 1993, the officer group gave the okay to continue with the study to see if it fit with existing manufacturing systems and if it could make money.

Victory Motorcycle Development[22,23]

An early decision was to determine which parts to make and which parts to buy. Dapper and Klancher explained that "they bought a Honda Shadow and a Harley-Davidson FXRS, took them completely apart, weighed, measured, and estimated the cost of every single part, and determined for each part whether they would make it or buy it."[24] After figuring manufacturer, dealer, profits, and sales volumes, the consultants and managers felt there was a good opportunity in the motorcycle business, and in February 1994, the officers group gave the okay to move forward and build a prototype.

A major boost to motorcycle development occurred in September 1994 when Geoff Burgess agreed to lead the Victory team. His extensive motorcycle industry experiences and emphasis on thorough analysis and design work set the direction for the Victory development. The Victory team took a very thorough, methodical, and analytical approach to research and development so the program didn't waste time, money, or valuable resources. Extensive computer-aided design was employed in building a prototype. "A lot of up-front thinking has saved us a lot of time on the back end," explained Parks.[25]

The Victory team began an in-depth benchmarking study by obtaining and extensively road testing a fleet of the competitors' cruisers in Minnesota, Tennessee, and Arizona. The Yamaha Royal Star and Virago, Honda Shadow ACE and Valkyrie, Harley-Davidson Road King, Ducati Monster, and BMW R1100RS were evaluated, compared, and ranked. The goal was not to copy the competition but to find the benchmarks for building a superior cruiser. The cost of producing the best features was also analyzed to ensure they could produce the motorcycle within their target price range.

The Victory team contacted Dunlop, manufacturer and tire supplier of Polaris ATVs, for information about motorcycle tires. Steve Paulos, a Dunlop test technician with an impressive motorcycle industry background, assisted the Victory team by sharing competitors' development and production process information. He accompanied the Victory team to Arizona and shared valuable insights about the benchmarked bikes.

In the early stages of the motorcycle project, the Victory staff determined the bike must excel in two key performance areas—handling and power. Marketing studies told Parks that the engine had to be a big V-twin, and it had to be US made; an American company like Polaris couldn't import the engine for a bike whose targeted buyers represented the red, white, and blue image of the cruiser culture. The group felt that the motorcycle needed to have its own signature engine. Talks with consulting firms with power-plant experts convinced the Polaris team that designing an engine would provide experience curve benefits that would be valuable when Victory Motorcycles broadened its model line to include other classes of bikes in the future. This fit well with Polaris's considerations of starting its own engine manufacturing operation.

Geoff Burgess first laid out the parameters for the Victory V92C engine in November 1994. Victory engineers refined the design, and in February 1995, a concept drawing was created. In March 1995, the Polaris engineering department visited England's Lotus, Cosworth, and Triumph plants, Italy's Ducati and Aprilia plants, and Germany's BMW operation. The team also benchmarked engines made by Fuji, Kawasaki motorcycles, and the Dodge Neon for manufacturing and assembly ideas.

From the Arizona test, the Victory team determined it should build a bigger engine than the competition. This would give it bragging rights for the biggest cruiser engine with the most horsepower on the market. The Arizona tests helped define handling goals as a top priority, so much so that chassis and frame were designed as desired, then the engine was reconfigured to fit in the available space in the frame.

The Arizona tests also convinced the team that the Victory engine should be oil-cooled. Since rows of cooling fins are an essential part of the cruiser look, the idea of using liquid cooling was rejected. Instead, a system was designed to circulate extra volumes of oil to enhance the fins' cooling effect. Steve Weinzierl, who had deep knowledge of aircraft-engineering history, strapped a Czech-built Velorex sidecar onto a prototype Victory bike and took it to Death Valley in California for worst-case cooling trials. At temperatures of 121 degrees Fahrenheit, he pulled within 10 inches of the Victory going 90 miles per hour, and handed the rider in the sidecar the wires from the thermocouple to test the cooling data. This method was used to test and enhance engine thermal stability.

Once the team had collected and analyzed loads of chassis data, "Francis the Mule," a crude prototype, wa created in May 1995. It was built with interchangea' clamps and drilled metal brackets so selected cor nents, such as its wheel base, steering-head angl rear-suspension geometry, could be mounted i positions and adjusted accordingly. The te test one thing at a time and meticulously evaluate the changes on subsequent test rides. They also used the Mule to focus on the chassis because it was a priority for the Victory to achieve optimal ride and handling. After hundreds of hours riding around on Frances and obtaining some assistance from Polaris engineers on the frame and chassis, the team agreed on a chassis design. This analysis helped reduce the weight of the frame by 20 pounds over the original prototype. In addition, the Victory team sought larger suspension forks to ensure that the chassis would have the desired rigidity and earn bragging rights for the biggest forks on the market.

Some elements of the V92C design were dictated by customer demand. It had to have some traits that are popular with, and familiar to, cruiser enthusiasts. Styling dictated a triangular rear swing-arm that simulated the "hard-tail" look of the unsuspended bikes of the 40s. A single shock mounted underneath the seat included an aluminum sub-frame supporting the seat and rear fender. They determined that a high-quality Fox shock was to be a standard feature. Polaris still owns several rear suspension patents as a result.

In May 1995, Mark Bader, who was familiar with compact, high-performance engines, was hired to lead the engine design staff. One of the first engine mock-ups was created from CAD drawings using the Victory rapid-prototyping machine and consisted of thousands of precisely cut pieces of paper glued together. These computer-generated mock-ups allow parts to be generated and test-fit without excessive costs. The first engine prototype via computer-aided design consisted of a tall, 1,507-cc V-twin with a 55-degree angle between its cylinders. This was too big to fit the frame, so the angle was narrowed to 50 degrees. After the frame and chassis were developed, the engine had to be shrunk. It seemed backwards to fit the engine to the frame and chassis, but Burgess felt it was appropriate for the V92C in order to deliver the ride and handling they wanted instead of the engine size determining the bike's size and layout. In addition, they decided to solid-mount the engine and utilize it as a stressed member or supportive of the frame and relatively more integral to the bike as a whole. As a result, the handling was greatly increased.

To develop the crankshaft, the team again benchmarked the performance of competitors' bikes. The Polaris team considered using Harley-style cylinder heads with push rods operating the valves, but chose a more modern overhead-camshaft design instead. The Victory team found it could eliminate virtually all traces of vibration, but it refused to do so because they felt it was a trademark of a cruiser. But they had to determine the proper balance of vibration. As described by Dapper and Klancher,

In the perfect world, there is imperfection. Without it, things just don't seem right. Motorcycles need to have personality; a little rumble here and tingle there lets you know that the machine underneath you is alive and kicking.[26]

The braking system was a concern of the Victory team so they set out to develop braking similar to high-performance sport bikes, rather than what's typically on cruisers. They chose Brembo hardware and worked with Brembo technicians to develop the desired feel and responsiveness. In addition, the Victory team decided to make its own master brake cylinder.

The Victory motorcycle team continued with numerous rigorous tests of the engine, chassis, and other components. The first prototype bikes with Victory engines were known as C bikes, and an early prototype cost approximately $250,000 to build. On November 7, 1996, the Victory concept bike C-1 (engine and chassis together for its first test ride) was first ridden at the Osceola, Wisconsin municipal airport. Eighteen people witnessed the event.

Victory Becomes a Reality[27,28]

Finally, on February 19, 1997, Polaris issued a press release announcing that it would be entering the motorcycle market. On June 26, 1997, the Victory was rolled out to the press at Planet Hollywood in the Mall of America in Bloomington, Minnesota. Al Unser Jr. rode a preproduction bike into the restaurant, and Victory team members fielded questions about the new bike. The next day, editors from several motorcycle magazines met the Victory staff in Osceola to learn more about the new American motorcycle.

Since the announcement, the Victory motorcycle has received universally positive reviews in the motorcycle press. It has also received coverage in newspapers such as the *Wall Street Journal, New York Times,* and *USA Today.* Parks appeared on CNN and CNBC promoting the bike. In August 1997, Victory made an appearance at the 57th Annual Sturgis Rally & Races in South Dakota. In January 1998, demonstration rides sponsored by dealers were given in Palm Springs, California, for the first time. Over 200 motorcyclists received demo rides on preproduction prototypes of Victory motorcycles during Daytona Bike Week in March 1998. After taking the bikes for a ride—experiencing street speeds, corners, and brakes—riders were given a questionnaire and interviewed by the Victory marketing staff. The riders' feedback indicated the bikes delivered outstanding handling and power. The Victory staff also made a few adjustments to the motorcycle based on customer feedback.[29]

The Victory team felt the bike was ready to roll and named the first model the V92C. "V" stood for the V-twin engine, "92" for the engine's 92-cubic inch displacement, and "C" indicated "cruiser." The V92C had the stiffest frame of any cruiser on the market (as stiff as some sport bikes), and utilized the engine as a stressed member (fundamental component) of the frame for increased strength and rigidity. Complementing the stiff frame were its large fork tubes with a rear suspension incorporating a stiff triangulated swing-arm controlled by a single shock absorber under the seat. The Victory V92C delivered up to 50 percent more horsepower than any of its direct competitors. Victory motorcycles were first produced in "Knock-Your-Socks-Off Blue" or "Antares Red."

"The first Victory V92C motorcycles rolled off the assembly line at the Polaris plant in Spirit Lake, Iowa, on the Fourth of July 1998, just over a year after unveiling the prototype."[30] Previously, in May 1998, *Cycle World*, the largest motorcycle magazine in North America, selected the Victory motorcycle as the "Best Cruiser of 1998" before the first bike was available to consumers.[31]

The Polaris team believed it could successfully produce a motorcycle because of its history of design, manufacturing, and distribution of recreational vehicles along with its engineering talent, business savvy, and loyal Polaris customers. Now former Polaris CEO W. Hall Wendel Jr. said at the time,

Entering the motorcycle market is a logical extension of our diversification strategy. We have the Polaris name, the engineering and marketing expertise, the manufacturing infrastructure, and the dealer and distributor network worldwide to effectively compete in this marketplace. Our main goal right now is to build the brand name recognition. When somebody says, "What kind of bike do you have?" we want the answer to be, "I have a Victory."[32]

Today, Victory motorcycles are lighter and have more torque, more storage, better engine performance, and a lower center of gravity than comparable Harley-Davidson bikes. Riders claim that Victory bikes are less "tippy," more stable going over bumps, and offer more control while riding than other cruisers and touring bikes. Victory enjoyed a 95 percent owner satisfaction rate in 2010.[33]

Manufacturing and Distribution[34,35]

In addition to developing a new, quality American motorcycle, another challenge was to develop high-quality manufacturing, distribution, and marketing plans. In determining how to best produce its bikes, the Victory team visited three European companies—Triumph Motorcycles in England, a company that made most of its engine parts; Aprilia of Italy, a scooter and small racing-bike builder; and BMW, a well-known German bike producer. As a result of these visits, Polaris decided to combine both outsourcing and original equipment manufacturing. Polaris would manufacture its own parts and components when it felt it could do a superior job, and outsource other components to good suppliers with requisite expertise.

The outsourced components of the Victory come from many sources. Wheels, pre-painted body parts, ignition coils, rear shock absorbers, and the lower end of the motor were purchased from reputable US suppliers. Brakes and front forks were supplied by companies in Italy. The electronic fuel-injection system was made by the British firm MBE, and pistons and cylinders were purchased from Mahle, a German company.

Victory motors are assembled at the Polaris plant in Osceola, Wisconsin, alongside lines where engines for PWCs and ATVs are made. Steel tubing for the bike's frames are also formed and fabricated in Osceola.

The engines and frame parts are then shipped to Spirit Lake, Iowa, where robots are used to weld the frames before being given a powder-coat treatment. Making the frames in-house is essential the company believes because it ensures the consistent geometry required to make each bike behave as the designers intended. Engines and all the other parts come together on an assembly line that consists of a carrier suspended from an overhead track. The bottom of the carrier is waist high so employees do not have to bend over. The assembly line is staffed by nine two-person teams, who walk from station to station on a padded surface covering the concrete floor, each building an entire motorcycle. At the end of the line, each bike is scrutinized by an optical measuring device called a laser theodolite that checks the chassis for misalignments that could hurt handling. Finally, a few test miles are put on each bike using a "rolling road" dynamometer. The Victory team knows the success of the Victory project depends on the quality of the bike. This philosophy was expressed by Spirit Lake plant manager, Chuck Crone, who said, "The interest is not to make them quick. The interest is to make them right."[36]

The Spirit Lake plant was already producing certain ATVs and PWC prior to assembling motorcycles and was chosen because it had production capacity and required Polaris to add only a handful of ne jobs. Assembling the Victory motorcycles at the Sr Lake site also allowed approximately 400 employe change from seasonal workers to year-round w and marked the first time that a motorcycle wa factured in Iowa for commercial distribution

Polaris managers planned to keep the motorcycle break-even point low and to start with conservative numbers to ensure quality, then eventually to expand internationally. Longer term, they expected Victory to become a significant part of the company's business. Managers planned initial production to be 2,000 to 3,000 units.

The first dealer shipments were rolled out in July 1998. To recognize the significance of Victory's entrance into the motorcycle market, Polaris numbered each of the first 1,500 bikes with a plate fastened to the handlebar clamp. Victory number 0001 was kept by the company to commemorate its history. Initially, motorcycles were manufactured and assembled in the spring and summer. However, over time, motorcycle manufacturing became a full time job.

Victory motorcycles are sold through the Polaris dealer network. The selection criteria for these dealers is very strict. Polaris dealers also sell lawn and garden equipment, marine products, motorcycles, and farm implements. The Victory was designed to eventually help Polaris leverage its existing engineering and manufacturing base, and provide cross-selling opportunities to its entire network of more than 2,000 dealers.[37]

Parks wanted dealers who were completely committed to the Victory brand. He felt that the company would be very well represented by dealers in all 50 states when the motorcycles became available. All dealers were fully trained in service and sales prior to receiving their motorcycles. The initial Victory rollout involved 200 dealers who each received approximately 10 bikes.

Victory Marketing[38,39,40,41]

One of the first public appearances of the production version of the Victory motorcycle was during "The Rock to Rock Victory" Tour. This tour was intended to showcase the quality, performance, and dependability of the Victory motorcycle by riding across America on a Victory motorcycle. "We're doing it to demonstrate the 'rock-solid engineering' of the new Victory V92C," said Mark Klein, owner of Big City Motorcycles in New York City.

Mark Klein's father, Joe, started the ride from a historic "rock" on one coast, the Statue of Liberty, and rode to another one on the opposite coast, Alcatraz in the San Francisco Bay. The tour started in Manhattan on October 2, 1998, and ended eight days and over 3,300 miles later in California. At the completion of the tour, Joe Klein said he had no problems with the ride. "I could hop on and ride the bike back home. That's how much confidence I have in the bike. I had a taillight bulb that went out and that was it," Klein said. "The gas mileage increased the further west we went,

and the bike just performed flawlessly. It was really great." The only other thing that had to be done to the bike was to adjust the clutch once. They named the support truck driver and mechanic the Maytag repairman because he seemingly was just along for the ride.

A billboard outside Polaris headquarters showed a pair of Victory bikes against the dramatic backdrop of Monument Valley, Arizona—a Harley-Davidson kind of scene. The message on the billboard states, "It's a free country. Act like it." The Victory trailers were also used to market the motorcycles. The graphic on the Victory trailers featured a huge photo of the V92C motorcycle and the image of the American flag provided the background on the truck's sides. The Victory fleet of semi-trailer trucks was honored by *Fleet Owner* magazine as winner of a 1998 *Fleet Owner* Vehicle Graphic Award.[42]

Assessing the Market[43]

Polaris managers felt the company's best opportunity for entering the motorcycle industry was the heavyweight segment. Heavyweight motorcycles were utilized as a mode of transportation as well as for recreational purposes. There are four sub-segments including cruisers, touring, sport bikes, and standards. Polaris analysts saw that US retail cruiser sales nearly doubled from 1993 to 1997. The company estimated that approximately 128,000 cruiser motorcycles were sold in the US market in 1997. Demand for cruisers at the time was strong. Sales were predicted to jump another 9 percent just prior to Polaris entering the market, to nearly 134,000 bikes. According to industry estimates, the worldwide market for cruiser motorcycles was more than 200,000 units annually in 1997–98.

In its annual report, Polaris predicted an 11 to 15 percent annual growth for the next five years in US cruiser sales. Polaris started distributing conservative quantities of bikes during the first few years of production. Due to a survey indicating that 30 percent of Polaris ATV and PWC owners also owned motorcycles, the company estimated that the first sales would be to existing Polaris customers. Polaris managers felt that re-entry customers were a major potential source of sales for Victory. Longer term, the company expected to expand internationally and broaden the product line to include models in all four motorcycle segments—cruisers, touring, sport bikes, and standards (see Exhibit 5). The expectation was for Victory bike sales to become a significant part of the overall company business. The worldwide motorcycle market was larger than that of snowmobiles or PWC, and Victory bikes were priced to sell at about twice the average price of other Polaris products.[44]

Exhibit 5 Victory Motorcycle Models

Touring		
Victory Vision Tour	**$23,199**	**luxury touring bike**
Victory Cross Roads	$14,999	customized touring bike
Victory Cross Country	$17,999	high cargo capacity/low seat

8-Ball Cruisers		
Vegas 8-Ball	$12,499	basic cruiser
Hammer 8-Ball	$14,499	performance cruiser
Kingpin 8-Ball	**$12,999**	**classic modern cruiser**
Victory Vision 8-Ball	$17,999	distance cruiser

Custom Cruisers		
Vegas Jackpot	**$18,499**	**custom chrome and graphics**
Kingpin	$14,999	custom performance cruiser
Vegas	$14,499	low profile cruiser

Muscle Cruisers		
Hammer	$17,799	precision performance cruiser
Hammer S	**$18,499**	**sport version of Hammer**

Ness Signature		
Arlen Ness Vision	**$27,999**	**customized version of Vision**
Cory Ness Cross Country	$24,999	customized touring bike
Zach Ness Vegas	$18,999	customized street bike

Source: http://www.polarisindustries.com/en-us/Victory-Motorcycles/Pages/home.aspx

"Our assumption all along has been that our target buyer is also a hard-core Polaris enthusiast," said Parks. "We asked them if they'd be interested in a motorcycle made by us, and they said 'absolutely.' We asked how many of our customers had owned or ridden motorcycles and 100 percent said yes." Parks said it was not targeting the youth market.

A major source of cruiser business is comeback riders. They've had careers, children, and mortgages and got out of bikes. Now they have empty nests, disposable income, and more leisure time, and they're getting back into riding.

Polaris marketing executives were initially targeting a rising cruiser wave fueled by baby boomers in their 30s and 40s. One Polaris dealer said his customers had two things in common, "They wanted another choice besides Harley-Davidson for an American cruiser ... and people want their money's worth. They

don't care what it costs as long as they get their money's worth."[45]

Polaris also intended to build strong owner loyalty through its Preferred Registered Owners (PRO) program, consisting of more than 600,000 members in 1998. Members were eligible for exclusive merchandise, competitive insurance rates for their Polaris vehicles, special group rides, and package tours. In return, these informed, responsible riders served as informal advocates for the Polaris brand. These customer groups provided valuable feedback on their riding habits and product demands. Dealer councils were formed to stay attuned to the market and retailer needs.

Polaris expected to recoup the money invested in Victory within three years. Victory was expected to break even on 4,000 bike sales a year, or about 3 percent of the market.

Managers believed that Victory would help Polaris's overall sales. With an initial retail price of $12,995 nearly all of the 2,000 to 3,000 bikes made in 1998 were pre-sold. For example, John Gardner at Mt. Hood Polaris sold 10 of his first 15 bikes sight unseen. Gardner said the number of customers was a surprise.

Industry Competition[46]

At the beginning of the twentieth century there were three big American manufacturers producing large displacement bikes: Harley-Davidson, Indian, and Excelsior-Henderson. These three accounted for 90 percent of the US market in 1930. The Great Depression devastated the industry, wiping out most of the smaller manufacturers. Starting in 1975 and continuing through the mid-80s, Japanese companies penetrated the custom motorcycle market with Harley look-alikes sporting V-twin engines. Harley struggled against Japanese competition in the 70s, but came back stronger than ever in the 80s. As the twentieth century ended, 1998 marked the first time since 1955 that Americans have had the choice of a large American-designed and manufactured motorcycle other than Harley-Davidson.[47] The introduction of the Victory marked the first time in 60 years that a new American motorcycle manufacturer introduced a "significant motorcycle" that would be widely distributed.

Victory aimed at grabbing market share from both the Japanese manufacturers (Honda, Yamaha, Kawasaki, and Suzuki) and Harley-Davidson. Victory's initial assessment of the attractiveness of entry into the motorcycle industry was based on its assessment of Harley's profit margins. When Victory was launched, Harley-Davidson had a nearly 54 percent share of the US market for heavyweight bikes and held an estimated 30 percent share of the $3 billion worldwide heavyweight market. Victory's goal was to take 5 percent of that market, or in other words, sales of approximately $150 million.[48] The heavyweight cruiser market had been growing and Harley-Davidson had been unable to satisfy demand in the US. By default, the Japanese producers were able to capture increasingly larger shares of the market. Some analysts felt that Victory bikes would take share from the Japanese but not from Harley-Davidson (see Exhibit 6).

Japanese Manufacturers: Honda, Yamaha, Kawasaki, and Suzuki[49]

Honda, Yamaha, Kawasaki, and Suzuki entered the US market in the 70s at the expense of both Harley-Davidson and the British motorcycle makers, and became the predominant world industry players. These longtime Japanese motorcycle powerhouses were strong competitors because they enjoyed large overall sales volume and diversified product lines.[50] Polaris had successfully taken on Japanese competitors in the past when it entered the Japanese-dominated market

Exhibit 6 North American Heavyweight Motorcycle Segment: 2008 Market Share

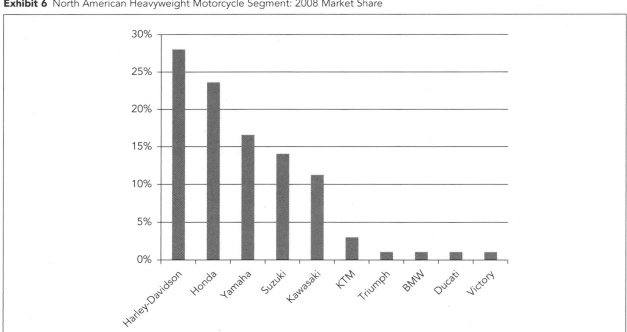

Source: Data for graph retrieved from Powersports Business, Market Data Book 2008, 44.

for ATVs in 1985 and started selling PWC in 1992. Polaris was now one of the biggest makers in each of those markets and was leading in terms of US market share in snowmobiles. Polaris regarded the Japanese as its significant competitors. At the time of the Victory launch, only two manufacturers, Polaris and Yamaha, competed in all four power-sports vehicle markets: snowmobiles, PWC, ATVs, and motorcycles. Polaris expected its success to continue with motorcycles. The Victory team also felt that US customers could be lured from Yamaha, Suzuki, Kawasaki, and Honda by exploiting the notion that the Japanese bikes were not American made.

However, by 2009, the Japanese bikes were as popular as ever, and the Japanese companies were showing no sign of retreating from the market. Honda was the world's largest producer of motorcycles in 2009. The Honda motorcycle line included everything from small scooters to the huge 1832cc Valkyrie Rune, one of the largest engines on the market. In 2009, Honda offered an extensive line of cruisers, as well as custom street, racing, and touring bikes. Its Shadow and VTX models were, in effect, Harley look-alikes. The Honda Gold Wing was still considered one of the best touring bikes as well. Honda and the other Japanese manufacturers seemed to be in the heavyweight segment to stay.

Harley-Davidson[51,52]

The Harley-Davidson Motor Company was founded in 1903 in Milwaukee, Wisconsin. During World War I, Harley-Davidson supplied the military with motorcycles and in 1918 became the largest motorcycle company in the world. In 1969, AMF (American Machine and Foundry), Inc. purchased Harley and poured money into the company. Some think the strategy used by AMF hurt Harley's quality while others thought AMF actually saved Harley from the Japanese because of its deep pockets. In 1982, a group of Harley managers led by Vaughn Beals and Jeffrey Bluestein purchased Harley from AMF and turned the company around. By 1988, Harley was *Fortune* Magazine's most admired transportation firm, and Harley had entrenched itself as a world leader in the heavyweight segment.

Harley-Davidson products include cruisers, factory custom and touring motorcycles, as well as police and military motorcycles. In 2009, Harley offered over 30 different motorcycle models. Harley-Davidson benefits from having one of the worlds most recognized and respected brand names and its motorcycle models— Sportster, Super Glide, Low Rider, Dyna Glide, Wide Glide, Softail, Road King, Electra Glide, and Tour Glide—are among the best-known in the industry.

Harley also supplies or licenses motorcycle replacement parts, accessories, as well as riding and fashion apparel and collectibles.

Harley-Davidson formed a riders, club in 1983, and by 2006, the Harley Owners Group (HOG) had in excess of 900,000 members worldwide. HOG is the industry's largest company-sponsored enthusiast organization. By comparison, Honda's Gold Wing Road Riders association has only 75,000 registered members.[53]

In 1993, Harley-Davidson took an equity stake in the Buell Motorcycle Co. of East Troy, Wisconsin, and began selling Buell cycles through its dealer network.[54] Erik Buell was a former Harley engineer who left the company to start a sport-bike business. Buells were racing bikes powered by modified Harley engines mounted on Harley frames, and were designed to appeal to younger riders. Harley-Davidson acquired 100 percent of the company in 1998, the same year Polaris launched Victory. Approximately 9,000 bikes were sold at its zenith in 2004 before sales both in the US and overseas started to decline.[55] In an attempt to continue to grow its sport-bike business, Harley acquired MV Agusta of Italy in 2009. Agusta makes sport bikes for both on- and off-road enthusiasts.

Harley-Davidson represents freedom and individuality. Harley views competitors as trying to imitate its motorcycles, but knows no one can copy the intangibles that make owning a Harley-Davidson a unique experience. Harley managers feel they are able to determine what is original and authentic in terms of the real riding experience. The quality of its bikes is very good and Harley is able to charge a price premium in the market. Prices range from approximately $8,000 for an entry-level Sportster to $30,000 for a top-of-the-line touring bike. Harleys tend to appeal to older riders with relatively more riding experience. In the 80s and 90s, Harleys became very popular with higher income groups such as accountants, lawyers, and doctors who were attracted by the prestige and image associated with owning a Harley.

With 1997 sales of $1.75 billion, Harley commands a 48 percent share of the growing North American market for heavy road bikes. Harley's product line is sold through a worldwide network of more than 1,000 dealers. Even though the number of motorcycles produced has increased, Harley-Davidson still can not meet the demand for its motorcycles. Customers worldwide who ordered a new Harley sometimes wait a year for delivery. For years, Harley had been building presold bikes, and some dealers have alienated customers by jacking up prices on scarce models. The wait is sometimes as long as two years for some models. This upsets dealers because they sometimes have no inventory and upsets customers because they have to wait so long for the product.

Now, primarily because of the introduction of Victory but also because the Japanese were planning to respond with improvements to their cruisers as well, Harley is facing a dogfight for the first time since 1983. As Harley's production catches up with the demand, the phenomenal resale value of the bikes has begun to decline. Rival producers saw opportunity in Harley-Davidson's production constraints. Honda, Kawasaki, Suzuki, and Yamaha all began chipping away at Harley's grip on the high-margin cruiser category. This began in the 90s and continued into 2000 and beyond.

By 2010, Harley production volume and sales had dropped to 2001 levels.[56] In 2008, the company made over 300,000 motorcycles but planned to cut production in 2009 to around 200,000 units. It also terminated the Buell line of sport bikes, sold the MV Agusta Italian motorcycle business back to the Agusta founder, and forced its labor unions into wage and benefit concessions by threatening to move factories out of Milwaukee. Its bike owners were getting old and few younger riders were attracted to Harley products. Harley sales peaked in 2006 at 349,000 units but because the bikes were no longer in short supply, demand hit a wall. As supply met demand, Harley became just another industry competitor and in the last quarter of 2009, it experienced its first quarterly loss in 16 years.[57]

Excelsior-Henderson and Indian[58,59]

Brothers Dave and Dan Hanlon attended a 1993 Sturgis bike rally in South Dakota and noticed nearly everyone owned a Harley or a Harley knockoff. Believing it made more sense to relaunch a brand rather than invent a new one, they decided to resurrect an American motorcycle manufacturing company and compete in the heavyweight segment. The brand they decided on was Excelsior-Henderson, a name with a rich, proud tradition. Originally founded in 1876, Excelsior Supply was a small but high-quality bicycle manufacturer. Ignatz Schwinn bought Excelsior in 1911 and another company, Henderson, in 1917. Soon thereafter Excelsior-Henderson began making motorcycles and, over time, gained a reputation for styling and speed. Excelsior-Henderson motorcycles were the first to break 100 miles per hour and were known for their quality, performance, and reliability. Charles Lindbergh and Henry Ford owned Excelsiors. Schwinn dropped motorcycle production in 1931 with the threat of the Great Depression

and low-priced autos, and the motorcycle brand was terminated.

The new Excelsior-Henderson Motorcycle Manufacturing Company headquarters and manufacturing plant were constructed in Belle Plaine, Minnesota, less than 100 miles away from the Victory plant. The original plan was to produce a single heavyweight cruiser, the Super X. Unlike Victory Motorcycles, which drew on the experience and resources of its corporate parent, Excelsior-Henderson booted up design, manufacturing, and marketing operations from scratch. The Hanlons initially signed up dealers, most of whom also sold Harleys. The Excelsior-Henderson Super X was priced at $17,500 in 1999, which was more than a comparable Harley. The first Super X production bike was shipped to a dealer on January 30, 1999.

Excelsior expected to compete with Japanese bikes, Harley-Davidson, and the new Victory even though it was charging a relatively higher price. The Hanlon brothers rode Super X prototypes to a hearty welcome by enthusiasts at Sturgis. Excelsior-Henderson appeared to have a strong brand name with historical cachet and a strong management team with some motorcycle-industry experience. Excelsior-Henderson was also an American brand.

Excelsior needed to sell 5,000 motorcycles a year to break even. They expected to produce 20,000 bikes per year in the Minnesota plant. However, production facilities never really materialized and sales were not forthcoming. The company went bankrupt in the year 2000.

Indian Motorcycles (Indian Motorcycle Manufacturing, Inc.) was the most recognizable American brand next to Harley-Davidson. Founded in 1901, Indian was the first American motorcycle company and its Indian Chief was a classic heavy cruiser highly desired by motorcycle enthusiasts worldwide. However, the company had been out of business since the British motorcycles knocked it out of the market in the 50s. There were several attempts to revive the brand in the 90s although none was successful in the long term.

However, a group of investors restarted the company in 2008, and so far, the future looks promising. The company offers at least two versions of the classic Indian Chief cruiser: the Chief Blackhawk and the Chief Dark Horse. The company reported annual sales increases in 2010 of 80 percent and an increase in the number of dealerships to 29. Indian managers projected growth into the apparel business and announced an event at Sturgis in 2011 to promote its new models. The company projected growth through 2011 despite the difficult economy.

Other Competitors[60]

BMW. In 1997, Germany's Bavarian Motor Works (BMW) unveiled a new heavyweight, low-slung cruiser designed to take on Harley. Over the years, BMW has continually developed high-quality/high-performing motorcycles for both comfort and style. BMW has the advantage of engineering that provides excellent handling characteristics. Known for extremely high quality and performance, BMW has been able to charge a price premium, sometimes up to 40 percent over similar bikes.

Big Dog. Big Dog Motorcycles are custom manufactured in Wichita, Kansas, and have a high cost of production and high retail prices.[39] Big Dog produces only five models—the Bulldog, Vintage Sport, ProSport, Vintage Classic, and Pitbull. Its V-Twin motors range from 88 to 107 cubic inches. Each bike is painted to customer specifications and built within 60 days from the time of the order. It has relatively few employees and produced only 300 bikes in 1997. Sheldon Coleman, president of Big Dog Motorcycles, built his first bike in 1993 and began the company the following year. Big Dog bikes are cruisers that provide customers with highly customized bikes at prices comparable to the mass producers.

New Markets and Emerging Technologies

There are many niches in heavyweight motorcycle market segment. *Dealernews* reports 77 different sellers of new "big twin" motorcycles, as well as numerous other custom and touring producers and sellers.[61] Companies such as Lifan, a Chinese motorcycle maker, have entered the industry by dominating countries where the Japanese were not present. Lifan marketed initially only in Iran, Nigeria, the Philippines, Vietnam, and Indonesia, but was preparing to move into more mature markets in the new millennium. Shanghai Motorcycle Works, another Chinese company, was ready to market its Xing-fu cycle worldwide. Xing-fu means "happiness" and is a very practical, energy-efficient, small bike targeted at commuters and large-city riders.

Traditional Italian bike makers like Bimota, Ducati, and Motto Guzzi were continuing to produce super bikes of extremely high quality and style. Bombardier, a Canadian firm, disrupted the market with a remarkably popular three-wheeled roadster. In addition, the British bike companies, Triumph and Norton, were creating very interesting and exciting new motorcycle models. Triumph was the fastest-growing

motorcycle brand, in terms of percentage sales growth, in the world in 2010.[62]

On top of all this, new entrepreneurial companies like Zero Motorcycles have been gaining notice in the business press and market. Zero produces electric dirt bikes and won praise from both *BusinessWeek* and *Fortune* for its products and business planning.[63] In June 2010, at the Bonneville Salt Flats in Utah, Mission One, another new company, had a rider set a world speed record of 150 miles per hour on a motorcycle with an electric motor.[64]

Victory: Preparing for the Next Decade

Mark Blackwell reflected on Victory's first 10 years and all the events surrounding the heavyweight motorcycle industry. His company's motorcycle had successfully taken on Harley-Davidson, an American icon. Victory sales had risen to $20.1 million in 2010, a 55 percent increase over 2009. Demand had improved across the entire Victory line, but particularly for the Cross Roads and Cross Country touring models. Markets outside North America were growing significantly, and sales of PG&A were also up 12 percent. Victory profits constituted over 7 percent of the parent company's bottom line[65] (see Exhibits 7 and 8).

Blackwell realized his motorcycles had received critical acclaim in the industry. Victory motorcycles were perceived as high-quality, technologically advanced bikes—especially compared to Harleys—and were offered at a very competitive price. Blackwell knew his bikes were good, but had they been marketed and distributed effectively? Was Victory successfully capturing the attractive profit margin potential of the heavyweight segment as it had planned?

Blackwell knew the announcement of the new Polaris on-road vehicle division had tremendous implications for both Victory and Polaris as a whole. He was also aware that current Polaris CEO, Scott Wine, wanted the company to grow into "adjacent" businesses. Did this mean the company would move into off-road bikes? Did this mean that Victory would engage in some sort of overseas expansion? Or perhaps some sort of energy-efficient scooter would make sense for Polaris? Perhaps the company was considering growth via acquisitions? Would it be in the market for an electric vehicle or some other alternative energy-related acquisition? From all indications, Victory's next decade was certainly shaping up to be as challenging and eventful as the first.

Exhibit 7 Polaris Industries Inc. Consolidated Balance Sheets

Period Ending						December 31,					
(In thousands, except per share data)	2009	2008	2007	2006	2005	2004	2003	2002	2001	2000	1999
ASSETS											
Current Assets:											
Cash and cash equivalents	$ 140,240	$ 27,127	$ 63,281	$ 19,566	$ 19,675	$ 138,469	$ 82,761	$ 81,193	$ 40,530	$ 2,369	$ 6,184
Trade receivables, net	90,405	98,598	82,884	63,815	78,350	71,172	51,885	51,001	56,119	56,130	53,293
Inventories, net	179,315	222,312	218,342	230,533	202,022	173,624	182,835	155,858	152,717	143,491	118,062
Prepaid expenses and other	20,638	14,924	17,643	19,940	13,330	12,090	10,718	10,136	10,203	4,922	6,175
Income taxes receivable	—	4,521	—	—	—	—	—	—	—	—	—
Deferred tax assets	60,902	76,130	65,406	59,107	60,498	65,489	59,517	45,471	45,748	34,000	31,000
Current assets from discontinued operations	—	—	—	—	113	4,811	—	—	—	—	—
Total current assets	491,500	443,612	447,556	392,961	373,988	465,655	387,716	343,659	305,317	240,912	214,714
Property and Equipment:											
Land, buildings and improvements	118,304	117,396	105,377	104,612	99,106	77,910	67,561	62,089	54,350	51,135	38,616
Equipment and tooling	454,023	478,793	463,757	422,482	415,446	386,575	337,297	325,042	305,647	267,484	236,951
	572,327	596,189	569,134	527,094	514,552	464,485	404,858	387,131	359,997	318,619	275,567
Less accumulated depreciation	(377,911)	(380,552)	(364,783)	(323,093)	(292,216)	(263,584)	(228,437)	(217,535)	(189,674)	—	—
Property and equipment, net	194,416	215,637	204,351	204,001	222,336	200,901	176,421	169,596	170,323	150,755	150,922
Investments in finance affiliate	41,332	51,565	53,801	55,629	59,601	98,386	79,578	65,185	52,963	167,864	38,310
Investments in manufacturing affiliates	10,536	15,641	32,110	99,433	87,772	2,877	—	—	—	45,468	—
Goodwill, net	25,869	24,693	26,447	25,040	25,039	24,798	24,295	24,267	27,199	24,558	—
Deferred tax assets	—	—	5,572	1,595	—	—	—	2,427	9,361	11,384	16,000
Intangible and other assets, net	—	—	44	132	220	308	3,342	3,512	—	—	22,081
Total Assets	$763,653	$751,148	$769,881	$778,791	$768,956	$792,925	$671,352	$608,646	$565,163	$490,186	$442,027

(Continued)

Exhibit 7 Polaris Industries Inc. Consolidated Balance Sheets (*Continued*)

LIABILITIES AND SHAREHOLDERS' EQUITY

Current Liabilities:											
Accounts payable	$ 91,805	$ 89,498	$ 101,554	$ 88,462	$ 65,987	$ 96,302	$ 97,065	$ 100,672	$ 90,045	$ 115,986	$ 75,657
Accrued Expenses:											
Compensation	35,291	30,747	34,615	35,572	39,730	50,815	51,022	42,333	55,465	56,567	55,313
Warranties	40,392	34,216	33,301	30,936	30,673	28,243	28,178	27,303	31,782	28,631	25,520
Sales promotions and incentives	19,999	41,792	95,280	39,460	63,481	59,348	62,227	65,226	79,233	75,211	67,055
Dealer holdback	—	—	—	73,651	73,561	78,214	84,707	80,546	83,867	80,941	72,229
Other	32,900	26,234	27,715	25,005	34,506	36,084	37,594	37,038	40,746	42,274	38,748
Income taxes payable	13,413	15,897	15,872	20,427	22,540	31,001	9,428	3,940	4,806	3,373	6,702
Current liabilities of discontinued operations	—	—	—	—	—	25,186	5,393	4,362	2,302	1,850	1,850
Total current liabilities	233,800	285,452	326,380	313,513	330,478	405,193	375,614	361,420	388,246	404,833	343,074
Long-term income taxes payable	—	—	—	—	—	—	—	—	8,653	5,103	4,988
Deferred income taxes	—	—	—	—	3,488	8,000	5,685	—	—	4,185	11,050
Borrowings under credit agreement	40,000	47,068	18,043	18,027	18,008	18,000	18,000	250,000	200,000	200,000	200,000
Total liabilities	273,800	285,452	326,380	331,540	351,974	431,193	399,299	611,420	596,899	614,121	559,112
Shareholders' Equity:											
Preferred stock	—	—	—	—	—	—	—	—	—	—	—
Common stock	242	235	229	446	434	427	417	355	342	325	326
Additional paid-in capital	8,987	—	—	—	—	—	—	—	—	—	9,992
Deferred compensation	(7,818)	(3,300)	(4,888)	(12,106)	(8,922)	(8,516)	(3,523)	—	—	—	—
Compensation payable in common stock	5,975	—	—	—	—	—	—	—	—	—	—
Retained earnings	160,841	207,613	248,634	289,433	330,205	366,345	375,193	152,219	146,763	140,559	191,399
Accumulated other comprehensive income, net	—	186	(5,192)	(667)	(2,339)	3,476	(2,430)	14,797	25,877	(3,857)	2,824
Total shareholders' equity	168,227	204,734	238,783	277,106	319,378	361,732	369,657	167,371	172,982	137,027	204,541
Total Liabilities and Shareholders' Equity	**$442,027**	**$490,186**	**$565,163**	**$608,646**	**$671,352**	**$792,925**	**$768,956**	**$778,791**	**$769,881**	**$751,148**	**$763,653**

Source: Polaris 2009, 2006, 2003, 2000, 1999 annual reports.

Exhibit 8 Polaris Industries Inc. Consolidated Statements of Income

Period Ending						For the Years Ended December 31,					
(In thousands, except per share data)	2009	2008	2007	2006	2005	2004	2003	2002	2001	2000	1999
Sales	$1,565,887	$1,948,254	$1,780,009	$1,656,518	$1,869,819	$1,773,206	$1,552,351	$1,468,170	$1,512,042	$1,425,678	$1,328,620
Cost of sales	1,172,668	1,502,546	1,386,989	1,297,159	1,458,787	1,348,943	1,189,475	1,135,738	1,167,668	1,097,574	1,030,570
Gross profit	393,219	445,708	393,020	359,359	411,032	424,263	362,876	332,432	344,374	328,104	298,050
Operating expenses											
Selling and marketing	111,137	137,035	123,897	108,890	108,395	105,984	92,321	81,620	119,905	122,028	112,116
Research and development	62,999	77,472	73,587	73,889	70,983	60,700	47,069	41,240	35,708	32,360	31,311
General and administrative	71,184	69,607	64,785	55,584	65,282	77,977	67,175	59,765	58,943	51,922	40,977
Total operating expenses	245,320	284,114	262,269	238,363	244,660	244,661	206,565	182,625	214,556	206,310	184,404
Income from financial services	17,071	21,205	45,285	47,061	38,640	32,035	23,587	14,643	—	—	—
Operating Income	164,970	182,799	176,036	168,057	205,012	211,637	179,898	164,450	129,818	121,794	113,646
Non-operating expense (Income):											
Interest expense	4,111	9,618	15,101	9,773	4,713	2,111	2,465	2,397	7,251	7,704	4,285
Impairment charge on securities held for sale	8,952	—	—	—	—	—	—	—	(14,355)	(14,123)	(9,495)
(Income) from manufacturing affiliates	—	—	—	(3,642)	(2,308)	—	—	—	—	—	—
(Gain) on sale of manufacturing affiliate shares	—	—	(6,222)	—	—	—	—	—	—	—	—
Other expense (Income), net	733	(3,881)	(3,179)	(1,853)	3,748	5,327	(83)	(3,634)	(2,641)	(173)	521
Income before income taxes	151,174	177,062	170,336	163,779	198,859	204,199	177,516	165,687	139,563	128,386	118,335
Provision for income taxes	50,157	59,667	57,738	50,988	61,138	67,386	57,693	54,357	48,149	45,577	42,009
Net Income from continuing operations	101,017	117,395	112,598	112,791	137,721	136,813	119,823	111,330	91,414	82,809	76,326
Loss from discontinued operations, net of tax	—	—	(948)	(812)	(1,007)	(8,457)	(8,894)	(7,738)	—	—	—
Loss on disposal of discontinued operations, net of tax	—	—	—	(5,401)	—	(23,852)	—	—	—	—	—
Cumulative effect of accounting change, net of tax	—	—	—	407	—	—	—	—	—	—	—
Net Income	$ 101,017	$ 117,395	$ 111,650	$ 106,985	$ 136,714	$ 104,504	$ 110,929	$ 103,592	$ 91,414	$ 82,809	$ 76,326

(Continued)

Exhibit 8 Polaris Industries Inc. Consolidated Statements of Income (*Continued*)

Basic Net Income per share											
Continuing operations	3.12	3.58	3.20	2.80	3.27	3.23	2.80	2.49	4.00	3.52	3.09
Loss from discontinued operations	—	—	(0.03)	(0.02)	(0.02)	(0.20)	(0.21)	(0.17)			
Loss on disposal of discontinued operations	—	—	—	(0.13)	—	(0.56)	—	—			
Cumulative effect of accounting change	—	—	—	0.01	—	—	—	—			
Net Income	$ 3.12	$ 3.58	$ 3.17	$ 2.65	$ 3.24	$ 2.47	$ 2.59	$ 2.32	$ 4.00	$ 3.52	$ 3.09
Diluted Net Income per share											
Continuing operations	3.05	3.50	3.10	2.72	3.15	3.04	2.66	2.36	3.88	3.50	3.07
Loss from discontinued operations	—	—	(0.03)	(0.02)	(0.02)	(0.19)	(0.20)	(0.17)			
Loss on disposal of discontinued operations	—	—	—	(0.13)	—	(0.53)	—	—			
Cumulative effect of accounting change	—	—	—	0.01	—	—	—	—			
Net Income	$ 3.05	$ 3.50	$ 3.07	$ 2.58	$ 3.12	$ 2.32	$ 2.46	$ 2.19	$ 3.88	$ 3.50	$ 3.07
Weighted average shares outstanding:											
Basic	32,399	32,770	35,236	40,324	42,131	42,318	42,905	44,623	22,864	23,501	24,732
Diluted	33,074	33,564	36,324	41,451	43,787	45,035	45,056	47,232	23,567	23,666	24,900

Sources: Polaris 2009, 2006, 2003, 2000, and 1999 annual reports.

NOTES

1. D. Johnson, 2009, *Dealernews*, Jan 16.
2. D. Johnson, 2008, From ho hum springs a radical vision: Victory Motorcycles enters its 10th year with a distinct lineup and a healthy reputation, *Big Twin Dealer*, Feb, 4–6.
3. *Dealernews*, May 22, 2009.
4. Polaris Industries, Form 10-K, US Securities and Exchange Commission, Dec 31, 1997, http://finance.yahoo.com// pr?s+PII+Profile
5. Polaris Industries Inc., Corporate Profile, http://www .polarisindustries.com
6. W. Ryberg, 1998, Polaris declares "Victory": A new motorcycle is joining the road—and it's made in Iowa, *Des Moines Sunday Register*, Aug 2, 1G–2G.
7. M. Dapper & L. Klancher, 1998, *The Victory Motorcycle: The Making of a New American Motorcycle*, Osceola, Wisconsin: MBI Publishing Company.
8. P. Klebnikov, 1997, Clear the roads, here comes the Victory, *Forbes*, Oct 20, 160(9): 162.
9. M. Dapper & L. Klancher, *op. cit.*
10. Polaris Industries Inc., Corporate Profile, *op. cit.*
11. *Ibid.*
12. http://www.bizjournals.com/milwaukee/news/2010/12/23/polarislay -offs-in-osceola-begin-march-1.html?ana=yfcpc
13. M. Dapper & L. Klancher, *op. cit.*
14. M. Stotts, 1999, Master's thesis, Iowa State University.
15. M. Dapper & L. Klancher, *op. cit.*
16. *Ibid.*
17. *Ibid.*
18. *Ibid.*
19. *Ibid.*
20. *Ibid.*
21. *Ibid.*
22. *Ibid.*
23. M. Stotts, *op. cit.*
24. M. Dapper & L. Klancher, *op. cit.*
25. *Ibid.*
26. *Ibid.*
27. *Ibid.*
28. M. Stotts, *op. cit.*
29. K. Mollet, Motorcyclists impressed by Victory performance during demo rides at Daytona bike week, http://www.victory-usa.com/ victory-usa/demo.htm
30. 1998, Polaris Industries' Victory motorcycles ready to roll, Jul 9, http://www.victory-usa.com/victory-usa/ready.htm
31. Polaris Victory Motorcycle Names "Best Cruiser" by Cycle World. May 12, 1998. http://www.victory-usa.com/victory-usa/cyclewld.htm
32. J. Murphy, 1997, Polaris enters the motorcycle market. *Dealernews*, Apr, 33(4): 36.
33. 2009, 2010 Victory Touring DVD, Victory: The New American Motorcycle, Polaris Industries.
34. M. Dapper & L. Klancher, *op. cit.*
35. M. Stotts, *op. cit.*
36. W. Ryberg, *op. cit.*
37. J. Miller, 1998, Polaris set to challenge Harley in motorcycle market, *Wall Street Journal*, Mar 11, B4.
38. M. Dapper & L. Klancher, *op. cit.*
39. M. Stotts, *op. cit.*
40. J. Miller, *op. cit.*
41. 1998, Historic cross-country Victory motorcycle tour—the Rock to Rock Victory Tour—begins with kick-off at New York dealership, http://www.victory-usa.com/victory-usa/mtour.htm
42. S. Worwa, 1998, Just like the motorcycle itself, Victory trucks are award winners, http://www.victory-usa.com/victory-usa/victruck.htm
43. M. Stotts, *op. cit.*
44. Polaris Industries Inc. 1997 Annual Report
45. P. Duchene, 1998, Minneapolis-based Polaris to fight Harley-Davidson in motorcycle market, *Knight-Rider/Tribune Business News*, May 13.
46. M. Stotts, *op. cit.*
47. J. Aker, 1998, And then there were three, and now there are three, *Winding Roads Motorcycle Times*, http://members.aol.com/JFA2/ three.html
48. R. Rose, 1997, Polaris is revving up to sell motorcycles in the US market, *Wall Street Journal*, Feb 20, B2.
49. M. Stotts, *op. cit.*
50. C. B. Shrader, F. R. David, & T. T. Dannels, 1997, Harley-Davidson.
51. M. Stotts, *op. cit.*
52. C. B. Shrader, F. R. David, & T. T. Dannels, *op. cit.*
53. R. Nolan & S. Kotha, 2006, Harley-Davidson: Preparing for the next century, Harvard Business School case, Apr 20.
54. 1997, That VROOM! you hear may not be a Harley, *BusinessWeek*, Oct 20, 159–160.
55. R. Nolan & S. Kotha, *op. cit.*
56. 2010, Harley shows its feminine side, *Bloomberg Businessweek*, Oct 4, 25–26.
57. A. Taylor, 2010, *Fortune*, Sep 17.
58. M. Stotts, *op. cit.*
59. The legend is back, Excelsior-Henderson Motorcycle Company promotional video.
60. M. Stotts, *op. cit.*
61. 2008, *Dealernews*, 44(12): 177.
62. N. Saiki, 2008, Zero motorcycles, *Fortune*, Jan 21, 28.
63. *Ibid.*
64. B. Dumaine, 2010, A motorcycle on a mission: To get investors to notice its software, a startup built the world's fastest electric bike, *Fortune*, Jun 14, 30.
65. http://www.motorcyclistcafe.com/forums/showthread.php?8995 -Victory-lives-up-to-its-name-for-Polaris-Q3

Ryan McVay/Getty Images

Seenu Brahmarouthu, Patrick Elliot, Deb Bartell, John Resch, Bradford Boyle, Katie Marion
Arizona State University

Tina Borja
Rice University

Introduction

As with any new, innovative company, there are many as-yet unanswered questions about Zipcar. Consumers are wondering if car sharing is the right fit for their lifestyle. Competitors are trying to identify the competitive advantage that is allowing Zipcar to acquire market share at such a fast pace. Investors are anxious to see if, considering the high overhead and an industry history of less than stellar attempts, Zipcar finally represents a profitable car sharing business model. Suppliers are wondering if they have a dependable and repeat customer. However, the biggest question plagues Zipcar itself—is the company's growth sustainable in the long term?

The car sharing industry is fraught with uncertainty and yet still ripe for competition. It is capital and resource intensive and, due to its lifecycle stages, requires constant modification and improvement to meet customer demand. Despite significant revenue growth in recent years, Zipcar has not yet posted a profit, largely due to the cost of its fleet. Fleet operations—the company's primary expenses—include lease expense, depreciation, parking, fuel, insurance, repairs, and maintenance among other costs, and consumed 71.2% of revenues in the first quarter of 2011.[1] Despite steady growth, there is concern that the company may soon reach the end of its potential market: Zipcar currently claims over 80% of the US car sharing market and half of all car sharing members worldwide.[2] Direct competitors and alternatives abound in the form of more traditional car ownership, car rental agencies, taxicabs, and public transportation. Consumer demand is critical to the long-term success of the car sharing market; thus Zipcar is working to secure future memberships through partnerships with universities, hoping that students will never see the need to own a car and become "Zipsters" for life (see Exhibit 1 for global car sharing statistics).

Which brings Zipcar to a final question. Having joined the "establishment" by becoming a public company in April 2011, will Zipcar lose its counter culture appeal: will it still be cool to be a Zipster? It is an important question to consider for a company that relies on customer satisfaction and the capitalization of the "green movement" to survive.

In the Driver's Seat

To deal with the overview of challenges mentioned above, the following key executives are in place. Their backgrounds and positions are provided.

Scott Griffith—Chairman of the Board and CEO

Griffith joined Zipcar in 2003, three years after its founding, replacing co-founder Robin Chase. He received his BS in engineering from Carnegie Mellon University and MBA from the University of Chicago. Prior to Zipcar, he held senior-level positions at Boeing, Information America, and The Parthenon Group. When he took over, Griffith thought the company was being run like a non-profit as opposed to a company with high-growth potential. With few concerns about the strong brand image and IT systems already in place, his immediate focus was on "getting things right" and turned his intense business acumen to Boston, Washington DC, and New York City (NYC). Griffith broke the cities into zones, expanded Zipcar's fleet, and talked to consumers and employees to figure out how to do it better. Griffith, unafraid to do whatever it took to drive Zipcar forward and eager to put some distance between what Zipcar

Exhibit 1 State of Car Sharing Worldwide

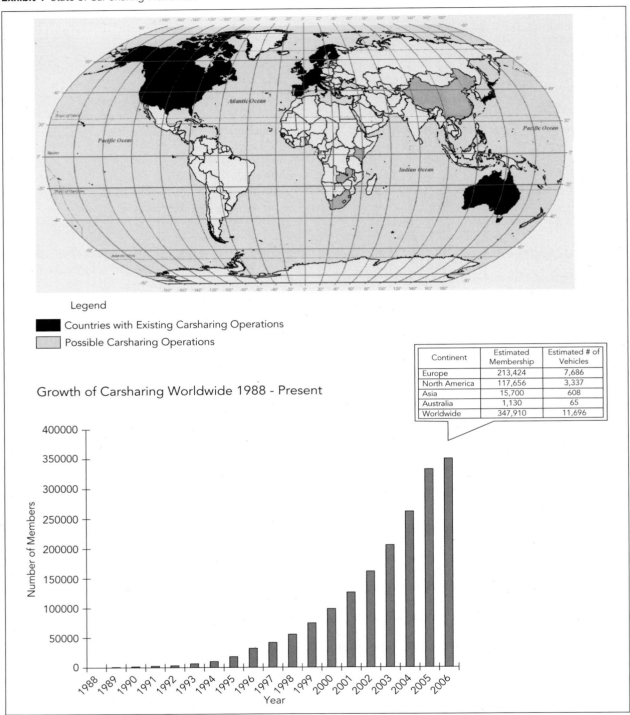

Legend

■ Countries with Existing Carsharing Operations

▨ Possible Carsharing Operations

Growth of Carsharing Worldwide 1988 - Present

Continent	Estimated Membership	Estimated # of Vehicles
Europe	213,424	7,686
North America	117,656	3,337
Asia	15,700	608
Australia	1,130	65
Worldwide	347,910	11,696

Source: S. A. Shaheen and A. P. Cohen. Worldwide Car Sharing Growth: An International Comparison. http://www.carsharing.net

had been and what; to become, all but one of Griffith's employees from the early days are now gone.[3] Even so, his leadership is credited with defining a new category of transportation.[4]

Steve Case—Board of Directors, Chair of Nominating and Governance Committee

As the co-founder of America Online in 1985, Case is a widely respected businessperson, being called "one of the nation's greatest entrepreneurs" by CNBC. He graduated from Williams College in Massachusetts in 1980 with a degree in political science before going on to lead AOL as it became the world's largest Internet company in the 90s. As the first Internet company to go public, AOL earned an 11,616% return on its stock. Case's accomplishments and entrepreneurial leadership style are an obvious fit for Zipcar. The company hopes to capitalize both on the respect that Case's association commands as well as his skill in handling emerging technologies.[5]

Ed Goldfinger—Chief Financial Officer

Goldfinger is a graduate of the Wharton undergraduate program at the University of Pennsylvania and worked as a CPA in Connecticut. His corporate credits include serving as the CFO of Spotfire—a business intelligence and analytics software company—KPMG, PepsiCo, CFO and then CEO at Empirix, and CFO at Sapient. His extensive experience brings technical savvy, financial education, and leadership skills in high growth firms to Zipcar. Zipcar's decision to replace former CFO Shaun Starbuck with Goldfinger was recognized as a move to focus on strategic growth initiatives—a facet that Goldfinger is well qualified to lead.[6]

Mark Norman—President and Chief Operating Officer

Norman, Flexcar's former CEO, joined Zipcar following the merger of the two in 2007. He has an undergraduate degree in economics from Rice University and an MBA from Harvard Business School. Norman's 20 years of executive experience in automotive industry—including roles as CEO of Flexcar and Chairman, President, and CEO of DaimlerChrysler-Canada—are invaluable to furthering Zipcar's strategic goals. Norman's ability to streamline the complex business model and operations while maintaining a focus on member experience will help Zipcar expand operations and sustain the company's entrepreneurial and customer focused approach.[7]

From the Beginning (History)

Zipcar took shape in 2000 with a handshake between founders Robin Chase and Antje Danielson in Cambridge, Massachusetts. Although several fledgling car sharing companies were already testing the waters with American consumers, Danielson hadn't heard of the concept before vacationing in Berlin. While Danielson, a carbon reduction strategy researcher, immediately recognized the potential environmental benefits of the industry, Chase "had no desire to create the car sharing equivalent of a community garden; she wanted to build the 'Whole Foods' of the car share industry." In other words, from the beginning, Zipcar was meant to be prof-

itable and prosperous. Chase raised the capital to start the business—$1.3 million from 14 investors. Once the start-up was funded, Chase quickly turned her focus to growth. However, her focus almost led to the company's early downfall when she prematurely spent $5 million in pledged investor money. When the investor fell through, the board forced her out and hired Scott Griffith to take over as CEO in 2003.[8] Griffith's senior level experience brought focused leadership to Zipcar, earning him a place on the annual "Best Leaders of 2006" list by *BusinessWeek*.[9]

In 2007, Zipcar acquired one of its main competitors, Flexcar. Zipcar merged the operations of the two companies to eliminate redundancies and fully benefit from the acquisition. In April 2010, Zipcar moved beyond its North American market (operations in Toronto commenced in 2005) when it purchased Streetcar Limited, a car sharing company in the UK, opening the door to growth via European operations.[10]

On April 14, 2011, Zipcar issued its highly anticipated IPO at $18.00 per share.[11] As a result of its acquisition of Flexcar, board member Steve Case's company, Revolution (Flexcar's former holding company), is the largest Zipcar shareholder. Silicon Valley firms Benchmark Capital and Greylock Partners, also with membership on the Zipcar board, are large stockholders as well.[12]

Today, Zipcar operates in 14 major metropolitan areas and on 230 college campuses in the US, Canada, and the UK and has focused its expansion on densely populated areas with parking challenges[13] (see Exhibit 2 for Zipcar locations).

What Zipcar Does

Zipcar has two product offerings—car sharing and fleet management. The car sharing product is marketed to individuals living in major metropolitan areas; college students, staff, and faculty at select universities; and organizations including private businesses and government entities. To become a Zipster, potential members must fill out an application and pay a small annual membership fee. If approved, the Zipster will receive a Zipcard that locks and unlocks vehicles reserved online or over the phone. The reserved car is parked in a local lot, often within walking distance of the member, and is ready for use with the keys in the ignition. The member pays a usage fee, which includes the cost of gas and insurance, and is automatically charged through Zipcar's proprietary technology system that requires little user interface beyond waving a Zipcard in front of the reader located on the windshield.

A key feature of the Zipcar product is the in-house technology developed to allow easy access for customers without compromising the security of its vehicles. The

Exhibit 2 Zipcar Locations

Zipcar Locations Serving All Customers		
Atlanta, GA	London, UK	San Francisco, CA
Baltimore, MD	New York, NY	Seattle, WA
Boston, MA	Philadelphia, PN	Toronto, Canada
Chicago, IL	Pittsburgh, PN	Vancouver, Canada
District of Columbia	Portland, OR	

Zipcar Locations Serving Students, Faculty, and Staff Only		
Amherst College	Hofstra University	University of AL
AZ State University	Holy Cross	University of CA, Irvine
Babson College	Hood College	University of CA, LA
Bates College	IN University	University of CA, Riverside
Baylor University	LaSalle University	University of CA, San Diego
Belmont University	Loyola Marymount University	University of CA, Santa Barbara
Boise State University	Marquette University	University of DE
Bowdoin College	MCPHS	University of FL
Brandeis University	Meredith College	University of IL
Brown University	MI State University	University of Miami
Bryn Mawr	Middlebury College	University of MI
Bucknell University	Monmouth University	University of MN, Twin Cities
Cal Poly, SLO	NC State University	University of NE
CA State Chico	North Central College	University of NH
CA State Long Beach	Occidental College	University of NC, Greensboro
CA State University, East Bay	Old Dominion University	University of Notre Dame
California University of PN	Pacific Lutheran University	University of Puget Sound
Caltech	Point Loma Nazarene University	University of Richmond
Chapman University	Pomona College	University of Rochester
Christopher Newport University	Purchase College	University of San Diego
Clark University	Rhodes College	University of Southern CA
Colby College	Rice University	University of TX, Austin
Columbus State University	San Diego State University	University of VA
CT College	Santa Clara University	University of WI, Milwaukee
Creighton University	Seton Hall University	University of NM, Albuquerque
Dartmouth College	Smith College	Vanderbilt University
Dickinson College	Stanford University	Vassar College
Drew University	SUNY Geneseo	VT Law School
Duke University	SUNY Oswego	VA Commonwealth University
East Carolina University	Syracuse University	Wake Forest University
Elmhurst College	College of William & Mary	Wellesley College
Elon University	Trinity College	Wesleyan University
Endicott College	University of CA, Davis	WV University
George Mason University	University of CA, Santa Cruz	Williams College
Green Mountain College	University of NC, Chapel Hill	Winona State University
Hamilton College	University at Buffalo	WPI
Hampshire College		Yale University

Source: zipcar.com

radio frequency identification (RFID) technology offers driver authentication and allows access to vehicles only when the holder has a reservation. In addition, RFID makes it possible for Zipcar to track the location of its cars for billing, security, inventory management, and maintenance purposes.[14] This entire system is known to the Zipcar community as the "Z3D Knowledge Center."

Zipcar's second product offering, FastFleet, is a fleet management software platform based on the one used by Zipcar that is licensed on a monthly basis to both private and public organizations that manage their own vehicle fleets.[15]

Getting From Here to There

For the cost conscious, environmentally aware, and carless individual looking to travel from point A to point B, public transportation has served as a mainstay.

Americans made 11 billion trips on US transit in 2008, a 50-year record. Use dropped only slightly in 2010 despite transit operators being forced to cut some routes and remove buses as the recession drove down local sales tax revenues needed for public transit.[16]

Public transit systems in most major metropolitan areas are open 24/7 with increased service during peak hours to accommodate the needs of their citizens.[17] Once largely considered the transit means for those that could not afford a vehicle, public transit in many cities is now being used by the same demographic of cost conscious, green thinking individuals sought by Zipcar. In many cases, consumers may view car sharing as a complement to public transit: in fact, people who car share are much more likely to use trains and buses than those who do not, holding annual passes to public transport at a rate of 60%.[18] Cities are so committed to encouraging the use of public transportation; as of 2010, over 73% of US buses had bike racks available for riders to use, thus solving the problem for those not within walking distance of the necessary bus stops of how to get to the bus and back again.[19]

In densely populated communities, taxicabs are the chief support for the carless looking to run errands farther than walking distance, to destinations not likely to provide parking, or that may require moving large items. With rates starting between $2.25 and $3.10 and rising by an average increment of .35 depending on distance and time spent in transit, taxicabs present a logical alternative for short trips within major metropolitan centers.[20] However, using a car sharing service for trips taken out of the city center may easily prove the wise choice. Additionally, for less densely populated cities, those with ample parking at typical destinations, or those simply spread farther out, taking a taxi is not as

simple as putting your hand in the air as you step to the curb and likely far less cost effective for a planned outing than car sharing.

Upon its inception, Zipcar set its sights on conquering the urban market. This market's receptiveness to the concept comes in part due to a forward thinking demographic, but also because of the impracticality of owning a vehicle in many city centers. For example, due to the proliferation of public transit and smaller neighborhood shops, it is estimated that Manhattan residents only need a personal vehicle once or twice a month, yet simply parking a vehicle in the city can cost individuals upwards of $500 per month or more.[21] Zipcar offers these urban dwellers the convenient use of a vehicle when they need it and, based on estimated use, for far less money than the cost of owning and parking a car.

Although owning and maintaining a car can be expensive and time consuming particularly within densely populated markets, it continues to be the most flexible transportation option for a majority of potential consumers. Additionally, as consumer demands have changed in America, car manufacturers have responded by producing smaller, lighter, safer, cars that get better gas mileage and use flex fuel, or are hybrid gas and electric. However, with the average price of a new car in the US approaching $30,000,[22] buying *any* car is a costly proposition, no less an eco-friendly car with prices ranging from $29,000 for the Toyota Prius to $59,000 for the Lexus sedan hybrid.[23] Car ownership in 2009 decreased 3.5%, but the fact remains that, with decades of consumer savvy marketing under their belts, the car companies have successfully embedded into the psyche of American consumers that freedom—an ideal that Americans view as a right and not a desire—cannot be fully achieved without at least one car in the garage. The success of this fabricated ideal is illustrated by the fact that Americans own more cars than there are licensed drivers in the US.

Marketing efforts aside, many college students have come to the logical conclusion that car ownership—in particular or at least while living on campus—is not worth the expense. Due to renter age restrictions mandated by insurance companies, college students have been largely shut out by car rental agencies, making Zipcar's lower age threshold of 18 a welcome addition on campus in recent years. For its academic customers, Zipcar provides fleet vehicles, insurance, and membership administration while the university typically supplies marketing, parking, and some financial guarantees. In return, the university benefits from an additional source of on- and off-campus transportation without having to shoulder the cost of buses and other forms of transportation, not to mention the fact that fewer students with cars on campus can result in the reduction of existing parking and the delay or elimination of costly plans for parking expansion. For example, MIT reports it has saved approximately $9 million in capital costs through the reduced need for parking structures by using alternative transportation programs.[24] On a more social level, it is becoming increasingly important for university administrators to demonstrate to students their commitment to the environment. A survey by the Princeton Review revealed that 63% of surveyed college applicants agreed that, "a college's commitment to the environment could affect their decision to attend." The article continues saying, "Students are looking into how sustainable their prospective colleges are, and if they don't make the grade, then they don't make the cut."[25] According to Zipcar's calculations, each Zipcar removes a minimum of 15 personally owned cars from the road, resulting in substantial decreases in CO_2 emissions—an appreciable effect in the eyes of college students.[26]

Many businesses have also seen the benefits of changing the status quo. Companies from Clear Channel to Twitter have contracted with Zipcar to use its fleet vehicles to cut back on capital costs and free up cash flow.[27] Zipcar offers these companies the ultimate in affordable, convenient flexibility and is particularly popular with businesses located in densely populated urban locations like San Francisco and NYC where an in-house fleet is cost prohibitive. Considering the cost of purchasing and/or leasing vehicles, maintenance, parking, insurance, fuel, and the staff to manage a fleet, Zipcar is often significantly less expensive for businesses in these locations. Additionally, many businesses leverage their alignment with sustainable companies like Zipcar to appeal to their own customers.

For those businesses not interested in disbanding their already established fleets, Zipcar makes its proprietary software—FastFleet—available for a monthly licensing fee. This software enabled the District of Columbia (Washington DC) to take 17% of its passenger cars out of its fleet within the first six months of use (due to increased scheduling efficiencies). The city estimates FastFleet will save the District $1 million in its first year and $6.6 million after five years.[28]

Who Wants a Piece of This Pie?

Zipcar offers an existing technology—a car—and an existing service—a rented car—in a completely new way. As such, the company has numerous big name competitors, primarily the more traditional car rental agencies. In addition, after letting Zipcar prove the viability of its business model and blaze the trail, new for-profit car sharing companies are beginning to enter the market.

Traditional car rental agencies are numerous and readily available to consumers. With a historic focus on customer service, convenience, variety, and price, these companies have been the consumer's go-to source for temporary vehicles. This transparent, mature market has high fixed costs and pitifully few big ideas to leverage to distinguish one company from all the others. As a result, car rental agencies compete on price, a fact that frequently spurs price wars between competitors. The two biggest players in the rental car market in the US are Enterprise and Hertz.

Enterprise Rent-A-Car Company

Founded in 1959, Enterprise Rent-A-Car Company is the largest of its kind in North America. Its substantial rental fleet boasts over 700,000 vehicles and its corporate servicing fleet has another 135,000 vehicles. Enterprise specializes in local opportunities and largely avoids the congested travel/airport segment by placing 8,100 offices within 15 miles of 90% of the American population. Enterprise caters to consumers who need temporary use of a vehicle while their car is being repaired or for a special event such as a business trip or weekend getaway. Enterprise was the first rental car agency to establish a 1-800 number for toll-free reservations. The company also coined the phrase "We'll pick you up," which became its marketing calling card in the 90s. Enterprise created a name for itself and, upon finally entering the airport market in the late 90s, enjoyed great success.[29]

Taking advantage of its size and widespread presence, in 2008, Enterprise became the first rental car company to offer car sharing with a program it calls *WeCar*. Says Sean Busking, executive director of the American Car Rental Association (ACRA),

I'm not surprised to see Enterprise taking the lead in the car rental industry and introducing its car sharing program across the country. Over the years, Enterprise has built an incredibly strong neighborhood presence in the US, so hourly rental and car sharing options are really a natural extension of its community-oriented business model. This is a smart move for Enterprise, which has a strong track record of responding to local customers and delivering services they need.[30]

Enterprise has rapidly expanded into this market, targeting college campuses, businesses, and government agencies. Enterprise is marketing WeCar as a convenient and easy to use way to meet the needs of consumers that value the resource saving capabilities that car sharing brings to a campus or corporation.[31] Not coincidentally, the majority of Enterprise's WeCars are hybrid vehicles.[32]

Hertz Global Holdings, Inc.

Hertz began as a small fleet of Model T Fords in 1918 and has since grown into the largest car rental company in the world with 555,000 vehicles at 6,500 locations in 140 countries. Over the years, Hertz has weathered many mergers and acquisitions and managed to capitalize on the popularization of air travel in the 60s by expanding its rental operations to airports. In more recent years, Hertz has grown into a diverse company offering heavy equipment rental, telecommunications services, claims management services, and various car rental segments. With a global presence unmatched in the industry, Hertz is now focused on expansion into emerging international markets including the Middle East and Russia.[33]

In an effort to enter community markets to serve clients that rent cars and other vehicles for business and personal use, gain market share with the insurance replacement segment, and expand beyond its airport locations, Hertz added 250 community locations in 2010 alone.[34] Hertz CEO Mark Frissora states, "Our revenues continue to expand at a double-digit rate in the off-airport market, and we are increasing our investment to meet anticipated demand."[35] To grow its share in the $10 billion off-airport market, Hertz is primarily co-locating with hotels, body shops, and other vehicle repair facilities.[36] Due to its size, Hertz has no difficulty competing on price. Like many rental car companies, however, rising gas and maintenance costs and high depreciation rates are taking their toll on business and Hertz has had to raise its rates in many key locations.[37] As of 2011, Hertz operated 1,900 non-airport locations in the US with pick up and drop off service, onboard GPS systems, and other customer friendly amenities. Additionally, more than 90% of the largest insurance companies use Hertz for their displaced customers.[38]

As car sharing has grown in popularity, Hertz has entered this market with *Connect by Hertz*. Hertz is new to this market and looks to expand by utilizing its existing locations and brand recognition.[39] Connect by Hertz has no annual membership fees, offers low hourly and daily rates, and GPS and Bluetooth connectivity in every car. In addition, it matches many Zipcar amenities including free gas, insurance, 24-hour roadside assistance, and up to 180 daily miles.[40] Like other car sharing companies, Hertz is appealing to the green movement by utilizing the Toyota Prius as its flagship car sharing fleet car.

Speaking of Green

Although Zipcar was very well received by investors through its IPO, selling at $30 a share, or 66% higher than its $18 a share IPO pricing, analysts are concerned about the company's financial performance.[41] Despite continued revenue growth achieved through member additions and acquisitions of other car sharing operations, Zipcar's net loss continues to grow: prior to its IPO, Zipcar had accumulated $65 million in debt with

no cash available to pay it down, and even a 48% leap in 2011 first quarter revenues did not preclude a net loss for the period of $6.1 million.[42] Concern has also been raised over the potential for profitability as annual operational cost per vehicle was reported to be approximately $15,500 in 2010—almost double the annual estimated cost of car ownership in the US, indicating that Zipcar is not yet enjoying economies of scale (see Exhibits 3, 4, and 5 for Zipcar financial data).

In its defense, Zipcar maintains that the losses are temporary growing pains related to the high initial costs of expanding its operations into new markets. One analyst points out that in Zipcar's four most established markets (Boston, NYC, Washington DC, and San Francisco), the company posted profits of $4.6 billion. For these markets, which account for more than half of revenues, Zipcar reported 17% profit margins and profit growth of 45% from the previous comparable quarter.[43] In theory, if the company continues to selectively target similar markets, it is reasonable to expect that, with more time, overall margins will be similar.

How It Is Done

Now that Griffith has taken Zipcar public, many investors are analyzing the company and looking for the keys to a successful growth plan. For a company with no history of profits to generate sizeable IPO buzz, substantial faith must be placed in Zipcar's strategy to bring long-term success. To instill confidence in investors and realize its goal of profitability, Griffith and the board are focused on maintaining Zipcar's culture of innovative service, staying tuned in to the customer experience, and expanding into new markets.[44]

Zipcar distinguishes itself as an original, green idea and is rapidly becoming a nationally known brand name synonymous with car sharing and sustainability. Zipcar is hoping that consumers interested in car sharing will be less attracted to car rental companies that will be seen as merely jumping on the bandwagon for profits and copycatting the Zipcar model. Zipcar also partners with lifestyle brands of its target demographic with innovative marketing efforts. For example, magnetic Starbucks placards were placed on Zipcar roofs in NYC; anyone who found a placard won a $5 Starbucks gift card.[45]

Zipcar keeps its organizational structure fairly flat to allow for efficient communication of employee and customer ideas and concerns to all levels of the organization. This helps the company remain flexible and able to respond easily and quickly to both internal and external changes in the environment.[46] Although Zipcar has greater flexibility than rental car agencies by removing the need for human interaction during pick up and drop off, the company has gone to great lengths to

Exhibit 3 Consolidated Statements of Operations Data/Zipcar

	Year Ended December 31,		
	2008	2009	2010
	(in thousands, except share and per share data)		
Revenue	$ 105,969	$ 131,182	$ 186,101
Cost and expenses			
Fleet operations	84,199	93,367	122,634
Member services and fulfillment	7,580	10,414	15,114
Research and development	1,549	2,314	3,170
Selling, general and administrative	25,324	29,973	49,172
Amortization of acquired intangible assets	1,226	990	3,414
Total operating expenses	119,878	137,058	193,504
Loss from operations	(13,909)	(5,876)	(7,403)
Interest income	429	60	47
Interest expense	(1,603)	(2,457)	(8,185)
Other income, net	568	3,690	1,731
Loss before income taxes	(14,515)	(4,583)	(13,810)
Provision for income taxes	—	84	311
Net loss	(14,515)	(4,667)	(14,121)
Less: Net loss attributable to redeemable noncontrolling interest	—	23	(4)
Net loss attributable to controlling interest	$ (14,515)	$ (4,644)	$ (14,125)
Net loss attributable to common stockholders per share-basic and diluted	$ (7.15)	$ (2.23)	$ (2.74)
Weighted average number of shares of common stock outstanding used in computing per share amounts-basic and diluted	2,028,986	2,083,943	5,148,559
Pro forma net loss per share-basic and diluted (unaudited)			$ (0.49)
Pro forma weighted average number of shares of common stock outstanding (unaudited)			29,031,776

Source: Zipcar, Inc. Prospectus Form 424B4. http://files.shareholder.com

Exhibit 4 Consolidated Balance Sheets/Zipcar

	December 31,		December 31, 2010
	2009	2010	Pro Forma
Assets	(in thousands, except share and per share data)		(Unaudited)
Current assets			
Cash and cash equivalents	$ 19,228	$ 43,005	$ 43,005
Accounts receivable, net of allowance for doubtful accounts of $319 and $541 as of December 31, 2009 and 2010	2,816	4,223	4,223
Restricted cash	48	900	900
Prepaid expenses and other current assets	5,037	9,905	9,905
Total current assets	27,129	58,033	58,033
Property and equipment, net	9,426	70,917	70,917
Goodwill	41,871	99,750	99,750
Intangible assets	1,385	8,527	8,527

(Continued)

Exhibit 4 Consolidated Balance Sheets/Zipcar (*Continued*)

	December 31		December 31, 2010
	2009	**2010**	**Pro Forma**
Restricted cash	5,750	3,503	3,503
Deposits and other noncurrent assets	4,346	8,198	8,198
Total assets	**$ 89,907**	**$248,928**	**$248,928**
Liabilities, Redeemable Convertible Preferred Stock and Stockholders' Equity (Deficit)			
Current liabilities			
Accounts payable	$ 3,953	$ 6,247	$ 6,247
Accrued expenses	8,207	16,594	16,594
Deferred revenue	9,763	14,261	14,261
Current portion of capital lease obligations and other debt	6,984	26,041	26,041
Total current liabilities	**28,907**	**63,143**	**63,143**
Capital lease obligations and other debt, net of current portion	8,228	68,022	68,022
Deferred revenue, net of current portion	3,145	3,651	3,651
Redeemable convertible preferred stock warrants	400	478	—
Other liabilities	764	1,975	1,975
Total liabilities	**41,444**	**137,269**	**136,791**
Commitments and contingencies (Note 9)			
Non-controlling interest	111	277	277
Redeemable convertible preferred stock, par value $0.001 per share:	95,715	116,683	—
Stockholders' (deficit) equity:			
Common stock, $0.001 par value: 72,500,000 and 100,000,000 shares authorized at 12/31/09 and 2010 respectively; 2,212,369 and 6,415,436 shares issued at 12/31/09 and 2010, respectively; 31,513,318 shares issued and outstanding pro forma at 12/31/10	2	6	32
Additional paid-in capital	4,019	59,647	176,782
Accumulated deficit	(51,093)	(65,380)	(65,380)
Accumulated other comprehensive loss	(291)	426	426
Total stockholders' (deficit) equity	**(47,363)**	**(5,301)**	**111,860**
Total liabilities, redeemable convertible preferred stock and stockholders' (deficit) equity	**$ 89,907**	**$248,928**	**$248,928**

Source: Zipcar, Inc. Prospectus Form 424B4. http://files.shareholder.com

Exhibit 5 Revenue/Zipcar

	Years Ended December 31,			Change in 2009		Change in 2010	
	2008	**2009**	**2010**	**$**	**%**	**$**	**%**
Vehicle usage revenue	$ 96,528	$117,553	$163,797	$21,025	21.80%	$46,244	39.30%
Fee revenue	8,972	13,503	22,085	4,531	50.50%	8,582	63.60%
Other revenue	469	126	219	(343)	(73.10)%	93	73.80%
Total	$105,969	$131,182	$186,101	$25,213	23.80%	$54,919	41.90%
	(amounts in thousands)						

Source: Zipcar, Inc. Prospectus Form 424B4. http://files.shareholder.com

ensure there is always someone available to help answer member questions and concerns. Zipcar prides itself on being extremely receptive to consumer needs by offering 24/7 customer service and empowering its employees to respond quickly with innovative solutions. Members can book reservations online, through apps on their wireless devices, or over the phone. If they have difficulty during their rental, they can contact the customer service center for assistance with mechanical issues, driving directions, or anything else they might need. This level of responsiveness has helped the company earn a reputation of consistency and reliability among members. Additionally, by conservative estimates, Zipcar members report saving $500 a month over car ownership[47] and spending, on average, about 6% of income on transportation, compared to the US average of 19%.[48]

Zipcar carefully selects the cities and universities in which it offers its services, knowing that urban markets will see the most value in car sharing. While separate financial data is not publicly available for its campus operations, Zipcar sees servicing the college market as insurance for the future: it believes that users who are exposed to car sharing and the Zipcar brand in college will be far less likely to switch alternative modes of transportation after graduation.

In addition to the individual user market, Zipcar's FastFleet allows businesses and government agencies to apply Zipcar's fleet management technology to manage their own vehicle fleets for a low monthly licensing fee. FastFleet tracks usage, location, and maintenance schedules of vehicles while reducing the human resources normally needed to do so.

Zipcar has recently grown domestically as well as internationally via acquisitions. By purchasing Flexcar in 2007, Zipcar solidified its US market dominance and, with its 2010 purchase of Streetcar, Zipcar launched into European operations.[49] Given the success of these two acquisitions and additional opportunities to acquire or merge with other car sharing ventures, Zipcar is likely to continue on this path.

Controlling Brand Image

Zipcar states that one of its competitive advantages is "low cost, word-of-mouth marketing" and relies on it to bring in new members. As found in a survey, 28% of new members who joined between March 2009 and 2010 learned about Zipcar from an existing member. While Zipcar reported marketing expenditures increased by $2 million in 2009 and $3.2 million in 2010, the cost per new account (defined as marketing expenses divided by gross new member additions) fell 6% from $52 in 2009 to $49 in 2010.[50]

The company's marketing is primarily targeted at member acquisitions. Zipcar takes a local approach to

marketing, posting ads on buses, bus stops, and subway stations in the neighborhoods of potential members as well as sending "street teams" to market block by block.[51] The company markets its car sharing service as more than just a mode of transportation.

We design our sales and marketing efforts to build a global lifestyle brand. Our brand is about more than cars, it is about fun and freedom and improving urban life for our Zipsters and the communities in which they live and work.[52]

Zipcar also uses social media such as Facebook and Twitter to share promotions with members and allow members to share their comments about Zipcar. This serves as both a marketing tool as well as a method for employees to stay in touch with member concerns.[53]

Defensive Driving: Challenges Ahead

Zipcar either leases or purchases fleet cars for two to three years before reselling the vehicles to dealers or at auction.[54] Due to rapid member expansion and its commitment to continually refresh its fleet of over 8,000 vehicles, the company relies heavily on discounts passed on by car manufacturers. According to Zipcar's prospectus,

…a decline in the economic and business prospects of car manufacturers, including any economic distress impacting the suppliers of car components to manufacturers, could also cause manufacturers to raise the prices we pay for vehicles and vehicle leases or potentially reduce their supply to us.[55]

The recent natural disasters in Japan are expected to raise Zipcar's costs as both Honda and Toyota experience supply shortages and manufacturing delays.[56] Additionally, as the owner of Hertz, Ford may opt to exert pricing power over Zipcar.

Zipcar is also confronted with the challenge of finding and keeping affordable and convenient parking for its vehicles. The company utilizes both publicly and privately owned real estate. Publicly owned lots allow Zipcar parking through the use of permits or meters whereas privately owned lots allow for pre-arranged monthly leases—often with very high costs in markets like NYC. With high and difficult to anticipate fluctuations in the cost of parking, Zipcar has had to pass the cost on to members through increased rates. In extreme cases, the availability of parking real estate has dictated whether Zipcar has been able to move into or stay in a neighborhood, thus limiting its ability to generate revenues. In NYC, 207 open-air lots were lost from 1999 to 2008. With the increasing scarcity of parking, Zipcar has had to get creative and recently began negotiating parking agreements in NYC at high schools and churches.[57] Without another solution, Zipcar's viability in these densely populated and land locked communities will continue to be dictated by the cost and availability of parking space.

As the average cost of owning a vehicle continues to rise (Exhibit 6), more consumers are likely to seek alternative forms of transportation such as car sharing. John Addison states in his article titled Ten Reasons for Drop in Car Ownership, "About 20% of a US car owner's disposable income is spent on the car, maintenance, insurance, and fuel. Oil prices have more than doubled since its bottom in March 2009. The era of cheap gasoline is over."[58] While lower rates of car ownership may seem to be a boon for Zipcar, the same costs that plague consumers, plague Zipcar. The average price to lease or purchase a car and the cost of gasoline have steadily increased and continue to spark political volatility in the US in regard to production, dependence on foreign oil, and natural resource usage[59] (see Exhibit 7 for gas cost data). With both Enterprise and Hertz able to leverage their built-in infrastructures and enjoy economies of scale that allow them to compete at much lower costs, Zipcar will have to work every other advantage it offers to its maximum

potential to keep its piece of market share from these giants.

More than ever, the happiness of Zipcar's customers is of primary concern. While recent declines in car ownership can be attributed to shifts in population to urban centers, greater use of public transportation and car sharing, and financial pressures from the recession,[60] to maintain this momentum, the increased planning necessary to be a mixed transit user will have to prove worth the estimated $8,000 annual cost savings for additional drivers to eschew car ownership. Consumers who choose Zipcar as their mode of transportation rely on the service to provide easy to use, readily available, safe, environmentally friendly vehicles. If members do not receive the experience they are looking for, they will show dissatisfaction by discontinuing their use of the service. With already established competitors and substitutions and 88% of Zipcar's reported 2010 revenues directly tied to vehicle usage revenue,[61] the needs of customers must be considered as key.

Additionally, although board members and related parties currently hold a significant portion of Zipcar's shares, shareholder concerns must now

Exhibit 6 Vehicular Capital Requirement

VOLKSWAGEN	MSRP	36-Mo Lease*
Jetta	$16,495.00	$270.68
Golf	$17,995.00	$295.29
Jetta SportsWagon	$19,995.00	$328.11
GTI	$23,695.00	$388.83
Tiguan	$23,720.00	$389.24
Routan	$26,930.00	$441.91
CC	$28,515.00	$467.92

HONDA	MSRP	36-Mo Lease*
Accord	$21,180.00	$347.55
Crosstour	$29,790.00	$488.84
Civic	$15,605.00	$256.07
CRV	$21,695.00	$356.01
CR-Z	$19,345.00	$317.44
Insight	$18,200.00	$298.65
Fit	$15,100.00	$247.78

*Monthly financing costs estimated on 6% sales tax, a 36-month lease, and $0 down at 5% interest rate.

Sources: http://www.vw.com/en/models.html; http://automobiles.honda.com

Exhibit 7 Sales Price of Transportation Fuel to End-Users (Current ¢ / gallon)

(As of January 2011)

Highway fuel (including taxes)	1980	1985	1990	1995	2000	2005	2006	2007	2008	2009
Gasoline, premium[b]	N	134.0	134.9	133.6	169.3	249.1	280.5	303.3	351.9	260.7
Gasoline, regular[b]	124.5	120.2	116.4	114.7	151.0	229.5	258.9	280.1	326.6	235.0
Gasoline, all types	122.1	119.6	121.7	120.5	156.3	233.8	263.5	284.9	331.7	240.1
Diesel no. 2 (excluding taxes)[a]	81.8	78.9	72.5	56.0	93.5	178.6	209.6	226.7	315.0	183.4

KEY: N = data do not exist.
[a]Sales to end-users (sales made directly to the ultimate consumer, incl bulk customers in agriculture, industry, and utility).
[b]Average retail price.

Source: US Department of Transportation, Research, and Innovative Technology Division. National Transportation Statistics. Table 3-11. http://www.bts.gov/publications/national_transportation_statistics/

also be considered in operations. The company must focus on achieving profitable growth. Of primary concern is Zipcar's ability to manage the inherently high costs of maintaining a fleet, including ever-rising gas prices. Additionally, while the college demographic may be receptive and currently underserved, it may also be risky as, according to the Insurance Institute for Highway Safety, teenager drivers have a crash rate four times higher than that of older drivers.[62] This means that insurance and liability expenses related to serving this market are high—an expenditure that, despite its long-term benefits, is unlikely to sit well with shareholders.

Secondly, although shareholders may be counting on Zipcar's rapid revenue growth to continue

unabated, it is possible the company will soon reach the end of its market potential. Its product is facing increased competition from industry rivals, a plentiful supply of substitute products, and a limited demographic that may already be tapped. Also of concern is whether taking Zipcar public has alienated some of Zipcar's original members who bought into the idea of an alternative lifestyle as opposed to a means of transportation.

Yet despite these concerns and as evidenced by its successful IPO, it would seem more than a few investors have pinned their hopes on the established and profitable markets of Boston, NYC, Washington DC, and San Francisco as proof that Zipcar's model is not inherently unprofitable. Can Zipcar prove them right?

NOTES

1. Zipcar announces 2011 first quarter results. 11 May 2011. *zipcar.com*. http://ir.zipcar.com/releasedetail.cfm?ReleaseID=576450
2. Wheels when you need them. 22 Sep 2010. *Economist.com*. http://www.economist.com/node/16945232?story_id=16945232
3. S. Clifford. 1 Mar 2008. How fast can this thing go, anyway? *Inc. Magazine*. http://www.inc.com/magazine/20080301/how-fast-can-this-thing-go-anyway.html
4. team: home office. *zipcar.com. op. cit.*
5. board of directors. *zipcar.com*. http://ir.zipcar.com/committees.cfm
6. team: home office. *zipcar.com. op. cit.*
7. *Ibid.*
8. M. Levine. Share my ride. 5 Mar 2009. *NY Times Magazine*. http://www.nytimes.com/2009/03/08/magazine/08Zipcar-t.html
9. team: home office. *zipcar.com*. http://www.zipcar.com/about/team
10. sec filings: Zipcar Prospectus Form 424B4. Filed 14 Apr 2011. *zipcar.com*. http://ir.zipcar.com/sec.cfm
11. Zipcar announces pricing of initial public offering. 13 Apr 2011. *zipcar.com*. http://ir.zipcar.com/releasedetail.cfm?ReleaseID=568924
12. A. Levy. LivingSocial is next bet for Steve Case after Zipcar IPO payoff. 16 Apr 2011. *Bloomberg Businessweek*. http://www.businessweek.com/news/2011-04-16/livingsocial-is-next-bet-for-steve-case-after-zipcar-ipo-payoff.html
13. sec filings: Zipcar Prospectus Form 424B4. *op. cit.*
14. M. K. Pratt. RFID: A Ticket to Ride. 18 Dec 2006. *ComputerWorld.com*. http://www.computerworld.com/s/article/269126/RFID_A_Ticket_to_Ride
15. sec filings: Zipcar Prospectus Form 424B4. *op. cit.*
16. J. Addison. Ten reasons for drop in car ownership. 9 Jan 2010. *Clean Fleet Report*. http://www.cleanfleetreport.com/clean-fleet-articles/car-ownership-declines/
17. A UITP position paper: Becoming a real mobility provider. Apr 2011. *International Association of Public Transport*. http://www.uitp.org/mos/focus/FPComMob-en.pdf
18. *Ibid.*
19. 2010 Public Transportation Fact Book. April 2010. *American Public Transportation Association*. http://www.apta.com/resources/statistics/Documents/FactBook/APTA_2010_Fact_Book.pdf
20. Passenger information. *City of Chicago*. http://www.cityofchicago.org/city/en/depts/bacp/supp_info/passenger_information.html. San Francisco taxi tips. *About.com*. http://sanfrancisco.about.com/od/gettingaroun1/qt/sftaxitips.htm. Passenger information - rate of fare. *New York City Taxi and Limousine Commission*. http://www.ny.com/frame?url=http://www.nyc.gov/html/tlc/html/passenger/taxicab_rate.shtml
21. Is zipcar for me? *zipcar.com*. http://www.zipcar.com/is-it/
22. B. Vlasic and N. Bunkley. A bad year for car bargains. 20 May 2011. *New York Times*. http://www.nytimes.com/2011/05/21/business/21auto.html
23. Competitive Comparison. *Chevrolet.com*. http://www.chevrolet.com/tools/comparator/compareVehicle.do?year=2011&pvc=500&comparisonVehicles=329591~329856~326538&snType=model
24. A. Frankel. Zipcar makes the leap. 1 Mar 2008. *Fast Company*. http://www.fastcompany.com/magazine/123/zipcar-makes-the-leap.html
25. G. Potthoff. Students control 'green,' eco-friendly movement on college campuses. 4 May 2010. *BG News*. http://bgnews.com/campus/students-control-green-eco-friendly-movement-on-college-campuses/
26. green benefits. *zipcar.com*. http://www.zipcar.com/is-it/greenbenefits
27. case studies. *zipcar.com*. http://www.zipcar.com/business/is-it/case-studies
28. FastFleet for the Public Sector. *FastFleet.net*. http://www.fastfleet.net/solutions
29. Enterprise Rent-A-Car Company. *Answers.com*. http://www.answers.com/topic/enterprise-rent-a-car-company
30. Enterprise expands car sharing program nationwide. 30 Sep 2008. *Reuters.com*. http://www.reuters.com/article/2008/09/30/idUS137976+30-Sep-2008+BW20080930
31. *Ibid.*
32. What is WeCar? *WeCar.com*. http://www.wecar.com/
33. The Hertz Corporation. *Answers.com*. http://www.answers.com/topic/the-hertz-corporation
34. Hertz opens 60 new local edition locations. 6 Oct 2010. *AutoRentalNews.com*. http://www.autorentalnews.com/News/Story/2010/10/Hertz-Opens-60-New-Local-Edition-Locations.aspx
35. The Hertz Corporation. *Answers.com. op. cit.*
36. Hertz opens 60 new local edition locations. *op. cit.*
37. A rise in Hertz rental car rates will not deter customers. 7 Oct 2010. *Internet Business Blog*. http://www.theinternetbusinessblog.com/a-rise-in-hertz-car-rental-rates-will-not-deter-customers.html
38. The Hertz Corporation. *Answers.com. op. cit.*
39. Hertz opens 60 new local edition locations. *op. cit.*
40. Hertz on demand – Rent spontaneously. *Hertz on Demand*. http://www.connectbyhertz.com/
41. S. Ovide. Zipcar IPO soars 66% out of the gate. *Wall Street Journal*. http://blogs.wsj.com/deals/2011/04/14/zipcar-ipo-soars-66-out-of-the-gate/

42. Zipcar announces 2011 first quarter results. *op. cit.*
43. R. A. Munarriz. Zipcar is a dangerous driver. 12 May 2011. *The Motley Fool.com.* http://www.fool.com/investing/general/2011/05/12/zipcar-is-a-dangerous-driver.aspx
44. sec filings: Zipcar Prospectus Form 424B4. *op. cit.*
45. *Ibid.*
46. Interview with Scott Griffith. Zipcar Organizational Structure. upload 1 Apr 2011. *YouTube.com.* http://www.youtube.com/watch?v=XfheAAlVBH0
47. Is zipcar for me? *zipcar.com. op. cit.*
48. S. Wright. Car sharing trend grows as urban dwellers seek inexpensive alternative to the high price of vehicle ownership. 7 Feb 2011. *Urban Travel, Sustainability & Accessibility.* http://urbantravelandaccessibility.blogspot.com/2011/01/car-sharing-trend-grows-as-urban_17.html
49. sec filings: Zipcar Prospectus Form 424B4. *op. cit.*
50. *Ibid.*
51. *Ibid.*
52. *Ibid.*
53. *Ibid.*
54. *Ibid.*
55. *Ibid.*
56. C. Zinsli. Zipcar braces for impact from Japanese disasters. 22 Mar 2011. *Wall Street Journal.* http://blogs.wsj.com/venturecapital/2011/03/22/zipcar-braces-for-impact-from-japanese-disasters/
57. A. Mindlin. Zipcar, zapped by parking. 27 Apr 2008. *New York Times.* http://www.nytimes.com/2008/04/27/nyregion/thecity/27zipc.html
58. J. Addison. Ten reasons for drop in car ownership. *op. cit.*
59. Local gas prices in the US. www.gasbuddy.com
60. J. Addison. Ten reasons for drop in car ownership. *op. cit.*
61. sec filings: Zipcar Prospectus Form 424B4. *op. cit.*
62. Fatality facts 2009: Teenagers. *Insurance Institute for Highway Safety.* http://www.iihs.org/research/fatality_facts_2009/teenagers.html

NAME INDEX

A

Abbott, M., 128n
Abdelnour, S., 258n
Abe, N., 31n
Abebe, M. A., 386n
Acharya, V. V., 319n, 322n
Ackerman, F., 67n
Acs, Z. J., 413n
Adamo, M., 399
Adams, M. B., 259n, 323n
Adams, R., 79
Addison, J. T., 323n
Adegbesan, J. A., 94n
Adhikari, D. R., 323n
Adithipyangkul, P., 323n
Adkins, B., 258n
Adkins, R., 371
Adler, P. S., 387n
Adner, R., 29n, 94n, 161n
Afuah, A., 126n, 415n
Afza, T., 189n
Agarwal, R., 29n, 128n, 188n, 288n, 320n, 355n, 414n
Aggarwal, V. A., 358n
Agle, B. A., 31n
Agle, B. R., 186n
Agrawal, A., 321n
Aguilera, R. V., 319n, 321n, 323n
Ahlstrom, D., 68n, 97n, 257n
Ahmad, S., 411n
Ahsan, M., 320n
Ahuja, G., 220n
Aiello, R. J., 222n
Aime, F., 94n
Akdogu, E., 219n
Akerson, D., 374
Albadvi, A., 128n
Albanese, T., 314
Alberti, G. F., 411n
Alcacer, J., 96n, 256n
Alcalde-Fradejas, N., 285n
Aldrich, H. E., 95n, 387n
Alegria, R., 258n
Alexander, D. E., 155
Alexander, M., 112, 186n

Alexiev, A. S., 387n
Allcock, D., 187n, 190n
Allen, M. R., 219n
Allen, S., 412n
Almieda, P., 95n
Alon, I., 258n, 323n
Alton, R., 219n, 415n
Alvarez, S. A., 387n, 388n, 411n, 415n
Alves, A., 200
Amason, A. C., 31n, 186n, 414n
Ambos, B., 259n, 414n
Ambrose, M. L., 387n
Ambrosini, V., 219n, 414n
Amburgey, T. L., 354n
Amess, K., 223n
Amit, R., 30n, 95n, 320n
Ammann, M., 186n
An, J., 97n, 358n
Anand, J., 29n, 158n, 220n, 258n, 287n, 288n, 388n
Andersen, P. H., 358n
Andersen, T. J., 259n, 355n
Anderson, B. S., 94n
Anderson, P., 96n
Anderson, R. C., 190n, 319n, 321n
Anginer, D., 322n
Angriawan, A., 386n
Annamalai, T. R., 255n
Anokhin, S., 288n, 358n
Anschober, M., 28n
Ante, E., 220n
Anthony, S. D., 388n
Apaydin, M., 128n
Apotheker, L., 78, 151–152, 361–362
Appelbaum, S. A., 256n
Appelbaum, S. H., 357n
Appelmaum, B., 320n
Arena, M. V., 388n
Argenti, P. A., 357n
Arikan, A. M., 95n, 387n
Arikan, A. T., 319n, 355n, 358n
Arino, A., 94n, 256n
Ariño, M. A., 32n, 68n

Arkan, A. T., 288n
Armour, S., 66n
Arndt, M., 188n
Arndt, N., 186n
Arregle, J.-L., 28n, 68n, 94n, 128n, 157n, 319n, 385n, 386n, 412n, 415n, 416n
Arrunada, B., 287n
Arthurs, J. D., 127n
Arvidsson, N., 354n
Arys, B., 160n
Asaba, S., 30n
Asakawa, K., 416n
Ash, M. K., 395
Ashford, W., 152
Ashforth, B. E., 319n, 388n
Ashmos Plowman, D., 128n
Aspinwall, M., 257n
Ataay, A., 256n, 358n
Atan, M. O., 66n
Athreye, S., 255n
Atkins, K., 288n
Atuahene-Gima, K., 414n
Audretsch, D. B., 28n, 29n, 128n, 355n, 411n
Auh, S., 414n
Aulakh, P. S., 257n, 288n
Autio, E., 288n, 358n, 412n, 413n
Avellaneda, C. N., 220n
Avery, G. C., 159n
Avolio, B. J., 385n
Aytac, B., 66n
Azadegan, A., 159n, 414n, 415n
Azar, J., 320n
Azeroual, B., 387n

B

Babüroglu, O. N., 28n, 157n
Backaler, J., 121
Baden-Fuller, C., 286n, 358n
Bae, J., 95n, 358n
Baghai, M., 126n
Bailom, F., 28n
Baiman, S., 357n
Bainbridge, S., 322n
Baja, V., 102

Baker, E., 399
Baker, G. P., 320n
Baker, L. T., 128n
Baker, M., 219n
Balasubramanian, B., 322n
Balasubramanian, S., 158n
Balboni, F., 66n
Baldan, C., 69n
Balfour, F., 257n
Balkundi, P., 384n
Ball, J., 36
Ballinger, G. A., 321n, 386n
Ballmer, S., 268, 286n
Balsvik, R., 258n
Banalieva, E. R., 256n
Bandelj, N., 258n
Bandyk, M., 257n
Bandyopadhyay, S., 152
Banerjee, S., 222n
Bansal, P., 96n
Bao, Y., 385n
Baraldi, E., 384n
Barboza, D., 9, 379
Barden, J. Q., 257n, 286n, 413n
Barkema, H. G., 221n, 222n, 413n, 415n
Barker, R. G., 256n
Barker, V. L., III, 320n, 386n
Barlett, C. A., 257n
Barnes, B., 415n
Barnett, M. L., 31n, 221n
Barney, J. B., 28n, 31n, 80, 94n, 96n, 126n, 186n, 221n, 288n, 356n, 358n, 387n, 388n, 411n, 415n
Baron, R. A., 385n, 412n, 413n
Barr, D. P. S., 411n
Barr, P. S., 65n, 157n, 386n
Barret, V., 152
Barreto, I., 385n
Barrick, M. R., 384n
Barringer, B. R., 128n, 157n, 411n
Barsoux, J.-L., 392
Barthelemy, J., 28n
Bartlett, C. A., 257n, 357n

Bartol, K. M., 322n, 385n, 388n
Barton, D. L., 97n
Basker, E., 159n
Bass, D., 189n
Bastian, B., 126n
Basu, C., 413n
Basu, K., 31n
Bates, T. W., 28n, 190n
Batjargal, B., 416n
Baucus, M. S., 287n
Bauer, R., 322n
Bauguess, S. W., 221n
Baum, J. A. C., 288n, 415n
Baumol, W. J., 411n
Baysinger, B., 321n
Bayus, B., 158n
Bayus, B. L., 288n
Beal, B. B., 159n
Beal, B. D., 255n
Beamish, P. W., 188n, 258n, 259n, 286n, 288n, 357n, 386n
Bebchuk, L. A., 322n
Beck, K. A., 357n
Beck, T. E., 128n
Becker, B. E., 387n, 388n
Becker, M. C., 160n, 286n
Beechler, S., 94n
Beer, J., 157n
Beer, M., 384n
Begley, J., 222n
Begley, T. M., 94n, 357n, 412n
Belausteguigoitia, I., 412n
Belderbos, R., 29n, 96n, 158n
Bellman, E., 358n
Bello, D. C., 97n, 257n
ben-Aaron, D., 269
Benbya, H., 65n
Bender, R., 167
Benito, G. R. G., 259n, 357n
Bennett, J., 65n, 285n
Benson, D., 411n
Berchicci, L., 68n, 259n
Berfield, S., 128n
Berggren, C., 413n
Bergh, D. D., 128n, 160n, 186n, 187n, 188n, 222n, 320n, 388n
Bergquist, N., 407
Bergsteiner, H., 159n
Berkman, H., 323n
Berle, A., 320n
Bernardo, A. E., 189n
Berrone, P., 31n, 322n
Berry, H., 255n
Berry, T. K., 320n
Best, A., 222n
Bettencourt, L. A., 127n, 128n, 413n
Bettencourt, S. L., 413n
Bettis, R. A., 160n
Bhardwaj, B. R., 411n
Bhattacharya, A. K., 259n
Bhattacharyya, S., 68n, 219n
Bhaumik, S., 258n
Bhaumik, S. K., 95n, 219n, 323n
Bian, X., 128n
Bianchi, M., 392

Bierly, P. E., III, 66n
Bierman, L., 129n, 159n, 256n, 321n, 386n, 387n, 412n
Bigley, G. A., 66n, 95n, 258n, 355n
Biller, S., 128n
Billings, S., 392, 414n
Bilotkach, V., 158n
Bin, S., 159n
Bingham, C. B., 354n
Birchall, J., 392, 415n
Bird, R., 257n
Birkinshaw, J. M., 354n, 355n, 357n, 385n, 389n, 392, 413n
Birnberg, J. G., 355n
Bitar, J., 96n
Bizjak, J. M., 190n, 320n
Black, B. S., 322n
Blakely, S., 410
Blasberg, J., 96n
Blasi, J. R., 414n
Bliss, R., 189n
Bloch, N., 257n
Block, J., 323n
Blomkvist, K., 128n
Boateng, A., 258n
Bobinski, P. A., 321n, 323n
Boeh, K., 68n, 220n
Boeker, W., 414n
Bogers, M., 126n, 411n
Bogle, J., 189n
Boivie, S., 159n, 319n
Bonardi, J. P., 65n
Bonazzi, L., 321n
Bono, 304
Booker, A., 226
Boone, C., 32n, 385n
Boreham, T., 315
Borgatti, S. P., 358n
Borza, A., 415n
Bosma, N., 413n
Bosse, D. A., 31n, 65n, 94n, 319n
Bossidy, L., 384n
Bou, J. C., 157n
Boubakri, N., 67n
Boudette, N. E., 255n
Boulding, W., 159n
Boulton, T. J., 319n
Bounds, G., 50
Bouquet, C., 258n, 385n, 392
Bouslimi, L., 67n
Boussebaa, M., 256n
Boutilier, R., 31n
Bowen, H. P., 255n, 258n, 320n, 357n
Bower, J. L., 188n, 357n
Bowerman, M., 96n, 321n
Bowman, C., 219n
Bowman, E. H., 30n
Bowonder, B., 286n
Boyacigiller, N. A., 94n
Boyd, B. K., 128n, 322n
Boyd, D. E., 257n
Boyd, D. P., 94n, 357n, 412n
Boyd, G., 386n
Boyd, J. L., 29n, 159n

Boyd, N. G., 30n
Boyer, K. K., 159n
Boyle, M., 386n
Boynton, A., 414n
Boyson, N. M., 322n
Braam, G. J. M., 356n
Bradley, B. H., 384n
Bradley, S. W., 95n
Bradmore, D., 187n
Bradshaw, T., 167, 189n, 194
Brady, D., 386n
Bragger, D., 387n
Bragger, J. D., 387n
Brandenburger, A., 69n
Brandes, P., 320n
Brannen, M. Y., 190n
Brannen, N. Y., 256n
Brant, J., 386n
Branzei, O., 258n
Braun, M., 412n
Brennan, R., 384n
Bresser, R. K. F., 29n, 159n
Brettel, M., 30n, 94n, 387n, 411n, 414n, 416n
Brewster, D., 321n
Bricker, R., 319n
Brief, A. P., 68n, 319n
Brietel, M., 127n
Briggs, T. W., 321n, 322n
Brin, D. W., 67n
Brinckmann, J., 96n
Brinsley, J., 67n
Britt, R., 189n
Brock, J. W., 220n
Brodie, R. J., 126n
Brodkin, J., 174
Broedner, P., 187n
Bromiley, P., 186n
Bross, M., 8
Brouthers, K. D., 258n
Brouwer, M. T., 189n
Brown, C. J., 319n
Brown, D. T., 223n
Brown, J. S., 28n, 66n
Brown, S. A., 67n
Browning, E. S., 66n
Brush, C. G., 30n
Brush, G. J., 126n
Brush, J. H., 358n
Brush, T. H., 29n, 97n, 186n
Bruton, G. D., 29n, 222n, 223n, 319n, 412n
Bruyaka, O., 411n
Bryant, A., 384n
Bryant, J., 298
Bryce, D. J., 29n
Bryon, E., 66n
Bucerius, M., 220n
Buchholtz, A. K., 319n, 356n, 386n
Buchholz, T. G., 384n
Buck, P., 71
Buck, T., 323n
Buckley, G., 398
Buckley, P. J., 67n, 256n
Bueno, R., 67n

Buisson, B., 413n
Bunderson, J. S., 385n, 387n
Burgelman, R. A., 384n, 387n, 412n, 413n
Burke, D., 36
Burkett, G., 338
Burkitt, L., 121, 158n
Burns, T., 355n
Burrows, P., 57, 66n, 160n, 356n
Busenitz, L. W., 95n, 220n, 222n, 223n, 412n
Bush, J., 67n
Bustillo, M., 112, 158n
Butt-Philip, A., 258n
Buyl, T., 32n, 385n
Byrne, J. A., 32n
Byrnes, N., 31n, 257n, 357n
Byron, E., 84, 322n

C
Cahoy, D. R., 257n
Cai, J., 322n
Calantone, R. J., 96n, 160n, 385n
Calart, A. A., 186n
Caldwell, C., 3, 31n, 326, 388n
Callaway, S. K., 29n
Calof, J., 66n
Camillus, J. C., 31n
Camp, S. M., 95n, 220n, 411n, 412n, 413n, 415n
Campagnolo, D., 286n
Campbell, A., 186n, 357n
Campbell, J., 68n, 157n
Campbell, J. T., 28n, 94n, 386n
Campbell, R., 310
Campbell, S. M., 190n
Camuffo, A., 286n
Cannella, A. A., Jr., 32n, 69n, 95n, 157n, 189n, 220n, 321n, 357n, 385n, 386n
Cantwell, J., 256n
Cao, Q., 32n, 387n
Capaldo, A., 29n, 288n
Capezio, A., 188n
Capon, L., 95n
Cappelli, P., 413n
Capron, L., 69n, 160n, 187n, 189n, 219n
Carbonell, P., 160n
Cardinal, L. B., 187n, 189n
Cardon, M. S., 412n, 414n
Cardona, M., 112
Carey, D., 321n
Cari, T., 68n
Carlson, B. D., 285n
Carlson, L. R., 321n
Carmeli, A., 387n
Carney, M., 255n
Carpenter, M. A., 189n, 219n, 222n, 322n, 386n
Carr, D., 174
Carroll, G. R., 159n
Carroll, J., 189n
Carroll, P. B., 189n
Carson, S. J., 95n

Carter, J. R., 159n, 414n
Carter, P. L., 159n, 414n
Carter, R., 187n
Carter, R. A., 158n
Carvalho, L., 413n
Casadesus-Masanell, R., 157n
Casey, A., 388n
Cashen, L. H., 320n
Cassar, G., 30n
Cassidy, J., 258n, 285n
Cassiman, B., 257n
Castañer, X., 412n
Castanias, R., 384n
Castellucci, F., 97n
Castleton, M. W., 189n
Castrogiovanni, G. J., 222n
Catan, T., 194
Caulfield, B., 132
Cavaliere, A., 392
Cavusgil, E., 413n
Cavusgil, S. T., 256n
Celuch, K., 29n
Cendrowski, S., 67n
Certo, S. T., 129n, 158n, 259n, 319n, 320n
Chacar, A., 65n
Chaharbaghi, K., 356n
Chahine, S., 319n, 321n
Chai, K., 132, 414n
Chaker, A. M., 127n
Chakrabarti, A., 188n
Chakrabarti, R., 220n, 255n
Chakravarthy, B., 126n
Chakravorti, B., 411n
Chambers, J., 78
Chambers, J. T., 337
Chambers, M., 315
Champlin, D. P., 188n
Chan, C. M., 67n
Chan, M., 304
Chandar, N., 319n
Chandler, A., 327–328, 330, 333, 355n
Chandler, D., 356n
Chandler, G. N., 28n
Chandy, R. K., 221n
Chang, H., 69n, 157n
Chang, S. J., 29n, 158n, 188n
Change, S.-C., 259n
Changhui, Z., 220n
Chao, L., 13
Chao, Y., 285n
Chapman, J., 220n
Chari, M. D. R., 186n, 187n
Charkha, J. P., 323n
Charny, B., 128n
Chatain, O., 69n, 128n
Chatterjee, A. K., 96n
Chatterjee, S., 187n, 188n, 221n, 222n
Chatterjee, S. J., 189n
Chatterji, A. J., 413n
Chattopadhyay, P., 65n
Chaturvedi, S., 294
Che, J., 258n

Chee, F. Y., 174
Chellappa, R., 157n
Chen, E. L., 66n, 157n
Chen, E.-T., 319n
Chen, G., 96n
Chen, J., 288n
Chen, J.-S., 256n
Chen, L.-Y., 259n
Chen, M., 157n
Chen, M. A., 321n
Chen, M.-J., 32n, 133, 134, 139, 157n, 158n, 159n, 160n, 285n, 387n
Chen, S.-F. S., 258n
Chen, X.-P., 68n, 412n
Chenevert, L., 176, 188n
Cheng, J. L. C., 158n
Cheng, S., 69n, 157n
Cheng, Y. K., 256n
Chen-Jui, H., 222n
Cherkas, L., 412n
Chesbrough, H. W., 160n, 186n, 391, 392, 414n
Chesney, J., 186n, 221n
Cheung, M-S., 127n
Cheung, Y.-L., 323n
Chhaochharia, V., 320n
Chi, J., 323n
Chi, T., 128n, 257n
Chiaroni, D., 392
Chiesa, V., 392
Child, J., 126n, 223n
Chin, Y. W., 220n
Chiu, S.-C., 320n
Chizema, A., 323n
Cho, H. J., 389n
Chod, J., 157n
Choi, B., 126n
Choi, C. J., 255n
Choi, S. B., 255n
Chon, G., 219n, 322n
Chong, L. C., 222n
Chou, J., 320n
Choudhury, A., 259n
Chow, R. P. M., 97n, 387n, 415n
Chowdhry, B., 189n
Chowdhury, S. D., 320n
Chrisman, J. L., 412n
Christen, M., 159n
Christensen, C. M., 29n, 75, 95n, 131, 132, 219n, 356n, 388n, 411n, 415n
Christensen, J., 57
Christensen, P. R., 358n
Christman, P., 415n
Christmann, P., 221n, 222n
Christophe, S. E., 259n, 357n
Chrusciel, D., 66n
Chu, R., 285n
Chu, W., 127n, 255n, 285n
Chua, C., 67n
Chum, R., 95n
Chung, C. C., 258n, 288n
Chung, C. N., 190n, 319n
Chung, W., 256n, 413n

Chvyrkov, O., 413n
Ciarione, A., 29n
Cimilluca, D., 189n, 219n
Cinquetti, C. A., 257n
Claburn, T., 152
Clark, D., 79, 222n, 294
Clark, E., 221n
Clark, K. D., 29n, 95n
Clarkson, G., 160n
Claro, D. P., 286n, 358n
Clarysse, B., 411n
Claver-Cortes, E., 65n
Cleary, M., 221n
Clegg, J., 67n
Clifford, S., 246
Coakley, L., 189n
Cochran, P. L., 31n, 388n
Cody, T., 223n
Coen, C. A., 96n
Coff, R. W., 96n, 188n, 189n
Coffee, J. C., 189n
Cohen, S. K., 128n, 413n
Cohen, S. S., 386n
Cohn, J., 372
Colbert, A. E., 384n
Colchester, M., 255n
Cole, R. A., 323n
Colella, A., 67n, 384n
Coles, J., 386n
Collier, N., 414n
Collins, C. G., 95n
Collins, C. J., 29n, 95n
Collins, J., 369
Collins, J. D., 159n, 388n
Collis, D., 186n, 188n, 356n
Colpan, A. M., 319n
Colquitt, J. A., 387n
Colvin, G., 50, 220n, 387n
Combs, J. G., 28n, 160n, 189n, 287n
Commandeur, H., 30n, 386n
Conduras, A., 413n
Conger, J. A., 31n
Connell, J., 288n
Connelly, B. L., 28n, 31n, 129n, 158n, 255n, 259n, 320n, 356n, 358n 384n
Contractor, F. J., 97n, 127n
Conyon, M. J., 322n
Cook, T., 293, 371
Cool, K., 219n
Coombes, S., 411n
Coombs, J. E., 322n
Cooper, A. C., 415n
Cooper, C. D., 414n
Cooper, R. W., 287n
Corbat, M., 209
Corbetta, G., 319n, 385n
Cordeiro, J. J., 189n
Cording, M., 221n, 222n, 415n
Core, J. E., 187n, 322n
Cornett, M., 219n
Corredoira, R. A., 257n
Costa, A. C., 388n
Coucke, K., 160n
Coughlan, J., 413n

Covey, F., 27
Covin, J. G., 97n, 223n, 286n, 354n, 355n, 356n, 388n, 413n, 414n
Cowan, A. P., 323n
Cowan, R., 127n, 288n, 414n, 415n
Cowen, A. P., 319n
Cox, R. A. K., 413n
Cox, R. K., 411n
Coyne, K. P., 66n
Craighead, M., 372
Crainer, S., 321n
Crane, A., 69n
Cronin, M. A., 414n
Crook, T. R., 28n, 160n
Crooks, E., 164, 220n
Cropanzano, R., 387n
Crosby, P. B., 159n
Crossan, M. M., 31n, 32n, 96n, 128n
Crossland, C., 259n
Crown, J., 186n
Croyle, R., 188n
Crystal, G., 307–308
Cuellar-Fernandez, B., 285n
Cuervo-Cazurra, A., 30n, 128n, 255n, 256n
Cuevas-Rodriguez, G., 97n
Cui, A. S., 385n
Cuiskey, K. J., 285n
Culpan, T., 379
Cunha, M. P. E., 256n
Cyr, M., 357n
Czipura, C., 286n

D

Dabal, A., 286n
Dacin, M. T., 68n, 97n, 257n, 415n
Dacin, T., 354n
Dagnino, G., 160n
Dagnino, G. B., 28n, 94n, 128n, 158n, 187n, 257n
Dahlvig, A., 128n
Daily, C. M., 223n, 386n
Daizadeh, I., 356n
Dalton, C. M., 319n, 321n
Dalton, D. R., 223n, 319n, 321n, 386n
Daly, R., 67n
Dalziel, T., 96n, 321n, 323n
Damanpour, F., 66n, 220n
Daneels, E., 387n
Daneke, G. A., 68n
Daniels, M., 371
Danneels, E., 94n, 96n, 414n
Dant, R. R., 97n
Darda, S. V., 413n
Darnell, N., 31n
Dart, M., 127n
Das, A., 189n, 219n
Das, S. S., 189n
Das, T. K., 68n, 257n, 285n, 288n, 289n
Dastidar, P., 256n

Datta, D. K., 223n, 321n, 386n, 412n
D'aunno, T., 258n
D'Aveni, R. A., 28n, 29n, 94n, 128n, 160n, 187n, 257n
David, P., 186n, 187n, 188n, 221n, 258n, 320n
David, R. J., 129n, 319n, 321n
Davidson, R., 222n
Davidson, W. N., 320n
Davidsson, P., 28n, 30n, 411n
Davies, G., 95n
Davis, G. E., 319n
Davis, J., 57
Davis, J. G., 126n
Davis, J. H., 31n, 386n
Davis, K. J., 221n
Davis-Blake, A., 95n
Davison, L., 28n, 66n
Davison, R. B., 219n, 322n
Davis-Sramek, B., 287n
Dawson, C., 262
Day, J. D., 355n
Day, M., 387n
De Abreu, P. G. F., 66n
de Bakker, F. G. A., 31n
De Benedetto, C. A., 220n
de Castilla, F., 157n
De Clercq, D., 412n, 414n
De Fontenay, C. C., 97n
de Graauw, H., 286n
de la Fuente Sabate, J. M., 69n
de la Torre, C., 323n
de Man, A.-P., 286n
de Queiroz, V., 323n
De Young, R., 155
Dean, X., 220n
Deaton, C., 371
DeCarolis, D. M., 30n
Dechenaux, E., 257n
Decker, C., 188n
Deephouse, D. L., 69n
Dekker, H. C., 288n
Del Brio, E. B., 319n
Del Brio, E. G., 319n
DelCarmen Triana, M., 67n
Delios, A., 188n, 188n, 221n, 222n, 258n, 320n
Dell, M., 329
Dellarocas, C., 66n
Delmas, M., 68n
Delmas, M. A., 28n, 30n, 126n
Deloof, M., 322n
DeLuca, F., 71
Deming, W. E., 159n
Demirbag, M., 256n
den Hond, F., 31n
Deng, F. J., 388n
DeNisi, A. S., 358n, 384n, 387n
Denison, D. R., 258n
Denning, L., 262
Denning, S., 112
DePass, D., 94n
Derfus, P. J., 157n
Derosby, D., 94n

DeRue, D. S., 223n
Desai, M. A., 356n
Desai, V., 95n
DeSarbo, W. S., 69n
Deshmukh, A., 255n
Deshpande, S. P., 323n
Dess, G. G., 29n, 160n, 388n
Desyllas, P., 415n
DeTienne, D. R., 414n
Deutsch, Y., 95n, 189n, 321n, 322n
Devaraj, S., 186n, 187n
Devers, C. E., 160n, 219n, 222n, 322n
Devos, E., 219n
Dewitt, R.-L., 320n, 388n
Dhanaraj, C., 257n, 286n, 287n, 358n, 415n
Dhanwadkar, R., 320n
Di Gregorio, D., 157n, 413n
Diamantopoulos, A., 66n, 189n
Dickler, J., 72
Dicolo, J. A., 128n
Diedrich, F. J., 356n
Dienhart, J. W., 323n
Dieroff, C., 68n
Diestre, L., 96n, 187n, 222n, 256n
Dikova, D., 258n, 259n
Diller, B., 186
Dimitratos, P., 67n
Dinc, I. S., 323n
Ding, D., 286n, 287n
D'Innocenzio, A., 246
Dino, R. H., 385n
DiPietro, J., 221n
Dirks, K. T., 414n
Disney, R., 148
Disney, W., 148
Dixon, S. E. A., 387n
Dobbs, R., 66n, 219n
Dobni, C. B., 355n
Dobrev, S. D., 159n
Doherty, A. M., 287n
Dokko, G., 289n
Dolan, M., 137, 412n
Dollinger, M., 221n
Domoto, H., 358n
Donaldson, L., 386n
Dong, Z., 322n
Donker, H., 221n
Donnelly, T., 222n
Dooley, K. J., 159n, 414n
Dooms, E., 187n
Dorfman, P. W., 386n, 387n
Dougherty, C., 66n
Douglas, A. V., 320n
Douglas, T. J., 30n
Doukas, J. A., 259n
Dowling, G. R., 160n
Doz, Y. L., 31n, 356n, 385n, 413n
Dranikoff, L., 223n
Driscoll, C., 388n
Drnevich, P. L., 30n, 94n, 127n, 414n
Droge, C., 96n, 160n
Drossos, D. A., 157n

Drovsek, M., 412n
Drucker, P. F., 333, 394, 411n
Du, Y., 322n
du Plessis, J., 314
Duan, Y., 65n, 66n
Dubelaar, C., 187n
Dubin, J. A., 95n
Dubuque, K., 221n
Duchin, R., 320n, 321n
Dudley, R., 35
Duffy, J., 338
Duhaime, I. M., 157n, 186n, 221n
Duncan, C., 222n
Dunlap-Hinkler, D., 29n, 94n, 127n, 414n
Durand, R., 411n
Dushnitsky, G., 319n, 415n
Dussauge, P., 287n, 358n
Dutta, P. K., 68n
Dutta, S., 96n
Dutton, J. E., 30n, 31n
Duysters, G., 285n, 415n
Dvir, T., 385n
Dwyer, L., 30n
Dwyer, R., 200
Dyer, J. H., 29n, 127n, 255n, 285n, 358n, 387n, 388n, 411n
Dykes, B. J., 158n, 219n

E
Earl, N., 223n
Easterwood, J., 223n
Eaton, K., 9
Eavis, P., 357n
Ebbers, H., 200
Ebbers, J. J., 96n, 288n
Ebbes, P., 69n
Echamabadi, R., 414n
Eckhardt, J. T., 415n
Eden, D., 32n, 385n
Eden, E., 323n
Eden, L. E., 158n, 160n, 256n, 258n, 358n, 386n, 415n
Ederhof, M., 322n
Edmondson, A. C., 30n
Edmondson, G., 389n
Edwards, C., 161n
Edwards, J., 323n
Ees, H., 323n
Eesley, C., 32n, 65n
Efrati, A., 194
Egelhoff, W. G., 357n
Eggers, J. P., 95n
Eiche, J., 257n, 258n
Eiche, J. J., 257n
Eichholtz, P., 322n
Einhorn, B., 68n
Eisenhardt, K. M., 32n, 66n, 126n, 157n, 187n, 188n, 220n, 286n, 288n, 354n, 356n, 387n, 414n, 415n
Eisenmann, T. R., 357n
Eisenstat, R., 188n, 384n
El Medi, I. K., 320n
Elango, B., 29n, 255n, 287n

Elbanna, S., 126n
Elenkov, D. S., 388n
Elfenbein, D., 415n
Elfenbein, H. A., 66n, 127n, 157n
Elfring, T., 412n
Elkind, P., 36
Elliott, S., 167
Ellis, D. K., 222n
Ellis, K. M., 221n
Ellis, P., 412n
Ellison, L., 197
Ellonen, H.-K., 220n, 287n
Elms, H., 68n
Elmuti, D., 128n
Elop, S., 268, 286n
Eng, T. Y., 127n
Engardio, P., 188n
Engelen, A., 414n
Engelland, B., 159n
Entin, E. E., 356n
Erakovic, L., 321n
Erikson, T., 127n
Ernst, H., 414n, 415n
Ertimur, Y., 321n
Ertug, G., 97n
Escrihuela-Villar, M., 286n
Espitia-Escuer, M., 285n
Esterl, M., 68n
Estrin, S., 95n, 219n, 258n
Ethiraj, S. K., 68n, 355n, 387n, 413n
Ethirau, S. K., 30n
Ethitaj, S. K., 157n
Euchner, J., 67n, 132
Evangelista, F., 285n
Evans, B., 355n
Evans, G., 128n
Evans, J., 145
Evans, J. D., 222n
Ewing, J., 357n
Exu, M., 66n
Eyring, M. J., 411n
Ezrati, M., 67n

F
Facchini, G., 258n
Fackler, M., 320n
Faems, D., 97n
Fahey, L., 65n, 67n
Fairbridge, R. W., 155
Fairclough, S., 256n
Faleye, O., 321n, 322n
Falkenberg, L., 95n
Fama, E. F., 190n, 319n
Fang, C., 357n
Fang, E., 259n, 415n
Fang, Y., 258n
Faruna, T., 49
Fee, C. E., 219n, 223n
Feils, D. J., 97n, 127n
Feinberg, K., 65
Feinberg, S., 357n
Feinberg, S. E., 29n, 68n
Feldman, A., 127n
Feldman, B., 399
Feldman, L. F., 30n

Felps, W., 66n, 95n
Feng-Jyh, L., 68n
Ferdowsi, A., 151–152
Fern, M. J., 187n
Fernandez-Araoz, C., 385n
Fernhaber, S. A., 412n
Ferri, F., 321n
Ferrier, W. J., 94n, 132, 157n, 158n, 160n, 388n
Fetter, T., 67n
Fey, C. F., 29n, 67n
Fiaharty, G., 372
Ficery, K. L., 222n
Fich, E. M., 322n
Fiedler, M., 257n
Fiet, J. O., 412n
Filatotchev, I., 187n, 190n, 259n, 319n, 321n, 356n
Finegold, D. L., 321n
Finkelstein, S., 32n, 96n, 365, 385n
Fiol, C. M., 95n
Fischer, B., 414n
Fischer, H. M., 322n
Fisher, D., 210
Fiss, P. C., 323n
Fitzsimmons, J., 28n
Fjeldstad, O. D., 31n, 127n
Flanagan, D. J., 223n
Fleisher, C. S., 69n
Fleury, A., 159n
Fleury, M., 159n
Flint, P., 219n
Flood, P., 385n
Flores, M., 412n
Florida, R., 72, 94n
Florou, G., 128n
Flynn, B., 127n
Foedermayr, E. K., 66n
Folta, T. B., 189n, 221n, 388n
Fong, E. A., 322n
Foo, M.-D., 412n
Foo, S., 66n
Foote, N., 188n
Forbes, D. P., 95n, 128n, 159n, 160n
Ford, D. L., 384n
Ford, H., 156
Ford, J. D., 95n
Ford, L. W., 95n
Forest, S. A., 188n
Fornes, G., 258n
Forsyth, M., 223n
Fortanier, F., 255n
Fortuna, N., 413n
Fosfuri, A., 159n
Fosu, A. K., 67n
Fouskas, K. G., 157n
Fowler, G. A., 13, 269, 407
Francis, J., 412n
Frankwick, G. L., 285n
Frattini, F., 392
Frazier, G., 187n
Frazier, M., 3, 326
Frechet, M., 285n, 288n

Fredrickson, J. W., 95n
Freeman, D., 220n
Freeman, R. E., 30n, 31n, 157n, 186n, 188n, 355n, 387n, 389n
French, S., 126n
Frenken, K., 286n
Friese, M., 189n
Froese, F. J., 222n
Frown, P. E., 126n
Fry, L. W., 31n
Fu, L. J., 323n
Fuentelsaz, L., 187n
Fuertes-Callen, Y., 285n
Fuller, D. B., 29n
Fulmer, I. S., 189n
Funk, C. A., 127n
Funk, J. L., 29n
Furr, N. R., 354n
Furu, P., 29n

G
Gaba, V., 414n
Gabrielsson, M., 257n
Gabrielsson, P., 257n
Gadiesh, O., 32n
Galagan, P., 223n
Galante, J., 338
Galbreath, J., 30n, 68n
Gallo, C., 18, 30n
Galper, J. P., 9
Galpin, T., 355n
Galunic, D. C., 188n
Galvin, B. M., 384n
Galvin, P., 30n, 68n
Gambardella, A., 255n
Ganco, M., 320n
Gani, L., 357n
Gannon, M. J., 159n
Ganotakis, P., 257n
Gans, J. S., 97n
Gao, S., 387n
Gapper, J., 194
Garces-Ayerbe, C., 31n, 65n
Garcia, M. F., 67n
Garcia, T., 385n
García-Canal, E., 219n
Garcia-Casarejos, N., 285n
García-Castro, R., 68n
Gardner, T., 160n
Garg, V. K., 66n
Garrette, B., 287n, 358n
Gartner, W. B., 66n
Garud, R., 416n
Gary, M. S., 95n, 387n
Gassman, O., 412n
Gates, M., 304
Geatson, A., 287n
Gebauer, H., 355n
Gedajlovic, E. R., 255n
Gehlhar, M. J., 127n
Geiger, S. W., 320n
Geletkanycz, M. A., 322n
Gemser, G., 414n

Gemünden, H. G., 356n
Genc, M. E., 255n
Gene, M., 256n
Gentry, R. J., 96n, 321n
George, G., 128n, 412n, 415n
Georgopoulos, G. J., 219n
Geppert, M., 221n
Geressy-Nilsen, K., 221n
Gerhard Dijkstra, S., 68n, 160n
Gerhart, B., 189n
Germain, R. N., 287n
Geroski, P. A., 95n
Gerwin, D., 160n
Ghalsasi, A., 152
Ghauri, P. N., 67n, 158n, 220n, 255n
Ghemawat, P., 68n, 256n, 355n
Ghosh, A., 322n
Ghosh, C., 310
Ghoshal, S., 257n, 357n
Ghosn, C., 261
Giachetti, C., 160n
Giacomin, J., 128n
Giarratana, M. S., 29n, 159n, 255n, 257n, 288n
Gibbert, M., 97n
Gibbons, P., 160n, 413n
Gibson, R., 221n
Giersch, C., 258n
Gietzmann, M., 320n
Gilad, B., 66n
Gilbert, B. A., 28n, 109, 113, 116, 187n, 288n, 357n, 411n, 412n
Gilbert, C. G., 411n
Gilbert, J. L., 32n
Gilbert, K., 68n
Gilley, K. M., 322n
Gilliland, T., 256n
Gilson, R., 189n
Gimeno, J., 28n, 95n, 127n, 158n, 159n, 187n, 255n, 320n
Gioia, D. A., 319n, 388n
Girod, S., 256n
Giroud, X., 319n
Givray, H. S., 384n
Gleason, K. C., 320n
Glick, W. H., 65n
Globerman, S., 258n, 323n
Glunk, U., 385n
Goddard, C. R., 258n
Goergen, M., 223n
Goerzen, A., 358n
Goes, J., 28n, 157n
Gogoi, P., 186n
Gold, D. L., 323n
Gold, R., 36
Goldberg, A. W., 9
Goldberg, S. R., 222n
Golden, B. R., 386n
Goldman, E. F., 384n, 388n
Goleman, D., 384n
Goll, I., 126n, 385n
Golovko, E., 255n, 257n
Gomez, C., 67n

Gomez, J., 187n
Gomez-Mejia, L. R., 31n, 97n, 186n, 319n, 320n, 322n, 414n
Gonzales-Benito, J., 127n
Gonzalez, I. S., 69n
Goodall, K., 256n
Goold, M., 186n, 188n, 356n, 357n
Goranova, M., 320n, 321n
Gore, A. K., 321n
Goteman, I., 128n
Goto, M., 66n
Gotsopoulos, A., 159n
Gottfredson, M., 29n
Gottschalg, O., 95n
Gove, S., 68n, 94n, 126n, 157n, 189n, 220n, 356n, 416n
Govindarajan, V., 388n
Gozubuyuk, R., 358n
Graebner, M. E., 187n, 219n, 220n, 222n, 321n, 415n
Graefe, A., 66n
Grant, A. M., 31n
Grant, R. M., 80
Gray, B., 287n, 413n
Gray, D., 128n
Gray, S. R., 189n
Greckhamer, T., 68n
Greco, J., 356n
Green, H., 126n
Green, K. M., 356n
Greenwood, R., 256n, 322n, 355n
Gregersen, H. B., 388n, 411n
Grégoire, D., 65n, 411n
Gregoriou, A., 323n
Greimel, H., 159n
Grenness, T., 67n
Greve, H. R., 96n, 126n, 158n, 159n, 219n, 222n, 288n, 415n
Greve, P., 355n
Grewal, D., 287n
Grewal, R., 69n
Griffin, D., 67n
Griffith, D. A., 385n
Grimm, C. M., 157n, 158n, 159n, 160n
Grimpe, C., 97n
Grinstein, Y., 320n
Groen, A. J., 30n, 387n
Gröne, F., 158n, 188n
Gross, D., 200
Grove, A. S., 384n
Gruber, M., 30n, 94n, 127n, 387n, 411n, 416n
Grundei, J., 160n
Gu, Q., 96n
Guay, W. R., 187n, 322n
Gudergan, S. P., 285n
Gudridge, K., 188n
Guedri, Z., 287n
Guerrera, F., 188n
Guidroz, A., 258n
Guillen, M. F., 219n, 255n
Guimaraes-Costs, N., 256n

Gul, F. A., 321n
Gulati, N., 246, 259n, 262
Gulati, R., 29n, 128n, 187n, 354n
Gulaty, R., 413n
Gulbrandsen, B., 219n
Gunkel, J. D., 389n
Gunther, M., 399
Guo, S., 221n
Gupta, A. K., 29n, 68n, 357n, 388n
Gupta, S., 187n
Gupta-Mukherjee, S, 255n
Gurnani, H., 257n
Guthrie, J. P., 223n
Gutierrez, C., 298

H
Haas, M. R., 95n
Hadani, M., 321n
Haeussler, C., 287n
Hafsi, T., 96n
Hagaoka, S., 257n
Hagedoorn, J., 415n
Hagel, J., III, 28n, 66n
Hagen, C., 127n
Hagerty, J. R., 221n, 252, 344, 399, 414n
Hagiwara, Y., 137, 256n
Hail, L., 256n
Hain-Cole, A., 67n
Hair, J. F. Jr., 126n
Haleblian, J., 158n, 189n, 219n, 222n, 322n
Hall, B. J., 320n
Hall, C., 160n
Hall, E., 167
Hall, J. K., 68n
Hall, S., 338
Haller, S. A., 258n
Hallikas, J., 126n
Hamari, M., 386n
Hambrick, C., 32n
Hambrick, D. C., 95n, 157n, 189n, 221n, 259n, 365, 385n, 386n
Hamel, G., 96n, 414n
Hamilton, B., 415n
Hamm, S., 97n
Hammer, M., 355n
Hammonds, K. H., 29n
Hamza, T., 219n
Han, X., 258n, 285n
Hanig, T. R., 31n
Hannah, S. T., 354n
Hanous, M. D., 258n
Hansen, M. H., 288n, 358n
Hansen, M. T., 95n
Hansen, M. W., 358n
Hanson, S., 65n
Hantula, D. A., 387n
Hanvanich, S., 96n, 160n
Hardaway, F., 102
Hardin, G., 155–156
Harding, R., 265
Hardy, Q., 407

Harper, N. W. C., 189n
Harrigan, K. R., 30n
Harrington, R. J., 31n, 126n
Harris, J., 68n
Harris, R., 223n
Harrison, D. A., 31n, 384n, 388n
Harrison, J. S., 30n, 31n, 65n, 94n, 157n, 186n, 188n, 188n, 189n, 219n, 220n, 221n, 222n, 257n, 319n, 355n, 387n, 388n, 389n, 415n
Harrison, S., 358n
Hartnett, K., 221n
Harvey, M., 288n, 386n
Hatch, N. W., 387n
Hatonen, J., 127n
Hau, L. N., 285n
Haugland, S. A., 219n, 285n
Haunschild, P., 286n
Hawawini, G., 30n
Hawes, J. M., 287n
Haxhi, I., 323n
Hayashi, A. M., 287n, 358n
Hayes, L. A., 388n
Haynes, K. T., 31n, 356n, 357n, 384n, 385n
Hayton, J. C., 220n
Hayward, M. L. A., 190n, 221n, 385n
Hayward, T., 35
He, X., 29n, 94n, 128n, 157n, 259n, 387n
Healey, J. R., 67n
Heames, J. T., 386n
Heath, N., 97n
Heavy, C., 127n, 384n
Hebert, L., 258n
Hecker, A., 97n
Heeley, M. B., 127n, 355n
Hefner, F., 222n
Hegarty, W. H., 258n
Heijitjes, M. G., 385n
Heimeriks, K. H., 285n
Heine, K., 96n
Heine, L., 414n
Heineman, B. W., Jr., 32n, 319n
Heinemann, F., 30n, 94n, 127n, 387n, 411n, 414n, 416n
Hekman, D. R., 32n
Helfat, C. E., 30n, 32n, 95n, 96n, 220n, 356n, 384n
Helman, C., 95n
Helms, M. M., 32n
Hemerling, J. W., 259n
Hempel, J., 407
Henderson, A. D., 159n
Hendricks, W., 385n
Hendrickx, M., 186n
Hendriks, W., 32n
Henriques, I., 31n
Heracleous, L., 189n, 319n
Herbert, T. T., 258n
Herd, T., 221n, 285n
Herko, R., 69n

Hermann, P., 32n, 97n, 385n
Hermel, P., 159n
Hermelo, F., 160n
Hernandez, E., 222n, 256n, 287n
Herper, M., 220n
Herrmann, P., 68n, 321n
Hess, A., 392, 416n
Hesseldahl, A., 362
Hesterly, W. S., 358n, 386n
Heugens, P. M. A. R., 255n
Higginbotham, S., 287n
Higgins, M. J., 94n
Higgins, T., 137
Hikino, T., 319n
Hill, C. W. L., 29n, 221n, 223n, 355n, 357n
Hill, D., 94n
Hill, L. A., 31n
Hill, S. A., 413n
Hille, K., 379
Hiller, N. J., 95n
Hillier, D., 223n, 323n
Hillman, A. J., 31n, 95n, 321n, 323n, 385n
Hilpirt, R., 355n
Hirai, K., 372
Hirasawa, K., 323n
Hitt, M. A., 28n, 29n, 30n, 31n, 32n, 68n, 88, 89, 94n, 95n, 96n, 97n, 109, 113, 116, 126n, 127n, 128n, 129n, 157n, 158n, 159n, 160n, 183, 186n, 187n, 188n, 189n, 219n, 220n, 221n, 222n, 223n, 226, 227, 232, 239, 246, 255n, 256n, 257n, 258n, 259n, 267, 271, 275, 280, 285n, 286n, 288n, 319n, 321n, 323n, 355n, 356n, 357n, 358n, 384n, 385n, 386n, 387n, 388n, 389n, 411n, 412n, 413n, 415n, 416n
Hmieleski, K. M., 385n, 412n
Ho, C., 68n
Hoang, H., 94n, 255n, 358n
Hodgson, G. M., 187n
Hoegl, M., 97n, 388n
Hoffmann, V. H., 68n
Hoffmann, W. H., 387n
Hofmann, D. A., 189n
Hoitash, R., 321n
Hoitash, U., 321n
Hoiweg, M., 159n
Holburn, G. I. F., 65n
Holburn, G. L. F., 67n, 255n
Holburne, G. F., 67n
Holcomb, T. R., 28n, 94n, 222n, 285n, 384n, 387n, 411n
Holland, R., 128n
Hollenbeck, G. P., 387n
Hollenbeck, J. R., 223n
Hollerer, M. A., 320n
Holloway, S. S., 94n
Holman, R., 392, 399

Holmes, E., 79, 286n
Holmes, M., 132
Holmes, R. M., Jr., 28n, 322n, 357n, 384n, 387n
Holt, D. H., 256n
Holt, D. T., 385n
Holtbrugge, D., 259n
Holzer, J., 308
Holzinger, I., 67n
Homburg, C., 220n
Hong, J., 355n
Hood, N., 389n
Hook, J., 67n
Hope, O., 200
Hopkins, M. S., 66n
Horn, J., 66n
Hornsby, J. S., 356n, 388n
Hosea, M., 399
Hoshino, Y., 257n
Hoskisson, R. E., 29n, 30n, 88, 89, 95n, 97n, 109, 113, 116, 126n, 127n, 159n, 183, 186n, 189n, 190n, 220n, 221n, 223n, 226, 227, 232, 239, 246, 255n, 257n, 259n, 267, 271, 275, 280, 288n, 319n, 320n, 321n, 323n, 355n, 356n, 357n, 358n, 385n, 386n, 388n, 389n, 412n, 415n, 416n
Hossain, M., 320n
Hotchkiss, E. S., 221n
Hough, J. R., 66n, 126n
House, R. J., 386n
Houston, D., 151–152
Hout, T. M., 68n
Howard, E., 222n
Howell, J. M., 413n
Howell, R. A., 357n
Hoy, F., 358n
Hoyer, W. D., 414n
Hsieh-Lung, L., 222n
Hsu, I.-C., 187n
Hsu, Y., 66n
Huafang, X., 386n
Huang, C.-H., 287n
Huang, X., 68n
Huang, Z., 258n, 285n
Huber, G. P., 65n
Hudomiet, P., 66n
Huff, A., 30n
Huggins, R., 69n
Hughes, A., 415n
Hughes, B., 371
Hughes, C. E., 370
Hughes, J., 210
Hughes, M., 257n, 411n, 416n
Huizingh, E. K. R. E., 392
Hull, J., 189n
Hulland, J., 222n
Hult, G. T. M., 30n, 66n, 126n, 354n, 355n, 387n
Humphery-Jenner, M. L., 322n
Hunbeling, S., 94n
Hung, J.-H., 189n

Hungeling, S., 127n, 387n, 411n, 416n
Hunt, M. S., 69n
Hunter, P., 36
Hurd, M., 361–362, 364
Hurlbert, M., 386n
Hurmelinna-Laukkanen, P., 159n
Hus, D. H., 286n
Huse, M., 319n, 321n
Huseby, T., 127n
Huselid, M. A., 387n, 388n
Hutchings, K., 67n
Hutchins, M. J., 68n
Hutt, M. D., 413n
Hutton, R., 287n
Hutzschenreuter, T., 158n, 188n
Huyghebaert, N., 160n

I

Iannotta, G., 320n
Ibarra, H., 31n
Icahn, C., 308–309, 310
Iger, R., 307
Ignatius, A., 67n, 308
Ihlwan, M., 127n
Ilgen, D. R., 223n
Im, S., 414n
Immelt, J., 9, 163, 327, 372
Inagaki, K., 255n
Inderst, R., 356n
Indjejikian, R. J., 188n
Inkpen, A. C., 30n, 358n
Insead, M. S., 355n
Iravani, S. M., 128n
Ireland, R. D., 28n, 29n, 30n, 32n, 88, 89, 94n, 95n, 109, 113, 116, 126n, 127n, 128n, 157n, 160n, 187n, 189n, 219n, 220n, 222n, 226, 227, 232, 239, 246, 257n, 258n, 267, 271, 275, 280, 285n, 287n, 288n, 354n, 355n, 356n, 357n, 358n, 384n, 387n, 388n, 411n, 412n, 413n, 415n, 416n
Isagawa, N., 323n
Islam, M. Z., 321n
Islam, S. M. N., 321n
Ismail, K. M., 384n
Isobe, T., 67n, 96n
Ito, K., 157n, 256n
Iverson, R. D., 94n, 222n, 223n
Iyer, B., 158n
Iyer, D. N., 322n
Iyer, G. R., 287n
Izosimov, A. V., 29n

J

Jackson, E. M., 96n
Jackson, S. E., 158n, 384n, 387n
Jacobides, M. G., 187n
Jacobson, R., 127n
Jacoby, S. M., 321n
Jaeger, J., 68n

Jain, S., 69n, 416n
Jain, S. C., 105
Janney, J. J., 29n, 189n
Jansen, J. J. P., 387n
Jansen, J. P., 31n
Janssens, M., 97n
Jantunen, A., 159n, 220n
Jardins, J. D., 416n
Jargon, J., 72, 102, 189n
Jaruzelski, B., 392, 399
Jarvis, L., 189n
Jarzabkowski, P., 354n
Javalgi, R. G., 287n
Javidan, M., 94n, 222n, 412n
Jawahar, D., 321n, 323n
Jayachandran, S., 158n
Jayaraman, N., 220n, 255n
Jenkins, M., 414n
Jensen, M., 320n, 385n
Jensen, M. C., 189n, 221n, 319n
Jensen, M. S., 320n
Jensen, P. D. O., 97n
Jeong, E., 387n
Jermias, J., 357n
Jia, H., 128n
Jian, X., 220n
Jiang, G.-L. F., 258n
Jiang, L., 29n, 412n, 413n
Jiang, M. S., 257n, 285n
Jiang, P., 323n
Jiang, R. J., 256n, 285n
Jiang, Y., 256n, 319n
Jianguo, Y., 386n
Jin, K., 96n
Jin, L-Y, 126n
Jindra, B., 356n
Jiraporn, P., 320n, 322n
Jobe, L. A., 128n, 187n, 219n, 415n
Jobs, S., 12, 18, 131, 293, 370, 371, 372
Jog, V., 220n
John, K., 219n
Johnson, J. E., 67n
Johnson, J. L., 288n
Johnson, M. D., 223n
Johnson, M. E., 188n
Johnson, M. W., 412n
Johnson, N. B., 126n
Johnson, R. A., 97n, 188n, 190n, 220n, 221n, 222n, 223n, 319n, 320n, 321n, 355n, 356n, 385n, 386n, 388n, 389n, 415n
Johnson, S., 94n
Johnson, S. G., 320n
Joiner, T. A., 356n
Joireman, J., 127n
Jolly, D. R., 286n
Jonard, N., 127n, 288n, 414n, 415n
Jones, C., 358n
Jones, F., 161n
Jones, T. M., 66n, 95n
Jonsson, S., 159n
Joogsan, O., 67n, 137
Jorissen, A., 322n

Joseph, J., 323n
Josephs, L., 161n
Joshi, A. M., 288n
Joshi, M. P., 355n
Judge, W., 319n, 388n
Julian, S. D., 32n
Julien, P.-A., 411n
Jundt, D. K., 223n
Jung, A., 347, 370
Justis, R. T., 32n
Jwu-Rong, J., 222n

K

Kabst, R., 257n, 258n
Kachi, H., 259n
Kachra, A., 158n
Kacperczyk, A., 65n, 221n, 323n
Kadapakkam, P.-R., 219n
Kaeufer, K., 128n
Kager, P., 188n
Kahai, S. S., 385n
Kahan, M., 190n
Kaiser, U., 97n
Kale, P., 30n
Kalla, A., 66n
Kalyta, P., 322n, 386n
Kambayashi, T., 66n
Kambil, A., 223n
Kamins, M. A., 95n
Kammel, B., 50
Kan, O. B., 259n
Kane, Y. I., 96n, 294, 407
Kang, W., 158n
Kangming, D., 379
Kant, S., 354n
Kanter, M., 338
Kao, J., 29n
Kaplan, R. S., 388n
Kaplan, S., 30n, 69n, 126n
Kaplan, S. N., 223n, 322n
Kapoor, R., 29n, 94n
Kappen, P., 128n, 255n
Kapur, S., 255n
Karakaya, F., 159n
Karandikar, H., 357n
Karim, S., 220n, 356n
Karlgaard, R., 160n
Karnani, A., 160n
Karp, J., 97n
Karri, R., 31n
Ka-shing, L., 168
Kashyap, A., 65n
Kasper, H., 256n
Kathuria, R., 355n
Katila, R., 66n, 157n, 220n, 412n
Kato, Y., 388n
Katsikeas, C. S., 97n, 257n
Katz, D. A., 294
Katz, J. A., 356n
Kaufman, L., 102
Kaufman, S. P., 356n
Kauppila, O.-P., 95n
Kawaller, I. G., 258n
Kay, N. M., 189n
Kayes, D. C., 388n

Keats, B. W., 355n, 386n
Kedia, B. L., 285n
Keels, J. K., 223n
Keil, M., 97n, 414n
Keil, T., 65n, 95n, 189n, 220n, 221n, 321n, 322n, 411n, 414n
Keim, G. D., 31n
Kein, P. G., 388n
Kelleher, H., 144–145
Keller, J. J., 321n
Kellermans, F. W., 385n
Kelley, D., 411n, 413n
Kellogg, A. P., 65n
Kemp, R., 68n, 160n
Kemp, S., 30n
Kempf, K. G., 66n
Kendrick, J., 344
Kennedy, W., 288n
Kenney, M., 222n
Kent, M. A., 304
Keramati, A., 128n
Kesner, I. F., 158n
Ketchen, D. J., 28n, 32n, 126n, 128n, 160n
Ketchen, D. J., Jr., 28n, 30n, 66n, 287n, 387n
Keupp, M. M., 412n
Keuslein, W., 189n
Kezdi, G., 66n
Khadem, R., 355n
Khan, R., 321n
Khanin, D. M., 322n, 388n
Khanna, P., 286n, 319n, 384n
Khanna, T., 188n, 258n
Khanna, V., 322n
Khoury, T. A., 68n, 255n
Khurana, R., 31n
Kidd, D., 385n
Kiechel, W., III, 223n
Kiessling, T., 288n, 386n
Kilduff, G. J., 66n, 127n, 157n
Kiley, D., 28n
Kim, D., 413n
Kim, H., 29n, 287n, 288n, 319n, 323n, 355n, 416n
Kim, J.-Y., 189n, 286n, 288n
Kim, K., 413n
Kim, P. H., 387n, 414n
Kim, W., 319n
Kim, Y. S., 95n, 288n, 320n
Kimberly, S., 167
Kimble, C., 128n, 357n
Kinc, M. H., 96n
King, A. W., 68n, 94n, 96n, 259n
King, D. R., 219n, 221n, 415n
King, R., 66n
Kinkel, S., 187n
Kinley, G., 222n
Kintana, M. L., 186n
Kirillova, O. M., 65n
Kirnan, J., 387n
Kistruck, G. M., 287n, 357n
Kitamura, M., 137, 256n
Klein, A., 387n
Klein, K. E., 127n, 411n, 416n

Klein, P. G., 411n
Kleinbaum, A. M., 355n
Klijn, E., 285n, 322n
Kline, J. P., 188n
Kling, K., 128n
Klonowski, D., 256n
Knapp, J. R., 323n
Knight, D., 385n
Knight, J. B., 67n
Knockaert, M., 411n
Knoedler, J. T., 188n
Ko, E., 255n
Kochhar, R., 387n, 412n
Kok, N., 322n
Koka, B. R., 415n
Koller, T., 223n
Koo, J., 95n, 358n
Koons, C., 286n
Koors, J. L., 321n
Kopczak, L. R., 188n
Kor, Y. Y., 157n
Kosnik, R., 322n
Kosonen, M., 31n, 356n, 385n
Kostova, T., 357n
Kotabe, M., 29n, 94n, 127n,
    128n, 358n, 414n
Kotha, R., 128n
Kotha, S., 160n
Kotter, J. P., 384n, 388n
Kowtha, S., 412n
Koxhikode, R. K., 159n
Koza, M. P., 256n, 358n
Kraaijenbrink, J., 30n, 387n
Kraatz, M., 223n, 388n
Kramer, K. R., 157n
Kratzer, J., 356n
Kretschmer, T., 97n
Kriauciunas, A. P., 30n, 94n,
    127n, 414n
Krishnamurthy, S., 219n
Krishnan, H. A., 219n, 222n,
    223n, 415n
Krishnan, M. S., 30n
Kristal, M., 68n
Kristof-Brown, A. L., 384n
Kroc, R., 364
Kroll, M., 30n, 96n, 321n
Kronborg, D., 287n
Krug, J. A., 322n, 386n
Kruschwitz, N., 66n
Kruse, D. L., 414n
Ksobe, T., 258n
Kubo, K., 323n
Kuemmerle, W., 411n
Kuenzi, M., 388n
Kuhn, T., 31n
Kulkarni, M., 128n
Kumar, M. V. S., 160n, 189n,
    320n
Kumar, N., 221n
Kumar, R., 68n, 289n
Kumar, S., 286n, 354n
Kumar, V. S. A., 97n, 127n, 161n,
    288n
Kumaraswamy, A., 416n

Kunc, M. H., 95n
Kundu, S. K., 97n, 127n
Kuo, Y. C., 189n
Kuratko, D. F., 28n, 354n, 356n,
    388n, 411n, 413n
Kuschel, J., 407
Kuss, M., 68n
Kutcher, E., 387n
Kwanghui, L., 160n
Kwon, S. W., 387n
Kyaw, N. A., 188n
Kyrgidou, L. P., 416n
Kyung-Tae, K., 67n, 137

L

Laamanen, T., 95n, 189n, 220n,
    321n, 322n
Lado, A. A., 30n, 97n
Lafley, A. G., 391
Lafontaine, F., 287n
Lahiri, S., 285n, 286n
Lainez-Gadea, J. A., 285n
Lam, M. L. L., 259n
Lam, S. S. K., 95n
Lamb, C. W. Jr., 126n
Lamberg, J. A., 28n, 66n,
    126n, 160n
Lamont, B. T., 221n, 222n
Lan, L. L., 189n, 319n
Lane, P. J., 29n, 96n, 187n,
    220n, 286n, 357n, 412n,
    414n, 415n
Lange, D., 159n, 319n
Langfield-Smith, K., 288n
Lankau, M. J., 31n, 186n
Lanzolla, G., 158n, 411n
Larcker, D. F., 357n
Larraza-Kintana, M., 320n, 322n
Laseter, T. M., 159n
Latham, S. F., 412n
Lau, A. W., 413n
Lau, C. M., 413n
LaValle, S., 66n
Lavie, D., 259n, 285n, 286n,
    287n, 288n, 358n, 415n
Lawler, E. E., III, 321n
Lawler, E. E., Jr., 386n
Lawrence, P. R., 187n, 355n
Lawson, E., 355n
Lawton, C., 187n
Lay, G., 187n
Layne, R., 164
Lazzarini, S. G., 67n, 159n,
    286n, 358n
Le Breton-Miller, I., 386n
Le Breton-Miller, S., 320n
Le Nadant, A.-L., 223n
Leana, C. R., 388n
Leask, G., 157n
Lechner, C., 287n
Lee, C., 158n
Lee, C.-G., 128n
Lee, C.-H., 187n
Lee, D., 188n, 222n
Lee, E., 379

Lee, G. K., 220n
Lee, H., 157n, 158n, 159n, 259n,
    323n, 357n, 387n, 413n
Lee, H. U., 97n, 385n, 413n
Lee, J., 67n, 69n, 255n, 357n
Lee, J. A., 344
Lee, J. S. Y., 97n, 387n, 415n
Lee, K., 69n, 186n
Lee, M., 31n
Lee, P. M., 96n, 223n, 323n
Lee, R., 411n
Lee, R. P., 288n
Lee, S., 158n, 188n, 356n, 411n
Lee, S. H., 29n, 255n, 258n,
    412n, 414n
Lee, S. K., 321n
Lee, S. M., 411n
Lee, Y.-H., 66n
Leenders, M. M., 414n
Legerer, P., 355n
Lehrer, M., 256n
Lei, D., 126n
Leiblein, M. J., 66n, 158n, 411n
Leiponen, A. E., 32n, 95n, 96n,
    288n, 411n
Lemak, D. J., 356n
Lemmon, M. L., 190n, 320n
Lenox, M. J., 32n, 65n, 68n, 127n
Lentz, P., 126n
Leonard, R. S., 388n
Leondis, A., 308
Leone, R., 161n
Lepak, D. P., 94n
Lepine, J. A., 68n
Leslie, K., 355n
Leslie, T. W. K., 287n
Lester, D. L., 95n
Lester, P. B., 354n
Lester, R. H., 95n, 320n,
    321n, 355n
Letterie, W., 415n
Leuz, C., 256n
Leung, S., 67n
Levicki, C., 356n
Levie, J., 413n
Levin, I. M., 386n
Levinthal, D., 161n, 355n
Levitas, E., 30n, 68n, 97n,
    128n, 257n, 287n, 320n,
    411n, 415n
Levy, M., 167
Levy, O., 94n
Lewin, A. Y., 32n, 127n, 259n
Lewis, M. W., 66n, 323n
Lewis, R., 127n
Ley, B., 388n
Li, D., 160n, 258n, 323n,
    358n, 415n
Li, H., 95n, 219n, 255n,
    385n, 414n
Li, J., 28n, 31n, 69n, 95n, 157n,
    159n, 258n, 287n, 320n,
    358n, 385n, 414n
Li, J. J., 157n, 256n, 288n, 387n

Li, L., 32n, 160n, 258n
Li, M., 258n
Li, P., 160n
Li, X., 222n
Li, Y., 95n, 97n, 255n, 288n
Li, Z., 152
Liao, J., 66n
Liao, S., 69n
Lichtenthaler, U., 257n, 415n
Lie, J. R., 160n
Lieberman, M. B., 30n,
    159n, 220n
Liebeskind, J. P., 223n
Light, J., 407
Lim, E. N.-K., 189n, 222n
Limpaphayom, P., 323n
Lin, H., 157n
Lin, L. H., 221n, 287n, 358n
Lin, X., 257n, 285n
Lin, Y., 285n, 286n
Lin, Z., 285n, 286n
Linebaugh, K., 137, 412n
Ling, H., 159n
Ling, X., 386n
Ling, Y., 384n, 385n
Liou, F.-M., 32n
LiPuma, J. A., 413n
Litan, R. E., 411n
Liu, C., 66n
Liu, J., 415n
Liu, R., 97n, 127n
Liu, Y., 97n, 126n, 288n,
    322n, 356n
Livengood, R. S., 158n
Ljungberg, J., 407
Ljungquist, U., 94n
Lloyd, M. E., 358n
Lo, W., 413n
Lobov, A., 200, 220n
Locander, W., 200, 258n
Locke, E. A., 385n
Locke, R., 97n
Lockett, A., 286n
Lococo, E., 9
Lodish, L. M., 95n
Loeb, M., 32n
Loftus, P., 288n
Lohr, S., 96n, 356n
Lokshin, B., 415n
Long, W. F., 223n
Loomis, C., 164
Lopez, E. J., 188n
Lopez-Duarte, C., 286n
Lopez-Gamero, M., 65n
López-Sánchez, J. I., 187n
Lorange, P., 126n
Lorenzoni, G., 358n
Lorsch, J. W., 355n
Loscher, P., 49
Lour, X., 319n
Louth, N., 13
Love, E. G., 223n, 388n
Love, J. H., 257n
Love, L. G., 157n, 355n, 357n
Loveday, E., 262

Lovvorn, A. S., 256n
Lowenstein, L., 189n
Lu, J. W., 96n, 379, 381
Lu, T., 323n
Lu, Y., 287n, 415n
Lubatkin, M., 68n, 128n, 187n, 188n
Lubatkin, M. H., 159n, 384n
Lubatkin, M. L., 385n
Lublin, J. S., 79, 94n, 294, 372
Lucas, M. T., 65n
Luce, R. A., 69n, 321n
Luckner, S., 66n
Ludema, R. D., 257n
Luffman, G., 355n
Lui, X., 323n
Lui, Y., 386n
Luk, C.-L., 97n, 387n, 415n
Lumineau, F., 285n, 288n, 319n
Lumpkin, G. T., 357n, 388n
Lundberg, D., 160n
Lunnan, R., 259n, 285n, 357n
Lunsford, J., 188n
Luo, X., 159n, 190n
Luo, Y., 29n, 32n, 257n, 358n, 388n
Lupton, N., 286n
Lursinsap, C., 286n
Lusch, R. F., 96n
Lutz, C., 68n, 160n
Lyandres, E., 157n
Lyles, M., 257n, 286n

M

Ma, J., 379, 381
Macauley, M., 288n
MacDuffie, J. P., 288n
MacFadyen, K., 194, 220n, 223n
Machold, S., 319n
Macintosh, G., 159n
Mackay, D., 298
Mackenzie, W. I., 96n
MacKenzie, W. J., 387n
Mackey, A., 31n, 188n, 319n, 384n
Mackey, T. B., 31n
MacMillan, D., 194
MacMillan, I. C., 126n, 149, 153, 158n, 160n, 319n, 385n, 388n, 412n
Madhaven, R., 188n, 222n
Madhok, A., 95n, 97n, 288n
Madsen, P. M., 95n
Madsen, T. L., 66n, 158n, 411n
Maestro, B. M. M., 68n, 385n
Maggitti, P. G., 157n
Magnusson, T., 413n
Mahate, A. A., 219n
Mahmood, I., 188n
Mahoney, D. M., 358n
Mahoney, J. T., 157n
Mahsud, R., 386n
Mainkar, A. V., 68n, 128n
Mair, J., 223n
Majid, S., 66n

Mak, S., 286n, 287n
Makadok, R., 68n, 158n
Makhija, M. V., 29n, 30n, 356n
Makino, S., 67n, 96n, 258n
Makri, M., 29n, 96n, 186n, 187n, 219n, 220n, 286n, 357n, 412n, 414n, 415n
Malhotra, D., 319n
Malhotra, S., 200, 258n
Malik, O., 9
Malone, C. B., 189n
Malone, S., 29n
Mandel, M., 357n
Mangalindan, J. P., 152
Mangematin, V., 411n
Manigart, S., 286n
Mann, J., 338
Manolova, T., 30n
Mansi, S. A., 186n
Manyika, J., 66n
Marathe, A., 288n
Marcel, J. J., 157n, 186n, 319n, 321n, 323n, 385n, 386n
Marchi, G., 160n
Marchick, D., 320n
Maremont, M., 357n
Marginso, D., 221n
Maritan, C. A., 96n
Markens, B., 158n
Markides, C. C., 221n, 357n
Markoczy, L., 385n
Marks, M., 221n
Marmenout, K., 222n
Marr, M., 188n
Marston, S., 152
Martijn Cremers, K. J., 219n
Martin, D., 355n
Martin, J. A., 187n, 221n
Martin, R. L., 294
Martin, S. L., 257n, 411n
Martin, X., 358n
Martin-Consuega Navarro, D., 255n
Martinez-Fernandez, M. T., 387n
Martynova, M., 219n, 322n
Marvel, M. R., 97n
Massey, P., 287n
Massimilian, D., 384n
Massini, S., 259n
Masulis, R. W., 322n
Mata, J., 95n
Mathews, B., 65n, 66n
Mathur, I., 320n
Matsa, D. A., 321n
Matsunaga, S., 321n
Matsusaka, J. G., 321n
Matta, E., 259n, 386n
Matthyssens, P., 32n, 385n
Matuson, R., 102
Matzler, K., 28n
Maula, M. V. J., 65n, 221n, 411n, 413n, 414n
Maurer, C. C., 96n
Maxfield, S., 126n

Maxwell, J. R., 355n
Maxwell, K., 286n
May, R. C., 66n
Mayer, D., 222n
Mayer, H., 411n
Mayer, K. J., 94n, 320n
Mayerowitz, S., 287n
Mayfield, C., 321n
Maynard, M., 412n
Mazzarol, T., 69n
McAulay, L., 221n
McCall, M. W., Jr., 387n
McCann, B. T., 255n
McCarthy, D. J., 29n, 413n
McClellan, B., 67n, 137
McClelland, P. L., 386n
McColgan, P., 223n
McConnon, A., 67n
McCracken, J., 9
McDaniel, C., 126n
McDonald, D., 210
McDonald, M. L., 219n, 222n, 319n, 321n, 384n, 385n
McDonald, R., 66n, 157n
McDonnell, J., 287n
McDougall, P. P., 223n, 411n, 412n
McDowell, M., 287n
McFadyen, M. A., 287n, 411n
McFarland, K., 222n
McGahan, A. M., 28n, 30n
McGee, S., 220n
McGrath, J., 78
McGrath, R. G., 388n, 412n
McGrath, R. S., 158n
McGregor, J., 28n, 126n
McGuire, J., 94n, 287n
McIntyre, D. P., 159n
McKee, A., 384n
McKee, M., 388n
McKee, S., 127n
McKelvie, A., 28n
McKendrick, D., 413n
McKenna, T. M., 66n
McKeown, A., 67n
McKinley, W., 222n
McLaughlin, K., 128n
McNamara, G. M., 69n, 158n, 160n, 219n, 222n, 322n
McNeill, L. S., 287n
McNerney, J., 398
McNulty, T., 321n
McVea, J., 31n
Means, G., 320n
Meek, W. R., 287n
Mehri, D., 127n
Mehta, M., 286n
Mela, C. F., 95n
Melcher, B. A., 159n
Mellahi, K., 159n
Mellewigt, M., 188n
Mendelow, A. L., 388n
Menguc, B., 31n, 414n
Mentzer, J. T., 127n
Merchant, H., 188n

Meschi, P.-X., 258n, 288n
Mesquita, L. F., 29n, 67n, 97n, 158n, 159n, 286n, 358n
Meulbroek, L. K., 322n
Meuleman, M., 223n, 286n, 287n
Meyer, A. D., 414n
Meyer, K., 95n
Meyer, K. E., 30n, 67n, 96n, 219n, 220n, 255n, 258n, 285n, 387n
Meyer, R. E., 320n
Mezias, J. M., 222n
Mialon, S. H., 356n
Michael, T. B., 187n, 189n
Michailova, S., 67n
Michalsin, M. D., 385n
Michel, J., 157n
Milanov, H., 358n
Miles, R. E., 354n
Milidonis, A., 320n
Millar, C. C. J. M., 255n
Miller, A. R., 321n
Miller, C. C., 102, 126n, 189n, 384n
Miller, D., 32n, 159n, 160n, 186n, 187n, 188n, 320n, 355n, 356n, 386n, 387n
Miller, D. J., 186n, 187n
Miller, J. S., 322n
Miller, K. D., 28n, 322n, 355n
Miller, S., 259n
Miller, S. R., 158n, 256n, 323n, 386n
Miller, T., 255n, 259n, 356n, 357n, 416n
Mills, P. K., 355n
Min, S., 159n
Miner, A. S., 288n
Minguela-Rata, B., 187n
Minichilli, A., 319n, 385n
Minow, N., 323n
Mirvis, P., 221n
Misangyi, V. F., Jr., 322n
Misangyl, V. F., 68n
Mische, M. A., 389n
Mishra, A., 66n
Mitchel, W., 287n
Mitchell, J. R., 386n, 411n
Mitchell, R. K., 411n
Mitchell, W., 160n, 219n, 356n, 358n
Mitra, S., 220n, 320n, 338, 415n
Mitsuhashi, H., 288n
Moatti, V., 287n, 358n
Mobley, W. H., 258n, 386n, 387n
Modell, S., 128n
Moeller, S. B., 221n
Moen, A., 269
Moesel, D. D., 220n, 319n, 356n, 415n
Moffett, S., 66n, 262, 286n
Mohr, A. T., 259n
Mol, J. M., 157n
Molina-Azorin, J., 65n
Molina-Morales, F. X., 387n
Moliterno, T. P., 94n, 358n, 384n

Molleman, E., 385n
Mollenkopf, D. A., 159n
Mollering, G., 384n
Momaya, K., 411n
Monatiriotis, V., 258n
Monks, R. A. G., 323n
Monteiro, L. F., 354n
Montgomery, C. A., 32n
Montgomery, D. B., 69n, 96n, 157n, 159n
Montoya-Weiss, M. M., 414n
Moon, S., 412n
Mooney, A. C., 32n
Moonves, L., 307
Mooradian, R. M., 322n
Moore, M. C., 69n, 157n
Moran, J., 372
Morck, R., 255n
Morecroft, J. D. W., 95n, 96n
Morehouse, J., 127n
Morgan, N. A., 126n, 128n
Morgan, R. E., 257n, 411n
Morris, M. H., 411n, 413n
Morris, T., 220n, 256n
Morrison, A., 385n
Morrison, D., 369
Morrison, N. J., 222n
Morrow, J. L., Jr., 94n, 222n, 285n, 384n, 411n
Mors, M., 413n
Morschett, D., 257n
Moschieri, C., 30n, 189n, 223n
Mountford, A., 67n
Moutinho, L., 128n
Moyer, L., 210
Mtar, M., 222n
Mu, S., 132, 414n
Muczyk, J. P., 385n
Mudambi, R., 29n, 94n, 96n, 127n, 255n, 414n
Mudambi, S. M., 95n, 97n, 286n
Mueller, H. M., 319n
Muhlbacher, J., 256n
Muim, C., 189n
Mukherjee, S., 220n
Mulcahy, A., 370
Muller, B., 256n
Muller, H. M., 356n
Muoi, N. P., 67n
Muriel, A., 128n
Murillo-Luna, J. L., 31n, 65n
Murphy, G. B., 29n, 78
Murray, G. C., 413n
Murray, J. Y., 128n
Murshed, F., 222n
Musteen, M., 412n
Muthusamy, S., 321n, 323n
Myers, M. B., 127n
Myers, R., 220n, 222n
Myers, S. C., 319n, 322n

N

Nachum, L., 28n, 255n, 256n, 285n
Nadeau, D., 357n

Nadkami, S., 97n
Nadkarni, S., 30n, 32n, 68n, 355n, 385n, 386n
Naidu, G. M., 413n
Naiker, V., 320n
Nain, A., 68n, 219n
Nair, V. B., 219n
Nakata, C., 414n
Nakazato, M., 323n
Nalebuff, B., 69n
Nanjad, L., 32n
Nanula, R., 255n
Narasimhan, O., 96n
Narayanan, M. P., 322n
Narayanan, V. K., 30n, 67n, 68n, 355n
Narula, R., 96n
Navarro, P., 188n
Naveen, L., 190n, 320n
Navissi, F., 320n
Nazir, M. S., 189n
Ncube, L. B., 388n
Ndofor, H., 157n
Ndofor, H. A., 30n, 94n, 128n, 259n, 387n
Neff, J., 158n, 194
Nemanich, L. A., 222n
Nerkar, A., 288n
Ness, H., 285n
Neubauer, S., 414n
Neville, B. A., 31n
Newbert, S. L., 30n, 160n
Newburry, W., 65n
Newman, N. C., 392
Ng, A. C., 321n
Ng, D. W., 158n, 188n
Ng, L., 320n
Nibler, M., 323n
Nicholas, S., 285n
Nichols-Nixon, C. L., 29n
Nickerson, J. A., 188n
Nicolai, A. T., 223n
Nicolaou, N., 412n
Nidamarthi, S., 357n
Niedermeyer, E., 262
Nielsen, B. B., 258n, 287n
Nielsen, S., 355n
Nielsen, T. M., 388n
Nieto, M. J., 255n, 287n, 288n
Nijssen, E. J., 126n, 356n
Nimeh, G., 158n
Ning, Li, 121–122
Nisar, T. M., 287n
Nishimura, J., 256n
Niththyananthan, K., 286n
Nittoli, J. M., 66n
Nix, N. W., 96n
Nixon, J., 32n
Nixon, R. D., 387n, 412n
Nobeoka, K., 358n
Noble, C. H., 67n, 159n, 411n
Nocera, G., 320n
Noe, R. A., 387n
Noel, M., 159n
Nohria, N., 31n

Nokelainen, T., 28n, 66n, 126n, 160n
Nolan, K., 358n
Nooyi, I. K., 48
Nord, W. R., 31n
Nordqvist, M., 319n
Norman, C., 78
Norris, G., 159n
Northcott, D., 321n
Norton, D. P., 388n
Nosowitz, D., 174, 188n
Novak, S., 187n
Nowland, J., 319n
Nutt, P. C., 95n
Nyberg, A. J., 189n, 222n

O

Obama, B., 35, 45–46, 163
Obermann, R., 197
Obloj, T., 160n
Obodru, O., 31n
O'Brien, J. P., 188n, 189n, 221n, 258n, 320n
Obst, N. P., 220n
Ocasio, W., 158n
O'Connell, A., 186n
O'Connell, V., 257n
O'Connor, E. J., 95n
O'Connor, G., 414n
O'Connor, J. P., 322n
O'Connor, P., 66n
O'Donnell, M., 188n
O'Donnell, S., 322n
Ofori-Dankwa, J. C., 32n
Ogasavara, M. H., 257n
Oh, C. H., 29n, 68n, 256n
Ohnsman, A., 137, 256n
Ojala, A., 257n, 259n
Ojo, B., 219n
Okamuro, H., 256n
O'Keeffe, K., 294
Okhmatovskiy, I., 319n, 321n
Okpara, J. O., 319n
Oldroyd, J. M., 413n
Oler, D. K., 219n
Olian, J. D., 385n
Oliva, R., 414n
Oliver, C., 67n
Olson, B. J., 385n
Olson, E. G., 157n
Olson, E. M., 126n, 354n, 355n
O'Mera, B., 127n
O'Neal, S., 121
O'Neill, H. M., 323n, 355n, 356n
Ong, V., 65n, 66n
Ordonez, L., 388n
Oriani, R., 258n, 287n, 412n
Orlik, T., 379
Ormanidhi, O., 127n
Ormiston, C., 257n
Orricchio, R., 174
Ortqvist, D., 288n, 358n
Ortutay, B., 174, 188n
Osawa, J., 255n, 285n
O'Shaughnessy, K. C., 223n

Osnos, P., 326
O'Sullivan, N., 223n
Otchere, I., 220n
O'Toole, J., 386n
Ouyang, H., 286n
Overall, J., 321n
Owen-Smith, J., 415n
Ozbas, O., 321n
Ozcan, P., 32n, 126n, 288n, 387n, 414n

P

Pacheco-de-Almeida, G., 28n, 159n, 160n
Paez, B. L., 188n
Pai, M., 254
Pak, Y. S., 222n
Pakdil, F., 159n
Palazzo, G., 31n
Palepu, K., 188n
Palich, L. E., 189n
Palmer, M., 189n
Palmer, N., 194
Palmer, T. B., 30n, 66n
Palmisano, S., 371, 372
Pan, X., 219n
Pan, Y., 257n, 285n
Pandit, V., 47–48, 208–210
Pangarkar, N., 160n
Panteva, N., 287n
Parayitam, S., 385n
Parente, R., 128n
Park, B. I., 67n, 158n, 220n
Park, C., 189n
Park, D., 68n, 222n, 223n
Park, J. H., 97n, 385n, 413n
Park, K., 188n, 356n
Park, S. H., 29n, 158n
Parkayastha, D., 338
Parke, Y., 258n
Parker, D., 157n
Parker, S. C., 385n, 414n
Parker, S. K., 95n
Parkhe, A., 415n
Parmigiani, A., 94n, 219n
Parnell, J. A., 95n
Parra-Bernal, G., 200
Paruchuri, S., 416n
Parvinen, P., 355n
Pascale, R. T., 31n
Pastoriza, D., 32n
Paswan, A. K., 287n
Patel, K., 68n
Patel, P. C., 414n
Patel, P. R., 30n
Patsalos-Fox, M., 321n
Pattison, P. E., 357n
Patton, K. M., 66n
Patton, L., 226
Paul, K. B., 399
Payne, A. F., 126n
Payne, G. T., 159n
Peaple, A., 36, 65n, 67n
Pearce, C. L., 385n
Pearce, J. A., II, 310, 322n

Pearson, D., 262, 286n
Pearson, S., 164
Pedersen, T., 97n, 127n, 358n
Peers, M., 219n
Peeters, C., 259n
Pehrsson, A., 186n, 187n
Pendrous, R., 50
Peneder, M. R., 68n
Peng, M. W., 68n, 69n, 95n, 186n, 188n, 219n, 255n, 256n, 257n, 258n, 319n, 323n, 358n, 413n
Peng, S., 68n
PengCheng, Z., 200
Penner-Hahn, J., 259n
Pepper, J., 49
Perdreau, F., 223n
Perez, E., 97n
Perez, P., 68n
Perez-Nordtvedt, L., 286n
Perry-Smith, J. E., 413n
Peteraf, M. A., 69n, 94n
Peters, B., 29n
Petersen, B., 358n
Peterson, A., 258n
Peterson, M. F., 190n
Petkova, A. P., 128n, 160n
Petrick, J. A., 385n
Petrou, A., 67n
Petrova, M., 310
Petruzzelli, A. M., 288n
Pfarrer, M. D., 96n, 322n, 388n
Pfeffer, J., 387n
Pfeiffer, T., 355n
Phan, P. H., 220n, 223n, 320n, 323n
Phelps, C. C., 30n, 289n, 358n
Phene, A., 95n
Philbin, B., 308
Phillips, R. A., 31n, 65n, 94n, 319n
Phillips, S., 29n
Picken, J., 160n
Pierce, A., 57
Pierce, L., 31n
Pil, F. K., 128n, 159n, 388n, 413n
Pinadado, J., 323n
Pinkham, B., 160n
Pinto, J., 388n
Pisano, V., 258n
Piselli, P., 29n
Pistre, N., 187n
Plakoyiannaki, F., 67n
Plambeck, J., 189n
Plambeck, N., 386n
Ployhart, R. E., 94n, 96n, 384n, 387n
Plumridge, H., 269
Podsada, J., 255n
Poletti, M., 159n
Poletti, T., 338
Polidoro, F., Jr., 94n
Pollock, T. G., 96n, 322n, 385n
Pomerantz, D., 132
Ponds, R., 286n

Poon, S. K., 126n
Poppo, L., 288n, 387n
Porac, F., 158n
Porrini, P., 222n
Porter, A. L., 392
Porter, M. E., 28n, 30n, 69n, 96n, 109, 113, 116, 126n, 127n, 157n, 186n, 187n, 231–233, 256n
Porth, S. J., 355n
Portugal, P., 95n
Post, J. E., 384n
Pouder, R. W., 356n
Powell, B., 379
Powell, R. G., 322n
Powell, T. C., 157n
Powell, W. W., 415n
Prabhu, J. C., 221n
Prada, P., 68n
Prahalad, C. K., 96n
Prashantham, S., 257n
Prazdnichnyky, A., 258n
Prechel, H., 220n
Prescott, J. E., 69n, 286n, 415n
Preston, L. E., 384n
Price, R., 412n
Priem, R. L., 66n, 126n, 157n, 322n, 355n, 357n
Priestland, A., 31n
Prince, C., 208–209
Prince, E. T., 387n
Prince, J. T., 287n
Probst, G., 28n, 389n
Prospero, M. A., 29n
Prossner, D., 294
Prussia, G. E., 386n
Pruthi, S., 220n, 258n
Pucik, V., 389n
Puffer, S. M., 29n, 413n
Puranam, P., 96n, 127n, 129n, 187n, 220n, 288n, 354n, 386n, 415n
Puryear, R., 29n
Puthod, D., 285n, 288n
Putz, F., 355n
Puumalainen, K., 159n
Pynnonen, M., 126n
Pyoria, P., 388n

Q

Qian, G., 68n, 255n
Qian, W., 258n
Qian, Z., 68n, 255n
Qiu, L. D., 287n
Qu, H., 69n
Quan, X., 385n
Quang, T., 187n
Quinlan, J. P., 29n
Quinn, J. B., 96n
Quinn, J. F., 385n
Quint, B., 188n

R

Rabinovich, E., 159n
Radner, R., 68n

Radulovich, L., 287n
Raes, A. M. L., 385n
Raff, H., 258n
Rafferty, A. E., 221n, 415n
Raghuvanshi, G., 286n
Rahman, M., 31n
Rahman, N., 285n
Raisch, S., 28n, 355n
Raj, T., 128n
Rajadhyaksha, U., 31n
Rajagopalan, N., 96n, 187n, 189n, 222n, 256n, 321n, 385n, 386n
Rajan, M. V., 357n
Rajan, R. G., 319n, 322n
Rajand, M., 223n
Rajgopal, S., 320n
Rajiv, S., 96n
Ralson, D. A., 256n
Raman, A. P., 96n, 200, 220n, 358n
Ramirez, C. C., 68n
Ramirez, G. G., 386n
Ramsey, M., 137, 412n
Ramseyer, J. M., 323n
Randall, T., 127n, 160n
Rangan, S., 257n
Rank, O. N., 357n
Ransbotham, S., 220n, 415n
Rao, V. R., 160n
Rapoport, H., 67n
Rappaport, A., 221n
Rasheed, A. A., 126n, 319n, 322n
Rauwald, C., 286n
Ravenscraft, D. J., 188n, 223n
Ravichandran, T., 356n
Rawley, E., 97n, 187n, 221n, 320n, 356n, 357n
Raynor, M. E., 186n, 188n
Raznick, J., 326
Ready, D. A., 31n
Reboud, S., 69n
Redding, G., 388n
Reddy, S., 66n
Redfern, K. A., 68n
Reeb, D. M., 186n, 319n, 321n
Reed, J. S., 208–209
Reed, R., 356n
Reese, A. K., 84
Regan, J., 370
Reger, R. K., 158n
Regmi, A., 127n
Regnér, P., 159n
Rego, L. L., 126n, 128n
Rehbein, K., 322n
Reid, E. A., 257n
Reilly, D., 320n
Reilly, W., 35
Reitzig, M., 97n, 127n
Remes, J., 66n
Remneland-Wikhamn, B., 407
Ren, H., 287n, 413n
Renn, R. W., 286n
Renneboog, L., 219n, 322n
Restburg, S. L. D., 221n, 415n

Restrepo, A., 66n
Reuer, J. J., 30n, 127n, 219n, 220n, 285n, 286n, 322n, 358n, 412n, 415n
Reus, T. H., 221n, 222n
Reutzel, C. R., 321n, 386n
Reynolds, S. J., 32n
Rezaee, Z., 320n
Reznichenko, A. A., 372
Rho, S., 69n
Ricadela, A., 68n, 152, 189n, 362
Ricart, J. E., 32n, 157n, 186n
Rice, T., 68n
Richardson, S., 28n
Rico, R., 385n
Ridge, J. W., 94n
Rieker, M., 210
Rigby, B., 174
Rindova, V. P., 94n, 96n, 128n, 132, 157n, 160n, 385n
Ring, P. S., 258n
Riposo, J., 388n
Rising, C., 219n, 415n
Ritala, P., 126n, 287n
Ritson, M., 160n
Rivera-Torres, P., 31n
Rivkin, J., 355n
Rivlin, G., 57
Roberson, Q., 387n
Roberts, D., 384n
Roberts, J., 256n, 321n
Roberts, K. H., 355n
Roberts, P. W., 160n
Robertson, P. L., 30n
Robinnson, S. L., 319n
Robins, G. L., 357n
Robinson, R. B., Jr., 310, 322n
Robinson, S. L., 388n
Robinson, W. T., 159n
Robson, M. J., 257n, 411n
Rocco, E., 158n
Roche, F., 258n, 285n
Rochelle, B., 327
Rock, E. B., 190n
Rockart, S. F., 32n, 127n
Rockoff, J. D., 219n, 287n, 415n
Rod, M., 288n
Rodrigues, S. B., 223n
Rodriguez, A. I., 160n, 255n, 287n
Rodriguez, P., 258n
Rodríguez-Duarte, A., 187n
Roe, R. A., 385n
Roese, J., 8
Rogers, J., 338
Roijakkers, N., 286n
Roll, R., 221n
Rometty, V., 371
Romis, M., 97n
Rooney, J., 72
Rose, E. I., 157n
Rose, E. L., 256n
Rose, L. C., 189n
Rose-Ackerman, S., 189n
Rosen, R. J., 189n, 221n

Rosenbaum, S., 3
Rosenbusch, N., 96n
Rosoff, M., 338
Ross, D., 188n
Ross, S. J., 23
Ross, T. W., 287n
Rosso, B. D., 31n
Rostker, B. D., 388n
Roth, A., 258n
Roth, K., 322n, 357n
Rothaermel, F. T., 94n, 128n, 187n, 219n, 255n, 358n, 392, 414n, 415n, 416n
Rottman, J. W., 289n
Roundy, P. T., 187n, 220n, 415n
Rowe, C., 355n
Rowe, G., 389n
Rowe, W. G., 356n
Rowley, C., 187n
Rowley, T. J., 288n
Roxburgh, C., 66n
Roy, M., 256n
Roy, R., 137
Rubineau, B., 356n
Rübsaamen, C., 414n
Ruckman, K., 322n
Rudea-Sabater, E., 94n
Ruefli, T. W., 94n
Rugman, A. M., 68n, 97n, 255n, 256n, 258n, 355n
Ruhe, J. A., 31n
Ruigrok, W., 355n
Ruiz-Mallorqui, M., 310
Rumelt, R. P., 127n, 166, 186n, 188n, 326, 354n, 356n, 388n
Rungtusanatham, M. J., 68n
Rupp, D. E., 323n
Russell, P., 36
Rust, K. G., 222n
Rutherford, M. A., 319n, 386n
Ryan, M., 258n
Ryman, J. A., 30n
Ryngaert, M., 310
Ryu, S., 288n

S

Sachitand, R., 67n
Sachs, S., 384n
Sacks, D., 167, 194
Sadorsky, P., 31n
Saebi, T., 358n
Sahay, A., 157n
Sahaym, A., 413n
Sahib, P. R., 259n
Saito, T., 323n
Saitto, S., 9
Sajid, K. M., 223n
Salamat, R., 68n
Salmador, M. P., 357n
Salmon, S., 356n
Salomon, R. M., 31n, 94n
Salvador, F., 68n
Sambamurthy, V., 157n
Sambharya, R., 385n

Samora, R., 200
Sanchez, C. M., 222n
Sanchez, R., 128n, 161n
Sanchez-Manzanares, M., 385n
Sandberg, S., 406
Sanders, P., 158n
Sanders, W. G., 95n, 323n
Sandulli, F. D., 187n
Sandvig, J. C., 189n
Sandvik, K., 219n
Sanna-Randaccio, F., 66n
Santala, M., 355n
Santamaria, L., 288n
Santana-Martin, D. J., 310
Santiago-Castro, M., 319n
Santoro, M. D., 66n, 256n, 285n
Santos, J., 413n
Santos, V., 385n
Sapienza, H. J., 30n, 411n, 412n
Saraf, N., 157n
Saran, C., 152
Sarin, S., 414n
Sarkar, M. B., 29n, 65n, 97n, 128n, 288n, 355n, 414n
Sarkar, M. G., 288n
Sasson, A., 31n, 127n
Satariano, A., 372
Sato, S., 411n
Satorra, A., 157n
Savetpanuvong, P., 286n
Sawyer, K., 288n
Sawyers, A., 137
Saxton, T., 221n
Sayles, L. R., 412n
Saylor, S., 68n
Scatz, A., 220n
Scharmer, C. O., 128n
Schechner, S., 79, 286n
Schegelmilch, B. B., 414n
Scheitzer, M. E., 388n
Schendel, D. E., 188n, 356n
Scherer, R. M., 188n
Schijven, M., 219n, 221n, 222n, 415n
Schildt, H., 221n, 414n
Schilling, M. A., 288n, 319n, 357n, 358n
Schindehutte, M., 411n
Schipani, C. A., 322n
Schivardi, F., 68n
Schlegelmilch, B. B., 259n
Schlingemann, F. P., 221n
Schlten, R., 310
Schmid, N. M., 357n
Schmidt, J. A., 221n
Schminke, M., 388n
Schnabel, C., 323n
Schnatterly, K., 320n
Schneider, A., 223n
Schneider, B., 399
Schneider, G., 355n
Schneider, M., 386n
Schoemaker, P. J. H., 30n, 95n
Schoenberg, R., 219n
Scholes, L., 223n

Scholes, M., 189n
Scholnick, B., 97n, 127n, 386n
Schoorman, F. D., 386n
Schrage, M., 157n
Schramm, C. J., 411n
Schramm-Klein, H., 257n
Schreyoegg, G., 285n
Schroeder, R. G., 68n, 411n
Schuker, A. E., 79
Schultz, F. C., 32n
Schultz, H., 101, 125, 225
Schulz, A., 223n
Schulze, W. S., 68n, 128n
Schuman, M., 256n
Schumpeter, J., 142, 158n, 395, 411n, 412n
Schwab, A., 288n
Schwarz, J. O., 66n
Schweitzer, J., 285n
Schwens, C., 257n, 258n
Sciascia, S., 411n
Scifres, E. L., 223n
Scott, P., 413n
Searcey, D., 28n
Sebora, T. C., 411n
Seboui, S., 320n
Sechler, B., 164, 355n
Selden, L., 126n
Selsky, J. W., 28n, 157n
Semadeni, M., 94n, 222n
Sen, B., 414n
Serpa, R., 31n, 356n, 357n, 384n
Seth, A., 223n, 257n
Seung-Kyu, R., 67n, 137
Seward, J. K., 190n
Sexton, D. L., 95n, 220n, 411n, 412n, 413n, 415n
Seyhun, H. N., 322n
Shabana, A., 413n
Shackleton, J., 128n
Shaffer, M. A., 157n, 355n
Shah, A., 344
Shah, O., 315
Shah, R. H., 415n
Shalley, C. E., 413n
Shambaugh, R., 32n
Shambora, J., 159n
Shamir, B., 385n
Shamsie, J., 30n, 160n
Shane, S. A., 412n, 415n
Shank, M., 94n
Shankar, R., 128n
Shankar, S., 257n
Shankar, V., 288n
Shanley, M., 69n
Shao, A. T., 157n
Shapira, Z., 319n
Shapiro, D. M., 258n, 323n
Sharfman, P., 386n
Sharma, D., 157n
Sharma, P., 255n, 412n
Sharma, S., 31n
Shaus, R., 257n
Shaver, J. M., 95n, 189n, 222n, 256n, 257n, 259n, 322n

Shaver, K. G., 66n
Shay, T., 93
Sheehan, N. T., 127n
Sheeran, J., 304
Shekshnia, S., 67n
Shen, M.-J., 252
Shen, W., 386n
Sheng, S., 256n
Shenkar, O., 257n, 412n
Shepherd, D. A., 65n, 95n, 219n, 258n, 286n, 356n, 358n, 386n, 411n
Sherman, E., 29n
Sherr, I., 96n, 152, 269
Shervani, T. A., 187n
Sherwood, A. L., 286n
Shevlin, T., 320n
Shewchuk, R., 69n
Shi, L. H., 256n
Shi, W., 286n
Shields, J., 188n
Shields, M. D., 355n, 388n
Shih, W. C., 356n
Shill, W., 322n, 386n
Shimizu, K., 30n, 126n, 129n, 189n, 219n, 221n, 223n, 256n, 387n, 412n, 415n
Shimizutani, S., 31n, 255n
Shin, H. H., 188n, 356n
Shin, J., 255n, 413n
Shin, N., 187n
Shin, S. J., 356n
Shipilov, A. V., 288n
Shirodkar, A., 286n
Shirodkar, S. A., 66n
Shirouzu, N., 286n
Shiryaevskaya, A., 288n
Shleifer, A., 188n
Shockley, R. L., 66n, 287n, 358n
Shook, C. L., 287n
Short, J. C., 28n, 30n, 66n, 159n, 186n, 221n, 287n, 356n
Shortell, S. M., 128n
Shrivastava, P., 30n
Shropshire, C., 321n, 323n
Shu, X., 323n
Shub, A. N., 355n
Shulman, J. M., 411n, 413n
Sibilkov, V., 320n
Siciliano, J. I., 31n
Sidel, R., 210
Sidhu, I., 326
Siebert, M., 370
Siegel, D. S., 221n, 223n
Siegler, M. G., 362
Siew Kien, S., 68n
Siggelkow, N., 355n, 358n
Silberzahn, P., 413n
Silver, S., 287n
Silver-Greenberg, J., 308
Simmering, M. J., 387n
Simms, J., 67n
Simon, B., 355n, 387n
Simon, D. H., 157n, 287n
Simons, K. L., 221n

Simons, T., 387n
Sims, H. P., 385n
Sims, K. T., 128n
Simsek, Z., 32n, 127n, 159n, 384n, 385n, 386n, 387n
Sin, L. Y. M., 97n, 387n, 415n
Singer, Z., 320n
Singh, H., 129n, 188n, 220n, 287n, 358n, 413n, 415n
Singh, J. V., 30n, 126n, 187n, 398, 412n, 413n
Singh, K., 188n
Singh, M., 320n
Singh, S., 97n
Sinha, K. K., 159n
Sinha, R. K., 67n, 159n, 322n, 411n
Sirkin, H. L., 259n
Sirmans, C. F., 310
Sirmon, D. G., 28n, 68n, 94n, 109, 113, 116, 126n, 128n, 157n, 187n, 189n, 222n, 259n, 285n, 288n, 319n, 321n, 357n, 384n, 385n, 386n, 387n, 388n, 411n, 412n, 416n
Sironi, A., 320n
Sirower, M. L., 221n
Skarmeas, D., 97n
Skill, M. S., 189n
Skovoroda, R., 323n
Slahudin, C., 189n
Slater, S. F., 126n, 354n, 355n, 387n
Sleuwaegen, L., 29n, 158n, 160n
Slevin, D. P., 355n, 356n
Slocum, J. W., Jr., 31n, 126n
Slotegraaf, R., 414n
Smallwood, N., 386n
Smart, S. B., 319n
Smisek, J., 196
Smit, S., 66n, 126n
Smith, J. B., 66n, 321n, 411n
Smith, K. A., 385n
Smith, K. G., 28n, 29n, 94n, 95n, 128n, 157n, 158n, 159n, 160n, 187n, 257n, 322n, 385n, 388n, 413n
Smith, K. T., 96n
Smith, M., 96n
Smith, R., 210
Smith, W. K., 66n
Snow, C. C., 32n, 354n
Sobczak, M., 319n
Sobero, M., 412n
Soda, G., 288n
Soh, C., 68n
Soh, P.-H., 286n, 288n, 384n
Sokoly, T., 322n
Som, A., 416n
Somaya, D., 95n, 288n
Somech, A., 414n
Song, J., 255n, 413n
Song, L. Z., 414n

Song, M., 96n, 160n, 220n, 414n
Song, S., 255n, 285n
Song, W., 221n
Song, Y., 69n
Sonka, S., 158n
Sonnenfeld, J. A., 31n, 186n, 190n
Sorcher, M., 386n
Sorensen, C., 132, 157n
Sorensen, L., 304
Sorescu, A. B., 221n
Souder, D., 322n
Souitaris, V., 68n, 385n
Speaker, B., 112
Spector, B., 3, 97n
Spector, T. D., 412n
Speh, T. W., 413n
Spekman, R. E., 257n
Spence, J., 67n
Spencer, J. W., 126n, 187n, 387n
Spencer, X. S. Y., 356n
Spender, J.-C., 30n, 387n
Spickett-Jones, J. G., 127n
Spiegel, F., 323n
Spillan, J. E., 95n
Spinosa, C., 354n
Spithoven, A., 411n
Srikanth, K., 96n, 187n, 220n, 288n, 415n
Srinidhi, B., 321n
Srinivasan, M., 188n
Srivastava, A., 159n, 385n
Srivastava, M., 67n, 269, 323n
Stahler, F., 258n
Stalk, G., Jr., 187n
Stalker, G. M., 355n
Stallkamp, T. T., 411n, 413n
Stam, W., 412n
Stanford, D., 50, 68n, 255n
Stanton, E. A., 67n
Staples, C. L., 322n
Stathopoulos, K., 320n
Statman, M., 28n
Staw, B. M., 66n, 157n
Staw, B. W., 127n
Steel, E., 287n
Steensma, H. K., 30n, 31n, 257n, 286n, 388n, 413n
Steers, R. M., 94n, 412n
Stefanou, S. E., 127n
Steffens, P., 28n
Stehr, C., 256n
Stein, J., 65n
Steinberg, B., 188n
Steindel, C., 189n
Stellin, S., 286n
Stephan, J., 356n
Stephan, U., 413n
Stephenson, R., 197
Stern, S., 187n
Sternin, J., 31n
Sternquist, B., 258n
Stevens, B., 31n
Stevens, J. M., 31n, 388n

Stewart, T. A., 96n, 358n
Stewart, W. H., 66n
Stieglitz, N., 96n, 414n
Stiles, P., 321n
Stimpert, J. L., 186n, 221n
Stinebaker, K., 96n
Stirling, D., 388n
Stone, B., 68n, 194, 407
Stonebraker, P. W., 355n
Storz, C., 256n
Strahan, P. E., 68n
Strang, S., 129n
Street, V. L., 32n
Stringa, O., 127n
Stringer, H., 372
Stromberg, P., 223n
Strumpf, D., 67n
Strutton, D., 255n
Stubben, S. R., 321n
Stulz, R. M., 28n
Sturman, M. C., 221n
Su, K.-H., 158n
Su, M., 160n
Su, Y., 323n
Suarez, F. F., 158n, 411n
Suarez-Gonzalez, I., 127n
Subramaniam, M., 32n, 69n, 157n, 220n, 414n
Subramanian, A. M., 132, 414n
Subramanian, V., 30n
Sudarsanam, S., 219n
Sueyoshi, T., 66n
Suh, Y. G., 222n
Sull, D. N., 66n, 354n
Sullivan, D. M., 57, 68n 97n
Sun, Q., 323n
Sun, S. L., 127n, 188n
Sung, H., 255n
Sung, T., 319n
Sunhaib, M., 128n
Surroca, J., 95n
Sushil, 411n
Sutcliffe, K. M., 159n, 387n
Sutherland, J. W., 68n
Sutter, C. J., 287n
Sutton, I., 362
Suur-Inkeroinen, H., 28n, 66n, 126n
Svejnar, J., 222n
Svobodina, L., 68n, 97n, 257n
Swaminathan, A., 219n
Swaminathan, V., 222n, 415n
Swoboda, B., 257n
Sydow, J., 285n

T
Takahashi, Y., 262
Takeishi, A., 415n
Takeuchi, R., 31n
Talaulicar, T., 160n
Talley, K., 94n
Tallman, S., 95n, 97n, 256n, 286n, 358n
Tam, P. W., 97n
Tamika, C., 220n

Tan, A., 319n
Tan, D., 285n
Tan, H., 67n
Tan, J., 29n, 69n, 285n, 412n, 413n
Tang, D., 132
Tang, E. Y., 413n
Tang, J., 413n
Tang, M., 219n
Tang, Y.-C., 31n, 32n, 95n, 258n, 385n
Tanlamai, U., 286n
Tanng, Y., 320n
Tanriverdi, H., 158n, 187n
Tanyeri, B., 219n
Tao, Q. T., 285n
Tarzijan, J. J., 68n
Tatoglu, E., 256n
Taylor, A., III, 137
Taylor, C. R., 255n
Taylor, K., 252, 256n
Taylor, M. S., 94n
Taylor, S., 94n
Teece, D. J., 188n, 219n, 356n
Tehranian, H., 219n
Teixeira, A., 413n
Tekleab, A. G., 97n
Tempel, A., 355n
Teng, B. S., 415n
Terjesen, S., 414n
Terlep, S., 94n, 137, 412n
Terpstra, R. H., 256n
Terziovski, M., 159n
Tesfatsion, L., 286n
Thang, L. C., 187n
Theerapatvong, T., 411n
Theodorou, P., 128n
Thirumalai, S., 159n
Thomas, A. R., 287n
Thomas, C., 385n
Thomas, D. E., 157n, 158n, 386n
Thomas, H., 158n
Thomas, J. R., 255n
Thomas, R. J., 387n
Thomas, S., 219n
Thomas, S. E., 223n
Thomas, T. W., 223n
Thomas, W., 200
Thomas-Solansky, S., 128n
Thompson, T. A., 319n
Thomsen, S., 287n
Thornhill, S., 129n, 412n
Thornton, E., 28n
Thottam, J., 187n
Thurm, S., 222n
Thursby, J., 257n
Thursby, M., 29n, 257n, 412n, 413n
Tianle, Y., 258n
Tibken, S., 79, 222n
Tihanyi, L., 31n, 129n, 158n, 190n, 223n, 255n, 257n, 258n, 259n, 286n, 320n, 321n, 355n, 356n, 385n
Tikkanen, H., 28n, 66n, 126n, 160n

Tita, B., 221n, 252, 344
Tiwana, A., 97n, 286n, 287n, 414n, 415n
Tjan, A. K., 31n, 126n
Todd, S. Y., 28n, 160n
Todo, Y., 255n
Toffel, M. W., 28n, 30n, 126n
Toffler, D. G., 388n
Toh, P. K., 94n, 160n
Tomas, G., 355n
Tomassen, S., 259n, 357n
Toms, S., 223n
Tong, T. W., 30n, 69n, 127n, 285n, 286n, 358n
Torrisi, S., 29n, 257n, 288n
Tortorici, V., 219n
Tosi, H. L., 322n
Tosolini, A., 135
Townsend, M., 226
Tozzi, J., 68n
Trachtenberg, J. A., 3, 96n, 97n
Trahms, C. A., 94n, 388n, 411n
Tran, A. L., 322n
Travis, D. V., 128n
Trebeschi, G., 29n
Trevino, L. J., 127n
Trevino, L. K., 32n, 319n, 388n
Trevor, C. O., 222n
Tribo, J. A., 95n
Tripodi, C., 411n
Tsai, K. H., 67n, 221n
Tsai, W., 158n, 412n
Tsai, W. H., 189n
Tsang, E. W. K., 257n, 413n
Tschang, C.-C., 384n
Tse, A. C. B., 97n, 387n, 415n
Tseng, C. Y., 220n
Tsiaplias, S., 67n
Tsui, A. S., 385n, 416n
Tsui-Auch, L. S., 384n
Tuan, N. P., 95n, 96n
Tucci, C. L., 259n
Tucci, L., 385n
Tuggle, C. S., 386n
Tuna, C., 152
Tunisini, A., 384n
Tuppura, A., 159n
Turck, T. A., 285n, 289n
Turner, E., 121
Turner, K. L., 356n
Turner, M., 200
Turner, S. F., 160n
Tuschke, A. C., 323n
Tushman, M. L., 355n
Tuunanen, M., 358n
Tyler, B. B., 68n

U

Ucbasaran, D., 412n
Uhlaner, L. M., 413n
Uhlenbruck, K., 30n, 129n, 222n, 256n, 258n, 387n, 412n
Ulrich, D., 386n, 388n
Ulwick, A. W., 127n, 128n
Un, C. A., 30n, 128n

Ungson, G. R., 355n
Uotila, J., 65n, 411n
Upadhyay, A., 321n
Urbany, J. E., 69n, 157n
Useem, M., 160n, 413n
Ushijima, T., 219n

V

Vaaler, P. M., 160n
Vafai, K., 319n
Vaghely, I. P., 411n
Vaidyanath, D., 285n, 415n
Vaidyanathan, G., 127n
Valenti, M. A., 321n
Valentini, G., 255n
Valikangas, L., 97n
Van Alstyne, M., 65n
van de Gucht, L. M., 160n
Van de Laar, M., 219n
Van den Abbeele, A., 288n
van den Bosch, F. A. J., 285n, 322n, 387n
Van der Laan, G., 31n, 386n
Van der Vegt, G. S., 385n
Van Ees, H., 31n
van Essen, M., 255n
Van Iddekinge, C. H., 96n, 387n
Van Looy, B, 97n
Van Oijen, A. A., 187n
van Olffen, W., 96n
van Oort, F., 286n
van Oosterhout, J., 255n
van Oyen, M. P., 128n
van Putten, B., 158n
van Witteloostuijn, A., 31n, 159n, 259n
Vance, A., 95n
Vanden Bergh, R. G., 65n, 67n
Varadarajan, P. R., 158n
Vassolo, R. S., 158n, 160n, 258n, 287n, 388n
Vasudeva, G., 288n
Vazquez, L., 287n
Veiga, J. F., 159n, 384n, 385n
Veiga, K. L., 384n
Veliyath, R., 189n
Veloso, F. M., 187n
Venkatesan, R., 161n
Venkatraman, N., 158n , 414n
Vera, D., 31n, 32n, 222n
Verbeke, A., 97n, 255n, 256n, 355n
Verbeke, W., 30n, 386n
Verdin, P., 30n
Verhofen, M., 186n
Vermeulen, F., 220n, 222n
Vernon, R., 228, 255n
Verwaal, E., 386n
Verwall, E., 30n
Veugelers, R., 66n
Vidal-Suarez, M. M., 286n
Vigano, R., 321n
Viguerie, P., 126n
Viguerie, S. P., 189n
Vilanova, L., 31n

Villalonga, B., 320n
Visconti, F., 411n
Vishny, R. W., 188n
Vishwanath, V., 96n
Vissa, B., 65n
Viviano, E., 68n
Vogt, C., 415n
Volberda, H. W., 97n, 285n, 322n, 387n
Vonortas, N. S., 95n, 288n
Voola, R., 288n
Vroom, G., 255n
Vuocolo, J., 189n
Vyas, D., 200

W

Waddock, S., 95n
Wade, J., 413n
Wade, J. B., 322n
Wagner, J., 355n
Wagner, S., 97n
Wagner, U., 255n
Wagner, W., 320n
Wahab, M. I. M., 128n
Wakeman, S., 286n
Waldeck, A., 219n, 415n
Walden, R., 220n
Waldman, D. A., 222n, 384n, 386n
Waldmeir, P., 121
Walgenbach, P., 355n
Walker, R. M., 220n
Wallace, J., 159n
Waller, E. R., 187n, 189n
Walsh, J. P., 31n, 68n, 190n, 222n, 319n, 322n
Walter, I., 357n
Walters, B. A., 66n, 96n, 321n
Wan, W. P., 30n, 159n, 186n, 190n, 220n, 221n, 255n, 288n, 323n, 356n
Wang, C., 322n
Wang, C. L., 257n, 285n
Wang, C.-F., 259n
Wang, E. Z., 320n
Wang, F., 159n, 255n
Wang, H. C., 128n, 186n, 357n, 385n
Wang, J.-C., 67n, 221n
Wang, K., 96n
Wang, Q., 320n
Wang, Y.-S., 187n, 258n, 285n
Ward, A. J., 31n, 186n, 190n
Ward, S., 30n
Warner, M., 187n
Warneryd, K., 356n
Wasburn, M. H., 388n
Wasserman, N., 190n
Wassmer, U., 286n
Wasti, S. A., 97n
Wasti, S. N., 97n
Waters, R., 194, 372
Watkins, M. D., 222n
Watson, N., 414n
Weaver, G. R., 32n, 388n

Webb, J. W., 29n, 128n, 157n, 287n, 319n, 355n, 358n, 385n, 388n, 411n, 412n, 416n
Webber, A. M., 96n
Webber, B., 158n
Weber, J., 320n
Weber, K., 386n
Weber, L., 320n
Webster, C., 414n
Wei, C.-P., 66n
Wei, D., 379
Wei, S.-J., 319n
Wei, Z., 97n
Weibel, A., 355n, 388n
Weick, K. E., 159n
Weigelt, C., 65n, 97n, 222n, 285n
Weil, P., 68n
Weill, S. I., 208–209
Weingart, L. R., 414n
Weinhardt, C., 66n
Weisbach, M. S., 322n
Weisman, J., 36
Weiss, R., 50
Welborne, T. M., 322n
Welch, J., 31n, 356n, 369, 372, 386n
Welch, S., 31n, 356n, 386n
Welpe, I. M., 257n
Wennberg, K., 414n
Werder, A. V., 160n
Werdigier, J., 386n
Werema, S., 223n
Wernerfelt, B., 160n, 189n
Werther, W. B., 385n
Westgren, R., 158n
Westhead, P., 412n
Westney, D. E., 256n
Westphal, J. D., 128n, 219n, 222n, 319n, 321n, 384n, 385n, 386n
Wezel, F. C., 95n, 358n
Whalen, J., 220n
Whelan, R., 286n
White, A., 414n
White, C., 256n
White, M. A., 66n
White, R. E., 129n, 158n, 190n, 223n, 355n
Whitford, D., 36
Whitman, M., 181, 370, 384
Whitney, J. O., 356n
Whittington, K. B., 415n
Whittome, J. R. M., 126n
Wiersema, M. F., 190n, 223n, 255n, 258n, 320n, 357n, 388n
Wiggins, J., 187n
Wiggins, R. R., 94n
Wijnberg, N. M., 96n, 157n, 288n
Wiklund, J., 219n, 258n, 286n, 358n, 414n
Wilkerson, D. B., 189n
Wilkinson, A., 159n
Wilkinson, T. J., 287n
Willatt, T., 68n
William, M., 67n

Williams, C., 158n, 255n, 411n, 412n, 414n
Williams, C. A., 323n
Williams, D., 69n
Williams, I., 67n
Williams, J. R., 160n, 188n, 286n
Williams, M. A., 187n, 189n
Williams, P., 223n
Williamson, I. O., 128n
Williamson, O. E., 187n, 188n, 221n, 319n, 356n
Williamson, P. J., 200, 220n, 357n, 413n
Willis, R. J., 66n
Wilstrom, P., 220n
Wiltbank, R., 94n, 132
Wincent, J., 288n, 358n, 412n
Wingfield, N., 13, 66n, 132, 194, 294
Winslow, G., 68n
Winter, S. G., 95n
Wiseman, R. M., 97n, 319n, 320n, 322n
Withers, M. C., 189n
Witt, P., 323n
Wittman, C. M., 287n
Woiceshyn, J., 95n
Wolf, J., 357n
Wolff, M. F., 357n
Wolfson, M., 189n
Wolter, C., 187n
Wong, P.-K., 384n
Woo, C. Y., 29n, 158n, 187n
Wood, G., 223n
Wood, M. S., 385n
Wood, R. E., 95n, 387n
Woods, T., 220n
Woodside, A., 187n
Woodward, J., 355n
Woody, T., 164
Woolley, J., 29n, 355n
Worthen, B., 13, 79, 152, 362, 372
Wowak, A. J., 189n, 386n
Woyke, E., 9
Wright, J., 287n
Wright, M., 28n, 126n, 220n, 223n, 258n, 259n, 286n, 287n, 412n
Wright, P. M., 30n, 96n, 321n, 356n, 388n

Wright, S., 69n
Wruck, K. H., 223n
Wu, D., 128n
Wu, F., 29n, 94n, 127n, 186n, 258n, 357n
Wu, H., 288n
Wu, J. B., 320n, 385n
Wu, S. D., 66n, 385n
Wu, T., 95n
Wu, X., 323n
Wu, Z., 222n
Wurgler, J., 219n
Wysocki, P., 256n

X

Xia, J., 285n
Xie, F., 322n
Xin, K. R., 385n
Xu, D., 158n, 188n, 320n, 323n
Xu, K., 69n, 387n
Xu, L., 385n
Xu, M., 65n
Xu, W., 220n

Y

Yago, G., 221n
Yam, R. M., 413n
Yan, Y., 286n, 287n
Yang, H., 30n, 188n, 285n, 286n
Yang, J., 323n, 344, 387n
Yang, R., 126n
Yannopoulos, P., 159n
Yao, J., 323n
Yao, X., 412n
Yarbrough, C., 288n
Yarrow, J., 362
Yasu, M., 372
Yau, O. H. M., 97n, 387n, 415n
Ybarra, C. E., 285n, 289n
Ye, J., 257n
Yeaple, S., 413n
Yeung, B., 255n
Yeung, P. C, 321n
Yi-Min, C., 68n
Yin, X., 356n
Yishi, T., 95n
Yiu, D., 30n, 319n, 386n, 389n
Yiu, D. W., 186n, 221n, 323n, 356n, 413n
Yiu, W., 220n
Yoo, J. W., 356n
York, J. G., 69n

Yoshi, T., 96n
Yoshikawa, T., 188n, 221n, 258n, 319n, 320n, 322n
You, H., 320n
Younassi, O., 388n
Young, C., 69n
Young, D., 186n, 188n, 356n
Young, G., 157n
Young, J. C. K., 95n
Young, M., 323n
Young, S., 257n
Yousuf, H., 226
Yu, L., 414n
Yu, T., 32n, 69n, 157n, 220n, 355n, 357n
Yuan, W., 97n
Yucel, E., 323n, 386n
Yueh, L., 67n
Yuening, J., 57, 68n
Yukl, G., 386n

Z

Zabinski, E., 220n
Zacharia, Z. G., 96n
Zack, M. H., 97n
Zaheer, A., 222n, 256n, 257n, 287n, 358n
Zaheer, S., 256n, 257n
Zahir, S., 221n
Zahra, S. A., 30n, 65n, 96n, 220n, 221n, 223n, 321n, 388n, 411n, 412n, 413n, 414n
Zaidi, K., 66n
Zajac, E. J., 320n, 323n, 356n, 358n, 385n, 386n
Zalewski, D. A., 188n
Zamaora, V., 320n
Zamiska, N., 257n
Zanarone, G., 287n
Zander, I., 128n
Zander, L., 97n, 220n
Zander, U., 97n, 220n
Zardkoohi, A., 95n, 321n
Zattoni, A., 321n
Zatzick, C. D., 94n, 222n, 223n
Zax, D., 164
Zeithaml, C. P., 96n
Zeller, T., 164
Zellweger, T., 319n
Zelner, B. A., 67n, 255n
Zemsky, P., 28n
Zen, F., 69n

Zenger, T. R., 188n
Zhang, H., 32n, 387n
Zhang, J., 152, 200, 286n, 358n, 384n
Zhang, L., 160n
Zhang, T., 323n
Zhang, X., 66n, 388n
Zhang, Y., 28n, 95n, 127n, 255n, 256n, 320n, 321n, 385n, 386n, 388n
Zhang, Z-X., 385n
Zhao, J., 222n
Zhao, M., 255n
Zhao, W., 321n
Zheng, P., 255n
Zheng, Y., 128n, 415n
Zhoa, X., 188n
Zhou, C., 159n, 200, 358n, 414n
Zhou, D., 158n
Zhou, H., 356n
Zhou, K. Z., 29n, 94n, 127n, 157n, 186n, 256n, 288n, 357n, 387n
Zhou, L., 415n
Zhou, L.-A., 95n, 255n
Zhou, Y., 222n
Zhou, Y. M., 187n, 221n, 357n
Zhu, D. H., 68n, 157n
Zhu, H., 219n
Zhu, P., 220n
Zhu, P.-C., 258n
Zied, G., 94n
Ziedonis, R. H., 411n
Zigmond, J., 67n
Ziobro, P., 30n
Zirpoli, F., 160n, 286n
Zmuda, N., 68n
Zolkiewski, J., 384n
Zollo, M., 95n, 129n, 219n, 220n, 221n, 415n
Zook, C., 32n, 355n
Zott, C., 30n, 96n, 127n
Zou, H., 255n, 259n, 323n
Zou, J., 96n
Zou, S., 256n, 259n
Zoumas, B. L., 127n
Zu, D., 257n
Zuckerman, G., 322n
Zuniga-Vicente, J. A., 69n
Zuoping, X., 31n
Zutter, C. J., 221n, 319n
Zweig, P. L., 188n

COMPANY INDEX

A

AB Volvo, 278
Ace Hardware, 277
Acer, 57, 104, 199
Adidas, 121–122
ADT, 144
Advance Publications Inc., 78
Aetna Inc., 58
AFC Enterprises, 214
Affiliated Computer Services, 202, 203
Airborne Express, 138
Airbus, 55, 58, 87, 142, 230, 244
AirTran, 218–219
Akamai, 147–148
Albertson's, 145
Alcatel-Lucent, 276
Alibaba, 378, 379
All Nippon Airways (ANA), 270
Altria Group Inc., 217, 218
Amazon.com, 3–4, 40, 47, 79–80, 91, 103, 104, 105, 111, 112, 114, 132, 151, 174, 194, 198, 325, 395
American Airlines, 108
Amerilink Telecom Corp, 8
AmerisourceBergen Corp., 217
Amylin Pharmaceuticals, 281
Ann Taylor, 120
Anne Fontaine, 120
AOL Inc., 174, 179, 218
Apple Inc., 3, 6, 11–13, 16, 39–40, 47, 56, 59, 83, 116, 131, 132, 133, 134, 141, 152, 173, 174, 181, 193, 293, 371, 391, 396, 401
Arkansas Best, 138
Asahi Group Holdings Ltd., 248
AstraZeneca, 407
AT&T, 197, 198
Auntie Anne's, 214
Automatic Data Processing Inc., 217
AutoNation, Inc., 137
Aviat Networks Inc., 218

Avis, 276
Avon, 347

B

Baidu Inc., 265
Bajaj Auto Ltd., 262, 272
Baker Hughes, 371
Banco do Brasil, 200
Banco Santander, 199
Barnes & Noble, 3–4, 91
Bavaria, 47
Best Buy, 180
BHP Billiton, 200
Big Lots Inc., 111
BMW Group, 137, 263
Boeing, 55, 58, 87, 142, 146, 230, 244
Borders, 3–6, 91, 325–326, 330
Boston Consulting Group (BCG), 185
BP Plc, 281, 282
Brazil national development bank (BNDES), 200
Bristol-Myers Squibb Co., 218
British Petroleum (BP), 35–36
Broadridge Financial Solutions Inc., 217
BSF AG, 315
Bucyrus International, Inc., 206
Burger King, 58

C

Cadbury, 153, 172
Cadillac, 137
Caesar's Entertainment, 104
CalPERS, 302, 309
Campbell Soup Co., 72, 168, 369
Canon, 131
Cardinal Health Inc., 218
CareFusion Corp., 218
Cargill, Inc., 49
Carrefour, 140, 228
Carvel, 214
Castle Lager, 47
Caterpillar, Inc., 82, 116, 140, 206

CEMEX, 235–236
Cephalon, 196, 201, 202, 206, 405
Champs Sports, 121
Chaparral Steel, 82
Chico's, 120
China National Chemical Corporation (ChemChina), 199–200
China National Tobacco Corporation (CNTC), 240
China YCT International, 313
Choice Hotels, 407
Chrysler Corporation, 135, 136, 262, 276
Chrysler Group LLC, 4, 38
Cinnabon, 214
Circuit City, 21
Cisco Systems, 78, 202, 203, 211–212, 279, 315, 336–337, 339, 407
Citi Holdings, 209, 210
Citicorp, 208, 209
CitiFinancial, 209
Citigroup, 47–48, 208–210, 213, 214
Clorox Co., 308–309, 391
Coach Inc., 118
Coca-Cola, 18, 53, 58, 87, 132, 138, 229
Colgate-Palmolive, 41, 53, 105
Comcast, 7
ConAgra, 391
Condé Nast, 78
Coniexpress S. A. Industrias Alimenticias, 47
Continental Airlines, 62, 108, 132, 195–196
Continental Lite, 108
Converteam, 163
Con-way Inc., 138
Costco, 111, 145
Covidien PLC, 217
Crate & Barrel, 82
CVC Capital Partners Ltd, 209
CVS, 354

D

DaimlerChrysler, 210
Danaher, 177
Darden Restaurants, Inc., 139
Dawning Information Industry, 391, 396
DB Realty, 313
Dell Inc., 52, 56–57, 59, 62, 147, 151, 173, 181, 199, 266, 329
Delta, 108, 132
Deutsche Bank, 205
Deutsche Lufthansa AG, 270
Deutsche Post World Net, 138
Deutsche Telekom AG, 197
Devon Energy, 200
DHL, 138, 173
Dimension Films, 175
Discover Financial Services, 217
Dollar General, 112
Dollar Store, 111, 114
Dollar Tree, 112
DoubleClick, Inc, 194
Dropbox, 151, 152
Drummond Company Inc., 266
Duferdofin, 267
Duferdofin - Nucor S.r.l., 267
Duke Energy Corp., 217
Dunkin Donuts, 125–126
DuPont, 200, 333

E

E. S. Kluft & Company, 75
Eastbay, 121
eBay, 47, 174, 179, 181, 193, 384
Edu-Science, 241
Electronic Arts (EA), 270, 272
Eli Lilly & Co., 281
Empresas ICA, 315
Enron, 313
Epocrates, 391, 396
Ericsson, 211
Ernst & Young, 200
EuroBank, 200
EW Scripps Co., 218
Exxon, 36

F

Facebook, 53, 57, 102, 104, 173, 174, 193, 194, 205, 391, 396, 406
Family Dollar, 112
FedEx, 138, 172–173, 205, 244, 276
Fiat SpA, 262, 276, 345
Fidelity National Information Services Inc., 218
Flextronics, 173
Foot Locker, 121
Ford Motor Company, 4, 18, 135, 136, 173, 184, 230, 345
Forestar Group Inc., 217
Fortis, 199
Fox, 186
Frito-Lay, 48, 50
Frontier Communications Corp., 218
Fujitsu Ltd., 264
Fujitsu Siemens Computers B.V., 264–265
Fujitsu Technology Solutions, 264

G

Gap Inc., 78
General Electric (GE), 7, 9, 163–164, 168, 171, 176, 184, 327, 368, 369, 372
General Mills Inc., 72, 274, 391
General Motors (GM), 4, 38, 45, 72, 135, 136, 137, 167, 173, 328, 333, 354, 374
Genzyme, 203, 205
Gillette, 39, 202, 203
GlaxoSmithKline, 391
Global Partner Network, 279
Godiva, 153
Goldman Sachs, 205
Google, 39–40, 56, 132, 134, 142, 173, 174, 193–194, 391, 396, 406
Goya Foods, 118
Green Mountain, 101, 102
Green Truck, 119
Greif & Company, 118
Greyhound Lines Inc., 110
Groupon, 174, 194, 391, 396
Guaranty Financial Group Inc., 217

H

H. J. Heinz Company, 47
Haier Group, 251–252
Halliburton Co., 36, 217
Hamilton Sundstrand, 202
Harley-Davidson, 54, 81
Harris Corp., 218
Hasbro, 272
HCL Technologies, 265
HealthSouth, 313
Hershey, 153

Hewlett-Packard (HP), 52, 56–57, 59, 62, 78–79, 118, 147, 150, 151–152, 172, 181, 199, 265, 337, 361–362, 367
Hill's Pet Nutrition, 105
Hitachi, 59
Hollywood Pictures, 175
Honda, 47, 54, 135, 172
HSN Inc., 186, 218
Huawei Technologies, 8–9, 337
Hugo Boss, 82
Hulu.com, 56, 268, 272, 284
Huntington Ingalls Industries Inc., 218
Hutchison Whampoa Limited (HWL), 168
Hyatt, 276
Hyundai Motor Corporation, 106, 136, 137, 143

I

IAC/InterActiveCorp., 186, 218
IBM, 52, 57, 82, 90, 147, 151, 152, 184, 199, 279, 371
IKEA, 119, 120, 228, 348
InfoSys, 254
Intel, 62, 173, 374, 399
International Aero Engines (IAE) consortium, 230
Interval Leisure Group Inc., 218
IronPort Systems Inc., 202
Itochu Corp., 266

J

JA Solar, 242
Jack in the Box, 254
Jaguar, 198
JBS, 200
JetBlue, 108, 132, 138
Juniper Networks, 337

K

Kazoo Toys, 119
KBR Inc., 217
Kellogg Company, 274, 298
Keystone Foods, 200
Kia Motors, 110
Kimberly-Clark, 391
Kodak, 131
Komatsu Ltd., 82, 140, 241
Kraft Foods Inc., 166, 217
Kroger, 145

L

Land Rover, 198
LDK Solar Co., 242
Lender Processing Services Inc., 218
Lenovo, 59, 199
Level 3 Communications, 147
Lexus, 233–234
LG Company, 153, 343, 344
Li Ning Company, 121–122
Limagrain, 241–242
Limelight Networks, 147

LinkedIn, 194, 406
Liz Claiborne, 120
LNP, 18
Lucent, 211

M

Mahindra & Mahindra Ltd., 262
Mail Boxes Etc., 205
Makhteshim Agan Industries, 200
Marathon Oil Corp., 218
Marathon Petroleum Corp., 218
Marfrig, 200
Mars, 153, 166, 172
Marshall & Ilsley Corp., 217
Mary Kay Cosmetics, 395
Matsushita, 59
McDonald's Corporation, 14, 18, 24, 49, 58, 71–72, 86, 200, 253, 351, 364
McKinsey & Co., 82, 116
Mead Johnson Nutrition Co., 218
Medtronic, 201
Mercedes, 137
Merck, 106, 149, 168, 180
Metavante Technologies Inc., 217
MetroJet, 107
Microsoft, 7, 39–40, 62, 82, 105, 132, 147, 173, 174, 179, 181, 193, 194, 268–269, 282, 284–285, 406
Millicom Ghana Ltd., 276
Minnesota Mining and Manufacturing Co., 398–399
Mitsubishi, 59, 210, 261
Moe's Southwest Grill, 214
Morgan Stanley, 205, 209, 217
Motorola, 8, 56
Motorola Mobility Holdings Inc., 218
Motorola Solutions Inc., 218
MSNBC, 7
MTV Networks, 78
Mustang Engineering, 86
MySpace, 102, 104, 406

N

Narang, 47
National Semiconductor, 195
NBC Universal, 7, 268
NCR Corp., 217
NEC, 59
Nestle, 153, 172
Netflix, 40, 56, 104, 174, 198, 391, 396
News Corporation, 268
Nike, 121–122, 391
Ningbo Bird, 199
Nintendo, 132, 142, 272
Nissan, 135, 261–262, 272, 274–275, 282, 391, 396
Nokia, 40, 56, 268–269, 282, 328, 399
Nomura Securities, 312
Nordstrom Inc., 82

Nortel, 211
Northrop Grumman Corp., 218
Novartis AG, 272
NTT DoCoMo Inc., 265
Nucor, 266, 267
NutraSweet, 55
NVR Inc., 273
Nycomed, 229

O

OAO Rosneft, 281, 282
OneWorld Alliance, 270, 284
Oprah Winfrey Network (OWN), 78
Oracle, 52, 57, 62, 151, 152, 197, 329
Oratech, 391
Otis Elevator Co., 82, 202

P

Palm, 152
Paramount Pictures, 186
Patriot Coal Corp., 217
Peabody Energy Corp., 77, 217
Penguin Group, 85
PepsiCo, 48, 53, 58, 87, 132, 138, 229
Petrobras, 200
Pfizer, 272
PharMerica Corp., 217
Philip Morris International (PMI), 40, 218, 240
Philips, 132
Pilgrim's Pride, 200
Ping An, 199
1020 Placecast, 276
Polaroid Corporation, 76
Porsche, 136, 381
Potash Corporation, 200
Pratt & Whitney, 202, 230, 278
Primerica, 209
Procter & Gamble (P&G), 7, 9, 39, 41, 49–50, 53, 82, 83–84, 87, 135, 168, 171, 194, 202, 203, 391, 392–393, 404
Providence Equity Partners, 268
PSA Peugeot Citroen, 345
Publicis Groupe S.A., 167, 168

Q

QEP Resources Inc., 218
Qingdao Refrigerator Company, 251
Quaker Foods North America, 274
Questar Corp., 218
QVC, 186

R

Ralcorp Holdings Inc., 274
Ralph Lauren Corp., 82, 116
Reliance ADA Group, 313
Reliance Industries, 36
Relsys, 197
Renault, 261–262, 272, 274–275, 282

Renault-Nissan, 273, 276
Research In Motion (RIM), 39, 56, 134
Rio Tinto Group, 228, 314–315
Roark Capital Partners, 214
Rosneft Corporation, 36
Royal Bank of Canada, 315

S

SABMiller, 47
Safeway, 145
SAIC, 199
Sajan, 199
Salesforce.com, 152
Sam's Club, 114
Samsung, 56, 59, 132, 153, 168
Samuel Electric, 273
Sanofi-Aventis, 203, 205
Santaris Pharma A/S, 272
SAP, 152, 329
Sara Lee, 181
SAS Institute, 106–107
Satyam, 313
Schlotzky's, 214
Scripps Networks Interactive Inc., 218
Sears Holdings, 341
Seattle's Best Coffee International, 214
Sementes Guerra, 241
Siemens AG, 49, 177, 264, 392
Sikorsky, 202
Silver Age Holdings, 242
Silver Lake, 193
SimpliSafe, 144
Singapore Airlines, 270
Skype, 179, 181, 193
SkyTeam Alliance, 62, 270, 284
Smith Barney, 209
Snaptu, 194
Solar Power Inc. (SPI), 242
Solar Silicon Valley Electronic Science and Technology Co., Ltd., 242
Song, 108

Sony, 59, 82, 131–132, 133, 142, 237, 372
Sony Ericsson, 132, 142
Southwest Airlines, 22–23, 86, 107–108, 132, 138, 145, 218–219
SPANX, 410
Spectra Energy Corp., 217
Sprint, 197
SsangYong Motor Company, 199
Stafford General Hospital, 318
Stanley Black & Decker, Inc., 392
Star Alliance, 62, 270, 284
Starbucks, 101–102, 106, 125, 225, 236
State Street Corporation, 209
Subway, 71–72, 79–80, 200
Sun Microsystems, 52, 57, 62, 151, 197
SunHealth Solutions, 391
Swift, 200
Synovus Financial Corp., 218

T

Takeda, 229
Tandberg, 202
Target, 85, 111, 112, 120, 145
Tata Motors, 137, 198
TE Connectivity Ltd., 217
Telefónica, 199
Temple-Inland Inc., 217
Teradata Corp., 217
Terex Corp., 206
Tesco, 40
Teva Pharmaceuticals, 196, 201, 202, 208, 405
Texas Instruments, 195
Textron Inc., 168, 343
Thales SA, 244
Thomson Consumer Electronics, 82, 199
3Leaf, 8
3M, 72, 398–399, 401, 404
TIAA-CREF, 309

Ticketmaster Entertainment Inc., 218
Time Warner, 23, 179, 218
Time Warner Cable Inc., 218
TLC Corporation, 199
T-Mobile, 197, 198
TomTom, 131
Toshiba Corp., 273
Total System Services Inc., 218
Touchstone Pictures, 175
Toyota, 47, 115–116, 131, 135, 136, 137, 143, 156, 233–234, 237, 244, 250, 350, 399
Trane Inc., 217
Transocean, 36
Travelers Group, 208, 209
Tree.com Inc., 218
Twitter, 53, 57, 194, 391, 396, 406
2Wire, 8
Tyco International Ltd., 217

U

Under Armour, 335
Unilever, 41, 50, 235
Unitech, 313
United Airlines, 62, 108, 132, 138, 195–196
United Parcel Service (UPS), 138, 166, 172–173, 205, 244
United Phosphorus (UPL), 199–200
United Shuttle, 108
United Technologies Corp. (UTC), 168, 176, 202, 203, 207
U.S. Airways, 107
U.S. Steel, 266
USAA, 103
UTC Fire & Security, 202
UTC Power, 202

V

Valeant Pharmaceuticals, 196, 206
Verizon, 197, 218

Vestas Wind Systems A/S, 315
Viacom Inc., 78, 307
Virgin Australia, 270
Virgin Group Ltd, 172
Vodaphone, 197
Volkswagen, 73–74, 273
Volkswagen-Porsche, 250
Volvo Aero, 278

W

WABCO Holdings Inc., 217
Walgreen, 354
Wal-Mart, 13, 50, 75, 82, 85, 110, 111, 112, 114–115, 131, 132, 133, 140–141, 142, 145, 244, 334
Walmart International, 244–246
Walt Disney Co., 148–149, 175, 237, 268, 307
Warburg Pincus LLC, 209
WellPoint Inc., 58
Wells Fargo, 209
Wendy's International, 58, 407
Western Forms Inc., 240
Williams-Sonoma, Inc., 407
Witt Gas Technology, 82
Wm. Wrigley Jr. Company, 165–166, 172
World Health Organization (WHO), 272
WorldCom, 313

X

Xerox, 131, 202, 203, 265

Y

Yahoo!, 174, 284–285, 406
YouTube, 174, 194
YRC Worldwide, 138

Z

Zappos.com, 93
Zara, 82, 121
Zynga, 391, 396

A

Ability, 140
Above-average returns, 4, 20, 75
Acquisitions
  corporate tax laws, 179
  cross-border, 198–201
  definition, 196
  effective, 211–213
  as form of entry into
      international markets,
      239, 245
  horizontal, 197
  innovation through, 405–407
  integration process, 370, 372
  as international entry mode,
      242–243
  versus mergers and takeovers,
      195–196
  popularity of, 195–196
  problems in achieving success,
      203–211
  reasons for, 196–203
  related, 198
  restructuring, 213–215
  vertical, 197
Activist hedge funds, 308
Activities
  integrated, 107–108
  sharing, 171
  support, 111
  value chain, 87–88, 113, 116
Activity maps, 107–108
Actor's reputation, 147
Adaptability in acquisitions,
  212
Advertising, 167, 275
Affiliation dimension of
  customer relationships, 105
African Americans, 46
Age structure, 42
Agency costs, 299–300
Agency relationships, 296–299
Aggressive pricing, 142
Airline industry, 107–108,
  269–270, 278
Alliance networks, 279–280

Antitrust regulation, 178–179
Asian Americans, 43, 46
Assessing, 41
  business-level cooperative
      strategies, 274–275
  corporate-level cooperative
      strategies, 277
Assets
  complementary, 212
  restructuring of, 177
Attack, likelihood of, 142–146
Automobile industry, 47
  cooperative strategies, 261–262
  economies of scale, 230
  horizontal complementary
      strategic alliances, 272
  integrated cost leadership/
      differentiation strategy,
      122
  international strategies, 250
  market commonality and
      resource similarity in,
      136–137
  second movers, 143
  uncertainty-reducing
      strategies, 273
Automobile parts suppliers, 107
Autonomous strategic behavior,
  400–401
Autonomy, 377
Average returns, 5, 20
Awareness, 139–140

B

Backward vertical
  integration, 197
Balanced scorecard, 380–381
Banks, 208–210, 311, 312
Bargaining power
  of buyers, 55, 113, 117
  of suppliers, 54–55, 113–114,
      117
Barriers to entry
  overcoming through
      acquisitions, 198–201
  types of, 52–54

Blockholders, 20–21
Boards of directors, 302–308,
  311, 367–368
  definition, 302
  enhancing effectiveness of,
      304–305
  ethical behavior, 313, 315
  responsibilities of, 293
Bonuses, 306
Brand loyalty, 117
Brazil, 200
Breakthrough innovation, 11,
  397–400
Broad markets, 109
Bureaucratic controls, 210–211
Business-level cooperative
  strategies, 270–275,
  350–351
Business-level strategies, 100–129
  and competitive rivalry, 133
  creating value, 75
  customers, 103–107
  definition, 24, 102
  for diversified corporations,
      164
  international, 231–234
  matches between functional
      structure and, 333–336
  purpose of, 107–108
  types of, 108–123
Buyer bargaining power, 55,
  113, 117

C

Canada, 48
Candy makers, 153–154
Capabilities, 17, 74, 81–84
  costly-to-imitate, 16, 84–87
  definition, 16
  developing through
      acquisitions, 203
  nonsubstitutable, 86–87
  rare, 85
  and resources, 79
  and strategic
      entrepreneurship, 408

valuable, 85
value chain analysis, 89
Capital
  financial, 373–374
  human, 22, 82, 204–205, 215,
      362–363, 374–375
  social, 89, 376
Capital gains, 178
Capital market allocation,
  175–177
Capital market stakeholders, 19,
  20–21
Capital requirements, 53
Capital structure change, 310
Cash flows, 178, 180, 298
Causally ambiguous links, 86
Centralization, 333, 335, 336
Cereal industry, 274
Chief executive officers (CEOs),
  18, 78–79, 293
  compensation, 305–308
  duality, 303–304, 367
  interim, 369
  as strategic leaders, 22
  succession, 368–372
  top management team and,
      367–368
Chief financial officers (CFOs),
  307
China
  Apple stores in, 12
  car sales, 47
  cigarette firms in, 240–241
  corporate governance in, 293,
      312–313
  cross-border acquisitions,
      199–200, 201, 242
  geographic distribution, 43
  in global economy, 7–9
  guanxi (personal connections),
      8–9, 46
  income distribution, 44
  population size and age, 42
  Starbucks in, 225
Cloud computing, 151–152
Coffee industry, 101–102, 225

Collaborative advantages, 262
Collusive strategies, 273–274
Combination structure, 347–348
Competencies
  identifying, 90–91
  misrepresentation of, 281
  strategic center firms, 350
  see also Core competencies
Competition
  five forces model of, 14
  multipoint, 172–173
  in strategic management
    process, 24
Competition response strategy,
  272–273
Competition-reducing alliances,
  275
Competition-reducing strategy,
  273–274
Competitive actions, 139–141,
  146
Competitive advantage, 7,
  74, 109
  from cooperative strategies,
    262
  definition, 4
  in resource-based model of
    above-average returns, 17
  sustainable, 84–87
Competitive aggressiveness, 377
Competitive agility, 374
Competitive behavior, 132
Competitive blind spots, 135
Competitive dynamics, 133,
  148–154
Competitive form of
  multidivisional structure,
  341–343
Competitive landscape, 6–14
Competitive responses, 139–141,
  146–148
Competitive risks
  with cooperative strategies,
    280–281
  of cost leadership strategy,
    114–115
  of differentiation strategy,
    117–118
  of focus strategies, 120
  of integrated cost leadership/
    differentiation strategy,
    123
Competitive rivalry, 132, 133,
  134–135
Competitive scope, 203
Competitive speed, 374
Competitiveness
  see Strategic competitiveness
Competitor analysis, 60–62,
  134–139
  definition, 39
  ethical considerations, 62–63
  market commonality, 135–138
  resource similarity, 138–139
Competitor environment, 38–39

Competitor intelligence, 61
Competitors, 133
  definition, 132
  intensity of rivalry among,
    57–59
  numerous or equally balanced,
    58
  rivalry with existing, 111–113,
    117
Complementary assets, 212
Complementary strategic
  alliances, 270–272, 274–275
Complementors, 62
Complexity
  affecting internal analysis,
    76–77
  of managing international
    strategies, 249–250
  social, and costly-to-imitate
    capabilities, 86
Computer manufacturers,
  264–265
Conglomerate discount, 176
Conglomerates, 168, 178, 214, 344
Consumer food manufacturers,
  153–154
Consumer markets, 105
Content delivery network (CDN)
  services, 147–148
Contingency workers, 46
Continuous learning, 14, 375
Cooperative form of
  multidivisional structure,
  337, 338–339, 342, 343
Cooperative strategies, 260–289,
  350–352, 376
  competitive risks with,
    280–281
  definition, 25, 262
  innovation through, 404–405
  managing, 281–283
  matches between network
    structures and, 348–350
  strategic alliances, 263–270
Coopetition, 138
Core competencies, 71, 73–75,
  82–84
  building, 84–90
  definition, 16
  determination of, 106–107
  exploiting and maintaining,
    374
  and value-creating
    diversification, 171–172
Core ideology, 372
Core rigidities, 73, 91
Core strategy, 103
Corporate charter amendments,
  310
Corporate entrepreneurship, 393
Corporate governance
  definition, 294
  and diversification, 182–183
  and ethical behavior, 313–315
  international, 310–313

Corporate relatedness, 169–172,
  175
Corporate-level cooperative
  strategies, 261–262, 275,
  276–277, 351
Corporate-level core
  competencies, 171–172
Corporate-level strategies, 25,
  162–165, 234–236, 336–343
Corruption, 242–243
Cost disadvantages independent
  of scale, 54
Cost leadership strategy,
  107–109, 110–115, 118–120,
  333–334
Cost minimization, 282
Costly-to-imitate capabilities, 16,
  84–87
Costs
  agency, 299–300
  fixed, 58
  and international
    strategies, 231
  of product development, 201
  storage, 58
  switching, 53–54, 59
Counterfeiting, 118
Creativity, 400
Cross-border acquisitions,
  198–201, 242–243
Cross-border strategic alliances,
  277–278
Cross-functional product
  development teams,
  402–403
Culture
  and benefits of international
    strategies, 231
  and international
    entrepreneurship,
    396–397
  see also Organizational culture
Currencies, 247
Customer perspective
  in balanced scorecard,
    380–381
Customer relationship
  management (CRM), 122
Customer service, 71, 103, 114–115
Customers, 103–107
  bargaining power of, 55,
    113, 117
  social capital, 89
  as stakeholders, 19, 21

D
Debt, 206, 212, 214
Decision-making specialists,
  296–297
Demand, 228, 232–233
Demographic segment, 42–44
Differentiation, 101–102, 108
  as barrier to entry, 53
  and cost leadership strategy,
    110

focus strategies, 118–120
  lack of, 59
Differentiation strategy, 109,
  115–120, 334–335
Diffuse ownership, 301
Direct transaction costs, 207
Disruptive innovation, 131–132
Disruptive technologies, 10–11
Distributed strategic networks,
  351–352
Distribution, 88, 113, 116
  capabilities in, 82
  channels, access to, 54
Diversification, 164–165,
  332–333, 336
  and acquisitions, 202
  as agency problem, 297–299
  excessive, 207–208
  and international strategies, 248
  levels of, 165–168
  reasons for, 168–170
  unrelated, 175–177
  value-creating, 170–175
  value-neutral, 178–181
  value-reducing, 182–183
Diversifying strategic alliances,
  275, 276
Divestiture, 213–214
Dodd-Frank Wall Street Reform
  and Consumer Protection
  Act (Dodd-Frank), 300, 308
Domestic-market strategies,
  231–233
Dominant-business
  diversification strategy, 166
Downscoping, 213–214, 215
Downsizing, 213, 214–215
Due diligence, 205–206, 212
Dynamic alliance networks, 280
Dynamic capability, 374
Dynamics
  competitive, 133, 148–154
  of international entry mode,
    244–246

E
Economic environment, 44
Economic risks, 246, 247
Economic segment, 44
Economies of scale, 52–53, 210,
  230–231
Economies of scope, 170–171,
  175, 210, 339
Emerging economies, 9, 177,
  228–229
Emerging markets, 167
Employee buyouts (EBOs), 214
Employees, 22, 72
Energy industry, 24, 35–36,
  77, 163
Entertainment business, 6–7, 268
Entrepreneurial mind-set,
  376–377, 395, 402
Entrepreneurial opportunities,
  393–394

Subject Index

Entrepreneurs, 395–396
Entrepreneurship, 393–394
  corporate, 393
  definition, 393
  international, 396–397, 408
  strategic, 376–377, 393, 407–408
Entry barriers
  see Barriers to entry
Entry modes, international, 239–246
Environment
  competitor, 38–39
  economic, 44
  general, 38–50
  industry, 38–39, 50–60
  physical, 48–50
  see also External environment
Environmental sustainability, 85
Environmental trends, 237–238
Environmental uncertainty, 77
Envisioned future, 372
Equally balanced competitors, 58
Equity strategic alliances, 265
Equity-based alliances, 242
Ethics, 18, 25, 62–63, 313–315, 377–379
Ethnic mix, 43
European sovereign-debt crisis, 45
European Union (EU), 7, 238
Evolutionary patterns of organizational structure and strategy, 330–333
Executive compensation, 182, 305–308, 314
Exit barriers, 59
Explicit collusion, 273
Exporting, 239–240, 244
External corporate governance mechanism, 295, 308–310
External environment, 24, 37
  analysis of, 5–6, 39–41
  ethical considerations, 62–63
External managerial labor market, 368–370

F

Family-owned businesses, 166, 296
Fast food industry, 14, 24, 71–72
Fast-cycle markets, 142, 149–153, 266–269
Finance, 89, 113, 116
Financial capital, 373–374
Financial controls, 207–208, 329, 340, 379–381
Financial economies, 175–177
Financial perspective, in balanced scorecard, 380–381
Financial resources, 80
Financial slack, 212
Financial supermarkets, 208–210
First mover, 142–144

Five forces model of competition, 51–55, 57–59
Fixed costs, 58
Flexibility
  and competitive actions, 145
  and integrated cost leadership/differentiation strategy, 122
  strategic, 13–14
  structural, 327
  and success of acquisitions, 212
Flexible manufacturing system (FMS), 122
Focus strategies, 118–120
Focused cost leadership strategy, 109, 119
Focused differentiation strategy, 109, 119–120
Follow-up service, 88, 113, 116
Food manufacturers, 153–154
Forecasting, 41
Foreignness, liability of, 237–238
Formalization, 333, 335, 336
Forward integration, 173
Franchising, 276–277, 351
Fraud, 379
Free cash flow, 178, 298
Friendly acquisitions, 212
Functional structure
  business-level strategies and, 333–336
  cost leadership strategy, 333–334
  definition, 332
  differentiation strategy, 334–335
  integrated cost leadership/differentiation strategy, 335–336
Future cash flows, 180

G

Game platform producers, 131–132, 141–142
General environment, 38–50
Generic strategies, 103
Geographic distribution, 43
Geographic diversification, 251–252
Geographically clustered firms, 279
Germany, 311–312
Global economy, 7–10
Global matrix design, 347–348
Global mind-set, 74
Global segment, 47–48
Global strategy, 235–236, 346–347
Globalfocusing, 48
Globalization, 9–10
Golden parachutes, 309, 310
Governance mechanisms
  see Corporate governance

Government policy, 54, 233, 250–251
Greenfield venture, 243–244
Greenmail, 310
Guanxi (personal connections), 8–9, 46

H

Headhunters, 370
Hedge funds, 308
Heterogeneous top management teams, 366, 369–370
Hispanic Americans, 43, 46
Historical conditions, unique, 86
Homogeneous top management teams, 369–370
Horizontal acquisitions, 197, 202
Horizontal complementary strategic alliances, 271, 272, 274–275, 350–351
Horizontal organizational structures, 402
Hostile takeovers, 308–310
Human capital
  and acquisitions, 204–205
  and capabilities, 82
  definition, 374
  developing, 374–375
  and strategic leadership, 22, 362–363
  when downsizing, 215
Human resources, 80–82, 89, 113, 116
Hybrid form of combination structure, 348
Hypercompetition, 7, 9, 268

I

Imitation, 115, 118, 143
  definition, 395
  and market type, 148–150, 152–153
Inbound logistics, 110–111
Income distribution, 43–44
Incremental innovation, 397–400
India
  corporate governance in, 293
  cross-border acquisitions, 199–200, 201
  energy industries, 36
  in global economy, 9
  income distribution, 44
  international strategies in, 229
  political/legal segment, 45
  population size, 42
Indirect transaction costs, 207
Induced strategic behavior, 401
Industrial markets, 105
Industrial organization (I/O) model of above-average returns, 14–17
Industry
  definition, 50–51
  in resource-based model of above-average returns, 17

Industry environment, 38–39, 50–60
Industry growth, 58
Information networks, 122
Information technology, 11–13
Information-based exchanges, 104–105
Inhwa (harmony), 48
Innovation, 12–13, 369, 394–395
  and acquisitions, 208, 212
  and bureaucratic controls, 210–211
  and competitive advantage, 72
  cost of, 201
  definition, 395
  and differentiation strategy, 115–116
  disruptive, 131–132
  entrepreneurial mind-set, 376–377
  in fast-cycle markets, 150
  by first movers, 142–143
  incremental, 397–400
  internal, 397–401
  and international strategy, 228, 249
  and licensing, 241
  open, 391–392, 399, 404–405
  and outsourcing, 90
  perpetual, 10–11
  promotion of by strategic leaders, 23
  radical, 397–400
  resources, 80
  in standard-cycle markets, 153
  through acquisitions, 405–407
  through cooperative strategies, 404–405
  and top management teams, 366–367
Innovativeness, 377
Insiders, 303–304
Institutional activism, 302
Institutional investors, 21
Institutional owners, 301–302
Intangible resources, 13, 80, 81, 172, 181
Integrated cost leadership/differentiation strategy, 109, 120–123, 335–336
Integration
  difficulties with after acquisitions, 205
  facilitating, 403
  vertical, 173, 174
Interfirm rivalry, 134, 141–148
Internal analysis, 5–6, 73–79
Internal business process, in balanced scorecard, 380–381
Internal capital market allocation, 175–177
Internal competition, 341–342
Internal corporate governance mechanisms, 295, 301–308

Internal corporate venturing, 400–401
Internal innovation, 397–404
Internal managerial labor market, 368–370
Internal organization
  analyzing, 5–6, 73–79
  resource-based model, 16–17
  in strategic management process, 5–6, 24
International business-level strategy, 225, 231–234
International cooperative strategies, 277–278, 282, 351–352
International corporate governance, 295, 310–313
International corporate-level strategy, 234–236
International diversification strategy, 248–252
International entrepreneurship, 396–397, 408
International strategies
  definition, 227
  incentives to use, 228–229
  matches with worldwide structure, 343–348
  types of, 231–236
Internet, 46–47, 56
  book sales, 3–4, 85
  and ease of exportation, 240
  and information age, 11, 13
  information-based exchanges over, 104–105
Internet Service Providers (ISPs), 13
Intraorganizational conflicts, 76–77
Invention, 395

J

Japan
  corporate governance in, 311–312
  economic environment, 44
  energy industries, 36
  population aging, 42
Joint ventures, 15, 243–245, 261, 263–265
Junk bonds, 206

K

Knowledge
  expanding base of, 375
  increasing intensity of, 13–14
  sharing, and international strategies, 230
Knowledge spillover, 13, 327
Korea, 48

L

Large-block shareholders, 301–302
Late movers, 144

Layoffs, 375
Learning and growth perspective, in balanced scorecard, 380–381
Leveraged buyouts (LBOs), 214, 215
Liability of foreignness, 237–238
Licensing, 239, 240–241, 244
Litigation, 310
Location advantages, international, 231
Logistics, 110–111
Long-term incentive plans, 305, 306
Long-term performance, 207–208
Long-term strategic direction, 372
Low-cost culture, 333
Loyalty, customer, 104, 117

M

Management buyouts (MBOs), 214
Management information systems, 82, 89, 113, 116
Managerial control, separation of ownership and, 295–300
Managerial defense tactics, 309–310
Managerial discretion, 364–365
Managerial employment risk, 298–299
Managerial hubris, 365–366
Managerial labor markets, 368–370
Managerial motives to diversify, 182–183
Managerial opportunism, 297
Managerial succession, 368–372
Manufacturing, 82
Market commonality, 135–138, 140
Market dependence, 147–148
Market for corporate control, 295, 308–310
Market leaders, 197
Market power, 172–174, 196–198
Market segmentation, 105
Market size, international, 229–230
Marketing, 82, 88, 113, 116
Markets
  fast-cycle, 142, 149–152, 153, 266–269
  segmentation, 105
  slow-cycle, 148–149, 266–267
  standard-cycle, 152–154, 266, 267, 269–270
  target, 109
Matrix organizations, 339
Mergers, 178, 179, 194–196
  see also Acquisitions
Mission, 18–19
Mobile ecosystems, 268–269
Modes of entry, international, 239–246

Monitoring, 40–41
Motivation, 140
Multidivisional (M-form) structure, 332–333, 336–343
Multidomestic strategy, 234–235, 251–252, 345–346
Multimarket competition, 133, 138, 140
Multinational companies, 305–306, 314–315
Multipoint competition, 172–173
Mutual forbearance, 274

N

Narrow market segments, 109
National advantage, 231–233
Network cooperative strategy, 279–280
Network structures, cooperative strategies and, 348–350
New entrants, 51–54
New wholly owned subsidiaries, 239, 243–244, 245
New York Stock Exchange, 303
Nonequity strategic alliances, 265–266
Nonsubstitutable capabilities, 16, 84–85, 86–87
North American Free Trade Agreement (NAFTA), 238

O

Offshoring, 90
Open innovation, 391–392, 399, 404–405
Operational relatedness, 169–170, 171, 175
Operations, 88, 113, 116
Opportunistic behaviors, 281, 297
Opportunities
  definition, 39
  global segment, 47
  identifying international, 227–231
  maximization management approach, 282–283
Organizational controls, 328–329, 378–381
Organizational culture, 22–23, 86, 376–377, 391–392
Organizational politics, 403
Organizational resources, 80
Organizational size, 144–145
Organizational slack, 143
Organizational stakeholders, 19, 22
Organizational structure, 233, 325–328
  definition, 327
  evolutionary patterns of, 330–333
  and strategy, 330
Outbound logistics, 110–111
Outsiders, 303–304, 305

Outsourcing, 90
  and cost leadership strategy, 111, 114
  in nonequity strategic alliances, 265–266
  strategic, 349–350
Overdiversification, 10, 207–208, 298
Ownership
  in German corporate governance system, 311
  in joint ventures, 264
  market for corporate control, 308–310
  separation of managerial control and, 295–300
Ownership concentration, 301–302

P

Patents, 11, 149, 395
Pension funds, 301
Perpetual innovation, 10–11
Pharmaceutical companies, 149, 180, 203, 272, 405
Physical environment segment, 48–50
Physical resources, 80
Poison pills, 309, 310
Political risks, 246–247
Political/legal segment, 44–45
Population size, 42
Potential entrants, 51–54, 114, 117
Price predators, 147
Price sensitivity, 117–118
Pricing
  aggressive, 142
  of ISPs, 13
Private synergy, 207
Privatization, 45
Proactiveness, 377
Product champion, 400
Product development
  cost of as reason for acquisitions, 201
  cross-functional teams, 402–403
Product differentiation, 53
Product diversification, 251–252, 297–299
Product innovation, 115–116
Product market stakeholders, 19, 21
Product quality dimensions, 145–146
Product substitutes, 55–57, 114, 117
Profit pools, 23–24
Profitability, 14, 15
Proprietary advantages, 148–149

Q

Quality
  definition, 145
  and likelihood of attack, 145–146

R

Race to learn, 350
Radical innovation, 11, 397–400
Rare capabilities, 16, 84–85, 87
Raw materials, 228
Reach dimension of customer
relationships, 104
Regionalization, 238
Related acquisitions, 198, 202
Related and supporting
industries, 233
Related constrained
diversification strategy,
166–168, 170–175, 338–339,
342
Related linked diversification
strategy, 166, 168, 170–175,
340–342
Related outsiders, 303
Relational advantages, 262
Relationship with customers,
104–105
Reputation
actor's, and likelihood of
response, 147
and differentiation strategy,
117
and diversification, 182
Reputational resources, 80, 81
Research and development (R&D)
capabilities in, 82
as core competence, 106–107
internal innovation, 397–401
and international strategies,
230–231, 249
and success of acquisitions, 212
Resource dissimilarity, 140–141
Resource portfolio, 373–376
Resource similarity, 136–139
Resource-based model of above-
average returns, 16–17
Resources, 79–81, 143, 281
creating value, 75
definition, 16
intangible, 13, 81
and internal analysis, 73–74
international strategies, 228
in I/O model of above-average
returns, 14
managing, 72–73
right, 91
sharing, and international
strategies, 230
tangible, 79–81
value-neutral diversification
and, 181
Restructuring, 213–215, 375
of assets, 177
changing organizational
culture and, 377
definition, 213
Returns, 87, 248, 249
above-average, 4, 20, 75
average, 5, 20
measuring, 4–5

Reverse engineering, 150
Richness dimension of customer
relationships, 104–105
Rigidities, core, 73, 91
Risk reduction as incentive to
diversify, 180–181
Risk taking in entrepreneurial
mind-set, 377
Risks
with cooperative strategies,
280–281
of cost leadership strategy,
114–115
definition, 4
of differentiation strategy,
117–118
for first movers, 143
of focus strategies, 120
of integrated cost leadership/
differentiation strategy,
123
international strategies,
246–247
investment, 296
lower, as reason for
acquisitions, 201–202
managerial employment,
298–299
related to globalization, 10
Rivalry
competitive, 130–161
with existing competitors,
111–113, 117
intensity of among
competitors, 57–59
and national advantage, 233
Russia
economic environment, 44
energy industries, 36
institutional instability, 247

S

Sarbanes-Oxley (SOX) Act, 300,
329
Scale competence, 84
Scanning, 40
Second movers, 143–144
Service-based companies, 177
Severance packages, 309, 310
Shared values, 403
Shareholders, 19–21, 296–303,
309, 311
Sharing activities, 171
Shipping industry, 138, 172–173
Simple structure, 331–332
Singapore, 295
Single-business diversification
strategy, 165–166
Slack, 143, 212
Slow-cycle markets, 148–149,
266–267
Social capital, 89, 376
Social networking, 102, 104,
405, 406
Sociocultural segment, 45–46

Soft infrastructure, 177
Software industry, 268–269
Spain, 199
Specialization, 333, 335, 336
Speed
competitive, 374
to market, 201
Spin-off, 213–214
Sportswear companies, 121,
122
Stable alliance networks, 280
Stakeholders, 17, 18, 19–22, 313
Standard-cycle markets,
152–154, 266, 267, 269–270
Standstill agreements, 310
Steel industry, 266–267
Stock option incentives,
305, 306
Strategic acquisitions, 201–202
Strategic actions, 5–6, 19,
141–142, 146
Strategic alliances, 239, 250–251,
261–262
assessing, 274–275
business-level cooperative
strategies, 350–351
complementary, 270–272
as cooperative strategies,
263–270, 405
definition, 263
diversifying, 276
dynamics of, 244
as international entry mode,
241–242
synergistic, 275, 276
Strategic behavior
autonomous, 400–401
induced, 401
Strategic business unit (SBU)
form, 340–343
Strategic center firms, 349–352
Strategic change, 366–367
Strategic competitiveness, 4, 5,
10, 248–249
Strategic context, 401
Strategic controls, 328–329,
340–341, 379–381
Strategic decisions, 90–91
Strategic direction, 372–373
Strategic entrepreneurship,
376–377, 393, 407–408
Strategic equivalents, 86
Strategic flexibility, 13–14
Strategic groups, 60
Strategic inputs, 5–6, 19
Strategic leaders, 22–24,
77–79
Strategic leadership, 362, 364,
372–381, 403
Strategic management process,
4–6, 24–25, 363
Strategic networks, 349–352
Strategic outsourcing, 349–350
Strategic responses, 141, 146
Strategic stakes, 59

Strategies, 5–6, 24–25, 103
definition, 4
evolutionary patterns of,
330–333
and organizational structure,
326–327, 330
Strengths, in internal analysis,
90–91
Structural change, 327–328
Structural flexibility, 327
Structural stability, 327
Substitute products, 55–57, 114,
117
Succession plans, 293, 368, 370–372
Suppliers
bargaining power of, 54–55,
113–114, 117
social capital, 89
as stakeholders, 21
Supply-chain management, 88,
113, 116
Support activities, 111
Support functions, 87–88, 113, 116
Sustainable competitive
advantage, 84–87
Switching costs, 53–54, 59
Synergistic strategic alliances,
275, 276
Synergy
after acquisitions, 207
definition, 180
as incentive to diversify, 180–181
and international strategies, 230

T

Tacit collusion, 273–274
Tactical actions, 141–142, 146
Tactical responses, 141, 146
Takeovers, 182, 195–196, 212,
308–310
Tangible resources, 79–81, 181
Target customers, 105
Target markets, 109
Tax laws, 178–179
Technological resources, 80
Technological segment, 46–47
Technology, 90, 228, 350
diffusion, 10–11, 150
disruptive, 10–11
increasing knowledge
intensity, 13–14
information, 11–13
Technology companies, 193–194
Telecommunications, 6–7, 8–9,
193, 268–269
Threats
definition, 39
in global segment, 47
of new entrants, 51–54
of substitute products, 55–57
Top management teams,
366–370
Top-level managers, 364–368
Total quality management
(TQM), 123

Trade agreements, 238
Transformational leadership, 364
Transnational strategy, 225, 236, 347–348
Transportation industry, 135, 138

U

Uncertain future cash flows, 180
Uncertainty affecting managerial internal analysis, 76–77
Uncertainty-reducing alliances, 275
Uncertainty-reducing strategy, 273
Unethical practices, 377, 379
Unions, 21
Unique historical conditions, 86
United Kingdom, 293
United States
    boards of directors, 293
    ethnic mix, 43, 46
    geographic distribution, 43
    global economy and, 8–9
    health care, 45–46
    Huawei in, 8–9
    income distribution, 43
    population, 42
Unrelated diversification strategy, 170, 175–177, 202
    competitive form of multidivisional structure, 341–343
    definition, 168
    financial controls, 329
    levels of diversification, 166

V

Valuable capabilities, 16, 84–85, 87
Value, 83–84, 403–404, 407–408
Value chain activities, 87–88, 113, 116
Value chain analysis, 87–90, 113, 116–117
Value chains in strategic networks, 350
Value-creating diversification, 169–175
Value-neutral diversification, 169, 178–181
Value-reducing diversification, 169, 182–183
Vertical acquisitions, 197
Vertical complementary strategic alliances, 270–272, 350–351
Vertical integration, 173, 174
Video game market, 131–132
Video on demand (VOD), 56–57, 132
Vision, 17–18, 23, 372

W

Weaknesses, in internal analysis, 90–91
Web-based retailing, 3–4, 85
Whistleblowers, 314–315
Whole-firm buyouts, 214, 215
Wholly owned subsidiaries, 239, 243–244, 245
Women
    entrepreneurship by, 408
    as strategic leaders, 370
Worldwide geographic area structure, 345–346
Worldwide product divisional structure, 346–347
Worldwide structure and international strategies, 343–348